The **Rough Guide** to

Italy

written and researched by

**Ros Belford, Martin Dunford,
Celia Woolfrey, Rob Andrews, Jules Brown,
Jonathan Buckley and Tim Jepson**

With additional contributions from
**Joe Fullman, Charles Hebbert, Jeffrey Kennedy,
Lucy Ratcliffe and Nick Woodford**

NEW YORK · LONDON · DELHI

www.roughguides.com

Contents

Italian food colour section following p.360

Italian football colour section following p.840

◀◀ Ponte Vecchio, Florence ◀ St Peter's Basilica, Rome

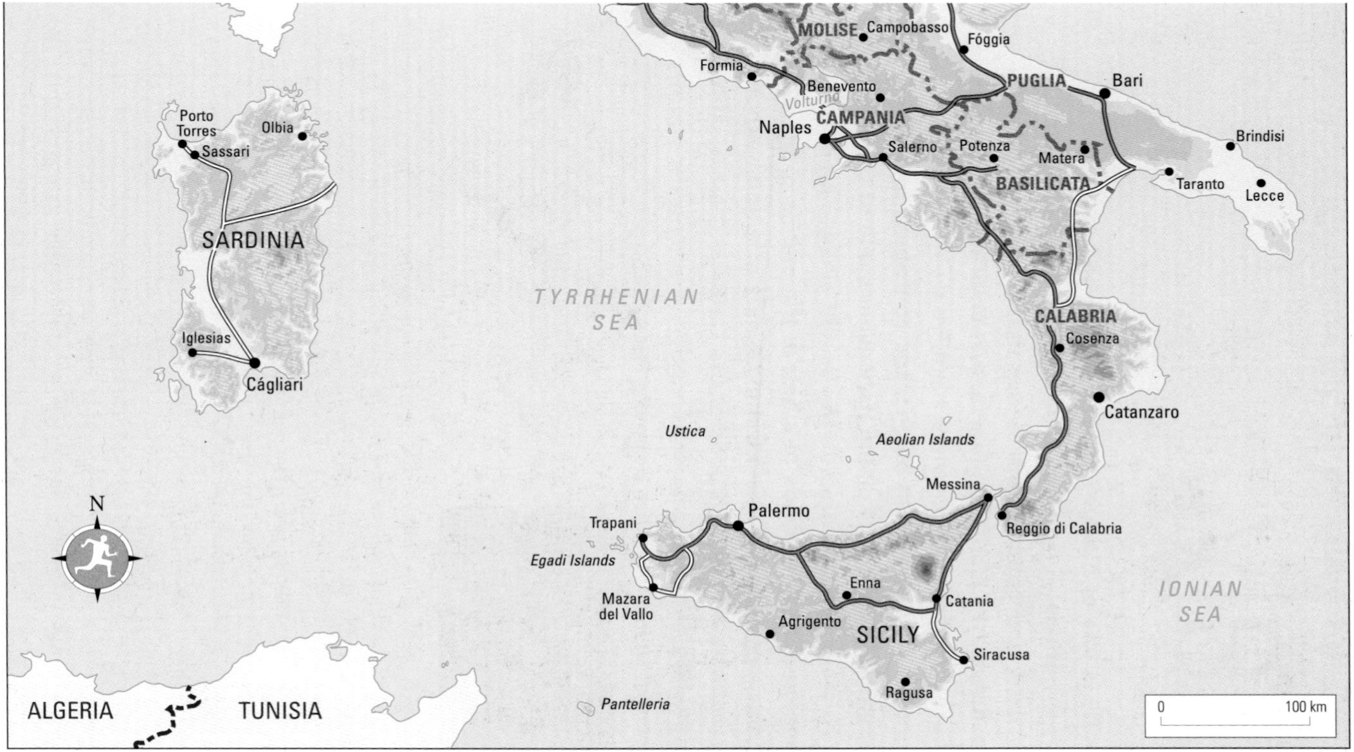
MOLISE
Campobasso
Fóggia
Formia
Benevento
Volturno
PUGLIA
Bari
CAMPANIA
Naples
Brindisi
Salerno
Potenza
Matera
Taranto
Lecce
BASILICATA
Porto Torres
Sassari
Olbia
SARDINIA
TYRRHENIAN SEA
CALABRIA
Cosenza
Iglesias
Cágliari
Catanzaro
Ustica
Aeolian Islands
Messina
Palermo
Trapani
Reggio di Calabria
Egadi Islands
Enna
Catania
Mazara del Vallo
Agrigento
SICILY
IONIAN SEA
Siracusa
Ragusa
Pantelleria
ALGERIA
TUNISIA
N
0
100 km

Introduction to

Italy

Italy is one of Europe's most complex and alluring destinations. A modern, industrialized nation, with an artistic and architectural legacy that few other countries can rival, it's also a Mediterranean country with a southern European sensibility, where traditional attitudes still prevail. Thriving small businesses contribute to strong regional identities, helping Italy avoid some of the bland effects of globalization. In towns and villages all over the country, life grinds to a halt in the middle of the day for a long lunch, and is strongly family-oriented, with an emphasis on the traditions of the Catholic Church, which, notwithstanding a growing scepticism among the country's youth, still dominates people's lives.

Above all, Italy provokes reaction. Its people are rarely indifferent, and on one and the same day you might encounter the kind of disdain dished out to tourist masses everywhere and an hour later be treated to embarrassingly generous hospitality. If there is a single national characteristic, it's to embrace life to the full: in the hundreds of local festivals taking place across the country on any given day, to celebrate a saint or the local harvest; in the importance placed on good food; in the obsession with clothes and image; and above all in the daily domestic ritual of the collective evening stroll or *passeggiata* – a sociable affair celebrated by young and old alike in every town and village across the country.

Italy only became a unified state in 1861, and, as a result, Italians often feel more loyalty to their region than to the nation as a whole – something manifest in different cuisines, dialects, landscape and often varying standards of living. There is also the country's enormous cultural legacy: Tuscany alone has more classified historical monuments than any country in the world; there are considerable remnants of the Roman Empire all over the country, notably in Rome itself; and every region retains its own relics of an artistic tradition generally acknowledged to be among the world's richest.

Yet there's no reason to be intimidated by all this. If you want to lie on a beach, there are any number of places to do so, from resorts filled with regimented rows of sun beds and umbrellas favoured by the Italians themselves, to secluded and less developed spots in the south. Mountains, too, run the country's length – from the Alps and Dolomites in the north right along the Apennines, which form the spine of the peninsula – and are an important reference-point for most Italians. Skiing and other winter sports are practised avidly, and in the national parks, protected from the national passion for hunting, wildlife of all sorts thrives.

Where to go

The north and central parts of the country constitute "discovered" Italy. The regions of **Piemonte** and **Lombardy**, in the northwest, make up the richest and most cosmopolitan part of the country, and the two main centres, Turin and Milan, are its wealthiest cities. In their southern reaches, these regions are flat and scenically dull, especially Lombardy, but in the north the presence of the Alps shapes the character of each: skiing and hiking are prime activities, and the lakes and mountains of Lombardy are time-honoured tourist territory. **Liguria**, the small coastal province to the south, has long been known as the "Italian Riviera" and is

▲ Taking a break, Courmáyer

Art

It's a safe bet that you're visiting the country with the world's greatest concentration of art treasures for just that – its art. And you won't be disappointed. **Northern Italy** on the whole has the country's richest crop, but wherever you're travelling, even the smallest country church can boast a masterpiece or two; remote monasteries and small country towns can hold enticing museums; and the big city galleries – the Uffizi in Florence, Milan's Brera, too many to mention in Rome – are stacked full of beautiful paintings and sculptures. Like food, you can find different styles – and the work of different artists – in distinct regions. Of the country's ancient art, the most obvious draws are the Roman mosaics and murals of Pompeii and Herculaneum, and the earlier funereal sculpture and applied arts of the Etruscans of northern Lazio. Siena was home to some of the earliest **Gothic** stylists of the fourteenth century; Florence bloomed most brightly during the **Renaissance** of the fifteenth century, and Rome's most characteristic style is the later **Baroque** look of the Counter-Reformation. Venice, not surprisingly, is the place to see the works of the great **Venetian** painters, Titian and Tintoretto. Your only problem will be having the time to take it all in.

accordingly crowded with sun-seeking holidaymakers for much of the summer season. Nonetheless, it's a beautiful stretch of coast, and its capital, Genoa, is a bustling port with a long seafaring tradition.

Much of the most dramatic mountain scenery lies within the smaller northern regions. In the far northwest, the tiny bilingual region of **Valle d'Aosta** is home to some of the country's most frequented ski resorts, and is bordered by the tallest of the Alps – the Matterhorn and Mont Blanc. In the northeast, **Trentino–Alto Adige**, another bilingual region and one in which the national boundary is especially blurred, marks the beginning of the Dolomites mountain range, where Italy's largest national park, the Stelvio, lies amid some of the country's most memorable landscapes.

The Dolomites stretch into the northeastern regions of the **Veneto and Friuli–Venezia Giulia**. However, here the main focus of interest is, of course, Venice; a unique city, and every bit as beautiful as its reputation would suggest (although this means you won't be alone in appreciating it). If the crowds are too much, there's also the arc of historic towns outside the city – Verona, Padua and Vicenza, all centres of interest in their own right, although rather overshadowed by their illustrious neighbour. To the south, the region of **Emilia-Romagna** has been at the heart of Italy's postwar industrial boom and has a standard of living on a par with Piemonte and Lombardy, although it's also a traditional stronghold of the Italian Left. Its coast is popular among Italians, and Rimini is about Italy's brashest (and trendiest) seaside resort, with a high reputation on the clubbing scene. You may do better to ignore the beaches altogether, however, and concentrate on the ancient centres of Ravenna, Ferrara, Parma and the regional capital of Bologna, one of Italy's liveliest, most historic but least appreciated cities – and traditionally Italy's gastronomic and academic capital.

Central Italy represents perhaps the most commonly perceived image of the country, and **Tuscany**, with its classic rolling countryside and the

▲ Cala Gonone, Sardinia

Fact file

• Italy is a peninsula, shaped rather like a boot, jutting out into the Mediterranean Sea. It covers a **surface area** of 301, 230 square km and includes the islands of Sardinia and Sicily. The distance from the tip of the country's "toe" to its northern border is about 1380km. Much of the land is mountainous, the **highest point** being Mont Blanc (4748m) in the north.

• Italy's **population** is just over 58 million, with just under 4 million living in the capital, Rome. The country is divided geographically and administratively into 15 regions and 5 autonomous regions. The dominant ethnic group is Italian, with small clusters of German-, French- and Slovene-Italians in the north and Albanian- and Greek-Italians in the south. There is also a growing Muslim immigrant community.

• Italy became a **nation state** in 1861, under King Vittorio Emanuele II, and has been a **democratic republic** since 1946, when the monarchy was abolished by popular referendum. The **parliament** consists of two houses, the Senate (315 seats) and the Chamber of Deputies (630 seats); both sit for five-year terms of office. The **president** is elected for a seven-year term by a joint session of parliament and regional representatives. Real power, however, is in the hands of the **prime minister**, who is generally the leader of the party with the biggest majority in the Chamber of Deputies.

art-packed towns of Florence, Pisa and Siena, to name only the three best-known centres, is one of its most visited regions. Neighbouring **Umbria** is similar in all but its tourist numbers, though it gets busier every year, as visitors flock into towns such as Perugia, Spoleto and Assisi. Further east still, the **Marche** has gone the same way, with old stone cottages being turned into foreign-owned holiday homes; the highlights of the region are the ancient towns of Urbino and Áscoli Piceno. South of the Marche, the hills begin

▲ Via dei Tribunali, Campania

Ice cream

The taste of real Italian ice cream, eaten in Italy, is absolutely unbeatable. **Gelato**, as it's known, is the country's favourite dessert, and there's no better way to end a day, as lots of Italians do, than with a stroll through the streets sampling a *gelato* while enjoying the cool of the evening. Italian ice cream really is better than any other, and like most Italian food this is down to the local insistence on using whole milk and eggs, and adding only naturally derived flavours. Everywhere but the tiniest village will have at least one *gelateria*, and many cafés serve ice cream as well. There will usually be at least a dozen flavours to choose from – and often many more – and you can try them either in a cone (*cono*) or tub (*coppa* or *copetta*); you can have as many scoops (*gusti*) as you want

– and as many flavours too. If you want to sample the very best, look for the signs saying "*produzione artiganale*", which means that the ice cream is produced according to strictly traditional methods, and "*produzione propria*" or "*nostra produzione*" which basically means it's home-made.

to pucker into mountains in the twin regions of **Abruzzo** and **Molise**, one of Italy's remotest areas, centring on one of the country's highest peaks – the Gran Sasso d'Italia. Molise, particularly, is a taster of the south, as is **Lazio** to the west, in part a poor and sometimes desolate region whose often rugged landscapes, particularly south of Rome, contrast with the more manicured beauty of the other central regions. Lazio's real focal point, though, is **Rome**, Italy's capital and the one city in the country that owes allegiance neither to the north or south, its people proudly aloof from the rest of the country's squabbles. Rome is a tremendous city quite unlike any other, and in terms of historical sights outstrips everywhere else in the country by some way.

The south proper begins with the region of **Campania**, to the south of Lazio. Its capital, Naples, is a unique, unforgettable city, the spiritual heart of the Italian south, and close to some of Italy's finest ancient sites in Pompeii and Herculaneum, not to mention the country's most spectacular stretch of coast around Amalfi. **Basilicata** and **Calabria**, which make up the instep and toe of Italy's boot, are harder territory but still rewarding, the emphasis less on art, more on the landscape and quiet, relatively unspoilt coastlines. **Puglia**, the "heel" of Italy, has underrated pleasures too, notably the landscape of its Gargano peninsula, the souk-like qualities of its capital

▲ Chianti vineyards, Tuscany

Roman Italy: the top 10 sites

Everyone who visits Italy wants to see the sites of **ancient Rome**, and these are easy enough to find – not least in **Rome** itself, where they literally litter the city centre: the **Forum**, the heart of the city during the Republic; the adjacent **Palatine Hill**, where the city's power-brokers lived; the **columns** and **plinths** of forums commemorating various Roman emperors, as well as the iconic bulk of the **Colosseum** could keep you occupied for a couple of days on their own – and, not far from here, the Baths of Caracalla, Domus Aurea and the ruins of Via Appia Antica, for a couple of days more. A short trip outside the city, the ruins of **Ostia**, Rome's former port, are strikingly well maintained, while to the south, the ruined towns of **Pompeii** and **Herculaneum**, simultaneously destroyed and preserved by the eruption of Vesuvius in 79 AD, are remarkable.

In the north of the country, Verona's **amphitheatre** continues to serve its purpose, hosting opera performances during the summer. Several other amphitheatres around the country are in various states of repair, while a number of triumphal **arches** – in Aosta, Rimini and Benevento – testify to the emperors' warlike activities all over the peninsula.

- Colosseum, Rome
- Ostia Antica
- Pompeii and Herculaneum, Campania
- Arch of Trajan, Benevento arch
- Amphitheatre, Verona
- Villa Adriana, Tivoli
- Saepinium, Abruzzo
- Cumae, Campania
- Arch of Augustus and Bridge of Tiberius, Rimini
- Piazza Armerina, Sicily

Bari, and the Baroque glories of Lecce in the far south, although it too is becoming more known as the years go by. As for **Sicily**, the island is really a place apart, with a wide mixture of attractions ranging from some of the finest preserved Hellenistic treasures in Europe, to a couple of Italy's most appealing beach resorts in Taormina and Cefalù, not to mention some gorgeous upland scenery. Come this far south and you're closer to Africa than Milan, and it shows – in the climate, the architecture and the cooking, with couscous featuring on many menus in the west of the island. **Sardinia**, too, feels far removed from the Italian mainland, especially in its relatively undiscovered interior, although you may be content to explore its fine beaches, which are among Italy's best.

When to go

I taly's **climate** is one of the most hospitable in the world, with a general pattern of warm, dry summers and mild winters. There are, however, marked regional variations, ranging from the more temperate northern part of the country to the firmly Mediterranean south. Summers are hot and dry along the coastal areas, especially as you move south, cool in the major mountain areas – the Alps and Apennines. Winters are mild in the south of the country, Rome and below, but in the north they can be at least as cold as anywhere in the northern hemisphere, sometimes worse, especially across the plains of Lombardy and Emilia-Romagna, which can be very inhospitable indeed in January.

As for **when to go**, if you're planning to visit fairly popular areas, especially beach resorts, avoid July and August, when the weather can be too hot and the crowds at their most congested. The first two weeks of August are when the Italians go on holiday, so expect the crush to be especially bad in the resorts and the scene in the major historic cities – Rome, Florence, Venice – to be slightly artificial, as the only people around are fellow tourists. The nicest time to visit, in terms of the weather and lack of crowds, is April to late June, or September and October. If you're planning to swim, however,

bear in mind that only the south of the country may be warm enough outside the May to September period.

Average temperatures

	Jan	Feb	Mar	Apr	May	Jun	Jul	Aug	Sep	Oct	Nov	Dec
Ancona												
°C	6	6	9	14	18	22	25	24	21	17	13	7
°F	43	43	48	57	64	72	77	75	70	63	55	45
Bari												
°C	8	9	11	14	18	22	25	24	22	18	15	10
°F	46	48	52	57	64	72	77	75	72	64	59	50
Bologna												
°C	2.5	3	9	14	18	23	26	25	21	15	10	4
°F	36	37	48	57	64	73	79	77	70	59	50	39
Cágliari												
°C	10.5	11	13	15	18.5	23	25.5	25.5	23	19	15	12.5
°F	51	52	55	59	65	73	78	78	73	66	59	55
Florence												
°C	6	7	10	13	17	22	25	24.5	21	16	11	6
°F	43	45	50	55	63	72	77	76	70	61	52	43
Genoa												
°C	8	9	11.5	14.5	18	22	25	25	22	18	18	13
°F	46	48	53	58	64	72	77	77	72	64	64	55
Milan												
°C	2	4	9	13	17	22	25	24	20	14	8.5	3
°F	35	39	48	55	63	72	77	75	69	57	47	37
Naples												
°C	9	9	11	14	18	22	25	25	22	18	14.5	10
°F	48	48	52	57	64	72	77	77	72	64	58	50
Palermo												
°C	10	10	13	16	19	23	25	25	23	19	16	13
°F	50	50	55	61	66	73	77	77	73	66	61	55
Rome												
°C	7	8	11.5	14	18	23	26	25.5	22	18	13	9
°F	45	46	53	57	64	73	79	78	72	64	55	48
Trieste												
°C	5	5	9	13	17	21	24	23	20	15	11	6
°F	41	41	48	55	63	70	75	73	69	59	52	43
Venice												
°C	4	4	8	13	17	21	24	23	20	15	10.5	5
°F	39	39	46	55	63	70	75	73	69	59	51	41

40

things not to miss

It's not possible to see everything that Italy has to offer in one trip – and we don't suggest you try. What follows is a selective taste, in no particular order, of the country's highlights: outstanding buildings and ancient sites, spectacular natural wonders, great food and colourful festivals. They're arranged in five colour-coded categories, which you can browse through to find the very best things to see and experience. All entries have a page reference to take you straight into the guide, where you can find out more.

01 Vatican Museums, Rome Page **793** • Put simply, this is the largest and richest collection of art and culture in the world. You'd be mad to miss it.

02 **Mantua** Page **209** • The Mantegna frescoes of Mantua's Palazzo Ducale, and the works of Guilio Romano in its Palazzo Te, make a visit to this ancient and alluring Lombard city hard to resist.

03 **Urbino** Page **691** • This so-called "ideal city" and art capital, created by Federico da Montefeltro, the ultimate Renaissance man, attracts people from miles around.

04 **Cinque Terre** Page **156** • These five fishing villages are shoehorned picturesquely into one of the most rugged parts of Liguria's coastline, and linked by a highly scenic coastal walking path.

05 **Truffles** Page **73** • The speciality of the region around Alba in Piemonte is the astonishingly expensive white truffle, shaved onto pasta and washed down with the excellent local Barolo or Barbaresco wine. The town hosts a huge truffle fair every November.

06 **Gubbio** Page **642** • The best-looking of Umbria's medieval hill-towns, and without Assisi's crowds and commercialism.

07 **Elba** Page **563** • This easily accessible, mountainous Tuscan island offers great beaches and some fantastic hiking opportunities.

08 **Cappella degli Scrovegni, Padua** Page

374 • The chapel frescoes here, by Giotto, constitute one of the great works of European art.

I ACTIVITIES I CONSUME I EVENTS I NATURE I SIGHTS I

09 **Skiing** Page **53** • Whether you opt for the Alps or the Dolomites in the north, or the Abruzzo or Aspromonte mountains in the south, you're never far from somewhere decent to ski in Italy.

10 Matera Page **1015** • A truly unique city, sliced by a ravine containing thousands of *sassi* – cave dwellings gouged out of the rock that were inhabited till the 1950s.

11 Parco Nazionale d'Abruzzo Page **860** • Italy's third-largest national park, and probably its wildest, with marvellous walking and wildlife.

12 Sardinia's beaches Page **1103** • There are plenty of places to sun-worship in Italy, but Sardinia's ranks among one of the most memorable coastlines.

13 Lecce Page **984** • This exuberant city of Baroque architecture and opulent churches is one of the must-sees of the Italian south.

14 Città Alta, Bergamo Page **238** • Bergamo's medieval high town is an impossibly romantic spot to spend an evening.

15 Sicily's Greek ruins Page **1031** • The ancient theatres at Siracusa and Taormina are magnificent summer stages for Greek drama, while the temple complex at nearby Agrigento is one of the finest such sites outside Greece itself.

I ACTIVITIES I CONSUME I EVENTS I NATURE I SIGHTS I

16 The Last Supper, Milan Page **193** • Leonardo da Vinci's mural for the refectory wall of the Santa Maria delle Grazie is one of the world's most resonant images.

17 Palio, Siena Page **574** • Perhaps the most fanatically followed and most violent horserace in the world – an amazing spectacle and a true slice of Sienese life.

18 Mount Etna Page **1065** • It's an eerie climb up the blackened lunar landscape of this smoking volcano, which dominates the landscape of eastern Sicily.

19 **Paestum** Page **940** • The majestic Greek temples of this Campanian site are the backdrop for a fine stretch of sandy beach.

21 **Duomo, Milan** Page **183** • The world's largest and perhaps most attention-grabbing Gothic cathedral.

22 **Duomo, Florence** Page **507** • Florence's cathedral dome is one of the most instantly recognizable images in the world – and one of its most significant engineering feats.

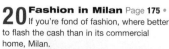

20 **Fashion in Milan** Page **175** • If you're fond of fashion, where better to flash the cash than in its commercial home, Milan.

24 **Ravenna's mosaics** Page **479** • Ravenna's Byzantine mosaics – in the churches Sant'Apollinare Nuovo and San Vitale – are a stunning testimony to the city's ranking as the capital of Europe fifteen hundred years ago.

23 **Genoa** Page **120** • An old port *par excellence*, Genoa's rabbit-warren of medieval streets, revitalized harbour and first-rate museums and churches make it one of Italy's most atmospheric cities.

25 Food in Emilia-Romagna
Page **444** • This region is known as Italy's gastronomic heart, home to Parma ham, Parmesan cheese, balsamic vinegar, great stuffed pasta dishes and underrated wines like Lambrusco, all on view at Bologna's marvellous indoor food market.

26 Basilica di San Francesco, Assisi Page **650**
• The burial place of St Francis and one of Italy's greatest church buildings, with frescoes by Giotto, Simone Martini and others.

27 Tuscan hill-towns Page **493**
• The campanile-spiked profile of a hill-town is what many people think of when they think of Italy. With Montepulciano, Montalcino and San Gimigniano, Tuscany in particular has some of the most beautiful, if sometimes also most touristy, examples of ancient hill-towns in the world.

28 Gran Paradiso National Park Page **109** • The first Italian
national park preserves an Alpine region of deep valleys and beautiful mountains that is home to ibex, chamois and golden eagles.

29 Pompeii and Herculaneum Pages **912** & **909**
• Probably the two best-preserved Roman sites in the country, destroyed and at the same time preserved by the eruption of Vesuvius in AD 79.

31 **Amalfi Coast** Page **932** • The views on the road that snakes along the Amalfi Coast, connecting the resorts of Positano, Amalfi and Ravello, can hardly be bettered anywhere in the world.

30 **Duomo, Orvieto** Page **680** • One of the country's finest – and best-sited – cathedrals, with a marvellous fresco cycle by Luca Signorelli.

32 **Museo Archeologico Nazionale, Naples** Page **899** • The finds from Pompeii and Herculaneum alone – including some erotic frescoes – make this superb museum worth a visit.

33 Carnival Page **367** • Venice's famous carnival is worth seeing for its costumes and crowds. But it's rather an exclusive affair, and events around the rest of the country – most notably in Verona, in the Veneto, in Ivrea in Piemonte and Viareggio, on the Tuscan coast – are more authentic and definitely more fun.

35 Cápri Page **919** • Stay the night if you can, when the day-trippers have departed, to make the most of the island, with its stunning scenery and clifftop walks.

34 Certosa di Pavia Page **205** • This Carthusian monastery is a fantastic construction, rising out of the rice fields near Pavia.

36 Centro Storico, Rome Page **759** • There's so much to see in Rome that aimlessly wandering the city's fantastic old centre can turn up a surprise at every turn – whether it's an ancient statue, a marvellous Baroque fountain or a bustling piazza.

37 **Basilica di San Marco, Venice** Page **327** • One of Europe's most exotic cathedrals, Venice's principal place of worship is a fabulous sight, with 4000 square metres of golden mosaics.

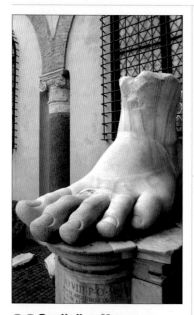

39 **Pizza** Page **882** • You can eat pizza all over Italy, but nowhere is it quite as good as in its home town of Naples, served sizzling hot straight from a wood-fired oven.

38 **Capitoline Museums, Rome** Page **758** • Separated by Michelangelo's elegant Campidoglio piazza, these make up the impressive home of some of Rome's finest ancient sculpture and paintings.

40 **The Uffizi, Florence** Page **514** • Italy's greatest collection of art, and – in a city not exactly short on things to see – perhaps the most essential attraction of them all.

Basics

Basics

Getting there

The easiest way to get to Italy from the UK and Ireland is to fly. The majority of flights go to Milan and Rome, with Bologna, Pisa, Turin and Venice in the second tier, as well as a number of regional cities – Pescara, Perugia, Rimini and several destinations in Sicily and Sardinia – that are increasingly served by low-cost carriers; there are also frequent onward flight connections to these and any number of other centres. From the US and Canada there are direct flights to Milan and Rome, although you could consider flying via London and picking up a cheap onward flight from there. There are no direct flights to Italy from Australia or New Zealand, but plenty of airlines fly to Milan and Rome via Asian or European cities.

Flights from the UK and Ireland

Of the scheduled **airlines** flying the Italian routes, British Airways (BA) and Alitalia regularly serve Turin, Milan, Rome, Bologna, Pisa, Verona, Venice, Naples and Catania. BA also fly from Manchester, Birmingham and Bristol to Milan. Aer Lingus has daily direct flights from Dublin to Rome and Milan, and Alitalia covers the same route three to five times a week depending on the season. It is possible to find deals **from Ireland** if you book early, but prices are usually significantly higher and unless you're in a hurry it can sometimes make more sense to pick up an inexpensive flight to London or Birmingham and get a connecting flight from there. Ryanair, Aer Lingus, British Midland (BMI) and British European operate regular daily flights from Dublin to London. Alternatively you could fly direct from Ireland to Brussels with Ryanair: they operate a cheap service from Brussels to Pisa, Venice and Rome.

Of the **low-cost carriers**, easyJet fly from London to Milan, Rome, Turin, Pisa, Rimini, Naples, Calgiari, Olbia and Palermo; Bristol to Rome, Venice and Pisa, East Midlands to Rome and Venice; and Newcastle to Rome. Ryanair fly London to Bologna, Bari, Bríndisi, Rome, Perugia, Palermo, Turin and Trieste; Dublin to Bologna (Forlì), Venice, Trápani, Rome, Alghero, Pisa and Milan; East Midlands to Rome, Rimini, Pisa, Alghero and Milan; Liverpool to Alghero; and Glasgow to Rome and Milan.

Prices depend on how far in advance you book and the popularity of the destination, although season is also a factor: a ticket to anywhere between June and August, when the weather is best, will cost more than in the depths of winter (excluding Christmas and New Year). Note also that it is generally more expensive to fly at weekends. As always, the cheapest scheduled tickets come with certain restrictions: any changes incur additional fees, and tickets are rarely valid for longer than a month. Book far enough in advance with one of the low-cost airlines and you can pick up a ticket for under £100 return plus taxes to somewhere like Rome, even in summer; book anything less than three weeks in advance and this could triple in price. Scheduled airline fares, booked within a month of travel, will cost cost around £120–160 out of season, and £250–300 in summer.

Flights from the US and Canada

Alitalia fly the widest choice of direct **routes** between the USA and Italy, with daily flights from New York, Miami, Chicago and Boston and Miami to Rome and Milan. Delta fly from New York to Rome and Milan direct, and from Chicago and LA with stopovers in New York. American Airlines fly direct from Chicago and LA to Milan. In addition, many European carriers fly to Italy (via their capitals) from all major US and Canadian cities – for example British Airways (via London), Lufthansa (via Frankfurt), KLM (via Amsterdam), and so on.

Fly less – stay longer! Travel and climate change

Climate change is a serious threat to the ecosystems that humans rely on, and air travel is among the fastest-growing contributors to the problem. Rough Guides regard travel, overall, as a global benefit, and feel strongly that the advantages to developing economies are important, as is the opportunity of greater contact and awareness among peoples. But we all have a responsibility to limit our personal impact on global warming, and that means giving thought to how often we fly, and what we can do to redress the harm that our trips create.

Flying and climate change

Pretty much every form of motorized travel generates CO_2 – the main cause of human-induced climate change – but planes also generate climate-warming contrails and cirrus clouds and emit oxides of nitrogen, which create ozone (another greenhouse gas) at flight levels. Furthermore, flying simply allows us to travel much further than we otherwise would do. The figures are frightening: one person taking a return flight between Europe and California produces the equivalent impact of 2.5 tonnes of CO_2 – similar to the yearly output of the average UK car.

Fuel-cell and other less harmful types of plane may emerge eventually. But until then, there are really just two options for concerned travellers: to reduce the amount we travel by air (take fewer trips – stay for longer!), and to make the trips we do take "climate neutral" via a carbon offset scheme.

Carbon offset schemes

Offset schemes run by ⓦwww.climatecare.org, ⓦwww.carbonneutral.com and others allow you to make up for some or all of the greenhouse gases that you are responsible for releasing. To do this, they provide "carbon calculators" for working out the global-warming contribution of a specific flight (or even your entire existence), and then let you contribute an appropriate amount of money to fund offsetting measures. These include rainforest reforestation and initiatives to reduce future energy demand – often run in conjunction with sustainable development schemes.

Rough Guides, together with Lonely Planet and other concerned partners in the travel industry, are supporting a **carbon offset scheme** run by climatecare.org. Please take the time to view our website and see how you can help to make your trip climate neutral.

ⓦwww.roughguides.com/climatechange

The **direct scheduled fares** charged by each airline don't vary as much as you might think, and you'll more often than not be basing your choice around things like flight timings, routes and gateway cities, ticket restrictions, and even the airline's reputation for comfort and service. The cheapest **round-trip fares** to Rome or Milan, travelling midweek in low season, start at around $550 from New York or Boston, rising to about $750 in spring and fall and over $1000 during the summer. Add another $100–200 for flights from LA, Miami and Chicago. Note that these prices do not include taxes.

Air Canada and Alitalia have **direct** flights from Toronto to Milan and Rome for a low-season fare of Can$650 midweek, increasing to around Can$1000 in high season without taxes.

Flights from Australia and New Zealand

Round-trip fares to Rome and Milan from the main cities in Australia go for A$1500–1850 in low season, and around A$2000 in high season. You are likely to get most flexibility by travelling with Alitalia, Malaysian, Thai, British Airways or Qantas, which offer a range of **discounted** Italian tour packages and air passes, although you can sometimes find cheaper offers with Garuda and Sri Lanka Airlines. There are no direct flights to

Italy from Australia. Round-trip fares to Rome from New Zealand cost from NZ$3000 depending on the season. Of the national carriers, Air New Zealand flies in conjunction with KLM and Alitalia, with stops in Japan and Amsterdam, to Rome and Milan; Alitalia with other carriers (from Auckland via Sydney and Bangkok/Singapore to Rome or Milan); British Airways to Rome from Auckland via Singapore/Bangkok or LA; Qantas to Rome from Auckland, Christchurch or Wellington via Sydney or Melbourne; JAL to Rome from Auckland (with inclusive overnight stop in Tokyo/Osaka); Malaysian and Thai to Rome from Auckland via Kuala Lumpur and Bangkok respectively.

Trains

Travelling **by train** to Italy from the UK won't save much money, but it can be an enjoyable and leisurely (and environmentally friendly) way of getting to the country, and you can stop off in other parts of Europe on the way. As you'd expect, the choice of routes and fares is hugely complex, but most trains pass through Paris and head down through France towards Milan. A return ticket from London to Milan (14hr), using **Eurostar** and then travelling by train from Paris, costs around £100, if you buy the very cheapest, non-refundable tickets at least two weeks in advance; the regular fare is around £160 return, more if you want to travel overnight by sleeper. For Rome you can expect to pay £120–180 (more if you travel on the Palatino sleeper from Paris to Rome), and the journey takes around 22 hours.

Advance booking is essential on these services (and can often save you quite a lot of money); there are also discounts (for under-26s) and in general special offers are legion. Using slower trains won't cut the cost very significantly and neither will the cross-Channel ferry route, which is now barely used and accordingly badly timetabled. Take into account also that if you travel via Paris on Eurostar you will have to change stations, which means lugging your bags on the metro from the Gare du Nord to the Gare de Lyon – although you could always take a taxi.

Details on all international **rail tickets and passes** are best obtained by calling personally at major train stations or by contacting the agents listed below. Don't expect much help from travel agents on planning routes, however, or indeed the Italian State Railways office to answer the phone. A good place to start looking is the excellent European rail website, ⓦwww.seat61.com. Rail passes include the **Interrail** and **Eurail** which offer a month's unlimited rail travel throughout Europe, but must be bought before leaving home. See "Getting Around" for details of all rail passes available, including those for use solely on the Italian rail network.

Rail contacts

Eurostar UK ☏ 0870/518 6186, ⓦwww.eurostar .com.
European Rail UK ☏ 020/7387 0444, ⓦwww .europeanrail.com.
International Rail ☏ 0870/084 1414, ⓦwww .international-rail.com.
Rail Europe ☏ 0870/837 1371, ⓦwww .raileurope.co.uk.
Trainseurope ☏ 0900/195 0101, ⓦwww .trainseurope.co.uk.
CIT Rail ⓦwww.fs-on-line.com.
Europrail International Canada ☏ 1-888/667-9734, ⓦwww.europrail.net.
Eurail ⓦwww.eurrail.com.
Italia Rail US 1-888-538-RAIL (7245), ⓦwww .italiarail.com.
Rail Europe US ☏ 1-877/257-2887, Canada ☏ 1-800/361-RAIL, ⓦwww.raileurope.com/us.
Rail Plus Australia ☏ 1300/555 003 or 03/9642 8644, ⓔ info@railplus.com.au.

Buses

It's difficult to see why anyone would want to travel to Italy by **bus,** unless they had a phobia of flying – and of trains. National Express Eurolines (☏0870/580 8080, ⓦwww.nationalexpress.com/eurolines) do, however, have occasional bargain offers, and regular tickets are in any case cheap – £69 to Milan or Rome if boo ked a week in advance, £98 for a fully refundable and flexible ticket. The Milan service departs four times a week and takes around 20 hours; Rome adds a gruelling 10 hours to the trip.

Airlines, online booking agents and operators

Online booking

ⓦwww.expedia.co.uk (UK)
ⓦwww.expedia.com (US)

ⓦwww.expedia.ca (Canada)
ⓦwww.lastminute.com (UK)
ⓦwww.opodo.co.uk (UK)
ⓦwww.orbitz.com (US)
ⓦwww.travelocity.co.uk (UK), ⓦwww
.travelocity.com (US), ⓦwww.travelocity
.ca (Canada), ⓦwww.zuji.com.au (Australia),
ⓦwww.zuji.co.nz (New Zealand)

Airlines

Aer Lingus Republic of Ireland ☎0818/365 000,
ⓦwww.aerlingus.ie.
Air Canada ☎1-888/247-2262, UK ☎0871/220
1111, Republic of Ireland ☎01/679 3958,
Australia ☎1300/655 767, New Zealand
☎0508/747 767; ⓦwww.aircanada.com.
Air New Zealand Australia ☎13 24 76, New
Zealand ☎0800/737 000; ⓦwww.airnz.co.nz.
Alitalia US ☎1-800/223-5730, Canada
☎1-800/361-8336, UK ☎0870/544 8259, Republic
of Ireland ☎01/677 5171, New Zealand ☎09/308
3357; South Africa ☎11/721 4500; ⓦwww.alitalia
.com.
American Airlines ☎1-800/433-7300, UK
☎0845/7789 789, Republic of Ireland ☎01/602
0550, Australia ☎1300/650 747, New Zealand
☎0800/887 997; ⓦwww.aa.com.

BMI UK ☎0870/607 0555 or ☎0870/607 0222,
Ireland ☎01/407 3036, US ☎1-800/788-0555;
ⓦwww.flybmi.com.
bmibaby UK ☎0871/224 0224, Republic of Ireland
☎1890/340 122; ⓦwww.bmibaby.com.
British Airways UK ☎0870/850 9850, Republic
of Ireland ☎1890/626 747, US & Canada
☎1-800/AIRWAYS, Australia ☎1300/767 177,
New Zealand ☎09/966 9777; ⓦwww.ba.com.
Delta US and Canada ☎1-800/221-1212, UK
☎0845/600 0950, Republic of Ireland ☎1850/882
031 or 01/407 3165, Australia ☎1300/302 849,
New Zealand ☎09/379 3370; ⓦwww.delta.com.
easyJet UK ☎0905/821 0905, Republic of Ireland
☎0870/600 0000; ⓦwww.easyjet.com.
Garuda Indonesia US ☎1-212/279-0756, UK
☎020/7467 8600, Australia ☎1300/365 330
or 02/9334 9944, New Zealand ☎09/366 1862;
ⓦwww.garuda-indonesia.com.
JAL (Japan Air Lines) US and Canada
☎1-800/525-3663, UK ☎0845/774 7700, Ireland
☎01/408 3757, Australia ☎02/9272 1111, New
Zealand ☎09/379 9906, South Africa ☎11/214
2560; ⓦwww.jal.com or ⓦwww.japanair.com.
KLM (Royal Dutch Airlines) See Northwest/
KLM. US and Canada ☎1-800/225-2525, UK
☎0870/507 4074, Republic of Ireland ☎1850/747
400, Australia ☎1300/392 192, New Zealand
☎09/921 6040, South Africa ☎11/961 6727;
ⓦwww.klm.com.
Lufthansa US ☎1-800/3995-838, Canada
☎1-800/563-5954, UK ☎0870/837 7747, Republic
of Ireland ☎01/844 5544, Australia ☎1300/655
727, New Zealand ☎0800/945 220, South Africa
☎0861/842 538; ⓦwww.lufthansa.com.
Malaysia Airlines US ☎1-800/5529-264, UK
☎0870/607 9090, Republic of Ireland ☎01/6761
561, Australia ☎.13 26 27, New Zealand
☎0800/777 747, South Africa ☎11/880 9614,
ⓦwww.malaysia-airlines.com.
Qantas Airways US and Canada ☎1-800/227-
4500, UK ☎0845/774 7767, Republic of Ireland
☎01/407 3278, Australia ☎13 13 13, New Zealand
☎0800/808 767 or 09/357 8900, South Africa
☎11/441 8550; ⓦwww.qantas.com.
Ryanair UK ☎0871/246 0000, Republic of Ireland
☎0818/303 030; ⓦwww.ryanair.com.
SriLankan Airlines US ☎1-877/915-2652,
Canada ☎1-416/227-9000, UK ☎020/8538
2001, Ireland ☎1/241 8000, Australia ☎02/9244
2234, New Zealand ☎09/308 3353, South Africa
☎11/289 8000; ⓦwww.srilankan.aero.
Thai Airways US ☎1-212/949-8424, UK
☎0870/606 0911, Australia ☎1300/651 960, New
Zealand ☎09/377 3886, South Africa ☎11/455
1018; ⓦwww.thaiair.com.

Packages and organized tour operators

Italy stands somewhat apart from other European package destinations: it's not especially cheap and has avoided the big hotel build-ups that have blighted parts of Spain and Greece. And it's as much a venue for specialist-interest and touring holidays as the standard sun-sand-sea packages. Having said that, there's no shortage of **travel-plus-accommodation** deals on the market, and if you're keen to stay in one (or two) places, they can work out to be very good value. Many companies offer travel at rates as competitive as you could find on your own, and any travel agent can fill you in on all the latest offers. Obviously it's cheapest to travel out of season, something we'd recommend anyway, as resorts and sights are much less crowded and the weather, in the south at least, is often still warm enough for swimming well into October. Restored **villas** and farmhouses are a popular option but are no bargain. A cheaper alternative is agriturismo accommodation (see p.42). An increasing number of operators organize **specialist holidays** to Italy – see below. These set up walking tours, art and archeology holidays, Italian food and wine jaunts, short breaks to coincide with opera festivals or even football matches. There's also a plethora of operators selling **short-break deals** to Italian cities. Finally, if you want to rent a car in Italy, it's well worth checking with tour operators (and flight agents) before you leave, as some **fly-drive** deals work out very cheaply.

Specialist tours

Abercromie and Kent ☏ +44 (0)845/0700 600, ⓦ www.abercromiekent.co.uk. Luxury cultural holidays.
Alternative Travel Group ☏ +44 (0)1865/315 678, ⓦ www. atg-oxford.co.uk. Walking and cycling holidays.
Martin Randall Travel ☏ +44 (0)20/8742 3355, ⓦ www.martinrandall.com. Cultural tours focusing on art, architecture, music, archeology, gastronomy and history.

Getting around

Italy is a big country with huge regional differences and unless you opt for a one-base holiday you will probably find yourself travelling around a fair bit. Naturally, you'll have most flexibility with your own transport, allowing you to journey at your own pace and to out of the way places. Roads are good in most of the country with excellent motorway links between cities, although these often come with heavy traffic and tolls. Off the main routes, most roads are quiet and well maintained, making cycling a very pleasant – and very popular – means of getting around.

In terms of **public transport**, the easiest way of travelling around Italy is by **train**. The Italian train system is one of the least expensive in Europe, reasonably comprehensive, and, in the north of the country at least, pretty efficient. It's also far preferable over long distances to the fragmented, localized and sometimes grindingly slow **bus** service. Local buses, though, can be very efficient, and where it's actually a better idea to take a bus, we've made this clear in the text.

Internal flights are coming down in price and there are some good deals to be had on flights to the islands. **Ferries** go to all the Italian islands, and also ply routes to Greece, Albania, Croatia, Malta, Yugoslavia, Corsica and Tunisia.

We've detailed train, bus and ferry frequencies in the "Travel details" sections at the end of each chapter of the Guide; note that these refer to regular working-day schedules (Monday to Saturday); services

Timetable reading

On timetables — and parking signs too — *Lavorativo* or *feriale* is the word for the Monday to Saturday service, represented by two crossed hammers; and *festivo* means that a train runs only on Sundays and holidays, symbolized by a Christian cross. Some other common terms on timetables are:

escluso sabato – not including Saturdays
si effettua fino all'... – running until
si effettua dal... – starting from
giornalmente – daily
prenotazione obbligatoria – reservation obligatory
estivo – summer
invernale – winter

can be much reduced or even non-existent on Sundays.

By train

Italian State Railways (Ferrovie dello Stato, or FS) operates a comprehensive network across the country with numerous types of trains. The **Eurostar Italia** (ES) runs between major cities, slightly faster and usually with newer rolling stock than the **Intercity** (IC) options. **Eurocity** (EC) and **Euronight** (EN) trains connect the major Italian cities with centres such as Paris, Vienna, Hamburg and Barcelona. Milan and Turin and Naples and Rome have recently been linked by a new high-speed service, the **Eurostar Alta Velocità**, which will eventually connect the north with the south of the country in record time. Reservations are usually required before you board the train for all of these services.

Diretto and **Interregionale** trains are the common-or-garden long-distance expresses, calling only at larger stations. Although reservations are not required for these trains, it's worth **reserving** seats if you're making a long journey, especially in summer, when they can get very crowded. Reservations can be made at any major train station or travel agent in Italy or via Italian State Railways agents in the UK, US or Australia (see p.29).

Lastly, there are the **Regionale** services, which stop at every place with a population higher than zero.

For **information** on all the above trains call ☏89.20.21, or visit the FS website at ⒲www.trenitalia.com.

In addition to the routes operated by FS, there are a number of **privately run** lines,

using separate stations though charging similar fares. Where they're worth using, these are detailed in the text.

Timetables

Timings and route information for the FS network are posted up at train stations, and we give a rough idea of frequencies and journey times in the "Travel details" sections at the end of each chapter. If you're travelling extensively it would be worth investing in a copy of the twice-yearly *In Treno In Tutt'Italia* timetable (€4.50), which covers the main routes and is sold at train-station newspaper stands.

Fares

Fares are inexpensive; they are calculated by the kilometre and easy to work out for each journey. The timetables give the prices per kilometre but as a rough guide, a second-class one-way fare for the four-hour trip from Rome to Milan currently costs about €47 by Eurostar. **Sleepers** (*cuccetta*) are available on many long-distance services, and prices vary according to the length of

Stamp it

All stations have yellow validating machines in which passengers must stamp their ticket before embarking on their journey. Look out for them as you come on to the platform: if you fail to **validate your ticket** you'll be given a hefty on-the-spot fine.

journey and whether or not you're sharing. **Children** aged 4–12 pay half price; under 4s (not occupying a seat) travel free. Return tickets are valid within two months of the outward journey, but as two one-way tickets cost the same it's hardly worth bothering.

Rail passes and discount cards

If you're travelling exclusively by train in Italy you might consider buying a **TrenItalia pass**, though you'd have to cover a lot of ground to make the price worth it and there are supplements for all the faster trains.

A rail pass is probably more worth considering if you plan to include Italy as part of a wider tour of Europe. The Europe-wide **InterRail** and **Eurail** passes give unlimited travel on the FS network, though again you'll be liable for supplements (€12 per journey on the faster trains).

If you're planning several trips to Italy or to use train travel for an extended period you might be interested in the various **discount cards** that are available. A **Verde Railplus** discount card is valid for one year for those under 26 and costs €40. It allows 10 percent off first- and second-class travel or a little more on some international routes. Those who are 60 and over are eligible for a **Carta Argento**, which costs €30 for a year and entitles the holder to 15 percent discount on first- and second-class tickets. A **Carta Blu** is for disabled passengers; it costs €5 and allows the holder and a companion to travel for the price of one full ticket. All the cards are available with proof of eligibility from ticket offices and stations.

TrenItalia pass

TrenItalia passes come in two forms – one for EU residents and one for non-residents – and must be bought before arriving in Italy. They can be bought for first- or second-class travel and are valid from four to ten days in a two-month period. Children from 4 to 12 years old are eligible for a fifty percent discount, youth (under-26) and group tickets are available. A second class four-day ticket costs £114 (US$189 for non-residents), a ten-day pass £191 (US$359). It also entitles the holder to discounts on some international ferries.

InterRail pass

InterRail passes (@ www.interrail.net) are only available to European residents, and you will be asked to provide proof of residency before being allowed to purchase one. They come in over-26 and (cheaper) under-26 versions, and cover 26 European countries (plus Turkey and Morocco) grouped together in zones:

A   Republic of Ireland/Britain
B   Norway, Sweden, Finland
C   Germany, Austria, Switzerland, Denmark
D   Czech & Slovak Republics, Poland, Hungary, Croatia
E   France, Belgium, Netherlands, Luxembourg
F   Spain, Portugal, Morocco
G   Italy, Greece, Turkey, Slovenia plus some ferry services between Italy and Greece
H   Bulgaria, Romania, Yugoslavia, Macedonia

The passes are available for 16 days for one zone only (€195, €286 over-26), 22 days for two zones (€275, €396 over-26), or one month for a global pass covering all zones (€385, €546 over-26).

InterRail passes do not include travel between Britain and the continent, although InterRail passholders are eligible for discounts on rail travel in Britain and Northern Ireland and cross-Channel ferries and free travel on the Brindisi–Patras ferry between Italy and Greece. The InterRail Pass also gives a discount on the London–Paris Eurostar service.

Eurail passes

A **Eurail Pass** is not likely to pay for itself if you're planning to stick to Italy. The pass, which must be purchased before arrival in Europe, allows unlimited free first-class train travel in Italy and sixteen other countries and is available in increments of 15 days, 21 days, 1 month, 2 months and 3 months. There are numerous small-group, youth and saver versions with details and prices given on @ www.raileurope.com. The passes can be purchased from the agents listed on p.29 under "Rail contacts".

By bus

Trains don't go everywhere and sooner or later you'll probably have to use **regional buses** (*autobus*). Nearly all places are connected by some kind of bus service, but in out-of-the-way towns and villages schedules can be sketchy and are drastically reduced – sometimes non-existent – at weekends, especially on Sundays. Bear in mind also that in rural areas schedules are often designed with the working and/or school day in mind – meaning a frighteningly early start if you want to catch that day's one bus out of town, and occasionally a complete absence of services during school holidays.

There's no national **bus company,** though a few regional ones do operate beyond their own immediate area. **Bus terminals** are often conveniently located next to the train station; wherever possible we've detailed their whereabouts in the text, but if you're not sure ask for directions to the *autostazione*. In smaller towns and villages, most buses pull in at the central piazza. **Timetables** are worth picking up from the local company's office, bus stations or on the bus. Buy **tickets** immediately before you travel from the bus station ticket office, or on the bus itself; on longer hauls you can try to buy them in advance direct from the bus company, but seat reservations are not normally possible. If you want to get off, ask *posso scendere?*; "the next stop" is *la prossima fermata*.

City buses are always cheap, usually costing a flat fare of around €1. **Tickets** are available from a variety of sources, commonly newsagents and tobacconists, but also from anywhere displaying a sticker saying tickets or *biglietti* including many campsite shops and hotel front desks. Once on board, you must register your ticket in the machine at the back of the bus. The whole system is based on trust, though in most cities checks for fare-dodging are regularly made, and hefty spot-fines are levied against offenders.

Pedestrians

Don't assume that as a **pedestrian** you're safe; even on crossings with traffic lights you can be subjected to some close calls. Look both ways before crossing the road even when there's a green light for you to go, and bear in mind that cars do not automatically stop at pedestrian crossings.

A useful site is ⓦwww.busstation.net/main/busita.htm, which has links to websites of hundreds of Italian bus companies.

By car

Travelling **by car** in Italy is relatively painless, though cities and their ring roads can be hard work. The roads are good, the *autostrada* (motorway) network very comprehensive, and the notorious Italian drivers rather less erratic than their reputation suggests. The best plan is to avoid driving in cities as much as possible; the congestion, proliferation of complex one-way systems and confusing signage can make it a nightmare.

Bear in mind that the **traffic** can be heavy on main roads (particularly over public holiday weekends and the first and last weekends of August) and appalling in city centres. Rush hour during the week usually runs from 7.30am to 9am and from 5pm to 9pm when roads in and around the major cities can be gridlocked.

Although Italians are by no means the world's worst drivers they don't win any **safety** prizes either. The secret is to make it very clear what you're going to do – and then do it. A particular danger for unaccustomed drivers is the large number of scooters that can appear suddenly from the blind spot or dash across junctions and red lights with alarming recklessness.

Fuel is pretty pricey in Italy – €1.30 per litre at the time of writing. Most petrol stations give you the choice of self-service (*Fai da te*) or, for a few centimes more per litre, someone will fill the tank and usually wipe down the windscreen while they're at it. Petrol stations often have the same working hours as shops, which means they'll be closed for a couple of hours at noon, shut up shop at around 7pm and are likely to be closed on Sundays. Outside these times many have a self-service facility payable into a machine between the pumps by bank note or, more rarely, credit card; these are often not well advertised so you might need to go on to the forecourt to check.

Rules of the road

Rules of the road are straightforward: drive on the right; at junctions, where there's any ambiguity, give precedence to vehicles coming from the right; observe the speed limits – 50kph in built-up areas, 110kph on dual carriage-ways and 130kph on motorways (for camper vans, these limits are 50kph, 80kph and 100kph respectively); and don't drink and drive. Drivers need to have their dipped headlights on while using any road outside a built-up.area.

As regards **documentation**, if you're bringing your own car, as well as current insurance, you need a valid driving licence and an international driving permit if you're a non-EU licence holder. If you hold a UK pre-1991 driving licence you'll need an international driving permit or to update your licence to a photocard version. It's compulsory to carry your car documents and passport while you're driving, and you can be fined on the spot if you cannot present them when stopped by the police – not an uncommon occurrence. It's also obligatory to carry a warning triangle and a fluorescent jacket in case of breakdown. For more information consult ⓦwww.theaa.com /allaboutcars/overseas/europeadvice.html.

Motorway driving

Most **motorways** are **toll-roads**. Take a ticket as you come on and pay on exit; in automatic booths the amount due is flashed up on a screen in front of you. Paying by cash is the most straightforward option but to pay by credit card follow the "*Viacard*" sign; queues are usually much shorter in the credit card lanes. Rates aren't especially high but they can mount up on a long journey. Since other roads can be frustratingly slow, tolls are well worth it over long distances but be prepared for queues at exits at peak times.

Parking

Parking can be a problem. Don't be surprised to see cars parked just about anywhere, notably on pavements, seemingly working tram lines and bus stops – it would be unwise to follow suit. Parking attendants are especially active in tourist areas and if you get fed up with driving around and settle for a space in a *zona di rimozione* (tow-away zone), don't expect your car to be there when you get back.

Most towns and villages have pay-and-display areas just outside the centre, but they can get very full during high season. An increasing number of towns operate a colour-coded parking scheme: **blue-zone** parking spaces (delineated by a blue line) usually have a maximum stay of one or two hours; they cost around €0.70–1.50 per hour (pay at meters, to attendants wearing authorizing badges or buy scratch-cards from local tobacconists) but are sometimes free after 8pm and on Sundays. Much coveted **white-zone** spaces (white lines) are free; **yellow-zone** areas (yellow lines) are reserved for residents. Note that walled towns that exclude cars often allow tourists to drive into the city to drop off baggage at a hotel.

Car parks, usually small, enclosed garages, are universally expensive, costing up to €20 a day in big cities; it's not unknown for hotels to state that they have parking and then direct you to the nearest paying garage. In smaller towns, it's handy to have a mini clock-like dial which you set and display in the windscreen, to indicate when you parked and that you're still within the allowed limit: rental cars generally come equipped with these, and some tourist offices have them too. Parking at night is easier than during the day, but make sure you're not parked in a street that turns into a market in the morning or on the one day of the week when it's cleaned in the small hours, otherwise you're likely to be towed.

Never leave anything visible in the car when you're not using it, including the radio. Certain economically depressed cities have appalling reputations for theft – in Naples, some rental agencies won't insure a car left anywhere except in a locked garage. If you're taking your own vehicle, consider installing a detachable car-radio, and depress your aerial and tuck in your wing mirrors when you park. Most cities and ports have **garages** where you can leave your car and which are a safer option.

Breakdown

If you **break down**, dial ⓣ116 and tell the operator where you are, the type of car you're in, and your registration number: the nearest office of the Automobile Club d'Italia (ACI) will send someone out to fix your car – however, it's not a free service and can work out very expensive if you need a tow. For this reason you might consider arranging cover with a motoring organization in your home country before you leave. Any ACI office in Italy can tell you where to get **spare parts** for your particular car.

Car rental

Car rental in Italy is pricey, especially in high season, at around €250–300 per week for a small hatchback, with unlimited mileage, if booked in advance. The major chains have offices in all the larger cities and at airports, train stations, and so on: addresses are detailed in the "Listings" sections at the end of city accounts throughout the Guide. Local firms can be less expensive and often have an office at the airport, but generally the best deals are to be had by arranging things in advance, through one of the agents listed below or with specialist tour operators when you book your flight or holiday. You need to be over 21 to rent a car in Italy and will need a credit card to act as a deposit when picking up your vehicle.

Car rental agencies

Avis UK ☎ 0870/606 0100, ⓦ www.avis.co.uk; Republic of Ireland ☎ 021/428 1111, ⓦ www.avis.ie; US ☎ 1-800/230-4898, Canada ☎ 1-800/272-5871, ⓦ www.avis.com; South Africa ☎ 11/923 3518, ⓦ www.avis.co.za; Australia ☎ 13 63 33, ⓦ www.avis.com.au; NZ ☎ 09/526 2847, ⓦ www.avis.co.nz.
Budget UK ☎ 0800/181 181, ⓦ www.budget.co.uk; Republic of Ireland ☎ 09/0662 7711, ⓦ www.budget.ie; US ☎ 1-800/527-0700, ⓦ www.budget.com; Australia ☎ 1300/362 848, ⓦ www.budget.com.au; NZ ☎ 09/976 2222, ⓦ www.budget.co.nz.
Europcar UK ☎ 0870/607 5000, Republic of Ireland ☎ 01/614 2800, US & Canada ☎ 1-877/940 6900, Australia ☎ 1300/131 390, ⓦ www.europcar.com; South Africa ☎ 11/574 4457, ⓦ www.europcar.co.za.
Hertz UK ☎ 0870/848 8848, ⓦ www.hertz.co.uk; Republic of Ireland ☎ 01/676 7476, ⓦ www.hertz.ie; US ☎ 1-800/654-3131, Canada ☎ 1-800/263-0600, ⓦ www.hertz.com; South Africa ☎ 21/935 4800, ⓦ www.hertz.co.za; Australia ☎ 13 30 39, ⓦ www.hertz.com.au; NZ ☎ 0800/654 321, ⓦ www.hertz.co.nz.
National UK ☎ 0870/536 5365, ⓦ www.nationalcar.co.uk; US ☎ 1-800/962-7070, ⓦ www.nationalcar.com; South Africa ☎ 011/570 1900, ⓦ www.national.co.za; Australia ☎ 13 10 45, ⓦ www.nationalcar.com.au; NZ ☎ 0800/800 115, ⓦ www.nationalcar.co.nz.
Thrifty UK ☎ 01494/751 600, ⓦ www.thrifty.co.uk; Republic of Ireland ☎ 1800/515 800, ⓦ www.thrifty.ie; US ☎ 1-800/847-4389, ⓦ www.thrifty.com; South Africa ☎ 0861/002 111, ⓦ www.thrifty.co.za; Australia ☎ 1300/367 227, ⓦ www.thrifty.com.au; NZ ☎ 09/309 0111, ⓦ www.thrifty.co.nz.

Campervan rental

Campervan or mobile home holidays are becoming increasingly popular in Italy and the rental market is opening up to meet the demand. To add to the obvious convenience of this type of holiday, facilities in campsites are usually dependable (see p.41), and more and more resorts have created free campervan parking areas (*sosta camper*). The following are just a selection of the companies offering new (or newish) quality vehicles for rent. Prices are usually around €1500 for a four-berth vehicle for a week in high season, with unlimited mileage.
Blu rent ☎ +39.0171.601.702, ⓦ www.blurent.com. Website available in English.
Comocaravan ☎ +39.031.521.215, ⓦ www.comocaravan.it.
DueDi ☎ +39.045.956.677, ⓦ www.duedicamper.it.
Maggiore ☎ +39.840.00.8840, ⓦ www.maggiorecamperrent.it.

By plane

In line with the rest of European airspace, internal air fares in Italy have been revolutionized in the last couple of years. Small companies have taken on the state airline and what used to be a form of business transport has become a good-value, convenient way of getting around the country.

Budget airlines open and close every season and there are often special deals being advertised; at the time of writing for example, Meridiana was offering Rome–Palermo for €20. Return fares are significantly more expensive with a Milan–Naples flight on Alitalia costing around €85 without airport taxes. It pays to shop around and, as always, book as far in advance as you can.

Airlines

Alitalia ☎ +39.199.20.70.80, ⓦ www.alitilia.it.

Meridiana ☎ 199.111.333 or +39.078.952.682, 🅦 www.meridiana.it.

Myair ☎ +39.899.5000.60, 🅦 www.myair.com

By ferry and hydrofoil

Italy has a well-developed network of **ferries** and **hydrofoils** operated by a number of different private companies. Large car ferries connect the major islands of Sardinia and Sicily with the mainland ports of Genoa, Livorno, La Spezia, Civitavecchia, Fiumicino and Naples, while the smaller island groupings – the Trémiti islands, the Bay of Naples islands, the Pontine Islands – are usually linked to a number of nearby mainland towns. The larger lakes in the north of the country are also well served with regular ferries in season, although they are drastically reduced in winter.

Fares are reasonable, and on some of the more popular services – to Sardinia, for example – you should book well in advance in summer, especially if you're taking a vehicle across. Remember, too, that sailings are cut outside the summer months, and some services stop altogether. You'll find a broad guide to journey times and frequencies in the "Travel details" section at the end of relevant chapters; for full up-to-date schedules and prices, check the Italian website 🅦 www.traghetti.com, which has links to all the main ferry companies, or contact one of the ferry agents below.

Agents for Italian ferries

SMS Travel ☎ +39.199.123.199, 🅦 www.siremar .it. Italian agents for Siremar and Tirrenia ferries.

Viamare Travel Limited ☎ 08704/106 040, 🅦 www.viamare.co.uk.

By bike

Cycling is a very popular sport and mode of transport in much of Italy. Italians in small towns and villages are welcoming to cyclists, and hotels and hostels will take your bike in overnight for safekeeping. On the islands, in the mountains, in major resorts and larger cities, it's usually possible to **rent** a bike, but in rural areas facilities for this are few and far between.

Serious cyclists might consider staying at one of a chain of hotels that cater specifically for cycling enthusiasts. Each hotel has a secure room for your bike, a maintenance workshop, overnight laundry facilities, suggested itineraries and group-tour possibilities, a doctor at hand and even dietary consultation. Contact ☎ +39/0541.660.410, 🅦 www.italybikehotels.it for further information and a list of hotels.

An alternative is to tour by **motorbike**, though again there are relatively few places to rent one. **Mopeds** and **scooters** are comparatively easy to find: everyone in Italy, from kids to grannies, rides one of these and although they're not really built for any kind of long-distance travel, for shooting around towns and islands they're ideal; we've detailed outlets in the chapters. Crash helmets are compulsory, though in the south at least it's a law that seems to be largely ignored.

Accommodation

Accommodation in Italy is fairly reliable and, while never especially cheap, is at least strictly regulated: hotels are star-rated and are required to post their prices clearly in each room. Most tourist offices have details of hotel rates in their town or region, and you can expect them to be broadly accurate.

Whatever happens, establish the full price of your room before you accept it. In popular resorts and the major cities booking ahead is advisable, particularly during July or August, while for Venice, Rome and Florence it's pretty much essential to book ahead from

Accommodation price codes

Hotels in this guide have been categorized according to the **price codes** outlined below. They represent the cheapest rates for a double room in high season (July & August), although in places like Florence and Venice you can expect high season rates from March to November.

❶ Under €50. The cheapest kind of one-star hotels; most rooms will have shared facilities and may be quite bleak. Places in this category can be heavily booked owing to the fact that they're often used as cheap permanent accommodation. Credit cards are rarely accepted.

❷ €51–75. The standard one-star hotel, normally with a mixture of rooms with shared and private facilities, and in most cases comfortable enough for a short stay. In Venice, Florence and some other northern cities and resorts, you'll be extremely lucky to find one-star places at this price.

❸ €76–100. Mainly two-star hotels, most with private facilities. Rooms will sometimes have a TV and telephone.

❹ €101–125. In Venice and Florence there are one-stars in this category. Elsewhere, this price will get you a room in an attractive two-star, or even a three-star hotel, generally with private bath, telephone and TV.

❺ €126–150. This should involve a room with private bath, TV and telephone pretty much everywhere in Italy, and in the south of the country and more remote places, you could be looking at something fairly swanky.

❻ €151–200. Usually a good three-star or moderate four-star, with high standards and a range of facilities including a pool and formal restaurant.

❼ €201–250. These should be special hotels, either by virtue of their location or facilities. Again, in Venice and Florence, you'll be paying this sort of price for rooms that would fall into one of the lower categories elsewhere.

❽ €251–300. We have only recommended somewhere in this category if it is really special, if it enjoys a wonderful location, a superb site or building – perhaps an old convent or manor house – or if the service and food are just too good to miss.

❾ Over €300. The sky's-the-limit category, populated by a select few of the most celebrated hotels in Italy.

Easter until late September and over Christmas and New Year. You can do this relatively painlessly with hotel booking services online or with travel and booking agents (see p.41), but we've given contact details throughout the Guide in case you want to reserve direct. Make sure you get confirmation of the booking by fax, email or letter – it's far from uncommon to arrive and find all knowledge of your booking is denied. The phrases on pp.1193–1194 should help you get over the language barrier, though in many places you should be able to find someone who speaks at least some English.

Hotels

Hotels in Italy come tagged with a confusing variety of names, and, although the differences have become minimal of late, you will still find a variety of names used for what are basically private hotel facilities. A **locanda** is historically the most basic option, although these days it is often used by boutique hotels and the like to conjure up images of simple, traditional hospitality. **Pensione**, **albergo** or **hotel** are all commonly used. **Prices** vary greatly between the south and north of Italy, as well as between tourist hotspots and more rural areas. The official star system is based on facilities (TV in rooms, swimming pool, and so on) rather than character or comfort – or even price.

In very busy places it's not unusual to have to stay for a minimum of three nights, and many proprietors will add the price of **breakfast** to your bill whether you want it or not; try to ask for accommodation only – you can always eat more cheaply in a bar. Be warned, too, that in major seaside resorts you will often be forced to take **half or full board** self-catering kitchens that enable you to cut costs further. In a few cases too – notably Castroreale in Sicily and Montagnana in the Veneto – the hostels are beautifully located and in many ways preferable to any hotel.

Virtually all of the Italian hostels are members of the official International Youth Hostel Federation, and you'll need to be a member of the organization in order to use them – you can join through your home country's youth hostelling organization (see p.41) or often at the hostel on arrival. You need to reserve well ahead in the summer, most efficiently by using Hostelling International's **International Booking Network** which, for a small fee, enables you to book (including online) at hostels in selected Italian cities from your home country up to six months in advance. For more out-of-the-way hostels, you need to contact them direct at least fifteen days in advance, sending approximately a thirty percent deposit with your booking. We've listed most of the hostels in the Guide, and you can find detailed information about each one on the Ostelli Online website, ⓦ www.ostellionline.org.

In some cities, including Rome, it's also possible to stay in **student accommodation** vacated by Italian students for the summer,

in high season. Note that people travelling alone may sometimes have to pay for the price of a double room even when they only need a single, though it can also work the other way round – if all their **single rooms** are taken, a hotelier may well put you in a double room but only charge the single rate.

Check out ⓦ www.venere.it, to access the Web pages of those hotels that have them – you can also book rooms online. Another good website is ⓦ www.room-service.co.uk – a dedicated booking service for hotels in all categories across most of northern and central Italy.

Hostels

There are plenty of official **HI youth hostels** in Italy, charging around €15 per night for a dormitory bed. You can easily base a tour of the country around them, although for two people travelling together they don't always represent a massive saving on the cheapest double hotel room – especially if you take into account the bus fare you might have to fork out to reach some of them. If you're travelling on your own, on the other hand, hostels are usually more sociable and can work out a lot cheaper; many have facilities such as inexpensive restaurants and

This is usually confined to July and August, but accommodation is generally in individual rooms and can work out a lot cheaper than a straight hotel room. Again you'll need to book in advance: we've listed possible places in the text, and you should contact them as far ahead as possible to be sure of a room.

You will also come across accommodation operated by **religious organizations** – convents (normally for women only), welcome houses and the like, again with a mixture of dormitory and individual rooms, which can sometimes be a way of cutting costs as well as meeting like-minded people. Most operate a curfew of some sort, and you should bear in mind that they don't always work out a great deal cheaper than a bottom-line one-star hotel. Information can be found in the local tourist offices.

Youth hostel associations

Australia ☏ 02/9261 1111, ⓦ www.yha.org.au.
Canada ☏ 1-800/663-5777, ⓦ www.hihostels.ca.
England & Wales ☏ 0870/770 8868, ⓦ www.yha.org.uk.
New Zealand ☏ 0800/278 299, ⓦ www.yha.co.nz.
Northern Ireland ☏ 028/9032 4733, ⓦ www.hini.org.uk.
Republic of Ireland ☏ 01/830 4555, ⓦ www.irelandyha.org.
Scotland ☏ 0870/155 3255, ⓦ www.syha.org.uk.
USA ☏ 301/495-1240, ⓦ www.hiayh.org.

Camping

Camping is popular in Italy and there are plenty of sites, mostly on the coast and in the mountains and generally open April to September (though winter "camping" – in caravans and camper vans – is common in ski areas). The majority are well equipped and often have bungalows, mainly with four to six beds. On the coast in high season you can expect to pay a daily rate of around €12 per person plus €10–15 per tent or caravan and €2.50 per vehicle. Local tourist offices have details of nearby sites, otherwise visit the Italian camping website, ⓦ www.camping.it, for information and booking facilities for campsites all over Italy.

Self-catering

Self-catering is becoming an increasingly feasible option for visitors to Italy's cities.

High prices mean that renting rooms or an **apartment** can be an attractive, cost-effective choice. Usually in well-located positions in city centres, and available for anything from a couple of nights to a month or so, they come equipped with bedding and kitchen utensils and there's nothing like shopping for supplies in a local market to you make feel part of Italian daily life, even on a short break.

If you're not intending to travel around a lot it might be worth renting a **villa** or farmhouse for a week or two. Most tend to be located in the affluent northern areas of Italy, especially Tuscany and Umbria, although attractive options are also available on Sicily and Sardinia and popping up in other rural locations too. They don't come cheap, but are of a high standard and often enjoy marvellous locations.

Villa and apartment companies

Bridgewater ☏ 0161/787 8587, ⓦ www.bridgewater-travel.co.uk. A company with over 25 years' experience sourcing apartments, agriturismo and country hotels throughout Italy.
Carefree Italy ☏ 01293/552 277, ⓦ www.carefree-italy.com. English company offering villas and apartments across the country.

41

Holiday Rentals ⓦ www.holiday-rentals.co.uk. This site puts you in touch directly with the owners of over 1000 Italian properties.

Ilios Travel ☏ 01444/880 350, ⓦ www.iliostravel .com. High-quality selection of country mansions and villas, in various parts of the country.

Italian Breaks ☏ 020/8660 0082, ⓦ www .italianbreaks.com. Accommodation to suit most budgets.

Italian Connection ☏ 01424/ 728 900, ⓦ www .italian-connection.co.uk. Major upmarket operator with an array of villas and smart apartments throughout the country.

Italian Homes ☏ 020/8878 1130, ⓦ www .Italian-homes.com. Apartments in Venice, Rome and Florence.

Livingitalia.com ☏ +39.06.321.10998, ⓦ www .livingitalia.com. Offers apartments in Florence and Rome.

Owners' Syndicate ☏ 020/7801 9807, ⓦ www .ownerssyndicate.co.uk. More than 200 properties around Tuscany and Umbria.

Rentxpress ☏ +39.02.805.3151, ⓦ www .rentxpress.com. English-speaking company with apartments for rent in various cities.

Bed and breakfast and agriturismo

Bed and breakfast schemes are a relatively new arrival, the best ones offering a way to get a flavour of Italian home life, though they're not necessarily cheaper than an inexpensive hotel, and they rarely accept credit cards. Some places going under the name are actually little different from private rooms, with the owners not living on the premises, but you'll invariably find them clean and well maintained. For an extensive list of Italy's B&Bs check out ⓦ www .bbitalia.it, ⓦ www.caffelletto.it or the links at ⓦ www.terranostra.it.

The **agriturismo** scheme which enables farmers to rent out converted barns and farm buildings to tourists has boomed in recent years. Usually these comprise a self-contained flat or building, though a few places just rent rooms on a bed-and-breakfast basis. While some rooms are still annexed to working farms or vineyards, many are smart, self-contained rural vacation properties; attractions may include home-grown food, swimming pools and a range of activities from walking and riding to archery and mountain biking. Many agriturismi have a minimum-stay requirement of one week in busy periods. Rates start at around €120 per night for self-contained places with two beds. Tourist offices keep lists of local properties; alternatively, you can search one of the growing number of agriturismo websites – there are hundreds of properties at ⓦ www.agriturismo.com, ⓦ www.agri -turismo.net, ⓦ www.agriitalia.it and ⓦ www .agriturist.it

Mountain refuges

If you're planning on hiking and climbing, it's worth checking out the **rifugi** network, consisting of about five hundred mountain huts, owned by the Club Alpino Italiano (**CAI** ☏ 02.205.7231, ⓦ www.cai.it). Non-members can use them for around €20 a night, though you should book at least ten days in advance. There are also private *rifugi* that charge around double this. Most are fairly spartan, with bunks in unheated dorms, but their settings can be magnificent and usually leave you well placed to continue your hike the next day. Bear in mind that the word *rifugio* can be used for anything from a smart chalet-hotel to a snack bar at the top of a cable-car line. We've indicated in the text where this is the case.

Eating and drinking

Although it has long been popular primarily for its cheapness and convenience, Italian cuisine also occupies a revered place as one of the world's greats. The southern Italian diet especially, with its emphasis on olive oil, fresh and plentiful fruit, vegetables and fish, is one of the healthiest in Europe, and there are few national cuisines that can boast so much variety in both ingredients and cooking methods. Italy's wines, too, are among the finest and most diverse in Europe.

The basics of Italian cuisine

The many **regions** of Italy still preserve their own distinctive cuisines, with, for example, the French influence in Piemonte, Austrian flavours in Alto Adige and even Greek contributions in Calabria: regional cuisine and specialities to seek out are highlighted in "Regional food and wine" boxes at the beginning of Guide chapters. Italy has remained largely untouched by the latter-day boom in non-indigenous eating, partly owing to its lack of any substantial colonial legacy but also because of the innate chauvinism of Italian eating habits. The exceptions are the Chinese restaurants that crop up in every town, the ubiquitous burger bars, and the Mexican, Japanese and North African cuisine found in more cosmopolitan cities, especially Rome and Milan. More often than not the most exotic option is to sample cooking from other parts of the country.

True to the stereotype that every Italian believes that Italian food is the best in the world and that mamma's is always the perfect example, many restaurants are simply an extension of the home dining table.

Perhaps the most striking thing about eating in Italy is how deeply embedded in the culture it really is. Food is celebrated with gusto: **traditional meals** tend to consist of many courses and can seem to last forever, starting with an antipasto, followed by a risotto or a pasta dish, leading on to a fish or meat course, cheese, and finished with fresh fruit and coffee. Even everyday meals are a scaled-down version of the full-blown affair.

Foods like bread and cheese are still made with an eye to quality. **Bread** is almost entirely made by small bakeries and tends to get heavier, crustier and saltier the further south you go (for eating with salty hams, salami and cheeses there is *pane senza sale*). Although of course there are some factory-produced **cheeses**, cheese-making also remains in the hands of local farmers working to traditional recipes and local tastes are much in evidence.

It was precisely this appreciation of good-quality local products that led to the development of the **Slow Food** movement (ⓦwww .slowfood.com) in 1986. An organization with increasing recognition worldwide, it seeks to promote the genuine pleasures of food and drink by encouraging high-quality gastronomic production and the protection of traditional cuisine in the face of the "aggressive advance of food and cultural standardization". Two excellent Slow Food publications, *Osterie d'Italia* and *Vini d'Italia,* are on sale in most Italian bookshops.

No smoking

In January 2005 a law prohibiting smoking in restaurants and bars came into force. Overnight, local neighbourhood bars became smoke-free zones; any establishment that wants to allow smoking has to follow very stringent rules in isolating a separate room – including doors and special air conditioning. Needless to say this is beyond the pocket of most places and so the majority remain no-smoking throughout. Don't worry, though, if you do want a puff with your coffee; the pavement outside has become a popular place.

Types of restaurants

Full **meals** are generally served in either a trattoria or a *ristorante*. Traditionally, a trattoria is a cheaper and more basic purveyor of homestyle cooking (*cucina casalinga*), while a *ristorante* is more upmarket, though the two are often interchangeable. Other types of eating places include those that bill themselves as everything – trattoria-ristorante-pizzeria – and perform no function very well, serving mediocre food that you could get at better prices elsewhere. Look out also for *spaghetterie*, bar-restaurants that serve basic pasta dishes and are often the hangout of the local youth. *Osterie* are common too, basically an old-fashioned restaurant or pub-like place specializing in home cooking, though some upmarket places with pretensions to established antiquity borrow the name. In all midrange establishments, pasta dishes go for €5–10, while the main fish or meat courses will normally cost between €7 and €15.

Understanding the menu

Traditionally, lunch (*pranzo*) and dinner (*cena*) start with **antipasto** (literally "before the meal"), a course consisting of various cold cuts of meat, seafood and cold vegetable dishes, generally costing €5–10. Some places offer self-service antipasto buffets. The next course, the **primo**, involves soup, risotto or pasta dish, and is followed by the **secondo** – the meat or fish course, usually served alone, except for perhaps a wedge of lemon or tomato. Watch out when ordering fish, which will either be served whole or by weight – 250g is usually plenty for one person – or ask to have a look at the fish before it's cooked. Note that by law, any ingredients that have been frozen need to be marked (usually with an asterix) on the menu; you might decide that it's better to try the local fish rather than one flown in from the South Atlantic, for example. Vegetables or salads – **contorni** – are ordered and served separately, and there often won't be much choice: potatoes will usually come as fries (*patate fritte*), but you can also find boiled

(*lesse*) or roast (*arrostite*) potatoes, while salads are either green (*verde*) or mixed (*mista*) and vegetables (*verdure*) usually come very well boiled. Afterwards, you nearly always get a choice of fresh local fruit (*frutta*) and a selection of **desserts** (*dolci*) – sometimes just ice cream or *macedonia* (fresh fruit salad), but often more elaborate home-made items, like apple or pear cake (*torta di mela/pera*), tiramisu, or *zuppa inglese* (trifle). **Cheeses** (*formaggi*) are always worth a shot if you have any room left; ask to try a selection of local varieties.

You will need quite an appetite to tackle all these courses and if your stomach — or wallet — isn't up to it, it's perfectly acceptable to have less. If you're not sure of the size of the portions, start with a pasta or rice dish and ask to order the *secondo* when you've finished the first course. And, although it's not a very Italian thing to do, don't feel shy about just having just an *antipasto* and a *primo*; they're probably the best way of trying local specialities anyway. If there's no menu, the verbal list of what's available can be bewildering; if you don't understand, just ask for what you want – if it's something simple they can usually rustle it up. Everywhere will have pasta with tomato sauce (*pomodoro*) or meat sauce (*al ragù*).

At the end of the meal ask for the bill (*il conto*); bear in mind that almost everywhere you'll pay a cover charge (*coperto*) of €1–5 a head. In many trattorias the bill amounts to little more than an illegible scrap of paper; if you want to check it, ask for a **receipt** (*ricevuta*). In more expensive places, service (*servizio*) will often be added on top of the cover charge, generally about ten percent. If service isn't included it's common just to leave a few coins as a **tip** unless you're particularly pleased with the service. In our listings, we've indicated the regular weekly **closing day**.

Breakfast

Most Italians start their day in a bar, their **breakfast** (*prima colazione*) consisting of a coffee and a *brioche* or *cornetto* – a croissant often filled with jam, custard or chocolate, which you usually help yourself to from the counter and eat standing at the bar. It will cost between €1.30 and €1.60. Breakfast in a hotel is often a limp affair of

There's a detailed **menu reader** of Italian terms on pp.1195–1199.

watery coffee, bread and processed meats, often not worth the price.

Pizza, snacks and ice cream

Pizza is now a worldwide phenomenon, but Italy remains the best place to eat it. When good, the creations served up here are wholly different from the soggy concoctions that have taken over the international fast-food market, and it has to be said that some of the joints in the tourist centres are inclined to feel that they can fob off undiscerning tourists with deeply inferior versions. For a quality pizza opt for somewhere with a wood-fired oven (*forno a legna*) rather than a squeaky-clean electric one, so that the pizzas arrive blasted and bubbling on the surface and with a distinctive charcoal taste. This adherence to tradition means that it's unusual to find a good pizzeria open at lunchtime; it takes hours for a wood-fired oven to heat up to the necessary temperature. In Italy pizza usually comes thin and flat, not deep-pan, and the choice of toppings is fairly limited, with none of the dubious pineapple and sweetcorn variations.

Pizzerias range from a stand-up counter selling slices to a fully fledged sit-down restaurant, and on the whole they don't sell much else besides pizza, soft drinks and beer. A basic cheese and tomato *margherita* costs around €6, a fancier variety €6–10, and it's quite acceptable to cut it into slices and eat it with your fingers. Consult our food glossary (see pp.1195–1199) for the different kinds of pizza.

For a lunchtime snack **sandwiches** (panini) can be pretty substantial, a bread stick or roll packed with any number of fillings. A sandwich bar (*paninoteca*) in larger towns and cities, and in smaller places a grocer's shop (*alimentari*), will normally make you up whatever you want. Bars may also offer *tramezzini*, ready-made sliced white bread with mixed fillings. Toasted sandwiches (*toast*) are common, too: in a *paninoteca* you can get whatever you want toasted; in ordinary bars it's more likely to be a variation on cheese or ham with tomato.

Other sources of quick snacks are **markets**, where fresh, flavoursome produce is sold, often including cheese, cold meats, warm spit-roast chicken, and *arancini* (deep-fried balls of rice with meat (*rosso*) or butter and cheese (*bianco*) filling. **Bread shops** (*panetteria*) often serve slices of pizza or *focacce* (bread with oil and salt topped with rosemary, olives or tomato). **Supermarkets**, also, are an obvious stop for a picnic lunch: the major chains, Esselunga, Carrefour and Auchan, are on the outskirts of larger towns, while *GS*, *Unes!* and *Sma* are often in the centre.

Italian **ice cream** (*gelato*) is justifiably famous and a cone (*un cono*) is an indispensable accessory to the evening *passeggiata*. Most bars have a fairly good selection, but for real choice go to a **gelateria**, where the range is a tribute to the Italian imagination and flair for display. There's no problem locating the finest *gelateria* in town – it's the one that draws the crowds – and we've noted the really special places throughout the Guide. If in doubt, go for the places that

---

Vegetarians and vegans

Although your diet will probably be based around pasta and pizza, Italy isn't a bad country to travel in if you're a **vegetarian**. As well as the ubiquitous tomato sauce there are numerous other pasta sauces without meat, some superb vegetable antipasti and, if you eat fish and seafood, you should have no problem at all. Salads, too, are fresh and good. The only real difficulty is one of comprehension: outside the cities and resorts Italians don't really understand someone not eating meat, and stating the obvious doesn't always get the point across. Saying you're a vegetarian (*Sono vegetariano/a*) and asking if a dish has meat in it (*C'è carne dentro?*) might still turn up a poultry or prosciutto dish. Asking for it "*senza carne e pesce*" should make things sufficiently clear.

Vegans will have a much harder time, though pizzas without cheese (*marinara* – nothing to do with fish – is a common option) are a good standby, vegetable soup (*minestrone*) is usually just that and the fruit is excellent.

make their own ice cream, denoted by the signs "*Produzione Propria*" outside. There's usually a veritable cornucopia of flavours ranging from those regarded as the classics – like lemon (*limone*) and pistachio (*pistacchio*) – through staples including *stracciatella* (vanilla with chocolate chips), strawberry (*fragola*) and *fiordilatte* (similar to vanilla), to house specialities that might include cinnamon (*cannella*), chocolate with chilli pepper (*cioccolato con peperoncino*) or even pumpkin (*zucca*).

Drinking

Although *un mezzo* (half-litre carafe of house wine) is a standard accompaniment to any meal, there's not a great emphasis on dedicated **drinking** in Italy. You'll rarely see drunks in public, young people don't devote their nights to getting wasted, and women especially are frowned on if they're seen to be overindulging. Nonetheless there's a wide choice of alcoholic drinks available, often at low prices; soft drinks come in multifarious hues; and, of course, there is always mineral water and crushed-ice drinks.

Where to drink

Traditional **bars** are less social centres than functional places and are all very similar to each other – brightly lit places, with a counter, a Gaggia coffee machine and a picture of the local football team on the wall. This is the place to come for a coffee in the morning, a quick beer or a cup of tea – people don't generally idle away evenings in bars. Indeed in some more rural areas it's difficult to find a bar open much after 8pm. Where these places do fit into the general Mediterranean pattern is with their lack of set licensing hours and the fact that children are always allowed in.

It's cheapest to drink standing at the counter, in which case you pay first at the cash desk (*la cassa*), present your receipt (*scontrino*) to the barperson and give your order. There's always a list of prices (*listino prezzi*) behind the bar and it's customary to leave a small coin on the counter as a tip for the barperson, although no one will object if you don't. If there's waiter service, just sit where you like, though bear in mind that to

do this will cost up to twice as much as positioning yourself at the bar, especially if you sit outside (*fuori*) – the difference is shown on the price list as *tavola* (table) or *terrazzo* (any outside seating area). Late-night bars and pubs rarely operate on the *scontrino* system; you may be asked to pay up front, in the British manner, or be presented with a bill. If not, head for the counter when you leave – the barperson will have kept a surprisingly accurate tally.

An **osteria** can be a more congenial setting, often a traditional place where you can usually try local specialities with a glass of wine. Real enthusiasts of the grape should head for an **enoteca**, though many of these are more oriented towards selling wine by the case than by the glass. Cities offer a much greater variety of places to sit and drink in the evening, sometimes with live music or DJs. The more energetic or late-opening of these have taken to calling themselves **pubs**, a spill-over from the outrageous success of Irish pubs, at least one of which you'll find, packed to the rafters, in almost every city. Beer, particularly in its draught form, *alla spina*, has become fashionable in recent years.

Coffee, tea and soft drinks

Always excellent, the basic choice of coffee is either small and black (*espresso*, or just *caffè*), which costs around €1 a cup, or white and frothy (*cappuccino*, for about €1.30), but there are scores of variations. If you want your espresso watered down, ask for a *caffè lungo* or, for something more like a filter coffee, an *Americano*; with a drop of milk is *caffè macchiato*; very milky is *caffè latte* (ordering just a "*latte*" in true New York-café style will get you a glass of milk!). Coffee with a shot of alcohol – and you can ask for just about anything – is *caffè corretto*. Many places also now sell decaffeinated coffee; while in summer you might want to have your coffee cold (*caffè freddo*).

If you don't like coffee, there's always **tea**. In summer you can drink this cold too (*tè freddo*) – excellent for taking the heat off. Hot tea (*tè caldo*) comes with lemon (*con limone*) unless you ask for milk (*con latte*). Milk itself is drunk hot as often as cold, or you can get it with a dash of coffee (*latte* *macchiato*) and sometimes as milk shakes – *frappe* or *frullati*. A small selection of herbal teas (*infusioni*) are generally available: camomile (*camomilla*) and peppermint (*menta*) are the most common.

Alternatively, there are various **soft drinks** (*analcolichi*) to choose from. Slightly fizzy, bitter drinks like San Bittèr or Crodine are common especially at *aperitvo* time. A **spremuta** is a fresh fruit juice, squeezed at the bar, usually orange, lemon or grapefruit. You might need to add sugar to the lemon juice (*di limone*), but the orange (*d'arancia*) is invariably sweet enough on its own, especially the crimson-red variety, made from blood oranges. There are also crushed-ice **granitas**, big in Sicily and offered in several flavours, available with or without whipped cream (*panna*) on top. Otherwise there's the usual range of fizzy drinks and concentrated juices: Coke is as prevalent as it is everywhere, though the diet or light versions less so; the home-grown Italian version, Chinotto, is less sweet and good with a slice of lemon. **Tap water** (*acqua normale*) is quite drinkable, and you won't pay for a glass in a bar, though Italians prefer **mineral water** (*acqua minerale*) and drink more of it than any other country in Europe. It can be drunk either still (*senza gas* or *naturale*) or sparkling (*con gas* or *frizzante*), and costs about €1.30 a bottle.

Beer and spirits

Beer (*birra*) is always a lager-type brew which usually comes in one-third or two-third litre bottles, or on tap (*alla spina*), measure for measure more expensive than the bottled variety. A small beer is a *piccola*, (20cl or 25cl), a larger one (usually 40cl) a *media*. The cheapest and most common brands are the Italian Moretti, Peroni and Dreher, all of which are very drinkable; if this is what you want, either state the brand name or ask for *birra nazionale* or *birra chiara* – otherwise you could end up with a more expensive imported beer. You may also come across darker beers (*birra nera* or *birra rossa*), which have a sweeter, maltier taste and in appearance resemble stout or bitter.

All the usual **spirits** are on sale and known mostly by their generic names. There are also Italian brands of the main varieties: the best Italian brandies are Stock and Vecchia Romagna. A generous shot of these costs about €1.50, imported stuff much more.

You'll also find **fortified wines** like Martini, Cinzano and Campari; ask for a Campari-soda and you'll get a ready-mixed version from a little bottle; a slice of lemon is a *spicchio di limone*, ice is *ghiaccio*. You might also try Cynar – believe it or not, an artichoke-based sherry often drunk as an aperitif with water. There's also a daunting selection of **liqueurs**. Amaro is a bitter after-dinner drink or *digestivo*, Amaretto much sweeter with a strong taste of almond, Sambuca a sticky-sweet aniseed concoction, traditionally served with a coffee bean in it and set on fire (though, increasingly, this is something put on to impress tourists). Another sweet alternative, originally from Sorrento, is *Limoncello* or *limoncino*, a lemon-based liqueur best drunk in a frozen vase-shaped glass. Strega is another drink you'll see behind every bar, yellow, herb-and-saffron based stuff in tall, elongated bottles: about as sweet as it looks but not unpleasant.

Wine

The labelling of Italian wine is confusing: there is no established system and there is often little geographical and varietal information to help you identify where a wine is from or what it is like. The **Denominazione d'Origine Controllata** (DOC) system was introduced in the 1960s as a way of guaranteeing the quality but it quickly became a mixed blessing. Denomination zones are set by governmental decree specifying where a certain named wine may be made, what grape varieties may be used, the maximum yield of grapes per hectare and for how long the wine should be aged. The **Denominazione d'Origine Controllata e Garantita** (DOCG) was established in the 1980s as one step up: wines sold under this label not only have to conform to the ordinary DOC laws, but are also tested by government-appointed inspectors. Though it's undoubtedly true that the DOC and DOCG system helped lift standards of Italian wines, the laws have come under fire from both growers and critics for their rigidity, constraints and anomalies. They leave no room for the experimentation and modern methods that northern Italy, for one, specializes in. Increasingly, producers eager to experiment began to disregard the regulations and make new wines that were sometimes among Italy's best, though they were only officially labelled table wine (*da tavola*). The **Indicazione Geografica Tipica** (IDT) was introduced in 1992 to enable producers to use geographical names and grape varieties on labels to help describe their wines – something that has benefited the less traditional producers in particular.

Just as Italy's food has suffered from stereotyped images, so too has its **wine**. Lambrusco was one of the first Italian wines to sell well overseas, despite (or because of) its reputation as cheap party plonk, while inexpensive Soave, Valpolicella and Chianti continue to shift units. Some of the finer wines are now well established abroad, though often the very best are kept for the home market. A few pointers in the right direction are given in the "Regional food and wine" box at the beginning of each chapter. Nudged along by the DOC laws, standards have been steadily increasing in recent years.

Many producers have been turning their hands to making higher **quality wines**, and besides the finer tuning of established names such as Barolo and Orvieto, there's a good deal of experimentation going on

everywhere. Sicilian wines are some of the best new additions to a wine-lover's choice with southern winemakers no longer content to see nearly all of their produce going north to beef up table-wine blends, while in Tuscany, Trentino-Alto Adige and Friuli-Venezia Giulia, French grape varieties such as Chardonnay, Sauvignon Blanc and the Pinots have joined old Italian favourites with startling success.

They don't waste drinking time in Italy with dialogue or veneration, however; nor is there much time for the snobbery often associated with "serious" wine drinking. Light **reds** such as those made from the dolcetto grape are hauled out of the fridge in hot weather, while some full-bodied **whites** are drunk at near room temperature. In restaurants you'll invariably be offered red (*rosso*) or white (*bianco*) – rarely rosé (*rosato*). If you're unsure about what to order, don't be afraid to try the local stuff (ask for *vino sfuso*, or simply *un mezzo* – a half litre – or *un quarto* – a quarter), sometimes served straight from the barrel, particularly down south. It's often very good, and inexpensive at an average of around €5 a litre. Bottled wine is pricier but still very good value; expect to pay €9–15 a bottle in a restaurant, and less than half that from a shop or supermarket. In bars you can buy a decent glass of wine for about €1–2.

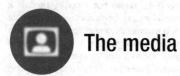

The media

Italy's decentralized press serves to emphasize the strength of regionalism in the country. Local TV is popular, too, in the light of little competition from the national channels. If you know where to look, journalistic standards can be high but you might find yourself turning to foreign TV channels or papers if you want an international outlook on events.

Newspapers

The **Italian press** is largely regionally based, with just a few newspapers available across the country. The centre-left *La Repubblica* and authoritative right-slanted *Corriere della*

Sera are the two most widely read, published nationwide with local supplements, but originating in Milan. Provincial newspapers include *La Stampa*, the daily of Turin, and *Il Messaggero* of Rome – both rather stuffy, establishment sheets. *Il Mattino* is the more readable publication of Naples and the Campania area, while other southern editions include the *Giornale di Sicilia* and *La Gazzetta del Sud*. Many of the imprints you see on newsstands are the official mouthpieces for political parties: *L'Unità* is the party organ of the former Communist Party, while *La Padania* is the press of the right-wing, regionalist Lega Nord party. The traditionally radical *Il Manifesto* has always been regarded as one of the most serious and influential sources of Italian journalism. Perhaps the most avidly read newspapers of all, however, are the specialist sports papers, most notably the *Corriere dello Sport* and the pink *Gazzetta dello Sport* (@www.gazzetta.it) – both essential reading if you want an insight into the Italian football scene.

English-language newspapers can be found for around three times their home cover price in all the larger cities and most resorts, usually a day late, though in Milan and Rome you can sometimes find papers on the day of publication. In remoter parts of the country it's not unusual for papers to be delayed by several days.

TV and radio

Italian **TV** is appalling, with ghastly quiz shows, mindless variety programmes and cathartic chat shows squeezed in between countless artless advertisements. Of the **three national channels**, RAI 1, 2 and 3, RAI 3 has the odd worthwhile programme, although the intelligent, satirical shows are often indecipherable to foreigners who have anything less than an encyclopedic knowledge of Italian politics from the last fifty years. **Satellite television** is fairly widely distributed, and three-star hotels and above usually offer a mix of BBC World, CNN and French-, German- and Spanish-language news channels, as well as MTV and Eurosport.

The situation in **radio** is if anything even more anarchic, with the FM waves crowded to the extent that you continually pick up new stations whether you want to or not – Catholic Radio Maria pops up with an uncanny frequency. This means there are generally some good stations if you search hard enough, but on the whole the RAI stations are again the more professional – though even with them daytime listening is virtually undiluted Euro-pop.

For **world service** stations check the following websites for details of their global frequencies:
BBC @ www.bbc.co.uk/worldservice
Radio Canada @ www.rcinet.ca
Voice of America @ www.voa.gov

Festivals

Whether for religious, traditional or cultural reasons, Italy has no shortage of festivals throughout the year, and at Christmas, Easter or during the summer months you are likely to come across at least one local festival celebrating an historic event, a patron saint's day, a town's local produce or some artistic talent.

Recently there's also been a revival of the carnival (*carnevale*), the last fling before Lent, although the anarchic fun that was enjoyed in the past has generally been replaced by elegant, self-conscious affairs, with ingenious costumes and handmade masks. The main places to head for are Venice, Viareggio in Tuscany and Arcireale in Sicily, although smaller towns also often put on a parade.

Perhaps the most widespread local event in Italy is the **religious procession**, which can be a very dramatic affair. **Good Friday** is celebrated in many towns and villages – particularly in the south – by parading

Festivals diary

There are literally thousands of festivals in Italy and sometimes the best ones are those that you come across unexpectedly in the smaller towns. Some of the highlights are listed below– we've detailed more throughout the Guide. Note that **dates change** from year to year, so it's best to contact the local tourist office for specific details.

January

Naples *San Silvestro*. New Year is welcomed in by bangers and fireworks on the streets and by throwing old furniture out of windows.

Milan *Epifania* (Jan 6). Costumed parade of the Three Kings from the duomo to Sant'Eustorgio, the resting place of the bones of the Magi.

Rome *Epifania* (Jan 6). Toy and sweet fair in Piazza Navona, to celebrate the *Befana*, the good witch who brings toys and sweets to children who've been good, and coal to those who haven't.

February

Sicily *Festa di Sant'Agata* (Feb 3–5) Riotous religious procession in Catania.

Carnevale Carnival festivities in Venice ⓦwww.venicecarnival.com, Viareggio ⓦwww.ilcarnevale.com, Foiano della Chiana (Arezzo), Cento (Ferrara) plus many towns throughout Italy.

Ivrea Battle of the Oranges. A messy couple of days when processions through the streets are an excuse to pelt each other with orange pulp ⓦwww.carnevalediivrea.it.

Agrigento Almond Blossom Festival (last two weeks of Feb).

March

Venice *Su e zo per i ponti* (second Sun). A marathon "up and down the bridges".

Milan *Salone Internazionale del Mobile* third week. The city becomes a showcase for the best of the world's furniture and industrial design.

April

Nocera Tirinese *Rito dei Battienti* (Easter Saturday). Macabre parade of flagellants whipping themselves with shards of glass.

Florence *Lo Scoppio del Carro* (Easter Day). A symbolic firework display outside the duomo after Mass.

May

Cocullo (*L'Aquila*) Festival of snakes (first week of May). One of the most ancient Italian festivals celebrating the patron saint, San Domenico Abate, in which his statue is draped with live snakes and paraded through the streets.

Gubbio *Corsa dei Ceri* (first Sun). Three 20ft-high wooden figures (*ceri*), representing three patron saints, are raced through the old town by *ceraioli* in medieval costume.

Camogli Fish festival of San Fortunato (second Sun). The patron saint of fishermen is celebrated with plenty of fried fish, fireworks and bonfires.

Florence *Festa del Grillo* (first, second & third Sun). Celebration of the cricket; contestants bring along highly ornate boxes containing crickets which are judged according to beauty and singing voice.

International Wine Day (last Sun). Wine estates all over Italy open their cellars to the public.

Siracusa Greek Drama festival (mid-May to mid-June).

Alba Truffle Festival (April 24 to May 2). Month-long opportunity to sample local delicacies as well as parades and a donkey *palio*.

June

Florence *Calcio Storico Fiorentino* (June 24). Medieval-style football match and other festivities to celebrate San Giovanni, the city's patron saint.

Spoleto *Festival dei Due Mondi*. Two months of theatre, concerts and street entertainment ⓦwww.spoletofestival.it.

Verona Verona Opera season starts ⓦ www.arena.it.
Positano Start of the Amalfi Coast Opera and Chamber Music Festival.

July
Siena *Palio* (July 2). Medieval bareback horse race in the *campo*.
Matera *Festa della Madonna della Bruna* (July 2). A statue of the town's patron saint is paraded on a float and then burned.
Palermo *Festino di Santa Rosalia* (second week). A five-day street party to celebrate the city's patron saint.
Perugia Umbria Jazz Festival ⓦ www.umbriajazz.com.
Bologna Porretta Soul Festival ⓦ www.porrettasoul.com.
Santarcangelo di Romagna Festival Internazionale del Teatro in Piazza ⓦ www .santarcangelofestival.com.

August
Ferragosto (Aug 15). National holiday with local festivals, water fights and fireworks all over Italy.
Siena (Aug 16). Second *Palio* horse race.
Pésaro Rossini Opera Festival (mid-month) ⓦ www.rossinioperafestival.it.
Ferrara Ferrara Buskers Festival. Gathering of some of the world's best street performers ⓦ www.ferrarabuskers.com.
Venice (end of month). Start of the oldest International Film Festival in the world ⓦ www.labiennaledivenezia.net.

September
Venice *La Regatta di Venezia* (first Sun). Gondola race in medieval costume along the Grand Canal.
Verona (Sept 12). Street entertainment and general partying to celebrate the birthday of the town's most famous lover, Juliet.
Naples *Festa di San Gennaro* (Sept 15). Festival for the city's patron saint with crowds gathering in the cathedral to witness the liquefaction of San Gennaro's blood.
San Giovanni Rotondo, Fóggia (Sept 23). Thousands of followers commemorate the death of Padre Pio.

October
Marino, Rome *Sagra del Vino* (first weekend). One of the most famous among hundreds of wine festivals across the country, with fountains literally flowing with wine.
Trieste *La Barcolana* (second Sun). Boat race ⓦ www.barcolana.it.
Perugia Eurochocolate (third & fourth weekend). Italy's chocolate city celebrates.
Acqualagna, Pésaro *Festa del Tartufo Bianco* (last Sun). Beginning of a month-long white truffle festival.

November
Olive oil Festivals all over Italy.

December
Stiffe, L'Aquila Bethlehem in the Grotto. Life-size statues from the nativity scene are carried into a 650-metre-deep grotto and positioned for the month among stalagmites and a natural waterfall.
Suvereto, Livorno *Festa del Cinghiale* (Dec 1–10). A ten-day festival in honour of the wild boar.
Milan *Oh Bej, Oh Bej!* (Dec 7) The city's patron saint, Sant'Ambrogio, is celebrated with a huge street market around his church and a day off work and school for all.
Santa Lucia (Dec 13). Opera season starts with an all-star opening night at La Scala.
Orvieto *Umbria Jazz Winter* (end of month) ⓦ www.umbriajazz.com.

models of Christ through the streets accompanied by white-robed, hooded figures singing penitential hymns. Many processions have strong pagan roots, marking important dates on the calendar and only relatively recently sanctified by the Church. Superstition and a desire for good luck are very much part of these events.

Despite the dwindling number of practising Catholics in Italy, there has been a revival of **pilgrimages** over the last couple of decades. These are as much social occasions as spiritual journeys with, for example, as many as a million pilgrims travelling through the night, mostly on foot, to the **Shrine of the Madonna di Polsi** in the inhospitable Aspromonte mountains in Calabria. Sardinia's biggest festival, the **Festa di Sant'Efisio**, sees a four-day march from Cágliari to Pula and back, to commemorate the saint's martyrdom.

There are many festivals that evoke local pride in **tradition**. Medieval contests like the **Palio** horse race in Siena perpetuate allegiances to certain competing clans, while other towns put on crossbow, jousting and flag-twirling contests, with marching bands in full costume accompanying the event with enthusiastic drumming. Far from staged affairs, these festivals are highly significant to those involved, with fierce rivalry between participants.

Food-inspired *feste* are lower-key, but no less enjoyable affairs, usually celebrating the local speciality of the region to the accompaniment of dancing, music from a local brass band and noisy fireworks at the end of the evening. There are literally hundreds of food festivals, sometimes advertised as **sagre**, and every region has them – look in the local papers or ask at the tourist office during summer and autumn and you're bound to find something going on. Most are modest affairs, primarily aimed at locals and little publicized, but there are a few exceptions.

The home-town pride that sparks off many of the food festivals also expresses itself in some of the **arts festivals** spread across Italy, particularly in the central part of the country – based in ancient amphitheatres or between medieval walls and occasionally marking the work of a native composer. Major concerts and opera are usually well advertised but also extremely popular, so you should book tickets well in advance.

One other type of festival to keep an eye out for are the summer **political** shindigs, like the *Festa de l'Unità*, advertised by posters all over the country. Begun initially to recruit members to the different political parties they have become something akin to a village fete but with a healthy Italian twist. Taking place mainly in the evenings, the food tents are a great way to try tasty local dishes washed down by a cup of wine for a couple of euro a dish. There's usually bingo going on in one corner, the sort of dancing that will make teenagers crimson with embarrassment and the odd coconut shy or the like. In larger towns these have become more sophisticated affairs with big-name national bands playing.

Sports and outdoor pursuits

Spectator sports are popular in Italy, especially the hallowed *calcio* (football), and there is undying national passion for frenetic motor and cycle races. When it comes to participation, though, there isn't the same compulsion to hit the hell out of a squash ball or sweat your way through an aerobics class after work as there is, say, in Britain or the States. Alternatively, the country's natural advantages provide possibly the best scope for keeping trim in the most enjoyable ways possible.

For visitors to Italy, the most accessible activities are centred around the **mountains** – where you can climb, ski, paraglide, raft or simply explore on foot or cycle – and the coastal regions, with plenty of opportunities for swimming, sailing and windsurfing; Campania, Calabria and Sicily are particularly popular for scuba diving and snorkelling.

You can get a guide and map suggesting **sailing itineraries** round the coast of southern Italy from the Italian State Tourist Office (see p.65).

Sports

Football – or **calcio** – is the national sport, followed fanatically by millions of Italians, and if you're at all interested in the game it would be a shame to leave the country without attending a *partita* or football match. The **season** starts around the middle of August, and finishes in June. **Il campionato** is split into four principal divisions, with the twenty teams in the Serie A being the most prestigious. Matches are normally played on Sunday afternoons, although Saturday, Sunday evening and Monday games are becoming more common. See Ⓦwww.lega -calcio.it for results, a calendar of events and English links to the official team websites. Inevitably **tickets** for Serie A matches are not cheap, starting at about €15–20 for "*Curva*" seats where the *tifosi* or hard-core fans go, rising to anything between €40 and €60 for "*Tribuna*" seats along the side of the pitch, and anything up to €100 for the more comfortable "*Poltroncina*" cushioned-seats in the centre of the Tribuna. We've given details of where to buy tickets for the major clubs and how to get to their grounds in the "Listings" sections at the end of major city

accounts. Once at the football match, get into the atmosphere of the occasion by knocking back *borghetti* – little vials of cold coffee with a drop of spirit added.

Italy's chosen sport after football is **basketball**, introduced from the United States after World War II. Most cities have a team, and Italy is now ranked among the foremost in the world. The teams vying for the top spot are Montepaschi Siena, Upea Capo d'Orlando, Benetton Treviso, Armani Jeans Milan and Vidivici Bologna. For more details on fixtures and the leagues, see Ⓦwww .eurobasket.com/ita.

In a country that has produced Ferrari, Maserati, Alfa Romeo and Fiat, it should come as no surprise that **motor racing** gives Italians such a buzz. There are grand prix tracks at Monza near Milan (home of the Italian Grand Prix) and at Ímola, where the San Marino Grand Prix is held.

The other sport popular with participants and crowds of spectators alike is **cycling**. At weekends especially, you'll often see a club group out, dressed in bright team kit, whirring along on their slender machines. The annual Giro d'Italia (Ⓦwww.ilgiroditalia.it) in the second half of May is a prestigious event that attracts scores of international participants each year, closing down roads and creating great excitement.

Outdoor pursuits

With the Alps right on the doorstep, it's easy to spend a weekend **skiing** or **snowboarding** from Milan, Turin or Venice. Some of the most popular ski resorts are Sestriere and Bardonecchia in Piemonte, Cervinia and Courmayeur in Val d'Aosta, and the Val Gardena and Val di Fassa in the stunning

Dolomite mountains of Trentino Alto Adige and Veneto – home to one of Italy's best known and most exclusive resorts, Cortina d'Ampezzo. Further south you can ski at the small resorts of Abetone and Amiata in Tuscany, Monte Vettore in the Marche, Gran Sasso and Maiella in Abruzzo and on Mount Etna in Sicily. Contact the regional tourist offices for information about accommodation, ski schools and prices of lift passes.

All of these mountain resorts are equally ideal as bases for summer **hiking** and **climbing**, and most areas have detailed maps with itineraries and marked paths. For less strenuous treks, the rolling hills of Tuscany and Umbria make perfect walking and **mountain bike** country and numerous tour operators offer independent or escorted tours throughout the region. Many tourist offices also publish booklets suggesting itineraries.

If the heat of the summer lures you towards the extensive Italian coast you can expect to find all the usual seaside resort activity and plenty of opportunities for **sailing** and **windsurfing**. **Scuba diving** is popular in Sicily and off most of the smaller islands – you can either join a diving school or hire equipment from one if you're an experienced diver.

Watersports aren't just restricted to the coast and can be found in places such as Lake Garda in the north and Trasimeno and Bolsena further south towards Rome. River **canoeing** and **rafting** are limited to the mountain areas of the north – contact the Monrosa rafting club near Turin, ⓦwww.monrosarafting.it, for details of their activities on the Sesia river.

Horse riding is becoming increasingly popular in rural areas of Italy and most tourist offices have lists of local stables (*maneggio*). Many agriturismi (see p.42) also have riding facilities and sometimes offer daily or weekly treks and night rides. Note that Italians rarely wear or provide riding hats.

Shopping

There is no shortage of temptation for shoppers and souvenir-hunters in Italy. Visitors can take advantage of Italy's traditional expertise in textiles, ceramics and leather and glassware in all price ranges; top-end Gucci garments, Murano glass or calf-skin footwear are often on sale just round the corner from somewhere offering rustic ceramics or gastronomic farm products. The regional variety of the country is reflected in the selection of goods available.

Much of Italy's manufacturing industry consists of small family-run companies producing consumerables for retail sale. This has led to factory outlets opening across the country, particularly for clothes and other textiles but also for pottery and glass; the Guide and local tourist offices will be able to point you in the right direction. Rural areas will usually have good basketware, local terracotta or ceramic items as well a veritable banquet of locally produced wine, olive oils, cheeses, hams and salamis. It's always worth rooting out the local speciality, even in urban centres: Turin is well known for its chocolate, Milan famous for designer clothes and furniture, Venice for glassware and lace, Florence for leather goods, Sicily and Perugia for ceramics.

Every large village and town has at least one weekly **market** (detailed in the Guide), and though these are usually geared towards household goods, they can be useful for picking up cheap clothing, basketware, ceramics and picnic ingredients.

Prices are mainly in line with most of Europe and are always a little higher in the

Clothing and shoe sizes

Women's dresses and skirts

American	4	6	8	10	12	14	16	18
British	8	10	12	14	16	18	20	22
Continental	38	40	42	44	46	48	50	52

Women's blouses and sweaters

American	6	8	10	12	14	16	18
British	30	32	34	36	38	40	42
Continental	40	42	44	46	48	50	52

Women's shoes

American	5	6	7	8	9	10	11
British	3	4	5	6	7	8	9
Continental	36	37	38	39	40	41	42

Men's suits

American	34	36	38	40	42	44	46	48
British	34	36	38	40	42	44	46	48
Continental	44	46	48	50	52	54	56	58

Men's shirts

American	14	15	15.5	16	16.5	17	17.5	18
British	14	15	15.5	16	16.5	17	17.5	18
Continental	36	38	39	41	42	43	44	45

Men's shoes

American	7	7.5	8	8.5	9.5	10	11	11.5
British	6.5	7	7.5	8	9	9.5	10.5	11
Continental	39	40	41	42	43.5	44	45	46.5

north of the country and urban areas. **Credit cards** are not widely used although most stores with pricey merchandise will accept them. **Haggling** is also uncommon in most of Italy but in more rural markets you might like try your luck; ask for *uno sconto* ("a discount") and see where it gets you. Bargaining is not practised when buying food, however, or in shops.

If you're resident outside the EU you are entitled to a rebate for the **VAT** (or *IVA*) paid on items over €180. You need to ask for a special receipt at the time of purchase and allow your goods to be checked at the airport and the receipt stamped when you leave the country. For more information, see Ⓦwww.globalrefund.com.

Travelling with children

Children are adored in Italy and will be made a fuss of in the street, and welcomed and catered for in bars and restaurants. Hotels normally charge around thirty percent extra to put a bed or cot in your room, though kids pay less on trains and can generally expect discounts for museum entry: prices vary, but 11–18 year-olds are usually admitted at half price on production of some form of ID (although sometimes this applies only to EU citizens). Under 11s – or sometimes only under 6s – have free entry.

Supplies for **babies** and small children are pricey: nappies and milk formula can cost up to three times as much as in other parts of Europe. Discreet breastfeeding is widely accepted – even smiled on – but nappy changing facilities are few and far between. Branches of the children's clothes and accessories chain, Prenatal, have changing facilities and a feeding area, but otherwise you may find you have to be creative. High-chairs are unusual too, although establish-ments in areas that see a high-volume of foreign visitors tend to be better equipped.

The only **hazards** when travelling with children to the Lakes are the heat and sun. Very high factor suncreams are quite difficult to find, although pharmacies usually sell sunblock. Bonnets or straw hats are plentiful in local markets. Take advantage of the periods of less intense sun – mornings and evenings – for travelling, and use the quiet of siesta-time to recover flagging energy. The rhythms of the southern climate soon modify established patterns, and you'll find it more natural carrying on later into the night, past normal bedtimes.

Internet resources

ⓦ **www.italyfamilyhotels.it** An organization of hotels across Italy geared up with facilities from cots and bottle warmers in rooms to baby sitters, play areas and special menus. New hotels are constantly joining.

ⓦ **www.travelforkids.com** Advice on planning holidays with children and tips on child-friendly tourist sights and activities, region by region.

Travel With Your Children 40 Fifth Ave, New York, NY 10011 ☏ 212/477-5524 or 1-888/822-4388. Publishes a regular newsletter, *Family Travel Times* (ⓦ www.familytraveltimes.com), as well as a series of books on travel with children.

Holidays With Kids ⓦ www.holidayswithkids .com.au. The website of the popular *Holidays With Kids* magazine, this site lists kid-friendly destinations and accommodation as well as providing advice to frazzled parents. You can book tours and holidays here, too.

Work and study in Italy

All EU citizens are eligible to work and study in Italy. Work permits are pretty impossible for non-EU citizens to obtain: you must have the firm promise of a job that no Italian could do before you can even apply to the Italian embassy in your home country.

Red tape

The main bureaucratic requirements to stay legally in Italy are a **Carta di Soggiorno** and a *codigo fiscale*, respectively a card proving your right to be in the country and a tax number. Available from the *questura* (police station), a *Carta di Soggiorno* requires you to produce a letter from your employer or place of study, or prove you have funds to maintain yourself. In reality, EU citizens can simply apply on the grounds of looking for work (*atessa di lavoro*) for which you'll need a passport and a photocopy, four passport photos, a current E111 and photocopy and a lot of patience. A **codigo fiscale** is essential for most things in Italy including buying a transport season pass, opening a bank account or renting a flat. It can be obtained from the local Ufficio delle Entrate although you can start the process online at ⓦ www.agenzieentrate.gov.it.

Work options

One obvious work option is to **teach English**, for which the demand has expanded enormously in recent years. You can do this in two ways: freelance private lessons, or through a language school. For the less reputable places, you can get away without any qualifications and a bit of bluff, but you'll need to show a TEFL (Teaching of English as a Foreign Language) certificate for the more professional establishments. For the main language schools, it's best to apply in writing before you leave (look for the ads in British newspapers the *Guardian* and *Times Education Supplement*), preferably before the summer, though you can also find openings in September. If you're looking on the spot, sift through the phone books and do the rounds on foot, asking to speak to the *direttore* or his/her secretary; don't bother to try in August when everything is closed. The best teaching jobs of all are with a university as a *lettore*, a job requiring fewer hours than the language schools and generally providing a fuller pay-packet. Universities require English-language teachers in most faculties, and you can write to the individual faculties. Strictly speaking you could get by without any knowledge of Italian while teaching, though it obviously helps, especially when setting up private classes.

If teaching's not up your street, there's the possibility of **holiday rep work** in the summer, especially around the seaside resorts. These are good places for finding **bar or restaurant work**, too – not the most lucrative of jobs, though you should make enough to keep you over the summer. You'll have to ask around for both types of work, and some knowledge of Italian is essential. **Au pairing** is another option: sift through the ads in *The Lady* magazine to find openings.

Study programmes

One way of spending time in Italy is to combine a visit with **learning the language**, enrolling in one of the many summer courses on Italian art and culture or joining an international work programme. There are many opportunities for studying Italian, either as part of an overseas study scheme or by applying directly to a language school when you arrive. Listed below are some useful contacts.

From the UK

British Council 10 Spring Gardens, London SW1A 2BN ☏ 020/7930 8466, ⓦ www.britishcouncil.org. Produces a free leaflet detailing study opportunities abroad. The Council's Central Management Direct

Teaching (☎ 020/7389 4931) recruits TEFL teachers for posts worldwide.

Earthwatch Institute 267 Banbury Rd, Oxford OX2 6HJ ☎ 01865/318 838, 🖰 www.earthwatch.org. Exchange programme organizing research trips, which sometimes include Italy.

International House 106 Piccadilly, London W1V 9NL ☎ 020/7518 6999, 🖰 www.ihlondon.com. Head office for reputable English-teaching organization which offers TEFL training and recruits for teaching positions in Italy.

Italian Cultural Institute 39 Belgrave Square, London SW1X 8NX ☎ 020/7235 1461, 🖰 www .italcultur.org.uk. The official Italian government agency for the promotion of cultural exchanges between Britain and Italy. A number of scholarships are available to British students wishing to study at Italian universities.

Socrates/Erasmus 🖰 www.ec.europa.eu. Europe-wide university-level initiative enabling students to study abroad for one year.

From the US

AFS Intercultural Programs 198 Madison Ave, 8th Floor, New York, NY 10016 ☎ 1-800/AFS-INFO or 212/299 9000, 🖰 www.afs.org/usa. Runs two-semester student exchange programmes.

American Institute for Foreign Study River Plaza, 9 West Broad St, Stamford, CT 06902-3788 ☎ 1-800/727-2437, 🖰 www.aifs.com. Language study and cultural immersion for the summer or school year.

Elderhostel 75 Federal St, Boston, MA 02110 ☎ 1/877-426-8056, 🖰 www.elderhostel.org. Runs activity programmes for over 60s, generally lasting a week or more and costs are in line with those of commercial tours.

From Australia

Australians Studying Abroad PO Box 285, Armadale, Victoria ☎ 1800/645 755 or 03/9509 1955, 🖰 www.asatravinfo.com.au. Study tours focusing on art and culture.

Travel essentials

Costs

The arrival of the euro, among other factors, has pushed up prices in Italy in recent years; accommodation costs in particular have soared. Generally you'll find the south much less expensive than the north. As a broad guide, expect to pay most in Venice, Milan, Florence and Bologna, less in Rome, while in Naples and Sicily prices come down quite a lot. Some **basics** are reasonably inexpensive, such as transport and, most notably, food: a pizza or plate of pasta with a beer or glass of wine (the staple cheap meal in a restaurant) will cost between €10 and €15 on average, and over most of the country you can eat and drink quite handsomely for €20–30 a head. As ever, in some of the larger, more visited cities – Florence and Venice, for example – it can be difficult to find appealing venues in the lower price ranges; Rome and Naples, on the other

hand, are never a problem. **Room rates** are now in line with much of the rest of Europe, at least in the major cities and resorts: reckon on paying €80–100 for the most basic double room in a one-star hotel in Rome, while Milan, Florence or Venice it's hard to find anything at all for under €120. A decent three star will set you back on average, countrywide, around €150 a night. **Drinking** is relatively pricey unless you stick to wine. Soft drinks and coffee cost around the same as in Britain and more than in North America; a large glass of beer costs around €4–6 if you decide to sit down. Overall, if watching your budget – camping or staying in hostels, buying food from shops and markets or living carefully on pizza and pasta – you could get by on around €50 a day, but a more realistic **average daily budget** – staying in one-star hotels, taking trains and eating one cheap meal out a day – would be approaching €75, perhaps a little less in the south; while to live reasonably well you probably need to spend at least €100 a day. Bear in mind, too, that the **time of year** can make a big difference. During the height of summer, in July and August when the Italians take their holidays, hotel prices can escalate; outside the season, however, you can often negotiate much lower rates. There are a few **reductions** and discounts for ISIC members, under-18s and over-65s, but only in the major cities and for entry into state museums and sites elsewhere.

Crime and personal safety

Despite what you hear about the Mafia, most of the crime you're likely to come across in Italy is of the small-time variety, prevalent in the major cities and the south of the country, where gangs of *scippatori* or "snatchers" operate. Crowded streets or markets and packed tourist sights are the places to be wary of; *scippatori* work on foot or on scooters, disappearing before you've had time to react. As well as handbags, they whip wallets, tear off visible jewellery and, if they're really adroit, unstrap watches. You can minimize the risk of this happening by being discreet: don't flash anything of value, keep a firm hand on your camera, and carry shoulderbags, as Italian women do, slung across your body. It's a good idea, too, to entrust money and credit cards to hotel managers. Never leave anything valuable in your car, and try to park in car parks on well-lit, well-used streets. On the whole it's common sense to avoid badly lit areas completely at night and deserted inner-city areas by day.

Confronted with a robber, your best bet is to submit meekly, but if the worst happens, you'll be forced to have some dealings with the **police. Carabinieri**, with their military-style uniforms and white shoulder belts, deal with general crime, public order and drug control, while the **Vigili Urbani** are mainly concerned with directing traffic and issuing parking fines; the **Polizia Stradale** patrol the motorways. These are the ones Italians are most rude about, but a lot of jokes concerning their supposed stupidity stem from the usual north-south prejudice. The

Carabinieri tend to come from southern Italy – joining the police is one way to escape the poverty trap – and they are posted away from home so as to be well out of the sphere of influence of their families.

The **Polizia Statale**, the other general crime-fighting force, enjoy a fierce rivalry with the **Carabinieri** and are the ones you'll perhaps have most chance of coming into contact with, since **thefts** should be reported to them. You'll find the address of the **Questura** or police station in the local telephone directory (in smaller places it may be just a local *commissariato*), and we've included details in the major city listings. The *Questura* is also where you're supposed to go to obtain a *permesso di soggiorno* **if you're staying** for any length of time, or a **visa extension** if you require one (see box below).

Disabled travellers

Facilities in Italy aren't geared towards disabled travellers, though people are helpful enough and progress is being made to make accommodation, transport and public buildings more accessible.

Public transport can be challenging, although low-level buses are gradually being introduced and some trains have disabled facilities (see p.33 for information on Carta Blu). There will be several appropriate accommodation options in most resorts and you might want to rope the local tourist office in to give you a hand with finding the most suitable but in more out of the way places it's rather potluck. Spacious, specially designed toilets are becoming increasingly common in bars

Emergencies

For help in an emergency, call one of the following national emergency telephone numbers:

☏ 112 for the police (Carabinieri).
☏ 113 for any emergency service, including ambulance (Soccorso Pubblico di Emergenza).
☏ 115 for the fire brigade (Vigili del Fuoco).
☏ 116 for road assistance (Soccorso Stradale).
☏ 118 for an ambulance (Ambulanza).

and restaurants as new legislation takes force. The cobbled streets in old town and village centres can present their own problems, as can access to sights including galleries and museums. Even in the larger cities high curbs, ad hoc parking and constant building works can make life difficult for those in wheelchairs and the partially sighted.

Contacts for travellers with disabilities

In Italy

Accessible Italy ☎ +39.378.941.108, ⊛ www .accessibleitaly.com. Italian operation offering organized tours or tailor-made trips to foreigners.

In the UK and Ireland

Holiday Care 2nd floor, Imperial Building, Victoria Rd, Horley, Surrey RH6 7PZ ☎ 01293/774 535, Minicom ☎ 01293/776 943, ⊛ www.holidaycare .org.uk. Provides free lists of accessible accommodation abroad and information on financial help for holidays.
Irish Wheelchair Association Blackheath Drive, Clontarf, Dublin 3 ☎ 01/833 8241, ⊛ www.iwa.ie. Useful information for wheelchair users about travelling abroad.
Tripscope ☎ 08457/585 641 (with caller announcement), ⊛ www.tripscope.org.uk. National information service with free advice on international transport for those with mobility problems.

In the US and Canada

Access-Able ⊛ www.access-able.com. Online resource for travellers with disabilities.
Accessible Journeys 35 West Sellers Av Ridley Park PA ☎ 1978-800/846-4537, ⊛ www.disability travel.com. Travel tips and programmes for groups or individual traveller including an Italian lakes tour.
Directions Unlimited 720 North Bedford Rd, Bedford Hills, NY 10507 ☎ 1-800/533-5343. Operator specializing in tours in Europe for people with disabilities.
Society for the Advancement of Travellers with Handicaps (SATH) 347 5th Ave, New York, NY 10016 ☎ 212/447-7284, ⊛ www.sath.org. Information on the accessibility of specific airlines and advice on travelling with certain conditions.
Travel Information Service ☎ 215/456-9600. Telephone-only information and referral service.

In Australia and New Zealand

Disabled Persons Assembly 4/173–175 Victoria St, Wellington, New Zealand ☎ 04/801 9100.

Resource centre with lists of travel agencies and tour operators for people with disabilities.
NICAN ⊛ www.ncan.com.au. Website including information about the Quantas Carers Concession card.
Spinal Injuries Australia ⊛ www.spinalcord injuries.com.au. Resource with links to Enterprise travel guides for tourists to Europe with disabilities.

Electricity

The supply is 220V, though anything requiring 240V will work. Most plugs have three round pins, though you'll find the older two-pin plug in some places: a travel plug adapter is useful.

Entry requirements

British, Irish and other EU citizens can enter Italy and stay as long as they like on production of a valid **passport**. Citizens of the United States, Canada, Australia and New Zealand need only a valid passport, too, but are limited to stays of three months. All other nationals should consult the relevant embassy about visa requirements. Legally, you're required to register with the police within three days of entering Italy, though if you're staying at a hotel this will be done for you. Although the police in some towns have become more punctilious about this, most would still be amazed at any attempt to register yourself down at the local police station while on holiday. However, if you're going to be living here for a while, you'd be advised to do it.

Italian embassies and consulates abroad

Australia Embassy: 12 Grey St, Deakin, Canberra, ACT 2600 ☎ 02/6273 3333, ⊛ www.ambcanberra .esteri.it. Consulates in Melbourne ☎ 03/9867 5744; Sydney ☎ 02/9392 7900; Adelaide ☎ 08/8337 0777; Brisbane ☎ 07/3299 8944.
Canada Embassy: 275 Slater St, Ottawa, ON, K1P 5H9 ☎ 613/232-2401, ⊛ www.ambottawa.esteri .it. Consulates in Montréal ☎ 514/849-8351 and Toronto ☎ 416/977-1566.
Ireland Embassy: 63–65 Northumberland Rd, Dublin 4 ☎ 01/660 1744, ⊛ www.ambdublino.esteri.it.
New Zealand Embassy: 34–38 Grant Rd, PO Box 463, Thorndon, Wellington ☎ 04/473-5339, ⊛ www.ambwellington.esteri.it.
South Africa Embassy: 796 George Ave, 0083 Arcadia, Pretoria ☎ 012/423 0000, ⊛ www .ambpretoria.esteri.it.

UK Embassy: 14 Three King's Yard, London W1Y 2EH ☏ 020/7312 2200, ⊛ www.amblondra.esteri.it. Consulate in Manchester ☏ 0161/236 9024. USA Embassy: 3000 Whitehaven St NW, Washington DC 20008 ☏ 202/612-4400, ⊛ www .ambwashingtondc.esteri.it/. Consulates in Boston ☏ 617/722-9201, Chicago ☏ 312/467-1550, New York ☏ 212/737-9100, San Francisco ☏ 415/931-4924 and other cities nationwide.

Gay and lesbian Italy

Homosexuality is legal in Italy, and the age of consent is 16. Attitudes are most tolerant in the northern cities: Bologna is generally regarded as the gay capital, and Milan, Turin and Rome all have well-developed gay scenes; there are also a few *spiagge gay* (gay beaches) dotted along the coast: the more popular gay resorts include Taormina and Rimini. Away from the big cities and resorts, though, activity is more covert. You'll notice, in the south especially, that overt displays of affection between (all) men – linking arms during the *passeggiata*, kissing in greeting and so on – are common. The line determining what's acceptable, however, is finely drawn. The **national gay organization**, ARCI-Gay ☏ 051.649.3055, ⊛ www .arcigay.it, is based in Bologna but has branches in most big towns. The ⊛ www .gay.it website has a wealth of information for gays and lesbians in Italy.

Health

As a member of the European Union, Italy has free reciprocal health agreements with other member states. EU citizens are entitled to free treatment within Italy's public health-care system on production of a **European Health Insurance Card** (EHIC), which British citizens can obtain by picking up a form at the post office, calling ☏ 0845/606 2030, or applying online at ⊛ www.dh.gov.uk. Allow up to 21 days for delivery. The EHIC is free of charge and valid for at least three years, and it basically entitles you to the same treatment as an insured person in Italy. The Australian Medicare system also has a reciprocal health-care arrangement with Italy. **Vaccinations** are not required, and Italy doesn't present any more health worries than anywhere else in Europe; the worst that's likely to happen to you is suffering from

the extreme heat in summer or from an upset stomach (shellfish is the usual culprit). The **water** is perfectly safe to drink and you'll find public fountains (usually button- or tap-operated) in squares and city streets everywhere, though look out for *acqua non potabile* signs, indicating that the water is unsafe to drink. It's worth taking **insect repellent**, as even inland towns, most notoriously Milan, suffer from a persistent mosquito problem, especially in summer. An Italian **pharmacist** (*farmacia*) is well qualified to give you advice on minor ailments and to dispense prescriptions; pharmacies are generally open all night in the bigger towns and cities. A rota system operates, and you should find the address of the one currently open on any *farmacia* door or listed in the local paper.

If you need **treatment**, go to a doctor (*medico*); every town and village has one. Ask at a pharmacy, or consult the local Yellow Pages (under *Azienda Unità Sanitaria Locale* or *Unità Sanitaria Locale*). The Italian Yellow Pages (*Pagine Gialle*) also lists some specialist practitioners in such fields as acupuncture and homeopathy, the latter much more common in Italy than in some countries. If you're eligible, take your EHIC with you to the doctor's: this should enable you to get free treatment and prescriptions for medicines at the local rate – about ten percent of the price of the medicine. For repeat medication, take any empty bottles or capsules with you to the doctor's – the brand names often differ. If you are seriously ill or involved in an accident, go straight to the *Pronto Soccorso* (casualty) of the nearest hospital, or phone ☏ 113 and ask for *ospedale* or *ambulanza*. Throughout the Guide, you'll find listings for pharmacies, hospitals and emergency services in all the major cities. Major train stations and airports also often have first-aid stations with qualified doctors on hand.

Incidentally, try to avoid going to the **dentist** (*dentista*) while you're in Italy. These aren't covered by your EHIC or the health service, and for the smallest problem you'll pay through the teeth. Take local advice, or consult the local Yellow Pages. If you don't have a spare pair of glasses, it's worth taking a copy of your prescription so that an optician (*ottico*) can make you up a new pair should you lose or damage them.

Insurance

Even though EU health care privileges apply in Italy, you'd do well to take out an **insurance policy** before travelling to cover against theft, loss, illness or injury. A typical policy usually provides cover for the loss of baggage, tickets and – up to a certain limit – cash or cheques, as well as cancellation or curtailment of your journey. Most policies exclude so-called dangerous sports unless an extra premium is paid; in Italy this can mean scuba-diving, windsurfing and trekking. Many policies can be chopped and changed to exclude coverage you don't need – for example, sickness and accident benefits can often be excluded or included at will. If you do take medical coverage, ascertain whether benefits will be paid as treatment proceeds or only after your return home, and whether there is a 24-hour medical emergency number. When securing baggage cover, make sure that the per-article limit – typically under £500 – will cover your most valuable possession. If you need to make a claim, you should keep receipts for medicines and medical treatment, and in the event you have anything stolen, you must obtain an official statement from the police (*polizia* or *carabinieri*).

Rough Guides has teamed up with Columbus Direct to offer you **travel insurance** that can be tailored to suit your needs. Products include a low-cost **backpacker option** for long stays; a **short break option** for city getaways; a typical **holiday package option**; and others. There are also annual **multi-trip policies** for those who travel regularly. Different sports and activities (such as trekking and skiing) can usually be covered if required. See our website (ⓦwww.rough guidesinsurance.com) for eligibility and purchasing options. Alternatively, UK residents should call ☏0870/033 9988; Australians, ☏1300/669 999 and New Zealanders, ☏0800/55 9911. All other nationalities should call ☏+44 870/890 2843.

Laundries

Coin-operated Laundromats, sometimes known as *tintorie*, are rare outside large cities, and even there, numbers are sparse; see the "Listings" sections of the main city accounts for addresses. More common is a *lavanderia*, a service-wash laundry, but this will be more expensive. Although you can usually get away with it, washing clothes in your hotel room can cause an international incident – simply because the room's plumbing often can't cope with all the water. It's better to ask if there's somewhere you can wash your clothes.

Mail

Post office opening hours are usually Monday–Saturday 8.30am–7.30pm, though branches in smaller towns tend to close at 1pm. Note too that offices close an hour earlier on the last working day of the month. **Stamps** (*francobolli*) are sold in *tabacchi*, too, as well as in some gift shops in the tourist resorts; they will often also weigh your letter. The Italian postal system is one of the slowest in Europe so if your letter is urgent make sure you send it "*posta prioritaria*", which has varying rates according to weight and destination. Letters can be sent *poste restante* to any Italian post office by addressing them "*Fermo Posta*" followed by the name of the town. When picking something up take your passport, and make sure they check under middle names and initials – and every other letter when all else fails – as filing is often diabolical.

Maps

The **town plans** throughout the Guide should be fine for most purposes, and practically all tourist offices give out maps of their local area for free. The clearest and best-value large-scale commercial **road map** of Italy is the Rough Guide 1:900,000 map, which covers the whole country including Sicily and Sardinia. There are also the 1:800,000 and 1:400,000 maps produced by the Touring Club Italiano, covering north, south and central Italy, and TCI also produces excellent 1:200,000 maps of the individual regions, which are indispensable if you are touring a specific area in depth.

For **hiking** you'll need at least a scale of 1:50,000. Studio FMB and the TCI cover the major mountain areas of northern Italy to this scale, but for more detailed, down-to-scale

1:25,000 maps, both the Istituto Geografico Centrale and Kompass series cover central and northwest Italy and the Alps. The Apennines and Tuscany are covered by Multigraphic (Firenze), easiest bought in Italy, while Tabacco produces a good series detailing the Dolomites and the northeast of the country. In Italy, the Club Alpino Italiano (@www.cai.it) is a good source of hiking maps; we've supplied details of branches throughout the Guide.

Money

Italy's currency is the **euro** (€). The euro is split into 100 cents. There are seven euro **notes** – in denominations of 500, 200, 100, 50, 20, 10, and 5 euros, each a different colour and size – and eight different **coin** denominations, including 2 and 1 euros, then 50, 20, 10, 5, 2, and 1 cents. Euro coins feature a common EU design on one face, but different country-specific designs on the other. At the time of writing the working **rate of exchange** is £1 = €1.52; US$1 = €0.76; Aus$1 = €0.60; NZ$1 = €0.53. In Italy, you'll get the best rate of exchange (*cambio*) at a **bank**. There are a few nationwide banking chains – the Banca Nazionale del Lavoro and Credito Italian, among others – and lots of regional chains like the Banca di Roma, Banco di Napoli or Banco di Sicilia. **Banking hours** are normally Monday to Friday mornings from 8.30am until 1.30pm, and for an hour in the afternoon (usually between 2.30pm and 4pm). There are local variations on this and banks are usually open only in the morning on the day before a public holiday. Outside banking hours, the larger **hotels** will change money or travellers' cheques, although if you're staying in a reasonably large city the rate is invariably better at the train station **exchange bureaux** – normally open evenings and weekends. Check the "Listings" sections of the main city accounts in the Guide.

Opening hours, public holidays

Most shops and businesses open Monday to Saturday from around 8am until 1pm, and from about 4pm until 7pm, though many close on Saturday afternoons and Monday mornings, and in the south the day can begin and end an hour later. In the north

Visiting churches and religious sites

The rules for visiting churches, cathedrals and religious buildings are much the same as they are all over the Mediterranean and are strictly enforced everywhere: **dress modestly**, which means no shorts (not even Bermuda-length ones) and covered shoulders for women, and try to avoid wandering around during a service.

some businesses work a 9-to-5 day to facilitate international dealings. Traditionally, everything except bars and restaurants closes on Sunday, though most towns have a *pasticceria* open in the mornings, while in large cities and tourist areas, Sunday shopping is becoming more common.

Churches, museums and archeological sites

Most churches open in the early morning, around 7 or 8am for Mass, and close around noon, opening up again at 4pm and closing at 7 or 8pm. In more remote places, some will only open for early morning and evening services, while others are closed at all times except Sundays and on religious holidays; if you're determined to take a look, you may have to ask around for the key.

Another problem is that lots of churches, monasteries, convents and oratories are **closed for restoration** (*chiuso per restauro*). We've indicated in the text the more long-term closures, though you might be able to persuade a workman or priest/curator to show you around even if there's scaffolding everywhere.

Opening hours for state-run **museums** are generally Tuesday to Saturday 9am until any time from 2pm until 7pm, and Sunday from 9am until 1pm. Most other museums

Closed Mondays

Most museums, archeological sites and tourist destinations throughout the country are closed on Mondays.

roughly follow this pattern too, although they are more likely to close for a couple of hours in the afternoon, and have shorter opening times in winter. Many large museums also run late-night openings in summer (till 10pm or later Tues–Sat, or 8pm Sun). The opening times of **archeological sites** are more flexible: most sites open every day, often including Sunday, from 9am until late evening – frequently specified as one hour before sunset, and thus changing according to the time of year. In winter, times are drastically cut, principally because of the darker evenings; 4pm is a common closing time.

Public holidays

Whereas it can be fun to stumble across a local festival, it's best to know when the national holidays are as almost everything will shut down. In **August**, particularly during the weeks either side of *Ferragosto* (August 15), when most of the country flees to the coast and mountains, many towns are left half-deserted, with shops, bars and restaurants closed and a reduced public transport service. Local religious holidays don't necessarily close down shops and businesses, but they do mean that accommodation space may be tight. The country's official **national holidays**, on the other hand, close everything down except bars and restaurants. A recent initiative has been to open national museums and monuments on public holidays to encourage Italians to make the most of their national heritage, although it's still best to check beforehand if you are planning a trip around one particular sight.

January 1 *Primo dell'anno*; New Year's Day
January 6 *Epifania*; Epiphany
Pasquetta Easter Monday
April 25 *Giorno della Liberazione*; Liberation Day
May 1 *Festa dei Lavoratori*; Labour Day
June 2 *Festa della Repubblica*; Republic Day

August 15 *Ferragosto*; Assumption of the Blessed Virgin Mary
November 1 *Ognissanti*; All Souls Day
December 8 *Immaccolata*; Immaculate Conception of the Blessed Virgin Mary
December 25 *Natale*; Christmas
December 26 *Santo Stefano*; St Stephen's Day

Phones

Public **telephones**, run by **Telecom Italia**, come in various forms, usually with clear instructions in English. Coin-operated machines are increasingly hard to find so you will probably have to buy a **telephone card** (*carta* or *scheda telefonica*), available from *tabacchi* and newsstands. **Telephone numbers** change with amazing frequency in Italy and codes are now an integral part of the number and always need to be dialled, regardless of whether or not you are in the zone you are telephoning. All telephone numbers listed in the Guide include the relevant code. Numbers beginning ☏800 are free, ☏170 will get you through to an English-speaking operator, ☏176 to international directory enquiries.

Phone **tariffs** are among the most expensive in Europe, especially if you're calling long-distance or internationally. You can cut costs hugely by buying a **phone card** – on sale for upwards of €5; you don't insert it into the phone but dial a central number and then a pin code given on the reverse of the card.

Time

Italy is always one hour ahead of Britain, seven hours ahead of US Eastern Standard Time and ten hours ahead of Pacific Time.

Tourist information

Before you leave, it may be worth contacting the Italian State Tourist Office (ENIT,

Calling home from abroad

UK and Northern Ireland international access code + 44 + city code.
Republic of Ireland international access code + 353 + city code.
USA and Canada international access code + 1 + area code.
Australia international access code + 61 + city code.
New Zealand international access code + 64 + city code.

www.enit.it) for a selection of maps and brochures, though you can usually pick up much the same information from tourist offices in Italy. Most towns, major train stations and airports in Italyhave a **tourist office** or "APT" (Azienda Promozione Turistica) or "IAT" (Ufficio Informazioni Accoglienza Turistica), all of which vary in degree of usefulness (and helpfulness) but usually provide at least a town plan and local listings guide. In smaller villages there is sometimes a "Pro Loco" office that has much the same kind of information, but the staff are unlikely to speak English.

Opening hours vary: larger city and resort offices are likely to be open Monday to Saturday 9am to 1pm and 4 to 7pm, and sometimes for a short period on Sunday mornings; smaller offices may open weekdays only, while Pro Loco times are notoriously erratic – some open for only a couple of hours a day, even in summer. If the tourist office isn't open and all else fails, the local telephone office, most hotels, and bars with phones should all have a copy of the local *Tuttocittà* or similar (a supplement to the main telephone directories), which carries listings and phone numbers of essential services and adverts for restaurants and shops, together with indexed maps of the appropriate city.

Italian State Tourist Offices abroad

Australia Level 4, 46 Market St, Sydney, NSW 2000 ☎ 02/926-21666, ✉ italia@italiatourism.com.
Canada 175 Bloor St East, Suite 907, South Tower, Toronto, ON M4W 3R8 ☎ 416/925-4882, ✉ enitto@italiantourism.com ⓦ www.italiantourism.com.
UK 1 Princes St, London W1R 2AY ☎ 0270/408 1254 or 00800/00482 542, ✉ Eitaly @italiantouristboard.co.uk.
US 630 Fifth Avenue, Suite 1565, New York, NY 10111 ☎ 212/245-4822, ✉ enitny@italiantourism .com; 12400 Wilshire Boulevard, Suite 550, Los Angeles, CA 90025 ☎ 310/820-1898, ✉ Eenitla @italiantourism.com, ⓦ www.italiantourism.com; 500 North Michigan Ave, Suite 2240, Chicago, IL 60611 ☎ 312/644-0996, ✉ Eenitch@atalian tourism.com, ⓦ www.italiantourism.com.

Guide

Guide

Piemonte and Valle d'Aosta

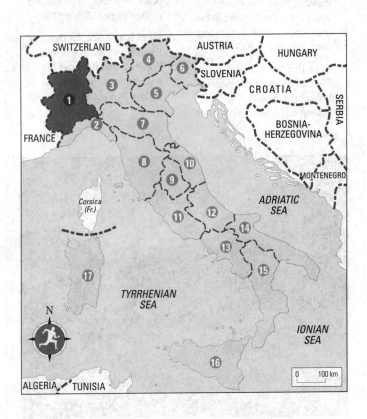

CHAPTER 1 **Highlights**

* Truffles The speciality of the Piemonte region is the very costly white truffle, shaved onto pasta and washed down with the excellent local Barolo or Barbaresco wine. **See p.73**

* Sacra di San Michele The views of the surrounding valley from this fortified abbey are more than worth the long climb up. **See p.90**

* Alba This hill-town is Piemonte's most captivating, boasting a beautiful, well-preserved historic centre and a bubblegum-pink Gothic Duomo with a fancifully decorated interior. **See p.96**

* Parco Nazionale del Gran Paradiso The first Italian national park preserves an Alpine region of deep valleys and beautiful mountains that is home to ibex, chamois and golden eagles. **See p.109**

* Mont Blanc (Monte Bianco) Excellent views of this awe-inspiring mountain can be enjoyed from the Testa d'Arpy. **See p.112**

△ Parco Nazionale del Gran Paradiso

Piemonte and Valle d'Aosta

I n the extreme northwest of Italy, fringed by the French and Swiss Alps and grooved with deep valleys, **Piemonte** and **Valle d'Aosta** are the least "Italian" regions. French was spoken in Piemonte until the end of the nineteenth century and still influences Piemontese dialects; Valle d'Aosta is bilingual and in some valleys the locals, whose ancestors emigrated from Switzerland, still speak a dialect based on German. Piemonte (literally "at the foot of the mountains") is one of Italy's wealthiest regions, known for its fine wines and food and for being home to huge Italian corporations such as Fiat and Olivetti. Italy's longest river, the mighty River Po, begins here, and the towns of its vast plain – which stretches right across northern Italy – have grown rich on both manufacturing and rice, cultivated in sweeping paddy fields.

Turin, on the main rail and road route from France to Milan, is the obvious first stop and, despite being Italy's second industrial city, retains a recently restored Baroque core and is well placed for days out. South of Turin, **Alba** and **Saluzzo** are perhaps the most enticing towns, the former a good base for visiting the region's wine cantinas, the latter convenient if you want to explore the western valleys. **Asti**, to the southeast, really comes to life during its famous medieval Palio, or horse race. For the rest of the region, winter sports and walking are the main activities; Sestriere is the main skiing centre, whilst the ascent of Monviso in the far west appeals to the climbing fraternity.

Greater challenges – and more spectacular views – are to be found in the adjoining region of **Valle d'Aosta**. Bordered by Europe's highest mountains, Mont Blanc, Monte Rosa and the Matterhorn, veined with valleys and studded with castles, Valle d'Aosta is undeniably picturesque. The central Aosta valley cuts right across the region, following the River Dora to the foot of Mont Blanc on the French border. Along the river are most of the feudal castles for which Valle d'Aosta is famed – the majority built by the Challant family, who ruled the region for seven centuries. Although the castles are pretty from the outside, and easily accessible by bus or train, few are absorbing enough to warrant a special trip into the region. But as skiing and walking country, Valle d'Aosta is unsurpassed. The main valley is rather bland, and it's in the more scenic tributary valleys that you'll want to spend most of your time. The eastern area is the most touristy, with ski resorts and narrow, winding roads that can get choked with holiday traffic – as well as with air pollution from Turin at times. If you're walking, head west for the

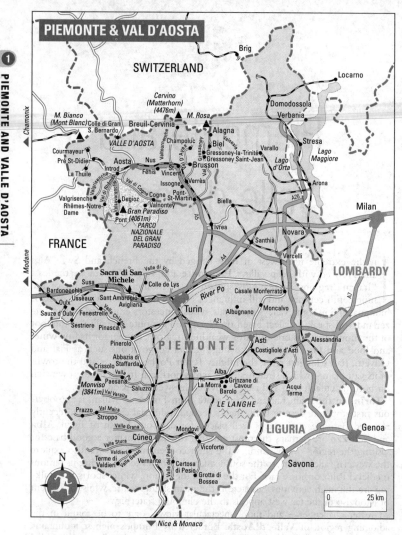

PIEMONTE & VAL D'AOSTA

protected zone of Italy's largest national park, the **Gran Paradiso**. The valleys here can also be busy – the mountain *rifugi* and hotels become packed in summer – but development is more restrained. **Aosta**, the regional capital, is the only town of any size and, with its attractive cobbled streets and good shopping, makes an excellent staging post on the way to the smaller mountain resorts.

Getting around Piemonte is fairly easy. The network of trains and buses is comprehensive, and your own transport is only necessary for the out-of-the-way places. You can get to most places from Turin; Alba makes a good base for exploring Le Langhe, Saluzzo for the western valleys.

Viewing the Valle d'Aosta on public transport is a bit trickier: buses run from Piemonte along the main valley past most of the castles, but services connecting

Piemonte and Valle d'Aosta are a paradise for gastronomes and connoisseurs of vintage wines. Rich Piemontese cuisine betrays close links with France through dishes like *fonduta* (fondue) and its preference for using **butter** and **cream** in cooking. Piemonte is perhaps most famous for its **white truffles**, the most exquisite of which come from around the town of Alba and are ferociously expensive. They are most often used in the form of shavings to subtly perfume a dish of pasta or a risotto. Watch out too for porcini mushrooms, chestnuts, and **bagna caöda** – a sauce of oil, anchovies, garlic, butter and cream, also served as a fondue. *Agnolotti* and *cappelletti* (pasta filled with meat or, more unusually, mushrooms) are the best-known dishes, followed by meat *buji* (boiled) or braised in wine. Cheeses to look out for are *tomini*, *robiole* and *tume*. The sweets, too, are marvellous, many of them invented in the Savoy kitchens to tempt the royal palates: among the decadent delights are *spumone piemontese*, a mousse of mascarpone cheese with rum; *panna cotta*, smooth cooked cream; and light pastries like *lingue di gatto* (cat's tongues) and *baci di dama* (lady's kisses). Turin is also credited as the home of *zabaglione*, an egg yolk, sugar and Marsala mixture used to fill *bignole*, or iced choux pastries. It was said to have been invented in the sixteenth century by Spanish friar San Pasquale Bayon, a gifted cook and parish priest of the city's church of San Tommaso.

The rolling vine-clad hills of Le Langhe and Monferrato produce traditional **wines** such as Barolo, Barbera and Nebbiolo. These fine reds need ageing, and Barolo in particular can be very expensive. More suitable for everyday drinking are wines made from the *dolcetto* grape, notably Dolcetto d'Alba, drunk young and lightly chilled. Probably the most famous is the sweet sparkling wine, Asti (wine makers dropped the "spumante" from the name in 1994 in a bid for a new image) – there has been a trend in recent years to make dry *spumante* too. Martini and Cinzano vermouths are also produced in and around Turin, a fusion of the region's wines with at least thirteen of the wild herbs that grow on its mountains. The traditional version to drink, now a brand name, is Punt e Mes ("point and a half") – one part bitter to half-a-part sweet.

the tributary valleys are infrequent, while trains are less regular and run only as far as Pré-St-Didier. For serious exploration of the quieter valleys, your own vehicle is a definite advantage. The road branches off at Aosta into Switzerland via the Grand-St-Bernard Pass and forks again some 30km further west at Pré-St-Didier: both branches run into France – the southern via the Petit-St-Bernard Pass to Chambéry, the northern to Chamonix through the Mont Blanc tunnel. As these roads link France and Italy, they are much used by long-distance lorries, which are something of an earache and eyesore. However, a tunnel between Bruzolo and St Jean de Maurienne, still in its early phases, will permit lorries to be transported by rail, and should dramatically reduce traffic and pollution by the year 2020.

Although the western shore of **Lago Maggiore** is actually in Piemonte, we've treated all the lakes as a region and covered them in the "Lombardy and the lakes" chapter; the Maggiore account starts on p.219.

Turin (Torino)

"Do you know Turin?" asked Nietzsche. "It is a city after my own heart . . . a princely residence of the seventeenth century, which has only one taste, giving commands to everything, the court and its nobility. Aristocratic calm is preserved in everything; there are no nasty suburbs." Although **TURIN**'s traffic-choked streets are no longer calm, and its suburbs are as dreary as any in Italy, the city centre's gracious Baroque thoroughfares, opulent palaces, sumptuous churches and splendid collections of Egyptian antiquities and northern European paintings are still there, as well as new pedestrian-only areas – a pleasant surprise to those who might have been expecting satanic factories and little else. Ever since the major spruce-up for the 2006 Winter Olympics, Turin's emphasis has been on promoting its historic urban charms, such as its genteel Belle Époque cafés and traditional chocolate treats (see box, p.85) – not to mention an array of walking tours that explore the city's extraordinary, vivid heritage (see Listings).

Some history

Although originally an ancient Roman settlement, it was the Savoy dynasty that left the largest impression on Turin: from 1563 the city was the seat of the Savoy dukes, who persecuted Piemonte's Protestants and Jews, censored the press and placed education of the nobles in the extreme hands of the Jesuits. The Savoys gained a royal title in 1713, and a few years later acquired Sardinia, which whetted their appetite for more territory. After more than a century of military and diplomatic wrangling with foreign powers, Duke Carlo Alberto di Savoia (who promised to "eat Italy like an artichoke") teamed up with the liberal politician of the Risorgimento, Cavour, who used the royal family to lend credibility to the Unification movement. In 1860 Garibaldi handed over Sicily and southern Italy to Vittorio Emanuele, successor to Carlo Alberto, and though it was to take a further ten years for him to seize the papal heart of the artichoke – Rome – he was declared king of Italy.

After a spell in Turin, then Florence, the capital was definitively moved to Rome in 1870, leaving Turin in the hands of the Piemontese nobility. It became a provincial backwater where a tenth of the 200,000 population worked as domestic servants, with a centre decked out in elaborate finery: its cafés were decorated with chandeliers, carved wood, frescoes and gilt – only slightly less ostentatious than the rooms of the Savoy palaces. World War I brought plenty of work but also food shortages and, in 1917, street riots erupted, establishing Turin as a focus of labour activism. Gramsci led occupations of the Fiat factory here, going on to found the Communist Party.

By the Fifties, Turin's population had soared to 700,000, mainly made up of migrant workers from the poor south, who were housed in shanty towns outside the city and shunned as peasants by the Torinesi. Blocks of flats were eventually built for the workers – the bleak Mirafiori housing estates – and by the Sixties' Fiat's workforce had grown to 130,000, with a further half million dependent on the company in some way. Not surprisingly, Turin became known as Fiatville. Today there are fewer people involved in the industry, and Fiat's famous Lingotto factory is now a shopping centre and conference centre; the gap left behind has been filled by some of the biggest names from other industries – Motorola, Einaudi, Ferrero and Martini – ensuring a continuation of Turin's industrial tradition and economic prosperity.

Arrival, information and city transport

Turin's **airport**, Caselle (information ☎011.567.6361 or 011.567.6362), is 15km north of the city, connected by buses every 30 to 45 minutes with Porta Susa and Porta Nuova train stations (40min; €5, €5.50 if you buy it on board). Turin's main **train station**, Porta Nuova, on Corso Vittorio Emanuele II at

A new Turin for the Winter Olympics 2006

As host of the Winter Olympics 2006 (Ⓦwww.torino2006.org), Piemonte interconnected seven of its eight major ski locations, now known collectively as **The Milky Way**, equipping them with new lodges, ski lifts and snow-making machines. Cesana, Pinerolo, Pragelato, Sauze d'Oulx, Sansicario, Claviere and Sestriere — with Bardonecchia unconnected to the continuum — welcomed a huge influx of visitors, a trend which seems set to continue. In Turin itself major changes have also come about: there are new sports arenas and an Olympic village — just behind the Lingotto Centre — and the city is revising its entire urban infrastructure. Some projects, such as one leg of the new metro line have been completed, while longer-term developments (to be finished in 2015 or so) include the regeneration of Porta Susa train station into a high-speed rail link connecting Turin and Lyon, and the renovation of some suburban districts. Whatever the time frame, the ultimate payback of the schemes will guarantee Turin's improvement, for locals and tourists alike. The city is already much more user-friendly, with many more pedestrian-only areas, face-lifted piazzas and attractions, efficient transport and excellent information services.

the southern end of Via Roma, is convenient for the city centre and hotels. Some trains also stop at Porta Susa on Corso Inghilterra, west of the centre and heralded as the city's primary hub in the near future (see box above). Close by, on the corner of Corso Inghilterra and Corso Vittorio Emanuele II, is the main **bus station** (Ⓣ800.333.444), the arrival and departure point for most intercity and all international buses; however, local buses to Saluzzo and Cúneo arrive at, and leave from, the top of Corso Marconi, near the junction with Via Nizza. The bus station is linked to Via Nizza (near Porta Nuova) and Porta Susa by bus #9.

The main **tourist office** is in one of the newfangled structures in the middle of Piazza Solferino, the Atrium 2006 building (daily 9am–7.30pm; Ⓣ011.535.181, Ⓦwww.turismotorino.org). There are further branches at the train station (daily 9.30am–7pm) and the airport (daily 8am–11pm); they can book accommodation, restaurants and guided tours, as well as supply you with the very reasonable **Torino card** (€16 for 48 hours, €18 for 72 hours or €30 for 5 days), allowing free entrance to some 140 museums and sights such as monuments, castles and royal residences in Turin and Piemonte, plus discounts on guided tours, theatre performances, concerts, opera, parking and even car rental. It also includes free use of urban transport, including the TurismoBus (see below) and the boats on the River Po.

Most of Turin's sights are within walking distance of Porta Nuova station, although if you're pushed for time you should take advantage of the city's fast and efficient **tram and bus** network (Ⓦwww.comune.torino.it/gtt/). Tickets, valid for 70min, must be bought before you board – they cost €0.90 each or €12.50 for fifteen from *tabacchi* and newsstands. Useful **routes** include tram #4, which heads north through the city from Porta Nuova along Via XX Settembre to Piazza della Repubblica; bus #1 between Porta Susa, Porta Nuova and the Lingotto centre; tram #15 from Porta Nuova to Via Pietro Micca; bus #61 from Porta Nuova across the river; and bus #34 from Porta Nuova to the Museo dell'Automobile. Alternatively, it's possible to explore the city by **TurismoBus** (daily 10am–7pm; €6 per day), which operates a hop-on-hop-off circular route that takes in the major sights. You can pick it up at Piazza Solferino, Piazza Castello, Piazza San Carlo and Via Lagrange among other places. Tickets can be bought on the bus. **Taxi** ranks are found on most of the main squares in the

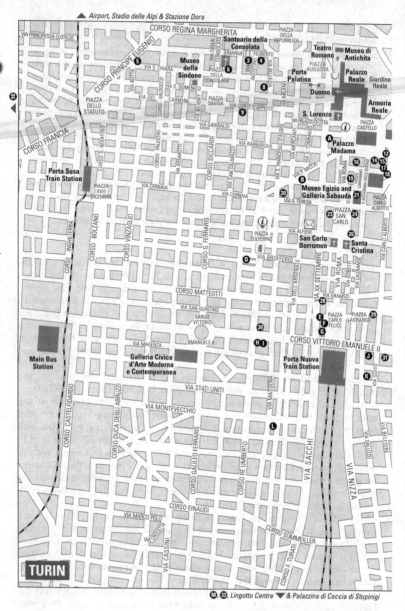

▲ *Airport, Stadio delle Alpi & Stazione Dora*

M, **33**, *Lingotto Centre* ▼ *& Palazzina di Caccia di Stupinigi*

centre of Turin, as well as at the bus and train stations and the airport, or dial ☎011.5730 or 011.5737.

Accommodation

Turin has a number of attractive **hotels** in every quarter. Demand is usually high, especially during the skiing season and trade fairs (when prices also rise), so it's a

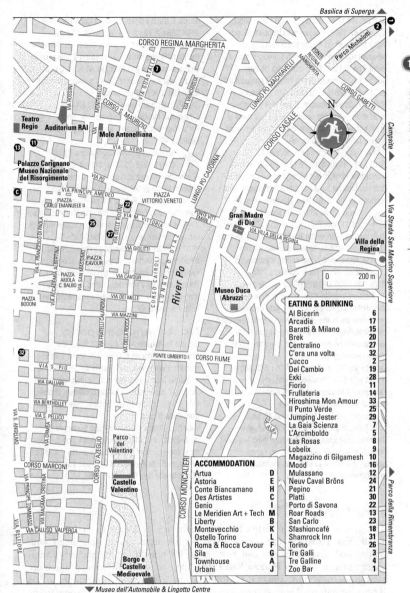

CORSO REGINA MARGHERITA

Parco Michelotti

FONTE REGINA MARGHERITA

CORSO GABETTI

Campsite ▶

LUNGO PO MACHIAVELLI

CORSO CASALE

Via Strada San Martino Superiore ▶

N

VIA ROSSINI
VIA GUASTALLA
MONTEBELLO
VIA GUASTALLA
CORSO S. MAURIZIO
VIA S. CIRIDO

❼

Teatro Regio Auditorium RAI
Mole Antonelliana
VIA G. VERDI

❽ ❶❶

Palazzo Carignano
Museo Nazionale del Risorgimento
VIA PO

LUNGO PO CADORNA

Ⓒ
VIA PRINCIPE AMEDEO
PIAZZA CARLO EMANUELE II
PIAZZA VITTORIO VENETO
❷❷
VIA M. VITTORIA
VIA DELLE ROSINE
❷❺
❷❼
VIA GIOLITTI
VIA S. FRANCESCO DA PAOLA
VIA ACCADEMIA ALBERTINA
VIA GIUSEPPE MASSIMO
PIAZZA CAVOUR
VIA CAVOUR
PIAZZA AIUOLA C. BALBO
PIAZZA BODONI
VIA DEI MILLE
VIA MAZZINI
VIA FRATELLI CALANDRA
VIA DELLA ROCCA
❸❷

PONTE VITT. EMAN. I

Gran Madre di Dio
VIA VILLA DELLA REGINA

Villa della Regina

0   200 m

PONTE UMBERTO I
CORSO FIUME

Museo Duca Abruzzi

River Po
CORSO CAIROLI
LUNGO PO DIAZ

VIA S. PIO
VIA GALLIARI
VIA BERTHOLLET
VIA S. PELLICO
VIA S. ANGELMO
VIA ORMEA

Parco del Valentino

CORSO MARCONI

Castello Valentino

CORSO D'AZEGLIO
CORSO MONCALIERI
VIA PRINCIPE TOMMASO
VIA MADAMA CRISTINA
VIA CALUSO VALPERGA
VIA BELFIORE

Borgo e Castello Medioevale

Parco della Rimembranza ▶

EATING & DRINKING

Al Bicerin	6
Arcadia	17
Baratti & Milano	15
Brek	20
Centralino	27
C'era una volta	32
Cucco	2
Del Cambio	19
Exki	28
Fiorio	11
Frullateria	14
Hiroshima Mon Amour	33
Il Punto Verde	25
Jumping Jester	29
La Gaia Scienza	7
L'Arcimboldo	5
Las Rosas	8
Lobelix	9
Magazzino di Gilgamesh	10
Mood	16
Mulassano	12
Neuv Caval Brôns	24
Pepino	21
Platti	30
Porto di Savona	22
Roar Roads	13
San Carlo	23
Sfashioncafé	18
Shamrock Inn	31
Torino	26
Tre Galli	3
Tre Galline	4
Zoo Bar	1

ACCOMMODATION

Artua	D
Astoria	E
Conte Biancamano	H
Des Artistes	C
Genio	I
Le Meridien Art + Tech	M
Liberty	B
Montevecchio	K
Ostello Torino	L
Roma & Rocca Cavour	F
Sila	G
Townhouse	A
Urbani	J

▼ Museo dell'Automobile & Lingotto Centre

good idea to phone in advance. Be aware that a few hotels close in August – which is low season for Turin – and virtually all of them offer special weekend packages.

Hotels

Artua Via Brofferio 3 ☏ 011.517.5301 or 11.561.3444, ☏ 011.517.5141 or 011.562.2241, ⓦ www.hotelartua.it or www.hotelsolferino.it.

Comfortable two-part hotel (with the neighbouring *Solferino*) with a/c, plus safe parking at extra charge. Very handy for major sights. ❻

Astoria Via XX Settembre 4 ☎011.562.0653, ⓕ011.562.5866, ⓦwww.astoriahotel.it. Good-value hotel just off Piazza Carlo Felice, with pleasant rooms and extremely friendly management. The traffic outside can get a bit noisy. ❹

Conte Biancamano Corso Vittorio Emanuele II 73 ☎011.562.3281, ⓕ011.562.3789, ⓦwww .hotelcontebiancamano.it. If you feel like staying in a rather grandiose setting, go for this hotel set in an old palace with panelled ceilings and large, freshly remodelled rooms. ❺

Des Artistes Via Principe Amedeao 21 ☎011.812.4416, ⓕ011.812.4466, ⓦwww .desartisteshotel.it. Not far from the main sights, this comfortable, spacious hotel has simple, smart rooms with the usual three-star amenities. ❺

🏃 Genio Corso Vittorio Emanuele II 47 ☎011.650.5771, ⓕ011.650.8264, ⓦwww .hotelgenio.it. Three-star Best Western just outside Porta Nuova station. Rooms are elegant and diverse, some even boast ceiling frescoes. ❺

Le Meridien Art + Tech Via Nizza 230 ☎011.664.2000, ⓕ011.664.2004, ⓦwww .lemeridien-lingotto.it. For a luxury treat head for this slightly out-of-the-way five-star designer emporium set in the old Fiat works and redesigned by Renzo Piano. You can go jogging on Fiat's ex-test track on the roof – and there are some lovely views too. ❼

Liberty Via Pietro Micca 15 ☎011.562.8801, ⓕ011.562.8163, ⓦwww.hotelliberty-torino.it. Relaxing Art Nouveau-style establishment on the edge of the medieval quarter. ❸

Montevecchio Via Montevecchio 13 bis ☎011.562.0023, ⓕ011.562.3047, ⓦwww .hotelmontevecchio.com. That rare thing – a quiet hotel near the train station. Though rather spartan, this one also has good facilities, with TV and telephone in all rooms. ❸

Roma & Rocca Cavour Piazza Carlo Felice 60 ☎011.561.2772, ⓕ011.562.8137, ⓦwww .romarocca.it. Old-style, family-run hotel in front of the Porta Nuova station, overlooking a noisy square with a small park and fountain. All in all, good value, with the choice of a very substantial buffet breakfast at €7.50 per person. ❷

Sila Piazza Carlo Felice 80 ☎011.544.086. Convenient location almost opposite the Porta Nuova train station, and offering decent facilities. ❷

🏃 Townhouse Via XX Settembre 70 ☎011.1970.0003, ⓕ011.1970.0188, ⓦwww.townhouse.it. A sleek, contemporary addition to the pedestrian-only zone just west of Piazza Castello. Rooms are plush and smartly contemporary in style, with every amenity; there's Wi-Fi in the soothingly decorated reception area. ❻

Urbani Via Saluzzo 7 ☎011.669.9047, ⓕ011.669.3226, ⓦwww.hotelurbani.it. Good choice for comfort and value in the station area, located on a quiet street a minute's walk from Porta Nuova. Very pleasant rooms, individually furnished, many with balconies overlooking the inner courtyard. ❸

Hostel and campsite

Ostello Torino Via Alby 1 ☎011.660.2939, ⓦwww.ostellotorino.it. Official HI hostel with clean modern dormitories, and dinners for €9. Wi-Fi is available. Members only. Closed Christmas to mid-Jan. €17 per person including breakfast. Doubles with private bath €19 per person. Take bus #52 from Porta Nuova.

Villa Rey Strada Val San Martino Superiore 27 ☎ & ⓕ011.819.0117, ⓦwww.actitorino.it. The most convenient of the city's campsites – take bus #61 from Porta Nuova, and then bus #54. Open late March to late Nov. From €10 daily.

The City

The grid street-plan of Turin's Baroque centre makes it easy to find your way about. **Via Roma** is the central spine of the city, a grand affair lined with rejuvenated designer shops and ritzy cafés. It's punctuated by the city's most elegant piazzas, notably **Piazza San Carlo**, close to which are some of the more prestigious museums. **Piazza Castello** forms a grandiose conclusion to Via Roma, with its royal palaces standing stately in a vast pedestrian-only zone. To the west lies a cluster of pedestrianized shopping streets, more relaxed than Via Roma and a good area to head for during the evening *passeggiata* in summer. North is the **Piazza della Repubblica**, a huge square with the largest open-air market in Europe. To the southeast, the porticoes of **Via Po** forge down to the river, where a short walk along brings you to the extensive **Parco del Valentino**, and some of the city's best nightlife just downriver at Murazzi. Beyond, the engaging **Museo dell'Automobile** and the **Lingotto centre** which houses the **Pinacoteca**

Giovanni e Marella Agnelli, an art gallery displaying the Fiat magnates' superb private collection, while the hills **across the river** – which are peppered with the Art Nouveau villas of the richest Torinesi – shelter the **Basilica di Superga**. South, beyond the city limits, lies the royal **Stupinigi Hunting-Lodge**.

Porta Nuova and around

The areas along the sides of the **Porta Nuova** station were still construction sites at the time of writing and the situation has only exacerbated the usual seediness endemic to all major train stations in Italy; it's a kind of no-man's-land haunt of prostitutes and petty criminals. The potentially elegant arcades (*portici*) of Via Nizza and Corso Vittorio Emanuele II are typical of Turin's measured symmetry – the city boasts over 40km of these colonnaded walkways.

To the west of here, the **Galleria Civica d'Arte Moderna e Contemporanea** (GAM) at Via Magenta 31 (Tues–Sun 10am–7pm; €7.50) features a good cross section of twentieth-century works by artists as varied as De Chirico, Morandi, Modigliani, Picasso, Klee and Warhol. The overall quality of the permanent collection is tempered by an unexciting floor-and-a-half of work mostly from the last two hundred years of the Torinese school, with the notable exception of a fine work by the nineteenth-century French Realist painter Gustave Courbet. However, as the gallery is on the international circuit for touring exhibitions and loans, there is often more than enough to compensate.

Back at Porta Nuova, crossing the road brings you to the neat gardens of **Piazza Carlo Felice**, beyond which lies **Via Roma**, the stamping ground of the well heeled.

Piazza San Carlo and around

Halfway down Via Roma, **Piazza San Carlo** is known with some justification as the parlour of Turin; it's a grand oval space fronted by Baroque facades, the porticoes of which house elegant cafés. Holding court is an equestrian statue of the Savoy duke Emanuele Filiberto raising his sword in triumph after securing Turin's independence from the French and Spanish at the battle of San Quintino in 1574. The entrance to the square is guarded by the twin Baroque churches of **San Carlo Borromeo** and **Santa Cristina**, behind which two gigantic Fascist-era reclining nudes represent Turin's two rivers, the Po and the Dora.

Around the corner from Piazza San Carlo, the newly refurbished **Museo Egizio**, Via Accademia delle Scienze 6 (Tues–Sun 8.30am–7.30pm; €6.50), holds a superb collection of Egyptian antiquities, begun under the aegis of Carlo Emanuele III in the mid-eighteenth century and added to over the ensuing centuries. Remodelled for the 2006 Winter Olympics, the building boasts some 30,000 artefacts and is second only to the Egyptian Museum of Cairo in size. You'll find decorated mummy cases, a fragment of painted canvas dated to 3500 BC and an intriguing assortment of everyday objects, including castanets, sandals, a linen tunic dating from 2300 BC, and even food – eggs, pomegranates and grain, recognizable despite their shrivelled, darkened state. The collection's most recent major acquisition is a small Nubian temple dedicated by Tutmosis III to Ellesija, although the undoubted overall highlights are a **statue of Ramses II** and the **Tomb of Kha and Mirit**. The tomb, discovered in 1906 at Deir-el-Medina, home of the architects, masons and painters of the nearby royal necropolis, is that of a 1400 BC architect, Kha, and his wife Mirit. The burial chamber contains the tools of Kha's trade – cubits, a case for balances, pens and a writing tablet – and more ordinary daily items: a bed with a headrest, clothes, generous rations of food and even a board game to while away the posthumous hours, as well as his own personal illustrated copy of the Egyptian Book of the

Dead. And to ensure that Mirit kept up appearances, she was provided with a cosmetic case, wig, comb and tweezers. Finally, and perhaps the most significant part of the museum's collection, is the vast array of papyri, which proved crucial to the definitive decoding of hieroglyphics in the early 1800s.

Above the museum, the **Galleria Sabauda** (Tues, Fri, Sat & Sun 8.30am–2pm, Wed & Thurs 2–7.30pm; closed Mon; €4) was built around the Savoys' private collection and is still firmly stamped with their taste: a crowded miscellany of Italian, Dutch and Flemish paintings punctuated by some real masterpieces. Of the Italian paintings downstairs, the most arresting is perhaps Botticelli's *Venus*. She is not nearly as elaborate as her Uffizi counterpart, but every bit as alluring. The fifteenth-century *Archangel Raphael and Tobias* by Antonio and Piero Pollaiuolo is one of the gallery's signature works, though it is not typical of the Pollaiuolo brothers' vigorous nude studies in human anatomy. Among the first artists to undertake such research, the brothers were once considered ahead of their time, but this image is more jaunty than muscular. Compare another painting in the collection by Pollaiuolo contemporary Filippino Lippi, which treats the same subject in a rarefied, almost ethereal way, displaying a much sweeter side to early Renaissance painting. The Dutch and Flemish section downstairs contains Van Eyck's *Stigmatization of St Francis*, a warmly human piece and the only panel by this artist in Italy, as well as works by Rembrandt, a bacchanalian *Amarilli and Mirtillo* by Van Dyck, and a thought-provoking *Vanity of Human Life* by Jan Brueghel. On a more austere level, yet filled with fanciful detail, Hans Memling's *Passion of Christ* depicts the key events of Christ's final days of suffering, though within the labyrinthine and anachronistic setting of a typical Italian Renaissance city. Upstairs, the collections of Emanuele Filiberto through to Carlo Felice are hung in a crowded, old-fashioned manner but it's worth seeking out Van Dyck's *The Children of Charles I of England* (a copy of which hangs in the Palazzo Reale) and some of the Venetian masterpieces, among them a couple of fine Veronese commissions including a rousing *Venus and Mars*. The gallery is expected eventually to move to a new location in Palazzo Reale, though no date has yet been suggested.

Piazza Castello and around

Via Roma continues north through the heart of Turin, passing near some of the significant monuments of the Savoys and Italian Unification. The **Museo Nazionale del Risorgimento Italiano**, Via Accademia della Scienze 5 (closed for restoration at the time of writing but set to reopen sometime in mid-2008), housed in the star-flecked **Palazzo Carignano**, birthplace of Vittorio Emanuele II, is worth a visit. The first meetings of the Italian parliament were held in the palace's circular Chamber of the Subalpine Parliament, and the building was the power base of leaders like Cavour, who ousted the more radical Garibaldi to an early retirement on the island of Caprera near Sardinia. It's ironic, then, that the most interesting sections of the museum are those dedicated to Garibaldi: portraits showing him as a scruffy, long-haired revolutionary, some of his clothes – an embroidered fez, a long stripy scarf and one of the famous red shirts – adopted during his exile in South America, where he trained himself by fighting in various wars of independence. These shirts became the uniform of his army of a thousand volunteers who seized southern Italy and Sicily from the Bourbons.

What Vittorio Emanuele II made of the eccentrically dressed revolutionary who secured half the kingdom for him is undocumented, but you feel sure that his residence, the sixteenth-century **Palazzo Reale** (Tues–Sun 8.30am–7.30pm; €6.50), at the head of the sprawling **Piazza Castello**, wouldn't have impressed Garibaldi. Designed by Castellamonte, this nouveau-riche palace with an unexceptional facade hides glitzy, semi-furnished rooms gilded virtually top-to-bottom and decorated with bombastic allegorical paintings. If this isn't enough, look in also on the seventeenth-century church of **San Lorenzo**, tucked behind the left wing of the palace. Designed by Guarini, who was also responsible for the Palazzo Carignano, it's scalloped with chapels, crowned by a complex dome supported on overlapping semicircles, and lined with multicoloured marble, frescoes and stucco festoons and statuettes.

On the right-hand side of the Palazzo Reale is the **Armeria Reale** (Tues–Sun 10am–7pm; €4), a collection of armour and weapons spanning seven centuries and several continents started by King Carlo Alberto in 1837. Pride of place is given to his stuffed horse, which stands among cases of guns and swords. There's also a gallery of suits of armour and an exotic, and rather chilling, collection of oriental arms, including gorgeously jewelled Turkish dagger sheaths and intimidating Japanese masks. The same building houses the **Biblioteca Reale** (Mon & Wed 8.15am–6.45pm, Tues & Thurs–Sat 8.15am–1.45pm; free; varying fees for temporary exhibitions), which, along with countless volumes and manuscripts, has a collection of drawings by artists including Leonardo da Vinci, Bellini, Raphael, Tiepolo and Rembrandt, part of it sometimes on display.

Across the square from the Palazzo Reale, the newly restored **Palazzo Madama** (☎011.443.3501, ⓦwww.palazzomadamatorino.it) is an altogether more appealing building, with an ornate Baroque facade by the early eighteenth-century architect Juvarra, who also redesigned the piazza and many of the streets leading off it. Inside, the originally fifteenth-century palace incorporates parts of a thirteenth-century castle and some Roman portal foundations – in effect it's an architectural cross section of the city's history. The most noteworthy architectural pieces are Juvarra's *Great Staircase* and the archeological excavations of the Medieval Court (Tues–Fri & Sun 9am–7pm, Sat 10am–8pm; free). It's worth visiting the **Museo Civico d'Arte Antica** (Tues–Fri & Sun 10am–6pm, Sat 10am–8pm; ticket office closes one hour before museum closing time; €7.50) – a collection of thousands of objects that includes everything from early Christian gold jewellery to an inlaid Gothic commode, rearranged into chronological order complete with excellent multilingual captions and multimedia displays.

The Duomo and around

Behind the Palazzo Reale – and reached through a small passage – is the fifteenth-century **Duomo** (daily 8am–noon & 3–7pm), on Via XX Settembre in Piazza San Giovanni. The only example of Renaissance architecture in Turin, it was severely damaged in a fire in 1997 but is open again to visitors and worshippers. However, the reconstruction of its fantastic Holy Shroud Chapel, designed by Guarini in 1668, will not be completed until at least 2010. Luckily, a quick-thinking fireman rescued from the blazing chapel what has been called "the most remarkable forgery in history", the **Turin Shroud** – a piece of cloth imprinted with the image of a man's body that has been claimed as the shroud in which Christ was wrapped after his crucifixion. One of the most famous medieval relics, it made world headlines in 1989 after carbon-dating tests carried out by three universities all concluded it was a fake, made between 1260 and 1390 – although no one is any the wiser about how the medieval forgers actually managed to create the image. Most of the time you can't see the shroud itself; it is locked away and officially only on display once every 25 years. However it is sometimes brought out for special occasions (it's worth checking at the tourist office). If you don't get to see the real thing, head to the left of the nave, where there's a photographic reproduction, on which the face of a bearded man, crowned with thorns, is clearly visible, together with marks supposed to have been left by a double-thonged whip, spear wounds and bruises that could have been caused carrying a cross. For those whose interest is still not satiated, there is a museum that covers the history and science of the shroud, **Museo della Sindone** (daily 9am–noon & 3–7pm; €5.50), on Via S. Domenico 28.

Relics of Turin's days as a small Roman colony are visible from outside the duomo: the scant remains of a **theatre** and the impressive Porta Palatina – two sixteen-sided towers flanking an arched passageway. Smaller archeological finds can be seen in the **Museo di Antichita** (Tues–Sun 8.30am–7.30pm; €4), behind the duomo, in what were the Palazzo Reale's orangeries. The first part of the museum displays objects found in the Piemonte region in an underground section organized in archeological layers; starting with medieval and working back chronologically to prehistoric times, its centrepiece is the renowned treasure-trove of the Roman silversmith's art, sculpture and other objects, unearthed in 1928 near the Piemontese town of Marengo. The rest of the exhibits are Etruscan, Greek and Cypriot finds collected by the House of Savoy.

Piazza della Repubblica and around

Northwest of the Duomo, the huge **Piazza della Repubblica**, otherwise known as Porta Palazzo, is home to Europe's largest outdoor market (Mon–Fri 8.30am–1.30pm, Sun 8.30am–6.30pm), selling mainly fruit and vegetables, but also some clothes and, in the indoor market hall, cheeses, bread and *salumi*. Behind the Porta Palazzo is the Saturday-morning Balôn, or **flea market**, home to black marketeers. On the second Sunday of each month there's a Gran Balôn on the same spot, with opportunities to buy collectable items including lace, toys, second-hand furniture and books.

West of Piazza della Repubblica stands Turin's most elaborate church, the royal **Santuario della Consolata**, built to house an ancient statue of the Madonna, Maria Consolatrice, the protector of the city. Designed by Guarini, its Neoclassical facade is pink and white, while the interior has an impressive decorative altar by Juvarra. Don't miss the vast array of votive objects devout Torinesi have offered to the statue, housed in an ancient crypt below the church. Not to be missed either is the series of paintings in the church, featuring people being "saved" from such disasters as being gored by a bull, cutting overhead electri-city cables with garden shears, exploding frying pans, and numerous accidents involving prams and trams. After all this, you may well want to head across the piazza to the beautiful old café, *Al Bicerin* (see p.86) for a pick-me-up. Historically, it was the city's only café where women could go in nineteenth-century post-Unification Turin without causing a scandal.

From Piazza Castello to the river

The porticoes of Via Po lead down to the river from Piazza Castello, ending just before the bridge in the vast arcaded Piazza Vittorio Veneto. Halfway down, a left onto Via Montebello brings you to the **Mole Antonelliana**, whose bishop's-hat dome, topped by a pagoda-like spire balancing on a mini-Greek temple, is a distinctive landmark and has been adopted as the city's emblem. Designed as a synagogue in the nineteenth century by the eccentric architect Antonelli, the building was ceded to the local council by Turin's Jewish community while still under construction because of escalating costs. The decision to house the new **Museo Nazionale del Cinema** (Tues–Fri & Sun 9am–8pm, Sat 9am–11pm; €5.20 or €6.80 with lift to top of Mole) in this rather unusual building seems a suitable way to celebrate the sheer spectacle of the place. Turin's involvement with cinema goes back to the early years of the twentieth century, when it was one of the first Italian cities to import and experiment with the new medium invented by the Lumière brothers. The interesting museum covers the early days of the magic lantern and experimental moving pictures, the development of the cinema as a global phenomenon, and twenty-first-century special effects.

Across the bridge from the Piazza Vittorio Veneto stands the Pantheon-like **Gran Madre di Dio** church, which, apart from being a useful landmark, is essentially unexciting. Behind the church, a path takes you up the hill to the **Museo Nazionale della Montagna "Duca degli Abruzzi"** at Via Giardino 39 (Tues–Sun 9am–7pm; €6), a fascinating museum dedicated to mountain environments, activities and people.

Parco del Valentino and the Museo dell'Automobile

South along the river from Piazza Vittorio Veneto, the riverside **Parco del Valentino** borders the site of a cluster of Turin's nightclubs – known as the **Murazzi** area; many of them are popular with the teen set, and the place can really come alive at night. In the daytime the huge park makes a pleasant place to wind down after the hum of the city centre, its curving lanes, formal flower beds and artificial hills covering half a million square metres – making it one of Italy's largest parks. Within the grounds are two castles, only one of which is the genuine article. The ornate **Castello Valentino** was another Savoy residence, used mainly for wedding feasts and other extravagant parties, and is nowadays the seat of the university's faculty of architecture. The **Borgo e Rocca Medioevale** date from an industrial exhibition held in 1884 and comprise a reconstructed medieval village (daily: April–Sept 9am–8pm; Oct–March 9am–7pm; free) whose houses are a synthesis of the best dwellings of medieval Piemonte and Valle d'Aosta, built with the same materials as the originals and using the same construction techniques. The centrepiece of the village is the Rocca (summer Tues–Sat 9am–8pm; winter Tues–Sun 9am–5pm; €5, free Tues), a fifteenth-century castle, which, although bogus, actually conjures up a picture of life in a medieval castle far better than many of the originals, kitted out with painstaking replicas of intricately carved Gothic furniture. The castle is based on the one at Fénis (see p.105), and the frescoes are reproductions of those at Manta (see p.93).

A three-kilometre walk from here, along the river, takes you to the **Museo dell'Automobile** at Corso Unità d'Italia 40 (Tues–Sun 10am–6.30pm; €5.50; ⓦ www.museoauto.org; bus #34 from Via Nizza), Italy's only motor museum. Even if you know nothing about cars this has some appeal – you'll spot models you haven't seen since your childhood and others familiar from films, as the museum traces the development from the early cars, handcrafted for a privileged minority, to the mass-produced family version. There's one of the first Fiats, a bulky 1899 model, near a far sleeker version built only two years later, and, just three decades later, the first small Fiat family-targeted vehicle, a design which was still on the streets in the Sixties. Take a look also at the gleaming Isotta Fraschini driven by Gloria Swanson in the film *Sunset Blvd.*, still with the initials of Norma Desmond, the character she played, on the side. The pride of the collection is the 1907 Itala, which won the Peking-to-Paris race in the same year; you can read of its adventures in Luigi Barzini's book *Peking to Paris*.

The Lingotto Centre

Walking 200 metres further on and turning right down Via Garessio takes you to what was the original Fiat factory, the **Lingotto Centre** at Via Nizza 250 (tram #1 or #18 from Porta Nuova). Fiat's headquarters are still here but the main part of the building, redesigned by Renzo Piano, houses a conference and exhibition space, a shopping centre, Turin University's automobile design department, a hotel (see p.78) and the **Pinacoteca Giovanni e Marella Agnelli** at no. 230 (Tues–Sun 10am–7pm; €4), a very small but priceless collection of artworks donated by the head of the Fiat dynasty, Gianni Agnelli, and his wife. The paintings are housed in a glass-and-metal gallery, which overlooks the test track on top of the former Fiat car works. The collection consists of mainly nineteenth- and twentieth-century masterpieces, including a number of Matisses and a couple of Picassos, as well as Modigliani's *Nu Couché* and Manet's *La Négresse*. The eighteenth century is represented by six Canalettos and Tiepolo's *Halberdier in a Landscape*.

Parco della Rimembranza and the Basilica di Superga

Southeast of the river, Turin fades into decrepit suburbs, beyond which lie the wooded hills concealing the fancy villas of the city's industrialists. For a taste of the views enjoyed by Turin's mega-rich, take bus #70 up to the **Parco della Rimembranza**, with 10,000 trees planted in honour of the Torinese victims of World War I and crowned with an enormous light-flashing statue of Victory. Northeast of the centre, you can take the **Sassi-Superga tram** (from Sassi, Mon & Wed–Fri 9am–5pm hourly on the hour, Sat 9am–8pm hourly on the hour, Sun 9am–8pm hourly on the hour and on the half-hour starting at 2.30pm; on Tues bus only; €3.10 return, weekends & holidays €4.13; free with the Torino card), complete with its original 1884 carriages, to the grandiose Baroque **Basilica di Superga**, from which there are fine panoramas across the city to the Alps (tram #15 from Piazza Castello to Sassi station).

The basilica (April–Sept 9am–noon & 3–5pm; Oct–March 9am–noon & 3–6pm; basilica free, €3; €9 to visit the basilica, the Savoy tombs and the royal apartments) yet another Filippo Juvarra design, stands high on a hill above the rest of the city, a position that is key to its existence. In 1706 Duke Vittorio Amedeo climbed the hill in order to study the positions of the French and Spanish armies who had been besieging the city for four months, and vowed that he would erect a temple to the Madonna on this site if she were to aid him in the coming battle. Turin was spared, and the duke immediately set Juvarra to work, flattening the top of the hill and producing over the next 25 years the circular basilica you see today. An elegant dome, pierced by windows and supported on pairs of white columns, is flanked by delicately scalloped onion-domed towers and rises above a Greek temple entrance, these days damaged by graffiti – names dating back to the beginning of the twentieth century scratched into the interior pillars. Many Torinesi come here not to pay homage to the Virgin, nor even to see the splendid tombs of the Savoys, but to visit the tomb of the 1949 Torino football team, all of whom were killed when their plane crashed into the side of the hill. If you happen to go to a match between Torino and Juventus, you may well hear the sinister chant from the Juventus supporters, "Superga, Superga".

The Stupinigi Palace

A nearby attraction worth the trip is the Savoy dynasty's luxurious hunting lodge, the **Palazzina di Caccia di Stupinigi** (closed for restoration at the time of writing; opening date set for late 2008). Another Juvarra creation, built in the 1730s and perhaps his finest work, this symmetrical fantasy with a generous dash of Rococo was awarded UNESCO World Heritage status in 1997. The exterior of the palace has been restored, while the interior is as luxurious as it ever was, also incorporating the **Museo di Arte e Ammobiliamento**, a collection of art and furniture from other Savoy palaces. The most extravagant room, the oval Salone Centrale, is a dizzying triumph of optical illusion that merges fake features with real in a superb trompe l'oeil. Other rooms are decorated with hunting motifs: Diana, goddess of hunting, bathes on bedroom ceilings; hunting scenes proceed across walls; and even the chapel is dedicated to St Uberto, patron saint of the hunt. And everywhere there are opulent wall-coverings – gilded brocades, hand-painted silk, carefully inked rice paper – and delicate eighteenth-century furniture, including gilded four-posters, inlaid desks and cabinets, even a marvellous marble bath, decorated with a relief of an imperial eagle, installed by Pauline Bonaparte. To get here, take bus #63 from Porta Nuova (bus stop #3492 "Porta Nuova FS" in Via Sacchi) then change at the stop after Piazza Caio Mario (bus stop #1080 "Impera") to bus #41; on the way you'll pass through the bleak Mirafiori suburbs on the west side of the city, built for workers at the nearby Fiat plant.

The Castello di Rivoli

Another rewarding trip is west to **RIVOLI** and its **Museo d'Arte Contemporanea** housed in the baroque Castello di Rivoli (Tues–Thurs 10am–5pm, Fri–Sun 10am–9pm; €6.50; @ www.castellodirivoli.org), one-time residence of the Savoy family. It's the most important collection of postwar art in Italy, ranging from works by Jeff Koons, Carl Andre and Claes Oldenburg to Arte Povera artists such as Mario Merz and Alighiero Boetti. On weekdays bus #36 (1hr) runs from Piazza Statuto, then it's a twenty-minute walk; at the weekend shuttle buses run infrequently from Piazza Castello direct to Rivoli.

Eating and drinking

It's worth taking your time over a drink, snack, pastry or ice cream in one of the fin-de-siècle **cafés** that are a Turin institution: prices are steep, but the elegant Belle Époque interiors – often with touches of Art Nouveau (known as "Liberty" style in Italy) – more than compensates. The city also has plenty of restaurants in which to sample local cuisine (see box, p.73), and standard Italian dishes.

Turin's chocolate

Make sure you leave some room to sample one of Turin's major products – **chocolate**. Best known is the hazelnut milk chocolate Gianduiotto, which dates back to the nineteenth century. Some even claim that it was the Torinesi who introduced chocolate to France when chocolate making for export began in 1678.

A good opportunity to sample it is during Turin's annual **chocolate fair**, held for three weeks in February and March (@ www.cioccola-to.com). At other times, there's the opportunity to indulge in the **ChocoPass**. You can taste samples (selected, not necessarily by you) of the finest chocolate products in all of Turin's historic establishments, confectionery shops and chocolate factories: Gianduiotti, pralines, various cakes, hot chocolate, and the distinctive *bicerin*, which is a bit like a cappuccino but fortified with brandy. The booklets of Chocopass vouchers offer ten samples in 24 hours (€10), or fifteen samples in 48 hours (€15). Otherwise, the favourite Torinese place to buy chocolate is listed on p.89.

Snacks, takeaways and self-service places

Brek Piazza Carlo Felice and Piazza Solferino. Part of a national chain of slick, high-quality self-service joints, with tables outside in summer. Main courses start at €5.

Exki Via XX Settembre 12. Natural, fresh and organic is the philosophy of this snack bar. Sandwiches, soups and drinks to eat in or take away. Closed Sun.

Frullateria Piazza Castello 44. Very central lunchtime option, with sandwiches and an array of fresh local and tropical fruits, ready for the liquidizer. Closed Sun.

Cafés

Al Bicerin Piazza della Consolata 5. This tiny, beautiful café is the place to try a *bicerin* – a Piemontese speciality of coffee fortified with brandy, cream and chocolate. Closed Wed & Aug.

Baratti & Milano Piazza Castello 27. Established in 1873 and preserving its nineteenth-century interior of mirrors, chandeliers and carved wood, where genteel Torinese ladies sip teas. Great hot chocolate. Closed Mon.

Fiorio Via Po 8. Turin's most historic café, once patronized by Nietzsche, presumably for its legendary *gelato* and its signature cappuccino, €3.

Mood Via Battisti 3. Books, coffee and aperitifs in the cosy Turin tradition, this is a relatively new, very attractive spot. Closed Sun & Mon morning.

Mulassano Piazza Castello 15. This cosy café first opened in 1900; it has marble fittings and a striking ceiling. Traditionally the favoured spot of actors and singers from the nearby Teatro Regio.

Neuv Caval'd Brôns Piazza San Carlo 155. A Torinese institution, this gustatory palace is known for its impressive help-yourself canapé selection. Closed Sat lunch & Sun.

Pepino Piazza Carignano 8. Ritzy café with summer garden, famed for its ice creams. Try the violet-flavoured *pinguino* or the outrageously rich cream-and-chocolate concoction of *pezzo duro*. Also offers an excellent Sunday brunch buffet menu for about €15. Closed Mon.

Platti Corso Vittorio Emanuele II 72. Art Nouveau-furnished café dating from 1870; hosts art exhibitions and occasional live music.

San Carlo Piazza San Carlo 156. Heroes of the Risorgimento once met in this café/restaurant/ice-cream parlour, now rather grandiosely restored with gilt pilasters and an immense chandelier.

Torino Piazza San Carlo 204. A good place for a leisurely aperitif or cocktail, of which the most popular is the Torinese "Elvira", made with Martini, vodka and various secret ingredients. Illustrious regulars have included writer Cesare Pavese and Luigi Einaudi (a Torinese economist who became the second President of the Italian Republic).

Restaurants

Arcadia Galleria Subalpina 16 (just off southeast corner of Piazza Castello) ☎011.561.3898. Try this place for an eclectic mix of Italian food and sushi. It's affordable at lunchtime, but pricier in the evening. Closed Sun & Aug.

C'era una volta Corso Vittorio Emanuele II 41 ☎011.650.4589. Simple, delicious Piemontese cuisine at moderate prices, and a good fixed menu for about €25. Closed Sun.

Cucco Corso Casale 89 ☎011.819.5536. A big Art Nouveau place near the river serving typical Piemontese cooking at moderate prices with a choice of around thirty antipasti. Closed Mon.

Del Cambio Piazza Carignano 2 ☎011.546.690. Historic, formal shrine to Piemontese food much frequented by expense-account types. A great opportunity to feast on traditional dishes such as Cavour's favourite of *fianziera* (veal, sweetbreads and *porcini*, cooked with butter and wine). Prices are suitably extravagant – starting around €25 for a main – and booking is advisable. Closed Sat, Sun & one week in Aug.

Il Punto Verde Via San Massimo 17 ☎011.885.543. Reasonably priced vegetarian restaurant with a good selection of dishes and a quiet outside terrace. Closed Sat dinner & Sun.

L'Arcimboldo Via Santa Chiara 54 ☎011.521.181. A simple restaurant specializing in *pasta fresca*, with a choice of a hundred sauces, all for around €8. Closed Sun.

La Gaia Scienza Via Guastalla 22 ☎011.812.3821. Old-style *osteria* serving wholesome traditional food. Expect to pay around €25 for a full meal. Closed Sunday.

Porto di Savona Piazza Vittorio Veneto 2 ☎011.817.3500. Cheap and cheerful restaurant, very popular with both students and business people, attracted primarily by the formula of *piatto unico* (single option main course) and dessert for €8–10. Closed all day Mon & Tues lunchtime.

Sfashioncafé Via Cesare Battisti 13 (Piazza Carlo Alberto) ☎011.516.0085. Enormous portions and great pizzas. Lunchtime bargains start at €8 and include a main course, a great house salad, drink and coffee or dessert. Colourful, friendly interior, plus sunny seating on the piazza.

Tre Galline Via Bellezia 37 ☎011.436.6553. The oldest restaurant in Turin, with a lovely panelled interior. Don't miss the *agrodolce* (sweet-and-sour) rabbit and reckon on €35 a head. Booking advisable. Closed all day Sun, Mon lunchtime & Aug.

△ Aperitivo in Turin

Nightlife and entertainment

Turin's cultural life is suitably comprehensive for a place of this size. The city's **opera** house, the Teatro Regio (℡011.881.5241, Ⓦwww.teatroregio .torino.it), is one of the best in the country and is recognizable from its pod-like Seventies architecture, while Il Teatro Stabile (Cavallerizza Reale ℡011.517.6246, Ⓦwww.teatrostabiletorino.it), one of Italy's principal publicly funded **theatre** companies, is acclaimed for its productions of major works by nineteenth- and twentieth-century European writers; performances are normally at the Carignano Theatre on Piazza Carignano. Turin is also home of the prestigious **RAI National Symphony Orchestra**, which performs in, among other locations, the Lingotto Centre. For most of September a major **festival** called, appropriately enough, Settembre Musica mixes jazz, world music, classical music and performance art (℡011.442.4777) at various venues around town. Check the website ⓦwww.comune.torino .it for listings. There are also four international **film** festivals held each year, including a women's film festival in March and a "cinema of homosexual themes" in April; contact the tourist office for details.

For **what's on listings** and opening hours, check the pages of the Turin daily, *La Stampa*, particularly its Friday supplements. The tourist office in the Atrium (see p.75) has a free **ticket reservation service**.

Turin's **nightlife** is more sedate than that of, say, Milan, but there's a reasonably varied mix of clubs and bars, with the liveliest spot down on the embankment bordered by the Parco del Valentino, known locally as the **Murazzi**. Its clubs are packed with a lively crowd at weekends so there's often a heavy police presence, and if you go, you should keep an eye on your belongings. The area is especially popular on summer weekends when a big crowd spills out of the bars and onto the riverfront jetties. Note that some **clubs** require membership cards, purchased when you enter and costing between €5 and €10, with your first drink usually included. After that, although drink prices can be inflated, measures are relatively generous – bar staff usually keep pouring until they think it looks big enough.

Getting down to the business of **drinking**, the old *birrerias* have been supplemented by new *vinerias* – wine bars – where you can also order a substantial snack (known as a *marenda sinoira*). Aside from the Murazzi, a good place to wander for a drink is the more tranquil medieval area, known as the **Quadrilatero Romano**, around Piazza Emanuele Filiberto and Via Santa Chiara.

Bars, birrerias, clubs and vinerias

Centralino Via delle Rosine 16. Basement club with jazz concerts and avant-garde productions; Sunday night is gay night; membership card required.

Hiroshima Mon Amour Via Bossoli 83. Live music, alternative theatre and cabaret in a converted school near the Lingotto centre. Cover charge depending on the event.

Jumping Jester Via Mazzini 2. Old-fashioned wooden interior with huge TV screen on which football matches are shown live. Serves a great pint of cold Caffreys or Tennants.

Las Rosas Via Bellezia 15. Trendy cantina-style *taqueria*. Drinks and tacos served until 2am. Drinks and tacos served until 2am to the sounds of ambeint music

Lobelix Via Corte d'Appello 15 (Piazza Savoia). Wine and cocktail bar with techno music, named for the obelisk that adorns the piazza. Closed Sun.

Magazzino di Gilgamesh Piazza Moncenisio 13b. *Birreria* and coffee shop, plus an international restaurant on the third floor, with jazz, Latin, classic and rock music in the background. Closed Sun.

Roar Roads Via Carlo Alberto 3. Despite the dubious name, this is a very passable pub just off Via Po that pulls in both locals and foreigners. Closed Sun.

Shamrock Inn Corso Vittorio Emanuele II 34. The place for an authentic pint of Irish stout. Good-value sandwiches too. Closed Sun.

Tre Galli Via Sant'Agostino 25. Busy *vineria* that used to be an Agnelli (Fiat founder) hangout, with a long wine list of local and Italian wines by the bottle or glass (for the latter, ask for a *mescita a calice*) as well as plates of cheeses, ham, salami and home-made *grissini* (breadsticks). Laid-back atmosphere and tables outside on the piazza in summer. Open until 2am. Closed Sun.

Zoo Bar Corso Casale 127. Out past the Ponte Regina Margherita, this loft bar hosts live rock and pop gigs. Closed Sun.

Listings

Bicycle rental You can rent bikes in summer in the following parks: Parco della Colletta, Parco del Valentino, Parco della Pellerina and Parco della Mandria.

Books and newspapers Libreria Luxembourg, Via Accademia delle Scienze 3, has an excellent range of British and American paperbacks and magazines. English-language newspapers can be bought from most newsagents in the city centre, in particular the one at the Porta Nuova station.

Car parks Central city parking spots and car parks are marked with blue lines on the road and cost €1 per hour. Parking lots, more expensive, also lie under some main piazzas.

Car rental Avis, Corso Turati 37 ☏011.669.9800; Europcar, Via Madama Cristina 72 ☏011.650.3603; Hertz, Via Magellano 12 ☏011.502.080. All these companies also have desks at the airport.

Chocolate *Confetteria Stratta* at Piazza San Carlo 191 is a Turin institution. Closed all day Sun & Mon morning. (See box, p.85).

Closing days Some shops are closed on Monday morning, and many establishments of every kind still follow the time-honoured Italian tradition and shut down during August.

Exchange Outside normal banking hours you can exchange money at Porta Nuova station (Mon–Sat 8am–8pm, Sun 10am–6pm).

Football Turin's two teams, Juventus and Torino, play on Saturday and Sunday afternoons at the new Stadio Olimpico, Via Filadelfia, until the Stadio dell' Alpi is restored – though it's rumoured that Torino may soon be moving to a new stadium. You can get to the Stadio Olimpico on Line #4 of the new Metropolitana Leggera. Although Juventus has been voted the most popular team in Italy, most of the locals support the underdogs, Torino.

Hospital Ospedale Molinette, Corso Bramante 88–90 ☏011.633.1633; for 24hr emergency medical attention call ☏5747, or simply ☏118 or ☏113, as throughout Italy.

Internet access Bu.Net Via San Quentino 13 (☏011.440.7517, ⓦ www.il-bu.net; 9am–1am; €0.06/min).

Laundries Vizzini, Via San Secondo 30; Lava Asciuga, Via de Nanni 84; and Blusurf, Piazza della Repubblica 1.

Markets In addition to the Porta Palazzo on Piazza della Repubblica, and the weekly Balôn and monthly Gran Balôn markets behind Porta Palazzo (see p.82), there's often heavily discounted designer fashion (the genuine thing, from end-of-line clearances) at the Crocetta market around Via Cassini and Via Marco Polo (Tues–Fri morning & all day Sat) – not exactly street market prices, but still much cheaper than in the shops.

Pharmacist Boniscontro, Corso Vittorio Emanuele II 66 (☏011.538.271), is an all-night chemist.

Police ☏113. City police station at Corso XI Febbraio 22. Dial ☏112 for Carabinieri.

Post office The central post office is at Via Alfieri 10 (Mon–Fri 8.30am–7pm, Sat 8.30am–1pm).

Shopping Via Roma is good for designer labels, and there's trendier, less expensive fare in the pedestrianized streets bordered by Via Garibaldi, Via Monte di Pietà, Via dei Mercanti and Via San Francesco d'Assisi. Sellers of secondhand clothes and costume jewellery, book binders and tailors cluster in the narrow streets around Via Barbaroux, Via San Tommaso and Via Monte di Pietà, off Via Garibaldi.

Walking tours Turin is pedestrian-friendly and a fine place to take a walking tour, with various themes on offer. Perhaps the most intriguing tour is based on the city's age-old reputation as one of the three great European centres of the occult (along with London and Prague). To visit some of the noted esoteric sites, relating to both black and white magic, check out ⓦ www.somewhere.it for their Magic Turin evening walking tour (Thurs & Sat; 9pm at Piazza Statuto; 2hr 30min tour; €20, reservations through the website). If the arcane is not your thing, they also offer several other tours, including Subterranean Turin and Jewish Turin.

West of Turin: the Susa and Chisone valleys

The main route to France from Turin runs through the **Susa Valley**, passing nearby the region's main ski resorts. You go through long tunnels most of the way, so don't expect to see much. The one real sight to spot is the **Sacra di San Michele**, a forbidding fortified abbey anchored atop a rocky hill; it's an easy day-trip from Turin. **Susa** itself, reached by a minor branch of the rail line, was once a modest Roman town and is now a modest provincial town – a pleasant stopover but with little else to lure you.

Sacra di San Michele

The closest town to the **Sacra di San Michele** (Ⓦwww.sacradisanmichele .com; mid-March to mid-Oct Tues–Sat 9.30am–12.30pm & 2.30–6pm, Sun 9.30am–noon & 2.40–6.30pm; weekday afternoons guided tours only; July, Aug & Sept also open Mon, same hours; mid-Oct to mid-March 9.30am–12.30pm & 2.30–5pm, Sun 9.30am–noon & 2.30–5pm; €4, €5 for an extended 1hr 45min guided tour on first Sat afternoon of each month, mid-March to mid-Oct begins at 5.30pm, otherwise at 4.30pm; Ⓣ011.939.130) is **SANT'AMBROGIO**, a small town at the foot of San Michele's hill. It's half an hour by train from Turin and connected with the abbey by a very steep ninety- to 120-minute hike. The walk is worth it, both for the views and for the opportunity to soak up the eerie atmosphere surrounding the glowering abbey, much of it in ruins. Climbing up to the abbey and hewn into the rock, a long flight of stairs – the *Scalone dei Morti* (Stairs of the Dead) – sets a morbid tone, for it was where corpses used to be laid out for local peasants to come and pay their respects. The sinister ambiance is augmented by the abbey buildings proper, from the Romanesque entrance arch carved with signs of the zodiac to the Gothic-Romanesque abbey church.

Susa

Some 25km down the valley from Sant'Ambrogio, **SUSA** is a likeable, rather scruffy old town with a few hotels, such as the *Du Parc*, Via Rocchetta 15 (Ⓣ0122.622.273, ❸), or the cheaper *Napoleon*, Via Mazzini 44 (Ⓣ0122.622.855; Ⓦwww.hotelnapoleon.it; ❸), which can be used as a base for exploring the area.

While most of Italy was ruled by the Romans, Susa and western Piemonte remained in the hands of the Gauls. The best-known of its Gaulish leaders, Cottius, was much admired by the Romans, with whom he reached a peaceful arrangement, and a handful of Gaulish/Roman remains cluster around the town centre, notably in **Piazza San Giusto**, where there's a redoubtable defensive gate. The adjacent Romanesque Cattedrale has a fine campanile, but its most interesting features are the external frescoes – a *Crucifixion* and an *Entry into Jerusalem*. Just above the piazza, Cottius erected the **Arco di Augusto** in honour of the Roman emperor, its top decorated with a processional frieze. Look through its broad arched opening frames for views down into a small park laid out around the remains of some **Roman baths**.

From Susa you can make an excursion to the **Abbey of Novalesa**, 10km away at the foot of Rocciamelone in the Cenischia Valley, close by the French border. The church here is a relatively recent, eighteenth-century structure, but parts of the cloister and walls date back to the eighth century, while the four chapels, one of which is decorated with frescoes, were built in the tenth century.

In the opposite direction, southeast, at the end of the Chisone Valley, **PINEROLO** was one of the Winter Olympics 2006 sites and is worth a short stop. It's a small town with a medieval centre that was for centuries the seat of the Acaia princedom, precursors of the House of Savoy. It's no longer possible to visit their palace, slowly deteriorating halfway up the hill, but you can visit the church of **San Maurizio**, burial place of the Acaia princes, decorated with fifteenth-century frescoes. In the town centre, there's a

Gothic Duomo, and the **Museo della Cavalleria** (Tues & Thurs 9–11.30am & 2–4pm, Sat & Sun 10am–noon & 3–6pm; free) gives a comprehensive sense of the town's glory days, with displays relating to the prestigious former cavalry school of Pinerolo.

The Piemontese ski resorts

Close to the French border, Piemonte's three main, purpose-built ski resorts – Bardonecchia, Sestriere and Sauze d'Oulx – are well used by British tour operators and, as co-hosts of the Winter Olympics 2006, have all had their facilities recently upgraded. Moreover, Sestriere, Sauze d'Oulx, Sansicario, Cesana and Claviere now collectively constitute some 400km of interconnected runs, more than 200 in all, known as **The Milky Way** (see box, p.75; ⓦwww .vialattea.it). You can gain access from Pragelato, thanks to the new cableway Pattemouche-Anfiteatro. One daily lift pass for all five runs is €32.

Modern **BARDONECCHIA** – unconnected to the Milky Way – is a weekenders' haunt, with small chalet-style hotels. **SAUZE D'OULX**, a little way south, is known as the "Benidorm of the Alps" and attracts hordes of youngsters who treat skiing as a hangover cure. Apart from a few winding streets of old houses, it's an ugly, sprawling place, and its lift-passes are expensive. **SESTRIERE** was the dream resort of Mussolini and the Fiat baron, Giovanni Agnelli, who conceived it as an aristocratic mountain retreat, favoured by the young and the beautiful. Nowadays, the reality is a bland resort that dribbles over a bleak mountain, dominated by two cylindrical towers, both owned by Club Med.

Taking the parallel Chisone Valley to the south back towards Turin, you will encounter a much more bucolic and less developed area, dotted along the way with small towns. If you don't have your own transport, you can take one of the **buses** that regularly service almost all the towns along the way. The picturesque slate-roofed hamlet of **USSEAUX** is worth discovering, its weather-worn old walls decorated with colourful murals. For lunch, the *Trattoria La Placette*, behind the church and on the village's edge overlooking the valley, is equipped with a sunny porch on which you can partake of hearty pastas, game and mountain cheeses.

Not far away, at an altitude of nearly 2000m, the impressive **Forte di Fenestrelle** (ⓦwww.fortedifenestrelle.com; daily July & Aug 10am–noon & 3–6pm; rest of year Mon & Thurs–Sun 10am–noon & 3–6pm; guided tours; ⓣ0121.83600 for reservations; €2–12, depending on choice of self-guided visit or seven-hour guided hike up and back, plus several other options), known as the Great Wall of Piemonte, has been recently restored and is an up-and-coming major attraction. It constitutes a gigantic fortified castle and dependent buildings, along with an adjoining massive 3km wall marching over the mountain. Built by the Savoys from 1728, it took some 122 years to complete, its purpose being to halt enemy invasions. Simply put, it's the largest defensive structure ever built in Europe. Much of the wall's length can now be visited, and the longest organized tour takes you up all of the 4000 steps and back, a strenuous seven-hour trek.

If you're tempted to spend some time in this idyllic area, note that one of the most welcoming **hotels** is the *Bella Baita*, Borgata Serre Marchetto, 1 Pinasca, nestled in a panoramic mountain forest high above the valley's villages (ⓣ339.750.3940, ⓦwww.bellabaita.com; ❷ including a hearty breakfast; half board also available). The hosts are very welcoming, knowledgeable about the area and they are trained professional chefs.

South to Saluzzo and the Valle Po

A flourishing medieval town, and later the seat of one of Piemonte's few Renaissance courts, **SALUZZO**, 57km south of Turin, retains much of its period appeal. Flaking ochre-washed terraces and Renaissance houses, their outside walls painted with trompe-l'oeil landscapes and scenes, line stepped

△ San Giovanni, Saluzzo

cobbled streets climbing up to a castle, from which you can enjoy views of the town. A pleasant place to stay, the town has the added attraction of regular bus services into the Po, Varaita and Maira valleys, which cut through the foothills of the Monviso mountain towards France.

There are a few things around town worth seeing. Just below the castle, the **Torre Civica** (March–Sept Thurs–Sun 9.30am–12.30pm & 2.30–6.30pm; Oct–Feb Sat & Sun same hours as above; €1.30) gives more great views over the town and surrounding areas. On the other side of the road, the Gothic church of **San Giovanni** has a number of thirteenth- and fourteenth-century frescoes and the tomb of the leading light of Renaissance Saluzzo, Marchese Ludovico II, anachronistically depicted as a medieval knight beneath a fancily carved canopy. Close by, the Gothic **Casa Cavassa**, Via San Giovanni 5, is a fifteenth-century palace with an arcaded courtyard that doubled as a home for one of Ludovico's ministers and now houses the town's **Museo Civico** (April–Sept Tues & Wed guided tours only, at 11am & 4pm, Thurs–Sun unaccompanied visits 10am–1pm & 2–6pm; Oct–March Tues & Wed guided tours only, at 11am & 3pm, Thurs–Sun unaccompanied visits 10am–1pm & 2–5pm; €4, combined ticket with Torre Civica €5). Inside are period furniture and paintings, including the gorgeously gilded *Madonna della Misericordia*, with the Madonna sheltering Ludovico, his wife and the population of Saluzzo in the folds of her cloak.

That's about all there is to the town centre, but just to the south of Saluzzo, a five-minute bus ride from outside the train station, there's the **Castello della Manta** – a medieval fortress that was transformed into a refined residence by the Saluzzo marquises in the fifteenth century (Tues–Sun 10am–5/6pm; €5, including audioguide). Though from the outside it's as plain and austere as Saluzzo's castle, it's worth visiting for the late-Gothic frescoes in the Baronial Hall. One of these illustrates the myth of the fountain of youth, elderly people processing towards the magical waters while others impatiently rip off their clothes to plunge in. The other, *Nine Heroes and Nine Heroines*, depicts chivalrous courtiers and exquisite damsels standing beneath stylized trees with coats of arms hanging from the branches.

Practicalities

Saluzzo's **tourist office**, on Piazzetta dei Mondagli 5, at the top of Via Volta (Mon–Sat 9am–1pm & 2.30–5.30pm, Sun until 6pm; ☎0175.46.710, ⓦwww .comune.saluzzo.cn.it), can provide information on the whole of the western valleys region. Among the town's **hotels**, the cheapest is the *Persico at Vicolo Mercati* 10 (☎0175.41.213; ②), which also has a very good **restaurant** serving traditional cuisine (closed Fri); or there are a couple of three-stars, the *Astor* at Piazza Garibaldi 39 (☎0175.45.506, ⓔastor@mtrade.com; ③) and the *Griselda* at Corso XXVII Aprile 13 (☎0175.47.484, ⓦwww.hotelgriselda.it; ④). If you want to **eat** in the old town, try the *Osteria dei Mondagli*, on Piazzetta dei Mondagli opposite the tourist office, which does a good fixed menu and has a beautiful summer terrace.

Valle Po

West of Saluzzo, close to the French border, lies the source of the River Po, which flows right across industrial northern Italy, gathering the waste from thousands of factories before finally discharging into the Adriatic. Towards the end of the valley is the Alpine-style resort of **CRISSOLO**, served by 2–4 buses daily from Paesana, farther down the valley, which in turn is served by buses from Saluzzo. From Crissolo you can hike 5km (or take a minibus in summer) to the **Pian del Re**, a grassy plain around the source of the Po. From here, it's possible to walk on to the entrance of the **Pertuis del Viso, aka Galleria delle Traversette**, a 75-metre-long tunnel (open roughly July–September, closed by snow rest of year) built by Saluzzo's Marquis Ludovico to ease the trading route into France for his mule trains. The pre-tunnel pass is said to have been used by Hannibal and his elephants.

Crissolo is also a good base for climbing **Monviso** (3841m), Piemonte's highest mountain; it's a long (about six hours) rocky scramble from the *Quintino Sella rifugio* (see below), two to three hours beyond the Pian del Re. Even if you don't want to scale the summit, the walk to the *rifugio* is lovely, passing a series of **mountain lakes**; or, if you prefer, it's possible to do a **circuit of the lakes**, turning off the main trail just before Lago Chiaretto, from where a path leads past Lago Superiore and back to Pian del Re. There are also **caves** near Crissolo, the **Grotta del Rio Martino** above the town, with stalactites and a subterranean lake and waterfall. The quick route here takes half an hour from Crissolo but is steep; the slower, easier route takes an hour. Unless you're an experienced caver, it's advisable to go with a guide, arranged through Crissolo's **tourist office** (June–Sept & Dec–Jan Mon–Sat 9.30am–12.30pm; ☎0175.940.131) at Via Umberto I 139.

Crissolo has a couple of average **hotels** open all year round: the *Monviso* at Piazza Umberto I 153 (☎0175.94.940; ❸) and the *Polo Nord* at Via Provinciale 22 (☎0175.94.908; ❷). Another small hotel at Pian del Re, the *Pian del Re* at Piazza Umberto I 186 (☎0175.94.967; ❷), is open mid-June to mid-September, while the *Quintino Sella rifugio*, near the Lago Grande del Viso, is open at Easter and from June 20 to September 20, and sometimes in winter; it's advisable to phone in advance (☎0175.94.943). The majority of **restaurants** are in the hotels, so you may find it both practical and economical to opt for half board.

Cúneo and around

There's not much to bring you to **CÚNEO** itself, the main town of southern Piemonte, although it has good bus and rail connections. Although the town's hilly setting is impressively attractive, its severely geometric modern centre and the old town – what there is left of it – is dark and gloomy. Even its one "sight", the **Museo Civico**, Via S. Maria 10 (Tues & Sat 8.30am–1pm & 2.30–5.30pm, Wed–Fri until 5pm, Sun 3–7pm; €2.60) in the restored Gothic convent of San Francesco behind the bus station, is only of limited interest, though the fifteenth-century portal of intricately carved stone is worth a look and the cloister is lush with plantings. The collection ranges from Roman archaeological remains to a folk section with traditional costumes, dolls, kitchen utensils and an ancient bike.

The **tourist office** is at Via Roma 28 (Mon–Sat 10am–12.30pm & 3–6.30pm; ☎0171.693.258, ⓦwww.cuneoholiday.com). There are a couple of reasonable **hotels**: the *Cavallo Nero* at Piazza Seminario 8 (☎0171.692.168; ❷) and the similarly priced *Ligure* at Via Savigliano 11 (☎0171.681.942; ❷), which also has a good **restaurant**.

The area has many sulphurous spas and valley resorts, which are the big draw. The **Valle Stura** is much visited by botanists for its many rare flowers. The **Valle Gesso** (meaning gypsum or chalk) is characterized by its vast walls of limestone, unusual in Piemonte. Some of it has been set aside as the huge **Parco Naturale dell'Argentera-Valle Gesso**, where you can stay in various refuges, take the waters at **TERME DI VALDIERI**, or visit the botanical gardens at **VALDIERI**. The **Valle del Pesio** shouldn't be missed, particularly in spring, when a waterfall, known for obvious reasons as the **Pis del Pesio**, is in full pelt; there's also a twelfth-century monastery, the **Certosa di Pesio**, with a missionary museum. Trains to France run through the verdant **Valle Vermenagna**, part of which is given over to the **Parco Naturale di Palanfre**, visitable from **VERNANTE**. Again, the appeal is mainly botanical, with over 800 species of trees and flowers growing at some 3000m above sea level.

Val Maira, northwest of Cúneo, is a quiet and narrow valley, known as the "Emerald Valley" for its greenery. There's not much beyond this, though the villages, with their traditional rubble and wood houses perched high above the river, are very picturesque, particularly **ELVA**, in the hills above **STROPPO** (ask in the cafés for the unofficial taxi driver). If you're walking, it's best to get a map from Saluzzo before heading out. There are no **hotels** in Stroppo, so the best base is the *Gentil Locanda* (☎0171.99.139; ❶), located at the Marmora Bridge, between Stroppo and the small village of Prazzo; it has clean rooms and a good-value restaurant. There's also a **campsite** (☎0171.99.143; open May to mid-Sept) at Marmora Bridge.

Mondoví and around

Half an hour by train east from Cúneo, **MONDOVÍ** isn't especially exciting, though it does give access to a sanctuary and some caves nearby. The town is split into two parts – modern Breo and the older, upper town of Piazza, where time is best spent. Piazza is built around a large square, Piazza Maggiore, where there's a turretted medieval palace and an exotic seventeenth-century Baroque church, the **Chiesa della Missione** – the interior is decorated with an incredible trompe l'oeil by Andrea Pozzo, a cloudy heaven with angels seemingly suspended in mid-air. You can laze around in the **Belvedere**, to the north of Piazza, a garden occupying the site of a thirteenth-century church. The campanile was used by a physicist in the eighteenth century to establish topographical measurements; though you can't climb up, the views from the garden stretch north to the hills of Le Langhe and south to the foothills of the Alps.

The Santuario di Vicoforte

Southeast of Mondoví and a twenty-minute bus ride (from the train station), the **Santuario di Vicoforte** (ⓦwww.santuariodivicoforte.com; daily 7am–noon & 2.30–7pm) is a popular trip from the town, an imposing Baroque church crowned by what is claimed to be the world's largest elliptical dome. It's liveliest on Sundays when churchgoers and pilgrims also pack out the nearby arcaded crescents housing restaurants, pastry, souvenir and clothes shops.

According to legend the sanctuary was constructed in honour of a Madonna and Child painted by a local artist on a pillar, which, when shot at by a hunter, began to bleed. The sanctuary was begun in 1598 on the orders of King Carlo Emanuele I, and eventually finished in 1890. The frescoed pillar is now the altarpiece beneath the 36-metre dome, and there's a kitsch museum featuring a haphazard collection of ecclesiastical bric-a-brac laid out in a labyrinth of rooms around the dome and towers. The exhibits range from gaudy treasures to ceremonial costumes and photos of those cured of their ailments by a visit here.

Grotta di Bossea

Twenty-four kilometres south of Vicoforte, and difficult to reach unless you have your own transport, the **Grotta di Bossea** (Mon–Sat 10am, 11.30am,

3pm & 4.30pm, Sun 10am, 11.30am, 2.30pm, 4pm & 5.30pm; €8) is a long-established subterranean tourist attraction filled with contorted stalactites and stalagmites, waterfalls and lakes, and an underground scientific laboratory, set up to monitor the caves' wildlife. On display is the skeleton of the *Ursus spelaeus*, an underground bear over 3m long and 2m high that lived here between 25,000 and 40,000 years ago.

Alba and Le Langhe

Northeast of Cúneo, the town of **Alba** and the surrounding **Le Langhe** hills signify two things to the Italians: white truffles and red wine. The **truffles** are more delicate and aromatic than the black variety found further south, and the **wines** range from the "King of Italian reds", Barolo, to the light and fragrant Nebbiolo. There are a number of wine museums and cantinas in the hill-villages around Alba, the best being those at Barolo, Annunziata and Grinzane di Cavour – buses from Alba are rather infrequent and not always direct, so your own transport is best for a thorough exploration.

Although the big cantinas all sell wine, you'll get a better deal at one of the smaller family-owned establishments scattered around the region. Most of the area's very different wines all come from the same grape, Nebbiolo, and the final taste is dependent on the soil: sandy soil produces the grapes for the light red **Nebbiolo**, calcium and mineral-rich soil for the more robust **Barolo**.

Alba

Whether or not you want to taste wine, **ALBA** is worth the visit for its alluring mix of red-brick medieval towers, Baroque and Renaissance palaces and cobbled streets lined with gastronomic shops. And if you come in October, you'll catch the town's hilarious annual donkey race – a skit on nearby Asti's prestigious Palio.

The town's only sight as such is its late-Gothic **Duomo**, standing confectionery pink on the central Piazza Risorgimento, gaudily restored and holding some fine Renaissance stalls, inlaid with cityscapes, musical instruments, and trompe-l'oeil cupboards whose contents appear to be on the verge of falling out. But Alba is primarily a place to stroll and eat. Leading up to the centre from Piazza Savona, the main drag of **Via Vittorio Emanuele** is a fine, bustling street, with the most tempting of Alba's local produce on display – wines, truffles, cheeses, weird and wonderful varieties of mushroom, and the wickedly sticky *nocciola*, a nutty, chocolatey cake. Via Cavour is a pleasant medieval street with plenty of wine shops, behind which the **donkey race** and displays of medieval pageantry attract the crowds during the festival at the beginning of October. There's also an annual **truffle festival** later in the month, when you could blow your whole budget on a knobbly truffle or a meal in one of the many swanky restaurants. At the end of April/beginning of May, the Vinum festival gives you the chance to taste five hundred local wines.

Practicalities

The **tourist office** (Dec–March Mon–Sat 9am–1pm & 2–6pm; March–June daily 9am–1pm & 2.30–6.30pm; June to mid–Sept Mon–Sat 9am–12.30pm & 2.30–6.30pm, Sun 9am–12.30pm; mid-Sept to Dec Mon–Thurs 9am–12.30pm & 2.30–6.30pm, Fri–Sun 9am–8pm; ☎0173.35.833, ⓦwww .langheroero.it) is at Piazza Risorgimento 2. If you want to **stay**, you could try the inexpensive and pleasant *Leon d'Oro*, Piazza Marconi 2 (T0173.440.536; not including breakfast, ❷), or the *Hotel Savona*, a decent three-star, located at Via Roma 1, handy for the train station (T0173.440.440, W www.hotelsavona .com; ❸), with good deals for triples. You'll need to plan ahead to be sure of a room, especially during the October festival. The best place to sample Albese cooking is the excellent *Osteria dell'Arco*, at Piazza Savona 5 (closed Sun & Mon), which has a particularly fine selection of local cheeses. For wine by the glass as well as excellent local dishes, try 🍴 *Vincafe*, Via Vittorio Emanuele 12 (W www.vincafe.com).

A ten-minute train ride away, the village of **NEIVE**, about 13km northeast of Alba, makes a good alternative overnight stop. Here *La Contea*, Piazza Cocito 8 (T0173.67.126, W www.la-contea.it; half board compulsory in high season; ❸), a **restaurant** with **rooms**, offers excellent food and some of the best Barbaresco, Dolcetto and Barolo wines from the vineyards around. Rooms are comfortable, with antique beds and whitewashed walls.

The hills of Le Langhe

Eight kilometres south of Alba, the castle of **Grinzane Cavour** was rented by the Cavour family in the nineteenth century and served as a weekend retreat for Camillo Cavour. Nowadays it's the seat of Piemonte's regional *enoteca*, or winery, and has a pricey restaurant serving local specialities. The upstairs **folk museum** (daily except Tues 10am–12.30pm & 2.30–6.30pm; closed Jan; free; T0173.262.159) holds various bits of Cavour trivia and an engaging display of agricultural equipment, ranging from a ferret trap and grappa distillery to winter boots made of hay and a contraption for cleaning the cocoons of silkworms. In the afternoons it holds **wine-tasting** sessions, and although there are inevitably some extremely expensive wines, many are affordable.

A few kilometres southwest of Grinzane, in the heart of Le Langhe, **BAROLO**, a small village with peach- and ochre-washed houses set among extensive vineyards, gives its name to one of the best-known Italian wines. Geared up to the steady stream of wealthy gastronomes and wine connoisseurs who invariably come here, the **Enoteca Regionale del Barolo**, housed in a flaking turreted castle on Piazza Falletti (daily except Thurs 10am–12.30pm & 3–6.30pm; T0173.562.277) is well worth a visit. Or indulge yourself with a night and a meal at the *Hotel Barolo*, Via Lomondo 2 (T0173.563.54, W www .hotelbarolo.it; ❷), whose restaurant – an imperious place with a smart dress code – is renowned locally.

Just north of Barolo, **LA MORRA** is a charming old village, with good views over the undulating vineyards from outside the *Belvedere* restaurant (closed all day Mon & Sun evening; T0173.50.190) at Piazza Castello 5, which offers classic Albese cooking, such as the wonderful *agnolotti*. The village is also home to the **Cantina Comunale di La Morra** (daily except Tues 10am–12.30pm & 2.30–6.30pm), in which you can taste and buy wine. There are some excellent food shops too, and if you're here on a Monday, you can pick up bargains at the market. As for **staying the night**, try the friendly *Italia* hotel at Via Roma 30 (T0173.50.609; ❷).

The Cantina Comunale has maps of **walks** through the vineyards, best of which is one to **ANNUNZIATA**, about half an hour down the hill to a private wine museum, the **Museo "Ratti" dei Vini d'Alba** at Abbazia dell'Annunziata (call T0173.50.183 to arrange a visit), housed in a Renaissance abbey next to the cantina. Laid out in a musty cellar, the museum has a number of intriguing exhibits including a letter from an Arctic explorer congratulating the local wine-producing Ratti family on the fact that their Barolo had stood up to the rigours of travel and climate on an expedition to the North Pole. Wine at the Ratti cantina is expensive, and you can only buy it in lots of six, so it's far cheaper bought in single bottles at the family cantina, *Oberto Severino*, 1km up the road back towards La Morra.

Asti and around

The wine continues to flow in Asti, 30km northeast of Alba. The capital of Italy's sparkling wine industry and the most famous producer of *spumante*, for most of the year Asti itself is fairly sedate; a small, averagely attractive town, it becomes the focus of attention in September every year as it gears up for its Palio. Though it's taken nothing like as seriously as Siena's famous event, and has been revived to some extent for tourists, you should make an effort to see it if you're near here at the right time. The surrounding area shelters a fine Romanesque abbey near **Albugnano**, and a rare glimpse of Italy's Jewish history in the grand synagogue of **Casale Monferrato**, but be aware that public transport is infrequent in the Piemonte hinterland and it's much easier with your own wheels.

Asti

In the run-up to its annual Palio, **ASTI** throws off its sedate air and hosts street banquets and a medieval market. On the day of the race itself, the third Sunday in September, there's a thousand-strong procession of citizens dressed as their fourteenth-century ancestors, before the frenetic bare-backed horse race around the arena of the Campo del Palio – followed by the awarding of the *palio* (banner) to the winner and all-night feasting and boozing.

The rest of the year the Campo del Palio is a vast, bleak car park, and there's frankly not a lot to see. The arcaded **Piazza Alfieri** is officially the centre of town, behind which is the **Collegiata di San Secondo** (daily 8.30am–noon & 3.30–6.30pm; free), dedicated to the city's patron saint and built on the site of the saint's martyrdom in the second century. There's nothing left of the second-century church but there is a fine sixth-century crypt, its columns so slender that they seem on the verge of toppling over. As for the rest of the church, it's a slick, early Gothic construction, with neat red-brick columns topped with tidily carved capitals and in the left aisle a polyptych by one of Asti's Renaissance artists, Gandolfino d'Asti. The Palio banners are also kept here, in a heavily ornate Baroque chapel, along with the *carroccio* – a sacred war chariot used in medieval times.

The main street, **Corso Alfieri**, slices through the town from the Piazza Alfieri, to the east of which lies the church of **San Pietro** at Corso Alfieri 2 (Tues–Sun 10am–1pm & 3/4–6/7pm). The church has a circular twelfth-century **Baptistry** (€2.50, €5 with the museum), now used as an exhibition space, and a **museum** housed in what was a pilgrim's hospice, displaying an odd – and badly labelled – assortment of Roman and Egyptian artefacts. At the other end of the Corso is the **Torre Rossa**, a medieval tower with a red and white chequered brick top, built on the remains of the sixteen-sided Roman tower in which San Secondo was imprisoned before his martyrdom. Secondo was a Roman officer of the patrician class, who converted to Christianity and defied imperial law by burying the martyred Saint Marcianus of Tortona, Piemonte's first bishop. After being held – and tortured – in the tower, he was beheaded on March 29 in 119 AD, during the reign of Emperor Hadrian. His relics are kept in the Asti cathedral.

Practicalities

Asti's **tourist office** is at Piazza Alfieri 29 (Mon–Sat 9am–1pm & 2.30–6.30pm, Sun 9am–1pm; ☎0141.530.357, ⓦwww.astiturismo.it). If you're intending to visit Asti on the Palio weekend, book a **room** well in advance; at other times there should be little problem. The best of the affordable options are the conveniently sited *Cavour* at Piazza Marconi 18 (☎0141.530.222, ⓦwww.hotelcavour-asti.com; ❷) and the slightly cheaper *Genova*, Corso Alessandria 26 (☎0141.593.197; ❷). Renowned for its food, Asti has a wide choice of **restaurants**, ranging from basic and cheap pizzerias like *Monna Laura*, Via Cavour 30 (closed Mon), to the excellent and rather pricey *Gener Neuv*, Lungotanaro dei Pescatori 4 (closed Sun eve & Mon), which serves delicious local cuisine. If you're into *spumante* or want to sample other wines from the region, come during the **wine festival**, the Festa della Douja d'Or, which is held from the second Friday to the third Sunday in September, with wine tastings in the piazzas from early evening until midnight. The rest of the year, you can always try the *Tre Bicchieri*, Piazza Statuto 37, an extremely well-stocked and fashionable wine bar.

Around Asti

CASALE MONFERRATO, 35km north of Asti, has the dubious distinction of being the cement capital of Italy, but it's also home to the country's most sumptuous **synagogue** (Sun 10am–noon & 3–6pm, or ring for an appointment on ☎0142.71.807), at Via Salomone Olper 44, the third right off the main Via Roma as you come from the cathedral. A rich, gold-encrusted affair with a voluptuously curving pulpit and a "museum of treasures" laid out in the closed-off women's gallery, the synagogue is a leftover from the days when there was a sizeable Jewish population in Piemonte, most of whom had fled from Spain in the sixteenth century to escape persecution. Casale was home to nearly 200 Jewish families, who lived here in peace until Mussolini's racial laws (brought in mainly to appease Hitler) forced many to leave.

Between Asti and Casale Monferrato is the small town of **MONCALVO**, tucked into a fold in the hills and surrounded by fields of sunflowers, vineyards and acres of corn. If you have the cash and want to spoil yourself in restful surroundings, head for the five-star *Locanda di Sant'Uffizio* (☎0141.916.292, ⓦwww.thi.it; ❾), 4km south of Moncalvo at Cioccaro di Penango, a luxury hotel housed in a seventeenth-century ecclesiastical palace, with antique-filled rooms, a gourmet restaurant and a swimming pool. There are also plenty of **agriturismo** places to eat at nearby, along with the *Ametista* at Piazza Antico Castello 14 (closed Wed) in Moncalvo itself, which offers country dishes such as pepperoni flan with *bagna caöda* sauce.

The **Abbazia di Vezzolano** (Tues–Sun 9am–12.30pm & 2–6.30pm), in the village of **ALBUGNANO**, deep in a valley to the northwest of Asti, represents some of the area's best late-Romanesque architecture. According to legend, the abbey was founded by Charlemagne, who experienced a religious vision on the site. Outside it has a fancy, arcaded and sculpted facade and a Romanesque cloister. Inside, there's a stone rood screen expressively carved with scenes from the life of Mary, and a row of rustic-looking saints.

Northern Piemonte: Biella, Varallo and Valsesia

The main attraction of northern Piemonte is the mountains, especially the dramatic Alpine **Valsesia**, which winds up to the foot of Monte Rosa on the Swiss border. On the way are two of the region's most visited sanctuaries, the **Santuario di Oropa** near **Biella** and the **Sacro Monte** at **Varallo**. From here you're well poised for either Piemonte's mountains or those of Valle d'Aosta, a few kilometres west. Worth a slight detour is the magical train ride that starts at **Domodossola**, conveniently en route if you're heading for Switzerland.

Biella and Ivrea

The sizeable but bland northern-Piemonte city of Novara is a useful place for transport connections but otherwise not really worth a stop. In passing through, you'll note that its central basilica, **San Gaudenzio**, has a striking tower, rather resembling a 122-metre Neoclassical cucumber. On a clear day the Alps, to which this city is a gateway (along with the Italian Lakes; see Chapter 3), make a stupendous backdrop. Otherwise, the area is mostly dominated by rice fields, soaking wet and heavily mosquito-infested in the warm months. A short train ride northwest from Novara brings you to the provincial capital of **BIELLA**, known for its wool industry, its periphery choked with mills and the hilltop upper town with the mansions and villas of wool barons. It's not an especially rewarding place either – apart from its small medieval quarter, reached by funicular – but it does give access to the **Santuario di Oropa** (Ⓦ www.santuariodi oropa.it; daily 8am–noon & 2–7pm; free, €3.50 for the museum), a forty-minute bus ride (#2 from the train station) about 11km northwest of Biella to the foot of Monte Mucrone. Founded in the fourth century by St Eusebio to house a black statue of the Madonna and Child, it's the most venerated of Piemonte's shrines, the main church an immense neo-Baroque concoction. It's a good starting-point for walks into the surrounding mountains, and a cable car runs regularly up Monte Mucrone from the sanctuary as far as the mountain refuge *Albergo Savoia* (Ⓣ 015.849.5131; half board ❷), which offers modest food and accommodation. A network of marked trails begins here: one of the nicest and easiest is to the **Lago Mucrone**, a small mountain lake. More energetic is the hike up to the summit of Monte Mucrone itself – a two-hour trek. If you wish, you can stay at the sanctuary, which has around 350 recently refurbished rooms – very austere unless you go for suites (Ⓣ 015.2555.1200; ❶).

Biella's **tourist office** is at Piazza Vittorio Veneto 3 (Mon–Fri 8.30am–1pm & 2.30–6pm, Sat 9.30am–12.30pm & 2.30–5.30pm; mid-June to mid-Sept also Sun 9am–12.30pm & 2.30–5.30pm; Ⓣ 015.351.128, Ⓦ www.atl.biella.it). If you need to **stay** overnight, try the clean and attractive *Bugella*, Via Cottolengo 65 (Ⓣ 015.406.607, Ⓦ www.hotelbugella.it; ❸). And check out *La Baracca* at Via San Eusebio 12 (closed Sat & Sun & mid-June to mid-July), a bar in a converted nineteenth-century factory building that serves authentic Piemonte meals for about €18; don't overlook the appealing antipasto buffet. Otherwise, *La Civetta*, at Piazza Cucco 10b (evenings only; closed Wed), turns out simple regional and Italian fare for €20–25.

IVREA, to the southwest of Biella, is well worth a visit in the week leading up to Shrove Tuesday, when there's a carnival – featuring piping, drumming, masked balls, historic processions and fireworks – that culminates in a bizarre three-day "Battle of the Oranges" when the whole town and hundreds of spectators turn out to pelt each other with oranges – you have to wear a red hat if you don't want to be a target. At the end of each day, the town is covered in a thick carpet of orange pulp, and the following morning there's a traditional handing out of polenta and cod. For a place to **stay**, try the small *Luca* at Corso Garibaldi 58 (℡0125.48.697; ❷), or head 3km northeast out of town to the four-star *Castello San Giuseppe* at Chiaverano d'Ivrea (℡0125.424.370, ⓦwww .castellosangiuseppe.it; ❻), set in a converted Carmelite monastery.

Varallo and Sacro Monte

VARALLO, some 50km by train north of Novara, marks the beginning of northern Piemonte's more picturesque reaches, surrounded by steep wooded hills and filled with Art Nouveau villas and Baroque *palazzi*. It's a pretty place, enjoyable for a short visit; most people come to see the sanctuary of **Sacro Monte** (see below), just outside the town and connected by cable car (Mon–Fri 9am–6.30pm, Sat & Sun 9am–7pm; €2.50 return ticket) from the top of Via Ferrari in the centre of town.

The centre is a five-minute walk from the train station; turn right along Via Durio or Corso Roma. On the way you pass the church of **San Gaudenzio**, anchored to a creeper-covered cliff and surrounded by arcades. Inside, there's a polyptych by the sixteenth-century Varallo-born artist Gaudenzio Ferrari, responsible for much of the work at Sacro Monte. The main street, **Corso Umberto I**, lined with shuttered and balconied palaces, winds through the town from here towards the River Serio. There's further work by Gaudenzio Ferrari in the church of **Madonna delle Grazie**, north of Corso Umberto I at the end of Via Don Maio, where an entire wall is covered with colourful and detailed scenes from the life of Christ.

The **tourist office** is at Corso Roma 38 (Mon–Fri 9am–1pm & 2.30–6.30pm, Sat 9.30am–1pm & 2.30–7pm; June–Aug open Sun, same hours as Sat; ℡0163.564.404, ⓦwww.turismovalsesiavercelli.it). If you want to **stay** in Varallo, head for the *Monte Rosa* at Via Regaldi 4 (℡0163.51.100, ⓦwww .albergomonterosa.it; ❷), a wonderful, friendly, rambling old hotel a brisk ten-minute walk away from the town centre. Or try the hostel, at Via Scarognini 37 (℡0163.51.036; €20 per person). For **food**, the restaurant *Il Tiglio*, opposite the station in Piazza Marconi 2, does good pizzas (closed Wed).

Sacro Monte

Crowning the hill above Varallo, **Sacro Monte** (ⓦwww.sacromontevarallo .com; in addition to regular services, Mon–Thurs 9am–12.30pm & 1–5pm; Fri 9am–noon; free) is a complex of 45 chapels, each housing a 3-D tableau of painted statues against frescoed scenery representing a scene from the life of Christ. Founded in the fifteenth century by a friar anxious to popularize Catholicism in a fiercely heretical region, Sacro Monte draws on sensationalism and spectacle, calculated to work on the emotions of the uneducated. The sanctuary is at its best when busy; to get a measure of its continuing popularity, you need to visit on a Sunday, when it's full of families, pensioners and nuns, all of whom picnic in the shady grounds after finishing their pilgrimage.

A bizarre spectacle, depicting the whole range of key biblical episodes from the Fall to Christ's birth, life and death, the tableaux don't pull any punches. The *Massacre of the Innocents* (#11) shows a floor littered with dead babies, while Herod's army prepares to spear, hack and slash more innocent victims. And the chapels (#30–41) that retell the events of Christ's passion are flagrant emotional manipulation, with crazed flagellators, spitting soldiers and a series of liberally blood-splattered Christs. By the time you reach the *Road to Calvary* (#36) you almost flinch at the sight of a flaked-out Christ being viciously kicked. Dominating the central piazza of the sanctuary, the Baroque Basilica offers some relief, the highlight being the cupola – a nice piece of optical trickery, encrusted with figures perched on bubblegum clouds.

Valsesia

From Varallo the main road follows the River Sesia to the foot of multipeaked Monte Rosa, whose massive bulk dominates four Italian valleys and spreads north into Switzerland. **VALSESIA**, the easternmost valley, is also the most dramatic – worth going for the ride even if you don't want to launch a hiking or skiing assault on the mountains.

Flanked by dark pine-wooded slopes topped with a toothed ridge of rock, the road winds up the valley, the perspective changing at every turn. It's a well-touristed area (mainly by Italians and Germans), where traditional houses with slate roofs and wood-slatted balconies mingle with Alpine-style villas and apartments. The villages are crowded for much of the summer, and with weekend skiers in the winter. September is the quietest month, when many of the hotels close, but the weather up the mountains is unpredictable then, and hiking can be hazardous.

The Valsesia villages were founded in the thirteenth century by religious sects from the Swiss Valais, known as Walser, in search of land and the freedom to worship. There are reckoned to be around 3000 true Walsers in the valleys of Monte Rosa, and in most bars and shops you'll still hear people speaking a dialect based on ancient German. If you want to see how these isolated communities lived and worked, visit the **Walser Museum** (July & Aug Tues–Sun 2–6pm; rest of the year Sat & Sun only; ℡0163.91.180; free), a traditionally furnished seventeenth-century house in the hamlet of **PEDEMONTE**, ten minutes' walk from Alagna.

ALAGNA, at the head of the valley, right below Monte Rosa, is the most convenient place to stay, whether you want to ski or hike. Popular and predominantly modern, it has a cluster of Walser houses, some of which still function as farms, with hay hanging to dry on the slats and wood stacked behind, while others are holiday homes, with geraniums tumbling from window boxes. The **tourist office** (Dec–May & mid-June to mid-Sept Wed–Mon 9am–noon & 3–6.30pm, Sat 9am–12.30pm & 2.30–7pm, Sun 9am–1pm & 3–6pm; otherwise Sat & Sun only; ℡0163.922.988, ⓦwww.turismovalsesiavercelli.it) is on Piazza Grober. Alagna's cheapest **hotel** is the Genzianella, Via Centro 33 (℡0163.923.205, ⓦwww.pensionegenzianella.com; not including breakfast, ❸).

There are lots of **walks** among the foothills near Alagna, all of which are well marked. If you're interested in seeing more than mountain scenery, follow a path 5km back down the valley to **RIVA VALDOBBIA**, whose church facade is covered with a colourful late sixteenth-century fresco, *The Last Judgement*. However, the toughest and most spectacular hikes are those on **Monte Rosa** itself. It's possible to save time and energy by taking the cable car up to Punta Indren (3260m), from where you can walk to one of the many *rifugi*; most of these are open from June to September and some are open all year, but check at the tourist office in Alagna before setting out. Failing that, you could walk down into the next valley, Val Gressoney in Valle d'Aosta (see opposite).

All these walks involve a good deal of scree-crossing and some sobering drops, and none is to be taken lightly – you'll need a good **map** (the IGC map of the four Monte Rosa valleys shows all paths, *rifugi* and pistes as does the Kompass Monte Rosa map) available in Alagna and Varallo, and you should monitor the weather carefully. There's also an ambitious long-distance circuit of Monte Rosa, starting at Alagna, taking in Val Gressoney, Val d'Ayas and Zermatt across the Swiss border: reckon on five days if you make use of ski lifts and cable cars, and a good deal longer if you don't.

Skiing in the area is organized by Monterosa Ski (☎0125.303.111; ⓦwww .monterosa-sky.com), which has an office in Alagna, and equipment is available for rent in the village. However, the runs are narrow, and though experienced skiers can cross into Val Gressoney, it involves walking as well as off-piste skiing. The valleys are also popular for canoeing and rafting, and several centres organize classes and excursions – try Hidronica (☎0163.735.301, ⓦwww .hidronica.com). Check ⓦwww.alagna.it for more information on summer and winter activities in and around Alagna.

Domodossola and over the border to Locarno

At the foot of the Simplon Pass, and handily situated on the main train line between Milan and Bern, in Switzerland (15 trains daily from Novara), is the little town of **DOMODOSSOLA**. With its arcaded medieval centre and market square, it warrants a visit in its own right, but is more famous as the starting point of a scenic train ride, La Vigezzina–Centovalli, that connects Domodossola with Locarno, across the border in Switzerland, taking in the vineyards and chestnut forests of the Val Vigezzo and Centovalli along the way. The scenery is gorgeous, and, although the ride is pricier than the regular train (one-way €19.80), it's well worth it; InterRail passes are valid. The journey to Locarno takes an hour and a half, but you can get off and explore at any of the pretty flower-strewn stations en route; when you want the next train to stop, just remember to raise the red and white signal on the platform.

The road to Aosta and the eastern valleys

The tributary valleys in **eastern Valle d'Aosta** (ⓦwww.regione.vda.it) have suffered most from the skiing industry since they are the easiest to access from Turin and Milan and therefore the most frequented. Experienced mountain hikers may be lured by the challenge of climbing Monte Rosa and the Matterhorn from **Valtournenche**, while less ambitious walkers will find most to do in the Val Gressoney, which still has a number of traditional villages settled by the Swiss Walsers. In the main Aosta valley you'll find one of the region's more interesting castles, **Fénis**.

Val Gressoney

The **Val Gressoney** is the first of the Valle d'Aosta valleys, but you could be forgiven for thinking you'd stepped into the stereotypical Switzerland. The grass is velvety green, the River Lys crystal clear, the traditional houses wood-slatted and the modern ones gleaming Alpine chalets, while the craggy head of the valley is overlooked by one of Monte Rosa's shimmering glaciers. As you might expect from such natural attractions, the valley gets busy, especially at weekends and holidays. The walking is good, and the skiing isn't bad either, with pistes laid out on rocky south-facing slopes that are great for catching the sun but which get a little slushy by the afternoon in late season.

At the mouth of the valley, **PONT-ST-MARTIN** is primarily useful as a transport interchange for heading into the Val Gressoney. The valley comes into its own at the popular but attractive resorts of **GRESSONEY-ST-JEAN** and especially the cheaper **GRESSONEY-LA-TRINITÉ**, which is close to the head of the valley and has some good, comfortable hotels. The latter also makes a convenient starting-point for walks, though be warned that the summer walking season doesn't start until late June: between Easter and then, most hotels are closed. If you want to do more than wander along the river, take the track from Orsia, 1km north of Gressoney-la-Trinité, which leads up to the lovely mountain lake, **Gabiet** – a two- to three-hour walk (the last leg of the walk is possible by ski lift, or you can take the cable car all the way up from Ciaval, 3km north of Gressoney-la-Trinité) – from where you can continue over the mountain into the Valsesia, doing the last part of the descent by cable car if you're tired. Val Gressoney's Walser settlements can be reached by footpaths from La Trinité. One of the nicest is **BIEL**, with some eighteenth-century houses (maps are available from La Trinité's tourist office; see below). The Walsers still speak their German dialect, along with French and Italian, a linguistic mixture evident in the area's trilingual signs.

Practicalities

La Trinité's **tourist office** (daily 9am–12.30pm & 2–6pm; ☎0125.366.143, Ⓦwww.aiatmonterosawalser.it) is at Piazza Tache 1, across the river from the bus stop. Most **hotels** in the area are quite expensive, but the *Gressoney*, at Via Lys 3 in St-Jean (☎0125.355.986, Ⓦwww.hotelsgressoney.com; ❺), has huge king-sized beds and is worth splashing out on if you feel like some four-star comfort (avoid eating here though and have a pizza in the village instead). At Gabiet you'll find the one-star *Del Ponte* (☎0125.366.180, Ⓦwww.albergodelponte .com; may insist on half board ❸); take the cable car as it's up at 2000m. There are a couple of places around St-Jean too, including *La Stella* at località Steina (☎0125.355.068, Ⓦwww.hotellastella.com; obligatory half board, minimum stay one week ❸). There's a **campsite** near St-Jean at località Schnacke 15: Camping Margherita (☎0125.355.370; open all year round).

Val d'Ayas

Branching off the main valley and headed by the huge mass of Monte Rosa, **Val d'Ayas** is one of the region's most beautiful valleys – large, open and flanked by thickly wooded slopes. As a result, it tends to be overwhelmed by visitors, with the tourist-geared villages chock-full of trippers and skiers at the weekend and during high season – and correspondingly dead at other times of the year.

The main ski resort, **CHAMPOLUC**, at the head of the valley, is the base for the tough ascent (4hr minimum; route #62) of the Testa Grigia (3315m), although you can cheat on this by taking the funicular and ski lift part of the way. From the top there's a superb view across the peaks of the Matterhorn to Mont Blanc; however, the climb is strictly for the experienced unless you can afford a guide (contact the Alpine Guide Association of Champoluc on ☎0125.366.139, or the Champoluc **tourist office**, at Via Varasc 16, Mon–Sat 9am–12.30pm & 3–5pm, Sun 9am–3pm; ☎0125.307.113, Ⓦwww.ayas-champoluc.com).

BRUSSON, further down the valley, is a better base for less demanding walks. There's a trail (3hr 30min; route #6) up to seven mountain lakes, starting with a long climb through a dense wood up to a waterfall – the water drops 30m, and is most impressive in spring when swollen by snowmelt.

The **hotel** *Beau Site* at Rue Trois Villages 4 (℡0125.300.144, ⓦ www.beausite .it; may insist on half board; one week minimum ➍), on the edge of Brusson, is clean, simple and has a good restaurant. In Champoluc hotels are expensive, but *Cré Forné* (℡0125.307.197, ⓦ www.creforne.champoluc.it; may insist on half board; minimum three days ➌) at Crest (connected with Champoluc by funicular) is a good alternative. There are also campsites between Brusson and Champoluc: try the *Camping Deans* (℡0125.300.297; open all year) in località Extrapieraz; facilities include a bar-restaurant.

Valtournenche and the Matterhorn (Cervino)

VALTOURNENCHE, headed by the Matterhorn at the north end and by the town of Chatillon at the southern central valley end, should be one of the most spectacular of Italy's mountain valleys, but unfortunately the main towns are overdeveloped and hydroelectric works ruin the views on the plains. The international ski resort **Breuil-Cervinia** is a functional, modern resort, and even the **Matterhorn** is a letdown, with tribes of skiers ensuring that its glacier is grubby for much of the year. That said, these are the Alps, and if you can't manage to carry on to the other valleys further west, you will at least get a taste of chocolate-box chalets and flower-covered meadows straight out of *Heidi*.

Breuil-Cervinia and the Matterhorn

BREUIL-CERVINIA was one of Italy's first ski resorts, built in the prewar years as part of Mussolini's drive for a healthy nation. In its heyday the ski lifts, soaring to 3500m, broke all records, and its grand hotels ensured the patronage of Europe's wealthy. Today the wealthy are cossetted in modern buildings outside the resort, leaving the tacky streets of the town for packaged hordes attracted by a large skiing area with lots of easy runs.

If you want to climb the **Matterhorn** (4478m), you should seriously consider approaching from Zermatt in Switzerland; the Italian route is strictly for experts. If undeterred, you'll need to acquire the IGC Matterhorn map and to be very well equipped. There are two overnight options on the way, the *rifugio Duca degli Abruzzi* (℡0166.949.145; mid-July to mid-Sept), 2hr 15min from Breuil in Orionde (2800m), and the bivouac *Jean A Carrel* (℡ same as for *Duca*; open all year) – where you need to take your own food and drink – four hours beyond (3850m). From the Carrel it's a tough climb to the summit, even with the ropes that have been fitted along the more dangerous stretches of the route.

Nus and the Castello di Fénis

Further up the main valley from Chatillon and overlooked by a ruined castle, the small, pretty village of **NUS** makes a good base for the **Castello di Fénis** 2km away (March–June & Sept 9am–6.30pm; July & Aug 9am–7.30pm; Jan–Feb Mon & Wed–Sat 10am–noon & 1.30–4.30pm; Sun 10am–noon & 1.30–5.30pm; €5). Backed by wooded hills and encircled by two rows of turreted walls, the castle is a fairy-tale cluster of towers decorated with scalloped arcades. These defences were primarily aesthetic, with the real job of protecting the valley being left to the less prettified fortresses of nearby Nus and Quart. Meanwhile, the Fénis branch of the Challant counts concentrated on refining their living quarters with fine Gothic frescoes; the best of these is in the courtyard, above the elaborate twin staircase that leads to the upper storeys. A courtly St George rescues a damsel in distress from the clutches of a tremendous dragon, overlooked by a tribe of protective saints brandishing moral statements on curling scrolls.

There's a **hotel** in Fénis – *La Chatelaine* (☎0165.764.264; ❷), in località Chez Sapin, open year-round. However, as Nus has a train station and is close to the main road for buses, you may find it more convenient to sleep there: the *Florian* at Via Risorgimento 3 (☎0165.767.968; ❸) has clean and comfortable doubles and is also open all year.

Aosta and around

The attractive mountain valley town of **AOSTA** was founded by the Romans in 25 BC after they disposed of the local tribe by auctioning them off in a slave market. The many Roman monuments, including the arch, the theatre and the forum bear testimony to this period, but Aosta was primarily an imperial military camp, vestiges of which can be seen in the extensive ruins of some towers and city walls. Remains of medieval Aosta predominate, its narrow cobbled streets and overhanging upper storeys giving the place a very alpine air. The town's key attraction is its position: encircled by the **Alps**, and with access to the lovely valleys of the **Parco Nazionale del Gran Paradiso**, the ski resorts of **Mont Blanc**, and a sprinkling of castles in between, it's an ideal base for exploring the northwest of the region.

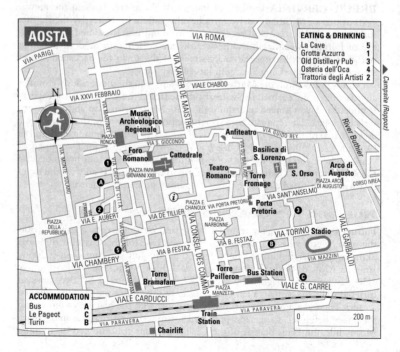

The Town

The large, elegant **Piazza E. Chanoux** and its pavement cafés form the centre of town, from where Via Porta Pretoria and Via Sant'Anselmo lead east – the principal streets for window-shopping and people-watching. In the middle, the **Porta Pretoria** is one of the town's most impressive sights: two parallel triple-arched gateways that served as the main entrance into the Roman town.

North of the gate is the **Teatro Romano** (daily: 9am–1hr before sunset; free); a section of the four-storeyed facade remains, 22m high and pierced with arched windows. Unfortunately since 2000 it has been hidden behind scaffolding, and no one will risk estimating a date for completion of the restoration. Close by, the medieval **Torre Fromage** at Via du Baillage is now sometimes used as a contemporary art exhibition space.

A short walk east of here, outside the main town walls off Via Sant' Anselmo, the church of **Sant'Orso** (daily: March–Sept 9am–7pm; Oct–Feb 10am–12.30pm & 1.30–5pm; free) houses a number of tenth-century frescoes behind its dull facade. They're hidden up in the roof where you can examine them at close quarters from specially constructed walkways – though you'll need to find the sacristan to get up there. If you can't find him, content yourself with the fifteenth-century choir stalls, carved with a menagerie of holy men and animals, ranging from bats and monkeys to a tonsured monk. There are even better carvings on the capitals of the Romanesque **cloisters** (daily: March–June & Sept 9am–7pm; July & Aug 9am–8pm; Oct–Feb 10am–12.30pm & 1.30–5pm; free) – mostly scenes from the story of Christ. The **priorate** has terracotta decorations on its outside walls and an octagonal tower which rises above the complex. Nearby are the fifth-century remains of the **Basilica of San Lorenzo** (same hours as cloisters; free), which are worth a peek on your way past.

At the far end of Via Sant'Anselmo, the **Arco di Augusto** was erected in 25 BC to celebrate the seizure of the territory from the local Salassi tribe and to honour Emperor Augustus, after whom the town was named Augusta Praetoria (Aosta is a corruption of Augusta). Though the arch loses something in being stranded in a sea of traffic and topped by a rustic eighteenth-century slate roof, it's a sturdy, dignified-looking monument. Beyond is a well-preserved **Roman bridge**, its single arch spanning the now dried-up bed of the River Buthier.

On the other side of town, the **Foro Romano** on Piazza Giovanni XXIII is the rather misleading name for another Roman relic, a vaulted passage (*cryptoporticus*) under the actual forum area, the purpose of which is not entirely clear, though it probably served as both a foundation for structures above ground and as a protected walkway. Nearby, the **Museo Archeologico Regionale** (daily 9am–7pm; free) has interesting exhibits on the settlements in and around Aosta since Neolithic times. Displays include artefacts of the Celtic Salassi tribe, who settled here in the second century BC and were defeated by the Romans in 25 BC, and conclude with finds dating to the fall of Rome in the fifth century AD. The nearby **cattedrale** looks unpromising from the outside, but masks a Gothic interior with fantastically carved choir stalls, with a mermaid, lion and a snail nestled among the saints. Remains of a fourth-century **baptistry** are visible through the floor; and there are mosaics on the presbytery pavement depicting the two rivers of earthly paradise and Christ, holding the sun and moon, surrounded by the symbols of the months. Like Sant'Orso, it has some impressive tenth-century frescoes hidden in the roof, saved for posterity by the lowering of the ceiling in the fourteenth century; you can visit these on a guided tour (several daily; €7.80). There are more treasures in the cathedral

museum (closed Mon; €2.10) – including gold-, silver- and gem-encrusted reliquaries and equally ornate chalices, crucifixes and caskets.

Practicalities

Aosta's **tourist office** (mid-June to Oct daily 9am–1pm & 2.30–8pm; Oct to mid-June Mon–Sat 9.30am–1pm & 3–6.30pm, Sun 9.30am–1pm; T0165.236.627, Wwww.regione.vda.it) is at Piazza E. Chanoux 2. You can get to most places within the region by **bus** from the bus station on Via G. Carrel, but some of the more remote valleys are served only by buses running at school times out of season (contact tourist office for printed timetables). The **train station** is on Piazza Manzetti, south of the centre.

The pleasant **hotel** *Le Pageot* at Via Carrel 31 (T165.32.433, F0165.33.217, Wwww.lepagot.it; ③) is handy for both train and bus and is near all the sights. Alternatively, the modern, good-quality *Hotel Bus*, Via Malherbes 18 (T0165.236.958, F0165.236.962, Wwww.hotelbus.it; ③), is just on the edge of the centre of town on the other side from the train station. A more upmarket and central option is the three-star *Turin* at Via E. Torino 14 (T0165.44.593, F0165.361.377, Wwww.hotelturin.it; ③).

There are a number of **campsites** nearby: *Milleluci*, about 1km away at località Porossan-Roppoz 15 (T0165.235.278, Wwww.campingmilleluci.com) is the nearest.

Finding somewhere to **eat** is no problem: try the locally popular ☽ *Grotta Azzurra*, Via Croce di Città 97 (closed Wed), for good-value pizza and other excellent dishes; the intimate *Trattoria degli Artisti* at Via Maillet 5/7 (closed Sun & Mon) for traditional Aostan fare, such as meat braised on stone; or the *Osteria dell'Oca* (closed Mon) in a quiet little square at Via E. Aubert 15, which again offers good local cuisine. Otherwise, Via E. Aubert and Via Porta Pretoria are the best streets to trawl. In the evening, a good place to relax with a glass of wine is *La Cave*, Via Challand 34, while ☽ *The Old Distillery Pub*, Via Près Fosses 7, offers a very welcoming nightlife scene for the anglophone crowd (open till 2am).

West from Aosta: Castello di Sarre

West from Aosta, the main valley holds a number of **castles**, the best of which is the thirteenth-century **Castello di Sarre** (March–July & Sept daily 9am–6.30pm, till 7.30pm July & Aug; Jan & Feb Tues–Sat 10am–noon & 1.30–4.30pm, Sun till 5.30pm; €5), accessible by bus or train from Aosta, some 5km away. It's a ten-minute walk up a hill covered with apple orchards from the St Maurice-Sarre train station; coming by bus, walk from the bus stop up the main road and take the unmarked turning just before the tollbooth. Sarre is the former hunting lodge of Vittorio Emanuele II, who, the story goes, actually bought the castle by mistake. He had set his sights on the property of Aymaville opposite, but the agent sent to buy the castle was confused about the direction in which the river flowed, and ended up buying Sarre instead.

Vittorio Emanuele made the best of a bad job, permanently stamping the halls of the castle with his astounding taste in interior decor, pushing the hunting-lodge motif to its limits, with horns of wild ibex lining the main gallery and thousands of white chamois skulls studding the stuccoed festoons. Pride of place is given to the first ibex slain by the king. The custodian claims that many died a natural death, but this was hardly the impression that Vittorio Emanuele, in his guise as macho huntsman, intended to convey. The castle has traditionally been a pilgrimage point for diehard Italian monarchists who used to come here to pay their respects to Savoy family trees. Now that the Italian royals have finally been allowed to return from Swiss exile, their fans have got the real deals to idolize, scandals and all.

North from Aosta: the Colle di Gran San Bernardo

Immediately north of Aosta, the **Colle di Gran San Bernardo** (2473m) leads the way into Switzerland. Named after the famous monastery that for centuries provided shelter to travellers on the main pilgrim route from Northern Europe to Rome, it was the home of the eponymous big brown-and-white dogs that rescued Alpine travellers in distress. The history of the mountain pass is well documented in the **museum** (June–Sept daily 9am–6pm; €5) housed in the monastery, although you'll need your passport to visit as it's situated just over the border in Switzerland. The spectacular pass is open only during summer, but the border is open year-round by way of a tunnel.

The Gran Paradiso National Park

For some of Valle d'Aosta's most beautiful mountains and valleys, make for the south, down to the **Parco Nazionale del Gran Paradiso** – Italy's first national park, spread around the valleys at the foot of 4061-metre-high Gran Paradiso mountain.

The park owes its foundation to King Vittorio Emanuele II, who donated his extensive hunting park to the state in 1922, ensuring that the population of ibex that he and his hunters had managed to reduce to near extinction survived. There are now around 3500 ibex here and about 6000 chamois, living most of the year above the tree line but descending to the valleys in winter and spring. The most dramatic sightings are during the mating season in November and December, when you may see pairs of males fighting it out for possession of a female. You might also spy golden eagles nesting, and there are a number of rare alpine flowers, most of which can be seen in the **botanical garden** in the Val di Cogne.

The park's three valleys – **Cogne**, **Valsavarenche** and **Val di Rhêmes** – are popular, but tourist development has been cautious and well organized. The hotels are good (you get far more for your money than you would in one of the nearby towns) and the campsites not too vast – camping outside of campsites is not permitted. There are a few mountain *rifugi* and *bivacchi* (unoccupied shelters) between which run well-marked footpaths. Though it's primarily a summer resort for walkers, the cross-country skiing is also good, and every winter a 45-kilometre **Gran Paradiso** trek is organized at Cogne (contact the tourist office in Cogne for details). The starting-point for the ascent of Gran Paradiso itself is **Pont** in the Valsavarenche, while Cogne gives access to the Alta Via 2, a long, high-level mountain trail.

Regular **buses** run throughout the year from Aosta to Cogne and Valsavarenche and along the Val di Rhêmes from mid-June to mid-September (see p.113). If you're using your own transport, access to either of these valleys is easiest from the village of **INTROD**, about 2km from **VILLENEUVE**, which is on the main bus route.

Val di Cogne

The **Val di Cogne** is the principal, most popular and most dramatic section of the park. Its lower reaches are narrow, the road running above the fast-flowing

Grand Eyvia River overlooked by sheer wavy-ridged mountains. Further on, the valley broadens out around the main village, **COGNE**, which is surrounded by gentle green meadows with glacier-covered mountains rising beyond.

The **tourist office**, in the centre of town at Via Bourgeois 34 (daily 9am–12.30pm & 3–5.30/6pm; ☎0165.74.040, ⓦwww.cogne.org), has maps with descriptions in English of walks, one of which is an easy, scenic stroll that follows the river, with the glaciers in view for most of the way. Before leaving the village of Cogne, it's worth visiting the **Maison de Gerard Dayné** (July & Aug 6 tours daily 10.40am–6.30pm; at other times of the year, ask at the tourist office or call ☎0165.749.264; free) a typical nineteenth-century Valdaostan house evocative of the traditional lifestyle.

The small village of **VALNONTEY** is the 2.5km from Cogne and starting-point for a steep, three-hour walk up to the *Rifugio V. Sella* (☎0165.74.310, ⓦwww.rifugiosella.com; Easter–Sept), a demanding hike that's incredibly popular on summer Sundays and in early August. The path passes a **botanical garden** (mid-June to mid-Sept daily 10am–6.30pm; €2.50), with rare Alpine flora, then zigzags up through a forest and onto exposed mountainside before reaching the *rifugio*, set on a grassy plateau. At the mountain tarn of Lago Loson, a fifteen-minute walk from the *rifugio*, you may well spot **ibex** or more timid **chamois**, especially at sunset and sunrise, when there are fewer people around. Hardened hikers who can cope with a stretch of climbing can press on over the **Colle de Lauson** to the Val di Rhêmes.

Practicalities

There's a campsite, *Vallée de Cogne*, close to Cogne village in località Fabrique Via Cavagnet 7 (☎0165.749.279; year-round), and two at Valnontey: *Lo Stambecco* (☎0165.74.152, ⓔcampingstambecco@tiscali.it; mid-May to mid-Sept) and *Gran Paradiso* (☎0165.749.204; mid-May to mid-Sept). As for **hotels**, Cogne's most reasonable are the *Stambecco*, Rue des Clementines 21 (☎0165.74.068, ⓕ0165.74.684; ❹), and the *Bouton d'Or* at Viale Cavagnet 15 (☎0165.74.268, ⓦwww.hotelboutondor.it; ❻). Both are open all year and get booked up quickly in high season, so call ahead. For a real treat you could stay in the *Bellevue* hotel on Rue Grand Paradis 22 (☎0165.74.825, ⓦwww.hotelbellevue.it; ❾), a luxury mountain chalet-style resort offering local health and beauty treatments and a choice of excellent restaurants. Groups of two to six people could consider staying in one of the *Bellevue* hotel's self-contained chalets which cost around €100 per person per night for half board – not a budget option, but the food is excellent.

Staying in Valnontey is a better bet if you want to do some walking. There is a handful of affordable **alberghi** among the cluster of stone and wood chalets that make up the village centre, but they may insist you take half board. Try *Herbetet* (☎0165.74.180, ⓦwww.hotelherbetet.com; mid-May to mid-Sept; ❹), the *Petit Dahu* (☎0165.74.146, ⓕ0165.74.146, ⓦwww.hotelpetitdahu.com; half board ❾) or the *Paradisia* (☎ & ⓕ0165.74.158; April–Oct; ❸). For **eating**, *La Barme* (☎0165.749.177, ⓦwww.hotellabarme.com; closed Oct & Nov) has set menus featuring local specialities, and the pinewood chalet, *Valnontey* (☎0165.74.154; Easter to Nov; closed Mon except in July & Aug), offers simple meals.

Cogne's choice of **restaurants** is a bit limited, since most people stay on a half-board basis. You could try the rustic and moderately pricey *Brasserie du Bon Bec* at Rue Bourgeois 72 (☎0165.749.288), the *Lou Ressignon* at Rue Mines de Cogne 22 (closed Mon dinner and all day Tues, end of May & Nov) where full meals run €20–30, or alternatively there are several delicatessens that will make up sandwiches for you.

Valsavarenche

Although not as spectacular as the Val di Cogne, **Valsavarenche**, the next valley west, has its own kind of beauty, attracting seasoned walkers rather than gentle amblers. The most popular route is the ascent of **Gran Paradiso**, from Pont at the end of the valley. Though reckoned to be the easiest of the higher Alps, it is nevertheless a climb rather than a hike, with no path marked beyond the *Rifugio Vittorio Emanuele II* (℡0165.95.920; mid-March to mid-Sept), two and a half hours from Pont.

If you feel safer walking along footpaths, the best of the hikes are from the main village of **Degioz**, otherwise known as Valsavarenche, up to the *Rifugio Orvielles* (2hr 30min; ℡0165.905.816) and then on to a series of high mountain lakes. This takes seven hours, but you can shorten it a bit by taking path #3a down to Pont. Less taxing is the two-hour walk from Pont towards the glacier **Grand Etret** at the head of the valley, although the first stretch is pretty boring.

Practicalities

The only **hotel** in Degioz is the *Parco Nazionale* (℡0165.905.706; Jan 1 & April–Sept; breakfast not included, ❸), while in Pont there is the *Genzianella* which may insist on half board (℡0165.95.393, ⓦwww.genzianella.aosta.it; June–Sept; breakfast not included, ❸). The area is well supplied with **campsites**, of which perhaps the nicest is Pont Breuil (℡0165.95.458; June–Sept), in Pont, with a well-stocked site shop (there's no other for kilometres around); ibex come down to graze on the grassy meadow around the tents. There's also a leafy campsite at località Plan de la Presse, Gran Paradiso (℡ & ⓕ0165.905.801; June–Sept). There are places to **eat** in Degioz, such as the *Pub Brasserie l'Abro de la Leuma* Frazione Degioz 93 (℡0165.905.732; closed Wed), but at Pont you'll have to cook for yourself or ask at one of the hotels.

Val di Rhêmes

The least touristed but most open of the valleys, Val di Rhêmes, is also headed by glaciers. The best place to stay is **BRUIL**, a hamlet at the end of the valley, from where most of the walks start.

There's a fairly easy path along the river to a waterfall, the Cascata di Goletta, at its most spectacular after the spring snowmelt, and from here you can continue to the mountain lake of Goletta and the *Rifugio Gian Federico Benevolo* (℡0165.936.143; March 6–Sept 20) taking in some splendid views on the way. Economical hotel options in Bruil include *Chez Lidia* (℡0165.936.103; breakfast not included, ❷) and the *Galisia* (℡ & ⓕ0165.936.100; breakfast not included, ❶); both are open all year.

Arvier and Valgrisenche

Valgrisenche, a few kilometres west from Val di Rhêmes, is the wildest and least accessible of Valle d'Aosta's valleys. Stunningly beautiful, it is narrow with rocky snow-dusted ridges rising above dark pine woods, although the upper reaches are defaced by the concrete dam of a reservoir. Buses into the Valgrisenche valley aren't very frequent, but buses and trains stop year-round at **ARVIER** at the mouth of the valley – one of the region's most appealing villages, with a small medieval core of twisting streets and stone houses alongside a gorge spanned by a Roman bridge. The town also produces L'Enfer d'Arvier, reckoned to be the region's best wine.

There are no **hotels** in the village of **VALGRISENCHE** itself, but the nearby hamlet of **BONNE** above the reservoir has the *Perret* (☎0165.97.107; not including breakfast, ❷) which boasts a restaurant, is open all year and makes a good starting point for **walks**. These include the ascent of the glaciated Testa del Rutor (3486m). There are many other walks, but none are easy – make sure you carry the Kompass *Gran Paradiso* map.

The northwest: around Mont Blanc

Dominated by the snowy peaks of **Mont Blanc** (Monte Bianco to the Italians), the northern reaches of Valle d'Aosta are spectacular and very popular. The most sensational views are from the cable cars that glide and swoop (at times, alarmingly so) across the mountain to Chamonix in France. However, the trip is expensive (about €55), even if you take a bus back to Italy through the eleven-kilometre-long Mont Blanc tunnel; the service is often suspended because of bad weather.

If the cable car seems too pricey, you can walk up to the **Testa d'Arpy** – a natural balcony with a bird's-eye view up the valley to Mont Blanc – from the sprawling resort of **LA THUILE**, on the road to the Petit-St-Bernard Pass into France. Buses run from Pré-St-Didier at the end of the Valle d'Aosta railway line to La Thuile, from where it's just over two hours' walk by path or road to the lodge *La Genzianella* hotel (☎0165.841.689, ⓦwww.hotelgenzianella.net; ❷) at the top of the Colle San Carlo. From here a path leads through woods to Testa d'Arpy in around ten minutes. It's well worth having a good map (IGC *Monte Bianco*), not so much to find your way as to identify the peaks and glaciers spread out before you.

La Thuile itself is a rather an overdeveloped resort but it's worth popping into the **tourist office**, at Via Collomb 4 (daily 9am–12.30pm & 3–6pm; ☎0165.884.179, ⓦwww.lathuile.it) for maps. The best **accommodation** is up the mountain at *Du Glacier*, Petite Golette 14 (July–Sept & Nov–April; phone in advance to check that there's room, and in high season they may only take bookings for a few days; ☎0165.884.137, ⓦwww.hotelduglacier.it; ❸). Of the walks starting from the hotel the most interesting is the 45-minute hike to **Lago d'Arpy**, from where a path leads down into La Thuile.

Courmayeur and Mont Blanc

COURMAYEUR is the smartest and most popular of Valle d'Aosta's ski resorts, much used by package-tour operators. The skiing is good, though there's little to challenge experts, and the scenery is magnificent, but, predictably, what remains of the old village is enmeshed in a web of ersatz Alpine chalets and après-ski hangouts. If you've come to hike or take the cable cars across to Chamonix, the most convenient place to stay is **LA PALUD**, 5km outside Courmayeur (three buses a day).

The **cable car** runs from La Palud to Punta Helbronner all year round, but continues to Chamonix only between July and September (Punta Hellbronner-Chamonix €39, Punta Hellbronner-Chamonix and return by coach €78). There are between ten and twelve departures a day, depending on the time of year, roughly hourly starting at 8.30am – although ultimately the regularity depends on the weather. To be sure of good views, you'll need to set out early since it's usually cloudy by midday; be sure also to get there in plenty of time, especially on summer weekends, as it's much used by summer skiers. Even if it's blazing hot in the valley, the temperature plunges to near freezing at the top, so come prepared.

There are good **walks** along the two valleys at the foot of the Mont Blanc glaciers, both of which have seasonal campsites accessible by bus from Courmayeur. Val Ferret to the west is the more interesting option – you can walk back from Frebouze over Monte de la Saxe, with some incredible views of Mont Blanc en route.

If you do spend a night in Courmayeur, note that one of the cheapest **hotels** is the *Venezia* at Via delle Villette 2 (☏ & ⓕ 0165.842.461; ❶); or there's the three-star Crampon, on the same street at no. 8 (☏0165.842.385, ⓕ0165.841.417, Ⓦ www.crampon.it; Christmas–April & July to mid-Sept; ❺). Hotels in La Palud include the charming *Chalet Joli* (☏0165.869.722, Ⓦ www.chaletjoli.com; ❹) and the extremely comfortable *Vallée Blanche* (☏0165.897.002, Ⓦ www .hotelvalleeblanche.com; ❺). Most of these hotels offer special pricing arrangements with local restaurants for their guests' main meals.

Travel details

Trains

Alba to: Asti (12 daily; 40min).
Aosta to: Pré-St-Didier (14 daily; 50min); St Maurice/Sarre (1 daily; 6min).
Asti to: Casale Monferrato (12 daily; 1hr).
Novara to: Biella (17 daily; 50min–3hr 30min); Varallo Pombia (10 daily; 25min–1hr); Varallo Sesia (20 daily; 1hr–1hr 30min).
Turin (all stations) to: Aosta (15 daily; 2–3hr); Asti (53 daily; 30min–1hr); Cúneo (26 daily; 1hr 30min); Milan Centrale (33 daily; 2hr); Modane (6 daily; 1hr 25min–3hr 10min); Novara (36 daily; 1hr 15min–4hr 30min); Sant'Ambrogio (23 daily; 30min–1hr).

Buses

Alba to: Barolo (Mon–Sat 2 daily; 30min); Grinzane (1 daily; 1hr).
Aosta to: Cogne (6–7 daily; 50min); Courmayeur (13–16 daily; 1hr); Gran San Bernardo (2–4 daily; 55min); Pont Valsavarenche (mid-June to mid-Sept 3 daily, mid-Sept to mid-June weekdays only; 1hr 10min); Rhêmes Notre Dame (mid-June to mid-Sept 3 daily; 1hr); Valgrisenche (mid-June to mid-Sept 3 daily; mid-Sept to mid-June schooldays only; 1hr).

Biella to: Ivrea (6 daily; 2hr 25min); Santuario di Oropa (7 daily; 40min).
Chatillon to: Breuil-Cervinia (6 daily; 1hr–1hr 30min).
Cogne to: Valnontey (July & early Sept 9 daily; Aug 22 daily; 15min).
Cúneo to: Dronero (Val Maira; 16 Mon–Sat, 6 Sun; 35min); Valle Stura (3 daily; 1hr–1hr 20min).
Mondoví to: Certosa Pesio (2 daily; 1hr); Santuario di Vicoforte (5 daily; 20min).
Pont-St-Martin to: Gressoney-La-Trinité (9–12 daily; 1hr 5min).
Pré-St-Didier to: Courmayeur (15 daily; 10–25min); La Thuile (11 daily; 25min).
Saluzzo to: Cúneo (17 daily; 1hr); Paesana (Valle Po; Mon–Sat 11 daily, 3 Sun; 2hr); Val Varaita (3 daily; 1hr 15min).
Turin (Corso Marconi) to: Cúneo (8 daily; 2hr 45min); Saluzzo (10 daily; 1hr 20min).
Turin (Corso Vittorio Emanuele II 131) to: Aosta (8 daily; 2–3hr); Cervinia (1 Sun; 2hr 15min); Champoluc (change at Verres); Courmayeur (7 daily; 4hr); Gressoney-La-Trinité (change at Pont St-Martin); Ivrea (12 daily; 1hr 15min).

Liguria

CHAPTER 2   # Highlights

✳ **Genoa** With its rabbit warren of medieval streets, revamped port area and clutch of first-rate museums and churches, Genoa could easily justify a week of your time. See p.120

✳ **The train from Genoa to Casella** An excellent way to escape the crowds on the coast and explore some of Italy's most spectacular mountain scenery. See p.139

✳ **San Remo** With its famous Art Nouveau casino, elegant palm-tree-lined seafront and characterful old quarter, San Remo affords a glimpse of old-style Riviera glamour. See p.141

✳ **Camogli** A collection of colourful trompe l'oeil cottages surrounding an idyllic harbour, Camogli is one of the coast's prettiest fishing villages. See p.150

✳ **Cinque Terre** Five picturesque villages shoehorned into one of the most rugged parts of Liguria's coastline and linked by a highly scenic coastal walking path. See p.156

△ San Remo casino

2

Liguria

S heltering on the seaward side of the mountains that divide Piemonte from the coast, **Liguria** is the classic introduction to Italy for travellers journeying overland through France. There's an unexpected change as you cross the border from Nice and Monaco: the **Italian Riviera** (as Liguria's commercially developed strip of coast is known) has more variety of

Regional food and wine

Liguria belongs geographically to the north, but its benign Mediterranean climate, and to some extent its cooking, belong further south. Traditionally, the recipes from this region make something out of nothing; this is a legacy of the hardships of life here in the past, and is mirrored by a reserve in the Ligurian character that has given the people an undeserved reputation among other Italians for meanness. The best-known of all Ligurian specialities is **pesto**. Invented by the Genoese to help their long-term sailors fight off scurvy, it's made with chopped basil, garlic, pine-nuts and grated sharp cheese (pecorino or parmesan) ground up together in olive oil – traditionally with a pestle and mortar, from where the name arises. It's used as a sauce for pasta (often flat *trenette* noodles, or knobbly little potato-flour shapes known as **trofie**), or stirred into soup to make *minestrone alla genovese*. Otherwise, **fish** dominates – not surprising in a region where more than two-thirds of the population live on the coast. Local **anchovies** are a common antipasto, while pasta with a variety of fish and seafood sauces appears everywhere (mussels, scampi, octopus and clams are all excellent); there's also a host of specific dishes such as *ciuppin* or fish soup, *burrida di seppie* (cuttlefish stew), or fish *in carpione* (marinated in vinegar and herbs). Salt **cod** (*bacalà*) and wind-dried cod (*stoccofisso*) are big local favourites, often served fried. Other dishes to look out for are *cima alla genovese* (cold, stuffed veal) and the widely available *torta pasqualina*, a spinach-and-cheese pie with eggs. The latter is served as fast food, as are other kinds of *torta* and golden **focaccia** bread, often flavoured with olives, sage or rosemary. Chickpeas grow abundantly along the coast and crop up in **farinata**, a kind of chickpea pancake displayed in broad, round baking trays that you'll see everywhere, and in *zuppa di ceci*, another dish rarely found outside Liguria. Pastries, too, are excellent: Genoa is famous for its **pandolce**, a sweet cake laced with dried fruit, nuts and candied peel.

Liguria's soil and aspect aren't well suited to vine-growing, although plenty of local **wine** – mainly white – is quite drinkable. The steep, terraced slopes of the Cinque Terre are home to an eponymous white wine and the sweet, expensive dessert wine called Sciacchetrà, made from partially dried grapes. From the Riviera di Ponente, look out for the crisp whites of Pigato (from Albenga) and Vermentino (from Imperia), as well as the acclaimed Rossese di Dolceacqua, Liguria's best red.

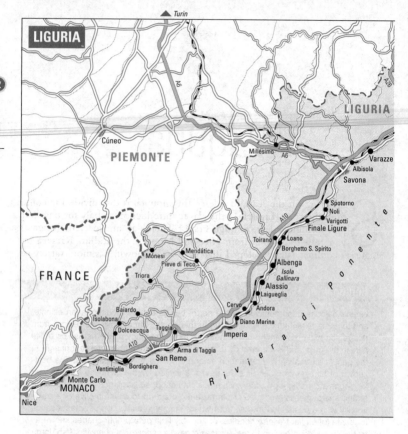

landscape and architecture than its French counterpart, and is generally less frenetic. The mountains, which in places drop sheer to the sea, are treated as an irrelevance by most visitors eager to press on to their chosen resort, but Liguria's lofty hinterland can offer respite from the standard format of beach, beach and more beach. Teetering on slopes carpeted with olives and vines are isolated mountain villages that retain their own rural culture and cuisine.

The chief city of the region is **Genoa**, an ancient, sprawling port often acclaimed as the most atmospheric of all Italian cities. It has a dense and fascinating old quarter that is complemented by a vibrant social and ethnic mix and a newly energized dockside district. The city stands midway along two distinct stretches of coastline. To the west is the **Riviera di Ponente**, one long ribbon of hotels packed out in summer with Italian families who book a year ahead to stay in their favourite spot. Picking your route carefully means you can avoid the worst of it. **San Remo**, the *grande-dame* of Riviera resorts, is flanked by hillsides covered with glasshouses, and is a major centre for the worldwide export of flowers; **Albenga** and **Noli** are attractive medieval centres that have also retained a good deal of character; and **Finale Ligure** is a thoroughly pleasant Mediterranean seaside town.

On Genoa's eastern side is the more rugged **Riviera di Levante**. Umbrella pines grow horizontally on the cliff-faces overlooking the water, and in the

evening a glassy calm falls over the little bays and inlets. Walks on **Monte di Portofino** and in the coastal scenery of the famed **Cinque Terre** take you through scrubland and vineyards for memorable vistas over broad gulfs and jutting headlands. This mix of mountains and fishing villages, accessible only by boat, appealed to the early nineteenth-century Romantics who "discovered" the Riviera, preparing the way for other artists and poets and the first package tourists. Now the whole area explodes into quite a ruck every July and August, with resorts like **Portofino** qualifying as among the most expensive in the country. Nearby **Santa Margherita Ligure** is unpretentious and elegant, and makes a great base for day-trips to Genoa, under an hour away, or for exploring the surrounding coastline by train or car. Visiting out of season, of course, is a peaceful way to enjoy the beauty without the hubbub.

In the summer months, though, the only real way to avoid the crowds is to travel inland. Minor roads and mule tracks link villages built spiral-fashion around hilltops, originally as protection against Saracen invasion. A testing long-distance footpath, the **Alta Via dei Monti Liguri**, runs from pass to mountain pass along the length of Liguria, but aside from the odd section accessible on public transport from the coast it's mainly for hardened pros. Nonetheless, high-altitude resorts such as **Santo Stefano d'Aveto** and **Torriglia** offer plenty of summer walking (and, in places, winter skiing) that can lift you a world away from the resorts down below on the sea. And the hills and mountains of the **Parco dell'Antola** (ⓦwww.parks.it/parco.antola) offer acres of protected landscape, with plenty of opportunities for walking, mountain biking and other outdoor pursuits.

In a **car**, the shore road is for the most part a disappointment: the coast is extremely built up, and in fact you get a much better sense of the beauty of the region by taking the east–west autostrada which cuts through the mountains a few kilometres inland by means of a mixture of tunnels and viaducts. Fleeting bursts of daylight between tunnels give glimpses of the string of resorts along the coast, silvery olive groves and a brilliant sea. However, the easiest way to take in the region is by **train:** there are regular services stopping just about every-where and, because the track is forced to squeeze along the narrow coastal strip, stations are almost invariably centrally located in towns and villages.

Liguria's regional **tourist office** is based at Piazza Matteotti 9, Genoa (ⓣ010.530.8201, ⓦwww.turismoinliguria.it) – check out their encyclope-dic website, which has information in English on every town and village in the region, plus the option to reserve at any hotel, campsite or agriturismo farmhouse. The excellent spiral-bound **Liguria Tourist Atlas**, published by the regional government in collaboration with cartographers DeAgostini, is invaluable if you're spending any time in the area and has useful detailed plans of town centres.

Genoa

GENOA (**Genova** in Italian) is "the most winding, incoherent of cities, the most entangled topographical ravel in the world". So said Henry James, and the city – Italy's fifth largest and home to 631,000 inhabitants – is still marvellously eclectic, full of pace and rough-edged style. Sprawled behind Italy's biggest port is a dense and fascinating warren of medieval alleyways and *caruggi* (tiny alleyways): "La Superba", as Rubens called Genoa, lays claim to being Europe's largest medieval town, and boasts more zest and intrigue than all the surround-ing coastal resorts put together. It's here that most of Genoa's important *palazzi* are to be found, built in the sixteenth and seventeenth centuries by the city's wealthy mercantile families and now masquerading as newly rejuvenated muse-ums and art galleries.

Some history

Genoa made its money at sea, through trade, colonial exploitation and piracy. By the thirteenth century, on the heels of a major role in the **Crusades**, the Genoese were roaming the Mediterranean, bringing back ideas as well as goods: the city's architects were using Arab pointed arches a century before the rest of Italy. The San Giorgio banking syndicate effectively controlled the city for much of the fifteenth century, and cold-shouldered **Columbus** (who had grown up in Genoa) when he sought funding for his voyages of exploration. With Spanish backing, he opened up new Atlantic trade routes that ironically reduced *Genova La Superba* to a backwater. Following foreign invasion, in 1768 the Banco di San Giorgio was forced to sell the Genoese colony of Corsica to the French, and a century later, the city became a hotbed of radicalism: **Mazzini**, one of the main protagonists of the Risorgimento, was born here, and in 1860 **Garibaldi** set sail for Sicily with his "Thousand" from the city's harbour. Around the same

△ Genoa old town

time, Italy's industrial revolution began in Genoa, with steelworks and shipyards spreading along the coast. These suffered heavy **bombing** in World War II, and the subsequent economic decline hobbled Genoa for decades.

Things started to look up in the 1990s. State funding to celebrate the 500th anniversary of Columbus's 1492 voyage paid to renovate many of the city's late-Renaissance palaces and the old port area, with Genoa's most famous son of modern times, **Renzo Piano** (best known as the co-designer of Paris's Pompidou Centre), taking a leading role. The results of a twelve-year, €46-million-euro programme, that saw Genoa becoming a **European Capital of Culture** in 2004, are evident all over the city.

The tidying-up hasn't sanitized the **old town**, however; the core of the city, between the two stations and the waterfront, is still dark and slightly threatening.

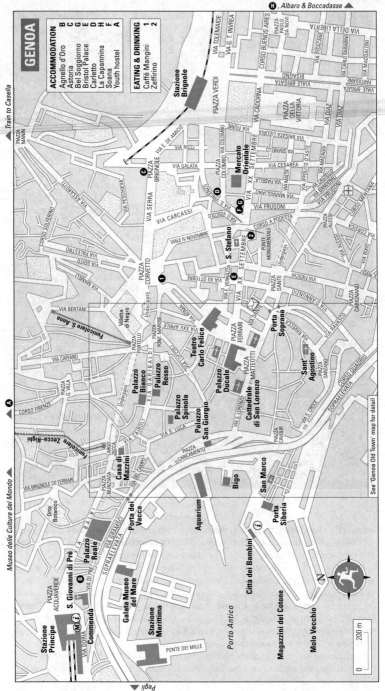

GENOA

ACCOMMODATION
Agnello d'Oro   B
Astoria   C
Bel Soggiorno   G
Bristol Palace   E
Carletto   D
La Capannina   H
Soana   F
Youth hostel   A

EATING & DRINKING
Caffè Mangini   1
Zeffirino   2

Train to Casella

Museo delle Culture del Mondo

Albaro & Boccadasse

Pegli

Stazione Brignole

PIAZZA VERDI

Stazione Principe

Stazione Marittima

Galata Museo del Mare

Palazzo Reale

Palazzo Bianco

Palazzo Rosso

Palazzo Spinola

Teatro Carlo Felice

Palazzo Ducale

Cattedrale di San Lorenzo

Porta Soprana

Sant'Agostino

Aquarium

Bigo

San Marco

Porta Siberia

Città dei Bambini

Porto Antico

Magazzini del Cotone

Molo Vecchio

Mercato Orientale

See 'Genoa Old Town' map for detail

0   200 m

PONTE DEI MILLE

But despite the sleaze, the overriding impression is of a buzzing hive of activity – food shops nestled in the portals of former palaces, carpenters' workshops sandwiched between designer furniture outlets, everything surrounded by a crush of people and the squashed vowels of the impenetrable Genoese dialect that has, over the centuries, absorbed elements of Neapolitan, Calabrese and Portuguese. Aside from the cosmopolitan street life, you should seek out the **Cattedrale di San Lorenzo** with its fabulous treasury, small medieval churches such as **San Donato** and **Santa Maria di Castello**, and the Renaissance *palazzi* that contain Genoa's **art** collections and furniture and decor from the grandest days of the city's illustrious past.

Arrival, transport and information

There are two main **train stations** in Genoa. **Stazione Principe**, on Piazza Acquaverde, just north of the port to the west of the centre, is the principal one, although a number of mainline trains also pass through **Stazione Brignole** on Piazza Verdi, to the east of the centre. Buses #33 and #37, among others, ply between the two. There's a staffed left-luggage office at Principe (daily 6am–10pm; €3 per piece for 12hr). If you're arriving at Principe after dark, cling on to your valuables while moving through the station and avoid the notorious Via di Prè alley nearby, which is the core territory of Genoa's lowlife. **Buses** heading to the city outskirts – the Riviera, and inland – arrive on Piazza della Vittoria, a few minutes' walk south of Brignole.

The **Aeroporto Cristoforo Colombo** (ⓦwww.aeroportodigenova.com) is 6km west of the city centre. Volabus #100 runs to Stazione Principe, Piazza de Ferrari, on the edge of the Old Town, and Piazza Verdi outside Stazione Brignole (every 30min; 25min; information ⓣ010.558.2414). Buy your €3 ticket – valid on all city buses for the whole day – from the driver.

Getting around the centre is best done **on foot**, resorting to Genoa's AMT **buses** (information ⓣ800.085.311, ⓦwww.amt.genova.it) only for trips to outlying sights. Public transport tickets, available from *tabacchi* and newspaper stands (€2 for ninety minutes, or €3.50 all day), are valid on buses, all the city's various **funiculars** and **lifts**, local trains between Voltri and Nervi (though not on the narrow-gauge mountain line to Casella; see p.139) and the expanding metro system which now winds its way from the suburban commuter belt to the city centre. There are currently six metro stations open – Brin, Dinegro, Principe, Darsena, San Giorgio and De Ferrari – with another four, including Brignole, due to become operational by 2010 (ⓦwww.genovametro.com). For a slightly more relaxed way of getting around the city, see the **boat** "Listings" on p.137.

The main **tourist office** is at Stazione Principe (Mon–Sun 9.30am–1pm & 2.30–6pm; ⓣ010.246.2633, ⓦwww.apt.genova.it), with branches at the Porto Antico in a small booth next to the Magazzini del Coteone (daily 9am–1pm & 2–6pm), on Piazza Matteotti next to the Palazzo Ducale (daily 9am–1pm

---

Genoa addresses

Genoa is one of the handful of Italian cities that, for some reason, has an unnecessarily complicated double system of street-numbering: commercial establishments, such as bars and restaurants, have **red** numbers (*rosso*), while all other buildings have **black** numbers (*nero*) – and the two systems don't run in tandem. This means, for example, that Via Banchi 35r might be next-door to Via Banchi 89n, but several hundred metres from Via Banchi 33n.

& 2–6pm) and at the airport (Mon–Sat 9.30am–1pm & 1.30–5pm, Sunday 10am–1.30pm and 2.30–5pm; ☎010.601.5247).

Accommodation

There's no shortage of **accommodation** in Genoa, but many of the budget hotels – especially those around the train stations – are grimy and depressing, and you need to look hard to find the exceptions. The area just west of Stazione Brignole (Piazza Colombo and Via XX Settembre) is preferable to anything around Stazione Principe. There's a handful of quality hotels in the old quarter – though you should steer clear of the one-star places down by the port (on and around Via di Prè), some of which are the haunts of drug-dealers and prostitutes. You'll need to reserve well in advance if your visit is to coincide with the annual **Salone Nautico Internazionale** (International Boat Show; Ⓦ www.fiera.ge.it), usually held in early October, when many of the city's hotels are booked solid.

Hotels

Agnello d'Oro Vico Monachette 6
☎010.246.2084, Ⓦ www.hotelagnellodoro.it.
Spacious, modernized rooms – some with balconies – in a seventeenth-century palace alongside the Palazzo Reale and within spitting distance of Stazione Principe. **❸**

Astoria Piazza Brignole 4 ☎010.873.316,
Ⓦ www.hotelastoria-ge.com. Characterful three-star, a short walk from Stazione Brignole. Large, atmospheric rooms – choose between "antique" or "restored" – and plenty of faded grandeur make this a reliable and interesting choice. **❻**

Bel Soggiorno Via XX Settembre 19/2
☎010.581.418, Ⓦ www.belsoggiornohotel.com.
Run by a gregarious German woman (who speaks English), this is a welcoming place, although the standard of the rooms – both en suite and not – doesn't quite measure up to the cosiness of the lobby and breakfast room. **❷–❸**

Bristol Palace Via XX Settembre 35
☎010.592.541, Ⓦ www.hotelbristolpalace.com.
Grand old pile near Stazione Brignole, full of antique furniture, old masters and an Edwardian sense of order and discretion. Rooms are large, attractive and air-conditioned. **❼**

Cairoli Via Cairoli 14/4 ☎010.246.1454,
Ⓦ www.hotelcairoligenova.com. A superior two-star, whose brightly furnished, modern,

en-suite rooms are soundproofed. There's also a roof terrace. One of the city's best deals. **❸**

Carletto Via Colombo 16/4 ☎010.588.412,
Ⓕ010.589.615. Less than ten minutes' walk from Stazione Brignole, just off busy Via San Vincenzo, this hotel has clean, ordinary rooms – some en suite. **❻**

Jolly Hotel Marina Ponte Calvi 5 ☎010.253.91,
Ⓦ www.jollyhotels.it. Great waterfront location a few steps from the aquarium makes up for the modern but slightly characterless rooms. Big discounts to be had during August. **❾**

La Capannina Via Tito Speri 7 ☎010.363.205,
Ⓦ www.lacapanninagenova.it. Down a side street off the river walkway near the charming fishing cove of Boccadasse, well east of the centre (bus #17). Characterful rooms and a tranquil location make this option well worth considering. **❸**

Major Vico Spada 4 ☎010.247.4174,
Ⓕ010.246.9898. A great location in the old town, just off Via Luccoli, along with clean and well-furnished rooms with TV and telephone, make this a great bargain. **❶**

Soana Via XX Settembre 23/8 ☎010.562.814,
Ⓦ www.hotelsoana.it. Very friendly service and a good location right by the Porta Monumentale make this hotchpotch of rooms – some are plain and basic, others are fully modernized – one of the best choices in the area. **❸**

Camping and hostels

The few **campsites** within the city boundaries include *Villa Doria* at Via al Campeggio Villa Doria 15 in Pegli (☎010.696.9600), though you'd do far better to stay at one of the coastal resorts and commute into town.

Genoa's HI **hostel** is clean and well run, although its out-of-town situation means you will be heavily reliant on buses. It's up in the hills of Righi, north of the centre, at Via Costanzi 120 (☎ & Ⓕ010.242.2457, Ⓦ www.hihostels.com;

check-in 3.30–6pm; closed late Dec & Jan). From Stazione Principe take bus #35, then switch at the fifth stop onto bus #40. Bed and breakfast costs €15, and there are cheap meals, as well as maps and information on offer.

The City

Genoa's atmospheric **Old Town** spreads outwards from the port in a confusion of tiny alleyways (*caruggi*), bordered by **Via Gramsci** along the waterfront and by **Via Balbi** and **Via Garibaldi** to the north. The *caruggi* are lined with high buildings, usually six or seven storeys, set very close together. Tiny grocers, textile workshops and bakeries jostle for position with boutiques, design outlets and goldsmiths amid a flurry of shouts, smells and scrawny cats. Not for nothing is Genoa the only European city to be mentioned in *Arabian Nights*.

The cramped layout of the area reflects its medieval politics. Around the thirteenth and fourteenth centuries, the city's principal families – Doria, Spinola, Grimaldi and Fieschi – marked out certain streets and squares as their territory, even extending their domains to include churches: to pray in someone else's chapel was to risk being stabbed in the back. New buildings on each family's patch had to be slotted in wherever they could, resulting in a maze of crooked alleyways that was the battleground of dynastic feuds which lasted well into the eighteenth century. Genoa has, however, remained relatively free of fire, not least because each building's kitchens were invariably placed on the topmost storey.

The Palazzo Ducale and around

From 1384 to 1515, except for brief periods of foreign domination, Genoa was ruled by a doge, resident at the **Palazzo Ducale** in Piazza Matteotti, right in the heart of the old town. The present building, with its huge vaulted atrium, was built in the sixteenth century and today makes a splendid exhibition hall (times and prices vary; ⓦwww.palazzoducale.genova.it). It also houses archives and libraries, and hosts shows and concerts. The **Gesù** church (daily 7am–noon & 4–5.30pm; free), across the square, was designed by Pellegrino Tibaldi at the end of the sixteenth century and contains a mass of marble and gilt stucco and some fine Baroque paintings, including Guido Reni's *Assumption* in the right aisle and two works by Rubens: *Miracles of St Ignatius* on the left and *Circumcision* on the high altar.

An alley between the two leads through to **Piazza de Ferrari**, overlooked by a statue of Garibaldi in front of the grand facade of the Carlo Felice opera house; from here, Via XX Settembre heads east towards Brignole, while Via Roma cuts north to skirt the old town.

Cattedrale di San Lorenzo

West of Piazza Matteotti, bulking out the north side of Via San Lorenzo which cuts down to the port, is the **Cattedrale di San Lorenzo** (7am–7pm; free).

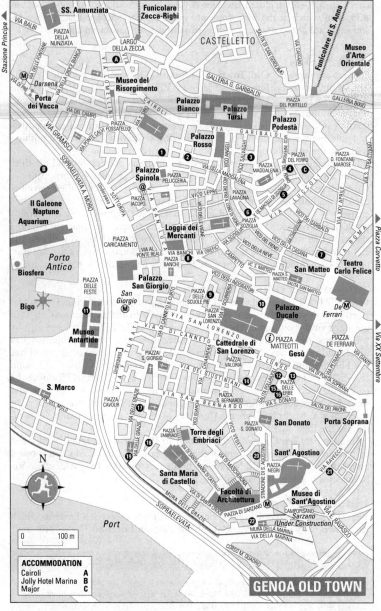

GENOA OLD TOWN

ACCOMMODATION

Cairoli	A
Jolly Hotel Marina	B
Major	C

EATING & DRINKING

Bar Berto	13	Caffetteria Orefici	8	I Tre Merli al Porto Antico	11
Britannia	7	Da Rina	19	Klainguti	6
Café La Madeleine	1	Eprîe Rosse	21	La Berlocca	5
Café Roger	20	Il Fado	16	La Bottega del Conte	17
Caffè degli Specchi	15	I Tre Merli	3	Louisiana Jazz Club	10
				Maxela	4

Östaja dö Castello	18
Pansön	12
Quaalude	22
Squarciafico	9
Ugo	14
Zeneise	2

There's an entrance from the street, but you should first go round to take in the main western **facade**, an elaborate confection of twisting, fluted columns and black-and-white striped stone – high-quality Carrara marble alternating with local slate – that was added by Gothic craftsmen from France in the early thirteenth century, a hundred years or so after the main building had been constructed. The **stripes** here, like other examples throughout the city, were a sign of prestige: families could use them only if they had a permit, awarded for "some illustrious deed to the advantage of their native city". While the rest of Genoa's churches were portioned out between the ruling dynasties, the cathedral – which lay between districts – remained freely open to all.

The **interior** houses the Renaissance chapel of St John the Baptist, whose ashes – legend has it – once rested in the thirteenth-century sarcophagus. After a particularly bad storm in medieval times, priests carried his casket through the city down to the port to placate the sea, and a commemorative procession still takes place each June 24 in honour of the saint. Note the ancient frescoes of the Last Judgement above the main entrance, painted at the beginning of the fourteenth century by an unknown Byzantine artist. The Baptist's reliquary is in the **Museo del Tesoro** (Mon–Sat 9am–noon & 3–6.30pm; €5.50), housed in an atmospheric crypt. Also on display are a polished quartz plate on which, legend says, Salome received John the Baptist's severed head, and a glass vessel said to have been given to Solomon by the Queen of Sheba and used at the Last Supper. Artefacts from Byzantine and later times include delicate jewelled crosses and reliquaries – along with a British artillery shell that was fired from the sea during World War II and fell through the roof, but miraculously failed to explode.

North of San Lorenzo

The district around the cathedral has changed dramatically in the last few years, with an influx of art shops and trendy fashion outlets along the main, pedestrianized, Via San Lorenzo. One block north, just off Piazza San Lorenzo, a narrow winding alley, **Vico del Filo**, doglegs its way down to Piazza Caricamento on the portside; a local insult for one who is particularly dim is to describe them as being "as stupid as the Vico del Filo".

An unnamed lane leads north from San Lorenzo through tiny **Piazza Invrea** to the rather swanky little shopping square of **Campetto** and adjacent **Via degli Orefici**, "Street of the Goldsmiths". Unlike the generic, machine-produced gold jewellery found in Florence, much of what is on offer in Genoa is still made by hand at upper-floor workshops in the area of Campetto, sold in shops such as *L'Oro degli Sforza* on the square at relatively affordable prices. Linked to Campetto is genteel **Piazza Soziglia**, with a good mixture of bars and places to eat, among them *Klainguti*, one of Genoa's oldest coffee houses (see p.135). From here **Via Luccoli** heads north, with glitzy boutiques and design outlets galore, while a few steps to the west is **Piazza Lavagna**, home to the thriving Mercato dei Pulci, the daily flea market. Via Garibaldi, with its sixteenth-century *palazzi* of Genoa's mercantile dynasties, is a short stroll north (see p.129).

A little east of Campetto and Piazza Soziglia is the city's prettiest small square, **Piazza San Matteo**. This lay in the territory of the Doria family, who went one step further than merely striping the twelfth-century church of **San Matteo** (Mon–Sat 7.30am–noon & 4–5.30pm; free) in black and white: they ordered elaborate testimonials to the family's worthiness to be carved on the facade of the church and their adjoining palaces. Andrea Doria, the most illustrious of the clan, lived in the building on the left corner of the square (the other palaces on the square were home to the rest of the family) before he built his lavish palace down on the waterfront (see p.131). He's now buried in the crypt, which the sacristan will open for you. Peek in too, at the pretty little cloister adjoining the church.

Piazza Banchi and Piazza Caricamento

Heading west from Campetto on Via degli Orefici brings you out into a thriving commercial zone centred on **Piazza Banchi**, a tiny enclosed market square of secondhand books, records, fruit and flowers which was once the heart of the medieval city. The little church of **San Pietro in Banchi**, overlooking the square, was built in the sixteenth century after a plague; with little money to spare, the city authorities sold plots of commercial space in arcades around the church terrace in order to fund construction of the main building, an economic model that is familiar today but was virtually unknown at the time.

It's a short stroll west from Piazza Banchi out into the open spaces of Genoa's port. The sea once came up to the vaulted arcades of Via Sottoripa, which runs alongside the main **Piazza Caricamento**; these days the waterfront is blocked off by containers and fences, but there's been a market here since the twelfth century, when small boats used to come ashore from galleys at anchor. Fruit and vegetable stalls still line the arcade, now interspersed with fly-pitches selling sunglasses and pirated CDs.

Towards the southern edge of the square is the **Palazzo di San Giorgio**, a brightly painted fortified palace built in 1260 from the stones of a captured Venetian fortress. After the great sea-battle of Curzola in 1298, the Genoese used the building to keep their Venetian prisoners under lock and key; among them was one **Marco Polo**, who met a Pisan writer named Rustichello inside and spun tales of adventure to him of worlds beyond the seas. After their release, Rustichello published the stories in a single volume that became one of the most famous books of all time, translated into English as *The Travels of Marco Polo*. In 1408, the building was taken over by the Banco di San Giorgio, a syndicate established to finance the war against Venice, which in the sixteenth century steered the city from trading to banking, thus turning Genoa into the leading financial centre of the day. These days, the *palazzo* is home to the harbour authorities, but you can ask the guardian on the door to let you in to see the medieval Sala dei Protettori and beautiful Sala Manica Lunga, whose decor was restored to its thirteenth-century grandeur following bomb damage in World War II.

The Galleria Nazionale di Palazzo Spinola

From Piazza Banchi, the animated medieval **Via San Luca** heads north, lined with shops selling counterfeit designer clothes and accessories. This street was in Spinola family territory, and their grand, former residence is now the excellent **Galleria Nazionale di Palazzo Spinola**, located beside Piazza Pellicceria (Tues–Sat 8.30am–7.30pm, Sun 1.30–7.30pm; €4, joint ticket with Palazzo Reale €6.50; Ⓦ www.palazzospinola.it). Exhibits include portraits by Van Dyck of Matthew, Mark, Luke and John as men of books, an intensely mournful *Ecce Homo* by the Sicilian master Antonello da Messina and the splendid *Adoration of the Magi* by Joos van Cleve, sawn into planks when stolen from the church of San Donato in the 1970s. Don't miss the little **terrace**, way up on the spine of the roof and shaded with orange and lemon trees.

Tucked away among surrounding buildings, the twelfth-century Baroque **Chiesa di San Luca** (Piazza San Luca; 9am–noon & 3–6pm; free) was rebuilt in the 1600s and remains privately owned by the Spinola family The building, shaped like a Greek cross, is notable for its seventeenth-century frescoes.

The way north passes through a hectic and rather seedy neighbourhood centred on the vibrant **Via della Maddalena** alley, crowded with shops and stalls that ring with shouts in French and Arabic from the predominantly West and North African street-traders, doing business alongside Genoa's thriving red-light trade, evidence of which is all too apparent on the neighbourhood's narrow alleys. Steep lanes rise north of Via della Maddalena, lifting you out of the mêlée and into the ordered calm of Via Garibaldi.

Along Via Garibaldi

When newly made fortunes encouraged Genoa's merchant bankers to move out of the cramped old town in the mid-sixteenth century, artisans' houses were pulled down to make way for the Strada Nuova, later named **Via Garibaldi**, on the northern fringe of the quarter. To walk along the surprisingly narrow street is to stroll through a Renaissance architect's drawing pad – sculpted facades, stuccowork and medallions decorate the exterior of the three-storey *palazzi*, while the big courtyards are almost like private squares. Take a look, for instance, at no. 7, the heavily stuccoed **Palazzo Podestà**, with its grotto and fountain on the far side of its small courtyard.

Three of the Via Garibaldis finest *palazzi* – Bianco, Rosso and Tursi – have been re-branded the **Musei di Strada Nuova** and together now hold the city's finest collection of old master paintings (€7 combined ticket). From the road's western end the first to come into view is the **Palazzo Bianco** (Tues–Fri 9am–7pm, Sat & Sun 10am–7pm; €5, Sun free; Ⓦ www .museopalazzobianco.it), built between 1530 and 1540 for the important Genoese family, the Grimaldis. Its gallery houses work by the Flemish and Dutch masters (Rubens, Memling, Van Dyck) as well as the largest collection of Genoese and Ligurian painting – including work by Castiglione and Castello – on public show.

Next door stands the splendid **Palazzo Tursi**, the largest of Genoa's palaces, which boasts a glassed-in main courtyard. It's the site of the town hall and, for the past couple of years, the **Sala Paganiniana** (Tues–Fri 9am–7pm, Sat & Sun 10am–7pm; free), a small museum dedicated to the great Italian violinist Niccolò Paganini, who was born in Genoa in 1782, although he spent most of his professional career in Lucca. The prime exhibit, displayed with an almost religious reverence, is the *cannone*, the great man's own violin made in 1743.

Across the road at Via Garibaldi 18 is the slightly less prestigious **Galleria di Palazzo Rosso** (Tues, Thurs & Fri 9am–1pm, Wed & Sat 9am–7pm, Sun 10am–6pm; Ⓦ www.museopalazzorosso.it) where every room on the top floor has been restored to its original Baroque grandeur, bedecked with chandeliers, mirrors and an excess of gilding. Frescoes cover the ceilings, and there's a series of splendid portraits by Van Dyck of the Brignole-Sale family, who built the palace in 1671.

Along Via Balbi

A few minutes' walk west of Via Garibaldi is the house at Via Lomellini 11 where Giuseppe Mazzini, one of the most influential activists of Italian Unification, was born in 1805; it now displays documents and relics from his life as the **Museo del Risorgimento** (Tues–Fri 9am–1pm, Sat 10am–7pm; €3.10). Past traffic-heavy Piazza della Nunziata, overlooked by the giant sixteenth-century church of **Santissima Annunziata del Vastato**, which boasts one of the most exuberantly decorated interiors in the city, you'll come to the main road of **Via Balbi**, laid out a few decades after Via Garibaldi.

The Palazzo Reale

At Via Balbi 10 stands the vast **Palazzo Reale** (Tues & Wed 9am–1.30pm, Thurs–Sun 9am–7pm; €5; @ www.palazzorealegenova.it), built by the Balbi family in the early seventeenth century and later occupied by the Durazzo dynasty and the Savoyard royals. Entering through the huge atrium that looks onto the elegant courtyard garden behind, you climb the grand staircase to the first big room, the **ballroom**, with gilt stucco ceilings and Chinese vases. To the left are four drawing rooms, featuring a huge watercolour of the crossing of the Red Sea painted on silk by Romanelli, grand marble fireplaces and bronze candelabra. These rooms lead through to the stunning hall of mirrors, where Joseph II, Emperor of Austria, is said to have remarked in 1784 – with a flourish of disingenuous flattery – that the palace appeared more of a royal residence than his own simple pad back in Vienna. The room was designed in the 1730s by Gerolamo Durazzo and the best of its statues are four exquisite works in marble and gold by Filippo Parodi: the first pair, facing each other nearest the door, are Hyacinth and Venus, while at the far end of the room are Adonis and Clizia. Doors lead through to the private quarters of the Duke of Genoa, with the **duke's bedchamber** featuring a sumptuous Baroque ceiling fresco and the duke's bathroom holding elegant furniture carved in England in the 1820s.

On the way back through to the east wing of the building, you pass along a **chapel gallery** behind the ballroom, covered in trompe-l'oeil frescoes by Lorenzo de Ferrari (1733). The adjacent **throne room**, its walls covered in deep red velvets and an excess of gold, is dotted with dozens of "C.A." monograms in honour of Carlo Alberto, King of Savoy. Continuing east, you come to the lavish **audience room**, with its dazzling Turkish carpet, silk curtains and a grand portrait of a tight-lipped Caterina Durazzo-Balbi painted by Van Dyck in 1624 during his six-year stay in Genoa. Alongside, the **king's bedchamber** has parquet wooden flooring, an exquisite Murano glass chandelier, and Van Dyck's first canvas of the Crucifixion, also dating from 1624, while the King's bathroom features the Savoyard motto *Je atans mon astre* ("I await my destiny" in archaic French) set into the floor. You then move into the **queen's quarters**, a series of rooms featuring a ghostly pale *Crucifixion* by the Neapolitan master Luca Giordano and a *St Lawrence* (1616) by Bernardo Strozzi. After another series of drawing rooms, one hung with Parisian tapestries of 1610, double-doors open onto the **grand terrace** which runs on three sides of a rectangle above the garden courtyard, giving airy views out over the port. Adjacent on the east side is the crumbling Teatro Falcone, where once the virtuoso Genoese violinist Paganini played.

Around Stazione Principe

Via Balbi continues west to the grandiose **Stazione Principe**, fronted by Piazza Acquaverde with a central statue of Columbus. Immediately below the train station, the drab run of portfront buildings is broken by the elegant loggia of the twelfth-century **Commendà**, a former convent, hospital and lodging house for crusading knights, now gutted and converted to a temporary exhibition space. The oddly double-apsed church of **San Giovanni di Prè**, whose landmark campanile was added in the late twelfth century, was originally reserved solely for the use of the Knights of Malta, or Knights Hospitallers, who ran the Commendà next door and who left behind them a host of Maltese crosses used as decoration on buildings all over town. From here, the busy and notoriously seedy **Via di Prè** runs parallel with the waterfront Via Gramsci and is the first real street of the old town; partway along is the Bagnaschi hardware shop, which occupies a former hospital dating from 1353. Via di Prè skirts the port as far as the twelfth-century **Porta dei Vacca**, from where alleys take you into the heart of the old quarter.

North of the station, and best reached via the lift from Via Balbi, is the **Museo delle Culture del Mondo** (April–Sept Tues–Sun 10am–6pm; Oct–March Tues–Sun 10am–5pm; €6; Ⓦwww.castellodalbertisgenova.it), or museum of world cultures. The museum is housed in the grand neo-Gothic home of the nineteenth-century adventurer Captain D'Albertis, who spent much of his later life filling its rooms with items picked up during voyages to the Americas, Africa and Oceania. It's an extremely eclectic but fascinating collection of items – masks, musical instruments, pottery, paintings, stuffed animals and more. Look out, in particular, for the room in which the eccentric D'Albertis made sundials, which he made a point of distributing around the world. The main purpose of the museum's recent renovation – other than to install a glass roof – was to water down the collection's former tone of colonial triumphalism in order to focus more on the lives and cultures of various indigenous peoples.

Back at the station, from Piazza Acquaverde, Via Doria runs west down to the ferry terminal, past the lavish gardens of the huge **Palazzo del Principe Doria Pamphilj** (May–July & Sept–Dec 25 Tues–Sun 10am–5pm; €6.20; Ⓦwww.palazzodelprincipe.it) built in the early 1530s by Andrea Doria, who made his reputation and fortune attacking Turkish fleets and Barbary pirates and liberating the Genoese republic from the French and Spanish. The gardens back onto the fin-de-siècle **Stazione Marittima**, which was once the departure point for steamers to New York and Buenos Aires, but nowadays handles ferries to Corsica, Sardinia and Sicily (see p.167). It was from the **Ponte dei Mille** (Jetty of the Thousand) in front of the ferry terminal that **Giuseppe Garibaldi**, ex-mercenary and spaghetti salesman, persuaded his thousand Red Shirts to set off for Sicily in two clapped-out paddle steamers, armed with just a few rifles and no ammunition. Their mission, to support a Sicilian uprising and unite the island with the mainland states, greatly annoyed some northern politicians, who didn't want anything to do with the undeveloped south – an attitude which echoes in Italian politics to this day. About 1km further round the port is Genoa's restored sixteenth-century lighthouse, the **Lanterna**, as well as the **Matitone**, a postmodern polygonal tower housing municipal offices which comes to a sharp point above the industrial area of the port – giving rise to its sardonic nickname "The Big Pencil".

Whale-watching

The waters off the Ligurian coast as far south as Corsica comprise a World Wildlife Fund-monitored **International Whale Sanctuary**, home to twelve species of whale as well as dolphins and plenty of other marine life. It's easy to join summer boat excursions from towns along the Riviera for whale-watching in open sea (June–Sept at least once a week). All must be **booked in advance** and comprise a full day on board, including a light lunch and commentary from local WWF experts.

Main operators are Alimar (Calata Zingari, Stazione Marittima; ℡010.256.775, Ⓦwww.alimar.ge.it) and Cooperativa Battellieri (Calata Zingari; ℡010.265.712, Ⓦwww.battellierigenova.it) – their boats start from **Genoa** and pick up from **Savona**; Alimar's also pick up from **Alassio**. Different boats depart from Porto Maurizio harbour in **Imperia** (℡0183.280.110, Ⓦwww.imperiamare.it), while from **San Remo** the operator is Riviera Line (℡0184.505.055, Ⓦwww.rivieraline.it). Prices change regularly so contact the companies for current information.

The Porto Antico

The *sopraelevata*, or elevated highway, shoots along the waterfront above Piazza Caricamento, dividing the city from the ancient port, or **Porto Antico**, long since finished as a commercial concern but pedestrianized and revitalized during the 1990s with the aim of bringing people down to the harbour again. Old warehouses have been converted into exhibition spaces, concert halls and museums. It's now a pleasant place to stroll, with cafés and pricey waterside bistros fronting the marina, albeit a rather sterile environment that seems artificially separated from the city centre's organic maze of shadowy alleyways.

The visual centrepiece of the development is the **Bigo** – a curious multi-armed contraption, brainchild of Renzo Piano, intended to recall the harbourside cranes of old. It consists of a tent-roofed exhibition/concert space where waterside performances are given in summer and an ice skating rink is set up in winter, next to which stands a circular elevator that ascends 60m in the air to let visitors see Genoa "as it is seen by the seagulls" (opening times vary, usually daily summer 10am–6pm; winter 10am–5pm, but be aware that it closes when it's windy – quite a common occurrence on the seafront; €3). East of the Bigo are two blocks of buildings, home to shops, restaurants, offices and, incongruously enough, the **Museo Nazionale dell' Antartide** (June–Sept Tues–Sun 10.30am–6.30pm; Oct–May Tues–Fri 9.45am–5.30pm; €5.30; ⓔmna@unige.it), the continent's only Antarctic museum, which has some interesting, if not overly spectacular, displays on the wildlife, geography and explorers of the South Pole.

Just west of here is the old Porta Siberia, with the **Molo Vecchio** (Old Wharf) beyond. This was formerly where condemned prisoners would be led, to take the Last Sacrament at the little church of **San Marco** halfway along, before arriving at the gallows overlooking Piazza Cavour. Continuing west, you reach a set of restored cotton warehouses that now house a shopping-cum-entertainment centre, the **Magazzini del Cotone**, with bars, cinemas and music stores. Its main attraction is the **Città dei Bambini** (Tues–Sun: July–Sept 11.30am–7.30pm; Oct–June 10am–6pm; adults €5, child €7; ⓦwww.cittadeibambini.net), a whiz-bang interactive children's science museum filled with gizmos and gadgets which should prove popular with its target audience. The museum is divided into separate areas: for 2- to 3-year-olds, 3- to 5-year-olds and 6- to 14-year-olds. Past the centre, you can enjoy grand sweeping views of the port from the end of the wharf.

North of the Bigo is the modern pride and joy of the city, the **Acquario di Genova** (July & Aug daily 9am–11pm; Sept–June Mon–Fri 9.30am–7.30pm, Sat & Sun 9.30am–8.30pm; last entry 1 1/2hr before closing; €14; ⓦwww.acquario.ge.it). This is Europe's largest aquarium, its 70 tanks housing sea creatures from all the world's major habitats, including the world's biggest reconstruction of a Caribbean coral reef, complete with moray eels, turtles and angelfish. Although the whole affair boasts a fashionably ecology-conscious slant and excellent background information (delivered in Italian and English), the larger beasts – including grey sharks, dolphins, seals and an enclosure containing a group of Humboldt penguins – can't help but seem pathetically subdued. Alongside the aquarium are a couple of new additions to the seafront area: the futuristic-looking **Biosfera**, to the south, a steel and glass Renzo Piano-designed sphere housing a small tropical ecosystem, complete with trees, flowers and insects (Tues–Sun 9.30am–sunset; €4) and, just north at the next pier opposite the *Jolly Hotel Marina*, **Il Galeone Neptune** (daily 10am–7pm; €5), a kitschy full-size replica of a seventeenth-century galleon with a huge, colourful Neptune figure head, and several decks to explore, which has become a popular family attraction.

A couple of minutes further north, housed in a giant glass building is the highly regarded **Galata, Museo del Mare** (Museum of the Sea; Tues–Sun: March–Oct 10am–7.30pm, last entry 6pm; Nov–Feb 10am–6pm, last entry 5pm; €10; Ⓦwww.galatamuseodelmare.it), which details the history of Genoa and its age-old relationship with the sea, following its evolution from the late medieval period, illustrated with plenty of nautical paraphernalia and even several full-size ships.

South of San Lorenzo

The section of the old town south of the Cattedrale di San Lorenzo is less visited than the attraction-packed districts to the north, and more residential. Many of Genoa's students and young professionals live in the upper floors of the old buildings lining Via dei Giustiniani and Via San Bernardo, generating a lively bar culture in the surrounding alleys.

From the cathedral and Piazza Matteotti, narrow **Salita Pollaiuoli** plunges you into the gloom between high buildings down to a crossroads with **Via San Bernardo**, built by the Romans and now one of Genoa's most characterful old-town streets, with grocers and bakers trading behind the portals of palaces decorated in the fifteenth and sixteenth centuries. On the south side of the crossroads is tiny **Piazza San Donato**, a quiet square overlooked by the church of San Donato, a crumbling, bare Romanesque church with a Roman architrave surviving over its door and an octagonal Byzantine-style campanile.

Piazza Sarzano and around

A shrine stuck on the side wall of San Donato faces up Stradone Sant'Agostino, laid out in the eighteenth century and now home to a quirky array of bars and workshops. Partway up, stairs lead you into the university's **architecture faculty**, designed by Ignazio Gardella; its tranquil internal garden courtyard gives expansive views over the city. At the top of the street is the long, narrow bulge of **Piazza Sarzano**, originally home to Genoa's many ropemaking workshops and, owing to its enormous length, still the scene for medieval-style jousting tournaments. The piazza is marked by the mosaic spire of the rebuilt church of **Sant'Agostino**, alongside which is the unique triangular cloister of the thirteenth-century monastery that now houses the **Museo di Sant'Agostino** (Tues–Fri 9am–7pm, Sat & Sun 10am–7pm; €4; Ⓦwww.museosantagostino.it), displaying Roman and Romanesque masonry fragments. The highlight is a fragment of the tomb of Margherita of Brabant, sculpted in 1312 by Giovanni Pisano.

Sneak down behind a remnant of the city wall at the southeastern corner of Piazza Sarzano alongside the church of San Antonio, and an alley lined with pretty houses will lead you down into the tranquil little enclosed piazza of **Campopisano**. It was here, during the wars between Genoa and Pisa, that Pisan prisoners were brought in chains, executed and buried; today, the pavement sports pretty mosaics in local *rissëu* style, using smooth white stones collected from the beach and black stones – or *serpentinita* – quarried from dark veins of slate that snake their way across nearby hillsides.

North from Piazza Sarzano streets connect to the **Porta Soprana**, a twin-towered stone gateway featuring impressive Gothic arches (surprisingly dating from as early as 1155) that now stands as the focus for a rather upmarket collection of bars and terrace cafés.

Modern Genoa

In the nineteenth century, Genoa began to expand beyond its old-town constraints. The newer districts begin with the large central **Piazza de Ferrari**, from where **Via XX Settembre** runs a straight course east through the commercial centre of the city towards Stazione Brignole. This grand boulevard features big department stores, shops selling designer clothes, and pavement cafés beneath its neon-lit arcades. There are prized delicatessens in the side streets around Stazione Brignole and Piazza Colombo, and a bustling covered **Mercato Orientale** partway along, in the cloisters of an old Augustinian monastery. At the eastern end of Via XX Settembre, the park outside the Brignole train station (hub for city buses) extends south into **Piazza della Vittoria**, a huge and dazzling white square built during the Fascist period that now serves as the long-distance bus station.

Walking north from Piazza de Ferrari takes you up to **Piazza Corvetto** – built by the Austrians in the nineteenth century and now a major confluence of traffic and people. Across the other side of the square, a thoughtful-looking statue of Giuseppe Mazzini marks the entrance to the **Villetta di Negro**, a lushly landscaped park whose artificial waterfalls and grottoes scale the hill. At the top, the **Museo d'Arte Orientale Edoardo Chiossone** (Tues, Fri, Sat & Sun 10am–7pm; €4; ⓦ www.musechiossenegenova.it) holds a collection of oriental art that includes eighteenth-century sculpture and paintings and samurai armour. Chiossone was a printer and engraver for the Italian mint, and, on the strength of his banknote engraving skills, he was invited by the Meiji dynasty to establish the Japanese Imperial Mint. He lived in Japan from 1875 until his death in Tokyo in 1898, building up a fascinating and extensive collection.

If you're not satisfied with the view from the Villetta di Negro, you can take the Art Nouveau-style public lift from **Piazza del Portello** up to the **Castelletto**, which offers a great panorama over the port and the roofs of the old town; a **funicular** also leaves from the same place up to the residential **Sant'Anna** district, although the views from here aren't as good (ordinary bus tickets are valid for both). When Genoa ran out of building space, plots for houses were hewn out of the hillside behind, like the steps of an amphitheatre, and the funicular enables you to see these at close quarters, as the carriages edge past people's front windows. Another funicular runs from Largo Zecca, further west, to the suburb of **Righi**, where you can admire vistas of the city below and wander off on any of a number of paths, although locals generally come here to sit in the various panoramic restaurants for extended sessions of family dining.

The outskirts: Albaro, Boccadasse and Staglieno

For a spot of relaxation, head out of town to the eastern waterfront suburb of **Albaro**, at the end of Corso Italia, a broad boulevard that runs along the seafront beyond the giant Fiera exhibition area (bus #31 from Stazione Brignole). This is the place to jog, stroll, pose at one of the private lidos, or watch the sun set from a café table. From Albaro, you can walk or take bus #42 to **Boccadasse**. Once an outlying fishing port, this village is now part of the city, with boats pulled up on the pebble beach, nets hanging out to dry, some arty shops, and costly restaurants in which to sample the catch of the day.

Another good outing is to the **Staglieno cemetery** (daily 7.30am–5pm; free), on a hill northeast of the centre above the Bisagno Valley. Bus #34 runs from Stazione Principe through Piazza Nunziata and Piazza Corvetto to the cemetery. This is still Genoa's major burial ground, laid out between 1844 and 1851, and is a veritable city of the dead, crammed with Neoclassical porticoes, Gothic chapels and statuary galore. The entrance gates lead you into a vast quadrangle dominated by a Neoclassical **Pantheon** holding monuments to a clutch of famous nineteenth-century Genoese, including **Nino Bixio**, second-in-command on Garibaldi's expedition to Sicily. Behind and to the right of the Pantheon is the mausoleum of **Giuseppe Mazzini**, fronted by two squat Doric columns. One of the most sentimental monuments is the statue of **Teresa Campodonico**, a seller of nuts, whose life savings went to reproduce her slight, bent figure; carved below is a poem recounting how she sold her nuts in sunshine and in rain so as to gain her daily bread and propel her image into future ages. In the Protestant section of the cemetery you'll find the grave of **Constance Lloyd**, Oscar Wilde's wife, who died in 1898 at the age of 40, less than a year after Wilde had been released from prison, having changed her name and the names of their two sons to Holland.

Eating, drinking and nightlife

You could spend several days checking out the scores of places to **eat** in Genoa, from basic trattorias to elegant nineteenth-century *caffès*. Piazza Caricamento is one of the best places for a **quick lunch** on the hoof, the arcades (*sottoripe*) along the edge of the piazza lined with cafés serving focaccia, panini and deep-fried seafood. There are also lots of places in the old town selling **farinata** (Genoa's home-grown bready snack, made from chickpea flour and olive oil) – two that stand out are *Antica Sciamadda* at Via Ravecca 19r (closed Mon), and *Tugnin* on Piazza Tommaseo. *Forno Patrone*, Via Ravecca 72r (closed Wed afternoon) is one of the city's top bakeries. Centuries of Turkish influence have produced Genoese variations on Middle Eastern confectionery, including candied fruit (best sampled at Romanengo in Via Soziglia) and slabs of *pandolce* as served up at *Profumo* in Via del Portello.

There are plenty of late-night **bars** along the seamy waterfront Via Gramsci, in between the strip joints and brothels, but more attractive places can be found in the Old Town around Piazza delle Erbe.

Bars and cafés

Bar Berto Piazza delle Erbe 6r. Narrow little stand-up café-bar founded in 1904 by Signor Berto who walked some 15km west to the ceramics centre of Albisola in order to collect colourful bits of broken tile to decorate the walls. There is some seating available outside on the pedestrianized square. A trendy spot for coffee, beer or a reasonably priced light meal.

Britannia Vico Casana 76r, off Piazza de Ferrari. English-style pub likely to appeal to home-sick Brits in search of a wide selection of beer and standard pub food.

Café La Madeleine Via della Maddalena 103r. A wonderful little café-theatre, haunt of writers, poets, musicians and story-tellers, with plenty of readings and small concerts. Closed Mon.

Café Roger Stradone di Sant'Agostino. A quirky spot designed in riotous style after the Frank Zappa song "The Dangerous Kitchen" – every shelf is wonky, fake meat-cleavers dangle overhead, plastic sharks rise out of the sink and so on. The staff, music and clientele make this a fun stop for a daytime coffee or evening beer.

Caffè degli Specchi Salita Pollaiuoli 43r. This has been a prime spot since 1917 for Genovese artists, writers and intellectuals to take coffee while admiring themselves in the mirrors (*specchi*) that cover

the magnificent tiled interior. It also offers a small selection of dishes, such as penne with tomato sauce and mozzarella (€7.50) and *carpaccio di manzo* (€13). Closed Sun.

Caffè Mangini Via Roma at Piazza Corvetto. One of Genoa's most venerable *pasticcerie*, in business since the early 1800s and still top-notch today. Daily until 7.30pm.

Caffetteria Orefici Via degli Orefici 25r. Tiny fragrant temple to the art of coffee-making, with a range of specialist coffees and perfect results every time. Closed Sun.

Eprie Rosse Via Ravecca 54r. A characterful wine-bar in the old town.

Klainguti Piazza Soziglia 98r. An Austrian-built *salon* dating from 1828, selling cakes, coffee and ice cream under chandeliers. They still produce the hazelnut croissant known as a *Falstaff*, which was much esteemed by Giuseppe Verdi, who spent forty winters in Genoa – "Thanks for the Falstaff, much better than mine," he wrote to the bakers. On cold days you can warm yourself up with a bowl of their excellent *minestrone alla Genovese* (€4.70).

La Bottega del Conte Via delle Grazie. This cocktail bar is a dimly lit Bohemian hangout in a street behind the Porto Antico. Once a delicatessen, antique culinary implements still adorn the walls. Live jazz on Tuesdays.

Zeneise Via della Maddalena 90r. With its distinctive orange decor, this atmospheric bar near the city's red light district has quickly become a popular hangout with the city's trendy crowd.

Restaurants

Da Rina Mura delle Grazie 3r ☎010.246.6475. Simple, high-quality, Genoese cooking in unpretentious surroundings down near the waterfront. Lots of fish and classic Ligurian dishes such as *cima alla genovese*. Moderately priced. Closed Mon and August.

Il Fado Via San Donato 9r ☎010.246.5171. As you might expect from the name, this restaurant is dedicated to all things Portuguese, specializing in fish and live melancholy fado performances. Closed Sun & Mon lunch.

I Tre Merli Via dietro il coro della Maddalena 6 ☎010.247.4095. Despite its "atmospheric" location in the heart of the red light district, this is one of the city's very best restaurants employing an innovative approach to Ligurian cuisine – try the *pappardelle nere all' astice* for €16. There are over 300 wines on the menu, all stored in a converted fourteenth-century well. Closed Sat lunch & all Sun. Equally good sister branch on the seafront, *I Tre Merli al Porto Antico*, Palazzina Millo ☎010.246.4416.

La Berlocca Via del Macelli di Soziglia 45r ☎010.247.4162. Sittiing opposite a magic shop in a narrow old town alleyway, this is a cosy bistro-style establishment with an open fire in winter and a menu featuring adventurous takes on traditional Ligurian dishes. Closed Mon.

Le Tre Finestre Scalinata di San Antonio 2a. A tiny old-time trattoria off Piazza Sarzano. There's no menu (the waitress will just rattle off the dishes of the day), and the food is cheap, plain and hearty. Join in the good old-fashioned accordion singalong on Friday nights. Closed Mon–Thurs eve & all day Sun.

Maxela Vico Inferiore del Ferro 9 ☎010.247.4209. There's been a restaurant in this building since 1790. The latest, *Maxela*, opened a few years ago and is an unashamed carnivore's delight with meat hooks hanging from the walls and a menu filled with bloody favourites, including *frattaglie* (offal), roasts and *sanguinacci* (blood sausages). Closed Sun.

Östaja dö Castello Salita Santa Maria di Castello 32r ☎010.246.8980. Great old-town, family-run trattoria serving fish and seafood specialities, such as *polpo con patate* (€8) and *gamberi alla griglia* (€8) Closed Sun.

Pansön Piazza delle Erbe 5r ☎010.246.8903. Venerable Genoese institution, in the same family since 1790; diners sitting in this attractive, tucked-away piazza choose from a mainly fishy menu priced high to keep the riff-raff away. Highly recommended. Closed Sun eve.

Squarciafico Piazza Invrea 3r ☎010.247.0823. Atmospheric cantina in the wine-cellar of a fifteenth-century mansion just off Piazza San Lorenzo. Modern decor and innovative, carefully prepared food complement each other perfectly; be prepared for €25 per person. Closed Aug.

Ugo Via Giustiniani 86r. Convivial trattoria in the heart of the student quarter near San Donato, with a boisterous, friendly group of regulars who pack in at shared tables to wolf down the Genoese and Ligurian dishes – heavy on pesto and seafood. A hearty meal for two comes in at a very reasonable €20. Closed Sun & Mon.

Zeffirino Via XX Settembre 20r ☎010.591.990. Expensive – expect to pay around €45 (excluding wine) for a three- to four-course meal of between-two-stools trad/mod cuisine – but this is where Frank Sinatra and Pavarotti have also dined and so has ineffable star quality. Closed Wed.

Entertainment and nightlife

If your Italian is up to it, use the best source of information on **nightlife**, which is the local daily paper *Il Secolo XIX*; in summer you can supplement this with *Genova by Night,* the tourist office's free what's-on guide. For **live music**, the *Louisiana Jazz Club* on Via San Sebastiano hosts trad jazz most nights from around 10pm, but you'll find more happening joints tucked away in the southern part of the old town. The *Quaalude*, beneath the "Massari" signboard at Piazza Sarzano 14, is an underground club that features live bands and dance parties on Fridays and Saturdays – ask around in local bars for the latest news.

The two main **theatres** in Genoa are the Teatro della Corte, Via E. F. Duca d'Aosta, and the Teatro Duse, Via Bacigalupo, who advertise their performances on the same hoardings around town and sell tickets to both venues (☎010.534.220). The Teatro Carlo Felice in Piazza de Ferrari (☎010.589.329,

@www.carlofelice.it) is Genoa's main **opera house**; its performances are often oversubscribed, but it's still worth an enquiry. Chamber-music concerts take place in some of Genoa's *palazzi* in summertime.

Listings

Airlines Alitalia ℗848.865.643; British Airways ℗199.712.266.

Airport ℗010.601.5410, @www .aeroportodigenova.com.

Banks Various branches next to Stazione Principe in Piazza Acquaverde, on Via Balbi, and on Via XX Settembre.

Boats Alimar (℗010.256.775, @www.alimar .ge.it) and Cooperativa Battellieri (℗010.265.712, @www.battellierigenova.it) offer 45min tours by boat around the port, departing from alongside the Aquarium (every 30min, daily 9am–5pm; €6). Alimar also do romantic tours by night (Aug, on request only). Both companies run plenty of summer excursions west and east along the Riviera (the reasonable prices vary), departing either from the Aquarium or from Calata Zingari next to the Stazione Marittima. Routings along the eastern coast are also operated by Golfo Paradiso, based in Camogli (℗0185.772.091, @www .golfoparadiso.it), whose boats depart from Calata Mandraccio, just south of the Bigo. For whale-watching see p.131.

Bookshops Feltrinelli (@www.feltrinelli.it), Via XX Settembre 233r, has some English-language paperbacks.

Car rental Europcar, at the airport ℗010.650.4881; Hertz, Via Casaregis 78 ℗010.570.2625, airport ℗010.651.2422; Maggiore, Corso Sardegna 275 ℗010.839.2153, airport ℗010.651.2467; Sixt, Via Montevideo 111r ℗010.315.166, airport ℗010.651.2111.

Consulates UK, Via di Francia 28 ℗010.416.958; USA, Via Dante 2 ℗010.584.492. **Doctor** Call ℗010.354.022 for a doctor on call (nights and holidays).

Ferries Any of the shipping agencies under the arcades along Piazza Caricamento can give current details of the long-distance ferries departing regularly to Bastia (Corsica), Olbia or Porto Torres (both Sardinia), Palermo (Sicily) and further afield to Barcelona, Tunis and around the Med. Main operators are: Grimaldi, Via Fieschi 17 ℗010.55.091, @www.grimaldi.it; Moby, Ferries Terminal at the port ℗010.254.1513, @www.mobylines.it; and Tirrenia, Ponte Colombo ℗010.254.3851, @www.tirrenia.it.

Football Genoa's premier side, Sampdoria, play at the Luigi Ferraris stadium, behind Stazione Brignole. They share the stadium with the city's other major team, Genoa – founded in 1893 as the Genoa Cricket and Athletic Club, originally for British expatriates only. Bus #12 from Piazza Caricamento, and bus #37 from Stazione Principe, both pass near the stadium, or you can walk it in 15–20min from Brignole.

Hospitals Ospedale Galliera, Mura delle Cappuccine 14 (℗010.56.321), is the city's most central hospital, situated just south of Piazza Vittoria, while Ospedale Evangelico, Corso Solferino 1a (℗010.55.221) is English-speaking. For an emergency ambulance, call ℗118.

Internet access World Communication, Via San Luca.

Parking There are a dozen or so central car parks, all of which cost €16–20 per day; the largest is beneath Piazza della Vittoria (open 24hr). The old quarter is barred to traffic.

Pharmacies Ponte Monumentale, Via XX Settembre 115r (℗010.564.430), and Farmacia Pescetto, Via Balbi 185r (℗010.246.2697), are both English-speaking and open 24hr.

Police Carabinieri ℗112; Polizia ℗113; coastguard police ℗010.27.771. Genoa's police HQ is at Via Armando Diaz 2 (℗010.53.661).

Post office Via Dante 4 (Mon–Sat 8am–6.30pm; two desks with English-speaking staff). Sub-post offices are at both train stations, open same hours.

Taxis Radio Taxi Genova ℗010.5966.

Train information ℗010.247.99.09.

Around Genoa

Genoa has spilled over its old city limits to sprawl some 30km along the coast, with good bus and train connections to most of its outlying parts, including the popular parks and promenades at **Nervi** to the east and **Pegli** to the west. If you can, though, head inland to the north, where the terraced hills are at their most verdant in spring, when the blossom is out and the vines are flourishing. Several small villages make good bases for scenic walking here, or you can sit back and let the train take the strain with an hour-long ride on a clanky old narrow-gauge line from Genoa up to the rustic hill-village of **Casella**.

Nervi

Genoa's mainly residential suburbs extend east to **NERVI** (accessible by local train from Stazione Brignole or bus #15 from Piazza Cavour), a neat resort spread around a small harbour. Walking left out of the train station brings you into the **Parco di Villa Gropallo**, with, alongside, the **Parco di Villa Serra**, which hosts an open-air cinema during August (information from the Genoa tourist office). The park slopes down to a romantic seafront promenade with a few bars and fish restaurants, while joining it to the east are the lavish rose-gardens of the **Parco di Villa Grimaldi**. Following the lovely **promenade** east around the cliffs of the Sant'Ilario headland brings you to the **Museo Civile G. Luxoro**, holding a small collection of furniture, textiles and clocks (Tues–Fri 9am–1pm, Sat 10am–1pm; €4; ⓦ www.museoluxoro.it). You can also buy a combined ticket for €7 to include the town's two other small museums, both of which hold collections of (mainly Italian) nineteenth- and twentieth-century art: the **Galleria d'Arte Moderna** in the Villa Saluzzo Serra (Tues–Sun 10am–7pm; €6), and the **Raccolte Frugone** in the Villa Grimaldi (Tues–Sun 10am–7pm; €4).

Pegli

West of Genoa lies **PEGLI**, and the romantic **Villa Durazzo-Pallavicini**, set in elegant grounds landscaped in the 1840s by Genovese architect Michele Canzio (gardens Tues–Sun: April–Sept 9am–7pm; Oct–March 9am–5pm;

> ## Walking the Alta Via
>
> The **Alta Via dei Monti Liguri** is a long-distance high-level trail covering the length of Liguria, from Ventimiglia in the west all across the ridge-tops to Ceparana on the Tuscan border above La Spezia in the east, a total distance of some 440km. The mountains, which form the connection between the Alps and the Apennines, aren't high – rarely more than 1500m – meaning that the scenic route, which makes full use of the many passes between peaks, is correspondingly easy-going. The whole thing would take weeks to complete in full, but has been divided up into 43 stages of between about two and four hours each, making it easy to dip in and out. Trail support and maintenance is generally good, with *rifugi* dotted along the path and distinctive waymarks (red-white-red "AV" signs).
>
> A sample walk starts from point 26 – **Crocetta d'Orero**, on the Genoa–Casella train line: heading east from Crocetta, an easy route covers 7.8km to point 27, **Colle di Creto** (2hr 30min, and served by Genoa buses), with a diversion along the way to a lovely flower-strewn path in and around the deserted hamlet of **Ciaé**. Another sample walk, the very first stage of all, from **Ventimiglia** to La Colla, sidelining to **Dolceacqua**, is outlined on p.141. Unfortunately, access from the main coastal towns to most other parts of the Alta Via can be tricky, and requires juggling with route itineraries and bus timetables.
>
> For information on the Alta Via, your best bet is the **Associazione Alta Via dei Monti Liguri**, ⓦ www.lig.camcom.it), which produces a full-colour wall-map of the route, along with detailed English descriptions and timings of all 43 stages (plus hotels and restaurants along the way). Books and an eight-pamphlet guide to the trail are on sale in bookshops. The same information is at ⓦ www.parks.it. **Club Alpino Italiano** offices in the major towns have information on *rifugi*, and the **Federazione Italiano Escursionismo** (FIE) publishes detailed guides to all the inland paths of Liguria.

☎010.666.864; €6). The villa houses the **Museo Civico di Archeologia Ligure** (Tues–Fri 9am–7pm, Sat & Sun 10am–7pm; €4; ⓦwww.museoarcheo logicogenova.it), where items unearthed from cave burials in the hills along the west coast include the skeleton of a "Young Prince" with seashell crown and ceremonial dagger. You can get here by local train from Stazione Brignole or slow buses #1, #2 or #3 from Piazza Caricamento.

Genoa's northern hinterland

Many Genoese escape the city in summer by heading for the hills. The Genoa tourist office has the useful *Antola and its Valleys* booklet in English, complete with itinerary suggestions, a map and details of walks; it is also downloadable from ⓦwww.apt.genova.it/inglese/depliant/depliant-menu.htm. AMT buses from Genoa's Piazza della Vittoria serve all the larger villages. Look out wherever you are for breads and pastas made with local chestnut flour, as well as *scarpignon*, ravioli stuffed with a meat and walnut paste.

Narrow-gauge FGC **trains** (☎010.837.321, ⓦwww.ferroviagenovacasella.it), dating back to 1929 and worth taking just for the pleasure of it, leave roughly hourly from a station in Genoa's Piazza Manin, connected to Brignole by bus #33 and Principe by bus #34. They start off climbing through the Val Bisagno and coil northwards up to **CASELLA**, in a wooded dell at the foot of Monte Maggio (55min from Genoa). Return fares to Casella are €6 and aren't covered by Genoa's normal bus tickets. Casella is the trailhead for a number of hiking routes in the picturesque **Valle Scrivia** (ⓦwww.altavallescrivia.it). The town has a couple of **hotels**, of which the *Magenta* at Piazza XXV Aprile 20 is the better bet if you're here in summer (☎010.967.7113; ❸; June–Sept only); and there are half-a-dozen **restaurants**, including *Camugin* (closed Mon) in front of the church, known for its fresh fish, and *Chiara* (closed Mon) with a wood-fired pizza oven. You can also take a dip at the pleasant public swimming baths, **Piscina Casella**, near the station (June & Sept 11am–6pm; July & Aug 10am–7pm; €8).

Northeast of Genoa, buses follow the SS225 road over the Passo di Scoffera to little **Torriglia**, which offers the photogenic ruins of a medieval castle and plenty of hiking trails into the mountains of the **Parco Naturale dell'Antola** (ⓦwww.parks.it). The **tourist office** is at Via N. S. della Provvidenza 3 (Tues–Sun 9.30am–12.30pm & 3–6pm; ☎010.944.175, ⓔlat.torriglia@apt.genova .it), and for accommodation there's the basic *Della Posta* **hotel** at Via Matteotti 39 (☎010.944.050; ❷). From Torriglia, the SS45 heads northeast along the Val Trebbia through **Montebruno**, famed for its richly decorated fifteenth-century Santuario dell'Assunta (containing a Byzantine carving of the Madonna) and its mushroom-shaped chocolates called *funghetti*. Minor roads from Montebruno serve the mountain community of **FONTANIGORDA**, set further east among beech and chestnut woods and famous for its thirteen fountains. A scenic walking trail from here heads up and over the Passo di Esola to Rezzoáglio, which lies within striking distance of **Santo Stefano d'Aveto**. Fontanigorda's **hotels** include the good-value *La Fontanella*, Piazza Roma 7 (☎010.952.000, ⓕ010.562.765; ❷), with en-suite and shared bathrooms, and the adequate *Augustus*, Via Fontana Vecchia 1 (☎010.952.014; ❷), both with **restaurants**.

Off to the west of Bolzaneto, a few kilometres north of Genoa, a minor road off the SS35 heads to the hilltop sanctuary of **Madonna della Guardia**, for centuries the prime pilgrimage spot for the Genoese. The SS35 continues north up the valley, with buses passing through tiny **Ronco Scrivia**, which has an attractive medieval bridge over the river with three pointed arches, and **Isole del Cantone**, where a minor road climbs right up a wild **side-valley** towards Vobbia. A few kilometres into the valley, high up on the left (north) side, you'll spot the towers of the **Castello della Pietra**, a thirteenth-century castle, which sits in a dramatic spot wedged between rock pinnacles above the thick forest; if you have the energy, climb the steep path up to it for spectacular valley views.

The Riviera di Ponente

The autostrada gives the most positive impression of the **Riviera di Ponente** (Western Riviera), the umbrella title for the stretch of Ligurian coast between the French border and Genoa. From its elevated viaducts, the marinas and resorts way below are mere specks in a stunning panorama of glittering sea and acres of glasshouses. If you exit the autostrada and venture down to the coastal road to see things close-up, you'll find that the Riviera towns are generally fairly functional places, occasionally sporting an attractive medieval quarter but always overflowing with hotels and apartment blocks. Yet these resorts have their good points – chiefly the sandy beaches, comparatively low prices and lack of pretentiousness.

Some of these places, the grand old resort of **San Remo**, for example, or the border town of **Ventimiglia**, also make good bases for travelling into the mountain areas behind the coast, where stone villages and agricultural communes reveal the more private side of the region. Walkers can explore sections of the Alta Via dei Monti Liguri (see box, p.138) or loop through attractive and little-visited hill-towns like **Taggia** or **Dolceacqua**.

For more information on the coast, check out Ⓦwww.inforiviera.it or call ⓉⓉ0182.64.711. An organization of local hoteliers, Consorzio Palmhotels (Ⓣ0184.66.698, Ⓦwww.palmhotels.it), with bases in Genoa and San Remo, also details accommodation along the coast.

Ventimiglia and around

The first stop inside Italy, barely 6km east of the French border, **VENTIMIGLIA** is an unexceptional frontier town that enjoyed several centuries of minor prosperity courtesy of the constant border traffic. However, it's been experiencing hard times since the 1995 Schengen agreement, permitting unchecked passage between France and Italy, rendered the town's time-honoured role as customs post and refreshment point redundant. The town does make a good base for country **walks** though, especially as the **hotels** offer considerably better value than those in other nearby resorts. The centre is quite lively with a handful of good restaurants and interesting delis, and the eastern side of town has a rather low-key **Area Archeologica**, where you can see some remains of a third-century Roman amphitheatre and baths. If you want to stay, the pleasant *Sea Gull*, Passeggiata Marconi 24 (Ⓣ0184.351.726, Ⓦwww.seagullhotel.it; ❸), has its own patch of beach below the crumbling medieval quarter, while the *XX Settembre*, Via Roma 16 (Ⓣ0184.351.222; ❷), is the pick of the low-end choices. For **food**, you could try the *Usteria d'a Porta Marina* (closed Tues eve & Wed), overlooking the river at Via Trossarelli 22: the celebrated *branzino* (sea bass) in local Rossese wine is expensive, but they have set menus for €18.

Mórtola Inferiore

From Via Cavour in front of Ventimiglia's train station, bus #1a (every hour, on the hour; no service between 3 & 4pm) heads west for 5km to the village of **MÓRTOLA INFERIORE**, famed for the spectacular hillside **Giardini Botanici "Hanbury"** (mid-June to Sept daily 9am–6pm; April to mid-June daily 10am–5pm; Oct daily 10am–6pm; Nov–March Mon, Tues & Thurs–Sun 10am–4pm; €7.50; ⓦwww.amicihanbury.com). These gardens were laid out in 1867 by Sir Thomas Hanbury, a London spice merchant who set up home here, and are highly atmospheric, with hidden corners and pergola-covered walks tumbling down to the sea. A half-hour walk further west along the coast road – or a few minutes on bus #1a – is the frontier post. A scramble down the hillside brings you to the caves of **Balzi Rossi** (Tues–Sun 9am–7pm; free), where remains of prehistoric civilizations dating back to the Paleolithic age were discovered; a small **Museo Preistorico** (same hours; €2) houses a collection of artefacts and crude fertility sculptures.

A walk to Dolceacqua
The area's best walk comprises Stage One of the **Alta Via dei Monti Liguri** hiking trail (see box, p.138). The ten-kilometre route (an easy 3hr romp) begins from Ventimiglia tourist office; walk east for a few minutes along Via Cavour, which becomes Corso Genova, and then duck north beneath the train tracks via an underpass that's marked with the first of the red-and-white "AV" waymarkers. From here, you climb out of the town through vineyards onto a ridge running between the valleys of the Roia and the Nervia, past the votive chapel of **San Giacomo**, through the ancient hamlet of **Ciaixe** and up to **La Colla**.

From La Colla, the trail continues along a side-path that takes you east down to the medieval riverside village of **DOLCEACQUA**, best known for its excellent Rossese red wine and its olive oil. Piles of black olives crowd the village at harvest time, spread out on cloths on the ground prior to processing. The Nervia, crossed by an elegant 33-metre single-span medieval bridge, runs from the new part of town, or **borgo**, alongside the valley road, to the steep, stone alleyways of the older quarter, the **terra**, which are arranged in concentric circles around slopes topped by the ruins of a castle that once belonged to the Doria family. A theatre festival and concerts are staged here every summer (contact the tourist office for details), and Dolceacqua is also the scene of a more ancient festival, rooted in fertility rites: on the Sunday nearest to January 20, a laurel tree hung with coloured Communion wafers is carried through the village as part of the procession of St Sebastian. For ideas on **walks** in the beautiful Upper Nervia Valley, ask at the **tourist office**, Via Patrioti Martiri 58 (daily 10am–1pm & 4–7pm; ⓣ0184.206.666, ⓦwww.dolceacqua.it). **Buses** run between Dolceacqua and Ventimiglia for those who don't fancy the walk.

San Remo and around
Set on a broad sweeping bay between twin headlands, **SAN REMO** had its heyday as a classy resort in the sixty years or so up to the outbreak of World War II, when the Empress Maria Alexandrovna headed a substantial Russian community in the town (Tchaikovsky completed *Eugene Onegin* and wrote his Fourth Symphony in San Remo in 1878) and wealthy Europeans paraded on the Corso Imperatrice. Some of the grand hotels overlooking the sea, especially those near the train station, are now grimy and crumbling, but others in the ritzier western parts of town are still in pristine condition, opening their doors to Europe's blue-rinse nobility season after season. San Remo is blessed with the Riviera's most famous **casino** after the one in Monte Carlo, and remains a showy and attractive town, with a good beach and a labyrinthine old town standing guard over the palm-laden walkways below.

The town has its fair share of events too. Every January the **Festival dei Fiori** (Festival of Flowers) sees flora-bedecked floats make their way through the town, displaying products by the area's horticulturists, while July's **Campionato Mondiale di Fuochi d'Artificio**, or World Fireworks Championship, is not for the jittery.

Arrival and information

San Remo's modern – and slightly confusing – **train station** is east of the town centre on Corso Cavallotti. The **tourist office** is in a striking building at Largo Nuvoloni 1 (Mon–Sat 8am–7pm, Sun 9am–1pm; ☎0184.59.059, ⓦwww.apt .rivieradeifiori.it). Five minutes' walk east from the train station along Corso Matteotti is the main **bus station** on Piazza Colombo. Local Riviera Trasporti (ⓦwww.rivieratrasporti.it) buses from here shuttle around town and up to Taggia (see p.144); one-hour tickets cost €1. **Boat** trips along the coast are run by Riviera Line, Molo di Levante 35 (March–Oct daily 10am & 3pm; lasts 1hr 30min; €11; ☎0184.505.055, ⓦwww.rivieraline.it); they also do whale-watching excursions (see p.131). Advice on **hiking** can be found at the Club Alpino Italiano office, Piazza Cassini 13 (Tues & Fri 9.30am–10.30pm, Wed & Sat 6–7pm; ⓦwww.cai.it).

Accommodation

Finding **accommodation** should be no problem, though most places insist on half- or full-board in high season. If you're looking for budget hotels, then the western end of the centre, on and between Corso Matteotti and Via Roma, is the area to head for. There's a **campsite**, *Villaggio dei Fiori*, west of town at Via Tiro a Volo 3 (☎0184.660.635, ⓦwww.villaggiodeifiori.it; open all year).

Al Dom Corso Mombello 13 ☎0184.501.460. Family-run choice, with large and airy but noisy rooms. ②

Alexander Corso Garibaldi 123 ☎0184.504.591, ⓕ0184.572.131. A characterful option, near the train station, in a beautiful Belle Époque building set back from the road. ③

Maristella Corso Imperatrice 77 ☎0184.667.881, ⓔhmcps@tin.it. Friendly place with attractive decor in a good spot, right by the sea. ③

Paradiso Via Roccasterone 12 ☎0184.571.211, ⓦwww.paradisohotel.it. In a quiet location above the town's bustle, with a secluded garden, pool and sunny, modern rooms. ⑤

Royal Hotel Corso Imperatrice 80 ☎0184.5391, ⓦwww.royalhotelsanremo.com. This expensive place scores highly for facilities and faded, old-fashioned opulence. It boasts three restaurants and a vast, heated, saltwater swimming pool set in a tropical garden. ⑨

The Town

The **Palazzo di Riviera**, where the tourist office is housed, is a prime example of the kind of floral architecture that lines the palm boulevard **Corso Imperatrice** that stretches along the seafront west of the centre. Directly opposite the *palazzo* is an onion-domed **Russian Orthodox church** (Tues–Sun 9.30am–12.30pm & 3–6.30pm; free), built in the 1920s and more impressive on the outside than within. About 100m further east you'll come to San Remo's landmark **Casino**, a white ornate palace with grand staircases and distinctive turrets that still stands as the epitome of the town's old-fashioned sense of monied leisure, playing an active part in its nightlife to this day. **Corso degli Inglesi** winds around and above the casino, home to dozens of villas in varying states of repair, including one close to the junction of Via Fratelli Asquascati complete with stained-glass irises and majolica tiles.

From the casino, the main **Corso Matteotti**, lined with cocktail bars, *gelaterie*, cinemas and clothes stores, heads east into the commercial centre of town. Lurid neon signs on side streets point to private clubs and by-the-hour hotels, all rubbing shoulders with a handful of expensive restaurants. The cross-street

Corso Mombello connects south to the Giardini Veneto on the seafront alongside the harbour, and north to the main central square **Piazza Eroi Sanremesi**. This huge, rambling space is partly taken up by market-stalls and terrace cafés, and partly backs onto the Gothic **Cattedrale di San Siro** (daily 7–11.15am & 3–6pm; free), which features unusual twelfth-century bas reliefs above its side doors and a processional black crucifix within. A short way east of the cathedral, at Corso Matteotti 143, is the impressive Renaissance Palazzo Borea d'Olmo, still owned by the family of the same name and now housing the **Museo Civico** (Tues–Sat 9am–noon & 3–6pm; €3), but its array of local finds and paintings is less memorable than the sumptuous frescoed interior. **Piazza Colombo** is just east of the museum, with Via Asquasciati heading down to the sea. If you follow the harbourside promenade east for 1km, you'll come to the marina and – on the north side of the tracks – the **Giardino Ormond** (daily 9am–7pm; free), which is filled with date palms, yuccas, olive trees, jacaranda, bougainvillea and even a grand cedar of Lebanon.

San Remo's most fascinating quarter – which stands in stark contrast to the glamour and bustle of the seafront districts – is its **old town**, accessible up steep lanes north of Piazza Eroi Sanremesi and Piazza Cassini. Known as **La Pigna** or the "Pine-Cone", its kasbah-like arched passageways and alleys leading nowhere come as a surprise after the busy, modern streets below. From the gardens at the highest peak you get excellent views across the whole of the town and surrounding countryside.

If you can drag yourself out of bed early enough, you will find that San Remo offers one of the liveliest and most engaging spectacles on the Riviera: the **wholesale flower market** at Mercato dei Fiori, Via Quinto Mansuino 12, Valle Armea, 4km east of town (Mon–Fri 3am–8am; visitors must arrive between 5am & 6am, Ⓦ www.sanremoflowermarket.it). Take the Taggia or Imperia-Diano Marina bus from the centre of town for the ten-minute ride. You'll know when you're approaching by the sight of waiters running around with trays of espresso, and the woven boxes for flowers attached to the vans and Vespas outside. Some eighty tonnes of flowers a day are shipped out of here, around Italy and the world. The market itself is strictly for trade, but no one minds bystanders as long as they don't get in the way.

Eating and drinking

San Remo is well served by **restaurants**, most of which offer the local speciality of *sardenàira*, a kind of cheese-less pizza topped with tomatoes, olives, capers, garlic and fresh oregano.

Bagatto Corso Matteotti 145 ☎0184.531.925. The most laid-back of San Remo's many formal restaurants. Closed Sun & July.

Don Fernando Via Bixio 77 ☎0184.508.484. Bright, modern and pretty decent, *Don Fernando* serves enormous pans of fresh pasta with the sauce of your choice. Closed Mon.

Lella's Place at Corso N. Sauro 25 ☎0184.502.141. Overlooking the old port and offering a fresh menu of salads, pizza and pasta, this is a good standby for a reasonably priced lunch. Closed Fri.

Vittorio Piazza Bresca 16 ☎0184.501.924. Dishes up an excellent selection of mid-price fish and seafood. Closed Wed.

Piccolo Mondo Via Piave 7 ☎0184.509.012. This archetypally charming little trattoria in an alley off the Corso Matteotti is the town centre's best-value choice, serving delicious Ligurian dishes. Closed Sun & Mon.

Solentiname Lungomare V. Emanuele 13 ☎0184.664.477. Cheerful place enjoying a wonderful waterfront setting and serving great pizza. Closed Mon.

Nightlife

Nightlife revolves around San Remo's famous **Casino** (daily 2.30pm–3am; ☏0184.59.51, ⓦwww.casinosanremo.it). Entrance is permitted only with your passport as ID; admission is free to the slot machines and from Monday to Thursday to the evocative Belle Époque gaming rooms (Fri–Sun €7.50). The dress code is jacket and tie for both American and French gaming rooms, but you can get away with more casual gear in the slot-machine area.

Elsewhere around town, there's no shortage of **clubs** and **bars** – *Zoo Bizarre* on Via Gaudio is a popular place serving wine and cocktails, and with a DJ on Saturdays; while *Newport Café*, Giardini Vittorio Veneto, has salads and sandwiches at lunchtime, and great cocktails served with a variety of snacks in the evening. In summer there are open-air jazz, blues and folk **concerts** around the harbour and in the various parks.

The Valle Argentina

The Valle Argentina heads inland from the bustling seaside resort of **Arma di Taggia**, 6km east of San Remo. Sleepy, crumbling **TAGGIA**, 3km north, is known for its sixteen-arched **Romanesque bridge**, the *taggiasca* black olive that is famed for giving top-quality oil, and a collection of work by Ligurian artists in the black-and-white stone convent church of **San Domenico** just outside the old walls (daily 9am–noon & 3–5pm; donation requested). If you can, time a visit for the third Sunday in July, when the ancient *festa* of the Magdalene culminates in a "Dance of Death" performed by two men, traditionally from the same two families, accompanied by the local brass and woodwind band.

Some 25km further up the valley is the tiny village of **TRIORA**. The trip here from San Remo (4 services daily from the main bus station) is worth doing in its own right, the bus wending its way past small settlements with ancient bridges and farms linked to the main road across the valley by a rope and pulley system. Triora is almost within sight of Monte Pietradura, which stays snow-capped until April. In 1588, after an unexpected famine, two hundred women in this isolated community were denounced by the Inquisition as **witches**: rumour has it that thirty were tortured, fourteen were burned at the stake, and one woman committed suicide before she could be executed. Documents from the trial are preserved in the **Museo Etnografico** in the village (May–Dec Mon–Sat 3–6.30pm, Sun 10.30am–noon & 3–6pm; Jan–April Sun only; €2), and a commemorative plaque adorns the overgrown Cabotina just outside the village, supposed scene of the witches' gatherings. Also worth seeking out is the celebrated Sienese painter Taddeo di Bartolo's *Baptism of Christ* (1397), hung in the baptistry of the Romanesque-Gothic **Collegiata** church. The village has a single **hotel**, the peaceful *Colomba d'Oro*, Corso Italia 66 (☏0184.94.051, ⓦwww.colombadoro.it; ❷), comfortably converted from an old monastery.

From San Remo to Genoa

Just about every settlement along the stretch of coast from San Remo to Genoa is a resort of some kind, either well-developed, family-targeted places like **Finale Ligure** or small, better-preserved villages like **Noli**, while the attractive medieval town of **Albenga** manages happily to fall somewhere in between.

Imperia, Alassio and Laigueglia

Some 30km east of San Remo is the provincial capital of **IMPERIA**, formed in 1923 when Mussolini linked twin townships on either side of the River Impero. Imposing **Porto Maurizio**, on the western bank, is the more attractive of the two, ascending the hillside in a series of zigzags from a marina and small beach, with its stepped old quarter dominated by a massive late-eighteenth-century cathedral and a series of Baroque churches and elegant villas. Quieter **Oneglia**, 2km east, is still very much wedded to the sea, with an active population of fisherfolk. Just behind its station at Via Garessio 13 is the **Museo dell'Olivo**, paid for by the town's leading olive-oil dynasty, the Fratelli Carli (daily 9am–12.30pm & 3–6.30pm; free; ⓦwww.museodellolivo.com), housing modern displays devoted to the history of Liguria's green nectar. The **tourist office** is at Viale Matteotti 37 in Porto Maurizio (Mon–Sat 9am–12.30pm & 3.30–7pm; ⓣ0183.660.140), where you'll also find the comfortable **hotels** *Croce di Malta*, overlooking the old harbour at Via Scarincio 148 (ⓣ0183.667.020, ⓦwww .hotelcrocedimalta.com; ❸), and *Corallo* (ⓣ0183.666.264, ⓦwww.corallo imperia.com; ❸), where all rooms have a sea view.

East of Imperia, olive plantations take over from flowers along what has been dubbed the **Riviera dei Olivi**. Two big beach resorts – Diano Marina and **ALASSIO**, the latter with a spectacular four-kilometre fine-sand beach and motorboat trips out to the Isola Gallinara island nature reserve – bookend a couple of slightly less frenetic spots: **Cervo** is a picturesque spiral of cottages that primps and preens itself for the tourist trade, while **LAIGUEGLIA**, a quiet ex-fishing port with a couple of porticoed streets to wander, offers a more palatable slice of beach life than its big-time neighbours.

A walk up the steps from the junction of Via Mimosa and the main Via Roma in Laigueglia takes you away from the coast through a cluster of holiday homes to the old **Roman road** near the top of the hill. From here, follow the *strada privata* into the woods and take the signposted path for about forty minutes to the ruins of the **Castello di Andora** and what is held to be one of the most important medieval monuments of the Riviera, the beautiful thirteenth-century church of SS Giacomo and Filippo. Even if you never get to the church

△ Alassio beach reserve

and castle, the walk along mule tracks between olive groves and woods is one of the most appealing parts of this bit of coast, with plenty of shaded places to dream away the afternoon. From the castle you can either backtrack or walk on through the outskirts of the village of **Andora** to its train station.

Albenga

Beyond Alassio the terrain grows more mountainous, and the rail line and road stick close to the sea for the eight-kilometre journey to the small market town of **ALBENGA**. With the silting up of the river estuary, Albenga long ago lost its port and merits a visit these days for its pleasingly business-like old quarter, still within medieval walls. The **train station** is 800m east of the old town via the twin parallel boulevards of Viale dei Mille and Viale Martiri della Libertà; the latter leads to the **tourist office** at no. 1 (Mon–Sat 9am–12.30pm & 3–6.30pm, Sun 9am–noon; ☎0182.558.444, ⓦwww.inforiviera.it), and on to **Piazza San Michele** at the heart of the old town. This small square is dominated by the elegant **cathedral**, the main part of which was built in the eleventh century and enlarged in the early fourteenth. Diagonally opposite in the Torre Comunale is the **Museo Civico Ingauno** (mid-Sept to mid-June Tues–Sun 10am–12.30pm & 4.30–6pm; mid-June to mid-Sept Tues–Sun 9.30am–noon & 3.30–7.30pm; €3; ⓦwww.iisl.it), displaying interesting ancient artefacts and providing access to Albenga's big draw, the **Baptistry**. This ingenious building went up alongside the cathedral in the fifth century, and combines an unusual ten-sided exterior with a more orthodox octagonal interior. Inside are fragmentary mosaics showing the Apostles represented by twelve doves.

Behind the baptistry to the north, the archbishop's palace houses the diverting **Museo Diocesano** (Tues–Sun 10am–noon & 3–6pm; donation requested). Taking pride of place are the remains of the fifteenth-century frescoes that adorned what used to be a chapel and the bishop's own bedchamber (the latter decorated by Provencal artists with a mixture of sombre and bright flower patterns to represent night and day). A few metres west, where Via Medaglie d'Oro crosses Via Ricci, is the thirteenth-century **Loggia dei Quattro Canti**, marking the town centre of Roman Albingaunum. Some 500m north of here, beyond Piazza Garibaldi and along Viale Pontelungo, you'll find the odd sight of an elegant, arched 150-metre bridge spanning nothing much – the **Pontelungo** was built here in the twelfth century to cross the river, which shifted course soon afterwards.

One of the cheapest **hotels** in the town is the pleasant, 1930-style *Italia*, Viale Martiri della Libertà 8 (☎0182.50.405, ⓔfaustocarrara@libero.it; ❶), with shared bathrooms only. Alternatively, down on the seafront *Sole Mare*, Lungomare Colombo 15 (☎0182.51.817, ⓕ0182.52.752; ❹), has a range of rooms. The *Lungomare* **campsite** is at the mouth of the river off Strada Vicinale Avarenna (☎0182.51.449, ⓕ0182.52.525; open all year). Albenga's least expensive **restaurants** are off Via Medaglie d'Oro on the alley Via Torlaro. *Da Puppo*, a characterful little place with a wood-burning pizza oven and good *farinata*, is at no. 20 (closed for lunch July & Aug), while at no. 13 is *Il Vecchio Mulino* (closed Thurs) serving basic trattoria food from €5. Pricey *Antica Osteria dei Leoni*, behind the Baptistry at Via Lengueglia 49 (closed Mon), has a good range of local dishes, while the popular *Babette*, Viale Pontelungo 26 (closed Mon & Tues), hosts Greek-, French- and Italian-themed dinners.

The caves of Toirano

Nurseries of artichokes and petunias, interspersed with garden centres and caravan sites, line the coast between Albenga and the town of **Borghetto Santo**

Spirito, transfer point for buses a few kilometres inland to the spectacular caves of **TOIRANO**, set halfway up a rocky hillside outside the well-preserved medieval village centre. There are three main cave complexes (daily: July & Aug 9.30am–12.30pm & 2–5.30pm; Sept–June 9.30am–12.30pm & 2–5pm; €9; ⓦwww.toirano.it). The stalactite-adorned **Grotta della Bàsura** – dialect for "The Witch's Cave" – was the home of Stone Age inhabitants some eighty thousand years ago. These early troglodytes apparently shared their cave-dwellings with local bears: there's a mass of bear bones in the underground Bear Cemetery, and dozens of prehistoric foot- and pawprints left in what was once mud. A path leads on to the **Grotta di Santa Lucia**, containing remarkable stalagmite and stalactite formations, with a natural spring that was dedicated in the Middle Ages to St Lucy, patron saint of eyesight, after several miraculous cures were effected here. Further on, guided tours around **Grotta del Colombo** lead you through the beautiful caverns formed in the limestone over millions of years by the action of water.

Finale Ligure

Though overly tourist-oriented, busy **FINALE LIGURE** nevertheless manages to remain an attractive place. The majority of visitors are Italian families who, by 10pm on summer nights, pack the outdoor restaurants, seafront fairground and open-air cinema, or take an extended *passeggiata* along the promenade and through the old alleys.

Of the town's three parts, **Finalmarina** is the main bit, with the **train station** at its western end, a good pebbly beach, a promenade lined with palms, and narrow shopping streets set back from the seafront that hold the **tourist office** at Via San Pietro 14 (Mon–Sat 9am–12.30pm & 3–6.30pm, plus Sun 9am–noon in summer; ☏019.681.019, ⓦwww.inforiviera.it). The bars in the vicinity of Piazza Vittorio Emanuele II and the adjoining Piazza di Spagna, the main public space in the centre of this spread-out resort, are the points to which everyone eventually gravitates.

Finalpia is a small district five minutes' walk to the east on the other side of the River Sciusa, focused around the twelfth-century church of Santa Maria di Pia (rebuilt in florid early eighteenth-century style) and its adjacent sixteenth-century cloistered abbey.

Finalborgo, the medieval walled quarter, sits on a slight hill 2km inland from Finalmarina, overlooked by bare rock-faces that are a favourite with free climbers who gather at *Bar Gelateria Centrale* in Finalborgo's Piazza Garibaldi at weekends. The area's wider fame comes from the **Grotte delle Arene Candide**, among Europe's most important caves for prehistoric remains; they're closed for excavation, but some finds are on display at the **Museo Civico** in Finalborgo's church of Santa Caterina (Tues–Sun: July & Aug 10am–noon & 4–7pm; Sept–June 9am–noon & 2.30–5pm; €3). The same church hosts an interesting antiques **market** on the first weekend of each month during summer.

The tourist office has information on picturesque inland **walks**, including the **Sentieri Parlanti** which zigzag across the hills past the excellent mid-priced ⚓ *Osteria La Briga* restaurant (☏019.698.579; closed Tues & Wed and in winter), where you can fill up on *ortica* (nettle) and *tartufo nero* (black truffle) lasagne. **Mountain bikes** can be rented on Via Brunenghi in Finalborgo, from Race-ware at no. 124, and R.C. Bike at no. 65.

Accommodation, eating and drinking
In high season virtually all the hotels insist on full board, and you'd do better staying up the coast at Noli, unless you opt for the excellent ⚓ *Castello Vuillermin*

HI **hostel** (one of the best in the country) which occupies an old castle high above the train station at Via Caviglia 46 and has marvellous views out to sea (☏019.690.515; €13 per person; mid-March to mid-Oct). *Eurocamping* is a well-run riverside **campsite** at Via Calvisio 37 in Finalpia (☏019.601.240, ⓦwww.eurocampingcalvisio.it; April–Sept).

The best places **to eat** need some hunting out. *Da Tonino*, Via Bolla 5, has outside seating and good pizzas. *Gabbri*, next to the church of San Giovanni Battisti at Via Pollupice 1 (closed Thurs), is a friendly trattoria whose atmosphere and reasonably priced menu feel a million miles away from the brash seafront pizza parlours. Up in Finalborgo, *Ai Torchi*, Via dell'Annunziata 12 (☏019.690.531; closed Tues except in Aug), occupies an ancient olive-oil factory and serves expensive pasta and fish dishes with care and some style.

Noli

The Via Aurelia heads northeast from Finale Ligure past the small Capo di Noli, where the sea is inviting and the inlets are accessible from the road. **NOLI**'s beaches aren't great but otherwise this is the most attractive resort along this part of the Riviera, topped by a castle whose battlements march down the hill to meet the walls of the small but pretty old town. To get here, take the train to Spotorno-Noli and then the bus (every 30min from Spotorno town centre, 5min). Aside from half-a-dozen medieval towers, Noli's grid of old streets hides the majestic Romanesque church of **San Paragorio**, notable for its crypt, frescoes, a thirteenth-century bishop's throne of inlaid wood kept behind glass in an interior chapel, and a twelfth-century *Volto Santo* (True Likeness of Christ) similar to the one at Lucca in Tuscany. The **tourist office** faces the sea at Corso Italia 8 (Mon–Sat 9am–12.30pm & 3–6.30pm, Sun 9am–noon; ☏019.749.9003), and a number of the town's thirteenth-century palaces have been converted into **hotels**, most of which have popular **restaurants** attached. *Albergo Triestina*, down a medieval street off the seafront at Via da Noli 16 (☏019.748.024, ⓦwww.hoteltriestina.com; ❹), offers a personal, welcoming ambience. The **beaches** are broad and sandy some 3km further up the coast at **SPOTORNO**, but otherwise this once-tranquil little place has lost just about all of the character it could claim in 1926, when D.H. Lawrence holed up here to write *Lady Chatterley's Lover*.

Savona

First impressions of **SAVONA**, 17km northeast of Noli, aren't up to much: it's a functional city much rebuilt after a hammering in World War II. However, its port infrastructure and ugly outskirts hide a picturesque **medieval centre** worth exploring – especially when it's taken over on summer Saturdays by a huge antiques and bric-a-brac market. The town's main claim to fame is as the *Città dei Papi*, City of Popes, after local boy Francesco Della Rovere who became **Pope Sixtus IV** in 1471 – and had a large private chapel built within the Vatican named the Sistine Chapel after himself – and his nephew Giuliano, who became **Pope Julius II** in 1503 – and commissioned Michelangelo to decorate the chapel's ceiling.

Savona lies at the southern end of a time-honoured route over the mountains, and the town's links with Turin are maintained to this day via the autostrada and main train line. The **train station** is in the west of town, across the River Letimbro from the old quarter, which nestles in the curve of the old port and bristles with medieval towers. Via Don Minzoni, to the left of the station as you walk out, heads east across the river to the parks of Piazza del Popolo, from where the main **Via Paleocapa**, lined with Art Nouveau arcades, continues east to the port. Savona's **tourist office** is at Corso Italia 157r (summer Mon–Sat 9.30am–1pm & 3–6.30pm, Sun 9.30am–12.30pm; winter Tues–Sat 9.30am–12.30pm & 3–6.30pm; ℡019.840.2321, Ⓦwww.inforiviera.it). The Dominican church of San Giovanni marks the point where Via Pia heads south into the atmospheric old quarter which is dominated by the **Duomo** and its attached **Cappella Sistina**, a Baroque extravaganza commissioned by Sixtus IV in memory of his parents.

Above the old town stands the huge **Priamàr** fortress, built in 1528 by the Genoese as a sign of their superiority over the defeated Savonese. These days it houses three major museums. The interesting **Museo d'Arte Sandro Pertini** (Sat & Sun 10am–noon), displaying modern Italian art collected by Pertini, one-time President of Italy, and the **Museo Renata Cúneo** (Mon–Sat 8.30am–12.30pm), housing contemporary sculpture by Cúneo, a Savona local, share a joint €2 admission ticket. Completing the array is the **Museo Storico-Archeologico** (winter Tues–Fri 9.30am–12.30pm & 3–5pm, Sat 10am–noon & 3–5pm, Sun 3–5pm; summer Tues–Sat 10am–noon & 5–7pm, Sun 5–7pm; €2, Ⓦwww.museoarcheosavona.it), which has Greek and Etruscan bits and bobs along with some Islamic and Byzantine ceramics. The **Pinacoteca Civica** at Palazzo Gavotti (Mon, Wed & Fri 8.30am–1pm, Tues & Thurs 2–7pm, Sat 8.30am–1pm & 3.30–6.30pm, Sun 9.30am–12.30pm; €4) houses mostly mediocre Baroque paintings, overshadowed by a striking Renaissance *Crucifixion* by Donato de Bardi.

There are no **hotels** in Savona's old town, but the decent *Riviera Suisse*, Via Paleocapa 24 (℡019.850.853, Ⓦwww.rivierasuissehotel.it; ❹), is very close by. The more convenient and enticing of Savona's two HI **hostels** is *Fortezza del Priamar* in the old fortress (℡019.812.653, Ⓔpriamarhostel @iol.it; €12; bus #2). The best **campsite** is *Buggi*, at Via N. S. del Monte 15 (℡019.804.573; April–Sept).

The Riviera di Levante

The glorious stretch of coast **east from Genoa**, dubbed the **Riviera di Levante**, is not the place to come for a relaxing beach holiday. Ports that once eked a living from fishing and coral diving have been transformed by thirty years of tourism – the coastline is still wild and extremely beautiful, but the sense of remoteness has gone. To experience the coast at its best, visit in spring or autumn, when the hordes have gone home, the coastal path has quietened and the scenery is at its spectacular best. Even in high season, though, there are quiet spots to be discovered.

Away from the resorts, the cliffs and bays are covered with pine and olive trees, best seen from the vantage points along the footpaths crisscrossing the headland of the **Monte di Portofino**. The harbour towns of **Camogli** on the **Golfo Paradiso** and **Santa Margherita Ligure** on the Golfo Tigullio are favourite subjects for arty picture postcards, while super-chic **Portofino** on the southern tip of the headland effortlessly pulls in the international jet set. Less exclusive nightlife is found at big, feisty resorts such as **Rapallo**. Further east, the main road heads inland, bypassing the spectacular **Cinque Terre** and joining the train line at the port of **La Spezia**, which stands at the head of the idyllic Golfo dei Poeti and gives access to romantic waterside villages such as **Portovénere**. From La Spezia, there's easy access by road or rail to Pisa or Parma, and by sea to Corsica.

Recco

Allied bombing in 1944 to cut the coastal rail line virtually destroyed **RECCO** – at the head of the gulf 18km east of Genoa – and the town that has sprung up in its place is unremarkable but for its gastronomy. People come here specifically to eat at some of the best **restaurants** in Liguria. If your wallet is fat, book a table at either *Da-ö Vittorió*, Via Roma 160 (☏0185.74.029, ⓦwww.daovittoria .it; ❷; closed Thurs), a renovated century-old building 500m north of the town centre, or the modern villa-style *Manuelina*, Via Roma 300 (☏0185.74.128, ⓦwww.manuelina.it; ❻; closed Wed), some 300m further north set in its own garden; both establishments are also hotels. They are acclaimed for their *focaccia al formaggio* (Recco's speciality), *minestrone alla genovese* and local *troffiette recchell-ine* (pasta with green beans, potatoes and pesto).

Camogli

CAMOGLI – 2km southeast of Recco – was the "saltiest, roughest, most piratical little place" according to Dickens when he visited the town. Though it still has the "smell of fish, and seaweed, and old rope" that the author relished, it's had its rough edges knocked off since his day, and is now one of the most attractive small resorts along this stretch of the coast, with a pretty collection of colourful cottages framing a small harbour and plenty of arts and crafts shops. As is common with many of the towns in this area, Camogli is built onto a steep hillside that ascends almost directly from the shore, and can be hard going on the legs.

The town's name, a contraction of *Casa Mogli* (House of Wives), comes from the days when voyages lasted for years and the women ran the port while the men were away. Though difficult to believe now, Camogli supported a huge fleet of 700 vessels in its day, which once saw off Napoleon. The town declined in the age of steam, but has been reborn in recent decades as a classy getaway without the exaggerated prices of further round the coast.

The **train station** is just inland and uphill of the beach; turn right towards the centre for the small **tourist office**, 50m north at Via XX Settembre 33 (Mon–Sat 9am–noon & 3–6pm, Sun 9am–12.30pm; ☏0185.771.066, ⓦwww .camogli.it). From here take the adjacent steps down to the seafront. Summer **boats** shuttle over from Genoa's Porto Antico several times a day, taking an hour (€8), using the old harbour on the north side of town, separated from the unimpressive pebble beach to the south by a promontory occupied by the medieval **Castello della Dragonara**.

Open or wrapped?

If you're visiting Camogli on the second Sunday in May, you won't be able to miss the **Sagra del Pesce**, preceded on the Saturday night by fireworks and a huge bonfire. This generous – and smelly – event has its origins in celebrating the munificence of the sea and retains its ancient resonance for Camogli's fisherfolk even today. Thousands of fish are plucked fresh from the waves, flipped into a giant frying-pan set up on the harbourfront and distributed free of charge to all and sundry as a demonstration of the sea's abundance (and in the hope for its continuation). In recent years the event has been beset by quibbles: bureaucrats have suggested that the frying-pan – some four metres across – is a health hazard, and there have even been allegations that frozen fish is defrosted out at sea and then passed off as fresh. For all that, local enthusiasm for the festival hasn't waned one bit.

The town's two best **hotels** neatly frame the town's vertical axis. On the seafront, the lavish *Cenobio dei Dogi*, Via Cúneo 34 (☎0185.7241, ⓦwww .cenobio.it; ❼), once the summer palace of Genoa's doges, has its own park, beach, pool, tennis courts and restaurants, while perched in woodland above the town in Ruta di Camogli, its sibling, the *Portofino Kulm* (☎0185.7241, ⓦwww .cenobio.it; ❼), has a refined secluded air, great views and provides easy access to the walks of the Portofino headland (see p.153). In the centre of Camogli, the *Hotel Casmona* (☎0185.770.015, ⓦwww.casmona.com; ❺) is housed in a seafront nineteenth-century villa and has light, airy rooms. Alternatively, try the good-value, family-run *Augusta,* Via Piero Schiaffino 100 (☎0185.770.592, ⓦwww.htlaugusta.com; ❹) with attractive air-conditioned rooms, all en suite. For **food**, the pricey *Vento Ariel* on the harbourfront (☎0185.771.080; closed Wed) serves fish directly from that day's nets (try the *insalate di mare* €13).

Fish aside, Camogli makes its living from **ferries** operated by Golfo Paradiso, Via Scalo 3 (☎0185.772.091, ⓦwww.golfoparadiso.it) from the little dock by the coastguard. Departures to tranquil **Punta Chiappa**, ideal for a spot of swimming and basking in the sun, and **San Fruttuoso** (see below), are most frequent (May–Sept at least hourly; Oct–April 3 weekdays, hourly at weekends; €6.50 to Punta Chiappa, €9 to San Fruttuoso), with a special **night excursion** offering the most romantic views of the gulf plus three hours in San Fruttuoso for dinner or a stroll (July & Aug 3 weekly; €9 return). There are also boats east to the **Cinque Terre** (July–Sept 2–4 weekly; €24 return), which stop en route at **Portofino** and continue to **Portovénere**, as well as plenty more west to **Recco** and **Genoa** (€10 return). You can also take **diving** trips and courses with the B&B Diving Center, just back from the harbour (☎0185.772.751, ⓦwww.bbdiving.it).

San Fruttuoso

The enchanting thousand-year-old abbey of **SAN FRUTTUOSO** is one of the principal draws along this stretch of the Riviera, occupying a picturesque little bay at the southern foot of Monte di Portofino. The only way to get there is **on foot** (see p.153) or **by boat**, dozens of which shuttle backwards and forwards from practically every harbour along the coast. On summer weekends, the tiny port and church may be uncomfortably crowded, but out of season (or at twilight, courtesy of the occasional night cruise), San Fruttuoso is a peaceful, excellent place for doing very little.

The **Abbazia di San Fruttuoso** (March, April & Oct Tues–Sun 10am–4pm; May & Sept daily 10am–6pm; Dec–Feb Sat & Sun 10am–4pm; €6) was originally built to house the relics of the third-century martyr St Fructuosus, which were brought here from Spain after the Moorish invasion in 711. It was rebuilt in 984 with an unusual Byzantine-style cupola and distinctive waterside arches and in later centuries it became a Benedictine abbey that exerted a sizeable degree of control over the surrounding countryside. The Doria family took over in the sixteenth century, adding the defensive **Torre dei Doria** nearby, and the small, elegant church, with its compact little cloister and half-dozen Doria tombs. Off the headland, a 1954 bronze statue known as the **Cristo degli Abissi** (Christ of the Depths) rests eight fathoms down on the sea bed, to honour the memory of divers who have lost their lives at sea and to protect those still working beneath the waves.

There are a handful of simple **restaurants** on San Fruttuoso's beach serving fish and steamed mussels, and one place **to stay** – the tiny and rather dingy *Da Giovanni* (☎0185.770.047; ❸).

Portofino and the Golfo del Tigullio

On the eastern side of Monte di Portofino headland stands the **Golfo del Tigullio**, a broad arc of a bay named after the local Tigullian tribe of pre-Roman antiquity. The gulf stretches 28km from the rocks and inlets around the millionaires' playground of **Portofino** and its friendlier neighbour **Santa Margherita Ligure** to head east along a dramatically beautiful – and densely touristed – coastline. In summer the main focus is the large resort of **Rapallo**.

The Consorzio Portofino Coast runs an **information** and hotel-booking service for the area, based at Via Lamarmora 17/6, Rapallo (☎0185.270.222, ⓦwww.portofinocoast.it).

Portofino

There's no denying the beauty of **PORTOFINO**, tucked into a protected inlet surrounded by lush cypress- and olive-clad slopes, yet it manages to be both attractive and off-putting at the same time. The village has been effortlessly drawing in Europe's jet set royals, film stars and other glitterati since the *dolce vita* days of Bogart and Bacall, Sophia Loren, Burton and Taylor, and Princess Grace, all of whom holidayed here – its snob rating remains impeccable.

The village lies at the end of a narrow and treacherously winding road 5km south from Santa Margherita, but thanks to continuous traffic the bus journey can take longer than the boats that shuttle regularly to and from all nearby ports. Once you've arrived, surveyed the expensive waterfront shops and restaurants and perhaps climbed up to Castello Brown, there's little to do other than watch the day's endless procession of tour groups do the same; bear in mind, though, that a couple of peaceful harbourside beers will leave you little change from €20.

To get a sense of Portofino's idyllic setting follow the footpath which heads south from the harbour up onto the headland. Five minutes from the village is the church of **San Giorgio**, said to contain relics of St George. A further ten minutes up is the spectacularly located **Castello Brown** (daily 10am–7pm; €3.50) from whose terrace there are breathtaking views of a pint-sized Portofino. The castle, which dates back to the Roman period and now frequently hosts art and photography exhibitions, is named after its former owner, British Consul Montague Yeats Brown, who bought it in 1867 and set about transforming it. In 1870 he planted two pines on the main terrace for his wedding; one for him and one for his wife, Agnes Bellingham. The sweeping pines are still a prominent feature today.

Boats on the Tigullio coast

Dozens of **boats** serve all points on the Tigullio coast, run by companies based in Genoa (see p.137), Camogli (see p.151) and La Spezia (see p.163), along with the main local operator, Servizio Marìttimo del Tigullio, Via Palestro 8/1b, Santa Margherita (☎0185.284.670, ⓦwww.traghettiportofino.it). You should **book ahead** to guarantee a place in high summer.

The most popular line shuttles to and fro between **Rapallo**, **Santa Margherita**, **Portofino** and **San Fruttuoso**, taking 15min between each (summer: hourly every day; winter: 2 on Sun). There are also lovely **night excursions** on the same route (July & Aug 2–8 weekly). The most you'll pay for a one-way fare is €.50. Boats also connect to the **Cinque Terre** (€15). Some continue to **Portovénere** and **Lérici** (€19). The best-value round-trip cruise ticket is the **Super Cinque Terre**, which gives stops of 1hr in Riomaggiore, 3hr for lunch in Monterosso and 1hr in Vernazza (June–Sept 2 weekly; €28.50).

Walks around Portofino

The Portofino headland – protected as the Parco Naturale Regionale di Portofino (wwww.parks.it) and encircled by cliffs and small coves – is one of the most rewarding areas for **walking** on the Riviera coast. At 612m, **Monte di Portofino** is high enough to be interesting but not so high as to demand any specialist hiking prowess. The trails cross slopes of wild thyme, pine and holm oak, enveloped in summer in the constant whirring of cicadas. From the summit, the view over successive headlands is breathtaking. Not many people walk these marked paths, maybe because their early stages are fairly steep – but they aren't particularly strenuous, levelling off later and with plenty of places to stop.

One of the best trails skirts the whole headland, beginning in Camogli, on the western side of the promontory. The path rises gently for 1km south to **San Rocco** (221m), then follows the coast south to a viewpoint above Punta Chiappa, before swinging east to the scenic **Passo del Bacio** (200m), rising to a ridge-top and then descending gently through the olive trees and palms to **San Fruttuoso** (3hr from Camogli). It continues east over a little headland and onto the wild and beautiful cliff-tops above **Punta Carega**, before passing through the hamlets of Prato, Olmi and Cappelletta and down steps to **Portofino** (4hr 30min from Camogli).

There are plenty of alternative routes. About 1km south of San Rocco, an easier path forks inland up to **Portofino Vetta** and **Pietre Strette** (452m), before leading down again through the foliage to San Fruttuoso (2hr 30min from Camogli). **Ruta** is a small village 250m up on the north side of Monte di Portofino, served by buses from Camogli, Santa Margherita and Rapallo; a peaceful, little-trod trail from Ruta heads up to the summit of the mountain (2hr), or diverts partway along to take you across country to Olmi and on to Portofino (2hr 30min from Ruta).

The scenic path continues south for a kilometre or so, down to the **Faro** (lighthouse) on the very tip of the promontory. The only way back is up the same path. Northwest from the village, steeply stepped paths head through vineyards and orchards to Olmi and on to San Fruttuoso. The best sandy **beach** is the sparkling cove at **Paraggi**, 3km north of Portofino on the corniche road (buses will stop on request) – not exactly remote, but less formal than Portofino, with a couple of bars set back from the water.

Practicalities

The **tourist office** is at Via Roma 35 (summer daily 10.30am–1.30pm & 2.30–7.30pm; winter Tues–Sun 10.30am–1.30pm & 2–4.30pm; ☎0185.269.024). **Accommodation** is absurdly expensive year-round. The *Eden* stands within its own delightful gardens in the centre at Vico Dritto 8 (☎0185.269.091, wwww .hoteledenportofino.com; ❼), but if money is no object, you'll want to shell out for a luxury room at the *Splendido*, Viale Baratta 16 (☎0185.269.551, wwww .hotelsplendido.com; ❾), with its fabulously lush grounds and stupendous views. Doubles are around €1000 a night, but this is generally regarded as one of Italy's best hotels, which is why it is regularly block booked by visiting sheikhs. **Eating out**, whether at the hotels or at the super-chic seafood restaurants, *Il Pitosforo* (☎0185.269.020) and *Chuflay Bar* (operated by the *Splendido*) on the harbour (☎0185.269.020; closed Mon & Tues), is best left to those who don't read their credit-card statements.

Santa Margherita Ligure

SANTA MARGHERITA LIGURE is a small, thoroughly attractive, palm-laden resort, tucked into an inlet and replete with grand hotels, garden villas and views of the glittering bay. In the daytime, trendy young Italians cruise the streets or whizz around the harbour on jetskis, while the rest of the family sunbathes or crams the *gelaterie*. Santa Margherita is far cheaper to stay in than Portofino and less crowded than Rapallo, and makes a good base both for taking boats and trains up and down the coast and for exploring the countryside on foot. The **train station** overlooks the harbour from the north; behind the waterfront Piazza Veneto 250m south is the **tourist office**, Via XXV Aprile 2b (Mon–Sat 9am–12.30pm & 3.30–6.30pm, Sun 9.30am–12.30pm; ☎0185.287.485).

The town is famous for its **watersports** – the European Dive-In Center, Via Canevaro 2 (☎0185.293.017, ⓦwww.europeandc.com), is one outfit offering waterskiing, sailing and diving; the tourist office has a list of others and there's a handful of places on the harbourfront offering **boats for rent**. **Walking** trails cross the Monte di Portofino headland: marked paths from Santa Margherita to Pietre Strette (1hr 30min) and Olmi (1hr 40min) link in with the trails outlined in the box on p.153. The best **beaches** are out of town, accessible by bus: south towards Portofino is Paraggi (see p.153), while to the north the road drops down to a patch of beach in the bay of **San Michele di Pagana**. In addition to its beach bars and crystal-clear water, a *Crucifixion* by Van Dyck in the church of San Michele may prove an added incentive for a visit.

Good mid-price **hotel** options include *Albergo Fasce* (☎0185.286.435, ⓦwww.hotelfasce.it; ❹), nicely located on a quiet side street, with a panoramic roof terrace. *Annabella*, Via Costasecca 10 (☎0185.286.531; ❷), has attractive rooms with shared bathrooms, and welcoming *Nuova Riviera*, Via Belvedere 10, off Piazza Mazzini (☎0185.287.403, ⓦwww.nuovariviera.com; ❸), is on a quiet residential street. For a splurge try the impressive, modern suite-style rooms at the seafront *Lido Palace*, Via Doria 3 (☎0185.285.821, ⓦwww.lidopalacehotel.com; ❻).

🍴 *Trattoria Baicin*, just back from the waterfront park at Via Algeria 5 (☎0185.286.763; closed Mon & Jan), is a very good (and very reasonably priced) family-run seafood **restaurant**, offering great Ligurian specialities, such as swordfish with tomato sauce and olives, and a three-course set menu for €18. Popular *Dal Baffo* at 56 Via Matteotti (☎0185.288.987) serves a great range of reasonably priced pizza, pasta and fish. Of the many seafront restaurants, one to aim for is *Da Alfredo*, Piazza Martiri 37 (☎0185.286.059; closed Tues), which does good pizzas. Head south behind the squat harbourfront *castello* to reach the old port, where you'll find a clutch of old-style fish restaurants, including *L'Ancora*, Via Maragliano 7 (closed Tues), an excellent-value, mid-priced place, and the waterfront *Dei Pescatori*, Via Bottaro 43 (☎0185.286.747). If you just fancy a snack, *Da Pezzi*, 29 Via Cavour, is a good *focacceria*, while opposite it the *bar-gelateria* can make up a big salad for €5.

Rapallo

RAPALLO is a highly developed resort town – three times bigger than Santa Margherita – with an expanse of glass-fronted restaurants and plush hotels crowding around a south-facing bay. In the early part of the twentieth century it was a backwater, and writers in particular came for the bay's extraordinary beauty, of which you now get an inkling only early in the morning or at dusk. Max Beerbohm lived in Rapallo for the second half of his life, and attracted a literary circle to the town; Ezra Pound wrote the first thirty of his *Cantos* here between 1925 and 1930, D.H. Lawrence stayed for a while and Hemingway also dropped by (but came away muttering that the sea was flat and boring). The resort's striking landmarks are the large **marina** and the **castle**, now converted into an exhibition space, stuck out at the end of a small causeway.

Unlike most of the Tigullio resorts, Rapallo does have an existence independent of its tourist trade, particularly around the **old town**, a grid of cobbled streets behind the stone Saline Gate: this is the commercial centre and venue for the Tuesday fish and vegetable market, while the busy Thursday market at Piazza Cile to the northwest of the centre beneath the train tracks is a good place to buy cheap clothing.

Practicalities

The **tourist office** is at Via Armanda Diaz 9 (Mon–Sun 9am–12.30pm & 3.30–7.30pm, Sun 9.30am–12.30pm; ℡0185.230.346), and can provide details of diving outfits in the town and places to rent boats. Rapallo's **hotels** are headed by the lavish *Excelsior Palace*, Via San Michele di Pagana 8 (℡0185.230.666, ⓦwww.thi.it; ➒). The polished *Riviera*, Lungomare Via Veneto 27 (℡0185.50.248, ⓦwww.hotelriviera.biz; ➐), overlooks the seafront and is where Hemingway wrote *Cat in the Rain*. Also overlooking the sea is *Hotel Miramare* (℡0185.230.261, ⓦwww.miramare-hotel.it; ➍), with spacious, spotless rooms. Cheaper is the welcoming *Stella*, Via Aurelia Ponente 6 (℡0185.50.367, ⓦwww.hotelstella-riviera.com; ➌), complete with roof terrace, though the busy main road outside can be noisy. Best bargain, if a little rough round the edges, is the *Bandoni*, in a fine old palazzo within sight and smell of the sea at Via Marsala 24 (℡0185.50.423, ℻0185.57.206; ➋). The Rapallo **campsite** is at Via San Lazzaro 4 (℡0185.262.018, ⓦwww.campingrapallo.it; June–Sept).

Many **restaurants** in Rapallo and along the Tigullio coast serve the local speciality *bagnun*, a dish based on anchovies, tomato, garlic, onion and white wine. You'll find good trattorias in the alleys behind the mediocre seafront restaurants: *Da Mario*, Piazza Garibaldi 23 (closed Wed), is moderately priced, with tables outside under medieval porticoes. *O Bansin*, Via Venezia 105 (closed Sun lunch), is an affordable old-town restaurant. *Nin Hao*, a pleasant Chinese place with its own garden at Piazza Molfino 4 (open daily), has good-value set menus. For just a drink or a snack, try the pub-like *Taverna Paradiso* down a side alley off Via Mazzini 73 (evenings only), the delightful *Il Castello* winebar at Lungomare Castello 6, with its waterfront terrace, or the *Gallo Nero* at Via Magenta 10. A couple of kilometres outside the town at Santa Maria del Campo 133, the 🕱 *Antica Cucina Genovese* (℡0185.206.009) serves some of the region's best vegetarian cuisine, and offers cookery classes.

Santuario di Montallegro

The best excursion from Rapallo is on the **cable car** (*funivia*; €8 return), which rises every thirty minutes from Via Castegneto, ten minutes' walk inland from Rapallo's castle, up to the **Santuario di Montallegro** (612m). The church was founded in 1557 when a Byzantine icon of the Madonna appeared miraculously in the hands of one Giovanni Chichizola, and it's in a superb setting overlooking a steep green valley, with views across the whole of the sparkling bay. A *festa* commemorating the miracle is held during the first three days of July, when the coffer of the Madonna is carried through Rapallo, and a fireworks contest culminates in the mock burning of the castle.

Alternative ways up to Montallegro include following a relatively easy footpath from Rapallo station (1hr). This continues to the summit of Monte Rosa above the church (another 30min), or diverts east across the hilltops and down to the quiet town of **Chiávari** (4hr 30min from Rapallo and also on the train line). Bus #92 runs from Rapallo station to Montallegro.

The Cinque Terre

The stupendous folded coastline of the **Cinque Terre** (Five Lands) stretches between the beach resort of Lévanto and the major port of La Spezia. The area is named for five tiny villages – **Monterosso**, **Vernazza**, **Corniglia**, **Manarola** and **Riomaggiore** – wedged into a series of coves between sheer cliffs; their comparative remoteness, and the dramatic nature of their position on a stunning coastline, make them the principal scenic highlight of the whole Riviera richly deserving of their recently acquired Unesco World Heritage status. They do inevitably get very crowded in summer and all the villages have lost some of their character to the tide of kitschy souvenir shops and overpriced, under-quality restaurants, but even in August you really shouldn't bypass the area – the scenery is breathtaking and there is some lovely walking between villages.

Principally fishing ports for centuries, in recent decades the five villages have diversified into **wine**. The Cinque Terre label is one of Liguria's better whites, but is less famous than the dessert wine Sciacchetrà, made from grapes which are left to dry on open-air racks until late autumn; they end up much sweeter than normal, like raisins, and in turn produce a full-bodied, heavily alcoholic and (because of the quantity of grapes that goes into it) expensive wine that you savour sip by sip, or dunk dry *biscotti* into after a meal.

Much of the area is now officially protected as the *Parco Nazionale delle Cinque Terre*, the website of which, Ⓦ www.cinqueterre.com, is especially

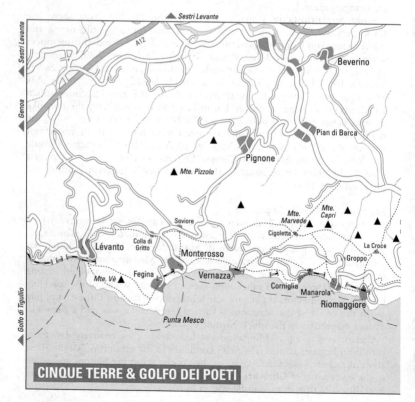

CINQUE TERRE & GOLFO DEI POETI

useful, as it operates a hotel booking service. You can also book **apartments and hotels** through Arbaspaa (☏0187.760.083, ⊛www.arbaspaa.com) based in Manarola.

The three principal ways to get to and around the villages of the Cinque Terre are trains, boats and on foot. If you're on a fast **train**, you'll zip through without seeing much more than a few tantalizing glimpses of turquoise water as the train speeds from one tunnel to the next. Regular slow trains, however, between Lévanto and La Spezia stop at every village. To make the most of your journey, you could think about investing in a **Cinque Terre Card**, which entitles the user to unlimited travel between all five villages and Lévanto, plus access to Path no. 2 of the national park (see p.158). It's available in one- (€5.40), three- (€12.40) or seven- (€19.50) day versions from the area's train stations and tourist information offices.

Boats from every company on the Riviera shuttle along this bit of coast all summer long. Make sure to confirm which of the four waterside villages you'll be stopping at (Corniglia has no harbour), and specify if you want a one-way ticket, rather than the more usual round-trip cruise tickets. Hopping between Cinque Terre villages by boat is easy, with between five and eight a day (April–Oct; sporadic service during winter months) going in both directions – although watch out for a lull between about noon and 2.30pm.

The most satisfactory way to get around is **on foot**: there's a network of trails (see box, p.158) linking the villages along the coast or up on the ridge-tops

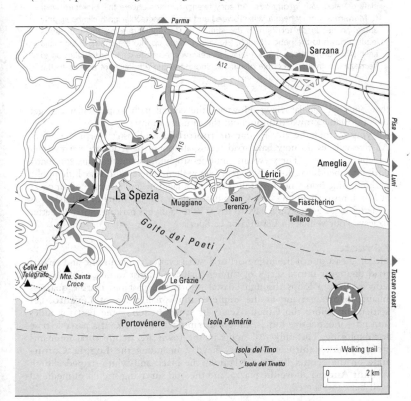

Walks in the Cinque Terre

There's plenty of excellent **walking** to be done in and around the Cinque Terre. However, if you're hoping to tackle the national park's most popular route, known as the Blue Route (Sentiero Azzurro), or Path no. 2, from Riomaggiore to Monterosso, you'll have to purchase a Cinque Terre Card for €3, either at the entrance to the path or at any local tourist office or train station (see p.157 for details of the card's travel options). The Red Route (Sentiero Rosso), or Path no. 1, is free. The tourist offices can also provide plenty of maps and information, and can advise on good itineraries. You should also note a couple of precautions before you set out. Most of the paths are unshaded, in summer temperatures can soar – wear a hat and carry a water bottle for even a short stroll – and walking shoes are advisable as paths are rocky and uneven at the best of times. Take note of weather forecasts in spring and autumn, as rainstorms can brew up rapidly and make paths treacherously slippery.

The 11km Blue Trail from Riomaggiore to Monterosso is signed either with blue waymarkers or as Path no. 2, and hugs the shoreline between all five villages, offering spectacular scenery the whole way along. Owing to the gradients, covering it from east to west (5hr) is considerably easier than from west to east; if you start early, walking west also means you'll have the sun behind you most of the way. Follow the red-and-white stripes painted on walls, trees and gates from **Riomaggiore** station to the start of the Blue Trail, a stretch called the **Via dell'Amore** (Lovers' Path), which winds above the waves past lemon trees in every backyard. In spring, before the sun has turned everything except the vines to dust, you'll walk beneath cliffs covered with wildflowers. An easy twenty minutes covers the kilometre west to **Manarola**, from where a less crowded and more spectacular path climbs slightly and then heads on for 3km to the station at **Corniglia**, passing rock-cut steps leading down to the pebbly beach. Steep steps lead up into the centre of Corniglia itself (1hr from Manarola). It's a fairly leisurely ninety-minute walk for the 4km on to **Vernazza**, with just a couple of difficult spots and the attraction of access to the

that offer spectacular views. However, the coastal path in particular can get uncomfortably crowded throughout the summer months.

Trying to tour the area by **car or motorbike** truly isn't worth the effort. All five villages do now have road access, although the roads are narrow and exceptionally steep. The views are in places stupendous, but there are too many corkscrew bends to allow you to truly enjoy them. There's also very little public parking, aside from one small toll area at Riomaggiore and a couple of car parks at Monterosso, including one on the beach. If staying at a hotel in Monterosso's pedestrianized zone, you'll have to pay €19 for a night's parking. You'd do better to leave your vehicle in Lévanto or La Spezia.

Lévanto

Heading east out of the big resort of Sestri Levante, the train line and coastal road disappear into a series of tunnels that last almost until La Spezia. The slow bus route loops through coastal resorts and past red marble quarries inland before arriving at the unpretentious small town of **Lévanto**, last settlement before the Cinque Terre. Its sandy **beach** – the best for miles around – inexpensive hotels and good transport links make it a passable base for exploring. The only real sights in the town are architectural remnants from Lévanto's thirteenth-century heyday, including the **Loggia Comunale** on the central Piazza del Popolo, the black-and-white striped church of **Sant'Andrea** above the piazza, and the odd surviving stretch of medieval wall here and there.

lovely beach at Guvano. Note that if you're attempting things in the other direction, the Vernazza–Corniglia walk is a tough-going 2hr-plus hike. The walk from Vernazza to **Monterosso** is the hardest westbound stretch, two hours to cover 3km, with first a steep climb up to 180m and then a sharp descent into Monterosso.

Other routes run perpendicular to the coastline, heading steeply up the slopes to give breathtaking coastal views, often passing old churches in the hills above each township. These routes link up with the long no. 1 Red Trail (Sentiero Rosso), that runs from Portovénere (east of Riomaggiore) along the ridge-tops to Lévanto, a full-day (9–10hr) hike covering some 23km. Nonetheless, it's easy to split things up manageably. As an example, trail no. 3 climbs from Riomaggiore past the Santuario di Montenero church up to the **Colle del Telegrafo** viewpoint (516m; 1hr 30min), from where trail no. 1 heads west, giving expansive views along the coast as far as Monterosso. Through the chestnut woods, some 3km west of Colle del Telegrafo, is **La Croce** (637m; 1hr), where no. 1 returns you steeply down to Riomaggiore (1hr). Another, even more scenic, option would be to follow trail no. 7 up from Vernazza – 3km through vineyards and past dry stone walls – to the church at San Bernardino, then Casa Fornacchi and the ridge-top at **Cigoletta** (612m; 1hr 30min). Cigoletta is another junction point on the Sentiero Rosso, from where a trail heads further up to the peak of **Monte Marvede** (667m; 45min) high above Corniglia, with panoramic vistas over the whole coast; the lovely trail no. 6 heads down from Marvede through more vineyards and patches of forest to Manarola (3.5km; 1hr 45min).

Another highly rewarding walk is trail no. 10, which leads from Monterosso station up through pine woods and onto a flight of steps that emerge at the San Antonio church on the high point of the **Punta Mesco** headland (1hr), giving a spectacular panorama along the length of the Cinque Terre coastline. The walk north along the tops from there to **Monte Vè o Focone**, and the descent on trail no. 14 into Lévanto, are both easy (total 3hr from Monterosso).

The **tourist office** is at the end of the main Via Roma at Piazza Mazzini 3 (Mon–Sat 9am–1pm & 3–6pm, Sun 9am–1pm; ☎0187.808.125), while the **train station** is ten minutes' walk inland from the seafront. Of the **hotels**, some of which insist on a minimum of two nights' stay and half board in high season, the finest is *Stella Maris*, Via Marconi 4 (☎0187.808.258, ⓦwww .hotelstellamaris.it; ❹), with a handful of characterful rooms in the nineteenth-century Palazzo Vannoni, plus some others in a more modern annexe on Piazza Staglieno. The *Europa*, Via Dante Alighieri 41 (☎0187.808.126, ⓕ0187.808.594; ❸), is another charmingly old-fashioned place with parking. The *Gentile*, a block back from the sea at Via Jacopo 27 (☎0187.808.551; ❷), is a popular cheaper option, with some private rooms. There's also a clean, modern and central **youth hostel** on Via San Nicolò (☎0187.802.562, ⓦwww .ospitaliadelmare.it; €16), with **Internet** access. The best of a handful of **camp-sites** is *Acqua Dolce*, Via Semenza 5 (☎&ⓕ0187.808.465, closed mid-Nov to mid-Dec & mid-Jan to Feb).

The town's best **restaurant** is the expensive *Araldo*, Via Jacopo 24 (closed Tues except in July & Aug), featuring fresh local ingredients beneath a vaulted, painted ceiling. Don't miss the specialities *gattafin*, deep-fried vegetable ravioli, and *cotolette di acciughe*, fried, stuffed anchovies.

Monterosso

Tucked into a bay on the east side of the jutting headland of Punta Mesco, **MONTEROSSO** is the chief village of the Cinque Terre. It's also the largest of the five – population 1800 – and most developed, with the modern beach resort of **Fegina** occupying the shore just west of the old village. Beaches, both free and toll, are broad and picturesque, separated from the narrow lanes of the old quarter by a hill, atop which is the seventeenth-century **Convento dei Cappuccini**. In the centre of the old village is the striped thirteenth-century church of **San Giovanni Battista**, while a more recent claim to fame is as the home town of the Nobel Prize-winning poet Eugenio Montale; his *Ossi di Seppia* (Cuttlefish Bones) is a collection of early poems about his youth in Monterosso.

Monterosso operates the Cinque Terre's main **tourist office**, in the station (summer 8am–10pm; winter 8am–8pm; ℡0187.817.059, ⓦwww .aptcinqueterre.sp.it), as well as a Pro Loco tourist association office at Via Fegina 38 (℡0187.817.506). Top **hotel** is the *Porto Roca*, Via Corone 1 (℡0187.817.502, ⓦwww.portoroca.it; March–Nov; ❽), which sits atop the rocks at the end of a narrow lane at the southern end of town. The public areas are decorated in rather dingy style with suits of armour and huge drab pictures, but the bedrooms come with sea views, terraces and sun loungers. *Villa Adriana*, Via IV Novembre 23 (℡0187.818.109, ⓦwww.villaadriana .info; ❺), has its own beach and even some car-parking space, while the *Amici*, at Via Buranco 36 (℡0187.817.544, ⓦwww.hotelamici.it; ❹), is tucked away from the hubbub and has a garden with views of the sea, as well as a good, characterful restaurant. Other **restaurant** highlights include *Ciak La Lampara*, off Via Roma, specializing in pricey but excellent local fish.

Vernazza

A few headlands east of Monterosso, **VERNAZZA**, loveliest of the five villages, throws a protective arm around the only natural harbour on this rocky coast. The narrow lanes with their tall, colourful houses are typical of the area, and the little cramped village is overlooked by stout medieval bastions and a watch-tower, built by the Genoese after they'd destroyed the previous castle in 1182 to punish the locals for piracy. Down beside the main piazza overlooking the sea is the Gothic church of **Santa Margherita di Antiochia**, with an elegant octagonal campanile.

There are two **hotels**: *Barbara*, Piazza Marconi 30 (℡ & ℻0187.812.398; ❸), has seven rooms – two with spectacular harbour views – on the top floor of an old building overlooking the main square, while the surly *Sorriso* is further up into the village at Via Gavino 4 (℡0187.812.224, ℻0187.821.198; ❸). A handful of places offer **rooms** – in summer – ask at the Monterosso tourist office in advance for details. Poor-value **restaurants** ring the main Piazza Marconi; the *Sorriso* hotel is better value and *Osteria Il Baretto*, Via Roma 31 (℡0187.812.381), may lack a sea view but has excellent *antipasti di mare* in recompense. Also on Via Roma is a sales outlet of the **Cooperativa Agricola Cinque Terre**, where you can sample the local wines.

Corniglia

CORNIGLIA is the smallest and remotest of the Cinque Terre villages, clinging to a high cliff 90m above the sea, its only access to the water (and the train station) via a long flight of steps. Floral-decorated squares fill the village, and the little Gothic church of **San Pietro** boasts an exquisite, marble rose window. There are no hotels, but plenty of places offering **rooms**, and a handful of unremarkable eateries. Oddly for a hilltop village, Corniglia stands out for its **beaches**. On the southern side of the village's rocky promontory is the **Spiaggone di Corniglia**, a narrow stretch of pebbles that has relatively easy access from the footpath towards Manarola. As with Monterosso, Corniglia's tourist office can be found in its train station (☎0187.812.523).

Manarola

MANAROLA is almost as enchanting as Vernazza, its pastel-shaded houses crowded impossibly up the sides of a prominent headland of dark rock. The fourteenth-century church of San Lorenzo in the village has another beautiful rose window. On the road from Manarola to Corniglia above the village is the hamlet of **Groppo**, home to the **Cooperativa Agricola Cinque Terre**, which offers tastings and direct sale of the local wines (Mon–Sat 10am–noon & 2–6pm; ☎0187.920.435).

Manarola's small **tourist office** is located in the train station and is only intermittently staffed (☎0187.760.511). The town has a handful of outstanding **accommodation** options. Family-run *Ca' d'Andrean*, Via Discovolo 101 (☎0187.920.040, ⓦwww.cadandrean.it; ❹), where breakfast is taken in the garden in summer, takes pride in its service and airy rooms (some with balcony). *Marina Piccola*, Via Birolli 120 (☎0187.920.103, ⓦwww.hotel marinapiccola.com; ❹; closed Nov to mid–Feb), has six elegant rooms, some with sea views. The small non-HI **hostel** *Ostello 5 Terre* is a clean, friendly place 300m up the hill from the station at Via Riccobaldi 21 (☎0187.920.215, ⓦwww.cinqueterre.net/ostello; €22); you may need to book several weeks ahead in summer. For **eating** options, try the restaurant of the *Marina Piccola* (see above), which offers a whole raft of reasonably priced fish dishes as well as outdoor seating, or join the locals just downhill at *La Scogliera* (☎0187.921.029; closed Sun), which serves some excellent Ligurian specialities – plenty of pesto and rabbit – and offers a pretty decent house wine; *primi* are around €7–9, *secondi* €10–13.

Riomaggiore

Lively **RIOMAGGIORE** is the easternmost of the Cinque Terre, with a relatively easy road link to the outside world that makes it also the most crowded of the five. Nonetheless, its vividly multicoloured houses piling up the steep slopes above the romantic little harbour, with no two on the same level, give the place a charm untempered by the café crowds, especially the higher you climb. Aside from the requisite rose window, the church of **San Giovanni Battista** houses a striking wooden *Crucifixion* by Maragliano. Riomaggiore is also the starting-point for the twenty-minute walk on the **Via dell'Amore** (Lovers' Path) to Manarola (see box, p.158).

As is common with several Cinque Terre towns, Riomaggiore's tourist office can be found in the train station (☎0187.760.091). The only **hotel** is the pleasantly modern *Villa Argentina*, in a lovely spot at Via De Gasperi 37 (☎ & ☎0187.920.213; ❹). Otherwise, your best bet is **private rooms**: English-speaking Roberto and Luciano Fazioli (Scalinata della Tagliata 6h; ☎0187.920.587; ❷) manage various properties in Riomaggiore and Manarola, from clean, simple rooms to self-catering apartments with terraced balconies overlooking the harbour. For **food**, *La Lanterna* (closed Tues in winter) has a good, moderately priced pasta and seafood menu, and a great location at the harbour (to get there, walk under the train line from the bottom of the main street). Otherwise, *Controvelaccio* (closed Sun) on Via Colombo has various inexpensive menus and delicious fresh anchovies, and *Ripa del Sole*, Via De Gasperi 4 (☎0187.920.143; closed Sun), serves acclaimed gourmet menus for €45.

△ Riomaggiore

The Golfo dei Poeti

After the beauty of the Golfo Paradiso and Golfo del Tigullio, and the drama of the Cinque Terre, Liguria still has a final flourish. Hard up against the Tuscan border is the majestic Golfo di La Spezia, an impressive sweeping panorama of islands and rough headlands renamed the **Golfo dei Poeti** in 1919 by Italian playwright Sam Benelli for the succession of romantic souls who fell in love with the place. Petrarch was the first; Shelley lived and died on these shores; Byron was another regular; and D.H. Lawrence passed the pre-World War I years here. The town at the head of the gulf is workaday **La Spezia**, a major naval and shipbuilding centre with a fine art gallery. Small resorts line the fringes of the bay, linked by buses that hug the twisting roads or boats that shuttle across the glittering blue water – **Portovénere**, sitting astride a spit of land to the southwest, and **Lérici**, on the southeastern shore, are both highly picturesque stopovers.

You enter through a twelfth-century towered **gate** built by the Genoese, who fortified this spot in opposition to Pisan forces that had taken Lérici across the bay. In the upper part of the village is the twelfth-century church of **San Lorenzo**, renowned for the remarkable treasures in its vestry, including four ivory caskets (three Syrian and one Byzantine) from about the year 1000. Higher up still is the sixteenth-century fortified **castello**, with panoramic views out over this most beautiful spot from its terraced gardens. Portovénere's characteristic rose- and yellow-painted tower-houses were aligned to form a defensive wall, now transformed into a trendy waterside strip known as the Palazzata, which continues to the end of the promontory and the church of **San Pietro**, built in the thirteenth century with a banded facade and an elegant campanile. The village got its name from the Latin *Portus Veneris*, or Port of Venus, and the church sits over the ruins of a Roman temple to the goddess of love. The views from the terrace in front of San Pietro out to the three islands and across to the Cinque Terre coast are magnificent. One of the rocky coves around the base of the church is the **Grotto Arpaia**, a favoured spot of Lord Byron; he swam across the bay from here to visit Shelley at San Terenzo (see below). To this day, the gulf has the nickname of the "Baia di Byron", but swimming is discouraged in favour of the **boats** that shuttle regularly to and from Lérici.

Boats from Portovénere also tour the three **islands** that lie south of the peninsula, all but the nearest of which lie in a military zone and so can only be viewed from the water. **Isola Palmária** is the largest, 500m south of Portovénere, with the Grotta Azzurra cave as its star attraction. Next is the **Isola del Tino**, a rocky islet marked with a lighthouse and the remains of a Romanesque abbey. Finally comes the even tinier **Isola del Tinetto**, also home to a monastic community in centuries gone by.

Practicalities

Portovénere's **tourist office**, at Piazza Bastreri 7 (Mon–Sat 9am–noon & 3–6pm, Sun 9am–noon; ☎0187.790.691, ⓦww.portovenere.it), has a list of the village's various bed and breakfast options and is located alongside the least expensive hotel, two-star *Genio* (☎ & ⓕ0187.790.611, ❹). Of the four upscale choices, the pick is the *Royal Sporting*, a short walk outside the village on the beach at Via dell'Olivo 345 (☎0187.790.326, ⓦwww.royalsporting.com; ❻). It has pleasant, cool interior courtyards, spectacular views and a huge saltwater swimming pool. In a different vein, *Locanda Lorena* offers half-a-dozen simple rooms that would be nothing special but for their remote location on the Isola Palmária, at Via Cavour 4 (☎0187.792.370; ❹; April–Sept).

There's a wealth of places to **eat** in town. The atmospheric, century-old *Antica Osteria del Carrugio* (closed Thurs) is at Via Capellini 66, in the shadow of the castle; its affordable specialities are anchovies, sheep's cheese and stuffed mussels (which are cultivated on poles in Portovénere's harbour). Down on the photogenic harbourfront, Calata Doria, are a handful of pricier places, including *La Taverna del Corsaro* (☎0187.900.622; closed Mon), famous for its version of Portovénere's *zuppa di datteri* (razor-clam soup), and the acclaimed *Iseo* (☎0187.790.610; closed Wed), in a prime waterfront location.

Lérici and around

East of La Spezia lie several kilometres of dockyards, foundries and thriving heavy industry, eventually brought to a stop at the boundary of a protected nature reserve which covers the southern half of the gulf shore.

First of the string of small resorts here is **SAN TERENZO**, marked by its prominent castle. There's a good sandy beach and a choice of accommodation, but, predictably, most of the **hotels** insist on full or half board in high season. The best deals are right on the seafront, at the *Nettuno*, Via Mantegazza 1 (☎0187.971.093, Ⓦwww.albergonettunolerici.it; ❸), and the *Trieste*, a few doors down at no. 13 (☎0187.970.610; ❶), alongside which is the **Villa Magni**, where Shelley spent some productive months in 1822, before setting off to meet Leigh Hunt at Livorno, "full of spirits and joy", according to Mary Shelley's account. On the way back, his boat, the *Ariel*, went down near Viareggio, and Shelley drowned, aged thirty. Long held plans to turn the house into a multimedia **Museo P. B. Shelley** are still on the drawing board.

About 2km south of San Terenzo lies **LÉRICI**, an upwardly mobile resort of garden villas, seafront bars, trattorias and gift shops. Piazza Garibaldi, behind the marina, acts as the bus station. The **tourist office** is on the seafront north of Piazza Garibaldi, at Via Biaggini 6 (Mon–Sat 9am–1pm & 2–8pm, Sun 10am–1pm; ☎0187.9601, Ⓦwww.aptcinqueterre.sp.it), and has details of the regular **boats** across to Portovénere (every hour). The circuitous route up to the Pisan-built castle from Piazza Garibaldi passes through **Via del Ghetto**, the old Jewish quarter once populated by Livornese merchants, and up the steep **Salita Arpara**, derived from a medieval word meaning "the place where hawks nest". At the top, the **castle** (Tues–Sun: July & Aug 10.30am–12.30pm & 6.30pm–midnight; Sept–June 10.30am–1pm & 2.30–5.30pm; €4.60) has fabulous views from the highest terrace right across to Portovénere and the three islands and back towards La Spezia. Inside, apart from a Gothic chapel, much of the interior is given over to a museum of geopaleontology, documenting prehistoric dinosaur life in the area.

Lérici's two most pleasant **hotels** are near the tourist office: the *Shelley & Delle Palme* is at Via Biaggini 5 (☎0187.968.204, Ⓦwww.hotelshelley.it; ❺) and the *Byron* at no. 19 (☎0187.965.699, Ⓦwww.byronhotel.com; ❹); both have suitably poetic sea views from balconied rooms. The sole inexpensive option is the unexceptional *Del Golfo*, inland at Via Gerini 37 (☎0187.967.400, Ⓦwww.hoteldelgolfo.com; ❷). When it comes to **eating**, the outdoor pizzerias that line Lérici's harbour provide an attractive setting as the sun goes down. Among many are the popular *Il Giogo*, Via Petriccioli 44 (closed Mon), where you can indulge in pizzas, seafood and home-made desserts; and the elegant *La Piccola Oasi*, Via Cavour 60 (closed Tues), which offers a simple set menu.

Travel details

Trains

Genoa to: Alassio (15 daily; 1hr 10min–1hr 25min); Albenga (16 daily; 1hr 10min–1hr 55min); Bologna (4 daily; 3–4hr); Camogli (every 20–30min; 30–50min); Finale Ligure (15 daily; 45min–1hr); Imperia (11 daily; 1hr 30min–2hr); La Spezia (hourly; 1hr 10min–2hr 10min); Milan (hourly; 2hr); Naples (every 2–3hr; 7–8hr); Pisa (14 daily; 2–3hr 30min); Rapallo (every 20min; 30min); Rome (every 1–2hr; 6hr); San Remo (hourly; 1hr 45min–2hr 40min); Santa Margherita (every 20min; 20min–1hr); Ventimiglia (every 30min; 2hr 55min).

Buses

Camogli to: Ruta (every 30min–1hr; 25min).
Chiávari to: Rezzoaglio (6 daily; 1hr 25min); Bologna (2 daily; 4hr).
Finale Ligure to: Borghetto Santo Spirito (every 15min; 25min).
Genoa to: Rovegno (5 daily; 1hr 50min); Torriglia (hourly; 1hr 10min).
La Spezia to: Lérici (every 10min; 20min); Portovénere (every 30min; 20min).
Rapallo to: Chiávari (hourly; 30min); Montallegro (every 2hr; 40min); Santa Margherita (every 20min; 10min).

San Remo to: Ventimiglia (every 15min; 20min).
Santa Margherita to: Portofino (every 15–20min; 15min).
Ventimiglia to: Dolceacqua (14 daily; 18min); La Mortola (9 daily; 15min).

Ferries

Genoa to: Bastia (1 weekly; 4hr 30min); Cágliari (2 weekly in summer; 20hr); Olbia (at least 7 weekly in summer; 9hr 30min); Palermo (4 weekly; 20hr); Porto Torres (7 weekly; 12hr).
La Spezia to: Porto Vecchio, Sardinia (one a week, summer only; 12 hr).
Santa Margherita to: Portofino (8 daily; 15min).

LIGURIA | Travel details

Lombardy and the lakes

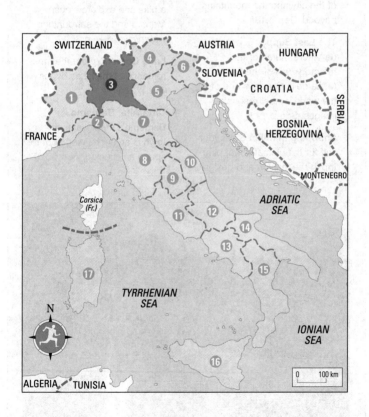

CHAPTER 3

Highlights

✳ **Ravioli alla zucca** Tuck into a plate of delicious pumpkin ravioli topped with sage butter. See p.174

✳ **Roof of Milan's Duomo** Wander around the roof of the world's largest Gothic cathedral with the best views of the city and the mountains beyond. See p.185

✳ **The Last Supper** Leonardo da Vinci's mural for the refectory wall of the Santa Maria delle Grazie is one of the world's most resonant images. See p.193

✳ **Shopping in Milan** Steel yourself for the ultimate shopping trip in the fashion and design capital of the world. See p.199

✳ **Certosa di Pavia** This Carthusian monastery is a fantastic construction rising out of the rice fields near Pavia. See p.205

✳ **Cycling round Mantua** Rent a bike and explore elegant Mantua and the surrounding waterways. See p.209

✳ **Lake Como** Explore the most romantic of the lakes by ferry. See p.226

✳ **Città Alta, Bergamo** Bergamo's medieval high town is an enchanting spot to spend an evening. See p.237

△ Cycling in Mantua

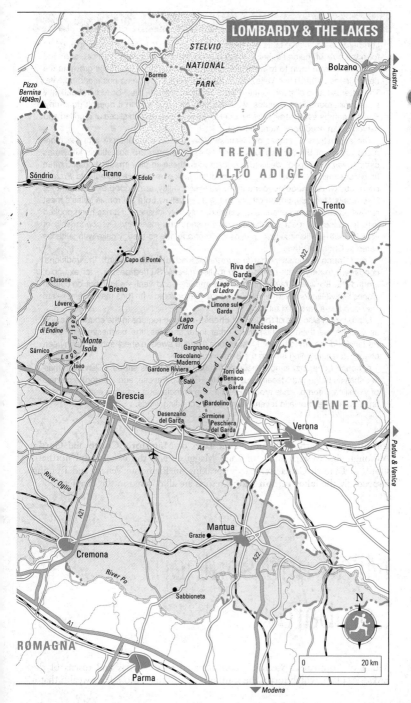

LOMBARDY & THE LAKES

STELVIO NATIONAL PARK

Bolzano

▶ Austria

Pizzo Bernina (4049m)

Bormio

Sóndrio   Tirano   Edolo

TRENTINO-
ALTO ADIGE

Trento

A22

Capo di Ponte

Clusone

Breno

Lóvere

Riva del Garda

Lago di Ledro   Torbole

Limone sul Garda

Lago d'Idro   Malcesine

Lago di Endine

Monte Isola

Sárnico

Lago d'Iseo

Iseo

Idro

Gargnano

Toscolano-Maderno

Gardone Riviera   Salò

Torri del Benaco

Garda

Bardolino

VENETO

Brescia

Desenzano del Garda   Sirmione

Peschiera del Garda

Verona

▶ Padua & Venice

A4   A22

River Oglio

Mantua

Grazie

A21

Cremona

River Po

Sabbioneta

N

ROMAGNA

0   20 km

Parma

▼ Modena

Regional food and wine

Lombardy is distinctive in its variations in culinary habits – **rice**, for example, might form the bulk of the diet in some areas but would rarely be eaten in others, and food varies even from town to town. The short-grain rice used for risottos is grown in the paddy fields of the Ticino Valley, and other staples include green pasta and polenta. The latter is found all over northern Italy: made from maize meal boiled and patiently stirred for around forty minutes, watched with an eagle eye so it doesn't go lumpy. Polenta can be eaten straightaway, or else left to cool and then sliced and grilled and served as an accompaniment to meat.

The sophisticated recipes of Milanese urbanites contrast sharply with the more rustic dishes of the Alpine foothills and lakes. The latter are sometimes known as *piatti poveri* (poor food): devised over centuries, these employ imagination and often time-consuming techniques to make up for the lack of expensive ingredients. *Pizzoccheri*, buckwheat **noodles** found in the Valtellina Valley, are a good example of this. *Risotto alla Milanese*, on the other hand, golden yellow from saffron, is Milan's most renowned culinary invention, and, it is said, only truly Milanese if it has been cooked with the juices of roast veal flavoured with sage and rosemary. *Ossobuco* (shin of veal) is another Milanese favourite, as is *Panettone*, the soft, eggy cake with sultanas eaten at Christmas time.

From Cremona comes *mostarda di frutta* (pickled fruit with mustard), the traditional condiment to serve with *bollito misto* (boiled meats). Stuffed pastas – for example, around the Po valley, ravioli filled with pumpkin – and veal – either hot or cold in dishes like *vitello tonnato* (thin slices of cold veal covered with tuna mayonnaise) – are also popular, as are wild fungi.

Lombardy is also one of the largest **cheese-making** regions in the country. As well as Gorgonzola there are numerous other local cheeses, the parmesan-like Grana Padano and the smooth, rich Mascarpone (used in sweet dishes) and the tangy soft cheese Taleggio being among the best known.

Although Lombardy is not renowned internationally for its **wines**, Milan supermarket shelves bulge with decent reds from the Oltrepò Pavese, and the northern areas of Valtellina, Inferno, while around Brescia, the Franciacorta area has earned more of an international profile in recent years for its sparkling wines.

and foreigners, particularly around the lakes of **Maggiore**, **Como** and **Garda**. Although the western shore of Lago Maggiore and the eastern and northern shores of Lago di Garda are, strictly speaking, in Piemonte, Veneto and Trentino respectively, the **lakes region** and its resorts are all covered in this chapter.

Milan and southern Lombardy

Much of Lombardy's wealth is concentrated in the cities and towns of the broad Po plain, which forms the southern belt of the region. It's a wealth that is obvious throughout the area in the well-preserved medieval towns and the industrial estates that surround them, not to mention in the well-pressed clothes and the new cars of its citizens.

Milan is an upbeat city, with layers of history epitomized by its spectacular cathedral, as well as world-famous designer stores and a lively night scene. It certainly needn't be as daunting as its reputation suggests; given time, and taken on its own contemporary terms, it is a stimulating place to be. **Pavia**, to the south, is a pretty medieval town that makes an attractive introduction to this part of Lombardy, its cobbled streets and ancient churches taking a firm back seat in terms of sights to its fabulous **Certosa**, just outside. In the east, **Cremona**, the birthplace of the violin and home of Stradivari, has a neat, well-preserved centre, but is not the kind of place that you'd want to stay long. **Mantua**, in the far eastern corner of the region, is Lombardy's most visually appealing city, although what you really come for are the remains of the powerful Gonzaga family, who ruled here for three hundred years from their extravagant ducal palace and later the Palazzo Te, on the outskirts of the city, which contains some of the finest (and most steamily erotic) fresco-painting of the entire Renaissance.

Milan

The dynamo behind the country's "economic miracle" in the Fifties, **MILAN** is an Italian city like no other. It's foggy in winter, muggy and mosquito-ridden in summer, and is closer in outlook, as well as distance, to London than to Palermo. This is no city of peeling *palazzi*, cobbled piazzas and *la dolce vita*, but one where consumerism and the work ethic rule the lives of its well-dressed citizens.

Because of this most people pass straight through, and if it's summer and you're keen for sun and sea this might well be the best thing you can do; the weather, in July and August especially, can be off-puttingly humid. But at any other time of year it's well worth giving Milan more of a chance. It's a historic city, with enough ancient churches and galleries to keep you busy for a week but there are also bars and cafés to relax in, and the contemporary aspects of the place represent the leading edge of Italy's fashion and design industry.

Arrival

Milan has two main **airports** – Malpensa and Linate – both of which are used by domestic and international traffic. It is also within easy reach of several smaller terminals: Bergamo-Orio al Serio (see p.235) is the best connected and the most convenient, while Brescia-Montichiari (see p.243) is a couple of hours' drive away.

Intercontinental **Malpensa** (☎02.7485.2200, ⓦ www.sea-aeroportimilano.it), 50km northwest of the city near Lago Maggiore, is connected by direct **bus** with the Stazione Centrale, Milan's main train station (every 20min 5.10am–11.30pm; 1hr; €5.50), and by a fast **train**, the Malpensa Express (every 30min 6.30am–1.30am; 40min; ☎02.8511.43382, ⓦ www.malpensaexpress.it; early morning and late evening services are replaced by a bus from Via Leopardi, just to the left of the station as you face it), with Milano Nord. Tickets cost €9 if bought beforehand, more if purchased on the train. Both the Stazione Centrale and Milano Nord are connected with the city's metro system. A **taxi** from Malpensa to the centre takes about forty minutes and costs around €80 when the traffic is not too heavy.

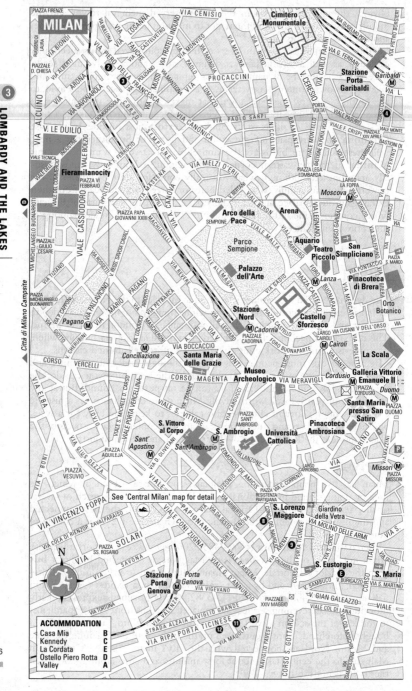

MILAN

PIAZZA FIRENZE

PIAZZALE
D. CHIESA

Città di Milano Campsite

Fieramilanocity

ACCOMMODATION

Casa Mia	B
Kennedy	C
La Cordata	E
Ostello Piero Rotta	D
Valley	A

See 'Central Milan' map for detail

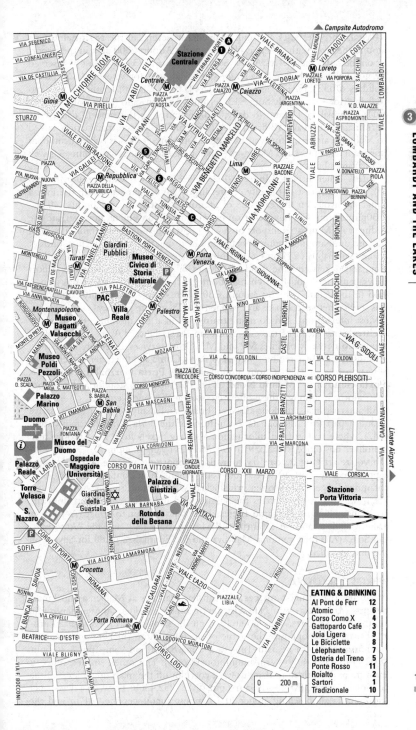

Campsite Autodromo ▲

Linate Airport ▲

EATING & DRINKING
Al Pont de Ferr	12
Atomic	6
Corso Como X	4
Gattopardo Café	3
Joia Ligera	9
Le Biciclette	8
Lelephante	7
Osteria del Treno	5
Ponte Rosso	11
Roialto	2
Sartori	1
Tradizionale	10

0   200 m

Regular private buses also link Malpensa to several of the **regional towns** around the lakes with tickets available from the Airport 2000 desk in the airport or on the buses themselves: Arona, Stresa and Verbania (5 daily; must be reserved by noon the day before travelling, 48hr in advance for weekends and public holidays ℡0323.552172, ⓦwww.safduemila.com; €10.50; Terminal 1); Como (6 daily Mon–Sat, 2 daily Sun; €13; Terminal 1); Menaggio (Mon–Sat 12.20pm; €11; Terminal 1); Lugano (8 daily; €20; Terminal 1); Bergamo (3 daily; €12; Terminal 2); and Pavia (2 daily; €14; Terminal 1). Gallarate train station, linked to Malpensa airport, 5km away by regular local bus services, is on the main train line from Milan to Lago Maggiore – including Arona, Stresa and Intra – as well as the Varese branch line.

Milan's other airport, **Linate** (℡02.7485.2200, ⓦwww.sea-aeroportimilano .it), is just 7km east of the city centre: airport buses connect it with the Piazza Luigi di Savoia, on the east side of Stazione Centrale (every 20min 5.40am– 9.30pm; 20min; €2; buy ticket on board). Just as convenient, however, are the ordinary ATM urban transport **buses** (#73), which run every ten minutes from 5.30am until around midnight between Linate and the city centre, just south of Piazza San Babila (€1) on Corso Europa. They take around the same length of time and tickets cost the standard €1 and should be bought from the airport newsagent, or, if you have change, from the ticket machine at the bus stop. A **taxi** to the centre will cost around €30. There's also a twice-daily connecting bus service between Linate and Malpensa, a 75-minute journey.

Most international and domestic **trains** pull in at the monumental **Stazione Centrale**, northeast of the city centre on Piazza Duca d'Aosta, at the hub of the metro network on lines M2 and M3. Other services, especially those from stations in the Milan region – Bergamo, Pavia, Como and the other western lakes – terminate at smaller stations around the city: **Porta Garibaldi**, **Lambrate**, **Porta Genova** and **Milano Nord**, all on M2 (the metro stop for Milano Nord is "Cadorna", although these often also stop at Stazione Centrale).

All international and long-distance **buses**, and many regional buses, arrive at and depart from the bus station in front of the Porta Garibaldi train station (M2), where you can get information and buy tickets from the Autostradale/ Eurolines bus office (℡02.3391.0794; Mon–Fri 9am–6.30pm).

If you're arriving by **car**, try to avoid the morning and evening rush hours (approximately 7.30–10am & 4.30–7pm) when Milan's outer ring road – the infamous Tangenziale, is often grid-locked. With copious signage, if not always clear, the ring road encircles the suburbs and industrial estates and links the main autostradas for Bergamo, Brescia, Lake Garda and on to Venice (A4), Varese, Lake Maggiore and on to Turin (A8), Lake Como (A9) and the "Autostrada del Sole" (A1) for Cremona, Mantova and the South. See p.180 for advice on parking in Milan.

Information

Milan has two **tourist offices**, plus smaller branches at Malpensa and Linate airports (daily 9am–4pm). The city centre office is hidden away underground on the edge of Piazza Duomo at 19/a, on the same side as the Galleria Vittorio Emanuele II, opposite the statue of the eponymous ruler trying to stay on his horse (Mon–Fri 8.45am–1pm & 2–6pm, Sat & Sun 9am–1pm & 2–6pm; ℡02.7740.4343, ⓦwww.milanoinfotourist.com). The other, smaller, office is even more difficult to find; it's down a corridor off the main upper level of the Stazione Centrale (Mon–Sat 9am–6pm; ℡02.7252.4360), between a newspaper kiosk and a shop selling amber (the signpost announces the "APT" and the neighbouring Telecom Italia office). The station office can phone ahead to make free hotel reservations for you.

For English-language **listings**, *Milano Mese*, a monthly booklet published by the tourist office, is good on exhibitions, while *Hello Milan* (Ⓦ www.hellomilano .it), available free in hotel lobbies and the city centre tourist office, gives comprehensive monthly rundowns of cultural events and is best for up-to-date opening hours of the major sights. The pullouts in *Corriere della Sera* on Wednesdays, and *La Repubblica* on Thursdays, are also valuable sources of listings – in Italian.

City transport

Milan's street-plan resembles a spider's web, with roads radiating out from the central Piazza Duomo. The city centre is, however, fairly compact, and most of what you'll want to see is within the first or second rings, each of them marking ancient city boundaries.

The streets can be smoggy, and at times you'll want to make use of the **public transport** system – an efficient network of trams, buses and metro. The **metro** is easy to master, and fast. It's made up of four lines, the red **M1**, green **M2**, yellow **M3** and blue *passante ferroviario*, that meet at the four main hubs of Stazione Centrale, Duomo, Cadorna and Loreto (see map below). It's also worth getting to grips with the well-organized **bus and tram system**. Bus stops display the route and direction, and as the tickets for all three forms of transport are integrated you can hop on and off at will. Buses, trams and the metro run from around 6am to midnight, after which **nightbuses** take over, following the metro routes until 1am. For all **public transport enquiries** (Ⓦ www.atm-mi.it) the information offices at the Duomo or Stazione Centrale metro stations are helpful, with invaluable route maps (€2) and English-speaking staff.

Tickets, valid for 75 minutes, cost €1 and can be used for one metro trip and as many bus and tram rides as you want. They are on sale at tobacconists, bars and at the metro station newsagents; most outlets close at 8pm so it's best to buy a few tickets in advance, or a *carnet* of ten for €8.70. Some stations have automatic ticket machines, although only the newer ones give change. You can also buy a one-day (€3) or two-day pass (€5.50) from the Stazione Centrale or Duomo metro stations. Remember to stamp your ticket when you enter the metro and board buses and trams, as inspections are common.

MILAN METRO

Taxis don't cruise the streets, so don't bother trying to flag one down. Either head for a taxi rank – on Piazza Duomo, Largo Cairoli, Piazza San Babila and Stazione Centrale, among others – or telephone (see p.202 for numbers).

Driving in the city is best avoided: the streets are congested and **parking** nigh on impossible. If you do drive, the useful SostaMilano scratch-card system is valid in parking spaces marked with blue paint: cards are available from bars and newspaper kiosks and you have to scratch off the date and time of arrival and display the card in your windscreen. Parking in prohibited zones is not worth it; you'll be fined if caught and have your car impounded by the police.

If you don't have much time you might want to try the hop-on, hop-off double-decker **bus tour** City Sighting Milano (Ⓦ www.milano.city-sightseeing .it), which has two different routes with a multilingual commentary, departing from Piazza Castello between 9.30am and 4pm; tickets cost €15 and are valid for 24hr. Alternatively Austostradale (Ⓦ www.autostradale.it; €50) and Zani Viaggi (Ⓦ www.zaniviaggi.it; €46) organize bus tours of the city with entrance fees to museums and *The Last Supper* (see p.193) included; the tourist offices will have the latest information about departure times.

Accommodation

Milan's **accommodation** is geared to the expense-account traveller: prices tend to be high and hotels are often anonymous as well as booked up for much of the year. If you want to be sure of a room, make your reservation in advance and get confirmation by fax or email.

The area around Stazione Centrale and across to Corso Buenos Aires is home to a good proportion of the city's cheaper hotels, and although many cater to the area's considerable red-light trade, you should be fine at any of the places below. As you go towards the centre, prices rise but there are still good deals to be had in some of the side streets off the city's main thoroughfares.

As many of the mid-range hotels are rather dingy you may want to look into **bed-and-breakfast** accommodation. The stylish, well-run rooms at 🏛 *Foresteria Monforte* (Ⓣ 340.237.0272, Ⓦ www.foresteriamonforte.it; ❹) are highly recommended, while *La Casa di Leonardo* is a central choice with an attractive sister option boasting a garden in *La Dolce Vita* (both Ⓣ 347.377.3044, Ⓦ www .ladolcevite.net; ❸); alternatively, if money is no object, head for the design-tastic *3 Rooms* at Corso Como 10 (Ⓣ 02.626.163, Ⓦ www.3rooms-10corsocomo.com; ❾) Look on Ⓦ www.bed-and-breakfast.it for further bed-and-breakfast establishments. The English-speaking outfit Rentxpress (Ⓣ 02.805.3151, Ⓦ www .rentxpress.com) has a selection of **apartments** to rent throughout the city – these can make an economical alternative for groups or families.

Hotels

Antica Locanda dei Mercanti Via San Tomaso 6 Ⓣ 02.805.4080, Ⓦ www.locanda.it. Tucked away between the Duomo and the castle, this quietly elegant *locanda* offers individually decorated rooms; four even have their own roof terraces. The *Alle Meraviglie* (Ⓦ www.allemeraviglie.it), next door at no.8, is run by the same people with similarly bright, tasteful rooms. M Cairoli. ❻

Antica Locanda Leonardo Corso Magenta 78 Ⓣ 02.463.327, Ⓦ www.leoloc.com. This charming little place is just steps away from *The Last Supper*

and has light and airy rooms overlooking a pretty internal garden. M Cadorna. ❻

Ariston Largo Carobbio 2 Ⓣ 02.7200.0914, Ⓦ www.brerahotels.com. This modern hotel prides itself on its ecological construction but the best thing about it is its position – within walking distance of the Duomo and the Navigli – and the free bicycles. Rooms are cramped but all en suite and there's a good breakfast included in the price. M Duomo, then tram #2, #3 or #14. ❼

Bulgari Via Fratelli Gabba 7b ☎02.058.051, ⓦwww.bulgarihotels.com. In a hidden corner of Brera, the city's top hotel has all the Milanese style you could wish for and none of the attitude you might expect. Staff are charming, facilities impeccable and the bar terrace and garden are an absolute treat. Rooms start at around €350 per night depending on special offers. M Montenapoleone. ❾

Casa Mia Viale Vittorio Veneto 30 ☎02.657.5249, ⓦwww.casamiahotel.it. A plain hotel with quiet en-suite rooms, just across from the Giardini Pubblici. All rooms have a/c and breakfast is included. M Repubblica. ❸

Cavour Via Fatebenefratelli 21 ☎02.620.001, ⓦwww.hotelcavour.it. A business-oriented hotel in a great position between the Giardini Pubblici and the Quadrilatero d'Oro. Service is well judged and the comfortable, soundproofed rooms are good value. M Montenapoleone or Turati. ❺

Kennedy Viale Tunisia 6, 6th floor ☎02.2940.0934, ⓦwww.kennedyhotel.it. A well-organized, friendly one-star with bright, simple rooms, some of which are en suite. Some rooms even have their own balconies overlooking the rooftops. M Repubblica or Pta Venezia. ❷

London Via Rovello 3 ☎02.720.166, ⓦwww.hotel-London-milan.com. A pleasant, family-run hotel in a good, central position. There's a choice of singles and doubles with or without en-suite shower; the decor is unexciting but all rooms have a/c. Closed Aug. M Cairoli. ❹

Mercure Milano Porta Venezia 1 ☎02.6610.1861, ⓦwww.mercure.com. One of the city's several branches of this French chain hotel with pleasing, comfortable rooms in a convenient location right on Porta Venezia. M Pta Venezia. ❻

Palazzo delle Stelline Corso Magenta 61 ☎02.481.8431, ⓦwww.palazzostelline.com. Pleasant business-like rooms are set around the attractive courtyard of a renovated seventeenth-century convent and offered at very good prices. The complex has an appealing garden where Leonardo da Vinci supposedly tended the vines while working on *The Last Supper*. M Cadorna. ❻

Rovello Via Rovello 18a ☎02.8646.4654, ⓦwww.hotel-rovello.it. Close to Castello Sforzesco, the pleasing rooms at this well-located hotel are spacious and air-conditioned. Prices may be negotiable in summer. Breakfast included. M Cairoli. ❻

Speronari Via Speronari 4 ☎02.8646.1125, ⓔhotelsperonari@inwind.it. Friendly little *pensione* overlooking Santa Maria presso San Satiro, a minute's walk from the Duomo. The clean, functional rooms are nothing to write home about; there are singles, doubles, triples and quads available – the majority en suite. M Duomo. ❸

Valley Via Soperga 19 ☎02.6698.7252 ⓦwww.hostelinmilan.it. Two minutes' walk north of the Stazione Centrale, this simple little spot is a good choice if you're catching an early train or arriving late at night. The airy, no-frills rooms are mainly en suite. M Centrale FS. ❸

Hostels and campsites

Autodromo Parco di Monza, Monza ☎039.387.771. A campsite in the huge royal hunting grounds just north of Milan, which also house the renowned Formula One circuit. Trains run from Stazione Centrale to Monza station, from where it's a short bus ride. Open from early May to the end of September only.

Città di Milano Via G. Airaghi 61 ☎02.4820.0134, ⓦwww.parcoacquatica.com. The nearest campsite to the centre, but still a metro trip and a bus ride away. M1 to De Angeli, then bus #72. Open all year.

La Cordata Via Burigozzo 11, off Corso Italia ☎02.5831.4675, ⓦwww.lacordata.it. Clean and basic in a very good central location, this is Milan's best hostel option by far. Bunks are in 6-, 10- or 16-bed dorms, each dorm with its own shower room. There's a large kitchen and communal room for residents' use. 12.30am curfew. €18 with sheets.

Ostello Piero Rotta Viale Salmoiraghi 1, on the corner of Via Martino Bassi ☎02.3926.7095. An institutional-feeling HI hostel out in an unsavoury corner northwest near the San Siro stadium. Open 7–9am and 3.30pm–1am. You can't book ahead, so it's best to arrive early, especially in summer. M1 to QT8, then a couple of hundred metres straight ahead and the hostel is on your right. €18.50 including breakfast.

The City

The obvious focal point of central Milan is Piazza Duomo, which, as well as being home to the city's iconic **Duomo**, leads on to the elegant **Galleria Vittorio Emanuele** and the Piazza della Scala, home to the world-famous **opera house**. Heading northwest along the shopping street of Via Dante takes

CENTRAL MILAN

0   200 m

you to the imperious **Castello Sforzesco** and the extensive **Parco Sempione** beyond. North, the well-heeled neighbourhoods of **Brera** and **Moscova** are the stomping ground of Milan's most style-conscious citizens. Here you'll find the fine art collection of the **Pinacoteca di Brera** and, nearby, the so-called **Quadrilatero d'Oro** (Golden Quadrangle), a concentration of top designer fashion boutiques. Slightly further north is Milan's most pleasant park, the **Giardini Pubblici**. Southwest of the Duomo, the shopping streets of Via Torino take you to the **Ticinese** district, a focal point at *aperitivo* time, and home to a couple of the city's most beautiful ancient churches. Continuing south on to the **Navigli** leads to the bar and restaurant area around the city's remaining canals. West of the cathedral stands the church of **Santa Maria delle Grazie** and the adjacent refectory building, holding Leonardo da Vinci's *The Last Supper*. The **Museo Archeologico** gives a taste of Roman Milan, while the basilica of Milan's Christian father, **Sant'Ambrogio**, is a couple of blocks away.

Piazza del Duomo and around

The hub of the city is **Piazza del Duomo**, a large, mostly pedestrianized square that's rarely quiet at any time of day, lorded over by the exaggerated spires of the **Duomo**, Milan's cathedral. The piazza was given its present form in 1860 when medieval buildings were demolished to allow grander, unobstructed views of the cathedral and the **Galleria Vittorio Emanuele II** was constructed to link the piazza with the showy new opera theatre, **La Scala**. South of the piazza there are several minor gems hidden among the shops and offices in the shape of the tiny church of **Santa Maria presso San Satiro** and the seventeenth-century **Pincacoteca Ambrosiana**.

The Duomo

The **Duomo** is the world's largest Gothic cathedral and the third-largest Roman Catholic church in the world – after St Peter's in Rome and Seville's cathedral. It was begun in 1386 under the Viscontis, but not completed until nearly five centuries later, when the finishing touches to the facade were added in 1813. Understandably, it is characterized by a hotchpotch of styles that range from Gothic to Neoclassical. From the **outside** at least, it's an incredible building, notable as much for its strange confection of Baroque and Gothic decoration, including 3500-odd statues, as its sheer size. The marble, chosen by the Viscontis in preference to the usual material of brick, was brought on specially built canals from the quarries of Candoglia, near Lake Maggiore, and continues to be used in renovation today.

The **interior** of the Duomo is striking for its dimension and atmosphere. The five aisles are separated by 52 towering piers, while a green, almost subterranean half-light filters through the stained-glass windows, lending the marble columns a bone-like hue that led the French writer Suarés to compare the interior to "the hollow of a colossal beast".

By the entrance, the narrow brass strip embedded in the pavement with the signs of the zodiac alongside is Europe's largest **sundial**, laid out in 1786. A beam of light still falls on it through the hole in the ceiling, though changes in the Earth's axis mean that it's no longer accurate. To the left of the entrance you'll find the archeological remains of a fourth-century **Battistero Paleocristiano** (daily 9.30am–5.15pm; €1.50), where the city's patron saint, Sant'Ambrogio, baptized St Augustine in 387 AD. Augustine had arrived in Milan three years earlier with his illegitimate son, and after sampling various religions, including paganism, was eventually converted to Christianity by Ambrose, then the city's bishop. The remains of the baptistery were discovered during excavations for a bomb shelter in the 1940s and also during work for the metro system in the 1950s, which revealed the foundations for the fourth-century basilica of Santa Tecla and some first-century Roman baths.

At the far end of the church, the large crucifix suspended high above the chancel contains the most important of the Duomo's holy relics – **a nail from Christ's cross**, which was also crafted into the bit for the bridle of Emperor Constantine's horse. The cross is lowered once a year, on September 14, the Feast of the Cross, by a device invented by Leonardo da Vinci. Close by, beneath the presbytery, is the **Scurolo di San Carlo** (daily 9.30am–1.30pm & 2–6pm), a crypt housing the remains of San Carlo Borromeo, the zealous sixteenth-century cardinal who was canonized for his unflinching work among the poor of the city, especially during the Plague of 1630. He lies here in a glass coffin, clothed, bejewelled, masked and gloved, wearing a gold crown attributed to Cellini. Borromeo was also responsible for the large altar in the north transept, erected in order to close off a door that was used by locals as a short cut to the market. Adjacent to Borromeo's resting place, the **treasury** (€1) features extravagant silverwork, Byzantine ivory carvings and heavily embroidered vestments. Here too is the Duomo's most surprising exhibit: a haunting video installation, the **Via Dolorosa**, by British artist Mark Wallinger. Commissioned by the diocese of Milan in a bold attempt to resurrect the role of the Church as a patron of the arts, it comprises a large screen showing the last eighteen minutes of Zeffirelli's *Jesus of Nazareth*, with ninety percent of the image blacked out leaving just a narrow frame visible round the sides.

△ Milan's Duomo

To the right of the chancel, by the door to the Palazzo Reale, the sixteenth-century statue of **St Bartholomew**, with his flayed skin thrown like a toga over his shoulder, is one of the church's more gruesome statues, its veins, muscles and bones sculpted with anatomical accuracy and the draped skin retaining the form of knee, foot, toes and toenails.

Outside again, from the northwest end of the cathedral you can get to the **cathedral roof** (daily: mid-Feb to mid-Nov 9am–5.20pm; mid-Nov to mid-Feb 9am–4.15pm; €4 to walk, €6 for the elevator), where you can stroll around the forest of tracery, pinnacles and statues while enjoying fine views of the city and on clear days even the Alps. The highlight is the central spire, its lacy marble crowned by a gilded statue of the Madonna – the *Madonnina*, the city's guardian – in summer looking out over the bodies of the roof top sunbathers.

Santa Maria presso San Satiro

The charming little church of **Santa Maria presso San Satiro** (daily 8–11am & 3.30–6.30pm), off the busy shopping street of Via Torino, is a study in ingenuity, commissioned from Milan's foremost Renaissance architect, Bramante, in 1478. Originally the oratory of the adjacent ninth-century church of San Satiro, it was transformed by Bramante into a long-naved basilica, by converting the long oblong oratory into the transept and adding a wonderful trompe l'oeil apse onto the back wall.

Pincoteca Ambrosiana

Five minutes west, just off Via Torino at Piazza Pio 2, the **Pinacoteca Ambrosiana** (Tues–Sun 10am–5.30pm; €7.50; Ⓦwww.ambrosiana.it) was founded by another member of the Borromeo family, Cardinal Federico Borromeo, in the early seventeenth century. In the face of Protestant reforms, the Cardinal was concerned enough to defend Catholic traditions not only through doctrine and liturgy, but also by educating the faithful about their Catholic origins. Thus he set about collecting ancient manuscripts, assembling one of the largest libraries in Europe (Mon–Fri 9.30am–5pm); the main draw though is his art collection, stamped with his taste for Jan Brueghel, sixteenth-century Venetians and some of the more kitsch followers of Leonardo. Among many mediocre works, there is a rare painting by Leonardo da Vinci, *Portrait of a Musician*, a cartoon by Raphael for the School of Athens, and a Caravaggio considered to be Italy's first ever still-life. The prize for the quirkiest exhibit is shared between a pair of white gloves that Napoleon reputedly wore when he met his Waterloo, and a lock of Lucrezia Borgia's hair – displayed for safe-keeping in a glass phial ever since Byron (having decided that her hair was the most beautiful he had ever seen) extracted a strand as a keepsake from the library downstairs, where it used to be kept unprotected.

Galleria Vittorio Emanuele II

Leading off to the north of Piazza Duomo is the gaudily opulent **Galleria Vittorio Emanuele II**, a cruciform glass-domed gallery designed in 1865 by Giuseppe Mengoni, who was killed when he fell from the roof a few days before the inaugural ceremony. The circular mosaic beneath the glass cupola is composed of the symbols that made up the cities of the newly unified Italy: Romulus and Remus for Rome, a fleur-de-lys for Florence, the white shield with a red cross for Milan and a bull for Turin – it's considered good luck to spin round three times on the bull's testicles, hence the indentation in the floor.

The *galleria* was designed as a covered walkway between the Piazza del Duomo and Piazza della Scala to the north, and, nicknamed the "*salotto*" – or

drawing room – of Milan, it used to be the focal point for the parading Milanese on their *passeggiata*. These days, visitors rather than locals are more likely
to swallow the extortionate prices at the gallery's cafés, which include the
historic *Zucca*, with its glorious 1920s tiled interior at one end, and the newer,
stylish *Gucci Café* – the label's first foray into catering – at the other. Shops, too,
are aimed at visitors to the city, with top designer labels sitting next to pricey
souvenir outlets. Somehow, however, the *galleria* still manages to retain most of
its original dignity, helped along by quietly elegant boutiques selling handmade
leather gloves or carefully turned hats, and the handsome eighty-year-old Prada
store in the centre.

Teatro alla Scala

The main branch of Galleria Vittorio Emanuele leads through to Piazza della
Scala fronted by the rather plain Neoclassical facade of the world-famous Teatro
alla Scala opera house, popularly know as **La Scala** (ⓦwww.teatroallascala
.org). The theatre was commissioned by Empress Maria Theresa of Austria from
the architect Piermarini and opened in 1778 with the opera *Europa Ricon-
sciuta* by Antonio Salieri. Many of the leading names in Italian opera had their
major works premiered here, including Bellini, Donizetti and Rossini, but it is
Giuseppe Verdi who is most closely associated with the opera house and whose
fame was consolidated here in 1842 with the first performance of *Nabucco* and its
perfectly timed patriotic sentiments. The post-World War II period saw another
breathtaking roll call of top composers and musical performers – among them
Schoenberg, Lucio Berio, Rudolf Nureyev and Maria Callas – while Toscanini,
perhaps the most influential conductor of all time, devoted more than fifty years
to the theatre. These days, however, La Scala is a bit at sea: no quality Italian
composers have emerged for over eighty years, the theatre is plagued by internal
political problems and the repertoire has become a touch predictable.

The opera house is still to a great extent the social and cultural centre of
Milan's elite and although protests in the 1960s led to a more open official
policy on the arts in Milan, unusually for opera-going in Italy it remains as
exclusive a venue as it ever was. Every year on the opening night – December 7,
the festival of Milan's patron saint, Sant'Ambrogio – when fur coats and dinner
jackets are out in force, it is the target for demonstrations from political and
social groups, ranging from animal rights' campaigners to local factory workers
complaining about redundancies. **Tickets** can be hard to come by, but if you
want to experience one of the world's most famous opera houses in action,
there are numerous avenues; see p.198 for ticket information.

Tucked in one corner of the theatre, a small **museum** (Tues–Sun 9am–noon
1.30–5pm; €5), features costumes, sets, composers' death masks, plaster casts of
conductors' hands, and a rugged statue of Puccini in a capacious overcoat. A
visit to the auditorium is included in the ticket, providing there is no rehearsal
taking place; times when the auditorium is empty are listed daily outside the
entrance to the museum.

The Castello Sforzesco and around

Northwest out of Piazza Duomo, at the start of Via Dante, lies **Piazza dei
Mercanti**, the commercial centre of medieval Milan. The square is dominated
by the thirteenth-century **Palazzo della Ragione**, where council meetings
and tribunals were held on the first floor and markets under the porticoes
below. The stone relief on the facade above the arcade shows the rather forlorn-
looking Oldrado di Tressano, the mayor who commissioned the building in
1228, astride his horse. Opposite, the striped black and white marble **Loggia**

degli Orsi, built in 1316, was where council proclamations were made and sentences announced. The coats of arms of the various districts of Milan are just about visible beneath the grime left by Milanese smog.

At the far end of the pedestrianized Via Dante, Castello Sforzesco rises imperiously from Foro Buonaparte, a road laid out by Napoleon in self-tribute. He had a vision of a grand new centre for the Italian capital, designed along Roman lines, but he only got as far as constructing an arena, a triumphal arch and these two semicircular roads before he lost Milan to the Austrians. The arena and triumphal arch still stand half forgotten behind the castle on the edges of the **Parco Sempione**, the city centre's largest patch of green and once the castle's garden and hunting grounds.

Castello Sforzesco

The red-brick castle, **Castello Sforzesco** (Ⓦ www.milanocastello.it), the result of numerous rebuildings, is, with its crenellated towers and fortified walls, one of Milan's most striking landmarks. Begun by the Viscontis, it was destroyed by mobs rebelling against their regime in 1447, and rebuilt by their successors, the Sforzas. Under Lodovico Sforza the court became one of the most powerful, luxurious and cultured of the Renaissance, renowned for its ostentatious wealth and court artists like Leonardo and Bramante. Lodovico's days of glory came to an end when Milan was invaded by the French in 1499, and from then until the end of the nineteenth century the castle was used as a barracks by successive occupying armies. Just over a century ago it was converted into a series of museums.

The *castello*'s buildings are grouped around three courtyards: through the **Filarete Tower** (rebuilt in 1905, having been destroyed in the sixteenth century by an explosion of gunpowder) you enter the larger of the three, the dusty-looking parade ground. It's not until you're through the gateway opposite that you begin to sense a Renaissance castle: this is the Corte Ducale, which formed the centre of the residential quarters and is now the home of the castle's museums. **The Rocchetta**, to your left, was the most secure part of the fortress and is now used for temporary exhibitions. The gateway ahead leads to the Parco Sempione.

The ticket office (Tues–Sun 9am–5.30pm; combined ticket €3), on your right as you enter the Corte Ducale, gives access to the **Museo d'Arte Antica** (Museum of Ancient Art), a succession of rooms containing an extensive collection of artefacts, saved from the city's churches and archeological excavations. More interesting than these, though, are the castle rooms themselves, especially the **Sala delle Asse**, designed by Leonardo da Vinci; his black-and-white preparatory sketches were discovered in the 1950s during the elegant reorganization of the museums by the architecture studio BBPR. After some rather dull armoury you reach the museum's star exhibit: Michelangelo's **Rondanini Pietà**, which the artist worked on for the last nine years of his life. It's an unfinished but oddly powerful work; much of the marble is unpolished and a third arm, indicating a change of position for Christ's body, hangs limply from a block of stone to his right.

Upstairs, the **Museo delle Arti Decorative** (Museum of Decorative Arts) exhibits furniture and decorative arts through the ages, including fascinating early works by the great twentieth-century Milanese designer, Gio Ponte. The Torre Falconiere (the Falconry Tower) next door holds the castle's **art collection** containing numerous paintings by Lombard artists, such as Foppa and Bramantino, as well as minor Venetian works, including some Canalettos. The best are all grouped together in Room XIII and include Antonello da Messina's *Saint Benedict*, originally part of a five-piece polyptych, of which two panels are in the Uffizi in Florence.

Across the courtyard, in the castle cellars, are two smaller collections: the **Egyptian collection,** with displays of mummies, sarcophagi and papyrus fragments from *The Book of the Dead*, while the deftly lit **prehistoric collection** consists of an assortment of finds from the Iron Age burial grounds of the Golasecca civilization, south of Lake Maggiore.

Parco Sempione

The **Parco Sempione** can make a refreshing break from the city's traffic-choked roads, but it does have its sleazy side and you might feel more comfortable visiting when the locals do – at the weekend, or early evening in summer. That said, there are several sights within the park itself, the most interesting of which is the Palazzo dell'Arte or **Triennnale** (Tues–Sun 10.30am–8.30pm; temporary exhibitions €8; ⓦwww.triennale.it), on the western reaches, at Viale Emilio Alemagna 6. The soaring lines of the building and its light airy interior are reason enough for a visit, but the Palazzo also holds good-quality temporary exhibitions of design, architecture and contemporary art, and there's a great café-bar, *Coffee Design* (see p.196), which overflows into the park as *Fiat Café* in the summer.

You might want to catch a bird's eye view of the city from the nearby **Torre Branca** (Wed 10.30am–12.30pm & 4–6.30pm, Sat 10.30am–1pm, 3–6.30pm & 8.30pm–midnight, Sun 10.30am–2pm & 2.30–7pm; €3), designed by Gio Ponte on the occasion of the fifth Triennale in 1933, or visit the newly reopened **Aquario Civico** (Tues–Sun 9am–1pm & 2–5.30pm; €3; ⓦwww.acquariocivico.mi.it), a pretty Liberty building with a small collection of tanks that will keep children entertained for a spell.

Next door is another monument to Napoleon's imperial aspirations in the **Arena Civica**, a Colosseum-inspired area where mock chariot races and naval battles were held. These days it's used for sports events and the odd lighter-waving, pop concert.

Brera and Moscova

Due north of Via Manzoni, **Via Brera** sets the tone for the city's arty quarter: small galleries and art shops nestle in the lanes surrounding the Accademia di Belle Arti and Milan's world famous art gallery, the **Pinacoteca Brera**. There's nothing resembling an artist's garret here, however: these cobbled streets are the terrain of the rich, reflected in the café prices and designer styles of those who can afford to sit outside them.

Across Via Fatebenefratelli, the stylish bars and traditional trattorias continue north through the neighbourhood of **Moscova**, renowned as the haunt of journalists – the offices of the *Corriere della Sera* are located here. A good area for shopping and browsing, Corso Garibaldi, Via Solferino and Via San Marco lead up to the bastion in Piazza XXV Aprile, which marks the beginning of **Corso Como**, a trendy street full of bars, clubs and chic shops, which in turn leads up to the train and bus station of Porto Garibaldi.

Pinacoteca di Brera

The Brera district gives its name to Milan's most prestigious art gallery, the **Pinacoteca di Brera**, at Via Brera 28 (Tues–Sun 8.30am–7.15pm; €5; ⓦwww.brera.beniculturali.it), originally opened to the public by Napoleon in 1809, who filled the building with works looted from the churches and aristocratic collections of French-occupied Italy. It's a fine gallery, Milan's best by far, but it's also rather large, and so your visit will probably be more enjoyable if you're selective, dipping into the collection guided by your own personal tastes. There's a good **audio guide** available (€3.50), although it does rather gallop through the highlights.

Not surprisingly, most of the museum's paintings are Italian and predate the twentieth century. The Brera does display some later work, including paintings by Modigliani, De Chirico and Carrà (Room X), but it's the Renaissance which comprises the museum's core. There's a good representation of Venetian painters – works by Bonifacio and, a century later, Paolo **Veronese**, the latter weighing in with *Supper in the House of Simon* (Room IX). The painting got him into trouble with the Inquisition, who considered the introduction of frolicking animals and unruly kids unsuitable subject matter for a religious painting. **Tintoretto's** *Pietà* (Room IX) was more in tune with requirements of the time, a scene of intense concentration and grief over Christ's body, painted in the 1560s. **Gentile Bellini's** *St Mark Preaching in St Euphemia Square* (Room VIII) introduces an exotic note: the square bustles with turbaned men, veiled women, camels and even a giraffe. There are also paintings by Gentile's follower, Carpaccio, namely *The Presentation of the Virgin* and *The Disputation of St Stephen* (Room VI), while the *Pietà* (Room VI) by Gentile's more talented brother, **Giovanni**, has been deemed "one of the most moving paintings in the history of art". Look out also for *The Dead Christ* (Room VI), a painting by Giovanni Bellini's brother-in-law, **Mantegna**: it's an ingenious composition – Christ, lying on a wooden slab, viewed from the wrinkled and pierced soles of his feet upwards. One of Mantegna's sons had died around the time he was working on this painting and it seems that the desolation in the women's faces and the powerful sense of bereavement emanating from the work were autobiographical.

Later rooms hold yet more quality work, of which **Piero della Francesca's** haunting *Madonna with Angels, Saints and Federigo da Montefeltro* (Room XXIV) is the most arresting. But take a look too at **Raphael's** *Marriage of the Virgin* (Room XXIV), whose lucid, languid Renaissance mood is in sharp contrast to the grim realism of **Caravaggio's** *Supper at Emmaus* (Room XXIX), which is set in a dark tavern. Less well known but equally lifelike are the paintings of Lombardy's brilliant eighteenth-century realist, Ceruti – known as **Il Pitochetto** (The Little Beggar) for his unfashionable sympathy with the poor, who stare out with reproachful dignity from his canvases (Room XXXVI). As his main champion, Roberto Longhi, said, his figures are "dangerously larger than life", not easily transformed into "gay drawing room ornaments", a description that could just as easily apply to the Canalettos and Crespis on the surrounding walls. **Francesco Hayez's** Romantic-era *The Kiss* (Room XXXVII) is one of the most reproduced of the gallery's paintings, but the artist's fine portrait of the writer Alessandro Manzoni, in the same room, is far less saccharine. The collection ends with the unfinished *Fuimaria* (Room XXXVII) by Giuseppe **Pelizza da Volpedo**, a composition revealing the artist's socialist ideals and an emerging consciousness of people-power – a theme that he returned to for *The Fourth Estate* (see p.190), adopted as an emblem of the power of the populace.

Quadrilatero d'Oro

The Roman thoroughfare **Via Manzoni** leads north from La Scala to Porta Nuova, one of the medieval entrances to the city forming one side of the **Quadrilatero d'Oro**. Comprising of a few hundred square metres bordered by Via Montenapoleone, Via Sant'Andrea, Via Spiga and Via Manzoni – the quarter is home to the shops of all the big international and Italian fashion names, along with design studios and contemporary art galleries. This is Milan in its element and the area is well worth a wander if only to see the city's better-heeled residents in their favourite habitat. For more on shopping in Milan, see p.199.

Museo Bagatti Valsecchi

In a house linking Via Santo Spirito with Via Gesù 5, just off Via Montenapoleone, is the **Museo Bagatti Valsecchi** (Tues–Sun 1–5.45pm; €6, Wed €3; ⓦ www.museobagattivalsecchi.org). Built by the Bagatti Valsecchi brothers in the nineteenth century in homage to Renaissance style it served as a home for their family and their collections. All the rooms are richly decorated with carved fireplaces, painted ceilings and heavy wall-hangings and paintings. The fireplace in the drawing room perfectly illustrates the brothers' eclectic approach to decoration: the main surround is sixteenth-century Venetian, the frescoes in the middle are from Cremona, while the whole ensemble is topped off with the Bagatti Valsecchi coat of arms. Modern conveniences were incorporated into the house but not allowed to ruin the harmony, so the shower in the bathroom is disguised in a niche, and the piano, which was not realised as an instrument until the eighteenth century, is incorporated within a cabinet. Among the miscellany of paintings, ceramics, armoury, ironwork and musical instruments are touching domestic items, such as the nursery furniture for Giuseppe's children.

Museo Poldi Pezzoli

Halfway between La Scala and Porta Nuova, the eclectic **Museo Poldi Pezzoli** at Via Manzoni 12 (Tues–Sun 10am–6pm; €7; ⓦ www.museopoldipezzoli.it) comprises pieces assembled by the nineteenth-century collector Gian Giacomo Poldi Pezzoli. Much of this is made up of rather dull rooms of clocks, watches, cutlery and jewellery, but the Salone Dorato upstairs contains a number of intriguing paintings, including a portrait of a portly San Nicola da Tolentino by Piero della Francesca, part of an altarpiece on which he worked intermittently for fifteen years. St Nicholas looks across at two works by Botticelli; one a gentle *Madonna del Libro*, among the many variations of the Madonna and Child theme which he produced at the end of the fifteenth century, and the other a mesmerizing *Deposition*, painted towards the end of his life in response to the monk Savonarola's crusade against his earlier, more humanistic canvases. Also in the room is the museum's best-known portrait, *Portrait of a Young Woman* by Pollaiuolo, whose anatomical studies are evidenced in the subtle suggestion of bone structure beneath the skin of this ideal Renaissance woman.

The Giardini Pubblici

At the top of Piazza Cavour, on the northern side of Porta Nuova, lie the **Giardini Pubblici**, Milan's most attractive park. Designed by Piermarini shortly after he completed La Scala, the gardens stretch from Piazza Cavour over to Porta Venezia. Re-landscaped in the nineteenth century to give it a more rustic look and to incorporate a now-defunct zoo, the park, with its shady avenues, children's play areas and small lake, is ideal for a break from the busy streets.

Across the road from the park, housed in the **Villa Reale**, or Villa Belgiojoso as it's also called after its architect, is the Museo dell'Ottocento, Via Palestro 16 (Tues–Sun 9.20am–1pm & 2–5.30pm; €3). Napoleon's former in-town residence has been refurbished recently to hold a rather lukewarm collection of Neoclassic and Romantic Italian art and sculpture, the only highlight being the huge canvas *Il Quarto Stato* by Giuseppe Pellizza da Volpedo, a member of the self-styled romantic *scapigliati* (wild-haired) movement of the late nineteenth century. Next door, the **Padiglione d'Arte Contemporanea** (PAC; Tues–Sun 9.30am–7pm, Thurs until 9pm; ⓦ www.comune.milano.it/pac; free) is a venue for decent, temporary exhibitions of contemporary art. Behind the art galleries, the **Giardini della Villa Reale** offer an urban oasis reserved for those with children under 13. With a small area of swings, lawns, shady trees and a little pond with ducks, turtles and giant carp, it makes a perfect bolthole.

The Ticinese district

Leading southwest away from the Duomo, past the chain stores of Via Torino, the city takes on a different, slightly more alternative air. The main thoroughfare of the Ticinese district, the Corso Porta Ticinese, has become a focus for fashion and is lined with small boutiques and bars. The area really comes into its own at *aperitivo* time, especially during summer when people spill on to the pedestrian streets from the numerous bars and cafés.

Towards the northern end of Corso Ticinese stands **San Lorenzo alle Colonne**, considered by Leonardo da Vinci to be the most beautiful church in Milan. It is indeed a graceful building with a quiet dignity, somewhat at odds with the skateboarding and partying that goes on in the piazza outside. One of the four churches founded by Sant'Ambrogio in the city in the fourth century, it was built with masonry salvaged from various Roman buildings, including the sixteen Corinthian columns outside – **the Colonne di San Lorenzo** – which were placed here as a portico to the church. To the right of the altar, the **Cappella di San Aquilino** (daily 7.30am–6pm; €2) was probably built as an imperial mausoleum. The lunettes in the Roman octagonal room hold beautiful fourth-century mosaics, which would originally have covered all the walls, while beneath the relics of Saint Aquilino steps lead down to what is left of the original foundations, a jigsaw of fragments of Roman architecture.

Heading south down Corso Ticinese, you come to **Sant'Eustorgio**, another fourth-century church, built to house the bones of the Magi, said to have been brought here by Sant'Ambrogio. It was rebuilt in the eleventh century, and in the twelfth century was virtually destroyed by Barbarossa, who seized the Magi's bones and deposited them in Cologne Cathedral. Some of the bones were returned in 1903 and are kept in a Roman sarcophagus tucked away in the right transept. The simple Romanesque body of the church and the medieval and Renaissance private chapels jostling for position on the right of the church are only half the story. A must-see while here is the **Portinari Chapel**, accessed round to the left of the main entrance (Tues–Sun 10am–6.30pm; €6). The beautiful chapel consciously recalls Brunelleschi's San Lorenzo in Florence, with two domed rooms, the smaller one housing the altar. It has been credited with being Milan's first real Renaissance building because of its simple geometric design and the mixture of Lombard terracotta sculpture and Florentine monochromatic simplicity makes an enchanting stylistic fusion of styles. It was commissioned from the Florentine architect Michelozzi in the 1460s by one Pigello Portinari, an agent of the Medici bank, to house the remains of St Peter the Martyr. One of Catholicism's less attractive saints, Peter, was excommunicated for allegedly entertaining women in his cell, then cleared of the charge and given a job as an Inquisitor. His death was particularly nasty – he was axed in the head by a member of the Cathar sect that he was persecuting near Lake Como – but the martyrdom led to almost immediate canonization and the dubious honour of being deemed Patron of Inquisitors.

The Navigli

The southern end of Corso di Porta Ticinese is guarded by the nineteenth-century **Arco di Porta Ticinese**, marking the beginning of Milan's canal – or **Navigli** – neighbourhood, once a bustling industrial area and these days a focus for the city's nightlife. Much lauded by tourist brochures, the area is scruffy and often disappointing in the harsh light of day. The best time to visit is in

Milan's canals

Comparisons with Amsterdam and Venice seem improbable these days, but less than fifty years ago Milan was still a viable port and less than one hundred years ago several of its main arteries – including Via Senato and Via San Marco – were busy waterways.

It was only logical for Milan's powers to want to harness the surrounding rivers for both trade and military purposes. In the twelfth century, the first **canals** linked irrigation channels and the various defensive moats of the city. Later, in 1386, the Naviglio Grande was opened, linking the city to the Ticino River and thus Lake Maggiore and Switzerland. It was Gian Galeazzo Visconti, however, who was really responsible for the development of the system in the fourteenth century. Looking for a way to transport the building materials for the Duomo, especially marble from Lake Maggiore, he invited proposals for solving the various logistical problems involved: Leonardo da Vinci is said to have had a hand in the invention of a system of locks developed to compensate for the different water levels of the canals.

Travellers were also seen on the canals: the ruling families of the North used them to visit one another, Prospero and Miranda escaped along the Navigli in *The Tempest*, and they were still plied by the Grand Tourists in the eighteenth century; Goethe, for example, describes the hazards of journeying by canal.

A number of rivers and canals were added to the system over the centuries; the Spanish developed the Darsena to the south in 1603 and under Napoleon's regime the Naviglio Pavese was made navigable all the way to Pavia and down to the Po, and so to the sea. During the Industrial Revolution, raw materials like coal, iron and silk were brought into the city, and hand-made products transported out with an efficiency that ensured Milan's commercial and economic dominance of the region. The process of covering over the canals began in the 1930s to make way for the city's trams and trolley buses. In the 1950s, desperately needed materials were floated in for reconstructing the badly bombed city but by the mid-1970s, only a handful of canals were left uncovered; the last working boat plied the waters in 1977.

The best way to explore Milan's waterways is on a relaxing **boat trip,** which run between April and mid-September when the canals are not being dredged or cleaned; for more information ask at the tourist office or check Ⓦwww.naviglilombardi.it. Alternatively, grab some mosquito repellent, don a pair of walking shoes or rent a bike (see p.201) and head off down the towpaths into the paddy fields of Lombardy.

the evening when the quarter's many restaurants and bars come alive, although the monthly Sunday street **antiques market** (closed July & Aug) also brings a vivacious focus to the waterways.

South from the Darsena (currently being remodelled), the **Naviglio Grande** and the **Naviglio Pavese**, respectively the first and last of the city's canals to be completed, lead into the plains of Lombardy. This was Milan with its sleeves rolled up, the working city at its grittiest. Some of the warehouses and traditional tenement blocks, or *case ringhere*, have been refurbished and become prime real estate but you'll still find plenty of unreconstructed corners. Craftsmen and artists have moved in and although the overpriced craft and antique shops won't hold your attention for long, a wander round the streets, popping into open courtyards, will give you a feel of the neighbourhood. Take a look at the prettified Vicolo dei Lavandai, or Washerwomen's Alleyway, near the beginning of the Naviglio Grande, where washerwomen scrubbed smalls in the murky canal waters.

Five minutes' walk west from the Naviglio Grande is **Porta Genova**, the train station for Milan's southern outskirts. It is also the name given to one of

Milan's up-and-coming areas. Across the tracks from the railway station, bars and restaurants have moved in and disused warehouses and factories are being reclaimed by photographers, fashion houses and designers. Giorgio Armani has an exhibition space and workshops here, as does Prada.

Santa Maria delle Grazie and around

Due west from the Duomo, on Corso Magenta, stands the attraction that brings most visitors to town – the beautiful terracotta-and-brick church of **Santa Maria delle Grazie**, famous for its mural of **The Last Supper** by Leonardo da Vinci. Originally built as a Gothic church by the architect, Solari, it was part of the Dominican monastery that headed the Inquisition in the fifteenth and sixteenth centuries. Soon after its completion however, Lodovico Sforza commissioned Bramante to rework and model the Gothic structure into a grand dynastic mauseoleum. Bramante promptly tore down the existing chancel and replaced it with a massive dome supported by an airy Renaissance cube. Lodovico also intended to replace the nave and facade, but was unable to do so before Milan fell to the French, leaving an odd combination of styles – Gothic vaults, decorated in powdery blues, reds and ochre, illuminated by the light that floods through the windows of Bramante's dome. A side door leads into Bramante's cool and tranquil cloisters, from which there's a good view of the sixteen-sided drum the architect placed around his dome.

The Last Supper

Leonardo's *The Last Supper* – signposted **Cenacolo Vinciano** – is one of the world's great paintings and most resonant images. However, getting to see art of this magnitude doesn't come easy: **visits must be booked** in advance, at least a month or more in summer and at weekends (English-speaking reservations line Mon–Fri 9am–6pm, Sat 9am–2pm; ☎02.8942.1146, ⓦwww.cenacolovinciano .it; viewing Tues–Sun 8am–7.30pm; €6.50, plus €1.50 obligatory booking fee). If it's fully booked when you ring, try asking about cancellations: people don't always turn up for the early morning viewings so it might be worth chancing your luck and going to the desk. At your allotted hour, once you've passed through a series of air-filtering systems, your fifteen-minute slot face-to-face with the masterpiece begins.

Henry James likened the painting to an "illustrious invalid" that people visited with "leave-taking sighs and almost death-bed or tip-toe precautions"; certainly it's hard, when you visit the fragile painting, not to feel that it's the last time you'll see it. A twenty-year restoration process has re-established the original colours using contemporary descriptions and copies, but that the work survived at all is something of a miracle. Leonardo's decision to use oil paint rather than the more usual faster-drying – and longer-lasting – fresco technique with watercolours led to the painting disintegrating within five years of its comple-tion. A couple of centuries later Napoleonic troops billeted here used the wall for target practice. And, in 1943, an Allied bomb destroyed the building, amaz-ingly leaving only *The Last Supper*'s wall standing.

A Last Supper was a conventional theme for refectory walls, but Leonardo's decision to capture the moment when Christ announces that one of his disciples will betray him imbues the work with an unprecedented sense of drama. Leonardo spent two years on the mural, wandering the streets of Milan searching for and sketching models. When the monks complained that the face of Judas was still unfinished, Leonardo replied that he had been searching for over a year among the city's criminals for a sufficiently evil visage, and that if he didn't find one he would use the face of the prior. Whether or not Judas is modelled on the prior is unrecorded, but Leonardo's Judas does seem, as Vasari wrote, "the very embodiment of treachery and inhumanity".

Goethe commented on how very Italian the painting was in that so much is conveyed through the expressions of the characters' hands; the group of Matthew, Thaddaeus and Simon on the far right of the mural could be discussing a football match or the latest government scandal in any bar in Italy today. The only disciple not gesticulating or protesting in some way is the recoiling Judas who has one hand clenched while a bread roll has just dropped dramatically out of the other. Christ is calmly reaching out to share his bread with him while his other hand falls open in a gesture of sacrifice.

If you feel you need any confirmation of the emotional tenor or accomplishment of the painting, take a look at the contemporary *Crucifixion* by Montorfano on the wall at other end of the refectory, not a bad fresco in itself, but destined always to pale in comparison with da Vinci's masterpiece.

Museo Archeologico and Roman remains

The **Museo Archeologico**, in the ex-Monastero Maggiore along the road at Corso Magenta 15 (Tues–Sun 9am–5.30pm; €2, free from 4.30pm daily & after 2pm on Fri), is worth a quick visit for a glimpse of the city's Roman heritage. The displays of glass phials, kitchen utensils and jewellery from Roman Milan are compelling, and though there's a scarcity of larger objects, you can see a colossal stone head of Jove, found near the castle, a carved torso of Hercules, and a smattering of mosaic pavements unearthed around the city. Perhaps the most interesting sight, though, is the 24-sided tower in the internal courtyard of the museum that was part of the Roman wall of the city.

One block east from the museum, Via Brisa runs south alongside the ruins of the imperial palace of the Roman emperor Maximian, unearthed after World War II bombing. South of here towards Via Torino, the medieval plan of the streets belies the Roman origins of the neighbourhood, where remnants of ancient mosaics and masonry are incorporated into the current buildings. The city's main street, the *decumanus maximus*, ran through here and there was a bath complex, as well as the huge arena – a corner of which is preserved in the quiet **Parco dell'Anfiteatro Romano** at Via Amicis 17 (Tues–Sat 9.30am–4.30pm, until 7pm in winter; free).

Sant'Ambrogio

A few minutes' walk southwest from Corso Magenta, the church of **Sant'Ambrogio** (Mon–Sat 7am–noon & 3–7pm, Sun 7am–1pm & 3.30–8pm) was founded in the fourth century by Milan's patron saint, St Ambrose, as he's known in English. Even today it's an important name in the city: the Milanese refer to themselves as Ambrosiani, have named a chain of banks after him, and celebrate his feast day, **December 7**, with the opening of the Scala season and a big street market around the church. The saint's remains still lie in the church's crypt, but there's nothing left of the original church in which his most famous convert, St Augustine, first heard him preach.

The present twelfth-century church, the blueprint for many of Lombardy's Romanesque basilicas, is, however, one of the city's loveliest, reached through a colonnaded quadrangle with column capitals carved with rearing horses, contorted dragons and an assortment of bizarre predators. Inside, to the left of the nave, a freestanding Byzantine pillar is topped with a "magic" bronze serpent, flicked into a loop and symbolizing Aaron's rod – an ancient tradition held that on the Day of Judgement it would crawl back to the Valley of Jesophat. Look, too, at the pulpit, a superb piece of Romanesque carving decorated with reliefs of wild animals and the occasional human, most of whom are intent on devouring one another. There are older relics further down the nave, notably the ciborium, reliefed with the figures of saints Gervasius and Protasius – martyred Roman soldiers whose clothed bodies flank that of St Ambrose in the crypt. A nineteenth-century autopsy revealed that they had been killed by having their throats cut. Similar investigations into St Ambrose's remains restored the reputation of the anonymous fifth-century artist responsible for the mosaic portrait of the saint in the Cappella di San Vittorio in Ciel d'Oro (to the right of the sacristy). Until then it had been assumed that Ambrose owed his crooked face to a slip of the artist's hand, but the examination of his skull revealed an abnormally deep-set tooth, suggesting that his face would indeed have been slightly deformed.

Outside (entrance to the left of the choir) is Bramante's unfinished **Cortile della Canonica**. The side that Bramante did complete, a novel concoction incorporating knobbly "tree trunk" columns and a triumphal arch, was shattered by a bomb in the last war and reconstructed from the fragments; the second side was added only in 1955. The adjacent Benedictine monastery that the Sforza family commissioned Bramante to restructure has housed the **Università Cattolica** since the 1920s.

Eating

There are **restaurants** and **cafés** in Milan to suit every pocket and a wider choice of cuisine than you'll find anywhere else in the country, apart from Rome. Whether you're looking for a neighbourhood trattoria, want to watch models pick at their salads or crave a bit of well-priced ethnic food, Milan has it all – usually within easy reach of wherever you're staying. If you don't fancy a sit-down meal, make the most of the Milanese custom of **aperitivo** (see below) to curb your hunger.

Lunch and snacks

There are **street markets** every day, except Sunday, scattered throughout the city, selling all the cheese, salami and fruit you need for a picnic lunch; a complete list is given daily in the *Corriere della Sera* under "Mercati". Alternatively, the *mercato communale* in Piazza Wagner sells similar fresh produce but under one, large colourful roof. Some of the handiest **supermarkets** are Standa at Via Torino 37, near the Duomo, Esselunga at Viale Piave 38, near Porta Venezia, and the over-priced Centro Commerciale in the Stazione Centrale (daily 5.30am–midnight).

Un aperitivo

An Italian custom that has been honed to a fine art in Milan is the **aperitivo**, or pre-dinner drink usually taken between 6 and 9pm. As well as another opportunity to preen and pose, *aperitivo*-time – or "happy hour" as it is also called – is a boon for budget travellers: counters are often laden with hot and cold food, all of which is included in the price of your drink (somewhere between €3 and €10, depending on the establishment). Take a plate and help yourself, although if you're really planning to fill up, it'll go down better if you go back several times rather than piling your plate high. If you choose your venue wisely you won't need to spend another penny on food all night. The food in most *aperitivo* bars winds up as the evening goes on: the lights dim and the volume of the music increases and you can settle in for the night. For reviews of the city's best *aperitivo* bars see p.198.

Café Design La Triennale, Viale Alemagne 6 ℡02.875.441. The chairs are all design classics in this spacious café with windows overlooking Parco Sempione. The good lunchtime menu (noon–2.30pm) features light dishes such as a trio of smoked fish or quiche and salad; Sunday brunch is a relaxed, civilized affair that you'll need to book for. In good weather, head outside to the *Fiat Café* to sip an *aperitivo* lounging around the sculptures by the likes of De Chirico and Toyo Ito. Closed Mon.

🏃 Da Claudio Via Ponte Vetrero 16. Mouth-wateringly fresh sashimi and shellfish served at the central bar amid the bustle of this traditional fishmongers on the edge of Brera. Lunch (noon–2.30pm) and *aperitivo*-time only (5–9pm). Closed Sun & Mon.

Luini Via S. Radegonda 16. A city institution that's been serving *panzerotti* (deep-fried mini *calzone*) round the corner from the Duomo for over 150 years. Grab a bench in nearby Piazza San Fedele if you want to eat sitting down. Closed Sun.

Palazzo Stelline Corso Magenta 61. This sunny bar terrace overlooking the garden of the convent where Leonardo stayed while painting the *Last Supper* is a relaxing spot for a salad or toasted *panino* (daily 9am–10pm). For something more filling, head down to the cellar to the self-service restaurant *buonappetito!*, with its tempting array of hot and cold dishes. Mon–Fri noon–2.15pm.

Vecchia Latteria Via dell'Unione 6. Delicious vegetarian dishes are prepared by the owners in this tiny neighbourhood café just off Via Torino. Closed Sun.

Cafés & gelaterie

Caffè Miani Piazza Duomo 21. Opened with the *Galleria* in 1867, *Caffè Miani*, also known as *Zucca in Galleria* and *Camparino*, was where David Campari invented Milan's famous sticky red drink. These days it's both expensive and touristy, but the price of a coffee standing at the tiled bar is easier to swallow. Closed Wed.

Chocolat Via Boccaccio 9. A small, modern bar, with comfy sofas, offering thirty different chocolate-flavoured ice creams plus some refreshing fruit ones, too; there's hot chocolate to die for in winter. Closed Sun morning.

Cova Via Montenapoleone 8. Fin-de-siècle surroundings set the scene for this elegant tearoom

dating from the Napoleonic era. Discreet service and starched linen accompany the mouthwatering chocolate delicacies, although naturally they don't come cheap.

🏃 Grom Via Santa Margherita 16. Practically opposite *La Scala,* the central branch of this specialist ice-cream chain serves up traditional flavours using top-quality organic ingredients.

Sartori Piazza Luigi di Savoia. Legendary kiosk up against one side of the Stazione Centrale (by the airport buses), serving some of the city's best ice cream, including avocado and lychee flavours. Closed Thurs.

Restaurants

Predictably, the **centre** of Milan has numerous pricey, expense-account establishments, but usually, just round the corner, there is somewhere more atmospheric or better value. To the south of the centre, the area around the **Ticinese** and **Navigli** is full of restaurants and cafés but although pleasant it's mainly a tourist preserve beyond Saturday and Sunday evenings. We've also included a couple of bargain places around the budget hotels near **Porta Venezia**.

🏃 Al Pont de Ferr Ripa di Porta Ticenese 55. An intimate restaurant right by the canal that offers an unusual take on local classics – try the delicious pumpkin risotto with pistachio. There's also an excellent cheese selection to complement the impressive wine list. Closed Aug.

Anema e Cozze Via Palermo 15 ℡02.8646.1646. Crisp, tasty Neapolitan-style pizzas are the main draw at this cheerful spot, although the fish dishes are popular too. Second branch at Alzaia Naviglio Grande 70.

Joia Ligera Corso di Porta Ticenese 106 ℡02.8940.4134. The new lighter version of the foodie haven (original branch Via P. Castaldi 18, ℡02.2952.2124 also recommended) serving highly imaginative combinations of vegetables and fish. The lunchtime menu is the best value otherwise – around €40 per person. Closed Sat lunch, Sun & Aug.

L'Osteria del Treno Via San Gregorio 46–48 ℡02.670.0479. The welcome couldn't be friendlier at this elegantly converted railworkers' canteen. Many diners opt for the delicious house platters of cold meats or cheese (€12), although the pasta dishes are recommended, too. Closed all day Sat & Sun evening.

La Latteria Via San Marco 24 ☎02.659.7653. This cosy trattoria is a favourite with the designer folk of the area. Delicious home-made pastas and roast meats are served up by the owner; reckon on around €15 for a main course. Closed Sat, Sun & Aug.

Oskar Via Palazzi 4. A popular restaurant with plenty of local atmosphere, serving fantastic-value pasta dishes in huge portions. Don't be put off by the voluble owners or the Mussolini memorabilia in the corners. Closed Sun.

Ponte Rosso Ripa di Porta Ticenese 23 ☎02.837.3132. One of the best spots in the canal area for a tasty, relaxed meal of local flavours. Good-value dishes and an impressive wine list. Closed all day Sun & Mon lunch.

Torre di Pisa Via Fiori Chiari 21 ☎02.874.877. An authentic Tuscan restaurant offering delicious antipasti (around €9) and great cuts of meat, in the very heart of pedestrian Brera. Closed Sun.

Tradizionale Ripa de Porta Ticenese 7. Tasty pizzas and mouth-watering fish dishes are on offer in the rustic atmosphere of this popular canal-side joint. There's another branch at Via de Amicis 26.

Trattoria Milanese Via Santa Marta 11 ☎02.8645.1991. An elegant but well-priced neighbourhood restaurant in the labyrinthine ancient streets ten minutes' walk west of the Duomo. Risotto and *osso buco* take pride of place among all that's best of Milanese cooking. Closed Tues.

Warsa Via Melzo 16 ☎02.201.673. An Eritrean restaurant near Porta Venezia serving delectable bargain food; good variety of vegetarian dishes as well as various meat options. Around €15 for a full meal. Closed Wed.

Nightlife: bars, clubs and live music

Milan is renowned as having some of the best **nightlife** in Italy, although it could hardly be described as cutting-edge. The scene currently centres on three main areas: the designer-label streets around Corso Como and south around Via Brera; the neighbourhood around Corso Sempione, which draws people after work for an *aperitivo* and keeps them there until the small hours; and the canal-side Navigli and the adjacent Ticinese quarter, south of the city, where a more mixed clientele enjoys the lively bars, restaurants and nightclubs, some hosting regular live bands. Some of the more popular bars and clubs that we have recommended out of town may require a bus or a quick taxi ride.

The city's **clubs** are at their hippest midweek – at weekends out-of-towners flood in and any self-respecting Milanese heads for the coast or mountains. Many clubs have obscure door policies, often dependent on the whim of the bouncer – this is Milan: dress to impress. Assuming you get in, you'll be given a **tessera** or card to be punched for each drink you buy, there's usually a minimum consumption and you settle the tab when you leave; you'll be charged extortionately if you lose the card.

As for **live music**, Milan scores high on jazz, and the pop scene is relatively good by Italian standards: there are regular gigs by local music groups, and the city is a stop on the circuit for big-name touring bands.

If you need an antidote to the expensive designer side of Milan's nightlife, check out the very healthy alternative scene, which revolves around the city's many **Centri Sociali**. Born out of the student protests of the late Sixties, these centres are essentially squatted buildings, where committees organize cheap, sometimes free, entertainment, such as concerts and film showings. They also contain bars and – often good – vegetarian restaurants. Check out the historic *Leoncavallo*, in recent years at Via Watteau 7, although that might change (☎02.670.5185, ⓦ www.leoncavallo.org), or look in the listings section of the newspaper *Il Manifesto* for other *centri*.

Bars

For the bars located in the fashion stores around the Quadrilatero d'Oro, see p.201.

Atomic Via Felice Casati 24. Refreshing spot just north of Porta Venezia where you can have an after-dinner drink and a dance in a cool but relaxed atmosphere – most un-Milanese. Closed Mon & Aug.

Bar Bianco Parco Sempione. Right in the heart of the park, this unassuming café kicks into action on summer nights as a late-night bar with thumping music. Closed Mon.

Bar Jamaica Via Brera 32. This bar, made famous by the Arté Povera set of the 1950s, is right in the heart of Brera. Pop in for a coffee or snack during the day or keep drinking well into the early hours.

Bhangrabar Corso Sempione 1. Opposite the Arco della Pace, this Indian-themed bar is a trendy option for *aperitivo*-time (6.30–9pm) or later, as the DJs crank up the latest electronic or world music.

Corso Como X Corso Como 10. The bar is the best bit of this chi-chi boutique, exhibition space, restaurant and a courtyard café-bar. Prices are extortionate but the atmosphere is very chic.

Cuore Via G Mora 3. Hidden away down a side street opposite San Lorenzo alle Colonne, this cool, friendly bar is well worth including in your night out. Good music with occasional live bands and DJs set the mixed crowd at their ease.

Gattopardo Café Via Piero della Francesca 47. This ultra-fashionable spot is located in a deconsecrated church and opens at 6pm. The door policy gets stricter after 10.30pm when the extensive *aperitivo* buffet is cleared away and the DJ turns up the music. Closed Mon.

Le Biciclette Conca del Naviglio 10. Smart young things prop up the bar in this swish modern joint in a leafy street near the Navigli. The definitive *aperitivo* bar.

Lelephante Via Melzo 22. Cocktails are the speciality at this good-time bar popular with a mixed crowd. Hardly a poseur in sight.

Roialto Via Piero della Francesca 55. This huge converted garage on various levels is done out in every conceivable style from 1930s colonial to chill-out lounge. Closed Mon.

Venues and clubs

Blue Note Via Borsieri 37 @ www.bluenotemilano .com. Newish jazz club located in the alternative neighbourhood of Isola, just north of Stazione Garibaldi. Big names and a relaxed atmosphere make this place a top venue. There's a small restaurant, as well as the bar.

Café L'Atlantique Viale Umbriale 42 @ www .cafeatlantique.com. Achingly Milanese spot where the slickest of Milan's slick meet. Commercial music and some of the most difficult doormen to pass in town.

Gasoline Via Bonnet 11a @ www.discogasoline.it. Small, dark, funky club near the bars of Brera and Corso Como playing, loud, hard music. On Sunday afternoons it becomes a popular gay club called *Bus Stop*.

Hollywood Corso Como 15 @ www.discoteca hollywood.com. Long established as the place to go (until dawn) if you want to be surrounded by beautiful people. Very Milanese but certainly no mould-breaker.

Magazzini Generali Via Pietrasanta 14 ℡ 02.5521.1313. Ex-warehouse that's become a Milan institution with a mixture of popular club nights (Friday is best) and live music.

Plastic Viale Umbria 120 @ www.thisisplastic.com. Time-honoured club that still draws in glam, quirky and chic crowds to dance til dawn to an eclectic mixture of sounds. Very strict door policy. Closed July–Sept.

Scimmie Via Ascanio Sforza 49 @ www.scimmie .it. Ticinese club that is one of Milan's most popular venues, with a different band every night and jazz-fusion predominating. Small and fun, with a decent restaurant – and a barge on the canal in summer.

Tunnel Via Sammartini 30 ℡ 02.6671.1370. With its eye firmly on what's happening abroad, this large club and venue located in an old warehouse near the Stazione Centrale is as close as Milan gets to having its finger on the pulse. Closed Mon.

Opera, theatre and cinema

Many of Milan's tourists are in the city for just one reason – **La Scala**, Via dei Filodrammatici 2, one of the world's most prestigious opera houses. The opera **season** runs from early December through to July, and there are usually also classical concerts and ballet between September and November. The average price of a ticket is about €60 and, not surprisingly, seats sell out months in advance. **Tickets** can be bought by phone or online (information

02.72.003.744, reservations 02.860.775, www.teatroallascala.org; the website has a useful seating-plan), or in person at the Galleria del Sagrato, just off the Piazza Del Duomo (daily noon–6pm; closed July 29 to Aug 28, Nov 1, December 8, 24, 25 & 26, Jan 1, 6 & 7, April 8, 9 & 25, May 1 & June 2). Alternatively, the ticket agency www.charta.it has an official quota of tickets. In addition, some tickets for each performance are reserved for sale on the day, from three hours before the start of the performance at the opera house; 140 tickets are available for operas and ballets, and 80 for concerts, with a maximum purchase of two tickets per person. Note that some performances, particularly of ballet and classical concerts, are held on the outskirts of the city in the rather less atmospheric Teatro Arcimboldi, which was built as the temporary home for the Scala during its restoration.

As for **cinema**, Sound and Motion Pictures (www.anteospaziocinema.com; €6) shows a selection of original language films at the following cinemas: the Arcobaleno, Viale Tunisia 11 (02.2940.6054; M Porta Venezia); the Anteo, Via Milazzo 9 (02.659.7732); and the Mexico, Via Savona 57 (02.4895.1802). In addition, the Fondazione Cineteca Italiana, based at the Spazio Oberdan (www.cinetecamilano.it), Viale Veneto 2, has a good programme of international art-house films.

Shopping

Milan is synonymous with **shopping**: whether you're here to indulge in the ultimate consumer experience or want to bag a designer bargain, there are few places on earth with more to offer. If your pockets are not that deep, you could always rummage through last season's leftovers at the many factory outlets around town, or check out the city's wide range of medium- and budget-range clothes shops. Milan also excels in furniture and **design**, with showrooms from the world's top companies, plus a handful of shops offering a selection of brands and labels under one roof.

Most shops **open** Tuesday to Saturday 10am to 12.30pm and 3.30 to 7pm plus Monday afternoons,

△ Indulge in some Milanese shopping

although some larger places also stay open at lunchtime and on Sunday afternoons. The summer **sale** usually lasts from early July through August, while the winter one starts around the second week of January and lasts for a month.

Fashion

The top-name fashion stores are mainly concentrated in three areas. The **Quadrilatero d'Oro** – Via Montenapoleone, Via della Spiga and around – is the place for Versace, Prada et al, while **Corso di Porta Ticinese** houses the funkier, more youth-oriented shops, with a handful of interesting, independent shops, as well as international names like Diesel, Carhartt and Stussy. If your budget is smaller, head to **Corso Vittorio Emanuele**, **Via Torino** or **Corso Buenos Aires** for large branches of Italian mid-range chainstores, including Max Mara, Benetton and Stefanel, plus international high-street giants H&M and Zara.

The following are just a taster of some of the best Milan has to offer in terms of the top-label shopping experience. These days the concept of a shop is being extended further and further: in-house cafés are springing up, as are exhibition spaces, spas, barbers' and even gyms.

Dolce & Gabbana Womenswear at Via della Spiga 26; D&G line including D&G junior, Corso Venezia 7; menswear, Corso Venezia 15. Go through to the courtyard on the ground floor of the eighteenth-century palace at Corso Venezia 15 to find a wonderful space dedicated to enhancing your shopping experience. There's an old-fashioned barber's, a small beautican's and the oh-so stylish *Bar Martini*, popular with beautiful people of all nationalities.

Gianfranco Ferré Via Sant'Andrea 15. The sculptural designs of this master of couture are mirrored by the decor of his new boutique with its stunning red resin wall, but it is the adjoining day-spa that makes it really special. Mon–Fri 10am–10pm, Sat 10am–9pm, Sun 11am–6pm.

Gianni Versace Via Montenapoleone 11. Unusually for Versace, this store, spread over five storeys, is nothing if not understated. The clean lines provide a perfect backdrop for the luxurious ostentation of the clothes, shoes and accessories in glinting gold and swirling colours.

Giorgio Armani Via Manzoni 31. This temple to all things Giorgio is more of a mini-shopping centre than a shop. There are boutiques for all his ranges – women's and menswear, furnishings and houseware – accompanied by *Armani Café*, a relaxed pavement café, and *Nobu*, a pricey, hi-tech Japanese restaurant with fantastically offhand service. With a book corner selling design and coffee-table books, an in-house florists and a chocolate counter offering monogrammed sugary confections, you really won't need to spend your money anywhere else in town.

Gucci Via Montenapoleone 5–7 & Galleria Vittorio Emanuele II. Every desirable fashion item imaginable is available in the warren of sleek show rooms in Montenapoleone, while the newer store in the Galleria Vittorio Emanuele II has the *Gucci Café*. Revitalize in an atmosphere of elegant minimalism with a freshly squeezed fruit juice or a coffee.

Just Cavalli Boutique Via della Spiga 30. The ultimate in bling. Cavalli's leopardskin-clad clientele feel wonderfully at home in the white-cloud lift or shimmering up and down the giant central staircase. The piece-de-resistance, however, is down in the café, *Just Cavalli Food*, where an aquarium swims with brightly coloured fish.

Prada Galleria Vittorio Emanuele II; accessories, including shoes, Via della Spiga 18; menswear, Via Montenapoleone 6; women, Via Montenapoleone 8; sportswear, Via Sant'Andrea 21. The original Prada store, dating from 1913, stands on a side corner in the centre of the Galleria Vittorio Emanuele II. Much of the elegant interior is original, including the monochrome marble floor and the polished wood display cabinets, but the best bit is the central staircase swirling down past the leather goods to the mens' and womens' collections in the basement.

Trussardi Women Via Sant'Andrea 3–7; accessories and home collection, Piazza della Scala 5. A spacious boutique across three floors with the uber-chic *Trussardi-Marino Alla Scala Café* on the ground floor and a huge video-wall to keep you entertained while you sip your coffee. On the floor above the soft leather bags and crisp linens is the formal but well-priced restaurant, and one floor higher still is a contemporary gallery space.

Factory outlets

There are **outlets** or factory shops galore in and around Milan for designer labels at affordable prices. A couple of these are centrally located: the multi-label D-Magazine, Via Montenapoleone 26; the hard-to-find Basement, entered through the door to the left of number 15 on Via Senato, with bargains from all the top labels; and DT Intrend, Galleria San Carlo 6, near the Duomo, offering discounts on the Max Mara brands. Others demand more of a hike, although the savings are higher: the grande dame of Milan's outlet stores is Il Salvagente, at Via Bronzetti 16, fifteen minutes east of San Babila by bus (#54 & 61), where, with a little rummaging, you can bag a designer label for around a third of its original price.

Design and furniture

To pick up Alessi, Gio Ponte or Castiglione **designer furniture**, make for the broad streets off San Babila: Corso Europa, Via Durini, Corso Venezia and Corso Monforte are home to the furniture and lighting showrooms that made Milan the design capital of the world in the 1950s.

For a more relaxed, but very Milanese, shopping experience, try a **concept store** that sells a bit of everything: High Tech, at Pizza XXV Aprile 12, is great for getting lost among designer, imitation and ethnic knick-knacks; while 10 Corso Como is an institution selling a few perfectly chosen design and fashion objects, as well as books and music, with a café and art gallery, too.

B&B Italia Via Durini 14 ⓦ www.bebitalia.it. International name that specializes in stylish contemporary furniture with collections by big names in Italian modern design.

Cassina Via Durini 16 ⓦ www.cassina.it. The showroom of this legendary Milanese company is always worth a visit for both new designs and their range of twentieth-century design classics including Eames, De Stijl and Rennie Mackintosh chairs.

De Padova Corso Venezia 14 ⓦ www.depadova .it. Two floors of elegant own-brand furniture and houseware artfully displayed in a light, stylish showroom. Their collections are designed by big names including Vico Magestretti and Patricia Urquiola.

Driade Via Manzoni 30 ⓦ www.driade.com. A wonderful multi-brand store with their own designs, as well as work by designers like Ron Arad and Philippe Starck. The collection includes furniture, tableware, kitchen and bathroom accessories, but the real treat here is the showroom housed in an elegant nineteenth-century *palazzo*.

Food and drink

Cotti Via Solferinio 42. A treasure trove of wines and liqueurs from across the country is accompanied by an array of gourmet treats – both sweet and savoury.

Cova Via Montenapoleone 8. Banks of irresistible cakes and confectionery are on offer at this famous tearoom dating back to the Napoleonic era.

Il Salumaio Via Montenapoleone 12. The selection of savoury delicacies and handmade pasta are to die for in this smart delicatessen, with a café and tables outside in the courtyard.

Peck Via Spadari 7–9. Three floors of top-priced Italian delicacies, from olive oil and home-made chocolate to mouth-watering prosciutto, cheeses and an impressive wine cellar. There's also a café on the first floor and a swish cocktail bar and restaurant round the corner at Via Cantù 3.

Listings

Airlines Alitalia, Piazzale Cadorna 14 ⓣ 02.2499.2500; British Airways, Corso Italia 8 ⓣ 199.712.266; Easyjet ⓣ 848.887.766; Ryanair ⓣ 899.967.8910.

Airport enquiries ⓣ 02.7485.2200 (daily 7am–11pm) for both Linate and Malpensa airports. **Bicycle rental** Despite the reputation of the city's traffic, central Milan is an enjoyable place to negotiate by bicycle: it's mainly flat and motorists show much more respect to cyclists than in London or New York. AWS rents town and mountain bikes at Via Ponte Seveso 33, to the northwest of the Stazione Centrale (Tues–Sun 9am–1pm & 3–7pm; ⓦwww.awsbici.com) and La Stazione (ⓦwww.piubici.org), by San Donato Milanese metro station offers hire, repair and storage services

Car rental Avis, Europcar, Hertz, Maggiore and all major operators have desks at Stazione Centrale, and at the airports.

Consulates Australia, Via Borgogna 2 ⓣ02.777.041; South Africa, Vicolo San Giovanni sul Muro 4 ⓣ02.885.8581; UK, Via San Paolo 7 ⓣ02.723.001; USA, Via Principe Amadeo 2/10 ⓣ02.290.351.

Doctors English-speaking doctors and dentists are available at the International Health Center (ⓣ02.7634.0720, ⓦwww.ihc.it), and The Milan Clinic (ⓣ02.7601.6047, ⓦwww.milanclinic.com).

Exchange Banks usually offer the best rates, but out of normal banking hours you can change money and travellers' cheques at the Stazione Centrale office (daily 7am–11pm), where there's also a 24-hour automatic currency-exchange machine. The airports all have exchange facilities.

Football Milan's two teams are Inter Milan and AC Milan. They play on alternate Sundays at the G. Meazza stadium (San Siro), Via Piccolomini 5 (ⓣ02.404.2432; MM Lotto, then a longish walk). There are hourly guided tours around the stadium (Mon–Sat 10am–5pm from Gate 21, Via Piccolomini 5; €12.50). You can buy match tickets here and, for AC Milan games (ⓦwww.acmilan.it), from Milan Point, on Via San Gottardo 2 (ⓣ02.8942.2711); and for Inter games (ⓦwww.inter.it), from Ticket One, Viale Vittorio Veneto 2 (ⓣ02.392.261, ⓦwww.ticketone.it), and branches of Banca Popolare Milano.

Gay and lesbian Milan Milan is one of the country's most gay-friendly cities, with little of the religious and socially fuelled homophobia of the south. Many of the city's nightspots welcome a mixed crowd, but they often hold specific gay nights, too. Naturally, see-and-be-seen venues are Milan's forte, though there is also a choice of more relaxed, as well as more hardcore establishments. The lesbian scene is less developed, with just a few dedicated venues. The focus of the Milan scene is the gay bookshop, Libreria Babele Galleria, at Via San Nicolao 10 (ⓦwww.libreriababele.it; M Cadorna), which has a gallery alongside a good selection of books and videos. This is also the place to pick up a copy of the Gay Milan map, detailing the city's saunas, clubs and cruising areas and details of **ArciUno Club Card** – an ID card

– which many establishments require as a condition of entry. In May, the city hosts an international **gay and lesbian film festival** (ⓦwww.cinema gaylesbico.com), which often has fringe activities organized around the same time.

Hospital There is a 24-hour casualty service at the Ospedale Maggiore Policlinico, Via Francesco Sforza 35 (ⓣ02.55.031), a short walk from Piazza Duomo.

Left luggage Stazione Centrale (daily 6am–midnight; €3.50 for 5 hours, then small increments up to a max of five days). Stazione Nord/Cadorna also has a number of lockers of various sizes for small bags and suitcases (daily 5am–11.30pm; small €3.50, med €4.50, large €6.50 for 2hr30min).

Pharmacy The Stazione Centrale (ⓣ02.669.0735), which has English-speaking assistants; and Carlo Erba, on Piazza Duomo (ⓣ02.8646.4832): both have 24-hour services. Rotas for other pharmacies are published in *Corriere della Sera*, and are usually posted on *farmacia* doors.

Police Phone ⓣ113.

Post office Via Cordusio 4, off Piazza Cordusio – not the building marked "Poste", but around the corner (Mon–Fri 8am–7pm, Sat 8.30am–noon). Corso Venezia, opposite the Giardini Pubblici (Mon–Fri 8am–7pm).

Swimming pools Covered pools: the monumental, Fascist-period Piscina Cozzi (ⓣ02.659.9703; M Repubblica/M Porta Venezia), at Viale Tunisia 35, is near to the Stazione Centrale; Piscina Solari (ⓣ02.459.5278; M S. Agostino), at Via Montevideo 20, lies to the south of the city; and the Lido di Milano (ⓣ02.392.791 or 02.66.100; M Lotto), which has both indoor and open-air pools, is out to the west. From June to mid-September, however, swimming becomes less a form of exercise and more a way of cooling down. The 1930s-built neighbourhood **open-air pools**, with their sunbathing areas, playgrounds and late-night bars, can get very crowded, especially during weekends and late afternoon, but are a great place to wash away the muggy heat of the Milanese summer. Among the nicest are Romano in Città Studi, at Via Ampère 20 (ⓣ02.7063.0825; M Piola); Argelati, at Via Segantini 6 (ⓣ02.5810.0012; M Pta Genova), by the Navigli; and Caimi on Via Botta (ⓣ02.5990.0754; M Pta Romana), near Porta Romana. Prices are €5 during the week and €5.50 at weekends; for opening hours see ⓦwww.milanosport.it.

Taxis Call one of the following numbers to book a taxi: ⓣ02.6767, 02.4040 or 02.8585.

Train enquiries ⓦwww.trenitalia.com; Ferrovie dello Stato ⓣ89.20.21 (daily 7am–9pm); Ferrovie Nord ⓣ02.20.222 (daily 9am–6pm).

South of Milan: Pavia and the Certosa

Fifty-five kilometres south of Milan and furthest west of the string of historic towns that spread across the Lombardy plain, **Pavia** is close enough to Milan to be seen on a day-trip, but still retains a clear identity of its own. A comfortable provincial town with an illustrious history, Pavia boasts one of the masterpieces of Italian architecture in the nearby Carthusian monastery, the **Certosa**.

Pavia

PAVIA was founded on an easily defendable stretch of land alongside the confluence of the Po and Ticino rivers and was always an important staging post en route to the Alps and beyond. Medieval Pavia was known as the city of a hundred towers, and although only a handful remain – one of the best collapsed in 1989 – the medieval aspect is still strong, with numerous Roman-esque and Gothic churches tucked away in a wanderable web of narrow streets and cobbled squares.

Pavia reached its zenith in the Dark Ages when it was capital of the Kingdom of the Lombards. After their downfall it remained a centre of power, and the succession of emperors – including Charlemagne in 774 and Frederick Barbarossa – in 1155, who ruled northern Italy continued to come to the town to receive the Lombards' traditional iron crown. This all came to an end in the fourteenth century when Pavia was handed over to the Viscontis and became a satellite of Milan. The Viscontis, and later the Sforzas, did, however, found the university and provide the town with its prime attraction – the nearby **Certosa di Pavia**.

Arrival and information

Regular **trains** make the thirty-minute journey between Pavia and Milan, but connections from Pavia to the other cities of the Lombardy plain are infrequent and slow. **Bus** services from Milan Famagosta metro station drop you at the bus station round the corner from the train station in Pavia, on the western edge of the town centre. Buses #3 and #6 connect the train station with the centre, or it's about a ten-minute walk down Corso Cavour to Piazza della Vittoria. The **tourist office** is round the corner from the bus station at Via F. Filzi 2 (Mon–Sat 8.30am–12.30pm & 2–6pm; ☎0382.22.156, ⓦwww.turismo .provincia.pv.it).

Accommodation

Pavia's **hotels** are an unexciting mix of business hotels and standard three-stars. Most are near the station, including the newly refurbished *Aurora*, at Via Vittorio Emanuele 25 (☎0382.23.664, ⓦwww.hotel-aurora.eu; ❷), and the city's smartest option, the *Moderno*, at Via Vittorio Emanuele 41 (☎0382.303.401, ⓦwww.hotelmoderno.it; ❺), which has a small spa centre and offer guests free use of bicycles.

The Town

Just wandering around town is the nicest way to spend time here: pick any side street and you're almost bound to stumble on something of interest – a lofty medieval tower, a pretty Romanesque or Gothic church, or just a silent, sleepy piazza. Getting lost is difficult, as the town is still based around its Roman axes. Corso Cavour – which becomes Corso Mazzini – runs east–west along the route of the *decamanus* and Strada Nuova runs north–south following the *cardus*. The Ticino river borders the south of the city centre.

The large cobbled rectangle of **Piazza della Vittoria**, lined with bars, *gelaterie* and restaurants, stands in the centre of the old town. At the square's southern end, the **Broletto**, medieval Pavia's town hall, abuts the rear of the rambling and unwieldy **Duomo**. An early Renaissance sprawl of protruding curves and jutting angles, the cathedral is best known for its huge nineteenth-century cupola, which dominates the skyline of the city. The facade was only added in 1933 and the exterior of the cathedral is still mainly unfinished. Most of the church is closed off for restoration and is not due to reopen until 2010. Beside the west front of the Duomo, facing **Piazza del Duomo**, are the remnants of the eleventh-century Torre Civica, a campanile that collapsed without warning in March 1989, killing four people.

Southwest of the piazza, the narrow, cobbled streets lead to the charming neighbourhood church of **San Teodoro** (daily 3–7pm). The twelfth-century basilica was clumsily restored at the end of the nineteenth century, and the main reason for visiting is to see the fresco on the left-hand side of the nave near the entrance: the *View of Pavia* by Bernardino Lanazani illustrates the city in 1522 with its hundreds of civic towers built by Pavia's noble families to show their superiority over their rivals. In the nineteenth century there were still eighty left, but these days, only three towers remain.

Also featured in the painting is the **Ponte Coperto**, the covered bridge over the Ticino just to the south of the basilica. The current bridge was rebuilt slightly downriver in the 1940s after the medieval one was bombed; you can still see remnants of the original jutting out into the water. The bridge leads over to the **Borgo Ticino**, the riverside neighbourhood traditionally inhabited by fishermen and *raniere* (frog catchers); these days there are several restaurants popular with locals. An open park runs along the shore of both banks west of the bridge, a popular sunbathing and picnic spot in summer.

The best of the town's churches is the beautiful Romanesque **San Michele**, a five-minute walk northeast from the bridge along via Capsoni. This is where the kings of Northern Italy were crowned and Federico I (or Barbarossa) came to receive the title here in 1155. The friezes and capitals on its broad sandstone facade are carved into a menagerie of snake-tailed fish, griffins, dragons and other beasts, some locked in a struggle with humans, representing the fight between good and evil. Sadly, despite restoration work in the 1960s, the sandstone is being worn away and some of the figures are being lost for good.

North of here lie the attractive courtyards and sandstone buildings of the **University of Pavia**, founded in 1361 by Galeazzo II Visconti, and particularly renowned for its medicine and law faculties. Crossing Piazza Castello, you reach the **Castello Visconteo** (March–June & Sept–Nov Tues–Fri 9am–1.30pm, Sat & Sun 10am–7pm; Dec–Feb, July & Aug Tues–Sat 9am–1.30pm Sun 9am–1pm; €6), also initiated by Galeazzo II Visconti in 1360, and added to by the Sforzas. The castle was used as a barracks until 1921, and although it's been restored, the rooms that remain are unremarkable. The **Museo Civico** inside includes an art gallery with a handful of Venetian paintings, an archeology collection with Roman jewellery, pottery and glassware, and a museum of sculpture displaying architectural fragments, mosaics and sculptures rescued from the town's demolished churches – most impressive of which are the reconstructed eleventh- and twelfth-century portals.

Eating and drinking

The best **restaurant** in town, with some of the most attractively located outdoor tables in summer, is in an alleyway by the church of San Michele. *Villaglori al San Michele*, Viccolo San Michele 4 (T03.8222.0716; closed

Mon & lunch Tues–Fri), offers excellently priced local wines to accompany interesting dishes like rabbit and asparagus lasagne or a mouth-watering selection of cold meats and cheeses in an elegant modern restaurant. Alternatively, across Corso Strada Nuova, the *Osteria della Madonna del Peo*, at Via Cardano 63 (℡0382.302.833; closed Sun), is a good central option serving local specialities, such as risotto with frogs' legs, in a cosy vaulted trattoria. If you'd prefer to grab a sandwich and head down to the river, the *Punto Bar*, Strada Nuova 9, is a first-rate *paninoteca*, with at least thirty varieties to tempt you.

The Certosa di Pavia

Ten kilometres from Pavia, the **Certosa di Pavia** (Charterhouse of Pavia; Tues–Sun: May–Sept 9–11.30am & 2.30–6pm; April closes 5.30pm; Oct–March closes 4.30pm; free) is one of the most extravagant monasteries in Europe, commissioned by the Duke of Milan, Gian Galeazzo Visconti, in 1396 as the family mausoleum. Visconti intended the church here to resemble Milan's late-Gothic cathedral and the same architects and craftsmen worked on the building throughout its construction. It took a century to build, and by the time it was finished tastes had changed – and the Viscontis had been replaced by the Sforzas. As a work of art the monastery is one of the most important testimonies to the transformation from late-Gothic to Renaissance and Mannerist styles, but it also affords a wonderful insight into the lives and beliefs of the Carthusian monks.

The Certosa is easily reachable from both Milan and Pavia, either by bus or by train. **Buses** are most frequent, hourly from Famagosta station (€3) in Milan or from Pavia's bus station, dropping you a fifteen-minute walk from the Certosa. Arriving by **train**, turn left out of the station and walk around the Certosa walls until you reach the entrance – also a fifteen-minute walk.

The complex

The monastery lies at the end of a tree-lined avenue, part of a former Visconti hunting range that stretched all the way from Pavia's *castello*. Encircled by a high wall, the complex is entered through a central gateway bearing a motif that reoccurs throughout the monastery – "GRA-CAR" or "Gratiarum Carthusiae", a reference to the fact that the Carthusian monastery is dedicated to Santa Maria delle Grazie, who appears in numerous works of art in the church. Beyond the gateway is a gracious courtyard with the seventeenth-century Ducal Palace on the right-hand side and outbuildings along the left. Rising up before you is the fantastical **facade** of the church, festooned with inlaid marble, twisted columns, statues and friezes. Despite more than a century's work by leading architects, the facade remains unfinished: the tympanum was never added to the top, thus giving the church its stocky, truncated look.

The Gothic **church** is no less splendid on the inside, its paintings, statues and vaults combining to create an almost ballroom glamour; look out for the tombs of Lodovico Il Moro and Gian Galeazzo Visconti, which are masterpieces of the early Renaissance. You can see the church unaccompanied but to visit the rest of the monastery you need to join a **guided tour** (free but contributions welcomed) of just under an hour, led by one of the monks released from the Carthusian strict vow of silence. It is in Italian, but well worth doing even if you don't understand a word as it allows you to explore the best parts of the monastery complex. The tour begins in the church when enough people have gathered together and then moves on to the **small cloister**, with fine terracotta decoration and a geometric garden around a fountain. The monks would wash at the terracotta and marble basin before entering the nearby **refectory** where they would eat together on Sundays and Holy days; the Bible was read throughout the silent meal from the pulpit (with a hidden entrance in the panelling). The dining room is divided by a blind wall, which allowed the monastery to feed lay workers and pilgrims staying in their guesthouse without compromising the rules of their closed order. Further on, the **great cloister** is stunning for its size and tranquillity, and also offers an insight into life in the complex. It is surrounded on three sides by the **monks' houses**, each consisting of two rooms, a chapel, a garden and a *loggia*, with a bedroom above. The hatches to the side of the entrances were designed to enable food to be passed through without any communication. The final call is the Certosa **shop**, stocked with honey, chocolate, souvenirs and the famous Chartreuse liqueur.

Cremona

A cosy provincial town situated bang in the middle of the Po plain, **CREMONA** is known for its violins. Ever since Andrea Amati established the first violin workshop here in 1566, and his son Nicolo and pupils Stradivari and Guarneri continued and expanded the industry, Cremona has been a focus for the instrument, attracting both tourists and musicians worldwide. Today there's an internationally famous school of violin-making here, while frequent classical concerts are held around town.

All this said, Cremona is a quiet, relatively unexciting town, and not an obvious place to spend a night, with most people treating it as a day-trip from Milan or as a stopover en route to the richer pickings of Mantua.

Arrival, information and accommodation

Cremona's **train station** is on Via Dante, on the northern edge of the city centre, ten minutes' walk from the focal Piazza del Comune; bus #1 runs regularly to the Piazza Cavour, also in the centre. Most intercity buses stop at the train station or at the **bus station** one block east.

The friendly **tourist office** is on the Piazza del Comune, opposite the Duomo (daily 9am–12.30pm & 3–6pm, June–Aug closed Sun pm; ☎0372.23.233, ⓦwww.aptcremona.it), and has leaflets, details of classical concerts and a list of violin makers.

Accommodation options include a **campsite**, the *Parco al Po*, on Via Lungo Po Europa (☎0372.21.268, ⓦwww.campingcremonapo.it; April–Sept; bus #1 from the train station, direction Viale Po), while the tourist office has lists of agriturismos and bed and breakfasts in and around town. Alternatively, the *Duomo* (☎0372.35.242, Ⓕ0372.458.392; ❷), just off the central square at Via Gonfalonieri 13, offers bright, clean, en-suite rooms with air conditioning. Cremona's top hotel is the slightly incongruous *Dellearti Design Hotel,* at Via Bonomelli 8 (☎0372.23131, ⓦwww.dellearti.com; ❺), more in keeping with Milan's design crowd than sleepy Cremona.

The Town

Alongside Cremona's musical connections, the town has some fine Renaissance and medieval buildings, and its cobbled streets make for some pleasant strolling. All the town's sights are within an easy twenty-minute walk of the main square.

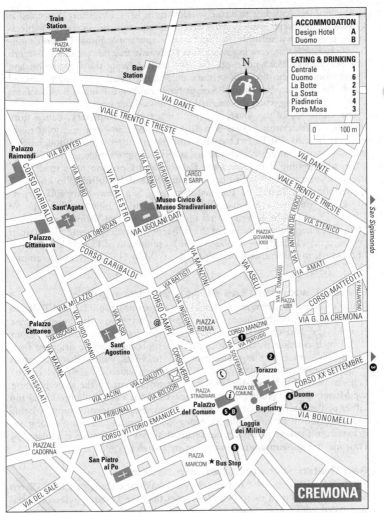

ACCOMMODATION
Design Hotel   A
Duomo   B

EATING & DRINKING
Centrale   1
Duomo   6
La Botte   2
La Sosta   5
Piadineria   4
Porta Mosa   3

0   100 m

CREMONA

▼ Parco al Po Campsite & River

Piazza del Comune

The centre of Cremona is **Piazza del Comune**, a slightly disjointed medieval square, with its west side formed by the red-brick **Loggia dei Militia** – formerly headquarters of the town's militia – and the arched **Palazzo del Comune**, and the northeast corner marked by the gawky Romanesque **Torazzo**. Built in the mid-thirteenth century and bearing a fine Renaissance clock dating from 1583, the Torazzo is 112m high, and claims to be Italy's highest medieval tower: there are excellent views over Cremona and its surroundings from the top (Tues–Sun 10am–1pm & 2.30–6pm; €2).

Next door, the **Duomo**, connected to the Torazzo by way of a Renaissance *loggia*, has a fine west facade made up of Classical, Romanesque and fancy

Gothic features, focusing on a rose window from 1274. Originally conceived as a basilica, its transepts were added when the Gothic style became more fashionable – presumably explaining its slightly squat appearance inside. Its most significant interior features are its sixteenth-century nave frescoes, including a superb trompe l'oeil by Pordenone on the west wall, showing the Crucifixion and Deposition, and the fifteenth-century pulpits, decorated with finely tortured reliefs. Recent excavations in the crypt have uncovered Roman mosaics from the fourth century, when the original church was built here.

The south side of the square features the octagonal **Baptistry**, dating from the late twelfth century (Tues–Sun 10am–1pm & 2.30–6pm; €2, joint ticket with the Torazzo €5). Its vast bare-brick interior is rather severe, although lightened by twin columns in each bay and a series of upper balconies.

Directly opposite the Duomo, the **Palazzo del Comune** has a small exhibition of nine historic violins in its upstairs **Sala dei Violini** (also known as Collezione degli Strumenti; Tues–Sat 9am–6pm, Sun 10am–6pm; €6), including a very early example made by Andrea Amati in 1566 for the court of Charles IX of France, as well as later instruments by Amati's son, Guarneri, and Stradivari. There are recordings of the different instruments being played or, at certain times of the day – as long as there's a minimum of 15 people – you can hear one of the instruments being played live (Mon 11.15am & noon; summer also 3.30pm).

Museo Civico and the Museo Stradivariano

If you've come to Cremona primarily for the violins, the pilastered **Palazzo Affaitati**, north of the square at Via Ugolani Dati 4, will also be of interest. It holds the **Museo Stradivariano** (Tues–Sat 9am–6pm, Sun 10am–6pm; €7), which contains models, paper patterns, tools and acoustic diagrams from Stradivari's workshop, along with more violins, violas, viols, cellos and guitars hanging impotently in glass cases; an informative video (English and Italian), helps to unravel the mysteries of the violin maker's art. In the same building, the **Museo Civico** (same hours; joint ticket €10) is a decidedly provincial and rather pedestrian collection of mainly Cremonese art, redeemed only by being well displayed in striking galleries. Alongside the art are changing exhibitions drawn from the bizarre artefacts and natural history specimens accumulated by Ponzone, the museum's nineteenth-century founder.

San Pietro al Po and San Sigismondo

Southwest of Piazza del Comune, on Via Tibaldi, the church of **San Pietro al Po** has better (and more visible) frescoes than the Duomo; indeed its walls are coated with paintings and intricate stuccos, also dating from the sixteenth century. It's all pretty excessive, but there's sophisticated optical trickery in the work of Antonio Campi in the transept vaults. Look in also on the refectory next door for Bernadino Gatti's hearty fresco *Feeding of the Five Thousand*.

If you like the church of San Pietro al Po, you'll love that of **San Sigismondo** on the eastern edge of town (bus #3 from the train station, bus #2 from Piazza Cavour). Built by Francesco and Bianca Sforza in 1441 to commemorate their wedding – Cremona was Bianca's dowry – its Mannerist decor is among Italy's best, ranging from Camillo Boccaccino's soaring apse fresco to the *Pentecost* by Giulio Campi in the third bay of the nave, plagiarized from Mantegna's ceiling in the Camera degli Sposi at Mantua. Other highlights include Giulio's *Annunciation* on the entrance wall, in which Gabriel is seemingly suspended in mid-air, and the gory *John the Baptist* in the second left chapel, by Giulio's younger brother Antonio.

Eating and drinking

Numerous cosy *osterie* dotted around town serve Cremona's excellent **local specialities**. Of special note is *bollito misto* – a mixture of boiled meats, served with Cremonese *mostarda di frutta*, fruit suspended in a sweet mustard syrup. The range of freshly produced flat-bread sandwiches at *Piadineria*, on Via Platina (Tues–Sun 11.30am–3pm & 6–11.30pm), on the far side of the Duomo from the tourist office, make a filling snack, while around Piazza del Comune and Piazza della Pace there are several very pleasant pavement **cafés** in which to while away the time, not least the *Portici del Comune* (closed Tues), with tables under the arches directly opposite the Duomo.

Centrale Via Pertusio 4, off Via Solferino ☎ 0372.28.701. An old staple that still serves well-priced traditional dishes. Closed Thurs.
Duomo Via Gonfalonieri 13, down the side of the Palazzo Comunale ☎ 0372.352.96. The tables outside this popular restaurant/pizzeria make a fine, sunny spot to tuck into a crispy pizza.
La Botte Via Porta Marzia 5. A youngish, local crowd come here for plates of *affittati* (cold meats and cheeses) and other specialities of the region. Closed Mon.

La Sosta Via Sicario 9 ☎ 0372.456.656. By the main piazza, this attractive *osteria* does a great line in Cremonese specialities at reasonable prices. Closed Sun evening & Mon.
Porta Mosa Via Santa Maria Bertlem 11 ☎ 0372.411.8903. A simple *osteria* serving delicious local dishes, washed down by well-chosen wines. Ten minutes' walk east from the Piazza del Comune. Closed Sun.

Mantua (Mantova) and around

Aldous Huxley called it the most romantic city in the world; and with an Arabian nights skyline rising above its three encircling lakes carpeted with lotus flowers in summer **MANTUA** (**MANTOVA**) is undeniably evocative. It was the scene of Verdi's *Rigoletto*, and its history is riddled with equally operatic plots, most of them perpetuated by the Gonzagas, one of Renaissance Italy's richest and most powerful families, who ruled the town for three centuries. Its centre of interlinking cobbled squares retains a medieval aspect, and there are two splendid palaces: the **Palazzo Ducale**, containing Mantegna's stunning fresco of the Gonzaga family and court, and **Palazzo Te**, whose frescoes by the flashy Mannerist Giulio Romano have entertained and outraged generations of visitors with their combination of steamy erotica and illusionistic fantasy.

Around Mantua the water and flat, agricultural plain offer numerous boat cruises and cycling routes, including a half-day trip to the quirky church at **Grazie** and the surrounding marsh lands. For those interested in urban planning, sixteenth-century **Sabbioneta**, to the southeast, will also provide an interesting diversion.

Some history

Mantova's renaissance began in 1459, when a visiting pope complained that the city was muddy, marshy and riddled with fever. This incited his host, **Lodovico II Gonzaga**, to give the city a facelift, ranging from paving the squares and repainting the shops to engaging **Andrea Mantegna** as court artist and calling in the prestigious architectural theorist **Leon Battista Alberti** to design the monumental church of Sant'Andrea, one of the most influential buildings of the early Renaissance. Later, Lodovico's grandson, **Francesco II** (1466–1519), swelled the family coffers by hiring himself out as a mercenary – money his wife, **Isabella d'Este**, spent amassing in a prestigious collection of paintings, sculpture and *objets d'art*.

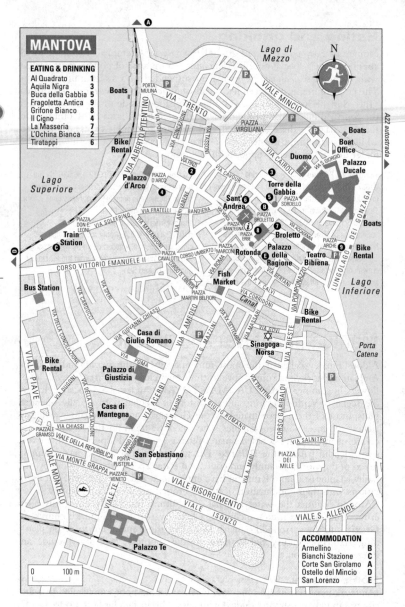

MANTOVA

EATING & DRINKING

Al Quadrato	1
Aquila Nigra	3
Buca della Gabbia	5
Fragoletta Antica	9
Grifone Bianco	8
Il Cigno	4
La Masseria	7
L'Ochina Bianca	2
Tiratappi	6

ACCOMMODATION

Armellino	B
Bianchi Stazione	C
Corte San Girolamo	A
Ostello del Mincio	D
San Lorenzo	E

Under Isabella's son, **Federico II**, Gonzaga fortunes reached their height; his marriage in 1531 to the heiress of the duchy of Monferrato procured a ducal title for the family, while he continued the policy of self-glorification by commissioning an out-of-town villa – the **Palazzo Te** – for himself and his mistress. Federico's descendants were for the most part less colourful characters, one notable exception being **Vincenzo I**, whose debauchery and corruption provided the inspiration for Verdi's licentious duke in *Rigoletto*. After Vincenzo's death in 1612, the then-bankrupt court was forced to sell many of the family treasures to Charles I of England (many are still in London's Victoria and Albert Museum), just three years before the arrival of the Habsburgs.

Arrival and information

Mantua's old centre is a ten-minute walk from the **train station** on Piazza Don E. Leoni, and the **bus station**, just beyond on Piazza Mondadori, off Corso Vittorio Emanuele II. Bus #1 runs from the train station to the centre of town. There are free parking places all along Viale Mincio as well as pay-and-display **parking** throughout the centre; note that Thursday is market day so check parking restriction signs carefully. The well-organized **tourist office**, in the centre of town at Piazza Mantegna 6 (daily 9am–7pm; ☎0376.432.432, Ⓦwww.turismo .mantova.it), has reams of useful information on the town and activities in the surrounding area including wine-tasting and local gastronomic festivals.

Accommodation

There is **accommodation** in Mantova to suit most budgets, though it gets booked up quickly, and it's advisable to phone ahead. If you're planning more than a fleeting visit, you might want to stay in one of the numerous relaxing **agriturismos** (Ⓦwww.agriturismomantova.it) in this part of Lombardy: the tourist office has an up-to-date list of both agriturismo and **bed-and-breakfast** establishments.

Armellino Via Cavour 67 ☎346.314.8060, Ⓦwww.bebarmellino.it. Three attractively furnished double rooms in an eighteenth-century palace right in the centre of town. There's a pretty garden for

drinks and breakfast is served in the period dining room. ❸
Bianchi Stazione Piazza Don E. Leoni 24 ☎0376.326.465, Ⓦwwwhotelbianchi.mantova.com.

Exploring Mantua

Mantua and its surrounding countryside are perfect for exploring on two wheels, and there are numerous well-signed **cycle** routes in the area, from a gentle circuit of the three lakes to a longer six-hour trip through the Parco del Mincio up to Peschiera on Lake Garda (40km). Bicycles can be rented by the hour or the day from La Rigola, on Via Trieste (☎0376.366.677), or at Mantova Bike, Viale Piave 22B (☎0376.220.909), nearer the station.

Local boatmen, the Barcaioli del Mincio (☎0376.349.292, Ⓦwww.fiumemincio.it) operate small craft upstream from Mantova on Lago Superiore to Grazie and Rivalta. Many of the **boats** accept bikes, so you can make a great day-trip – a morning on the boat, a picnic lunch at, say, Rivalta, then a gentle cycle-ride back in the afternoon.

Cruising around
Several companies offer **cruises** on Mantova's lakes – bulges in the course of the River Mincio – and on the river itself down to its confluence with the Po. All run daily but must be **booked in advance**: usually a day ahead, but sometimes an hour or so will do. The leading company is Motonavi Andes Negrini, whose information and ticket office is at Via San Giorgio 2 (☎0376.322.875, Ⓦwww.motonaviandes .it), three minutes' walk from its jetty on Lago Inferiore beside the castle. Navi Andes (☎0376.324.506, Ⓦwww.naviandes.com), a separate concern, with its booking office at its jetty on Lago di Mezzo opposite the castle, runs much the same trips for similar prices. These can often be busy excursions, on large boats.

A pleasant, family-run hotel by the station with plain rooms and small suites arranged around an appealing garden in the *cortile*. ④

Corte San Girolamo ⓣ & ⓕ 0276.39018, ⓦ www.agriturismo-sangirolamo.it. Housed in a renovated watermill 3km out of town on the cycle route from Mantova to Lago di Garda, this serene agriturismo has en-suite doubles with disabled facilities plus one four-person apartment. Bicycles are available. ③

Ostello del Mincio via Porto 23/25, Rodigo ⓣ 0376.653.924, ⓦ www.ostellodelmincio.org. Seventeen kilometres west of town, this brand new youth hostel holds an idyllic position on the banks of the Mincio in a sleepy village. There are two six-bed bunk rooms and two two-bed rooms plus a bar; canoes are available for rent and boat trips can be arranged. The #13 bus runs an hourly service from Mantova bus station (ⓦ www .apam.it) and there are also regular bus links with Brescia. ①

San Lorenzo Piazza Concordia 14 ⓣ 0376.220.500, ⓦ www.hotelsanlorenzo.it. The top hotel in town, right in the centre opposite the Rotonda, boasts simple but elegantly furnished rooms with balconies overlooking the town. ⑦

The City

The centre of Mantova is made up of four modestly sized but very attractive squares, each connected to the next. Lively Piazza Mantegna is overlooked by the massive **Sant'Andrea** church. Beside it is the lovely Piazza Erbe, with fine arcades facing the medieval **Rotonda** church and Palazzo della Ragione. To the north, through medieval passageways and across Piazza Broletto, the long, cobbled slope of Piazza Sordello is dominated by the **Palazzo Ducale**, the fortress and residence of the Gonzaga, packed with Renaissance art – not least Mantegna's frescoes in the **Camera degli Sposi**.

Mantova's other great palace stands in its own gardens 1.5km south through the historic centre. **Palazzo Te** is, if anything, even more impressive than the Palazzo Ducale, with superb frescoes in the **Sala dei Giganti** and **Sala di Amore**.

Sant'Andrea

Dominating **Piazza Mantegna** is the facade of Alberti's church of **Sant'Andrea**, an unfinished basilica that effectively reflects the ego of Lodovico II Gonzaga, who commissioned it. He felt that the existing medieval church was neither impressive enough to represent the splendour of his state nor large enough to hold the droves of people who flocked to Sant'Andrea every Ascension Day to see the holy relic of Christ's blood which had been found on the site. The relic is still there, and after years of dispute about its authenticity (it was supposed to have been brought to Mantua by the soldier who pierced Christ's side), Pope Pius II settled the matter in the fifteenth century by declaring it had miraculously cured him of gout.

Work started on the church in 1472, with the court architect, Luca Fancelli, somewhat resentfully overseeing Alberti's plans. There was a bitchy rivalry between the two, and when, on one of his many visits, Alberti fell and hurt a testicle, Fancelli gleefully told him that "God lets men punish themselves in the place where they sin". **Inside**, the church is roofed with one immense barrel vault, echoing the triumphal arch of the facade, which gives it a rather cool and calculated feel. The octagonal balustrade at the crossing stands above the crypt where the holy relic is kept in two vases, copies of originals designed by Cellini and stolen by the Austrians in 1846; to see them, ask the sacristan. The painter Mantegna is buried in the first chapel on the left, his tomb topped with a bust of the artist that's said to be a self-portrait; the wall-paintings in the chapel were designed by the artist and executed by students, one of whom was Correggio.

Piazza dell'Erbe and around

Opposite Sant'Andrea, sunk below the present level of the adjoining **Piazza dell'Erbe**, is Mantua's oldest church, the eleventh-century **Rotonda** (daily 10am–1pm & 2–6pm), which narrowly escaped destruction under Lodovico's city-improvement plans only to be partially demolished in the sixteenth century and used as a courtyard by the surrounding houses. Rebuilt at the beginning of the last century and beautifully restored in recent years, it still contains traces of twelfth- and thirteenth-century frescoes.

Piazza dell'Erbe itself is one of the town's most characterful squares, with a small daily market and cafés and restaurants sheltering in the arcades below the thirteenth-century **Palazzo della Ragione**. At the north end of the square, a passage leads under the red-brick **Broletto**, or medieval town hall, into the smaller **Piazza Broletto**, where you can view two reminders of how "criminals" were treated under the Gonzagas. The bridge to the right has metal rings embedded in its vault, to which victims were chained by the wrists, before being hauled up by a pulley and suspended in mid-air; while on your far left – actually on the corner of Piazza Sordello – the tall medieval **Torre della Gabbia** has a cage attached in which prisoners were displayed. The Broletto itself is more generous to deserving Mantuans, and is dedicated to the city's two most famous sons: Virgil, a statue of whom overlooks the square, and Tazio Nuvolari, Italy's most celebrated racing driver, whose career is mapped in a small **museum** (Tues, Wed & Fri–Sun 10am–1pm & 3.30–6.30pm; closed Jan–March; €3).

If you have the time, it's worth making a short diversion off Via Broletto up Via Accademia to the eighteenth-century **Teatro Scientifico** or **Bibiena** (Tues–Sun 9.30am–12.30pm & 3–6pm; €2), the work of Antonio Bibiena, whose brother designed the Bayreuth Opera House. This is a much smaller theatre, at once intimate and splendid, its curved walls lined with boxes calculated to make their occupants more conspicuous than the performers. A 13-year-old Mozart gave the inaugural concert here: his impression is unrecorded, but his father was fulsome in his praise for the building, writing that he had never in his life seen anything more beautiful. Concerts are still held here – pick up details from the theatre or tourist office.

Piazza Sordello and the Palazzo Ducale

Northeast of Piazza Broletto, **Piazza Sordello** is a large, sombre square, headed by the Baroque facade of the **Duomo**. Flanked by touristy pavement cafés and grim crenellated palaces built by the Bonalcosi (the Gonzagas' predecessors) the Duomo conceals a rich interior, designed by Giulio Romano after the church had been gutted by fire. Every year on the patron saint's day, March 18, the uncorrupted, clothed corpse of San Anselmo is wheeled out to worshippers.

Opposite, the Palazzo del Capitano and Magna Domus were taken by Luigi Gonzaga when he seized Mantua from the Bonalcosi in 1328, beginning three hundred years of Gonzaga rule: they now form the core of the **Palazzo Ducale**, an enormous complex that was once the largest palace in Europe. At its height it covered 34,000 square metres, had a population of over a thousand, and when it was sacked by the Habsburgs in 1630 eighty carriages were needed to carry the two thousand works of art contained in its five hundred rooms.

Palazzo practicalities

Only a proportion of the rooms in Palazzo Ducale are open to visitors (Tues–Sun 8.45am–7.15pm, last entrance 6.30pm; €6.50; Ⓦ www.mantovaducale.it). In **winter** (Nov–March), don't miss the free guided tour: these start from the ticket desk roughly every quarter-hour, or when twenty people have gathered, and take ninety minutes.

For conservation reasons, only 1500 people a day are allowed to visit the highlight of the complex, the **Camera degli Sposi** (also called the **Camera Picta**). In the peak season for school trips (March 15 to June 15 & Sept 1 to Oct 15), individuals must book in advance for a timed slot for admission to this room, on ☎041.241.1897 (press 1 for English-speaking operators; Mon–Fri 9am–6pm, Sat 9am–2pm). Booking costs €1 extra, payable on arrival.

The Palazzo interior

The first rooms of the palace are the least impressive, with the highlight being the fragments of a half-finished fresco by Pisanello, discovered in 1969 behind two layers of plaster and thought to depict either an episode from an Arthurian romance or the (idealized) military exploits of the first marquis, Gianfrancesco Gonzaga. Whatever its subject, it's a powerful piece of work, charged with energy, in which faces, costumes and landscape are minutely observed.

The splendid Neoclassical **Sala dei Specchi** ("Hall of Mirrors"; room 6) was originally an open *loggia*, bricked up in 1773; teams of horses are being driven across the barrel-vaulted ceiling from Night to Day. In the **Sala degli Arcieri** next door ("Hall of Archers"; room 7), the Flemish sixteenth-century artist, Ruben's huge canvas shows the Gonzaga family of 1604 seated comfortably in the presence of the Holy Trinity; notice Vincenzo with his handlebar moustache. The picture was originally part of a huge triptych, but Napoleonic troops carried off two-thirds of it in 1797 (one part is now in Antwerp, the other in Nancy) and chopped the remaining third into saleable chunks of portraiture; some gaps remain. Around the room is a curious frieze of horses, glimpsed behind curtains. Beyond the **Sala del Labirinto** (room 9), named for the maze on its painted and gilded wooden ceiling, adorned with *forse che si, forse che no* ("maybe yes, maybe no"), the **Sala di Amore e Psiche** (room 11) is an intimate space with a wooden floor and an eighteenth-century *tondo* of Cupid and Psyche in the ceiling.

From here follow signs along several corridors, down the stairs, over a moat and into the fourteenth-century **Castello di San Giorgio**, which contains the palace's principal treasure: Mantegna's frescoes of the Gonzaga family in the so-called **Camera degli Sposi** (during busy periods entrance restricted to five minutes in groups of twenty). They're naturalistic pieces of work, giving a vivid impression of the Marquis Lodovico, his wife Barbara and their family, and of the relationships between them. In the main fresco Lodovico discusses a letter with a courtier while his wife looks on; their youngest daughter leans on her mother's lap, about to bite into an apple, while an older son and daughter (possibly Barbarina) look towards the door, where an ambassador from another court is being welcomed – lending some credence to the theory that negotiations are about to take place for Barbarina's marriage. The other fresco, *The Meeting*, divided into three sections by fake pilasters, shows Gonzagan retainers with dogs and a horse in attendance on Lodovico, who is welcoming his son Francesco back from Rome. In the background are the Holy Roman Emperor Frederick III and the King of Denmark – a selection which apparently annoyed the Duke of Milan, who was incensed that the "two most wretched men in the world" had been included while he had been omitted. Lodovico's excuse was that he would have included the duke had he not objected so strongly to Mantegna's uncompromising portrait style. If you have time before the guide sweeps you out, have a look at the ceiling, another nice piece of trompe l'oeil, in which two women, peering down from a balustrade, have balanced a tub of plants on a pole and appear to be on the verge of letting it tumble into the room. This kind of illusionism was to be crucial in the development of the Gonzagas' next resident artist of any note, Giulio Romano, whose Palazzo Te – see below – should not be missed.

On exiting this part of the castle, you enter the sixteenth-century Corte Nuova wing, designed by Giulio Romano for Federico II Gonzaga. After several formal audience rooms you come to the **Sala di Troia** (room 22), decorated with Romano's brilliantly colourful scenes from the *Iliad* and *Aeneid*. The adjacent **Galleria dei Marmi** (room 23), with delicate floral and wildlife motifs, looks out over the Cortile della Cavallerizza (Courtyard of the Riding School). Along the courtyard's long side runs the immense **Galleria della Mostra** (room 24), once hung with paintings by Titian, Caravaggio, Breughel and others, all now dispersed; in their place are 64 Roman marble busts. Push on through the smaller rooms and up more stairs to the stunning **Sala dello Zodiaco** (room 33), whose late sixteenth-century ceiling is spangled with stars and constellations. The adjoining Rococo **Sala dei Fiumi** (room 34) features an elaborate painted allegory of Mantova's six rivers, flanked at either end by a mock garden complete with painted creepers and two ghastly stucco-and-mosaic fountains. The hanging gardens outside the window are considerably more attractive.

Save some wonder for rooms 35–37, beside the Sala dello Zodiaco. These comprise the **Stanze degli Arazzi**, three rooms (and a small chapel) altered in the eighteenth century to house a set of nine sixteenth-century Flemish tapestries of exceptional virtuosity, made from Raphael's cartoons (now in the V&A in London) for the Sistine Chapel and depicting stories from the Acts of the Apostles.

South of the centre

A twenty-minute walk from the centre of Mantua, at the end of the long spine of Via Principe Amedeo and Via Acerbi, the Palazzo Te is the later of the city's two Gonzaga palaces, and equally compelling in its way; you can take in a few of Mantua's more minor attractions on the way there.

The first thing to look at on the way is Giulio Romano's **Fish Market**, to the left off Piazza Martiri Belfiori, a short covered bridge over the river, which is still used as a market building. Following Via Principe Amedeo south, the **Casa di Giulio Romano**, off to the right at Via Poma 18, overshadowed by the monster-studded Palazzo di Giustizia, was also designed by Romano – like much of his Mantuan work, it was meant to impress the sophisticated, who would have found the licence taken with the Classical rules of architecture witty and amusing. A five-minute walk away on busy Via Giovanni Acerbi, the more austere brick **Casa del Mantegna** was also designed by the artist, both as a home and private museum, and is now used as a contemporary art-space and conference centre (during exhibitions daily 10am–12.30pm & 3–6pm). Across the road, the church of **San Sebastiano** (mid-March to mid-Nov Tues–Sun 10.30am–12.30pm & 3–5pm; €1.50) was the work of Alberti, and is famous as the first Renaissance church to be built on a central Greek cross plan, described as "curiously pagan" by Nikolaus Pevsner. Lodovico II's son was less polite: "I could not understand whether it was meant to turn out as a church, a mosque or a synagogue." Its days as a consecrated building are over and it now contains commemorative plaques forming a monument to the fallen Mantuan soldiers of World War II.

Palazzo Te

At the end of Via Giovanni Acerbi, across Viale Te, the **Palazzo Te** (Mon 1–6.30pm, Tues–Sun 9am–6pm, last entrance 5.30pm; €8) was designed for playboy Federico Gonzaga and his mistress, Isabella Boschetta, by Giulio Romano; it's the artist/architect's greatest work and a renowned Renaissance pleasure dome. When the palace was built, Te, or Tejeto, as it used to be known – was an island connected to the mainland by bridge, an ideal location for an amorous retreat away from Federico's wife and the restrictions of life in the Palazzo Ducale. Built around a square courtyard originally occupied by a labyrinth, these days it houses modest but appealing collections of Egyptian artefacts and modern art, although the main reason for visiting is to see Giulio's amazing decorative scheme.

A tour of the palace is like a voyage around Giulio's imagination, a sumptuous world where very little is what it seems. In the **Camera del Sole e delle Luna**, the sun and the moon are represented by a pair of horse-drawn chariots viewed from below, giving a fine array of bottoms on the ceiling; in the **Sala dei Cavalli**, dedicated to the prime specimens from the Gonzaga stud-farm (which was also on the island), portraits of horses stand before an illusionistic background in which simulated marble, fake pilasters and mock reliefs surround views of painted landscapes through nonexistent windows. The function of the **Sala di Psiche**, further on, is undocumented, but the sultry frescoes, and the proximity to Federico's private quarters, might give a few clues, the ceiling paintings telling the story of Cupid and Psyche with some more dizzying "*sotto in su*" (from the bottom up) works by Giulio, among others clumsily executed by his pupils. The walls are more than a little racey, too, covered with orgiastic wedding-feast scenes, at which drunk and languishing gods in various states of undress are attended by a menagerie of real and mythical beasts. Don't miss the severely incontinent river-god in the background, included either as a punning reference to Giulio's second name, Pippi (The Pisser), or as encouragement to Federico who, according to his doctors, suffered from the "obstinate retention of urine". Other scenes show Mars and Venus having a bath, Olympia about to be raped by a half-serpentine Jupiter and Pasiphae disguising herself as a cow in order to seduce a bull – all watched over by the giant Polyphemus, perched above the fireplace, clutching the pan-pipes with which he sang of his love for Galatea before murdering her lover.

Polyphemus and his fellow giants are revenged in the extraordinary **Sala dei Giganti** beyond – "the most fantastic and frightening creation of the whole Renaissance", according to the critic Frederick Hartt – showing the destruction of the giants by the gods. As if at some kind of advanced disaster movie, the destruction appears to be all around: cracking pillars, toppling brickwork and screaming giants, mangled and crushed by great chunks of architecture, appearing to crash down into the room. Stamp your feet and you'll discover another parallel to twentieth-century cinema – the sound effects that Giulio created by making the room into an echo chamber.

Eating and drinking

Mantua has plenty of excellent, reasonably priced restaurants, many serving Mantuan **specialities** like *spezzatino di Mantova* (donkey stew), *agnoli in brodo* (pasta stuffed with cheese and sausage in broth) or the delicious *tortelli di zucca* (pasta stuffed with pumpkin). If you want a **snack**, try the *kioskos* in the park just off Viale Isonzo, which serve a wide choice of *piadine* and panini, with a view of Palazzo Te. In town the wine bar *Buca della Gabbia*, at Via Cavour 98, is a good spot for an *aperitivo* in winter or something stonger after dinner.

Al Quadrato Piazza Virgiliana 49. A tranquil spot away from the fray, overlooking the Piazza Virgiliana park; good pizzas and tasty fish dishes. Closed Mon.

Aquila Nigra Vicolo Bonaclosi 4 ☏0376.327.180. One of the top places in town, this formal restaurant, housed in an elegant *palazzo* just off Piazza Sordello, serves delicious seasonal fare complemented by an impressive wine list. Closed Sun, Mon & Aug.

Fragoletta Antica Piazza Arche 5a ☏0376.323.300. Over towards the Lago Inferiore, this lively *osteria* has been around since 1748 and remains popular with locals for its well-priced regional cuisine with creative touches. *Primi* are around €7–8, *secondi* around €10. Closed Mon.

Grifone Bianco Piazza dell'Erbe 6 ☏0376.365.423. The pick of the restaurants on this stretch of the Piazza, serving excellent local specialities at moderate prices. Closed Tues, Wed & late July.

Il Cigno (Trattoria dei Martini) Piazza d'Arco 1 ☏0376.327.101. Exceptional restaurant occupying a sixteenth-century mansion in a quiet corner away from the centre. The tasteful old dining room overlooks a beautiful private garden and the local ingredients are served up with style by the welcoming owners. Expect well over €50 per head plus wine. Closed Mon, Tues & Aug.

La Masseria Piazza Broletto 7 ☏0376.365.303. A popular, lively place with good pizzas as well as a wide selection of other dishes served at outside tables. Closed Thurs.

L'Ochina Bianca Via Finzi 2 ☏0376.323.700. Cosy *osteria* where friendly staff serve tasty Mantovan dishes – this is a mainstay of the Italian "Slow Food" movement, dedicated to promoting quality and conviviality (see p.43). Five minutes' walk west from Piazza Erbe. Closed Mon.

Tirattappi Piazza Alberti 30 ☏0376.322.366. Atmospheric old wine-bar on this little-visited square, down a concealed passageway beside the Sant'Andrea church off Piazza Mantegna. Wine and produce are all local: reasonably priced specialities are served with care. Closed Tues.

Grazie and Sabbioneta

A ten-minute bus ride west of Mantova at **GRAZIE**, the church of **Santa Maria delle Grazie** has an interior chock-full of votive offerings, with wax and wooden mannequins, their clothes petrified with age, standing in niches surrounded by wooden hearts, breasts, hands and feet nailed up by the recipients of miracle cures. There's even a stuffed crocodile hanging from the ceiling. Alongside the church, a path leads down to the marshes, rich in rare birds and wildlife. See p.211 and p.212 for details of boat trips and the new youth hostel 2km to the north.

Further out, fifty minutes by bus from Mantua bus station (3–7 daily), **SABBIONETA** is a more interesting target, an odd little place with the air of an abandoned film set, where imperious Renaissance palaces gaze blankly over deserted and dusty piazzas. The town is the work of the Vespasiano Gonzaga, member of a minor branch of the Mantuan family, who dreamed of creating the ideal city; sadly it has now been abandoned by all but the oldest inhabitants, a handful of agricultural workers and the tourist board. The tourist office at Piazza D'Armi 1 (Tues–Sat 10am–1pm & 2–5pm; ☏0375.221.044, ⊛www.comune.sabbioneta.mn.it), arrange guided tours around the most important buildings (Tues–Sun 10am–1pm & 2.30–6pm; €8, or €3 for individual monuments).

Even as it was being built, Sabbioneta was an anachronism. In the sixteenth century it was no more than an agricultural village, nominal capital of an insignificant state on the Mantuan border struggling to maintain its independence from the foreign powers who had colonized most of Lombardy. Unperturbed, its ruler, Duke Vespasiano, was keen to create an ideal state on the model of ancient Athens and Rome. He uprooted his subjects from their farm cottages, forcing them to build and then inhabit the new city, which held a Greek and Latin Academy and a Palladian theatre as well as a couple of ducal residences. After Vespasiano's death, Sabbioneta returned to – and has remained in – its former state: a small agricultural village like hundreds of others throughout Italy.

Tours start with the **Palazzo del Giardino** – Vespasiano's private residence – decorated with frescoed models ranging from Roman emperors to the Three Graces. Next stop is the **Teatro Olimpico**, copied from Palladio's theatre of the same name in Vicenza, in which the only spectators are pallid marble gods, fake-bronze emperors and ghostly painted courtiers. The **Palazzo Ducale**, around the corner, holds painted wooden statues of four of the Gonzagas, including Vespasiano (with the ruffle and beard), sitting imperiously on horse-back. What remains of the palace's decor is likewise concerned with the show of strength – frescoed elephants and friezes of eagles and lions. Close by, the **Chiesa dell'Incoronata** (Sun & public holidays only 3–6pm) is remarkable mainly for its trompe l'oeil roof, which appears to be three times higher in than out – perhaps an apt comment on Vespasiano himself, a bronze statue of whom sits beneath, dressed as a Roman emperor and looking reluctant to leave his dream city.

Northern Lombardy: lakes and mountains

"One can't describe the beauty of the **Italian lakes**, nor would one try if one could." Henry James's sentiment hasn't stopped generations of writers trying to do just that in pages of purple prose. In fact, the lakes just about deserve it: their beauty is extravagant, and it's not surprising that the most melodramatic and romantic of Italy's opera composers – Verdi, Rossini and Bellini – rented lakeside villas in which to work. British and German Romantic poets also enthused about the area, and in doing so implanted it firmly in northern European imaginations. The result is a massive influx every summer of tourists from cooler climes, come to savour the Italian dream and to take large gulps at what Keats called "the beaker of the warm south".

Garda is the largest lake, and one of the best centres in Europe for windsurfing and sailing, although you'll have to share the water with large numbers of like-minded enthusiasts. If watersports don't appeal, **Como** is the most scenically stunning of the lakes: surrounded by tall peaks that rise more or less directly from the water's edge, the luxuriance of its vegetation is equalled by the opulence of the local villas and *palazzi*; and when such things begin to cloy, there are good hikes in its mountainous hinterland. The shores of **Maggiore** are much flatter, and many of its *fin-de-siècle* resorts are rather sedate. There are, however, some good walks, and you shouldn't miss the gardens on Isola Bella. Though the picture-postcard charms of Orta San Giulio, the main village on **Lago d'Orta**, ensure that it is thronged with people at Easter and in summer, it's a romantic base in spring or autumn, and while the other minor lakes – **Lago d'Iseo** and **Lago Ledro** – are subdued in comparison, you might want to spend some time relaxing on Iseo's islet, Monte Isola.

The hilly terrain between the lakes is sliced up by **mountain valleys**: their lower reaches are largely residential and harbour light industry, with their rivers frequently reduced to a trickle by hydroelectric works, but the upper reaches are mainly untouched, with plenty of possibilities for hikes. There are also numerous small ski resorts, but none worth going out of your way for. Of the two main cities, **Brescia** is best as a daytrip; **Bergamo** makes a much nicer place to stay, with an old walled hilltop centre that ranks as one of the loveliest in Italy. If you're lucky enough to find a room there, it's also a good base for trips to lakes Como and Iseo and the mountainous country in between.

Getting around the lakes

The three biggest lakes are all well served by ferries, which zigzag from shore to shore, docking at jetties that are usually conveniently positioned on the main lakeside piazzas or in the centre of the larger towns' promenades. Some of the regular boats are pretty slow, and if you're in a hurry, you can pay extra for a hydrofoil. **Car ferries** also operate on Lago Maggiore (Verbania–Laveno), Lago Como (Menaggio–Bellagio–Varenna) and Lago Garda (Toscalano–Maderno–Torri del Benaco). These can be a good way to minimize driving along slow, traffic-congested lakeside roads.

Timetables and fares are available at all tourist offices and the ticket booths on the jetties themselves. Prices vary, but fares are relatively inexpensive: Como to Bellagio, for example, is €6.20 one-way. There are some discounts for EU citizens over 65 and for children; deals on passes are constantly changing but if you plan to travel a lot it's worth enquiring at tourist offices. For full up-to-date schedules and prices, check ⓦwww.navigazionelaghi.it, which covers the services on the three main lakes, and ⓦwww.navigazionelagoiseo.it for information on the service on Lago d'Iseo.

In addition, there are fairly regular **buses** up and down the shores, a cheaper but far less interesting way of travelling. Timetables are usually posted on bus stops, and again the better-organized tourist offices have copies. Be warned, though, that in Garda and Maggiore, which have one shoreline in Lombardy and another in, respectively, Veneto and Piemonte, it can be impossible to get hold of timetables for the "rival" region's buses.

Lago Maggiore and Lago d'Orta

For generations of overland travellers, **Lago Maggiore** has been the first taste of Italy. Road and railway from Switzerland run between the shores of Maggiore and **Lago d'Orta** and, for travellers weary of the journey and the cool grandeur of the Alps, the first glimpse of Maggiore's limpid waters, gentle green hills and the hint of exotic vegetation can seem a promising taster of the country. Unmistakably Mediterranean in atmosphere, with palms and oleanders lining the lakeside proms and a peaceful, serene air, this is not somewhere for thrill-seekers, but is a relaxing place. Tourists come to see the orange blossom, vines, clear air and the verbena that flourishes on its shores, and you'll need to book in advance in peak season. Note that between October and Easter the resorts all practically close down and accommodation is hard to find.

The western shore

The majority of tourists who flock to Lago Maggiore head for the western shore, from where you can easily get to the lake, the sumptuous gardens and villas of the **Isole Borromee**. Miraculously, however, the area has not completely lost its charm and the *fin-de-siècle* resort of **Stresa** is still a popular base for a visit to the area. It is the last lakeside stop on the trainline to Domodossola (see p.103), a bus ride away from Lago d'Orta and, most importantly, has fantastic views and access to the lake's islands. Further north, **Verbania** has ferry links to the eastern shore, plus the lake's only youth hostel, while enchanting **Cannobio**, the last stop before Switzerland, is a younger resort that's popular with families and a convenient place from which to explore Maggiore's hilly hinterland.

All the resorts on the western shore of the lake are connected by regular **bus** and **ferry** services. The train line goes inland after Stresa but in season, the combined rail-and-ferry **Lago Maggiore Express** allows you to catch the train up to Domodossola, change to a private rail link to Locarno, just over the border in Switzerland, then get the ferry back to Stresa. The route is stunning, passing through some beautiful mountain scenery with magnificent lake views. You can stop off wherever you want en route and two-day passes are available: prices vary according to whether there are restaurant facilities on board. For details of prices and schedules, check ⓦwww.lagomaggioreexpress.com or at local tourist offices.

Stresa

The Maggiore of the tourist brochures begins at **STRESA**, whose popularity as a resort began in 1906 with the construction of the Simplon Tunnel (the railroad connecting Domodossola to Brig in Switzerland). Its elegant lakeside promenade is now trodden by elderly visitors for whose benefit the main square in its mellow old centre is filled with ranks of café tables dedicated to the mass consumption of outsize ice-cream sundaes.

After strolling up and down the promenade past the *Grand Hotel des Iles Borromees*, a location in Hemingway's *A Farewell to Arms*, you might want to catch the cable car up **Monte Mottarone** (daily every 20min 9.30am–5.20pm; €9 return) from the Lido. It's hardly the most sensational of hills, but undeserving of Ruskin's derision – he referred to it as "the stupidest of mountains" and thought the views of the Alps dull. Ruskin's mood or the weather must have been bad, for the views are impressive, stretching from Monte Rosa on the Valle d'Aosta/Swiss border across to the Adamello. Its wooded western slopes are now a favourite destination for family outings, and on summer Sundays the roadside is lined with picnickers; the tourist office has leaflets detailing walks in the area. You can rent mountain bikes near the summit (€22 per day), or walk down to Lago d'Orta on the other side of the mountain, though it's a fairly dull three-hour tramp.

Practicalities

Stresa's well-organized **tourist office**, by the ferry jetty at Piazza Marconi 16 (March–Oct daily 10am–12.30pm & 3–6.30pm; Nov–Feb Mon–Fri 10am–12.30pm & 3–6.30pm; ☎0323.31.308, ⓦwww.lagomaggiore.it), provides useful local information, as well as programmes for the prestigious **international music festival** held annually in late July and early August.

Stresa's top **hotel** is the lakefront *Grand Hotel des Iles Borromees* (☎0323.938.938, ⓦwww.borromees.it; ⓐ), whose opulent surroundings and every conceivable comfort make it popular with Brits and Americans. At the other end of the scale, the friendly little *Albergo Ristorante Luina*, at Via Garibaldi 21 (☎0323.30.285, ⓦwww.stresa.org; ⓐ), is right in the centre of the village, with diminutive en-suite rooms and a good-value restaurant serving home cooking. Also in the centre, the two-star *Hotel Fiorentino* (☎0323.30.254, ⓦwww.hotelfiorentino .com; ⓐ), at Via A.M. Bolongaro 9, has comfortable en-suite rooms above a family-run restaurant with a sunny courtyard. The most atmospheric option in this area, however, is the *Albergo Ristorante Verbano* (☎0323.30.408, ⓦwww .hotelverbano.it; ⓐ) on the Isola dei Pescatori. The handsomely furnished rooms in this small, romantic hotel have wonderful lake views and make a perfect bolthole at any time of year.

The best place to try regional Piemontese **food** is in the snug *La Botte* (T0323.30.462; closed Thurs) on Via Mazzini 6/8, right in the village centre, where the friendly host serves up local game as well as a variety of tasty pasta dishes. A couple of doors away, at no. 25, the pricier *Pietmontese* (T0323.30.235; closed Mon & Nov to mid-Feb) offers a more refined atmosphere in its elegant dining room or pleasant garden. Alternatively, the *Osteria degli Amici*, at Via A.M. Bolongaro 27 (T0323.30.453; closed Wed), on the other side of the main square, is a simple place with an attractive vine-covered terrace, where a very tasty *risotto alle scampetti* is served, though service can be slow.

The Isole Borromee

The three visitable **Isole Borromee** (W wsw.borromeoturismo.it) are all served by regular ferries from Stresa, either from Piazza Marconi or Piazzale Lido, further up the lakeside promenade; ignore the hard-sell skippers unless you want to go on a private launch. **Isola Bella** is home to a villa (March 25 to Oct 22 daily 9am–5.30pm; gardens 9am–6.15pm; €10, €15 with Isola Madre), reckoned by Robert Southey to be "one of the most costly efforts of bad taste in all Italy". It is best known, however, for being the most gloriously excessive of all the lakes' gardens, though three centuries ago it was little more than a barren rock. In the seventeenth century Count Carlo III Borromeo decided to create an island paradise for his wife Isabella, and commissioned the architect, Angelo Crivelli, to transform it into a sumptuous Baroque oasis. Tons of soil were brought across from the mainland, a villa, fountains and statues were built, white peacocks imported, and ten terraces of orange and lemon trees, camellias, magnolias, box trees, laurels and cypresses carved out. The centrepiece, however, is a four-tiered confection of shell-, mirror- and marble-encrusted grottoes, topped with a suitably melodramatic unicorn, mini-obelisks, and various Greek gods and cute cherubs in attendance. Inside, ritzy rooms are opulently furnished, and there are more artificial grottoes and a collection of eighteenth-century marionettes in the cellar. Isola Bella really is worth seeing, though as Maggiore's main tourist attraction, every inch of the island not occupied by the palace and garden is taken up by restaurants with multilingual menus and stalls selling lace, pottery and the ubiquitous Pinochio puppet.

Hemingway's favourite island, **Isola dei Pescatori** (or Isola Superiore), once an island of fishermen, retains a certain charm, despite the regular invasions of sightseers. Along with the obligatory trinket stands and restaurants there are a few ordinary bars and shops, and it's a good spot for a picnic; see also the hotel option on p.220. Ferries move on to **Isola Madre**, larger but less visited than Isola Bella, with a small, tasteful *palazzo* (March 25 to Oct 22 9am–5.30pm; €9, €15 with Isola Bella), stacked with portraits of the Borromeos in a luxuriant but less formal garden. Tiny **San Giovanni**, the fourth Borromean island, has a villa once owned by Toscanini, but is closed to the public.

Verbania

Half way up the lake is **PALLANZA**, which along with the industrial quarters of Suna and Intra makes up the town of **VERBANIA**, whose name recalls *Verbanum* – the name used by the Romans for the whole, verbena-shored lake. Verbania's winter climate is the mildest on the lake, which enabled a retired Scottish soldier, Captain Neil McEachern, to create in the 1930s the most botanically prestigious garden of all the lakes, at the **Villa Táranto**. The splendid grounds (April–Nov daily 8.30am–7.30pm, last admission 6.30pm; €8.50;

ⓦwww.villataranto.it) contain 20,000 species of plant – including giant Amazonian lilies, lotus blossoms, Japanese maple, and *Melia azederach*, a sacred Indian tree – laid out with cool geometric accuracy around fountains and pools.

A half-hour walk south of Villa Táranto, Pallanza's lakefront is lined with manicured flower beds and dapper *gelaterie*, bars and hotels, but on the hill behind there's a more down-to-earth quarter in which the souvenir shops are almost outnumbered by *alimentari*, fruit shops and *pasticcerie*. The **tourist office** is on Corso Zanitello 8 (Mon–Fri 9am–12.30pm & 3–6pm, Sat 9am–12.30pm; May–Sept also Sat afternoon & Sun morning; ⓣ & ⓕ0323.503.249, ⓦwww .verbania-turismo.it). From just north of the entrance to the villa, the lake's only **car ferry** links the east Piemonte coast with the western Lombardy shores at the town of Laveno (see p.224). Pallanza also boasts the lake's only **youth hostel** (ⓣ0323.501.648, ⓔostello-verbania@libero.it; €14.50; March–Oct), at Via alle Rose 7, a signposted ten-minute uphill walk from Piazza Gramsci where the bus drops you. It's a friendly place set in an old villa with singles, doubles and small dorms; the staff also organize activities in the area.

Cannobio

CANNOBIO is the most appealing place to stay on the western shore of the lake, its lakefront road of pastel-washed houses giving on to a series of stepped alleyways leading into a tightly tangled old village of stone houses. The town's only sight as such is the **Santuario della Pietà**, a Bramante-inspired church beside the landing stage with a curious openwork cupola, built to house a painting of the Pietà which supposedly began to bleed in 1522.

At the head of Via Marconi is the SS34 coast road, Viale Vittorio Veneto, on which you'll find the **tourist office** (Mon–Sat 9am–noon & 4.30–7pm, Sun 9am–noon; Oct–March closed Thurs; ⓣ0323.71.212, ⓦwww.cannobio.net) and a couple of supermarkets. At the northern end of the lakefront, past the car park, between the town and most of the campsites, lies the blue-flag winning public beach, backed by a pleasant grassy area with trees, picnic tables, showers; you can hire watersports equipment here. On Sundays, the local market takes over the waterfront area selling anything from fresh produce to leather and tacky brand goods.

The cheapest **accommodation** in Cannobio is offered by the various lakeside campsites to the north of town, many of which have bungalows and caravans to rent; there are also plenty of rooms advertised along the main road. Recently redecorated with plush, over-the-top furnishings, the *Hotel Cannobio* (ⓣ0323.739.639, ⓦwww.hotelcannobio.com; ⓺) has a splendid position on the lakefront, though a better option is the serene and friendly *Hotel Pironi*, Via G. Marconi 35 (ⓣ0323.706.24, ⓦwww.pironihotel.it; March–Nov; ⓹), a converted fifteenth-century convent tucked among the streets winding up from the lakeside. Residents can use the swimming pool at its sister hotel, the modern *Villa Belvedere* (ⓣ0323.70.159, ⓦwww.villabelvederehotel.it; ⓸), just out of town on the road to the Val Cannobina. A cheaper but still appealing choice is the *Antica Stallera*, Via P. Zacchero 7 (ⓣ0323.715.95, ⓦwww .anticastallera.com; ⓷), with a vine-covered garden restaurant overlooked by simple, modern en-suite rooms. Cannobio's very popular **campsite**, *Residence Campagna* (ⓣ0323.70.100, ⓦwww.campingcampagna.it; March–Oct), is out of town on the SS34, just past the River Cannobino; as well as tent pitches, it also has rooms in a clean, modern villa (⓶).

Lo Scalo (closed Mon), on a corner site on the lakefront opposite the ferry port, is arguably the best **restaurant** in town and is certainly one of the smartest. The inventive food is based on Piemontese specialities; you'll pay around €80 a head for a full meal with wine. If you're keeping to a tighter budget, try *Osteria La Streccia*, up a narrow cobbled alley off the lakefront (closed Tues), which offers good food in a rustic, low-ceilinged dining room; head for the garden at the *Antica Stallera* (see opposite). In summer the *gelaterie* along the lakefront are great for a **snack** or cappuccino, while the bar below the *Hotel Pironi* (see opposite) is a cosy spot for a **drink** in cooler weather.

Inland along the Val Cannobina

Extending behind the town, the wooded **Val Cannobina** offers beautiful views, little-visited stone-built hamlets and a clutch of good countryside restaurants (see below). Buses climb high into the valley, on one route to **Falmenta**, marooned in the jagged shadow of Monte Vadà (1836m), and on another to **Cúrsolo**, from where a scenic seven-kilometre walk heads past Finero to **Malesco** in the Val Vigezzo, a stop on the Domodossola–Locarno train line. The tourist office has details of many walks, including along the Linea Cadorna, a well-preserved World War I defence line that snaked across the peaks from the Val d'Ossola down to Cannobio.

Only 2.5km into the valley from central Cannobio, near Traffiume, a turn-off signs the **Orrido di Sant'Anna**, a spectacular rocky gorge surrounded by wooded slopes that is a popular picnic spot. Beside the Roman bridge and the chapel is a small river beach and a wonderfully sited restaurant, the *Sant'Anna* (℡0323.70.682; closed Mon), which offers tasty and reasonably priced food. An attractive cycle route runs along the riverside from the centre of Cannobio; you can rent bikes from the shop on Viale Veneto, opposite the tourist office.

The eastern shore

In general there is little of great interest on the eastern side of Lago Maggiore, although any of the smaller centres make feasible bases for the rest of the lake, or for hiking into the hills behind. From **MACCAGNO**, an improbably steep track leads straight out from the village into the hills, from where there are paths to tiny Lago Delio. Most interestingly, you can walk to the village of Curiglia, beyond which, from Ponte di Piero, an acute mule track climbs to the picturesque village of **Monteviasco**, 500m above. There's no road to Monteviasco, and until the recent arrival of a cable car, the mule track was its only link with the world. For drivers, a road also climbs from Maccagno through the woods to Lake Delio; the views looking back at Cannobio, 1000m below on the lake are breathtaking.

Four kilometres south, you'll find appealing places **to stay** in the area: the *Hotel Camin Colmegna* (℡03332.510.855, Ⓦ www.camin-hotels.com; ❺), a friendly family-run hotel right on the waterfront. It's uncomfortably close to the main road, but on a sunny day the extensive lakeside gardens and swimming areas are difficult to beat.

One and half kilometres further south, the sizeable town of **LUINO** is besieged on Wednesdays by tourists from all the lake's resorts visiting Maggiore's biggest market, an unappealing mixture of local produce, plastic toys and cheap shoes. The *centro storico* (follow sign off the main road to the left of the *imbarcadero*) is no great shakes but is reasonably well stocked with food and especially wine shops. If you've spent any time in Lombardy's art galleries you may already be familiar with the work of Bernardino Luino, one of Leonardo's followers. It's assumed that he hailed from Luino, and if you like his work, you should take a look at his frescoes on the campanile at the oratory of **SS Pietro e Paolo**. Luino's **tourist office** (Mon–Sat 9am–noon & 2.30–6.30pm; ℡0332.530.019) is across the road from the jetty and can provide a list of places to stay.

Twenty-five kilometres south of Luino, **LAVENO** is also accessible by car ferry from Intra (€2 per person plus €5.10 for an average-sized car; 20min). From Laveno a cable car climbs up to the **Sasso del Ferro** for great views of the Alps. On its southern slopes, but visible only from the lake, is the **Santuario di Santa Caterina del Sasso** (April–Oct daily 8.30am–noon & 2–6pm; rest of the year 9am–noon & 2–5pm; free; ⓦ www.provincia.va.it/santacaterina). In the early twelfth century a wealthy moneylender, Alberto Besozzi, was sailing on the lake when his boat sank. He prayed to St Catherine of Alexandria and was safely washed up on shore, afterwards giving up usury and becoming a hermit in a cave on the hillside. When his prayers averted a plague the locals built a church; this became popular with pilgrims, especially after a boulder fell on the roof but was miraculously wedged just above the altar instead of falling on the priest. The boulder finally crashed through in 1910.

Lago d'Orta

The locals call **Lago d'Orta** "Cinderella", capturing perfectly the reticent beauty of this small lake with its deep blue waters and intriguing island. Occupying the tip of a peninsula on the lake's eastern shore, **ORTA SAN GIULIO** is a romantic little village where narrow cobbled streets run between pastel-washed houses and palaces with elaborate wrought-iron balconies. It is, not surprisingly, the lake's main attraction, and on summer Sundays the approach roads are jammed with traffic, though in the evenings the charm returns. The village is at its best mid-week or out of season.

Life in Orta San Giullio centres on two piazzas: **Piazzetta Ernesto Ragazzoni** and **Piazza Motta**, which open to the lake and look directly onto Isola San Giulio. Somewhat out of place among the pavement cafés is the **Palazzo della Comunità**, the diminutive town hall, decorated with faded frescoes and supported on an arcaded *loggia*. From here, you can take Via Giovanetti out of the village for a stroll or a sunbathe on the lakeside promenade, or catch a boat out to the island (see below).

Above the town is a *Santuario*, with a **Sacro Monte**, 21 chapels dedicated to St Francis of Assisi and containing some awful tableaux of painted terracotta statues acting out scenes from the saint's life against frescoed B-movie backgrounds. The chapels make up a devotional route still followed by pilgrims, though as many visitors come simply to picnic, admire the views of the lake and inhale the pine-scented air. From the piazza, simply follow the signposts uphill to the *Santuario*.

Isola San Giulio

Lago d'Orta's highlight is the **Isola San Giulio**, a tiny island dominated by a white seminary and the tower of its twelfth-century basilica. Boats leave from Orta San Giullio's Piazza Motta every fifteen minutes, and the return journey costs €3; the last boat back is at 7.30pm. No vehicles are allowed on the island and it takes about twenty minutes to walk round the island on its one cobbled lane. There are a couple of shops, a restaurant and several potential picnic spots with views across the lake.

San Giulio was a priest who in 390 AD decided to found a sanctuary on the island. The locals refused to row him over, however as the island was supposedly seething with monsters and snakes, and Giulio is said to have crossed on foot using his staff as a rudder and his cloak as a sail. Once there, he banished the snakes, founded his sanctuary and earned himself a sainthood. The **Basilica** (May–Sept Mon–Sat 9.30am–noon & 2–6.45pm, Sun 9.30am–12.15pm &

2–6.45pm; Oct–April closes 5.30pm) has a redoubtable pulpit, carved from local serpentine stone with symbols of the four evangelists and images of good winning over evil: note the crocodile locked in battle with the phoenix.

Arrival and information

Orta-Misiano **station** (on the Novara–Domodossola branch line) is around 3km out of town: turn left out of the station on to the main road and continue downhill for about twenty minutes to the village. On the way, you'll pass the well-organized **tourist office**, on Via Panoramica (Tues–Sun 10am–1pm & 3–6.30pm; ☎0322.905.6163, ⓦwww.lagodorta.net). The village is entirely car-free and there are extensive car parks (worth paying for the covered one in summer) at the end of the road.

Accommodation

Orta's **accommodation** is generally good, but limited: you should always **book in advance**, at any budget. Hotels aside, you can **rent en-suite rooms** or self-catering apartments from a handful of places, notably the little office at Via Olina 40 (☎0322.905.656, ⓦwww.ortainfo.com). The **campsite**, *Camping Orta* (☎ & ⓕ0322.90.267, ⓦwww.campingorta.it), with its own beach, is a little out of town sandwiched between the main road and the lake – it's about a fifteen-minute walk downhill from the station (turn right at the main crossroads opposite *Hotel Crespi*).

Contrada dei Monti Via dei Monti 10 ☎0322.905.114, ⓦwww.orta.net /lacontradadeimonti. Situated on one of the steep lanes leading off the main drag, this comfortable little hotel has rooms that open onto a tiny enclosed courtyard where breakfast is served in summer. Closed Jan. ❹
Hotel Aracoeli Piazza Motta 34 ☎0322.905.173, ⓦwww.ortainfo.com. An idiosyncratic contemporary hotel run by the family that owns another hotel, *Olina*, a restaurant and also rooms for rent (see below). Located on one corner of the main square, the rooms are individually themed ❺
Leon d'Oro Piazza Motta 42 ☎0322.911.991, ⓦwww.orta.net/leondoro. Just off the main square, the rooms in this recently renovated three-star are

somewhat over decorated but many offer great lake views. ❹
Orta Piazza Motta 1 ☎0322.90.253, ⓦwww .hotelorta.it. A traditional hotel on the main square that's been in the same family since 1864. The en-suite rooms saw better days in the 1970s, though many have lake views and if you can bag one of the three suites facing the island, with private terraces over the water, you'll be in heaven. Closed Nov–March. ❸
San Rocco Via Gippini 11 ☎0322.911.977, ⓦwww.hotelsanrocco.it. This fantastically sited four star at one end of village should be the best place in town, but its rooms are tired and dated. There is, however, a wonderful lakeside swimming pool. ❻–❼

Eating and drinking

For a picnic on the island or on one of the various jetties overhanging the water, the *gastronomia* in the centre of the main piazza makes good panini. Alternatively, *Taverna Boeuc*, on Via Bersani, serves tasty **snacks** to accompany well-chosen wine. For more of a sit-down **meal**, the *Olina*, Via Olina 40 (closed Wed), serves excellent local specialities and thoughtful extras like aperitifs on the house, while the smarter *Antico Agnello*, at Via Olina 18 (☎0322.90.259; closed Tues), offers tasty Lombard and Piedmont dishes, great puddings and congenial service. The lakeside *Leon d'Oro* has a wisteria-covered terrace looking out to the island (☎0322.911.991), and features a carefully chosen, moderately priced menu of local specialities. There's also a friendly little restaurant *Sacro Monte* (☎0322.90220; closed Tues & Jan) inside the grounds of the Sacro Monte, with a cosy interior and attractive alfresco tables.

Lago di Como

Of all the Italian lakes, it's the forked **Lago di Como** that comes most heavily praised: Wordsworth thought it "a treasure which the earth keeps to itself". Today, despite the influx of tourists, the lake is still surrounded by abundant vegetation and zigzagging across the water on a steamer can seem almost ridiculously romantic. In addition to indulging in *belle époque* dreams, you could try one of the several great walks through the lake's mountainous hinterland. The principal towns – **Como** and **Lecco** – are on the southern shores of the two "forks" of the lake, while of the other towns and villages, three are outstanding: **Varenna** and **Bellagio** for unrepentant romantics, and **Menaggio** if you want a pleasant, affordable base for walking, swimming or cycling.

Como Town

COMO can be a rather dispiriting place to arrive, with little of the picture-postcard prettiness you would expect from a lakeside town. As the nearest resort to Milan and a popular stop-off on the main road into Switzerland, it's both heavily touristed and, on the outskirts at least, fairly industrialized. Although the main industry is a rarefied one – Como is the main silk-supplier for Milan's fashion designers – it doesn't make the factories any more endearing. The old walled town, however, is pleasant to wander or eat in, and the funicular ride has wonderful views across the water, but really you'd do best using the town as a transport hub and moving on to one of the lake's more attractive resorts.

Lakeside **Piazza Cavour** is bounded by modern hotels and banks. To the northwest, a little waterfront park is set around a curious temple, now the **Museo Alessandro Volta** (Tues–Sun 10am–noon, also April–Sept & 3–6pm; Oct–March 2–4pm; €3), dedicated to Como's most useful son, a pioneer in

△ A villa on Lake Como

electricity who gave his name to the volt – some of the instruments he used to conduct his experiments are displayed inside. Beyond, compellingly illuminated at night, is the **Villa Olmo** (Mon–Sat 9.30am–noon & 3–6pm; free), an eighteenth-century Neoclassical pile in magnificent grounds. The villa itself hosts conferences and art exhibitions, but it is the **gardens** that are the biggest draw (Mon–Sat: summer 8am–11pm; winter 7am–7pm; free).

From Piazza Cavour, Via Plinio leads up to the **Broletto**, prettily striped in pink, white and grey, and with a fifteenth-century balcony designed for municipal orators. Next door, the splendid **Duomo** (daily 7.30am–noon & 3–7pm) was begun at the end of the fourteenth century but wasn't completed until the eighteenth, when the Baroque genius Juvarra added its cupola. The church is reckoned to be Italy's best example of Gothic-Renaissance fusion: the Gothic spirit clear in the fairy-tale pinnacles, rose windows and buffoonish gargoyles; that of the Renaissance in its portals (with rounded rather than ogival arches) and in the presence of the two pagans flanking the main west door – the Elder and Younger Plinys, both of whom were born in Como. There was nothing unusual in the sequestration of classical figures by Christians in the Renaissance, but the presence, especially of Pliny Junior, does seem somewhat inappropriate, since his only connection with Christianity was to order the assassination of two deaconesses. Inside, the Gothic aisles are hung with rich Renaissance tapestries (some woven with perspective scenes) and if you've a few spare coins you could illuminate a heavy-lidded Leonardoesque *Madonna* and an *Adoration of the Magi* by Luini, and a languid *Flight to Egypt* by Gaudenzio Ferrari.

Behind the Duomo, on the other side of the railway tracks in Piazza del Popolo, is the definitive example of Rationalist architecture by Como-born Giuseppe Terragni. Built as the headquarters for the local Fascist party in the 1930s it has been rechristened the **Palazzo Terragni** and is now home to the area Guardia di Finanza.

Once you've tired of the town, head down to the lake shore to the right of Piazza Cavour, by Como Lago Nord station, and take the **funicular** (roughly every 30min 6am–10.30pm, until midnight in summer; €4.10 return) to **Brunate**. The railway chugs up for about seven minutes alongside the gardens of superb nineteenth-century villas to a small hilltop resort that has a few bars and restaurants and great views of the lake. It is also a good starting-point for hikes; the tourist office has free leaflets detailing routes.

Practicalities

Como has three **train stations**: the most important is Como San Giovanni, on the main line from Milano Centrale to Chiaso/Lugano, and Como Borghi and Como Lago Nord, from where trains run to Milan Nord (Cadorna), Saronno, Varese Nord and Novara Nord. Como Lago is, as its name suggests, on the lakeshore, across the road from the **bus station**. Bus C250 operated by SPT (ⓦwww.sptcomo.it) runs to Como direct from Malpensa airport. Como San Giovanni station, ten minutes' walk west from the walled old centre, is connected with the jetty (and the bus station) by buses #4 and #7. Como Borghi is on the southern side of the town centre, a short walk down Via Sirtori from Viale Battisti. Como San Giovanni has a small **tourist office**, but the main office is situated on Piazza Cavour (Mon–Sat 9am–1pm & 2.30–6pm, also June–Sept Sun 9.30am–12.30pm; ⓣ031.269.712, ⓦwww.lakecomo.org).

One of the more attractive **places to stay** in Como's centre is the comfortable *Del Duca* at Piazza Mazzini 12 (ⓣ031.264.859, ⓦwww.albergodelduca .it; ●) where most of the small pleasant rooms overlook a pretty piazza a few blocks back from the waterfront. In the adjacent Piazza Volta, Terragni's austere

facade on the *Albergo Ristorante Posta* (☎031.26.6012, ⓦwww.hotelposta
.net; ❷) matches its clean, utilitarian, en-suite rooms, including some triples
and a quad. Over the other side of town near the funicular, *Hotel Quarcino*,
at Salita Quarcino 4 (☎031.303.934, ⓦwww.hotelquarcino.it; ❷), is a family-
run hotel with quiet rooms, many with balconies overlooking the hillside.
The family rooms and suites are particularly good value and there is residents parking available. To get to Como's **youth hostel**, Via Bellinzona 2
(☎031.573.800, ⓦwww.ostellionline.org; €4; March–Nov), take bus #1 or
#6 from Como San Giovanni or walk for twenty minutes along Via Borgo
Vico (on the left as you walk down the steps from the main train station). The
hostel serves dinner (€9), has laundry facilities, rents out bikes, and provides a
discount on the funicular.

There are many definitively average **places to eat** in Como centre but the
moderately priced *Antica Trattoria da Angela*, Via Foscolo 16, near the bus station,
serves inspired regional cuisine using local ingredients, while the family-run
Del Duca in the corner of Piazza Mazzini is a pleasant spot to settle down for a
tasty pasta or crispy pizza. Alternatively, down one side of the Duomo, the *Teatro
Sociale*, at Via Maestri Comacini, serves a decent set meal for €15 (closed Tues).
For an *aperitivo* or evening **drink**, the atmospheric wine bar *Osteria del Gallo*, at
Via Vitani 16, serves a choice of tasty nibbles with a fine selection of wines. If
you'd prefer something livelier, head for the bars on the waterfront Lungo Lario
Triest, by the funicular station.

The western shore

The lower reaches of the western shore are the stuff of tourist brochures:
wooded mountain slopes protect the lake from extremes of temperature and
lush gardens abound. Many of the opulent villas that line the lakeside are still
privately owned by Italian industrialists and international celebrities (George
Clooney among them) and on summer weekends the lakeside road is solid
with day-trippers. The lake's only island, Isola Comacina, lies at the narrowest
point of the lake, just before the waters open up to the warm climes of the
nineteenth-century resorts of the Tremezzina. **Menaggio**, a little further north,
makes a good base for trips into the mountains behind or across to Bellagio (see
p.232) and Varenna (see p.231). As you skirt the lakeshore, it becomes rockier
and less accessible until the water spreads out into the marshes and flatter territory that accommodates campsites and windsurfers around **Gravedona**.

Ferries and the C10 **bus** regularly ply their way from Como to Colico, and,
from Cadenabbia and Menaggio, car and passenger **ferries** shuttle across to the
central and eastern shores of the lake.

Cernobbio and Isola Comacina

The first port of call by steamer on the western shore of Lake Como is
Cernobbio (also accessible by frequent bus from Como's Piazza Matteotti),
whose main claim to fame is the palatial sixteenth-century **Villa d'Este** hotel
(☎031.3481, ⓦwww.villadeste.it; ❾). The extravagant gardens with statues,
fountains and grottoes and the atmosphere of moneyed comfort make the hotel
very popular with ageing Americans and celebrities, although the service far
from lives up to its reputation.

A little further north lies **Isola Comacina**, Como's only island and, previously, another retreat for the well heeled. Uninhabited save for a handful
of artists, this is a wild place where you can wander through the ruins of
nine abandoned churches. One of the earliest settlements on the lake, it was

conquered by the Romans, and, later, when the barbarians invaded, it became a refuge. It developed into a centre of resistance, and in the turmoil of the Middle Ages attracted an eclectic mix of dethroned monarchs, future saints and the pirate Federico Barbarossa. Eventually it allied with Milan against Como, an unfortunate move that led to the island being sacked by Como and razed to the ground. Abandoned for centuries, it was bought by a local, Auguste Caprini, who outraged Italy by selling it to the King of Belgium after World War I. Diplomatically, the king decided to return it, and the island is now administered by a joint Belgian-Italian commission. Bring a **picnic**, as the snack bar by the jetty is pricey even for simple sandwiches. In the evening the island's only **restaurant**, the *Locanda dell'Isola* (☎0344.55.083), offers an elaborate "exorcism by fire" show, which is not as tacky as it sounds – involving essentially flambéed liquer coffee – and stems from a curse supposedly laid on the island in 1169 by the Bishop of Como. The price for a good-quality meal also (€55) includes a return boat ride.

The Tremezzina

Sheltered by a headland, the shore above Isola Comacina, known as the **Tremezzina**, is where Como's climate is at its gentlest, the lake at its most tranquil and the vegetation at its most lush. Lined with cypresses and palms, it's lovely at any time of year, but unbeatable in spring, when it's awash with colour and heady with the scent of flowering bushes.

Inland at **MEZZEGRA**, in 1944, two families of evacuees staying at the Villa Belmonte witnessed a less tranquil scene from their windows. A car drew up and a burly man in a black beret, nervously clutching the lapels of his coat, got out, followed by a woman and a tall pale man with a machine gun. The burly man was Mussolini, the woman his mistress, Claretta Petacci, and the tall man the partisan leader, Walter Audisio. Audisio pulled the trigger and Claretta flew at him, grasping the barrel of the gun; Audisio shot twice more, but the trigger jammed. He took his driver's machine gun and pointed it at Mussolini, who said "Shoot me in the chest"; Audisio shot first at Claretta, killing her outright, and then complied with Mussolini's last request. The bodies were bundled in a car headed for Piazza Duomo in Milan but a frenzied mob heard the news, stopped the car and the dictator and his mistress were strung up in Piazza Loretto for all to see.

TREMEZZO, like Como's other resorts, has its fair share of *belle époque* palaces, villas and hotels, but overall it's a sedate, rather middle-aged place. The main reason to stop here is to visit the **Villa Carlotta** (daily: April–Sept 9am–6pm; March & Oct 9–11.30am & 2–4.30pm; €7.50; ⓦ www.villacarlotta .it), which has its own *imbarcadero* between Tremezzo and Cadenabbia. Pink, white and Neoclassical, it was bought by a Prussian princess for her daughter, Carlotta, and now houses a collection of pompous eighteenth-century statues, including Canova's overly romantic *Cupid & Psyche* and a frieze of Alexander entering Babylon commissioned by Napoleon – though he was exiled before he could pay for it. The bill was picked up by a count, who in return got himself included as a member of Alexander's army (he's at the end, along with the artist). The villa's greatest attraction, however, is the fourteen-acre **garden**, a beautifully ordered collection of camellias, rhododendrons and azaleas.

Menaggio

MENAGGIO, 5km north, a bustling and lively village resort, is a good base for hiking and cycling in the mountains as well as sunbathing and swimming. The **ferry jetty** is about five minutes' walk from the main square, Piazza

Garibaldi, in and around which you'll find most of Menaggio's lakeside cafés and restaurants. The **tourist office** here (Mon–Sat 9am–noon & 3–6pm; ℡0344.32.924, ⓦwww.menaggio.com) is unusually well organized, with practical information on the town and maps on walks in the area and **Internet** access. Swimming in the lake is safe, and there's a beach and vast pool at the **Lido** (late June to mid-Sept daily 9am–7pm), as well as **water-skiing** and other waterborne activities at the Centro Lago Service on Via Lago Castelli (℡0344.32.003). There's a good selection of **hikes** in the countryside around Menaggio, ranging from a two-and-a-half hour walk to the pretty village of Codogna, to the fifty-kilometre *Sentiero delle 4 Valli*, which leads through four valleys to Lago Lugano. The tourist office can provide descriptions of the routes in English, including details of how to get to the various starting-points by public transport, but take a map as well.

Menaggio's **youth hostel**, the *Ostello La Primula*, Via IV Novembre 86 (℡0344.32.356, ⓦwww.menaggiohostel.com; €14 including breakfast; March–Oct), is just outside the village, overlooking the main road, with small, clean dorms and a couple of family rooms: reservations are essential. The hostel is well run with a friendly atmosphere, its own small beach and **bikes** for rent. It also serves excellent meals for €12, organizes hikes and can arrange discounts on boat rental. The nicer of the two **campsites** is the *Lido* (℡0344.31.150; May–Sept), on the road heading north out of town; the slightly cheaper *Europa* (℡0344.31.187; April–Sept) is just before. If you'd prefer a **hotel**, the three-star *Bellavista*, Via IV Novembre 21 (℡0344.32.136, ⓦwww.hotel-bellavista.org; ❺; April–Oct), is on the lake with its own pool, while the *Garni Corona*, Largo Cavour 3 (℡0344.32.006, ⓦwww.hotelgarnicorona.com; ❷; March–Nov), is a plain, family-run option with some lake-view rooms.

The lakeside has several **restaurants** serving set menus, but for something less touristy, *Vecchia Menaggio* at Via al Lago 13 (closed Tues) dishes up simple, good-value meals, as do *Il Vapore*, Piazza Grossi 3 (closed Wed; no credit cards), just back from the waterfront, and *Osteria Il Pozzo*, Via Carlo Porta 3 (closed Wed), just off Piazza Garibaldi.

Gravedona and around

The next major steamer stop is **GRAVEDONA**, not a particularly pretty place but one of the few towns on the lake as old as Como. Wordsworth set off on a moonlight hike from here, got lost, and, stuck on a rock in the middle of nowhere, was unable to sleep because he was "tormented by the stings of insects". Medieval Gravedona, along with nearby Dongo and Sorico, formed part of an independent republic, victimized in the fifteenth century by the inquisitor Peter of Verona for daring to doubt that the pope was God's earthly representative. The people got rid of Peter by hacking him to death, but the pope rewarded him for his devotion to duty by swiftly canonizing him and deeming him Patron of Inquisitors. There's a prophetic twelfth-century carving in the lakeside church of **Santa Maria del Tiglio** (generally open but, if not, get the key from the green house on the road) – a centaur pursuing a deer, an early Christian symbol for the persecution of the Church.

Boats dock at the main Piazza Garibaldi; running one block back is the narrow, attractive Via Sabbati, just off which is the simple *Lauro*, Via Tagliaferri 12 (℡0344.89.070; ❶) – a two-star **hotel** and **restaurant**. Beyond Gravedona, the terrain flattens out and the winds provide good **sailing** and **windsurfing**: see ⓦwww.gravedona.it for details of a number of **campsites** and cheap, modern **hotels** in the vicinity.

The eastern shore and Bellagio

The **eastern shore** of the lake, stretching from the flat marshes of the north to **Lago Lecco**, is – as a consequence of being overshadowed by the saw-like ridge of Monte Resegone – often sunless and consequently less visited than the western shore. The triangle of land between the two branches – the **central zone** – is lusher and sunnier, busy on the coast but with plenty of quiet villages and three small lakes inland. There are fewer places to stay, however, and these are not easily accessible, except Colico, Bellano and **Varenna** on the main shore and **Bellagio** on the central triangle, all served by ferries. The **C30** bus shuttles from Como to Bellagio and the **D20** bus runs between Lecco and Colico.

The north

At the top end of the lake's eastern shore – opposite Gravedona – **COLICO** is the final stop for Como steamers, a small industrial centre whose only attraction is a restored eleventh-century abbey, the **Abbazia di Piona** (daily 9am–noon & 2–6pm), on the tip of the promontory just above the steamer landing. From here, steamers and hydrofoils head back down the eastern shore, stopping off at **BELLANO**, a small workaday town of silk and cotton mills. From opposite the ferry jetty, follow the signs for the three-minute walk up behind Piazza San Giorgio to the **Orrido do Bellano** (April–Sept daily 10am–noon & 2–11.30pm; Oct–March Sat & Sun 10am–12.30pm & 2–7pm; €2.50), a steep gorge with a series of walkways suspended above a roaring river.

Varenna

Five kilometres further south, **VARENNA** is arguably the nicest place on the lake. Shaded by pines and planes, and almost completely free of souvenir shops, the village falls down steep narrow alleyways to the lakefront.

Arrival, information and accommodation

Varenna's **tourist office** is on the main Piazza San Giorgio (April–Sept Tues–Sat 10am–noon & 2.30–5.30pm; Oct–March Sun 10am–noon; ☎0341.830.367, ⓦwww.varennaitaly.com), at the top of the town, just opposite the main **bus** stop. The **station**, with regular direct trains to Milan, is a ten-minute walk away at the other end of town above the *Beretta* bar and hotel (see below). There's no shortage of **accommodation** in Varenna, though you'll need to book ahead in high season.

Beretta Via per Esino 1 ☎0341.830.132. This friendly chintzy place near the train station is the best of the cheaper options. It's also the hotel most likely to have room if you haven't booked ahead. ❷

Del Sole Piazza San Giorgio 21 ☎0341.815.218, Ⓔalbergo.sole@virgilio.it. Good family-run hotel in the village centre overlooking the piazza. Rooms are light, airy and modern – some with lake views. ❹

Du Lac Via del Prestino 4 ☎0341.830.238, ⓦwww.albergodulac.com. Varenna's top hotel, hidden away in a corner of the village right on the

waterfront, offers spacious rooms and an attractive terrace. ❻

Milano Via XX Settembre 29 ☎0341.830.298, ⓦwww.varenna.net. A real treat run by a charming couple, this romantic place has great views from the rooms and breakfast terrace. The evening meals are lovingly prepared. ❺

Olivedo Piazza Martiri 4 ☎0341.830.115, ⓦwww.olivedo.it. Eccentric little family-run hotel near the landing stage, stuffed with old prints and knickknacks. ❺

The Village

If you are feeling energetic, you could choose the brisk twenty-minute climb up the path opposite Villa Monastero for some great views from the semi-ruined **Castello de Vezio** (June–Sept daily 10am–10pm; April, May & Oct

10am–sunset; Feb & March Sat & Sun 10am–4pm, Nov & Dec Sun only; free), allegedly founded by the Lombard Queen Theodolinda in the first century. If you're not, head down to the waterfront from the square and drink in the peaceful views at one of the cafés or from the walkway which runs along to the ferry stop.

The other sights in town are botanical: now a hotel, the nineteenth-century **Villa Cipressi** (March to mid-Nov daily 9am–8pm; €2, or €3.50 including Monastero, see below; @www.hotelvillacipressi.it; ❹), on the southern fringe of the village, has swooningly scented terraced gardens tumbling down to the lake, that make a perfect spot to relax with a book in the afternoon sun. The gardens of the next-door **Villa Monastero** (April–Oct daily 9am–7pm; €2) are even more lavish: wandering here feels like a secret discovery. The splendid house is now used as a conference centre; when meetings are on, the gardens are closed.

Eating

Varenna's best place to **eat** is also its smallest. Hidden away in the thicket of narrow lanes off the main piazza is the tiny *Il Cavatappi* (☎0341.815.349; closed Wed), with just five tables. Booking is essential for this delightful little restaurant, where the owner/manager/chef takes the time to discuss the menu with you before turning out simple, beautifully cooked dishes with first-class ingredients. A meal is around €25 a head. *Vecchia Varenna* (☎0341.830.793; closed Mon) is in an unbeatable location, tucked beneath the arcades on the lakeside promenade and the food is good if not outstanding. The pizzeria attached to *Albergo del Sole* (closed Wed), on the main piazza, is another sound choice, with good, inexpensive fare and an attractive summer garden.

Bellagio

Cradled by cypress-spiked hills on the tip of the triangle separating Como's two "legs", **BELLAGIO** has been called the most beautiful town in Italy. With a promenade planted with oleanders and limes, *fin-de-siècle* hotels painted shades of butterscotch, peach and cream, and a hilly old centre of steep cobbled streets and alleyways – to say nothing of its tremendous location – it's easy to see why Bellagio has become so popular. These days, the streets are lined with upmarket souvenir shops and village life undoubtably plays second fiddle to the tourists but this is still an attractive resort, and outside the summer season, a relaxing, pleasant one to visit.

Arrival, information and accommodation

Bellagio's **tourist office**, in the *imbarcadero* on lakefront Piazza Mazzini (April–Oct Mon & Wed–Sat 9am–noon & 3–6pm; Nov–Easter Mon & Wed–Sat same hours; ☎031.951.555, @www.bellagiolakecomo.com), is a helpful source of information on activities in the area including hiking, horse riding, mountain biking and watersports. **Car ferries** pull into the jetty by the main car park, which is also the end of the line for the spectacular C30 bus route from Como.

As well as a full range of accommodation options, there's a small, relaxed **campsite**, *Camping Clarke*, about ten minutes' drive out of town on Via Valassina (☎031.951.325, @www.bellagio-camping.com; June–Sept) run by an English woman and her Italian husband.

Bellagio Salita Grandi 6 ☎031.950.424, @www .hotelbellagio.it. An appealing hotel in one of Bellagio's tallest buildings with huge picture windows. Go for the rooftop vistas from the fourth floor; the cheaper rooms lower down have less dreamy views. ❹

Belvedere Via Valassina 31 ☎031.950.410, @www.belvederebellagio.com. A modern

three-star hotel in its own grounds at the top of the village, with a swimming pool and wonderful views over the Lecco arm of the lake. April–Nov. ❹
Giardinetto Via Roncati 12 ☎031.950.168. Friendly one-star place at the top of Bellagio: some of the rooms have lake views and there's a garden where you can picnic. Best of the budget options. No credit cards. March–Oct. ❷

🏃 **La Pergola** Piazza del Porto 4, Pescallo ☎031.950.263, ⓦwww.lapergolabellagio.it. Stylish, en-suite rooms with balconies overlooking the lake and the vine-covered restaurant below in this enchanting fishing hamlet. It's a good fifteen-minute walk over the hill from Bellagio, so you'll need your own transport or a taxi when arriving with luggage. April–Nov. ❹
Silvio Via Carcano 12 ☎031.950.322, ⓦwww .bellagiosilvio.com. Just out of town, this bright two-star has rooms with lake views, and an excellent restaurant serving home-made dishes featuring fish freshly caught by the friendly owner. April–Oct. ❸

The Village

The village is blessed with luxuriant gardens and it's well worth making the effort to book onto a guided tour around the gorgeous gardens of the **Villa Serbelloni**, splendidly sited on a hill above the town. Built on the site of one of Pliny the Younger's residences, now owned by the Rockefeller Foundation, the villa was once a favourite haunt of European monarchs, and it's not hard to imagine them strolling among the grottoes and statues of the extravagant garden and gushing over the lake views. The sumptuously frescoed interior is closed to visitors, but there are guided tours around the **gardens** (April–Oct Tues–Sun 11am & 4pm; book at the tourist office; €6). At the foot of the hill is a pricey hotel, also called *Villa Serbelloni* (☎031.950.216, ⓦwww.villaserbelloni.it; ❾), whose guests numbered Churchill, JFK and Prince Rainier of Monaco as well as Clark Gable and Michael Schumacher.

The lake is clean enough **to swim**, which you can do from the Lido (Easter–Oct daily 8am–midnight; €7) at the end of the promenade, or if you can't stand the piped music, copy the local kids and have a dip at the tiny harbour less than 1km out of town in the other direction; follow the signs to the *Ristorante La Punta*.

Just beyond the Lido, the lake promenade continues for about 500m to the gardens of the **Villa Melzi** (April–Oct daily 9am–6pm; €6), a luxuriant affair crammed with azaleas, rhododendrons, ornamental lemon trees, cypresses, palms, camellias and even a sequoia. The gardens extend to the characterful harbourside hamlet of **LÓPPIA**, a relatively quiet retreat after Bellagio.

About ten minutes' walk east of Bellagio on an attractive footpath through vineyards is the enchanting little harbour of **PESCALLO**, a fishing port since Roman times, with a tremendous view of the Grigne mountains looming over the Lecco branch of the lake.

Eating

Like everything in Bellagio, **restaurants** can be pricey and you should **book** ahead to be sure of a table. One of the best options is *La Punta* (☎031.951.888), five minutes' walk north of town, which serves excellent food at good prices and has lovely views over the lake. Other attractive locations are *Bilacus*, at the top of Salita Serbelloni (☎031.950.480), for tasty local dishes under a pretty pergola; the wonderful fish restaurant *Silvio* (see above) overlooking the lake; and the authentic waterside restaurant at *La Pergola* (see above). The best places for **ice cream** are *Il Sorbetto* at the top of Salita Serbelloni and the *Gelateria del Borgo* at Via Garibaldi 46.

Lecco and around

Flanked by mountains of scored granite, Como's austere, fjord-like eastern fork is at its most atmospheric in the morning mists. The villages wedged along the shoreline are far more humdrum than those of the rest of the lake, and **LECCO**, at its foot, is a frantic commercial centre. You almost certainly won't want to stay in Lecco, but its public transport connections are good, and there are some challenging hikes in the nearby mountains. Trains run to Como, Milan and Bergamo, and back up the eastern shore by way of Varenna to Sondrio, and there are buses into the mountain villages. **Buses** leave from outside the **train station**, from where it's a brisk five-minute walk to the **ferry station** (go straight down the central street, Via Cavour, and across Piazza Garibaldi, to the shore and turn right). Lecco's business-like **tourist office** is on Via Nazario Sauro 6, off Piazza Garibaldi (Mon–Sat 9am–12.30pm & 2.30–6.30pm; June also Sun 9am–12.30pm; ℡0341.362.360, Ⓦwww.turismo.provincia.lecco.it), with detailed information on hikes in the natural parks above the town.

If you've time to kill you could pop into Lecco's **Basilica**, which boasts a set of fourteenth-century Giottesque frescoes. **Villa Manzoni**, on Via Amendola, the birthplace of Alessandro Manzoni, author of the great nineteenth-century novel *I Promessi Sposi* ("The Betrothed"), is open as a museum (Tues–Sun 9.30am–5.30pm; €4). To get there, head left out of the station along Via Sassi then Via Marconi. On display is Manzoni's study and chapel, decorated as they would have been when he sold the house in 1818.

The Valchiavenna and Valtellina

Trains run north of Colico into the **Valchiavenna**, a flat-bottomed valley into which Lake Como extended right up until Roman times. The main place to aim for is **CHIAVENNA**, at the end of the train line, to visit one of the many *crotti*, natural cellars in the rocks (across the rail line), which for centuries have been used for maturing wine, salami, cured meats and cheeses. Most are now inns and restaurants, one of the most authentic of which is the *Crotto al Prato*, on Via Picchi 13 (follow signs to the "*campo polisportivo*"), where you can sit at outdoor tables by the boules pitch with wonderful mountain views, or in the cosy stone interior. The town is otherwise a quiet mountain resort and the very friendly **tourist office** (daily 10am–12.30pm & 3–7pm; ℡0343.37.485, Ⓦwww.valchiavenna.com), on the main Via Consol Chiavennaschi, can provide information on things to see.

For somewhere **to stay** try the pleasant little *Flora* at Via Don Guanella 10 (℡0343.32.254, Ⓦwww.florahotel.com; ❷), 150m right of the station as you leave, or the three-star *Crimea*, Via Pratogiano 16 (℡0343.34.343, Ⓦwww.hotel-crimea.com; ❸). Alternatively there's an attractive **campsite** (℡0343.36.7555, Ⓦwww.campingacquafraggia.com), 3km north of town, next to the impressive Acquafraggia waterfall.

You can take some interesting walks up to the **Marmitte dei Giganti**, potholes formed by glaciation. Buses run to St Moritz in **Switzerland**, from where the *trenino rosso* (Ⓦwww.treninorosso.it) takes a scenic mountain route back across the border to Tirano.

Unless you're a keen skier, or are heading for eastern Switzerland or Trentino, there's little to draw you to the **Valtellina**, east of Lake Como, one of Italy's less appealing Alpine valleys. Cut through by road and rail, it's mined for minerals and iron ore and is prone to landslides. The train continues up from Lake Como to the region's main centre, **SONDRIO**, a modern and undistinguished town, known for its wine, which is on sale in many of its shops. Further up the valley, **BORMIO**, a prestigious, snooty resort – one of Europe's largest areas for summer skiing – was once an important stopover on the trade routes between Venice and Switzerland. It retains an attractive cobblestoned core, with a number of fifteenth-century frescoes palaces interspersed in the sprawl of hotels. Close by, the huge **Parco Nazionale dello Stelvio** is a good place for walks and challenging climbs, as well as skiing. Details can be gleaned from the **tourist office** in Bormio at Via Roma 131b (mid-June to mid-Sept Tues–Sun 9am–1pm & 3–7pm, Aug also Mon; ☎0342.903.300, ⓦwww.bormio.info) – where you can also pick up maps, details of *rifugi*, and information on the town – or from the national park **visitors' centre**, Via Roma 26 (Mon–Fri 9am–1pm & 2.30–6.30pm, until 5pm on Fri; plus Sat & Sun in summer 9am–12.30pm & 2–7pm; ☎0342.908.645, ⓦwww.stelviopark.it).

Bergamo

Just 50km northeast of Milan, yet much closer to the mountains in look and feel, **BERGAMO** is made up of two distinct parts – **Bergamo Bassa**, the lower, nineteenth- and twentieth-century centre, and medieval **Bergamo Alta**, clinging to the hill above the Lombardian plain. Bergamo Bassa is an odd mixture of Neoclassical and Fascist town planning and medieval cobbled streets, but Bergamo Alta is one of northern Italy's loveliest city centres, with fresh mountain air, wanderable lanes and a lively, easy-going pace of life.

Bergamo owes much of its magic to the Venetians, who ruled the town for over 350 years, adorning many a facade and open space with the Venetian lion – symbol of the republic. The most striking feature, however, is the ring of gated walls. Now worn, mellow and overgrown with creepers, these kept alien armies out until 1796, when French Revolutionary troops successfully stormed the city, throwing off centuries of Venetian rule. The best way to enjoy the Città Alta is to roam the alleyways which weave around the **Piazza Vecchia** and adjacent church of **Santa Maria Maggiore**. Just outside the walls in the Città Bassa, the **Accademia Carrara** holds one of Italy's leading provincial art collections.

Arrival and information

Bergamo's international **airport**, Orio al Serio (☎035.326.111, ⓦwww .orioaeroporto.it), lies 5km southeast of town; regular buses connect to the bus station and Città Alta in Bergamo (every 30min Mon–Sat 6am–midnight, 8 buses on Sun 9.15am–7.15pm; €1.55; ⓦwww.atb.bergamo.it) and the Stazione Centrale in Milan (4.30am–1am every half-hour; €6.90; ⓦwww.autostradale.it). Tickets can be bought on the bus if the office to the right of Arrivals is closed.

The **train station** is at the end of Bergamo Bassa's central avenue, Viale Giovanni XXIII, which becomes Via Vittorio Emanuele II. Opposite is the **bus station** for SAB buses, serving the northern mountains and valleys, and the Stazione Autolinee, for all other destinations. Bus #1 runs from right outside the train station to the **funicular station** at the foot of the hill, from where you can make the ascent by cable car to Piazza Mercato delle Scarpe for no extra charge as long as you show your bus ticket – otherwise it costs €1. Alternatively, you can stay on the bus until the end of the line at the northwestern gate of Porto Alessandro at Largo Colle Aperto, at the other end of the main drag in Bergamo Alta. **Bus tickets** are available from any newspaper stand in town; the most convenient if arriving by train is just inside the station on the left as you leave.

There are two branches of the **tourist office**, one on Piazzale Marconi (Mon–Fri 9am–12.30pm & 2–5.30pm; ☎035.210.204, ⓦwww.apt.bergamo.it),

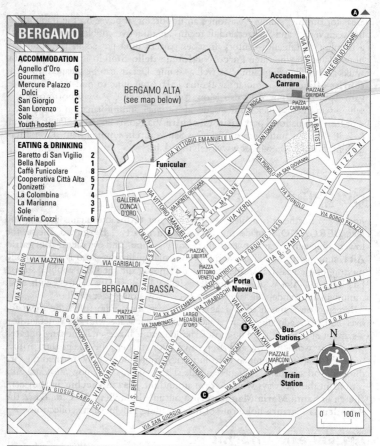

BERGAMO

ACCOMMODATION

Agnello d'Oro	G
Gourmet	D
Mercure Palazzo Dolci	B
San Giorgio	C
San Lorenzo	E
Sole	F
Youth hostel	A

EATING & DRINKING

Baretto di San Vigilio	2
Bella Napoli	1
Caffè Funicolare	8
Cooperativa Città Alta	5
Donizetti	7
La Colombina	4
La Marianna	3
Sole	F
Vineria Cozzi	6

BERGAMO ALTA
(see map below)

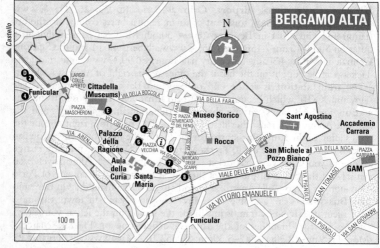

BERGAMO ALTA

in front of the train station, and the main office up in Bergamo Alta in the tower at Via Gombito 13 (daily 9am–12.30pm & 2–5.30pm).

Accommodation

Bergamo is not somewhere to arrive without a reservation, even out of season: **accommodation** is pricey and, in the centre, fairly limited. The lower town has several business hotels, while the upper town's options are atmospheric but the quality is not spectacular. It's worth also checking out the B&B options at ⓦ www .bed-and-breakfast.it as some are located in attractive buildings in Città Alta.

Agnello d'Oro Via Gombito 22 ☏ 035.249.883, ⓔ hotel@agnellodoro.it. In the heart of the upper town, this cosy hotel offers plain but comfortable en-suite rooms. Some have balconies overlooking the tiny square below. Breakfast included. ❸

Gourmet Via San Vigilio 1 ☏ 035.437.3004, ⓦ www.gourmet-bg.it. Just above Città Alta, with spacious but characterless modern rooms boasting wonderful views; there are also two mini-apartments and a restaurant serving local staples below. ❸

Mercure Palazzo Dolci Viale Papa Giovanni XXIII 100 ☏ 035.227.411, ⓦ www.mercure.com. Four-star, contemporary chain hotel a short walk from the station. Anonymous but comfortable, convenient and excellent value, it also has good soundproofing. Parking at the adjacent underground garage is discounted. ❺

San Giorgio Via San Giorgio 10, the continuation of Via Paleocapa ☏ 035.212.043, ⓦ www .sangiorgioalbergo.it. A well-run and friendly hostel-like option, a five-minute walk from the station in the lower-town. Various sized rooms with or without bathrooms are available, all spotless and decently furnished. ❷

San Lorenzo Piazza Mascheroni 9a ☏ 035.237.383, ⓦ www.hotelsanlorenzobg.it. Pleasant four-star hotel in a great location at the top of the old town near the Colle Aperto, with parking on the square in front. Some of the 24 rooms have balconies facing the mountains; there's a rather unromantic archeological pit of overgrown Medieval remains just in front of the hotel. ❻

Sole Via B Colleoni 1 ☏ 035.218.238, ⓕ 035.240.011. In an unbeatable location just off the main square in Città Alta, this bright and breezy traditional hotel offers simple en-suite two-star rooms with little balconies looking over a back courtyard or the private garden. ❷

Youth hostel Via G. Ferraris 1 ☏ 035.361.724, ⓦ www.ostellodibergamo.it. Although a fair hike from the city centre, this hostel has won awards for its facilities which include bathrooms and balconies in every room, bicycles for rent (€11 per day), a roof-top terrace with a great view of Città Alta, a garden to flop in, canteen meals plus facilities for the disabled. You can catch bus #3 from Piazza Mercato delle Scarpe in the Città Alta directly to the front door. Alternatively, take bus #6 from Porta Nuova (direction Monterosso), and get off at the stop named Ostello, just after the modern church. The hostel is at the top of the rather steep steps on the right. €15.50 per person for dorm, €20 per person for a double, triple or quad room (❶), breakfast and sheets included.

The City

However you get to Bergamo, you'll arrive in **BERGAMO BASSA**, which spreads north from the railway station in a comfortable blend of Neoclassical ostentation, Fascist severity and tree-lined elegance. At the heart of things are the mock-Doric temples of the **Porta Nuova** with Via XX Settembre, the city's main shopping drag, full of high-street names and little boutiques, leading off to the west.

Bergamo's main appeal, however, lies in the upper town – **BERGAMO ALTA**, easily reached using the **funicular** at the top end of Viale Vittorio Emanuele II, or by taking the bus (see p.235). If your calf muscles are up to it though, the half-hour uphill walk is well worthwhile. Head up Via Pignolo, lined with sixteenth- and seventeeth-century *palazzi*, to Porta Sant'Agostino in the city walls. Follow Viale delle Mura round – with views over the orchards and private gardens of the villas – until you feel like diving into the heart of the upper town proper.

Bergamo Alta

With its narrow, steep streets, flanked by high facades of Bergamo's upper town, **BERGAMO ALTA** remains largely as it was in the Middle Ages, but the main public spaces – **Piazza Vecchia** and adjacent **Piazza del Duomo** – combine medieval austerity with the grace of later, Renaissance design. The main street, beginning as Via Gombito and continuing as **Via Colleoni**, follows the line of the Roman *decumanus maximus*, topped and tailed by evidence of Bergamo's military past – the **Rocca** to the east, the **Cittadella** to the west. From **Colle Aperto** at the top of town, a steep road and a second funicular lead up to the neighbourhood of **San Vigilio** with the ruins of the city's castle.

Piazza Vecchia and Piazza del Duomo

From Piazza Mercato delle Scarpe, where the funicular arrives, Via Gombito leads up to **Piazza Vecchia**, enclosed by a harmonious miscellany of buildings, ranging from wrought-iron-balconied houses containing cafés and restaurants to the opulent Palladian-style civic library. Stendhal rather enthusiastically dubbed the square "the most beautiful place on earth", and certainly it's a striking open space. The most imposing building is the medieval **Palazzo della Ragione**, a Venetian-Gothic-style structure that stretches right across the piazza opposite the Palazzo Nuovo, lending a somewhat stagey feel to things, especially at night when the wrought-iron lamps are switched on. Court cases used to be heard under the open arcades that form the ground floor, and, following a guilty verdict, condemned criminals were exhibited there. The piazza itself was the scene of more joyous celebrations in 1797, when the French formed the Republic of Bergamo: a "tree of liberty" was erected, and the square, carpeted with tapestries, was transformed into an open-air ballroom in which – as a symbol of the new democracy – dances were led by an aristocrat partnered by a butcher.

To the right of the Palazzo della Ragione is the entrance to the massive **Torre Civica**, or Torre del Campanone, which you can ascend by lift (April–Oct Tues–Sun 9.30am–7pm, Sat until 9.30pm; Nov–March Sat & Sun 9.30am–4.30pm; €1). Its seventeenth-century bell, which narrowly escaped being melted down by the Germans to make arms during World War II, still tolls every half-hour. Walk beneath the Palazzo's arcades to the **Piazza del Duomo** and the **Duomo** (under renovation) – though this is of less interest than the church of **Santa Maria Maggiore** opposite, a rambling Romanesque church with a scalloped Gothic porch. Inside, Santa Maria is a perfect example of high Baroque, its ceiling marzipanned with ornament, encrusted with gilded stucco, painted vignettes and languishing statues. There's a piece of nineteenth-century kitsch too – a monument to Donizetti, the Bergamo-based composer of highly popular romantic comedies with memorable melodies and predictable plots, who died from syphilis here in 1848. As the town's most famous son, his death was much grieved, and bas-relief *putti* stamp their feet and smash their lyres in misery over the event. More subtly, the intarsia biblical scenes on the choir stalls – designed by Lorenzo Lotto, and executed by a local craftsman – are remarkable not only for their intricacy but also for the incredible colour-range of the natural wood.

Even the glitziness of Santa Maria is overshadowed by the Renaissance decoration of the **Cappella Colleoni** next door (Tues–Sun: March–Oct 9am–12.30pm & 2–6.30pm; Nov–March until 4.30pm). Built onto the church in the 1470s, the chapel is a gorgeously extravagant confection of pastel-coloured marble carved into an abundance of miniature arcades, balustrades and twisted columns, and capped with a mosque-like dome. Commissioned by Bartolomeo

Colleoni, a Bergamo mercenary in the pay of Venice, it was designed by the Pavian sculptor Amadeo – responsible for the equally excessive Certosa di Pavia (see p.205). The interior is almost as opulent, with a ceiling frescoed in the eighteenth century by Tiepolo sheltering Colleoni's sarcophagus, topped with a gleaming gilded equestrian statue. There's also the more modest tomb of his daughter, Medea, who died aged 15. Note Colleoni's coat of arms on the gate as you enter; the smoothness of the decorative third "testicle" (supposedly biologically accurate) bears witness to the local tradition that rubbing it will bring you luck.

The **Baptistry**, on the square outside, was removed from the interior of Santa Maria Maggiore in the seventeenth century when christenings were transferred to the Duomo. After some time in storage it was eventually reconstructed outside the **Aula della Curia** ("Bishop's Court"; Mon–Fri 9am–12.30pm; free), alongside the Cappella Colleoni. You'll find the bulging and recently restored **Tempietto di Santa Croce** behind, at the back of Santa Maria Maggiore, dating from the tenth century, although it's still closed to the public.

Museo Donizettiano

From the south door of Santa Maria Maggiore, **Via Arena** climbs towards the west end of the Città Alta. Partway up at number 9, a frescoed doorway opens into the grounds of the Santa Grata monastery, where the Palazzo della Misericordia is home to the **Museo Donizettiano** (Tues–Sun 10am–1pm & 2.30–5.30pm; Oct–May mornings only; free; ⓦwww.gaetanodonizetti .net). One of the masters of the "bel canto" opera style along with Bellini and Rossini, Gaetano Donizetti (1797–1848), who was born and died in Bergamo, is celebrated for his melodramatic lyricism, which reached a peak in *Lucia di Lammermoor*, and his comedies such as *Don Pasquale*. The museum contains portraits of the maestro, original letters and scores, as well as his fortepianos and imperial-style bed.

Via Colleoni to the Cittadella

Leading northwest out of Piazza Vecchia, the narrow **Via Colleoni** is one of the upper city's main pedestrian thoroughfares, leading to the brink of Bergamo Alta, lined with delicatessens and pastry shops selling sweet polenta cakes topped with chocolate birds. Make sure to pop into the Teatro Sociale, at via Colleoni 4, if it's open. Built at the beginning of the nineteenth century the atmospheric, three-tiered wooden theatre was left to crumble away when it closed in the 1920s; the decline has been halted but while discussions continue about what to do with it, the main stage is open for temporary exhibitions and art installations.

At the end of Via Colleoni, Piazza Mascheroni lies at the entrance to the **Cittadella**, a military stronghold built by Barnabo Visconti that originally occupied the entire western headland. The remaining buildings now house a small theatre and two well-organized, didactic (Italian only) **museums**: one of **archeology** (Tues–Sun 9am–noon & 2–6pm; free) and the other of **natural history** (Tues–Fri 9am–12.30pm & 2.30–5.30pm, Sat & Sun 9am–7.30pm; free).

Colle Aperto and San Vigilio

Passing through the opposite gateway of the Cittadella brings you out to the **Colle Aperto**, where there are good vistas. For really outstanding views, however, you need to walk up to the **Castello**, perched on the summit of **San Vigilio**, which rises up from Porta Sant'Alessandro. A short funicular journey will take you to the top but the walk is pleasant, up a steep, narrow road over-looking the gardens of Bergamo's most desirable properties, and past a handful of very attractive but rather pricey restaurants. In the grounds of the castle there's a maze of underground passages to explore that used to run right down to Bergamo Alta. **Guided tours** of the tunnels are organized by the Gruppo Speleologico Le Nottole (℡035.251.233, Ⓦwww.nottole.it; hours and price vary according to season and size of group).

Museo Storico and the Rocca

Returning to the Colle Aperto, you can either walk back through the city or follow the old **walls** around its circumference – the whole circuit takes a couple of hours. The most picturesque stretch lies between the Colle Aperto and Porta San Giacomo, from where a long flight of steps leads down into the lower city. Alternatively, returning through the upper city to Piazza Mercato delle Scarpe, you can turn down Via San Pancrazio and then into Piazza Mercato del Fieno, to see the **Museo Storico** (Tues–Sun 9.30am–1pm & 2–5.30pm; free). Housed in the ex-convent of San Francesco, with a beautiful thirteenth-century cloister, it currently spans the history of the city during the Unification, but there are plans to display the rest of the collection. Following Via Solata east from here you'll climb to Via Rocca, which leads up to the grounds of the Rocca, where there is little to attract your attention apart from the sensational view over eastern Bergamo.

The Accademia Carrara

Just below the upper town, close to the city walls, the **Accademia Carrara** (Tues–Sun 10–1pm & 2.30–5.30pm; €2.60; Ⓦwww.accademiacarrara.bergamo .it), in Piazza Giacomo Carrara, is Bergamo's most important museum and among Lombardy's best collections of art. You can walk down here from the old city, along the steep Via Porta Dipinta and through the Porta Sant'Agostino, to see works by Pisanello, Botticelli, Giovanni Bellini, Crivelli, Carpaccio and Lotto – all carefully and imaginatively displayed. There are also paintings by the Lombard realists Foppa and Bergognone, Spanish-style portraits by Moroni, an elegant idealized *St Sebastian* by Raphael and canvases by Titian and Palma il Vecchio. Don't miss the room dedicated to works by the twentieth-century Bergamo-born sculptor Giacomo Manzù, best known for his stylized bronzes of cardinals. The **Galleria d'Arte Moderna e Contemporanea** (Ⓦwww .gamec.it; prices and times vary according to each exhibition), across the road, hosts top-quality touring exhibitions of work by modern artists and designers.

Eating and drinking

One of the pleasures of Bergamo is its food, easily enjoyable whether you're on a tight budget and restricted to assembling picnics from the many *salumerie* and bakeries in the old town, or can afford to graze around the city's **osterie**, many of which line Via Colleoni in Città Alta. The town's culinary attractions are headed by game – hunting the local wildlife is a major pastime in these parts – as well as the signature dishes of polenta and *casoncelli*, ravioli stuffed with sausage meat and served with sage butter. At the restaurants given below, it's always worth **booking ahead** – essential at weekends.

For **picnic food**, stock up on rustic-style pies at the Salumeria Mangili at Via Gombito 8, or on *pane greco* (bread topped with aubergine and tomato) from Forno tre Soldi, Via Colleoni 13a, and decadent pastries at Nessi, Via Gombito 34, in Bergamo Bassa. You'll find the best **ice cream** under the luxuriant balconies of *La Marianna*, in the corner of Colle Aperto in the Città Alta; they also have a branch at Orio al Serio airport for your last fling before heading home.

Baretto di San Vigilio Via Castello 1 ☏ 035.253.191. An unbeatable choice of excellent dishes on an attractive vine-covered terrace with spectacular views. Prices reflect the location so expect to pay more than €50 per head.

Bella Napoli Via Taramelli 5/7/9 ☏ 035.242.308. A wide choice of decent, wood-oven-cooked pizzas in a bright, modern pizzeria near the station. Useful if you find yourself hanging around for a train or a bus. Eat in or take away.

Caffè Funicolare In the funicular station on Piazza Mercato delle Scarpe. Good-value snacks and drinks served on a terrace with a great view over Città Bassa. Open until 2am. Closed Tues.

Cooperativa Città Alta Vicolo Sant'Agata, clearly signposted off Via Colleoni. A cheery amalgam of café, restaurant and bar, open until 2am. This co-operative venture in Bergamo Alta boasts low prices, a happy hour on Thursdays, and a garden

where you can idle away your time admiring the distant hills. Closed Wed.

Donizetti Via Gombito 17a ☏ 035.242.661. Excellent place for a slap-up meal or a *degustazione* platter of local meats and cheeses washed down with fine wine. Inside is warm and welcoming; in summer tables are laid out in the covered market space.

La Colombina Via Borgo Canale 12 ☏ 035.261.402. A wonderful little trattoria with tasty, good-value Bergamasco food and glorious views (ask for a table by the window when you book). Closed Mon & Aug.

Sole Via B. Colleoni 1 ☏ 035.218.238. A very popular restaurant attached to the eponymous hotel, serving traditional local specialities and fish in an attractive garden in summer.

Vineria Cozzi Via Colleoni 22a. A classy wine bar in Bergamo Alta with around three hundred wines to choose from and an excellent cold buffet. Closed Wed.

Lago d'Iseo and the Val Camonica

Pretty little **Lago d'Iseo** may be the least-known of the lakes, but any notion that it had escaped either tourist exploitation or industrialization would be misled. The western shore around Lovere sees heavy industry and slow lorries heading down from the mountains, while holiday apartments and campsites are strewn rather indiscriminately around the southern reaches; all around the lake traffic is slow and heavy. **Iseo town**, however, on the Brescia shore, is an appealing little resort that's an easy access point for the lake's main attraction, **Monte Isola**, a small, steep island rising up out of the water. The town also makes a decent base for a visit to the Bronze Age rock-carvings in **Val Camónica**, forty kilometres to the north.

Iseo town and Monte Isola

ISEO town is easily accessed by train and bus from Brescia as well as seasonal buses from Bergamo. The town's **tourist office** at Lungolago Marconi 2 (Mon–Sat 9am–12.30pm & 3–6pm, Sun 9am–noon; closed Sat pm & Sun in winter; ☏ 030.980.209, ⓦ www.lagodiseo.org) has maps and details of walks around the lake and in the mountains behind. Iseo's attractive waterfront offers a couple of decent **accommodation** options, the best of which is the *Milano*, Lungolago Marconi 4 (☏ 030.980.449, ⓦ www.hotelmilano.info; ❷), which has pleasant en-suite rooms, some with balconies and lake views.

The real highlight in this area, however, is the traffic-free **Monte Isola** (ⓦ www.monteisola.com), Italy's largest lake-island at over 3km long and 600m high. At the south of the lake, it's accessible by an hourly **ferry** from Iseo, and also from Sulzano in season (ⓦ www.navigazionelagoiseo.it). As a magnet for local day-trippers in summer and at weekends, it's unlikely to provide much solitude, but out of season it's well worth a visit, to walk or cycle round the edge of the island, and for great views across the lake. **Bicycles** are available for rent for €3.50 per hour in Peschiera (March–Oct; ☎030.982.5228) or Carzano (☎030.982.5144).

The island also has a couple of appealing **hotels**, both with their own restaurants serving tasty regional dishes: the *Bellavista* (☎030.988.6106, Ⓦwww.albergo-bellavista.it; restaurant closed Tues; ❷) in the village of **SIVIANO** on the northwest corner of the island, and the waterfront *La Foresta* (☎030.988.6210, Ⓕ988.6455; restaurant closed Wed; ❷), five minutes' walk outside Peschiera. The campsite (☎030.982.5221; April–Oct) is at **CARZANO** on Monte Iseo's northeast tip.

Val Camonica

Road and railway run up from the lake, following the River Oglio through the spa town of Boario to **CAPO DI PONTE**, famous for its prehistoric **rock art**. There are carvings throughout the valley, but the most concentrated group is in the **national park** (Tues–Sun: March to mid-Oct 8.30am–7.30pm, mid-Oct to Feb closes 4.30pm; €4), a fifteen-minute walk uphill from the station (turn left out of the station and left again a couple of hundred metres further on when you see a sign). Here, prehistoric engravings span an incredible 8000 years – remnants from the culture of the Camuni tribe who holed up here to escape northern invaders from 5000 BC until the Romans colonized the area several thousand years later, together with the even older works that inspired the Camuni's art. Begin with the **Great Rock** in front of the site's shop, where a set of simple, matchstick-men figures gives a taste of Camuni life over a thousand-year period. There are hunters, agricultural workers, a religious ceremony presided over by priests, and a depiction of a Bronze Age burial in which the corpse is surrounded by his weapons and tools. To see how the civilization developed into the Iron Age, head for Rock 35, carved with a blacksmith, and Rock 23, with a four-wheeled wagon transporting an urn. Carvings in other parts of the valley include some in the hamlet of **BEDOLINO** outside **CEMMO**, about 2km above Capo di Ponte on the other side of the Oglio, where, in someone's garden, there's a rock with a carving of a **Bronze Age map** showing huts, fields, walls, streams, canals and the *Rosa Camuna*, which has been adopted as the symbol of Lombardy.

Brescia and around

Located between two lakes and surrounded by vine-covered hills, the ancient settlement of **BRESCIA** is a wealthy town, boasting valuable Roman remains, Renaissance squares and a Medieval city centre juxtaposed with important twentieth-century architecture. Yet for all this, it lacks the elegance and charm of other northern Italian cities and you'd do best to visit its sights in a day and then head on your way – easy as the town is well connected with onward public transport and motorway connections. The gentle hills to the west, known as the **Franciacorta**, give their name to renowned wines made on the hillsides.

Arrival, information and accommodation

Brescia's main advantage is the convenience of its transport connections: it is on the main Milan–Verona railway line and motorway, giving access to the cities of the Veneto as well as those of Lombardy. The rest of the province,

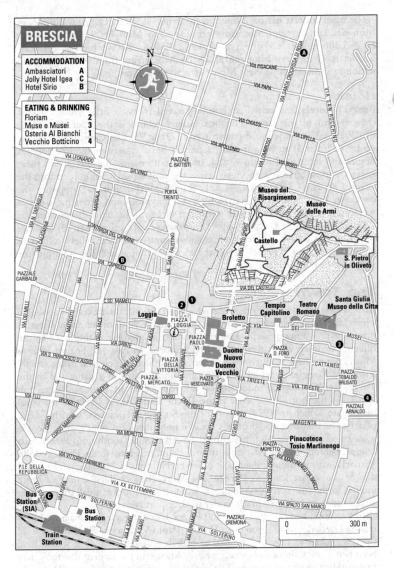

BRESCIA

ACCOMMODATION
Ambasciatori	A
Jolly Hotel Igea	C
Hotel Sirio	B

EATING & DRINKING
Floriam	2
Muse e Musei	3
Osteria Al Bianchi	1
Vecchio Botticino	4

including the main resorts of Garda, Cremona and Mantova and several more distant destinations, is covered by direct buses, which leave from the two bus terminals (Ⓦwww.trasportibrescia.it) on either side of the train station, a short bus ride (#1 or #2) or fifteen-minute walk south of the city centre. The international **airport** is at Montichiari (Ⓣ030.965.6599, Ⓦwww.aeroportobrescia .it), 23km southeast, where flights are met by shuttle buses to Brescia (30min; €7.50 return) and to Verona's Porta Nuova train station (45min; €11; stopping at Peschiara on Lago di Garda on request). Alternatively, a taxi to Brescia should cost around €30.

The main **tourist office**, located in the centre at Piazza Loggia 6 (June–Sept Mon–Sat 9am–6.30pm, Sun 9am–1pm; Oct–May Mon–Fri 9.30am–12.30pm & 2–5.30pm, Sat 9.30am–1pm; ℡030.297.8988, Ⓦwww.bresciatourism.it), has details of the **free bike rental** scheme, which runs from outside the train station in summer (June–Sept Mon–Sat 7.30am–7.30pm).

Hotels

Brescia's **hotels** are aimed at business travellers, with little choice at the cheaper end of the range. The best budget option is the basic *Hotel Sirio* (℡030.375.0706, Ⓦwww.albergosirio.com; ❷), at Via Elia Capriolo 24, in the centre of town. Run by a friendly family, it has a variety of spotless doubles, singles and multi-bed rooms – with or without en-suite facilites – and there is even a small terrace with views across the roof tops. For more comfort, the chain *Jolly Hotel Igea* (℡030.44.221, Ⓦwww.jollyhotels.it; ❻), opposite the station at Viale Stazione 15, is clean and anonymous and often has deals at weekends. While, a little further north out of town, the ugly *Ambasciatori*, Via Crocefissa di Rosa 90 (℡030.399.114, Ⓦwww.ambasciatori.net; ❺) belies a fine, well-run four-star hotel, with spacious rooms and an excellent restaurant (count on around €40 per head); there's free parking, and bus #1 from the station stops outside.

The Town

Brescia's centre comprises a compact cluster of piazzas linked by cobbled streets stretching out east to what was the centre of the Roman town. Brescia's main square – **Piazza della Loggia** – is also its prettiest, dating back to the fifteenth century, when the city invited Venice in to rule and protect it from Milan's power-hungry Viscontis. The Venetian influence is clearest in the fancily festooned **Loggia**, in which both Palladio and Titian had a hand, and in the **Torre dell'Orologio**, modelled on the campanile in Venice's Piazza San Marco. In the northeast corner is the **Porta Bruciata**, a defensive medieval tower-gate, which in 1974, as part of the Strategy of Tension, was the scene of a Fascist bomb attack during a trade union march, in which eight people were killed and over a hundred injured. Streets connect south from Piazza della Loggia, behind the tourist office, into the austere, Fascist-built **Piazza della Vittoria** with its monumental post office building at via 24 Maggio. The south side of the square leads to **Piazza del Mercato**, a cobbled square of more interest to the stomach than the eye: as well as a supermarket, small shops selling local salamis and cheeses nestle under its dark porticoes.

Passages from Piazza della Loggia and Piazza della Vittoria lead east across galleried Via Dieci Giornate through to **Piazza Paolo VI Piazza Paolo VI**, one of the few squares in Italy to have two cathedrals – though, frankly, it would have been better off without the second, a heavy Mannerist monument that took over two hundred years to complete. The old twelfth-century cathedral, or **Rotonda** (April–Oct Tues–Sun 9am–noon & 3–7pm; Nov–March Sat & Sun 10am–noon & 3–5pm), is quite a different matter, a simple circular building of local stone, sunk below the current level of the piazza. Inside, glass set into the transept pavement reveals the remains of Roman baths (a wall and geometrical mosaics) and the apse of an eighth-century basilica, which burned down in 1097.

Behind Piazza del Duomo, Via Mazzini leads to Via dei Musei – the *decumanus maximus* of the Roman town of Brixia, with Via Gallo the *cardus*. A short walk east brings you to what was the centre of Roman Brixia, **Piazza del Foro**, built over the ancient forum (which was substantially larger than the current square). Dominating the area are the tall columns of the **Tempio Capitolino** (Tues–Sun 10am–1pm & 2–5pm; free), a Roman temple built in 73 AD, now partly reconstructed with red brick. Behind are three reconstructed *celle*, probably temples to the Capitoline trinity of Jupiter, Juno and Minerva. Adjacent to the east, reached by dodging around a side street, is a part-excavated Roman **theatre**; ongoing archeological work has revealed frescoes and remnants of an older temple beneath the current one. Moves are afoot to rationalize this whole area and create a new museum.

Further along Via dei Musei is the rewarding civic museum housed in the sprawling ex-Benedictine convent of San Salvatore and **Santa Giulia** (Tues– Sun 10am–6pm; Oct–May 9.30am–5.30pm; €8; Ⓦ www.bresciamusei.com) over what was, during the Roman period, a residential quarter of frescoed villas. Inside are three churches: the oldest being San Salvatore, whose present structure dates back to the twelfth century but includes the remains of an original crypt built in 762 to house the relics of St Julia; Santa Maria in Solario, built in the twelfth century as a private chapel for the Benedictine nuns who lived at the abbey, is covered in frescoes painted mainly by the Renaissance artist Floriano Ferramola; and the late-sixteenth-century church of Santa Giulia with further frescoes by Ferramola. The museum holds a collection of artefacts chronicling the city's history from the Bronze Age to the end of the twentieth century. The highlights are undoubtedly the Roman rooms containing bronze objects found by the Capitolium including the life-sized winged *Victory* and the beautifully preserved mosaic floors of several Roman *domus* discovered *in situ* under the complex. The complex also plays host to major modern art exhibitions; see Ⓦ www.lineadombra.it for details.

Behind the museum, Via Piamarta climbs up the **Cydnean Hill**, the core of early Roman Brixia, mentioned by Catullus, though again the remains are scanty. There are a few fragments of a gate just before you reach the sixteenth-century church of **San Pietro in Oliveto**, so-called because of the olive grove surrounding it, and the hill itself is crowned by the **Castello** (daily 8am–8pm; free) – a monument to Brescia's various overlords, begun in the fifteenth century by Luchino Visconti and added to by the Venetians, French and Austrians over the years. The resulting confusion of towers, ramparts, halls and courtyards makes a good place for an atmospheric picnic, and holds a complex of museums including the large **Museo delle Armi** (Tues–Sun 10am–1pm & 2.30–5pm; €3), and the **Museo del Risorgimento** (same hours; free).

More appealing perhaps is Brescia's main art gallery, the **Pinacoteca Tosio-Martinengo** at Via Martinengo da Barco 1 (Tues–Sun: June–Sept 10am–5pm; Oct–May 9.30am–1pm & 2.30–5pm; €3), which consists of a well-laid-out collection mainly made up of the works of local artists, including Foppa, Savoldo, Romanino and Lotto, plus a couple of small, beautiful Raphaels. **Room 2.5**, holds the single most disturbing painting in the gallery, Moretto's chilling *Passion* (c.1550), with a pale Christ slouched on a flight of steps, with a frozen, reproachful look in his eyes.

Eating and drinking

Brescia has a good selection of reasonably priced **places to eat** in the centre of town, specializing in local dishes such as *casoncei* (large meat-filled ravioli) or game. One very pleasant central option is *Floriam*, Via Gasparo da Salò 3 (Ⓣ 030.41.314; closed Tues), a little café-restaurant just off Piazza Loggia offering an innovative mix of lake and land cuisine, with outside tables in summer. Another central option, *Osteria Al Bianchi* on Via Gasparo de Saló 42 (closed

Tues eve & Wed), just by Piazza della Loggia, serves tasty dishes and is very popular with locals. When it comes to **aperitivo-time**, the town-centre bars fill up or you could head for Piazzale Arnaldo to the east of the centre where, at number 6, *Vecchio Botticino* (closed Sun) is a funky place to watch the town unwind with a glass or two of local wine. Alternatively, just a few steps from the Santa Giulia museum, *Muse e Musei*, in Piazza Brusato (closed Wed) is a laid-back wine-bar-cum-jazz-club serving light meals.

Around Brescia

The area between Brescia and Lago d'Iseo is known as the **Franciacorta** – a hilly wine-producing district, rising from the bland built-up lowlands around the city, which got its name from the religious communities that lived there from the eleventh century onwards. These communes and their land were exempt from tax and known as the Corti Franche, or free courts. The wine-producers soon moved in, attracted by the possibility of owning vineyards in a duty-free haven, and though the Franciacorta is no longer tax-free, the **wine** continues to flow – and is available from shops all over the region. The best is the Franciacorta DOCG, Italy's most refined sparkling wine, produced according to Champagne methods – and light-years ahead of humdrum *spumante*. There are also very drinkable reds and whites that can be sampled at various visitable vineyards and the regions' many restaurants. For more information and details of vineyards and tasting cellars, pick up the **Strada del Vino Franciacorta** map from tourist offices or look at the website Ⓦ www.stradadelfranciacorta.it.

Val Trompia, Lago d'Idro and Lago di Ledro

Brescia is famous for its arms industry, the impact of which is unavoidable directly north of the city around the **Val Trompia**. The industry dates back over four hundred years, and was started by the Venetians, keen to utilize the rich iron ore deposits of the area and to whom it became so indispensable that during the sixteenth-century restrictions were actually placed on people's movements out of the region. The centre of today's (much diminished) arms industry is **GARDONE VAL TROMPIA**, where the Beretta company – makers of 007's favourite gun – has its headquarters.

The valley beyond Gardone is crammed with industry as far as Lavone, and hiking becomes possible only at **BOVEGNO**. From this small village, paths lead up to Monte Muffetto (4hr) and, even better, to Monte Crestoso and its tiny tarns (5hr 30min), though you'll need a tent, as there are no *rifugi*. There are two *rifugi* further on however, *Croce Domini* (1992m) at the head of the valley, and *Bonardi* (1743m) above the lovely Passo del Maniva. From either base you can walk down to Lago d'Idro or climb Monte Colombino, again with a couple of tarns. The map to get is the Kompass Carta Turistica, *Le Tre Valli Bresciane*. There are also a few cheap hotels at the ski resorts of **Collio** and **San Colombano** (Ⓦ www.valtrompiaturismo.it).

From close to the *rifugio Croce Domini* a steep track climbs over into the broad Valle della Berga and up to attractive **BAGOLINO** (Ⓦ www.bagolinoinfo .it) on the road to Lago d'Idro. Bagolino is captivating, preserving many of its medieval houses and a church, **San Rocco**, that has a startlingly realistic cycle of fifteenth-century frescoes. If you want to avoid Idro's unremarkable resorts,

Al Tempo Perduto (☎0365.99.665, ⓦ www.altempoperduto.it; ❷) is the place to stay: it's a lovely hotel and restaurant in an historic building on the main street, with buses running fairly frequently to and from the lake.

Lago d'Idro is a reasonably pretty lake, except for its marshy upper reaches where the effect is spoiled by a sand-dredger. There's no road running along the upper reaches of the east shore, so you should be able to find a quiet beach there, despite the family-orientated tourism. Idro's resorts are uniformly bland, but if you want to stay over, go to *Al Lago*, Via Lago 10 (☎ & ⓕ 0365.809.026; closed Oct–March; ❶), at Anfo, which has cheap doubles. The most convenient **campsites** include the lakeside *Pilù* (☎0365.809.037, ⓦ www.pilu.it; closed Oct–March) at Anfo, and *Vantone Pineta* (☎0365.823.385; closed Nov–Feb) at Vantone on the east shore: both are on the bus route from Brescia.

Northeast from Idro, via Ponte Caffaro, you reach the point where the Austrian border ran through until 1918. From here a road leads to tranquil **Lago di Ledro** in the Val Sabbia, only 2km long and slightly less across, and a good bolt hole if you want to get away from the frantic northwest of Lake Garda. Quieter than Idro, and far preferable, it has a couple of **campsites**, including the attractive *Al Sole* (☎0464.508.496, ⓦ www.campingalsole.it) right on the lakeside, and a good **hotel** – the three-star *Mezzolago* (☎0464.508.181, ⓦ www.hotelmezzolago.com; ❷), with balconies over the lake.

Lago di Garda

Lago di Garda is the largest and cleanest of the Italian lakes, and also the most popular. Each year its resorts are invaded by a fair number of package-holiday clients, as well as huge numbers of Germans, Austrians and Italians attracted by the variety of **sports** available on the water and the mountains around. Winters are mild, summers tempered by breezes – the northern *sover*, which blows down the lake from midnight and through the morning, and the *ova*, blowing from the south in the afternoon and evening. On the most sheltered stretch of the western shore are lush groves of olives, vines and citrus trees – fruits used for Garda's main products: olive oil, citrus syrups and Bardolino, Soave and Valpolicella wines. Scenically the shores of the lake are varied: the rich vegetation of its middle reaches gives way to the rugged north, where the lake narrows and is tightly enclosed by craggy mountains; the southern shores, 16km at their widest, are backed by gentle plains.

The waters of the lake lap onto the shores of three distinct administrative regions: the western shore, north to Limone del Garda, is in **Lombardy** (ⓦ www.bresciatourism.it), the top of the lake is in **Trentino** (ⓦ www.gardatrentino.it), and the west side of the lake from Malcesine to Peschiera is in the **Veneto** (ⓦ www.tourism.verona.it).

The one-lane road round the lake can be traffic-bound during the summer months – especially at weekends – and you may want to leave the driving to someone else: regular **buses** ply their way between Desenzano and Riva on one shore and Riva and Peschiera on the other. The passenger **ferry**, however, is the most relaxing option; it serves a similar service between Sirmione and Riva, with a car ferry crossing the middle of the lake between Toscolano-Maderno and Torri del Benaco. Although there is plenty of **accommodation** around the lake – from world-class hotels to campsites and a youth hostel – things can get very busy. Between June and September it's advisable to book ahead or bag a room early in the day.

The southern shore

Within easy striking distance of the Milan–Venice autostrada and railway and with regular buses from the main Lombardian towns, the **southern shore** of Lake Garda is predictably well touristed. **DESENZANO DEL GARDA**, the lake's largest town, serves as a major rail junction and therefore a good starting-point for visiting Garda. Buses tend to connect with trains, and there are several ferries daily up to Riva stopping off at other resorts on the way. The town itself holds little to detain you. The lakefront, lined with bars and restaurants, is quite attractive, though it's hard to ignore the busy main road running alongside. If you do end up with time to fill, head for the **castle**, from where there are spectacular views, or the **Roman villa** on Via Crocifisso: a formerly large and luxurious home that preserves some good mosaics (Tues–Sun: 8.30am–7.30pm; Nov to Feb closes 5pm; €2).

SIRMIONE, 9km east, is spread along a narrow promontory protruding 4km into the lake. It is a popular spot, in a beautiful setting, though these days it's suffocated with hotels, souvenir stands and tourists many of whom come to take the waters: Sirmione has Lake Garda's only mineral spring. You're unlikely to want to stay, and in any case most of the hotels are usually fully booked by package tours, but it's worth a brief visit to take in the town's handful of sights and laze around on the surrounding lidos.

Inside the battlements of the traffic-free town stands the **Rocca Scaligera** (Tues–Sun 9am–7pm; Oct–March closes 4.30pm; €4), a fairy-tale castle with boxy turreted towers almost entirely surrounded by water, built by the Veronese Scaligeri family in the thirteenth century when they ruled Garda. There's not much to see inside, although the views from its battlements are wonderful. You can escape the crowds by walking out beyond town to the peninsula's triangular, hilly head, covered in cypresses and olive groves. A path leads along the edge of the peninsula, passing bubbling hot sulphur springs, to the **Spiaggia Lido delle Bionde** (May–Oct daily 8am–midnight) where you can eat and drink, swim in the lake or sunbathe on the pontoon or nearby rocks. If you continue, you'll reach a fenced-off area at the tip of the peninsula. The signs warn of landslides, but most people ignore these since the flat rocks are good for sun-soaking. Swimming or paddling is tricky, however, as underwater the rocks are slippery. There's a gate here up to the **Grotte di Catullo** (Tues–Sun 8.30am–7pm; Nov–Feb closes 4.30pm; €4), touted as Catullus's villa, although the white ruins are actually of a Roman spa. Catullus did, however, retire to the town, coming all the way from the Black Sea by boat, hauling it overland when necessary so that he could keep it on the lake. The ruins, scattered on the hillside among ancient olive trees, are lovely, and there are superb views across the lake to the mountains. There's a small antiquarium with fragments of mosaics and frescoes, and below the site, though not accessible from it, a beach.

For more information, and a list of rooms if you're tempted to stay, head for the **tourist office** (Easter–Oct daily 9am–12.30pm & 3–6pm; Nov–Easter Mon–Fri same hours, Sat 9am–12.30pm; ℡030.916.114, 🖳www.gardariviera.com), outside the bridge into the old quarter, by the bus station and main car park.

The western shore

The rolling hills of the Valtenesi overlooking the **western shore** are a good place to stock up on local produce, as much of the area is dedicated to vine and olive growing. In addition, down by the lake, there are plenty of campsites which make for a cheap stay if you're just here overnight. A little further north from the old Venetian town of **Salò** stands the exuberant residence. **Il Vittoriale** (see below), just outside the sedate resort of **Gardone Riviera**. Beyond **Gargnano** – the most attractive and unspoilt of the lake villages – the shoreline has been dubbed the Riviera del Limone because of the citrus cultivation that lines the steep hillsides. The crop was reportedly introduced here by the Franciscans in the fourteenth century and was cultivated in the *lemonaias* that are still strewn across the landscape, although most are now abandoned. As the terrain gets more mountainous, the tortuous winding road offers tantalizing glimpses of the sparkling lake from between *gallerie* and lemon trees, but there is little reason to stop until you reach the nineteenth-century resort of **Riva del Garda** at the head of the lake.

Garda's only **car ferry** at Toscolano-Maderno, halfway up the shore, regularly plies across the lake to the eastern shore's most attractive village, Torri del Benaco (see p.254).

Saló and Gardone

SALÓ, splendidly sited on a bay at the foot of the luxuriant Riviera Bresciana, is worth a brief stop. The town gave its name to Mussolini's short-lived last republic, instituted here in September 1943 after his rescue from the Abruzzi by the Nazis. It's a handsome town, retaining a handful of buildings from the fifteenth century – notably the Duomo and town hall – when it was the Venetian Empire's main garrison town. They are set back from an attractive *lungolago* (Lakefront road) full of tourist-oriented cafés and *gelaterie*.

A couple of kilometres further up the shore, **GARDONE RIVIERA**, once the most fashionable of Garda's resorts, still retains its symbols of sophistication, though the elegant promenade, lush gardens, opulent villas and ritzy hotels now have to compete with more recent – less tasteful – tourist tack. Famous for the consistency of its climate, it boasts Garda's most exotic botanical garden, the **Giardino Botanico Hruska** (mid-March to mid-Oct daily 9am–7pm; €6), laid out among artificial cliffs and streams. The main sight in town is the eye-popping **Il Vittoriale**, spread across the hillside just above the resort.

Il Vittoriale

Rising up above the lakeside road, **Il Vittoriale** (Tues–Sun: April–Sept 9.30am–7pm; Oct–March 9am–1pm & 2–5pm; ⓦwww.vittoriale.it; €16) was the home of Italy's most notorious and extravagant twentieth-century writer, **Gabriele D'Annunzio**. Weight of numbers means that tickets for the house

---

Gabriele D'Annunzio

Born in 1863, Gaetano Rapagnetta – who took the name **Gabriele D'Annunzio** (Gabriel of the Annunciation) – is often acclaimed as one of Italy's greatest poets. He did pen some exquisite poetry and a number of novels, but became better known as a soldier and socialite, leading his own private army and indulging in much-publicized affairs with numerous women, including the actress Eleonora Duse. When berated by his friends for treating her cruelly, he simply replied, "I gave her everything, even suffering." He was a fervent supporter of Mussolini, providing the Fascist Party with their (meaningless) war cry *"eia! eia! alalá!"* – though Mussolini eventually found his excessive exhibitionism an embarrassment (D'Annunzio's boasts of eating roast babies, certainly, were bad publicity). In 1921 Mussolini presented D'Annunzio with the Vittoriale villa – ostensibly as a reward for his patriotism, in reality to shut him up. D'Annunzio spent the next years expanding the villa, redesigning its interiors and acquiring neighbouring land. He died in the house in 1938, suffering a brain haemorrhage while sitting at his desk in the Zambracca room, which remains untouched.

itself are restricted at peak times (Sun, national holidays, some days in July & Aug), when you must arrive well before the opening hours to be sure of entry – even then, be prepared for a scrum. Once tickets for the house are sold out, you can only visit the grounds, the mausoleum, a small war museum and the ship *Puglia*, beached incongruously among cypress trees in the park; the ticket for the grounds only is €7.

D'Annunzio's personality makes itself felt from the start in the **house** in the two reception rooms – one a chilly and formal room for guests he didn't like, the other warm and inviting for those he did. Il Duce was apparently shown to the former, where the mirror has an inscription reputedly aimed at him – "Remember that you are made of glass and I of steel." Dining with D'Annunzio was never a reassuring experience: roast baby may not have featured on the menu, but in the glitzy dining room, as a warning to greedy guests, pride of place was given to a gilded and embalmed tortoise who had died of overeating. In fact D'Annunzio rarely ate with his guests, retreating instead to the Sala di Lebbroso, where he would lie on a bier surrounded by leopard skins and contemplate death. The rest of the house is no less bizarre – or gloomy (D'Annunzio reportedly had an eye condition which meant daylight was painful to him): the bathroom has a bathtub hemmed in by hundreds of objects, ranging from Persian ceramic tiles, through Buddhas, to toy animals; and the Sala del Mappamondo, as well as the huge globe for which it is named, contains an Austrian machine gun and an immense version of *The Divine Comedy*. Suspended from the ceiling of the auditorium adjoining the house is the biplane that D'Annunzio used in a daring flight over Vienna in World War I.

Outside is the prow of the battleship *Puglia* used in D'Annunzio's so-called "Fiume adventure". Fiume (now Rijeka), on the North Adriatic, had been promised to Italy before they entered World War I, but was eventually handed over to Yugoslavia instead. Incensed, D'Annunzio gathered together his army, occupied Fiume, and returned home a national hero.

Practicalities

Gardone's **tourist office** is at Corso Repubblica 39, the cobbled street that runs parallel with the lakefront (June–Sept daily 9.30am–12.30pm & 3–6.30pm; Oct–May Mon–Sat 9am–12.30pm & 2.15–6pm; T & F 0365.20.347). To complement the town's signature opulent **hotels** – with price tags to match – there are a couple of mid-range options: the lakefront *Hotel du Lac*, Via Repubblica 58 (T 0365.21.558, W www.gardalake.it/hotel-dulac; ❹), offers rooms with balconies right on the lakefront, while *Locanda Agli Angeli*, at Piazzetta Garibaldi 2 (T 0365.20.832, W www.agliangeli.com; ❸), on the hillside near Il Vittoriale, has simple rooms, a verandah, a restaurant (see below) and peace and quiet. Down on the lakeside there are numerous cafés where you can settle down for a coffee or a *gelato*. For **restaurants**, however, you're better off heading up to the old village around Il Vittoriale, where *La Stalla* (T 0365.21.038; closed Wed), on Via dei Colli, signposted off the road down from Il Vittoriale, serves well-priced staples in a tranquil garden. For a treat, *Agli Angeli* (see above; closed Mon & Tues), has interesting pasta and fish courses.

Above Gardone

The mountains above Gardone offer lovely walks with some splendid views. The little Alpine hamlet of **SAN MICHELE** is linked by six buses daily to Gardone and Saló, or it's a steep one- to two-hour signposted walk. The family-run *Colomber Hotel* (T 0365.21.108, W www.colomber.com; ❷), 500m inland, has comfortable en-suite rooms, some with balconies overlooking the hills, a swimming pool and a decent restaurant serving local specialities. It's a good base if you want to hike to the springs and waterfalls in the surrounding hills; the owners can give suggestions for **walks**, but for more ambitious hikes, pick up maps marked with footpaths from CAI, Via San Carlo 17, in Saló. Halfway up the hill at Via Panoramica 8, the *Borgo degli Ulivi* (☎0365.20.652 Ⓦwww .residenceborgodegliulivi.it; from ❹), clinging to the mountainside with spectacular views from its neat little apartments, swimming pools and garden, makes a good base for a lake holiday.

Gargnano

Twelve kilometres up the coast is **GARGNANO**, the prettiest village on the lake, now famous for its annual sailing race – the Centomiglia – but once the headquarters of Mussolini's puppet Republic of Saló. The puppeteers were the Nazis, who placed him here in Villa Feltrinelli largely to keep him out of harm's way. The dictator had by this time lost all credibility and he sank into depression; although he installed his mistress, Claretta Petacci, in nearby Gardone, the cold, damp rooms and heavy Nazi presence in the woods outside put paid to any passion.

Gargnano, tumbling down the hillside from the main road to the little fishing port, is still more a working village than a resort. It's the perfect spot to unwind for a day or two and wander around the abandoned olive factory or the lakefront villas with their boathouses, or just to relax with an ice cream or a drink in one of the waterfront cafés. It was here that D.H. Lawrence stayed while writing *Twilight in Italy*, a work which is beautifully evocative of the lake's attractions.

The main sight in the village is the thirteenth-century church of **San Francesco** – the columns in its cloisters are carved with citrus fruits, a reference to the Franciscans' introduction of the crop to Europe. A three-kilometre-stroll along the road which leads north from the port takes you through olive and lemon groves, past Il Duce's final home, the *Villa Feltrinelli* (see below), to the eleventh-century chapel of **San Giacoma Calina**. On the side facing the lake, under the portico where the fishermen keep their equipment, is a thirteenth-century fresco of St Christopher, incredible for the fact that it is still visible despite the obvious lack of attention.

Practicalities

Gargnano's **tourist office** (April–Oct Mon–Thurs 9am–noon, Fri 4–7pm; ☎0365.71.222, Ⓦwww.comune.gargnano.brescia.it) is housed in the ex-Palazzo Comunale; two cannonballs wedged in the lakeside of the building serve as a reminder of the naval bombings suffered in July 1866 during the War of Independence from the Austrians. Shining among the numerous **accommodation** options in Gargnano is the fabulous ⚑ *Villa Feltrinelli* (☎0365.798.000, Ⓦwww.villafeltrinelli.com; closed Nov–March; ❾) – one of the world's top hotels. Every detail has been considered in this elegant eleven-roomed villa with an enviable lakeside position; it's worth pawning all your worldly possessions for the view from the baths alone. Also on the lakefront, and more realistically priced, the very pleasant *Gardenia*, Via Colletta 53, Villa di Gargnano (☎0365.71.195, Ⓦwww.hotel-gardenia.it; closed Nov–March; ❸) offers simple comforts in an attractive garden villa, while the friendly *Tiziana-Garnì*, on Via Dosso 51 (☎0365.71.342, Ⓦwww.albergotiziana.com; ❷), has basic but comfortable modern rooms, most with lake views, though it's a little close to the main road. There is also a campsite, *Rucc*, at Via Rimembranze 23 (☎0365.71.805), near the local beach.

Gargnano is also well served for good **places to eat**. Various places around the harbour serve snacks and ice cream, and there's an idyllically located bar, 1km south along the lakeside lanes to the smaller port, known as "*porto*". Just across the little piazza here, the *Osteria del Restauro* (closed Wed), serves good, inexpensive local cuisine at outdoor tables. Back in the centre, by the *imbarcadero*, the *Miralago*, overlooking the lake, offers excellent food at good prices, while just behind on via XXIV Maggio, the cosy *La Tortuga* (☎0365.71.251; eve only; closed Mon & Tues), is a Michelin-starred restaurant offering top food in a formal atmosphere (expect to pay around €60 per head).

Limone

Seventeen kilometres further north among citrus groves lies **LIMONE SUL GARDA**, a pretty, stone-built village jammed on the slopes between the mountains and the lake. Unfortunately, it's ruined by tourism, the steep cobbled streets lined with stalls selling souvenirs, leather jackets and sequined T-shirts, the old stone facades studded with plastic signs advertising restaurants and hotels. As you elbow your way through the crowds you'll dig into more German and British than Italian ribs, and unless you're aching to eat chicken and chips, frankfurters and sauerkraut, you're best off staying away.

Riva del Garda

At the northwest tip of the lake, **RIVA DEL GARDA** is the best known of the lake's resorts. It started attracting visitors in the late-nineteenth century and retains some stylish pastel-painted hotels. Dramatically located under sheer cliffs, the old town is pleasant enough despite being overrun with tourists and it is also cheaper than most of the other lake resorts; this, coupled with the fact that it boasts Garda's only youth hostel, makes the town a good base for a budget holiday.

There's not a great deal to see, except for the severe moated **castle** (daily 9.30am–12.30pm & 2.30–5.30pm; €3) alongside the port, which contains a modest collection of local art. The entry ticket also allows you to climb the **Torre Apponale** in the main Piazza 3 Novembre, which provides wonderful views of the lake (Tues–Sun: mid-June to mid-Sept 9.30am–6pm; mid-March to mid-June & mid-Sept to Oct 9.30am–12.45pm & 2.15–5.30pm).

Practicalities

Grab a map of Riva from the well-equipped **tourist office** in the Giardini di Porta Orientale on the far side of the castle (Easter to Oct Mon–Sat 9am–noon & 3–6pm, June–Aug also Sun 10am–noon & 3.30–6.30pm; Nov–Easter Mon–Fri 9am–noon & 2.30–5pm; ☎0464.554.444, ⓦwww.gardatrentino .it) – staff here can give you information on everything the town has to offer including a free, guided walking tour. For **accommodation**, the very central **youth hostel** at Piazza Cavour 10 (☎0464.554.911, ⓦwww.ostelloriva.com; €14; April–Oct), has two-, four- and six-bed rooms plus one larger dorm, and is a good choice. Alternatively, the *Albergo Ancora* (☎0464.522.131, ⓦwww .albergoancona.net; ❸), just west of Piazza Cavour at Via Montanara 2, has reasonably priced, comfortable rooms. A walk away from the centre, *Bellariva*, at via Franz Kafka 13 (☎0464.553.620, ⓦwww.rivadelgarda.com/bellariva; ❺), is a modest holiday hotel near the town's beaches, with a peaceful lakeside lawn.

The lakefront is lined with **gelaterie and pizzerias**, and there are numerous bars open in the evening. If you want a more local experience, head for *Osteria del Gallo* under the portico in the corner of Piazza San Rocco, west off the main piazza. There's a short menu of simple local mountain staples and the owner will

Sports and activities on Lake Garda

There are **watersports** on offer all round Lake Garda but the northern shore around Riva – and especially Tòrbole – is the area's main centre. All prices below are approximate; tourist offices keep contact details and flyers for all operators.

A clutch of local outfits offer **windsurfing** for first-timers (€60–65 for 3hr), and there are group lessons at various grades (around €70 for 3hr). If you are already proficient, you can rent a board for about €40–50 per day. **Sailing** is also popular, with beginners' courses (around €125 for 4hr) and rental (€60–120 per day, depending on the size of boat). Shop around: local operators include ⓦ www.pierwindsurf .it, ⓦ www.vascorenna.com, ⓦ www.sailingdulac.com, ⓦ www.surfsegnana.it, ⓦ www .surflb.com and ⓦ www.windsurfconca.com. **Kiteboarding** is also on offer; check out ⓦ www.swiss-kiteboarding.com for beginners' courses (€260; 9hr total). You can **rent canoes** (for one person €18/day; for two people €29/day) at the Sabbioni beach in Riva.

With over a dozen fine locations within easy reach of the lake, **canyoning** is a good bet (April–Oct only). Half-day trips around €35–50, full-day trips about €65–105; leading operators include ⓦ www.canyonadv.com and ⓦ www.wetway.it. Several companies offer more traditional **Alpine activities** – ice-climbing, *via ferrata* trekking and so on; check out ⓦ www.alpinguide.com and ⓦ www.guidealpinearco.com for more. **Paragliding** – notably off Monte Baldo above Malcésine – is a fantastic way to get spectacular, eagle-eye views of the lake: Volo Libero (ⓦ www.timetofly.net) runs tandem paragliding flights, where you're strapped to an instructor, for €60–80; see also ⓦ www.condorfly.com.

reel off many more dishes. The good wine list of Trento wines and the relaxed atmosphere make this a fine spot to settle down for the evening. Alternatively, *Osteria Pane Saleme*, at via Marocco 22, in the tiny backstreet parallel west of Via Fiume, has well-priced simple fare and wine by the glass.

The eastern shore

Overlooked by the mountains of the Monte Baldo chain, the main resorts of Garda's **eastern shore** are heavily touristed and have little of the faded charm of the western side. **Torbole** in the north is the place to head if you're a keen windsurfer or attracted by any of the myriad of other outdoor activities on offer. Along the shore to the south, **Malcesine**'s appealing centre is nowadays hidden under postcard stands and trilingual pizza menus. It is, however, still a good base for escapes by bike or on foot into the mountains. Further south still lies **Torri del Benaco**, a lovely old village, popular but not yet ruined by tourism, while **Garda** and **Bardolino** are bustling resorts, the former a favourite haunt of Italian holiday-makers.

Torbole

TORBOLE, at the top of the lake, 4km east of Riva, played an important role in the fifteenth-century war between the Viscontis and the Venetians, when a fleet of warships was dragged overland here and launched into the lake. Nowadays it's still the water that dominates, since Torbole's main diversions are sailing and windsurfing, and the place has a fresh, youthful feeling. This is a good place to stay if you're into sports, with numerous activities on offer both on the water and in the mountains behind. Windsurfing enthusiasts come here from all over Europe, attracted by the ideal wind conditions. It's also a good place for beginners, and in the mornings, when the wind is gentler, the water is full of wobbling novices attempting to circle their instructors. See box, p.253 for a rundown of good watersports outfitters.

Practicalities

The **tourist office** (mid-June to mid-Sept Mon–Sat 9am–noon & 3–6.30pm, Sun 10am–noon & 4–6.30pm; April to mid-June & mid-Sept to mid-Oct Mon–Sat 9am–noon & 3–6.15pm; Nov to end March Mon–Fri 9am–noon & 2.30–5.15pm; ℡0464.505.177, Ⓦwww.gardatrentino.it) stands between the town centre and the landing centre; it has a huge range of information on different courses, places to rent bikes and boards, and routes for every imaginable sport. There are dozens of **hotels**, including *Lido Blu*, Via Foci del Sarca 1 (℡0464.505.180, Ⓦwww.lidoblu.com; ❺), by the mouth of the River Sarca, next to the beaches, which is popular with families, and *Casa Romani*, at Via Pescicoltura 35 (℡0464.505.113, Ⓦwww.torbole.com/casaromani; ❷), behind the tourist office, featuring two pools, a garden of olive trees and views over the lake.

Malcesine

Backed by the slopes of Monte Baldo and blessed with the same windsurfer-friendly winds as Torbole, **MALCESINE**, 14km further south, is inundated with British and German package tourists and consequently the crowds temper much of the appeal of the historic, old town. The main sight is a thirteenth-century turreted **Castello** (April–Oct daily 9am–9pm; Nov–March Sat & Sun only; €4), built, like Sirmione's, by the Scaligeri family. Goethe was imprisoned here briefly in 1786, having been arrested on suspicion of being a spy – he'd been caught making sketches of the lake castle's towers.

For land-based active pursuits you need to head up Monte Baldo. Although there are well-marked walking trails up the mountain, you can save energy by taking the **funicular** (daily: April–Oct every 30min 8am–6pm; €16 return), but be prepared for long queues in summer. For those who want to make the panoramic descent on **mountain bike**, there are wheels for hire at G. Furioli in Piazza Matteotti, who even transport the bikes to the top; you can also take your own bike up on one of the four trips – three in the morning and one at lunchtime – designed especially for cyclists.

Practicalities

The **tourist office** at Via Capitanato 6–8 (Mon–Sat 9am–1pm & 3–7pm; May–Oct also Sun 9am–1pm; ℡045.740.0044, Ⓦwww.malcesinepiu.it), north along the lake from the port, has maps of signposted walks in the hills behind town. Most **hotels** in Malcesine get filled by package companies, so the choice is limited, but *Hotel Europa* (℡045.740.0022, Ⓦwww.europa-hotel.net; ❹), a three-star hotel right on the lake, five minute's walk north of town, is a pleasant choice with a pool. Most of Malcesine's **restaurants** are very poor indeed, but the *Trattoria Vecchia Malcesine* (℡045.740.0469, Ⓦwww.vecchiamalcesine.com) breaks the mould, serving creative dishes using local ingredients on a relaxing terrace. It's at via Pisort 6, five minutes' walk south of the tourist office.

Torri del Benaco

Twenty kilometres south of Malcesine, **TORRI DEL BENACO** is the prettiest and least spoilt of the villages on this side of the lake. Its old centre consists simply of one long cobbled street, Corso Dante, crisscrossed with tunnelling alleyways and lined with mellow stone *palazzi*. At one end of the street is the **castle**, illuminated at night and with a long glasshouse – or *lemonia* – built along one side to protect the lemon trees inside during cold weather. Next to the castle, the port area is a *piazza* planted with limes and chestnuts, at night the focus of the *passeggiata*. At the other end of town, along the *lungholagho,* the town's **beach** comprises 100m of white pebbles and shallow water. On the corner, known as Punto Cavallo, a quiet, walled **park** provides a pleasant grassy patch of shade, a children's playground, and a locals' bar.

Practicalities

The **tourist office** is by the castle, just off the main road (April–Sept Mon–Sat 9am–1pm & 3–7pm, Tues & Thurs closes 6.30pm, Sun 9am–1pm only; ☎045.722.5120; ⓦwww.tourism.verona.it). Torri is a fine place to stay; the best **hotel** is the *Onda*, located on Via per Albisano, two minutes' walk from the village centre (☎045.722.5895, ⓦwww.garnionda.com; closed Nov–April; ➋). Each spotless room has its own balcony or terrace and the friendly owners provide a first-rate breakfast and helpful advice on the area. If there's no space, try the *Baia dei Pini* (☎045.722.5215, ⓦwww.baiadeipini.com; closed Nov–April; ➎), overlooking the town beach, which offers contemporary, stylish and comfortable rooms a short walk from the village centre. The best hotel in town is the elegant *Gardesana* (☎045.722.5411, ⓦwww.hotel-gardesana.com; closed Nov–March; ➏) right on the harbour at Piazza Calderini 20.

The *Gardesana* also boasts the town's top **restaurant** (closed Tues & Nov–Feb), where you can splash out on a romantic meal overlooking the lake. The other decent place to eat in the village is practically next door, *Trattoria Bell'Arrivo* (☎045.629.9028), on Piazza Calderini. It's a cosy spot with unusually good food, served at tables in an attractive little garden. There are numerous other options among the warren of streets and along the waterfront, although in general the lake-view spots are overpriced and poor quality. For excellent food in unbeatable surroundings, head a couple of kilometres above town into the hills towards Albisano where the 🍴 *Trattoria agli Olivi* (☎045.722.5483) serves delicious dishes at bargain prices on a splendid lake-view terrace amid olive groves.

Punta San Vigilio

A few kilometres south, the appealing **Punta San Vigilio** juts into the lake, offering a well-equipped pay beach (May–Sept €10) with sun loungers, picnic tables and children's equipment scattered on grassy slopes planted with pines

---

Theme parks: Gardaland and Canevaworld

If you have kids to amuse, or just fancy a daft day out, head for one of the **theme parks** along Lake Garda's eastern shore between Peschiera and Lazise. The biggest is **GARDALAND** (daily: mid-March to Sept 9.30am–6pm; late June to early Sept 9am–midnight, plus weekends in Oct & Dec; ☎045.644.9777, ⓦwww.gardaland.it; €24, children under 10 €20). It's pricey, and you pay extra for some of the attractions, but its rides and themed entertainments are exciting and well presented.

Just to the north is **CANEVAWORLD** (☎045.696.9900, ⓦwww.canevaworld.it), comprising two parks side by side: **Movie Studios Park** (mid-March to June & Sept daily 10am–6pm; July & Aug Mon–Fri 10am–7pm, Sat 10am–11pm, Sun 10am–6pm; plus weekends in Oct), with fake movie sets and shows revealing the secrets of special effects; and **Aqua Paradise Park** (daily mid-May to mid-Sept 10am–6pm, July & Aug until 7pm), with slides, flumes, pools and a pirate island. Admission costs €18 for one park (€15 if you are less than 1.40m high), or €23/19 for both. Free **buses** shuttle at least hourly to Gardaland and Canevaworld from Peschiera train station.

and olive trees. Just over the headland, there's a charming, diminutive harbour with a pricey bar/restaurant, the *Punto San Vigilio* (March–Nov daily noon–1pm & 8–10pm) and an exclusive hotel, *San Vigilio* (℡045.725.6688, Ⓦwww .punta-sanvigilio.it; Ⓔ), which numbers Churchill, Laurence Olivier and Prince Charles among its former guests.

Garda, Bardolino and Lazise

Like many of its neighbours, the ancient fishing village of **GARDA**, 8km south, has seen its narrow, winding alleys and cottages encroached on by snack bars, cheap leather and souvenir shops. Even the fifteenth-century **Loggia della Losa**, originally a dock for the palace behind, is now a *gelateria*. If you want to stay, visit the **tourist office**, on the waterfront at Lungolago 3 (April–Sept Mon–Sat 9am–7pm, Sun 9am–1pm; Oct–March Mon–Sat 9am–1pm & 3–6pm; ℡045.627.0384, Ⓦwww.tourism.verona.it), which has daily updated information on available accommodation and can also provide leaflets on walks in the hills behind.

Three kilometres away is the spruce little resort of **BARDOLINO**, popular with British and German visitors, and, as you might have guessed, the home of the light, red Bardolino wine; the town is at its most animated between mid-September and mid-October, during the *Festa di Uva* (Festival of the Grape). At other times of year, the unlikely-looking bar on Via Cesare Battisti, which has no name outside but is commonly known as *Da Romaldi*, is a good place to sample local vintages or try the ice cream at *Cristallo* on the lakefront near the ferry jetty, renowned as one of the lake's best *gelaterie*.

The walled village of **LAZISE**, further down the shore, was once a major Venetian port and retains a (privately owned) **castle** and, on the harbour, an arcaded medieval **customs house**. Originally used for building and repairing boats for the Venetian fleet, it later served as a shelter for sheep, whose urine was used to make nitrogen, a vital ingredient in gunpowder. Nowadays Lazise is crammed with cafés, pizzerias and *gelaterie* and plenty of summer visitors, but it's not a bad place to visit out of season, when it reverts to being a sleepy lakeside village. The **tourist office** (Mon–Sat: April–Oct 9am–1pm & 3–7pm; Nov–March 9am–1pm & 3–6pm; ℡045.758.0114), on Via F. Fontana near the harbour, has maps and leaflets about the village.

Travel details

You can find a very useful site combining timetables for different forms of public transport in Lombardy at Ⓦwww.infopoint.it/trl_index.htm. The downside is that it sticks strictly to the administrative region of Lombardy and so the eastern shore of Lake Garda and the western shores of Lago Maggiore and Lago d'Orta are not included.

Trains

Bergamo to: Brescia (hourly; 50min); Cremona (3 daily; 1hr 30min); Lecco (hourly; 35min); Milan (every 40min; 50min); Verona (1 daily; 1hr 30min).

Brescia to: Capo di Ponte (5 daily; 1hr 55min); Cremona (every 2hr; 50min); Desenzo-Sirmione (every 30min; 20min); Milan (every 30min; 1hr); Parma (9 daily; 1hr 30min–1hr 50min); Verona (every 30min; 45min).

Cremona to: Brescia (every 2hr; 50min); Mantua (hourly; 55min); Milan (6 daily; 1hr 10min).

Lecco to: Bergamo (hourly; 45min); Milan (hourly; 45min); Sondrio (hourly; 1hr 25min).

Mantua to: Bologna (2 daily; 1hr 35min); Milan (6 daily; 2hr); Modena (every 30min; 45min); Padua (2 daily; 1hr 55min); Rome (Mon–Sat

1 daily; 4hr 15min); Venezia (Mon–Sat 1 daily; 2hr 45min); Verona (hourly; 50min).

Milan Centrale to: Bergamo (hourly; 50min); Brescia (every 30min; 1hr 20min); Certosa di Pavia (6 daily; 25min); Como (hourly; 40min); Desenzano (hourly; 1hr 15min); Lecco (hourly; 1hr); Pavia (every 15min; 25min); Peschiera (hourly; 1hr 20min); Stresa (hourly; 1hr 10min); Varenna (every 2hr; 1hr 20min); Verona (hourly; 1hr 35min).

Milan Lambrate to: Certosa di Pavia (9 daily; 20min); Cremona (3 daily; 1hr 35min); Pavia (every 15min; 25min).

Milan Porta Garibaldi to: Bergamo (every 40min; 55min); Streaa (8 daily; 1hr 30min); Varese (17 daily; 1hr).

Milan Porta Genova to: Vigévano (hourly; 35min).

Pavia to: Certosa di Pavia (14 daily; 10min); Cremona (11 daily; 2hr 20min); Mantua (6 daily; 3hr); Milan (hourly; 25min).

Sondrio to: Tirano (every 50min; 35min).

Buses

Brescia to: Gardone Riviera (every 25min; 1hr 5min); Iseo (4 daily; 45min); Mantua (hourly; 1hr 25min).

Como to: Bellagio (every 30min; 1hr 10min); Cernobbio (every 30min; 20min); Colico (5 daily; 2hr 20min); Menaggio (every 20min; 1hr 10min); Tremezzo (14 daily; 1hr); Varese (38 daily; 1hr 10min).

Cremona to: Bergamo (4 daily; 2hr 30min); Brescia (hourly; 1hr 15min); Milan (1 daily; 1hr 15min).

Gardone Riviera to: Brescia (every 30min; 1hr); Limone (3 daily; 1hr); Riva del Garda (5 daily; 1hr 15min).

Mantua to: Brescia (hourly; 1hr 35min); Peschiera (6 daily; 1hr 10min); Sabbioneta (3 daily; 50min); Sirmione (1 daily; 1hr 20min); Verona (6 daily; 1hr 20min).

Menaggio to: Lugano (9 daily; 1hr).

Milan (Metro Famogosta) to: Certosa (Mon–Sat every 45min, Sun 7 daily; 30min).

Pavia to: Certosa (Mon–Sat every 30min, Sun hourly; 20min); Milan (Mon–Sat every 30min, Sun 7 daily; 1hr).

Tirano to: Bormio (15 daily; 1hr).

Ferries

The frequencies below are for summer sailings; for other times of year consult Ⓦ www .navigazionelaghi.it.

Cadenabbia to: Bellagio (every 25min; 10min); Varenna (every 25min; 25min).

Como to: Bellagio (6 daily; 2hr 10min); Cernobbio (every 20min; 15min); Colico (5 daily; 4hr); Menaggio (6 daily; 2hr 25min); Varenna (6 daily; 2hr 40min).

Desenzano to: Garda (8 daily; 1hr 15min); Gardone Riviera (7 daily; 1hr 15min); Gargnano (3 daily; 2hr); Malcesine (5 daily; 3hr 15min); Riva del Garda (8 daily; 3hr 30min); Saló (5 daily; 1hr 30min); Sirmione (every 45min; 20min).

Intra to: Laveno (every 30min; 20min); Stresa (every 30min; 55min).

Maderno to: Torri (every 35min; 30min).

Stresa to: Intra (every 30min; 55min); Isola Bella (every 30min; 10min); Isola dei Pescatori (every 30min; 15min); Isola Madre (every 30min; 30min); Pallanza (every 30min; 35min); Villa Táranto (hourly; 45min).

Trentino-Alto Adige

CHAPTER 4

Highlights

* **Trento's Piazza Duomo**
Trento's pleasant central
square, with its backdrop
of mountains, is ringed by
arcades, shops and cafés.
See p.269

* **Strada di Vino** Follow the
"wine road" through the Adige
valley and sample some of the
region's best food and wine.
See p.272

* **Ice Man** The chief exhibit in
Bolzano's Museo Archeologico
is the superbly preserved "Ice
Man", an early Copper Age
male, found in the Ötzaler Alps
in 1991. See p.289

* **Castello Róncolo** A
thirteenth-century castle
decorated with beautiful frescoes of courtly life. See p.290

* **The Dolomites** The glamorous Olympic resort of Cortina
makes an excellent base for
skiing and hiking in the
Dolomites. See p.301

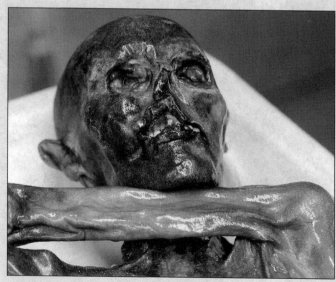

△ Ice Man

Trentino-Alto Adige

"and to dream in a vague way of those mystic mountains beyond Verona which we knew of, somewhat indefinitely, as the Dolomites."

Amelia B. Edwards (1831–92; adventurer)

Despite the boom in tourism since the development of winter sports in the 1950s and 1960s, Italy's northernmost region, Trentino–Alto Adige, still remains the mysterious area of untrodden peaks and infrequented valleys that Amelia Edwards spoke of in her travel adventures. It is a unique **German–Italian** region, made up of two autonomous provinces, much of which has only been part of Italy since 1919. Before then, Alto Adige was known as the South Tyrol (Südtirol) and was part of Austria. At the end of World War I, Austria ceded South Tyrol to the Italians, and, in a bid to make the new territory instantly Italian, Mussolini turned the name on its head, naming it after the upper reaches of the Adige river, which bisects the region. Many Tyroleans opted for resettlement in Germany, but others stayed and have clung tenaciously to their language, culture and traditions.

Even now, one of the first things you'll notice about **Alto Adige** (also known as Südtirol) is its German character. Gothic onion-domed churches dot the landscape of vineyards and forests, street signs are in German, and there's sauerkraut and strudel on the menu. By contrast **Trentino**, just to the south, is 98 percent Italian-speaking, and the food and architecture belong more to the Mediterranean world than to the Alps. Both parts of the region enjoy autonomy from central government, along with one of the highest standards of living in Italy, a consequence of special grants and aid they receive from Rome – intended to defuse the ethnic tension that has existed ever since enforced union took place.

If some German speakers are unwilling to remain part of Italy, there are right-wing Italian speakers who would be equally pleased to see them go. Friction between the two camps flared up in the 1960s, when Germanic activists staged disturbances. Talks between the Austrian and Italian governments brought about a package of concessions and promises from central government, known as the *pachetto*, all the provisions of which have now been implemented. These days, the **political climate** has shifted slightly and many German speakers have moved away from the extreme nationalist Union Für Südtirol towards the Lega Nord. The Italian government, too, has finally acquiesced to some of the South Tyrolean demands for independent status. In February 2001, a reorganization of the region led to power being invested in the two provinces separately rather than jointly, with each wielding greater political clout, though they remain linked, if only by their official name.

Tourism (chiefly skiing and hiking), farming and wine production are the mainstays of the economy, and there are plenty of good, reasonably cheap

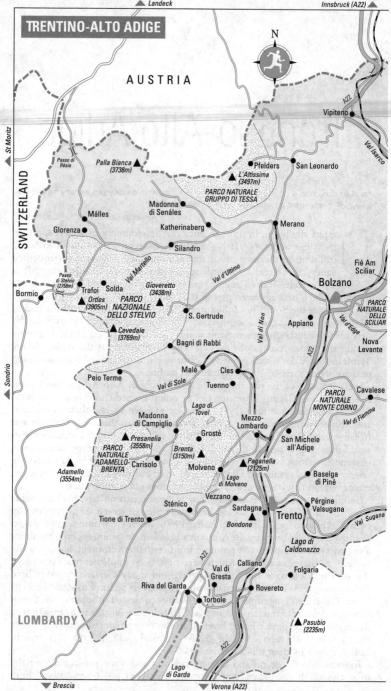

TRENTINO-ALTO ADIGE

Landeck

Innsbruck (A22)

N

AUSTRIA

Vipiteno

A22

Val d'Isarco

St Moritz

SWITZERLAND

Passo di Résia

Palla Bianca
(3738m)

Pfelders

San Leonardo

L'Altissima
(3497m)

PARCO NATURALE
GRUPPO DI TESSA

Málles

Madonna
di Senáles

Glorenza

Katherinaberg

Merano

Silandro

Fié Am
Sciliar

Val Martello

Val d'Ultimo

Bolzano

Passo
di Stelvio
(2758m)

Trafoi

Solda

Gioveretto
(3438m)

PARCO
NATURALE
DELLO
SCILIAR

Sondrio

Bormio

Ortles
(3905m)

PARCO
NAZIONALE
DELLO STELVIO

S. Gertrude

Val d'Edge

Nova
Levante

Cevedale
(3769m)

Appiano

Bagni di Rabbi

Val di Non

Peio Terme

Malé

Cles

Val di Sole

Tuenno

PARCO
NATURALE
MONTE CORNO

Cavalese

Madonna
di Campiglio

Lago di
Tovel

Grostè

Mezzo-
Lombardo

Val di Fiemme

Presanella
(3558m)

Brenta
(3150m)

San Michele
all'Adige

PARCO
NATURALE
ADAMELLO-
BRENTA

Carisolo

Molveno

Paganella
(2125m)

Baselga
di Piné

Adamello
(3554m)

Lago
di Molveno

Vezzano

Pérgine
Valsugana

Sténico

Sardagna

Trento

Tione di Trento

Bondone

Lago di
Caldonazzo

Val Sugana

Calliano

Folgaria

Val di
Gresta

Riva del Garda

Rovereto

Torbole

LOMBARDY

Pasubio
(2235m)

Lago
di Garda

Brescia

Verona (A22)

Passo di
Brénnero
(1357m)
▲ Gran Pilastro
(3510m)

AUSTRIA

Campo Túres

Fúndres
Selva dei
Molini

Val Pusteria

Brunico

San Lorenzo

Villabassa

PARCO NATURALE FÁNES-
SÉNNES-BRÁIES

Novacella

San Vigilio

Dobbiaco

Bressanone

PARCO NATURALE
DOLOMITI DI SESTO

Fortezza

Pederú

Croda Rossa
(3139m) ▲

Chiusa
Val di Funes

PARCO
NATURALE
OLDE

Cristallo
(3221m) ▲

Lago
di Misurina

▲ Tre Cime di Lavaredo
(2999m)

Santa Maddalena
Ortisei

Pedráces
La Villa

Tofane
(3243m) ▲

Passo Tre
Croci (1814m)

Auronzo
di Cadore

Val Gardena

Passo di Gardena
(2121m)

San Cassiano

Siusi

Passo di
Sella (2234m)

Corvara

Cortina
d'Ampezzo

Sasso Lungo
(3179m) ▲

Selle (3151m)

Passo di
Valparola

Passo di
Falzarego

Antelao
(3263m) ▲

Alpe di Siusi

Arabba

Pieve di Cadore

Rosengarten/
Catinaccio
(2981m) ▲

Passo
Pordoi
(2239m)

Canazei

Caprile

Vigo
di Fassa

Marmolada
(3343m) ▲

Alleghe

Carezza
al Lago

Passo di Costalunga
(1745m)

Moena

Passo di San
Pellegrino (1918m)

Civetta
(3218m) ▲

FRIULI-

Val di Fassa

Predazzo

Panevéggio

Pale di San
Martino (3192m)

VENEZIA

GIULIA

Tésero

Passo
di Rolle
(1970m)

San Martino

PARCO
NATURALE
PANEVÉGGIO

Passo di Cereda
(1369m)

Cima d'Asta
(2847m) ▲

Fiera di Primiero
Mezzano

Belluno

Imer

Fonzaso

Feltre

Vittório
Veneto

VENETO

A27

0   10 km

▶ Lienz & Salzburg

▶ Udine

▶ Trieste

▼ Venice

guesthouses and agriturismi in the mountains and vineyards. Although the region's resorts can be sleepy, the landscape, dominated by the stark and jagged **Dolomites**, is among the most beautiful in the country. Circling the spiked towers of rock that characterize the range, a network of trails follows the ridges, varying in length from a day's walk to a two-week trek; the long-distance trails, called *alte vie*, can be picked up from the small resorts.

The chief towns of **Trento** and **Bolzano** are the transport hubs for the region. Trento gives access to most of the western Dolomites: the **Pale di San Martino**, a cluster of enormous peaks encircling the high, rocky plain above San Martino di Castrozza; the **Catinaccio** (or Rosengarten) range between the Val di Fassa and Bolzano; the **Gruppo di Sella**, with its *vie ferrate* (see box, p.267); and the glacier-topped **Marmolada**. Still in the western Dolomites, but with easier access from Bolzano, are the **Alpe di Siusi**, a magical plateau of grass and wetland, high above the valley. The *alpe* are enclosed by the peaks of **Sasso Lungo** (or Langkofel) and **Sciliar** (or Schlern); to the north is the quieter Odle (or Geisler Gruppe). Even further to the west, on the other side of Trento, are the **Dolomiti di Brenta**, a collection of wild peaks above the meadows of Valle Rendena.

Regional food and wine

Trentino-Alto Adige, as its name suggests, is really two regions: Alto Adige with its unreservedly Germanic traditions, and Trentino, which mixes mountain influences with more Italian flavours from the south. Another influence is the weather: in this mountainous region, with only a couple of snow-free months a year, the diet tends to be dominated by carbohydrates. There's no such thing as a light supper in Trentino.

A **typical meal** starts with some kind of salami (*lucanicche* in local dialect), often paper-thin slices of salt beef, followed by Tyrolean *canederli* – bread dumplings flavoured with *speck* (smoked ham) and accompanied by a melted butter dressing – or *strangolapreti*, bread and spinach gnocchi. Game and rabbit with polenta are popular as *secondi*. Desserts are often based on apples, pears or plums, readily available from the local orchards. Other sweet treats include *Soffiato alla Trentina*, a meringue trifle, and *Zelten Trentino*, a rich fruitcake flavoured with grappa and usually eaten at Christmas.

As you travel north into Alto Adige the menu becomes more Germanic, with *knödel* (dumplings) and goulash, sausages with horseradish sauce (*salsa al cren*), sauerkraut, *apfel strudel*, *sachertorte* and all manner of sweet tarts and pastries. If you're really keen to sample some of Alto Adige's cuisine, try to co-ordinate your visit with the Törggelen season (see box, p.291).

Vines have been cultivated here since Roman times, and Trentino-Alto Adige produces more **DOC wines** than any other region in Italy. Most famous are the Pinot Grigios and Chardonnays, which are bright and aromatic from being grown at high altitudes and in cool conditions. These also provide wine makers with the raw material for some outstanding traditional-method sparkling wines, often marketed under the *spumante Trentino Classico* label. Despite the excellence of the whites, local wine makers actually make more reds, achieving considerable success with local varieties like Teróldego and Schiava (known as Vernatsch in German-speaking areas). Red wines made from Schiava are good when young: look out for the pale-red Kalterersee (Caldaro) and the fuller, more fruity St Magdalene (Santa Maddalena); those made from the Lagrein grape variety are more robust, such as the strong, dark Lagrein Dunkel, or the Kretzer rosé from Bolzano's vineyards at Gries. Also worth seeking out is the rare **vin santo** from Trentino's Valle dei Laghi – a luscious dessert wine made from local Nosiola grapes.

The eastern Dolomites start on the opposite side of the Adige Valley, past Passo di Campolongo and Corvara, with activity focusing on **Cortina d'Ampezzo**, self-styled "Queen of the Dolomite resorts" – though actually just across the regional border in the Veneto. In summer, avoid the overpopulated peaks like the **Tre Cime di Lavaredo** and head for **Sorapiss** or **Monte Pelmo** to the south, or **Le Tofane** and the mountains of the **Fánes-Sénnes-Bráies** group to the west. In winter, Cortina comes into its own as an upmarket ski resort with excellent, if expensive, facilities.

It's worth noting that provincial **bus** companies stick fairly rigidly to towns within their territory, so that some places which look like they should be easy to get to from Bolzano, say, often are not. For example, there are more frequent buses to Canazei from Trento, and this is the case for other towns in the northern part of Trentino. If you're **driving** outside the summer months, be aware that many passes can remain closed until well after Easter. Approach roads all have signs indicating whether the pass is open, or you can call Bolzano's information line on ℡0471.999.999. The Südtirol's official **website** ⊛www .suedtirol.com has some useful links and reams of information about the province, with pages devoted to individual towns and resorts.

Hiking and skiing

The official **hiking** season lasts from June 20 to September 20; this is when most refuges (see p.266) and cable cars are open, though there will be local variations and you'll find some also have a winter season. The refuges are the best place to phone for local information on cable cars and weather conditions.

Routes are well established, with a large number of well-marked day walks and a series of longer trails, known as **alte vie**. Four of these run north–south between the Val Pusteria (Pustertal) and the Veneto, and four from the Val d'Isarco (Eisacktal) south, each stage requiring five to eight hours' walking from one mountain refuge to the next. Some of the initial ascents are strenuous, but once you are up on the ridges the paths level out and give superb views across the valleys and glaciers. (As a rule of thumb, an averagely fit person takes around three hours to ascend 1000m.) Parts of the trails are exposed, or have snowfields across them, but alternative routes are always available. Alta Via 1, between the Lago di Bráies (Pragser Wildsee) and Belluno, is the most popular, so much so that you should think twice about going between mid-July and August because of the crowds, not to mention the summer heat.

There aren't many guides to the trails in English. Tourist offices usually have information on the day walks in the locality, often quite detailed and with good maps. The larger branches sometimes have guides to Alte Vie 1 and 2; Martin Collins's *Alta Via: High Level Walks in the Dolomites* (Cicerone) details walks along Alte Vie 1 and 2; and if you read Italian or German, Alpina Verlag's *Dolomite Alte Vie/Dolomiten Hohenwegel 1–10* is an extremely thorough option – available free from larger tourist offices. As for maps, the *alte vie* are marked on the Kompass 1:50,000 and Tabacco 1:25,000 maps, along with the multitude of other shorter trails that can be followed without guides. These maps are on sale everywhere in the Dolomites.

As for **skiing and winter sports**, Trento's excellent *Snow Info* brochure and Bolzano's skiing booklet (published by the provincial tourist offices) give details of chair lifts, altitude and length of runs in each resort, plus maps. From December, you can get the latest on snow conditions in Trentino at ⊛www .meteotrentino.it and in Bolzano on ℡0471.271.177; Bolzano's weather website, ⊛www.provinz.bz.it/meteo, is very useful. *Settimane Bianche* ("White

Skiing and Dolomiti Superski

If you take a car and want to ski at more than one resort, the **Dolomiti Superski** gives you access to 1220km of runs, 450 cable cars and chair lifts, and costs, in high season, €40 per day, €214 per a week or €368 per fortnight. The vast ski circus is made up of twelve smaller areas: see Ⓦ www.dolomitisuperski for a full list. The individual areas or resorts often represent a group of villages strung along a valley, and lifts link them together. Some areas are joined up to create circuits including the famous **"Sella Ronda"** that takes you around the **Marmolada** (3342m). Ski buses are free in some places, and are useful in areas not linked into the rest of the circuit by the lifts. The slopes are open from late December to late April depending on snow; snow machines can help when snowfall has been low. The sheer size of the area inevitably means there are slopes for all abilities but it is its status as a regular fixture on the FIS World Cup ski race, taking in Val Gardena most years, for which the area is most talked about. However, of seemingly more interest to most Italians are the mountain restaurants which dot the slopes, where sun drenched terraces host delicious multi-course lunches that can go on for several hours.

Several **ski schools** operate out of each resort, covering all disciplines of skiing and snowboarding. A six-day course (three hours of tuition per day in a group of around fifteen people) costs about €140. Private lessons average €30–50 per hour. In more expensive resorts, such as Cortina, prices can be higher.

Scuola italiana di sci is the main Italian ski school (Ⓦ www.amsi.it) and most resorts have their own office: Arraba Ⓦ www.scuolasciarabba.com; Colfosco Ⓦ www .scuolascicolfosco.it; Canazei Ⓦ www.scuolascicanazei.com. All the resorts in the area have ski and snowboard rental shops; allow €20–40 per day for equipment depending on the level and quality of the material you choose.

Weeks") are bargain package deals offering full or half board and a ski-pass: information is available from Italian tourist offices before you leave, and also from regional offices in Italy. For specific details of places to stay and prices, ask for the information leaflets published each October by local tourist offices.

Rifugi

If you're seriously into hiking or skiing, the most convenient places to stay once you're high up are the **rifugi** (refuges). Solidly constructed, usually two- or three-storey buildings, they provide dormitory accommodation (or sometimes double rooms), meals and a bar. Some have hot showers, but just as many have only freezing cold water. Blankets are provided, and sheets can be rented for a nominal charge. All are open from June until around September or October, and some also operate in the skiing season; we've given opening periods as a guide, but these are still subject to prevailing weather conditions. If you're planning a long trek that relies on refuges for accommodation, you should definitely call ahead; at the same time, you can check that the place isn't likely to be packed out by a large party – nobody is ever turned away, but overflow accommodation is either on a mattress in the bar or even in the hen house. If you are a member of the Club Alpino Italiano (Ⓦ www.cai.it) the overnight rate is around €10; if not, expect to pay around €18. In high season, you may only be accepted if you agree to half board: count on paying €30–40 for a bunk, breakfast and dinner. **Emergency calls** can be made from most refuges; to call Soccorso Alpino (Alpine Rescue), dial ☏118. A full list of refuges, with phone numbers, is available from the provincial tourist offices in Bolzano and Trento. For more on *rifugi*, see "Accommodation" in Basics, p.47 or check the official website Ⓦ www.rifugi.it.

Vie ferrate

Vie ferrate (literally "iron ways") are a peculiarly Italian phenomenon. The easiest way to describe them is as aided rock-climbs. Consisting of permanently fixed metal ladders, pegs and cables, onto which climbers' karabiners can be clipped, they provide access to routes that would otherwise be too difficult. Many *vie ferrate* were begun as far back as the late nineteenth century as mountaineering really took off in Europe; others were put in place by the Alpini troops during World War I to assist the climbs that were a matter of survival for the soldiers fighting in the mountains. Many more have been created since by volunteers from local *Club Alpino Italiano* groups.

All are clearly marked on both Kompass and Tabacco maps as a line of little black dots or crosses, but *vie ferrate* are definitely not for beginners or vertigo-sufferers. You need to be confident belaying, have the proper equipment (including helmet, ropes, two self-locking karabiners and a chest- or seat-harness) – and you must know what you're doing. Incidentally, it's not advisable to climb a *via ferrata* in a thunderstorm either; it might just become one long lightning conductor.

Of course, once you've done a few straightforward paths up in the mountains you may be inspired to tackle some *ferrate*, and there are plenty of people around who will teach you. Individual guides charge by the hour, and so become more affordable if you can assemble a small group. Otherwise, enrol on a mountain skills course: both Trentino and Alto Adige provincial tourist offices keep lists of guides and mountaineering schools, but you'll need to book well in advance.

Guides and mountaineering schools

Alpinschule Südtirol Jungmannstrasse 8, Campo Túres ☎0474.690.012, ⓦwww .kammerlander.com. Courses throughout the Dolomites, from ice-climbing to *vie ferrate*. The school is run by the famous mountaineer Hans Kammerlander.

Collegio Guide Alpine Via Manci 57, Trento ☎0461.981.207, ⓦwww.guidealpine trentino.it – central number for Alpine guides in the province of Trentino; for Alto Adige, call ☎0471.976.357, ⓦwww.guidealpine.altoadige.info.

Scuola Alpinismo Orizzonti Trentini Via Sotteri 93b ☎0461.421.008, ⓦwww .orizzontitrentini.com. Trento-based guides, with another branch in Besenello, Via Manzoni 3 ☎0464.835.449.

For those who shudder at the idea of walking boots and rucksacks, the region is also famous for its many varied and beautiful castles, some of which have fascinating Gothic fresco cycles. A handy publication is the *Guide to the Castles of Trentino* available from the tourist office in Trento.

Trento

Straddling the Adige Valley, **TRENTO**, just three hours from Venice by train, is a quiet provincial centre that makes one of the best bases for exploring the region, not least because of its bus services to the mountains. It's a lovely city, all fading frescoes and cobblestones, narrow streets and café-speckled piazze. Overshadowed by the dramatic Monte Bedone just 13km away, it's beautifully sited, too, encircled by mountains and exuding a relaxed pace of life. It wasn't always so, however. From the tenth to the eighteenth centuries, Trento was a powerful bishopric ruled by a dynasty of princes; it was the venue of the Council of Trent in the sixteenth century, when the Catholic Church, threatened by the Reformation in northern Europe, met to plan its countermeasures – meetings that spanned a total of

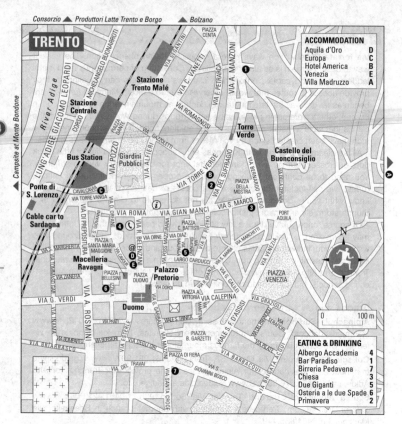

eighteen years. Later, throughout the nineteenth century, ownership of the city, which remained in Austrian hands, was hotly contested, and it only became properly part of Italy in 1919, after the conclusion of World War I.

These days, the city makes an interesting destination in itself, and also an excellent base for exploring the surrounding Alpine landscapes, with minor attractions such as the ethnographic museum at **San Michele all'Adige** and the castle at **Calliano**, as well as the **MART**, Italy's largest modern art museum, just 25km south.

Arrival and information

Trento's main **bus and train stations** are almost next door to each other at Piazza Dante and Via Pozzo. A secondary, combined station – **Trento-Malé**, run by a private company – is on Via Dogana, just beyond the train station, with trains up to Cles in the Val di Non, Malé in the Val di Sole and buses to Madonna di Campiglio and Molveno. Tickets and information on Trento-Malé connections can be had from the office at the station (T0461.238.350, W www.fertm.it).

The useful **tourist office**, close to the main train station at Via Manci 2 (daily 9am–7pm; T0461.216.000, W www.apt.trento.it), stocks *Trentino Mese*, the city's monthly listings guide, plus several excellent publications including *Renaissance Trento*, a guide to the city's palaces, and *Walking Through the Painted*

City, a set of ambulant itineraries highlighting the art, history and culture of Trento. It also sells the extremely useful **Trento Card** (€9/24hr, €14/48hr), which allows unlimited travel on all local transportation (including cable cars), free bike rental (check with tourist office for participating outlets; photo ID required), free entry into all the city's museums and aquarium (plus, with the 48hr card, Castel Beseno, the ethnographic museum in San Michele all'Adige, and the MART in Rovereto), and a ten percent discount in many restaurants, shops and sports facilities. The **regional information centre** (contactable by phone/Web only: ☎0461.405.405, ⓦwww.trentino.to) has details on mountain refuges, transport, hiking, skiing and agriturismi; its informative website features a searchable accommodation database and regional listings, and staff will happily mail out information.

Accommodation
There is a good range of places to stay for all budgets in and around Trentino but it is advisable to book ahead before and during Christmas and New Year. Drop into Trentino Agritur on via Aconcio 13 (☎0461.235.323) for information on B&Bs and farm accommodation outside the town, or for camping try the *Campeggio Malga Mezavia* Loc. Malga Mezavia (☎0461.948.178) at Monte Bondone. In the town good options are:

Aquila d'Oro Via Belenzani 76 ☎0461.986.282, ⓦwww.aquiladoro.it. An old pink town house in a central location a stone's throw from the Duomo; modern, clean but soulless rooms. ❺
Europa Via Torrevange 9, 500m to your right beyond the station ☎0461.263.484, ⓦwww.gayaproject.org. For visitors on a budget this friendly hostel offers singles and doubles (€20 per person) as well as dorm beds from €13.50. ❶
Hotel America Via Torre Verde 50 ☎0461.983.010, ⓦwww.hotelamerica.it. Affordable, close to the main station and a short walk away from the action. Ask for an upper-floor room for wonderful views over the rooftops to the mountains. ❹
Venezia Piazza Duomo 45 ☎0461.234.559, ⓦwww.hotelveneziatn.it. The cheapest hotel close to the centre. Comfortable if rather shabby, with a few rooms overlooking the piazza and others in a thirteenth-century tower. ❷
Villa Madruzzo Via Ponte Alto 26 ☎0461.986.220, ⓦwww.villamadruzzo.it. Situated further out in Cagnola, in the hills overlooking Trento to the east, you can reach this hotel by bus #9 (20min); it's good value and serves regional cuisine. ❸

The City
Trento was known as Tridentum to the Romans, a name celebrated by the eighteenth-century Neptune fountain in the central **Piazza Duomo**, a pleasant square ringed by arcades, shops and cafés and giving on to streets – notably Via Belanzani – lined with frescoed palaces, many of them built in the sixteenth century when Trento was an important market town. There's an excellent guide to the palaces, *Renaissance Trento*, available from the tourist information office.

The three most significant meetings of the Council of Trent – convened to confront the growth of Protestantism and to establish the so-called Counter-Reformation – took place in the **Duomo** between 1545 and 1563. The building itself was begun in the thirteenth century, but wasn't completed until the sixteenth. Inside, the arched, colonnaded steps flanking the nave are a dramatic touch on an otherwise plain building. There are fresco fragments in the nave and an enormous carved marble baldachin over the altar – a replica of the one in St Peter's, Rome – although the most interesting part lies under the church, where a medieval crypt and foundations of an early Christian basilica (built over the tomb of St Vigilio, the third bishop of Trento) were discovered in 1977. The neighbouring **Museo Diocesano Tridentino e Basilica Paleocristiana** (daily except Tues 9.30am–12.30pm & 2–5.30pm; €4; Ⓦ www.museodiocesano tridentino.it), housed in the Palazzo Pretorio, includes large annotated paintings of the sessions of the Council of Trent and some carved altarpieces from the church of San Zeno in the Val di Non. Hidden away in cell-like side rooms are some ornate reliquaries and an impressive cycle of fifteenth-century Flemish tapestries. The building is appealing in itself, too, with its fishtail battlements, heavy studded doors and a view from the upper floor of the frescoed palaces around the square.

Also of particular interest is the **Tridentum** on Piazza Cesare Battisti (Tues–Sun: June–Aug 10am–noon & 2.30–7pm; Sept–May 9am–noon & 2.30–6pm; €2), a recently uncovered section of Roman Trento dating from between 1000BC and 400AD. In the 1990s, when the Teatro Sociale was being restored, archeologists discovered around 1700 square metres of a Roman road complete with sewage system, buildings, city walls, the remains of a tower, private court-yards and more. Nowadays, you can see it all from a newly constructed visitor centre, built on a level with the existing road.

The most powerful of the Trento princes was Bernardo Clesio, who in the late fifteenth and early sixteenth centuries built up much of the city's art collec-tion, a good proportion of which is held in the **Castello del Buonconsiglio** (Tues–Sun: Nov–May 9.30am–5pm; Jun–Oct 10am–6pm; closed Mon; €6; Ⓦ www.buonconsiglio.it), another venue of the Council of Trent, a short walk from Piazza Duomo on the eastern side of the city centre. It's two castles really: the thirteenth-century **Castelvecchio** and the extension built in 1530 called the **Magno Palazzo**, in which several rooms frescoed with classical subjects by the Dossi Family and Romanino lead off a quiet inner courtyard. Upstairs is the **Museo Provinciale d'Arte**, whose highlight is the *Ciclo dei Mesi* ("Cycle of the Months"), hidden at the end of a narrow passageway in the Torre d'Aquila (a tour costs an extra €1 and must be booked in advance, Tues–Fri only, on

△ Piazza Duomo, Trento

⊕0461.492.840). These frescoes, dating from 1400, show details from farming and courtly life and – reflecting the castle's role in the nineteenth century – soldiers confined to barracks; in a case of life imitating art, soldiers also added their own touches by scribbling on the borders and drawing in beards.

The ditch around the castle was the place of execution for two celebrated Trentese, Cesare Battisti and his comrade Fabio Filzi. Born in 1875, Battisti was a man of his times, a combination of romantic idealist and guerrilla fighter. He set up the socialist-irredentist newspaper *Il Popolo* as a forum for protest against Austrian rule, and used Italy's entry into World War I as an opportunity to step up his campaign to eject Austrian forces from the Tyrol. The stratagem was unsuccessful: in 1916 he led an attempt to take Monte Pasubio to the south of Trento, but he was arrested by the Austrians and shot as a traitor. You can visit his and Filzi's cells in the castle, as well as a small museum to the Risorgimento and Liberation of Trentino.

Eating, drinking and nightlife

You can **eat** well in Trento and the surrounding area, feasting on unfussy local specialities. There are also a couple of good *rosticcerie* on Via Santa Croce, near the market. The porticos and arcades teem with shops selling Trento delicacies: *Macelleria Ravagni* on Piazza Duomo sells locally produced salamis and cured meats while *Consorzio Produttori Latte Trento e Borgo*, via Campotrentino 9, sells cheese made on the premises. Christmas is an excellent time for shopping; from late November hundreds of traditional wooden kiosk stalls fill the streets to celebrate the feast of St Lucy.

Trento doesn't resound with nightlife, but has a couple of good bars that stay open late. *Bar Paradiso*, on Largo Nazario Sauro 33 (⊕0461.980.147), has a DJ on Friday nights and live music on Saturdays, and the small microbrewery, *Birreria Pedavena*, Piazza Fiera 13 (⊕0461.98.62), features interesting beers.

Restaurants

Chiesa Via San Marco ⊕0461.238.766. An eighteenth-century palazzo with barrel-vaulted ceilings. Specializes in Trentino cuisine; try the excellent local trout. Closed Sun.

Due Giganti Via Simonino 14. Charming, good-value self-service chain with tagliatelle dishes from €3. Closed Sun lunch & Mon evening.

Osteria a le due Spade Via Don Arcangelo Rizzi 11 ⊕0461.234.343. Gourmands will appreciate the special four-course menus (€30–40) with sophisticated dishes to savour in a low-ceilinged, wood-panelled room. It's west of the Duomo off Via G. Verdi, and there has been an eatery on this spot for 460 years. Closed Sun & Mon lunch.

Pedavena Via Santa Croce 15. This lively restaurant stays open until midnight and serves excellent, cheap Trentese dishes such as *canederli* and *strangolapreti* (spinach gnocchi). Closed Aug.

Primavera at Via Suffragio 92. Popular for inexpensive Italian standards, with outside seating under the arches.

Ristorante Araliki Vicolo Collico 6, off Piazza Santa Maria Maggiore ⊕0461.981.580. You can get marvellous, but quite expensive, local specialities such as *luganega con formai e fonghi trifoladi* – local sausage with cheese and mushrooms. The restaurant is attached to the Albergo Accademia.

Listings

Banks Banca Commerciale Italiana, Via Mantova 2; Banca di Trento e Bolzano, Via Mantova 19; Cassa Rurale di Trento, Piazza Fiera 1 and Via Manci 87. **Car rental** Avis, 53 Via Brennero, ⊕0461.420.276; Sixte, Piazza Leonardo da Vinci 3 ⊕0461.263.467; Hertz, Lung'Adige Apuleio 20 ⊕0461.421.555. **Doctor** Health Doctors, Via Malta 8 ⊕0461.915.809.

Travelling the wine road

Wine enthusiasts are well catered for in Trentino, with a wine road (**Strada di Vino** or Südtiroler Weinstrasse) that enables you to indulge in a happy combination of sight-seeing and **sampling local food and wine**. Head out of Trento on the trunk road to Bolzano, and take the right turning, signposted for Lavis, from where the wine road is clearly marked; Trento tourist office has a good guide to local grape types and wine producers.

The vines are often strung on wide pergolas, the traditional method of viticulture here since Roman times, which allows the breezes blowing up the Adige Valley from Lago di Garda to circulate around the grapes, giving a beneficial cooling effect. Farmers and wine makers who are part of the agriturismo network advertise their establishments with a **yellow sign**: anything with a farm name and a knife and fork symbol is usually worth investigating. Often the owners will have converted a room in their farmhouse into a small informal restaurant, and will serve a set meal, accompanied by their own (or local) wine for around €12. Most of the goodies will be home-made: *nostra produzione* is the phrase to look out for, applied across the menu to anything from salami and sausages to goat's cheese. It helps to have a few words of Italian or German at your disposal so you can chat – you will probably be shown around the farm or *cantina* (winery) if you express an interest.

Hospitals San Camillo, Via Giovanelli ☎0461.216.111; Santa Chiara, Largo Medaglie d'Oro 9 ☎0461.903.111.
Internet Call Me, Via Belenzani 58 (€4/hr).
Pharmacies Dall'Armi, Piazza Duomo 10; Madonna, Via Manci 42; S. Chiara, Via S. Croce 57; ⓦwww.farmacietrentino.it for emergency pharmacy opening times.

Police In an emergency, dial ☎113; otherwise the station is on Via Fratelli Bronzetti (☎0461.916.111).
Post office Piazza A. Vittoria 20 ☎0461.984.714.
Taxis Radiotaxi, Via Degasperi 27 ☎0461.930.002.

Around Trento

Trento's **cycle path** network is excellent, and with free bike rental if you purchase a Trento card, it's well worth exploring as an alternative to crowded buses and cable cars. The city is linked via the grander Adige Cycle Path to Bolzano to the north and Verona to the south, with many charming towns and villages along either route.

Cable cars run from Ponte San Lorenzo, near Trento's bus station (every 15–30min; €0.90), to **SARDAGNA**, on the lower slopes of the towering Monte Bondone. There's some skiing in winter, and a scattering of holiday homes belonging mostly to Trentese; for committed **campers** there's *Camping Mezavia* (☎0461.948.178; June–Sept & Dec–April), two hours' trek from the top of the cable car. Also popular with locals are the resorts of **Lavarone** and **Folgaria** to the south, or **Pérgine** to the west near **Lago di Caldonazzo**, where there is a free beach and lido (buses from Trento).

An enjoyable half-day trip from the city (and reachable by local bus or train, or along the cycle path) is a visit to the **ethnographic museum** (Museo degli Usi e Costumi della Gente Trentina; Tues–Sat 9am–12.30pm & 2.30–6pm; €4, free with 48hr Trento card, see p.269; ⓦwww.museosanmichele.it) at **SAN MICHELE ALL'ADIGE**, 15km northeast of Trento. One of the largest of its kind in Europe, with exhibits ranging from re-creations of village houses (complete with muddy boots drying by the stove) to displays on hunting, grazing and wine making, the museum gives a real flavour of what life in Trentino was like until the twentieth century.

The rail line south from Trento runs between the scree-covered slopes of the Adige Valley, where the only sight for miles might be a station platform in the middle of nowhere or the blank fortifications of a castle or World War I stronghold. Hanging on an outcrop above the village of **CALLIANO**, around 15km from Trento, **Castel Beseno** is one of the few castles that have been restored and opened to the public (March–Oct 9am–noon & 2–5pm, closed Mon; €3.50, free with 48hr Trento card, see p.269; ⊕0464.834.600).

It's more of a fortified town than a castle in fact, spreading across the hilltop at the valley entrance and once providing a bulwark between the Venetians and the Tyrolese. A bloody but decisive battle was fought here in 1487, after which the Venetians gave up all hope of seizing Trentino at all. The castle is a twenty-minute walk from the village of **Besenello**, which is connected with Trento by bus and the Adige cycle path. At weekends buses run all the way to the castle from Besenello's main piazza.

Monte Pasubio and Sentiero della Pace

Some of the bloodiest engagements of World War I took place around **Monte Pasubio**, to the southeast of Calliano. A total of 460,000 lives were lost – many from the cold – and 947,000 were wounded on the Italian side alone. The recently created **Sentiero della Pace** ("Path of Peace") follows the front, from the Órtles mountains east across the ranges to Marmolada, the trail littered with old bullets and barbed wire. Tourist offices can provide free maps (Kompass, 1:50,000) of the entire route. The opposing armies dug fortresses in the rock and cut tunnels into the glaciers, but protection from enemy fire did not ensure safety – in the winter of 1916, one of the hardest in living memory, around 10,000 soldiers died in avalanches. The Campana dei Caduti, made out of melted-down cannon, tolls every evening in memory of the dead of both sides, from the Colle di Miravalle, a hill just outside the nearby town of Rovereto.

MART

If you're interested in contemporary art, it's worth considering a trip out to the **MART**, Italy's largest modern art museum, just 25km south of Trento at Corso Bettini 43 in Rovereto (daily 10am–6pm, closed Mon; €8, free with 48hr Trento card, see p.269; ⓦwww.mart.trento.it). Designed by Mario Botta and opened in December 2002, the museum boasts 5500 square metres of exhibition space and hosts a permanent collection of over 9000 paintings, designs and sculptures as well as an exciting programme of temporary exhibitions. Particularly strong are its collections of Futurist and twentieth-century avant-garde art: Italian futurist Fortunato Depero bequeathed his 3000-strong collection of drawings, tapestries and sculpture. National art is obviously to the fore: major pieces by Osvaldo Licini, Massimo Campigli and Mario Sironi are featured, along with works by Fausto Melotti and Toti Scialoja, among others. Recent acquisitions have been somewhat more international in scale and the museum has made especially important purchases of American Pop Art, including works by Lichtenstein, Rauschenberg and Warhol, and more contemporary pieces by the likes of Naumann, Gursky and Höfer. MART is accessible by local bus #301 from Trento, by train from Bolzano, or on the cycle track along the river Adige.

The Dolomiti di Brenta

The sawtoothed peaks and glaciers of the **Dolomiti di Brenta**, northwest of Trento, give these ranges a rougher character than the rest of the Dolomites, yet throughout you can choose your own level of walking. While steep, few peaks rise above 3000m, and the paths are easy to follow but strenuous, while less demanding trails circle the side valleys. The range is circled by a good but slow and winding road, the southern half of which passes through the quiet lake resort of **Molveno** before it is joined by the road from Trento. The circuit then turns north passing the frescoed churches and wooded valleys of the **Valle Rendena** before arriving at the main resort of **Madonna di Campiglio**, the best base for climbing, walking or skiing in the area. The northern half of the Brenta is bounded by **Val di Non** and **Val di Sole**, both served by the private Trento–Malé railway line and home to a smattering of castles and other sights.

Climbers come here for the towers of Cima Tosa and Cima Brenta, the original reason for *vie delle bochette* – iron ladders knocked into the rock to give access to these ascents; their position, clinging tenaciously to the rock walls, is sensational (see box, p.267 for more on the *vie ferrate*). There are enough regular, marked footpaths for two or three days' high-altitude walking; Kompass produces the best map for the area. Trento's tourist office has a free guide to the Dolomiti di Brenta in English.

Up the Valle Rendena

Buses from Trento to Madonna di Campiglio skirt Monte Bondone and wind their way past a series of patchy hills and villages, passing **Lago di Toblino**, just outside **VEZZANO**, where **Castel Toblino** – now a restaurant – sits on a spit of land jutting into the lake. The castle is steeped in the legend of a medieval love affair between one Claudia Particella and Carlo Emanuele Madruzzo, Prince-Bishop of Trento. The bishop apparently asked the pope, in vain, to allow him to leave the Church, but was refused. Undeterred, the two lovers returned to the castle, but one night, during a trip on the lake, they mysteriously drowned. Whether it was murder, accident or suicide is unknown. In the **restaurant**, a four-course meal is about €35, but there's also a lakeside bar selling beer, coffee and sandwiches for a fraction of the price.

From Lago di Toblino, the road continues west, turning into the **Valle Rendena** at Tione di Trento, where a more remote landscape of pasture and forest begins. This quiet valley is a good place to rest, with a wonderfully eccentric roadside **hotel**, *Pub da Giorgio* (℡0465.321.541, ⓦwww.pubdagiorgio .it; ❷), at Iavré, 6km north of Tione, which the proprietor has packed with more than 5000 historical objects and curiosities including a collection of old keys and a watch that was recovered from the wreck of the *Titanic*. There are also a couple of small **campsites** reasonably close to villages; one of these is *Faè della Val Rendena* (℡0465.507.178; June–Sept & Dec–April), north of Pinzolo, near **Sant'Antonio di Mavignola**.

Small churches like the lone Sant'Antonio, just before Borzago, are decorated with fresco cycles by Baschenis, one of the many Bergamasque artists who worked in the area. At **CARISOLO**, the church of **Santo Stefano** has frescoes of the *danse macabre* on an outside wall, and others inside depicting the legend of Charlemagne's passage through the Val di Campiglio on the way to his coronation in Rome. Before Madonna, several turnings off the main road lead high up west into the Adamello range, the most beautiful being the **Val di Genova**, which begins 2km from Carisolo. The road follows the cascading river up through a pine forest, along a deteriorating road past several waterfalls, spectacular in spring when the snow begins to melt. Most impressive is the **Cascata di Nárdis**, 4km from the turn-off, where several channels spill down the granite rock walls of the mountainside. Facing the waterfall is the *Albergo Cascate Nardis* (℡0465.501.454; ❷), with a restaurant; it's a good place to stop, though busy with day-trippers in summer. From here, it's another 13km to **BÉDOLE** (1614m), and a further two to three hours' hike from there along trail 212 to the *Rifugio Città di Trento* (℡0465.501.193; open April & June–Sept) at 2480m, within reach of the Adamello glaciers.

A short way before Carisolo, at **CADERZONE**, a turning off the Valle Rendena follows a much less trodden trail (221) which heads steeply up to the small lakes of **San Giuliano** and **Garzone** (two-and-a-half hours' walk). There's a small, very basic refuge between the two, and a second path (230) heads north then descends to the ski village of **PINZOLO** (two hours' descent). It's much smaller than its neighbour Madonna di Campiglio (ski-lift passes cover both resorts), but well worth a look for its church of San Vigilio, decorated with another sixteenth-century fresco of the *danse macabre* by Simone Baschenis.

Madonna di Campiglio

The major village in the Valle Rendena is **MADONNA DI CAMPIGLIO**, an upmarket ski resort with plenty of chair lifts and runs for all levels of skiing. It's also a fairly pleasant place to spend a day or two relaxing. Eight or nine buses a day run from Trento to the main square, while thrice-daily trains head to Malé, 23km north, from where handily timed bus connections will take you to Madonna. The helpful **tourist office**, not far from the main square on Via Pradalago 4 (Mon–Sat 9am–12.30pm & 2–6pm; ℡0465.442.000, ⓦwww.campiglio.to), can provide bus, train and cable car timetables, accommodation information and detailed maps of day hikes from Madonna. Nearby, on Piazza Brenta Alta 16, the **Alpine Guide** office (daily 10am–noon & 4–8pm; ℡0465.442.634, ⓦwww.guidealpinecampiglio.it) has useful information on hiking trails and *vie ferrate* and offers a wide variety of climbing courses and mountain excursions during the summer. **Internet** facilities are available at the library (Mon–Sat afternoons) upstairs at the lakeside sports centre.

In summer, the climbing and walking in the Dolomiti di Brenta are superb, and you may want to stay at Madonna, if only to reach the trailheads. Luckily, out of the skiing season, the village tends to be deserted except for a sprinkling of walkers, and there are often good off-season deals to be had in three-star **hotels**. Much of the accommodation in this area insists on a seven-night minimum stay in high season, three nights at other times of year. The best value for money – though it may insist on a seven-night stay in high season – is the *Hotel Cristiania* (℡0465.441.470, ⓦwww.hotelcristiania.it; ❹), a four-star B&B with sun terrace and bar. A more luxurious option, keeping an eye on ecology, is *Bio-Hotel Hermitage* (℡0465.441.558, ⓦwww.chalethermitage.com; €180 per person, half board only). A similar ten-minute stroll from town is *Fortini* (℡0465.441.508, ⓦwww.albergofortini.it; ❷) while nearby, and cheapest of all, is *Garni Bucaneve* (℡0465.441.271, ⓦwww.hotelbucaneve.com; ❷).

The best way to approach the trailheads is by cable car from **Carlo Magno**, 3km north of the village centre, to Grostè (daily: late June to mid-Sept 8.30am–12.30pm & 2–5pm; middle two weeks in Aug from 8am; €8 one way, €13 return) – see overleaf. Another possibility is to head west, taking Funvia Cinque Laghi (mid-July to early Sept daily 8.30am–12.50pm & 2–5.20pm; €6 one way, €8 return) from the centre of the village to *Rifugio Pancugolo* (no accommodation) at 2064m, in the Presanella group. From the refuge, paths include a five-hour route via **Lago Ritorto** and **Lago Gelato** back down to the valley. A six-day summer lift ticket is €45, while a winter Madonna only ski-lift pass is €35 per day and €185 for seven days.

Trails from Grostè

Once you're at **GROSTÈ** (2437m) you can plan your own routes as long as you have a decent hiking map, such as the one produced by Kompass. By the cable-car terminus is the *Rifugio Graffer*, at 2261m (℡0465.441.358, ⓦwww .graffer.com; June 20–Sept 20 & Dec–April). It is close to the trails and has overnight accommodation and a restaurant. From the cable-car station, trail 316 sets out across boulder-strewn slopes towards refuges *Sella* and *Tuckett* at 2272m (both ℡0465.507.287, Ⓔrifugiotuckett.campiglio@tin.it; June 20–Sept 20), about 5km away, where you can eat a large meal and bask on the veranda, thousands of feet above the valley.

Trail 328, which later becomes 318 (called the Sentiero Bogani), starts just past the refuges; there are difficult boulders to negotiate at first, but then there's an easy path that has been blasted out of the side of the rock walls. A shrine in a small overhang commemorates the lives lost in these peaks, but by this time, about four hours from Grostè, the *Rifugio Brentei* (℡0465.441.244; June 20–Sept 20), set at 2176m, is in sight, midway between Cima Brenta and Cima Tosa. There are some difficult ascents a short distance from the refuge, but it's more than likely that by this stage you won't be capable of anything other than staring across the vast ravine at the Adamello glaciers in the distance. Next day, if you can cope with snowfields, you could either trek up to the **Bocca di Brenta** and cross over the ridge to meet trail 319 down to Molveno (see below; 3hr 30min), or simply return to Madonna via trails 318 and 316 (3hr 30min).

Molveno and Andalo

The lakeside village of **MOLVENO**, surrounded by the peaks of the Brenta Alta, is a marginally cheaper place to stay than Madonna. Although the cheapest places go quickly, particularly in high season, the **tourist office** here, above the lake in the small town centre, at Piazza Marconi 5 (Mon–Sat 9am–12.30pm & 3.30–7pm, Sun 9.30am–12.30pm; ℡0461.586.924, ⓦwww.molveno.it), should be able to help you find a **room** for the night. On Via Lungolago, the three-star *Ariston* (℡0461.586.907, ⓦwww.aristonmolveno.it; €68 per person, full board only) has great views of the lake, as does the simpler *Garni Alpenrose* (℡0461.586.169, ⓦwww.alpenrosemolveno.it, ❷). Failing these, there's a swish **campsite**, *Campeggio Spiaggia Lago di Molveno* (℡0461.586.978, ⓦwww .molveno.it/camping; €16 per tent), on the water's edge, with a restaurant, bar, Internet access and shop.

Five kilometres away by road, or 4km by a beautiful wooded trail, is the town of **ANDALO**. Bigger than Molveno and somewhat less touristy, it often has hotel rooms available when Molveno's are full. Try the cosy *Milano* (℡0461.585.731, ⓦwww.hotelmilano.org; €65 per person full board only in summer), which offers short treks into the mountains with trained Alpine guides (€3), or the B&B-only *Garni Fiordaliso* (℡0461.589.027, ⓦwww .hotelfiordaliso.com; ❸). There's also a **campsite**, *Camping Andalo*, Viale del Parco 4 (℡0461.585.753, ⓦwww.andalovacanze.com). For other accommodation options, the tourist office on Piazza Dolomiti 1 (Mon–Sat 9am–noon & 2–5pm, Sun 9am–noon; ℡0469.585.836, ⓦwww.aptdolomitipaganella.com) should be able to help. There's **Internet access** at *Oli-info*, Viale Ponte Lambin 17 (daily 9am–noon, 4–7pm; €0.39 per minute).

There are few **easy trails** from Molveno into the Brenta massif – paths often disappear into nothing but *vie ferrate* across the rocks; fortunately these are all marked on maps, so you just need to plan your route carefully. If you decide to approach the Brenta group from this side you can use a cable car, which runs from the village to **Pradel** (1500m), where there's an *albergo*, *Rifugio Pradel* (☎0461.586.903; June–Sept), and from where trails lead through the beeches and pines of the **Val delle Seghe** in the shadow of Croz dell'Altissimo (2339m). An easy circular route winds back to Molveno (2hr 30min), or more demanding paths take you higher up, past *Rifugio Tosa* at 2439m, and *Rifugio Tommaso Pedrotti* at 2491m (both ☎0461.948.115; June–Sept).

The most prodigious of nineteenth-century climbers, Francis Fox Tuckett, opened up a difficult new route to Cima Brenta from Molveno, now known as the **Bochetta di Tuckett**. As ice axes hadn't been invented, he negotiated snowfields with a ladder and alpenstock, and carried joints of meat and bottles of wine for mountaintop breakfasts. The landscape where he "roamed amongst toppling rocks, and spires of white and brown and bronze coloured stone" is almost unchanged but for the *bochetta*, descending from the pass down to the *Tuckett* and *Sella* refuges (see opposite). More paths skirt Cima Tosa and lead to Pinzolo via *Rifugio Dodici Apostoli* (☎0465.501.309, ⓦwww.salvaterra.biz; June–Sept), a stone-built refuge for the hardy set at 2498m, with only cold water to wash in. From Molveno, the road follows the lake south, then descends down to **Ponte Arche**, where you can pick up buses on the Madonna–Trento route. It's a beautiful trip through a valley which hasn't benefited from, or been blighted by, ski tourism, but there are only two buses daily.

The land around Molveno and Andalo is known for its quality **mushrooms**, and many Italians come here to pick them. To do so, you must have a mushrooming licence (€10 per day, €24 per week), available from the tourist offices. You can only pick 2kg of *funghi* a day, and only between 7am and 7pm.

Finally, those travelling with children might like to consider the **Brown Bear Area** in Spormaggiore (mid-June to mid-Sept daily 9.30am–6.30pm; €2.50, €1.50 for under 14s, free for under 6; ⓦwww.prolocospormaggiore .tn.it), about nine miles northeast of Molveno. A reintroduction project begun collaboratively in 1999 by the Italian Wildlife Institute, the province of Trentino and the Adamello Brenta Natural Park, the *Life Ursus* project has created a "natural habitat" for a declining bear population, with bears taken from Italian zoos to prepare them for reintroduction into the wild. The enclosed outdoor area (follow the signs for the *area orsi*) lets you walk around and watch brown bears in their natural habitat, and is well worth a visit – though the stars of the show spend a lot of time sleeping. An informative **visitor centre** back in the village (late June to mid-Sept daily 9.30am–12.30pm & 2–6pm; mid-Sept to mid-Oct Sat & Sun only 10am–noon & 2–6pm; combined ticket with Brown Bear Area; ⓦwww.parcodamellobrenta.tn.it), tells the story of the project and has an exhibit on the bears. The site is accessible by bus from Molveno and Andalo.

East of Trento

To the **east of Trento**, the **Valsugana** and the **Val di Fiemme** are joined by road, making a wide loop. Halfway around, a group of stunning pinnacles and bare peaks called the **Pale di San Martino** appears: formed as a coral reef sixty million years ago, their rock is so pale it glares even at dawn. It is now incorporated in the **Parco Naturale Panevéggio**, a gentler, wooded area with many walks, trails and campsites. The nearest resort to the Pale is **San Martino di Castrozzo**, the terminus for buses travelling the loop in both directions.

Valsugana

Most people take the bus along the **Valsugana** to get to a market in one of its modern and busy towns, such as Caldonazzo. There's nothing to see between the towns except rows of fruit trees and vineyards, and later, as the Brenta Valley closes in to become a narrow gorge, a succession of hydroelectric plants. What makes the trip interesting is the terrain to the north, in particular the **Cima d'Asta**, a mountain dotted with bright-blue, icy tarns and crossed by the Sentiero della Pace ("Path of Peace", see p.273). You reach the westerly part of this from **Panarotta**, in the mountains above Lago di Caldonazzo, from where the trail – at this point an ancient ridgeway path and wartime patrol route – follows a course across the peaks towards Passo di Rolle (see "Parco Naturale Panevéggio", p.280).

If you're travelling by public transport from Trento to San Martino di Castrozza you have no choice but to go the long way round, via Fonzaso in the Veneto; most services head east by **train** from Trento to Primolano, where you have to change for the **bus** on to San Martino. By **car**, though, there's a short cut if you turn off at Borgo Valsugana and cut through the foothills, climbing through an increasingly Alpine landscape to rejoin the main road at Imer.

Imer, Mezzano and Fiera di Primiero

IMER and, a couple of kilometres east, **MEZZANO** are archetypal tourist villages, decked out with geraniums and credit-card stickers, attracting people by the busload, but away from the main roads you can easily escape the crowds. The valley itself is wide, with hay meadows spreading either side, and, outside from the main tourist centres, makes a good place to rest, with easy paths running into the foothills. One possibility is the path east from Imer along the lush **Val Noana** to the reservoir under the slopes of Monte Pavione (a 3hr 30min round trip). As far as **accommodation** goes, self-sufficiency is an advantage, as you'll be competing with bus tours for the cheap hotels. An alternative to Alpine-style hotels in the villages is *Camping Calavise*, a (well-signposted) couple of kilometres off the main valley road which has a bar and playground (℡0439.67.468, ⓦwww.campingcalavise.it; €18 per tent) or, further up the valley, *Rifugio Fonteghi* (℡0439.67.043), a 45-minute walk along the path on the south side of the reservoir.

About 4km further on from Imer, **FIERA DI PRIMIERO** is a larger resort and market town with a **tourist office** (Mon–Sat 9am–noon & 3.20–7pm, Sun 9.30am–12.30pm; ℡0439.62.407). It's a major crossroads in the area, from where buses run up to the beginning of the Val Canali and to Passo Cereda (1369m). The mountains around Fiera were worked for silver from the thirteenth century, and local miners paid for the town's fifteenth-century church. Now the ranges are crossed by hiking trails.

Trails to the north of Passo Cereda take you up into the high plateau of the **Pale di San Martino**. One path follows a long ridge of rock before passing down into **Val Canali**, described by Amelia Edwards in the nineteenth century as the most "lonely, desolate and tremendous scene . . . to be found this side of the Andes". Things have changed since the arrival of Alta Via 2 – followed by a bar, visitor centre, refuge and campsite – but the valley retains a feeling of isolation. The official campsite, the *Castelpietra* (℡0439.62.426, ⓦwww.castelpietra.it; June–Oct

& Nov–April; €12.40 per tent), is opposite the National Park centre, and there are further places to camp at the head of the glen. *Rifugio Treviso* (☎0439.62.311; late June to Sept) is a possible overnight stop, while the more luxurious *Cant del Gal* (☎0439.62.997; ❷), further down the valley, also has a good restaurant specializing in game and wild mushrooms, though it's fairly expensive.

A stiff ascent from *Rifugio Treviso* brings you onto the **Altopiano delle Pale** at Passo di Pradidali, where eagles can be seen circling above the barren plateau and the silence is broken every so often by a trickle of falling stones. Once you are at this altitude, there are many possibilities for linking up with other trails across the stark upland; local tourist offices publish a useful 1:35,000 map which shows the various paths, though you shouldn't rely on it for navigation. *Rifugio Pedrotti alla Rosetta* (☎0439.68.308; June–Sept), at 2581m, is the nearest place with accommodation (a 2hr 30min hike north); facilities include cold-water washbasins, a restaurant and bar. The *rifugio* is also the base of the Orizzonti Trentini alpine guides (see "Vie ferrate" box, p.267).

San Martino di Castrozza and around

The road into **SAN MARTINO DI CASTROZZA** twists and turns, and you feel like you're in the middle of nowhere until the resort's new hotels appear around the corner; the sensation is even more marked if you're heading up over the Passo di Rolle (see p.280). After Cortina d'Ampezzo, San Martino is one of the smarter Dolomite resorts, but it has a more relaxed atmosphere in its cafés and a less pretentious way of going about things. The **tourist office**, next to the bus stop at Via Passo Rolle 165 (Mon–Sat 9am–noon & 3.30–7pm, Sun 9am–12.30pm; ☎0439.768.867, ⓦwww.sanmartino.com) has a great walking map of the area, with detailed information about refuges, difficulty levels, approximate times and so on. It may be able to help with finding a cheapish **room**. Otherwise, try the pretty *Albergo Fratazza* on Via Passo Rolle (☎0439.682.23, ⓦwww.albergofratazza.com; €50 per person, half board only) or the slightly more expensive *Suisse* (☎0439.68.087; ❷); on Via Dolomiti, which runs off the main square just up from the tourist office. The alternative is to pitch a tent at the village **campsite**, *Sass Maòr* (☎0439.68.347), about 1km from the centre. There's also a **youth hostel**, *Albergo per la Gioventù Montana* (☎0439.769.166; €25 dorm bed). Heading out of San Martino, **buses** south to Fiera di Primiero and Imer run at least hourly. The service north over the Passo di Rolle runs less often, but you can count on at least six daily for much of the summer.

A number of **trails**, chair lifts and cable cars head off into the mountains, making San Martino one of the best bases in the area. The strongest attraction is again the **Pale di San Martino**; a cable-car ride from San Martino (daily 8am–5pm; journey up €9.50, down €8.50, return trip €16) takes you up to *Rifugio Pedrotti alla Rosetta*, perched on the edge of the Altopiano – see above for details. The Colverde cable car from the village runs to the foot of the Pale, from where the Rosetta cable car takes you up to the highland.

Up on the summits, even in the summer, you should be prepared for snow, wind and rain – as well as scorching sun and the most stupendous views. From the chair-lift terminus, you can make for *Rifugio Pradidali* at 2278m (☎0439.64.180; June 20–Sept 20), a walk and descent of three hours. A more ambitious walk would be to continue on from the refuge over the **Passo di Ball**, returning from there to San Martino or descending over into **Val Canali** at *Rifugio Cant del Gal* (see above). If you prefer the relative security of a guided trek, ask at the desk of the Gruppo Guide Alpine (daily 5–7pm;

☎0461.768.795), in the same building as the tourist office; they run graded excursions most days in July and August.

Parco Naturale Panevéggio

Out of San Martino, traffic files up to **Passo di Rolle**, a beautiful stretch of high moorland dotted with avalanche breaks and a few sheep. There are only two buses a day, so a car really helps here. At the pass, a chair lift takes you up to Baita Segantini, a log-cabin bar from where you can see **Cimon della Pala**'s summit. It takes thirty minutes or so to walk back down to the pass, where there are several more bars and restaurants.

The Passo di Rolle falls within the **Parco Naturale Panevéggio** (ⓦwww .parcopan.org), an area of firs, rowan and larch that once provided timber for the Venetian fleet and wood for Stradivarius violins. Skirted by nature trails, there are three **visitors' centres**: in San Martino (June 20–Sept 5 daily 9am–12.30pm & 3–7pm; ☎0439.768.859); in the Villa Welsperg in Tonadico (June 6–Sept 30 daily 9am–12.30pm & 3–6pm; ☎0439.765.973); and 7km on from the pass, outside **PANEVÉGGIO** village (June 6–Sept 19 daily 9am–12.30pm & 1.30–5.30pm; ☎0462.576.283). The Paneveggio branch has excellent displays on the area's wildlife and offers guided walks into the forest (€1.70). In the remoter parts of the park you might catch a glimpse of white alpine hare or marmot – a creature resembling a large guinea pig, which stands up on its hind legs to act as sentinel for the burrow and emits a distinctive screech. There's an unusually pleasant **camping area** next to Lago Paneveggio, though it's less appealing when the lake is dry. The entrance is at the end of the track marked "Area della Sosta", just past the village; facilities are minimal and stays are limited to 24 hours. There's a proper campsite, *Bellamonte* (☎0462.576.119, ⓦwww.campingbellamonte.it; €15.60 per tent), 4km down the road to Predazzo (see below).

Val di Fiemme

Once you're out of the confines of the park, **PREDAZZO** is the first town you come to in the **Val di Fiemme**, at the turn-off for the Val di Fassa. The town itself has become something of a pilgrimage site for geologists, owing to the extensive collection of local rocks and fossils in the newly enlarged **Museo Civico Geologia e Etnografia** on Piazza Santi Filippo e Giacomo (☎0462.500.366; Tues–Sun 10am–6pm; €2.50). Surprisingly accessible to non-experts, the displays include samples of the Dolomitic calcite rock first identified by, and named after, the French mineralogist Dieudonné Sylvain Guy Tancrède de Gratet de Dolomieu.

Predazzo is a useful place to stay, and **bus** connections to Trento and Bolzano are reasonable. A good **hotel**, though it may insist on half board, is the *Maria* (☎0462.501.203, ⓦwww.hmaria.it; ❷), five minutes' walk from the centre on the main Corso Dolomiti, with a lovely garden. *Camping Valle Verde* (☎0462.502.394, ⓦwww.campingvalleverde.it; €13.60 per tent) is a thirty-minute walk east from the central bus station, but has spectacular views, and facilities include a restaurant and shop. The **tourist information office** at Via Cesare Battisti 4 (Mon–Sat 9am–noon & 3.30–7pm, July & Aug also Sun 9am–noon; ☎0462.501.237, ⓔinfo.predazzo@valdifiemme.info) can help you out if both places are full.

Throughout the valley, hotel hoardings are ubiquitous, and even the tiniest villages hereabouts have a plan of the mountain ranges with chair lifts marked, but behind the modern Dolomites tourist industry, this is an ancient region that from the twelfth to the seventeenth centuries was virtually autonomous. A local parliament met at the *Banco de la reson*, a circle of stone benches surrounded by trees in **CAVALESE**, the next town along, and the Magnifica Comunità of Cavalese is still relatively powerful, administering extensive communal land. A short way beyond the town centre, at Via Fratelli Bronzetti 60, the road to Tésero, is a small **tourist office** (Mon–Sat 9am–noon & 3.30–7pm; July & Aug also Sun 9am–noon; ☎0462.241.111, ⓦwww.valdifiemme.info) that can arrange visits to the medieval **Palazzo della Magnifica Comunità**. This was the Bishop of Trento's summer palace, and now houses a small **museum and gallery** (guided tours only; July & Aug daily 4.30, 5.30 & 6.30pm; rest of year for hours contact the tourist office; free). Wood-panelled rooms redolent of sawdust and polish, with fine wooden ceilings and painted friezes, contain the original valley statutes, together with some unremarkable paintings by local seventeenth-century artists. The building's lack of fortifications indicates that Trento's bishop felt safe from the armed rebellions that had plagued him in the city, and its exterior is covered in frescoes depicting St Vigilio (Trento's patron saint) enthroned in the centre of a trompe-l'oeil pediment.

Many people pause at Cavalese simply to stroll the cobbled streets, grazing at some of the cake and ice-cream shops, or to take the cable car up to the **Catena dei Lagorai**. This mountain chain, concealing a string of lakes, is accessible on foot from any of the small villages along the main road. There was a tragic accident here in February 1998, in which a number of skiers were killed when a low-flying US airforce aeroplane sliced through the wires of their cable car; the lift has since reopened (July, Aug & Dec–Easter; €12.50 return). Leisurely day-trips are feasible, but if you feel inspired once you're up on the ridges, either follow the paths towards Passo di Rolle, or go west. A day or two of walking west (via refuges) brings you to the Val dei Mócheni, which was colonized in medieval times by German farmers travelling south, and has kept its own language and Gothic script. The first farmers were joined later by speculators searching for the rich seams of copper and silver that lay in the mountains. For somewhere to **stay**, head for the recently refitted *Laurino* (☎0462.340.151, ⓦwww.hotelgarnilaurino.com; ❸) in Cavalese.

TÉSERO, 4km from Cavalese on the higher road, is, for most people, simply a staging post on their way to the mountains. The town's only attraction is the parish church, frescoed with *Cristo della Domenica* (Christ of the Sabbath) who stands in the middle surrounded by more than thirty symbols depicting everything that's banned on a Sunday including drinking, work and commerce.

The Catinaccio and Gruppo di Sella

North of Predazzo, the Val di Fassa penetrates deep into the western Dolomites, passing through one of the heartlands of **Ladino** culture (see box, p.283). Access to the famously roseate peaks of the **Catinaccio** (Rosengarten) range is simple enough from **Vigo di Fassa**, the valley's main resort. The area is popular with German walkers, drawn to the dramatic serrated peaks, but once you're above the whine of the cable cars there's plenty of wilderness to lose yourself in.

At the head of the Val di Fass, **Canazei** makes a good springboard for the high plateaux of the **Gruppo di Sella**, and the gentler trail of the **Viel del Pan**, which leads down to the tiny resort of **Arabba**. On the northern side of the Sella group, **Corvara** is a much larger resort with a sizeable Ladino population.

Catinaccio

The long belt of sheer rock walls and towers which makes up the **Catinaccio** (**Rosengarten**) range is an awesome sight, described by local judge and nineteenth-century writer Theodor Christomannos as a "gigantic fortification ...the gate into the kingdom of immortal ghosts, of high-flying giants". Rosengarten gets its German name from the roses that legend says used to grow here. King Laurino, saddened when his daughter married and left him alone, put a spell on the roses so that no one would see them again by day or night, but forgot to include dawn and dusk in his curse, which is when the low sun gives the rock a roseate glow.

The trails across the range cater for all levels of hiking ability, but the going gets tough on the ridges, from where you can see as far as the Stubaier Alps, on the border with Austria. The most popular approach to Catinaccio is from the hamlet of **VIGO DI FASSA**. The village, with a bus stop on the Trento–Canazei route, has a few three-star **hotels**; try the good-value *Renato*, Strada di Solar 27 (℡0462.764.006, Ⓦwww.hotelrenato.it; €79 per person, half board only) with its new wellness centre, pool and many rooms with balconies; the *Gambrinus*, Via Nuova 2 (℡0462.764.159, Ⓦwww.hotel-gambrinus.it; €55 per person, half board only) which has a sauna and runs guided walks; or the slightly more luxurious *Vael* at Strada Rezia 29 (℡0462.764.110, Ⓦwww.hotelvael.it; €60 per person, half board only) with a pool, solarium and bar – be warned that this last may insist on a week-long minimum stay. Alternatively, there's the *Rifugio Roda di Vael* (℡0462.764.450, Ⓦwww.rodadivael.it; June–Sept), a ninety-minute walk away from the village along trails 547 and 545. Should you need further help, try the **tourist office** on Strada Rezia, 10 (Mon–Sat 8.30am–12.10pm & 3–6.30pm, Sun 10am–12.30pm; ℡0462.609.700, Ⓦwww.fassa.com).

The trek to **Torri del Vajolet** from Vigo di Fassa is the preferred route up onto the range – and on the way you'll cross into Südtirol. The cable car from the village to *Rifugio Ciampedie* (℡0462.764.432; mid-June to mid-Oct) covers most of the ascent; a well-beaten trail leads from the terminus through the woods to the basic *Rifugio Gardeccia* (℡0462.763.152, Ⓦwww.gardeccia.it; mid-June to mid-Oct). From here it's a steep walk up to a refuge under the Torri, although the severity of the ascent doesn't discourage hordes of summer Sunday walkers. A stiff zigzagging climb from here brings you to *Rifugio Re Alberto* (℡0462.763.428, Ⓦwww.rifugiorealberto.com; June–Sept), three hours from *Rifugio Ciampedie*; there's also alternative accommodation nearby at the *Rifugio Passo Santner* (℡0471.642.230; June–Sept) or the *Rifugio Vàiolet* (℡0462.763.292, Ⓦwww.rifugiovajolet.com; mid-June to Sept).

Paths lead **south** across the range and eventually down to Passo di Costalunga and the Lago di Carezza, a beautiful little lake reflecting the peaks of the Latemar range, from where you can catch a bus to Bolzano. There are more choices to the **north**, where there are a number of trails onto Monte Sciliar (Schlern), with variations in height of no more than around 500m. *Rifugio Bolzano* (*Schlern Haus*; ℡0471.612.024, Ⓦwww.schlernhaus.it; June–Sept), near the summit of Monte Sciliar, is a good two days' trek from *Rifugio Re Alberto*; you can stop overnight at *Rifugio Alpe di Tires* (*Tierser Alptheütte*; ℡0471.727.958, Ⓦwww.tierseralpl.com), in between the two. From Sciliar, paths descend onto the wetland plateau of the Alpe di Siusi (see p.296).

For a change of pace, head to the **Istitut Cultural Ladin** (Mon–Thur 9am–noon & 2–5pm, Fri 9am–noon; €3; Ⓦwww.istladin.net) for an excellent introduction to Ladino culture (see box opposite). Located in a renovated hayloft next to the parsonage of the parish church of San Giovanni, the tiny village next to Vigo di Fassa (within walking distance), the museum has intriguing exhibits on the myths and rites of the Ladini.

Canazei

CANAZEI is a relatively modern town at the head of the Val di Fassa and a buzzing summer and winter resort. It's from here that you head for the high passes – the **Gruppo di Sella** for hard trails, or the easier **Viel del Pan**, opposite Marmolada. The Sella Ronda Card entitles you to use a selection of lifts and public transport (buses run by the SAD company) around the Gruppo di Sella and is available at ski lifts and the **tourist office** on Piaz Marconi 5 (℡0462.609.600, ⓦwww.fassa.com) for €16. Canazei itself makes a good base to stay: *La Zondra* (℡0462.601.233, ⓦwww.lazondra.com; ❸), with balconied rooms, and the pleasant one-star *Ciamorc* (℡0462.602.426, ⓔalbergogarni ciamorc@libero.it; ❷) are both on Via Pareda, while the *Giardino delle Rose* (℡0462.602.221; ❷) is located on Via Dolomiti, in the middle of the village; *Villa Mozart* (℡0462.601.254, ⓦwww.hotelvillamozart.com; ❷) is also central, on Strada Roma. From Canazei a switchback road (of 27 bends) climbs relentlessly for 12km and is often busy with busloads of tourists heading for the scenic Great Dolomites Road (see p.303) and determined cyclists making the thousand-metre ascent.

Ladino country

The meeting-point of Trentino, Alto Adige and the Veneto is home to a distinct cultural group, the **Ladini**. Their language, Ladin, was once spoken over a wide area, from Austria down to the River Po (in what's now Emilia-Romagna), but now survives only in a few valleys in the Dolomites, and in Swiss Engadine, preserved by the relative remoteness of the mountainous territory. There are around 40,000 speakers, but Ladin is especially prevalent in the area around the Sella group – the Val di Fassa, the Val Badia, the Val Gardena and Livinallongo.

The history of the Ladini is recorded in their epics, which recount tales of battles, treachery and reversals of fortune. Around 400 AD, the Ladini were constantly threatened with invasion by Germanic tribes from the north and others from the Po Valley. Christianity later emerged as a major threat, but the Ladini absorbed and transformed the new religion, investing the new saints with the powers of more ancient female divinities. The rudimentary Castello di Thurn at San Martino di Badia, a bleak outpost of the bishop-princes of Bressanone, is testimony to the Church's attempt to keep the Val di Badia under its control. In 1452, Bishop Nicolo Cusano railed against a woman from the Val di Fassa who said she had met the goddess Diana in the woods, and there was a strong pagan undercurrent to the cult of Santa Giuliana, whose sword-wielding image is painted on the plaster of houses in the Fassa and Badia valleys.

The Cësa di Ladins, in **Ortisei** (see p.297), and the Istitut Cultural Ladin, near **Vigo di Fassa** (see opposite), are excellent places to find out more. Meanwhile, villages in the area around Vigo contain sections of the museum devoted to working life in Ladino country (mid-June to mid-Sept Mon–Sat 8.30am–noon & 3.30–7pm; for outside season opening hours call tourist information in Vigo di Fassa (℡0462.764.093, ⓦwww.fassa.com). **Moena** is home to a restored nineteenth-century cooperage (*Botega da Pinter*) at Via Dolomiti 3; **Pera di Fassa** houses a restored watermill (*Molin de Pezol*) at Via Jumela 6; and a working, antique sawmill (*La Sia*) can be seen at Via Pian Trevisan at Penia, just outside Canazei. Tourist offices, notably the one in Corvara (see p.285), have details of occasional festivals, exhibitions and events.

Halfway up the switchback road out of Canazei, the cable car at Pradel leads to **Passo Sella** (2240m), one of the most impressive of the Dolomite passes. Paths climb from here onto the jagged peaks of the **Sasso Lungo** (Langkofel) and follow the ridges down onto the Alpe di Siusi. Even up on the summits, saxifrage grows between cracks in the rock, and the silence is broken only by the occasional buzzing of a beetle. It takes two days to walk from the Sella pass, via *Rifugio Vicenza* (☎0471.792.323, ⊛www.rifugiovicenza.com; June–Sept), into the Val Gardena (Grödnertal), where there are buses to Bolzano.

Just past Pradel the road forks. The right-hand turning takes you up to **Passo Pordoi** (2242m), an astonishing vantage point between the Gruppo di Sella and Marmolada and at 3246m the highest Dolomite with its rounded peak permanently shrouded by a glacier. From here, peaks radiate in every direction, giving you a chance to identify the distinctive shapes of each of the main Dolomite ranges. In the foreground, the Sasso Lungo mountains look like a jagged, gloved hand, flanked by two prominent peaks; the Gruppo di Sella is squat and chunky; and Sciliar (Schlern), just visible in the distance, comprises a flat rocky tabletop, culminating in two peaks. A small road winds downwards to Passo Folzarego, and ultimately Cortina d'Ampezzo, but Passo Pordoi itself is where many of the trails start. It's also another occasion for joining Alta Via 2, which dips down to the main road here. Most of the tourist buses stop at this point, and a collection of cafés and stalls have taken advantage of their location around the trailheads to charge rather inflated prices; the **hotels** here may insist on half board; try the *Pordoi* (☎0462.601.115; €60 per person, half board only).

The Gruppo di Sella

The **Gruppo di Sella** lies to the north of Passo Pordoi and resembles a lunar landscape, with an arid plateau surrounded by pink, dolomitic peaks and crisscrossed by many fairly difficult trails. For less confident walkers, there's a choice of two physically less demanding paths: either stick to the Alta Via 2, which crosses from one edge of the massif to the other, or break away at Sass de Mesdi, from where a trail circles down to the Sella pass. Both routes take a couple of

△ Passo Pordoi, Gruppo di Sella

days, with overnight stops at *Rifugio Cavazza* (*Pisciaduhutte*; ☎0471.836.292; July–Sept) or *Rifugio Boè* (*Boè Hutte*; ☎0471.847.303; June–Sept). The Gruppo di Sella is an excellent place to walk, with views across the ranges down to Passo Gardena (Sellajoch, 2137m), from where Corvara and the Val Badia are within striking distance, as are the Odle (Geisler) group across the valley. There are bus services to Sella Ronda, and you can also pick up buses to Bolzano from **Selva**, 11km away in the Val Gardena.

Viel del Pan

Some much less ambitious walking can be undertaken from Passo Pordoi, starting just past the *Albergo Savoia*, again following the route of Alta Via 2 but in the opposite direction. A narrow path cut into the turf traverses the mountainside opposite Marmolada, where Austrian battalions hid under the glacier in 8km of gallery during World War I. Even if you're not a great walker, a twenty-minute stroll along this easy trail is worthwhile for the views of the Dolomites, which are far better than those from the road.

From the seventeenth century this path was on the grain-smuggling route called the **Viel del Pan** ("trail of bread" in Venetian dialect), and it remained busy enough in the nineteenth century for the Guardia di Finanza to set up armed patrols along it. The contrast between the glacier on Marmolada and the peaks of the Sella group – 360 degrees of mountain – is superb. The path descends to **Lago Fedaia**, from where there are irregular buses in summer back to Canazei. The *Rifugio Marmolada Castiglioni* (☎0462.601.117) is on the edge of the reservoir.

On the northern side of the ridge lies **ARABBA**, a small resort with family-run hotels in the centre and scattered in the peaceful pastures around, from where a cable-car system runs up to the Dolomites. For somewhere to **stay**, the *Albergo Posta* (☎0436.79.105; ❷) is basic but central and ageing gracefully, with a gorgeous terrace and an in-house pizzeria, while the *Garni Emma* (☎0436.79.116, garniemma@virgilio.it; ❷) has a family atmosphere and sits beside a small stream. The larger, more professional *Garni Marilena* (☎0436.79.128, ⓦwww.hotel-marilena.it; ❸) is right at the foot of the cable car. The only bus service from here goes from Belluno to Corvara.

Corvara and around

The central town of the Ladini (see box, p.283), **CORVARA** is primarily a ski resort, and the most visible sign of the language is a page or two in Ladin in local newspapers. Corvara also makes a good base for the excellent trails of the nearby Fánes Park, a bus ride away, where most of the Ladini legends are based. The **tourist office** at Strada Col Alt 36 (Mon–Sat 8am–noon & 3–7pm, Sun 10am–noon & 4–6pm; ☎0471.836.176, ⓦwww.altabadia.org) has details of **hotels and rooms** in private houses. The chalet-style *Monti Pallidi*, Strada Col Alt 75 (☎0471.836.081, ⓦwww.montipallidi.net; ❶), has excellent value, modern rooms most with a kitchenette.

A few buses leave for Brunico and Belluno (see p.405) from outside the tourist office. Some 4.5km north of Corvara is **LA VILLA**, a small village with a fairy-tale sixteenth-century castle. **SAN CASSIANO**, 4km further east, towards the Paso di Valparola, is home to the luxurious *Rosa Alpina* (☎0471.849.500, ⓦwww.rosalpina.it; ❸), a comfortable spa hotel where you can treat yourself to relaxing post-hike beauty treatments. These villages make up the northern Alta Badia part of the Dolomiti Superski (see box, p.266).

Bolzano (Bozen)

Situated on the junction of the rivers Talvera (Talfer) and Isarco (Eisack) near the southern limit of the province, **BOLZANO** (largely known by its German name, Bozen) is Alto Adige's chief town. In both winter and summer, the town is a busy tourist resort, and its pavement cafés and generally relaxed pace of life make it a good, if uneventful, place to rest or use as a base for trips into the mountains. Located in a predominantly sunny, sheltered bowl, for centuries Bolzano was a valley market town and way station whose fortunes in the Middle Ages vacillated as the Counts of Tyrol and the Bishops of Trento competed for power. The town passed to the Habsburgs in the fourteenth century, then at the beginning of the nineteenth century Bavaria took control, opposed by Tyrolese patriot and military leader Andreas Hofer. His battle in 1809 to keep the Tyrol under Austrian rule was only temporarily successful, as in the same year the Austrian Emperor ceded the Tyrol to the Napoleonic kingdom of Italy. More changes followed, as Bolzano was handed back to Austria until after World War I, whereupon it passed, like the rest of the province, to Italy.

An unmissable pleasure is the local wine: Bolzano is at the head of the wine road (Strada di Vino/Südtiroler Weinstrasse; see box, p.272), which runs south to the border with Trentino, and it's especially well known for its Chardonnay.

Arrival, information and accommodation

Bolzano's **bus station**, centrally placed at Via Perathoner 4, serves most of the small villages and resorts in the province; the **train station** is a few minutes' walk south of here through the park down Via Stazione. There is a city **tourist office** at Piazza Walther 8 (Mon–Fri 9am–6.30pm, Sat 9am–noon; ☎0471.307.000, ⓦwww.bolzano-bozen.it). For **regional information**, it's best to visit the regularly updated website, ⓦwww.suedtirol.info, where you can request brochures, book accommodation and more. The *Club Alpino Italiano* at Piazza Erbe 46 (Tues–Fri 11am–1pm & 5–7pm; ☎0471.978.172, ⓦwww.caibolzano.it), on the top end of the square, is a good source of local hiking information.

Accommodation

The best option for budget **accommodation** is to take a room in a private house or a local farmhouse; you can get a list from the tourist office. *Moosbauer* campsite (☎0471.918.492, ⓦwww.moosbauer.com) is on the main Bolzano–Merano road and is €21 per tent.

Gatto Nero St. Magdalena 2 (Schwarze Katz) ☎0471.975.417. Calm and pleasant, this is a conventional and cheap albergo. ➋

Hotel Greif Waltherplatz ☎0471.318.000, ⓦwww.greif.it. Hip and luxurious boutique hotel where rooms are designed by local artists and come with a/c, laptops and use of the park and pool at their elegant sister hotel, the Parkhotel Laurin (see below). ➏

Hotel Regina Via Renon 1 ☎0471.972.195, ⓦwww.hotelreginabz.it. Great location opposite the train station. Inexpensive, but a little characterless. ➌

Kolpinghaus Via Ospedale 3, off Piazza Walther ☎0471.308.400, ⓦwww.kolping.it/bz. An imposing residence with single and twin rooms. ➌

Parkhotel Laurin ☎0471.311.000, ⓦwww.laurin.it. An extremely genteel establishment set in a secluded park on Via Laurin in the pedestrian area of town – some rooms have terraces, others balconies, and the fanciest boast a sauna or Jacuzzi too. ➏

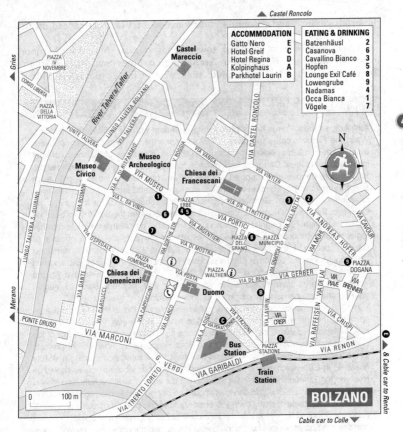

▲ Castel Roncolo

ACCOMMODATION		EATING & DRINKING	
Gatto Nero	E	Batzenhäusl	2
Hotel Greif	C	Casanova	6
Hotel Regina	D	Cavallino Bianco	3
Kolpinghaus	A	Hopfen	5
Parkhotel Laurin	B	Lounge Exil Café	8
		Lowengrube	9
		Nadamas	4
		Occa Bianca	1
		Vögele	7

Cable car to Colle ▼

The Town

Central Bolzano definitely looks like a part of the German-speaking world. Restaurants serve *speck*, *gulasch* and *knödel*, and bakers sell black bread and *sachertorte*. The centre of town is **Piazza Walther**, whose pavement cafés, around its statue of the *minnesinger* (troubadour) Walther von der Vogelweide, are the town's favoured meeting places. Converted into a cathedral as recently as 1964, the **Duomo** (Dom) sits on the edge of the square; built in the fourteenth and fifteenth centuries, and restored after being bombed in World War II, it has a striking green-and-yellow mosaic roof and elaborately carved spire. The fourteenth-century **Franciscan church** on Via dei Francescani is also worth seeking out, embellished with a carved wooden altarpiece by Hans Klocher and with elegant, frescoed cloisters from the same period.

A couple of streets west of Piazza Walther, on Via Cappuccini, the **Chiesa dei Domenicani** (Dominican monastery) has frescoes of fifteenth-century courtly life painted on the walls of the decaying cloisters, framed by a growth of stone tracery. The **Cappella di San Giovanni**, built at the beginning of the fourteenth century, retains frescoes by painters of the Giotto school, including a *Triumph of Death* underneath a starry vault. Follow the street north to **Piazza Erbe**, site of a daily fruit and vegetable market, from where

287

the oriel windows and eleventh-century arcades of **Via Portici** lead off to the right.

On the west side of the old town stands one of Alto Adige's more important museums, the **Museo Archeologico** (Tues–Sun 10am–5.30pm, Ⓦ www.iceman.it; €9), a ten-minute walk west of the centre at Via Museo

The history of Alto Adige

Alto Adige (Südtirol) was Italy's prize for co-operation with the Allies in World War I. When the Fascists came to power in 1923, despite the fact that German speakers outnumbered Italian speakers by about ten to one, a process of Italianization was imposed on the area. Cartographers remade maps, substituting Italian place names for German; people were stripped of their own names and forced to adopt Italian ones; the teaching of German in schools was banned and stonemasons were even brought to chip away German inscriptions from tombstones. Most telling was the change of the region's name and orientation – what had been the *South* Tyrol became the *Upper* Adige. But colonization wasn't just linguistic, as Italian workers from other regions were encouraged to settle, particularly in the towns. A large number of German speakers took the hint and emigrated, but after World War II many remained – along with the rival claims of Austria and Italy for control over the area. Both parties came to an agreement ratified under the Paris Peace Treaty of 1946 that Austria would give up its claim to the region on condition that Italy took steps to redress some of the cultural damage perpetrated under Fascism.

In 1948 some fancy footwork by the Italian government led to the union of Italian-speaking Trentino with German-speaking Alto Adige. In the new Trentino-Alto Adige region, German speakers were a minority and, as such, were entitled to very few of the compensatory measures agreed under the Paris Peace Treaty. After violent protests in the 1960s, a package of concessions was hastily put together, including a statute drawn up in 1971 which deemed that two-thirds of all public jobs and houses should be reserved for German speakers (a fair reflection of the ethnic mix at the time, and indeed to this date) and that all public servants should be bilingual in German and Italian. This has since been upheld, partly owing to pressure from the SVP (Südtiroler Volkspartei). Funds have been channelled into the area by successive governments, with the result that the unemployment rate here is the lowest in Italy, and per capita income high. There have been tricky patches, however. Stability here was particularly fragile during the 1980s, when the neo-fascist MSI (Movimento Sociale Italiano – now the Alleanza Nazionale), which argued for repeal of the 1971 act, gained enough strength to command something like fifty percent of the local Italian vote. In 1987 it secured the election of its first-ever local deputy to government, a lawyer who declared Mussolini "a great man", and actively encouraged neo-fascist sympathizers to move into the province to swell their numbers. However, the tide had evidently turned by November 1998, when 96 percent of the eligible population turned out for the provincial governmental elections, voting overwhelmingly for the SVP and denying the MSI a seat on the assembly.

February 2001 saw the region of Trentino-Alto Adige divested of much of its power, which was then divided between the new autonomous provinces of Trentino and Alto Adige. The region still exists for administrative purposes, but Alto Adige now enjoys more independence than ever before and much greater say in local law. Today, every child is enrolled in a school that teaches in his or her mother tongue (either German or Italian), with the other taught as a "second" language, and increasingly it is German that is the language of preference in Alto Adige. Over the last few years, Italy has moved closer into the European Union, and its central and regional governments have had to become more tolerant of ethnic diversity. But while political pressures may have declined, on social occasions the two groups remain surprisingly separate – some bars and restaurants, particularly in Bolzano, make their allegiances clear.

(Museumstrasse) 43. Once the seat of the Austro-Hungarian National Bank, and then the Banco d'Italia, the building's four floors trace the region's history and developing culture from the end of the last Ice Age to the early Middle Ages, through exhibits, reconstructions, models and multimedia presentations. At the heart of the museum is the Ice Man, nicknamed "Ötzi", the superbly preserved mummy of an early Copper Age male discovered in the ice of the Ötzaler Alps in 1991. Visitors can only view the mummy through a small window in a high-tech refrigeration unit; its preservation depends on remaining in an identical climate to the one in which it was discovered. At around 5300 years old, "Ötzi", his clothing, and his attendant possessions provide an unprecedented insight into the everyday culture of his time. What the museum won't tell you is that "Ötzi" was found by Austrians on the Italo–Austrian border; Italy only won custody after an unseemly legal battle with Austria in the 1990s. The Bolzano **museum card** (available from the tourist office; €2.50) is valid for a year and gives the holder discounted entry to museums in Bolzano as well as the **Castello Róncolo** (see p.290).

Continuing westwards down Via Museo takes you to a pleasant park along-side the River Talvera (Talfer). Bolzano's German and Gothic quarter ends on the other side of the Ponte Talvera, where **Piazza della Vittoria** signals the edge of the Italian town, much of it laid out by Mussolini's favourite architect, Marcello Piacentini. The epic triumphal arch on the square was commis-sioned by Mussolini in 1928 and is something of a controversial monument. Until a recent cleanup, it was covered with graffiti and surrounded by low railings, and was even bombed by German-speaking separatists in the late 1980s. The piazza is now the site of relatively sedate activity, hosting a big general market on Saturdays.

Eating, drinking and nightlife

If you're just after a lunchtime snack, try *wurstel* and *apfel strudel,* the common-est **street foods**, available from stalls on Piazza Erbe, Piazza del Grano and Via Stazione, and the cafés of Via dei Portici. Via Museo is a good source of decent local **restaurants**. It's worth noting that despite being a tourist destina-tion, Bolzano practically closes down on Sunday, most supermarkets included, though on Sunday evenings, and late every night, it's possible to get **pizza** and ice cream from *Subito*, on Piazza Erbe.

If you're after **nightlife,** downtown Bolzano is rather dull, with only four venues (see p.290). Still, that means it's easy to meet young people, and they tend to spill out onto the streets, beers in hand, at the weekend. The scene hots up a little in the industrial zone, and if you really want to dance, keep an eye out for flyers advertising the ever-changing venues for weekend parties.

Restaurants

Batzenhäusl Via A. Hofer 30 ℡ 0471.050.950. Old wine bar with a lively atmosphere. Closed Tues.
Cavallino Bianco (Weisses Rössel) Via Museo 6 ℡ 0471.973.267. With mains from €11, this *bierkeller* features a menu heavy on Tyrolean specialities. Closed July.
Hopfen Obstplatz 17 ℡ 0471.300.788. On the corner of the fruit market at Piazza Erbe; highly recommended for its beer brewed on the premises and huge plates of meaty Tyrolean specialities.

Lowengrube Piazza Dogana 3, a *bierlokal* with good food and *weissbier* on tap.
Occa Bianca Via Museo 17a, along Via dei Bottai. Offers a good-value set lunch. Closed Sun.
Vögele Goethestrasse 3 ℡ 0471.923.938. Probably the best restaurant in town, Vögele's big oak tables and wood panelling, abundant candles and charming staff make it the perfect place to sample local wines and delicacies. Set three-course menus are €17–29. Closed Sun & June 20–July 10.

Bars

Alumix Voltastraße, 9. Some nights feature live music, others disco. Located in the South Bolzano area. Entrance is €9 (one drink included).
Casanova Erbsengasse 8 ☏ 0471.301.897. Bolzano's only gay bar.

Lounge Exil Café Piazza del Grano 2a ☏ 0471.971.814. A young urban hangout in an industrial-style café.
Nadamas Piazza Erbe 44 ☏ 0471.980.684. International-themed restaurant with a huge variety of snacks.

Listings

Airport Aeroporto Bolzano Dolomiti ☏ 0471.255.255.
Car rental Hertz, Piazza Verdi 42 ☏ 0471.981.411; Alamo Via Garabaldi 2 ☏ 0471.971.531.
Hospitals Ospedale Centrale di Bolzano, Via Lorenz Böhler 5 ☏ 0471.908.111.
Internet *Multi Culti*, Via Doctor Streiter 9.
Parking Parcheggio Piazza Walther; Central Parking, Piazza Stazione; Bolzano Centro, Via Mayr-Nusser.

Pharmacies Don Bosco, Don Bosco Platz 6B ☏ 0471.915.239; Paris, Florenzstrasse 56 ☏ 0471.917.384; Gires, Telser Durchgang 8 ☏ 0471.285.096.
Police station Via Marconi 23 ☏ 0471.997.788.
Post office Piazza Parrocchia 13 ☏ 0471.322.211.
Taxis Radio Taxi ☏ 0471.981.111.

Around Bolzano

Bolzano is hemmed in by mountains terraced high with vineyards, across which a couple of footpaths wind up from the valley basin and present a brief taster of the countryside. The **Passeggiata del Guncinà** starts at the end of Via Knoller near Gries' Parrocchiale, while the other, the **Passeggiata Sant'Osvaldo**, begins at Via Rencio, behind the train station, traverses some hillside terraces, and brings you down to the path next to the River Talvera.

Just north of the town centre, the thirteenth-century **Castello Róncolo** (Schloss Runkelstein; Tues–Sun 10am–6pm; €8), reachable by bus #12 from the station, is covered with frescoes of courtly life showing people hunting and dancing as well as the legendary lovers Tristan and Isolde. Look out for a fresco showing a group of nobles fishing in the Sala del Torneo. In the background a noble is offering a fish to a lady – the medieval equivalent of an indecent proposal. The Castello also has an excellent trattoria in its courtyard.

There's a whole clutch of castles just southwest of Bolzano at **APPIANO** (Eppan An Der Weinstrasse). One of the few that hasn't fallen to rack and ruin or been turned into a hotel or restaurant is **Schloss Moos Schulthaus** (mid-April to Oct Tues–Sun, tours 10am, 11am, 4pm & 5pm; ☏ 0471.660.139; €4), which was saved from crumbling away just in time and turned into a museum. Its original Tyrolean kitchen, complete with a huge great hearth, has been kept intact, and there are some newly uncovered frescoes depicting "the war of cats and mice".

From the ruined battlements of nearby **Schloss Hocheppan** (now a restaurant, April–June & Sept–Nov daily except Tues 9am–5pm; July daily 9am–5pm; tours at 10am, 11am, 4pm & 5pm; ☏ 0471.636.081) you can see thirty or so other fortresses and castles, testifying to the cut and thrust of medieval politics in these parts. Hocheppan was the stronghold of the Counts of Eppan, rulers of the area until the powerful Counts of Tyrol took over after a series of bloody battles. The Hocheppan chapel by the side of the ruins is worth a look for its secular frescoes: women flirting at the altar, and one of the earliest representations of the ubiquitous *knödel*, or dumpling, which still features heavily on most South Tyrolean menus.

Törggelen

To get a flavour of Alto Adige's edible specialities, it's well worth timing your visit for the **Törggelen season**. This roughly coincides with the grape harvest, from about the end of September to the beginning of December, and traditionally marked the passage of the year – celebrating a golden time of clear autumnal weather before winter really set in.

Farmers and innkeepers lay on a spread of *speck* (smoked ham), local cheese and roast chestnuts, accompanied by wines from the surrounding hills, to which you apply yourself after a walk (or just a cable-car ride) up the mountain. Good areas to embark on your Törggelen expedition are just south of Bolzano, around the wine road (see p.272), and the villages of Termano (Tramin), Caldaro (Kaltern) and Appiano (Eppan), or the Valle d'Isarco (Eisacktal) around Bressanone (Brixen). Just a few suggestions to whet your appetite: *Törglkeller* at Località Bichl 2 at Caldaro (closed Sun); *Loosmannhof* (☎0471.365.551), Località Signato/Signat; and *Wieser* (☎0471.662.376; closed Wed) at Appiano (Eppan).

A trip up **Monte Renòn** (Rittner) gives a small taste of the high peaks that surround Bolzano. A cable car (open all year dawn to dusk; every 20min) ascends from Via Renòn (Rittnerstrasse) to Soprabolzano (Oberbozen), from where a tram service and footpaths lead to some of the other small villages, past a forest of eroded earth pillars, thirty minutes' walk north of Collalbo. A good time to come up here is in summer, around St Bartholomew's Day (August 24), when hundreds of farmers from outlying villages congregate on Renòn for the annual horse fair.

You might also visit the area south of Bolzano to eat; some of the farmhouses serve typical South Tyrolean dishes in their wood-panelled dining rooms (see box above).

Merano and the Giogáia di Tessa

MERANO (Meran), an hour north by train from Bolzano, lies close to two great mountain ranges. The closest, the **Giogáia di Tessa** (Texelgruppe), less than 10km away, is characterized by steep traverses across pastureland, with old snow still on the slopes in summer; watercourses irrigate the south-facing slopes, planted below with vines, peach and apple trees. Further west, the **Ortles** mountains – an unbelievable expanse of glaciers and rocky spurs – straddle the border with Valtellina and are included within the Parco Nazionale dello Stelvio, one of Italy's major national parks (see p.294). Both ranges offer isolated trails, away from tourist routes, with bus services to most villages.

Merano itself sits on a bend in the River Passirio, a handsome, sedate spa town surrounded by a ring of mountains, and, incongruously, by semitropical plants. Mild spring and autumn weather attracted Central Europeans at the beginning of the last century, and a resort of fin-de-siècle hotels, neat gardens and promenades evolved. The town's old nucleus is **Via dei Portici**, running west from the Gothic **Duomo** and fifteenth-century castle; around it are plenty of shopping streets and the Thermal Centre, which still provides radioactive water cures. It's mainly a retirement resort, but you may decide to stay in Merano for bus connections to the Parco Naturale di Tessa to the north, or the Ortles mountains to the southwest. If so, make sure to try the **Sentiero di Sissi** (Sisi's Walk), named for the Empress Elisabeth of Austria who often holidayed here.

It winds up from the old Spa House (*Kurhaus*) on the Kurpromenade to the **Trauttmansdorff botanical gardens** at Via Valentino 51 (daily: mid-March to mid-Nov 9am–6pm; mid-May to mid-Sept 9am–9pm; €9.50, €4.50 after 6pm); an English-language booklet available from the tourist office explains the significance of the various monuments you pass on the way. The gardens themselves are a charming place to while away an hour or two, and have great views over the valleys below.

If you're here on Easter Monday, head for the hippodrome to the south of the centre, where Tyrolean musicians astride huge Haflinger horses parade around the stadium, with much horn-blowing and flag-waving before the actual races start. In summer, twice-weekly classical concerts are held – some in atmospheric castles. Perhaps more tempting, though, is the **grape fest** in the third week of October, marked by a procession, concerts and stands groaning under the weight of gastronomic delights.

Buses arrive and leave directly outside the **train station** on Piazza Stazione, ten minutes' walk from the centre of town. If you plan to stay in Merano more than three days you may find the **Meran Card** useful (ⓦ www.merancard.com; three-day card €27, seven-day card €48), as it gives free access to museums, buses and lifts. It is available from the **tourist office** at Corso Libertà 45 (Jan & Feb Mon–Fri 9am–12.30pm & 2–6.30pm; March–Sept Mon–Fri 9am–6pm, Sat 9.30am–12.30pm; Dec Mon–Fri 9am–12.30pm & 2–5pm, Sat 10am–5pm, Sun 10.30am–4pm; ⓣ 0473.272.000, ⓦ www.meraninfo.it). Three of the least expensive central **hotels** are the nineteenth-century *Hotel Westend*, right on the river at Speckbacherstrasse 9 (ⓣ 0473.447.654, ⓦ www.westend.it; ❷), most of whose rooms have balconies; *Tyrol*, a quiet hotel with a garden, closer to the train station at Via XXX Aprile 8 (ⓣ 0473.449.719; ❷); and *Villa Betty*, just across the river from the station, on Via Petrarca (ⓣ 0473.233.949; ❹). For a really special place to stay, check out *Castel Fragsburg* (ⓣ 0473.244.071, ⓦ www .fragsburg.com; ❽) on Via Fragsburg in the hills above the city, with gorgeous, light, modern rooms, excellent food, spa services and tremendous views – especially from the outdoor pool. At the other extreme, there's the new **youth hostel** at Carduccistrasse 77 (ⓣ 0473.201.475, ⓦ www.jugendherberge.it), with en-suite rooms, a laundry and TV room, and a workshop for bicycle repairs; dorm beds are €19.50 per night, with a €2 surcharge for staying just one night. **Campers** should use *Camping di Merano,* Via Piave 44 (ⓣ 0473.231.249; Easter–Nov), which has a swimming pool: turn right out of the station, cross the river by way of Via Rezia and Via Petrarca, and Via Piave is the third turning on the right.

The best place to **eat** in town is the expensive *Sissi*, at Galileistrasse 44 (ⓣ 0473.23.10.62), where renowned Italian chef Andrea Fenoglio puts modern twists on traditional dishes. Less fancy, but good nonetheless, is *Weinstube Hais-rainer,* Via dei Portici 100, serving Italian and Tyrolean dishes. For **hiking** advice and information, consult the Club Alpino Italiano office, Via Carlo Wolff 15 (ⓣ 0473.448.944, ⓦ www.caimerano.it), or Merano's Alpine association, the Alpenverein Südtirol, at Galileistraße 45 (Mon–Fri 9–11.45am; ⓣ 0473.237.134, ⓦ www.alpenverein.it).

Parco Naturale Gruppo di Tessa (Naturpark Texelgruppe)

The mountain chains around Merano belong to a separate geological period from the Dolomites, and are actually part of the Zillertaler and Ötztaler ranges of the eastern Alps. Their foothills, called the **Giogáia di Tessa** (Texelgruppe), begin immediately north of the town. Two high-level paths, the north and south sections of the **Meraner Höhenweg**, encircle this massif. The gentler **southern route** (marked as route 24 on signs) overlooks Merano, the hikers' haven of Val Venosta (Vinschgau), and the neighbouring peaks, and is crowded even out of season. The total walking time is 24 hours, and every few kilometres there's a dairy farm offering bed and breakfast or a *rifugio* for overnight stops. **Buses** go from Merano to the beginning of the route at Hof Unterpferl in Katharinaberg (#21), and continue to Ulfas just west of San Leonardo, where the route ends – plus several points along the way, including **Castel Tirolo** (mid-March to mid-Nov Tues–Sun 10am–5pm; ☎0473.220.221, ⓦwww .schlosstirol.it; €6, guide an extra €2), where a cable car ascends to a couple of *rifugi* and souvenir shops at **Hochmuter**. The castle's tenth-century frescoed chapel is worth the visit, if you can fight your way through the crowds of other tourists who pack the lanes around. Below Tirolo Castle is **Brunnenburg**, a neo-Gothic pile that's all fishtail battlements and conical towers, where American poet Ezra Pound spent the last years of his life. It's now home to the Ezra Pound Center for Literature, a beloved haunt of many creative writing students, and an **agricultural museum**, encompassing ethnology, folklore and folk art. Pound's grandson now runs a rather bizarre **art gallery** in the same building (April–Oct daily except Tues 9am–5pm; ☎0473.923.533; €3), all its works being linked by the theme "bread".

The **northern** stretch of the Meraner Höhenweg is an entirely different trail, running at a higher altitude but still below the snowline, through isolated pastures and rocky terrain. The comparative scarcity of *rifugi* makes it necessary to plan overnight stops in advance. The first section of the trail, Katherinaberg–Montfert–Eishof, is a walk of four hours; you then pick up the path from Eishof to *Rifugio Stettiner* (no accommodation; 3hr 30min); Stettiner to Pfelders (3hr 30min) is the last part. For places to stay in **KATHERINABERG**, try the *Hotel Am Fels* (☎0473.679.139, ⓦwww.hotel-amfels.it; ❶), which has a swimming pool and sauna; in **PFELDERS**, there's *Edelweiss* (☎0473.646.713, ⓦwww.residence-edelweiss.it; ❷), with compact, well-appointed self-catering apartments, and the small and friendly *Panorama* (☎0473.646.727, ⓦwww .panorama-pfelders.com; ❶).

From *Rifugio Stettiner* there's another option, the **Pfelderer Höhenweg**, which runs east to the Zwickauer Shelter, crosses the path here, and traverses the pastures of Obere Schneid. There are some sheer drops down to the valley, and you need crampons above the snowline, but this is an excellent walk, which gives a hint of how isolated these small valleys were until recently. If you don't feel equipped for this, but want to extend the route, continue past Pfelders to Ulfas (4hr), and from there on to Vipiteno (2–3 days), where you either link up with the main Bolzano to Innsbruck railway or carry on eastwards along the **Pfunderer Höhenweg** (see p.301).

A bus travels north from Merano to **SAN LEONARDO** along the Val Passiria (Sankt Leonhard), skirting the edge of the Texelgruppe, and, on the other side, Merano's ski resorts on the slopes of Punta Cervina (Hirzer Spitze). A network of paths cross the summer pastures around Sankt Leonhard: one of these leaves **San Martino** (Sankt Martino), 4km south of San Leonardo, and makes the steep ascent (2hr 30min) to **Pfandleralm**, the home village of Andreas Hofer. Originally an innkeeper, wine merchant and cattle dealer, he fought for the Tyrol's return to Austria after it had been ceded to Bavaria in 1805. After successful uprisings against occupying Bavarian and Napoleonic troops, he became self-styled commander in chief of the South Tyrol, attracting strong popular support. However, larger political forces overtook him.

When the Tyrol was ceded to the French by Austria's Emperor Francis I, Hofer was arrested in 1810 and executed under Napoleon's orders in Mantua. At Pfandleralm a memorial to him stands on the edge of the meadow, and in the Sandwirt guesthouse at San Leonardo, there's a small "Hofer" **museum** (March–Nov Tues–Sun 10am–6pm; Ⓦwww.museum.passeier.it, €5).

❹ Parco Nazionale dello Stelvio

The **Parco Nazionale dello Stelvio** (or the Stilfser National Park) is one of Italy's major national parks; it covers the whole **Ortles** range, and is topped by one of Europe's largest glaciers (the Ghiaccciaio dei Forni) and crossed by the Passo dello Stelvio, which misses being the highest pass in the Alps by just twelve metres. Tourism has made its mark, and the park is as crisscrossed by ski lifts as anywhere in the Alps. But it's still a remarkable place. People come here for the high trails and glacier skiing in summer, or for the chance of seeing species such as the red and roe deer, elk, chamois, golden eagles and ibex. One of the best valleys for spotting wildlife is the sheer-sided Val Zebrù, off the Valfurva, the smallest of the valleys, accessible from Bormio (see p.234). If you're driving, consider approaching over the **Passo dello Stelvio**; this amazingly convoluted route through the park consists of over forty switchbacks and turns but is well worth it – for both the thrill and the view.

There are buses to the park's various points of access but perhaps the place to head for first is **SILANDRO** (Schlanders), in the long, relatively wide Val Venosta (Vinschgau), with its **Tourism Association** on Vinschgau Kapuzinerstraße 10 (summer Mon–Fri 8.30am–7pm, Sat 9am–noon; winter Mon–Fri 8.30am–noon & 2–6pm; ℡0473.737.000, Ⓦwww.schlanders.suedtirol.com) who provide information on *rifugi* and trails. If you're all hiked out, there's a interesting castle, **Coira**, but more frequently known by its German name of **Churburg**, 20km away on the road to Malles (Mals; buses from Merano). It was owned by the Lords of Matsch at the beginning of the thirteenth century, when it was just one castle in a whole chain stretching from Bavaria to just north of Milan and was battled over by various knights in armour – whose suits, some weighing nearly 25kg, can be seen in the **armoury** (March 20–Oct 31 Tues–Sun 10am–noon & 2–4.30pm; ℡0473.615.241, Ⓦwww.churburg.com; €6) – the largest private collection in Europe.

The valleys

Three main valley roads thread their way from the Val Venosta (Vinschgau) into the foothills of the Ortles range: Val d'Ultimo (Ultental), Val Martello (Martelltal) and Val di Solda (Suldental). A traditional place of hiding in an area renowned for mountain warfare, the isolated **Val d'Ultimo** was opened up in the last century, and buses now run from Merano to the village of **SAN GERTRUDE** (Sankt Gertraud). Around the lower slopes are startling green pastures and some ancient larches, but the main attraction in coming here is higher up, where trails lead over rock-strewn moorland to *Rifugio Canziani* (*Höchster Hütte*; 3hr; no accommodation), dramatically surrounded by the glaciers and peaks of **Zufrittspitze**. If you're feeling less energetic, the valley is still a good place for some shorter walks, using the village as base. *Utnerhof*, Hauptstrasse 114 (℡0473.798.117; ❷), is one of a handful of **hotels** in the village, and most rooms have balconies, while for **food** you should splash out at *Genziana*, Via Fontana Bianca 116 – enjoy amazing meals for around €20 a head.

Further west, **Val Martello** (Martelltal) is equally beautiful, its lower slopes covered with silver birches. A bus travels from Merano to Silandro, and another from Silandro into Val Martello, passing the ruins of Cartel Montani and an aviary for falcons at Morter. At the head of the valley, **PARADISO DEL CEVEDALE** (2088m) is one of the busiest bases for climbers and cross-country skiers, lying close to Monte Cevedale (Zufall Spitze; 3757m); other trails lead through high passes to Val d'Ultimo and Val di Solda. One of the main roads through the park is the awe-inspiring route over the **Passo dello Stelvio** (2758m), one of the highest and last to open – it is known to stay closed until July. A single bus from Merano makes the journey to the pass (late June to mid-Sept), going past the turn-off to the Val di Solda on the way; an alternative route is to take the frequent service from Merano to **Spondigna** and wait for one of the two afternoon buses from Malles there. **TRAFOI**, up at 1543m, is a beautifully situated hamlet perched by the side of the road towards the beginning of the main climb. The views from here are stupendous, and the slopes remarkably unsullied by tourism. The *Hotel Bella Vista* (☏0473.611.716, ⓦwww.bellavista-suedtirol.com; €57 per person, half board only) lives up to its name, boasting uninterrupted views of the Ortles range. The home of Olympic gold medallist Gustav Thöni, it has large, Scandinavian-style rooms, most with balconies, a sauna and Turkish bath and a pleasant play area outside. Cheaper alternatives include the charming and very reasonable *Tuckett* (☏0473.611.722, ⓦwww.gasthof-tuckett.com; ❷).

A cable car leads up to *Rifugio Forcola* (no accommodation), at 2250m, from where a fine path continues up and round to the Passo dello Stelvio (4hr). The pass marked the frontier between Italy, Switzerland and Austria until 1918, and **Pizzo Garibaldi** (Dreisprachenspitze), a spur of rock fifteen minutes' walk from the pass, is the symbolic meeting place for the three main languages of the area. The road continues down through switchbacks and startling gradients to Bormio.

Just short of Trafoi is the turn-off for **SOLDA** (Sülden), 8km west. Set in an isolated tributary valley hanging over the main road, it's been a major climbing and skiing centre since the nineteenth century – there's even a tiny, eccentric **museum** (daily 9am–7pm; free) celebrating Solda's existence as a mountain resort. There's also a helpful **tourist office** at Via Principale 72 (Mon–Fri 8am–noon & 3–6pm, Sat 9am–noon, Aug also Sat 3–6pm; ☏0473.737.060, ⓦwww.ortlergebiet.it) and a large range of **accommodation**. In the lower town, best for restaurants and services, are *Paulmichl* (☏0473.613.064, ⓦwww .pensionpaulmichl.com; ❸), right next to the tourist office, and *Ortlerhof*, the first hotel on the way into town (☏0473.613.052, ⓦwww.ortlerhof-sulden .com; ❶; June–Sept), where B&B accommodation in an en-suite room with balcony comes at an incredibly low price. Ten minutes' walk away, in the upper part of town, the ⚡ *Garni des Alpes* (☏0473.613.062, ⓦwww.garnidesalpes .com; ❷) is excellent value and has a resident climbing/skiing guide. Although Solda attracts fairly serious climbers and skiers, you don't have to be experienced to attempt some of the trails. There are easy paths (2hr) up to *Rifugio-Albergo Città di Milano* (*Schaubach Hütte*; ☏0473.613.002; June–Sept) at 2581m, or more difficult trails to *Rifugio Payer* (☏0473.613.010; July–Sept) at 3020m, a fantastic viewpoint and base for the ascent of **Ortles** (3905m).

Record-breaking climber **Reinhold Messner** is from Südtirol, and has interests all over the area. This Solda **restaurant**, *Yak e Yeti*, at Suldenstrasse 55 (☏0473.613.266; closed Mon; around €30 for a three course meal), is one of the most celebrated in the Val Venosta, with Messner's own yaks resident below, while his very reasonable *osteria* (☏0473.668.238; daily noon–3pm & 7–10pm) at his castle near Naturno, Juval, has hearty local, organic food and wines. Dancing on the sturdy wooden tables is not uncommon – for a more genteel evening, try eating in the shady garden.

Blessed by three hundred days of sunshine a year, the Val Venosta region is rich in fresh fruit and vegetables, and every weekend during July and August one or other of the villages celebrates summer with a **street festival**, with live music, beer gardens and fresh produce. One of the best is the Marmor & Marillen (Marble & Apricots) festival in early August in the tiny village of Laas, which fêtes the local fruit-growing and marble industries, and where you can sample delicious *marillenknödel*, sweet potato dough dumplings filled with whole apricots and rolled in toasted breadcrumbs, sugar and cinnamon.

Alpe di Siusi (Seiser Alm)

The grasslands of the **Alpe di Siusi** (Seiser Alm), to the east of Bolzano, are Europe's largest Alpine plateau, extending over sixty square kilometres high above the rest of the valley under the peaks of **Sciliar** (Schlern) national park. The valley roads give you little idea of what lies above.

The bus from Bolzano goes to Siusi, from where another service ascends to the Alpe. On the way, the road climbs through a series of loops past the Hauenstein forest, the ruins of a castle which was once the home of Osvald of Wolkenstein (1377–1445) – the last *minnesinger* (troubadour) of the South Tyrol – and the onion-domed church of **San Valentino** (Sankt Valentiskirchlein). Buses terminate at **SALTRIA** (Saltner), at the heart of the wetlands in an area that's increasingly popular with German walkers but still relatively unspoilt, where the main evidence of human activity is dairy farming and some logging in the woods. Horses graze on the tough grass, picking their way between the bogs and streams, and small huts and clumps of pine are dotted across the plateau. Paths lead off the Alpe di Siusi to *rifugi* in the peaks, and there is a smattering of **hotels** that are more or less the only buildings at Saltria: *Almgasthof Tirler* is one of the better-value (℡0471.727.927; Ⓦwww.tirler.it; €56 per person, half board only) with good sized rooms and friendly service. Along with a **tourist information office** (Mon–Sat 9am–5pm, Sun 9am–noon; ℡0471.727.904, Ⓦwww.seiseralm.net), there's much more accommodation in the tourist-heavy Alpe di Siusi proper, including the luxurious *Plaza* (℡0471.727.973, Ⓦwww.seiseralm.com; €74 per person, half board only) and the simpler *Anemone Seiseralm*, with en-suite rooms and balconies (℡0471.727.963, Ⓦwww.anemone-seiseralm.com; €63 per person, half board only). It's also the starting point for many excellent day-hikes, such as the two-and-a-half-hour trek up to *Tierser Alpl* (℡0471.707.460 or 727.958, Ⓦwww.tierseralpl.com) at 2440m, a cute, red-roofed refuge with amazing views.

Sciliar (Schlern) and Sasso Lungo (Langkofel)

The **Parco Nazionale dello Sciliar**, which spreads over this area, is named after **Sciliar** (Schlern), a flat-topped, sheer mountain which splits off at one end into two peaks, Cima Euringer and Santner. Trails lead onto Sciliar from Tires (Tiers), Fié Am Sciliar (Völs Am Schlern) or Siusi (Seis), all involving long, steep climbs up to the summit (2563m). In the heyday of the spa resort, **FIÉ AM SCILIAR** was famous for its curative hay baths – presumably only beneficial if you didn't suffer from hayfever. Schloss Prösels, the fairly simple **castle** (guided tours daily: April–Oct 11am, 2 & 3pm; ℡0471.601.062, ⊛www .schloss-proesels.it; €4) here, was once the seat of the Lords of Völs, patrons of the arts and staunch campaigners against witchcraft and superstition. Nowadays, it has its own owl.

Just before the peak of Sciliar is *Rifugio Bolzano al Monte Pez* (*Schlernhaus*; ℡0471.612.024, ⊛www.schlernhaus.it; June–Oct), one of the original Alpine huts from the 1880s. The cable car from Hoferalp, above Umes di Fiè (Ums), cuts out 1000m of ascent. In summer, paths can be crowded, but the day-trippers tend to disappear back down into the valley by evening, when the teeth of **Sasso Lungo** (Langkofel) become blunted by cloud.

Trails onto Sasso Lungo spring from the path between Saltria and **Monte Pana**, above Santa Cristina in the Val Gardena (see below). Half a day's walking brings you to *Rifugio Vicenza* (*Langkofelhütte*; ℡0471.792.323; June 20–Sept 20); from here paths lead across the mountain down to Passo di Sella (Sellajoch).

Val Gardena (Grödnertal)

Trails and chair lifts connect the Alpe with the **Val Gardena** (Grödnertal), a valley of squeaky-clean guesthouses and a continuous stream of tourist buses. The main village in the valley, **ORTISEI** (Sankt Ulrich), has for centuries been a big producer of religious sculpture and, more recently, hand-carved wooden toys, with several families each perpetuating a particular design. Three thousand woodcarvers in the valley still make furniture and religious statues, but Ortisei, like the neighbouring villages of **Santa Cristina** (Sankt Christina) and **Selva** (Wolkenstein), is now mainly a ski resort, within easy reach of the **Sella Ronda**, a route of ski-runs and lifts encircling the Gruppo di Sella that make up the heart of the Dolomite skiing area. The massive circuit takes at least a day to complete. For information about skiing and accommodation, contact Ortisei's **tourist office** at Reziastrasse 1 (Mon–Sat 8.30am–12.30pm & 2.30–6.30pm, Sun in summer 8.30am–noon & 5–6.30pm, Sun in winter 10am–noon & 5–6.30pm; ℡0471.777.600, ⊛www.valgardena.it). There's another **branch** at Santa Christina, on Dursan Strasse 78 bis (same hours; ℡0471.777.800). The **Museum di Gherdëina** in the **Cësa di Ladins** at Reziastrasse 83 (June & Sept to mid-Oct Tues–Fri 2–6pm, Wed 10am–noon & 2–6pm; Jul & Aug Mon–Fri 10am–noon, Sun 2–6pm; €4) celebrates local Ladino culture (see box, p.283), the natural history of the area and local-boy-made-good Luis Trenker, a documentary filmmaker in the 1930s. **Buses** make the journey back to Bolzano, or you can drive in the other direction towards the Passo di Sella or Passo di Gardena.

Valle d'Isarco and Val Pusteria

The attraction of the four-hour bus trip from Bolzano to Cortina d'Ampezzo isn't so much what you see of the **Valle d'Isarco** (Eisacktal) and **Val Pusteria** (Pusertal), but the access it gives to the beginning of the *alte vie* and quieter routes into the **Val di Funes** (Villnöss), the Odle group, and the isolated ridges to the north of Val Pusteria. Largely untouched by tourism, these are great places to walk. In the side valleys dippers dart in and out of the streams and the sawing of timber cuts through the air. Higher up, you're likely to see marmots, and chamois betray their presence with a tumbling of stones.

Valle d'Isarco (Eisacktal) and around

The main village of the southern Valle d'Isarco (Eisacktal), **CHIUSA** (Klausen), is served by trains from Bolzano and Bressanone (Brixen), and by buses that continue into the **Val di Funes**, a little to the north. **SANTA MADDALENA** (Sankt Magdalena), surrounded by tracts of pasture, lies 10km into the valley, at the base of Le Odle. This quiet village is a good place for an overnight stop with a few reasonable **hotels**, such as the three-star *Gasthof Hofmann* on Hofmann Johann (☏0474.948.014, ⓦ www.hotelhofmann.com; €59 per person, half board only), boasting spacious rooms, many with balconies, and a health club with sauna, solarium and Turkish bath. Another bus climbs halfway up the mountain to Zanseralm, from where it's one hour's walk to *Rifugio Genova* (☏0472.840.132; July–Oct) at 2301m. The level paths take you above the larch forests that fill the valley, and give fantastic views of the peaks. A four-hour circular trail called the Sentiero delle Odle (Adolf Munkel Weg) traverses the grass slopes beneath the teeth of the range, from Zanseralm via Saint Renon or to Brogles-Alm, and back down to the valley. Alta Via 2 is a short walk from Saint Renon.

Bressanone (Brixen)

Alta Via 2 can also be picked up in the foothills above **BRESSANONE** (Brixen), whose bishops – in constant rivalry with the neighbouring Counts of Tyrol – ruled the area as an independent state for a thousand years. The complex of buildings that made up their base is still the focus of the town, centred on Piazza del Duomo (Dom Platz), and preserves a medieval character, though rather diluted by bourgeois tidiness.

The **Duomo** (9am–noon & 3–6pm; free), originally from the tenth century but destroyed by fire in the eleventh and rebuilt in its current Baroque style in the eighteenth, is the most imposing building in the complex: the interesting part lies to the side, in the fantastically ornate cloisters, which were frescoed in the fourteenth century and depict the evolution of medieval art. The cathedral **treasury** is now kept in the Museo Diocesano (see below), where vestments belonging to Bressanone's bishop-princes are hung. Their strong influence in the region is evident from the present given by Emperor Henry II to Bishop Albuino: a tenth-century Byzantine silk cloak, spread with the stylized eagle that was the bishop's personal emblem. The bishop's palace, next to the Duomo, houses the **Museo Diocesano** (mid-March to Oct Tues–Sun 10am–5pm; Dec–Jan daily 2–5pm; closed Nov and Feb to mid-March; €5; ⓦ www .dioezesanmuseum.bz.it), furnished in predictably grand style, with an overwhelming collection of crib scenes in the **crypt** (same ticket as Museo Diocesano). For more secular pleasures, head for the **Novacella Monastery** (Kloster Neustift), 3km away and reachable by bus (at least hourly), which produces well-regarded wine and sells direct to the public via its own cellar in the old smithy. If you have the time, take a guided tour around the beautiful, frescoed medieval **cloisters** (Mon–Sat: Nov–Easter 11am & 3pm; mid-July to mid-Sept noon & 1pm; Jan–March Mon by appointment only; €5; ☏0472.836.189, ⓦ www.kloster-neustift.it).

Just north of the Duomo lies Via Portici Maggiore, where you'll find a fascinating hotchpotch of shopping arcades and the seventeenth-century Porta de San Michele; this opens onto Via Ponte Aquila, which leads down to the river and boasts a gem of a museum at no. 4a. The **Pharmaziemuseum** (Tues–Wed 2–6pm, Sat 11am–4pm, Aug open Mon–Fri same hours; €3.50; ☏0472.209.112, ⓦ www.pharmazie.it) is located on the second floor (follow the painted snakes) and boasts a weird and wonderful selection of antique vials and pillboxes, pharmaceutical apparatuses, and sumptuously illustrated medical manuals from the late sixteenth century. The excellent audiovisual display is currently available in German and Italian only.

Bressanone's **tourist office** (Mon–Sat 8.30am–12.30pm & 2.30–6pm; ☎0472.836.401, ⓦwww.brixen.org), opposite the bus station, has information on trails around the town and further afield. There are some excellent, inexpensive **places to stay** in the old town, including *Tallero*, Via Mercato Vecchio 35 (☎0472.830.577, ⓦwww.tallero.it; ❸), and the small, family-run *Mayrhofer*, Via Tratten 17 (☎0472.836.327, ⓦwww.mayrhofer.it; ❸). Moving upmarket, the *Elephant*, Via Rio Bianco 4 (☎0472.832.750, ⓦwww.hotelelephant.com; ❻), is one of the longest-established grand hotels in the Dolomites, furnished in elegant Tyrolean style, with a good restaurant (see below), while the *Goldene Krone Vital Stadthotel* on Via Fienili 4 (☎0472.835.154, ⓦwww.goldenekrone .com; ❺) is one of the newest, with an emphasis on light cuisine and wellbeing. There are two **campsites** 5km north in Varna (Vahrn): the *Leone* (*Löwenhof*) is at Via Lago di Varna 60 (☎0472.836.216, ⓦwww.loewenhof.it; €29 per tent; closed Nov), while the other, *Al Lago* (*Zum See*), is near Lake Varna, at Via Lago di Varna 129 (☎0472.832.169; April–Oct); several buses travel here on weekdays, fewer at weekends. The best **restaurants** in town are *Finsterwirt* at Vicolo del Duomo 3 (☎0472.835.343; closed Mon, mid-Jan to mid-Feb and two weeks in July or Aug), serving excellent local specialities and wine (€30), and the restaurant at the *Elephant* hotel (☎0472.836.579; closed Thurs mid-March to July, and all Nov & Feb) for expertly prepared regional cuisine, including a vegetarian option (three-course menu is €31–52). For picnics, try the shops in the old arcades or the Monday market on Via Brennero; alternatively grab a slice of freshly made pizza from *Pizza da Nando* on Via Fienili.

Val Pusteria (Pusertal)

The road through the **Val Pusteria** (Pusertal), a wide valley of maize fields and hay meadows, sweeps around the northern edge of the Dolomites. Most of the *alte vie* start from points along the main road through the valley, which is served by bus from Brunico. The train route branches off the main Bolzano–Innsbruck line at Fortezza, heading on to Bressanone and Brunico on its way to Innichen. For walkers, many of the *alte vie* start in the Val Pusteria: Alta Via 1 starts from Lago di Bráies (Pragser Wildsee), Alta Via 3 from Villabassa (Niederdorf), Alta Via 4 from San Cándido (Innichen) and Alta Via 5 from Sesto (Sexten). There are also lesser-known trails to the north, for example the Alta Via Val di Fundres (Pfunderer Höhenweg) – see p.301 for details.

Brunico (Bruneck)

An influx of people from the surrounding villages arrives daily in the otherwise sleepy market town of **BRUNICO** (Bruneck), which is also the transport centre of the region, with buses along the valley and to most of the small places higher up in the hills. Brunico was the home of the painter and sculptor Michael Pacher (c1435–98); if you have some time to kill, go and look at his *Vine Madonna* in the parish church of the village of San Lorenzo, 4km southwest of town. Pacher is probably the most famous Tyrolean painter and woodcarver, straddling German Gothic and the more spare Italian styles; there's something vaguely unsavoury about this particular Madonna and her pudgy child, gripping a bunch of black grapes, but it's refreshing to see work in its original setting rather than in a museum.

The Brunico **tourist office**, Rathausplatz 7 (Mon–Fri 9am–12.30pm & 2–6pm, Sat 9am–noon; ☎0474.555.722, ⓦwww.bruneck.com), has details of **places to stay**. Reasonable options include the cute, cosy and central *Blitzburg*, Via Europa 10 (☎0474.555.837, ⓦwww.blitzburg.it; €60 per person, half board only), and *Haus Ragen*, at Brüder-Willemstrasse 29 (☎0474.410.972; ❷), with a garden. For **campers** there's the *Camping Schiesstand*, Via Dobbiaco 4 (☎0474.401.326; May–Sept). A stopping **train** makes the journey along the Val Pusteria from here to the end of the line at Dobbiaco.

Vipiteno (Sterzing)

Situated on the busy route north from Bolzano to Innsbruck, **VIPITENO** (Sterzing) is easy enough to get to. This close to the Austrian border it's hardly surprising that much of Vipiteno is typically Tyrolean, with geranium-filled balconies and wood-panelled old inns. The porticoed main street, however, **Via Città Nuova** (Neustadtstrasse), is more reminiscent of places further south, lined with elegant, battlemented *palazzi* erected in Renaissance times by a locally based Florentine bank. At one end, the **Torre di Città** was rebuilt in 1867 after fire destroyed the fifteenth-century original. The late-Gothic **Palazzo Comunale** on the square behind is worth a visit for its attractive galleried courtyard and a collection of fifteenth- and sixteenth-century paintings and sculptures (Mon–Sat 8.30am–noon & 2.30–5.30pm; free). Try also to get to the **Museo Civico**, on Via della Commenda (April–Oct Tues–Sat 9.30am–12.30pm & 2–6pm; €3), five minutes' walk from the centre, near the hospital. The museum is essentially an exhibition of local carving, the highlight being an altarpiece by Hans Multscher, a fifteenth-century sculptor and painter from Ulm. His work shows a keen sense of realism, as exemplified in an altarpiece of 1459. Several of his carved wooden figures can be seen in the nearby parish church of **Santa Maria in Vibitin**.

The **tourist office** is at Piazza Città 3 (daily 8.30am–12.30pm & 2.30–6pm; ☎0472.765.325, ⓦwww.infovipiteno.it). If you decide to **stay** in Vipiteno, the elegant, friendly *Wipptalerhof*, Via Città Nuova 4 (☎0472.765.428, ⓦwww .wipptalerhof.it; ❷), is undoubtedly the first choice. If it's fully booked, the tranquil *Pension Schneider*, Eduard Ploner Strasse 1 (☎0472.765.288; ❷), is well situated on a quiet side street just above Via Città Vecchia, the extension of Via Città Nuova.

Parco Naturale Fánes-Sénnes-Bráies

If you have a limited amount of time to spend in the **Parco Naturale Fánes-Sénnes-Bráies**, east of Brunico, you should aim for the upper slopes of **Alpe di Fánes**, where you pick up some of the best ridgeway paths. You can get here by taking a bus from either Corvara (see p.285) or Brunico to **Longega** (Zwischenwasser), and then walking 4km to **San Vigilio Di Marebbe**, in a side valley, where the tourist office can advise on routes up into the mountains. A regular jeep-taxi service runs from San Vigilio to *Rifugio Fánes* (Dec 20–April 30 & June 10–Oct 15; ☎0474.501.097, ⓦwww.rifugiofanes.com) and *Rifugio La Varella* (March 19–April 25 & June 19–Oct 19; ☎0474.501.079, ⓦwww.lavarella.it), both around 2000m up on the Alpe di Fánes Piccola. Footpaths cross the grassy plateaus, passing small tarns and the rocks of **Castel de Fánes**, home of Dolasilla, the mythical princess of the Ladini. The lakes are fed by underground streams, which you can sometimes hear, burbling deep beneath your feet.

Perhaps the best way to see the park, however, is to walk the section of Alta Via 1 that runs through it, a hike which takes three to four days, with overnight stops at refuges. The trail starts at **Lago di Bráies** (Pragser Wildsee), a deep-green lake surrounded by pines, 8km off the main road through the Val Pusteria – an extraordinary place (according to legend, the lake is a gateway to underground caverns), although you should avoid it in July and August, when crowds descend on the trails. To get here, take a bus from **Corvara** to **Brunico** and then another bus towards **Dobbiaco** (Toblach), asking the driver to drop you at the turn-off, which is between **Monguelfo** (Welsberg) and **Villabassa** (Niederdorf), around thirty minutes out of Brunico; buses also go all the way to the lake from Dobbiaco.

Also accessible from Brunico by cable car (€10 return) is the **Plan de Coro-nes**, surrounded by jagged peaks. Here, legend has it, Dolasilla was crowned at the top of the mountain with the *raïëta* – a crystal that harnessed powerful forces.

Alta Via Val di Fundres (Pfunderer Höhenweg)

The high-level **Alta Via Val di Fundres** (Pfunderer Höhenweg) follows the ridges north of Brunico. Although it's in the lower part of the Zillertal Alps, the path gives a feeling of the high mountains, with views across to the glaciers of Gran Pilastro (Hochfeiler) on the Austrian border. It's an exhilarating area, often subject to snow, ice and scorching sun in the same day. Access to the path is at Kleines Tor (2374m) on Monte Sommo (Sambock), a steep climb along path 29 from **Selva Dei Molini** (Mühlwald), 24km from Brunico. The walk takes four to five days, with overnight stops in *rifugi* or *bivacci*. The nearest big village is **CAMPO TURES** (Sand In Taufers), where the wonderfully evocative medieval castle, **Schloss Taufers** (daily 10am–5pm; ☎0474.678.053; closed Nov; €5), has dozens of wood-panelled rooms, including one haunted by a woman whose husband was murdered on their wedding day. The dungeons boast a particularly gruesome array of torture instruments, but perhaps the most appealing aspect of the castle is its setting: stark grey walls, bristling with towers, stand in contrast to the glistening backdrop of the Zillertal glaciers.

From Kleines Tor the path drops down to the Winnebach Valley, then climbs to *Fritz Walde Hütte*. A steep path crosses the Hochsagescharte Col (2650m), falls to Passenjoch (2410m) and then, after a westerly descent to *Gampes Hütte* (2223m), makes a spectacular traverse across steep pasture that eventually descends to the Eisbrugger Valley. The end of the route at **Vipiteno** (see opposite) is reached via **Boden** and the Weitenber Valley. Early on the last day you can be descend-ing across snowcapped pasture, and in the evening be eating pizza in town. It's possible to do half of the walk by joining the path above **Fundres**, or the top of the Val di Valles (Valser Tal), where there's accommodation at *Brixner Hütte* (☎0472.547.131; mid-June to Oct).

Cortina d'Ampezzo and around

The 1956 Winter Olympics, staged at **CORTINA D'AMPEZZO**, kickstarted the town's transformation from a small resort to a city in the mountains. Its main reason for existing now is the **skiing** season – roughly Christmas to Easter – when the population rises from 7000 to around 40,000, packing out the art galleries, designer boutiques and antiques shops, as well as the slopes around the city. Cortina is the Italian equivalent of Saint Moritz, attracting actors, artists and all manner of rich, beautiful people. The place encourages a kind of Holly-wood existence: taking sleighs down the mountain after a meal at a glamorous restaurant, or renting helicopters to seek out off-piste skiing. There's a summer season, too, between July and September when the cable cars operate, although it's much more subdued, attracting mainly Italian and keen European hikers. As a base for either walking or skiing, the place is hard to beat: the setting is stunning, surrounded by a great circle of mountains which includes Monte Pelmo and Antelao, the Gruppo delle Marmarole, and Monte Sorapiss, Cristallo and Tofane. The Pista Olimpica di Bob, built for the Olympics, now plays host to the **Cortina Adrenalin Center** (℡0436.860.808, 🌐www.adrenalincenter.it), a mountain-activities organization offering rafting, hydrospeeding, kayaking, mountain biking and more.

Arrival and information

Apart from the tortuous **bus** routes via Bolzano and Belluno, there are long-distance services to Cortina from Milan, Padua and Bologna; the **bus station** is on Via Marconi, above town. The nearest **train station** is Calalzo, 32km east; a connecting bus runs every hour.

Cortina's **tourist office** is at Piazzetta San Francisco 8 (daily 9am–12.30pm & 3.30–6.30pm; ℡0436.3231, 🌐www.infodolomiti.it). Its hiking map, also available from many hotels, is good, with refuge phone numbers and an indication as to how long trails take to walk. Alternatively, you can rent **bikes** from several places downtown – the cheapest is Cicli Cortina on Via Majon 148 (℡0436.867.215; €25 a day). **Internet** facilites are available at *Videoteca Piller* at Via C. Battisti 43 or at the *Aquila* hotel opposite the pharmacy on Corso Italia.

Accommodation

The bad news is that **staying** in Cortina is expensive: prices climb exponentially in August and during the peak ski season. However, the tourist board has a list of **rooms to rent**, and in summer there's the option of **camping** at one of several well-equipped sites, all with bar and shop. Try *Olympia,* 5km north at Fiames (℡0436.5057, 🌐www.campingolympiacortina.it; €24 per tent), which also has a swimming pool, and *Rochetta*, 2km south of Cortina at Campo (℡0436.5063, 🌐www.campingrocchetta.it; €24 per tent).

Hotel de La Poste Piazza Roma 14
℡0436.42.71, 🌐www.delaposte.it. This upmarket, atmospheric hotel could not be more cental on the square opposite the church. The sweeping marble corridors enhance the decadent feel. ⑥
Hotel Villa Resy Via Riva 50 ℡0436.3303, 🌐www.cortina.dolomiti.org/villaresy. A twenty-minute walk from the centre along the charming, well-lit passeggiata, this friendly hotel has simply decorated, but characterful rooms, some with balconies – just make sure you ask for one away from the main road – and there's a relaxing garden

and a great bar and restaurant, *Smokey Joe* (see opposite) on site. ④
🏃 **Lago Ghedina** 5km west of the village
℡0436.860.876, 🌐www.cortinadampezzo.it/lagoghedina. If you really want to get away from it all, stay at this magical restaurant and *pensionè* situated by a lake that reflects the Dolomite mountains, surrounded by tall firs. From the lake, you can eat the delicious fresh trout for dinner. ⑤
Menardi Via Majon 110 ℡0436.24.00, 🌐www.hotelmenardi.it. Family-run hotel in an old farm, 2km from the village. €115 per person, half board only.

Eating and drinking

Eating choices in downtown Cortina are somewhat limited, with most of the restaurants attached to hotels. Several good cafés serve simple but tasty local fare. *Ai due forni* at Via C. Battisti 18 is a decent pizza place with takeaway by the slice, and there's also an excellent supermarket, *Cooperativa* (closed Sun except in high season) on Corso Italia in the centre of town.

Bar Dolomiti Via Roma 50. A café perfect for people-watching on the main pedestrian high street.

Ciarlis Largo Delle Poste 35. A slow food restaurant that morphs into a disco most nights in high season and at weekends during the rest of the year.

Leone y Anna 2km out of town on Alverà 112 ☏ 0436.2768. Perfectly executed

Sardinian cuisine in a great chalet atmosphere. Try *malureddus*, home-made dumplings with tomato and Sardinian salami sauce.

Smokey Joe 5km west of the village. Serving local specialities such as *casunziei all'ampezzana*, or beetroot ravioli.

Around Cortina

Cortina is better known for trips by road and cable car than for mountain trails, with many drivers heading for the **Great Dolomites Road** (a scenic route between Cortina and Bolzano) and its passes. In summer there are buses to the small lake at **Misurina** (3 or 4 daily) and to the **Tre Cime di Lavaredo**, three extraordinary mountain peaks to the northeast of the city – both extremely busy areas in high season.

One of the alternatives is to head south by bus towards Belluno in the Veneto, passing through Titian's home town of **PIEVE DI CADORE**, with many paintings attributed to him and his family in the Parrocchiale. The one most likely to be authentic is in the third chapel on the left, and the altarpiece of the Last Supper, by his cousin Cesare, is rather fine. **Titian's birthplace** is represented by a stone and wood house on Via Arsenale (late June to mid-Sept Tues–Sun 10am–12.30pm & 3–7pm; €2). Although it has been equipped with furniture and a fireplace from the fifteenth century, the present structure dates from the 1800s.

The most comfortable of Pieve di Cadore's inexpensive **hotels** is *Sporting*, Piazza Municipio 21 (☏0435.31.262; ❸); the **tourist office** (Mon–Wed & Fri–Sat 9am–12.30pm & 3.30–6.30pm, Sun 10am–12.30pm; ☏0435.31.644, ⓦwww.infodolomiti.it), just down the road in a village called **TAI DI CADORE**, has the full list of accommodation. Among the handful of cafés and **bars**, *Caffè Tiziano* (closed Mon), in the vaults of the old Palazzo della Magnifica Comunità Cadorina, offers snacks, great cocktails and pool on full-size tables.

Cable cars connect Cortina to Faloria (€15), Mandres (€8), Col Druscié (€12), Ra Valles (€18) and Tofana (€24); prices are for a return trip – for a single journey, estimate about three-quarters of the fare.

Alleghe and Monte Civetta

Without your own vehicle, it can be difficult to reach the most interesting mountains in these parts. One place you can get to by bus is the small village of **ALLEGHE**. The lake here was created after a huge rock avalanche in the eighteenth century – a common occurrence in the area. Now a peaceful summer and winter resort, Alleghe borders the northeastern edge of the lake, its aquamarine waters reflecting the pine forests around. Towering above is Monte Civetta, essentially Alleghe's main attraction, and the village makes a good base in between walks or climbs. The best of several two-star **hotels** in Alleghe is the central *La Nava*, Corso Italia 43 (☏0437.523.340; ❸), in a good position right by the lake. Also lakeside, but rather more upmarket, is the three-star *Savoia* (☏0437.523.323; ❸), with its own garden and sun loungers available to guests. *Camping Alleghe*, 2km away at Masarè (☏0437.732.737; June–Sept & Dec–April), is open for the summer and skiing. **Places to eat** in town include *Enoteca Alleghe*, a great wine bar with good, reasonably priced local cuisine on Piazza J.F. Kennedy (closed Tues); don't miss the cakes and strudel at the *pasticceria* on the same square. Here you'll also find the **tourist office** (Mon–Sat

9am–12.30pm & 3.30–6.30pm, July & Aug Sun same hours; ℡0437.523.333), geared up to provide information on cable cars and difficulty of footpaths; it also sometimes has English-language guides to the *alta via* routes.

For trips around the lake, the *Hotel Alleghe* at the bottom of town rents out mountain **bikes** at reasonable rates. But the classic trip from Alleghe is the walk up to **Monte Civetta**, or Owl Mountain: from Fontanive just above the village take footpath 564 all the way up through steep meadows and summer pastures until you join Alta Via 1 at the Pian dei Sech. From here it's a last haul (about an hour) to *Rifugio Sonino* at Coldai (also signposted as *Rifugio Coldai*; ℡0437.789.160; late June to mid-Sept) at 2132m. If avoiding the three- or four-hour slog up the mountain appeals, then take the **cable car** from the town to Piani di Pezze and the **chair lift** from here to Col dei Baldi (July–Aug daily 8.30am–5.30pm; €9 return). If you're lucky enough to be at the Col on a clear evening, head for Lago Coldai just beyond the refuge for views of the great rock wall of Civetta, rippling with rock chimneys and pipes, glowing red in the sunset.

Hardened hikers can continue on Alta Via 1; the next day takes you across small snowfields and past windows in the rock that offer dizzying glimpses of the valley and the Dolomite groups. A couple of hours from Coldai, *Rifugio Tissi* is perched improbably on an incline, on a vast slab of rock, and is cheerfully shambolic, with accommodation available (℡0437.721.644; late June to mid-Sept). From here you can continue on Alta Via 1, past *Rifugio Vazzoler* down to Listolade in the valley (5hr; hourly buses to Alleghe), or head straight down the steep trail 563 for three hours to Masare (20min walk from Alleghe), dipping your feet in a waterfall on the way.

Travel details

Trains

Bolzano to: Bressanone (23 daily; 30min); Merano (16 daily; 40min); Trento (32 daily; 1hr or 29min express); Vipiteno (12 daily; 55min).
Brunico to: Dobbiaco (16 daily; 30min).
Fortezza to: Brunico (16 daily; 35min); Dobbiaco (16 daily; 1hr).
Trento to: Bologna (20 daily; 4hr 15min or 2hr 15min express); Bolzano (31 daily; 35min); Cles (Trento-Malé line; 13 daily; 1hr); Malé (Trento-Malé line; 13 daily; 1hr 10min); Rovereto (32 daily; 13min); Venice (27 daily; 3hr 40min or 2hr 30min express); Verona (30 daily; 1hr 5min).

Buses

Note that buses are significantly less frequent on Saturdays, and rare on Sundays and public holidays.
Bolzano to: Alpe di Suisi (2 daily; 1hr 20min); Canazei (4 daily; 3hr 10min or 1hr 45min express); Corvara (7 daily; 3hr 35min or 2hr 40min express); Fiè (26 daily; 30min); Merano (9 daily; 1hr); Predazzo (7 daily; 2hr); Selva (16 daily; 1hr 15min);

Siusi (every 30min; 40min); Vigo di Fassa (3 daily; 1hr 20min).
Bressanone to: Brunico (29 daily; 50min); San Pietro (4 daily; 40min); Santa Maddalena (4 daily; 45min); Siusi (9 daily; 40min).
Brunico to: Bressanone (29 daily; 50min); Campo Túres (33 daily; 30min); Corvara (11 daily; 1hr 10min); Dobbiaco (12 daily; 40min); Plan de Corones cable-car terminal (2 daily; 15min); San Vigilio di Marebbe (6 daily; 35min); Siusi (10 daily; 3hr 56min or 1hr 50min express).
Cortina d'Ampezzo to: Belluno (6 daily; 2hr); Calalzo (10 daily; 1hr); Dobbiaco (6 daily; 45min); Pieve di Cadore (10 daily; 50min).
Corvara to: Belluno (2 daily; 2hr 45min); Longega (11 daily; 45min).
Dobbiaco to: Brunico (12 daily; 40min); Cortina d'Ampezzo (6 daily; 45min); Lago Bráies (5 daily; 23min); Villabassa (18 daily; 5min).
Fiera di Primiero to: Passo di Cereda (1–2 daily; 25min).
Merano to: Katharinaberg (5 daily; 1hr 10min); Moso (at least hourly; 1hr 10min); Passo Stelvio (3 daily; 3hr); San Gertrude (8 daily; 1hr 25min);

San Leonardo (25 daily; 50min); Silandro (30 daily; 1hr 5min); Solda (2 daily; 2hr 40min).

San Martino di Castrozza to: Feltre, Veneto (8 daily; 1hr 20min); Fiera di Primiero (8 daily; 30min); Imer (8 daily; 40min); Predazzo (2 daily; 1hr).

Siusi to: Ortisei (12 daily; 30min–1hr 30min); Santa Cristina (17 daily; 1hr 45min or 45min express); Selva (17 daily; 1hr 45min or 45min express); Tires (7 daily; 40min).

Trento to: Belluno (1 daily; 2hr 40min); Canazei (2 daily, bus and train connection; 2hr 45min); Fiera di Primiero (6 daily, bus and train connection; 2hr); Madonna di Campiglio (12 daily; 2hr 15min); Molveno (9 daily; 1hr 40min); Predazzo (6 daily; 1hr 45min); Rovereto (hourly; 40min); San Martino di Castrozza (6 daily, bus and train connection; 2hr 15min); Tione (11 daily; 1hr); Vigo di Fassa (6 daily; 2hr 15min).

Venice and
the Veneto

CHAPTER 5 # Highlights

* **San Marco, Venice** San Marco is an amazing sight with its 4000 square metres of golden mosaics – all you have to work out is how to beat the queues. See p.327

* **Itinerari Segreti del Palazzo Ducale** A fascinating tour that takes you behind the scenes of Venice's superb Gothic palace. See p.333

* **The Accademia** Masterpieces by Titian, Bellini, Veronese and Tintoretto feature strongly in the world's best collection of Venetian painting. See p.336

* **Giotto frescoes** Giotto's frescoes in Padua's Cappella degli Scrovegni constitute one of the pivotal works in the history of European art. See p.374

* **Vicenza** The well-heeled city of Vicenza is renowned above all for the buildings of Palladio, perhaps the most influential architect ever. See p.379

* **Verona** Cradled in a wide curve of the Adige river, Verona is a fabulously handsome city. See p.385

* **Carnivals** Venice's carnival is famous for its costumes and crowds, but if you want a more local event, head for Verona, where the whole town turns out for a procession of more than eighty floats. See p.395

△ Venetian gondola, under Rialto Bridge

5

Venice and
the Veneto

T he first-time visitor to **Venice** arrives with a heavy freight of expectations, most of which turn out to be well founded. All the photographs
you've seen of the Palazzo Ducale, of the Basilica di San Marco, of the
palaces along the Canal Grande – they've simply been recording the
extraordinary truth. All the bad things you've heard about the city turn out
to be right as well. Economically and socially ossified, it is losing hundreds of

Regional food and wine

The Veneto vies with Lombardy for the risotto-making crown, while Venice specializes
in fish and **seafood**, together with exotic ingredients like pomegranates, pine nuts
and raisins, harking back to its days as a port and merchant city. The **risottos** tend
to be more liquid than those to the west, usually with a seafood base although peas
(*bisi* in the local dialect) are also common, as are other seasonal vegetables including
spinach, asparagus and pumpkin. The red salad leaf raddichio also has its home in
the Veneto, as does the renowned Italian dessert, **tiramisù**. Polenta is eaten too, while
pork in all forms features strongly, together with heavy **soups** of beans, rice and root
vegetables. Gnocchi tend to be served in an unusual sweet-sour sauce.

Pastries and **sweets** are also an area of Venetian expertise. Look out for the thin
oval biscuits called *baicoli*, the ring-shaped cinnamon-flavoured *bussolai* (a speciality of the Venetian island of Burano) and *mandolato*, a cross between nougat and
toffee, made with almonds. The Austrian occupation left its mark in the form of the
ubiquitous strudel and the cream- or jam-filled *krapfen* (doughnuts).

The Veneto has been very successful at developing **wines** with French and German
grape varieties, notably Merlot, Cabernet, Pinot Bianco, Pinot Grigio, Müller-Thurgau,
Riesling, Chardonnay and Gewürztraminer. The quintessentially Italian Bardolino,
Valpolicella and Soave are all from the Verona region and, like so many Italian wines,
taste better near their region of origin. This is also true of the more rarely exported
Prosecco, a light champagne-like wine from the area around Conegliano: don't miss
the chance to sample Prosecco Rosé and the delicious Cartizze, the finest type of
Prosecco. Grappa, the local firewater, is associated particularly with the upland town
of Bassano di Grappa, where every *alimentari* is stocked with a dozen varieties. Made
from grape husks, juniper berries or plums, grappa is very much an acquired taste,
but beware – the acquisition can be a damaging process.

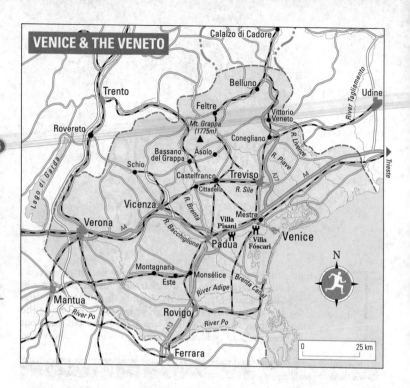

VENICE & THE VENETO

Calalzo di Cadore

Belluno

Trento

Feltre

Udine

River Tagliamento

Vittorio
Veneto

Mt. Grappa
(1775m)

Rovereto

Conegliano

R. Livenza

Bassano
del Grappa

Ásolo

Schio

Castelfranco

Treviso

A27

R. Piave

Cittadella

R. Sile

A4

Vicenza

R. Brenta

R. Bacchiglione

Mestre

Villa
Pisani

Verona

A4

Padua

Villa
Fóscari

Venice

N

Montagnana

Monsélice

Este

Brenta Canal

Mantua

River Adige

River Po

Rovigo

River Po

Lago di Garda

A13

Ferrara

0   25 km

▶ Trieste

people by the year and playing virtually no part in the life of modern Italy. It's deluged with tourists – the annual influx exceeding Venice's population two-hundredfold – and occasionally things get so bad that entry into the city is barred to those who haven't already booked a room. And it's expensive – the price of a good meal almost anywhere else in Italy will get you a lousy one in Venice, and its hoteliers make the most of a situation where demand will always far outstrip supply.

As soon as you begin to explore Venice, though, every day will bring its surprises, for this is an urban landscape so rich that you can't walk for a minute without coming across something that's worth a stop. And although it's true that the city can be unbearably crowded, things aren't so bad beyond the magnetic field of San Marco and the kitsch-sellers of the vicinity, and in the off-season (October to Christmas and January to Easter, excluding Carnevale) it's even possible to have parts of the centre virtually to yourself. As for keeping your costs down, Venice has plenty of markets in addition to the celebrated Rialto, there are some good-value eating places, and you can, with planning, find a bed without spending a fortune.

Tourism is far from being the only strand to the economy of the **Veneto**, however. The rich, flat land around the Po supports some of Italy's most productive farms and vineyards, and industrial development around the main towns rivals even the better-known areas around Milan, making the region one of the richest in Europe. At Marghera, just over the lagoon from Venice, the Veneto has the largest industrial complex in the country, albeit one that is now in decline. But tourism is important, and the region has more tourist accommodation than any other in Italy. After Venice, it's **Padua** and **Verona** that are the main attractions, with their masterpieces by Giotto, Donatello and Mantegna and a profusion of great buildings from Roman times to the Renaissance. None of the other towns of the Veneto can match the cultural wealth of these two former rivals to Venice, but there are nonetheless plenty of places between the plains of Polésine in the south and the mountains in the north that justify a detour – the Palladian city of **Vicenza**, for instance, the fortified settlements of **Castelfranco** and **Cittadella**, and the idyllic upland town of **Ásolo**.

For outdoor types, much of the Veneto is dull, consisting of flatlands interrupted by gentle outcrops around Padua and Vicenza. The interesting terrain lies in its northern part, especially in the area above **Belluno** and **Vittorio Veneto**, where the wooded slopes of the foothills – excellent for walking – soon give way to the savage precipices of the eastern Dolomites. Because most of the high peaks of the Dolomites lie within Trentino-Alto Adige, and the mountains of the eastern Dolomites are most easily explored as part of a tour of the range as a whole, the area of the Veneto to the north of Belluno is covered in the "Trentino-Alto Adige" chapter. Similarly, the eastern shore of Lago di Garda is covered as part of the lakes region in the "Lombardy and the Lakes" chapter.

Venice (Venezia)

The monuments that draw the largest crowds in Venice are the **Basilica di San Marco** – the mausoleum of the city's patron saint – and the **Palazzo Ducale** – the home of the doge and all the governing councils. Certainly these are the most dramatic structures in the city: the first a mosaic-clad emblem of Venice's Byzantine origins, the second perhaps the finest of all secular Gothic buildings. But every parish rewards exploration, and a roll-call of the churches worth visiting would feature over fifty names, and a list of the important paintings and sculptures they contain would be twice as long. Two of the distinctively Venetian institutions known as the **scuole** retain some of the outstanding examples of Italian Renaissance art – the **Scuola di San Rocco**, with its sequence of pictures by Tintoretto, and the **Scuola di San Giorgio degli Schiavoni**, decorated with a gorgeous sequence by Carpaccio.

Although many of the city's treasures remain in the buildings for which they were created, a sizeable number have been removed to one or other of Venice's **museums**. The one that should not be missed is the **Accademia**, an assembly of Venetian painting that consists of virtually nothing but masterpieces; other prominent collections include the museum of eighteenth-century art in the **Ca'Rezzonico**, and the **Museo Correr**, the civic museum of Venice – but again, a comprehensive list would fill a page.

The cultural heritage preserved in the museums and churches is a source of endless fascination, but you should discard your worthy itineraries for a day and just wander – the anonymous parts of Venice reveal as much of the city's essence as the highlighted attractions. And equally indispensable for a full understanding of Venice's way of life and development are expeditions to the

northern and southern islands of the lagoon, where the incursions of the tourist industry are on the whole less obtrusive.

A brief history

Small groups of fishermen and hunters were living on the mudbanks of the Venetian lagoon at the start of the Christian era, but it was with the barbarian invasions of the fifth century that sizeable communities began to settle on the mudbanks. The first mass migration was provoked by the arrival in the Veneto of **Attila the Hun**'s hordes in 453, and the rate of settlement accelerated a century later, when, in 568, the **Lombards** swept into northern Italy.

The loose confederation of island communes that began to develop in the sixth century owed political allegiance to Byzantium, and until the end of the seventh century its senior officials were effectively controlled by the Byzantine hierarchy of Ravenna. But with the steep increase in the population of the islands that resulted from the strengthening of the Lombard grip on the Veneto in the later seventh century, the ties with the empire grew weaker, and in 726 the settlers chose their own leader of the provincial government – the first **doge**.

The control of Byzantium soon became no more than nominal, and the inhabitants of the lagoon signalled their independence through one great symbolic act – the theft of the body of **St Mark** from Alexandria in 828. St Mark displaced Byzantium's St Theodore as the city's patron, and a basilica was built alongside the doge's castle to accommodate the relics. These two buildings – the **Basilica di San Marco** and the **Palazzo Ducale** – were to remain the emblems of the Venetian state and the repository of power within the city for almost one thousand years.

Before the close of the tenth century the Venetian **trading networks** were well established through concessions granted by Byzantium in the markets of the East and the exploitation of the waterways of northern Italy to distribute the goods from the Levant. By the early twelfth century Venetian merchants had won exemption from all tolls within the eastern empire and were profiting from the chaos that followed the **First Crusade**, which had been launched in 1095. Prosperity found expression in the fabric of the city: the present-day basilica and many of its mosaics are from this period; and at the end of the century the Piazza was brought to something close to its modern shape. The **Fourth Crusade**, diverted to Constantinople by the Venetians, set the seal on their maritime empire. They brought back shiploads of treasure (including the horses of San Marco) from the **Sack of Constantinople** in 1204, but more significant was the division of the territorial spoils, which left "one quarter and half a quarter" of the Roman Empire under Venice's sway and gave the Republic a chain of ports that stretched almost without a break from the lagoon to the Black Sea.

Venetian foreign policy was predominantly eastward-looking from the start, but a degree of intervention on the mainland was necessary to maintain its continental trade routes. By the middle of the fifteenth century, Venice was in possession of a mainland empire that was to survive virtually intact until the coming of Napoleon. But while Venice was advancing at home, the **Ottoman Turks** were emerging as a threat to the colonial empire. Constantinople fell to the Sultan's army in 1453, and with their capture of the main fortresses of the Morea (Peloponnese) in 1499, the Turks gained control of the access to the Adriatic.

After the **Sack of Rome** in 1527 the whole Italian peninsula, with the sole exception of Venice, came under the domination of Emperor Charles V. Hemmed in at home, Venice saw its overseas territory further whittled away by the Turks as the century progressed: by 1529 the Ottoman Empire extended right along the southern Mediterranean to Morocco, and even the great naval success at **Lépanto** in **1571** was quickly followed by the surrender of Cyprus.

The decline continued throughout the 1600s and by the eighteenth century Venice had become a political nonentity, reduced to pursuing a policy of unarmed neutrality. Politically moribund and constitutionally ossified, Venice was renowned not as one of the great powers of Europe, but rather as its playground, a city of casinos and perpetual festivals. **Napoleon** brought the show to an end. On May 12, 1797, the Maggior Consiglio met for the last time, voting to accede to Napoleon's demand that it dismantle the machinery of government. In October, Napoleon relinquished Venice to the Austrians, but returned in 1805 to join the city to his Kingdom of Italy, and it stayed under French rule until after Waterloo. It then passed back to the Austrians and remained a Habsburg province until united with the Kingdom of Italy in 1866.

It was the need for a more substantial economic base that led, in the wake of World War I, to the construction of the industrial complex on the marshland across the lagoon from Venice, at **Marghera**, a processing and refining centre to which raw materials would be brought by sea. In 1933 a road link was built to carry the workforce between Venice and the steadily expanding complex, but it was not until after World War II that Marghera's growth accelerated. The factories of Marghera are essential to the economy of the province, but they have caused terrible problems too: apart from polluting the environment of the lagoon, they have siphoned many people out of Venice and into the cheaper housing of Mestre, making Mestre-Marghera today more than three times larger than the historic centre of Venice, where the population has dropped since World War II from around 170,000 to about 80,000. No city has suffered more from the tourist industry than Venice – about ten million people visit the city each year, and around half of those don't even stay a night – though without them Venice would barely survive at all.

Arrival

Arriving **by air**, you'll touch down in one of two airports: **Treviso**, 30km inland, or at Venice's Marco Polo airport. The former is used chiefly by charter companies, many of whom provide a bus link from the airport into Venice – the ATVO bus that meets Ryanair flights, for example, costs €5 single and takes 1hr 10min. If such a service isn't provided, take the #6 bus (tickets from the bar across the road or from the driver) from right outside the arrivals building into Treviso (20min), from where there are regular bus and train connections to Venice.

Most **scheduled** flights and some charters arrive at the recently enlarged and smartened **Marco Polo**, around 7km north of Venice, on the edge of the lagoon. If you're on a package holiday, the cost of transport to the city centre, either by land or by water, might already be covered. If it's not, the most inexpensive transport is provided by the two road-going **bus services** to the terminal at Piazzale Roma: the ATVO (*Azienda Trasporti Veneto Orientale*) coach, which departs every half-hour and takes around twenty minutes (€3), or the ACTV (*Azienda del Consorzio Trasporti Veneziano*; Ⓦwww.actv.it) bus #5/5D, which is equally frequent, usually takes just five minutes longer (it's a local bus service, so it picks up and puts down passengers between the airport and Piazzale Roma), and costs €2. If you'd prefer to approach the city by water, you could take one of Alilaguna **water buses**, which operate on three routes, all taking about

Madonna
dell'Orto

Ghetto

CANNAREGIO

Tronchetto
Car Park

Train Station

CANAL GRANDE

Ca'
d'Oro

SANTA CROCE

Rialto

Piazzale Roma
(Car Park &
Bus Station)

CAMPO
S. POLO

Stazione
Marittima

Rio Nuovo

Frari

SAN POLO

S. Rocco

Rio Fóscari

SAN
MARCO

CAMPO
S. MARGHERITA

CAMPO
S.STEFANO

Ca' Rezzonico

S. M.
del Giglio

DORSODURO

S. Sebastiano

Accademia

Salute

Guggenheim
Collection

Redentore

La Giudecca

an hour to reach San Marco: Murano (€6) – Lido – Arsenale – San Marco
– Záttere (all €11; service hourly 6.15am–12.15am); Murano – Fondamente
Nove (€6) – Lido – San Zaccaria – San Marco (hourly 9.45am–11.45pm); and
directly to San Zaccaria and then San Marco (hourly 9.30am–5.30pm). Ticket
offices for water buses and land buses are in the arrivals hall; in addition to single
tickets, you can also get ACTV passes and Venice Cards here (see p.317) – a wise
investment for almost all visitors. There's also a ticket machine right by the #5
bus stop, but you'll need the exact change for it. Note that ACTV passes are not
valid on the Alilaguna service nor on the ATVO bus.

The most luxurious way to arrive is by **water taxi**, which offers the best
views of the city – and you can't beat the thrill of arriving at the water door

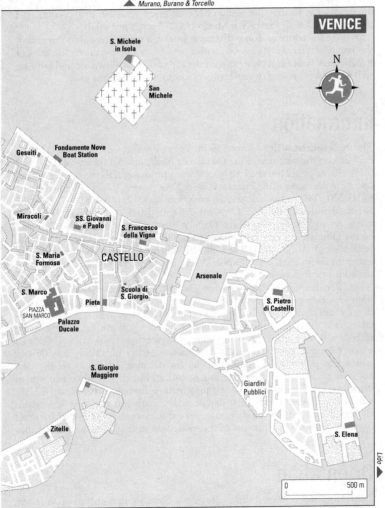

of a hotel by taxi. The drivers tout for business in and around the arrivals hall and will charge around €90 for up to six people. Ordinary **car taxis** are ranked outside the arrivals hall, and cost about €35 to Piazzale Roma, site of the Venice bus terminal.

Visitors arriving **by car** must leave their vehicle either on the mainland or in one of the city's car parks – at Piazzale Roma or the ever-expanding Tronchetto, Europe's largest car park. Prices at these two vary according to the time of year, the length of stay and the size of car, but it's never a cheap option, and in summer the tailbacks can be horrendous. It's better to use either the less expensive open-air San Giuliano car park at **Mestre** on the mainland (open summer, Easter and during the Carnevale), linked by ACTV buses with central Venice, or the terminal at **Fusina**, just south of Mestre (open year-round) and connected by water buses with Piazza San Marco (ACTV passes not valid).

Arriving **by train or long-distance bus**, you simply get off at the end of the line. The Piazzale Roma bus station and Santa Lucia train station are just five minutes' walk from each other, at the top of the Canal Grande, and both are well served by *vaporetto* (water-bus) services to the core of the city.

Information

The main **tourist office** – known as the Venice Pavilion – occupies the Palazzina del Santi, on the west side of the Giardinetti Reali, within a minute of the Piazza (daily 10am–6pm; ☎041.529.8711, ⓦ www.turismovenezia.it); smaller offices operate in the corner of the Piazza at Calle dell'Ascensione 71/f (daily 9am–3.30pm; ☎041.520.8740), at the train station (daily 8am–6.30pm; ☎041.529.8727), in the airport arrivals area (Mon–Sat 9.30am–7.30pm; ☎041.541.5887), at the multi-storey car park at Piazzale Roma (daily 9.30am–6.30pm; ☎041.529.8746) and on the Lido at Gran Viale S.M. Elisabetta 6 (June–Sept daily 9.30am–12.30pm & 3.30–6pm; ☎041.526.5721). The Calle dell'Ascensione office is also the city's main outlet for information on the whole Veneto. These offices produce free listings of museums, exhibitions and concerts.

The free English–Italian magazine *Un Ospite di Venezia* (ⓦ www.unospite divenezia.it), produced fortnightly in summer and monthly in winter, gives slightly fuller information on special events, plus extras such as *vaporetto* time-tables; it is distributed through upmarket hotels – just ask for a copy at the reception desk. For listings of nightlife and events the bimonthly *Venezia da Vivere* (ⓦ www.veneziadavivere.it) is useful, as is the bimonthly *Leo Bussola*, which also publishes interesting articles (in Italian and English) on the city; both are available free from the tourist offices, but they tend to run out of stock quickly. The fullest source of information, though, is *VE:News* (€2.20), which is published on the first day of each month and is sold at newsstands all over the city; it has good coverage of exhibitions, cultural events, bars and restaurants, with a fair amount of text presented in English as well as Italian.

Orientation

The 118 islands of central Venice are divided into six districts known as *sestieri*, and the houses within each *sestiere* are numbered in a sequence that makes sense solely to the functionaries of the post office – this explains how buildings facing each other across an alleyway can have numbers that are separated by hundreds.

Venice's main thoroughfare is the **Canal Grande**. Almost four kilometres long and between thirty and seventy metres wide (but at no point much deeper than five metres), it divides the city in half – three *sestieri* to the west and three to the east. The majority of the most important palaces in Venice stand on the Canal Grande, and the main facades of all of them are on the canalside, many properly visible only from the water.

On the east side of the Canal Grande is the *sestiere* of **San Marco**, the zone where the majority of the essential sights are clustered, and accordingly the most expensive and most crowded district of the city. To the east is **Castello**, and on the north is **Cannaregio** – both of which become more residential, and poorer and quieter, the further you get from the centre. On the other side of the Canal

The Venice and Rolling Venice cards

The **Venice Card** comes in two forms and is valid for either one, three or seven days, with a discount for the under-30s. The **blue** card (1-day €17, €15 with discount; 3-day €34/€30; 7-day €52/€47) gives unlimited use of all ACTV public transport, and free access to some public toilets, most usefully those at Piazzale Roma, Campo San Bartolomeo, the Piazza (off the west side) and the Giardinetti Reali (by the tourist office). The **orange** card (1-day €29/€22; 3-day €54/€45; 7-day €76/€67) in addition gives free access to all the museums covered by the Museum Pass and the Chorus Pass (see p.326). For a €20 supplement you can buy a version of the blue and orange cards that's valid on Alilaguna services to and from the airport. Note that children under 6 get free museum entrance but only under-4s get free travel on public transport – so an orange card for an under-6-year-old is a pointless investment. You can buy Venice Cards from the tourist offices, the VeLa/ACTV offices at the airport, train station and Piazzale Roma, and the Alilaguna desk at the airport. Alternatively, you can order the card a minimum of 48 hours in advance on ⓦ www.venicecard.it (which gives a discount of up to €2.50) or by calling ⓣ 899.909.090 (within Italy – it's a free number) or ⓣ 00.39.041.2424 (from abroad). You will be given a code number which you will need to present when you turn up to collect your ticket from any of the offices listed above.

If you're aged between 14 and 29, you are eligible for a **Rolling Venice** card, which entitles you to discounts at some shops, restaurants, hostels, campsites, museums, concerts and exhibitions, plus a discount on the 72-hour ACTV travel pass; details are given in a leaflet that comes with the card. The card costs €5, is valid until the end of the year in which it's bought, and is worth buying if you're in town for at least a week and aim to make the most of every minute. The tourist offices and ACTV/VeLa offices issue it, on production of a passport or similar ID.

Grande, the largest of the *sestieri* is Dorsoduro, stretching from the fashionable quarter at the southern tip of the canal to the docks in the west. **Santa Croce**, named after a now-demolished church, roughly follows the curve of the Canal Grande from Piazzale Roma to a point just short of the Rialto, where it joins the smartest and commercially most active of the districts on this bank – **San Polo**.

City transport

Venice has two interlocking street systems, the canals and the pavements, and contrary to what you might expect, you'll be using the latter most of the time. In general, the speediest way of **getting around** is on foot – distances between major sights are extremely short and you can cross the whole city in an hour. However, you will want to get on to the water at least once during your trip and a fairly comprehensive system of water-based transport exists to accommodate this and to get you to further-flung places. Services are run by ACTV (ⓦ www.actv.it).

The water buses

Apart from the #1 and #82 and a couple of other peak-time services, which cut through the city along the Canal Grande, water buses skirt the city centre, connecting points on the periphery and the outer islands. There are two basic types of boat: the **vaporetti**, which are the lumbering workhorses used on the Canal Grande stopping service and other heavily used routes, and the

motoscafi, smaller vessels employed on routes where the volume of traffic isn't as great. The standard **fare** is €5 for a single journey; the ticket is valid for sixty minutes. Should you have more than one piece of large luggage, you're supposed to pay €5 per additional item. Children under 4 travel free on all water buses. **Tickets** are available from most landing stages, from *tabacchi*, from shops displaying the ACTV sign, from the tourist offices, and the ACTV office at Piazzale Roma (daily: summer 6am–midnight; winter 6am–8pm). Tickets can also be bought on board at the standard price, as long as you ask the attendant as soon as you get on board; if you delay, you could be liable for a €30 spot-fine on top of the fare.

Unless you intend to walk all day, you'll almost certainly save money by buying some sort of **travel card** as soon as you arrive. ACTV produces a **24-hour** ticket (€12) and a **72-hour** ticket (€25), which can be used on all ACTV services within Venice (including ACTV land buses from the airport). For seven days of unrestricted travel, you have to buy a Venice Card (see box, p.317).

If you buy one of these unrestricted travel tickets at the train station or Piazzale Roma, the train station, San Zaccaria or San Marco it will be automatically **validated** with a time-stamp unless you specifically request a

Water bus routes

What follows is a run-through of the **water bus routes** that visitors are most likely to find useful; a fully comprehensive (and free) timetable can usually be picked at the major *vaporetto* stops: Piazzale Roma, Ferrovia, San Marco, San Zaccaria, Accademia, Fondamente Nove. Be warned that so many services call at San Marco, San Zaccaria, Rialto and the train station that the stops at these points are spread out over a long stretch of waterfront, so you might have to walk past several stops before finding the one you need. Note that the main San Marco stop is also known as San Marco Vallaresso, or plain Vallaresso, and that the San Zaccaria stop is as close to the Basilica as is the Vallaresso stop.

#1: The #1 is the workhorse of the system, and the one you'll use most often; it's also one of the very few routes that seems to be exempt from alterations. It starts at the Piazzale Roma, calls at every stop on the Canal Grande except San Samuele, works its way along the San Marco waterfront to Sant'Elena, then goes over to the Lido. The #1 runs every 20min between 5 and 6.30am, every 10min between 6.30am and 9.45pm, and every 20min between 9.45 and 11.45pm. For the night service, see #N.

#3: The quickest service down the Canal Grande, running every 20min from Tronchetto to San Marco between 8.30am and 12.50pm, calling at Piazzale Roma, Ferrovia, San Samuele and Accademia en route.

#82: The #82 is in effect a speeded-up version of the #1, as it makes fewer stops on the Canal Grande. Its clockwise route takes it from San Zaccaria to San Giorgio Maggiore, Giudecca (Zitelle, Redentore and Palanca), Záttere, San Basilio, Sacca Fisola, Tronchetto, Piazzale Roma, the train station, then down the Canal Grande (usually calling at Rialto, Sant'Angelo, San Tomà, San Samuele and Accademia; from around 4–8pm it calls at San Marcuola) to San Marco (Vallaresso); the anti-clockwise version calls at the same stops. From Monday to Friday the #82 runs along most of the route (in both directions) every 10min from 6am to 8.30pm, then every 20min until 11pm, but for the section between Rialto and San Marco the bus runs only every 20min through the day and is even less frequent before 8am and after 8.30pm; at weekends the #82 runs every 20min for the whole route. In summer the #82 is extended from San Zaccaria to the Lido. For the night service see #N.

#41/42: The circular service, running right round the core of Venice, with a short detour at the northern end to San Michele and Murano. The #41 travels non-validated one; the same goes for ordinary tickets. When using a **non-validated** ticket or pass (such as the Venice Card) you must validate it before embarking, by inserting it into one of the machines at the entrance to the vaporetto stop or on board the bus; the ticket is valid from that moment, and you need to validate it just once.

Traghetti

Pending completion of the much-delayed Calatrava bridge that's planned for Piazzale Roma, there are only three bridges on the Canal Grande – at the train station, Rialto and Accademia – so the **traghetti** (gondola ferries) that cross it can be useful time-savers. Costing just €0.50, they are also the only cheap way of getting a ride on a gondola – though it's *de rigueur* to stand in a *traghetto* rather than sit. Routes are: San Marco–Salute; Santa Maria del Giglio–Salute; San Barnaba–San Samuele; San Tomà–Santo Stefano; Riva del Carbon–Riva del Vin (near Rialto); Santa Sofia–Pescerìa; San Marcuola–Fondaco dei Turchi; train station–San Simeone. All *traghetti* run Mon–Sat from early morning to noon, while those on the routes Santa Maria del Giglio–Salute, San Tomà–Santo

anticlockwise, the #42 clockwise and both run every 20min from 6.30am until around 8pm; after that, the #41/42 together act as a shuttle service between Murano and Fondamente Nove, running every 20min until around 11.30pm.

#51/52: Similar to the #41/42, this route also circles Venice, but heads out to the Lido (rather than Murano) at the easternmost end of the circle. The #51 runs anticlockwise, the #52 clockwise, and both run fast through the Giudecca canal, stopping only at Záttere and Santa Marta between San Zaccaria and Piazzale Roma. Both run every 20min for most of the day. In the early morning and late evening (4.30–6am & 8.30–11pm) the #51 doesn't do a complete lap of the city – instead it departs every 20min from Fondamenta Nove and proceeds via the train station to the Lido, where it terminates; similarly, from about 8–11pm the #52 (which starts operating at 6am) shuttles between the Lido and Fondamente Nove in the opposite direction, and from 11pm to around 12.20am goes no farther than the train station.

#LN: For most of the day the "Laguna Nord" runs every half-hour from Fondamente Nove (approximately hourly from 7.40pm to 11.20pm), calling first at Murano-Faro before heading on to Mazzorbo, Burano (from where there is a connecting half-hourly **#T** shuttle to Torcello), Treporti, Punta Sabbioni, the Lido and San Zaccaria (the Pietà stop); it runs with the same frequency in the opposite direction.

#DM: From around 8am to 6pm the "Diretto Murano" runs from Tronchetto via Piazzale Roma and Ferrovia to Murano, where it always calls at Colonna and Museo, and often at other Murano stops too.

#N: This night service (11.30pm–4.30am) is a selective fusion of the #1 and #82 routes, running from the Lido to Giardini, San Zaccaria, San Marco (Vallaresso), Canal Grande (Accademia, San Samuele, San Tomà, Rialto, Ca' d'Oro, San Stae, San Marcuola), train station, Piazzale Roma, Tronchetto, Sacca Fisola, San Basilio, Záttere, Giudecca (Palanca, Redentore and Zitelle), San Giorgio and San Zaccaria – and vice versa. It runs along the whole of the route in both directions roughly every 30min, and along the Rialto to Tronchetto part every 20min. Another night service connects Venice with Murano and Burano, running to and from Fondamente Nove every 30min between midnight and 4am.

Stefano and Santa Sofia–Pescerìa run till around 7–9pm daily, the last two on Sundays, as well; in the winter months some *traghetti* stop running earlier, while others are suspended altogether.

Water taxis

Venice's **water taxis** are sleek and speedy vehicles that can penetrate most of the city's canals. Unfortunately they are possibly the most expensive form of taxi in western Europe: the clock starts at €8.70 and goes up €1.30 every minute. All sorts of additional surcharges are levied as well – €1.60 for each extra person if there are more than four in the party; €1.50 for each piece of luggage over 50cm long; €5.50 for a ride between 10pm and 7am. There are three ways of getting a taxi: go to one of the main stands (in front of the Piazzetta and at the airport), find one in the process of disgorging its passengers, or call one by phone (℡041.522.2303 or 041.723.112). If you use the phone, there is also a call charge of €6.

Gondolas

The famous Venetian **gondola** is no longer a form of transport but rather an adjunct of the tourist industry. That said, it can be a delightful way of relishing the sheer sense of being in Venice, and the cost isn't all that off-putting when split among a small group. To hire one costs €73 per fifty minutes for up to six passengers, rising to €91 between 8pm and 8am; you pay an extra €37 for every additional 25min, or €47 from 8pm to 8am. Further hefty surcharges will be levied should you require the services of an on-board accordionist or tenor – and a surprising number of people do. Even though the tariff is set by the local authorities, it's been known for some gondoliers to try to extort even higher rates than these – if you do decide to go for a ride, establish the charge before setting off.

To minimize the chances of being ripped off, only take a boat from one of the following **official gondola stands**: west of Piazza San Marco at Calle Vallaresso, Campo San Moisè or Campo Santa Maria del Giglio; immediately north of the Piazza at Bacino Orseolo; on the Molo, in front of the Palazzo Ducale; outside the *Danieli* hotel on Riva degli Schiavoni; at the train station; at Piazzale Roma; at Campo Santa Sofia, near the Ca' d'Oro; at San Tomà; or by the Rialto Bridge on Riva Carbon.

Accommodation

Demand for holiday accommodation in Venice outstrips supply to such a degree that this city is the most expensive in western Europe, with some one-star hotels charging in excess of €150 for a double room in high season. What's more, the **high season** here is longer than anywhere else in the country – it is officially classified as running from March 15 to November 15 and then from December 21 to January 6, but many places don't recognize the existence of a low season any more. (A few hotels, on the other hand, lower their prices in August, a month in which trade can take a bit of a dip; as every Italian knows, Venice can be hellishly hot and clogged with day-trippers during that month.)

It's never a good idea to turn up in Venice without reserving your accommodation first, and if you intend to stay here at any time during the official high season (or Carnevale) it's wisest to book your place at least three months in advance. If your first-choice hotel is fully booked, go to the tourist office's website (Ⓦwww.turismovenezia.it), which gives details of accommodation of all types, or try the websites of the Venetian Hoteliers' Association (AVA) – Ⓦwww.veniceinfo.it and Ⓦwww.veneziasi.it – which lists hundreds of hotels.

Finally, should you bowl into town with nowhere to stay, you could call in at one of the AVA **booking offices**: at the **train station** (daily: summer 8am–9pm; winter 8am–7pm); on the **Tronchetto** (9am–8pm); in the multi-storey car park at **Piazzale Roma** (9am–9pm); and at **Marco Polo airport** (summer 9am–7pm; winter noon–7pm). They only deal with hotels (not hostels or B&Bs) and take a deposit that's deductible from your first night's bill.

Hotels

Venice has well in excess of two hundred hotels, ranging from spartan one-star joints to five-star establishments. Though there are some anomalies, the star system is a broadly reliable indicator of quality, but always bear in mind that you pay through the nose for your proximity to the **Piazza San Marco**. So if you want maximum comfort for your money, decide how much you can afford and then look for a place outside the San Marco *sestiere* – after all, it's not far to walk, wherever you're staying.

Breakfast is nearly always included in the room rate; if it isn't, you're best advised to take breakfast in a café, where the quality will probably be better and the price certainly lower. In 2000 Italy's laws relating to tourist accommodation were relaxed, which resulted in the opening of several guesthouses called **locande**, and the appearance of a number of private houses offering bed and breakfast (see p.324). The prefix *locanda* doesn't necessarily indicate an inexpensive place: some upmarket hotels use the label to give their image a more homely finish. The majority of *locande*, however, are small family-run establishments, offering a standard of accommodation equivalent to three- or even four-star hotels (24-hour room service is just about the only facility they don't provide), but often at considerably lower cost.

San Marco

Ai Do Mori Calle Larga S. Marzo 658
☎041.520.4817, Ⓦwww.hotelaidomori.com. Very friendly, and situated a few paces off the Piazza, this is a top recommendation for budget travellers. The top-floor room has a private terrace looking over the roofs of the Basilica and the Torre dell'Orologio, and is one of the most attractive (and, of course, expensive) one-star rooms in the city. All rooms have their own bathroom. Non-smoking. ❹

Ala Campo S. Maria del Giglio 2494
☎041.520.8333, Ⓦwww.hotelala.it. The three-star family-run *Ala* has spacious rooms (choose between modern and traditional Venetian) and a perfect location, on a square that opens out onto the mouth of the Canal Grande. Often has good special offers, and with 85 rooms it often has vacancies. ❽

Al Gambero Calle dei Fabbri 4687
☎041.522.4384, Ⓦwww.locandaalgambero.com. Twenty-six-room three-star hotel in an excellent position a short distance off the north side of the Piazza; many of the rooms overlook a canal that's on the standard gondola route from the Bacino Orseolo. There's a boisterous Franco–Italian bistro on the ground floor. ❼

Art Deco Calle delle Botteghe 2966
☎041.277.0558, Ⓦwww.locandaartdeco.com. This three-star locanda has a seventeenth-century palazzo setting, but the pristinely white bedrooms rooms have modern wrought-iron furniture. ❻

Casa Petrarca Calle delle Schiavini 4386
☎041.520.0430, Ⓔcasapetrarca@yahoo .it. A very hospitable one-star, one of the cheapest hotels within a stone's throw of the Piazza – but make sure you phone first, as it only has seven rooms, including a tiny single. No credit cards. ❸

Fiorita Campiello Nuovo 3457 ☎041.523.4754, Ⓦwww.locandafiorita.com. Welcoming one-star with just ten rooms, so again it's crucial to book well in advance. ❹

Kette Piscina S. Moisè 2053 ☎041.520.7766, Ⓦwww.hotelkette.com. A four-star favourite with the upper-bracket tour companies, mainly on account of its quiet location, in an alleyway parallel to Calle Larga XXII Marzo. In season there's nothing under €300, but out of season prices are much more reasonable. **9**

Noemi Calle dei Fabbri 909 ☏041.523.8144, ⓦwww.hotelnoemi.com. *Noemi* is right in the thick of the action, just a minute's walk north of the Piazza, so it's hardly surprising that its prices are higher than nearly all the other one-stars. Out of season, though, it has doubles for as little as €60. Decor is eighteenth-century Venetian and nearly all its fifteen rooms have private bathrooms. **6**

Novecento Calle del Dose 2683 ☏041.241.3765, ⓦwww.novecento.biz. Beautiful boutique-style three-star hotel with nine individually decorated doubles and excellent bathrooms. Styling is ethnic/eclectic (furnishings from Morocco, China, Japan and Egypt), and there's a small courtyard for breakfast. **7**

Orseolo Corte Zorzi 1083 ☏041.520.4827, ⓦwww.locandaorseolo.com. Friendly non-smoking family-run *locanda* abutting the Orseolo canal, fifty metres north of Piazza S. Marco. Rooms are spacious and light, breakfasts substantial. Entrance is through an iron gate in Campo S. Gallo. **7**

Dorsoduro

Accademia Villa Maravege Fondamenta Bollani 1058 ☏041.521.0188, ⓦwww.pensione accademia.it. Once the Russian embassy, this three-star seventeenth-century villa has a devoted following, not least on account of its garden, which occupies a promontory at the convergence of two canals and has a view of a small section of the Canal Grande. To be sure of a room, get your booking in at least three months ahead. The owners also run two three-star hotels in the middle of San Marco and the management has been known to try to palm off people with those if the Villa is full, but they lack the charm and calm of this place. **8**

Agli Alboretti Rio Terrà Foscarini 884 ☏041.523.0058, ⓦwww.aglialboretti.com. Friendly and comparatively inexpensive three-star well situated right next to the Accademia. All rooms have a/c and TV. Avoid murky room 19 and you can't go wrong. **6**

Antico Capon Campo S. Margherita 3004/b ☏041.528.5292, ⓦwww.anticocapon.com. Seven simply furnished small rooms without a/c above a pizzeria-restaurant on an atmospheric square in the heart of the student district, plus a few rooms in a nearby annexe. Pleasant staff. **3**

Ca' Fóscari Calle della Frescada 3887/B ☏041.710.401, ⓦwww.locandacafoscari.com. Quiet and well-decorated one-star, tucked away in a micro-alley near S. Tomà. Just eleven rooms (seven with shower), so it's quickly booked out. Its

hours are somewhat hostel-like: check-in is from 2pm, check-out by 10am. **3**

Ca' Pisani Rio Terà Foscarini 979a ☏041.240.1411, ⓦwww.capisanihotel.it. This very glamorous 29-room four-star, just a few metres from the Accademia, created quite a stir when it opened in 2000, partly because of its location, on the opposite side of the Canal Grande from its top-echelon peers, but chiefly because of its high-class retro look. Taking its cue from the style of the 1930s and 1940s, the *Ca' Pisani* makes heavy use of dark wood and chrome, a refreshing break from the Renaissance and Rococo tones that tend to prevail in Venice's upmarket establishments. **9**

DD 724 Ramo da Mula 724 ☏041.277.0262, ⓦwww.dd724.com. In a city awash with nostalgia, the high-grade modernist style of this new boutique hotel, right by the Guggenheim, comes as a refreshing change. It has just seven rooms, each of them impeccably cool and luxurious – and not a Murano chandelier in sight. **7**

La Calcina Zàttere ai Gesuati 780 ☏041.520.6466, ⓦwww.lacalcina.com. Charismatic three-star hotel in the house where Ruskin wrote much of *The Stones of Venice*. From the more expensive rooms you can gaze across to the Redentore, a church that gave him apoplexy. All rooms are no-smoking and have parquet floors – unusual in Venice. No TV or minibar in the rooms either – a management decision indicative of the desire to maintain the building's character. Its restaurant is good too. **6**

Locanda San Barnaba Calle del Traghetto 2785 ☏041.241.1233, ⓦwww.locanda-sanbarnaba .com. Exceptionally pleasant three-star hotel right by the Ca' Rezzonico. Well-equipped rooms – some have eighteenth-century frescoes, and one has an enormous family-size bath. **6**

Messner Rio Terrà dei Catacumeni 216 ☏041.522.7443, ⓦwww.hotelmessner.it. In an excellent, quiet location close to the Salute vaporetto stop, the *Messner* has modern, smart rooms and is run by friendly staff. The one-star annexe round the corner has rooms that are slightly cheaper but more appealing than those in the two-star main building. **5**

Montin Fondamenta di Borgo 1147 ☏041.522.7151, ⓦwww.locandamontin.com. The *Montin* is known principally for its upmarket and once-fashionable restaurant; few people realize that it offers some of Venice's best budget accommodation. Only eleven rooms, three of them without private bathroom; the best rooms are spacious and balconied. **5**

Tivoli Crosera S. Pantalon 3838 ☏041.524.2460, ⓦwww.hoteltivoli.it. This two-star is the biggest low-priced hotel in the immediate vicinity of the Frari and S. Rocco, and often has space when the rest are full. ❹

San Polo and Santa Croce

🏃 **Ca' Arco Antico** Calle del Forno, San Polo 1451 ☏041.241.1227, ⓦwww.arcoanti covenice.com. Owners Gianfranco and Marco have done a fine job of making this eight-room guest house an attractive mix of the traditional and the modern. With big rooms, great location, and excellent breakfast (a rarity in itself), Ca' Arco Antico offers some of the best-value accommodation in the city. ❻

Casa Peron Salizzada S. Pantalon, Santa Croce 84 ☏041.710.021, ⓦwww.casaperon.com. A plain, very inexpensive and congenial one-star in the heart of university district, very close to San Rocco and the Frari. Most rooms have showers, but few have their own toilet. ❷

San Cassiano-Ca' Favretto Calle della Rosa, Santa Croce 2232 ☏041.524.1768, ⓦwww .sancassiano.it. Beautiful 35-room three-star, with some rooms looking across the Canal Grande towards the Ca' d'Oro. Has very helpful staff, a nice courtyard garden and a grand entrance hall. ❽

Cannaregio

Abbazia Calle Priuli 68 ☏041.717.333, ⓦwww .abbaziahotel.com. Walking away from the train station, turn left immediately after the Scalzi church and you'll arrive at Cannaregio's most restful hotel. Occupying a former Carmelite monastery (the monks attached to the Scalzi still live in a building adjoining the hotel), the light-filled *Abbazia* provides three-star amenities without losing its air of quasi-monastic austerity. There's a delightful garden too. ❼

Adua Lista di Spagna 233/a ☏041.716.184, ⓦwww.aduahotel.com. Thirteen-room two-star with friendly management and benign prices. One of the best hotels in this bustling area of the city. ❹

🏃 **Bernardi Semenzato** Calle dell'Oca 4366 ☏041.522.7257, ⓦwww.hotelbernardi .com. Very well-priced two-star in a prime location (in a tiny alleyway close to Campo S. Apostoli), with immensely helpful owners who speak excellent English. Has five singles for as little as €40 (with a shared bathroom). ❹

Casa Martini Rio Terrà San Leonardo 1314 ☏041.717.512, ⓦwww.casamartini.it. Delightful small hotel near the Cannaregio canal. Nine pleasantly furnished a/c rooms, with breakfast terrace at the back, and a kitchen for guests' use. ❺

Hesperia Calle Riello 459 ☏041.715.251, ⓦwww .hotelhesperia.com. Very friendly sixteen-room two-star in a secluded alleyway just beyond the Palazzo Savorgnan, close to the Cannaregio canal. Rooms are small but homely, and come complete with Murano glass fittings (not the garish variety). ❻

Locanda Ai Santi Apostoli Strada Nova 4391a ☏041.521.2612, ⓦwww.locandasantiapostoli .com. Occupying the top floor of a *palazzo* opposite the Rialto market, this ten-room three-star is one of the pricier *locande*, but there aren't many better rooms in this price than the pair overlooking the Canal Grande – and if you want one of these, you'd better get your request in early. ❽

Locanda Leon Bianco Corte Leon Bianco 5629 ☏041.523.3572, ⓦwww.leonbianco.it. Friendly and charming three-star in a superb location not far from the Rialto Bridge, tucked away beside the decaying Ca' da Mosto. Only eight rooms, but three of them overlook the Canal Grande (you pay a €50 premium for these) and four of the others are spacious and tastefully furnished in eighteenth-century style – one even has a huge fresco copied from a Tiepolo ceiling. ❻

Villa Rosa Calle della Misericordia 389 ☏041.718.976, ⓦwww.villarosahotel.com. Clean and fairly rooms at this 31-room one-star, with a/c and private bathrooms – the best even have a small balcony. There is a large terrace at the back for breakfast. ❹

Castello

Canada Campo S. Lio 5659 ☏041.522.9912, ⓦwww.canadavenice.com. Well-kept and friendly second-floor two-star; book well in advance for the double room with a roof terrace. ❻

Caneva Corte Rubbi 5515 ☏041.522.8118, ⓦwww.hotelcaneva.com. A well-appointed and peaceful one-star tucked away behind the church of Santa Maria della Fava, close to Campo S. Bartolomeo. Most of the 23 rooms have a/c and private bathrooms. ❹

Casa Verardo Calle della Chiesa 4765 ☏041.528.6127, ⓦwww.casaverardo.it. Very fine, well-refurbished three-star hotel just a couple of minutes from San Marco and Campo Santa Maria Formosa. Twenty three very well-equipped rooms with a breakfast terrace downstairs, a sun lounge at the top and another terrace attached to one of the rooms. ❽

Danieli Riva degli Schiavoni 4196 ☏041.522.6480, ⓦwww.luxurycollection.com /danieli. No longer the most expensive hotel in Venice (the *Cipriani* has that title), but no other place can compete with the glamour of the *Danieli*. Balzac stayed here, as did George Sand, Wagner and Dickens. This magnificent Gothic *palazzo* affords just about the most sybaritic hotel experience on the continent – provided you book a room in the old part of the building, not the modern extension. Cheapest doubles are €600 out of season; the best double, in summer, will set you back more than €1300 per night. **⑨**

La Residenza Campo Bandiera e Moro 3608 ⓣ041.528.5315, ⓦwww.venicelaresidenza .com. This fourteenth-century palazzo is a mid-budget gem (in Venetian terms), occupying much of one side of a tranquil square just off the main waterfront. It was once a tad pricier than the average two-star, but the rest of the pack have raised their tariffs more in recent years, making *La Residenza* a clear top choice. The recently refurbished rooms are very spacious (rare at this price) and elegant, and

the management extremely *simpatico*. Payment in cash is preferred for short stays. **⑤**

Locanda Casa Querini Campo San Giovanni Novo 4388 ⓣ041.241.1294, ⓦwww.locandaquerini .com. Friendly *locanda* occupying parts of two houses in a quiet courtyard near the Piazza. Eleven smallish but nicely furnished a/c rooms. **⑥**

Scandinavia Campo S. Maria Formosa 5240 ⓣ041.522.3507, ⓦwww.scandinaviahotel.com. Sizeable and comfortable three-star hotel on one of the city's most lively and spacious squares. Decorated mainly in eighteenth-century style (lots of Murano glass and floral motifs), its 34 rooms offer an unusually wide variety of accommodation, ranging from large suites to rooms with private but not en-suite bathroom. Huge reductions in the quiet months. **⑦**

Bed and breakfast

The Italian tourism authorities define a **bed and breakfast** as a private dwelling in which a maximum of three bedrooms are available to paying guests, with a minimum of one shared bathroom for guests' exclusive use. The places listed below are all officially registered B&Bs; guesthouses are included in the hotel listings. The tourist office has lists of around 150 officially registered B&Bs, and the number is growing with each year. Some of these – as you may expect in a city where you could charge €100 for the privilege of sleeping on a mattress in the attic – are not terribly attractive. Our selection is taken from those whose rooms are viewable online; for full listings of Venice's B&Bs, go to ⓦwww .turismovenezia.it.

San Marco

A Le Boteghe Calle delle Botteghe 3438 ⓦwww .aleboteghe.it. **④**

Ca' del Pozzo Calle Lavezzera 2612 ⓦwww .cadelpozzo.com. **⑥**

Ca' Moroni Campo Sant' Angelo 3824 ⓦwww .camoroni.it **⑤**

Casa de' Uscoli Campo Pisani San Marco 2818 ⓦwww.casadeuscoli.com. **⑥**

Palazzo Duodo Gregolin Ramo Duodo 1014 ⓦwww.palazzoduodo.com. **⑥**

Dorsoduro

Ai Mendicoli Campiello Tron 1902 ⓦwww .aimendicoli.com. **⑤**

Almaviva House Fondamenta delle Romite 1348 ⓦwww.palazzopompeo.com. **⑥**

Ca' Arzere Corte Maggiore 2314 ⓦwww .bbveneziarzere.com. **⑤**

Ca' Turelli Fondamenta di Borgo 1162 ⓦwww.caturelli.it. **⑤**

Corte Contarini Corte Contarini 3488r ⓦwww.cortecontarini.it. **③**

Fujiyama Calle Lungo San Barnabà 2727a ⓦwww.bedandbreakfast-fujiyama.it. **⑤**

La Colonna Gotica Campo Angelo Raffaele 1710 ⓦwww.veneziabedandbreakfast.it. **⑤**

Palazzo dal Carlo Fondamenta di Borgo 1163 ⓦwww.palazzodalcarlo.com. **⑤**

San Polo & Santa Croce

Al Campaniel Calle del Campaniel 2889 ⓦwww.alcampaniel.com. **④**

Al Campiello dei Meloni Campiello dei Meloni 1419a ⓦwww.ciprea.info. **③**

Corte 1321 Campiello ca' Bernardi ⓦwww .cabernardi.com. **⑦**

Cannaregio

Al Palazzetto Calle delle Vele 4057 ⓦwww .guesthouse.it. **⑥**

Al Saor Ca' d'Oro Calle Zotti 3904a ⓦwww .alsaor.com. **④**

At Home a Palazzo Calle Priuli 3764 ⓦwww .athomeapalazzo.com. **⑥**

Ca' Pier Calle Bembo 4357 ⓦwww.capier.com. **⑥**

Castello

Ai Greci Calle del Magazen 3338 ⓦ www
.aigreci.com. ⑥
Campiello Santa Giustina Calle Due Porte 6499
ⓦ www.campiellogiustina.com. ④
Gli Angeli Campo della Tana 2161 ⓦ www
.gliangeli.net. ⑥
San Marco Fondamenta San Giorgio degli
Schiavoni 3385 ☏ 041.522.7589, ⓦ www
.realvenice.it/smarco. ⑤

La Giudecca

Casa Eden Corte Mosto 25 ⓦ www
.casaeden.it. ④
Casa Genoveffa Calle del Forno 472 ⓦ www
.casagenoveffa.com. ⑥
Corte Grande dei Sette Camini Corte Grande
501 ⓦ www.cortegrandi.it. ⑥

Hostels and institutions

Venice has a large HI **hostel** and a few hostel-like establishments run by
religious foundations, which are generally available to tourists during the
university's summer vacation – during term time they double as student accommodation. Bona-fide students looking for a room for an extended stay during
the summer vacation should check out ⓦ www.esuvenezia.it, which gives
details of rooms in the various accommodation blocks of Venice's university.

Domus Ciliota Calle delle Muneghe, S. Marco
2976 ☏ 041.520.4888, ⓦ www.ciliota.it; map on
pp.330–331. Welcoming but expensive hostel-style
accommodation, close to Campo S. Stefano. Open
mid-June to mid-Sept. Singles from €70; doubles
from €100.
Domus Civica Calle Campazzo, San Polo 3082
☏ 041.721.103, ⓦ www.domuscivica.com. A
student house in winter, open to female visitors
from mid-June to Sept. A little awkward to find: it's
off Calle della Lacca, to the west of San Giovanni
Evangelista. Most rooms are doubles; showers
free; no breakfast; 11.30pm curfew. €30 per
night, with reductions for ISIC and Rolling Venice
card holders.
Foresteria Valdese S. Maria Formosa, Castello
5170 ☏ 041.528.6797, ⓦ www.diaconiavaldese
.org. Run by Waldensians, this hostel is installed in a
wonderful palazzo at the end of Calle Lunga S. Maria
Formosa, with flaking frescoes in the rooms, a large
salon and cheap Internet access. It has several large
dorms, plus bedrooms that can accommodate up to
eight people. Reservations by phone only; dorm beds
cannot be booked in advance, except by groups.
Registration 9am–1pm & 6–8pm. Prices average out
at around €22 per night.

Ostello Santa Fosca S. Maria dei Servi,
Cannaregio 2372, ☏ 041.715.733, ⓦ www
.santafosca.com. Student-run hostel in an atmospheric former Servite convent in a quiet part of
Cannaregio, with dorm beds and double rooms, all
with shared bathrooms. Check-in 5–8pm; 12.30pm
curfew. Cheap Internet point. €20 per night on
average. They take bookings one week ahead
only, and only by phone; it's essential to book in
summer.
Ostello Venezia Fondamenta delle Zitelle,
Giudecca 86 ☏ 041.523.8211, ℮ vehostel@tin.it.
The city's HI hostel occupies a superb location
looking over to San Marco, but it's run with a
certain briskness. Registration opens at 1.30pm in
summer and 4pm in winter. Curfew at 11.30pm,
chucking-out time 9.30am. Gets so busy in July
and August that written reservations must be made
by April; written reservations are required all year.
Breakfast and sheets included in the price – but
remember to add the expense of the boat over to
Giudecca (the nearest stop is Zitelle). No kitchen,
but full (and good) meals for around €10. From
€18.50 per dorm bed, breakfast included; HI card
necessary, but you can join on the spot.

Camping

If you're coming from the airport and want to pitch your tent promptly, you
could settle for the four-star *Alba d'Oro*, Via Triestina 214/b (open all year;
☏ 041.541.5102, ⓦ www.ecvacanza.it; €14 per tent plus €8 per person per
night, or €60 per night for a chalet), just beyond the airport (take bus #15 to
Cánoghera, the fourth stop after the airport). Plenty of sites are to be found on
the outer edge of the lagoon on the **Litorale del Cavallino**, which stretches

from the Punta Sabbioni to Jésolo and has a total of around 60,000 pitches, many of them quite luxuriously appointed. Vaporetto #LN, from Fondamente Nove or San Zaccaria to the Punta, stops close to the two-star *Miramare*, Lungomare Dante Alighieri 29 (April–Oct; ☎041.966.150, @www.camping-miramare.it; €4–25 per tent plus €3.50–10.50 per person per night); a bit further away there's the more luxurious four-star *Marina di Venezia*, Via Montello 6 (May–Sept; ☎041.966.146, @www.marinadivenezia.it; €9.20–24.20 per tent plus €3–9 per person per night). Bear in mind, though, that it's a forty-minute boat trip into the city from here.

Alternatively, back on the mainland there's a two-star site at **Fusina**, Via Moranzani 93 (open all year; ☎041.547.0064); it has almost 1000 places, and charges €9–12 per tent plus €8–9 per person. A *Linea Fusina* waterbus links Fusina to the Záttere in central Venice (ACTV tickets not valid), taking 25 minutes, with an hourly service from 8am till until around 10pm from late May to the end of September, and till around 8pm for the rest of the year. Alternatively, you can get a bus to Mestre and change there for the #1 bus or a train.

The City

Venice's heart and tourist hub lies in and around Piazza San Marco and it's here, with the best-known symbols of the city's former glories, that the account

---

Museum and church passes

In an attempt to make sure that tourists go to see more than just the big central monuments, a couple of **Museum Cards** have been introduced for the city's civic museums (@www.museiciviciveneziani.it). The card for I **Musei di Piazza San Marco**, costing €12 (€6.50 for ages 6–14, students under 30, EU citizens over 65 & Rolling Venice Card holders), allows you to visit the Palazzo Ducale, Museo Correr, Museo Archeologico and the Biblioteca Marciana. The **Museum Pass**, costing €18/€12, covers all the museums listed above, plus Ca' Rezzonico, Casa Goldoni, Palazzo Mocenigo, Museo Fortuny, Ca' Pésaro (the modern art and oriental museums), the Museo del Merletto (Burano) and the Museo del Vetro (Murano). Passes are valid for six months, allow one visit to each attraction, and are available from any of the participating museums. The **Musei di Piazza San Marco** can only be visited with a card; at the other places you have the option of paying an entry charge just for that attraction. Note also the orange version of the Venice Card (see box, p.317) covers all of the museums covered by the Museum Pass, and that accompanied disabled people have free access to all of these museums. There is also a combined ticket for the city's **state museums** (the Accademia, Ca' d'Oro and Museo Orientale), costing €11/5.50.

Sixteen churches are now part of the ever-expanding **Chorus Pass** scheme (@www.chorusvenezia.org), whereby an €8 **ticket** allows one visit to each of the churches over a one-year period. All of the proceeds from the scheme are ploughed back into the maintenance of the buildings. The individual entrance fee at each of the participating churches is €2.50, and all the churches (except for the Frari) observe the same opening hours: Monday to Saturday 10am to 5pm. The churches involved are: the Frari (Mon–Sat 9am–6pm, Sun 1–6pm); the Gesuati; Madonna dell'Orto; the Redentore; San Giacomo dell'Orio; San Giobbe; San Giovanni Elemosinario; San Pietro di Castello; San Polo; San Sebastiano; San Stae; Sant'Alvise; Santa Maria dei Miracoli; Santa Maria del Giglio; Santa Maria Formosa; and Santo Stefano. The Chorus Pass is available at each of these churches; the orange Venice Card gives free admission to all of them.

below begins. The undoubted appeal of the area is matched in the quieter *sestieri* too where your chances of getting lost in the jumble of streets is almost guaranteed and provides one of the joys of any visit, offering the possibility of stumbling on some hidden gem of a square or tranquil side canal.

San Marco

The section of Venice enclosed by the lower loop of the Canal Grande – a rectangle smaller than 1000 metres by 500 – is, in essence, the Venice of the travel brochures. The plush hotels are concentrated here, in the *sestiere* of **SAN MARCO**, as are the swankier shops and the best-known cultural attractions of the city. But small though this area is, you can still lose the hordes within it.

"The finest drawing-room in Europe" was how Napoleon described its focal point, the **Piazza San Marco** – the only piazza in Venice, all other squares being *campi* or *campielli*. Less genteel phrases might seem appropriate on a suffocating summer afternoon, but you can take some slight consolation from the knowledge that the Piazza has always been congested. Neither is the influx of foreigners a modern phenomenon – its parades, festivities and markets have always drawn visitors from all over the Continent and beyond, the biggest attraction being a huge international trade fair known as the **Fiera della Sensa**, which kept the Piazza buzzing for the fortnight following the Ascension Day ceremony of the marriage of Venice to the sea. The coffee shops of the Piazza were a vital component of eighteenth-century high society, and the two survivors from that period – *Florian* and *Quadri* – are still the smartest and most expensive in town.

The Basilica di San Marco

The **Basilica di San Marco** is the most exotic of Europe's cathedrals, and no visitor can remain dispassionate when confronted by it. Herbert Spencer found it loathsome – "a fine sample of barbaric architecture", but to John Ruskin it was a "treasure-heap ...a confusion of delight". Delightful or not, it's certainly confusing, increasingly so as you come nearer and the details emerge; some knowledge of the history of the building helps bring a little order out of chaos.

San Marco is open to tourists Monday to Saturday 9.45am–5.30pm (4.30pm from October to April) and Sunday 2–4pm, though the Loggia dei Cavalli is open on Sunday morning. Entrance to the main part of the church is free, but admission fees totalling €6.50 are charged for certain parts of the church. You cannot take large bags into the church – they have to be left, free of charge, at nearby Calle San Basso 315a. If you're visiting San Marco in summer, get there early – by midday the queues are enormous.

The story of the Basilica

According to the **legend of St Mark's annunciation**, the Evangelist was moored in the lagoon, on his way to Rome, when an angel appeared and told him that his body would rest there. (The angel's salute – *Pax tibi, Marce evangelista meus* – is the text cut into the book that the Lion of St Mark is always shown holding.) The founders of Venice, having persuaded themselves of the sacred ordination of their city, duly went about fulfilling the angelic prophecy, and in 828 the body of St Mark was stolen from Alexandria and brought here.

Modelled on Constantinople's Church of the Twelve Apostles, the shrine of St Mark was consecrated in 832, but in 976 both the church and the Palazzo Ducale were ruined by fire during an uprising against the doge. The present basilica was originally finished in 1094 and embellished over the succeeding centuries. Every trophy that the doge stuck onto his church (and bear in mind

△ Basilica di San Marco

this church was not the cathedral of Venice but the doge's own chapel) was proof of Venice's secular might and so of the spiritual power of St Mark.

The exterior, narthex and Loggia dei Cavalli

Of the exterior features that can be seen easily from the ground, the **Romanesque carvings** of the **central door** demand the closest attention – especially the middle arch's figures of the months and seasons and outer arch's series of *The Trades of Venice*. The carvings were begun around 1225 and finished in the early fourteenth century. Take a look also at the mosaic above the doorway on the far left – *The Arrival of the Body of St Mark* – which was made around 1260 (the only early mosaic left on the main facade) and includes the oldest known image of the basilica.

From the Piazza you pass into the vestibule known as the **narthex**, decorated with the first of the church's **mosaics**: Old Testament scenes on the domes and arches, together with *The Madonna with Apostles and Evangelists* in the niches of the bay in front of the main door – dating from the 1060s, the oldest mosaics in San Marco.

A steep staircase goes from the church's main door up to the **Museo Marciano** and the Loggia dei Cavalli (daily: May–Sept 9.45am–5pm; Oct–April 9.45am–4pm; €3). Apart from giving you an all-round view, the loggia is also the best place from which to inspect the Gothic carvings along the apex of the facade. The **horses** outside are replicas, the genuine articles having been removed inside to the **Galleria**, along with oddments of mosaic and a fine polyptych by Paolo Veneziano. Thieved from the Hippodrome of Constantinople in 1204 during the Fourth Crusade, the horses are probably Roman works of the second century – the only such ancient group, or *quadriga*, to have survived.

The interior

With its undulating floor of twelfth-century patterned marble, its plates of eastern stone on the lower walls, and its 4000 square metres of **mosaics** covering every other inch of wall and vaulting, the interior of San Marco is the most opulent of any cathedral. One visit is not enough – there's too much to take in at one go, and the shifting light reveals and hides parts of the decoration as the day progresses; try calling in for half an hour at the beginning and end of a couple of days.

The majority of the mosaics were in position by the middle of the thirteenth century; some date from the fourteenth and fifteenth centuries, and others were created in the sixteenth to replace damaged early sections. A thorough guide to them would take volumes, but an inventory of the very best might include the following. On the west wall, above the door – *Christ, the Virgin and St Mark*; west dome – *Pentecost*; arch between west and central domes – *Crucifixion, Resurrection*; central dome – *Ascension*; east dome – *Religion of Christ Foretold by the Prophets*; between windows of apse – *Four Patron Saints of Venice*; north transept's dome – *Acts of St John the Evangelist*; arch to west of north transept's dome (and continued on upper part of adjacent wall) – *Life of the Virgin and Life of the Infant Christ*; wall of south aisle – *The Agony in the Garden*; west wall of south transept – *Rediscovery of the Body of St Mark*. This last scene refers to the story that St Mark's body was hidden during the rebuilding of the basilica in 1063 and was not found again until 1094, when it miraculously broke through the pillar in which it had been buried.

From the south transept you can enter the **Sanctuary** (May–Sept Mon–Sat 9.45am–5pm, Sun 2–4pm; Oct–April Mon–Sat 9.45am–4pm, Sun 2–4pm; €1.50), where, behind the altar, you'll find the most precious of San Marco's treasures – the **Pala d'Oro** (Golden Altar Panel). Commissioned in 976 in Constantinople, the Pala was enlarged, enriched and rearranged by Byzantine goldsmiths in 1105, then by Venetians in 1209 (to incorporate some less cumbersome loot from the Fourth Crusade) and again (finally) in 1345. The completed screen holds 83 enamel plaques, 74 enamelled roundels, 38 chiselled figures, 300 sapphires, 300 emeralds, 400 garnets, 15 rubies, 1300 pearls and a couple of hundred other stones.

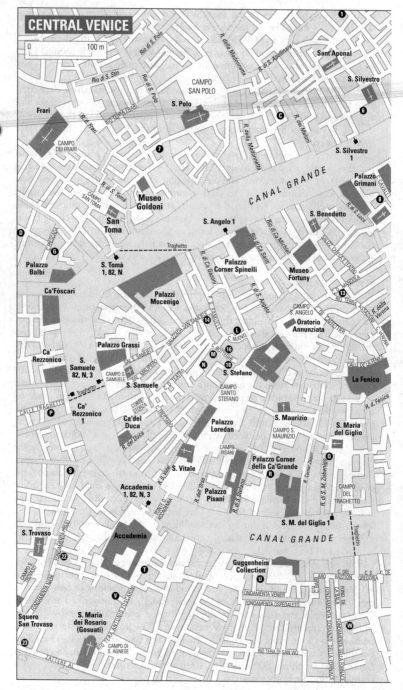

CENTRAL VENICE

0   100 m

Sant'Aponal

S. Silvestro

Rio di S. Polo

R. della Madonnetta

R. di S. Apollinare

Rio di S. Polo

Rio di S. Stin

Rio di S. Polo

Rio di S. Stin

CAMPO SAN POLO

S. Polo

Frari

CAMPO DEI FRARI

R. d. Frari

RIO TERA' FRARI

R. della Madonnetta

R. dei Meloni

S. Silvestro 1

CANAL GRANDE

Palazzo Grimani

CAVALLI

R. di S. Luca

Museo Goldoni

R. di S. Tomà

CAMPO SAN TOMA

S. Angelo 1

R. di Ca' Michiel

S. Benedetto

SALIZ. DEL TEATRO

San Tomà

Traghetto

S. Tomà 1, 82, N

Palazzo Corner Spinelli

R. di Ca' Garzoni

R. di S. Angelo

Museo Fortuny

MANDOLA

RIO TERA' ASSASSINI

R. della Verona

Palazzo Balbi

CRESSADA

Palazzi Mocenigo

SALIZADA SAN SAMUELE

Ca'Fóscari

Palazzo Grassi

S. Samuele 82, N, 3

CAMPO S. SAMUELE

SAL. S. SAMUELE

SAL. MALIPIERO

C.P.O TEATRO

S. Samuele

Ca'del Duca

CORTE STORTA

R. del Duca

C. BELLOTTO

CAMPO S. ANGELO

Oratorio Annunziata

C.TE DEI CATTETTIER

CALLE DE LA MANDOLA

C.V. VERONA

Ca' Rezzonico

CAMPO SANTO STEFANO

S. Stefano

C. NUOVO

C. BOTTEGHE

Traghetto

CALLE TRAGHETTO

Ca' Rezzonico 1

S. Maurizio

CAMPO S. MAURIZIO

CALLE DE LA MANDOLA

La Fenice

R. d. Fenice

Palazzo Loredan

Palazzo Corner della Ca'Grande

R. Corner Zaguri

S. Maria del Giglio

R. di S. M. Zobenigo

S. Vitale

R. S. Vidal

CAMPO PISANI

Palazzo Pisani

R. di S. Stefano

S. M. del Giglio 1

CAMPO DEL TRAGHETTO

Accademia 1, 82, N, 3

PONTE D. ACCADEMIA

S. Trovaso

CAMPO S. TROVASO

FONDAMENTA NANI

Accademia

RIO TERA' ANTONIO FOSCARINI

FONDAMENTA PRIULI

CANAL GRANDE

Traghetto

Guggenheim Collection

FONDAMENTA VENIER

FONDAMENTA OSPEDALETTO

CAMPO S. VIO

C. DEL BASTION

C.S. S. DE

C. DE CRISTO

FOND. DE CA' BALA

FONDAMENTA SORANZO DELLA FORNACE

Squero San Trovaso

S. Maria dei Rosario (Gesuati)

RIO TERA' ANTONIO FOSCARINI

CAMPO DI S. AGNESE

RIO TERA' DI SAN VIO

ZATTERE AL

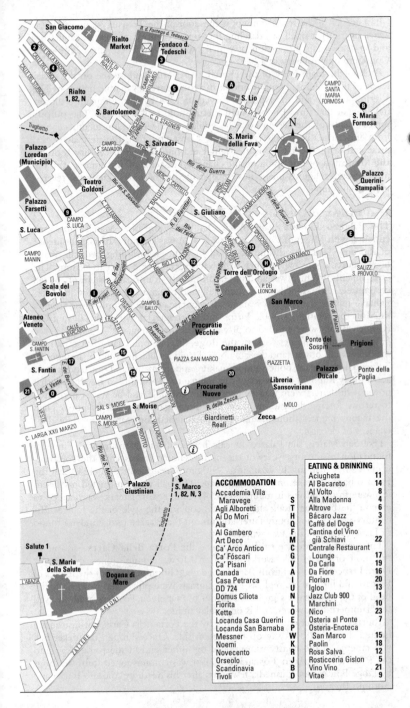

ACCOMMODATION

Accademia Villa Maravege	S
Agli Alboretti	T
Ai Do Mori	H
Ala	Q
Al Gambero	F
Art Deco	M
Ca' Arco Antico	C
Ca' Fóscari	G
Ca' Pisani	V
Canada	A
Casa Petrarca	I
DD 724	U
Domus Ciliota	N
Fiorita	L
Kette	O
Locanda Casa Querini	E
Locanda San Barnaba	P
Messner	W
Noemi	K
Novecento	R
Orseolo	J
Scandinavia	B
Tivoli	D

EATING & DRINKING

Aciugheta	11
Al Bacareto	14
Al Volto	8
Alla Madonna	4
Altrove	6
Bácaro Jazz	3
Caffè del Doge	2
Cantina del Vino già Schiavi	22
Centrale Restaurant Lounge	17
Da Carla	19
Da Fiore	16
Florian	20
Igloo	13
Jazz Club 900	1
Marchini	10
Nico	23
Osteria al Ponte	7
Osteria-Enoteca San Marco	15
Paolin	18
Rosa Salva	12
Rosticceria Gislon	5
Vino Vino	21
Vitae	9

In a corner of the south transept is the door of the **Treasury** (same times as Sanctuary; €2), a small but dazzling line-up of chalices, reliquaries, candelabra and so on – a fair proportion of which owe their presence here to the great Constantinople robbery of 1204.

Back in the main body of the church, there's still more to see on the lower levels of the building. Don't overlook the **rood screen**'s marble figures of The Virgin, St Mark and the Apostles, carved in 1394 by the dominant sculptors in Venice at that time, Jacobello and Pietro Paolo Dalle Masegne. The **pulpits** on each side of the screen were assembled in the early fourteenth century from miscellaneous panels (some from Constantinople); the new doge was presented to the people from the right-hand one. The tenth-century **Icon of the Madonna of Nicopeia** (in the chapel on east side of north transept) is the most revered religious image in Venice; it used to be one of the most revered in Constantinople.

The Palazzo Ducale

The **Palazzo Ducale** (daily: April–Oct 9am–7pm; Nov–March 9am–5pm; entrance with Museum Card – see box, p.326) was far more than the residence of the doge – it was the home of all of Venice's governing councils, many of its courts, a sizeable number of its civil servants and even its prisons. The government of Venice was administered through an intricate system of elected committees and councils – a system designed to limit the power of any individual – but for the last 500 years of the republic's existence only those families listed in the register of noble births and marriages known as the *Libro d'Oro* (Golden Book) were entitled to play a part in the system.

At the head of the network sat the **doge**, the one politician to sit on all the major councils of state and the only one elected for life; he could be immensely influential in steering policy and in making appointments, and restrictions were accordingly imposed on his actions to reduce the possibility of his abusing that power – his letters were read by censors, for example, and he wasn't permitted to receive foreign delegations alone. The privileges of the job far outweighed the inconveniences though, and men campaigned for years to increase their chances of election.

Like San Marco, the Palazzo Ducale has been rebuilt many times since its foundation in the first years of the ninth century. It was with the construction of a new hall for the Maggior Consiglio (Great Council) in 1340 that the Palazzo began to take on its present shape. The hall was constructed parallel to the waterfront and was inaugurated in 1419; three years later, it was decided to extend the building along the Piazzetta, copying the style of the fourteenth-century work – the slightly fatter column on the Piazzetta side, under a tondo of Justice, is where the two wings meet.

The principal entrance to the Palazzo – the **Porta della Carta** – is one of the most ornate Gothic works in the city. It was commissioned in 1438 by Doge Francesco Fóscari from Bartolomeo and Giovanni Bon, but the figures of Fóscari and his lion are replicas – the originals were pulverized in 1797 by the head of the stonemasons' guild, as a favour to Napoleon. Fóscari's head survived the hammering, however, and is on display inside.

Tourists no longer enter the building by the Porta della Carta, but instead are herded through a doorway on the lagoon side. Once through the ticket hall you emerge in the courtyard, opposite the other end of the passageway into the Palazzo – the **Arco Fóscari**. This also was commissioned from the Bons by Doge Fóscari but finished a few years after his death by Antonio Rizzo and Antonio Bregno.

The itinerary begins on the left side of the courtyard, where the finest of the capitals from the Palazzo's exterior arcade are displayed in the **Museo dell'Opera**. Upstairs, the route takes you through the doge's private apartments then on to the **Anticollegio**, the room in which embassies had to wait before being admitted to the presence of the doge and his cabinet. As regards the quality of its paintings, this is one of the richest rooms in the Palazzo Ducale: four pictures by Tintoretto hang on the door walls, and facing the windows is Veronese's *Rape of Europa*.

The cycle of paintings on the ceiling of the adjoining **Sala del Collegio** is also by Veronese, and he features strongly again in the most stupendous room in the building – the **Sala del Maggior Consiglio**. Veronese's ceiling panel of *The Apotheosis of Venice* is suspended over the dais from which the doge oversaw the sessions of the city's general assembly; the backdrop is **Tintoretto**'s immense *Paradiso*, painted towards the end of his life, with the aid of his son, Domenico. At the opposite end there's a curiosity: the frieze of portraits of the first 76 doges (the series continues in the Sala dello Scrutinio – through the door at the far end) is interrupted by a painted black veil, marking the place where **Doge Marin Falier** would have been honoured had he not conspired against the state in 1355 and been beheaded for his crime.

A couple of rooms later you descend quickly to the underbelly of the Venetian state, crossing the **Ponte dei Sospiri** (Bridge of Sighs) to the prisons. Before the construction of these cells in the early seventeenth century all prisoners were kept in the Piombi (the Leads), under the roof of the Palazzo Ducale, or in the Pozzi (the Wells) in the bottom two storeys; the new block was occupied mainly by petty criminals. The route finishes with a detour through the Pozzi, but if you want to see the Piombi, and the rooms in which the day-to-day administration of Venice took place, you have to go on the **Itinerari Segreti del Palazzo Ducale**, an intriguing guided tour through the warren of offices and passageways that interlocks with the public rooms of the building. It's not cheap (€16, or €10 if you have a Venice Card or Museum Pass or I Musei di Piazza San Marco card), but well worth the price, and covers entry to the whole palace. Tickets can be booked up to 48hr in advance on ☏041.520.9070; for visits on the next or same day go in person to Palazzo Ducale ticket desk to check availability; the tour is held in English every day at 9.55am, 10.45am and 11.35am.

The Campanile and Torre dell'Orologio

Most of the landscape of the Piazza dates from the great period of urban renewal that began at the end of the fifteenth century and went on for much of the following century. The one exception – excluding San Marco itself – is the **Campanile** (daily: April–June, Sept & Oct 9am–7.45pm; July & Aug 9am–9pm; Nov–March 9.30am–4.15pm; €6; usually closed for 3 weeks after Christmas), which began life as a lighthouse in the ninth century and was modified frequently up to the early sixteenth. The present structure is in fact a reconstruction: the original tower collapsed on July 14, 1902 – a catastrophe that injured nobody (except a cat) and is commemorated by faked postcard photos ostensibly taken at the very instant of the disaster. The collapse reduced to rubble the **Loggetta** at the base of the campanile, but somehow it was pieced together again; built between 1537 and 1549 by Sansovino, it has served as a meeting-room for the nobility, a guardhouse and the place at which the state lottery was drawn. At 99 metres, the campanile is the tallest structure in the city, and from the top (there is a lift) you can make out virtually every building, but not a single canal.

The other tower in the Piazza, the **Torre dell'Orologio**, was built between 1496 and 1506. A restoration lasting several years has prevented people from taking the staircase up past the innards of the clock and onto the terrace on which the stand the two bronze figures known locally as the Moors.

The Procuratie and Museo Correr

Away to the left of the Torre dell'Orologio stretches the **Procuratie Vecchie**; begun around 1500 by Codussi, this block housed the offices of the **Procurators of St Mark**, a committee of nine men whose responsibilities included the upkeep of the basilica and other public buildings. A century or so after taking possession, the procurators were moved to the opposite side of the Piazza, into the **Procuratie Nuove**. Napoleon converted these apartments into a royal palace and then, having realized that the building lacked a ballroom, remedied the deficiency by smashing down the church of San Geminiano in order to connect the two Procuratie with a new wing for dancing.

Generally known as the **Ala Napoleonica**, this short side of the Piazza is partly occupied by the **Museo Correr** (daily: April–Oct 9am–7pm; Nov–March 9am–5pm; entrance with Museum Card – see box, p.326), an immense triple-decker museum with a vast **historical collection** of coins, weapons, regalia, prints, paintings and miscellanea. Much of this is heavy going unless you have an intense interest in Venetian history, though there's an appealing exhibition of Venetian applied arts, and one show-stopping item in the form of the original blocks and a print of Jacopo de'Barbari's astonishing aerial view of Venice, engraved in 1500. The **Quadreria** on the second floor is no rival for the Accademia's collection, but it does set out clearly the evolution of painting in Venice from the thirteenth century to around 1500 (though not all of its pictures are by Venetians), and it contains some gems – the most famous being the **Carpaccio** picture usually known as *The Courtesans*, although its subjects are really a couple of bored-looking bourgeois ladies dressed in a style at which none of their contemporaries would have raised an eyebrow. The section of the Correr devoted to the **Museo del Risorgimento** is largely given over to the 1848 rebellion against the Austrians, but is often *in restauro*.

Accessed from within the Correr, the **Museo Archeologico** is a somewhat scrappy museum, with cases of Roman coins and gems, fragments of sarcophagi and inscriptions, miscellaneous headless statues and bodiless heads interspersed with the odd Bronze Age, Egyptian or Assyrian relic, generally presented in a manner that isn't very inspiring. From the archeological museum you pass into the hall of the **Libreria Sansoviniana**, described by Palladio as "perhaps the richest and most ornate building to be created since the times of ancient Greece and Rome". Paintings by Veronese, Tintoretto, Andrea Schiavone and others cover the walls and ceiling, gazing down on reproductions of some of the more precious of the library's volumes; Titian's *Allegory of Wisdom* occupies the central panel of the ceiling of the anteroom, beyond which lies the intended approach to the library, a magnificent staircase encrusted with stuccowork by Vittoria.

The Piazzetta

The **Piazzetta** – the open space between San Marco and the waterfront pavement known as the Molo – was the area where the politicians used to gather before meetings. Facing the Palazzo Ducale is Sansovino's masterpiece, the **Libreria Sansoviniana** (see above), which is attached to Sansovino's first major building in Venice, the **Zecca** (Mint), built between 1537 and 1545 on the site of the thirteenth-century mint. By the beginning of the fifteenth century the city's prosperity was such that the Venetian coinage was in use in every European exchange, and the doge could with some justification call Venice "the mistress of all the gold in Christendom".

The Piazzetta's two **columns** were brought here from the Levant at the end of the twelfth century, in company with a third, which fell off the barge and still lies somewhere just off the Molo. The figures perched on top are St Theodore (it's a copy – the original is in the Palazzo Ducale), patron saint of Venice when it was dependent on Byzantium, and a Chimera, customized to look like the Lion of St Mark. Public executions were carried out between the columns, the techniques employed ranging from straightforward hanging to burial alive, head downwards. Superstitious Venetians avoid passing between them.

North of the Piazza

The Mercerie, a chain of streets that starts under the clock tower and finishes at the Campo San Bartolomeo, is the most direct route between the Rialto and San Marco and has therefore always been the main land thoroughfare of the city and a prime site for its shopkeepers. For those immune to the charms of window-shopping there's little reason to linger until you reach the church of **San Salvador** (Mon–Sat 9am–noon & 3–7pm), an early sixteenth-century church cleverly planned in the form of three Greek crosses placed end to end. It has a couple of Titian paintings – an altarpiece of the Transfiguration (1560) and an *Annunciation* (1566), whose awkward angel is often blamed on the great man's assistants. The end of the south transept is filled by the tomb of Caterina Cornaro, who for a while was Queen of Cyprus before being manoeuvred into surrendering the island to Venice (see p.401).

The **Campo San Bartolomeo**, close to the foot of the Rialto Bridge, is at its best in the evening, when it's as packed as any bar in town. If the crush gets a bit too much, you can retire to the nearby **Campo San Luca**, another focus of after-work gatherings but not as much of a pressure-cooker as San Bartolomeo.

Beyond Campo San Luca is **Campo Manin**, on the south side of which is a sign for the spiral staircase known as the **Scala del Bovolo** (*bovolo* means "snail shell" in Venetian dialect), a piece of flamboyant engineering dating from around 1500 (April–Oct daily 10am–6pm; Nov–March Sat & Sun 10am–4pm; €3.50). The **Museo Fortuny** is also close at hand, similarly tucked away in a spot you'd never accidentally pass. In addition to making his famous silk dresses, which were said to be fine enough to be threaded through a wedding ring, Mariano Fortuny (1871–1949) was a painter, architect, engraver, photographer, theatre designer and sculptor, and the museum reflects his versatility. Design and photography exhibitions are held regularly here (the Venice Card is valid for these), and how much of the building you get to see depends on how extensive the show is – often only a couple of rooms are used. And in high season you'll have to queue, as the Palazzo is so fragile that only 75 people are allowed in at a time.

West of the Piazza

Although it too has its share of fashionable shops – much of the broad Calle Larga XXII Marzo, for example, is dedicated to the beautification of the well heeled and their dwellings – the area to the **west of the Piazza** is less frenetic than the streets to the north. None of the first-division tourist sights is here, but the walk from the Piazza to the Accademia Bridge, through a succession of *campi* each quite unlike its predecessor, isn't lacking in worthwhile diversions.

Heading west from the Piazza, you soon reach the hypnotically dreadful **San Moisè** (daily 3.30–7pm, plus Sun 9am–noon), runaway winner of any poll for the ugliest church in Venice. The facade sculpture, featuring a species of camel unknown to zoology, was created in 1668 by Heinrich Meyring – and if you think this is in dubious taste, wait till you see his altarpiece *Mount Sinai with Moses Receiving the Tablets*.

Halfway along the Calle Larga XXII Marzo, on the right, is the Calle del Sartor da Veste, which takes you over a canal and into the Campo San Fantin, where the Renaissance church of **San Fantin** has a graceful domed apse by Sansovino. Across the campo is Venice's largest and oldest theatre, **La Fenice**, opened in December 1792, rebuilt in 1836 after the place had been wrecked by fire, but devastated by yet another fire on the night of January 29, 1996, just as a phase of restoration was coming to a close. The rebuilding was fraught with problems and intrigue, and was made more difficult by the demand that better fireproofing be installed while retaining the superb acoustics of the original opera house.

Back on the main road to the Accademia, another very odd church awaits – **Santa Maria del Giglio**, otherwise known as Santa Maria del Zobenigo (Mon–Sat 10am–5pm, Sun 1–5pm; €2.50 or Chorus Pass). You can stare at this all day and still not find a single Christian image. The statues are of the five Barbaro brothers who financed the rebuilding of the church in 1678; Virtue, Honour, Fame and Wisdom hover respectfully around them; and the maps in relief depict the towns the brothers graced in the course of their exemplary military and diplomatic careers.

The tilting campanile that soon looms into view over the vapid church of San Maurizio belongs to Santo Stefano, which stands at the end of the next *campo* – the **Campo Santo Stefano**. Large enough to hold several clusters of tourists and locals plus a kids' football match or two, it's a lively place but never feels crowded, and has, in *Paolin*, one of the best ice-cream places in Venice. To those few non-Venetians to whom his name means anything, Francesco Morosini is known as the man who lobbed a missile through the roof of the Parthenon during a Venetian assault on Turkish-controlled Athens towards the end of the seventeenth century. He lived at the Canal Grande end of the campo (no. 2802) and is buried in **Santo Stefano** (Mon–Sat 10am–5pm, Sun 1–5pm), a thirteenth-century church that was rebuilt in the fourteenth and altered again in the first half of the fifteenth; the Gothic doorway and the ship's keel roof both belong to this last phase. The best paintings are in the sacristy (€2.50 or Chorus Pass) – *The Agony in the Garden*, *The Last Supper* and *The Washing of the Disciples' Feet*, all late works by Tintoretto.

Dorsoduro

Some of the finest architecture in Venice, both domestic and public, is to be found in the *sestiere* of **DORSODURO**, a situation partly attributable to the stability of its sandbanks – Dorsoduro means "hard back". Yet for all its attractions, not many visitors wander off the strip that runs between the main sights of the area – the Ca' Rezzonico, the Accademia and the Salute.

The Galleria dell'Accademia

The **Galleria dell'Accademia** (Mon 8.15am–2pm, Tues–Sun 8.15am–7.15pm; €6.50; @www.gallerieaccademia.org) is one of the finest specialist collections of European art, following the history of Venetian painting from the fourteenth to the eighteenth centuries. When it was established in 1807, its exhibits came largely from churches and convents that were then being suppressed; indeed, the buildings that the Accademia has occupied since then include two former religious buildings – the church of Santa Maria della Carità, rebuilt by Bartolomeo Bon in the 1440s, and the incomplete Convento dei Canonici Lateranensi, partly built by Palladio in 1561.

The Accademia is the third component – with San Marco and the Palazzo Ducale – of the triad of obligatory tourist sights in Venice, but admissions are restricted to batches of 300 people at a time. This may change with the completion of the expansion programme that's under way, but for now you should expect to queue if you're visiting in high summer.

The early Renaissance

The gallery is laid out in a roughly chronological succession of rooms going anticlockwise. The first room at the top of the stairs is the fifteenth-century assembly room of the Scuola and houses works by the earliest known individual Venetian painters. **Paolo Veneziano** (from the first half of the fourteenth century) and his follower **Lorenzo Veneziano** are the most absorbing.

Room 2 moves on to works from the late fifteenth and early sixteenth centuries, with large altarpieces that are contemplative even when the scenes are far from calm. **Carpaccio**'s strange and gruesome *Crucifixion and Glorification of the Ten Thousand Martyrs of Mount Ararat* (painted around 1512) and his *Presentation of Jesus in the Temple* accompany works by **Giovanni Bellini** and **Cima da Conegliano**.

In the west room you can observe the emergence of the characteristically Venetian treatment of colour, but there's nothing here as exciting as the small paintings in rooms 4 and 5, a high point of the collection. Apart from an exquisite *St George* by **Mantegna** and a series of **Giovanni Bellini** Madonnas, this section contains **Giorgione**'s enigmatic *Tempest*.

The High Renaissance

Rooms 6 to 8 introduce the heavyweights of Venetian painting, Jacopo Robusti, known as **Tintoretto**, **Titian** (Tiziano Vecellio) and **Lorenzo Lotto**. Room 10 is dominated by epic productions, and an entire wall is filled by **Paolo Veronese**'s *Christ in the House of Levi*. Originally called *The Last Supper*, this picture provoked a stern reaction from the Court of the Holy Office: it was too irreverent for such a holy subject, they insisted – why were there "Germans and buffoons and such-like things in this picture? Does it appear to you fitting that at our Lord's last supper you should paint buffoons, drunkards, Germans, dwarfs, and similar indecencies?" Veronese fielded all their questions and responded simply by changing the title, which made the work acceptable. The pieces by **Tintoretto** in here include three legends of St Mark: *St Mark Rescues a Slave* (1548), which was the painting that made his reputation, *The Theft of the Body of St Mark* and *St Mark Saves a Saracen* (both 1560s). All of these show Tintoretto's love of energy and drama – from the physical or psychological drama of the subject matter, emphasized by the twisting poses of the people depicted, to the technical energy of his brush strokes, perception of colour and use of light. Opposite is an emotional late **Titian**, a pietà (1570s) intended for his own tomb in the Frari.

The eighteenth century

Room 11 contains a number of works by **Giambattista Tiepolo**, the most prominent painter of eighteenth-century Venice, including two shaped fragments rescued from the wreckage of the Scalzi (1743–45) and *The Translation of the Holy House of Loreto* (1743), a sketch for the same ceiling. There's also more from **Tintoretto**; the *Madonna dei Tesorieri* (1566), with its sumptuously painted velvets, shows facial types still found in Venice today.

The following stretch of seventeenth- and eighteenth-century paintings isn't too enthralling – the highlights are portraits by Rosalba Carriera and interiors by Pietro Longhi in room 17. Carriera's work popularized the use of pastel as a medium; look for her moving *Self-Portrait in Old Age* (1740s), executed just before she went blind. Longhi is not the most brilliant of painters in the Accademia, but his illustrative work is fascinating for its reportage on eighteenth-century Venice.

The Vivarinis, the Bellinis and Carpaccio

Around the corner and to the right are more works from the fifteenth and early sixteenth centuries. Pieces by the Vivarini family feature strongly; **Alvise Vivarini**'s *Santa Chiara* is outstanding. **Giovanni Bellini** is represented by four triptychs painted, with workshop assistance, for this church in the 1460s. The extraordinary *Blessed Lorenzo Giustinian* is by his brother, **Gentile**; one of the oldest surviving Venetian canvases, and Gentile's earliest signed work, it was possibly used as a standard in processions, which would account for its state.

The magnificent cycle of pictures painted around 1500 for the Scuola di San Giovanni Evangelista, mainly illustrating the miracles of the Relic of the Cross, is displayed in room 20, off a corridor to the left. All of the paintings are replete with fascinating local details, but particularly rich are **Carpaccio**'s *Cure of a Lunatic* and **Gentile Bellini**'s *Recovery of the Relic from the Canale di San Lorenzo* and *Procession of the Relic in the Piazza*. The next room contains a complete cycle of pictures by **Carpaccio** illustrating the Story of St Ursula, painted for the Scuola di Sant'Orsola at San Zanipolo (1490–94). Restored in the mid-1980s, the paintings form one of Italy's most unforgettable groups. The legend is that Hereus, a British prince, proposed marriage to Ursula, a Breton princess. She accepted on two conditions: that Hereus convert to Christianity, and that he should wait for three years, while she went on a pilgrimage. The pilgrimage, undertaken with a company of 11,000 virgins, ended with a massacre near Cologne by the Huns – as Ursula had been forewarned in a dream.

Finally, in room 24 (the former hostel of the Scuola), there's **Titian**'s *Presentation of the Virgin* (dating from 1539). It was painted for the place where it hangs, as was the triptych by **Antonio Vivarini** and **Giovanni d'Alemagna** (1446), another of the oldest Venetian canvases.

The Guggenheim and the Salute

Within five minutes' walk of the Accademia, east beyond the Campo San Vio, is the unfinished Palazzo Venier dei Leoni, home of Peggy Guggenheim for thirty years until her death in 1979 and now the base for the **Guggenheim Collection** (daily except Tues 10am–6pm; June–July open Sat till 10pm; €10; Ⓦ www .guggenheim.org). Her private collection is an eclectic, quirky choice of mainly excellent pieces from her favourite modernist movements and artists. Prime pieces include Brancusi's *Bird in Space* and *Maestra*, De Chirico's *Red Tower* and *Nostalgia of the Poet*, Max Ernst's *Robing of the Bride*, sculpture by Laurens and Lipchitz, paintings by Malevich and collages by Schwitters.

Continuing along the line of the Canal Grande, you come to Santa Maria della Salute, better known simply as the **Salute** (daily 9am–noon & 3–6.30pm; closes 5.30pm in winter), built to fulfil a Senate decree of October 22, 1630, that a new church would be dedicated to Mary if the city were delivered from the plague that was ravaging it – an outbreak that was to kill about a third of the population. Work began in 1631 on **Baldessare Longhena**'s design and was completed in 1681, though the church was not consecrated until November 9, 1687, five years before Longhena's death. Thereafter, every November 21, the Signoria headed a procession from San Marco to the Salute, over a specially constructed pontoon bridge, to give thanks for the city's good health (*salute* meaning "health" and "salvation") – even today the festival of the Salute is a major event in the Venetian calendar.

In 1656, a hoard of **Titian** paintings from the suppressed church of Santo Spirito was moved here and is now housed in the sacristy (€1.50). The most prominent of these is the altarpiece *St Mark Enthroned with Saints Cosmas, Damian, Sebastian and Rocco* (the plague saints). The *Marriage at Cana*, with its dramatic lighting and perspective, is by **Tintoretto** (1561), and features likenesses of a number of the artist's friends.

The **Dogana di Mare** (Customs House), with its Doric facade (1676–82), occupies the spur formed by the meeting of the Canal Grande with the Giudecca canal. Known as the Punta della Dogana, the very tip of the promontory is a great spot to have a picnic, particularly at sunset. The gold ball, noticeable from anywhere on this busy stretch of water, is a weathervane, topped by a figure representing either Justice or Fortune.

Along the Záttere to San Sebastiano

Stretching along Dorsoduro's southern waterfront from the Punta della Dogana to the Stazione Maríttima, the **Záttere** (Rafts) was originally the place where most of the bulky goods coming into Venice were unloaded, and is now a popular place for a picnic lunch or a Sunday stroll. Its principal sight is the church of Santa Maria del Rosario, invariably known as the **Gesuati** (Mon–Sat 10am–5pm, Sun 1–5pm; €2.50, or Chorus Pass); it's worth a call for its paintings by **Giambattista Tiepolo**: three ceiling frescoes called *Scenes from the Life of St Dominic* and an altarpiece, *Madonna with three Dominican Saints*.

A diversion to the right straight after the Gesuati takes you past the **squero di San Trovaso**, most famous of the very few gondola workshops left in Venice, and on to the church of **San Trovaso** (Mon–Sat 3–6pm; free). Venetian folklore has it that this church was the only neutral ground between the rival working-class factions of the Nicolotti and the Castellani, who would celebrate intermarriages and other services here, but came and went through separate doors. Its paintings include a fine pair by **Tintoretto** (*The Temptation of St Anthony* and *The Last Supper*), and two large scenes that were begun by Tintoretto at the very end of his life and completed by his son and other assistants: *The Adoration of the Magi* and *The Expulsion from the Temple*.

The church of **San Sebastiano** (Mon–Sat 10am–5pm, Sun 1–5pm; €2.50, or Chorus Pass), right up by the Stazione Maríttima was built between 1505 and 1545 and was the parish church of **Paolo Veronese**, who provided most of its paintings and is buried here. He was first brought in to paint the ceiling of the sacristy with a *Coronation of the Virgin* and the *Four Evangelists*, followed by the *Scenes from the Life of St Esther* on the ceiling of the church. He then painted the dome of the chancel (since destroyed), and with the help of his brother, Benedetto, moved on to the walls of the church and the nuns' choir. The paintings around the high altar and the organ came last, painted in the 1560s.

Ca' Rezzonico and Ca' Fóscari

From San Sebastiano it's a straightforward walk back towards the Canal Grande along Calle Avogaria and Calle Lunga San Barnaba, a route that deposits you in Campo San Barnaba, just yards from the **Ca' Rezzonico**, now the **Museo del Settecento Veneziano** (April–Oct 10am–6pm; Nov–March 10am–5pm; closed Tues; €6.50). Having acquired the Ca' Rezzonico in 1934, the *comune* of Venice set about furnishing and decorating it with eighteenth-century items and materials (or their closest modern equivalent), so giving the place the feel of a well-appointed house rather than of a formal museum.

On the applied arts side of the collection, the plentiful and outlandish carvings by **Andrea Brustolon** are as likely to elicit revulsion as admiration. As for the paintings, the highlights are **Pietro Longhi**'s affectionate illustrations of Venice social life and pictures by **Giambattista and Giandomenico Tiepolo** – the latter's frescoes of clowns and carnival scenes (created for his own house) are his best-known images.

Immediately north of Ca' Rezzonico, the cluster of Gothic palaces fronting the Canal Grande constitutes one of the city's architectural glories. Built in 1435, the **Ca' Fóscari**, which Ruskin thought "the noblest example in Venice" of late Gothic, was the home of Doge Francesco Fóscari, whose extraordinarily long term of office came to an end with his forced resignation, an event partly attributable to the unrelenting feud conducted against him by the Loredan family and its allies. He died in 1457, only weeks after leaving the Palazzo Ducale. Adjoining the Ca' Fóscari are a pair of joined buildings of the same period – the **Palazzi Giustinian**. Wagner wrote the second act of *Tristan and Isolde* while living here.

Campo Santa Margherita and around

The nearby **Campo Santa Margherita** is the social heart of Dorsoduro, and the largest square on this side of the Canal Grande. It's spacious and at the same time modest, with no grandiose architecture – the tone is set instead by its cluster of market stalls and its plethora of bars and cafés, which draw much of their custom from the nearby university. The **Scuola Grande dei Carmini** (daily: April–Oct 10am–5pm; Nov–March 10am–4pm; €5), in the southwest corner of the *campo*, is a showcase for Giambattista Tiepolo, whose ceiling paintings in the main upstairs hall, painted in the early 1740s, centre on the panel *The Virgin in Glory*.

To the north of the campo stands the church of **San Pantaleone** (Mon–Sat 8–10am & 4–6pm), which possesses a *Coronation of the Virgin* by Antonio Vivarini and Giovanni d'Alemagna (in the chapel to the left of the chancel) and Veronese's last painting, *San Pantaleone Healing a Boy* (second chapel on right). The church also boasts the most melodramatic ceiling in the city: *The Martyrdom and Apotheosis of San Pantaleone*. It kept Gian Antonio Fumiani busy from 1680 to 1704 but he never got the chance to bask in the glory of his labours – he died in a fall from the scaffolding on which he'd been working.

San Polo and Santa Croce

Two *sestieri* are covered in this section: **San Polo** *sestiere*, which extends from the Rialto market to the Frari area; and **Santa Croce**, a far less sight-heavy district which lies to the north of San Polo and reaches right across to Piazzale Roma. There are two main routes through the district, each following approximately the curve of the Canal Grande – one runs between the Rialto and the Scalzi bridge, the other takes you in the opposite direction from the Rialto, down towards the Accademia. Virtually all the essential sights lie on, or just off, one of these two routes.

The Rialto Bridge

The famous **Ponte di Rialto** (Rialto Bridge) is the bustling link between San Marco and San Polo *sestieri*, standing at a bend in the Canal Grande as it curves its way through the city, lined with shops and constantly thronged with locals and tourists. The current structure superseded a succession of wooden and sometimes unreliable structures – in 1444 a forerunner collapsed under the weight of the crowd gathered to watch the wedding procession of the Marquis of Ferrara; and one of Carpaccio's *Miracles of the True Cross*, in the Accademia, shows what the next drawbridge looked like. The decision to construct a stone bridge was taken in 1524, and over the following sixty years proposals by Michelangelo, Vignola, Sansovino and Palladio were considered and rejected. Eventually the job was awarded to the aptly named **Antonio da Ponte**, whose top-heavy design was described by Edward Gibbon as "a fine bridge, spoilt by two rows of houses upon it". Until 1854, when the first Accademia Bridge was built, this was the only point at which the Canal Grande could be crossed on foot.

From the Rialto to Ca' Pésaro

West of the Rialto Bridge, the relatively stable building land and good defensive position of the area drew some of the earliest lagoon settlers to the high bank (*rivo alto*) that was to develop into the **Rialto** district. While the political centre of the new city grew up around San Marco, the Rialto became the commercial zone. In the twelfth century, Europe's first state bank was opened here, and the financiers of the district were the weightiest figures on the international exchanges for the next three centuries and more. The state offices that oversaw all maritime business were here as well, and in the early sixteenth century the offices of the exchequer were installed in the new **Palazzo dei Camerlenghi**, at the foot of the Rialto Bridge.

The connection between wealth and moral turpitude was exemplified by the Rialto, where the fleshpots were as busy as the cash desks. A late sixteenth-century survey showed that there were about 3000 patrician women in the city, but well over 11,000 prostitutes, the majority of them based in the banking quarter. One Rialto brothel, the Casteletto, was especially esteemed for the literary, musical and sexual talents of its staff, and a perennial Venetian bestseller was a catalogue giving the addresses and prices of the city's most alluring courtesans.

It was through the markets of the Rialto that Venice earned its reputation as the bazaar of Europe. Virtually anything could be bought or sold here: Italian fabrics, precious stones, silver plate and gold jewellery, and spices and dyes from the Orient. Trading had been going on here for over 400 years when, in 1514, a fire destroyed everything in the area except the church. The possibility of relocating the business centre was discussed but found little favour, so reconstruction began almost straight away, the **Fabbriche Vecchie** (the arcaded buildings along the Ruga degli Orefici and around the Campo San Giacomo) being finished eight years after the fire, and Sansovino's **Fabbriche Nuove** (running along the Canal Grande from Campo Cesare Battisti) following about thirty years later.

Today's Rialto market is tamer than that of Venice at its peak, but it's still one of the liveliest spots in the city, and one of the few places where it's possible to stand in a crowd and hear nothing but Italian spoken. There's a shoal of memento-sellers by the church and along the Ruga degli Orefici; the market proper lies between them and the Canal Grande – mainly fruit stalls around the **Campo San Giacomo**, vegetable stalls and butchers' shops as you go through to the Campo Battisti, after which you come to the fish market. (The fish market and many of the other stalls close for the day at 1pm, but some reopen in the late afternoon.)

A popular Venetian legend asserts that the city was founded on Friday, March 25, 421 AD at exactly midday; from the same legend derives the claim that the church of **San Giacomo di Rialto** (Mon–Sat 9.30–noon & 4–6pm) was founded in that year, and is thus the oldest church in Venice. Whether it is or not, what is not disputed is that the church was rebuilt in 1071 and that parts of

VENICE AND THE VENETO | The City

the present structure date from then – for instance, the interior's six columns of ancient Greek marble have eleventh-century Veneto-Byzantine capitals.

The church of **San Cassiano** (daily 9am–noon & 5–7pm) is a building you're bound to pass as you wander west from the Rialto. Don't be put off by its barn-like appearance: it contains three paintings by **Tintoretto**, *The Resurrection, The Descent into Limbo* and *The Crucifixion.* The first two have been mauled by restorers, but the third is one of the greatest pictures in Venice, a startling composition dominated not by the cross but by the ladder on which the executioners stand.

Nearby, and signposted from San Cassiano, is the **Ca' Pésaro**, in which you'll find both the **Galleria d'Arte Moderna** and **Museo Orientale** (Tues–Sun: April–Oct 10am–6pm; Nov–March 10am–5pm; €5.50, or Museum Pass/Venice Card). Pieces bought from the Biennale make up the core of the modern art collection, with Italian artists predominating, few of them much known to the wider world. As for the oriental galleries, the jumble of lacquer work, armour, screens, weaponry and so forth has long been awaiting an overhaul.

Campo San Polo

The largest square in Venice after the Piazza, the **Campo San Polo** used to be the city's favourite bullfighting arena as well as the site of weekly markets and occasional fairs. Nowadays it's a combination of outdoor social centre and children's sports stadium.

The bleak interior of **San Polo** church (Mon–Sat 10am–5pm, Sun 1–5pm; €2.50, or Chorus Pass) should be visited for *The Last Supper* by **Tintoretto** and **Giandomenico Tiepolo**'s paintings *The Stations of the Cross*, a series painted when the artist was only 20. The sober piety of these pictures will come as a surprise if you've been to the Ca' Rezzonico, though it often seems that his interest was less in the central drama than in the society portraits that occupy the edges of the stage.

The Frari

The Franciscans were granted a large plot of land near San Polo in about 1250, not long after the death of St Francis. Replacement of their first church by the present Santa Maria Gloriosa dei Frari – more generally known simply as the **Frari** (Mon–Sat 9am–6pm, Sun 1–6pm; €2.50, or Chorus Pass) – began in the mid-fourteenth century and took over a hundred years. This mountain of brick is not an immediately attractive building but its collection of paintings, sculptures and monuments make it a guaranteed highlight of anyone's visit.

Venice is relatively impoverished as far as major paintings by **Titian** are concerned: apart from the Salute and the Accademia, the Frari is the only building in Venice with more than a single significant work by him. One of these – the *Assumption*, painted in 1518 – you will see almost immediately as you look towards the altar through the fifteenth-century monks' choir, a swirling, dazzling piece of compositional and colouristic bravura for which there was no precedent in Venetian art. The other Titian masterpiece here, the *Madonna di Ca' Pésaro*, was equally innovative in its displacement of the figure of the Virgin from the centre of the picture.

Wherever you stand in the Frari, you'll be facing something that deserves your attention. Two funerary monuments embodying the emergence in Venice of Renaissance sculptural technique flank the Titian *Assumption*: on the left the **tomb of Doge Niccolò Tron**, by **Antonio Rizzo** and assistants, dating from 1476; on the right, the more chaotic **tomb of Doge Francesco Fóscari**, carved by **Antonio and Paolo Bregno** shortly after Fóscari's death in 1457.

The wooden statue of St John the Baptist, in the first chapel to the right, was commissioned from **Donatello** in 1438 by Florentine merchants in Padua; recent work has restored its luridly naturalistic appearance. Still moving to the right, the third chapel houses a typically vivid *Christ on the Sarcophagus* by **Bartolomeo Vivarini**. Head through the door on the right for the sacristy, where on the altar (the site for which it was created) is a picture that alone would justify a visit to the Frari – the *Madonna and Child with Saints Nicholas of Bari, Peter, Mark and Benedict*, painted in 1488 by **Giovanni Bellini**. In the words of Henry James, "it is as solemn as it is gorgeous and as simple as it is deep".

Two massive tombs take up much of the nave. One is the bombastic monument to Titian, built in the mid-nineteenth century on the supposed site of his grave. He died in the 1576 plague epidemic, in around his ninetieth year, and was the only casualty of that outbreak to be given a church burial. Opposite is a tomb of similarly pompous dimensions but of redeeming peculiarity: the Mausoleum of Canova, erected in 1827 by pupils of the sculptor, following a design he had made for the tomb of Titian.

The Scuola Grande di San Rocco and San Rocco church

At the rear of the Frari is a place you should on no account miss: the **Scuola Grande di San Rocco** (daily: April–Oct 9am–5.30pm; Nov–March 10am–5pm; €5.50). St Rocco (St Roch) was attributed with the power to cure the plague and other serious illnesses, so when the saint's body was brought to Venice in 1485, this *scuola* began to profit from donations from people wishing to invoke his aid. In 1515 it commissioned this prestigious new building, and soon after its completion in 1560, work began on the decorative scheme that was to put the Scuola's rivals in the shade – a cycle of more than fifty major paintings by **Tintoretto**.

The Tintoretto paintings

To appreciate the evolution of Tintoretto's art you have to begin in the smaller room on the upper storey, the **Sala dell'Albergo**. In 1564 the Scuola held a competition for the contract to paint its first picture. The subject was to be the glorification of St Roch, and Tintoretto won the contest by rigging up a finished painting in the very place for which the winning picture was destined – the centre of the ceiling. The protests of his rivals, who had simply submitted sketches, were to no avail. Virtually an entire wall of the Sala is occupied by the stupendous *Crucifixion*, a painting that reduced Ruskin to a state of dumbfounded wonder. His loquacious guide to the cycle concludes: "I must leave this picture to work its will on the spectator; for it is beyond all analysis, and above all praise." The pictures on the entrance wall – *Christ before Pilate*, *Christ Crowned with Thorns* and *The Way to Calvary* – inevitably suffer from such company, but they deserve close scrutiny.

Tintoretto finished the Sala in 1567 and eight years later he started on the main upper hall, a project he completed in 1581. The Old Testament subjects depicted in the three large panels of the **ceiling**, with their references to the alleviation of physical suffering, are coded declarations of the Scuola's charitable activities: *Moses Striking Water from the Rock*, *The Miracle of the Brazen Serpent* and *The Miraculous Fall of Manna*. The paintings around the walls, all based on the New Testament, are an amazing feat of sustained inventiveness, in which every convention of perspective, lighting, colour and even anatomy is defied. A caricature of the irascible Tintoretto (with a jarful of paint brushes) is incorporated into the trompe-l'oeil carvings by the seventeenth-century sculptor Francesco Pianta.

Displayed on easels, either in the *sala* or main hall – they are often moved – are a handful of paintings that are understandably missed by many visitors, given the competition. *Christ Carrying the Cross* is now generally thought to be an early **Titian**, though some still maintain Giorgione's authorship; Titian's *Annunciation* is similarly influenced by the earlier master. Two early **Tiepolo** paintings, also on easels, relieve the eyes with a wash of airy colour.

The paintings on the ground floor were created between 1583 and 1587, when Tintoretto was in his late 60s. The turbulent *Annunciation* is one of the most arresting images of the event ever painted, and there are few Renaissance landscapes to match those of *The Flight into Egypt* and the small paintings of *St Mary Magdalen* and *St Mary of Egypt*.

The church

Yet more paintings by Tintoretto adorn the neighbouring church of **San Rocco** (8am–12.30pm & 3–5pm). On the south wall of the nave you'll find *St Roch Taken to Prison*, and below it *The Pool of Bethesda* – though only the latter is definitely by Tintoretto. In the chancel are four large works, all of them difficult to see properly: the best are *St Roch Curing the Plague Victims* (lower right) and *St Roch in Prison* (lower left); the two higher pictures are *St Roch in Solitude* and *St Roch Healing the Animals*, though the second is again a doubtful attribution.

Cannaregio

In the northernmost section of Venice, **CANNAREGIO**, you can go from the bustle of the train station and the execrable Lista di Spagna to areas which, although no longer rural (Cannaregio comes from *canna*, meaning "reed") are still among the quietest and prettiest parts of the whole city. The district also has the dubious distinction of containing the world's original ghetto.

The station area

The first building worth a look in the vicinity of the station is to the left as you come out of it – the **Scalzi** church, also called Santa Maria di Nazareth (daily 7–noon & 4–7pm; free). Built in the 1670s for the barefoot (*scalzi*) order of Carmelites, the interior, by Baldessare Longhena, is a joy for aficionados of the Baroque. There are frescoes by Giambattista Tiepolo in the first chapel on the left and the second on the right, but his major work in the church, the ceiling, was destroyed in 1915 by an Austrian bomb. A couple of fragments, now in the Accademia, were all that was salvaged.

Foreign embassies used to be concentrated in this area, so that the Venetian authorities could keep an eye on them all together, and the **Lista di Spagna** takes its name from the Spanish embassy, which used to be at no. 168. The street is now completely given over to the tourist trade, with shops and stalls, bars, restaurants and hotels all competing for the same desperate trade. If you are hunting for trinkets, food or a bed, you'll find better elsewhere.

The church of **San Geremia** (Mon–Sat 8.30am–noon & 4–6.30pm, Sun 9.15am–12.15pm & 5.30–6.30pm) is chiefly notable for being the present home of **St Lucy**, martyred in Syracuse in 304, stolen from Constantinople by Venetian crusaders in 1204, and ousted from her own Palladian church in 1863 when it was demolished to build the station. Lucy tore her own eyes out after an unwanted suitor kept complimenting her on their beauty, and hence became the patron saint of eyesight: the glass case on the high altar contains her desiccated body. Architecturally, the church's main point of interest is the twelfth-century campanile, one of the oldest in the city.

The ballroom of the **Palazzo Labia**, next door to the church, contains frescoes by Giambattista Tiepolo and his assistants (1745–50), illustrating the story of Antony and Cleopatra. The present owners, RAI (the state radio service), allow the public in to see them on Wednesdays, Thursdays and Fridays 3–4pm).

The **Canale di Cannaregio** was the main entrance to Venice before the road and rail bridges were built; walk along it to get to the church of **San Giobbe** (Mon–Sat 10am–5pm, Sun 1–5pm; €2.50, or Chorus Pass). The physical afflictions with which God permitted Satan to test the faith of Job – he was smitten with "sore boils from the sole of his foot unto his crown" – made Job particularly popular with the Venetians, who suffered regularly from malaria, plague and a plethora of damp-related diseases. The church was built on the site of an oratory by the Venetian Gothic architect Antonio Gambello, later assisted by Pietro Lombardo, who introduced Tuscan Renaissance elements. Lombardo's contribution, his first work in Venice, consists of the doorway and, inside, the statues of SS Anthony, Bernardino and Louis and the chancel. Its choicest paintings – Giovanni Bellini's *Madonna Enthroned with Saints* and Carpaccio's *Presentation in the Temple* – have been removed to the drier atmosphere of the Accademia.

The Ghetto

The Venetian **Ghetto** was, in a sense, the first in the world: the word comes from the Venetian dialect *getar* (to found), or *geto* (foundry), which is what this area was until 1390. It was in 1516 that all the city's Jews were ordered to move to the island of the Ghetto Nuovo, an enclave that was sealed at night by Christian curfew guards – whose wages were paid for by the Jews. Distinctive badges or caps had to be worn by all Jews, and there were various economic and social restraints on the community, although oppression was lighter in Venice than in most other parts of Europe (it was one of the few states to tolerate the Jewish religion). When Jews were expelled en masse from Spain in 1492 and Portugal in 1497, many of them came here.

Each wave of Jewish immigrants established its own synagogues with their distinctive rites. The **Scola Levantina**, founded in 1538, and the **Scola Spagnola**, possibly founded about twenty years later, reflect the wealth of these particular groups, who were important traders within the Venetian state; the latter was redesigned around 1584 by Longhena (the profession of architect was barred to Jews), a project that influenced the alteration of the other synagogues. These two are still used today for services, the former in summer and the latter in winter, and, together with the beautiful Scola al Canton and the Scola Italiana, can be viewed in a fascinating hourly tour of the area organized by the **Jewish Museum** in Campo Ghetto Nuovo (daily except Sat & Jewish hols: June–Sept 10am–7pm; Oct–May 10am–5.30pm; €3, or free with tour, which costs €8.50; tours in English on the half-hour; last tour June–Sept 5.30pm, Oct–May 4.30pm); the collection in the museum itself is mainly of silverware, embroidery and other liturgical objects.

The Jewish population grew to about 5000 and, even though they were allowed to spread into the **Ghetto Vecchio** (called the "old ghetto" because that's where the foundries used to be) and the **Ghetto Nuovissima**, there was gross overcrowding. As the Ghetto buildings were not allowed to be more than one-third higher than the surrounding houses, the result was a stack of low-ceilinged storeys – seven is the usual number. Napoleon removed the gates of the Ghetto in 1797 but Venice's Jews didn't achieve equal rights with other Venetians until Unification with Italy in 1866. The Ghetto came close to extinction during World War II: in a corner of the campo a series of reliefs by **Arbit Blatas** commemorate the two hundred Venetian Jews deported to the death camps in 1943 and 1944, whose names and ages are inscribed on a separate memorial entitled *The Last Train*. Today Venice's Jewish population of around six hundred (which includes a recent influx of young Italians and North Americans belonging to the Lubavitch sect) is spread all over the city, but the Ghetto remains the centre of the community.

Sant'Alvise, Madonna dell'Orto and around

The area northeast of the Ghetto is one of the most restful parts of Venice. The long *fondamente*, dotted with food shops, bars and trattorias; the red walls and green shutters of the houses; the blue and yellow hulls of the boats – together they create a scene reminiscent of Henry James's vision of the essence of Venice: "I simply see a narrow canal in the heart of the city – a patch of green water and a surface of pink wall."

A few minutes north of the Ghetto stands the church of **Sant'Alvise** (Mon–Sat 10am–5pm & Sun 1–5pm; €2.50, or Chorus Pass). Commissioned by Antonia Venier, daughter of Doge Antonio Venier, after the saint appeared to her in a vision in 1388, the church has one outstanding picture, *The Road to Calvary* by Giambattista Tiepolo, painted in 1743. His *Crown of Thorns* and *Flagellation*, slightly earlier works, are on the right-hand wall of the nave. Normally under the nuns' choir, to the right as you enter the church, but on view in the sacristy while restoration work is ongoing, are eight small tempera paintings, generally known as *The Baby Carpaccios* thanks to Ruskin's speculative attribution; they do date from Carpaccio's infancy (around 1470), but they're not actually by him.

A circuitous stroll eastwards brings you to the Gothic church of **Madonna dell'Orto** (Mon–Sat 10am–5pm & Sun 1–5pm; €2.50, or Chorus Pass). Dedicated to St Christopher in about 1350, the church was renamed after a large stone Madonna by Giovanni de'Santi, found discarded in a local vegetable garden (*orto*), began to work miracles. Brought inside the church in 1377, the figure can still be seen (now heavily restored) in the Cappella di San Mauro through a door at the front end of the right aisle. The main sculpture on the facade is a fifteenth-century *St Christopher* by the Florentine Nicolò di Giovanni; Bartolomeo Bon designed the portal in 1460, shortly before his death. The **interior** was messed around with in the 1860s and although some of the overpainting was removed during restoration work in the 1930s, its appearance still owes much to nineteenth-century interference. Scraps of fresco on the arches and the painted beams give an idea of how it must have looked in the sixteenth century.

This was also Tintoretto's parish church: he's buried in the chapel to the right of the high altar. So too are his son and daughter, Domenico and Marietta. And there are a number of paintings by the artist here as well, notably the colossal *Making of the Golden Calf* and *The Last Judgement*, which flank the main altar. Others include Tintoretto's *The Presentation of the Virgin in the Temple*, at the end of the right aisle; *The Vision of the Cross to St Peter* and *The Beheading of St Paul*, on each side of the chancel's *Annunciation* by Palma il Giovane; and *St John the Baptist and Other Saints* by Cima da Conegliano on the first altar on the right. In the first chapel on the left there should also be a *Madonna and Child* by Giovanni Bellini, but it was stolen in 1993.

From the Ca' d'Oro to the Gesuiti

Back towards the Canal Grande, the main thoroughfare of eastern Cannaregio, the **Strada Nova**, was carved through the houses in 1871–72, and is now a bustling and eclectic shopping street where you can buy anything from spaghetti to surgical trusses. Nearly halfway along is the inconspicuous *calle* named after, and leading to, the **Ca' d'Oro** – a Gothic palace much altered by restoration, and whose finest feature, the facade, is best seen from the water. Inside, the main attraction of the **Galleria Giorgio Franchetti** (Mon 8.15am–2pm, Tues–Sat 8.15am–7.15pm; €5) is undoubtedly the *St Sebastian* painted by **Mantegna** shortly before his death in 1506. Many of the big names of Venetian art are found on the second floor, but the canvases by Titian and Tintoretto are not among their best, and Pordenone's fragmentary frescoes from Santo Stefano require a considerable feat of imaginative reconstruction, as do the remains of Giorgione and Titian's work from the exterior of the Fondaco dei Tedeschi. The Ca' d'Oro's collection of sculpture, though far less extensive than the array of paintings, has more outstanding items, notably **Tullio Lombardo**'s beautifully carved *Young Couple*, and superb portrait busts by Bernini and Alessandro Vittoria.

At the eastern end of the Strada Nova you come to the Campo dei Santi Apostoli, a general meeting-point and crossroads, and the church of **Santi Apostoli** (daily 7.30–11.30am & 5–7pm). The exterior is unexceptional, other than the curious 24-hour clock on the campanile, but give the interior a look for the Cappella Corner: the design of the chapel is attributed to Mauro Codussi, the altar painting of the *Communion of St Lucy* is by Giambattista Tiepolo, and the tomb of Marco Corner (father of Caterina Cornaro, see p.401) is attributed to Tullio Lombardo.

Just inland from the Fondamente Nove, the northern edge of this zone, is the **Gesuiti** church, as Santa Maria Assunta is familiarly known (daily 10am–noon & 4–6pm). The Jesuits began work on their church in 1714, and it took fifteen years to inlay the marble walls of the interior and carve its marble "curtains", with a result that is jaw-droppingly impressive even if you hate Baroque architecture. The *Martyrdom of St Lawrence* by Titian, on the first altar on the left, is a night scene made doubly obscure by the lighting arrangements.

San Giovanni Crisostomo and the Miracoli

In the southeastern corner of Cannaregio you'll find the cosy church of **San Giovanni Crisostomo** (Mon–Sat 8.15am–12.15pm & 3–7pm, Sun 3–7pm), which was built around 1500 to designs by Mauro Codussi, and has two fine paintings: Giovanni Bellini's late *Saints Jerome, Christopher and Augustine* and Sebastiano del Piombo's *St John Chrysostom with Saints John the Baptist, Liberale, Mary Magdalene, Agnes and Catherine*. Round the back of the church is the Corte Seconda del Milion, a tiny courtyard hemmed in by ancient buildings, one of which – though nobody is sure which – was Marco Polo's family home.

Sitting on the lip of a canal just a minute to the north of Corte Seconda del Milion, the church of Santa Maria dei Miracoli – known simply as the **Miracoli** (Mon–Sat 10am–5pm & Sun 1–5pm; €2.50, or Chorus Pass) – is one of the most attractive buildings in Europe. It was built in the 1480s to house a painting of the Madonna (still the altarpiece) that was believed to have performed a number of miracles, such as reviving a man who'd spent half an hour lying at the bottom of the Giudecca canal. The church is thought to have been designed by Pietro Lombardo; certainly he and his two sons Tullio and Antonio oversaw the building and executed much of the carving. Typically for Renaissance architecture in Venice, richness of effect takes precedence over classical correctness – the Corinthian pilasters are set below the Ionic, so that the viewer can better appreciate the carving on the Corinthian.

The marble-lined interior contains some of the most intricate decorative sculpture to be seen in Venice. The half-length figures of two saints and

△ Market in front of Santa Maria dei Miracoli

the *Annunciation* on the balustrade of the raised galleries at the east end are attributed to Tullio Lombardo; the rest of the attributions for the carvings at this end are arguable between the two brothers and their father. Ruskin was greatly distressed by the children's heads carved to the side of the top of the altar steps: "The man who could carve a child's head so perfectly must have been wanting in all human feeling, to cut it off, and tie it by the hair to a vine leaf."

Castello

Bordering both San Marco and Cannaregio, and spreading right across the city to the housing estates of Sant'Elena in the east, Castello is the largest of the *sestieri*. In terms of its tourist appeal, centre stage is occupied by the huge **Santi Giovanni e Paolo**, a place saturated with the history and mythology of Venice. Within a few minutes' walk of here are two other fascinating churches, **Santa Maria Formosa** and **San Zaccaria**, as well as the beguiling Carpaccio paintings in the Scuola di San Giorgio degli Schiavoni.

Much of the eastern section of the Castello *sestiere* is given over to the **Arsenale**, once the industrial hub of the city and the largest manufacturing site in Europe. Beyond it lies a predominantly residential quarter that has little to offer of cultural significance, except when the Biennale art and architecture shows are on, though its open spaces – the **Giardini Garibaldi**, **Giardini Pubblici** and **Parco della Rimembranza** – offer an antidote to the claustrophobia that overtakes most visitors to Venice at some point.

Campo Santi Giovanni e Paolo

After the Piazza, the Campo Santi Giovanni e Paolo – or, in its Venetian dialect form, San Zanipolo – is the most impressive open space in Venice. Dominated by the huge brick church from which it gets its name, it also has the most beautiful facade of any of the *scuole grande* and one of the finest Renaissance equestrian monuments.

The Colleoni statue and the Scuola Grande di San Marco

When the *condottiere* mercenary **Bartolomeo Colleoni** died, he left a handsome legacy to the republic on condition that a monument should be erected to him in the square before San Marco, an impossible proposition to Venice's rulers, with their cult of anonymity. They got around this dilemma with a splendid piece of disingenuousness, interpreting the will in a way that allowed them to raise the monument before the Scuola Grande di San Marco, rather than the basilica, and still claim the money. In 1481 the commission for the monument was won by **Andrea Verrocchio**, who was working on the piece when he died at the end of June 1488. **Alessandro Leopardi** was called in to finish the work and produce the plinth for it, which he gladly did – even adding his signature on the horse's girth and appending *del Cavallo* to his name.

A spectacular backdrop to Colleoni, the **Scuola Grande di San Marco** has provided a sumptuous facade and foyer for the Ospedale Civile since its suppression in the early nineteenth century. The facade was started by Pietro Lombardo and Giovanni Buora in 1487, and finished in 1495 by Mauro Codussi.

The church of Santi Giovanni e Paolo

The church of **Santi Giovanni e Paolo** (Mon–Sat 7.30am–7pm, Sun 7.30am–6pm; €2.50) is the Dominican equivalent of the Frari, founded in 1246, rebuilt and enlarged from 1333, and finally consecrated in 1430. The sarcophagus of Doge Giacomo Tiepolo, who originally gave the site to the Dominicans, is on the left of the door outside.

Approximately 90 metres long, 38 metres wide at the transepts and 33 metres high in the centre, the **interior** is stunning for its sheer size, and is more spacious than it would have beenup to 1682, when the wooden choir was demolished. The simplicity of the design, a nave with two aisles and gracefully soaring arches, is offset by the huge number of tombs and monuments around the walls. Contrary to the impression created, not all of the doges are buried here, just 25 of them.

The **west wall** is devoted to the Mocenigo family: above the door is the tomb of Doge Alvise Mocenigo and his wife by Pietro Lombardo; to the right is the monument to Doge Giovanni Mocenigo by Tullio Lombardo; and on the left the superb monument to Doge Pietro Mocenigo by Pietro Lombardo, assisted by his sons.

In the **south aisle**, after the first altar, is the monument to the Venetian military commander Marcantonio Bragadin, to which is attached one of Venice's grisliest stories. In 1571 Bragadin was double-crossed by the Turks to whom he had been obliged to surrender Famagusta: tortured and humiliated for days by his captors, he was eventually skinned alive. Some years later the skin was brought back to Venice, and today it sits in that urn high up on the wall.

Giovanni Bellini's superb polyptych *St Vincent Ferrer, with Saints Christopher and Sebastian*, with an *Annunciation* and pietà above, occupies the next altar. At the far end of this aisle, before you turn into the transept, you'll see a small shrine with the **foot of St Catherine of Siena**: most of her body is in Rome, her head is in her house in Siena, one foot's here, and other little relics are scattered about Italy.

The **south transept** has a painting by Alvise Vivarini, *Christ Carrying the Cross* (1474), and Lorenzo Lotto's *St Antonine* (1542), painted in return for nothing more than his expenses and permission to be buried in the church. Sadly, Lotto was eventually driven from his home town by the jealousies and plots of other artists (including Titian), and died in the monastery at Loreto.

On the right of the chancel is the tomb of Doge Michele Morosini, selected by Ruskin as "the richest monument of the Gothic period in Venice". The tomb of Doge Andrea Vendramin, opposite, was singled out as its antithesis – only the half of the effigy's head that would be visible from below was completed by the artist, a short cut denounced by Ruskin as indicative of "an extreme of intellectual and moral degradation". Tullio Lombardo is thought to have been the culprit, with help from others – maybe his father and brother.

In 1867 a fire wrecked the **Cappella del Rosario**, at the end of the north transept, destroying paintings by Tintoretto, Palma il Giovane and others; of their replacements, the best are **Veronese**'s ceiling panels and *Adoration*. Funerary sculpture is the main attraction of the north aisle. To the left of the sacristy door is the monument to Doge Pasquale Malipiero by Pietro Lombardo, one of the earliest in Renaissance style in Venice.

Santa Maria Formosa and around

South of San Zanipolo lies Campo di Santa Maria Formosa, an atmospheric square with a modest but mouthwatering morning market. The church of **Santa Maria Formosa** (Mon–Sat 10am–5pm & Sun 1–5pm; €2.50, or Chorus Pass) was built by San Magno, Bishop of Oderzo, in the seventh century, who was inspired by a dream in which he saw a buxom (*formosa*) figure of the Madonna. The present building is another Codussi effort, dating from 1492. Palma il Vecchio's altarpiece *St Barbara*, the church's outstanding picture, was admired by George Eliot as "an almost unique presentation of a hero-woman". Bartolomeo Vivarini's *Madonna della Misericordia*, in a side chapel, is a fine example of one of the warmest Catholic symbols – here she's shown sheltering a group of parishioners under her cloak.

The Renaissance Palazzo Querini-Stampalia, just round the corner from Santa Maria Formosa, houses the **Pinacoteca Querini-Stampalia** (Tues–Thurs & Sun 10am–6pm, Fri & Sat 10am–10pm; €8). Unless you have a voracious appetite for seventeenth- and eighteenth-century Venetian painting, you'll get most pleasure from earlier pieces such as Palma il Vecchio's portraits *Francesco*

Querini and *Paola Priuli Querini* and Giovanni Bellini's *The Presentation in the Temple*. Apart from that, the main interest is in the eighteenth-century decor of the rooms, especially the library. It's worth taking advantage of the unusual late opening times at the weekend, when you can often savour the atmosphere of the palace in peace or take in a classical concert (included in the price).

San Zaccaria and the Riva

The Campo San Zaccaria, a few yards off the waterfront, has a more torrid past than most – the convent here was notorious for its libidinous goings-on (officials were once sent to close down the nuns' parlour, only to be met with a barrage of bricks), and in 864 Doge Pietro Tradonico was murdered here as he returned from vespers. The towering church of **San Zaccaria** (daily 10am–noon & 4–6pm), a pleasing mixture of Gothic and Renaissance, was started by Antonio Gambello and finished after his death in 1481 by Mauro Codussi, who was responsible for the facade from the first storey upwards. Inside is one of the city's most stunning altarpieces, a *Madonna and Four Saints* by Giovanni Bellini. A fee of €1 gets you into the rebuilt remnants of the old church, the Cappella di Sant'Atanasio and Cappella di San Tarasio, where you'll find an early Tintoretto, *The Birth of John the Baptist*, and three wonderful altarpieces by Antonio Vivarini and Giovanni d'Alemagna. Floor mosaics from the ninth and twelfth centuries can be seen through panels in the present floor level, and downstairs is a spooky, waterlogged, ninth-century crypt.

The principal waterfront of the area, the **Riva degli Schiavoni**, stretches right back to the Molo. It's a favourite walk, particularly as the sun goes down, and many notables have lived or stayed in houses and hotels here: Petrarch and his daughter lived at no. 4145 for a while, Henry James stayed nearby at no. 4161 when he was finishing *The Portrait of a Lady*, and the *Hotel Danieli*, at the far end, has accommodated George Sand, Charles Dickens, Proust, Wagner and the ever-present Ruskin.

Halfway along the Riva stands the **Pietà** church (or Santa Maria della Visi-tazione), famous as the place where Vivaldi was choirmaster – he was also violin teacher to the attached orphanage. Giorgio Massari won a competition to redesign the church in 1736, and it's possible that he consulted with Vivaldi on its acoustics; building didn't actually begin until 1745, and the facade was even more delayed – it was only finished in 1906. The church is still used for concerts, and when the box office is open you can sometimes peer over the ropes at the interior, which looks like a wedding cake turned inside out and has one of Venice's most ostentatious ceiling paintings, Giambattista Tiepolo's *The Glory of Paradise*.

The Greek quarter and the Scuola di San Giorgio degli Schiavoni

Stroll north along the flank of the Pietà and you'll enter the quarter of Venice's Greek community, identifiable from a distance by the alarmingly tilted campanile of **San Giorgio dei Greci**. The Greek presence was strong in Venice from the eleventh century, and grew stronger after Constantinople's capture by the Turks in 1453; by the close of the fifteenth century they had founded their own church, college and school here. The present *scuola*, designed (like the college) by Longhena in the seventeenth century, now houses the **Museo Dipinti Sacri Bizantini** (daily 9am–5pm; €4). Although many of the most beautiful of the exhibited works (mainly fifteenth to eighteenth century) maintain the traditions of icon painting in terms of composition and use of symbolic figures rather than attempts at realism, it's fascinating to see how some of the artists absorbed Western influences. The **church** contains icons dating back to the twelfth century and a lot of work by Michael Danaskinàs, a sixteenth-century Cretan artist.

From here it's a hundred metres or so to the **Scuola di San Giorgio degli Schiavoni**, whose ground-floor hall (April–Oct Tues–Sat 9.30am–12.30pm & 3.30–6.30pm, Sun 9.30am–12.30pm; Nov–March Tues–Sat 10am–12.30pm & 3–6pm, Sun 10am–12.30pm; €3) would get onto anyone's list of the ten most beautiful rooms in Europe. Venice's resident Slavs (*Schiavoni*), most of whom were traders, set up a *scuola* to look after their interests in 1451; the present building dates from the early sixteenth century, and the whole interior looks more or less as it would have then. Entering it, you step straight from the street into the superb lower hall, the walls of which are decorated with a cycle created by Vittore Carpaccio between 1502 and 1509. Originally painted for the upstairs room, but moved here when the building was rearranged in 1551, the sequence of pictures consists chiefly of scenes from the lives of SS George, Tryphone and Jerome (the Dalmatian patron saints). Outstanding among them is *The Vision of St Augustine*, depicting the moment that Augustine, while writing to St Jerome, was told in a vision of Jerome's death.

San Francesco della Vigna

Somewhat stranded on the northern edge of Castello, the church of **San Francesco della Vigna** (daily 8am–12.30pm & 3–6.30pm) takes its name from the vineyard that was here when the Franciscans were given the site in 1253. The present church building was begun in 1534, designed and supervised by Sansovino, but the design was modified during construction, and Palladio was later brought in to provide the facade. Although smaller than the two great mendicant churches of San Zanipolo and the Frari, it feels less welcoming – probably attributable to the cold colouring added to the more calculated Renaissance architecture. However, there are some fine works of art that make the trek worthwhile – but be sure to have a pocketful of coins for the light boxes. The ones you shouldn't miss are: *Saints Jerome, Bernard and Ludovic*, attributed to Antonio Vivarini (left of main door); the sculptures of Prophets and Evangelists by the Lombardo family (in the chapel left of the chancel); and a *Sacra Conversazione* by Veronese (fifth chapel on the north side).

The Arsenale and Museo Storico Navale

A corruption of the Arabic *darsin'a* (house of industry), the very name of the **Arsenale** is indicative of the strength of Venice's trading links with the eastern Mediterranean, and the workers of these dockyards and factories were the foundations on which the city's mercantile and military supremacy rested. Construction of the Arsenale commenced in the early years of the twelfth century, and by the third decade of the fifteenth century it had become the base for some 300 shipping companies, operating around 3000 vessels in excess of 200 tons. The productivity of the Arsenale was legendary: for the visit of Henry III of France in 1574 a complete ship was built while the state reception for the king was in progress.

Expansion of the Arsenale continued into the sixteenth century – Sanmicheli's covered dock for the state barge (the *Bucintoro*) was built in the 1540s, for example, and da Ponte's gigantic rope-factory (the Tana) in 1579. By then, though, the maritime strength of Venice was past its peak; militarily, too, despite the conspicuous success at Lépanto in 1571, Venice was on the wane, and the recapture of the Morea at the end of the seventeenth century was little more than a glorious interlude in a longer story of decline. When Napoleon took over the city in 1797 he burned down the wharves, sank the last *Bucintoro* and confiscated the remnant of the Venetian navy.

There's no public access to the Arsenale complex except during the Biennale, but you can get a look at part of it from the bridge connecting the Campo Arsenale and the Fondamenta dell'Arsenale. The main **gateway**, built by Antonio Gambello in 1460, was the first structure in Venice to employ the classical vocabulary of Renaissance architecture. The four **lions** to the side of the gateway must be the most photographed in the city: the two on the right were probably taken from Delos (at an unknown date), the left-hand one of the pair being positioned here to mark the recapture of Corfu in 1716; the larger pair were brought back from Piraeus in 1687 by Francesco Morosini after the reconquest of the Morea.

Nearby, on the other side of the Rio dell'Arsenale and facing the lagoon, is the **Museo Storico Navale** (Mon–Fri 8.45am–1.30pm, Sat 8.45am–1pm; €1.60). Chiefly of interest for its models of Venetian craft from the gondola to the *Bucintoro* (these models were the equivalents of blueprints), the museum gives a comprehensive picture of the working life of the Arsenale and the smaller boatyards of Venice.

San Pietro di Castello

In 1808 the greater part of the canal connecting the Bacino di San Marco to the broad inlet of the Canale di San Pietro was filled in to form what is now **Via Garibaldi**, the widest street in the city and the busiest commercial area in the eastern district. Head along the right-hand side of the street and you'll soon cross the Ponte di Quintavalle onto the island of **San Pietro**, once the ecclesiastical centre of Venice, but nowadays a slightly down-at-heel place where the chief activity is the repairing of boats.

As with the Arsenale, the hidden history of San Pietro is perhaps more interesting than what you can actually see. The church (Mon–Sat 10am–5pm, Sun 1–5pm; €2.50, or Chorus Pass) – which takes its name from the castle that used to stand here – is basically a grandiose derivative of a plan by Palladio and has little to recommend it. The most intriguing object inside is the so-called Throne of St Peter (in the south aisle), a marble seat made from an Arabic funeral stone inscribed with texts from the Koran. The lurching campanile, rebuilt by Codussi in the 1480s, was the first tower in Venice to be clad in stone.

Sant'Elena

Located at the eastern limit of the city, the island of **Sant'Elena** was enlarged tenfold during the Austrian administration, partly to form exercise grounds for the troops. Much of the island used to be covered by the meadow of Sant'Elena, a favourite recreation area in the nineteenth century but since usurped by houses, leaving only a strip of park along the waterfront. Still, the walk out here is the nearest you'll get to country pleasures in Venice, and the **church of Sant'Elena** – next to the city's football stadium – is worth a visit.

A church was first erected here in the thirteenth century, following the acquisition of the body of St Helena (the mother of Constantine), and substantially rebuilt in 1435. The spartan Gothic interior has recently been restored, as have the cloister and campanile, but the main attraction is the doorway to the church, an ensemble created in the 1470s by Antonio Rizzo. The sculptural group in the lunette – a monument to Comandante Vittore Cappello, showing him kneeling before St Helena – is the district's one major work of art.

The northern islands

The islands lying to the north of Venice – **San Michele**, **Murano**, **Burano** and **Torcello** – are the places to visit when the throng of tourists in the main part of the city becomes too oppressive, and are the source of much of the glass and lace work you see in many shops in the city.

To get to the northern islands, the main **vaporetto stop** is **Fondamente Nove** (or Nuove), as most of the island services start here or call here. For **San Michele and Murano only** the circular #41 and #42 *vaporetti* both run every twenty minutes, circling Murano before heading back towards Venice; the #41 follows an anticlockwise route around the city, the #42 a clockwise route. Murano can also be reached by the #DM ("Diretto Murano"), which from around 8am to 6pm runs to the island from Tronchetto via Piazzale Roma and the train station. For **Murano, Burano and Torcello** the #LN (Laguna Nord) leaves every half-hour from Fondamente Nove for most of the day (hourly early in the morning and evenings), calling first at Murano-Faro before heading on to Mazzorbo and Burano, from where it proceeds, via Treporti, to Punta Sabbioni and the Lido. A shuttle boat runs every half-hour between Burano and Torcello, timed to fit in with Venice boat arrivals and departures at the Burano stop.

San Michele

The high brick wall around the cemetery island of San Michele gives way by the landing stage to the elegant white facade of **San Michele in Isola** (daily 7.30am–12.15pm & 3–4pm), designed by Mauro Codussi in 1469. With this building, Codussi not only helped introduce Renaissance architecture to Venice, but also promoted the use of Istrian stone. Easy to carve yet resistant to water, it had been used as damp-proofing at ground level, but never before for a complete facade; it was to be used on the facades of most major buildings in Venice from the Renaissance onwards.

The main part of the island, through the cloisters, is the city **cemetery** (daily: April–Sept 7.30am–6pm; Oct–March 7.30am–4pm), established by Napoleonic decree and nowadays maintained by the Franciscans, as is the church. The majority of Venetians lie here for just ten years or so, when their bones are dug up and removed to an ossuary and the land recycled. Only those who can afford it stay longer. The cemetery is laid out in sections, the most dilapidated of which is for the Protestants (no. XV), **Ezra Pound**'s final resting place. In section XIV are the Greek and Russian Orthodox graves, including the restrained memorial stones of **Igor and Vera Stravinsky** and the more elaborate tomb of **Serge Diaghilev** – always strewn with flowers.

Even with the grave-rotation system, the island is reaching full capacity, so in 1998 a competition was held for the **redevelopment** of San Michele. The winning entry, from English architect David Chipperfield, places a sequence of formal courtyards alongside a new funerary chapel and crematorium (the Church's line on space-saving cremation having become more flexible of late). Chipperfield's creation promises to be an austerely beautiful place – and there's a certain appropriateness to the fact that the twenty-first century's first large-scale addition to the Venetian cityscape will be a cross between a necropolis and a philosopher's retreat.

Murano

Chiefly famed now as the home of Venice's **glass-blowing** industry, **Murano**'s main *fondamente* are crowded with shops selling the mostly revolting products of the furnaces. However, don't despair: Murano does have other things to offer.

The glass furnaces were moved to here from Venice as a safety measure in 1291, and so jealously did the Muranese guard their industrial secrets that for a long while they had the European monopoly on glass mirror-making. The glass-blowers of Murano were accorded various privileges not allowed to other artisans, such as being able to wear swords. From 1376 the offspring of a marriage between a Venetian nobleman and the daughter of a glass-worker were allowed to be entered into the *Libro d'Oro*, unlike the children of other cross-class matches.

Far more interesting than most of the finished products is the performance of their manufacture. There are numerous **furnaces** to visit, all free of charge on the assumption that you will then want to buy something. Many of the workshops are to be found along Fondamenta dei Vetrai, traditionally a glass-working centre, as the name suggests.

When the Venetian Republic fell to Napoleon in 1797, there were seventeen churches on Murano; today only two are open. The first is **San Pietro Martire** (daily 9am–noon & 3–6pm), a Dominican Gothic church begun in 1363 and largely rebuilt after a fire in 1474. Its main attraction is a pair of paintings by Giovanni Bellini hanging on the right wall: on the left is the large and elegant *Madonna and Child with Saints Mark and Augustine, and Doge Barbarigo*, and on the right an *Assumption*.

The Glass Museum

Close by, along Riva Longa, you'll find the **Museo del Vetro** (April–Oct 10am–5pm; Nov–March 10am–4pm; closed Wed; €4 or Museum/Venice card). Perhaps the finest single item is the dark-blue Barovier marriage cup, dating from around 1470; it's on show in room 1 on the first floor, along with some splendid Renaissance enamelled and painted glass. But every room contains some amazing creations: glass beakers that look as if they are made from veined stone; sixteenth-century platters that look like discs of crackled ice; stupendously ugly nineteenth-century decorative pieces, with fat little birds enmeshed in trellises of glass. A separate room contains a fascinating exhibition on the history of Murano glass techniques, this time fully explained in English.

Santi Maria e Donato

Murano's finest building is the Veneto-Byzantine church of **Santi Maria e Donato**, which was founded in the seventh century and rebuilt in the twelfth (daily 8am–noon & 4–7pm). Its beautiful **mosaic floor**, dated 1141 in the nave, mingles abstract patterns with images of beasts and birds – an eagle carries off a deer; two roosters carry off a fox, slung from a pole. The church was originally dedicated to Mary, but in 1125 was rededicated when the relics of St Donato were brought here from the Greek Island, Kefalonia. Four splendid bones from an unfortunate dragon that was slain by the holy spit of Donato are now hanging behind the altar. Above these, in the apse, is a twelfth-century **mosaic of the Madonna** and fifteenth-century frescoes of the Evangelists.

Burano

The main route into **Burano** is a narrow street full of lace shops which soon opens out to reveal the brightly painted houses of the village itself; the colours used to be symbolic, but the meanings have become muddled over time and people now paint their houses whatever colour takes their fancy.

This is still largely a fishing community, the lagoon's main yield being shell-fish of various kinds, such as *vongole* (tiny clams) and small crabs. (The catch can be bought either here, on the Fondamenta Pescheria, or back in Venice, at the Rialto.) The lives of the women of Burano used to be dominated by the **lace** industry, but the production of handmade lace is no longer a large-scale enterprise, and much of stuff sold in the shops lining the narrow street lead-ing into the village from the vaporetto stop is produced by machine. Making Burano-point and Venetian-point lace is extremely exacting work, both highly skilled and mind-bendingly repetitive, taking an enormous toll on the eyesight. Each woman specializes in one particular stitch, and as there are seven stitches in all, each piece is passed from woman to woman during its construction. An average-size table centre requires about a month of work.

The skills of lacemaking are still taught at Burano's **Scuola del Merletto** (April–Oct 10am–5pm; Nov–March 10am–4pm; closed Tues; €4, or Museum Pass/Venice Card), on Piazza Baldassare Galuppi. Although the *scuola* has not operated as a full-time school since the late 1960s and is now almost mori-bund, a few courses are still held here, and on weekdays you might see a few local women at work on their cylindrical cushions. Pieces produced here are displayed in the attached museum, along with specimens dating back to the sixteenth century; after even a quick tour you'll have no problems distinguish-ing the real thing from the machine-made and imported lace that fills the Burano shops.

Torcello

Torcello was settled as early as the fifth century, became the seat of the Bishop of Altinum from 638, and the home of about 20,000 people by the fourteenth century, before being eclipsed by Venice – by the end of the fifteenth century Torcello was largely deserted and today only about thirty people remain in residence. The main reason people come here today is to visit Venice's first cathedral, **Santa Maria dell'Assunta** (daily: March–Oct 10.30am–5pm; Nov–Feb 10am–4.30pm; €3, joint ticket with campanile or museum €5.50, or €8 with museum and campanile). An early church on the site became a cathedral after the Bishop of Altinum arrived with other emigrants from the mainland. The present Veneto-Byzantine building is on pretty much the same plan as the seventh-century one, but it was largely rebuilt in the 860s and altered again in 1008. Inside, the waterlogged crypt is the only survivor of the original church; the baptistery also dates from the seventh century, but circular foundations in front of the main doors are all that remain of it.

The dominant tones of the interior are created by pink brick, gold-based mosaics and the watery green-grey marble of its columns and panelling; the mosaic floor is eleventh century, but two wooden panels lift to reveal the original floor underneath. A stunning twelfth-century **mosaic** of the Madonna and Child, on a pure gold background, covers the semi-dome of the apse, resting on an eleventh-century mosaic frieze of the Apostles. In the centre of the frieze, below the window, is an image of St Heliodorus, the first Bishop of Altinum, whose remains were brought here by the first settlers. It's interesting to compare this image with the gold-plated face mask given to his remains in a Roman sarcophagus in front of the original seventh-century altar. Ruskin described the view from the **campanile** as "one of the most notable scenes in this wide world", a verdict you can test for yourself as the campanile has now been reinforced, cleaned and reopened, after thirty years' service as a pigeon-loft (daily: March–Oct 10.30am–5.30pm; Nov–Feb 10am–5pm; €3).

The church of **Santa Fosca** (same hours as Santa Maria; free) was built in the eleventh and twelfth centuries to house the body of the eponymous saint, brought to Torcello from Libya some time before 1011 and now resting under the altar. Much restored, the church retains the Greek cross form and a fine exterior apse, and inside, the elegant brick arches and cornerings leading up to its wooden dome. Despite the tourists, both these churches manage to maintain a meditative calm.

In the square outside sits the curious **chair of Attila**. Local legend has it that if you sit in it you will be wed within a year. Behind it, in two buildings round the square, is the **Museo di Torcello** (Tues–Sun: March–Oct 10.30am–5pm; Nov–Feb 10am–4.30pm; €3), which includes nicely displayed thirteenth-century beaten gold figures, sections of mosaic heads, and jewellery.

The southern islands

The section of the lagoon to the south of the city, enclosed by the long islands of the **Lido** and **Pellestrina**, has far fewer outcrops of solid land than the northern half: once you get past **Giudecca** and **San Giorgio Maggiore** – in effect detached pieces of central Venice, served by water buses #82, and #82 plus #41/42 respectively – and clear of the smaller islands that dot the water off the middle section of the Lido, you could, on certain days, look in the direction of the mainland and think you were out in the open sea. The nearer islands are the more interesting: the farther-flung settlements of the southern lagoon have played as significant a role in the history of Venice as the better-known northern islands but nowadays they have little going for them other than the pleasure of the trip.

San Giorgio Maggiore

The prominence of Palladio's church of **San Giorgio Maggiore** (daily: May–Sept 9.30am–12.30pm & 2–5.30pm; Oct–April 9.30am–12.30pm & 2.30–5pm) almost forces you to have an opinion as to its architectural merits. Ruskin didn't much care for it: "It is impossible to conceive a design more gross, more barbarous, more childish in conception, more servile in plagiarism, more insipid in result, more contemptible under every point of rational regard." Palladio's successors were more impressed, though, and it was to prove one of the most influential Renaissance church designs.

The finely calculated proportions and Counter-Reformation austerity of the interior reminded Ruskin merely of an assembly room; in his opinion, its paintings were what justified opening the door. Two pictures by Tintoretto hang in the chancel: *The Fall of Manna* and *The Last Supper*, perhaps the most famous of all his images. They were painted as a pair in 1592–94, the last years of the artist's life; another Tintoretto of the same date – a *Deposition* – hangs in the Cappella dei Morti, approached through the door on the right of the choir.

On the left of the choir a corridor leads to the **campanile** (€3). Rebuilt in 1791 after the collapse of its predecessor, it's the best vantage point in the city, with the whole of Venice spread out before you.

The ex-Benedictine monastery next door to the church, now the base of the combined arts research institute, craft school and naval college known as the **Fondazione Giorgio Cini** (Ⓦ www.cini.it), is one of the architectural gems of Venice, and a regular venue for exhibitions (the only time when the Fondazione is open to the public). It incorporates a 128-metre-long dormitory, designed by

Giovanni Buora around 1494, a double staircase and a library by Longhena, a magnificent refectory by Palladio and two adjoining cloisters, one planned by Giovanni Buora and built by his son, the other designed by Palladio.

La Giudecca

In the earliest records of Venice, the island of **La Giudecca** was known as Spina Longa, a name clearly derived from its shape; the modern name might refer to the Jews (*Giudei*) who were based here from the late thirteenth century until their removal to the Ghetto, or to the disruptive noble families who, from the ninth century, were shoved onto this chain of islets to keep them out of mischief (*giudicati* meaning "judged"). Before the banks of the Brenta became the prestigious site for one's summer abode, the Giudecca was where the wealthiest aristocrats of early Renaissance Venice built their villas, and in places you can still see traces of their gardens. The present-day suburb is a strange mixture of decrepitude and vitality: at the western edge is the neo-Gothic fortress of the Mulino Stucky, a long-derelict flour mill built in 1895 that is now being converted into a Hilton hotel, and at the other stands the *Cipriani*, the most expensive hotel in Venice.

The Franciscan church of the **Redentore** (Mon–Sat 10am–5pm, Sun 1–5pm; €2, or Chorus Pass), designed by Palladio in 1577, is Giudecca's main monument. In 1575–76 Venice suffered an outbreak of bubonic plague that annihilated nearly 50,000 people – virtually a third of the city's population. The Redentore was built in thanks for Venice's deliverance, and every year until the downfall of the republic the doge and his senators attended a Mass in the church on the Feast of the Redentore to express their continuing gratitude. The procession walked to the church over a pontoon bridge from the Záttere, a ceremony perpetuated by the people of Venice on the third Sunday in July.

Recently restored, the bright plasterwork of the interior manipulates the different intensities of light in the various parts of the church to draw the eye – and the mind – inward and upward. As the architect wrote, "Among all colours, none can be more suitable for temples than white because the purity of the colour is more acceptable to God." The best paintings in the church, including a *Madonna with Child and Angels* by Alvise Vivarini, are in the sacristy, which is rarely opened.

San Lazzaro degli Armeni

No foreign community has a longer pedigree in Venice than the Armenians: they were established by the end of the thirteenth century, and for around five hundred years have had a church within a few yards of the Piazza (in Calle degli Armeni). They are far less numerous now, and the most conspicuous sign of their presence is the Armenian island by the Lido, **San Lazzaro degli Armeni**, identifiable from the city by the onion-shaped top of its campanile. The Roman Catholic Armenian monastery here was founded in 1717 by Manug di Pietro (known as Mechitar, "The Consoler"), and derived its name from the island's past function as a leper colony – Lazarus being the patron saint of lepers. Visitors are received here daily from 3.25pm to 5.25pm, admission is €6 and the connecting #20 *motoscafo* leaves San Zaccaria at 3.10pm, returning within ten minutes of the end of the guided tour

The Armenian monks have always had a reputation as scholars and linguists, and the monastery's collection of precious books and manuscripts, some going back to the fifth century, is a highlight of the tour, along with a Tiepolo ceiling panel and the room in which Byron stayed while lending a hand with the preparation of an Armenian–English dictionary.

The Lido

For about eight centuries, the **Lido** was the focus of the annual hullaballoo of Venice's "Marriage to the Sea", when the doge went out to the Porto di Lido to drop a gold ring into the brine and then disembarked for Mass at San Nicolò al Lido. It was then an unspoilt strip of land, and remained so into the nineteenth century. By the twentieth century, however, it had become the smartest bathing resort in Italy, and although it's no longer as chic as it was when Thomas Mann set *Death in Venice* here, there's less room on its beaches now than ever before. But unless you're staying at one of the flashy hotels that stand shoulder to shoulder along the seafront, or are prepared to pay a ludicrous fee to rent one of their beach huts for the day, you won't be allowed to get the choicest Lido sand between your toes. The ungroomed public beaches are at the northern and southern ends of the island – though why people would want to jeopardize their health in these filthy waters is a mystery.

Eating and drinking

Not long ago the reliable judges of the Accademia della Cucina ventured that it was "a rare privilege" to eat well in Venice, and there's more than an element of truth to Venice's reputation as a place where mass tourism has produced monotonous menus, cynical service and slapdash standards in the kitchen. Venice has fewer good moderately priced **restaurants** than any other major Italian city, but things have been improving in recent years, due in part to the efforts of the Ristorante della Buona Accoglienza, an association of restaurateurs determined to present the best of genuine Venetian cuisine at sensible prices – which in the Venetian context means in the region of €35 per person.

A distinctive aspect of the Venetian social scene is the **bácaro**, which in its purest form is a bar that offers a range of snacks called **cicheti** (some times spelled *ciccheti*); the array will typically include *polpette* (small beef and garlic meatballs), *carciofini* (artichoke hearts), hard-boiled eggs, anchovies, *polipi* (baby octopus or squid) and sun-dried tomatoes, peppers and courgettes cooked in oil. Some *bácari* also produce one or two more substantial dishes each day, such as risotto or seafood pasta. Excellent food is also served at many of Venice's **osterie** (or *ostarie*), the simplest of which are indistinguishable from *bácari*, while others have sizeable dining areas. We've classified our bars and restaurants according to which aspect of the business draws most of the customers, but if you're looking for a simple meal in a particular area of the city, be sure to check both sets of listings.

Restaurants

Virtually every budget restaurant in Venice advertises a set-price **menù turistico**, which can be a cheap way of sampling Venetian specialities, but the quality and certainly the quantity won't be up to the mark of an **à la carte** meal, and frequently won't even be acceptable. Value for money tends to increase with the distance from San Marco; plenty of restaurants within a short radius of the Piazza offer menus that seem to be reasonable, but you'll probably find the food unappetizing, the portions tiny and the service abrupt. There are two notable concentrations of good-value restaurants: around San Barnaba in Dorsoduro, with several recommended places on Calle Lunga San Barnaba; and the area between the Cannaregio canal and Sant'Alvise, with the Ghetto at its centre.

We've supplied the day of the week on which each restaurant is closed (in the vast majority of cases this day is Sunday or Monday), but bear in mind that many restaurateurs take their annual holiday in August, and that quite a few places close down on unscheduled days in the dead weeks of winter. In most cases, booking a table is advisable in high season, and you should also be aware that Venetians tend to eat early and that restaurateurs routinely close early if trade is slack, so if you're in town at a quiet time, don't turn up later than 8.30pm, unless you're dining at one of the city's more expensive restaurants, which tend to keep longer hours.

San Marco

Al Bacareto Calle Crosera San Samuele 3447 ☎041.528.9336. This place has been recommendable for many years, but recently has been getting smarter, and a little more expensive. Dishes such as the excellent risottos can be eaten either in the dining room or standing at the bar area (the cheaper option). You can sit outside in summer. Closed Sun.

Da Carla Sottoportego Corte Contarina 1535a ☎041.523.7855. Tiny bar-trattoria hidden down a *sottoportego* off the west side of Frezzeria, a few paces from the Piazza. The battered old sign is somewhat misleading, as the place has recently undergone a makeover, but it's still packed at lunchtimes with workers dropping in for sandwiches, simple pasta dishes and salads. One of the best places for a quick bite close to the Piazza. Closed Sun.

Da Fiore Calle delle Botteghe 3461 ☎041.523.5310. Established in the mid-1990s, this popular restaurant offers genuine Venetian cuisine in a classy trattoria-style setting. The anteroom is a nice small bar that does very good *cicheti*. Closed Tues.

Harry's Bar Calle Vallaresso 1323 ☎041.528.5777. Often described as the most reliable of the city's gourmet restaurants (*carpaccio* – raw strips of thin beef – was first created here), though there are many who think the place's reputation has more to do with glamour than cuisine. The bar itself has been fashionable since time immemorial, and is famed in equal measure for its cocktails, its sandwiches and its prices. Open daily till 1am.

Osteria-Enoteca San Marco Frezzeria 1610 ☎041.528.5242. As you'd expect for a place so close to the Piazza, this classy modern *osteria* is not cheap, but prices are not madly unreasonable for the quality of the food – and the wine list is very good. Closed Sun.

Rosticceria Gislon Calle della Bissa 5424a. Downstairs it's a sort of glorified snack bar,

serving pizzas and set meals starting at around €10 – the trick is to first grab a place at the long tables along the windows, then order from the counter. Good if you need to refuel quickly and cheaply, but can't face another pizza. There's a less rudimentary restaurant upstairs, where prices are considerably higher for no great increase in quality. Daily 9am–9.30pm.

Dorsoduro

Ae Oche Zàttere al Ponte Lungo 1414 ☎041.520.6601. Sibling of the *Ae Oche* near San Giacomo, this is essentially a huge pizzeria, with a big dining room and waterfront tables too; it does a few other basic dishes, but the huge repertoire of pizzas is what people come for. Open daily noon–3pm & 7pm–midnight (1am Fri & Sat).

Ai Carmini Rio Terrà de la Scoazzera 2894 ☎041.523.1115. A basic good-value trattoria, just off the west end of Campo S. Margherita; the friendly service makes up for a lack of ambience. Closed Sun.

Ai Quattro Ferri Calle Lunga S. Barnaba 2754a ☎041.520.6978. Popular and very highly recommended *osteria* just off Campo S. Barnaba with a menu that changes daily but often consists entirely of fish and seafood. Closed Sun. No credit cards. Booking essential in high season. Moderate.

Casin dei Nobili Calle Lombardo 2765 ☎041.241.1841. Popular with both locals and tourists, this place serves excellent pizzas (from 7pm) plus a varied menu that includes local specialities such as eel. Good two-course menu with water and wine €24. Separate dining area for smokers. *Casin* or *casino* means brothel, as you'll gather from the place mats – not to be confused with *casinò*, which means casino. Closed Mon.

Do Farai Calle Cappeller 3278 ☎041.277.0369. Tucked into an alley close to Ca' Rezzonico, *Do Farai* is a fine *osteria*, serving good steaks and other meat dishes, plus excellent seafood and fish – the speciality is a delicious *carpaccio* of sea bass. In summer it spreads out into the neighbouring *campo*. Closed Sun.

L'Avogaria Calle dell'Avogaria 1629 ℡041.296.0491. The ultra-refined *Avogaria* styles itself as a lounge, restaurant, café and style shop, which gives you an idea of its self-image. The presence of *orrechiette* (thick little pasta "ears") on the menu is a clue to the Puglian origins of the proprietors, who give a distinctive twist to Venetian seafood – this must be the only restaurant in town that marinades its prawns in grappa. Closed Tues.

La Bitta Calle Lunga S. Barnaba 2753a ℡041.523.0531. Innovative fare on a menu that's remarkable for featuring no fish dishes. Marcellino runs the kitchen while his wife Debora serves and cajoles the guests, offering expert guidance on the impressive wine and grappa list. Delicious cheese platter, served with honey and fruit chutney. Tiny dining room (and garden), so booking is essential. Mon–Sat 6.30–11pm. No credit cards.

San Polo and Santa Croce

Alla Madonna Calle della Madonna 594 ℡041.5522.3824. Roomy, loud and bustling seafood restaurant that's been going strong for four decades. Little finesse but very good value for money, and many locals rate its kitchen as one of the city's best. Closed Wed.

Al Nono Risorto Sottoportego de Siora Bettina 2338 ℡041.524.1169. Located just off Campo S. Cassiano, the "Resurrected Grandad" is a pizzeria-restaurant with a predominantly 20-something following. It often has live jazz and blues, and a pleasant small garden is a further attraction. Open noon–2pm & 7pm–midnight; closed Wed and Thurs lunch. No credit cards.

Da Fiore Calle del Scaleter 2202a ℡041.731.308. Refined, elegant restaurant off Campo San Polo; prides itself on its seafood, regional cheeses, desserts, home-made bread and wine list. Generally considered among the very best in Venice, and service is faultless. You can also drop into the tiny front room bar for a quality snack. Closed Sun & Mon.

Il Refolo Campiello del Piovan 1459 ℡041.524.0016. Run by the son of the owner of the famous *Da Fiore*, this excellent canalside pizzeria fills up the tiny square that fronts the church of San Giacomo dell'Orio. The pizzas are perhaps the best in Venice – and are certainly the most expensive. There's also a small menu of (not inexpensive) restaurant dishes, featuring terrific salads. Closed Nov–March; rest of year closed all Mon and Tues lunch.

Jazz Club 900 Campiello del Sansoni 900 ℡041.522.6565. Just off Ruga Vecchia S. Giovanni, the dark-pannelled *Novecento* serves some of the best pizzas in the city, accompanied by non-stop jazz (live once a week, except in summer). Open until midnight or later. Closed Mon.

Osteria al Ponte, "La Patatina" Calle dei Saoneri 2741a ℡041.523.7238. This bustling *osteria*, sibling of *Al Pantalon*, similarly serves excellent *cicheti* and other Venetian specialities, alongside full-meal menus that change regularly. Closed Sun.

Cannaregio

Ai 40 Ladroni Fondamenta della Sensa 3253 ℡041.715.736. Very successful and very busy *osteria*, with high-quality *cicheti* at the bar, and similarly good Venetian standards served at the tables. Tues–Sun 10am–midnight.

Alla Fontana Fondamenta Cannaregio 1102 ℡041.715.077. Once primarily a bar, *Alla Fontana* has tranformed itself into a very good trattoria, offering a small menu of classic Venetian maritime dishes; tables beside the canal are an added attraction in summer. Mon–Sat 6.30–11pm, closes 10pm in winter.

Alla Vedova Calle del Pistor 3912 ℡041.528.5324. Located in an alley directly opposite the one leading to the Ca' d'Oro, this long-established little restaurant is fronted by a bar offering a mouthwatering selection of *cicheti* (the *polpette* are famous) and a good range of wines. Strangely, *Alla Vedova* does not serve coffee, and the only *dolci* is sweet wine with biscuits. Closed all Thurs & Sun lunch. No credit cards.

Anice Stellato Fondamenta della Sensa 3272 ℡041.720.744. Hugely popular with Venetians for the superb, reasonably priced meals and unfussy atmosphere. Situated by one of the northernmost Cannaregio canals, it's rather too remote for most tourists. If you can't get a table – it's frequently booked solid – at least drop by for the excellent *cicheti* at the bar. Usually closed Mon & Tues, but occasionally Tues & Wed.

Da Rioba Fondamenta della Misericordia 2553 ℡041.524.4379. This smartly austere *osteria* is another excellent northern Cannaregio eatery; often full to bursting, especially in summer, when tables are set beside the canal, but the management always keeps the atmosphere relaxed. Closed Mon.

Vini da Gigio Fondamenta S. Felice 3628a ℡041.528.5140. Until a few years ago most of the customers at this popular, family-run wine bar-trattoria were locals; it's now on the tourist map yet it retains its authenticity and is still, by Venetian standards, excellent value, even if prices have crept up in recent years. As the name suggests, the wine list is remarkable. Closed Mon.

Castello

Aciugheta Campo SS. Filippo e Giacomo 4357 ☎041.522.4292. A bar with a sizeable pizzeria-trattoria attached. The closest spot to San Marco to eat without paying through the nose, it draws a lot of its custom from water-bus staff and gondoliers. Good bar food – in fact, it's generally better than you get in the restaurant section. The name translates as "the little anchovy" and there are pictures of anchovies on the wall. Closed Wed.

Bandierette Barbaria delle Tole 6671 ☎041.522.0619. Nice seafood dishes served by nice people at nice prices – around €35 a head. It has a loyal local following, so it's best to book your table. Closed Mon evening & all Tues.

Corte Sconta Calle del Pestrin 3886 ☎041.522.7024. Secreted in a lane to the east of San Giovanni in Brágora, on the route to San Martino, this restaurant is a candidate for the title of Venice's finest. The exceptionally pleasant staff tend to make it difficult to resist ordering the day's specials, which could easily result in a bill in the region of €70 each – and it would be just about the best meal you could get in Venice for that price. If expenditure is an issue, check the menu in the window carefully before going in (often the waiters will simply recite what's on offer rather than give you anything printed). Booking several days in advance essential for most of the year. Closed Sun & Mon.

Da Remigio Salizzada dei Greci 3416 ☎041.523.0089. Superb upmarket trattoria, serving excellent fish dishes and gorgeous home-made *gnocchi*. The wine list is outstanding too. Be sure to book – the locals (and increasing numbers of tourists) pack this place every night. Closed Mon evening & all Tues.

Dai Tosi Calle Secco Marina 738 ☎041.523.7102. Not to be confused with the establishment of the same name in the same street, this is a lively pizzeria-trattoria with a devoted local clientele – you'd be well advised to book at the weekend. There's a bar in front of the small dining room, where they mix the house aperitif: *sgropino*, a delicious mingling of vodka, peach juice, Aperol and prosecco. Open till 11.30pm; closed Wed, and the kitchen often also closes Mon, Tues and/or Thurs in winter.

Burano

Al Gatto Nero Fondamenta Giudecca 88 ☎041.730.120, Burano. Outstanding local trattoria, just a few minutes' walk from the busy Via Galuppi, opposite the Pescheria. Max, the owner, is a keen fisherman, and what he doesn't know about the marine delicacies of Venice isn't worth knowing. Closed Mon.

La Giudecca

Harry's Dolci Fondamenta S. Biagio 773 ☎041.522.4844. Despite the name, sweets aren't the only things on offer here – the kitchen of this offshoot of the legendary *Harry's* is rated by many as the equal of its ancestor. It's appreciably less expensive than *Harry's Bar* (even though many of the dishes are identical), but you're nonetheless talking about a place where you'll be spending in the region of €70 a head, drink excluded. Still, if you want to experience Venetian culinary refinement at its most exquisite, this is it. Open April–Oct; closed Tues. Very expensive.

Mistrà Giudecca 212a ☎041.522.0743. Occupying the light-filled upper storey of a former factory right in the thick of the Giudecca boatyards, *Mistrà* caters mostly to local dockyard workers at lunchtime, when the menu is very brief, very plain and very cheap. In the evenings you'll find a somewhat more refined offering of Venetian fish and seafood, at prices that are higher than the midday dishes, but still extremely reasonable. Closed Mon evening & all Tues.

Bars

One of the most appealing aspects of Venetian social life is encapsulated in the phrase "*andemo a ombra*", which translates literally as an invitation to go into the shade, but is in fact an invitation for a drink – more specifically, a small glass of wine (an *ombra*), customarily downed in one. (The phrase is a vestige of the time when wines were unloaded on the Riva degli Schiavoni and then sold at a shaded kiosk at the base of the Campanile; the kiosk was shifted as the sun moved round, so as to stay in the shade.) Most bars serve some kind of **food**, their counters usually bearing trays of the characteristically Venetian fat little crustless sandwiches called *tramezzini*, which are stuffed with delicious fillings such as eggs and mushrooms, eggs and anchovies, or Parma ham and artichokes.

Many bars will have a selection of *cicheti* as well, and even a choice of two or three more substantial dishes each day.

San Marco

Al Volto Calle Cavalli 4081. This dark little bar is an *enoteca* in the true sense of the word – 1300 wines from Italy and elsewhere, some cheap, many not; good snacks, too. Open till 10pm. Closed Sun.

Bácaro Jazz Salizzada Fondaco dei Tedeschi 5546. A jazz-themed bar-restaurant that's proving a big hit with Venetian kids, mainly on account of its late hours; there's food, but it's far from the best quality. Open 4pm–3am. Closed Wed.

Centrale Restaurant Lounge Piscina Frezzeria 1659b, ☏041.296.0664. The spacious, transatlantic-style *Centrale* touts itself as the best-designed and coolest bar-restaurant in town, and few would argue with the claim. The food is very expensive (you'll pay around €70 per person), but you might be tempted to blow a few euros for the pleasure of sinking into one of the sumptuous leather sofas, cocktail in hand, and listening to late-night jazz or chilled-out music. Open 6.30pm–2am; closed Tues.

Vino Vino Ponte delle Veste 2007. Very close to the Fenice opera house, this wine bar stocks more than 350 wines. It also serves relatively inexpensive meals as well, and the quality has improved markedly of late. Open 10am–midnight; closed Tues.

Vitae Calle Sant'Antonio 4118. Trendy bar between Campo San Luca and Campo San Manin, serving terrific cocktails and good snacks to the city's bright young things. Open 9am–2am. Closed Sun.

Dorsoduro

Al Chioschetto Záttere al Ponte Lungo 1406a. This canalside bar, as its name suggests, is just a kiosk with outdoor tables. An excellent place to sit with your spritz and a sandwich and watch the sun set over Giudecca. Has a DJ on Fri from 6.30pm in summer. Open till midnight in summer, until 5pm in winter. Open daily – unless the weather's bad, in which case it might not open at all.

Café Blue Calle dei Preti 3778. Lively student haunt where afternoon teas and cakes are on offer as well as whiskies and good cocktails. Puts on art exhibitions, has a DJ on Wednesdays, and hosts local rock bands on many Friday nights. Free internet access too. Mon–Fri 8am–2am, Sat & Sun 5pm–2am.

Café Noir Crosera San Pantalon 3805. This is another favourite student bar, with a cosmopolitan all-day crowd chatting over a *spritz* or coffee. Open Mon–Sat 7am–2am, Sun 9am–2am.

🏃 **Cantina del Vino già Schiavi** Fondamenta Nani 992. Great bar and wine shop opposite San Trovaso – do some sampling before you buy.

Excellent *cicheti* and the generously filled *panini* too. Mon–Sat 8.30am–2.15pm & 3.30–8.30pm; Sun closes 1pm.

Margaret DuChamp Campo S. Margherita 3019. Until Orange opened for business opposite, *Du Champ* was undisputedly the first-choice bar for the style-conscious, and even with the competition across the street it's still kept its edge. Open till 2am. Closed Tues.

San Polo & Santa Croce

Altrove Campo San Silvestro 1105. A very slick young bar, with DJs or bands on Tuesday nights, and a decent kitchen. Mon–Sat 8am–1am.

🏃 **Bancogiro** Sottoportego del Banco Giro 122. Very popular small *osteria*, in a splendid location in the midst of the Rialto market. Come here to nurse a glass of fine wine beside the Canal Grande, or nip upstairs to the dining room for a well-priced and well-prepared meal. Tues–Sun noon–2am.

🏃 **Do Mori** Calle Do Mori 429. Hidden just off Ruga Vecchia S. Giovanni, this is the most authentic old-style Venetian bar in the market area – some would say in the entire city. It's a single narrow room, with no seating, packed every evening with home-bound shopworkers, Rialto porters, and locals just out for a stroll. Delicious snacks, great range of wines and terrific atmosphere. Mon–Sat 8.30am–8.30pm.

Cannaregio

Al Ponte Calle Larga G. Gallina 6378. Brilliant *osteria* between the Miracoli and Santi Giovanni e Paolo: one of the best in the area for a glass of wine and a light meal or snack. Open till 8.30pm. Closed Sun.

Cantina Vecia Carbonera Rio Terrà della Maddalena 2329. Old-style *bácaro* atmosphere and a chilled-out playlist attracts a young, stylish clientele. Good wine, excellent snacks and plenty of space to sit down. Open till 11pm most nights. Closed Mon.

Iguana Fondamenta della Misericordia 2517. This cross between a *bácaro* and a Mexican cantina serves reasonably priced Mexican fare to a young crowd. Live music (Latin, rock and jazz) Tues 9–11pm and some weekends. Tues–Sun till 2am; happy hour 6–8pm.

Castello

Al Portego Calle Malvasia 6015. In the middle of the day this bar is crammed with customers eating cicheti, and in the evening there's often a queue for a place at one of the tiny tables, where some well-prepared basics (pasta, risotto) are served. No reservations are taken, and the kitchen closes at 9.30pm. Closed Sun.

Enoteca Mascareta Calle Lunga Santa Maria Formosa 5183. Always busy wine bar with delicious snacks. Mon–Sat 6pm–1am.

Cafés, pasticcerie and ice cream

As in every Italian city, Venice's **cafés** are central to its social life, and you'll never be more than a couple of minutes from a decent one. In addition to their marvellous local confections, many **pasticcerie** also serve coffee, but will have at most a few bar stools. Strict budgeting is further jeopardized by Venice's terrific **gelaterie**.

San Marco

Florian Piazza S. Marco 56–59. Opened in 1720 and decorated in a passable pastiche of that period, this has long been the café to be seen in. A simple *cappuccino* at a table will set you back around €8 and you'll have to take out a mortgage for a cocktail; if the "orchestra" is playing, you'll be taxed another €5.50 for the privilege of hearing them. Closed Wed in winter.

Igloo Calle della Mandola 3651. Luscious home-made ice cream. Closed Jan & Dec; rest of year open daily.

Marchini Calle Spadaria 676. The most delicious and most expensive of Venetian *pasticciere*, where people come on Sunday morning to buy family treats. The cakes are fabulous, as is the *Marchini* chocolate. Daily 9am–8pm.

Paolin Campo S. Stefano 2962. Some of the best ice cream in Venice, and the outside tables have one of the finest settings in the city. Closed Fri.

Dorsoduro

Causin Campo S. Margherita 2996. The ice cream created by Davide Causin rates among the best in all of Italy, and each year he adds a new flavour to his repertoire – such as *manna*, derived from the sap of ash trees. His café has seating on the *campo*. Closed Sun and most of August.

Il Caffè Campo S. Margherita 2963. Known as *Caffè Rosso* for its big red sign, this small, atmospheric, old-fashioned café-bar is a student favourite. Good sandwiches, and lots of seats outside in the campo. Mon–Sat 8am–2am.

Nico Zàttere ai Gesuati 922. A high-point of a wander in the area, celebrated for an artery-clogging creation called a *gianduiotto* – ask for one *da passeggio* (to take out) and you'll be given a paper cup with a block of praline ice cream drowned in whipped cream. Closed Thurs.

San Polo and Santa Croce

Alaska Calle Larga dei Bari 1159. Superb *gelateria*, dishing out adventurous flavours such as artichoke and fennel amid the more traditional concoctions.

Caffè del Doge Calle dei Cinque 609. Fantastically good coffee (they supply many of the city's bars and restaurants), served in a chic minimalist set-up very close to the Rialto Bridge. Daily 7am–7pm.

Cannaregio

Boscolo Calle del Pistor 1818. Established in the 1930s, *Boscolo* is still going strong: the pastries are excellent, and they turn out some interesting novelties, such as chocolate Kama Sutra figures and chocolate toolkits. Closed Mon.

Il Gelatone Rio Terà Maddalena 2063. The best ice creams in Cannaregio. Closed mid-Dec to mid-Jan; rest of year open daily.

Castello

Didovich Campo Marina 5910. A highly regarded *pasticceria* – some say with the city's best tiramisù and *pastine* (aubergine, pumpkin and other savoury tarts). Standing room only inside, but has outdoor tables. Open till 8pm. Closed Sun.

La Boutique del Gelato Salizzada S. Lio 5727. Top-grade ice creams at this small outlet. Closed Jan–Dec; rest of year open daily.

Rosa Salva Campo Santi Giovanni e Paolo. With its marble-topped bar and outside tables within the shadow of Zanipolo, this is the most characterful of the three Rosa Salva branches (the others are at Calle Fiubera 951 & Merceria S. Salvador 5020, both San Marco). The coffee and home-made ice cream are superb. Closed Wed.

Markets and shops

The *campi*, parks and canalside steps make **picnicking** a pleasant alternative to a restaurant in Venice, and if you're venturing off to the outer islands it's often the only way of refuelling. Don't try to picnic in the *campi*, though – the by-laws against it are strictly enforced.

Open-air **markets** for fruit and vegetables are held in various squares every day except Sunday; check out Santa Maria Formosa, Santa Margherita, Campiello dell'Anconetta, Rio Terrà San Leonardo and the barge moored by Campo San Barnaba. The market of markets, however, is the one at the Rialto, where you can buy everything you need for an impromptu feast – it's open Monday to Saturday 8am to 1pm, with a few stalls opening again in the late afternoon.

Virtually every parish has its **alimentari** and most of them are good; one worth singling out is Aliani Gastronomia in Ruga Vecchia S. Giovanni (San Polo) – scores of cheeses, meats and salads that'll have you drooling. Alternatively, you could get everything from one of Venice's well-hidden **supermarkets**, the most central of which is *Su.Ve*, on the corner of Salizzada San Lio and Calle Mondo Nuovo (Castello). Best of the rest are as follows: *Punto Sma*, tucked between houses 3019 and 3112 on Campo Santa Margherita (Dorsoduro); *Billa* at Záttere Ponte Lungo 1491, by the San Basilio *vaporetto* stop (Dorsoduro) and at Strada Nova 3660, near San Felice (Cannaregio); and the large *Co-Op* by the Piazzale Roma vaporetto stop for services to Murano. Most are open daily 8.30am–8/8.30pm, though some of the smaller ones close for a couple of hours in the middle of the day, and on Sunday.

Nightlife

Though quite a few of Venice's bars stay open reasonably late, Venice after dark is pretty tame, and locals tend to head to Mestre and Lido di Jesolo for nightlife. In Venice itself there are just a couple of tiny **clubs**, the better of which is the members-only Club Malvasia Vecchia (Oct–June Wed–Sat 11pm–4am or later; ☎041.522.5883), hidden in Corte Malatina, a tiny courtyard at the back of the Fenice; on-the-door membership is just €15, the bar is reasonable, and the owner-DJ keeps the place buzzing for as long as people want to dance. The other club – even tinier – is the studenty Round Midnight, near Campo Santa Margherita at Fondamenta del Squero 3102 (Oct–June Fri & Sat, plus some Thursdays, midnight–4am).

Concerts and cinema

Music in Venice, to all intents and purposes, means classical music – though the Teatro Malibran does stage concerts by Italian rock outfits from time to time, bands rarely come nearer than Padua, and the biggest names tend to favour Verona.

La Fenice (ⓦwww.teatrolafenice.it) might be the third-ranking Italian opera house (after Milan's La Scala and Naples' San Carlo) and Venice's top music venue, yet its prices are far from exclusive: the cheapest seats (from a mere €10) give no view of the stage, but very good seats can be had for a reasonable €50–60 on most nights. You'll pay around twice as much for the opening night of a production as you would for the same seat later in the run (midweek prices are the lowest). The opera season runs from late November to the end of June, punctuated by ballet performances. Tickets can be bought at the Fenice box office, the Piazza tourist office, the VeLa/ACTV offices at Piazzale Roma and the train station, and at Vivaldi Store, opposite the post office in Salizzada Fontego dei Tedeschi.

The city's major venues for classical music concerts are the Sale Apollinee in La Fenice, and the recently restored **Teatro Malibran**, behind the church of San Giovanni Crisostomo. Tickets for the Malibran can be bought in advance from the same outlets as tickets for the Fenice. The Malibran's own ticket office sells tickets only on the night of the concert, from around one hour before the start.

Music performances at the **Goldoni** (box office Mon–Sat 9.30am–12.30pm & 4–6pm; ☎041.520.5422, ⓦwww.teatrostabileveneto.it) are somewhat less frequent than at La Fenice and the Malibran; the repertoire here tends to be more populist, with a jazz series cropping up every now and then. For most of the year the Goldoni specializes in the works of the eponymous writer.

Classical concerts, with a very strong bias towards the eighteenth century (and Vivaldi in particular – hardly a week goes by without a performance of *The Four Seasons*) – are also performed at the Palazzo Prigione Vecchie, the Scuola Grande di San Giovanni Evangelista, the Scuola Grande di San Rocco, Palazzo Mocenigo (San Stae) and the churches of Santo Stefano, the Frari, San Stae, San Samuele, San Vidal, San Giacomo di Rialto, San Bartolomeo, Zitelle, San Barnaba, the Ospedaletto and the Pietà (the most regularly used). The average ticket price for these concerts is around €25 (usually with a reduction for students and children). The state radio service sometimes records concerts at the Palazzo Labia, to which the public are admitted free of charge, as long as seats are reserved in advance (☎041.716.666).

The only **cinema** in central Venice is the small two-screen Giorgione at Rio Terrà dei Franceschi 4612a, Cannaregio (☎041.522.6298); non-dubbed English-language films are shown on Tuesdays from October to May, but otherwise the basic fare consists of dubbed general release movies. From around mid-July to the end of August an open-air cinema in Campo S. Polo shows dubbed or Italian-language films to a high-spirited local audience. Films start each night at around 9pm, and it's worth an evening of anyone's holiday, if only for the atmosphere. For information check ⓦwww.comune.venezia.it/cinema.

Exhibitions – and the Biennale

Venice has numerous venues for temporary shows, of which **Palazzo Grassi** (ⓦwww.palazzograssi.it) maintains the highest standards. There's also the **Venice Biennale** (ⓦwww.labiennale.org), set up in 1895 as a showpiece for international contemporary art and held from June to September of every odd-numbered year. Its permanent site in the Giardini Pubblici has pavilions for about forty countries (the largest for Italy's representatives), plus space for a thematic international exhibition. Supplementing this central part are events at venues all over the city: the salt warehouses on the Záttere, for instance, or the Corderie in the Arsenale. In even-numbered years the city hosts an architecture Biennale, a smaller-scale event which runs from the second week in September to mid-November.

Festivals

The *Carnevale* and the Film Festival might be the best publicized of the city's festivals, but the calendar is strewn with other special events, most of them with religious or commemorative origins.

Carnevale

Venice's **Carnevale** occupies the ten days leading up to Lent, finishing on Shrove Tuesday with a masked ball for the glitterati and dancing in the Piazza for the plebs. After falling out of fashion for many years, it was revived in 1979 and is now supported by the city authorities who organize various pageants and performances. Apart from these events, Carnevale is an endless parade where during the day people don costumes and go to the Piazza to be photographed, while business types can be seen doing their shopping in the classic white mask, black cloak and tricorn hat. In the evening some congregate in the remoter squares, while those who have spent hundreds of pounds on their costumes install themselves in the windows of *Florian* and pose for a while. Masks are on sale throughout the year in Venice, but special mask and costume shops magically appear during Carnevale, and Campo San Maurizio sprouts a marquee with mask-making demonstrations and a variety of designs for sale.

La Sensa

The feast of **La Sensa** happens in May on the Sunday after Ascension Day – the latter the day on which the doge performed the wedding of Venice to the sea. The ritual has recently been revived – a distinctly feeble procession that ends with the mayor and a gang of other dignitaries getting into a present-day approximation of the *Bucintoro* (the state barge) and sailing off to the Lido. Of more interest is the **Vogalonga** (long row), held on the same day. Open to any crew in any class of rowing boat, it covers a 32-kilometre course from the Bacino di San Marco out to Burano and back; the competitors arrive at the mouth of the Canal Grande between about 11am and 3pm.

Santa Maria della Salute

Named after the church of the Salute, this centuries-old feast day is a reminder of the devastating plague of 1630–31. The church was built in thanks for deliverance from the outbreak, and every November 21 since then the Venetians have processed over a pontoon bridge across the Canal Grande to give thanks for their good health, or to pray for sick friends and relatives. It offers the only chance to see the church as it was designed to be seen – with its main doors open, and with hundreds of people milling up the steps and round the building.

La Festa del Redentore

Another plague-related festival, this time to mark the end of the 1576 epidemic. Celebrated on the third Sunday in July, the day is centred on Palladio's church of the Redentore, which was built by way of thanksgiving for the city's escape. A bridge of boats is strung across the Giudecca canal to allow the faithful to walk over to the church, and on the Saturday night hundreds of people row out for a picnic on the water. The night ends with a grand fireworks display, after which it's traditional to make for the Lido to watch the sun rise.

The Regata Storica

Held on the first Sunday in September, the **Regata Storica** is the annual trial of strength and skill for the city's gondoliers and other expert rowers. It starts with a procession of richly decorated historic craft along the Canal Grande course, their crews all decked out in period dress. Bystanders are expected to support contestants in the main event, and may even be issued with appropriate colours.

The Film Festival

The **Venice Film Festival** – the world's oldest, founded in 1932 – takes place on the Lido every year in late August and early September. The tourist office will have the festival programme a few weeks in advance. Tickets are available for the general public, but you have to go along and queue for them on the day of performance.

Listings

ACTV enquiries Piazzale Roma daily 7.30am–8pm; English-language information from Hello Venezia (daily 7.30am–8pm) on ☏041.2424 or ⓦ www.actv.it or ⓦ www.hellovenezia.it.

Airlines Alitalia international flights ☏848.865.642, domestic flights ☏848.865.641, ⓦ www.alitalia.it; British Airways information ☏041.260.6428, tickets ☏199.712.266, ⓦ www .britishairways.com; British Midland ☏199.400.044, ⓦ www.british-midland.com; Easyjet ☏848.887.766, ⓦ www.easyjet.com; Ryanair ☏899.889.973, ⓦ www.ryanair.com.

Airport enquiries Marco Polo airport ☏041.260.9260, ⓦ www.veniceairport.com; Treviso airport ☏0422.315.211, ⓦ www.trevisoairport.it.

Banks Banks in Venice are concentrated on Calle Larga XXII Marzo, San Marco, west of the Piazza, and along a chain of squares and alleyways between Campo S. Bartolomeo and Campo Manin. There is not much to choose between them in terms of commission and exchange rates, and their hours are generally Mon–Fri 8.30am–1.30pm & 2.30–3.30pm

Car rental At Marco Polo airport: Hertz ☏041.541.6075; Europcar ☏041.541.5654; Maggiore Budget ☏041.541.5040. At Piazzale Roma: Avis ☏041.522.5825; Europcar ☏041.523.8616; Hertz ☏041.528.3524; Mattiazzo ☏041.522.0884.

Consulates and embassies The British consulate is on the mainland in the Palazzo Donatori di Sangue 2/5, Mestre ☏041.505.5990; this office is staffed by an honorary consul – the closest full consulate is in Milan. The nearest US consulate is also in Milan. Travellers from Ireland, Australia, New Zealand and Canada should contact their Rome embassies (see p.808).

Exchange There are clusters of exchange bureaux (*cambios*) where most tourists gather – near San Marco, the Rialto and the train station. Open late every day of the week, they can be useful in emergencies, but their rates of commission and exchange tend to be steep, with the notable exception of Travelex, which can be found at no. 142 on the Piazza, at Riva del Ferro 5126 (by the Rialto Bridge), and at the airport.

Hospital Ospedale Civile, Campo SS. Giovanni e Paolo; ☏041.529.4111.

Internet access Dozens of dedicated Internet points have opened in the last few years; most charge €6–8 per hour, though rates usually drop the longer you stay online. Places are opening and closing all the time, but you should find the following still in operation:

San Marco: *Internet Point*, Campo S. Stefano 2958 (daily 10am–11pm); *Venetian Navigator*, Calle dei Stagneri 5239 (daily 10am–8.30pm).

Dorsoduro: *Internet Point*, Crosera S.Pantalon 3812a (daily 10am–11pm).

San Polo: *Venice Connection*, Calle del Campaniel (Mon–Sat 10am–10pm, Sun 11am–10pm).

Cannaregio: *Planet Internet*, Rio Terà San Leonardo 1519 (daily 9am–11pm) by the Ponte delle Guglie; *Internet Station*, Sottoportego Falier 5640 (daily 10am–1pm & 3–11pm).

Castello: *Internet Corner*, Calle del Cafetier 6661a (Mon–Sat 10am–10pm, Sun 1–9pm); *Internet Point*, Calle della Sacrestia 4502 (daily 10am–11pm); *Internet Service*, Corte dei Preti 3546a (daily 10am–1pm, 3–8pm & 9–11pm); *Venetian Navigator*, Casselleria 5300 (daily: summer 10am–10pm; winter 10am–7.30pm) & Calle delle Bande 5269 (same hours).

Laundries *Speedy Wash*, Rio Terà San Leonardo, Cannaregio 1520 (daily 8am–11pm); at Ruga Giuffa, Castello 4826 (daily 8.30am–11pm), off Campo S. Maria Formosa; *Bea Vita* at Campiello delle Muneghe 665, Santa Croce (daily 7am–10pm); *Laundry Self-Service*, Calle delle Chioverette 665, Santa Croce (daily 7.30am–10.30pm); and at Fondamenta delle Zitelle 65, on Giudecca (daily 7am–10pm). You'll pay around €5 for an 8kg wash and €4 for a dryer. All over the city you'll find drycleaners, many of which will take in laundry for a service wash.

Left luggage The desk at the end of platform 14 in the train station (6am–midnight) charges €3.80 per item for five hours, then €0.60 for each of the next six hours, and €0.20 per hour thereafter. The office on Piazzale Roma (6am–9pm) charges €3.50 per item per 24hr.

Lost property If you lose anything on the train or at the station, call ☏041.785.238; on the buses, call ☏041.272.2838; at the airport, call ☏041.260.6436; on the *vaporetti*, call ☏041.272.2179; and anywhere in the city itself, call the town hall on ☏041.274.8225.

Police To notify police of a theft or lost passport, report to the Questura on Piazzale Roma (☏041.271.5511); in the event of an emergency, ring ☏113.

Post offices Venice's main post office is in the Fondaco dei Tedeschi, near the Rialto bridge (Mon–Sat 8.30am–6.30pm). Any poste restante should be addressed to Fermo Posta, Fondaco dei Tedeschi, 80100 Venezia; take your passport with when collecting your post. The principal branch post offices are in Calle dell'Ascensione, at Zàttere 1406, and by the Piazzale Roma vaporetto stops (Mon–Fri 8.30am–2pm, Sat 8.30am–1pm). Stamps can also be bought in tabacchi, as well as in some gift shops.

Public toilets There are toilets on or very near to most of the main squares. You'll need a €1 coin, but the toilets are usually staffed, so you can get change; note that the Venice Card (see box, p.317) gives free access to many staffed toilets. The main facilities are at the train station, at Piazzale Roma, on the west side of the Accademia bridge, by the main tourist office at the Giardinetti Reali, off the west side of the Piazza, off Campo S. Bartolomeo, on Campo Rialto Nuovo, on Campo S. Leonardo, on Campo S. Angelo and on Campo S. Margherita. Toilets are to be found in most of the city's bars as well; it's diplomatic, to say the least, to buy a drink before availing yourself.

Telephones Most of Venice's public call-boxes accept coins, and all of them take phone cards, which can be bought from tabacchi and some other shops (look for the Telecom Italia sticker), as well as from machines by the Telecom Italia phone booths in Strada Nova (near S. Felice), Piazzale Roma and adjoining the main post office building near the Rialto Bridge. You're never far from a pay phone – every sizeable campo has at least one, and there are phones by most vaporetto stops.

The Veneto

Virtually every acre of the Veneto bears the imprint of Venetian rule. In **Belluno**, right under the crags of the Dolomites, the style of the buildings declares the town's former allegiance, while the Lion of St Mark looks over the market square of **Verona**, on the Veneto's western edge. On the flatlands of the Po basin (the southern border of the region) and on farming estates all over the Veneto, the elegant **villas** of the Venetian nobility are still standing.

Yet the Veneto is as diverse culturally as it is geographically. The aspects of Verona that make the city so attractive were created long before the expansion of Venice's terra firma empire, and in **Padua** – a university seat since the thirteenth century – the civilization of the Renaissance displays a character quite distinct from that which evolved in Venice. Even in **Vicenza**, which reached its present form mainly during its long period of subservience, the very appearance of the streets is proof of a fundamental independence.

Nowadays this is one of Italy's wealthiest regions. Verona, Padua, Vicenza and **Treviso**, 30km north of Venice, are all major industrial and commercial centres, while intensive dairies, fruit farms and vineyards (around Conegliano, for example) have made the Veneto a leading agricultural producer too.

The Veneto's densest concentration of industry is at **Mestre** and **Marghera**, the grim conurbation through which all road and rail lines from Venice pass before spreading out over the mainland. It's less a city than an economic life-support system for Venice, and the negative impression you get on your way through is entirely valid. Some people trim their holiday expenses by staying in Mestre's cheaper hotels (Venice's tourist offices will supply addresses), but venturing further inland is a more pleasurable cost-cutting exercise.

The Brenta

The southernmost of the three main rivers that empty into the Venetian lagoon, the **Brenta** caused no end of trouble for the earliest settlers on both the mainland and the islands, with its frequent flooding and its deposits of silt. By the sixteenth century, though, the canalization of the river had brought it under control, and it became a favoured building site for the Venetian aristocracy. Some of these Venetian villas were built as a combination of summer residence and farmhouse – many, however, were intended solely for the former function. The period from mid-June to mid-November was the season of the *villeggiatura*, when the patrician families of Venice would load their best furniture onto barges and set off for the relative coolness of the Brenta.

Around one hundred **villas** are left standing on the river between Padua and Venice: some are derelict, a large number are still inhabited and a handful are open to the public. Of this last category, two are outstanding – the **Villa Fóscari** and the **Villa Pisani** – both of which are easily accessible by bus from Venice: four ACTV buses go to the former (€1), and the hourly buses between Padua and Venice (ACTV bus going via Dolo, not the SITA bus that goes on the motorway) go past both (€2.90). Don't be tempted by the widely advertised boat trips along the Brenta – they cost around €70 and stop longer for lunch than at any of the villas.

Villa Fóscari

The **VILLA FÓSCARI** at Malcontenta (April–Oct Tues & Sat 9am–noon; €7) was designed in 1559 by Palladio (see box, p.381) and is the nearest of his villas to Venice. Most of Palladio's villas fall into two broad groups: those built on cohesive farming estates, with a central low block for living quarters and wings for storage and associated uses (the Villa Barbaro at Masèr); and the large, single-block villas, built for landowners whose fields were dispersed or in some way unsuitable for the construction of a major building. The Villa Fóscari is the masterpiece of this second group, powerfully evoking the architecture of ancient Rome by its heavily rusticated exterior, its massive Ionic portico and its two-storey main hall – a space inspired by the baths of the imperial capital.

The frescoes in the living rooms include what is said to be a portrait of a woman of the Fóscari family who was exiled here as punishment for an amorous escapade, and whose subsequent misery, according to legend, was the source of the name Malcontenta. The reality is more prosaic – the area was known by that name long before the Fóscari arrived, either because of some local discontent over the development of the land or because of the political *malcontenti* who used to hide out in the nearby salt marshes.

The Villa Pisani

The **VILLA PISANI** (or Nazionale) at Stra (Tues–Sun: April–Oct 8.30am–7pm; Nov–March 9am–4pm; €5 for house and garden, €2.50 for garden only), virtually on the outskirts of Padua (on the bus ask the driver where to get off), looks more like a product of the *ancien régime* than a house for the Venetian gentry. Commissioned by way of celebration when Alvise Pisani was elected Doge of Venice in 1735, it was the biggest such residence to be built in Venetian territory during that century. It has appealed to megalomaniacs ever since: Napoleon bought it off the Pisani in 1807 and handed it over to Eugène Beauharnais, his stepson and Viceroy of Italy; and in 1934 it was the place chosen for the first meeting of Mussolini and Hitler.

Most of what you see is unexciting and sparsely furnished, but stick with it for the ballroom, its ceiling covered with a dazzling fresco, *The Apotheosis of the Pisani Family*, painted by Giambattista **Tiepolo** at the age of 66. And if you're trying to puzzle out what's going on – the Pisani family, accompanied by Venice, are being courted by the Arts, Sciences and Spirits of Peace, while Fame plays a fanfare in praise of the Pisani and the Madonna looks on with appropriate pride.

In the **grounds**, the long fish-pond ends in front of a stable-block which from a distance might be mistaken for another grand house. Off to the right there's an impressive maze – unless a blizzard is blowing, it'll be packed with coachloads of Italian schoolkids. The immaculate citrus garden, restored on the basis of years of historical research, is in stark contrast to the neglect of the house.

Padua

Extensively reconstructed after the damage caused by bombing in World War II, and hemmed in by the sprawl that has accompanied its development as the most important economic centre of the Veneto, **PADUA** (Padova) is not immediately the most alluring city in northern Italy. It is, however, one of the most ancient, and plentiful evidence remains of its impressive lineage. A large student population creates a young, vibrant atmosphere, and yet in spite of having two big attractions – the **Giotto frescoes** and **relics of St Antony** – Padua has the feel of a town that is just getting on with its own business. And indeed, for many people Padua's main appeal is as a base from which to make day-trips to its overcrowded neighbour, Venice.

A Roman municipium from 45 BC, the city thrived until the barbarian onslaughts and the subsequent Lombard invasion at the start of the seventh century. Recovery was slow, but by the middle of the twelfth century, when it became a free commune, Padua was prosperous once again. The university was founded in 1221, and a decade later the city became a place of pilgrimage following the death here of St Anthony.

In 1337 the **Da Carrara** family established control. Under their domination, Padua's cultural eminence was secured – Giotto, Dante and Petrarch were among those attracted here – but Carraresi territorial ambitions led to conflict with Venice, and in 1405 the city's independence ended with its conquest by the neighbouring republic. Though politically nullified, Padua remained an artistic and intellectual centre: Donatello and Mantegna both worked here, and in the seventeenth century Galileo researched at the university, where the medical faculty was one of the most ambitious in Europe. With the fall of the Venetian Republic the city passed to Napoleon, who handed it over to the Austrians, after whose regime Padua was annexed to Italy in 1866.

Arrival and information

Trains arrive in the north of the town, just a few minutes' walk up Corso del Popolo from the old city walls. The main **bus station** is at Piazzale Boschetti, immediately north of the walls to the east of the Corso; however, local buses for the city and nearby towns such as Ábano and Montegrotto leave from outside the train station. A new system of electric **trams** (Metrobus) is very gradually being introduced to the city; the first line to be completed runs between the station and Prato della Valle. There are **tourist offices** at Piazzetta Pedrocchi in the town centre (Mon–Sat 9am–1.30pm & 3–7pm; T049.876.7927, W www .turismopadova.it), at the train station, on the right as you exit (June–Aug

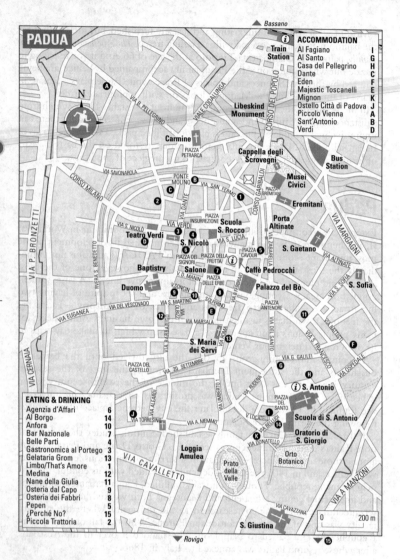

PADUA

ACCOMMODATION
Al Fagiano   I
Al Santo   H
Casa del Pellegrino C
Dante   F
Eden   E
Majestic Toscanelli K
Mignon   J
Ostello Città di Padova A
Piccolo Vienna   B
Sant'Antonio   B
Verdi   D

Train Station

Bassano

Carmine

PIAZZA PETRARCA

Libeskind Monument

Cappella degli Scrovegni

Bus Station

PONTE MOLINO

Musei Civici

Eremitani

Porta Altinate

Scuola S. Rocco

Teatro Verdi

S. Nicolò

S. Gaetano

Baptistry

Salone

Caffè Pedrocchi

S. Sofia

Duomo

Palazzo del Bò

S. Maria dei Servi

Loggia Amulea

S. Antonio

Scuola di S. Antonio

Oratorio di S. Giorgio

Orto Botanico

Prato della Valle

S. Giustina

Rovigo

0   200 m

EATING & DRINKING
Agenzia d'Affari   6
Al Borgo   14
Anfora   10
Bar Nazionale   7
Belle Parti   4
Gastronomica al Portego   3
Gelataria Grom   13
Limbo/That's Amore   1
Medina   12
Nane della Giulia   11
Osteria dal Capo   9
Osteria dei Fabbri   8
Pepen   5
¿Perché No?   15
Piccola Trattoria   2

Mon–Sat 9am–7pm, Sun 9.15am–noon; Sept–May Mon–Sat 9.15am–7pm, Sun 9.15am–noon; ☏049.875.2077), and on Piazza del Santo (April–Oct Mon–Sat 9am–1pm & 3–6pm, Sun 9am–1pm; ☏049.875.3087).You can rent **bikes** at the station (discounts with Padovacard), and **Internet** access is available east of the centre at Internet Point Padova, via Altinate 145, opposite Santa Sofia church.

Accommodation

Though rooms are cheaper in Padua than Venice, availability can be a problem, especially during high season or during festivals. Don't despair, however – Padua has plenty of reasonably priced hotels and a growing number of bed and

Padovacard

Costing €14, and valid for 48 hours, the **Padovacard** allows one visit for one adult and one child under 12 to 24 sites in the city, including the Musei Civici degli Eremitani, Scrovegni Chapel (plus €1 booking fee), and Palazzo della Ragione. There are further discounts on the other main attractions in the city and region, as well as free parking in the three main car parks, free travel on the APS buses, free bicycle hire and discounts on some bed and breakfast schemes. It's available from the tourist office and participating museums and monuments. Note that advance booking is required for the Scrovegni Chapel (see p.374).

breakfasts. The tourist office has a full list of both, or for B&Bs you can go through the scheme operated by *Kokonor* (℡049.864.3394, ⓦ www.bbkokonor .it); at some places you can also get a small reduction on stays of more than two nights with the Padovacard – see above. Many of the B&Bs are out in the suburbs, but they usually have good links to the centre.

Hotels

Al Fagiano Via Locatelli 45 ℡049.875.0073, ⓦ www.alfagiano.com. Whacky decorations in a friendly two-star, which has forty rooms over three floors, each floor decorated in a different colour. The rooms are on the small side, but have a/c, TV and hair dryers. Close to the Basilica. ❸

Al Santo Via del Santo 147 ℡049.875.2131, ⓦ www.alsanto.it. Located virtually next door to the Basilica, this hotel has been recently refurbished (rather austerely, but comfortably) and upgraded to a three-star. ❸

Casa del Pellegrino Via M. Cesarotti 21 ℡049.823.9711, ⓦ www.casadelpellegrino.com. Large, inexpensive two-star popular with groups coming to pay their respects to St Antony across the road – after all, it is the "Pilgrim's House". Its 157 rooms are simply furnished and come with or without bathrooms. ❷

Dante Via San Polo 5 ℡049.876.0408, ⓔ hotel .dante@virgilio.it. Well placed, inside the inner city walls but in a quieter quarter. The friendly signora speaks no English but she keeps her one-star establishment clean. Eight big rooms, not all en suite. ❶

Eden Via C. Battisti 255 ℡ & ℻049.650.484, ⓦ www.hoteledenpadova.it. A cut above other one-stars, though offers something of a mixed bag of rooms. All doubles have showers, but avoid the coffin-like singles. Situated in a good location near Piazza del Santo, in the university quarter. ❷

Majestic Toscanelli Via dell'Arco 2 ℡049.663.244, ⓦ www.toscanelli.com. The most appealing of the city's four-stars, probably the hotel of choice if you want to stay in style, with glitzy, nicely equipped rooms; it's located in the old Jewish quarter just south of Piazza delle Erbe, off Via SS. Martino e Solferino. ❻

Mignon Via Luca Belludi 22 ℡049.661.722, ℻049.661.221, ⓦ www.italiadiscovery.it/pd /hotelmignon. Lying between the Prato della Valle and the Botanical Garden, this is a simple but comfortable two-star. It has 23 rooms, including some that sleep three and four. ❷

Piccolo Vienna Via Beato Pellegrino 133℡049.871.6331, ⓦ www.hotelpiccolovienna.it. One of the cheapest hotels in Padua, a 10-minute walk northwest from the centre. Simply furnished rooms with or without bathrooms – those at the back are quieter. ❷

Sant'Antonio Via San Fermo 118 ℡049.875.1393, ⓦ www.hotelsantantonio.it. Two-star with large and modern, if slightly faded, rooms; those at the back have views over the canal and the lovely Ponte Molino, and are better than the street-facing rooms. Start the day with fresh orange juice and coffee next door at the cheerful *Albabar*. ❸

Verdi Via Dondi dall'Orologio 7 ℡049.836.4163, ⓦ www.albergoverdipadova.it. A recently opened and fully modernized small three-star. In a quiet street near the Teatro Verde, it is light, airy and very acceptable. ❸

Hostel and campsite

Montegrotto Terme Via Roma 123/25 ℡049.793.400, ⓦ www.sportingcenter.it. This is the nearest campsite to Padua – 15km south from the city centre, but frequent trains take around 15min; a very upmarket site, it not only has a swimming pool but thermal baths too. Open March–early Nov. €11.50 per tent and €7.50 per person per night.

Ostello Città di Padova Via A. Aleardi 30 ℡049.875.2219, ⓦ www.ostellopadova.it. Padua's quiet and friendly HI hostel is a good 30min walk from the train station. Alternatively, take bus #3, #8, #12 or #18 (#32 on Sun) to Prato della Valle, from where it's a short walk northwest. Reception is closed between 9am and 4pm and there's an 11pm curfew. Dorm beds cost €16.50.

The City

From the train station, the Corso del Popolo and its extension Corso Garibaldi lead south passing the seventeen-metre-tall structure of glass and steel designed by the architect Daniel Libeskind, as a memorial to the victims of the September 11 attacks. A couple of minutes walk further on is the Cappella degli Scrovegni and Musei Civici degli Eremitani. For many people the **Giotto frescoes** in the Scrovegni, considered to be a key work in the development of European art, are the reason for coming to Padua, but even if you're no expert the chapel exerts an extraordinary presence. However, anyone limiting their visit to Giotto would be missing out on Padua's other delights, from the fine old monuments and buildings such as the *Salone* or the duomo baptistry, to its busy, narrow streets and bustling market squares. Padua's thirteenth-century university is the second oldest in Italy, and the town has also been a major centre of pilgrimage for almost as long.

The Capella degli Scrovegni

The **Capella degli Scrovegni** (Scrovegni Chapel; daily 9am–10pm, closes 7pm Jan to mid-Feb; €12, or Padovacard, see box, p.373, reduced to €8 on Mon and after 7pm; after 7pm you can book a "doppia turno" ticket for €12, which allows an extra 20min in the chapel) was commissioned in 1303 by Enrico Scrovegni in atonement for his father's usury, which was so vicious that he was denied a Christian burial. As soon as the walls were built, Giotto was commissioned to cover them with illustrations of the life of Mary, the life of Jesus and the story of the Passion; the finished cycle, arranged in three tightly knit tiers and painted against a backdrop of saturated blue, is one of the high points in the development of European art. The Scrovegni series is a marvellous demonstration of Giotto's innovative attention to the inner nature of his subjects. In terms of sheer physical presence and the relationships between the figures and their environment, Giotto's work takes the first important strides towards realism and humanism. The Joachim series on the top row of the north wall (on your right as you walk in) is particularly powerful – note the exchange of looks between the two shepherds in the *Arrival of Joachim*. Beneath the main pictures are shown the vices and virtues in human (usually female) form, while on the wall above the door is a *Last Judgement* – in rather poor condition and now thought to be only partly by Giotto – with rivers of fire leading from God to hell. Directly above the door is a portrait of Scrovegni presenting the chapel; his tomb is at the far end, behind the altar with its statues by **Giovanni Pisano**.

The number of visitors permitted each day is strictly limited, and **tickets** have to be reserved at least 24 hours in advance at the ticket office, by phoning ☎049.201.0020 (Mon–Fri 9am–7pm, Sat 9am–6pm), or by booking online at ⓦ www.cappelladegliscrovegni.it. Such is the demand, it's advisable to book tickets at least three or four days in advance, especially in summer, but it's still worth turning up even if you haven't reserved, as there may be space. Tickets must be picked up from the museum ticket office an hour before your timed entry; be at the chapel waiting room five minutes before your allotted time. Before going in, you should visit the **Sala Multimediale** in the museum and watch the short film – in English – which gives you an excellent introduction to the frescoes.

Groups of 25 are admitted to the chapel every quarter of an hour, and if you miss your slot you have to book and pay again. Once inside, a high-tech system adjusts the air humidity of the waiting room down to that of the chapel itself and filters away the worst of the spores and pollution you've brought in. Fourteen minutes later another door leading to the chapel itself opens and you have exactly a quarter of an hour to take in the frescoes before being ejected through a third glass door back into the grounds of the museum.

The Musei Civici degli Eremitani

Next to the chapel, the **Musei Civici degli Eremitani** (Tues–Sun 9am–7pm; €10, free with Padovacard), formerly the monastery of the Eremitani, is a superbly presented three-part museum complex. The archeological collection, on the ground floor, has a vast array of pre-Roman, Roman and paleo-Christian objects. Upstairs, the vast **Museo d'Arte** houses an extensive assembly of fourteenth- to nineteenth-century art from the Veneto and further afield. The collection is arranged in chronological order, and it's a fairly long walk through tracts of workaday stuff, but works by names such as Titian, Tintoretto and Tiepolo leaven the mix. Spectacular highlights are provided by the Giotto *Crucifixion* that was once in the Scrovegni chapel, and a fine *Portrait of a Young Senator* by Bellini. The Capodilista collection, an offshoot of the main gallery, has a pair of mysterious Titian and Giorgione landscapes, and some good Luca Giordano grotesques. The **Museo Bottacin**, for more specialist tastes, was founded in 1865 and contains over 50,000 coins, medals and seals, making it one of the most important museums of its type in the world.

The Chiesa degli Eremitani

The neighbouring church of the **Eremitani** (Mon–Sat 9am–1pm & 3.30–7pm, Sun 9.30–12.30 & 4–6pm; free), built at the turn of the fourteenth century, was almost completely wrecked by an Allied bombing raid in 1944 but has been fastidiously rebuilt. Photographs to the left of the apse show the extent of the damage, the worst aspect of which was the near-total destruction of Mantegna's frescoes of the lives of St James and St Christopher – the war's most severe blow to Italy's artistic heritage.

Produced between 1454 and 1457, when Mantegna was in his mid-20s, the frescoes were unprecedented in the thoroughness with which they exploited fixed-point perspective – a concept central to Renaissance humanism, with its emphasis on the primacy of individual perception. The extent of his achievement can now be assessed only from the fuzzy photographs and the sad fragments preserved in the chapel to the right of the high altar. On the left wall is the *Martyrdom of St James*, put together from fragments found in the rubble; and on the right is the *Martyrdom of St Christopher*, which had been removed from the wall before the war.

The central squares

Walking back to the Corso Garibaldi and turning left leads you past the **Caffè Pedrocchi**, which used to be the city's main intellectual salon; it's no longer that, but it does have a multiplicity of functions – chic café, with old ladies in their best hats, concert hall and conference centre. Just beyond, the **Piazza della Frutta** and **Piazza delle Erbe**, the sites of Padua's daily markets, are lined with bars, restaurants and shops. Separating them is the extraordinary **Palazzo della Ragione** or **Salone** (Tues–Sun: Feb–Oct 9am–7pm; Nov–Jan 9am–6pm; €4, free with Padovacard), which you enter by the stairs on the Piazza delle Erbe side at the eastern end of the building. At the time of its construction in the

1210s, this vast hall was the largest room to have been built on top of another storey. Its decoration would once have been as astounding as its size, but the original frescoes by Giotto and his assistants were destroyed by fire in 1420, though some by Giusto de'Menabuoi have survived. Most of the extant frescoes are by Nicola Miretto (1425–40) depicting an astrological calendar distinctively medieval in its complexity. Mainly used as the city council's assembly hall, it was also a place where Padua's citizens could plead for justice – hence the appellation *della Ragione*, meaning "of reason". The large wooden horse with disproportionately gigantic gonads is modelled on Donatello's *Gattamelata*, and was made for a joust in 1466.

The Duomo and baptistry

Padua's **Duomo** (Mon–Sat 7.30am–noon & 3.30–7.30pm, Sun 8am–1pm & 3.45–8.30pm; free) is an unlovely church whose architect took his design from drawings by Michelangelo. The adjacent Romanesque **baptistry**, however, is one of the unproclaimed delights of the city (daily 10am–6pm; €2.50, or €1 with Padovacard). Built by the Da Carraras in the thirteenth century, and still in use today, it's lined with fourteenth-century frescoes by Giusto de'Menabuoi, a cycle which makes a fascinating comparison with Giotto's in the Cappella degli Scrovegni. The influence of Giotto is plain, but in striving for greater realism Giusto has lost Giotto's monumentality and made some of his figures awkward and unconvincing. Yet many of the scenes are delightful, and the vibrancy of their colours, coupled with the size and relative quiet of the building, make for a memorable visit.

To the university

The area just southeast of *Caffè Pedrocchi* is dominated by the main block of the **university**, the **Palazzo del Bò** ("the Ox", named after an inn that used to stand here). Established in September 1221, the University of Padua is older than any other in Italy except that of Bologna, and the coats of arms that encrust the courtyard and Great Hall attest to the social and intellectual rank of its alumni. The first permanent **anatomy theatre** was built here in 1594, a facility that doubtless greatly helped William Harvey, who went on to develop the theory of blood circulation after taking his degree here in 1602. Galileo taught physics at the university from 1592 to 1610, declaiming from a lectern that is still on show. And in 1678 Elena Lucrezia Corner Piscopia became the first woman in the world to collect a university degree when she was awarded her doctorate in philosophy here – there's a statue of her in the courtyard. The Bò is only open for guided visits (March–Oct Mon, Wed & Fri 3.15, 4.15 & 5.15pm, Tues, Thurs & Sat 9.15, 10.15 & 11.15am; Nov–Feb Mon, Wed & Fri 3.15 & 4.15pm, Tues, Thurs & Sat 10.15 & 11.15am; €5); at present, tours set off from the bar, signposted in the courtyard, but it's best to check with the tourist office. A special Paduan tradition takes place in the square in front of the Palazzo in February, May and September when, to mark their graduation, students are given a poster-sized, caricatured account of their college life and achievements to read out in front of family and friends while drinking a bottle of wine and performing feats or forfeits those around them dare them to do. They are then crowned with a wreath of laurels and cheered with cries of "*dottore, dottore*".

The Prato della Valle and Santa Giustina

Past the *palazzo*, Via VIII Febbraio turns into Via Roma and then Via Umberto I, before opening up into the sprawling **Prato della Valle**, claimed to be the largest town square in Italy. It's a generally cheerless area, ringed by very wide roads, but the vast Saturday market and the summer funfair do a lot to make it jollier. As the number of ice-cream vendors might suggest, it's also a favourite place for the *passeggiata* on summer evenings. One side is fronted by the sixteenth-century **Basilica di Santa Giustina** (daily 7.30am–noon & 3–8pm; free). A pair of fifteenth-century griffins, one holding a knight and the other a lion, are the only notable adornments to the unclad brick facade; the interior has little of interest except a huge *Martyrdom of St Justina* by Paolo Veronese (in the apse), some highly proficient carving on the choir stalls, and the sarcophagus which once contained the relics of Luke the Evangelist (apse of left transept).

More appealing are the vestiges of the church's earlier incarnations. In the right transept a stone arch opens onto the **Martyrs' Corridor**, a composite of fifth- to twelfth-century architectural fragments that leads to the **Sacellum di Santa Maria e San Prosdocimo**, burial place of St Prosdocimus. He was the first bishop of Padua back in the fourth century, when the church was founded, and is depicted here on a fifth-century panel. The fifteenth-century **old choir**, reached by a chain of corridors from the left-hand chapel of the right transept, has choir stalls inset with splendid marquetry panels.

Il Santo

At the far end of Via Belludi on Piazza del Santo towers the Basilica di San Antonio, or **Il Santo** (daily 6.30am–7.45pm; ⓦ www.basilicadelsanto.it; free). Within eighteen months of his death in 1231, St Anthony had been canonized and his tomb was attracting enough pilgrims to warrant the building of the basilica. It was not until the start of the fourteenth century that the church reached a state that enabled the saint's body to be placed in the **Cappella del Santo** (in the left transept). Plastered with such votive offerings as photographs of healed limbs and car crashes survived with the saint's intervention, the shrine has an uneasy, irresistible pull. The chapel's more formal decoration includes the most important series of relief sculpture created in sixteenth-century Italy, a sequence of nine marble panels showing scenes from the life of St Anthony. Carved between 1505 and 1577, most have the names of their sculptors incised into the base, Antonio Lombardo, Tullio Lombardo and Jacopo Sansovino being among the most famous.

Adjoining the chapel is the Cappella della Madonna Mora (named after its fourteenth-century French altar statue), which in turn gives onto the Cappella del Beato Luca, whose fourteenth-century frescoes include a lovely image of St James lifting a prison tower to free a prisoner. Back in the aisle, just outside the Cappella del Santo, is Padua's finest work by Pietro Lombardo, the monument to Antonio Roselli (1467). More impressive still are the high altar's bronze sculptures and reliefs by Donatello (1444–45), the works that introduced Renaissance classicism to Padua. Built onto the farthest point of the ambulatory, the **Cappella del Tesoro** (daily 9am–1pm & 2.30–6.30pm) houses the tongue and vocal chords of St Anthony, as well as a host of lesser relics. For more on St Anthony and the basilica, enter the cloisters (on the south side of the basilica) and follow the signs for the **Museo Antoniano** (daily 9am–1pm & 2.30–6.30pm; €2.50, €1.50 with Padovacard), which includes the **Mostra Antoniana** (closes 30min earlier). The former, on the first floor, is a collection of paintings (including the fresco of St Anthony and St Bernardino by **Mantegna**), ornate incense holders, ceremonial robes and other paraphernalia linked to the basilica; the latter, on the ground floor, is a history of votive gifts.

In the shadow of the basilica stands Donatello's **Monument to Gattamelata** (which translates literally as "The Honeyed Cat"), as the *condottiere* Erasmo da

Narni was known. He died in 1443 and this monument was raised ten years later, the earliest large bronze sculpture of the Renaissance. A direct precursor to Verrocchio's monument to Colleoni in Venice (see p.349), it could hardly be more different: Gattamelata was known for his honesty and dignity, and Donatello has given us an image of comparative sensitivity and restraint, quite unlike Verrocchio's image of power through force.

South of Il Santo

To the left as you leave the basilica are the **Oratorio di San Giorgio** and **Scoletta del Santo** (daily 9am–12.30pm & 2.30–7pm but closes 5pm Nov–March; €2, or €1.50 with Padovacard). The oratory was founded in 1377 as a mortuary chapel, and its frescoes by Altichiero di Zevio and Jacopo Avanzi were completed soon after. One wall is adorned by the wonderfully titled *St Lucy Remains Immovable at an Attempt to Drag Her with the Help of Oxen to a House of Ill Repute*.

The Scoletta was founded soon after Anthony's canonization, though this building only goes back as far as the early fifteenth century. The ground floor is still used for religious purposes, while upstairs is maintained to look pretty much as it would have in the sixteenth century, with its fine ceiling and paintings dating mainly from 1509–15. Four of the pictures are said to be by Titian.

One way to relax is to stroll round the corner to the oldest botanic gardens in Europe, the **Orto Botanico**, on Via Donatello (summer daily 9am–1pm & 3–6pm; winter Mon–Sat 9am–1pm; €4, free with Padovacard). Planted in 1545 by the university's medical faculty as a collection of medicinal herbs, the gardens are laid out much as they were originally, and the specimens on show haven't changed too much either. Goethe came here in 1786 to see a palm tree that had been planted in 1585; the selfsame tree still stands.

Eating, drinking and nightlife

Catering for the midday stampede of ravenous students, Padua's **bars** generally produce weightier **snacks** than the routine *tramezzini* – slabs of pizza and sandwiches vast enough to satisfy a glutton are standard; you'll find several amid the food stalls underneath the Palazzo della Ragione. Several self-service **restaurants** offer good-value full menus, open for lunch and dinner, but they turn off their hotplates by 9pm. For a *passeggiata* and a place to sit and watch the world go by, the main areas to head for are Piazza dell' Erbe, Piazza Duomo, Piazza Cavour and Prato della Valle, but for the real action the studenty bars in the narrow streets around these piazzas and the University are the liveliest. For the most exquisite ice cream in the city hurry to Gelateria Grom, Via Roma 101 (open daily till midnight), the chain that started in Turin and is set to conquer the world.

Restaurants

Al Borgo Via L. Belludi 56. Wood-fired oven pizzeria with tables outside looking onto the Piazza del Santo; popular with locals and tourists alike. Closed Tues.
Anfora Via dei Soncin 13 ⊕049.656.629. Boisterous and very reasonable bohemian restaurant that doubles up as a bar between restaurant hours (12.30–3.15pm & 8–11.30pm), with delicious snacks all day. Get there early or book in advance. Closed Sun.
Belle Parti Via Belle Parti 11 ⊕049.875.1822. On a tiny street running between Via Verdi and

Via Santa Lucia, this place has an excellent menu (upwards of €35 a head) and a relaxed atmosphere. Closed Mon lunch & Sun.
Gastronomica al Portego Via Dante 9. High-grade yet inexpensive self-service restaurant with local dishes. Closed Sun evening and all day Mon.
Medina Via S.G. Barbarigo 18. Small, bustling pizzeria, often packed with students enjoying excellent pizza and salads. Closed Tues.
Nane della Giulia Via Santa Sofia 1. An unusual mix of trendy and unpretentious in this

5

gay-friendly spot. Go for the reasonably priced Veneto and vegetarian specialities earlier in the evening and the bar atmosphere later. Live piano Wed & Thurs. No credit cards. Open evenings only, closed Mon.

Osteria dal Capo Via Obizzi 2. ℗049.663.105. In a street just off Piazza Duomo is this small restaurant renowned among the locals.Home-made cuisine, regional fish dishes a speciality, and a wide range of pasta such as duck tagliatelle. Booking advised. Closed all day Sun and Mon lunchtime.

Osteria dei Fabbri Via dei Fabbri 13 ℗049.650.336. Excellent mid-range trattoria; you'll be lucky to get a seat if you haven't booked. Closed Sun.

Pepen Piazza Cavour 15. With a wonderful range of pizzas and seats on the square in the summer, this is one of Padua's best-sited pizzerias. Closed Sun.

Piccola Trattoria Via R Da Piazzola 21 ⓦwww .piccolatrattoria.it. Friendly place full of locals, serving pasta with unusual sauces and good main courses – suckling pig and lamb with lemon. You can eat for about €40 per person.

Bars and nightlife

Your best bet, as usual, is to head for the centre and follow the throng. A good place to start is around the unmarked *Bar Nazionale*, at Piazza delle Erbe 40, on the northeast corner (closed Sun). The bar closes at 9pm but the crowds linger for long after, before dispersing – mostly to out-of-town clubs, though the places listed below tend to stay pretty lively until at least 2am during university term time. The *Anfora* (see opposite) also serves as a popular bar, spilling out on to the street.

Padua's main theatre is the **Teatro Verdi** (closed in summer) on Corso Milano, hosting opera and big-name dramatists; details of the season's events can be obtained from the tourist office or in the bilingual information booklet *Padova Today*, distributed in some bars and most hotels. Of the local newspapers, the most comprehensive for listings is *Il Mattino*, but for more offbeat events check out the posters up around the **city**, particularly in the university area.

Agenzia d'Affari Via Dante 16. Close to Piazza dei Signori. One of a fast-growing number of designer wine bars in town. Open until midnight, it has a penchant for inventive tapas, including raw fish varieties. DJs are also on hand Wed & Fri evenings.

Extra Extra Via Ciamician 5. Padua's flashiest disco to the west of town gets buzzing after 2am from Thursday to Saturday, but is dead the rest of the time. If you can't get a taxi, it's an inadvisable

thirty-minute walk back to the centre by way of Via Sório. Closed in summer.

Limbo/That's Amore Via San Fermo 44. Popular disco-pub that's open until 3am. Open Fri–Sun.

¿Perché no? Via Manzoni 4. Padua's main gay bar, a small, friendly place just beyond the city walls: head along Via Cavazzana out through the walls, turn right and the bar is just before the second major crossroads. Open till 2am daily.

Vicenza

Europe's largest producer of textiles and the focus of Italy's "Silicon Valley", **VICENZA** is a very sleek city, where it can seem that every second car is a BMW. Prosperity hasn't ruined the look of the city though, and the centre, still partly enclosed by medieval walls, is an amalgam of Gothic and Classical buildings that today looks much as it did when the last major phase of construction came to an end at the close of the eighteenth century. This historic core is compact enough to be explored in a day, but the city and its environs really require a short stay to do them justice.

In 1404 Vicenza was absorbed by Venice, and the city's numerous Gothic palaces reflect its status as a Venetian satellite. But in the latter half of the sixteenth century the city was transformed by the work of an architect who owed nothing to Venice and whose rigorous but flexible style was to influence every succeeding generation – Andrea di Pietro (or della Gondola), alias Palladio.

Arrival, information and accommodation

The **train station** and **bus terminus** are a ten-minute walk southwest of the historic centre; head straight ahead through the park to reach Piazza del Castello. The very helpful **tourist office** is at the far end of Corso Palladio, alongside the entrance to the Teatro Olimpico, at Piazza Matteotti 12 (daily 9am–1pm & 3–6pm; ☎0444.320.854, ⓦwww.vicenzae.org). There's another office on Piazza Signori (daily 10am–12.30pm & 2.30–6.30pm). For listings, pick up a copy of the local papers *Il Gazzettino* or *Il Giornale di Vicenza*. **Internet** access can be found in Matrix at Piazza della Biade 11a (daily 10am–11pm except Wed & Sun 2–11pm). You can hire **bikes** at the friendly Pronto Bici at Contra pedemuro San Biagio 11 (mobile ☎328.357.0365).

Accommodation

Vicenza is a big conference destination, and many of its **hotels** are stuck out in characterless suburbs, so it pays to be careful where you book. Wherever you decide to stay, phone ahead in summer or early autumn – some places close in August and the main conference season is in September.

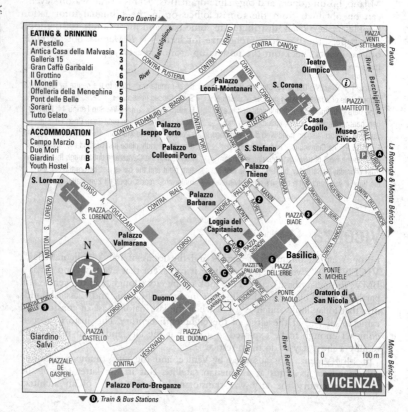

EATING & DRINKING

Al Pestello	1
Antica Casa della Malvasia	2
Galleria 15	3
Gran Caffè Garibaldi	4
Il Grottino	6
I Monelli	10
Offelleria della Meneghina	5
Pont delle Belle	9
Sorarù	8
Tutto Gelato	7

ACCOMMODATION

Campo Marzio	D
Due Mori	C
Giardini	B
Youth Hostel	A

VICENZA

0 — 100 m

▼ **D**, Train & Bus Stations

Campo Marzio Viale Roma ☎0444.545.700, Ⓦ www.hotelcampomarzio.com. Overlooking the large park that lies between the station and Piazza Castello, this is the only four-star in the historic centre. A modern block but with luxurious period décor, out of season prices drop massively. ❺

🏃 **Due Mori** Contrà Do Rode 26 ☎0444.321.886, Ⓦ www.hotelduemori .com. With some beautifully furnished and spacious rooms – especially the ground floor room with disabled access – it also has a disabled parking space in front of the hotel, this graceful hotel offers excellent value, and it is within a few metres of the Piazza dei Signori. It is only a two-star, but feels better than that. ❸

Giardini Via Giuriolo 10 ☎0444.326.458, Ⓦ www .hotelgiardini.com. A three-star modern hotel at the southern end of Piazza Matteotti that has comfortable air-conditioned rooms – go for the quieter ones at the back. ❺

Youth hostel Viale Giuriolo 7 ☎0444.540.222. The only budget place in the centre of town is in a superb position just off Piazza Matteotti; a dorm bed costs €16, doubles €17.

The City

The main street of Vicenza, the **Corso Andrea Palladio**, cuts right through the old centre from the Piazza del Castello down to the Piazza Matteotti, and is lined with palaces, all of them now occupied by shops, offices and banks. Palladio's last palace, the fragmentary **Palazzo Porto-Breganze**, stands on the southern side of Piazza Castello; no. 163 on the Corso, the **Casa Cogollo**, is confusingly known as the Casa del Palladio, though he never lived here and few people think he designed it.

Palladio

Born in Padua in 1508, Andrea di Pietro (or della Gondola) began his career as an apprentice stonemason in Vicenza. At 30 he became the protégé of a local nobleman, Count Giangiorgio Trissino, the leading light of the humanist Accademia Olimpico – a learned society that still meets in Vicenza. Trissino gave the architect his classicized name, **Palladio**, directed his architectural training, brought him into contact with the dominant class of Vicenza and, perhaps most crucially, took him to Rome – the first of many trips he made through Italy, sketching Imperial Roman remains.

Between 1540 and his death in 1580, Palladio created around a dozen palaces and public buildings in Vicenza, nearly twenty villas in the countryside of the Veneto and two important religious buildings in Venice. But unlike the pioneers of Renaissance Classicism – architects such as Alberti, Brunelleschi and Bramante – Palladio's reputation does not rest on a particular transformation of architectural style. Instead, his fame – and he is arguably the most influential architect in the world – rests on the way he is considered to have perfected existing values of harmony and proportion.

In particular, his lasting influence stems from *I Quattro Libri dell'Architettura* or "The Four Books of Architecture", a treatise he published in 1570, towards the end of his career. Other architects had written important works of theory, but Palladio's is unique in its practical applicability, serving almost as a textbook for Classical architecture. As the style spread into the rest of Europe and beyond, it was to Palladio's book that architects like Inigo Jones (and later, Thomas Jefferson) turned, finding both inspiration and guidance in his examples.

Today, Palladio has perhaps become the victim of his own success. The ubiquity of neo-Classicism in second-rate churches and third-rate bank buildings can make it hard to sense the freshness and brilliance of his designs, though it still shines through in masterpieces like the Basilica in Vicenza, the Villa Barbaro near Ásolo and the churches of the Redentore and San Giorgio Maggiore in Venice. Even if you're inclined to agree with Herbert Read's opinion that "in the back of every dying civilization there sticks a bloody Doric column", you might leave the region converted.

The Museo Civico and Teatro Olimpico

The Corso ends with one of the architect's most imperious buildings, the **Palazzo Chiericati** (begun in 1550), now home of the Museo Civico, also known as the Pinacoteca (Tues–Sun 9am–5pm; see Vicenza museum box opposite for ticket info). The core of the picture collection is made up of Vicentine artists, none of whose work will knock you flat on your back; it's left to a few more celebrated names – Memling, Tintoretto, Veronese, Tiepolo – and some fine fifteenth-century painting to make the visit memorable.

Across the Piazza Matteotti is the one building in Vicenza you shouldn't fail to go into – the **Teatro Olimpico**, the oldest indoor theatre in Europe (Tues–Sun: July & Aug 9am–7pm; Sept–June 9am–5pm; see Vicenza museum box opposite for entry). Approached in 1579 by the members of the Olympic Academy (a society dedicated to the study of the humanities) to produce a design for a permanent theatre, Palladio devised a covered amphitheatre derived from his reading of Vitruvius and his studies of Roman structures in Italy and France. He died soon after work commenced, and the scheme was then overseen by Scamozzi, who added to Palladio's design the backstage perspective of a classical city, creating the illusion of long urban vistas by tilting the "streets" at an alarming angle. The theatre opened on March 3, 1585, with an extravagant production of *Oedipus Rex*, and is still used for plays and concerts.

The Piazza dei Signori

At the hub of the city, the **Piazza dei Signori**, stands the most awesome of Palladio's creations – the **Basilica**. Designed in the late 1540s (but not finished until the second decade of the next century), this was Palladio's first public project and the one that secured his reputation. The monumental regularity of the basilica disguises the fact that the Palladian building is effectively a stupendous piece of buttressing – the Doric and Ionic colonnades enclose the fifteenth-century hall of the city council, an unstable structure that had defied a number of attempts to prop it up before Palladio's solution was put into effect. The vast Gothic hall is often used for good contemporary architecture exhibitions. On Tuesdays and Thursdays a vast market fills the streets between the basilica and the duomo, though if you're shopping for picnic food, you'll save money by going down the slope and over the river, where the shops are a good bit cheaper.

A late Palladian building, the unfinished **Loggia del Capitaniato**, faces the basilica across the Piazza dei Signori. Built as accommodation for the Venetian military commander of the city, it's decorated with reliefs in celebration of the Venetian victory over the Turks at Lepanto in 1571.

The churches

The **Duomo** was bombed flat in 1944 and, though carefully reconstructed after the war, it's a rather gloomy place, chiefly distinguished as one of the few Italian cathedrals to be overwhelmed by its secular surroundings. Far more interesting is **Santa Corona** (Mon 4–6pm, Tues–Fri 8.30am–noon & 3–6pm, Sat & Sun 3–5pm; free) on the other side of the Corso Palladio (at the Piazza Matteotti end), a Dominican church dating from the mid-thirteenth century. Here you'll find two of the three great church paintings in Vicenza – *The Baptism of Christ*, a late work by Giovanni Bellini, and *The Adoration of the Magi*, painted in 1573 by Paolo Veronese. The cloisters now house a run-of-the-mill **Museo Naturalistico-Archeologico** (Tues–Sun 9am–5pm; see box opposite for admission prices).

The nearby **Santo Stefano** (Mon–Sat 8.30–9.45am & 5–6.30pm, Sun 8.30–9.45am; free) contains the third of the city's fine church paintings: Palma Vecchio's typically stolid and voluptuous *Madonna and Child with Saints George and Lucy*.

The palazzi and the parks

Santo Stefano faces a corner of the huge **Palazzo Thiene**, another of Palladio's palaces (May, June & Sept Wed & Fri 9am–noon & 3–6pm, Sat 9am–noon; Oct–April Tues & Wed 9am–noon & 3–6pm; closed July & Aug; admission free, by advance booking only, on ℡0444.542.131). It was planned to occupy the entire block down to Corso Palladio, but in the end work progressed no further than the addition of this wing to the existing fifteenth-century house. The facade of the old building is in Contrà Porti, a street that amply demonstrates the way in which the builders of Vicenza grafted new houses onto old without disrupting the symmetry of the street; the palaces here span two centuries, yet the overall impression is one of cohesion. Facing Palazzo Thiene is the **Palazzo Barbarano** which houses a research institute for Palladian architecture and often has excellent exhibitions, usually, but not always, on classical architects.

Outstanding buildings on Contrà Porti are the fourteenth-century **Palazzo Colleoni Porto** (no. 19) and Palladio's neighbouring **Palazzo Iseppo da Porto**, designed a few years after the Thiene palace. The parallel Corso A. Fogazzaro completes the itinerary of major Palladian buildings with the Palazzo Valmarana (no. 16), perhaps the most eccentric of Palladio's projects – notice the gigantic stucco figures at the sides of the facade, where you'd expect columns to be.

At the end of Contrà Santa Corona, two blocks east of Contrà Porti, the **Palazzo Leoni-Montanari** (Tues–Sun 10am–6pm; €4; Ⓦwww .palazzomontanari.com) houses a rather specialized gallery with a collection of art from the Veneto that is respectable enough, if not up to the standards of Venice, or even Padua. Eighteenth-century painting is best represented, including landscape works by Canaletto and Guardi, and there's a rather surprising collection of Russian icons.

Contrà Porti takes you towards the Pusteria Bridge and the **Parco Querini**, the biggest expanse of green in the city, enlivened by a decorative hillock populated by ducks, rabbits and peacocks. Vicenza's other refuge for the brick-weary, the **Giardino Salvi** (at the end of the road running straight up from the train station), is a more modest, artificial affair of winding gravel paths and fountains.

The outskirts – Monte Bérico and the villas

In 1426 Vicenza was struck by bubonic plague, during the course of which outbreak the Virgin is said to have appeared twice at the summit of Monte Bérico – the hill on the southern edge of the city – to announce the city's deliverance. The chapel raised on the site of her appearance became a place of pilgrimage, and at the end of the seventeenth century it was replaced by the present **Basilica di Monte Bérico**. On foot it takes around half an hour from the centre of town. Sadly, public transport is patchy: the only direct bus service from the centre is on Sundays – bus #18 – which climbs the hill every thirty

Vicenza's museums

To visit the Teatro Olimpico, Museo Civico and Museo Naturalistico-Archeologico you'll need to buy the €8 **Card Musei** (€12 for a family card), which also gives admission to the Museo del Risorgimento, a rather specialized museum a long way out. The Card Musei can be bought at the tourist office or any of the sights it covers, and is valid for three days.

minutes or so. On weekdays you'll have to go to the bus station and catch a long distance bus, #6 bound for Barbarano Vicentino and get off at Monte Bérico.

Pilgrims regularly arrive here by the busload, and the glossy interior of the church is immaculately maintained to receive them; a well-stocked shop in the cloister sells devotional trinkets to the faithful. Those in search of artistic fulfilment should venture into the church for Montagna's pietà (in the chapel to the right of the apse) and *The Supper of St Gregory the Great* by Veronese (in the refectory). The latter, the prototype of *The Feast in the House of Levi* in Venice's Accademia, was used for bayonet practice by Austrian troops in 1848 – the small reproduction nearby shows what a thorough job the vandals and subsequent restorers did.

Carry on towards the summit of the hill and you come to the **Museo del Risorgimento e della Resistenza,** some ten minutes' walk beyond the basilica. The museum houses an impressive display paying particular attention to Vicenza's resistance to the Austrians in the mid-nineteenth century and to the efforts of the anti-fascist Alpine fighters a century later, but for many visitors the main attraction will be the extensive wooded parkland laid out on the slopes below the Villa Guiccioli, the main building (Tues–Sun 9am–1pm & 2.15–5pm; €3, or Card Musei: see box, p.383).

The Villa Valmarana

Ten minutes' walk away from Monte Bérico is the **Villa Valmarana "ai Nani"** – go back down the hill, head along Via M. D'Azeglio for 100m, then turn right into the cobbled Via S. Bastiano, which ends at the villa. This is an undistinguished house made extraordinary by the decorations of Giambattista and Giandomenico Tiepolo (March 15–Nov 5 Tues–Sun 10am–noon & 3–6pm; rest of year Sat & Sun 10am–noon & 2–4pm; €6). *Nani*, by the way, means "dwarfs", the significance of which becomes clear when you see the garden wall.

There are two parts to the house: the Palazzina, containing six rooms frescoed with brilliant virtuosity by Giambattista (scenes based on Virgil, Tasso and Ariosto – you're handed a brief guide to the paintings at the entrance); and the Foresteria, one room of which is frescoed by Giambattista and six by Giandomenico, whose predilections are a little less heroic than his father's.

La Rotonda

From the Villa Valmarana the narrow Strada Valmarana descends the slope to one of Europe's most imitated buildings – Palladio's Villa Capra, known to most people as **La Rotonda** (grounds & villa mid-March to mid-Nov Wed 10am–noon & 3–6pm, €10; grounds Tues–Sun same weeks and hours, plus Nov–March Tues–Sun 10am–noon & 2.30–5pm; €5), because of its centrally planned structure: the square outer walls symbolize the physical world while the circle within represents the idea of divine perfection. More obviously, the villa's shape and hilltop position emphasize its domination of the surrounding countryside. La Rotonda is unique among Palladio's villas (see box, p.381) in that it was designed not as the main building of a farm but as a pavilion in which entertainments could be held and the landscape enjoyed. Only a tour of the lavishly decorated interior will fully reveal the subtleties of the Rotonda; the grounds are little more than an attractive belt of grass from which to view the villa and surrounding countryside.

Eating and drinking

Central Vicenza has a delightful buzz in the evening, as the populace gathers in the Piazza dei Signori or just saunters up and down the Corso Palladio. And there is no shortage of **bars** and **cafés** if you want to pause and watch the crowds. While **restaurants** are not numerous in the *centro storico,* standards are high – all of which means you'll need to book or get there early for a table. You should also remember that many places close their kitchens by 11pm – and many shut up shop altogether in August. Popular specialities include *baccalà alla Vicentina* (*baccalà* elsewhere in Italy is salted cod, whereas *baccalà alla vicentina* is made by marinating dried cod in milk and oil, a recipe that dates back to the 13th century) and *sopressa*, a kind of salami from the Pasubio and Recoaro valleys, generally eaten with a slice of grilled polenta. The best **ice creams** in town are at *Tutto Gelato*, contra Frasche del Gambero 26 (between the basilica and the Duomo), though the *Gran Caffè Garibaldi* runs a close second.

Cafés and restaurants

Al Pestello Contrà S. Stefano 3 ☎0444.323.721. Sophisticated small restaurant behind San Stefano that's good for *baccalà alla vicentina* and other specialities of the city. Worth booking (closed all day Sun & Mon lunch).

Antica Casa della Malvasia Contrà delle Morette 5. A popular budget choice; a bustling, roomy inn just off Piazza dei Signori. The quality of the food can vary but there's live music on Tuesday and it's open till at least 1am on Friday and Saturday.

Gran Caffè Garibaldi Piazza dei Signori. The largest of the cafés overlooking the basilica, with the largest terrace, this is always likely to have space. Also serves ice cream inside and heaps of food upstairs.

I Monelli Contra Ponte San Paolo 13 ☎0444.540.400. Small, atmospheric *osteria* that attracts the crowds for its good local fare and

moderate prices. It lies across the bridge down from Piazza delle Erbe (closed Mon).

Offelleria della Meneghina Contrà Cavour 18. Another of the elegant cafés around the main Piazza, this has been going since 1791.

Sorarù Piazzetta Andrea Palladio. Highly recommended *pasticceria* café, where the nineteenth-century interior vies with the cakes for your attention. The location is also unbeatable: it's right in front of the Basilica.

Trattoria Ponte delle Bele Contrà Ponte delle Bele 5 ☎0444.320.647. Specializes in Trentine and South Tyrolean cuisine, but also does Vicentine specialities in a friendly rustic atmosphere. Closed Sun & mid-Aug.

Tutto Gelato Contrà Frasche del Gambero 26 (between the basilica and the Duomo). You can find the best ice creams in town here, though the *Gran Caffè Garibaldi* (see above) runs a close second.

Bars

Galleria 15 Piazza delle Biade 15. Atmospheric bar with live music or a DJ on Friday and Saturday and is open till 2am (closed Mon).

Il Grottino Piazza delle Erbe 2. Situated under the basilica, *Il Grottino* has a good range of wines

and some snacks, stays open till 2am and has a DJ playing jazz and lounge music on Thursday (closed Mon).

Verona

With its wealth of Roman sites and streets of pink-hued medieval buildings, the easy-going city of **VERONA** has more in the way of sights than any other place in the Veneto except Venice itself. It even hosts one of the major cultural events in the region, when the Roman Arena becomes a magical setting for an outdoor opera festival in July and August. Unlike Venice, though, it's not a city overwhelmed by the tourist industry, important though that is to the local economy. Verona is the largest city of the mainland Veneto, its economic success largely due to its position at the crossing of the major routes from Germany and Austria to central Italy and from the west to Venice and Trieste.

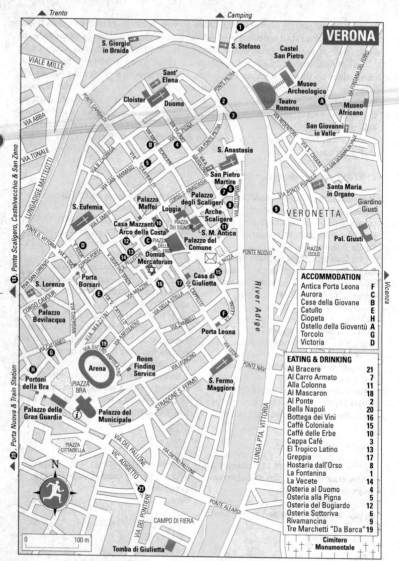

▲ Trento   ▲ Camping

VERONA

S. Giorgio in Braida
S. Stefano
Castel San Pietro
VIALE MILLE
VIA ABBA
Sant' Elena
Cloister
Duomo
PONTE GARIBALDI
PONTE PIETRA
Museo Archeologico
Teatro Romano
Museo Africano
San Giovanni in Valle
VIA REDENTORE
VIA S. CHIARA
VIA SAN GIOVANNI VALLE
VIA FONTANA DEL FERRO
VIA TONALE
LUNGADIGE MATTEOTTI
Ponte Scaligero, Castelvecchio & San Zeno
VIA PIGNA
VIA DIANO
VIA PONTE PIETRA
S. Anastasia
San Pietro Martire
Palazzo Maffei
Palazzo degli Scaligeri
Arche Scaligere
S. M. Antica
Palazzo del Comune
Santa Maria in Organo
Giardino Giusti
VERONETTA
Pal. Giusti
S. Eufemia
Casa Mazzanti
Arco della Costa
Loggia
PIAZZA DEI SIGNORI
Domus Mercatorum
PIAZZA DELLE ERBE
Casa di Giulietta
PIAZZA ISOLO
PONTE NUOVO
PONTE G. VITTORIA
RIVA SAN LORENZO
S. Lorenzo
Porta Borsari
CORSO PORTA BORSARI
VIA S. PELLICO
VIA MAZZINI
VIA CAPPELLO
River Adige
CORSO CAVOUR
Palazzo Bevilacqua
VIA OBERDAN
VIA DELLA STELLA
VIA ZAMBELLI
Porta Leona
VIA DIETRO PALLONE
VIA CATTANEO
VIA MAZZINI
VIA STELLA
Arena
Room Finding Service
VIA LEONI
PONTE NAVI
PONTE ALEARDI
Portoni della Bra
PIAZZA BRA
S. Fermo Maggiore
STRADONE S. FERMO
LUNGA PTA. VITTORIA
Palazzo della Gran Guardia
Palazzo del Municipale
VIA DEL PALLONE
VIA DIETRO PALLONE
PIAZZA CITTADELLA
N
CAMPO DI FIERA
Tomba di Giulietta
Cimitero Monumentale

▲ Porta Nuova & Train Station

▲ Vicenza

0 100 m

ACCOMMODATION

Antica Porta Leona	F
Aurora	C
Casa della Giovane	B
Catullo	E
Ciopeta	H
Ostello della Gioventù	A
Torcolo	G
Victoria	D

EATING & DRINKING

Al Bracere	21
Al Carro Armato	7
Alla Colonna	11
Al Mascaron	18
Al Ponte	2
Bella Napoli	20
Bottega dei Vini	16
Caffè Coloniale	15
Caffé delle Erbe	10
Cappa Café	3
El Tropico Latino	13
Greppia	17
Hostaria dall'Orso	8
La Fontanina	1
La Vecete	14
Osteria al Duomo	4
Osteria alla Pigna	5
Osteria del Bugiardo	12
Osteria Sottoriva	6
Rivamancina	9
Tre Marchetti "Da Barca"	19

Verona's initial development as a **Roman** settlement was similarly due to its straddling the main east–west and north–south lines of communication. A period of decline in the wake of the disintegration of the Roman Empire was followed by revival under the Ostrogoths, who in turn were succeeded by the Franks: Charlemagne's son, Pepin, ruled his kingdom from here. By the twelfth century Verona had become a city-state, and in the following century approached the zenith of its independent existence with the rise of the Scaligers. Ruthless in the exercise of power, the Scaligers were at the same time energetic patrons of the arts, and many of Verona's finest buildings date from their rule.

With the fall of their dynasty a time of upheaval ensued, Gian Galeazzo Visconti of Milan emerging in control of the city. Absorption into the Venetian Empire came in 1405, and Verona was governed from Venice until the arrival of Napoleon. Verona's history then shadowed that of Venice: a prolonged interlude of Austrian rule, brought to an end by the Unification of Italy in 1866.

Arrival, information and accommodation

If you're flying to Verona's Valerio Catullo **airport** at Villafranca, 10km away, you can get into the city by a regular APT bus (every 20min 7am–11.30pm; €4.50) from the airport to the train station and Piazza Cittadella, near the city centre. Flights to **Montichiari**, 23km southeast of Brescia, also called Brescia or, optimistically, Verona, are served by a daily shuttle bus (€11) that takes an hour; a taxi costs around €90. For more information on both airports, go to ⓦwww .aeroportoverona.it. Buses to both leave from in front of the station, and tickets can be bought on board.

The **train** and **bus stations** are a fifteen-minute walk from the centre. (Note that Verona Porta Nuova is the town's main station, not Porta Vescovo.) To walk to the centre from here, turn right outside the train station (keeping to the right-hand side of the road) then left at the main junction with the broad Corso Porta Nuova, which leads straight to Piazza Bra, site of the Arena and the hub of Verona. If you don't fancy the walk, you can get a bus; tickets must be bought before boarding, either from the machines alongside bay A or from the *tabacchi* inside the train station ticket hall. They cost €1 and are valid for any number of journeys within an hour.

The main **tourist office** is by the central Piazza Bra at Via degli Alpini 9, within the old town walls beside the Palazzo Municipale (Mon–Sat 9am–7pm & Sun 9am–3pm; ⓣ045.806.8680, ⓦwww.tourism.verona.it). There are additional offices at the train station (daily 9am–6pm; ⓣ045.800.0861) and at the airport. You can **rent bikes** from Zanchi, Corso Cavour 13a, near the Porta Borsari (Mon 3.30–7.30pm, Tues–Sat 9am–12.30pm & 3.30–7.30pm). There's **Internet** access at Internet Train, Via Roma 19 (Mon–Fri 10am–10pm, Sat & Sun 4–8pm), and Via 4 Spade 3b (daily 2.30–8.30pm).

Accommodation is hard to find during the opera season (late June to early Sept) so you'll need to book ahead. You could try the room-finding service, Cooperativa Albergatori Veronesi (CAV), at Via Patuzzi 5 (May to mid-Nov Mon–Sat 10am–7pm; mid-Nov to April Mon–Fri 10am–6pm; closed mid-Dec to mid-Jan; ⓣ045.800.9844 ⓦwww.veronapass.com).

Hotels

Antica Porta Leona Via Corticlla Leoni 3 ⓣ045.595.499, ⓦwww.anticaportaleona.com. Spacious rooms in this large three-star, all with a/c, some with balconies. Has plenty of single rooms ❹

Aurora Piazzetta XIV Novembre 2 ⓣ045.594.717, ⓦwww.hotelaurora.biz. Upmarket two-star hotel with a welcoming atmosphere and many rooms overlooking the Piazza delle Erbe. The staff are friendly and knowledgeable, and speak good English. Excellent buffet breakfast. ❹

Catullo Via Valerio Catullo 1 ⓣ045.800.2786, ⓔlocandacatullo@tiscali.it. The cheapest – if not the friendliest – hotel in the centre, just off the

main shopping artery of Via Mazzini. The large rooms are rather shabby but have plenty of light, and some have a private bathroom. ❷

Ciopeta Vicolo Teatro Filarmonica 2 ⓣ045.800.6843, ⓦwww.ciopeta.it. Very friendly, family-run establishment located in an alley parallel to Via Roma. Book ahead, as this one-star only has five rooms (all with shared bathrooms). Excellent restaurant, too, which spreads out into the alley in summer. ❷

Torcolo Vicolo Listone 3 ⓣ045.800.7512, ⓦwww.hoteltorcolo.it. Nicely turned-out two-star hotel within 100m of the Arena, just off Piazza Bra. Extremely welcoming owners – and a favourite with the opera crowds, so book ahead. ❸

Victoria Via Adua 8, ☎045.590.566, ⓦwww
.hotelvictoria.it. Housed in a complex of old buildings, this four-star has a snazzy modern foyer,
well-equipped rooms and gymnasium. If you
want to treat yourself, the superior doubles are
gorgeous. Good deals out of season. ❼

Hostels and campsites

Casa della Giovane Via Pigna 7 ☎045.596.880,
ⓕ045.800.5449, ⓦwww.casadellagiovane.com.
Spartan but friendly convent-run hostel for women,
with an 11pm curfew, although there is some flexibility for guests with opera tickets. Reservations by
fax only. €13 in dorms, plus some double rooms at
€16 per head.
Ostello della Gioventù Salita Fontana del Ferro
15 ☎045.590.360. The official HI hostel is in
Villa Francescatti, a beautiful old building behind

the Teatro Romano; as it's quite a walk from the
centre, it's best to take a bus (#73, or #90 on Sun)
to Piazza Isolo, then walk up the hill. No reservations, but with over 200 beds, there should be
room. The 11.30pm curfew is extended for guests
with concert tickets. HI membership not essential
if you're staying for just one night. €15 per night;
reasonably priced evening meals are available. At
the bottom of the hill there's a sister hostel, the
Santa Chiara, which is new and better equipped,
but tends to be open only when the main hostel
is full.
Campeggio Castel San Pietro Via Castel S. Pietro
2 ☎045.592.037, ⓦwww.campingcastelsanpietro
.com. A pleasant site out by the old city walls, the
only place to camp near the centre of Verona; take
a bus to Via Marsala and then it is a steep walk up
the hill. Open mid-June to Sept.

The City

Coming from the train station, you pass Verona's south gate, the **Porta Nuova**,
and come onto the long Corso Porta Nuova, which ends at the battlemented
arches that precede the **Piazza Bra**. Here stands the mightiest of Verona's
Roman monuments, the Arena, marking the edge of the old city that nestles in
the bend of the river Adige and is crisscrossed by a neat grid of streets around
the old Roman forum. Most of the sights are in this old centre, though it's
worth venturing across the river to the Veronetta district for a clutch of sights,
including the archaeology museum.

The Arena

Dating from the first century AD, the **Arena** has survived in remarkable
condition, despite the twelfth-century earthquake that destroyed all but four
of the arches of the outer wall. The interior (Mon 1.45–7.30pm, Tues–Sun
9am–7.30pm, but closes 3.30pm during the opera season; €4, or Verona Card
– see box opposite; free on first Sun of month) was scarcely damaged by the
tremor, and where once crowds of around 20,000 packed the benches for gladiatorial contests and the like – nowadays audiences come to watch gargantuan
opera productions. Originally measuring 152m by 123m overall, and thus the
third largest of all Roman amphitheatres, the Arena remains an awesome sight
– and as an added treat offers a tremendous urban panorama from the topmost
of the 44 pink marble tiers.

The Casa di Giulietta and San Fermo

North of the arena, **Via Mazzini** is a narrow traffic-free street lined with
generally expensive clothes, shoe and jewellery shops. A left turn at the end
leads to the Piazza delle Erbe, while a right takes you into **Via Cappello**, a
street named after the family that Shakespeare turned into the Capulets – and
on the left, at no. 23, is the **Casa di Giulietta** or Juliet's House (Mon 1.30–
7.30pm, Tues–Sun 9am–7.30pm; €4). In fact, although the "Capulets" and the
"Montagues" (Montecchi) did exist, Romeo and Juliet were entirely fictional
creations. The house itself, constructed at the start of the fourteenth century,
is in a fine state of preservation, but is largely empty. It's said that if you stand
under the balcony and make a wish about love it will come true.

A **biglietto unico**, costing €5, allows one visit each to San Zeno, San Lorenzo, the Duomo (but not the Museo Canonicale), Sant'Anastasia and San Fermo. The ticket can be bought at any of these churches, which individually charge €2 for admission. If you're planning to be very busy, it might be worth getting the **Verona Card**, which gives access to all the sights listed above, including the Museo Canonicale, plus the Arena, the Torre dei Lamberti, the Museo Lapidario, Castelvecchio, the Casa di Giulietta, the Tomba di Giulietta and the Roman Theatre, as well as free travel on city buses. A one-day Verona card costs €8, the three-day €12. You can buy it at *tabacchi* and in theory at the museums and monuments too, though sometimes they run out of stock. Note that many museums are closed on Monday mornings.

Via Cappello leads into Via Leoni with its Roman gate, the **Porta Leona**, and a segment of excavated Roman street, exposed 3m below today's street level. At the end of Via Leoni and across the road rises the red-brick **San Fermo** church (March–Oct Mon–Sat 10am–6pm, Sun 1–6pm; Nov–Feb Tues–Sat 10am–1pm & 1.30–4pm, Sun 1–5pm; €2.50 or *biglietto unico*/Verona Card – see box above), whose inconsistent exterior betrays the fact that it consists of two churches combined. Flooding forced the Benedictines to superimpose a second church on the one founded in the eighth century. The Gothic upper church has no outstanding works of art but is graceful enough; the Romanesque lower church, entered from the left of the choir, has impressive low vaulting, sometimes obscured by exhibitions.

Piazza delle Erbe and Piazza dei Signori

Originally a major Roman crossroads and the site of the forum, **Piazza delle Erbe** is still the heart of the city. As the name suggests, the market used to sell mainly vegetables, but nowadays it has been largely taken over by ugly, semi-permanent booths selling clothes, souvenirs, antiques and fast food. The rich variety of buildings framing the square is far more attractive. Most striking are the **Domus Mercatorum** (on the left as you look from the Via Cappello end), which was founded in 1301 as a merchants' warehouse and exchange, the fourteenth-century **Torre del Gardello** and, to the right of the tower, the **Casa Mazzanti**, whose sixteenth-century murals are best seen after dark, under enhancing spotlights.

The neighbouring **Piazza dei Signori** used to be the chief public square of Verona. Much of the right side is taken up by the **Palazzo del Capitano**, which is separated from the Palazzo del Comune by a stretch of excavated Roman street. Facing you as you come into the square is the medieval **Palazzo degli Scaligeri**, residence of the Scaligers; a monument to more democratic times extends from it at a right angle – the fifteenth-century **Loggia del Consiglio**, former assembly hall of the city council and Verona's outstanding early-Renaissance building. The rank of Roman notables along the roof includes Verona's most illustrious native poet, Catullus. For a dizzying view of the city, take a sharp right as soon as you come into the square, and go up the twelfth-century **Torre dei Lamberti** (closed for restoration until 2007; Mon 1.30–7pm, Tues–Sun 9.30am–7.30pm; €3 by lift, €2 on foot, or Verona Card – see box above).

The Scaligeri tombs

Passing under the arch linking the Palazzo degli Scaligeri to the Palazzo del Capitano, you come to the little Romanesque church of Santa Maria Antica, in front of which are ranged the **Arche Scaligeri**, some of the most elaborate Gothic funerary monuments in Italy. Over the side entrance to the church, an equestrian statue of **Cangrande I** ("Big Dog"; died 1329) gawps down from his tomb's pyramidal roof; the statue is a copy, the original being displayed in the Castelvecchio (see opposite). The canopied tombs of the rest of the clan are enclosed within a wrought-iron palisade decorated with ladder motifs, the emblem of the Scaligers – the family name was della Scala, "*scala*" meaning ladder. **Mastino I** ("Mastiff"; died 1277), founder of the dynasty, is buried in the simple tomb against the wall of the church; Mastino II (died 1351) is to the left of the entrance, opposite the most florid of the tombs, that of **Cansignorio** ("Top Dog"; died 1375). From June to September a €4 joint ticket with the Torre dei Lamberti (bought at the tower) lets you in to inspect the tombs more closely.

Sant'Anastasia, San Pietro Martire and the Duomo

Going on past the Arche Scaligeri, and turning left along Via San Pietro, you come to **Sant'Anastasia** (March–Oct Mon–Sat 9am–6pm, Sun 1–6pm; Nov–Feb Tues–Sat 10am–1pm & 1.30–4pm, Sun 1–5pm; €2.50 or *biglietto unico*/Verona Card – see box, p.389), Verona's largest church. Started in 1290 and completed in 1481, it's mainly Gothic in style, with undertones of the Roman-esque. The fourteenth-century carvings of New Testament scenes around the doors are the most arresting feature of its bare exterior; the interior's highlight is Pisanello's delicately coloured fresco *St George and the Princess* (high above the chapel to the right of the altar), a work in which the normally martial saint appears as something of a dandy.

To the left of Sant'Anastasia's facade is an eye-catching tomb, a free-standing monument to one Guglielmo di Castelbarco (1320) by Enrico di Rigino. To its left, on one side of the little piazza fronting Sant'Anastasia, stands **San Pietro Martire** (open occasionally in the afternoon and for concerts), deconsecrated since its ransacking by Napoleon. Numerous patches of fresco dot the walls, making for an atmospheric interior, though the highlight is the vast lunette fresco on the east wall. Easily the strangest picture in Verona, it's thought to be an allegorical account of the Virgin's Assumption, though the bizarre collection of animals appears to have little connection with a bemused-looking Madonna.

Verona's red-and-white-striped **Duomo** (March–Oct Mon–Sat 9.30am–5.30pm, Sun 1.30–5.30pm; Nov–Feb Tues–Sat 11am–1pm & 1.30–4pm, Sun 1.30–5pm; €2.50 or *biglietto unico*/Verona Card – see box, p.389) lies just round the river's bend, past the Roman Ponte Pietra. Consecrated in 1187, it's Romanesque in its lower parts, developing into Gothic as it goes up; the two doorways are twelfth century – look for the story of Jonah and the whale on the south porch, and the statues of Roland and Oliver, two of Charlemagne's pala-dins, on the west. The interior has fascinating architectural details around each chapel and on the columns – particularly fine is the Cappella Mazzanti (last on the right). In the first chapel on the left, an *Assumption* by Titian occupies an architectural frame by Sansovino, who also designed the choir.

To the Castelvecchio

After the Arena and the Teatro Romano, Verona's most impressive Roman remnant is the **Porta dei Borsari** (on the junction of Via Diaz and Corso Porta Borsari), a structure that was as great an influence on the city's Renais-sance architects as the amphitheatre. Now reduced to a monumental screen straddling the road, it used to be Verona's largest Roman gate; the inscription dates it at 265, but it's almost certainly older than that.

Heading down Corso Cavour from Porta dei Borsari, past the small twelfth-century **San Lorenzo** (March–Oct Mon–Sat 10am–6pm & Sun 1–6pm; Nov–Feb Tues–Sat 10am–1pm & 1.30–4pm, Sun 1–5pm; €2.50 or *biglietto unico*/Verona Card – see box, p.389), you come to the **Arco dei Gavi**, a first-century Roman triumphal arch that was rebuilt in 1930 after Napoleon's troops tore down the original. This is your best vantage point from which to admire the **Ponte Scaligero**, built by Cangrande II between 1355 and 1375. It was the turn of the German army to indulge in wanton destruction this time: they blew up the bridge in 1945, but the salvaged material was used for reconstruction. The stretch of shingle on the opposite bank is a popular spot for picnics, sunbathing and just watching the water flow by, rich in colour from the glacial deposits upstream.

The fortress from which the bridge springs, the **Castelvecchio** (Mon 1.30–7.30pm, Tues–Sun 8.30am–7.30pm; €4 or Verona Card, free on first Sun of month), was commissioned by Cangrande II at around the same time and became the stronghold for Verona's subsequent rulers. Opened as the city museum in 1925, it was damaged by bombing during World War II, but opened again in 1964 after scrupulous restoration. The Castelvecchio's collection of paintings, jewellery, weapons and other artefacts flows through a labyrinth of chambers, courtyards and passages that is fascinating to explore in itself. The equestrian figure Cangrande I, removed from his tomb, is strikingly displayed on an outdoor pedestal; his expression is disconcerting at close range, the simpleton's grin being difficult to reconcile with the image of the ruthless warlord. Outstanding among the paintings are two works by Jacopo Bellini, two Madonnas by Giovanni Bellini, another Madonna by Pisanello, Veronese's *Descent from the Cross*, a Tintoretto *Nativity*, a Lotto portrait and works by Giambattista and Giandomenico Tiepolo. The real joy of the museum, however, is in wandering round the medieval pieces: beautiful sculpture and frescoes by the often nameless artists of the late Middle Ages. And look out for the extraordinary painting by Francesco Caroto of a beaming boy holding up a drawing – a rare depiction of a child's work in medieval painting.

San Zeno Maggiore

A little over 1km northwest of the Castelvecchio is the **Basilica di San Zeno Maggiore** (March–Oct Mon–Sat 8.30am–6pm, Sun 1–6pm; Nov–Feb Tues–Sat 10am–1pm & 1.30–4pm, Sun 1–5pm; €2.50 or *biglietto unico*/Verona Card, see box, p.389), one of the most significant Romanesque churches in northern Italy. A church was founded here, above the tomb of the city's patron saint, as early as the fifth century, but the present building and its campanile were put up in the first half of the twelfth century, with additions continuing up to the end of the fourteenth. Its large rose window, representing the Wheel of Fortune, dates from the early twelfth century, as does the magnificent portal, whose lintels bear relief sculptures representing the months – look also for St Zeno trampling the devil. The reliefs to the side of the portal are also from the twelfth century and show scenes from the Old Testament on the right, and scenes from the New Testament on the left (except for the bottom two on both sides, which depict scenes from the life of Theodoric). Extraordinary bronze panels on the doors depict scenes from the Bible and the *Miracles of San Zeno*, their style influenced by Byzantine art; most of those on the left are from around 1100, and most of the right-hand panels date from a century or so later. Areas of the lofty and simple interior are covered with frescoes, some superimposed on others, some defaced by ancient graffiti. Diverting though these are, the one compulsive image in the church is the high altar's luminous *Madonna and Saints* by Mantegna.

△ Basilica di San Zeno Maggiore

Across the Adige

On the other side of Ponte Garibaldi, and right along the embankments or through the public gardens, is **San Giorgio in Braida**, in terms of its works of art the richest of Verona's churches. A *Baptism* by Tintoretto hangs over the door, while the main altar, designed by Sanmicheli, incorporates a marvellous piece by Paolo **Veronese** – *The Martyrdom of St George*.

It's a short walk along the embankments, past the twelfth-century church of Santo Stefano and the Ponte Pietra, to the first-century-BC **Teatro Romano** (Mon 1.30–7.30pm, Tues–Sun 8.30am–7.30pm; €3 or Verona Card, see box, p.389, free on first Sun of month); much restored, the theatre is now used for concerts and plays. High above it, and reached by a rickety looking lift, the **Museo Archeologico** (same hours & ticket) occupies the buildings of an old convent. Its well-arranged collection features a number of Greek, Roman and Etruscan finds, including a magnificent Roman bronze head; from the old frescoed chapel at the top the views across the town are magnificent.

If you've the energy to walk up hill again, there are two sites nearby. The **Museo Africano** (summer Thurs–Sat 10am–1pm, 2–6pm, first Sun of the month till 7pm; winter Tues–Sat 10am–1pm, 2–6pm Sun till 7pm; €4), off Via San Giovanni in Valle at Vicolo Pozzo 1, has a brightly lit and well-displayed collection of musical instruments, fetishes and masks brought back over the years by missionaries as well as photos of the continent. Its information sheets on the role of spiritual healers and voodoo make interesting reading. Further up Via San Giovanni in Valle, just below the youth hotel, stands the small Romanesque church of **San Giovanni in Valle** (daily 9am–noon), which was founded in the eighth century and rebuilt in the twelfth after earthquake damage. Bombing in 1944 destroyed the decoration of the interior, but the crypt escaped pretty well unscathed.

Back down at river level is one of the treats of the city: the church of **Santa Maria in Organo** (daily 8am–noon & 2.30–6pm; free), which possesses what Vasari praised as the finest choir stall in Italy. Dating from the 1490s, this marquetry was the work of a Benedictine monk, one Fra Giovanni, and is astonishing in its precision – in depicting animals – and use of perspective. There's more of his work in the sacristy, while in the crypt you can see reused upside-down Roman columns. Further down Via Santa Chiara you'll come to the finest formal gardens in Verona, the **Giardino Giusti** at Via Giardino Giusti 2 (daily: summer 9am–8pm; winter 9am–sunset; €5). Full of fountains and shady corners, the Giusti provides the city's most pleasant respite from the streets.

Eating, drinking and entertainment

The Veronese have a reputation for liking their food – one story the people of Vicenza tell is that the gluttonous Veronese defenders of castle during the 13th century opened their gates when they heard that the besiegers were cooking *baccalà*, dried cod – although that was more likely a sign of their desperation. You can certainly eat well in the city: if the local speciality of horse meat is not to your taste you can try the local salamis, pumpkin ravioli or *bigoli*, a handmade thick version of spaghetti. The best **restaurants** in Verona tend to be packed after 9pm, so it's best to book or go out early. Your money goes a lot further in Verona than it does in Venice, with numerous trattorias offering full meals for under €20 (especially in the Veronetta district, on the east side of the river). As the Veneto produces more DOC **wine** than any other region in Italy, it's not surprising that Italy's main wine fair, Vinitaly, is held in Verona; it takes place in April and offers abundant sampling opportunities. For non-alcoholic pleasures, sit outside one of the *gelaterie* in Piazza delle Erbe and indulge in an incredible concoction of fruit, cream and ice cream; or head for the best ice cream in the city at *Balu*, at Corso Porta Borsari 57 just inside the Roman gate (takeaway only, open till 8pm, closed Mon). In the week before and after the Arena season (July and August) you may find places close early or shut completely as the city takes a rest.

Restaurants

Al Bracere Via Adigetto 6a. Pleasant, busy pizzeria through the city walls behind the tourist office. Extensive menu includes generous pizzas baked in a wood-fired oven. Open daily to midnight.

Alla Colonna Largo Pescheria Vecchia 4 ☎045.596.718. Almost impossible to get into, as the food is simple but superb and the prices excellent (€13 menu). Tables are often packed with savvy locals. Serves until 2am. Closed Sun.

Bella Napoli Via Marconi 14. Serves the best pizza – and the largest – in Verona – in a distinctly Neapolitan atmosphere. Open till 1am, or later on Fri–Sat.

Bottega del Vino Vicolo Scudo di Francia 3a ☎045.597.945, ☺www.bottegavini.it. One of the top restaurants in Verona, with flamboyant antique décor and one of the largest selection of wines you'll find anywhere in Italy – though it's slightly touristy. A dish to look out for is the *risotto all'Amarone* – rice braised in the local wine. Open till midnight and closed Tues.

Greppia Vicolo Samaritana 3 ☎045.800.4577, ☺www.ristorantegreppia.com. This small family-run trattoria near the Piazza dell'Erbe has an excellent reputation yet low prices. Local specialities include *bollito misto con la peará*, boiled meats (which are better than they sound in English) in a

typical peppery Veronese sauce. Worth booking, especially during the opera season. Closed Mon.

Hostaria dall'Orso Via Sottoriva 3c ☎045.597.214. Friendly place under the atmospheric arches of Via Sottoriva serving good salads and local dishes. The resident English novelist Tim Parks is the father of one of the staff – which explains the large number of his books on the shelves. Lunch menu €14. Open till midnight Mon–Sat.

La Fontanina Piazzetta Fontanina, Veronetta ☎045.913.305, ☺www.ristorantelafontanina.com. One of the best old-world *osterie* on the left bank of the Adige. Exclusive atmosphere (and prices to match – it has a Michelin star, after all), with tables hidden among crates of wine and decorated screens. Closed all day Sun, Mon lunch & all Aug.

Osteria alla Pigna Via Pigna 4 ☎045.800.4080, ☺www.osteriapigna.it. Elegant traditional restaurant between the duomo and Piazza dell'Erbe. One of the best of the *osterie tipiche* dotted around the historic centre. Closed Mon lunch & Sun.

Osteria del Bugiardo Corso Porta Borsari 17a ☎045.591.1869. Small, new establishment with an excellent range of dishes. Its high tables are packed at lunchtime with locals grabbing a quick lunch. Closed Mon.

Tre Marchetti "Da Barca" Vicolo Tre Marchetti 19b ☎045.803.0463. A couple of steps north of the Arena, this place is perfect for a pre- or post-opera meal of Veronese specialities, such as tortelloni stuffed with Veronese white celery, bigoli, or veal braised in Amarone – but you should book a table. Closed Sun & Mon lunch (closed all day Mon in July & Aug).

Bars and cafés

Al Carro Armato Vicolo Gatto 2a. One of the most atmospheric *osterie* in the city, with a counter full of delicious *antipasti* for you to choose from, such as *polpetti*, *sfilacci* (fine slices of horse) and beans with onions. Live music on some Sundays. Open until 2am; summer, closed Mon evening and all day Tues, winter closed Mon.

Al Mascaron Piazza San Zeno 16. Fine wines and an urbane atmosphere early in the evening, popular disco-bar later. Five minutes' walk west from Castelvecchio. Open until 1am; closed Mon.

Al Ponte Via Ponte Pietra 26. Sip a glass on the terrace here and enjoy a marvellous view of Ponte Pietra and the Teatro Romano. Open until 3am; closed Wed.

Caffè Coloniale Piazzetta Viviani 14c. The best hot chocolate in the city, and good snacks in a mock-colonial setting, with attractive outdoor terrace. Open 7am–midnight. Closed Sun in Aug.

Caffè delle Erbe Piazza delle Erbe 32. Known universally as Mazzanti, this is the loudest, youngest and coolest of the late-opening bars on the square. Open until midnight. Closed Mon.

Cappa Café Piazzetta Bra Molinari 1a. Large bar with eastern trappings, floor cushions, riverfront terrace and live jazz on Sundays. Open till 2am daily.

El Tropico Latino Via Pellicciai 20. Steer clear of the Tex-Mex food, and head for the cocktails and buzzing bar, which keeps going until 2am. Closed Tues and usually takes break in Aug.

Le Vecete Via Pellicciai 32. Atmospheric *osteria* with a delicious selection of the savoury tartlets known as *bocconcini*, and good lunches. Its wine list is excellent, ranging from cheap to very, very expensive. Open till midnight, or later during the opera season. Closed Sun.

Osteria al Duomo Via Duomo 7a. Best of the city's bars, little changed by modern fashion, and enlivened by live music on Wednesday afternoons from Sept to June. Interesting small menu, too, with local specialities such as *bigoli* with a donkey sauce (*sugo d'asino*). Open 4pm–midnight; closed Sun.

Osteria Sottoriva Via Sottoriva 9. Verona's traditional *osterie* don't come much more authentic than this: it's rumbustious, full of locals, and serves delicious food. In summer you can sit outside under the arches. Open 10.30am–10.30pm; closed Wed.

Rivamancina Vicolo Quadrelli 1, Veronetta. Lively late bar on the left bank of the Adige, with trendy music and contemporary cocktails. Mon–Sat 8pm–2am.

Nightlife and entertainment

Music and theatre are the dominant art forms in the cultural life of Verona. The city's renowned **opera festival**, held in the Arena during July and August, is a major draw, always featuring a no-expense-spared production of *Aida*. To get the best (or last-minute) seats, call in at the office on Via Dietro Anfiteatro 6b, which opens late on performance nights; if you can't make it in person you can book by phone or online (℡045.800.5151, ⓦ www.arena.it). Big rock events crop up on the Arena's calendar too. A season of ballet and of Shakespeare and other dramatists in Italian is the principal summer fare at the **Teatro Romano**. Some of the Teatro events are free; for the rest, cheapskates who don't mind inferior acoustics can park themselves on the steps going up the hill alongside the theatre. The box office at the Teatro Romano also sells tickets for the Arena and vice versa.

From October to May **English-language films** are shown at the Cinema Stimate in Piazza Cittadella. The **disco** scene is much livelier than in Venice, but venues come and go fast, and many of them are outside the centre; look in the local paper, *L'Arena* (there's a copy in every bar), to find out where they are and what days they're open. A very popular and enduring club is *Alter Ego*, a couple of kilometres north of the centre across the Ponte Pietra at Via Torricelle 9 – best reached by taxi. The *Spettacoli* section of *L'Arena* is the best source of up-to-date information on entertainment in Verona (in Italian only).

One of the most enjoyable days in the calendar is Verona's **Carnevale**, during which, on the Friday before Shrove Tuesday, a huge procession of more than eighty floats winds through the centre from Piazza Bra. Totally unlike its Venice counterpart, this is a local event with none of the masks and posing – just lots of people dressing up, loud music and confetti everywhere – though you need to steer clear of the kids who get carried away spraying white foam everywhere. The procession is led by a large character called the Papa del Gnocco, hence why most of the city's restaurants serve *gnocchi* on that Friday.

Treviso

One of the undiscovered gems in the Veneto is **TREVISO**, a charming, quiet town that makes an ideal jumping-off point both for Venice and the northern Veneto. Treviso was an important town long before its assimilation by Venice in 1389, and plenty of evidence of its early status survives in the form of Gothic churches, public buildings and, most dramatically of all, the paintings of **Tomaso da Modena** (1325–79), the major artist in northern Italy in the years immediately after Giotto's death. The general townscape within Treviso's sixteenth-century walls is often appealing too – long porticoes and frescoed house facades give many of the streets an appearance quite distinct from those of other towns in the region.

Arrival and accommodation

Arriving at the **train station**, head straight across the bridge, bending slightly left at the first roundabout to reach the centre. Ryanair lays on buses to meet its **flights** to Treviso but these only go to Venice – to get into town take bus #6 from the bus stop on the main road (tickets from the bar across the road or on the bus; 20min, every 20min). If you arrive on the late flight take a taxi, which should cost around €15. There's **Internet** access at Servicepoint, Via Toniolo 19 (Mon–Fri 8.30am–12.30am, 3–7pm) in the centre of town. The **tourist office** is right in the centre, at Piazza Monte di Pietà 8 (Mon 9am–12.30pm, Tues–Sat 9am–12.30pm & 2–6pm, Sun 9.30am–12.30pm & 3–6pm; ☎0422.547.632, ⓦwww.turismo.provincia.treviso.it); it dispenses useful leaflets not just on Treviso but on attractions throughout Treviso province.

Accommodation

Though the tourist office valiantly promotes Treviso as one of Italy's under-valued cities, the town isn't really geared up for tourists, its main problem being that most of its hotels are characterless or somewhat down-at-heel Eurobusiness places. The tourist office can help with B&B accommodation.

Carlton Largo Porta Altinia 15 ☎0422.411.661, ⓦwww.hotelcarlton.it. Large, but friendly, business-orientated four-star that's situated near the railway station. ❹
Continental Via Roma 16 ☎0422.411.216 ⓦwww.hcontinental.it. Virtually next door to the *Continental*, this four-star hotel is predominantly geared to business clientele. ❸
Il Focolare Piazza Ancilotto 4 ☎ & ⓕ0422.56601 ⓦwww.albergoilfocolare.net. Close to the tourist office, *Il Focolare* is a small and reasonably priced two-star hotel, with an annex near San Nicolò. ❸

The City

These features are well preserved in the main street of the centre, **Calmaggiore**, where modern commerce has reached the sort of compromise with the past that the Italians seem to arrange better than anyone else. Contemporary building techniques have played a larger part than you might think in shaping that compromise – Treviso was pounded during both world wars and on Good Friday 1944 was half-destroyed in a single bombing raid.

At the bottom of Calmaggiore, on one side of the **Piazza dei Signori**, the early thirteenth-century **Palazzo dei Trecento** was one casualty of 1944 – a line round the exterior shows where the restoration began. The lengthy restoration of its surviving frescoes has just been finished – check at the tourist office to see if they can be visited yet. The adjoining **Palazzo del Podestà** is a nineteenth-century structure, concocted in an appropriate style.

Of more interest are the two churches at the back of the block: San Vito and Santa Lucia (usually open daily 9am–noon; free). The tiny, dark chapel of Santa Lucia has extensive frescoes by Tomaso da Modena and his followers; San Vito has even older paintings in the alcove through which you enter from Santa Lucia, though they're not in a good state. The duomo of Treviso, **San Pietro**, stands at the end of Calmaggiore (Mon–Sat 7.30am–noon & 3.30–7pm, Sun 7.30am–1pm & 3.30–8pm; free). Founded in the twelfth century, San Pietro was much altered in succeeding centuries, and then rebuilt to rectify the damage of 1944. The interior is chiefly notable for the crypt – a thicket of twelfth-century columns with scraps of medieval mosaics – and the Cappella Malchiostro, with fragmentary frescoes by Pordenone and an *Annunciation* by Titian.

Just over the River Sile from the railway station is the severe Dominican church of **San Nicolò** (Mon–Fri 8am–noon & 3.30–7pm; free), which has frescoes dating from the thirteenth to the sixteenth centuries. Some of the columns are decorated with paintings by Tomaso da Modena and his school, of which the best are the *SS Jerome* and *Agnes* (by Tomaso) on the first column on your right as you enter; there's also a towering *St Christopher*, on the wall of the right aisle, painted around 1410 and attributed to Antonio da Treviso. Equally striking, but far more graceful, is the composite *Tomb of Agostino d'Onigo* on the north wall of the chancel, created in 1500 by Antonio Rizzo (who did the sculpture) and Lorenzo Lotto (who painted the attendant pages). The figures of Agnes and Jerome are an excellent introduction to Tomaso da Modena, but for a comprehensive demonstration of his talents you have to visit the neighbouring **Seminario**, where the chapterhouse, to the left of the entrance, is decorated with forty *Portraits of Members of the Dominican Order*, painted in 1352 (Mon–Fri: summer 8am–6pm; winter 8am–12.30pm & 3–5.30pm; free – you may need to ring the bell to get in).

The Santa Caterina district

On the other side of town from San Nicolò there's another brilliant fresco cycle by Tomaso da Modena, *The Story of the Life of Saint Ursula*, in the deconsecrated church of **Santa Caterina** (Tues–Sun 9am–12.30pm, 2.30–6pm; €3) behind Piazza Giacomo Matteotti on Via Santa Caterina. Painted for the now extinct church of Santa Margherita sul Sile, the frescoes were detached from the walls in the late nineteenth century shortly before the church was destroyed. As the old **Museo Civico** is closed, its works are gradually being brought over to Santa Caterina and the adjoining cloister buildings.

The district around the church is a pleasant one, with its antiques sellers and furniture restorers and the hubbub of the stalls around the market in Piazza Matteotti. There are a couple of other churches worth a look, too. To the north of Santa Caterina is the rebuilt thirteenth-century church of **San Francesco** (daily 8am–noon & 3–7pm), an airy building with a ship's keel roof and patches of fresco, including a *Madonna and Saints* by Tomaso da Modena (chapel to north of chancel). To the south, at the end of Via Carlo Alberto, stands the **Basilica di Santa Maria Maggiore** (daily 6.30–11.45am & 3–7.30pm), which houses the most venerated image in Treviso, a fresco of the Madonna originally painted by Tomaso but subsequently retouched. Beyond the church on the banks of the Sile is the brand-new **university**, one of the forces behind a rash of building and restoration work in town.

Eating, drinking and nightlife

Treviso's **restaurants** have a far higher reputation that its hotels, while the **bars** and **cafés** clustered underneath and around the Palazzo dei Trecento are always buzzing. Regular features on the city menus are *radicchio*, the bitter red lettuce that is remarkably popular, and *tiramisu*, which as every local knows comes from here. Treviso's **nightlife** is very low-key, though this may change as the university population grows. Currently, if you want to dance you have to head 3km out of town to the places along the Via Fonderia, but the trendier Trevisans stay in town for a drink at *Sottoportico* (Mon–Sat till 2am) under the arcades at Sottoportico dei Buranelli 29 or *Al Tocai* (Tues–Sun till 1am) in Piazzetta Lombardi, south of Piazza dei Signori.

Restaurants and bars

Dai Naneti Vicolo Brolo 2. Round the corner from the Palazzo Trecento, Beppe and Fabio preside over a small bar that is packed with locals sampling the wine, food and congenial atmosphere. Closed all Sun & Wed eve.

La Pausa Via d'Annunzio 3b. The best late-night bar in town, *La Pausa*, attracts a laid-back clientele and sometimes has live music on Saturday evening. Closed Mon & Sun.

Muscoli's Via Pescheria 23. The alleyway below the tourist office leads down to this marvellous bar, where the customers spill out onto the fish market island opposite when the weather permits. Excellent snacks – such as the fig and blue cheese *crostini*. At lunchtime, the stern lady behind the bar occasionally breaks into song, accompanied by the old men at the counter. Closed Sun.

Osteria al Canevon Piazza San Vito 18 ☎0422.540.208. You'll find adventurous cuisine and high standards in this friendly restaurant centrally placed on the square behind the tourist office. Specializes in fish. Closed Thurs.

Osteria al Dante Piazza Garibaldi 6. For basic trattoria fare at very reasonable prices head for this bustling place down by the river, next to the Ponte Dante. Closed Sun.

Osteria Arman Via Manzoni 27. An old family-run bar behind San Francesco that sells its own *prosecco* to accompany generous helpings of pasta. Closed Thurs all day & Sun lunchtime.

Toni del Spin Via Inferiore 7 ☎0422.543.829. A few steps from the church of San Vito, the recently refurbished Toni del Spin provides superb Trevisan cuisine for around €30 per head; open till 11pm, closed all Sun & Mon lunchtime.

Castelfranco Veneto and Cittadella

CASTELFRANCO VENETO once stood on the western edge of Treviso's territory, and battlemented brick walls that the Trevisans threw round the town in 1199 to protect it against the Paduans still encircle most of the old centre (or *castello*). Of all the walled towns of the Veneto, few bear comparison with Castelfranco, and the place would merit a visit on the strength of this alone. But Castelfranco was also the birthplace of **Giorgione** and possesses a painting that single-handedly vindicates Vasari's judgement that Giorgione's place in Venetian art is equivalent to Leonardo da Vinci's in that of Florence.

Known simply as the **Castelfranco Madonna,** Giorgione's *Madonna and Child with St Francis and St Liberale* hangs in the eighteenth-century Duomo (daily 9am–noon & 3.30–6pm), in a chapel to the right of the chancel. Giorgione is the most elusive of all the great figures of the Renaissance: only six surviving paintings can indisputably be attributed to him, and so little is known about his life that legends have proliferated to fill the gaps – for instance, the one that attributes his death in 1510, aged not more than 34, to his catching bubonic plague from a mistress.

Next to the duomo, the Casa Giorgione is a bizarre disappointment hardly worth the entry fee (Tues–Sun 10am–12.30pm, 3–6.30pm; €2.50). Its beautifully restored rooms are totally empty, except for a chiaroscuro frieze in one of the first-floor rooms that has been hopefully attributed to Giorgione. Far more interesting is the interior of ✻ *Alle Mura* restaurant, nearby at Via Preti 69 (☎0423.498.098; closed Thurs), which is crammed with an extraordinary array of Polynesian artefacts – such as row upon row of handbags hanging from the ceiling – and the terrace, tucked in a gap in city walls is similarly fabulous. It specializes in seafood – go for the two-course lunches (*menu veloce*) for €12–15, which are delicious and supremely good value.

To get from the train station to the centre, turn left as you leave the station, then follow the curve of the road to the right, heading straight up Borgo Pieve to the southeast corner of the town walls.

When Treviso turned Castelfranco into a garrison, the Paduans promptly retaliated by reinforcing the defences of **CITTADELLA**, 15km to the west, on the train line to Vicenza. The fortified walls of Cittadella were built in the first quarter of the thirteenth century, and are even more impressive than those of its neighbour. You enter the town through one of four rugged brick gateways; if you're coming from the train station it'll be the Porta Padova, the most daunting of the four, flanked by the **Torre di Malta**. The tower was built as a prison and torture chamber by the monstrous Ezzelino da Romano, known to those he terrorized in this region in the mid-thirteenth century as "The Son of Satan". His atrocities earned him a place in the seventh circle of Dante's *Inferno*, where he's condemned to boil eternally in a river of blood. There's not much else to Cittadella, but it's definitely worth hopping off the train for a quick circuit of the walls.

Bassano del Grappa

Situated on the River Brenta, **BASSANO** has expanded rapidly over the last few decades, though its historic centre remains largely unspoiled. It's better known for its manufacturers and produce, and for the events of the two world wars (see opposite), than for any outstanding architecture or monuments, but the airy situation on the edge of the mountains and the quiet charm of the old streets make it well worth the trip. For centuries a major producer of ceramics and wrought iron, Bassano is also renowned for its **grappa** distilleries and culinary delicacies such as porcini mushrooms, white asparagus and honey.

Arrival and accommodation

Bassano's **tourist office** is just within the easternmost ambit of the town walls, at Largo Corona d'Italia 35 (Mon–Sat 9am–1pm & 2–6pm; closed Sat pm; ☎0424.524.351, ⊛www.comune.bassano.vi.it). On the website you can also find information about the town's summer opera festival. From the tourist office you go through the city walls and turn right for the **bus station** on Piazzale Trento – you buy tickets at the newspaper kiosk; for the train station, go straight across the main road and down Via Chilesotti.

Accommodation

Al Castello Via Bonamigo 19
☎ & ℱ 0424.228665, ⓦ www.hotelalcastello.it.
The only hotel in the old centre, this three-star is right by the castle. ❸

Brennero Via Torino 7 ☎ 0424.228.538 ⓦ www .hotelbrennero.com. Easy walking distance to the centre, the three-star Brennero lies just east of the walls. ❸

Ostello Don Cremona Via Chini 6
☎ & ℱ 0424.219.137, ⓦ www.ostellobassanodel grappa.it. For a low-budget stay, just south of the centre is the youth hostel with 90 beds. €13 for a dorm bed, doubles €24 per person.

Victoria Viale Diaz 33 ☎ 0424.503.620, ⓦ www .hotelvictoria-bassano.com. Three-star hotel situated on the west bank of the Brenta; you can walk to the centre with ease from this hotel. ❸

🏃 **Villa Brocchi Colonna** Contra' San Giorgio 98 ☎ 0424.501.580,
ⓦ www.villabrocchicolonna.it. If you have your own transport you can stay in this charming place 2km from the centre on the western edge of town. The welcoming mother and daughter team offer very comfortable rooms and the breakfast – with pancakes and a fantastic array of jams made from produce in the orchard – is delectable. ❹

The Town

Almost all of Bassano's sights lie between the Brenta and the train station. Walking away from the station, you cross the orbital Viale delle Fosse to get to **Piazza Garibaldi**, one of the two main squares. Here, the cloister of the fourteenth-century church of San Francesco now houses the **Museo Civico** (Tues–Sat 9am–6.30pm, Sun 3.30–6.30pm; ⓦ www.museobassano.it; €4.50, ticket includes the Palazzo Sturm – see below), devoted to Roman finds and paintings by the da Ponte family (better known as the Bassano family). Jacopo Bassano is the most famous, though his works can be sentimental and derivative; his son Francesco is better represented by some brooding portraits. Don't miss the tucked-away medieval rooms concealing a couple of typically luminous Bartolomeo Vivarini works. Other rooms are devoted to a number of plaster works by Canova and to the great baritone Tito Gobbi, who was born in Bassano.

Overlooking the other side of the piazza is the **Torre Civica**, once a lookout tower for the twelfth-century inner walls, now a clock tower with spurious nineteenth-century battlements and windows (Sat–Sun 10am–noon & 2–5pm; €2). Beyond the adjacent Piazza Libertà, Piazzetta Montevecchio leads to a little jumble of streets and stairways running down to the river and the **Ponte degli Alpini**, designed by Palladio in 1568. Nardini, a **grappa** distillery founded in 1779 (daily 8am–8pm), stands at this end of the bridge; these days the distilling process takes place elsewhere, but there's still the original shop and bar where you can sample before you select your bottle.

From here, if you follow Via Ferracina downstream for a couple of minutes you'll come to the eighteenth-century **Palazzo Sturm** (April–Oct Tues–Sat 9am–12.30pm, Sun 3.30–6.30pm; Nov–March Fri 9am–12.30pm, Sat & Sun 3.30–6.30pm; same ticket as Museo Civico – see above), a showcase for the town's famed majolica ware.

Various streets and squares in Bassano commemorate the dead of the two world wars. In 1944 resistance fighters were rounded up and hanged from trees along the street now called Viale dei Martiri. The major **war memorial**, however, is out of town on **Monte Grappa**, an hour's drive away, access by car only at present – ask the tourist office if the bus has been revived. The Fascists built the vast, circular, tiered edifice with its "Via Eroica" in 1935. It is rather over the top, but then it does hold 12,000 Italian and 10,000 Austro-Hungarian dead and marks the setting for the Italians' desperate and successful fight to repulse the Austrians' final offensive in 1917. There is a museum just below the top

(9am–noon, 1.30–6pm), and you can walk down the old tunnels quarried into the rock. From the top the views – 1775 metres – are astounding; on a clear day you can see Venice.

Eating, drinking and nightlife

Bassano del Grappa is naturally best known for its *grappa*, the Italian firewater, and – this being Italy – where there is good alcohol you'll find good food not far behind. The town's one other speciality is white asparagus, which, the story goes, was the result of an accident in the 16th century, and which can be found in many restaurants in spring. Bassano's central streets and squares come alive at the end of the siesta and the **bars** and **restaurants** around the main square have a real buzz by the early evening.

Restaurants and bars

Al Caneseo Via Vendramini 20 ⊤ 0424.228.524. The bright lighting might give a slightly impersonal feel at first impression but both the food and the atmosphere are very good in this small restaurant, which serves dishes from Abruzzo and the Veneto. Closed Mon & all Aug.

Alla Riviera Via San Giorgio 17 ⊤ 0424.503.700. On the western fringe of the town, this friendly restaurant serves good range of well-cooked regional specialities, including white asparagus, rabbit, local salamis and Asiago cheese. The choices are recited at your table in Italian or English – there is no written menu. Covered summertime terrace. Popular with locals. Closed Sun evening and all day Mon.

Antica Osteria Via Matteotti 7. Old-fashioned *osteria* that has a strong local following, and serves traditional fare, as well as good bar snacks (closed Mon).

Del Borgo Via Margnan 7 ⊤ 0424.522.155. Classy establishment with its own garden, *Del Borgo* is very popular and comes highly recommended. It is a short walk downhill north of the old centre. Closed Wed.

La Caneva Via Matteotti 34. Cosy bar that does delicious snacks as well as more substantial dishes. Has tables out in the street when the weather permits.

Nardini right on the bridge head at Ponte Vecchio 2. Once a distillery and now a period-piece bar and *grappa* shop. The bar spills out onto the bridge in summer as the populace engage in the *passegiata*. Closed Mon.

Osteria Terraglio on Piazza Terraglio. Excellent wine and delicious salads at this friendly bar/ restaurant, which has a large terrace in the square; there's also jazz on Tuesdays (Oct–May, best to book tables). Tues–Sun open till 2am.

Asolo and the Villa Barbaro

Known as *la Città dai cento orizzonti* ("the city with a hundred horizons"), the medieval hilltop town of **ÁSOLO** presides over a tightly grouped range of nearly thirty gentle peaks in the foothills of the Dolomites. In 1234 Ezzelino da Romano wrested the town from the Bishop of Treviso; on his death in 1259 the townspeople ensured that the dynasty died with him by massacring the rest of his family, who were at that time in nearby San Zenone.

The end of the fifteenth century was marked by the arrival of Caterina Cornaro (see opposite) – her celebrated court was attended by the likes of Cardinal Bembo, one of the most eminent literary figures of his day, who coined the verb *Asolare* to describe the experience of spending one's time in pleasurable aimlessness. Later writers and artists found the atmosphere equally convivial: Gabriele d'Annunzio wrote about the town, and Robert Browning's last published work – *Asolando* – was written here.

There are regular **buses** to Ásolo from Bassano; if you want to get here from Venice, it's quickest to take a train to Treviso, from where there are buses at least hourly (some change at Montebelluna) – all the buses to Bassano go via Ásolo and Masèr (see p.402).

The Town

The bus drops you at the foot of the hill, from where a connecting minibus (€1 return) shuttles you up into the town. Memorabilia of Ásolo's celebrated residents are gathered in the Museo Civico in Piazza Maggiore (Sat & Sun 10am–noon, 3–7pm; €4). Especially diverting are the portraits, photos and personal effects of Elenora Duse. An actress in the Sarah Bernhardt mould, Duse was almost as well known for her tempestuous love life as for her roles in Shakespeare, Hugo and Ibsen, and she came to Ásolo to seek refuge from public gossip. Although she died in Pittsburgh while on tour in 1924, her wish was to be buried in Ásolo, and so her body was transported back here, to the church of Sant'Anna. The main interest of the art collection is provided by a pair of dubiously attributed Bellinis, a portrait of Ezzelino painted a good couple of centuries after his death and a brace of large sculptures by Canova.

Via Canova leads west away from the town centre past Eleonora Duse's house (no. 306), near the Porta Santa Caterina. The church of **Santa Caterina** (May–Sept daily 9am–6.30pm; Oct–April Sat & Sun only 9am–4.30pm) next to the *Carabinieri*, is deconsecrated but open to allow visitors to see its fifteenth-century frescoes. The **Rocca** above the town – which offers excellent views – was from 1489 to 1509 the home of **Caterina Cornaro**, one of the very few women to have played a major part in Venetian history. Born into one of Venice's most powerful families, Caterina was married to Jacques II, King of Cyprus. Within a year of the wedding Jacques was dead, and there followed nearly a decade of political pressure from Venice's rulers, who wanted to get their hands on the strategically vital island. In 1489 she was finally forced to abdicate in order to gain much-needed weapons and ships against a Turkish attack. Brought back to Venice to sign a deed "freely giving" Cyprus to the Republic, she was given the region of Ásolo as a sign of Venice's indebtedness. Eventually Ásolo too was taken away from her by the Emperor Maximilian, and she sought asylum in Venice, where she died soon after, in 1510.

Practicalities

The **tourist office** is at Piazza G. D'Annunzio 2 (daily 9.30am–12.30pm Thurs–Sat 3–6pm; ☎0423.529.046, ⓦwww.asolo.it). Accommodation is all but impossible to find. The cheapest of the three hotels is the *Duse*, a reasonable-quality three-star at the bottom of the main square at Via Browning 190 (☎0423.55.241, ⓦwww.hotelduse.com; ❹); the place is booked solid on the second Sunday of every month, when the antiques fair takes over the centre of town. The four-star *Albergo al Sole*, Via Collegio 33 (☎0423.952.332, ⓦwww.albergoalsole.com; ❻) has a gym and a breathtaking view from the breakfast terrace, but top of the price range is the sybaritic *Villa Cipriani*, Via Canova 298 (☎0423.523.411, ⓦwww.sheraton.com/villacipriani; ❾), long a favourite with Europe's crowned heads and showbiz types.

The best **restaurant** in town is the *Ca'Derton*, Piazza G. D'Annunzio (☎0423.529.648, ⓦwww.caderton.com; closed Sun eve & Mon), which has an excellent menu at around €35 for two courses; booking is essential. You can sample the same fuel cooking at around half the price in the more informal *Enoteca di Nino e Antonietta* next door. The more basic *Cornaro*, just off Piazza Garibaldi in Via Regina Cornaro (closed Mon), has the standard *primi* and *secondi*. Or slightly further from the main square, opposite Santa Caterina church, the *Hostaria alla Rocca* at Via Canova 288 is a friendly, cheap bar-restaurant that does delicious food and specializes in its own pork (closed Tues eve and all day Wed).

The Villa Barbaro at Masèr

Touring the villas of the Veneto, you become used to mismatches between the quality of the architecture and the quality of the decoration, but at the **VILLA BARBARO** at **MASÈR** (Tues, Sat & Sun: summer 3–6pm; winter 2.30–5pm; €5; Ⓦ www.villadimaser.it), a few kilometres northeast of Ásolo, you'll see the best of two of the central figures of Italian civilization in the sixteenth century – **Palladio** (see box, p.381) and **Paolo Veronese**, whose careers crossed here and nowhere else. If you're reliant on public transport, a visit is best made by bus from Bassano via Ásolo or from Treviso – the services from Treviso to Ásolo all pass through Masèr.

The **villa** was built in the 1550s for Daniele and Marcantonio Barbaro, men whose humanist training and diverse cultural interests made the process of designing the house far more of a collaborative venture than most of Palladio's other projects. The entire ground floor was given over to farm functions with dovecotes in the end pavilions, stables and storage space under the arcades, administrative offices on the lower floor of the central block. The avenue of trees, the sculptures and the very structure of the villa draw you in from the fields, down the projecting central axis of the building and through to the extravagant nymphaeum watered by a spring – the source of the fertility of the land.

This theme of fertility is echoed again and again in the living quarters of the *piano nobile* – the decorated public rooms that usually form the first "noble" floor of Venetian villas – in a series of **frescoes** by Veronese that has no equal in northern Italy. The more abstruse scenes are decoded in an excellent guidebook on sale in the villa, but most of the paintings require no footnotes. The walls of the Villa Barbaro are the most resourceful display of trompe l'oeil you'll ever see: servants peer round painted doors, a dog sniffs along the base of a flat balustrade in front of a landscape of ruins, a huntsman (probably Veronese himself) steps into the house through an entrance that's a solid wall. It's speculated that the woman facing the hunter at the other end of the house was Veronese's mistress.

In the grounds in front of the villa (but now separated by a busy main road) stands Palladio's Tempietto (currently closed for restoration).

Conegliano

North of Treviso, around the amiable town of **CONEGLIANO**, the landscape ceases to be boring. The surrounding hills are patched with vineyards, and the production of wine (*prosecco* in particular) is central to the economy of the district. Italy's first wine-growers' college was set up in Conegliano in 1876, and there's a large grape festival in the last weekend of September, with parades and a banquet. It's a rewarding place for tourists, too, as a couple of well-established **wine routes** meet here: the Strada dei Vini del Piave, which runs for 68km southeast to Oderzo, and the more rewarding Strada del Prosecco, the first to be established in Italy, a 42-kilometre journey west to Valdobbiádene (Ⓦ www .prosecco.it). Access to Conegliano itself is straightforward, as nearly all the regular Venice–Udine trains stop here.

The old centre of Conegliano is right in front of you as you come out of the station; just follow the road ahead and climb the steps to Via XX Settembre.

This is the original main street, whose most decorative feature is the unusual facade of the **Duomo**: a fourteenth-century portico, frescoed in the sixteenth century, which joins seamlessly to the buildings on each side. The interior of the church has been much rebuilt, but retains fragments of fifteenth-century frescoes; the major adornment of the church, though, is the magnificent altarpiece *The Madonna and Child with Saints and Angels*, painted in 1493 by Giambattista Cima, the most famous native of Conegliano. Cima's birthplace, no. 24 Via G.B. Cima (at the rear of the duomo), has now been converted into the **Casa Museo di G. B. Cima** (book on ℡0438.21.660; €1), which consists mainly of reproductions of his paintings and archeological finds made during the restoration of the house.

The **Museo Civico** (Tues–Sun 10am–12.30pm & 3.30–6.30pm; €2) is housed in the tallest surviving tower of the reconstructed *castello* on top of the hill. It's reached most quickly – though it is still a long climb – by the steep and cobbled Calle Madonna della Neve, which begins at the end of Via Accademia, the street beside the palatial Accademia cinema, and follows the town's most impressive stretch of ancient wall. The museum has some damaged frescoes by Pordenone and a small bronze horse by Giambologna, but most of the paintings are "Workshop of . . . " or "School of . . . ", and the displays of coins, maps, archaeological finds, armour and so forth are no more fascinating than you'd expect. But it's a lovingly maintained place, and the climb through the floors culminates on the tower's roof, from where you get a fine panorama the gentle vine-clad landscape. You can also enjoy the view from the terrace of the neighbouring *Al Castello* bar, which looks towards the Dolomites.

Practicalities

Conegliano's **tourist office** is at Via XX Settembre 61 (daily 9.30am–12.30pm, Thurs–Sat 3–6pm; ℡0438.21.230, ⓦwww.turismo.provincia.treviso.it), and has details of *prosecco* routes. The three-star *Canon d'Oro* **hotel**, at Via XX Settembre 129 (℡0438.34.246, ⓦwww.hotelcanondoro.it; ❸), is the best base for a tour of the vineyards. The same street has all you'll need in the way of cafés, bars and food shops. Top recommendations for low-cost **eating** are the excellent fish menu of the *Trattoria Città di Venezia*, Via XX Settembre 77 (℡0438.23.186; closed Sun eve & Mon), which will take you into the region of €45 (the cheaper ♣ *Osteria La Bea Venezia* next door has similarly high standards), and the cosy *Al Bacareto*, Via Cavour 6 (closed Mon). The main square is given over to a medieval pageant in mid-June, the **Dama Castellana**, and the streets of Conegliano host a major **wine festival** in September.

Vittorio Veneto

The name **VITTORIO VENETO** first appeared on the map in 1866 when, to mark the Unification of Italy and honour the first king of the new country (Vittorio Emanuele II), the neighbouring towns of Cèneda and Serravalle (not previously the best of friends) were knotted together and rechristened. A new town hall was built midway along the avenue connecting the two towns, and the train station was constructed opposite, thus ensuring that the visitor steps straight from the train into a sort of no-man's-land. It's here, too, that you'll find the tourist office and bus station. Bus #1 runs between the two towns every fifteen minutes.

Cèneda

CÈNEDA, the commercial centre of Vittorio Veneto, is primarily worth a visit for the **Museo della Battaglia** (Tues–Sun: May–Sept 9.30am–12.30pm & 4–7pm; Oct–April 9.30am–12.30pm & 2–5pm; €3, or €5 joint ticket with the Museo del Cenedese) at Piazza G. Paolo 1, whose *loggia* was built by Sansovino. The dull cathedral is right next door; turn right out of the station and keep going until you see the sign for the centre. The museum is dedicated to the climactic Battle of Vittorio; fought in October 1918, this was the final engagement of World War I for the Italian Army and marked the end of the Austro-Hungarian empire, which is why most towns in Italy have a Via Vittorio Veneto.

Overlooking the town is the imposing Castello di San Martino, once a Lombard stronghold and now the bishop's palace, which is why you won't be allowed in. The only other building that merits a look in Cèneda is the church of **Santa Maria del Meschio**, where you'll find a splendid *Annunciation* by Andrea Previtali, a pupil of Giovanni Bellini. If you turn left off the Cèneda–Serravalle road instead of going right for the cathedral square, you'll soon come across it.

Serravalle

SERRAVALLE, wedged up against the mouth of a gorge, is an entirely different proposition from its reluctant twin. Once through its southern gate you are into a town that has scarcely seen a demolition since the sixteenth century, though the effect is spoiled by the main road tearing right through the centre. Most of the buildings along Via Martiri della Libertà, Via Roma and Via Mazzini, and around the stage-like Piazza Marcantonio Flaminio, date from the fifteenth and sixteenth centuries – the handsomest being the shield-encrusted Loggia Serravallese. This is now home of the **Museo del Cenedese** (see Museo della Battaglia above for times and price), a jumble of sculptural and archeological bits and pieces, detached frescoes and minor paintings. The **Palazzo Minucci de Carlo** (daily 9am–noon; €5.50; ☎0438.571.93) has a ragbag collection of minor paintings, tapestries and old furniture, but you'll need to make an appointment to get inside.

Your time will be more profitably spent in the church of **San Lorenzo dei Battuti** (same ticket as Museo del Cenedese and Museo della Battaglia), immediately inside the south gate, which is decorated with frescoes painted around 1450. Uncovered in 1953 and restored to rectify the damage done when Napoleon's lads used the chapel as a kitchen, this is one of the best-preserved fresco cycles in the Veneto. If it's closed, ask at the museum.

Practicalities

The tourist office, midway between the two halves at Viale della Vittoria 10 (daily 9.30am–12.30pm & Thurs–Sat 3–6pm; ☎0438.57.243), is good for information on the ski resorts and walking terrain around the town, as well as accommodation. The town's **hotels** are mainly geared towards businesspeople; as comfortable as any other three-star is the *Terme*, on the Serravalle–Cèneda road at Via delle Terme 4 (☎0438.554.345, ⓦwww.hotelterme.tv; ❸). The best food in town is served at *Al Postiglione*, Via Cavour 39 (☎0438.556.924; closed Tues), at the southern end of Serravalle: wild boar and mushrooms feature prominently on a reasonably priced menu – with menus for €22–35.

Belluno

The northernmost of the major towns of the Veneto, **BELLUNO** was once a strategically important ally of Venice, and today is the capital of a province that extends mainly over the eastern Dolomites. Although the urban centres to the south are not far away, Belluno's focus of attention lies clearly to the north – the network of the Dolomiti-Bus company radiates out from here, trains run regularly up the Piave Valley to Calalzo, and the tourist handouts are geared mostly to hikers and skiers. Just one train a day runs from Venice to Belluno directly, but it's just as quick anyway to go from Venice to Conegliano and change there; from Padua there are twelve trains daily.

Its position is Belluno's main attraction, but the old centre calls for an hour or two's exploration if you're passing through. The hub of the modern town, and where you'll find its most popular bars and cafés, is the wide **Piazza dei Martiri**, off the south side of which a road leads to the Piazza del Duomo, the kernel of the old town. The sixteenth-century **Duomo**, an amalgam of the Gothic and Classical, and built in the pale yellow stone that is a feature of the buildings in Belluno, was designed by Tullio Lombardo; it has had to be reconstructed twice after earthquake damage, in 1873 and 1936. There are a couple of good paintings inside: one by Andrea Schiavone (first altar on right) and one by Jacopo Bassano (third altar on right). The stately **campanile**, designed in 1743 by Filippo Juvarra, is unfortunately closed to the public.

Occupying one complete side of the Piazza del Duomo is the residence of the Venetian administrators of the town, the **Palazzo dei Rettori**, a frilly late-fifteenth-century building dolled up with Baroque trimmings. A relic of more independent times stands on the right – the twelfth-century **Torre Civica**, all that's left of the medieval castle. Continuing round the piazza, in Via Duomo, along the side of the town hall, you'll find the **Museo Civico** (April–Sept Tues–Sun 10am–1pm & 4–7pm; Oct–March Mon–Sat 10am–1pm plus Thurs–Sun 3–6pm; €2.30): the collection is strong on the work of Belluno's three best-known artists – the painters Sebastiano and Marco Ricci and the sculptor-woodcarver **Andrea Brustolon** – all of whom were born here between 1659 and 1673.

Via Duomo ends at the **Piazza del Mercato**, a tiny square hemmed in by porticoed Renaissance buildings. The principal street of the old town, **Via Mezzaterra**, goes down to the medieval **Porta Rugo** (veer left along the cobbled Via Santa Croce about 50m from the end), from where the view up into the mountains provides some compensation if you haven't managed to find the campanile open.

Practicalities

The **tourist office**, at Piazza Duomo 2 (daily 9am–12.30pm & 3.30–6.30pm, Sun 10am–12.30pm; ☎0437.940.083, Ⓦwww.infodolomiti.it), is a good source of leaflets on Belluno and its province. The most central of the town's **hotels** are the *Cappello e Cadore*, just off the main square at Via Ricci 8 (☎0437.940.246, Ⓦwww.albergocappello.com; ❸ – the more expensive rooms have Jacuzzis), and the *Astor*, Piazza dei Martiri 26/e (☎0437.942.094, Ⓦwww.astorhotelbelluno .com; ❸), which has great views. Of the town's **restaurants** the *Terracotta*, near the train station at Borgo Garibaldi 61 (☎0437.942.644; closed Tues eve & Wed) is an old favourite, with moderate prices, though it has just come under new management.

Travel details

Trains

Belluno to: Conegliano (8 daily; 55min); Vittorio Veneto (8 daily; 35min).

Castelfranco to: Padua (every 30min; 35min); Treviso (10 daily; 35min); Venice (every 30min; 55min).

Conegliano to: Belluno (8 daily; 55min); Udine (every 30min; 1hr 15min); Venice (every 30min; 1hr); Vittorio Veneto (15 daily; 25min).

Padua to: Bassano (hourly; 1hr 5min); Belluno (12 daily; 2hr); Milan (25 daily; 2hr 30min); Venice (every 30min; 35min); Verona (every 30min; 55min); Vicenza (every 20min; 20min).

Treviso to: Udine (hourly; 1hr 10min–1hr 30min); Venice (every 20min; 30min); Vicenza (hourly; 1hr).

Venice to: Bassano (14 daily; 1hr); Belluno (1 daily; 2hr); Conegliano (every 30min; 1hr); Milan (25 daily; 2hr 50min–3hr 50min); Padua (every 30min; 35min); Treviso (every 20min; 30min); Trieste (every 30min; 2hr 10min); Udine (every 30min; 2hr); Verona (every 30min; 1hr 30min); Vicenza (every 30min; 55min); Vittorio Veneto (6 daily; 1–2hr).

Verona to: Milan (every 30min; 1hr 40min); Padua (every 30min; 50min); Venice (every 30min; 1hr 30min); Vicenza (every 30min; 30min).

Vicenza to: Castelfranco (hourly; 40min); Cittadella (hourly; 30min); Milan (30 daily; 1hr 40min); Padua (25 daily; 20min); Treviso (hourly; 1hr); Venice (every 30min; 55min); Verona (every 30min; 30min).

Buses

Bassano to: Ásolo (15 daily; 30min); Masèr (8 daily; 40min); Possagno (every 1–2hr; 40min).

Padua to: Bassano (every 30min; 1hr 15min).

Treviso to: Ásolo (hourly; 50min); Bassano (hourly; 1hr 20min); Padua (every 30min; 1hr 10min); Venice (every 20min; 55min).

Venice to: Malcontenta (hourly; 20min); Strà (every 30min; 45min).

Vicenza to: Bassano (hourly; 1hr 10min).

Friuli-Venezia Giulia

CHAPTER 6 # Highlights

✳ **Trieste's Panorama** The view from the castle atop the San Giusto hill takes in the entirety of this elegant and inviting maritime city. See p.414

✳ **Grotta Gigante** The world's largest accessible cave. See p.419

✳ **Osmizze** Lunch at an *osmizza* is the best way to experience the Slovene culture of the Carso. See p.419

✳ **Aquileia's Basilica** This glorious basilica, with its mosaic pavements by Theodore, ranks among the most important monuments of early Christendom. See p.424

✳ **Udine's Piazza della Libertà** The central piazza of Friuli-Venezia Giulia's second town is a perfect ensemble of well-preserved historic buildings. See p.430

✳ **Tiepolo paintings** Outstanding frescoes by Tiepolo cover every surface of the Gallerie del Tiepolo in Udine. See p.431

✳ **Tempietto Longobardo** The exquisite statues in this tiny chapel are among the most splendid surviving works of art from the ninth century. See p.433

✳ **The Carnia** The lakes and mountains of the Carnia region offer the perfect backdrop to some gentle hiking. See p.435

△ Upper lake in Tarvisio, Udine

Friuli-Venezia Giulia

The geographical complexity of **Friuli-Venezia Giulia** – around eight thousand square kilometres of alps, limestone plateaux, alluvial plain and shelving coastlands – is mirrored in its social diversity. The mountainous north is ethnically and linguistically Alpine; the old peasant culture of Friuli, though now waning, still gives a degree of coherence to the area south of the mountains; **Udine** seems Venetian, and **Grado**, slumbering in its Adriatic lagoons, Byzantine-Venetian; while **Aquileia**, a few kilometres north of Grado, is still redolent of its Roman and early Christian past. **Trieste**, the regional capital, is a Habsburg city, developed by Austria to be the empire's great southern port. In spirit and appearance it is somewhat central European, in some ways more like Ljubljana in Slovenia than anywhere else in the region with the possible exception of **Gorizia**.

If one thing unites the different parts of the region, it's how far removed they are from the conventional image of Italy, a remoteness that intensifies

Regional food and wine

Unlike many other regions of Italy, Friuli-Venezia Giulia is not famous for its cuisine. **Local food** reflects the cultural eclecticism of the place and veers towards the simple and hearty, from thick soups to warming stews, often – and unusually – combining sweet and savoury ingredients. One such dish is *cialzons*, a ravioli-type pasta filled with spinach, chocolate, raisins and nutmeg, among other dubious delights, while less challenging menu choices include polenta accompanied by *squazeto alla friulana* (lamb casserole), *jota friulana*, a thick meat, beans and cabbage stew, and *brovada*, another distinct speciality, made from wine-fermented turnips. Definitely worth seeking out is the delicious prosciutto from the town of San Daniele, salted and cured raw ham that melts in the mouth. Desserts head very much eastwards, with rich, Central European-influenced cakes filled with nuts and dried fruit – look out for *presnitz* and *gubana*.

If Friuli-Venezia Giulia does have something to sing about, it's the region's classy **wines**, especially its whites. Melding modern technology and ancient traditions, the region is second only to Trentino-Alto Adige for DOC wines, with the mix of Alpine and Adriatic air creating excellent conditions, most notably in Collio Goriziano and Colli Orientali del Friuli, two areas running up against the Slovenian border. Tocai is the best-known white (but local government is locked in an ongoing dispute with the EU over the similarity of its name to Hungarian Tokaj), while Picolit, a sweet white wine hugely popular two centuries ago, is making a comeback to widespread acclaim. Reds, though not as prestigious, include Refosco and the highly drinkable Terrano.

the further east you travel. This area has always been a bridge between the Mediterranean world and Central Europe – that hazy multinational entity which begins, according to Eric Newby at least, at Monfalcone, north of Trieste. It has been invaded – sometimes enriched, often laid waste – from east and west and north, by the Romans, Huns, Goths, Lombards, Nazis and even the Cossacks. Venice in its heyday controlled the coast and plain as far as Udine; Napoleonic France succeeded the Venetian Republic, to be supplanted in turn by the Habsburgs. Later, the region saw some of the fiercest fighting of World War I on the **Carso** (the plateau inland from Trieste), where artillery shells splintered the limestone into deadly shrapnel. Today the hills are still scarred with trenches, and vast war memorials and ossuaries punctuate the landscape.

There was less loss of life in World War II, but Fascism in Trieste was especially virulent, and the city held one of Italy's two death camps. One of the strangest sideshows of the war was staged north of Udine: Cossack troops, led by White Russian officers, made an alliance with the Nazis and invaded Carnia, on the promise of a Cossack homeland among the Carnian mountains once the Reich was secure. The area also saw the invasion of Tito at the end of the war, which brought just as much terror and atrocities that resulted in mass graves for an estimated 10,000. No more invading armies have taken this road, but the last border dispute between Italy and Yugoslavia was not settled until the 1970s, and when neighbouring Slovenia became independent in June 1991 the border posts with Italy were the scene of brief but fierce confrontations between Slovene and Yugoslav troops. Despite Italian fears, however, the fighting did not spill across the border.

While the Friulani want Italian nationality, they don't care for the baggage of Italian identity. Respect for Rome and the government is in short supply, and enthusiasm for the separatist north Italian Lega Nord movement has spread from Lombardy in the last decade. It is unlikely that this marks the birth of Friulian separatism, but there's no doubt that the people here have their own ways and traditions, fostering a strong sense of identity. The local dialect, *Friulano*, is undergoing something of an official revival – many road signs are in Italian and *Friulano*, while studies of the dialect's history and many local variants are published by the Società Filologica Friulana in Udine. Economically the region is in fairly good shape: Udine and Pordenone are thriving, while Trieste is a focus for container traffic that has helped the city to retain its role as a port.

Tourism is growing too. Increasing numbers of visitors, mostly Italian and German, are discovering places that almost rival the claims of neighbouring Veneto, with none of the crowds or the cynical attitudes to tourists. **Trieste** makes a good base for walking trips into the extraordinary, cave-riven landscape of the Carso, with the option of a day at one of the purpose-built beach resorts along the classy **Triestine Riviera**. **Udine**, with its beautiful Venetian centre and excellent art collections, is within easy reach to the north, as is tiny **Cividale del Friuli**, which preserves a picturesque historic centre perched on the gorge of the Natisone, as well as some fascinating Lombard remains. The archeologically minded will head straight for **Aquileia**, however, which has some of the most important Roman and early Christian remains in Italy, and is fifteen minutes from the lagoon resort of **Grado**, which conceals a tiny early Christian centre amid the beach hotels. Further north, towards the Austrian border, the **Carnia** is struggling to develop itself as a rival to the Dolomites for skiing and hiking, though in truth it has little over its neighbour other than peace and quiet.

Trieste

Backed by the green and white cliffs of a limestone plateau and facing the blue Adriatic, sparkling **TRIESTE** has an idyllic setting with an atmosphere of grandeur and welcome. Its main squares are adorned with spectacular Neoclassical buildings, and the canal, clustered with open-air cafés, is a reminder that, just like Venice around the lagoon, this city has had its glorious seafaring history. The city itself is fascinating and rather strange: an imperial creation built to play a role that no longer exists, though like so many ports in Europe, the seediness that long prevailed is now giving way to optimism. Trieste was Tergeste to the Romans, who captured it in 178 BC, but although signs of their occupancy are scattered throughout the city, what strikes you straightaway is its modernity. With the exception of the castle and cathedral of San Giusto, and the tiny medieval quarter below it, the city's whole pre-nineteenth-century history seems dim and vague beside the massive Neoclassical architecture of the **Borgo Teresiano** – the name given to the modern city centre, after Empress Maria Theresa (1740–80), who initiated the development.

Trieste was constructed largely with Austrian capital to serve as the Habsburg Empire's southern port. It briefly eclipsed Venice as the Adriatic's northern port, but its short-lived heyday drew to a close after 1918, when it finally became

TRIESTE

EATING & DRINKING

Ai Fiori	19
Antica Trattoria Suban	1
Buffet Pepi	8
Café Gourmet	12
Caffè degli Specchi	11
Caffè Pasticceria Pirona	18
Caffè San Marco	2
Caffè Tommaseo	7
Circus	9
Corallo	16
Cremcaffè	10
Da Giovanni	5
El Fornel	14
Il Barattolo	4
La Piazzetta	15
La Triestina	17
L'Osmiza	13
Naima	3
Osteria da Libero	20
Zampolli	6

ACCOMMODATION

Alabarda	B
Capitelli	G
Continentale	E
James Joyce	F
Marta	C
Nuovo Albergo Centro	D
Porta Cavana	A
Youth Hostel	A

412

▲ Train & Bus Stations

▲ Campsite & Opicina

▲ Risiera San Sabba

0   100 m

N

Porto Vecchio

MOLO IV

MOLO AUDACE

Stazione Marittima

PIAZZA DUCA D'ABRUZZI

PIAZZA VITTORIA VENETO

PIAZZA DALMAZIA

PIAZZA OBERDAN

Tranvia

VIA GALATTI

VIA MILANO

VIA ROMA

VIA TRENTO

VIA MACHIAVELLI

VIA TORREBIANCA

VIA FABIO FILZI

VIA XXX OTTOBRE

VIA GIUSTINIANO

VIA SAN FRANCESCO

VIA DEL CORONGO

PIAZZA GOTTI

VIA ROSSETTI

VIA GIOTTO

VIA CRISPI

PICCARDI

VIA DONIZETTI

VIA C. BATTISTI

VIALE XX SETTEMBRE

VIA FRANCESCO CRISPI

VIA GINNASTICA

VIA TIMEUS

PIAZZA DELL'OSPITALE

VIA DELLA

PIAZZA GARIBALDI

VIA PASCOLI

V.G. FOSCHIATTI

V. ORIANI

VIA DEL BOSCO

VIA DELLA MADONNA

LARGO BARRIERA VECCHIA

VIA G. CARDUCCI

VIA VALDIRIVO

VIA GIOVANNI

PIAZZA SAN GIOVANNI

Museo Morpurgo

S. Antonio Thaumaturgo

VIA IMBRIANI

VIA MAZZINI

PIAZZA GOLDONI

VIA DEL MONTE CAPITOLINA

VIA S. FELICE

VIA LAZZARO

Canal Grande

BORGO TERESIANO

VIA BELLINI

VIA ROSSINI

CORSO TRE NOVEMBRE CAVOUR

PIAZZA PONTEROSSO

PIAZZA SANT'ANTONIO

VIA PAGANINI

S. Spiridione

VIA S. SPIRIDIONE

VIA DANTE ALIGHIERI

VIA NICOLO

VIA GENOVA

VIA CASSA DI RISPARMIO

PIAZZA BORSA

PIAZZA TOMMASEO

CORSO ITALIA

Teatro Romano

VIA DEL TEATRO ROMANO

Castello

Roman Forum

VIA CAPITOLINA

V. S. GIUSTO

VIA T. GROSSI

VIA P. RISORTA

S. Giusto

PIAZZA DELLA CATTEDRALE

Museo di Storia ed Arte

VIA DELLA CATTEDRALE

VIA S. MICHELE

S. Maria Maggiore

S. Silvestro

PIAZZA BARBACAN

PIAZZA UNITÀ D'ITALIA

Municipio

Teatro Verdi

RIVA TRE NOVEMBRE

VIA PUNTO DEL FORNO

VD MERCATO VECCHIO

VIA CAVANA

VIA FELICE VENEZIAN

VIA MADONNA DEL MARE

Basilica Paleocristiana

CITTÀ VECCHIA

VIA ARMANDO DIAZ

RIVA DEL MANDRACCHIO

VIA S. GIORGIO

PIAZZA VENEZIA

Museo Revoltella

Museo Sartorio

Museo Joyce

VIA TORINO

VIA DI CAVANA

VIA HORTIS

RIVA N. SAURO

VIA L. CADORNA

Italian and discovered that, for all its good intentions, Italy had no economic use for it. The city languished for over sixty years, but recently things have picked up. The large container port to the south of the centre has seen an increase in seaborne trade; tourism plays an increasingly important role in the economy and has prompted an attractive facelift for the labyrinthine medieval quarter; and the €650-million redevelopment of the Porto Vecchio is providing new leisure and business facilities in the heart of the town.

Lying on the political and ethnic fault-line between the Latin and Slavic worlds, Trieste has long been a city of political extremes. In the nineteenth century it was a hotbed of *irredentismo* – an Italian nationalist movement to "redeem" the Austrian lands of Trieste, Istria and the Trentino. After 1918 the tensions increased, leading to a strong Fascist presence in Friuli Venezia Giulia. Yugoslavia and the Allies fought over Trieste until 1954, when the city and a connecting strip of coast were secured for Italy, though a definitive border settlement was not reached until 1975. Tito kept the Istrian peninsula, whose fearful Italian population emigrated in huge numbers: Fiume (Rijeka), for example, lost 58,000 of its 60,000 Italians. The Slovene population of the area around Trieste, previously in the majority, suddenly found itself treated as second-class citizens, with Italians dominant politically and culturally; nationalist parties built support on the back of the tensions between the two communities. There is even now little interaction between Slovenes and Italians.

Yet nationalism has long provoked the development of its antithesis and there is an intense socialist and cosmopolitan intellectual tradition which is intimately connected with the city's ever-burgeoning café culture. Numerous foreign writers based themselves around Trieste, most famously James Joyce (see box, p.415) and Rainer Maria Rilke, and native literati included Umberto Saba and Italo Svevo.

Freud also spent some time researching in Trieste as a medical student, and the city became the first Italian centre of psychoanalytical thought under Freud's pupil Edoardo Weiss. More recently, in 1980, Trieste became the first city in Italy to completely close its old psychiatric hospital. The city's alternative care programme in the community pioneered by Dr Franco Basaglia in the 1970s is now considered an exemplar in its field.

Arrival and information

Trieste's Piazza Libertà **bus station** is right by the central **train station**, ten minutes' walk from the town centre. The nearest **airport** is at Ronchi dei Legionari (☎048.177.3224, ⊛www.aeroporto.fvg.it), 33km northwest of the city, connected to the bus station by APT bus #51 (every 30min; 50min; €2.75 from the machine directly outside Arrivals, €1 surcharge if ticket bought on bus; ☎040.425.020). The helpful main **tourist office** is on the central Piazza Unità d'Italia 4e (daily 9am–7pm; ☎040.347.8312, ⊛www.triestetourism.it). When you arrive in town, consider buying the "**T for You**" card (€8 for 4hr, €10 for 48hr). Among other advantages, it entitles you to discounts at many hotels and restaurants, as well as free access to all civic museums and free use of public transport. The card is available at hotels and at the tourist office.

Accommodation

Recent years have seen an improvement in the **accommodation** available in Trieste. The cheapest decent **hotels** are all still between the train station and the town centre, but boutique hotels in the restored old quarter provide atmospheric alternatives. All the hotels listed below include breakfast in their prices.

The **HI hostel** is 7km out of the city at Viale Miramare 331 (℡ 040.224.102, ⓦ www.ostellionline.org; €13) – take bus #36 from the station to Grignano and get off at Bivio al Miramare, from where it's a five-minute walk. The facilities are basic but it has stunning sea views, and is just 500m from Castello Miramare (see p.423). The nearest **campsite** is the *Obelisco* (℡ 040.211.655, ⓔ campeggioclubtrieste@tin.it), on an airy site 7km away in the hills below Opicina, from Piazza Oberdan take either bus #4 or the *tranvia* (cable tramway), which runs up to 8pm: stop at the obelisk, cross over the tracks and you'll see a sign to the campsite which is a minute's walk away.

Alabarda Via Valdirivo 22 ℡ 040.630.269, ⓦ www .hotelalabarda.it. Located in the heart of the new town, the *Alabarda* is a good, inexpensive option with TVs in all its eighteen clean rooms, plus Internet facilities. Double glazing keeps out most of the noise from the busy street outside. **❷**

Capitelli Via Trauner 1, corner Via Capitelli ℡ 040.305.947, ⓦ www.hotelcapitelli.it. This recently done-up hotel in the historic centre stands right next to an ancient Roman arch. The accommodation is fresh, light and spacious at the same time as charming and cosy. **❸**

Continentale Via San Nicolò 25 ℡ 040.631.717, ⓦ www.goldengrouphotel.com. On a quiet pedestrianized street in the city centre, this is the best of Trieste's four-stars. Rooms are simple but classy, while staff are helpful and attentive. **❻**

🏃 **James Joyce** Via dei Cavazzeni 7 ℡ 040.311.023, ⓦ www.hoteljamesjoyce .com. In the newly done-up heart of the medieval quarter, this enticing little place has retained its wood-beamed ceilings and its spiral stone staircase without compromising on comforts, such as an elevator and a/c. Guests are greeted by a life-size image of the eponymous author. **❸**

Marta Via Valdirivo 11 ℡ 040.660.242, ⓦ www.hotelmarta.it. Nicely furnished and clean rooms, all with TV, and at a bargain rate. Internet available. **❷**

🏃 **Nuovo Albergo Centro** Via Roma 13 ℡ 040.347.8790, ⓦ www.hotelcentrotrieste .it. Bright and spotlessly clean rooms in this, the most pleasant moderately priced place in town. Ten percent discount for guests showing a copy of this book. Ask for a room at the back to get away from the noise of the street. New, equally excellent facility run by the same family on the floor above. **❷**

Porta Cavana Via F. Venezian 14 ℡ 040.301.313, ⓦ www.hotelportacavana.it. Another beautiful addition to the old quarter, warmly and richly decorated, with each room uniquely designed. **❺**

The City

Trieste's modern life takes place in the grid-like streets of the **Borgo Teresiano**, but the focal point of the city's pre-modern history, and its prime tourist site, is the hill of **San Giusto**, named after the patron saint of the city. Scattered elsewhere around the old town are some interesting museums and a clutch of churches and Roman remains that can easily take up a day's strolling.

San Giusto and the Old Town

At the very summit of the San Giusto hill, overlooking the remnants of the Roman forum, is the **Castello** (daily: April–Sept 9am–7pm; Oct–March 9am–5pm; €1.50), a fifteenth-century Venetian fortress. There's nothing much to see inside, but a walk round the ramparts offers fine views of the new town and the busy port below, while beyond the city confines the high escarpment of the Carso looms over the Adriatic. Its **museum** (Tues–Sun 9am–1pm; €2) houses a small collection of archeological finds, including antique weaponry.

More interesting is the **Cattedrale di San Giusto** (Mon–Sun 8am–noon & 3.30–7.30pm, closes one hour later am & pm in summer; free), built on the ruins of a first-century AD Roman structure. Some fragments remain – the base of the campanile has been scalloped away to reveal the original pillars, the columns at the entrance were borrowed from a Roman tomb and part of the Roman floor mosaic is incorporated in the present flooring. In around 1050 an earlier Christian chapel was replaced by two churches, the Basilica di Santa

Joyce in Trieste

From 1905 to 1915, and again in 1919–20, **James Joyce** and his wife Nora lived in Trieste. After staying at Piazza Ponterosso 3 for a month, they moved to the third-floor flat at Via San Nicolò 30. (In 1919 the poet Umberto Saba bought a bookshop on the ground floor at the same address. The two writers seem never to have met, though they had a common friend in the novelist Italo Svevo.) There's a plaque in Via San Nicolò, and one at Via Bramante 4, quoting the postcard that Joyce despatched in 1915 to his brother Stanislaus, whose Irredentist sympathies had landed him in an Austrian internment camp. The postcard announced that the first chapter of James's new work, *Ulysses*, was finished. For Joyce fans the tourist office publishes a leaflet listing places associated with him, and there's a museum (Mon–Fri 10am–noon; free) in Piazza Hortis though, at present, it only holds a small collection of Joyce-related exhibits, including images of some of his female pupils who reportedly idolized him. No Joyce devotee should miss the bronze statue of the writer, strolling bemusedly across the little canal bridge of Via Roma.

Maria Assunta and the Capella di San Giusto. The site was further expanded in the early thirteenth century in an extraordinary stroke of pragmatic architectural genius: the two adjacent buildings were bridged by a high-beamed vault, forming the current cathedral nave and leaving a double aisle on each side. The complex history of the building becomes clearer if you study the arches in the interior, or look down on the apse from the castle wall behind. As it stands today, the cathedral is a typically Triestine synthesis of styles, with a serene, largely Romanesque interior only marred by an ugly modern choir. The **Cappella di Santa Maria Assunta** (north aisle) has fine Venetian-Ravennan mosaics of the Coronation of the Virgin, revealing the Byzantine roots of the style, while the **Cappella di San Giusto** (south aisle) has thirteenth-century frescoes of the life of the saint, framed between Byzantine pillars. The facade is predominantly Romanesque, but includes a Gothic rose window.

The tiny remnant of the **Città Vecchia** (Old Town) lies between the castle and the Stazione Maritima below. On the cobbled Via della Cattedrale, the **Museo Civico di Storia ed Arte** (Tues & Thurs–Sun 9am–1pm, Wed open late until 7pm; €2) houses a collection of cultural plunder that embraces Himalayan sculpture, Egyptian manuscripts and Roman glass. Behind the museum, and accessible from Piazza della Cattedrale, is the **Orto Lapidario**, a pleasant environment in which fragments of classical statuary, pottery and inscriptions are arranged on benches and against walls, among cow-parsley and miniature palm trees. The little Corinthian temple on the upper level contains the remains of J.J. Winckelmann (1717–68), the German archeologist and theorist of Neoclassicism, who was murdered in Trieste by a man to whom he had shown off his collection of antique coins.

Further down Via della Cattedrale are a couple of ill-matched churches. The imposing **Santa Maria Maggiore** (Mon–Sat 8am–noon & 4–6.45pm, Sun 8am–12.45pm; free) is little more than another brutish Baroque creation, but its tiny early Romanesque neighbour, **San Silvestro** (Thurs & Fri 10am–noon; free), is worth a look for its unusual state of preservation; it's now used by adherents of the rare Helvetic-Waldensian sect. A short way below are the heavily restored remains of the Roman theatre where performances are staged during the city's spring–autmun festival season. There's little else of monumental note in the old city – though some of the older buildings are now being nicely renovated – but mosaic enthusiasts may want to stop off at the remains of the **Basilica Paleocristiana** (Thurs 10am–noon, or by appointment ☎040.43.631;

free) under the building at Via Madonna del Mare 11. The modest **Arco di Riccardo**, on the nearby Piazza Barbacan, is a remnant of the Roman walls dating from 33 BC, while excavation works nearby are revealing more traces of the city's ancient imperial past and will eventually form part of an archeological tourist trail from San Giusto down to Piazza Unità (see below).

The Borgo Teresiano and around

To the north of the old centre, Trieste's new town, the **Borgo Teresiano**, is dominated by heavy Neoclassical architecture imported from nineteenth-century Vienna, with wide boulevards and a waterfront spoilt by a busy main road. The focus of the main grid of streets is **Piazza Sant'Antonio Nuovo**, with its small yacht basin overlooked by cafés and dominated by two churches: the Neoclassical hulk of San Antonio Thaumaturgo and the smaller, more appealing Serbian Orthodox San Spiridione. The real heart of town, however, is the grandiose **Piazza Unità d'Italia**, directly below the hill of San Giusto. Built mostly by Giuseppe Bruni in the late nineteenth century, the expanse of flagstones with one side open to the water is deliberately reminiscent of Venice's Piazza and Piazzetta – Trieste had commercially eclipsed the older city some years before. Projecting into the harbour nearby, the **Molo Audace**, named after the first boat of Italian soldiers to land here in 1918, is the venue for the evening *passeggiata*.

Trieste's principal museum is the **Revoltella** (mid-July to Aug Mon & Wed–Sat 9am–1.30pm & 4–11pm, Sun 9am–2pm; Sept to mid-July Mon & Wed–Sat 9am–6pm, Sun 10am–6pm; €5, €2 more for special exhibitions; ⓦwww .museorevoltella.it), Via Armando Diaz 27, housed in a Viennese-style *palazzo* bequeathed to the city by the financier Baron Pasquale Revoltella in 1869. Its combined display of nineteenth-century stately home furnishings and Triestine paintings is well worth a look and the adjacent palace, redesigned by the architect Carlo Scarpa, houses an extensive collection of modern art. The nearby **Museo Sartorio**, in Largo Papa Giovanni XXIII (℡040.310.500; Tues–Sun 9am–1pm; €3), has ceramics and icons downstairs and oppressive private rooms upstairs, but its highlight, the early fourteenth-century Santa Chiara triptych, is well worth a visit. The central panel contains 36 beautifully restored miniature scenes from the life of Christ. There is also an important collection of drawings by Tiepolo.

A more pleasant domestic interior is the **Museo Morpurgo**, north of San Giusto at Via Imbriani 5 (Tues & Thurs–Sun 9am–1pm, Wed open late until 7pm; €2). The *palazzo* was left to the city by the merchant and banker Mario Morpurgo di Nilma, and its apartments have not really been touched since their first decoration in the 1880s. With its sepia photographs and other memorabilia, it feels less like a museum than like a home whose owners went on holiday and never came back.

One of the ugliest episodes of recent European history is embodied by the **Risiera di San Sabba**, overlooking the southern flank of Trieste's port at Ratto della Pileria 43 (daily 9am–7pm; free), on the #8 and #10 bus routes. Once a rice-hulling plant, this was one of only two concentration camps in Italy (the other was near Carpi in Emilia-Romagna) and now houses a permanent exhibition that serves as a reminder of Fascist crimes in the region. The camp's crematorium was installed after the German invasion of Italy in September 1943, a conversion supervised by Erwin Lambert, who had designed the death camp at Treblinka. Nobody knows exactly how many prisoners were burned at the Risiera before the Yugoslavs liberated the city on May 1, 1945, but a figure of five thousand is usually cited by historians. Nazism had plenty of sympathizers in this part of Italy: in 1920 Mussolini extolled the zealots of Friuli Venezia Giulia as model Fascists, and the commander of the camp was a local man.

Eating and drinking

Triestine **cuisine** is as mixed as its population, with goulash, potato noodles and cheese dumplings on many menus, as well as some superb fish dishes. The local *terrano*, a very sharp red wine grown only on the limestone highlands, was reputedly the favourite of the Roman empress Livia and is supposed to be good for the blood. It's delicious in any event and should be tried, ideally as an accompaniment to the heavy Triestine food. For less stolid meals, investigate the **osmizze** (see box, p.419), impromptu eating places, often in the hinterland of the Carso, which offer the simplest of local produce at rock-bottom prices. Trieste is most famous in Italy for its **coffee**, imported and even roasted here – you'll be pushed to find a better or a stronger cup anywhere. Via C. Battisti, east of Sant'Antonio, is a good street for **food shops** – cheeses, cooked meats, olives and pasta in its many guises are piled high in the windows.

Cafés and gelaterie

Trieste's association with **coffee** dates back to the mid-eighteenth century, when trading began and when the first coffee shops opened in emulation of Vienna. Even now it's the leading coffee port in the Mediterranean – most of Italy's coffee arrives here, and the former city mayor and now provincial governor is one Riccardo Illy, from the famous Illy coffee clan. One of the pleasures of walking around the city centre is the unexpected scent of roasting beans that wafts through the streets and there are several places – known as *torrefazioni* – that roast and sell their own beans. **Ice cream** lovers, too, are well catered for, with a host of places tempting you to try their products – the best area to head for is leafy, pedestrian-only Viale XX Settembre, known as the *Acquedotto* ("aqueduct"), where citizens stroll in the evening.

Caffè degli Specchi Piazza Unità. Better for its excellent position on Trieste's main square than its slightly soulless interior, the city's most famous café is still the place to sip your wine and people-watch.
Caffè Pasticceria Pirona Largo Barriera Vecchia. Superior cakeshop that's the place to head for a quick pastry fix – James Joyce was a regular.

🏃 **Caffè San Marco** Via C. Battisti. Trieste's favourite café has occupied its premises for some eighty years. It's a huge, relaxed place with a clientele of all ages chatting and playing chess in the mahogany and mirrored Art Nouveau-style interior. Closed Wed.

Caffè Tommaseo Piazza Tommaseo. Much of the historic style of this café – a rendezvous for Italian nationalists in the nineteenth century – was lost in a recent refurbishment, but it has a nice setting and frequent live music.
Crèmcaffè Piazza Goldoni 10. Excellent *torrefazione* near the junction with Via Mazzini.
La Triestina Via di Cavana 2. Another great, central choice to load up on caffeine, where they roast their own coffee beans in the great Triestine tradition.

🏃 **Zampolli** Viale XX Settembre. Of the many ice-cream parlours on this street, *Zampolli* is probably the best; try the unforgettable *bacio bianco*.

Restaurants

Trieste has a huge range of good-value **cafés** and **restaurants** scattered around both the new and old town. Especially attractive is the pedestrian-only thoroughfare Viale XX Settembre, which sports a number of lively places among its bars and cinemas. More expensive choices tend to specialize in fish, of which *branzino* and *sogliola* (sea bass and sole) are local favourites. Booking is not usually necessary.

Ai Fiori Piazza Hortis 7. Excellent, classy, gourmet trattoria on a leafy square between the Riva and the castle hill. Closed Sun & Mon.

Antica Trattoria Suban Via Comici 2. Way out to the east of the city, this prestigious and pricey restaurant is worth the taxi ride for its superb meat

dishes, particularly the steak. Closed Mon, Tues &
part of Aug.

Buffet Pepi Via Cassa di Risparmio 3. Student
option that's the perfect place for snack meals and
lunches. Cooking emphasizes Trieste's Austrian
connections with excellent sausages, gammon and
bowls of steaming sauerkraut. Closed Sun.

Corallo Via Vidali 12. Pizzas the way the locals
like them. Try the house version, loaded up with
prosciutto, funghi, artichokes, ricotta, hard-boiled
egg and *prosciutto crudo*. Closed Wed.

Da Giovanni Via S. Lazzaro 14. Simple meals
served at bench tables, with hams hanging from
the ceiling and barrels of wine behind the bar lending it a distinctly rustic air. Closed Sun.

El Fornel Via dei Fornelli 1. Very popular place that
concentrates on the food – mostly fish and seafood
– rather than the decor. Closed Sun.

Il Barattolo Piazza Sant'Antonio. Deservedly popular
place, with friendly staff, tasty southern Italian-style
food, and pleasant outdoor seating in this pretty
square in the summer. Closed Mon in winter.

L'Osmiza Via della Torretta. Feast on
products straight from the Carso countryside, including *prosciutto crudo*, olives and eggs.
Closed every eight days, according to tradition.

La Piazzetta Piazza Cavana 1b. Extremely good
value, with fish as a speciality in this cosy find
towards the old quarter. Closed Mon.

Bars

Many of the city's **bars** are as glossy as the top-notch cafés, though there is
one survivor of old Trieste, the *Osteria da Libero*, on the castle hill at Via Risorta
7 (closed Sun), which can hardly have changed in a hundred years. The *Café
Gourmet* in the Galleria Protti has a Thirties' nightclub feel, while nearby *Circus*,
Via San Lazzaro 9 (closed Sun), is a trendy, buzzing wine bar. *Naima*, at
Via Rosetti 6 (daily 7.30pm–3am), off Viale XX Settembre, is younger and
more studenty than most, and has occasional live music. For late drinking,
Via Madonna del Mare, on the castle hill, has a number of bars whose names,
managements and popularity come and go each year – it's best to follow your
ears to where the crowds are.

Listings

Airport information ☎0481.773.224, ⊚www
.aeroporto.fvg.it.

Bus information Freephone ☎800.0166.75.
Timetables and tickets can be bought from automatic machines at main stops or from newsagents
and *tabacchi*; a ten-ticket *bloquetto* saves a couple
of euros and is more convenient than buying
individual tickets. Town buses cost €0.90 for any
journey made within an hour of purchase; provincial buses cost a standard €1, except private APT
services which depend on distance.

Car rental Avis, Molo dei Bersaglieri 3
☎040.300.820; Europcar, ☎800.014.410, Airport
☎0481.778.920; Hertz, Molo dei Bersaglieri 3
☎040.322.0098.

Club Alpino Italiano Via Donota 2 ☎040.630.464.

Consulates UK, Via Dante Alighieri 7 (Tues 10am–
noon, Fri 2.30–4.30pm; ☎040.347.8303); US
Consular Agent, Via Roma 15 (Mon–Fri 10am–noon;
☎040.660.177).

Festivals and events From spring to autumn
there are programmes of events across Trieste,
including at the Teatro Verdi (☎040.672.2111,

⊚www.teatroverdi-trieste.com), which also has
operas and musicals throughout the year. Check for
details in *Il Piccolo*, Trieste's daily paper – which
should also have details of the festivals in the
Carso villages – or at the tourist office.

Hospital Ospedale Maggiore, Piazza dell'Ospedale
☎040.399.1111; in an emergency dial ☎118.

Internet access Smilenet, Piazza Squero Vecchio
1c, just west of Piazza Unità (daily 10am–9pm);
OneNET Internet Point, Via San Francesco 28c
(Mon, Wed & Sat 10am–1pm & 4–9pm, Tues, Thurs
& Fri 4–9pm; ⊚www.onenet.it).

Police The *Questura* is at Via Tor Bandena 6
☎040.379.0111. Otherwise ring ☎113.

Post office The main post office is in Piazza
Vittorio Veneto 1 (Mon–Sat 8.30am–7pm).

Taxis Radio Taxi ☎040.307.730.

Train information ☎147.888.088.

Travel agent Agemar, Piazza Duca degli Abruzzi
1a ☎040.363.737, ⊚www.agemar.it – for ferry
tickets to Grado and Ligano, Pirano (Slovenia),
Brioni and Rovigno (Croatia).

Around Trieste: the Carso

The **Carso** is the Italian name for the limestone uplands that rise from the plain of the Veneto south of Monfalcone and eventually merge into the Istrian plateau. Although within thirty minutes' bus ride of Trieste, it feels like an entirely different country, and is geologically, botanically and socially distinct from anywhere else in Italy. Most of the Carso now lies within Slovenia (its Slovene name is Kras), and even the narrow strip inside Italy, though supporting a population of just 20,000, remains distinctively Slovene in culture, boasting villages with names like Zagradec and Koludrovica. The dour villages of thick-walled houses seem to hunker down against the *bora*, the northeasterly wind which can blast this area at any time of year – when it's especially fierce, ropes are strung along the steeper streets in Trieste.

Like all limestone country, the environment is harsh: arid in summer and sometimes snowbound in winter. The surface of the plateau is studded with sink-holes left by streams which have slowly carved their way underground, sometimes reappearing miles away on the coast. The abundance of caves has even led to the German name for the area, *karst*, becoming the standard geographical term for this type of landscape. In other places – near Aurisina, for instance – the land is scarred with World War I trenches.

The distinctive landscape and natural environment have led to proposals for creating a National Park. There is fine **walking** to be had, and several bus services run to the Carso from Trieste, including the #42 and #44. The tourist office publishes a useful map of the network of numbered footpaths in the Carso; it shouldn't be used for serious navigation, but is a useful guide to what's possible – and it would be difficult to get yourself seriously lost. If the scenery isn't as grand as the Dolomites, the pace is gentler, especially if you can break your expedition at an *osmizza* (see box below).

Grotta Gigante and Rupingrande

The most picturesque way up into the Carso is to take the *tranvia* (cable tramway; 7.30am–8pm; every 20min; €0.90, same ticket as for buses) from Trieste's Piazza Oberdan to the village of Opicina, at the edge of the plateau. From the tram stop, cross the square and take bus #42 (which you can also take all the

---

Osmizze

Perhaps the best way to experience the Slovene culture of the Carso is to find an **osmizza** (see opposite for one in Trieste itself), an informal restaurant where farmers sell their own produce, such as home-cured meats, cheese, olives, hard-boiled eggs, bread and wine. The name comes from the Slovene word *osem* "eight days", which was the period of time allowed by imperial edict for the peasants to sell their wares. The goods are usually very cheap, and a frequent bonus is a stunning view over the bay of Trieste or the limestone hills behind the city. The problem with *osmizze* is that they are often temporary, don't advertise, and usually lie off the beaten track – which makes them all the more worth tracking down. Your best bet is to ask the tourist office for a list or look at ⑩ www.interware.it/tsr/Ambiente/carso/osmizze.htm (Italian only). Otherwise, as long as you don't mind taking a few detours, just take a #44 bus from outside the station in Trieste, get off at the villages Prosecco or Contovello, and start asking if there is an *osmizza* nearby. You'll know you are getting warm when you see arrows on clumps of leaves suspended from archways and lampposts: they point the way to the nearest *osmizza*.

△ Grotta Gigante

way from Trieste) to one of the Carso's highlights, the **Grotta Gigante** (guided visits daily: April–Sept every 30min 10am–6pm; March & Oct hourly 10am–4pm; Nov–Feb hourly 10am–noon & 2–4pm; €7.50; Ⓦwww.grottagigante .it), the world's largest accessible cave, and the second-largest natural chamber anywhere in the world (the largest is in Malaysia). As it's 107m deep by 208m broad, the dome of St Peter's would fit comfortably inside. It's a steady 11°C inside, so come prepared.

The cave is impressive in scale and, like most of the caves in the Carso, was created by the erosive action of a river, in this case the Timavo, which sank deeper and deeper underground before changing course (the cave is now dry). The stalactites and stalagmites grew later, formed by deposits of calcium carbonate and colourful metal oxides. Much more recently, ferns and moss have started to grow in what was previously a lifeless environment, thanks to photosynthesis triggered by electric lighting. The two long "pillars" in the centre of the cave are in fact wires sheathed in plastic. At the bottom end two super-accurate pendulums are suspended, used to measure seismic shifts in isolation from surface noise and air currents.

If the tour of the cave has given you an appetite, visit the nearby **trattoria** *Milic* (closed Mon), close to the bus stop, which serves tasty and reasonably priced meals.

Apart from the Grotta Gigante, the main sights to head for are in and around the village of **RUPINGRANDE**, just 3km northeast of the cave and also on the #42 bus route. A short walk east of the village is a fortress built in the fourteenth century to defend the area from Turkish incursions, while in Rupingrande itself the **Casa Carsica** (April–Nov Sun & hols 11am–12.30pm & 3–5pm, or by appointment; ℡040.327.122; free) exhibits old furniture and nineteenth-century peasant costumes, as well as works by local artisans. The Casa Carso is signposted from the central crossroads in Rupingrande. Every two years (2007, 2009, and so on) the village hosts an important Slovene folk festival, the **Nozze carsiche** (Carsic wedding), on the four days leading up to the last Sunday in August.

Strada Vicentina and Val Rosandra

Two walking areas near the city can be particularly recommended. The **Strada Vicentina** (or Napoleonica) is some 2km long, curving along the hillside above the city, between the *Obelisco* campsite and the hamlet of **BORGO NAZARIO** (near Prosecco). It's a scenic but unstrenuous walk, partly shadowed by trees and partly cut through almost sheer limestone cliffs. Roughly halfway along is the truncated pyramid (nicknamed the "Little Cheese") of the **Tempio Mariano** at Monte Grisa, built in 1967 on the site of a local place of pilgrimage. The structure isn't exactly easy on the eye, but the interior is impressive, if stark, and on a clear day the views are superb. Access to the Strada Vicentina couldn't be simpler: *Obelisco* is a stop on the *tranvia*, and the Borgo Nazario end is near Via San Nazario, where the #42 bus stops on its way back to Trieste station.

The other area, the **Val Rosandra**, is very different. This miniature wilderness of limestone cliffs and sumac trees is the local rock-climbing headquarters and is crisscrossed with paths. Take bus #40 from Trieste's bus station to **BAGNOLI DELLA ROSANDRA** and follow the road at the back of the square northeast towards the hills. After about 500m or so the tarmac gives way to a path bordered on the right by a miniature Roman aqueduct – now resembling little more than a stone-lined ditch – and on the left by a stream with pools for bathing. After thirty minutes the little sanctuary church of Santa Maria in Siaris appears, perched on a spur of rock high on the right. You can climb up to it easily enough and a steep path continues up to the top of the plateau beyond. Beyond this is a waterfall, accessible by a steep path, then the tiny hamlet of Bottazzo – the last habitation before Slovenia. At the border a sign advertises a friendship path linking communities on either side of the frontier. Don't be tempted to investigate; only locals are allowed to cross unpatrolled borders, and the military are fairly active in the area as it's a busy crossing point for illegal immigrants.

Other paths lead across the valley and up to the villages of **Mocco**, where there's a ruined castle. The most rewarding expedition, although strenuous, is across the slopes of **Monte Carso**. It's simplest to begin at **SAN DORLIGO DELLA VALLE**, where bus #40 terminates. Walk uphill through town past the general store until you leave the village. At a T-junction with a major road cross the road to the fountain and national park signs where there's a signpost to the beginning of the walk. After 100m, the unsurfaced track divides into two paths at a small spring. Take the left fork here and follow the path marked #46 as it rises gently across the contours of Monte Carso. After about an hour the trail steepens to bring you out onto the plateau. Be wary of taking the smaller paths that branch uphill off the main trail; these are local shortcuts, but often peter out among faded signs warning of old mines – the explosive type. At the top of the mountain is a beautiful undulating plateau of mixed woodland and grasses, the path running within metres of the Slovene border. A number of roughly marked steep paths turn down into Val Rosandra, but you'll need good grip and a head for heights; the last, #17, probably has the gentlest gradient.

The Triestine Riviera

The thirty-odd kilometres of coastline either side of Trieste, from Múggia to the south and as far as Duino in the north, are optimistically known as the **Triestine Riviera**. While beaches aren't as good as you'll find further down the Adriatic, or even at nearby Grado, some fine walks, historic sites and castles are worth a day-trip from Trieste. Frequent **buses** trace the coast road and, in summer, **ferries** (see p.438) call at all the coastal towns.

Múggia

Directly south across the bay from Trieste, 11km away by road, **MÚGGIA**, the last remnant of Venice's Istrian possessions, is now reduced to little more than a popular spot for lunch expeditions from Trieste, though the town comes into its own during carnival time. The ferry-trip across the bay from Trieste (summer only) can be a good enough reason in itself to visit, but there are also appealing signs of the past, particularly in the brightly painted buildings on the main square. On the east side of the piazza, the fifteenth-century **Duomo** reveals its origins in its Venetian–Gothic arches and a bas-relief of Christ Pantocrator in the lunette above the main door; the handsome **Palazzo dei Rettori**, on the north side of the square, displays the tell-tale *leone marciano*, the lion of St Mark, symbol of Venice's former control here. The piazza is backed by a handful of narrow streets and tumbledown houses, many of which date back to Venetian times.

On the seaward side of the piazza, the tiny *mandracchio* is now used as a basin for pleasure boats, while the working harbour just beyond is spoilt only by the unrivalled view of Trieste's industrial backside. Múggia's handful of **fish restaurants** are all within spitting distance of the water. Top recommendation, and not just for the name, is the *Trattoria Lilibontempo* (closed Tues), at Riva Nazario Sauro 10, known as the "ex-Hitler" after the former proprietor, who bore an unnerving resemblance to the Nazi dictator. Further along the harbour front and with sea views, *Trattoria Risorta* (closed Sun & Mon) does tasty fish dishes for around €12, or try the *Due Leoni* (closed Mon), opposite on the jetty, which serves similar food at slightly cheaper prices.

At Via Roma 20, in front of the **tourist office** (℡040.273.259; open Carnevale & July & Aug only), as well as from the port, you can pick up bus #20, which runs back to Trieste every 30min, but it's worth visiting **Múggia Vecchia**, on the hilltop hard against the Slovene border and less than 20km from Croatia. It's a steep twenty-minute walk past Múggia's fourteenth-century castle and town walls, but bus #50 from outside the **bus station**, 100m inland from the main road, runs every hour or so for those who don't fancy the climb. The old village has a few oddments of ancient foundations, but the main reason to visit is the lovely **Santuario di Santa Maria Assunta**, a largely tenth-century structure, though much rebuilt in the twelfth and fifteenth centuries. Inside, there is just enough light coming through the narrow Romanesque windows to illuminate some peeling Venetian-Byzantine frescoes, mostly from the thirteenth century, and an unusual pulpit supported on four slender, carved columns. From the hill behind the sanctuary on a clear day you can see as far as Fiume (Rijeka) and Grado.

Barcola and Miramare

BARCOLA, 2km northwest of Trieste and connected to the city by bus #36 from the bus station, is the nearest beach resort. Developed during Trieste's great days at the end of the nineteenth century, it is now really a suburb that comes to life in summer, when all Trieste seems to come here to chat, play cards, sunbathe and swim. Despite the cargo ships and tankers moored in the harbour, the water is moderately clean. Just short of the resort, perched on the slope of the limestone escarpment and offering stunning views along the coast, is the **Faro della Vittoria** (April–Sept daily except Wed 9–11am & 4–6pm;

Oct–March Sun & hols 10am–3pm; free), the second-tallest lighthouse in the world after New York's Statue of Liberty.

Standing at the tip of a rocky promontory 7km from Trieste, the salt-white castle of **MIRAMARE** is the area's prime tourist attraction. The Archduke Ferdinand Maximilian, Emperor Franz Josef's younger brother, was once forced ashore here by a squall, and resolved to buy the site. He built his dream castle and laid out its grounds between 1856 and 1870, but never lived to see it completed – having accepted Napoleon III's offer to make him the Emperor of Mexico, Maximilian was executed by his Mexican opponents in 1867, in the line of imperial duty. His wife Carlotta later went mad, and the legend was born that anyone who spends a night in Miramare will come to a bad end.

The park makes an excellent spot for a picnic, but the real draw is the castle's kitsch **interior** (daily 9am–7pm; €4), a remarkable example of regal decadence, and carved, gilded, and inlaid in every way possible. The Monarchs' Salon, for instance, is embellished with portraits of a King of Norway, the Emperor of Brazil, a Czar of Russia – anyone, no matter how fraudulent or despotic, as long as they're nominal monarchs. This softens you up for the bedroom and its images of the most important events in the history of this area, pride of place going to the construction of the castle, of course. Other rooms are panelled and furnished like a ship's quarters, reflecting Maximilian's devotion to the Austrian Navy.

There are a number of ways **to get to Miramare**, of which the simplest is to take the #36 bus from Piazza Oberdan, though the private APT service from the bus station is quicker. Trains heading west from Trieste also stop, and in summer there's a boat service from the harbour. In July and August a *son et lumière* called "the Romance of Maximilian of Mexico and Charlotte of Habsburg" is performed beside the sea, with a regular performance in English; check with Trieste's tourist office or the castle (☎040.224.143, ⓦ www.castello -miramare.it) for information on dates and times.

Duino and Sistiana

The village of **DUINO**, 14km northwest along the coast from Trieste, is dominated by its two castles, the **Castello Vecchio**, built around the tenth century and now just a ruined eyrie above the sea, and the early fifteenth-century **Castello Nuovo**, seat of the princes of Thurn and Taxis down to the present day. The latter and its grounds opened to the public in 2003 (March–Sept Mon & Wed–Sun 9.30am–5.30pm; Oct Mon & Wed–Sun 9.30am–4.30pm; Nov Sat & Sun 9.30am–4pm; €6; ☎040.208.120, ⓦ www.castellodiduino.it) and visitors can now stroll through the lavishly decorated rooms, take a look at a massive doll's house given to the family by Napoleon III's widow and a history of the family's eighteenth-century pan-European postal service, and admire the fantastic coastal views from the beautiful gardens and the top of the third-century Roman tower. A small **café** in the grounds offers refreshments or, down by the harbour, a couple of **restaurants** serve more substantial fare – turn left out of the castle and head downhill.

A pleasant footpath, the Sentiero Rilke – named after Rainer Maria Rilke who began the famous *Duino Elegies* while visiting the castle – runs 3km back along the coast to the **campsite** (April–Sept; ☎040.299.264, ⓦ www.camping .it/friuli/marepinetabaiasistiana) at **SISTIANA**, where there's a large harbour backed by woods, and a **beach**. Bus #44 and the faster APT bus #51 run from Trieste's Piazza Oberdan and bus station to Sistiana and Duino. There are also three ferries a day to Duino harbour in summer (see p.438).

Aquileia, Grado and around

Bordered by the Tagliamento in the west and the Isonzo in the east, and drained by other rivers flowing into the sandy, shallow waters at the head of the Adriatic, the triangle of flatlands west of Trieste and south of Udine seems unpromising territory for a visitor – mile upon mile of maize fields, punctuated by telegraph poles, streams, level roads and newish villages. Yet at **Aquileia**, the dull fields of this secretive region have yielded up a wealth of Roman remains, while the glorious **Basilica** ranks among the most important monuments of early Christendom. Tucked away in the lagoons, just to the south, the popular resort of **Grado** with its beaches and crowds of holiday-makers has a completely different atmosphere, though it too preserves some beautiful early Christian remains. If you don't have your own transport, **buses** are the way to explore the region: they leave Udine for Grado at least every hour, calling at Palmanova and Aquileia on the way; from Trieste, change at **Monfalcone**, from where buses leave hourly for Aquileia and Grado or take the summer-only **ferry** from Trieste's Molo Pescheria to Grado's Molo Torpediniere (see p.438)

Aquileia

Forty-five kilometres west of Trieste, **AQUILEIA** was established as a **Roman colony** in 181 BC, its location at the eastern edge of the Venetian plain – on the bank of a navigable river a few kilometres from the sea – being ideal for defensive and trading purposes. It became the nexus for all Rome's dealings with points east and north, and by 10 BC, when the Emperor Augustus received Herod the Great here, Aquileia was the capital of the Regio Venetia et Histria and the fourth most important city in Italy, after Rome, Milan and Cápua. In 314 the Patriarchate of Aquileia was founded, and under the first patriarch, Theodore, a great basilica was built. Sacked by Attila in 452 and again by the Lombards in 568, Aquileia lost the patriarchate to Grado, which was protected from invasion by its lagoons. It regained its primacy in the early eleventh century under **Patriarch Poppo**, who rebuilt the basilica and erected the campanile, a landmark for miles around. But regional power inevitably passed to Venice, and in 1751 Aquileia lost its patriarchate for the last time, to Udine. The sea has long since retreated, the River Natissa is a reed-clogged stream, and Aquileia is now a quiet little town of 3500 people.

Aquileia's rich history is made visible in the layers of the vast **Basilica** (daily: summer 9am–7pm; winter Mon–Fri 9am–1pm & 2–5pm, Sat & Sun 9am–5pm; free), just east of the main road. The earliest part, Theodore's extraordinary **mosaic pavement**, was discovered below the nave floor at the beginning of the twentieth century and is thought to be the earliest surviving remnant of any Christian church. The mosaic undulates the full length of the nave in a riot-ous sequence of colours, patterns and images, many of which draw on Roman iconography. As far as the red line extending across the nave aisle there is no explicitly Christian imagery, though pagan symbolism was frequently adopted and adapted by the early Church. Look for the blond angel bearing the laurel wreath and palm frond – whether it represents the Pax Romana or Christian Victory, no one is sure. Beyond the line the Biblical story of Jonah begins, complete with waves, whale and fish everywhere – a motif not unconnected to the nearby Adriatic. Other mosaics from Theodore's original basilica, depicting a whole bestiary, have been discovered around the base of the campanile (access from inside the basilica). Next door, a climb up the **bell tower** (March–Oct daily 9.30am–1pm & 2.30–6pm; €1.10) gives a new perspective on the basilica as well as views stretching from the mountains to the coast.

In 1348 an earthquake destroyed much of Poppo's work, but the building is still superb, the Gothic elements of the reconstruction – all points above the capitals – harmonizing perfectly with the Romanesque below. The fine nave ceiling, like the steeple of the campanile, dates from the early sixteenth century. The ninth-century **crypt** under the chancel (€3) has very faded twelfth-century frescoes telling the story of St Hermagora, the legendary first bishop of Aquileia, including a gory beheading scene and a moving descent from the cross.

A couple of minutes' walk west from the basilica, on the other side of the main road, on Via Roma, is the **Museo Archeologico** (Mon 8.30am–2pm, Tues–Sun 8.30am–7.30pm; €4). Worked stone and everyday items litter the fields around Aquileia, but the finer pieces have been collected here, ranging from precise surgical needles, delicate coloured glass and precious stones to great piles of jumbled masonry. The two courtyards, in particular, resemble a junkyard of Roman stone, with hundreds of funerary monuments, including urns piled in neat pyramids; concerts are occasionally held here in summer. It's worth persevering up to the top floor of the museum where two extraordinary bronze heads are displayed side by side. One is a fantastical relief in the Hellenistic style, the other a naturalistic bust that may portray a dictator of the third century AD; the cruel expression certainly supports the speculation. On the ground floor rows of marble sculptures and busts mostly derive from the Roman tombs that once lined the roads into Aquileia.

The **Museo Paleocristiano** (Tues–Sun 8.30am–1.45pm; free), housed in the shell of a Benedictine monastery in the northern part of the town, opposite the campsite on Via Germina, is recommended solely to those insatiable for more mosaic pavements. There's also a miscellany of early Christian carving and sculpture, but the fifteen-minute riverside walk to the museum from the basilica is perhaps the best reason to go, taking you past the sad remnants of the quays of Aquileia. From the museum you can loop back along the main road, past the forum, to the basilica.

The **tourist office** is at the Via Iulia Augusta bus terminal (Mon–Fri 9am–7pm, Sat & Sun 10am–1pm & 2–5pm; ☎0431.91.491, ⓦwww.aquileiaturismo .info). The Pro Loco office beside the basilica does not provide tourist information. In the newer part of town, past the main road past the Museo Archeologico, you'll find the cheaper of Aquileia's two three-star **hotels**, the *Aquila Nera*, Piazza Garibaldi 5 (☎0431.91.045, ⓦwww.hotelaquilanera.com; ❷), with an excellent **restaurant** attached. The slightly more upmarket *Hotel Patriarchi* sits on the main road not far from the bus terminal (☎0431.919595, ⓦwww .hotelpatriarchi.it; ❸). There's also a decent **HI hostel**, *Domus Augusta*, Via Roma 25 (☎043.191.024, ⓦwww.ostelloaquileia.it; €15.50) and a **campsite**, *Camping Aquileia* Via Gemina 10 (☎0431.91.042, ⓦwww.campingaquileia .it; mid-May to mid-Sept), with bungalows as well as tent sites. Of the area's **restaurants**, *Alla Basilica*, Via Della Stazione 2, serves decent pizzas, and the agriturismo *La Pergola*, on the main road at Località Beligna 4, serves good home cooking and home-produced wines.

Grado and around

Some 11km south of Aquileia, isolated among lagoons at the end of a causeway, is the ancient island-town of **GRADO**, through which Aquileia once traded with Syria, Cyprus, Arabia and Asia Minor. But Grado is no miniature Venice, despite its parallel history and situation, the tiny historic centre being all but lost among the concrete buildings of the large, modern resort.

For relaxing on the **beach**, however, this is one of the best places in the northern Adriatic, the resort extending eastwards along the length of the sandy island. The water is safe and warm as a bath, and almost as shallow – indeed, the name of the town comes from the gentle angle of its shore. The free beaches are at the eastern and western end; if you want a locker, deckchair and shower facilities, you have to pay a few euros to one of the businesses on the Lungomare Adriatico.

It's worth seeking out the **historic centre**, however, for its three early-Christian buildings, grouped close together in the heart of a miniature network of old streets. The exteriors are of fairly rustic brick construction, though enlivened by fragments of carved Roman marble. The sixth-century **Basilica** (daily 8.30am–6.15pm; free) was heavily restored between the 1930s and 1950s, but preserves a bizarre parade of ill-matched nave pillars topped by an assortment of Corinthian capitals; it's thought that these were borrowed from various Roman buildings in Aquileia. The pulpit is of similarly hybrid origins, perched on six slender Roman columns under a Venetian canopy that resembles an oriental tent. Venice's presence is also felt in the fourteenth-century silver *pala* on the high altar. The mosaic pavement, while not as impressive as Aquileia's, is beautiful, the pattern being formed by an endless knot.

The adjacent octagonal **Baptistry** (erratic opening hours) also dates back to the fifth century and the arrival of the first Christians in the lagoon. The church of **Santa Maria delle Grazie** (daily 8.30am–6.15pm; free), on its far side, is from the same period and has another mongrel collection of columns and capitals. From the outside it's possible to see how the ground level has sunk over the centuries.

Grado's **tourist office**, at Viale Dante Alighieri 72 (April–Sept daily 8am–1pm & 3–7pm; Oct–March Mon–Thurs 8am–1pm & 2–5pm, Fri 8am–1pm; ℡0431.877.111, ⓦwww.gradoturismo.info), has details of **hotels**, the majority of which are fairly expensive and sometimes insist on your taking full pension. Three cheaper options are the *Villa Marin*, Via dei Provveditori 20 (℡0431.80.789, ⓔvillamarin@grado.it; ❸), overlooking the seafront wall between the two beaches; *Villa Romana Meublé*, Viale Dante Alighieri 20 (℡0431.82.604; ❷; May–Sept), just east of the historic centre and one street back from the beach; and *Al Sole Meublé*, Viale del Sole 31 (℡ & ℻0431.80.370; ❷; April–Oct), which is near the beach, at its free, eastern end, a good ten-minute walk from the centre. The best local **campsites** are at Grado Pineta, around 3km east of the town and served by regular buses: *Camping al Bosco*, Via Strada della Rotta 4 (℡0431.80.485, ⓦwww.campingalbosco.it; May–Sept), the three-star *Camping Punta Spin* Via Monfalcone 10 (℡0431.80.732, ⓦwww .puntaspin.it; April–Sept), which has a swimming pool, and *Villaggio Turistico Europa* Via Monfalcone 12 (℡0431.80.877, ⓦwww.villaggioeuropa.it; mid-April to mid-Sept).

A cluster of good **restaurants** can be found in the old streets around Santa Maria. The tiny *Santa Lucia* (closed Tues in low season), secreted in an alleyway at Campo Porta Nuova 1, serves good pizzas, while the *Enoteca In Sentina*, at 1b, is good for wine and snacks. Nearby the cosy *Tavernetta all'Androna* (closed Tues) is expensive and not especially good value but has a lovely courtyard under Santa Maria's east wall. For Grado's fish specialities, head just west to *Trattoria de Toni*, Piazza Duca d'Aosta 37, or the *Trattoria Alla Borsa*, Via Conte di Grado 1, behind the marina.

Gorizia and around

As with other towns in this region, the tranquillity of present-day **GORIZIA** – virtually midway along the Trieste–Udine rail line – belies the turbulence of its past. The castle that dominates the old centre was the power-base of the dukes of Gorizia, who ruled the area for four centuries. After their eclipse, Venice briefly ruled the town at the start of the sixteenth century, before the Habsburgs took over. It was controlled from Vienna uninterruptedly until August 8, 1916, when the Italian army occupied it – but only until the rout at Caporetto (now Kobarid in Slovenia), some 50km north. **War cemeteries** in the area attest to the violent struggles fought over the territory. The border settlement after World War II literally split houses in Gorizia down the middle. Italy kept the town proper, but lost its eastern perimeter to what was then Yugoslavia, where the new regime resolved to build its own Gorizia: **Nova Gorica** – New Gorizia – is the result.

The town's appearance, like that of Trieste, is distinctly central European, stamped with the authority of Empress Maria Theresa. Numerous parks and gardens – thriving in the area's mild climate – further enhance the *fin-de-siècle* atmosphere. Again like Trieste, it's a major shopping town for Slovenes, which explains the large number of electrical, clothes and food shops, and the cafés and restaurants.

The main sight in town is the **Borgo Castello**, the quarter built round the castle by the Venetians, mostly in the sixteenth century. It's a pleasant place to wander, but the view from the castle walls is more inspiring. The graceful rooms of the **Castle** itself (Tues–Sun: April–Sept 9.30am–1pm & 3–7.30pm; Oct–March 9.30am–6pm; €3, more with exhibitions and special events) hold an unexceptional collection of musical instruments, weaponry, and paintings and models of the castle and town. The **Museo Provinciali** (Tues–Sun 10am–7pm; €3.50), in the Borgo just down from the castle entrance, is again fairly dry, with collections on textiles, fashion and World War I.

One of the finest of Gorizia's Neoclassical buildings is the **Palazzo Attems** (Tues–Sun 9am–7pm; €6) in Piazza De Amicis, northwest of the castle, built by Nicolo Pacassi, Maria Theresa's favourite architect. Part of the Museo Provinciali, it shows temporary exhibitions on themes such as fashion and modern art. Behind the *palazzo*, in what was once the Jewish quarter, the **Synagogue**, at Via Ascoli 19 (Tues & Thurs 5–7pm, also second Sun of month 10am–1pm; free), is also of Neoclassical design; the serene interior resembles those in Venice's Ghetto.

Probably the strangest sight in Gorizia is the crypt in the Franciscan monastery at **Castagnavizza** – Kostanjevica, rather, for the **monastery** (Mon–Sat 9am–noon & 3–5pm, Sun 3–5pm) lies across the border in Slovenian Nova Gorica. This is the burial place of the last of the French Bourbons, Charles X. After being ousted by the bloodless revolution of July 1830, the Bourbons were exiled from France, the family eventually arriving in Gorizia in 1836, where the Habsburgs allowed them to stay, though Charles died of cholera just seventeen days after his arrival. The Bourbon Institute has asked for the return to France of the family but both the monks and the Slovenian government have refused, asserting that the royal relics now form part of Slovenia's history. The monastery was also home to Brother Stanislav Skrabec (1844–1918), an important Slovene linguist, and the library of 11,000 books (open to large groups by appointment only; ☎386.5330.7750) includes a rare copy of the first Slovene grammar book, inscribed by its author, Adam Bohoric (1584). The easiest way **to get there** is to cross the border on Via San Gabriele, in the northeast part of town (take your

FRIULI-VENEZIA GIULIA | Gorizia and around

passport as there's usually someone checking), cross the railway line and follow the signs uphill – it's about a ten-minute walk from the border. Once there, ring the bell; there's no charge, but a donation of €1.50 is expected.

Practicalities

Gorizia's **tourist office** is at Corso Italia 9 (daily 9.30am–6.30pm; ℡0481.535.764, ⓦwww.turismo.fvg.it). For **accommodation**, try the excellent and welcoming one-star *Sandro*, at Via S. Chiara 18 (℡0481.533.223; ❷, including breakfast), not far from the central Piazza della Vittoria. If that's full, the comfortable but more expensive *Alla Transalpina*, at Via Caprin 30 (℡0481.530.291, ⓦwww.hotel-transalpina.com; ❷, breakfast included), is newly restructured; the restaurant is overpriced, and it's a good 2km northeast of the centre, right on the Slovene border, but bus #1 runs every fifteen minutes from the train station through town, terminating opposite the hotel.

Gorizia is better served by **places to eat**. The *Osteria Panesale*, Corso Verdi 11 (closed Mon), on the way into the old ghetto, serves good local food in simple surroundings, as does *Alle Lune*, Via Oberdan 13 (closed Sun eve & Mon). But the best option in town is the excellent *Ai Tre Soldi Goriziana* (closed Sun eve & Mon), up an alley off Corso Italia 38. It has a lovely garden-eating area in summer and serves up a wide range of beautifully cooked Friulian specialities and local wines – try the *menù degustazione* for €22.

The war cemeteries

Three sobering reminders of Friuli-Venezia Giulia's violent past stand close to Gorizia. Three kilometres north of the town, across the River Isonzo, is the **Sacrario di Oslavia cemetery** (Tues–Sun 8.30am–noon & 1.30–5pm; free), built in 1938 and containing the remains of around sixty thousand soldiers from World War I. To get here take bus #2 or #4 to the first stop after the river, then follow Via Bella Veduta north – it's about a ten-minute walk.

Twelve kilometres southwest of Gorizia, and accessible by train to its eponymous station, the **cemetery at Redipuglia** (daily dawn–dusk; free) is Italy's largest war memorial. A massive example of Fascist architecture, inaugurated in the same year as its counterpart in Oslavia, it holds the bones of 100,000 dead, some 60,000 of whom are unidentified. A monumental set of steps leads up to a chapel, surmounted by three bronze crosses, from where there are panoramic views of the Carso – scene of so much fighting – while a small **museum** displays relics and documents related to the conflict (April–Sept Tues–Sun 8.30am–noon & 1.30–5pm; Oct–March Tues–Sat same hours; free). One kilometre west of Redipuglia lies another cemetery (winter 9.30am–12.30pm & 3.30–6.30pm; summer 9.30am–12.30pm & 3.30–7pm; free), this one for 15,000 troops of the Austro-Hungarian armies who died in the area.

Udine and around

It is fitting that the best artworks in **UDINE**, 71km northwest of Trieste, are by Giambattista Tiepolo: his airy brilliance suits this town. Running beside and beneath the streets are little canals called *roggie*, diverted from the Torre and Cormor rivers, and these bright streams reflect light onto the walls and through the roadside greenery. Comfortable and bourgeois, Udine is the second city of Friuli-Venezia Giulia, and some say that although it has less than half the

△ Cavour Street, Udine

population of Trieste, it will gain the ascendancy sooner or later. Despite the rather sullen suburbs, it's certainly an attractive spot with fine churches, galleries and well-preserved historic buildings around Piazza della Libertà.

Some history

Along with Cividale (see p.432), Tricesimo and Zuglio, Udine was one of the frontier bastions of Imperial Rome, and by the sixth century AD it was far more than a garrison colony. Legend has it that the castle-topped hill at the heart of Udine was built by Attila's hordes, using their helmets as buckets, so that their leader could relish the spectacle of Aquileia in flames, 36km away. But it was not until the thirteenth century that it started to become a regional centre.

Patriarch Bertoldo di Andechs (1218–51) can be seen as the father of Udine – he established two markets (the old market in Via Mercatovecchio, and the new one in Piazza Matteotti, still a marketplace), moved the patriarchate from Cividale to the castle of Udine, and set up a city council. In 1362 the dukes of Austria acquired the place by treaty, but not for long: Venice, now hungry for territory, captured Udine in 1420, after several assaults and sieges. The city was ruled by Venetian governors for almost 400 years – until 1797, when the Venetian Republic surrendered to Napoleon. Even now, the old aristocracy of Udine speak a version of Venetian dialect, while the humbler Udinese, many of whom have migrated from the countryside, speak *friulano*.

Arrival, information and accommodation

Udine's **train** and **bus stations** are close together in the south of the town, on Viale Europa Unità; Via Roma and its continuation Via Dante Alighieri lead from the train station into the centre. The **tourist office**, at Piazza I (primo) Maggio 7 (Mon–Sat 8.30am–6.30pm, Sun 10am–4pm; ☎0432.295.972, ⓦwww.comune.udine.it), sells the **Card Udine Museale** (€6), which allows discounted entry to at least five civic museums and exhibitions. **Internet** access can be found in the centre of town, at *Internetplay*, Via San Francesco 33 (closed daily 12.45–3.30pm), near the duomo.

Hotel options are surprisingly limited, but some attractive new options have sprung up in recent years near the centre.

Al Cappello Via Sarpi 5 at ☎0432.299.327, ⓦwww.osteriaalcappello.it. This traditional welcoming *osteria* also offers a small *locanda* with a few rooms. Very central, with popular Piazza Matteotti just around the corner. ❷

Allegria Vicolo Chiuso 1 ☎0432.201.116, ⓦwww.hotelallegria.it. On a quiet pedestrianized street just a block from the city centre, this is the best of the city's newest hotels. Everything is stylish and state-of-the-art, including a car elevator to the underground garage, in a carefully restored medieval building. ❺, including breakfast.

Astoria Piazza XX Settembre 24 ☎0432.505.091, ⓦwww.hotelastoria.udine.it. This plush and very central modern choice has everything you'd expect from a four-star, and weekend offers see rates fall by almost half. ❼, breakfast included.

Principe Viale Europa Unità 51 ☎0432.506.000, ⓦwww.principe-hotel.it. Directly across from the train station and just next door to the bus terminal, this modern and efficient choice is set back in its own courtyard to ensure quiet. Free parking, choice of non-smoking rooms. ❸, including breakfast.

The City

The place to start any exploration of Udine is at the foot of the hill, in the **Piazza della Libertà**, a square whose architectural ensemble is matched by few cities in Italy. The fifteenth-century **Palazzo del Comune** is a clear homage to the Palazzo Ducale in Venice, and the clock-tower facing the *palazzo*, built in 1527, similarly has a Venetian model – the lion on the facade and the bronze Moors who strike the hours on top of the tower are explicit references to the Torre dell'Orologio in Piazza San Marco. The statue at the north end of the square is a bad allegory called *Peace*, donated to the town by Emperor Franz I to commemorate the Habsburg acquisition of Udine.

To walk up to the **castello**, go through the **Arco Bollani**, designed by Palladio, and onwards up the graceful Venetian Gothic gallery, the **Loggia del Lippomano** on the right. The sixteenth-century *castello*, decorated by local artists and once the seat of the Friulian parliament, now houses an excellent **Galleria d'Arte Antica** (Tues–Sat 9.30am–12.30pm & 3–6pm, Sun 9.30am–12.30pm; €2.60, free Sun), containing works by Carpaccio, Bronzino and Tiepolo, as well as an indifferent Caravaggio and an interesting historical painting by Palma Il Giovanni showing St Mark putting the city under the patronage of St Hermagora, first bishop of Aquileia; Piazza della Libertà is clearly visible on the right. The best-known painting in its collection is Tiepolo's *Consilium in Arena*, showing a meeting of the Order of the Knights of Malta, said to be a faithful rendering, amazingly painted entirely on the basis of written accounts given to the artist.

North from the Piazza della Libertà is **Via Mercatovecchio**, once the mercantile heart of the city and now the town's busiest shopping street. The little chapel of **Santa Maria**, incorporated into the Palazzo del Monte di Pietà in Via Mercatovecchio, is a beauty: viewed through the glass booth from the street, the interior, with its cloudy Baroque frescoes by Giulio Quaglio (1694), has a pristine, subaqueous appearance.

Due west lies the **Piazza** Matteotti, with galleries on three sides and the fine Baroque facade of San Giacomo on the fourth. The square's importance as the centre of public life in Udine is proved by the outside altar on the first-floor balcony of **San Giacomo**; mass was celebrated here on Saturdays so that selling and buying could go on uninterrupted in the market below. As well as being the town's main market, this was the setting for tournaments, plays and carnivals, and still sees summer festivals today. The fountain in the middle of the square was designed in 1543 by Giovanni da Udine, a pupil of Raphael, who also had a hand in building the castle.

Off the south side of Piazza della Libertà is the **Duomo** (daily 7am–noon & 4–8pm; free), a Romanesque construction that was given a Baroque refit in the eighteenth century. Altarpieces and frescoes by Giambattista Tiepolo are the main attraction – they decorate the first two chapels on the right and the chapel of the Sacrament, a little way beyond. A series of frescoes painted by Tiepolo in collaboration with his son, Giandomenico, can be seen in the tiny **Oratorio della Purità** opposite – ask the sacristan in the Duomo to show you.

But Udine's outstanding works of art are the Giambattista Tiepolo frescoes in the nearby **Gallerie del Tiepolo** in the beautifully furnished **Palazzo Arcivescovile** (Wed–Sun 10am–noon & 3.30–6.30pm; €5, including Museo Diocesano – see below). Painted in the late 1720s, these luminous and consummately theatrical scenes add up to a sort of Rococo epic of the Old Testament. *Fall of the Rebel Angels* is the first work you see as you climb the staircase, while the finest room, the Gallery, is at the top, immediately on your right. Every surface is painted with either trompe-l'oeil architectural details or scenes from the story of Abraham, Isaac and Jacob. To the left is a sequence of rooms decorated in rich colours: watch for Tiepolo's *Judgement of Solomon* in the Red Room, and Bambini's wonderful *Triumph of Wisdom* in the serene Delfino library. Also inside the Palazzo Arcivescovile and arranged around the Tiepolo galleries is the **Museo Diocesano**, with an assortment of sculpture and funerary monuments, as well as an exhibition of naive art – popular sculptures from Friuli's churches spanning the Gothic, Renaissance and Baroque periods.

The new **Galleria d'Arte Moderna**, Piazzale Paolo Diacono 22 (Tues–Sat 9.30am–12.30pm & 3–6pm, Sun 9.30am–12.30pm; €2.60) aims to give an overview of Italian art in the twentieth century, with a few foreign greats thrown in for good measure. Works include those by Martini, Guttuso, Fontana and de Kooning.

Eating, drinking and entertainment

Udine's thriving café society means there are scores of **cafés** and **bars** to choose from. The town can also boast dozens of **restaurants**, many of the most appealing clustered in the southwest corner of the old town. Most menus display a decidedly Central European bent.

In summer there's a busy programme of **cultural events** – theatre, outdoor cinema, music, dance – in and around the town: ask the tourist office for the fortnightly listings of events. Throughout the year the Ferroviario arts cinema at Via Cernaia 2 is always worth checking out for films in their original language.

Cafés and bars

Birrificio Udinese Via Caccia 5, at the top of Via Gemona and across Piazzale Osoppo. This microbrewery features regional beers – all organic – and frequent live music. Tuesday is jazz night.

Bistrot Piazza Matteotti 18. One of the hottest spots in this very happening square, at the centre of the city's nightlife.

Caffè Caucigh Via Gemona 36. A comfy Irish pub enlivened with occasional live music, usually on Fridays.

Caffè Contarena Via Cavour 1. Located next to the *palazzo* in Piazza Libertà, a visit here is a classy way to start the day, with coffee and a light breakfast.

M. de Luisa Via Roma 46. Just across from the train station, this little *pasticceria* has been turning out delicious regional treats, such as marbleized *gubana* cake, for three generations.

Osteria Al Cappello Via Sarpi 5. A lively spot featuring rustic regional cookery in a rousing atmosphere like none other. Just north of Piazza Matteotti.

Piccolo Bar Via Rialto 2. This stylish option, on Piazza della Libertà, is an intimate wine bar just right for starting the evening off.

Restaurants

Al Vecchio Stallo Via Viola 7. Just west of the centre, near Piazzale XXVI Luglio, this traditional *osteria* features local dishes at reasonable prices in a converted stables. Closed Wed.

Alla Tavernetta Via Artico di Prampero 2. Centrally located, just south of the Duomo, this cosy, traditional place serves hearty regional dishes, such as barley and bean soup and prosciutto of various kinds. Moderate prices. Closed Sun & Mon.

Pan e Vino e San Daniele Piazza Lionello 12. Just west of Piazza della Libertà, a variety of moderately priced dishes on offer, including, of course, the excellent San Daniele ham. Closed Sun.

Sbarco dei Pirati Via Bartolini 12. Just north of the centre, enjoying a beautiful setting built over a *roggia*, this lively *osteria* offers a welcoming atmosphere and traditional regional fare. Closed Sun.

Spaghetteria da Ciccio Via Grazzano 11, southeast of Piazza della Libertà. Famously vast portions of inexpensive pasta dishes served to an appreciative studenty crowd. Closed Wed.

Trattoria alla Ghiacciaia Via Zanon 13b. Cosy little place serving good-value dishes with an attractive canal-side garden. Closed Mon.

Cividale del Friuli

Lying only 17km east of Udine and connected to it by train and bus, **CIVIDALE DEL FRIULI** is a gem of a town, much prized by the Friulani but pretty well unknown to outsiders. It was founded in 50 BC by Julius Caesar where the Natisone Valley opens into the plain, and in the sixth century AD became the capital of the first Lombard duchy. In the eighth century the Patriarch of Aquileia moved here, inaugurating Cividale's most prosperous period.

The Town

The old town lies between the rail and coach stations and the Natisone, and the visitor need never cross the river, though a walk over the Ponte del Diavolo (Devil's Bridge, see opposite) is *de rigueur*. Just strolling around the town, within the oval ring bisected by Via Carlo Alberto and Corso Mazzini, is a pleasure; the pace of life is provincially serene, and there are some remarkable tourist sights, too. Cividale has been the main market town in the Natisone Valley for two hundred years, and today you hear Italian, *friulano* and Slovene dialects spoken in the street.

The tiny **Tempietto Longobardo** (Oct–March Mon–Sat 9.30am–12.30pm & 3–5pm, Sun 9.30am–12.30pm & 2.30–6pm; April–Sept Mon–Sat 9.30am–12.30pm & 3–6.30pm, Sun 9.30am–1pm & 3–7.30pm; €2), poised above the Natisone off Piazza San Biagio, is a uniquely fine example of Lombard art. Constructed in the ninth century, largely from older fragments, much of the elaborate stuccowork inside the chapel was reduced to rubble in the terrible earthquake of 1222. The delicate interior preserves faded frescoes and carved stalls from its use as a convent chapel in the late fourteenth century, but the eye is drawn to the east wall where an exquisite stucco arch is flanked by six female figures. Whether they represent saints, queens or nuns is uncertain, but the luminous, smiling statues are among the most splendid surviving works of art from the ninth century.

Two other beautiful Lombard pieces are in the **Museo Cristiano** (Mon 9am–2pm, Tues–Sun 8.30am–7.30pm; €2, including the Museo Archeologico, see below), housed in the precincts of the fifteenth-century Duomo. The Altar of Ratchis was carved for Ratchis, Duke of Cividale and King of the Lombards at Pavia, who died as a Benedictine monk at Montecassino in 759; the reliefs of Christ in Triumph and the Adoration of the Magi are delicate and haunting. The other highlight is the Baptistry of Callisto, named after Callisto de Treviso, the first Patriarch of Aquileia to move to Cividale. He lived here from 730 to 756 and initiated the building of the patriarchal palace, the cathedral and this octagonal baptistry, which used to stand beside the cathedral. It's constructed from older Lombard fragments, the columns and capitals dating from the fifth century.

The **Duomo** itself (Mon 9am–2pm, Tues–Sun 8.30am–7.30pm) houses a twelfth-century masterpiece of silversmithery: the *pala* (altarpiece) named after Pellegrino II, the patriarch who commissioned and donated it to the town; it depicts the Virgin seated between the archangels Michael and Gabriel, who are flanked by 25 saints and framed by more saints, prophets and the patron himself. Also in Piazza del Duomo is the **Museo Archeologico** (same hours and ticket as the Museo Cristiano, see above), which houses an excellent exhibition on the Lombards on the first floor, incorporating local finds including some beautiful gold brooches. On the ground floor is a hotchpotch of late Roman and early Christian pieces, the highlight being a second-century mosaic of a wild-eyed head identified as Neptune.

East of the piazza, on Via Monastero Maggiore, is a cellar-like cavern called the **Ipogeo Celtico** (Oct–March Mon–Sat 9.30am–12.30pm & 3–7pm, Sun 9.30am–12.30pm & 2.30–6pm; April–Sept Mon–Sat 9.30am–12.30pm & 3–6.30pm, Sun 9am–1pm & 3–6.30pm; key from the bar *All'Ipogeo* next door; donation requested). The hypogeum was probably used as a tomb for Celtic leaders between the fifth and second centuries BC, but there is still some dispute as to whether it's artificial or was merely adapted by its users. Either way, the spectral faces carved on the walls make it a most unsettling place.

Just beyond the Ipogeo, and spanning the Natisone, the **Ponte del Diavolo** (Devil's Bridge) is a reconstruction of the original fifteenth-century structure that was destroyed during World War I. Of many legends concerning the bridge's demonic name, a favourite involves the devil agreeing to aid the speedy construction of the bridge in return for the soul of the first living thing to cross it – Cividale's wily inhabitants sent an unfortunate dog.

Practicalities

The **tourist office**, five minute's walk northwest of Piazza Duomo at Piazza Diacono 10 (Mon & Fri 9.30am–12.30pm & 4–7pm, Tues & Thurs

9.30am–12.30pm, Sat & Sun 10am–12.30pm & 4–7pm; ☎0432.710.422, ⓦwww.cividale.net), has details on Mittelfest, an annual summer celebration of Central European culture with concerts, theatre and dance. Most visitors are day-trippers from Udine, but for an overnight stay head for the beautiful and comfortable ⟁ *Locanda al Castello*,Via del Castello 12 (☎0432.733.242, ⓦwww .alcastello.net; ❺, including breakfast), 1km southwest of town, on a hill above the road to Tarcento and Faedis. The restaurant too is recommended, especially on a sunny day when its terrace is the best place for a leisurely lunch.

The town's smartest **café** is the *San Marco*, Via Gemona 31, opposite the duomo in the loggia of the sixteenth-century town hall. Good though pricey **restaurants** include *Zorutti*, Via Borgo di Ponte 7 (closed Mon), situated just across the Natisone by the Ponte del Diavolo; and *Alla Frasca*, Stretta de Rubeis 8 (closed Mon), one block west from Piazza Duomo and boasting a vast array of truffle and mushroom dishes. A favourite with discerning locals is the excellent *Trattorie Dominissini*, at Stretta Stellini 18 (closed Mon) – take a right just short of the Ponte del Diavolo.

Codroipo and Pordenone

Heading west through **Codroipo** to **Pordenone**, a workaday provincial capital best known for its favourite son, the architect of the same name, you might think there's little reason to get off the train, particularly with the attractions of the Veneto waiting just a few minutes away. But the frequency of trains – they run hourly from Udine to Venice – means that it's possible to hop on and off, and in the pleasantly low-key towns you'll have most of the sites to yourself.

Codroipo

CODROIPO is a peaceful little town on the main railway line, midway between Udine and Pordenone, that would have nothing to recommend it were the huge **Villa Manin** not just 3km to the southeast, where it completely dominates the little village of Passariano. As the only public transport to the villa from Codroipo consists of three daily buses, the best way to get here is to walk: straight ahead from the station, and bear left in the main square.

Friuli's best-known country house, the Villa Manin was built in 1738 and later enlarged for Lodovico Manin, the pitiful last doge of Venice. In 1797 Napoleon stayed here when he signed the Treaty of Campoformio, which gave Venice to Austria. The greater part of the interior, much of it coated in run-of-the-mill frescoes, is impressive solely for its size; the arena created by its great frontal galleries, frequently compared to St Peter's Square in Rome, is used for open-air concerts. The villa is now a centre for contemporary art, with three or more special exhibitions annually, as well as occasional concerts (Tues–Fri 9.30am–12.30pm & 2.30–6pm, Sat & Sun 10am–6.30pm; free; ☎0432.906.509, ⓦwww .villamanincontemporanea.it). The accompanying **sculpture park** offers a taste of some of the bigger names in contemporary Italian art like Patrick Tuttofuocco and Paola Pivi (Easter–Oct Tues–Fri 9.30am–6pm, Sat & Sun 10am–6.30pm; free), as well as being an attractive place for an afternoon doze.

Pordenone

The westernmost of Friuli-Venezia Giulia's three large towns, **PORDENONE** was once a thriving river port, but is now the region's main manufacturing centre, specializing in light industries, especially textiles and ceramics. As such, the town is hardly set up for tourism, with few specific sights, but the historic centre is carefully preserved and worth a visit. From the train station go straight ahead along Via Mazzini, then take the third right down arcaded and shop-filled **Corso Vittorio Emanuele** to the Gothic-Renaissance **Palazzo Comunale**.

Over the road is the **Museo Civico d'Arte** in Palazzo Ricchieri, Corso Vittorio Emanuele II 51 (Tues–Sat 3–7pm, Sun 10am–1pm & 3–7pm; Ⓦ http://museoarte.comune.pordenone.it; €1); it's predominantly a second-string collection of Venetian art, but it does have a clutch of works by the finest local artist, Giovanni Antonio de' Sacchis, better known simply as Il Pordenone. Many of the paintings in the museum were removed from the Duomo after the 1976 earthquake. The **Duomo** itself (daily 7am–noon & 4–7pm), mainly a late-Gothic structure, is notable only for its Romanesque campanile and some works by Pordenone – the first altarpiece on the right, and the two (not three, whatever the sign may say) least damaged frescoes belonging to the right-hand pillar at the end of the nave.

If you want to see more of Pordenone's work in his home town, search out the parish churches of Roraigrande, Torre, Villanova and Vallenoncello – for information about access, ask at the helpful **tourist office**, Via Damiani 2c (Mon–Fri: May–Sept 9am–1pm & 3–6pm; Oct–April 9am–1pm & 3–5pm; ℡ 0434.520.381, Ⓦ www.pordenone-turismo.com). The town's **hotels** tend to be business-oriented with no special charms. You might try the swish *Hotel Moderno*, Viale Martelli 1, a triumphant piece of Fascist-era architecture (℡ 0434.28.215, Ⓦ www.eahotels.it; ❹), or the nearby *Minerva*, Piazza XX Settembre 5 (℡ 0434.26.066, Ⓦ www.hotelminerva.it; ❺, breakfast included), smart enough, if not exactly cosy.

The choices for **eating** are better: *La Vecia Osteria del Moro,* Via Castello 2 (℡ 0434.28.658; closed Sun) is an expensive and beautiful old restaurant on a side street a step away from the Palazzo Comunale where you can eat superbly for around €45 a head. For budget meals, *Da Zelina* (closed Mon), just behind the Palazzo, serves good pizza and more.

Gemona and the Carnia

The peak district in the north of Friuli is known as the **Carnia**, a name given to it by the Celtic tribes who settled here in the fourth century BC. If you're approaching the area by road or rail from Udine, you could make a stop at **GEMONA** (tourist information ℡ 0432.981.441), a little town that was largely destroyed in the 1976 earthquake, when almost 1000 people were killed and around 15,000 houses destroyed. The historic centre, on the steep-sided hilltop, has been devotedly reconstructed and feels disconcertingly like a film set. The cathedral, once a marvellous Romanesque-Gothic specimen, is notable for the enormous fourteenth-century statue of St Christopher on the facade.

Gemona is a good staging post on the way into the Carnia, with a couple of fine and inexpensive **hotels**. The better one is the *Agli Amici*, a couple of kilometres out of the centre at Via Godo 160 (℡ 0432.981.013; ❷) – turn right outside the station then head along Via Piovega, following the yellow signs; the alternative is the *Si-Si*, Via Piovega 15 (℡ 0432.981.158, Ⓦ www.hotelsisi.it; ❷). There's an excellent **trattoria** at the *Agli Amici*, while *Al Falomo*, Via Cavour 17 (closed Wed), on the main street just down from the Duomo, has pizzas and an inexpensive tourist menu.

The Carnia proper begins north of Gemona, around the headwaters of the River Tagliamento, and comprises two distinct areas. To the west, hay meadows and orchards give way to the Alpine uplands and pastures of the **Alpi Carniche**, which share the culture of the eastern Dolomites. To the east, the high, sheer and often barren limestone peaks of the **Alpi Giulie** are divided by deep, forested valleys that radiate towards the borders with Austria in the north and Slovenia in the east. Both of these ranges are hardly known even within Italy, yet the area has a lot to offer the hiker and climber. Linguists should get a kick out of it too, as the villagers speak strange variants of *friulano*, German and Slovene.

If you want to plan a Carnia **walking trip** in advance, call in at the Udine office of the *Società Alpina Friulana*, Via Odorico da Pordenone 3 (Mon–Fri 5–7.30pm plus Thurs 9–10.30pm; ☎0432.504.290, Ⓦwww.scuolecaifvg.spin .it). A useful website on Carnia is Ⓦwww.carnia.it.

Western Carnia

The lush valleys and flower-filled meadows of the **western Carnia** attract hundreds of **walkers** from June to September, when the numerous *rifugi* are open for business. One of the best bases for the northern part of this region is the village of **ARTA TERME**, about 35km north of Gemona – there are buses direct from Udine and services from Gemona, changing at Tolmezzo. There's cheap **accommodation** at the central *Miramonti* at Via Umberto I 22 (☎0433.92.076, Ⓦwww.albergo-miramonti.it; ❷, breakfast included) and *Comune Rustico* at Via Fontana 14 (☎0433.92.218; ❶, breakfast included), with slightly dearer rooms at the *Grand Hotel Gortani* at Via Umberto I 43 (☎0433.928.754, Ⓦwww.gortani.it; ❹, half board required). At **PIANO D'ARTA**, 1km away, you'll find another option – *Pensione Cozzi* at Via Marconi 13–15 (☎0433.92.039, Ⓕ0433.928.957; ❶). The **tourist office**, Via Umberto I 15 (May–Sept Mon–Sat 9am–noon & 4–7pm, Sun 9am–1pm; Oct–April Mon–Sat 9am–noon & 3–6pm, Sun 9am–1pm; ☎0433.929.290), has masses of information on the beautifully secluded local refuges and on the fourteen waymarked Club Alpino walks in the surrounding highlands. If these **treks** sound too energetic, you could always just spend €4.65 on a visit to the **thermal pool** of the pagoda-style spa complex close to the tourist office.

Between **Tolmezzo**, where you're likely to have to change buses, and **FORNI DI SOPRA** is a thickly wooded area. After the rural peasantry moved out to the cities and the trees moved in, the area was designated the **Parco Naturale Dolomite Friulane**. The Forni **tourist office**, at Via Cadore 1 (summer 9am–noon & 4–7pm; winter 9am–noon & 3.30–6pm; ☎0433.88.553, Ⓦwww.fornidisopra.org), has lots of information on activities such as mountain biking, horse-riding and **hikes**. They can also help with *rifugi*, as well as provide lists of **accommodation** in town. The cluster of villages that comprises Forni lies about 70km northwest of Gemona, at the foot of the Passo di Mauria, the mountain pass between the Carnia and the eastern Dolomites. It really feels like the end of the road; seven buses arrive here direct from Udine every day but the services onwards are sporadic. In Forni itself, the *Albergo Centrale*, Piazza del Comune 9 (☎0433.88.062, Ⓔcentraleforni @libero.it; closed Oct & Nov; ❸, half board required, minimum three nights) is a good choice. The only **campsite** hereabouts is the *Tornerai* (☎0433.88.035, Ⓔtornerai@tiscali.it), 2km away in **STINSANS**.

The Forni region is celebrated for its **food**, with many of its dishes incorporating some of the wild plants found in the vicinity. The mountain refuges are excellent places to sample these local specialities. Especially good is the nearby and spectacularly sited *Varmost* (June–Sept), on the slopes of Monte Crusicalas – there's a cable car in operation (July–Aug & Dec–March; €7 return ticket). In Forni itself, the **places to eat** are *Varmost* (closed Wed), with polenta and *frico* (a cheese and potato dish) or hearty sausages and goulash to eat in or take away, or the *Bar Pizzeria Alle Alpi* (no regular closing day); both are on the main road through town, Via Nazionale. Forni also has a branch of the *Club Alpino Italiano* at Via Vittorio Veneto 9, on the square behind the bus stop (July & Aug daily 5–7pm; Sept–June Fri, Sat & Sun 5–7pm), which organizes walks of varying degrees of difficulty.

Eastern Carnia

The place to head for in the **eastern Carnia** is **TARVISIO**, a small mountain resort 65km northeast of Gemona and just 6km from the Austrian border. Four **buses** a day come here from Udine, and eleven **trains** (some services involving a transfer to bus).

The town receives a steady flow of Austrian visitors who pour in for the cheap Italian booze, the strange mix of *bierkeller* and café nightlife, and the first-rate ski slopes. More robust types set off from here on the Carnia's one high-level **long-distance trail**, the *Traversata Carnica*, which runs all the way to Sesto, just below the border. Information on this and all other healthy Tarvisio pursuits is available from the extremely helpful **tourist office** at Via Roma 10 (Mon–Sat 9am–12.30pm & 3.30–7pm, Sun 10am–12.30pm & 4–7pm; ℡0428.2135, ⓦ www.tarvisiano.org) – ask about the detailed leaflets in English on local walks. The nicest place **to stay** in Tarvisio is the *Albergo Valle Verde*, just outside the village at Via Priesnig 12 (℡0428.2342, ⓦ www.hotelvalleverde.com; ❸, breakfast included) – it has a wonderful **restaurant** too, serving local specialities. There are a couple of cheaper but decent places in Tarvisio itself: the *Al Cacciatore* at Via Dante 9 (℡0428.2082; ❶) and *Al Mangart* at Via Vittorio Veneto 39 (℡0428.2246; closed Feb; ❶); both have popular restaurants too.

For a taste of the splendours of the **Parco Regionale delle Alpi Giulie**, you could hop onto one of the summer buses to the **Laghi di Fusine** – two peaceful, wooded, blue-green lakes within 9km of Tarvisio. The smaller of the pair, and the nearer to Tarvisio, is **Lago Inferiore**, where there's **accommodation** at the *Capanna Edelweiss* (℡0428.61.050; ⓦ www.albergo-edelweiss.com; ❷). However, the best walks are from **Lago Superiore**, a short distance up the road, from where there's a marked five-hour circular trail via the *Rifugio Zacchi* (℡0428.61.195; June–Sept).

Travel details

Trains

Trieste to: Gorizia (up to 27 daily; 45min); Redipuglia (up to 5 daily; 40min); Udine (up to 26 daily; 1hr 20min); Venice (up to 17 daily; 1hr 40min).
Udine to: Cividale (hourly; 20min); Conegliano (up to 38 daily; 1hr 15min); Gemona (14 daily; 30min); Gorizia (up to 30 daily; 30min); Pordenone (up to 37 daily; 30min); Redipuglia (up to 8 daily; 50min); Tarvisio (up to 16 daily, many including transfer to bus at Carnia; 2hr); Trieste (up to 33 daily; 1hr 30min); Venice (hourly; 1hr 45min–2hr 15min).

Buses

Gemona to: Tolmezzo (3 daily; 30min).
Gorizia to: Cividale (4 daily; 1hr).
Grado to: Gorizia (up to 22 daily; 1hr 20min).
Tolmezzo to: Arta Terme (10 daily; 20min); Forni di Sopra (7 daily; 1hr 20min).

Trieste to: Duino (hourly; 30min–1hr); Grado (14 daily; 1hr–1hr 30min); Monfalcone (for Aquileia and Grado; hourly; 45 min); Tolmezzo (1 daily; 3hr); Udine (27 daily; 1hr 15min).

Udine to: Aquileia (16 daily; 40min); Arta Terme (10 daily; 1hr); Cividale (at least 21 daily; 20min); Codroipo (hourly; 20min); Forni di Sopra (7 daily; 2hr); Gemona (6 daily; 50min); Grado (12 daily; 1hr); Pordenone (hourly; 40min); Tarvisio (4 daily; 2hr 20min); Tolmezzo (6 daily; 50min); Trieste (9 daily; 1hr).

Ferries

Trieste to: Barcola (July to mid-Sept hourly; 30min); Duino (July–Sept 3 daily via Grignano and Sistiana; 1hr 45min); Grado (mid-June to Aug 3 daily; 1hr 30min–2hr); Múggia (mid-June to Oct every 90min; 30min); CROATIA: Brioni (June–Sept Tues–Sun; 4hr); Rovigno (June–Sept Tues–Sun; 3hr 10min); SLOVENIA: Pirano (Wed, Fri & Sun; 1 daily; 1hr 50min).

Emilia-Romagna

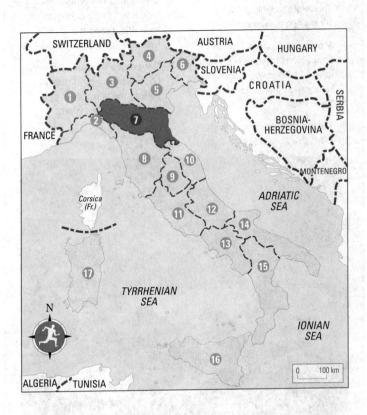

CHAPTER 7   # Highlights

* **Bologna food market** In the gastronomic capital of Italy everything begins at the market, a bustling and magical mix of sights and smells. **See p.449**

* **Hot chocolate** On a cold day, there's no better way to warm up than with a mug of fine hot chocolate in Bologna's La Torinese bar. **See p.454**

* **Modena's Duomo** One of the finest Romanesque buildings in Italy, with some magnificent decoration inside and out. **See p.459**

* **Parma and its food** Parma is inextricably linked to two great delicacies, Parma ham and Parmesan cheese, both of which can be sampled in the city or in the surrounding region. **See p.464**

* **Rocca Viscontea** Northern Emilia Romagna's most majestic castle. **See p.470**

* **Brisighella festivals** This medieval village is known for its truffle, polenta and olive festivals in autumn. **See p.472**

* **Ravenna's mosaics** Unrivalled both in beauty and preservation, these mosaics are unmissable. **See p.483**

△ Café culture in Bologna

Emilia-Romagna

S et between Lombardy and Tuscany, and stretching from the Adriatic coast almost to the shores of the Mediterranean, **Emilia-Romagna** is the heartland of northern Italy. Once two provinces – Emilia to the west and the Romagna to the east – they formed the Papal States until joined together after Unification. Before the papacy took charge in the area, it was a patchwork of ducal territories, ruled over by a handful of families – the Este in Ferrara and Modena, the Farnese in Parma, and lesser dynasties in Ravenna and Rimini – who created sparkling Renaissance courts, combining autocracy with patronage of the arts alongside a continual jockeying for power with the Church. Their castles and fortresses remain, preserved in small villages and towns with restored medieval centres which, apart from a few notable exceptions, are relatively off the tourist track, since many visitors are put off by the extreme weather (searingly hot in summer, close to freezing in winter), or are sidetracked by the more immediate pleasures of Tuscany and Umbria.

The region's **landscape** is a varied one, ranging from the foothills of the Apennine mountains in the south to the flat fields of the northern plain, the Pianura Padana, interrupted only by windbreaks of poplars, shimmering in the breeze. The area has grown wheat since Roman times, and nowadays its industry and agribusinesses are among Italy's most advanced and Emilia-Romagna is one of the richest regions in the country.

Carving a dead-straight route through the heart of Emilia-Romagna, from Piacenza to Rimini on the coast, the **Via Emilia** (or more prosaically the A1 and A14 roads) is a central and obvious reference point, a Roman military road constructed in 187 BC that was part of the medieval pilgrim's route to Rome, and the way east to Ravenna and Venice. The towns that grew up along here are among Emilia's most compelling. **Bologna**, the region's capital, is one of Italy's largest cities and a place that, despite having one of the most beautifully preserved city centres in the country and some of its finest food, has been relatively neglected by tourists – a pity as it makes a great base for regional exploration and is a destination in its own right.

Easily accessible from Bologna are places like **Modena** and **Parma** (each just an hour or so away by train), wealthy provincial towns that form the smug core of Emilia and hold some of its finest and most atmospheric architecture, as well as giving access to routes south into the **Apennines**. With a car you can dip into the foothills at will from any of these points, sampling local cuisine and joining in the festivals; and even by bus it's possible to get a taste of this beautiful area, far removed from the functional plain to the north. If you're a keen hiker, you might be tempted by the Grand Escursione Apenninica, a 25-day-long trek

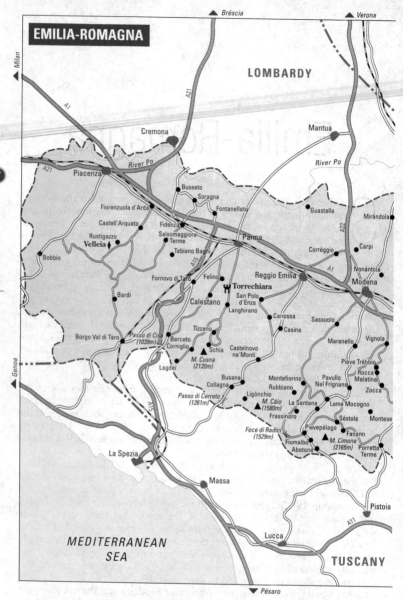

EMILIA-ROMAGNA

LOMBARDY

Bréscia
Verona
Milan
Cremona
Mantua
River Po
River Po
Piacenza
Busseto
Soragna
Fontanellato
Guastalla
Mirándola
Fiorenzuola d'Arda
Castell'Arquato
Fidenza
Salsomaggiore
Terme
Parma
Corréggio
Carpi
Rustigazzo
Velleia
Tabiano Bagni
Nonántola
Bobbio
Fornovo di Taro
Felino
Reggio Emilia
Modena
Torrechiara
Bardi
San Polo
d'Enza
Calestano
Langhirano
Canossa
Sassuolo
Borgo Val di Taro
Tizzano
Casina
Maranello
Vignola
Passo di Cisa
(1039m)
Berceto
Corniglio
Schia
Castelnovo
ne'Monti
Pieve Trébbio
Rocca
Malatina
Lagdei
M. Cusna
(2120m)
Busana
Montefiorino
Pavullo
Nel Frignano
Zocca
Collagna
Rubbiano
Passo di Cerreto
(1261m)
Ligónchio
M. Cáio
(1580m)
La Santana
Lama Mocogno
Frassinoro
Séstola
Montese
Foce di Radici
(1529m)
Pievepélago
Fanano
Fiumalbo
M. Cimone
(2165m)
Porretta
Terme
La Spezia
Abetone
Genoa
Massa
Pistoia
MEDITERRANEAN
SEA
Lucca
Pésaro
TUSCANY

following the backbone of the range from refuge to refuge, and which can be
accessed from the foothills south of **Reggio Emilia**.

The north of Emilia-Romagna is less interesting than the Via Emilia stretch,
the Po disgorging into the Adriatic from its bleak **delta** (which it shares with
the Veneto), a melancholic region of marshland and lagoons that is mainly of
appeal to birdwatchers. However, **Ferrara**, just half an hour north of Bologna,

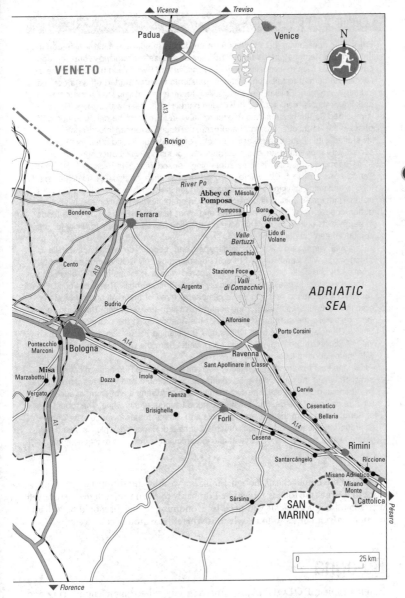

is one of the most important Renaissance centres in Italy, formerly under the tutelage of the Este family; and **Ravenna**, a short way east, preserves probably the finest set of Byzantine mosaics in the world in its churches and mausoleums. The coast south is an overdeveloped ribbon of settlement, although **Rimini**, at its southern end, provides a spark of interest, with its wild seaside strip concealing a surprisingly historic town centre.

Regional food and wine

Emilia-Romagna has a just reputation for producing the richest, most lavish food in Italy, with its famous specialities of **parmesan** cheese (*parmigiano-reggiano*), egg pasta, **Parma ham** (generically known as *prosciutto di Parma*) and balsamic vinegar. Despite its current foodie connotations, **balsamic vinegar** started off as a cottage industry, with many Emilian families distilling and then redistilling local wine to form a dark liquor that is then matured in wooden barrels for at least twelve years. Bologna is regarded as the gastronomic capital of Italy, and Emilia is the only true home of **pasta** in the North: often lovingly handmade, the dough is formed into lasagne, tortellini stuffed with ricotta cheese and spinach, pumpkin or pork, and other fresh pastas served with *ragù* (meat sauce), cream sauces or simply with butter and parmesan – *alla parmigiana* usually denotes something cooked with parmesan. Modena and Parma specialize in *bollito misto* – boiled **meats**, such as flank of beef, trotters, tongue and spicy sausage – while another Modenese dish is *zampone* – stuffed pig's trotter. Romagna's cuisine is more Southern in orientation. While ingredients such as butter, cheese, mushrooms, chestnuts and meat feature in Emilia, Romagna tends more towards onions, garlic and olive oil; the region is second only to Sicily for the amount of **fish** caught in its waters.

Regional **wines** are, like the landscapes and people, quite distinct. Emilia is synonymous with **Lambrusco**, but don't despair: buy only DOC Lambrusco and be amazed by the dark, often blackberry-coloured wine that foams into the glass and cuts through the fattiness of the typically meaty Emilian meal. There are four DOC zones for Lambrusco and you get a glimpse of three of them, all around Modena, from the Via Emilia, each supporting neat rows of high-trellised vines. The fourth zone extends across the plains and foothills of the Apennines, in the province of Reggio Emilia. Other wines to try, both whites, are Trebbianino Val Trebbia and Monterosso Val D'Arda, while the lively Malvasia (also white) from the Colli di Parma goes well with the celebrated local ham.

Heading east towards the Adriatic coast, you come to the Romagna, a flatter, drier province where the wines have less exuberance but more body and are dominated by Albana and Sangiovese. The sweeter versions of **Albana** are often more successful at bringing out the peachy, toasted-almond flavours of this white. The robust red of **Sangiovese**, from the hills around Ímola and Rimini, comes in various "weights" – all around the heavy mark. Much lighter is Cagnina di Romagna, which is best drunk young (within six months of harvest) and is particularly good with roast chestnuts.

None of this comes cheap, though: Emilia is a wealthy area that makes few concessions to tourists; the tone is, rather like Lombardy to the north, well mannered, well dressed and comfortable. If you need to economize, though, it would be a shame to stint when it comes to food, which is where the region excels.

Bologna

Emilia's capital, **BOLOGNA**, is a thriving city, whose light engineering and high-tech industries have brought conspicuous wealth to the old brick palaces and porticoed streets and squares. It's well known for its food – undeniably the richest in the country – and for its politics. "Red Bologna" became the Italian Left's stronghold and spiritual home, having evolved out of the resistance movement to German occupation during World War II. Consequently, Bologna's train station was singled out by Fascist groups in 1980 for a bomb attack in Italy's worst postwar terrorist atrocity. A glassed-in jagged gash in the station

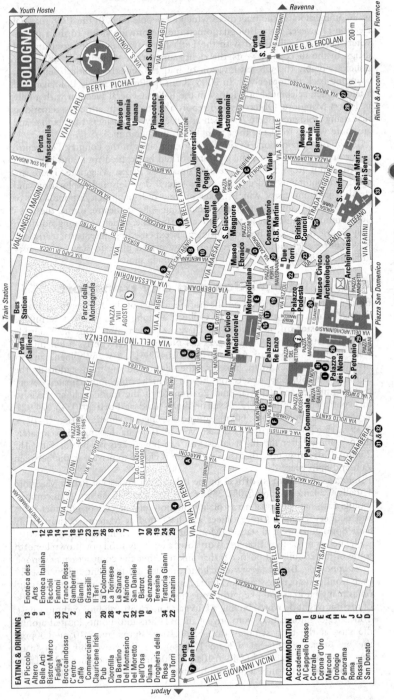

wall commemorates the tragedy in which 84 people died. In the 1998 mayoral elections, however, even Bologna joined the nationwide swing to the right, as voters became disillusioned with the Left's failure to handle rising crime and drugs. In the succeeding years, the right's support for some hugely unpopular policies, notably the US-led invasion of Iraq, has sent the political pendulum swinging back the other way. In 2006, Romano Prodi, a native Bolognan and a left-winger, celebrated his victory in the Italian General Election with a rally in Piazza Maggiore. Observers also report a slight shift in attitudes, remarking that many Bolognese seem less open and friendly to outsiders than before and are more willing to blame their troubles on immigration.

Bologna is certainly one of the best-looking cities in the country. The centre is startlingly medieval in plan, a jumble of red brick, tiled roofs and balconies radiating out from the great central square of Piazza Maggiore. There are enough monuments and curiosities for several days' leisured exploration, and thanks to its university, which makes up one-fifth of the city's population of 500,000, there's always something happening – be it theatre, music, the city's lively summer festival, or just the café and bar scene, which is among northern Italy's most convivial. The only problem is expense; nightlife, particularly, can leave your wallet empty, and finding a low-priced place to stay can be very difficult, especially during one of the major trade shows.

Arrival, information and city transport

Bologna's **train station** lies on the northern edge of the city centre at Piazza delle Medaglie d'Oro, near Porta Galliera; all long-distance buses terminate at the **bus station**, next door on Piazza XX Settembre. Bus #25 outside the train station takes you to Piazza del Nettuno otherwise it's a ten-minute walk. Bologna's **Marconi Airport** (℡051.647.9615, ⓦwww.bologna-airport .it) lies northwest of town, linked to the centre and the train station by the Aerobus (€4.50; buy tickets on board), which runs approximately every twenty minutes and takes around 25 minutes if the traffic is light. Taxis to the centre cost around €17. Ryanair flights land at **Forlí** (℡0543.474.921, ⓦwww.forliairport.com), 60km southeast. Special shuttle buses (E-BUS; ℡199.115.577) are on hand to take you to Bologna, leaving approximately thirty minutes after the flight lands; you can buy tickets on board (€10; 1hr 25min). If **driving**, note that the city centre is closed to private traffic between 7am and 8pm every day.

Bologna's main **tourist office**, in the Palazzo del Podestà at Piazza Maggiore 1 (daily 9.30am–7.30pm; ℡051.239.660 or 051.251.947, ⓦhttp://iat.comune .bologna.it), has the usual array of information, plus details of gourmet tours and cookery courses. Other offices can be found at Marconi Airport (daily 8am–8pm) and the train station (Mon–Sat 9am–7pm, Sun 9am–3pm).

The best way to enjoy Bologna is **on foot**: a leisurely stroll downtown beneath some of the 25 miles of porticoes that link together the compact *centro storico* is most appealing. **Buses** (ⓦwww.atc.bo.it) are fast and frequent; tickets cost €1 each from *tabacchi*, newsstands, ATCittà centres or ticket machines and are valid on as many buses as you like within one hour. If you plan to make frequent use of them it might be worth buying a Citypass for €6.50, valid for eight journeys. You can get information from any of the ATCittà info points located around the city: at the train station (Mon–Sat 6.10am–8pm, Sun 7.10am–8.30pm); the bus station (Mon–Sat 6.20am–1.40pm); Via IV Novembre 16/a (daily 7am–8pm); Via Rizzoli 1d (daily 6.10am–7.50pm) and the corner of Via Lame and Via Marconi (Mon–Sat 5.40am–8.30pm, Sun 7am–8pm). The ATCittà info points also sell tickets for the new open-top, hop-on hop-off Giro Tp Tram-Bus (€10; ☎800.281.281 tollfree, ⓦwww.trambusopen.com) **tour** of the city. There are ten departures daily between 10am and 4pm from Viale Pietramellara in front of the train station.

Accommodation

Bologna's accommodation mostly caters for business travellers, and has with just a few inexpensive **hotels**, and no handily placed campsite. During the trade fair peak (March to early May & Sept–Dec) prices can more than double. Many hotels prefer to take block bookings during these times and making an individual reservation can be tricky. In July and August prices are far lower. The tourist offices have hotel lists, and the Centre for Tourist Services, next to the tourist office desk at Piazza Maggiore 6 (Mon–Sat 10am–2pm & 3–7pm, Sun 10am–2pm; ☎051.648.7607 or 800.856.065 tollfree, ⓦwww.cst.bo.it), can book rooms for you at no charge.

The city's official **youth hostel**, *San Sisto-Due Torri*, is at Via Viadagola 5 and 14 (☎051.501.810, ⓔhostelbologna@hotmail.com), 6km outside the centre of town. To get there take bus #93 from Via Marconi (last service 10.45pm) or #301 from the bus station on Sundays. It opens at 3.30pm and there's a curfew at 11.30pm. Beds are €15.50 per head in a dorm, and there are also double rooms (❶). It's a busy place so book in advance.

Accademia Via Belle Arti 6 ☎051.232.318, ⓦwww.hotelaccademia.it. In the heart of the university quarter, this large two-star hotel has modest-sized doubles (a mixture of private and shared bathrooms), some with balconies. Most rooms have air conditioning; those without are slightly cheaper. ❸

Al Cappello Rosso Via de' Fusari 9 ☎051.261.891, ⓦwww.alcappellorosso.it. Comfy and unfussy furnishings with efficient four-star luxury in one of the city's oldest hotels. It has an atmospheric and central location too. ❻

Centrale Via della Zecca 2 ☎051.225.114, ⓦwww.albergocentralebologna.it. Good-value two-star in the heart of the city. All of the 25 spacious rooms come with bathrooms and a/c, and there are great views from the top floor. ❸

Corona d'Oro Via Oberdan 12 ☎051.236.456, ⓦwww.corona.hotel-bologna.net. Four-star opulence in a recently refurbished *palazzo* close to the twin towers and graced with a lovely wooden portico. ❻

Marconi Via Marconi 18 ☎051.262.832. Although the stairway up to this friendly one-star on the first floor of a modern block is not particularly inviting, the rooms inside are clean and recently refurbished, if basic (some have private bathrooms). It's on a major road, so you might want to ask for a room at the back. No credit cards. ❷

Orologio Via IV Novembre 10 ☎051.231.253, ⓦwww.orologio.hotel-bologna.net. Overlooking a corner of Piazza Maggiore, this is the most appealing of Bologna's hotels, with an air of understated luxury, well-equipped rooms and helpful staff. Free Internet access too. Book well in advance. ❽

Galeazza

Forty minutes by car north of Bologna, near Crevalcore, stands the medieval castle of Galeazza (Via Provanone 8585 ☎051.985.170, ⓦwww.galeazza.com; ❶), that's now best described as a residential cultural centre – the brainchild of a young American, Clark Lawrence. Frescoed rooms can accommodate up to ten guests, everyone pitches in with cleaning and cooking duties, and there's an ongoing cultural programme, known throughout the area, of art exhibitions, classical and jazz concerts and readings, plus impromptu parties and other events that keep the atmosphere lively. With a stimulating mix of Italians and foreigners, it makes an excellent base from which to explore Ferrara, Bologna and Modena, which are all about 40 minutes away.

Panorama Via Livraghi 1 ☏ 051.221.802, ⊚ www
.hotelpanoramabologna.it. Just off Via Ugo Bassi
(no sign), offering a range of accommodation, from
three- and four-bedded rooms to ordinary doubles
– all sharing clean and pleasant bathrooms down
the corridor. Helpful owners. ②
Roma Via D'Azeglio 9 ☏ 051.226.322, ⊚ www
.hotelroma.biz. On one of the centre's major
pedestrian arteries, this place is friendly, quiet
and refined, though the chintzy decor won't be to
everyone's taste. ⑤

Rossini Via Bibiena 11 ☏ 051.237.716,
℻ 051.268.035. In the student quarter, just off
Piazza Verdi, a friendly two-star hotel with comfortable though basic rooms, some with bath. ②
San Donato Via Zamboni 16 ☏ 051.235.395,
⊚ www.hotelsandonato.it. Even though the rooms
don't quite match the elegance of the first-floor
lobby, this is a very comfortable four-star. The
rooms overlooking the square have fabulous views
of the two towers, and there's also a breakfast
terrace. ⑥

❼ The City

Bologna's city centre is compact with most sights within easy reach of the main
ring road. Lined with shops and bars, **Via dell'Indipendenza** runs from the
train station to the centre, finishing up at the linked central squares of **Piazza
Maggiore** and **Piazza del Nettuno**. West of here is the commercial district,
bordered by the office blocks of Via G. Marconi, while to the east lies the
university quarter. The one thing you soon notice is how well preserved the
central area actually is, and what a joy it is to stroll around. The famous medieval, ochre-coloured porticoes, built high enough to accommodate people on
horseback, make a vivid first impression, especially at night, while by day they
provide an unofficial catwalk for Bologna's well-turned-out residents.

Piazza Maggiore, Piazza del Nettuno and around

Piazza Maggiore and the adjacent **Piazza del Nettuno** hold the city's principal secular and religious buildings: the church of San Petronio, Palazzo Re
Enzo and Palazzo Comunale – all impressive for their bulk alone, with heavy
studded doors and walls pitted with holes from the original scaffolding.

At the centre of Piazza del Nettuno, the **Neptune Fountain** is a symbol of the
city, styled in extravagant fashion by Giambologna in the late sixteenth century.
Beside the fountain is a wall lined with photographs of partisans who died in
World War II, near another memorial to those killed in the 1980 train station
bombing. Across the square, the **Palazzo Re Enzo** takes its name from its time
as the prison-home of Enzo, king of Sicily, confined here by papal supporters
for two decades after the Battle of Fossalta in 1249. Next door to the Palazzo
Re Enzo, **Palazzo Podestà** fills the northern side of Piazza Maggiore, built
at the behest of the Bentivoglio clan, who ruled the city during the fifteenth
century, before papal rule was re-established. Both *palazzi* open occasionally for
special exhibitions. On the piazza's western edge, the **Palazzo Comunale** gives
some indication of the political shifts in power, its facade adorned by a huge
statue of Pope Gregory XIII as an affirmation of papal authority. Inside are two
art collections: the **Collezioni Comunali d'Arte** (Tues–Fri 9am–3pm, Sat
& Sun 10am–6.30pm; free), whose galleries of ornate furniture and paintings
include works by Vitale da Bologna, Simone dei Crocifissi and others of the

Bologna museum card

You don't need to do much sightseeing to make the *Carta Bologna dei Musei*
worthwhile: available for either one (€6) or three days (€8), the pass grants free and
reduced access to the city's main sights. You can buy the card at tourist offices,
museums and at Bologna's main train station.

Bolognese School; and the **Museo Morandi** (Tues–Fri 9am–3pm, Sat & Sun 10am–6.30pm; ⓦ www.museomorandi.it; free), devoted to the life and works of one of Italy's most important twentieth-century painters. Two hundred works and a faithful reconstruction of Morandi's studio offer a fascinating glimpse into the artist best known for his Futurist works.

On the southern side of Piazza Maggiore stands the church of **San Petronio** (daily: winter 7.30am–1pm & 2.30–6pm; summer 7.45am–12.30pm & 3.30–6pm), one of the finest Gothic brick buildings in Italy. This enormous structure was originally intended to have been larger than St Peter's in Rome, but money and land for the side aisle were diverted by the pope's man in Bologna towards a new university and plans had to be modified. The end result looks a little strange at first glance, with the beginnings of the planned aisles on both sides of the building clearly visible – when they stopped work they sliced through the window arches and left only the bottom third of the facade decorated with the marble geometric patterns intended to cover the whole. There are models of what the church was supposed to look like in the museum (Mon–Sat 9.30am–12.30pm & 2.30–5.30pm, Sun pm only; free). Notwithstanding its curtailment, San Petronio is a fine example of late fourteenth-century architecture. Above the central portal is a beautiful carving of the Madonna and Child by visiting artist Jacopo della Quercia that certainly catches the eye, although the most unusual feature is the large sundial.

The ornately decorated building next door to San Petronio is the Palazzo dei Notai ("Notaries"), a fourteenth-century reminder of Bologna's legal scholars who laid the first foundations of contemporary European law. In the opposite direction, across Via dell'Archiginnasio from San Petronio, the **Palazzo dei Banchi** is more of a set piece than a *palazzo*, basically a facade designed by the Renaissance architect Vignola to unify a set of medieval houses that didn't really fit with the rest of the square. Adjacent, the **Museo Civico Archeologico** (Tues–Fri 9am–3pm, Sat & Sun 10am–6.30pm; €4) is rather stuffy, but has good displays of Egyptian and Roman antiquities, and an Etruscan section that is one of the best outside Lazio, with finds drawn from the settlement of Felsina, which predated Bologna; there are reliefs from tombs, vases and a bronze *situla*, richly decorated, from the fifth century BC. English audioguides are available for €4.

Just north of the museum, **Via Clavature** – together with nearby Via Pescerie Vecchie and Via Draperie – is home to a grouping of **market stalls** and shops that makes for one of the city's most enticing sights and provides proof positive of Bologna's gourmet proclivities. In autumn, especially, the market is a visual and aural feast, with fat porcini mushrooms, truffles in baskets of rice, thick rolls of mortadella, hanging pheasants, ducks and hares, and skinned frogs by the kilo. The church of **Santa Maria della Vita** (daily 7.30am–6.30pm; free), in Via Clavature, is worth a look for its outstanding pietà by Nicola dell'Arca – seven life-sized terracotta figures that are among the most dramatic examples of Renaissance sculpture you'll see.

Down the street in the other direction, Bologna's old university – the **Archiginnasio** – was founded at more or less the same time as Piazza Maggiore was laid out, predating the rest of Europe's universities, although it didn't get a special building until 1565, when Antonio Morandi was commissioned to construct the present building on the site until then reserved for San Petronio. Centralizing the university on one site was a way of maintaining control over students at a time when the Church felt particularly threatened by the Reformation. You can wander freely into the main courtyard, covered with the coats of arms of its more famous graduates, and perhaps even attend a lecture. In the mornings it's also possible to visit the main upstairs **library**, and, most interestingly, the **Teatro Anatomico** (Mon–Fri 9am–6.30pm, Sat 9am–1.30pm; ☎051.236.488; free), the original medical faculty dissection theatre. Tiers of seats surround an extraordinary professor's chair, covered with a canopy supported by figures known as *gli spellati* – "the skinned ones". Not many dissections went on, owing to prohibitions of the Church, but when they

△ The Due Torri

did (usually around carnival time), artists and the general public used to turn up as much for the social occasion as for studying the body.

Outside the old university, **Piazza Galvani** remembers the physicist Luigi Galvani with a statue. One of Bologna's more successful scientists, Galvani discovered electrical currents in animals, thereby lending his name to the English language in the word "galvanize". A few minutes south, down Via Garibaldi, is **Piazza San Domenico**, with its strange canopied tombs holding the bones of medieval law scholars. Bologna was instrumental in sorting out wrangles between the pope and the Holy Roman emperor in the tenth and eleventh centuries, earning itself the title of *La Dotta* ("The Learned") and forming the basis for the university's prominent law faculties. The church of **San Domenico** was built in 1221 to house the relics of St Dominic, which were placed in the so-called *Arca di San Domenico*: a fifteenth-century work that was ostensibly the creation of Nicola Pisano – though in reality many artists contributed to it. One of Pisano's pupils was **Michelangelo** and it was his hands that sculpted the angel resting on St Dominic's tomb. While you're in the church, try also to see the **Museo di San Domenico** (Mon–Fri 9.30am–12.30pm & 3.30–6.30pm, Sat & Sun 3–5.30pm; free) displaying a very fine polychrome terracotta bust of St Dominic by Nicolò dell'Arca along with paintings, reliquaries and vestments, and, beyond, the intricately inlaid mid-sixteenth-century choir stalls.

The university quarter

Bordered by Via Oberdan to the west and Strada Maggiore to the south, the eastern section of Bologna's *centro storico* preserves many of the older **university** departments, housed for the most part in large seventeenth- and eighteenth-century palaces. Bookshops, cafés and vegetarian restaurants make this atmospheric slice of studentville perfect for idling away an afternoon but be aware that after dark the city's heroin addicts use the porticoes here for makeshift homes. Police presence has minimized any danger but care should still be taken along along Via Zamboni.

Via Rizzoli leads into the district from Piazza Maggiore, ending up at Piazza di Porta Ravegnana, where the **Torre degli Asinelli** (daily 9am–6pm; closes 5pm in winter; €3), and the perilously leaning **Torre Garisenda** next to it, are together known as the **Due Torri**, the only two remaining of hundreds of towers that were scattered across the city in the Middle Ages. The former makes a good place from which to get an overview of the city centre and beyond, out over the red-tiled roofs across the hazy, flat plains and southern hills beyond.

Southeast of the Due Torri, Via Santo Stefano leads down to its medieval gateway, past a complex of four – but originally seven – churches, collectively known as **Santo Stefano**. It's an attractive complex set in a wide piazza at the conjunction of several narrow porticoed streets. Three of the churches face onto the piazza, of which the striking polygonal church of **San Sepolcro** (daily 9am–12.15pm & 3.30–6pm; free), reached through the church of **Crocifisso**, is about the most interesting. The basin in its courtyard, called "Pilate's Bowl", dates from the eighth century, while on the inside the bones of St Petronius, held in a tomb modelled on the church of the holy sepulchre in Jerusalem, provide a macabre focus typical of the relic-obsessed Middle Ages. A doorway leads from here through to **Santi Vitale e Agricola**, Bologna's oldest church, built from discarded Roman fragments in the fifth century.

From here, follow Via Gerusalemme up to Strada Maggiore, where, a little way down on the right, stands the elegant fourteenth-century **Santa Maria dei Servi**, filled with frescoes by Vitale da Bologna – it's a rare chance to see the work of the so-called "father" of Bolognese painting *in situ*. The beautiful portico holds a festive market during the Christmas season. Across the street stands the **Museo Davia Bargellini** (Tues–Sun 9am–2pm, closes 1pm on Sun; free), made up of the eclectic art collection of the Davia family, as well as textiles, glassware and furniture. Further north from here, Via Petroni leads through to **Piazza Verdi**, at the heart of the university district. On summer evenings it draws the crowds with its open-air bars and live music. **Via Zamboni** bisects Piazza Verdi, around and along which are many of the old palaces housing various parts of the university. A large number of these buildings were decorated by members of the Bolognese academies, which were prominent in Italian art after 1600. Tibaldi, better known as an architect, turned his hand to fresco in the main building, the **Palazzo Poggi** at no. 33, where you'll find many of the university's specialist museums (Mon–Fri 10am–1pm & 2–4pm, Sat & Sun 10.30am–1.30pm & 2.30–5.30pm, but times frequently change so check on ☎051.209.9360, ⓦwww.unibo.it/musei-universitari; free). Tibaldi's fresco of Ulysses here was influenced by Michelangelo's Sistine Chapel and has played a part in the much-publicized row over the latter's restoration, with art historians using Tibaldi's fresco as proof that they have got Michelangelo's colours right. On the fourth floor of the building, the fascinating 300-year-old **Specola**, or observatory, draws most people here. Its small **Museo di Astronomia** (Mon–Fri 9am–2pm by appointment only; free) is home to a number of eighteenth-century instruments and a frescoed map of the constellations – painted just seventy years after Galileo was imprisoned for his heretical statements about the cosmos.

The **Museo della Cera Anatomiche ("Luigi Cattaneo")**, a short distance north at Via Irnerio 48 (Mon–Fri 9am–5pm, after 2pm by appointment only; ☎051.244.217, ⓦwww.museocereanatomiche.it; free), might seem an odd place to visit, but it would be a shame to leave Bologna without seeing its highly idiosyncratic (and beautiful) **waxworks**. These were used until the nineteenth century for medical demonstration, and are as startling as any art or sculpture in the city. There were two Italian schools of waxworks: the Florentine method, where they used limbs, organs and bones to make moulds to cast the wax; and the Bolognese, where everything was sculpted, even tiny veins and capillaries, which were rolled like Plasticine. The boundaries between "art" and "science" were not rigidly drawn, and in Bologna in the early eighteenth century the workshops of Anna Morandi Mazzolini and Ercole Lelli turned out figures that were much more than just clinical aids. Mazzolini, for example, created a self-portrait in the midst of a brain dissection, pulling back a scalp with wispy hairs attached; other figures, unnervingly displayed in glass cases, are modelled like classical statues, one carrying a sickle, the other a scythe.

Close by, the collection of paintings in the **Pinacoteca Nazionale** at Via delle Belle Arti 56 (Tues–Sun 9am–7pm, ⓦwww.pinacotecabologna.it; €4) may provide some light relief, concentrating mainly on the work of Bolognese artists. There are canvases by the fourteenth-century painter Vitale da Bologna with later works by Francia and Tibaldi, and paintings from the city's most productive artistic period, the early seventeenth century.

Back towards the centre down Via Zamboni, in Piazza Rossini, is the church of **San Giacomo Maggiore** (daily 7am–noon & 3.30–6.30pm; free), a Romanesque structure begun in 1267 and enlarged over the centuries. The target here is the Bentivoglio Chapel, decorated with funds provided by one Annibale Bentivoglio to celebrate the family's victory in a local feud in 1488. Lorenzo Costa painted frescoes called *Apocalypse*, *Triumph of Death* and *Madonna Enthroned* as some well as of the Bentivoglio family – a deceptively pious-looking lot, captured in what was a fairly innovative picture in its time for the careful characterizations of its patrons. Further frescoes by Costa, along with Francesco Francia, decorate the **Oratorio di Santa Cecilia** (daily 9.30am–1pm & 2–6pm; free); they show episodes from the lives of saints Cecilia and Valerian.

Piazza Rossini is named after the nineteenth-century composer, who studied at the **Conservatorio G.B. Martini** on the square. The library here is among the most important music libraries in Europe (free entrance but visits must be arranged; ☎051.221.483) with some original manuscripts on display, along with a few paintings. On the other side of Via Zamboni at Via Valdonica 1/5 is the **Museo Ebraico** (Mon–Thurs & Sun 10am–6pm, Fri 10am–4pm; ⓦwww .museomusicabologna.it; €4). Situated in the old Jewish ghetto, it's the best Jewish museum in the province and presents the history of the once-thriving Jewish community in Emilia-Romagna.

The Metropolitana, Museo Civico and the basilica of San Francesco

There's much less of interest to the north and west of Bologna's central squares. A couple of blocks north of Piazza Nettuno, the city's cathedral, the **Metropolitana di San Pietro** (daily 8am–noon and 4–6.15pm), was originally a tenth-century building but has been rebuilt many times and is these days more enjoyable for its stately atmosphere than any particular features. The **Museo Civico Medioevale e dal Rinascimento** (Tues–Fri 9am–3pm, Sat and Sun 10am–6.30pm; €4), opposite, is of more interest, housed in the Renaissance Palazzo Fava at Via Manzoni 4 and decorated with frescoes by Carracci and members of the Bolognese School depicting the History of Europa, Jason's Feats and scenes from the *Aeneid*. The museum collection itself includes bits of armour, ceramics, numerous tombs and busts of various popes and other dignitaries, and a *Madonna and Saints* by Jacopo della Quercia.

West of Piazza del Nettuno, at the end of Via Ugo Bassi, the basilica of **San Francesco** (daily 6.30am–noon & 3–7pm) is a huge Gothic brick pile supported by flying buttresses that was heavily restored in the 1920s and partly rebuilt after World War II. Inside there are a beautiful and very ornate altarpiece from 1392 and a pleasant cloister.

Eating, drinking and entertainment

Eating and **drinking** are the mainstays of Bologna's social life. Eating especially is important to the Bolognese: the city is known as *La Grassa* ("The Fat One"), the result of a rich culinary tradition, and the emphasis on food here can be taken to extremes. People travel a long way to eat at the top restaurants, which are said to be the best in Italy, and even the simplest restaurants and the many **osterie** often serve dishes of a very high standard. Handmade lasagne, tagliatelle and tortellini (small, shaped pasta with a stuffing of ham, sausage, chopped chicken, pork and veal, eggs, nutmeg and parmesan) are excellent and regarded with great affection by Bologna's inhabitants, to the extent that elaborate stories explain their origin: the first tortellini are said to have been made by a Bolognese innkeeper trying to recreate the beauty of Venus's navel.

Bologna's **bar culture** thrives thanks to its huge student population with most drinking places centred on and around Via Zamboni. **Clubs** are plentiful and varied – some popular places are mentioned on p.455, and the tourist office has a free pamphlet called "2night" (ⓦwww.2night.it) for details of life in the city after dark.

As for the **arts and cultural attractions**, Bologna has tried to curb the July and August exodus by mounting a summer arts festival, called Viva Bologna, with evening concerts and cinema screenings in the courtyards of the civic buildings. Ferragosto in August is an especially good time to be here, when everyone takes to the hills for all-night revelry in one of the parks outside town. One of the main venues for opera and classical music is the Teatro Comunale on Piazza Verdi (ⓦ www.comunalebologna.it).

For listings there's the useful *Bologna Spettacolo* available from bookshops with details of forthcoming gigs, theatre productions and events. There's also *City* and *BolognaBologna* for information on entertainment in the city – you can pick them up in bars and cafés. And for concerts and venues, you could try asking at the Rock Shop, Via Mazzini 146, or looking in the weekly supplement of the national newspaper *La Repubblica*.

Snacks, bars, cafés and ice cream

Al Piccolo Bar Piazza Verdi 1. As small as its name suggests, revellers spill out of this famous student hangout onto the piazza in the summer, when it stays open into the early hours.

Altero Via dell'Indipendenza 33. This *mensa*-style place is the best choice for pizza by the slice; it's located halfway between the centre and the station. Open till 1am daily.

Caffè Commercianti Strada Maggiore 23c. Atmospheric bar that serves everything from coffee and ice cream to aperitifs. Try their version of *café frappé* served in a wine glass – perfect for hot days. Open till 8pm; closed Sun.

Clauricane Irish Pub Via Zamboni 18. Perhaps the largest bar in town, very popular with students from the university up the road, with punters spilling out onto the street on hot evenings. Open daily till 3am.

Enoteca des Arts Via San Felice 9. Tiny, dark and atmospheric bar serving cheap, local wine. Open Mon–Sat 4.30pm–2am.

Enoteca Italiana Via Marsala 2b. Just off Via dell'Indipendenza, this place has a range of excellent Italian wines and good snacks. Open till 8pm; closed Sun.

Faccioli Via Altabella 15b. It's been described as a discreet library of a bar, with bottles, not books, lining the walls. Very pleasant place to taste wines and nibble snacks in the shadow of one of the city's towers. Open from 6pm; closed Sun, & Sat in July & Aug.

Gamberini Ugo Bassi 12. Decent coffee and cake pit-stop under Ugo Bassi's arcades, just far enough away from the central hubbub to be relaxing.

Gianni Via Montegrappa 11. Fine spot to eat some of the best ice cream in town, with tables outside in the summer. Open noon–1am.

La Torinese Piazza Re Enzo 1. Hot chocolate to die for and ice cream to drool over are just some of the treats in this old-fashioned bar in a great central spot.

Le Stanze Via Borgo di San Pietro 1/A. Elegant place to unwind and sip wine and cocktails in the airy splendour of a converted Bentivoglio *palazzo*. The sixteenth-century frescoed ceilings, romantic candles and occasional art exhibition produce an evocative atmosphere lapped up by its chic clientele.

San Daniele bistrot Via Altabella 3a. Excellent wines, cheeses and hams and generally good snacks in a relaxed atmosphere. Open daily till 1am.

Zanarini Piazza Galvani 1. Where the chic Bolognese gather for their *aperitivi* and therefore suitably smart and expensive. Closed Mon.

Restaurants

Belle Arti Via Belle Arti 14. Vibrant, popular place with friendly service, extra-large pizzas and other southern specialities. Eat in the atmospheric wood-beamed interior or on the pavement terrace fringed with hanging flowers. Closed Wed.

Bistrot Marco Fadiga Via Rialto 23/c ☎051.220.118. Intimate place in the heart of Bologna's theatrical quarter with a French bias alongside more typically Emilian cuisine. Signature pudding of biscuits served with a sauce made of a Cuban cigar infusion mixed with honey is just one indication of the pricey menu's character. Closed Sun eve & Mon.

Broccaindosso Via Broccaindosso 7a ☎051.234.153. There's little in the way of signs to alert you to the existence of this friendly and eccentric restaurant, and you'll need to ring a bell to get in. The waiters bring no menu, just a succession of fantastic antipasti and desserts; you can have pasta too, if you need it. Very good value and worth booking. Open 8.30pm–2am; closed Sun.

C'entro Via dell'Indipendenza 45. Large self-service restaurant with a wide range of cheap quality food, including as much salad as you can pile onto your plate. Open between 11.45am–3pm and 6.30–9.30pm. Closed Sun.

Clorofilla Strada Maggiore 64c. A brightly lit, almost sterile, non-smoking vegetarian restaurant – just the place if the "fat of Bologna" has been weighing you down. Good value at around €10 for a meal. Open till midnight; closed Sun.

Da Bertino Via Delle Lame 55. The place to come for no-nonsense Bolognese peasant-style cooking, including *bollito* and *arrosto* (boiled and roast meats), accompanied by traditional relishes. Open till 10.30pm; closed Sun, Sat evenings in summer & Mon in winter.

Del Montesino Via del Pratello 74b. One of many bars on this welcoming street, a chatty, convivial place serving snacks, including substantial, southern-inspired salads and good *crostini* (various toppings spread on toasted bread). The house wine is very drinkable too. Closed Sun.

Del Moretto Via San Mamolo 5 ☎051.580.284. One of Bologna's best *osterie*, especially favoured by musicians and artists. Open evenings only 7pm–3am.

Dell'Orsa Via Mentana 1f. The mainly meat-based dishes here are fairly pricey, but stick with the bruschetta for a good-value snack. There's live jazz during the winter. Closed Mon.

Diana Via dell' Independenza 24 ☎051.231.302. About as fancy a dining experience as Bologna offers, this large 1920s establishment – all chandeliers and bow-tied waiters – has an excellent menu, specializing in roasts. Reservations recommended.

Drogheria della Rosa Via Cartoleria 10 ☎051.222.529. This converted grocery store/pharmacy still retains many of its original features but now serves hearty prescriptions of Bolognan cuisine. It's all a bit ad hoc with a changing (and often unwritten) menu, but it's won numerous awards. Closed Sun.

Due Torri Via De' Giudei 6. Five minutes from the landmarks of the same name is this super cheap self-service place that's busy and friendly, and has vegetarian options. Open for lunch only between noon and 3pm. Cash only. Closed Sun.

🏃 **Fantoni** Via del Pratello 11. Family-style Bolognese food that's highly popular with locals. Amazing value for money with lunchtime pasta dishes starting at €3.50 and an adventurous dinner menu with some fish specialities. Closed Sun & Mon eve.

Franco Rossi Via Goito 3 ☎051.238.818. Run by two brothers, this cosy one room place offers light inventive interpretations of heavy Romagnan staples. Closed Sun.

Grassilli Via del Luzzo 3 ☎051.222.961. Emilian dishes adapted with flair to suit modern tastes, accompanied by exceptionally good service. Walls decorated with pictures of opera singers who dined here add to the glam ambience. An experience to remember, though you'll need to book and it's above averagely priced. Open till 10.30pm. Closed Wed & Sun eve.

Il Tarì Via Collegio di Spagna 13. A trattoria and pizzeria featuring fish dishes, such as delicious *spaghetti allo scoglio* – with seafood and *galletti* mushrooms. Enormous servings of everything. Open till midnight. Closed Thurs.

La Colombina Vicolo Colombina 5 ☎051.231.706. Very attractive and fairly expensive, but excellent value if you're looking for authentic Bolognese specialities. Open till 11pm; closed Tues.

Marione Via San Felice 137. Old, smoky and dark *osteria*, with good wine and snacks, served under the watchful eye of Mario. Open till 2am; closed Wed.

Senzanome Via Senzanome 42a. Off Via Saragozza, this was a favourite drinking place for cart drivers in the seventeenth century when the *osteria* was famed for its sausage – made, it is claimed, from bulls' testicles. The place now serves good home-made pasta and has a wide choice of beers and wines. Open evenings only; closed Mon.

Teresina Via Oberdan 4 ☎051.228.985. A great family-run restaurant serving regional dishes as well as very good southern Italian food for around €30 a head for a full meal. Worth booking. Open till 10.30pm; closed Sun.

Trattoria Gianni Via Clavature 18 ☎051.229.434. One of the top options in Bologna: try the ultra-traditional *bolliti*, a variety of meats boiled in the Emilian way, or the fantastic home-made tortellini. Moderate prices. Closed Sun eve & Mon.

Clubs and live music venues

Café Caracol Piazza Galileo, 6. Centrally placed Mexican theme bar that's open until 2am, serves great food, and has a small dance floor. Cheap cocktails too during the club's happy hour (6–7pm). Free entrance. Closed Sun.

🏃 **Cantina Bentivoglio** Via Mascarella 4b ☎051.265.416, ⓦ www.cantinabentivoglio .it. As much an *osteria* as a bar, this place has live jazz from around 10pm in the cellars of this sixteenth-century *palazzo*, where the food (snacks to full meals) and wine are excellent. Open daily but closed Sun in summer.

Cassero Via Don Minzoni 18 ☎051.649.4416, ⓦ www.cassero.it. Housed downstairs in La Salara, one of the old city fortifications, this is the best of Bologna's gay bars, open every day from 9pm with bar and entertainment (Thursday night is lesbian night). It also has an archive, counselling centre and meeting point (Mon–Fri 10am–1pm & 2–7pm). **Chet Baker** Via Polese 7a ⊤051.223.795, ⓦwww.chetbaker.it. One of the city's most popular jazz venues attracting international names. Closed Sun.

Link Via Fioravanti. This *centro sociale* has a bar upstairs and enormous dance floor downstairs, with avant-garde performance art and live bands

early on, and ambient and techno sounds later. No entrance fee, except for gigs. Daily 10pm–5am. **Made in Bo** V. del Fonditore 16, ⓦwww.madeinbo .it. Bus #25 takes revellers to this large venue north of the centre, off Via Stalingrado. Massive rock festivals are held in summer. **Transilvania** Via Zamboni 16 ⓦwww.transilvania .it. Bologna's goths congregate at this tiny rock horror café done up in a crypt style with a rocky soundtrack.

Listings

Books Huge selection of English books and magazines from Feltrinelli International, Via Zamboni 7.
Car rental Avis, Viale Pietramellara 27d ⊤051.255.024; Europcar, Via Amendola 12f ⊤051.247.101; Hertz, Via Amendola 16a ⊤051.254.830; Maggiore, Via Cairoli 4 ⊤051.252.525. All the major companies also have desks at the airport.
Cinema Nosadella, Via Nosadella 21 (ⓦwww .nosadella.it), shows films in their original language on Monday; Arena Puccini, Via Serlio 25, is a summer-only outdoor cinema; Lumiere, Via Pietralata 55a, is an excellent film club that occasionally offers non-dubbed alternative movies.
Gay and lesbian Bologna Gay-friendly places abound in Bologna – the city has the largest homosexual community in Italy. Friendly places are listed in the free *Cassero Magazine* available from the tourist office. Specific gay places, however, are few but popular hangouts include Tuesday night at *Sushi Café* (Piazza Malpighi) and Sunday aperitifs at *Stile Libero* at Via Lame 108. Gay saunas include Steam at Via Ferrarese 22/1 and New Vigor at Via San Felice 6b – *Caffè Casablanca* next door is also popular (closed Sun).
Hospital In an emergency, dial ⊤118; or go to the Pronto Soccorso (24hr casualty) at the Ospedale San Orsola Generale, Via Massarenti 9 (⊤051.636.3111); bus #14 from Via Rizzoli.
Internet access There are numerous Internet cafés all over Bologna. Two reasonably central

options include Easy Internet Café on Via Rizzoli 9 (daily 9am–11pm) and Happynet, Via Oberdan 17/b (⊤051.1998.4179; Mon–Fri 9am–11pm, Sat and Sun 10am–11pm).
Laundry Laundromat, Via Petroni 38, is the most central coin-op/drop-service laundry.
Markets There are a couple of great food markets in the city centre: the large and lively Mercato delle Erbe, Via Ugo Bassi 2 (Mon–Sat 7am–1.15pm & 5–7.30pm, closed Thurs & Sat pm); and the Mercato di Mezzo on Via Pescherie Vecchie (Mon–Sat 7am–1pm & 4.15–7.30pm; closed Thurs am). For a huge range of new and secondhand clothes, handicrafts and textiles head to La Piazzola market on Piazza VIII Agosto on Fridays and Saturdays (dawn to dusk).
Pharmacy Farmacia Comunale in Piazza Maggiore is open 24 hours.
Police Main *questura* is at Piazza Galileo 7 ⊤051.640.1111.
Post office The main post office is on Piazza Minghetti (Mon–Fri 8am–6.30pm, Sat 8am–12.30pm).
Shops Some of Bologna's most colourful sights are inside its many food stores, particularly those between Piazza Maggiore and the Due Torri, epitomized by Tamburini at Via Caprarie 1. The most convenient supermarket is the Co-op, at Via Montebello 2, behind the train station.
Taxis Cooperativa Taxisti Bologna, ⊤051.372.727. Consorzio Autonomo Taxista, ⊤051.534.141.
Travel agents CTS, Largo Respighi 2g ⊤051.261.802; and Via C.Battisti 17 ⊤051.296.0764.

South of Bologna

In the heat of the summer the hills that start almost as soon as you leave Bologna's gates take you high enough to catch some cooling breezes. The most obvious destination for a short trip is the eighteenth-century shrine of **Santuario di Madonna di San Luca** (7am–12.30pm and 2.30–5pm (until 7pm in

Italian food

Food is a passion in Italy. It dominates every aspect of Italian life and makes visiting the country a fantastic gastronomic experience. Not only does the food taste better on its home soil, but there's a regional variety that makes travelling from place to place a source of pure, indulgent culinary pleasure. Italy wasn't a unified country until the late nineteenth century and its cuisine serves only to highlight this fact: it's created from a patchwork of ingredients and cooking methods that even now keep a parochial distance from each other. Every region thinks their way of cooking is the best, and will argue fiercely as to why. However, the one thing that every Italian you meet will agree on is that the food in Italy is the best in the world. For more on each region's cuisine, see the box at the beginning of the Guide chapters. Buon Appetito!

The north

The northern regions are home to the country's richest cuisine: home to the Slow Food movement (see box), **Piemonte** is famous for its meat dishes in rich, creamy sauces, as well as its white truffles, most celebrated in the area around Alba (which has a huge truffle festival every year in November), and some excellent red wines – Barolo, Dolcetto d'Alba and Barbaresco. In **Lombardy** you're as likely to eat risotto as pasta as a starter, and meat dishes may come with polenta – boiled corn

▲ A Ligurian speciality – fresh fish

grits – instead of potatoes. The neighbouring region, **Veneto**, is well known for its crisp white wine, Soave, and light red Valpolicella, and the emphasis not surprisingly is on fish – manifest in fantastic risottos and black, squid-ink flavoured pasta. Fish also features strongly in the food of **Liguria**, where you should make sure to try the *stoccafisso* or fish stew and shellfish soups. But the coast here also gives the first taste of the kind of food you will eat further south: its valleys produce the olive oil, pine nuts and basil that go to make its ubiquitous green pasta sauce, pesto.

Central Italy

Emilia-Romagna is celebrated for being the Italian culinary heartland, known for its salami and cheeses, pork dishes, rich pasta sauces and fresh filled

> It's hard to over-emphasize just how menus change from region to region...

pasta, as well as Parma ham and Parmesan cheese – products from the rich farmlands of the nearby Po plains. In opposition, the cuisine of **Tuscany** and to some extent neighbouring **Umbria** is simple: the trademark dish in both regions is *bistecca alla fiorentina*, chargrilled steaks from the cattle of Tuscany's Maremma plain. As in the south, olive oil rather than butter is used for cooking, but you're still not in pasta country, and the pasta you find, as in Emilia-Romagna, tends to be fresh rather than the more common dried variety or *pasta asciutta*, delicious washed down with some of the country's best wines – Chianti, Brunello di Montalcino and

◄ Parmesan cheese from Bologna

Vino Nobile di Montepulciano. Umbria, **Marche** and **Abruzzo** are known for their game, and the cheese of choice in all these central regions is sheep's milk *pecorino*, which varies from the young and sweet to the sharp, salty crumble of *pecorino Romano* – in Rome they use it in cooking instead of Parmesan. In these central regions, you'll also find *porchetta*, or pork stuffed with herbs and roasted on a spit – especially at outdoor gatherings where it's munched between thick hunks of rustic bread.

Rome forms the boundary between the Italian north and south in many ways, and food is no

exception. Its denizens favour pasta dishes, thick spaghetti and noodles mainly, with rough, peasant sauces. Some of the most well-known pasta sauces hail from here; *alla carbonarara* and *alla amatriciana* are Roman varieties. The city is also known for its Italian-Jewish specialities – deep-fried courgette flowers, offal dishes and *baccalà* (deep-fried cod).

The south

Southern Italy's staples include pasta, olive oil, fresh fruit and vegetables, particularly tomatoes, and fish and seafood – perhaps Italy's healthiest diet. Yet the cuisine of the south is just as complex as that of the north, and its regions as diverse. Flat breads originated here, notably foccaccia, though this has spread all over the country, much like Naples' signature pasta dish of *spaghetti al pomodoro*: a simple delight of which the mayor of Naples said, "The angels in paradise eat nothing but *pasta al pomodoro*."

Cheese is also the **Campania** region's big attraction, most notably – and deliciously – the soft white mozzarella made from the milk of the buffalo that are kept on farms south of Naples. This delicacy can now be found all over Italy, but it's best eaten here. Also made from buffalo milk are the harder *cacicocavallo* and *provolone* – bulbous balls that can be eaten plain or smoked.

Further south, the food reflects the influence of Arabs and Greeks, who between

▼ Fresh fruit and veg in Naples

them brought great sweets and desserts, and a liking for spicier food. **Puglia** is a huge wine-growing region, and lamb, as in **Abruzzo**, is the meat of choice. **Sicily**, meanwhile, has a cuisine almost of its own: ultra-sweet pastries like cream-filled *cannoli predomi nate*, while in some parts north African couscous features. **Sardinia**, too, has a number of unique delicacies – really pungent *pecorino*, and its own peculiar, wafer-thin flat bread, *carta di musica*.

The glorious variety of pasta

Garibaldi swore that **pasta** would unite Italy, and he could have been right. There are literally hundreds of different pasta shapes, each of which are designated a number. Some, like spaghetti (number 12 in case you were wondering), you will find more or less everywhere; others are less common and usually indigenous to one particular part of the country. Incidentally, the theory that Marco Polo brought pasta back from China in the thirteenth century probably isn't true: there are records of people eating dried pasta in the Italian peninsula decades before his return.

Agnolotti Literally "lambs' ears" – semicircular filled pasta pockets.

Capelli d'angeli Very thin noodles, literally "angels' hair".

Conchigliette Small shell-like shapes often used in soup.

Gemelli Loose spirals of pasta.

Manicotti Large ridged tubes, often stuffed.

Orzo Pasta shaped like grains of rice.

Paccheri Large tubes of pasta.

Rotini Tight spirals of pasta.

Strozzapreti Literally "strangled priests" – twisted flat noodles.

Trofie Teardrops of potato and pasta, usually served with pesto in Liguria.

Vermicelli Thin strand pasta often served in soup – literally "little worms".

Ziti Narrow tubes of pasta.

summer), close on 4km outside the city but connected by way of the world's longest portico, which meanders across the hillside in a series of 666 arches – a shelter for pilgrims on the trek to the top. Bus #20 from the station drops you at the start of the route, by Porta Saragozza southwest of the centre. Further south, the N325 passes through **PONTECCHIO MARCONI**, where the physicist Guglielmo Marconi lived in the late nineteenth century, and from where, in 1895, he sent the first radio message ever – to his brother on the other side of the hill. Marconi now lies in a specially designed mausoleum in the village.

The route on from here towards Pistoia is a beautiful one, taking you above the Setta Valley, past chestnut groves and small villages. It's a well-trafficked road, though, and the back roads are the greatest attraction. **MARZABOTTO**, a few kilometres on from Sasso Marconi and accessible by direct bus from Bologna, is known as the site of the massacre by the Nazis of 1800 people during World War II. It also holds the remains of an Etruscan town, **Misa** (daily 8am –7pm; free), just outside. The site marks out the residential areas, the city gates, streets and drains, and fragments of foundations from temples and some tombs remain. The **museum** (daily 9am–noon & 3–6.30pm; €2) contains a variety of finds, from the remains of the piped water system to household objects inscribed *mi Venelus* ("I belong to Venel") and *mi Sualus* ("I belong to Sualu").

Modena and around

Though only thirty minutes northwest by train, **MODENA** has a quite distinct identity from Bologna. It proclaims itself the "spiritual capital" of Emilia, highlighting the two cities' long and sometimes intense rivalry. Indeed, Modena does have a number of claims to fame: its outskirts are fringed with prosperous industry – knitwear and ceramics factories on the surrounding plain make a healthy profit, and great car names such as Ferrari, Lamborghini and Maserati are tied to the town (celebrated in *Modena Terra di Motori* in April/May, when the piazzas are filled with classic models); Pavarotti is a native of Modena and gives regular concerts in May in the Parco Novi Sad; the area's balsamic vinegar has become a cult product in kitchens around the world, duly celebrated in the Balsamica festival in May; and the cathedral is considered one of the finest Romanesque buildings in Italy. Of things to see, top of most people's list are the rich collections of paintings and manuscripts built up by the Este family, who decamped here from Ferrara in 1598, after it was annexed by the Papal States, and ruled the town until the nineteenth century. But really the appeal of Modena is in wandering its labyrinthine old centre, finishing off the day with some good food.

Arrival and information

Modena's centre, marked by the main Piazza Grande, is a ten-minute walk southwest from the **train station** on Piazza Dante Alighieri, down the wide Corso Vittorio Emanuele II. Buses #7 and # 11 connect the train station with the main street of Via Emilia. The **bus station** for villages on the plain or in the Apennines is on Via Fabriani, off Viale Monte Kosica, ten minutes' walk west from the train station and northeast from the centre of town. The **tourist office** is just off the main Piazza Grande at Via Scudari 12 (Mon 3–6pm, Tues–Sat 9am–1pm & 3–6pm, Sun 9.30am–12.30pm; ☎059.206.660, ⓦwww .comune.modena.it/infoturismo). If you want to see balsamic vinegar being created, contact the *Modenatur* office next door at no. 8/10 (☎059.220.022, ⓦwww.modenatur.net) for information on trips to *aceteria* (these are free but

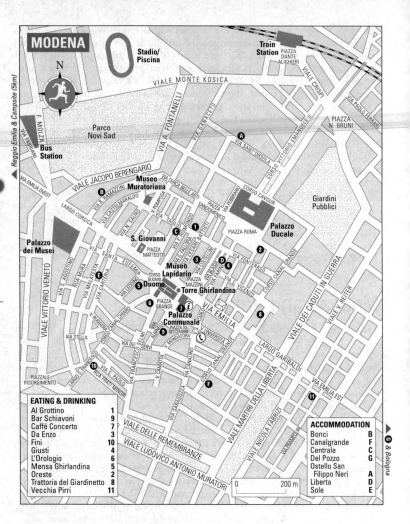

MODENA

Stadio/
Piscina

Train
Station PIAZZA
DANTE
ALIGHIERI

N

Reggio Emilia & Campsite (5km)

VIALE MONTE KOSICA

Parco
Novi Sad

PIAZZA
N. BRUNI

Bus
Station

VIALE JACOPO BERENGARIO

Museo
Muratoriana

Giardini
Pubblici

Palazzo
dei Musei

S. Giovanni

PIAZZA
ROMA

Palazzo
Ducale

Museo
Lapidario

Duomo

Torre Ghirlandina

PIAZZA
GRANDE

Palazzo
Communale

VIA EMILIA

PIAZZALE
RISORGIMENTO

LARGO GARIBALDI

VIA EMILIA EST

EATING & DRINKING	
Al Grottino	1
Bar Schiavoni	9
Caffè Concerto	7
Da Enzo	3
Fini	10
Giusti	4
L'Orologio	6
Mensa Ghirlandina	5
Oreste	2
Trattoria del Giardinetto	8
Vecchia Pirri	11

VIALE DELLE REMEMBRANZE

VIALE LUDOVICO ANTONIO MURATORI

ACCOMMODATION	
Bonci	B
Canalgrande	F
Centrale	C
Del Pozzo	G
Ostello San Filippo Neri	A
Liberta	D
Sole	E

0   200 m

& Bologna

being private establishments visits depend on owners' schedules). They also have
information on Lambrusco tours and cookery courses. You can go **online** at
Piazza Grande 17 (Mon–Sat 9am–1pm & 3–7pm, closed Wed pm and Sundays).
There's **free parking** inside the stadium at Parco Novi Sad, though most
hotels in the centre either have a garage or can give you free parking permits;
driving in the centre's one-way system during weekdays can be something of
a nightmare though.

Accommodation

Modena makes a relaxing place to stay for a night or two, and there are a few
reasonably priced **hotels** in the centre: these fill up quickly so you'll need to
book in advance.

To save a bit of money, it's worth investing in Modena's **museum card**, which for just €6 enables to holder to make unlimited visits to the *Museo Lapidario* and the collections of the *Palazzo de Musei* over a two-day period. It's available at all the participating sites.

The city's **hostel** is the clean and pleasant *Ostello San Filippo Neri*, with two- and three-bed rooms. It's conveniently located for both the centre and the train station at Via Sant'Orsola 52 (lockout 10am–2pm, midnight curfew; ⓣ & Ⓕ059.234.598, Ⓔhostelmodena@hotmail.com; €15.50).

The nearest **campsite** is *International Camping Modena* at Via Cave di Ramo 111 (ⓣ059.332.252), Località Bruciata, 5km from Modena on the way to Reggio Emilia, though the nearby motorway makes it noisy. To get there take bus #19 from Viale Monte Kosica, close by the train station, to Emilia Ovest 1006, from where it's a ten-minute walk: head up Via Rosmini, turn left at the end and follow the road under the motorway approach road.

Hotels

Bonci Via Ramazzini 59 ⓣ059.223.634. A friendly but basic place, a fair walk from the centre. ❷
Canalgrande Corso Canalgrande 6 ⓣ059.217.160, Ⓦwww.canalgrandehotel.it. Close to the main piazza and the place to go if you're after full Modenese elegance complete with a garden terrace for chic breakfasting. ❻
Centrale Via Rismondo 55 ⓣ059.218.808, Ⓦwww.hotelcentrale.com. One of the smarter hotels in as convenient a location as its name suggests and offering spacious and air-conditioned rooms with or without private bath. Garage parking available too (€10). ❸
Del Pozzo Via del Pozzo 72a ⓣ059.360.350. An economical option with basic but good-sized rooms (with or without bathrooms). ❶
Liberta Via Blasia 10 ⓣ059.222.365, Ⓦwww .hotelliberta.it. Just off Piazza Mazzini lies this well positioned and chic three-star with comfortable furnishings. ❺
Sole Via Malatesta 45 ⓣ059.214.245. Rather basic one-star offering rooms with shared bathrooms. ❷

The Town

Modena's small, concentric medieval centre is bisected by **Via Emilia**, which runs past the edge of **Piazza Grande**, the nominal centre of town, its stone buildings and arcades forming the focus of much of its life. Dominating the square, the twelfth-century **Duomo** (daily 7am–12.20pm & 3.30–7pm; Ⓦwww.duomodimodena.it; free) is one of the finest products of the Romanesque period in Italy and is on the Unesco world heritage list. Its most striking feature is the west facade, just off the piazza, whose portal is supported by two fierce-looking lions and fringed with marvellous reliefs – the work of one **Wiligelmo**, who also did the larger reliefs that run along the wall. Inside, the choir, supported by more lions and crouched figures, is friezed with polychrome reliefs depicting New Testament stories – the *Last Supper* stands out particularly. Under the choir is the plain stone coffin of St Geminianus, the patron saint of Modena – on his feast day, January 31, crowds come to visit his coffin, and a big market is held out in the main square. Have a look too at Begarelli's terracotta tableaux, *Shepherds*, in the south aisle.

Beside the main entrance to the duomo, the **Museo Lapidario** (Tues–Sun 9.30am–12.30pm & 3.30–6.30pm; €3 or see box above for combined tickets) includes Roman-age marbles from the duomo, while on the other side of the church lurches the 83-metre high **Torre Ghirlandina** (April–July & Sept–Oct

.30pm & 3–7pm; €1), begun at the same time as the duomo
...eted until two hundred years later.

... main focus for your wanderings is at the far, northwestern end of
...ia, where the **Palazzo dei Musei** houses the city museums and art
...es. Through an archway lined with Roman tombstones – nearby Piazza
...teotti was the site of a necropolis – a staircase leads off to the right up to the
...iblioteca Estense, on the first floor (Mon–Sat 9am–1pm; €2.60). This is only
partly open to non-students, but what is on display is worth a look: letters sent
by monarchs, popes and despots, with great wax seals, old maps, and the prize
treasure, Borso d'Este's bible – the *Bibbia di Borso d'Este* – arguably the most
decorated book in the world. The **Museo Civico Archeologico Etnologia**
(Tues–Fri 9am–noon, Sat & Sun 10am–1pm & 3–6pm); €4 or see box, p.459
for combined tickets), on the second floor, is the newest part of the museum,
with a large collection of artefacts of archeological and artistic significance,
while on the top floor, the **Galleria Estense** (Tues–Sun 8.30am–7.30pm;
Ⓦ www.galleriaestense.it; €4 or see box, p.459 for combined tickets) is perhaps
the highlight of all the exhibits. Made up of the picture collection of the Este
family, it contains paintings of the local schools, from the early Renaissance
through to the works of the Carraccis, Guercino and Guido Reni, a sculpture
of St Monica in terracotta attributed to Nicolo Dell'Arca, as well as portable
altars, Madonnas and triptychs by lesser-known Emilian artists like Cosmè Tura,
who painted the Palazzo Schifanoia in Ferrara (see p.476). There's also a bust
of Francesco I d'Este by Bernini, a portrait of the same man by Velázquez, and
Venetian works by Tintoretto and Veronese.

Eating, drinking and nightlife

Modena is packed with places to **eat**, with a large array of restaurants in all price
ranges. Try to sample some of the local pork-based specialities, like *ciccioli* – flaky
pork scratchings laid out in bars in the evening – or, in a restaurant, *zampone*
(pig's trotters, boned and filled with minced meat) or *cotechino* – the same thing,
but stuffed inside an animal bladder.

Al Grottino Via del Taglio 26. Dependable mid-priced place that gets packed out with crowds coming for the *gigante* pizzas that more than live up to their name. Big on pastas and fish with the creamy *risotto ai funghi porcini* is especially recommended. Closed Wed.

Bar Schiavoni Via Albinelli 13. Good choice for a great coffee and delectable and inventive panini for around €3 (open during market hours) at this tiny, busy place right by the market.

Caffè Concerto Piazza Grande. Large, elegant place that operates as café, restaurant and bar although its main role is as Modena's most celebrated meeting place and premier evening spot. Closed Tues.

Da Enzo Via Coltellini 17 ☎059.225.177. Pleasant, slightly old-fashioned place serving Modenese specialities – though not especially cheap. Closed Mon.

Fini Via Albareto 211, off Largo San Francesco ☎059.223.314. Classy, pricey hotel restaurant serving delectable food, from tortellini to prosciutto. Closed Mon & Tues.

Giusti Via Farini 75. At the bottom end of the price scale, this place has been a delicatessen since the seventeenth century and is a good source of picnic food. Open lunchtimes only. Closed Sun & Mon.

L'Orologio Piazette delle Ova 4. Indulge in a rich cappuccino at this stylish place in a prime spot by Piazza Grande and you'll see why this was recently voted best café in Italy. The adventurous might also like to try their Pavarotti Martini – a blend of balsamic vinegar and vodka. Closed Wed.

Mensa Ghirlandina Via Leodino 9. Dedicated to feeding impoverished students, this place offers reasonable quality food at low prices. Open noon–2pm. Closed Sun.

Oreste Piazza Roma 31 ☎059.243.324. This superb Michelin-starred affair is one of Pavarotti's favourite restaurants. Specialities include pumpkin ravioli. The decor is fusty but charming. Closed Sun.

Trattoria del Giardinetto Piazzale Boschetti 1. Buzzy place where people come in droves for the *gnocco e tigelle* – a platter of cold meats and fresh vegetables served with light puff-pastry diamonds, little scones and a variety of dips that is a meal in itself. Open until midnight, closed for lunch on Sat and all day Sun.

Vecchia Pirri Via Prampolini 8 ☎ 059.235.324. Don't be alarmed by the television screens and tacky lampshades, this restaurant serves up imaginative, handmade pasta with the freshest ingredients, at only slightly higher than average prices. Closed Mon.

Around Modena

The area immediately around Modena looks rather bland and uninviting with its discount furniture and lighting stores, garages, crumbling farmhouses and factories. Worth a look, however, is **CARPI**, around 15km north of Modena. The town's central **Piazza dei Martiri** is an enormous and impressive open space, almost worth the trip alone, and the sixteenth-century **Castello del Pio**, a mass of ornamental turrets and towers, holds an interesting museum inside – the **Museo al Deportato** (Thurs, Sat, Sun & public hols 10am–12.30pm & 3.30–7pm; €3). Occupying German forces in World War II held prisoners awaiting deportation to concentration camps at a site in Fóssoli, 6km to the north – the camp sheds still stand, dilapidated, in a field – and the museum has displays on the camps and the conditions in which the prisoners were held, putting them into context with information on political and racial exile. The most sobering aspect of the museum is its layout; you progress through the almost bare rooms accompanied by a long ribbon of quotes painted on the walls, taken from prisoners' letters.

The activity outside in the square provides some welcome relief with slick clothing stores running the length of its sixteenth-century red-brick **Portico Lungo**. At one end of the square are a couple of cafés and the bright ochre **Teatro Comunale**, at the other the Renaissance **Cattedrale** with a Baroque facade. The rest of Carpi is unexciting, so it's unlikely that you'll want to hang around town. There are trains and buses every hour to Modena, but if you do want to stay try the **rooms** at *Albergo da Giorgio* at Via G. Rocca 1–5 (☎059.685.365; ❸).

Also worth a detour is the **Galleria Ferrari**, at Via Dino Ferrari 43 in **MARANELLO**, around 23km south of Modena (daily: Oct–April 9.30am–6pm; May–Sept 9.30am–7pm; ⓦ www.galleria.ferrari.com; €12), an exhibition centre dedicated to the racing dynasty. On display are the cups and trophies won by the Ferrari team over the years, an assortment of Ferrari engines, along with vintage and contemporary examples of the cars themselves and a reconstruction of Enzo Ferrari's study.

Further **south of Modena** lie the foothills of the Apennines, covered by turkey oak, hornbeam and hazel woods. Narrow roads corkscrew into the mountains, from which you can climb by foot onto the *crinale* – the backbone of the Apennine range. Trails lead along the succession of peaks above the treeline, steep slopes on either side, to some glacial lakes, although the routes are most impressive for the views they give across the breadth of Italy on either side.

For many, the main attraction of the **small villages** in the foothills is **food**. The tourist office can advise you on "gourmet itineraries" to find the real Modenese cuisine, but they're not really necessary: restaurant signs by the side of the road invite you in to try cuisine "*alla tua nonna*" – "like grandma used to make" – often involving mortadella, salami or *crescente* (a kind of pitta bread eaten with a mixture of oil, garlic, rosemary and parmesan). Higher in the mountains you can still find *ciacci* – chestnut-flour pancakes, filled with ricotta and sugar – and walnuts that go to make *nocino* liqueur.

The best time to head to **VIGNOLA**, 20km southeast of Modena, is in April when the spring festival sees the place bathed in blossom as the town celebrates its famed cherries. Outside of the festival, Vignola is rather too industrial to be a conventional sightseeing stop although the well-preserved, ivy-infused castle, the **Rocca di Vignola** (summer Tues–Sat 9am–noon & 3.30–7pm, Sun 10am–noon & 3.30–7pm; winter Tues–Sat 9am–noon & 2–6pm, Sun 1am–noon & 2–6pm; free) is a definite highlight. One of many built in the fifteenth and sixteenth centuries to defend the crossings along the River Panaro into the neighbouring state of Bologna, it's a mammoth specimen, with enormous watchtowers on each corner, and fancy brickwork.

Vignola isn't really somewhere to **stay** – the only hotel is the recently improved but still pretty uninviting *Eden*, Via Cesare Battisti 49 (☎059.772.847, ⓦ www.eden-hotel.it; ❷) – but there are plenty of decent places to **eat**, especially at the foot of the castle. For a special treat, though, head for **Tavernelle**, 3km southwest on the road to Pavullo nel Frignano where you'll find the moderately priced *Antico Trattoria Moretto*, Via Frignanese (☎059.772.785; closed Mon), a barn of a place, packed with people of all ages enthusiastically tucking into some of the best local fare around.

Reggio Emilia and around

About 25km northwest, up the Via Emilia from Modena, is **REGGIO EMILIA**, nicknamed "the red town" – in 1960 five protestors were killed by police during demonstrations designed to prevent Fascists joining the government. You wouldn't credit such a revolutionary past wandering round this quiet, pleasant place now, more associated today with fashion house MaxMara.

The town is built around two central squares, **Piazza Prampolini** and **Piazza San Prospero**, and the **Palazzo del Municipio** that comes alive on market days (Tues & Fri). Stalls specialize in rather tacky clothes – the shops surrounding the market are far more interesting, many of them crammed with a mighty range of local produce such as salami and *parmigiano-reggiano*. Around the square, the buildings squeeze up so close to the church of **San Prospero** that they seem to have pushed it off-balance so that it now lurches to one side. Built in the sixteenth century, it's guarded by six lions in rose-coloured Verona marble – a marked contrast to the unclad octagonal campanile next to it. Via Broletto leads through into **Piazza Prampolini**, skirting the side of the **Duomo**, which displays an awkward amalgamation of styles. Underneath the marble tacked on in the sixteenth century, it's possible to see the church's Romanesque facade, with incongruously Mannerist statues of Adam and Eve lounging over the medieval portal, although all else that remains of the original building are the apse and enormous crypt.

At right angles to the duomo is the sugar-pink **Palazzo del Capitano del Popolo**. The Italian tricolour of red, white and green was proclaimed here as the official national flag of Italy when Napoleon's Cispadane Republic was formed in 1797. North of here on the edge of Piazza della Vittoria are the **Musei Civici** (Sept–May Mon–Fri 9am–noon, Sat 9am–noon & 3–7pm, Sun & hols 10am–1pm & 3–7pm; free), containing an eighteenth-century private collection of archeological finds, fossils and paintings. In the corner of the square, the **Galleria Parmeggiani** (Mon–Fri 9am–noon, Sat 9am–noon & 3–7pm; Sun & hols 10am–1pm & 3–7pm; free) houses an important collection of Spanish, Flemish and Italian art, including sculptures and bronzes, as well as costumes and textiles. Nearby stands the church of **Madonna della Ghiara**, built in the seventeenth century and decorated with Bolognese School frescoes of scenes from the Old Testament and a *Crucifixion* by Guercino.

Practicalities

Reggio is on the main rail line between Bologna and Milan. The **train station** is on Piazza Marconi I, just east of the old centre; the **bus station** is on the west side of the public gardens on Via Raimondo Franchetti. The **tourist office** is in the main Piazza Prampolini (Mon–Sat 8.30am–1pm & 2.30–6pm, Sun 9am–noon; ℡0522.451.152, ⓦwww.municipio.re.it/turismo), while the helpful **Club Alpino Italiano** office at Viale Mille 32 (℡0522.436.685) has information on walking in the nearby hills (Tues, Wed & Fri 6–7.30pm, Thurs & Sat 8.30–10.30pm; closed most of August). For **Internet** access head for *Qui Qua Navigator*, Piazza Fontanesi 4 (Mon–Sat 9am–7.30pm).

If you're planning **to stay**, hotel space is often limited so book ahead. The *Ariosto* on Via San Rocco 12 (℡0522.437.320, Ⓕf0522.452.514; ❷) is a central and reasonably priced hotel, while the *Posta*, Piazza del Monte 2 (℡0522.432.944, ⓦwww.hotelposta.re.it; ❻), is in the historic Palazzo del Capitano del Popolo and is the choice for anyone desiring a taste of fabulous luxury. There's an attractive **youth hostel**, *Ostello Basilica della Ghiara*, 1km from the train station at Via Guasco 6 (℡0522.452.323, but prefer reservations by fax Ⓕf0522.454.795; no lock-out or curfew; €15 with breakfast).

Food and drink options are relatively good. *Caffe Arti E Mestieri*, Via Emilia S. Pietro 14 (closed Sun & Mon), is a rather smart restaurant with a menu of stylishly updated classic dishes from the region (expect to pay around €35–40 for two courses with wine), while *Canossa*, at Via Roma 37 (closed Wed), specializes in various ham antipasti and is consistently popular with locals (€25–30 for two courses). *La Casseruola*, not far from the central piazza at Via S. Carlo 5a (closed Tues), is a bustling pizzeria, with tables outside.

Around Reggio

The foothills **south of Reggio** are cheese country. Signs along the roadside advertise the local *parmigiano-reggiano* and the village of **CASINA**, 27km outside Reggio on the N63 to La Spezia, holds a popular Festa del Parmigiano in August, when the vats of cheese mixture are stirred with enormous wooden paddles.

With your own transport, you can take the side road leading from Casina to **CANOSSA**. This was the seat of the powerful Da Canossa family, whose most famous member, the Countess Mathilda of Tuscany (La Gran Contessa), was a big name here in the eleventh century – unusually so in a society largely controlled by warlords and the clergy. She was known for donning armour and leading troops into battle herself, and at the age of 43 scandalized the nobility by marrying a youth of 17. The remains of the **Castle** (summer Tues–Sun 9am–12.30pm & 3–7pm; winter 9am–4.30pm; free) are largely thirteenth century, but it's really the location – on a rocky outcrop looking towards the mountains in one direction and over the neighbouring castle at Rossena and the towns strung out over the plain in the other – which is impressive. People from the surrounding towns are fond of coming out here at weekends to eat in the local **restaurants**, and it's a popular area for **hiking** or cross-country skiing. You may also see people armed with baskets for collecting **mushrooms** (legally, only baskets can be used, so as to allow the mushroom spores to fall back to the ground), or filling bottles with mineral water from the springs off the mountains.

High in the surrounding hills paths lead onto the mountain *crinale*, with **Castelnovo Ne'Monti** a possible base for local walks. Further on, at **Busana**, a road forks to the left, descending through a series of hairpin bends bordered by plenty of falling rock signs, in the Secchia Valley, climbing back up the other side through Cinquecerri to **Ligonchio** – another good starting-point for walks away from cable cars and ski lifts onto nearby **Monte Cusna** (2120m). Close by here are the Prati di Sara, a windswept expanse of grassland with small tarns and the occasional tree. As you ascend, you have more of a view across the layers of ridges, often half-obscured in the mist. It's possible to stay overnight in some of the refuges that group along the **Grand Escursione Apenninica** route, a 25-day trek that weaves its way back and forth across the border between Emilia and Tuscany. The Club Alpino Italiano office in Reggio (see p.463) should have information on this route.

Parma

Generally reckoned to have one of the highest standards of living in Italy, **PARMA**, about 30km along the Via Emilia northwest of Reggio, is about as

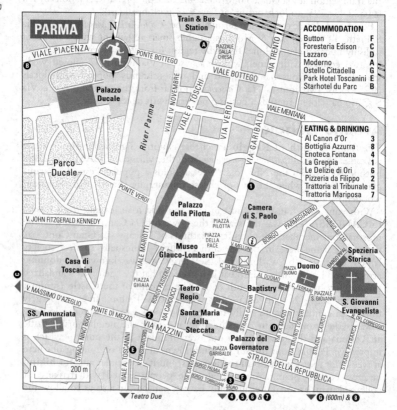

comfortable a town as you could wish for. The measured pace of its streets, the abundance of its restaurants and the general air of affluence are almost cloying, especially if you've arrived from the south. Not surprisingly, if you're travelling on a tight budget, Parma presents a few difficulties. That said, it's a friendly enough place, with plenty to see. A visit to the opera can be an experience – the audience are considered one of the toughest outside Milan's La Scala and don't pull any punches if they consider a singer to be performing badly – and the city's works of art include the legacy of two great artists, Correggio and Parmigianino.

Arrival and information

Parma's **train and bus stations** are fifteen minutes' walk from the central Piazza Garibaldi, or a short ride on buses #8 & #9. The **tourist office** is at Via Melloni 1a (Mon–Sat 9am–7pm, Sun 9am–1pm; closed Wed 1–3pm; ⓣ0521.218.855, ⓦhttp://turismo.comune.parma.it). Internet access is available at the old *Fiaccadori* bookshop on Strada Duomo 8a or at *Polidoro Web* (Mon–Sat 10am–8pm) in the Galleria Polidoro, a mall on the corner of Via Mazzini by the river.

Accommodation

If you're planning a trip during spring or the run-up to Christmas, be sure to book in advance as this is also trade-fair season in Parma. You really need to plan ahead for the town's cheaper **hotels** too, although there's a good alternative in the HI **hostel**, *Ostello Cittadella*, just south of the town centre in a converted castle in the Parco della Cittadella (ⓣ0521.961.434; €11; April–Oct) with a campsite attached – take bus #2, #12, #15 or #18 from the station. Alternatively there's the upmarket *Foresteria Edison* hostel, Largo VIII Marzo (ⓣ0521.924.368; reception closed 1–7pm; €25 including breakfast), attached to a cultural centre with gallery, theatre and open-air cinema. It's across the river to the southwest – to get there take bus #2 from the station to the last stop.

Button Borgo Salina 7 ⓣ0521.208.039, ⓔhotelbutton@tin.it. Small but very well-appointed and pretty decent value three-star with air-conditioned rooms. ❸
Lazzaro Via XX Marzo 14 ⓣ0521.208.944. A tiny, homely establishment offering basic rooms with bathrooms above its own, very good restaurant. ❷
Moderno Via A. Cecchi 4 ⓣ0521.772.647. Inexpensive two-star near the station, offering spacious rooms, with or without private baths. It can suffer from street noise though. ❷

Park Hotel Toscanini Viale Toscanini 4 ⓣ0521.289.141, ⓦwww.hoteltoscanini.com. Lavish four-star that's home to the Italian football team whenever they are in town. Great position sandwiched between the river and most of the main sights. ❹
Starhotel du Parc Viale Piacenza 12c ⓣ0521.292.929, ⓦwww.starhotels.it. Luxurious conversion of an old palace on the north side of the Parco Ducale, complete with fitness room, Internet access and two restaurants. ❾

The Town

Parma's main street, **Via Mazzini**, and its continuation, **Strada della Repubblica**, run east from the river, past **Piazza Garibaldi** which, together with the narrow streets and alleyways that wind to the south and west, forms the fulcrum of Parma. The majority of the town's museums and churches lie to the north of here, with a few points of interest, worthy of a stroll, lying across the river.

Piazza Garibaldi and Piazza Duomo

The mustard-coloured **Palazzo del Governatore** forms the backdrop of Piazza Garibaldi, behind which the Renaissance church of **Santa Maria della Steccata** (daily 9am–noon & 3–6pm; free) was apparently built using Bramante's original plan for St Peter's as a model. Inside there are frescoes by a number of sixteenth-century painters, notably **Parmigianino**, who spent the last ten years of his life on this work, eventually being sacked for breach of contract by the disgruntled church authorities. A year later he was dead, aged 37, "an almost savage or wild man" who had become obsessed with alchemy, according to Vasari.

Five minutes' walk away – turn right off Strada Cavour – the slightly gloomy **Piazza Duomo** forms part of the old *centro episcopale*, away from the shopping streets of the commercial centre. The Lombard–Romanesque **Duomo** (daily 9am–12.30pm & 3–7pm; free), dating from the eleventh century, holds earlier work by Parmigianino in its south transept, executed when the artist was a pupil of **Correggio** – who painted the fresco of the Assumption in the central cupola. Finished in 1534, this is among the most famous of Correggio's works, the Virgin Mary floating up through a sea of limbs, faces and swirling drapery, which attracted some bemused comments at the time. One contemporary compared it to a "hash of frogs' legs", while Dickens, visiting much later, thought it a sight that "no operative surgeon gone mad could imagine in his wildest delirium". Correggio was paid for the painting with a sackful of small change to annoy him, since he was known to be a great miser. The story goes that he carried the sack of coins home in the heat, caught a fever and died at the age of 40. Before you leave, take a look at the relief of the Deposition on the west wall of the south transept, an impressive work by the architect Benedetto Antelami that dates from 1178.

There's a more significant work by Antelami outside the duomo, in the form of the beautiful octagonal **Baptistry** (daily 9am–12.30pm & 3–6.30pm; €4), its sugary pink Verona marble rising four storeys high, encircled by a band of sculpture and topped off with some slim turrets. The three elaborately carved portals serve as a meeting place in the evening. Bridging the gap between the Romanesque and Gothic styles, this is considered Antelami's finest work; starting in 1196, the architect sculpted the frieze that surrounds the building and was also responsible for the reliefs inside, including the polychrome figures above the door and a series of sculptures representing the months and seasons that have been painstakingly scrubbed down and restored. There's more work by Correggio in the cupola of the church of **San Giovanni Evangelista** behind the duomo (daily 8am–noon & 3.30–6pm; free) – a fresco of the Vision of St John at Patmos. Next door, the **Spezieria Storica di San Giovanni Evangelista**, at Borgo Pipa 1 (daily 8.30am–1.45pm; €2), is a thirteenth-century pharmacy that preserves its medieval interior.

Via Garibaldi and around

A short walk northwest from Piazza Duomo, the **Camera di San Paolo** in the former Benedictine Convent off Via Garibaldi on Via Melloni (daily 9am–1.45pm; €2) houses more frescoes by Correggio executed in 1519; above the fireplace, the abbess who commissioned the work is portrayed by Correggio as the goddess Diana. Around the corner on Piazza della Pace, the **Museo Glauco-Lombardi** at Via Garibaldi 15 (Tues–Sat 10am–3pm, Sun 9am–1pm; €4) has a display of memorabilia relating to Marie-Louise of Austria, who reigned here after the defeat of her husband Napoleon at Waterloo. She set herself up with another suitor (much to the chagrin of her exiled spouse) and expanded the Parma violet perfume industry.

Across the street from here, it's hard to miss Parma's biggest monument, the **Palazzo della Pilotta**, surrounded by vast expanses of wonderfully green lawn set off by modern fountains. Begun for Alessandro Farnese – the wily Pope Paul III – in the sixteenth century, the building was reduced to a shell by World War II bombing, but has been rebuilt and now houses a number of Parma's museums, including the main art gallery, the **Galleria Nazionale** (Tues–Sun 9am–1.45pm; €6, including the Teatro Farnese), a modern, high-tech display that includes more work by Correggio and Parmigianino, and the remarkable *Apostles at the Sepulchre* and *Funeral of the Virgin* by Carracci – massive, overwhelming canvases, suspended either side of a gantry at the top of the building.

The **Teatro Farnese** (same times as gallery; €2, €6 including the Galleria Nazionale), which you pass through to get to the gallery, in the former arms room of the palace, was almost entirely destroyed by bombing in 1944. The restored theatre, still used occasionally, has an extended semicircle of seats three tiers high, made completely of wood, in a facsimile of Palladio's Teatro Olympico at Vicenza, and also houses Italy's first revolving stage. On the lower floor, the **Museo Archeologico Nazionale** (daily 9am–7.30pm; €2) is a less essential stop but still worth a glance, with finds from the prehistoric lake villages around Parma, as well as the table top on which the Emperor Trajan notched up a record of his gifts to the poor.

Across the river

Behind the *palazzo*, the Ponte Verdi crosses the River Parma, bringing you to the **Parco Ducale** (April–Oct 6am–midnight; Nov–March 7am–8pm; free), a set of eighteenth-century formal gardens arranged to offset the sixteenth-century **Palazzo Ducale** (Mon–Sat 9.30am–noon; €3) built for Ottaviano Farnese and filled with frescoes by Carracci. Just south, the **Casa di Toscanini** on Via R. Tanzi (Tues–Sat 9am–1pm & 2–6pm, Sun 10am–1pm; €1.50) is the birthplace of the conductor who debuted in the Teatro Regio here (see p.468), and just one of the sights that recall Parma's strong musical heritage. Further south still, on the same side of the river, the embalmed body of the violinist Niccolo Paganini rests under a canopy in the **Cimitero della Villetta** (daily: summer 8am–12.30pm & 4–7pm; winter 8am–12.30pm & 2.30–5pm; free).

Eating and drinking

Many **restaurants** in Parma – especially the ones in the centre – can be rather pricey, though less expensive options do exist, most noticeably on Via Garibaldi and Strada Farini. Local specialities include the obvious Parma ham (prosciutto) and *parmigiano reggiano* – which are often served together as an antipasto – as well as *guancia di manzo*, cheek of beef. For snacks, prosciutto stuffed into pastries and other local delights are available for around €2 from the many bakeries, and picnic supplies can be bought at the market by the river on Piazza Ghiaia (Wed & Sat).

Al Canon d'Or Via N. Sauro 3a. Slightly pricey place, housed in a former palace. Parmesan-flavoured specialities figure highly and there are over thirty wines on offer. Closed Wed.

Bottiglia Azzurra Borgo Felino 63. This place has a good choice of wines and hot snacks and stays open until 2am. Closed Sun.

Enoteca Fontana Strada Farini 24. Great authentic old bar, with long wooden tables, a huge choice of wines from all over the region and a menu that includes great sandwiches and steaming bowls of pasta – all reasonably priced. Closed Sun & Mon.

La Greppia Via Garibaldi 39a ⓣ0521.233.686. Even by Parma's elegant, expensive standards, this is a cut above offering dishes such as risotto with strawberries and chicken. Wine buffs will be spoilt for choice with almost 600 wines available. Closed Mon & Tues.

Le Delizie di Ori Strada Farini 19a. Prize-winning, well-priced café, crammed with mouthwatering cakes and *gelati*.

Pizzeria da Filippo Via Mazzini 41a. Very cheap and central option near the river with comfortable dining, both inside and out. Pizzas are the main thing but it also serves some of the best-priced local specialities around – try the *risotto alla parmigiana*. Closed Sun.

Trattoria al Tribunale Vicolo Politi 5b, up an alley-way off Strada Farini ☎0521.285.527. Affordable gourmet option that serves large plates of creamy pink prosciutto and other antipasti delights. More adventurous diners might like to try the braised veal cheek. Closed Tues.

Trattoria Mariposa B. Garimberti 27. Tucked away in a side street off Strada Farini, the butterfly is a comfortable restaurant, decorated with 1950s black and white photography. The light and flaky *crostini* is a must. Closed Sun & Mon eve.

7 Entertainment

For nightlife in refined Parma, **opera** and **theatre** take precedence over clubs. Fans of the former should head to the **Teatro Regio**, at Via Garibaldi 16a (☎0521.218.678, ⊕www.teatroregioparma.org). **Teatro Due**, next to the river on Viale Basetti, is the home of one of the top theatre companies in Europe, the **Colletivo di Parma**, who perform between October and April (☎0521.230.242, ⊕www.teatrodue.org) and in the Palazzo della Pilotta in June and July – their shows draw on a tradition of comedy and political theatre. In summer the city's entertainment options become more diverse – the piazzas host live jazz bands and during July and August locals flock to the garden behind **Camera di San Paolo** for a free season on Wednesday nights of old horror movies, dubbed in Italian (⊕www.ufficiocinema.it).

In addition to all its highbrow cultural offerings, Parma also had in the 1990s a Uefa cup-winning **football** team, which was bankrolled by the Tanzi family, owner of the dairy company Parmalat, the local industrial giant. A criminal investigation into the company in 2003, however, led to its collapse and a large reversal in its dependent team's fortunes. Though still in Serie A, the Italian first division, the team no longer competes for top honours and often struggles to fill its stadium, which, happily from a tourist perspective, at least makes it that much easier to visit. Tickets are often available throughout the season, even for matches with the bigger clubs such as AC Milan. Buses #8 and #9 link the train station with the Stadio Ennio Tardini, which lies around a fifteen-minute ride from the centre at Viale Partigiani d'Italia (☎0521.505.111, ⊕www.fcparma.com).

South of Parma

The countryside **around Parma** is a strange mixture: some of the major roads follow bleak gorges, skirting the edge of blank rock walls for miles; others look as if they will lead precisely nowhere before emerging into meadows and orchards with rich farmland stretching into the distance.

Prime targets are any of the **medieval castles** strung out across the foothills. There are around twenty, many built by the powerful Farnese dynasty. The website ⊕www.castellidelducato.it has a useful map locating all the castles and can help you plan a tour. It's also worth buying a Castelli del Ducato card (€1) available from tourist offices or the castles themselves that will give you a twenty percent reduction on admission fees. One of the best-sited castles is at **TORRECHIARA**, about 18km south of Parma and connected by hourly buses. The castle provides a superb vantage point over the surrounding area and also has frescoes by Bembo in the **Camera d'Oro**

(April–Sept Tues–Sun 9am–7.30pm; Oct–March Tues–Fri 9am–4pm, Sat & Sun 9am–5pm; €3).

One of the most famous Parma hams (*Prosciutto di Langhirano*) comes from the foothills around **LANGHIRANO**, which is a few kilometres further on and also linked by regular bus with Parma. The experts say the ham cures so successfully here because of the unique mixture of clear mountain air and sea breezes blowing over the Apennines from Liguria; it is served simply with butter, so as not to mask the fine flavour. The town itself has grown into a mass of stainless steel warehouses – there's no reason to come unless you want to carry a haunch of meat round with you for the rest of your holiday. But the countryside around, particularly near Calestano, is beautiful. Apart from the rail route, the fast way over the mountains is by **autostrada**, the A15, which snakes its way in and out of a succession of tunnels, giving glimpses of lush, hidden valleys, vines and orchards.

The slower N62 gives access to the *crinale* of the mountains: the trails are a popular attraction for walkers these days, but served a quite different purpose in the last war, when adults and children made the long journey by foot, carrying sacks of salt from the coast to trade for food. The writer Eric Newby was hidden by villagers in these mountains as an escaped prisoner of war in 1943, and the book chronicling his experiences, *Love and War in the Apennines*, captures the beauty of the region

CORNIGLIO, reached by bus from Parma, is a centre for hiking and skiing; try the atmospheric, *Ostello Corniglio.it* (℡0521.881.012, ⓦwww.ostello corniglio.it; €10) if you want to stay. More buses squeeze themselves round the tight bends to the small villages of Monchio (16km), Trefiumi (20km) and Prato Spilla (23km from Corniglio), leaving you on the lower slopes of **Monte Malpasso** (1716m) – glistening with small lakes and tarns. Buses also run to **Lagdei** (14km), a starting point for further walks.

West of Parma

The Via Emilia continues west from Parma, with small towns mushrooming out from the edges of the road, mostly just a ribbon of shops and roadside cafés. **FIDENZA**, the first place of any size, has a Lombard-Romanesque **cathedral** with a richly decorated facade worked on by followers of the Parma master, Antelami. As Fidenza was a major staging post on the pilgrimage route to Rome, the carvings depict pilgrims as well as more domestic subjects – strings of sausages festoon one figure, while elsewhere there are hunting scenes. The building itself is an important and relatively rare example of architecture from the Romanesque-Gothic transition period.

The countryside **to the north** of here is the *bassa*, flat, low country (where Parmese-born Bertolucci filmed the epic *1900*) cut by drainage ditches and open fields growing wheat and corn, sugar beet and vines. In summer it's scorching hot and almost silent, with an odd, still beauty all its own, but generally it's a place to pass through on your way to somewhere else. The small towns and villages of the region are quiet and mainly undistinguished. **SORAGNA** is a good place to be at the end of April/first weekend in May for its grand agricultural *festa*, with local wine, cheese and salami tasting. At any time of year, the aroma wafting out of the *salumerie* in the main square may tempt you to sample its array of local produce, also available at *Ristorante Stella d'Oro*, in the side alley Via Mazzini. The small market town is dominated by the tenth-century palace of **Rocca Meli Lupi di Soragna** (Tues–Sun: March–Oct 9–11am & 3–6pm; Nov–Feb 9–11am & 2.30–5pm; Ⓦwww .roccadisoranga.com; €7), still owned by the local Meli Lupi family who ran the town between the fourteenth and eighteenth centuries. The dozen or so rooms are furnished with the original sixteenth-century pieces and decorated with frescoes, some by Parmigianino.

The attractive village of **FONTANELLATO**, a few kilometres northeast of Fidenza, was the site of the camp where Eric Newby was imprisoned, but is perhaps better known as a centre for the production of parmesan cheese. Its central square is dominated by the **Rocca Sanvitale** (April–Oct daily 9.30am–12.30pm & 3–6pm; Nov–March Tues–Sun 9.30am–12.30pm & 3–6pm; by tour only, in Italian, last tour an hour before closing; €3.80), a fifteenth-century moated castle that the Sanvitale family called home until the onset of World War II. Inside there are some ancient pieces of furniture and a fresco of the legend of Diana and Acteon by Parmigianino.

Five kilometres to the north, the small village of **LE RONCOLE** marks the start of **Verdi** country. By the main road on Piazza Giovannino Guareschi – named after the author of the Don Camillo books who also lived here – you can visit the humble **house** where the great composer was born (Tues–Sun: April–Sept 9.30am–12.30pm & 3–7pm; Oct & Nov 9.30am–12.30pm & 2.30–5.30pm; €4). Some 5km up the road is **BUSSETO**, the childhood home of Verdi and the centre of the Verdi industry that has grown up around the composer, with regular opera performances during summer. It's an appealing little battlemented town, but the main attractions are strictly for Verdi pilgrims. The **Salone Barezzi** (Tues–Sun: April–Sept 10am–12.30pm & 3–6.30pm; Oct–March 10am–12.30pm & 2.30–5.30pm; €3) on the main street, Via Roma 119, now a Verdi museum, was the home of Antonio Barezzi, a wealthy merchant who spotted the young Verdi's talent and brought him in as a teacher for his daughter. Verdi lived here for a while and later married his pupil, Margherita. Now restored to its nineteenth-century state, the museum contains the piano that Verdi played on, the first portrait of the maestro and memorabilia such as the baton that Toscanini used to conduct his Verdi memorial concert in 1926. The rather unfriendly tourist office in Busseto's old *rocca* at Piazza Verdi 10 (Ⓣ0524.92.487, Ⓦwww.bussetolive.com) may give you information about the sights and about tickets for concerts in the **Verdi Theatre**. You'll need private transport to get to the last of the Verdi sights, the composer's **villa**, a couple of kilometres west of Busseto at **SANT'AGATA DI VILLANOVA**. The villa (Ⓦwww.villaverdiorg), which contains a mock-up of the Milan hotel room where Verdi died, is open for guided tours, lasting 45 minutes (Tues–Sun: April–Sept 9–11.45am & 3–6.45pm; Oct–March 9.30–11.45am & 2.30–5.30pm; €6).

A little way south of here is the beautiful **CASTELL'ARQUATO**, a nicely restored medieval town set on a hillside overlooking the Arda Valley. At the top of the town is Piazza del Municipio, lined with some stunning buildings. The thirteenth-century **Palazzo del Podestà** isn't open to the public, but you can visit the **Basilica**, a magnificently preserved Romanesque monument with an eighth-century baptismal font in the right-hand apse. The newly restored tower of the fourteenth-century **Rocca Viscontea** (Tues–Sun: March–Oct 10am–noon & 3–6pm; Nov–Feb 10am–noon & 3–5pm; €3) offers amazing views of the surrounding countryside.

The **tourist office** (March–Oct Tues–Sat 9.30am–12.30pm, Sun 10am–noon & 3–4.30pm; Nov–Feb Tues–Sat 9.30am–12.30pm; Ⓣ0523.803.091, Ⓦwww .comune.castellarquato.pc.it) is in a hut by the bridge over the river.

Accommodation is thin on the ground; try the friendly, comfortable *Leon d'Oro* at Piazza Europa 6 (☎0523.803.651; ❷) at the bottom of the town, which has simply furnished doubles. **Restaurants and cafés** on the other hand are plentiful: *La Falconiere* (closed Mon) serves local specialities in the atmospheric surroundings of the castle. For more humble dining there's *Osteria La Cantina*, on Vicolo Riorzo 1, which does big salads and *primi* from around €6. For snacks and pastries you can't beat the thriving bakery/café *La Casa del Pane* on Piazza Europa.

East along the Via Emilia from Bologna

East of Bologna, the Via Emilia passes through a clutch of small towns – some of them industrialized and mostly postwar, like Forlì, the unappealing administrative capital of the region, others, like **Faenza**, with medieval piazzas surrounded by towers and battlements. Both started life as Roman way-stations and were under the rule of the Papal States for much of their subsequent history. The **lowlands** to the north are farmed intensively, while on the southern side lie hilly vineyards and pastures, narrow gorges that lead up into the mountains and a couple of ski resorts around Monte Fumaiolo (1407m).

Faenza

Travelling east, cypress trees and umbrella pines, gentler hills and vineyards signal the fact that you're leaving Emilia and entering the Romagna – although strictly speaking there's no distinct boundary between the two regions. **FAENZA**, 50km from Bologna, gives its name to the faïence-ware it has been producing for the last six hundred years. This style of decorated ceramic ware reached its zenith in the fifteenth and sixteenth centuries, and the town is worth a visit for the vast **Museo Internazionale delle Ceramiche** alone (April–Oct Tues–Sat 9am–7pm, Sun 9.30am–1pm & 3–7pm; Nov–March Tues–Fri 9am–1.30pm, Sat 9.30am–1.30pm & 3–6pm, Sun 9am–1pm & 3–6pm; €6); it's at Viale Baccarini 19 – take Corso D. Baccarini from the station, and it's on the left. The massive collection includes early work painted in the characteristic blue and ochre, and later, more colourful work, often incorporating portraits and landscapes with exhibits from the Far East and Middle East too. The overall highlight is perhaps the Sala Europa, featuring ceramic art by Picasso, Matisse and Chagall.

Faenza is still home to one of Italy's leading ceramics schools, teaching techniques of tin-glazing first introduced in the fourteenth century – the ceramics are decorated after glazing and are given a final lead-based, lustrous wash. The town is also a major production centre, with small workshops down most of its side streets; details of where to buy are available from the **tourist office** in Piazza del Popolo 1 (May–Sept Mon–Sat 9.30am–12.30pm & 3.30–6.30pm, Sun 9.30am–12.30pm; Oct–April Tues–Sat 9.30am–12.30pm & 3.30–5.30pm, closed Thurs pm; ☎0546.25.231, ⊛www.prolocofaenza.it).

The rest of Faenza is an attractive town with buildings garnished with ceramic art and an appealing medieval centre formed by the long, crenellated **Palazzo del Podestà**, the **Piazza del Popolo** and the **Piazza della Libertà**, which is the scene of much activity on market days (Tuesday, Thursday and Saturday). **Piazza Martiri della Libertà** – through an archway from Piazza del Popolo – is where you'll find more stalls selling cheese and other local foodstuffs. In the summer local *bambini* turn entrepreneur hosting their own colourful **children's market** on Thursday afternoons in Piazza del Popolo until around 8pm, selling toys, books and bric-à-brac. Another good time to be in Faenza is for the **Palio del Niballo** (ⓦwww.racine.ra.it/niballo), which takes place on the last Sunday in June. If you want to **stay** here, you might consider a bed-and-breakfast, around half the price of a hotel – ask the tourist office for the list of *affittacamere*. The best hotel in town is the *Vittoria*, Corso Garibaldi 23 (ⓣ0546.21.508; ②), a few blocks north of Piazza del Popolo, featuring nineteenth-century decor and a dining room with a frescoed ceiling. **Eating** prospects are mainly centred around the Piazza del Popolo but the *Osteria del Mercato* in the Piazza Martiri della Libertà is a good, lively place, frequented by locals.

Brisighella

South of Faenza, and accessible by train, the village of **BRISIGHELLA**, half-way up a hillside, is famed for its restaurants (visited by people from as far afield as Milan) and its **Via degli Asini** – a raised, covered lane once part of the town fortifications, used to protect mule trains carrying olive oil and clay for making ceramics. The medieval fortress topping the cliffs over the town was held first by the local Manfredi family, then successively by Cesare Borgia, the Venetians and the pope. The thirteenth-century **Torre dell'Orologio** sits on a spur of rock opposite, while below the town, down by the River Lamone, is the **Pieve del Tho**, an eleventh-century church, built on top of the remains of an earlier temple to Jupiter. It's worth coming here at carnival time and in mid-July for the Feste Medievali (ⓦwww.festemedioevali.org). Other high points in the year are the Sagra (festival) della Polenta (October), del Tartufo (truffle) and dell' Ulivo (both in November).

One of Brisighella's best **restaurants** is *La Grotta Osteria con Uso di Cucina* serving excellent Romagnolo dishes; it's not cheap, but does have an affordable fixed-price menu (ⓣ0546.81.829; closed Tues). Or there's the *Cantina del Bonsignore*, at Via Recuperati 4 (ⓣ0546.81.889; open till midnight, closed Thurs), offering an interesting menu and good wine in a romantic setting. You'll need to book well in advance if you wish to **stay** in the old town, especially during the food festivals in November. Top choice is the imposing *Albergo Gigiole* on the main square at Piazza Carducci 5 (ⓣ0546.81.209, ⓦwww.gigiole.it; ⑤), offering four-star luxury; the chef here started the whole food thing off when his restaurant (closed Mon) proved a magnet for aspiring chefs. *La Rocca*, just up the hill at Via delle Volte 10 (ⓣ0546.81.180, ⓦwww.albergo-larocca.com; ②), has cheaper and simpler rooms, and a pretty decent restaurant, or you can stay in one of the numerous agriturismo places, details of which are available at the very helpful **tourist office** at Porta Gabolo 5 (April–Oct Mon–Fri 9.30am–12.30pm & 4–6pm, Sat 3–5pm; Nov–March Mon–Fri 10.30am–12.30pm; open Sun during holiday season; ⓣ0546.81.166, ⓦwww.racine.ra.it/sda).

Ferrara

Thirty minutes' train ride north of Bologna, **FERRARA** was the residence of the Este dukes, an eccentric dynasty that ranked as a major political force throughout Renaissance times. The Este kept the main artists of the day in commissions and built a town which, despite a relatively small population, was – and still is – one of the most elegant urban creations of the period.

At the end of the sixteenth century, with no heir to inherit their lands, the Este were forced to hand over Ferrara to the papacy and leave for good. Life in the city effectively collapsed: eighteenth-century travellers found a ghost town

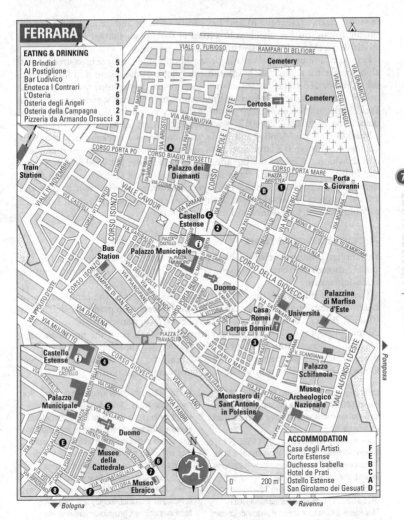

FERRARA

EATING & DRINKING
Al Brindisi	5
Al Postiglione	4
Bar Ludivico	1
Enoteca I Contrari	7
L'Osteria	6
Osteria degli Angeli	8
Osteria della Campagna	2
Pizzeria da Armando Orsucci	3

ACCOMMODATION
Casa degli Artisti	F
Corte Estense	E
Duchessa Isabella	B
Hotel de Prati	C
Ostello Estense	A
San Girolamo dei Gesuati	D

▼ Bologna   ▼ Ravenna

of empty streets and clogged-up canals infested with mosquitoes. Since then Ferrara has picked itself up, dusted itself down, and is now the centre of a key fruit-producing area, to which the expanse of neat, pollarded trees outside town testifies. It's a popular stop for tourists travelling up from Bologna to Venice, but they rarely stay, leaving the city centre enjoyably peaceful in the evenings.

Arrival and information

Ferrara's **train station** is west of the city walls, a fifteen-minute walk along Viale Cavour to the centre of town, or take bus #1, #2, #9 or #3C (#2 is the most direct). The **bus station** lies just southwest of the main square, on Corso Isonzo. The main **tourist office** can be found in the *castello* courtyard (Mon–Sat 9am–1pm & 2–6pm, Sun 9.30am–1pm & 2–5.20pm; ☎0532.299.303,

Ⓦwww.ferraraterraeacqua.it) and has plenty of maps and general information on the town. You can check your **email** at the *Ferrara Internet Point*, Via degli Adelardi 17 (Mon–Fri 11am–1pm & Sat 3.30–5pm).

Ferrara is famous as a *città della bicicletta*. Although the city's cobbled streets don't always make for a particularly smooth ride, much of the centre is at least closed off to motorized traffic, so you won't have to spend your time weaving in and out of cars. Bikes can be rented at the station (to the left as you come out, from Pirani e Bagni Ⓣ0532.772.190 or inside the city walls from Cicli Romanelli, Via della Luna 10 (Ⓣ0532.206.017, Ⓦwwwferraracicli.it) for around €2 per hour.

Market days are Monday and Friday and on the first weekend of the month (except Aug) there is a large **antiques** market in the centre between the *castello* and the duomo. One of the big annual events, held the last weekend in May, is the **Palio**, smaller than the famous Siena race, but still an exciting time to be here (Ⓦwww.paliodiferrara.it). In August, the streets of the town ring to the annual **buskers' festival** (Ⓦwww.ferrarabuskers.com), with musical offerings ranging from African drums to Dixieland bands.

Accommodation

Ferrara has a number of affordable **hotels**, most of them handily placed in the centre, though booking is advised, especially during the spring and autumn trade-fair season.

The town's HI **hostel**, the *Ostello Estense*, is northwest of the centre at Corso Biagio Rossetti 24, and has huge, spotlessly clean rooms with grand wooden beams (Ⓣ0532.204.227, Ⓔhostelferrara@hotmail.com; reception closed 10am–3.30pm; curfew 11.30pm; €17). The nearest **campsite**, *Estense*, is on the northeast edge of town at Via Gramicia 76 (Ⓣ0532.752.396, Ⓔcampeggio.estense@libero.it; open all year; €5 per person); take bus #1 from the train station to Piazzale San Giovanni by the walls, from where it's a ten-minute walk north.

Casa degli Artisti Via Vittoria 66 Ⓣ0532.761.038. Friendly, budget option in a modern block in the medieval quarter. Rooms available with or without bathrooms. ❶

Corte Estense Via Correggiari 4a Ⓣ0532.242.176, Ⓦwww.corteestense.it. This grand option with its elegant courtyard and spacious rooms is centrally located, close to the duomo. ❹

Duchessa Isabella Via Palestro 70 Ⓣ0532.202.121, Ⓦwww.duchessaisabella.it. This Relais & Chateaux affiliated sixteenth-century building filled with bright frescoes is the top choice for five-star luxury. Closed Aug. ❽

Hotel de Prati Via Padiglioni 5 Ⓣ0532.241.905, Ⓦwww.hoteldeprati.com. Close by the *castello*, this central option is draped with modern paintings and offers comfortable rooms with antique furniture. Prices rise during trade-fair season. ❸

San Girolamo dei Gesuati Via Madama 40a Ⓣ0532.207.448, Ⓦwww.sangirolamo deigesuati.com. Quiet, friendly and good-value hotel overlooking a green courtyard near the Palazzo Schifanoia. ❸

The Town

Ferrara's main sights are clustered together in an area that's easily explored on foot. The castle is the main focus of interest, but several other palaces and museums offer reminders of the town's more glorious past.

The Castello Estense

The bulky, moated **Castello Estense** (Tues–Sun 9.30am–5.30pm, last entry 4.45pm; €6) dominates the centre of Ferrara, built in response to a late-fourteenth-century uprising and generally held at the time to be a major feat of military engineering. Behind its impenetrable brick walls, the Este court

△ Castello Estense

thrived, supporting artists like Pisanello, Jacopo Bellini, Mantegna, and the poets Ariosto and Tasso. The Este dukes' coffers were kept flowing by imaginative and not always respectable means such as the selling of official titles, putting up the tolls for traffic along the Po, and supplying troops for the rulers of Naples, Milan and Florence.

The first of the **Este** to live here was Nicolò II, who commissioned the castle, though his descendants were responsible for its decoration. One of the most famous later members of the family was Nicolò III d'Este, who took over in 1393. Nicolò was a well-known patron of the arts and notorious for his amorous liaisons. He was also a ruthless man who is said to have murdered his wife Parisina and his son by another woman, Ugo, when he discovered that they were having an affair. Three other sons, Leonello, Borso and Ercole (Nicolò's heir), also made their mark and oversaw some of Ferrara's most civilized years. When Ercole's children, Beatrice and Isabella, married into the Sforza and Gonzaga families, the Este's status as one of the most glittering of Renaissance dynasties was assured. Ercole's grandson, Alfonso I, married **Lucrezia Borgia**, who continued to support the retinue of artists and poets, patronizing Titian and Ariosto – as did the last Este duke, Alfonso II, who invited Tasso and Guarini to his court. It's hard to credit all this as you walk through the castle now, most of which is used as offices and inaccessible to the public. The few rooms that you can see go some way to bringing back the days of Este magnificence, especially the *saletta* and Salone dei Giochi, or games rooms, decorated by Sebastiano Filippi with vigorous scenes of wrestling, discus-throwing, ball-tossing and chariot-racing. There's also the less-innocent poison room which was apparently mainly used as a toxic pharmacy for the Este's political enemies.

Piazza Municipio and the Duomo

Just south of here, the crenellated **Palazzo Municipale**, built in 1243 but much altered and restored since, holds statues of Nicolò III and son, Borso, on its facade – though they're actually twentieth-century reproductions. Walk through the arch into the pretty, enclosed square of **Piazza Municipio** for a view of the rest of the building. Opposite the Palazzo Municipio, the **Duomo** is a mixture of Romanesque and Gothic styles and has a monumental facade, focused on a carved central portal that was begun in the mid-twelfth century and finished a century or so later. Much of the carving depicts the Last Judgement, with the damned souls grimacing on the central frieze and hell itself depicted on the central lunette, while below the frieze bodies climb out of their coffins. Inside, the main part of the church has the grandeur of a ballroom, with sparkling chandeliers, but is much less intriguing than the exterior carving, and it's in the **Museo della Cattedrale**, housed in the former church of San Romano across the square (Tues–Sun 9.30am–noon & 3–6pm; €5), that the real treasures are kept. The highlight of the collection is a set of bas-reliefs illustrating the labours of the months, which formerly adorned the outside of the cathedral, and a beautiful *Madonna* by della Quercia.

The medieval quarter

The long arcaded south side of the duomo flanks **Piazza Trento e Trieste**, whose rickety-looking rows of shops herald the arcades of the appealing **Via San Romano** that runs off the far side of the square past the museum. Beyond this lies the labyrinth of alleyways that make up Ferrara's medieval quarter; the arched **Via delle Volte**, a long street running east, parallel to Via Carlo Mayr, is one of the most characteristic. At Via Mazzini 95 a couple of **synagogues** and the **Museo Ebraico di Ferrara**, the town's small **Jewish** museum (visits by guided tour only Sun–Thurs 10am, 11am & noon; €4), with a display of ritual objects, preserve the memory of the town's small Jewish community. On the wider streets above the tangled medieval district are a number of the Renaissance palaces once inhabited by Ferrara's better-heeled families with most of them now closed to the public. The **Casa Romei**, at Via Savonarola 30 (Tues–Sun 8.30am–7.30pm; €2), is a typical building of the time, with frescoes and graceful courtyards alongside artefacts rescued from various local churches. Just beyond is the house, at no. 19, where the monk Savonarola was born and lived for twenty years, while behind the palace, the monastery church of **Corpus Domini** at Via Pergolato 4 (Mon–Fri 9.30–11.30am & 3.30–5.30pm; free but contributions accepted) holds the tombs of Alfonso I and II d'Este and **Lucrezia Borgia**.

The southeast town centre

Two minutes southeast of Corpus Domini, the **Palazzo Schifanoia** – the "Palace of Joy" – at Via Scandiana 23 (Tues–Sun 9am–6pm; €5) is one of the grandest of Ferrara's palaces. It belonged to the Este family, and Cosimo Tura's frescoes inside transplanted their court to Arcadia. In the Salone dei Mesi (the "rooms of the months"), the blinds are kept closed to protect the colours, and the room seems silent and empty compared with what's happening on the walls. Borso features in many of the court scenes on the lowest of the three bands of frescoes, surrounded by friends and hunting dogs, along with groups of musicians, weavers and embroiderers with white rabbits nibbling the grass at their feet. Above, each section is topped with a sign of the zodiac and, above that, various mythological scenes.

On nearby Corso della Giovecca, at no. 170, the **Palazzina di Marfisa d'Este** (Tues–Sun 9am–1pm & 3–6pm; €3) has more frescoes, this time by Filippi, and although its gloomy interior is less impressive than the Schifanoia complex, in summer the loggia and orange grove are a welcome refuge from the heat. In the other direction, to the south, the **Museo Archeologico Nazionale**, Via XX Settembre 124 (Tues–Sun 9am–2pm; €4), holds the city's well-organized archeological collections, with finds from Spina, the Greco-Etruscan seaport and trading colony near Comacchio.

Down in the southeast corner of the town is a gem of a place: the **Monastero di Sant'Antonio in Polesine**, with exquisite frescoes (Mon–Sat 9.30–11.30am & 3–5pm, Sat 9.30–11.15am & 3–4pm; donations expected). Knock at the door of the convent and the nuns shepherd you into a chapel covered with works by the school of Giotto, including a rare *Flight from Egypt* in which Joseph carries Jesus on his shoulders.

North of the castle

There are some more impressive palaces north of the *castello*, on and around **Corso Ercole I d'Este** – named after Ercole I, who succeeded to the throne in 1441 after his father Nicolò III died, probably poisoned, and who promptly disposed of anyone likely to pose a threat. His reputation for coldness earned him nicknames such as "North Wind" and "Diamond" and his huge ambition led him to order the extension of the northern quarter of the city, the so-called "Herculean Addition", on such a grand scale that Ferrara was doubled, incorporating a planning system that was considered at the time to be boldly avant-garde. The **Palazzo dei Diamanti**, a little way down the Corso on the left, named after the 8500 pink and white marble ashlars in the form of pyramids (or diamonds) that stud its facade, was at the heart of Ercole's town plan and is nowadays used for temporary modern art exhibitions as well as being home to the recommended **Pinacoteca Nazionale** (daily 9am–7pm; €4), holding works from the Ferrara and Bologna schools, notably paintings by Dossi, Garofalo and Guercino, and a spirited St Christopher by "Il Bastianino" (Sebastiano Filippi). Next door is the small **Museo Michelangelo Antonioni** (Tues–Sun 9am–1pm & 3–6pm; €2) created to celebrate the Ferrarese film-maker's talent as a portrait, watercolour and oil painter. Upstairs is the main part of *The Enchanted Mountains* – the director compares the process of enlargement in this series as similar in operation to his most celebrated movie *Blow Up*.

Eating and drinking

Ferrara has a good range of **restaurants** and trattorias with prices to suit most pockets, plus a few bars in which to while away the evening with the locals.

Al Brindisi Via degli Adelardi 11. Around the back of the Duomo, this unprepossessing exterior – all chipped plaster and frayed posters – conceals Ferrara's oldest *osteria*, once frequented by the likes of Cellini and Titian. The food is reasonable and reasonably priced, but some of the vintages in the magnificent wine collection are among Italy's finest and priced accordingly. Closed Mon.
Al Postiglione Vicolo del Teatro 4. Tucked up a small alleyway opposite the castle, this *paninoteca*

serves up many different sandwich combinations, hot and cold, as well as home-made pasta and local wines. Open until midnight. Closed Tues & Sun eve.

Bar Ludivico Piazza Ariostea 7. Welcoming café/bar off a pretty piazza and full of gossiping locals. Great inventive salads and jumbo panini take their place alongside a large drinks menu.

Enoteca I Contrari Via Contrari 50. Friendly drinking place with outdoor seating and a happy atmosphere. Daily 6pm–1am, plus Mon–Fri noon–3pm.

L'Osteria Via Romei 51 ☎0532.207.673. Rather expensive but worth treating yourself – the *tortelli di zucca* (pumpkin ravioli) is something special. Closed Mon.

Osteria degli Angeli Via delle Volte 4. A convivial place, with lots of different wines and good food. Moderately priced with *primi* 7–8pm, *secondi* 9–10pm. Open 7–10pm. Closed lunch.

Osteria della Campana Via Borgo dei Leoni 26 ☎0532.241.256. Romantic but rather pricey

osteria near the *castello*. Goose sausages with raspberries and cheese and truffle flavoured *rigatoni* are just two choices from an interesting menu. Closed Mon.

Pizzeria da Armando Orsucci Via Saraceno 116. Low on prices but high on charm, this place's speciality – besides pizza – is *torta di ceci*, a chickpea-flour pie eaten straight out of the oven. Open till 1am; closed Thurs.

Ristorante Tassi Viale Repubblica 23, Bondeno ☎0532.893.030. Some 20km west of Ferrara – accessible by the "Bondeno" bus from the bus station – this place is a food lover's heaven. There's no menu; you just let Signor Tassi lead you through an amazing succession of fine dishes. It's not cheap (€30 per head without drinks) but it is unforgettable, and if you're wise, you'll book one of the comfortable large rooms upstairs (②) so you don't have too far to stagger to bed.

The Po Delta

East of Ferrara lies the **Po Delta**, an expanse of marshland and lagoons where the River Po splits into several channels, trickling to the sea, and small fingers of land poke out into the Adriatic. Etruscan traders set up the port of Spina here between the fourth and third centuries BC, when the sea covered much of the land from Comacchio to Ravenna. Partly owing to drainage schemes, the briny waters have since retreated by 12km, and the area becomes a bit less marshy each year – an advantage for local farmers but a threat to the many varieties of sea and shore **birds** that inhabit the area. The two main lagoons of **Valli di Comacchio** and **Valle Bertuzzi** have been designated as nature reserves to protect at least some of the wetlands and now constitute one of Europe's most highly regarded birdwatching areas, providing a habitat for nesting and migrating birds, including herons, egrets, curlews, avocets and terns.

The most evocative way of seeing the delta is by **boat**. There are a number of locals in the surrounding area who run guided tours. Signor Schiavi Vincenzino, Via Vicolo del Farol (☎0533.999.815), or Signor Dante Passarella, c/o *Ristorante USPA* (☎0533.999.817), both in Gorino, take out boats in summer if enough people are interested. And between April and October voluntary groups run free boat tours on a typical marshland boat called a *batane* from its mooring at the fish market of Trepponti in Comacchio – call ☎0523.312.516 or 0523.312.892 for more information. Two-hour boat trips also set off from the harbour of Stazione Foce, south of Comacchio (daily April–Oct at 9am, 11am, 3pm & 5pm; ☎0348.471.0332, ⊛www.vallidicomacchio.it/indexe.htm; €9.20, accessible by car only; follow signs for "Museo delle Valli". More information is available at the tourist office in Comacchio (see below).

Comacchio

The region's main centre, **COMACCHIO** is a small fishing town intersected by a network of canals, with a famous local attraction in its triple-bridge or **Trepponti**, built in 1634, which crosses three of the canals. Comacchio is an eel port and a good time to visit is in October when the Festival of the Eel sees wriggling masses of the creatures fished out of the canals on their way to the Sargasso Sea. Eel (*anguille*) unsurprisingly takes centre stage in many local restaurants with other regional dishes like fish risotto and *fritto misto* particularly recommended. Call in at the **tourist office** at Piazza Folegatti 28 (June–Oct Mon–Sat, 9.30am–12.30pm & 4–7pm, Sun 10am–12.30pm & 4–6.30pm; T0533.310.111, Wwww.comune.comacchio.fe.it) for more information.

Pomposa Abbey

About 20km north of Comacchio, and connected by buses from the port, the **Abbey of Pomposa** (daily 8.30am–7pm; €4) is about all the area has to offer in the way of orthodox sights, a lonely collection of buildings, saved from complete oblivion by numerous bus tours in summer. At the centre of a complex that includes a Lombard-Romanesque campanile, a chapterhouse and refectory, is an eighth-century **Basilica** containing frescoes by Vitale di Bologna and the Bolognese School. The abbey is better known for one of its monks, Guido d'Arezzo, who in the early eleventh century invented the musical scale here.

Only a few hundred years after Pomposa was built, it went into decline, the delta becoming marshier and malarial, and those who weren't killed off by the disease were left to scratch a living from hunting and fishing. The monks finally abandoned their abbey in the seventeenth century.

Ravenna and around

When **RAVENNA** became capital of the Western Roman Empire sixteen hundred years ago, it was more by quirk of fate than design. The Emperor Honorius, alarmed by armies invading from the north, moved his court from Milan to this obscure town on the Romagna coast around 402; it was easy to defend, surrounded by marshland, and was situated close to the port of Classis – at the time the biggest Roman naval base on the Adriatic. After enjoying a period of great monumental adornment as chief city of the empire, Ravenna was conquered by the Goths in 476. However, the new conquerors were also Christians and continued to embellish the city lavishly, particularly the Ostrogoth Theodoric, making it one of the most sought-after towns in the Mediterranean. In the mid-sixth century Byzantine forces annexed the city to the Eastern Empire and made it into an exarchate, under the rule of Constantinople.

The Byzantine rulers were responsible for Ravenna's most glorious era, keen to outdo rival cities with magnificent palaces, churches and art, and the city became one of the most compelling cultural centres in the world. The sixteenth century saw the sack of the city and its absorption into the Papal States, since when the Adriatic shoreline has receded, and an eleven-kilometre-long canal through a vast industrial complex now links Ravenna's port to the sea. But remnants of the dazzling Byzantine era are still thick on the ground – not least a set of mosaics at San Vitale that is generally acknowledged to be the crowning achievement of Byzantine art extant anywhere in the world. No fewer than eight of Ravenna's buildings have been designated World Heritage sites by Unesco.

Unlike Florence or Venice, say, tourism seems almost incidental to the life of the town, although the nearby **Mirabilandia**, (T0544.651.156, Wwww .mirabilandia.it) a Disneyesque theme park, helps bring in the crowds during summer. You can see the park's big wheel rising above the surrounding flat countryside as you approach the city. For a city that has such historic monuments,

Ravenna's centre feels surprisingly modern – a combination of Mussolini's building programme and allied bombs that levelled much of the city in World War II. It's a pleasant enough place to spend a couple of day and, though it has some excellent bars and restaurants, it's the churches and mosaics that will monopolize your time. Nightlife is sparse, but the lido towns a dozen or so kilometres away provide some excitement in summer.

Arrival and information

From the **train station** on Piazza Farini in the east of town, it's only a five-minute walk along Viale Farini and Via Armando Diaz to Ravenna's central square, **Piazza del Popolo**, which with the adjoining streets makes up the compact old centre. The **bus station** is across the tracks behind the train station, in Piazzale Aldo Moro.

Ravenna is not simply best explored on foot, with much of the centre pedestrianized, there's a good deal that can only be explored that way unless you opt for two wheels. **Bikes** can be hired from the Cooperativa San Vitale (Mon–Sat 7am–8pm; ☎0544.370.31), the green building next to the train station, for €1 per hour or €7.75 per day; it also gives out maps and holds left luggage. The helpful **tourist office** is at Via Salara 8 (Mon–Sat 8.30am–6/7pm, Sun 10am–4pm; ☎0544.35.404, ⓦwww.turismo.ravenna.it). You can go **online** at the *Rock Café*, Via Castel San Pietro 9 – the road after Via G. Mazzini.

Accommodation

There isn't a great deal of affordable **accommodation** in Ravenna. **Bed-and-breakfast** is a cheap option – the tourist office can recommend places close to the centre. *Ostello Dante Alighieri*, Via Nicolodi 12 (☎ & ⓔhostelravenna@hotmail .com; lockout between 10am & 5pm; 11.30pm curfew; €16), is the HI **hostel**, located east of the station handily opposite a large Co-op supermarket. You can get there on bus #1 #70 or from outside the train station, or it's a ten-minute walk – south out of the station, east under the tracks, follow Via Candiano and then head southeast down Via T. Gulli; Via Nicolodi goes off to the right.

The closest **campsite** to Ravenna is *Camping Adriano* (☎0544.438.510), Via dei Campeggi 7, in the nearby coastal resort of Punta Marina Terme 8km away. To get there take bus #1 or #70 that leaves from Piazzale Farini in front of the train station.

Al Giaciglio Via Rocca Brancaleone 42 ☎0544.39.403, ⓦwww.albergoalgiaciglio .com. One of Ravenna's cheapest hotels is this small, basic but friendly place near the station. Rooms come with or without bathrooms. Its restaurant offers tourist menus for €6, €7 and €13. ❷

🏃 **Cappello** Via IV Novembre 41 ☎0544 219.813, ⓦwww.albergocappello.it. Old *palazzo* that's been turned into an extremely stylish small hotel with just seven chic rooms and an excellent restaurant. **⑥**

Centrale Byron Via IV Novembre 14 ☎0544.212.225, ⓦwww.hotelbyron.com. Comfortable place, right in the historic centre, with satellite TV in the rooms and air conditioning in summer. **③**

Ostello Galletti Abbiosi Via di Roma 140 ☎0544.215.127, ⓦwww.galletti.ra.it. Stylish hotel with comfortable air-conditioned singles and doubles. Some of the large rooms have fine painted ceilings and attractive marble floors. **③**

The City

The centre of Ravenna is the **Piazza del Popolo**, an elegant open space, arcaded in one corner, that was laid out by the Venetians in the fifteenth century and is now filled with café tables. A few blocks south of the square, across Piazza Garibaldi on Via Alighieri, the **Tomba di Dante** is a site of local pride, a small Neoclassical building which was put up in the eighteenth century to enclose the tomb of Dante. The poet had been chased out of Florence by the time he arrived in Ravenna, and he was sheltered here by the Da Polenta family – then

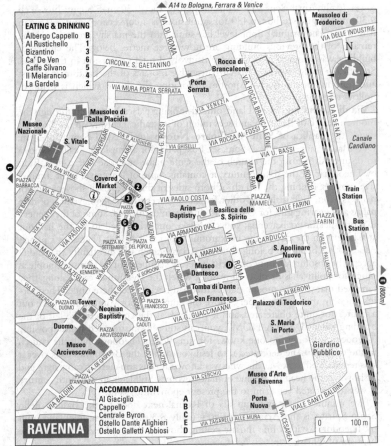

in control of the city – while he finished his *Divine Comedy*. He died in 1321 and was laid to rest in the adjoining church of **San Francesco**, a much-restored building, elements of which date from the fourth century. File down the stairs towards the tenth-century waterlogged crypt complete with the surreal touch of swimming goldfish and remnants of a mosaic floor. The **Museo Dantesco**, situated in San Francesco's cloister on Via Alighieri (daily 9.30am–noon & 3.30–6pm; €2) is for devotees only.

A couple of minutes' walk west of here, a group of buildings around **Piazza del Duomo** shelters the **Duomo** itself, with its cylindrical – and slightly tipsy – tower. Originally a fifth-century building, it was completely destroyed by an earthquake in 1733 and rebuilt in unexceptional style soon after. More interesting is the **Museo Arcivescovile** in the Bishop's Palace behind, with fragments of mosaics from around the city and the palace's sixth-century Oratorio Sant'Andrea, which is adorned with mosaics of birds in a meadow above a Christ dressed in the armour, cloak and gilded leather skirt of a Roman centurion (daily: April–Sept 9am–7pm; March & Oct 9.30am–5.30pm; Nov–Feb 9.30am–4.30pm; see box, p.480 for admission details).

The **Neonian Baptistry**, on the same side of the duomo, by the bell-tower (daily: April–Sept 9am–7pm; March & Oct 9.30am–5.30pm; Nov–Feb 9.30am–4.30pm; see box, p.480 for admission) is a conversion from a Roman bathhouse. The original floor level has sunk into the marshy ground, and the remains of the previous building are now three metres below. The choice of building was a logical one as baptisms involved total immersion in those days. Stylistically it also works well with attractive mosaics of the baptism of Christ and portraits of the twelve Apostles decorating the dome, which is made of hollow terracotta tubes.

Via di Roma, lined with bland, official-looking palaces, cuts right through the modern centre of Ravenna and sees much of its traffic. Halfway up on the right stands the basilica of **Sant'Apollinare Nuovo** (daily: April–Sept 9am–7pm; Oct–March 9am–noon & 2–5pm; see box, p.480 for admission) – called Nuovo to distinguish it from the church of the same name at Classe (see p.485). Built by Theodoric in the sixth century, it contains some of Ravenna's most impressive mosaics, running the length of both sides of the nave. Each shows a line of martyrs – one side male, the other female – processing through avenues of date palms and bearing gifts for Christ and the Virgin enthroned. Some of the scenery is more specific to Ravenna: you can make out what used to be the harbour at Classe with the city in the background, from which rises Theodoric's palace. As a Goth, Theodoric belonged to the Arian branch of Christianity that didn't accept the absolute divinity of Christ, a heresy stamped out by Constantinople as much for political as theological reasons. When the Byzantines came along, they removed many of the mosaic figures that had been placed here under Theodoric's reign. In the mosaic drapery above the entrance door you can just make out a figure, not quite obliterated, and if you look at the columns to the left of the building labelled "PALA TIUM", you can still see outstretched hands, possibly Theodoric's, though no one knows for sure. When Theodoric built the church in the early 500s, he dedicated it to Jesus, but when the Byzantines took over it was rededicated to St Martin, who was known for his anti-heretic campaigns and is shown at the head of the line of male devotees. Still later, in the ninth century, it was rededicated yet again to the present eponymous saint.

Five minutes' walk away up Via di Roma, next door to the Basilica dello Santo Spirito, is the **Arian Baptistry** (daily 8.30am–7.30pm; free), also built by Theodoric, with a fine mosaic ceiling showing the twelve Apostles and the baptism of Christ.

San Vitale and around

In terms of monuments, Ravenna's biggest draw is the area ten minutes' walk northwest of the city centre, around the basilica of San Vitale, which holds the finest of the mosaics and is now gathered together into one big complex, including the mausoleum of Galla Placidia and the National Museum.

San Vitale (daily: April–Sept 9.30am–6.30pm; March & Oct 9.30am–5.30pm; Nov–Feb 9.30am–4.30pm; see box, p.480 for admission), which was begun in 525 under the Roman emperor Theodoric and finished in 548 under the Byzantine ruler Justinian, remains unique for an Italian building. Created to an Eastern-inspired arrangement of void and solid and dark and light, Byzantine architecture was influenced by mathematics and the evidence here is clear. Based on two concentric octagons, its central dome supported by eight columns, and with eight recesses extending from each side – one of which is a semicircular apse that glitters with mosaic. The design was the basis for the great church of Aghia Sofia in Istanbul, built fifteen years later.

There were definite rules about who appeared where in **mosaics** – the higher up and further to the east, the more important or holy the subject. The series in the basilica starts with Old Testament scenes spread across the semi circular lunettes of the choir; the triumphal arch shows Christ, the Apostles and sons of St Vitalis. Further in, on the semi-dome of the apse, a beardless Christ stands between two angels, presenting a model of the church to St Vitalis and Bishop Ecclesius. But what could have been simply a rigid hierarchy preserved in stone is enlivened by fields and rivers teeming with frogs, herons and dolphins. Of the mosaics on the side walls of the apse, the two processional panels are the best surviving portraits of the Emperor Justinian and his wife Theodora – he's on the left and she's on the right – and a rich example of Byzantine mosaic technique. The small glass *tesserae* are laid in sections, alternate rows set at slightly different angles to vary the reflection of light and give an impression of depth. Colour is used emblematically, too, with gold backgrounds denoting either holiness or high status.

Theodora looks a harsh figure under her finery, and she certainly had a reputation for calculated cruelty, arranging "disappearances" of anyone who went against her. According to the sixth-century chronicler Procopius, in his *Secret History* of the court, her rise to power was meteoric. When young she made a living as a child prostitute and circus performer with her two sisters, and later became a courtesan and an actress in bizarre sex shows. She travelled the Middle East, and when she returned brought herself to the attention of the emperor, Justinian. To the horror of the court, he rejected the well brought-up daughters of his Roman peers and lived with Theodora, giving her the rank of patrician. He was unable to marry her until his mother, the empress, was dead and the law changed; the two then embarked on a reign of staggering corruption and legalized looting.

Across the grass from the basilica is the tiny **Mausoleo di Galla Placidia** (daily: April–Sept 9.30am–6.30pm; March & Oct 9.30am–5.30pm; Nov–Feb 9.30am–4.30pm; see box, p.480 for admission) named after the half-sister of Honorius. The emperor's frequent absences left Galla in charge of the city and she was responsible for much of the grandeur of Ravenna's early days. Despite the name and the three sarcophagi inside, it's unlikely that the building ever held her bones. Galla Placidia was taken hostage when the Goths sacked Rome, and caused a scandal by marrying one of her kidnappers, Ataulf. She went into battle with him as his army forged south, and later they reigned jointly over the Gothic kingdom. When Ataulf was assassinated the Romans took her back for a ransom of corn, after which she was obliged to marry a Roman general, Constantius. Their son formally became the Emperor Valentinian III at the age of 6, and as his regent, Galla Placidia assumed control of the Western Empire.

Inside the *mausoleo*, filtered through thin alabaster windows, the light falls on mosaics that glow with a deep blue lustre, most in an earlier style than those of San Vitale, full of Roman and naturalistic motifs. Stars around a golden cross spread across the vaulted ceiling; the Gospels are four volumes on the shelves of a small cupboard, and there are symbolic representations of the Apostles – the lion of St Mark and the ox of St Luke are set in the sky at the points where you would expect to see the constellations of Leo and Taurus. At each end are representations of St Lawrence, with the gridiron on which he was martyred, and at the entrance end is a depiction of the Good Shepherd, with one of his flock.

Adjacent to San Vitale on the southern side, housed in the former cloisters of the church, the **Museo Nazionale** (Tues–Sun 8.30am–6.30pm; €4 or see box, p.480 for joint tickets) contains various items from this and later periods – fifteenth-century icons, early Byzantine glass and embroidery from Florence. Among the most eye-catching exhibits is a sixth-century statue of Hercules capturing a stag, possibly a copy of a Greek original. Still within Ravenna, but a bit of a hike north of the train station, lies one more early sixth-century monument that's worth visiting: the **Mausoleo di Teodorico** (daily 8.30am–7pm; €2 or see box, p.480 for joint tickets). This ten-sided curiosity is unique in Western architecture owing much to Syrian models of its day, and constructed of Istrian limestone. The 300-tonne cupola is a single, if cracked, chunk and no one knows exactly how it was manoeuvred into place. Inside the decagonal second storey sits an ancient porphyry bathtub, pressed into use as the royal sarcophagus.

Eating, drinking and entertainment

Central Ravenna is not exactly filled with **places to eat**, and you need to know where to go to avoid fruitless wandering. The covered market on Piazza A. Costa is open from 7am to 1.30pm and is a good source of picnic supplies.

The **Ravenna Festival** in June and July attracts big names in the classical music world (ⓦwww.ravennafestival.org) like Philip Glass, and the Jazz Festival in July and August also draws international stars.

Albergo Cappello Refined, slightly pricey, spot with excellent daily pasta specials and mouth-watering selection of appetizers at the bar for upmarket grazing. Seats outside are great for people-watching in this central spot. Closed Sun and Mon lunchtimes.

Al Rustichello Via Maggiore 21/23 ☎0544.36.043. Consistently popular and inexpensive place where the owner tells you the menu (in English too) with food that an Italian grandmother would be proud of – the *cappelletti* with asparagus is recommended. Booking advised.

Bizantino Piazza A. Costa. Self-service place, just inside the market, with excellent value (lunch only) hot and cold dishes including some vegetarian options. Pick up three courses here for under €10.

Ca' De Ven Via C. Ricci 24. Stunning wood-panelled *enoteca* with painted ceilings and wine racks seemingly covering every other available space. It offers a simple changing menu of a few pizza and pasta dishes and a huge range of vintages to sample by the glass from €1 upwards (and upwards). Closed Mon.

Caffè Silvano Piazza Einaudi 7. Popular place with tourists offering simple meals and good sandwiches, and with a covered seating area on the square. Closed Sun.

Il Melarancio Via Mentana 33. Good sightseeing pit-stop offering freshly made and generously filled *piadine* and panini. Queues out of the door are common. Come evening, it turns into a popular bar.

La Gardela Via Ponte Marino 3. Central place across from the Torre Civica (Ravenna's own leaning tower) with a varied menu of fish dishes and home-made pasta, all at moderate prices – *primi* €5–6, *secondi* €6.50–15. Closed Thurs.

Sant'Apollinare in Classe and Ravenna's seaside resorts

About 6km south of Ravenna by train or buses #4 and #44 from the station, the remains of the old port of Classe (daily 9am–dusk; €2) are very thin indeed – the buildings have been looted for stone and the ancient harbour has now completely disappeared under the silt of the River Uniti. One building, however, does survive – the church of **Sant'Apollinare in Classe** on Via Romea Sud (Mon–Sat 8.30am–7.30pm, Sun 1–7.30pm; €2 or see box, p.480 for combined tickets), spared because it was the burial place of Ravenna's patron saint. It's a typical basilical church with more fine mosaics including a marvellous allegorical depiction of the Transfiguration in the apse, with Christ represented by a large cross in a star-spangled universe. Overall, it's an odd site with an otherworldly feel quite at odds with its position close to the autostrada.

There's easy access by bus through Ravenna's heavy industry belt to the nine lido towns nearby totalling 35 kilometres of coast. **Marina di Ravenna** and **Punta Marina** are both crowded, lively places; or for something quieter head north to the beaches at **Porto Corsini**, **Casalborsetti** and **Marina Romea**. **PORTO CORSINI**, between Marina Romea and Marina di Ravenna, is also interesting for its working port, large and modern enough to take tankers but still with old-fashioned cantilevered nets used for fishing the side channels. Just before the port, you pass the **Capanno Garibaldi**, a reconstruction of the hut in which Garibaldi hid on his epic 800-kilometre march from Rome after the fall of the short-lived Roman republic in 1849. Garibaldi's life-long partner Anita, who often fought alongside him, died on the way and he was unable to stop for long enough to bury her. With your own vehicle you can take a left through the pinewoods after Marina Romea towards the Strada Romea (SS309), where you'll find places to picnic under the umbrella pines, well away from the sight of the industrial area – as well as some places for viewing the bird life that still frequents the lagoon, which is part of the Po Delta nature reserve (see p.478).

Rimini

RIMINI is the archetypal seaside resort, with a reputation for good if slightly sleazy fun. It's a traditional family resort, to which some Italians return year after year, to stay in their customary *pensione* and be looked after by a hardworking *padrona di casa* as if they were relatives. The resort is best avoided in August, unless you have a penchant for teeming crowds. Out of season, however, it's a pleasant enough town, though bear in mind that many hotels, restaurants and shops are closed and the atmosphere is almost eerily quiet.

There's a less savoury side to the town too. Rimini is known across Italy for its fast-living and chancy nightlife, and there's a thriving hetero- and transsexual prostitution scene alongside the town's more wholesome attractions. The road between the train station and the beach and on the coast to the south of the centre can be particularly full of kerb crawlers, and, although it's rarely dangerous, women on their own – after dark at any rate – should be wary in this part of town.

Given Rimini's reputation and the 95 percent destruction it suffered in the last war, it's surprising to find that the town has a much-ignored old centre that is worth at least a morning of your time. But it's the beach, the crowds and the wild nights that you really come for: Rimini is still the country's best place to party.

Arrival, information and transport

Rimini's **train** and **bus station** is situated in the centre of town, on Piazzale Cesare Battisti, ten minutes' walk from both the sea and the old centre. From the airport (T0541.715711, Wwww.riminiairport.com), 8km south of Rimini, bus #9 goes to the train station every 25–30 minutes; tickets cost €1, and can be bought at the airport bar and kiosks. A taxi costs around €17. There are several places to turn for more information on Rimini including a helpful **tourist office** right outside the train station to the left (March–Oct Mon–Sat 8.30am–7pm, Sun 9.30am–12.30pm; Nov–Feb Mon–Sat 10am–4pm; T0541.51.331), which has a list of hotels and can help you find a room, or pass you on to the hotel booking office (see "Accommodation"). The main tourist office, at Piazza Federico Fellini 3 on the seafront (April–Sept Mon–Sat 8.30am–7pm, Sun 9.30am–12.30pm; Oct–March Mon–Sat 9.30am–12.30pm & 3.30–6.30pm; T0541.438.211, Wwww.riminiturismo.it), offers the same service and has a board outside showing vacancies when everything else is closed.

Getting around is best done on foot, at least within the town centre. But if you need to use the buses, buy an orange ticket from a tobacconist or newsstand; it gives 24 hours' unlimited travel in Rimini and the surrounding area (including Santarcángelo, Riccione and Bellaria) for €3. There are also a couple of nightbus services (see "Nightlife" on p.488).

Accommodation

Despite 1300 hotels, **accommodation** can be a problem in Rimini, and in summer especially you may have to take the expensive option of full board. Out of season few hotels open and they will be mainly geared to business travellers. And with no hostel around you may find yourself sharing your hotel with a school group whatever the season – check before if this will be a problem. You can book accommodation through the tourist office or the town's hotel booking office (June to early Sept, daily 8.15am–2pm & 2.15–7.45pm; T0541.24.760, Eriminibooking@iper.net) next to the tourist office by the train station.

All the hotels listed below are within a five-minute walk of the beach. To get to the beach area from the station, exit to the right – northwest – all the way to the end of the plane trees, and then turn right again – northeast – through the underpass. The name of the beach area's main artery changes every ten blocks or so, but the section nearest the station underpass is called Viale Amerigo Vespucci.

Among the **campsites** all reachable by bus #4 from Rimini station, *Torre Pedrera* at Via S. Salvador 200 is open mid-March to October (T0541.720.437). An alternative is *Camping Italia International,* 2km along the coast at Via Toscanelli 112, Viserba (T0541.732.882, Wwww.campingitaliarimini.it; late May to late Sept); and *Camping Belvedere*, 5km up the coast at Via Grazia Verenin 9, Viserbella (T0541.720.960, Wwww.iper.net/belvedere; June–Sept). The nearest campsite open all year is *Happy Camping Village* on Via Panzini 228 in Bellaria (T0541.346.102, Wwww.happycamping.it).

Bel Ami Via Metastasio 4 T0541.381.643. Located in a peaceful, shady side street, three blocks south of Piazzale B. Croce, this place has rather simple but comfortable rooms. ❷
Donau Viale Alfieri 12 T0541.381.302, Wwww .hoteldonau.it. On a leafy side street between Piazzale Tripoli and Piazzale B. Croce this is a welcoming, if rather basic, option. It is, however, open all year round. ❷

Gradisca Viale Fiume 1 T0541.25.200, Wwww .hotellagradisca.it. Located down the main thoroughfare towards the south lies this luxurious four-star, where the decor inside and out is like the over-the-top set of a Fellini film. ❻
Grand Hotel Parco Federico Fellini T0541.560.000, Wwww.grandhotelrimini .com. More Fellini-esque swank at this histori-cal hotel, right by the sea, where the rooms are

decorated with Venetian and French antiques. **6**

Nancy Viale Leopardi 11 ⓣ0541.381.731, ⓕ0541.387.374. Attractive villa in a lush garden with a good breakfast buffet. **3**

Verudella Viale Tripoli 238 ⓣ0541.391.124, ⓔhotelverudella@libero.it. A few blocks south from the *Gradisca*, this is one of the best of Rimini's affordable options. It's attractively smart and run by a friendly brother-and-sister management. Open all year round. **2**

Villa Adriatica Viale Vespucci 3 ⓣ0541.54.599, ⓦwww.villaadriatica.it. Part of the Ambient hotel group, this is a very stylish choice close to the beach with a swimming pool. The swankiest rooms come with wooden floors, large beds and air conditioning. **4**

Villa Lalla Viale Vittorio Veneto 22 ⓣ0541.55.155, ⓦwww.villalalla.com. Along a quiet tree-lined street, this bright friendly place has neat white rooms with modern decor (lots of uplighting) and a pleasant veranda for an evening drink. **2**

The Town

Rimini divides into two parts: a belt of land east of the railway line taken up by clean **beaches**, holiday accommodation and a brash main drag crammed with souvenir shops, restaurants and video arcades; and the **old town**, inland, an often unseen part of Rimini, made up of old stone buildings clustered around the twin squares of Piazza Tre Martiri and Piazza Cavour, and bordered by the port-canal and town ramparts.

On the southern and northern edges of the old centre respectively sit the **Arco d'Augusto** and **Ponte Tiberio**, testifying to Rimini's importance as a Roman colony. The patched-up Arco was built at the beginning of the first century AD at the point where Via Emilia joined Via Flaminia. Rimini's other Roman remains consist of the **Anfiteatro**, of which there are sparse foundations off Via Roma, just south of the train station.

Just south of the Ponte Tiberio, **Piazza Tre Martiri** and **Piazza Cavour** are the two main squares. Piazza Cavour has a statue of Pope Paul V and the Gothic **Palazzo del Podestà**; the square was rebuilt in the 1920s, and purists argue that it was ruined, although the fishtail battlements are still impressive enough. Opposite, beyond the sixteenth-century fountain incorporating Roman reliefs, the beautiful **old fish market** often shades antiques stalls worth a browse. The **Museo della Città** at Via L. Tonini 1 (mid-June to mid-Sept Tues–Sat 10am–12.30pm & 4.30–7.30pm, Sun 4.30–7.30pm; mid-Sept to mid-June Tues–Sat 8.30am–12.30pm & 5–7pm, Sun 4–7pm; €4) has a collection of works of art dating from the fourteenth to the nineteenth centuries, the highlight of which is Giovanni Bellini's Pietà.

Just east of here on Via 4 Novembre is Rimini's best-known monument, the recently restored **Tempio Malatestiano** (Mon–Sat 8am–12.30pm & 3.30–7pm, Sun 9am–1pm & 3.30–7pm; free), which serves as the town's cathedral. Built by the Guelph family of Malatesta, it was originally a Franciscan Gothic church before being transformed in 1450 into a monument to Sigismondo Malatesta, a notorious *condottiere* whose long list of alleged crimes included rape, incest and looting. Understandably, the pope of the time, Pius II, was less than impressed and publicly consigned an ambivalent Sigismondo to hell. Sigismondo was more concerned with his great love, Isotta degli Atti, and treated the *tempio* as a private memorial chapel to her. Their initials are linked in emblems all over the building, and the Malatesta family's favourite heraldic animal – trumpeting elephants – appears almost as often. There are a number of fine artworks, now restored, to look out for, including a *Crucifix* attributed to Giotto, friezes and reliefs by Agostino di Duccio and a fresco by Piero della Francesca of Sigismondo himself. It's an appropriate attraction for Rimini, its qualities of pleasurable extravagance almost an emblem for a town that thrives on excess.

There's more homegrown hedonism on offer a short way south at the tiny **Museo Fellini**, Via Clementini 2 (Tues–Fri 4–7pm, Sat & Sun 10am–noon & 4–7pm; free), which celebrates the director's career with exhibits ranging from his drawings – the director began his career as a cartoon illustrator – to movie posters.

Eating and drinking

Rimini is not the best place to eat cheaply with even snack places being rather pricey. The seafront and Via Tripoli have some cheap pizza bars but many eating options on Rimini's seaside quarter demand formal dress and high prices. Less ritzy restaurants can be found in the old town and for the truly impoverished there's a large Standa supermarket handily located on Via Vespucci 133.

Acero Rosso Viale Tiberio 11 ☏ 0541.535.77. Expensive (around €20 for main courses) but excellent restaurant specializing in fish and meat dishes. Closed Mon.

Dalla Maria Via Grazie 81. Dependable Romagnolo cooking for around €25 per person. To get there take the same route as to *Paradiso* (see "Nightlife" below). Closed Mon.

La Baracca Via Marecchiese 312, Spadarolo (5km out of town, take bus #20) ☏ 0541.727.155. This place is worth the journey out of town for its well-priced regional cooking. Closed Wed.

Lo Squero Lungomare Tintori 7. One of the best restaurants on the seafront offering great shellfish

on a leafy terrace right on the harbour. Summer only; closed Tues.

Osteria de Börg Via Forzieri 12. Relaxed and moderately priced place serving innovative regional cooking, such as *cappelletti* (filled pasta) in carrot sauce, fish kebabs, meat roasted over an open fire and a dozen different vegetable dishes. Closed Mon.

Pic-Nic Via Tempio Malatestiano 30. Perennially popular place thanks to its reasonably priced pizzas, pasta, crêpes and game. Vegetarian specials too. Closed Mon.

Rimini Key Piazzale B. Croce. Good-value set menus and pizzas, in a prime location for observing Rimini's evening *passeggiata* along the seafront. Closed Tues.

Nightlife

Rimini's **nightlife** is mainly concentrated on the seafront with most **clubs** to the south of the centre, though there are a few places to the north as well. Clubbing is a seasonal activity here. As full-on as things get in summer, you'll find few places open come winter. Even on a balmy July evening, things tend to start late with crowds cruising the bars from about 11pm onwards before driving to the first club at around 1am. If you haven't got a car, or are drinking, use a nightbus called the Blue Line, which acts as Rimini's club shuttle. It operates through the night (10.30pm–6am) and serves two routes: the first along the length of the coast, from Bellariva to Cattólica; the second from Rimini to Covignano for club *Paradiso*. Pick up either route at Piazzale Kennedy; nightly bus passes cost €3, tickets available on board. For up-to-date information on the Rimini club scene, check the **listings** in the Italian weekly *Chiamami Città* (free in the tourist office or click on ⓦ www.chiamamicitta.com) or in *X-Tra*, which is also free from the tourist office. Another useful website is ⓦ www.riminilive .com, with information on places and transport.

Byblos Piazza Castell 24 ☏ 0541.690.252, ⓦ www.byblosclub.com. Summer-only club that's big on house music.

Cinema Arena Astra Viale Vespucci 133, Misano Adriatico ☏ 0541.391.702. Shows alternative and re-run movies in the open air in July and August.

Le Cocoricò Via Chieti 44 ☏ 0541.605.183, ⓦ www.cocorico.it. One of Italy's most celebrated

clubs where thousands congregate every weekend under an enormous glass pyramid to rave to the latest in Italian techno.

Paradiso Via Covignano 260 ☏ 0541.751.132, ⓦ www.paradisoclub.it. Perhaps the most consistently popular club, helped in part by its stunning hillside location overlooking the sea. The multi-roomed complex has a large central dance floor, a restaurant and seven bars. Along with its regular club nights, it also stages fashion shows and art-based events and draws top DJs from across Europe.

Prince Via Tre Baci 49 ☎0541.691.209. A swimming pool adds to the delights at this club. Music is mostly techno and house.

Listings

Airport ☎0541.715.711, ⓦwww.riminiairport.com.
Car rental Avis, Viale Trieste 16d ☎0541.51.256; Europcar, Via Giovanni XXIII 126 ☎0541.54.746; Mondaini, Viale Tripoli 16 ☎0541.782.646.
Doctor ☎118, or Infermi hospital ☎0541.705.111.
Internet access The tourist office has a list of Internet cafés – two good ones are the Email Beach at Viale Vespucci 29c (Mon–Sat 2–8pm) and Cyber Pub at Viale Mantova 70 (daily 8pm–midnight, closed Sun in winter) in Rivazzurre, south of the centre.

Laundry Lavanderia Carla Ekoclean, 180 Via Tripoli.
Pharmacy Via IV Novembre 39/41 (daily except Thurs 8.30am–12.30pm & 4–8pm; ☎0541.24.414); when closed, details of all-night services are posted outside.
Post office Main office on Largo Giulio Cesare (Mon–Fri 8.15am–5.30pm, Sat 8.15am–1pm); smaller branch at Piazzale Tripoli 4 (Mon–Fri 8.10am–1.30pm, Sat 8.10–11.50am).
Taxis Radiotaxi Cooperative ☎0541.50.020; 24hr rank outside the train station.

Around Rimini: Santarcángelo and San Marino

The attractive countryside around Rimini is dotted with small hilltop towns and lush gentle valleys covered with firs and chestnuts. **SANTARCÁNGELO**, 11km inland and accessible by bus #9 and #114 or train from Rimini, is worth the short trip for its steep medieval streets and thirteenth-century **fortress** (open the first Saturday of each month 2–4pm; €3). Carved into the hillside on the edge of the village are some artificial caves, the origins of which are largely unknown, though it's thought they were once used for a local cult. The **tourist office**, at Via C. Battisti 5 (daily: May–Sept 9.30am–12.30pm & 3–7.30pm; Oct–April 9.30am–12.30pm & 3–6.30pm; ☎0541.624.270), has information on accommodation options if you decide to stay. It's also worth visiting Santarcángelo for the village's **restaurants**, of which *Da Lazarou*, at Via del Platano 21, is recommended for its warm atmosphere and classic dishes such as ravioli with aubergine. *Osteria della Violina*, Vicolo d'Enzi 4 (booking advisable, ☎0541.620.416; open Wed–Sun), occupies a seventeenth-century *palazzo* with an internal courtyard, and has a cheaper section downstairs serving *piatti poveri* ("poor dishes"), which are chalked up on a board and washed down with Sangiovese wine.

Santarcángelo is very different from the region's second tourist attraction (after the beach), the **REPUBLIC OF SAN MARINO** – an unashamed, though not entirely unpleasant, tourist destination that trades on its nearly two millennia of precariously maintained autonomy. Said to have been founded around 300 AD by a monk fleeing the persecutions of Diocletian, it has its own mint, produces its own postage stamps, and has an army of around a thousand men. The ramparts and medieval-style buildings of the citadel above Borgomaggiore, also called "San Marino", restored in the last century, are mildly interesting; there's a **waxworks museum** in Via Lapicidi Marini 17 (daily: April–Sept 8.30am–6.30pm; Oct–March 8.30am–12.30pm & 2–5.30pm; €5) as well as tacky souvenir shops and restaurants. And you can also get your passport officially stamped, for only €2.50, by the border guards or at the **information** office at Contrada del Collegio (Mon–Fri 8.30am–6.30pm, Sat & Sun 8.30am–1.30/2pm & 1.30/2–6pm; ☎0549.882.914). All the touristy tawdriness aside, however, it's a good place just to stroll around; the walk up through town to the

rocce, battlemented castles along the highest three ridges, is worth the effort for the all-round views. Below, in Borgomaggiore, is Giovanni Michelucci's "fearless and controversial" modernist church, built in the 1960s, with a roof that seems to cascade down in waves.

Travel details

Trains

Bologna to: Ancona (hourly; 2hr 15min); Faenza (hourly; 35min); Ferrara (frequent; 25–55min); Fidenza (hourly; 1hr 10min); Florence (hourly; 1hr 10min); Forlì (hourly; 45min); Milan (frequent; 1hr 45min–2hr 30min); Modena (every 30min; 20min); Parma (frequent; 55min); Ravenna (hourly; 1hr 20min); Reggio Emilia (frequent; 40min); Rimini (every 20min; 1hr 10min–2hr 30min).
Faenza to: Brisighella (hourly; 10–20min).
Ferrara to: Ravenna (hourly; 1hr); Rimini (every 30min; 2hr–2hr 20min).
Fidenza to: Busseto (hourly; 12min); Cremona (hourly; 35min).
Modena to: Carpi (hourly; 12–20min); Mantua (hourly; 1hr–1hr 10min); Verona (9 daily; 2hr).
Parma to: Brescia (hourly; 1hr 45min–2hr 20min); La Spezia (8 daily; 2hr 15min).
Rimini to: Santarcángelo (6 daily; 8min).

Buses

Bologna to: Marzabotto (hourly; 15min); Pontecchio Marconi (every 15min; 45min); Vignola (hourly; 1hr).
Ferrara to: Comacchio (10 daily; 1hr 10min).
Fidenza to: Fontanellato (3 daily; 25min); Soragna (10 daily; 20min).
Modena to: Carpi (20 daily; 40min); Maranello (hourly; 30min); Vignola (6 daily; 40min).
Parma to: Busseto/Le Roncole (5 daily; 1hr); Fontanellato (6 daily; 35min); Langhirano (hourly; 45min); Roncole Verdi (5 daily; 50min); Soragna (5 daily; 40min).
Ravenna to: Classe (every 30min; 10min); Marina di Ravenna (every 30min; 20min); Marina Romea (10 daily; 20min); Mésola (1 daily; 1hr 40min).
Reggio Emilia to: Casina (17 daily; 50min).
Rimini to: Rome (2 daily in summer, 2 weekly in winter; 5hr 30min); San Marino (hourly; 30min); Santarcángelo (hourly; 30min).

8

Tuscany

CHAPTER 8 **Highlights**

✳ **The Duomo, Florence** Climbing Brunelleschi's dome, the city's signature building, is a must. See p.507

✳ **The Uffizi** The world's greatest collection of Italian Renaissance paintings. See p.514

✳ **Medici villas** Explore the country houses of Florence's pre-eminent family. See p.537

✳ **Chianti** The country's most famous vineyards. See p.538

✳ **The Leaning Tower, Pisa** Still defying gravity, still drawing the crowds and still continuing to amaze. Now saved from imminent collapse, the tower is once again open to visitors. See p.547

✳ **Lucca** A stunning array of Romanesque churches in this most urbane of Tuscan towns. See p.553

✳ **The Palio** Siena's historic, chaotic horse race, run over three frenetic laps of the Campo. See p.579

✳ **Tuscan hill-towns** Tuscany's hill-towns epitomize the region for many visitors, with San Gimignano the most popular. See p.591

△ Saints on Lucca Cathedral

Tuscany

T uscany harbours the classic landscapes of Italy, familiar from Renaissance paintings and TV travel shows alike, and its medieval hill-towns, rows of slender cypress trees, vineyards and olive groves, and artfully sited villas and farmhouses have long held an irresistible attraction for northern Europeans.

The expat's perspective may be distorted, but Tuscany is indeed the essence of Italy in many ways. The national language evolved from the Tuscan dialect, a supremacy ensured by Dante – who wrote the *Divine Comedy* in the vernacular of his birthplace, Florence – and Tuscan writers such as Petrarch and Boccaccio. But what makes this area pivotal to the culture of Italy and all of Europe is the **Renaissance**, which fostered painting, sculpture and architecture that comprise an intrinsic part of a Tuscan tour. The very name by which we refer to this extraordinarily creative era was coined by a Tuscan, Giorgio Vasari, who wrote in the sixteenth century of the "rebirth" of the arts. **Florence** was the most active centre of the Renaissance, flourishing principally through the all-powerful patronage of the Medici dynasty. Every eminent artistic figure from Giotto onwards – Masaccio, Brunelleschi, Alberti, Donatello, Botticelli, Leonardo da Vinci, Michelangelo – is represented here, in an unrivalled gathering of churches, galleries and museums.

Few people react entirely positively to Florence's crowds and its rather draining commercialism. **Siena** provokes less-ambiguous responses. This is one of the great medieval cities of Europe, almost perfectly preserved, and with superb works of art in its religious and secular buildings. Its beautiful Campo – the central, scallop-shaped market square – is the scene, too, of Tuscany's one unmissable festival, the **Palio**, which sees bareback horse-riders careering around the cobbles amid the brightest display of pageantry this side of Rome. Other major cities, **Pisa** and **Lucca**, provide convenient entry points to the region, either by air (via Pisa's airport) or along the coastal rail route from Genoa. **Arezzo** serves as the classic introduction to Tuscany if you're approaching from the south (Rome) or east (Perugia). All three have their splendours – Pisa its Leaning Tower, Lucca a string of Romanesque churches, Arezzo an outstanding fresco cycle by Piero della Francesca.

Tucked away to the west and south of Siena are dozens of small **hill-towns** that, for many, epitomize the region. **San Gimignano** is the best known, and is worth visiting as much for its spectacular array of frescoes as for its much-photographed bristle of medieval tower-houses, though it's now a little too popular for its own good. **Montepulciano**, **Pienza** and **Cortona** are each superbly located and dripping with atmosphere, but the best candidates for a Tuscan hill-town escape are little-mentioned places such as **Volterra**, **Massa**

Tuscan cooking, with its emphasis on simple dishes using fresh, quality, local ingredients, has had a seminal influence on Italian cuisine. Classic Tuscan *antipasti* are peasant fare: bruschetta is stale bread, toasted and dressed with oil and garlic; *crostini* is toast and pâté. **Olive oil** is the essential flavouring, used as a dressing for salads, a medium for frying and to drizzle over bread or vegetables and into soups and stews just before serving.

Soups are very popular – Tuscan menus always include either *ribollita*, a hearty stew of vegetables, beans and chunks of bread, or *zuppa di farro*, thick soup with spelt (a barley-like grain). Fish restaurants around the region try to copy *cacciucco*, a spiced fish and seafood soup, but the best place in Italy to try it is the town of its birth, Livorno. White cannellini **beans** (*fagioli*) are another favourite, turning up in salads, with pasta (*tuoni e lampo*) or just dressed with olive oil. Tuscany is not known for its **pasta**, but many towns in the south serve *pici*, a local variety of thick spaghetti. **Meat** is kept plain, often grilled, and Florentines profess to liking nothing better than a good *bistecca alla fiorentina* (rare char-grilled steak), or the simple rustic dishes of *arista* (roast pork loin stuffed with rosemary and garlic) or *pollo alla diavola* (chicken flattened, marinated and then grilled with herbs). Hunters' fare such as *cinghiale* (wild boar) and *coniglio* (rabbit) often turns up in hill-town trattorias. Spinach is often married with ricotta and gnocchi, used as a pasta filling, and in *crespoline* (pancakes) or between two chunks of *focaccia* and eaten as a snack. Sheep's milk *pecorino* is the most widespread Tuscan **cheese** (best in Pienza), but the most famous is the oval *marzolino* from the Chianti region, which is eaten either fresh or ripened. **Dessert** menus will often include *cantuccini*, hard, almond-flavoured biscuits to be dipped in a glass of Vinsanto (sweet dessert wine) – best known as *biscottini* in Prato – but Siena is the main source of sweet treats, including almond macaroons and *panforte*, a rich and sticky cake full of nuts and fruit.

Tuscany has some of Italy's finest **wines**. Three top names, which all bear the exclusive DOCG mark (and price tags to match), are Chianti Classico, Brunello di Montalcino and Vino Nobile di Montepulciano – not the sort of thing you'd knock back at a trattoria. There are dozens of other Chianti varieties, most of them excellent, but it can be difficult to find a bargain. Both Montalcino and Montepulciano produce *rosso* varieties that are more pocket-friendly, and other names to look for include Carmignano and Rosso delle Colline Lucchesi. Two notable whites are dry Vernaccia di San Gimignano and the fresh Galestro. Tuscany is also renowned for Vinsanto, a sweet, strong dessert wine made from grapes left to dry in the sun.

Maríttima or **Pitigliano**, in each of which tourism has yet to undermine local character.

If the Tuscan **countryside** has a fault, it's the popularity that its seductiveness has brought, and you may find lesser-known sights proving most memorable – remote monasteries like **Monte Oliveto Maggiore** and **San Galgano**, the sulphur spa of **Bagno Vignoni**, or the striking open-air art gallery of the **Tarot Garden**. The one area where Tuscany fails to impress is its over-developed **coast**, with uninspired beach-umbrella compounds filling every last scrap of sand. The Tuscan **Islands** have rather more going for them – **Elba** may be a victim of its own allure, but the smaller Islands such as **Capraia** retain a tranquil isolation.

Tuscany's **tourist office** is based in Villa Fabbricotti, Via Vittorio Emanuele 62–64, Firenze (℡055.462.801, ⊛www.toscanapromozione.it), but mainly serves to promote the area overseas. The website linking all fifteen of Tuscany's local tourist offices is more useful and has a comprehensive accommodation database (⊛www.turismo.toscana.it). Finding **accommodation** can be a major problem in the summer so you should definitely reserve in advance. **Agriturismo** is big

business, with a plethora of family-run places dotted around the countryside offering anything from budget rooms in a farmhouse to luxury apartments in restored castles or Renaissance villas; the regional government's website (Ⓦwww .agriturismo.regione.toscana.it) has plenty of information.

Florence (Firenze)

Since the early nineteenth century **FLORENCE** has been celebrated by many as the most beautiful city in Italy. Stendhal staggered around its streets in a perpetual stupor of delight; the Brownings sighed over its idyllic charms; and E.M. Forster's *Room with a View* portrayed it as the great southern antidote to the sterility of

Anglo-Saxon life. The pinnacle of Brunelleschi's stupendous cathedral dome dominates the cityscape, and the close-up view is even more breathtaking, with the multicoloured **Duomo** rising beside the marble-clad **Baptistry**. Wander from here down towards the River Arno and the attraction still holds: beyond the broad Piazza della Signoria, site of the towering **Palazzo Vecchio**, the river is spanned by the medieval, shop-lined **Ponte Vecchio**, with the gorgeous church of **San Miniato al Monte** glistening on the hill behind it.

Yet after registering these marvellous sights, it's hard to stave off a sense of disappointment, for much of Florence is a city of narrow streets and heavy-set *palazzi* that show only iron-barred windows and massive, studded doors to the outside world.

The fact is that the best of Florence is to be seen indoors. The development of the Renaissance can be plotted in the vast picture collection of the **Uffizi** and in the sculpture of the **Bargello** and the **Museo dell'Opera del Duomo**. Equally revelatory are the fabulously decorated chapels of **Santa Croce** and **Santa Maria Novella**, forerunners of such astonishing creations as Masaccio's superb frescoes in the **Cappella Brancacci**. The Renaissance emphasis on harmony and rational design is expressed with unrivalled eloquence in Brunelleschi's architecture, specifically in the churches of **San Lorenzo**, **Santo Spirito** and the **Cappella dei Pazzi**. While the full genius of Michelangelo, the dominant creative figure of sixteenth-century Italy, is on display in the fluid design of San Lorenzo's **Biblioteca Laurenziana** and the marble statuary of the **Cappelle Medicee** and the **Accademia** – home of the *David*, every quarter of Florence can boast a church or collection worth an extended call, and the enormous **Palazzo Pitti** south of the river constitutes a museum district on its own.

Some history

The Roman colony of Florentia was established in 59 BC and expansion was rapid, based on trade along the Arno. In the sixth century AD the city fell to the barbarian hordes of Totila, then the Lombards and then Charlemagne's Franks. In 1078 Countess Mathilda of Tuscia supervised the construction of new fortifications, and in the year of her death – 1115 – granted Florence the status of an independent city. Around 1200, the first Arti (Guilds) were formed to promote the interests of traders and bankers in the face of conflict between the pro-imperial Ghibelline faction and the pro-papal Guelphs. The exclusion of the nobility from government in 1293 was the most dramatic measure in a programme of political reform that invested power in the Signoria, a council drawn from the major guilds. The mighty Palazzo della Signoria – now known as the Palazzo Vecchio – was raised as a visible demonstration of authority over a huge city: at this time, Florence had a population around 100,000, a thriving mercantile sector and

Planning a visit

Three days is the minimum to get a feel for Florence and its trappings. Since many museums close on Mondays, and many churches close to tourists on Sundays, it's best to schedule a midweek visit. Watch out, too, for **opening-times**: some museums only open in the mornings, the Baptistry only opens in the afternoons, and almost all churches close in the middle of the day. The famous sights, notably the Duomo and the Uffizi, can get absurdly overcrowded – on a whistle-stop visit, it makes sense to reject them in favour of the under-visited Bargello, Cappella Brancacci and Cappelle Medicee. Booking entry to museums in advance is strongly recommended (see p.506).

a highly developed banking system (the florin was common currency across Europe). Strife within the Guelph camp marked the start of the fourteenth century, and then in the 1340s the two largest banks collapsed and the Black Death struck, destroying up to half the city's population.

The political rise of **Cosimo de' Medici**, later dubbed Cosimo il Vecchio ("the Old"), was to some extent due to his family's sympathies with the smaller guilds. The **Medici** fortune had been made by the banking prowess of Cosimo's father, Giovanni Bicci de' Medici, and Cosimo used the power conferred by wealth to great effect. Through his patronage of such figures as Brunelleschi and Donatello, Florence became the centre of artistic activity in Italy.

The ascendancy continued under Cosimo's grandson **Lorenzo il Magnifico**, who ruled the city at the height of its artistic prowess. Before Lorenzo's death in 1492, the Medici bank failed, and in 1494 Lorenzo's son Piero was obliged to flee. Florentine hearts and minds were seized by the charismatic Dominican monk, **Girolamo Savonarola**, who preached against the decadence and corruption of the city. Artists departed in droves as Savonarola and his child spies, in a symbolic demonstration of the new order, collected all the trappings of Florence's Medicean culture – books, paintings, tapestries, fancy furniture and clothes – and piled them high in Piazza della Signoria in a **Bonfire of the Vanities**. But such a graphic assault on the past signalled a turning point and, within a year, Savonarola had been found guilty of heresy and treason, and was burned alive on the same spot.

After Savonarola, the city functioned peaceably under a republican constitution headed by Piero Soderini, whose chief adviser was his friend **Niccolò Machiavelli**. In 1512 the Medici returned, and in 1516, Giovanni de' Medici became **Pope Leo X**, granting Michelangelo and Leonardo da Vinci major commissions. After the assassination of the tyrannical transvestite Alessandro de' Medici in 1537, Florentine power was handed to a new Cosimo, who seized the Republic of Siena and, in 1569, took the title **Cosimo I**, Grand Duke of Tuscany. The great traditions of Florentine art descended into farce as sycophants such as **Giorgio Vasari** plastered the city with fawning images of Medici power and glory.

Florence's decline was slow and painful. Each of the later Medicis was more ridiculous than the last: **Francesco** spent most of his thirteen-year reign indoors, obsessed by alchemy; **Ferdinando II** sat back as harvests failed, plagues ran riot and banking and textiles slumped to nothing; the virulently anti-Semitic **Cosimo III** spent 53 years in power cracking down on dissidents; and **Gian Gastone** spent virtually all his time drunk in bed. When Gastone died, in 1737, the Medici line died with him.

Under the terms of a treaty signed by Gian Gastone's sister, **Anna Maria Ludovica**, Florence – and the whole Grand Duchy of Tuscany – passed to Francesco of Lorraine, the future Francis I of Austria. Austrian rule lasted until the coming of the French in 1799; after a fifteen-year interval of French control, the Lorraine dynasty was brought back, remaining in residence until being overthrown in the Risorgimento upheavals of 1859. Absorbed into the united Italian state in the following year, Florence became the **capital** of the Kingdom of Italy in 1861, a position it held until 1875.

At the end of the nineteenth century, large areas of the medieval city were **demolished** by government officials and developers; buildings that had stood in the area of what is now Piazza della Repubblica since the early Middle Ages were pulled down to make way for undistinguished office blocks, and old quarters around Santa Croce and Santa Maria Novella were razed. In 1944, the retreating German army blew up all the city's bridges except the Ponte Vecchio and

FLORENCE

ACCOMMODATION

Azzi	F
Benvenuti	B
Camping Michelangelo	K
Liana	G
Monna Lisa	H
Ostello Villa Camerata	A
Pio X	J
Regency	I
Residenza Johanna	C
Villa Betania	L
Villa Il Castagno	D
Villino La Magnolia	E

EATING & DRINKING

Alla Vecchia Bettola	3
Cibrèo	1
Frilli	5
Fuori Porta	6
I Tarocchi	4
Il Pizzaiuolo	2

Stadio Comunale

Fiesole

Museo Stibert

Prato & Pistoia

Stazione Campo di Marte

VIA DELLE SETTE

VIALE DEI MILLE

VIA MANEL

VIA MASACCIO

PIAZZA G. VASARI

VIA ANDREA DEL CASTAGNO

VIA DEGLI ARTISTI

VIA GIUSEPPE PII

Innocenti

Cimitero degli Inglesi

VIA V. FRE

PIAZZALE DONATELLO

VIA BORGO PINTI

VIA MASACCIO

VIALE GIACOMO MATTEOTTI

VIALE GINO CAPPONI

PIAZZA SAVONAROLA

VIA FRA BARTOLOMMEO

Giardino della Gherardesca

VIA GIUSEPPE GIUSTI

PIAZZA DELLA LIBERTA

VIA G. LA PIRA

Museo Botanico

Giardino dei Semplici

Museo Archeologico

VIA DELLA COLONNA

VIA SAN GALLO

VIA CAMILLO CAVOUR

SS. Annunziata

PIAZZA SANTISSIMA ANNUNZIATA

SANTISSIMA ANNUNZIATA

Spedale degli Innocenti

Scalzo

VIA SANTA REPARATA

Museo di San Marco

PIAZZA SAN MARCO

VIA RICASOLI

Accademia

River Mugnone

VIALE SPARTACO LAVAGNINI

VIA SAN ZANOBI

VIA NAZIONALE

VIA XXVII APRILE

VIA DI SANTA CATERINA D'ALESSANDRIA

VIA GUELFA

VIA BONIFACIO LUPI

Sant'Apollonia

VIA CAMILLO CAVOUR

VIA DEI GINORI

VIALE GIOVANNI MILTON

VIALE DI CADORNA

PIAZZA DELL'INDIPENDENZA

PIAZZA MERCATO CENTRALE

VIA FAENZA

Cenacolo di Foligno

VIALE FILIPPO STROZZI

Palazzo dei Congressi

VIA VALFONDA

VIA NAZIONALE

VIA

Palazzo delle Mostre Fortezza da Basso

VIA DELLO STATUTO

PIAZZA ADUA

Stazione Santa Maria Novella

PIAZZA DELLA STAZIONE

VIA DEL ROMITO

VIA GUASTI

VIA DEL ROMITO

VIALE FILIPPO STROZZI

VIA LUIGI ALAMANNI

VIALE BELFIORE

See 'Central Florence' map for detail

Bus Station

N

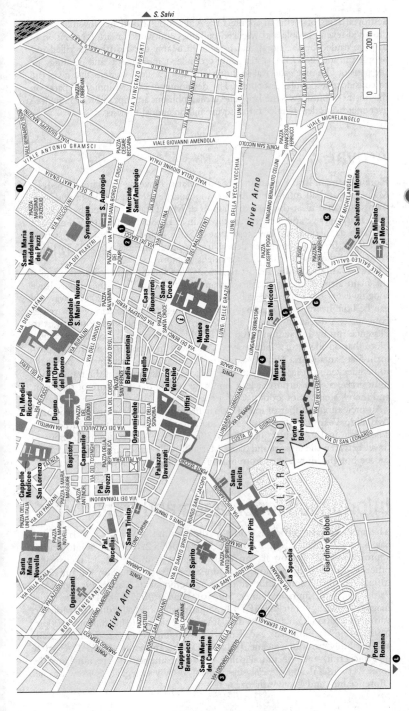

▲ S. Salvi

8

TUSCANY

0   200 m

River Arno

Viale Michelangelo

San Salvatore al Monte

San Miniato al Monte

Ⓚ

Piazza Giuseppe Poggi

Piazzale Michelangelo

Viale Galileo Galilei

Viale G. Poggi

Ⓖ

San Niccolò

Ⓗ

Lungarno Serristori

Lungarno Benvenuto Cellini

Ponte San Niccolò

Piazza Francesco Ferrucci

Lung. della Vecca Vecchia

Viale della Giovine Italia

Lung. del Tempio

Via Giovanni Gherardi

Via dell'Agnolo

Via Ghibellina

Via dei Macci

Borgo La Croce

Via Pietrapiana

S. Ambrogio

Mercato Sant'Ambrogio

Ⓐ

Synagogue

Via dei Pilastri

Santa Maria Maddalena dei Pazzi

Ⓘ

Piazza Massimo d'Azeglio

Via dei Della Mattonaia

Viale Antonio Gramsci

Viale Bernardo Segni

Viale Giuseppe Mazzini

Piazza G. Oberdan

Via Vincenzo Gioberti

Via Fra' Giovanni Angelico

Via Fra' Paolo Sarpi

Via Giampaolo Orsini

Via Luigi Carlo Farini

Viale Giovanni Amendola

Piazza Cesare Beccaria

Piazza dei Ciompi

②

①

Casa Buonarroti

Via Ghibellina

Via dell'Oriuolo

Via Buonarroti

Via dei Benci

Borgo degli Albizi

Via del Corso

Via del Proconsolo

Via dei Servi

Via degli Alfani

Ospedale S. Maria Nuova

Museo dell'Opera del Duomo

Pal. Medici Riccardi

Duomo

Baptistry

Campanile

Orsanmichele

Badia Fiorentina

Bargello

Palazzo Vecchio

Uffizi

Santa Croce

ⓘ

Museo Horne

Piazza Salvemini

Piazza Santa Croce

Piazza Giuseppe Verdi

Lung. delle Grazie

Ponte alle Grazie

Ⓓ

Museo Bardini

Via San Niccolò

Via de' Bardi

Costa di S. Giorgio

Via di Belvedere

Via di San Leonardo

Forte di Belvedere

Piazza del Duomo

Via dei Calzaiuoli

Piazza della Repubblica

Piazza San Firenze

Piazza della Signoria

Via dei Tosinghi

Via dei Tornabuoni

Via della Vigna Nuova

Via Porta Rossa

Via Martelli

Cappelle Medicee

San Lorenzo

Pal. Strozzi

Palazzo Davanzati

Piazza Santa Maria Maggiore

Piazza dell'Unità Italia

Via Faenza

Via dei Panzani

Via Cerretani

Piazza Antinori

Santa Trinita

Pal. Rucellai

Lung. Corsini

Piazza Santa Maria Novella

Santa Maria Novella

Ognissanti

Piazza Santa Maria Novella

Via della Scala

Via del Palazzuolo

Borgo Ognissanti

Lungarno Amerigo Vespucci

Ponte Amerigo Vespucci

River Arno

Lungarno Corsini

Ponte alla Carraia

Piazza C. Goldoni

Ponte Santa Trinita

Borgo Santi Apostoli

Borgo San Jacopo

Ponte Vecchio

Santa Felicita

Via de' Guicciardini

Via Maggio

Palazzo Pitti

La Specola

Piazza San Spirito

Via Santo Spirito

Via Sant'Agostino

Via Sant'Agostino

Santo Spirito

Via Romana

OLTRARNO

Giardino di Bóboli

Via dei Serragli

Ⓙ

Piazza del Carmine

Borgo San Frediano

Via del Leone

Via della Chiesa

Via dell'Ardiglione

Via Camaldoli

Via del Campuccio

Ponte alla Vittoria

Piazza Castello

Cappella Brancacci

Santa Maria del Carmine

③

Porta Romana

Ⓛ

▼

499

destroyed acres of medieval architecture. A disastrous **flood** in November 1966 drowned several people and wrecked buildings and works of art. Restoration of damage caused by the flood, and by a 1993 **Mafia car-bomb** that killed five people outside the Uffizi, is still going on. Indeed, monuments and paintings are the basis of Florence's survival in the new century, a state of affairs that gives rise to considerable popular discontent. The development of new industrial parks on the northern outskirts is the latest and most ambitious attempt to break Florence's ever-increasing dependence on its seven million annual tourists.

Arrival

Florence's main **train station** is Santa Maria Novella, or "Firenze SMN". Many city and all inter-urban **buses** stop outside. Between 1.30am and 4am, trains stop instead at the eastern Campo di Marte station, served by nightbus #70. **Buses** arrive and depart from the main SITA bus terminal on Via di Santa Caterina da Siena, just a few steps west of Santa Maria Novella railway station; after 9pm, however, the buses depart from outside the Bar Cristallo in Largo Alinari, off the eastern side of Piazza della Stazione.

Pisa's Galileo Galilei airport (see p.534) lies 95km west of Florence and is the main airport for flights into Tuscany. Direct trains from the airport leave roughly every hour and take an hour and a half; tickets cost €5.20 one-way and can be bought from the window next to left luggage at the end of the arrivals concourse. A direct bus service also runs every hour or so from Pisa airport to Florence run by Terravision (℡06.3212.0011, ⓦwww.terravision.it; €8 single). Note that on the return journey you can check in with some airlines by platform 5 at Santa Maria Novella station in Florence (daily 7am–5pm) – bags have to be checked in at least thirty minutes before the departure of the train, which must arrive at Pisa airport at least one hour before the departure of the flight, and there's a charge of around €3 for the service.

An increasing number of international air services use Florence's **Aeroporto Amerigo Vespucci** (ⓦwww.aeroporto.firenze.it), 5km northwest in Perétola. The "Vola in Bus" shuttle bus (every 30min; €4.50) takes around 20mins to travel between the airport and Santa Maria Novella station in Florence. Tickets can be bought on board or from machines at the airport and bus station.

Information, orientation and transport

The main **tourist office** is north of the Duomo at Via Cavour 1r (Mon–Sat 8.30am–6.30pm, Sun 8.30am–1.30pm; ℡055.290.832/3, ⓔinfoturismo @provincia.fi.it). Handy if you're arriving by train or bus is the smaller office at Piazza della Stazione 4 (Mon–Sat 8.30am–7pm, Sun 8.30am–2pm; ℡055.212.245). There's another office at Borgo Santa Croce 29r (Mon–Sat 9am–7pm, until 5pm in winter, Sun 9am–2pm; ℡055.234.0444), an information counter within the APT's headquarters at Via Manzoni 16 (Mon–Fri 9am–1pm; ℡055.23.320) and a desk at Vespucci airport (daily 8.30am–8.30pm; ℡055.315.874). Florence's excellent what's-on guide is *Firenze Spettacolo*, available monthly from newsagents (€1.60). On the **Internet**, the APT (ⓦwww .provincia.fi.it) and the municipality (ⓦwww.comune.fi.it) are outclassed by some very useful commercial sites, notably ⓦwww.mega.it, ⓦwww.arca.net /florence.htm and ⓦwww.firenze.net.

Finding your way around the centre of town is very easy – it's just ten minutes' walk along Via de' Panzani and Via de' Cerretani from Santa Maria Novella to the central Piazza del Duomo, from where the great majority of the major sights are an easy stroll away.

Within the historic centre walking is generally the most efficient way of getting around, but to cross town quickly or get to outlying sights the best form of transport is the ATAF **buses**. They have a wide range of tickets: €1.20 for 1hr, €5 for 24hr, €12 for 3 days and €16 for 7 days. A *biglietto multiplo* allows for four one-hour rides for €4.50, while the *Firenze Passepartour* entitles the holder to 24 hours of bus travel, including rides on the open-top red sightseeing buses, for €22. These can all be bought from the main **ticket and information office** (daily 7.15am–1.15pm & 1.45–7.45pm; freephone ☎800.424.500) in the bays to the east of Santa Maria Novella train station, from shops and stalls displaying the ATAF sign, and from automatic machines all over Florence. Most routes originate at or pass by the train station, where you can get more information from the ATAF kiosk in Piazza della Stazione (freephone ☎800.424.500, ⓦ www.ataf.net).

Accommodation

Florence's **accommodation** is generally over-priced and the welcome and service you receive are often not on a par with that of other places in Italy. You should definitely **book in advance**, especially between March and October, though if you leave it to the last minute, the easiest solution is to queue up at the **Consorzio Informazioni Turistiche Alberghiere** (ITA) inside the train station (Mon–Sat 8.30am–7pm, Sun 9am–5.30pm; ☎055.282.893, ⓕ055.288.429) – they charge from €2 upwards, according to the class of hotel, and only take bookings over the counter. The other option is to save money staying outside Florence, at Fiesole, Prato, Pistoia, Empoli or Greve in Chianti, all of which are within a thirty-minute radius of Florence by bus or train.

Hotels

The further from the centre you're prepared to stay, the better value for money you will find. South of the river and west of the centre are good areas for some local atmosphere without so many crowds if you don't mind not being on the doorsteps of the biggest sights and museums.

Florence addresses

Street numbering in Florence runs in relation to the river. If the street or square is parallel to the river, numbers start from the east and proceed west. If the street is perpendicular to the river, the numbering starts from the end nearest the river. Odd numbers are on the left side of the street, even on the right.

However, beware that Florence has a complicated double system of street numbering: commercial establishments (such as bars and restaurants) have **red** numbers (*rosso*), while private buildings have black or blue numbers – and the two systems don't run in tandem. This means, for example, that Via Mosca 35r might be next door to Via Mosca 89, but several hundred metres from Via Mosca 33. There's no logic or purpose to it at all.

The central area

Alessandra Borgo Santi Apostoli 17 ☎055.283.438, ⓦwww.hotelalessandra.com. Occupying a sixteenth-century *palazzo*, steps from the Uffizi, this stylish two-star, with 25 rooms (16 with bathroom) furnished in a mixture of antique and modern styles, is justifiably popular. ❹

Bavaria Borgo degli Albizi 26 ☎055.234.0313, ⓦwww.hotelbavariafirenze.it. Installed in a sixteenth-century *palazzo*, this is a simple one-star with wooden ceilings and nine rooms, all but one with shared bathroom. No credit cards. ❷

Dali Via dell'Oriuolo 17 ☎055.234.0706, ⓦwww.hoteldali.com. Discreet little one-star, just behind the Duomo, with nine plain and rather basic rooms (three en suite), a peaceful courtyard and limited parking. The friendly young owners speak good English. ❸

Firenze Piazza dei Donati 4 ☎055.214.203, ⓦwww.hotelfirenze-fi.it. Modernized one-star bang in the heart of things, with 57 clean, en-suite, generic doubles, spread over five floors. ❹

Hermitage Vicolo Marzio 1 ☎055.287.216, ⓦwww.hermitagehotel.com. This swanky three-star is steps from the Ponte Vecchio. Reception is alongside the roof garden, while above-averagely elegant guest rooms fill the front of the lower floors, some with river views. ❼

Orchidea Borgo degli Albizi 11 ☎055.248.0346, ⓦwww.hotelorchideaflorence.it. Little *locanda* in a twelfth-century *palazzo* run by a friendly Anglo-Italian couple. Four doubles and three singles, with shared bathrooms. ❸

Scoti Via Tornabuoni 7 ☎055.292.128, ⓦwww.hotelscoti.com. An effusively friendly hotel with bags of character and a superb central location. The lounge features amazing floor-to-ceiling frescoes and the en-suite rooms are light and spacious. ❸

The western city centre

Azzi Via Faenza 56 ☎055.213.806, ⓦwww.hotelazzi.com. With most of its rooms overlooking the garden, the *Azzi* is the most pleasant of the six one-stars occupying the upper floors of this building, but it tends to get block-booked by a tour operator. Of the others, *Anna's* (☎055.230.2714, ⓦwww.hotelannas.com) is the most tolerable. ❷

Desirée Via Fiume 20 ☎055.238.2382, ⓦwww.desireehotel.com. A comfortable two-star with stained-glass windows, simulated antique furniture, and a bath in every room. ❹

Elite Via della Scala 12 ☎055.215.395, Ⓕ055.213.832. Usefully located, tiny two-star with pleasant, friendly management and occasional bargain prices. ❸

Ferretti Via delle Belle Donne 17 ☎055.238.1328, ⓦwww.emmeti.it/Hferretti. Comfortable little place, with clean bathrooms, better-than-average breakfasts, helpful and informative staff and free Internet access. ❸

The northern city centre

Casci Via Cavour 13 ☎055.211.686, ⓦwww.hotelcasci.com. A welcoming, excellent, family-run two-star. Only two of its 26 rooms face onto busy Via Cavour, both of which are triple-glazed; some of the others look onto the peaceful rear garden. Big buffet breakfast, library of guidebooks and free Internet access. ❹

Loggiato dei Servi Piazza Santissima Annunziata 3 ☎055.289.592, ⓦwww.loggiatodeiservitihotel.it. An elegant, converted monastery, overlooking one of Florence's loveliest squares, with vaulted ceilings, original antiques and all mod cons. ❺

Residenza Johanna Via Bonifacio Lupi 14 ☎055.481.896, ⓦwww.johanna.it. Comfortable old place on a residential street offering peace and quiet in en-suite rooms, which come with Internet access. The owners now have four other similar *residenze* around town. ❹

South of the river

Bandini Piazza Santo Spirito 9 ☎055.215.308, Ⓔpensionebandini@tiscali.it. The rooms at this *pensione* range from beautifully decorated to grim so make sure you inspect before paying. One of its main assets is the grandstand views from the top-deck loggia of the piazza below. ❹

Lungarno Borgo San Jacopo 14 ☎055.27.261, ⓦwww.lungarnohotels.com. Picture windows in all public rooms take full advantage of the romantic Arno view, as do the balconies attached to the best of the blue-and-cream liveried guest rooms. There are also apartments, complete with kitchens. ❾

Villa Betania Viale Poggio Imperiale 23 ☎055.222.243, ⓦwww.villabetania.it. Fifteenth-century villa 1km south of Porta Romana that has its own lush gardens and private parking. Ten percent student discount (July, Aug & Nov–Feb). Bus #11. ❺

Further north and east

Benvenuti Via Cavour 112 ☎055.572.141, Ⓔbensecc@iol.it. A first-choice two-star in the university quarter, on the corner of Piazza Libertà and Via Matteotti. Bus #1 or #7 to Libertà. ❸

Liana Via V. Alfieri 18 ☎055.245.5303, ⓦwww.hotelliana.com. A small nineteenth-century hotel that was once the British Embassy and maintains a similar tone, with refined interiors and a cool, discreet atmosphere. Bus #6 to D'Azeglio. ❻

Monna Lisa Borgo Pinti 27 ☏ 055.247.9751, ⓦ www.monnalisa.it. A grim facade conceals a charming and elegant hotel, furnished with original antiques and decor. Go for one of the larger rooms overlooking the lovely internal garden. Bus #6 to Colonna. ❽

Regency Piazza M. D'Azeglio 3 ☏ 055.245.247, ⓦ www.regency-hotel.com. Decent five-star choice in a converted nineteenth-century town house on a quiet residential square. The service is helpful, the rooms large and vaguely Art Deco-ish, but the highlight is the leafy breakfast garden adorned with local works of art. Bus #6 to D'Azeglio. ❾

Villa Il Castagno Via A. del Castagno 31 ☏ 055.571.701, ⓦ www.hotelvillailcastagno .com. Pleasant two-star in a residential area, with plenty of on-street parking. Rooms are standard but comfortable. Bus #10, #11 or #17 to Ponte al Pino. ❸

Villino La Magnolia Via Mannelli 135 ☏ 055.246.6015, ⓦ www.villinolamagnolia.it. Tasteful conversion of a family home near Campo di Marte, with marble floors, spacious high-ceilinged guest rooms and modern bathrooms. Internet access and easy parking too. Bus #12 to Campo Marte. ❹

Hostels and campsites

In the absence of many inexpensive hotels, **hostels**, several of them in historic buildings, are a good option for a stay in the city. As well as hostels, Florence has student houses, some of them run by religious bodies, which are open to young tourists in summer (June–Oct) – ⓦ www.florencerooms.net has details. **Camping** is another possibility, with a couple of excellent sites within easy reach of the centre.

Hostels

Istituto Gould Via dei Serragli 49 ☏ 055.212.576, ⓦ www.istitutogould.it. Excellent place occupying part of a seventeenth-century *palazzo* near Santo Spirito: ask for a quieter back room. Singles are €41/36, doubles €28/25 per person; also triples and quads available. Fixed price meals are offered too. Check in Mon–Fri 8.45am–1pm & 3–7.30pm, Sat 9am–1.30pm. Bus #36 or #37 from the train station to Serragli.

Ostello Villa Camerata Viale Righi 2–4 ☏ 055.601.451, ⓕ 055.610.300. HI hostel occupy-ing a sixteenth-century frescoed villa in a beautiful park below Fiesole. Films in English; inexpensive meals; midnight curfew. Dorms €18.50 per person per night including breakfast. There's a small, basic, year-round campsite in the grounds too. Bus #17b from the train station, plus a walk up the hill. **Pio X** Via dei Serragli 106 ☏ 055.225.044, ⓦ www .hostelpiox.it. Quality hostel with friendly, relaxed staff. Aim to arrive by 9am if you haven't got a reservation as its 64 beds soon get snapped up. From €17 per person per night. Midnight curfew.

Santa Monaca Via Santa Monaca 6 ☏ 055.268.338, ⓦ www.ostello.it. Very popular 115-bed non-HI hostel near Santo Spirito. Separate male and female dorms, kitchen and laundry facilities, free hot showers and inexpensive meals. €17 for a dorm bed. Maximum stay seven nights. Credit cards accepted. It's open to check-in 6am–1pm and 2pm–12.30am. Curfew 1am. Bus #11, #36 or #37 to Serragli.

Campsites

Michelangelo Viale Michelangelo 80 ☏ 055.681.1977, ⓦ www.ecvacanze.it. Always crowded, owing to a superb hillside location and regular late-night disco, this place offers kitchen facilities, a shop, restaurant and cash machine. Two-person "housetents" are also available for rent. Bus #13 from the station.

Panoramico Via Peramonda 1, Fiesole ☏ 055 599.069, ⓦ www.florencecamping.com. The area's best campsite has a swimming pool and great views. See p.523.

The City

Greater Florence now spreads several kilometres down the Arno Valley and onto the hills north and south of the city, but the major sights are contained in an area that can be crossed on foot in under thirty minutes.

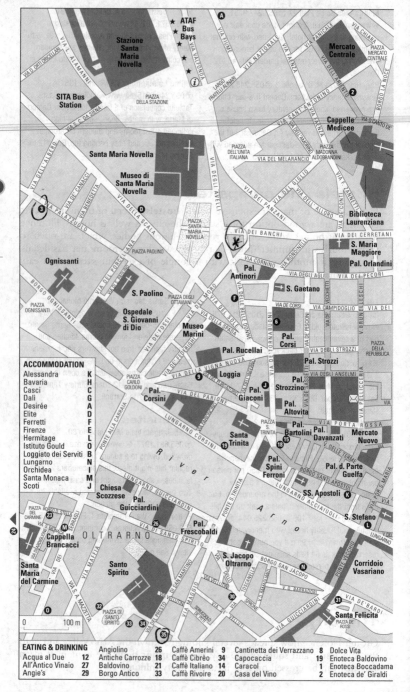

TUSCANY

8

504

ACCOMMODATION

Alessandra	K
Bavaria	H
Casci	C
Dali	G
Desirée	A
Elite	D
Ferretti	F
Firenze	E
Hermitage	L
Istituto Gould	O
Loggiato dei Servliti	B
Lungarno	N
Orchidea	I
Santa Monica	M
Scoti	J

EATING & DRINKING

Acqua al Due	12	Angiolino	26	Caffè Amerini	9	Cantinetta dei Verrazzano	8	Dolce Vita
All'Antico Vinaio	27	Antiche Carrozze	18	Caffè Cibrèo	34	Capocaccia	19	Enoteca Baldovino
Angie's	29	Baldovino	21	Caffè Italiano	14	Caracol	1	Enoteca Boccadama
		Borgo Antico	33	Caffè Rivoire	20	Casa del Vino		Enoteca de' Giraldi	2

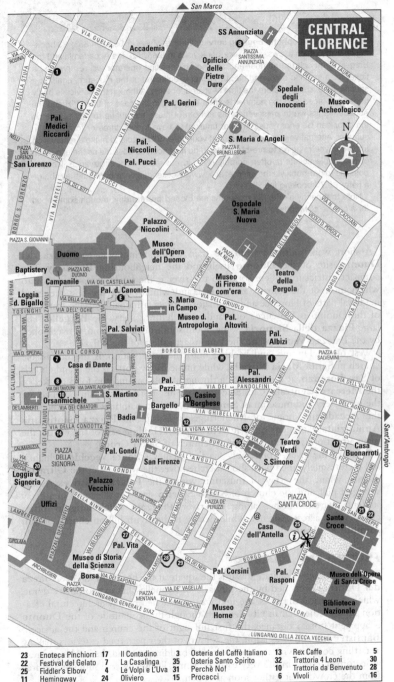

CENTRAL FLORENCE

San Marco

VIA GUELFA
Accademia
SS Annunziata
PIAZZA SANTISSIMA ANNUNZIATA
Opificio delle Pietre Dure
VIA FAENZA
VIA DELLA STUFA
VIA TADDEA
VIA ROSINA
VIA DE' GINORI
VIA CAVOUR
VIA RICASOLI
VIA DEI SERVI
VIA DELLA COLONNA
VIA LAURA
Pal. Gerini
Spedale degli Innocenti
Museo Archeologico
N
Pal. Medici Riccardi
Pal. Niccolini
Pal. Pucci
S. Maria d. Angeli
PIAZZA F. BRUNELLESCHI
NELLI
PIAZZA SAN LORENZO
San Lorenzo
VIA DE' GORI
VIA DEI PUCCI
VIA DEL CASTELLACCIO
VIA DEGLI ALFANI
VIA MARTELLI
VIA DEI BIFFI
BORGO S. LORENZO
PIAZZA S. GIOVANNI
Palazzo Niccolini
Museo dell'Opera del Duomo
Ospedale S. Maria Nuova
VIA BUFALINI
PIAZZA S. MARIA NUOVA
VIA DELLA PERGOLA
BORGO PINTI
Duomo
Baptistery
PIAZZA DEL DUOMO
Campanile
VIA DEI CASTELLANI
Museo di Firenze com'era
Teatro della Pergola
VIA FIORAVANTI
VIA SANT'EGIDIO
VIA FIESOLANA
Loggia d. Bigallo
VIA ROMA
VIA DEGLI SPEZIALI
TOSINGHI
Pal. d. Canonici
VIA DELLA CANONICA
VIA DELL'OCHE
VIA S. ELISABETTA
S. Maria in Campo
Museo d. Antropologia
VIA DELL'ORIUOLO
Pal. Altoviti
Pal. Albizi
PIAZZA G. SALVEMINI
Pal. Salviati
VIA DEL CORSO
VIA DEI CALZAIUOLI
BORGO DEGLI ALBIZI
Pal. Alessandri
VIA PALMIERI
VIA DELL'ULIVO
Casa di Dante
VIA DEL PRESTO
VIA DELLO STUDIO
VIA DEL PROCONSOLO
Pal. Pazzi
VIA DEI PANDOLFINI
VIA GIUSEPPE VERDI
VIA DELL'AGNOLO
Orsanmichele
S. Martino
Badia
Bargello
Casino Borghese
VIA GHIBELLINA
VIA DELLE CASINE
DE' LAMBERTI
VIA DEI CIMATORI
VIA DELLA CONDOTTA
VIA DELLA VIGNA VECCHIA
Teatro Verdi
Casa Buonarroti
VIA G. P. VERRAZZANO
VIA DE' PEPI
CALIMARUZZA
PIAZZA SAN FIRENZE
VIA D. BURELLA
S. Simone
VIA G. FINIGUERRA
VIA DE' FICO
VIA VACCHE-RECCIA
Pal. Gondi
San Firenze
VIA DELL'ANGUILLARA
VIA ISOLA DELLE STINCHE
VIA D. LAVATOI
VIA TORTA
VIA G. PISTOLI
Loggia d. Signoria
PIAZZA DELLA SIGNORIA
VIA DE' MAGAZZINI
BORGO DEI GRECI
PIAZZA SANTA CROCE
BORGO ALLEGRI
Palazzo Vecchio
VIA DELLA NINNA
VIA DEI LEONI
VIA VINEGIA
PIAZZA DE' PERUZZI
VIA DE' PINZOCHERE
VIA DI SAN GIUSEPPE
Uffizi
PIAZZALE DEGLI UFFIZI
VIA DE' NERI
Casa dell'Antella
Santa Croce
LAMBERTESCA
VIA DI CASTELLANI
Pal. Vita
VIA DEL BENCI
BORGO S. CROCE
VIA MAGLIABECHI
GIROLAMI
ARCHIBUSIERI
Museo di Storia della Scienza
Borsa
VIA DE' SAPONAI
Pal. Corsini
Pal. Rasponi
Museo dell'Opera di Santa Croce
PIAZZA DE' GIUDICI
VIA DE' VAGELLAI
VIA V. MALENCHINI
Museo Horne
Biblioteca Nazionale
PIAZZA MENTANA
LUNGARNO GENERALE DIAZ
CORSO DEI TINTORI
LUNGARNO DELLA ZECCA VECCHIA

Sant'Ambrogio

TUSCANY

8

23	Enoteca Pinchiorri	17	Il Contadino	3	Osteria del Caffè Italiano	13	Rex Caffe	5
22	Festival del Gelato	7	La Casalinga	35	Osteria Santo Spirito	32	Trattoria 4 Leoni	30
25	Fiddler's Elbow	4	Le Volpi e L'Uva	31	Perchè No!	10	Trattoria da Benvenuto	28
11	Hemingway	24	Oliviero	15	Procacci	6	Vivoli	16

505

* Il Piccolo

Florence has a **telephone booking service**, Firenze Musei (℡ 055.294.883; €3 booking charge), which allows you to pre-book visits to the Uffizi, the Accademia and the Bargello. You call the number and an English-speaking operator will reserve you a ticket for a specific day and time; the ticket is collected at the museum, again at a specific time, shortly before the time allocated for entry. Although the service is badly under-resourced and the number is often engaged, in the case of the Uffizi and the Accademia it's worth persevering, as at both of these the queue to buy tickets on the door can be enormous – it's not unusual to have to wait three or four hours in summer. Alternatively, you may find that your hotel will be able to make a reservation for you. If you're going to pre-book a visit, do it as soon as possible as the allocation of reservable tickets is often completely sold out many days in advance. It's also possible to pre-book via the Internet at ⓦ www.weekendafirenze.com but they charge a hefty €5.70 booking fee.

Note that nearly all the big museums are **closed on Monday**, though some open for a couple of Mondays each month.

A short walk southeast from the train station brings you to **Piazza del Duomo**, site of the **Duomo** itself and the neighbouring **Baptistry**. The compact district from here south to the river is the inner core, the area into which most of the tourists are packed, and which boasts the best-preserved medieval parts of Florence and the majority of its fashionable streets. Just south of the Duomo is Florence's outstanding sculpture gallery, the **Bargello**. The large **Piazza della Signoria**, some 300m south of the Duomo, is overlooked by the **Palazzo Vecchio** and the famous art gallery of the **Uffizi**.

West of the Duomo, and backing onto the train station, is the unmissable church of **Santa Maria Novella**, while immediately north is the grand church of **San Lorenzo**, at the heart of a throng of stalls around the food market of the **Mercato Centrale**. Clustered together just northeast of San Lorenzo are the monastery and museum of **San Marco**, with its paintings by Fra'Angelico; the **Accademia**, home of Michelangelo's *David*; and **Piazza Santissima Annunziata**, Florence's most attractive square. Heading east of the centre, the main attraction is the vast Franciscan church of **Santa Croce**.

South of the river – preferably via the medieval **Ponte Vecchio**, which is still picturesquely lined with shops perched over the water – lies the **Oltrarno** district, where the array of museums within the **Palazzo Pitti** exerts the strongest pull, and the church of **Santo Spirito** stands at the focus of a lively student quarter. Further along the river, **Piazzale Michelangelo** offers classic views across Florence while nearby is the lavish hilltop church of **San Miniato al Monte**.

Piazza del Duomo

Traffic and people gravitate towards the square at the heart of Florence, **Piazza del Duomo**, beckoned by the pinnacle of Brunelleschi's extraordinary dome, which dominates the cityscape in a way unmatched by any architectural creation in any other Italian city. Yet even though the magnitude of the **Duomo** is apparent from a distance, the first full sight of the church and the adjacent **Baptistry** still comes as a jolt, the colours of their patterned exteriors making a startling contrast with the dun-coloured buildings around them. The square is at its romantic best in the very early morning, lit by low, pale sunlight and free from the crowds that gather soon after 8am.

The Duomo (Santa Maria del Fiore) and around

It was sometime in the seventh century when the seat of the Bishop of Florence was transferred from San Lorenzo to the ancient church that stood on the site of the **Duomo**. In the thirteenth century, it was decided that a new cathedral was required, to better reflect the wealth of the city and to put the Pisans and Sienese in their place. **Arnolfo di Cambio**, entrusted with the project in 1294, designed a massive vaulted basilica focused on a domed tribune embraced by three polygonal tribunes. He died eight years later, but by 1418 everything was in place to bear the weight of the dome that he had envisaged as the church's crown. The conception was magnificent: the dome

△ The campanile, Piazza del Duomo

was to span a distance of nearly 42m and rise from a base some 54m above the floor of the nave. It was to be the largest dome ever constructed – but nobody had yet worked out how to build it.

A committee of the masons' guild was set up to ponder the problem, and it was to them that **Filippo Brunelleschi** presented himself. Some seventeen years before, in 1401, Brunelleschi had been defeated by Ghiberti in the competition to design the Baptistry doors (see opposite), and had spent the intervening time studying classical architecture and developing new theories of engineering. He won the commission on condition that he worked jointly with Ghiberti – a partnership that did not last long (though Ghiberti's contribution to the project was probably more significant than his colleague ever admitted). The key to the dome's success was the construction of two shells: a light outer shell about one metre thick, and an inner shell four times thicker. Brunelleschi's genius was to lay the brickwork in a herringbone pattern in cantilevered rings, thus allowing the massively heavy dome to support itself as it grew, without the use of scaffolding. On March 25, 1436 – Annunciation Day, and the Florentine New Year – the completion of the dome was marked by the papal consecration of the cathedral.

The duomo's overblown and pernickety main **facade** is a nineteenth-century imitation of a Gothic front, its marble cladding quarried from the same sources as the first builders used – white stone from Carrara (see p.560), red from the Maremma, green from Prato. The south side is the oldest part, but the most attractive adornment is the **Porta della Mandorla**, on the north side. This takes its name from the almond-shaped frame that contains the relief *The Assumption of the Virgin*, sculpted by Nanni di Banco around 1420. Note that limited numbers of people are permitted inside the duomo at any one time, and long **queues** often form outside. If you can, come early.

Inside the Duomo

The duomo's **interior** (Mon–Wed & Fri 10am–5pm, Thurs 10am–3.30pm, Sat 10am–4.45pm, Sun 1.30–4.45pm, closes 3.30pm on first Sat of month) is a vast enclosure of bare masonry in stark contrast to the fussy exterior. Today the fourth-largest church in Europe, it once held a congregation of ten thousand to hear Savonarola preach and the ambience is still more that of a public assembly hall than of a devotional building. Initially, the most conspicuous pieces of decoration are two memorials to *condottieri* (mercenary commanders) in the north aisle – Uccello's monument to **Sir John Hawkwood**, painted in 1436, and Castagno's monument to **Niccolò da Tolentino**, created twenty years later. Just beyond, Domenico do Michelino's *Dante Explaining the Divine Comedy* makes the dome only marginally less prominent than the mountain of Purgatory. The enamelled terracotta reliefs over the doorways to the two **sacristies**, on each side of the altar, are by Luca della Robbia, who also cast the bronze doors of the north sacristy. Judged by mere size, the major work of art in the duomo is the fresco of *The Last Judgement* inside the dome, though a substantial number of Florentines are of the opinion that Vasari's and Zuccari's 1572–79 effort does nothing but deface Brunelleschi's masterpiece and want it stripped away. Below the fresco are seven stained-glass roundels designed by Uccello, Ghiberti, Castagno and Donatello; they are best inspected from the gallery immediately below them, which forms part of the route up **inside the dome** from a separate side entrance (Mon–Fri 8.30am–7pm, Sat 8.30am–5.40pm; first Sat of the month 8.30am–4pm; €6). The gallery is the queasiest part of the climb, most of which winds between the brick walls of the outer and inner shells of the dome, up to the very summit with its stunning views over the city.

In the 1960s remnants of the duomo's predecessor, the **Cripta di Santa Reparata**, were uncovered beneath the west end of the **nave** (Mon–Wed & Fri 10am–5pm, Thur 10–3.30pm, Sat 10–4.45pm, first Sat of the month 10–3.30pm; €3). A detailed model helps make sense of the jigsaw of Roman, early Christian and Romanesque remains, areas of mosaic and patches of fourteenth-century frescoes. Also down here is the **tomb of Brunelleschi**, one of the few Florentines ever honoured with burial inside the duomo.

The Campanile
Alongside Italy's most impressive cathedral dome is perhaps its most elegant bell tower. The **Campanile** (daily 8.30am–7.30pm; €6) was begun in 1334 by **Giotto**, who was no engineer: after his death in 1337 Andrea Pisano and Francesco Talenti took over the teetering, half-built edifice, and immediately doubled the thickness of the walls to stop it collapsing. The first storey is studded with two rows of remarkable bas-reliefs; the lower, *The Creation of Man* and the *Arts and Industries*, was carved by Pisano himself, the upper by his pupils. The figures of *Prophets* and *Sibyls* in the second-storey niches were created by Donatello and others. The parapet at the top of the tower has the advantage of letting you view the dome as a foreground counterpoint to Florence's cityscape.

The Baptistry
The **Baptistry** (Mon–Sat noon–7pm, Sun 8.30am–2pm; €3) is the oldest building in Florence, generally thought to date from the sixth or seventh century. Although its mysterious origins lie in the depths of the Dark Ages, no building better illustrates the special relationship between Florence and the Roman world. Throughout the Middle Ages the Florentines chose to believe that the baptistry was originally a Roman temple to Mars, a belief bolstered by the interior's inclusion of Roman granite columns. The pattern of its marble cladding, applied in the eleventh and twelfth centuries, is clearly classical in inspiration, and the baptistry's most famous embellishments – its gilded bronze doors – mark the emergence of a self-conscious interest in the art of the ancient world, the birth of the Renaissance.

After Andrea Pisano's success with the **south doors** in 1336, the merchants' guild held a competition in 1401 for the job of making a new set of doors. The two finalists were Brunelleschi and **Lorenzo Ghiberti** – and the latter won the day. Ghiberti's **north doors** show a new naturalism and classical sense of harmony, but their innovation is timid in comparison with his sublime **east doors**. Unprecedented in the subtlety of their modelling, these Old Testament scenes are a primer of early Renaissance art, using perspective, gesture and sophisticated grouping of their subjects to convey the human drama of each scene. Ghiberti has included a self-portrait in the frame of the left-hand door – his is the fourth head from the top of the right-hand band. All the panels now set in the door are replicas, with the originals on display in the Museo dell'Opera (see p.510); the original competition entries are in the Bargello (see p.511).

Inside, both the semi-abstract mosaic floor and the magnificent mosaic ceiling – including a fearsome platoon of demons at the feet of Christ in judgement – were created in the thirteenth century. To the right of the altar is the **tomb of John XXIII**, the schismatic pope who died in Florence in 1419. The monument, draped by an illusionistic marble canopy, is the work of Donatello and his pupil Michelozzo.

8

TUSCANY | Florence (Firenze) • The City

The Museo dell'Opera del Duomo

At Piazza del Duomo 9, behind the east end of the duomo, is the **Museo dell'Opera del Duomo** (Mon–Sat 9am–7.30pm, Sun 9am–1.45pm; €6), second only in size to the Bargello and far easier to take in on a single visit. In the large ground-floor hall are four seated figures of the Evangelists (including **Donatello**'s fine *St John*) wrenched from the Duomo's demolished sixteenth-century facade. On the mezzanine is the highlight of the museum – **Michelangelo**'s angular and anguished pietà. This was one of his last works, carved when he was almost 80 and intended for his own tomb: Vasari records that the face of the hooded Nicodemus is a self-portrait. **Upstairs** in room II are **Donatello**'s figures for the campanile, the most powerful of which is the prophet *Habbakuk*, the intensity of whose gaze allegedly prompted the sculptor to seize it and yell "Speak, speak!" Donatello also created one of the ornate *cantorie* (choir-lofts) here, competing with **Luca della Robbia**'s opposite, created at the same time and featuring crowds of laughing, dancing children. Room III is dominated by a very different side of Donatello: his haggard wooden figure of Mary Magdalene stares into the middle distance, a wild presence amid cases full of rich vestments, jewelled reliquaries, and a huge silver-gilt **altar** from the Baptistry. Returning through room II leads you along a corridor lined with ropes and pulleys used in the construction of the dome (as well as Brunelleschi's **death mask**) to a room full of wooden models submitted as part of a 1588 facade-designing competition.

You return to ground level into the newly covered **courtyard** – where Michelangelo worked from 1501 to 1504 on his *David*. Today, it displays, in sealed cases of nitrogen, Ghiberti's original **bronze panels** for the baptistry's east doors.

Orsanmichele and the Badìa

The main route south from Piazza del Duomo is the arrow-straight **Via dei Calzaiuoli**, Florence's main street, today – as in Roman times – a catwalk for the Florentine *passeggiata* between the campanile and Piazza della Signoria. Halfway down the street is the opening into **Piazza della Repubblica**, created in the nineteenth century by razing the old Jewish quarter and markets which once stood here in an attempt to give Florence a grand public square. It's a characterless place, impressive solely for its size.

Partway along Via dei Calzaiuoli is the church of **Orsanmichele** (closed for restoration at time of writing). Often unintentionally bypassed by visitors dazzled by the ice-cream parlours and shoe-shops, it stands three storeys high like a military tower. From the ninth century, the church of *San Michele ad Hortum* ("at the garden") stood here, replaced in 1240 by a grain market and after a fire in 1304 by a merchants' loggia. In 1380 the loggia was walled in and dedicated exclusively to religious functions, while two upper storeys were added for use as emergency grain stores. Its **exterior** has some impressive sculpture: outstanding on the east side (Via dei Calzaiuoli) is *John the Baptist* by Ghiberti, the first life-size bronze statue of the Renaissance; on the north side Donatello's *St George*; and on the west side *St Matthew* and *St Stephen* by Ghiberti.

Opposite Orsanmichele, the narrow Via Tavolini heads east a few blocks to **Via del Proconsolo**, the other main route between Piazza del Duomo and Piazza della Signoria. On the corner, more or less across the road from the Museo del Bargello, is the huge **Badìa Fiorentina**, a tenth-century Benedictine abbey finally approaching the end of a lengthy restoration. Tourist visits are allowed on Monday afternoons (3–6pm); at other times the church is open for prayer only. The **interior** is deliciously musty and gloomy. Immediately on the left as you enter is Filippino Lippi's *Madonna and St Bernard*. An unmarked door from the choir, immediately right of the high altar, leads to a staircase giving access to the upper storey of the tranquil, fifteenth-century **Chiostro degli Aranci** (Cloister of Oranges – named after the fruit trees that the monks cultivated here), the walls of which are brightened by a vivid fresco cycle of the life of St Benedict, thought to be the work of Giovanni di Consalvo, a Portuguese contemporary of Fra Angelico.

The Bargello

To get a comprehensive idea of the Renaissance achievement in Florence, two museum calls are essential: one to the Uffizi and one to the **Museo Nazionale del Bargello** (Tues–Sat 8.15am–1.50pm; also open on second & fourth Sun, and first, third & fifth Mon of month same times; €4). This outstanding museum is installed in the dauntingly fortress-like Palazzo del Bargello on Via del Proconsolo, halfway between the Duomo and the Palazzo Vecchio. Nowhere else in Italy is there so full a collection of sculpture from the period, and yet the Bargello is normally uncrowded, visitors preferring to throng the Uffizi instead. The palazzo was built in 1255, and soon became the seat of the *Podestà*, the chief magistrate. Numerous malefactors were tried, sentenced and executed here and the building acquired its present name in the sixteenth century, after the resident *Bargello*, or police chief.

The courtyard and ground floor

From the ticket desk, you enter the beautiful Gothic **courtyard**, which is plastered with the coats of arms of the *Podestà* and contains, among many other pieces, six allegorical figures by **Ammannati**. At the foot of the courtyard steps is the **Michelangelo Room** (room B) containing his first major sculpture, a tipsy, soft-bellied figure of Bacchus, carved at the age of 22 – a year before his great pietà in Rome. A decade later, Michelangelo's style had evolved into something less immediately seductive, as is shown by the *Pitti Tondo*, the stern grandeur of which prefigures the prophets of the Sistine Chapel ceiling, on which he was then about to start work. The square-jawed bust of Brutus, Michelangelo's sole work in the genre, is a coded celebration of anti-Medicean republicanism, having been made in 1540 soon after the murder of the tyrannical Duke Alessandro de' Medici. Works by Michelangelo's followers and contemporaries are ranged in the immediate vicinity; some would command prolonged attention in different company, including **Cellini**'s *Bust of Cosimo I*, and **Giambologna**'s voluptuous *Florence Defeating Pisa*, eclipsed by his more famous *Mercury*. Comic relief is provided by the reliably awful **Bandinelli**, whose coiffured *Adam and Eve* look like a grandee and his wife taking a stroll through their estate *au naturel*.

The upper floors

At the top of the courtyard staircase, the **loggia** has been turned into an aviary for Giambologna's bronze birds, brought here from the Medici villa at Castello (see p.537). The doorway to the right at the top of the stairs opens into the fourteenth-century Salone del Consiglio Generale (room H), where the presiding genius is **Donatello**. Vestiges of the sinuous Gothic manner are evident in the drapery of his marble *David*, placed against the left wall, but there's nothing antiquated in the alert, tense *St George*, carved just eight years later for the tabernacle of the armourers' guild at Orsanmichele and installed in a replica of its original niche at the far end of the room. In front stands Donatello's sexually ambiguous bronze *David*, cast in the early 1430s as the first freestanding nude figure since classical times and memorably described by Mary McCarthy as "a transvestite's and fetishist's dream". Back opposite the entrance door is Donatello's strange, jubilant figure known as *Amor Atys*, dating from the end of the 1430s, while his breathtakingly vivid bust of Niccolò da Uzzano nearby shows that he was just as comfortable with portraiture. The less complex humanism of **Luca della Robbia** is embodied in the glazed terracotta Madonnas set round the walls, while Donatello's master, **Ghiberti**, is represented by his relief *The Sacrifice of Isaac*, his successful entry in the competition for the baptistry doors. The treatment of the same theme submitted by **Brunelleschi** – and rejected – is displayed close by. Most of the rest of this floor is occupied by a collection of **European and Islamic applied art**, of so high a standard that it would constitute an engrossing museum in its own right. Elsewhere on this floor is dazzling carved **ivory** from Byzantium and medieval France.

The sculptural display resumes on the next floor up, with **Giovanni della Robbia**'s pietà and **Andrea della Robbia**'s exquisite busts of a young woman and a boy. The Sala dei Bronzetti (room P) is Italy's best assembly of small Renaissance bronzes, with plentiful evidence of Giambologna's virtuosity at table-top scale. Lastly, rooms Q and R are devoted mainly to Renaissance portrait busts, including a small bronze group called *Hercules and Antaeus* by **Antonio Pollaiuolo**, possessing a power out of all proportion to its size.

Piazza della Signoria

Even though it sets the stage for the **Palazzo Vecchio** and the **Uffizi**, Florence's main civic square – the frenetic **Piazza della Signoria** – doesn't quite live up to its role. Too many of its buildings are bland nineteenth-century efforts, and the surface of the square resembles the deck of an aircraft carrier. In the 1970s, it was decided to restore the piazza's ancient paving stones, but when the "restorers" returned the first batch, it was found that they had sandblasted chunks off them rather than rinsing them carefully. Some of the original stones

---

Secret passageways

The so-called **Secret Passageways** (guided tours daily; €9, includes ticket to Palazzo Vecchio) allow access to parts of the Palazzo Vecchio that are normally off limits. Most visually impressive is the trip up through the palace and into the Attic of the Salone del Cinquecento. From the vantage point of a balcony high above the hall, the guide describes the complex way in which Vasari created such a huge space within the medieval structure, and explains the allegorical meaning of the paintings. You are then led up into the vast attic itself, where a forest of pungent timber supports the roof above and the ceiling below.

Less magnificent, but still worth it for the guides' commentary, is the route leading from the street outside up through the secret Stairway of the Duke of Athens. The doorway was knocked through the exterior wall of the Palazzo in 1342 as an emergency escape route for the Duke, who briefly took up the reins of power here. He never in fact used the staircase, but only because his fall from grace came rather sooner than he had imagined.

How many tours are given in English depends on demand: during quieter periods it's likely that you'll have a guide to yourself, but in high season and at weekends it's worth booking in advance at the main ticket office in the Palazzo Vecchio (☎055.276.8224).

then turned up in the yard of a builders' merchant and on the front drives of a number of Tuscan villas.

What little charm the Piazza della Signoria does possess comes from its peculiar array of **statuary**, a miscellany collected at the foot of the Palazzo Vecchio. The line-up starts with Giambologna's equestrian statue of Cosimo I and continues with Ammannati's fatuous *Neptune Fountain* and copies of Donatello's *Marzocco* (the city's heraldic lion), his *Judith and Holofernes* and Michelangelo's *David*. Near Ammannati's fountain is a small plaque set into the pavement to mark the location of Savonarola's **Bonfire of the Vanities** (see p.497) and his execution pyre. The square's **Loggia della Signoria** was built in the late fourteenth century as a dais for city officials during ceremonies; only in the late eighteenth century did it become a showcase for some of the city's more melodramatic sculpture.

The Palazzo Vecchio

Florence's fortress-like town hall, looming above the square as an icon of the city's power and authority, is the **Palazzo Vecchio** (Mon–Wed & Fri–Sun 9am–7pm, Thurs 9am–2pm; €6, combined ticket with Capella Brancacci €8; ⓦwww.palazzovecchio.it). The building was begun in 1299 to serve as the home of the Signoria, the highest tier of the city's republican government. Local folklore has it that its misshapen plan was due to the fact that the Guelph government refused to encroach on land previously owned by the hated Ghibellines, and so squeezed the building instead. The most radical overhaul came in 1540, when **Cosimo I** – recently installed as Duke of Florence – moved his retinue here from the Palazzo Medici. The Medici were only in residence for nine years before moving to the Palazzo Pitti, but the enlargement and refurbishment instigated by Cosimo continued throughout the period of his rule. The **entrance**, which is alongside the copy of Michelangelo's *David* mobbed night and day by snap-happy crowds, leads into a lovely internal **courtyard** designed by Michelozzo.

Giorgio Vasari, court architect from 1555 until his death in 1574, was responsible for much of the sycophantic decor in the state apartments. His limited talents were given full rein in the huge **Salone dei Cinquecento** at the top of the stairs, built at the end of the fifteenth century as a council assembly hall. This room might have become one of Italy's most extraordinary showcases of Renaissance art, when in 1503 Leonardo da Vinci and Michelangelo were commissioned to fresco opposite walls of the chamber. Unfortunately, Leonardo abandoned the project after his experimental fresco technique went wrong, and Michelangelo's ideas existed only on paper when he was summoned to Rome by Pope Julius II. A few decades later Vasari stepped in, and painted over Leonardo's failed attempts with drearily bombastic murals celebrating Cosimo's military prowess. Michelangelo's *Victory*, facing the entrance door, was sculpted for Julius's tomb but was donated to the Medici by the artist's nephew.

Stairs rise from the corridor past an intriguing fireworks fresco of 1558 showing the Piazza della Signoria during celebrations for the feast of John the Baptist. Turn left at the top and you enter the **Quartiere degli Elementi** – the decor plays second fiddle to the romantic rooftop views from the terrace. Back at the top of the stairs, head straight on and you cross a gallery at the rear of the Salone dei Cinquecento into the private apartments of **Eleanor**, Cosimo I's wife. Star turn here is the tiny and exquisite **chapel**, superbly and vividly decorated by Bronzino in the 1540s.

The **Sala dei Gigli** takes its name from the lilies (*gigli*) that adorn most of its surfaces. The room has another splendid ceiling by the Maiano brothers, and frescoes by Domenico Ghirlandaio, but the highlight is **Donatello**'s original *Judith and Holofernes*, a copy of which sits down below in the piazza. Commissioned by Cosimo il Vecchio, the piece originally served as a fountain in the Palazzo Medici. Donatello froze the action at the moment Judith's arm begins the scything stroke that is to cut off Holofernes' head, a dramatic conception that no other sculptor of the period would have attempted.

The two small side-rooms are the Cancellaria, **Machiavelli**'s office for fifteen years and now containing a bust and portrait of the much-maligned political thinker; and the lovely **Sala delle Carte**, decorated with 57 maps painted in 1563 by the Medici court astronomer Fra' Ignazio Danti, depicting in some detail what was then the entire known world.

The Museo di Storia della Scienza

Towards the river, **Piazza dei Giudici**, so called because of the tribunal that met here, now houses the **Museo di Storia della Scienza** (June–Sept Mon & Wed–Fri 9.30am–5pm, Tues & Sat 9.30am–1pm; Oct–May Tues 9.30am–1pm, Wed–Sat 9.30am–5.30pm, second Sun of month 10am–1pm; €6.50), which offers a glimpse of the Renaissance that includes neither heroic male nudes nor tortured saintly visages.

Long after Florence had declined from its artistic apogee, the intellectual reputation of the city was maintained by its scientists. Grand Duke Ferdinando II and his brother Leopoldo, both of whom studied with **Galileo**, founded the Academy of Experiment at the Pitti in 1657, and the instruments made and acquired by this academy form the core of the museum, which has extensive English notes. The **first floor** features timepieces and measuring instruments (such as beautiful Arab astrolabes), as well as a massive armillary sphere made for Ferdinando I to prove the fallacy of Copernicus's heliocentric universe. Galileo's original instruments are on show here, including the lens with which he discovered the four moons of Jupiter. On the **top floor** is the huge lens made for Cosimo III, with which Faraday and Davy managed to ignite a diamond by focusing the rays of the sun. The medical section is full of alarming surgical instruments and wax anatomical models for teaching obstetrics.

The Uffizi

Ranged around a grand U-shaped courtyard between Piazza della Signoria and the river, the **Galleria degli Uffizi** (Tues–Sun 8.15am–7pm, €6.50, free to under-18s & over-65s; see box, p.506 for details of advance reservations; Ⓦwww.uffizi.firenze.it) holds Italy's greatest art collection, with plenty of instantly recognisable iconic images, such as Botticelli's *Birth of Venus*. Its status as the city's key attraction is perhaps the reason why the gallery's directors feel no shame in making you queue for two hours or more for admission. Should you fancy a spot of refreshment after a long wait to get in, there's an expensive rooftop café with excellent views.

The main picture rooms open off a corridor that runs all the way round the uppermost level of the U-shaped building, and which, crammed higgledy-piggledy with **classical statuary** and with a **ceiling** decorated in ornate Grotesque style, is an artwork in itself. The paintings are hung chronologically, with each block of rooms forming a neat, self-contained unit. So many masterpieces are collected here that you should put aside **three or four hours** as the minimum to be able to take in the gallery's key works. If time or energy is short, it makes sense to limit yourself to an hour or two exploring the first fifteen rooms, where the Florentine Renaissance works are concentrated.

The elongated building originated in 1560, when Duke Cosimo I ordered **Giorgio Vasari** to design a block of government offices (*uffizi*) to fill a site between the Palazzo Vecchio and the river that was, at that time, occupied by houses and a church. After Vasari's death, work was continued by **Buontalenti**, who – under orders from Francesco I – glazed the upper storey so that it could house his art collection. Each of the succeeding Medici added to the family's trove of art treasures, and the accumulated collection was preserved for public inspection by the last member of the family, Anna Maria Lodovica, whose will specified that it should be left to the people of Florence and never be allowed to leave the city. During the nineteenth century, a large proportion of the sculpture was transferred to the Bargello, while many of the antiquities went to the Museo Archeologico, leaving the Uffizi itself as essentially a gallery of paintings.

Rooms 1–9: from Cimabue to Fra' Filippo Lippi

Room 1 (often closed) houses an assembly of antique sculpture, used as a source-book by Renaissance artists. The gestation period of the Renaissance can be studied in **room 2**, where three altarpieces of the Maestà (Madonna Enthroned) by Cimabue, Duccio and Giotto dwarf everything around them, and demonstrate the softening of the Byzantine style into a more tactile form of representation. A high point in the comparatively conservative art of fourteenth-century Siena (room 3) is Martini's *Annunciation*, with its eloquently expansive background of plain gold. Florence's only first-rank Gothic painter, Lorenzo Monaco, features amid the collection of other *trecento* artists (**rooms 5 & 6**), with a majestic *Coronation of the Virgin* and an *Adoration of the Magi*; the spangled version of the latter subject by Gentile da Fabriano is the epitome of International Gothic, cramming every inch of the flattened picture plane with often highly naturalistic detail.

In **room 7**, Piero della Francesca is represented by the paired portraits *Federico da Montefeltro* and *Battista Sforza*. The panels are backed by images of the Duke surrounded by the cardinal virtues and his wife by the theological virtues. Paolo Uccello's curiously measured *Battle of San Romano* once hung in Lorenzo il Magnifico's bedchamber, in company with depictions of the same skirmish that now reside in the Louvre and London's National Gallery. Among the plentiful works by Fra' Filippo Lippi in **room 8** is his celebrated *Madonna and Child with Two Angels*. Close by there's a fine *Madonna* by Botticelli.

Rooms 10–16: from Botticelli to Leonardo da Vinci

Botticelli's reputation rests on the works gathered in the merged **rooms 10–14**: *Primavera*, *The Birth of Venus*, *Adoration of the Magi* and *The Madonna of the Magnificat*. *The Birth of Venus* shows a radiantly beautiful Venus being blown to shore by Zephyrus, god of the west wind, and the nymph Cloris; she is about to step – with oddly filth-lined toenails – onto land, to be clothed by Hora, daughter of Aurora, goddess of the dawn. The *Primavera* on the nearby wall is generally held to show the triumph of Venus, who stands as the central focus of the painting. Zephyrus, on the right, chases Cloris and transmutes her into Flora, symbol of natural fertility (who is endowed with one of the most reproduced smiles in the history of art). The Three Graces, expressions of physical beauty, dance together while Mercury, tantalizingly clad only in a loose robe, chases away the clouds of winter.

Though the Uffizi doesn't own a finished painting entirely by Leonardo da Vinci, works in **room 15** comprise a full sketch of his career. From his formative years there's the celebrated and precisely handled *Annunciation* (mainly by

Leonardo) along with the landscape and single angel in profile that he painted aged 18 in Verrocchio's *Baptism*. The incomplete sketch for *The Adoration of the Magi* in the same room encapsulates Leonardo's later radicalism, with its vortex of figures round Mary and the infant Christ. **Room 16**, the enigmatically titled Map Room, is usually kept closed.

Rooms 17–24: from Bronzino to Holbein

Room 18, the octagonal **Tribuna**, was the original Medici gallery and now houses the most important of the Medici sculptures, principal among which is the *Medici Venus*, a first-century BC copy of the Praxitelean Aphrodite of Cnidos. Also in this room are del Sarto's flirtatious *Portrait of a Girl* and some chillingly precise portraits by Bronzino – especially compelling are *Bartolomeo Panciatichi*, *Lucrezia Panciatichi* and *Eleanor of Toledo with Giovanni de' Medici*. Vasari's portrait of Lorenzo il Magnifico and Bronzino's of Cosimo il Vecchio are deceptively immediate – each was painted long after the death of its subject.

Room 20 is largely devoted to Cranach and Dürer, including the latter's *Portrait of the Artist's Father*, his earliest authenticated painting. Highlights in the following sequence of rooms (**21–23**) are a perplexing *Sacred Allegory* by Giovanni Bellini and Holbein's *Portrait of Sir Richard Southwell*.

Rooms 25–45: from Michelangelo to Goya

The main attraction in **room 25** is Michelangelo's only completed easel painting, the virtuoso *Holy Family*, widely known as the "Doni Tondo" (a tondo – a circular artwork – commissioned by the Doni family). An unusually robust and powerful, bare-armed Mary reaches back to take the Christ child from Joseph, watched by a young John the Baptist in an animal skin. The contorted gestures and cold, almost metallic, colours were revolutionary for the time, as was the innovation of including nude figures in an ostensibly religious painting. The *maniera*, or style and execution, of this work was studied and imitated by Florentine painters of the sixteenth century in what became known as the Mannerism movement – as can be gauged from *Moses Defending the Daughters of Jethro* in **room 27** by Rosso Fiorentino, one of the pivotal figures of Mannerism, and works by Bronzino and the mercurial Pontormo. Separating the two Mannerist groups is **room 26** containing Andrea del Sarto's sultry *Madonna of the Harpies* and a number of compositions by Raphael, including the lovely *Madonna of the Goldfinch* and *Pope Leo X with Cardinals Giulio dei Medici and Luigi de' Rossi* – as shifty a group of ecclesiastics as ever was gathered in one frame. **Room 28** is almost entirely given over to another of the titanic figures of sixteenth-century art, Titian. His *Flora* and *A Knight of Malta* are stunning, but most eyes tend to swivel towards the famous *Venus of Urbino*, just about the most fleshy and provocative of all Renaissance nudes.

A brief diversion through the painters of the sixteenth-century Emilian school follows, centred on Parmigianino, whose *Madonna of the Long Neck* is one of the definitive Mannerist creations. **Rooms 31 to 35** feature artists from Venice and the Veneto, with outstanding paintings by Paolo Veronese (*Holy Family with St Barbara*), Tintoretto (*Leda*) and G.B. Moroni (*Count Pietro Secco Suardi*). Sebastiano del Piombo's *Death of Adonis* which was formerly hung here was torn to shreds in 1993 by a Mafia bomb and is still being pieced together.

In **room 41**, dominated by Rubens and Van Dyck, it is one of the less demonstrative items that makes the biggest impact – Rubens' *Portrait of Isabella Brandt*. His equally theatrical contemporary, Caravaggio, has a cluster of pieces in **room 43**, including a sultry, come-hither *Bacchus*. Next is a showcase for the portraiture of Rembrandt – the *Self-Portrait as an Old Man*, painted five years or so before his death, is one of his most melancholic works, its poignancy enhanced by the proximity of another self-portrait from decades earlier. Portraits also seize the attention in the following room of eighteenth-century works (**room 45**), especially the two of Maria Theresa painted by Goya. **Room 42**, between these, is an impressively ceilinged hall packed with classical statuary, while in an alcove at the top of the exit stairs – misleadingly entitled **rooms 36 & 37** – squats one of Florence's talismans, the *Wild Boar*, a Roman copy of third-century-BC Hellenistic sculpture. This tusked beast was the model for the *Porcellino*, which stands today in the Mercato Nuovo.

The Corridoio Vasariano

A door on the west corridor between rooms 25 and 34 opens onto the **Corridoio Vasariano**, a passageway built by Vasari to link the Palazzo Vecchio to the Palazzo Pitti through the Uffizi. Winding its way down to the river, over the Ponte Vecchio on an upper level, through the church of Santa Felicità and into the Giardino di Bóboli, it gives a fascinating series of clandestine views of the city, and is completely lined with paintings, the larger portion of which comprises a **gallery of self-portraits**. Once you're past the portrait of Vasari, the series proceeds chronologically, its roll call littered with illustrious names: Andrea del Sarto, Bronzino, Bernini, Rubens, Rembrandt, van Dyck, Velázquez, Hogarth, Reynolds, Delacroix, Ingres and others.

  Guided tours (€8.50) have to be arranged by phone (T055.265.4321) or at the gallery's ticket office. Tours are conducted in the morning, usually on Wednesday and Friday only, with the precise time varying with the availability of staff. The numbers are limited to thirty people on each tour, so the tours tend to get booked up months in advance.

The western city centre

Several streets in central Florence retain their medieval character, especially in the district west of Piazza della Signoria. Forming a gateway to this quarter is the **Mercato Nuovo** (summer daily 9am–7pm; winter Tues–Sat 9am–5pm), whose souvenir stalls are probably the busiest in the city; there's been a market here since the eleventh century, though the present loggia dates from the sixteenth. Usually a small group is gathered round the bronze boar known as **Il Porcellino**, trying to gain some good luck by getting a coin to fall from the animal's mouth through the grill below his head. An aimless amble through the streets beyond will give you some idea of the feel of Florence in the Middle Ages, when every important house was an urban fortress.

Santa Trinità and around

Via Porta Rossa culminates at Piazza Santa Trinità, not so much a square as a widening of the city's classiest street, **Via de' Tornabuoni**, which heads south across the Arno on the city's most stylish bridge, the **Ponte Santa Trinità**. This was ostensibly designed by Ammannati, but the curve of its arches so closely resembles the arc of Michelangelo's Medici tombs that the credit probably should be his; it was rebuilt stone by stone after the retreating Nazis had blown up the original in 1944. **Santa Trinità** (Mon–Sat 8am–noon & 4–6pm, Sun 4–6pm; free) was founded in the eleventh century, but piecemeal additions have lent it a pleasantly hybrid air: the largely Gothic interior contrasts with Buontalenti's Mannerist facade of 1594. The interior is notable for **Ghirlandaio**'s decoration of the **Cappella Sassetti** (second to the right of the altar). His frescoes *Life of*

St Francis are concerned as much with a portrayal of fifteenth-century Florence as with their religious themes. Elsewhere in the church is **Luca della Robbia**'s powerful composition for the tomb of Benozzo Federighi, Bishop of Fiesole, occupying a wall of the chapel second to the left of the altar and framed by a ceramic border of flowers and greenery.

Heading north from Santa Trìnita is **Via de' Tornabuoni**, home to Cartier, Versace, Armani and the famous local firms Ferragamo and Gucci. Conspicuous wealth is nothing new here, for looming above everything is the vast **Palazzo Strozzi**, the last, the largest and the least subtle of Florentine Renaissance palaces. Filippo Strozzi bought and demolished a dozen town houses to make space for Giuliano da Sangallo's strongbox in stone (1536). Part of the building is now used for interesting and sometimes high-profile exhibitions – see Ⓦ www.palazzostrozzi.info for details.

The church of San Pancrazio, nearby on Via della Spada, has been converted into the slick **Museo Marino Marini** (Mon–Sat 10am–5pm; closed Sat in June, July & Aug; €4). Marini (1901–80) was one of Italy's foremost sculptors of the twentieth century, and this spacious conversion displays variations on his familiar horse-and-rider theme.

Ognissanti

In medieval times a major area of cloth production – the foundation of the Florentine economy – lay in the west of the city. **Ognissanti** (daily 7.30am–12.30pm & 3.30–7.30pm; free), or All Saints, the main church of this quarter located on Borgo Ognissanti, five minutes' walk west of Via de' Tornabuoni, was founded in 1256 by a Benedictine order who wove woollen cloth. Three hundred years later the Franciscans took it over and renovated it in Baroque style; inside is the habit worn by St Francis of Assisi when he received the stigmata atop Monte Verna in September 1224. The young face squeezed between the Madonna and the dark-cloaked man in **Ghirlandaio**'s *Madonna della Misericordia* fresco, over the second altar on the right, is said to be that of Amerigo Vespucci – later to set sail on voyages that would give his name to America. Just beyond this, on opposite sides of the nave, are mounted **Botticelli**'s *St Augustine* and Ghirlandaio's more earthbound *St Jerome*, both painted in 1480. In the same year Ghirlandaio painted the bucolic *Last Supper* that covers one wall of the **refectory**, reached through the cloister entered to the left of the church (Mon, Tues & Sat 9am–noon; free).

Santa Maria Novella

The focus of the western city centre is the large, pleasant **Piazza Santa Maria Novella** in front of the church it was named after, which has a lethargic backwater atmosphere, favoured as a spot for picnic lunches and after-dark loitering.

From the beguiling green, white and pink patterns of its marble facade, you'd never guess that the church of **Santa Maria Novella** was the Florentine base of the Dominican order, fearsome vigilantes of thirteenth-century Catholicism. The architects of the Gothic **interior** (Mon–Thurs 9.30am–5pm, Fri & Sun 1–5pm; €2.50) were capable of great ingenuity – the distance between the columns diminishes with proximity to the altar, a device to make the nave appear from the entrance to be longer than it is. **Masaccio**'s extraordinary 1427 fresco *The Trinity*, one of the earliest works in which perspective and classical proportion were rigorously employed, is painted onto the wall halfway down the left aisle. **Filippino Lippi**'s frescoes for the **Cappella di Filippo Strozzi** (immediately to the right of the chancel) are a fantasy vision of classical ruins in which the narrative often seems to take second place, and one of the first examples of an archeological interest in Roman culture. As a chronicle of fifteenth-century life in Florence, no series of frescoes is more fascinating than **Domenico Ghirlandaio**'s behind the high altar; the work was commissioned by Giovanni Tornabuoni – which explains why certain ladies of the Tornabuoni family are present at the birth of John the Baptist and of the Virgin. **Brunelleschi**'s *Crucifix*, popularly supposed to have been carved as a response to Donatello's uncouth version at Santa Croce, hangs in the Cappella Gondi, left of the chancel. At the end of the left transept is the raised **Cappella Strozzi**, whose faded frescoes by Nardo di Cione (1350s) include an entire wall of visual commentary on Dante's *Inferno*. The magnificent altarpiece by Nardo's brother Andrea (better known as **Orcagna**) is a piece of propaganda for the Dominicans – Christ is shown bestowing favour simultaneously on St Peter and St Thomas Aquinas, a figure second only to St Dominic in the order's hierarchy.

The Museo di Santa Maria Novella

More remarkable paintings are on display in the spacious Romanesque conventual buildings to the left of the church, entered through a separate door into the **Museo di Santa Maria Novella** (Mon–Thurs & Sat 9am–5pm, Sun 9am–2pm; €2.70). The cloisters, just beyond the ticket desk, are more richly decorated than any others in Florence. The first set, the Romanesque **Chiostro Verde**, features the frescoes *Stories from Genesis* by **Paolo Uccello** and his workshop.

Off the cloister opens what was once the chapterhouse of the immensely rich convent the **Cappellone degli Spagnuoli** (Spanish Chapel), which received its new name after Eleanor of Toledo reserved it for the use of her Spanish entourage. Its fresco cycle by Andrea di Firenze, an extended depiction of the triumph of the Catholic Church, was described by Ruskin as "the most noble piece of pictorial philosophy in Italy". The left wall depicts the Triumph of Divine Wisdom: Thomas Aquinas is enthroned below the Virgin and Apostles amid winged Virtues and biblical notables. The more spectacular right wall depicts the Triumph of the Church, and includes at the bottom a building supposed to be Florence's cathedral, a pinky-purple creation imagined eighty years before its actual completion.

The northern city centre

The busy quarter north of the Duomo and east of the train station is packed with shops and commerce. Focus of the area is Florence's main food market, the vast covered **Mercato Centrale** (Mon–Sat 7am–2pm; winter also Sat 4–8pm). Butchers, *alimentari*, tripe sellers, greengrocers, pasta stalls and bars are all gathered under one roof, charging prices lower than you'll find elsewhere. All around is a hectic **street market** (Mon–Sat 8.30am–7pm; Ⓦ www .sanlorenzomarket.com), thronged with stalls selling leather bags, belts, clothes and shoes – plus racks of cut-price replica football shirts from all the most famous teams in Europe.

San Lorenzo

Founded in the fourth century, **San Lorenzo**, on the piazza of the same name (Mon–Sat 10am–5pm; €2.50), has a claim to be the oldest church in Florence – though the current building dates from the 1420s – and was the city's cathedral for almost three centuries. Although Michelangelo sweated to produce a scheme for San Lorenzo's facade, the bare brick of the exterior has never been clad; it's a stark, inappropriate prelude to the powerful simplicity of Brunelleschi's interior, one of the earliest Renaissance church designs. Inside are two striking **bronze pulpits** by **Donatello**. Covered in densely populated and disquieting reliefs, chiefly of scenes preceding and following the Crucifixion, these are the artist's last works and were completed by his pupils. Close by, at the foot of the altar steps, a large disc of multicoloured marble marks the grave of Cosimo il Vecchio, the artist's main patron. Further pieces by Donatello (who is buried here) adorn the **Sagrestia Vecchia** off the left transept.

At the top of the left aisle of San Lorenzo a door leads out to the cloister, and the staircase immediately on the right goes up to the **Biblioteca Laurenziana** (Mon–Sat 8.30am–1.30pm; free, except during special exhibitions). Wishing to create a suitably grandiose home for the precious manuscripts assembled by Cosimo il Vecchio and Lorenzo il Magnifico, Pope Clement VII (Lorenzo's nephew) asked **Michelangelo** to design a new Medici library in 1524. The vestibule of the building he came up with is a revolutionary showpiece of Mannerist architecture, delighting in paradoxical display – brackets that support nothing, columns that sink into the walls rather than stand out from them, and a flight of steps so large that it almost fills the room, spilling down like a solidified lava flow. You pass from this deliberately eccentric space into the tranquil, architecturally correct reading room. Almost everything here is the work of Michelangelo, even the inlaid desks.

In the summer of 2004 a project to exhume the bodies of the Medici family discovered a secret crypt under the stone floor of San Lorenzo containing the bodies of Grand Duke Gian Gastone, another adult and seven unknown children, who it is believed may have been the Duke's illegitimate offspring, although it will take a DNA test to establish their identity for certain.

The Cappelle Medicee

Some of Michelangelo's most celebrated Florentine works are in San Lorenzo's Sagrestia Nuova, part of the **Cappelle Medicee** (Tues–Sat 8.15am–5pm, plus same hours first, third & fifth Sun and second & fourth Mon of month; €4). The entrance to the chapels is round the back of San Lorenzo, on Piazza Madonna degli Aldobrandini, and leads directly into the low-vaulted **crypt**, last resting place of a clutch of minor Medici tossed down here in 1791 by Ferdinand III. After filing through the crypt, you climb steps into the **Cappella dei Principi** (Chapel of the Princes), a gloomy, marble-plated octagonal hall built as a mausoleum for Cosimo I and his ancestors. Morbid and dowdy, it was the most expensive building project ever financed by the family.

Follow the corridor leading on to the **Sagrestia Nuova**, one of the earliest Mannerist buildings, begun by Michelangelo in 1520 and intended as a tribute to, and subversion of, Brunelleschi's Sagrestia Vecchia in San Lorenzo (see above). Architectural connoisseurs go into raptures over the complex cornices of the alcoves and other such sophistications, but you might be more drawn to the fabulous **Medici tombs**, carved by Michelangelo. To the left is the **tomb of Lorenzo**, Duke of Urbino, grandson of Lorenzo il Magnifico. Opposite is the **tomb of Giuliano**, Duke of Nemours, youngest son of Lorenzo il Magnifico. Their effigies were intended to face the equally grand tombs of Lorenzo il Magnifico and his brother Giuliano, two Medici who had genuine claims to fame and honour, but the only part of the project realized by Michelangelo is the serene **Madonna and Child**, the last image of the Madonna he ever sculpted and one of the most affecting, now flanked by *Cosmas* and *Damian*, patron saints of doctors (*medici*) and thus of the dynasty.

The Palazzo Medici-Riccardi

On the northeastern edge of Piazza San Lorenzo stands the **Palazzo Medici-Riccardi** (Mon, Tues & Thurs–Sun 9am–7pm; €5; Ⓦ www.palzzo-medici.it), built by Michelozzo in the 1440s for Cosimo il Vecchio and for a century or more the principal seat of the Medici in the city. With its heavily rusticated exterior, this monolithic palace was the prototype for such houses as the Palazzo Pitti and Palazzo Strozzi, but was greatly altered in the seventeenth century by its new owners, the Riccardi family, who took over after Cosimo I moved out. Thanks to its restored Gozzoli **frescoes** – some of the most charming in all Florence – it now rates as a major sight. However, as only fifteen people are allowed to view these paintings at any one time, the queues can be overwhelming. If time allows, visit the ticket office (through the palace courtyard to the rear) or call ℡ 055.276.0340 to book a timed visit in advance.

Of Michelozzo's original scheme, only the upstairs **chapel** remains intact, its interior covered by brilliantly colourful narrative frescoes *Procession of the Magi*, painted around 1460 by Benozzo Gozzoli. A second staircase ascends from the courtyard to the **Sala di Luca Giordano**, a gilded and mirrored gallery notable for its *Madonna and Child* by Fra' Filippo Lippi, kept in a grotesque black metal box to the left of the door. Luca Giordano's overblown ceiling fresco *The Apotheosis of the Medici*, painted after the Riccardi family had bought the building in 1659, is either deftly tongue-in-cheek or utterly shameless.

The Accademia

Florence's, and indeed Europe's, first Academy of Drawing was founded northeast of San Lorenzo on Via Ricasoli in the mid-sixteenth century by Bronzino, Ammannati and Vasari. In 1784, Grand Duke Pietro Leopoldo opened the onsite **Galleria dell'Accademia** (Tues–Sun 8.15am–6.50pm; €6.50). The gallery has an impressive collection of paintings, especially of Florentine altarpieces from the fourteenth to the early sixteenth centuries – but the pictures are not what pull the crowds. Everyone comes here to see the most famous sculpture in the world, **Michelangelo's** *David*.

Seeing the *David* for the first time can be something of a shock. The conception of the piece was revolutionary. Instead of, as was common, portraying a static warrior David in full armour, with the head of Goliath lying trophy-like at his feet, Michelangelo chose to emphasize human thought and motivation. This David, as well as breaking with tradition by being completely nude (thus recalling classical statuary), is frozen in mid-movement. He is gazing intently over his left shoulder with a stone in his other hand, sizing up Goliath while shifting his weight onto his right foot prior to loading his sling and firing off the stone. The poise of the figure comes in its balance between head and hands, between thought and action.

Michelangelo spent almost three years working beneath a temporary shelter set up in the courtyard of the Opera del Duomo, sculpting the *David* from a narrow block of flawed Carrara marble that had already been partly worked by others and abandoned. He finished it, the largest nude to have been sculpted since classical times, in early 1504 at the age of 29. It was then carted on a four-day procession through the city to its display site in front of the Palazzo Vecchio, suffering attacks as it went from pro-Medici supporters who saw it as symbolizing the recent overthrow of Medicean and Savonarolan rule. Since then, the *David* has become an emblem of the city's pride and of the illimitable ambition of the Renaissance artist. In 1873, it was moved to this specially designed tribune in the Accademia for conservation reasons, and was replaced outside the Palazzo Vecchio by a marble copy.

But herein lies the shock of a first viewing, which so upsets many in the scrum that gathers at *David*'s feet. Michelangelo seems blithely to have abandoned all normal human **proportion**. *David*'s head and hands are far too big, his arms are too long, his legs are too short. Laser-wielding scientists even determined in 2000 that he is wall-eyed. Without the benefit of being able to view the work from a position well back as Michelangelo envisaged – which would give the illusion of lengthening the legs and shortening the trunk and arms – the *David* appears hopelessly gangling. Equally, scrutinizing a close-up, full-face image of *David*'s frowning features is a modern preoccupation: from below, in profile and at a distance, the eyes that do in fact point in slightly different directions appear perfectly focused. In the words of Marc Levoy, the scientist from Stanford University who discovered the squint, "He optimized each eye for its appearance as seen from the side – it's a typical Michelangelo trick." Proportion, it seems, is in the eye of the beholder.

Michelangelo once described the process of sculpting as being the liberation of the form from within the stone, a notion that seems to be embodied by the stunning unfinished **Slaves** that line the approach to *David*. His procedure, clearly demonstrated here, was to cut the block as if it were a deep relief, and then to free the three-dimensional figure. Carved in the 1520s and 1530s, these immensely powerful creations were intended for the tomb of Pope Julius II, but in 1564 the artist's nephew gave them to the Medici, who installed them in the grotto of the Bòboli gardens.

The Museo di San Marco

Just north of the Accademia is the lively **Piazza San Marco**, a meeting-place for Florence's many art students. One side of the square is taken up by the Dominican convent and church of San Marco, now deconsecrated to house the **Museo di San Marco** (Tues–Fri 8.15am–1.50pm, Sat 8.15am–7pm, plus first, third & fifth Mon of each month 8.15am–1.50pm, and second & fourth Sun 8.15am–7pm; €4). In the 1430s, the convent was the recipient of Cosimo il Vecchio's most lavish patronage: he financed Michelozzo's enlargement of the buildings, and went on to establish a vast public library here. Ironically, the convent became the centre of resistance to the Medici later in the century – Savonarola was prior of San Marco from 1491. Meanwhile, as Michelozzo was altering and expanding the convent, its walls were being decorated by one of its friars, **Fra' Angelico**, a painter in whom a medieval simplicity of faith was uniquely allied to a Renaissance sophistication of manner.

The **Ospizio dei Pellegrini** (Pilgrims' Hospice) contains around twenty paintings by Fra' Angelico, most brought here from other churches in Florence. A *Deposition* and a small *Last Judgement* are outstanding – the former remarkable for its aura of tranquillity, as though the minds of its protagonists were already fixed on the Resurrection. The key work, for the drama of its setting and the lucidity of its composition, is the famous **Annunciation** at the summit of the main staircase. All round this upper floor are ranged 44 tiny **dormitory cells**, each frescoed either by Angelico himself or by his assistants – don't miss the *Noli me tangere* (*Touch me not*; cell 1), the *Annunciation* (cell 3), the *Transfiguration* (cell 6) and the *Coronation of the Virgin* (cell 9).

The **church** of San Marco, greatly altered since Michelozzo's intervention, is worth a visit for two works on the second and third altars on the right: a *Madonna and Saints*, painted in 1509 by Fra' Bartolommeo (like Fra' Angelico, a friar at the convent), and an eighth-century mosaic called *The Madonna in Prayer*, brought here from Constantinople.

Piazza Santissima Annunziata

The Accademia stands between Piazza San Marco to the west and, to the east, **Piazza Santissima Annunziata**, the locals' favourite square on account of its lovely porticoes and church. Until the seventeenth century the Florentine year used to begin on March 25, the Feast of the Annunciation, and the day is still marked by a huge fair in the square and the streets leading off it.

The tone of the square is set by Brunelleschi's **Spedale degli Innocenti** (daily except Wed 8.30am–2pm; €3), opened in 1445 as the first foundlings' hospital in Europe and still incorporating an orphanage – Luca della Robbia's ceramic tondi of swaddled babies advertise the building's function. The convent, centred on two beautiful cloisters, now also contains a miscellany of Florentine Renaissance art including one of Luca della Robbia's most charming Madonnas and an incident-packed *Adoration of the Magi* by Ghirlandaio.

The church of **Santissima Annunziata** (daily 7am–12.30pm & 4–6.30pm; free) is the mother church of the Servite order, which was founded by seven Florentine aristocrats in 1234. Its dedication took place in the fourteenth century, in recognition of a miraculous image of the Virgin which, left unfinished by the monastic artist, was purportedly completed by an angel. It attracted so many pilgrims that the Medici commissioned **Michelozzo** to rebuild the church in the second half of the fifteenth century in order to accommodate them. In the Chiostro dei Voti, the atrium that Michelozzo built onto the church, are some beautiful frescoes mainly painted in the 1510s, including a *Visitation* by **Pontormo** and a series by **Andrea del Sarto**, whose *Birth of the Virgin* achieves a perfect balance of spontaneity and geometrical order. The adjoining Chiostro dei Morti, entered from the left transept, is worth visiting for Andrea del Sarto's calculatedly informal *Madonna del Sacco*, painted over the door.

The Museo Archeologico

Just off the square is the **Museo Archeologico**, Via della Colonna 38 (Mon 2–7pm, Tues & Thurs 8.30am–7pm, Wed & Fri–Sun 8.30am–2pm; €4; see box, p.506 for details of advance reservations), the pre-eminent museum of its kind in northern Italy with an especially strong **Etruscan** collection. On the ground floor, pride of place goes to the *François Vase*, an Attic bowl from the sixth century BC. It's been restored twice – once after its discovery in Chiusi in 1845, and again after a butter-fingered member of staff converted it into a 638-piece jigsaw in 1900. The two upper floors are arranged with variable clarity. Outstanding among the **Roman** pieces is the nude known as the *Idolino*, probably a copy of a fifth-century BC original. The **Greek** head of a horse, in the same room, once adorned the garden of the Palazzo Medici, where it was studied by Donatello and Verrocchio. In the long gallery, highlights of the Etruscan collection include the *Arringatore* (Orator), the only known Etruscan large bronze from the Hellenistic period; and a *Chimera*, a bizarre triple-headed bronze monster of the fifth century BC discovered at Arezzo and much admired by Cosimo I's retinue of Mannerist artists.

The eastern city centre

The 1966 flood permanently changed the character of the eastern city centre. Before the deluge it had been one of the more densely populated districts of the city, packed with tenements and small workshops. But **Piazza Santa Croce**, a short stroll east of Piazza della Signoria, and the streets around it lie lower than the surrounding area, and were devastated when the Arno burst its banks. Many of the residents moved out permanently in the following years and today, though traditional leather shops and jewellers are still in evidence, souvenir stalls are a more conspicuous presence.

The piazza has traditionally been one of the city's main arenas: the Medici used it for self-aggrandizing pageants, and under Savonarola it was the principal site for the ceremonial execution of heretics. It's still sometimes used for the **Gioco di Calcio Storico**, a football tournament between the city's four *quartieri*; the game is held three times in St John's week (the last week of June), and is characterized by incomprehensible rules and a degree of violence from which the heavy sixteenth-century costumes offer inadequate protection.

Santa Croce

Florence's two most lavish churches after the Duomo were the headquarters of the two preaching orders: the Dominicans occupied Santa Maria Novella, while the Franciscans were based at the giant church of **Santa Croce** (Mon–Sat 9.30am–5.30pm, Sun 1–5.30pm; €5; ⓦ www.santacroce.firenze.it), famed as the mausoleum of Florence's eminent citizens. Over 270 tombstones pave the floor of the church, while grander monuments commemorate the likes of Ghiberti, Michelangelo, Machiavelli and Galileo. **Dante** has a monument in the church as well as a supremely dramatic statue overlooking the piazza outside – although he is actually buried in Ravenna, where he died.

Inside the door is Vasari's monument to **Michelangelo**, whose body was brought back from Rome to Florence in July 1574; he requested this position so that when the graves of the dead fly open on Judgement Day, the first thing to catch his eye would be Brunelleschi's cathedral dome. At the end of the left aisle is the tomb of **Galileo**, made in 1737, when it was finally agreed to give the great scientist a Christian burial. Also in this aisle, **Ghiberti**, the creator of the Baptistry's doors, has a tomb laid into the floor. Back in the right aisle, the Neoclassical cenotaph to **Dante** is immediately after the second altar, with Machiavelli's tomb on the same side.

The dazzling chapels at the east end of Santa Croce are a compendium of Florentine fourteenth-century art, showing the extent of Giotto's influence and the full diversity of his followers. The two immediately to the right of the chancel are entirely covered with frescoes by **Giotto**: beside the chancel is the **Cappella Bardi**, featuring scenes from the life of St Francis, while next to it is the **Cappella Peruzzi** with a cycle on the lives of St John the Baptist and John the Evangelist. On the south side of the right transept is the **Cappella Baroncelli**, featuring the first night-scene in Western painting, Taddeo Gaddi's *Annunciation to the Shepherds*. On the north side of the left transept, the second **Cappella Bardi** houses a wooden *Crucifix* by **Donatello** – supposedly criticized by Brunelleschi as resembling a "peasant on the Cross".

The Museo dell'Opera di Santa Croce

Santa Croce's most celebrated attractions have been hived off to form the separate, and little-explored, **Museo dell'Opera di Santa Croce** (entry included with ticket to church), entered to the right of the main steps of the church. Standing at the far end of the **Primo Chiostro**, a peaceful expanse of grass hard up against the church wall, is one of Florence's architectural gems, Brunelleschi's **Cappella dei Pazzi**. If one building could be said to typify the spirit of the early Renaissance, this is it. Brunelleschi designed the chapel in the 1430s and worked on it between 1442 and 1446, though it was only completed after his death. The building is geometrically perfect without seeming pedantic, and is exemplary in the way its decorative detail harmonizes with the design. The polychrome lining of the portico's shallow cupola is by **Luca**

della Robbia, as is the tondo of St Andrew over the door; inside, Luca also produced the blue-and-white tondi of the Apostles.

As you exit the chapel, to your left hides Santa Croce's spacious **Secondo Chiostro**, also by Brunelleschi, and perhaps the most peaceful spot in the centre of Florence (although restoration means access is often restricted). A building between the two houses a damaged *Crucifixion* by **Cimabue** on the right wall, which has become the emblem of the havoc caused by the 1966 flood – six metres of filthy water surged into the church, tearing the artwork from its mounting. Also in this room are Taddeo Gaddi's fresco of the Last Supper and *Crucifixion*, and **Donatello**'s enormous gilded *St Louis of Toulouse*, made for Orsanmichele.

South of the river

Visitors to Florence might perceive the Arno as merely a brief interruption in the urban fabric, but Florentines talk as though a ravine divides their city. North of the river is *Arno di quà* ("over here"), while the south side is *Arno di là* ("over there"), also known as the **Oltrarno**, literally "Beyond the Arno". Though traditionally an artisans' quarter, the Oltrarno has always contained prosperous enclaves, and many of the ruling families chose to settle in this area. Nowadays some of the city's swankiest shops line Borgo San Jacopo, while the windows of Via Maggio are an amazing display of palatial furnishings. The main attraction is the Palazzo Pitti and its astounding art collections, though a number of churches also grace the area and are well worth seeking out.

The Ponte Vecchio

The direct route from the city centre to the heart of Oltrarno crosses the river on the **Ponte Vecchio**, the only bridge not mined by the retreating Nazis in 1944. Built in 1345 to replace an ancient wooden bridge, the bustling thoroughfare has always been loaded with shops propped over the water. Up until the sixteenth century, butchers, fishmongers and tanners occupied the bridge, but in 1565 the Medici had the Corridoio Vasariano (see p.517) constructed over the arcades as a private passageway between the Palazzo Vecchio and the Palazzo Pitti. For a generation, the noble nostrils suffered the stench rising from the bridge, until in 1593 Ferdinando I ejected the butchers and installed goldsmiths instead. Today, still replete with jewellery firms, the bridge is crammed with sightseers and big-spending shoppers during the day, and also remains busy after the shutters come down, when street traders set out their stalls and the local lads hang around the bust of Cellini.

The Palazzo Pitti

Although the Medici later took possession of the largest palace in Florence – the **Palazzo Pitti** – it still bears the name of the man for whom it was built. Luca Pitti was a prominent rival of Cosimo il Vecchio, and much of the impetus behind the building of his new house came from a desire to trump the Medici. No sooner was the palace completed, however, than the Pitti's fortunes began to decline and by 1549 they were forced to sell to their former rivals. The palace then became the Medici's family pile, growing in bulk until the seventeenth century, when it achieved its present gargantuan proportions. Today, the *palazzo* and the pavilions of the grand **Giardino di Bóboli** hold eight museums, ranging from the essential to the purely specialist.

Many of the paintings gathered by the Medici in the seventeenth century are now arranged in the **Galleria Palatina**, a labyrinthine suite of 26 rooms in the right-side upper-floor wing of the palace (Tues–Sun 8.15am–6.50pm; €8.50, including admission to the Appartamenti Reali and the Galleria d'Arte Moderna). The ticket office is on the ground floor, just off the main courtyard; once inside allow a couple of hours to do the gallery justice. There are half a dozen excellent works by **Raphael**, including, in room 5, portraits of Angelo Doni and his wife Maddalena – her pose copied directly from the *Mona Lisa* – and the celebrated *Madonna della Seggiola*, or Madonna of the Chair, in which the figures are curved into the rounded shape of the picture with no sense of artificiality. An even larger contingent of supreme works by **Titian** includes a number of his most trenchant portraits – among them *Pietro Aretino*, the preening *Cardinal Ippolito de' Medici*, and the disconcerting *Portrait of an Englishman* in room 2, a picture that makes the viewer feel as closely scrutinized as was the subject. **Rubens**' *Consequences of War* packs more of a punch than most other Baroque allegories, while the gallery's outstanding sculpture is **Canova**'s *Venus Italica* in room 1, commissioned by Napoleon.

Much of the rest of this floor comprises the **Appartamenti Reali** – the Pitti's state rooms, renovated by the dukes of Lorraine in the eighteenth century, and then again by King Vittorio Emanuele when Florence became Italy's capital. On the floor above is the **Galleria d'Arte Moderna** (Tues–Sat 8.15am–6.50pm; entry included with Galleria Palatine ticket). Displaying a chronological survey of primarily Tuscan art from the mid-eighteenth century to 1945, the most rewarding exhibits are the products of the Macchiaioli, the Italian division of the Impressionist movement, while the most startling are the sublime specimens of sculptural kitsch, such as Antonio Ciseri's *Pregnant Nun*. The left-side wing of the palace is given over to the **Museo degli Argenti** (Silver Museum), entered from the garden courtyard (same hours and ticket as Giardino di Bóboli, see below) – a collection of luxury artefacts, including Lorenzo il Magnifico's trove of antique vases, displayed in one of the four splendidly frescoed reception rooms on the ground floor. The **Galleria del Costume** (Tues–Sat 8.15am–1.50pm; also open on first, fourth & fifth Sun and second & fourth Mon of month; €8 includes entry to the Giardino di Bóboli) is housed in the Palazzina della Meridiana, the eighteenth-century southern wing of the Pitti, and across the palace gardens is the **Museo delle Porcellane** (Museum of Porcelain; same hours as Giardino di Bóboli; included in ticket for Giardino di Bóboli, see below).

The Bóboli Gardens and the Belvedere

The **Giardino di Bóboli** is the Pitti's enormous formal garden (Jan–Feb & Nov–Dec 8.15am–4.30pm; March 8.15am–5.30pm; April–May & Sept–Oct 8.15am–6.30pm; June–Aug 8.15am–7.30pm; closed first & last Mon of month; €8, includes entry to the Galleria del Costume, see above). Created when the Medici took possession of the Palazzo Pitti, it continued to expand into the early seventeenth century. Today, it is the only extensive area of greenery in the centre of the city, and thus tends to get crowded in the areas close to the gates; it gets quieter in the heart of the garden, however, as the sharp gradients of its avenues take their toll. Of all the garden's Mannerist embellishments, the most celebrated is the **Grotta del Buontalenti**, close to the entrance to the left of the palace facade, beyond the turtle-back figure of Cosimo I's court dwarf (as seen on a thousand postcards). In among the fake stalactites are shepherds and sheep that look like calcified sponges, while embedded in the corners are replicas of Michelangelo's *Slaves*, replacing the originals that were here until 1908. In the deepest recesses of the cave stands Giambologna's *Venus Emerging from her Bath*, leered at by attendant imps.

△ Bóboli Gardens

It's sometimes possible to leave the gardens by the gate in their southeast corner that leads to the precincts of the **Forte di Belvedere**. This star-shaped fortress was built on the orders of Ferdinando I in 1590, ostensibly for the city's protection but really to intimidate the Grand Duke's fellow Florentines. The **urban panorama** from here is superb and art exhibitions are sometimes held in the box-like palace in the centre of the fortress. East from the Belvedere, and also accessible on Costa San Giorgio which coils up from Piazza Santa Felìcita, stretches the best-preserved section of Florence's fortified walls, an attractive if tiring route to San Miniato (see p.543).

Santo Spirito

The charming **Piazza Santo Spirito**, south of the Ponte Santa Trinità, encapsulates the self-sufficient character of the quarter, with its students, market stalls and cafés, and neighbouring streets with their furniture workshops and antiques showrooms. Don't be deterred by the vacant facade of the church of **Santo Spirito** (Mon–Sat 10am–noon & 4–5.30pm, closed Wed afternoon, Sun 11.30am–noon; free) – the interior, one of Brunelleschi's last projects, prompted Bernini to describe it as "the most beautiful church in the world". It's so perfectly proportioned it seems artless, yet the plan is extremely sophisticated – a Latin cross with a continuous chain of 38 chapels round the outside and a line of 35 columns running in parallel right round the building. Unfortunately a Baroque baldachin covers the high altar, but this is the sole disruption of Brunelleschi's arrangement.

The Cappella Brancacci

In 1771 fire wrecked the Carmelite convent and church of **Santa Maria del Carmine** some 300m west of Santo Spirito, but somehow the flames did not damage the frescoes of the church's **Cappella Brancacci**, a cycle of paintings that is one of the essential sights of Florence (Mon & Wed–Sat 10am–5pm, Sun 1–5pm; €6). The frescoes adorn one side-chapel of the Carmine, which is barricaded off from the chancel and nave and has to be entered on a back route through the cloister. The ticket office is to the right of the church entrance.

The decoration of the chapel was begun in 1424 by **Masolino** and **Masaccio**, the former aged 41 and the latter 22. Within a short time the elder was taking lessons from the younger, whose grasp of the texture of the real world, of the principles of perspective, and of the dramatic potential of the biblical texts they were illustrating far exceeded that of his precursors. Three or four years later Masaccio was dead, according to one report from poisoning, though he may have been a victim of the plague. In the words of Vasari, "All the most celebrated sculptors and painters since Masaccio's day have become excellent and illustrious by studying their art in this chapel." Michelangelo used to come here to make drawings of Masaccio's scenes – and had his nose broken on the chapel steps by a young sculptor whom he enraged with his condescending attitude.

The Brancacci frescoes are as startling a spectacle as the Sistine Chapel in Rome, the brightness and delicacy of their colours and the solidity of the figures exemplifying what Bernard Berenson singled out as the tactile quality of Florentine art. The small scene on the left of the entrance arch is the quintessence of Masaccio's art. Depictions of **The Expulsion of Adam and Eve** had never before captured the desolation of the sinners so graphically – Adam presses his hands to his face in bottomless despair, Eve raises her head and screams. In contrast to the emotional charge of Masaccio's couple, Masolino's almost dainty *Adam and Eve* on the opposite arch pose as if to have their portraits painted.

St Peter is chief protagonist of most of the remaining scenes, two of which are especially compelling. The *Tribute Money* on the upper left wall is the most widely praised, a complex narrative by Masaccio showing Peter, under Christ's instruction, fetching money from the mouth of a fish to pay a sum demanded by the city authorities of Capernaum. Masaccio's *St Peter Healing the Sick*, to the left of the altar, depicts the shadow of the stern saint curing the infirm as it passes over them, a miracle invested with the aura of a solemn ceremonial.

The cycle was suspended in 1427 when Masaccio left for Rome, where he died, and work did not resume until 1480, when the frescoes were completed by **Filippino Lippi**. He finished the *Raising of Theophilus's Son and St Peter Enthroned* (lower left wall), which depicts St Peter bringing the son of the Prefect of Antioch to life and then preaching to the people of the city from a throne. The three figures to the right of the throne are thought to be portraits of Masaccio, Alberti and Brunelleschi. Masaccio originally painted himself touching Peter's robe, but Lippi considered such physical contact to be improper and painted out the offending limb – you can still clearly see where the arm used to be.

San Miniato al Monte

The brilliant, multicoloured facade of **San Miniato al Monte** on a steep hillside in the Oltrarno lures troupes of visitors up from the south bank of the Arno. Most routes pass through or alongside the broad **Piazzale Michelangelo** just below the church: buses #12 and #13 stop here, there's free parking or it's twenty minutes' walk from the city centre. The spectacular views from here of Brunelleschi's dome floating above the city are worth a special journey in themselves.

The church itself more than fulfils the promise of its appearance from a distance: **San Miniato** is the finest Romanesque church in Tuscany. The church's dedicatee, St Minias, belonged to a Christian community that settled in Florence in the third century; according to legend, after his martyrdom his corpse was seen to carry his severed head over the river and up the hill to this spot, where a shrine was subsequently erected to him. Construction of the present building began in 1013 with the foundation of a Cluniac monastery. The gorgeous marble facade – alluding to the baptistry in its geometrical patterning – was added towards the end of that century, though the external mosaic *Christ between the Virgin and St Minias* dates from the thirteenth. The **interior** (summer daily 8am–7.30pm; winter Mon–Sat 8am–noon & 3–6pm, Sun 3–8pm; free) is like no other in the city, with the choir raised on a platform above the large crypt; its general form has changed little since the mid-eleventh century. The main structural addition is the Cappella del Cardinale del Portogallo, a paragon of artistic collaboration: the basic design was by Antonio Manetti (a pupil of Brunelleschi), the tomb was carved by Antonio Rossellino, and the terracotta decoration of the ceiling is by Luca della Robbia. The majority of the frescoes along the aisle walls were painted in the fifteenth century; the most extensive are the sacristy's *Scenes from the Life of St Benedict*, painted in the 1380s by Spinello Aretino. Nearby, the Renaissance church of **San Salvatore**, built by Simone del Pollaiolo between 1499 and 1504, has a choir specializing in Gregorian chants that accompanies Sunday evening mass.

Eating, drinking and entertainment

Florence's gastronomic reputation has suffered under the pressure of mass tourism, and many locals swear there's scarcely a single genuine Tuscan **restaurant** left in the city. But don't despair – this is an exaggeration and a decent meal isn't hard to come by if you explore away from the touristy central streets.

Florentines have always seemed to prefer wine to coffee, and the city can't really claim to have a **café** tradition like that of Rome or Turin – **bars** are both more plentiful and generally more attractive places to rest weary limbs. The university and the annual influx of language students and other young visitors keep the **nightlife** lively, while **classical music** events such as the prestigious Maggio Musicale maintain Florence's standing as the cultural focus of Tuscany.

Restaurants, pizzerias and snack bars

In gastronomic circles, Florentine cuisine is often accorded as much reverence as Florentine art, but quality cooking doesn't come cheap. However, there are some more affordable and congenial places in districts that have a bit of local colour to them, such as Santa Croce and around Santo Spirito. One thing to be aware of is that many restaurants in Florence will only serve full meals – check the menu outside if you're thinking of just popping in for a quick lunchtime plate of pasta.

We've divided the listings below by price: **expensive** means an average full meal (excluding wine) costs €40–60 per person; **inexpensive** means you can eat for €18 or less; **moderate** is between the two. **Reservations** are not usually necessary so we've given phone numbers only where they are.

Inexpensive

Cantinetta dei Verrazzano Via dei Tavolini 18–20r. Great elegant and central place for pizza, sandwiches or pastries, owned by a prestigious Chianti vineyard. Take away fresh bread, sit at the counter for a coffee, or grab a table in the pleasant rooms at the back to sample the wine. Mon–Sat 8am–9pm. Closed Aug.

I Tarocchi Via dei Renai 12/14 ☎055.234.3912. Often packed with locals – always a good sign in this most touristy of cities – this serves thin and crispy pizzas with good quality toppings. Closed Mon.

Il Contadino Via Palazzuolo 69r. Very basic but good cheap meals, Il Contadino offers a fixed price two-course menu for €9.50 lunch, €10.50 dinner. Expect to find lots of backpackers waiting to get in. Closes 9.30pm. Closed Sun & Aug.

Il Pizzaiuolo Via de' Macci 113r ☎055.241.171. Many Florentines reckon the pizzas at this tiny side street Neapolitan-owned restaurant are the best in the city. The ambience is friendly but space is at a premium so book in advance, especially in the evening. No credit cards. Closed Sun & Aug.

La Casalinga Via del Michelozzo 9r ☎055.218.624. Long-established, traditional trattoria that serves up some of the best low-cost (*primi* €4.50, *secondi* €6–7) authentic Tuscan dishes in town. Paper tablecloths and brisk service add to the allure. Closed Sun & Aug.

Trattoria da Benvenuto Via della Mosca 16r, corner Via de' Neri ☎055.214.833. Good, unpretentious Tuscan dishes in a simple setting – try the delicious ravioli with rocket sauce and *arista* (roast pork loin). Closed Sun.

Moderate

Acqua al Due Via della Vigna Vecchia 40r ☎055.284.170. Always packed, chiefly on account of its *assaggio di primi* – a succession of pasta dishes shared by everyone at the table. *Primi* €7, *secondi* €12–13. Open till 1am daily.

Alla Vecchia Bettola Viale Lodovico Ariosto 32–34r ☎055.224.158. South of the river, this former drinking den – the long marble-topped tables help retain some of the atmosphere – has a good repertoire of Tuscan meat dishes. Closed Sun & Mon.

Angiolino Via Santo Spirito 36r ☎055.239.8976. One of the city's prettiest trattorias, with window displays of flowers, fruit and meat, a brick-vaulted ceiling and red-checked tablecloths. The menu is short and Tuscan (expect plenty of boar and tripe), though quality can be erratic. *Primi* €6–7, *secondi* €12–14. Closed Mon.

Antiche Carrozze Borgo Santi Apostoli 66r. Despite its location on the main tourist beat, this multi-roomed affair is a popular local haunt and a good place to pop in for a lunchtime bowl of pasta. They do a very generous *bruschetta* for €4.50. Closed Mon.

Baldovino Via San Giuseppe 22r ☎055.241.773. Next to Santa Croce with outdoor seating by the church, this stylish restaurant is especially known for pizzas – try the Lombardo with truffles for €10 – but the menu is chock-full of other excellent Tuscan and Italian dishes. *Primi* €6–8, *secondi* €12–15.50. Closed Mon.

Borgo Antico Piazza Santo Spirito 6r ☎055.210.437. A popular and boisterous trattoria, with quieter tables outside in summer. Choose from twelve different pizzas (all €7), great salads, a daily set-price menu or a range of Tuscan standards. Servings are generous, queues frequent. Closed Sun.

Osteria del Caffè Italiano Via Isola delle Stinche 11–13r ☎055.289.020. This rambling wood-panelled place, with casual lunch parlour, wine bar and smarter restaurant sections, serves first-rate Tuscan food. Closed Mon.

Osteria Santo Spirito Piazza Santo Spirito 16r ☎055.238.2383. Trendy, modern-looking *osteria* serving simple, hearty Tuscan dishes with contemporary flair. There's no problem ordering a snack or single course, and it has outside tables in summer.

Trattoria 4 Leoni Via Vellutini 1r ☎055.218.562. A young, relaxed place arranged around an impressive three-room medieval interior. They only serve full meals, and direct you across the road to the *Caffè degli Artigiani* if you just want a snack. The menu is very Florentine: as a starter try the *finocchiona*, a type of Tuscan salami. *Primi* €6–8, *secondi* €9–12. Closed Wed in winter.

Expensive

Cibrèo Via de'Macci 118r ☎055.234.1100. Serves a superb selection of Tuscan classics (the *pappa* – Tuscan tomato and bread soup is recommended) in a relaxed, tasteful dining room. You need to book days in advance for the main restaurant, but the next door trattoria-bar has virtually the same food and prices are far lower. Closed Sun, Mon & Aug.

Enoteca Pinchiorri Via Ghibellina 87 ☎055.242.777. Located on the ground floor of the very grand *Relais Santa Croce* hotel, Florence's best restaurant has three Michelin stars, sublime, sophisticated food, and 80,000 different bottles of wine. None of this comes cheap – the steak Fiorentina is €100 for two – but there's nowhere better for a never-to-be repeated Florentine treat. Closed Aug & all day Sun & Mon plus lunch on Tues & Wed.

Oliviero Via delle Terme 52r ☎055.240.618. *Oliviero's* reputation for exclusivity is heightened by its tucked-away side street location. Its serves up some of Florence's best food – including a range of innovative Tuscan dishes and puddings, as well as fresh fish when available, something of a rarity in Florence – but at a price. Closed Sun & Aug.

8

TUSCANY | Florence (Firenze) • Eating, drinking and entertainment

Cafés, gelaterie, bars and pubs

Pavement **cafés** are not really part of the Florentine scene. Smaller, less ostentatious venues are more the city's style – one-room cafés, bars or *pasticcerie*, or places that combine the functions of all three. Devotees of Italian **ice cream** will find plenty of *gelaterie* in Florence to sample some wacky concoctions without straying far off the main drags. The city has a fair spread of **bars** and **pubs** to fuel an evening's entertainment, and classier, specialist **wine bars** are coming back into fashion after a hiatus: one of the focal points of a Florentine parish is the *vinaio*, an institution that's part wine cellar, part snack bar and part social centre.

Cafés

Caffè Amerini Via della Vigna Nuova 63r. As stylish as the clothes of the surrounding fashion boutiques, *Amerini* has a clientele as eclectic as its medieval/Art Deco/modern decor. Ideal for an expensive snack lunch, *aperitivo*, or, to make the most of your money, lingering on a rainy afternoon. Closed Sun.

Caffè Cibrèo Via A. del Verrocchio 5r. It's a long way to come just for a drink, but the glorious wood-panelled interior is the prettiest in the city, and the cakes and desserts are outstanding. Tues–Sat 8am–1am.

Caffè Italiano Via della Condotta 56r. A veritable oasis just steps away from the madness of Via dei Calzaiuoli. Elegant downstairs bar with ornate, filigree iron stools, silver teapots and wonderful cakes, and a secret little room upstairs with red velvet banquettes. Simple lunches such as bean soup or pasta are good too. Closed Sun.

Caffè Rivoire Piazza Signoria 5r. If you want to people-watch on Florence's main square, this smart café is the place to go. Founded in 1872, its main claim to fame is the thick hot chocolate, but in summer go for the refreshing *aperitivo della casa* (Campari, Martini, tonic and Punt e Mes). Closed Mon.

Hemingway Piazza Piattellina 9r. Chocolate is the owners' passion (they're big shots in the Chocolate Appreciation Society, and offer desserts to die for), and the ranges of speciality teas, gourmet coffees, cocktails, food and wines are all excellent, too. Tues–Fri 4pm–1/2am, Sun 11am–8pm.

Procacci Via de' Tornabuoni 64r. Famous café-shop that doesn't serve coffee, just cold drinks. Its fame comes from the extraordinary truffle rolls (*panini tartufati*), which are delicious if not very filling. Closed Mon.

Gelaterie

Festival del Gelato Via del Corso 75r. Over 100 varieties, with some exotic combinations (including carrot and spinach) and good *semifreddi*. Closed Mon.

Frilli Via del Monte alle Croci 5. Excellent ice creams made from seasonal fruit in what claims to be Florence's oldest *gelateria*. Closed Wed.

Perchè No! Via dei' Tavolini 19r. Very central and highly regarded *gelateria* with a vast range of flavours; go for the juicy *mirtillo* (blueberry) or the nuttily delicious pistacchio. Closed Tues.

Buying picnic food

One way to cut eating costs is to retire with a **picnic** to the Bóboli gardens or squares such as Santissima Annunziata, Santa Croce or Santa Maria Novella. The easiest option is to call in at San Lorenzo's **Mercato Centrale** (see p.519), though almost as comprehensive, and even cheaper, is the **Mercato Sant'Ambrogio** by Santa Croce (Mon–Fri 7am–2pm), while the American bakery Mr Jimmy's, Via San Niccolò 47, has bagels, brownies, muffins, banana bread and cheesecake. In the centre, Via dei Tavolini, off Via dei Calzaiuoli, is a good street in which to assemble a picnic: Grana Market at no. 11r has cheeses, and Semelino at no. 18r bakes wonderful bread. Every district has its *alimentari*, selling the choicest Tuscan produce, and the unnamed one close to Santa Trinità, at Via Parione 19, prepares delicious sandwiches and has a few seats too. Vera, at the southern end of Ponte Santa Trinità at Piazza Frescobaldi 3r, takes the prize for the ultimate Florentine deli, while other excellent central *alimentari* include Tassini at Borgo Santi Apostoli 24r and Alessi Paride at Via delle Oche 27–29r.

Vivoli Via Isola delle Stinche 7r. Operating from unprepossessing premises in a side street close to Santa Croce, this is the best ice-cream maker in Florence – some say in Italy. An institution, creating subtle and sublime flavours. Closed Mon & Aug.

Pubs, bars and wine bars

All'Antico Vinaio Via de' Neri 65r. Traditional place that preserves much of the rough-and-ready atmosphere that's made it one of Florence's most popular wine bars for the last hundred years. Tues–Sat 8am–8pm, Sun 8am–1pm.

Angie's Via dei Neri 35r. Seemingly always packed with people, this tiny pub is the place to come if you want to put the world to rights. Expect loud, animated conversations.

Capocaccia Lungarno Corsini 12–14r. Voted locals' favourite night-time rendezvous, this trendy riverfront haunt doubles as a daytime café and evening snackery, while there's a DJ Tues–Thurs. The street tables outside are almost always packed with Italians in designer shades. Tues–Sat noon–4pm & 6pm–1am.

Caracol Via Ginori 10r. Cheery, bumptious Mexican restaurant with a long wooden bar and ranks of tequila bottles, serving big bowls of chili to share for €13. Happy hour is Tues–Wed 6–12pm, Thurs–Sun 6–8pm, when all cocktails are €3.50. Closed Mon.

Casa del Vino Via dell'Ariento 16r. Wine bar located just west of the Mercato Centrale where Florentines pitch up for a drink, a natter and an assault on a fine range of panini and *crostini*. Mon–Fri 8am–2.30pm & 5–8pm, Sat 9am–2.30pm. Closed Aug.

Dolce Vita Piazza del Carmine 6r. Trendy, modern-looking bar, with seating on the square, that's often a venue for small-scale art exhibitions. Summer Mon–Sat 10.30am–1.30am, Sun 6pm–1.30am; winter daily 6pm–1.30am.

Enoteca Baldovino Via San Giuseppe 18r. Bright, modern and painted in warm ochre tones, this is a stylish, friendly place for buying a range of gastronomic goodies and sampling wines by the bottle or glass. Summer daily noon–midnight; winter Tues–Sun noon–4pm & 6pm–midnight.

Enoteca Boccadama Piazza Santa Croce 25–26r. With outdoor seating right in front of Santa Croce, this is a slick, welcoming wine bar offering plenty of fine Italian vintages. As an accompaniment, try the selection of Tuscan salamis with cheese and liver canapés or, for a vegetarian alternative, the cheese, fresh fruit and honey platter (both €9). Closed Mon.

Enoteca de' Giraldi Via de' Giraldi 4r. Old-fashioned central wine bar and bistro, with vaulted ceilings, stone columns and marble-topped tables, that concentrates on local wines. Mon–Sat noon–4pm & 7pm–1am.

Fiddler's Elbow Piazza Santa Maria Novella. Florence's most popular Irish pub is an invariably heaving affair, though fortunately outside tables relieve the crush. Mon–Thurs 3pm–1am, Fri 3pm–2am, Sat 2pm–2am, Sun 2pm–1am.

Fuori Porta 10r Via del Monte alle Croci. If you're climbing up to San Miniato you could take a breather at Florence's most famous wine bar. There are over 400 wines by the bottle – the choice by the glass changes every few days – and a wide selection of grappas and malt whiskies. Also a good place for a light lunch, with tables outside. Mon–Sat 12.30–3.30pm & 7pm–12.30am.

Le Volpi e L'Uva Piazza dei Rossi 1r. This discreet little place just over the Ponte Vecchio typifies the atmosphere of the Oltrarno – relaxed, mellow and welcoming. The owners concentrate on the interesting wines of small producers, and provide high-quality snacks to accompany them – the cheeses are tremendous, as are the spicy Calabrian *crostini*. Mon–Sat 11am–8pm.

Rex Caffe Via Fiesolana 25r. Long-established night-time fixture with eye-catching decor and a friendly atmosphere. Cocktails are good, tapas are excellent and DJs provide the sounds at weekends. Mon–Thurs & Sun 5pm–1.30am, Fri & Sat 5pm–2.30am. Closed June–Aug.

Nightlife and entertainment

Florentine **nightlife** has a reputation for catering primarily to the middle-aged and affluent, but like every university town it has its pockets of activity, and by talking to people and keeping an eye out for posters around the San Marco or Santo Spirito quarters you should pick up news of any impromptu events. Florence's **gay and lesbian** scene is small but lively – see Listings on p.534. The city's sizeable population of British and American students ensures a supply of English-language **films**, and the highbrow cultural calendar is filled out with seasons of **classical music, opera and dance** to rival the best in Europe.

You can find **information** in English about concerts and shows at the kiosks in Piazza della Repubblica and inside the Palazzo Vecchio; otherwise, get hold of the *Firenze Spettacolo* monthly listings magazine (see p.500). The **ticket agency** Box Office, at Via Alamanni 39 (℡055.210.804, Ⓦwww.boxol.it) and Chiasso de' Solderini 8r off Via Porta Rossa (℡055.219.402), has information and tickets for all events, concerts and festivals – but permanently busy phones.

Clubs and live music venues

Central Park Via Fosso Macinante 2, Parco delle Cascine. Currently one of the city's best clubs, with adventurous, wide-ranging music and a superb sound system. A card system operates for drinks, and the first drink is included in the admission, around €18. Note that the park outside is unsafe, especially for women. Summer Tues–Sat 11pm–4am; winter Fri & Sat same hours.

Chiodo Fisso Via Dante Alighieri 16r. Good central venue for folk and sometimes jazz music. Open nightly.

Flog Auditorium Via M. Michele 24b. Popular live venue in the north of the city, this specializes in up-and-coming acts preparing to make the step up to the big time of the Tenax stage.

Jazz Club Via Nuova de' Caccini 3. Florence's foremost jazz venue has been a fixture for years in this side street off Borgo Pinti. The €6 annual membership fee gets you down into the medieval brick-vaulted cellar, where the atmosphere is informal and there's live music most nights. Closed Sun.

Tenax Via Pratese 46 ℡055.308.160. *Tenax* is the city's leading venue for new and established bands as well as big-name international acts. Keep an eye out for posters around town or call here or at the tourist office for upcoming gigs. The place is enormous but easy-going, doubles as a club after hours, and has ranks of bars, pool tables, computer games and plenty of seating.

Film

Of the **cinemas** showing undubbed movies, Cinema Astro, in Piazza San Simone, near Santa Croce (no phone), screens English-language films six nights weekly, while Cinema Goldoni, Via dei Serragli 109 (℡055.222.437), and Odeon Original Sound, Via Sassetti 1 (℡055.214.068, Ⓦwww.cinehall.it), run VO (original-language) films once or twice a week. Most cinemas close in the summer months, when **open-air screens** take over – usually at the Forte Belvedere, above the Bóboli gardens, and at the Palazzo dei Congressi, near the train station on Viale Strozzi.

Classical music, opera and dance

The **Maggio Musicale Fiorentino** is one of Europe's leading festivals of **opera** and **classical music**, lasting from late April to early July. Events are staged at the Teatro Comunale, the tiny Teatro Goldoni, the Teatro della Pergola, the Palazzo dei Congressi, and occasionally in the Bóboli gardens. Information and tickets are available from the Teatro Comunale box office, Corso Italia 16 (℡055.211.158 or 055.213.535, Ⓦwww.maggiofiorentino.com).

The Teatro Comunale is the city's major concert venue, hosting the **symphony orchestra**, which performs a new programme every week during the winter concert season (Jan–March), as well as a prestigious **opera and ballet** season in the autumn (Sept–Dec). The Teatro della Pergola, at Via della Pergola 18 (℡055.247.9651), built in 1656 and believed to be Italy's oldest theatre, hosts seasons of **chamber concerts** by the Amici della Musica that draw in world-class performers (Oct–April), while the Florence Chamber Orchestra (℡055.783.374, Ⓦwww.videosoft.it/orchest) performs every two weeks (April–June, Sept & Oct) in Orsanmichele church. The **Estate Fiesolana** summer festival concentrates on chamber and symphonic music, with most events held in Fiesole's open-air Teatro Romano (see p.535). July's three-week **Florence Dance Festival** showcases first-rate classical, traditional and contemporary dance; get tickets and information from the festival offices at Borgo Stella 23r (℡055.289.276, ⓦwww.florencedance.org) or the Box Office agency (see p.533).

Listings

Airlines For airlines flying into Pisa, see p.539. Alitalia ℡055.27.881; British Airways ℡199.712.266; Lufthansa ℡199.400.044; Meridiana ℡055.318.530.

Airport information Aeroporto Galileo Galilei, Pisa ℡050.500.707, ⓦwww.pisa-airport.com (information also from the check-in desk at Santa Maria Novella train station, platform 5; daily 7am–8pm). Peretola-Amerigo Vespucci airport, Via del Termine 11, Florence ℡055.373.498, ⓦwww .aeroporto.firenze.it.

Banks and exchange Florence's main banks are on or around Piazza della Repubblica but exchange booths (*cambio*) and ATM cash machines (*banco-mat*) can be found across the city. Banks generally open Mon–Fri 8.20am–1.20pm and 2.35–3.35pm, though some are open longer hours. The main Thomas Cook branch is at Lungarno Acciaiuoli 6–12 (Mon–Sat 9am–6pm, Sunday 9am–2pm; ℡055.289.781); American Express is at Via Dante Alighieri 22r (Mon–Fri 9am–5.30pm, Sat 9am–12.30pm; ℡055.50.981).

Bike, scooter and moped rental Alinari, Via Guelfa 85r ℡055.280.500; Florence by Bike, Via San Zanobi 120–122r ℡055.488.992, ⓦwww .florencebybike.it. Bicycle Tuscany (℡055.222.580, ⓦwww.bicycletuscany.com) and Tuscany Bike Tours (℡339.116.3495, ⓦwww.tuscany-biketours .com) both offer day-trip tours into the Chianti hills.

Books The chain bookshop, Feltrinelli, Via Cavour 12r, has a large English language section, including several guidebooks, as does the nearby Libreria Martelli, Via dei Martelli 22. Otherwise, good general outlets include the Paperback Exchange, Via dell Oche 4r, and Il Viaggio, Borgo degli Albizi 41r, which specializes in travel books, guides and maps.

Car rental All the following are either on Borgo Ognissanti or Via Maso Finiguerra. Avis ℡055.213.629; Europcar ℡055.290.437/8; Hertz ℡055.282.260; Italy by Car/Thrifty ℡055.287.161; Maggiore ℡055.210.238.

Consulates UK, Lungarno Corsini 2 ℡055.284.133; USA, Lungarno Vespucci 38 ℡055.239.8276.

Emergencies Police ℡112 or 113; Fire ℡115; car breakdown ℡116; First aid ℡118.

Gay and lesbian life Florence's past is scattered with some of history's greatest gay and bisexual artists (Michelangelo, Leonardo and Botticelli, among others). The leading gay venue these days is *Crisco Bar*, Via S. Egidio 43r (Mon & Wed–Sun 10/11pm until late; ℡055.248.0580, ⓦwww .crisco.it), though the ambience can be a bit heavy for some tastes. *Il Piccolo Caffè*, Borgo Santa Croce 23r (daily 5pm until late; ℡055.241.704), has a more chilled-out atmosphere, while *Y.A.G.B@r*, also near Santa Croce at Via de' Macci 8r (Mon–Sat 9pm–3am, Sun 5pm–3am; ℡055.246.9022, ⓦwww.yagbar.com), is stylish and draws a trendy, mixed crowd. The key bar-club is the pioneering *Tabasco*, which has been going for more than thirty years at Piazza Santa Cecilia 3r, just by Piazza della Signoria (daily 10pm until late, with music Thurs–Sun; ℡055.213.000, ⓦwww.tabascogay.it). For lesbian visitors to the city, the women's bookshop Libreria delle Donne, Via Fiesolana 2b, is the place to head for contacts and information.

Internet access Florence has dozens of cyber-cafés. Prices are a touch expensive, at around €5 per hour, though discounts can bring it down considerably. The two biggest companies, with branches all over the city, are TheNetGate (ⓦwww .thenetgate.it) and Internet Train (ⓦwww.internet train.it), both of which operate a rechargeable card-based system, which you can use in any branch. Internet Train will also copy digital photos onto CD.

Laundry Wash & Dry (Via Ghibellina 143r, Via Nazionale 129r, Via della Scala 52r, Via dei Serragli 87r, Via dei Servi 105r and Via Morgangi 21r) is open daily 8am–10pm.

Left luggage There's a staffed counter at the train station, near platform 16 (daily 6am–midnight).

Lost property The city office, Via Circondaria 19 (Mon–Wed, Fri & Sat 9am–noon; ℡055.367.943), receives property handed in to police or the railway police; take bus #23 to Viale Corsica. There's also a lost property office at Santa Maria Novella station, on platform 16 next to left luggage; open daily 4.15am–1.30am (℡055.235.2190).

Medical facilities The Tourist Medical Service (IAMAT) is a private service that has doctors on call 24 hours a day. Call ℡055.475.411 or visit their clinic at Via Lorenzo il Magnifico 59 (Mon–Fri 11am–noon & 5–6pm, Sat 11am–noon). Note that you need insurance cover to recoup the cost of a consultation, which will be at least €50.

Alternatively, Florence's central hospital is on Piazza Santa Maria Nuova.

Parking The only legal street parking is in a blue space (max 2hr, 8am–8pm) for which you should buy a *Gratta e Sosta* (Scratch and Park) card for €1, marking on the time and date that you parked your car. Alternatively you can buy a ticket from a machine. Firenze Parcheggi (☎055.272.011, ⓦ www.firenzeparcheggi.it) controls all city car parks, including the 24-hour guarded car park, Parterre, at Piazza della Libertà; with a chit from your hotel you pay €18 for 24 hours here. The most central parking is on Piazza Brunelleschi, northeast of the Duomo, and you can also park in the centre of the Piazza della Liberta (if you can find your way in); both €1 per hour. There's free parking south of the river at Piazzale Michelangelo – watch out for a long-running scam whereby bogus parking attendants direct you into a free space, thus implying there's a charge (there isn't). If you've been towed, phone ☎055.308.249 and be prepared for a cash fine of around €80.

Pharmacies Comunale della Stazione inside the train station (☎055.289.435) and All'Insegna del Moro, Piazza San Giovanni 20r (☎055.284.013), are both open 24hr. All pharmacies display a late-night roster in their window; otherwise ring ☎182 for information.

Police The Questura, where you should report a lost passport or a theft, is at Via Zara 2 (daily 8.30am–12.30pm; ☎055.49.771; dedicated foreigners' office ☎055.497.7235). The special Tourist Aid Police may be useful if you're having communication problems: Via Pietrapiana 50 (Mon–Fri 8.30am–7.30pm, Sat 8.30am–1.30pm; ☎055.203.911).

Post office Central post office is at Via Pellicceria 8 (Mon–Fri 8.15am–6pm, Sat 8.15am–noon; telegram office open 24hr; *poste restante* is through the door immediately on the left as you enter from the street). Other post offices are at Via Pietrapiana 53 and Via Cavour 71r (same hours).

Taxis Radio taxis are on ☎055.4798, 055.4242 and 055.4390. Main stands are the train station and Piazza della Repubblica.

Train information ☎89.20.21, ⓦ www.treniitalia .com.

Around Florence

The Greater Florence area has a number of towns and attractions to entice you on a day-trip from the city or even act as a base for exploring the region. City buses run northeast to the hill-village of **Fiesole** and to the nearest of the various **Medici villas** – originally country retreats, now all but consumed by the suburbs – while to the south towards Siena lie the hills and vineyards of **Chianti**, Italy's premier wine region. Around thirty minutes northwest of Florence on the train or bus route towards Lucca lie the neighbours of **Prato** and **Pistoia**, both of them full of art and historic architecture, whereas west towards Pisa, there are worthwhile diversions to **Vinci** – Leonardo's birthplace – and hilltop **San Miniato**.

Fiesole

A long-established Florentine retreat from the summer heat and crowds, **FIESOLE** spreads over a cluster of hilltops 8km northeast of the city. It predates Florence by several millennia: the Etruscans held out so long up here that the Romans were forced to set up permanent camp in the valley below – thus creating the beginnings of the settlement that was to become Florence. The **views** of Florence, which highlight just how extraordinary Brunelleschi's cathedral dome is, are unmissable, and the airiness of the place makes it great for kicking back.

The slightly unkempt-looking central square of Fiesole, **Piazza Mino**, is named after the fifteenth-century sculptor Mino da Fiesole, who has two fine pieces in the **Duomo** that dominates the north side of the square. Nineteenth-century restoration ruined the Duomo's exterior, and the interior is something like a stripped-down version of Florence's San Miniato, although there's relief

Florence has an alphabet soup of **bus companies** operating on different routes to destinations within Tuscany and in the neighbouring regions. All of them are headquartered at one or other of the bays around Santa Maria Novella train station. ATAF offers information on all local buses; for anything longer distance you'll have to enquire with the relevant company.

ATAF, Piazza Stazione ☏055.565.0222, ⑩www.ataf.net; **CAP**, Largo Alinari 9 ☏055.214.637, ⑩www.capautolinee.it; **CLAP**, c/o Lazzi, Piazza Stazione 1 ☏0583.587.897; **COPIT**, Largo Alinari 9 ☏0571.74.194; **Eurolines**, c/o Lazzi Express ☏055.215.155; **Lazzi**, Piazza Stazione ☏055.215.155, ⑩www.lazzi.it; **LFI**, c/o Lazzi, Piazza Stazione 1 ☏0575.39.881; **RAMA**, c/o Lazzi, Piazza Stazione 1 ☏0564.454.169; **SITA**, Via Santa Caterina da Siena 15 (local and regional ☏800.373.760, long-haul ☏055.214.721); **SULGA**, Piazza Adua ☏075.500.9641, ⑩www.sulga.it.

Arezzo SITA	Pistoia COPIT, Lazzi
Assisi SULGA	Poggibonsi† SITA
Bettoll* LFI	Poggio a Caiano CLAP
Empoli Lazzi	Prato **CAP** Lazzi
Fiesole ATAF	Sansepolcro SITA
Greve in Chianti SITA	Siena SITA
Grosseto RAMA	Viareggio Lazzi
Livorno Lazzi	Vinci COPIT
Lucca CLAP, Lazzi	Volterra SITA
Perugia Lazzi, SITA, SULGA	* change for Montepulciano
Pisa Lazzi	† change for San Gimignano

from the austerity in the Cappella Salutati, to the right of the choir: it contains Mino's panel *Madonna and Saints*. Behind the Duomo lie the **Museo Archeologico** (summer daily 9.30am–7pm; winter Mon & Wed–Sun 9.30am–5pm), containing pieces excavated from the Teatro Romano; and the **Museo Bandini** (hours as Museo Archeologico; €6.20, includes entrance to Fiesole's other museums), housing a local canon's collection of medieval Florentine and Tuscan art. Gates give onto the Area Archeologica behind (hours as Museo Archeologico), featuring a 2,000-seat **Teatro Romano** built in the first century BC, a baths complex and an **Etruscan temple** dedicated to Minerva.

Fiesole's two other major churches are reached by the very narrow Via San Francesco, which rises steeply from Piazza Mino, partway up broadening into a terrace giving a spectacular panorama of Florence. **Sant'Alessandro** (daily 10am–noon & 3–5pm; free) was founded in the sixth century on the site of Etruscan and Roman temples and has beautiful *marmorino cipollino* (onion marble) columns adorning its basilical interior. The Gothic church of **San Francesco** occupies the site of the acropolis; across one of the tiny cloisters there's a chaotic museum of pieces brought back from Egypt and China by missionaries. An alternative to retracing your steps to Piazza Mino is through the public park, entered by a gate facing San Francesco's facade. Another lovely walk heads southwest from Piazza Mino for 1.5km down the narrow, winding Via Vecchia Fiesolana (which branches off the main road) to the hamlet of **SAN DOMENICO**. Fra' Angelico was once prior of the Dominican **monastery** here and the church retains a 1420 *Madonna and Angels* by him (first chapel on the left), while the chapterhouse also has the Fra' Angelico fresco *The Crucifixion* (ring the bell at no. 4 for entry).

Practicalities

ATAF city **bus** #7 runs every fifteen minutes from Florence's train station through Piazza San Marco and on to Fiesole's Piazza Mino. The **tourist office** is just off the square, behind the cathedral on Via Portigiani 3 (daily 9am–6pm, Sun 10am–1pm; ☎055.598.720, ⓦwww.comune.fiesole.fi.it).

Best of Fiesole's few **hotels** is the stunning but hugely expensive *Villa San Michele*, a fifteenth-century former monastery at Via Doccia 4 (☎055.567.8200, ⓦwww.villasanmichele.orient-express.com; ❾), surrounded by gorgeous parkland and with a great restaurant, offering glorious views of the grand sweep of Florence. Similarly gorgeous views, at rather less outrageous prices, are provided by the delightful ⚜ *Pension Bencistà* (☎055.591.63, ⓦwww.bencista .com; ❸), another converted former monastery whose rambling network of rooms are littered with antiques. The cheapest option closest to the centre is the pleasant, unfussy *Villa Sorriso*, Via Gramsci 21 (☎055.59.027, ⓦwww .albergovillasorriso.com; ❷). The **campsite** *Panoramico*, 3km east at Via Peramonda 1 (☎055.599.069, ⓦwww.florencecamping.com), is Florence's best with a pool, great views over the city and bungalows for those who don't fancy sleeping in a tent. *San Domenico Pizzeria e Ristorante*, at Piazza San Domenico 11, is popular with students and academics, and also has good views down over Florence.

The Medici villas

The finest country houses of the Florentine hinterland are, predictably enough, those built for the **Medici**. The earliest of these grand villas were intended as fortified refuges to which the family could withdraw when the political temperature in the city became a little too hot, but as the Medici became established and the risk of challenge lessened, the villas became more ostentatious, signifying the might of the dynasty through their sheer luxuriousness. The **northern outskirts** of Florence hold a clutch of them, all boasting beautiful gardens, though reaching them these days is often through unattractive industrial sprawl.

The **Villa Medicea La Petraia** (☎055.451.208; Jan–Feb & Nov–Dec 8.15am–5pm; March & Oct 8.15am–6pm; April, May & Sept 8.15am–7pm; June–Aug 8.15am–8pm; closed first & third Mon of month; free, including gardens of Villa di Castello; bus #28 from train station to Castello) was adapted from a medieval castle in the 1570s and 1580s by Buontalenti. Vittorio Emanuele II glassed over the interior courtyard – its walls covered by a seventeenth-century fresco glorifying the Medici – to convert it into a ballroom. Giambologna's bronze statue of Venus, now transplanted to a small room indoors, used to adorn the marble fountain on the upper terrace of the magnificent **garden**. A little under 1km northwest down the hill from La Petraia stands the Baroque **Villa di Castello** (villa closed to public; gardens same hours and ticket as Villa della Petraia; free). This house was bought in 1477 by Lorenzo and Giovanni de' Medici, principal patrons of Botticelli – the *Birth of Venus* and *Primavera* both used to hang here. The fame of the villa rests on its spectacular **garden**: Montaigne was delighted by its labyrinths, fountains and myriad tricks, and judged it the best garden in Europe. The outstanding eccentricities are Ammannati's shivering figure *January*, the triple-bowled fountain topped by the same artist's *Hercules and Antaeus*, and the Grotto degli Animali, an artificial cave against whose walls stands a menagerie of sculpted creatures.

In the small town of **POGGIO A CAIANO**, 18km northwest of Florence and 7km south of Prato, is the romantic **Villa Medici di Poggio a Caiano** (☎055.877.012; daily: Jan–Feb & Nov–Dec 8.15am–5pm; March & Oct

8.15am–6pm; April, May & Sept 8.15am–7pm; June–Aug 8.15am–8pm; closed second & third Mon of month; free). A COPIT bus leaves from Piazza Santa Maria Novella every half-hour, and takes around 30min to get there; an alternative approach is the #M local CAP service from Prato.

Lorenzo il Magnifico bought a farmhouse on this site in 1480 and had it rebuilt as a grand rural palace by Giuliano da Sangallo. An impressive double-staircase sweeps up to the imposing entrance loggia, commissioned by Lorenzo's son Giovanni, the future Pope Leo X. Inside, the focal point is the double-height *salone*, which the architect made out of the original courtyard; its sixteenth-century frescoes include works by Pontormo and del Sarto. The **gardens**, modified by the Lorraine princes into an English-style landscape, contain some magnificent old trees. To cap the afternoon in style, take a local bus 5km west to the village of **CARMIGNANO** where, in the church of San Michele, hangs Pontormo's *Visitazione* (c.1530), one of the outstanding works of the Mannerist period: its combination of superbly realized colour in the women's drapes, profound emotion and the mesmeric quality of all four faces is electrifying.

The Chianti region

Ask a sample of northern Europeans to describe their idea of paradise, and the odds are it will sound much like **Chianti**, the territory of vineyards and hilltowns that stretches between Florence and Siena. The climate is drenched in luminescent sunlight during the long summer and rarely grim even in the pit of winter. And to cap it all, there's the **wine** – the one Italian vintage everyone's heard of (ⓦwww.chianticlassico.com). Visitors from Britain and other similarly ill-favoured climes were long ago alerted to Chianti's charms, and the rate of immigration has been so rapid since the 1960s that the region is now wryly dubbed **Chiantishire**. Yet it would be an exaggeration to say that Chianti is losing its character in the way that many of Italy's coastal towns have lost theirs. The tone of certain parts has been altered, but concessions to tourism have been more or less successfully absorbed into the rhythm of local life.

If you're relying on **buses**, the best targets are the two main towns, **Greve in Chianti** and **Radda in Chianti**. Three SITA **buses** a day run from Florence through Greve and Castellina to Radda. Five TRA-IN buses a day run from Radda through Castellina (but not Greve) to Siena. But the only realistic way to get to know the region is with **your own transport**, following the Strada "Chiantigiana", the SS222 that snakes its way between Florence and Siena through the most beautiful parts of Chianti. The Florence APT's excellent *Il Chianti cartoguida turistica* 1:70,000 contour map pinpoints every lane and farmhouse.

Greve in Chianti and around

The "Chiantigiana" road meanders south through picture-pretty wine-villages for 28km to the amiable market town of **GREVE IN CHIANTI**. The venue for Chianti's biggest **wine fair** (usually held during the second weekend in September), this is a town with wine for sale on every street: the best outlets are the Enoteca di Gallo Nero, Piazzetta Santa Croce 8, and the Cantinetta di Checucci Sandro, Via Vittorio Veneto. Its hub is the attractive central **Piazza Matteotti**, a long, sloping triangle that hosts the regular Saturday market, overlooked by a statue of local boy **Giovanni da Verrazzano**, who became, in 1524, the first European to see Manhattan Island.

Greve's vineyard-oriented **tourist office** in Via Luca Cini (Mon–Sat 10am–1pm & 2–5pm; ☏055.854.5243, ⓦwww.comune.greve-in-chianti.fi.it) can give information on accommodation in local farmhouses and trekking in Chianti. There are also a number of interesting **villas** a stone's throw from Greve, including **Verrazzano**, beyond Greti, 5km to the north, and **Vignamaggio**, just south of Greve, where Kenneth Branagh filmed *Much Ado about Nothing*.

Comfortable **accommodation** on Piazza Matteotti is offered by *Del Chianti* at no. 86 (℡055.853.763, ⓦwww.albergodelchianti.it; ❸) and *Da Verrazzano* at no. 28 (℡055.853.189, ⓦwww.verrazzano.it; ❸). The latter also has a very good **restaurant**, at around €35 for a full meal (closed Mon & mid-Jan to mid-Feb). There are several decent pizzeria-restaurants too: *Gallo Nero*, Via Cesare Battista 9; *La Cantina*, Piazza Trento; and *Torre delle Civette*, Via Veneto.

Other good accommodation alternatives in the area include the *Villa San Michele*, at Via Casole 42, in Lucolena (℡055.851.034, ⓦwww.villasanmichele .it; €12), 10km east of Greve, where a selection of apartments, private rooms and very comfortable dormitories are arranged in attractive grounds around a swimming pool. Just outside the village of Figline Valdarno, one of the region's best value (and oldest) **agritourismo** concerns, ⚒ *Locanda Casanuova* (℡055.950.0027, ⓦwww.casanuova-toscana.it; ❷), is run by a charming German couple. Set amid rolling vineyards, it offers a hotch-potch collection of different sized rooms in its converted farmhouse and hearty meals made with home-grown produce.

Radda in Chianti

A ridge 22km south of Greve is occupied by the well-heeled town of **Castellina in Chianti**; its walls, fortress and the covered perimeter walkway all bear testimony to an embattled past on the frontline between Florence and Siena, which lies a further 21km south. From Castellina, the SS429 branches east 22km to **RADDA IN CHIANTI**. The street plan of this minuscule but historic town is focused on **Piazza Ferrucci**, where the frescoed and shield-studded Palazzo Comunale faces a church raised on a high platform.

Close to the piazza, at Via Roma 41, there is the simple one-star *Girarrosto* **hotel and restaurant** (℡0577.738.010; restaurant closed Wed; ❶). Fairly pricey meals are served at the *Vignale*, Via XX Settembre 23 (℡0577.738.094; closed Thurs & mid-Jan to mid-March), but for consistently better food, and spectacular scenery, visit either *Le Vigne* (℡0577.738.640), just off the road between Villa a Radda and Radda in Chianti, where you'll pay around €30, or the restaurant of the three-star *Vescine* hotel (℡0577.741.144, ⓦwww.vescine.it; ❾), on the road to Castellina, where meals cost about €10 more.

If you have your own transport, Radda can make a good base for exploring the **Parco Sculture del Chianti** (℡0577.357.151, ⓦwww.chiantisculpturepark .it; €7), to the southwest in Pievasciata, 11km out of Siena. This is an outdoor exhibition of over twenty modern sculptures, rendered in a variety of different materials – including stone, metal and plastic – and styles, all drawn from the collection of the founder, Piero Giadrossi, and distributed throughout a picturesque oak woodland.

Prato

Taking its name from the meadow (*prato*) where a great market was held in antiquity, **PRATO** – capital of its own little province 15km northwest of Florence – has been Italy's chief textile city since the early Middle Ages. Even though recent recession has cut into export sales, it still produces three-quarters of all Italy's woollen cloth and its proximity to Florence (just half-an-hour away) makes it feasible as a cut-price alternative base.

The City

Prato's *centro storico* is enclosed within a rough hexagon of walls, making orientation straightforward. From the square in front of Stazione Centrale, cross the bridge to Piazza Europa and continue on Viale Vittorio Veneto to Piazza San Marco, which is framed by the city walls. Directly ahead, past the prominent **Henry Moore** sculpture *Square Form with Cut* (1974) in the centre of the piazza, rises the white-walled **Castello Imperatore** (Mon & Wed–Sun 9am–1pm and 4–7pm; €2.50, €6 *biglietto unico*, with Museo dell'Opera del Duomo & Museo di Pittura Murale), built in the thirteenth century for Emperor Frederick II. Concerts are held in the courtyard in summer, and the ramparts offer fine views. Just below the castle to the north is Prato's major Renaissance monument, Giuliano Sangallo's church of **Santa Maria delle Carceri** (daily 7am–noon & 4–7pm; free), which makes a decorative gesture towards the Romanesque with its bands of green and white marble. The interior is lightened by an Andrea della Robbia frieze.

Piazza Duomo, one block north of Piazza del Comune, forms an effective space for the Pisan-Romanesque facade of the **Duomo** (July–Sept daily 7.30am–12.30pm & 4–7pm, Sun 4–7pm; free), distinguished by an Andrea della Robbia terracotta over the portal and Donatello and Michelozzo's beautiful **Pulpit of the Sacred Girdle**. This unique addition was constructed for the ceremonial display of the girdle of the Madonna, a garment handed to the ever-incredulous apostle Thomas at her Assumption. The girdle (or *Sacro Cingolo*) was supposedly bequeathed by Thomas to a priest, one of whose descendants married a crusader from Prato, who in turn brought it back to his home town in the twelfth century. It's displayed five times a year: on Easter Sunday, May 1, August 15, September 8 and Christmas Day.

The sensuous frescoes behind the high altar were created between 1452 and 1466 by **Fra' Filippo Lippi**, and depict the martyrdoms of St John the Baptist and St Stephen. During the period of his work, Lippi – though nominally a monk – became infatuated with a young nun called Lucrezia, eventually having a child, Filippino, with her. Lucrezia is said to be the model for the dancing figure of Salome, while Filippo has painted himself as one of those mourning St Stephen; he's third from the right. For several years the Lippi cycle has been undergoing restoration, but at weekends it's possible to view the pictures at close range, from the restorers' scaffolding, if you book a ticket in advance at the tourist office (see below), either in person or by phone; the fee is €8 per person.

Housed alongside the Duomo, around the cloister of the bishop's palace, the **Museo dell'Opera del Duomo** (Mon & Wed–Sat 9.30am–12.30pm & 3–6.30pm, Sun 9.30am–12.30pm; €4 or €6, with Castello & Museo Pittura Murale) contains Donatello's panels of gambolling children taken from the duomo's pulpit (they've been replaced by replicas). The museum's other main treasure is Maso di Bartolomeo's tiny reliquary for the Sacred Girdle, while further important works by Filippo Lippi, including his *Madonna del Ceppo*, are housed in the **Museo di Pittura Murale** (Mon & Wed–Sat 10am–6pm, Sun 10am–1pm; €6, includes entrance to the Museo dell'Opera del Duomo & Castello), a five-minute walk west of the duomo.

Practicalities

All **trains** stop at Stazione Centrale; slow Florence–Pistoia trains also stop at the more convenient Stazione Porta al Serraglio, 150m north of Piazza Duomo. CAP and Lazzi **buses** from Florence stop at Piazza Duomo, while Lazzi buses from Pistoia, Lucca and local villages pass through both train station forecourts. The **tourist office** (Mon–Fri 9am–1.30pm & 2–6.30pm, Sat 9am–1.30pm

& 2–6pm; ℡0574.24.112, ⓦwww.comune.prato.it) is on Piazza delle Carceri, 500m west of Stazione Centrale in the centre of the old town.

At the budget end of the **accommodation** scale are the one-star *Roma*, outside the southern gate at Via Carradori 1 (℡0574.31.777; ❷), and two two-stars: *Il Giglio* at Piazza San Marco 14 (℡0574.37.049, Ⓕ0574.604.351; ❷) and *La Toscana* at Piazza Ciardi 3 (℡0574.28.096, Ⓕ0574.25.163; ⓦwww.hoteltoscana .prato.it; ❷). Prato's more expensive hotels tend to be featureless concrete blocks, catering for business visitors, though one exception is the three-star *Flora*, Via Cairoli 31 (℡0574.33521, ⓦwww.hotelflora.info; ❸), which occupies a handsome nineteenth-century building very close to the Piazza del Comune. Of the rest, the pick is the *Giardino*, Via Magnolfi 2–6 (℡0574.606.588, ⓦwww.giardinohotel .com; ❸), which has the advantage of being just twenty metres from the Duomo.

Prato has a strong team of decent **restaurants**. *Lo Scoglio*, Via Verdi 42 (℡0574.22.760; closed Mon), does good pizzas and inexpensive fish dishes, while the slightly pricier *Il Baghino*, Via dell'Accademia 9 (℡0574.27.920; closed Sun eve & Mon lunch), is a long-standing local favourite, serving Prato specialities, such as bread soup and rabbit, in a traditional atmosphere. *Enoteca Barni*, near Piazza San Marco at Via Ferrucci 22 (℡0574.607.845; closed all Sat & Sun lunch), is an excellent family-run restaurant/wine bar, where you'll spend in the region of €30–40 a head; a similar bill can be expected at the homely *Osteria 900*, at Via Banchelli 14 (℡0574.24.353; closed Mon lunch).

Pistoia

PISTOIA, 18km northwest of Prato and also capital of its own province, is one of the least visited cities in Tuscany – an unjustified ranking for this quiet, well-preserved medieval city just 35 minutes by train from Florence (and about the same by bus). Pistoia was known throughout medieval times for its feuding and was condemned by Dante, Machiavelli and others; Michelangelo referred to the Pistoiese as "the enemies of heaven". An important metalworking centre, it left a legacy to the world in the *pistole*, originally the name of a dagger but later the title given to the first local firearms.

Piazza Duomo and around

The superb medieval complex of **Piazza Duomo** is the heart of the town and scene of many events and celebrations throughout Pistoia's July festival (see p.543). If you've arrived from Pisa or Lucca, the style of the **Duomo** itself will be immediately familiar, with its tiered arcades and striped decoration of black and white marble. Set into this soberly refined front is a tunnel-vault portico of bright terracotta tiles by Andrea della Robbia, creator also of the *Madonna and Child* above the door. The **interior** (daily 8.30am–12.30pm & 3.30–7pm; free) has an outstanding array of sculptural pieces, one of which is part of the entrance wall – a font designed by Benedetto da Maiano, showing incidents from the life of John the Baptist. Off the right aisle is the Cappella di San Jacopo (€3.62), endowed with one of the richest pieces of silverwork to be seen in Italy, the **Altarpiece of St James**. Weighing almost a ton and populated with 628 figures, it was begun in 1287 and completed by Brunelleschi in 1456.

Adjoining the duomo is the Palazzo dei Vescovi housing the **Museo di San Zeno** (guided tours summer Tues, Thurs & Fri 10am, 11.30am & 3.30pm; winter second Sun of month 4.30pm; €3.62; book ahead at the tourist office, maximum 20 people). The chief exhibit is the huge golden **reliquary of St James** by Lorenzo Ghiberti (1407), and there's a modest archeological collection, with relics from the Roman settlement.

Opposite is the dapper Gothic **Baptistry**, the Battistero San Giovanni (Tues–Sun 10am–6pm; free); there's nothing under the vast conical brick ceiling but a font made by Lanfranco da Como in 1226, though the emptiness is sometimes filled by shows of contemporary art. On the opposite side of the piazza, the Palazzo Comunale contains the **Museo Civico** (Tues–Sat 10am–6pm, until 5pm in winter, Sun 9am–12.30pm; €3.50, €6.50 *biglietto cumulativo*, including the Diocesan, Marini & Rospigliosi museums), where the customary Tuscan welter of medieval and Renaissance pieces is bolstered by an impressive showing of Baroque hyperactivity. To the side of the Palazzo Comunale, the Palazzo Rospigliosi on Via Ripa del Sale houses the combined **Museo Diocesano** and **Museo Rospigliosi** (Tues–Sat 10am–1pm & 4–7pm; also the second Sun of the month, same hours; €3.50, €6.50 *biglietto cumulativo*, including Museo Civico & Marini museum), a typical small-town collection of historical and ecclesiastical oddments.

The rest of the town

Barely 100m south of the baptistry, Via Cavour is now the main street of the city's inner core, but was once the settlement's outer limit – as the name of the majestic **San Giovanni Fuorcivitas** ("outside the city") proclaims. The church was founded in the eighth century, but rebuilt between the twelfth and fourteenth centuries, when it received the dazzlingly striped green-and-white flank that serves as its facade. The interior (daily 7.30am–noon & 5–6.30pm; free), though lit only feebly by the slit windows, is just as remarkable for its pulpit, another of Pistoia's exquisite thirteenth-century trio, carved in 1270 by a pupil of Nicola Pisano.

Via Crispi leads due south to Piazza Garibaldi, where the **Cappella del Tau** (Mon–Sat 9am–1pm; free) preserves a chaos of fourteenth- and fifteenth-century frescoes. A couple of doors away, in the Palazzo del Tau, is the **Museo Marino Marini** (Mon–Sat 10am–6pm; €3.50, €6.50 *biglietto cumulativo*, including Museo Civico & Diocesan and Rospigliosi museums), showing a selection of etchings, engravings, sculptures, drawings and watercolours by this important modern artist and Pistoia local.

Practicalities

Trains and **buses** from Florence drop you just a couple of minutes' walk south of the historic centre – Viale XX Settembre points the way north to Piazza Treviso and the gate into the old town. The **tourist office** is at Piazza del Duomo 4 (Tues–Sun 9am–1pm & 3–6pm; ☎0573.21.622, ⓦ www.comune.pistoia.it).

The city's low tourist profile means there is a dearth of **accommodation** so if you plan to stay, phone ahead. There's just one one-star hotel, the clean and friendly *Albergo Autisti*, Viale Pacinotti 89 (☎0573.21.771; ❶), and only one two-star within the city walls, the *Albergo Firenze*, a short walk west of Piazza del Duomo at Via Curtatone e Montanara 42 (☎ & ⓕ0573.231.141; ❸). Central alternatives are the three-star *Leon Bianco*, Via Panciatichi 2 (☎0573.26.675, ⓦ www.hotelleonbianco.it; ❹), or the *Patria*, Via Crispi 6 (☎0573.25.187, ⓕ0573.368.168; ❹) – both are within a minute of San Giovanni Fuorcivitas.

There are two excellent **osterie** in Via del Lastrone, off Piazza della Sala: *La Bottegaia*, at no. 4 (closed Sun lunch & all Mon), which has a terrific range of *crostini* and bruschetta in addition to its more substantial offerings; and *Lo Storno*, at no. 8, where the food is somewhat more robust (tripe and *baccalà*, for example), and the emphasis is on lunch (open for lunch daily, but only Wed & Sat eve). There's also a straightforward, inexpensive and good-quality Tuscan menu at *S. Jacopo*, Via Crispi 15 (closed all Mon & Tues lunch).

Key festival is the **Luglio Pistoiese**, a programme of concerts and events throughout July that includes open-air performances in Piazza Duomo by world-class jazz and blues acts. The *Giostra dell'Orso* medieval pageant and joust is on July 25.

West to Pisa

Two main roads and rail lines head west from Florence. The A11 autostrada shadows the train track northwest through Prato and Pistoia to Lucca. An alternative is the SS67 road, which heads due west from Florence down the valley of the Arno to Pisa, a pleasant enough journey of an hour or so, passing through the industrial town of **Empoli** that marks the turn-off into the hills north to **Vinci**. A little west of Empoli, past the turning south to Siena and across the border in the Provincia di Pisa, is the medieval village of **San Miniato**, perched high on its rock above the pretty Valdarno.

Vinci

Occupying the picturesque vine- and olive-planted southern slopes of Montalbano 11km north of the industrial town of Empoli, **VINCI** is inextricably associated with **Leonardo da Vinci**, who was born on April 15, 1452, in nearby Anchiano and baptized in Vinci's church of Santa Croce. Vinci itself is a torpid little village that suffers from a surfeit of tour groups (especially at weekends). The main sight is the thirteenth-century castle, now home to the **Museo Leonardiano** (Jan–Feb & Nov–Dec 9.30am–6pm, March–Oct 9.30am–7pm; ⓦ www.museoleonardo.it; €5), packed with models reconstructed from Leonardo's notebook drawings – his celebrated bicycle, helicopter and multi-barrelled machine gun are all on display.

San Miniato

The strategic hilltop village of **SAN MINIATO**, midway between Pisa and Florence, was given its landmark fortress by the Holy Roman Emperor Frederick II in 1236. Today it's an attractive mid-journey stop, split between a modern valley settlement with train and bus stations and the original medieval village on its hill with a warren of attractive cobbled alleys. Dominating the old quarter's central **Piazza del Popolo** is the fourteenth-century church of **San Domenico**; its windows, glazed with odd greenish-yellow glass, do nothing to aid appreciation of its frescoes and trompe-l'oeil decoration. There's a market in its cloisters every Sunday. A narrow street climbs to **Piazza della Repubblica**, which is jazzed up by seventeenth-century *sgraffiti* on the long facade of the religious seminary; part of the ground floor is a row of rare, restored fourteenth-century shops. Opposite the seminary a flight of steps rises to the **Prato del Duomo**, where a tower of the imperial fortress now houses the three-star *Miravalle* hotel (Piazza del Castello 3, ☎0571.418.075, ⓦ www.albergomiravalle.com; ❸) with its restaurant next door on the site of the **Palazzo dei Vicari dell'Imperatore**. The red-brick **Duomo** itself, dedicated to St Genesius, the patron saint of actors, is hacked-about Romanesque, with an interior of Baroque gilding and marbling. Next door, the tiny **Museo Diocesano** (April–Nov Tues–Sun 10am–1pm & 3–7pm; Dec–March Sat & Sun same hours; €5 combination ticket for eight museums, valid for one year, ⓦ www.sanminiatomuseums.notlong.com for details) has a *Crucifixion* by Fra' Filippo Lippi and a terracotta bust of Christ by Verrocchio. From the Prato del Duomo it's a short walk up to the tower of the **Rocca** (Tues–Sun 10am–7pm), which was restored after damage in World War II; the spectacular view from the top is worth the climb. Dante's *Inferno* perpetuates the memory of Pier della Vigna, treasurer to Frederick II, who was imprisoned and blinded here, a fate that drove him to suicide by jumping from the tower – as the inscription on a graffitied stone at the base of the tower records.

The **train station**, down in the Arno valley, is a ten-minute walk from the modern part of town, **San Miniato Basso**, from where it's a steep 4km climb to **San Miniato Alto**, the old quarter. An orange **bus** runs to the latter from the train station every thirty minutes or so (daily 6.30–10.30am & 3.45–7.30pm; €1.50). It deposits you just below the walls in **Piazzale Dante Alighieri**, which is also the place to park. Beyond the town gate, down the road on the right, is Piazza del Popolo and the **tourist office** (summer daily 9am–1pm & 4–7.30pm; winter Mon–Sat 10am–1pm & 3–6.30pm; ☎0571.42.745, ⓦwww .comune.san-miniato.pi.it).

Pisa, Lucca and the coast

Thanks to its Leaning Tower, **Pisa** is known by name to just about every visitor to Italy, though it remains an underrated place, seen by most people on a whistle-stop day-trip that takes in little of its majestic architecture, less of its atmospheric medieval quarters, and none of its street life. Genteel **Lucca** nearby, its walled old town crammed with Romanesque churches, is even less explored.

Tuscany's **coast** is a mixed bag, generally too over-developed to be consistently attractive. North of Pisa, the succession of beach resorts enjoys the backdrop of the mighty Alpi Apuane, which harbour the marble quarries of Carrara. South from Pisa, past the untouristed port of **Livorno**, are a hundred scrubby strips of hotels and campsites. The Tuscan shoreline is at its best in the **Maremma** region, where you'll find the protected **Monti dell'Uccellina** reserve and the wild, wooded peninsula of **Monte Argentario**. Tuscany's **islands** also offer a breath of fresh air, from the scenic walks on **Elba** to the remoteness of little **Capraia**.

Pisa

Since the beginning of tourism, **PISA** has been known for just one thing – the **Leaning Tower**, which serves around the world as a shorthand image for Italy. It is indeed a freakishly beautiful building, a sight whose impact no amount of prior knowledge can blunt. Yet it is just a single component of Pisa's breathtaking **Campo dei Miracoli**, or Field of Miracles, where the **Duomo**, **Baptistry** and **Camposanto** complete a dazzling architectural ensemble. These, and a dozen or so churches and *palazzi* scattered about the historic centre, belong to Pisa's Golden Age, from the eleventh to the thirteenth centuries, when the city was one of the maritime powers of the Mediterranean. The so-called Pisan-Romanesque **architecture** of this period, with its black and white marble facades inspired by the Moorish designs of Andalucia, is complemented by some of the finest medieval **sculpture** in Italy, much of it from the workshops of Nicola and Giovanni Pisano. The city's political zenith came late in the eleventh century with a series of victories over the **Saracens**: the Pisans brought back from Arab cultures long-forgotten ideas of science, architecture and philosophy. Decline set in with defeat by the Genoese in 1284, followed by the silting-up of Pisa's harbour. From 1406 the city was governed by Florence, whose Medici rulers re-established the University of Pisa, one of the great intellectual establishments of the Renaissance; **Galileo** was teacher here. Subsequent centuries saw Pisa fade into provinciality, though landmarks from its glory days bring in hundreds of thousands of visitors a year, and the combination of tourism and a large student population give the contemporary city a lively feel.

Arrival, information and orientation

Pisa Centrale **train station** (information ☎1478.88.088) is about 1km south of the Arno. Lazzi **buses** from Florence, Prato, Pistoia and Carrara arrive at the

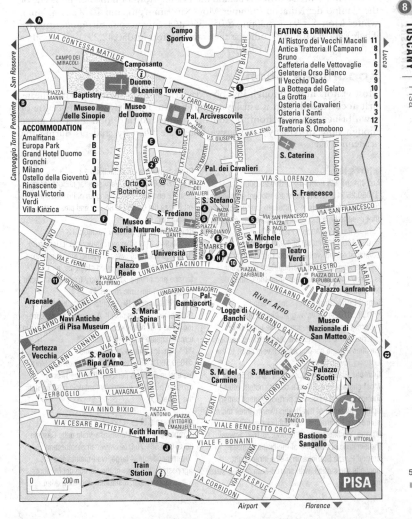

EATING & DRINKING
Al Ristoro dei Vecchi Macelli 11
Antica Trattoria Il Campano 8
Bruno 1
Caffeteria delle Vettovaglie 6
Gelateria Orso Bianco 2
Il Vecchio Dado 9
La Bottega del Gelato 10
La Grotta 5
Osteria dei Cavalieri 4
Osteria I Santi 3
Taverna Kostas 12
Trattoria S. Omobono 7

ACCOMMODATION
Amalfitana F
Europa Park B
Grand Hotel Duomo E
Gronchi D
Milano J
Ostello della Gioventù A
Rinascente G
Royal Victoria H
Verdi I
Villa Kinzica C

Airport ▼   Florence ▼

nearby Piazza Vittorio Emanuele II, while other buses from Volterra, Lucca and Livorno arrive at Piazza San Antonio alongside it. From here, the Leaning Tower is about 25 minutes' walk north, or a ride on CPT city bus #1 from outside the station. Alternatively, you could hop on a **local train** for the five-minute journey to the more convenient Pisa San Rossore station, 200m west of Piazza Manin (also served by local trains from Lucca and some from Viareggio).

Pisa's **Aeroporto Galileo Galilei** (information ⓣ050.500.707, ⓦwww .pisa-airport.com) is 2km south of Centrale station. Hourly trains run from Pisa Aeroporto station to Pisa Centrale in just five minutes (€1.10), and then on to Florence (see p.495). CPT city bus #3 departs from the airport every fifteen minutes (€0.85), and passes the train station, runs along the south bank of the Arno, over Ponte Solferino, to Piazza Manin. A taxi to the centre costs around €6.

Pisa's APT **tourist office** is behind the Leaning Tower on the northern side of the Campo dei Miracoli (summer Mon–Sat 9am–7pm, Sun 10.30am–4.30pm; winter Mon–Sat 9am–5.30pm; ⓣ050.560.464, ⓦwww.pisa.turismo.toscana.it). There's also a small APT office at the **train station** (ⓣ050.42.291), and another at the **airport** (ⓣ050.503.700).

Accommodation

Most visitors hurry through Pisa on a day-trip – this is their loss, but it means that **accommodation** is usually not too hard to find. Staying in the centre of town brings you away from the touristy haunts and into local life a bit more, though note that many inexpensive hotels are filled by students during the academic year.

Hotels

Amalfitana Via Roma 44 ⓣ050.29.000, ⓕ050.25.218. Rooms here are modern and a little bland but the setting, in a fifteenth-century building that used to be a monastery, is a fine one. ❷

Europa Park Via Andrea Pisano 23 ⓣ050.500.732, ⓕ050.554.930. Smallish, comfortable and well-run modern three-star hotel, with parking. It's on a characterless street, but is barely two minutes' stroll from the Campo dei Miracoli. ❸

Grand Hotel Duomo Via Santa Maria 94 ⓣ050.561.894, ⓦwww.grandhotelduomo.it. A decent, modern four-star whose ugly 1970s exterior belies an elegant if slightly dated interior. Facilties include parking and it's very close to the Leaning Tower. ❻

Gronchi Piazza Arcivescovado 1 ⓣ050.561.823. Most characterful of Pisa's budget hotels, offering exceptional value in a perfect position within spitting distance of the Tower. Twenty-three rooms share four bathrooms. Midnight curfew. ❶

Milano Via Mascagni 14 ⓣ050.23.162, ⓦwww .hotelmilano.pisa.it. One of the better choices around Piazza Stazione, in a side street right opposite the station, with shared-bath and en-suite rooms. ❷

Rinascente Via del Castelletto 28 ⓣ & ⓕ050.580.460. Very popular budget rooms – some en suite – occupying an old *palazzo* just off Piazza dei Cavalieri. Roomy and pleasantly dilapidated. ❷

Royal Victoria Lungarno Pacinotti 12 ⓣ050.940.111, ⓦwww.royalvictoria.it. Tastefully furnished spacious *palazzo* overlooking the Arno, with character, old-fashioned elegance, a roof terrace and private parking. Very friendly and some bargain non-en-suite rooms. ❸

Verdi Piazza della Repubblica 5/6 ⓣ050.598.947, ⓔhotelverdi@sirius.pisa.it. A competent, welcoming three-star hotel occupying a restored *palazzo* in a quiet square near San Matteo. ❸

Villa Kinzica Piazza Arcivescovado 2 ⓣ050.560.419, ⓦwww.hotelvillakinzica.it. More expensive and less personal than the nearby *Gronchi*, but with an equally fantastic position near the Tower. ❹

Campsite and hostel

Campeggio Torre Pendente Viale delle Cascine 86 ⓣ050.561.704, ⓦwww.campingtoscana .it/torrependente. A large, well-maintained site, signposted 1km west of the Campo dei Miracoli, with a laundry, bar, restaurant and shop. Mini apartments also available. From €6.50 per person. Open April to mid-Oct.

Ostello della Gioventù Via Pietrasantina 15 ⓣ & ⓕ 050.890.622. Despite the misleading signs, this non-HI hostel is a 45-minute hike from Campo dei Miracoli; take bus #3 from the station or Piazza Manin, which stops outside. There's a supermarket and pizzeria nearby. Make sure you have mosquito repellent in summer, as it's right by a marsh.

The City

Laid out in the mid-eleventh century, Pisa's ecclesiastical centre is known as the **Campo dei Miracoli** (Field of Miracles; also Piazza dei Miracoli or Piazza Duomo; ⓦ www.opapisa.it). The four major buildings – the **Duomo**, its bell-tower (which almost immediately slipped to become the **Leaning Tower**), the **Baptistry** and the monumental cemetery of the **Camposanto** – were built on a broad swath of grassy lawn just within the northern walls of the city. Unfortunately, the turf rests on highly unstable sandy soil, which accounts for the tower's lean; take a look at the baptistry and you'll see that it leans the other way from the tower.

These days visiting the campo is rarely a gentle, reflective experience. As fine a sight as the buildings make, with their gleaming marble neatly contrasting with the surrounding greenery, they are too often engulfed in a tourist maelstrom – tour groups marching up and down the nave of the Duomo, lines of photographers in front of the tower getting that all important pushing over/holding up snap, and surrounding it all a mass of stallholders.

Thankfully, the rest of the city centre makes for some fine and much less hectic wandering, through alleys that have largely retained their medieval appearance. Southeast, on the river, is the **Museo Nazionale di San Matteo**, a fine collection of ecclesiastical art and sculpture, while west along the Arno is the lavish **Palazzo Reale** and the huge **Arsenale**, the latter currently housing a display of items taken from ongoing excavations at the site of Pisa's ancient harbour. One of Pisa's biggest surprises lurks in a barely noticed piazza near the train station where, covering one wall of the bus station, is the last-ever mural by US artist **Keith Haring** (see p.551).

The Leaning Tower of Pisa

The view from the Porta Nuova gate over the serene architectural ensemble laid out on the Campo dei Miracoli would be memorable enough, even without the desperately comic sight of the **Leaning Tower** (April–Sept 8.30am–8.30pm; March 9am–6pm; Oct 9am–7pm; Nov–Feb 9.30am–5pm; guided tours only; €15) sticking out jauntily from behind the Duomo, wearing its rakishly angled bell-chamber like a pork-pie hat. It is a lunatic vision, slouched over far enough to topple any second – or so it seems.

Two of the most telling facts about the tower (*Torre Pendente* in Italian) are that it has always tilted, and that no one ever put their name to the project, as though

Campo dei Miracoli's ticketing system

The five museums and monuments in and around Campo dei Miracoli – the Duomo, Baptistry, Museo dell'Opera, Camposanto and Museo delle Sinopie – share a complicated system of **ticketing**. Admission to the Duomo costs €2. Admission to any one other sight costs €5. Admission to any two sights, including the Duomo, costs €6. Admission to any three sights, including the Duomo, costs €8. Admission to all five costs €10.50. You can get tickets from the **ticket office** next to the tourist office in the Campo dei Miracoli.

the masons involved somehow knew it was doomed. Twelve years after work began on the tower in 1173, it started to subside, but in the opposite direction from the current lean. Masons inserted wedge-shaped stones to correct the problem, whereupon the whole tower tilted crazily the other way. Work was halted when it was only three storeys high. A century or so later, after much calculation, architects added three more uneven storeys, tilted to counterbalance the lean, and then in 1350 Tommaso Pisano completed the stack with a lopsided bell-chamber. A couple of centuries later, **Galileo** exploited the overhang in one of his celebrated experiments, dropping items of different mass off the top to demonstrate the constancy of gravity.

An ill-advised attempt to correct the southerly lean in the mid-nineteenth century involved digging a trench all the way round the base of the tower; this made things considerably worse and, along with the lowering of the water table, brought the structure to the edge of crisis. By 1990, the top leant more than

△ The Leaning Tower of Pisa

five metres from vertical and the tower was finally declared off-limits to visitors. Scientists and engineers joined forces to save the world-famous monument, the main operation using **drills** to remove silt and sand from beneath the foundations on the north side, in effect causing the ground to subside the other way. The tower slowly began to correct its lean and settle and eleven years and $30 million dollars later the tower was officially reopened to the public in November 2001, its overhang now reduced by 50cm – back to how it was in 1838.

Tours to the top of the tower take place every forty minutes with a maximum of thirty people per group; no under-8s are allowed. You can save yourself a long wait by booking tickets in advance on Ⓦ www.opapisa.it (€2 booking fee). Otherwise book at the office in the northeast corner of the Campo as early as possible. No bags are allowed in the tower – there are left luggage lockers at the booking office. The narrow climb up 294 worn steps at a five degree angle can be fairly disorienting, and sadly you can no longer step out onto the surrounding balconies, but you do get good views of Pisa's spires and rooftops, with the Monte Pisano hills in the background.

The Duomo

Pisa's breathtaking **Duomo** (daily: April–Sept 10am–8pm; March 10am–6pm; Oct 10am–7pm; Nov–Feb 10am–1pm and 3–5pm; €2; see box, p.547 for details of combined tickets) was begun in 1064 and completed around a century later. With its four levels of variegated colonnades and its subtle interplay of dark-grey marble and white stone, the building is the archetype of Pisan-Romanesque, a model often imitated in buildings across Tuscany, but never surpassed. Squares and discs of coloured marble are set into the magnificent facade, but the soberly graceful effect of the primary grey and white is such that you notice these strong tones only when you look closely.

Entry is through the bronze door on the right-hand side of the facade (note, that "The Entrance for the Masses" is for services not the general populace). The vast interior is defined by the crisp black-and-white marble of the long arcades, which recalls the Moorish architecture of Cordoba. A notable survivor from the medieval period is the apse mosaic *Christ in Majesty*, completed by Cimabue in 1302. The acknowledged highlight, however, is the **pulpit** sculpted by **Giovanni Pisano**. This was packed away after a 1595 fire and only rediscovered in 1926. The last of the great series of three pulpits created in Tuscany by Giovanni and his father Nicola (the others are in Siena and Pistoia), it is a work of amazing virtuosity with, for instance, the story of the Passion condensed into a single panel.

The rest of the Campo dei Miracoli

Leaving the duomo at the main western facade, directly ahead is the circular **Baptistry** (daily: April–Sept 8am–8pm; March 9am–6pm; Oct 9am–7pm; Nov–Feb 10am–7pm; €5), a bizarre but pleasing building with its three storeys of Romanesque arcades peaking in a crest of Gothic pinnacles and a dome shaped like the end of a lemon. This is the largest baptistry in Italy, begun in 1152 by a certain Deotisalvi ("Godsaveyou"), who left his name on a column to the left of the door; it was worked on in the thirteenth century by Nicola and Giovanni Pisano, and completed late in the fourteenth century. Inside you're immediately struck by the plainness of the vast interior, with its unadorned arcades and bare dome, and by its astonishing acoustics. Overlooking the massive raised font is Nicola Pisano's **pulpit**, sculpted in 1260, half a century before his son's work in the cathedral. There are **stairs** to the upper gallery, and more stairs from there up inside the dome.

The screen of sepulchral white marble running along the north edge of the Campo dei Miracoli is the perimeter wall of what has been called the most beautiful cemetery in the world – the **Camposanto** (same hours as baptistry; €5). According to legend, the Archbishop Ubaldo Lanfranchi had Pisan knights on the Fourth Crusade of 1203 bring a cargo of soil back to Pisa from the hill of Golgotha, in order that eminent Pisans might be buried in holy earth. The building enclosing this sanctified site was completed almost a century later and takes the form of an enormous Gothic cloister. However, when Ruskin described the Camposanto as one of the most precious buildings in Italy, it was the **frescoes** that he was praising. Paintings once covered over two thousand metres of cloister wall, but now the brickwork is mostly bare: **incendiary bombs** dropped by Allied planes on July 27, 1944, set the roofing on fire and drenched the frescoes in molten lead. The most important survivor is the remarkable *Triumph of Death* cycle, a ruthless catalogue of morbid horrors painted within months of the arrival of the Black Death in 1348.

Near the Leaning Tower is the absorbing **Museo dell'Opera del Duomo** (daily: same hours as Baptistry; €5). Room 7 contains Giovanni Pisano's affecting *Madonna del Colloquio* (*Madonna of the Conversation*), so called because of the intensity of the gazes exchanged by the Madonna and Child suggest communication. In room 11 is the *Pisan Cross*, which incited the Pisan contingent on the First Crusade to invade Jerusalem. Upstairs, room 15 has beautiful examples of intarsia, the art of inlaid wood, much practised in Pisa in the fifteenth and sixteenth centuries.

On the south side of the Campo, the only gap in the souvenir stalls is for the **Museo delle Sinopie** (same hours as Baptistry; €5). After the damage wreaked on the Camposanto, restorers removed its *sinopie* (a monochrome sketch over which a fresco is painted) and these great plates of plaster now hang from the walls of this high-tech museum.

Piazza dei Cavalieri and the eastern quarters

Away from the Campo dei Miracoli, Pisa takes on a very different character. Few tourists penetrate far into its squares and arcaded streets, with their Romanesque churches and – especially along the Arno's banks – ranks of fine palazzi. With the large student population it can be a lively place, particularly during the summer festivals and the monthly market, when the main streets on either side of the river become one continuous bazaar.

Piazza dei Cavalieri opens unexpectedly from the narrow backstreets, the central civic square of medieval Pisa. The curving **Palazzo dei Cavalieri**, covered in sgraffiti and topped with busts of the Medici, adjoins the church of **Santo Stefano**, which still houses banners captured from Turkish ships by the Knights of St Stephen – a grand title for a gang of state-sponsored pirates. On the other side of the square is the Renaissance-adapted **Palazzo dell'Orologio**, in whose tower the military leader Ugolino della Gherardesca was starved to death with his sons and grandsons in 1208, as punishment for his alleged duplicity with the Genoese enemy – as described in Dante's *Inferno* and Shelley's *Tower of Famine*. Via Dini heads east to the arcaded **Borgo Stretto**, Pisa's smartest street, its windows glittering with consumer desirables that seem out of kilter with the city's unshowy style. Much more typically Pisan is the lively but down to earth market in **Piazza Vettovaglie** and the atmospheric, narrow streets that surround it (Mon–Fri am & all day Sat). The Borgo meets the river at the traffic-knotted **Piazza Garibaldi**, at the foot of the Ponte di Mezzo.

At the eastern end of the riverfront road Lungarno Mediceo is the **Museo Nazionale di San Matteo** (Tues–Sat 8.30am–7pm, Sun 8.30am–1pm; €4, joint ticket with Palazzo Reale €6.50). Most of the major works of art from Pisa's churches are now gathered here, including a *St Paul* by a young Masaccio, an oddly festive *Crucifixion* by Gozzoli, and another *Crucifixion* by Turino Vanni that clearly shows the Leaning Tower. The sculpture collection is led by two outstanding works – Donatello's gilded bronze bust, the introspective *San Lussorio*, and Andrea and Nino Pisano's *Madonna del Latte*, a touchingly crafted work showing Mary breastfeeding the baby Jesus.

The western quarters

A main route south from the Campo dei Miracoli is **Via Santa Maria**, which starts out clogged with touristy shops. Where Via dei Mille heads east for Piazza dei Cavalieri, the smaller Via Ghini cuts west to the gate of the **Orto Botanico**, the oldest university botanical gardens in the world, founded in 1543 (Mon–Sat 8am–1pm; free). Via Santa Maria continues south in a much more subdued vein, crooking its way down to meet the river alongside the second of Pisa's leaning towers, the campanile of **San Nicola**, which starts off cylindrical, then becomes octagonal, and finally hexagonal on top.

Alongside San Nicola, fronting onto the Arno, is the **Museo Nazionale di Palazzo Reale**, Lungarno Pacinotti 46 (Mon–Fri 9am–2pm; €6, joint ticket with San Matteo €12), displaying painting, sculpture and furniture belonging to the Medici, Lorraine and Savoy dynasties which occupied the house. Lavish sixteenth-century Flemish tapestries share space with antique weaponry, ivory miniatures and porcelain. A largely undistinguished collection of paintings is led by **Bronzino**'s famous portrait of Cosimo I's wife, Eleanor of Toledo. Just as memorable, however, is the lovely river **view** from the balcony.

West along the Arno is the vast **Arsenale**, built in the late sixteenth century to house the ships of the Order of St Stephen. In a twist of fate, it is again housing a naval fleet, though one from much earlier. In December 1998, during excavations to expand Pisa San Rossore train station, archeologists stumbled on the extensive, well-preserved remains of port facilities and ships dating from Etruscan and Roman times. Sixteen ships were uncovered, dating from between the first century BC and the sixth century AD – one of which may turn out to be the only complete Roman warship yet discovered – along with a vast hoard of artefacts. The maritime museum, known as **Le Navi Antiche di Pisa**, occupies one wing of the arsenal, but is closed indefinitely while being refurbished.

Just west of the arsenal rises the **Torre Guelfa** of the Fortezza Vecchia or Cittadella Vecchia (June–Aug Tues–Fri 2–6pm, Sat & Sun 11am–1.30pm & 3.30–7pm; April, May & Sept Tues–Fri 2–5pm, Sat & Sun 2–7pm; Oct–March Sat & Sun 2–5pm; €2, joint ticket with Santa Maria della Spina €2.50). This ancient fortress, originally built in the thirteenth century, once stood guard over Pisa's harbour but now punctuates an otherwise little-explored district. Pisa is a low-rise city, and the **view** from the tower is spectacular.

South of the river

The middle of the **Ponte di Mezzo**, the city's central bridge, is a perfect spot from which to admire the sweep of Pisa's *palazzo*-lined waterfront and the **Logge di Banchi** on the south side of the bridge. Formerly the city's silk and wool market, this is now the scene for student gatherings and assignations after dark; it stands at the head of the main **Corso Italia**, a street that gets progressively shabbier as it nears the train station. On the church of San Antonio, just off Piazza Vittorio Emanuele II, is the last work of US artist **Keith Haring**. Haring completed the vibrant, imaginative mural in a week in June 1989 while seriously ill; he died eight months later. His bendy, cartoonish figures radiate colour above what is now the bus station, tragically unregarded, and indeed quite often obscured by parked buses.

A five-minute walk west of the Ponte di Mezzo is the turreted oratory of **Santa Maria della Spina**. The little church dates from 1230, but was rebuilt in 1323 in the finest flourish of Pisan Gothic by a merchant who had acquired a thorn (*spina*) of Christ's crown. The tiny single-naved **interior** (same hours as Torre Guelfa; €1.50, joint ticket with Torre Guelfa €2.50) has mullioned windows on the riverside, but has lost most of its furnishings.

Eating and drinking

Restaurants in the environs of the Leaning Tower are not good value (although the many **bars** and **cafés** benefit from the views). A few blocks south, around Piazza Cavalieri and Piazza Dante, you'll find predominantly local places, many with prices reflecting student finances. There are many excellent small restaurants and bars in the narrow streets of the market area around Piazza delle Vettovaglie too. Although most kitchens serve up standard Tuscan fare, you'll also find Pisan dishes including *baccalà alla Pisana* (dried cod) and plenty of seafood.

Al Ristoro dei Vecchi Macelli Via Volturno 49 ☎050.20.424. Acclaimed as Pisa's best restaurant, with a wide range of sophisticated, innovative takes on Tuscany's gourmet traditions – choose from meat or fish set menus for upwards of €40. Closed Sun lunch & Wed.

Antica Trattoria Il Campano Via Cavalca 19 ☎050.580.585. Excellent traditional Tuscan cuisine in a smart local restaurant with copious quantities of wine on its shelves. Closed Wed & Thurs lunch.

Bruno Via Luigi Bianchi 12 ☎050.560.818. Outside the historic centre, northeast of the Leaning Tower, this traditional trattoria is known for its top-notch, if pricey, Pisan cuisine. Closed Mon eve & Tues.

Caffeteria delle Vettovaglie Piazza delle Vettovaglie 33. A touch rough and ready in the day, an inevitable consequence of its proximity to market, come *aperitivo* hour this is the place to be – trendy young Pisani sit out on the square with glasses of wine and plastic plates piled high with bruschetta and antipasti. Closed Sun.

Gelateria Orso Bianco Via S Maria 54. On the corner of Piazza Felice Cavallotti, this offers a good selection of home-made ice cream – try the chocolate and walnut.

Il Vecchio Dado Lungarno Pacinotti 21. Quality pizzeria on the waterfront with a friendly welcome, a good selection of fish and seafood dishes (such as their excellent *fritto di gamberi e totonai* €11) and lively atmosphere. Closed Wed & Thurs lunch.

La Bottega del Gelato Piazza Garibaldi 11–12. In a fantastic position, a stone's throw from the Ponte di Mezzo, this popular *gelateria* has a great selection of ice creams.

La Grotta Via San Francesco 103 ☎050.578.105. Comfortable and welcoming old *osteria* with a cave-like ceiling and the motto "wine, bread and company". Locals crowd the benches to sample unfussy Tuscan nosh, such as *tagliatelle sulla lepre* €8; try the house *antipasti* (€9) for a selection. Closed for lunch & all day Sun.

🎿 **Osteria dei Cavalieri** Via San Frediano 16 ☎050.580.858. Outstanding quality, with English-speaking staff and a tranquil atmosphere. The fish is exquisite, Tuscan meat and game dishes are expertly prepared (try the Tuscan steak, roast "*scamorza*" cheese and grilled vegetables for €12), and their vegetarian options are excellent. Eat à la carte or choose the €26, €30 or €32 set menu. Closed Sat lunch & Sun.

Osteria I Santi Via S Maria 71/73 ☎050.28.081. Less than five minutes' walk from the Campo, *I Santi* caters mainly to Italians in the evening, but also offers a tourist menu for €9.50 at lunch. The unusually good house wine is the restaurant's own production.

Taverna Kostas Via del Borghetto 39, left off Lungarno Buozzi between Ponte Fortezza and Ponte delle Vittoria. Longstanding local favourite, offering a mix of Greek and Mediterranean cooking, as well as Pisan seafood. Closed Sun lunch & Mon.

Trattoria S. Omobono Piazza S Omobono 6. Tucked in the corner of a market, this is a simple, no-nonsense sort of a place serving local specialities – such as *trippa alla Pisana* €8 – to hungry traders. Closed Sun.

Entertainment

Pisa's big traditional event is the **Gioco del Ponte**, held on the last Sunday in June every year, when twelve teams from the north and south banks of the city stage a series of battles, pushing a seven-tonne carriage over the Ponte di Mezzo. The event, first mentioned in 1568, is still held in medieval costume with much ceremony. June 17 sees the **Regata di San Ranieri**, where four rowing teams race in costume in honour of the patron saint of Pisa; it's preceded the night before by the **Luminaria di San Ranieri**, when all the waterfront buildings and the Leaning Tower are illuminated. Italy's four great maritime republics (Amalfi, Pisa, Genoa and Venice) take turns to host the **Regata delle Antiche Repubbliche Marinare**, which next comes round to Pisa in late May/early June 2010. Four eight-man crews from each of the cities race against each other on the Arno, in between festivities and parades.

Look out for **concerts** at the Teatro Comunale Verdi, Via Palestro 40, and for more offbeat and contemporary shows (even the odd rock concert) held in a former church at the end of Via San Zeno. The city also has an adventurous **arts cinema**, Cinema Nuove, in Piazza Stazione.

Listings

Airlines Air Dolomiti ℡ 02.3030.1000; Air France ℡ 848.884.466; Alitalia ℡ 848.865.643; British Airways ℡ 199.712.266; Lufthansa ℡ 02.3030.1000; Ryanair ℡ 050.503.770; Transavia Airlines ℡ 02.218.981.

Airport information Aeroporto Galileo Galilei, Pisa ℡ 050.849.300, ⓦ www.pisa-airport.com.

Books Libreria Ghibellina, Borgo Streto 37, stocks English books.

Car rental The following are all based at the airport. Autoeuropa ℡ 050.506.883; Avis ℡ 050.42.028; Europcar ℡ 050.41.017; Hertz ℡ 050.43.220; Liberty Rent ℡ 050.48.088; National/Maggiore ℡ 050.42.574; Program ℡ 050.500.296; Sixt ℡ 050.46.209; Thrifty ℡ 050.45.490; Travelcar ℡ 050.44.424.

Hospital Santa Chiara, Via Roma 67 ℡ 050.992.111.

Internet access Internet Planet, Piazza Cavallotti 3; Internet Point, Via dei Mille 3. Internet Surf, Via Carducci 5.

Laundry OndaBlu, Via San Francesco 8a.

Left luggage At the airport (daily 10am–8pm; ℡ 050.500.707).

Lost property At the airport ℡ 050.849.400.

Parking There are car parks outside the Porta Nuova, just west of the Campo dei Miracoli, and west of the train station on Via Battisti. Parking in the historic centre is severely restricted: yellow spaces are off-limits, blue spaces are charged by the hour, day and night, and white spaces are free only if you display a chit from your hotel, signed, stamped and dated. The airport long-term car park P2 is free.

Police The *Questura* is at Via Mario Lalli 1 ℡ 050.583.511.

Post office Piazza Vittorio Emanuele II (Mon–Fri 8.15am–7pm, Sat 8.15am–noon).

Taxi Radio Taxi ℡ 050.541.600.

Lucca

LUCCA, 17km northeast of Pisa, is the most graceful of Tuscany's provincial capitals, set inside an imposing ring of Renaissance walls fronted by gardens and huge bastions. Charming and quiet out of season, Lucca's narrow streets rapidly reach full tourist capacity during the summer months, when you may find yourself traipsing around its attractions as part of a great camera-clicking procession.

The city lies at the heart of one of Italy's richest agricultural regions, and has prospered since Roman times. Its heyday was the eleventh to fourteenth centuries, when the silk trade brought wealth and, for a time, political power. Lucca first lost its independence to Pisa in 1314, then, under Castruccio Castracani, forged an empire in the west of Tuscany. Pisa and Pistoia both fell,

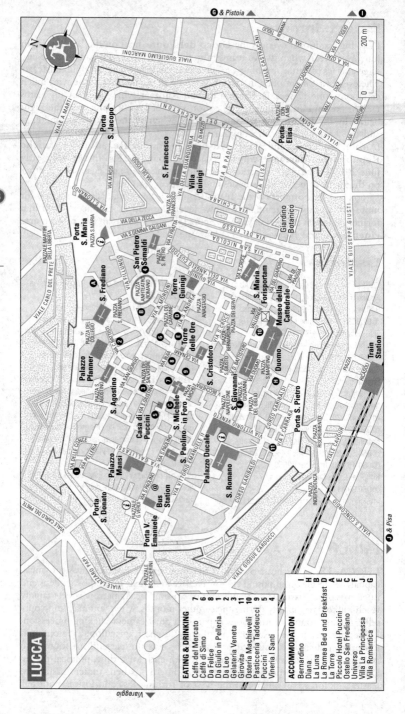

8

TUSCANY | Lucca

Viareggio

G & Pistoia

I

Porta S. Jacopo

VIALE GUGLIELMO MARCONI

VIALE A. MARTI

VIA M. ROSI

VALLE FOSSO

VIA DELLA ZECCA

VIA S. GEMMA GALGANI

Porta S. Maria

PIAZZALE MARTIRI DELLA LIBERTÀ

VIALE CARLO DEL PRETE

VIA DEL FOSSO

VIA DELLA QUARQUONIA

V DI MEZZO

S. Francesco

PIAZZA S. FRANCESCO

Villa Guinigi

VIA S. CHIARA

VIA ELISA

Porta Elisa

VIALE GIUSEPPE GIUSTI

Giardino Botanico

VIA S. CROCE

VIA SAN NICOLAO

VIA DEL FOSSO

S. Maria Forisportam

VIA DELLA QUARQUONIA

VIALE CASTRACANI

VIA DI TIGLIO

VIA G. PACINI

PIAZZALE DON ALDO MEI

VIA A. CONTINE

San Pietro • 4 Somaldi

PIAZZA ANFITEATRO ROMANO

Torre Guinigi

Torre delle Ore

VIA A. TORDINI

VIA FILLUNGO

S. Frediano A

PIAZZA S. FREDIANO

Palazzo Pfanner

PIAZZA DEL COLLEGIO

S. Agostino

PIAZZA S. AGOSTINO

Casa di Via S. Agostino 3

S. Michele in Foro 5

S. Paolino 6

Palazzo Ducale

Palazzo Mansi

Porta S. Donato

Porta V. Emanuele

Bus Station @

S. Romano

S. Cristoforo

S. Giovanni F

Duomo

Museo della Cattedrale

Porta S. Pietro

Train Station

J & Pisa

Viareggio

EATING & DRINKING

Caffè del Mercato	7
Caffè di Simo	6
Da Felice	8
Da Giulio in Pelleria	1
Da Leo	2
Gelateria Veneta	3
Girovita	11
Osteria Machiavelli	10
Pasticceria Taddeucci	9
Puccini	5
Vineria I Santi	4

ACCOMMODATION

Bernardino	I
Diana	H
La Luna	B
La Romea Bed and Breakfast	D
La Torre	A
Piccolo Hotel Puccini	E
Ostello San Frediano	C
Universo	F
Villa La Principessa	J
Villa Romantica	G

LUCCA

0   200 m

and, but for Castracani's untimely death in 1325, Lucca might well have taken Florence. In subsequent centuries it remained largely independent until falling into the hands of Napoleon and then the Bourbons. The city's most famous son, composer **Giacomo Puccini**, was born here in 1858. Today Lucca is among the wealthiest and most conservative cities in Tuscany, its prosperity gained largely through **silk** and high-quality **olive oil**.

Arrival and information

Lucca's **train station** (☎1478.88.088) is just south of the city walls. Frequent Lazzi and CLAP **buses** from Florence, and Lazzi ones from Pisa and Livorno, arrive at the western Piazzale Verdi.

Lucca's large and very helpul main **tourist office** is in the north of town, at Piazza Santa Maria 35 (daily: April–Sept 9am–7pm; Oct–March 9am–5pm; ☎0583.919.931, ⓦwww.luccaturismo.it). It has public toilets. Other offices are in the Cortile degli Svizzeri, behind Piazza Napoleone (same times; ☎0583.4171), and on Piazzale Verdi (daily: April–Sept 9am–7pm; Oct–March 9am–2pm; ☎0583.419.689). They all have (English) **audioguides** for a self-guided town walk (€10) which lasts eighty minutes. Two-hour guided tours of the town in English leave everyday from the Palazzo Pretorio on Piazza San Michele at 2.45pm; they cost €10 per person.

Accommodation

Accommodation can be difficult at almost any time of year – the number of hotels has failed to keep pace with the town's growing popularity – so if you turn up without a booking, be prepared to move on to one of the nearby towns, or even out to Pisa or Pistoia. There are few **hotels** within the walls, although some good-value **private rooms** ease the burden (consult the tourist office). Lucca has one HI hostel, the **Ostello San Frediano**, Via della Cavallerizza 12 (☎0583.469.957, ⓦwww.ostellolucca.it; midnight curfew; €16.50, double rooms ❶), which is conveniently located just inside the walls.

Bernardino Via di Tiglio 108 ☎0583.953.356, ⓦwww.hotelbernardino.it. A plain two-star, 5min east of Porta Elisa, with plain but comfortable rooms, all en suite and with TV. ❸

Diana Via del Molinetto 11 ☎0583.492.202, ⓦwww.albergodiana.com. A block west of the Duomo, this unfussy, nine-room place has seven double rooms with private bathroom and two singles without. A nearby annexe has smarter, more expensive rooms (❸) and a studio apartment. ❷

La Luna Corte Compagni 12 ☎0583.493.634, ⓦwww.hotellaluna.com. A smart and welcoming 29-room three-star within the walls, with characterful rooms ranged around an internal courtyard and free parking. ❹

La Romea Bed and Breakfast Vicolo delle Ventaglie 2 ☎0583.464.175, ⓦwww.laromea.com. Notwithstanding its imposing black gates, La Romea, just off Via San Andrea, is one of the the friendliest and most sophisticated places in town. The five rooms are stylishly designed and an excellent home-made breakfast is served in the spacious hall. ❹

La Torre 1, 2 and 3 Reception at Piazza del Carmine 11 ☎ & ⓕ0583.957.044, ⓦwww .roomslatorre.com. These three places are all close together in a quiet part of town. Service can be brusque but rooms are big and good value, especially those with shared bathrooms. ❷

Piccolo Hotel Puccini Via di Poggio 9 ☎0583.55.421, ⓦwww.hotelpuccini.com. Friendly three-star steps from the Casa di Puccini and San Michele. The 14 standard en-suite rooms are less stunning than the location. ❸

Universo Piazza del Giglio 1 ☎0583.493.678, ⓦwww.universolucca.com. A venerable and spacious old three-star, right in the centre complete with red carpet and grand, golden chairs. The varying set of rooms matches the staff for unpredictable charm. ❺

Villa La Principessa SS del Brennero 1616, Massa Pisana ☎0583.370.037, ⓦwww .hotelprincipessa.com. A beautifully appointed nineteenth-century country villa set in lovely grounds (with pool), 3km south of town. ❼

Villa Romantica Via N Barbantini 246, corner
of Via Inigo Campioni ☎0583.496.872,
ⓦwww.villaromantica.it. An attractive Liberty-style
town house outside the city walls near the easily
spotted stadium, with a swimming pool and six
nicely maintained rooms. ❺

The City

Lucca is a delightful place simply to wander in randomly, with much of the
centre free from traffic, although you will have to keep any eye out for the many
cyclists weaving through the crowds (or perhaps even join them, see listings on
p.559). The focus of Lucca's compact *centro storico* is the vast Piazza Napoleone,
but its social heart is **Piazza San Michele** just to the north. The "long thread",
Via Fillungo, heads northeast to the extraordinary circular **Piazza Anfiteatro**,
while further east, beyond the Fosso ("ditch"), lies San Francesco and Lucca's
major art museum, housed in the **Villa Guinigi**.

San Michele and around

The historical heart of town, and once the site of the Roman forum, is now
a lively square fringed with shops and cafés that plays host to a daily market
(clothes, bags, sweets tourist knick-knacks etc) that sits alongside **San Michele
in Foro** (daily 7.40am–noon & 3–6pm; free), a church with one of Tuscany's
most exquisite **facades**. Most of the present structure dates from the century
after 1070, but the church is unfinished, as the money ran out before the body
of the building could be raised to the level of the facade. The effect is wonderful,
the upper loggias and the windows fronting air. Its Pisan-inspired intricacy is a
triumph of poetic eccentricity: each of its myriad columns is different – some
twisted, others sculpted or candy-striped. The impressive **campanile** is Lucca's
tallest. It would be hard to follow this act and the **interior** barely tries; the best
work of art is a beautifully framed painting called *Saints Jerome, Sebastian, Roch
and Helena* by Filippino Lippi in the right-hand nave.

   The composer **Giacomo Puccini** was born about a block away, on December 22, 1858, at Corte San Lorenzo 9; his father and grandfather had both been
organists at San Michele. The family home, the **Casa di Puccini** (ⓦwww
.puccini.it) is currently closed for renovation and is not due to reopen till
2010. Just west of here is the **Museo Nazionale di Palazzo Mansi**, Via Galli
Tassi 43 (Tues–Sat 8.30am–7.30pm, Sun 8.30am–1.30pm; €4; joint ticket with
Museo Guinigi €6.50). This seventeenth-century *palazzo* is worth seeing for
its magnificent Rococo decor: from a vast, frescoed **Music Salon**, you pass
through three drawing rooms hung with seventeenth-century Flemish tapestries to a gilded **bridal suite**, complete with lavish canopied bed. Rooms
11–14 in the far wing hold an indifferent **Pinacoteca**, the highlight of which
is Pontormo's portrait of Alessandro de' Medici.

The Duomo and around

It needs a double-take before you realize why the **Duomo** (also known as the
Cattedrale di San Martino) looks odd. The building is fronted by a severely asym-
metric facade – its right-hand arch and loggias are squeezed by the belltower,
which was already in place from an earlier building. Nonetheless, little detracts
from its overall grandeur, created by the repetition of tiny columns and loggias
and by the stunning **atrium**, whose bas-reliefs are some of the finest sculptures
in the city. The carvings over the left-hand door – a *Deposition, Annunciation,
Nativity* and *Adoration of the Magi* – are by **Nicola Pisano**. Other panels display
a symbolic labyrinth, a Tree of Life (with Adam and Eve at the bottom and
Christ at the top), a bestiary of grotesques and the months of the year.

The **interior** (daily: summer 9.30am–7pm; winter 9.30am–5pm; free) is best known for the contribution of **Matteo Civitali** (1435–1501), who is represented here most famously by the *Tempietto*, a gilt-and-marble octagon halfway down the church. Some fanatically intense acts of devotion are performed in front of it, directed at the **Volto Santo** (Holy Face) within, a cedarwood crucifix with bulging eyes and dark brown skin popularly said to be a true effigy of Christ carved by Nicodemus, an eyewitness to the Crucifixion. Legend has it that the *Volto Santo* came to Lucca of its own volition, first journeying by boat from the Holy Land, and then brought by oxen guided by divine will. The effigy attracted pilgrims from all over Europe, including kings – William II of England used to swear by it ("*Per sanctum vultum de Lucca!*"). The **Tomb of Ilaria del Carretto** (1410) in the sacristy is considered the masterpiece of Sienese sculptor **Jacopo della Quercia**. It consists of a raised dais and the sculpted body of Ilaria, second wife of Paolo Guinigi, one of Lucca's medieval big shots. In a touching, almost sentimental gesture, the artist has carved the family dog at her feet. Also within the sacristy is a superb *Madonna Enthroned* by **Ghirlandaio**.

Occupying a converted twelfth-century building opposite the Duomo is the **Museo della Cattedrale** (mid-March to Oct daily 10am–6pm; Nov to mid-March Mon–Fri 10am–2pm, Sat & Sun 10am–5pm; €4, or €6 with the cathedral sacristy & San Giovanni). This contains some unnerving Romanesque stone heads, human and equine, and, in room II on the upper floor, a reliquary from Limoges decorated with stories from the life of St Thomas à Becket alongside the *Croce dei Pisani*, an ornate fifteenth-century gold crucifix. West of the Duomo is the church of **San Giovanni** (same hours; €2.50; combined ticket with Tomb of Ilaria & Museo della Cattedrale €5.50). This was Lucca's cathedral until 715, and excavations here have unearthed a tangle of remains, from Roman mosaics to traces of a Carolingian church.

North to San Frediano

Via Cenami leads from the duomo north to the **Torre delle Ore**, the city's clock tower since 1471. From here, **Via Fillungo** cuts through Lucca's luxury shopping district.

San Frediano, between Via Fillungo and the northwest city walls, is again Pisan-Romanesque, featuring the magnificent thirteenth-century exterior mosaic *Christ in Majesty*, with the Apostles gathered below. The **interior** (Mon–Sat 8.30am–noon & 3–5pm, Sun 10.30am–5pm except during services; free) lives up to the facade's promise – a delicately lit, hall-like basilica. Facing the door is the **Fonta Lustrale**, a huge twelfth-century font executed by three unknown craftsmen. Set behind the font is an *Annunciation* by Andrea della Robbia, festooned with trailing garlands of ceramic fruit. The left-hand of the two rear chapels houses the apparently incorrupt body of **St Zita** (died 1278), a Lucchese maidservant who achieved sainthood from a white lie: she used to give bread from her household to the poor, and when challenged one day by her boss as to the contents of her apron, she replied "only roses and flowers" – into which the bread was transformed. She is commemorated on April 27 by a flower market outside the church. Lucca's best frescoes – **Amico Aspertini**'s sixteenth-century scenes of the Arrival of the Volto Santo, the Life of St Augustine and The Miracle of St Frediano – occupy the second chapel of the left aisle. Frediano, an Irish monk, is said to have brought Christianity to Lucca in the sixth century and is depicted here saving the city from flood.

A short distance west, at Via degli Asili 33, is the **Palazzo Pfanner** (March–Oct 10am–6pm; garden €2.50, garden and palace €4). The *palazzo*, housing a textiles collection, is less interesting than its rear loggia and exquisite statued gardens with fountain. They can be seen to good effect from the city walls just nearby, which also yield a good overview of another fine church, **Sant'Agostino**.

East of San Frediano is the remarkable **Piazza Anfiteatro**. This ramshackle circuit of medieval buildings, built on the foundations of the Roman amphitheatre that once stood here (arches and columns of which can still be discerned), is now ringed by cafés. South past a covered market looms the **Torre Guinigi**, which once belonged to Lucca's eponymous, leading fifteenth-century family and is one of the strangest sights in town – its battlemented tower is surmounted, 44m up, by a **holm oak** whose roots have grown into the room below. You can climb the tower from Via Sant'Andrea (daily: May to Sept 9am–midnight; Oct to Feb 9.30am–5pm; March to April 9.30am–7pm; €3.50).

East to San Francesco

Running from north to south across town is a canal and Via del Fosso, across which is the church of **San Francesco**, fronted by a relatively simple facade and adjoining a crumbling brick convent. Behind the church is Lucca's key collection of painting, sculpture, furniture and applied arts, the **Museo Nazionale di Villa Guinigi**, housed in the family's much-restored mansion (Tues–Sat 8.30am–7.30pm, Sun 8.30am–1.30pm; €4, or €6.50 combined ticket with Palazzo Mansi). Its lower floor has mainly sculpture and archeological finds, with numerous Romanesque pieces and works by della Quercia and Matteo Civitali. Upstairs are lots of big sixteenth-century paintings and more impressive works by early Lucchese and Sienese masters, as well as fine Renaissance offerings from such as Fra' Bartolommeo.

Eating, drinking and entertainment

Lucca has some high-quality **restaurants**, and local specialities worth keeping an eye out for include *zuppa di farro*, a thick soup made with spelt (a type of grain), *torta di spinaci*, a sweet tart made with spinach, and *capretto*, mountain goat, often roasted.

The town's **food shops** are equally good and make great places to stock up for a picnic. *La Cacioteca*, Via Fillungo 242, sells a wide variety of cheeses; *Forno Amedeo Giusti*, Via Santa Lucia 18, and *Forno Casali*, Via Guinigi 32, are two of the town's top bakeries; both sell delicious fresh *focaccia*. *Caniparoli* in Via San Paolina is a wonderful chocolate shop.

The **Lucchese Settembre** festival features plenty of activity throughout September, centred on a **candlelit procession** on the 13th, when the bejewelled *Volto Santo* (see p.557) is carried through the streets from San Frediano to the Duomo. Consult the tourist office for details of affiliated September events, such as **classical concerts** (including performances of a Puccini opera) at the intimate, four-tiered Teatro Comunale in Piazza del Giglio, as well as **jazz** happenings and **art** exhibitions. Another key musical event is the Summer Festival (ⓦwww.summer-festival.com) often featuring big-name international stars performing in Piazza Anfiteatro.

Cafés, bars and gelaterie

Caffe del Mercato Piazza San Michele. The most alluring of the bars around the main piazza, particularly as the church keeps it nice and shady throughout lunch.

Caffè di Simo Via Fillungo 58. Lucca's most famous café-bar was Puccini's favourite haunt and retains an appealing late nineteenth-century ambience. It serves a decent array of cakes as well as a few simple hot dishes for €6–8.

Gelateria Veneta Via Vittorio Veneto 74. It's been serving some of Lucca's best ice cream since 1927 and is open conveniently late. Five scoops for €2.30. Closed Tues.

Girovita Piazza Antelminelli 2. With tables outside in the quiet piazza opposite the cathedral, trendy *Girovita* is the place to come for an *aperitivo* or a lengthy afternoon coffee.

Pasticceria Taddeucci Piazza San Michele 34 ℡0583.494.933. A stunning interior of wood-panelling and mosaic tiles match the selection of cakey delights and great coffee.

Vineria I Santi Via dell'Anfiteatro 29a. Inventive, well-prepared dishes, such as goose live paté with marmalade accompany the wine list at this bar, which has tables outside on a small piazza behind the amphitheatre. Closed Wed.

Restaurants

Da Felice Via Buia 12. Overspilling with locals at lunchtime, this tiny little place serves delicious melt-in-the-mouth pizza by the slice. Closed Sun.

Da Giulio in Pelleria Via della Conce 45 ℡0583.55.948. A lively trattoria always packed in the evenings – the food is not exceptional, but the prices are very reasonable (*primi* €4.50–6, *secondi* 5–7) and the atmosphere makes it worth it. Closed Sun & Mon.

Da Leo Via Tegrimi 1 ℡0583.492.236. Small, inexpensive locals' haunt with solid (and solidly meaty) Tuscan cooking. *Primi* €5.50, *secondi* €8–10.50. Closed Sun.

Osteria Machiavelli Via Cesare Battisti 28. Great family-run place with a jovial air of controlled chaos, fantastic food and unbeatable prices of around €10 for two courses. Closed Sun.

Puccini Corte San Lorenzo 1 ℡0583.316.116. Opposite the composer's house, this place has a light touch and classy approach to its dishes, which include macaroni with chestnuts and mushrooms. It's not cheap (*primi* €10–12, *secondi* €17–19), but is the top choice for a lunch to remember or a romantic dinner date. Closed Tues & Wed lunch in summer, all day Tues in winter.

Listings

Bike rental Cycling the perimeter walls is one of Lucca's great pleasures and though many roads through the town are barred to two-wheeled traffic, locals seem to happily ignore this rule. Rental places include the tourist office in Piazzale Verdi; Barbetti Cicli, Via dell'Anfiteatro 23; Cicli Bizzarri or Biciclette Poli, either side of the tourist office in Piazza Santa Maria. Prices are around €2.50 an hour.

Hospital Campo di Marte, in Via dell'Ospedale ℡0583.9701.

Internet access Tourist office at Piazza Santa Maria or any of the many outlets on Via San Paolino.

Lost property c/o Comune di Lucca, Via Battisti 10 ℡0583.442.388.

Parking Outside the walls, parking is free for all; inside, only hotel customers can park for free.

Police The *Questura* is at Via Cavour 38 ℡0583.4551.

Post office Via Vallisneri 2 (Mon–Fri 8.15am–7pm, Sat 8.15am–12.30pm).

North of Pisa

The coast from near Pisa north to the Ligurian border is a solid strip of unattractive beach resorts. This **Riviera della Versilia** ought to be otherwise, given the dramatic backdrop of the **Alpi Apuane** mountains, but the beaches share the coastal plain with a railway, autostrada and clogged urban roads – and, on top of this, the sea is not the cleanest in Italy. The resort of **Viareggio** provides a lively diversion on a coastal journey north to the stunning Cinque Terre. Otherwise, the only real appeal lies inland, hiking in the Alpi Apuane and exploring the famed marble-quarrying centre of **Carrara**.

Viareggio

VIAREGGIO, 22km northwest of Pisa, tends not to feature highly on most independent travellers' Tuscan itineraries. These days everyone wants picturesque former fishing villages and converted farmhouses – the old and functional converted for modern tourist use – not tailor-made attractions. But Viareggio has never been anything other than what it is – a purpose built seaside resort. This can make visiting problematic. Many hotels insist on at least half board in summer, and most of the beach has been parceled up into private strips controlled by the hotels – who can charge up to €20 for the use of a sun lounger and an umbrella for the day. However, to regard Viareggio as package holiday haunt to be avoided would be to do it a disservice. It's a lot better than that. The town has some very neat 1920s Art Deco buildings here unlike anything else in the province, as well as a good selection of bars and restaurants, best sampled on a night-time stroll along its three lane wide, several kilometre long seafront boulevard, which, on a balmy summer evening, has a strip-like neon-lit aesthetic more American in feel than Tuscan. To see Viareggio at its liveliest, come for its famously boisterous **Carnevale** in February, when for four consecutive Sundays there's an amazing parade of floats, or *carri* – colossal, lavishly designed papier-mâché models of politicians and celebrities (@www.viareggio.ilcarnevale.com).

The **train station** is 600m back from the seafront. **Buses** (Lazzi, CAT and CLAP) stop nearer the centre; along the seafront, turn right past Piazza Mazzini, to find the **tourist office**, at Viale Carducci 10 (Mon–Fri 9am–1pm & 3–6.30pm, Sat 9.30am–12.30pm & 3.30–6.30pm, Sun 10am–noon; ℡0584.962.233). The town has literally hundreds of **hotels** in all price brackets; one inexpensive option is *Villa Amadei*, just west of the tourist office at Via F. Gioia 23 (℡0584.45.517, @www.hotelamadei.it; ❷). For the best **restaurant** in town head for the Michelin-starred *Romano*, Via Mazzini 120 (℡0584.31.382; closed Mon), for sublime fish and seafood.

Carrara

The capital of Massa-Carrara, Tuscany's northernmost province, is **Massa**, a modern, unappealing town that is more or less merged with its adjacent beach resort of **Marina di Massa** in a sprawl of undistinguished holiday development. Nearby **CARRARA** sits just inside the Ligurian border, 28km north of Viareggio, and enjoys a fame that far outstrips its modest size. For the mountains here have been a principal source of **marble** since the Roman period and everyone from Michelangelo to Henry Moore has tramped up here in search of the perfect block. Carrara is still the world's largest producer and exporter of

---

Walks in the Alpi Apuane

There are **walks** throughout the **Alpi Apuane**, which loom behind the Riviera della Versilia and are now protected as a Parco Regionale. Altitudes are relatively low (the summits crest at 1900m), conditions are easy and distances are short – you're never very far from civilization. **Ufficio Promozione del Parco delle Apuane**, Via Corrado del Greco 11 in Seravezza, partway between Viareggio and Massa, has leaflets, maps and guidance for walkers (Mon–Sat 10am–noon; ℡0584.756.144, @www.parks.it/parco.alpi.apuane).

One access point is the lovely village of **STAZZEMA**, served by bus from Pietrasanta and with the simple **hotel** *Procinto*, Via IV Novembre 21 (℡0584.777.004; ❶). Trail #5 is a gentle climb from Stazzema through chestnut woods to the Procinto, a huge tabletop crag, below which is the **Rifugio Forte dei Marmi** (open daily June 5 to Sept 5; rest of the year, weekends only; ℡0584.777.051; bed only €12). This is an easy day-trip, with time to explore above the *rifugio* and drop in for a snack on the way back down to Stazzema on trails #121 or #126.

marble, shipping out 1.5 million tonnes a year from the container port plumb in the middle of **Marina di Carrara**. But quiet Carrara itself has a pleasant, rural feel and comes as a relief after the holiday coast.

From the central **Piazza Matteotti**, the pedestrianized Via Roma heads north to the attractive Piazza Accademia, with steps down (west) to the old town and Carrara's Romanesque-Gothic **Duomo**, graced with a lovely Pisan-style marble facade. Heart of the old town is gracious **Piazza Alberica**, the focus for the town's display of contemporary marble sculpture, the biennial **Scolpire all'Aperto** (late July to early Oct), when the town invites internationally renowned artists to create new works in public. For the low-down on marble, there's an impressive **Museo Civico di Marmo** on Viale XX Settembre, 2km south of town (July & Aug Mon–Sat 10am–8pm; May, June & Sept Mon–Sat 10am–6pm; Oct–April 9am–5pm; ☎0585.845.746; €4.50), served by CAT buses from Piazza Matteotti.

Any short trip into the interior brings you to the startling sight of the marble **quarries**. To get a closer view, take a bus (hourly from Via Minzoni) towards **Colonnata**, 8km northeast of Carrara, and get off before the village at the *Visita Cave* signs by the mine – if you're driving, follow the *Cava di Marmo* signs from the Colonnata. You'll see a huge, blindingly white marble basin, its floor and sides perfectly squared by the enormous wire saws used to cut the blocks that litter the surroundings.

Practicalities

Carrara-Avenza **train station** is close to the Marina di Carrara seafront, and is served by regular **buses** that run 4km inland to drop off at Carrara's central Piazza Matteotti. The town has a summer-only **tourist office** at Via XX Settembre 46 (daily 9am–7pm; ☎0585.844.403), though you'll find more information on the coast at Marina di Carrara, from where Navigazione Golfo dei Poeti (see p.162) runs **boats** to Portovenere and the Cinque Terre (June–Sept daily; around €18). Carrara's two **hotels** are the spartan *Da Roberto*, on Via Apuana (☎0585.70.634; ❶), and the more salubrious *Michelangelo*, Corso Fratelli Rosselli 3 (☎0585.777.161, ✉hm.carrara@tin.it; ❸), with parking and a jolly manager. The HI **hostel**, *Ostello Albergo Apuano per la Gioventù* (☎0585.780.034, ✉aig@uni.net; mid-March to mid-Sept; curfew 11.30pm; €8.26), is on the seafront between Marina di Carrara and Marina di Massa at Via delle Pinete 237, alongside plenty of **campsites**. The excellent *Il Via* **restaurant**, Via Roma 17 (☎0585.779.423; closed Sun in winter), has a quality meat or fish menu at moderate prices. Elsewhere are the moderately priced *Roma*, Piazza Cesare Battisti 1 (closed Sat), and *Osteria della Contrada*, Via Ulivi 2 (☎0585.776.961; closed Mon). A good little spot for a drink is the *Bar Fuori Porta* at Piazza Battisti 1 (closed Sun), which also serves inexpensive snacks.

Livorno

LIVORNO, 18km southwest of Pisa, is Tuscany's third-largest city and one of Italy's largest ports – a status that invited blanket bombing during World War II. Its rebuilt commercial centre is not pretty, but a poke around the back streets will reveal a network of picturesque canals and hump-backed bridges, a lively streetlife that benefits from a very un-Tuscan ethnic diversity, and plenty of places to sample top-quality **seafood**. What you won't find are the very things Tuscany is famous for: art, architecture and tourists.

Livorno's port was developed under the **Medici**. In 1618, they declared it a **free port** and instituted a liberal constitution that prompted an influx of Jews, Greeks, Spanish Muslims, English Catholics and a cosmopolitan throng of other refugees. Livorno flourished, and attracted a community of English expatriates (including Shelley) whose cack-handed anglicization of the city's name into **Leghorn** is still in use.

The City

The old **Porto Mediceo** has fishing boats spilling back into the canal quarter and often a cruise liner blocking the view out to sea. Sangallo's **Fortezza Vecchia** flanks the harbour, about 100m north of Livorno's sole surviving nod to Renaissance art – the statue of the **Quattro Mori**, overlooking the busy waterfront road at Piazza Micheli. This bizarre work decorates an inept 1595 statue of Ferdinando I with the addition of four chained Moors by Pietro Tacca (1623), tacked on either as a celebration of the success of Tuscan raids against North African shipping, or merely as slaves cowering beneath Medici glory. Either way they stand as a poignant and shocking harbourside symbol for this multiracial city. The **Museo Civico Giovanni Fattori**, devoted to Fattori and the late-nineteenth-century Macchiaioli movement, Italy's milk-and-water version of Impressionism, is housed in the extravagant Villa Mimbelli, 1km south at Via San Jacopo in Acquaviva 65 (⊕0586.808.001; Tues–Sun 10am–1pm & 4–7pm; €4; bus #1).

The broad Via Grande heads inland to **Piazza Grande**, which features the **Duomo**, a postwar reconstruction. Via Cairoli curls around the duomo and, partway along, Via Buontalenti leads off to the ochre **Mercato Centrale** that stands at the heart of a boisterous street market. The canal near here was the

Ferries from Livorno

There are dozens of **ferry** sailings from Livorno, to **Corsica** (Bastia or Porto Vecchio), **Sardinia** (Olbia, Golfo Aranci or Cágliari), **Sicily** (Palermo) and the Tuscan Islands. Nearly all ferries to Corsica and Sardinia leave from alongside the **Stazione Marittima**, west of the centre behind the Fortezza Vecchia, although some (and boats to Sicily) depart from **Varco Galvani**, a long way west of town. Ferries to Capraia leave from the central **Porto Mediceo**. Check with the tourist office and the companies themselves for times and prices, and **reserve** well ahead in summer. If you're taking a car to Sardinia, note that most companies offer discount deals if you cross to Corsica and drive the 180km to the southern tip of the Island – and often the subsequent ferry to Sardinia is free. For a full list of ferries to Sardinia, see p.1105 and to Elba, see p.564.

Ferry companies

Corsica Ferries/Sardinia Ferries Stazione Marittima, Calata Carrara ⊕0586.881.380, ⓦwww.corsicaferries.com. To Bastia (Corsica) and Golfo Aranci (Sardinia).

Corsica Marittima Stazione Marittima, Calata Carrara ⊕0586.210.507. To Bastia, Porto Vecchio and Olbia (Sardinia).

Grandi Navi Veloci (Grimaldi) Varco Galvani, Calata Tripoli, Porto Nuovo ⊕010.589.331, ⓦwww.grimaldi.it. To Palermo (Sicily).

Lloyd Sardegna/Linea dei Golfi Varco Galvani, Calata Assab, Porto Industriale ⊕0565.222.300, ⓦwww.lloydsardegna.it. To Olbia and Cágliari (Sardinia).

Moby Lines Stazione Marittima, Calata Carrara ⊕0586.826.823, ⓦwww.mobylines .it. To Bastia (Corsica) and Olbia (Sardinia).

Toremar Porto Mediceo ⊕892.123, ⓦwww.toremar.it To Gorgona and Capraia.

limit of the Medici port city; follow it northeast to the ugly treeless expanse of Piazza della Repubblica on one side, and Piazza XX Settembre on the other. The latter is the home of the **Mercatino Americano** – a cultural endowment of stationed American troops – that sells army surplus clothing, fishing and camping gear and flick-knives. From the Mercato Centrale, Via della Madonna strikes north into the **Venezia** district, Livorno's most attractive quarter, with crumbling old tenement buildings and the Fortezza Nuova ringed around by a network of quiet canals. August sees the area come alive for the *Effetto Venezia*, a free **street carnival** of jazz and world music.

Practicalities

The **train station** is 2km east of the centre with buses #1 or #2 connecting it to Piazza Grande. ATL **buses** from Piombino drop off on Piazza Grande; Lazzi buses from Florence, Pisa and Lucca arrive on Piazza Manin. The main **tourist office** is on Piazza Municipio (daily 8.30am–12.30pm & 2–6pm; ☎0586.204.611). There's also an information office at the station.

The best **hotel** is the eighteenth-century villa *La Vedetta*, on the Montenero hill at Via della Lecceta 5 (☎0586.579.957, ⓦwww.hotellavedetta.it; ❷), with modern decor, parking and spectacular panoramic views. Livorno has a rash of cheap hotels, some of which – around the harbour and station – are grim dives. The *Villa Morazzana*, at Via di Collinet 86 in the hills above town (☎0586.500.076, ⓦwww.villamorazzana.it; ❷), is a pleasant exception with strikingly designed colourful rooms in an eighteenth-century building that also offers **hostel** accommodation. The large **campsite** *Miramare*, Via del Littorale 220 (☎0586.580.402, ⓦwww.campingmiramare.com; April–Oct), a short way south of town, has a shingle beach.

Italians travel to Livorno just to eat seafood and, specifically, to feast on the local dish *cacciucco*, a spicy seafood stew served with garlic toast. A choice **restaurant** if you can spare €35 a head is *La Chiave*, Scali delle Cantine 52 (☎0586.888.609; closed Wed). There are dozens of more affordable options: *Antico Moro*, Via Bartelloni 59 (☎0586.884.659; closed Wed & lunchtime), is a pleasant locals' haunt with excellent *cacciucco*. *Café d'Etoile*, Via Indipendenza 13 (☎0586.210.667; closed Sun), off Piazza Cavour, serves fresh salads and snacks. On Venezia's canalsides you'll find the moderately priced couscous-house *Mediterraneo*, Scali Ponte di Marmo 14 with occasional live music (☎0586.829.799; closed Tues), and *The Barge*, a waterside pub with English beers and food, Scali Ancore 6 (closed Sun).

Elba

Mountainous **ELBA** is Italy's third-largest island – 29km long by some 19km wide – and since captivating Napoleon, has attracted visitors ever since. It has exceptionally clear water, fine white-sand beaches, and a lush, wooded interior, superb for walking, and though it's now well and truly embracing package tourism, almost everyone comes for the beach resorts – even in the height of summer, inland villages remain mostly quiet. **Portoferraio** is very much the capital, a characterful port overlooked by a warren of old alleys. Elsewhere, the most attractive towns are **Capoliveri** and **Porto Azzurro** in the southeast and little **Marciana** in the west, the last of these providing access to woodland hikes and the impressive chair lift up to **Monte Capanne** (1018m). **Biòdola** occupies an idyllic sweeping bay near Portoferraio that is largely free from the Island's otherwise remorseless beach culture. You can also take a ferry from

The main port of departure to Elba is **PIOMBINO**, 75km south of Livorno – not a great place to stay, since it was flattened in World War II and these days makes its living from a giant steelworks. If you're arriving by train, you'll probably have to change at **Campiglia Marittima** station, from where connecting trains run through the town to Piombino Marittima. At the port, you'll find plenty of ticket outlets for all ferry companies. Most people head to Elba's Portoferraio, to where Toremar and Moby **ferries** run every day of the year, the first around 6am and the last around 9pm (earlier and later in high summer; one-way €26 for a car and driver, €6.50 for additional passengers and foot passengers, plus €8.90 tax; summer every 30min; winter every 2hr; 1hr). If you're looking to cut costs get the slightly cheaper ferry to Rio Marina on the Island's east coast with Toremar. Port taxes add a few euros. Note that you should book your return ticket from Elba as soon as possible in summer.

From Piombino Toremar also serves Rio Marina (2–3 daily) and Porto Azzurro (summer 1 daily). Toremar's **rapid ferry**, or *linea veloce*, serves Portoferraio (summer 2 daily; takes 40min) and Rio Marina (summer 3 daily; 30min). Toremar's **hydrofoil**, or *aliscafo*, glides to Cavo (summer 5 daily; winter 3 daily; 20min) and Portoferraio (summer 4 daily; takes 30min).

Ferry company offices

Moby Nuova Stazione Marittima, Piombino ☎0565.225.211; Via Ninci 1, Portoferraio ☎0565.9361; or Viale Elba 4, Portoferraio ☎0565.914.133, ⓦwww.mobylines.it.

Toremar Nuova Stazione Marittima, Piombino ☎0565.31.100, ⓦwww.toremar-elba.it; Calata Italia 23, Portoferraio ☎0565.918.080; Calata Voltoni 20, Rio Marina ☎0565.962.073; Banchina IV Novembre 26, Porto Azzurro ☎0565.95.004; or Via Michelangelo 54, Cavo ☎0565.949.871.

Portoferraio or Porto Azzurro to the largely unspoilt Island of **Capraia**, some 30km off Elba (see p.570).

Historically, Elba has been well out of the mainstream. The principal industry from ancient times until World War II was **mining**, both of iron ore and of the extensive mineral deposits. The **Romans** wrote of "the Island of good wines" (Elban wines are still among Tuscany's finest). In later centuries control passed from Pisa to Genoa and on to the Medici, Spain, Turkey and finally France – a cosmopolitan mix that has left its legacy on both architecture and cultivation. Most people know the Island as the place of exile for **Napoleon**, who, after he was banished here in May 1814, revamped education and the legal system, built roads and modernized the economy before escaping back to France in February 1815. The epic "Hundred Days" that followed culminated in his final defeat at Waterloo.

All seven Tuscan Islands, and the seas around them, form the **Parco Nazionale dell'Arcipelago Toscano**, the largest protected marine park in Europe, with a helpful, slick and high-tech new **information office** at Calata Italia 31 (☎0565.919.411, ⓦwww.isoleditoscana.it), just along from the main tourist information office in Portoferraio (see p.566). It's here that you should also enquire about the possibility of visiting the beautiful Island of **Pianosa**, only recently opened up to limited numbers of visitors after a past as a military base. The rocky island has good beaches, abundant wildlife and no resident humans.

Getting around Elba

ATL **buses** serve just about every settlement on the island (no service after 8pm). One-way **fares** are between €0.80 and €3.10 depending on distance,

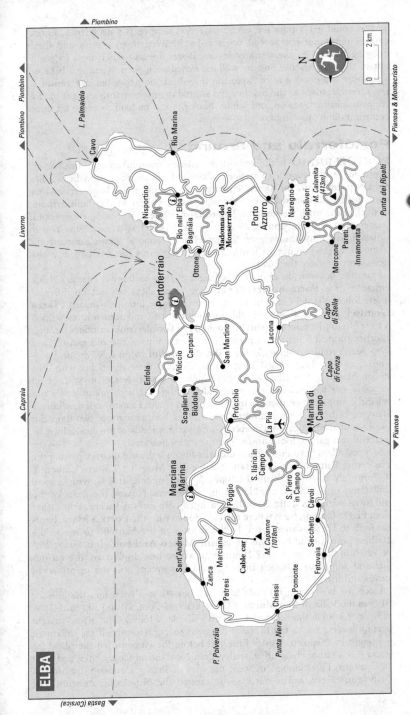

ELBA

Piombino

Piombino

Piombino

Livorno

Capraia

Bastia (Corsica)

Pianosa & Montecristo

Punta dei Ripalti

Pianosa

N

0   2 km

I. Palmaiola

Cavo

Rio Marina

Nisportino

Rio nell' Elba

Bagnàia

Madonna del
Monserrato

Porto
Azzurro

Naregno

Capoliveri

M. Calamita
(413m)

Ottone

Morcone

Pareti

Innamorata

Portoferraio

Capo
di Stella

Carpani

San Martino

Lacona

Capo
di Fonza

Viticcio

Enfola

Scaglieri

Biòdola

Pròcchio

La Pila

Marina di
Campo

Marciana
Marina

Pòggio

S. Ilário in
Campo

Sant'Andrea

Zanca

Marciana

Cable car

M. Capanne
(1018m)

S. Piero
in Campo

Càvoli

Secchéto

Fetovaia

Patresi

Chiessi

Pomonte

P. Polvéraia

Punta Nera

or you could get a **pass** for €6.50 (one day) or €18 (six days). In addition, council minibuses run several times a day between town centres and their outlying beaches in the summer season. **Boats** are also much used to reach out-of-the-way beaches, and are well advertised at all ports. Renting a **bike** or a **scooter** is a good way of exploring the island, see p.568, but **car rental** is less advisable: roads to the beaches and around the major resorts can get nastily congested in high season, and winter bookings can be hard to come by, since companies don't pay insurance off-season.

Portoferraio and around

PORTOFERRAIO is the hub of the Island's transport system, but has an atmospheric old quarter of stepped alleys and old churches, and lives a life quite separate from the hectic comings-and-goings of the huge ferries that dock nearby. All **boats** slide past the old quarter with its Medici-built harbour to dock at the main Calata Italia. The **tourist office** (summer daily 8am–8pm; winter Mon–Sat 8am–2pm & 3–6pm; ☎0565.914.671, ⓦwww.aptelba.it) is at Calata Italia 23, and the websites ⓦwww.elbalink.it and ⓦwww.elbatuttanatura .com are a good source of information. Hiking maps can be bought at the newsagent opposite the bus stop.

From the quayside, head up a short flight of steps to the old quarter's "back entrance", the **Porta a Terra**. From here, steep alleys fan out on different levels; follow Via del Carmine up to the picturesque little tree-shaded **Piazza Gramsci**, perched above the old port with a café and romantic views. Via Victor Hugo (the novelist spent his boyhood in Portoferraio) continues through another tunnelled gateway up to the highest point of the old quarter and Napoleon's residence-in-exile, the **Villa dei Mulini** (Mon & Wed–Sun 9am–7pm, Sun 9am–1pm; closed Tues; €5 or €9 joint three-day ticket with Villa di San Martino). The villa was purpose-built on a well-chosen site with grand views of the bay, and is a fair-sized old building – though undoubtedly not what the emperor was used to. Inside is a gallery with Empire-style furniture, a Baroque bedroom with an absurdly over-gilded bed, a library of two thousand books sent over from Fontainebleau, and various items of memorabilia. The peaceful rear garden looks down over the rocky headland.

Stepped alleys head down from the villa through the old quarter, passing the arts centre **Pinacoteca Foresiana** (Easter–July Mon–Sat 9.30am–12noon & 4–7pm; July & Aug 9.30am–12.30pm & 6pm–midnight; €4), with a small collection of paintings and Napoleonic ephemera. Nearby, the heart of the old town is **Piazza della Repubblica**, lined with cafés. Adjacent is the rather drab Piazza Cavour, from where the old Medici gate, the **Porta a Mare**, heads through to the U-shaped port. In the shadow of the Martello tower on the farthest point of the U is the fascinating **Museo Archeologico** (Tues, Wed & Fri–Sun 9am–1pm & 4–7.30pm; €2), whose best displays are the various jars and amphorae salvaged from Roman shipwrecks, still full of preserved olives and fish.

From the bus station on Viale Elba take bus #1 southwest into the hills for 5km to the **Villa di San Martino** (Tues–Fri 9am–7pm, Sat and Sun 9am–1pm; €5, or €9 joint three-day ticket with Villa dei Mulini). The arrow-straight avenue leading up to the house is designed to impress, even if the villa itself – bought by Napoleon's sister Elise just before the emperor left the island for good – is a rather chilly affair, with a drab Neoclassical facade enlivened with "N" motifs. The monograms were the idea of Prince Demidoff, husband of Napoleon's niece, and it was he who created the Napoleonic museum. The interior halls of the *palazzo* are devoted to temporary art exhibitions. Head left of the facade to the ticket office, and then up flights of stairs to the back of the site where you'll find Napoleon's modest summer retreat. Of the handful of Empire-style rooms, the best is the **Sala Egizio**, decorated with Nilotic scenes to commemorate the Egyptian campaign.

West of Portoferraio, buses head 7km to **ÉNFOLA**, a headland flanked by sandy beaches, and then wind above the coast to the village at the end of the road, **VITICCIO**. From here a footpath covers ground inaccessible to vehicles for 2km south across a prominent headland to picturesque **SCAGLIERI**, fronted by a shop, a bar (which rents bikes and mopeds) and a pizzeria-restaurant. The beaches here are some of the best on the Island. Just round the bay sits **BIODOLA** – little more than a road, a couple of hotels and a superb stretch of white sand. The main town of the area, **PROCCHIO**, lies around the next headland to the south: with its traffic, buzzing bars and shops, it's not a place to get away from it all, but the sea is welcoming and the clean white sand similarly appealing.

Practicalities

The Associazione Albergatori, Calata Italia 20 (Mon–Fri 9am–1pm & 3.30–7pm, Sat 9.30am–12.30pm; ☎0565.914.754, ⓦwww.albergatorielbani.it), will phone around to help find **accommodation**. Otherwise, you could ask in bars about **private rooms** or book a self-catering **apartment** through the tourist office. The best **hotel** in the area for its sense of exclusive isolation and impeccable service is the *Park-Hotel Napoleone*, a nineteenth-century mansion beside the emperor's villa at San Martino (☎0565.911.111, ⓦwww.parkhotelnapoleone.com; ❼). The white-sand beach at Biodola is overlooked by the luxury *Hermitage* with a golf club, tennis club and swimming pool (☎0565.974.811, ⓦwww.elba4star.it; ❾); north along this coast is the decent *Danila* in Scaglieri (☎0565.969.915, ⓦwww.hoteldanila .it; ❹). Portoferraio's best choices are the comfortably decorated *Ape Elbana*, Salita Cosimo dei Medici 2 (☎0565.914.245, ⓔapelbana@elba2000.it; ❷); pleasant *Villa Ombrosa*, Viale De Gasperi 3, facing Le Ghiaie beach (☎0565.914.363, ⓦwww .villaombrosa.it; ❺); and clean but spartan *Nobel*, Via Manganaro 72 (☎0565.915.217, ⓔnobel@elbalink.it; ❷).

The Associazione Campeggi (FAITA), Viale Elba 7 (☎0565.930.208, ⓦwww .campingelba.net), can help out with bookings for the Island's **campsites**. The shaded *Enfola* (☎0565.939.001, ⓦwww.campingenfola.it; April to mid-Oct) is west from Portoferraio on the scenic coast road. On the hillside above Biodola beach is *Scaglieri* (☎0565.969.940, ⓦwww.campingscaglieri.it; April to mid-Oct). Lacona, Elba's camping hotspot on the coast 7km south of Portoferraio, has a flat foreshore crowded with bars and discos and the nearby site of *Lacona* (☎0565.964.161, ⓦwww.camping-lacona.it), set in pine woods. You can also camp by the beach at *Camping le Foce* (☎0565.976.456, ⓦwww.campinglafoce .com) in Marino di Campo, further west. Both Lacona and Scaglieri campsites also have bungalows and apartments.

Portoferraio's **restaurants** can be poor value. Notable exceptions include the characterful, mid-priced *Osteria Libertaria*, on the Medici harbourfront at Calata Matteotti 12 (closed Mon), and *Trattoria La Barca*, one street back at Via Guerrazzi 60 (☎0565.918.036; closed Wed), considered the best restaurant in town. For a real treat, book well ahead at the expensive terrace restaurant of the *Park-Hotel Napoleone* at San Martino (☎0565.918.502; closed in winter); the classic Tuscan cuisine is exquisite, but the multilingual maître d's service really stands out as something special. Back in town, upmarket *Caffè Roma* fronts the harbour, a bright, lively place open all day for coffee and snacks, before turning into a **bar** in the evening.

Listings

Bike, scooter, car and boat rental Main agencies are all near the quay: TWN, Viale Elba 32 ℡0565.914.666, ⊛www.twn-rent.it; BW's, Via Manganaro 15 ℡0565.930.491; Rent Chiappi, Piazza Citi 5 ℡0565.913.524, ⊛www.rentchiappi.it; and Tesi (Maggiore/Budget), Calata Italia 8 ℡0565.930.222. Cicli Brandi (Via Carducci 33 ℡0565.914.128) is a mountain-bike specialist. From any of these outlets, the per-day rate for a small car is around €40–60, a 50cc scooter €35, a mountain-bike €15, and an ordinary bike €9. A 5-metre boat costs €70–100 a day (no licence needed).

Internet access Joinelba, Via Concia di Terra 40 ℡0565.919.178.

Left luggage In the bus station (daily 8am–8pm).

Markets Behind Piazza Cavour is the covered food market (Mon–Sat 7am–1pm & 4–8pm, Sun 7am–1pm) which, aside from fruit and veg, has bottles of Elba's acclaimed DOC wines, *rosso* and *bianco*. The weekly Friday market in Piazza della Repubblica focuses on clothes and bric-à-brac.

Parking The car park opposite the bus station on Viale Elba is free. Cars are banned from the old quarter during the summer.

Pharmacy Centrale, Via Cavour 20 ℡0565.914.026.

Post office Piazza della Repubblica in the old town (Mon–Fri 8.15am–7pm, Sat 8.15am–12.30pm).

Eastern Elba

Eastern Elba comprises two tongues of land, each of them dominated by mountain ridges. The northeast corner was formerly mining country, as the reddish rocks bear testament, but is these days given over entirely to beach tourism. The main road east from Portoferraio heads through **Rio nell'Elba**, once the major mining town of the east, to **RIO MARINA**. Tourism and ferry links have replaced iron ore as the town's principal source of revenue; if you're stuck here, the one **hotel** is the *Rio*, Via Palestro 31 (℡0565.924.225, ⊛www.hotelriomarina.it; ➌), next to the public gardens overlooking the port. Some boats stop at picturesque **CAVO**, 9km north of Rio Marina; its clutch of **hotels** includes the three-star *Maristella* on the waterfront at Lungomare Kennedy 3 (℡0565.949.859, ⊛www.hotelmaristella.com; April–Sept; ➌), and one of its best **restaurants** is mid-priced La Scogliera (℡0565.949.638), with tables overlooking the beach. The southeast tip of the Island has some good beaches and interesting towns but is relatively developed.

Porto Azzurro and Capoliveri

The busy resort of **PORTO AZZURRO** was heavily fortified by Philip III of Spain in 1603. Today his fortress is the Island's prison; a walk round the outer ramparts brings you to a shop selling crafts made by the inmates. The town's small, pretty old quarter – closed to traffic – centres on bustling **Via d'Alarcon**. Choice of the lacklustre **hotels** is Belmare, Banchina IV Novembre 21 (℡0564.95.012, ⊛www.elba-hotelbelmare.it; ➍). The *Arrighi* **campsite** north of town at Barbarossa (℡0565.95.568, ⊛www.campingarrighi.it; April–Nov) gives straight onto the beach. Busy town **restaurants** serve standard pasta-based nosh, including the friendly *Lo Scoglio*, Via Cavour 15 (closed Wed in winter). *All'Arco Antico* on Via d'Alarcon has snacks and pizzas from €4. Plenty of places rent **bikes**, boats and scooters, including BW's, Via Provinciale 10 (℡0565.920.196). Motorboats shuttle across the bay to the sandy beach at **Naregno**.

CAPOLIVERI, 3.5km southwest of Porto Azzurro and overlooked by Monte Calamita, is the best of the towns on Elba's eastern fringe, a prosperous inland centre whose close-knit lanes have made few concessions to tourism. Capoliveri makes an ideal base for visits south to the fine **beaches** at Morcone, Pareti and Innamorata, but **accommodation** is limited: try the comfortable two-star *Villa*

Miramare in Pareti (☎0565.968.673, ⓦwww.hotelvillamiramare.it; ❸). The *Sugar Reef* **bar** and music venue 1km south of Capoliveri at La Trappola (ⓦwww .sugar-reef.com) feeds the town's nightlife, with dance parties all summer long (daily 11pm–5am). In summer, municipal minibuses run hourly between Capoliveri and nearby beach towns until 1am.

Western Elba

The main road west from Portoferraio heads to prim **MARCIANA MARINA**, whose traffic-filled promenade of bars, restaurants and trinket shops does little to lure you into staying. However, you can **rent a bike** or scooter for a trip inland from TWN, Via Dussol 45 (☎0565.997.027), and access the **Internet** at Foto Berti, Via Cavour 5 (daily 9am–1pm, 5–8pm & 9–11.30pm; ☎0565.997.053). Aquavision (☎0328.709.5470) operates sea trips on the **M/N Nautilus**, which has glass panels below the waterline.

A winding road heads south for 5km into the hills to **POGGIO**, a village renowned for its mineral water and medieval centre, with decorated doorways and a patchwork of cheerful gardens. One of Elba's leading **restaurants**, *Da Publius*, Piazza XX Settembre 13 (☎0565.99.208; closed Mon), has great views and steep prices for its classic Elban cooking (including *cacciucco* and wild boar with mushrooms).

Marciana and Monte Capanne

The high, isolated village of **MARCIANA**, up 4km of switchbacks from Poggio, is the oldest settlement and most alluring place on Elba, perfectly located between great beaches and the mountainous interior. Its steep **old quarter** is a delight of narrow alleys, arches, belvederes and stone stairs festooned with flowers and climbing plants that culminate at the twelfth-century **Fortezza Pisano** (closed to the public, but with great views from its lofty location). The best **restaurant** is the award-winning *Osteria del Noce*, high up at Via della Madonna 19 (☎0565.901.284; open daily March–Sept; ⓦwww.osteriadelnoce .it), with excellent mid-priced food and a terrace with spectacular views. Way up beside the Fortezza at Via del Pretorio 64 is little *Monilli*, a bar and *paninoteca* open daily until 2am, perched over a wooded hillside.

Walks around Marciana

Various **walking** trails head out from Marciana, both up to Monte Capanne and on scenic, quiet routes down to the coast. Before setting off, you should pick up the local *Comunità Montana* **map** from the Portoferraio tourist office (see p.566), and make sure you have water and a sunhat.

Trail #1 is a circular route starting from the southern end of the village, which passes the fifteenth-century **Oratorio di San Cerbone** (1hr) and continues beyond the junction with trail #6 up to the summit of the mountain (where you could take the *cabinovia* down again); you then retrace your steps and take trail #6 west across open country to La Stretta, then skirt Monte Giove back to Marciana (total 8.5km; 4hr 30min).

A different route heads uphill west of Marciana – the path begins at the *Osteria del Noce* – for about 30min to the **Santuario della Madonna del Monte**, the Island's most celebrated shrine, a Renaissance church built to house a stone mysteriously painted with an image of the Virgin. From the church, trail #3 again skirts round Monte Giove to La Stretta, then continues jigging on switchbacks west and down through fragrant woodland and scrub to hit the coast at **Chiessi** (total 12km; 6hr).

The main draw of Marciana is 500m south of the village – the base-station of a **cabinovia** (cable car) that climbs 650m to the summit of **Monte Capanne** (1018m), Elba's highest point (daily: June–Sept 10am–12.15pm & 2.30–6pm; Oct–May 10am–12.15pm & 2.30–5.30pm; €12 return). Note that "cable car" is something of a misnomer: it's a series of small exposed cages, each of which is big enough for two people to stand up in, hooked onto a continually running cable: the open-air ride might give you the jitters lifting you slowly above the wooded hills and eventually above the tree line to a levelled platform with a café. From here, it's a short scramble to the summit, from where the views are suitably stupendous. Another local attraction is one of Tuscany's very few **vegetarian restaurants**, *Vegetariano alla Cabinovia* (☏0565.901.029; closed in winter), by a brook in the woods alongside the *cabinovia* base-station, which boasts an affordable menu including falafel, wholewheat pasta and organic wine.

The western coast and Marina di Campo

The spread-out village of **SANT'ANDREA**, 6km northwest of Marciana, just off the coast road, is one of Elba's trendiest retreats, with divers drawn here by the crystal-clear seas. **Hotels** are not expensive, most of them discreetly set amid near-tropical vegetation; just above the beach is the eco-friendly *Ilio* (☏0565.908.018, ⓦwww.ilio.it; ❸), which uses all biodegradable materials and has a helpful manager and delicious breakfasts and dinners. A little west, the road hugs the coast for a lonely, scenic drive round to **CHIESSI** and **POMONTE**, each with a small stony beach, beautifully clear water and little commercialism. By **FETOVAIA** on the southwestern tip of the Island you're back to beach development, but the sandy beach is superb – and a big car park prevents some of the chaos of other Elban resorts. About 2km east of Fetovaia is a stretch of **nudist** beach.

    MARINA DI CAMPO was the first resort on Elba and is now the largest. The huge white **beach** and clean water are what make the place suffocatingly popular. There's also all the tourist frippery and nightlife you'd expect in any major seaside centre, as well as a **tourist office**, Piazza dei Granatieri (Mon–Wed, Fri & Sat 8am–8pm; ☏0565.977.969). Internet Planet on Via Carducci has **Internet** access (daily 10am–midnight). The moderately priced **restaurant** *L'Aragosta*, Via Bologna 3 (closed winter), has fresh fish served daily, while *Il Gazebo*, Piazzetta Torino, is a **bar** specializing in wholewheat panini, pizzas, *calzoni* and hot-dogs.

Capraia

CAPRAIA, 30km northwest of Elba, is a lovely and largely unspoilt island. Its former use as a penal colony (up until 1996) ensured that the terrain remained largely untouched, and the local council has since backed environmental protection. The scrubby, almost tree-less island has a knobbly spine of 400m hills, with the eastern slope shallow and riven with valleys, and the western coast featuring cliffs rising almost sheer from the sea. Most people come for the excellent deep-sea **diving**. Toremar **ferries** run from Livorno (at least 1 daily; takes 2hr 30min; €10) – their pre-sunrise service (Thurs 4.50am summer only) is a memorable way to make the crossing. You can also make the crossing with Linee di Navigazione Arcipelago Toscano from Porto Azzurro (☏0565.921.009, ⓦwww.elbacrociere.com) or from Portoferraio (☏0565.914.797).

    From the harbour to the village of **CAPRAIA ISOLA**, overlooked by the **Fortezza di San Giorgio**, is a gentle walk. The Pro Loco **tourist office** is on

Via Assunzione (no fixed hours; ☎0586.905.138).The Cooperativa Parco Naturale, Via Assunzione 42 (☎0586.905.071, ✉agparco@tin.it), **rents out boats**.
The Capraia Diving Service at Via Assunzione 72 (☎0586.905.137, ⓦwww
.capraiadiving.it) has equipment for rent and organizes courses and dives to
some excellent sites off the island's east coast.The main **hotel** is the comfortable four-star *Il Saracino*, Via L. Cibo 40 (☎0586.905.018, ⓕ0586.905.062;
❹), although there's also the small, attractive *Pensione Da Beppone* near the
water (☎0586.905.001, ⓕ0586.905.842; ❸), numerous private rooms, and
the **campsite** *Le Sughere* (☎ & ⓕ0586.905.066, ⓦwww.campeggiolesughere
.it; May–Sept) behind the church. One of the best **restaurants** is the
moderately priced *Vecchio Scorfano*, Via Assunzione 44 (closed winter). A
good, well-signposted **walk** leads up from the village into the uninhabited
interior, passing springs and – on a branch trail – an isolated tarn known as
Lo Stagnone.The path goes up to **Il Semaforo**, just below the summit of
Monte Arpagna (410m), where a ravine between peaks gives a stunning view
westwards across open water to Corsica.The rough trail heads steeply down
to a lighthouse on the rugged western coast. Alongside a watchtower on the
southernmost tip of land is the narrow inlet of **Cala Rossa** – a spectacular
place to swim, in sparkling clear water beneath cliffs of fiery red.

The Maremma coast

The **Maremma** is a term derived from *maríttima* and refers to the coastal strip
and inland hills of the Provincia di Grosseto, Tuscany's southernmost province.
This was the northern heartland of the Etruscans but was depopulated in the
Middle Ages as wars disrupted the drainage schemes and allowed malarial
swamps to build up behind the dunes.The area became almost synonymous
with disease, and nineteenth-century guides advised strongly against a visit
– even so, *butteri* cowboys roamed freely then, as now, taking care of the region's
half-feral horses and its celebrated white cattle.Today, the provincial capital of
Grosseto remains pretty uninspiring, though there are some patches of fine
scenery – notably the **Monti dell'Uccellina**, protected in the **Parco Naturale
della Maremma**, and the wooded peninsula of **Monte Argentario**.

Grosseto and around

Until the mid-nineteenth century, **GROSSETO** was a malaria-ridden back-
water.The draining of the marshes, however, which was finally effected under
Mussolini, began the transformation of the town into a provincial capital for
the Maremma. Grosseto was rebuilt after the war with a rash of dreary condo-
miniums and is deservedly undervisited, though you may well find yourself
passing through.

Piazza Dante, at the heart of the old town, has a quirky statue showing
Leopoldo II protecting Mother Maremma and crushing the serpent malaria
under his foot.The adjacent **Duomo** was started in 1294 but virtually nothing
is left to suggest antiquity: the white-and-pink marble facade is a product of the
nineteenth century, while the interior has suffered repeated modifications. Its
finest artworks are on display in the **Museo Archeologico**, Piazza Baccarini
3 (May–Oct Tues–Sun 10am–1pm & 5–8pm; Nov–Feb Tues–Fri 9am–1pm,
Sat & Sun 9am–1pm & 4–6pm; March & April Tues–Sun 9am–1pm & 4–6pm;
€8). Most interest is in rooms 24–34, the **Museo d'Arte Sacra**, with a handful of good Sienese paintings, notably Sassetta's *Madonna of the Cherries* and a

Byzantine *Last Judgement* by Guido da Siena. The church of **San Francesco**, just north of the museum, has a few patches of fresco and an early crucifix by Duccio, and from here you can walk round the **walls**, a trip of about forty minutes and one of the more rewarding things Grosseto has to offer.

Most mainline **trains** on the Pisa–Rome coastal line stop in Grosseto, where you can change for Siena or Orbetello. The **tourist office** is inconveniently situated out of town at Via Monterosa 206 (Mon–Fri 8.30am–2.30pm & 3–6pm, Sat 8.30am–12.30pm; ☎0564.462.611, ⓦwww.grosseto.turismo .toscana.it); they have information on the whole province. To reach the **old town**, head up Via Roma from the station past a Fascist-era post office and piazza. Central **hotels** include the *Appennino*, Viale Mameli 1 (☎0564.23.009, ⓕ0564.416.134; ➋).

The Monti dell'Uccellina

The hills and coastline of the **Monti dell'Uccellina**, 12km south of Grosseto, are protected as the **Parco Naturale Regionale della Maremma** (ⓦwww .parco-maremma.it), set to be upgraded to a Parco Nazionale – recognition for an area that, it is claimed, is the last virgin coastal landscape on the Italian peninsula. This breathtaking piece of countryside combines cliffs, coastal marsh, *macchia*, forest-covered hills, pristine beaches and some of the most beautiful stands of umbrella pines in the country. It is a microcosm of all that's best in the Maremma, devoid of the bars, marinas, hotels, roads and half-finished houses that have destroyed much of the Italian littoral. There's no public road access – all drivers should park in **ALBERESE** (scene, in August, of a *butteri* rodeo), near the Visitors' Centre on Via del Fante (☎0564.407.098, ⓔparcomar@gol .grosseto.it). RAMA city **buses** #15, #16 and #17 run irregularly from Grosseto station to Alberese (Mon–Sat); otherwise, take a taxi (€15).

Admission to the park (daily: July to Sept 7.30am–dusk; Oct–June 9am–dusk; €6) secures a basic **map** and a place on an hourly bus that runs from the entrance, 10km into the hills, dropping you at the trailhead at **Pratini**. From Pratini, you're left to your own devices, or you can book ahead for a place on a three- or five-hour **guided walk** (summer only; tour in English Friday 4.30pm; €8). Most people head straight onto the *Strada degli Olivi*, which leads to the superb **beach**, an idyllic curving bay backed by cliffs and wooded hills. The circular **Trail A1** (*San Rabano*; 6km; 5hr) climbs a ridge and passes the ivy-covered eleventh-century ruined abbey of San Rabano. The last return buses from Pratini or Alberese are around 6.30pm in summer, earlier in winter. For **horse riding**, **canoeing** or **bike rental** in the park contact Il Rialto Centro Turismo Equestre (☎0565.407.102, ⓔilrialto@katamail.com).

Monte Argentario

The high, rocky terrain of **Monte Argentario** (ⓦwww.monteargentario.it), 37km south of Grosseto, is as close to wilderness as southern Tuscany comes. The interior is mountainous, reaching 635m at its highest point, and the coast is sectioned dramatically into headlands, bays and shingle beaches. Much of the area is still uninhabited scrub and woodland, badly prone to forest fires but still excellent walking country.

Long ago, Monte Argentario was an island. Over several thousand years, inshore currents built up two narrow sand spits (*tomboli*) between the mountain and the mainland, creating a lagoon between them. The ancient town of **Orbetello** occupied a peninsula sticking out into the lagoon; then the Romans built a causeway to link Orbetello to the Argentario, forming a third spit of land

The Tarot Garden

Bang on the Lazio border 20km east of Orbetello, in a landscape of dust, scrub and clammy heat, is one of the oddest and most engaging works of modern art in the region. The Gaudi-esque **Giardino dei Tarocchi**, or Tarot Garden, is the life-long dream of Niki de St-Phalle, wife of the late Swiss artist Jean Tinguely. Since 1978, St-Phalle has been devoting herself to constructing this physical interpretation of the tarot deck – chunky, brightly coloured cartoon figures of the **Devil**, the **Guardian Angel**, the **Hanged Man** and others loom well above the treetops, arranged around a curvaceous, arcaded **courtyard** tiled in shards of mirror and shimmering, multi-coloured plastic. The symbolism of the garden may be obscure, but kids of all ages will love it. The garden has limited **opening hours** (April to mid-Oct daily 2.30–7.30pm; €10.50; mid-Oct to March first Sat of month 9am–1pm; free; ☎0564.895.122, ⓦwww .nikidesaintphalle.com). There's no public **transport**, but the sculptures are visible about 1km north of the main Livorno–Rome "Via Aurelia" highway, near the village of Pescia Fiorentina. The nearest **train station** is Chiarone, 4km south – a **taxi** from here will save on the €25 fare you're likely to run up if you come from Orbetello.

and dividing the lagoon in two. Orbetello's strange location is the most exciting thing about it, and on summer weekends the roads over the northern Tombolo della Giannella sandbar and through Orbetello become bottlenecks as tourists pile in to resorts such as **Porto Ercole**.

Orbetello and around

ORBETELLO is an unassuming place, graced with palm trees, the pastel-coloured remnants of its Spanish walls, and a lively *passeggiata* each evening along its main street, Corso Italia. It was probably Etruria's leading port, though little evidence of an ancient past remains: the sixteenth-century Spanish fortifications are the town's most conspicuous feature. The **train station** is 4km east at Orbetello Scalo. **Buses** originating in Rome or Grosseto run from Orbetello station to the bus stops near the **tourist office** at Piazza della Repubblica 1 (Mon–Sat 10am–12.30pm & 4.30–8.30pm; ☎0564.860.447, ⓦwww.proloco-orbetello.it). Best **hotel** is the simple, friendly and very central *Piccolo Parigi*, Corso Italia 169 (☎0564.867.233, ⓕ0564.867.211; ❷). Most of the area's thirteen **campsites** are on and around the lagoon; plump for the *Feniglia* (☎0564.831.090, open all year), the only site on the southern Tombolo di Feniglia. One of Orbetello's best fish **restaurants** is the moderately priced *Osteria il Nocchino*, just behind Piazza della Repubblica on Via Furio Lenzi (☎0564.860.329; open weekends only in winter), otherwise there's plenty of choice on and around the main Corso Italia.

Roads from Orbetello head north and south around the base of Monte Argentario. On the south side is intimate **PORTO ERCOLE**, with an attractive old quarter and a fishing-village atmosphere. Though founded by the Romans, its chief historical monuments are two **Spanish fortresses**, facing each other across the harbour. At the entrance to the old town, a plaque on the stone gate commemorates the painter **Caravaggio**, who in 1610 keeled over with sunstroke on a beach nearby and died of a fever; he was buried in the parish church of Sant'Erasmo. From the village, you can easily **walk** across the Tombolo di Feniglia, which is barred to traffic and is a prime spot for birdwatching over the lagoon. Finest **restaurant** for fish and seafood is the classy *Gambero Rosso*, Lungomare Andrea Doria (☎0564.832.650; closed Wed).

8

TUSCANY | The Maremma coast

573

Siena and around

SIENA is the perfect antidote to Florence, a unified, modern city at ease with its medieval aspect, ambience and traditions – indeed, exultant about them. It's a place not easily read by outsiders, and to get anything meaningful from a visit you'll need to stay at least one night; too many visitors breeze through on a day-trip.

Self-contained behind its medieval walls, Siena's great attraction is its cityscape, a majestic Gothic ensemble that could be enjoyed without venturing into a single museum. The physical and spiritual heart of the city is the great scallop-shaped piazza **Il Campo**, loveliest of all Italian squares and scene of the thrilling **Palio** bareback horserace. Siena's **Duomo** and **Palazzo Pubblico** are two of the purest examples of Italian Gothic architecture, and the best of the city's paintings – collected in the **Museo Civico** and **Pinacoteca Nazionale** – are in the same tradition; the finest example of Sienese Gothic is Duccio's *Maestà*, on show in the outstanding **Museo dell'Opera Metropolitana**. More frescoes fill the halls of **Santa Maria della Scala**, the city's hospital for over 900 years and now its premier exhibition space.

The most popular trip from Siena is northwest to the picturesque multi-towered village of **San Gimignano**. Far fewer people take the trouble to sample the ancient Etruscan town of **Volterra**, a highly rewarding stop en route west from Siena to Pisa.

Some history

Though established as a Roman colony by Augustus, it wasn't until the twelfth and thirteenth centuries that Siena, for a hundred years or so, became one of the major cities of Europe. Virtually the size of Paris, it controlled most of southern Tuscany and its wool industry, dominated the trade routes between France and Rome, and maintained Italy's richest pre-Medici banks. This era reached an apotheosis with the defeat of a much superior Florentine army at the battle of **Montaperti** in 1260. Although the result was reversed permanently nine years later, Siena embarked on an unrivalled urban development under the guidance of its mercantile governors, the **Council of Nine**. From 1287 to 1355 the city underwrote the completion of its cathedral and then the Campo and its exuberant Palazzo Pubblico. The prosperity came to an abrupt halt with the **Black Death**, which reached Siena in May 1348; by October, two-thirds of the 100,000 population had died. The city never fully recovered (the population today is 60,000) and its politics, always factional, descended into chaos. In 1557 Philip II gave up Siena to **Cosimo de' Medici** in lieu of war services, and the city subsequently became part of Cosimo's Grand Duchy of Tuscany. The lack of subsequent development explains Siena's astonishing state of preservation: little was built and still less demolished. Since World War II, Siena has again become prosperous, owing partly to **tourism** and partly to the resurgence of the **Monte dei Paschi di Siena**. This bank, founded in Siena in 1472 and currently the city's largest employer, is one of the major players in Italian finance. It today sponsors much of Siena's cultural life, coexisting, apparently easily, with one of Italy's strongest left-wing councils.

Arrival and information

Siena's **train station** is 2km northwest of town. It has a counter selling city bus tickets (Mon–Sat 5.50am–7.30pm; €0.75). To get into town, you can either walk, which takes a good 20–25 minutes, or cross the road and take just about any city **bus** heading left (#3, #9 to Tozzi; #4, #7, #8, #14, #17, #77 to Garibaldi/Sale; #10 to Gramsci), all of which drop off at Piazza Gramsci on the northern edge of the centre. Most **intercity buses** arrive on Viale Tozzi, the road running alongside Piazza Gramsci, or at La Lizza nearby, but note that many now avoid the centre and terminate at the train station instead. Coming from Florence **by train**, you may need to change at Empoli (takes 1hr 45min); **by bus**, there are hourly TRA-IN or SITA expresses (takes 1hr 15min). The **tourist office** is at no. 56 on the Campo (Mon–Sun 9am–7pm; ☏0577.280.551, ⓦwww.terresiena.it).

Accommodation

Finding **accommodation** is barely less of a struggle than in Florence. An alternative to contacting hotels directly is to let **Siena Hotels Promotion** do the work for you – phone, fax or email bookings through them for any of the city's thirty-odd hotels are free (☏0577.288.084, ⓦwww.hotelsiena.com). If you arrive without a reservation, go to their booth on Piazza Madre Teresa di Calcutta in front of San Domenico (Mon–Sat 9am–8pm; winter closes 7pm), where over-the-counter bookings for the same night cost €1.55. **Vacanze Senesi** offers a similar service, based within the Parcheggio Il Campo parking garage, south of the centre at Via Fontanella 9 (Mon–Fri 9am–1pm & 3–7pm, Sat 9am–1pm; ☏0577.45.900, ⓦwww.vacanzesenesi.it). Note that hotels are booked solid at **Palio** time (early July & mid-Aug). Hotels tend to be rather plain, knowing that they can largely rely on the city's attractions for customers.

Hotels

Bernini Via della Sapienza 15 ☏0577.289.047, ⓦwww.albergobernini.com. Friendly, well-situated one-star hotel near San Domenico, with good-value rooms – some with shared bathrooms – and a roof terrace with a fantastic view over Siena. Midnight curfew. ❷

Cannon d'Oro Via Montanini 28 ☏0577.44.321, ⓦwww.cannondoro.com. A stylish, friendly and well-maintained thirty-room hotel, tucked down an alleyway east of Piazza Matteotti. ❸

Centrale Via C Angiolieri 26 ☏0577.280.379, ⓔhotelcentrale.siena@libero.it. A block north of the Campo, up on the third floor, this place has friendly staff and a good location, but no lift. ❸

Certosa di Maggiano Via Certosa 82 ☏0577.288.180, ⓦwww.certosadi maggiano.com. Surely Siena's most beautiful hotel, this former monastery in the countryside 1km southeast of the centre is absolutely stunning with large, elegant rooms surrounding the central cloister, above which peers the (still functioning) belltower. There's also a library, a swimming pool and a fantastically swanky restaurant. Prices are equally fantastic. ❾

Chiusarelli Viale Curtatone 15 ☏0577.280.562, ⓦwww.chiusarelli.com. Pleasant and friendly old three-star hotel with fifty airy rooms, a garden and private parking, steps from Piazza Matteotti. ❹

Duomo Via Stalloreggi 38 ☏0577.289.088, ⓦwww.hotelduomo.it. Pleasant hotel in a grand old building, located in a residential area. Rooms have air conditioning but are unremarkable, other than those with rooftop views of the Duomo. Free parking at Parcheggio Il Campo. ❹

Garibaldi Via Duprè 18 ☏0577.284.204. Seven no-nonsense rooms above a quality low-price trattoria just a few strides south of the Campo. Midnight curfew. ❸

La Perla Via delle Terme 25 ☏0577.47.144, ⓦwww.hotellaperlasiena.com. Regular one-star *pensione* with all en-suite rooms, in a very central location overlooking Piazza Indipendenza. Curfew 1am. ❶

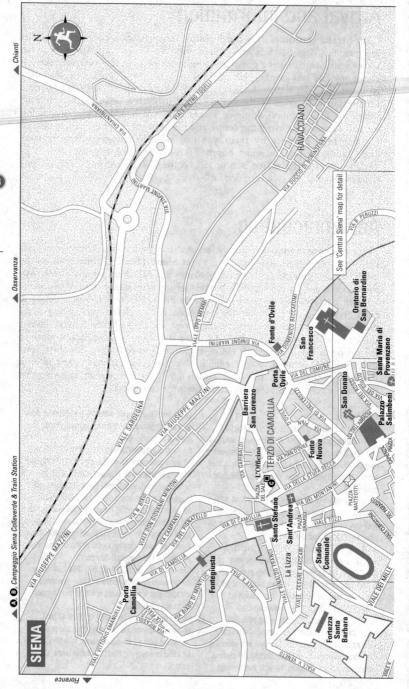

576

SIENA

N

▲ Chianti

▲ Osservanza

▲ ▲, ⓐ, ⓑ Campeggio Siena Colleverde & Train Station

◀ Florence

VIA CHIANTIGIANA

VIALE PIETRO TOSELLI

VIA DUCCIO DI BONINSEGNA

RAVACCIANO

VIA B. PERUZZI

VIALE SIMONE MARTINI

See 'Central Siena' map for detail

Oratorio di
San Bernardino

Santa Maria di
Provenzano

VIA LIPPO MEMMI

VIA SIMONE MARTINI

Fonte d'Ovile

VIA DOMENICO BECCAFUMI

San
Francesco

San Donato

Palazzo
Salimbeni

VIALE GIUSEPPE MAZZINI

VIALE SARDEGNA

VIA GIUSEPPE MAZZINI

Barriera
San Lorenzo

VIA DEL COMUNE

Porta
Ovile

VIA DEL GIGLIO

VIA DEI ROSSI

VIA BANCHI DI SOPRA

PIAZZA
SALIMBENI

VIA GARIBALDI

TERZO DI CAMOLLIA

VIA DI VALLEROZZI

VIA DI PIAN D'OVILE

VIA PIAN

L'Officina

PIAZZA
DEL SALE

Fonte
Nuova

VIA DELLA STUFA SECCA

VIALE DON GIOVANNI MINZONI

VIA N. BIXIO

VIA CAMPANSI

VIA DEL PIGNATTELLO

VIA DI CAMOLLIA

Santo Stefano

Sant'Andrea

PIAZZA
GRAMSCI

VIA DEI MONTANINI

PIAZZA
MATTEOTTI

VIALE TOZZI

DEI PARADISO

VIA DI CAMOLLIA

La Lizza

Stadio
Comunale

VIALE CARLO PISACANE

VIALE X SETTEMBRE

VIALE DEI MILLE

VIALE RINALDO FRANCI

Porta
Camollia

Fontegiusta

VIA FONTEBRANDA

VIA DI DIACCETO DI MONTLUC

VIALE CESARE MACCARI

VIALE V. VENETO

Fortezza
Santa Barbara

VIALE VITTORIO EMANUELE II

VIA RIPA DI SOTTO

VIA RIPA D'SOPRA

VIALE

ⓒ

▲ Arezzo

▼ Buonconvento

▼ Autostrada

▼ Autostrada

ACCOMMODATION

Certosa di Maggiano	F
Ostello Guidoriccio	B
Palazzo Ravizza	D
Piccolo Hotel Il Palio	C
Santa Caterina	E
Villa Scacciapensieri	A

0   200 m

VIA ENEA SILVIO PICCOLOMINI

Porta Pispini

San Raimondo

Santo Spirito

San Giovannino
della Staffa

Palazzo Piccolomini

Logge del Papa

San Martino

San Giorgio

Palazzo
Bianchi

Santa Maria
dei Servi

Porta
Romana

TERZO DI SAN MARTINO

San Cristoforo

San Virgilio

Loggia d.
Mercanzia

Palazzo
Pubblico

IL CAMPO

Museo
dell'Opera
del Duomo

Palazzo
delle
Papesse

Pinacoteca
Nazionale

San Giuseppe

San
Pietro

Sant'Agostino

Parcheggio
Il Campo

Orto
Botanico

Porta Tufi

VIA ROMA

VIA DEI PISPINI

VIA DI SALICOTTO

VIA DI PORTA GIUSTIZIA

Santa
Caterina

Fonte-
branda

San
Domenico

Porta
Fontebranda

Duomo

Ospedale di
Santa Maria
della Scala

San Sebastiano

TERZO DI CITTÀ

Palazzo
Pollini

Santa Maria
del Carmine

Parcheggio
Il Duomo

Porta
Laterina

Porta S. Marco

San Niccolò
e Lucia

VIA DELLA SPERANDIE

VIA DI S. QUIRICO

Palazzo Bruchi Via Pantaneto 105
ⓣ0577.287.342, ⓦwww.palazzobruchi.it. Housed
in a seventeenth century *palazzo*, this is a real
bargain run by a friendly mother and daughter
team. Lovely bright rooms. ❷

Palazzo Ravizza Pian dei Mantellini 34
ⓣ0577.280.462, ⓦwww.palazzoravizza.it. Genteel
old-style hotel in a pleasant backwater of town. It
has a quality restaurant and charming little garden
for afternoon tea. Free parking. ❹

Piccolo Hotel Etruria Via delle Donzelle 3
ⓣ0577.288.088, ⓦwww.hoteletruria.com.
Small, central place, with some poky rooms and a
12.30am curfew, but with parking nearby. ❸

Piccolo Hotel Il Palio Piazza del Sale 19
ⓣ0577.281.131, ⓦwww.piccolohotelilpalio.it.
Perfectly located for bus arrivals (right near all
the bus stops), but 200m north of the centre, with
clean, good-sized rooms and extremely friendly
staff. ❹

Santa Caterina Via E.S. Piccolomini 7
ⓣ0577.221.105, ⓦwww.hscsiena.it. A three-star

hotel, ten minutes' walk southeast of the Campo,
with the benefit of air conditioning and private
parking. ❻

Villa Scacciapensieri Via di Scacciapensieri 10
ⓣ0577.41.441, ⓦwww.villascacciapensieri.it.
Converted country villa 3km north of Siena, with
great views and every luxury including a pool. ❼

Hostel and campsite

Campeggio Siena Colleverde Strada di
Scacciapensieri 47 ⓣ0577.280.044,
ⓕ0577.333.298. Secure, well-maintained
campsite, 2km north of town (bus #3 or #8), with
a pool. Mid-March to mid-Nov.

Ostello Guidoriccio Via Fiorentina 89, Stellino
ⓣ0577.52.212, ⓔsiena.aighostel@virgilio.it.
Non-HI 111-bed hostel, 2km northwest of the
centre; take bus #3, #10 or #15 from Piazza
Matteotti or, if you're coming from Florence, ask
the bus driver to let you off at "Lo Stellino" (just
after the Siena city sign). Curfew 11pm.

The City

Everything is easily walkable from Siena's great central square, **Il Campo**,
which is built at the intersection of a configuration of hills that looks, on the
map, like an upside-down Y. Each arm of the Y counts as one of the city's *terzi*,
or thirds, and each has its principal thoroughfare, leading out from the Campo
on elevated ridges: humdrum **Banchi di Sotto** in the Terzo di San Martino
on the southeast; bustling, shop-lined **Via di Città** in the Terzo di Città on the
southwest; and elegant **Banchi di Sopra** in the Terzo di Camollia on the north.
The central core of alleys – almost entirely medieval in plan and appearance, and
closed to traffic – can get a little disorienting, and it's surprisingly easy to lose
your fix on the Campo, masked as it is by high buildings. The huge **Duomo**

Siena's museums

Siena has a full deck of excellent-value discounted **museum passes**. They're on sale
at all of the participating museums, but all permit only a single entry to each place.

Two-day passes
Museo Civico (not the tower), Santa Maria della Scala, Palazzo delle Papesse – €10.
Winter Art Itinerary (Nov to mid-March): Museo Civico (not the tower), Santa Maria
della Scala, Palazzo delle Papesse, Museo dell'Opera Metropolitana, Duomo and
Libreria Piccolomini, Baptistry – €13.

Seven-day passes
Summer Art Itinerary (mid-March to Oct): everything included in the two-day pass, plus
Chiesa di Sant'Agostino, Oratorio di San Bernardino and Museo Diocesano – €16.

   The **Pinacoteca Nazionale** is run by a separate body from all the above, and is not
included on any of the passes.

The **Siena Palio** (Ⓦwww.comune.siena.it) is the most spectacular festival event in Italy: a twice-yearly bareback horse race around the Campo, preceded by days of preparation, medieval pageantry and chicanery. Only ten of the seventeen *contrade* can take part in any one race; these are chosen by lot, and their horses and jockeys are also assigned at random. The seven that miss out are automatically entitled to run in the following year's race. The only rule is that riders cannot interfere with each others' reins. Otherwise, anything goes: each *contrada* has a traditional rival, and ensuring that it loses is as important as winning oneself. Jockeys may be bribed to throw the race or whip a rival or a rival's horse; *contrade* have been known to drug horses and even to ambush a jockey on his way to the race. This is primarily a show for the Sienese; for visitors, in fact, the undercurrent of brutality and the bragging, days-long celebration of victory can be quite a shock.

The race has been held since at least the thirteenth century. Originally it followed a circuit through the town, but since the sixteenth century it has consisted of three laps of the **Campo**, around a track covered with sand and padded with mattresses to minimize injury to riders and horses (though this does occur, and the Palio is a passionate subject for animal-rights supporters). There are two Palios a year, with the following build-up:

June 29 and August 13: The year's horses are presented in the morning at the town hall and drawn by lot. At 7.15pm the first trial race is held in the Campo.

June 30 and August 14: Further trial races at 9am and 7.45pm.

July 1 and August 15: Two more trial races at 9am and 7.45pm, followed by a street banquet in each of the *contrade*.

July 2 and August 16: The day of the Palio opens with the *messa del Fantino* (jockeys' mass), held by the archbishop in the chapel beside the Palazzo Pubblico, before a final trial at 9am. In the early afternoon each *contrada* takes its horse to be blessed in its church (it's a good omen if the horse shits). At around 5pm the Palazzo Publico's bell begins to ring and riders and *comparse* – equerries, ensigns, pages and drummers in medieval costume – proceed to the Campo for a display of flag-twirling and other pageantry. The **race** itself begins at 7.45pm on July 2, or 7pm on August 16, and lasts little more than ninety seconds. There's no PA system to tell you what's going on. At the start (in the northwest corner of the Campo) all the horses except one are penned between two ropes; the free one charges the group from behind, when its rivals least expect it, and the race is on. It's a hectic and violent spectacle; a horse that throws its rider is still eligible to win. The jockeys don't stop at the finishing line but keep going at top speed out of the Campo, pursued by a frenzied mass of supporters. The **palio** – a silk banner – is subsequently presented to the winner.

There are viciously expensive stands for dignitaries and the rich (booked months ahead), but most spectators crowd for free into the centre of the Campo. For the **best view**, you need to have found a position on the inner rail by 2pm (ideally at the start/finish line), but be prepared to stand your ground; people keep pouring in right up until a few minutes before the race, and the swell of the crowd can be quite overwhelming. Toilets, shade and refreshments are minimal, and you won't be able to leave the Campo until at least 8.30pm. **Hotel rooms** are extremely difficult to find, and if you haven't booked, reckon on either staying up all night or travelling in from a neighbouring town. The races are shown live on national TV and repeated endlessly all evening.

The Cinema Moderno on Piazza Tolomei (May–Oct Mon–Sat) regularly screens a twenty-minute **film** explaining the history and drama of the race, dubbed into various languages.

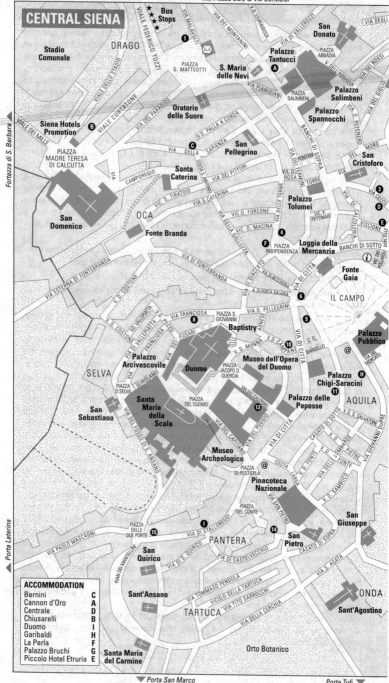

CENTRAL SIENA

Piazza Gramsci & La Lizza

Piazza Sale & Via Garibaldi

Stadio Comunale

DRAGO

Bus Stops

San Donato

PIAZZA ABBADIA

VIA DEL ROSSI

VIALE FEDERICO TOZZI

VIA MALAVOLTI

VIA DEI MONTANINI

VIA DI VALLEROZZI

VIA DEGLI

VIA DI RUFFASCA

PIAZZA G. MATTEOTTI

Palazzo Tantucci **A**

S. Maria delle Nevi

VIALE DELLO STADIO

VIA PIANIGIANI

PIAZZA SALIMBENI

Palazzo Salimbeni

Palazzo Spannocchi

VIA DEL GIGLIO

VIA DI REGENRO

VIALE DEI MILLE

Forteza di S. Barbara

Siena Hotels Promotion **B**

VIALE CURTATONE

VIA DEL PARADISO

Oratorio delle Suore

V.D. PALLA A CORDA

V.D. SAPIENZA

VIA DELLA

San Pellegrino

BANCHI DI SOPRA

VIA DEL MORO

San Cristoforo

PIAZZA MADRE TERESA DI CALCUTTA

VIA CAMPOREGIO

VIA DELLA SAPIENZA

COSTA S. ANTONIO

VIA DEI PITTORI

Santa Caterina

VIA DELLE TERME

VIA PONTANI

VIL D. TERMINI

VIA DI CECCO **3**

VIA DI CALZOLERIA

D

E

VISCIONE

San Domenico

OCA

VIC. D. TIRATOIO

VIA S. CATERINA

VIA DELLA GALLUZZA

VIC. D. FORCONE

VIC. D. MACINA

Palazzo Tolomei

TORRE

VIC. P. PETTINAIO

4

Loggia della Mercanzia

BANCHI DI SOTTO

VIC. DI PIAZZI

i

Fonte Branda

VIA DI FONTEBRANDA

PIAZZA INDIPENDENZA

F

VIA DI DIACCETO

VIA DI BECCHERIA

VIA DI CITTA

Fonte Gaia

VIA ESTERNA DI FONTEBRANDA

V.D. COSTONE

A. DI PORTA SALARIA

6

IL CAMPO

Porta Laterina

VIA FRANCIOSA

VO. VALLEPIATTA

V.D. POZZO

V.D. COSTONE

FRANCIOSA

VIA DEI FUSARI

PIAZZA S. GIOVANNI

Baptistry

V.D. MONNA

V.D. AGNESE

8

9

VIA DI CITTA

C. Q.

BARGELLO

Palazzo Pubblico

SELVA

Palazzo Arcivescovile

PIAZZA JACOPO D. QUERCIA

Duomo

10

Museo dell'Opera del Duomo

H

@

VIA DEL MERCO

San Sebastiano

PIAZZA D.SELVA

PIAZZA D. GIROLAMO

Santa Maria della Scala

PIAZZA DEL DUOMO

12

VIA DEL CASTORO

Palazzo delle Papesse

Palazzo Chigi-Saracini

11

AQUILA

V.D. S. SALVATORE

San Pietro

VIA DEL FOSSO DI S. ANSANO

Museo Archeologico

VIA DEL CAPITANO

VIA DEL POGGIO

VIA DI CITTA

CASATO DI SOTTO

V.D. GIOVANNI DUPRE

PIAZZA DI POSTIERLA

@

Pinacoteca Nazionale

COSTA LARGA

V.D. FONTE

VIA DELLE FONTE

V.D. LOMBARDI

PIETRE

V.D. SAMBUCO

San Giuseppe

PIAZZA DEL CONTE

VIA SAN PIETRO

PIAZZA DELLE DUE PORTE

15

I

VIA DI STALLOREGGI

14

San Pietro

CASATO DI SOPRA

San Quirico

PIAN DEI MANTELLINI

VIA PAOLO MASCAGNI

VIA DI S. QUIRICO

PANTERA

VIA DI CASTELVECCHIO

VIA S. AGATA

Sant'Ansano

VIA TOMMASO PENDOLA

VICOLO DELLA TARTUCA

VIA TITO SARROCCHI

TARTUCA

VIA DELLA CERCHIA

ONDA

Sant'Agostino

Santa Maria del Carmine

Orto Botanico

Porta San Marco

Porta Tufi

8

TUSCANY

ACCOMMODATION

Bernini	C
Cannon d'Oro	A
Centrale	D
Chiusarelli	B
Duomo	I
Garibaldi	H
La Perla	F
Palazzo Bruchi	G
Piccolo Hotel Etruria	E

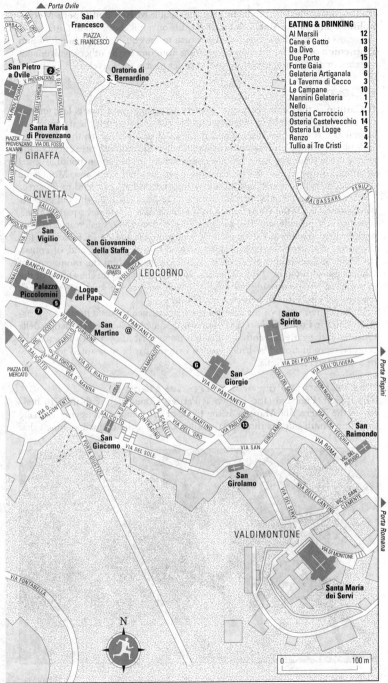

▲ Porta Ovile

San Francesco
PIAZZA S. FRANCESCO

San Pietro a Ovile

Oratorio di S. Bernardino

Santa Maria di Provenzano

GIRAFFA

CIVETTA

San Vigilio

San Giovannino della Staffa

PIAZZA GRASSI

LEOCORNO

Palazzo Piccolomini

Logge del Papa

San Martino

VIA DI PANTANETO

Santo Spirito

San Giorgio

VIA DI PANTANETO

San Raimondo

San Giacomo

San Girolamo

VALDIMONTONE

Santa Maria dei Servi

▶ Porta Pispini

▶ Porta Romana

EATING & DRINKING

Al Marsili	12
Cane e Gatto	13
Da Divo	8
Due Porte	15
Fonte Gaia	9
Gelateria Artiganala	6
La Taverna di Cecco	3
Le Campane	10
Nannini Gelateria	1
Nello	7
Osteria Carroccio	11
Osteria Castelvecchio	14
Osteria Le Logge	5
Renzo	4
Tullio ai Tre Cristi	2

N

0   100 m

(and attendant museums, including the unmissable **Museo dell'Opera Metro-politana** and **Santa Maria della Scala**) sits on a hill above Via di Città, looking across the deep Fontebranda valley north to the equally huge church of **San Domenico** occupying its own hill; getting from one to the other involves a lot of stairs, or a big semicircular detour in order to stay on a level.

Il Campo

Il Campo is the centre of Siena in every sense: the main streets lead into it, the Palio is held around its perimeter, and in the evenings it is the natural place to gravitate towards, for visitors and residents alike. Don't spurn the chance to soak up the atmosphere last thing at night, when the amphitheatre curve of the piazza throws the low hum of café conversation around in an invisible spiral of sound, drowned out in the daytime. Four hundred years ago, Montaigne described it as the most beautiful square in the world; it's still hard to disagree.

When the Council of Nine were planning the piazza in 1293, this old market-place, which lay at the convergence of the city quarters but was a part of none, was the only possible site. The piazza, completed in 1349, was created in nine segments in honour of the council. It was, from the start, a focus of city life, the scene of executions, bullfights, communal boxing matches, and, of course, the Palio. St Bernardino preached here, holding before him the monogram of Christ's name in Greek ("IHS"), which the council placed on the facade of the Palazzo Pubblico, alongside the city's she-wolf symbol – a reference to Siena's legendary foundation by Senius, son of Remus.

At the highest point of the Campo the Renaissance makes a fleeting appearance with the **Fonte Gaia** (Gay Fountain), designed and carved by Jacopo della Quercia in the early fifteenth century but now replaced by a poor nineteenth-century reproduction. The badly eroded original has been restored for display in Santa Maria della Scala.

The Museo Civico and Torre del Mangia

The Palazzo Pubblico (also known as Palazzo Comunale), with its 97m bell-tower, the **Torre del Mangia**, is the focus of the Campo, occupying virtually the entire south side. Its three-part windows pleased the council so much that

△ Siena's Palio

they ordered their emulation on all other buildings on the square. The *palazzo* is still in use as Siena's town hall, but its principal rooms have been converted into the **Museo Civico** (daily: mid-March to Oct 10am–7pm; Nov & Feb to mid-March 10am–6.30pm; Dec & Jan 10am–5.30pm; €7, or €10 with Torre del Mangia; Ⓦ www.comune.siena.it/museocivico) – a series of grand halls frescoed with themes integral to the secular life of the medieval city. If you have time or inclination for only one of Siena's museums, make it this one.

At the top of the stairs, you're directed through a disappointing five-room picture gallery to the **Sala del Risorgimento**, painted with nineteenth-century scenes of Vittorio Emanuele, first king of Italy. Across the corridor is a series of frescoed rooms, the **Sala di Balìa** (or dei Priori; room 10), the **Anticamera del Concistoro**, and the grand **Sala del Concistoro**. Room 13, the **Vestibolo**, holds the gilded bronze *She-Wolf suckling Romulus and Remus* (1429), an allusion to Siena's mythical founding. Alongside is the **Anticappella**, decorated between 1407 and 1414 by Taddeo di Bartolo. Behind a majestic wrought-iron screen by Jacopo della Quercia is the **Cappella del Consiglio**, also frescoed by di Bartolo and holding an exceptional altarpiece by Sodoma and exquisite inlaid choir stalls.

All these are little more than a warm-up for room 16, the great **Sala del Mappamondo**. Taking its name from the now scarcely visible frescoed cosmology – a circular map by Lorenzetti – the room was used for several centuries as the city's law court, and contains one of the greatest of all Italian frescoes. Simone Martini's fabulous *Maestà* (Virgin in Majesty) is a painting of almost translucent colour, painted in 1315 when Martini was 30. The richly decorative style is archetypal Sienese Gothic and Martini's great innovation was the use of a canopy and a frieze of medallions to frame and organize the figures – lending a sense of space and hint of perspective that suggest a knowledge of Giotto's work. The fresco on the opposite wall, the *Equestrian Portrait of Guidoriccio da Fogliano*, is a motif for medieval chivalric Siena and was, until recently, also credited to Martini. Art historians, however, have long puzzled over the anachronistic castles, which are of a much later style than the painting's signed date of 1328. A number of historians – led by the American Gordon Moran (whom the city council accused of being a CIA agent and for a while banned from the building) – interpret the *Guidoriccio* as a sixteenth-century fake, while others maintain that it is a genuine Martini overpainted by subsequent restorers. A fresco below the portrait, of two figures in front of a castle, is meanwhile variously attributed to Martini, Duccio and Pietro Lorenzetti.

The adjacent **Sala della Pace** holds Ambrogio Lorenzetti's *Allegories of Good and Bad Government*, frescoes commissioned in 1338 to remind the councillors of their duties. This is one of Europe's most important cycles of medieval secular painting, and includes the first-known panorama in Western art. The walled city shown is clearly Siena, and the paintings are full of details of medieval life; their moral theme is expressed in a complex iconography of allegorical virtues and figures. *Good Government* (the better-preserved half) is dominated by a throned figure representing the *comune*, flanked by the Virtues and with Faith, Hope and Charity buzzing about his head. To the left, Justice (with Wisdom in the air above) dispenses rewards and punishments, while below her throne Concordia advises the Republic's councillors on their duties. *Bad Government* is ruled by a horned demon, while over the city flies the figure of Fear, whose scroll reads: "Because he looks for his own good in the world, he places justice beneath tyranny. So nobody walks this road without Fear: robbery thrives inside and outside the city gates."

Some fine panel paintings by Lorenzetti's contemporaries are displayed in the **Sala dei Pilastri** to one side. Take time to climb the stairs up to the rear **loggia**, where you can crane your neck to see the current council chambers, also frescoed. From the loggia you can see how abruptly the town ends: buildings rise to the right and left for a few hundred metres along the ridges of the Terzo di San Martino and Terzo di Città, holding a rural valley in their embrace.

Off to the left of the Palazzo Pubblico's internal courtyard, opposite the entrance to the Museo Civico, a door gives access to the 503 steps of the **Torre del Mangia** (daily: mid-March to Oct 10am–7pm; Nov to mid-March 10am–4pm; €6, €10 with Museo Civico), which gives fabulous views across the town and surrounding countryside. The tower takes its name from its first watchman – a slothful glutton (*mangiaguadagni*) who is commemorated by a statue in the courtyard. Note that there is a maximum of fifty people allowed in the tower at one time and that at the merest hint of rain it closes for safety reasons.

The Loggia della Mercanzia and around

Gaps between buildings behind the Fonte Gaia lead up to the junction-point of the three main streets of Siena, marked by the fifteenth-century **Loggia della Mercanzia** – reluctantly Renaissance, with its Gothic niches for the saints – that was designed as a tribune house for merchants to do their deals. From here, Banchi di Sopra heads north (see p.587), and Via di Città curves west (see p.587). If you follow **Banchi di Sotto** east, you soon reach the **Logge del Papa** with, alongside it, the **Palazzo Piccolomini**, a committed Renaissance building by Bernardo Rossellino, the architect employed at Pienza by the Sienese Pope Pius II (Aeneas Sylvius Piccolomini).

The Duomo and around

Few buildings reveal so much of a city's history and aspirations as Siena's **Duomo**. Complete to virtually its present size around 1215, it was subjected to constant plans for expansion. An initial project, early in the fourteenth century, attempted to double its extent by building a baptistry on the slope below and using this as a foundation for a rebuilt nave, but the work ground to a halt as walls and joints gaped under the pressure. Eventually the chapter hit on a new scheme to reorient the cathedral, using the existing nave as a transept and building a **new nave** out towards the Campo. Again cracks appeared, and then, in 1348, came the Black Death. With the population decimated and funds suddenly cut off, the plan was abandoned once and for all. The part-extension still stands at the north end of the square – a vast structure that would have created the largest church in Italy outside Rome. Despite all the abandoned plans, the duomo is a delight, its style an amazing conglomeration of Romanesque and Gothic, delineated by bands of black and white marble. The **facade** was designed in 1284 by Giovanni Pisano, who with his workshop created much of the statuary – philosophers, patriarchs and prophets, now replaced by copies. In the next century the **Campanile** and a Gothic **rose window** were added. The mosaics in the gables, however, had to wait until the nineteenth century, when money was found to employ Venetian artists.

The use of black and white decoration is continued in the sgraffito marble **pavement**, which begins outside the church and takes off into a startling sequence of 56 panels adorning the **interior** (March–May & Sept & Oct Mon–Sat 10.30am–7.30pm, Sun 1.30–5.30pm; June–Aug Mon–Sat 10.30am–8pm, Sun 1.30–6pm; Nov–Feb Mon–Sat 10.30am–6.30pm, Sun 1.30–5.30pm,

€3). They were completed between 1349 and 1547, with virtually every artist who worked in the city trying his hand on a design. The finest are reckoned to be Beccafumi's *Moses Striking Water from a Rock* and *Sacrifice of Isaac*, just beyond the dome area. However, you're unlikely to see much of the pavement, which is now protected by boarding for all but a few weeks a year in August, when the full effect is on show (exact dates vary so ask at the tourist office). The zebra-striped interior is equally arresting above floor level, with its line of popes' heads set above the pillars, the same hollow-cheeked scowls cropping up repeatedly. The greatest individual artistic treasure is Nicola Pisano's **pulpit**, with its elaborate high-relief detail of the Life of Jesus and Last Judgement. In the north transept is a bronze statue by **Donatello**, the emaciated *St John the Baptist*, companion piece to his equally ragged *Mary Magdalene* in Florence (see p.510), and the Renaissance High Altar is flanked by superb candelabra-carrying angels by Beccafumi.

Midway along the nave, on the left, is the entrance to the stunning **Libreria Piccolomini**. The library was commissioned by Francesco Piccolomini (who for ten days was Pius III) to house the books of his uncle Aeneas (Pius II), and to celebrate Aeneas's life in a series of crystal-sharp, brilliantly colourful frescoes by Pinturicchio. The cycle begins to the right of the window, with Aeneas attending the Council of Basel as a secretary, then, in subsequent panels around the walls, presenting himself as envoy to James II of Scotland; being crowned poet laureate by Holy Roman Emperor, Frederick II; representing Frederick on a visit to Pope Eugenius IV; and then – as Bishop of Siena – presiding over the meeting of Frederick III and his bride-to-be Eleanora outside Siena's Porta Camollia. The next panels show Aeneas being made a cardinal in 1456; being elected pope two years later; and then launching a call for a crusade against the Turks, who had just seized Constantinople. His best-remembered action was the canonization of St Catherine, shown in the penultimate panel. The last fresco shows his death at Ancona.

Santa Maria della Scala

Opposite the duomo is the **Ospedale di Santa Maria della Scala** (daily: mid-March to Oct 10.30am–6pm; Nov to mid-March 10.30am–4.30pm; €6; for information on museum passes see p.578; ⓦ www.santamaria.comune.siena .it). For nine hundred years up until the 1980s, this vast complex served as the city's main hospital. Today its wonderful interiors are being gradually converted into a major centre for art and culture, revealing works that have been inaccessible to all but the ill and most determined of visitors for centuries.

To the left of the ticket desk is the church of **Santissima Annunziata** (also with its own door onto the piazza), blandly remodelled in the fifteenth century but with a bronze statue on the high altar of the *Risen Christ* by Vecchietta, with features so gaunt the veins show through the skin. The other way from the ticket desk leads into a vestibule, the **Cappella del Manto**, with the strikingly beautiful fresco *St Anne and St Joachim* (1512) – parents of the Virgin – by Beccafumi. Having failed to conceive during twenty years of marriage, the pair are each told by an angel to meet at Jerusalem's Golden Gate and kiss (the scene depicted in the fresco), a moment which symbolizes the Immaculate Conception of their daughter. Adjacent is a long hall, partly used as a bookshop; left off this hall is the vast **Sala del Pellegrinaio**, formerly used as the main hospital ward and entirely frescoed with scenes intended to record the hospital's history and promote the notion of charity toward the sick and orphaned. Their almost entirely secular content was extraordinary at the time they were painted (after 1440). Off to the left, in room 12, is the frescoed **Cappella del Sacro Chiodo** (also known as the Sagrestia Vecchia), which once housed a nail (*chiodo*) from the Passion.

Stairs lead down to the **Oratorio di Santa Caterina della Notte**, an oratory that belonged to one of a number of medieval confraternities that maintained places of worship in the basement vaults of the hospital. It's a dark and strangely spooky place, despite the plethora of decoration – you can easily imagine St Catherine passing nocturnal vigils down here. Also on this level is a series of rooms devoted to documenting the continuing restoration of the original **Fonte Gaia** from the Campo. Stairs lead down again to the oratory and meeting-room of the **Società di Esecutori di Pie Disposizioni** (Executors of Benevolent Legacies), oldest of the lay confraternities, which house a wooden crucifix said to be the one that inspired St Bernadino to become a monk.

The Museo dell'Opera Metropolitana

Tucked into a corner of the proposed new nave of the duomo is the impressive **Museo dell'Opera Metropolitana** (daily mid–March to May & Sept–Oct 9.30am–7pm; June–August 9.30am–8pm; Nov–Feb 10am–5pm; €6; ⓦwww .operaduomo.siena.it). A tour starts on the top floor where room 1 houses the haunting Byzantine icon known as the **Madonna dagli Occhi Grossi** (of the Big Eyes), the duomo's original altarpiece, as well as panels depicting St Bernardino preaching in the Campo and Piazza San Francesco. Pass through to the tiny entrance to the **Panorama dal Facciatone** – this leads to steep spiral stairs climbing the walls of the abandoned nave. The sensational view is worth the two-stage climb, but beware that the topmost walkway is narrow and scarily exposed.

Downstairs is the work that alone merits the museum admission: Duccio's vast and justly celebrated **Maestà**, which was the duomo's altarpiece from 1311 until 1505. This is one of the superlative works of Sienese art, its iconic, Byzantine spirituality accentuated by Duccio's flowing composition, his realization of the space in which action takes place, and a new attention to narrative detail in the panels of the predella and the reverse of the altarpiece which are now displayed to its side. Downstairs again, back on ground-floor level, is the **Galleria delle Statue**, with Donatello's delicate ochre *Madonna and Child* flanked by huge, elongated, twisting figures by Giovanni Pisano. You exit the museum through the atmospheric, late-Baroque church of **San Niccolò in Sasso**, emerging onto Via del Poggio in front of a handy little café.

Along Via di Città

Via di Città is the main thoroughfare linking the duomo with the Campo, and is lined with shops and plenty of explorable side-alleys, as well as being fronted by some of Siena's finest private *palazzi*. The **Palazzo Chigi-Saracini**, at no. 82, is a Gothic beauty, with its curved facade and rear courtyard. Almost opposite, at Via di Città 126, is the fifteenth-century **Palazzo delle Papesse**, Siena's museum of contemporary art (Tues–Sun 11am–7pm; €5; ⓦ www.papesse.org). Its four airy floors house excellent temporary exhibits covering anything from architecture to video art, displayed in rooms, some with nineteenth-century frescoes, that still conserve many of their original Renaissance structural and decorative features.

Via di Città continues to a small piazza from where Via San Pietro leads south to the fourteenth-century Palazzo Buonsignori, now the home of the **Pinacoteca Nazionale** (Mon 8.30am–1.30pm, Tues–Sat 8.15am–7.15pm, Sun 8.15am–1.30pm; €4.30). The collection is a roll of honour of Sienese Gothic painting. The first rooms – two storeys up – hold a host of gilded, thirteenth-century Madonnas; in rooms 7–8, two tiny panels recently attributed to Sassetta – *City by the Sea* and *Castle by a Lake* – are described as the first-ever landscape paintings entirely devoid of religious purpose. Down one flight are Renaissance works by such as Sodoma, whose panel of the *Deposition* (room 32) and frescoes from Sant'Agostino (room 37) show his characteristic drama and delight in costume and landscape. The gallery's topmost storey is devoted to the **Collezione Spannocchi**, a miscellany of Italian, German and Flemish works, including the only painting in the museum by a female artist – *Bernardo Campi Painting Sofonisba's Portrait* by Sofonisba Anguissola, a neat little joke in which the artist excels in her portrait of Campi, but depicts his portrait of her as a flat stereotype.

South of the Pinacoteca Nazionale is the church of **Sant'Agostino** (mid-March to Oct daily 10.30am–1.30pm & 3–5.30pm; €2), with outstanding paintings by Perugino (a *Crucifixion* in the second altar of the south aisle) and Sodoma (*Adoration of the Magi* in the Cappella Piccolomini). A nice walk loops southwest along Via della Cerchia into a studentish area around the church of **Santa Maria del Carmine** (which contains a hermaphrodite *St Michael and the Devil* by Beccafumi). Via del Fosso di San Ansano, north of the Carmine square, is a country lane above terraced vineyards that leads to the Selva (Rhinoceros) *contrada*'s square, from where the stepped Vicolo di San Girolamo leads up to the duomo.

North of the Campo

Exploring only slightly beyond the touristed central alleys between the Campo and the duomo reveals much more of the bustling everyday life of the city. North of the Campo, the main street **Banchi di Sopra** leads through the commercial heart of town to **Piazza Matteotti**, home of the main post office, north of which lies the workaday neighbourhood of the Terzi di Camollia. The church of **Santo Stefano** fronts one of the nicest *contrada* squares in the city, home of the Istrici (Porcupine), while the road emerges from the walls at the northern Porta Camollia, inscribed "Siena opens her heart to you wider than this gate." The northwest corner of the city is occupied by a stadium and the gardens of **La Lizza**, which lead up to the bastions of the **Fortezza di Santa Barbara**, rebuilt by the Medici and now housing the comprehensive wine collection of the *Enoteca Italiana* (see p.590).

San Domenico

Monasteries were essentially rural until the beginning of the thirteenth century, when the idea of an exclusively meditative retreat was displaced by the

St Catherine of Siena was born on March 25, 1347, the 24th child of Jacopo Beninscasa, a dyer, and Lapa di Duccio de' Piacenti. Her path to beatification began early, with a vision aged 6 of Christ as pope, followed a year later by a vow of perpetual virginity. Her family tried to drill some sense into her by forcing her to work at household chores, but when her father discovered her at prayer one day with a dove fluttering above her head, he realized her holy destiny. Catherine took the Dominican habit aged 16, and then began charitable works in post-plague Siena before turning her hand to politics. She prevented Siena and Pisa from joining Florence in rising against Pope Urban V (then absent in Avignon), and then, in 1376, travelled herself to Avignon to persuade Pope Gregory XI to return to Rome. It was a fulfilment of the ultimate Dominican ideal – a union of the practical and mystical life. Catherine returned to Siena to a life of contemplation, retaining a political role in her attempts to reconcile the 1378 schism between the Popes and Antipopes. She died in Rome in 1380, and was the first woman ever to be **canonized** – by Pius II in 1461. Pius IX made her **co-patron of Rome** in 1866; Pius XII raised her to be **co-patron of Italy** (alongside St Francis) in 1939; and then John Paul II declared her **co-patron of Europe** in 1999.

preaching orders of friars. Suddenly, in the space of a few decades, orders began to found monasteries on the periphery of the major Italian cities. In Siena the two greatest orders, the Dominicans and Franciscans, located themselves respectively to the west and east. **San Domenico**, a vast brick church west of Piazza Matteotti (daily: April–Oct 7.30am–1pm & 3–6.30pm; Nov–March 9am–1pm & 3–6pm; free), was founded in 1125 and is closely identified with St Catherine of Siena (see box above). Inside on the right is a raised chapel with a contemporary portrait of the saint by her friend Andrea Vanni. Her own chapel, on the south side of the enormous, airy nave, has frescoes by Sodoma of her swooning (to the left of the altar) and in ecstasy (to the right), as well as a reliquary containing her head.

The **Casa Santuario di Santa Caterina** – St Catherine's family house, where she lived as a Dominican nun – is just south of the church, down the hill on Via Santa Caterina (daily: 9am–12.30pm & 3–6pm; free). The building has been much adapted, with a Renaissance loggia and a series of oratories – one on the site of her cell. At the bottom of the hill, through the Oca (Goose) *contrada*, is the **Fonte Branda**, the best-preserved of Siena's medieval fountains and, according to Sienese folklore, the haunt of werewolves, who would throw themselves into the water at dawn to return in human form.

The Oratorio di San Bernardino

St Bernardino, born in the year of St Catherine's death, began his preaching life at the chill monastic church of **San Francesco**, across the city to the east. Alongside the church is the **Oratorio di San Bernardino** (mid-March to Oct daily 10.30am–1.30pm & 3–5.30pm; €3; for museum passes see box on p.578), with a beautifully wood-panelled upper chapel frescoed by Sodoma and Beccafumi. In the lower chapel are seventeenth-century scenes from the saint's life, which was taken up by incessant travel throughout Italy, preaching against usury and denouncing political strife; his sermons in the Campo, it is said, frequently went on for the best part of a day. He was canonized in 1444, and – because of his dictum on rhetoric, "make it clear, short and to the point" – was made patron saint of advertising in the 1980s. The attached **Museo Diocesano di Arte Sacra** (same hours and ticket) contains an array of devotional art from the thirteenth to the seventeenth centuries.

Eating, drinking and nightlife

Although Siena has no shortage of places in which to **eat** well, the city feels distinctly provincial after Florence. The main action of an evening is the *passeggiata* from Piazza Matteotti along Banchi di Sopra to the Campo – and there's not much in the way of **nightlife** after that. For most visitors, though, the Campo, the city's universal gathering place, provides diversion enough, while the presence of the university ensures a bit of life in the **bars**.

Putting together a **picnic** in the Campo or elsewhere is easy: you can buy pizza by weight from many central hole-in-the-wall places, or phone an order ahead for quality, fresh-baked pizza (whole or by the slice) from *Mister Pizza*, Via delle Terme 94 (℡0577.221.746; closed Sun). Gourmet supplies are at the extravagantly stocked food store *Manganelli*, Via di Città 71. The **covered market** south of the Campo in Piazza del Mercato (Mon–Sat mornings) is also good for picnic provisions, and every quarter has its bakery.

Restaurants

Siena used to have a poor reputation for **restaurants** but over the last few years a range of new, imaginative *osterie* has signalled a general rise in standards. Food is often heavy so expect plenty of wild boar and rabbit. Local **specialities** include *pici* (thick, hand-rolled spaghetti with toasted breadcrumbs), *finocchiona* (minced pork flavoured with fennel), *pappa col pomodoro* (bread and tomato soup) and *fagioli all'uccelletto* (white bean and sausage stew).

Al Marsili Via del Castoro 3 ℡0577.47.154. Elegant, upmarket restaurant serving some exellent meat dishes (including grilled lamb and steak with three pepper sauce, both €17) and a few vegetarian choices (such as grilled vegetables with *scamorza* cheese, €17). Attentive service. Closed Mon.

Cane e Gatto Via Pagliaresi 6 ℡0577.287.545. Don't be put off by the absence of a menu – this restaurant serves superb if expensive Tuscan cuisine on its seven-course *menu degustazione*. Allow around €50 per person. Evening only & closed Thurs.

Da Divo Via Franciosa 29 ℡0577.286.054. Book a table in the atmospheric subterranean dining room to savour hearty Tuscan food that is generally above average. Allow around €50 per person. Closed Sun in winter.

Due Porte Via di Stalloreggi 62 ℡0577.221.887. This place has pizza and a large Tuscan menu, lower prices than you'd expect – pizza €5, *primi* €6–7, *secondi* €8–12 – and an open terrace at the back on which to enjoy them. Closed Mon.

La Taverna di Cecco Via Cecco Angiolieri 19 ℡0577.288.518. Attentive service, moderate prices and heavenly rabbit and rocket salad. Good pasta dishes too, including tagliatelle with walnuts and cream. Closed Wed.

Le Campane Via delle Campane 6 ℡0577.284.035. High-quality Sienese cuisine at a small, formal restaurant just below the duomo. *Primi* €8.50, *secondi* €10–13. Closed Mon.

Nello Via del Porrione 28 ℡0577.289.043. Sienese specialities at their best: try red chicory and smoked cheese ravioli in leek sauce, roast rabbit, or beef fillet

Sweet treats

Most Sienese buy **ice cream** at one or the other end of the *passeggiata* – either at the *Nannini Gelateria*, in Piazza Giacomo Matteotti, or *Gelateria Artiganala*, on the Via di Città. Siena is also famous for a whole range of **cakes**, including the trademark **panforte** – a dense and delicious wedge of nuts, fruit and honey – and biscuits like *cavallucci* (aniseed, nut and spice) and *ricciarelli* (almond). All are best bought fresh by the *etto* (100g) in any of the bakeries or *pasticcerie* along Banchi di Sopra; the gift-packaged boxes aren't as good.

with rocket and *pecorino* for around €19–23 for two courses. Closed Sun.

Osteria Carroccio Via Casato di Sotto 32 ☎0577.411.65. Popular little *osteria* offering good Sienese dishes (such as *pappardelle* with hare and *tagliatelle al cinghiale*, both €7) and an extensive wine list for reasonable prices – around €18–20 for two courses. The whole package let down by the slightly off-hand service. Closed Wed.

Osteria Castelvecchio Via di Castelvecchio 65 ☎0577.49.586. First-rate, adventurous and nicely informal *osteria* with a barrel vaulted brick ceiling and good choices for vegetarians. Menus change daily; average price around €25 for two courses. Closed Sun.

Osteria Le Logge Via del Porrione 33 ☎0577.48.013. The best-looking restaurant in Siena, in an old cabinet-lined pharmacy off the Campo. Good pasta and some unusual *secondi*, but at a price – around €50 a head. Closed Sun.

Renzo Piazza Indipendenza ☎0577.289.296. This friendly *spaghetteria* offers light, uncomplicated meals at terrace tables on a quiet enclosed piazza off Via di Città. The large menu includes a few pizzas. Closed Thurs.

Tullio ai Tre Cristi Vicolo Provenzano 1 ☎0577.280.608. A Sienese institution since 1830, this is the neighbourhood restaurant of the Giraffa *contrada* and is draped with heraldic banners between the frescoes and arches to accompany its traditional fare – roast boar, steaks, tripe, plenty of fish and some pastas. The seasonal menu is around €40. Closed Wed.

Bars and cafés

There are pleasant **bars** all over town. *L'Officina*, north of the centre at Piazza del Sale 3a, has around a hundred bottled beers and others on tap, and sometimes live music. Of the terrace **cafés** ringing the Campo, *Caffè Fonte Gaia* stays open later than most, but otherwise they're much of a muchness, and rather expensive – expect to pay €7 for a large beer. The garden of the *Palazzo Ravizza* hotel, Pian dei Mantellini 34, is a lovely tranquil spot for a cup of tea on a hot afternoon. The *Enoteca Italiana* inside the Fortezza (Mon noon–8pm, Tues–Sat noon–1am; ☎0577.228.811, ⓦwww.enoteca-italiana.it) is the country's only national **wine** collection. Its cellar stocks and exhibits every single Italian wine (well over a thousand of them) and there's a **bar** – at its best in the early evening – where you can order by the glass or bottle. At various times of year it stages promotions highlighting particular wine regions, and even hosts the odd concert.

Nightlife and entertainment

You'll spot posters for city **events** at Piazza Matteotti, and the Siena supplement of *La Nazione* newspaper has details of the day's concerts and films. **Live bands** play at *L'Officina* bar, Piazza del Sale 3a, and at the disco-bar *Al Cambio*, Via di Pantaneto 48, but otherwise your only chances are at the low-key **Siena Jazz** in the last week of July and the gigs organized for the PDS-Communist Party **Festa dell'Unità** throughout the summer.

Siena has prestigious **classical** concerts throughout the year. The Accademia Musicale Chigiana is the driving force, staging the *Estate Musicale Chigiana* cycle all summer, and the *Settimana Musicale Senese* in late July, often featuring a major opera production. Venues vary from the duomo and Sant'Agostino to out-of-town locations such as the atmospheric ruined abbey of San Galgano. Tickets start at €11, bookable through the tourist office or from mid-June onwards in person at the Accademia Musicale Chigiana, Via di Città 89 (daily 3–7pm; ☎0577.22.091, ⓦwww.chigiana.it).

Listings

Bike rental DF Bike, Via Massetana Romana 54 ⊕ 0577.271.905, ⊛ www.dfbike.it; Perozzi Automotocicli, Via del Gazzani 16 ⊕ 0577.223.157, ⊛ www.perozzi.it.

Bus information Ticket offices beneath Piazza Gramsci have information on all routes. The Sienese bus company is called TRA-IN (⊕ 800.905.183, ⊛ www.trainspa.it) – and despite appearances has nothing to do with trains. They run roughly half-hourly to Poggibonsi, where you must change for San Gimignano (buy a through ticket), and eight times daily to Montalcino, more to Montepulciano (though with most you have to change at Buonconvento). Note that some buses to the hill-towns south of Siena depart from the train station, not from Piazza Gramsci. TRA-IN and SITA also run regularly to Florence (take an express).

Car rental Avis, Via Simone Martini 36 ⊕ 0577.270.305; Hertz, Viale Sardegna 37 ⊕ 0577.45.085.

Guided walks "Ecco Siena" walking tours (in English) start from outside San Domenico (April–Oct Mon–Sat 3pm; €15; 2hr 30min). The tours only cost €5 if pre-booked through Siena Hotels Promotion, Piazza Madre Teresa di Calcutta ⊕ 0577.288.084, ⊛ www.hotelsiena.com, before 2.45pm on the same day.

Hospital Loc. Le Scotte ⊕ 0577.585.111.

Internet access Internet Train, Via di Città 121, and Via Pantaneto 54; MegaWeb, Via Pantaneto 132; Interfast Net, Via Casato di Sotto 1. All have long opening hours and charge around €1.50 for 15min (less for students).

Laundry Wash & Dry, Via Pantaneto 38 (daily 8am–9pm); OndaBlu, Casato di Sotto 17 (daily 8am–10pm); both are self-service.

Left luggage At the TRA-IN bus information centre below Piazza Gramsci (daily 7am–7.45pm; €3.50 per piece for one day only). At the train station, there are self-service lockers on platform 1.

Lost property Comune di Siena, Casato di Sotto 23 (Mon–Fri 9am–12.30pm, Tues & Thurs also 3–5pm).

Market A huge weekly market sprawls over La Lizza (Wed 8am–1pm).

Parking The two biggest parking garages – run by the same company and clearly signposted – charge around €1.50 per hour (daily 7am–11pm) but are misleadingly named: "Parcheggio Il Campo" and "Parcheggio Il duomo" are a long way south of either the Campo or the Duomo, just inside the Porta Tufi and Porta San Marco respectively (⊛ www.sienaparcheggi.com). Parking outside the city gates is free. Tourists are permitted to drive through the old town alleys only in order to check in at their hotel.

Police The *Questura* is on Via del Castoro ⊕ 05.

Post office Piazza Matteotti (Mon–Sat 8.15am–7pm).

Taxi Radio Taxi ⊕ 0577.49.222; taxis wait on Piazza Matteotti.

Train information ⊕ 89.20.21, ⊛ www.trenitalia.it.

San Gimignano

SAN GIMIGNANO, 27km northwest of Siena, is perhaps the most visited small village in Italy. Its stunning hilltop skyline of towers, built in aristocratic rivalry by the feuding nobles of the twelfth and thirteenth centuries, evokes the appearance of medieval Tuscany more than any other sight. And the town is all that it's cracked up to be: quietly monumental, very well preserved, enticingly rural, and with a fine array of religious and secular frescoes. However, from Easter until October, San Gimignano has very little life of its own, with hordes of day-trippers traipsing up and down its narrow streets and filing in and out of its innumerable olive oil, wine and souvenir shops. If you want to reach beyond its facade of quaintness, try to come well out of season; if you can't, then aim to spend the night here – the town takes on a very different pace and atmosphere in the evenings.

San Gimignano was quite a force to be reckoned with in the early Middle Ages. It was controlled by two great families – the Ardinghelli and the Salvucci – and its 15,000 population (twice the present number) prospered on agricultural holdings and its position on the Lombardy-to-Rome pilgrim

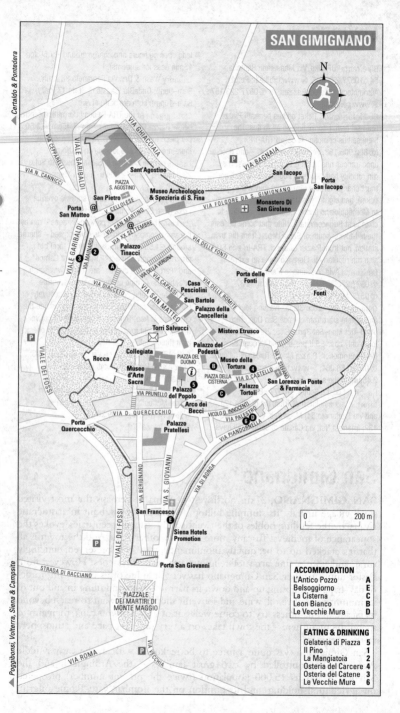

route. At its heyday, the town's walls enclosed five monasteries, four hospitals, public baths and a brothel. **Feuds**, however, had long wreaked havoc: the first Ardinghelli–Salvucci conflict erupted in 1246. Whenever the town itself was united, it picked fights with Volterra, Poggibonsi and other neighbours. These were halted only by the **Black Death**, which devastated the population and, as the pilgrim trade collapsed, the economy. Subjection to Florence broke the power of the nobles and so their tower-houses, symbolic in other towns of real control, were not torn down; today, 15 of an original 72 survive. At the beginning of the nineteenth century, travellers spoke of San Gimignano as "miserably poor"; its postwar history, however, has been one of ever-increasing affluence, thanks to **tourism** and the production of an old-established but recently rejuvenated white **wine**, Vernaccia. The famous *Festival Internazionale* (Ⓦwww .fts.toscana.it) fills a couple of weeks in late July with **opera**, **ballet** and concerts of symphonic and chamber **music** on an open-air stage in Piazza Duomo; consult the tourist office for full details.

Arrival, information and accommodation

Although tour buses arrive throughout the day from Siena, San Gimignano welcomes very few direct public buses from anywhere other than **Colle Val d'Elsa** and the ugly industrial town of **Poggibonsi**: you're likely to have to transfer here. There's an hourly connecting bus from Poggibonsi train station (on the Florence–Empoli–Siena line) that drops off at both of San Gimignano's main gates, **Porta San Giovanni** in the south and **Porta San Matteo** in the north. From each, the main streets Via San Giovanni and Via San Matteo climb to meet in the middle of town at the interlocking squares of **Piazza Duomo** and **Piazza della Cisterna**, where you'll find the Pro Loco **tourist office**, Piazza Duomo 1 (daily 9am–1pm & 3–7pm; ℡0577.940.008, Ⓦwww .sangimignano.com).

Accommodation is bookable for free from the tourist office or through a branch of Siena Hotels Promotion, located just inside the southern gate at Via San Giovanni 125 (Mon–Sat: summer 9am–7pm; winter 9.30am–12.30pm & 3–6pm; ℡0577.940.809, Ⓦwww.hotelsiena.com). They can also give details of **private rooms**, an especially good option for those looking for cheaper accommodation, otherwise thin on the ground. Try at the house of the Boldrini family, 95 Via San Matteo; ℡0577.940.908.

Hotels

Belsoggiorno Via San Giovanni 91 ℡0577.940.375, Ⓦwww.hotelbelsoggiorno.it. Twenty-one smallish but beautifully appointed rooms on the town's main shopping drag. ❺

L'Antico Pozzo Via San Matteo 87 ℡0577.942.014, Ⓦwww.anticopozzo.com. An upmarket, eighteen-room three-star, occupying a fifteenth-century town house. ❻

La Cisterna Piazza Cisterna 24 ℡0577.940.328, Ⓦwww.hotelcisterna.it. Elegant ivy-clad hotel (established 1919), built into a medieval ensemble; some rooms have views onto the piazza or over the valley. Good restaurant – *Le Terrazze*. ❸

Le Vecchie Mura Via Piandornella 13 ℡0577.940.270, Ⓔvecchiemura@tin.it. Three doubles above a restaurant with superb views over vineyards and rolling Tuscan countryside. Free parking on the other side of town. ❷

Leon Bianco Piazza Cisterna 13 ℡0577.941.294, Ⓔleonbianco@joli.it. Tasteful three-star hotel, in a fourteenth-century town mansion opposite the *Cisterna*. Also with a roof terrace for breakfast, drinks and lounging. Rooms without a view are considerably cheaper. ❹

Campsite

Campeggio Boschetto di Piemma ℡0577.940.352, Ⓦwww.boschettodipiemma .it. The nearest campsite (with bar, restaurant and pool), 3km downhill from Porta San Giovanni at Santa Lucia, off the Volterra road. €7.80 per person high season.

The Town

You could walk from one end of San Gimignano to the other in about twenty minutes. It deserves at least a day, however, both for its frescoes and for its lovely surrounding countryside. From the southern gate, **Porta San Giovanni**, the *palazzo*-lined **Via San Giovanni** leads to the interlocking main squares, the Piazza del Duomo and the Piazza della Cisterna. On the right of the street, about 100m up, is the former church of San Francesco – a Romanesque building converted, like many of the *palazzi*, to a wine shop. You enter the **Piazza della Cisterna** through another gateway, the **Arco dei Becci**, part of the original fortifications built before the town expanded in the twelfth century. The square itself is flanked by an anarchic cluster of towers and *palazzi*, and is named after the thirteenth-century public cistern, still functioning in the centre. Northwest of the square is one of the old Ardinghelli towers; a Salvucci rival rears up behind. An arch leads through to the more austere **Piazza Duomo**, with further towers and civic *palazzi*.

The Collegiata

The plain facade of the Duomo, or more properly the **Collegiata**, since San Gimignano no longer has a bishop, could hardly provide a greater contrast

△ The towers of San Gimignano

with its interior (April–Oct Mon–Fri 9.30am–7pm, Sat 9.30am–5pm, Sun 12.30–5pm; March & Nov to mid-Jan Mon–Sat 9.30am–5pm, Sun 12.30–5pm; mid-Jan to Feb open for religious celebrations only; €3.50; for details of combined entry ticket see box opposite). This is one of the most comprehensively frescoed churches in Tuscany, with cycles of paintings filling every available space, their brilliant colours set off by Pisan-Romanesque arcades of black and white striped marble. Entrance is from the side courtyard, where you'll also find the small **Museo d'Arte Sacra** (same hours as Collegiata; €3; for details of combined entry ticket see box opposite). Less spectacular than the Collegiata, it's nevertheless worth a look for its rescued religious art.

The Collegiata's three principal **fresco cycles** fill the north and south walls, plus two short side walls which protrude from the east (exit) wall of the facade. The **Old Testament** scenes on the north wall, completed by Bartolo di Fredi around 1367, are full of medieval detail in the costumes, activities and interiors. They are also quirkily naturalistic: there are few odder frescoes than the depiction of Noah exposing himself in a drunken stupor. The cycle (which reads from left to right, top to bottom) follows the story of the **Flood** with those of **Abraham and Lot** (their trip to Canaan), **Joseph** (his dream; being let down the well; having his brothers arrested, and being recognized by them), **Moses** (changing a stick into a serpent before the Pharaoh; the Red Sea; Mount Sinai) and **Job** (temptation; the devil killing his herds; thanking God; being consoled). Above, note the beautiful fresco depicting the Creation of Eve, in which Eve emerges from the rib of the sleeping Adam. The **New Testament** scenes opposite (begun 1333) have a disputed attribution – either Barna da Siena or Lippo Memmi. They impress most by the intensity of their emotional expression: in *The Kiss of Judas*, the focus of eyes is startlingly immediate. One of the most dramatic scenes is the *Resurrection of Lazarus*, in which a dumbstruck crowd witnesses the removal of a door to reveal the living Lazarus in the winding bandages of burial. An altogether different vision pervades Taddeo di Bartolo's **Last Judgement** (1410), with paradise to the left and hell to the right. This is one of the most gruesome depictions of a customarily lurid subject, with no-holds-barred illustrations of the Seven Deadly Sins.

On the north side of the Collegiata, San Gimignano's most important Renaissance artwork is the superb fresco cycle made by Domenico Ghirlandaio for the small **Cappella di Santa Fina**. The subject is a local saint, born in 1238, who was struck by a dreadful and incurable disease at the age of 10. She gave herself immediately to God, repented her sins (the worst seems to have been accepting an orange from a boy), and insisted on spending the five agonizing years until her death lying on a plank on the floor. The fresco of the right-hand lunette shows Fina experiencing a vision of St Gregory. Opposite it is an even more accomplished work, the *Funeral of St Fina* – Raphael is said to have been especially impressed with it – showing the saint on her deathbed with the towers of San Gimignano in the background. Ghirlandaio left a self-portrait: he's the figure behind the bishop who is saying Mass.

The Pinacoteca

The Palazzo Popolo, the other key component of Piazza Duomo, is partly given over to council offices, but most of the building is devoted to the **Pinacoteca** and the **Torre Grossa**, the only one of San Gimignano's towers which you can climb for great views of the Val d'Elsa (daily: March–Oct 9.30am–7pm; Nov–Feb 10am–5pm; €5, for details of combined tickets see box opposite).

The lovely courtyard was built in 1323. A loggia opens on the right, from which judicial and public decrees were occasionally proclaimed (hence the subject matter of its frescoes). Stairs lead up to a picturesque little balcony and the ticket office. The first room, frescoed with hunting scenes, is the **Sala di Dante** – the poet visited as Florence's ambassador to the town in 1299, making a plea here for Guelph unity. Most of the paintings are Sienese in origin or inspiration, and the highlight is Lippo Memmi's *Maestà* (1317). Off the Sala di Dante are busts of a winsome Santa Fina (1496) and San Gregorio by Pietro Torrigiano. Highlights upstairs include two outstanding tondi by **Filippino Lippi**. Rooms off to the right hold a triptych by **Taddeo di Bartolo**, the *Scenes from the Life of St Gimignano* (1393) – with the saint holding the eponymous town on his lap – and **Lorenzo di Niccolò's** *Scenes from the Life of St Bartholomew* (1401), which includes a graphic depiction of the saint being flayed alive. The most enjoyable paintings are hidden away in a small room off the stairs, frescoes of wedding scenes completed in the 1320s by the Sienese painter Memmo di Filipuccio that are unique in their subject matter: they show a tournament where the wife rides on her husband's back, followed by the lovers taking a shared bath and then climbing into bed – the man managing to keep on the same red hat throughout.

The rest of the town

A few steps east of Piazza della Cisterna at Via del Castello 1 is the **Museo della Tortura** (daily: mid-July to mid-Sept 9am–midnight; mid-Sept to mid-July 10am–6, 7 or 8pm; €8), part of a chain with branches in several Tuscan towns, which combines an array of instruments – everything from thumbscrews to chastity belts – with an air of a distasteful, seedy prurience. Via di Castello continues east past the Romanesque **San Lorenzo in Ponte** (with fragments of a dramatic fresco of the Last Judgement) to a rural lane that winds down between vineyards to the city walls; just beyond the public wellhouse or **Fonti** stretches open countryside.

A signposted lane leads from Piazza Duomo up to the **Rocca**, the old fortress, with its one surviving tower and wonderful views. It was built, at local expense, by the Florentines "in order to remove every cause of evil thinking from the inhabitants" after their union with the *comune*. Later, its purpose presumably fulfilled, it was dismantled by Cosimo de' Medici. Nowadays it encloses an orchard-like public garden, with figs, olives and a central well.

Via San Matteo is one of the grandest and best preserved of the city streets, running north from Piazza Duomo to the main **Porta San Matteo** gate. Before the gate, Via XX Settembre heads east to the former convent of Santa Chiara, which now houses both the **Galleria d'Arte Contemporaneo**, with work by nineteenth- and twentieth-century Tuscan artists, and the interesting **Museo Archeologico** (both open daily 11am–5.30pm; closed from Jan–March; €3.50 or see box, p.594 for combined entry tickets). In the same complex is the **Spezieria di Santa Fina**, fragrant halls filled with exhibits from the sixteenth-century spice and herb pharmacy of the town's Santa Fina hospital. The northernmost corner of town is occupied by the large church of **Sant'Agostino** (daily 7am–noon & 3–7pm; Nov–March closes 6pm), with an outstanding fresco cycle behind the high altar by Benozzo Gozzoli, the *Life of St Augustine* (1465), which provides an amazing record of life in Renaissance Florence. Read from low down on the left, the panels depict the saint – who was born in what is now Tunisia in 354 – being taken to school and being flogged by his teacher, studying grammar at Carthage university, crossing the sea to Italy, his teaching in Rome and Milan and being received by Emperor Theodosius. Then comes the turning-point, when he hears St Ambrose preach and, while reading St Paul, hears a child's voice extolling him "*Tolle, lege*" (take and read). After this, he was baptized and returned to Africa to found a monastic community. The depiction of his death almost exactly prefigures Ghirlandaio's Collegiata fresco of the death of St Fina.

Eating and drinking

San Gimignano isn't famous for its **food** – there are too many tourists and too few locals to ensure high standards. However, the tables set out on the car-free squares and lanes, and the good local wines, make for pleasant dining. The recommended places below are all moderately priced. Good **bars** are similarly thin on the ground, though there are one or two on each of the main piazzas which are pleasant enough places from where to watch the world go by.

The little but extraordinarily popular ⚒ *Gelateria di Piazza*, Piazza della Cisterna 4, has arguably the best **ice cream** in Tuscany. Owner Sergio has certainly won enough competitions, including the *Gelato del Mondo* in 2006. Framed plaudits cover the walls. His incomparable pistachio flavour is made from finest-quality Sicilian nuts, and his trademark *crema di Santa Fina* is perfumed with saffron, but you'd be hard-pushed on a hot afternoon to beat the trio of peach, champagne with grapefruit, and *vernaccia*, the last a fragrant sorbet made from the crisp local white wine for €2.50.

Restaurants

Il Pino Via San Matteo 102 ☏0577.942.225. First choice for eating, with a lovely interior, and a specialist focus on *antipasti* (all €12) and dishes sprinkled with truffle. Closed Thurs.

La Mangiatoia Via Mainardi 5 ☏0577.945.28. Classical music and stained glass compete for attention with some imaginative pasta dishes and wild boar stew. Mains €12–15. Closed Tues.

⚒ Le Vecchie Mura Via Piandornella 15 ☏0577.940.270. The restaurant is housed in an old vaulted stable and serves decent fare (*primi* €6–9, *secondi* €10–12), but it's the terrace

across the road which is the real draw offering the best views in town out across the surrounding countryside. Closed Tues & lunch.

Osteria del Carcere Via del Castello 13 ☏0577.941.905. Award-winning place run by young owners, serving Tuscan cuisine with an innovative edge. Closed Wed.

Osteria del Catene Via Mainardi 18 ☏0577.941.966. Thoroughly reliable spot for straightforward Tuscan cooking, plus an extensive wine list. Offers increasingly more elaborate set menus for €13, €19, €21 and €31. Closed Wed.

Listings

Bike and scooter rental Bruno Bellini, Via Roma 41 ☏0577.940.201, ⊛www.bellinibruno.com.
Bus information You can buy tickets and get timetables from the tourist office in Piazza Duomo. Last buses to Poggibonsi and Colle leave from Porta San Giovanni about 8.30pm.
Internet access Cartoleria La Tuscia, just outside Porta San Matteo, or the craft shop at Via XX Settembre 24b.

Market Piazza Duomo and Piazza Cisterna (Thurs morning).
Parking There are four pay car-parks dotted around the walls, which fill up quickly in summer. Aim to get there early. Driving within the walls is forbidden unless you have a chit from your hotel, and the police will ticket you if you try.
Taxis ☏0577.940.499 and ☏0577.940.049.

Volterra

The dramatic location of **VOLTERRA** – built on a high plateau enclosed by volcanic hills midway between Siena and the sea – prompted D.H. Lawrence to write that "it gets all the wind and sees all the world – a sort of inland Island",

Alabaster is a form of crystallized chalk that has a delicate, milky texture and lends itself to the sculpture of fine, flowing lines and close ornamental detail. In even quite large blocks, it is translucent. The Etruscans and Romans extensively mined Volterra's alabaster for sculpting and up until the 1960s, there were large alabaster factories throughout the town centre, but – not least because of the quantity of dust they threw up – large-scale production was moved to outlying areas. These days, only about a dozen artisans are permitted to maintain workshops in the centre of town, and Volterra's famous art school is the only one in Europe to train students to work alabaster.

You'll spot plenty of alabaster shops dotted around the centre – most are outlets for factories that produce machined pieces from the tasteful to the tacky. *Alab'Arte*, down the alley alongside the Museo Guarnacci at Via Orti S. Agostino 28 (☏0588.87.968), is one of the few to stick to hand production, turning out sculpted pieces for just a few euros.

and indeed, you can often find seashells embedded in the paving of streets and squares. Touristy but still atmospheric, the town's walled medieval core is made from the yellow-grey stone *panchino*. **Etruscan** Volterra (Velathri) flourished through a combination of its alabaster mines and an impregnable position, attributes that ensured its survival through the Roman era and beyond. Its isolation was, however, its downfall. Under **Florentine** control from 1360, it proved unable to keep pace with changing and expanding patterns of trade, and the town itself began to subside, its walls and houses slipping away to the west over the **Balze** cliffs, which form a dramatic prospect from the Pisa road. Today, Volterra – part of the Provincia di Pisa – occupies less than a third of its ancient extent.

The Town

Dominating the almost totally medieval square of **Piazza dei Priori**, the **Palazzo dei Priori** is the oldest town hall in Tuscany, begun in 1208, which may have served as the model for Florence's Palazzo Vecchio. Upstairs inside the *palazzo* (March–Oct daily 10.30am–5.30pm; Nov–Feb Sat & Sun 11am–5pm; €1) is the **Sala del Consiglio**, used as the town's council chamber without interruption since 1257. Its end wall is frescoed with a huge *Annunciation* by Orcagna.

Leaving the square west past the tourist office, you come to a crossroads overlooked by the **Torre Buomparenti**. South (left) at Via Roma 13 is the **Museo d'Arte Sacra**, a rich four-room collection (daily: March–Oct 9am–1pm & 3–6pm; Nov–Feb 9am–1pm; joint ticket with Museo Guarnacci and Pinacoteca €8), which includes a silver reliquary bust of St Ottaviano by Antonio del Pollaiuolo and a beautiful sixteenth-century alabaster ciborium. Via Roma continues into the slightly down-at-heel cathedral square, with the Pisan-Romanesque **Duomo**, consecrated in 1120 (daily 8am–12.30pm & 3–5pm) and **Baptistry** (late-thirteenth century). The best of the duomo's works is a sculpture of the Deposition (1228) in the south transept, disarmingly repainted in its original bright colours. Behind the baptistry is an old foundling's hospital decorated by della Robbia. Via Marchesi heads south uphill to a lush area of grass, trees and shade known as the **Parco Archeologico** (March–Oct daily 10.30am–5.30pm; Nov–Feb Sat & Sun 11am–4pm; free). There's not much archeology about the place – a few odd lumps of rock, said to be part of a Roman bathhouse – but it's a beautiful part of the town to walk around for a few hours. Overlooking the park to the east is the Medicean **Rocca**, with rounded bastions and a central tower; it's one of the great examples of Italian military architecture and for the last 150 years has been a prison. The first turning off Via Marchesi is Via Porta dell'Arco, which runs downhill to the **Arco Etrusco**, an Etruscan gateway, third-century BC in origin, built in cyclopean blocks of stone. The gate was narrowly saved from destruction in the last war during a ten-day battle between the partisans and Nazis.

North from the Torre Buomparenti at Via dei Sarti 1 is the beautiful Renaissance Palazzo Minucci-Solaini, now housing the **Pinacoteca e Museo Civico** (daily: March–Oct 9am–7pm; Nov–Feb 8.30am–1.45pm; €8 joint ticket with Museo Guarnacci and Museo d'Arte Sacra). The key works are Florentine: Ghirlandaio's marvellous *Christ in Glory*, Luca Signorelli's *Annunciation* and, best of all, Rosso Fiorentino's extraordinary *Deposition*. This is one of the masterpieces of Mannerism, its figures, without any central focus, creating an agitated tension from sharp lines and blocks of discordant colour. The building also contains the **Eco-Museo dell'Alabastro** (April–Oct daily 11am–5pm; Nov–March Sat & Sun 9am–1.30pm; €3), which provides an overview of alabaster working in the area from Etruscan times to the present day and has a replica sculptor's workshop.

On the same street as the Pinacoteca is **Palazzo Viti**, Via dei Sarti 41 (April–Oct daily 10am–1pm & 2.30–6.30pm; Nov–March by appointment only; €4; ☎0588.840.47), an extensively frescoed Renaissance mansion filled with alabaster, everything from two-metre-high candelabras to tiles laid in the floor of the ballroom.

The Museo Etrusco Guarnacci

The **Museo Etrusco Guarnacci**, 500m east of Piazza dei Priori at Via Don Minzoni 15 (same hours and ticket as Pinacoteca), is one of Italy's major archeological museums. On display are entirely local finds, including some six hundred Etruscan **funerary urns**. Carved in alabaster, terracotta or local sandstone or limestone, they date from the fourth to first centuries BC, and follow a standard pattern: below a reclining figure of the subject (always leaning on their left side), bas-reliefs depict domestic events, Greek myths or simply a symbolic flower – one for a young person, two for middle-aged, three for elderly. The vast collection is organized by theme, with informative notes in each room. Key highlights are **upstairs**: past a large Roman mosaic transferred here from Volterra's baths is the **Urna degli Sposi**, a rare and artistically unique clay urn lid which features a disturbing double portrait of a husband and wife, all piercing eyes and dreadful looks. The star piece is the exceptional **Ombra della Sera** ("Evening Shadow"), an elongated nude that is unique in that it has been personalized and individualized – most of the figurines in nearby cases are generic. This piece was much admired by the twentieth-century Swiss sculptor Alberto Giacometti, who drew inspiration for his famous elongated figures from this Etruscan artist's visualization of the long evening shadows cast in hilltop Volterra.

The Balze cliffs

To reach the much-photographed eroded **Balze** cliffs, follow the Via Ricciarelli northwest from the Piazza dei Priori. As Via San Lino, this passes the church of **San Francesco**, with fifteenth-century frescoes of the Legend of the True Cross by Cenni di Cenni, before leaving town through the Porta San Francesco. From here, follow Borgo Santo Stefano and its continuation, Borgo San Giusto, past the Baroque church and former abbey of **San Giusto**, its dilapidated but striking facade framed by an avenue of cypress trees. At the Balze (almost 2km west of Piazza dei Priori) you gain a real sense of the extent of Etruscan Volterra, whose old walls drop away into the chasms. Gashes in the slopes and the natural erosion of sand and clay are made more dramatic by alabaster mines, ancient and modern. Below are buried great tracts of the Etruscan and Roman city, and landslips continue – as evidenced by the ruined eleventh-century **Badia** monastery ebbing away over the precipice.

Practicalities

Irregular **buses** run to Volterra from Larderello, Pisa and Colle Val d'Elsa. All arrive on the south side of the walls at Piazza Martiri, from where it's a two-minute walk to the central Piazza dei Priori and the helpful **tourist office** at no. 20 (daily: April–Oct 9am–1pm & 2–8pm; Nov–March 10am–1pm & 2–6pm; ⊤0588.87.257, ⓦwww.volterratur.it). They can book accommodation for free, sell you museum tickets and rent you an **audioguide** (€5), available in English, for a self-guided town tour. There are free **car parks** on the northern side of the walls, and a pay-by-the-hour underground car park just to the south. Walking and mountain-bike tours are run by the COOP Viaggio Antico (⊤0588.81.527, ⓦwww.viaggioantico.com) – or contact the tourist office. There's an **Internet point** at *Web e Wine*, just south off the Piazza dei Priori, which stays open late.

Volterra's most attractive **hotel** is the sixteenth-century *Villa Nencini*, in a peaceful, panoramic setting west of the centre at Borgo Santo Stefano 55 (⊤0588.86.386, ⓦwww.villanencini.it; ❸). Housed in a restored fifteenth-century convent, the *Hotel San Lino*, Via San Lino 26, just inside the walls in the north of the town, has comfortable rooms and a swimming pool (⊤0588.85.250, ⓦwww.hotelsanlino.com; ❸). Anyone can stay in a cell-with-a-view at the *Sant'Andrea* **convent** in the northeast outskirts (⊤0588.86.028; €36 for a room). The **campsite** *Le Balze* is 1km west of town at Via di Mandringa 15 (⊤0588.87.880, ⓦwww.campinglebalze.com; April–Sept).

As a renowned centre for hunting, Volterra's **restaurant** menus are dominated by wild boar (*cinghiale*), hare (*lepre*) and rabbit (*coniglio*). Most places are moderately priced, often offering fixed price menus for around €12. *Ombra della Sera*, Via Gramsci 70 (closed Mon), is a pleasant local haunt, while the vaulted gloom of *Vecchia Osteria dei Poeti*, Via Matteotti 55 (closed Thurs), is the most characterful spot for Volterra's gamey cuisine. The brighter, airier *Don Beta*, Via Matteotti 39, serves all the main staples (pasta, pizza, steak etc), but with added truffles (closed Mon).

Southern Tuscany

The inland hills of **southern Tuscany** are the region at its best, an infinite gradation of trees and vineyards that encompasses the *crete* – a sparsely populated region of pale clay hillsides – before climbing into the hills around Monte Amiata. Southwest of Siena towards the sea is gentle **Massa Maríttima**, a memorable but little-visited hill-town that presides over a marshy coastal plain. Magnificent monastic architecture survives in the tranquil settings of **San Galgano** and, a short distance east, **Monte Oliveto Maggiore**, which boasts the additional attraction of some marvellous frescoes. The finest of the hill-towns to the south of Siena is **Montepulciano**, with its superb wines and an ensemble of Renaissance architecture that rivals neighbouring **Pienza**.

Further south, the tourist crush is noticeably eased in smaller towns and villages that are often overlooked by visitors gorged on Florentine art and Sienese countryside. Wild **Monte Amiata** offers scenic mountain walks, **Saturnia** has some remarkable sulphur springs, and isolated **Pitigliano** is one of the most dramatically sited medieval towns in the region, nurturing the amazing story – and scant remains – of what was once Tuscany's strongest Jewish community.

Massa Maríttima

The road south from Volterra over the mountains to **MASSA MARÍTTIMA** is scenically magnificent yet little explored: classic Tuscan countryside which is given an added surreal quality around **Larderello** by the presence of *soffioni* (hot steam geysers), huge silver pipes snaking across the fields, and sulphurous smoke rising from chimneys amid the foliage. There are three **buses** daily to Massa from Volterra (change at Lardarello), one from Grosseto and three from Siena. It sees none of the crowds of San Gimignano, and even Volterra looks crowded in comparison.

Massa, like Volterra, has been a wealthy **mining** town since Etruscan times. In 1225, on the heels of a declaration of independence, it passed Europe's first-ever charter for the protection of miners; in the century afterwards, before Siena took over in 1335, its exquisite **Duomo** went up and the population doubled. The trend was reversed in the sixteenth century, and by 1737, after bouts of plague and malaria, it was a virtual ghost town. Massa gained its "Maríttima" suffix in the Middle Ages when it became the leading hill-town of this coastal region, even though the sea is 20km distant across a silty plain. Its recovery began with the draining of coastal marshes in the 1830s. Today, it's a quiet but well-off town, where the effects of mining are less evident than agriculture and low-profile tourism.

Blocks of new buildings mar the approach, but the medieval splendour of **Piazza Garibaldi**, just up from the bus stops, more than compensates. This perfect example of Tuscan town planning showcases the thirteenth-century **Duomo**, set on broad steps at a dramatically oblique angle to the square. The cathedral is dedicated to the sixth-century St Cerbone, whose claim to fame was to persuade a flock of geese to follow him when summoned to Rome on heresy charges. Its airy **interior** (irregular hours but approximately 8.30am–noon & 3–6pm; free) features eleventh-century carvings of grinning, cross-eyed faces – powerful and primitive, in dramatic contrast to the severe, polished Roman sarcophagus nearby. A modest **Museo Archeologico** occupies the Palazzo del Podestà opposite (April–Oct Tues–Sun 10am–12.30pm & 3.30–7pm; Nov–March closes 5pm; €3) – worth visiting for the town's undisputed masterpiece, a superb *Maestà* altarpiece by Ambrogio Lorenzetti, coloured in vivid pink, green and tangerine, with Cerbone and his geese lurking in the corner. Off the other side of the piazza is the **Collezione Martini**, Via Goldoni 5 (Tues–Sat 10.30am–12.30pm & 3–5pm; €2), which includes an engaging collection of late-nineteenth-century painting.

Otherwise, barring a couple of limited-interest museums devoted to mining, aim for the picturesque lane Via Moncini, which climbs steeply to the quiet Gothic **upper town**: as you emerge beneath an impressive but militarily useless arch onto **Piazza Matteotti**, facing you is the **Torre del Candeliere**, part of the thirteenth-century *Fortilizio Senese*. The tower is climbable for a stupendous panorama (summer daily 10am–1pm & 3–6pm; €2.50).

Practicalities

The helpful **tourist office** is just below Piazza Garibaldi at Via Todini 3/5 (daily 9am–1pm & 3–7.30pm; April, May & Nov closed Sun pm, Dec–March closed all Sun; ℡0566.902.756, ⓦwww.altamaremmaturismo.it). Massa's only central **hotel** is the comfortable *Il Sole*, Corso della Libertà 43 (℡0566.901.971, ⓔhotel@ilsolehotel.it; ❷); otherwise go for the pleasant, refurbished *Duca del Mare*, just below town at Piazza Dante Alighieri 1 (℡0566.902.284, ⓦwww .ducadelmare.it; ❸). There's also a good **hostel**, Ostello Massa Marittima, in the higher part of town, converted from a school at Via Gramsci 3 (℡0566.901.115, ⓔleclarisse@libero.it; €15 per person; 9am–noon & 5pm–midnight). Better **restaurants** than those lining Piazza Garibaldi include the characterful *Trattoria dei Cavalieri*, Via Norma Parenti 35 (℡0566.902.093; closed Thurs), with moderately priced Tuscan staples, and *Osteria da Tronca* at Vicolo Porte 5 (℡0566.901.991; closed lunch & Wed), offering inexpensive *osteria*-style fare in a rustic stone wall setting. *Pizzeria Barbablu*, up at Piazza Matteotti 5, has excellent and spectacular *pizza gialla* (a pizza base sprinkled with saffron, scamorza and parmesan cheeses, and rocket) and outside tables. There's also an extensive and very reasonable pasta menu. Opposite hotel *Il Sole*, the **pub** *Del Priore*, Via Libertà 34, has good beer and a blues jukebox.

Make time in summer for the **Toscana Foto Festival** (℡0566.901.526, ⓦwww.toscanafotofestival.com), with photo exhibits and workshops at venues around town in late July, and a prestigious show of the cream of the crop running until late August.

The crete

South of Siena stretches classic Tuscan countryside known as the *crete* – a sparsely populated region of pale clay hillsides dotted with sheep, cypresses and the odd monumental-looking farmhouse. These tranquil lands were one of the heartlands of medieval monasticism in Tuscany. The Vallombrosan order maintained their main house at Torri just south of Siena, the Benedictine order had theirs at Sant'Ántimo near Montalcino (see p.611), while the Cistercians founded the convent and abbey of **San Galgano**; now ruined, this is one of the most alluring sights in Tuscany, complete with its hilltop chapel housing a "sword in the stone". The region's grandest monastery is southeast of Siena at **Monte Oliveto Maggiore**.

San Galgano

The **Abbazia di San Galgano**, 26km northeast of Massa Maríttima in a peaceful rural setting, is perhaps the most evocative Gothic building in all Italy – roofless, with a grass field for a nave, nebulous patches of fresco amid the vegetation, and panoramas of the sky, clouds and hills through a rose window. In the twelfth and thirteenth centuries, local **Cistercian** monks were the leading power in Tuscany. The abbots exercised powers of arbitration in city disputes, and at Siena the monks were the city's accountants. Through them, the ideas of Gothic building were imported to Italy. The order began a hilltop **church** and monastical buildings here in 1218, but their project to build a grand abbey on the fertile land below was doomed to failure. Building work took seventy years up to 1288, but then famine struck in 1329, the Black Death in 1348, and mercenaries ran amok in subsequent decades. By 1500, all the monks had moved to the security of Siena. The buildings mouldered until 1786, when the belltower was struck by lightning and collapsed. Three years later, the church was deconsecrated, and the complex was abandoned for good.

These days, the main appeal of the **abbey** (open all day and illuminated at night until 11.30pm) is its state of ruin, although work to halt the advance of Mother Nature is under way and there are concerts of classical music held from late July to late August (see p.590 for more).

On the hill above, the unusual round Romanesque church of **Monte Siepi** commemorates the spot where Galgano – a local twelfth-century knight – renounced his violent past by thrusting his sword into a stone. Amazingly enough, Galgano's **sword in the stone** has survived, protected under glass as an object of veneration. A side chapel preserves the decaying remains of a man's hands: local legend has it that two wolves – companions of Galgano – tore them from a robber who had broken into the saint's tomb.

There are two or three **buses** daily between Massa Maríttima and Siena that pass within sight of the abbey and you can ask to be dropped off. To one side of the abbey building, in the old vaulted scriptorium, is a small **tourist office** (daily: summer 10.30am–6pm; winter 10.30am–1.30pm & 3–5pm; ☎0577.756.738, ⓦwww.prolocochiusdino.it). The small café on the approach to the abbey, run by the *Cooperativa Agricola San Galgano*, has **rooms** (☎0577.756.292; ❶), and produces sandwiches and simple meals as well as selling local produce. In its grounds is the **Centro Italiano Rapaci**, or Raptor Centre; it's open all summer with unreliable opening times (call ☎0347.704.9732 for more information), but restricts displays of falconry to August only.

Monte Oliveto Maggiore

It takes some effort to visit the **Abbazia di Monte Oliveto Maggiore**, but the rewards are clear: Tuscany's grandest monastery is sited 26km southeast of Siena in one of the most beautiful tracts of Sienese countryside, and houses one of the most absorbing Renaissance **frescoes** you'll find anywhere. By car, you can approach from the crossroads town of Buonconvento, climbing quickly into forests of pine, oak and cypress, and then into the olive groves that enclose the monastery. One afternoon **bus** daily from Siena's train station goes to the village of Chiusure, 2km east of the abbey.

When Pius II visited in 1463, it was the overall scene that impressed him: the architecture, in honey-coloured Sienese brick, merging into the woods and gardens that the **Olivetan** or White Benedictine monks had created from the eroded hills of the *crete*. Within six years, the pope recognized the order and over the following two centuries this, their principal house, was transformed into one of the most powerful monasteries in the land. It was only in 1810, when the monastery was suppressed by Napoleon, that it fell from influence. Today it's maintained by a small group of Olivetan monks, who supplement their state income with a high-tech centre for the restoration of ancient books. At the **gatehouse**, there's a good café-restaurant, *La Torre* (☎0577.707.022; closed Tues), from where an avenue of cypresses leads down the hill to the abbey. Signs at the bottom of the slope direct you along a walk to **Blessed Bernardo's grotto** – a chapel built on the site where the founder lived as a hermit – and there's also a **shop** selling herbal cures and liquors (Mon–Sat

10am–noon & 3.45–6pm, Sun 9.30–10.45am & 3.45–6pm), and a small **tourist office** (Tues–Sun 10am–1pm & 2.30–5.30pm).

The **abbey** (daily 9.15am–noon & 3.15–6pm; winter closes 5pm) is a huge complex, though much of it remains off-limits to visitors. The entrance leads to the **Chiostro Grande**, covered by a series of frescoes depicting the Life of St Benedict, the man traditionally regarded as the founder of Christian monasticism. The cycle begins on the east wall, just on the right of the door into the church, and was begun in 1497 by Luca Signorelli who painted nine panels in the middle of the series that start with the depiction of a collapsing house. The colourful Antonio Bazzi, known as Il Sodoma, painted the remaining 27 scenes between 1505 and 1508. He was by all accounts a lively presence, bringing with him part of his menagerie of pets, which included badgers, depicted at his feet in a self-portrait in the third panel. There's a sensuality in many of the secular figures, especially the young men – as befits the artist's nickname – but also the "evil women" (originally nudes, until protests from the abbot). The **church** (entered off the Chiostro Grande) was given a Baroque remodelling in the eighteenth century and some superb stained glass in the twentieth. Its main treasure is the choir stalls, inlaid by Giovanni di Verona and others with architectural, landscape and domestic scenes (including a nod to Sodoma's pets with a cat in a window). Stairs lead from the cloister up to the **library**, again with carving by Giovanni; sadly, it has had to be viewed from the door since the theft of sixteen of its twenty codices in 1975.

BUONCONVENTO, 9km southwest, has unappealing outskirts but a perfectly preserved medieval village at its heart, sheltering the **hotel-restaurant** *Roma* (℡0577.806.021, ℻0577.807.284; ❷; restaurant closed Mon). Regular **buses** from Siena's train station to Buonconvento head on to Montalcino, or to Pienza and Montepulciano.

Montepulciano and around

The highest of the Tuscan hill-towns, at more than 600m, **MONTEPUL-CIANO** is built on a long, narrow ridge 65km southeast of Siena, along which coils the main street, the **Corso**, flanked by a series of dark alleys that drop away to the walls, providing slivers of views between Renaissance *palazzi* out over the rolling countryside. Henry James, who compared the town to a ship, spent most of his time here drinking – a sound policy, in view of the excellent local table wine and the more refined and much-celebrated **Vino Nobile**. The town is set in superb walking country and is not yet overrun by day-trippers, while a short distance east is the little Etruscan town of **Chiusi**.

Arrival, information and accommodation

TRA-IN **buses** run roughly every hour between Buonconvento, Torrenieri (change for Montalcino), San Quírico d'Órcia, Pienza and Montepulciano – some of them begin from Siena – while LFI buses run regularly between Montepulciano, Chiusi and its **train** station.

Montepulciano's spiralling, tortuous streets are pretty steep, and **orientation** can get confusing. The main entrance to the town – at the lowest point – is the northern gate, the **Porta al Prato**, terminus of most buses; from here, the Corso climbs south through the town (changing its name from Via di Gracciano to Via di Voltaia, then to Via dell'Opio) until it reaches the southern gate, the **Porta delle Farine**, where intercity buses also drop off. From here, the main

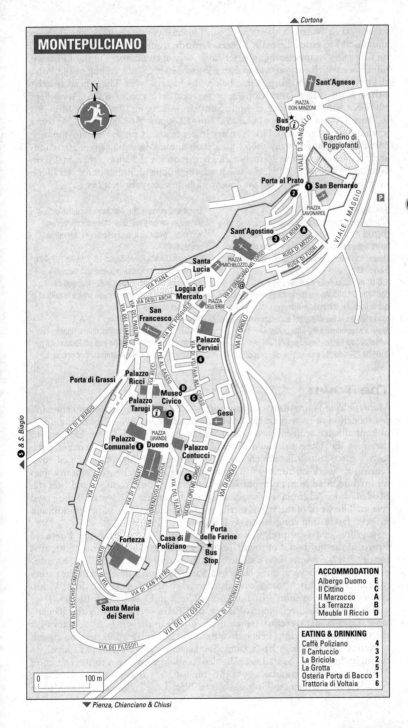

MONTEPULCIANO

▲ Cortona

N

Sant'Agnese

PIAZZA
DON MINZONI

Bus
Stop ℹ

Giardino di
Poggiofanti

Porta al Prato ●1 San Bernardo
●2

PIAZZA
SAVONAROL

Sant'Agostino

●3 VIA ROMA Ⓐ

RUGA DI MEZZO

RUGA DI FUORI

VIALE D. SANGALLO

VIALE I MAGGIO

P

🅟

Santa
Lucia

PIAZZA
MICHELOZZO

VIA DI GIACOMO DEL CORSO

Loggia di
Mercato

PIAZZA
DELL'ERBE

@

VIA PIANA

VIA DEGLI ARCHI

VIA DEL PAOLINO

VIA DEL GIARDINO

San
Francesco

VIA DEL POGGIOLO

VIA DI ORIOLO

VIA RICCI

VIA PIE AL SASSO

Palazzo
Cervini
Ⓐ4

VIA DI VOLTAIA NEL CORSO

Porta di Grassi

Palazzo
Ricci

Palazzo
Tarugi

Museo
Ⓑ
Civico
Ⓒ

ℹ Ⓓ

Gesù

VIA DI S. BIAGIO

Palazzo
Comunale Ⓔ

PIAZZA
GRANDE
Duomo

Palazzo
Contucci

●6

VIA DI ORIOLO

◀ ⑤ & S. Biagio

VIA DI COLLAZZI

VIA DI S. DONATO

VIA FIORENZUOLA VECCHIA

VIA DEL TEATRO

VIA DELL'OPIO NEL CORSO

Porta
delle Farine
★
Bus
Stop

Fortezza

Casa di
Poliziano

VIA DI S. DONATO

VIA DI SAN PIETRO

VIA DI CIRCONVALLAZIONE

Santa Maria
dei Servi

VIA DEL VECCHIO CIMITERO

VIA DEI FILOSOFI

VIA DEI FILOSOFI

8

▼ Pienza, Chianciano & Chiusi

ACCOMMODATION
Albergo Duomo	E
Il Cittino	C
Il Marzocco	A
La Terrazza	B
Meuble Il Riccio	D

EATING & DRINKING
Caffè Poliziano	4
Il Cantuccio	3
La Briciola	2
La Grotta	5
Osteria Porta di Bacco	1
Trattoria di Voltaia	6

0   100 m

605

street (Via di Poliziano, then Via di San Donato) continues its coiling path up and around to enter the main **Piazza Grande** from the south. The stiff climb on foot takes an unrelenting quarter-hour; or you could resort to the LFI town minibuses which run on a loop every 20min, starting and ending at the Porta al Prato (€0.75). **Parking** is free below the eastern walls. The official **tourist office** is on Piazza Don Minzoni at the northern end of town (April–Sept Mon–Sat 9am–12.30pm & 3–8pm, Sun 9am–12.30pm; Oct–March Mon–Sat 9.30am–12.30pm & 3–6pm, Sun 9.30am–12.30pm; ☏0578.757.341, ⓦwww .comune.montepulciano.si.it). It offers Internet access for €1 per 15 minutes. More central, and equally useful for details about Montepulciano's attractions and facilities, as well as Vino Nobile, is the Strada del Vino office in Piazza Grande 7 (☏0578.717.484, ⓦwww.stradavinonobile.it). Either office can advise on private rooms, otherwise the following hotels are your best bet.

Hotels

Albergo Duomo Via San Donato 14 ☏0578.757.473, ⓔalbergoduomo@libero.it. A short distance from Piazza Grande, the three star *Duomo* has excellent facilities and smart clean rooms. ❸

Il Cittino Vicolo della Via Nuova 2 ☏0578.757.335. Above the restaurant of the same name (look for the handwritten sign stating "also rooms"), this is the cheapest accommodation in town. It's welcoming if a little basic. ❶

Il Marzocco Piazza Savonarola 18 ☏0578.757.262, ⓦwww.albergoilmarzocco.it.

Large and elegant, the *Marzocco* occupies a sixteenth-century building. There's a restaurant and café downstairs, and relatively plain rooms upstairs. ❸

La Terrazza Via Piè al Sasso 16 ☏0578.757.440, ⓦwww.laterrazzadimontepulciano.it. Recently renovated, the friendly and well-equipped *La Terrazza* has a leafy roof terrace where breakfast is served in summer. ❸

Meuble Il Riccio Via Talosa 21 ☏ & ⓕ0578.757.713, ⓦwww.ilriccio.net. Housed in a cloistered medieval building just off Piazza Grande, *Il Riccio* enjoys a central, atmospheric option. ❸

The Town

Montepulciano's unusually consistent array of Renaissance *palazzi* and churches is a reflection of its remarkable development after 1511, when, following intermittent alliance with Siena, the town finally threw in its lot with Florence. In that year the Florentines sent **Antonio Sangallo the Elder** to rebuild the town's gates and walls, which he did so impressively that the council took him on to work on the town hall and a series of churches. The local nobles meanwhile hired him, his nephew, Antonio Sangallo the Younger, and later the Modena-born **Vignola** – a founding figure of Baroque – to work on their own *palazzi*. The work of this trio is totally assured in conception and execution, and makes a fascinating comparison with Rossellino's Pienza.

Sangallo's first commission was Montepulciano's main gate, the **Porta al Prato**, at the north end of town. Inside the gate the **Corso** begins. In the first square, Piazza Savonarola, is a stone column bearing the heraldic lion (*marzocco*) of Florence. Just beyond is the church of **Sant'Agostino**, designed by the earlier Medici protégé, Michelozzo, who also carved the relief above the door. Within are good Sienese paintings by Lorenzo di Credi and Giovanni di Paolo.

About 100m further along is **Piazza dell'Erbe** overlooked by the Renaissance **Loggia di Mercato**, which marks a fork in the street. A right turn off the Corso brings you up steeply to a beautiful little piazza fronting the church of **Santa Lucia**, which has a fabulous *Madonna* by Signorelli in a chapel on the right. Just below Santa Lucia, Via del Poggiolo runs down to the church of San Francesco and continues – as the imposing Via Ricci – up to the Piazza Grande past the Sienese-Gothic Palazzo Neri-Orselli, home to the **Museo**

Civico (Tues–Sat 10am–1pm & 3–7pm, Sun 10am–7pm; €4.13), an extensive collection of small-town Gothic and Renaissance works.

Piazza Grande, Montepulciano's theatrical flourish of a main square, is built on the highest point of the ridge, and is worth the climb. Its most distinctive building is the **Palazzo Comunale**, a thirteenth-century Gothic mansion to which Michelozzo added a tower and rustication in imitation of the Palazzo Vecchio in Florence. You can climb the **tower** (daily 10am–6pm; €1.55) – though disappointingly not right to the top – and on clear days the view supposedly stretches to Siena. Down below, two of the *palazzi* on the square were designed by Sangallo. The **Palazzo Tarugi**, by the lion and griffin fountain, is a highly innovative building, with a public loggia cut through one corner; it originally had an extension on the top floor, though this has been bricked in. Headier pleasures await at the **Palazzo Contucci**, one of many buildings scattered about the town that serve as *cantine* for the wine trade, offering free *degustazione* (tastings) and sale of the Vino Nobile. Sangallo and his contemporaries never got around to building a facade for the plain brick **Duomo** across the square (daily 9am–1pm & 3.30–7pm; free). Its interior is an elegant Renaissance design, scattered with superb sculptures by Michelozzo, while the finest of its paintings is the Sienese **Taddeo di Bartolo**'s iridescent 1401 altarpiece of the Assumption, a favourite subject among Sienese artists.

Sangallo's greatest commission came in 1518, when he was invited to design the pilgrimage church of **San Biagio** on the hillside below the town. It's a fifteen-minute walk from the centre: aim for the Porta di Grassi, a couple of levels below the north side of Piazza Grande, from where Via San Biagio slopes down to the church. This was the second-largest church project of its time after St Peter's in Rome, and exercised Antonio until his death in 1534. The result is one of the most serene Renaissance creations in Italy, constructed from a porous travertine whose soft honey-coloured stone blends perfectly into its niche in the landscape. Its major architectural novelty was the use of freestanding towers to flank the facade (only one was completed). The interior is spoilt a little by Baroque trompe-l'oeil decoration, but remains supremely harmonious. Scarcely less perfect is the nearby **Canonica** (rectory), endowed by Sangallo with a graceful portico and double-tiered loggia.

Eating, drinking and entertainment

Vino Nobile di Montepulciano has been acclaimed since medieval times and today boasts a top-rated DOCG mark; something the townspeople have not been shy in exploiting. Montepulciano's streets are filled with wine shops selling gift sets, and local vineyards often offer tastings in the town (generally free, but usually requiring advance notice). Every restaurant can provide a range of vintages, the very cheapest of which will still set you back at least €20. The tourist office has a complete list of the town's wine outlets, and can organize a **wine-tasting** ramble for you. Some of the many places to check out include the venerable *Contucci*, Via San Donato 15 (☎0578.757.006, ⓦwww.contucci .it), which can trace the family line in Montepulciano back a thousand years, and the *Cantina Del Redi*, Via di Collazi 5 (☎0578.716.092, ⓦwww .cantinadelredi.com). Even if you can't afford Vino Nobile, ordering a cheap carafe of house *rosso* anywhere in Montepulciano will turn up a fragrant, silky smooth and highly memorable wine.

Every July, the three-week **Cantiere Internazionale d'Arte** (☎0578.757.089, ⓦwww.cantiere.toscana.nu) presents exhibitions and concerts around town, and the last Sunday in August sees the **Bravìo delle Botti**, a barrel-race in medieval costume. Just south of the Piazza Grande, the **Palazzo Ricci**, designed by Baldasarre Peruzzi, a pupil of Sangallo, is now home to the German-run European Academy of Music and Art (*Europäische Academie für Musik und Darstellende Kunst*, ☎0578.765.022, ⓦwww.palazzoricci.com), which occasionally stages public performances of classical music and opera.

Cafés and restaurants

Caffè Poliziano Via di Voltaia nel Corso 27. An 1868 tearoom restored to a classic Art Nouveau design; it serves pastries and pots of tea, while its adjoining restaurant, *Il Grifin d'Oro*, serves somewhat pricey meals, such as *pici* (fat spaghetti) with wild boar *ragù* for €9.90, and offers great views from a small terrace. Daily 7am–midnight.

Il Cantuccio Via delle Cantine 1 ☎0578.757.870. A standard Tuscan menu is enlivened by items such as *boarconcini di cinghiale* (little bites of wild boar). Mains range from €8 to €15. Closed Mon.

La Briciola Via delle Cantine. Quality wood-fired pizza, as well as a range of hearty Tuscan *primi* (€8) and *secondi* (€10–12). Closed Wed.

La Grotta Via di San Biagio ☎0578.757.607. Opposite San Biagio church, about 1km outside the city walls, brick-vaulted *La Grotta* serves pricey classic Tuscan cuisine in a sixteenth-century building with its own garden. Closed Wed.

Osteria Porta di Bacco Via di Gracciano nel Corso 106 ☎0578.757.948. Just inside the Porta al Prato, this quiet, characterful old stone-arched place is one of a clutch of moderately priced options, offering a set three-course menu for €12. Closed Tues.

Trattoria di Cagnano Via dell Opio Nel Corso 30 ☎0578.758.757. Popular and bustling, this offers a wide range of pizzas, from the simple €4.50 *margherita* to the €7.50 *estate* (mozzarella, tomatoes, rocket, prosciutto and parmesan), as well as outside seating. Closed Sat.

Chiusi

CHIUSI, 14km southeast of Montepulciano, is a useful transport hub, but this sleepy place is also worth more than an hour or two's stopover – its quietly extraordinary cathedral, Christian catacombs and an Etruscan labyrinth could well entice you into delaying an onward journey. **Chiusi Scalo**, an unattractive suburb, is the default stop for all intercity buses, and is where the train station is located. The town centre, **Chiusi Città**, is 2km west; it's a short walk from the bus stop up Via Marconi to the main street, **Via Porsenna**, named after a semi-mythical Etruscan king of the sixth century BC. Here you'll find the modest (if not modestly named) **Museo Archeologico Nazionale** (daily 9am–8pm; €4), dedicated mainly to Etruscan relics, with numerous sarcophagi, a few terracottas with traces of ancient paint, and the odd treasure – notably the enigmatic Gualandi Urn. If you're interested in seeing some of the Etruscan **tombs** outside town, ask one of the museum guards to take you (they hold the keys); the famous frescoed Tomba della Scimmia (of the Monkey), can be visited on prebooked guided tours (Tues, Thurs & Sat 11am & 4pm; ☎0578.20.177).

Outside the museum is Piazza Duomo, an elegant little square paved in glittering marble with the Romanesque **Duomo**, one of Tuscany's oldest, which was built in the sixth century almost entirely from Etruscan and Roman blocks. Inside is a wealth of decoration; although much of the mosaic work on the walls is nineteenth-century, the marble columns – each with a different capital – the mosaic floor and the alabaster font are all Roman. The **Museo della Cattedrale** alongside (daily: June to mid-Oct 9.30am–1pm & 4–7pm; mid-Oct to May Mon–Sat 9.30am–12.45pm, Sun 9.30am–12.45pm & 3–6pm; €2) has a small collection of silverware and codices, and gives access to the **Labirinto di Porsenna** ("Labyrinth of Porsenna", €3, or €4 combined ticket), which leads you through the atmospheric tunnels of the Etruscan water-catchment system below the piazza to a huge Roman cistern and then up inside the twelfth-century campanile. You can also arrange here to meet a guide at the entrance to the **Catacomba Cristiana di Santa Mustiola** ("Christian Catacombs of Santa Mustiola"), 2km east of town, which were used by early Christians in the fourth and fifth centuries (tours daily 11am; June to mid-Oct also 5pm; €6).

Practicalities

Chiusi's **tourist office** (Mon–Sat 9.30am–1pm & 3.30–6.30pm, Sun 9.30am–1pm; usually closed afternoons in winter; ☎0578.227.667, ⊛www.comune .chiusi.siena.it) is opposite the Duomo. There's one central **hotel**, the basic *La Sfinge*, Via Marconi 2 (☎0578.20.157, ⊛www.albergolasfinge.it; ❸), with more options at Chiusi Scalo. The best **restaurant** is *La Solita Zuppa*, Via Porsenna 21 (☎0578.21.006; closed Tues), with an inventive menu offering lots of soups and items such as *tagliolini al ginger*. The more traditional *Zaira*, nearby at Via Arunte 12 (☎0578.20.260; closed Mon in winter), offers "Etruscan" fare – boar, rabbit, trout and the like.

Pienza and around

PIENZA, 11km west of Montepulciano, is as complete a Renaissance creation as any in Italy, established in an act of considerable vanity by **Pope Pius II** as a Utopian "New Town". The transformation of the village of Cortignano, where Pius was born, began in 1459 under the architect **Bernardo Rossellino**. The cost was astronomical, but the cathedral, papal and bishop's palaces, and the core of a town (renamed in Pius's honour), were completed in just three years. Pius lived just two more years, and of his successors only his nephew paid Pienza any regard: the city, intended to spread across the hill, stayed village-sized. Today, with a population of 2500, it still has an air of emptiness and folly – a natural stage set, where Zeffirelli filmed *Romeo and Juliet*.

Hikes in the Parco della Val d'Orcia

There are plenty of interesting **hikes** in the area around San Quírico and Montalcino comprising the **Parco della Val d'Orcia**, full details of which are in *Walking the Val d'Orcia*, an English pamphlet by the Touring Club Italiano, available at the park office, at Piazza Chigi in San Quírico (☎0577.899.711, ⊛www.parcodellavaldorcia.com).

A moderately challenging trail runs from **Bagno Vignoni** out to the castle restaurant at Ripa d'Orcia and back (12km; 4hr). From 100m before the car park, a cart-track rises through vineyards and olive groves to Rocca di Vignoni, the hamlet of Vignoni and on to Podere Bellaria, after which is a junction. One route heads right (north) to San Quírico, the other left (south) through a scenic landscape up to the castle. Backtracking 500m down the castle hill you'll find a signposted path leading right, down through foliage to a broken bridge over the Orcia river; don't cross, but follow the left-hand riverbank back to Bagno Vignoni.

There's an easy trail from **Montalcino** to San Quírico, crossing shadeless clay hills and dipping through vineyards (13km; 4hr), or you could cycle it, with rental bikes from *Lorenzo Minocci*, Viale Strozzi in Montalcino (☎0577.848.282). From the northern Porta Burelli, a track drops down to Gli Angeli and crosses the paved road in front of Podere La Casaccia, heading into an area of hummocks until you reach the provincial highway. Follow the road right for a few hundred metres, coming off at Podere Fiesole and heading east across clay ground to Podere Casello and Poderi Pian dell'Asso. Cross the train track and a couple of streams before climbing to Podere Belladonna and the chapel of Madonna di Riguardo. A rising and falling path covers the last 1.5km into San Quírico.

Traffic converges on **Piazza Dante**, just outside the main gate, Porta al Murello, and from here the **Corso** leads straight to Rossellino's centrepiece, **Piazza Pio II**, which deliberately juxtaposes civic and religious buildings – the Duomo, Palazzo Piccolomini (papal palace), Bishop's Palace and Palazzo Pubblico – to underline the balance between church and town. The square makes the usual medieval nod to Florence in its town hall, but is otherwise entirely Renaissance in conception.

The **Duomo** has one of the earliest Renaissance facades in Tuscany; the interior, on Pius's orders, took inspiration from the German hall-churches he had seen on his travels, and remains essentially Gothic. The chapels house an outstanding series of Sienese altarpieces, commissioned from the major paint-ers of the age – Giovanni di Paolo, Matteo di Giovanni, Vecchietta and Sano di Pietro. How long the building itself will remain standing is uncertain though. Even before completion a crack appeared, and after an earthquake in the nineteenth century it has required much buttressing – the nave currently dips crazily towards the back of the church. The airy **crypt**, with a separate entrance (Mon, Tues & Thurs–Sat 10am–noon & 3.30–5.30pm; €1), displays some sixteenth-century tapestries. Pius's residence, the recently restored **Palazzo Piccolomini**, sits alongside the duomo. You're free to walk into the courtyard and through to the original "hanging garden" behind to the left, with a triple-tiered loggia offering a superb view over the valley. The **apartments** above (Tues–Sun 10am–12.30pm & 3–6pm; €3, €7 including guided tour) include Pius II's bedroom, library and other rooms filled with collections of weap-ons and medals. Further mementoes of the pope – notably his English-made embroidered cope – are across the piazza in the excellent **Museo Diocesano** (mid-March to Oct 10am–1pm & 3–6.30pm; Nov to mid-March Sat & Sun 10am–1pm & 3–6pm; €4).

Practicalities

Regular **buses** between Montepulciano and Buonconvento pass through Pienza and San Quírico d'Orcia. Pienza is also a gentle day's **walk** from Montepulciano on an old cross-country route through the walled village of Monticchiello. The very helpful **tourist office** (Mon–Sat 9.30am–1pm & 3–6.30pm; ☎0578.748.359, ⓦwww.comunepienza.it), at Piazza Dante Aligh-ieri 18, by the Porta al Murello at the entrance to the town, offers a self-guided fifty-minute audio tour of the town (€5). Pienza has pleasant rooms and self-catering apartments at *Giardino Segreto*, Via Condotti 13 (☎0578.748.539, ⓦwww.ilgiardinosegreto.toscana.nu; ❸), and the fabulously romantic hotel *Relais Il Chiostro di Pienza*, a converted Franciscan monastery at Corso Rossel-lino 26 (☎0578.748.400, ⓦwww.relaisilchiostrodipienza.com; ❺). Non-guests are welcome to visit the cloisters. Its **restaurant**, *La Terrazza* (same telephone number; closed Mon), with expansive views, is the best in Pienza, but pricier than most – there's an Internet café, *Pienza Internet*, next door. More afford-able eating options include *Dal Falco*, a simple trattoria in Piazza Dante with a pleasantly leafy outdoor eating area (☎0578.748.551; closed Fri), and the friendly *Latte di Luna*, (although it can get pricey if you go for the house speciality – *maialino arrosto*, roast suckling pig), just inside the walls at Via San Carlo 2 (☎0578.748.606; closed Tues), again with a good outside seating area. You can get sandwiches and wine at the *Enoteca Le Crete* on Piazza Martiri, and there's plenty of **picnic food**: Pienza is centre of a region producing pecorino sheep's cheese, and has gone overboard on natural food shops: cheesy smells await around every corner.

San Quírico d'Orcia and Bagno Vignoni

SAN QUÍRICO D'ORCIA, a rambling old village, stands at a crossroads 8km west of Pienza. Despite being a major stop for TRA-IN (Siena–Montepulciano), RAMA (Siena–Arcidosso) and SIRA (Montalcino–Rome) buses, its old town is quiet and rather decayed, with an exceptionally pretty Romanesque **Collegiata** church. If you've got your own transport, you can head for the stunning *Castello Ripa d'Orcia*, an isolated castle **hotel-restaurant** 5km southwest of town down a gravel road (℡0577.897.376, ⓦwww .castelloripadorcia.com; minimum stay two nights; ❸; from €515 per week in one of the castle's self-catering apartments).

You can **rent bikes** from Cicloposse, Via Primo Maggio 27 in Pienza (℡0578.749.983, ⓦwww.cicloposse.com), to follow a country track south to the medieval baths at **BAGNO VIGNONI**, 6km southeast of San Quírico (also served by bus). Its central square is occupied by an arcaded Roman *piscina*, or open pool; the springs still bubble up at a steamy 51°C, and the old, flooded piazza with its backdrop of the Tuscan hills and Renaissance **loggia** – built by the Medici, who, like St Catherine of Siena, took the sulphur cure here – made a memorable scene in Tarkovsky's film *Nostalgia*. The *piscina* has been out of bounds for bathing for some years, but you can bathe in the sulphur springs at the *Piscina Val di Sole*, a modern bathing complex at the characterful *Posta Marcucci* **hotel** just below the village (℡0577.887.112, ⓦwww.hotelpostamarcucci .it; ❺; pool free to guests, €10 per day to others). Pius II's fifteenth-century summer retreat overlooking the *piscina* is now the romantic *Albergo Le Terme* (℡0577.887.150, ⓦwww.albergoleterme.it; ❹). Best **restaurant** is the excellent *Antica Osteria del Leone*, Via dei Mulini 3 (℡0577.877.300; closed Mon).

Montalcino

MONTALCINO is another classic Tuscan hill-town, 20km west of Pienza. Set within a full circuit of walls and watched over by a *rocca*, it looks tremendous from below – and from above, the surrounding countryside strewn with vineyards, orchards and olive groves is equally impressive. Montalcino produces a top-notch DOCG **wine**, Brunello di Montalcino, reckoned by many to be the finest in Italy, and is a quiet place, affluent in an unshowy way from its tourist trade. For a time in the fifteenth century, though, the town was of great symbolic importance: it was the last of the Sienese *comune* to hold out against the Medici, the French and the Spanish after Siena itself had capitulated. This role is acknowledged at the Siena Palio, where the Montalcino contingent – under its medieval banner proclaiming "The Republic of Siena in Montalcino" – takes pride of place.

The main street, Via Mazzini, leads from **Piazza Cavour** at the north end of town to the **Piazza del Popolo**, an odd little square set beneath the elongated tower of the town hall, based in all but its dimensions on that of Siena. An elegant double loggia occupies another side with, opposite, a wonderful and rather Germanic nineteenth-century café, the *Fiaschetteria Italiana*, which is very much the heart of town life. Steps (Scale di Via Bandi) near the café lead up to the excellent **Museo Civico e Diocesano d'Arte Sacra** (Tues–Sun: April–Dec 10am–6pm; Jan–March 10am–1pm & 2–5.30pm; €4.50 or €6 joint ticket with the Rocca fortress). The quality of the art on show is out of all proportion to the size of the town, and takes in a wealth of Sienese painting and early sculpture. Following Via Ricasoli south brings you to the **Rocca** fortress (daily

9am–8pm; winter closes 6pm; €1.50 or €6 joint ticket with Museo Civico). Impressively complete, this encloses a public park and plush *enoteca*. You can also get access to the ramparts from here.

Practicalities

Regular **buses** arrive from Buonconvento and Siena, most of which pass first through Torrenieri, from where connections head to Pienza and Montepulciano, and to Arcidosso and Abbadia San Salvatore. Montalcino's bus stop is at the north end of town in Piazza Cavour. The Pro Loco **tourist office** is in the town hall, just off the Piazza del Popolo at Costa del Municipio 8 (winter Tues–Sun 10am–1pm & 2–5.40pm; summer daily 10am–1pm & 2–5.50pm; ☏0577.849.331, ⓦwww.prolocomontalcino.it). **Hotels** are not particularly oustanding with the *Giardino*, Via Cavour 2 (☏ & ⑤0577.848.257; ❷), prone to street noise and offering saggy beds; although *Il Giglio*, Via Saloni 49 (☏0577.848.167, ⓦwww.gigliohotel.com; ❸), does have a certain charm and a decent restaurant with a terrace providing views over the valley. It's worth looking into the option of **private rooms**: try *Palazzina Cesira*, Via Soccorso Saloni, 2 (☏0577.846.055, ⓔecesira@montalcinoitaly.com; ❷ including breakfast); *Le Camere di Bacco*, Via Mazzini 65 (☏0577.849.356, ⓦwww.lecameredibacco .com; ❷ with breakfast), or ask at tourist information. The best **restaurant** is *Il Re di Macchia*, Via Soccorzo Saloni 21 (☏0577.846.116; closed Thurs), although it is a tad pretentious; *Grappolo Blu*, Via Scale di Moglio 1, a *taverna* off Via Mazzini (☏0577.847.150; closed Fri), is more down-to-earth. Best pizza in town is at *San Giorgio* on Via Soccorzo Saloni (☏0577.848.507; closed Wed), while *Agrodolce*, Via Matteotti 19 (☏0577.847.207; closed Wed), serves fantastic *crostone,* home-made pastas and other traditional Tuscan dishes prepared with lots of care and attention and has a large wine list. Mains are around €8 and there are a few sought-after tables on the street. *Caffè Mariuccia*, Via Matteotti 31, makes exquisitely delicious Sienese patisserie, especially the sublime *ricchiarelli* (soft almond biscuits). *Enoteca Osteria Osticcio*, Via Matteotti 23 (Mon–Sat 9am–8pm; ☏0577.848.271, ⓦwww.osticcio.com), is a slickly beautiful wine shop with tables for tasters and views over a spectacular Tuscan landscape.

Monte Amiata

At 1738m, the extinct volcano of **Monte Amiata** is the highest point in southern Tuscany. Rising from the comparative desolation of the *crete* in a succession of hills forested in chestnut and fir, it's visible for miles around. A circle of towns rings its lower slopes, but the only one worth visiting for its own sake is **Abbadia San Salvatore**; nonetheless, old castles and bucolic countryside make the area a good detour. Towns such as Abbadia and, on the western slope, **Arcidosso** are refreshingly cool for summer walking, and in winter are the nearest ski resorts to Rome. **Buses** serve Abbadia San Salvatore from Siena, Buonconvento, Chiusi and Montepulciano; those from Rome and Grosseto to Abbadia pass first through Arcidosso. Avoid the Monte Amiata **train** station – it's 45km away.

The centre of activity is **ABBADIA SAN SALVATORE**, which shelters at its heart a perfect, self-contained medieval quarter. The Benedictine **abbey**, around which the village developed, was founded under the Lombards and rebuilt in 1036. Today a mere fraction remains of the original, and most remnants date from the Middle Ages; the highlight is a large and beautiful eighth-century **crypt**, its 35 columns decorated with Lombard motifs. The town sees plenty of summer visitors, up here for the landscape, cool breezes and some good easy walks: best is the **Anello della Montagna**, a 29km path which circles the mountain between 900m and 1300m – a long day's walk, or easily manageable in sections round to Arcidosso. In July and August, buses shuttle up to the **summit**, offering a panorama that stretches to the sea. The **tourist office**, Via Adua 25 (Mon–Sat 9am–1pm & 4–6pm; ☎0577.775.811, ⓦwww .amiataturismo.it), is headquarters for the Amiata region. Best of the numerous **hotels** are the *Cesaretti*, Via Trento 37–43 (☎0577.778.198; ❶), and the central *San Marco*, Via Matteotti 19 (☎ & Ⓕ0577.778.089; ❷).

ARCIDOSSO is another summer walking centre, with prosperous new development surrounding a well-preserved medieval quarter. Six buses daily connect to Abbadia. The *Gatto d'Oro* is a modern **hotel** at Aia dei Venti (☎ & Ⓕ0564.967.074; ❷), and there's a new **tourist office** at Piazza Indipendenza 30 (☎0564.966.438, ⓦwww.comune.arcidosso.gr.it). Good **walks** include a ramble to the village of Montelaterone, 3km northwest, passing the Romanesque **Abbadia Santa Maria ad Lamulas**. More demanding is the hike up **Monte Labbro** (1193m) 10km south (also accessible by dirt road), which has, on its summit, the ruins of a church established by Davide Lazzaretti, founder of the Jurisdavidical Church, a Christian movement which campaigned for social reform in the turbulent 1870s. Lazzaretti was murdered by the Carabinieri in 1878, and is still remembered by locals.

Pitigliano and around

Tuscany's deep south, on the Lazio border, is its least-touristed corner. **PITIGLIANO**, the largest town of the area, is best approached along the road from Manciano, 15km west. As you draw close, the town soars above you on a spectacular outcrop of tufa, its quarters linked by the arches of an immense aqueduct. **Etruscan** tombs honeycomb the cliffs, but the town was known for

8

TUSCANY | Pitigliano and around

The Jews of Pitigliano

Jews began moving to Pitigliano from Rome in the thirteenth century and the community flourished until the annexation of the area by the Medici in 1608, when new laws forced the Jews to live in a **ghetto** and wear red clothing as a mark of identification. The granting of **religious freedom** throughout Tuscany by the last Medici ruler, Gian Gastone, in 1735, gave the town a new lease of life. Over the next 125 years, Jewish workshops and artisans on present-day **Via Zuccarelli** thrived, and there was even a Jewish university that attracted students from around Europe. By 1860, a third of the town, or some 2200 people, were Jewish.

It was Italian **Unification** that brought about the end. In the new Italy, individuals felt freer than before to marry across religious lines, and the removal of a Catholic Papal State in central Italy gave Jews a new freedom to travel; many headed to the southern ports to take ships bound for Palestine. By 1900, there were barely a hundred Jews left in Pitigliano. During the Second World War, the town's Jews were forced into **hiding**, and virtually all were protected from the Nazis by local Christian families. But by 1945 most felt unable to stay on, and departed for Rome, Livorno and Florence (all of which have large Jewish communities). Pitigliano's **synagogue** closed in the late 1950s, and today, in what was formerly one of the centres of Jewish learning in southern Europe, there are almost no Jewish residents left.

centuries for its flourishing **Jewish** community (see box, p.613). Today it has a slightly grim grandeur, owing to its mighty **fortress** and the tall and largely unaltered alleys of the old Jewish ghetto.

Immediately through the main city gate is **Piazza Garibaldi**, flanked by the fortress (1459–62) and aqueduct (1543) and with views across houses wedged against the cliffside. Within the fortress is the Renaissance **Palazzo Orsini** (Tues–Sun 10am–1pm & 3–7pm; winter closes 5pm; €4), its lovely interiors filled with jewellery and ecclesiastical ephemera; also in the fortress is the **Museo Civico** (same hours; €2.50), with an interesting collection of Etruscan vases and trinkets. The fortress backs onto **Piazza della Repubblica**, Pitigliano's elongated main square. Beyond lies the old town proper, a tight huddle of arches and medieval alleys. This is where you'll find the old Jewish Quarter, centred on the Via Zuccarelli, which has been turned into a sort of outdoor museum known as *La Piccolo Gerusalemme* (The Little Jerusalem), with a kosher baker, butcher, a **synagogue** and a small attached Jewish Museum, the **Mostra Ebraico** (Mon–Fri & Sun 10am–12.30pm & 3–5.30pm; €2.50). Pitigliano's eighteenth-century synagogue part-collapsed in the 1960s, and lay derelict until renovation in 1995. The grand stone arch and the stairs leading up to the women's gallery are the only survivors of the old building, along with plaques commemorating visits made by grand dukes Ferdinand III in 1823 and Leopold II in 1829. Although the Jewish community is virtually gone, Florentine, Livornese and even American couples still choose to tie the knot here. Staff are happy to show you around the old ghetto, which includes a **bakery** on Via Marghera with a Star of David in its barred window. A few minutes' walk beyond, at the western end of town, you can see traces of the **Etruscan wall** below the Porta Capisotto.

Three RAMA **buses** daily from Manciano and Grosseto, two from Orbetello and one from Siena drop off on **Piazza Pettruccioli** just outside the city gate. The helpful **tourist office** at Piazza Garibaldi 51 (Tues–Sat 10am–1pm & 3.30–7pm; ☎0564.617.111, ⓦwww .comune.pitigliano.gr.it) has maps of the *Vie Cave*, ancient Etruscan paths that weave between tombs and cliffside caves all around the town. With its untouristed lanes and the drama of its cliff-edge site, Pitigliano makes a memorable overnight

△ Pitigliano's fortress walls

stop. The only **hotel** is *Guastini*, Piazza Petruccioli 16/34 (☎0564.616.065, ⓦwww.albergoguastini.it; ❹), with a good **restaurant**. Also check out the award-winning, mid-priced *Osteria Il Tufo Allegro*, carved into the cliffs at Vicolo della Costituzione 2 (☎0564.616.192; closed all Tues & Wed lunch).

Terme di Saturnia

SATURNIA, 23km northwest of Pitigliano, is renowned for its sulphurous **hot springs**. Several daily buses run from Pitigliano to Orbetello on the coast (see p.572), and there are three daily **buses** north along the minor road from Manciano to Saturnia. Be sure to get off at the springs (*Le Terme*) and not at Saturnia village. The last return bus is at 1pm, so you might end up spending the night. The large **spa resort**, with fierce admission charges, a vast pool and a four-star hotel (☎0564.600.111, ⓦwww.termedisaturnia.it; ❾), is 6km north of the village of Montemerano; some 200m before it (as the road takes a sharp curve) follow a dirt track off to the right, unsignposted but usually signalled by a cluster of cars and vans. Two minutes' walk from here brings you to the **cascatelle**, sulphur springs that burst from the ground, forming natural rock-pools of warm, turquoise water, in which you can lie around for hours submerged up to your neck. Entrance is unrestricted and free, but you'll need a shower to wash off the sulphur smell, which can linger for days. The nearest **hotel** is the excellent *Albergo-Ristorante Stellata* (☎0564.602.978; ❹), in an isolated spot 1km down from the springs on the road to Manciano, while the **campsite** *Poggio alle Querce* (☎0564.602.568; open all year) is at Montemerano.

Eastern Tuscany

The Valdarno, or Arno Valley, upstream from Florence is a solidly industrial-ized district, with no compelling stop before you reach the provincial capital, **Arezzo**, visited by foreigners in their thousands for its Piero della Francesca frescoes, and by Italians in even greater numbers for its antiques trade. South of Arezzo is the ancient hill-town of **Cortona**, whose picturesquely steep streets and sense of hilltop isolation make it an irresistible place for a stopover.

Arezzo

AREZZO, 65km southeast of Florence, has a charming old quarter, unspoilt enough to catch the eye a few years back of local folk-hero and clown of Italian cinema **Roberto Benigni**. Many key scenes in his Oscar-winning *La Vita è Bella* (*Life is Beautiful*) were filmed in Arezzo, and strolling on its quiet streets is like a breath of fresh air after days spent doing battle with Florence's big-city grind.

Arezzo was a major Etruscan and Roman city, and was a prosperous inde-pendent republic in the Middle Ages, until, in 1289, its Ghibelline loyalties precipitated military defeat at the hands of Guelph Florentines. In the arts, Petrarch, Pietro Aretino and Vasari, all native Aretines, brought lasting prestige to the city, yet it was an outsider who gave Arezzo its permanent Renaissance monument – **Piero della Francesca**, whose extraordinary **frescoes** are in the same league as Masaccio's in Florence and Michelangelo's in Rome. Today, the local economy relies on innumerable jewellers and goldsmiths (the city has the world's largest gold manufacturing plant) and on the **antiques** trade: Piazza Grande has showrooms filled with the sort of furniture you put in a bank vault rather than in your living room and once a month – on the first Sunday and the Saturday preceding it – a vast **Fiera Antiquaria** occupies the square. The array of some 600 stalls is fun to browse, but don't expect any bargains.

Arrival, information and accommodation

Arezzo is a major stop for **trains** between Florence and Rome, and is also served by a branch line from Perugia. **Buses** from Siena and elsewhere arrive diagonally opposite the train station. The main **tourist office** is on the right as you come out of the train station, at Piazza della Repubblica 28 (April–Sept Mon–Sat 9am–1pm & 3–7pm, Sun 9am–1pm; Oct–March Mon–Sat 9am–12.30pm & 3–6.30pm, 1st Sun of month 9am–1pm; ☎0575.377.678, Ⓦwww.apt.arezzo.it); the helpful staff speak English, have masses of information on Arezzo and its province, and will book accommodation. There's also an equally helpful *Centro Accoglienza e Informazioni Turistico* on Via Ricasoli

ACCOMMODATION	
Cavaliere Palace	D
Cecco	E
Continental	F
La Toscana	B
Patio	C
Villa Severi	A

EATING & DRINKING	
Antica Osteria L'Agania	1
Fiaschetteria de' Redi	4
Il Cantuccio	7
Il Gelato	6
Il Saraceno	8
La Buca di San Francesco	2
Liquidbar	5

(☎0575.377.829), which hires out audioguides of the town for €6. The **post office** is at Via Guido Monaco 34.

Accommodation can be hard to come by – especially on the first weekend of every month when the antiques fair is on. In addition, the town is booked solid at the end of August and beginning of September, when the choir competition, the *Concorso Polifonico Guido d'Arezzo* (Ⓦ www.polifonico.org), and the *Giostra del Saracino* (Ⓦ www.giostradelsaracino.arezzo.it), the "Joust of the Saracens", a medieval-themed pagent and fair, follow in quick succession. It pays to book ahead as far in advance as possible.

Cavaliere Palace Via Madonna del Prato 83 ☎0575.26.836, Ⓦ www.cavalierehotels.com /arezzo. One of Arezzo's smartest hotels, the four-star *Palace* is efficient and well equipped, but a little businesslike. ❺

Cecco Corso Italia 215 ☎0575.20.986, Ⓦ www .hotelcecco.com. Plain but good-value modern rooms above a restaurant on a busy shopping street. ❷

Continental Piazza Guido Monaco 7 ☎0575.20.251, Ⓦ www.hotelcontinentale.com. This new town hotel is modern but a bit soulless – a little like the new town itself. Rooms are generically comfortable and come with sound-proofing and Internet access. The highlight is the roof terrace. ❸

Patio Via Cavour 23 ☎0575.401.962, Ⓦ www.hotelpatio.it. Arezzo's best (and unbeatably central) hotel, the stylish *Patio* has colourfully themed rooms loosely based on the life and works of writer Bruce Chatwin. ❻

Villa Severi Via Francesco Redi 13 ☎0575.299.047, Ⓦ www.peterpan.it/ostello.htm. Arezzo's excellent hostel is 1km east of the old town. €15 a night per person, half (€27) and full board (€35) also available.

The Town

Arezzo divides into two distinct parts: the **old town** stands on the higher parts of the hill and is where the majority of interest lies, while the new town, which is of interest mainly for its shopping opportunities, occupies the gentler slopes directly in front of the train station. The Via Roma marking the border between the two. If you want to spare your legs – it's quite a climb from the station to the top of the old town – you'd be best off driving and arriving at the car park at the north end of town. A series of escalators (and a stair lift) now link the car park with the Duomo, greatly improving the town's disabled access.

The Basilica di San Francesco

In the heart of the old town, west of the main Corso Italia, stands the church of **San Francesco**, home to Piero della Francesca's celebrated **fresco** cycle in the choir. After centuries of damp and neglect, and some poor restoration early in the twentieth century that did more harm than good, work began in 1985 to consolidate and restore the badly damaged frescoes, and in 2000 the brilliantly coloured pieces were revealed in full, with details visible that had been obscured by dust and grime for centuries.

You can see the frescoes from the nave of the church (Nov–March 9am–6pm; April–Oct 9am–7pm), but you need to get closer to really appreciate them, and you're not allowed any closer than the altar steps unless you've bought a ticket: **visits** are limited to 25 people at a time (Mon–Fri 9am–6pm, Sat 9am–5.30pm, Sun 1–5.30pm; €6), and to thirty minutes per group, and tickets must be booked in advance (☎0575.352.727, Ⓦ www.pierodellafrancesca.it) – outside the peak summer months you can usually make a reservation in person, an hour or so ahead, at the ticket office beside the church. Tickets must be collected at least half an hour before your entrance slot.

Built after 1322, the plain basilica earned its renown in the early 1450s, when the local Bacci family commissioned **Piero della Francesca** to continue the decoration of the choir. The theme chosen was **The Legend of the True Cross**, a story in which the wood of the Cross forms the link in the cycle of redemption that begins with humanity's original sin. Piero painted the series in narrative sequence, working continuously until about 1457. However, he preferred to arrange them according to the precepts of symmetry: the two battle scenes, for example, face each other across the chapel, rather than coming where the story dictates. As is always the case with this mystical painter, smaller-scale symmetries are present in every part of the work: the retinue of the Queen of Sheba (middle right wall) appears twice, in mirror-image arrangement, and the face of the queen is the same as that of the Empress Helena (middle left wall). This orderliness, combined with the pale light and the statuesque quality of the figures, creates an atmosphere of spirituality that is unique to Piero, a sense of each incident as a part of a greater plan.

The fresco cycle

The complex story begins with the **Death of Adam** (top right wall), when a sprig from the Tree of Knowledge is planted in Adam's mouth. Below (to the left), **Solomon** orders a bridge to be built from wood taken from the tree that grew from Adam's grave. The visiting **Queen of Sheba** kneels, sensing the holiness of the wood, and then later (to the right) tells Solomon of her prophecy that the same wood will be used to crucify a man. Solomon then orders the beam to be buried (back wall, middle right).

The two most striking scenes have benefited hugely from cleaning. With the encrustation of dirt over the centuries, the **Dream of Constantine** (back wall, lower right) was always thought to be a night scene, but restoration has shown it in fact to depict early morning. As the angel descends to the tent of the sleeping emperor, bringing a vision of victory under the sign of the Cross, dawn is breaking behind the mountains to banish the constellation of Ursa Minor. Constantine's stolid guards keep watch, waiting, stiff with cold, for sunrise. Alongside, the **Victory of Constantine** (lower right wall) shows the emperor's defeat of his rival Maxentius, and his later baptism; part of the wall is damaged, but the sky is suffused with what the critic Sir Kenneth Clark has called "the most perfect morning light in all Renaissance painting".

Under torture, **Judas the Levite** (back wall, middle left) reveals to St Helena, mother of Constantine, the burial places of the three crosses from Golgotha, and then the three are excavated (middle left wall); the **True Cross** is recognized when it brings about a man's resurrection. Arezzo appears as Jerusalem in the top left. Then the Persian king Chosroes, who had stolen the Cross, is defeated by Emperor **Heraclius** (lower left wall); on the right he kneels awaiting execution. Heraclius returns the Cross to Jerusalem (upper left wall).

The rest of the town

Piero della Francesca's frescoes are the main reason to visit Arezzo, but the town's other highlights fit nicely into a pleasant afternoon stroll through the hilly lanes. Further up the Corso northeast of San Francesco is the steeply sloping **Piazza Grande**, which may look familiar from the film *La Vita è Bella*. The grand, imposing piazza is bordered on the east side by wooden balconied apartments and on the west by the apse of Santa Maria (see below) and the tiered facade of the **Palazzetto della Fraternità dei Laici**, with a Gothic ground floor and fifteenth-century upper storeys. The northern side is formed by the beautiful **Loggia di Vasari**, designed in the sixteenth century by Giorgio Vasari, court architect to the Medici. Backing onto the square is the twelfth-century **Santa Maria della Pieve** (daily: summer 8am–noon & 3–7pm; winter closes 6pm;

free) with its unmistakable fourteenth-century campanile, known locally as "the tower of the hundred holes" for its many double-arched windows. The arcaded facade, elaborate yet severe, belongs to a Romanesque type associated more with Pisa and western Tuscany, and the church is doubly unusual in presenting its front to a narrow street rather than to the town's main square. The carvings of the months over the portal are a perfect Romanesque group, dating from the 1210s; in the tranquil interior, the raised sanctuary – the oldest section of the church – supports Pietro Lorenzetti's *Madonna and Saints* polyptych, painted in 1320 and restored rather nastily.

At the highest point of town looms the large and unfussy **Duomo** (daily 7am–12.30pm & 3–6.30pm; free), its harmonious appearance belying its history. Begun in the late thirteenth century, it was virtually finished by the sixteenth, but the campanile comes from the nineteenth and the facade from the twentieth. The stained-glass windows, made by Guillaume de Marcillat around 1520, let in so little light that his other contributions to the interior – the paintings on the first three bays of the nave – are virtually invisible. The tiny fresco nestled against the right side of the tomb is **Piero della Francesca**'s *Maddalena*, his only work in the town outside San Francesco.

A short distance west of the duomo is the thirteenth-century church of **San Domenico** (daily 8.30am–7pm; free). The high altar has a *Crucifix* painted by a 20-year-old **Cimabue** in 1260 and well restored, and there are tatters of frescoes all round the walls. Signs point the way to the nearby **Casa Vasari**, Via XX Settembre 55 (Mon & Wed–Sat 8.30am–7.30pm, Sun 8.30am–1pm; €2), designed in lurid style by the celebrated biographer–architect–painter for himself. Down the slope, at Via San Lorentino 8, the fifteenth-century Palazzo Bruni-Ciocchi houses the **Museo Statale d'Arte Medioevale e Moderna** (Tues–Sun 8.30am–7.30pm; €4), with a collection of paintings by local artists and majolica work dating from the thirteenth to the eighteenth centuries.

All the principal sights are in the upper part of town, with the exception of the **Museo Archeologico** (daily 8.30am–7.30pm; €4), which occupies part of a monastery built into the wall of the town's Roman amphitheatre, to the right of the station at Via Margaritone 10. Most impressive are the marvellously coloured coralline vases produced here in the first century BC – their skill and artistry demonstrate how the Aretines achieved a reputation throughout the Roman world as consummate craftspeople.

Eating and drinking

Arezzo's **restaurants** are some of Tuscany's best. The busiest **bars** and **cafés** are around piazzas Guido Monaco, Grande and San Francesco, and along Corso Italia.

Antica Osteria L'Agania Via Mazzini 10 ☏ 0575.295.381. A cosy side street restaurant with fantastic rustic-style food, at around €5–10. Closed Mon.

Fiaschetteria de' Redi Via de' Redi 10 ☏ 0575.355.012. Busy stone-floored, wooden-beamed wine-bar-cum-*osteria* on a road with lots of eating options. Simple but excellent dishes start at €6. Closed Mon.

Il Cantuccio Via Madonna Del Prato 76 ☏ 0575.26.830. Just on the border of Arezzo's old/new town, this family-run (by three generations)

trattoria serves great simple Tuscan cooking, such as wild boar *carpaccio*. Primi €8, *secondi* €8–12.

Il Gelato Via de' Cenci 24. On the corner of Via San Francesco, this place has Arezzo's best ice cream.

Il Saraceno Via Mazzini 6a ☏ 0575.27.644. Another good option for excellent traditional Tuscan cuisine, *Il Saraceno* has been open since 1946. Allow around €20 for a two-course meal. Closed Wed.

La Buca di San Francesco Via di San Francesco 1 ☏ 0575.23.271. Housed in a fourteenth-century building, this is a pricier spot for Tuscan cooking and a little tourist-oriented, but still very good – count on around €45 per head. Closed Mon eve & Tues.

Liquidbar Via di Tolletta 5. Popular but rather small bar where people seem to do as much drinking outside as in. Open till 2am Thurs–Sat.

Cortona

Travelling south from Arezzo you enter the **Valdichiana**, reclaimed swampland that is now prosperous cattle country, producing the much-prized Florentine *bistecca*. From the valley floor a long road winds up through terraces of vines and olives from the hill-town of **CORTONA**, 20km south of Arezzo, from whose heights you can see Lago Trasimeno. A scattering of Etruscan tombs aside, the steep streets are dominated by medieval architecture that claws its way around a knife-edge ridge, with barely a patch of level ground anywhere. Official city maps make a point of proudly highlighting what little flat land there is. Traffic is restricted, which accentuates the sense of hilltop isolation – although the quantity of summer visitors can diminish the atmosphere. Even without its art treasures, Cortona would be a good place to rest up, with pleasant hotels, excellent restaurants, and an amazing view at night of the villages of southern Tuscany glittering in the distance.

Arrival and information

There are hourly LFI **buses** between Arezzo and Cortona dropping off in Piazza Garibaldi. **Trains** from Arezzo call at Camucia-Cortona station (6km), from where a shuttle (roughly every half an hour) takes ten minutes to run up to the old town. Buy tickets at the station bar. The fast Florence–Rome trains stop at Teróntola, 10km south, which is also served by a shuttle roughly every hour (25 minutes to Cortona's Piazza Garibaldi); Teróntola is the station to get off at if you are approaching from Umbria. The centre is closed to traffic, so if you're driving you should park in Giardini del Mercato, in Piazza Mazzini by Porta Colonia, in Piazza Garibaldi (the most convenient and therefore busiest), or in front of Santa Margherita below the Fortezza, though this leaves quite a walk back uphill from the centre of town.

The **tourist office** is at Via Nazionale 42 (May–Sept Mon–Sat 9am–1pm & 3–7pm, Sun 9am–1pm; Oct–April Mon–Fri 9am–1pm & 3–6pm, Sat 9am–1pm; ☎0575.630.352, ⓔinfocortona@apt.arezzo.it). There is an **Internet** point which doubles as a phone centre at Via Roma 20.

Accommodation

There are half a dozen **hotels** in the historic centre and an excellent **youth hostel**. Places often fill up quickly so booking ahead is advisable, especially if arriving after lunch.

Italia Via Ghibellina 5 ☎0575.630.254, ⓔhotel .italia@planhotel.com. A decent three-star in a 15th-century mansion near the Piazza della Repubblica. Some of the rustically decorated rooms are a bit small, but all have good showers. Great roof-top breakfast room. ❸
Le Gelosie Via Dardano 6 ☎0575.630.005, ⓦwww.legelosie.com. With stylish rooms and

suites, this is one of the town's best B&B options. It also offers self-catering apartments. ❸
Oasi Neumann Via delle Contesse 1 ☎0575.630.354, ⓦwww.hoteloasi.org; open mid-March to mid-Dec. An atmospheric alternative to the central hotels, this charismatic three-star is located about twenty minutes' walk south from Via Garibaldi and occupies a converted

monastic complex. They sometimes accept guests only on a full-board or half-board basis – no great hardship, as its restaurant is good. ❹ **Ostello San Marco** Via G. Maffei 57 ☎0575.601.765, ⊛www.cortonahostel.com. Cortona's hostel is a clean and spacious old monastery in the heart of town, with fantastic views from the dormitories and friendly management. Open mid-March to mid-Oct 7–10am & 3.30pm–midnight, though the curfew is sometimes flexible. €12.50 for a dorm bed and breakfast (and extra €9 for dinner). Doubles and family rooms (€16.50 per person) are available too.

Sabrina Via Roma 37 ☎0575.630.397, ⓔinfo @cortonastorica.com. Another good mid-range mid-town option. The breakfasts are excellent and it has a nice family atmosphere. ❸ **San Luca** Piazza Garibaldi 2 ☎0575.630.460, ⊛www.sanlucacortona.com. This large four-star hotel is a charmless modern building, but many of its rooms have lovely views over the Valdichiana. ❹ **San Michele** Via Guelfa 15 ☎0575.604.348, ⊛www.hotelsanmichele.net. The most luxurious choice in town is a handsome four-star converted from a patrician medieval town house. Several of its rooms have whirlpool baths. ❺

The Town

From **Piazza Garibaldi** Via Nazionale, the only level street in town, connects to **Piazza della Repubblica**, which is overlooked by the grandstand staircase of the squat Palazzo del Comune. Just behind is **Piazza Signorelli**, named after Luca Signorelli (1441–1523), Cortona's most famous son, and site of the **Museo dell'Accademia Etrusca** (April–Oct daily 10am–7pm; Nov–March Tues–Sun 10am–5pm; €4.20), where an enormous hall contains cabinets of prized Etruscan stuff, surrounded by second-rate paintings. The major exhibit – honoured with its own bijou temple – is an Etruscan bronze lamp from the fifth century BC, its circumference decorated with alternating male and female squatting figures. The painter Gino Severini (1883–1966), another native of Cortona and an acolyte of the Futurist firebrand Filippo Marinetti, gets a room to himself. With pre-booking (☎0575.630.415), museum experts can guide you around a handful of Etruscan tombs outside town.

Piazza Signorelli links with Piazza Duomo, where the **Duomo** sits hard up against the city walls, overlooking the precipice. It was raised on the ruins of a pagan temple, but progressive rebuilding work has muffled the original Renaissance construction. To the right of the altar is an illuminated vitrine holding a reliquary said to contain a fragment of the True Cross. Across the little piazza, a couple of churches have been knocked together to form the **Museo Diocesano** (April–Oct daily 10am–7pm; Nov–March Tues–Sun 10am–5pm; €5), with a small collection of Renaissance art plus a fine Roman sarcophagus, carved with fighting centaurs.

Climbing from Piazza della Repubblica on Via Santucci and then Via Berrettini brings you into the upper town. A work by Signorelli can be found in the unassuming church of **San Nicolò**, reached by veering right across Piazza della Pescaia at the far end of Via Berettini, then heading up the stepped Via San Nicolò. Ring the bell on the left-hand side wall, and the caretaker will take you to Signorelli's double-sided altarpiece, revealed by a neat hydraulic system that swivels the picture away from the wall. Signorelli's fresco called *Madonna, Child and Saints* on the left is reminiscent of his more famous work in Orvieto.

From Piazza della Pescaia, a steep path leads up to **Santa Margherita**, resting place of St Margaret of Cortona, the town's patron saint. The daughter of a local farmer, she spent her long years of widowhood helping the poor and sick of Cortona, founding a hospital that stood close to the site of this church. Her tomb, with marble angels lifting the lid of her sarcophagus, was created in the mid-fourteenth century, and is now mounted on the wall to the left of the chancel, while her remains are on display in a glass coffin directly behind the chancel.

Eating and drinking

Cortona has numerous **restaurants**, several of which are highly recommended. Most of those offering outside seating have had to create a series of step terraces in order to cope with the town's everpresent slope. Good for a quick lunch or a light evening meal is the very large *Taverna Pane e Vino*, at Piazza Signorelli 27 (℡0575.631.010; closed Mon & Jan), offering a wide selection of salamis and cheeses, plus a few more substantial dishes – and the wine list runs to 550 vintages. For a fuller meal, you can't beat the *Osteria del Teatro*, just round the corner at Via Maffei 5 (℡0575.630.556; closed Wed). Set in a handsome and rambling old house, it's a good-naturedly busy place, featuring delicious home-made pastas on a meat-heavy menu; count on around €18 for a two-course meal. Good alternatives include *Tonino*, on Piazza Garibaldi (℡0575.630.500; closed Tues), where there's the bonus of a panoramic view from the terrace; and *Fufluns* (℡0575.604.140), which serves over twenty types of pizza, none costing more than €6.

On summer evenings a favourite hangout is the *Caffè del Teatro*, on the terrace of the Teatro Signorelli, with live music from Friday to Sunday. You'll occasionally get music at the glossy *Caffè La Saletta*, on Via Nazionale, which also does excellent crêpes and ice cream, and has a terrific wine list. At night many of Cortona's young people gather inside and (mostly) outside *Route 66*, a bar at Via Nazionale 78.

East of Arezzo

Arezzo is the springboard for the Piero della Francesca art itinerary. Once you've taken in della Francesca's paired portraits of the Duke and Duchess of Urbino in the Uffizi in Florence, and the *Legend of the True Cross* and *Maddalena* in Arezzo, head east into the attractive Valtiberina (Tiber Valley) for more.

MONTERCHI is famous as the home of the *Madonna del Parto*, the only representation of the pregnant Madonna in Renaissance art. The village is off the main SS73 road to Sansepolcro, and is served by four buses daily from Arezzo. Signposts direct you to a former school on Via della Reglia, the painting's new home (Tues–Sun: April–Sept 9am–1pm & 2–7pm; Oct–March closes 6pm; €3.20 or free to pregnant women). Della Francesca shows two attendant angels drawing back the flap of a small pavilion to reveal the pregnant Virgin, who places her hand on the upper curve of her belly, her eyes downcast. No other Renaissance artist produced anything comparable to its poise and gravity. Note that the picture is an object of pilgrimage and attendants clear the museum of visitors when local pregnant women come to pray to the Madonna.

SANSEPOLCRO, 25km northeast of Arezzo by regular SITA **buses** (also served by **trains** from Perugia and Città di Castello), makes its living as a manufacturer of lace (or more specifically drawn-thread work) and Buitoni pasta. Piero della Francesca was born here in the 1410s, and, despite short periods away, he spent much of his life in the town. Sansepolcro's modest **Museo Civico**, in the centre at Via Aggiunti 65 (daily: June–Sept 9am–1.30pm & 2.30–7.30pm; Oct–May 9.30am–1pm & 2.30–6pm; €6.20), houses what is perhaps della Francesca's greatest painting, the spectral *Resurrection*. Originally painted for the adjoining town hall in the 1450s and moved here in the sixteenth century, it's an image that has occasioned plenty of enthusiastic prose – Aldous Huxley called it the best painting in the world – and even some pretty dramatic actions. In the Second World War during an allied offensive Capt.

Anthony Clark ordered his troops to stop bombing the town lest they damage the picture, even at the risk of allowing the Germans to regroup. The good captain's overwhelming love of art prompted a grateful town to name a road after him – Via A. Clark. Elsewhere in the museum, an earlier della Francesca masterpiece, the *Madonna della Misericordia* polyptych, epitomizes the graceful solemnity of his work. Other pieces that attract attention are a sadistic *Martyrdom of St Quentin* by Pontormo and a painted standard by Luca Signorelli, a student of della Francesca.

Around the town, lesser art treasures are to be found in the **Duomo**, with its tenth-century carved image of the crucified Christ, and in the church of **San Lorenzo**, which has a *Deposition* by Rosso Fiorentino, painted within half-a-century of della Francesca's last works but seeming to belong to another world.

Sansepolcro's little **tourist office** is on Piazza Garibaldi behind the museum (daily: April–Oct 9.30am–noon & 2–7pm; Nov–March 10am–noon & 2–6pm; ☎0575.730.231, ⓦwww.sansepolcro.net). Best **hotel** is the welcoming ⚐ *Fiorentino*, Via Pacioli 60 (☎0575.740.350, ⓦwww.albergofiorentino.com; ❷), in business since 1807 and with rooms both en suite and not. It also has a characterful **restaurant** (closed Fri), in which you can expect to pay around €35. Other excellent restaurants in the same price range include the family-run *Da Ventura*, Via Niccolò Aggiunti 30 (☎0575.742.560; closed Sun eve & Mon, plus Aug & 2 weeks in Jan), and the ever-expanding ⚐ *L'Osteria in Aboca* (☎0575.749.125), a couple of kilometres from the centre on the Rimini Road, which serves fantastic *crespelle* and steaks.

Travel details

Trains

Arezzo to: Assisi (12 daily; 1hr 35min); Bibbiena (hourly; 45min); Bolzano (3 daily; 5–7hr); Camucia-Cortona (hourly; 20min); Chiusi (hourly; 1hr); Florence (hourly; 1hr); Foligno (every 2hr; 1hr 45min); Orvieto (hourly; 50min–1hr 20min); Perugia (8 daily; 1hr 10min); Poppi (hourly; 1hr); Rome (hourly; 1hr 40min); Teróntola-Cortona (hourly; 25min); Trento (3 daily; 7hr); Udine (5 daily; 5hr 30min–7hr); Venice (5 daily; 5hr); Verona (3 daily; 3hr 30min–4hr 45min).

Empoli to: Florence (every 30min; 35min); Pisa (every 30min; 30–55min); Siena (every 30min; 55min–1hr 10min).

Florence to: Arezzo (hourly; 1hr); Assisi (8 daily; 2hr–2hr 30min); Bari (15 daily; 7hr–9hr 30min, change at Bologna or Rome); Bologna (every 30min; 1hr–1hr 40min); Bolzano (5 daily; 4hr–4hr 30min); Empoli (every 20min; 30min); Foligno (6 daily; 2hr 40min); Genoa (2 daily; 3hr 10min); Lecce (13 daily; 9hr 10min–15hr, change at Bologna or Rome); Livorno (12 daily; 1hr 30min); Lucca (every 30min; 1hr 15min–1hr 45min); Milan (hourly; 2hr 45min–3hr 30min); Naples (hourly; 3hr 30min–5hr); Perugia (8 daily; 1hr 35min–2hr

10min); Pisa Airport (hourly; 1hr 15min); Pisa Central (every 30min; 1hr–1hr 30min); Pistoia (every 30min; 35–55min); Prato (every 20min; 15–30min); Reggio Calabria (from Campo Marte 5 direct trains daily; 9hr 15min–11hr; from Santa Maria Novella, changing at Rome 6 daily; 8hr 10min–10hr); Rimini (hourly; 2hr 20min–3hr 30min, change at Bologna); Rome (every 20min; 1hr 45min–3hr 40min); Siena (hourly; 1hr 30min–2hr); Trieste (3 daily; 4hr 40min–6hr 20min); Udine (3 daily; 4hr 20min–6hr); Venice (9 daily; 2hr 50min–3hr 45min); Venice-Mestre (10 daily; 2hr 35min–3hr 30min); Verona (6 daily; 2hr 20min–2hr 45min); Viareggio (14 daily; 1hr 20min–1hr 55min).

Grosseto to: Cécina (17 daily; 45min–1hr 20min); Florence (6 daily; 3hr); Livorno (hourly; 1hr 10min–2hr); Orbetello (16 daily; 20–30min); Pisa (hourly; 1hr 20min–2hr 20min); Rome (hourly; 1hr 40min–2hr 20min); Siena (9 daily; 1hr 20min–1hr 45min).

Livorno to: Florence (12 daily; 1hr 30min); La Spezia (hourly; 1hr–1hr 30min); Pisa (every 20min; 15min); Rome (19 daily; 2hr 45min–3hr 45min).

Lucca to: Florence (every 30min; 1hr 15min–1hr 45min); Pisa (hourly; 20min); Pistoia (every 30min; 45min); Prato (every 30min; 50min–1hr 15min); Viareggio (hourly; 20min).

Pisa to: Empoli (every 30min; 30–55min); Florence (every 30min; 1hr–1hr 30min); Livorno (every 20min; 15min); Lucca (hourly; 20–30min); Viareggio (every 30min; 15–20min).

Pistoia to: Bologna (hourly; 1hr 20min–1hr 50min); Florence (30min; 35–55min); Lucca (every 30min; 40–50min); Viareggio (11 daily; 1hr–1hr 30min).

Prato to: Bologna (every 30min; 50min–1hr 15min); Florence (every 20min; 15–30min); Lucca (every 30min; 50min–1hr 15min); Pistoia (every 30min; 15min); Viareggio (hourly; 1hr 15min).

Siena to: Asciano (11 daily; 30min); Buonconvento (9 daily; 20–30min); Chiusi (hourly; 1hr 30min); Empoli (every 30min; 55min–1hr 10min); Grosseto (9 daily; 1hr 20min–1hr 45min).

Buses

Arezzo to: Città di Castello (12–15 daily; 1hr 30min); Cortona (hourly; 1hr); Sansepolcro (17 daily; 1hr); Siena (5 daily Mon–Fri; 2hr).

Chiusi to: Montepulciano (14 daily; 45min).

Cortona to: Arezzo (hourly; 50min); Chianciano (4 daily; 1hr), changing for Montepulciano.

Florence to: Bibbiena (8 daily; 2hr 15min); Castellina in Chianti (3 daily; 1hr 35min); Greve in Chianti (3 daily; 1hr 5min); Poggibonsi (10 daily; 1hr 20min); Poppi (9 daily; 2hr 5min); Radda in Chianti (1 daily Mon–Sat; 1hr 40min); Siena (12 express daily, plus 9 stopping services; 1hr 15min express); Volterra (6 daily; 2hr 25min). In addition to these state-owned SITA services, numerous independent bus companies operate from Florence to most Tuscan towns, including Arezzo, Grosseto, Lucca, Pisa, Pistoia, Prato, Sansepolcro and Viareggio.

Livorno to: Piombino (8 daily; 2hr); Pisa (every 30min; 20min).

Lucca to: Florence (30 daily; 1hr 15min); La Spezia (7 daily; 2hr 20min); Livorno (3 daily; 1hr 20min); Pisa (35 daily; 40min); Pisa Airport (3 daily; 1hr 30min); Prato (9 daily; 2hr 15min); Viareggio (30 daily; 40min).

Massa Marittima to: Piombino (2 daily; 25min); San Galgano (2 daily; 1hr); Siena (2 daily; 1hr 40min).

Montalcino to: Buonconvento (hourly; 35min); Monte Amiata (2 daily; 1hr); Siena (6 daily; 1hr).

Montepulciano to: Buonconvento (7 daily; 1hr); Chianciano (every 30min; 25min); Chiusi (every 30min; 50min); Pienza (7 daily; 20min); San Quírico (7 daily; 40min); Torrenieri (7 daily; 50min).

Pisa to: Florence (hourly; 1hr 10min); La Spezia (7 daily; 1hr 20min); Livorno (every 30min; 20min); Viareggio (hourly; 20min).

San Gimignano to: Poggibonsi (hourly; 35min).

Siena to: Abbadia San Salvatore (3 daily; 1hr 20min); Arezzo (4 daily; 2hr); Buonconvento (10 daily; 35min); Florence (30 daily; 1hr 30min–3hr); Grosseto (4 daily; 2hr); Massa Maríttima (3 daily; 1hr 20min); Montalcino (6 daily; 1hr); Montepulciano (4 daily; 1hr 20min); San Galgano (3 daily; 40min); San Gimignano (16 daily; 1hr–1hr 30min); Volterra (6 daily; 2hr).

Viareggio to: Pisa (every 30min; 35min).

Volterra to: Colle Val d'Elsa (for connections to Florence & Siena; 4 daily); Pisa (1 daily).

Ferries

Livorno to: Capraia (1–2 daily; 3hr); Portoferraio (1 daily; 4hr).

Piombino to: Portoferraio (10–18 daily; 1hr).

9

Umbria

SWITZERLAND   AUSTRIA   HUNGARY

①

③

②

⑦

⑧

⑤

④

⑥   SLOVENIA

CROATIA

SERBIA

BOSNIA-
HERZEGOVINA

FRANCE

Corsica
(Fr.)

⑨

⑩

⑫

⑪

⑭

⑬

⑮

MONTENEGRO

ADRIATIC
SEA

⑰

TYRRHENIAN
SEA

IONIAN
SEA

⑯

N

ALGERIA   TUNISIA

0   100 km

625

CHAPTER 9 ## Highlights

* **Galleria Nazionale dell'Umbria** The region's finest and largest collection of medieval and Renaissance Umbrian paintings. **See p.633**

* **Gubbio** Best-looking of Umbria's medieval hill towns, and without Assisi's crowds and commercialism. **See p.642**

* **Basilica di San Francesco** Burial place of St Francis and one of Italy's great buildings, with frescoes by Giotto and Simone Martini. **See p.650**

* **Valle di Spoleto** A swathe of country with four of the region's most compelling villages: Spello, Bevagna, Trevi and Montefalco. **See p.654**

* **San Francesco, Montefalco** One of Umbria's best small galleries, with a major fresco cycle by Benozzo Gozzoli. **See p.657**

* **Valnerina** A verdant, mountain-edged valley dotted with hill-villages and spectacular views. **See p.667**

* **Piano Grande** A glorious upland plain, the centrepiece of the Monti Sibillini national park. **See p.668**

* **Duomo, Orvieto** On a par with the cathedrals in Milan and Siena, Orvieto's duomo has a glorious facade and a majestic fresco cycle by Luca Signorelli. **See p.680**

△ Gubbio, Umbria

9

Umbria

O ften referred to as "the green heart of Italy", Umbria is a predominantly beautiful and – despite the growing number of visitors – a
largely unspoiled region of rolling hills, woods, streams and valleys.
Within its borders it also contains a dozen or so classic hill-towns,
each resolutely individual and crammed with artistic and architectural treasures
to rival bigger and more famous cities. To the east, pastoral countryside gives
way to more rugged scenery, none better than the dramatic twists and turns
of the Valnerina and the high mountain landscapes of the Parco Nazionale dei
Monti Sibellini.

Umbria was named by the Romans after the mysterious **Umbrii**, a tribe
cited by Pliny as the oldest in Italy, and one that controlled territory reaching
into present-day Tuscany and Marche. Although there is scant archeological
evidence about them, it seems that their influence was mainly confined to
the east of the Tiber; the darker and more sombre towns to the west – such
as Perugia and Orvieto – were founded by the **Etruscans**, whose rise forced
the Umbrii to retreat into the eastern hills. Roman domination was eventually undermined by the so-called barbarian invasions, in the face of which the
Umbrians withdrew into fortified hill-towns, paving the way for a pattern of
bloody rivalry between independent city-states that continued through the
Middle Ages. Weakened by constant warfare, most towns eventually fell to the
papacy, entering a period of economic and cultural stagnation that continued
to the very recent past.

Historically, however, Umbria is best known as the birthplace of several saints,
St Benedict and **St Francis of Assisi** being the most famous, and for a religious tradition that earned the region such names as *Umbra santa, Umbra mistica*
and *la terra dei santi* ("the land of saints"). The landscape itself has contributed
much to this mystical reputation, and even on a fleeting trip it's impossible to
miss the strange quality of the Umbrian light, an oddly luminous silver haze that
hangs over the gentle curves of the land.

After years as an impoverished backwater, Umbria has begun to capitalize
on its charms. Foreign acquisition of rural property is now as rapid as it was
in Tuscany thirty years ago, though outsiders have done nothing to curb the
region's renewed sense of identity and youthful enthusiasm, nor to blunt the
artistic initiatives that have turned Umbria into one of the most flourishing
cultural centres in Italy. Headline-grabbing earthquakes in 1997 briefly dented
tourist numbers, but they have had a negligible long-term effect – at least as far
as visitors are concerned – as the majority of sights suffered little damage.

Most visitors head for **Perugia**, **Assisi** – the latter with its extraordinary frescoes by Giotto in the Basilica di San Francesco – or **Orvieto**, whose duomo is

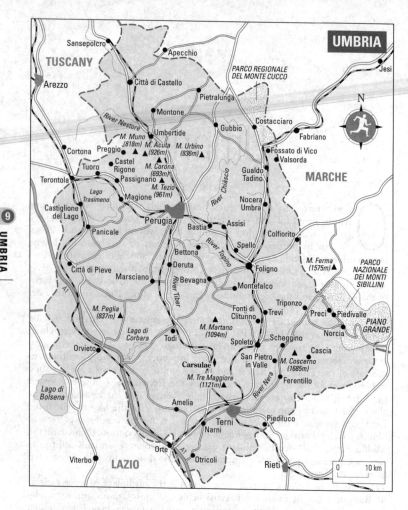

one of the greatest Gothic buildings in the country. For a taste of the region's more understated qualities, it's best to concentrate on lesser-known places such as **Todi**, **Gubbio**, ranked as the most perfect medieval centre in Italy, and **Spoleto**, for many people the outstanding Umbrian town. Although there are few unattractive parts of the Umbrian landscape (the factories of Terni and the Tiber Valley being the largest blots), some districts are especially enticing: principally the mountainous **Valnerina**, **Piano Grande** and **Lago Trasimeno**, the last of which is the largest lake in the Italian peninsula, with plenty of opportunities for swimming and watersports.

   Getting around the region by public transport presents no problems. Distances between the main sights are short, and there are excellent rail links both within the region and to Florence and Rome. The official tourist board **websites** on the area are ⓦ www.umbria-turismo.it and ⓦ www.umbria2000 .it; the latter offers links to individual major tourist offices around the region.

The cuisine of landlocked, hilly Umbria relies heavily on rustic staples – pastas and roast meats – and in the past tended to be simple and homely. The region is also the only area outside Piemonte where **truffles** are found in any abundance, and their perfumed shavings, particularly in the east of the region, find their way onto eggs, pasta, fish and meat – but at a price that prohibits overindulgence.

Meat plays a leading role – especially **lamb** and **pork**, which is made into hams, sausage, salami and, most famously, *la porchetta*, whole suckling pig stuffed with rosemary or sage, roasted on a spit. **Game** may also crop up on some menus, most often as pigeon, pheasant or guinea fowl. The range of **fish** is restricted by the lack of a coast, but trout is pulled out of the Nera, Clitunno and Scordo rivers, while the lakes of Piediluco and Trasimeno yield eels, pike, tench and grey mullet. **Vegetable** delicacies include tiny lentils from Castelluccio, beans from Trasimeno, and celery and cardoons from around Trevi. Umbrian **olive oil**, though less hyped than Tuscan oils, has a high reputation, particularly that from around Trevi and Spoleto.

As for desserts, Perugia is renowned for its **chocolate** and pastries. **Cheeses** tend to be standard issue, although some smaller producers survive in the mountains around Norcia and Gubbio.

Umbria used to be best known outside Italy for fresh, dry white **wines**. Orvieto, once predominantly a medium-sweet wine, has been revived in a dry style, though the original *abboccato* is still available. However, the pre-eminence of Orvieto in the domestic market has been successfully challenged by Grechetto, an inexpensive and almost unfailingly good wine made by countless producers across the region. Umbria's quest for quality is also increasingly reflected in a growing number of small producers, many of which have followed the lead of Giorgio Lungarotti, one of the pioneers of Umbrian viticulture (any wine with his name on is reliable), and in some outstanding reds, notably the tiny Montefalco DOCG region close to Spoleto.

Also useful are Ⓦ www.bellaumbria.net, Ⓦ www.umbria.org, Ⓦ www.comune
.perugia.it and Ⓦ www.umbriaonline.com. For train and transport information,
visit Ⓦ www.umbriatrasporti.it and Ⓦ www.tourinumbria.com for information
for travellers with disabilities.

Perugia

The provincial capital, **PERUGIA** is the most obvious, if not the most pictur-esque, base to kick off a tour of Umbria. Although the centre of town is still medieval, it's surrounded by ugly suburbs and a considerable amount of industry. In summer, the streets become claustrophobic and exhausting, so you probably won't want to spend a lot of time here. On the other hand, there's at least a day's worth of good sightseeing, and it's not a bad place to base yourself if you want to explore the surrounding area: it has big-city amenities and trains run to all the major highlights, complemented by fast new roads and an extensive bus network.

The town's main cultural draw in summer is **Umbria Jazz**, Italy's foremost jazz event, whose line-ups may well tempt you into staying – past stars have included Sting, Stan Getz, Gil Evans and Wynton Marsalis. Information and tickets are best acquired well in advance from the tourist office (see below) or via the website (Ⓦ www.umbriajazz.com).

The presence of the **Università Italiana per Stranieri** (the Italian University for Foreigners) is another plus. Set up by Mussolini to improve the image of Italy abroad, it's now run as a private concern and gives the town a welcome dash of style and an unexpectedly cosmopolitan flavour. The big state university also means there's an above-average number of films, concerts and miscellaneous cultural events, which can be somewhat lacking in the rest of the region.

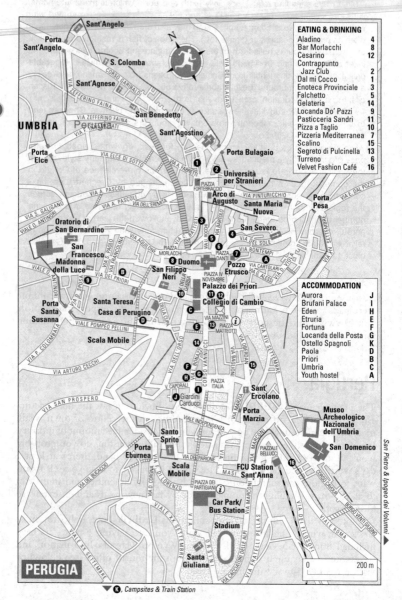

EATING & DRINKING

Aladino	4
Bar Morlacchi	8
Cesarino	12
Contrappunto Jazz Club	2
Dal mi Cocco	1
Enoteca Provinciale	3
Falchetto	5
Gelateria	14
Locanda Do' Pazzi	9
Pasticceria Sandri	11
Pizza a Taglio	10
Pizzeria Mediterranea	7
Scalino	15
Segreto di Pulcinella	13
Turreno	6
Velvet Fashion Café	16

ACCOMMODATION

Aurora	J
Brufani Palace	I
Eden	H
Etruria	E
Fortuna	F
Locanda della Posta	G
Ostello Spagnoli	K
Paola	D
Priori	B
Umbria	C
Youth hostel	A

UMBRIA

Perugia

9

Arrival and information

Arriving on the state train network you'll find yourself to the southwest of the centre at **Piazza Vittorio Veneto**: from here it's a fifteen-minute ride by bus (bus #6, #7, #9 or #11 – anything to Piazza Italia or Piazza Matteotti will do). City **bus tickets** (€1 for any number of journeys in 70min) are available from the station newsagents (turn right as you enter the ticket hall from the platforms) or a small booth over to the left as you exit the station. You can also purchase tickets on board the bus for €1.50, but you must have the right change. A tourist ticket, the **Carta Turistico** (also sometimes called a Card Turistico), valid for 24 hours, costs €3.60, though you're unlikely to be using enough buses to make it worthwhile. You'll probably want to avoid walking to the centre – it's a steep haul on busy roads. If you're coming on the private FCU (Ferrovie Centrale Umbra) lines from Todi or Terni to the south, or from Città di Castello or Sansepolcro to the north, you'll arrive at the much more central **Stazione Sant'Anna**, near the bus terminal at **Piazza dei Partigiani**. From this large square you can jump on a *scala mobile* (escalator) as it wends its way through weird subterranean streets to **Piazza Italia**.

If you're arriving by **car** be prepared for considerable hassle: all the town's approaches are up steep hills and the signposting leaves plenty to be desired. The centre is closed to traffic at peak times, and you'll do best to leave your car at the main train station and take a bus. Alternatively you could head towards one of the big peripheral car parks – Piazza dei Partigiani is the largest and most convenient. For details and a map of central **car parks**, contact Sipa (⌾075.572.1938, ⓦwww.sipaonline.it).

There's a **tourist office** in the Loggia dei Linari on the east side of Piazza Matteotti at no. 18 (May–Sept Mon–Sat 8.30am–6.30pm, Sun 9am–1pm; Oct–April Mon–Sat 8.30am–1.30pm & 3.30–6.30pm, Sun 9am–1pm; ⌾075.573.6458 or 075.577.2686, ⓦwww.paesaggi.umbria2000.it). Another good official site for Perugia is ⓦtourism.comune.perugia.it. The tourist office provides a good map, advice on city events and help in finding accommodation. There is also a private information office, the **Infotourist Point** (also known as InfoUmbria) on the northeast corner of Piazza dei Partigiani (Mon–Fri 9am–1pm & 2.30–6.30pm, Sat 9am–1pm; ⌾075.5757, ⓦwww.infoumbria .com), which is a useful source of information on organized half-day and day tours and operates as a **box office** for many events and concerts; it also has a left-luggage facility and **Internet access** during office hours. The Perugia council also runs InformaGiovani (⌾075.572.0646), which offers a wealth of information to travellers, students and other young people.

Accommodation

Perugia has plenty of **accommodation** in all price ranges, although during term time long-stay students tend to monopolize the cheapest options. As in most of Umbria's main towns, it's a good idea to book in advance, especially during the Jazz festival in July, when room rates may well be raised.

Hotels

Aurora Viale Indipendenza 21 ⌾ & ⌾075.572.4819, ⓔalbergoaurora@virgilio .it. Basic, clean and pleasant two-star hotel with 14 rooms, though on a busy street. ❷

Brufani Palace Piazza Italia 12 ⌾075.573.2541, ⓦwww.brufanipalace.com. Perugia's smartest and most luxurious option is right in the centre of town by Piazza Italia. ❾

Eden Via C. Caporali 9 ⌾075.572.8102, ⌾075.572.0342. A two-star with eighteen rooms, all with private bathroom, in a quiet location close to the Corso. ❷

Etruria Via della Luna 21 ⌾075.572.3730. A

one-star with just eight rooms (seven with private bathrooms) in an unbeatable position immediately off the Corso. **②**

Fortuna Via Bonazzi 19 ⊕075.572.2845, ⓦwww .umbriahotels.com. A central two-star in an historic thirteenth-century palazzo with frescoed ceilings in some rooms and a roof garden with good views of the old city. **③**

🏃 **Locanda della Posta** Corso Vannucci 97
⊕075.572.8925, ⓦwww.umbriatravel .com/locandadellaposta. Perugia's first choice if you want an upmarket treat, not as slick as the *Brufani* but just as central and a historic building where the likes of Goethe and Hans Christian Andersen once stayed. **⑥**

Paola Via della Canapina 5 ⊕075.572.3816. Popular place with eight nice rooms, all with shared bathrooms. Hard to find – follow signs for the *Umbria* (see below) off the Corso and then bear left. **②**

Priori Via Vermiglioni 3 ⊕075.572.3378, ⓦwww .hotelpriori.it. Perugia's first-choice mid-range two-star hotel. The 49 rooms (all with private bathroom) are tastefully fitted out and there's a terrace overlooking the rooftops. The rooms vary greatly so ask to see a selection. **②**

Umbria Via Boncambi 37 ⊕075.572.1203. Basic, centrally located two-star; all of the eighteen rooms have private bathrooms. **③**

Hostels and camping

The town's original **youth hostel**, the Centro Internazionale di Accoglienza per la Gioventù, is two minutes from the duomo, at Via Bontempi 13 (⊕075.572.2880, ⓦwww.ostello.perugia.it; closed 9.30am–4pm & mid-Dec to mid-Jan; dorm beds €15). It has 134 beds in four-, six- and eight-bed dorms, and is perfectly situated. The newer **Ostello per la Gioventù Maria Luisa Spagnoli**, Via Cortonese 4, Località Pian di Massiano (⊕075.501.1366, ⓦwww.ostellionline.org; €15; open year round), is down near the main station and has its own restaurant and 186 beds in 33 four- and six-bed dorms.

The **campsites** *Il Rocolo*, Strada Fontana 1n (⊕ & ⓕ075.517.8550, ⓦwww .ilrocolo.it; 1 April to 15 Oct), and *Paradise d'Été*, Via del Mercato 29a, Strada Fontana (⊕075.517.3121, ⓦwww.emmeti.it; March to end Oct), are 5km out of town at Località Colle della Trinità (Sulga bus marked "Colle della Trinità" from Piazza Italia or #9 bus from the station and a short uphill walk from the crossroads), but you're perhaps better off heading to the more rural sites on Lago Trasimeno (see p.638).

The Town

Once you're safely in Piazza Italia **orientation** is straightforward. The town hinges around a single street, the Corso Vannucci, one of the country's greatest people-watching streets, packed from dawn through to the early hours with a parade of tourists and Umbria's trendsetters. Named after the city's most celebrated artist, Pietro Vannucci, better known simply as Perugino, the Corso contains several of the key sights and a couple of Perugia's most atmospheric little cafés.

Piazza IV Novembre and the Palazzo dei Priori

At the far end of the Corso Vannucci is the big and austere **Piazza IV Novembre** (once a Roman reservoir), backed by the plain-faced **Duomo**, fully restored after damage caused by the 1983 earthquake. While the Baroque interior is big

Two **passes** are available for all major museums and sights in Perugia. One "Card" (€7) is valid for any four sights within a four-hour period and can be purchased from any of the participating sights. The second "Card" (€12) is valid for all sights over three days and can be purchased from the Palazzo Baldeschi, a council-owned building at Corso Vannucci 76.

on size, it's pretty small on works of art and comes as a disappointment after the fifteenth-century facade. As a change from pieces of the True Cross, the chapel almost immediately on your right as you enter, behind a heavy metal grille, contains the Virgin's "wedding ring", an unwieldy 2cm-diameter piece of agate that apparently changes colour according to the character of the person wearing it. The Perugians keep it locked up in fifteen boxes fitted into one another like Russian dolls, each opened with a key held by a different person. It's brought out for general public edification once a year on July 30. In one of the transepts there's an urn holding the ashes of Pope Martin IV, who died in the city after eating too many eels. Urban IV's remains are here too – he was reputedly poisoned with *aquetta*, an imaginative brew made by rubbing white arsenic into pork fat and distilling the unpleasantness that oozes out.

Outside in the piazza (which is the town's main hangout), the centrepiece is the **Fontana Maggiore**, designed by Fra' Bevignate, a monk, and sculpted by the father-and-son team, Nicola and Giovanni Pisano. Sculptures and bas-reliefs – depicting episodes from the Old Testament, classical myth, Aesop's fables and the twelve months of the year – on the two polygonal basins were part of a carefully conceived decorative scheme designed to illustrate the city's glory and achievements. By some canny design work they never line up directly, encouraging you to walk round the fountain chasing a point of repose that never comes.

Just opposite rises the gaunt mass of the **Palazzo dei Priori**, often – and rightly – described as one of the greatest public palaces in Italy. Sheer bulk aside, it's certainly impressive – with rows of trefoil windows (from which convicted criminals were once thrown to their deaths), majestic Gothic doorway, and business-like Guelph crenellations – though the overall effect is rather forbidding; its real beauty derives from the harmony set up by the medieval buildings around it. The lawyers' meeting hall, the **Sala dei Notari** (daily 9am–1pm & 3–7pm; closed Mon Oct–June; free), at the top of the fan-shaped steps, is noted for its frescoes portraying scenes from the Bible, Aesop's fables and the coats of arms of medieval civic worthies: lots of colour, fancy flags, swirls and no substance – but certainly worth a glance.

The small **Collegio della Mercanzia** (March–Oct & 20 Dec to 6 Jan Tues–Sat 9am–1pm & 2.30–5.30pm, Sun 9am–1pm; rest of year Tues, Thurs & Fri 8am–2pm, Wed & Sat 8am–4.30pm, Sun 9am–1pm; €1.50, or €4.50 with Collegio di Cambio) lies further down the Corso side of the palace at Corso Vannucci 15 hidden behind an innocuous door. The seat of the Merchants' Guild, it is covered entirely in intricate and beautiful fifteenth-century panelling. A few doors down at Corso Vannucci 25, the impressive **Collegio di Cambio** (mid-March–Oct Mon–Sat 9am–12.30pm & 2.30–5.30pm, Sun 9am–1pm; rest of year closed Mon 2.30–5.30pm; €4.50, including Collegio della Mercanzia) was the town's money exchange in medieval times. The superb frescoes on the walls were executed by Perugino at the height of his powers and are considered the artist's masterpiece; in true Renaissance fashion, they attempt to fuse ancient and Christian culture. Up on the door-side wall there's a famous but unremarkable self-portrait in which the artist looks like he had a bad lunch. The small chapel to the right of the Collegio is frescoed by Giannicola di Paolo (1519), the last important Umbrian painter influenced by Perugino.

The **Galleria Nazionale dell'Umbria** (daily 8.30am–7.30pm, closed first Mon of every month; €6.50) is on the upper floor of the palace complex (lift or stairs), with the entrance through its opulently carved **doorway**. One of central Italy's best and most charming galleries, this takes you on a romp through the history of Umbrian painting, with masterpieces by Perugino,

Pinturicchio and many others, plus one or two stunning Tuscan masterpieces (Duccio, Fra' Angelico, Piero della Francesca) thrown in for good measure. The entrance is worth every cent if you're the slightest bit interested in early and mid-Renaissance art, and the paintings are further enhanced by a recent restoration of the rooms. Plans are also in hand to extend the gallery across a large part of the palace's lower floors.

Just east of Piazza Danti behind the cathedral at Piazza Piccinino 1 lies the entrance to the **Pozzo Etrusco** (April–Aug daily 10am–1.30pm & 2.30–6.30pm; Sept–Oct same hours, closed Tues; Nov–March daily except Tues 10.30am–1.30pm & 2.30–4.30pm; €2.50, includes admission to San Severo & Cassero di Porta di Sant'Angelo), a massive and extraordinary well that does more than hint at the dazzling engineering and technical skills of its Etruscan builders.

A few minutes' walk farther east along Via del Sole brings you to the church of **San Severo** (same hours and ticket as Pozzo Etrusco) in Piazza Raffaello, known for its painting *Holy Trinity and Saints* by Raphael, who spent some five formative years in Umbria. Today it's the only **painting** by him still left in the region – Napoleon carted many of the artist's works off to France – except for a painted banner in the art gallery in Città di Castello (see p.640). The lower third of the painting, *Six Saints*, was completed in 1521 after Raphael's death by Perugino, his erstwhile teacher.

North and west of Corso Vannucci

The best streets to wander around for a feel of the old city are to the east and west of the duomo, **Via dei Priori** being the most characteristic. Just behind the Palazzo dei Priori in Via della Gabbia there once hung a large iron cage used to imprison thieves and sometimes even clergy. In January 1442, according to a medieval chronicler, priest Angelo di Ferolo "was put back into the cage at midday, and it was very cold and there was much snow, and he remained there until the first day of February both night and day and that same day he was brought out dead". You can still make out long spikes on some of the

△ Piazza IV Novembre

lower walls, used as hooks for the heads of executed criminals. Medieval Perugia was evidently a hell of a place to be. "The most warlike of the people of Italy", wrote the historian Sismondi, "who always preferred Mars to the Muse." Male citizens played a game (and this was for pleasure) in which two teams, thickly padded in clothes stuffed with deer hair and wearing beaked helmets, stoned each other mercilessly until the majority of the other side were dead or wounded. Children were encouraged to join in for the first two hours to promote "application and aggression".

In 1265 Perugia was also the birthplace of the **Flagellants**, who had half of Europe whipping itself into a frenzy before the movement was declared heretical. In addition to some hearty scourging they took to the streets on moonlit nights, groaning and wailing, dancing in white sheets, singing dirges and clattering human bones together, all as expiation for sin and the wrongs of the world. Then there were the infamous **Baglioni**, the medieval family who misruled the city for several generations, their spell-binding history – full of vendetta, incest and mass-slaughter – the stuff of great medieval soap opera.

Via dei Priori passes the rarely open **Madonna della Luce** on the north side after the medieval Torre degli Scirri, little more than a chapel dominated by an impressive altarpiece by G. B. Caporali, a follower of Perugino. The church takes its name from the story that in 1513 a young barber swore so profusely on losing at cards that a Madonna in a wayside shrine closed her eyes in horror and kept them closed for four days. The miracle prompted celebrations, processions and the building of a new church. Some way beyond, as the street bears right, is a nice patch of grass perfectly placed for relaxing with the crowd from the art school next door or for admiring Agostino di Duccio's colourful **Oratorio di San Bernardino**, whose richly embellished facade (1461) is far and away the best piece of sculpture in the city. Again to the north is what's left of San Francesco, once a colossal church, now ruined by centuries of earthquakes, but with a curiously jumbled and striking facade still just about standing.

From here you can wander along the rather uninspiring Via A. Pascoli, under the much-photographed Acquedotto (a raised walkway from the old centre to the north of the city – well worth taking for the views) and past the hideous university buildings, to the **Università Italiana per Stranieri** (℡075.57.461, ⓦ www.unistrapg.it) in Piazza Fortebraccio. The big patched-up gateway here is the **Arco di Augusto**, its lowest section one of the few remaining monuments of Etruscan Perugia. The Romans added the upper remnant when they captured the city in 40 BC. Terms run from April to December, and posters around the place give details of concerts and English films (especially in the summer).

About a minute's walk north on Corso Garibaldi is **Sant'Agostino**, once Romanesque, now botched Baroque and filled with wistful signs explaining what paintings used to hang in the church before they were spirited to France by light-fingered Napoleonic troops. The church, however, is not entirely ruined: there's a beautiful choir (probably based on a drawing by Perugino) and a couple of patches of fresco on the left-hand (north) wall, giving a tantalizing idea of what the place must once have been. Next door to the north side is the fifteenth-century **Oratorio di Sant'Agostino**, its ludicrously ornate ceiling looking as if it's about to erupt in an explosion of gilt, stucco and chubby plaster cherubs. Fifteen minutes' walk up the street is the fifth-century church of **Sant'Angelo**, situated in a tranquil spot (with a pretty little patch of grass and trees – perfect for picnics and siestas) and based on a circular pagan temple; the 24 columns, each made from a different stone, are from the earlier building. Finally, at the northern end of Corso Garibaldi is the **Cassero di Porta di Sant'Angelo** (daily: April–Oct 11am–1.30pm & 3–6.30pm; Nov–Mar

11am–1.30pm & 3–5pm; closed Tues, except April & Aug; same ticket as Pozzo Etrusco – see p.634), a medieval tower with good city views.

Corso Cavour

The rest of Perugia's highlights are on the other side of town, grouped together on **Corso Cavour**, a busy and dustily unpleasant road in the summer. On the way over you could join the smooching couples in the small but well-kept **Giardini Carducci** (by Piazza Italia) to see why Henry James called Perugia the "little city of the infinite views". When the usual cloak of haze lifts on crisp winter mornings, half of Umbria is laid out before you, with the mountains of Tuscany in the distance.

Below the piazza stands the strange octagonal, rarely open, church of **Sant'Ercolano** – built on the site where the head of Perugia's first bishop miraculously re-attached itself to his body after the Goths chopped it off. It's worth taking a short walk past here to look into the Porta Marzia, where a subterranean road of medieval houses, **Via Baglioni Sotteranea**, leads under the ruins of the Rocca Paolina, a once-enormous papal fortress destroyed by the Perugians at Unification. This amazing underground labyrinth can also be accessed from the escalators to Piazza dei Partigiani from the west side of Piazza Italia.

Continuing on to Corso Cavour and heading south, you come to **San Domenico**, Umbria's biggest church. It has a desolate and unfinished air from the outside, with pigeons nesting where they shouldn't and grass growing from the pinky-orange marble, but it's also appealing in a big and rather melancholy sort of way. The original Romanesque interior collapsed in the sixteenth century and the Baroque replacement is vast, cold and bare. Like Sant'Agostino, however, it's full of hints as to how beautiful it must have been – nowhere more so than in the fourth chapel on the right, where a superb **carved arch** by Agostino di Duccio is spoilt only by a doll-like Madonna. In the east transept, to the right of the altar, is the **tomb of Benedict XI** (1324), another pope who died in Perugia, this time from eating poisoned figs. It's an elegant and well-preserved piece by one of the period's three leading sculptors: Pisano, Lorenzo Maitani or Arnolfo di Cambio, no one knows which. There's also another good choir, together with some impressive **stained-glass** windows – the second biggest in Italy after those in Milan's duomo and a welcome splash of colour in the midst of all the mud-coloured paint.

Housed in the church's cloisters is the **Museo Archeologico Nazionale dell'Umbria** (Mon 10am–7.30pm, Tues–Sun 8.30am–7.30pm; €4). Before being hammered by Augustus, Perugia was a big shot in the twelve-strong Etruscan federation of cities, which is why the city has one of the most extensive Etruscan collections around. The museum has recently undergone a major overhaul, turning what had been a dusty and uninspiring set of displays into a far brighter and more appealing ensemble. The place is definitely worth a visit, even if the Etruscans normally leave you cold, for there's far more here than the usual run of urns and funerary monuments. Particularly compelling are the Carri Etruschi di Castel San Marino, some exquisite sixth-century bronze chariots; a witty collection of eye-opening artefacts devoted to fashion and beauty in the Etruscan era; and the bewildering **Bellucci Collection**. The last is a private hoard of charms and amulets through the ages: everything from the obvious – lucky horseshoes – to strange and often sinister charms such as snakeskins and dried animals. The exhibits span several thousand years, and form a unique and oddly poignant picture of people's fears and superstitious hopes across the millennia.

If the Etruscans get you going you might try the outstanding local tombs, the **Ipogeo dei Volumni** (daily: July & Aug 9am–12.30 & 4.30–7pm; Sept–June 9am–1pm & 3.30–6.30pm; €3), 7km east of the town at Via Assisana 53, Ponte San Giovanni (bus or train to Ponte San Giovanni and then a short walk). Though the best in Umbria, they're quite small and without any of the racy paintings found in some Tuscan tombs; and certainly not a patch on the graves at Tarquinia or Cerveteri (see p.816 & p.815). Visits are also restricted to a maximum of seven people at a time and you're only officially allowed five minutes in the tombs themselves.

Farther down Corso Cavour, advertised by a rocket-shaped belltower, is the tenth-century basilica of **San Pietro**, the most idiosyncratic of all the town's churches. Tangled up in a group of buildings belonging to the university's agriculture department, the none-too-obvious entrance is through a frescoed doorway in the far left-hand corner of the first courtyard off the road. Few churches can be so sumptuously decorated: every inch of available space is covered in gilt, paint or marble, though a guiding sense of taste seems to have prevailed, and in the candle-lit gloom it actually feels like the sacred place it's meant to be. All the woodwork is extraordinary; the **choir** has been called the best in Italy, and there is a host of works by Perugino, Fiorenzo di Lorenzo and others.

Eating and drinking

Perugia's student population ensures that there is a plethora of reasonably priced **places to eat** out, from the many snack bars around the centre of town to simple *osterie* serving traditional Umbrian cuisine. Local dishes feature wild mushrooms, truffles and game often succulently combined with home-made egg pasta.

Pizzerias and restaurants

Aladino Via della Prome 11 ☎075.572.0938. Just up Via del Sole from Piazza Danti and the cathedral, this well-regarded restaurant serves an inspired mixture of Umbrian and Sardinian cooking and has an interesting wine list. Mains cost about €13. You'll need to book. Open daily for dinner only.

Cesarino Piazza IV Novembre 45 ☎075.572.8974. A great central restaurant and a Perugia tradition which hasn't suffered too much from a recent interior redecoration. Meals from around €27. Booking advised. Closed Wed.

Dal mi Cocco Corso Garibaldi 12 ☎075.573.2511. Good-value traditional dishes with a variety of set menus from €14. Closed Mon.

Falchetto Via Bartolo 20, just off Piazza Danti. A reliably good and easy-going place with a medieval interior. A full meal costs around €25. Closed Mon.

Locanda Do' Pazzi Via della Sposa 1b ☎075.572.0565. Atmospheric spot off the western end of Via dei Priori in the cellar of a former medieval church, with ancient vaults and food from across Italy. Closed Sun.

Pizza a Taglio Via dei Priori 3, corner Via della Gabbia. A little place just a few steps from Corso Vannucci for inexpensive pizza by the slice to take away. Open daily.

Pizzeria Mediterranea Piazza Piccinino 11 ☎075.572.1322. Simple and tasteful pizzeria with small wood-fired oven and a couple of brick-vaulted rooms a few steps beyond the entrance to the Pozzo Etrusco. Open daily.

Scalino Via Sant'Ercolano. Authentic old-fashioned pizzeria and trattoria, staffed by little old ladies and patronized almost entirely by locals. Fabulous brick-vaulted dining room and very reasonable prices. Closed Fri.

Segreto di Pulcinella Via Larga 8 ☎075.573.6284. A bustling pizzeria that's very popular with students.

Turreno Piazza Danti 16 ☎075.572.1976. Superb, central *tavola calda* that offers a handful of light meals (around €10, with soft drink) and snacks daily to eat in (there are tables to the rear) or take away. Lunch only. Closed Sat.

Cafés and nightlife

The city's liveliest **cafés** are clustered on Corso Vannucci, with the atmospheric old-world *Pasticceria Sandri* at no. 32 (closed Mon) a high spot for the sweet-toothed. For **ice cream** in more-than-generous helpings, join the queues at the *gelateria* at Via Bonazzi 3 on the corner of Piazza della Repubblica. The best place to indulge in local wines is at the *Enoteca Provinciale* at Via Ulisse Rocchi 16–18 (closed Sun pm), which also does good light snacks in a room to the rear. Several places lay on **live music**: two of the longest-established places are the *Bar Morlacchi*, Piazza Morlacchi 6–8 (closed Sun), and the *Contrappunto Jazz Club*, Via Scortici 4a (closed Mon), open until 1am and 2am respectively. The only real in-town club is the sleek *Velvet Fashion Café*, Viale Roma 20 (closed Mon & Tues), which offers smart dining, drinking and occasional live music. The majority of big **clubs** and discos are out in the suburbs: ask at the tourist office for the latest hotspots.

Lago Trasimeno

The most tempting option around Perugia – whose surroundings are generally pretty bleak – is **LAGO TRASIMENO**, an ideal spot to hole up in for a few days, and particularly recommended if you want to get in some swimming, windsurfing or sailing. The lake is about 30km from Perugia and is well served by both train and bus. It's the biggest inland stretch of water on the Italian peninsula, the fourth largest in Italy overall, and, though you wouldn't think so to look at it, never deeper than 7m – hence bath-like warm water in summer. And, because the tourist and fishing industries are the economic bread and butter of the surrounding towns, it's also clean. Large banks of weed drift in during the summer, but the council takes care of these, dumping them with little subtlety on the shore.

A winning combination of tree-covered hills to the north, Umbria's subtle light, and placid lapping water produces some magical moments, but on overcast and squally days the mood can turn melancholy. Not all the reed-lined shore is uniformly pretty either; steer clear of the northern coast and head for the stretches south of Magione and Castiglione if you're after relative peace and quiet. Be warned, too, that **unofficial camping** is not as easy as it looks, partly because a lot of the immediate shoreline is marshy, but mainly because most of the good spots have already been grabbed by locals.

There's some good **walking** in the vicinity, with treks possible up Monte Castiglione on the mule track from the Passo di Gosparani (7km north of Tuoro); up Monte Acuto from Montacuto (15km northeast on the Umbértide road); or up Monte Murlo from **Preggio**, a hill-village 7km north of Castel Rigone and worth a visit in its own right. If you feel less adventurous, you could try some of the twelve waymarked trails around the lake, starting from centres such as Panicale, Passignano and Castiglione del Lago; pick up the map-brochure *Itinerari Turistici del Trasimeno* from tourist offices.

For visitors with a car, this area is also a good point to cross the border into Tuscany to visit Cortona (see p.620).

Passignano

Strung out along the northern shore, **PASSIGNANO**, a newish town with a medieval heart, is the lake's most accessible point, served by seven daily buses and hourly trains from Perugia and Terontola. In summer it can get a bit clogged with traffic, but in the evenings, the joint is jumping, with bars, discos and fish restaurants aplenty. There's a **tourist office** at Piazza Trento e Trieste 6 (June–Sept Mon–Sat 10.30am–12.30pm & 4–7pm, Sun 10am–12.30pm; Oct–May Fri &

Sat 3–6.30pm, Sun 10am–12.30pm; ☎075.827.635), and about a dozen **hotels** – the best value of which are the fifteen-room, one-star *Florida*, Via II Giugno 2 (☎075.827.228; ❷), and, for around €13 more, the larger, smarter three-star *Trasimeno*, Via Roma 16a (☎075.829.355, ⓦwww.hoteltrasimeno.it; ❷).

Somewhere along the lakeshore towards Tuoro, probably at Sanguineto ("the Place of Blood") or Ossaia ("the Place of Bones"), is the spot where the Romans suffered their famous clobbering at the hands of **Hannibal** in 217 BC. Hannibal was headed for Rome, having just crossed the Alps, when he was met by a Roman force under the Consul Flaminius. Things might have gone better for Flaminius if he'd heeded the omens that piled up on the morning of battle. First he fell off his horse, next the legionary standards had to be dug out of the mud, then – and this really should have raised suspicions – the sacred chickens refused their breakfast. Poultry accompanied all Roman armies and, by some means presumably known to the legionnaire in charge of chickens, communicated the will of the gods to waiting commanders in the field. With the chickens against him Flaminius didn't stand a chance. Hannibal lured him into a masterful ambush, with the only escape a muddy retreat into the lake. Sixteen thousand Romans, including the hapless commander, were killed.

Tuoro and Castel Rigone

The rambling village of **TUORO**, 4km west of Passignano and a three-kilometre walk from the Trasimeno battlefield, is a quiet, dull little place giving road access into the desolate, beautiful mountains north of the lake – the best of the scenery within easy reach of Perugia. A hard-to-find drive and walkway have been laid out, starting and finishing just west of the village on the road to Cortona, that take in salient features of the old battlefield. Accommodation here is relatively restricted, with the best-value **hotel**, the eight-roomed *Volante Inn*, at Via Sette Martiri 52 (☎075.826.107, ⓔvolanteinn@libero.it; ❶), plus a **campsite**, the *Punta Navaccia*, Via Navaccia 4 (☎075.826.357, ⓔnavaccia @camping.it; April–Sept), in the nearby hamlet of **Punta Navaccia**.

The village of **CASTEL RIGONE**, 8km northeast of Passignano, sits in the mountains, with superb views and a small, geranium-strewn medieval centre. There are two smart, rather staid, hotels, the better of which is the immediately obvious four-star *Relais La Fattoria*, Via Rigone 1 (☎075.845.322, ⓦwww .relaislafattoria.com; ❺). The restaurants at the hotels are the only places for a bite to eat, though neither is terribly good.

Castiglione del Lago

CASTIGLIONE DEL LAGO is the most appealing town on the lake and cuts a fine silhouette from other points around the shore, jutting out into the water on a fortified promontory. In the event it doesn't really live up to its distant promise, but is still a friendly, unpretentious place with enough charm and action to hold anyone's interest for a couple of days – longer if all you want to do is crash out on a (albeit modest) beach. It's easy to reach by slow train either from Chiusi (heading north) or Terontola if you're coming from Arezzo or Perugia. There are also nine buses daily from Perugia.

There's a good **tourist office** at no. 10 in the main Piazza Mazzini (Mon–Fri 8.30am–1pm & 3.30–7pm, Sat 9am–1pm & 3.30–7pm, Sun 9am–1pm & 4–7pm; ☎075.965.2484 or 075.965.2738, ⓔinfo@iat.castiglione-del-lago.pg.it), whose flashiness in such a small place gives a good idea of the town's considerable appeal to tourists. It has a lot of reasonable but generally characterless **rooms** on its books and apartments to rent weekly, usually a cheaper option if you can get a party together. Among the **hotels**, top dog is the three-star *Duca della Corgna*, Via B. Buozzi 143 (℡075.953.238, Ⓔhotelcorgna@trasinet.com; ❷), with the *Trasimeno*, Via Roma 174 (℡075.965.2494, Ⓕ075.952.5258; ❷), hot on its heels; more atmospheric is the *Miralago*, Piazza Mazzini 6 (℡075.951.157 or 075.953.063, Ⓦwww.hotelmiralago.com; ❺), with views of the lake behind. Most of the **campsites** are off the main road some way north or south of the town. The most highly rated is the *Badiaccia*, Via Trasimeno I 91, Località Badiaccia (℡075.965.9097, Ⓦwww.badiaccia.com). Aside from the summer-only **restaurants** on the promenade, the place to eat game, fish fresh from the lake and other dishes is the mid-priced *L'Acquario*, Via Vittorio Emanuele II 69 (℡075.965.2432; closed Wed, also Tues in winter) on the old town's single main street (mains around €10). Or try the *Vinolento*, Via VIttorio Emanuele 112 (℡075.952.5262), a good little wine bar, or the long-established *Cantina* in the same street at no. 93 (℡075.965.2463; closed Mon except in summer). The best **swimming** is at the public lido on the southern side of the promontory.

Regular boats make the trip out to the **Isola Maggiore**, one of the lake's three islands, a fun ride if you don't mind the summer crowds. There's a pretty walk round the edge of the island, and you should have no problem discreetly pitching a tent once everyone else has packed up and gone home. If not, there's one good, popular **hotel**, the three-star *Da Sauro*, Via Guglielmi 1 (℡075.826.168, Ⓕ075.825.130; ❹), which also doubles as a fine restaurant that's especially known for its fish.

The Upper Tiber

Rome's great river, the Tiber, actually spends most of its short life in Umbria, rising in the Alpe della Luna above Sansepolcro. In its moderately pretty but rather unexciting upper reaches north of Perugia – largely given over to sheep and fields of tobacco – you're faced with the familiar problem that everything you don't want to see is easily accessible and everything you do is out of reach without your own transport. The **Ferrovia Centrale Umbra** and the fast N3 to Sansepolcro are perfect for **Città di Castello**, the area's only town of note, after which you'll probably want to strike east on the N257 across the mountains to Urbino (70km). The best reason to follow the Tiber is to stay on the trail of **Piero della Francesca's** mysterious and unsettling masterpieces at Sansepolcro, Arezzo and Monterchi.

The region's best aspect, in fact, is not the valley but the desolate countryside on either side, areas that, like the Valnerina in the east, give the lie to the notion of Umbria as some sort of pastoral idyll. With few roads and fewer villages, but thousands of hectares of natural woodland and abandoned pasture, it teems with wildlife, including many rare species of birds, deer, wild boar and even wolves, now apparently pushing further up the Italian peninsula every year. **Pietralunga** and **Apecchio** to the north are the best exploring bases.

Città di Castello and around

CITTÀ DI CASTELLO is a charming and little-visited town, with a sedate and ordered medieval centre that's well worth a few hours of your time. It's also increasingly the focus for visitors staying in the many rented villas and farmhouses in hills to the east and west. In August and early September the town becomes busier than usual during its renowned **Festival of Chamber Music** (further information ℡075.852.2823 or 075.852.4357, Ⓦwww.festivalnazioni.com).

Once an important Roman centre – the grid-iron of streets is the only legacy – today the plain-bound site preserves just a handful of fairly mediocre medieval monuments. The town's main attractions are a trio of museums and an art gallery, along with some quiet, pleasant medieval streets and a bargain restaurant (see below). Foremost among the museums is the **Pinacoteca** at the southern edge of town at Via della Cannoniera 22 (Tues–Sun: April–Oct 10am–1pm & 2.30–6.30pm; Nov–March 10am–12.30pm & 2–5.30pm; ☎075.855.4202; €5), one of the region's best art galleries after Perugia's. The collection makes up in quality what it lacks in quantity, taking in works by **Raphael**, **Signorelli**, **Ghirlandaio** and **Lorenzetti**, plus a wondrous *Maestà* by the anonymous four-teenth-century Maestro di Città di Castello. There are also several sculptures, the most notable by Ghiberti, and a glittering reliquary of Florentine origin, dating from 1420.

The banal reworked **Duomo** in Piazza Gabriotti warrants a call for its smart and newly revamped museum, the **Museo del Duomo**, entered to the right of the church (Tues–Sun 10am–1pm & 3–6.30pm; ☎075.855.4705; €5). It contains a completely unexpected collection of big-name paintings, including major works by Rosso Fiorentino, Giulio Romano and Pinturicchio. Even better is the **treasure of** Canoscio, a precious hoard of sixth-century silver chalices dug up in 1932.

The third of the town's triumvirate of museums is the fascinating **Collezi-one Tessile di Tele Umbra**, just off the main square at Via Sant'Antonio 3 (Tues–Sat 10am–noon & 3.30–5.30pm, Sun 10.30am–1pm & 3–6pm, Nov–March Sun closes 5.30pm; ☎075.554.337; €3.50). The museum is annexed to a small textile factory set up in 1908 by the Franchetti, a local aristocratic family determined to keep alive the centuries-old traditions of linen-making in the region. The museum traces the history of textiles in the Upper Tiber valley, though in many ways the more interesting part of the concern is the original workshop, which continues to employ local women and still – almost uniquely in Italy – uses traditional hand-worked looms (workshop open museum hours Mon–Fri only; €1 in addition to museum entrance).

Just north of the Collezione Tessile is the **Palazzo Albizzini** (Tues–Sat: April–Oct 9am–12.30pm & 2.30–6pm; Nov–March 10.30am–12.30pm & 3–6pm; Sun 10.30am–12.30pm & 3–5pm; ☎075.855.4649; €5) at Via degli Albizzini 1, off Piazza Garibaldi. It's home to the Collezione Burri, a medley of large sculptural works by local artist Alberto Burri. If you have come to the town from the south you'll probably have seen some distinctive and colossal buildings (on Via Pierucci) once used to dry tobacco: today they house some of Burri's larger works (same ticket and hours April–Oct only).

Città di Castello's **tourist office** in the Logge Bufalini just off Piazza Matte-otti (Mon–Fri 9am–1pm & 3.30–6.30pm, Sat 9.30am–12.30pm & 3.30–6pm, Sun 9.30am–12.30pm; ☎075.855.4922, @info@iat.citta-di-castello.pg.it) deals with the whole Upper Tiber region and so is a useful stop if you're spending any time locally. Best place to stay on a budget is the excellent, modern, two-star **hotel** *Umbria*, Via dei Galanti 4, off Via Sant'Antonio (☎075.855.4925, @umbria@hotelumbria.net; ❷), just inside the medieval walls, in the east of the old centre. Top of the range is the central four-star *Tiferno*, Piazza Raffaello Sanzio 13 (☎075.855.0331, @www.hoteltiferno.it; ❺). There's also a pleas-ant, rural **campsite** at La Montesca, 1km west of town on the minor road to Monte San Marina – the *Montesca* (☎075.855.8566, @www.lamontesca .it; May–Sept). Best of several good **restaurants** is ⚘ *Amici Miei*, downstairs in a medieval cellar at Via del Monte 2 (☎075.855.9904; closed Wed), off Corso Garibaldi just south of the main Piazza Matteotti: there's no choice, but the menu changes daily and you get four wonderful courses, excluding wine, for under €20. For about the same price there's the equally good *Il Cacciatore*,Via della Braccina 10 (℡075.852.0882; closed Tues), a new but traditionally styled *osteria* with simple regional food. Alternatively, try *Lea*, an equally reasonable locals' favourite at Via San Florido 28 (℡075.852.1678; closed Mon), a short way south of the cathedral.

A couple of kilometres south of Città di Castello, in the hamlet of **GARAVELLE**, is one of Umbria's best **folk museums**, the Centro delle Tradizioni Popolari (Tues–Sun: April–Oct 8.30am–12.30pm & 3–7pm; Nov–March 8.30am–12.30pm & 2–6pm; €3.50). It's located in an eighteenth-century farmhouse, preserved with all the accoutrements of daily life – pots, pans, furniture and so forth, plus a range of exhibits covering rural activities such as wine making and weaving.

Gubbio

GUBBIO is the most thoroughly medieval of the Umbrian towns, an immediately likeable place that's hung on to its charm despite an ever-increasing influx of tourists.The streets are picture-book pretty, with houses of rosy-pink stone and seas of orange-tiled roofs; the setting is equally gorgeous with the forest-clad mountains of the Apennines rearing up behind. A broad and largely unspoilt plain stretches out in front of the town, and the whole ensemble – especially on grey, windswept days – maintains Gubbio's tough, mountain outpost atmosphere.

A powerful medieval commune, and always important as the gateway to Ravenna and the Adriatic (it was a key point on the Roman Via Flaminia), these days it's a town apart, not really part of Umbria,Tuscany or Marche – the reason it's been spared the onslaught of modernity.

Arrival and accommodation

Gubbio is easiest approached by **bus** from Perugia on the intermittently pretty cross-country SS298 **road**.The nearest **train station** is at Fossato di Vico, 19km south on the Rome–Foligno–Ancona line; there are ten connecting shuttle buses to Gubbio from Monday to Saturday, six on Sundays.

You shouldn't have any problem **staying** in Gubbio, though the place does get busy, and many of the hotels and restaurants are rather smart affairs aimed at well-heeled Italians. Check for cheap **rooms** in private houses with the **tourist office**, Piazza Odersi 6 (Mon–Fri 8.30am–1.45pm & 3.30–6pm, Sat 9am–1pm & 3.30–6pm, Sun 9.30am–12.30pm; ℡075.922.0790 or 075.922.0693, Ⓦwww.gubbio.com).

Hotels

Albergo dei Consoli Via dei Consoli 59 ℡075.927.3335, Ⓦwww.urbaniweb.com. Formerly a rather humble hotel that has been transformed into a four-star; has the advantage of a great position just a few steps down the hill from the Palazzo dei Consoli. ❺

Bosone Via XX Settembre 22 ℡075.922.0688, Ⓕ075.922.0552. A long-established and traditional three-star hotel in a medieval palace with frescoed ceilings and lots of antiques. There's a good restaurant garden, too. ❹

Gattapone Via G. Ansidei 6 ℡075.927.2489, Ⓔhotel.gattapone@libero.it. The best-priced of the town's three-star options with a peaceful garden and a central setting, but beware the bells of the nearby church if you're a light sleeper. ❸

Grotta dell'Angelo Via Gioia 47 ℡075.927.1747, Ⓕ075.927.3438. A reliable two-star option in a

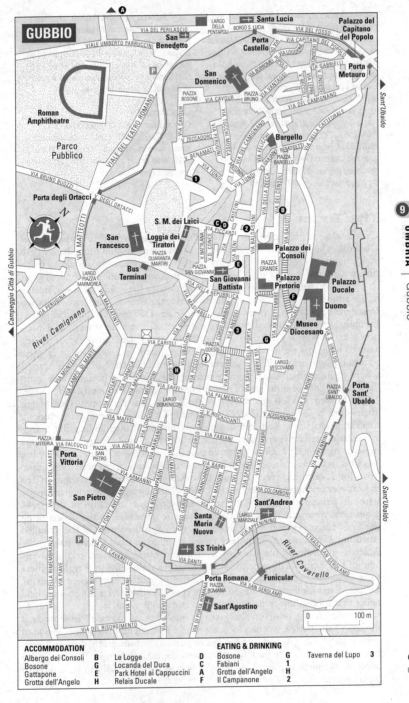

GUBBIO

Roman Amphitheatre

Parco Pubblico

VIALE UMBERTO PARRUCCINI

VIA DEL PERILASCIO

LARGO DELLA PENTAPOLI

BORGO S. LUCIA

Santa Lucia

Porta Castello

VIA DEL FOSSO

VIA CAPITANO DEL POPOLO

Palazzo del Capitano del Popolo

Porta Metauro

V. GABRIELLI

VIA BORROMEO

VIA LOGGIONE

V. BECCHI

V. ONDEDEI

BERNINO P. DE' FALCI

San Benedetto

PIAZZA BOSONE

VIA CAVOUR

San Domenico

PIAZZA BRUNO

VIA VANTAGGI

V. LEPRE

VIA DEL CAMIGNANO

VIA DELLA CATTEDRALE

VIA PERUGINA

VIA ZECCADORO

V. BENAMATI

VIA CAVOUR

VICOLO MOSCA

VIA DEL TEATRO ROMANO

VIA FELUCHI

REMOSELLI

VIA GIULIANO

PIAZZA BARGELLO

Bargello

VIA TONDI

VIA TONDI

ANTINORI

VIA DELLA RECCA

VIA DEI CONSOLI

VIA BRUNO BUOZZI

①

VIA CRISTINI

VIA BALDASSINI

ⓑ

Porta degli Ortacci

VIA DEGLI ORTACCI

S. M. dei Laici

VIA PICCARDI

ⓒ ⓓ

②

VIA GALEOTTI

VIA MATTEOTTI

San Francesco

Loggia dei Tiratori

PIAZZA QUARANTA MARTIRI

V.D. CONCE

V. BATTILANA

VIA BENI

V.D. BENI

ⓔ

Palazzo dei Consoli

PIAZZA GRANDE

Bus Terminal

LARGO PIAZZA MARMOREA

PIAZZA SAN GIOVANNI

San Giovanni Battista

VIA DELLA REPUBBLICA

Palazzo Pretorio

ⓕ

Palazzo Ducale

Duomo

VIA PERUGINA

VIA MAZZATINTI

VIA MASSARELLI

CORSO GARIBALDI

VIA ANSIDEI

VIA XX SETTEMBRE

VIA DUCALE

Museo Diocesano

VIA S. GEROLAMO

VIA MONTELLO

VIA GIOIA

VIA UBALDINI

③

VIA SAVELLI DELLA PORTA

ⓖ

River Camignano

VIA CAMPO DI MARTE

VIA CARIOLI

PIAZZA ODESSI

VIA ANSIDEI

LARGO VESCOVADO

VIA REPSAI

VIA MAZZINI

VIA PICCOTTI

ⓗ

ⓘ

VIA SAFFI

VIA MENFRINI

VIA CONSOLI

VIA GOIA

VIA PALMERUCCI

VIA DEL MONTE

PIAZZA SANT' UBALDO

Porta Sant' Ubaldo

VIA FORMICA

LARGO DOMENICONI

CORSO GARIBALDI

V. RISCACCIANTI

V. ALESSANDRINI

VIA MAFFEI

VIA MARIANELI

VIA FABIANI

VIA APPENNINO

PIAZZA VITTORIA

VIA FALCUCCI

VIA AQUILANTE

PIAZZA SAN PIETRO

VIA VITANTONIELLI

VIA BARBI

VIA XX SETTEMBRE

Porta Vittoria

VIA CAMPO DEL MARTE

VIA ARMANNI

VIA FRANCIARINI

VIA MARIONI

VIA SAVELLI DELLA PORTA

VIA SFERELI

VIA COLOMBONI

San Pietro

VIA FONTE AVELLANA

VIA BONCOMPAGNI

CORSO GARIBALDI

VIA NELLI

LARGO S. MARZIALE

Sant'Andrea

STRADA SAN GEROLAMO

VIALE DELLA RIMEMBRANZA

VIA PIAVE

VIA BIXIO

VIA DEL CAVARELLO

VIA PISCANE

Santa Maria Nuova

VIA APPENNINO

River Cavarello

VIA G. DEVUTO

SS Trinità

VIA DANTE

Porta Romana

PIAZZA ROMANA

Funicular

VIA SAN GEROLAMO

VIA DEL RISORGIMENTO

VIA DI PORTA ROMANA

Sant'Agostino

0   100 m

▲ Ⓐ

▲ Sant'Ubaldo

▲ Sant'Ubaldo

◀ Campeggio Città di Gubbio

9

UMBRIA | Gubbio

ACCOMMODATION

Albergo dei Consoli	**B**
Bosone	**G**
Gattapone	**E**
Grotta dell'Angelo	**H**
Le Logge	**D**
Locanda del Duca	**C**
Park Hotel ai Cappuccini	**A**
Relais Ducale	**F**

EATING & DRINKING

Bosone	**G**
Fabiani	**1**
Grotta dell'Angelo	**H**
Il Campanone	**2**
Taverna del Lupo	**3**

peaceful side street; there's also an excellent and moderately priced restaurant. ❷

Le Logge Via Piccardi 7–9 ⊕075.927.7574. Great rooms in the same street as the *Locanda del Duca* (see below), and a nicer proposition thanks to the pleasant owners, homely feel and pretty garden. ❷

Locanda del Duca Via Piccardi 1 ⊕075.927.7753. Seven decent one-star en-suite rooms in a convenient position just off the big Piazza Quaranta Martiri in a quiet side street. ❷

Park Hotel ai Cappuccini Via Tifernate ⊕075.9234, ⓦwww.parkhotelaicappuccini.it. A large and elegantly converted fourteenth-century monastery in parkland just outside the town, boasting a pool, gym, sauna and garden. ❼

🏃 **Relais Ducale** ⊕075.922.0157, ⓦwww .relaisducale.com. A classy four-star just below the cathedral and entered from one of two tiny alleys – Via Ducale or Via Galleotti (signed off the east side of Piazza Grande. A better bet for a treat than the *Park* (above) thanks to its superior location and greater intimacy. ❼

Campsite

Città di Gubbio Località Ortoguidone ⊕ & ⓕ075.927.2037, ⓔinfo@gubbiocamping .com. Less than 2km south of town just off the SS298 road, and in a pleasant setting with a swimming pool. April–Sept.

The Town

Centre-stage is the immense and austere fourteenth-century **Palazzo dei Consoli**, whose crenellated outline and 98-metre campanile immediately grab your attention. Probably designed by Matteo Gattapone, who was also responsible for Spoleto's Ponte delle Torri, the palace took a couple of hundred years to build and required the levelling of vast tracts of the medieval town, mainly to accommodate the huge and windswept Piazza Grande. The lesser **Palazzo Pretorio** opposite was built to the same plan. Deliberately dominating and humbling, it was what medieval civic pride was all about, an attempt to express power and supremacy in bricks and mortar. Behind a plain square facade (there's a small hole top right where criminals were hung in a cage called *la gogna* – from *vergogna* or "shame") is a cavernous baronial hall, the Salone dell'Arengo, where council officials and leading citizens met to discuss business. The word "harangue" derives from *arengo*, suggesting proceedings frequently boiled over.

The **Museo Civico** (daily: April–Sept 10am–1pm & 3–6pm; Oct–March 10am–1pm & 2–5pm; ⊕075.927.4298; €5) is also based here and includes a small archeological collection, entered from the rear of the building; this houses a typical miscellany, unremarkable except for the famous **Eugubine Tablets** (upstairs to the left), Umbria's most important archeological find. Discovered in 1444 by an illiterate shepherd, later conned into swapping his priceless treasure trove for a worthless piece of land, the seven bronze tablets are more or less the only extant record of the ancient Umbrian language, a vernacular tongue without written characters. The bastardized Etruscan and Latin of their religious texts were aimed at producing a phonetic translation of the dialect using the main languages of the day. Gubbio was close to the shrine of the so-called Apennine Jove, a major pagan deity visited by pilgrims from all over Italy, so the tablets were probably the work of Roman and Etruscan priests taking advantage of the established order to impose their religious cults in a region where their languages weren't understood. Most importantly, they suggest Romans, Etruscans and Umbrians achieved some sort of coexistence, refuting a long-held belief that succeeding civilizations wiped one another out.

Admission to the museum also gets you into the five-roomed **Pinacoteca** at the top of the palace, worth a look for works by the Gubbian School – one of central Italy's earliest, and a collection of ponderous fourteenth-century furniture. Try the door at the back for views from the palace's **loggia**. The palace also boasted 26 toilets; apparently it was the first in medieval Italy to have interior piped water.

To the north of the Piazza Grande lurks a not very inspiring thirteenth-century **Duomo**, partly redeemed by the odd fresco, twelfth-century stained glass, and some arches gracefully curved apparently to emulate the meeting of hands in prayer. There are also a pair of carved **organ lofts** that for once don't look as if they'd be more at home in a fairground. The adjoining **Museo Diocesano** (daily: April–Oct 9am–7pm; Nov–March 10am–6pm; €4.50; ☎075.922.0904, ⓦwww.museogubbio.it), to the right as you face the facade at the corner of Via Federico da Monefeltro, is well worth a few minutes, mainly for a florid Flemish cope, presented to the cathedral by Pope Marcellus II, who was born in Gubbio.

The plain-faced Gothic cathedral is overshadowed by the **Palazzo Ducale** in Via Federico da Montefeltro opposite (Tues–Sun 8.30am–7.30pm; ☎075.927.5872; €6), built over an earlier Lombard palace by the Dukes of Montefeltro as a scaled-down copy of their more famous palace in Urbino. The **courtyard** is particularly attractive, but the interior, stripped of most of its original furniture and other trappings, is a trifle dull, despite some fine views from the windows and the harmonious scale of the rooms.

On the hillside above the town stands the **Basilica of Sant'Ubaldo**, which has some great views (even better ones if you climb up to the **Rocca**). There's not much to see in the basilica itself, except the body of the town's patron saint, St Ubaldo, missing three fingers – they were hacked off by his manservant as a religious keepsake. You can't miss the big wooden pillars (*ceri*) featured in Gubbio's annual **Corsa dei Ceri** (May 15), little known outside Italy but second only to Siena's Palio in terms of exuberance and bizarre pageantry. The rules and rigmarole of the 900-year-old ceremony are mind-boggling, but they boil down to three teams racing from Piazza della Signoria to the basilica, carrying the *ceri* (each representing a different saint) on wooden stretchers. By iron-clad tradition, the *cero* of St Ubaldo always wins, the other teams having to ensure they're in the basilica before the doors are shut by the leaders. There's hours of involved ritual at either end, vast crowds and plenty of drinking. A scholarly debate rages as to whether the whole thing's intrinsically religious (commemorating the day in 1155 Ubaldo talked Barbarossa out of flattening Gubbio), or a hangover from some pagan fertility rite. Nowadays the Church, not surprisingly, claims it as its own, but judging by the very phallic *ceri*, and the roar that goes up when they're raised to the vertical, there's something more than religion at play here.

There are several ways up to the basilica, one being via the steep track that strikes off from behind the duomo. However, it's quicker and far more fun – unless you have no head for heights – to take the **funicular** (hours vary considerably, but generally summer 8.30/9.30am–7.30pm; winter reduced hours; return €5) from Porta Romana, over on the eastern side of town; you jump on small two-person cradles, which then dangle precariously over the woods and crags below as you shudder slowly upwards. While you're waiting you could take in more of Ottaviano Nelli's paintings, tucked away in the thirteenth-century **Sant'Agostino** and **Santa Maria Nuova** nearby. The unusually lovely *Madonna del Belvedere* (1408) in the latter is a masterpiece of the detailed and highly decorative style for which he was famous. His most majestic efforts – seventeen frescoes on the life of the Virgin – are in **San Francesco**, the big church that dominates the Piazza dei Quaranta Martiri – the bus terminal – at the foot of the town. The piazza's named in memory of forty citizens shot by the Germans in 1944, a reprisal for partisan attacks in the surrounding hills.

Gubbio's **Porte della Morte**, the "doors of death", are as controversial as the phallic *ceri*. Almost unique to the town (there are a few others in Assisi and southern France), these are narrow, bricked-up doorways wedged into the facades of its medieval town houses (with the best examples in Via dei Consoli). The party line is that they were used to carry a coffin out of a house, and then, having been tainted with death, were sealed up out of superstitious fear. Nice theory, and very Italian, but judging by the constricted stairways behind the doors, their purpose was probably defensive – the main door could be barricaded, leaving the more easily defended passageway as the only entrance.

There are dozens of picturesque odds and ends around the streets, which are as wonderfully explorable as any in the region. The **Bargello** in Via dei Consoli – the main medieval street (and home to most of the ceramic shops) – the medieval police station, is worth tracking down and gives you the chance to survey the adjacent **Fontana dei Matti** (the "fountain of the mad"), undistinguished but for the tradition that anyone walking round it three times will wind up mad. There's usually someone wondering whether to give it a go.

Eating

Gubbio boasts a good selection of restaurants, with some high-quality, if rather expensive, options close to the Palazzo dei Consoli. Cheaper places for snacks, sandwiches or *pizza taglia* are found in the grid of streets to the south, and towards the northern end of Via dei Consoli.

Bosone Via XX Settembre 22 ☎075.922.0688. The restaurant of the *Bosone* hotel (see p.642) is open to non-patrons, and, thanks to its garden, is the nicest place to eat outdoors in the summer. Prices are little over the average for the town, at around €12 for mains.

Fabiani Piazza Quaranta Martiri 26a/b ☎075.927.4639. Fine, friendly place, with several dining rooms set in part of the elegant Palazzo Fabiani; attractive terrace for summer alfresco dining. Good value (meals from around €30) given the quality of the cooking. Closed Tuesday.

Grotta dell'Angelo Via Gioia 47 ☎075.927.3438. Annexed to the *Grotta dell'Angelo* hotel (see p.642), offering very tasty and reasonably priced basic meals in a wonderful dining room. Closed Tues.

Il Campanone Via Piccardi 22 on the corner with Via Baldassini ☎075.927.6011. Fine local food, moderate prices and several attractive medieval vaulted dining rooms.

Taverna del Lupo Via Ansidei 21 ☎075.927.4368. A smart and long-established place in a medieval setting, well worth a splurge (mains around €15) for its classic Umbrian dishes and excellent truffle risotto. Closed Mon.

Gualdo Tadino and around

GUALDO TADINO, like Gubbio, is distinct from the rest of Umbria and has a similarly rugged mountain-outpost character. Much the same goes for **Nocera Umbra**, 15km to the south, but it was devasted by the 1997 earthquake and will be under scaffolding for years to come. Sprawling over the lower slopes of the Apennines, Gualdo Tadino has a bleakly medieval centre, hedged about with light industry and unplanned housing. Its single historical claim to fame is as witness to the death of Totila the Hun, who was slain by the Romans under the town walls.

The only remarkable thing about the thirteenth-century Gothic **Duomo** is that the facade has two tiers instead of Umbria's usual three; the interior, done to death in the nineteenth century, has absolutely nothing to recommend it. The **Museo Civico** (Mon–Fri 10am–1pm & 3–7pm, Sat & Sun 10am–7pm; €7) in the Rocca Flea, a thirteenth-century castle in Via della Rocca. Space is given to archeological finds, a collection of ceramics on the upper floor, and to local painters such as fifteenth-century Matteo da Gualdo: the centrepiece is a polyptych by **Nicolò Alunno**, considered unsurpassed among the central

Italian artists before Perugino. Without the sugary quality of some Umbrian offerings – all soft-focus saints and dewy-eyed Madonnas – Alunno has a harder edge and a wider and more genuine range of emotion.

With little to detain you, you could easily soak up the atmosphere of the place between the frequent trains from Foligno and Fabriano. The cheapest **accommodation**, however, if you need it, is at the two-star *Centro Sociale Verde Soggiorno*, Via Bosco 50 (℡075.916.263, ℮verdesoggiorno@libero.it; ❷), or the two-star *Dal Bottaio*, Via Casimiri 17 (℡075.913.230; ❶), which also has a restaurant. For **pizzas** in the old centre, visit *Baccus* in Via R. Calai (℡075.910.235; closed Mon). The **tourist office** *Pro Tadino* at Via Calai 39 (daily 9am–noon & 4–7pm; ℡075.912.172) will fill in the gaps.

Parco Regionale del Monte Cucco

Some of Umbria's best upland scenery is to be found in the mountains east and north of Gualdo on the border with Marche, much of it protected by the **Parco Regionale del Monte Cucco**. Where this area really scores is in its organized trails and backup for outdoor activities of every kind; if you want to don walking boots without too much fuss, this is one of the areas to do it – and **access** is easy, with buses from Gualdo to Valsorda and from Perugia, Gualdo, Gubbio and Assisi to Costacciaro.

The southernmost base for exploration of the park is the resort of **VALSORDA** (1000m), 8km northeast of Gualdo on the park's southern extremity. You can tackle the straightforward trek (1hr) up **Serra Santa** (1421m) on a track of motorway proportions carved out by pilgrims over the years. From the summit you could drop into the spectacular **Valle del Fonno** gorge and follow it down to Gualdo. Paths follow the main ridge from Valsorda north and south, and it's feasible to walk all the way to Nocera Umbra (6hr). Accommodation is thin on the ground, but there's a **campsite**, the *Valsorda* (℡075.913.261; June–Sept).

To get closer to the heart of the mountains head to the unpretentious and appealing **COSTACCIARO**, centre for all the park's outdoor pursuits and access point for the **Grotta di Monte Cucco**, at 922m the fifth-deepest cave system in the world. Above, the huge, bare-sloped Monte Cucco (1566m) is the main playground for **walkers**. The best place to go if you want to get seriously wet or muddy, or just tag along with a tour party, is the **Centro Nazionale di Speleologia**, Via Galeazzi 5 (off Corso Mazzini; ℡ & ℉075.917.0400 for details of tours; ⓦwww.cens.it), one of the country's most energetic and organized outdoor centres; in the past the *centro* has also offered hostel accommodation, but call ahead for current status.

There are several places **to stay** in and around Costacciaro, the best of them being the two-star *Monte Cucco da Tobia* in the Val di Ranco (℡075.917.7194, ⓦwww.albergomontecucco.it; ❶; Easter–Oct), a fabled mountaineers' and cavers' hangout (with an inexpensive restaurant). The nearest **campsite** is the *Rio Verde* (℡075.917.0138, ⓦwww.campingrioverde.it; April–Sept) at **Fornace**, 3km north of Costacciaro. Freelance camping is prohibited within the *parco regionale*, but elsewhere you'll have few problems finding a discreet pitch for a tent.

Assisi

ASSISI is already too well known, thanks to **St Francis**, Italy's premier saint and founder of the Franciscan order, which, with its various splinter groups, forms the world's biggest order. Had the man not been born here in 1182 the town wouldn't be thronged with tourists and pilgrims for ten months of the year, but then neither would it have the **Basilica of St Francis**, one of the greatest monuments to thirteenth- and fourteenth-century Italian art. You'll probably feel it's worth putting up with the crowds and increasingly overwhelming commercialism, but you may not want to hang around once you've seen all there is to see – something which can easily be done in a day. That said, Assisi quietens down in the evening, and it does retain considerable medieval hill-town charm.

Arrival and information

Getting here is easy. **Buses** connect regularly with surrounding towns – especially Perugia – putting down and picking up in Piazza Matteotti, in the east of the town above the duomo. In addition, one bus a day leaves for Rome and two for Florence, from Piazza Unità d'Italia. There are very frequent (at least hourly) **trains** to Foligno (via Spello) and Terontola (via Perugia), with connecting half-hourly bus services between the town and the station, which is 5km away to the southwest

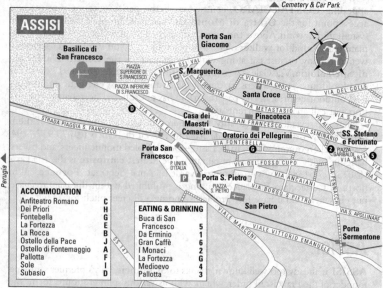

of the centre. If you are **driving**, however, note that the centre of town is closed to traffic. Your best bet is to park either in Piazza Matteotti at the top (eastern) end of the town, or below the basilica in Piazza Unità d'Italia; either way, you will have a stiff uphill walk if you explore the whole town. The staff at the **tourist office**, at the western end of Piazza del Comune (April–Oct Mon–Sat 8am–6.30pm, Sun 9am–1pm; Nov–March Mon–Fri 8am–2pm & 3–6pm, Sat 9am–1pm & 3–6pm, Sun 9am–1pm; ☎075.812.534, ✉info@iat.assisi.pg.it), do their best to help with accommodation and provide some useful maps and pamphlets.

Accommodation

Assisi offers a wide range of **accommodation**, but the supply is often only just adequate for the number of visitors, so advance booking is highly advisable, and essential if you plan to visit over Easter or during the Festa di San Francesco (Oct 3–4) or Calendimaggio (May 21–22). The tourist office has a full list of lodgings, including over fifty **rooms** for rent, and will make reservations for you, too. Spello is close enough to make seeing Assisi easy, and see below for options just outside town. Wherever you choose to stay, try to avoid the concentration of rooms and hotels in Santa Maria degli Angeli or the grim village of Bastia, 4km out of Assisi.

Hotels in Assisi

Anfiteatro Romano Via Anfiteatro 4 ☎075.813.025, ✉hotelanfiteatro@libero.it. A good-value one-star in a very pleasant part of town. Choice of rooms with or without bathrooms. ❷

Dei Priori Corso Mazzini 15 ☎075.812.237, ℻075.816.804. A three-star slightly east of Piazza del Comune. Rooms vary greatly. ❹

Fontebella Via Fontebella 25 ☎075.812.883, ⓦwww.fontebella.com. The town's most elegant

and intimate choice. Ask for a room on one of the top floors for great panoramas. ❾

La Fortezza Vicolo della Fortezza 19b ☎075.812.418, ⓦwww.lafortezzahotel.com. Friendly two-star with just seven rooms in a perfect position next to Piazza del Comune; the co-owned restaurant is also excellent. ❷

La Rocca Via di Porta Perlici 27 ☎ & ℻075.812.284. A one-star situated at the end of the street beyond the duomo. Quiet rooms, some with views, most have private bathrooms. ❶

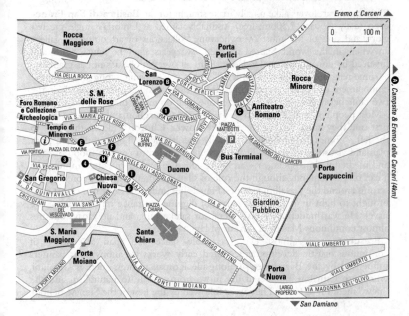

Eremo d. Carceri ▲

0   100 m

▶ ◢ Campsite & Eremo delle Carceri (4km)

▼ San Damiano

Pallotta Via San Rufino 6
☎ & ℻ 075.812.307, ⓦ www.pallottaassisi
.it. A two-star in a good location between the
duomo and Piazza del Comune; also has a first-
rate co-owned *trattoria* just off Piazza del Comune
(see p.654). ❷
Sole Corso Mazzini 35 ☎ 075.812.373, ⓦ www
.assisihotelsole.com. Recently renovated but fairly
functional two-star one minute's walk from the
Basilica di Santa Chiara. Good option if everywhere
else is full. ❷
Subasio Via Frate Elia 2 ☎ 075.821.206, ⓦ www
.hotelsubasio.com. Assisi's four-star grande dame,
old-world comfort with valley views and an

enviable position – right next to the porticoes of the
Basilica di San Francesco. ❽

Hotels outside Assisi

Castello di Petrata Pieve San Nicolò 22
☎ & ℻ 075.815.451, ⓦ www.castellopetrata.com.
An elegantly converted medieval castle, 6km north
of Assisi, with wonderful views over the valley and
its own fine restaurant. ❼

Relais La Corte di Bettona Via Santa
Caterina 2, Bettona ☎ 075.987.114,
ⓦ www.relaisbettona.com. Very comfortable
converted medieval building, with an excellent
restaurant, and a complementary bus shuttle
service to both Assisi and Perugia. ❻

Rooms, hostels and camping

Assisi has rooms for rent, but they change from year to year. Lists are available
from the tourist office, which can also supply details of **pilgrim hostels**. There
are two **regular hostels**: the *Ostello di Fontemaggio*, 3km east of town on Via
San Rufino Campagna, the road to the Eremo delle Carceri (☎075.813.636
or 075.812.317, ℻075.813.749; €20), with a **campsite**; and the larger 66-bed
Ostello della Pace at Via di Valecchie 177 (☎075.816.767, ⓦ www.assisihostel
.com; €14), off Viale Marconi, a ten-minute downhill walk from Piazza Unità
d'Italia – follow Viale Marconi until it bends sharp right, at which point a
minor road leads off left (ignore the minor road straight on at the same point)
and downhill, passing the *Country House* hotel on the left after five minutes and
reaching the hostel on the right shortly afterwards.

The Basilica di San Francesco

Pilgrims and art lovers alike usually make straight for the **Basilica di San Francesco** (daily 6.30am–7.30pm; free) justifiably famed as Umbria's single greatest
glory, and one of the most overwhelming collections of art outside a gallery
anywhere in the world. Started in 1228, two years after the saint's death, and
financed by donations that flooded in from all over Europe, it's not as grandiose
as some religious shrines, though it still strikes you as being a long way from the
embodiment of Franciscan principles. If you don't mind compromised ideals, the
two churches making up the basilica – one built on top of the other – are a treat.

Most people start with Giotto in the **Upper Church**, mainly because it's the
first one they come to, but the sombre **Lower Church** – down the steps to
the left – comes earlier, both structurally and artistically. The complicated floor
plan and claustrophobic low-lit vaults were intended to create a mood of calm
and meditative introspection – an effect added to by brown-robed monks and
a ban on photography, though the rule of silence is pretty much ignored by the
scrums around the Cavallini frescoes. Francis lies under the floor in a **crypt** only
brought to light in 1818 after 52 days of digging (entrance midway down the
nave). He was hidden after his funeral for safekeeping, and nowadays endures
almost continuous Masses in dozens of languages.

Frescoes cover almost every available space and span a century of
continuous artistic development. Stilted early works by anonymous painters
influenced by the Byzantines sit alongside Roman painters such as Cavallini,
who with Cimabue pioneered the move from mosaic to naturalism and the
"new" medium of fresco. They were followed by the best of the Sienese School,

St Francis is the most extraordinary figure that the Italian church has produced, a revolutionary spirit who took Christianity back to basics. The impact that he had on the evolution of the Catholic Church stands without parallel, and everything he accomplished in his short life was achieved by nothing more persuasive than the power of preaching and personal example. Dante placed him alongside another Messianic figure, John the Baptist, and his appeal has remained undiminished – Mussolini called him "*il piu santo dei santi*" (the most saintly of the saints).

The events of his life, though doubtless embellished by myth, are well chronicled. He was born in Assisi in 1182, the son of a wealthy merchant and a Provençal woman – which is why he replaced his baptismal name, Giovanni, with Francesco (Little Frenchman). The Occitan literature of Provence, with its troubadour songs and courtly love poems, was later to be the making of Francis as a poet and speaker. One of the earliest writers in the vernacular, Francis laid the foundation of a great Franciscan literary tradition – his Fioretti and famous Canticle to the Sun ("brother sun...sister moon") stand comparison with the best of medieval verse.

In line with the early life of most male saints, his formative years were full of drinking and womanizing; he was, says one chronicler, "the first instigator of evil, and behind none in foolishness". Illness and imprisonment in a Perugian jail incubated the first seeds of contemplation. Abstinence and solitary wanderings soon followed. The call from God, the culmination of several visions, came in Assisi in 1209, when the crucifix in San Damiano bowed to him and told him to repair God's Church. Francis took the injunction literally, sold his father's stock of cloth and gave the money to Damiano's priest, who refused it.

Francis subsequently renounced his inheritance in the Piazza del Comune: before a large crowd and his outraged father, he stripped naked in a symbolic rejection of wealth and worldly shackles. Adopting the peasant's grey sackcloth (the brown Franciscan habit came later), he began to beg, preach and mix with lepers, a deliberate embodiment of Christ's invocation to the Apostles "to heal the sick, and carry neither purse, nor scrip [money], nor shoes". His message was disarmingly simple: throw out the materialistic trappings of daily life and return to a love of God rooted in poverty, chastity and obedience. Furthermore, learn to see in the beauty and profusion of the natural world the all-pervasive hand of the Divine – a keystone of humanist thought and a departure from the doom-laden strictures of the Dark Ages.

In time he gathered his own twelve apostles and, after some difficulty, obtained permission from Pope Innocent III to found an order that espoused no dogma and maintained no rule. Francis himself never became a priest. In 1212 he was instrumental in the creation of a second order for women, the Poor Clares, and continued the vast peregrinations that took him as far as the Holy Land with the armies of the Crusades. In Egypt he confronted the sultan, Melek el-Kamel, offering to undergo a trial by fire to prove his faith. In 1224 Francis received the stigmata on the mountaintop at La Verna. Two years later, nursing his exhausted body, he died on the mud floor of his hovel in Assisi, having scorned the offer of grander accommodation at the bishop's palace. His canonization followed swiftly, in 1228, in a service conducted by Pope Gregory.

However, a split in the Franciscan order was inevitable. Francis's message and movement had few sympathizers in the wealthy and morally bankrupt papacy of the time, and while his popularity had obliged the Vatican to applaud while he was alive, the papacy quickly moved in to quash the purist elements and encourage more "moderate" tendencies. Gradually it shaped the movement to its own designs, institutionalizing Francis's message in the process.

Despite this, Francis's achievement as the first man to fracture the rigid orthodoxy of the hierarchical Church remains beyond question. Moreover, the Franciscans have not lost their ideological edge, and their views on the primacy of poverty are thought by many to be out of favour with the present Vatican administration.

Simone Martini and Pietro Lorenzetti, whose paintings are the ones to make a real point of seeing.

Martini's frescoes are in the Cappella di San Martino (1322–26), the first chapel on the left as you enter the nave. He was given free rein in the chapel, and every detail, right down to the floor and stained glass, follows his drawings, adding up to a unified scheme that's unique in Italy. Lorenzetti's works, dominated by a powerful *Crucifixion*, are in the transept to the left of the main altar. Vaults above the altar itself contain four magnificent frescoes, complicated but colourful allegories of the virtues on which Francis founded his order: Poverty, Chastity and Obedience. Once thought to have been the work of Giotto, they're now attributed to one of the church's army of unknown artists. The big feature in the right transept is Cimabue's over-restored *Madonna, Child and Angels with St Francis*, a painting Ruskin described as "the noblest depiction of the Virgin in Christendom." Look out for the famous portrait of Francis and for the much-reproduced fresco of St Clare on the wall to its left.

The more straightforward Upper Church, built to a light and airy Gothic plan – that was to be followed for countless Franciscan churches – is a completely different experience. It's less a church than an excuse to show off Giotto's dazzling frescoes on the life of St Francis. *Francis Preaching to the Birds* and *Driving the Devils from Arezzo* are just two of the famous scenes reproduced worldwide on cards and posters. The cycle starts on the right-hand wall up by the main altar and continues clockwise. Giotto was still in his 20s when he accepted the commission, having been recommended for the job by Cimabue, whose own frescoes – almost ruined now by the oxidation of badly chosen pigments and further damaged in the 1997 'quake – fill large parts of the apse and transepts. In the vaults, several harsh areas of bare plaster stand as graphic monuments to the collapse of that year.

If time allows check out the cloisters, accessible from the rear right-hand side of the Lower Church, and the Treasury, or Museo del Tesoro e Collezioni F. M. Perkins (April–Oct Mon–Sat 9.30am–5pm; donation), reached via the apse of the Lower Church. The latter, often passed by, contains a rich collection of paintings – including works by Pietro Lorenzetti and Masolino da Panicale.

The rest of the town

Via San Francesco leads back to the town centre from the basilica. Partway along the street on the left is the Palazzo Vallemani, the new site of Assisi's excellent Pinacoteca (daily: mid-March to June & Sept to mid-Oct 10am–1pm & 2–6pm; July–Aug 10am–1pm & 2.30–7pm; mid-Oct to mid-March 10am–1pm & 2–5pm; €3.50; joint ticket with Foro Romano & Rocca Maggiore €4.50). It would be easy to ignore this after the rich artistic pickings of the basilica, but the gallery is well worth the admission, not least for the wonderful paintings moved here semi-permanently from the earthquake-ravaged gallery in Nocera Umbra, near Gualdo Tadino. These include the impressive *Immaculate Conception of the Virgin* (1495–1505) by Matteo da Gualdo, a work complemented by many detached frescoes rescued from churches and other buildings around Assisi, among them important works by the Gubbian artist Ottaviano Nelli. The displays are enhanced by good English commentaries.

A little farther down the street on the right are the remains of the fifteenth-century Oratorio dei Pellegrini (daily 9am–noon & 3–8pm; free), the hospice for pilgrims, frescoed inside and out by local painters Mezzastris and Matteo da Gualdo – appealing but modest offerings after the basilica (and often out of bounds because of praying nuns).

Of more limited appeal is the **Foro Romano e Collezione Archeologica** entered just off Piazza del Comune at Via Portica 2 (same hours as Pinacoteca; €3.50; joint ticket with Pinacoteca & Rocca Maggiore €4.50), housed in the crypt of the now defunct church of San Nicolò. The classical remains include an excavated street – probably part of the old Roman forum – buried under the Piazza del Comune. The piazza itself is dominated by the so-called **Tempio di Minerva**, an enticing and perfectly preserved classical facade from the first century, concealing a dull, if beautifully restored, seventeenth-century Baroque conversion; it was the only thing Goethe was bothered about seeing when he came to Assisi – the basilica he avoided, calling it a "Babylonian pile". Francis's birthplace lies just south of the piazza, marked by the Chiesa Nuova, a dreary church.

A short hike in the other direction up the steep Via di San Rufino brings you to the thirteenth-century **Duomo** (daily 7/8am–noon & 2–7pm; free) with a typical and very lovely three-tiered Umbrian facade and sumptuously carved central doorway. The only point of interest in a boring interior is the font used to baptize St Francis, St Clare and – by a historical freak – the future Emperor Frederick II, born prematurely in a field outside the town. Off the right (south) nave, there's the small **Museo Capitolare**, or **Museo della Cattedrale** (daily: April–Oct 10am–1pm & 3–6pm; Oct–Nov 10am–1pm & 2.30–5.30pm, but closed Nov–March some years; €3), with a handful of good paintings, including a 1470 work by Nicolò Alunno, and an atmospheric **crypt**, the **Cripta di San Rufino** (same hours & ticket), entered outside down steps to the right of the facade. The cathedral makes a good point from which to strike off for the **Rocca Maggiore** (daily 10am–dusk; €3.50, €4.50 with Pinacoteca & Foro Romano), one of the bigger and better preserved in the region, with some all-embracing views the reward after a stiff climb.

Below the duomo, on the pedestrianized Piazza Santa Chiara, stands the **Basilica di Santa Chiara** (daily 6.30/7am–noon & 2pm–dusk; free), burial place of St Francis's devoted early companion, who at the age of 17 founded the Order of the Poor Clares, the female wing of the Franciscans. By some peculiar and not terribly dignified quirk she's also the patron saint of television. The church was consecrated in 1265 and is a virtual facsimile of the basilica up the road, down to the simple facade and opulent rose window. Its engineering wasn't up to the same standards, however, and arches had to be added in 1351 to prevent the whole thing being undermined by crumbling foundations. Instead of art, the scantily decorated interior has the once-withered (it was restored by a specialist in Rome) and macabrely blackened body of St Clare herself and the Byzantine crucifix famous for having bowed to Francis and commanded him to embark on his sacred mission to repair God's Church (see box, p.651).

You're not long off the Francis trail in Assisi. **San Damiano** (daily 10am–noon & 2–6pm, closes 4.30pm in winter; free), a peaceful spot of genuine monastic charm, is one of its highlights, and is easily reached by taking the Via Borgo Aretino beyond the basilica and following signs from the Porta Nuova, a steep downhill walk of about fifteen minutes. Original home to the Poor Clares, and one of St Francis's favourite spots (he is thought to have written his well-known *Canticle to the Sun* here), the church, cloisters and rustic setting preserve – almost uniquely in Assisi – a sense of the original Franciscan ideals of humility and simplicity often absent in the rest of the town.

From the train station you can see the town's other major attraction, the vast and majestically uninspiring **Santa Maria degli Angeli** (daily: April–June 6.30am–7.30pm; July–Sept 6.30am–10/11pm; Nov–March 6.30am–12.30pm & 2–7.30pm; free), built in the seventeenth century and rebuilt after an earthquake in 1832. Somewhere in its Baroque bowels are the remains of the

Porzuincola, a tiny chapel that was effectively the first Franciscan monastery. Francis lived here after founding the order in 1208, attracted by its then remote and wooded surroundings, and in time was joined by other monks and hermits who built a series of cells and mud huts in the vicinity. Today the church is crammed full of largely fourth-rate works of art and bears no relation to the Franciscan ideal.

After you've exhausted the myriad Francis connections, Assisi has the usual wonderful back streets, churches, Roman remains and miscellaneous odds and ends that characterize most Italian towns of similar age. If you have time you could check out the **Roman amphitheatre** near Porta Perlici (east of the duomo) or the Romanesque church of **San Pietro**, brilliantly restored for once, in Piazza San Pietro.

Eating and drinking

Multilingual tourist menus proliferate in the town's **restaurants**, and prices can be steep. For straight pizzas there's the superb *I Monaci*, Scaletti del Metastasio, whose entrance is in a stepped alley off the north side of Via Fontebella, a few steps down from Piazzetta Garibaldi (closed Wed). The excellent *Pallotta*, just south of Piazza del Comune at Via Volta Piana 2 (⏲075.812.307; closed Tues), is an unpretentious and welcoming mid-priced trattoria – arrive early for a table at lunch. More upmarket, *La Fortezza*, Vicolo della Fortezza 2 (reservations essential in summer, ⏲075.812.418; closed Thurs & Feb), has great food but slightly slow service. *Medioevo*, Via dell'Arco dei Priori 4b (booking advised, ⏲075.813.068; closed Wed, Jan & July 1–21), just south off the Piazza del Comune, is highly recommended for a splurge (mains around €18) on some eclectic cuisine that draws its inspiration from France, Germany and Austria as well as Italy. Slightly less expensive is the long-established *Buca di San Francesco*, Via Brizzi 1 (⏲075.812.204; closed Mon), though food can be variable here: excellent one day, middling the next. At the other end of town, above the duomo in a quiet corner, is *Da Erminio*, Via Montecavallo 19 (⏲075.812.506; closed Thurs, Jan & Feb & a period in July); it's very good value, with full meals at around €20. For wonderful **ice cream** and mouthwatering **pastries**, head for the *Gran Caffè*, Corso Mazzini 16a.

Spello to Trevi

Ranged on broad terraces above the Vale of Spoleto, medieval and pink-stoned **SPELLO** is the best place for a taste of small-town Umbria if you haven't time or means to explore further, being easy to reach by road and rail (20min from Assisi or Spoleto). Emperor Augustus gave land in the adjacent valley to faithful legionnaires who had reached the end of their careers, turning the town (Hispellum) into a sort of Roman retirement home in the process, an ambience it still rather retains.

The walls and three gateways are the most obvious Roman remnants. Don't bother walking out to the paltry and overgrown remains of the old amphitheatre hidden away beyond the main highway to Assisi: you can see all you need to from the top of the town. By far the most distinguished sight is **Pinturicchio's fresco cycle** in the thirteenth-century church of Santa Maria Maggiore (daily: April–Oct 8.30am–12.30pm & 3–7pm; Nov–March 8.30am–12.30pm & 3–6pm; free), about a third of the way up the town's winding and steep main street on Piazza G. Matteotti. The number-two Umbrian painter after Perugino, he left other important works in Siena (the duomo), Rome (the Sistine Chapel, Borgia apartments) and a host of churches scattered over central Italy. The frescoes themselves are fresh and glowing from restoration, with Pinturicchio's famous details and colouring brought out to stunning effect. Unfortunately they're behind glass, which also means you can't get a closer look at the chapel's praised but faded fifteenth-century **ceramic pavement**. Almost immediately to the north of the church stands an excellent little art gallery, the **Pinacoteca Civica** (Tues–Sun: Oct–March 10.30am–12.30pm & 3–5pm; April–Sep 10.30am–1pm & 3–6.30pm; €2.60). It contains a handful of masterpieces by local Umbrian painters, notably Nicolò Alunno, as well as several rare pieces of sculpture. Look out in particular for the figure of Christ with movable arms, once common, now extremely rare: during Holy Week the arms could be raised for ceremonies involving depictions of the Crucifixion and lowered for those depicting the Deposition and Resurrection. Farther up the busy, steep main street on the right stands **Sant'Andrea**, a striking Gothic church with another Pinturicchio painting in the right transept brightening up the gloomy interior. Also look out for the looming crucifix attributed to the school of Giotto. The little streets at the top of the street and the many small alleys off it are a pleasing antidote to the busy main drag.

Spello makes a reasonable base for visiting Assisi, with a good range of **accommodation**, fair restaurants and a small **tourist office** at the northern end of Piazza Matteotti at no. 3 (daily 9.30am–12.30pm & 3.30–5.30pm; ☎0742.301.009). *Il Cacciatore*, Via Giulia 42 (☎0742.651.141, ⓦwww.ilcacciatorehotel.com; ❸), is a reasonable-value two-star hotel, with fine views from some rooms and potentially noisier rooms looking out over the street. Above the *Pinturicchio* restaurant (see below) at the top of the main street on the left is the *Residence San Jacopo* (☎0742.301.260, ⓦwww.residencesanjacopo.it), with a warm welcome and seven excellent mini-apartments at €72 nightly, with kitchenettes for self-catering. At the smarter four-star *La Bastiglia*, Via dei Molini 17 (☎0742.651.277, ⓦwww.labastiglia.com; ❼), most of the rooms command a fine view and there's a good if expensive Michelin-starred restaurant (reckon on about €50 for three courses; closed Wed & Thurs lunchtimes).

Otherwise, Spello's most appealing **restaurant**, set in a vaulted medieval town house, is *Il Molino*, a few steps up from Santa Maria Maggiore at Piazza Matteotti 6–7 (☎0742.651.305; closed Tues), a fairly smart place (mains from €15) serving plenty of regional specialities – and wonderful fresh pasta – but with the unfortunate odd pretension. *Il Cacciatore* (closed Mon), attached to the hotel (see above), has middling and less expensive food and service but a great terrace for alfresco dining. Farther up the main street, the *Hosteria de Dadà*, at no. 47, on the left is a tiny place with a handful of shared tables and is good for cheap, light meals at lunch or dinner (daily April–Oct noon–4pm & 7pm–midnight). Towards the top of the main street, look out for *Bar Giardino* on the right at no. 12, with a vast garden and panoramic terrace at the back. A little farther along, opposite the church of San Lorenzo, sits the *Pinturicchio*, a cheap and reliable trattoria; the *Bar Tullia*, to its left, is also good and has outside tables from which to take in the street life.

Foligno

To move on anywhere from Spello by public transport means a trip to **FOLIGNO** and a lull in proceedings, because it's a large modern town and flat in every sense of the word. Most of its star-turns were bombed out of existence in the war, and the place is now a mediocre provincial backwater sprawled over an unattractive plain. Its appearance wasn't helped by the 1997 earthquake, which hit the town relatively hard. However, much of what's left is conveniently grouped together in the central **Piazza della Repubblica**, and as you're likely to be passing through, a quick look isn't going to hurt. The town's also brimful of hotels and acts as a nodal point for trains and local village buses.

For the **tourist office** – at Corso Cavour 126 (Mon–Sat 9am–1pm & 4–6/7pm, Sun 9am–1pm; ℡0742.354.459, ✉info@iat.foligno.pg.it) – and bus station (Porta Romana), follow Viale Mezzetti west from the train station to Piazzale Alunno, and the office is on the southernmost corner. Continue up Corso Cavour and you hit the historic centre two minutes later. The graceful twelfth-century **Duomo** has two good Romanesque facades, but the interior was finished off in the eighteenth century to predictable effect. The nearby **Palazzo Trinci** is the only thing worth making a real effort to see. The Trincis were Foligno's medieval big shots, with territory and influence extending over great swaths of Umbria, and their palace is an art-filled monument to wealth and power – all frescoed stairways, carved ceilings and general opulence, most of it restored in the 1990s. Inside are a small **Museo Archeologico Comunale** (Tues–Sun 10am–7pm; €6) and a **pinacoteca** (same hours & ticket) with good frescoes by the fifteenth-century Gubbian painter Ottaviano Nelli.

The only other monument that hints at Foligno's former glory is **Santa Maria Infraportas** (off Piazza San Domenico), a church of pagan origins in which St Peter himself is said to have conducted a Mass. The oldest part of the current building (eighth century) is the Cappella dell'Assunta off the left nave, dominated by the town's most precious piece of art, a twelfth-century Byzantine mural.

If you need **to stay**, try the pleasant *Valentini Hotel*, Via Flavio Ottaviani 19 (℡0742.353.990, ℻0742.356.243; ❷), just to the right of the station as you come out, on the same piazza. There's also a **hostel**, the *Pierantoni*, Via Pierantoni 23 (℡0742.342.566, ✉folhostel@tiscalinet.it; €17). For snacks and full **meals**, *La Bottega Barbanera*, right next to the side facade of the duomo, at Piazza della Repubblica 34 (℡0742.350.672), serves gourmet dishes at moderate prices in charming surroundings. If you're stuck at the station between trains, note that the peaceful *Da Remo*, Via Filzi 10 (℡0742.340.522; closed Sun dinner & Mon), is close by, with full meals, including Folignese specialities like *stranghozzi* pasta, from about €20.

Bevagna

The serene, attractive backwater of **BEVAGNA** is quieter and less visited than Spello, with a windswept **central square** of stark perfection. Flanked by two of Umbria's finest Romanesque churches – both untouched and creaking with age – the Piazza S. Silvestri dates from around the thirteenth century. The only exception is the fountain, which, while blending perfectly, was installed in 1889. Look out particularly for the surreal gargoyles over the doorway of the larger church, San Michele. Also worth seeking out is the impressive **Roman mosaic** (north side of Via Porta Guelfa; free), once part of a bath complex. This fine work shows octopus, lobsters, sea-centaurs and other creatures. To get to see it you'll need to find a guide at the small **Museo di Bevagna** to take you there (April–Oct daily 10.30am–1pm & 2.30–5pm; same hours rest of the year but closed Mon; €3.50). Located at Corso G. Matteotti 70, the museum is devoted to the history of the village and divided into three modest sections: archeological displays, art and history, and maps, letters and other documents. The museum and mosaic joint ticket also gives access to the delightful little nineteenth-century **Torti theatre**, formerly the Palazzo Comunale, just off the main square.

There's not a lot else to the town, other than the quaint attractiveness of the streets, but Bevagna does boast three charming **hotels**. The most central is the one-star *Il Chiostro di Bevagna*, Corso G. Matteotti 103 (℡0742.361.987, ℻0742.369.231; ❸), just off Piazza S. Silvestro, in an atmospheric renovated Dominican convent, with an original cloister. Down the same street, the three-star *Palazzo Brunamonti*, Corso G. Matteotti 79 (℡0742.361.932, ⓦwww .brunamonti.com; ❸), is a sumptuous place with a period setting and trompe l'oeil decorations. *L'Orto degli Angeli* (℡0742.360.130, ⓦwww.ortoangeli .it; ❼), just off the Corso G. Matteotti at the eastern end of town, is the most luxurious and historic of them all; the mansion, with porticoes, gardens and a popular gourmet restaurant, *Redibis* (closed Tues), has been in the same family since 1788. There are also a few good **restaurants** in town: try the mid-priced *Ottavio*, Via del Gonfalone 4, immediately south of Piazza S. Silvestri in the square in which the buses from Foligno and Montefalco stop; or the *Enoteca di Piazza Onofri*, just behind the Palazzo Comunale at Piazza Onofri 1 (closed Wed, lunchtimes except at weekends & late July to early Aug), perfect for light meals or a snack and a glass of wine. Also appealing is the *Osteria del Podestà*, Corso Matteotti 67 (℡0742.361.832; closed Tues), a small, central *osteria* with full meals at around €27; main courses are traditional to Umbria, puddings a little more adventurous, and the rustic surroundings – stone walls and ceiling – a definite bonus.

Montefalco

Bus is the only means of public transport from Foligno to **MONTEFALCO**, a pleasing and intimate medieval village that's home to a superb collection of paintings. Its name, meaning Falcon's Mount, was glorified with the appendage *la ringhiera dell'Umbria* – "the balcony of Umbria" – a tribute to its wonderful views. It was also the birthplace of eight saints, good going even by Italian standards. Nowadays the town's sleepy rather than holy, with only a stupendously ugly water tower and very slight urban sprawl to take the edge off its medieval appeal. The strong, blackberry-flavoured **local wine**, *Sagrantino Passito*, made from a grape variety found nowhere else in Europe, is well worth a try; it's available in many shops around town. Recommended producers are Adanti and Caprai, also makers of the excellent Rosso di Montefalco.

The town's lofty location was a godsend to Spoleto's papal governors, left high, dry and terrified by the fourteenth-century defection of the popes to Avignon. They took refuge here, and their cowering presence accounts for some of the rich decoration of Montefalco's churches, a richness out of all proportion to the town's size. The cavernous ex-church of San Francesco, off the central Piazza del Comune at Via Ringhiera Umbra 6, is now the **Museo Civico di San Francesco** (June–Aug daily 10.30am–1pm & 3–7pm, Aug open until 7.30pm; March–May, Sept & Oct daily 10.30am–1pm & 2–6pm; Nov–Feb Tues–Sun 10.30am–1pm & 2.30–5pm; €5), housing the town's big feature, Benozzo Gozzoli's sumptuous **fresco cycle** on the life of St Francis. With Fra' Angelico, Gozzoli was one of the most prolific and influential Florentine painters to come south and show the backward Umbrians what the Renaissance was all about. Resplendent with colour and detail, the cycle copies many of the ideas and episodes from Giotto's Assisi cycle but, with two hundred years of artistic know-how to draw on, is more sophisticated and more immediately appealing, if lacking Giotto's austere dignity. Among numerous other paintings in the church and excellent adjoining gallery are works by most of the leading Umbrians (Perugino, Nicolò Alunno, Tiberio d'Assisi), as well as a host of more minor efforts by local fifteenth-century artists. There are more early frescoes in **Sant'Agostino** across the main piazza in Via Umberto I.

The rest of the town is relatively low key but nice for a wander. Probably the most bizarre sight is the mummified body of **St Clare** (St Chiara), which languishes in the otherwise dismal church of the same name, five minutes' walk from San Francesco in Via Verdi (this is a second St Clare, not to be confused with the one in Assisi). Ring the bell and, if the nuns aren't deep in prayer, they may show you round the adjoining convent: in what turns out to be a fascinating behind-the-scenes look at monastic life, you're shown the remains of the saint's heart and the scissors used to hack it out. The story goes that Christ appeared to Clare, saying the burden of carrying the cross was becoming too heavy; Clare replied she would help by carrying it in her heart. When she was opened up after her death, a cross-shaped piece of tissue was duly found on her heart. Other strange exhibits include three of her kidney stones and a tree that miraculously grew from a staff planted in the garden here by Christ, during one of his appearances to Clare; the berries are used to make rosaries and are said to have powerful medicinal qualities.

Fifty metres beyond the church, preceded by a triple-arched Renaissance porch, is the chapel of **Sant'Illuminata**, strikingly if not terribly well frescoed by local painter Melanzio and others in 1510. Keep on heading out of town, turn left at the T-junction, and fifteen minutes of tedious walking brings you to **San Fortunato**, nicely situated among ilex woods and noted for the frescoes by Tiberio d'Assisi (1512), in the Cappella delle Rose (left of the main courtyard).

Practicalities

There's no need to spend more than a morning in Montefalco, but if you do decide **to stay** – and it's a peaceful spot to rest up – try the *Hotel "Degli Affreschi"*, Via G. Mameli 45 (T0742.379.243, F0742.379.643; ❷), not far from the main square. Residents have use of the swimming pool at the ugly modern sister hotel *Hotel Nuovo Mondo*, 2km outside of town on the main road. The best restaurant is the mid-priced *Coccorone*, on the corner of Largo Tempestivi and Via Fabbri (T0742.379.535; closed Wed except in summer) – the *crespelle* (stuffed pancakes) and the *tiramisù* are especially good. Otherwise, the main square has a couple of cafés and wine bars for drinks and snacks.

If you want more **information** on the town, contact the tourist desk inside San Francesco (same hours as Museo Civico; T0742.379.598).

Trevi

The best way to move southwards without your own transport from Foligno is by train, which skirts the plain of Spoleto and whisks past the light industrial sites that blight the whole stretch of the valley towards Terni and beyond. Not many people stop before Spoleto itself, giving **TREVI** and its towering position no more than an admiring glance. Its daunting inaccessibility is one of the reasons for its easy-going, old-fashioned charm; the feeling is of a pleasant, ordinary provincial town, unspoilt but just beginning to feel the first effects of tourism. All around it lie vast expanses of olive groves, renowned for producing central Italy's finest oil.

The medieval centre, looming high on its hill, is 4km from the station, connected by bus. The main square inside the walls, Piazza Mazzini, has a small and obliging Pro Loco **tourist office** at no. 6 (daily 9am–1pm & 3–6/7pm;

ⓣ0742.781.150, ⓦwww.protrevi.com), supplemented in a corner of the same piazza by a very helpful Tourist Co-Op (Mon–Sat 9am–1pm; ⓣ0742.780.066). The latter can organize all manner of accommodation locally, from rooms to villas, as well as a variety of tours and activities: despite the official afternoon closing times, there is generally someone in the office most of the day.

The key sight in town is the superb **Pinacoteca Comunale** (April–May & Sept Tues–Sun 10.30am–1pm & 2.30–6pm; June–July Tues–Sun 10.30am–1pm & 3.30–7pm; Aug daily 10.30am–1pm & 3–7.30pm; Oct–March Fri–Sun 10.30am–1pm & 2.30–5pm; €3) in Largo Don Bosco, in the former Convento di San Francesco, reached by taking Via di San Francesco from the northern end of Piazza Mazzini. It houses a well-presented display of coins, ceramics and Roman fragments, several paintings by Umbrian masters and one outstanding work, a *Coronation of the Virgin* (1522) by Lo Spagna. Trevi's medieval governors commissioned this last painting as a copy of a more famous work by the Florentine Ghirlandaio, mainly because they couldn't afford the real thing. In the same complex is the **Museo della Civiltà dell'Ulivo** (same hours and ticket), a smart museum devoted to history of the olive and olive oil production. It's packed with interesting information, in English as well as Italian, though the number of exhibits is small.

Accommodation is limited, though recent new hotels further underline the changes taking place in the town. The best central bet is the very polished *Antica Dimora alla Rocca*, Piazza della Rocca (ⓣ0742.38.541, ⓦwww.hotelallarocca .it; ❹), part of a historic 1650 building with frescoed ceilings and other period features, all beautifully restored. Aim to be in the main hotel, with nineteen rooms, rather than the seven-room annexe. Hotel alternatives include the rather bland but adequate three-star *Trevi*, at the southern edge of town at Via Fantosati 2 (ⓣ0742.780.922, ⓕ0742.780.772; ❸), and the more recent two-star *Il Terziere* (ⓣ & ⓕ0742.78.359, ⓦwww.ilterziere.com; ❸), which has the bonus of a pleasant garden: it lies east of the vast square and car park by which you enter Trevi on its eastern side at Via Salerno 1. The tourist offices (see opposite) will be able to come up with **private rooms** to rent in and around town.

For **food** try the *Osteria La Vecchia Posta*, Piazza Mazzini 14 (closed Thurs except in July & Aug), or the more expensive, and half-hidden, *La Prepositura*, Vicolo Oscura 2a, just below Piazza della Rocca, which has lovely medieval dining areas and full set meals, excluding wine, from €25 per person. At about the same price is *Maggiolini*, midway between the Municipio and San Francesco at Via San Francesco 20 (ⓣ0742.381.534; closed Tues), with good Umbrian staples and housed in part of a sixteenth-century wine cellar.

Fonti di Clitunno

A short hop from Trevi on the road south are the sacred **FONTI DI CLITUNNO** (daily: March–April & Sept–Oct 9am–6/6.30pm; May–Aug 8.30am–8pm; Nov–Feb 10am–5.30pm; €2), an unexpected beauty spot given the pockmarked surroundings. There's a certain amount of commercialized fuss and bother at the entrance, but the springs, streams and willow-shaded lake beyond – painted by Corot and an inspiration to poets from Virgil to Byron – are pure, languid romanticism. Unfortunately, the proximity of the noisy road, with its roaring trucks and buses, comes very close to ruining the effect. The spa waters have attracted people since Roman times – the likes of Caligula and Claudius came here to party – but their major curative effect is allegedly the dubious one of completely extinguishing any appetite for alcohol. Earthquakes over the years have upset many of the underground springs, so the waters aren't as plentiful as they were, but they still flow as limpid as they did in Byron's day, the "sweetest wave of the most living crystal . . . the purest god of gentle waters . . . most serene of aspect and most clear . . . a mirror and a bath for Beauty's youngest daughters". A mini tourist office doles out background information in the summer.

A few hundred metres north is the so-called **Tempietto di Clitunno** (Tues–Sun: April–Oct 8am–8pm; Nov–March 8am–6pm; free), looking for all the world like a miniature Greek temple but actually an eighth-century Christian church, cobbled together with a mixture of idiosyncrasy, wishful thinking and old Roman columns. It's only a small, one-off novelty, but still evocative, and with the bonus inside of some faded frescoes said to be the oldest in Umbria.

Spoleto

SPOLETO is perhaps Umbria's most charming town, divided into the medieval and hill-top Upper Town, home to the duomo and most of the key museums and galleries, and the predominantly modern Lower Town, which nonetheless preserves a handful of Romanesque churches and Roman ruins. Known these days mainly for its big **summer festival** (see box, p.662), it's also remarkable for its thorough-going medievalism, an extremely scenic setting, and several of Italy's most ancient Romanesque **churches**. Far more graceful and provincial a city than Perugia, nowadays it plays second fiddle politically to its long-time historical enemy, though for several centuries it was among the most influential of Italian towns. Two kilometres of well-preserved walls stand as testament to the one-time grandeur of its Roman colony, though its real importance dates from the sixth century when the Lombards made it the capital of one of their three Italian dukedoms. The autonomous **Duchy of Spoleto** eventually stretched to Rome, and by 890 its rulers had become powerful enough to lay claim to the imperial throne itself, making Spoleto, for a short time at least, the capital of the entire Holy Roman Empire. Barbarossa flattened the city in a fit of pique in 1155, and in 1499 the 19-year-old Lucrezia Borgia was appointed governor by her father, Pope Alexander VI. After that it was one long decline until about forty years ago and the arrival of the festival.

Arrival and information

Spoleto is easily reached by **train**, with regular services on the main Rome–Ancona line and local links with Foligno, Terni, Orte and elsewhere. The train station is just northwest of the lower town; shuttle buses to the centre depart from outside the station – buy tickets (€0.80) from the station newspaper stand – as do services for Norcia (see p.667); other **buses** leave from central Piazza Libertà and Piazza Garibaldi in the north of the town. The Spoleto **tourist office** is at Piazza Libertà 7 (Mon–Fri 9am–1pm & 4–7pm, Sat & Sun 10am–1pm & 4–7pm; Nov–March weekday afternoon hours 3.30–6.30pm; T0743.220.311 or 0743.238.920, E info@iat.spoleto.pg.it).

Accommodation

There is an inexpensive **hotel** in the lower town, the *Villa Redenta*, Via di Villa Redenta 1 (T0743.224.936, evillaredenta@hotmail.com; ●), though its location makes this very much a second choice. From the station walk the length of Viale Trento e Trieste and turn left at the end on Via Flaminia Vecchia: the simple hotel is another seven or eight minutes' walk on the left almost opposite Via delle

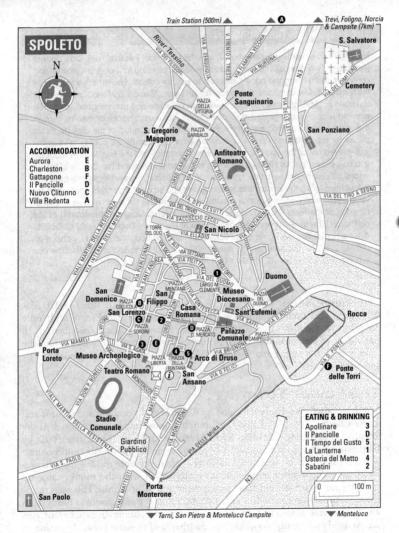

SPOLETO

N

Train Station (500m) ▲

▲ **⒜**

▲ Trevi, Foligno, Norcia & Campsite (7km)

S. Salvatore

VIA D. CERQUIGLIA

River Tessino

VIA DEL TESSINO

V. TRENTO E TRIESTE

VIA FLAMINIA VECCHIA

VIA NURSINA

VIA DEL CIMITERO

Cemetery

Ponte
Sanguinario

PIAZZA
DELLA
VITTORIA

VIA DELLE LETTERE

San Ponziano

S. Gregorio
Maggiore

PIAZZA
GARIBALDI

VIA CACCIATORI D. ALPI

CORSO GARIBALDI

VIA NUOVA

Anfiteatro
Romano

VIA DELL'ANFITEATRO

VIA DEL TIRO A SEGNO

VIA POSTERNA

VIA DEL TRIVIO

VIA DEI GESUITI

VIA PONZIANINA

P. TORRE
DEL OLIO

VIA SACCOCCIO CECILI

VIA ELLADIO

San Nicolò

VIA PIERLEONE

VIA ALÒ

VIA SETTANI

VIA DELL'ORTI

VIA SANT'ANDREA

VIA SDRUC. FILITTERIA

Duomo

VIA DEL
DUOMO

PIAZZA
DEL
DUOMO

ACCOMMODATION
Aurora   E
Charleston   B
Gattapone   F
Il Panciolle D
Nuovo Clitunno C
Villa Redenta A

VIA INTERNA DELLE MURA

VIALE MARTIRI DELLA RESISTENZA

San
Domenico

PIAZZA
COLLICOLA

PIAZZA
MENTANA

LARGO B.
CLEMENTE

San
Filippo

VIA FONTESECCA

Museo
Diocesano

Museo
Diocesano

VIA MONTEROZZO

CORSO MATTEOTTI

Casa
Romana

Sant'Eufemia

VIA SAFFI

Rocca

San
Lorenzo

PIAZZA
SORDINI

PIAZZA
D. MERCATO

Palazzo
Comunale

PIAZZA
CAMPELLO

VIA D. PONTE

VIA MAMELI

VIA S. AGATA

VIA VITTORIO

Porta
Loreto

Museo Archeologico

PIAZZA
LIBERTÀ

PIAZZA
DELLA
FONTANA

Arco di Druso

San
Ansano

VIA O. FELICI

VIA BRIGNONE

Ponte
delle Torri

Teatro Romano

VIA DON P. BONELLI

VIALE MATTEOTTI

VIALE MONTERONE

VIALE DELLE MURA

N3

VIALE MARTIRI DELLA RESISTENZA

Stadio
Comunale

Giardino
Pubblico

EATING & DRINKING
Apollinare   3
Il Panciolle   D
Il Tempo del Gusto 5
La Lanterna   1
Osteria del Matto 4
Sabatini   2

VIA S. PAOLO

San Paolo

Porta
Monterone

0   100 m

▼ Terni, San Pietro & Monteluco Campsite

▼ Monteluco

9

UMBRIA | Spoleto

Lettere. Other inexpensive **rooms** are hard to come by when the festival's in full swing, but at other times you shouldn't have too many problems.

The best reasonably priced rooms in town are at the central *Aurora*, a perfectly situated two-star in an alley off Piazza Libertà at Via dell'Apollinare 3 (☎0743.220.315, ⓦwww.hotelauroraspoleto.it; ❸), or the seven good rooms above *Il Panciolle* restaurant (though outdoor eating can make staying here a noisy option in summer) at Via del Duomo 4 (☎0743.45.677; ❷). The best of the central three-stars is the *Nuovo Clitunno*, Piazza Sordini 6 (☎0743.223.340, ⓦwww.hotelclitunno.com; ❸), followed by the *Charleston*, Piazza Collicola 10 (☎0743.220.052, ⓦwww.hotelcharleston.it; ❸), by the church of San Domenico. Finally, for a treat, top choice is the ⚘ *Gattapone*, Via del Ponte 6 (☎0743.223.447, ⓦwww.hotelgattapone.it; ❺), spectacularly situated above the gorge and almost alongside the Ponte delle Torri.

The Festival dei Due Mondi

Hosting Italy's leading international arts festival, the **Festival dei Due Mondi** (Festival of Two Worlds), has been a double-edged blessing for Spoleto – crowds and commercialism being the price it has had to pay for culture. Having already rejected thirty other Italian locations, the influential arts guru Giancarlo Menotti plumped for the town in 1958, attracted by its scenery, small venues and general good vibes. The ensuing jamboree is a great attraction if you're into music, dance or theatre, though the place forgoes a good part of its charm as a result. On top of the crowds, ticket prices for top companies and world-class performers can be off-putting, as can the well-heeled cut of the audiences. Be warned too that while the festival is in progress you can expect packed hotels, madness in the restaurants and the chance of higher prices all round. At the same time there's an Edinburgh-type fringe and plenty of fellow travellers (plus lots of films jazz, buskers and so on). Organizers, moreover, are increasingly looking to more avant-garde acts and wacky shows to recover the artistic edge of the festival's early days. Check out **information** from the **tourist office** on Piazza Libertà or the festival's own **office** at Piazza del Duomo 8 (T0743.45.028, Wwww.spoletofestival.it). Advance tickets can also be bought online or by phone on T0743.220.320 (or free phone in Italy T800.565.600) or in Spoleto itself at the box office at Piazza Libertà 12 (T0743.44.700, F0743.46.416).

For **campers** the closest site is *Camping Monteluco* (T0743.220.358, Ecampeggiomonteluco@libero.it; April–Sept), behind San Pietro, with only 35 places. *Il Girasole* (T & F0743.51.335, Ecampingilgirasole@libero.it) in the village of **Petrognano** (10km northwest of Spoleto; hourly buses from the train station) is a bigger and flashier affair, with a public swimming pool nearby and tennis courts.

The Lower Town

The lower town was badly damaged by World War II bombing and its only real interest lies in a couple of first-rate churches, most impressive of which is the fourth-century paleo-Christian **San Salvatore** (daily 7am–5pm; free), built by Christian monks from the eastern Mediterranean in the fourth century, since when it's hardly been touched. Conceived when the only models for religious buildings were Roman temples, that's pretty much what the monks came up with, the net result leaning more to paganism than Christianity. The walls inside are bare, the floors covered in fallen stone, and the dusty gloom is heavy with an almost eerie antiquity. Crumbling Corinthian columns from different ages are wedged awkwardly alongside one another, and at some point the arches in the nave were filled in to prevent total collapse.

A few moments' walk to the southwest, off Via del Cimitero, is **San Ponziano**, unremarkable but for its distinctive Romanesque facade and a beautiful tenth-century crypt, which you should be able to visit by calling on the caretaker at the house on the left of the facade as you face it. The lower town's other attraction, in a prominent position on the main Piazza Garibaldi, is the church of **San Gregorio Maggiore** (daily 9am–noon & 3.30–6pm), started in 1069. The tower and intriguing portico are made from a patchwork of fragments clearly pinched from earlier Roman remains, but it's the interior that commands most attention. Stripped back to their Romanesque state, the walls are dotted with substantial patches of fresco and interrupted by a series of unusual stone confessionals. The presbytery is raised several metres above the level of the naves to allow for a masterful little crypt, supported by dozens of tiny pillars.

Tradition has it that somewhere under the church are the bones of ten thousand Christian martyrs killed by the Romans in the **amphitheatre** close by in the military barracks on Via dell'Anfiteatro. No one seems to mind if you just walk straight in; bear right from the gateway for the best of the amphitheatre's remains. The ever-ingenious Romans apparently constructed special gutters to drain blood from the arena into the nearby Torrente Tessino, which ran crimson as a result.

The Upper Town

There's really no single central piazza in Spoleto, but the place to head for is **Piazza Libertà**. Here you'll find the much-restored first-century **Roman theatre**, complete enough, if overshadowed by the gaudily painted buildings on all sides. The worst of these offenders, the church and convent of **Sant'Agata**, were built over much of the stage area in the Middle Ages, and houses, among other things, the **Museo Archeologico** (daily 8.30am–7.30pm; €4), entered from Via Sant'Agata, the street that drops west from the piazza. The museum ticket gives access to the small theatre stage, used for festival and other performances throughout the summer. Its past includes a grisly episode in 1319 when four hundred Guelph supporters were rounded up by the Spoletans and dumped on the stage with their throats cut; the corpses were then pushed into a pile and burnt. The highlights of the little museum are the *Lex Spoletina*, two Roman inscriptions that forbade the chopping down of trees in the sacred woods of **Monteluco**. The injunction must have worked because the forests, home to hermits in the second century and later to St Francis, are still there, 8km east of the town. Take one of the hourly #9 buses from Piazza Libertà if you're not up to the very long, stiff walk, and head away from the hotel-restaurant complex and accompanying crowds into the footpaths that cross the woods. You don't have to walk far before you're alone. The views are great on a good day, and it's a welcome relief from the summer maelstrom in Spoleto itself.

Cutting into the adjoining **Piazza della Fontana** are more Roman remains, all far humbler than the tourist hype leads you to expect. Of the town's many arches from the period, the **Arco di Druso** (23 AD) straddling the entrance to the Piazza del Mercato is the only one not embedded in a wall. It was intended as a triumphal gateway to the old forum, and built to honour what, given the gate's rather modest dimensions, must have been very minor campaign victories on the part of Drusus, son of Tiberius. The patched-up walls behind it are the city's oldest, built in the sixth century BC by the Umbrians. To the right of the arch is what is described as a **Roman temple**, but unless you've a vivid imagination it's difficult to see it as anything other than a ditch. Pop into the adjacent church of **San Ansano** for a look at more of the temple and the wonderful fresco-covered crypt (down the stairs to the left of the high altar), originally the home of sixth-century monks.

Nowhere do you get a better sense of Spoleto's market-town roots than in the homely **Piazza del Mercato** beyond, whose two bars on the west side offer a fine opportunity to take in some streetlife. Old women wash fruit and vegetables in a fountain, its crown embellished with an impressive clock, the men drink in the bars and swap unintelligible stall-holders' gossip, and tourists make barely a dent in the proceedings. The *alimentari* on all sides are a cornucopia of goodies, with a definite bias towards truffles and sticky liqueurs.

Leaving the piazza to the north and turning right on Via A. Saffi brings you to the **Duomo** (daily: March–Oct 7.30am–12.30pm & 3–6pm; Nov–Feb closes 5pm; free), whose facade of restrained elegance is one of the most memorable in the region. The careful balance of Romanesque and Renaissance elements is framed by a gently sloping piazza and lovely hanging gardens, but the broad background of sky and open countryside is what sets the seal on the whole thing. The church suffered like many in Italy from the desire of rich communities to make their wealth and power conspicuous, a desire usually realized by tearing the guts out of old churches and remodelling them in the latest style. This worked well on the thirteenth-century **facade**, which has an arched portico tacked on in 1491, but less well in the interior where Pope Urban VIII's architect, Luigi Arrigucci, applied great dollops of Baroque midway through the seventeenth century. His "improvements", luckily, are eclipsed by the apse's superlative **frescoes** by the great Florentine artist Fra' Filippo Lippi, dominated by his final masterpiece, a *Coronation of the Virgin* (1469).

The artist died shortly after their completion, the rumour being that he was poisoned for seducing the daughter of a local noble family, his position as a monk having had no bearing on his sexual appetite. The Spoletans, not too perturbed by moral laxity, were delighted at having someone famous to put in their cathedral, being, as Vasari put it, "poorly provided with ornaments, above all with distinguished men", and so refused to send the dead artist back to Lorenzo de' Medici, his Florentine patron. Interred in a **tomb** designed by his son, Filippino Lippi (now in the right transept), the corpse disappeared during restoration two centuries later, the popular theory being that it was spirited away by descendants of the compromised girl – a sort of vendetta beyond the grave.

You should also make a point of seeing the **Erioli Chapels** at the beginning of the right nave, primarily for a faded *Madonna and Child* (with Lago di Trasimeno in the background) by Pinturicchio (1497), and for the cruder frescoes in the adjoining chapel by the Sicilian artist Jacopo Santori. There's also a good **Cosmati marble floor**; Umbria's earliest documented painting (a *Crucifix* of 1187, by Alberto Sotio, behind glass at the beginning of the left nave); a colourful chapel further down the left nave containing a framed letter written by St Francis (one of only two to survive); and the inevitable **icon**, which Barbarossa gave to the town in 1185 to try to make amends for having flattened it thirty years earlier.

The **Pinacoteca**, usually housed in the Palazzo Comunale, has been moved temporarily into eight rooms of the Palazzo Rosari-Spada, Piazza Sordini 5-Vicolo IIIc, off Corso Mazzini (mid-March to mid-Oct daily 10.30am–1pm & 3–6.30pm; mid-Oct to mid-March daily except Tues 10.30am–1pm & 2.30–5pm; €3, or €6 for combined ticket with Casa Romana & Galleria Civica d'Arte Moderna). The paintings include a couple of big canvases by a follower of Perugino, Lo Spagna, one of several local Renaissance artists represented.

In a tiny side street below the Palazzo Comunale is the **Casa Romana**, Via di Visiale (daily: mid-March to mid-Oct 10am–8pm; rest of year 10am–6pm; €2, or €6 combined ticket), a dark and atmospheric little corner that contains the impressive remains of a Roman house. The unexciting **Galleria Civica d'Arte Moderna**, to the west across Corso Mazzini at Palazzo Collicola on Piazza Collicola (same hours as Pinacoteca; €4, or €6 combined ticket), is devoted primarily to modern Italian artists, though it contains some works by foreigners who have been connected with the Spoleto Festival over the years, among them Alexander Calder, the man responsible for the large sculpture by the railway station.

Very close to the Palazzo Comunale's back entrance is the medieval town's most celebrated **church**, the twelfth-century **Sant'Eufemia** (seen with Museo Diocesano – see opposite), architecturally unique in Umbria for its *matronei*, high-arched galleries above the side-naves that segregated women from the men in the main body of the church. It was built over the site of the eighth-century Lombard ducal palace and appears to have been partly constructed from the remains of this and earlier Roman monuments; one or two of the completely mismatched columns are carved with distinctive Lombard motifs. The general dank solemnity of the place clearly points to an early foundation.

Sant'Eufemia is visited in conjunction with the outstanding **Museo Dioc-esano**, located in the same courtyard as the church (April–Sept Tues–Fri 10am–1pm & 3–6pm, Sat & Sun 10am–6pm; Oct–March Wed–Sun 10am–1pm & 3–5pm; €3). The half-dozen rooms contain several surprisingly good paint-ings, including a *Madonna* by Fra' Filippo Lippi and an early Beccafumi, a room of old wooden statues and some wonderfully graphic votive panels offering thanks for salvation from a host of vividly illustrated mishaps.

The Rocca, Ponte delle Torri and San Pietro

If you do nothing else in Spoleto you should take the short walk out to the **Ponte delle Torri**, the town's picture-postcard favourite and an astonishing piece of medieval engineering. It's best taken in as part of a circular walk around the base of the Rocca or on the longer trek out to San Pietro (see p.666). Within a minute of leaving shady gardens in Piazza Campello you suddenly find yourself looking out over superb countryside, with a dramatic panorama across the Tessino gorge and south to the mountains of Castelmonte. There's an informal little bar, on the left before the bend, to help you enjoy the views.

The **Rocca**, everyone's idea of a cartoon castle, with towers, crenellations and sheer walls, was another in the chain of fortresses with which the tireless Cardinal Albornoz hoped to re-establish Church domination in central Italy, a primacy lost during the fourteenth-century papal exile to Avignon. It served until the early 1980s as a high-security prison – testimony to the skill of its medieval builders – and was home to, among others, Pope John Paul II's would-be assassin and leading members of the Red Brigade. It's approaching the end of some fifteen years of restoration, and will house, among other things, a museum devoted to the Duchy of Spoleto, but despite prodding from the EU – who put up much of the money for restoration – no date has been set for the grand opening. In the meantime it's possible to visit on roughly hourly **guided tours** (mid- to end March Mon–Fri 10am–1pm & 3–6pm, Sat & Sun 10am–6pm; April to mid-June & mid-Sept–Oct Mon–Fri 10am–1pm & 3–7pm, Sat & Sun 10am–7pm; mid-June to mid-Sept daily 10am–8pm; Nov to mid-March Mon–Fri 2.30–5pm, Sat & Sun 10am–5pm; €5). The tours last 45 minutes and depart from the gate at the edge of Piazza Campello: the ticket includes a mini-bus ride and a guide with limited English, though in the event there is little to be explained: the best bits of the tour are the superb views, the imposing twin courtyards and the sheer scale of the building.

The **bridge**, too, is a genuinely impressive affair, with a 240-metre span supported by ten eighty-metre arches that have been used as a launching pad by jilted lovers for six centuries. Designed by the Gubbian architect Gattapone, who was also responsible for Gubbio's Palazzo dei Consoli, it was initially planned as an aqueduct to bring water from Monteluco, replacing an earlier Roman causeway whose design Gattapone probably borrowed and enlarged upon. In time it also became used as an escape from the Rocca when Spoleto was under siege. The remains of what used to be a covered passageway connect-ing the two are still visible straggling down the hillside.

It's well worth crossing the bridge and picking up the **footpath**, which zigzags up from the left-hand side of the road and then contours left into peaceful countryside within a few hundred metres, giving great views back

△ Ponte delle Torre

over the gorge. Alternatively, turn right on the road and make for the church of **San Pietro**, whose facade beckons from a not-too-distant hillside. If the idea of another church doesn't appeal you can easily double back to town on the circular Via della Rocca.

Though the walk to San Pietro is a longish one (2km), it's pleasantly shady with some good glimpses of Spoleto; the only thing to beware of on the country road (no pavements) are crazed drivers taking the bends too fast. The church would be undistinguished were it not for the splendid **sculptures** adorning its facade. Taken with Maitani's bas-reliefs in Orvieto, they are the best Romanesque carvings in Umbria, partly Lombard in their inspiration, and drawing variously on the Gospels and medieval legend for their complicated narrative and symbolic purpose. A particularly juicy scene to look out for includes the *Death of a Sinner* (left series, second from the top) where the Archangel Michael abandons the sinner to a couple of demons who bind and torture him before bringing in the burning oil to finish the job. Fourth panel from the top (right series) shows a wolf disguised as a friar before a fleeing ram – a dig at dodgy monastic morals.

Eating and drinking

The best place for light **meals** and a glass of wine is the *Osteria del Matto* (℡0743.225.506), a few steps west of Piazza del Mercato at Vicolo del Mercato 3: the single room is dark and snug and the owner very welcoming. A good basic trattoria is *Il Panciolle*, at Via del Duomo 3 (℡0743.221.241, ⓦwww.ristoranteilpanciollespoleto.com; closed Wed), which has a wonderful terrace for alfresco meals, though service can be slow; reckon on around €25 for a full meal. Another mid-priced option is *La Lanterna* (closed Wed), a convivial, central place on a side street left off the hill between Piazza della Libertà and Piazza Fontana, with meals at about €15. For something more special, head to the town's smartest spot, the occasionally precious *Sabatini*, at Corso Mazzini 54 (closed Mon), with outside tables to the rear and meals at around €45, or the preferable ⚔ *Apollinare*, Via Sant'Agata 14 (closed Tues), which has superb meals around the €40 mark. A recent newcomer to the ranks of Spoleto's better restaurants is *Il Tempio del Gusto*, Via Arco del Druso 11 (☎0743.47.121; closed Thurs), but reckon on up to €70 for a full meal with all the trimmings.

The Valnerina and Norcia

The **VALNERINA** is the most beautiful part of Umbria. Strictly translated as the "little valley of the Nera", it effectively refers to the whole eastern part of the region, a self-contained area of high mountains, poor communications, steep wooded valleys, upland villages and vast stretches of barren nothingness. Wolves still roam the summit ridges and the area is a genuine "forgotten corner", deserted farms everywhere bearing witness to a century of emigration.

The region is best explored with a car, as **public transport** is limited. The easiest way to get to the region without a car is by bus from Spoleto: five to seven daily run from Spoleto station to Norcia (1hr 15min), calling at Piedipaterno (2 daily connections to Monteleone), Borgo Cerreto, Serravalle and villages in between (timetables from the tourist office in Spoleto; see p.660). A new road tunnel links Spoleto to the valley, but for scenery stick to the old and tortuous N395 from Spoleto until you hit the "main" SS209 and the more pastoral run up the Nera Valley towards Norcia. Mountains roundabout are around 1500m high, with excellent walking, creeping up as you move east to about 2500m in the **Monti Sibillini**. It's difficult to explore with any sort of plan (unless you stick to the Nera), and the best approach is to follow your nose, poking into small valleys, tracing high country lanes to remote hamlets.

More deliberately, you could make for **VALLO DI NERA**, the most archetypal of the **fortified villages** that pop up along the Lower Nera. Medieval **TRIPONZO** is a natural focus of communications, little more than a quaint staging post and fortified tower (and a better target than modernish Cerreto nearby). **MONTELEONE** is the only place of any size for miles, with a fine church, and popular with trippers.

CASCIA figures large on the map, but is disappointing in actuality – largely modern, thanks to countless earthquakes over the years – and only recommendable to pilgrims in search of **St Rita**, whose presence, enshrined in the stupendously ugly twentieth-century **basilica**, dominates both the new and earthquake-damaged hill-town.

Norcia

The very pleasant mountain retreat of **NORCIA** is the only place of any size or substance in the Valnerina. Noted on the one hand as the birthplace of **St Benedict** – founder of Western monasticism – and on the other as the producer of Italy's top **salami**, it has an air of charming dereliction, and its low, sturdy houses (built to be earthquake-resistant) are a world away from the pastoral, fairy-tale cities to the west. If transport allows, it could be the base for some good trips into neighbouring territory, particularly the famed Piano Grande (see p.668) and the mountains to the east and north. A big new road through the mountains into Marche has opened and should bring in more visitors – good news for local employment, which is scarce, but a possible challenge to the environment. Hang-gliders and winter-sports enthusiasts have also recently discovered the area, another mixed blessing. There is no tourist office, but the intermittently open Casa del Parco, an office for the Parco Nazionale dei Sibillini, at Via del Solferino 22 (☎0743.817.090), has some information; alternatively, you can visit Ⓦ www.norcia.com, a private site.

It doesn't take long to see the town, but you may want to stay on for the pleasant atmosphere and the surrounding scenery. Most of the action is in the central **Piazza San Benedetto**, site of the Roman forum and presided over by a statue of Benedict. Apart from its facade, you can largely forget about the **Duomo** – destroyed by several earthquakes (the last big one was in 1979), and patched up to look like nothing on earth. The **Castellina** is more captivating: a papal fortress full of gaunt medieval echoes, it contains a fine little **museum** (May–Sept Tues–Sun 10am–1pm & 4–7.30pm; €3) with fascinating old wooden sculptures and several surprisingly accomplished paintings. Unfortunately it keeps irregular hours, especially in winter, when it is often closed for the duration. The fortress makes a strange bedfellow for the labyrinthine church of **San Benedetto**, which supposedly was built over the saint's birthplace but was probably raised from the ruins of an earlier Roman temple. Inside there are a few paltry frescoes, nothing more, though the crypt contains the remains of a Roman-era house.

Meat-eaters would be daft not to try the deservedly famous **local pork products**. Anything that can be done to a pig, the Norcians apparently do – and supposedly better than anyone else. Even today, you still see butchers in other parts of Italy called *un nurcino*, after the town. If finances stretch, you could also indulge in the area's prized black **truffle**. The season runs from January to April (though you may come across the lesser prized summer truffles too). Plenty of shops, an attraction in themselves, are on hand to sell you all manner of local specialities, not just truffles, but also hams, the famed lentils of Castelluccio (see below) and lots of rare mountain cheeses.

A decent **hostel**, the *Ostello Norcia* (☎0743.817.487, Ⓦ www.montepatino .com), offers beds (in two-, four-, five- and ten-bed rooms) at €15, including breakfast, but you must book in advance. It's in the northeast corner of town at Via Ufente 1b (take Via Anicia from behind San Benedetto and turn left at Piazza Palatina). Moderate **hotels** comprise the central eight-roomed *Da Benito*, Via Marconi 4 (☎0743.816.670, Ⓔ ristorante.benito@libero.it; ❷), and the bigger *Casa Religiosa San Benedetto*, Via delle Vergini 13 (☎ & Ⓕ0743.828.208; ❶), located at the far northwest corner of the upper town, open to all even though it's still a working convent. For a very comfortable modern option, try the *Salicone*, Via Montedoro (☎0743.828.076, Ⓦ www.bianconi.com; ❻) just outside the walls. Under the same management is the *Grotta Azzurra*, a comfortable three-star on Via Alfieri 12 (☎0743.816.513, Ⓕ0743.817.342; ❹), whose restaurant – *the Granaro del Monte* – is *the* best place to **eat** in Norcia; it's relatively inexpensive and set in large medieval banqueting halls (a former papal granary) complete with suits of armour and huge, roaring fires. Otherwise, *Beccofino* (☎0743.816.086; closed Wed except in summer), on the main Piazza San Benedetto, offers good light meals from €20.

Around Norcia – the Piano Grande and Preci

The eerie, expansive **Piano Grande**, 20km east of Norcia, is an extraordinary prairie ringed by bare, whaleback mountains and stretching, uninterrupted by tree, hedge or habitation, for miles and miles. It's much photographed – especially in spring when it's ablaze with poppies – and was used by Zeffirelli as a setting in his Franciscan film *Brother Sun, Sister Moon*. The desperately isolated village of **CASTELLUCCIO** hangs above it at around 1400m, and although no longer the sole preserve of shepherds, it remains an unspoilt base and the ideal starting point for any number of straightforward mountain walks. To plan routes, get hold of the 1:50,000 Kompass map no. 666 or the more detailed 1:25,000 CAI maps (the latter are often available in Norcia or Castelluccio's bars). There's no public transport into the area (save for one bus in and out on a Thursday, market day in Norcia), though you might try your luck at catching lifts in high season. Rough **camping** is generally no problem, and there are a couple of two-star **hotel–restaurants** convenient for the plain and many walks: *La Sibilla*, in Castelluccio itself (booking advised, ☎0743.821.113; ❸), which has an excellent restaurant, and the *Forca Canapine* (☎0743.823.005, ⓦwww.hotelcanapine.com; ❷), a big and comfortable ski-hotel (but with some tiny rooms and even tinier bathrooms) on the Norcia–Arquata road, above the southern edge of the Piano Grande.

If you can't get out here the smaller **Piano di Santa Scolastica**, due south of Norcia, will give you a very watered-down idea of what you're missing. Another worthwhile trip, if you're short of time to spend in aimless exploration, is the road north to **PRECI** and thus to Visso in Marche. Walled and castled Preci was known throughout Europe in the sixteenth century as a school for surgeons, their main trade being removal of kidney stones. However, they had a more notorious sideline – castrating young boys who were foolish enough to show operatic potential. The town has a good place to **eat**: *Il Castoro*, Via Roma (☎0743.939.248; Oct–June closed Thurs), which offers pizza or good local food such as boar, trout or chewy *stringozzi* pasta. Full meals start at about €22. A kilometre above nearby **PIEDIVALLE** is the beautifully sited Abbey of San Eutizio, one of the cradles of the Benedictine movement. Now only a pretty – if over-restored – twelfth-century Romanesque church stands on the site, but in its day the community of monks held sway over more than a hundred castles and local churches. Above the church you can still see the caves used by the earliest hermits and by Benedict himself, who discovered his vocation while visiting the hermits from Norcia.

Terni and around

TERNI was the unlikely birthplace of one of the world's most famous saints, **St Valentine**, bishop of the town until his martyrdom in 273 and now entombed in his personal basilica at San Valentino, a village 2km to the southwest. A less romantic city, however, would be hard to imagine. Terni's important arms and steel industries made it a natural target for Allied bombing in 1944, and eighty percent of the town was reduced to rubble, including, sadly, the best part of its Roman and medieval heritage. Rebuilding replaced what was lost with a grey grid-iron city straight out of postwar eastern Europe; it also put the arms industry back on its feet – the gun used to assassinate Kennedy was made here – and though the town no longer lives up to its nineteenth-century nickname of "the Manchester of Italy", hi-tech weaponry and the stench of chemicals aren't the most enticing of prospects. The **tourist office** (Mon–Sat 9am–1pm & 4–7pm; ☎0744.423.047, ⓔinfo@iat.terni.it), should you need it, is at Viale Battisti 7a – take Viale della Stazione from the station, and Viale Battisti 300m up, on the right, at the first major piazza.

The Marmore waterfall

The best place to make for locally is the **Cascate delle Marmore** (train or bus from Terni), created by the Romans in 271 BC when they diverted the River

Velino into the Nera during drainage of marshlands to the south. The highest waterfall in Europe (at 165m), it was boosted by the damming of Lago di Piediluco in the 1930s to satisfy the demands of industry for cheap hydroelectric power. Pictures of the falls in full spate adorn most Umbrian tourist offices, but what they neglect to tell you is that the water can be turned off at the flick of a switch (in favour of electric turbines), leaving a none-too-spectacular trickle. Running times vary considerably from year to year, and month to month. Summer weekends are usually a good bet, but most main tourist offices in southern Umbria carry details of current times. The observation platforms are below on the SS209 and above in the village of Marmore, with a steep path between the two (plus bus shuttle in summer when the falls are running). The green and luxuriant setting, tumbling water and expanses of gleaming polished marble add up to a spectacular show – shame about the factories round the corner, though.

The Abbazia di San Pietro in Valle

A worthwhile excursion from Terni, particularly if you're making for Norcia and the Valnerina from the south rather than Spoleto, is the **Abbazia di San Pietro in Valle** (daily 10am–noon & 2–5pm; free), 18km from Terni and signposted from Colleponte. Buses make the run up to **Triponzo**, passing the abbey en route. Founded by the Lombard duke Faroaldo II, who retired to monastic life after being deposed by his son in 720, the abbey was among the most powerful religious houses in Umbro-Romano, controlling vast tracts of land and dominating the lives of thousands of people. It's set high on the hill-side near a thickly wooded cleft, the first impression being of a dull blockhouse affair, with nothing to hint at the splendour of the Lombard and Byzantine art inside. The faded frescoes (1190) that cover the body of the main church are the first tentative attempts to create a distinctively Italian art and move away from the stylized influence of Byzantine painting, an influence that nonethe-less was to prevail until the advent of Pietro Cavallini, Cimabue and Giotto a century later. The **altar**, beautifully set off by the rose-coloured stone and rich Romanesque display all around, is a rare and important example of Lombard sculpture, carved with what look like pagan, almost Celtic figures and motifs. To each side are well-preserved Roman sarcophagi, backed by a profusion of gorgeously coloured frescoes. A doorway (not always open) leads to the twelfth-century campanile, a Lombard import of a type common in Rome and Lazio and distinguished by fragments and reliefs salvaged from the eighth-century church. There's also a faultless double-tiered cloister from the twelfth century, though access to this may be restricted as the complex's private owners – only the church belongs to the state – have opened a very appealing **hotel** (⊕0744.780.129, ⓦwww.sanpietroinvalle.com; ❹) in part of the abbey.

By following the SS209 past the walled, medieval village of **SCHEGGINO** you can pick up the Spoleto road into the Valnerina, a route covered on p.667. If you need to **stay** locally, Scheggino's *Albergo-Trattoria del Ponte*, Via del Borgo 17 (⊕0743.61.253, ⓔmarco.ronca@virgilio.it; ❸), is the best bet. Even if you're just passing through, give its excellent **restaurant** (closed Mon & Sept 1–15) a try – the trout dishes with truffles, in particular, are superb.

Carsulae

The building of the Via Flaminia in 220 BC between Rome and Ancona cemented Umbria's strategic importance as the crossroads of central Italy. Staging-posts and fully fledged colonies sprang up along its route, turning into modern-day Narni, Terni, Spoleto and Spello. Some settlements, however, such as **CARSULAE**, 15km north of Terni, were subsequently abandoned in the wake of earthquakes and civil war. In its day this particular pile of stones was known as the Pompeii of central Italy, and both Tacitus and Pliny the Younger praised its beauty.

The surrounding plain, though rustic and peaceful, has little real interest, but the excavated remains are surprisingly impressive. The freely accessible site – the largest Roman site in Umbria – is dominated by a church, **San Damiano**, made from materials filched from the ruins (other stones and precious marbles went to build local houses), behind which runs a stretch of the original Via Flaminia, complete with grooves made by carts and chariots, part of the arched northern gate, tombs, baths, wells, an amphitheatre and all the other trappings of an ex-Roman town.

Narni and around

It's an easy thirty-minute hop on the train from Terni to **NARNI**, which claims to be the geographical centre of Italy, with a hilltop site jutting into the Nera Valley on a majestic spur and crowned by another of Albornoz's formidable papal fortresses. Commanding one end of a steep gorge (about ten minutes of fairly spectacular train travel), it was once the gateway into Umbria, the last post before the Tiber Valley and the undefended road to Rome. However, while the town retains a fine medieval character, the views from its heights are marred by steel and chemical works around **Narni Scalo**, the new town that's grown up in the valley below. The trick is to keep your gaze firmly fixed on the gorge side of the walls and pretend the factories don't exist.

The heart of the **old town** (bus from the train station) has all the standard fittings: the medieval piazzas, the warren of streets, a modest art gallery, the usual crop of Romanesque churches, and a huge *rocca*, currently being restored. There's a **Roman bridge** on the outskirts, the subject of considerable local hype. Goethe arrived in Narni in the middle of the night and was peeved not to have seen it; he was only missing a solitary arch in the middle of the river – just as easily viewed from the train.

In what's an appealing but relatively low-key centre, things revolve around the narrow **Piazza dei Priori**, where pride of place goes to the fourteenth-century **Palazzo dei Priori**, now council offices, unremarkable except for a fountain and graceful **loggia** designed by the Gubbian architect Gattapone. Inside on the first floor is a superlative and much-copied canvas by Ghirlandaio. The gaunt and somewhat eccentric building opposite is the **Palazzo del Podestà**, cobbled together by amalgamating three town houses and adding some token decoration. The thirteenth-century Romanesque sculptures above the main door are worth a glance.

The bulk of the town's paintings are housed in a tiny but charming **Pinacoteca Comunale** (Tues–Thurs 11am–1pm & 3–7pm, Fri–Sun 10am–1.30pm & 2.30–7pm; €2) in the old Palazzo Vescovile (Bishops' Palace) at Piazza Cavour 8, just south of Piazza dei Priori. The collection includes key works by Benozzo Gozzoli and Fiorenzo di Lorenzo, plus fourteenth- to sixteenth-century frescoes removed from churches in surrounding villages. On the town's main street, on the other side of Piazza dei Priori, is the tiny and easily overlooked church of **Santa Maria in Pensole**, unaltered since 1175 – you can still see the date above the door – and adorned across the width of its facade with a marvellous carved frieze.

Some of Narni's most captivating sights lie beneath the streets, parts of Roman cisterns, eighth-century chapels and more, all of which can be seen on a handful of one-hour **guided tours** led by an outfit called Narni Sotterranea (April–Oct Sat 3pm & 6pm, Sun 10am, 1pm, 3pm & 5pm; Nov–March Sun 11am, 1pm, 3pm & 5pm; €4; ☎0744.722.292, ⓦwww.narnisotterranea.it).

There's no real reason for staying overnight in Narni, but should you want to your best bet would be the cosy, central *Dei Priori*, Vicolo del Comune 4 (☎0744.726.843, ⓦwww.loggiadeipriori.it; ❷), which offers first-class meals at the lovely *La Loggia* restaurant (closed Mon & second half of July). Far cheaper is the *Casa di Accoglienza* (☎0744.715.217; €17 per person), run by the nuns of Sant'Anna at Via Gattemelata 74, close to the walls in the northeast fringe of the old town. There's also a collection of cheap but deeply uninspiring **rooms** around the station, and a **campsite** 5km south of town at Strada di Borgaria 22, Monte del Sole (☎ & ⓕ0744.796.336, ⓔmontesole@libero.it; April–Sept). The **tourist office** is at Piazza dei Priori 3 (summer daily 9.30am–12.30pm & 3.30–6/7pm; ☎0744.747.247 or 0744.715.362, ⓦwww.comune.narni.tr.it).

Amelia

AMELIA, 11km northwest of Narni and plonked on top of a sugar-loaf hilltop, is by far the most tempting local excursion if the ruins don't appeal. Though not big on monuments, it's fairly interesting and unvisited, noted mainly for its extraordinary cyclopean walls, claimed as some of the oldest and mightiest in Italy. Supported by their own weight and comprising vast polygonal blocks up to 7m across, they reach a height of over 20m in places and date back, according to early Roman historians, to the Umbrian settlement of the eleventh century BC. The best of the town's archeological artifacts (and a handful of paintings) are collected in the **Museo Archeologico**, Piazza Augusto Vera 10 (April, May, June & Sept Tues–Sun 10.30am–1pm & 4–7pm; July & Aug Tues–Sun 10.30am–1pm & 4.30–7.30pm; Oct–March Fri–Sun 10.30am–1pm & 3–6pm; €5; ☎0744.978.120), most notably a superb bronze of the Roman general Germanicus, found locally in 1963. If you're in town at the weekend, be sure to explore the Roman cisterns under Piazza Matteotti (April–Oct Sat 4.30–7.30pm, Sun 10.30am–12.30pm & 4.30–7.30pm; Nov–March Sat 3–6pm, Sun 10.30am–12.30pm & 3–6pm; €2; ☎0744.978.436, ⓦwww.ameliasotterranea.it).

Most of the town's churches were ruined in the nineteenth century, and art's thin on the ground – San Giacomo's **double cloister** and a **tomb** by **Agostino di Duccio** are the only highlights – but Amelia's charm is the typically Umbrian mixture of good views, medieval streets and lovely countryside close at hand.

The **tourist office** is at Via Orvieto 1 (mid-June to mid-Sept Mon & Sun 9.30am–12.30pm, Tues–Sat 9.30am–12.30pm & 3.30–7.30pm; mid-Sept to mid-June Mon & Sat 9am–12.30pm, Tues–Fri 9am–12.30pm & 3.30–6.30pm; ☎0744.981.453, ⓔinfo@iat.amelia.tr.it). The local culinary speciality is a tooth-rotting combination of white figs, chocolate and crushed nuts (only available in winter), but for more substantial fare there are two good **restaurants**, both with **rooms** to rent: the three-star *Anita*, Via Roma 31 (☎0744.982.146, ⓕ0744.983.079; ❷; restaurant closed Mon); and, just 1km north of town, *Le Colonne*, Via Roma 191 (☎0744.983.529; ❷; restaurant closed Wed). There is a good **hostel** at Piazza Mazzini 9 (☎0744.978.673, ⓦwww.ostellogiustiniani.it; dorm beds €14.50). The nicest place to stay, however, if you can afford it, is the small fourteen-room *Il Carleni*, Via Pellegrino Carleni 21 (☎0744.983.925; ❹), with a pretty garden, good views and a mid-priced restaurant. For food, also try the more expensive *Gabelletta*, Str Tuderte Amerina 20 (℡0744.982.159; closed Mon), in an elegant villa 3.5km northeast, on the road to Montecastrilli.

The drive on to Orvieto along the back roads is a treat: plenty of oak forests and fine walks, and the chance to catch one of Umbria's Romanesque highlights, the twelfth-century church of **Santa Maria Assunata** at Lugnano in Teverina.

Otricoli

OTRICOLI, 15km south of Narni, is almost the last town in Umbria before you enter Lazio and a reasonable miniature of all the region's hill-towns. Its medieval delights, though, are eclipsed by the remains of Roman **Otriculum**, a ramshackle collection of ruins within easy walking distance of the village. To reach them get on the main road that bypasses the village, head downhill for 200m and take the signposted track that strikes off right towards the Tiber. So far no more than a trickle of tourists visits the colony – still largely unexcavated and evocatively draped in clinging undergrowth – but plans by the state to make them the centre of a vast archeological park mean they're headed for the big time. Finds from the site are collected in a small **Museo Archeologico** (Sat, Sun & public holidays: April–Sept 10.30am–12.30pm & 3.30–6pm; Oct–March 10.30am–12.30pm; €2) at Via Vittorio Emanuele II 13–15.

Unusually, the settlement has no walls, mainly because it was more a pleasure garden than a defensive site, built as a sort of holiday village for Rome's hoi polloi, who travelled up from the capital by boat on the then still navigable Tiber. Turner stopped off to paint a picture (now in the Clore wing of Tate Britain in London), and in the sixteenth century Montaigne described the spot as "infinitely pleasant". You can find **rooms** up in Otricoli at the small *Umbria*, Via Roma 72 (℡0744.709.013; ❶).

Todi

TODI is one of the best-known Umbrian hill-towns, at heart still a thriving and insular agricultural centre, but also a favoured trendy retreat for foreign expats and Rome's arts and media types. In the way of these things the tourists haven't been far behind, but neither fact should deter you from making a day-trip: few places beat it for sheer location – its hilltop position is stunning – and fairy-tale medievalism.

Getting there by public transport and sussing out how to fit it into an itinerary are likely to be your biggest problems. Basically you come either from Terni on the hourly FCU train or from Perugia, again by FCU, or on one of the regular buses that stop below the town by the church of Santa Maria della Consolazione or higher up, just off the main square near San Fortunato. Moving on, in addition to the train, you have the option of a daily bus to Orvieto. Todi's **train stations** (there are two) are both in the middle of nowhere, and **buses** to the centre don't always connect with the trains. Ponte Rio is the station to go for; Ponte Naia, 5km distant, is marginally closer, but fewer trains stop there, bus shuttles are few and far between, and the uphill walk to town is one very, very long slog. If you want to book a **taxi**, call ℡075.894.2375, 075.894.2525 or 0347.774.8321.

The Town

The central **Piazza del Popolo** is widely held to be the most perfect medieval piazza in Italy and is the reason why most people come here. The **Duomo** (daily 8.30am–12.30pm & 2.30–6.30pm; church free, museum €1) at the far (northern) end, atop a broad flight of steps, is the main feature – a meeting point of the last of the Romanesque and the first of the Gothic forms filtering up from France in the early fourteenth century. The square, three-tiered **facade** is inspired simplicity; just a sumptuous rose window (1520) and ornately carved doorway to embellish the pinky weathered marble – the classic example of a form found all over Umbria. Inevitably the interior is less impressive. There's some delicate nineteenth-century stained glass in the arched nave on the right, and a good altarpiece by Giannicolo di Paolo (a follower of Perugino), but an appalling sixteenth-century *Last Judgement*, loosely derived from Michelangelo's, defaces the back wall. The strikingly carved **choir** (1530) – of incredible delicacy and precision – is the region's best, with panels at floor level near the front depicting the tools used to carve the piece. The crypt and small museum contains a rambling collection of ancient Roman – and possibly Etruscan – fragments and religious ephemera.

Back in the piazza, the other key buildings are the three **public palaces**, squared off near the Duomo in deliberately provocative fashion as an expression of medieval civic pride – definitely trying to put one over on the Church. The adjoining Palazzo del Capitano (1290) and adjacent Palazzo del Popolo (begun 1213) are most prominent, thanks mainly to the stone staircase that looks like the setting for a thousand B-movie sword fights. Several films *have* actually been shot in Todi, filmmakers lured by its relative proximity to Rome's Cinecittà and scenographic "authenticity".

The Palazzo del Capitano houses a superb museum, the **Museo-Pinacoteca e Museo della Città** (Tues–Sun: April–Aug 10.30am–1pm & 2.30–6.30pm; Oct–Feb 10.30am–1pm & 2–4.30pm; Oct–Feb 10.30am–1pm & 2–4.30pm; March & Sept 10.30am–1pm & 2–5pm; €3.50, or €6 for a combined ticket with the Cisterne Romane & Campanile di San Fortunato; see below), which brilliantly weaves an open-plan sequence of rooms into the existing medieval structure. The first section of the museum delves into Todi's history, followed by rooms devoted to archeology, coins and medallions, fabrics, ceramics and a picture gallery. In many cases the rooms are more alluring than their displays – particularly the lovely frescoed salon devoted to ceramics – but numerous individual exhibits merit a closer look, none more so than the museum's star painting: the sumptuous *Coronation of the Virgin* (1507) by Lo Spagna.

The **Palazzo dei Priori** (1293–1337) is the southernmost building in the square, with all the various crenellations, battlements and mullioned windows of the other palaces but with the difference that they've been recently restored. It's been the seat of all the town's various rulers and today is still the town hall; if you can look as if you're on council business you should be able to peep inside. The best place to enjoy the streetlife is from the **bar** down on its right-hand side, more of a locals' local than the flashy place halfway down the piazza (but which does do a good line in sandwiches). Close to this latter bar, a small side street leads off the west side of the piazza to the **Cisterne Romane** (April–Oct Tues–Sun 10.30am–1pm & 2.30–6.30pm; Nov–March Sat & Sun 10.30am–1pm & 2–4.30pm; €2, or €6 combined ticket with Museo della Città & Campanile di San Fortunato), a massive Roman cistern, which offers a graphic illustration of the Romans' prodigious engineering abilities.

Streets to the right of the duomo are quiet and dozy and worth a wander, though the single most celebrated sight in town after the piazza is the church of **San Fortunato** (daily 9.30am–12.30pm & 3–6pm; free), set above some half-hearted gardens a very short stroll from the centre. It's an enormous thing given the size of the town – testimony to Todi's medieval wealth and importance. The squat, messy and clearly unfinished facade, an amalgam of Romanesque and Gothic styles, reflects the time it took to build (1292–1462) and at first glance doesn't exactly raise expectations. A florid **Gothic doorway** of arched swirls and carved craziness, however, is the first of several surprises, second of which is the enormous light, airy interior, recently highlighted by cleaning and several dazzling coats of whitewash. It marks the pinnacle of the Umbrian tradition for large vaulted churches, a style based on the smaller and basic "barn churches" common in Tuscany, which were distinguished by a single, low-pitched roof and naves and aisles of equal height. (San Domenico in Perugia, p.636, is another example.) It also marks a trend for side-chapels, a habit picked up from Catalonia and southern France in the thirteenth century and made necessary by the rising demand for daily Masses as the Franciscans became a more ministering order. There's another good **choir**, heavier and with more hints of the Baroque than the one in the Duomo, as well as a few scant patches of Sienese fresco. The fresco by **Masolino di Panicale** in the fourth chapel on the right is a good example of this rare painter's work, though a bit battered. Some lovely **cloisters** to the rear (outside and to the right) round off a distinctive and worthwhile church. Climb the **Campanile** (Tues–Sun: April–Oct 10.30am–1pm & 3–6.30pm; Nov–March 10.30am–1pm & 2.30–5pm; €1.50, or €6 combined ticket with Museo della Città & Cisterne Romane) for sweeping views over the town and surrounding countryside.

Santa Maria della Consolazione (closed daily 1–3pm), completed in 1607, is thought to have been based on an earlier Bramante draft for St Peter's in Rome; the alternating window types in the cupola are a Bramante trademark. Victorian writers called it the best Renaissance church in Italy (pretty close to saying the best in the world). It's worth a look to judge for yourself, but doesn't merit a special journey.

An ideal place for a siesta is the rambling **Giardino Pubblico**, full of shady nooks and narrow pathways, and a cut above the normal town plot. There's also a kids' playground and a very small **Rocca**, both less noteworthy than the views, which are extensive though usually hazy. The gardens are best tackled via the stony track to the right of San Fortunato, less of a sweat than the path that comes up from Piazza Oberdan.

Todi's tourist offerings are soon exhausted, but if you want to go the whole hog, check the so-called **niches** in Piazza del Vecchio Mercato, all that's left of the Roman colony. The town's proud of them, but they don't amount to much: four big and slightly overgrown arches of completely unknown purpose. Two minutes' walk down the lane in the lowest corner of the piazza brings you to the tiny **San Carlo** or **Ilario** (1020), an ancient Lombard chapel well off the beaten track that's all too often locked to protect a set of frescoes by Lo Spagna. A few metres beyond the church, and next to a crumbling flower-strewn arbour, is the **Fonte Scarnabecco** (1241), an unusual arched fountain that was the town's lifeblood and social meeting place until the advent of piped water. In your wanderings look out for the **three sets of walls**, concentric rings that mark Todi's Umbrian, Roman and medieval limits; they're seen to best effect on Via Matteotti.

Practicalities

The **tourist office** has shifted around town over the last four or five years, but currently is in the southeast corner of Piazza del Popolo at no. 36 (April–Oct daily 10am–1pm & 4–7pm; Nov–March Mon–Sat 10am–1pm & 3–5pm, Sun 10am–1pm; ☏075.894.5416, ⓦwww.comune.todi.pg.it). **Hotels** are in demand, especially during the increasingly popular **Todi Festival** (first ten days of Sept; ⓦ www.todiartefestival.it), and with a couple of exceptions are characterless, modern affairs some way out of town. Those exceptions are the very nice but expensive four-star, the 🏆 *Fonte Cesia*, Via Lorenzo Leoni 3 (ⓣ 075.894.3737, ⓦ www.fontecesia.it; ⑥), and the less sumptuous *Bramante*, just beyond Santa Maria della Consolazione at Via Orvietana 48 (ⓣ 075.894.8381; ⓦ www .hotelbramante.it; ⑥). Ten minutes' dispiriting walk straight down the main road from Porta Romana brings you to the *Tuder*, Via Maestà dei Lombardi 13 (ⓣ 075.894.2184, ⓔ hoteltuder@libero.it; ④), an overpriced and functional place in an uninspiring spot. A short distance beyond it is the rather fancy and marginally better located *Villa Luisa*, Via Angelo Cortesi 147 (ⓣ 075.894.8571, ⓦ www.villaluisa.it; ④). The best alternative is a set of six central rooms, *San Lorenzo Tre*, Via San Lorenzo 3 (ⓣ 075.894.4555; closed Jan & Feb; ④). They're not cheap, but the rooms are lovely, you sleep on linen sheets, and the breakfast, which is included, is excellent.

The town's best-known **restaurant** is the *Umbria*, Via San Bonaventura (ⓣ 075.894.2737; closed Tue), beneath the museum; prices are high (€25 and up for a full meal) and service can be slapdash, but the panorama from the terrace makes it all worthwhile; in season, book to be sure of an outside table. Cheaper alternatives (reckon on €15 for a basic meal) include the unpretentious *Cavour* at Corso Cavour 21 (closed Wed) – just a shame about the piped music – and the basic *Pizzeria Giubilei Italo*, off Corso Cavour in Piazza B. d'Alviano (closed Mon after 8pm). More recent is *Pane e Vino*, just off the main square at Via Ciuffelli 33 (ⓣ 075.894.5448; closed Wed), perfect for simple lunches and suppers (from €20 for three courses): there's a tremendous choice of *antipasti*. Opposite this is a good **bar** with outside tables, the *Pianiggiana*, though the bars in the main square give you more to look at with your drink or ice cream.

Deruta and the Tiber Valley

North of Todi, the Tiber Valley broadens out into a flat plain edged with moderately pretty low hills and dotted with light industry. It's not somewhere you'll want to spend a lot of time, but there are one or two things worth catching if you're in no hurry to get to Perugia, though Marsciano, the area's main town, certainly isn't one of them.

Instead try to take in some of the **hill-villages** along the route – almost any you choose will boast a Romanesque church. Most are built over the graves of early monks and martyrs, the Tiber and Naia valleys having been among the earliest to be colonized by Christians fleeing Roman persecution, and thus the springboard of Umbria's powerful monastic tradition. The most rewarding churches are those you come on by accident, in crumbling hamlets or in the midst of the ilex woods that blanket surrounding hills, but if you prefer to plan a visit you should make the following a priority: Viepri, Villa di San Faustino, Santa Maria in Partano, San Teranzano and the Abbazia di San Fidenzo.

If you don't get to the peripheral villages, head for **Madonna dei Bagni**, the one church on the main N3 that's definitely worth a look. Its walls are covered with hundreds of votive tiles left by pilgrims over three hundred years, constituting a unique social document and giving occasionally wacky insights into the peculiarities of religious belief. Day-to-day life in the fields, the insides of houses, transport (from horse to carriage to car), clothes and so on are represented almost as cartoons, though the most entertaining tiles are those offered as thanks for "miraculous" escapes from dangerous and not so dangerous corners – a fall from a cow, a bite from a donkey, fire, flood and famine. A hundred tiles were stolen in 1980, and opening times have been curtailed to reduce the risk of a recurrence. The best time to try is Saturday morning, when it's not unknown for bus tours to show up; otherwise ask at the tourist office in Deruta, 2km up the road.

Deruta

The town of **DERUTA** is best known for its **ceramics** and seems to be devoted to nothing else. Some of the stuff is mass-produced trash, and some pieces so big you'd need a trailer to get them home, but most are beautiful – hand-made, hand-painted and, by general consent, Italy's best. The Romans worked local clay, but it was the discovery of distinctive blue and yellow glazes in the fifteenth century, allied with the Moorish-influenced designs of southern Spain, that put the town on the map. Some fifty workshops traded as far afield as Britain, and pieces from the period have found their way into most of the world's major museums. Designs these days are mainly copies, with little original work, though it's still very much the place for browsing and buying; avoid the roadside stalls and head for the workshops of the new town for the best choice and prices.

The **old town** on the hill isn't particularly compelling, but there's a slick **Museo Regionale della Ceramica** next to the church of San Francesco (April–June daily 10.30am–1pm & 3–6pm; July–Aug 10am–1pm & 3.30–7pm; Oct–March Wed–Mon 10.30am–1pm & 2.30–5pm; €3), which traces the history of ceramic production in the town: one of the highlights is a tiled floor (1524) lifted wholesale from the town's parish church. For more on the town, including ceramics outlets, visit the **tourist office** at Piazza dei Consoli 4 (April–Sept Mon–Sat 9am–noon & 3–6.30pm, Sun 9am–noon; Nov–March closes 5pm; ☎075.971.1143).

Orvieto

Out on a limb from the rest of Umbria, **ORVIETO** is perfectly placed between Rome and Florence to serve as a historical picnic for tour operators. Visitors flood into the town in their millions, drawn by the **Duomo**, one of the greatest Gothic buildings in Italy. However, once its facade and Signorelli's frescoes have been admired, the town's not quite as exciting as guides and word of mouth make out. This is partly to do with the gloominess of the dark volcanic rock (*tufa*) from which it's built, and, more poetically, because it harbours something of the characteristic brooding atmosphere of Etruscan towns (it was one of the twelve-strong federation of Etruscan cities). Two thousand years on, it's not difficult to detect a more laid-back atmosphere in the cities east of the Tiber – founded by the Umbrians, a sunnier and easier-going people. All the same Orvieto is likeable, the setting superb, the duomo unmissable, and the rest of the town good for a couple of hours' visit. And you could always indulge in its renowned white **wine** if you're stuck with time on your hands.

Arrival and information

First impressions of Orvieto from afar tend to be the ones that linger; its position is almost as remarkable and famous as its cathedral. The town, rising 300m sheer

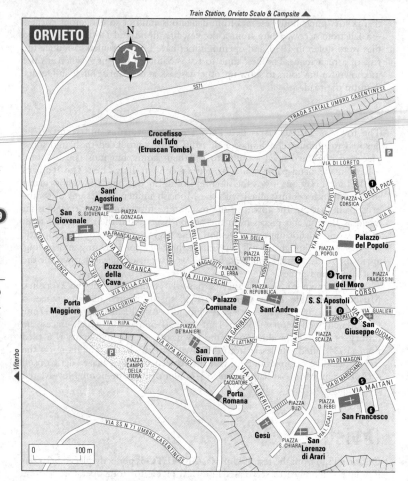

ORVIETO

N

UMBRIA | Orvieto

9

◄ Viterbo

Crocefisso
del Tufo
(Etruscan Tombs)

Sant'
Agostino

San
Giovenale

PIAZZA
S. GIOVENALE

PIAZZA
G. GONZAGA

Pozzo
della
Cava

Porta
Maggiore

PIAZZA
D. POPOLO

Palazzo
del Popolo

Torre
del Moro

S. S. Apostoli

San
Giuseppe

Palazzo
Comunale

Sant'Andrea

San
Giovanni

Porta
Romana

San Francesco

Gesù

San
Lorenzo
di Arari

0   100 m

from the valley floor, sits on a tabletop plug of volcanic lava, one of four such
remnants in the vicinity. Without a doubt, the best approach is by car through
the hills to the southwest (from Bolsena, see p.826). It starts to look fairly average
again from the dismal town around the train station, but hit the twisting three-
kilometre road up to the old centre and you begin to get a sense of its drama and
one-off weirdness. If you arrive by train, take the restored nineteenth-century
funicular (tickets at €0.80 from the funicular ticket office or station newsagent
or bar) from the station forecourt to Piazza Cahen: it's a pleasant walk along
Corso Cavour to the centre of town (allow 5–10min), or you can take one of
the regular minibus shuttles (tickets €0.80) that stop outside the funicular every
few minutes for the run to Piazza del Duomo. Buses replace the funicular when
it closes at 8.30pm. Inter-town buses take you directly to Piazza Cahen, Piazza
XXIX Marzo, or Piazza della Repubblica, depending on the service.

The **tourist office** is at Piazza del Duomo 24 (Mon–Fri 8.15am–2pm & 4–7pm,
Sat & Sun 10am–1pm & 3–6pm; ☎0763.341.772, ⓦwww.comune.orvieto.tr.it).

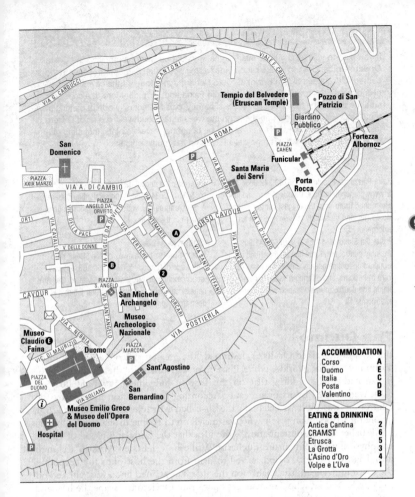

ACCOMMODATION

Corso	A
Duomo	E
Italia	C
Posta	D
Valentino	B

EATING & DRINKING

Antica Cantina	2
CRAMST	6
Etrusca	5
La Grotta	3
L'Asino d'Oro	4
Volpe e L'Uva	1

Check your **email** at *Caffè Montanucci*, Corso Cavour 19–23 (8am–midnight, closed Wed; €6.20 hr).

Accommodation

Most of the town's budget **rooms** – and nightlife – are in Orvieto Scalo, the unlovely district around the station, but this is very much a position of last resort, and our **hotel** recommendations are all in the upper old town.

Hotels

Corso Corso Cavour 343 ☎ & ⓕ 0763.342.020, ⓦ www.hotelcorso.net. A little way from the centre, and therefore relatively quiet, but still within easy walking distance of everything, with good-value and well-appointed rooms. ❸

Duomo Via Vicolo di Maurizio 7 ☎ 0763.341.887, ⓦ www.orvietohotelduomo.com. This three-star in a comfortable restructured medieval building is extremely central and convenient for the duomo, which is less than a minute's walk away. ❹

Italia Piazza del Popolo 13 ☎ 0763.342.065, ⒲ www.grandhotelitalia.it. Unexceptional and long-established three-star; the biggest central place (45 rooms) and thus likely to have space in an emergency. ❹

Posta Via Signorelli 18 ☎ & ⒻAX 0763.341.909. The only central hotel that can be described as a budget option; pleasantly dated, two minutes from the duomo, and offering a wide range of single and double rooms with and without private bathrooms. ❶

Valentino Via Angelo da Orvieto 30–32 ☎ & ⒻAX 0743.342.464, Ⓔ hotelvalentino@libero.it. A reliable three-star with nineteen rooms a 5min walk from the duomo. ❸

Campsite

Scacco Matto 10km away on the SS448 road near Lago di Corbora ☎ 0744.950.163, ⒲ www .scaccomatto.net (bus to Baschi/Civitella). Orvieto's nearest campsite is a lowly one-star job that is open from April to October.

The Duomo

Burckhardt described Orvieto's duomo as "the greatest and richest polychrome monument in the world", while Pope Leo XIII called it "the Golden Lily of Italian cathedrals", adding that on the Day of Judgement it would float up to heaven carried by its own beauty. According to a tradition fostered by the Church, it was built to celebrate the so-called **Miracle of Bolsena** (1263), involving a Bohemian priest who was travelling to Rome to shake off a heretical disbelief in transubstantiation – the idea that the body and blood of Christ are physically present in the Eucharist. While he celebrated Mass in a church near Lago di Bolsena, blood started to drip from the host onto the corporale, the cloth underneath the chalice on the altar. The stained linen was whisked off to Pope Urban IV, who like many a pope was in Orvieto to escape the heat and political hassle of Rome. He immediately proclaimed a miracle, and a year later Thomas Aquinas, no less, drew up a papal bull instigating the feast of **Corpus Domini**. The Church at the time, however, was in retreat, and the Umbrian towns were at the height of their civic expansion. It's likely that the building of an awe-inspiring cathedral in one of the region's most powerful *comuni* was less an act to commemorate a miracle than a shrewd piece of political opportunism designed to remind errant citizens of the papacy's power.

It was miraculous that the duomo was built at all. Medieval Orvieto was so violent that at times the population thought about giving up on it altogether. Dante wrote that its family feuds were worse than those between Verona's Montagues and Capulets – the original inspiration for *Romeo and Juliet*. The building was also dogged by a committee approach to design – even the plans took thirty years to draw up. Yet though construction dragged on for three centuries and exhausted 33 architects, 152 sculptors, 68 painters and 90 mosaicists, the final product is a surprisingly unified example of the transitional Romanesque-Gothic style. Credit for guiding the work at its most important stage goes to the Sienese

△ The duomo's facade

architect **Lorenzo Maitani** (c1270–1330), with the initial plans probably drawn up by Arnolfo di Cambio, architect of Florence's Palazzo Vecchio.

The facade

The facade is the star-turn, owing its undeniable impact to a decorative richness just the right side of overkill. It's a riot of columns, spires, bas-reliefs,

sculptures, dazzling and almost overpowering use of colour, colossally emphasized doorways and hundreds of capricious details just about held together by
four enormous fluted columns. Stunning from the dwarfed piazza, particularly
at sunset or under floodlights, it's not all superficial gloss. The **four pillars**
at the base, one of the highlights of fourteenth-century Italian sculpture, are
well worth a close look. The work of Maitani and his pupils, they describe
episodes from the Old and New Testaments in staggering detail: lashings of
plague, famine, martyrdoms, grotesque mutilation, mad and emaciated figures,
the Flagellation, the Massacre of the Innocents, strange visitations, Cain slaying
Abel (particularly juicy), and only the occasional touch of light relief. In its
day it was there to point an accusing finger at Orvieto's moral slackers, as the
none-too-cheerful final panel makes clear, with the damned packed off to fire,
brimstone and eternal misery.

The interior

The inside (daily: 7.30am–12.45pm & 2.30–7.15pm; March & Oct closes
6.15pm; Nov–March 5.15pm; free) is a disappointment at least at first glance, as
if the facade either took all the enthusiasm or all the money and the church was
tacked on merely to prop everything else up. Adorned with alternating stripes
of coloured marble similar to those found in the cathedrals of Siena, Florence
and Pisa, it's mainly distinguished by **Luca Signorelli's** fresco cycle, *The Last
Judgement* (1499–1504), in a chapel at the end of the south nave. Some claim it
surpasses even Michelangelo's similar cycle in the Sistine Chapel, painted forty
years later and obviously heavily influenced by Signorelli's earlier treatment.
The cycle is on view again after years of restoration, and though you now
have to pay for the privilege of seeing it, the admission's more than worth it
(April–June Mon–Sat 9am–12.45pm & 2.30–7.15pm, Sun 2.30–5.45pm; July–
Aug same hours but closes 6.45pm on Sun; Nov–Feb Mon–Sat 9am–12.45pm
& 2.30–5.15pm, Sun 2.30–5.45pm; March & Oct Mon–Sat 9am–12.45pm
& 2.30–6.15pm, Sun 2.30–5.45pm; €5, also includes Museo dell'Opera &
Sant'Agostino). Tickets are not available in the cathedral, but must be bought
from the tourist office.

Several painters, including Perugino and Fra' Angelico (who completed
two ceiling panels), tackled the chapel before Signorelli – a free-thinking and
singular artist from nearby Cortona – was commissioned to finish it off. All
but the lower walls are crowded with the movement of passionate and beautifully observed muscular figures, creating an effect that's realistic and almost
grotesquely fantastic at the same time. Draughtsmanship and a delight in the
human form are the frescoes' most obvious attributes, but there are plenty
of bizarre details to hold the narrative interest. A mass of monstrous lechery
and naked writhing flesh fills the *Inferno* panel, including that of the painter's
unfaithful mistress, immortalized in hell for all to see. In another an unfortunate is having his ear bitten off by a green-buttocked demon. Signorelli,
suitably clad in black, has painted himself with Fra' Angelico in the lower left
corner of *The Sermon of the Antichrist*, both calmly looking on as someone is
garrotted at their feet.

All this overshadows the twin **Cappella del Corporale**, which contains
the sacred corporale itself, locked away in a massive, jewel-encrusted casket
(designed as a deliberate copy of the facade), plus some appealing frescoes by
local fourteenth-century painter Ugolino di Prete, describing events connected
with the Miracle of Bolsena. The entire apse is covered in more frescoes by
Ugolino, many of which were partly restored by Pinturicchio, who was eventually kicked off the job for "consuming too much gold, too much azure and

too much wine". Also worth a mention are an easily missed *Madonna and Child* by Gentile da Fabriano and a beautifully delicate fifteenth-century font, both near the main doors.

The rest of the town

Next to the duomo on the right as you look at it is the **Museo dell'Opera del duomo** (Wed–Thurs: April–June & Sept–Oct 10am–6pm; July & Aug 10am–1pm & 3–7pm; Nov–March 10am–5pm; €5, includes admission to Signorelli frescoes in the duomo & church of Sant'Agostino). Highlights are paintings by Martini and Pastura (an artist from Viterbo influenced by Perugino), several important thirteenth-century sculptures by Arnolfo di Cambio and Andrea Pisano, and a lovely font filled with Escher-like carved fishes. The **Emilio Greco** section of the museum (daily: April–Sept 10.30am–1pm & 2–6pm; Oct–March 10.30am–1pm & 2.30–5.30pm; €2.50, €5.50 for Biglietto Cumulativo, which includes Il Pozzo di San Patrizio) comprises nearly a hundred works donated to the city by the artist who created the duomo's bronze doors in the 1960s, none of them profoundly interesting – peek through the door beyond the ground-floor ticket office and you'll see enough of the exhibits to know if you want a closer look.

The wonderfully restored **Museo Claudio Faina** (incorporating the Museo Civico and Museo dei Ragazzi) opposite the duomo (April–Sept daily 9.30am–6pm; Oct–March Tues–Sun 10am–5pm; €4.50; ⓦ www.museofaina.it) has a predictable but superbly displayed collection of vases and fragments excavated from local tombs (it also offers some great **views** of the cathedral facade). These sixth-century-BC **tombs** (daily: summer 9am–7pm; winter closes 1hr before dusk; €2) are still visible just off the road which drops towards the station from Piazza Cahen and are worth tracking down for their rows of massive and sombre stone graves – though none has the grandeur or paintings of the more famous necropoli in Cerveteri and Tarquinia (see p.815 & p.816). Before leaving Piazza del Duomo enquire at the tourist office (see p.678) for details of the fascinating **Orvieto Underground** tours into the vast labyrinth of **tunnels**, caves and store rooms that riddle the soft volcanic rock on which Orvieto is built: most date back to medieval times, some to the Etruscan era. Tours leave from the tourist office daily (except Feb, when they run at weekends only) at 11am, 12.15pm, 4pm and 5.15pm (€5.50), but there is some flexibility: ask at the separate desk in the tourist office, call ⓣ0763.344.891 or 0339.733.2764, or visit ⓦ www.orvietounderground.it for details and bookings.

As far as the town's **churches** go, they all naturally pale beside the duomo, though most have something worthwhile to see. The tiny Romanesque **San Lorenzo di Arari** was built in 1291 on the site of a church destroyed by monks from nearby San Francesco because the sound of its bells got on their nerves. Four recently restored **frescoes** on the left of the nave depict typically traumatic scenes from the life of St Lawrence. There's also an Etruscan sacrificial slab, which rather oddly serves as the Christian altar (*arari* meaning "altar").

From Piazzale Cacciatore there's a decent **walk** around the city's southern walls (Via Ripa Medici) with views over to a prominent outcrop of rock in the middle distance, part of the old volcanic crater. Ten minutes or so brings you to **San Giovenale**, whose rustic surroundings, on the very western tip of the *rupa*, Orvieto's volcanic plateau, are a far cry from the bustle of the duomo. It's not much to look at from the outside, but the musty **medieval interior** is the best (and oldest) in the town, though virtually no one makes the trek out to see it. The thirteenth-century Gothic transept, with its two pointed arches, rather oddly stands a metre above the rounded Romanesque nave, making for a hybrid and distinctive church, all of it exhaustively decorated with thirteenth- and fifteenth-century **frescoes**. Check out the *Tree of Life* fresco right of the main door and the macabre *Calendar of Funeral Anniversaries* partly covered by the side entrance.

From the church back to the centre of town Via Malabranca and Via Filippeschi are the best of the **medieval streets**, all tantalizing doorways and tiled roofs, but second-rate by the standards of neighbouring hill-towns. For an overview, climb the **Torre del Moro**, a medieval tower in Corso Cavour just south of Piazza del Popolo (daily: March–April & Sept–Oct 10am–7pm; May–Oct 10am–8pm; Nov–Feb 10.30am–1pm & 2.30–5pm; €2.60).

The central **Sant' Andrea** on Piazza della Repubblica is worth a mention, more for its strange twelve-sided **campanile** than the bits and pieces of the Roman and Etruscan city in the crypt. In the Piazza del Popolo, further up Corso Cavour (the town's pedestrianized main drag), there's a daily fruit and veg market plus the odd craft stall – in front of the restored and impressive **Palazzo del Popolo** (closed to the public).

Il Pozzo di San Patrizio (daily: March–Sept 10am–6.45pm; Oct–Feb 10am–5.45pm; €4.50 with the Emilio Greco museum), just off Piazzale Cahen, is the town's novelty act, a huge cylindrical well commissioned in 1527 by Pope Clement VII to guarantee the town's water supply during an expected siege by the Imperial Army (which never came). Water was brought to the surface by donkeys on two broad staircases, cannily designed never to intersect. It's a striking piece of engineering, 13m wide and 62m deep, named after its supposed similarity to the Irish cave where St Patrick died in 493, aged 133.

Eating and drinking

There are plenty of places to **eat** in Orvieto, though nowhere that stands out gastronomically. For a tourist town, though, many restaurants offer very good value and tasty Umbrian food. **Restaurants** are grouped together at the bottom (eastern end) of Corso Cavour, though one of the best places on this street, *Antica Cantina*, popular with locals, is midway down in Piazza Monaldeschi 18–19 (☏0763.344.746; closed Wed eve). It's reasonably priced (€15 will buy a good, light meal) and succeeds in reproducing the old-fashioned trattoria atmosphere and simple, but well-cooked staples. Even better-value – though less atmospheric – eating can be found close to the duomo at the cooperatively run *CRAMST*, Via Maitani 15 (open daily). Again deservedly popular with locals for its excellent value, it's a 450-seat canteen affair, offering a choice between restaurant and self-service pizzeria. *La Grotta*, Via Signorelli 5 (☏0763.341.348; closed Tues), is reasonable value (€20 and up for a meal), friendly and has been around longer than most.

A touch cheaper and with better food to boot is the *Volpe e L'Uva*, Via Ripa Corsica 1 (☏0763.341.612; closed all day Mon & Tues lunch), tucked away off Via della Pace north of Piazza del Popolo. Similar is *L'Asino d'Oro*, Vicolo del Popolo (☏0763.344.406; closed Mon), with the welcoming atmosphere and simple, hearty food of a traditional *osteria* (three courses from €23). In summer you can eat at a handful of tables on the narrow street outside. Equally traditional, and guaranteed to give you a memorable meal in old-world surround- ings, is the *Etrusca*, Via Maitani 10 (☏0763.344.016; closed Mon).

The **wine bars** around the duomo are an expensive way of sampling the well-known Orvietan white. For great **ice cream** head for *Gelateria Pasqualetti*, an ivy-covered *gelateria* in the main piazza, to the north side of the duomo; it also has an outlet at Corso Cavour 56.

Around Orvieto

Moving on from Orvieto, you have are plenty of choices of destination. The obvious targets are Rome and Florence, both about ninety minutes away by train, but if you're in no hurry you might just as well head west. There are buses from Piazza Cahen to Viterbo (see p.820) and Bolsena (see p.826), both in Lazio. The road to Bolsena has some of the best views of Orvieto: it's where the postcard shots are taken from and was also where Turner set up his easel (the resulting picture's now in the Clore wing of London's Tate Britain). The wooded pocket of countryside west of Orvieto around Castel Giorgio is pretty enough, but probably only worth bothering with if you're in a car. Depending on the route you've taken so far you could stay in Umbria and take a slow train north through **Città della Pieve** or follow one of two good routes east to Todi. The first of these runs through **Monte Peglia**, some of the region's classic hill country.

Monte Peglia

Monte Peglia is the generic name for the triangular expanse of land that rises between the Chiani Valley in the west and the Tevere in the east. It's wild, sparse and timeless countryside, with hilltop hamlets, olives, vines, herds of white oxen and miles of deserted roads and tracks – the archetype of the pastoral lowlands you find all over the region. Although the map marks several villages, most turn out to be no more than scattered farms, many of them abandoned. The only realistic way of tackling the remoteness is with your own transport.

You'll get the best quick taste of the area on the circuitous and beautifully deserted N79 from Orvieto Scalo to Todi; most of the traffic these days takes the newer and infinitely quicker route south of Lago di Corbara. Superb initial views of Orvieto peter out as the road climbs through many a hairpin into densely wooded hill country, with occasional glimpses (haze allowing) as far as Perugia.

The best of the scenery is north of the road, where the area's woods, rivers and fields are a haven for **wildlife**. It's about the only place in Umbria you'll see otters, for example, and is well known for the variety of its birds, who owe their immunity from the Sunday morning blast-anything-that-flies fraternity to an ancient tract of land – *una bandita demeniale di caccia* – where hunting has traditionally been forbidden.

It's quicker and almost equally scenic to take the N448 to Todi, which after meandering along the flattish southern shore of Lago di Corbara takes off into an unexpectedly dramatic **gorge** for the rest of the run onto Todi. Nobody seems keen to swim in the lake, and it's not used for any sort of watersports – and to be honest it doesn't actually look that inviting. Further on things get better, when the strange purple-red rocks of the gorge, along with sheer cliffs and forested slopes, add up to a more enticing package. The road's pretty quiet, with plenty of free-style **camping** and **picnic** opportunities as the valley flattens out towards Todi.

Città della Pieve

Città della Pieve is most famous as the birthplace of Perugino (1445–1523), but it has a modicum of charm that merits a short visit in its own right. Again, you're better off in a car, for the station is a long haul from the town and it's the sort of place that can easily be seen in an hour. From below, the town looks vaguely and mysteriously enticing as it straggles along a distant ridge to the east, but once up close it lacks the impact of other Umbrian towns, the chief appeal being the tiny red-bricked houses (there was no local building stone), old women knitting, and geraniums in profusion at every window. One of the streets, Via della Baciadonna, claims to be the narrowest in Italy, the width of a "woman's kiss", the translation suggests.

Otherwise its only real interest lies in the handful of **Perugino's paintings**, which lie scattered around the town's churches, palaces and oratories, some of which – the **Palazzo della Corgna**, the church of **Sant'Agostino** and the **Oratorio di Santa Maria dei Bianchi** – have been united in a self-contained "circuit" known as the **Museo Aperto** with a single-ticket admission, available from any of the relevant attractions (daily: June–Sept 9.30am–1pm & 4–7.30pm; Oct–April 10am–12.30pm & 3–6pm; €3). The town's small **tourist office** is at Piazza Matteotti 4 (May–Sept Mon–Fri 10am–1pm & 3–7pm, Sat & Sun 10am–7pm; Oct–March daily 10am–12.30pm & 3.30–6pm; ☎0578.299.375).

The cathedral itself has a couple of late works that show **Perugino** in his worst light. The painter's reputation today, though still very high, is lower than it was in his own time, when contemporaries spoke of him in the same breath as Leonardo and Michelangelo. He trained with Leonardo da Vinci in Florence but largely remained faithful to the tenets of the Umbrian School – sublime misty landscapes behind ethereal religious subjects. His great facility enabled him to produce vast numbers of dewy-eyed saints and Madonnas, whose occasional absence of genuine religious sentiment horrified those who demanded sincerity above all else in devotional art. What in his youth had been profound and innovative gradually came to seem stilted and repetitive. Accused of merely replicating a successful formula, he also did nothing to discourage pupils finishing his works, adding his signature to some real shockers – especially in old age. He remains, however, one of the most influential of the Renaissance painters. The painting not to miss is *The Adoration of the Magi* in Santa Maria dei Bianchi, considered his greatest work still resident in Italy (Napoleon removed many to the Louvre in Paris), with lesser paintings in nearby **San Antonio Abate**, **San Pietro** and **Santa Maria dei Servi**.

Travel details

Trains

Assisi to: Foligno (18–24 daily; 17min); Perugia (18–24 daily; 30min); Spello (18–24 daily; 9min); Terontola (18–24 daily; connections to Chiusi, Orvieto, Arezzo, Florence and Rome; 1hr).

Città di Castello to: Perugia (hourly; 50min); Sansepolcro (hourly; 15min).

Foligno to: Ancona (13 daily; 1hr 30min–2hr); Assisi (18–24 daily; 17min); Fabriano (14 daily; 40min–1hr); Fossato di Vico (for Gubbio, 14 daily; 40min); Gualdo Tadino (8–11 daily; 40min); Narni (12–16 daily; 1hr 10min); Orte (hourly; 1hr–1hr 10min); Perugia (18–24 daily; 40min); Rome (16 daily; 1hr 55min); Spello (18–24 daily; 9min); Spoleto (12–18 daily; 20min); Terni (12–18 daily; 55min); Terontola (18–24 daily; connections for Chiusi, Orvieto, Arezzo, Florence and Rome; 1hr

15min); Trevi (12–16 daily; 7min); Tuoro sul Trasimeno (18–24 daily; 1hr 10min).

Orvieto to: Arezzo (14–20 daily; 1hr 20min); Chiusi (14–20 daily; 40min; connections to Siena, 1hr 30min); Florence (14–20 daily; 1hr 30min); Orte (14–20 daily; connections to Narni, Terni, Spoleto and Foligno; 40min); Rome (14–20 daily; 1hr 20min); Terontola (7–10 daily; connections to Perugia; 50min).

Perugia to: Assisi (18–24 daily; 30min); Città di Castello (hourly; 50min); Deruta (hourly; 30min); Florence (6 daily; 2hr 15min); Foligno (18–24 daily; 40min); Sansepolcro (hourly; 1hr 30min); Spello (18–24 daily; 30min); Terni (hourly; 1hr 40min); Terontola (18–24 daily; 35min); Todi (hourly; 50min).

Spoleto to: Arezzo (8 daily; 2hr 10min); Florence direct (8 daily; 2hr 30min); Foligno via Trevi

(12–18 daily; connections for Assisi, Spello, Perugia, Terontola and Florence; 20min); Fossato di Vico (10 daily; 50min); Narni (10–17 daily; 40min); Nocera Umbra (6 daily; 35min); Perugia direct (15–20 daily; 45min); Rome (10–17 daily; 1hr 15min–1hr 45min); Terni (10–17 daily; 30min).

Terni to: Città di Castello (FCU line hourly; 2hr 30min); Foligno (18–23 daily; connections to Spello, Assisi, Gualdo Tadino, Fossato di Vico and Perugia; 40min); Narni (17 daily; 15min); Orte (12–16 daily; connections to Rome, Orvieto, Chiusi, Arezzo and Florence; 30min); Perugia (FCU line; 10–16 daily; connections at FCU Sant'Anna station in Perugia for Città di Castello and Sansepolcro, shared FCU and FS/Trenitalia station at Ponte San Giovanni for connections to Foligno and Terontola; 1hr 20min); Sansepolcro (FCU line; 10–16 daily via Perugia Sant'Anna; 3hr); Spoleto (12 daily; 20min); Todi (FCU line; 10–16; 40min).

Buses

Assisi to: Bettona (1 daily; 50min); Foligno (4 daily Mon–Sat; 50min); Gualdo Tadino (1 daily; 1hr); Norcia and the Valnerina (1 daily; Mon–Sat, from Santa Maria degli Angeli; Perugia (7–10 daily; 40min); Rome (1 daily; 3hr 30min); Spello (10 daily; 40min).

Bevagna to: Foligno (5 daily Mon–Sat; 30min); Montefalco (4 daily; 40min).

Foligno to: Assisi (4 daily Mon–Sat; 50min); Bevagna (3 daily Mon–Fri; 20min); Gualdo Tadino (3 daily Mon–Sat; 50min); Montefalco (8 daily; 35min); Norcia (1 daily Mon–Sat; 1hr 35min); Perugia (4 daily; 1hr 10min); Rome (2–3 daily 1hr 35min); Spello (7 daily; 15min); Spoleto (4–8 daily; 50min); Trevi (4 daily Mon–Sat; 23min).

Gubbio to: Fossato di Vico (10 daily; 30min); Perugia (10 daily Mon–Sat, 4 daily Sun; 1hr 10min); Rome (1 daily; 2hr 40min).

Montefalco to: Bevagna (4 daily Mon–Sat; 20min).

Narni to: Amelia (4–12 daily; 15min); Orvieto (5 daily; 1hr); Otricoli (7–10 daily; 40min); Terni (4–6 daily; 30min).

Norcia to: Castelluccio (1 daily Thurs only; 50min); Perugia (1 daily Mon–Sat; 1hr 30min); Rome

(2 daily Mon–Sat, 1 on Sun; 3hr); Spoleto (5–7 daily Mon–Sat, 3 on Sun; 1hr 10min); Terni (1 daily; 1hr).

Orvieto to: Amelia (5–7 daily Mon–Sat; 1hr 15min); Baschi (5–7 daily; 30min); Bolsena (2 daily Mon–Sat; 50min); Lugnano in Tevere (7 daily Mon–Sat; 1hr); Narni (5 daily Mon–Sat; 40min); Perugia (1 daily; 2hr); Terni (5 daily Mon–Sat; 2hr); Todi (1 daily Mon–Sat; 1hr 30min).

Perugia to: Áscoli Piceno (1–4 daily; 3hr); Assisi (3–12 daily; 30min); Bettona (2 daily; 40min); Castiglione del Lago (7–9 daily Mon–Sat; 1hr 15min); Chiusi (5 daily Mon–Sat; 1hr 45min); Florence (1 daily; 2hr); Foligno (4 daily; 1hr 10min); Gubbio (10 daily Mon–Sat, 4 daily Sun; 1hr 10min); Norcia (1 daily; 2hr 50min); Orvieto (1 daily; 2hr 25min); Passignano (7 daily Mon–Sat; 1hr 30min); Rome (2–6 daily; 2hr 30min); Rome Fiumicino airport (1–3 daily; 3hr); Siena (3–7 daily; 1hr 30min); Spello (4 daily Mon–Sat; 55min); Spoleto (1 direct daily Mon–Sat; 1hr 20min); Todi (via Deruta; 5–7 daily; 1hr).

Spoleto to: Cascia with connection at Serravalle (5–7 daily Mon–Sat, 3 on Sun; 1hr 5min); Foligno (Mon–Sat 4 daily; 50min); Fonti di Clitunno (7 daily; 20min); Montefalco (3–4 daily Mon–Sat; 1hr); Monteleone (via Valle di Nero and Gavelli; 1 daily in winter; 1hr 30min); Norcia via Sant'Anatolia di Narco (5–7 daily Mon–Sat; 3 on Sun; 1hr 10min); Perugia (5 daily; 1hr 20min); Rome (1 daily; 2hr 20min); Scheggino (5 daily; 1hr 10min); Terni (6 daily; 45min); Trevi (7 daily; 25min).

Terni to: Amelia (10 or more daily Mon–Sat, 1 on Sun; 50min); Cascata delle Marmore (15-plus daily Mon–Sat, 11 on Sun; 40min); Ferentillo (17 daily Mon–Sat, 12 on Sun; 40min); Orvieto (via Baschi, Guardea, Montecchio and Amelia; 5 daily Mon–Sat; 2hr); Scheggino (8 daily Mon–Sat, 5 on Sun; 50min); Todi (via Sangemini, Acquasparta or Avigliano; 3 daily Mon–Sat; 1hr); Also long-distance services to Bolsena (connection at Orvieto) and Rome.

Todi to: Deruta (3 daily Mon–Sat; 40min); Marsciano (2 daily; 30min); Orvieto (1 daily Mon–Sat; 1hr 30min); Perugia (3 daily; 1hr); Terni (3 daily Mon–Sat; 1hr).

Marche

CHAPTER 10   # Highlights

* **Urbino** "Ideal city" and art capital created by Federico da Montefeltro, the ultimate Renaissance man.
See opposite

* **San Leo** This spectacular ancient town on a rocky outcrop is a landmark for miles around. See p.701

* **Lorenzo Lotto** Don't miss paintings by the Renaissance's best portraitist at Jesi, Loreto, Ancona and Recanati. See p.711, p.715 p.708 & p.718

* **Conero promontory** Cliffy coastline ideal for walking, cycling and swimming in one of several small bays. See p.712

* **Macerata and the road to Sarnano** Catch a summer opera in this appealing old university town before driving south through some of central Italy's most beautiful countryside. See p.719 & p.724

* **Monti Sibillini** A hiker's mountain paradise. See p.727

* **Áscoli Piceno** Interesting food and architectural gems in this relatively undiscovered medieval town. See p.730

△ Lorenzo Lotto: *Madonna and Child with Saints Flavin and Onuphrius*

Marche

ying between the Apennines and the Adriatic, **Marche** (sometimes anglicized as The Marches) is a varied region, and one you could spend weeks exploring. Large areas of it are unspoilt, particularly in the south-west, where stone hill-villages make atmospheric bases for hikes into the stunning **Monti Sibillini** range. Not that all of Marche is free from tourism: English and German tourists have been buying and renovating cottages in the countryside, and much of the coastline is studded with modern resorts. The area also has a fair amount of industry – in particular light engineering, shoe manufacturing and ceramics – heaviest around the port of **Ancona** and along the main road and rail route from Umbria.

Of Marche's old-fashioned and slightly forgotten seaside resorts, **Pésaro** is the largest, with a Renaissance centre maintaining its dignity behind the package-tour seafront. For more interesting sunning and swimming, head south of Ancona to the **Cónero Riviera**, a dramatic stretch of coast, with small beaches nestling beneath the craggy cliffs of Monte Conero. San Benedetto del Tronto has six kilometres of sand, five thousand palm trees, and numerous discos, but is not exactly a happening place compared with say Rimini. The most appealing – and best known – of Marche's sights are the small hilltop town of **Urbino**, with its spectacular Renaissance palace, and the dramatic fortress of **San Leo**, just across the border from San Marino. Further south, **Macerata** is a sleepy university town surrounded by lovely countryside, and, right on the regional border, the fascinat-ing city of **Áscoli Piceno** is a worthy stop-off on the way into Abruzzo.

Getting around on public transport is relatively easy, though your own vehicle is useful in the more remote areas. There are two main **rail routes**: along the coast on the Milan–Bari line or across Italy on the Ancona–Rome service. The provincial capitals – Urbino, Pésaro, Macerata, Ancona and Áscoli Piceno – are all well served by public transport, and Ancona is also a major port for **ferries** to Greece and Croatia. For hiking in the Sibillini, **Amándola** has the best bus service; if you don't mind relying on fewer buses, **Montefortino** is a prettier base.

Urbino and around

URBINO is Marche's most immediately likeable town, a walled hilltop jumble of Renaissance and medieval houses, churches and *palazzi* dominated by the tremendous Palazzo Ducale. During the second half of the fifteenth century, it was one of the most prestigious courts in Europe, ruled by the remarkable Federico da Montefeltro, who employed some of the greatest artists and

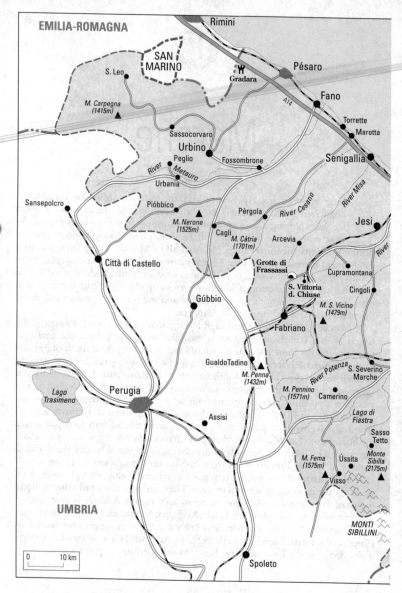

architects of the time to build and decorate his palace in the town. Baldassarre Castiglione, whose sixteenth-century handbook of courtly behaviour, *Il Cortegiane* (The Courtier), is set in the palace, reckoned it to be the most beautiful in all Italy, and it does seem from contemporary accounts that fifteenth-century Urbino was an extraordinarily civilized place, a measured and urbane society in which life was lived without indulgence.

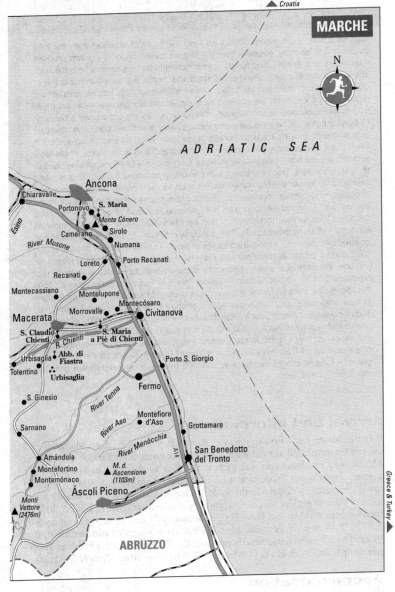

ADRIATIC SEA

Chiaravalle
Ancona
Portonovo
S. Maria
Monte Cónero
Camerano
Sirolo
Esino
Numana
River Musone
Loreto
Porto Recanati
Recanati
Montecassiano
Montelupone
Montecósaro
Macerata
Morrovalle
Civitanova
S. Claudio
Chienti
S. Maria
a Piè di Chienti
R. Chienti
Porto S. Giorgio
Urbisaglia
Abb. di
Fiastra
Tolentino
Urbisaglia
S. Ginesio
River Tenna
Fermo
River Aso
Montefiore
d'Aso
Grottamare
Sarnano
River Menócchia
San Benedotto
del Tronto
Amándola
M. d.
Ascensione
(1103m)
Montefortino
Montemónaco
Áscoli Piceno
Monti
Vettore
(2476m)
A14

ABRUZZO

Nowadays Urbino is saved from an existence as a museum piece by its lively university. There's a refreshing, energetic feel to the place, plenty of places to eat and drink; its nightlife is hardly wild, but a few bars host local bands and the like. Although a new town has grown up in the valley below, it's in the walled **upper town** that you'll want to spend your time.

Marche is very much a rural region, its food a mixture of **seafood** from the long coastline and **country cooking** from the interior, based on locally grown produce – tomatoes and fennel – and funghi, game, nuts and herbs gathered from the wild. The most distinctive dish, often served at summer *festas*, is a sweet-and-sour mix of olives stuffed with meat and fried, then served with *crema fritta*, little squares of fried cream. Rabbit and lamb are popular, as is *papardelle alla papara*, wide, flat pasta with duck sauce, and, as in many other regions, truffles are considered a delicacy. Unfamiliar items on the antipasti menu include *lonza* (salt-cured pork) and *ciauscolo* (a pork-based spread). Meat grilled *alla brace* (over wood embers) is ubiquitous in the Marche, and you may even come across the grand dish of *porchetta*, whole roast suckling pig, both in its original large-scale form and in a fast-food version used to fill crisp bread rolls. Don't confuse it with *coniglio in porchetta* though – this is rabbit cooked with fennel. Baked, stuffed dishes such as *vincisgrassi*, a rich layered dish of pasta, minced meat, mushrooms, giblets, brain, bechamel and truffles, are found everywhere. A typical seafood dish from Ancona is *zuppa di pesce*, a fish soup flavoured with saffron, though you'll find excellent fish broths – known simply as *brodetto* – all along the coast. Puddings include *cicerchiata*, balls of pasta fried and covered in honey, and *frappe*, fried leaves of filo-like pastry dusted with icing sugar.

Although it produces many drinkable **wines**, the Marche region is best known for just one, **Verdicchio**, a greeny-gold white, excellent with fish, which is instantly recognizable from its amphora-shaped bottle. This is in fact a hangover from a 1950s marketing ploy inspired by the ancient Greek custom of shipping wine from Ancona in clay amphorae, and, reputedly, by the shape of the actress Gina Lollobrigida. Today, however, many producers sell their best Verdicchio in standard bottles – the one to look out for is Verdicchio dei Castelli di Jesi (see p.711). Lesser known **reds** include one of Italy's finest, Rosso Conero, a light wine based on the Montepulciano grape and full of fruit; more common is Rosso Piceno, based on the Sangiovese grape. A Marche aperitif now back in fashion is **mistrà**, an aniseed liqueur generally drunk with coffee.

Arrival and information

Regular **buses** from Pésaro – where they depart from Piazzale Matteotti and the train station until around 8pm – and slower buses from Fano stop in Borgo Mercatale, a terminus-cum-car park at the foot of the Palazzo Ducale in the modern lower town. From here a lift (daily 8am–8pm) takes you up to the old town, depositing you outside the Palazzo Ducale. Outside these hours it's a five minute walk along Via Mazzini, or you could take a taxi (☏0722.327.949). The **tourist office** (Mon–Sat 9am–1pm & 3–6pm, July & Aug may also open Sun; ☏0722.2613, ⒲www.comune.urbino.ps.it & www.urbinoculturaturismo.it) is at Piazza Duca Federico 35, directly opposite the Palazzo Ducale. There's an **Internet point**, 2000Net, at Via G. Mazzini 17 (Mon–Sat 10am–2pm & 5–11pm).

Accommodation

Urbino's **accommodation** options run from comfortable hotels and B&Bs to student halls (June–October only) and hostels. With your own vehicle, and especially during the oppressive heat of summer, a hotel outside the city is an option. An economical alternative if staying for a week or more is a **room in a private house** – ask the tourist office for a list and, during term time when you'll be competing for places with students, book in advance. Expect to pay about the same as for a two-star hotel (❷–❸). You could also try the **university hostel**,

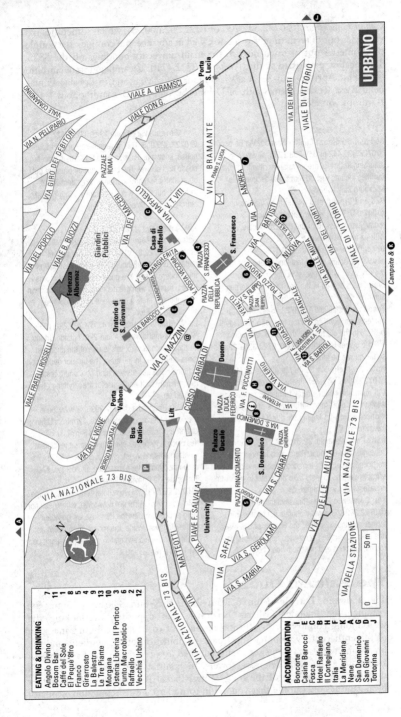

URBINO

EATING & DRINKING

Angolo Divino	7
Bosom Bar	11
Caffè del Sole	1
El Pequè'8fro	8
Franco	5
Girarrosto	4
La Balestra	9
Le Tre Piante	13
Morgana	10
Osteria Libreria Il Portico	3
Punto Macrobiotico	6
Raffaello	2
Vecchia Urbino	12

ACCOMMODATION

Boncorte	I
Casina Barocci	E
Fosca	C
Hotel Raffaello	B
Il Cortegiano	H
Italia	F
La Meridiana	K
Nene	A
San Domenico	G
San Giovanni	D
Tortorina	J

MARCHE | Urbino and around

▶ Campsite & **K**

10

695

Collegi Universitari (☎0722.302.700 or 0722.302.600; ❶), which sometimes has vacancies out of term time if you book well in advance; the complex is a couple of kilometres out of town next to the main university buildings off the SS73. The nearest **campsite** is the *Pineta* (☎0722.4710, ⓔcampeggiopinetaurbino @email.it; April to mid-Sept) at Via S Donato Ca'Mignone, in Località Fonta-nelle Bassa Cesana, 2km south of Urbino beyond San Bernardino; bus #4 or #7 drops you close by.

City hotels

Bed and Breakfast Casina Barocci Via Barocci 9 ☎0722.320.442 or 348.293.1265, ⓦwww .bburbino.it. One-bedroom apartment with cooking facilities located just off Piazza Rinascimentale. Minimum stay two nights. ❸

Bed and Breakfast Il Cortegiano Via Veterani 1 ☎347.047.7214, ⓦwww.ilcortegiano.it. Two sunny rooms just across from the Palazzo Ducale, each with its own bathroom. ❷

Boncorte Via delle Mura 28 ☎0722.2463, ⓦwww.viphotels.it. Old-fashioned hotel just inside the city walls with views over the countryside. Breakfast is served in the tiny courtyard garden in summer. ❹

Fosca Via Raffaello 67 ☎0722.2542. Small, studenty *pensione* on the top floor of a residential *palazzo* in the old town, with shared bathrooms – if the owner isn't there, call ☎0722.329.622 and someone will be along. ❶

Hotel Raffaello Via Santa Margherita 38/40 ☎0722.4896, ⓦwww.albergoraffaello.com. Old town hotel with simply furnished rooms and wide views over the pantiled roofs of Urbino. It offers a pick-up facility for guests from the lower town. ❸

Italia Corso Garibaldi 32 ☎0722.2701, ⓦwww .albergo-italia-urbino.it. Renovated albergo in a porticoed street, with terracotta floors and plain but attractive rooms. Guests take breakfast in the small private garden in summer. ❹

San Domenico Piazza Rinascimento 3 ☎0722.2626, ⓦwww.viphotels.it. Located in a former religious complex, the interior of this place has been extensively renovated and offers large rooms, big beds and polished wood floors. ❻

San Giovanni Via Barocci 13 ☎0722.2827, ⓕ0722.329.055. This sixteenth-century Patrician house, known as Palazzo della Spillara, is drab but cheap and central. The owner can be brusque but other staff are more courteous. Breakfast is not included, but there is a restaurant serving typical Marche dishes. Closed July. ❷

Outside the city

Balcone sul Metauro Via Manzoni 20 Peglio, near Urbania ☎0722.310.104, ⓦwww.balconesul metauro.com A half-hour drive southwest of Urbino, this modern option is a good choice. Most rooms have balconies with great views over the little town of Peglio and there's good food and an open-air swimming pool too. ❷

La Meridiana Via Urbinate 43 ☎0722.320.169, ⓦwww.la-meridiana.it. About 2km outside Urbino on the road to Pésaro, this is one of the cheapest three-star hotels in the area. The interior decoration is bland but it has a swimming pool and a restaurant, friendly staff and is useful if everything else is booked up. ❸

Nene Via Biancalana ☎0722.2996, ⓦwww.nene urbino.com. Restored stone house, 2km from Urbino, just off the "*strada rossa*" towards Fermignano, this place is visited as much for its great restaurant – with interesting vegetarian options – as for its accommodation. There's an open-air pool too. ❷

Tortorina Via Ottaviano Petrucci 4 ☎0722.327.715, ⓦwww.hotel-tortorina.it. A large hotel complex in Urbino's new town, whose exterior is an anticlimax after the Renaissance grandeur of the old town. Inside, the rooms are modern and facilities include a swimming pool, a fully-equipped gym and a restaurant. ❸

The Palazzo Ducale

The **Palazzo Ducale** (Mon 8.30am–2pm, Tues–Sun 8.30am–7.15pm; €4; entrance fee includes Galleria Nazionale, see opposite), overlooking the surrounding countryside, is a fitting monument to Federico, the urbane ruler of fifteenth-century Urbino. An elegant combination of the aesthetic and the practical, the facade comprises a triple-decked *loggia* in the form of a triumphal arch flanked by twin defensive towers. In contrast, the Palazzo's bare south side, forming one side of the long central Piazza Rinascimento, looks rather bleak, and it's only inside that you begin to understand its reputation as one of

△ Palazzo Ducale, Urbino

the finest buildings of the Renaissance. Although the Palazzo now houses the **Galleria Nazionale delle Marche**, only the few remaining original Urbino works justify much attention, and until you hit these it's the building itself that makes the biggest impression.

The courtyard and ground floor

Just inside the entrance, the **Cortile d'Onore** is your first real taste of what Urbino is about. The courtyard is not immediately striking – in fact the rest of Italy has a host of similar ones – but this is a prototype of the genre. Designed by Dalmatian-born Luciano Laurana, who was selected by Federico after he'd failed to find a suitably bold artist in Florence, it's at once elegant and restrained. Although each element, from the furling Corinthian capitals to the inscription proclaiming Federico's virtues, is exquisitely crafted, it's the way they work together that is Laurana's real achievement. Pilasters on the first floor echo columns on the ground floor, pale stone alternates with dark, and the whole is enhanced by the subtle interplay of light and shadow.

Off the Cortile is the room that housed Federico's **library**, which in its day was more comprehensive than Oxford University's Bodleian Library. He spent fourteen years and over thirty thousand ducats gathering books from all over Europe, and employed forty scribes to make illuminated copies on kidskin, which were then covered in crimson and decorated with silver. They disappeared into the vaults of the Vatican after Urbino fell to the papacy in 1631, and all that's left of the room's former grandeur is one of the more outrageous representations of Federico's power – the Eagle of the Montefeltros surrounded by tongues of fire, symbolizing the artistic and spiritual gifts bestowed by Federico.

Federico da Montefeltro

Federico (ruled from 1442 to1482) was a formidable soldier, a shrewd and humane ruler, and a genuine intellectual – qualities that were due in part to his education at the Mantua school of the most prestigious Renaissance teacher, Vittorino da Feltre. Poor scholars and young nobles were educated together in Vittorino's classes and were taught self-discipline and frugal living as well as the more usual Latin, maths, literature and the courtly skills of riding, dancing and swordsmanship.

As the elder but illegitimate son of the Montefeltro family, Federico only became ruler of Urbino after his tyrannical half-brother Oddantonio fell victim to an assassin during a popular rebellion. Federico promptly arrived on the scene – fuelling rumours that he'd engineered the uprising himself – and was elected to office after promising not to punish those responsible for Oddantonio's death, to cut taxes, to provide an educational and medical service, and to allow the people some say in the election of magistrates.

Urbino was a small state with few natural resources and a long way from any major trading routes, so selling the military services of his army and himself was Federico's only way of keeping Urbino solvent. In high demand because of his exceptional loyalty to his employers, Federico's mercenary activities yielded an annual income equivalent to £7,000,000/US$12,200,000, a substantial portion of which was used to keep taxes low, thus reducing the likelihood of social discontent during his long absences. When he was at home, he seems to have been a remarkably accessible ruler: he would leave his door open at mealtimes so that any member of his 500-strong court might speak to him between courses, and used to move around his state unarmed (unusual in a time when assassination was common), checking the welfare of his people.

Between military and political commitments, Federico also found time to indulge his interest in the arts. Though he delighted in music, his first love was architecture, which he considered to be the highest form of intellectual and aesthetic activity. He was a friend of the leading architectural theorist, Alberti, and according to his biographer, Vespasiano di Bisticci, Federico's knowledge of the art was unequalled. The Dalmatian architect Luciano Laurana was scarcely known until taken up by Federico, while his later commissions included works from the more established Francesco di Giorgio Martini and one of the greatest of all painters and theorists of architecture, Piero della Francesca.

The first floor

A monumental staircase, one of the first ever built in Italy, takes you up to the first floor. Wandering through the white, airy rooms, you'll see wooden doors inlaid with everything from gyroscopes and mandolins to armour, representing the various facets of Federico's personality. On carved marble fireplaces, sphinxes are juxtaposed with angels and palm trees with dolphins, while ceilings are stuccoed with such symbols of Montefeltro power as ermines, eagles and exploding grenades.

A famous portrait of Federico da Montefeltro by the Spanish artist **Pedro Berruguete** is worth seeking out (it's been moved about in recent years). Painted, as he always was, in profile (having lost his right eye in battle), Federico is shown as warrior, ruler, scholar and dynast; wearing an ermine-fringed gown over his armour, he sits reading a book, with his pale and delicate son, Guidobaldo, standing at his feet.

The most elaborately decorated part of the *palazzo* is the suite of rooms known as the **Appartamento del Duca**. On display here are **Piero della Francesca**'s two great works: the *Madonna of Senigallia*, a haunting depiction of foreboding in which Mary, flanked by two angels, offers up her child; and the more perplexing *Flagellation*, where at the back of a cubic room Christ is being almost casually beaten, while in the foreground stand three figures: a beautiful youth and two older men. The most persuasive interpretation of this much debated painting identifies the foreground figure on the left as Ottaviano Ubaldini (Federico Montefeltro's senior counsellor), while the one on the right is Ludovico Gonzaga (grandfather of Federico's son-in-law), both of whom had been bereaved at the time the picture was commissioned. By this account the beautiful youth is the idealized projection of the boys they were mourning, and the picture as a whole is a meditation on the consolations of Christian faith. Also here is Raphael's compelling portrait of a gentlewoman, *La Muta*.

Still in the Appartamento del Duca, no painting better embodies the notion of perfection held by Urbino's elite than *The Ideal City*, long attributed to Piero but now thought to be by one of his followers. Probably intended as a design for a stage set, this famous display of perspective skill depicts a perfectly symmetrical and utterly deserted cityscape, expressing the desire for a civic order that mirrors that of the heavens.

Paolo Uccello's last work, the six-panelled *Profanation of the Host*, tells the story of a woman who sold a consecrated host to a Jewish merchant. She was hanged, and the merchant and his family were burned at the stake – the angels and devils are arguing over the custody of the woman's soul. The morbid theme and fairy-tale atmosphere that pervade the work may reflect the artist's depression at getting old: shortly after completing it, he filled in his tax return with the statement, "I am old, infirm and unemployed, and my wife is ill."

It's the next three rooms of the Duke's apartment that give you the best insight into Federico's personality. A spiral staircase descends to two adjoining chapels, one dedicated to Apollo and the Muses, the other to the Christian God. This dualism typifies a strand of Renaissance thought in which mythology and Christianity were reconciled by positing a universe in which pagan deities were seen as aspects of the omnipotent Christian deity.

Back on the main floor you come to the most interesting and best preserved of the palace's rooms, Federico's **Studiolo**, a triumph of illusory perspective created not with paint but with intarsia (inlaid wood). Shelves laden with geometrical instruments appear to protrude from the walls, cupboard doors seem to swing open to reveal lines of books, a letter lies in an apparently half-open drawer. Even more remarkable are the delicately hued landscapes of Urbino as if viewed from one of the surrounding hills, and the lifelike squirrel next to an equally realistic bowl of fruit. The upper half of the room is covered with 28 portraits of great men ranging from Homer and Petrarch to Solomon and St Ambrose – another example of Federico's eclecticism.

The rest of the town

Urbino is a lively place, and its bustling streets can be a refreshing antidote to the rarefied atmosphere of the Palazzo Ducale. Next door to the palace, the town's **Duomo** is a pompous Neoclassical replacement for Francesco di Giorgio Martini's Renaissance church, destroyed in an earthquake in 1789. There's a **museum** inside (daily 9am–1pm & 2.30–6.30pm; €3), but the only reason for going in would be to see Barocci's *Last Supper*, with Christ surrounded by the chaos of washers-up, dogs and angels.

A trek up to the gardens dominated by the sixteenth-century fortress, **Fortezza Albornoz** (9am–6pm; free), is rewarded with great views of the town and the countryside. Close by is the **Oratorio di San Giovanni**

(Mon–Sat 10am–12.30pm & 3–5.30pm, Sun 10am–12.30pm; winter mornings only; €2), behind whose unfortunate modern facade is a stunning cycle of early fourteenth-century frescoes, depicting the life of St John the Baptist and the Crucifixion. Vividly coloured and full of expressive detail, so different from the cool economy of later Renaissance artists, the frescoes are at their liveliest in such incidental details as the boozy picnic in the background of the *Baptism of the Multitude*, or the child trying to escape from its mother in the *Crucifixion*.

On Via Raffaello, the **Casa Natale di Raffaello**, birthplace (in 1483) of Urbino's most famous son, the painter Raphael (summer Mon–Sat 9am–1pm & 3–7pm, Sun 10am–1pm; winter Mon–Sat 9am–2pm, Sun 10am–1pm; €3), proudly displays the "stone" where Raphael and his father Giovanni Santi mixed their pigments and sizes. There's one work by Raphael, an early *Madonna and Child*, otherwise the walls are covered with reproductions and minor works by his contemporaries.

Eating, drinking and nightlife

There are plenty of reasonable places to **eat** in Urbino, with dozens of fast-food and inexpensive self-service places aimed at student budgets – the university *mensa* on Piazza San Filippo, which is open to student ID card-holders only, is the best deal. There's also more refined cooking typical of the province in a selection of more formal restaurants.

During term time when students are in town, Urbino's late-night **bars** see a brisk trade, and there are reasonable dancing and live-music options on offer too.

Restaurants

Angolo Divino Via San Andrea 14 ☏0722.327.559. Geranium-covered on the outside, and atmospheric within, this *osteria* is located in an ancient *palazzo* near the Botanical Gardens. It's well known for regional delicacies (including home-made pasta) and there are some good vegetarian choices as well. Closed Sun eve and Mon lunch.

Franco Via del Poggio 1 ☏0722.2492. Self-service place at lunchtime and a restaurant in the evening, serving *primi* such as home-made *strozzapreti* – "strangled priests" (one can only assume that its twisted shape is supposed to be resonant of a strangled neck), with vegetables, and *secondi* including rabbit cooked with fennel, all at reasonable prices. Closed Sun.

Girarrosto Piazza San Francesco 3 ☏0722.4445. Tempting smells of grilled meats and truffles lead you to this small restaurant, open in summer only, where you can dine outside in the busy square. There are plenty of pasta dishes, *funghi porcini* in season and a few veggie options too, at moderate prices. Closed Mon and winter.

La Balestra Via Valerio 16 ☏0722.2942 Unpretentious and good-value restaurant with tables inside and out and serving typical local food (game and truffles) and pizzas until 3am.

Le Tre Piante Corner of Via Foro Posterula 1 and Via Voltaccia della Vecchia ☏0722.4863. Hidden away just off Via Budassi, this restaurant is worth seeking out for its small terrace overlooking the hills. Pasta dishes such as *strozzapreti* – with sausage, cream, mushrooms and peppers – or tagliatelle with lemon and prawns, are excellently done, as is the *carne alla braccia*, grilled meat. Moderately priced and highly recommended. Closed Mon.

Morgana Via Nuova 3 ☏0722.2528. Another inexpensive choice, especially good for healthy salads, unusual pizza combos and more traditional pasta dishes, such as *tagliatelle con erbe selvatica*, wild herbs and greens. Closed Mon.

Punto Macrobiotico Via Pozzo Nuova 6 ☏0722. 329.790. Students pack out this 120-seater, self-service restaurant for its bargain vegetarian dishes, made from home-grown cereals and vegetables. Closed Sun.

Raffaello Via Raffaello 41. Café-bar serving sit-down or takeaway *piadine* (cheese- or ham-filled flat bread) and *crescia sfogliata* (a bit like a pizza folded in half). Closed Sun.

Vecchia Urbino Via Vasari 3/5 ☏0722.4447. Elegant and upmarket place with a traditional menu including baby squid in olive oil, *raviolono al tartufo bianco* (a large, hand-made ravioli with white truffle) and marinated home-made sausage and olives as well as meat and fish grilled *alla brace* – over a wood fire – and marinated slow-cooked rabbit (*coniglio al coccio*).

The puddings are excellent too and the wine list is good value. Expect to pay around €50 a head. Booking advisable. Closed Tues and 10 days in July.

Bars, clubs and live music venues

Bosom Pub Via Budassi 24 ☏0722.4783. Stone-vaulted, if garishly lit, pub with a well-stocked bar, including Belgian beers, and "giraffes" – tall contraptions full of several litres for a group to share. Plays mainstream Latin, House, pop and rock. Decent sandwiches available too.

Bus Bar Via Nazionale Bocca Trabaria 16. Outside the city centre on the main road between the Borgo Mercatale and the University, this is Urbino's most popular nightclub, catering for students.

Caffe del Sole Via Mazzini 34. Up from the bus station, on the main drag into town, this alternative café-bar is open from morning till the early hours. It has a laid-back atmosphere, comfy couches and live jazz on selected nights. Call in for details or phone ☏0722.2619.

El Pequèro Via San Domenico 1 ☏0722.327.463. Pub-restaurant that has more of an emphasis on eating than drinking, and is centrally located in a side street round the corner from the tourist office and Palazzo Ducale.

Osteria Libreria Il Portico An intriguing venue in an archway at the top of Via Mazzini that bills itself as bookshop, rum bar, pub, café and pizzeria. You can browse the shelves by day – when they serve panini and snacks – or head here at night when it turns into a club open til 2am. Closed Mon.

Sassocorvaro and San Leo

The villages of northern Marche, though pleasant enough, cannot compete with the crumbling hill-settlements further south, and the rarity of buses makes exploration by public transport something of an ordeal. Two places, however, **Sassocorvaro** and **San Leo**, are worth the trip and reward your efforts getting there with splendid medieval strongholds.

Sassocorvaro

Perched above a twee artificial lake some 30km northwest of Urbino by road, **SASSOCORVARO** is dominated by one of Francesco di Giorgio Martini's most ambitious **fortresses** (April–Sept daily 9.30am–12.30pm & 3.30–7pm; Oct–March Sat & Sun 9.30am–12.30pm & 2.30–6pm; €4). Built on the orders of Federico da Montefeltro for one of his *condottieri* (mercenary soldiers), Ottaviano degli Ubaldini, like San Leo (see below) it was designed to withstand the onslaught of cannon. Unfortunately the site lacked San Leo's natural advantages and Francesco was forced to seek a strictly architectural solution, doing away with straight walls and building a grim fortress bulging with hourglass towers. After the exterior, the inside comes as something of a surprise, with an elegant Renaissance courtyard and an intimate and frescoed theatre. It's a tribute to the strength of Francesco's architecture that the fortress was selected as a safe house for some of Italy's greatest works of art during World War II, including Piero della Francesca's *Flagellation* and Giorgione's *La Tempesta*, reproductions of which are on show.

There's also a museum of **folk life** (same hours and admission ticket as the castle), with displays of traditional weaving, winemaking equipment and a mock-up of an old kitchen.

San Leo

The menacing fortress of **SAN LEO** (Nov–Feb Mon–Fri 9am–noon & 2.30–6pm; March–Oct daily 9am–6pm; €8), clamped to the summit of a dizzying precipice in the northern tip of the Marche, has staggered generations of visitors with its intimidating beauty. Machiavelli praised it, Dante modelled the terrain of his Purgatory on it, and Pietro Bembo considered it Italy's "most beautiful implement of war". In fact it's not as impregnable as it seems, and one of the few invaders to have actually been repelled was Cesare Borgia, despite his having first persuaded a weak-willed retainer to give him the key.

There's been a fortress at San Leo since the Romans founded a city on the rock. Later colonizers added to it until the fifteenth century, when Federico da Montefeltro realized that it was no match for the new gunpowder-charged weapons, and set his military architect, Francesco di Giorgio Martini, the task of creating a new one. The walls were built on a slight inward slope and backed with earth, thus reducing the impact of cannonballs and providing a rampart. Three large squares were incorporated for the manoeuvring of heavy cannons, and every point was defended with firing posts. San Leo's greatest advantage, however, remained its position, which allowed unwelcome visitors to be spotted from a great distance.

From the eighteenth century San Leo was used as a prison for enemies of the Vatican, of whom the most notorious was the womanizing Count of Cagliostro, a self-proclaimed alchemist, miracle doctor and necromancer. At first the charismatic heretic was incarcerated in a regular prison, but on the insistence of his guards, who were terrified of his diabolic powers, he was moved to the so-called **Pozzetto di Cagliostro** (Cagliostro's Well), now the fortress's most memorable sight. The only entrance was through a trap door in the ceiling, so that food could be lowered to him without the warden running the risk of engaging Cagliostro's evil eye. There was one window, triple-barred and placed so that the prisoner couldn't avoid seeing San Leo's twin churches. Not that this had any effect – Cagliostro died of an apoplectic attack, unrepentant after four years of being virtually buried alive.

As well as the fortress, there's the pleasant old **village** to explore. St Leo arrived in the third century and converted the local population to Christianity, and the two village churches, though they failed to impress Cagliostro, are worth a visit. The **Pieve** was built in the ninth century, with material salvaged from a Roman temple to Jupiter, by Byzantine-influenced architects from Ravenna. The capitals, dimly lit by tiny windows, are carved with stylized foliage; also notable is the raised sanctuary, designed to impress on the common worshippers the elevated position of their social superiors. Sunk into the ground behind the church is a sixth-century chapel founded by and later dedicated to St Leo, whose body lay here until 1014 when Henry II, emperor of Germany, calling in at the town on his way home from defeating the Greeks and Saracens in Rome, decided to remove it to Germany. His plans were thwarted by the horses bearing the saint's body – after a short distance they refused to go any further, so St Leo's body was left in the small village of Voghenza near Ferrara.

The heavy lid of the sarcophagus remains in the twelfth-century **duomo**, dedicated to the saint. Like the Pieve it's built of local sandstone and incorporates fragments from the Jupiter temple, on whose site it was raised. The best of these are the Corinthian capitals sitting on the stubby Roman columns in the raised sanctuary, above which vaults are supported on the heads of crouching caryatids. The lid of St Leo's sarcophagus is in the crypt (not always open), which is far older than the church and was perhaps once used for pagan worship, as evidenced by the primitive carvings on the wall behind the altar.

Getting to San Leo on public transport is a pain: you need to travel up the coast to Rimini, then catch a bus (approximately hourly, Mon–Sat only) to Novafeltria, getting off at Pietracuta. From here a minibus goes up to San Leo twice a day at 9.15am and 1.40pm. If there's no sign of it, call the driver (T333.909.1537) or hitch a lift. Once here, there's a **tourist office** at Piazza Dante 14 (daily 9am–6pm, open later in summer; T0541.916.306, Wwww .conmune.san-leo.ps.it). There are two **hotels** in San Leo: the rambling *La Rocca*, Via G. Leopardi 16 (T0541.916.241, Wwww.paginegialle.it /laroccasanleo; ②), which has a rustic **restaurant** beneath its seven rooms, and the spick-and-span *Castello*, Piazza Dante Alighieri 11/12 (⊤0541.916.214, ⓌWwww.hotelristorantecastellosanleo.com; ❷), a family-run hotel, bar and restaurant on the main square. Camper vans are allowed to make overnight stops in the car park below the main square. There are also six nice rooms with private bathroom to rent in the heart of town at the little guesthouse *Affitacamera Dorres*, Genoveffa Mercedes, Via Montefeltro 6 (⊤0541.916.284, ⊤334.196.5576; ❶).

Pésaro and around

Most of the tourists who come to **PÉSARO** visit for a beach holiday, attracted by the string of affordable three-star hotels and the low-key family fun on offer. Germans and Brits arrive on cheap package holidays but it's a popular place with Italians too, going through the daily ritual of beach, lunch, beach, *passeggiata* and ice cream before dinner back at the hotel. A lot of Pésaro dates from the 1920s and 1930s, and the town today is a bit of a backwater but pleasant enough nonetheless, with its long stretch of sandy **beach** and an old centre full of small craft and design shops. And with regular transport connections to lesser-known towns like Gradara and Fano, it makes a feasible base from which to explore the northern Marche.

The Town

The centre of town is the dignified **Piazza del Popolo**, in which the rituals of the pavement café scene are played out against the sharp lines of sundry Fascist-period buildings and the Renaissance restraint of the **Palazzo Ducale**.

The most significant relic of Renaissance Pésaro, however, is Giovanni Bellini's magnificent *Coronation of the Virgin* polyptych, housed in the art gallery of the **Museo Civico** at Piazza Toschi Mosca 29 (July & Aug Wed & Fri–Sun 9.30am–12.30pm & 4–7pm, Tues & Thurs 9.30am–12.30pm & 4–10.30pm; Sept–June Tues & Wed 9.30am–12.30pm, Thurs–Sun 9.30am–12.30pm & 4–7pm; €4, €7 with Casa Rossini). Painted in the 1470s for a church now known as Madonna delle Grazie (in Via San Francesco), the altarpiece situates the coronation not in some starry heaven but in the countryside around Pésaro, dominated by the castle of Gradara. Portraits of saints flank the central scene, ranging from the hesitant St Lawrence to the dreamy St Anthony, and below are a nativity and scenes from the saints' lives. Renaissance Pésaro was famous for its ceramics, and the museum houses a fine collection – ranging from a *Madonna and Child* surrounded by pine cones, lemons and bilberries from the workshop of Andrea della Robbia, to plates decorated with an Arabian bandit. The most striking piece, however, stands above the entrance to the museum – a ferocious snake-haired *Medusa* by the local artist Ferruccio Mengaroni. A couple of steps from the museum on Via Rossini is Pésaro's Romanesque **cattedrale**, with a large mosaic on two levels showing incredibly intricate geometric Byzantine and medieval designs. Also on Via Rossini, at no. 34, the **Casa Rossini** (same hours as Museo Civico; €4, €7 with Museo Civico) houses a growing shrine of memorabilia to the composer, who was born here in 1792. The Teatro Rossini on Piazza Lazzarini hosts an opera festival in his honour every August.

Heading north, the old and narrow Via Castelfidardo leads down to Pésaro's most attractive street, the porticoed **Corso XI Settembre**. If you want to do more than just browse in its shops, take a look inside the church of **Sant'Agostino** – the choir stalls are inlaid with landscapes, Renaissance cityscapes, and, displaying a wit to rival the *studiolo* in the Palazzo Ducale in Urbino, half-open cupboards and protruding stacks of books.

On Via Mazza, the continuation of Via Castelfidardo, Pésaro's archeological museum, the **Museo Oliveriano** (July & Aug Mon–Sat 4–7pm; Sept–June Mon–Sat 9am–noon on request at the adjacent library; ☎0721.33344; free), is housed in the Palazzo Almerici and has a small but unusual collection of local finds. Among the relics from an Iron Age necropolis at nearby Novilara are a child's tomb filled with miniature domestic utensils and a tomb slab carved with pear-shaped figures rowing a square-sailed boat into battle. Even more intriguing is the collection of ex-votives – breasts, feet, heads and even a dog – collected not from an early Catholic church but from a Roman sacred grove at San Veneranda (3km from Pésaro), consecrated in the second century BC. Pride of place, however, goes to a bronze statue of a Grecian youth, exquisite even though it's a facsimile of a Roman copy of a fifth-century-BC Greek original.

A tree-lined grid of stucco hotels and gleaming apartments marks Pésaro's long sandy **beachfront**, punctuated by a handful of Art Deco villas, including one on Piazzale della Libertà whose eaves are supported by white plaster lobsters.

Practicalities

Viale Risorgimento leads from the **train station** to the town's main axis, Via Branca–Via Rossini–Viale della Repubblica, which cuts straight through the historical town to the beach. Bisecting it at Piazza del Popolo are Corso XI Settembre, scene of the evening *passeggiata*, and Via San Francesco, which leads to the **bus station** on Piazzale Matteotti. The main **tourist office** (summer Mon–Sat 8.30am–1.30pm & 3–7pm, Sun 8.30am–1pm; winter Mon–Sat 9am–1pm, Tues & Thurs 9am–1pm & 3–6pm; ☎0721.69.341, ⓦ www.turismo .pesarourbino.it) is on the seafront on Piazzale della Libertà, at the end of Viale della Repubblica.

Among the many reasonably priced and convenient **hotels** along the seafront are *Caravelle*, Viale Trieste 269 (☎0721.370.450, ⓦ www.hotel-caravelle.net; closed Oct–April; ❸), a light, airy place with a swimming pool, bikes, a games room, and room prices that drop by almost a half in May and September. One of the few hotels to stay open all year is the *Des Bains*, Viale Trieste 221 (☎0721.34.957, ⓦ www.innitalia.com; ❷), dating back to 1905 and, though modernized many times since then, still with something of the "belle époque" about it. *Napoleon*, Viale Fiume 118 (☎0721.31.160, ⓦ www.hotelnapoleonpesaro .it; ❷), is a summer-only hotel, geared up for families with its mini-suites, bikes, play room and pool with water slides. Other hotels line the avenues which run parallel to the sea: at the less expensive end of the scale, *Clipper*, Viale Marconi 53 (☎0721.30.915, ⓦ www.hotelclipper.it; ❸), is relaxed and friendly and offers an alfresco buffet breakfast on the terrace (open May–Sept). On the edge of town on the road south to Fano, 🍴 *Villa Serena* at Via S. Nicola 6/3 (☎0721.55.211, ⓦ www.villa-serena.it; ❺) is an atmospheric family-owned hotel stuffed full of antiques and heirlooms, with a handful of guest rooms and a swimming pool in the rambling garden (closed Jan & Feb).

The best budget choice is the cheerful *Ostello Sejore*, Strada Panoramica Ardizio (☎0721.390.030, ⓦ www.ostellosejore.it), 6km south of the city in Località Fosso Sejore where the bus between Pésaro and Fano will drop you off. It costs €14 per person per night in a room with between four and seven beds; a small additional charge is made for bedding and towels. The nearest **campsites** to Pésaro are at Fano (see p.706) and, 7km north, the *Panorama* campsite (☎0721.208.145; May–Sept) in a beautiful setting at Fiorenzuola.

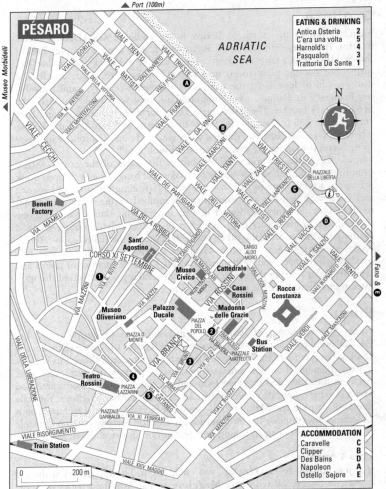

ADRIATIC
SEA

▲ Museo Morbidelli

EATING & DRINKING
Antica Osteria	2
C'era una volta	5
Harnold's	4
Pasqualon	3
Trattoria Da Sante	1

VIALE GORIZIA
VIALE TRENTO
VIALE C. BATTISTI
VIALE ROVERETO
VIALE TRIESTE
VIALE DELLA VITTORIA
VIA M. PATERINI
VIA MONTEFELTRONE
VIALE FIUME
VIALE L. DA VINCI
VIALE MARCONI
VIALE DANTE
VIALE ZARA
VIALE TRIESTE
VIALE DEI PARTIGIANI
VIALE DELLA VITTORIA
VIALE C. BATTISTI
VIALE LANFRANCO
VIALE D. REPUBBLICA
PIAZZALE DELLA LIBERTA
VIALE CECCHI
VIA DELLA ROBBIA
VIA MAMELI

Benelli Factory

VIA CASTELGOLARDO
VIALE R. SANZIO
VIALE VACCAI

Sant' Agostino

CORSO XI SETTEMBRE

LARGO ALDO MORO

VIALE BUONARROTTI

VIALE TRENTO

▶ Fano & E

VIA G. BOVIO
VIA MAZZA
PIAZZA DEL POPOLO

Museo Civico **Cattedrale**

Casa Rossini

Rocca Constanza

Museo Oliveriano **Palazzo Ducale** **Madonna delle Grazie**

VIA ROSSINI
VIA DON MINZONI

PIAZZA D. MONTE

VIA BRANCA
VIA DIAZ
VIA BAVIERA
S. FRANCESCO
PIAZZALE MATTEOTTI

Bus Station

VIALE VERDI
VIALE MASSIGNI

VIALE DELLA LIBERAZIONE

Teatro Rossini

PIAZZA LAZZARINI

VIA ABBATI
VIA G. BRUNO
VIA CATTANEO

VIA BUOZZI
VIA MANZONI

PIAZZALE GARIBALDI

VIALE RISORGIMENTO

Train Station

VIA XI FEBBRAIO
VIALE XXIV MAGGIO

0   200 m

ACCOMMODATION
Caravelle	C
Clipper	B
Des Bains	D
Napoleon	A
Ostello Sejore	E

There's no shortage of affordable places to **eat**. For food on your feet, try the excellent panini at *Harnold's* on Piazza Lazzarini (℡0721.65.155; closed Sun in winter). For pizzas, *C'era una volta*, at Via Cattaneo 26 (℡0721.30.911; closed Mon), is good, cheap and popular – so long as you don't mind rustic decor and loud rock music. There's a fine *osteria* called *Pasqualon* at Via G. Bruno 37 (℡0721.371.108; closed Sun) where you can eat home-made pasta, while among notable fish restaurants, *Trattoria Da Sante*, on Via G. Bovio (℡0721.33.676; closed Mon), in the east of town serves a great fish soup (*brodetto*) for €9. *Antica Osteria La Guercia* at Via Baviera 33, just off the Piazza del Popolo (℡0721.33.463; closed Sun), does amazing pasta and fish dishes and is very reasonably priced; try *maltagliati con ceci e vongole*, home-made pasta with chickpeas and clams.

Gradara

Inland, 15km to the north of Pésaro, is the castle of **GRADARA** (Mon 8.30am–1pm, Tues–Sun 8.30am–6.30pm; July & Aug same hours plus Thurs–Sun 9–11pm; €4), a fairy-tale confection of mellow red-brick and swallow-tail turrets but not the place to go in season if you want to avoid crowds. The castle is said to have been the scene of a thirteenth-century scandal involving Francesca da Rimini, who committed adultery with Paolo da Malatesta, her husband's brother. The lovers were killed for their transgression and later consigned to hell by Dante – he meets their spirits in Canto V of the *Inferno*, where they are caught in a ceaseless whirlwind – though Francesca's unhappy spirit is said to wander the castle when the moon is full.

Inside the castle is a room decked out as the scene of the crime, with a sumptuously refurbished four-poster bed, fake wall hangings and an open book – Francesca tells Dante in hell that it was while reading the story of Lancelot and Guinevere that she and Paolo first succumbed to their passion. Further reminders of the story are found in two nineteenth-century paintings: one showing the lovers (either dead or in a state of post-coital collapse) watched by the crippled husband; the other, less ambiguous, of the naked couple. Other rooms are furnished as a torture chamber, complete with spiked iron ball, handcuffs and lances, and as the guards' room, a strange mixture of tavern and armoury. After touring the castle, it's well worth taking a walk round the walls for the fine views over the surrounding hills.

Fano

Fifteen minutes south of Pésaro (by half-hourly bus or hourly trains) lies **FANO**, no longer quite the haven it was when Robert Browning came here in 1848, seeking relief from the heat and crowds of Florence. Although its beaches remain splendid, they now attract thousands of package tourists every year. Between the sandy and sheltered Lido and the long, pebbly Sassonia are good stretches where you don't have to pay, and there are further beaches at the little resorts of Torrette and Marotta to the south, both easily reached by bus. Fano is a pleasant enough place if a little humdrum, and comfortably combines its role as resort with that of small fishing port and minor historical town.

The Town

If you're coming to Fano by bus, you could ask to be dropped off at the old town gate, the crenellated **Porta Maggiore**, to start you sight-seeing with the remnants of the medieval defensive walls, on the southwestern side of the town centre. Behind them is a Roman gate, the **Arco di Augusto**, impressive despite having been truncated in the fifteenth century when Federico da Montefeltro blasted away its upper storey. You can see what it used to look like in a relief on the facade of the adjacent church of San Michele.

The Roman precursor of Fano, named Fanum Fortunae after its Temple of Fortune, stood at the eastern end of the Via Flaminia, which cut across the Apennines to Rome. The town is still built around a Roman crossroads plan: Via Arco di Augusto and Corso Matteotti follow the routes of the *cardus* and *decumanus*, and their junction is marked with a copy of a Roman milestone stating its distance from the capital (195.4 Roman miles). There are few other relics of Roman Fano, although the fifteenth-century **fountain** in the main square, along Via Mazzini, is dedicated to Fortune.

Overlooking the fountain are the reconstructed thirteenth-century Palazzo della Ragione and the fifteenth-century **Corte Malatestiana**, dating from the time Fano was ruled by the Malatesta family. Its most notorious member was Sigismondo, whose disagreements with the pope led to the siege of Fano (when the Arco di Augusto lost its top) and his excommunication. After the death of his first wife – whom he was suspected of having poisoned – Sigismondo remarried in Fano in 1449, holding a three-day banquet in the Corte Malatestiana. Rumours about Sigismondo's sinister interest in his wives' diet revived when, seven years later, his second wife also died unexpectedly, leaving him free to marry his long-time mistress, Isotta degli Atti. The Corte is at its best nowadays on summer evenings, when its loggias, turrets and trefoil windows provide a backdrop for concerts. Inside there's a small **museum and art gallery** (Tues–Sat 9.30am–12.30pm & 4–7pm, Sun 10am–1pm, usually with extended hours in summer; €3), whose most striking exhibit is a mosaic of a winged figure riding a panther. Upstairs, the art gallery is worth visiting for an insight into the Victorian psyche, as it's here that you'll find Guercino's *The Guardian Angel*, a painting that entranced Browning during his stay here and inspired a poem of the same title. Expressing a wistful desire to take the place of the child depicted here learning how to pray, the gushingly sentimental poem became incredibly popular, and Italy was flooded with reproductions of the painting for holidaying Browning fans. The keenest disciples set up a club, membership of which was gained by travelling to Fano and sending the founder a postcard.

Less saccharine paintings are to be found in the Renaissance church of **Santa Maria Nuova** on Via de Pili, off the main square. The two works by Perugino, a *Madonna, Child and Saints* and an *Annunciation*, are both suffused with a calm luminosity.

Practicalities

The **train station**, where buses also stop, is ten minutes' walk from the seafront, at the end of Via Cavallotti. Fano's **tourist office**, at Via C. Battisti 10 (June to mid-Sept Mon, Wed & Fri 9am–1pm, Tues & Thurs 9am–1pm & 3–6pm, Sat & Sun 9am–1pm; ℡0721.803.534, ⓦwww.turismofano.com), is well organized, with additional offices at the nearby resorts of Torrette (Via Boscomarina 10) and Marotta (Via Viale C. Colombo 31) during July and August.

One of the most reasonably priced **hotels** is *Mare*, Viale Colombo 20 (℡0721.805.667; ❷), an easy-going, family-run pension with a shady garden and verandah a few blocks back from the sea. It offers good home cooking and an excellent full-board deal. Alternatively try the more formal *Corallo* at Via Leonardo da Vinci 3 (℡0721.804.200, ⓦwww.hotelcorallo-fano.it; ❸), on the seafront. If you have your own transport, you could stay at *Borgo della Luca* (℡0721.885.763, ⓦwww.borgodellaluca.it; ❷), a lovely **country B&B** in an old stone house around 5.5km inland from Fano towards Pésaro; it's at Strada Madonna degli Angeli, Località Sant'Andrea in Villis 95/A. Plenty of **campsites** line the coast between Pésaro and Fano: both *Norina* (℡0721.55.792; April–Sept) and *Marinella* (℡0721.55.795, ⓦwww.campingmarinella.it; April–Sept) are easily reached by bus from both towns.

For **eating**, as well as numerous pizzerias and snack bars, there's a fairly reasonable fish trattoria, *Alla Quinta*, in the harbour at Viale Adriatico 42 (closed Sun). Just around the corner from the port, don't miss one of the best budget places to eat in the province: ⚑ *Self Service "Al Pesce Azzurro"*, at Viale Adriatico 48 (℡0721.803.165; May–Oct closed Mon), is run by a cooperative of fishermen's wives and offers great-value three-course set meals (lunch and dinner) of the freshest *pesce azzurro*, oily fish such as anchovies, sardines and mackerel, for just €9.50 a head.

Senigallia

Further down the coast, **SENIGALLIA** is an unprepossessing family resort with a good beach and most of its tourist activity packed into a short season. It makes an easy day-trip from Pésaro, which is a just a twenty-minute train ride away (roughly every 30min). The town centre focuses on the rickety **Foro Annonario**, a semicircular Neoclassical marketplace, behind which stands the imposing thirteenth-century **Rocca Roveresca** (daily 8.30am–7.30pm; €2). The *rocca*, or castle, was built for Federico da Montefeltro's son-in-law by Luciano Laurana, architect of the Palazzo Ducale in Urbino. Below the elegant Renaissance halls lies an underground warren of vaulted storage rooms and dungeons. Upstairs, the fireplaces and beautiful spiral staircase show little sign of use. The cells, however, are a different matter: converted from cannon positions when the region fell to the pope, they have tiny air holes designed to inflict a slow and agonizing suffocation on their occupants. Fine views are to be had from the towers, built in the fifteenth century when the Adriatic coast was plagued by Turkish bandits.

Ancona and around

Severely damaged by war and earthquakes, workaday **ANCONA** has few historical monuments embedded in its tangle of commercial buildings. The modern centre is a grid of broad avenues and palm-shaded piazzas, while the station area, with its heavy trucks travelling noisily to and from the port, will probably make you want to take the next train out. However, as one of the Adriatic's largest ports it's a convenient departure point, and you may well pass through in order to catch one of the regular ferries to Greece and Croatia. These days the city is even more of a gateway to the Marche region with Ryanair's direct flights from the UK to Falconara airport, 10km away.

Arrival and information

Via Marconi and its continuation, Via XXIX Settembre, run along the coast from the train station to the port and the centre of town. Via XXIX Settembre ends in the adjacent piazzas of Kennedy and Repubblica, from which the modern centre's three parallel avenues – Corso Stamira, Corso Garibaldi and Corso Mazzini – slice up to Piazza Cavour, while Via della Loggia runs up above the port to the alleyways of the old town. The main **bus terminus** is Piazza Cavour, connected by regular bus with the **train station** on Piazza Rosselli. The **Stazione Marittima**, where ferries dock, is also connected with the train station by bus. Monday to Saturday a bus (℡071.280.2092, ⑥www .cormerobus.it) also connects the airport with the train station, taking around thirty minutes. Buy your ticket (€1) before boarding from any bar or newspaper kiosk. The bus is J on weekdays (and runs roughly hourly until 6.45pm). Note that there is no service on Sundays and public holidays, and a taxi will cost a steep €35 (℡071.43.321).

The main **tourist office** for Ancona and the Marche region is at Via Thaon de Revel 4 at the end of Viale della Vittoria (summer Mon–Fri 9am–2pm & 3–6.30pm, Sat 9am–1pm & 3.30–6.30pm, Sun 9am–1pm; rest of year Mon–Fri 9am–2pm & 3.30–6pm, Sat 9am–1pm & 3.30–6pm; ℡071.358.991, ⑥www .turismo.marche.it). There's also a seasonal office at the Stazione Marittima (July & Aug daily 9am–7pm; opens 9.30am and closes 1–2pm at beginning and end of this period; ⑥iat.ancona@regione.marche.it).

Accommodation

If you want to **stay** the night in Ancona you will find no shortage of cheap and cheerful places opposite the station. Ancona's **youth hostel** is 100m from the station at Via Lamaticci 7 (⊕071.42.257, ⓔ aigancona@tiscalinet.it; €14 without bathroom, €25 with bathroom); note that there's a lock-out between 11.30am and 4.30pm.

Gino Via Flaminia 4 ⊕071.42.562, ⓔ hotel.gino @tiscalinet.it. Popular with truck drivers, this is a lively place with its own restaurant. ❶

Grand Hotel Passetto Via Thaon de Revel 1 ⊕071.31.307, ⓦ www.hotelpassetto.it. Luxurious establishment with a pool, cocktail bar and health club. ❻

Hotel della Rosa Piazza Rosselli 3 ⊕071.42.651, ⓦ www.hoteldellarosa.it. Clean and shiny hotel with a professional air. ❸

Milano Via Montebello 1 ⊕071.201.147. Clean, appealing and centrally located bargain of a place. Popular so book ahead. ❶

Roma e Pace Via G. Leopardi 1 ⊕071.202.007, ⓦ www.hotelromaepace .it. The most interesting of the mid-range hotels abounds with original fittings and faded 1930s elegance – entering this place is like stepping into an Agatha Christie novel. ❸

The Town

Regular buses run along the seafront from the train station to the port, passing the pentagonal **Lazzaretto**, built within the harbour in the eighteenth century as a quarantine station for immigrants. The port itself is headed by a well-preserved Roman arch, the **Arco di Traiano**, raised in honour of Emperor Trajan, under whose rule Ancona first became a major port. Behind it is the **Arco Clementino**, a piece of architectural self-congratulation by Pope Clement XII, who made Ancona a free port in the eighteenth century and thus considered himself Trajan's equal.

On a steep hill overlooking the port rises the town's Romanesque duomo, while what survives of old Ancona is spread out below. At the foot of the hill is Piazza della Repubblica, from which Via della Loggia leads past the **Loggia dei Mercanti**, whose Gothic splendours include figures of medieval dignitaries and horsemen below its elaborately carved windows. Walk along the narrow road into Piazza del Plebiscito and you come to the **Museo della Città** (closed for restoration), with models, paintings, sculptures and original documents showing key events in Ancona from 2000BC to 2000AD. Backtracking to Piazza della Repubblica, take a left into Corso Mazzini, where there's a long sixteenth-century **fountain** with thirteen spouting heads, all with interesting expressions, attributed to the sixteenth-century sculptor Pellegrino Tibaldi.

Equally appealing, a short walk away on Piazzetta S. Maria (walk straight ahead until you hit the train line, then turn right), is the Romanesque church of **Santa Maria della Piazza**, its facade a fantasia of blind loggias and its portal carved with chunky figures and elegant birds. Behind the church, on Via Pizzecolli, is the town's **Pinacoteca Comunale** (Mon 9am–1pm, Tues–Fri 9am–7pm, Sat 8.30am–6pm, Sun 3–7pm; €4.40). The highlight here is Titian's *Apparition of the Virgin*, a sombre yet impassioned work, with the Virgin appearing to a rotund and fluffy-bearded bishop in a stormy sunset sky. There's also a glorious *Holy Conversation* by Lotto, a view of sixteenth-century Ancona by Andrea Lilli, and an exquisite yet chilling *Madonna and Child* by Carlo Crivelli, with a mean-looking Mary pinching the toe of a rather pained Christ.

Beyond the gallery is the church of **San Francesco delle Scale**, named for the steps leading up to it. Titian's *Apparition* was painted for this church, but today its most remarkable work is an almost orgasmic *Assumption* by Lotto.

Further up the hill, still on Via Pizzecolli, the **Museo Archeologico** is not a bad place to spend an hour (Tues–Sun 8.30am–7.30pm; closed Tues July–Sept; €4), its wacky moulded ceilings vaulting over a collection of finds ranging from red- and black-figure Greek craters to a stunning Celtic gold crown.

From here, passing the remains of the Roman amphitheatre, you can climb up to the pink-and-white **duomo**, San Ciriaco. Though mostly built in a restrained Romanesque style, there's an outburst of Gothic exuberance in the doorway's cluster of slender columns, some plain, others twisted and carved. The simple and calm interior is built on a Greek-cross plan, enlivened by a cupola that from below resembles an elongated umbrella. The most memorable feature, however, is a screen along the edge of the raised right transept, one section of which is carved with eagles, fantastic birds and storks entwined in a tree, the other with saints.

Eating and drinking

You can eat well in Ancona, particularly in the family-run fish restaurants scattered around town. Afterwards, Piazza Roma is the place to hang out – there are plenty of cafés with tables outside in the pedestrianized cobbled square.

Onwards to Croatia, Albania, Greece and Turkey

Ferries leave from the Stazione Marittima, a couple of kilometres north of the train station (bus #1 or #1/4), close to the centre of town. For the best at-a-glance idea of timetables and routes, visit ⓦ www.doricaportservices.it. Each of the main ferry lines has a ticket office (closed 1–3pm) and you can also buy tickets from the agencies all around the port. Alternatively, book online with Superfast/BlueStar, Jadrolinija and Adria Ferries.

Among the main **ferry companies** are Blue Star and Superfast (ⓣ071.202.033 or 071.202.034, ⓦ www.superfast.com) that have now combined operations and sail to Igoumenitsa (15hr 30min) and Patras (21hr). Minoan (ⓣ071.201.708, ⓦ www.minoan.it) and Anek (ⓦ www.ferries.gr) also operate along this route. Jadrolinija (ⓣ071.204.305, ⓦ www.jadrolinija.it) sails to Croatia and the Dalmatian Islands (8–9hr), and Marmaris Lines (ⓣ071.207.6165, ⓦ www.amatori.com) sails to Çesme in southwest Turkey (2 days). A company called Miatrade (ⓣ071.562.16, ⓦ www.amatori.com) operates a fast catamaran service to Zadar/Bozara and Hvar/Bol in Croatia – the crossing takes just over three hours and costs €60–80 one-way. Adria Ferries (ⓣ071.5021.1621) sails three times a week year-round to Durazzo in Albania (18hr).

Ticket prices depend on the speed of the crossing, with one-way fares starting at around €44 per person to Croatia; if you're taking a car add another €57.50. For the 21-hour overnight journey to Patras in July and August, reckon on paying €74 for deck class (cabins are available at additional cost), with an extra €118 for a car. For the mammoth crossing to Turkey (43hr 15min to 55hr) with Marmaris Lines, you can expect to pay €165 for a Pullman seat plus €195 for a car one-way in high season. Most of the shipping lines offer some good five-adult/one-car deals. There are no discounts for holders of InterRail and Eurail passes, but outside high season prices drop by 15–20 percent. There are also 20 percent discounts on return journeys, and some lines will give a student discount if you show proof of status. Check whether boarding taxes are included in your ticket; sometimes an additional fuel tax is payable to the port agency at the time of embarkation for a car. You should book in advance, and you should always aim to arrive at the Stazione Marittima two hours before your ferry is due to depart (three hours beforehand if you're taking a camper van).

Caffè Giuliani Via del Traffico. For a good, inexpensive spread of roasted vegetables, pasta and seafood salads, go for the lunchtime buffet here (closed Sat and Sun).

Clarice Via del Traffico 6 ☎071.20.29.26. First choice among Ancona's restaurants, an old-style, family place in a cobbled alleyway off Corso Garibaldi (on the right as you walk up from the sea). It serves traditional, very reasonably priced food, with many local dishes such as *seppie e piselli* (cuttlefish and peas) and *stoccafisso al patate* (salt cod baked with potatoes). Closed Sat eve and Sun.

Enopolis Palazzo Jona, Corso Mazzini 7 ☎071.207.1505. This wine-bar-cum-restaurant in one of the main streets between the sea and Piazza Roma is a great option for a drink. A *crostini* and a glass of wine goes for as little as €5, though a full blow-out will set you back around €45. Closed Tues.

La Cantineta Via Gramsci 1c ☎071.201.107. This place, just off Piazza del Plebiscito, may look unprepossessing but their speciality, *stoccafisso all'Anconetana*, a traditional recipe involving salt cod, is well worth sampling. Closed Mon eve.

La Luna al Passetto ☎338.853.5005. Take the bus to the beach, Spiaggio di Passetto, at the end of Viale della Vittoria for excellent seafood, including a fishy, fixed-price *degustazione* menu for €35 that will probably be more than you can eat. Open May–August; from September to April they move to Via Trieste 5 and call themselves *La Luna d'Inverno*.

Osteria del Pozzo Via Bonda 2c ☎071.207.3996. A small, traditional restaurant on a narrow lane off Piazza del Plebiscito, where you can tuck into seafood and pasta dishes. If you call in advance, they'll make you a *brodetto*, fish soup, or oven-baked *baccala*. Closed Sun.

Roma e Pace Via G. Leopardi 1. A popular restaurant from the same era as the above-mentioned hotel (see p.709), with white linen tablecloths and pizzas cooked in a wood-fired oven.

Inland: the Esino Valley

West of Ancona and cutting right across the Marche, the **Esino Valley** is broad and bland in the east, but narrows to a dramatic limestone gorge – the Gola di Rossa – just before the town of **FABRIANO** and the border with Umbria. Famous for two things – paper-making and Gentile da Fabriano, the best of the International Gothic artists – Fabriano is now heavily industrialized and a pretty dismal town – one you're likely to pass straight through on your way to Umbria and Rome. Although Fabriano and **Jesi** (a production centre for the famous Marche wine, Verdicchio di Jesi) are built up, most of the valley is given over to agriculture and is best known for **Verdicchio**, a dry white wine produced in the hilltop villages around Jesi. What most visitors come for, however, are the vast **Frasassi caves**.

Jesi

Though its industrial development has led to **JESI** (served by frequent buses from Ancona) being known as "the little Milan of the Marche", the historic centre of the town is well preserved. Clinging to a long ridge, it's fringed by medieval walls and retains a scattering of Renaissance and Baroque palaces. One of the most majestic of these, the Palazzo Pianetti, is home to the **Pinacoteca Civica** (mid-June to Sept Tues–Sun 10am–8pm; Oct to mid-June Tues–Sat 9am–1pm & 4–7pm, Sun 10am–1pm & 5–8pm; €5.50). The highlight of its opulent interior is the magnificent 72-metre-long stuccoed, gilded and frescoed gallery – a Rococo fantasy of shells, flowers and festoons framing cloud-backed allegorical figures. The collection of paintings is best known for some late works by **Lorenzo Lotto**, who, unlike his contemporaries Titian and Giorgione, chose to be an outsider from the Venetian artworld. As a result his work was long-neglected, though his use of colour and the expressive intensity of his portraits is exceptional, and he was unique in combining this meticulous realism with the southern European traditions of the High Renaissance. If you're interested, note that you can buy a joint ticket here for €7.80 that admits you to several other galleries in the Marche showing work by Lotto – visit ⓦ www.lorenzo-lotto.it for more details.

In two graceful *Annunciation* panels (once part of a triptych), a hurried angel Gabriel delivers the news to a more than slightly taken aback Virgin; and in the *Visitation*, the setting is a simple domestic interior. Scenes from the life of St Lucy show Lotto's freshness of colour; the *Madonna delle Rose* is interesting for its naturalistic setting – with a baby Jesus trying to jump into the arms of a grandfatherly St Joseph – as well as its allusions to Christian mysticism.

A stroll around town takes you past the **Teatro Pergolesi**, a vast eighteenth-century opera house in Piazza della Repubblica, named after local-born composer Giovanni Battista Pergolesi. Encircling the town are the massive **ramparts**, restructured in the fourteenth century and built on top of the foundations of Roman walls – an escalator takes you through the ramparts, several metres thick, from the lower town to the upper town (with steps back down again).

The village of **CUPRAMONTANA** in the hills above Jesi is known as the capital of Verdicchio country. The best time to visit (7 daily buses from Jesi) is on the first Sunday in October, when there's a parade and dancing, and the village streets are lined with stalls of wine and food for the **grape festival**. Theoretically, this marks the eve of the harvest but, owing to hangovers, it's usually a couple of days before anyone feels fit enough to start work. A *cantina aperta* ("open cellar") day at the end of May gives you the chance to sample the fruits of the winemakers' labours – if you're interested in knowing more about producers and vineyards, check out ⓦ www.assivip.it. The regional Enoteca, Via Federico Conti 5 (daily: April–Oct 11am–1pm & 5.30–9.30pm; Nov–March 5–9pm; ⓣ 0731.213.386) in Jesi's historic centre (near the top of the escalator), holds tasting sessions of local wines every Monday.

The Frasassi caves

Further up the Esino Valley, just after the Gola di Rossa, a road leads up from Genga train station to the Frasassi gorge, carved by the River Sentino, which was also responsible for creating the eighteen kilometres of caves beneath it. The largest of the Grotte di Frasassi, or **Frasassi caves**, (March–July & Sept–Nov guided tours 9.30am, 11am, 12.30pm, 3pm, 4.30pm, 6pm; Aug open 8am–6.30pm, with tours leaving every 10min; €12; ⓦ www.frasassi.com) was discovered only in 1971, and just over a kilometre of its caverns and tunnels is now open to the public on tours that last seventy minutes – note that the average temperature inside is 14°C so bring a sweater.

Inevitably, the most remarkable stalactite and stalagmite formations have been named: there's a petrified Niagara Falls, a giant's head with a wonderfully Roman profile, a cave whose floor is covered with candles complete with holders, and a set of organ pipes. The vast Cave of the Great Wind, at 240m high, is one of the biggest in Europe – large enough to contain Milan Cathedral – and has been used for a series of experiments, ranging from sensory deprivation (as a possible treatment for drug addicts) to a subterranean version of *Big Brother* when a group of people were shut away for a month.

Sadly there is no public transport to the caves, so you need your own vehicle to get here.

The Cónero Riviera

Just south of Ancona the white cliffs of **Monte Conero** plunge straight into the sea, forming the northern Adriatic's most spectacular and enjoyable stretch of coastline. It's easily accessible, with the major resorts of **Portonovo**, **Sirolo** and

△ Monte Conero

Numana all linked by bus from Ancona, either from the train station or Piazza Cavour. Sirolo and Numana are now as crowded in July and August as the rest of the Adriatic resorts, the main difference being that their cliff-backed beaches are more picturesque. The most stunning stretch of coast, a series of tiny coves at the base of Monte Conero between Portonovo and Sirolo, is best explored by boat – they leave from both bays. You can go just for the scenery or ask to be dropped off somewhere along the way and be picked up a few hours later. The return journey should cost around €10.

This stretch of coast is the home of Rosso Conero wine, made from the same Montepulciano grape as Chianti, though less well known than its Tuscan counterpart. Rarely found outside Italy, there's a chance to sample it at the Rosso Conero **festival** at Camerano, 8km inland from Monte Conero, in the first week in September.

Portonovo

Only 11km from Ancona, **PORTONOVO**, nestling beneath Monte Conero, is a pleasant resort made up of a couple of campsites and a clutch of expensive hotels, one of which is sited in the Napoleonic fort that dominates the bay. The main attraction is the unbeatable scenery and the transparent water, and though the main pebbly pay-beach gets very busy in summer, it's easy enough to escape by walking about 1km to Mezzavalle beach (free) just north of Portonovo Bay or clambering over rocks to the few tiny beaches to the south. On the walk south, there's a lovely Romanesque church, **Santa Maria** (Tues–Sun 4.30–6.30pm; free) perched above the shore at the end of an oleander-lined path. The clear light reflected from the sea bathes it in a golden glow, the shadows adding to the delicate interplay of arcades and wavily tiled roof. There are lots of **trails** across Monte Conero of varying degrees of difficulty. Ask at the tourist offices or, if you understand Italian, look at ⓦ www.conero.net. The tourist office at Sirolo has maps, as do many souvenir shops in the area.

Portonovo is linked with Ancona by regular urban **buses** – from mid-June to the end of August, they run every twenty minutes. **Accommodation** is stylish rather than budget: *Emilia*, Via Collina di Portonovo (ⓣ071.801.117, ⓦ www .hotelemilia.com; ❸), is a five-minute car journey inland – and uphill – from the beach. A light, modern hotel, the walls are covered with a huge contemporary art collection, a legacy of the Fifties and Sixties when artists paid for their stay with a piece of work; the filmmaker Nanni Moretti has also been a long-term guest. The hotel also has a pool, rents out electric bikes for exploring the Mont Conero Park and offers a shuttle service to the beach. Down by the seashore the *Fortino Napoleonico* (ⓣ071.801.450, ⓦ www.hotelfortino.it; ❼) was built on the orders of Napoleon to stop the English landing to take on fresh water from Monte Conero's springs. The upmarket hotel retains some military touches in the suites but generally is rather chi-chi and grand. Otherwise there are two **campsites**: *Camping Club Adriatico* (ⓣ071.801.170; May to mid-Sept) is slightly cheaper; if it's full, try the *Camping Comunale La Torre* (ⓣ071.801.257; June to mid-Sept). As for **eating**, there's no better place to watch the sun go down than from the fashionable beach bar and restaurant *Il Clandestino* (March/April to Sept/Oct depending on the weather; to find it, follow the "Torre" signs). *Susci Italiano* is on the menu – like sushi in concept but using speciality olive oils and balsamic vinegar rather than wasabi and soy sauce. *Da Anna*, on the beach (summer only), is a great family-run fish restaurant.

Sirolo

Further south, **SIROLO** has an old centre of terraced cottages divided by neat cobbled streets. The main square, Piazza Veneto, is on the clifftop, with good views of the coast and Monte Conero. What used to be a quiet bolt hole has taken off in the last few years and the place is now packed-out on weekends from June to September. In season, buses run roughly every half-hour to the two **beaches** below: Sassi Neri, a wide, long, black-pebbled strand of beach, and San Michele, an attractive, narrow sandy stretch. A third and particularly inviting beach is the small white-pebble one with two jagged sea-stacks in front of it known as the Due Sorelle, but you can only get to it by boat from Numana (see opposite) or a difficult hike down the mountainside.

The **tourist office** is on Piazza Vittorio Veneto (daily: May–Oct 9am–1pm & 4–8pm, July & Aug same hours plus 9–11pm; ⓣ071.933.0611, ⓔ iat.sirolo @regione.marche.it). There's a good choice of **accommodation**: beach lovers should head for *Arturo*, Via Spiaggia 1 (ⓣ071.933.0975, ⓦ www.arturo residencesirolo.com; ❸–❺; June–Sept), right on the white shingle strand, with four rooms and two studio apartments with cooking facilities that open out onto small balconies and the sea. It's a bus ride from Sirolo proper (or a long walk down and then back uphill), but it's one of the least expensive options in town. It has its own restaurant with live music down on the beach. At the other end of the scale is ⚘ *Rocco*, Via Torrioni 1 (ⓣ071.933.0558, ⓦ www.locandarocco .it; ❹), built into the town gate and a short walk down the main street of Corso Italia from the piazza. Once a thirteenth-century inn where St Francis is said to have slept, it's now a stylish seven-room hotel with an upmarket restaurant (closed Tues in winter) serving refined, imaginative and relatively expensive food. At Via Giulietti 9 is *Stella* (ⓣ071.933.0704, ⓦ www.hotelstellasirolo.it; ❷), and a short walk away behind the main town car park is *Emiliana*, Via Raffaello Sanzio

2 (℡071.933.0932, @www.hotelemiliana.it; ②), both pleasant, modern hotels. A few Sirolese are offering **B&B** these days – look out for the *"camere"* signs around town or try ✲ *B&B Zaratan*, Via Cavour 43 (℡071.736.0432 & 349.269.3757, @www.zaratan.it; ②), a welcoming place in an old stone village house signposted off Corso Italia. Sirolo's closest **campsite** is the *Internazionale* (℡071.933.0884, @www.camping.it/marche/internazionale/; April–Sept), set on a terraced, wooded hillside below Piazza Veneto, within sight and sound of the sea.

If you can afford to splurge in Sirolo, do it on a **meal** at the hotel ✲ *Rocco* (see opposite; closed Tues in winter), which offers a tasting menu and à la carte options such as goat's cheese mousse with pesto and cherry tomatoes. *Il Grottino* (closed Mon) on Via Ospedale, just off Via Italia, is a moderately priced place specializing in fish under its stone vaults. Otherwise there's *La Taverna* (℡071.9331.1382; booking advisable; closed Mon in winter), Via Italia 10, offering *enogastronomia*: local wine and several fish and pasta combinations plus the local cheese, *formaggio di Fossa*. At *Trattoria Sara* next door at number 9 (℡071.933.0716; closed Wed in winter) diners can sample robust dishes in a no-nonsense atmosphere; the seafood antipasti, risotto and tagliatelle with fish sauce are especially recommended. Take-away food for a beach picnic can be bought at the *Rosticceria* at Corso Italia 21–23 (closed Mon & Thurs pm). For cocktails and **ice creams** with a sea view head to *Il Grillo*, on Via Giulietti, just below Piazza Veneto.

Numana

NUMANA, a small port with a large pebble beach, is where you can take a boat to the offshore islets of **Due Sorelle** (June–Sept roughly hourly 9am–3pm, rest of the year twice-daily; €15 return) for a spot of swimming and sunbathing. There's also the added attraction of a **museum** (daily 8.30am–7pm; €2), filled mostly with relics of the Piceni tribe, who occupied the area between Senigallia and Pescara from the seventh century BC; the extent to which they were influenced by the Greeks, who set up a trading post nearby, is clearly visible in the red-and-black pots decorated with scenes from Greek mythology. If you want **to stay**, try *Sorriso*, 50m from the beach at Via Flaminia 109 (℡071.933.0645, @www.hotelsorrisonumana.it; ❶–❷), which has good food and a shady garden, or the *Scogliera*, Via del Golfo 21 (℡071.933.0622, 🖷071.933.1403; ❸), a modern, appealing place on a small headland at the northern edge of the bay. Both are open April to October.

Loreto

One of Italy's most popular sites of pilgrimage, attracting four million visitors every year, **LORETO** owes its existence to one of the Catholic Church's more surreal legends. The story goes that in 1292, when the Muslims kicked the Crusaders out of Palestine, a band of angels flew the **house of Mary** from Nazareth to Dalmatia, and then, a few years later, whisked it across the Adriatic to Loreto. In the face of growing scepticism, the Vatican came up with the more plausible story that the Holy House was transported to Loreto on board a Crusader ship. Not surprisingly, though, this new theory doesn't have the same hold on the Catholic imagination, and the Madonna of Loreto continues to be viewed as the patron of aviators: Lindbergh took an image of her on his landmark Atlantic flight in 1927, and a medallion inscribed with her image also accompanied the crew of Apollo 9. Among the Madonna of Loreto's more unlikely fans were Galileo, denounced and imprisoned as a heretic, and Descartes, who reckoned she'd helped him refine his philosophical method. For centuries she was also credited with military victories (presumably she was thought to have power over projectiles), though the builders of Loreto's basilica, aware that the site was vulnerable to Turkish pirates, decided not to rely on the Madonna's defensive capabilities, and accordingly constructed a formidable fortified church here.

Loreto's treasures were indeed covetable, the most costly and idiosyncratic being a golden baby donated by Louis XIII of France, weighing exactly the same as his long-awaited heir, the future Louis XIV. The basilica was ransacked in 1798 by Napoleonic troops, most of the plunder ending up on the shelves of the Louvre in Paris. Following Napoleon's demise, subsequent popes managed to retrieve many of the valuables, but the majority were stolen again in 1974 in what became known as the "holy theft of the century".

Numbering among its contributors such figures as Bramante, Antonio da Sangallo, Sansovino, Lotto and Luca Signorelli, the basilica is a must for anyone even mildly interested in the Renaissance. However, for the non-believer the atmosphere of devotional hard-sell can soon become stifling. Loreto can also be a distressing or moving place, depending on your attitude to faith – between April and October so-called "white trains" bring the sick and terminally ill on three-day missions of hope, the main event being a Mass in Piazza della Madonna, outside the basilica.

The pilgrimage site

Had it been completed according to Bramante's design, the **Piazza della Madonna** would have been an ideal Renaissance square. It still looks pretty good, although Bramante's **Palazzo Apostolico** has only two of its projected three wings, and his low facade for the basilica, designed to make its elegant dome the piazza's focal point, was never built. Instead, the dome, masked by a fluid late-Renaissance facade, is best seen from the back. Here you can see how Baccio Pontelli, who had a hand in most of the Marche's fifteenth-century military architecture, fortified the church – the loggia that runs along the sides and around the nine apses has a dual role as a walkway for meditating monks and a battlement, looking down over the sturdy defensive walls.

Inside the basilica

The church's **interior** (daily: April–Sept 6.15am–8pm; Oct–March 6.45am–7pm) is the jumbled result of Bramante's, Sansovino's and Sangallo's attempts to graft Renaissance elements onto the late-Gothic structure. Clashing with the pointed arches of the nave, Loreto's raison d'être, the **Santa Casa** (Holy House), is encased in a marble cuboid designed by Bramante and encrusted with statues and reliefs. With typical Renaissance panache, pagan sibyls are juxtaposed with Old Testament prophets, all sharing in the honour of foreseeing Mary's life, scenes from which decorate the rest of the walls. The best are by Sansovino: a *Nativity* on the south side and an *Annunciation* on the front.

You may not be able to look around the Holy House itself as a service is usually being conducted for visiting pilgrims and it is closed from 12.30pm to 2.30pm. A primitive stone building, it has no foundations and only three walls – cited by believers as proof of its authenticity (the basement and fourth wall were formed by a grotto which can still be seen in Nazareth), but seen by sceptics simply as evidence of the research undertaken by its fakers. Pride of place is given to a copy of the famous *Black Madonna of Loreto*; the medieval original, once crazily attributed to St Luke, was destroyed in a fire in 1921. Madonna and Child are usually swathed in an ornate but ill-fitting wrap known as a dalmatic, a practice started by Pope Pius VII in 1801 in celebration of the statue's return from the Louvre. Pope Julius II contributed the cannon shell hanging on the right-hand wall, attributing his miraculous escape from it to the Madonna of Loreto's missile-deflecting powers.

One of the most recent of the church's 25 chapels is the **Cappella Americana**, featuring a plane in recognition of the Madonna's role as patron of aviators. Of more artistic interest is the **Cappella del Crocifisso**, whose wooden *Crucifixion* is a triumph of Baroque ingenuity: viewed from the left, Christ appears to be still alive; from the centre, to be drawing his last agonized breath; and from the right, to be dead. Less theatrical is the **Sagrestia di San Giovanni**, frescoed by Luca Signorelli – most striking is the Conversion of St Paul, with its panic-stricken courtiers. The sacristy's inlaid cupboards, featuring a jumble of trompe-l'oeil bric-a-brac, are influenced by those in the *studiolo* of Urbino's palace (see p.699).

Next door, in the **Cappella dei Duchi di Urbino**, commissioned by the last duke, Francesco Maria II della Rovere, is an *Annunciation* by Barocci, taking place before an open window through which the Palazzo Ducale can be seen. By far the most entertaining chapel, however, is the **Sagrestia di San Marco**, where vaulted frescoes feature prophets who seem to be resolving the knotty problem of the sex of angels by peering up their skirts. Ezekiel looks appalled, Zacharias flushed and embarrassed, Jeremiah delighted, and David utterly overwhelmed.

To the left of the Chapel of the Crucifix, a corridor leads to the sumptuously stuccoed atrium and the **Treasury**, its vault unremarkably frescoed by Pomerancio. The artist won the competition for the commission in 1604 thanks to Vatican manoeuvring, much to the chagrin of the loser, Caravaggio, who hired a cut-throat to slash Pomerancio's face.

The Museo-Pinacoteca

The items left behind in the treasury after the 1974 burglary are now kept in the **Museo-Pinacoteca** (Tues–Sun: April–Oct 9am–1pm & 4–7pm; Nov–March 10am–1pm & 3–6pm; donations requested) housed in the west wing of the Palazzo Apostolico. It shouldn't be missed, principally for the eight paintings by Lorenzo Lotto that are held here, nearly all dated between 1549 and 1556, including his final work, *The Presentation in the Temple*. Plagued by neurosis and lack of money, Lotto finally joined the religious community at Loreto, painted some of the canvases shown here, and died here in 1556. Looking at *The Presentation*, with its rotund, crumbling priest and frail, almost skeletal nun, it would appear that he never found much inner peace. *Christ and the Adulteress* is an even more powerful work, with Christ surrounded by maniacally intense men and a swooning adulteress. For some light relief, take a look at the best of all the depictions of the Holy House's angel-powered flight – a copy of a fluffy-clouded fantasy by Giambattista Tiepolo.

Practicalities

Loreto is easily accessible by **train** from Ancona; the station is some way out of town but connected with the centre by regular buses. The busiest pilgrimage periods are December 8–12 (the anniversary of the legendary flight), August 1–20, September 5–10, Easter, and from Christmas through to January 7; it's also pretty crowded throughout the summer, and finding accommodation can be difficult so it's worth visiting ⓦwww.turismo.marche.it or the **tourist**

office at Via Solari 3 (Mon–Fri 9am–1pm & 4–6.30pm, Sat 9am–1pm; ☎071.970.276, ✉iat.loreto@regione.marche.it) for a complete list. The one-star **hotels** are run by religious orders, among them the *Sorelle Francescane*, Via Marconi 26 (☎071.970.306; ❶). For something less spartan, try the central *Il Giardinetto*, just inside the Porta Romana in a mellow stone building on Corso Boccalini, which also has parking for €8 a night in its nearby garage (☎071.977.135, ⓦwww.hotelgiardinetto.it; ❷), or *Centrale*, Via Solari 7 (☎071.970.173, ✉hotelcentrale@girarrosto.it; ❷), a comfortable two-star with good reductions in low season and a vast and popular restaurant, *Girarrosto* (see below). Within the city walls there are good deals in low season at the *Pellegrino e Pace* on the edge of the main square at Piazza della Madonna 5 (☎071.977.106, ⓦwww.hotelpellegrinoepace.it; ❷). Leading away from the piazza, at Corso Boccalini 69, is *Delfino Azzurro* (☎071.977.283, ⓦwww.delfinoazzurro.it; ❷), a friendly two-star with a private garage. The **youth hostel** is at Via Aldo Moro 46 (☎071.750.1026, ⓦwww.ostelloloreto.it), a short walk from Piazza Basile, with beds from €15 to €22).

Your best bet for places to **eat** are the *Girarrosto* in the *Centrale* hotel on Via Solari, which serves antipasti typical of the Conero peninsula, or, for great pizza, the *Garibaldi*, further down the same street (closed Wed), or the *Euthymia* set in an atmospheric old house on Via Papa Benedetto XV (☎071.750.1006).

Recanati and Porto Recanati

A few kilometres along the Macerata road from Loreto is **RECANATI**, a small town that makes a comfortable living from having been the birthplace of the opera singer Beniamino Gigli and the nineteenth-century poet Giacomo Leopardi, and its coastal satellite, the resort of **Porto Recanati**. Visitors can wallow in Gigli memorabilia in Recanti's civic art gallery, or visit places that feature in Leopardi's poems; if such acts of homage don't appeal, there's little point in coming to Recanati. Those who do want to visit can get here by bus from Ancona, Macerata or Loreto.

Recanati

On the central Piazza Leopardi, the **Museo Beniamino Gigli** (Tues–Sun 10am–1pm & 3–6pm; €2.50) is housed in the nineteenth-century **Palazzo Comunale**, a fussy mock-Renaissance symbol of Recanatese obtuseness – in order to build it they ripped down a fine medieval palace. All that remains of the original palace is the vast **Torre del Borgo**, glowering down on the municipal architecture that surrounds it. Once inside the gallery you can forget all this and lose yourself in Gigli's world, evoked by costumes worn by the great tenor, presents received by him (including a dagger from D'Annunzio), and, best of all, a replica of his dressing room. A crackly recording of his voice is often playing on a wind-up gramophone as a fitting accompaniment to the exhibits. It's worth dropping in, too, at the patrician house on Via Gregorio XII where the **Museo Civico Villa Colloredo Mels** (Tues–Sun 9am–noon & 3–6pm; open until 7pm in summer, €4.50) is housed, with four paintings by **Lotto** the highlight of the small collection. Among them there's a polyptych, a *Transfiguration* and a haunting *Annunciation*, better known as *The Madonna of the Cat* for the cat scuttling between the Madonna and angel – thought by some critics to represent the devil.

Left out of Piazza Leopardi, the main street leads down to the **Palazzo Leopardi** where the poet was born in 1798 and which still contains his vast library of over 25,000 volumes. The odd name of the square in front of it, **Piaz-zuola Sabato del Villagio**, comes from one of Leopardi's poems, in which he observes a typical Recanati Saturday, with "a swarm of children shouting on the piazzuola". You're almost certain to meet crowds of schoolkids here – Leopardi is required reading in Italian schools – but their elation tends to come from relief at finishing the tedious tour of Leopardi's gloomy house. Leopardi himself sought solace in the view from the edge of town – on a good day it extends as far as the Apennines. The lower hills, which seem to roll endlessly towards the mountains, inspired his most famous poem, *L'Infinito* (Infinite Hills), and a plaque with a line from it has been stuck on a wall, above a heap of rocks from Naples, where he died and is buried.

Porto Recanati

If you're not a fan of either Gigli or Leopardi, you may well head straight to **PORTO RECANATI**, the nearest resort to Loreto. Its main street, Corso Matteotti, is headed by the turreted tower of a medieval castle; off it is a tiny old quarter of terraced cottages surrounded by hotels and apartment buildings. Apart from the long sandy **beach**, limited attractions include a **sailing and windsurfing school** (June–Aug) – details from the **tourist office** (summer daily 9am–12.30pm & 4.30–7pm; winter Tues and Thurs only 9am–1pm; ☏071.979.9084, ⊛www.portorecanatiturismo.it) on the Corso – and various beach bars and discos. If you tire of the beach, pay a visit to the art gallery inside the **castle** (Mon–Fri 4–7pm; free): among the sixteenth and seventeenth-century works are pieces by Luca Giordano, a Baroque artist so prolific that he was known as Luca Fa-Presto ("Luca Works-Fast"). The castle itself has been completely restored and in the keep (Tues–Sun 4–8pm; free) is a collection of statuary excavated from the remains of the nearby Roman city of Potentia. Even better, the castle courtyard has an **arena** – a wonderfully atmospheric place to see films and theatre (see ⊛www.portorecanatiturismo .it for programmes).

There are two mid-range **hotels** in town: the seventeen-room *Bianchi Nicola*, Piazza Brancondi (☏071.979.9016, ⊛www.hotelbianchi.com; ❸), and the *Bianchi Vincenzo* at Via Garibaldi 15 (☏071.979.9040; ❸), in a central but quiet position with one-, two- and three-room apartments overlooking the sea. In high season they're let by the week only and the price includes your own beach umbrella and sun loungers on the sand. *Enzo* at Corso Matteotti 21/23 (☏071.759.0734, ⊛www.hotelenzo.it; ❺) is a glossy four-star. The *Il Vascello* **campsite**, to the south on Viale della Repubblica (☏071.759.1322), is simple and reasonably convenient.

Porto Recanati is best known for its *brodetto*, a classy fish soup cooked with nine varieties of fish, spiced with saffron and served with squares of toast. One of the best places to try it is the **restaurant** inside the *Bianchi Vincenzo* hotel (see above; closed to non-residents Mon) on the seafront – the chef is justifiably known as the *l'uomo del brodetto* (the "brodetto man"). The *mago del brodetto*, however (the "brodetto magician"), is the chef at the other Bianchi family hotel, *Bianchi Nicola* (closed Nov–March, and in summer to non-residents Mon).

Macerata

A little-known provincial capital surrounded by Marche's loveliest countryside, **MACERATA** is one of the region's liveliest historical towns, thanks to its ancient university. Easy-paced and unpretentious, it's an ideal place to wind down in the evenings after exploring the province. For opera and ballet fans, its annual *Stagione Lirica* (mid-July to mid-Aug; for info Ⓦ www.sferisterio.it), held in Italy's best open-air venue outside Verona, is a must: in recent years it has drawn such heavyweights as Placido Domingo, Birgit Nilsson and José Carreras. And if you're the slightest bit interested in contemporary art, Macerata has a gallery that alone is reason enough for visiting the town.

Arrival and information

Old Macerata is wrapped around a hill, surrounded by modern suburbs that are home to the **train station**, a ten-minute walk south down Viale Don Bosco and connected to central Piazza della Libertà by frequent **buses**. Most stop at the Giardini Diaz, directly below the old town on the western side, across Viale Puccinotti; some continue to a more convenient stop, from where it's a five-minute climb up stepped Piaggia delle Torre to Piazza della Libertà.

The **tourist office** is on Piazza della Libertà (July to mid-Sept daily 9am–1pm & 3–7pm; mid-Sept to June closed Sat pm and Sun; ☏ 0733.234.807, Ⓔ iat.macerata @regione.marche.it). The website for the province is Ⓦ www.provincia.mc.it.

For **Internet** access, try the Internet Center at Piazza Mazzini 52 (summer daily 10am–1pm & 4–8pm; winter Mon–Sat 9.30am–1pm & 3.30–8pm; July & Aug closed Mon).

Accommodation

There are just a handful of **hotels** in Macerata, and if you're looking for somewhere inexpensive you should book in advance, especially during the opera season (mid-July to mid-Aug). Top budget choice is the **youth hostel**, Via dell'Asilo 36 (☏ 0733.232.515; €14 including breakfast), housed in a converted nineteenth-century *palazzo* that once contained Macerata's first infant school. It's centrally located in the old town, right next to the Sferisterio, and offers ninety beds in a choice of dorms or smaller rooms. Among the central hotel choices is the appealing *Arcadia* on Via P. Matteo Ricci (☏ 0733.235.961, Ⓦ www.hotelarcadia.it; ❸), a quiet cobbled street in the historic centre between Piazza della Libertà and Piazza Mazzini. Rooms come with mini-kitchens and there's a small bar downstairs. The friendly *Arena* at Vicolo Sferisterio, off Piazza Mazzini (☏ 0733.230.931, Ⓔ albergoarenamc @libero.it; ❷), is tucked away in a small courtyard behind the opera arena and has an interior done out in rustic style in keeping with its ancient stone structure. Otherwise there's the *Hotel Lauri* at Via T. Lauri 6 (☏ 0733.232.376, Ⓦ www.hotellauri.com; ❷), also central and reached via Corso Matteotti; its rooms are quite plain but nicely decorated with whitewashed walls, terracotta tile floors and old prints. Macerata's four-star option is *Hotel Claudiani*, at Via Ulissi 8 (☏ 0733.261.400, Ⓦ www.hotelclaudiani.it; ❸), just off Corso Matteotti in the historic centre; its bedrooms are "hotel style" rather than "antique palazzo". A pleasant option **out of town** is *Il Vecchio Granaio*, località Chiaravalle, Passo di Treia (☏ 0733.843.488, Ⓦ www.ilvecchiogranaio.it; ❷), an agriturismo complex, a twenty-minute drive from Macerata on the SS361 at the km 40,500 marker (there are five buses a day to Passo di Treia from Macerata). The large guest rooms are decorated with antiques and hunting prints, and there are superlative views of the hills from the communal sun terrace. There's a large swimming pool too and the restaurant serves excellent marchigiana food such as *gnocchi alla paparo* (gnocchi with duck).

The Town

Piazza della Libertà is the heart of the old town, an odd square in which the disparate buildings vie for supremacy. The Renaissance **Loggia dei Mercanti** was supplied by Alessandro Farnese, better known as Pope Paul III, the instigator of many architectural improvements to sixteenth-century Rome; sadly he did nothing else for the square, and the loggia is elbowed out by the bland **Palazzo del Comune** and overlooked by the dull **Torre del Comune**. The dreariest feature, however, is the mournful brick facade of **San Paolo**, a deconsecrated seventeenth-century church now used as an exhibition space.

Things pick up along the main *passeggiata* route, the boutique- and bar-lined **Corso della Repubblica**, which ends at **Piazza Vittorio Veneto** and the **Pinacoteca Civica** (daily: July & Aug 9am–1pm & 4–7pm, Sept–June Mon 4–7pm; Tues–Sat 9am–1pm & 4–7pm; Sun 9am–1pm; free). The collection here, ranging from the Renaissance perfectionist Crivelli to Ancona-born futurist Cagli, isn't bad, but you might find the twentieth-century artworks on show in the **Palazzo Ricci** (summer only daily 10am–1pm & 4–8pm; free), off the square on Via Ricci, more stimulating. There are two thrilling sculptures in the piazza by Francesco Messina – a nerve-tingling nude of a dancer putting on her shoes, and a leaping horse. Enrico Baj's *Military Head* depicts a general decorated with assorted fabric on a background of upholstery material, and you might see a similarly satiric intent in Manzu's bronze bas-relief of a clutch of cardinals. There's also a good cross section of work by the Italian futurists, followed by de Chirico's weird *Worried Muse*; de Chirico's brother, Alberto Savinio, provides the gallery's jokiest piece of social satire in the form of a painting of a richly dressed society woman whose long neck ends in a goose's head.

Seeing the rest of Macerata's sights doesn't take long. Via Ricci leads along towards the bleak **Piazza Mazzini**, below which is the Neoclassical **Sferisterio**, built in the early nineteenth century as an arena for *sphaera*, a traditional game that involved bashing a ball with a spiked iron glove. It was also used for bullfights, horse racing and mock jousts until 1921 when the opera festival was inaugurated and the musicians took over.

Up Via Ciccarelli from Piazza Mazzini, the town's **duomo** on Piazza Strambi is no architectural showpiece either – a workaday chunk of Baroque, which might have looked slightly more appealing had its facade been finished. Inside there's a statue of Macerata's patron saint, Giuliano, whose path to sainthood sounds like something out of a Sunday tabloid. He arrived home to find two people in his bed and, thinking they were his wife and her lover, promptly killed them. Discovering he'd murdered his parents, he hacked one of his arms off in remorse – the severed limb is now kept in a church strongroom, encased in a sleeve of gold and silver. The relic is displayed on request, but a day's notice is required.

Eating, drinking and nightlife

Macerata's student population ensures that there's a good supply of cheap and interesting places to **eat** and **drink**, and there are some excellent, more upscale restaurants serving the specialities of the region too.

For lunchtime food locals head for *Il Ghiottone*, a self-service restaurant at Via Gramsci 30 (℡0733.234.319; closed Mon), which runs between the tourist office and Palazzo Ricci. The student *mensa* at Viale Don Bosco 12, outside the centre on the Piazza Mazzini side of town, is open Monday to Friday for lunch (noon–2.15pm) and dinner (7–8pm), and Saturday and Sunday lunch only (noon–1pm). *Da Silvano* on Piazza delle Torre, just off Piazza della Libertà (℡0733.260.216; closed Mon and most of May), is a good pizzeria, as is *Il*

Sorriso, Vicolo Sferisterio 2 (☎0733.232567; closed Wed), close to the youth hostel and the opera arena. For beautiful home-made pasta (try the ravioli with ricotta and lemon) and in season, funghi porcini and truffles, head for *Da Rosa* at Via Armaroli 17 (☎0733.260.124; closed Sun), where you can eat and drink well for under €25. *Trattoria da Ezio*, Via Crescimbeni 65 (☎0733.232.366; closed Sun), serves very reasonably priced food with gnocchi the speciality on Thursday, fish on Friday, and *vincisgrassi*, the rich Marche version of lasagna, on Saturday. For a more indulgent meal, head for Macerata's most famous restaurant, ✴ *Da Secondo*, on Via Pescheria Vecchia (☎0733.260.912; closed Mon); they do a fabulous *vincisgrassi*, along with excellent roast lamb and pigeon.

For a small town there's a surprising amount of **nightlife**. There's the *Roxi Bar*, Via Garibaldi 57, for live music, poetry readings and Brazilian and Cuban theme nights, and the popular *Il Pozzo*, Via Costa 5 (off Piazza Oberdan), an alternative pub-*birreria* dating back to 1984 where you can eat simple local food and listen to recorded jazz. As for dancing, *Number One* at Vicolo Coltelli 13 (☎0733.408.025) is a disco-pub that goes on until 5 or 6am at the weekend, while you can sometimes catch live music at *Terminal-Music* at Via Fontemaggiore 25 (☎0733.239.482), just outside the city walls by Porta San Giuliano (you can eat well here too). Seats for the **opera** are bookable at the Biglietteria dell'Arena Sferisterio, Piazza Mazzini 10 (Mon–Sat 9.30am–1pm & 4–8pm; ☎0733.230.735 or 0733.233.508, ⓦwww.sferisterio.it). Ticket prices range from €15 in the balcony (not bookable) to €130 (plus ten percent booking fee) in the front stalls.

Around Macerata

With its hills rising from the coast and rippling towards the Apennines, its medieval villages and scattering of Romanesque abbeys and churches, the area around Macerata is well worth a good chunk of time. Most villages we list below are well served by bus (approximately hourly) from Macerata's terminal on Piazza Pizzarello (☎0733.261.594). You can get to and back from most places by bus within a day, though you may be charmed into sleeping over.

The Chienti Valley

From Macerata the road and rail lines run east to the coast through the **Chienti Valley**, taking in some of the region's most characteristic hill-towns and two of its finest churches. About 10km from Macerata, close to the turn-off for Morrovalle, is the Romanesque church of **San Claudio al Chienti**, approached along a cypress-lined avenue. Carefully restored after years of use as a farm outbuilding, the church appears to be none the worse for its undignified past – you'd certainly never guess that the two cylindrical towers flanking its facade used to serve as grain silos. The upper storey, intended for church dignitaries, was entered through the elegant marble portal, while lesser mortals were directed to the tunnel-like door on the ground floor. The marble for the portal, like much of the church's fabric, was scavenged from a Roman village, Pausula, which once stood in the adjacent field.

Morrovalle and Montelupone

Above San Claudio is the hill-village of **MORROVALLE**, skirted by a stepped street that disappears through arched gates. Hemmed inside the main piazza at the top of the village is the squat Palazzo del Podestà, where Italy's first pawnshop was set up by St Bernard in 1428. The building next to it is the Palazzo Lazzarini, seat of the ruling family who survived their internecine battle for the privilege of ruling Morrovalle. The *palazzo*, though built in the fourteenth century, incorporates an earlier Romanesque-Gothic portal, possibly taken from a local church.

The even more remote **MONTELUPONE** has few bus connections, so is best visited by car. Once there, you'll be rewarded with fine views from Monte Conero across to the most beautiful of the Apennines, the Monti Sibillini. A good time to go is during the *passeggiata*, when the stone buildings look handsome in the early evening sun, and the village is at its liveliest.

Santa Maria a Piè di Chienti

Back in the valley, road and rail pass the ex-monastery of **Santa Maria a Piè di Chienti** (daily 8am–8pm; free) just after the fork for Montecosaro. It was built by Cluniac monks who came to the area in the tenth century, draining the flood-prone river into channels and creating fertile land out of what had been a fever-ridden marsh. Situated close to the coast, the monastery was vulnerable to Saracen invasions, so the monks encircled it with ditches, which could be flooded in the event of a raid. The monastery survived until the early nineteenth century, when it was destroyed by Napoleonic troops, and now all that remains is the church itself. The facade was rebuilt in the eighteenth century, and the church's best external features are now its apses, decorated with fake pilasters and scalloped arcades. However, it's the interior (ask for the key from the adjacent bar) that's really special, its columns and arches bathed in the half-light that falls from the windowpanes of alabaster. After wandering around the vaulted chamber beneath the raised presbytery, and up the stairs to the galleries (narrow to ensure that they were climbed slowly, with a prayer on every step), you'll need to switch the lights on (by the right transept) to see the fifteenth-century frescoes properly. The best-preserved are in the apse, showing New Testament scenes in Renaissance settings, framed by fake mosaics and dominated by a stony-faced Christ.

West of Macerata

Heading southwest of Macerata towards the Sibillini mountain range, you might stop off briefly at the little town of **TOLENTINO** to see the **Basilica di San Nicola** (daily 8.30am–noon & 3.30–6.30pm; free). Its west front is a real feast for the eyes – a curly Baroque facade with a grinning sun instead of a rose window and a fancily twisting Gothic portal topped by an oriental-style arch enclosing a dragon-slaying saint. Inside, the most intriguing feature is the **Cappellone di San Nicola**, a large chapel whose Gothic frescoes create a kaleidoscope of colourful scenes of medieval life. In fact, they are episodes from the life of Christ, painted in the fourteenth century by one of Giotto's followers, known only as the "Maestro di Tolentino". The most striking are *The Wedding at Cana*, with hefty servants carrying massive jugs of wine on their shoulders, *The Slaughter of the Innocents* and *The Entry into Jerusalem*, in which an attempt at perspective is made by peopling the trees with miniature figures.

Just east of Tolentino is the imposing, fourteenth-century **Castello della Rancia** (mid-March to mid-Oct Tues–Sun 10am–12.30pm & 3.30–6.30pm; mid-Oct to mid-March Sat & Sun 10am–12.30pm & 3–6.30pm; €2.50). This vast fort was the main grain store for the Cistercian abbey of Fiastra (see p.724) back in the twelfth century. Transformed into a castle in the fourteenth century, it became the focal point for a number of armed clashes, at one time harbouring the notorious Renaissance mercenary Sir John Hawkwood.

San Severino Marche

Twelve kilometres northwest of Tolentino lies the ancient town of **SAN SEVERINO MARCHE**, a pretty little place whose modern centre converges on an unusual elliptical square, **Piazza del Popolo**, surrounded by porticoes. Just above the piazza on Via Salimbeni, the town's art gallery, known as the **Pinacoteca Tacchi e Venturi** after a local historian (July & Aug Tues–Sun 9am–1pm & 4.30–6.30pm; Oct–June Tues–Sat 9am–1pm; €2), is as good a reason as any for a visit, with a memorable assembly of pieces. A gilded polyptych of saints by Paolo Veneziano is followed by an even more sumptuous altarpiece by Vittore Crivelli, which centres on a china-doll Madonna weighed down in heavy gold embroidery. It's the frame that really catches your eye, though – an opulent confection of scalloped arches topped with urns from which spring gesticulating ecclesiastics. Other highlights are the works by the Salimbeni brothers, the region's undervalued early Renaissance painters who were born and worked in San Severino in the fifteenth century; they are represented by delicate and expressive frescoes detached from local churches and the wooden polyptych *The Marriage of St Catherine*.

Other works by the Salimbeni brothers adorn two of San Severino's churches. One of these, the ancient **San Lorenzo in Doliolo**, at the top of Via Salimbeni, looks slightly odd thanks to a medieval brick tower standing on top of its stone portal. The Salimbeni frescoes, illustrating the story of St Andrew, are on the vault of the tenth-century crypt, looking far older and more primitive than they really are because of their antique surroundings; the back part of the crypt is thought to be a pagan temple dating back to the time of the refugees from Septempeda (see below).

The other church – actually the old cathedral – is up in **CASTELLO**, the upper part of San Severino, a long and steep walk, although there are occasional buses from the main square. The **Duomo Vecchio** was founded in the tenth century but has a Romanesque-Gothic facade, simple Gothic cloisters, and a much rebuilt interior. Not surprisingly, it's lost a bit of atmosphere with all the reconstructions, but the baptistry vault still has its Salimbeni frescoes. Also worth a look are the inlaid choir stalls and tomb of the town's patron, St Severinus. Finds in the nearby **Museo Archeologico** on Via Castello al Monte (winter Tues–Sun 9am–1pm; summer Tues–Sun 9am–1pm & 4–7pm; €2) were excavated from the Roman valley town of Septempeda, whose inhabitants, driven out by barbarian invasions in the sixth century, escaped up here to found San Severino. Close to the old cathedral's thirteenth-century walls, sheltered by a Gothic portico, is the **Fontana dei Sette Canelle**, a seven-spouted fountain where you'll occasionally see women doing their washing.

For a congenial **place to stay** above town in the Castello, head for the *Due Torri*, Via San Francesco 21 (℡0733.645.419, ⓦ www.duetorri.it; ❷), which is run by the third generation of the Severini family; it has spotless bedrooms in an old stone wing with tiled floors and simple furnishings. There's a popular restaurant attached, which doubles as a shop, selling local delicacies, wines and spirits.

South of Macerata: the road to Sarnano

With the Sibillini mountains on the horizon, snowcapped for most of the year, the route south from Macerata towards the spa town of Sarnano ranks as one of the Marche's most beautiful. Ten kilometres along the road, on the edge of a dense wood, is the Romanesque-Gothic complex of the **Abbazia di Fiastra** (mid-June to mid-Sept daily 10am–12.30pm & 3–7pm; mid-Sept to mid-June Sat, Sun and the public holidays 10am–12.30pm & 3–5.30pm; €4 for abbey and museum), a Cistercian abbey with a simple, pantiled brick cloister and monastic quarters adjoining a grandiose aisled church. The latter is lit by an impressive rose window and contains fifteenth-century frescoes *Crucifixion with St Benedict and St Bernard*. From the typically Cistercian central cloister, doors lead into side rooms, among them the refectory, with a vaulted roof resting on seven columns borrowed from the ancient Roman colony of Urbs Salvia a few kilometres down the road. Other buildings in the complex include the eighteenth-century **Palazzo Giustiniani-Bandini**, where Wagner once stayed and whose wedding-cake facade was modelled on Buckingham Palace.

Just as interesting as the bricks and mortar is the vivid picture you get of the monks' influence on the surrounding area: it was they who first drained the marshy land back in the twelfth century and started farming here. Their huge granary, the Castello della Rancia (see p.723), can still be seen by the roadside on the way to Tolentino, giving some clue as to the size of their domain. At the height of their power there were more than two hundred monks here and the abbey was an important religious centre for three centuries. In the fifteenth century the abbey was ransacked by mercenaries but today it is once again occupied by monks who can occasionally be seen flitting across the cloister in their white hooded robes.

The abbey complex is a popular day out with a steady stream of visitors looking round the building and its grounds, now a nature reserve. The trails through the woods are a popular Sunday stroll, and you should take time to see the **Museo della Civiltà Contadina** (open summer only, same times as abbey, see above; €1 for museum or €4 for abbey and museum), a folk museum laid out in the abbey's low-vaulted outhouses. Among the agricultural and weaving equipment is a decorated wagon such as most farming families would have owned right up until the middle of the twentieth century, using it as a manure cart, a wedding carriage, or whatever form of transport was needed. For some insight into women's work, take a look at the spinning wheels and looms. Note that there's nowhere to eat here, so you might want to bring a picnic.

A five-minute bus ride away is the site of **Urbisaglia** (March to mid-June Sat, Sun & public holidays 10am–1pm & 3–6pm; mid-June to mid-Sept daily 10am–1pm & 3–7pm; mid-Sept to Feb Sat, Sun & public holidays 10am–1pm & 3–4.30pm; guided tours €2 for a single monument, €5 for three and €7 for everything). Urbs Salvia, as it was known, was one of the Marche's most important Roman towns and home to 30,000 people until it was sacked by Alaric in 409 AD. The Lourdes of its day (Urbs Salvia means "city of health"), its fame continued into the Middle Ages, when Dante invoked it as an example of a city fallen from glory in his *Paradiso*. So far an amphitheatre, theatre, baths and parts of the walls have been excavated, and frescoes of hunting scenes have been discovered in a *cryptoportico* (underpassage). The theatre was one of the largest in Italy, and could seat 12,600 spectators. The best parts of the site are scattered either side of the main road and up the hillside so it's worth paying for an English-speaking guide (find them at the main-road entrance) to take you round, particularly for their gruesome stories about fights in the amphitheatre between gladiators and bears and the re-enactments of naval battles (the arena was flooded from the cistern up in the town) in which slaves were lashed to their rowing positions so that they drowned when boats were capsized. Up in modern Urbisaglia, there's also a small **archeological museum** (same hours), visitable on the same ticket, containing finds from the site such as the egg-shaped stone omphalos, or "navel of the world", a direct copy of the Greek one at Delphi.

South of Urbisaglia, the hill-town health resort of **SAN GINESIO** is justifiably known as the balcony of the Sibillini: the panoramic view from the gardens of the Colle Ascarano, just outside the town walls, stretches from the Adriatic and Monte Conero to the Sibillini mountains and the highest of the Apennines, the Gran Sasso in Abruzzo. There's a fair amount to see in the town itself: its central piazza is dominated by one of the Marche's most unusual churches, the **Collegiata della Annunziata**, whose late-Gothic facade is decorated with filigree-like terracotta moulding. Rising above it are two campaniles, one capped by an onion dome and the other by what looks like a manicured cactus. Gothic frescoes adorn some of the chapels, and the crypt has frescoes by the Salimbeni brothers – including a pietà in which Mary looks completely demented and Christ is so covered with nail-holes that he appears to have chicken pox.

Sarnano

SARNANO, south of San Ginesio, was once a poor and virtually abandoned village. In the last couple of decades or so, however, the town has woken up to the potential of its radioactive springs, known since Roman times to have wide-ranging curative properties, and has begun to develop itself into a spa resort and weekend day-trip destination. The medieval core, coiling in concentric circles around a gentle hill, has been subtly restored, and though it's now more of a showpiece than a living village, its narrow interconnecting cobbled streets and picturesque old houses make it an ideal place for an undemanding day's wandering. On the last weekend in May until mid-June every year, an arts and crafts fair draws in the crowds, with work by Italian craftsmen on sale at scores of temporary shops/exhibition spaces in and around the historic centre.

It's worth getting a map from the **tourist office** at Lago Enrico Ricciardi 1, just off Piazza della Libertà in the new town (Mon–Fri 9am–1pm & 3–6pm, Sat 9am–1pm; ☎0733.657.144, ⓦwww.sarnano.com), before heading up through **Porta Brunforte** into old Sarnano. Just inside the gate is the fourteenth-century church of **San Francesco**, decorated with Palestinian plates, thought to have been brought to Sarnano by souvenir-collecting crusaders. On Via G. Leopardi is a fine **Pinacoteca** (summer hours yet to be decided; winter open in the mornings on request by calling the *comune* at Via Leopardi 1, ☎0733.859.911; €3), the major item being a *Madonna and Child* by Vittore Crivelli.

Continue climbing to the summit of the town and you hit **Piazza Alta**, once the political and religious centre. When Sarnano fell under papal rule in the sixteenth century, the limitation of local power made participation in public life lose its allure; eventually, in the nineteenth century, the underused fourteenth-century **Palazzo del Popolo** was converted into a theatre. It also proved increasingly difficult to ordain priors, as Rome refused to accept those chosen by the people, and the **Palazzo dei Priori** became the prison. These and the square's other medieval buildings have all been restored in recent years and are worth a look; keys are held by the *comune* (see above). At present the most interesting of the piazza's buildings is the thirteenth-century church of **Santa Maria di Piazza**, whose fifteenth-century frescoes include a figure known as the *Madonna with Angels*, for the host of celestial musicians and choristers surrounding her. The wooden statue of Christ on the altar has been saddled with one of popular tradition's strangest myths – if it's about to rain, his beard is supposed to grow. On the second Sunday in August, Santa Maria is the starting-point for Sarnano's annual medieval knees-up, or *palio* – though apart from the costumes and processions, it has more in common with a kids' sports day, featuring a tug-of-war, pole climbing, and a race in which the competitors have to balance jugs of water on their heads.

For an overnight stay, the two most affordable **hotels** in Sarnano are *Villa*, Via Rimembranza 46 (☎0733.657.218, ⓦwww.hrlavilla.com; ❶), a shuttered villa in its own substantial garden 300m uphill from the tourist office, and *Ai Pini*, Via F. Corridoni 101 (☎0733.657.183; ❶), a small, welcoming family-run hotel between the public gardens and the town car park.

Southeast of Macerata: Fermo and Porto San Giorgio

Southeast of Macerata, a short distance from the coast, is the attractive old town of **FERMO**. Its web of streets is lined with graceful medieval and Renaissance buildings, erupting out of which is a wooded peak crowned with a Romanesque-Gothic cathedral. The town's most spectacular monument, however, is hidden from view – a first-century underground complex of thirty filter beds known as the **Cisterne Romane** (winter Tues–Sun 10am–1pm & 3.30–6pm; summer Tues–Sun 10am–1pm & 3.30–7pm; €3), originally designed to supply the Roman Imperial fleet with fresh water when it docked at the nearby port. It's worth joining one of the guided tours (no additional charge) that leave Fermo's small museum every hour; the night tours are especially atmospheric (9pm, 10pm & 11pm every Thurs in July and daily from mid- to late-August). Entered from Via Aceti, off the main Piazza del Popolo, the cistern is something akin to a flooded cathedral, with its well-preserved vault and arches subtly lit and reflected in the dark, still water. If by this time you've worked up something of an appetite, make for *L'Osteria Il Frantoio* on a steep street in the medieval quarter at Via Migliorati 19, and sample various types of bruschetta, simple pasta and wood-grilled meat, local Marchiagiana cheeses and salami and carefully selected local wines. From Fermo a road descends to the resort of **PORTO SAN GIORGIO**, with a small fishing and sailing port and a long sandy beach.

The Monti Sibillini National Park

With a mountain lake reddened by the blood of the devil, a narrow pass known as the gorge of hell and a cave reputed to have been the lair of an enchantress, the **Monti Sibillini** are not only the most beautiful section of the Apennines, but they teem with ancient legends too. Wolves, chamois and brown bear all have a home in the national park and even if you don't come across one of these, you may be lucky enough to see an equally rare golden eagle instead.

The best way to experience the park is by walking, cycling or horse-riding, and if you're up for a challenge there's *Il Grande Anello dei Sibillini* (the Big Sibillini Circuit), 120km of signposted footpaths that take nine days to walk, or four to five days to cover by mountain bike. Maps and accommodation details, including several new mountain refuges, are listed on ⓦwww.sibillini.net. There are shorter trails too, through meadows filled with wild flowers, for which the most agreeable bases are the medieval hill-villages that crown the Sibillini foothills. Most villages are served by buses, but they're generally few and far between and it's best to have your own transport.

Amándola and around

The small village of **AMÁNDOLA** is fairly easy to get to on public transport, making it a good base for seeing the region. Its main sight is a new

Museo (summer daily 9.30am–12.30pm & 3.30–6.30pm; winter Tues–Fri 9.30am–12.30pm, Sat & Sun 9.30am–12.30pm & 3.30–6.30pm; €3) housed in the ex-convent of the church of San Francesco and packed full of interactive exhibits about the wildlife and legends of the park. Amándola's other attraction is an excellent week-long international **theatre festival** in the first week of September. Low on pretension and high on participation, the festival overcomes language barriers with mime and movement performances and workshops – the atmosphere is irresistible, and it's well worth sticking around for the whole week.

Otherwise, Amándola is a great place to unwind after a day's hiking in the Sibillini. It has an excellent **hostel** in a converted eighteenth-century *palazzo*, the *Casa per Ferie*, Via Indipendenza 73 (☎0736.848.598, ⓦwww.montesibillini .it; ❶; Oct–Easter for groups of 20 or more only). Also recommended is the very welcoming **B&B** 🍴 *Il Palazzo*, Via Indipendenza 59–61 (☎0736.847.082 or 0333.331.0878, ⓦwww.palazzopecci.com; ❷), in a fifteenth-century mansion two minutes' walk from the main square.

Montefortino

A few kilometres south of Amándola, the hill-village of **MONTEFORTINO** is perhaps a prettier base than Amándola though less well served by buses and touristy in season. Primarily a place to wander and admire the Sibillini views, the town also has a small **Pinacoteca** (open on request, ☎0736.859.491; free), whose chief attractions are a polyptych by Alemanno – a follower of the Crivelli who took as much delight in painting embroidery as they did – and an arresting twelfth-century portrait of a man with a pipe and candle emerging from the darkness. Appropriately, given the necromantic traditions of this area, there's also an eighteenth-century painting of Circe with her occult apparatus. A lovely place **to stay** in the historic centre is the French-owned B&B 🍴 *Tabart Inn*, Via Papiri 24 (☎0736.859.054 or 339.122.6465, ⓦwww.tabart-inn.com; ❸), a sixteenth-century house with three light, spacious and elegant beamed rooms and lovely terraces overlooking the mountains. The nicest **restaurant** is *Da Benito*, Via Tenna 9 (☎0736.859.515; closed Mon), a wonderful place in autumn to eat wild mushrooms and truffles.

Montemónaco and around

A short way south of Montefortino, **MONTEMÓNACO**, a walled medieval village of cobbled streets and yellow stone houses, is close to some of the Sibillini's most legendary sights. One, the **cave of the sibyl**, whose occupant gave her name to the mountain group, is a two-hour walk west from the village, though periodic rockfalls can block the way. The other, through the **Gola dell'Infernaccio** (Gorge of Hell), a few kilometres southwest of the village, is an easy and spectacular hike in summer. You can take a bus from Montefortino to the Infernaccio fork, from where it's a three-hour walk to the gorge along a well-defined path. The approach through a narrow valley is atmospheric: silent, except for the distant roar of the River Tenna, with memorial plaques on the cliffs at the entrance to commemorate climbers who've died scaling the walls. The path squeezes its way under jagged rocks, accompanied by the deafening sound of raging water. Once past a second bridge it forks, the lower path leading to the tranquil source of the Tenna while the upper brings you, in about half an hour, to the **Hermitage of San Leonardo**, occupied by a solitary monk.

Back down in the valley, *Agriturismo La Cittadella* (☎0736.856.361, ⓦwww .cittadelladeisibillini.it; ❷), 2.5km down an dirt road from the northern end of

Montemónaco, is a peaceful place for an overnight stay; their restaurant serves great local dishes such as *tagliatellini ai funghi porcini* (thin tagliatellie with ceps) and *coniglio in porchetta* (rabbit cooked with fennel), and you can buy apples and chestnuts in season. For local information call the *comune* at Montemónaco (℡0736.856.141) or the seasonal Pro Loco office on ℡0736.856.411. If you're going to attempt a climb up Monte Sibilla, the *Rifugio Monte Sibilla* (June to mid-July & mid- to end Sept Sat & Sun; mid-July to mid-Sept daily; ℡0736.856.422, 338.829.2399 or 338.469.0730; ❶) is the best base. It lies about 6km east of Montemónaco along the path that eventually leads to the cave of the sibyl (see opposite). As the path is only barely visible you'd be advised to take the Kompass *Monti Sibillini* map which can be bought locally.

To do the best of the Sibillini treks, however, you need to drive or take a taxi 8km east from Montemónaco to the quiet village of **FOCE**, where you can stay and eat well in the *Taverna della Montagna* (℡0736.856.327; ❶). There's also a spot to pitch a tent or park your camper for a nominal fee at the end of the village: no comforts, but magnificent views. The hike, through the **Valle del Lago di Pilato** and up to the **Lago di Pilato** (Pilate's Lake) and **Pizzo di Diavolo** (Devil's Peak), is fairly tough; allow a whole day, take the Kompass map and only attempt it in good conditions during the high summer months as the snow doesn't melt until June. Here, guarding the entrance to Umbria, stands **Monte Vettore** (2476m), the highest of the Sibillini peaks.

According to the legend of the lake, Pilate's body was dispatched from Rome on a cart pulled by two wild oxen who climbed up into the Sibillini and ditched the corpse in the water here. In the Middle Ages it became a favourite haunt for necromancers seeking dialogues with the devil – stones inscribed with occult symbols have been found on its shores. Deciding they wanted to be rid of the magicians, one night the local lords put soldiers on guard around its shores. Nothing happened until the morning, when the soldiers discovered that the lake had turned red; assuming it was with the devil's blood, they fled. What in fact turned the water red was a mass of minuscule red *Chircephalus marchesonii*, a species of fish indigenous to Asia; a shoal was stranded here millions of years ago when the sea receded, and its descendants still thrive.

Visso, Ússita and hiking territory

Close to the border with Umbria, **VISSO** (reachable by bus from Macerata) is the western gateway to the national park. A pleasant village with narrow streets bordered by medieval stone houses, Visso was more prominent back in the fifteenth and sixteenth centuries when it was at a strategic point on the route between Marche and Umbria. There's good food, including *funghi porcini* and truffles in season, to be had at *Trattoria da Richetta*, Piazza Garibaldi 7 (℡0737.972.033; closed Mon), and the **Casa del Parco** at Via Galliano 4 (June, July & Sept daily 9.30am–12.30pm & 3.30–6.30pm; August daily 9.30am–1pm & 3.30–7pm; rest of year mornings only; ℡0737.968.026, ⓦwww.sibillini.net) has information on walks and wildlife. For access to the **mountain hiking** trails, you'll need to head up the narrow valley to **ÚSSITA**, a rather anonymous winter sports resort at the foot of Monte Bove. Several walks start from the basic *Rifugio Forcella del Fargno* (June & Oct Sat only; July & Sept Sat & Sun; Aug daily; ℡0733.230.812, 330.280.690 or 338.629.5107). Among them is the ascent of the three-peaked mountain known as the **Pizzo Tre Vescovi** because it resembles three mitred bishops. The going can be tricky, as the upper peaks are covered in snow for most of the year, so you'll need a good map (Kompass 666 is the best).

If you have your own transport you can also head up to the **Santuario di Macereto** (daily 7.30am–12.30pm & 3.30–7pm; free), set on a wild, high plain above Ússita. It's no rustic chapel but an elegant Bramantesque church built in the sixteenth century as a spiritual stopover for shepherds bringing their flocks up from their winter grazing grounds in the south.

Áscoli Piceno and the coast

Áscoli Piceno owes its existence to a woodpecker that led a band of nomadic shepherds to the wedge of land between two rivers on which the city now stands. At least, that's one of the many legends to have grown up around the origins of Ascoli and the Piceni tribe for whom it is named; other versions replace the woodpecker-guide with Diomedes or the son of Saturn, and the nomadic shepherds with veterans of the Trojan War or Greek traders. Whatever the truth, the Piceni were real enough, and the relics of their civilization suggest that they were a pretty emotional and impetuous lot: writing curses on missiles, gauging grief by measuring the volume of tears, and losing a critical battle against the Romans when they interpreted an earthquake as a sign of divine wrath and abandoned the fight.

Today the Ascolani seem initially to be reserved, as if in obedience to the aphorisms urging moderation, hard work and reticence that are inscribed on many of their houses. However, one taste of the exuberance that fills the central piazza of this good-looking medieval town in the early evening is enough to dispel such an impression. If you come for Mardi Gras, you'll be able to participate in the Marche's most flamboyant carnival, while on the second Saturday in July and first Sunday in August there's the Quintana, a medieval festival that incorporates a spectacular joust.

Arrival and information

Ascoli's **train station** is just east of the town centre, ten minutes' walk along Viale Indipendenza and Corso Vittorio Emanuele. **Buses** from other towns stop outside the train station. The **tourist office** is in the centre on the ground floor of the Palazzo dei Capitani del Popolo on Piazza del Popolo (Oct–March Mon–Fri 9am–1.30pm, Tues & Thurs also 3–6pm, Sat 9am–1pm; longer hours in summer; ☎0736.253.045, ✉iat.ascolipiceno@regione.marche.it).

There's **Internet access** at the Libreria Cattolica on Piazza Arringo (Mon–Sat 8.30am–12.30pm & 4–8pm; ☎0736.259679).

Accommodation

Áscoli Piceno has enough attractions to merit an overnight stay. The most affordable option is a **youth hostel**, the *Ostello de' Longobardi*, open all year round and located in a spooky medieval tower bang in the historic centre at Via Soderini 16 (☎0736.261.862, ⓦwww.ostellionline.it; €16). A few streets away *Cantina dell'Arte*, Rua della Lupa 8 (☎0736.255.620, ⓦwww.cantinadellarte .it; ❶), is a great-value, cheerful, well-kept **hotel** with eleven small rooms and five apartments in an annexe, along with a very reasonably priced restaurant. At the other end of the price scale, *Palazzo Guiderocchi*, Via Cesare Battisti 3 (☎0736.244.011, ⓦwww.palazzoguiderocchi.com; ❹–❼), a restored palace in the old town, offers huge rooms with high ceilings and every comfort – it often has good deals in low season. *Gioli*, Viale de Gasperi 14 (☎0736.255.550; ❸), just outside the historic centre, is a smart hotel catering mostly for the business market. If you have a car, note there are good **agriturismo** places to stay

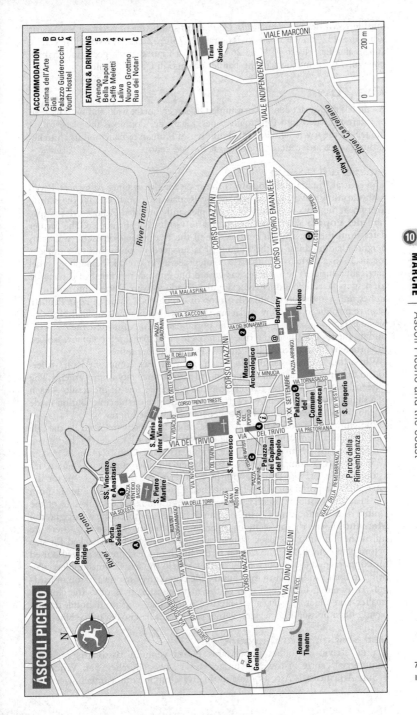

ÁSCOLI PICENO

N

ACCOMMODATION
Cantina dell'Arte	B
Gioli	D
Palazzo Guiderocchi	C
Youth Hostel	A

EATING & DRINKING
Arengo	5
Bella Napoli	3
Caffè Meletti	4
Laliva	2
Nuovo Grottino	1
Rua dei Notari	C

Roman Bridge

River Tronto

River Tronto

Porta Solestà

SS. Vincenzo e Anastasio

S. Pietro Martire

S. Maria Inter Vineas

S. Francesco

Palazzo dei Capitani del Popolo

Palazzo del Comune (Pinacoteca)

S. Gregorio

Museo Archeologica

Baptistry

Duomo

Parco della Rimembranza

Roman Theatre

Porta Gemina

Train Station

City Walls

River Castellano

VIA MALASPINA

VIA SACCONI

VIA DEI BONAPARTE

VIALE MARCONI

VIALE INDIPENDENZA

CORSO MAZZINI

CORSO VITTORIO EMANUELE

VIALE ALCIDE DE GASPERI

CORSO MAZZINI

CORSO MAZZINI

CORSO TRENTO TRIESTE

VIA DEL TRIVIO

VIA DEL TRIVIO

VIA XX SETTEMBRE

VIA TORNASACCO

VIA PRETORIANA

VIA DI VESTA

V MINUCIA

PIAZZA ARRINGO

PIAZZA DEL POPOLO

PIAZZA GIACOMINI

R DELLA LUPA

VIA DELLE CANTERINE

VIA V DIACILIO

VIA NICOLO IV

DEL TEATRO

PIAZZA A. BONFINE

PIAZZA GIOSUÈ BATTISTI

VIA MANILIA

VIA DEL FLOGRAMMARIO

VIA DELLE TORRI

PIAZZA SAN AGOSTINO

CORSO MAZZINI

VIA DINO ANGELINI

VIA F. RICCI

VIALE DELLA REMEMBRANZA

PIAZZA VENTIDIO BASSO

VIA SOLESTÀ

0   200 m

outside town, among them *Villa Cicchi*, 2km southwest of Ascoli at Via Salaria superiore 137, on the road to Rosara (☎0736.252.272, ⓦwww.villacicchi.it; ❸–❺), and *Le Sorgenti* (☎0736.263.725; ❷), a farm keeping goats and making olive oil 7km from town in the hamlet of Lago di Castel Trosino.

The Town

Ascoli has a compact centre, surrounded by largely intact walls and with its areas of interest divided into four main zones. Piazza del Popolo is the place to get the feel of the town, while its small number of Roman remains and its churches and museums are scattered throughout the old centre.

Piazza del Popolo

The central **Piazza del Popolo** is the stage for the evening *passeggiata*. Paved with gleaming travertine and flanked by Renaissance porticoes, it's the setting for two of the city's finest buildings, the pleasantly jumbled **Palazzo dei Capitani del Popolo** and the refined Romano-Gothic San Francesco. The former dates from the late twelfth century, when the free *comune* of Ascoli was at its height. That anything of the building has survived is something of a miracle, for in 1535 a certain Giambattista Quieti set it on fire to incinerate a rebel barricaded inside. The interior was gutted but enough remained of the facade for a swift facelift to suffice. Rectangular windows were slotted into medieval arches, and a grand portal affixed, on top of which sits a statue to Pope Paul III, who reintroduced peace by replacing Quieti with a neutral outsider. Not that peace lasted long; a few years after the portal had been completed, the Ascolani, finding themselves under the rule of an overbearing papal representative, solved the problem by murdering him in the sacristy of the duomo.

When they weren't slaughtering each other, at least some of Ascoli's rulers found time to collect public money in order to finance city improvements. The sixteenth-century **loggias** that enclose the piazza are one of the results – each of a slightly different width, to correspond to the size of the contribution made by the various merchants and shopkeepers who worked here.

The church of **San Francesco**, on the other hand, was financed by the sale of a Franciscan convent outside the city, after Pope Alexander IV had given the Franciscans permission to move within its walls. Construction started in 1258 but wasn't completed until 1549, when the low cupola was added. It's a somewhat restrained church, with little to seize the attention except for the intricate west portal on Via del Trivio, but a good place to take a break from the heat and bustle of Ascoli's narrow streets. Adjoining the south side of the church and overlooking Corso Mazzini is the sixteenth-century **Loggia dei Mercanti**. Formerly the scene of commercial wheeling and dealing, there are still niches cut into the back wall in which bricks could be checked for size before being purchased. The cloister to the north of the church is now also used for commerce as the site of a daily market, where the female smallholders who bring in their produce from the countryside could give anyone a lesson in hard-sell. An opening in the end wall of the main cloister gives onto the church's smaller and older cloister, a far prettier place that remains tranquil, despite having been pressed into service as the garden of a Fascist-era office block.

San Vincenzo and around

Via del Trivio continues up towards Piazza Ventidio Basso, the medieval commercial centre of town, of interest for its two churches. **San Vincenzo e San Anastasio** is Ascoli's most distinctive church, with a fifteenth-century chessboard facade that was once filled out with frescoes. Beneath the mainly eleventh-century body of the building is a primitive crypt erected over a spring that was supposed to have leprosy-curing properties. Although the plunge bath is still there, the spring was diverted elsewhere in the last century.

Across the square, **San Pietro Martire** is a far less appealing building, erected by Dominican monks in the thirteenth century in order not to be outdone by their Franciscan rivals down the road. It's as austere and intimidating as Saint Peter the Martyr himself, who, between founding Dominican communities like that at Ascoli, gained such a reputation as a persecutor of religious sects that he became the patron of inquisitors after his murder by a couple of so-called heretics.

The dark **Via Soderini**, leading west out of the square, forms the spine of Ascoli's riverside medieval quarter. Lined with buildings out of which the occasional defensive tower sprouts, it's an evocative street, giving a clear idea of how rigorously the town was defended. Tiny streets fan out from it, many of them spanned by covered passages that in times of siege served as escape routes and as stations from which to pour oil down onto the heads of attackers. Of the defensive tower houses, one of the best preserved is the **Palazzetto Longobardi**, a virtually windowless twelfth-century building, now converted into a youth hostel (see p.730).

After exploring the quarter you can cut through to the river and the thirteenth-century gate, the **Porta Solestà**, from which one of Italy's largest and most impressively preserved **Roman bridges** spans the river. An underpassage tunnels through it, which unfortunately has flooded with water and is currently being restored, though groups can visit by arrangement at the tourist office. It's worth trying this if you can, as much for the uncanny experience of walking across an unseen river with traffic crossing just above your head as for the opportunity to examine colossal Roman masonry at close quarters.

San Gregorio and around
There's little else of Roman Ascoli to see, except some sparse remains of a **Roman theatre**, on the southwest edge of town, close to the Roman **Porta Gemina**, or twin gate, at the beginning of the road to Rome. From the theatre a road leads up to the **Parco della Rimembranza**, for a great rooftop view of the town, and on to the steep and picturesque **Via Pretoriana**, whose small craft shops make it a good hunting ground for gifts. Close by, the fourteenth-century church of **San Gregorio** was ingeniously built around the remains of a Roman temple. Incorporated into the facade are two lofty Corinthian columns, originally imported by the Romans from Greece, and patches of *opus reticulatum* (diamond brickwork). In the adjoining convent is a tiny revolving door with the inscription *Qui si depositano gli innocenti* ("Here you deposit the innocent"), designed so that parents could remain anonymous when leaving unwanted children to the care of priests and nuns.

The Duomo, Pinacoteca and Museo Archeologico
With the pregnant caryatids on the facade of the **Palazzo del Comune** overlooked by the pompous **duomo**, **Piazza Arringo** is a testimony to the flamboyance of Ascoli's Baroque architects. However, as the duomo shelters what is reckoned to be Carlo Crivelli's best work, and the Palazzo del Comune is one of the Marche's best art galleries, the square's eccentric architecture does have its positive side.

The duomo's flashy interior holds chandeliers suspended on strings of illuminated beads, an apse painted with a fake Persian carpet, gaudily gilded pillar capitals and vault ribs, and a cupola decorated with late nineteenth-century frescoes of obscure Ascolani saints. In the midst of this, the **Crivelli polyptych**, in the Cappella del Sacramento, is worth seeking out. Even if his penchant for rarefied opulence isn't to your taste, this work's style and psychological insight are impressive. The most arresting of the ten panels is the central pietà, in which the haggard expression of Mary, the torment that distorts Christ's face, and the Magdalene's horror as she examines the wound in his hand are given heightened impact by the strict semicircular composition.

The **Pinacoteca Civica** in the Palazzo Comunale (daily 9am–1pm & 3–7pm; €5) contains other pieces by Crivelli, and though they are in poor condition and not as sophisticated as the duomo's polyptych, they are engaging nonetheless. One shows the sprawling baby Christ, chin in hand, apparently mesmerized by an apple. Pietro Alemanno, Crivelli's follower, contributes an *Annunciation* featuring a view of medieval Ascoli bristling with towers, and there are also a few foreign works, most notably a *Portrait of a Woman* by Van Dyck.

If you want to know more about ancient Ascoli, visit the evocative **Museo Archeologico** (Tues–Sun 8.30am–7.30pm; €2), across the square. The collection includes Piceni projectiles inscribed with curses against their Roman enemies, jewellery, heavy bronze rings that were placed on the stomachs of dead women, and small test-tube-like containers used to assess the quality of grief by measuring the volume of tears.

Eating and drinking

You don't have to spend a lot to **eat** well in Ascoli, particularly at ⚑ *Trattoria dell'Arengo*, Via Tornasacco 5 (℡333.471.3333; closed Mon) off Piazza Arringo, which serves hearty local food such as wild boar, mushrooms and a mixed grill of meats and vegetables. There's no written menu but they'll tell you (in English) the specials of the day that might include *pasta al ceppo* (shaped in the old days around a knitting needle) with tomato and ham. The lively *Bella Napoli*, Via Bonaparte 18–20 (evenings only, closed Thurs), is the town's best pizzeria, while Ascoli's most imaginative cooking is at ⚑ *Trattoria Laliva*, Piazza della Viola 13 (℡0736.259.358; closed Tues eve & Wed), where chef Marinella Filiponia offers a modern take on Marchegiana cuisine with dishes such as *Le Sibille*, lasagna baked with parma ham, herbs, artichokes and chilli, and, her latest innovation, sugar candied olives (which taste a lot better than you might imagine). *Trattoria Nuovo Grottino*, Piazza Ventidio Basso 2, is a popular neighbourhood place for grilled meat (they also do a good tagliatelle with *funghi porcini*). Alternatively, for more refined cuisine, try *Ristorante Rua dei Notari*, Via Cesare Battisti 3 (closed Thurs). For a **drink**, there are many places to linger over a coffee or a cocktail in Piazza del Popolo. Among them is the famous Art Nouveau-style *Caffè Meletti* that makes its own superb *amaro* and anisette and is lined with mahogany cases filled with obscure bottles.

The Áscoli coast

Easily accessible by bus or train from Áscoli Piceno, **SAN BENEDETTO DEL TRONTO** is the most extravagant of the Marche's resorts. Known as the "Riviera delle Palme" for the five thousand palms that shade its promenade, and with 6km of sandy white beach, it makes a nice break on a hot afternoon if you're in Ascoli and fancy a swim. There are around 120 **hotels**, details of which are available on the database at ⓦwww.turismo.marche.it or from the **tourist office** on Viale delle Tamerici (Mon, Wed & Fri 9am–1pm, Tues & Thurs 9am–1pm & 3–6pm, Sun 9am–noon; ℡0735.592.237, ℮iat.sanbenedetto@regione.marche.it). Note that most places insist on full board in August.

GROTTAMARE, a few minutes further up the coastal rail line, is a lower-key resort on the same model, but without San Benedetto's panache. If you have a car head instead the 8km inland to *La Campana*, at Contrada Menocchia 39, 6km from the hill-town of Montefiore d'Aso (☎0734.939.012, ⓦwww.lacampana .it; ❸–❺), an agriturismo complex made up of a farm that breeds sheep and rabbits, and old stone buildings containing guest rooms. The swimming pool is on a terrace overlooking the Adriatic, while meals (bed and breakfast from May to December, full board from late-July to late-August) are made from home-produced vegetables, meat, cheese and buttermilk.

Travel details

Trains

Ancona to: Bologna (32 daily; 1hr 55min); Jesi (18 daily; 25min); Loreto (16 daily; 20min); Porto San Giorgio (24 daily; 30–45min); Rome (10 daily; 3–4hr); San Benedetto (29 daily; 1hr 10min); Senigallia (33 daily; 20–25min).
Áscoli Piceno to: San Benedetto del Tronto (16 daily; 35min–1hr).
Macerata to: San Severino Marche (15 daily; 25–45min); Tolentino (15 daily; 20min).
Pésaro to: Ancona (39 daily; 35–50min); Fabriano (17 daily; 1hr 30min–2hr 30min).

Buses

All services are much reduced on Sundays and public holidays. Extra buses may be provided in high summer to seaside resorts.
Amándola to: Áscoli Piceno (4 daily Mon–Sat; 1hr 10min); Fermo (4 daily; 1hr); Montefortino (5 daily; 10min); Montemónaco (5 daily; 20–25min); Porto San Giorgio (4 daily; 1hr 15min); Sarnano (7 daily; 30min).
Ancona to: Jesi (25 daily; 45min); Loreto (6 daily Mon–Sat; 1hr 20min); Macerata (10 daily; 1hr 30min); Numana (16 daily, 9 on Sun; 40min); Porto Recanati (5 daily Mon–Sat; 1hr 5min); Portonovo (mid-June–Aug every 20min; 25–30min); Sirolo (16 daily, 9 on Sun; 35min).
Áscoli Piceno to: Amándola (4 daily Mon–Sat; 1hr 10min); Montefortino (5 daily Mon–Sat; 1hr 20min); Montemónaco (5 daily Mon–Sat; 1hr 30min); Rome

(5 daily; 3hr); San Benedetto del Tronto (every 30min; hourly on Sun; 1hr).
Macerata to: Abbazia di Fiastra and Urbisaglia (12 daily; 10min); Amándola (6 daily; 1hr 15–20min); Ancona (10 daily; 1hr 30min); Loreto (10 daily; 50min); Naples (1 daily; 5hr 30min); Porto Recanati (11 daily; 1hr); Recanati (11 daily; 35min); Rome (5 daily; 4hr); San Severino (5 daily; 35min); Sarnano (12 daily; 55min–1hr 25min); Tolentino (12 daily; 30min); Visso (5 daily; 1hr 45min).
Pésaro to: Fabriano (3 daily; 2hr); Fano (approximately every 30min; 15min); Gradara (hourly; 55min); Sassocorvaro (5 daily; 1hr); Torrette (7 daily; 15min); Urbino (10 daily Mon–Fri, 6 Sun; 1hr).
Porto San Giorgio to: Fermo (every 30min; 15–20min).
San Leo to: Rimini (2 daily; 45min).
Urbino to: Fano (8 daily; 1hr 10–15min); Pésaro (11 daily Mon–Fri; 6 Sun; 1hr).

International ferries

Ancona to: Durazzo, Albania (3 weekly; 18 hr); Bar, Montenegro (1 weekly June–Sept; 15hr); Zadar/ Bozara, Hvar/Bol and Split, Stari Gad and Korcula in Croatia (summer 4–5 weekly; winter 2 weekly; ferry from 8–9hr; catamaran from 3hr); Igoumenitsa (at least 1 daily; 15hr 30min); Patras (at least 1 daily; 21hr); Çesme, Turkey (April–Nov 1 weekly, Sat departure; 43–55hr).

⑪

Rome and Lazio

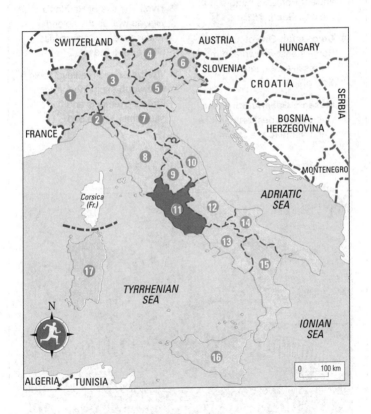

CHAPTER 11

Highlights

* **Capitoline Museums** The august and impressive home of some of Rome's finest ancient sculpture and paintings. See p.758

* **Pantheon** The most complete ancient Roman structure in the city. See p.761

* **Colosseum** One of ancient Rome's best-known and most impressive monuments. See p.780

* **Museo e Galleria Borghese** One of city's best art galleries – and home to the cream of the work of the city's favourite sculptor, Bernini. See p.784

* **Vatican Museums** Quite simply the largest and richest collection of art in the world. See p.795

* **Tivoli** The site of Hadrian's villa, as well as the splendid landscaped gardens of Villa d'Este. See p.811

* **Viterbo** An old medieval town well worth exploring for its Etruscan remains and museums. See p.820

△ St Peter's Square, the Vatican

Rome and Lazio

Rome is the most fascinating city in Italy, which makes it arguably the most fascinating city in the world. An ancient place packed with the relics of over two thousand years of inhabitation, you could spend a month here and still only scratch the surface. Yet it's so much more than an open-air museum: its culture, its food, its people make up a modern, vibrant city that would be worthy of a visit irrespective of its past. As a historic place, it is special enough; as a contemporary European capital, it is utterly unique.

Evenly placed between north and south, Rome is perhaps the perfect Italian capital. Former heart of the mighty Roman Empire, and still the home of the papacy, Rome is seen as a place somewhat apart from the rest of the country, spending money made elsewhere on the bloated government machine. Romans, the thinking seems to go, are a lazy lot, not to be trusted and living very nicely off the fat of the rest of the land. For the traveller of course, this is much less evident than the sheer weight of history that the city supports. First, of course, are Rome's classical features, most visibly the Colosseum, and the Forum and Palatine Hill; but from here there's an almost uninterrupted sequence of monuments – from early Christian basilicas and Romanesque churches to Renaissance palaces and the fountains and churches of the Baroque period, which perhaps more than any other era has determined the look of the city today. There is the modern epoch, too, from the ponderous neoclassical architecture of the post-Unification period to the self-publicizing edifices of the Mussolini years. These various eras crowd in on one another to an almost overwhelming degree: there are medieval churches atop ancient basilicas above Roman palaces, houses and apartment blocks that incorporate fragments of eroded Roman columns, carvings and inscriptions, roads and piazzas which follow the lines of ancient amphitheatres and stadiums.

All of this means that the capital is not an easy place to absorb on one visit, and you need to take things slowly, even if you only have a few days here. Most of the city's sights can be approached from a variety of directions, and it's part of Rome's allure to stumble across things by accident, gradually piecing together the whole, rather than marching around to a timetable on a predetermined route.

Beyond Rome, the region of **Lazio** inevitably pales in comparison, with relatively few centres of note and a landscape that varies from the gently undulating green hills of its northern reaches to the more inhospitable mountains to the south and east. It's a relatively poor region, its lack of identity the butt of a number of Italian jokes, and it's the closest you'll get to the feel of the Italian south without catching the train to Naples. Much, however, can be easily seen on a day-trip from the capital, not least the ancient sites of **Ostia Antica** and the Roman Emperor Hadrian's villa at **Tivoli** – two of the area's

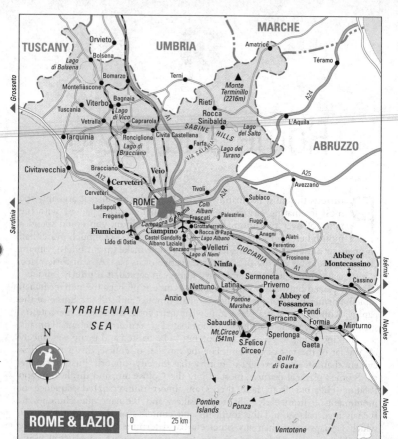

most important ancient sites. Further afield, in the north of Lazio, the Etruscan sites of **Tarquinia** and **Cerveteri** provide the most obvious tourist focus, and are again just about visitable on a day-trip, but you'd do better to use the pleasant provincial town of **Viterbo** as a base. Romans, meanwhile, head out at weekends to soak up the gentle beauty of lakes **Bracciano**, **Vico** and **Bolsena**. The region east of Rome is sparsely populated and poor, though scenically appealing, its high hills unfolding beyond the rather dull regional centre of **Rieti**. The south arguably holds Lazio's most appealing enclaves, and you might want to beat a leisurely path to Naples via small towns like **Anzio** and **Nettuno** (although these are again easily accessible on day-trips, and make the best places to swim while based in the capital). The coast beyond is home to unpretentious resorts like **Terracina** and **Sperlonga** – relatively unknown outside Italy; and the island of **Ponza**, accessible from Terracina and **Formia**, further down the coast, is – out of season at least – one of the most alluring spots on the entire western seaboard. Inland, much is mountainous and fairly inaccessible, but that's part of its appeal: the monasteries at **Subiaco** and **Montecassino** are just two worthwhile stops on what might be a rewarding and original route south.

Roman cooking is traditionally dominated by the earthy cuisine of the working classes, with a little influence from the city's centuries-old Jewish population thrown in. Although you'll find all sorts of pasta served in Roman restaurants, spaghetti is common, as is the local speciality of *bucatini* or thick-cut spaghetti (sometimes called *tonarelli*), as they stand up well to the coarse, gutsy sauces the Romans prefer: *aglio e olio* (garlic and oil), *cacio e pepe* (pecorino and ground black pepper), *alla carbonara* (with beaten eggs, cubes of pan-fried *guanciale* – cured pork jowl – or bacon, and pecorino or parmesan), and *alle vongole* (with baby clams). Fish is an integral, though usually pricey, part of Roman cuisine, and features most frequently in Rome as salt cod – *baccalà*; best eaten Jewish-style, deep-fried. Offal is also key, and although it has been ousted from many of the more refined city-centre restaurants, you'll still find it on the menus of more traditional places, especially those in Testaccio. Most favoured is *pajata*, the intestines of an unweaned calf, but you'll also find *lingua* (tongue), *rognone* (kidney), *milza* (spleen) – delicious as a paté on toasted bread) and *trippa* (tripe). Look out too for *coda alla vaccinara*, oxtail stewed in a rich sauce of tomato and celery; *testerelle d'abbacchio*, lamb's head baked in the oven with herbs and oil; and *coratella*, lamb's heart, liver, lungs and spleen cooked in olive oil with lots of black pepper and onions. More conventional meat dishes include *abbacchio*, milk-fed lamb roasted to melting tenderness with rosemary, sage and garlic; *scottadito*, grilled lamb chops eaten with the fingers; and *saltimbocca alla romana*, thin slices of veal cooked with a slice of prosciutto and sage on top. Artichokes (*carciofi*) are the quintessential Roman vegetable, served *alla romana* (stuffed with garlic and roman mint and stewed) and in all their unadulterated glory as *alla giudea* – flattened and deep fried in olive oil. Another not-to-be-missed side dish is *fiori di zucca* – batter-fried courgette blossom, stuffed with mozzarella and a sliver of marinated anchovy. Roman pizza has a thin crust and is best when baked in a wood-burning oven (*a legna*), but you can also find lots of great pizza by the slice (*pizza al taglio*), always sold by weight.

    Wine comes mainly from the Castelli Romani (most famously Frascati) to the south, and from around Montefiascone (Est! Est! Est!) in the north. Both are basic, straightforward whites, fine for sunny lunchtimes but otherwise not all that noteworthy. However, in most places you'll find a complete selection of Italy's best and most famous wines.

Rome

You won't enjoy Rome if you spend most of your time trying to tick off sights. However, there are some places that it would be a pity to leave the city without seeing. The **Vatican** is perhaps the most obvious one, most notably **St Peter's** and the amazing stock of loot in the Vatican Museums; and the star attractions of the ancient city – the **Forum** and **Palatine**, the **Colosseum**, Nero's **Domus Aurea** – are worth a day or two in their own right. There are also the churches, fountains and works of art from the period that can be said to most define Rome, the Baroque, and in particular the works of Borromini and Bernini, whose efforts compete for space and attention throughout the city. Bernini was responsible for the Fountain of the Four Rivers in the city's most famous square, **Piazza Navona**, among other things; but arguably his best sculptural work is in the **Galleria Borghese**, or in various churches, like his statue of St Theresa in Santa Maria in Vittoria. Borromini, his great rival at the time, built the churches of San Carlo alle Quattro Fontane and Sant'Ivo, both buildings intricately squeezed into small sites – Borromini's trademark. There are other great palaces that are themselves treasure troves of great art, like the **Doria-Pamphilj** and **Palazzo Barberini**; and unmissable museums, like the august galleries of the Capitoline, and the main collections of the **Museo Nazionale Romano** in the Palazzo Altemps and Palazzo Massimo, all of which hold staggering and beautifully displayed collections of the cream of the city's ancient art and sculpture. And finally there's the city beneath all this: stroll through the *centro storico* in the early morning, through Trastevere at sunset, or gaze down at the roofs and domes from the Janiculum Hill on a clear day, and you'll quickly realize that there's no place in Italy like it.

Some history

Rome's early **history** is caked with legend. Rea Silvia, a vestal virgin and daughter of a local king, Numitor, had twin sons – the product, she alleged, of a rape by Mars. The two boys were abandoned and found by a wolf, who nursed them until their adoption by a shepherd, who named them **Romulus and Remus**. As they grew into manhood, under the protection of the gods, they became leaders in the small community, and later laid out the boundaries of the city on the Palatine Hill. However, it soon became apparent that there was only room for one ruler, and they quarrelled, Romulus killing Remus and becoming in 753 BC the city's first **monarch**, to be followed by six further kings.

The Roman Republic and Empire

Whatever the truth of this story, there's no doubt that Rome was an obvious spot to build a city: the Palatine and Capitoline hills provided security, and there was, of course, the river Tiber, which could easily be crossed here by way of the Isola. Rome as a kingdom lasted until about 507 BC, when the people rose up against the tyrannical King Tarquinius and established a **Republic**. The city prospered, growing greatly in size and subduing the various tribes of the surrounding areas: the **Etruscans** to the north, the **Sabines** to the east, the **Samnites** to the south. By the time it had fought and won the third Punic War against its principal rival, **Carthage**, in 146 BC, it had become the dominant power in the Mediterranean.

The history of the Republic was, however, also one of **internal strife**, marked by factional fighting among the patrician ruling classes, and the ordinary people, or plebeians, enjoying little more justice than they had under the Roman monarchs. This all came to a head in 44 BC, when **Julius Caesar**, having proclaimed himself dictator, was murdered by conspirators concerned at the growing concentration of power into one man's hands. A brief period of turmoil ensued, giving way, in 27 BC, to the founding of the **Empire** under **Augustus** – a triumph for the new democrats over the old guard. Augustus heaved Rome into the Imperial era: he was determined to turn the city – as he claimed – from one of stone to one of marble, building arches, theatres and monuments of a magnificence suited to the capital of an expanding empire. Under Augustus, and his successors, the city swelled to a population of a million or more, its people housed in cramped apartment blocks or *insulae*; crime in the city was rife, and the traffic problem apparently on a par with today's, leading one contemporary writer to complain that the din on the streets made it impossible to get a good night's sleep. But it was a time of peace and prosperity too, with the empire's borders being ever more extended, reaching their maximum limits under the Emperor Trajan, who died in 117 AD. This period constitutes the heyday of the Roman Empire, a time that the historian Gibbon called "the happiest times in the history of humanity".

The **decline of Rome** is hard to date precisely, but it could be said to have started with the Emperor Diocletian, who assumed power in 284 and divided the empire into two parts, east and west. The first Christian emperor, **Constantine**, shifted the seat of power to Byzantium in 330, and Rome's period as capital of the world was over; the wealthier members of the population moved east and a series of invasions by Goths in 410 and Vandals about forty years later served only to quicken the city's ruin. By the sixth century Rome was a devastated and infection-ridden shadow of its former self.

The Papal City

After the fall of the empire, the **pope** – based in Rome owing to the fact that St Peter (the Apostle and first pope) was martyred here in 64 AD – became the temporal ruler over much of Italy, and it was the papacy, under Pope **Gregory I** ("the Great") in 590, that rescued Rome from its demise. By sending missions all over Europe to spread the word of the Church and publicize its holy relics, he drew pilgrims, and their money, back to the city, in time making the papacy the natural authority in Rome. The pope took the name "Pontifex Maximus" after the title of the high priest of classical times (literally "the keeper of the bridges", which were vital to the city's wellbeing). The crowning a couple of centuries later of **Charlemagne** as Holy Roman Emperor, with dominions spread Europe-wide but answerable to the pope, intensified the city's revival, and the pope and city became recognized as head of the Christian world.

There were times over the next few hundred years when the power of Rome and the papacy was weakened as disputes between the city and the papacy led to a series of popes relocating to Viterbo; in 1308 the French-born Pope **Clement V** transferred his court to Avignon, while in the mid-fourteenth century **Cola di Rienzo** seized power, setting himself up as the people's saviour and forming a new Roman republic. But the increasingly autocratic ways of the new ruler soon lost popularity; Cola di Rienzo was deposed, and in 1376 Pope **Gregory XI** returned to Rome. As time went on, power gradually became concentrated in a handful of **families**, who swapped the top jobs, including the papacy itself, between them. Under the burgeoning power of the pope, the city began to take on a new aspect: churches were built, the city's pagan monuments rediscovered and preserved, and artists began to arrive in Rome to work on commissions for the latest pope, who would invariably try to outdo his predecessor's efforts with ever more glorious buildings and works of art. This process reached a head during the Renaissance; Bramante, Raphael and Michelangelo all worked in the city throughout their careers, and the reigns of **Pope Julius II**, and his successor, **Leo X**, were something of a golden age – the city was once again the centre of cultural and artistic life. However, in 1527 all this was brought abruptly to an end, when the armies of the Habsburg monarch, Charles V, swept into the city, occupying it for a year, while Pope **Clement VII** cowered in the Castel Sant'Angelo.

The ensuing years were ones of yet more restoration, and perhaps because of this it's the **seventeenth century** that has left the most tangible impression on Rome today, the vigour of the **Counter-Reformation** throwing up huge sensational monuments like the Gesù church that were designed to confound the scepticism of the new Protestant thinking. This period also saw the completion of St Peter's under **Paul V**, and the ascendancy of Gian Lorenzo

Bernini as the city's principal architect and sculptor. The **eighteenth century** witnessed the decline of the papacy as a political force, a phenomenon marked by the seventeen-year occupation of the city in 1798 by Napoleon, after which, papal rule was restored.

The post-Unification city

Thirty-four years later a pro-Unification caucus under **Mazzini** declared the city a republic but was soon chased out, and Rome had to wait until troops stormed the walls in 1870 to join the unified country – symbolically the most important part of the Italian peninsula to do so. "Roma o morte", **Garibaldi** had cried, and he wasted no time in declaring the city the capital of the new kingdom – under **Vittorio Emanuele II** – and confining the by now quite powerless pontiff, **Pius IX**, to the Vatican until agreement was reached on a way to coexist. The Piemontese rulers of the new kingdom set about building a city fit to govern from, cutting new streets through Rome's central core (Via Nazionale, Via del Tritone) and constructing grandiose buildings like the Altar of the Nation. **Mussolini** took over in 1922, and in 1929 signed the **Lateran Pact** with Pope **Pius XI**, a compromise which forced the Vatican to accept the new Italian state and in return recognized the Vatican City as sovereign territory, independent of Italy, together with the key basilicas and papal palaces in Rome – these remain technically independent of Italy to this day.

The contemporary city

During **World War II**, Mussolini famously made Rome his centre of operations, making declamatory speeches to the crowds from the balcony of the Palazzo Venezia until his resignation as leader in July 1943. The city was eventually liberated by Allied forces in June 1944. The Italian republic since then has been a mixed affair, changing its government (if not its leaders) every few months until a series of scandals forced the old guard from office. Since then things have continued in much the same vein, with the city symbolizing, to the rest of the country at least, the inertia of their nation's government. In spite of this the city's growth has been phenomenal, its population soaring to getting on for four million, with a marked increase in its immigrant numbers. Depite being famous in the Sixties as the home of Fellini's *Dolce Vita* and Italy's bright young things, it is still a relatively provincial place, by northern Italian standards at least. However, changes to the city made for the jubilee year of 2000 mean it is looking sprucer, and more vibrant, than it has done for some time, and there are even plans afoot to deal with the city centre's chronic traffic problem, with the construction of a third metro line well under way and other improvements in progress. In short, the city is more cosmopolitan (and more expensive) than ever before, and despite the crowds, which seem to increase every year, there's never been a better time to visit.

Arrival

Rome has two **airports**: Leonardo da Vinci, better known as Fiumicino, which handles the majority of scheduled flights, and Ciampino, where you'll arrive if you're travelling with one of the low-cost airlines or on a charter flight. **Taxis** to the city centre from Fiumicino cost €40 and Ciampino €30 and take 20–30 minutes and 30–40 minutes respectively. Otherwise the public transport connections are reasonable. **Fiumicino** is linked to the centre of Rome by direct trains, which take thirty minutes to get to Termini and cost €11; services begin at 6.35am and then leave half-hourly until 11.35pm. Alternatively, there are more frequent but slower trains to Ostiense and Tiburtina stations, each on the edge of the city centre; tickets to these stations cost €5 and Tiburtina and Ostiense are both stops on Rome's metro (see below). There are no direct connections between the city centre and **Ciampino**, and if you're travelling with one of the low-cost airlines the best thing you can do is take the *Terravision* shuttle bus, timed to coincide with arrivals and departures to Termini (€8 single, €14 return). Otherwise ATRAL buses run from the airport to the Anagnina metro station, at the end of line #A, every forty minutes (€1), from where it's a twenty-minute ride into the centre (a further €1).

Travelling by **train** from most places in Italy, or indeed Europe, you arrive at **Stazione Termini**, centrally placed for all parts of the city and meeting-point of the two metro lines and many city-bus routes. There are **left-luggage** facilities here, by platform 1 and platform 24 (daily 7am–midnight; €2.50–3 per piece). As for **other train stations** in Rome, Tiburtina is a stop for some north–south intercity trains; selected routes around Lazio are handled by the Regionali platforms of Stazione Termini (a further five-minute walk beyond the end of the regular platforms); and there's also the Roma-Nord line station on Piazzale Flaminio, which runs to Viterbo.

Arriving by **bus** can leave you in any one of a number of places around the city. The main station for trains from outside the Rome region is Tiburtina. Others include Ponte Mammolo (trains from Tivoli and Subiaco); Lepanto (Cerveteri, Civitavecchia, Bracciano area); EUR Fermi (Nettuno, Anzio, southern Lazio coast); Anagnina (Castelli Romani); Saxa Rubra (Viterbo and around). All of these stations are on a metro line, except Saxa Rubra, which is on the Roma-Nord line and connected by trains every fifteen minutes with the station at Piazzale Flaminio, on metro line A.

Coming into the city by **road** can be quite confusing. If you are on the A1 highway coming from the north take the exit "Roma Nord"; from the south, follow exit "Roma Est". Both lead you to the Grande Raccordo Anulare, which circles the city and is connected with all the major arteries into the city centre.

City transport

Like most Italian cities, even the larger ones, the best way to get around Rome is to **walk**. Rome wasn't built for motor traffic, and it shows in the congestion. Despite that, its ATAC-run **bus service** is on the whole pretty good – cheap, reliable and as quick as the clogged streets allow. There are also four **tram** lines, and Rome's **metro** operates from 5.30am to 11.30pm, although its two lines cater more for commuters from the suburbs than tourists in the city centre. Nonetheless, there are a few useful city-centre stations: Termini is the hub of both lines, and there are stops at the Colosseum, Piazza Barberini and Pizza di Spagna. When the buses and the metro stop – at around midnight – a network of **night buses** comes into service, accessing most parts of the city and operating until about 5am; they are easily identified by the owl symbol above the *bus notturno* schedule.

Flat-fare **tickets** on all forms of transport currently cost €1 each and are good for any number of bus rides and one metro ride within 75 minutes of validating them – bus tickets should be stamped in machines on board the bus. You can buy tickets from *tabacchi*, newsstands and ticket machines located in all metro stations and at major bus stops, as well as from machines on the buses themselves. If you're using transport extensively it's worth getting a **season ticket**: either a day pass (BIG), valid on all city transport until midnight of the day purchased, for €4; a three-day pass for €11 (BTI) or a seven-day pass (CIS) for €16. Ⓦ www.atac.roma.it has more information, some in English.

The easiest way to get a **taxi** is to find the nearest taxi stand (*fermata dei taxi*) – central ones include Termini, Piazza Venezia, Largo Argentina, Piazza San Silvestro, Piazza di Spagna and Piazza Barberini. Alternatively, you can simply

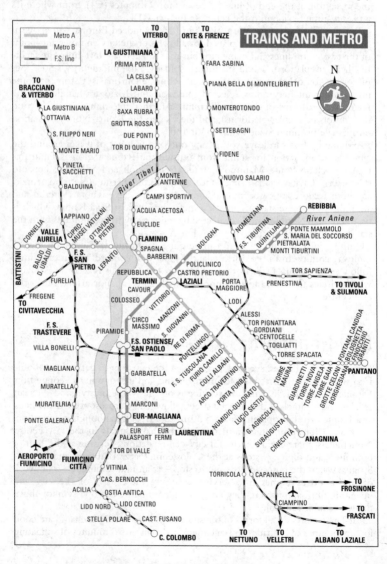

⓫

ROME AND LAZIO | City transport

call a taxi (☎06.3570, 06.4157, 06.6645, 06.8822 or 06.5551), but bear in mind that these usually cost more, as the meter starts ticking the moment the taxi is dispatched to collect you. Most cabs are white, and a journey from one side of the city centre to the other should cost around €10, or around €15 on Sunday or at night. Note that all taxis carry a rate card in English giving the current tariff.

Useful transport routes

Buses

#23 Piazza Clodio–Piazza Risorgimento–Ponte Vittorio Emanuele II–Ponte Garibaldi–Via Marmorata–Piazzale Ostiense–Centrale Montemartini–Basilica di S. Paolo.

#40 (Express) Termini–Via Nazionale–Piazza Venezia–Largo Argentina–Piazza Pia.

#64 Termini–Piazza della Repubblica–Via Nazionale–Piazza Venezia–Largo Argentina–Corso Vittorio Emanuele II–Stazione S. Pietro.

#175 Termini–Piazza Barberini–Via del Corso–Piazza Venezia–Colosseo–Circo Massimo–Aventine–Stazione Ostiense.

#492 Stazione Tiburtina–Piazzale Verano–Termini–Piazza Barberini–Via del Corso–Piazza Venezia–Largo Argentina–Corso del Rinascimento–Piazza Cavour–Piazza Risorgimento–Cipro.

#660 Largo Colli Albani–Via Appia Nuova–Via Appia Pignatelli–Via Appia Antica.

#714 Termini–Santa Maria Maggiore–Via Merulana–San Giovanni in Laterano–Viale Terme di Caracalla–EUR.

#910 Termini–Piazza della Repubblica–Via Piemonte–Via Pinciana (Villa Borghese)–Piazza Euclide–Palazzetto dello Sport–Piazza Mancini.

Minibuses

These **small buses** negotiate circular routes through the narrow streets of Rome's centre.

#116 Porta Pinciana–Via Veneto–Via del Tritone–Piazza di Spagna–Piazza San Silvestro–Corso Rinascimento–Campo de'Fiori–Piazza Farnese–Lungotevere Sangallo–Terminal Gianicolo.

#117 San Giovanni in Laterano–Piazza Celimontana–Via Due Macelli–Via del Babuino–Piazza del Popolo–Via del Corso–Piazza Venezia–Via Nazionale–Via dei Serpenti–Colosseo–Via Labicana.

#119 Piazza del Popolo–Via del Corso–Piazza Venezia–Largo Argentina–Via del Tritone–Piazza Barberini–Via Veneto–Porta Pinciana–Piazza Barberini–Piazza di Spagna–Via del Babuino–Piazza del Popolo.

Trams

#3 Stazione Trastevere–Via Marmorata–Piramide–Circo Massimo–Colosseum–San Giovanni–San Lorenzo–Via Nomentana–Parioli–Viale Belle Arti.

#8 Casaletto–Stazione Trastevere–Piazza Mastai–Viale Trastevere–Largo Argentina.

#19 Porto Maggiore–Piazzale Verano–Viale Regina Margherita–Viale Belle Arti–Via Flaminia–Ottaviano–Piazza Risorgimento.

Line #110

Good for general orientation and a quick glance at the sights is the ATAC-run **#110 tour bus** with guided commentary. It leaves from Stazione Termini and stops at all the major sights, including Piazza di Spagna, Castel Sant'Angelo, the Vatican and Appia Antica. The whole round trip takes about two hours. In summer, departures are every half-hour from 9am until 8pm daily, including holidays and Sundays. Tickets cost €13 and allow you to hop on and off throughout the day.

Passes

You can visit the three main museums that make up the **Museo Nazionale Romano** on one ticket, valid for seven days, which costs €7, and is available from any of the three locations – Palazzo Altemps, Palazzo Massimo and the Museo delle Terme di Diocleziano. The **Roma Pass** (℡06.8205.9127, ⓦwww.romapass.it) costs €20 and is valid for 3 days. Available from major sights and tourist information kiosks, it entitles you to travel for free on buses, trams and the metro, free admission to two and reduced entry to quite a few of the city's major sights and museums, and, perhaps most importantly, the opportunity not to queue at the first two sights you visit – quite a lifesaver at the Colosseum and one or two others. Finally some sites and museums give discounts or even free admission to **students and EU citizens under 18 or over 65** – make sure you have the relevant ID.

Information

There are **tourist information booths** at Fiumicino, terminal B (daily 8.15am–7pm) and by platform 4 at Termini (daily 8am–9pm), although the long queues that often develop at both mean you're usually better off heading straight for the main **tourist office** at Via Parigi 5 (Mon–Sat 9am–7pm; ℡06.8205.9127, ⓦwww.romaturismo.it), five minutes' walk from Termini. They have free maps that – together with our own – should be ample for finding your way around, and they can help with accommodation if necessary. You'll also find information kiosks (see box below) in key locations around the city centre (daily 9am–6pm); these are useful for free maps, directions (the staff usually speak English) and details about nearby sights. Another good source of information is the privately run **Enjoy Rome**, Via Margherita 8a (Mon–Fri 8.30am–7pm, Sat 8.30am–2pm; ℡06.445.1843, ⓦwww.enjoyrome.com), whose friendly, English-speaking staff hand out lots of free information; they also operate a free room-finding service, organize tours, and have a left-luggage service for customers, and run a shuttle bus to Fiumicino.

The city's best source of **listings** is the weekly *Romac'è* (€1.20), which has a helpful section in English giving information on tours, clubs, restaurants, services and weekly events, and a decent website – ⓦwww.romace.it. The twice-monthly English expat magazine, *Wanted in Rome* (€0.75) – ⓦwww.wantedinrome.com – is also a useful source, especially if you're looking for an apartment or work. Both are available at most newsstands. Those with a bit of

Information kiosks

Castel Sant'Angelo Piazza Pia ℡06.6880.9707.
Fontana di Trevi Via Minghetti ℡06.678.2988
Fori Imperiali Piazza del Tempio della Pace ℡06.6992.4307.
Piazza Navona Piazza delle Cinque Lune ℡06.6880.9240.
San Giovanni Piazza San Giovanni in Laterano ℡06.7720.3535.
Santa Maria Maggiore Via dell'Olmata ℡06.474.0955.
Trastevere Piazza Sonnino ℡06.5833.3457.
Via del Corso Largo Goldoni ℡06.6813.6061.
Via Nazionale Palazzo delle Esposizioni ℡06.4782.4525.

748

Italian should check the daily arts pages of the Rome **newspaper**, *Il Messaggero*, which lists movies, plays and major musical events, along with *La Repubblica*, which includes the "Trova Roma" supplement in its Thursday edition, another handy guide to current offerings.

Accommodation

There's plenty of **accommodation** in Rome, and for much of the year you can usually expect to find something, although it's always worth booking in advance, especially when the city is at its busiest – from Easter to the end of October, and over the Christmas period. If you haven't booked, the official tourist office or the Enjoy Rome office (see opposite) are your best bets. The rooms offered by touts at Termini are rarely a good deal, and can often be rather unsavoury – only use them as a last resort and be sure to establish the full price beforehand, in writing if possible.

Hotels and pensions

Many of the city's cheaper places are located close to **Termini** station, and you could do worse than hole up in one of these, so long as you can tolerate the relative seediness of the district. The streets both sides of the station – Via Amendola, Via Principe Amedeo, Via Marghera, Via Magenta, Via Palestro – are stacked full of bargain hotels, and some buildings have several pensions to choose from. If you want to stay somewhere more central and picturesque, go for one of the many hotels in the **centro storico** or around **Camp de'Fiori**, some of them not that expensive, but they fill quickly – it's best to phone in advance. For more luxury surroundings, the area **east of Via del Corso**, towards Via Veneto and around the Spanish Steps is the city's prime hunting ground for beautiful, upscale accommodation – although there are a few affordable options close by Piazza di Spagna. Consider also staying across the river in **Prati**, a pleasant neighbourhood, nicely distanced from the hubbub of the city centre proper, and handy for the Vatican, or in the lively streets of **Trastevere**, again on the west side of the river but an easy walk into the centre of town. The following are shown on the maps on p.750, p.756 and p.760.

Centro Storico and Campo de' Fiori

Abruzzi Piazza della Rotonda 69 ☏ 06.9784.1351, ⓦ www.hotelabruzzi.it. This hotel used to be a very old-fashioned *pensione* right in the heart of the *centro storico*, but it's been updated into something a bit more comfortable. The knockout views of the Pantheon are still the main reason to stay here. ❼

Arenula Via S. Maria de' Calderari 47 ☏ 06.687.9454, ⓦ www.hotelarenula.com. Simple, clean rooms, each with its own bath, TV and telephone. No lift, and top-floor rooms are quite a climb, but it's in a good location. ❺

Campo de' Fiori Via del Biscione 6 ☏ 06.6880.6865, ⓦ www.hotelcampodefiori.com. A friendly place in a nice location with clean and pleasant rooms that come in all shapes and colours.

The large roof terrace has some great views, and the hotel also owns a number of small apartments nearby for those keen to self-cater. ❺–❻

Cesàri Via di Pietra 89a ☏ 06.674.9701, ⓦ www.albergocesari.it. In a perfect position close to the Pantheon, this has been a hotel since 1787 – as they will be sure to tell you – but has also been very recently renovated. The rooms are quiet and comfortable, and are charming enough while having all the modern touches. ❼

Due Torri Vicolo del Leonetto 23 ☏ 06.6880.6956, 06.687.6983 or 06.687.5765, ⓦ www.hoteldue torriroma.com. Quietly elegant, this little hotel was once a residence for cardinals, following which it served as a brothel. Completely remodelled, it retains a homely feel and some rooms have private terraces with rooftop views. A good location just north of Piazza Navona. ❻

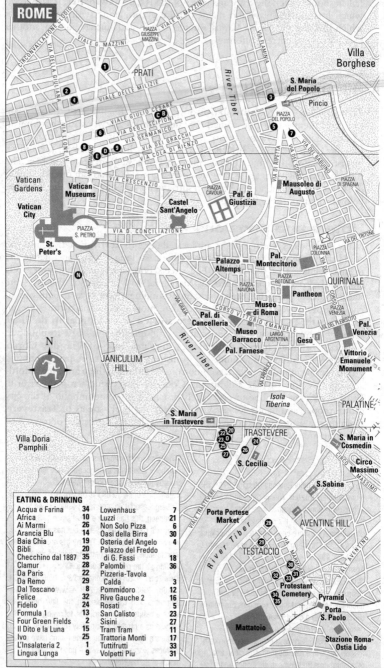

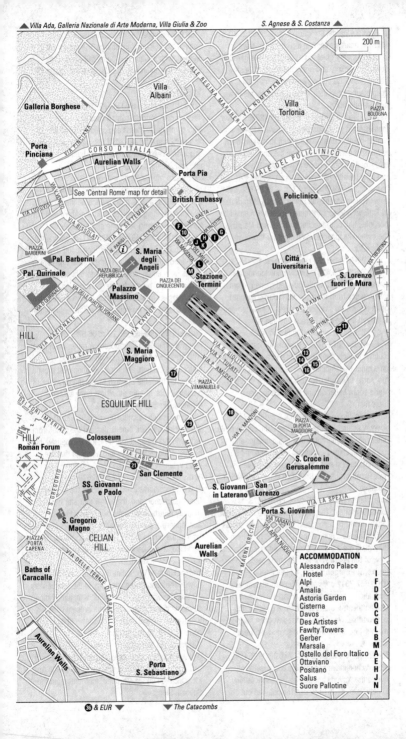

Galleria Borghese

Villa Albani

Villa Torlonia

PIAZZA BOLOGNA

Porta Pinciana

CORSO D'ITALIA

Aurelian Walls

Porta Pia

VIALE DEL POLICLINICO

Policlinico

British Embassy

See 'Central Rome' map for detail

PIAZZA BARBERINI

Pal. Barberini

Pal. Quirinale

S. Maria degli Angeli

PIAZZA DELLA REPUBBLICA

PIAZZA DEI CINQUECENTO

Palazzo Massimo

Stazione Termini

Città Universitaria

S. Lorenzo fuori le Mura

HILL

S. Maria Maggiore

ESQUILINE HILL

PIAZZA V. EMANUELE II

Colosseum

Roman Forum

San Clemente

SS. Giovanni e Paolo

S. Gregorio Magno

CELIAN HILL

S. Giovanni in Laterano

San Lorenzo

S. Croce in Gerusalemme

Porta S. Giovanni

Baths of Caracalla

Aurelian Walls

Aurelian Walls

Porta S. Sebastiano

PIAZZA DI PORTA MAGGIORE

ACCOMMODATION

Alessandro Palace Hostel	I
Alpi	F
Amalia	D
Astoria Garden	K
Cisterna	O
Davos	C
Des Artistes	G
Fawlty Towers	L
Gerber	B
Marsala	M
Ostello del Foro Italico	A
Ottaviano	E
Positano	H
Salus	J
Suore Pallotine	N

ROME AND LAZIO

751

▼ The Catacombs

In Parione Via dei Chiávari 32 ☎06.6880.2560, ⓦwww.inparione.com. In a nice part of town, central but very quiet, many of the rooms here look down to a bakery and enjoy the smell of freshly baked bread. Run by a sweet, efficient Italian couple, who keep their clean if basic rooms to a high standard. ❹

Navona Via dei Sediari 8 ☎06.686.4203, ⓦwww .hotelnavona.com. Completely renovated *pensione*-turned-hotel housed in a building that dates back to the first century AD, built on the ancient Roman baths of Agrippa. Very close to Piazza Navona and run by a friendly Italian-Australian couple. ❺

Pomezia Via dei Chiávari 13 ☎ & ⓕ06.686.1371, ⓦwww.hotelpomezia.it. Down the street from the *In Parione*, and slightly more expensive. A small bar occupies half of the reception area, and Maurizio, the owner, keeps it open all night for those who want it. ❹

🏃 **Portoghesi** Via dei Portoghesi 1 ☎06.686.4231, ⓦwww.hotelportoghesi roma.com. Decent, well-equipped modern rooms, five minutes from most places you might want to go in the *centro storico*. Breakfast is included and is served on the roof terrace upstairs. ❻

🏃 **Santa Chiara** Via Santa Chiara 21 ☎06.687.2979, ⓦwww.albergosantachiara .com. A friendly, family-run hotel in a great location, on a quiet piazza behind the Pantheon. Nice rooms too, some of which overlook the church of Santa Maria sopra Minerva, and the price includes breakfast. ❼

Smeraldo Vicolo dei Chiodaroli 9 ☎06.687.5929, ⓦwww.smeraldoroma.com. Clean and comfortable hotel with a modern if rather bland interior and rooms with shiny new baths, televisions and a/c. The terrace and some rooms have lovely views over Rome's rooftops. Breakfast is not included in the price. ❺

Sole Via del Biscione 76 ☎06.6880.6873, ⓦwww .solealbiscione.it. This place enjoys one of the best locations in the centre, and has reasonable rooms with televisions and phones. The real treat here, though, is the small roof terrace with a spectacular view of the nearby domes. No credit cards. ❺

Teatro di Pompeo Largo del Pallaro 8 ☎06.687.2812 , ⓦwww.hotelteatrodipompeo.it. Built above the remains of Pompey's ancient Roman theatre, the rooms here are classy and comfortable, with high-beamed wooden ceilings, marble-topped furniture and some with great views. ❻

Zanardelli Via G. Zanardelli 7 ☎06.6821.1392, ⓦwww.hotelnavona.com. The more lavish alternative to the *Navona* and run by the same family. Located just north of Piazza Navona, the building

used to be a papal residence and has many original fixtures and furnishings. The rooms are elegant, with antique iron beds, silk-lined walls, and modern amenities, but still decently priced. ❻

Tridente

Condotti Via Mario de' Fiori 37 ☎06.679.4661, ⓦwww.hotelcondotti.com. A cosy and inviting hotel with comfortable rooms equipped with satellite TV and minibars. A bit devoid of personality, although this is somewhat compensated for by the cheerful and welcoming staff. ❻

De Russie Via del Babuino 9 ☎06.328.881, ⓦwww.roccofortehotels.com. Since opening in 2000, the *Russie* has quickly become the abode of choice for visiting movie stars in-the-know and hip travellers spending someone else's money. ❾

Eden Via Ludovisi 49 ☎06.478.121, ⓦwww.hotel -eden.it. This former private residence, on a quiet tree-lined street, is one of Rome's most enchanting hotels, with an understated, comfortable lobby decorated and rooms that have everything you would expect from a luxury hotel. Even if you can't afford to stay, the rooftop bar or restaurant is worth a visit. ❾

Erdarelli Via due Macelli 28 ☎06.679.1265, ⓦwww.erdarelliromehotel.com. A rather plain hotel with no-frills rooms, but it's family-run and welcoming enough, and for its location, just around the corner from the Spanish Steps, the prices can't be beat. Most, but not all, rooms have en-suite facilities. ❹

Firenze Via due Macelli 106 ☎06.679.7240, ⓦwww.hotelfirenzeroma.it. Just up the street from Erdarelli, this three-star is a bit more expensive but has large rooms with TVs and minibars that are good value for money. ❺

Homs Via della Vite 71–72 ☎06.679.2976, ⓦwww.hotelhoms.it. In the heart of the Spanish Steps neighbourhood, this small four-star has recently refurbished rooms and a very friendly atmosphere – something that's not always guaran- teed in the hotels of this ritzy neighbourhood. They also have a two-bedroom rooftop apartment for around €250 a night. ❻

Internazionale Via Sistina 79 ☎06.6994.1823, ⓦwww.hotelinternazionale.com. In the first century AD this site was part of Lucullus' villa, and original elements can still be seen in the present hotel, which is very good value for this level of style and comfort, with TV, miinbar and wi-fi. ❻

Manfredi Via Margutta 61 ☎06.320.7676, ⓦwww.hotelmanfredi.com. Occupying a sixteenth- century building, this is a first-class hotel with an ideal location on Via Margutta, moments from the Spanish Steps. ❼

Margutta Via Laurina 34 ☎06.322.3674, ⓦwww
.hotelmargutta.it. Popular hotel, handily located in
the Corso/Piazza del Popolo shopping area. Three
rooms have tiny private balconies. Reserve well
ahead. ⑤

Termini

Alpi Via Castelfidardo 84 ☎06.444.1235, ⓦwww
.hotelalpi.com. One of the more peaceful yet
convenient options close to Termini, recently
renovated, and within easy walking distance of the
station. Pleasant, if somewhat small, rooms with
bathrooms, and a great buffet breakfast – much
better than you would normally expect in a hotel of
this category. ⑤

Astoria Garden Via Bachelet 8 ☎06.446.9908,
ⓦwww.hotelastoriagarden.it. In a calm area east
of Termini, this recently renovated hotel was once
the home of an Italian count. Rooms are pleasant,
quiet and some have balconies that look onto the
large garden below. ⑤

Daphne Via di San Basilio 55, Via degli
Avignonesi 20 ☎06.8745.0087, ⓦwww
.daphne-rome.com. Two wonderfully welcoming
pensioni run by an American woman and her
Roman husband. Bright, beautifully renovated
modern rooms in two great locations close to
Piazza Barberini, and as much advice as you need
on how to spend your time in Rome. Some rooms
have shared bathrooms, some are en suite. ④

Des Artistes Via Villafranca 20 ☎06.445.4365,
ⓦwww.hoteldesartistes.com. One of the better
hotels in the Termini area. Exceptionally good value,
spotlessly clean, and with a wide range of rooms,
including dorm beds for around €25. Eat breakfast
or recover from a long day of sightseeing on the
breezy roof terrace. Doubles go for €140–160 for
most of the year, although rooms are much
cheaper in low season. ⑤

Elide Via Firenze 50 ☎06.488.3977, ⓦwww
.hotelelide.com. A *pensione* for over fifty years, and
about as cheap a private bed as you'll find in the
city, with clean, simple rooms and friendly staff.
Several of the rooms are right on a busy street,
though; if noise bothers you, ask for a room at the
back. ③

Fawlty Towers Via Magenta 39 ☎06.445.4802,
ⓦwww.fawltytowers.org. Playfully named accommodation, this place has both dorm beds for
around €25 and clean and comfortable hotel
rooms, some with private bath. There's a
communal kitchen, Internet access, and a pleasant
roof terrace. ③

Grifo Via del Boschetto 144 ☎06.487.1395,
ⓦwww.hotelgrifo.com. A new addition to the Monti
district, the decor is crisply functional and modern,

although the roof terrace overlooks a timeless
scene of medieval Rome at its most picturesque. ④

Positano Via Palestro 49 ☎06.490.360, ⓦwww
.hotelpositano.it. Not glamorous, but certainly
reasonably priced at €100 for a double, this place
has comfortable rooms two minutes' walk from
Termini. Helpful management too. ③

Salus Piazza Indipendenza 13 ☎06.444.0330,
ⓦwww.hotelsalus.crimar.it. This modest establishment has the virtues of being attractive, clean,
efficiently run and friendly – things that can't always
be said for the hotels in this neighbourhood – and it
also has an internal garden for guests' use. ③

Trastevere and Prati

Amalia Via Germanico 66 ☎06.3972.3356,
ⓦwww.hotelamalia.com. Located on an attractive
corner of the busy shopping zone of Prati, this is an
extremely good-value option, with four-star
amenities at three-star prices. ⑥

Arcangelo Via Boezio 15 ☎06.687.4143,
ⓦwww.travel.it/oma/arcangelo. Clean, reliable
hotel, with comfortable, elegant rooms in a quiet
street not far from the Vatican. The lounges have a
warm, clubby feel. ⑥

Cisterna Via della Cisterna 7–9 ☎06.581.7212,
ⓦwww.cisternahotel.it. Welcoming two-star with a
homely feel, bang in the middle of Trastevere.
Twenty rooms, some with colourful tiled floors and
wooden beamed ceilings, and all with private
bathrooms. The peaceful terrace garden out the
back is a treat when the weather is good. ④

Colors Via Boezio 31 ☎06.687.4030, ⓦwww
.colorshotel.com. Run by the friendly people from
Enjoy Rome, this is a smaller version of their
popular *Fawlty Towers* (see above), a hostel/hotel in
a quiet neighbourhood near the Vatican. Dorm beds
(€25) and private rooms are available. There are
kitchen facilities, a lounge with satellite TV, and a
small terrace, and the same organization rents out
self-catering apartments too. ③–④

Davos Via degli Scipioni 239 ☎06.321.7012,
Ⓕ06.323.0367. Simple, affordable *pensione* on a
quiet street. Rooms are basic but clean; but all
except one have a private bath. No credit cards. ②

Gerber Via degli Scipioni 241 ☎06.321.9986,
ⓦwww.hotelgerber.it. Friendly staff and elegant,
comfortable rooms make this hotel great value for
its convenient location on a quiet street not far
from the Vatican. Even better, they give a ten
percent discount to *Rough Guide* readers. ⑤

La Rovere Vicolo San Onofrio 4–5
☎06.6880.6739, ⓦwww.hotellarovere.com. Just
round the corner from St Peter's and across the
bridge from Piazza Navona, this attractive boutique
hotel is tucked quietly away from all the bustle and

offers a terrace garden and antique-filled setting for its guests to relax in. ⑥

Santa Maria Vicolo dei Piede 2 ☎06.5894626, ⓦwww.hotelsantamaria.info. A few yards off Piazza Santa Maria in the heart of Trastevere, the rooms of this small three-star surround an orange-tree-filled garden, giving the feel of a place far removed from the hubbub of the city. ⑥

Hostels, convents and student accommodation

If your budget doesn't stretch to a hotel room, you can still bag a bed at one of a number of **hostels**. The official HI hostel is comfortable and well run, although it's a bus ride from most of the sights. There are, however, a handful of city centre options, and women travellers might want to consider the single-sex alternatives offered by Rome's various religious organizations.

Alessandro Palace Hostel Via Vicenza 42 ☎06.4938.0534, ⓦwww.hostelsalessandro.com. This place has been voted one of the top hostels in Europe, and it sparkles with creative style. Pluses include no lock-out or curfew, a good bar with free pizza every night, Internet access and satellite TV. A few blocks away, on the city centre side of Termini, you'll also find *Alessandro Downtown*, Via C. Cattaneo 23 (☎06.4434.0147). Beds go for €22–30, doubles €1, with bath €3.

Ostello del Foro Italico Viale delle Olimpiadi 61 ☎06.323.6267, ⓦwww.ostellionline.org. Rome's official HI hostel, though not particularly central or easy to get to from Termini – take bus #32, 69, 224 or 280 and ask the driver for the "*ostello*". You can call ahead to check out availability, but they won't take phone bookings. Beds cost €18 including breakfast. You can join here if you're not a HI member already, and facilities include a restaurant and bar.

Ottaviano Via Ottaviano 6 ☎06.3973.8138, ⓦwww.pensioneottaviano.com. A simple *pensione*-cum-hostel near to the Vatican that's very popular with the backpacking crowd; book well in advance, fluent English spoken. Dorm beds for around €20; doubles ❷ with shared bath.

Suore Pallotine Viale della Mura Aurelie 7B ☎06.393.6351, ⓦwww.procuramissionarie pallottine.it. Simple, clean accommodation near the Vatican, run by nuns, but open to women and men. Midnight curfew April–September, 11pm in winter. Singles cost €47 for a room without bath, €62 with bath, Doubles ❸. Breakfast is included.

YWCA Via C. Balbo 4 ☎06.488.0460, 🖷06.487.1028. Open to women and men, and conveniently situated just ten minutes' walk from Termini, although the market outside may get you up earlier than you might want. A range of singles (from €37), doubles (from €62), triples and quads (€26 per person), without bath; all rooms include breakfast except Sun mornings and August. Curfew 11pm.

Camping

All Rome's **campsites** are some way out of the city, but are easy enough to get to. The closest site is *Camping Flaminio*, 8km north of the centre at Via Flaminia Nuova 821 (March–Oct; ☎06.333.2604, ⓦwww.villageflaminio.it); it also has bungalows for rent and a swimming pool, restaurant and lots of facilities. To get there from the city centre, either take the Roma-Nord service from Piazzale Flaminio to Due Ponti, or take bus #910 to Piazza Mancini and transfer to bus #200 (ask the driver to drop you at the "*fermata più vicina al campeggio*"). Camping Tiber, on Via Tiberina at Km1400 (March–Oct; ☎06.3361.0733, ⓦwww.campingtiber.com), is another good bet – right beside the Tiber, quiet, spacious and friendly, with a bar/pizzeria, a swimming pool and really hot showers; and it too has bungalows as well as camping spaces. It has a free shuttle service (every 30min between 8am and 11pm) to and from the nearby Prima Porta station, where you can catch the Roma-Nord train service to Piazzale Flaminio (about 20min).

The City

Rome's **city centre** is divided neatly into distinct blocks. The warren of streets that makes up the **centro storico** occupies the hook of land on the left bank of the River Tiber, bordered to the east by Via del Corso and to the north and south by water. From here Rome's central core spreads south and east: down towards the old quarter around Campo de'Fiori; across Via del Corso to the major shopping streets and alleys around the **Spanish Steps**; to the major sites of the **ancient city** to the south; and to the expanse of the **Villa Borghese** park to the north. The left bank of the river is a little more distanced from the main hum of the city centre, home to the **Vatican** and **Saint Peter's**, and, to the south of these, **Trastevere** – even in ancient times a distinct entity from the city proper, as well as the focus of much of the city's nightlife.

Piazza Venezia

Piazza Venezia is not so much a square as a road junction, and a busy one at that. But it's a good central place to start your wanderings, close to both the medieval and Renaissance centre of Rome and the bulk of the ruins of the ancient city. Flanked on all sides by imposing buildings, it's a dignified focal point for the city in spite of the traffic, and a spot you'll find yourself returning to time and again.

Palazzo Venezia and the church of San Marco

Forming the western side of the piazza, the **Palazzo Venezia** (Tues–Sun 8.30am–7.30pm; €4) was the first large Renaissance palace in the city, built for the Venetian Pope Paul II in the mid-fifteenth century and for a long time the embassy of the Venetian Republic. More famously, Mussolini moved in here while in power, occupying the vast Sala del Mappamondo and making his declamatory speeches to the huge crowds below from the small balcony facing on to the piazza. Nowadays it's a venue for great exhibitions and home to the **Museo Nazionale di Palazzo Venezia**, a museum of Renaissance arts and crafts, with a number of fifteenth-century devotional paintings, bronzes and sculpture.

Adjacent to the palace on its southern side, the church of **San Marco**, accessible from Piazza San Marco (daily 8am–noon & 4–7pm; closed Mon morning & Wed afternoon), is the Venetian church in Rome – and one of its most ancient basilicas. Standing on the spot where the apostle is supposed to have lived while in the city, it was rebuilt in 833 and added to by various Renaissance and eighteenth-century popes. Look out for the apse mosaic dating from the ninth century and showing Pope Gregory offering his church to Christ.

The Vittorio Emanuele Monument

Everything pales into insignificance beside the marble monstrosity rearing up across the street – the **Vittorio Emanuele Monument** (daily 9.30–6pm; free), erected at the beginning of the twentieth century as the "Altar of the Nation" to commemorate Italian Unification. Variously likened in the past to a typewriter (because of its shape), and, by American GIs, to a wedding cake (the marble used will never mellow with age), King Vittorio Emanuele II, who it's in part supposed to honour, probably wouldn't have thought much of it – he was by all accounts a modest man; indeed, the only person who seems to have benefited from the building is the prime minister at the time, who was a deputy for Brescia, from where the marble was supplied. The Vittoriano – as it's known – was closed

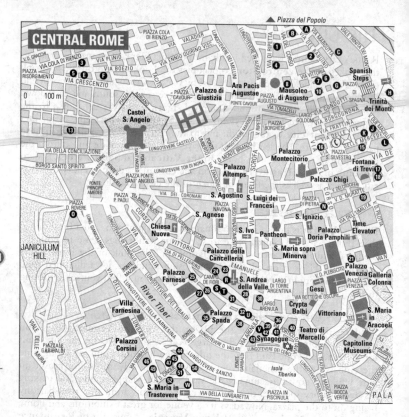

to the public for years but is now fully open, and it's great to clamber up and down the sweeping terraces and flights of steps. There are things to see inside (principally a large Unification museum), but the main interest is on the outside: the Tomb of the Unknown Soldier at the top of the first flight of steps; the equestrian statue of Vittorio Emanuele 11, one of the world's largest, on the next level; and the huge sweeping gallery at the top, beyond which you can cut through to a café and to Piazza del Campidoglio. Needless to say, the views from the top are magnificent – not least because it's the one place in the city you can't see the Vittoriano.

The Capitoline Hill

The real pity about the Vittorio Emanuele Monument is that it obscures views of the **Capitoline Hill** behind – once the spiritual and political centre of the Roman Empire. Apart from anything else, this hill has contributed key words to the English language, including, of course, "capitol", and "money", which comes from the temple to Juno Moneta that once stood up here and housed the Roman mint. The Capitoline also played a significant role in medieval and Renaissance times: the flamboyant fourteenth-century dictator Cola di Rienzo stood here in triumph in 1347, and was murdered here by an angry mob seven years later – a humble statue marks the spot.

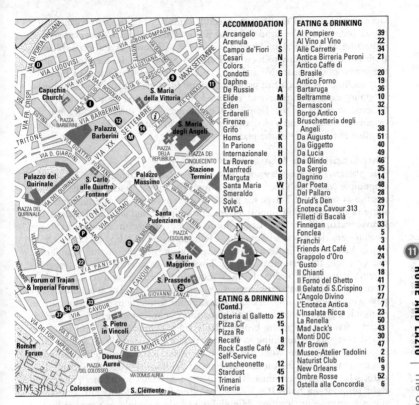

Santa Maria in Aracoeli

The church of **Santa Maria in Aracoeli** (daily 9am–12.30pm & 3–6.30pm) crowns the highest point on the Capitoline Hill, built on the site of a temple where, according to legend, the Tiburtine Sybil foretold the birth of Christ. You can reach it by a steep flight of steps erected by Cola di Rienzo in 1348, or by cutting through from the Vittoriano, and it's one of Rome's most ancient basilicas, with, in the first chapel on the right, some fine frescoes by Pinturicchio recording the life of San Bernardino – realistic tableaux of landscapes and bustling town scenes. The church is also known for its role as keeper of the "Bambino", a small statue of the Christ child, carved from the wood of a Gethsemane olive tree. It's said to have healing powers and was traditionally called out to the sickbeds of the ill and dying all over the city, its coach commanding instant right of way through the heavy Rome traffic. The statue was stolen in 1994, however, and a copy now stands in its place, in a small chapel to the left of the high altar.

Piazza del Campidoglio

Next door to the steps up to Santa Maria is the **cordonata**, an elegant, gently rising ramp, topped with two Roman statues of Castor and Pollux, leading to **Piazza del Campidoglio**, one of Rome's most elegant squares. Designed by Michelangelo in the last years of his life for Pope Paul III, the square wasn't in fact completed until the late seventeenth century. Michelangelo balanced the piazza, redesigning the facade of what is now **Palazzo dei Conservatori** and projecting an identical building across the way, known as **Palazzo Nuovo**. Both are angled slightly to focus on **Palazzo Senatorio**, Rome's town hall. In the centre of the square Michelangelo placed an equestrian statue of Emperor Marcus Aurelius, which had previously stood for years outside San Giovanni in Laterano; early Christians had refrained from melting it down because they believed it to be of the Emperor Constantine. After careful restoration, the original is now behind a glass wall in the Palazzo Nuovo, and a copy has taken its place at the centre of the piazza.

The Capitoline Museums

The Palazzo dei Conservatori and Palazzo Nuovo together make up the Capitoline Museums (Tues–Sun 9am–8pm; €6.50, €8.50 for Centrale Monte-martini as well, valid 7 days; see p.788; ⓦ www.museicapitolini.org), containing some of the city's most important ancient sculpture and art. The **Palazzo dei Conservatori** holds the larger, more varied collection. Among its many treasures are the so-called Spinario, a Roman statue of a boy picking a thorn out of his foot; the Etruscan bronze she-wolf nursing the mythic founders of the city, and the Hannibal Room, covered in wonderfully vivid fifteenth-century paintings recording Rome's wars with Carthage, and so named for a rendering of Hannibal seated impressively on an elephant. The wonderfully airy new wing holds the original of Marcus Aurelius, formerly in the square outside, alongside a giant bronze statue of Constantine, or at least its head, hand and orb. Nearby stands the rippling bronze of Hercules, behind which are part of the foundations and a retaining wall from the original temple of Jupiter here, discovered when the work for the new wing was undertaken. And when museum fatigue sets in you can climb up to the floor above to the second floor **café**, whose terrace commands one of the best views in Rome. The second floor **pinacoteca** holds Renaissance painting from the fourteenth century to the late seventeenth century. Highlights include a couple of portraits by Van Dyck, a penetrating *Portrait of a Crossbowman* by Lorenzo Lotto, a pair of paintings from 1590 by Tintoretto, and a very fine early work by Lodovico Carracci, *Head of a Boy*. In one of the two large main galleries, there's a vast picture by Guercino, depicting the Burial of Santa Petronilla (an early Roman martyr who was the supposed daughter of St Peter), and two paintings by Caravaggio, one a replica of the young *John the Baptist* which hangs in the Palazzo Doria-Pamphilj, the other an early work known as *The Fortune-Teller*.

The **Palazzo Nuovo** across the square – also accessible by way of an under-ground walkway that takes in good views of the Roman Forum just below – is the more manageable of the two museums, with some of the best of the city's Roman sculpture crammed into half a dozen or so rooms. Among them is the remarkable, controlled statue *Dying Gaul*, as well as a *Satyr Resting* that was the inspiration for Hawthorne's book the *Marble Faun*; and the red marble *Laughing Silenus*. There are also busts and statues of Roman emperors and other famous names: a young Augustus, a cruel Caracalla, and, the centrepiece, a life-size portrait of Helena, the mother of Constantine, reclining gracefully. Don't miss the coy, delicate *Capitoline Venus*, housed in a room on its own.

The Tarpeian Rock and San Pietro in Carcere

Behind the Palazzo Senatorio, Via del Monte Tarpeio follows, as its name suggests, the brink of the old **Tarpeian Rock**, from which traitors would be thrown in ancient times – so-called after Tarpeia, who betrayed the city to the

Sabines. On the left side of the Palazzo Senatorio (as you face it from the Campidoglio) steps lead down to the little church of **San Pietro in Carcere** (daily 10am–7pm; donation expected for the prison), built above the ancient Mamertine Prison, where spies, vanquished soldiers and other enemies of the Roman state were incarcerated, and where St Peter himself was held. Steps lead down into the murky depths of the jail, where you can see the bars to which he was chained, along with the spring the saint is said to have created to baptize the other prisoners down here. At the top of the staircase, hollowed out of the honeycomb of stone, is an imprint claimed to be of St Peter's head as he tumbled down the stairs (though when the prison was in use, the only access was through a hole in the ceiling). It's an unappealing place even now, and you won't be sorry to leave – through an exit cunningly placed to lead you through the gift shop.

The Centro Storico

Immediately north of Piazza Venezia is the real heart of Rome – the **centro storico** (historic centre), which makes up most of the triangular knob of land that bulges into a bend in the Tiber. This area, known in ancient Roman times as the Campus Martius, was outside the ancient city centre, a low-lying area that was mostly given over to barracks and sporting arenas, together with several temples, including the Pantheon. Later it became the heart of the Renaissance city, and nowadays it's the part of the town that is densest in interest, an unruly knot of narrow streets and alleys that holds some of the best of Rome's classical and Baroque heritage and its most vivacious street- and nightlife. It's here that most people find the Rome they have been looking for – a city of small crumbling piazzas, Renaissance churches and fountains, blind alleys and streets humming with scooters and foot-traffic. Whichever direction you wander in there's something to see; indeed it's part of the appeal of the centre of Rome that even the most aimless ambling leads you past some breathlessly beautiful and historic spots.

Via del Corso

The boundary of the historic centre to the east, **Via del Corso** is Rome's main thoroughfare, leading all the way from Piazza Venezia at its southern end up to the Piazza del Popolo to the north. On its eastern side, it gives onto the swish shopping streets that lead up to Piazza di Spagna; on the western side the web of streets tangles its way right down to the Tiber. It is Rome's principal shopping street, home to a mixture of upmarket boutiques and chain stores that make it a busy stretch during the day, full of hurrying pedestrians and crammed buses, but a relatively dead one come the evening. The good news is that the top end, beyond Piazza Colonna, where the bulk of the shops are, is pedestrian-ized, so shopping and strolling is much easier and more enjoyable.

Galleria Doria Pamphilj

North of Piazza Venezia, the first building on the left of Via del Corso is the Palazzo Doria Pamphilj, one of the city's finest Rococo palaces. Inside, through an entrance on Piazza di Collegio Romano, the **Galleria Doria Pamphilj** (Mon–Wed & Fri–Sun 10am–5pm; €8, including audio guide in English; private apartments tours every 30min 10.30am–12.30pm; €3.50; ⓦwww .doriapamphilj.it) is one of Rome's best private late-Renaissance art collections. The Doria Pamphilj family still lives in part of the building, and the first part of the gallery is made up of a series of **private apartments**, furnished in the

CENTRO STORICO

EATING & DRINKING

Anima	15
Armando al Pantheon	12
Bar del Fico	11
Bar della Pace	9
Bloom	19
Caffè Sant'Eustachio	21
Camilloni	20
Capranica	4
Cul de Sac	22
Da Alfredo e Ada	6
Da Baffetto	23
Da Francesco	13
Da Tonino	16
Enoteca Corsi	24
Giolitti	2
Il Forno di Campo	26
Jonathan's Angels	14
La Curia di Bacco	27
La Tazza d'Oro	8
Le Cornacchie	5
Lo Zozzone	17
Maccheroni	3
Miscellanea	7
Myosotis	1
Pascucci	25
Tre Salini	10
Trinity College	18

ACCOMMODATION

Abruzzi	D
Due Torri	A
Navona	H
Pomezia	B
Portoghesi	F
Santa Chiara	G
Teatro di Pompeo	E
Zanardelli	C

River Tiber

Castel Sant'Angelo

Palazzo di Giustizia

Palazzo Primoli

San Giovanni dei Fiorentini

Oratorio dei Filippini

Chiesa Nuova

Santa Maria della Pace

Santa Maria dell'Anima

Palazzo Altemps

Torre della Scimmia

Sant'Agostino

San Lorenzo in Lucina

Palazzo Montecitorio

Palazzo Wedekind

San Silvestro

Main Post Office

Central Bus Terminal

Palazzo Chigi

Galleria Sordi

Sant'Ignazio

San Luigi dei Francesi

Palazzo Madama

Sant'Ivo

Sant'Agnese

Santa Maria Sopra Minerva

The Pantheon

Teatro Argentina

Museo di Roma

Museo Barracco

San Andrea della Valle

Palazzo Cancelleria

Galleria Doria-Pamphilj

Palazzo Altieri

Gesù

St. Ignatius Rooms

Palazzo Venezia

San Marco

SS. Apostoli

Palazzo Colonna

250 m

style of the original palace, through which you're guided by way of a free audio-tour narrated by the urbane Jonathan Pamphilj. Beyond here, the **picture gallery** extends around a courtyard, the paintings displayed in old-fashioned style, crammed in frame-to-frame, floor-to-ceiling. Just inside, at the corner of the courtyard, there's a badly cracked bust of Innocent X by Bernini, which the sculptor apparently replaced in a week with the more famous version down the hall, in a room off to the left – Bernini appears to have captured the pope about to erupt into laughter. In this room also, Velázquez's famous painting of the same man is quite different, depicting a rather irritable character regarding the viewer with impatience. The rest of the collection is just as rich in interest, including perhaps Rome's best concentration of Dutch and Flemish paintings, with a rare Italian work by Brueghel the Elder showing a naval battle being fought outside Naples, a highly realistic portrait of two old men, by Quentin Metsys, and a Hans Memling *Deposition*, in the furthest rooms, as well as another Metsys painting – the fabulously ugly *Moneylenders and their Clients* – in the main gallery. There's also Carracci's bucolic *Flight into Egypt*, painted shortly before the artist's death; two paintings by Caravaggio, *Mary Magdalene* and *John the Baptist*, and *Salome with the head of St John* by Titian. All in all it's a marvellous collection of work, displayed in a wonderfully appropriate setting.

Sant'Ignazio

The next left off Via del Corso after the palace leads into **Piazza Sant'Ignazio**, a lovely little square, laid out like a theatre set and dominated by the facade of the Jesuit church of **Sant'Ignazio** (daily 7.30am–12.30pm & 4–7.15pm). The saint isn't actually buried here; appropriately, for the founder of the Jesuit order, he's in the Gesù church a little way south. It's a spacious structure, built during the late seventeeth century, and worth visiting for the marvellous Baroque ceiling by Andrea del Pozzo showing the entry of St Ignatius into paradise, a spectacular work that employs sledgehammer trompe-l'oeil effects, notably in the mock cupola painted into the dome of the crossing. Stand on the disc in the centre of the nave, the focal point for the ingenious rendering of perspective: figures in various states of action and repose, conversation and silence, fix you with stares from their classical pediment.

The Pantheon

Via del Seminario leads down to Piazza della Rotonda, where the main focus of interest is the **Pantheon** (Mon–Sat 8.30am–7.30pm, Sun 9am–6pm; free), easily the most complete ancient Roman structure in the city and, along with the Colosseum, visually the most impressive. Though originally a temple that formed part of Marcus Agrippa's redesign of the Campus Martius in around 27 BC – hence the inscription – it's since been proved that the building was entirely rebuilt by the Emperor Hadrian and finished around the year 125 AD. It's a formidable architectural achievement even now, although, like the city's other Roman monuments, it would have been much more sumptuous in its day. Consecrated as a Christian site in 609 AD and dedicated to Santa Maria ai Martiri in allusion to the Christian bones that were found here, a thousand years later, its bronze roof was stripped from the ceiling of the portico by Pope Urban VIII, to be melted down for the baldacchino in St Peter's and the cannons of the Castel Sant'Angelo. Some of the "stolen" bronze later found its way back here when, after Unification, the cannons were in turn melted down to provide materials for the tombs of two Italian kings, which are housed in the right and left chapels. Inside, you get the best impression of the engineering expertise of Hadrian: the diameter is precisely equal to its height (43m), the hole in the centre of the dome – from which shafts of sunlight descend to illuminate the musty interior – a full 9m across. Most impressively, there are no visible arches or vaults to hold the whole thing up; instead they're sunk into the concrete of the walls of the building. Again, it would have been richly decorated, the coffered ceiling heavily stuccoed and the niches filled with the statues of gods. Now, apart from the sheer size of the place, the main thing of interest is the tomb of Raphael, between the second and third chapel on the left, with an inscription by the humanist bishop Pietro Bembo: "Living, great Nature feared he might outvie Her works, and dying, fears herself may die." The same kind of sentiments might well have been reserved for the Pantheon itself.

Santa Maria Sopra Minerva

There's more artistic splendour on view behind the Pantheon, though Bernini's **Elephant Statue** doesn't really prepare you for the church of Santa Maria Sopra Minerva beyond. The statue is Bernini's most endearing piece of work, if not his most characteristic: a cheery elephant trumpeting under the weight of the obelisk he carries on his back – a reference to Pope Alexander VII's reign and supposed to illustrate the fact that strength should support wisdom. **Santa Maria Sopra Minerva** (Mon–Sat 7am–7pm, Sun 8am–7pm) is Rome's only Gothic church, and worth a look just for that, though its soaring lines have since been overburdened by marble and frescoes. Built in the late thirteenth century on the ruins of a temple to Minerva, it's also one of Rome's art-treasure churches, crammed with the tombs and self-indulgences of wealthy Roman families. Of these, the Carafa chapel, in the south transept, is the best known, holding Filippino Lippi's fresco of the Assumption, a bright, effervescent piece of work, below which one painting shows a hopeful Carafa (the religious zealot, Pope Paul IV) being presented to the Virgin Mary by Thomas Aquinas; another depicts Aquinas confounding the heretics in the sight of two beautiful young boys – the future Medici popes Leo X and Clement VII (the equestrian statue of Marcus Aurelius, destined for the Capitoline Hill, is just visible in the background). The lives of Leo and Clement come full circle in the church, where they are both buried, and remembered by two very grand tombs either side of the high altar – Leo on the left, Clement on the right, close by which is the figure of Christ Bearing the Cross, a serene work that Michelangelo completed for the church in 1521.

Sant'Ivo

A few steps west of the Pantheon, on Corso del Rinascimento, the rather blank facade of the **Palazzo della Sapienza** cradles the church of **Sant'Ivo** (Mon–Fri 8.30am–5pm, Sat & Sun 9am–noon) – from the outside at least, one of Rome's most impressive churches, with a playful facade designed by Borromini. Though originally built for the Barberini pope, Urban VIII, the building actually spans the reign of three pontiffs. Each of the two small towers is topped with the weird pyramidal groupings that are the symbol of the Chigi family (representing the hills of Monti di Paschi di Siena), and the central cupola spirals helter-skelter fashion to its zenith, crowned with flames that are supposed to represent the sting of the Barberini bee, their family symbol. The inside, too, is very cleverly designed, light and spacious given the small space the church is squeezed into, rising to the tall parabolic cupola.

San Luigi dei Francesi

A short walk from here, at the bottom of Via della Scrofa, the French national church of **San Luigi dei Francesi** (daily except Thurs afternoon 8.30am–12.30pm & 3.30–7pm) is worth a look, mainly for its works by Caravaggio. In the last chapel on the left are three paintings: *The Calling of St Matthew*, in which Christ points to Matthew, who is illuminated by a shaft of sunlight; The Inspiration of St Matthew, where Matthew is visited by an angel as he writes the Gospel; and the Martyrdom of St Matthew. Caravaggio's first public commission, these paintings were actually rejected at first, partly on grounds of indecorum, and it took considerable reworking by the artist before they were finally accepted.

Piazza Navona and around

Just west of San Luigi dei Francesi lies **Piazza Navona**, Rome's most famous square. Lined with cafés and restaurants, and often thronged with tourists, street artists and pigeons, it is as picturesque – and as vibrant, day and night – as any piazza in Italy. It takes its shape from the first-century AD Stadium of Domitian, the principal venue of the athletic events and later chariot races that took place in the Campus Martius. Until the mid-fifteenth century the ruins of the arena were still here, overgrown and disused, but the square was given a facelift in the mid-seventeenth century by Pope Innocent X, who built most of the grandiose palaces that surround it and commissioned Borromini to design the facade of the church of **Sant'Agnese in Agone** on the piazza's western side (daily 9.30am–12.30pm & 4–7pm). The story goes that the 13-year-old St Agnes was stripped naked before the crowds in the stadium as punishment for refusing to marry, whereupon she miraculously grew hair to cover herself. The church, typically squeezed into the tightest of spaces by Borromini, is supposedly built on the spot where it all happened.

Opposite, the **Fontana dei Quattro Fiumi**, one of three that punctuate the square, is a masterpiece by Bernini, Borromini's arch-rival. Each figure represents one of the four great rivers of the world – the Nile, Danube, Ganges and Plate – though only the horse, symbolizing the Danube, was actually carved by Bernini himself. It's said that all the figures are shielding their eyes in horror from Borromini's church facade (Bernini was an arrogant man who never had time for the work of the less successful Borromini, and their rivalry is well documented), but the fountain had actually been completed before the facade was begun. The grand complexity of rock is topped with an Egyptian obelisk, brought here by Pope Innocent X from the Circus of Maxentius. Bernini also had a hand in the fountain at the southern end of the square, the so-called **Fontana del Moro**, designing the central figure of the Moor in what is another fantastically playful piece of work, surrounded by toothsome dolphins and other marine figures.

Museo di Roma

Overlooking the south side of Piazza Navona, the eighteenth-century Palazzo Braschi is the home of the **Museo di Roma** (Tues–Sun 9am–7pm; €6.50; ⓦ www.museodiroma.comune.roma.it), which has a permanent collection relating to the history of the city from the Middle Ages to the present day. The building itself is probably the main attraction – particularly the magnificent Sala Nobile where you enter, the main staircase, and one or two of the renovated rooms – but some of the paintings are of interest, showing the city during different eras, and frescoes from demolished palaces provide decent enough highlights.

Piazza Pasquino and Via del Governo Vecchio

The nearby triangular space of **Piazza Pasquino** is named after the small battered torso that still stands in the corner. Pasquino is perhaps the best-known of Rome's "talking statues" of the Middle Ages and Renaissance times, on which anonymous comments on the affairs of the day would be attached – comments that had a serious as well as a humorous intent, and gave us our word "pasquinade". **Via del Governo Vecchio** leads west from here, and is home – along with the narrow streets around – to some of the *centro storico's* liveliest restaurants and bars.

Palazzo Altemps

Just across the street from the north end of Piazza Navona, Piazza Sant'Apollinare is home to the beautifully restored **Palazzo Altemps** (Tues–Sun 9am–7pm; €7, includes Palazzo Massimo, Terme Diocletian, Crypta Balbi, valid 3 days, for combined ticket see box, p.748), nowadays home to part of the Museo Nazionale Romano (the other main section is in the Palazzo Massimo, see p.774), and the cream of its collections of Roman statuary. On the ground floor at the far end of the courtyard's loggia is a statue of the Emperor Antoninus Pius, and, around the corner, a couple of marvellous heads of Zeus and Pluto, a bust of Julia, the daughter of the Emperor Augustus, and a likeness of the philosopher Demosthenes, from the second century AD. There are two almost identical statues of Apollo the Lyrist, a magnificent statue of Athena taming a serpent, pieced together from fragments found near the church of Santa Maria Sopra Minerva, an Aphrodite from an original by Praxiteles, and, in the far corner of the courtyard, a shameless Dionysus with a satyr and panther, found on the Quirinal Hill. Upstairs you get a slightly better sense of the original sumptuousness of the building – some of the frescoes remain and the north loggia retains its original, late-sixteenth-century decoration, simulating a vine-laden pergola. Among the objects on display there's a fine statue of Hermes, a wonderful statue of a warrior at rest, and, most engagingly, a charmingly sensitive portrayal of Orestes and Electra, from the first century AD by a sculptor called Menelaus – his name is carved at the base of one of the figures. In a later room stands a colossal head of Hera, and – what some consider the highlight of the entire collection – the famous Ludovisi throne: an original fifth-century BC Greek work embellished with a delicate relief portraying the birth of Aphrodite. Further on, the Fireplace Salon – whose huge fireplace is embellished with caryatids and lurking ibex, the symbol of the Altemps family – has the so-called Suicide of Galatian, apparently commissioned by Julius Caesar to adorn his Quirinal estate. At the other end of the room, an incredible sarcophagus depicts a battle between the Romans and barbarians in graphic, almost viscerally sculptural, detail.

Via dei Coronari

West of Palazzo Altemps, narrow **Via dei Coronari**, and some of the streets around, are the fulcrum of Rome's antiques trade, and, although the prices are as high as you might expect in such a location, there's a huge number of shops (Via dei Coronari consists of virtually nothing else) selling a tremendous variety of stuff, and a browse along here makes for an absorbing bit of sightseeing.

Sant'Agostino

Just east of Palazzo Altemps, through an arch, the Renaissance facade of the church of **Sant'Agostino** (daily 7.45am–noon & 4–7.30pm; free) takes up one side of a drab piazza of the same name. It's not much to look at from the outside, but a handful of art treasures might draw you in. Just inside the door, the serene statue of the Madonna del Parto, by Sansovino, is traditionally invoked during pregnancy, and is accordingly surrounded by photos of newborn babes and their blissful parents. Further into the church, take a look at Raphael's vibrant fresco of Isaiah, on the third pillar on the left, beneath which is another work by

Sansovino, a craggy *St Ann, Virgin and Child*. But the biggest crowds gather around the first chapel on the left, where the *Madonna and Pilgrims* by Caravaggio – a characteristic work of what was at the time almost revolutionary realism – shows two peasants with dirty clothes praying at the feet of a sensuous Mary and Child.

Piazza Montecitorio and around

A short walk east from Sant' Agostino, **Piazza Montecitorio** takes its name from the bulky **Palazzo di Montecitorio** on its northern side, home since 1871 to the Italian parliament – though the building itself is a Bernini creation from 1650. The obelisk in the centre of the square was brought to Rome by Augustus and set up in the Campus Martius, where it formed the gnomon of a giant sundial. Just beyond, off Via del Corso, the **Palazzo Chigi** flanks the north side of **Piazza Colonna**, official residence of the prime minister. The **Column of Marcus Aurelius**, which gives the square its name, was erected between 180 and 190 AD to commemorate military victories in northern Europe, and, like the column of Trajan that inspired it, is decorated with reliefs depicting scenes from the campaigns.

Campo de' Fiori, the Ghetto and around

Just south of the *centro storico* proper, this is Rome's old centre part two, a similar neighbourhood of cramped, wanderable streets opening out into small squares flanked by churches. However, it's less monumental and more of a working quarter as evidenced by its main focus, Campo de' Fiori, whose fruit and veg stalls are a marked contrast to the pavement artists of Piazza Navona. Close by are the dark alleys of the old Jewish Ghetto, and the busy traffic junction of Largo di Torre Argentina.

Largo di Torre Argentina and around

Largo di Torre Argentina is a large square, frantic with traffic circling around the ruins of four Republican-era temples and the channel of an ancient public lavatory, now home to a thriving colony of cats. On the far side of the square, the **Teatro Argentina** was in 1816 the venue for the first performance of Rossini's *Barber of Seville*, not a success at all on the night: Rossini was apparently booed into taking refuge in Bernasconi's pastry shop which used to be next door. Built in 1731, it's one of the city's most important theatres, and has a small museum that can be visited by appointment. Nowadays, however, the **Crypta Balbi**, around the corner at Via delle Botteghe Oscure 31 (Mon & Wed–Sun 9am–7.45pm; €4), is the area's principal point of interest, housed on the site of an old Roman imperial theatre and with displays covering the period from the fall of the Roman Empire to the late Middle Ages.

The Gesù and Rooms of St Ignatius

Just east of Largo Argentina, the church of **Gesù** is a huge structure (daily 6am–12.30pm & 4–7.15pm; free), the headquarters of the Jesuits and ideal for the large and fervent congregations the order wanted to attract – indeed, high and wide, with a single-aisled nave and short transepts edging out under a huge dome, it has since served as the model for Jesuit churches everywhere. The facade is by Giacomo della Porta, the interior the work of Vignola. The glitzy tomb of the order's founder, St Ignatius, is topped by a huge globe of lapis lazuli – the largest piece in existence – opposite which the tomb of the sixteenth-century Jesuit missionary St Francis Xavier, decorated with a painting by Carlo

Maratta showing his death on a Chinese island, holds a reliquary containing the saint's arm, severed from the rest of his (incorruptible) body, which remains a focus of pilgrimage in Goa, India. Otherwise it's the staggering richness of the church's interior that you remember, especially the paintings by the Genoese painter Baciccia in the dome and the nave, the *Triumph in the Name of Jesus*, which oozes out of its frame in a tangle of writhing bodies, flowing drapery and stucco angels stuck like limpets.

Next door, the **Rooms of St Ignatius** (Mon–Sat 4–6pm, Sun 10am–noon; free) occupy part of the first floor of the Jesuit headquarters, and are basically the rooms – recently restored – where St Ignatius lived from 1544 until his death in 1556. There are bits and pieces of furniture and memorabilia relating to the saint, but the true draw is the decorative corridor just outside, decorated by Andrea Pozzo in 1680 – a superb exercise in perspective on a minimized scale, giving an illusion of a grand hall in what is a relatively small space.

Piazza Campo de' Fiori

On the other side of Largo Argentina, **Piazza Campo de' Fiori** is in many ways Rome's most appealing square, home to a lively fruit and vegetable market (Mon–Sat 8am–1pm), and flanked by restaurants and cafés. No one really knows how the square came by its name, which means "field of flowers", but one theory holds that it was derived from the Roman Campus Martius, which used to cover most of this part of town; another claims it is after Flora, the mistress of Pompey, whose theatre used to stand on what is now the northeast corner of the square – a huge complex by all accounts, which stretched right over to Largo Argentina. You can still see the foundations in the basement of the Da Pancrazio restaurant, on the tiny Piazza del Biscione, and the semicircular Via di Grotta Pinta retains the rounded shape of the theatre. Later, Campo de' Fiori was an important point on papal processions between the Vatican and the major basilicas of Rome (notably San Giovanni in Laterano) and a site of public executions. The most notorious killing was of Giordano Bruno, a late-sixteenth-century freethinker who followed the teachings of Copernicus and was denounced to the Inquisition; his trial lasted for years under a succession of different popes, and finally, when he refused to renounce his philosophical beliefs, he was burned at the stake. His death is commemorated by a statue in the middle of the square.

Palazzo Farnese and Galleria Spada

Just south of Campo de' Fiori, **Piazza Farnese** is a quite different square, with great fountains spurting out of lilies – the Farnese emblem – into marble tubs brought from the Baths of Caracalla, and the sober bulk of the **Palazzo Farnese** itself, begun in 1514 by Antonio da Sangallo the Younger and finished off after the architect's death by Michelangelo, who added the top tier of windows and cornice. The building now houses the French Embassy but is open to those organized enough to make an appointment (closed late July to early Sept and end Dec: Mon & Thurs visits in French or Italian at 3pm, 4pm, 5pm; free; book in advance at Via Giulia 250, on ☏06.688.92818 or at ✉visitfarnese@france -italia.it) – worth doing to see the amazing Baroque ceiling frescoes of Annibale Carracci in one of the rear reception rooms.

If you can't make it to the Palazzo Farnese, make do instead with the Palazzo Spada, back towards Via Arenula at Piazza Capo di Ferro 3, and the **Galleria Spada** inside (Tues–Sun 8.30am–7.30pm; €5); walk right through the courtyard to the back of the building. Its four rooms, decorated in the manner of a Roman noble family's home, aren't spectacularly interesting unless you're a connoisseur of seventeenth- and eighteenth-century Italian painting. But there are two portraits of Cardinal Bernadino Spada by Reni and Guercino, and the building itself is a treat: its facade is frilled with stucco adornments, and, left off the small courtyard, there's a crafty trompe l'oeil by Borromini – a tunnel whose actual length is multiplied about four times through the architect's tricks with perspective – though to see this you have to wait for one of the guided tours.

Via Giulia

Via Giulia runs parallel to the Tiber from the Ponte Sisto, and was laid out by Julius II to connect the bridge with the Vatican. The street was conceived as the centre of papal Rome, and Julius commissioned Bramante to line it with imposing palaces. Bramante didn't get very far with the plan, as Julius was soon succeeded by Leo X, but the street soon became a popular residence for wealthier Roman families, and is still packed full with stylish palazzi and antique shops and as such makes for a nice wander, with features such as the playful Fontana del Mascherone right behind the Farnese palace and topped with the Farnese emblem, to tickle your interest along the way.

Via Portico d'Ottavia and around

Cross over to the far side of Via Arenula and you're in what was once the city's **Jewish Ghetto**, a crumbling area of old narrow, switchback streets and alleys, easy to lose your way in. There was a Jewish population in Rome as far back as the second century BC, and although much depleted now, it still numbers 16,000 (around half Italy's total). This is nowadays spread all over the city, but a couple of kosher restaurants and butchers remain on and around the main artery of the Jewish area, **Via Portico d'Ottavia**. This leads down to the **Portico d'Ottavia**, a not terribly well-preserved second-century BC gate, rebuilt by Augustus and dedicated to his sister in 23 BC, that was the entranceway to the adjacent amphitheatre of the **Teatro di Marcello** (summer daily 9am–7pm, winter daily 9am–6pm; free). This has served many purposes over the years: begun by Julius Caesar, finished by Augustus, it was pillaged in the fourth century and not properly restored until the Middle Ages, after which it became a formidable fortified palace for a succession of different rulers, including the Orsini family. Crossing to the other side of Via Portico d'Ottavia, follow your nose to **Piazza Mattei**, whose **Fontana delle Tartarughe**, or "turtle fountain", is a delightful late-sixteenth-century creation, perhaps restored by Bernini.

The Synagogue

The Ghetto's principal Jewish sight is the huge **Synagogue** by the river (Sun–Thurs 10am–5pm, Fri 9am–2pm; closed Sat & Jewish holidays; €7.50; ⓦwww .museoebraico.it), built in 1904 and very much dominating all around with its bulk – not to mention the carabinieri who stand guard 24 hours a day. The only way to see the building is on one of the short guided tours it runs in English, afterwards taking in the small two-room museum. The interior of the building is impressive, rising to a high, rainbow-hued dome, and the tours, which are included in the price and leave very regularly, are excellent, giving good background on the building and Rome's Jewish community in general.

Isola Tiberina

Almost opposite the syngagogue, the **Ponte Fabricio** crosses the river to **Isola Tiberina**. Built in 62 BC, it's the only classical bridge to remain intact without help from the restorers (the Ponte Cestio, on the other side of the island, was partially rebuilt in the nineteenth century). As for the island, it's a calm respite from the city centre proper, with its originally tenth-century church of **San Bartolomeo**, worth a peep inside for its ancient columns and an ancient wellhead on the altar steps, carved with figures relating to the founding of the church; the figures include St Bartholomew himself, who also features in the painting above the altar, hands tied above his head, on the point of being skinned alive – his famous and gruesome mode of martyrdom. Beyond the island, you can see the Ponte Rotto (Broken Bridge) – all that remains of the first stone bridge to span the Tiber, originally built between 179 and 142 BC.

Piazza Bocca della Verità and around

Further along the river from the Synagogue lies **Piazza Bocca della Verità**, home to two of the city's better-preserved Roman temples, the **Temple of Portunus** and the **Temple of Hercules Victor** – the oldest surviving marble structure in Rome and long known as the temple of Vesta because, like all vestal temples, it's circular. Both date from the end of the second century BC, and although you can't get inside, they're worth a look as fine examples of republican-era places of worship.

More interesting is the church of **Santa Maria in Cosmedin** on the far side of the square (daily 10am–5pm), a typically Roman medieval basilica with a huge marble altar and a colourful and ingenious Cosmati-work marble mosaic floor – one of the city's finest. Outside in the portico, and giving the square its name, is the **Bocca della Verità** (Mouth of Truth), an ancient Roman drain cover in the shape of an enormous face that in medieval times would apparently swallow the hand of anyone who hadn't told the truth. It was particularly popular with husbands anxious to test the faithfulness of their wives; now it is one of the city's biggest tour-bus attractions.

On the northern side, the square peters out peacefully at the **Arch of Janus**, perhaps Rome's most weathered triumphal arch, beyond which the campanile of the church of **San Giorgio in Velabro** (daily 10am–12.30pm & 4–6.30pm) is a stunted echo of that of Santa Maria across the way. The interior is one of the city's barest and most beautiful ancient basilicas; only the late-twelfth-century fresco in the apse, the work of Pietro Cavallini, lightens the melancholy mood. Cavallini's fresco shows Christ, his mother and various saints, including St George on the left, to whom the church is dedicated – and whose cranial bones lie in the reliquary under the high altar canopy, placed here in 749 AD, shortly after the original basilica was built.

Tridente

The northern part of Rome's centre is sometimes known as **Tridente** on account of the trident shape of the roads leading down from the apex of Piazza del Popolo – Via di Ripetta, Via del Corso and Via del Babuino. The area east of Via del Corso, focusing on Piazza di Spagna, is travellers' Rome, historically the artistic quarter of the city, for which eighteenth- and nineteenth-century Grand Tourists would make in search of the colourful, exotic city. Keats and Giorgio de Chirico are just two of those who lived on Piazza di Spagna; Goethe had lodgings on Via del Corso; and institutions like *Caffè Greco* and *Babington's Tea Rooms* were the meeting-places of a local artistic and expat community for close on a couple of centuries. Today these institutions have given ground to more latter-day traps for the tourist dollar: American Express and *McDonald's* have settled in, while Via dei Condotti and around is these days strictly international designer territory, with some of Rome's fanciest stores – local residents are more likely to be investment bankers than artists or poets.

Piazza del Popolo

The oval-shaped expanse of **Piazza del Popolo** is a dignified meeting of roads, now pedestrianized, that was laid out in 1538 by Pope Paul III (Alessandro Farnese) to make an impressive entrance to the city. The monumental **Porta del Popolo** went up in 1655, and was the work of Bernini, whose patron Alexander VII's Chigi family symbol – the heap of hills surmounted by a star – can clearly be seen above the main gateway. During summer, the steps around the obelisk and fountain, and the cafés on either side of the square, are popular hangouts. But the square's real attraction is the unbroken view it gives all the way down Via del Corso, to the central columns of the Vittorio Emanuele Monument. If you get to choose your first view of the centre of Rome, make it this one.

On the far side of the piazza, hard against the city walls, **Santa Maria del Popolo** (Mon–Sat 7am–noon & 4–7pm, Sun 8am–1.30pm & 4.30–7.30pm) holds some of the best Renaissance art of any Roman church. It was originally erected here in 1099 over the supposed burial place of Nero, in order to sanctify what was believed to be an evil place, but took its present form in the fifteenth century. Inside there are lovely frescoes by Pinturicchio in the first and third chapels of the south aisle, and the same artist also did some work in the Bramante-designed apse, which in turn boasts two fine tombs by Andrea Sansovino. The Chigi chapel, the second from the entrance in the northern aisle, was designed by Raphael for Agostino Chigi in 1516, though most of the work was actually undertaken by other artists and not finished until the seventeenth century. Michelangelo's protégé, Sebastiano del Piombo, was responsible for the altarpiece, and two of the sculptures in the corner niches, of Daniel and Habakkuk, are by Bernini. But it's two pictures by Caravaggio in the left-hand chapel of the north transept that attract the most attention. These are typically dramatic works – one, the *Conversion of St Paul*, showing Paul and horse bathed in a beatific radiance; the other, the *Crucifixion of St Peter*, depicting Peter as an aged but strong figure, dominated by the muscular figures hoisting him up.

The Mausoleum of Augustus

Via Ripetta runs southwest from Piazza del Popolo into **Piazza del Augusta Imperatore**, an odd square of largely Mussolini-era buildings, dominated by the massive **Mausoleum of Augustus**, burial place of the emperor and his family. These days not much more than a peaceful ring of cypresses, circled by paths, flowering shrubs and the debris of tramps, the mausoleum (visitable by appointment only daily Mon–Sat 9am–6pm; €2.50) has been transformed into many buildings over the years, not least a fortress, like Hadrian's mausoleum across the river. Inside, the passageways and central crypt, where the ashes of the members of the Augustan dynasty were kept, don't add much to the picture you get from the outside.

Ara Pacis Augustae

On the far side of the square, the **Ara Pacis Augustae** or "Altar of Augustan Peace" is now enclosed in a controversial purpose-built structure designed by the New York-based architect Richard Meier, its angular lines and sheer white surfaces dominating the river side of the square (daily 9am–7pm; €6.50, audio guide €3.50). The altar is a more substantially recognizable Roman remain than the mausoleum, a marble block enclosed by sculpted walls built in 13 BC, probably to celebrate Augustus's victory over Spain and Gaul and the peace it heralded. Much of it had been dug up piecemeal over the years, but the bulk of it was found during the middle half of the last century, about a few hundred yards south in the heart of the Campus Martius where it had originally stood. It is a superb example of imperial Roman sculpture, particularly in the victory procession itself on the mauseoleum side of the altar. This is a picture of a family at the height of its power, with little inkling of the scandal and tragedy that would afflict it in years to come. The first part is almost completely gone, but the head of Augustus is complete, as are the figures that follow – first the priests with their skull-cap headgear, then, behind the figure carrying an axe, Agrippa, hooded, clutching a rolled piece of parchment, with his son Gaius pulling on his toga. Then, respectively, come Augustus's wife Livia, followed by her son – and Augustus's eventual successor – Tiberius and niece Antonia, the latter caught simply and realistically turning to her husband, Drusus, while holding the hand of her son Germanicus. Of the various other children clutching the togas of the elders, the last is said to be the young Claudius, while the old man towards the end is perhaps the figure of Maecenas, Augustus's most trusted advisor during his heyday.

Piazza di Spagna and the Keats-Shelley Memorial House

Via del Babuino leads down from Piazza del Popolo to **Piazza di Spagna**, a long straggle of a square almost entirely enclosed by buildings and centring on the distinctive boat-shaped **Barcaccia** fountain, the last work of Bernini's father. It apparently remembers the great flood of Christmas Day 1598, when a barge from the Tiber was washed up on the slopes of Pincio Hill here.

Fronting the square, opposite the fountain, is the house where the poet John Keats died in 1821. It now serves as the **Keats-Shelley Memorial House** (Mon–Fri 9am–1pm & 3–6pm, Sat 11am–2pm & 3–6pm, Sun closed; €3.50; Ⓦ www.keats-shelley-house.org), an archive of English-language literary and historical works and a museum of manuscripts and literary memorabilia relating to the Keats circle of the early nineteenth century – namely the poet himself, Shelley and Mary Shelley, and Byron (who at one time lived across the square). Among many bits of manuscript, letters and the like, there's a silver scallop shell reliquary containing locks of Milton's and Elizabeth Barrett Browning's hair, while Keats's death mask, stored in the room where he died, captures a resigned grimace. Keats didn't really enjoy his time in Rome, referring to it as his "posthumous life": he was tormented by his love for Fanny Browne, and spent months in pain before he died, confined to the rooming house with his artist friend Joseph Severn, to whom he remarked that he could already feel "the flowers growing over him".

The Spanish Steps

The only thing Spanish about the **Spanish Steps** is the fact that they lead down to the Spanish Embassy, which also gave the piazza its name. Sweeping down in a cascade of balustrades and balconies, in the nineteenth century they were the hangout of young hopefuls waiting to be chosen as artists' models. Nowadays the scene is not much changed, with the steps providing the venue for international posing and fast pick-ups late into the summer nights. At the top is the **Trinità dei Monti**, a largely sixteenth-century church designed by Carlo Maderno and paid for by the French king. Its rose-coloured Baroque facade overlooks the rest of Rome from its hilltop site, and it's worth clambering up just for the views. While here you may as well pop your head around the door for a couple of faded works by Daniele da Volterra, notably a soft, flowing fresco of the Assumption in the third chapel on the right, which includes a portrait of his teacher Michelangelo, and a poorly lit *Deposition* across the nave.

Fontana di Trevi

In the opposite direction from the Spanish Steps, across Via del Tritone, is one of Rome's more surprising sights, easy to stumble on by accident – the **Fontana di Trevi**, a huge, very Baroque gush of water over statues and rocks built onto the backside of a Renaissance palace and fed by the same source that surfaces at the Barcaccia fountain in Piazza di Spagna. There was a previous Trevi fountain, designed by Alberti, around the corner in Via dei Crociferi, a smaller, more modest affair by all accounts, but Urban VIII decided to upgrade it in line with his other grandiose schemes of the time and employed Bernini, among others, to design an alternative. Work didn't begin, however, until 1732, when Niccolò Salvi won a competition held by Clement XII to design the fountain, and even then it took thirty years to finish the project. Salvi died in the process, his lungs destroyed by the time spent in the dank waterworks of his construction. The Trevi fountain is now a popular hangout and, of course, the place you come to chuck in a coin if you want to guarantee your return to Rome. You might also remember Anita Ekberg throwing herself into it in *La Dolce Vita*, though any attempt at recreating the scene is discouraged by the police presence here.

Galleria Colonna and the Time Elevator Roma

A short stroll south from the Fontana di Trevi brings you to the **Galleria Colonna**, at Via della Pilotta 17 (Sat 9am–1pm, closed Aug; €7), part of the Palazzo Colonna complex and worth forty minutes or so if you happen by when it's open, if only for the chandelier-decked Great Hall where most of the paintings are displayed. Best is the gallery's collection of landscapes by Dughet (Poussin's brother-in-law), but other works that stand out are Carracci's early – and unusually spontaneous – *Bean Eater* (though this attribution has been questioned), a *Narcissus* by Tintoretto and a *Portrait of a Venetian Gentleman* caught in supremely confident pose by Veronese.

Near Galleria Colonna at Via SS. Apostoli 20 is the **Time Elevator Roma** (daily 10.30am–7.30pm; €11), a multimedia film show of the history of Rome from its founding to the present day. With visitors strapped into a chair that moves around a bit like a flight simulator, it takes you on a "ride" through time; it lasts an hour and is a fun introduction if you don't know much about the history of the city.

In the opposite direction, the **Museo delle Cere** (daily 9am–8pm; €5) is a quirky first-floor museum of waxworks that hosts a diverse array of characters from history and Italian culture: not essential viewing by any means but certainly different from anything else you'll see in Rome, with wax figures of everyone from Mussolini to Francesco Totti.

The Quirinale and East Central Rome

Of the hills that rise up on the eastern side of the centre of Rome, the **Quirinale** is perhaps the most appealing, home to some of the city's greatest palaces, but also to some of Rome's greatest collections, not least in the amazing Palazzo Massimo. It's an area that you may spend quite a bit of time in anyway, as it's home to the area that includes Termini station and the hotels and restaurants that surround it.

Piazza Barberini

Piazza Barberini, a frenetic traffic junction at the top end of the busy shopping street of Via del Tritone, was named after Bernini's **Fontana del Tritone**, which gushes a high jet of water in the centre of the square. Traditionally, this was the Barberini family's quarter of the city; they were the greatest patrons of Gian Lorenzo Bernini, and the sculptor's works in their honour are thick on the ground around here. He finished the Tritone fountain in 1644, going on shortly after to design the **Fontana delle Api** ("Fountain of the Bees") at the bottom end of Via Veneto. Unlike the Tritone fountain you could walk right past this; it's a smaller, quirkier work, with a broad scallop shell studded with the bees that were the symbol of the Barberini.

Via Veneto and the Capuchin Cemetery

Via Veneto bends north from Piazza Barberini up to the southern edge of the Borghese gardens, its pricey bars and restaurants lining a street that was once the haunt of Rome's Beautiful People, made famous by Fellini's *La Dolce Vita*. They left a long time ago, however, and Via Veneto isn't really any different from other busy streets in central Rome – a pretty, tree-lined road, but with a fair share of high-class tack trying to cash in on departed glory.

A little way up on the right, the Capuchin church of **Santa Maria della Concezione** (daily 9am–noon & 3–6pm) was another sponsored creation of the Barberini, though it's not a particularly significant building in itself, only numbering Guido Reni's androgynous *St Michael Trampling on the Devil* among its treasures. The devil in the picture is said to be a portrait of Innocent X, whom the artist despised and who was apparently a sworn enemy of the Barberini family. The church is currently under restoration but when open its main attraction is its **Capuchin cemetery** (same times; donation expected), one of the more macabre and bizarre sights of Rome. Here, the bones of 4000 monks are set into the walls of a series of chapels, a monument to "Our Sister of Bodily Death" in the words of St Francis, that was erected in 1793. The bones appear in abstract or Christian patterns or as fully clothed skeletons, their faces peering out of their cowls in various twisted expressions of agony.

Palazzo Barberini

On the other side of Piazza Barberini, the **Palazzo Barberini**, at Via Barberini 18, is home to the **Galleria di Arte Antica** (Tues–Sun 8.30am– 7.30pm; €6; apartment tours leave every 45min), still undergoing a long-running restoration, but consisting of a rich patchwork of mainly Italian art from the early Renaissance to late Baroque period. It's an impressive collection, highlighted by works by Titian, El Greco and Caravaggio, but perhaps the most impressive feature of the gallery is the building itself, worked on at different times by the most favoured architects of the day – Bernini, Borromini and Maderno. The first floor Gran Salone is dominated by Pietro da Cortona's manic fresco *The Triumph of Divine Providence*, one of the best examples anywhere of exuberant Baroque trompe-l'oeil work – it almost crawls down the walls to meet you. Of the paintings, be sure to see Caravaggio's *Judith Beheading Holofernes*; Fra' Filippo Lippi's warmly maternal *Madonna and Child*, painted in 1437 and introducing background details, notably architecture, into Italian religious painting for the first time; Raphael's beguiling *Fornarina*, a painting of the daughter of a Trasteveran baker thought to have been Raphael's mistress (Raphael's name appears clearly on the woman's bracelet); Bronzino's rendering of the marvellously erect *Stefano Colonna*; and a portrait of Henry VIII by Hans Holbein. You can visit the **Barberini apartments** on regular guided tours, and it's just about worth it for the glimpse you get of Borromini's staircase – a spiral riposte to the main Bernini staircase on the other side of the building.

San Carlo, Sant' Andrea and the Palazzo del Quirinale
Heading southeast of Palazzo Barberini, along Via delle Quattro Fontane, brings you to a seventeenth-century landmark, the church of **San Carlo alle Quattro Fontane** (Mon–Sat 10am–1pm & 3–6pm, Sat noon–1pm). This was Borromini's first real design commission, and in it he displays all the ingenuity he later became famous for, cramming the church elegantly into a tiny and awkwardly shaped site that apparently covers roughly the same surface area as one of the dome-supporting piers inside St Peter's. Tucked in beside the church, the cloister is also squeezed into a tight but elegant oblong, topped with a charming balustrade. Outside the church are the four **fountains** that give the street and church their name, each cut into a niche in a corner of the crossroads that marks this, the highest point on the Quirinal Hill, while to the left is the featureless wall of the **Palazzo del Quirinale** (Sun 8.30am–noon; €5; www.quirinale .it), a sixteenth-century structure that was the official summer residence of the popes until Unification, when it became the royal palace. It's now the home of Italy's president, and worth braving the security for a glimpse of the style in which popes, despots, kings and now presidents like to live, with a fine set of state rooms and some very accomplished works of art.

You can appreciate its exceptional siting from the **Piazza del Quirinale**, from which views stretch right across the centre of Rome. The main feature of the piazza is the huge statue of the Dioscuri, or Castor and Pollux – massive five-metre-high Roman copies of classical Greek statues, showing the two godlike twins, sons of Jupiter, who according to legend won victory for the Romans in an important battle. Nearby, there's another piece of design ingenuity on Via del Quirinale: the domed church of **Sant'Andrea al Quirinale** (Mon–Sat 8.30am–noon & 3.30–7pm, Sun 9am–noon & 3.30–7.30pm), which Bernini planned as a kind of flat oval shape to fit into its wide but shallow site. Like San Carlo, it's unusual and ingenious inside, and the upstairs rooms where the Polish saint, St Stanislaus Kostka, lived (and died) in 1568, focus on a disturbingly lifelike painted statue of Stanislaus lying on his deathbed.

Via XX Settembre and Santa Maria della Vittoria
Via XX Settembre spears out towards the Aurelian Wall from Via del Quirinale – not Rome's most appealing thoroughfare by any means, flanked by the deliberately faceless bureaucracies of the national government, erected after Unification in anticipation of Rome's ascension as a new world capital. It was, however, the route by which Italian troops entered the city on September 20, 1870, and the place where they breached the wall is marked with a column. The church of **Santa Maria della Vittoria** here (daily 7am–noon & 3.30–7pm) was built by the Baroque-era architect Carlo Maderno and its interior is one of the most elaborate examples of Baroque decoration in Rome: almost shockingly excessive to modern eyes, its ceiling and walls are pitted with carving, and statues are crammed into remote corners as in an over-stuffed attic. The church's best-known feature, Bernini's carving the *Ecstasy of St Theresa*, the centrepiece of the sepulchral chapel of Cardinal Cornaro, continues the histrionics – a deliberately melodramatic work featuring a theatrically posed St Theresa, who lays back in groaning submission beneath a mass of dishevelled garments in front of the murmuring cardinals.

Via Nazionale and Piazza della Repubblica

A couple of minutes' walk from Via XX Settembre, **Via Nazionale** connects Piazza Venezia and the centre of town with the area around Termini and the eastern districts beyond. A focus for much development after Unification, its heavy, overbearing buildings were constructed to give Rome some semblance of modern sophistication when it became capital, but most are now occupied by hotels and bland shops and boutiques. At the top of Via Nazionale, **Piazza della Repubblica** is typical of Rome's nineteenth-century regeneration, a stern and dignified semicircle of buildings that was until recently rather dilapidated but is now – with the help of the new and very stylish *Hotel Exedra* – once again resurgent, centring on a fountain surrounded by languishing nymphs and sea monsters.

Santa Maria degli Angeli and the Aula Ottagona

Piazza della Republica actually follows the outlines of the exedra of the Baths of Diocletian, the remains of which lie across the piazza and are partially contained in the church of **Santa Maria degli Angeli** (Mon–Sat 7am–6.30pm, Sun 7am–7.30pm) – one of Rome's least welcoming churches but giving the best impression of the size and grandeur of Diocletian's baths complex. It's a huge, open building, with an interior standardized by Vanvitelli into a rich eighteenth-century confection after a couple of centuries of piecemeal adaptation (started by an aged Michelangelo). The pink granite pillars, at nine feet in diameter the largest in Rome, are original, and the main transept formed the main hall of the baths; only the crescent shape of the facade remains from the original caldarium (it had previously been hidden by a newer facing), the vestibule (the tepidarium) and main transept. The meridian that strikes diagonally across the floor here was, until 1846, the regulator of time for Romans (now a cannon shot is fired daily at noon from the Janiculum Hill).

The exit channels you through the sacristy – and a small exhibition on the history of the baths and church – to Via Cernaia; behind is another remnant of the baths, the **Aula Ottagona** (Octagonal Hall), part of the Museo Nazionale Romano (Mon–Sat 9am–2pm, Sun 9am–1pm; same ticket), which contains marble statues taken from the baths of Caracalla and Diocletian, and two remarkable statues of a boxer and athlete from the Quirinale Hill. Excavations underground – accessible by stairs – show the furnaces for heating water for the baths and the foundations of another building from the time of Diocletian.

Museo delle Terme di Diocleziano

Behind Santa Maria degli Angeli, the huge halls and courtyards of Diocletian's baths have been renovated and they and an attached Carthusian monastery now hold what is probably the least interesting part of the Museo Nazionale Romano (Tues–Sun 9am–7pm; €7, includes Palazzo Altemps, Palazzo Massimo, Crypta Balbi, valid 3 days). The museum's most evocative part is the large cloister of the church whose sides are crammed with statuary, funerary monuments and sarcophagi and fragments from all over Rome. The galleries that wrap around the cloister hold a reasonable if rather academically presented collection of pre-Roman and Roman finds: busts, terracotta statues, armour and weapons found in Roman tombs – hardly compulsory viewing.

Palazzo Massimo

Across from Santa Maria degli Angeli, through a seedy little park, the **Palazzo Massimo**, Largo Perretti 1 (Tues–Sun 9am–7pm; €7, includes Palazzo Altemps, Terme Diocletian, Crypta Balbi, valid 3 days, €4 for the audio guide), is home to one of the two principal parts of the Museo Nazionale Romano (the other is in the Palazzo Altemps) – a superb collection of Greek and Roman antiquities (second only to the Vatican's). As one of the great museums of Rome, there are too many highlights to do justice here, and there is something worth seeing on every floor. Start at the **basement** where there are displays of exquisite gold jewellery from the second century AD, and the mummified remains of an 8-year-old girl, along with a fantastic coin collection. The **ground floor** is devoted to statuary of the early Empire, including a gallery with an unparalleled selection of unidentified busts found all over Rome – amazing pieces of portraiture, and as vivid a representation of patrician Roman life as you'll find. There are also identifiable faces – a bronze of Germanicus, a marvellous small bust of Caligula, several representations of Livia and a hooded statue of Augustus. Note the superb examples of Roman copies of Greek statuary – an altar found on Via Nomentana stands out, decorated with figures relating to the cult of Bacchus, as well as statues of Aphrodite and Melponome. The museum really gets going on the **first floor**, with groupings of the various Imperial dynasties in roughly chronological order, starting with the Flavian emperors – the craggy determination of Vespasian, the pinched nobility of Nerva – and leading on to Trajan, who appears with his wife Plotina as Hercules, next to a bust of his cousin Hadrian. The collection continues with the Antonine emperors – Antoninus Pius in a heroic nude pose and in several busts, flanked by likenesses of his daughter Faustina Minor. Faustina was the wife of Antoninus's successor, Marcus Aurelius, who appears in the next room. Further on are the Severans, with the fierce-looking Caracalla looking across past his father Septimius Severus to his brother Geta, whom he later murdered. Finally there's the **second floor**, which takes in some of the finest Roman frescoes and mosaics ever found. There's a stunning set of frescoes from the Villa di Livia, depicting an orchard dense with fruit and flowers and patrolled by partridges and doves, wall paintings rescued from what was perhaps the riverside villa of Augustus's daughter Julia and Marcus Agrippa, and mosaics showing four chariot drivers and their horses, so finely crafted that from a distance they look as if they've been painted.

Stazione Termini

Across the street is the low white facade of **Stazione Termini** (so named for its proximity to the Baths or "Terme" of Diocletian) and the vast, bus-crammed hubbub that is Piazza dei Cinquecento in front. The station is an ambitious piece of modern architectural design that was completed in 1950 and still entirely dominates the streets around with its low-slung, self-consciously futuristic lines. The cavernous ticket hall is occupied by retail and restaurant space and is a nice spot for a browse and a wander, and a marvellous place to catch a train. As for **Piazza dei Cinquecento**, it's a good place to find buses and taxis, but otherwise it and the areas around are pretty much low-life territory and, although not especially dangerous, not a place to hang around for long either.

Via Nomentana

At the north end of Via XX Settembre, the **Porta Pia** was one of the last works of Michelangelo, erected under Pope Pius IV in 1561, beyond which the wide boulevard of **Via Nomentana** leads up eventually to the church of **Sant'Agnese fuori le Mura** (Mon 9am–noon, Tues–Sat 9am–noon & 4–6pm, Sun 4–6pm), served by bus #36 from Termini, or #60 from Piazza Venezia. Dedicated to the same saint who was martyred in Domitian's Stadium in 303 AD, the church was built by Honorius I in the seventh century, when he reworked Constantine's original structure. The apse mosaic is Byzantine in style and contemporary with

Honorius's building, showing Agnes next to the pope, who holds a model of his church. Out of the narthex the custodian will lead you down into the **catacombs** (same hours as church; €5) that sprawl below the church and are among the best-preserved and most crowd-free of all the city's catacombs.

The guide will then show you a further part of the small complex of early Christian structures, the church of **Santa Constanza** (usually open the same hours as Sant'Agnese; free), which perhaps more than any other building in Rome illustrates the transition from the pagan to Christian city in its decorative and architectural features. Built in 350 AD as a mausoleum for Constantia and Helena, the daughters of the Emperor Constantine, it's a round structure that follows the traditional shape of the great pagan tombs, and the mosaics on the vaulting of its circular ambulatory – fourth-century depictions of vines, leaves and birds – would have been as at home on the floor of a Roman *domus* as they were in a Christian church.

San Lorenzo fuori le Mura

South and east of Via Nomentana, a short walk from Termini, the studenty neighbourhood of San Lorenzo takes its name from the basilica of **San Lorenzo fuori le Mura** – one of the great pilgrimage churches of Rome, and a typical Roman basilica, fronted by a columned portico and with a lovely twelfth-century cloister to its side (daily: summer 7am–noon & 4–7.30pm; winter closes 5.30pm). The original church here was built over the site of St Lawrence's martyrdom by Constantine – the saint was reputedly burned to death on a gridiron, halfway through his ordeal apparently uttering the immortal words, "Turn me, I am done on this side." Where the church of San Lorenzo differs is that it is actually a combination of three churches built at different periods – one a sixth-century reconstruction of Constantine's church by Pelagius II, which now forms the chancel, another a fifth-century church from the time of Sixtus III, both joined by a basilica from the thirteenth century by Honorius II. Because of its proximity to Rome's rail yards, the church was bombed heavily during World War II, but it has been rebuilt with sensitivity, and remains much as it was originally. Inside there are features from all periods: a Cosmetic floor, thirteenth-century pulpits and a Paschal candlestick. The mosaic on the inside of the triumphal arch is a sixth-century depiction of Pelagius offering his church to Christ, while below stairs, catacombs (currently closed for restoration) – where St Lawrence was apparently buried – sit among pillars from Constantine's original structure. There's also a Romanesque cloister with a well-tended garden that you can enter via the sacristy.

Ancient Rome

There are remnants of the ancient Roman era all over the city, but the most concentrated and central grouping – which for simplicity's sake we've called Ancient Rome – is the area that stretches southeast from the Capitoline Hill. It's a reasonably traffic-free and self-contained part of the city, but it wasn't always

Visiting the Forum, Palatine and Colosseum

The Forum, Palatine and Colosseum are open daily: summer 8.30am–6pm; winter 9am–4.30pm. Entry to the Forum is free but entry to the Palatine and Colosseum costs €11 for both if you visit on the same day and buy your ticket by 1.30pm. A visitor centre, opposite the church of Santi Cosma e Damiano (daily 9.30am–6.30pm), has information if you need it, and a café to rest your aching feet.

like this. Mussolini ploughed Via dei Fori Imperiali through here in the 1930s, with the intention of turning it into one giant archeological park, and this to some extent is what it is. You could spend a good half-day or longer picking your way through the rubble of what was once the heart of the ancient world.

The Imperial Forums and around

One of the major victims of Mussolini's plan was the **Forum of Trajan** on the north side of Via dei Fori Imperiali (Tues–Sun 9am–6pm; €3), a complex of basilicas, monuments, apartments and shops that was, in its day, the most sumptuous of the imperial forums, built here after the Forum proper had become too small at what was probably the very pinnacle of Roman power and prestige. It's currently fairly unrecognizable, the main section no more than a sunken area of scattered columns to the left of the road, fronting the semicircle of **Markets of Trajan,** a tiered ancient Roman shopping centre that's also accessible from Via IV Novembre but is currently under restoration. Down below the markets, the **Basilica Ulpia** was a central part of the Forum of Trajan, an immense structure, now mostly hidden below ground level. It had five aisles and a huge apse at either end, and measured 176m by 59m. At the head of the basilica, the enormous **Column of Trajan** was erected to celebrate the emperor's victories in Dacia (modern Romania) in 112 AD, and is covered from top to bottom with reliefs commemorating the highlights of the campaign. The carving on the base shows the trophies brought back and there's an inscription saying that the column was dedicated by the Senate and People of Rome in 113 AD in honour of Trajan. Behind the Forum of Trajan, the **Torre delle Milizie** is fondly imagined to be the tower from which Nero watched Rome burning, although it's actually a twelfth-century fortification left over from the days when Rome was divided into warring factions within the city walls.

Back on Via dei Fori Imperiali, to the left, the round brick facade here was once part of the **Forum of Augustus.** You can get up closer to the ruins here by way of a metal walkway, which also takes you through to the lower streets of the Monti district, or just continue on down past the various other imperial forums to the visitor centre, and the church of **Santi Cosma e Damiano** opposite (daily 8am–1pm & 3–7pm), originally created from the Temple of Romulus in the Forum, and you can look down into this from the nave of the church. The main features are the mosaics in the apse, while outside the cloister is wonderfully peaceful and has a Neapolitan **presepio** or giant Christmas crib displayed in a room in the corner (April–Oct daily 10am–1pm & 3–6.30pm; Nov–March Tues–Thurs 10am–1pm, Fri–Sun 10am–1pm & 3–5.30pm; €1), a huge piece of work with literally hundreds of figures spread among the ruins of ancient Rome.

The Roman Forum

The five or so acres that make up the **Roman Forum** were once the heart of the Mediterranean world and, although the glories of ancient Rome are hard to glimpse here now, there's a symbolic allure to the place, and at certain times of day a desolate drama, that make it one of the most compelling sets of ruins anywhere in the world. You need an imagination and a little history to really appreciate the place but the public spaces are easy enough to discern, especially the spinal **Via Sacra**, the best-known street of ancient Rome, along which victorious emperors and generals would ride in procession to give thanks at the Capitoline's Temple of Juno. Towards the Capitoline Hill end of the Via Sacra, the large cube-shaped building is the **Curia**, built on the orders of Julius Caesar as part of his programme for expanding the Forum, although what you see now is a 3rd-century AD reconstruction. The Senate met here, and inside three wide stairs rise left and right, on which about 300 senators could be accommodated with their folding chairs. In the centre is the speaker's platform, with a porphyry statue of a togaed figure. Nearby, the **Arch of Septimius Severus** was constructed in the early third century AD by his sons Caracalla and Galba to mark their father's victories in what is now Iran. The friezes on it recall Severus and in particular Caracalla, who ruled Rome with a reign of undisciplined terror for seven years. Next to the arch, the low brown wall is the **Rostra**, from which important speeches were made (it was from here that Mark Anthony most likely spoke about Caesar after his death), to the left of which are the long stairs of the **Basilica Julia**, built by Julius Caesar in the 50s BC after he returned from the Gallic wars. A bit further along, on the right, rails mark the site of the **Lacus Curtius**, the spot where, according to legend, a chasm opened during the earliest days of the city and the soothsayers determined that it would only be closed once Rome had sacrificed its most valuable possession into it. Marcus Curtius, a Roman soldier who declared that Rome's most valuable possession was a loyal citizen, hurled himself and his horse into the void and it duly closed. Next to the Basilica Julia, the enormous pile of rubble topped by three graceful Corinthian columns is the **Temple of Castor and Pollux**, dedicated in 484 BC to the divine twins or Dioscuri, who appeared miraculously to ensure victory for the Romans in a key battle. Beyond here, the **House of the Vestal Virgins** is a second-century AD reconstruction of a building originally built by Nero: four floors of rooms around a central courtyard, still with its pool in the centre and fringed by the statues or inscribed pedestals of the women themselves, with the round Temple of Vesta at the near end. Almost opposite, across the Via Sacra, a shady walkway to the left leads to the **Basilica of Maxentius**, sometimes called the Basilica of Constantine, in terms of size and ingenuity probably the Forum's most impressive remains. Begun by Maxentius, it was continued by his co-emperor and rival, Constantine, after he had defeated him at the Battle of the Milvian Bridge in 312 AD. Back on the Via Sacra, past the church of Santa Maria Nova, the **Antiquarium of the**

△ The Roman Forum

Forum (closed at the time of writing) houses a collection of statue fragments, capitals, mosaics and other bits and pieces found around the Forum, past which the hill climbs more steeply to the **Arch of Titus**, built by Titus's brother, Domitian, after the emperor's death in 81 AD, to commemorate his victories in Judea in 70 AD, and his triumphal return from that campaign. It's a long-standing tradition that Jews don't pass under this arch.

The Palatine Hill

Rising above the Roman Forum, the **Palatine** (daily 8.30am–6pm; €11, includes the Colosseum, valid the same day if bought before 1.30pm; guided tours in English at noon €3.50) is supposedly where the city of Rome was founded, and is home to some of its most ancient remains. In a way it's a more pleasant site to tour than the Forum, and a good place to have a picnic and relax after the rigours of the ruins below. In the days of the Republic, the Palatine was the most desirable address in Rome (the word "palace" is derived from Palatine), and big names continued to colonize it during the Imperial era, trying to outdo each other with ever larger and more magnificent dwellings.

Along the main path up from the Forum, the **Domus Flavia** was once one of the most splendid residences, and, to the left, the top level of the gargantuan **Domus Augustana** spreads to the far brink of the hill – not the home of Augustus as its name suggests, but the private house of any emperor (or "Augustus"). You can look down from here on its vast central courtyard with fountain and wander to the brink of the deep trench of the **Stadium**. On the far side of the stadium, the ruins of the Domus and **Baths of Septimius Severus** cling to the side of the hill, while the large grey building nearby houses the **Museo Palatino** (daily 9am–6pm), which contains an assortment of statuary, pottery and architectural fragments that have been excavated on the Palatine during the last 150 years. In the opposite direction from the Domus Flavia is the **Cryptoporticus**, a long passage built by Nero to link the vestibule of his Domus Aurea (see p.781) with the Palatine palaces, and decorated along with well-preserved Roman stuccowork at the far end, towards the **House of Livia**, originally believed to have been the residence of Livia, the wife of Augustus, though now identified as simply part of **House of Augustus** – the set of ruins beyond, next to which are the remains of the Palatine **Temple of Apollo**, dedicated by Augustus himself in 28 BC. Climb up the steps by the entrance to the Cryptoporticus and you're in the bottom corner of the **Farnese Gardens**, among the first botanical gardens in Europe, laid out by Cardinal Alessandro Farnese in the mid-sixteenth century and now a tidily planted, shady retreat from the exposed heat of the ruins. At the far end of the gardens are the traces of an **Iron Age village** that perhaps marks the real centre of Rome's ancient beginnings.

The Arch of Constantine

Leaving the Roman Forum by way of the Via Sacra, the huge **Arch of Constantine** on your right was placed here in the early decades of the fourth century AD after Constantine had consolidated his power as sole emperor. The arch demonstrates the deterioration of the arts during the late stages of the Roman Empire – most of the sculptural decoration here had to be removed from other monuments, and the builders were probably quite ignorant of the significance of the pieces they borrowed: the round medallions are taken from a temple dedicated to the emperor Hadrian's lover, Antinous, and show Antinous and Hadrian engaged in a hunt. The other pieces, taken from the Forum of Trajan, show Dacian prisoners captured in Trajan's war.

The Colosseum

The **Colosseum** (daily 8.30am–6pm; €11, includes the Palatine, valid the same day if bought before 1.30pm) is perhaps Rome's most awe-inspiring ancient monument, an enormous structure that despite the depredations of nearly 2000 years of earthquakes, fires, riots, wars and, not least, plundering for its seemingly inexhaustible supply of ready-cut travertine blocks, still stands relatively intact – a recognizable symbol not just of the city of Rome, but of the entire ancient world. It's not much more than a shell now, eaten away by pollution and cracked by the vibrations of cars and the metro, but the basic structure is easy to see, and has served as a model for stadiums around the world ever since. You'll not be alone in appreciating it and during summer the combination of people and scaffolding can make a visit more like touring a contemporary building-site than an ancient monument. But visit late in the evening or early morning before the tour buses have arrived, and the arena can seem more like the marvel it really is.

Originally known as the Flavian Amphitheatre (the name Colosseum is a much later invention), it was begun around 72 AD by the emperor Vespasian. Inside, there was room for a total of around 60,000 people seated and 10,000 or so standing. The seating was allocated strictly, with the emperor and his attendants naturally occupying the best seats in the house, and the social class of the spectators diminishing as you got nearer the top. There was a labyrinth below that was covered with a wooden floor and punctuated at various places for trap doors that could be opened as required, and lifts to raise and lower the animals that were to take part in the games. The floor was covered with canvas to make it waterproof and the canvas was covered with several centimetres of sand to absorb blood; in fact, our word "arena" is derived from the Latin word for sand.

Monti and San Giovanni

Immediately north of the Colosseum, the **Esquiline Hill** is the highest and largest of the city's seven hills. Formerly one of the most fashionable residential quarters of ancient Rome, it's nowadays a mixed area that together with the adjacent Viminale Hill make up the district known as Monti, an appealing and to some extent up-and-coming quarter of cobbled streets and neighbourhood bars and restaurants. It's also an area that most travellers to Rome encounter at some point – not just because of key sights

△ The Roman Forum

like Nero's Domus Aurea and the basilica of Santa Maria Maggiore, but also because of its proximity to Termini, whose environs shelter the lion's share of Rome's budget hotels.

The Domus Aurea

One of the Esquiline Hill's most intriguing sights is without doubt Nero's **Domus Aurea**, though unfortunately this is currently closed due to flooding. Once covering a vast area between the Palatine and Esquiline, it wasn't in fact intended to be a residence at all, but a series of banqueting rooms, small baths, terraces and gardens, facing a lake fed by underground springs and streams. Rome was accustomed to Nero's excesses, but it had never seen anything like the Golden House before; the facade was supposed to have been coated in solid gold, there was hot and cold running water in the baths, and the grounds, which covered a full square mile, held vineyards and game. Nero didn't get to enjoy it for long – he died a couple of years after it was finished, and later emperors were determined to erase it from Rome's cityscape – Vespasian built the Colosseum over the lake and Trajan built his baths on top of the rest of the complex – and it was pretty much forgotten until its wall paintings were discovered by Renaissance artists, including Raphael. Tours start by taking you down a long corridor into the excavated rooms of the palace where the temperature always hovers around 10°C so bring a sweater or jacket even in the middle of summer. You quickly become aware of just how much Trajan set out to obliterate the place – his baths' foundations merge into parts of the palace, and vice versa – but a free plan, not to mention the guide, helps you imagine how it once looked. Most spectacular is the domed Octagonal Room, with a hole in the middle, which is supposed to have rotated as the day progressed to emulate the passage of the sun. Elsewhere there are paintings depicting people looking back through windows at the viewer, garlands of flowers and foliage, interspersed with mythical animals, and, best of all, a room illustrating Homer's story of Achilles being sent to the island of Skyros disguised as a woman to prevent him being drawn into the Trojan wars.

San Pietro in Vincoli

Recently restored, **San Pietro in Vincoli** (daily 8am–12.30pm & 3–7pm) is one of Rome's most delightfully plain churches. It was built to house an important relic, the chains (*vincoli*) that bound St Peter when imprisoned in Jerusalem and those that held him in the Mamertime Prison, which miraculously fused together when they were brought into contact with each other. The chains can still be seen in the *confessio* beneath the high altar, but most people come for the tomb of Pope Julius II at the far end of the southern aisle. The tomb occupied Michelangelo on and off for much of his career and was the cause of many a dispute with Julius and his successors. The artist eventually and reluctantly gave it up to paint the Sistine Chapel – the only statues that he managed to complete are the *Moses*, *Leah* and *Rachel*, which remain here, and two *Dying Slaves* which are now in the Louvre. The figures are among the artist's most captivating works, especially *Moses*: because of a medieval mistranslation of scripture, he is depicted with satyr's horns instead of the "radiance of the Lord" that Exodus tells us shone around his head. Nonetheless this powerful statue is so lifelike that Michelangelo is alleged to have struck its knee with his hammer and shouted "Speak, damn you!"

Via Cavour and Santa Maria Maggiore

Steps lead down from San Pietro in Vincoli to **Via Cavour**, a busy central thoroughfare that carves a route between the Colosseum and Termini station.

ROME AND LAZIO | The City

After about half a kilometre, the street widens to reveal the basilica of **Santa Maria Maggiore** (daily 7am–7pm; free), one of the city's greatest basilicas, and with one of Rome's best-preserved Byzantine interiors – a fact belied by its dull eighteenth-century exterior. Unlike the other great places of pilgrimage in Rome, Santa Maria Maggiore was not built on any special Constantinian site, but instead went up during the fifth century after the Council of Ephesus recognized the cult of the Virgin, and churches venerating Our Lady began to spring up all over the Christian world. According to legend, the Virgin Mary appeared to Pope Liberius in a dream on the night of August 4, 352 AD, telling him to build a church on the Esquiline hill, on a spot where he would find a patch of newly fallen snow the next morning. The snow would outline exactly the plan of the church that should be built there in her honour – which of course is exactly what happened, and the first church here was called Santa Maria della Neve ("of the snow"). The present structure dates from about 420 AD, and was completed during the reign of Sixtus III, and survives remarkably intact, the broad nave fringed on both sides with strikingly well-kept mosaics, most of which date from the church's construction and recount incidents from the Old Testament. The chapel in the right transept holds the elaborate tomb of Sixtus V – another, less famous, Sistine Chapel, decorated with frescoes and stucco reliefs portraying events from his reign. Outside this is the tomb of the Bernini family, including Gian Lorenzo himself, while opposite, the Pauline Chapel is even more sumptuous than the Vatican's Sistine Chapel, home to the tombs of the Borghese pope, Paul V, and his immediate predecessor Clement VIII. The floor, in the *opus sectile* style of mosaic work, contains the Borghese arms, an eagle and dragon, while the magnificently gilded ceiling shows glimpses of heaven. Between the two chapels, the *confessio* contains a kneeling statue of Pope Pius IX, and, beneath it, a reliquary that is said to contain fragments of the crib of Christ. The high altar, above it, contains the relics of St Matthew, among other Christian martyrs, but it's the mosaics of the arch that really dazzle, a vivid representation of scenes from the life of Christ. There's a **museum** underneath the basilica that sports what even by Roman standards is a wide variety of relics (daily 9am–6.30pm; €4), and a **loggia** above the main entrance whose thirteenth-century mosaics of the legend "of the snow" are worth seeing (tours daily at 9am & 1pm, bookable in advance; €3).

Santa Prassede and Santa Pudenziana

South of Santa Maria Maggiore, off Via Merulana, the ninth-century church of **Santa Prassede** (daily 7am–noon & 4–6.30pm) occupies an ancient site, where it's claimed St Prassede harboured Christians on the run from the Roman persecutions. She apparently collected the blood and remains of the martyrs and placed them in a well where she herself was later buried; a red marble disc in the floor of the nave marks the spot. In the southern aisle, the Chapel of Saint Zeno was built by Pope Paschal I as a mausoleum for his mother, Theodora, and is decorated with marvellous ninth-century mosaics that make it glitter like a jewel-encrusted bowl. The chapel also contains a fragment of a column supposed to be the one to which Christ was tied when he was scourged.

On the other side of Via Cavour, the church of **Santa Pudenziana** on Via Urbana (daily 8am–noon & 4–6pm) has equally ancient origins, dedicated to St Prassede's supposed sister and for many years believed to have been built on the site where St Peter lived and worshipped – though this has since been entirely discredited. There were for years two relics in the church, the chair that St Peter used as his throne and the table at which he said Mass, though both have long gone – to the Vatican and the Lateran, respectively. But the church still has one feature of ancient origin, the superb fifth-century apse mosaics – some of the oldest Christian figurative mosaics in Rome, though they've been tampered with and restored over the years.

San Giovanni in Laterano

At the opposite end of Via Merulana from Santa Maria Maggiore, a ten-minute walk, the basilica of **San Giovanni in Laterano** (daily 7am–6.30pm) lends its name to the district that surrounds it. Officially Rome's cathedral and the seat of the pope as bishop of Rome, this was for centuries the main papal residence. However, when the papacy returned from Avignon at the end of the fourteenth century, the pope moved across town to the Vatican, where he has remained ever since. There has been a church on this site since the fourth century, the first established by Constantine, and the present building, reworked by Borromini in the mid-seventeenth century, evokes Rome's staggering wealth of history, with a host of features from different periods. The doors to the church were taken from the Curia of the Roman Forum, while much of what you see inside dates from 1600, when Clement VIII had the church remodelled for that Holy Year. The first pillar on the left of the right-hand aisle shows a fragment of Giotto's fresco of Boniface VIII, proclaiming the first Holy Year in 1300. Further on, a more recent monument commemorates Sylvester I – "the magician pope", Bishop of Rome during much of Constantine's reign – and incorporates part of his original tomb, said to sweat and rattle its bones when a pope is about to die. Kept secure behind the papal altar are the heads of St Peter and St Paul, the church's prize relics. Outside, the **cloisters** (daily 9am–6pm; €2) are one of the most pleasing parts of the complex, decorated with early thirteenth-century Cosmati work and with fragments of the original basilica arranged around in no particular order, including a remarkable papal throne assembly and various papal artefacts (not least the vestments of Boniface VIII) in a room off to the side. Next door, the **Baptistry** (daily 7am–12.30pm & 4–7.30pm; free) has been carefully restored, along with the side of the church itself, after a car bombing in 1993. It's the oldest surviving baptistry in the Christian world, a mosaic-lined, octagonal structure built during the fifth century that has been the model for many such buildings since. There are more ancient remains on the other side of the church, on Piazza di Porta San Giovanni, foremost of which is the **Scala Santa** (April–Sept daily 6.15am–noon & 3.30–6.45pm; Oct–March daily 6.15am–noon & 3–6.15pm; free), claimed to be the staircase from Pontius Pilate's house down which Christ walked after his trial. The 28 steps are protected by boards, and the only way you're allowed to climb them is on your knees, which pilgrims do regularly – although there is also a staircase to the side for the less penitent. At the top, the Sancta Sanctorum or chapel of **San Lorenzo** holds an ancient (sixth- or seventh-century) painting of Christ said to be the work of an angel, hence its name – *acheiropoeton*, or "not done by human hands".

San Clemente

A short walk from San Giovanni, back towards the Colosseum, is the church of **San Clemente** (Mon–Sat 9am–12.30pm & 3–6pm, Sun 10am–12.30pm & 3–6pm; €5 for the lower church and temple), a cream-coloured twelfth-century basilica that's a conglomeration of three places of worship, encapsulating perhaps better than any other the continuity of history in the city. The ground-floor church is a superb example of a medieval basilica: its facade and courtyard face east in the archaic fashion, and there are some fine, warm mosaics in the apse and – perhaps the highlight of the main church – a chapel with frescoes by Masolino, showing scenes from the life of St Catherine. Downstairs there's the nave of an earlier church, dating to 392 AD, with a frescoed narthex depicting, among other things, the Miracle of San Clemente. And at the eastern end of this church, steps lead down to a third level: a labyrinthine set of rooms including a dank Mithraic temple of the late second century, set among several rooms of a Roman house built after the fire of 64 AD. A statue of Mithras slaying the bull and the seats on which the worshippers sat during their ceremonies are preserved in the temple. The underground river that formerly fed the lake in front of the Domus Aurea can be heard rushing to its destination in the Tiber, behind the Circo Massimo, a reminder that Rome is built on very shaky foundations indeed.

Santa Croce in Gerusalemme

Five minutes' walk from San Giovanni in the opposite direction lies another key Roman church, **Santa Croce in Gerusalemme**, one of the seven pilgrimage churches of Rome (daily 6.45am–7.30pm). Despite its later Renaissance and Baroque adornments, it feels very ancient – as indeed it is, supposedly standing on the site of the palace of Constantine's mother St Helena. It houses the relics of the true cross she brought back from Jerusalem, stored in a surreal Mussolini-era chapel up some steps at the end of the left aisle. The Renaissance apse frescoes show the discovery of the fragments, under a seated Christ, and are very fine indeed. Steps behind lead down to the original level of Helena's house – now a chapel dedicated to the saint and decorated with Renaissance mosaics.

The Pincio and Villa Borghese

The terrace and gardens of the **Pincio**, immediately above Piazza del Popolo, were laid out by Valadier in the early nineteenth century, and, fringed with dilapidated busts of classical and Italian heroes, give fine views over the roofs, domes and TV antennae of central Rome, right across to St Peter's and the Janiculum Hill. Beyond lie the collection of parks and gardens that forms Rome's largest central open space, the **Villa Borghese**, made up of the grounds of the seventeenth-century pleasure palace of Scipione Borghese, which were bought by the city at the beginning of the last century. It's a huge area, with its woods, lakes and lawns offering respite from the bustle of the city centre, and any number of attractions – including some of the city's finest museums – for those who want to do more than just stroll or sunbathe.

Museo e Galleria Borghese

Situated on the far eastern edge of the Villa Borghese park is the wonderful **Museo e Galleria Borghese** (Tues–Sun 9am–7pm; €8.50; pre-booked visits are obligatory as a limited number of people are allowed in every 2hr; ☎06.32.810, ⓦ www.galleriaborghese.it). Built in the early seventeenth century by Cardinal Scipione Borghese and turned over to the state when the gardens became city property in 1902, today it's one of Rome's great treasure houses and should not be missed.

The **ground floor museo** contains mainly sculpture: a mixture of ancient Roman items and seventeenth-century works, roughly linked together with late-eighteenth-century ceiling paintings showing scenes from the Trojan War. Highlights include, in the first room off the entrance hall, Canova's famously erotic statue *Paolina Borghese* – sister of Napoleon and married (reluctantly) to the reigning Prince Borghese – posed as Venus. Next door, there's a marvellous statue of David by Bernini, the face of which is a self-portrait of the sculptor, and, further on, a dramatic, poised statue of Apollo and Daphne that captures the split second when Daphne is transformed into a laurel tree, with her fingers becoming leaves and her legs tree trunks. Next door, the walls of the Room of the Emperors are flanked by seventeenth- and eighteenth-century busts of Roman emperors, facing another Bernini sculpture, *The Rape of Persephone*, dating from 1622, a coolly virtuosic work that shows in melodramatic form the story of the abduction to the underworld of the beautiful nymph Persephone. Finally, the so-called Room of Silenus contains a variety of paintings by Cardinal Scipione's protege Caravaggio, notably the *Madonna of the Grooms* from 1605, a painting that at the time was considered to have depicted Christ far too realistically to hang in a central Rome church. Look also at *St Jerome*, captured writing at a table lit only by a source of light that streams in from the upper left of the picture, and his *David holding the Head of Goliath*, sent by Caravaggio to Cardinal Scipione from exile in Malta, where he had fled to escape capital punishment for various crimes, and perhaps the last painting he ever did.

The **upstairs galleria** is literally one of the richest small collections of paintings in the world. In the first room are several important paintings by Raphael – including his *Deposition*, painted in 1507 for a noble of Perugia in memory of her son – his teacher Perugino and other masters of the Umbrian school from the late fifteenth and early sixteenth centuries. Look out also for *Lady with a Unicorn* and *Portrait of a Man* by Perugino, and a copy of the artist's tired-out Julius II, painted in the last year of the pope's life, 1513. In further rooms there are more early sixteenth-century paintings; prominent works include Cranach's *Venus and Cupid with a Honeycomb*, Lorenzo Lotto's touching *Portrait of a Man*, and in the opposite direction a series of self-portraits by Bernini at various stages of his long life. Next to these are a lifelike bust of Cardinal Scipione executed by Bernini in 1632, portraying him as the worldly connoisseur of fine art and fine living that he was, and a smaller bust of Pope Paul V, also by Bernini. Beyond here, in a further room, is a painting of Diana by Domechino, depicting the goddess and her attendants doing a bit of target practice, and Titian's *Sacred and Profane Love*, painted in 1514 when he was about 25 years old, to celebrate the marriage of the Venetian noble Nicolò Aurelio.

Galleria Nazionale d'Arte Moderna

The Villa Borghese's two other major museums are situated on the other side of the park, about 1km away along the Viale delle Belle Arti, and of these, the **Galleria Nazionale d'Arte Moderna**, at no. 131 (Tues–Sun 8.30am–7.30pm; €6.50), is probably the least compulsory; it's a lumbering, Neoclassical building housing a collection made up of a wide selection of nineteenth- and twentieth-century Italian (and a few foreign) names. The nineteenth-century collection, on the lower floor, contains a lot of minor Italian painters, most notably the work of the Macchiaioli School of Tuscan impressionists, as well as paintings by Courbet, Cézanne and Van Gogh, while the twentieth-century collection upstairs includes work by Modigliani, De Chirico, Giacomo Balla, Boccione and the Futurists, along with the odd Mondrian and Klimt, and some postwar canvases by the likes of Mark Rothko, Jackson Pollock and Cy Twombly, who lived in Rome for much of his life.

Museo Nazionale Etrusco di Villa Giulia

A harmonious collection of courtyards, loggias, gardens and temples put together in a playful Mannerist style for Pope Julius III in the mid-sixteenth century, the Villa Giulia now houses the **Museo Nazionale Etrusco di Villa**

Giulia (Tues–Sun 8.30am–7.30pm; €4), the world's primary collection of Etruscan treasures (along with the Etruscan collection in the Vatican). Not much is known about the Etruscans, but they were a creative and civilized people, evidenced here by a wealth of sensual sculpture, jewellery and art. The most famous exhibit, in the octagonal room in the east wing, is the remarkable *Sarcophagus of the Married Couple* (dating from the sixth century BC, and actually containing the ashes of the deceased) from Cerveteri – a touchingly lifelike portrayal of a husband and wife lying on a couch. Look also at the delicate and beautiful *cistae,* drum-like objects, engraved and adorned with figures, that were supposed to hold all the things needed for the care of the body after death. In the same room are marvellously intricate pieces of gold jewellery, delicately worked into tiny horses, birds, camels and other animals, as well as mirrors, candelabra, religious statues and tools used in everyday life, including a realistic bronze statuette of a ploughman at work. Further on you'll find a drinking horn in the shape of a dog's head that is so lifelike you almost expect it to bark; a *holmos*, or small table, to which the maker attached 24 little pendants around the edge; and a bronze disc breastplate from the seventh century BC decorated with a weird, almost modern abstract pattern of galloping creatures.

The Celian, Aventine and South Central Rome

The area south of the Forum and Palatine has some of the city's most compelling Christian and ancient sights, from the relatively central **Circo Massimo** and **Baths of Caracalla** to the famous **catacombs** on the fringe of the city on Via Appia Antica. It also has one of Rome's leafiest and most peaceful corners in the **Aventine Hill**, along with its funkiest neighbourhoods in gentrified **Testaccio** and up-and-coming **Ostiense**.

The Celian Hill

Some of the animals that were to die in the Colosseum were kept in a zoo up on the Celian Hill, just behind the arena, the furthest south of Rome's seven hills and probably still its most peaceful, with the **Villa Celimontana** park at its heart. At its summit, the church of **Santi Giovanni e Paolo** (daily 8.30am–noon & 3.30–6.30pm), marked by its colourful campanile, is dedicated to two government officials who were beheaded here in 316 AD after refusing military service; a railed-off tablet in mid-nave marks the shrine where the saints were martyred and buried. The remains of what is believed to be their house, the **Case Romane**, are around the corner on Clivio di Scauro (daily except Tues & Wed 10am–1pm & 3–6pm; €6). Around twenty rooms are open in all, patchily frescoed with pagan and Christian subjects, including the *Casa dei Genii*, with winged youths and cupids, and the courtyard or nymphaeum, which has a marvellous fresco of a goddess being attended on.

The road descends from the church and Roman house to the church of **San Gregorio Magno** on the left (daily 8.30am–12.30pm & 3–6.30pm), founded by Saint Gregory who was a monk here before becoming pope in 590 AD. Gregory was an important pope, stabilizing the city after the fall of the empire and effectively establishing the powerful papal role that would endure for the best part of the following 1500 years. Today's rather ordinary Baroque interior doesn't really do justice to the historical importance of the church, but the lovely Cosmati floor remains intact, and the chapel of the saint at the end of the south aisle has a beautifully carved bath showing scenes from St Gregory's life along with his marble throne, a beaten-up specimen that actually predates the saint by 500 years.

Circo Massimo and the Aventine Hill

On its southern side, the Palatine Hill drops down to the **Circo Massimo**, a long, thin, green expanse bordered by heavily trafficked roads that was the ancient city's main venue for chariot races. At one time this arena had a capacity of up to 400,000 spectators, and if it were still intact it would no doubt match the Colosseum for grandeur. As it is, a litter of stones at the Viale Aventino end is all that remains, together with – at the southern end – a little medieval tower built by the Frangipani family.

On the far side of the Circo Massimo is the **Aventine Hill**, the southernmost of the city's seven hills and the heart of plebeian Rome in ancient times. These days the working-class quarters of the city are further south, and the Aventine is in fact one of the city's more upscale residential areas, covered with villas and gardens and one of the few places in the city where you can escape the traffic. A short way up Via Santa Sabina, the church of **Santa Sabina** (daily 6.30am–12.45pm & 4–7pm) is a strong contender for Rome's most beautiful basilica: high and wide, its nave and portico were restored back to their fifth-century appearance in the 1930s. Look especially at the main doors, which are contemporary with the church and boast eighteen panels carved with Christian scenes, forming a complete illustrated Bible that includes one of the oldest representations of the Crucifixion in existence. Santa Sabina is also the principal church of the Dominicans, and it's claimed that the orange trees in the garden outside, which you can glimpse on your way to the restrained cloister, are descendants of those planted by St Dominic himself. Whatever the truth of this, the views from the gardens are splendid – right across the Tiber to the centre of Rome and St Peter's.

The Baths of Caracalla

Across the far side of Piazza di Porta Capena, the **Baths of Caracalla**, Viale Terme di Caracalla 52 (Mon 9am–1pm, Tues–Sun 9am–sunset; €6, includes the Tomb of Cecilia Metella and the Villa dei Quintilli, valid 7 days), are much better preserved and give a far better sense of the scale and monumentality of Roman architecture than most of the extant ruins in the city – so much so that Shelley was moved to write *Prometheus Unbound* here in 1819. The baths are no more than a shell now, but the walls still rise to very nearly their original height. There are many fragments of mosaics – none spectacular, but quite a few bright and well preserved – and it's easy to discern a floor plan. As for Caracalla, he was one of Rome's worst rulers, and it's no wonder there's nothing else in the city built by him. Nowadays the baths are used for occasional opera performances during the summer – one of Mussolini's better ideas.

Testaccio

Across the Aventine, on the far side of Via Marmorata, the solid working-class neighbourhood of **TESTACCIO** groups around a couple of main squares, a tight-knit community with a market and a number of bars and small trattorias that was for many years synonymous with the slaughterhouse that sprawls down to the Tiber just beyond. In recent years the area has become a trendy place to live, property prices have soared, and some uneasy contradictions have emerged, with vegetarian restaurants opening their doors in an area still known for the offal dishes served in its traditional trattorias, and gay and alternative clubs standing cheek-by-jowl with the car-repair shops gouged into Monte Testaccio.

The slaughterhouse, or **Mattatoio**, once the area's main employer, is used for concerts, raves and exhibitions now, along with stabling for the city's horse-and-carriage drivers and a branch of the **Museum of Contemporary Art of**

Rome (MACRO; Tues–Sun 4pm–midnight), where a couple of large pavilions stage temporary exhibitions of a radical and adventurous nature. Opposite, **Monte Testaccio** gives the area its name, a 35-metre-high mound created out of the shards of Roman amphorae that were dumped here. The ancients were not aware of the fact that the terracotta amphorae could be recycled, and consequently broke them up into small shards and laid them down in an orderly manner, sprinkling quicklime on them to dissolve the residual wine or oil and so creating the mountain you see today. It's an odd sight, the ceramic curls visible through the tufts of grass that crown its higher reaches, with bars and restaurants hollowed out of the slopes below.

The Protestant Cemetery

Via Zabaglia leads from Monte Testaccio to Via Caio Cestio, a left turn up which takes you to the entrance of the **Protestant Cemetery** (Mon–Sat 9am–5pm; donation expected), one of the shrines to the English in Rome and a fitting conclusion to a visit to the Keats-Shelley Memorial House, since it is here that both poets are buried, along with a handful of other well-known names. In fact, the cemetery's title is a misnomer – the cemetery is reserved for non-Roman Catholics so you'll also find famous Italian atheists, Christians of the Orthodox persuasion, and the odd Jew or Muslim buried here. Most visitors come here to see the grave of Keats, who lies next to his friend, the painter Joseph Severn, in the furthest corner of the less crowded, older part of the cemetery, his stone inscribed as he wished with the words "Here lies one whose name was writ in water." Severn died much later than Keats but asked to be laid here nonetheless, together with his brushes and palette. Shelley's ashes were brought here at Mary Shelley's request and interred, after much obstruction by the papal authorities, in the newer part of the cemetery, at the opposite end. The Shelleys had visited several years earlier, the poet praising it as "the most beautiful and solemn cemetery I ever beheld". It had been intended that Shelley should rest with his young son, William, who was also buried here, but his remains couldn't be found (although his small headstone lies nearby). Among other famous internees, Edward Trelawny, friend and literary associate of Byron and Shelley, lies next to him, the political writer and activist, Gramsci, on the far right-hand side in the middle, to name just two – though if you're at all interested in star-spotting you should ask to have a look at the English booklet at the entrance.

The Piramide Cestia

The most distinctive landmark in this part of town is the mossy pyramidal tomb of one Caius Cestius, who died in 12 BC. Cestius had spent some time in Egypt, and part of his will decreed that all his slaves should be freed – the white pyramid you see today was thrown up by them in only 330 days of what must have been joyful building. It's open to the public on the second and fourth Saturday of each month, though you can visit the cats who live here, and the volunteers who care for them, any afternoon between 2.30pm and 4.30pm.

Centrale Montemartini

It's a ten-minute walk south down Via Ostiense to the former electricity generating station of **Centrale Montemartini** at Via Ostiense 106 (Tues–Sun 9am–7pm; €4.50, €8.50 for Capitoline Museums as well, valid 7 days), which was requisitioned to display the cream of the Capitoline Museums' sculpture while the main buildings were being renovated. It became so popular that it's now a permanent outpost, attracting visitors south to the formerly industrial area of Ostiense. The huge rooms of the power station are ideally suited to showing ancient sculpture, although checking out the massive turbines and furnaces has a fascination of its own, and more than competes for your attention. Among many compelling objects, there are the head, feet and an arm from a colossal statue, once 8m high, found in Largo Argentina; a large Roman copy of *Athena*; a fragmented mosaic of hunting scenes; and an amazingly naturalistic statue of a girl seated on a stool with her legs crossed, from the third century BC. There's also a figure of Hercules and next to it the soft *Muse Polymnia*, the former braced for activity, the latter leaning on a rock and staring thoughtfully into the distance.

San Paolo fuori le Mura

Two kilometres or so south of the Porta San Paolo, the basilica of **San Paolo fuori le Mura** (summer daily 7am–6.30pm; winter until 6pm); is one of the four patriarchal basilicas of Rome, occupying the supposed site of St Paul's tomb, where he was laid to rest after being beheaded nearby. Of the four, this basilica has probably fared the least well over the years, and from apparently being the grandest of them all, a devastating fire in 1823 means that the church you see now is largely a nineteenth-century reconstruction. For all that, it's a very successful, if somewhat clinical, rehash of the former church: whether you enter by way of the cloisters or the west door, it's impossible not to be awed by the space of the building inside, its crowds of columns topped by round-arched arcading. Some parts of the building did survive the fire. In the south transept, the paschal candlestick is a remarkable piece of Romanesque carving, supported by half-human beasts and rising through entwined tendrils and strangely human limbs and bodies to scenes from Christ's life, the figures crowding in together as if for a photocall. The bronze aisle doors date from 1070 and were also rescued from the old basilica, as was the thirteenth-century tabernacle by Arnolfo di Cambio. The arch across the apse is original too, embellished with mosaics donated by the Byzantine queen Galla Placidia in the sixth century that show angels, Christ giving a blessing, the symbols of the Gospels, and saints Peter and Paul. There's also the cloister, just behind here – probably Rome's finest piece of Cosmatesque work, its spiralling, mosaic-encrusted columns enclosing a peaceful rose garden. You can get here on bus #23 from Piazzale Ostiense, or from the city centre by taking metro line #B and walking two minutes to the eastern entrance, or by taking bus #271 from Piazza Venezia – it stops outside the west entrance – though this doesn't run at weekends.

EUR

EUR (pronounced "eh-oor", the acronym for the district built for the Esposizione Universale Roma in 1942) is not so much a neighbourhood as a statement in stone. Planned by Mussolini for the aborted World's Fair and not finished until well after the war, it's a soulless grid of square buildings, long vistas and wide processional boulevards. It's worth a visit for some of its numerous museums or if you have a yen for modern city architecture and planning. Of the museums, the most interesting is the **Museo della Civiltà Romana**, Piazza Agnelli 10 (Tues–Sat 9am–2pm, Sun 9am–1.30pm; €6.50, €8.50 including planetarium), which has, among numerous ancient Roman finds, a large-scale model of the fourth-century city – perfect for setting the rest of the city in context – and also shares the building with Rome's **Planetarium** (Tues–Fri 9am–2pm, Sat & Sun 9am–7pm; €6.50, €8.50 including the Roman museum).

Via Appia Antica: the catacombs

Starting at the Porta San Sebastiano, the **Via Appia Antica** is the most famous of Rome's consular roads that used to strike out in every direction from the ancient city. It was built by one Appio Claudio in 312 BC, and is the only Roman landmark mentioned in the Bible. During classical times it was the most important of all the Roman trade routes, carrying supplies through Campania to the port of Bríndisi. It's no longer the main route south out of the city – that's Via Appia Nuova from nearby Porta San Giovanni – but it remains an important part of early Christian Rome, its verges lined with numerous pagan and Christian sites, including most famously the underground burial cemeteries or catacombs of the first Christians. The best way to get to Via Appia Antica is by bus – take #118 from Piazzale Ostiense, #218 from Piazza Porta San Giovanni or #660 from Colli Albani metro station (on line A).

About 500m from Porta San Sebastiano, where the road forks, the church of **Domine Quo Vadis** is the first obvious sight on Via Appia. Legend has this as the place where St Peter saw Christ while fleeing from certain death in Rome and asked "Where goest thou, Lord?" (*Domine quo vadis?*), to which Christ replied that he was going to be crucified once more, leading Peter to turn around and accept his fate. The small church is ordinary enough inside, except for its replica of a piece of marble that is said to be marked with the footprints of Christ (the original is in the church of San Sebastian, see below).

Continuing on for 1km or so, the **Catacombs of San Callisto** (daily except Wed 9am–noon & 2–5pm; €5) are the largest of Rome's catacombs, founded in the second century AD; many of the early popes (of whom St Callisto was one) are buried here. The site also features some well-preserved seventh- and eighth-century frescoes, and the crypt of Santa Cecilia, who was buried here after her martyrdom, before being shifted to the church dedicated to her in Trastevere.

The **Catacombs of San Sebastiano**, 500m further on (daily except Sun 9am–noon & 2.30–5pm; €5), are situated under a much renovated basilica that was originally built by Constantine on the spot where the bodies of the apostles Peter and Paul are said to have been laid for a time. Half-hour tours take in paintings of doves and fish, a contemporary carved oil lamp and inscriptions dating the tombs themselves. The most striking features, however, are not Christian at all, but three pagan tombs (one painted, two stuccoed) discovered when archeologists were burrowing beneath the floor of the basilica upstairs. Just above here, Constantine is said to have raised his chapel to Peter and Paul, and although St Peter was later removed to the Vatican, and St Paul to San Paolo fuori le Mura, the graffiti above records the fact that this was indeed, albeit temporarily, where the two Apostles' remains rested.

Trastevere

Across the river from the centre of town, on the right bank of the Tiber, the district of **TRASTEVERE** was the artisan area of the city in classical times, neatly placed for the trade that came upriver from Ostia and was unloaded nearby. Outside the city walls, Trastevere (the name means "across the Tiber") was for centuries heavily populated by immigrants, and this separation lent the neighbourhood a strong identity that lasted well into the last century. Nowadays the area is a long way from the working-class quarter it used to be, with its bars and restaurants at night thronged with tourists, lured by the charm of its narrow streets and closeted squares. However, even if the local *Festa de' Noantri* ("celebration of we others"), held every July, seems to symbolize the slow decline of local spirit rather than celebrate its existence, there is good reason to come to Trastevere. It is among the more pleasant places to stroll in Rome, particularly peaceful in the morning, lively come the evening, as dozens of trattorias set tables out along the cobblestone streets, and still buzzing late at night when its bars and clubs provide a focus for one of Rome's most dyanamic night-time scenes.

Porta Portese

Trastevere at its most disreputable, but also its most characteristic, can be witnessed on Sunday, when the **Porta Portese** flea market stretches down from the Porta Portese gate down Via Portuense to Trastevere train station in a congested medley of antiques, old motor spares, cheap clothing, trendy clothing, cheap *and* trendy clothing, household goods, bric-a-brac and antiques and assorted junk. Haggling is the rule, and keep a good hold of your wallet or purse. Come early if you want to buy, or even move – most of the bargains, not to mention the stolen goods, have gone by 10am, by which time the crush of people can be intense.

Santa Cecilia in Trastevere

Further north, on Via Anicia, is the church of **Santa Cecilia in Trastevere** (daily 9.30am–12.30pm & 4–6.30pm), a cream-coloured, rather sterile church – apart from a pretty front courtyard – whose antiseptic eighteenth-century appearance belies its historical associations. A church was originally built here over the site of the second-century home of St Cecilia, whose husband Valerian was executed for refusing to worship Roman gods and who herself was subsequently persecuted for Christian beliefs. The story has it that Cecilia was locked in the caldarium of her own baths for several days but refused to die, singing her way through the ordeal (Cecilia is patron saint of music). Her head was finally half hacked off with an axe, though it took several blows before she finally succumbed. Below the high altar, Stefano Maderno's limp, almost modern statue of the saint shows her incorruptible body as it was found when exhumed in 1599, with three deep cuts in her neck – a fragile, intensely human piece of work that has helped make Cecilia one of the most revered Roman saints. Downstairs, excavations of the baths and the rest of the Roman house are on view in the crypt (€2.50), but more alluring by far is the singing gallery above the nave of the church (Mon–Sat 10.15am–12.15pm, Sun 11.15am–12.15pm; €2.50, ring the bell to the left of the church door to get in), where Pietro Cavallini's late-thirteenth-century fresco of the Last Judgement – all that remains of the decoration that once covered the entire church – is a powerful, amazingly naturalistic piece of work for its time, centring on Christ in quiet, meditative majesty, flanked by angels.

Santa Maria in Trastevere

The heart of Trastevere lies across Viale Trastevere, the wide boulevard that cuts through the centre of the district, where **Piazza Santa Maria in Trastevere** constitutes the district's de facto centre. The square takes its name from the church of **Santa Maria in Trastevere** in its northwest corner (daily 7am–9pm), supposed to be the first Christian place of worship in Rome, built on a site where a fountain of oil is said to have sprung on the day of Christ's birth. The church's mosaics are among the city's most impressive: those on the cornice by Cavallini were completed a century or so after the rebuilding and show the Madonna surrounded by ten female figures with lamps – once thought to represent the Wise and Foolish Virgins. Inside, there's a nineteenth-century copy of a Cosmatesque pavement of spirals and circles, and more twelfth-century mosaics in the apse– Byzantine-inspired works depicting a solemn yet sensitive parade of saints thronged around Christ and Mary, while underneath a series of panels shows scenes from the life of the Virgin by the painter Pietro Cavallini. Beneath the high altar on the right, an inscription – "FONS OLEI" – marks the spot where the oil is supposed to have sprung up.

Galleria Nazionale di Palazzo Corsini and the Orto Botanico

Cutting north through the backstreets towards the Tiber, you'll come to the **Galleria Nazionale d'Arte di Palazzo Corsini** at Via della Lungara 10 (Tues–Sun 8.30am–2pm; €4), an unexpected cultural attraction on this side of the river. It's a relatively small collection, and only takes up a few rooms of the giant palace, which was a fitting final home for Queen Christina of Sweden, who renounced Protestantism and with it the Swedish throne in 1655, bringing her library and fortune to Rome, to the delight of the Chigi pope, Alexander VII. Among the highlights are works by Rubens, van Dyck, Guido Reni and Caravaggio, and the curious Corsini Throne, thought to be a Roman copy of an Etruscan throne of the second or first century. Cut out of marble, its back is carved with warriors in armour and helmets, below which is a boar hunt, with wild boars the size of horses pursued by hunters.

The park of the Palazzo Corsini is now the site of the **Orto Botanico** (Tues–Sat 9.30am–6.30pm; €4), which are a good example of eighteenth-century garden design but by no means among the top tier of Europe's botanical gardens. Nonetheless it's a pleasantly neglected expanse, covering the side of the Janiculum Hill with stands of bamboo, a wood of century-old oaks, cedars and conifers, and a grove of acclimatized palm trees.

Villa Farnesina

Across the road from the Palazzo Corsini is the **Villa Farnesina** (Mon–Sat 9am–1pm; €5), built during the early sixteenth century by Baldassare Peruzzi for the banker Agostino Chigi. It's one of the earliest Renaissance villas and its opulent rooms are decorated with frescoes by some of the masters of the period. Most people come to view the Raphael-designed painting *Cupid and Psyche* in the now glassed-in loggia, completed in 1517 by the artist's assistants. The painter and art historian Vasari claims Raphael didn't complete the work because his infatuation with his mistress – "La Fornarina", whose father's bakery was situated nearby – was making it difficult to concentrate. Nonetheless it's mightily impressive: a flowing, animated work bursting with muscular men and bare-bosomed women. He did, however, apparently manage to finish the *Galatea* in the room next door, whose bucolic country scenes are interspersed with Galatea on her scallop-shell chariot and a giant head once said to have been painted by Michelangelo in one of the lunettes. The ceiling illustrates Chigi's horoscope constellations, frescoed by the architect of the building, Peruzzi, who also decorated the upstairs Salone delle Prospettive, where trompe-l'oeil balconies give views onto contemporary Rome – one of the earliest examples of the technique.

The Janiculum Hill

It's about a fifteen-minute walk up Via Garibaldi from the centre of Trastevere to the summit of the Janiculum Hill – not one of the original seven hills of Rome, but the one with the best and most accessible views of the centre. Follow Vicolo del Cedro from Via della Scala and take the steps up from the end, cross the main road, and continue on the steps that lead up to **San Pietro in Montorio**, best known for the Renaissance architect Bramante's little **Tempietto** in its courtyard. Head up from here to the Passeggiata del Gianicolo and follow the ridge to **Piazzale Garibaldi**, where there's an equestrian monument to Garibaldi – an ostentatious work from 1895. Just below is the spot from which a cannon is fired at noon each day for Romans to check their watches. Further on, the statue of Anita Garibaldi recalls the important part she

Italian
football

Calcio – football, or soccer – is Italy's national sport, and enjoys a fanatical following across the country. It's usually possible to get tickets to see one of the big sides – as long as they're not playing each other – and although not especially cheap, it's one of the best introductions to modern Italian culture you'll find; and the shirts and banners that you can buy outside the grounds make great souvenirs.

▲ Flag-waving Italians

Oddly enough, Italian football is an English invention. The first club, Genoa, was created by a group of English expats in the late 1890s, and formed the first league with three clubs from Turin in 1898. Genoa regularly won the championship in the early years of the twentieth century; however, as more clubs joined, their influence waned, and the first national league, formed in 1929, was won by Internazionale of Milan. Since World War II, Italian football has been dominated by Internazionale, AC Milan and Juventus, who have between them won the *scudetto* (championship) 54 times. It's a testament to the English origins that AC Milan, as well as Genoa, continue to uphold their English names, and to sport the cross of St George in their insignia. Unfortunately the other thing that has been copied from the English is hooliganism, which is rife in Italian football. It led to the death of a policeman at a Catania game in February 2007 – following which the entire league programme was cancelled.

The teams

The northwestern triumvirate of **Juventus** (Turin), **AC Milan** and **Internazionale Milano** are traditionally two of the country's strongest teams, even in the light of the match-fixing scandal of 2006. In the northeast, Venice's hometown club, **Venezia**, was once a contender but has been consigned to the lower divisions after falling foul of one of the first match-fixing scandals, this one in the late 1990s. In the same region, **Chievo Verona** and **Udinese** remain unfashionable but strong and stable clubs. In Tuscany, **Fiorentina** reckon themselves among the big teams, but are languishing near the bottom of Serie A after being implicated in the big scandal of 2006. Emilia-Romagna's big club is **Parma**, who remain in Serie A but don't enjoy the top billing they had in the 1990s. In Rome, **AS Roma** and **SS Lazio** are the two biggest teams – both in Serie A and both regular contenders for the *scudetto*, although Lazio's star has faded after a period of massive investment came to an end and their fans became perceived as one of the worst examples of Italy's right-wing lunatic fringe. Further south, **Napoli** still revel in their Eighties "glory days", when they

◄ Fiorentinas stadium

Talking football

Italy's daily newspapers are relatively light on sports coverage, but if you speak a little bit of Italian and are a keen football fan it can be worth getting hold of a copy of one of the three big Italian daily sports papers: the pink *Gazzeto dell Sport*, *Tuttosport* or the *Corriere dello Sport*. Coverage focuses on football, giving you the chance to learn some of the words you'll need to know for a proper appreciation of the Italian national game. Here are some to get you started:

* Corner — Angolo
* Foul — Fallo
* Goalkeeper — Portiere
* Manager — Allenatore
* Match — Partita
* Midfielder — Centrocampista
* Offside — Fuorigiocco
* Pitch — Campo
* Referee — Arbitro

were led by Diego Maradona. They need to keep their spirits up though – currently sitting in Serie B, they struggle to fill their giant 80,000 capacity stadium. Conversely, the other big southern clubs, **Palermo** and **Catania** of Siciliy, and **Cagliari** of Sardinia, thrive – comfortably placed in the middle to upper reaches of Serie A.

Going to a game

Going to see one of the top teams, either at Juventus's Stadio delle Alpi (which they share with their big city rival, Torino) or at the San Siro in Milan, where both AC and Inter play, may be one of the highlights of your trip. And because of the number of teams – both professional and semi-pro – there's always likely to be a game on close to where you're staying.

Serie A games are played on Sunday afternoons, though there are also evening kick-offs on Saturday and Sunday, while most Serie B games take place

◀ Cheering them on

▲ Flying the flag

on Saturday afternoons, with evening games on Friday and Monday. Serie A tickets cost around €20 for seats in the *curva* (end) stands, although these can sometimes be hard to get as they're usually snapped up by diehard fans or *tifosi*. The corner seats, in the so-called *distinti* stands, may be easier to find and are not greatly more expensive at €25–40, while seats in the *tribuna* (side stands) start at around €60 and go up to around €100 for the very best seats. Most clubs sell tickets online, but many also have club shops in city centres; alternatively, tickets are sold direct from the stadium. As for sustenance during the match, you should try **borghetti** – little vials of cold coffee "corrected" with a stiff spirit. And, of course, there's the ubiquitous beer and snacks.

We've given details of the big city clubs in the Guide, but wherever you are, grab a paper and see what's on. There are companies that put together packages to see Serie A games: try their websites at ⓦwww.fanfare-events.com or ⓦwww.footballencounters.co.uk.

Scandal!

2006 saw Italian football reach the lowest point in its history, when Juventus and a number of other top clubs (Lazio, Fiorentina and Milan among them) were implicated in a **match-fixing** scandal that rocked football worldwide: Juventus director, Luciano Moggi, was found guilty of making sure friendly referees were assigned to Juventus games. Other Italian clubs had long suspected that referees were kinder to Juventus than

▼ Luciano Moggi

other clubs, and there had been a row as far back as 1998 when Inter had had blatant penalty claims turned down in a crunch game against Juve. On that occasion they got away with it. However, in May 2006 Moggi and the entire Juve board was forced to resign, and Juventus were stripped of the *scudetto* they had just won (it was later awarded to Inter who came second). In true Italian style there were many other resignations as the sleazefest unravelled, including the president and vice-president of the Italian FA, the president of the Italian referees association, and even a television presenter, Aldo Biscardi. who after hosting the popular football chat show, *Il Processo*, for 26 years, was accused of presenting Juve in a better light than other teams. After a series of investigations, Juventus's punishment was to be relegated to Serie B and the docking of 30 points at the start of the season (later commuted to 9 points). Other clubs were, after appeal, allowed to stay in Serie A but docked points – from 15 points (for Fiorentina) to 8 points for AC Milan, and 3 points for Lazio – and they look like they will survive. But the credibility of Italian football has been seriously damaged, not least among its fans, and will take years to recover.

played in an encounter with the French in 1849 – a fiery, melodramatic work that also marks her grave. Spread out before her are some of the best views in Rome, taking in pretty much the whole of the city.

The Vatican

Situated on the west bank of the Tiber, just across from the city centre, **Vatican City** was established as a sovereign state in 1929, a tiny territory surrounded by high walls on its far western side and on the near side opening its doors to the rest of the city and its pilgrims in the form of St Peter's and its colonnaded piazza. The city-state's 1000 inhabitants have their own radio station, daily newspaper, postal service, and indeed security service in the colourfully dressed Swiss Guards. It's believed that St Peter was buried in a pagan cemetery on the Vatican hill, giving rise to the building of a basilica to venerate his name and the siting of the headquarters of the Catholic Church here. St Peter's is obviously one of the highlights, but the only part of the Vatican Palace itself that you can visit independently is the Vatican Museums – quite simply, the largest, richest, most compelling and perhaps most exhausting museum complex in the world. Otherwise, apart from visiting St Peter's or the museums, you wouldn't know at any point that you had left Rome and entered the Vatican; indeed the area around it, known as the Borgo, is also one of the most cosmopolitan districts, full of hotels and restaurants, and scurrying tourists and pilgrims. You may find yourself staying in one of many mid-range hotels located here, or in the neighbouring nineteenth-century district of Prati, although you may prefer to base yourself in the city centre and travel back and forth on the useful bus #64. However much you try, one visit is never anywhere near enough.

Castel Sant'Angelo

The great circular hulk of the **Castel Sant'Angelo** (Tues–Sun 9am–7.30pm; €8) marks the edge of the Vatican, designed and built by Hadrian as his own mausoleum. Renamed in the sixth century, when Pope Gregory the Great witnessed a vision of St Michael here that ended a terrible plague, the papal authorities converted the building for use as a fortress and built a passageway to link it with the Vatican as a refuge in times of siege or invasion. Inside, a spiral ramp leads up into the centre of the mausoleum, over a drawbridge, to the main level at the top, where a small palace was built to house the papal residents in appropriate splendour. Pope Paul III had some especially fine renovations made, including the beautiful Sala Paolina, whose gilded ceiling displays the Farnese family arms. You'll also notice Paul III's personal motto, *Festina Lenta* ("make haste slowly"), scattered throughout the ceilings and in various corners of all his rooms. Elsewhere, the rooms hold swords, armour, guns and the like, some lavishly decorated (don't miss the bathroom of Clement VII on the second floor, with its prototype hot and cold water taps and mildly erotic frescoes). Below are dungeons and storerooms that can be glimpsed from the spiralling ramp, testament to the castle's grisly past as the city's most notorious Renaissance prison. From the quiet bar upstairs you'll also get one of the best views of Rome and an excellent cup of coffee.

Piazza San Pietro

Perhaps the most famous of Rome's many piazzas, Bernini's **Piazza San Pietro** doesn't disappoint, although its size isn't really apparent until you're right on top of it, its colonnade arms symbolically welcoming the world into the lap of the Catholic Church. The obelisk in the centre was brought to Rome by Caligula in 36 AD, and was moved here in 1586, when Sixtus V ordered that it be erected in front of the basilica, a task that took four months and was apparently done in silence, on pain of death. The matching fountains on either side are the work of Carlo Maderno (on the right) and Bernini (on the left). In between the obelisk and each fountain, a circular stone set into the pavement marks the focal points of an ellipse, from which the four rows of columns on the perimeter of the piazza line up perfectly, making the colonnade appear to be supported by a single line of columns.

Basilica di San Pietro

The Basilica di San Pietro, better known to many as **St Peter's** (daily: April–Sept 7am–7pm; Oct–March 7am–6pm), is the principal shrine of the Catholic Church, built on the site of St Peter's tomb, and worked on by the greatest Italian architects of the sixteenth and seventeenth centuries. One of the channels on the right side of the piazza funnels you into the basilica (the other two lead to the underground grottoes or the ascent to the dome – see opposite). Bear in mind that whichever you opt for first, you need to be properly dressed to enter, which means no bare knees or shoulders – a rule that is very strictly enforced.

Going straight into the **church**, the first thing you see is Michelangelo's graceful *Pietà* on the right, completed when he was just 24. Following an attack by a vandal, it sits behind glass, strangely remote from the life of the rest of the building. Further into the church, the dome is breathtakingly imposing, rising high above the supposed site of St Peter's tomb. With a diameter of 41.5 metres it is Rome's largest dome, supported by four enormous piers, decorated with reliefs depicting the basilica's so-called "major relics": St Veronica's handkerchief, which was used to wipe the face of Christ; the lance of St Longinus, which pierced Christ's side; and a piece of the True Cross. On the right side of the nave, the bronze statue of St Peter is another of the most venerated monuments in the basilica, its right foot polished smooth by the attentions of pilgrims. Bronze was also the material used in Bernini's wild spiralling baldachino, a

△ St. Peter's Basilica

massive 26m high, cast out of 927 tonnes of metal removed from the Pantheon roof in 1633. Bernini's feverish sculpting decorates the apse, too, his bronze *Cattedra* enclosing the supposed chair of St Peter, though more interesting is his monument to Alexander VII in the south transept, with its winged skeleton struggling underneath the heavy marble drapes, upon which the Chigi pope is kneeling in prayer.

An entrance off the aisle leads to the **treasury** (daily: summer 9am–6pm; winter 9am–5pm; €6), which has among many treasures the late-fifteenth-century bronze tomb of Pope Sixtus IV by Pollaiuolo, viewable from above and said to be a very accurate portrait. The **grottoes** (daily: summer 8am–6pm; winter 7am–5pm), which you can opt to visit first outside, emerging in the basilica at the central crossing, is where a good number of popes are buried, including the last one, John Paul II. Also accessible by one of three main outside entrances, the ascent to the **roof and dome** (daily: May–Sept 8am–6pm; Oct–April 8am–5pm; €7 with lift, €4 using the stairs) is well worth making. The views from the gallery around the interior of the dome give you a sense of the enormity of the church, and from there the roof grants views from behind the huge statues onto the piazza below, before the (challenging) ascent to the lantern at the top of the dome, from which the views over the city are as glorious as you'd expect. You emerge in the north aisle of the basilica.

The Vatican Museums

If you've found any of Rome's other museums disappointing, the **Vatican Museums**, on Viale Vaticano, a fifteen-minute walk from St Peter's, out of the north side of Piazza San Pietro (March–Oct Mon–Fri 8.45am–3.20pm, Sat 8.45am–1.20pm; Nov–Feb Mon–Sat 8.45am–12.30pm, last exit 1.45pm; closed Sun, holidays & religious holidays, except the last Sun of each month when admission is free; €12, reduced rate €8, audioguides €6; ⓦ www.vatican.va), are probably the reason why. So much booty from the city's history has ended up here, from both classical and later times, and so many of the Renaissance's finest artists were in the employ of the pope, that not surprisingly the result is a set of museums stuffed with enough exhibits to put most other European collections to shame.

As its name suggests, the complex actually holds a series of museums on very diverse subjects – displays of classical statuary, Renaissance painting, Etruscan relics, Egyptian artefacts, not to mention the furnishings and decoration of the building itself. There's no point in trying to see everything, at least not on one visit, and the only features you really shouldn't miss are the Raphael Stanze and the Sistine Chapel. Above all, decide how long you want to spend here, and what you want to see, before you start; you could spend anything from an hour to the better part of a day here, and it's easy to collapse from museum fatigue before you've even got to your most important target of interest. Also, bear in mind that the collections are in a constant state of restoration, and are often closed and shifted around with little or no notice – so check the website above.

Museo Pio-Clementino

To the left of the entrance, the **Museo Pio-Clementino** is home to some of the best of the Vatican's classical statuary, including two statues that influenced Renaissance artists more than any others, the serene *Apollo Belvedere*, a Roman copy of a fourth-century BC original, and the first century BC *Laocoön*, which shows a Trojan priest being crushed by serpents for warning of the danger of the Trojan horse – perhaps the most famous classical statue ever. There are also busts and statues of the Roman emperors, fantastic Roman floor mosaics, and the so-called *Venus of Cnidos*, the first known representation of the goddess.

Museo Gregoriano Egizio

The **Museo Gregoriano Egizio** isn't one of the Vatican's main highlights, but it has a distinguished collection of ancient Egyptian artefacts, including some vividly painted mummy cases (and two mummies), along with *canopi*, the alabaster vessels into which the entrails of the deceased were placed. There's also a partial reconstruction of the Temple of Serapis from Hadrian's Villa near Tivoli, along with another statue of his lover, Antinous, who drowned close to the original temple in Egypt and so inspired Hadrian to build his replica.

Museo Gregoriano Etrusco

The **Museo Gregoriano Etrusco** holds sculpture, funerary art and applied art from the sites of southern Etruria – a good complement to Rome's specialist Etruscan collection in the Villa Giulia. Especially worth seeing are the finds from the Regolini-Galassi tomb, from the seventh century BC, discovered near Cerveteri, which contained the remains of three Etruscan nobles, two men and a woman; the breastplate of the woman and her huge *fibia* (clasp) are of gold. There's also armour, a bronze bedstead, a funeral chariot and a wagon, as well as a great number of enormous storage jars, in which food, oil and wine were contained for use in the afterlife.

Galleria dei Candelabri, Galleria degli Arazzi and Galleria delle Carte Geografiche

Outside the Etruscan Museum, a large monumental staircase leads back down to the **Galleria dei Candelabri**, the niches of which are adorned with huge candelabra taken from Imperial Roman villas. Beyond here the **Galleria degli Arazzi** (Tapestries) has Belgian tapestries to designs by the school of Raphael and tapestries made in Rome at the Barberini workshops during the 1600s. Next, the **Galleria delle Carte Geografiche** (Maps), which is as long (175m) as the previous two galleries put together, was decorated in the late sixteenth century at the behest of Pope Gregory XIII to show all of Italy, the major islands in the Mediterranean, the papal possessions in France, as well as large-scale maps of the maritime republics of Venice and Genoa. This gallery is considered by many to be the most beautiful in the entire Vatican Museums, and its ceiling frescoes, illustrating scenes that took place in the area depicted in each adjacent map, are perhaps another reason why.

Braccio Nuovo and Museo Chiaramonti

The **Braccio Nuovo** and **Museo Chiaramonti** both hold classical sculpture, although be warned that they are the Vatican at its most overwhelming – close on a thousand statues crammed into two long galleries. The Braccio Nuovo was built in the early 1800s to display classical statuary that was particularly prized, and it contains, among other things, probably the most famous extant image of Augustus, and a bizarre-looking statue depicting the Nile, whose yearly flooding was essential to the fertility of the Egyptian soil. The 300-metre-long Chiaramonti gallery is especially unnerving, lined as it is with the chill marble busts of hundreds of nameless, blank-eyed ancient Romans, along with the odd deity. It pays to have a leisurely wander, for there are some real characters here: sour, thin-lipped matrons with their hair tortured into pleats, curls and spirals; kids, caught in a sulk or mid-chortle; and ancient old men with flesh sagging and wrinkling to reveal the skull beneath.

Raphael Stanze (Raphael Rooms)

The **Raphael Rooms** formed the private apartments of Pope Julius II, and when he moved in here he commissioned Raphael to redecorate them in a style more in tune with the times. Raphael died in 1520 before the scheme was complete, but the two rooms that were painted by him, as well as others completed by pupils, stand as one of the highlights of the Renaissance. The Stanza di Eliodoro, the first room you come to, was painted by three of Raphael's students five years after his death, and is best known for its painting the *Mass of Bolsena* which relates a miracle that occurred in the town in northern Lazio in the 1260s, and, on the window wall opposite, the *Deliverance of St Peter*, showing the saint being assisted in a jail-break by the Angel of the Lord. The other main room, the Stanza della Segnatura or Pope's study, was painted in the years 1508–11, when Raphael first came to Rome, and comes close to the peak of the painter's art. The *School of Athens*, on the near wall as you come in, steals the show, a representation of the triumph of scientific truth in which all the great minds from antiquity are represented. It pairs with the *Disputation of the Sacrament* opposite, which is a reassertion of religious dogma – an allegorical mass of popes, cardinals, bishops, doctors and even the poet Dante.

The Appartamento Borgia

Outside the Raphael Stanze, the **Appartamento Borgia** was inhabited by Julius II's hated predecessor, Alexander VI and is nowadays host to a large collection of modern religious art, although its ceiling frescoes, the work of Pinturicchio in the years 1492–95, are really the main reason to visit.

The Sistine Chapel

Steps lead from the Raphael Rooms to the **Sistine Chapel**, a huge barn-like structure that serves as the pope's official private chapel and the scene of the conclaves of cardinals for the election of each new pontiff. The ceiling frescoes here, and painting of the Last Judgement on the altar wall, are probably the most viewed paintings in the world: it's estimated that on an average day about 15,000 people trudge through here to take a look. It's useful to carry a pair of binoculars with you to view the ceiling, but bear in mind that photography is strictly prohibited and it's also officially forbidden to speak – although this rule is rampantly ignored.

The walls of the chapel were decorated by several prominent painters of the Renaissance – Pinturicchio, Perugino, Botticelli and Ghirlandaio. Recently restored, they would be studied very closely anywhere else. As it is, they are entirely overshadowed by Michelangelo's more famous **ceiling frescoes**, commissioned by Pope Julius II in 1508. They depict scenes from the Old Testament, from the Creation of Light at the altar end to the Drunkenness of Noah over the door. Entering from behind the altar, you are supposed, as you look up, to imagine that you are looking into heaven through the arches of the fictive architecture that springs from the sides of the chapel, supported by little putti caryatids and *ignudi* or nudes. Look at the pagan sibyls and biblical prophets which Michelangelo also incorporated in his scheme – some of the most dramatic figures in the entire work, and all clearly labelled by the painter, from the sensitive figure of the Delphic Sybil, to the hag-like Cumaean Sybil. Look out too for the figure of the prophet Jeremiah – a brooding self-portrait of an exhausted-looking Michelangelo. The **Last Judgement**, on the altar wall of the chapel, was painted by the artist more than twenty years later. Michelangelo wasn't especially keen to work on this either but Pope Paul III, an old acquaintance, was eager to complete the decoration of the chapel. The painting took five years, again single-handed, and is probably the most inspired and homogeneous large-scale painting you're ever likely to see, the technical virtuosity of Michelangelo taking a back seat to the sheer exuberance of the work. The centre is occupied by Christ, turning angrily as he gestures the condemned to the underworld. St Peter, carrying his gold and silver keys, looks on in astonishment, while Mary averts her eyes from the scene. Below Christ a group of angels blasts their trumpets to summon the dead from their sleep. On the left, the dead awaken from graves, tombs and sarcophagi and are levitating into the heavens or being pulled by ropes and the napes of their necks by angels who take them before Christ. At the bottom right, Charon, keeper of the underworld, swings his oar at the damned souls as they fall off the boat into the waiting gates of hell.

The Pinacoteca

The **Pinacoteca** is housed in a separate building on the far side of the Vatican Museums' main spine and ranks highly among Rome's picture galleries, with works from the early to High Renaissance right up to the nineteenth century.

Julius II and the painting of the Sistine Chapel ceiling

The pope responsible for the Sistine Chapel ceiling, **Julius II**, was an avid collector and patron of the arts, and he summoned to Rome the best artists and architects of the day. Among these was Michelangelo, who, through a series of political intrigues orchestrated by Bramante and Raphael, was assigned the task of decorating the Sistine Chapel. Work commenced in 1508. Oddly enough, Michelangelo hadn't wanted to do the work at all: he considered himself a sculptor, not a painter, and was more eager to get on with carving Julius II's tomb (now in San Pietro in Vincoli) than the ceiling, which he regarded as a chore. Pope Julius II, however, had other plans, drawing up a design of the twelve Apostles for the vault and hiring Bramante to design a scaffold for the artist from which to work. Michelangelo was apparently an awkward, solitary character: he had barely begun painting when he rejected Bramante's scaffold as unusable, fired all his staff, and dumped the pope's scheme for the ceiling in favour of his own. But the pope was easily his match, and there are tales of the two men clashing while the work was going on – Michelangelo would lock the doors at crucial points, ignoring the pope's demands to see how it was progressing – and legend has the two men at loggerheads at the top of the scaffold one day, resulting in the pope striking the artist in frustration.

Julius II lived only a few months after the ceiling was finished, but the fame of the work he had commissioned soon spread far and wide. Certainly, it's staggeringly impressive, all the more so for its recent restoration (financed by a Japanese TV company to the tune of $3 million in return for three years' world TV rights), which has lifted centuries of accumulated soot and candle grime off the paintings to reveal a much brighter, more vivid painting than anyone thought existed. The restorers have also been able to chart the progress of Michelangelo as he moved across the vault. Images on fresco must be completed before the plaster dries, and each day a fresh layer of plaster would have been laid, on which Michelangelo would have had around eight hours or so before having to finish for the day. Comparing the different areas of plaster, it seems the figure of Adam, in the key Creation of Adam scene, took just four days; God, in the same fresco, took three days. You can also see the development of Michelangelo as a painter when you look at the paintings in reverse order. The first painting, over the door, the *Drunkenness of Noah*, is done in a stiff and formal style, and is vastly different from the last painting he did, over the altar, *The Creation of Light*, which shows the artist at his best, the perfect master of the technique of fresco painting.

Among early works is the stunning Simoneschi triptych by Giotto, the *Martyrdom of SS Peter and Paul*, painted in the early 1300s for the old St Peter's, Masolino, Fra Angelico and Filippo Lippi, and Melozzo de Forlí's musical angels – fragments of a fresco commissioned for the church of Santi Apostoli. Further on are the rich backdrops and elegantly clad figures of the Umbrian School painters, Perugino and Pinturicchio. Raphael has a room to himself, where you'll find his *Transfiguration*, which he had nearly completed when he died in 1520, the *Coronation of the Virgin*, done when he was only 19 years old, and, on the left, the *Madonna of Foglino*, showing saints John the Baptist, Francis of Assisi, and Jerome. Leonardo's *St Jerome*, in the next room, is a remarkable piece of work with the saint a rake-like ascetic torn between suffering and a good meal, while Caravaggio's *Descent from the Cross*, in the next room but one, is a warts-and-all canvas that unusually shows the Virgin Mary as a middle-aged mother grieving over her dead son. Take a look also at the most gruesome painting in the collection, Poussin's *Martyrdom of St Erasmus*, which shows the saint stretched out on a table with his hands bound above his head in the process of having his small intestine wound onto a drum – basically being "drawn" prior to "quartering".

The Musei Gregoriano Profano, Pio Cristiano and Missionario Etnologico

Next door to the Pinacoteca, the **Museo Gregoriano Profano** holds more classical sculpture, mounted on scaffolds for all-round viewing, including mosaics of athletes from the Baths of Caracalla, and Roman funerary work, notably the Haterii tomb friezes, which show backdrops of ancient Rome and realistic portrayals of contemporary life. The adjacent **Museo Pio Cristiano** has intricate early Christian sarcophagi and, most famously, an expressive third-century AD statue called the *Good Shepherd*. And the **Museo Missionario Etnologico** displays art and artefacts from all over the world, collected by Catholic missionaries.

Eating and drinking

Rome is a great place to **eat**: its denizens know a good deal about freshness and authenticity, and can be very demanding when it comes to the quality of the dishes they are served. Consequently, eating out is a major, often hours-long, activity, and the meals you'll enjoy generally range from good to truly remarkable. Most city-centre **restaurants** offer standard Italian menus, with the emphasis on traditional Roman dishes, although a few more adventurous places have been popping up of late; plus there are numerous establishments dedicated to a variety of regional cuisines, and a reasonable number of ethnic restaurants. The city is also blessed with an abundance of good **pizzerias**, churning out thin, crispy-baked pizza from wood-fired ovens. We've also listed a range of places serving **snacks** and included a rundown of the city's best **ice-cream joints** and **bakeries**. One final caveat: although generally speaking it's hard to find truly bad food in Rome, it may be wise to avoid places that are adjacent to major monuments such as the Pantheon, Piazza Navona or the Vatican.

Coffee, snacks and lunch spots

Rome has plenty of places in which to refuel during a long day's sightseeing, and it's easy to find places that aren't just targeted at tourists. Most bars sell panini and *tramezzini*, and there are plenty of stand-up *rosticerrie* for roast chicken and the like. The following are some of our favourite places for a good-quality, unpretentious **lunch or snack**, but if you just want a refreshing ice cream and milk shakes see also the box, p.801.

Centro Storico

Antico Forno Via delle Muratte 8. The last thing you'd expect just by the Trevi Fountain: fresh pizza, a sandwich bar, a bakery and grocery store, all rolled into one – and open on Sundays.

Caffè Sant'Eustachio Piazza Sant'Eustachio 82. Just behind the Pantheon you'll find what many feel is absolutely Rome's best coffee, usually served Neapolitan-style – that is, very, very sweet.

Camilloni Piazza Sant'Eustachio 54 ☎06.686.4995. Bus #63 or #492. Tues–Sun 8.30am–midnight. The rival for Rome's best coffee, larger than the Sant'Eustachio, across the square, and with great cakes.

Enoteca Corsi Via del Gesú 87–88. Old-fashioned trattoria and wine shop that serves up only what they happen to have cooked that morning. Lunch only, and costing around €7.50 for a main course.

La Tazza d'Oro Via degli Orfani 84–86 ☎06.679.2768. Bus #63, 492. Mon–Sat 7am–8pm. Straight off Piazza del Pantheon, this place is well named, since it is by common consent the home of one of Rome's best cups of coffee, plus decent iced coffee and sinfully rich *granita di caffè*, with double dollops of whipped cream.

Lo Zozzone Via del Teatro Pace 32. This Rome legend, just around the corner from Piazza Navona and with outside seating, serves the best *pizza bianca* in town, by general consent – as well as lots of delicious *pizza al taglio* choices. Mon–Fri 9am–9pm, Sat 10am–11pm.

Campo de' Fiori

🏃 **Bernasconi** Piazza Cairoli 16. Great, long-established *pasticceria* and café with *sfogiatelle* (flaky, custard-filled pastries) to die for and a host of other goodies.

Bruschetteria degli Angeli Piazza Benedetto Cairoli 2a. Lovely and large birreria that does a great line on large bruschette with all kinds of toppings. Lots of other choices, too. You'll pay €8 or so for a large bruschetta, which is enough for two as a snack.

Il Forno di Campo de' Fiori Campo de' Fiori 22. Great bakery in the corner of Campo de'Fiori that does all sorts of baked goodies, including fantastic *pizza al taglio*.

Tridente

Museo-Atelier Tadolini Via del Babuino 150a. It's a bit odd eating here among the grand sculptures of this café-cum-museum, and certainly not cheap. But it provides one of the few places to sit down along this busy street, and decent sandwiches, salads, and simple pasta dishes. A few outside tables too to watch the designer clothes-horses bustle by.

Pizzeria-Tavola Calda Piazzale Flaminia. Right by the #2 tram stop outside the Porta del Popolo, the *pizza al taglio*, roast chicken, roast potatoes and various *fritti* items at this long-established *tavola calda* are a godsend in a part of town lacking in good snack places. A few tables outside, too, though it's not the quietest place to eat.

Quirinale and Termini

Dagnino Galleria Esedra, Via E.Orlando 75 ☎06.481.8660. Good for both a coffee and snack or light lunch, this long-established Sicilian bakery is a peaceful retreat in the Termini area, with tables outside on a small shopping arcade.

Self-Service Luncheonette Salita di San Nicola da Tolentino 19–21. Just up from Bernini's spouting Triton fountain, this place has great food served cafeteria-style.

Trimani Via Cernaia 37b. Classy wine bar (Rome's biggest selection of Italian regional vintages), good for a lunchtime tipple and gastronomic indulgence.

Monti and San Giovanni

Antico Caffè di Brasile Via dei Serpenti 23. Reliable old Monti stand-by that has been selling great coffee, sandwiches, snacks and cakes for over a century.

Enoteca Cavour 313 Via Cavour 313. This lovely old wine bar makes a handy retreat after seeing the ancient sites. Lots of wines and delicious (though not cheap) snacks and salads.

Testaccio

🏃 **Volpetti Piu** Via A. Volta 8. Testaccio *tavola calda* that's attached to the famous deli of the same name around the corner at Via Marmorata 47. Pizza, chicken, *supplli* – all the usual fare.

Trastevere

Bibli Via dei Fienaroli 28. Bookstore and café that serves up a decent Sunday brunch.

Fidelio Via degli Stefaneschi 3–7. Just off Viale Trastevere, this old-fashioned wine bar serves salads, sandwiches and typical wine bar fare, such as cold cuts and cheese plates.

Friends Art Café Piazza Trilussa 34. Fashionable bar with decent salads and light lunches.

La Renella Via del Moro 15. Arguably the best bakery in Rome, right in the heart of Trastevere, with great foccaccia and superb *pizza al taglio*. Takeaway or eat on the premises at its long counter.

Sisini Via San Francesco a Ripa 137. Hole-in-the-wall pizzeria that does great slices, as well as roast chickens and potatoes, *suppli* and all the usual *rosticceria* fare.

Prati and the Vatican

Franchi Via Cola di Rienzo 200. One of the best delis in Rome, great for making up a picnic, with plenty of hot and cold food to go.

Non Solo Pizza Via degli Scipioni 95–97. Try a slice of pizza with sausage and broccoli. There's also the whole range of Roman fritters – *suppli*, *olive ascolane*, *fiori di zucca*, *crocchette* – and a selection of hot dishes.

Restaurants and pizzerias

There are lots of good restaurants in the **centro storico**, and it's surprisingly easy to find places that are not tourist traps – prices in all but the really swanky places remain pretty uniform throughout the city. The area around **Via Cavour** and **Termini** is packed with inexpensive places, although some of them are of dubious cleanliness; if you're not in a hurry, you might do better heading up to the nearby student area of **San Lorenzo**, where you can often eat far better for the same money. South of the centre, the **Testaccio** neighbourhood is also well endowed with good, inexpensive trattorias, as is **Trastevere**, across the river, Rome's traditional restaurant enclave.

Centro Storico

Armando al Pantheon Salita de' Crescenzi 30 ℡06.6880.3034. Unpretentious surroundings and hearty food at good prices. Closed Sat pm & all day Sun.

Capranica Piazza Capranica 104 ℡06.679.0860. Restaurant, taverna and pizzeria all in one serving standard fare that's well prepared and averagely priced.

Da Alfredo e Ada Via dei Banchi Nuovi 14 ℡06.687.8842. There's no menu, and precious little choice at this city centre stalwart, but Ada

presides over an appreciative clientele of regulars who come for the hearty Roman home cooking.

Da Baffetto Via del Governo Vecchio 114 ℡06.686.1617. A tiny, highly authentic pizzeria that has long been a Rome institution. It's still good value, and has tables outside in summer, though you'll always have to queue.

Da Francesco Piazza del Fico 29 ℡06.686.4009. Not just delectable pizzas in this full-on pizzeria in the heart of trendy night-time Rome, but good *antipasti*, *primi* and *secondi* too. Slapdash service, but the food is excellent and relatively inexpensive.

Ice cream and fruit shakes

Giolitti Via Uffici del Vicario 40. An Italian institution that once had a reputation – now lost – for the country's top ice cream. Still pretty good, however, with a choice of seventy flavours.

Il Gelato di San Crispino Via della Panetteria 42. Considered by many to be the best ice cream in Rome. Wonderful flavours – all natural – will make the other *gelato* you've tasted pale by comparison.

Palazzo del Freddo di Giovanni Fassi Via Principe Eugenio 65–67. A wonderful, large 1920s ice-cream parlour not far from Termini, with brilliant fruit ice creams and good milkshakes.

Pascucci Via di Torre Argentina 20. The best *frullati* place in town. Your choice of fresh fruit whipped up with ice and milk – the ultimate Roman refreshment on a hot day.

Tre Scalini Piazza Navona 30. Bus #64 or #492. Piazza Navona institution that is renowned for its famous *tartufo* – death by dark chocolate.

Da Tonino Via del Governo Vecchio 18–19
ⓣ06.333.587.0779. There are no menus in this unmarked *centro storico* favourite, but usually they'll just tell you what they've got that day – basic Roman food, always freshly cooked, and always delicious, although the service can be a bit slow. Closed Sun.

L'Insalata Ricca Largo dei Chiávari 85–86
ⓣ06.6880.3656. An Anglo-American presence in a relaxed and slightly out-of-the-ordinary place, although it is just one of a Roman chain of six. Interesting, big salads, as the name suggests, wholefood options and reasonably priced Italian fare.

Le Cornacchie Piazza Rondanini 53
ⓣ06.6819.2096. Classic Roman dishes served on this quiet piazza bang in the centre of the city. The cooking is good, the service fast, and the prices moderate.

Maccheroni Piazza delle Coppelle 44
ⓣ06.6830.7895. Spartan yet comfy restaurant that enjoys a perfect location on this quiet *Centro Storico* square. It serves good, basic Italian fare at affordable prices. Closed Sun.

Myosotis Via della Vaccarella 3–5 ⓣ06.686.5554. Excellent food, service and value at this upscale restaurant a short walk from the Pantheon. Try the *maltagliati* or *stracci* if you like fresh pasta. Closed Sun.

Campo de' Fiori and the Ghetto

Al Pompiere Via Santa Maria de' Calderari 38
ⓣ06.686.8377. Housed in a frescoed old palace in the heart of the Ghetto, this is a great, if rather fusty old place to sample the city's most authentic Roman-Jewish food. Moderate to expensive prices.

🏃 **Da Giggetto** Via del Portico d'Ottavia 21–22
ⓣ06.686.1105. Roman-Jewish fare featuring deep-fried artichokes, baccalà, and offal-based rigatoni con pajata, along with good non-offal pasta dishes, eaten outside in summer by the ruins of the Portico d'Ottavia. Not cheap, but worth it. Closed Mon.

🏃 **Da Sergio** Via delle Grotte 27
ⓣ06.686.4293. An out-of-the-way, cosy trattoria with a traditional, limited menu and the deeply authentic feel of old Rome. Outdoor seating in summer. Closed Sun.

Del Pallaro Largo del Pallaro 15 ⓣ06.6880.1488. An old-fashioned trattoria serving a set daily menu for €21, including wine. Located in a quiet piazza between Campo de' Fiori and Largo Argentina. No credit cards. Closed Mon.

Filetti di Baccalà Largo dei Librari 88. A fish-and-chip shop without the chips. Paper-covered

Formica tables (outdoors in summer), cheap wine, beer and fried cod, a timeless Roman speciality. Closed in August.

Grappolo d'Oro Piazza della Cancelleria 80
ⓣ06.686.4118. This place has had a bit of a facelift but still remains relatively untouched by the hordes in nearby Campo de' Fiori, and serves imaginative Roman cuisine in traditional trattoria atmosphere at moderate prices. Closed Sun.

🏃 **Osteria al Galletto** Piazza Farnese 102
ⓣ06.686.1704. In spite of its location just off one Rome's trendiest streets and one of its trendiest piazzas, this place retains the feel of a provincial trattoria, serving good wholesome Roman food at very decent prices.

Tridente

Antica Birreria Peroni Via San Marcello 19
ⓣ06.679.5310. Big bustling birreria with an excellent menu of moderately priced simple food that's meant to soak up lots of beer.

Beltramme Via della Croce 39. This very old-fashioned *fiaschetteria* (originally it sold only wine, by the fiasco or flask) is always packed and fairly pricey, but if you want authentic Roman food, atmosphere and service the way it used to be, this is the place. No credit cards.

'Gusto Piazza Augusto Imperatore 9
ⓣ06.322.6273. A slick establishment that's a restaurant, pizzeria and wine bar rolled into one. Its reasonably priced Mediterranean buffet is good value for lunch at €8 a head.

Il Chianti Via del Lavatore 81–82a
ⓣ06.678.7550. This Tuscan restaurant and wine bar is quite a find with good spreads of cold meats and cheeses, and full meals of pasta, pizza and beef dishes.

L'Enoteca Antica Via della Croce 76b
ⓣ06.679.0896. An old Spanish Steps-area wine bar with a selection of hot and cold dishes, including soups and tempting desserts.

Naturist Club Via della Vite 14 ⓣ06.679.2509. A friendly, well-priced vegetarian fourth floor restaurant, with wholegrain risottos, vegetable pies and fresh juices, wonderful organic wines, home-made ice creams and other delicious desserts. Lunch €10 a head, dinner €20. Closed Sun.

🏃 **Otello alla Concordia** Via della Croce 81
ⓣ06.678.1454. This place used to be one of Fellini's favourites – he lived just a few blocks away on Via Margutta – and remains an elegant, yet affordable choice in the heart of Rome. Closed Sun.

Pizza Cir Via della Mercede 43–45
ⓣ06.678.6015. A big, friendly pizza place that also

has first courses, main courses and desserts. Try the *linguine al cir*, which comes with seafood. Just up from Piazza San Silvestro.

Pizza Re Via di Ripetta 14 ℡06.321.1468. Authentic Neapolitan pizzeria made in a wood-stoked oven, along with other dishes. Cheap and busy, so book. Closed Sun lunch.

Recafé Piazza Augusto Imperatore 9 ℡06.6813.4730. The entrance on Via del Corso is a Neapolitan café, while on Piazza Augusta Impera-tore you can enjoy proper Neapolitan pizzas, good pasta and salad dishes and excellent grilled *secondi* for moderate prices – €9 or so for a *primo*, €12–18 for a *secondo*. Neapolitan sweets and *fritti* too.

Quirinale, Termini, San Lorenzo

Africa Via Gaeta 26 ℡06.494.1077. Arguably the city's most interesting (Eritrean) food, testimony to its significant Ethiopian and Somalian population. No credit cards. Closed Sat.

Arancia Blu Via dei Latini 57 ℡06.445.4105. Bus #71, 492 or Tram #3, #19. Daily 8.30pm–midnight. This ultra-trendy San Lorenzo vegetarian restaurant reckons itself a cut above. But in a city with very few vegetarians it doesn't have to try too hard. Good food using fresh ingredients in an imaginative fashion: specialities include various stuffed veggie pasta dishes – ravioli, cannelloni and the like – and decent salads.

Formula 1 Via degli Equi 13 ℡06.445.3866. Justifiably popular San Lorenzo pizzeria, with tables outside in summer. Closed Sun.

Il Dito e la Luna Via dei Sabelli 49–51 ℡06.494.0726. Creative Sicilian cuisine in a bistro-like San Lorenzo restaurant popular with 30-something-ish Romans. Closed Sun.

Pommidoro Piazza dei Sanniti 44 ℡06.445.2692. A typical, family-run Roman trattoria, with a breezy open veranda in summer and a fireplace in winter. Closed Sun.

Tram Tram Via dei Reti 44–46 ℡06.490.416. A grungy location but a cosy spot, this trendy, animated San Lorenzo restaurant, serves good Pugliese pasta dishes, fish and seafood and unusual salads. Closed Mon.

Monti and San Giovanni

Alle Carrette Via Madonna dei Monti 95 ℡06.679.2770. Inexpensive pizza joint that also does great desserts.

Baia Chia Via Machiavelli 5 ℡06.7045.3452. Just off Via Merulana, this Sardinian restaurant offers lots of good fish starters and tasty first courses. Closed Sun.

Luzzi Midway between San Giovanni in Laterano and the Colosseum, this bustling restaurant is a good choice amid the tourist joints of the neighbourhood. The food is hearty and simple, if unspectacular. There's outside seating and it's extremely cheap – *secondi* go for €6–9. There are pizzas, too, but only in the evening.

Monti DOC Via G. Lanza 93 ℡06.487.2696. Comfortable Santa Maria Maggiore neighbourhood wine bar, with a good wine list and some nice food: cold cuts and cheese, soups and salads and pasta, including some delicious veggie dishes. Closed Mon.

Trattoria Monti Via di San Vito 13a ℡06.446.6573. Small, family-run restaurant that specializes in the cuisine of the Marche region – which means great pasta, interesting cabbage-wrapped starters and mainly meaty *secondi*. Very much a neighbourhood place, and moderately priced too.

Testaccio

Acqua e Farina? Piazza O. Giustiniani 2 ℡06.574.1382. Bus #23, #30, #75, #95, #170, #280, #716, #781 or Tram #3. Daily noon–3pm & 8pm–midnight. Very reasonable Testaccio restau-rant serving dishes that are unique: everything, from starters to desserts, is a variation on the theme of pastry creations – hence the name, "Water & Flour?". Ideal for a light meal, lunch or dinner, for as little as €10 a head. A very busy place in the middle of an area bustling with streetlife, especially in summer.

Checchino dal 1887 Via Monte Testaccio 30 ℡06.574.6318. Bus #23, #30, #75, #95, #170, #280, #716, #781 or Tram #3. Tues–Sat noon–3pm & 8–11.30pm. A historic symbol of Testaccio cookery, with an excellent wine cellar, too. Go to the end of Via Galvani to find the road that circles Monte Testaccio, lined with restaurants and night-spots. Expensive.

Da Remo Piazza Santa Maria in Liberatrice 44 ℡06.574.6270. No-nonsense pizzeria serving some of the crispiest thin-crust Roman pizzas you'll find.

Felice Via Mastro Giorgio 29 ℡06.574.6800. Bus #23, #30, #75, #95, #170, #280, #716, #781 or Tram #3. Mon–Sat 12.30–2.45pm & 8–10.30pm. Don't be put off by the "*riservato*" signs on the tables – the owner likes to "select" his customers. Smile and make Felice understand that you're hungry and fond of Roman cooking. Try *bucatini cacio e pepe*, or lamb, and, in winter, artichokes.

Tuttifrutti Via Luca della Robbia 3a ℡06.575.7902. This Testaccio favourite is pretty much the perfect restaurant – family-run, with good food, decent prices and lots of customers. The menu changes daily, and offers interesting variations on traditional Roman dishes. Recommended. Closed Mon.

Trastevere

Ai Marmi Viale Trastevere 53–59 ℗06.580.0919. Nicknamed "the mortuary" because of its stark interior and marble tables, this place serves unique "*supplì al telefono*" (deep-fried rice balls, so named because of the string of mozzarella it forms when you take a bite), fresh *baccalà* and the best pizza in Trastevere. A lively feel of the real Rome. Closed Wed.

Da Augusto Piazza de Renzi 15 ℗06.580.3798. Diner-style neighbourhood staple serving Roman basics in an unpretentious, bustling atmosphere. Good pasta and soup starters and daily meat and fish specials.

Da Lucia Vicolo del Mettonate 2 ℗06.580.3601. Bus #23, #75, #280, #630, #780, H or Tram #8. Tues–Sun noon–3pm & 7.30–11.30pm. Outdoor Trastevere dining in summer is at its traditional peak at this wonderful old Roman trattoria. *Spaghetti cacio e pepe* is the great speciality here – get here early for a table outside.

Da Olindo Vicolo della Scala 8 ℗06.581.8835. Great, family-run Trastevere trattoria with traditional Roman fare. There's a small menu of staples, and prices are easy: *primi* cost €7, *secondi* €9

Da Paris Piazza San Callisto 7a ℗06.581.5378. Fine Roman Jewish cookery and other traditional dishes in one of Trastevere's most atmospheric piazzas. Closed Sun.

Dar Poeta Vicolo del Bologna 45 ℗06.588.0516. One of the top-ten pizzerias in Rome, though don't expect the typical crusty Roman pizza here; the

margherita (ask for it *con basilico* – with basil) comes out of the oven soft and with plenty of good mozzarella on top. Be prepared to wait for a table, and you might prefer to sit outside as the noise within can be deafening. Closed Mon.

Ivo Via di San Francesco a Ripa 158 ℗06.581.7082. The archetypal Trastevere pizzeria, almost in danger of becoming a caricature, but still good. Arrive early to avoid a chaotic queue. Closed Tues.

Prati and the Vatican

Borgo Antico Borgo Pio 21. Great old-fasioned wine bar right by St Peter's Square that does (mainly cold) food and great wine.

Dal Toscano, Via Germanico 58–60 ℗06.3972.5717. Long-established Tuscan eatery that specializes in thick Tuscan steaks – charcoal-grilled at very affordable prices.

L'Insalatiera 2 Via Trionfale 94 ℗06.3974.2975. A vegetarian restaurant specializing in regional Italian cuisine. Everything is home-made, including the wonderful desserts, such as chocolate and ricotta pie. No smoking. Closed Sun.

Lingua Lunga Piazza dell' Unitá 25–27 ℗06.3260.0166. A good menu for those paralysed by indecision after the rigours of the Vatican Museums. Lots of *fritti* and *bruschette* and a full menu of pizzas and classic pasta dishes, plus steaks in various forms, make it good choice for lunch. The food is nothing special, but the location handy.

Osteria del Angelo Via G. Bettolo 24 ℗06.372.9470. Above-average and reasonably priced Roman cooking, from a highly popular restaurant run by an ex-rugby player. Lots of very authentic Roman specialities.

Bars

There are plenty of **bars** in Rome, and although, as with the rest of Italy, most are functional daytime haunts and not at all the kinds of places you'd want to spend an evening, there are plenty of more conducive bars and pubs nowadays – and there's an Irish pub practically on every corner in central Rome. There's also been a recent upsurge in **wine bars** (*enoteche* or *vinerie*); the old ones have gained new cachet, and newer ones, with wine lists the size of dictionaries, are weighing in too, often with accompanying gourmet menus, or just plates of salami and cheese.

Bear in mind that there is sometimes considerable **crossover** between Rome's bars, restaurants and clubs. For the most part, the places listed below are drinking spots, but you can eat, sometimes quite substantially, at many of them, and several could be classed just as easily as nightclubs, with loud music and occasionally even an entrance charge. Although we've divided these listings into **neighbourhoods**, the truth is the areas around Campo de' Fiori, Trastevere and Testaccio are the densest and most happening parts of town.

Centro Storico

Anima Via Santa Maria dell' Anima 57. At present one of the most popular spots in town, tricked out in post-modern-*Flintstones* chic and offering an assortment of elegant snacks to go with your cocktails. Music tends towards chill-out, lounge and softer soul stuff.

Bar del Fico Piazza del Fico 26–28. Currently one of several hotspots in the area – just around the corner from Bar della Pace, and slightly cheaper. Outdoor heating in winter.

Bar della Pace Via della Pace 5. Just off Piazza Navona, this is *the* summer bar, with outside tables full of Rome's self-consciously Beautiful People.

Bloom Via del Teatro Pace 29. One of central Rome's coolest bars, from its leather banquettes to its curvy zinc counter. It serves food, but you'd do better to just turn up late and sample one of the excellent, if pricey, cocktails.

Cul de Sac Piazza Pasquino 73. Busy, long-running wine bar with an excellent wine list, a great city-centre location with outside seating, and decent wine-bar food – cold meats, cheeses, salads and soups. One of the best *centro storico* locations for a snack.

Jonathan's Angels Via della Fossa 18. This quirky bar, just behind Piazza Navona, certainly wins the "most decorated" award. Every inch (even the toilet, which is worth a visit on its own) is plastered, painted or tricked out in outlandish style by the artist-proprietor.

Miscellanea Via delle Paste 110a. This place was the first American-style bar in Rome, a boozy hangout of US students, and inevitably packed at night. Reasonable prices and the best-value sandwiches in town.

Trinity College Via del Collegio Romano 6. A warm and inviting establishment offering international beers and food, the latter served until 1am.

Campo de' Fiori and the Ghetto

Bartaruga Piazza Mattei 7. Wonderfully camp bar furnished with all sorts of eighteenth-century bits and pieces that, not surprisingly, make it a favourite with the thespian set.

L'Angolo Divino Via dei Balestri 12. A peaceful haven after the furore of Campo de' Fiori, this wine bar has a large selection of wine, and simple wine-bar food fare – bread, cheese, cold cuts, soups and the like.

La Curia di Bacco Via del Biscione 79. This bustling place was hollowed out of the ruins of the ancient Teatro di Pompeii, near Campo de' Fiori. A very young crowd, some good wines and inter-esting snacks.

Mad Jack's Via Arenula 20. One of the nicest and most authentic of Rome's army of Irish pubs. The Guinness is decent, and it's not just frequented by expats and tourists.

Rock Castle Café Via B. Cenci 8. In the Jewish Ghetto, just across from Trastevere, this is a basement student hangout consisting of six medieval-style rooms, all for dancing and mingling.

Vineria Campo de' Fiori 15. Long-established bar right on the Campo, patronized by devoted regulars, although it's now been refurbished, and also offers light meals.

Tridente

L'Enoteca Antica Via della Croce 76b. An old Spanish Steps-area wine bar, recently refurbished, with a selection of hot and cold dishes, including soups and attractive desserts. Intriguing trompe l'oeil decorations inside, majolica-topped tables outside.

Lowenhaus Via della Fontanella 16d. Metro A Spagna or Bus #52, #53, #61, #71, #80, #85, #95, #116, #119, #160, #850. Daily 11am–2am. Just off Piazza del Popolo, a Bavarian-style drinking establishment with beer and snacks to match. Live jazz from 10pm onwards on Fridays.

Rosati Piazza del Popolo 5. This bar hosted left-wingers, bohemians and writers in years gone by, and although that's no longer really the case its cocktails and food still draw the crowds. A nice place from which to watch the action on Piazza del Popolo.

Quirinale, Termini, San Lorenzo

New Orleans Via XX Settembre 52. More or less a regular Italian bar by day, but a loud and boozy pub by night, with American food, good German beer and live jazz.

Rive Gauche 2 Via dei Sabelli 43. The San Lorenzo district's mythic dive, this is a smoky, noisy, cavernous evocation of intellectual Left Bank Paris. Happy hour till 9pm.

Monti and San Giovanni

Al Vino al Vino Via dei Serpenti 19. Seriously good wine bar situated on the Monti district's most happening street. Snacks too – generally Sicilian specialities.

Druid's Den Via San Martino ai Monti 28. Appealing Irish pub with a genuine Celtic feel (and owners) and a mixed expat/Italian clientele. Live Irish music every Mon.

Finnegan Via Madonna dei Monti 28. Decent Irish pub with live football on TV, pool, and a friendly ex-pat crowd. Seating outside as well on this bustling Monti street.

Testaccio

Clamur Piazza del'Emporio 1. Large yet cosy Irish pub, on the trendy Testaccio side of the Porta Portese (Trastevere) bridge, offering the usual beers plus snacks.

🏃 **Oasi della Birra** Piazza Testaccio 41. Subterranean Testaccio bar with a beer selection that would rival anywhere in the world and plenty of wine to choose from as well. For nibbles there are generous plates of cheese and salami.

Trastevere

Accademia Vicolo della Renella 90 ℡06.589.6321. A huge and popular Trastevere eatery-cum-party spot for a youngish crowd. Live rock Mon & Wed, otherwise a DJ.

Mr Brown Vicolo del Cinque 29. This popular hangout is one of Trastevere's most charming detours, with a young, fun-loving crowd, happy hour from 9pm to 10pm daily, cheap beers, and an assortment of salads, sandwiches and crepes. Closed Sun.

🏃 **Ombre Rosse** Piazza Sant'Egidio 12. A people-watching spot that has become a

Trastevere institution, especially for a morning cappuccino, but also for interesting light meals.

RipArte Café Via Orti di Trastevere 7 ℡06.586.1852. Cool, elegantly modern hotel bar with live music at 11pm every evening.

🏃 **San Calisto** Piazza San Calisto 4. A Trastevere bar which attracts a huge crowd of just about everybody on late summer nights; the booze is cheap, and you can sit at outside tables for no extra cost. Things are slightly less demi-monde during the day, when it's simply a great spot to sip a cappuccino, read and take the sun.

Stardust Vicolo de' Renzi 4. One of Trastevere's most authentic haunts, and just the place for all-night partying, with occasional live jazz.

Prati and the Vatican

Fonclea Via Crescenzio 82a. Busy and happening bar in the Vatican area that hosts regular live music – usually jazz, soul and funk.

Four Green Fields Via C. Morin 42. Mixed crowds visit this long-running, versatile Vatican area pub, which also has a cocktail bar. Live music in the basement every night starting at 9.30pm. Free admission.

Nightlife

Roman **nightlife** retains some of the smart-set style satirized in Fellini's film *La Dolce Vita* – designer dressing-up is still very much a part of the mainstream scene and entry-prices to the big **clubs** tend to be high. But there are a few, smaller and more alternative nightspots where your travel-crumpled clothes will be more acceptable, and a **live music scene** that is nothing if not unpretentious, although the chances of catching any big names are virtually nonexistent – Rome just doesn't figure on the promoters' circuit. The city is also a bit of a backwater for the **performing arts**, and very few international performers of renown in any of the arts regularly put in an appearance here. Nevertheless, there is cultural entertainment available, and the quality is sometimes better than you might expect. In any case, what the arts here may lack in professionalism, they often make up for in the charm of the setting. Rome's **summer festival** (*Estate Romana*) means that there's a good range of classical music and opera running throughout the warm months, often in picturesque locations, and when that's over there's the *Notte Bianca* event, when music and theatre events are held all over the city all night on a Saturday in mid-September.

Clubs

Alien Via Velletri 13–19 ℡06.841.2212, ⓦwww.aliendisco.it. The two halls here feature starkly contrasting decor, one redolent of maharaja plushness, the other done up in

modernistic black and white. Music is a mixture of house and techno. It also has a summer venue, *Alien 2 Mare*, at the nearby seaside resort of Fregene, at Piazzale Fregene 5 ℡06.6656.4761.

Black Out Via Saturnia 18 ☎ 06.7049.6791. Murky San Giovanni club that plays punk, heavy metal and Goth music, with occasional gigs by US and UK bands. Closed in summer.

Classico Village Via Libetta 3 ☎ 06.5728.8857. Industrial Ostiense location with a big dance floor, a venue for live music, and a restaurant.

Gilda Via Mario de' Fiori 97 ☎ 06.678.4838, ⓦ www.gildabar.it A few blocks from the Spanish Steps, this slick, stylish and expensive club is the focus for the city's minor celebs and wannabes. Jacket required. Their summer venue, *Gilda-on-the-Beach*, is in Fregene, at Lungomare di Ponente 11 ☎ 06.6656.0649, ⓦ www.gildaonthebeach.it.

Goa Via Libetta 13 ☎ 06.574.8277. Long-running Ostiense club that was opened by famous local DJ Giancarlino and is still playing techno, house and jungle; *Goa* also has sofas to help you recover after high-energy dancing.

La Maison Vicolo dei Granari 4 ☎ 06.683.3312. Ritzy club whose chandeliers and glossy décor attract Rome's gilded youth. Sunday – gay night – is the one to go for.

Piper Via Tagliamento 9 ☎ 06.855.5398. Established back in the 1970s, but still going strong, Piper has different nightly events and a wide variety of music. The summer venue by the sea is *Aquapiper di Guidonia*, Via Maremmana ☎ 0774.326.538.

Qube Via Portonaccio 212 ☎ 06.4358.7454. *Bi Tiburtina* club hosts a variety of different nights each week, including live music. Not the most original for music but its Friday gay and drag night draw a big crowd.

Zoobar Via Bencivenga 1 ☎ 339.27.27.995. This club is now in a new location out near Nomentana station but still plays a wide range of different music – oldies, ska, funk, R&B and much more.

Rock and pop venues

Alpheus Via del Commercio 36 ☎ 06.574.7826, ⓦ www.alpheus.it. Housed in an ex-factory off Via Ostiense, a little way beyond Testaccio, the *Alpheus* has space for three simultaneous events – usually a disco, concert and exhibition or piece of theatre. Saturday is Gorgeous – gay night.

Blue Knight Via delle Fornaci 8–10 ☎ 06.630.011. Right near St Peter's, the main floor here is a bar and

gelateria, while downstairs there are concerts – almost always acoustic music, ranging from rock to blues to pop, featuring some of Rome's best musicians and occasional foreign acts. Concerts usually start at 10.30pm.

Circolo degli Artisti Via Casilina Vecchia 42 ☎ 06.7030.5684, ⓦ www.circoloartisti.it. A very large venue, located beyond Porta Maggiore, that was one of the first of the city's co-called *centri sociali*. A good range of bands, with frequent discos and theme nights from hip-hop to ska. Fridays it hosts Omogenic – gay night. Bus #105 from Termini, or #810 from Piazza Venezia.

Il Locale Vicolo del Fico 3 ☎ 06.687.9075. Centrally located close to Piazza Navona, this trendy joint enjoys a lively, if not chaotic, atmosphere, and English and American alternative bands and Italian folk-rock. Not the trendsetter it once was, but still a fun, central venue.

Villaggio Globale Lungotevere Testaccio 22 ☎ 06.575.7233. Situated in the old slaughterhouse along the river, the "global village" has something on almost every night, whether it's world music, indie rock or avant-garde performance art, in its Spazio Boario. Closed Aug.

△ Patrytime

Jazz, blues and Latin-American venues

Alexanderplatz Via Ostia 9 ⓣ06.5833.5781, ⓦwww.alexanderplatz.it. Rome's top live jazz club/restaurant with reasonable membership (€10) and free entry, except when there's star-billing. Reservations recommended. Doors open at 8pm.

Big Mama Vicolo San Francesco a Ripa 18 ⓣ06.581.2551, ⓦwww.bigmama.it. Trastevere-based jazz/blues club of long standing, hosting nightly acts. Membership €8, and free entry except for star attractions (when it's important to book ahead). Doors open 9pm.

Caffè Latino Via Monte Testaccio 96 ⓣ06.5728.8556. Multi-event Testaccio club with varied live music almost every night, as well as cartoons, films, and cabaret. There's also a disco playing a selection of funky, acid jazz and R&B music. Best at weekends when it gets more crowded. Admission €6–10. Tues–Sun 10pm–3am.

Gregory's Via Gregoriana 54d ⓣ06.679.6386. Just up the Spanish Steps and to the right, this elegant nightspot pulls in the crowds with its live jazz, improvised by Roman and international musicians. Tues–Sun 5.30pm–3am.

Classical music and opera

Under new directors, Rome's **orchestras** of late are approaching international standards, and although the city attracts far fewer prestigious artists than you might expect of a capital, it is becoming more and more a magnet for contemporary works – a sea change that has been inspired by the completion of the new *Auditorium*. Check the listings and keep a look-out for posters advertising little-known concerts – a wide range of choral, chamber and organ recitals – in churches or other often spectacular venues, sometimes including the private halls in Renaissance or Baroque palaces. The city's **opera** scene has long been overshadowed by that of Milan, Parma and even Naples, grand opera's acknowledged birthplace, but it is improving. In summer, opera moves outdoors and ticket prices come down: performances are now once again held in the stunning setting at the ancient Baths of Caracalla, as well as in the courtyard of the San Clemente basilica and in other churches and venues all around Rome.

Gay bars, restaurants and clubs

Asinocotto Via dei Vascellari 48 ⓣ06.589.8985. Gay-friendly Trastevere restaurant with a great, Proust-inspired menu of moderately priced pasta, meat and fish dishes. Worth a visit whatever your non-culinary preferences.

Coming Out Via San Giovanni in Laterano 8 ⓣ06.700.9871. If any area is developing as Rome's gay zone, it may be the stretch between the Colosseum and Piazza Vittorio. This little pub is the newest addition to the scene, frequented mostly by a younger clientele.

Garbo Vicolo di Santa Margherita 1a ⓣ06.581.6700. Friendly Trastevere bar, just behind the main piazza, with a relaxed atmosphere and a nice setting.

L'Alibi Via Monte Testaccio 44 ⓣ06.574.3448. Predominantly – but by no means exclusively – male venue that's one of Rome's oldest and best gay clubs. Downstairs there's a multi-room cellar disco, upstairs an open-air bar, and there's a big terrace to enjoy in the warm months.

L'Hangar Via in Selci 29 ⓣ06.4881.3971. About halfway between Termini and the Roman Foru m, just off Via Cavour, this is one of Rome's oldest and least expensive gay spots. Saturday night it's almost impossible to get in the door it's so jammed.

La Buca di Bacco Via San Francesco a Ripa 165 ⓣ0348.764.7388. This cocktail bar, wine bar and tea room is one of the new breed of openly gay establishments. Quiet during the day, gayer by night.

Classical music and opera venues

Auditorium/Parco della Musica Via P. de Coubertin 15 ℡199.109.783, ⒲www.auditorium.com. This new landmark musical complex is Rome's most prestigious venue. home to its premier orchestra, the Accademia Nazionale di Santa Cecilia, who are resident part of the year in its largest hall. Two smaller venues host smaller chamber, choral, recital and experimental works. The complex also hosts major rock and jazz names when they come to town. Daily 11am–6pm to visit; guided tours available €9. Box office Mon–Sun 11am–6pm.

Aula Magna dell'Università la Sapienza Piazzale Aldo Moro 5 ℡06.3600.1511. The university's music institute is deliberately experimental and eclectic, with musical offerings ranging from Mozart to Miles Davis, and from Ravel to Kurt Weill.

Oratorio del Gonfalone Via del Gonfalone 32a ℡06.687.5952. This lovethly eatre stages performances of chamber music, with an emphasis on the Baroque.

Teatro dell'Opera di Roma Piazza Beniamino Gigli 1 ℡06.481.601, ⒲www.operaroma.it. Nobody compares it to La Scala, but cheap tickets are a lot easier to come by at Rome's opera and ballet venue – they start at around €20 for opera, less for ballet – and important artists do sometimes perform here. Box office Mon–Sat 9am–5pm, Sun 9am–1.30pm.

Teatro Olimpico Piazza Gentile da Fabriano 17 ℡06.320.1752, ⒲www.teatroolimpico.it. Classical standards, chamber music and ballet are performed here, by resident orchestra Accademia Filarmonica Romana, as well as occasional contemporary work. Tickets are cheap and relatively easy to come by. Bus #910 from Termini.

Film

There tends to be more **English-language cinema** on offer in Rome these days, partly due to foreign demand, though if your Italian is up to it, you'll naturally also find current Italian language productions available all over town.

Alcazar Via Merry del Val 14 ℡06.588.0099. Trastevere cinema featuring mainstream American and English films, with the occasional weird one slipping in.

Metropolitan Via del Corso 7 ℡06.320.0933. The city centre's largest multi-screen cinema, with four screens showing blockbusters and all general-release films.

Nuovo Olimpia Via in Lucina 16 ℡06.686.1068. Very central, just off Via del Corso, with two screens; tickets here cost €6. They sometimes feature at least one foreign film in the original language.

Nuovo Sacher Largo Ascianghi 1 ℡06.581.8116. Another Trastevere location, this movie house shows their current film – mainly foreign independent movies – in its original version on Mondays.

Pasquino Piazza Sant'Egidio 10 ℡06.580.3622. Long-established in Trastevere as Rome's premier English-language cinema, with three screens showing recent general releases and the odd indie. The programme changes every Friday, and they also mount their own mini-festivals from time to time.

Listings

Airlines Many of the big airline offices are located on and around Via Bissolati/Piazza Barberini. Air Canada ℡06.6501.0991; Alitalia domestic ℡06.2222; American ℡06.6605.3169; British Airways ℡199.712.266; Delta ℡800.477.999; EasyJet ℡848.887.766; Ryanair ℡899.88.99.73.

Airport enquiries Fiumicino ℡06.6595.3640, Ciampino ℡06.794.941, ⒲www.adr.it.

American Express Piazza di Spagna 38 ℡06.67641 (Mon–Fri 9am–5.30pm, Sat 9am–12.30pm).

Bike and scooter rental Barberini Villa della Purificazione 84 ℡06.488.5485 rents out bikes,

mopeds and scooters. Bikes cost €10 per day, mopeds €30, scooters €50.

Books All of the following are excellent English-language bookshops: Anglo-American Bookshop Via delle Vite 102 ℡06.679.5222; Almost Corner Bookshop Via del Moro 45 ℡06.583.6942: Lion Bookshop, Via dei Greci 33 ℡03.3265.4007.

Car rental All the usual suspects have desks at Fiumicino, Ciampino, Termini and elsewhere in the city. Avis ℡199.100.133 Ciampino ℡06.7934.0368, Fiumicino ℡06.6501.1531; Europcar ℡800.014410 Ciampino ℡06.7934,0387, Fiumicino ℡06.6501.0879; Hertz ℡199.112211 Ciampino ℡06.7934.0616,

Fiumicino ☎06.6501.1553; Maggiore ☎848.867.067.

Car repair Call ☎116 for emergency breakdown service. Otherwise, consult the Yellow Pages (*Pagine Gialle*) under "*Autoriparazioni*" for specialized repair shops.

Dentist Absolute Dentistry, Dr Andrea Chiantini, Via G.Pisanelli 1–3, has a 24-hour emergency service ☎06.3600,3837 or 339.250.7016.

Embassies Australia, Via Bosio 5 ☎06.852,721; Britain, Via XX Settembre 80a ☎06.4220.0001; Canada, Via G.B. de Rossi 30 ☎06.445.981; Ireland, Piazza Campitelli 3 ☎06.697.9121; New Zealand, Via Zara 28 ☎06.441.7171; USA, Via Veneto 119a ☎06.46.741.

Emergencies Police ☎113; Carabinieri ☎112; Fire ☎115; Ambulance ☎118. Fire ☎115. Both the police and the *carabinieri* have offices in Termini. Otherwise the most central police office is off Via del Corso in Piazza del Collegio Romano 3 (☎06.46.86), and there's a *carabinieri* office in Piazza Venezia.

Exchange American Express (see p.809); Thomas Cook, Piazza Barberini 21a (Mon–Sat 9am–8pm, Sun 9.30am–5pm) and Via della Conciliazione 23 (Mon–Sat 8.30am–7.30pm, Sun 9.30am–5pm). Post offices will exchange American Express travellers' cheques and cash commission-free. The last resort should be any of the many Ufficio Cambio, almost always offering the worst rates (despite "no commission" signs).

Football Rome's two big teams, Roma and Lazio, play on alternate Sundays between September and May at the Olympic Stadium, northwest of the city centre. You can reach this by taking tram #2 from Piazzale Flaminio to Piazza Mancini and then walking across the river to the stadium. Lazio fans traditionally occupy the Curva Nord, the northern end of the ground, and Roma fans the Curva Sud, and tickets in these areas cost €15–25 (if you can get one). It's usually easier to pick up seats in the corner stands, or *distinti*, for €25–35; seats in the side stands, or *tribuna*, cost €60–100. Except for the really big games, you can get tickets at the ground. Or try the Lazio store, Via Farini 34 (☎06.482.6768, ⓦwww.sslazio.it), or the AS Roma store, Piazza Colonna 360 (☎06. 6920.0642, ⓦwww.asromacalcio.it).

Gay contacts ARCI-GayOra, Via Goito 35b (☎06.6450.102, ⓦwww.arcigayroma.it), is the Rome branch of the nationwide gay organization and has a help line available on ☎800.713.713 (Mon & Wed 5–9pm, Sat 4–8pm.).

Hospitals In an emergency call ambulance ☎118, police ☎113, fire ☎115. Otherwise the most central hospitals with emergency facilities are: Santo Spirito, Lungotevere in Sassia 1 (☎06.68.351), near the Vatican, and Fatebenefratelli, Isola Tiberina (☎06.683.7299). The Rome American Hospital, Via E. Longoni 81 (☎06.22.551) is a private multi-speciality hospital with bilingual staff and has a 24hr emergency line.

Internet access Bibli, Via dei Fienaroli 28 (Tues–Sun 11am–midnight, Mon 5.30pm–midnight); Easy Internet Café Via Barberini 2 (daily 7am–1am); Internet Train Piazza Sant'Andrea delle Valle 3 (Mon–Fri 10am–11pm, Sat 10am–8pm, Sun noon–8pm); Internet Café, Via Cavour 213 (daily 9am–1am; ☎06.4782.3051, Pole2Pole Via Santa Maria Maggiore 129 (daily 9am–11pm).

Laundry Onda Blu, Via Vespasiano 50, near the Vatican (daily 8am–10pm); Wash and Dry, Via Della Pelliccia 35 & Via della Chiesa Nuova 15–16 (both daily 8am–10pm). All offer a wash including soap and tumble-drying for €7–10 for a 6kg (15lb) load.

Lost property For property lost on a train call ☎06.4730.6682 (daily 7am–11pm); on a bus ☎06.581.6040 (Mon & Fri 8.30am–1pm, Tues–Thurs 2.30–6pm); on the metro ☎06.487.4309.

Pharmacies The following pharmacies are all open 24hr, year-round: Internazionale, Piazza Barberini 49 ☎06.4825456; Piram, Via Nazionale 228 ☎06.488.0754; and Farmacia della Stazione, Piazza dei Cinquecento 51 ☎06.488.0019.

Post offices Rome's main poffiost ce is on Piazza San Silvestro (Mon–Fri 9am–6.30pm, Sat 9am–2pm).

Swimming pools La Piscina della Rose, Viale America 20 (☎06.592.6717) is central Rome's largest public pool (June–Sept 9am–7pm) – a swim costs about €10. Otherwise try one of the big hotel pools, which they'll let you use for around €50 a day.

Train enquiries General enquiries ⓦwww .trenitalia.it; Termini ☎06.892.021, ⓦwww .romatermini.it.

Travel agents For discount tickets try the CTS offices at Via Genova 16 ☎06.462.0431 and Corso Vittorio Emanuele II 297 ☎06.687.2672, both open Saturday mornings, when other travel agents are closed. Other good places to try are Viaggiare, Via San Nicola da Tolentino 15 ☎06.421.171, who have some English-speaking staff, and Elsy Viaggi, Via di Torre Argentina 80 ☎06.689.6460.

Out from the city: Tivoli and Ostia Antica

You may find there's quite enough in Rome to keep you occupied during your stay, but Rome can be a hot, oppressive city, its surfeit of churches and museums intensely wearying, and if you're around long enough you really shouldn't feel any guilt about getting out to see something of the countryside around. Two of the main attractions visitable on a day-trip are, it's true, Roman sites, but just the process of getting to them can be energizing. **Tivoli**, about an hour by bus east of Rome, is a small town famous for the travertine quarries nearby, the landscaped gardens and parks of its Renaissance villas, and a fine ancient Roman villa just outside. **Ostia**, in the opposite direction from the city near the sea, and similarly easy to reach on public transport, is nowadays the city's main seaside resort (though one worth avoiding; see p.740 for more attractive options just a little further south), but it was home to the port of Rome in classical times, and the site is well preserved and worth seeing. Bear in mind, too, that a number of **other places in Lazio** – the Etruscan sites north of Rome, the Castelli Romani, Palestrina and Subiaco, and parts of the southern coast – are close enough to the city to make a feasible day-trip, especially if you have access to a car.

Tivoli

Just 40km from Rome, perched high on a hill and looking back over the plain, **TIVOLI** has always been something of a retreat from the city. In classical days it was a retirement town for wealthy Romans; later, during Renaissance times, it again became the playground of the moneyed classes, attracting some of the city's most well-to-do families, who built their country villas out here. Nowadays the leisured classes have mostly gone, but Tivoli does very nicely on the fruits of its still-thriving travertine business, exporting the precious stone worldwide (the quarries line the main road into town from Rome), and supports a small airy centre that preserves a number of relics from its ritzier days. To do justice to the gardens and villas – especially if Villa Adriana is on your list, as indeed it should be – you'll need time, so it's worth setting out early.

Villa d'Este and Villa Gregoriana

Most people head first for **Villa d'Este** (summer daily 9am–1hr before sunset; winter Tues–Sun 9am–1hr before sunset; €6.50), across the main square of Largo Garibaldi – the country retreat of Cardinal Ippolito d'Este that was transformed from a convent by Pirro Ligorio in 1550, and is now often thronged with visitors even outside peak season. They mainly come to see the fountains of the landscaped gardens, but the restored ground-floor apartments alone make the trip worthwhile, frescoed with scenes of mythology and the history of Tivoli by Girolamo Muziano and Federico Zuccari in 1555–60. Unfortunately, restoration is still going on in the gardens below, and you may find many of the famous fountains are temporarily closed. However, you can see the theatrical, magnificent Organ Fountain, which has been returned to its original glory and makes a most imposing sight as it gushes millions of gallons of water down the hillside. Among the other fountains you can see are the Fontana dell'Ovato, near the Organ Fountain, fringed with statues, behind which is a rather dank arcade, and the Rometta or "Little Rome", on the opposite side of the garden, which has reproductions of the city's major buildings. Finally a word of warning: be sure to drink only from those fountains marked *acqua potabile*, and don't wade or splash in the other fountains – the water is basically sewage from the town above.

Tivoli's other main attraction is **Villa Gregoriana** (April–Oct daily 10am–6.30pm; €4), a park with waterfalls created when Pope Gregory XVI diverted the flow of the river here to ease the periodic flooding of the town in 1831. Less well known and less touristed than the d'Este estate, it has none of the latter's conceits – its vegetation is lush and overgrown, descending into a gashed-out gorge over 60m deep. There are two main **waterfalls** – the larger Grande Cascata on the far side, and a small Bernini-designed one at the neck of the gorge. The path winds down to the bottom of the canyon, scaling the drop on the other side past two grottoes, where you can get up close to the pounding water, the dark, torn shapes of the rock glowering overhead. It's harder work than the Villa d'Este – if you blithely saunter down to the bottom of the gorge, you'll find that it's a long way back up the other side – but in many ways more rewarding; the path leads up on the far side to an exit and the substantial remains of a **Temple of Vesta**, which you'll have seen clinging to the side of the hill. This is now incorporated into the gardens of a restaurant, but it's all right to walk through and take a look, and the view is probably Tivoli's best – down into the chasm and across to the high green hills that ring the town.

Villa Adriana

Once you've seen these two sights you've really seen Tivoli – the rest of the town is nice enough but there's not that much to it. But just outside town, at the bottom of the hill, fifteen minutes' walk off the main Rome road (ask the Rome–Tivoli bus to drop you or take the local CAT #4 from Largo Garibaldi), **Villa Adriana** (Hadrian's Villa; daily 9am–1hr before sunset; €6.50) casts the invention of the Tivoli popes and cardinals very much into the shade. This was probably the largest and most sumptuous villa in the Roman Empire, the retirement home of the Emperor Hadrian for a short while between 135 AD and his death three years later, and it occupies an enormous site. You need time to see it all; there's no point in doing it at a gallop and, taken with the rest of Tivoli, it makes for a long day's sightseeing. Spending €3.81 on the large-scale map they sell at the bookstore near the ticket booth helps make it all manageable and comprehensive.

The site is one of the most soothing spots around Rome, its stones almost the epitome of romantic, civilized ruins. The imperial palace buildings proper are in fact one of the least well-preserved parts of the complex, but much else is clearly recognizable. Hadrian was a great traveller and a keen architect, and parts of the villa were inspired by buildings he had seen throughout the empire. The massive Pecile, for instance, through which you enter, is a reproduction of a building in

Athens; and the Canopus, on the opposite side of the site, is a liberal copy of the sanctuary of Serapis near Alexandria, its long, elegant channel of water fringed by sporadic columns and statues leading up to a Temple of Serapis at the far end. Nearby, a museum displays the latest finds from the ongoing excavations, though most of the extensive original discoveries have found their way back to Rome. Walking back towards the entrance, make your way across the upper storey of the so-called Pretorio, a former warehouse, and down to the remains of two bath complexes. Beyond is a fishpond with a *cryptoporticus* (underground passageway) winding around underneath, and behind that the relics of the emperor's imperial apartments. The Teatro Maríttimo, adjacent, with its island in the middle of a circular pond, is the place to which it's believed Hadrian would retire at siesta time to be sure of being alone.

Practicalities

Buses leave Rome for Tivoli and Villa Adriana every twenty minutes from Ponte Mammolo metro station (line B) – journey-time fifty minutes. In Tivoli, the **bus station** is in Piazza Massimo near the Villa Gregoriana, though you can get off earlier, on the main square of Largo Garibaldi, where you'll find the **tourist office** (Mon & Sat 9am–3pm, Tues–Fri 9am–6.30pm; ☎0774.334.522), which has free maps and information on **accommodation**.

Ostia Antica

There are two Ostias: one a rather over-visited seaside resort, **Lido di Ostia**, which is best avoided; the other, one of the finest ancient Roman sites – the excavations of **OSTIA ANTICA** – which are on a par with anything you'll see in Rome itself and easily merit the half-day journey out. The stop before Lido di Ostia on the train from Rome, the site of Ostia Antica marked the coastline in classical times, and the town which grew up here was the port of ancient Rome, a thriving place whose commercial activities were vital to the city further upstream. The **excavations** are relatively free of tourists (April–Oct Tues–Sun 8.30am–6pm; March 8.30am–5pm; Nov–Feb 8.30am–4pm; €4), and it's much easier to reconstruct a Roman town from these than from any amount of pottering around the Forum. It's also very spread out, so be prepared for a fair amount of walking.

The **Decumanus Maximus** is the main street, leading west from the entrance, past the **Baths of Neptune** on the right (where there's an interesting mosaic) to the town's commercial centre, otherwise known as the **Piazzale delle Corporazioni**, for the remains of shops and trading offices that still fringe the central square. These represented commercial enterprises from all over the ancient world, and the mosaics just in front denote their trade – grain merchants, ship-fitters, ropemakers and the like. Flanking one side of the square, the **theatre** has been much restored but is nonetheless impressive, enlarged by Septimius Severus in the second century AD to hold up to 4000 people. On the left of the square, the **House of Apulius** preserves mosaic floors and, beyond, a dark-aisled *mithraeum* with more mosaics illustrating the cult's practices. Behind here – past the substantial remains of the *horrea* or warehouses that once stood all over the city – the **Casa di Diana** is probably the best-preserved private house in Ostia, with a dark, mysterious set of rooms around a central courtyard, and again with a *mithraeum* at the back. You can climb up to its roof for a fine view of the rest of the site, afterwards crossing the road to the **Thermopolium** – an ancient Roman café, complete with seats outside, a high counter, display shelves and even wall paintings of parts of the menu. North of the Casa di Diana, the **museum** (Tues–Sat 9am–4.30pm, Sun 9am–1pm; entry with ticket for the excavations – see p.813) holds a variety of articles from the site, including a statue of Mithras killing a bull, wall paintings depicting domestic life in Ostia, and some fine sarcophagi and statuary from the imperial period. Left from here, the **Forum** centres on the **Capitol** building, reached by a wide flight of steps, and is fringed by the remains of baths and a basilica. Further on down the main street, more **horrea**, superbly preserved and complete with pediment and names inscribed on the marble, merit a detour off to the right; although you can't enter, you can peer into the courtyard. Beyond, the **House of Cupid and Psyche** has a courtyard you can walk into, its rooms clearly discernible on one side, a colourful marbled floor on the other.

Northern Lazio

Northern Lazio, or "Alto Lazio", is quite a different entity from the region south of the capital and is well worth a visit. Green and wooded in the centre, its steadily more undulating hills hint at the landscapes of Tuscany and Umbria further north. Few large towns exist, however, and, with determination (and, in some cases, a car), you can see much of it on day trips from Rome. Foremost among the area's attractions is the legacy of the **Etruscans**, a sophisticated pre-Roman people swathed in mystery. To the west, some of their most important sites are readily accessible by road or rail – necropolises mainly, the only remains of a civilization that ruled this region for nearly one thousand years. To the east, the **Sabine Hills** hold picturesque olive groves, unspoilt villages and religious centres like Farfa, once the most powerful abbey in Europe. The **coast** is of very little appeal until **Tarquinia Lido**, the first of several popular beaches stretching up to the Tuscan border. Alternatively, swimmers can head inland to the lakes **Vico** or **Bolsena** – playgrounds for hot and bothered Romans on summer weekends. **Viterbo**, the medieval "city of popes", can serve as a base if you're thinking of a two or three day visit, particularly if you're touring without a car. It's close to some fine examples of the region's **Mannerist villas and gardens** and a good source of information on Etruscan sites and local museums. Over to the east, **Rieti** is the big centre, a rather bland and somewhat deservedly unvisited town on the way to Abruzzo. Beyond it lie the **lakes and mountains** of Terminillo and Amatrice, scenically spectacular, but again difficult to reach without a vehicle.

Etruria and the coast

D.H. Lawrence had pretty much the last word on the plain, low hills stretching **north from Rome** towards the Tuscan border. "A peculiarly forlorn coast," he lamented, "the sea peculiarly flat and sunken, lifeless looking, the land as if it had given up its last gasp and was now forever inert." His *Etruscan Places*, published in 1932, is one of the best introductions to this pre-Roman civilization and their cities, which, one or two beaches excepted, are the main reasons for venturing out here.

Cerveteri

CERVETERI provides the most accessible Etruscan taster, travelling from Rome's Lepanto station by COTRAL **bus** (line A; every 40min; 80min) to Piazza Aldo Moro. The same Roma-Cerverteri bus also links to the train station 7km away at **LADISPOLI**, incidentally the best of the uninspiring seaside resorts just outside the capital. Swimming spots exist about ten minutes' walk from the station, although the best is further north, around half an hour away at the **Torre Flavia** – a medieval construction restored in 1565 by an Orsini cardinal but now collapsing elegantly into the water in four equal parts.

The settlement here dates back to the tenth century BC and was once a trading heavyweight, one of the Mediterranean's largest centres. Cerveteri, also known as *Caere*, ranked among the top three cities in the twelve-strong Etruscan federation, its wealth derived largely from the mineral-rich **Tolfa hills** to the northeast – a gentle range that gives the plain a much-needed touch of scenic colour. In its heyday, the town spread over 8km (something like thirty times its present size), controlling territory 50km up the coast. Rot set in from 351 BC, when Romans assumed control without granting full citizenship rights.

The present town is a thirteenth-century creation, dismissed by D.H. Lawrence – and you really can't blame him – as "forlorn beyond words". On arrival, make straight for the Etruscan **necropolis** (May–Sept Tues–Sun 9am–7pm; Oct–April Tues–Sun 9am–4pm; €4, €6.50 including museum), just 1km away in Banditaccia and signposted from the central piazza. From the seventh to first century BC, the Etruscans constructed a literal city of the dead here, weird and fantastically well preserved, with complete streets and homes. Some tombs are strange round pillboxes carved from cliffs; others are covered in earth to create the tumuli effect that ripples the surrounding plateau. Archeologists speculate that women were buried in separate small chambers within the "house" – easy to distinguish – while the men were laid on deathbeds (occasionally in sarcophagi) hewn directly from the stone. Indeed archeological evidence suggests that the position of women in Etruscan society was roughly on a par with that of men. Also, cremated slaves lay in urns alongside their masters – civilized by comparison with the Romans, who simply threw them into mass burial pits. The twelve or so show-tombs, lying between the two main roads, close in random rotation. Don't miss the **Tomba Bella** (Tomb of the Bas-Reliefs), **Tomba dei Letti Funebri** (Tomb of the Funeral Beds) and the **Tomba dei Capitelli**.

You could spend several hours wandering about, but you might be better off heading back into town to the **Museo Nazionale di Cerveteri**, at the top of the old quarter in the sixteenth-century **Castello Ruspoli** (Tues–Sun 9am–7pm; €4). This has two large rooms containing a fraction of the huge wealth that was buried with the Etruscan dead – vases, terracottas and a run of miscellaneous day-to-day objects; most of the best stuff though has been whisked away to Villa Giulia in Rome. En route, quench your appetite at the little **trattoria**, *Tukulcha*, on the necropolis road, where they serve hearty country-style food backed up by crisp Cerveteri white wines (no credit cards; closed Mon).

Civitavecchia

The only reasons to break a journey in **CIVITAVECCHIA**, 30km north of Cerveteri, are to change trains or catch a **ferry** to Sardinia (see p.844 for details of crossings); a night crossing saves the dubious pleasure of exploring town, although its worth knowing that for many years it was the home of the nineteenth-century French writer Stendhal. The **docks** are in the city centre at the end of Viale Garibaldi, ten minutes' walk from the **train station**. Between the two, the **tourist office** at Viale Garibaldi 40 (Mon–Sat 8.30am–1pm, Tues & Fri also 3–6pm; ☎0766.25.348) sells ferry tickets, but travel agents can make reservations (essential in the summer months); head for *Laboratorio Viaggi*, Porto Turistico Riva di Traiano (☎0766.217.11, ⓦ www.ciaoetruria.it), or *Dock & Discover*, Largo Plebiscito 23–26 (☎0766.581.574, ⓦ www.dockdiscover.com). Should you get stuck downtown, try the *Hotel Roma* at Via Monte Grappa 27 (☎0766.31.020) or, failing that, the modern *Hotel Medusa* (☎0766.24.327; ❹), which is near the 68,300km marker on Via Aurelia and has tidy, respectable rooms. As for **eating**, try *Trattoria Sora Maria*, off Largo Plebiscito on Via Zara (Mon, Tues, Sun lunch, Thurs, Fri, Sat lunch and dinner; closed Wed), known for its fish, or for decent pizza go around the corner to the *Pizzeria del Ghetto* (evenings only; also closed Wed).

Tarquinia

TARQUINIA, about 15km further north, is the most touted of the Etruscan necropolises, and with good reason. When not overrun with fellow visitors, the site is quite evocative and the actual town, partial walls containing a crop of medieval towers, is a pleasant place to pass an afternoon. The museum is the region's finest outside Rome and is unmissable.

The Town

The old fortified district contains a twelfth-century Romanesque church, **Santa Maria di Castello**, noted for its rib vaulting, the first known example in Italy. Otherwise it's the **Museo Nazionale Tarquiniense**, right on the main square of Piazza Cavour (Tues–Sun 8.30am–7.30pm; €4, €6.50, including necropolis), that draws the crowds. Though not large, the collection is choice and sensitively housed in an attractive Gothic-Renaissance *palazzo*. The ground floor exhibits superb sculpted sarcophagi, many decorated with warm and human portraits of the deceased. Upstairs are displays of exquisite Etruscan gold jewellery, painted ceramics, bronzes, candlesticks, heads and figures, including the renowned winged horses (fourth century BC), probably from a temple frieze – a striking example of the Etruscans' skill in decorative terracotta. The impressive top floor boasts wall paintings, removed from the necropolis to prevent deterioration, as well as fine views of the countryside and sea.

The site

Regular buses connect Piazza Cavour and the **necropolis** (summer Tues–Sun 8.30am–7.30pm; winter 8.30am–2pm; €4, €6.50 including museum), the real reason for a visit here, with its vividly painted tombs unmissable masterpieces. The walk is just fifteen minutes, though: take Via Umberto I from Piazza Cavour, pass through the Porta Romana, cross Piazza Europa, follow Via IV Novembre/Via delle Croci up the hill, and the site is on the left.

Once the artistic, cultural and probably political capital of Etruria, the wooden city has now all but vanished. Founded in the tenth century BC, its population peaked around 100,000, but the Roman juggernaut triggered its decline six hundred years later and only a warren of graves remains, cut into a plateau, on the southeast edge of the modern town. Excavations started in 1489, the first recorded in modern times, since when 6000 tombs have been uncovered (900 in 1958 alone), with many more to go. Grave robbing is common (thieves are known as *i tombaroli*). Fresh air and humidity have also damaged the **wall paintings** but improved conservation keeps the fourteen major tombs open more often than not. Etruscan burial places often mimicked neighbourhoods and houses (though less literally here than at Cerveteri). Some frescoes may depict the inhabitants' expectations of the afterlife: scenes of banqueting, hunting and even a ménage à trois. The famed **Tomba dei Demoni Blu** makes a darker prediction with demons greeting the deceased in the Underworld. The earliest paintings emphasize mythical and ritualistic scenes, but the sixth to fourth-century works – in the Orco, Auguri, Della Caccia and Della Pescia tombs – show greater social realism. This style is a mixture of Greek, indigenous Etruscan and eastern influences: the ease and fluidity points to a civilization at its peak. Especially important are the echoes of Hellenistic monumental painting – few traces remain of this form. Later efforts grow increasingly morbid with purely necromantic drawings, enough to discourage picnic lunches on the pleasant, grassy site.

You might be better off trying this at the **acropolis**, the remains of the living city across the valley, but you'll need a car. Continue along the road away from Tarquinia, which soon ends at the SS1bis, the main highway between Viterbo and Civitavecchia. Turn left towards Viterbo and after a couple of kilometres you come to a Roman aqueduct that follows the highway; you should see a turning to your left with a sign for the acropolis, and from there it's about another kilometre along a gravel road. The site has been fenced off to discourage grazing sheep and contemporary *tombaroli* with their metal detectors, and to be honest there's not an awful lot to see, but there's an impressive view down the valley to the town and the sea, giving a feel for the grandeur of the whole enterprise.

Practicalities

Tarquinia's **train station** is 2km below the town centre, connected with the central Barriera San Giusto, hard up against the city walls, by regular local shuttles; **buses** from Viterbo and Rome also stop here. There's a **tourist office** just through the city gate at Piazza Cavour 13 (daily 8am–2pm & 3–6pm; ℡0766.856.384, Ⓔinfotarquinia@apt.viterbo.it), and another on the main square, Piazza Trento e Trieste, in the centre of town – Etruscan Viaggi (℡0766.857.750, Ⓔetruscaviaggi@hotmail.com), where you can also get a list of bed-and-breakfast accommodation – useful in a town where **accommodation** is limited. The serene and gracious *Hotel San Marco* at Piazza Cavour 18 (℡0766.842.234, Ⓦwww.san-marco.com; ❹) is about the best option, and you can **dine** at the hotel's upscale restaurant, serving exotic meats like bison, ostrich and kangaroo (closed Mon), or the cosy trattoria-pizzeria, *Napule e*, nearby at Piazza Cavour 11 (closed Mon). Perhaps the most atmospheric place to **drink** is *Osterina il Grottino*, a cave-like bar at Alberata Dante Alighieri 8 that serves wine siphoned out of barrels piled in the corner.

Tarquinia Lido

TARQUINIA LIDO, reachable by hourly bus from Barriera San Giusto via the train station, is home to the area's flashy action. The helpful **information office**, a shack on the corner of Via Porto Clementino and Viale Mediterraneo, is open in summer and sells bus tickets (9.30am–12.30pm, also July & Aug 2.30–7.30pm; ℡0339.308.4825). The *Nautilis Miramare*, Viale dei Tirreni 36 (℡0766.864.020, but no phone bookings accepted, Ⓔnautilis-miramar@libero .it; ❷), has tidy en suites with a mishmash of antiques and 1970s plywood furnishings. Towels and sheet charges pad the prices, but at least the **hotel** is across from the free beach. You might find a spot at the Antica Salina bed and breakfast (℡0766.864.172 or 380.712.2628). Head south for 1km along the road to Saline and you'll see it on your left, just before you get to the salt marshes, which have been turned into a nature reserve and bird sanctuary. Three huge **campsites** – plus those at Riva di Tarquinia to the north – host great herds of holidaymakers. **Eat** at the locals' favourite, *Falcioni*, serving fried fish from €15, on Lungotevere del Tirreni 5 (look for the turquoise rowboat submerged in the sand). The **beaches** are heavily developed – with restaurants, discos, sports facilities, "pubs" and even cinemas – but might just hit the spot after sedate Tarquinia proper. The best bet, though, is to round off a day-trip with a quick dip and head back to the station.

Lago di Vico and Caprarola

The smallest, but most appealing of northern Lazio's lakes is the only one deemed worthy of nature reserve status. **LAGO DI VICO** is a former volcanic crater, ringed by appreciable mountains, the highest of which, Monte Fogliano, rises to 963m on the western shore. The **Via Cimina** traverses the summit ridges and is a popular scenic drive, dotted with restaurants, but there's a quieter road (closed to cars) near the shoreline. The flatter northern edge, marshy in places, is the spot for discreet unofficial **camping**.

Getting around this part of Lazio is difficult without private transport. But there are plenty of buses between Viterbo and the **Saxa Rubra** station in Rome which skirt the area. For the lake, pick up the bus that follows the Via Cimina from Rome to Viterbo via **Ronciglione**, and there's a stop a couple of kilometres north of the town that drops you at the lakeshore. There's also a bus service to **Caprarola** from Saxa Rubra, but the most reliable service is from Viterbo (see p.820). Don't be fooled by the rail line marked on the map that runs between Capranica and Caprarola: there are stations (a good 5km from the actual towns), but no longer any trains.

Caprarola: the Palazzo Farnese

Over and above the lake's sheer prettiness, there's not much besides the odd attractive village and a scattering of Roman and Etruscan remains – none terribly interesting in their own right, but worthwhile if you can string several together. More deserving of individual attention is the **Palazzo Farnese** at **CAPRAROLA**, which, like the villas at Bagnaia and Bomarzo, ranks among the high points of seventeenth-century Italian Mannerism.

The **palace** stands huge and imposing at the top of the town's steep main street (Tues–Sun 8.30am–6.45pm, gardens 9am–4.30pm in winter; €3, palace and gardens). The complex is clearly a masterpiece; Stendhal described it as the place where "architecture married Nature". Begun by Antonio da Sangallo the Younger for Pierluigi Farnese in the early 1520s, it was originally more a castle than a palace, situated at the centre of the Farnese family lands. Later, Cardinal Alessandro Farnese took up residence here, in 1559 hiring Vignola to modify the building while retaining its peculiar pentagonal floor-plan. Vignola was an inspired choice: apprenticed at Fontainebleau in France he was among the most accomplished architects of the late Renaissance, and his creation here exemplifies the Mannerist style at its best. Caprarola celebrates the period's values of superiority of art over nature and style over substance, together with a self-satisfied, almost gloating eulogizing of the patron's virtues.

Of the palace's five floors only the *piano nobile* is open to the public. Although all the furniture has gone, the interior is still impressive. There are frescoes from

1560, most of them by the brothers Zuccari, chronicling the Farnese family's greatness, much lauded as the building's highlight (though some are embarrassingly crude and others terribly knocked about), and a monumental spiral staircase up to a circular courtyard. The courtyard gives onto the main rooms of the piano nobile, huge and heavy with its thirty pairs of columns, but nevertheless considered one of Vignola's finest moments. The first and last rooms are perhaps the best, however. The former has a super-embellished grotto-like fireplace and pictures of local communities like Caprarola itself (the central scene is an imaginary one). The latter, the Sala del Mappamondo, boasts huge painted maps of the known world and a wonderful ceiling fresco of the constellations.

Outside there are twin **gardens** (guided tours Tues–Sun 10am, 11am, noon & 3pm), divided into a south-facing summer terrace and an east-facing winter terrace, with plants and design appropriate to each. Look out for the artificial grotto and the stalactites, imported from a real cave. The palace also hosts free summer concerts (℡0335.628.4128).

Practicalities

Without your own car, it's best to use Viterbo (see p.820) as a base and take one of the seven **buses** a day from here to Caprarola. This entails a very pleasant 45-minute ride through the wooded hills of the Monti Cimini that leaves you at the foot of the main street, from where it's a ten-minute walk to the palace at the top. In any case, Caprarola has few **hotels**, the *Farnese* (℡0761.646.029; ❷), a modern place way out on Via Circonvallazione (the bus to Viterbo goes right past) should be used in emergencies only, or you could try the *La Rocca* bed and breakfast at Piazza Romeo Romei 7 (℡0761.646.411, ✉bblarocca @bblarocca.it; ❷). For **food**, there's the *Trattoria del Cimino* midway down the main street at Via F. Nicolai 44 (closed Mon; ℡0761.646.173), and a *pizzeria* off to the left of Piazza Romei in front of the palace (closed Sun).

Bracciano

The closest of northern Lazio's lakes to Rome, **Lago di Bracciano** fills an enormous volcanic crater, a smooth, roughly circular expanse of water that's popular – but not too popular – with Romans keen to escape the summer heat of the city. It's nothing spectacular, with few real sights and a landscape of rather plain, rolling countryside, but its shores are fairly peaceful even on summer Sundays, and you can eat excellent lake fish in its restaurants.

The lake's main settlement is **BRACCIANO** on the western shore, about half an hour by train from Rome San Pietro (direction Viterbo), a small town that was caterpulted into the news when Tom Cruise and Katie Holmes got married here in 2006. The couple tied the knot at the imposing **Castello Orsini-Odelscalchi** (April–Sept Tues–Sat 10am–12.30pm & 3–6pm, Sun 9am–12.30pm & 3–6.30pm; Oct–March Tues–Sat 10am–noon & 3–5pm, Sun 9am–noon & 3–5.30pm; tours every 30min; €6), which dominates the town, a late-fifteenth-century structure now privately owned by the Odelschalchi family. The outer walls, now mostly disappeared, contained the rectangular piazza of the medieval town; nowadays it's a little rundown, its interior home to rusting suits of armour and faded frescoes, but the view from the ramparts is worth the admission price alone.

The best place to **swim** in the lake is from the beach at Lungolago Argenti, below Bracciano town. You can rent a boat and picnic on the beach, and the nearby trattorias are good and inexpensive – try *Da Tonino* at no.18 right on the beach, which serves good pasta and fish. The shore between Trevignano and Anguillara also boasts fine swimming spots, as well as good **restaurants** in both of the towns. One of the best is the *Casina Bianca*, Via della Rena 100 (closed Mon), Trevignano, which also serves fresh fish on a terrace overlooking the lake.

Viterbo and around

The capital of its province, and indeed of northern Lazio as a whole, **VITERBO** is easily the region's most historic centre, a medieval town that during the thirteenth century was once something of a rival to Rome. It was, for a time, the residence of popes, a succession of whom relocated here after friction in the capital. Today there are some vestiges of its vanquished prestige – a handful of grand palaces and numerous medieval churches, enclosed by an intact set of walls. The town is a well-kept place and refreshingly untouched by much tourist traffic, but only really worth staying in if you're keen to visit the surrounding area. Otherwise, buses and trains run frequently to Rome (buses are quicker) and you can comfortably see the town in a day.

Arrival, information and accommodation

Unusually for a small town, Viterbo has three **train stations**: the first, and probably the quickest and least complicated for trips from Rome, is just outside its namesake Porta Romana to the centre's south, around fifteen minutes from Piazza del Plebiscito. It's on the FM3 line from Rome, which connects Roma Ostiense, Trastevere and San Pietro, and also with the metropolitana at Valle Aurelia. There are at least hourly departures throughout the day, less frequent at night, and the journey time is 80 minutes. Viterbo's second, Porta Fiorentina, is on Viale Trento, close by Piazza della Rocca and handier for hotels. This line runs via **Montefiascone** to **Orte**, a stop on the main north–south line that runs the length of Italy. Virtually any train travelling to the major northern cities from Rome's **Stazione Termini** stops at Orte. The third is the terminus for the Roma-Nord line and is next door to Porta Fiorentina station, the last stop on a picturesque but lengthy ride through just about every small town between Rome and Viterbo, which you pick up from Rome's **Piazzale Flaminia** station. One of the first stops this train makes on the way out of Rome is at **Saxa Rubra,** where there's a bus depot for the **COTRAL** bus network that serves Bagnaia, Bomarzo and Tuscania and Lago di Vico and Caprarola (see p.822). The main depot in Viterbo is a ten-minute walk from the centre, out past Porta Fiorentina on Via Amadeo Cerasa.

For **information**, there's a tourist office inside the Porta Romana train station (Mon–Sat 10am–1pm, 4–6pm; ☎0761.304795), and another on Via Ascenti 4 (hours as above, ☎0761.325992, ✉infotuscia@libero.it). Both should be able to give you the good free guide for the area, "Ospitalità Tuscia", in both Italian and English, which has all the basics you need.

Close by, Via della Cava winds its way up to Piazza della Rocca and has a couple of inexpensive **hotels**, such as the down-at-heel *Roma,* Via della Cava 26 (☎0761.226.474; ❷), or the more welcoming *Leon D'Oro,* at no.36 (☎0761.344.444; ❷). Forgive the lounge's clashing upholstery and rugs, as the rooms are more restful. The *Tuscia* on Via Cairoli, just off Piazza della Rocca (☎0761.344.400; ❷), is bright and friendly and its air-conditioned rooms are newly renovated, or there's a cheap but slightly dingy alternative in the *Trieste*, across from the Roma-Nord station at Via N. Sauro 32 (☎0761.341.882; ❷).

The Town

If there is a centre to Viterbo, it's **Piazza del Plebiscito**, an appropriately named square girdled almost entirely by the fifteenth- and sixteenth-century buildings that make up the town's council offices. The lions and palm trees that reflect each other across the square are the city's symbols, repeated, with grandiose echoes of Venice, all over town. Peek into the fine Renaissance courtyard of the main, arcaded building of the **Palazzo dei Priori**. The council chamber is decorated with a series of murals depicting Viterbo's history right back to Etruscan times in a weird mixture of pagan and Christian motifs – a melange continued across the square in the church of **Sant'Angelo**.

Roads fork in many directions from the piazza. Most interesting is **Via San Lorenzo** to the right, which sweeps past the pretty Piazza di Gesù to the macabrely named **Piazza del Morte** – the "Square of Death", after the paupers and abandoned corpses that were buried here by the monks. A left from here leads to Viterbo's oldest district, the **Quartiere San Pellegrino** – a tight mess of hilly streets, home to a number of art and antique shops. In the opposite direction, **Piazza San Lorenzo** is flanked by the town's most historic buildings, notably the **Palazzo Papale** itself, a thirteenth-century structure whose impressive site, looking over the green gorge that cuts into central Viterbo, is best appreciated from its open Gothic loggia. You can glimpse the Great Hall, venue of the election of half a dozen or so popes, but otherwise the palace is closed to the public. Content yourself with a wander into the **Duomo** opposite, a plain Romanesque church that has an elegant striped floor and an understated beauty unusual among Italian churches.

East of Piazza del Plebiscito, Via Roma joins **Corso Italia** at **Piazza dell'Erbe**, Viterbo's main shopping area and the scene of a busy *passeggiata* of an evening. At its far end, steps lead up from Piazza Verdi to the nineteenth-century church of **Santa Rosa**, where the desiccated corpse of the town's patron saint can be seen in a south aisle chapel – a faintly grotesque, doll-like figure with a forced grin, dressed up in a nun's habit. A good time to be in Viterbo is September 3 during the **festa**, when the *macchina di Santa Rosa* – a huge three-storey platform and altarpiece holding the icon – is carried through the streets on the backs of *facchini*, to the accompaniment of much revelry and, later, fireworks.

After Santa Rosa, the rest of Viterbo can't help but seem sinister, and in any case, you've seen it all except for one quarter, which is at the top of the hill above Piazza Verdi. Follow Via Matteotti up to **Piazza della Rocca**, a large square dominated by the fierce-looking **Rocca Albornoz**, home of the small **Museo Nazionale** (Tues–Sun 8.30am–6.30pm; €4), whose archeological collection includes displays of locally unearthed Roman and Etruscan artefacts. Just off the opposite side of the square, the church of **San Francesco** is also worth a quick look. The high, unusually plain Gothic church is the burial place of two of Viterbo's popes – Clement IV and Adrian V – both laid in now heavily restored, but impressive, Cosmatesque tombs on either side of the main altar.

Outside the walls is the twelfth-century church of **Santa Maria della Verità**, whose fine, early Renaissance frescoes by little-known master Lorenzo da Viterbo in the Capella Mazzatosta were recently restored. In the convent next door is the **Museo Civico**, with artefacts from the Iron Age to the Roman Imperial period, and an art gallery that focuses on the Viterbo school and includes a *Pietà* by

Sebastiano del Piombo. Unfortunately, and for no apparent reason, a wing of the building collapsed about a year ago, the only casualty an expensive Mercedes parked on the street below, and it has shown no recent signs of reopening.

Terme

Accessible by local bus from the station in **Piazza Martiri D'Ungheria** (refered to locally as "Sacrario"), Viterbo's various *terme*, or "hot baths", are a couple of kilomtres west of the city, the most famous of which, *Bulicame*, gets a mention in Dante's *Inferno*. Unfortunately this is closed at the moment, but you can take the #2F bus along the Fosso Faul gorge to the **Terme dei Papi** (℡0761.3501; €15), a popular spot with the locals at which you spend a very relaxing few hours lounging poolside or floating in the 35-degree water; plus there are a range of therapeutic treatments on offer – sulphur baths, mud baths, a steam grotto and suchlike. For the same experience but free of charge, stay on the bus until just before the **Strada Tuscanese**, where the parked cars and rising steam around the *pozzi* on your left hand side signal a similar hotspot but one yet to be developed.

Eating and drinking

Finding **somewhere to eat** in Viterbo is no problem. *Schenardi*, Corso Italia 11 (closed Wed), with its regilded Art Nouveau interior, is one of the nicest places for a lunchtime snack or tea. The *Taverna Etrusca*, Via Annio 10 (℡0766.226.694, closed Sun), does excellent pizzas. The Porta Romana, in Via della Bonta, does good local food and is supremely friendly. Otherwise, try *Tre Re*, Via Marcel Gattesco 3 (closed Thurs), off Piazza delle Erbe – a cosy place, popular with locals and a good venue for trying regional specialities. Or splurge on exquisite "slow food" at *Enoteca la Torre*, Via della Torre 5 (℡0761.226.467; evenings only, closed Sun). Viterbo's culinary highlight is slightly precious, but not overly costly, if you select sparingly from the five or six courses on offer – and go easy on the huge and pricey wine list. For a bit of nightlife, try *Bar Lucio*, Via San Pellegrino 13, where Viterbo's burgeoning student population hang out.

Around Viterbo: San Martino al Cimino Bagnaia, Bomarzo and Tuscania

Viterbo makes by far the best base (besides Rome) for seeing much of Northern Lazio, especially the places that aren't really feasible on a day-trip from the capital. If you're without a car, don't worry. The **COTRAL** bus network is extensive, and, once you tune in to its eccentricities, virtually everywhere worth going to is accessible. The Mannerist villas of **Caprarola** (see p.818) and **Bagnaia** are a short distance away and easily reached on public transport, as are – from the same era – the bizarre gardens of **Bomarzo** and the shores of **Lago di Bolsena** (see p.825). Less excitingly, Viterbo is also connected by regular bus with **Tuscania**.

San Martino al Cimino

One outing easily done from Viterbo is **SAN MARTINO AL CIMINO**, a pretty little walled village a few kilomtres south that was once the country seat of the Pamphilj family, one of Rome's big papal families. The #11 bus from Piazza Martiri D'Ungheria winds up the hill and drops you by the fountain in **Piazza Mariano Buratti**, the main square, from where you can stroll up to the dominating **Chiesa Abbaziale** – originally a Cistercian monastery founded in the thirteenth century by friars from Pontigny in France. The interior retains some of its unfussy gothic lines, despite a considerable Baroque revamping, and there's a nice view west towards the Tyrrhenian Sea from the large terrace. The **Palazzo Doria Pamphilj**, across the street, has been turned into a conference centre and is worth a peek if it's open (actual conferences seem rare). It also houses the provincial **tourist office** and if you follow the winding staircase up to the second floor you should be able to get some free glossies on all the local sites, although all in Italian. Back down **Via Doria** towards the main square, the *Widman Bed and Breakfast* at (℡0761.379.709 or 340.325.7387, Ⓔonofri_@libero.it) has clean, cheerful and reasonably priced rooms. Across the street from the *Widman* there's a *Bar Gelateria* with wonderful home-made pastries and an atmosphere little changed from the 1950s, while for a real gastronomic treat La Pergoletta, Via Doria 38 (℡0761.378.666, Ⓦwww .lapergoletta.it; closed Wed), has great local cooking – not cheap, but excellent value for money. Bear in mind, if you've got a car, that it's a short and scenic drive from the village up over the mountain to **Lago di Vico** (see p.818).

Bagnaia

About 5km east of Viterbo, **BAGNAIA** isn't much of a town, but like Caprarola further south it's completely dominated by a sixteenth-century palace, the **Villa Lante**, whose small but superb estate is considered Vignola's masterpiece and a supreme creation of Renaissance garden art. Sacheverell Sitwell pronounced it "the most lovely place of the physical beauty of nature in all Italy or in all the world". The villa is easily visited from Viterbo using the hourly **bus #6** from Piazza Martiri dei Ungheria or from the stop at the beginning of Viale Trento, or the less frequent trains of the Roma-Nord line.

A short walk uphill from the main square, the **villa** is actually two buildings, built twenty years apart for different cardinals, but symmetrically aligned as part of the same architectural plan. They are closed to the public, but there's nothing much to write home about anyway; in contrast to Caprarola, it's the **gardens** (Tues–Sun 8.30am–1hr before sunset; €2) that take pride of place – some of the period's best preserved and a summing up of Mannerist aspirations. The main group lies behind the villas, ranged over five gently sloping terraces, and are only visitable in the company of a guide (℡0761.288.008). An attempt at a stylized interpretation of the natural world, they were an ambitious project even by the standards of the time, depicting the progress of a river from its source in the hills to its outlet in the sea – represented here by a large parterre. The route takes in various watery adventures – waterfalls, lakes and the like – and among numerous fountains and low hedges surface plenty of humorous (or plain silly) touches. Look for the maiden whose breasts spout water, a cascade designed as an elongated crayfish, and the so-called "wetting sports" – hidden sprays of water that drenched unsuspecting onlookers and were a big favourite of Mannerist pranksters. Only the guide gets to play with these, however.

The adjoining **park** (hours and prices as for the villa), through which you can wander at will, has an even more ambitious narrative, attempting to describe through horticulture civilization's progress from primitive times to the glories of the sixteenth century. In true Mannerist style, almost as much weight is given to allegory as to architecture, both here and on the villas. The various square motifs, for example, supposedly represented the perfection of heaven brought to earth.

Bomarzo

Twelve kilometres northeast of Bagnaia, the village of **BOMARZO** is home to another Mannerist creation, the **Parco dei Mostri** (daily 8am–1hr before sunset; €8) and a greater contrast to the former's restrained elegance would be hard to find. The "Monster Park" is still ostensibly a garden, but one look at the tangled wood and its huge, completely crazed sculptures demonstrates that this is Mannerism gone mad. Salvador Dalí loved the surreal flavour of the place, even making a film here, and its strange otherworldly qualities – like a sixteenth-century theme park of fantasy and horror – have made it one of northern Lazio's primary tourist attractions.

Built in 1552 by the hunchbacked Duke of Orsini, the *Sacro Bosco* – "Sacred Wood", as he called it – set out to parody Mannerist self-glorification by deliberate vulgarity. The design mocks intellectual pretensions, idealized Arcadian retreats and Art's supposed "triumph" over Nature, by making a calculated bid at sensationalism, typical of the time. Apparently built by Turkish prisoners captured at the Battle of Lepanto (though this smacks of a Christian rationalization of "heretical" features), the park has an Etruscan influence, manifest in the plentiful urns and pinecones. A popular epic – Ariosto's *Orlando Furioso*, a tale of insanity – may have induced its more bizarre monuments. The giant warrior at the entrance, tearing apart a woodcutter, represented Orlando's madness. Deeper into the park, an English prince pours Orlando's brains down an elephant's trunk – another symbol apparently, this time of the restoration of sanity. There are many other dank, mossy sculptures of tortoises, elephants, a whale, a mad laughing mask, dragons, nymphs, butterflies and plenty more. Highlights include a perfect octagonal temple, dedicated to Orsini's wife, and a crooked, slanting house that makes your head spin. Numerous cryptic inscriptions dot the park and add to the mystery.

Eight **buses** a day run from Viterbo to Bomarzo, from where the Parco dei Mostri is a signposted ten-minute walk. You can also get here by **train** – the nearest station is Attigliano-Bomarzo, on the Orte–Montefiascone–Viterbo link, five kilometres away. The site has a self-service cafeteria, bar and ample picnic tables.

Tuscania

Only sheep break the monotony of the wide, desolate country between Viterbo and Tarquinia until the towers of **TUSCANIA** appear – an impressive sight, especially bathed in the early morning sun. Franco Zefferelli filmed *Romeo and Juliet* and *The Taming of the Shrew* here, but in 1971 an earthquake flattened the atmospheric medieval town, killing several hundred people. Today, Tuscania's a very tidy and clean reconstruction of its former self – and well worth a wander. There's a helpful **tourist shack** on Piazzale Trieste (☎0761/436.371).

The real draw, however, lies in two justly celebrated **Romanesque churches** on the eastern edge of town, close to the rocky outcrop of the old Etruscan settlement. From the central Piazza Basile, take the Via Clodia until the unmistakable bulk of **San Pietro** (daily: summer 9am–1pm & 3–7pm; winter 9am–1pm & 2–5pm; free) looms into view. Considered one of the gems of the Italian Romanesque, it's an essentially thirteenth-century construction with eighth-century fragments of Lombard origin. Fronted by a threadbare grass piazza, which produces an odd courtyard effect, it's also flanked by the remains of a Bishop's Palace and two sturdy towers – the whole church was once fortified as part of the town's defensive scheme. The facade's marble carvings are a bizarre mix of mythological figures and Christian symbolism – look out for the dancer and a three-headed man spewing out a twisting vine – and may well come from an Etruscan temple. The interior is solemn and cavernous, with huge blunt pillars supporting curious notched arches, a feature known in Italian as *dentati* (literally "toothed"), a spiralling Cosmatesque pavement and some early twelfth-century frescoes in the transept, somewhat the worse for wear post-quake. Steps lead underneath the chancel to a mosque-like crypt of 28 columns and ribbed vaulting.

The town's other focal point, **Santa Maria Maggiore** (same hours as San Pietro) is a stone's throw down the hill, a less gracious affair, though built slightly earlier in the same style. Pisan sculptors probably added the arched marble doorway in the twelfth century, now surmounted by an almost naive white-marble Madonna and Child, and flanked by saints and biblical scenes. The rest of the ruddy stone facade is largely Gothic, only the left portal preserving the zigzags of Norman motif. Inside is the usual bare simplicity of the Romanesque – stone walls, the odd fresco (including entertaining scenes of the Last Judgment in the apse, now, alas, fading fast) and, most remarkably, a font designed for total immersion.

Montefiascone, Lago di Bolsena and around

Heading north from Viterbo by road, you've little choice but to take the Via Cassia to **MONTEFIASCONE**, an unattractive journey, not improved by the train, which runs alongside. However, the hill-town, high on the rim of an old volcanic crater, justifies the trip.

Montefiascone was possibly the site of a huge temple to Voltumna – a sort of parliament for the heads of the twelve-city Etruscan Federation. The seventeenth-century **Cathedral of Santa Margherita** is immediately striking, its huge octagonal pile dominating the skyline. The dome is Italy's third largest, though the structure is overall less riveting than the twelfth-century **San Flaviano**, just outside town towards Orvieto. Two interconnected but opposite-facing basilicas form this extraordinary Romanesque work. The lower church contains frescoes, as well as the tomb of Bishop Giovanni Fugger, who reputedly died from a surfeit of the local wine, called Est! Est!! Est!!! The **tourist office** on Largo Plebiscito (daily 9am–noon; ☎0761.832.060, ✉info@commune.montefiascone.vt.it) regales guests with other unlikely legends surrounding this potable brew. For something **to eat**, *La Cavalla*, Via Bandita 25 (☎0761.826.3780), has a good selection of fish dishes and great views of Lago di Bolsena. The simpler *Ristorante Dante*, Via Nazionale 2, just off the main piazza, has a handwritten menu in childish notebooks, but chic guests beg for tables (closed Mon). Standout dishes include roasted lake eels and *porcini fettucine* at €6.50. Appeal to the matriarch for a **room** upstairs: upper storyes boast lake views (☎0761.826.015; ❶). Hearty travellers may prefer the *Amalasunta* **campsite**, Via del Lago 77 (☎0761.825.294), 5km down the Marta road at Prato Roncone.

Buses run from Montefiascone to Orvieto and to most points on **LAGO DI BOLSENA** – a popular destination, though rarely overcrowded. The western shore is better for camping rough and more picturesque into the bargain. The lake occupies the remains of a broad volcanic crater and is the largest of its kind in Europe. The immensely fertile soil and super-mild microclimate spur farmers and vintners to great heights. Dante praised the quality of its eels, though fishermen today are hampered by the so-called *sesse* – odd tide-like variations in the lake's level.

CAPODIMONTE, on the southern shore, is one of the more developed spots, an attractive town that pushes into the lake on a partly forested peninsula.

There are any number of nice **walks** you can take around around the lake, one of which is just a few kilometres and easily do-able if you have your own transport to get to the traihead. Follow the signposts for Valentano out of Capodimonte; after a few kilometres, take the fork to the right (signposted Gradoli) and park a little further up the hill. From here, you can walk up to a small **chapel** on the left, and, beyond, skirt a small farmhouse and follow the trail through through some woods to emerge at the summit of the hill where there are impressive views of the **lake**, Isola Bisentina, Capodimonte and the surrounding countryside. Steps leads down from here. Follow them, duck under a low arch in the rock and you'll find yourself inside a *tomba a columbaio*, an Etruscan funerary cave with a square, honeycomb design etched into the rock, all that remains of the once great Etruscan city of *Bisenzio*, or *Visentium*, as it is marked on the map. As always with this lost civilization, it's a funny mix of the magical, the slightly creepy and the spectacular. Once you're back in the car, continue down the main road to a long beach beside the lake, where you can take a quick dip to wash off all the Etruscan cobwebs, and then stop off at *Trattorio da Massimo*, further down on the left (only open Fri–Sun; ☎0761.870.148), where you can have a reasonably priced supper of lake fish washed down with a bottle or two of Est! Est!! Est!!!

The only sight worth a mention is the sixteenth-century **Castello Farnese** (open Mon only 9am–noon), an octagonal tower commanding the tip of the promontory, but there's enjoyable **swimming** from the tree-lined shore, or you can take a boat to **Isola Bisentina** (April–Sept 11am & 5pm; also 11am, 3pm & 7pm Sun & holidays; €11 inclusive of guide; book ahead for English ☎0761.870.760, ⓦwww.navigabolsena.com). The verdant island sports Etruscan tombs, five frescoed chapels and another Farnese villa – the summer retreat of several popes. The nearest **campsite** is 1.5km away at Località San Lorenzo, *Camping Bisenzio* (☎0761.871.202; May–Sept).

On the opposite shore of the lake, **BOLSENA** is the main focus, a relaxed and likeable place that's worth a brief stop. Medieval nooks and alleyways run off the main drag, Via Cassia, with the well-preserved fourteenth-century Monaldeschi **castle** perched over the western end. Inside is the local **museum** (summer Tues–Sun 10am–1pm & 4–8pm; winter Tues–Fri 10am–1pm & 3–6pm; €3.50) with modest displays on underwater archeology and Villanovan and Etruscan finds, plus stunning views from the ramparts. The deconsecrated thirteenth-century church of **San Francesco** adds character to the town's main Piazza Matteotti and occasionally hosts concerts and small exhibitions, while the eleventh-century **Santa Cristina** conceals a good Romanesque interior behind a wide Renaissance facade added in 1494. Cristina, daughter of the town's third-century Roman prefect, was tortured by her father for her Christian beliefs, eventually being thrown into the lake with a stone round her ankles. Miraculously the rock floated, though Cristina later died aged 12 as a result of further mistreatment. The stone, marked with the imprint of her feet, is the altar of the Cappella del Miracolo, off the left-hand aisle. Adjoining the chapel is the Grotta di Santa Cristina, once part of early Christian **catacombs** (summer daily 9am–noon & 3.30–6.30pm; winter daily 9am–noon & 3–5pm; €4).

Set back 1km from the lake, the town itself tends to shut down come nightfall, when the **bars and restaurants** on the shore get into full swing. For food head to *Trattoria da Picchietto* at Via Fiorentina 15 (☎0761.799.158; closed Mon). The closest of the **campsites**, most of which are a short walk out of town, is the *Campeggio Il Lago International*, less than 1km away at Viale Cadorna 6 (T0761.799.191, E anna.bruti@libero.it; March–Sept). *La Pineta* is a similar distance from town at Viale Diaz 48 (T0761.799.801; May–Sept). The cheapest **hotel** is the *Pensione Italia*, Corso Cavour 53 (T0761.799.193; ❷). For full details, call in at the **tourist office** at Piazza Matteotti 12 (summer Mon–Sat 9.30am–12.30pm & 4–7pm; winter Thurs–Sun 9.30am–12.30pm & 4–8pm; T0761.799.923, E ufficioturistico@comunebolsena.it).

Rieti and around

Pleasantly situated but rather dull, **RIETI** is the capital of Lazio's largest province, occupying the plumb geographical centre of Italy – and with a plaque in Piazza di San Rufo to prove it. In Roman times, this was a key region, the so-called *Umbilicus Italiae*, and the Via Salaria formed an essential route for trading salt (extracted from the Tiber estuary) with the Sabines, who lived in these hills. Nowadays the area's on its last legs, with the second-lowest population density in the country (after Aosta) and adrift from the land that's more typical of the south. Three-quarters of the rural population has moved from the countryside since 1950, most to Rome, and the trend continues. Poor communications have deterred any sort of industrial initiative – something that is to the visitors', if not the locals', advantage – leaving Rieti's mountain-ringed plain almost entirely unscarred by factories or housing.

The Town

Rieti is really just somewhere to while away an hour waiting for a bus – or use a base for hikes. Despite the tourist office's artful pictures of medieval walls and arches, the only traces are the **Duomo** and the **Palazzo Vescovile** off the main street and a short stretch of twelfth-century wall to the north of the centre. For those planning serious walking or camping trips, it's worth visiting the main **tourist office** on Piazza Vittorio Emanuele II (Tues–Fri 9am–1pm & 3–6pm, Sat 9am–1pm & 3–5pm, Sun 9am–1pm; T0746.203.220, W www.apt.rieti.it), which has maps of the town and, more importantly, detailed routes for high-level walks around Terminillo (see p.828). With their help you also shouldn't have problems planning a tour of the four **Franciscan monasteries** around Rieti (T0746.201.146, W www.camminodifrancesco.it) – a scenic route, although without an abiding interest in their patron you may not find them terribly exciting. The most famous is at **GRECCIO**, where St Francis created the first ever Christmas crib (*presepio*), a real-life nativity scene complete with cows; this is re-enacted every year on December 24, December 26 and Epiphany on January 6.

Practicalities

Rieti's **train station** is just north of the town centre on the far side of Viale L. Morroni. By **train** from Rome it's around three hours to Rieti: there's no direct link and you have to change at Terni (and sometimes Orte) for a line that eventually continues to L'Aquila and Sulmona. The **bus station** is in Via Fratelli Sebastiani off Via Salaria, and several **buses** a day ply back and forth to Rome (a 2hr journey). For somewhere **to stay**, the *Serena*, Viale della Gioventù 17 (T0746.270.930; ❷), is probably the cheapest option close to the centre of town, and has a few rooms without baths. You can **eat** inexpensively at *Pizzeria Il Pappamondo*, Piazza Cavour 63 (closed Tues), or, for a little more money, at *Bistrot*, on Piazza San Rufo 25 (closed Sun), where an adventurous menu is served up in an elegant monochromatic setting.

Terminillo and Amatrice

Less than 20km from Rieti, reachable by way of a heart-stopping bus ride, **TERMINILLO** lies amid 2000-metre-high mountains and scenery of almost Alpine splendour. This ski-resort considers itself an elite tourist centre and, as such, it's dominated by clusters of big modern hotels, ski lifts and associated winter-sports paraphernalia. It's not an especially attractive place, more a string of ski-centres than a town, but there's plenty of off-season scope for walking and climbing in the hills, including a series of refuges, if you want to do more than stroll.

Advice on ski conditions and accommodation is available from the **tourist office** at Via dei Villini 33 in Pian de Valli (Tues–Fri 9am–1pm & 3–7pm, Sat 9am–1pm & 3–5pm, Sun 8.30am–12.30pm; ☎0746.261.121). There's a **youth hostel**, the *Ostello della Neve*, at Anello Panoramico 15, Campoforogna (☎0746.261.169; €13 per person). Contact the **Club Alpino Italiano**, Via Garibaldi 264b, in Rome (☎06.686.1011), for advance information on some of the most challenging hikes in the countryside. One tremendous low-level route is by way of **La Valle Scura**, 12km across country to Sigillo. If you plan on wilderness trekking, bear in mind that many slopes away from the ski-runs are thickly wooded, especially in the Vallonina towards Leonessa, and you often have to climb quite high before finding open country.

Another good base for hikes is **AMATRICE**, 65km northeast of Rieti, a rather drab grid-iron town laid out in 1529, famous only as the birthplace of *spaghetti all'Amatriciana*, pasta with a spicy bacon and tomato sauce. Behind, the Monti della Laga rise to seriously high peaks – 2400m – that continue into Abruzzo's Gran Sasso range. The **tourist office** at Corso Umberto I 98 (July & August daily 10am–1pm & 4.30–7pm; June & Sept–May daily 9am–1pm; ☎0746.826.344) issues a detailed map with several marked paths, most of which start from rough roads above the hamlets of San Martino and Cappricchia. Stay at the two-star **hotel** *La Conca* at Via della Madonnella 24 (☎0746.826.891; ❷).

The Sabine Hills

The **Sabine Hills**, south of Rieti, are an altogether softer option. For an area so close to Rome, this sees only a trickle of tourism – partly because there are no big sights and partly because transportation is tricky among the small villages and secondary roads. The best scenery is east of the Via Salaria around **Lago del Turano** and **Lago del Salto**, where the village of **ROCCA SINIBALDA** provides a focus – though it's really no more than a fortified castle, surrounded by high wooded hills. Northeast lies a great swath of desolate country centred around Monte Nuria (1888m) and Monte Moro (1524m) – walking and backpacking territory mostly, with the small **Lago Rascino** providing a wild and unspoilt destination, especially good for camping.

On the other side of the Via Salaria, many villages have been decimated, first in the Fifties by people emigrating to the capital, and then – ironically – by richer Romans returning to buy up holiday homes. Varying degrees of medieval character are about all they've got going for them, though the rolling countryside is moderately pretty. One undoubted highlight in a lacklustre area is the old Benedictine abbey at **FARFA**, situated in fine olive-covered terrain 6km from Faro village. Bus connections are difficult, but the Rieti tourist office provides the latest schedules. Founded in the fifth century and endowed by Charlemagne, it once numbered among the most powerful abbeys in Europe, with a huge economic base, a merchant fleet, even its own army, and rights to Aquila, Molise, Viterbo, Spoleto, Tarquinia and Civitavecchia – central Italy in effect. By the end of the Middle Ages, however, it was in decline, then fifteenth- and sixteenth-century additions submerged most of its early medieval splendour. The **Abbey Church** (guided tours daily at 10.30am, 11.30am, 4pm & 5pm, Sat & Sun 10am, 11am, noon, 1pm, 3.30pm, 4.30pm, 5.30pm; donation expected; Ⓦwww.abbaziadifarfa.it) is stacked with various treasures, including parts of the Carolingian pavement, the sculptural relief forming the pulpit base and a few eleventh-century frescoes in the belltower, an ancient library, and, most fascinating, the Cures Pillar, found in a local riverbed in 1982 and with a sixth-century BC inscription that is the only known example of Sabine. Still undeciphered, it remains an emblem for studies of this largely ignored indigenous culture.

Southern Lazio

The saying goes that the Italian South begins with the first petrol station below Rome, and certainly there's a radically different feel here. Green wooded hills give way to flat marshy land and harsh unyielding mountains that possess a poor, almost desperate, look in places – most travellers skate straight through en route to Naples. But the **coast** merits a more unhurried route south – its resorts, especially **Terracina** and **Sperlonga**, are fine places to take it easy after the rigours of the capital. And the **Pontine Islands**, a couple of hours offshore, are – out of high season, at least – among Italy's undiscovered treasures. **Inland**, too, the landscape can be rewarding: the day-trip towns of the **Castelli Romani** attractively encircle Lago Albano. **Subiaco** to the east and the **Ciocaria** region to the south are more remote, but hold some of Lazio's most inspiring scenery – broad tree-clad hills and valleys sheltering small, unassuming towns.

The Castelli Romani and Alban Hills

Just free of the sprawling southern suburbs of Rome, the thirteen towns that make up the **Castelli Romani** date back to medieval times. These hills – the **Colli Albani** – have long cooled rich and powerful urbanites, who also treasure the area's extraordinary white wines, inspired by the rich volcanic soil. The region is now pretty heavily built-up, with most of the historic centres ringed by unprepossessing suburbs, and summer weekends see traffic jams of Romans trooping out to local trattorias. But off-peak, it's worth the journey, either as an excursion from Rome or a stop on the way south. By car, there are two obvious routes, both starting with Frascati and Grottaferrata and then spearing off at Marino along either the eastern or western side of Lago Albano. COTRAL **buses** serve the area (every 30min; 35min) from Rome's Anagnina metro station (line A).

Frascati and around

At just 20km from Rome, **FRASCATI** is the nearest of the Castelli towns and also the most striking, dominated by the majestic **Villa Aldobrandini**, designed by Giacomo della Porta at the turn of the sixteenth century. The Baroque *palazzo* is off-limits, but the **gardens** are open (Mon–Fri: summer 9am–1pm & 3–6pm; winter 9am–1pm & 3–5pm; €2). Sadly the elaborate water theatre, where statues once played flutes, no longer spouts in top form, but the view from the front terrace is superb, with Rome visible on a clear day.

Frascati's main square, **Piazza Marconi**, is right beneath the Aldobrandini villa, and home to a **tourist office** (Tues–Fri 8am–2pm & 4–7pm, Sat 8am–2pm; ☎06.942.0331). Just beyond here is the pedestrianized old centre, which revolves around the two squares of **Piazza San Pietro** and **Piazza del Mercato** just beyond. Frascati is also about the most famous of the Colli Albani wine towns: ask at the tourist office for details of winery tours and tastings, or simply indulge at one of the many trattorias in town. Better yet, pick up a *porchetta* (roast pork) sandwich from one of the stands on **Piazza del Mercato** and take the greasy bundle into a *cantine*, where wine is sold from giant wooden barrels for just 50c a glass. Try the *Antica Osteria di Castello*, just off Piazza del Mercato, or *Grappolo d'Oro*, just off Piazza del Gesù. For **accommodation**, the *Pinocchio*, Piazza del Mercato 21, has affordable, stylish rooms, the warm tones offsetting all the black lacquer (☎06.941.7883, ⓦwww.hotelpinocchio.it; ❷), and its **restaurant** specializes in porcini mushrooms and duck.

Tusculum, beautifully sited on a nearby hill, was an Etruscan centre overrun by Roman patricians. The Emperor Tiberius and orator Cicero both had villas here, but Pope Celestine III destroyed the resort in 1191 and the inhabitants moved down to modern-day Frascati. Undergrowth has submerged most of the Roman remains, but there's a small theatre, and the views, again, are fine.

North of Lago Albano

Three kilometres or so down the road, **GROTTAFERRATA** is also known for its wine and its eleventh-century **Abbey** – a fortified Basilian (Greek Orthodox) monastery surrounded by high defensive walls and a now empty moat (daily: summer 6am–12.30pm & 3.30–7pm: winter 6am–12.30pm & 3.30pm–sunset; free). Within the complex, the little church of Santa Maria has Byzantine-style interior decorated with thirteenth-century mosaics and, in the chapel of St Nilo off the right aisle, frescoes by Domenichino. Through the inner courtyard there's a small museum (closed for restoration) displaying classical and medieval sculptures.

MARINO, another 4km further on, is a pleasant little town set around a pretty main square, Piazza Matteoti, and its wine is perhaps the region's best after Frascati. On Piazza Matteoti, the Fontana dei Mori has mermaids and manacled Moors commemorating the Battle of Lepanto, and spouts *vino* on special occasions such as the first Sunday of October during its Sagra dell'Uva festival, while at other times of years you can simply sample the local wine in the *For de Porta* vineria in the corner of the square; or the food at the *Rotonda* restaurant in the opoosite corner.

East of Lago Albano

The scenic Via dei Laghi skirts the eastern rim of **Lago Albano** until a winding road leads up to **Monte Cavo** (949m), the second highest of the Colli Albani and topped with the masts and satellite dishes of the Italian military – who operate from nearby Ciampino airport. There used to be a hotel here, a former Passionist convent, but the building is now derelict, and the summit is much less of a tourist attraction than it used to be. A temple to Jupiter once stood here, but now the only extant antiquity is the Via Sacra, which, about 1000m from the top, emerges from dense undergrowth, snaking down through the woods for a kilometre or so before disappearing again into thick bush.

On the far side of Monte Cavo, the road bears right for **ROCCA DI PAPA**, at 680m the loftiest Castelli Romani town and one of the most picturesque, with a medieval quarter tumbling down the hill in haphazard terraces, and motor traffic kept to a strictly enforced minimum. Make for the small Piazza Garibaldi, a lively place in summer with a bar and restaurant, and soak up the views.

West of Lago Albano and Lago di Nemi

Leaving Marino, the road joins up with the ancient Roman Via Appia, which travels straight as an arrow down the west side of Lago Albano. **CASTEL GANDOLFO** is the first significant stop, best known as the pope's summer retreat. Four hundred metres above the lake, it's a pleasantly airy place, and enjoys great views over the entire lake from its terraces close by the main piazza della Libertá, a pleasant oblong of cafés and papal souvenir shops, at the end of which is the imposing bulk of the Papal Palace itself. Inevitably Vatican business predominates, especially on Sundays between July and September when the pope traditionally gives a midday address from the palace. If it's hot, you can take good advantage of the lake here: there's a pleasant lido just below town, with lots of restaurants and pizzerias and a small stretch of grey beach from where you could stroll the whole shoreline in about two hours. The road leads down from the main road, just north of Castel Gandolfo's old centre.

From Castel Gandolfo a panoramic road leads to **ALBANO LAZIALE**, one of the larger and in some ways more appealing of the towns along the ancient Via Appia. Its strategic position has left it with lots of Roman remnants: a crumbled old amphitheatre, once with room for 15,000 spectators, fragments of a gate right in the town centre and the foundations of the Roman garrison's baths behind the church of **San Pietro**, on the main street, Corso Matteotti. In one direction on Corso Matteotti, busy Piazza Mazzini looks south over Villa Comunale park, where there are sketchy remains of a villa that once belonged to Pompey, while in the other direction, off to the right down Via della Stella, the **Tomb of Horatii and the Curiatii**, whose strange "chimneys" – giant truncated cones resembling Etruscan funerary urns – date from the Republican era. You can get the lowdown on all this in the nearby **Museo Civico**, Viale Risorgimento 3 (Mon–Sun 9am–1pm, plus Wed & Thurs 4–7pm; €2.50), which has lots of information and a small but high-quality archeological collection.

There are much nicer places to stay than Albano, but if you're hungry, *Sesto*, a bar and *tavola calda* on the main street at no.40, is a good place for either a snack or full lunch, with outdoor seating out the back. Otherwise the Via Appia continues on to **ARICCIA**, across the nineteenth-century **Ponte di Ariccia** – whose Roman viaduct arches are visible below – into the town's central piazza, a well-proportioned square embellished with Bernini's round church of **Santa Maria dell'Assunzione**. Ariccia, incidentally, is famous for *porchetta* – roast pork, as well as being the site of the **Palazzo Chigi** at Piazza di Corte 14 (Tues–Fri guided tours at 11am, 4pm & 5.30pm, Sat & Sun hourly 10.30am–6pm; €7), also built by Bernini for Pope Alexander VII.

Beyond here, **GENZANO** was once the seat of the Sforzas and is still dominated by the **Castello Sforza-Cesarini** at the top of the town, a decrepit building whose grounds now form the pleasantly bucolic **Parco Sforza** (daily

10am–1pm & 3–8pm; free); its wooded paths and ponds give wonderful views over the Lago di Nemi. There's a great **restaurant** here, right opposite the castle, *La Scuderia*, Piazza Sforza Cesarini 1 (℡06.939.0521; closed Mon), whose impeccable service and superb, moderately priced local food is absolutely worth stopping for.

A detour east will take you to **NEMI**, built high above the tiny crater **lake** of the same name. The village itself isn't much to write home about, but a cobbled road leads down to fields of strawberries that lie between the steep walls of the crater and the shores of the lake and make a good place to picnic. The town is known for its year-round strawberry harvest, in fact, and celebrates this on the first Sunday in June in the *Sagra delle Fragole*. On the northern shore of the lake you'll notice a large hangar-like building, the local **museum** (daily 9am–6pm; €2), which contains the scanty remains of two Roman pleasure boats said to have been built by Caligula. In ancient times they caught fire and sank. They were raised in the 1930s by the Mussolini government and placed in the specially constructed hangars, prime examples of reinforced concrete engineering and fascist architecture. In the last days of the German occupation in 1944 they were set on fire again so what you see is the ruins of a ruin. Much of the bronze fittings of these boats have been transferred to Palazzo Massimo in Rome but there are always interesting exhibitions of recent local archeological finds on display.

Further southeast, **VELLETRI**, though larger, is scarcely more interesting, its largely modern centre rebuilt after extensive war damage and with a Baroque cathedral, the fourteenth-century Torre del Trivio and a small archeological museum among its scant sights.

Palestrina, Subiaco and the Ciociaria

Considering its proximity to the capital, it's a surprise that the **southeastern section of Lazio**, tucked in the foothills of the Abruzzo mountains, is so neglected and generally bypassed on the fast Autostrada del Sole heading south. For those who take the time, the area yields some real gems, from a masterpiece mosaic in **Palestrina** and Belle Époque beauty at **Fiuggi**, to the cave of St Benedict in **Subiaco** and the infamous World War II battleground at **Cassino**.

Palestrina

PALESTRINA was built on the site of the ancient Praeneste, originally an Etruscan settlement and later a favoured resort for patrician Romans. "Cool Praeneste", as Horace called it, was the site of an enormous Temple of Fortune, whose foundations more or less determine the modern centre, that steps up the hillside in a series of terraces, echoing the levels of the once vast edifice – its ruins appear at every turn.

The bus trip from Rome takes 45 minutes (and departs about as frequently), terminating at Via degli Arcioni from where the trudge up to the town is a steep one. The main square, **Piazza Regina Margherita**, gives a chance to catch your breath and is home to the town's **Duomo**, which has a copy of Michelangelo's chunky and rather modern-looking *Pietà di Palestrina* in the left aisle – the original is now in Florence. Take a look also at the **Area Sacra** (March–Oct daily 9am–5pm; Nov–Feb 9am–4pm; free), in the corner of the square, where there are a few fragments of ancient Roman floor mosaic showing sea creatures of various kinds.

The stepped streets around encourage casual strolling, but you need to save your energy for Palestrina's real attraction, right on top of the hill, the **Palazzo Colonna-Barberini**, which houses the **Museo Nazionale Archeologico Prenestino** (daily 9am–8pm; €3), originally built in the eleventh century and greatly modified in 1640. The palace and the terraces below were carved out of a Republican temple which previously stood on this site, and the views are magnificent from the top, surveying the countryside around as far as the eye can see. The palace, too, follows the shape and retaining walls of the temple inside. Among the collection's highlights are a number of ancient Roman pieces found locally: a torso of Fortune in slate-grey marble; the *Triade Capitolina*, showing Juno, Jupiter and Minerva, which was illegally excavated relatively recently and narrowly apprehended in the Stelvio Pass on its way out of the country; Etruscan funerary *cistae*; tiny clay votive offerings emulating faces and parts of the body (feet, finger, tongues, whatever was afflicted); and, the museum's prize possession, a marvellous late-second-century BC *Mosaic of the Nile* housed at the very top of the building, which traces the flooding river from source to delta, chronicling everyday Egyptian life en route. Look closely at the wealth of detail: a banquet under vines to the left, soldiers and priests outside a Serepaeum to the right, and a hunting scene at the top.

There's a **tourist office** on Piazza Santa Maria degli Angeli, and another next door to the Palazzo Barberini (both Mon–Fri 9am–12.30pm & 3–7pm, Sat 9am–1pm; ☎06.953.4019). If you decide to stay, the rather gloomy 1950s-style **hotel** *Stella*, just past the cathedral at Piazzale della Liberazione 3, is good enough (☎06.953.8172, ⓦwww.hotelstella.it; ❸), and has a decent restaurant. Or, for **food**, grab a pizza or local dish at *Antica Palestrina* (☎06.9531.0069) on Piazza Santa Maria degli Angeli.

Subiaco

Around 15km northeast of Palestrina, **SUBIACO** is beautifully set, pyramided around a hill topped by the Rocca Abbazia castle, and close to Monte Liviato – one of Lazio's premier ski resorts. Purpose-built for workmen on Nero's grand villa (very meagre traces of which survive), Subiaco became the contemplative base of St Benedict in the fifth century. The hermit dwelt in a mountain cave here for three years, before leaving to found the monastery at Montecassino, but his legacy continues today in the shape of two monastic complexes just outside town.

The **Abbazia di Santa Scolastica** (daily 9am–12.30pm & 3.30–7pm; free) is the closer (and larger) complex, where the first book to be printed in Italy came off the press in 1465. It's a pleasant four-kilometre walk along the Jenne road from the main bus stop – follow the signs left before the bridge. Dedicated to Benedict's sister, the complex has been heavily restored over the years: the facade, with the Benedictine motto *Ora et Labora* over the entrance, isn't original and the interior's only notable features are two *cipolino* marble pillars from Nero's villa. The three cloisters, though, are delightful. The first is from the Renaissance period; the second, one of the oldest Gothic works in Italy, lushly planted and fragrant; and the third a Cosmati work with lovely arcades of pillars.

Fifteen minutes up the same road, the landscape grows more dramatic as it approaches the craggy **Abbazia di San Benedetto**, nicknamed the "swallow's nest" (daily 9am–12.30pm & 3–6pm; free). This is much the more interesting monastery: the church's upper part has frescoes of the fourteenth-century Sienese school and fifteenth-century Perugian school and the lower levels incorporate Benedict's cave, all raw authentic rock except for a serene statue by Raggi, a disciple of Bernini. From here a spiral staircase leads up to the chapel of San Gregorio, containing a thirteenth-century picture of St Francis that's reckoned to be the first portrait of the saint painted from life. In the other direction, stairs descend to the chapel where Benedict preached to shepherds, and a terrace that overlooks the so-called "Holy Rose Tree" – in fact, a three-forked bush allegedly created by St Francis from a bramble.

Practicalities

Subiaco and its monasteries are a comfortable **day-trip** from Rome's Ponte Mammolo station (2hr 30min; last bus 8.30pm, Sun 7.30pm). Five daily buses also service Frosinone, a transport hub, if you're heading **south** to Campania.

The town's location may, however, make you want to linger and you can book a central **room** at the *Aniene*, at Via Cavour 21 (☎0774.85.565; ❷), which also has an adequate **restaurant**. The bargain *Villino Michela B&B* at Contrada Rapello 4, 1.5km outside town towards Fiuggi, offers a warm welcome, lush garden, and free pickup from Subiaco (☎0774.84.750, 📧villino.michela@virgilo.it; ❷). The *Maratta* bakery serves the local delicacy "chocolate salami" – a loaf of sugary bread, entirely vegetarian – and take-away pizza (Via V. Veneto 2). The **tourist office** at Via Cadorna 59 (Mon 8am–2pm, Tues–Sat 8am–2pm & 3.30–6.30pm; ☎0774.822.013) is eager to advise. Just downhill, towards the fourteenth-century humpbacked bridge of **San Francesco**, is a new booth promoting the **Monte Simbruini Park**, popular among climbers, kayakers, skiers and hikers.

The Ciociaria

From Subiaco the road heads south into **Ciociaria**, a relatively remote corner of Lazio that takes its name from the bark sandals (*ciocie*) worn here in antiquity. Italic tribes – the Hernici, Equii, Volscians and Sanniti – settled this hilly land and built inaccessible, heavily fortified towns several centuries before the Romans. The extraordinary cyclopean walls, unique in Italy, can still be seen, owing to their shrewd foreign policy of allying with Rome.

FIUGGI is a spa resort, which also pumps out a popular brand of bottled mineral water. Health-conscious Italians clog the lower **Fonte** quarter – a grim modern grid – in summer. The bright and breezy **historic centre**, however, has medieval alleys, genteel cafés, panoramic views of the chestnut-clad hills and a positively giddy Art Nouveau theatre. The **tourist office** is near the train station and spa below (Piazza Frascara 4; ☎0775.515.019; daily 8am–1pm & 3.30–5.30pm). **Dine** just off Piazza Trento e Trieste at *La Grotta*, an appealing pizzeria, decorated with old farm tools, that serves €5–9 mains like *scaloppa al vino* (Via Garibaldi 2; ☎0775.514.072; closed Thurs).

From Fiuggi, head west to Anagni or south to Alatri. **ANAGNI**, a former Hernici stronghold, is a well-preserved old place that produced a number of medieval popes from its powerful Segni family, including Boniface VIII. He tried to assert the papacy's absolute authority, provoking representatives of Philip IV of France to attack his **palace** (daily 9am–12.30pm & 3–6pm; €2) here in 1303. Visit the room where Colonna, one of Philip's henchmen, allegedly slapped Boniface – a statue of whom stands outside Anagni's **Duomo**, an imposing Romanesque basilica dating from the eleventh century. Inside there's a fine Cosmatesque pavement, a thirteenth-century baldachino, some important proto-Renaissance thirteenth-century frescoes in the crypt and a treasury containing some of Boniface's pontifical effects. Piazza Innocenzo III is home to the **tourist office** (summer 9am–1pm & 4–7pm; winter 9am–1pm & 3–6pm; ☎0775.727.852).

In the opposite direction, **ALATRI** – the Hernici Aletrium – preserves its cyclopean walls from the sixth-century BC acropolis. Built long before sophisticated Roman stone-cutting techniques, they are still very much intact – most impressively, perhaps, in the Porta di Falli, with its strident fertility symbols carved on the lintel. The town's streets wind around the citadel beneath the walls, cut by two square gateways (the arch hadn't yet been invented in Europe), inside of which the cathedral and Episcopal Palace stand on the site of the Hernici's ancient temples, since lost. The views, incidentally, are terrific.

FERENTINO, 10km west, also sports a good set of walls, though a hybrid one, modified by the Romans. You can get up to the old citadel here too, though it's 5km from the modern town's station (the Frosinone-Genazzano and Rocchi-Frosinone routes both stop here a dozen times a day). The cathedral is open regularly. **FROSINONE**, 10km or so further south, is the main town of the Ciociaria. This bland sprawling hub – with barely any remains of the Hernici settlement – is of little interest. Buses run west to Priverno and nearby lies the Fossanova abbey and train station (out of town, shuttle connection) with services to Naples, Cassino, Caserta and points north.

Further south: Cassino and the Abbey of Montecassino

The town of **CASSINO**, fifty minutes down the railway line from Frosinone, is the site of another important monastery, the **Abbey of Montecassino** (daily 8.30am–noon & 3–6pm; free; ⓦ www.osb.org). Three ravens guided St Benedict to this spot, after he left Subiaco in 529. He founded one of the most important and influential Christian complexes in the world. Its monks spread the word as far away as Britain and Scandinavia, while developing the tradition

△ Abbey of Montecassino

of culture and learning that was at the core of the Benedictine order. Ironically, its strategically vital position, perched high on a mountaintop between Rome and Naples, was the abbey's downfall. A succession of invaders coveted and fought over this vantage point, and the buildings were repeatedly destroyed.

During World War II, the abbey came to be the lynchpin of the German presence in this part of Italy. After a battle that lasted almost six months, the Allies – a mixture of Poles, New Zealanders and Indian troops – eventually bombed it to ruins in May 1944, sacrificing several thousand lives in the process. The austere medieval architecture has been faithfully recreated, but it's really more impressive for its position. Much is not open to the public, and its sterile white central courtyard is engaging only for the views of the surrounding hills and the Polish war cemetery below. The hideously ornate Baroque church has a small **museum** (same hours as abbey; €1.50) containing incunabula, old manuscripts and suchlike. Yet you can't help but feel that Montecassino's glory days ended firmly with the war.

The **town** below was fairly comprehensively destroyed, too, and has very little appeal (except for Fiat enthusiasts, who coo over the factory). There's a **tourist office** at Piazza de Gasperi 10 (Mon–Sat 8.30am–1pm & 3.30–6.30pm, Sun 9am–noon; ☏0776.21.292, ⓦwww.apt.frosinone.it), on the opposite side of the centre to the train and bus station, and another at Corso della Repubblica 23 (Mon–Sat 9am–noon & 4–7pm; ☏0776.26.842). Buses scale the mountain to the abbey from Piazza San Benedetto twice daily. If you need to stay, you'll find that **hotels** are at least inexpensive: the central *La Pace* delivers Neapolitan-style pizza right to the faded but spacious rooms and has Internet access (Via Abruzzi 16; special deals on ⓦwww.cassinohotel.it; ☏0776.313.630; ❸).

The southern Lazio coast

The **Lazio coast to the south** of Rome is a more attractive proposition than the northern stretches. Its towns have a bit more charm, the water is cleaner, and in the further reaches, beyond the flats of the Pontine Marshes and Monte Circeo, the shoreline begins to pucker into cliffs and coves that hint gently at the glories of Campania – all good either for day-trips and overnight outings from the city, or for a pleasingly wayward route to Naples.

Anzio and Nettuno

About 40km south of Rome, and easily seen on a day-trip, **ANZIO** is the first town of any note, centre of a lengthy spread of settlement that focuses on a lively central square and a busy fishing industry. Much of the town was damaged during a difficult Allied landing here on January 22, 1944, to which two military cemeteries (one British, on the road to Aprilia, and another, American, just outside nearby Nettuno) bear testimony, as does a small museum. Despite thorough rebuilding, it's a likeable resort, still depending as much on fish as tourists for its livelihood.

In town, the seafood **restaurants** that crowd together along the harbour are not unreasonably priced: *La Cicala*, right by the water at Riviera Zanardelli 11 (☏06.984.6747; closed Wed), is as good as any; *Pierino*, a couple of blocks inland at Piazza C. Battisti 3 (☏06.984.5683; closed Mon), is a cut above the rest. The **beaches**, which edge the coast on either side, are sandy and not unbearably thronged outside August, and stretch right up to the ruins of the **Villa di Nerone** to the north. Anzio is also a possible route to Ponza; **hydrofoils** leave

daily April–August from Via Porto Innocenziano (℡06.984.5083; ⓦwww.vetor
.it). For timings and other information, ask at the **tourist office** at Piazza Pia
19 (Tues–Sat 9am–1pm, Wed & Thurs also 3–6pm; ℡06.984.5147).

NETTUNO, a couple of kilometres down the coast (walkable by the
shoreline road), is more of the same, but with slightly smaller beaches, and water
less clear and calm. Again, it's a mostly modern town, but there's a well-preserved
old quarter, still walled, with a couple of decent **trattorias** on the main square –
information from the **tourist office** at the port (Mon–Fri 10am–12.30pm &
5–7.30pm, Sat 10am–12.30pm & 5.30–7pm; ℡06.980.3335).

The Pontine Marshes: Latina, Sermoneta, Priverno

Beyond Anzio and Nettuno lie the **Pontine Marshes**, until seventy-odd years
ago a boggy plain prone to malaria and populated by only a few inhabitants and
water buffalo. Julius Caesar hoped to drain the area, but was assassinated before
he could carry out the plan. Instead Mussolini reclaimed the region in 1928 –
building a series of spanking new towns and exposing fertile, fresh farmland.

At the centre of the development lies **LATINA**, the provincial capital, founded
in 1932, and heart of the lively, local agricultural economy, though of little interest
save for its transport connections. Buses zigzag up to the medieval town of
SERMONETA, remarkable for its walls erected to safeguard against the Saracens
and later struggles between the papacy and Naples, which raged throughout the
Middle Ages. The outer ramparts have a massive gleaming white aspect that's
reminiscent of Fascist architecture, but Cesare Borgia built them in the late 1400s,
when his father Alexander VI awarded this town to him. The earlier defences
surround the historical centre and the well-preserved **castle** (April–Oct daily
except Thurs 10am–noon & 3–6pm; Nov–March daily 10am–noon & 2–4pm;
€4). Erected in the 1200s by the feudal Caetani family, it's a near-perfect example
of the medieval system of moats, portcullises, drawbridges and tunnels designed
to render the place practically impregnable. As well as all the martial architecture,
there is a huge display of arms, armour, catapults and ancient cannons, plus the
vast siege cisterns and silos. To get a feel for Sermoneta, it's worth staying over, and
the *Ostello San Nicola* is the place, at Via G. Matteotti 1 (℡0773.30.381, ⓦwww
.sannicola-hostel.com; ❶), a thirteenth-century convent with Gothic church and
fading frescoes, plus a mixture of dorm beds and private rooms, and communal
kitchen. To **eat**, the family-run *Birreria Ghost* serves standard, tasty fare under the
imposing castle walls, (Via Sotto il Forte 2; ℡0773.303.38). The chic *Enoteca
Simposio*, Via della Condutture 2 (℡0773.623.896), brings gastronomy to the
masses, offering a pasta and glass of wine for just €6. Weather permitting, sit in
the walled garden.

Several **buses** a day run from Rome's EUR Fermi (Metro line B) with a stop
at **NINFA**. This other Caetani stronghold and its enchanting gardens huddle at
the base of the cliff. The tranquil nook inspired the poetry of Pliny the Elder:
the oasis – surrounding a temple to the nymphs – later grew into a thriving
fortified village in the twelfth century. Bandits, mercenaries and malaria
destroyed Ninfa, dubbed the "Pompeii of the Middle Ages" by the nineteenth-
century historian Gregorovius. The citizens fled to Sermoneta: their ruins
became the backdrop of spectacular landscaping in the early twentieth century.
Wild and domestic flowers, shrubs and trees flourish among charming rivulets,
waterfalls and ponds: the design is spontaneous, whimsical and entirely
enchanting (April–Oct; open first weekend of each month; guided tours only,
last admission at 6pm; €8; ℡0773.633.935).

Buses from Latina take about fifty minutes to reach **PRIVERNO**, another hilltop town. Mythology claims the virgin warrior Camilla, celebrated in Virgil's *Aeneid*, was queen of the Volsci tribe here. The pretty main square is flanked by a Gothic town hall and a 1283 cathedral, which apparently holds the relics of St Thomas Aquinas. About 5km south – an hour or so walk or short bus ride from Piazza XX Settembre – the **Abbey of Fossanova** (daily: summer 7am–noon & 4–7.30pm; winter 7am–noon & 3–5.30pm; free) was where Aquinas died in 1274, travelling between Naples and Lyon. This Cistercian monastery is a good diversion for travellers waiting at Priverno-Fossanova train station, 2km beyond. Although it has been rather heavily restored, the simplicity of its thirteenth-century Burgundian Gothic church is refreshing after the gaudiness of its Baroque counterparts. A door opens onto a plain Romanesque cloister, garden and chapter house. Lay brothers once watched the services through these wide windows (the corridor on the far side was for their use). The left-hand door leads through another courtyard to the guest wing, where, at the northern end, St Thomas supposedly breathed his last.

Sabaudia, Monte Circeo and San Felice Circeo

The area around **SABAUDIA**, 20km from Latina, gives some impression of the terrain's native sogginess, poised between two lagoons. Fascist propaganda claims the town was built in just 253 days. Architectural highlights include the austere rationalist-style town hall **tower**, the mosaiced exterior of **SS Annunziata church** and the quirky, asymmetrical **post office**. The **tourist office** is at Piazza del Commune 18 (open Mon–Sat 9.15am–12.45pm & 4–8pm, Sun 9am–10m; ☎0773.515.046).

A bridge leads from Sabaudia across the lagoon to the coast, where the beaches are unspoilt and empty most of the time except during high season. Although there are plenty of beachfront properties, there are lots of places to access the sand, and parking spaces alongside. The road cuts through the dunes between the sea and the coastals lakes, leading towards the huge bulk of **Monte Circeo** to the south, which together with offshore Zannone island forms the **Parco Nazionale del Circeo**. Created in 1934, this preserves something of the marshes' wildlife and almost sinister natural beauty (the information office is in San Felice Circeo, see below). It's a fine spot for birds: all kinds of aquatic species can be seen here – herons, buzzards, storks, fish hawks, and rare breeds like the peregrine falcon and Cavaliere d'Italia. Flora includes eucalyptus groves, oaks, elms, ash and wild flowers in spring. The beaches are fine all the way along, until you reach the crumbling, sixteenth-century **Torre Paola**, perched at the entrance of a canal that links the lake and sea: a group of fishermen usually occupy the little pier. Here the road turns inland and skirts the mountain's slopes, passing through splendid woods. Sabaudia is well supplied with campsites and inexpensive **hotels**: an atmospheric B&B stands 1.5km from the tower. *Bahia di Buzios* is in a verdant glade, two minutes from the sea (Via delle Querce 18; ☎0773.596.815, ⓦwww.bahiadibuzios.it; ➋)

About 4km from the tower, a road branches right and rounds the mountain to emerge at **SAN FELICE CIRCEO**, a picturesque village of pretty stone houses bleached yellow by the sun and clinging to the side of the mountain. In summer, the spot's fairly trendy: the lower town's marina chock-a-block with fancy motor launches and yachts, its sandy beaches crowded with oiled bodies and roads clogged with flashy cars. In season you can rent a boat (☎0773.543.263) to the famous **Grotta della Maga Circe**. Or explore on foot: take a left at the lighthouse (*Faro di Torre Cervia*) for the **Grotto delle Capre** or continue straight a few kilometres to a secluded and rocky swimming spot, also great for snorkelling.

Most of San Felice's accommodation is in the lower town, but you can nab a half-board **room** with sea views in the upper town at Albergo *Giardino degli Ulivi* (Via XXIV Maggio 13; ☎0773.548.034; ❷). Families, widows and motor-cyclists crowd together for ample dinners, then linger chatting under the vine canopy in the courtyard. A few yards from here along the main road, *Trattoria Il Grottino* backs on to the upper town's main Piazza Vittorio Veneto (☎0773.548.446), and has good views along the coast back Terracina, as well as serving decently priced seafood. Its bustling atmosphere is infectious, as it is the terrace of *Il Principe*, across the other side of the square, which also does good seafood pasta dishes and fish main courses. Just off Piazza V. Veneto, Piazza Lanzuisi is home to the Municipio, and a **tourist office** that also serves as an office for the **Monte Circeo park** (Mon–Sat 8am–2.30pm; ☎0773.549.038, ☯www.parcocirceo.it). Walk through the arch to the main road, which winds up to the summit of Monte Circeo to an ancient **temple**. The views from here are marvellous: there's a large car park at the top, with a summer bar; nearby, there are sparse relics of a Roman town – *Circeii* – and its rather better preserved cyclopean walls, not unlike the constructions in the Ciociaria.

Terracina

A further 15km down the coast from San Felice (hourly buses from Rome Laurentina; also on the coastal train route from Rome's EUR Fermi), **TERRACINA** is an immediately likeable little town, divided between a tumble-down old quarter high on the hill and a lively newer area by the sea. During classical times, it was an important staging-post on the Appian Way, which meets the ocean here; nowadays it's primarily a seaside resort and one of the nicest along this stretch of coast, with good, ample beaches and frequent connections with the other points of interest, including twice-daily ferries to Ponza (one on Sunday), run by Snap (☎0773.790.055, ☯www.snapnavigazione.it).

The centre of the old quarter is **Piazza Municipio**, which occupies the site of the Roman forum – complete with the original steps and slabs – and now focuses on the colonnade of the town's **Duomo**, with its elegant mossy campanile. An endearing church with a fine mosaic floor and a beautiful tile-studded pulpit and twisted mosaic candlestick, it was built within the shell of a Roman temple dedicated to Augustus. Also on the square, the three rooms of the **Museo Civico Pio Capponi** (Tues–Sat 9.30am–1.30pm & 3–8pm, Sun 10am–1pm & 5–9pm; €1.55) has finds from the Roman town.

Terracina's main attraction, and rightly so, is the **Temple of Jupiter Anxurus**, which crowns the hill. Take the steps up from Piazza Municipio onto Via Anxur and follow this for 200m, from where a road winds to the top (40min). You can also take bus line #L from Via Roma or Piazzale Marconi; it runs every hour. The temple may date back to the first century BC and was connected to Terracina by some lengthy walls, and it's these days an impressive if rather ruinous complex, with tremendous views both ways up the coast. You can walk right through the vaulted arches of the temple and scramble around among the remains of the acropolis, and finishing off with a coffee in the temple's café.

Practicalities

Apart from the scrubby oval of sand fringing the centre, Terracina's **beaches** stretch west pretty much indefinitely from the main harbour and are large enough to be uncrowded. The town's **tourist office** is five minutes' walk from the sea in the new part of town, just off Via G. Leopardi, in the park behind Piazza Mazzini (summer Mon–Sat 9am–1pm & 5–8pm, Sun 9am–1pm; winter Mon–Sat 9am–1pm, Tues & Thurs also 3–6pm; ⓣ0773.727.759), has information, hotel lists and maps. One of the best places to **stay** is the *Hegelberger*, up in the old town at Via San Domenico 2 (ⓣ0773.701.697; ❷), a very informal *pensione* with guest rooms off the owner's lounge; though basic, there's a self-catering kitchen and a spacious balcony with a spectacular view. The nearest **campsite** is the *Costazzurra* (ⓣ0773.702.589), a fifteen-minute walk south along the coast road, and there are numerous others outside town, especially on the stretch called Salito di Fondi. As for **eating**, in the lower town, *Il Tempio*, on Piazza della Repubblica, at the end of the main Via Roma (ⓣ0773.702.424), does great seafood pasta dishes and pizzas too, with *secondi* for around €9. Across the other side of the square, at Piazza dell Repubblica 41 (ⓣ0773.702.352), *Da Pino* serves up superb Neapolitan-style pizzas. Up in the old town, ⚐ *St Patrick's*, Corso Garibaldi 56 (ⓣ0773.703.170), is a wine bar and restaurant that offers excellent food – try the lasagne – while a few doors along *Ai Trioni* (ⓣ0773.702.613) has local specialities – lots of porcini mushroom dishes and game – and styles itself as the town's top restaurant, despite its moderate prices.

Sperlonga

The coast south of Terracina is probably Lazio's prettiest stretch, the cliff punctured by tiny beaches signposted enticingly from the road. **SPERLONGA**, built high on a rocky promontory, is a fashionable spot for Roman and Neapolitan families, its whitewashed houses, arched alleys and stepped narrow streets almost Moorish in feel. Both the old upper town and modern lower district are almost given over entirely to tourists during summer, but it's still a pleasant place, and cars are not allowed into the old centre. A couple of kilometres south, the remains of the **Villa of Tiberius** (daily 8.30am–7.30pm; €2) are the only real sight of note and well worth the walk along the beach. There's a small and extremely engaging museum with finds from the villa and its attached fish farm – basically a cave fronting on to the sea and filled with monumental sculptural objects depicting scenes from Homer's *Odyssey*, the remains of which have been partially reconstructed. The villa is right by the beach, and you can stroll around the excavations, as well as walking into the cave to see the plinths on which the statues stood – one of which is submerged – and watch the fish darting about in the water beneath. Beyond Sperlonga the coast steepens markedly, with yet more appealing beaches and any number of handy campsites.

The **beaches** run either side of Sperlonga's headland, but a lot of space is taken up by pre-sited umbrellas. The modern *Grazie* **hotel** at Via M. A. Colonna 10 (ⓣ0771.548.223; ❸), a block from the beach at the northern end of the beachfront strip, is a good choice with nice modern rooms. The *Corallo*, just off Piazza della Repubblica at Corso Leone 3 (ⓣ0771.548.060; ❺), is a nice option if you want to be up in the old town. Another possibility are the many **rooms and apartments** rented during peak season; ask at the **tourist office** on the road that winds round the headland to the left of the main beach (Mon–Sat 9am–noon & 3–6pm; ⓣ0771.557.341). There's also a **youth hostel**, on the Terracina road out of town, Via Fiorelle (ⓣ0771.557.031). As for **food**, the *Torre Truglia* restaurant enjoys the most handsome location (Via Torre Truglia; ⓣ0771.549.474), overlooking the sea from the prow of the promontory, but it's considered locally to be more show than substance and it's shunned in favour of humble *L'Angolo* (ⓣ0771.548.808) on the sandy southern **beach**. Try the €10 maritime *scoglieri bruschette*, toast topped with clams, squid, mussels and octopus. In the modern centre, *Tropical*, Via C. Colombo 27 (℡0771.549.621), does pizzas and other food and has a bar.

Formia, Gaeta and Minturno

Some 20km around the bay, hard under the glowering backdrop of the Monti Aurunci, lies **FORMIA**. This largely modern town, which proudly touts its 1500 parking spaces, was an important resort during Roman times. In 44 AD, Mark Antony's soldiers murdered Cicero here for his opposition to the triumvirate that succeeded Caesar. There are good **beaches** to the north and a **tourist office** at Viale Unita d'Italia 30–40 (summer Mon–Sat 8.30am–2pm & 5–8pm, Sun 9am–1pm; winter Mon, Wed & Fri–Sun 8.30am–2pm, Tues & Thurs 8.30am–2pm & 5–8pm; ℡0771.771.490). Otherwise Formia is a place to stopover rather than a stay, with plentiful connections to Naples, Rome and Cassino, and regular ferries and hydrofoils to Ponza (see p.842). The *Del Golfo*, Piazzale Stazione Ferroviaria 1 (℡0771.790.037; ❷), is the town's most central and cheapest **hotel**, and convenient if you're taking an early ferry to Ponza; or there's the *Miramare*, on the southern edge of the centre at Via Appia 44 (℡0771.320047; ❹), which is good value and has a decent restaurant and a swimming pool. The nearby restaurant, *Zi Anna Mare* on Largo Paone (closed Tues), is also a great choice for **food**, with fresh fish and pizzas served on a terrace.

The towers, cliffs and fortifications of **GAETA**, 5km southwest, glow golden at sunset – a fine sight for motorists stuck in the inevitable A-1 traffic jam here. Once a marine republic and last bastion of the Bourbons, the city now teems with American servicemen from a base here. Burgers and beer dominate the lively port, but Gaeta has an atmospheric medieval quarter too, dominated by a stocky cliff-side **castle**. Behind the gothic church, SS Annuziata, lies the chapel of the **Golden Grotto** with its shimmering gilded barrel vault and alleged handprint of the Minotaur. Another myth claims Mount Orlando trembled and split in half when Jesus died.

MINTURNO is the last town before the Campania border, 15km east of Formia, a maze of tiny lanes and vaulted streets oddly reminiscent of an Arab *medina*. A massive crumbling **castle**, formerly owned by the Carraciolo-Carafa dynasty, dominates the main square. Behind, the town's **Duomo** is a Norman structure not unlike those of nearby Sessa Arunca or Ravello, with a similar colourful mosaic pulpit. About 4km south of town are the ruins of the ancient Roman port of **Minturnae** (daily 9am–7pm; €3), a once flourishing town decimated as this low-lying area became malarial. Most striking are the remains of a restored amphitheatre (still used for concerts in summer), below which there's a small antiquarium and a broken-down aqueduct that runs for 2km southwest. Though the views are striking, Minturno doesn't merit the slog on public transport (the **train** station is below the hill-town proper).

The Pontine Islands

Scattered across the sea between Rome and Naples, these islands are some of Italy's least known. Volcanic in origin, only two are inhabited: **Ventotene** and **Ponza**. The latter bustles with tourists between mid-June and the end of August, as people seek an alternative to crowded Cápri; at any other time, the island is yours for the asking.

As for **transport**, Formia has year-round service to Ponza (twice-daily ferry & hydrofoil, except Wed; ⓦwww.caremar.it), as does **Terracina** (once daily;

more in summer) and **Anzio** between June and September (at least twice daily; Ⓦ www.vetor.it). Fares are similar from all ports, with ferries around €15 one-way and hydrofoils about €25 per person one way – although the journey time is easily halved. Departures from **Naples** are more expensive (Ⓦ www.snav.it) €40–50 per person. You can reach **Ventotene** from **Formia** or **Anzio**: ferries run once daily; hydrofoils run twice daily except Tuesday. You can also travel **between the islands** of Ponza and Ventotene using the services of Cooperativa Barcaioli Ponzesi (Ⓣ 0771.809.929, Ⓦ www.ponza.com/barcaioli).

Ponza

Even **PONZA**, the group's main island, is manageably small: the sharp, rocky hunk of land is only 8km long and 2km across, at its widest point. Beautiful **PONZA TOWN** is heaped around the bay in a series of neat pastel-coloured pyramids, its flat-roofed houses radiate out from the pink semicircle that curls around the fishing harbour. This town makes a marvellous place to rest, having so far escaped the clutches of designer boutiques and souvenir shops. Although the island lacks specific sights, Ponza is great for aimless wanderings; locals indulge too in the early evening, as crowds parade along the yellow-painted **Municipio** arcade of shops and cafés. For lazing and swimming, there's a small, clean **cove** in the town and the **Chiaia di Luna** beach, a ten-minute walk away, across the island. A slender rim of sand edges the sheer sickle cliff – though be warned that the waves here are much choppier than on the sheltered side facing the mainland, and the beach is intermittently closed for safety reasons.

The only other real settlement on the island is **LA FORNA**, a wide green bay dotted with huddles of homes. The beach here is small and grubby, so instead, follow the path down from the road, around the bay to the rocks: the water of the so-called **Piscina Naturale** is lovely and clear, perfect for sheltered swimming when the fishing boats have finished for the day. For really secluded sea frolicking, take a boat from here (€5 per person return) around the headland to **Spiaggia Santa Lucia**. The settlement straggles on from La Forna towards the sharp northern end of the island, where the road ends abruptly and a steep stony path (to the right) leads down to more rocks where you can swim.

Practicalities

The **tourist office** on Via Molo Musco in Ponza Town (Mon–Sat 9am–1pm & 4.30–7.30pm, Sun 9am–1pm; Ⓣ 0771.80.031) has maps and accommodation lists. You may well be accosted with offers of **rooms** as you get off the ferry: if so, a fair price is around the €30–50 mark; otherwise, the woman at Via Chiaia di Luna 8 (Ⓣ 0771.80.043) takes in visitors for a negotiable fee. **Hotels** are pricier; the cheapest is *Pensione Silvia*, a cheerful golden structure presiding over row-boat-strewn sands (200m through the spooky Roman tunnel on the Santa Maria waterfront; Via Marina; closed Oct–April; Ⓣ 0771.80.075; ❸). *Gennarino al Mare* at Via Dante 64 (Ⓣ 0771.80.071, Ⓦ www.emmeti.it /Gennarino; ❼) is next to the town beach. The sky-blue hotel – great for a splurge – nestles on a dock: all the rooms have elegant decor, private wrought-iron balconies and great seascape views. You might also try the helpful people at *TouristCasa*, Via Roma 2 (Ⓣ 0771.809.886), who rent out rooms and apartments year-round.

A **bus service** connects the port with other points on the island, roughly hourly. In La Forna, the serene and chic *Ortensia* (Ⓣ 0771.808.922, Ⓦ www .ponzahotel.it; ❹) is the best and most convenient option location-wise. **Rent scooters** along Ponza Town's harbour. **Boats**, too, are a good (sometimes the

⑪

only) way of seeing the most dramatic parts of the island. Barcaioli (see opposite) charges about €5 per person for water-taxi service. Motorboat hire costs around €45 a day (any number of harbour outlets), or there's always room for negotiation with Signora Lucia (☎0771.80.516). For **food**, you're spoilt for choice: Ponza Town has plenty of restaurants and most are good, albeit expensive. Try *Al Aragosta* in the harbour, which serves the local speciality of *zuppa di lenticchie* (lentil soup); the *Ippocampo*, in the Municipio above, does good pasta and fish; or check out the restaurant attached to the *Gennarino al Mare* hotel (see opposite).

Ventotene

The only other inhabited Pontine island, **VENTOTENE** is situated a fair way south: flatter, smaller and drabber than Ponza, it has reddish-brown soil dotted with cacti and shrubs. Roman politicians exiled embarrassing wives and daughters here. Later San Stefano, a half-mile offshore, housed a dramatic horseshoe-shaped prison, designed by Carpi in the eighteenth century.

Although it makes a nice stop on a leisurely route to Naples, Ventotene is unlikely to detain anyone long. However, if you decide to linger, there are a couple of places renting out rooms. The single town – village really – has a population of around 500, and its dusty piazza is home to a **museum** displaying finds from an imperial-era villa, remains of which blanket the headland to the left of the village. On the other side, there's a small **beach** of grey volcanic sand.

Travel details

Trains

Frosinone to: Caserta (8 daily; 1hr 10min); Cassino (12 daily; 50min).
Priverno-Fossanova to: Terracina (6 daily; 30min).
Rome (Termini) to: Ancona (8 daily; 4hr); Anzio/Nettuno (hourly; 1hr); Bologna (12 daily; 3hr 30min); Cerveteri* (hourly; 45min); Civitavecchia* (hourly; 1hr); Florence (hourly; 1hr 30min–2hr 30min); Formia (hourly; 1hr 25min); Latina (hourly; 35min); Milan (12 daily; 3hr–5hr 40min); Naples (hourly; 2hr 30min); Pescara (4 daily; 3hr 40min); Priverno-Fossanova (hourly; 1hr); Tarquinia* (6 daily; 1hr 20min).
Rome (Roma-Nord line) to: Viterbo (5 daily; 2hr 45min).
Rome (San Pietro) to: Bracciano* (12 daily; 1hr); Viterbo* (12 daily; 1hr 30min).
* Trains also run from Rome Trastevere.

Buses

Frosinone to: Priverno (hourly; 50min).
Latina to: Sermoneta (Mon–Sat 12 daily, Sun 6 daily; 1hr).

Rome (Anagnina) to: Palestrina (16 daily; 45min).
Rome (EUR Fermi) to: Sabaudia (12 daily; 2hr 15min); San Felice (12 daily; 2hr 15min); Terracina (12 daily; 2hr 30min).
Rome (Ponte Mammolo) to: Subiaco (18 daily; 1hr 15min); Tivoli (every 20min; 1hr).
Rome (Saxa Rubra) to: Viterbo, via Sutri and Vetralla (every 30min; 1hr 30min).
Rome (Via Lepanto) to: Blera, via Barbarano Romano (Mon–Sat 6 daily, Sun 2 daily; 2hr); Cerveteri (every 30min; 1hr 20min); Civita Castellana (via Nepi and Castel S. Elia) (12 daily; 1hr 30min); Civitavecchia (20 daily; 1hr 50min); Tarquinia (10 daily; 2hr 15min).
Rome (Tiburtina) to: Rieti (every 20min; 1hr 50min).
Subiaco to: Frosinone (3 daily; 2hr).
Terracina to: Cassino (3 daily; 2hr 30min); Formia (every 30min; 1hr 10min); Sabaudia (8 daily; 1hr 20min); San Felice Circeo (17 daily; 30min); Sperlonga (every 30min; 1hr).
Viterbo to: Bagnaia (11 daily; 20min); Bomarzo (6 daily; 30min); Caprarola (7 daily; 45min); Civitavecchia (8 daily; 1hr 30min); Tarquinia (11 daily; 1hr); Tuscania (14 daily; 30min).

Ferries

Anzio to: Ponza (1 daily; 1hr 45min).
Civitavecchia to: Cágliari (1 daily; 13hr); Golfo
Aranci (2 daily; 9hr); Olbia (1 daily; 7hr).
Formia to: Ponza (2 daily; 2hr 30min); Ventotene
(2 daily; 2hr 10min).
Terracina to: Ponza (2 daily; 1hr).

Hydrofoils (aliscafi)

Anzio to: Ponza (2 daily; 1hr 10min); Ventotene
(1 daily; 1hr 10min).
Formia to: Ponza (2 daily; 1hr 15min); Ventotene
(2 daily; 1hr 15min).
Ponza to: Ventotene (2 daily; 40min).

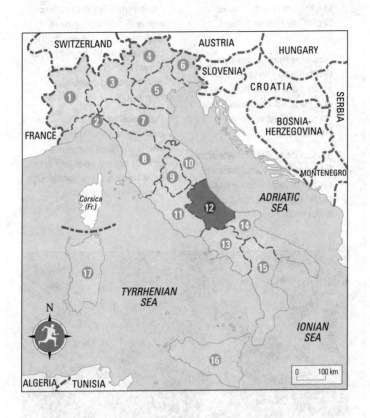

12

Abruzzo and Molise

CHAPTER 12

Highlights

* **Corno Grande** Hike in the wild and craggy Gran Sasso massif, out of which rises Italy's highest peak, the Corno Grande. See p.853

* **Monte Majella** Seek out the rocky hermitages that earned Majella the name "Domus Christi" or House of God. See p.857

* **National Park of Abruzzo** Get back to nature in this lovely park which has around one hundred indigenous species of fauna and flora. See p.862

* **Museo delle Genti d'Abruzzo, Pescara** Poetry and intricately carved objects bear witness to the industry of Abruzzo's shepherds. See p.866

* **Archeological Museum at Chieti** Head here for the best and most comprehensive display of Abruzzese antiquities, including the unique Capestrano warrior. See p.869

* **Saepinum** This enchanting archeological site in rural Sepino is a throwback to the original Grand Tour, with over-grown Roman ruins dotted with inhabited dwellings. See p.874

* **Bull race at Ururi** The ordinary town of Ururi turns into a scene of frenetic activity once a year as horses, bulls and carts career through the streets. See p.876

△ Rocca di Calascio in the Gran Sasso National Park

Abruzzo and Molise

A bruzzo and Molise, one region until 1963 known simply as the Abruzzi, together make Italy's transition from north to south. Both are sparsely populated mountainous regions prone to earthquakes, and both have always been outside the mainstream of Italian affairs. You could spend a whole holiday exploring the **Abruzzo**. Bordered by the Apennines, it holds some of Italy's wildest terrain: silent valleys, abandoned hill-villages and vast untamed mountain plains, once roamed by wolves, bears and chamois. Legends of werewolves and witches abound and there's a strong sense of the provincial. There are villages where life is hard and strangers something of a novelty and, although the region's costumes, crafts and festivals naturally appeal to visitors, there is little hype or sham. The Abruzzesi have done much to pull their region out of the poverty trap, developing resorts on the long, sandy Adriatic coastline and exploiting the tourist potential of a large, mountainous national park and some great historic towns. Most visited are **L'Aquila**, at the foot of **Gran Sasso** – the Apennines' highest peak – and Sulmona to the southeast. Both are good bases: Sulmona is more convenient if you're coming by train from Rome, L'Aquila if you're approaching from Umbria. The hill-villages around L'Aquila are worth visiting too if you're based here for any length of time. Those below the Gran Sasso are deeply rural places, where time seems to have stopped somewhere in the fifteenth century; **Bominaco**, to the east, has two impressive churches, one a perfect and pristine example of the Romanesque, the other covered with Byzantine-style frescoes. The rail route from the Marche runs down the coast through Abruzzo's numerous grid-plan **resorts** – few of them anything special, but adequate sun-and-sand stopovers. The best of them is **Vasto**, with a gently shelving sandy beach and bus connections inland to the lively old centre. Among other hill-towns worth visiting is **Atri**, whose cathedral contains a stunning cycle of frescoes.

South of Sulmona, Abruzzo feels more traditional. In **Scanno** elderly women wear costumes that originated in Asia Minor, and make intricate lace on cylindrical cushions known as *tomboli*. Just down the road, the scruffy hill-village of **Cocullo** hosts one of Europe's most bizarre religious festivals, in which a statue of the local saint is draped with live snakes before being paraded through the streets.

Gentler, less rugged and somewhat poorer than Abruzzo, **Molise** has more in common with southern than central Italy. Much of the region still seems to be struggling out of its past, its towns and villages victims of either economic neglect or hurried modern development. The cities, **Isernia** and **Campobasso**, are large and bland, rebuilt after earthquakes and fringed with factories erected by northern money that has been lured here by the low price of land and labour.

But Molise has its compensations. Just as the modern-day industrial tycoons have invaded the area, so, over two thousand years ago, the Romans charged into the region, forcing the native Italic Samnite tribes to leave their small villages and live in formula-built settlements. Molise still has a scattering of low-key Roman ruins – most interestingly at **Saepinum**, Italy's most complete example of a Roman provincial town and a site that's still well off the tourist track. Wandering among the ruins, and looking out over the green fields to the mountains beyond, you get some inkling of what it must have been like to be Italy's first Grand Tourists. A less-refined but equally interesting attraction takes place in the village of **Ururi**, settled by Albanian refugees in the fourteenth century, where the annual chariot race is as barbaric as anything the Romans dreamed up.

Finally there's the sheer physical aspect of the place. Forty percent of Molise is covered by **mountains**, and although they are less dramatic than Abruzzo's, there are masses of possibilities for hiking. A must is the trail up **Monte La Gallinola** in the **Matese mountains**, from where on a clear day the whole of the peninsula, from the Bay of Naples to the Adriatic, stretches out before you. Visitors are also starting to explore the area's ancient sheep-droving routes, known as *tratturi*, which are gaining new life as mountain-bike or horseback-riding trails, served by occasional farmhouse guesthouses and riding stables along the way.

Don't expect to rush through Abruzzo and Molise if you're relying on public transport; in both regions, **getting around** on bus and train demands patience and the careful studying of timetables.

Abruzzo is a mountainous region where agriculture is difficult and sheep-farming dominates. Consequently, **lamb** tends to feature strongly in the local cuisine. You'll come across *abbacchio*, unweaned baby lamb that is usually cut into chunks and roasted; and *castrato*, castrated lamb, when the meat is often cooked as a casserole with tomatoes, wine, herbs, onion and celery (*intingolo di castrato*), while the innards are typically roasted in the oven (*alenoto di castrato*). Look out as well for *agnello a cutturo*, an aromatic herby casserole served with bread. The region has a good variety of sausages and salamis such as the *aquilano*, usually with a strip of lard down the centre to keep the salami moist, and the *fegato*.

The other crucial ingredient in the region's cuisine is **chilli** (*peperoncino* in the rest of Italy, but known locally as *pepedinie* or *diavolini*), used liberally in all kinds of dishes and believed by many locals to be a cure for ailments ranging from neuralgia to arthritis; around L'Aquila in particular saffron (*zafferano*) is also found widely in sweet and savoury dishes.

Probably Abruzzo's most famous dish is *maccheroni alla chitarra*, made by pressing a sheet of **pasta** over a wooden frame wired like a guitar, and usually served with a tomato or lamb sauce. Other local pastas include the roughly cut *strangozze* and *maltagliati*, both inevitably served with a lamb sauce. Cheese tends to be *pecorino* – most often mature and grainy like parmesan, but you may come across young cheeses that are still mild, soft and milky. Also worth seeking out is *ricotta al fumo di ginepro*, an aromatic smoked version of the soft cheese.

The **wines** of Molise are rarely found outside the region. The most interesting vintages come from the Biferno Valley between Larino and Guglionesi, where a hearty Biferno red is made from a combination of the Montepulciano, Trebbiano Toscano and Aglianico grapes. The best-known wine of Abruzzo is Montepulciano d'Abruzzo, a heavy **red** made from the Montepulciano grape with up to fifteen percent Sangiovese, commonly found as house red in the restaurants of Abruzzo, Molise and Rome. Montepulciano d'Abruzzo Cerasuola is a light **rosé** made from the same grapes; and Trebbiano d'Abruzzo is an often insipid dry **white** made from the Trebbiano d'Abruzzo and Trebbiano Toscano grapes. There are, however, a few quality producers: look out for wines from the Azienda Agricola Illuminati Dino and from the Azienda Agricola Pepe Emidio, both in the province of Téramo, in the north of Abruzzo.

⑫

L'Aquila and around

The pleasant town of **L'AQUILA** is an appealing blend of ancient and modern, with a university, smart shops, bustling streets and a daily market where you can buy anything from black-market cassettes to traditional Abruzzese craftwork. It was founded in 1242 when the Holy Roman Emperor Frederick II drew together the populations from 99 Abruzzesi villages to form a new city. Each village built its own church, piazza and quarter: there's a medieval fountain with 99 spouts, and the town-hall clock still chimes 99 times every night. These days only two churches remain, albeit magnificent ones. The town is overlooked by the bulk of the **Gran Sasso** mountain range and is the main access point to the national park of the same name.

Arrival, information and accommodation

L'Aquila's **train station** is a good way downhill from the centre, connected with the main part of town by regular buses. Long-distance **buses** stop on

Piazza Battaglione Alpini at the beginning of the old centre's main street, Corso Vittorio Emanuele. The **information booth** there has bus timetables covering L'Aquila province and connections to Rome. The main **tourist office** is at Piazza Santa Maria Paganica 5, just south of the bus station (Mon–Fri 9am–1pm & 3–6pm, Sat 9am–1pm; ℡0862.410.808, Ⓦwww.abruzzoturismo.it). There's an **Internet** café, *Internauti*, at Via Cimino 51 (Tues–Sat 6pm–1am).

The main drawback of L'Aquila is its lack of cheap **accommodation**, and you should definitely book in advance if you're planning to stay. Of the B&Bs, the one run by Giovanni Ranieri at Viale Duca degli Abruzzi 23 (℡0862.25.945, Ⓦwww.laquilahotel.it; ❷) is a well-appointed central and clean place with free parking. Of the hotels, the *Duomo*, Via Dragonetti 6 (℡0862.410.893, Ⓦwww.hotel-duomo.it; ❸), is your best bet, a three-star housed in a quiet, eighteenth-century palace with great views over Piazza del Duomo, and even better views of the mountains. Otherwise try the *Castello*, Piazza Battaglione Alpini

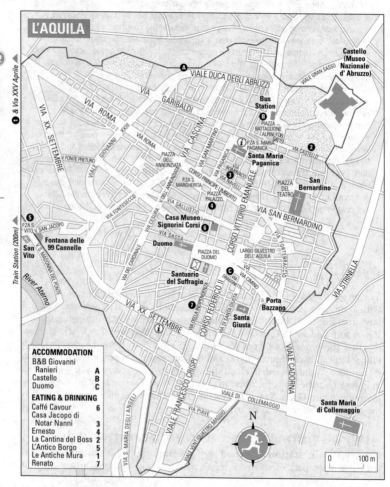

ACCOMMODATION
B&B Giovanni
  Ranieri   A
Castello   B
Duomo   C

EATING & DRINKING
Caffé Cavour   6
Casa Jacopo di
  Notar Nanni   3
Ernesto   4
La Cantina del Boss 2
L'Antico Borgo   5
Le Antiche Mura   1
Renato   7

(☎0862.419.147, ⓦ www.hotelcastelloaq.com; ❹), a swish business hotel from the 1960s that has been revamped and offers stylish, attractive rooms.

The City

L'Aquila's centre is relatively compact and easily seen on foot. Marking the northeastern entrance to the city centre is **Piazza Battaglione Alpini**, with the unusual Fontana Luminosa at its centre, best seen at night when it's lit up by multicoloured lights. Viale delle Medaglie d'Oro leads to the formidable **Castello**, built by the Spanish in the sixteenth century to keep the citizens of L'Aquila in order after an uprising. The Spanish forced the *Aquilani* to pay for the castle by imposing an annual tax and heavy fines. In the Fascist period the castle's surroundings were landscaped as a park, and, following the devastation wreaked by the Nazis in 1943, the building was renovated and the **Museo Nazionale d'Abruzzo** (Tues–Sun 8.30am–7pm; €4) established in the former barracks. The most popular exhibit here is the skeleton of a prehistoric mammoth found about 14km from L'Aquila in the 1950s, but the collection of works of art rescued from abandoned and earthquake-ravaged churches is also worth a visit. Among the polychrome wooden Madonnas, those by Silvestro dell'Aquila stand out, while the best of the paintings are the dreamy and mystical works attributed to Andrea Delitio, a fifteenth-century Abruzzese artist responsible for the region's best fresco cycle in the cathedral at Atri. The exhibit with the most sensational history is an elaborate silver crucifix by Nicola da Guardiagrele – after being stolen from L'Aquila's duomo and auctioned at Sotheby's, it's now kept for safety in the museum. The museum also hosts concerts throughout the year; check with the tourist office for details.

From Piazza Battaglione Alpini, arcaded **Corso Vittorio Emanuele** is L'Aquila's main street, lined with upmarket clothes shops, jewellers and cafés, and liveliest in the evenings when L'Aquila's youth turn out for the *passeggiata*. To the left down Via San Bernardino, the church of **San Bernardino** (daily 8.30am–noon & 3–6pm; free) has a sumptuous facade, with three magnificent white tiers bedecked with classical columns, pediments, friezes and inscriptions. Inside, the ceiling is luxuriously gilded and skilfully carved, while the glazed blue and white terracotta altarpiece by Andrea della Robbia – on the right as you enter – is very fine, as is San Bernardino's mausoleum, sculpted by Silvestro dell'Aquila. San Bernardino was originally from Siena but died in L'Aquila, where his relics remain, ritually visited every year on his feast day by Sienese bearing gifts of Tuscan oil.

On the opposite side of the Corso, Via Sallustio leads to Via Patini and the **Casa Museo Signorini Corsi** (Mon–Fri 4–7pm, Sat & Sun 10am–1pm & 4–7pm; €3), a sixteenth-century *palazzo* whose intimate rooms aim for a lived-in look. Along with displays of decorative items and period furniture, there are several religious paintings, mainly from the fifteenth to seventeenth centuries, including an appealing *Madonna with Cat* and a luminous *Holy Family* attributed to Botticelli. The main Corso carries on up to the central **Piazza del Duomo**, more noted for its **market** (Mon–Sat 8am–2pm) and as the focus for the *passeggiata* than for its architecture; the numerous surrounding cafés make a pleasant spot for a coffee and a snack. The **duomo**, having been destroyed on several occasions by earthquakes, now features a tedious Neoclassical front. The facade of the eighteenth-century **Santuario del Suffragio**, by contrast, is a voluptuous combination of curves, topped by a flamboyant honeycombed alcove. Tumbling down the hill below the piazza, steep-stepped streets of ancient houses lead down to **Porta Bazzano**, one of the old city gates. Rather than heading straight there, take time to wander the abutting streets, lined with

Renaissance and Baroque palaces. Some of these are still opulent, others decaying, and all provide an evocative backdrop for the church of **Santa Giusta**, whose rose window is decorated with twelve figures representing the various artisans who contributed to the building.

From Porta Bazzano, Via Porta Bazzano leads to the church of **Santa Maria di Collemaggio** (daily 8.30am–noon & 3–6pm free). One of Abruzzo's most distinctive churches, its massive rectangular bulk is faced with a geometric jigsaw of pink and white stone, more redolent of a mosque than a church, pierced by delicate, lacy rose windows and entered through a fancy Romanesque arch. It was founded in the thirteenth century by Pietro of Morrone, a hermit unwillingly dragged from his mountain retreat to be made pope by power-hungry cardinals who reckoned he would be easy to manipulate. When he turned out to be too naive even for the uses of the cardinals, he was forced to resign and was posthumously compensated for the ordeal by being canonized. Thieves stole his relics in April 1988, intending to hold them to ransom, but they were soon safely retrieved and returned to their grandiose Palladian-style sarcophagus. One of the few things Peter managed to do during his short reign was to install a Holy Door in the church – opened every year on August 28, when sinners pass through it to procure absolution.

Finally there's L'Aquila's best-known sight, the **Fontana delle 99 Cannelle**, outside the town centre close to the train station, tucked behind the medieval **Porta Riviera**. Set around three sides of a sunken piazza and overlooked by abandoned houses and the tiny church of **San Vito**, each water spout is a symbol for one of the villages that formed the city. This constant supply of fresh water sustained the *Aquilani* through the plagues, earthquakes and sieges to which the city was subjected, and was used for washing clothes until after the war.

Eating, drinking and nightlife

L'Aquila has a decent selection of good, reasonably priced **places to eat**, ranging from restaurants serving traditional Abruzzese fare to cheap and cheerful pizzerias catering for the town's student population. Alternatively, several shops on Via Patini (between Piazza Palazzo and Piazza del Duomo) or the market in Piazza del Duomo have all you need for a good picnic or lunch on the go.

As a university city, L'Aquila also has some good **cafés** and **pubs** in the streets and piazzas from Piazza del Duomo to Piazza S. Biagio to the northwest. A particular favourite among the young is *Caffè Cavour*, Via Cavour 16, where live music is played on some nights.

Casa Jacopo di Notar Nanni Via Bominaco 24 ☎0862.61.141. Housed in part of a fifteenth-century *palazzo*, this place has good antipasto with local salmais and cheeses, and typical local dishes such as lentil and spelt soup (*zuppa di farro e lenticchie*) and *spaghetti alla chitarra* with saffron, basil, cherry tomatoes and parmesan. Closed Sun eve and Mon.

Ernesto Piazza Palazzo ☎0862.21.094. Family-run place good for a treat: try the home-made *pasta sagnarelli* with ricotta, mushroom, ham and local *pecorino*, or a soup of *farro* (spelt) for around €6. Closed Sat eve & Sun.

La Cantina del Boss Via Castello 3 ☎0862.413.393. Bustling wine bar with a good selection of local and national wines and great filled *foccaccia* for €3.50. Closed Sat eve & Sun.

L'Antico Borgo Piazza San Vito 1 ☎0862.22.005. Tasty fish dishes in a peaceful spot make this a great choice for lunch outside in summer. Try the *grano e sapori di bosco* (wheat berries cooked as in a risotto with *funghi porcini, zafferano e tartufo*) for €8. Open daily.

Le Antiche Mura Via XXV Aprile 2 ☎0862.62.422. Traditional restaurant with a wide variety of local specialities – try *ceci e castagne* (chickpeas and chestnuts) or *coniglio allo zafferano* (rabbit scented with saffron). If you want to try everything, there's a *degustazione* menu for €33. Closed Sun.

Renato Via della Indipendenza 9 ☎0862.25.596. The waiter will reel off the specials of the day based on produce from the market nearby; try their *maccheroni alla chitarra con zafferano* for €8. Closed Sun.

The Gran Sasso and Campo Imperatore plain

Whether you approach Abruzzo from Marche in the north or Rome in the west, your arrival will be signalled by the spectacular bulk of the **Gran Sasso** massif, containing by far the highest of the Apennine peaks, and these days a **national park** with hiking trails. If you come by autostrada from Marche, you'll actually travel underneath the mountains, through a ten-kilometre tunnel, passing the entrance to a trailblazing particle-physics research laboratory bored into the very heart of the mountain range.

The massif itself consists of two parallel chains, flanking the vast **Campo Imperatore** plain that stretches for 27km at over 2000m above sea level. This is a bleak but atmospheric place, overlooked by abandoned and semi-abandoned hill-villages, its rolling grassland in places laid bare to reveal rocks, carved into moonscape ripples by the wind.

The itinerary below is an easy day's drive from L'Aquila. If you're dependent on public transport, it will take two days and you may have to content yourself with viewing the plain by cable car and taking buses up to the hill-villages from L'Aquila via the less interesting southern route.

Fonte Cerreto and the Corno Grande

Bus #6 from L'Aquila's Corso Vittorio Emanuele runs regularly up to **FONTE CERRETO**, the gateway to Campo Imperatore – basically two hotels, a restaurant and a campsite clustered around a cable-car station. Most of these were built in the Thirties as part of Mussolini's scheme to keep Italians fit by encouraging them to take exercise in the mountains. Ironically, he was imprisoned here in 1943, first at the *Villetta* inn in Fonte Cerreto, and then at the *Albergo Campo Imperatore*, a grim hotel at the top of the cable-car route. Apparently it was with some trepidation that Mussolini stepped into the cable car, enquiring whether it was safe and then hastily covering his cowardice by adding, "Not for my sake, you understand, because my life is over. But for those who accompany me." *Il Duce* supposedly spent his days at the hotel on a diet of eggs, rice, boiled onions and grapes, contemplating suicide. Hitler came to his rescue, dispatching an ace pilot to airlift him out in a tiny plane that is said to have terrified Mussolini almost as much as the cable car.

The **cable car** that so spooked Mussolini has been replaced by a new one (June to late Sept daily 8am–7pm; winter daily 8.30am–5pm, but service depends on snowfall; return journey €10). A small **information office** (July & Aug daily 9am–1pm; ☎0862.606.829) near the *Villetta* hotel has details of walks and wildlife to be seen in the Gran Sasso park. You can still stay at the *Villetta* (☎0862.606.171, ⓦwww.fiordigigli.com; ❸), though it's now a pleasantly modernized **hotel** over a snack bar; alternatively, try *Villetta*'s larger sister hotel, the *Fiordigigli* (same details; ❸), also at the base of the cable car. There's cheaper accommodation in two **mountain refuges** run by CAI; one of these is the *Ostello Campo Imperatore* (☎0862.400.011; €17, or €33 for dinner, bed and breakfast), which occupies the old cable-car station; the other is the *Duca degli Abruzzi rifugio* (☎0347.623.2101; €16 for a bed; June to mid-Sept;), several metres beyond. It's now the most popular starting-point for assaults on the Gran Sasso's highest peak, the **Corno Grande** (2912m).

Outside the summer months, **the ascent** of Corno Grande should only be attempted by experienced climbers, and at all times includes some fairly strenuous scree-climbing and alarming descents. Perhaps the most challenging route is the tough trek from the *Ostello Campo Imperatore* right across the mountain range, taking

△ Walking in the Gran Sasso, in front of Corno Grande

in the Corno Grande, sleeping over at the *Rifugio Franchetti* (☎0861.959.634 or 333.232.4474, ⓦ www.rifugiofranchetti.it; €17, or €40 for dinner, bed and breakfast; June–Sept), and then walking across to the Arapietra ridge. From here a ski lift will take you down to the ugly ski resort of **Prati di Tivo** – which nevertheless offers some of the best views of Gran Sasso – from where you can get a bus to the town of Teramo. If you're going to do any of the Gran Sasso trails, you'll need the CAI *Gran Sasso d'Italia* **map** (on sale in newsagents around town), and should check out **weather conditions** from either the tourist office or the CAI office at Via Sassa 34 in L'Aquila (☎0862.24.342, ⓦ www.cailaquila.it).

The Campo Imperatore plain

For non-hikers the road continues from Fonte Cerreto across **Campo Imperatore**, backed by awesome rocky massifs that have been prime locations for film-makers over the years, masquerading as everything from the surface of Mars to a remote region of Tibet. Film crews and the occasional hiker apart, the only people you're likely to meet here are **nomadic shepherds**, who bring their flocks up to the plain for summer grazing after wintering in the south – a practice that has been going on since Roman times. Although the sheep are now transported by lorry rather than on foot, the shepherds' shacks sprinkled across the plain suggest that their living standards have changed very little.

South to Sulmona: Bominaco

From L'Aquila, the SS17 follows the ancient route of the local shepherds across the saffron fields south to Sulmona. If you have your own transport, it's worth making a short detour on the way to see two of Abruzzo's most beautiful churches at **BOMINACO** (also accessible by bus from L'Aquila). The village itself is an inauspicious knot of grubby houses, but the endearingly askew and lichen-mottled facade of **San Pellegrino**, founded by Charlemagne, conceals floor-to-ceiling frescoes in vivid hues reminiscent of a peacock's plume (opened on request, see below). The brilliant thirteenth-century frescoes include pictures of the life of Christ, the Virgin and a huge St Christopher, as well as an intriguing calendar with signs of the zodiac. If you put your ear to the hole at the side of the altar, tradition says you'll hear the heartbeat of San Pellegrino buried below.

The church of **Santa Maria dell'Assunta** (opened on request, see below), just beyond, stands on the foundations of a Roman temple to Venus. It has a more coolly refined exterior, but its aloofness is tempered by monsters carved at the bases of the windows – notably a chimera with the face of a diabolic lion, flexing its talons and flicking its serpentine tail. Inside, the creamy-white carvings are so exquisitely precise that it seems the mason has only just put down his chisel; in fact they're eight hundred years old and though there's been some restoration, this is scarcely discernible, and the lack of the usual cracks and crumblings is uncanny. Particularly striking is the extraordinary free-standing column, consisting of two entwined rolls of stone so supple and sensuous that you expect them to dimple to the touch. If the churches are closed, you can get the keys from Signora Alessandrina Tiberi at Via Ripa 4 (℡0862.93.756).

Sulmona and around

Flanked by bleak mountains and bristling with legends about its most famous son, Ovid, **SULMONA** is a rich and comfortable provincial town owing its wealth to gold jewellery and sugared almonds. An atmospheric little place, with a dark tangle of a historical centre lined with imposing palaces, its sights can be seen in a day, but the town makes a good base for exploring the surroundings – from ancient hermitages to towns with snake-infested festivals – and you may want to stay longer.

Arrival, information and accommodation

Buses arrive in Sulmona at the Parco Fluviale, just down the hill from the western end of the main street, Corso Ovidio. The **train station** is about 1km outside the centre of town; bus #A runs from the station along Corso Ovidio. The **tourist office** (June–Sept Mon–Sat 9am–1pm & 4–7pm, Sun 9am–1pm; Oct–May Mon–Fri 9am–1pm & 3–6pm, Sat 9am–1pm; ℡0864.53.276) is at Corso Ovidio 208. There's a second information office in the old pharmacy of the Palazzo SS Annunziata with very helpful staff, maps and details of Sulmona's churches and palaces (daily 9am–12.30pm & 3.30–7pm; ℡0864.210.216, ⓦwww.comune.sulmona.aq.it).

There's a good choice of **accommodation** and the town is well worth a stay. The most atmospheric of the affordable hotels is the *Italia*, on Piazza Salvatore Tommasi, just behind Piazza XX Settembre (℡0864.52.308, ⓔgianlucadicamillo @libero.it; no credit cards; ❷). It's a little ramshackle, but has plenty of person-ality and a friendly owner. Another good option is the newly refurbished *Stella*, Via Mazara 18 (℡0864.52.653, ⓦwww.hasr.it; ❷), a relaxed, family-run establishment that's deservedly popular, so book ahead. At Via Matteotti 14, *Il Celestino* (℡0864.56.549; ❷) offers simple, neat rooms in a former school, as well as hostel dorms for €30 a head. For something more upmarket, head to *Amandos*, Via Montenero 15 (℡0864.210.783, ⓦwww.hotelarmandos.it; ❸), a smart, well-equipped choice on the edge of town.

The Town

Corso Ovidio, Sulmona's main street, cuts through the centre from the park-side bus terminus, leading up to the intimate square **Piazza XX Settembre**. A couple of minutes back up Corso Ovidio stands Sulmona's architectural showpiece, the **Annunziata**, a Gothic-Renaissance *palazzo* adjoining a flamboyant Baroque church. These days, its steps are a hangout for the town's young men during the evening *passeggiata*, but once they would have been crowded with Sulmona's ill and destitute: the Annunziata housed a hospital, a pharmacy and a store of grain, donated by the rich and shared out to the needy. It was established by a confraternity to take care of the citizens from birth until death, and most of the external decoration is designed to remind onlookers of the life process. Around the first door is a tree of life; an allegorical frieze with scenes from the cultivation of the vine representing birth, marriage and death stretches across the facade; a sunburst-style wheel of life stands above a window; and statues of saints gaze piously down from pedestals, firmly placing the symbolism in a Christian context. The most intriguing statue, however, is just inside the entrance: Ovid, metamorphosed from pagan poet of love into an ascetic friar. Inside the Annunziata are three **museums**: one (undergoing a lengthy restoration) with exhibits on local costumes and transhumance – the practice of moving sheep to summer pastures – and examples of work by Sulmona's Renaissance goldsmiths, a trade that continues here today, as evidenced by the number of jewellers' shops along the Corso; another, the **Museo Civico** (June–Oct Tues–Thurs 9am–1pm, Fri, Sat & Sun 9am–1pm & 3–7pm; €2), has local sculpture and paintings from the sixteenth to seventeenth centuries; and a third, the **Museo "in situ"** (Wed & Fri 10am–1pm; free), shows the excavations of a Roman villa inhabited from the first century BC to the second century AD, abandoned suddenly along with many other houses in the valley when a landslide or an earthquake struck. Among the fragments of fabulously coloured wall painting are depictions of Pan, Eros, Dionysus and Ariadne, and there are several floor mosaics, all well labelled.

As well as gold, the Corso's **shops** are full of Sulmona's other great product – *confetti*, originally a confection of sugared almonds, but nowadays consisting of sugar-coated chocolate and hazelnuts wired into elaborate flowers with the aid of coloured cellophane, crêpe paper and ribbons. Through ingenious marketing the Sulmonese *confetti* barons have made gifts of their intricate sculptures *de rigueur* at christenings and confirmations throughout Catholic Europe, while at Abruzzese weddings, bride and groom are painfully pelted with loose white *confetti*.

At the end of the Corso is Piazza del Carmine, where the weighty Romanesque portal of **San Francesco della Scarpa** was the only part of the church solid enough to withstand a 1703 earthquake. The church gets its name – della Scarpa (of the shoe) – from the fact that Franciscans wore shoes instead of the sandals worn by other monastic orders. Opposite, the impressive Gothic **aqueduct**, built to supply water to the town and power to its wool mills, ends at a small fifteenth-century fountain, the **Fontana del Vecchio**, named for the bust of a chubby-cheeked old man on top. On the other side of the aqueduct is **Piazza Garibaldi**, a vast square dominated by the austere slopes of **Monte Morrone**, on which the hermit Pietro Morrone lived until he was dragged away to be made pope. There's a former nunnery in the corner – take a look at the courtyard, where there's a tiny door at which unmarried mothers were permitted to abandon their babies.

Eating and drinking

Sulmona has some excellent reasonably priced **restaurants**, with mains generally around the €6–7 mark. *Cesidio*, Via Solimo 25 (T0864.52.724; closed
Mon eve), is a popular local place with some great home-made pasta dishes
including *alla chitarra* (try it *spazzocamini*, with capers, olives, tomato and herbs).
On the same street, at no. 20, *Mafalda* (T0864.34.538; closed Sun in winter)
is particularly enjoyable in summer, when you can eat dishes like home-made
maccheroni alla chitarra outside in its walled garden. *Al Quadrivio*, Via Mazara
38 (T0864.55.533; closed Wed), serves up some simple but delicious dishes
such as home-made *pasta con pomodoro e basilico* (tomato and basil) or with
funghi porcini in season. Warmly recommended is ⅍ *Clemente*, Vico Quercia 20
(T0864.52.284; closed Thurs), a bright, family-run place in an old *palazzo* that's
been serving home-produced salami and dishes such as *cosciotto d'agnello alle erbe*,
slow cooked lamb with herbs, for over fifty years.

For **ice cream** both *Schiazza* and *di Marzio*, along Corso Ovidio, are worth a
try during the *passeggiata*, but for a *gelato* with a view try *Gelateria La Rotonda*,
above the remains of the aqueduct and with amazing mountain panoramas. For
an excellent choice of **wines** head for *La Cantina di Biffi*, an elegantly countri-
fied place in Via Barbato off Corso Ovidio (closed Mon), where you can eat as
well; or try the quintessentially Italian *Black Bull* (closed Sun), across the river
by the Ponte Capograssi.

East of Sulmona: the Majella

The **Parco Nazionale della Majella**, 30km to the east of Sulmona, is named
after the mountain – **Monte Majella** – that dominates the area. Dedicated
to the Goddess Maja, the mountain was held sacred by the ancient people of
Abruzzo, and during the Middle Ages the region around it was named Domus
Christi by Petrarch, or the "House of God", for its proliferation of hermitages
and abbeys. Over a hundred **hermits** made their retreat here in the Middle
Ages, among them the man who was to become Pope Celestine V. While some
hermits reused cave dwellings, others built hermitages and churches into the
rock, haunting constructions to this day. There's detailed information on the
park's website Ⓦ www.parcomajella.it.

Of the **hermitages**, the two most famous, as well as being relatively easy
to reach, are San Bartolomeo and Santo Spirito. To visit them, your own
transport is advisable as you'll need to get to **Roccamorice**, a small village a
fifty-kilometre drive from Sulmona, or take a train or bus to Scafa and change
there for infrequent connections to Roccamorice. For **San Bartolomeo**, a
hermitage that Celestine V reconstructed in the 1200s, follow the road out of
Roccamorice for the Majelletta for about 3km, then turn off to the right on
a tarmac road. After a few metres you'll come to the path that leads to San
Bartolomeo. From here you'll have to go down on foot, keeping to the left,
until you find the stairs to the hermitage, which has recently been reoccupied
by a religious community.

For **Santo Spirito**, don't turn off the tarmac road but keep straight on by car
for about 4km through the woods, where you'll find the hermitage, which has
recently been reoccupied by a religious community.

West of Sulmona: Cocullo

A tatty hill-village, connected with Sulmona by infrequent trains and even less
frequent buses, **COCULLO** is understandably neglected by outsiders for 364

days of the year. However, on the first Thursday in May it's invaded by what seems like half the population of central Italy, coming to celebrate the weird **festival of snakes**, an annual event held in memory of St Dominic, the patron saint of the village, who allegedly rid the area of venomous snakes back in the eleventh century.

The festival is an odd mixture of the modern and archaic. Everyone pours into the main square, while a wailing Mass is relayed from the church over aged speakers. After the service a number of snake-charmers in the crowd drape a wooden statue of St Dominic with a writhing mass of live but harmless snakes, which is then paraded through the streets in a bizarre celebration of the saint's unique powers (he was apparently good at curing snake-bites too). It's actually thought that Cocullo's preoccupation with serpents dates back to before the advent of the saint when in the pre-Christian era local tribes worshipped their goddess Angitia with offerings of snakes. Scholars have attempted to rationalize the festival by drawing a parallel between snakes shedding their skins and the ancient Cocullans shedding their paganism for Christianity – but whatever the origins, Cocullo's festival is today more than anything a celebration of St Dominic's power to attract enough tourist money in a day to keep the village going for a year. Incidentally, if you're suffering from toothache, he's also reckoned to have the power to cure it, the only snag being that you have to ring the church bell with the rope in your teeth.

South of Sulmona: Scanno

Twenty kilometres down the road, and accessible by bus from Sulmona, Scanno is another popular tourist destination, reached by passing through the narrow and rocky **Saggitario Gorge**, a spectacular drive along galleries of rock and around blind hairpin bends that widen out at the glassy green **Lago di Scanno**. Perched over the lake is a church, **Madonna del Lago**, with the cliff as its back wall, and nearby there are boats and pedalos for rent, and a good restaurant, the *Trattoria sul Lago*. If you're planning on staying there's a **campsite** *I Lupi* (☎0864.740.100, ⓦwww.campingilupi.it; open all year), 2km away at Villalago, and on the shores of the lake, but be warned that it gets packed out in summer.

A couple of kilometres beyond, **SCANNO** itself is a well-preserved medieval village encircled by mountains. The **traditional costumes** immortalized by photographer Henri Cartier-Bresson in 1953 are still to be seen in everyday use, though the custom is dying fast. Just a few of the elderly women of the village wear the long, dark, pleated skirts and bodices, with either a patterned apron for daywear or a brocade skirt and embroidered fez with coils of cord looped behind to conceal the hair on special occasions (with a white skirt for weddings). The skirts are made of wool – the village's staple industry in former times – and weigh around 12 kilos, but their heaviness doesn't prevent them from being worn for household tasks. The hat, and the fact that at Scannese weddings the tradition was for women to squat on the floor of the church, has led scholars to believe that the Scannese originated in Asia Minor; Scannese jewellery also has something of the Orient about it – large, delicately filigreed earrings, and a star, known as a *presuntuosa*, given to fiancées to ward off other men. If you want to see the costume and jewellery at close quarters head for the shop at Strada Silla 32.

It's a pleasure strolling around the **old town**, built into the steep hillside, the squares and alleyways lined with solid stone houses built by wool barons when business was good. Though shepherding as a way of life has virtually finished

△ Woman in traditional mourning dress, Scanno

and the population has dwindled, it's a living village, with enough work available in Sulmona and in tourism to keep people from moving away. A **chair lift**, signposted 300m from the centre (undergoing restoration, but due to reopen early 2007; call the *Comune* on ℡0864.74.545 if you need to check) ,takes **skiers** up to a handful of runs on Monte Rotondo, operating also in the short summer season when it's worth going up just for the view of lake and mountains, especially at sunset.

If you're around in August, you might catch Scanno's **classical music festival**, with a series of concerts held throughout the month (see ⓦ www.scanno .org), and on January 17 there's a **lasagne festival** – more properly called the Festa di San Antonio Abate, involving the cooking of a great cauldron of lasagne and beans outside the door of the church, which is then blessed and doled out with a somewhat unholy amount of pushing and shoving.

Scanno practicalities

The **tourist office** (mid-May to mid-Sept Mon–Sat 9am–1pm & 4–7pm, Sun 9am–1pm; rest of year Mon–Fri 9am–1pm & 3–6pm, Sat 9am–1pm; ⓣ 0864.74.317, ⓦ www.abruzzoturismo.it) is at Piazza Santa Maria della Valle 12.

    Accommodation options include *Mille Pini*, next to the chair lift at Via Pescara 2 (ⓣ 0864.74.387, ⓦ www.millepiniscanno.it; ❸), a large chalet overlooking the village and the most atmospheric place to stay. Between the lake and the village, *Albergo Nilde*, Viale del Lago 101 (ⓣ 0864.74.359, ⓦ www.ilrifugiodellupo.it; no credit cards; ❷), is a simple family-run place with great views. They also have a slightly more upmarket place out of town towards the lake, the *Albergo Rifugio del Lupo* (ⓣ 0864.74.397; ❷), or try the central and modern *Seggiovia*, Via D. Tanturri 42 (ⓣ 0864.74.371, ⓦ www.albergoseggiovia.it; ❷).

    For **eating**, *Gli Archetti* (ⓣ 0864.74.645), on Via Silla inside the Porta della Croce entrance to the old town, cooks up imaginative variations on traditional Abruzzese fare, and *Birreria La Baita* (ⓣ 0864.747.826; July–Oct daily; Nov–June Sat only) above the village near the chair lift, serves excellent pasta dishes, with occasional live music. It also has some cabin rooms available (❷).

Southwest Abruzzo and the Abruzzo national park

Heading west towards Rome from Sulmona, road and railway skirt the **Fucino Plain**, an endless, unreal and utterly flat expanse of agricultural land whose only landmarks are the satellite dishes of Telespazio, Italy's biggest telecommunications complex. On its western fringe, you'll find the well-preserved Roman remains of the town of **Alba Fucens**, though the main attraction of this part of the region is undoubtedly the **Parco Nazionale d'Abruzzo** in the mountains to the south, one of the few areas in western Europe where bears and wolves still roam free.

The Fucino plain

The Fucino was once Italy's third-largest lake, and is the largest lake in the world to have been artificially drained. Attempts to empty it began nearly two thousand years ago. The Marsi people who lived on its shores, fed up with the fact that it flooded every time the mountain snows melted, managed to persuade Emperor Claudius to build a six-kilometre-long outlet tunnel, designed to transfer the water from the lake into a nearby valley. On the day of the draining, the shores and surrounding mountains were packed with spectators: the proceedings were inaugurated by a mechanical Triton who rose up from the lake blowing a trumpet, whence a mock battle ensued, with warships manned by condemned criminals, after which Claudius gave the signal for the outlet gates to be opened. Unfortunately, the tunnel couldn't cope with the vast volume of water, and thousands of spectators, including members of the imperial

Fauna and flora in the Abruzzo National Park

There are around a hundred indigenous species of **fauna and flora** in the Abruzzo National Park, making this an area of exception biodiversity. Many of the larger mammals can be seen in nature reserves next to dedicated museums, such as the wolf museum at Civitella Alfadena; others can be seen close up at the fascinating clinic and natural history museum in Pescasseroli; to try and see them in the wild, ask locals where they have been sighted.

One of the most important **animals** in the park is the Marsican brown bear. Until recently an endangered species, there are now around fifty in the park and the best time to watch for them is the crack of dawn or around 8 or 9pm – the bear should not be any danger as its first instinct on scenting humans is to flee, but make sure you don't come between a mother and her cubs. Another key park inhabitant is the Appenine Wolf, of which there are around forty. As with the bears, it offers no danger to humans. Look out too for the chamois d'Abruzzo, deer and roe deer, wildcats, martens, otters, badgers, polecats and the edible dormouse.

Among **birds**, the park's species include the golden eagle, the peregrine hawk, the goshawk and the rare white-backed woodpecker. Higher up are snow finches, alpine accentors and rock partridges.

The park's **flora** includes many local orchids, among which the most important variety is Venus's little shoe or Our Lady's slipper, which thrives on the chalky soil in the park. There are also gentians, peonies, violets, irises and columbines, and black pine woods at Villetta Barrea and the Camosciara.

party, only narrowly escaped being washed away. Frederick II attempted to open up the tunnel in 1240, but the lake was only finally drained in 1875, as much to gain agricultural land as to solve the flooding problem – though it has brought associated problems. The climate has grown humid, misty and mosquito-ridden, and it's clear that lakeside tourist developments would have been far more profitable than agriculture.

Celano and Avezzano

Fringing the plain is **CELANO**, a pretty village crowned by the turreted toytown Castello Piccolomini, home of the **Museo d'Arte Sacra** (Mon, Wed & Fri–Sun 9am–2pm, Tues & Thurs 9am–5pm; €3), which displays a range of medieval paintings, sculpture and vestments. More interesting, but difficult to reach without your own transport, is the striking, turf-roofed **Museo della Preistoria d'Abruzzo**, south of Celano, 3km from the Aielli–Celano exit off the A25 (Mon, Wed & Fri–Sat 8am–2pm, Tues & Thurs 8am–5pm; free; ☎0863.790.357). Finds from a nearby Bronze Age lake village and tomb reconstructions are well displayed, as are intricate bone artefacts, the best and largest of which is a complete funeral jar from the first century BC. If you need **accommodation** in Celano, *Hotel Le Gole* on Borgo Sardellino (☎0863.711.009, ⓦwww.hotellegole.it; ❸) makes an excellent overnight stop and also has great food at reasonable prices in its *Da Guerrinuccio* **restaurant**. It's situated on the Aielli–Celano road off the A25 autostrada.

A little further west is **AVEZZANO**, destroyed – along with ten thousand inhabitants – by an earthquake in 1915. It was rebuilt, but flattened again by World War II bombings. It's since been reconstructed, but there are only two reasons to stop here: to get a bus (from outside the train station) south to the Parco Nazionale d'Abruzzo; or to get a bus to Alba Fucens, Abruzzo's most significant archeological site.

Alba Fucens

A once important Roman town and military stronghold, **ALBA FUCENS**, 5km north of Avezzano, contains a series of well-preserved and surprisingly untouristed **excavations**. The site nearly went under the hammer in a recent sale of Italian state property and though rescued by the Abruzzo Region, it's still at risk with open access day and night (free) contributing to the theft of mosaics, columns and sundry other "souvenirs".

Coming on public **transport** from Avezzano, you'll have to spend half a day here (buses do a round trip Mon–Sat from Avezzano to Alba Fucens at 6.30am, 8am and 11.30am, returning from Alba Fucens to Avezzano at 1pm, 2.10pm, 6.10pm and 7.20pm). There's an **information office** in Alba Fucens' main square (T0863.445.642, Wwww.albafucens.info) where you can get a useful map (€1) and guide to the site's history. In the summer there are theatre and music performances in the amphitheatre, check out the website for details.

From the entrance to the right of the information office, you enter the centre of the **Roman town**, with the overgrown forum to your left – still not excavated – and, to your right, a basilica, market place and a series of squares nestled between two hills that were once topped with fourth-century BC **temples**. One, the Temple of Pettorino, is no more than a few stones on the hillside, but the other, the Temple of Apollo, is now a church, San Pietro.

Turning right down the main road you come to a substantial **domus** or villa on your right, with internal courtyards. Up the hill to your right is one of the highlights, a slightly crumbling first-century BC **amphitheatre** – scale the moss-covered seats for a stupendous view of the Roman town and hills around. Leaving the amphitheatre, to the left are the remains of another villa that once boasted interesting frescoes and mosaics but which have sadly vanished. Further up the hill you'll come to San Pietro. From this vantage point you may be able to make out the dip in the land where the theatre once stood in the opposite hill. It was used as a stone quarry and nothing is left.

The Parco Nazionale d'Abruzzo

At four hundred square kilometres, the **PARCO NAZIONALE D'ABRUZZO** is Italy's third-largest national park and holds some of its wildest mountain land, providing great walking and a hunter-free haven for wolves, brown bears, chamois, deer, lynx, wild boar and three or four pairs of royal eagles. The central village, **PESCASSEROLI**, is the most commercialized spot, liberally decorated with the park's logo – a cuddly brown bear – and surrounded by campsites, holiday apartments and hotels.

The best way to get away from the town is to **hike**, and if you're not up for this there's not much point in coming here. The trick is to take advantage of the comprehensive information service, and get walking as quickly as possible: as soon as you get away from the vicinity of the tourist villages, the wild Apennine beauty really makes itself felt.

Information

There's a **tourist office** in Pescasseroli, opposite the police station on Via Piave (summer Mon–Sat 9am–1pm & 4–7pm, Sun 9am–1pm; winter Mon–Sat 9am–1pm & 3–6pm, Sun 10am–1pm; T0863.910.097). The village also has an excellent **natural history museum** on Viale Santa Lucia (summer daily 10am–1pm & 3–7pm; winter Tues–Sun 10am–1pm & 2–5pm; €6), which fills you in on the park's flora and fauna and acts as a clinic for sick animals. The helpful **Centro Accoglienza Turistica** (daily: summer 10am–1pm & 3–7pm; winter 2–5pm;

⊤0863.911.3242, ⓦ www.parcoabruzzo.it), behind the *municipio* (town hall), offers information on hiking in the park and has a good map you can refer to.

There are other tourist offices in **Opi** (same hours as Pescasseroli; ⊤0863.910.622), which also has a **chamois museum** (Easter & June–Sept daily 10am–1pm & 3–7pm; free); **Villetta Barrea** (same hours as Pescasseroli; ⊤0864.89.333); and **Barrea** (summer only daily 9am–1pm & 4–8pm; ⊤0864.88.227). All have leaflets outlining popular walks that take less than an hour. Nearby in **Civitella Alfadena** there's tourist information on the park attached to the interesting **wolf museum,** the Museo del Lupo (Tues–Sun: summer 10am–1pm & 3–7pm; winter 10am–1pm and 2–5pm; €3) which discusses the bad press the wolf has received as well as showing how the animal lives; the attached nature reserve currently has two wolves, one male and one female.

Walking routes

The tourist offices can also sell you a map (€6.50) on which all **walking routes** in the park are marked, along with an indication of the difficulty involved (M=moderate, D=difficult), the time needed, and the flora and fauna you're likely to see on the way. There are nearly 150 different routes, starting from 25 letter-coded points, so making a choice can be difficult. The following are just suggestions, taking into account the ease of reaching the starting-point by bus.

From point #F2, 1km southeast of Opi on the SS83 (car park available) there's a two-and-a-half-hour walk through the **Valle Fondillo** – one of the loveliest parts of the park. This route is best followed very early in the morning, to avoid other hikers and have a small chance of seeing bears and chamois. Off this path runs #F1 via which you can climb **Monte Amaro** (1862m) for great views over to Lake Barrea. Another good climb is up **Monte Tranquillo** (route #C3, about 2hr) about 1km out of Pescasseroli, taking the road to the left on entering the village, past the campsite *Panoramica*. The mountain (1841m) is crowned by a small sanctuary, dedicated to the black Madonna of Monte Tranquillo. From the summit you can either retrace your steps or take path #Q3 into the next valley, where you'll probably meet fewer fellow walkers. Your best chance of seeing some of the park's chamois is to take path #I1, turning left just before the youth hostel at Civitella Alfedena, and through the forested **Val di Rosa**, until the forest gives way to the grassy slopes where the chamois graze. A path zigzags from here up the slope to **Passo Cavuto**, and beyond to the *Rifugio Forca Resuni*. From here #K6 descends into the **Valle Iannanghera** – where you may see bears – and back to Civitella Alfedena. This circuit should take six hours.

The **Camosciara** #G7 off the SS83 from Opi to Villetta Barrea is another recommended route; the park has closed the road that used to end near the gentle half-hour walk to the waterfall (Le Cascate) at #G5, so there's now a 3–4km hike to the start of the route.

After Barrea take the SS83 towards Alfedena and turn off at #K. Lagovivo means living lake, and it is formed when the snows melt in spring; it dries up every summer and in the autumn the area becomes a mating ground for deer. Take #K6 then #K5 through the ominous-sounding Valle dell'Inferno to the lake and circuit round following #K7.

Note that from July 1 to September 15, the three most popular routes – #F1 to Monte Amaro, #I1 through Val di Rosa and #K6 to Valle Iannanghera – are open by **reservation only**. For #F1, book onto a guided tour with park staff (in English by request; €8) at the Ufficio dell'Ente Parco in Pescasseroli (⊤0863.911.3242). Access to #I1 is free in June but restricted from July 8 to

ABRUZZO AND MOLISE | Southwest Abruzzo and the national park

September 10 to fifty walkers per day and a hundred on Sundays and holidays. From September 16 to November 5 it is free to walk #I1 during the week, but access is restricted at weekends; book in person at the information point at Civitella Alfedena (€8). During the rest of the year these three routes are open without restriction or fee, though guided tours can still be arranged.

Accommodation

Pescasseroli is fairly well served by **buses** (from Avezzano, from Castel di Sangro on the border with Molise, and one bus daily to Rome in summer), so you may find it a convenient place to stay. In high season, there's little chance of finding a **room** on arrival; you need to book at least a month in advance and be prepared for compulsory half board in August. If you're coming here for a week or more, you might consider B&B accommodation in a private house or an apartment rental – the tourist office can supply you with a list.

Campers should manage to find space on one of the **campsites**, though be warned that temperatures are low even in summer. The simplest to reach is the *Dell'Orso* (☎0863.91.955), which also has a *rifugio* (€5), on the main approach road (SS83) – a fairly basic affair in a nice location. *Sant'Andrea* (☎0863.912.173) is further into town off the SS83, and more built-up. *Panoramica* (☎0863.912.257), which has impressive views, is out of the village at the foot of the *funivia* (cable car) up to Monte Vitelle. Otherwise at nearby **Civitella Alfadena** there's the simply equipped *Wolf* (☎0864.890.360; July–Sept), 300m from the centre. At **Barrea** *La Genziana* campsite (☎0864.88.101), which has an on-site bar, is convenient for walk-point #K and five minutes' walk from the town.

Al Castello Via Gabriele d'Annunzio, Pescasseroli ☎ & ℱ0863.910.757. Off the main piazza, this small, stone-built guesthouse comes with squeakily clean and pretty rooms. ❶

Degli Olmi Via Fossata 8b, Villetta Barrea ☎0864.89.159, ⊛www.hotel-olmi.it. Highly polished and quiet hotel, with compulsory half board. ❶

La Torre Via Castello, Civitella Alfadena ☎0864.890.121,⊛www.albergolatorre.com.

Small, jolly hotel where the owner speaks good Scottish. ❷

Paradiso Via Fonte Fracassi 4, Pescasseroli ☎0863.910.422, ⊛www.albergo-paradiso.it. Delightful hotel run by the Scottish Geraldine and her Italian husband Marco, with warm rustic decor and good country cooking. Ask to see Geraldine's pub. ❷

Peppe di Sora Viale B. Croce, Pescasseroli ☎0863.91.908, ℱ0863.910.023. Welcoming place, across the river from the main town. ❷

Eating and entertainment

Eating out in most of the park's villages means fairly cheap pizza and pasta, and general stores that will make up sandwiches for picnics. For local specialities try *Plistia* at Principe di Napoli 28 (☎0863.910.732; closed Mon), where you can eat hearty mountain fare such as soup with local vegetables and pulses, or, in spring, gnocchi with asparagus and saffron. Otherwise try *La Baita*, on Piazzale Cabinovia (☎0863.910.434; closed Tues); dishes include *spaghetti alla chitarra* and polenta. Slightly more expensive is *Il Pescatore* in Villetta Barrea on Via Roma (☎0864.89.347), a large restaurant where you can feast on superlative fresh trout from the lake and home-made pasta dishes.

Two **festivals** worth trying to coincide a trip with are the Festa della Transhumanza, on September 8/9, commemorating the work of local nomadic shepherds by retracing their routes on foot or on horse, followed by a tasting of local products in Pescasseroli's main square. The town's Festa della Madonna, on July 16, sees the black Madonna carried 9km from her sanctuary on Monte Tranquillo to Pescasseroli and back to celebrate the town's miraculous escape from being bombed during the last war after prayers were offered to the Madonna.

Northeast Abruzzo: Téramo and around

Rising from the Adriatic and rolling towards the eastern slopes of the Gran Sasso, the landscape of **northeast Abruzzo** is gentle, and its inland towns are usually ignored in favour of its long, sandy and highly popular coastline. **TÉRAMO**, capital of the province of the same name, is a modern town with an elegant centre harbouring the remains of a Roman amphitheatre, theatre and baths and a treasure-filled cathedral. The town also has good bus and train connections with the northern Abruzzo coast, and if you're heading for the sea you may well pass through.

The Town

Téramo's main attraction, the **duomo**, at the top of Corso San Giorgio, is currently closed for restoration, so you may wish to give the town a miss till it reopens (check with the tourist office on ☎0861.244.222, ⓦwww.abruzzoturismo.it). When it does, you'll find that behind its patchy facade lies a remarkable silver **altarfront**. Crafted by the fifteenth-century Abruzzese silversmith Nicola da Guardiagrele – also responsible for the statues of Mary and Gabriel that flank the church doorway – it has 35 panels with lively reliefs of religious scenes, starting with the *Annunciation* and moving through the New Testament, punctuating the narrative with portraits of various saints. Nicola was famous enough to feature in a sumptuous polyptych by a Venetian artist, Jacobello del Fiore, in a Baroque chapel to the left. Set into an ornate gilded frame are static portraits of saints, in rich blue, red and gold gowns, flanking the *Coronation of the Virgin*, and beneath it a model of Téramo, set against a gilded sky, with Nicola wearing a monk's habit on the left, Jacobello in the red gown on the right.

To the right of the duomo, Via Irelli leads to the heart of Roman Téramo, with fragments of the **amphitheatre**, and the more substantial walls of the **theatre**, where two of the original twenty entrance arches remain. Just behind Piazza Garibaldi at Viale Bovio 1 is the town's modest **Pinacoteca** (Tues–Sun 9am–1pm & 3–6pm; €4 joint ticket with the Museo Archeologico). The collection of local art over the centuries is best represented by the *Madonna Enthroned with Saints* – a polyptych in which the colours are lucid and the forms almost sculpted, the work of local fifteenth-century artist Giacomo da Campli. The **Museo Archeologico** off Via Carducci on Via Delfico (same hours as the Pinacoteca; €4 for joint ticket with Pinacoteca) is strong on Roman finds from excavations in Téramo and includes a first-century mosaic of a lion among the forum columns and marble busts.

Practicalities

Buses to Téramo stop at Piazza Garibaldi, with which the **train station** is linked by regular city buses. To reach the **tourist office** (Mon–Fri 9am–1pm & 3–6pm, Sat 9am–1pm; ☎0861.244.222, ⓦwww.abruzzoturismo.it) at Via Carducci 17, take Corso San Giorgio from Piazza Garibaldi and then turn right. In the other direction off the piazza, at Via del Castello 62, is a reasonable **hotel**, the *Castello* (☎ & ℉0861.247.582; no credit cards; ❶), which has simple, old-fashioned rooms and its own restaurant. **Restaurants** include *Antico Cantinone*, at Via Ciotti 5 (☎0861.248.863; closed Sun), which has good local fare, and the bustling ⚔ *Enoteca Centrale*, Corso Cerulli 24–26, where a great wine list is backed up by excellent food, such as *scripelle*, a broth with little pancakes. If you don't want to stay in Téramo itself, you could head for the hill-village of

CIVITELLA DEL TRONTO, between Téramo and Áscoli Piceno in Marche, where *Zunica*, Piazza Filippi Pepe 14 (☏0861.91.319, ⓦwww.hotelzunica .it; ❸), has small, modern rooms, superb food in the restaurant, and a lively locals' bar on the ground floor. Regular buses run to Civitella del Tronto from Piazza Garibaldi in Téramo, taking around forty minutes.

The northern Abruzzo coast

The **northern Abruzzo coastline** isn't at first sight the region's most appealing stretch, its ribbon of sand hugged for most of its considerable length by road and railway, studded with grids of beach umbrellas and flimsy cabins and lined with concrete-box apartment blocks and hotels. However, the beaches are popular and frequently palm-fringed, and there are plenty of campsites and hotels, which you should book well in advance.

More of interest lies in **Pescara**, the main town in Abruzzo, where designer shops vie with the brilliant museum of the Abruzzo people for your attention, as well as in the neighbouring town **Chieti**'s superb archeological museum, and inland from the resorts in places like **Atri**, a town caught in a time-warp and with a church brilliantly frescoed by Andrea Delitio.

Pescara

The main town and resort of the Abruzzo coast is **PESCARA**, a bustling, modern place that's the region's most commercial and expensive city. If you're looking for somewhere to sunbathe there are much quieter places than Pescara's sixteen-kilometre beach; but if you're aiming to take a ferry over to Croatia or the islands of the Dalmatian coast, you might find yourself using the city as a departure point. It's also the nearest to the new Abruzzo airport where low-cost flights from the UK touch down.

The Town

Pescara was heavily bombed in World War II and architecturally there's little of distinction here. Opposite the new train station, the main street, **Corso Umberto**, is lined with designer boutiques and packed with the label-conscious Pescarese, who also hang out in the elegant cafés on **Piazza Rinascita**, known as Pescara's *salone*. In the little that remains of its historic streets, the town boasts an excellent museum, the **Museo delle Genti d'Abruzzo** at Via delle Caserme 22 (Mon–Sat 9am–4pm, Sun 9am–2pm, longer hours in summer; €5), dedicated to the life and popular traditions of the region. There's a run-down of local festivals tracing their pre-Christian roots, though perhaps the most enchanting room is one devoted to the nomadic shepherds, containing books of their poetry, carved objects and volumes of Ariosto's chivalric romance *Orlando Furioso*.

Admirers of Mussolini's poet and mentor, **Gabriele d'Annunzio** (see p.249), may want to visit his birthplace at Corso Manthonè 101 (daily 9am–1.30pm; €2), while devotees of Art Nouveau and later twentieth-century art should head for the **Museo e Pinacoteca Cascella** at Viale G. Marconi 45 (Mon, Wed & Fri–Sat 9am–1pm, Tues & Thurs 9am–1pm & 4–6pm; €2.50) home to five hundred lithographic prints, paintings, ceramics and sculptures, including a stunning set of portraits (mounted on dinner plates) by the prolific Cascella family who lived and worked here.

Practicalities

Pescara has two **train stations**, though unless you're leaving the country you only need to use one, Stazione Centrale, at Piazza della Repubblica (the other, Porta Nuova, is only for ferry connections). Conveniently, **buses** to Rome (quicker than the train) and Naples, as well as regional buses, leave from outside Stazione Centrale. Ryanair **flights** from London Stansted touch down at **Abruzzo Airport** (ⓦwww.abruzzo-airport.it), around 5km southwest of the city; from the airport, the #38 bus leaves for Piazza della Repubblica every ten minutes. The **tourist office** is on the first floor at Via Paolucci (June–Sept Mon–Sat 9am–1pm & 4–7pm, Sun 9am–1pm; Oct–May Mon–Fri 9am–1pm & 3–6pm, Sat 9am–1pm; ⓣ085.421.9981, ⓦwww.abruzzoturismo.it), close to the seafront.

Most **hotels** are on the beach front, north of the river and the old town. The *Alba*, Via M. Forti 14 (ⓣ085.389.145, ⓦwww.hotelalba.pescara.it ❷), is a fairly upmarket choice – the rooms here have a baroque touch that takes them beyond the average business hotel. The *Corso*, opposite the train station at Corso Vittorio Emanuele 292 (ⓣ085.422.4210; no credit cards; ❷), is the oldest hotel in Pescara, offering simple rooms with high ceilings, while the *Marisa*, Via Regina Margherita 39 (ⓣ & ⓕ085.273.45; ❷), is a friendly, family-run place two blocks in from the sea, and just a short walk from the train station. The nearest **campsites** are *Francavilla* (ⓣ085.810.715; June–Sept) and *Paola* (ⓣ085.817.525; June–Sept), 10km south of Pescara at Francavilla al Mare – buses #1 and #2 stop outside.

For meals and nightlife, head for the little that remains of the old town of Pescara near the river. Along Corso Manthonè and Via delle Caserme there are more than fifty **bars** and **restaurants**. Recommended is the *Cantina di Jozz* at Via delle Caserme 61 (ⓣ085.451.8800; closed all day Mon & Sun eve), which does great Abruzzese food such as *maialino arrosto* (roast suckling pig) for around €11. Otherwise, try the slow-food advocate *La Lumaca*, just down the road from the *Cantina* at no. 51 (ⓣ085.451.0880; evenings only; closed Tues) – one of their best dishes is *agnello porchettato* (lamb cooked like an aromatic hog roast) – or the 🍴 *Locanda Manthonè*, Corso Manthonè 58 (ⓣ085.454.9039; closed Sun), loved by the Pescarese for its reasonably priced quality food, such as slow-cooked lamb with saffron. A few doors away at no. 46 is the *Taverna 58* (ⓣ085.690.724; closed Sat lunch and Sun) where you can eat innovative dishes such as *baccala al cartoccio*, salt cod baked in a parcel with a sweet onion marmalade or a slow cooked lamb stew scented with mountain herbs.

Atri

The approach to **ATRI**, a slow-paced, pretty little town 30km north of Pescara, is like travelling through the background of a Renaissance painting, with gently undulating hills planted with orderly olive groves giving way to occasional sleek clay gullies known as *calanchi*, water-eroded into smooth ripples, wrinkles and folds. Atri's duomo contains Abruzzo's greatest cycle of frescoes, but it is currently undergoing restoration. Still, the town itself, with its narrow stepped and bridged streets, is one you're likely to be reluctant to leave.

Regular **buses** make the trip from Pescara and Téramo and drop you at the start of **Corso Elio Adriano**, the main thoroughfare, which leads up to the central piazza, dominated by the thirteenth-century **duomo**. Its facade is understated, pierced by a rose window and perforated by the holes in which scaffolding beams were slotted during construction. The inside is similarly simple, with patches of frescoes on the brick columns and – visible through glass set into the floor of the apse – an octagonal mosaic pavement decorated with sea horses, dolphins and fish, from the Roman baths over which the church was built. The duomo's highlight, however, is the cycle of **fifteenth-century frescoes** by Andrea Delitio on the apse walls. Delitio has been called the "Piero della Francesca" of Abruzzo for his sophisticated use of architecture and landscape; but in contrast to Piero's cool intellectualism and obscure symbolism, Delitio places the religious scenes in realistic contexts. *The Birth of Mary*, for example, has servants giving the newly born baby a bath; in the apse vault the four Evangelists are placed in natural settings, the animals that are the emblems of the saints behaving as domestic pets; and back on the walls, the lives of the rich – especially in the *Wedding at Cana* and *Presentation in the Temple* – contrast with the lives of the poor, notably Mary, Joseph and the shepherds in the *Nativity*. The most emotionally charged scene is the *Slaughter of the Innocents*, in which the horror is intensified by the refined Renaissance architectural setting and the fact that the massacre is coolly observed from a balcony by Herod's party of civic bigwigs.

For a touch of light relief, head back up the right-hand aisle to see a piece of Renaissance kitsch – a font with four oversized frogs clinging to the basin. The attached **museum** (daily except Wed: summer 10am–noon & 4–8pm; winter 10am–noon & 3–5pm; €2.58) reveals large, seventeenth-century majolica dishes and jugs, silverware and baptismal shells. It also lets you into the cloisters, the site of a cavernous Roman cistern. Concentrating on more recent history, the **Museo Civico Etnografico** (Tues–Sat: summer 10am–1pm & 5–8pm; winter 10am–1pm; €1.55), near the post office in Via S. Pietro, is good on old radiograms, prams, nineteenth-century costume and shoes, and has an intriguing 1950s machine for making liquorice. If you've had your fill of museums simply sit in a café and watch the small-town life around you, or head to the *Alla Corte* **restaurant** (☎085.870.305; closed Wed) where you can eat reasonably priced local dishes such as *spaghetti alla chitarra* with little meatballs.

Loreto Aprutino

One of the most important market towns in the region is **LORETO APRU-TINO**, a quiet hilltop settlement with medieval origins 24km inland from Pescara. The labyrinthine old town is home to a couple of **artisans' workshops**, open to the public (daily 4–7pm) and making knives, copper and iron pots and items in terracotta and decorated glass. There are also tiny *cantinas* in the old town selling **olive oil**, for which the area has been awarded a DOP (*denominazione di origine protetta*), the equivalent of the DOC designation for wine. Loreto heaves with people on **market day** (Thurs until 1pm) and in the evenings during the late-running *passeggiata*, when it's a pleasure to simply do nothing and soak up the atmosphere. If you want a focus for your wanderings, head just outside town to the fourteenth-century church of **Santa Maria in Piano** (daily 8am–noon & 3–7pm; free). It's noted for its series of **frescoes** in the right aisle, painted in diverse styles dating from the fourteenth to sixteenth centuries and celebrating the devotions of saints and apostles, including St Thomas of Aquinas, protector of the city. At the top of the old town, on the end of a row of nineteenth-century *palazzi*, stands the church of **San Pietro Apostolo**. The church dates from the fifteenth and sixteenth centuries, with a Renaissance doorway decorated with the coat of arms of the Borboni, who chose this as their castle abbey.

Practicalities

Regular **buses** make the trip from Pescara, dropping you near the **tourist office** at Via dei Normanni 8 (Tues–Sat 9am–1pm & 3.30–5.30pm, Sun 8.30am–12.30pm; ℡085.829.0213). There are plenty of decent **places to stay** in town. The ⚑ *Lauretum*, Via del Baio 3 (℡085.829.2000, ⓦwww.bedbreak fastlauretum.com ❷), is fantastic value for money, with accommodation in a family house near the Castello (see below). The huge frescoed rooms come with antique furniture and there's a dedicated billiards room too. Another nice B&B is the airy, centrally located *Loreblick*, Via Fiorano 42 (℡ & ℉085.829.0323, ⓦwww.bedandbreakfastloreblick.com ❷), which also has a good restaurant. Considerably grander is the stately *Castello Chiola* (℡085.829.0690, ⓦwww .castellochiola.com; ❺), occupying the ninth-century castle topping the town, where facilities include a swimming pool (open May–Sept) overlooking the countryside. Outside town at Contrada da Fiorano 83 is the agriturismo ⚑ *Le Magnolie* (℡085.828.9534, ⓦwww.lemagnolie.com; ❷), with tasteful rooms and apartments (and excellent home-cooked meals) on a farm growing olives, fruit, vegetables and cereal crops. It's on a minor road between the SS151 between Penne and Loreto Aprutino, and the SS81 between Penne and Pianella; look out for the signposts. For **food**, you can eat very well at hotel-restaurant *La Bilancia*, Contrada da Palazzo 11 (℡085.828.9321; closed Mon), or try the pub-restaurant *New Evo*, Via Pretara 9.

Chieti

Twenty minutes by train southwest of Pescara, the relaxed and appealing town of **CHIETI** is a more attractive place to stop over between trains. Spread over a curving ridge, the town offers great views of the Majella and Gran Sasso mountains and – when it's clear – out to sea. It also holds Abruzzo's best archeological museum by far.

If you arrive by bus you'll be dropped on Piazza Vittorio Emanuele alongside the chunky and much-reconstructed **cathedral**, from where the main **Corso Marrucini** cuts through the town centre to Piazza Trento e Trieste. Behind the post office, off Via Spaventa, are the remains of three little **Roman temples**. However, it's the **Museo Archeologico Nazionale di Abruzzo** (Tues–Sun 9am–8pm; €4) that is of most interest, beyond Piazza Trento e Trieste and laid out in the dignified Villa Comunale. It holds finds from Abruzzo's major sites: a massive and muscular white-marble Hercules from a temple at Alba Fucens and an elegant bone funeral bed from a tomb at Amiternum, near L'Aquila. There's also a striking bronze Hercules from a sanctuary outside Sulmona and the *Capestrano Warrior*, a statue of a Bronze Age warrior prince with strangely female thighs. It dates back to the time (sixth century BC) when a deified, hero-worshipped warrior leader was key to Bronze Age society. Statues like these in characteristic pose with the arms across the torso were set on the top of burial mounds to mark territory throughout the Adriatic and Central Europe and must have made an awesome feature on the landscape. Remains of the occupants of Bronze Age tombs are laid out in the adjacent rooms – the men buried with armour and weapons, the women with jewellery, kitchen utensils, spindles, and in one case even a nail-brush.

Further digs in Chieti have uncovered the core of **Teate** – the main town of the Marrucini, an Italic tribe – that became a Roman colony in the first century BC. The site lies on the edge of central Chieti at the **Civitella archeological park** (Tues–Sun 9am–8pm; €4) and includes the remains of temples, theatre, amphitheatre, thermal baths and a new museum.

Practicalities

The **train** drops you at Chieti Scalo, down in the valley, from where it's a short journey on bus #1 up the hill to Chieti proper, 5km away. **Buses** arrive at Piazza Vittorio Emanuele, alongside the cathedral. Chieti's **tourist office** is at Via Spaventa 29, just off Corso Marrucino (May–Sept Mon–Sat 9am–1pm & 4–7pm, Sun 9am–1pm; Oct–April Mon, Tues & Thurs 9am–1pm & 3–6pm, Wed & Fri 9am–1pm; ☎0871.63.640). For **accommodation**, try *Garibaldi*, Piazza Garibaldi 25 (☎ & ℻0871.345.318; ❷), which has affordable and central, if ordinary rooms. Otherwise, ⚲ *Il Quadrifoglio*, Strada Licini 22, Colle Marcone (☎0871.63.400, ⓦwww.agriturismoilquadrifoglio.com; ❷), is an excellent working farmhouse, 3km southwest of Chieti, with pleasant rooms, cookery courses and home-cooked food – for non-residents too. They can also pick up from the airport.

Very good-value **meals** can also be had in central Chieti at *Trattoria Nino*, Via Principessa di Piemonte 7 (☎0871.63.781; closed Fri), near Piazza Trento e Trieste, where the service is slow but the family atmosphere and regional specialities at around €7 compensate, and at *Primavera*, Viale B. Croce 69 (☎0871.560.157; closed Sun), in Chieti Scalo, the lower town, where you'll find good fish dishes for €10.

The southern Abruzzo coast

The coast south of Pescara is less developed than the northern stretch, though the long ribbon of sand continues, followed by the train line and punctuated with mostly small resorts. **ORTONA**, further along, is of most interest for its daily summer ferries to the Trémiti islands, its mainly reconstructed centre dominated by the shell of a castle and the massive dome of its cathedral.

Twenty kilometres south of Ortona lies the small and charming resort of **FOSSACÉSIA MARINA**, where there are only three **hotels** so it's advisable to book well ahead in summer; be prepared for compulsory half board in July and August. The *Levante* hotel is right on the beach (☎0872.60.169, ⓦwww.hotellevante.it; ❸), while 3km inland at Via S. Giovanni in Venere 40 is the *Golfo di Venere* (☎ & ℻0872.60.541, ⓦwww.golfodivenere.com; compulsory half board in August; ❷) and a **campsite**, *Valle di Venere* (☎0872.608.291; open all year). Another campsite, *La Foce* (☎0872.609.110; open all year), lies 4km up the coast next to the beach, just off the SS16 at the Km 484.3 mark, and is well equipped with shady pitches, bar and sailing and surfing facilities. On the way inland to Fossacesia itself is the creamy-gold Romanesque church of **San Giovanni in Venere** (Venere is Italian for Venus), which owes its name to the fact that it was built over a Roman temple dedicated to Venus the Conciliator and is visited by anyone seeking the return of peace within their family. The church, with its finely carved sandstone door and triple apse, is superbly sited among the undulating fields above the coast and is still a favourite outing for Abruzzese families – harmony now being found in a hearty meal in the restaurant outside the church. If you're visiting at the weekend or during holidays and want the church to yourself, aim to get there at lunchtime, while everyone else is safely ensconced behind plates of pasta.

Vasto

VASTO, further south and close to the border with Molise, is a fine old city, built on the site of the Roman town Histonium and overlooking the resort of **VASTO MARINA**. There are boats in the summer to the Trémiti islands, plenty of campsites, and a handful of reasonable hotels along the broad sandy **beach** – palm-lined and beach-hutted in the centre, wilder and rockier to the north (the free beach area is central).

Vasto is all about the beach, though if you're here for a day or so you should definitely get a bus from the train station on the seafront to the **upper town** (#4 or #1 for the Marina and Vasto Centro, roughly every 30min; 10min), whose rooftops and campaniles rise above palms and olive groves. The centre of town is **Piazza Rossetti**, its gardens dominated by the massive **Castello Calderesco**. The piazza is named after Gabriele Rossetti, a local eighteenth-century poet who is better known as the father of the Pre-Raphaelite poet Dante Gabriele Rossetti.

Just off the piazza, next to the small duomo, stands the Renaissance **Palazzo d'Avalos** and its enchanting Neapolitan garden, a courtyard affair with orange trees and pillars and gorgeous sea views. The Palazzo was once the home of the poet and friend of Michelangelo, Vittoria Colonna, who was famous in her time for the bleak sonnets she wrote after her husband's death; nowadays it houses the town **museum** (Tues–Sun: July & Aug 8am–midnight; Sept–June 9.30am–12.30pm & 4.30–8.30pm; €1.05 for the archeological museum, €3.65 for the art gallery, €1.05 for the costume museum, or €5.15 for the whole lot), a somewhat sparse collection of archeological objects and beautiful old clothes, as well as some paintings by the Palizzi brothers. The best of its exhibits are some bellicose second-century bronzes, a third-century warrior with an arm missing and a collection of Greek coins – evidence of Vasto's early importance as an international trading centre.

Piazza del Popolo opens onto a panoramic promenade that takes you to Vasto's most memorable sight, the door of the church of **San Pietro**, surrounded by Romanesque twists and zigzags, standing isolated against a backdrop of sky, sea and trees, the rest of the church having been destroyed in a landslide in 1956. Along the coast path to your left are the remains of some Roman baths, whose mosaics are covered with a makeshift tin roof.

Practicalities

The **tourist office** (mid-May to Sept Mon–Sat 9am–1pm & 4–7pm, Sun 9am–1pm; rest of year Mon–Sat 9am–1pm & 3–6pm, Sun 9am–1pm; ☎0873.367.312) is on Piazza del Popolo.

Pleasant as the upper town is, it doesn't offer much in the way of **accommodation**. A couple of places to try are *Palizzi*, a large two-star with all mod cons at Corso Mazzini 14 (☎0873.367.361, ⊛www.milanoanteprime.it; ❷), and *Dei Sette*, Via San Michele 66 (☎0873.362.819, ⊛www.hoteldei7.it; ❷), a basic, clean two-star which also has some apartments for hire, a ten-minute walk out of the centre past the stadium and the public gardens. Otherwise, most of the action is down by the beach **in Vasto Marina**; note that hotels insist on half board in July and August. The nicest place to stay hereabouts is the *Villa Vignola* (☎0873.310.050, ⊛www.villavignola.it; ❺), a small white villa outside town with a tiny pebble beach, a garden for lounging in and a romantic terrace restaurant serving such delicacies as stuffed baby squid (at least €45 a head). If your budget won't stretch that far, *La Bitta*, Lungomare Cordella 18 (☎ & ⊠0873.801.979; no credit cards; ❷), is a spacious and welcoming hotel (open April–Sept) close to the free beach, with good home cooking. There are also numerous **campsites** along the coast. Most of them are off the SS16 towards Fóggia. *Il Piopetto* is right on the beach and has pine trees for shade (☎0873.801.466, ⊛www.ilpiopetti.it; mid-May to mid-Sept).

For **eating and drinking**, there are loads of pizzerias and pubs in Vasto Marina, although you might prefer to consider splashing out at *Villa Vignola* (see above).

Isernia and around

ISERNIA, inland from Vasto, is a useful entry point into western Molise, with good train connections from Rome and Naples. It was severely damaged for the eighth time by an earthquake in 1984, but after a slow recovery it has rebuilt its commercial centre so that it's now comparatively busy and bustling. Historically the city hasn't had much luck: much of the centre was destroyed in a bombing raid on September 10, 1943, and a monument to the four thousand who were killed – an anguished nude ankle-deep in fractured tiles, bricks and gutters – is the centrepiece of the square called, understandably, Piazza X Settembre.

Given its past, it's not surprising that little of old Isernia survives. The city's main attraction is the **Museo Nazionale Santa Maria delle Monache** (daily except first and third Mon of the month 8.30am–7pm; €2), in the heart of the old town at Piazza Santa Maria 8. In 1979 local road-builders unearthed traces of a Palaeolithic settlement at least 700,000 years old – the most ancient signs of human life yet found in Europe. The exhibits are backed up by a video in English, which reconstructs the settlement and puts the ancient civilization in context. Contrary to the misleading publicity, there were no human remains found, just weapons, traps, traces of pigment thought to have been used as body paint, and animal bones, laid out to create a solid platform on the marshy land for the village.

The rest of Isernia, though unbeguiling in itself, can be a good starting-point for exploring the rest of Molise: **buses** to local villages leave from Via XXIV Maggio, parallel with the main street, Corso Garibaldi, and longer-distance buses, including those to Rome and Naples, from outside the **train station**. The **tourist office** is at Via Farinacci 1 (Mon–Sat 8am–2pm; ☎0865.3992). You probably won't need **to stay** over, but if you do, head for *Sayonara*, a swish modern three-star at Via G. Berti 131 (☎0865.50.992, ⓦwww.sayonara.is.it; ❷) and the only central hotel. As for **eating**, try *Ristorante Paradiso*, near the cathedral on Piazza Mercato (☎0865.414.847), where you can eat good, cheap, honest local fare such as *tagliatelle ai fagioli* (tagliatelle with beans).

Around Isernia

The countryside **around Isernia** is lush and gentle, and at its best in spring, when the meadows are sprinkled with wild flowers. The valleys are headed by hill-villages, most of them run-down places ringed with new housing estates, and the rewards of exploring are principally those of being the first foreigner to have visited in ages. Getting around, though, isn't easy. Buses are often organized around the school day, which means you'll have to leave either very early in the morning or at around 2pm – after that there may be no other bus until the next day, so having your own transport is a distinct advantage.

Just outside the village of **PIETRABBONDANTE**, 25km northeast of Isernia, are the remains of a pre-Roman Samnite village, notably a well-preserved theatre (Mon–Sat 8.30am until 1hr before dusk; €2) set in a green field at the foot of Monte Caraceno. Further along the road, **AGNONE** is best known for having produced church bells for over a thousand years. The **Marinelli Pontifical Foundry** still makes bells in the traditional way, using a priest to bless the molten bronze as it's poured into the mould, which supposedly ensures that the bell's tones will be pure. A small **museum** can be visited (booking essential ☎0865.78235; guided tours Mon–Sat noon–4pm; €4.50). Agnone is also famous for its coppersmiths, most of whom work on the main street.

To the west of Isernia, the bus calls at **Cerro al Volturno**, crowned by one of Molise's more spectacular castles, almost growing out of the grey rock on which it is perched. A few kilometres further on is **CASTEL SAN VINCENZO**, another pretty-from-a-distance hill-village: get off the bus below the village at the Cartiera (paper mill) and walk along the road to the left for about 1km, until you come to the abbey of **San Vincenzo al Volturno** (☎0865.955.246, ⒲www .sanvincenzoabbey.org) – a much-reconstructed complex now run by American nuns, with a crypt covered by a complete cycle of ninth-century frescoes in rich Byzantine colours, the only surviving example of ninth-century Benedictine art. Unfortunately the frescoes are not generally open to the public; to see them you need to contact the abbey well in advance to make an appointment. At the **zona archeologico** nearby are the remains of a seventh-century monastery (call ☎0865.951.006 or 338.174.2486 for access; guided tours only €2.50).

About 20km to the south, but most easily accessible by train from Isernia, is the village of **VENAFRO**, topped by a derelict castle and with a Roman amphitheatre (just by the railway station) that was converted into an oval piazza in the Middle Ages. Most of the local finds are on display in the **Museo Archeologico Santa Chiara** (Tues–Sat 9am–7pm; €2) on Via Garibaldi.

Campobasso, Saepinum and the Matese mountains

Home of a top-security prison and the National Carabinieri School, **CAMPO-BASSO**, Molise's regional capital, is about as appealing as you'd expect – a modern, rather faceless town that was once known for its cutlery industry. It's a good base, though, for the remarkable ruins at **Saepinum**, and if you're around in early June, don't miss the town's spectacular Corpus Christi *Sagra dei Misteri* **procession**, in which citizens are dressed as saints, angels and devils, inserted into fantastic contraptions and transported, seemingly suspended in mid-air, through the streets.

At any other time of the year the most notable attraction is the **Samnite Museum** (daily 8.30am–6pm; free) at Via Chiarizia 12, with statues and a scattering of archeological finds from the area, most notably the haunting contents of a Longobard tomb, a warrior buried alongside his horse. Steep alleys of the small, old **upper town** lead up to a couple of Romanesque churches – **San Bartolomeo**, which has eerily contorted figures carved around its main door, and **San Giorgio**, whose entrance displays a dragon surrounded by stylized flowers. There's little point in carrying on up the hill to the monastery and sixteenth-century castle: the monastery is modern, and the castle now a weather station. The **tourist office** (Mon–Sat 8am–2pm; ☎0874.415.662) at Piazza Vittoria 14 in the new town has details of local events and bus routes to elsewhere in the province.

Until recently Campobasso had just a few old-fashioned, down-at-heel business **hotels**, but two huge and characterful four-stars have recently opened: *San Giorgio*, Via Insorti d'Ungheria (☎0874.493.620, ⒲www.hotelsangiorgio.org; ⑤), a Renaissance-style place that's beautifully furnished and has a welcoming lounge and bar; and the similar *Rinascimento*, Via Labanca (☎0874.481.455,

@grandhotelrinascimento@virgilio.it; ❸). Other options include the *Tricolore* (⊕0874.63.190, Ⓦwww.hoteltricolore.it; ❷), an old-fashioned two-star on the road to Térmoli, with all en-suite rooms.

As a business city it's not surprising that there are some excellent places **to eat**. Among them, *Trattoria La Grotta* (also known as *Zia Concetta*), Via Larino 7 (⊕0874.311.378, closed Sat & Sun), does a set menu of solid home cooking for around €20, and if you're lucky you'll get some of the family's home-produced salami. Otherwise, *Miseria e Nobiltà'*, Viale del Castello 16–18 (⊕0874.94.268; closed Sun), does excellent, innovative local fare.

Saepinum

It's **SAEPINUM**, a ruined **Roman town** to the south, close to the border with Puglia, that makes the stopover in Campobasso worthwhile. Three kilometres from the nearest village and surrounded by a lush plain fringed with the foothills of the Matese mountains, it's the best example in Italy of a provincial Roman town.

The main reason Saepinum is so intact is that it was never very important: nothing much happened here, and after the fall of the Roman Empire it carried on as the sleepy backwater it had always been – until the ninth century when it was sacked by Saracens. Over the centuries its inhabitants added only a handful of farms and cottages, incorporating the odd Roman column, and eventually moved south to the more secure hilltop site of present-day Sepino. Some have now moved back and rebuilt the farms and cottages on Saepinum's peripheries, contributing if anything to the site's appeal. Their sheep graze below an ancient mausoleum, chickens scratch around the walls, and the only sounds are the tinkling of cowbells.

Saepinum is accessible by **bus** from Campobasso – either catch one of the two services that stop at Altilia (right outside the site) which leave the Campo Sportivo daily except Sunday at 7.50am and 1pm, or get a bus to **Sepino** (10 daily except Sun; to check schedules call ⊕0874.64.744) and walk the remaining 3km to Saepinum. Buses return to Campobasso from the archeological site at 8.15am and 1.35pm. By road, look for signs to Sepino. There's **information** and a good **restaurant** at the Centro Turistico Il Grifo, though be prepared for large school parties. There are also two bar-restaurants at the Porta Boiano and the Porta Tammaro (see below).

The site

Depending on whether you arrive by bus or by car, the entrance to Saepinum (always open; free) is through the **Porta Terravecchia** or the **Porta Tammaro**, two of the town's four gates. The site is bisected by the *cardo maximus* (main road), still paved with the original stones and crossed by the *decumanus maximus* (the other main road in Roman towns), centre of town and home to the public buildings and trading quarters. On the left, grass spills through the cracks in the pavement of the **forum**, now used by the few local kids as a football pitch, bordered by the foundations of various municipal buildings: the *comitium* (assembly place), the *curia* (senate house), a temple, baths, and in the centre a fountain with a relief of a griffin. Beyond the forum, on the left of the *decumanus*, the **Casa Impluvio Sannitico** contains a vat to collect rainwater, a remnant from the Samnite town that stood on the site before the Romans sacked it in 293 BC. Until quite recently the village was passed through, as it had been for over two thousand years, by nomadic shepherds, moving their flocks between their winter grazing lands in the south and summer pastures in Abruzzo. The *trattura*, as it's called, still takes place, but in much reduced form by lorry and motorway. Further along the road is what must have been a welcome, if bizarre, landmark for generations of shepherds – an enormous stone cylinder resembling a modern water tower that is in fact the mausoleum of one of Saepinum's Roman citizens.

Back down the *decumanus* on the other side of the crossroads is the well-preserved **basilica** that served as the main courthouse. Beyond is the most interesting part of the town – the octagonal *macellum* (marketplace), with its small stone stalls and central rain-collecting dish, and a series of houses fronted by workshops, with the small living quarters behind. This leads down to the best-preserved gate, the **Porta Boiano**, flanked by cylindrical towers with a relief showing two barbarians and chained prisoners.

The Matese mountains

One of Italy's least visited mountain ranges, scattered with high plains, forests and lakes, the **Matese** stretches between Molise and Campania. Wolves still wander its woods, and the peaks are home to eagles, falcons and hawks, while the streams are well stocked with fish and the valleys full of the much-coveted porcini mushrooms.

Trains running between Isernia and Campobasso stop at **BOIANO**, a pleasant town overlooked by a densely wooded hill crowned with the remains of a castle. If you want to stay, try the *Hotel Mary* at Via Barcellona 21 (T & F0874.778.375; **❶**), a central hotel where all rooms are en suite and have TV. The town is a handy starting-point for the hike up **Monte Gallinola** (1923m; around 2hr) – best done on a clear day when the views take in Italy's eastern and western coastlines. The road leads from beyond the central Piazza Pasquino up to a *rifugio*; from here a steep road, later a footpath, climbs through forest to the Costa Alta, a mile-high pass whose views are good – though nothing compared to what you'll see when you get to the summit. The path then leads across ski-slopes to the base of Monte Gallinola, where a track heads up to the top, from which you look down over the Lago del Matese, and, if weather permits, get the much-touted panoramic view.

You can see something of the Matese in more comfort by taking a bus to the winter-sports centre of **CAMPITELLO MATESE** from either Boiano or Campobasso; or by staying over at the *Matese* (T0874.780.378, Wwww.hotel matese.it; **❷**), 9km from Campitello Matese at **SAN MASSIMO**, northwest of Boiano. From Boiano, take the road marked Castellone and San Massimo, and, coming down from the mountains, take the left branch when the road forks.

Towards the coast: Larino and the Albanian villages

Halfway between Campobasso and Térmoli, **LARINO** is considerably more attractive than most Molise towns, its medieval centre clasped in a valley, relatively untouched by the concrete and pace of the modern industrial town that supports it. The highlight is its cathedral, but there are also some minor Roman relics in its small museum and a neglected amphitheatre in the modern town.

To the left of the **train station**, Via Gramsci leads down to **old Larino**. The main street widens out at Piazza Vittorio Emanuele, backing onto which is the **Palazzo Ducale**, whose **museum** (closed for restoration until late 2007) contains large Roman mosaics and a hoard of coins. On Via Gramsci, about halfway between the station and the *centro storico*, there's a garden that also has **Roman ruins**, including capitals and columns, and a sacrificial altar called the Ara Frentana. Close by is the **duomo**, a lovely building with an intricately carved Gothic portal built in the early fourteenth century just after the town had been flattened by an earthquake and sacked by the Saracens.

The oldest part of the town starts beyond the duomo, but, appealing as the houses and steep alleys are, it is the glimpses of centuries-old streetlife that are more memorable – women making lace and preparing vegetables outside their houses, while the kids play at their feet.

If you take a bus from Piazza Vittorio Emanuele to the upper city, you'll jump a couple of centuries in five minutes. **Modern Larino** is a bustling place, built on the site of the original Samnite/Roman town. The large and overgrown **amphitheatre** off Via Viadotto Frentano is visible from the street (free access) and gives some idea of the importance of early second-century BC Larinum. If you want to **stay**, your only choice is the *Park Hotel Campitelli 2* (℡0874.823.541, ⓦwww.parkhotelcampitelli.it; ❷) at Via San Benedetto 1, an air-conditioned four-star, about 1km from the station.

The Albanian villages

URURI, 12km from Larino, and **PORTOCANNONE**, closer to the coast, are isolated villages, most easily reached by bus from Térmoli. Their isolation is such that, six hundred years after their ancestors emigrated from Albania, the locals still speak an Albanian-Italian dialect incomprehensible to outsiders. Portocannone's Romanesque church contains an icon of the Madonna of Constantinople, brought over by the original émigrés, and in Ururi, at the beginning of May, a **festival** is staged: a fierce and furious race through the village streets on gladiator-style carts, pulled by bulls and pushed by men on horseback with spiked poles. It's a ruthless business: the horses are fed beer before the race to excite them, and although the riders are supposed to push only the back of the carts, they are not averse to prodding the flanks of the bulls, who have already been given electric shocks to liven them up. The race itself is terrifying, but unforgettable, with bulls, carts and spikes hurtling past the frenzied crowds, nowadays protected by wire fences. There are almost inevitably injuries, and at least one person has been killed. If you want to go, the tourist offices at Campobasso and Térmoli will have the precise date.

The Molise coast

The brief stretch of the **Molise coast** is less developed than Abruzzo's and its only real town, **TÉRMOLI**, a fishing port and quiet, undistinguished resort, makes for a relaxing place to spend a day. The beach is long and sandy and the old town, walled and guarded by a castle, has an interesting cathedral. It's also a departure point for ferries to the Trémiti islands (see p.962).

Térmoli is the place where Italian and Central European time is set – from the observatory inside the stark castle built above the beach in 1247 by Frederick II. Beyond the castle the road follows the old walls around the headland, holding what's left of the old town, focus of which is the **duomo**. This is most notable for its Romanesque exterior, decorated all the way round with a series of blind arcades and windows – a feature introduced by Frederick II's Norman-influenced architects. Inside are the relics of St Timothy, best known for the letters he received from St Paul, who advised him on how to go about converting the Greeks. That he ended up in Térmoli is thanks to Termolese Crusaders, who brought his bones back from Constantinople as a souvenir. The Termolese hid them, fearing that if the Turks ever succeeded in penetrating the city they would seize and destroy them. In fact the relics were hidden so well they weren't discovered until 1945, during restoration work to repair bomb damage (the sacristan will show you them).

Practicalities

Long-distance **buses** pull up in Via Martiri della Resistenza, 1km from Térmoli's centre and the **train station**. The **tourist office** (Mon–Fri 8am–2pm & 5–6.30pm, Sat 8am–12.30pm, longer hours in summer; ℡0875.706.754) on Piazza M. Bega is difficult to find, tucked into a grotty car park behind a Benetton shop and opposite the local bus station. There's a second office open (usually just in the evening) in summer run by the *Comune* in Piazza Duomo in the old town, which promotes local crafts and Molise in general.

Central **accommodation** includes *Rosary*, Lungomare Corso Colombo 24 (℡0875.84.944, ℻0875.84.947; ➋), 200m from the train station, with plenty of rooms and balconies facing the beach, and *Corona*, (℡0875.84.041, ℻0875.84.043; ➌), a spacious but pricey place, opposite the station. The cheapest hotel is *Al Caminetto*, Via Europa 2 (℡ & ℻0875.52.139; no credit cards; half board compulsory in July & Aug; ➋), 4km from the town centre off the SS16 in Villaggio Airone and served in high season by rare buses from the station. On the same bus route are two **campsites**: *Campeggio Cala Saracena* (℡0875.52.193; June to mid-Sept), with a private beach, bar and small supermarket, and *Campeggio Azzurra* (℡0875.52.404; June–Sept), near Cala Saracena, by a free beach, with bar, restaurant and mini-market.

While here you should certainly have a meal in one of Térmoli's seafood **restaurants**. Of these, *Z'Bass* on Via Oberdan 8 (℡0875.706.703; closed Mon) does excellent, reasonably priced fresh fish – leave room for their home-made *pasticceria secca* (sweet pastries) and fruit served on ice. There are plenty of pizzerias and simple trattorias along Via Fratelli Brigada, the seafront and the parallel Via V. Emanuele III; later on try the wine bar *Spirito di Vino* on Largo Pie di Castello 27.

Travel details

Trains	Buses
Campobasso to: Térmoli (8 daily; 1hr 45min).	**Atri** to: Pescara (10 daily; 1hr).
Isernia to: Campobasso (10 daily; 1hr).	**Avezzano** to: Alba Fucens (3 daily; 30min);
L'Aquila to: Sulmona (10 daily; 1hr); Terni	Pescasseroli (8 daily; 1hr 30min).
(10 daily; 2hr).	**Chieti** to: Rome (8 daily; 2hr 30min).
Pescara to: Ancona (25 daily; 1hr 30min–2hr);	**Isernia** to: Campobasso (4–5 daily; 45min).
Rome (6 daily; 3hr 30min); Sulmona (18 daily;	**L'Aquila** to: Bominaco (4 daily; 1hr); Rome
1hr–1hr 20min); Térmoli (hourly; 1hr); Vasto	(20 daily; 1hr 40min); Sulmona (7 daily; 1hr
(10 daily; 55min).	30min); Téramo (6 daily; 1hr 20min).
Sulmona to: Avezzano (10 daily; 1hr 15min);	**Pescara** to: Áscoli Piceno (7 daily; 3hr); Atri
Celano (9 daily; 1hr); L'Aquila (11 daily; 1hr).	(10 daily; 1hr); Chieti (every 20min; 40min);
Térmoli to: Fóggia (11 daily; 1hr).	L'Aquila (9 daily; 1hr 50min); Loreto Aprutino

(6 daily; 45min); Rome (9 daily; 3–4hr); Sulmona (4 daily; 1hr 30min).

Sulmona to: Cocullo (1 daily; 45min); Scanno (7 daily; 1hr).

Téramo to: Atri (3 daily; 1hr 10min).

Térmoli to: Campobasso (hourly; 1hr 10min); Pescara (3 daily; 2hr 20min).

Ferries

Pescara to: Bol and Stari Grad (1 weekly; 4hr 40min & 5hr 30min); Hvar, Bol and Stari Grad (1 weekly; 4hr 15min, 5hr 15min & 6hr); Spalato and Stari Grad (1 weekly; 4hr 30min & 5hr 45min); Vela Luka and Stari Grad (2 weekly; 4hr 30min & 6hr 15min).

Ortona via Vasto to: Trémiti islands (1 daily; 2hr).

Térmoli to: Trémiti islands (2 ferries & 3 hydrofoils daily summer, 1 ferry daily in winter; 40min–1hr 40min).

Vasto to: Stari Grad (1 weekly; 4hr).

Campania

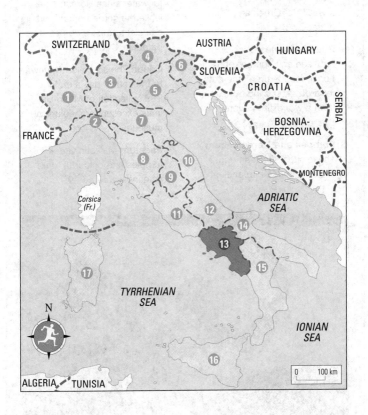

CHAPTER 13

Highlights

* **Miracle of San Gennaro**
The liquefaction of the saint's blood in Naples' cathedral is an occasion charged with emotion and accompanied by much festivity. See p.893

* **Museo Archeologico Nazionale** A superb museum with a wealth of Greek and Roman artifacts. See p.899

* **Pizza in Naples** Choose between any number of traditional, family-run restaurants for a pizza, sizzling hot straight from a wood-fired oven. See p.903

* **Pompeii and Herculaneum** These sites afford an unparalleled glimpse into ancient Roman daily life and architecture. See p.912 & p.909

* **Cápri** A jewel of an island with stunning scenery and cliff walks. See p.919

* **Ischia** The island's spa baths have been providing healthful water since Roman times, while the garden of La Mortella can claim to be a corner of paradise. See p.924

* **Cápua** The so-called "gateway to the south" has a matchless collection of Madri Dei in its excellent archeological museum. See p.930

* **Paestum** Majestic Greek temples and colourful tomb paintings. See p.940

△ Engraving at Paestum

Campania

The region immediately south of Lazio, **Campania**, marks the real beginning of the Italian south or *mezzogiorno*. It's the part of the south too, perhaps inevitably, that most people see, as it's easily accessible from Rome and home to some of the area's (indeed Italy's) most notable features – Roman sites, spectacular stretches of coast, tiny islands. It's always been a sought-after region, first named by the Romans, who tagged it the

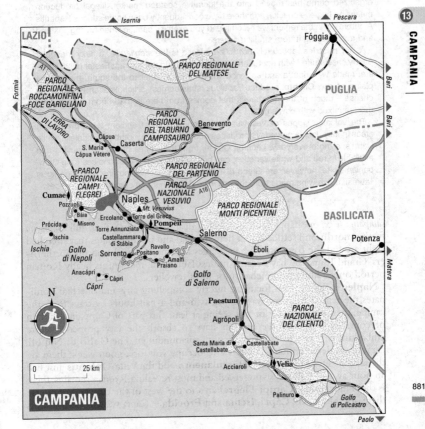

CAMPANIA

The flavour of Naples dominates the whole of Campania. Nowhere else in Italy is street food so much part of the culture. Most importantly, perhaps, Naples is the true home of the pizza, rapidly baked in searingly hot wood-fired ovens and running with olive oil. There's no such thing as "Pizza Napoletana" here; in Naples, the crucial one is the marinara – not, as you might think, anything to do with seafood, but the basic Neapolitan pizza, topped with just tomato, garlic and a leaf or two of basil, no cheese. Street food also comprises fried pizzas – *pizzette* – topped with a smear of tomato and a square of mozzarella, and calzone, a stuffed fried pizza with ham and cheese or vegetables. *Friggitorie* sell other fried food: heavenly *krocche* (potato croquettes), *arancini* (rice balls) and *fiorilli* (courgette flowers in batter).

Naples is also the home of pasta and tomato sauce, made with fresh tomatoes and basil, and laced with garlic; it's a curious aspect of Neapolitan sauces that garlic, onion and parmesan are rarely combined. Aubergines and courgettes turn up endlessly in **pasta sauces**, as does the tomato-**mozzarella** pairing (the regions to the north and east of Naples are both big mozzarella-producing regions), the latter particularly good with *gnocchi*. **Seafood** is excellent all along the coast: clams combine with garlic and oil for superb *spaghetti alle vongole*; mussels are prepared as *zuppa di cozze* (with hot pepper sauce); fresh squid and octopus are ubiquitous. A word of warning though: after police cracked down on illegally imported cigarettes, organized crime has moved into the lucrative seafood market. Illegal production means no hygiene checks, and there have consequently been some serious Hepatitis A outbreaks in the region; we recommend you exercise caution when buying seafood and avoid buying it from strolling sellers.

As for **pastries**, absolutely not to be missed is the *sfogliatella*, a flaky triangular pastry case stuffed with ricotta and candied peel, and the fragrant Easter cake, *pastiera*, made with ricotta and softened wheat grain. Further to the south, the marshy plains of the **Cilento** produce fabulous strawberries, artichokes and mozzarella cheese – much of the mozzarella that comes from here is made from pure buffalo milk, unmixed with cow's milk.

The volcanic slopes of Vesuvius are among the most ancient **wine-producing** areas in Italy: Ischia nowadays produces good **white** wine, notably Biancolella, while Cápri's is more everyday. Lacrima Christi, from the slopes of Mount Vesuvius and available in red and white varieties, can be reasonable. The best choices for a Campanian white, however, are Greco di Tufo and Fiano di Avellino; the **red** to go for is Taurasi, a rich wine made from the *aglianico* grape that can command high prices.

campania felix, or "happy land" (to distinguish it from the rather dull *campagna* further north), and settled down here in villas and palatial estates that stretched right around the bay. Later, when Naples became the final stop on northerners' Grand Tours, the bay became no less fabled, the relics of its heady Roman period only adding to the charm for most travellers.

Naples is the obvious focus, an utterly compelling city and one that dominates the region in every way. At just two-and-a-half hours by train from the capital, there's no excuse for not seeing at least this part of Campania, though of course you need three or four days to absorb the city properly, before embarking on the remarkable attractions surrounding it. The **Golfo di Napoli**, certainly, is dense enough in interest to occupy you for a good week: there are the ancient sites of **Pompeii**, **Herculaneum** and the **Villa Oplontis**, just half an hour away – Italy's best-preserved and most revealing Roman remains; there is the odd, volcanic **Campi Flegrei** area to the west of the city; and of course there are the islands, **Cápri**, **Ischia** and **Prócida** – Cápri swarms with visitors but is so beautiful that a day here is by no means time squandered, while Ischia, which is the largest island and absorbs tourists more readily, is a lively and attractive world in which to while away an entire holiday.

Inland Campania is, by contrast, a poor, unknown region for the most part, though the towns of **Cápua** and **Benevento**, an old stop on the Roman route to Brindisi, repay a visit. The area **south of Naples**, however, has more immediate appeal. **Sorrento**, at the far east end of the bay, is a major package-holiday destination but a cheery and likeable place for all that; and the **Amalfi coast**, across the peninsula, is probably Europe's most dramatic stretch of coastline, harbouring some fantastically enticing – if exclusive – beach resorts. Further south, the lively port of **Salerno** gives access to the Hellenistic site of **Paestum** and the uncrowded coastline of the **Cilento** just beyond.

Naples

Whatever your real interest in Campania, the chances are that you'll wind up in **NAPLES** – capital of the region and, indeed, of the whole Italian south. It's the kind of city that is laden with visitors' preconceptions, and it rarely disappoints: it is filthy, it is very large and overbearing, it is crime-infested, and it is most definitely like nowhere else in Italy – something the inhabitants will be keener than anyone to tell you. In all these things lies the city's charm. Perhaps the feeling that you're somewhere unique makes it possible to endure the noise and harassment, perhaps it's the feeling that in less than three hours you've travelled from an ordinary part of Europe to somewhere akin to an Arab bazaar. One thing, though, is certain: a couple of days here and you're likely to be as staunch a defender of the place as its most devoted inhabitants. Few cities on earth inspire such fierce loyalties.

In Naples, all the pride and resentment of the Italian south, all the historical differences between the two wildly disparate halves of Italy, are sharply brought into focus. This is the true heart of the *mezzogiorno*, a lawless, petulant city that has its own way of doing things. It's a city of extremes, fiercely Catholic, its streets punctuated by bright neon Madonnas cut into niches, its miraculous cults regulating the lives of the people much as they have always done. Football, too, is something of a religion here, though support is not as fanatical as it used to be since the demise of the club from Italy's *serie* A to C1 status after going bankrupt. Now renamed Napoli Soccer and under the ownership of movie mogul Aurelio De Laurentiis, the team's ongoing ambition is to get into *serie* B as soon as possible.

Music, also, has played a key part in the city's identity: there's long been a Naples style, bound up with the city's strange, harsh dialect – and, to some extent, the long-established presence of the US military: American jazz lent a flavour to Neapolitan traditional songs in the 1950s, and the 1970s saw one of Italy's most concentrated musical movements in the urban blues scene of Pino Daniele and the music around the radical Alfa Romeo factory out at Pomigliano. In the 1990s came Neapolitan rap, a fusion of traditional Neapolitan sounds and African and American influences, with groups such as Almamagretta, Bisca and 99 Posse using their music to comment on the state of Naples and Italian society in general. More recently an offshoot of the workers' groups at the Alfa Romeo factory, Spaccanapoli, had a hit album, *Aneme Perze* (*Lost Souls*), which combines serious social critique with modern dance music and traditional Neapolitan forms.

△ View of Naples bay, from Castel Sant'Elmo

Some history

There was a settlement here, **Parthenope**, as early as the ninth century BC, but it was superseded by a colony formed by the Greek settlers at nearby Cumae, who established an outpost here in 750 BC, giving it the name Neapolis. It prospered during Greek and later Roman times, escaping the disasters that befell the cities around and eventually declaring itself independent in 763 – which it remained for close on 400 years, until the **Normans** took the city in 1139. The Normans weren't here for long: like the rest of this region, the city soon came under the rule of the Hohenstaufen dynasty, who stayed rather half-heartedly until 1269, when their last king, Conradin, was beheaded in what's now Piazza del Mercato, and the **Angevins** took over the city. With one exception – Robert the Wise, who was a gentle and enlightened ruler and made the city a great centre for the arts – the Angevin kings ruled badly, in the end losing Naples to Alfonso I of Aragon in 1422, thus establishing a **Spanish** connection for the city for the next 300 years. Following the War of the Spanish Succession, Naples was briefly ceded to the Austrians, before being taken, to general rejoicing, by **Charles of Bourbon** in 1734. Charles was a cultivated and judicious monarch, but his dissolute son Ferdinand presided over a shambolic period in the city's history, abandoning it to the republican French. Their "Parthenopean Republic" here was short-lived, and the British reinstalled the Bourbon monarch, carrying out vicious reprisals against the rebels. The instigator of these reprisals was Admiral Nelson – fresh from his victory at the Battle of the Nile – who was famously having an affair with Lady Hamilton, the wife of the British ambassador to Naples. Under continuing Bourbon rule, or more accurately misrule, the city became one of the most populated in Europe, and one of the most iniquitous, setting a trend which still holds good today. For the rest of Europe, Naples was the requisite final stop on the **Grand Tour**, a position it enjoyed not so much for its proximity to the major classical sites as for the ready availability of sex. The city was for a long time the prostitution capital of the Continent, and its reputation drew people from far and wide, giving new meaning (in the days when syphilis was rife) to the phrase "see Naples and die".

More recently, Naples and its surrounding area have been the recipient of much of the money that has poured into the south under the **Cassa per il Mezzogiorno** scheme, and its industry is spreading, if not exactly booming. But the real power in the area is still in the hands of organized crime or the **Camorra**: much of the coastline west of the city – to Bagnoli – was built by Camorra money, and, although it's not at all publicized, little happens that matters here without the nod of the larger families. Not surprisingly, much government money has found its way into their hands too, with the result that there's been little real improvement in the living standards of the average Neapolitan: a very high percentage remain unemployed, and a disgraceful number still inhabit the typically Neapolitan one-room *bassi* – slums really, letting in no light and housing many in appallingly overcrowded conditions, particularly in the Quartieri Spagnoli area, widely held to be the most dangerous part of town. In the late 1970s there was a cholera outbreak in part of the city, and until recently it was thought that the same thing could happen again. However, **Antonio Bassolino**, mayor of the city from 1993 until 2000 and currently president of Campania, has done much to promote Naples and its attractions. Bassolino feels confident that supporting Naples' cultural strengths will continue to boost local pride. Scores of neglected churches, museums and palaces were restored and are now open for visits, at least occasionally, but in some cases only in the month of May, during a festival called Maggio dei Monumenti, or during the annual autumnal Notte Bianco (White Night), when the city parties all night long. There's been a burst of creative activity from local filmmakers, songwriters, artists and playwrights, and saying that you are from Naples gives you instant credibility in the rest of Italy.

From time to time, however, Mafia violence raises its ugly head, as in 2000 when an alliance between the Camorra families concocted by godmother Maria Licciardi, known as "La Madrina", resulted in the death of sixty people in a series of tit-for-tat killings. Licciardi was arrested in June 2001, since when violent activity has quietened down.

Arrival, information and city transport

Naples' Capodichino **airport** (℡081.789.6259, ⓦ www.gesac.it) is around 7km north of the city centre. It is connected with Piazza Garibaldi (the stop

13

CAMPANIA | Naples

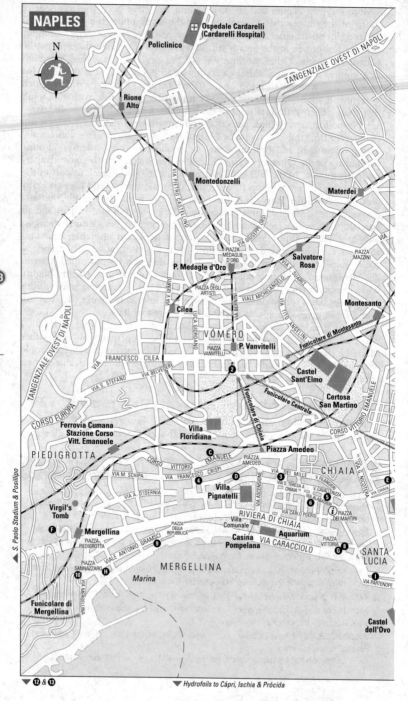

N

Ospedale Cardarelli
(Cardarelli Hospital)

Policlinico

TANGENZIALE OVEST DI NAPOLI

Rione
Alto

Montedonzelli

Materdei

VIA PIETRO CASTELLINO

VIA GIUSEPPE ORSI

PIAZZA
MAZZINI

VIA

PIAZZA
MEDAGLIE
D'ORO

Salvatore
Rosa

P. Medaglie d'Oro

VIA S. SUAREZ

VIA A. SUAREZ

PIAZZA DEGLI
ARTISTI

VIALE MICHELANGELO

Montesanto

VIA V. GEMITO

Cilea

LUCA GIORDANO

VIA BERNINI

VIA TITO ANGELINI

Funicolare di Montesanto

VOMERO

FRANCESCO CILEA

PIAZZA
VANVITELLI

P. Vanvitelli

Castel
Sant'Elmo

CORSO VITTORIO EMANUELE

VIA S. STEFANO

VIA BELVEDERE

Funicolare di Chiaia

Funicolare Centrale

Certosa
San Martino

CORSO EUROPA

Ferrovia Cumana
Stazione Corso
Vitt. Emanuele

Villa
Floridiana

Piazza Amedeo

CORSO VITTORIO EMANUELE

PIEDIGROTTA

CORSO   VITTORIO   EMANUELE

C

PIAZZA
AMEDEO

VIA DEI MILLE

V. FILANGIERI

CHIAIA

VIA G. NICOTERA

VIA M. SCHIPA

VIA FRANCESCO CRISPI

VIA S. TERESA A
CHIAIA

V. CAVALLERIZZA

VIA CHIAIA

E

VIA A. D'ISERNIA

Villa
Pignatelli

4   D

VIA ASCENSIONE

3   VIA ALABARDIERI

5

6   i

PIAZZA
DEI MARTIRI

Virgil's
Tomb

F

VIA CARLO POERIO

RIVIERA DI CHIAIA

Mergellina

Villa
Comunale

Aquarium

PIAZZA
DELLA
REPUBBLICA

9

PIAZZA
PIEDIGROTTA

VIALE ANTONIO GRAMSCI

Casina
Pompeiana

VIA CARACCIOLO

PIAZZA
VITTORIA

G   8

SANTA
LUCIA

PIAZZA
SANNAZZARO

H

MERGELLINA

Marina

VIA PARTENOPE

I

10

VIA MERGELLINA

Funicolare di
Mergellina

Castel
dell'Ovo

12 & 13

Hydrofoils to Cápri, Ischia & Prócida

S. Paolo Stadium & Posillipo

13

CAMPANIA

TANGENZIALE OVEST DI NAPOLI

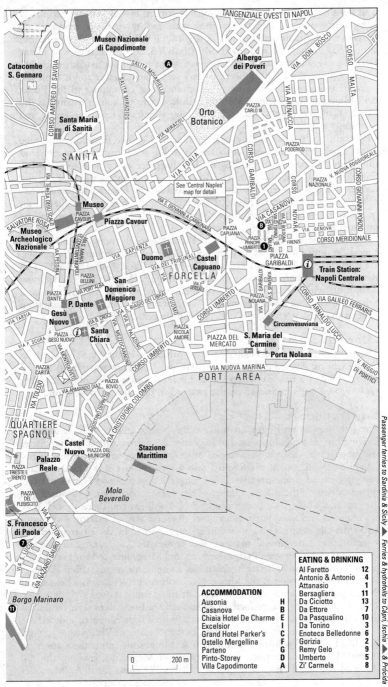

Passenger ferries to Sardinia & Sicily ▶ Ferries & hydrofoils to Capri, Ischia ▶ & Procida

ACCOMMODATION

Ausonia	H
Casanova	B
Chiaia Hotel De Charme	E
Excelsior	I
Grand Hotel Parker's	C
Ostello Mergellina	F
Parteno	G
Pinto-Storey	D
Villa Capodimonte	A

EATING & DRINKING

Al Faretto	12
Antonio & Antonio	4
Attanasio	1
Bersagliera	11
Da Ciciotto	13
Da Ettore	7
Da Pasqualino	10
Da Tonino	3
Enoteca Belledonne	6
Gorizia	2
Remy Gelo	9
Umberto	5
Zi' Carmela	8

0   200 m

is in front of the station at the McDonald's corner) by bus #3S approximately every thirty minutes, and the journey takes twenty to thirty minutes; buy tickets (€1) from the *tabacchi* in the departures hall. There is also an official airport bus, *Alibus*, operated by ANM (☎081.763.2177), which runs to Piazza Garibaldi every twenty minutes between 6.30am and 11.30pm (6am–midnight in the opposite direction), although it isn't very much quicker and is triple the price (€3); however, it does have the advantage of continuing to the Piazza del Municipio and Stazione Marittima, from where hydrofoils depart for the islands. Taxis, too, tend to take almost as long as buses to reach the centre, and cost up to €20.

By train, you're most likely to arrive at Napoli Centrale, situated on the edge of the city centre at one end of Piazza Garibaldi, at the main hub of city (and suburban) transport services; there's a **left luggage** office here (open 24hr). Some trains also pull into Stazione Mergellina, on the opposite side of the city centre, which is connected with Piazza Garibaldi by the underground *metropolitana*. For train enquiries phone ☎848.888.088, check ⓦwww.trenitalia.com or go to the information booths at Napoli Centrale (daily 7am–9pm) and be prepared to queue.

City and suburban **buses** also stop on Piazza Garibaldi, though you'll need to check the stops carefully as they are not well signed and are subject to change. CTP (☎081.700.1111) run buses to Caserta and FABN (☎800.127.157) to Benevento from here, but the main company, SITA (☎081.552.2176, ⓦwww .sitabus.it), which connects with Pompeii, Sorrento, the Amalfi coast and Salerno, leaves from Via G. Ferraris, just south of the Stazione Centrale and from their main office at Via Pisanelli 3/7, just off Piazza Municipio.

Information

The most convenient of Naples' **tourist offices** is in the Stazione Centrale (Mon–Sat 8am–8pm, Sun 9am–2pm; ☎081.268.779, ⓦwww.inaples.it), a good place to pick up a free **city map** and an English-language copy of the monthly *Qui Napoli*, a useful reference on the city and an indicator of **what's on**.

City transport

The only way to really **get around** central Naples and stay sane is to **walk**. Driving can be a nightmare, and to negotiate the narrow streets, hectic squares and racetrack boulevards on a moped or scooter takes years of training. In any case, *not* to walk would mean you'd miss a lot – Naples is the kind of place best appreciated from street level. For longer journeys – and Naples is a big, spread-out city – there are a number of alternatives, both for the city itself and the bay as a whole. City **buses** run by ANM will get you there, though they are crowded and slow, but remain much the best way of making short hops across the city centre. The bus system is supplemented by the **metropolitana**, a small-scale underground network that crosses the city centre, stopping at about four places between Piazza Garibaldi and Mergellina, and runs eventually out to Pozzuoli and Solfatara in about half an hour; the metro station at Piazza Dante has a useful stop at the Museo Nazionale Archeologico. As a bonus, you should get to see some of the modern art installations thoughtfully provided at metro stations by the council. In addition, three **funiculars** scale the hill of the Vómero: one, the Funicolare di Chiaia, from Piazza Amedeo; another, the Funicolare Centrale, from the station at the bottom of Via Mattia, just off Via Toledo; and a third, the Funicolare di Montesanto, from the station on Piazza Montesanto. Another, the Funicolare di Mergellina, runs up the hill above Mergellina from Via Mergellina. *Uniconapoli* **tickets** for all ANM modes of transport cost a flat €1 (valid 90min) and must be bought in advance from such places as *tabacchi*, newsstands, stations, or the transport booth on Piazza Garibaldi; an all-day ticket costs €3. Any combination of journeys by bus, tram, metro, funicular, Ferrovia Cumana and Circumflegrea lines is allowed.

If you need to take a **taxi** make sure the driver switches on the meter when you start (they often don't); fares start at €2.58 for the initial journey – minimum fare €4.15. Note that journeys to and from the airport incur an extra charge of €2.60; trips after 10pm or before 7am cost an extra €2.10; and those on public holidays an extra €1.60; all of which gives plenty of scope for confusion, and even resident Neapolitans are wary of the stunts taxi drivers pull to get a higher fare. There are taxi ranks at the train station, on Piazza Dante and Piazza Trieste e Trento, or phone ☏081.556.4444 or 081.556.0202.

For solely **out-of-town trips** – around the bay in either direction – there are three more rail systems. The **Circumvesuviana** runs from its own station on Corso Garibaldi, behind the main station of Napoli Centrale, and goes right round the Bay of Naples about every thirty minutes, stopping everywhere, as far south as Sorrento, which it reaches in about an hour. The **Ferrovia Cumana** operates every ten minutes from its terminus station in Piazza Montesanto west to Pozzuoli and Baia. And the **Circumflegrea** line runs every twenty minutes, again from Piazza Montesanto, west to Cuma. Uniconapoli **tickets** are valid for all such suburban lines except the Circumvesuviana, for which tickets can be bought at any train station.

Accommodation

Accommodation **prices** in Naples may come as a refreshing change after the north of Italy, but they're still not cheap, and the city being the kind of place it is you need to choose carefully from among the cheaper dives. A good many of these are situated around Piazza Garibaldi, spitting distance from the train station but rather insalubrious and noisy, and poorly placed for going out at night; a better bet is the lively and more atmospheric group in the *centro storico*, near the university. If you can, try to **book in advance**, as the city does get crowded, or ask on arrival at the station tourist office. Don't go with one of the touts hanging around the station: quite apart from safety issues, you'll be charged commission.

Hotels

Ausonia Via Caracciolo 11 ☏081.682.278, ⓦ www.hotelausonianapoli.com. A two-star with bay views, decorated to give the impression you're on board a yacht, neatly placed in Mergellina, next to the stop for hydrofoils to the islands. Bus #R3 or #152. ④

🏃 **Bella Cápri** Via Melisurgo 4 ☏081.552.9494, ⓦ www.bellacapri.it. Cheapest rooms with views over the bay in town and right by the port. Very welcoming staff who can help you find bargains for island visits, too. Ten percent discount on your room with this book. ③

Caravaggio Piazza Cardinale Sisto Riario Sforza 157 48 ☏081.211.0066, ⓦ www.caravaggiohotel .it. Right in the thick of things in the old centre, but removed enough to be quiet. Some of the elegant

rooms in this impeccably restored seventeenth-century building have views of the impressive *guglia* that adorns the square. ⑥

Casanova Via Venezia 2 ☏081.268.287, ⓦ www .hotelcasanova.com. Best of the station-area budget options, this creeper-clad hotel is quiet, run by an affable team, has pleasant rooms and a communal roof terrace. ②

Chiaia Hotel De Charme Via Chiaia 216 ☏081.415.555, ⓦ www.hotelchiaia.it. Lovely, old fashioned, well-furnished hotel near Piazza del Plebiscito. ⑤

Des Artistes Via Duomo 61 ☏081.446.155, ⓦ www.hoteldesartistesnaples.it. Simple, comfortable rooms, friendly staff, and perfectly located for exploring the historic centre. ④

🏃 **Duomo** Via Duomo 228 ☏081.265.988, ⓦ www.hotelduomonapoli.it. Newly and stylishly done up, but prices are still among the lowest in town. Ideal location for seeing all the major sights of Spaccanapoli, as well as the Archaeological Museum and, of course, the Duomo. Very welcoming. ❷

Excelsior Via Partenope 48 ☎ 081.764.0111, ⓦwww.excelsior.it. An extremely plush period hotel, wonderfully situated on the waterfront opposite the Castel dell'Ovo. ❾

Grand Hotel Parker's Corso Vittorio Emanuele 135 ☎081.761.2474, ⓦwww.grandhotelparkers.it. This upmarket and extremely comfortable hotel claims to be the oldest in Naples, and has hosted Oscar Wilde and Virginia Woolf, as well as King Vittorio Emanuele himself. With an exalted vantage point over the city, the views from the dining room over the bay and east to Vesuvius are unparalleled. ❾

Le Orchidee Corso Umberto I 7 ☎081.551.0721, ⓦwww.hotelleorchidee.com. A good central location, not far from the ferry port and just a short bus ride from Stazione Centrale. Large and elegantly furnished rooms, all with private bath. ❸

🏃 **Parteno** Via Partenope 1 ☎081.245.2095, ⓦwww.parteno.it. Seven individually designed and beautifully furnished rooms in an eighteenth-century building on the waterfront. Great breakfasts and wonderful attention to detail by owners. ❺

Pinto-Storey Via Martucci 72 ☎081.681.260, ⓦwww.pintostorey.it. An evocative period Art Nouveau building in one of Naples' most pleasant areas, near parks and the sea. Many rooms have views of the bay. ❸

Villa Capodimonte Via Moiariello 66 ☎081.459.000, ⓦwww.villacapodimonte.it. Ideally sited for seeing the Palazzo Reale di Capodimonte, this modern option is very comfortable, and attractively located. It sits above the Sanità district, which can be dangerous. ❼

Hostels

Hostel Bella Cápri Via Melisurgo 4 ☎081.552.9494, ⓦwww.bellacapri.it. Spanking new upper floor hostel, including free Internet and a large, light and airy breakfast room. Right on the port so perfect for accessing the islands. Beds are in small dorms of seven or four beds, with adjoining bathrooms. Beds run at €20 in high season; ten percent discount with this book. ❷

Hostel of the Sun Via Melisurgo 15 ☎081.420.6393, ⓦwww.hostelnapoli.com. Clean, colourful hostel with kitchen, probably the best and friendliest in Naples and next to the main ferry dock. Well placed for going out: ask for Luca's nightlife suggestions. No curfew. Breakfast included. Dorm beds €20, rooms of various configurations; ten percent discount on hotel rooms with this book. ❷

Ostello Mergellina Salita della Grotta 23 ☎081.761.2346, ⓦwww.hihostels.com. Popular HI site with a view of the bay, conveniently located not far from the Mergellina metro station, There's a 12.30am curfew, but ask for a double room and they are more flexible. Breakfast included. Three-day maximum stay in July & Aug. Dorm beds €14–16. ❷

Campsites

There are a number of **campsites** within a feasible distance of Naples. The closest is the excellent and beautiful 🏃 *Vulcano Solfatara* site in Pozzuoli at Via Solfatara 47 (☎081.526.7413, ⓦwww.solfatara.it; April–Oct; €9 per person, ❶ for double bungalow); take the *metropolitana* to Pozzuoli and walk ten minutes up the hill. When this is closed, you're probably best off going to one of the other sites around the bay – perhaps at Pompeii, or, rather nicer, Sorrento, neither of which is more than an hour out from the city.

The City

Naples is a large, sprawling city, with a centre that has many different focuses. The area between Piazza Garibaldi and Via Toledo, roughly corresponding to the old Roman Neapolis (much of which is still unexcavated below the ground), makes up the old part of the city – the **centro storico** – the main streets still following the path of the old Roman roads. This is much the liveliest and most teeming part of town, an open-air kasbah of hawking, yelling humanity that makes up in energy what it lacks in grace. Buildings rise high on either side of the narrow, crowded streets, cobwebbed with washing; there's little light, not even much sense of the rest of the city outside – certainly not of the proximity of the sea.

But the insularity of the *centro storico* is deceptive, and in reality there's another, quite different side to Naples, one that's much more like the sunwashed Bay of Naples murals you've seen in cheap restaurants back home. **Via Toledo**, the main street of the city, edges the old centre from the **Palazzo Reale** up to the **Museo Nazionale Archeologico** and the heights of **Capodimonte**; to the left rises the **Vómero**, with its fancy housing and museums, and the smug neighbourhood of **Chiaia**, beyond which lies the long green boulevard of **Riviera de Chiaia**, stretching around to the districts of **Mergellina** and **Posillipo**: all neighbourhoods that exert quite a different kind of pull – that of an airy waterfront city, with views, seafood eaten *al fresco* and peace and quiet.

Piazza Garibaldi to Via Toledo: the centro storico

However you actually get to Naples, there's a good chance that the first place you'll see is **Piazza Garibaldi**, a long, wide square crisscrossed by traffic lanes and currently choked with construction sites, that cuts into the city centre from the modern train station. It's the city's transport hub – most of the city buses leave from here, as do the *metropolitana* and Circumvesuviana lines – and one of its most hectic junctions; indeed it's Piazza Garibaldi, perhaps more so than any other part of the city, that puts people off Naples. The entire piazza is currently a vast construction site due to work on the new underground system; pedestrians are blocked by steel walls and challenged by traffic at every turn, especially when trying to reach the bus stops at the opposite side of the piazza. Of late, the area around here has also become a centre for Naples' growing African community, with a number of African restaurants and Moroccan groceries, and don't be surprised to hear Slavic accents too – many Ukrainians find their way here to work as housekeepers in the city.

Forcella and around

Piazza Garibaldi is good preparation for the noise and confusion that make up the rest of the city centre – especially in the streets around the station, which are sleazy and best avoided. The other side of the square, the *centro storico* spreads west as far as Via Toledo – the tangled heart of Naples and its most characteristic quarter. Off the right corner of the square, the **Porta Capuana** is one of several relics from the Aragonese city walls, a sturdy defensive gate dating from 1490, delicately decorated on one side in Florentine Renaissance style. Across the road, the white and much renovated **Castel Capuano** was the residence of the Norman king William I, and later, under the Spanish, became a courthouse – which it still is.

Behind here, the **FORCELLA** quarter, which spreads down to Corso Umberto I, is the main city-centre stronghold of the Camorra and home to its

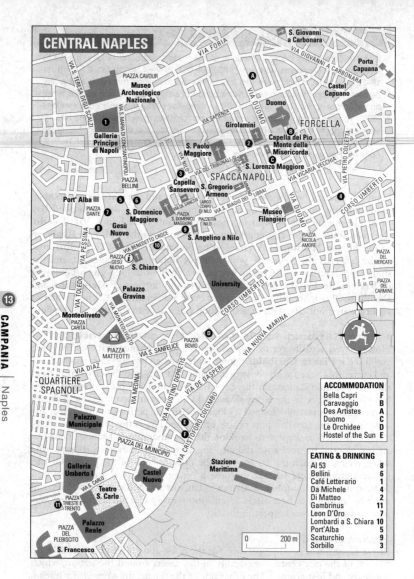

most important families. It's also the city's open-air **market**, stamping-ground of CD and sunglasses hawkers, contraband seafood sellers (one of the Camorra's new trades after a lengthy police campaign against black-market cigarettes), and a quantity of food stalls – chickens sit in boxes waiting for the chop, after which they'll be plucked and cleaned up while you wait. The two main streets of the *centro storico* are **Via dei Tribunali** and **Via San Biagio dei Librai** – narrow thoroughfares, lined with old arcaded buildings, which lead due west on the path of the *decumanus maximus* and *decumanus inferiore* of Roman times, both charged with atmosphere throughout the day, a maelstrom of hurrying pedestrians, revving cars and buzzing, dodging scooters. Via dei Tribunali cuts up to **Via Duomo**, which ploughs straight through the old town to meet Corso Umberto I and Piazza Nicola Amore, laid out after a cholera epidemic in 1884 decimated this part of the city. On Via Tribunali, just before Via Duomo, you can't miss the **Cappella del Pio Monte della Misericordia** (Mon–Sat 9am–1pm; free) – a beautiful octagonal chapel, with paintings by, among others, Caravaggio and Luca Giordano. The chapel was founded in the sixteenth century as a charity to raise money to ransom Christians held in the so-called Barbary States.

The Duomo

The **Duomo** (Mon–Sat 8.30am–noon & 4.30–6pm; free), sharp on the right and tucked away unassumingly from the main street, is a Gothic building from the early thirteenth century (though with a late nineteenth-century neo-Gothic facade) dedicated to the patron saint of the city, San Gennaro. The church – and saint – are key reference points for Neapolitans: San Gennaro was martyred at Pozzuoli, just outside Naples, in 305 AD under the purges of Diocletian. Tradition has it that, when his body was transferred here, two phials of his blood liquefied in the bishop's hands, since which time the "miracle" has continued to repeat itself no fewer than three times a year – on the first Saturday in May (when a procession leads from the church of Santa Chiara to the cathedral) and on September 19 and December 16. There is still a great deal of superstition surrounding this event: San Gennaro is seen as the saviour and protector of Naples, and if the blood refuses to liquefy – which luckily is rare – disaster is supposed to befall the city, and many still wait with bated breath to see if the miracle has occurred. Interestingly, one of the few occasions in recent times that Gennaro's blood hasn't turned was in 1944, an event followed by Vesuvius's last eruption. The last times were in 1980, the year of the earthquake, and in 1988, the day after which Naples lost an important football match to their rivals, Milan.

The miraculous liquefaction takes place during a special Mass in full view of the congregation – a service it's perfectly possible to attend (see box below), though the church authorities have yet to allow any close scientific examination

---

The miracle of San Gennaro

If you're in Naples at the right time it's possible to attend the service to witness the liquefaction of San Gennaro's blood, but you must be sure to arrive at the cathedral early. The Mass starts at 9am, and queues begin to form two hours before that; arrive much after 7am and there's a chance you won't get in. Once the line of Carabinieri have opened up the church everyone will make a dash for the front; for a good view of the proceedings you'll have to join them – and pushing and shoving is, incidentally, very much part of the procedure. The atmosphere in the church throughout the service is a boisterous one. The preliminary Mass goes on for some time, the chancel of the church ringed by armed policemen and flanked by a determined press and photographic corps, until a procession leads out of the saint's chapel holding the (still solid) phial of the blood aloft, to much applause and neck-craning, and cries of *"Viva San Gennaro"*. After ten minutes or so of emotional imprecations the reliquary is taken down from its holder and inspected – at which point, hopefully, it is declared to tumultuous applause and cheering that the saint's blood is indeed now liquid, and the phial is shaken to prove the point. Afterwards the atmosphere is a festive one, stallholders setting up outside the church and the devout queuing up to kiss the phial containing the liquefied blood – a process that goes on for a week.

of the blood or the "miraculous" process. Whatever the truth of the miracle, there's no question it's still a significant event in the Neapolitan calendar, and one of the more bizarre of the city's institutions.

The first chapel on the right as you walk into the cathedral is dedicated to San Gennaro. It's an eye-bogglingly ornate affair, practically a church in its own right, containing the precious phials of the saint's blood and his skull in a silver bust-reliquary from 1305 (stored behind the altar except for ceremonies). On the other side of the cathedral, the basilica of **Santa Restituta** actually is a separate church, officially the oldest structure in Naples, erected by Constantine in 324 and supported by columns that were taken from a temple to Apollo on this site. The **Baptistry**, too (Mon–Sat 9am–noon & 4.30–6pm, Sun 9am–noon; €3), contains relics from very early Christian times, including a late fifth-century chamber preserving fragments of contemporary mosaics and a font believed to have been taken from a temple to Dionysus. Downstairs, the **crypt** (same ticket as for the baptistry) of San Gennaro is one of the finest examples of Renaissance art in Naples, founded by Cardinal Carafa and holding the tombs of both San Gennaro and Pope Innocent IV.

Spaccanapoli

Across Via Duomo, Via Tribunali continues on past **Piazza Girolamini**, on which a plaque marks the house where, in 1668, Giambattista Vico was born – now the home of a well-known Camorra family. Vico was a late-Renaissance Neapolitan philosopher who advanced theories of cyclical history that were far ahead of their time and still echo through twentieth-century thinking: James Joyce's *Finnegan's Wake* was based on his writings. Vico lived all his life in this district and was buried in the church of **Girolamini** (entrance on Via Duomo). Next door, you can look in on the impressive **Chiostro dei Girolamini**, built around a courtyard containing orange and medlar trees, and the **Quadreria dei Girolamini** (Mon–Fri 9am–2pm, Sat 9am–noon; free), a gallery containing paintings by Ribera, Solimena and Dürer, among many others.

Further down Via Tribunali, on the left, the church of **San Lorenzo Maggiore** is a light, spacious Gothic church, unspoiled by later additions and with a soaring Gothic ambulatory at its apse – unusual in Italy, even more so in Naples, where garishly embellished church interiors are the order of the day. It's a mainly thirteenth- and fourteenth-century building, though with a much later facade, built during the reign of the Angevin king Robert the Wise on the site of a Roman basilica – remains of which are in the cloisters. In a way it was at the centre of the golden age that Naples enjoyed under Robert, the focus of its cultural activity. Petrarch stayed for a while in the adjacent convent, and Boccaccio is said to have met the model for his Fiammetta, believed to be Robert's daughter, during Mass here in 1334.

Excavations beneath the church (Mon–Sat 10am–5pm, Sun 10am–1.30pm; €4) have revealed what was once the Roman forum and, before that, the Greek agora. You can walk along the old Roman pavement, passing a barrel-vaulted bakery, a laundry and an area of sloping stone banquettes that were warmed underneath by a fire, where it is thought that people reclined and debated the great issues of the day. What was likely to have been the town's treasury shows a remarkable resemblance to a contemporary bank, with visitors having to negotiate a security-conscious double doorway before reaching the main area for business. The great tufa foundations of the Roman forum were built over the earlier Greek agora; a scale model shows how the latter was laid out, with the circular tholos, where some goods were sold, at its centre. It's a rare chance to see exactly how the layers of the city were built up over the centuries, and to get some idea of how Naples must have looked back in the fifth century BC.

You're now in the city's busiest and most architecturally rich quarter, the so-called **Spaccanapoli** or "split-Naples" that's the real heart of the old city. Cut down to its other main axis, **Via San Biagio dei Librai**, by way of **Via San Gregorio Armeno**, one of the old city's most picturesque streets, lined with places specializing in the making of *presepi* or Christmas cribs (see box above) – the last courtyard on the left is a good place to see one of them in action.

Almost opposite is the arched portal of the church of **San Gregorio Armeno** (Mon & Wed–Fri 9am–noon, Tues 9am–12.45pm, Sat & Sun 9am–12.30pm), a sumptuous Baroque edifice with frescoes by the late seventeenth-century Neapolitan artist Luca Giordano, not to mention two stupendously ornate gilded organs, one on each side of the nave. Up above the south aisle, you'll notice a series of grilles through which the Benedictine nuns of the **Chiostro di San Gregorio** Armeno next door would view the services. You can visit the courtyard of the convent (entrance up the street and on the left; daily 9.30–11.30am; free), which is a wonderfully peaceful haven from the noise outside, planted with limes and busy with nuns quietly going about their duties.

There's more work by Giordano back on Via Duomo, at no. 288 in the **Museo Filangieri**, which unfortunately is closed indefinitely for restoration; contact the tourist office for updates.

Heading west down Via San Biagio leads to the **Largo di Corpo di Nilo**, where you'll find a Roman statue of a reclining old man, sculpted in Nero's time; it's a representation of the Nile and has a habit, it's claimed, of whisper-ing to women as they walk by. The church nearby, **Sant'Angelo a Nilo**, has sculptures by Michelozzo and Donatello, the first Renaissance work to be seen in Naples. Further on, **Piazza San Domenico Maggiore** is marked by the **Guglia di San Domenico**, built in 1737 – one of the whimsical Baroque obelisks that were originally put up after times of plague or disease or to celebrate the Virgin. The **church** (daily 8.30am–noon & 4.30–7pm; free) of the same name flanks the north side of the square, an originally – though much messed about – Gothic building from 1289, one of whose chapels holds a miraculous painting of the Crucifixion which is said to have spoken to St Thomas Aquinas during his time at the adjacent monastery.

North of here, Via de Sanctis leads off right to one of the city's odder monu-ments, the **Capella Sansevero** (Mon & Wed–Sat 10am–5.40pm, closes 5pm in winter, Sun 10am–1.10pm; €5), the tomb-chapel of the di Sangro family, deco-rated by the sculptor Giuseppe Sammartino in the mid-eighteenth century. The decoration, at least, is extraordinary, the centrepiece a carving of a dead Christ, laid out flat and covered with a veil of stark and remarkable realism, not least because it was carved out of a single piece of marble. Even more accomplished

⑬

CAMPANIA | Naples

is the veiled figure of Modesty on the left, and, on the right, its twin Disillusionment, in the form of a woeful figure struggling with the marble netting of his own disenchantment. Look, too, at the effusive *Deposition* on the altar and the memorial above the doorway, which shows one Cecco di Sangro climbing out of his tomb, sword in hand. You might also want to venture downstairs. The man responsible for the chapel, Prince Raimondo, was a well-known eighteenth-century alchemist, and down here are the results of some of his experiments: bodies of an upright man and woman, behind glass, their capillaries and most of their organs preserved by a mysterious liquid developed by the prince – who, incidentally, was excommunicated by the pope for such practices. Even now the black entanglements make for a gruesome sight.

Continuing west, Via San Biagio becomes Via San Benedetto Croce, named after the twentieth-century philosopher who spent much of his life in this neighbourhood, living in the palace at no. 12. A little way down, the street broadens out at Piazza del Gesù Nuovo, centring on another ornate **Guglia**, much larger than the San Domenico one and dating from 1750. On the right, the **Gesù Nuovo** (daily 7am–12.30pm & 4–7.30pm; free) church is most notable for its lava-stone facade, originally part of a fifteenth-century palace which stood here, prickled with pyramids that give it an impregnable, prison-like air. The inside is as gaudy as you might expect, in part decorated by the Neapolitan-Spanish painter Ribera.

Facing the Gesù church, the church of **Santa Chiara** (daily 8am–12.30pm & 4.30–7.30pm; free) is quite different: a Provençal-Gothic structure built in 1328 that was completely destroyed by Allied bombs during the last war and on rebuilding returned to its original bare Gothic austerity, quite pleasing after the excesses opposite. There's not very much to see inside, but the medieval tombs of the Angevin monarchs are very fine and include that of Robert the Wise at the altar, showing the king in a monk's habit. The attached convent, established by Robert's wife, Sancia, has a **cloister** (entrance to the left of the church; Mon–Sat 9.30am–1pm & 2.30–5.30pm, Sun 9.30am–1pm; €4) that is truly one of the gems of the city, a shady haven planted with neatly clipped box hedges, and most notably furnished with benches and low walls covered with colourful majolica tiles depicting bucolic scenes of life outside.

Corso Umberto I, Piazza Municipio and the Palazzo Reale

Off the far left corner of Piazza Garibaldi, **Via Garibaldi** runs down to the sea, past the main Circumvesuviana terminal and, on the right, the **Porta Nolana**, a solid-looking Aragonese gateway that signals the entrance to Naples' main fish market – a grouping of streets lined with a wonderful array of stalls piled high with displays of wriggling fish and seafood. Behind, towards the water, the church of **Santa Maria del Carmine** dates back to the thirteenth century and is traditionally the church of the poor in Naples, particularly fishermen and mariners – the main port area is close by. Axel Munthe, the Swedish writer and resident of Cápri, used to sleep here after tending to victims of the 1884 cholera outbreak.

Just west, the still war-damaged **Piazza del Mercato** was for centuries home to the city's scaffold, and is a bleak, dusty square even now. There's little to detain you in this part of town, and you may as well cut back up to **Corso Umberto I**, which spears through the old part of the city, a long straight journey from the seedy gatherings of prostitutes and kerb crawlers at its Piazza Garibaldi end, past many of the city's more mainstream shops, to the symmetrical **Piazza Bovio**. The piazza is currently disrupted by the construction of the new subway system, but it used to be home to the elegant seventeenth-century Fontana del Nettuno, which has now been returned to its original site at the beginning of Via Medina.

From Piazza Bovio it's a short walk down to **Piazza del Municipio**, a busy traffic junction that stretches from the ferry terminal on the water up to the Palazzo Municipale at the top, dominated by the brooding hulk of the **Castel Nuovo** opposite – the "Maschio Angioino" – erected in 1282 by the Angevins and later converted as the royal residence of the Aragon monarchs. The entrance incorporates a triumphal arch from 1454 that commemorates the taking of the city by Alfonso I, the first Aragon ruler, and shows details of his triumph topped by a rousing statue of St Michael. These days the castle is mainly taken up by the offices of the Naples and Campania councils, but part is given over to the **Museo Civico** (Mon–Sat 9am–7pm; €5). On the first floor is a collection of fourteenth- to sixteenth-century religious paintings and sculpture, along with, perhaps most intriguingly, the original bronze doors cast in 1468 and showing scenes from Ferdinand of Aragon's struggle against the local barons. The cannonball wedged in the lower left-hand panel dates from a naval battle in 1495 between the French and the Genoese that took place while the former were pillaging the doors from the castle. On the upper floor are very charming and revealing secular works by eighteenth- to twentieth-century Neapolitan painters and sculptors. Two additional rooms worth a look are the Sala dei Baroni, with its magnificent umbrella-ribbed vaults and fragments of frescoes by Giotto, and the Gothic Capella Palatina, with fine fourteenth- to sixteenth-century frescoes, Renaissance sculptures and fifteenth-century marble portal and rose window.

Just beyond the castle, on the left, the **Teatro San Carlo** is an oddly unimpressive building from the outside; inside, however, you can see why this theatre was the envy of Europe when it opened in 1737 in time for Charles of Bourbon's birthday, for whom it was built. Destroyed by fire in 1816 and quickly rebuilt, it's one of the largest opera houses in Italy and one of the most distinguished in the world. Opposite, the **Galleria Umberto I** has fared less well over the years, its high arcades, erected in 1887, comparatively empty of the teeming life that characterizes the rest of Naples, and in the evening even something of a danger spot.

Come out of the Galleria and you're on **Piazza Trieste e Trento**, more a roundabout than a piazza, whose life you can watch while sipping a pricey drink on the terrace of the sleekly historic **Caffè Gambrinus**. To the left, **Piazza del Plebiscito** is another attempt at civic grandeur, with a curve of columns modelled on Bernini's piazza for Saint Peter's in Rome and a favourite place to stroll of an evening. Art installations here have included a monumental pyramid of salt by Mimmo Paladino, a mountain of ancient furniture, armoires and kitchen tables by Jannis Kounellis and low-key son et lumière events. The church of **San Francesco di Paola** is floodlit at night, when it is at its most impressive. At other times its attempts at classical majesty (it's a copy of the Pantheon in Rome) only really work once you're standing under its enormous dome.

Opposite, the **Palazzo Reale** (daily except Wed 9am–9pm; last entry 7pm; €4) manages better than most of the buildings around here to retain some semblance of its former glories, though it's a bland, derivative building for the most part and even a bit of a fake, thrown up hurriedly in 1602 to accommodate Philip III on a visit here and never actually occupied by a monarch long term. Indeed it's more of a monument to monarchies than monarchs, with the various dynasties that ruled Naples by proxy for so long represented in the niches of the facade, from Roger the Norman to Vittorio Emanuele II, taking in among others Alfonso I and a slightly comic Murat on the way. Upstairs, by way of a exaggerated white marble double-staircase, the palace's first-floor rooms are decorated with fine Baroque excesses of gilded furniture, trompe-l'oeil ceilings, great overbearing tapestries, impressive French Empire pieces and lots and lots of quite creditable seventeenth- and eighteenth-century paintings, including works by Guercino, Carraci and Titian, as well as Flemish old masters. Best bits are the chapel, on the far side of the central square (you may have to ask someone to open this for you), with its finely worked altarpiece; the little theatre – the first room on the right – which is refreshingly restrained after the rest of the palace; and the terrace, which gives good views over the port and the forbidding Castel Nuovo.

Just south of Piazza del Plebiscito, the road curves around towards the sea. Via Santa Lucia is the main artery of the **SANTA LUCIA** district – for years the city's most famed and characteristic neighbourhood, site of a lively fish market and source of most of the *O Sole Mio*-type clichés about Naples you've ever heard. It's a much less neighbourly place now, home to most of the city's poshest hotels, in fact, on the streets around and along the seafront Via Partenope, though one or two decent restaurants make it a better than average place to come and eat. Down on the waterfront, the grey mass of the **Castel dell'Ovo** or "egg-castle" (Mon–Sat 9am–6pm, Sun 9am–2pm; free) takes its name from the whimsical legend that it was built over an egg placed here by Virgil in Roman times: it is believed that if the egg breaks, Naples will fall. Actually it was built by the Hohenstaufen king Frederick II and extended by the Angevins. You can walk over the short causeway that connects its small island to the mainland and eat at one of the surrounding restaurants in the evening.

From Piazza Trieste e Trento to Capodimonte

Piazza Trieste e Trento marks the beginning of the city's main shopping street, **Via Toledo** – or, to give it its official name, Via Roma – which leads north in a dead straight line, climbing the hill up to the national archeological museum and separating two very different parts of Naples. To its right, across as far as Piazza del Gesù Nuovo, the streets and buildings are modern and spacious, centring on the unmistakable mass of the Fascist-era central **Post Office**. The streets to the left, on the other hand, scaling the footslopes of the Vómero, are some of the city's most narrow and crowded, a grid of alleys that was laid out to house Spanish troops during the seventeenth century and hence now known as the **Quartieri Spagnoli**. It's an enticing area, at least for visitors, in that it's what you expect to find when you come to Naples, with the buildings so close together as to barely admit any sunlight. But it's as poor a part of Italy as you'll find, home to the notorious Neapolitan *bassi* – one-room windowless dwellings that open directly onto the street – and as such a national disgrace.

Further up Via Toledo, just north of Piazza Carità on the edge of the old part of the city, the church of **Monteoliveto** (Tues–Sat 8.30am–12.30pm) was rebuilt after a sound wartime bombing, but it holds some of the city's finest Renaissance art, including a sacristy frescoed by Vasari, a rather startling almost life-size pietà of eight figures by Guido Mazzoni (the faces are said to be portraits) and two sculptural works by Antonio Rossellino – a nativity scene and the tomb of Mary of Aragon, daughter of Ferdinand I.

Continuing on up the hill, you come to **Piazza Dante**, designed by Luigi Vanvitelli during the eighteenth century and cutting an elegant semicircle off to the right of the main road that focuses on a statue of the poet. There are a couple of restaurants here, and it's a turnaround point for buses, but otherwise – unless you want to take a right through the seventeenth-century **Port'Alba** into the very appealing **Piazza Bellini** and the old part of the city – you may as well push on up the street to the archeological museum, housed in a grandiose, late-sixteenth-century army barracks on the corner of Piazza Cavour.

The Museo Archeologico Nazionale

Naples is a city with a couple of Italy's most important museums – although for many there's more on the streets that's worth observing on the whole, and most displays of interest are kept *in situ* in churches, palaces and the like. However, the **Museo Archeologico Nazionale** (daily except Tues 9am–7.30pm; €6.50; from Piazza Garibaldi take bus #C40 or the *metropolitana*) is simply exceptional, home to the Farnese collection of antiquities from Lazio and Campania and the best of the finds from the nearby Roman sites of Pompeii and Herculaneum. You'd be mad to miss seeing them; it's worth investing in a guidebook (€7.75) or an audio guide (€4), both in English, to get the most out of your visit, and allow yourself at least half a day to see everything.

The ground floor of the museum concentrates on sculpture from the **Farnese collection**, displayed at its best in the mighty Great Hall, which holds imperial-era figures like the *Farnese Bull* and *Farnese Hercules* from the Baths of Caracalla in Rome – the former the largest piece of classical sculpture ever found. Don't miss *Ephesian Artemis*, an alabaster and bronze statue with rows of bulbous objects peeling off her chest – variously interpreted as breasts, eggs, bulls' scrota, dates or pollen sacs, and bees, mini-beasts and sphinxes adorning her lower half. The mezzanine floor holds the museum's collection of **mosaics** – remarkably preserved works all, giving a superb insight into ordinary Roman customs, beliefs and humour. All are worth looking at – images of fish, crustacea, wildlife on the banks of the Nile, a cheeky cat and quail with still-life beneath, masks and simple abstract decoration. But some highlights include a realistic *Battle Scene* (no. 10020); the *Three Musicians with Dwarf* (no. 9985); an urbane meeting of the Platonic Academy (no. 124545); and a marvellously captured scene from a comedy, *The Consultation of the Fattucchiera* (no. 9987), with a soothsayer giving a dour and doomy prediction.

At the far end of the mezzanine is the fascinating **Gabinetto Segreto** (Secret Room), containing erotic material taken from the brothels, baths, houses and taverns of Pompeii and Herculaneum; to see the display, which lurks tantalizingly behind a grilled gate, you need to be sure to obtain a timed ticket upon entering the museum (no extra charge) in the entrance hall. The objects in the collection weren't always segregated in this way; it was the shocked Duke of Calabria who, having taken his wife and daughter to view the museum, decided that the offending objects should be removed from the gaze of ladies. From then until the time of Garibaldi they were kept under lock and key, disappearing again from public view in the twentieth century for long periods. The artefacts, from languidly sensual wall paintings to preposterously phallic lamps, bear testimony to Roman licentiousness, although the phallus was often used as a kind of lucky charm rather than as a sexual symbol – cheerfully hung outside taverns and bakeries to ward off the evil eye. Free English-language tours of the Gabinetto are admirably serious and smut-free, though it is hard to repress a giggle at the sculpture of a man whose toga is failing to mask an erection, or at the graphic but elegantly executed marble of Pan "seducing" a goat.

Upstairs through the Salone della Meridiana, which holds a sparse but fine assortment of Roman figures (notably a wonderfully strained *Atlas* and a demure *Venus* adjusting her sandal – Roman replicas of Greek originals), a series of rooms holds the **Campanian wall paintings**, lifted from the villas of

Pompeii and Herculaneum, and rich in colour and invention. There are plenty here, and it's worth devoting some time to this section, which includes works from the Sacrarium – part of Pompeii's Egyptian temple of Isis, the most celebrated mystery cult of antiquity – the discovery of which gave a major boost to Egyptomania at the end of the eighteenth century. In the next series of rooms, some of the smallest and most easily missed works are among the most exquisite. Among those to look out for are a paternal *Achilles and Chirone* (no. 9109); the *Sacrifice of Iphiginia* (no. 9112) in the next room, one of the best preserved of all the murals; the dignified *Dido abandoned by Aeneas and the Personification of Africa* (no. 8998); and the series of frescoes telling the story of the Trojan horse. Look out too for the group of four small pictures, the best of which is a depiction of a woman gathering flowers entitled *Allegoria della Primavera* – a fluid, impressionistic piece of work capturing both the gentleness of spring and the graceful beauty of the woman.

Beyond the murals are the actual **finds from the Campanian cities** – everyday items like glass, silver, ceramics, charred pieces of rope, even foodstuffs (petrified cakes, figs, fruit and nuts), together with a model layout of Pompeii in cork. On the other side of the first floor, there are finds from one particular house, the **Villa dei Papiri** in Herculaneum – sculptures in bronze mainly. The *Hermes at Rest* in the centre of the second room is perhaps the most arresting item, boyishly rapt and naked except for wings on his feet. All around are other adept statues – of athletes, suffused with movement, a languid *Resting Satyr*, the convincingly woozy *Drunken Silenus*, a pair of youthful *Runners* and, in the final room, portrait busts of soldiers and various local big cheeses.

Piazza Cavour and Sanità

To the left of the archeological museum as you come out, **Piazza Cavour** is a busy traffic junction and bus stop. A short walk east, at 223 Via Foria, lies the **Orto Botanico** (Mon–Sat 9am–2pm, by appointment only; ☎081.449.759), founded in 1807 by Joseph Bonaparte and a detour worth making if you're interested in such things. Perhaps more intriguing is the enormously long facade, actually only one-fifth of the originally conceived size, of the **Albergo dei Poveri** alongside, a workhouse built in 1751 that has been empty for years and forms a vast, oddly derelict landmark along the top side of **Piazza Carlo III**.

North of Piazza Cavour, you can stroll up through the old quarter of **SANITÀ**, following the tangle of streets for ten minutes or so up to the church of **Santa Maria della Sanità** on the piazza of the same name, a Dominican church from the early seventeenth century whose design was based loosely on Bramante's for Saint Peter's in Rome. There are paintings by Giordano and other Neapolitan artists inside, if you can get in, although perhaps of more interest are the **Catacombe di San Gaudioso** (guided tours by appointment only ☎081.544.1305; €5) underneath, an intriguing early Christian burial ground full of skeletons and the fifth-century tomb of St Gaudioso, a bishop known as the "African", as he was from North Africa.

Lifts link Sanità with Corso Amedeo up above, the main road up to Capodimonte. Walk under the bridge through to the rest of the teeming district, home to a couple of the city centre's larger hospitals and, close by one of them, another burial place, the **Catacombe di San Gennaro** (currently closed for restoration; ring ☎081.741.1071 for times of guided visits) behind the huge Madre del Buon Consiglio church. These were only discovered relatively recently, next to the original eighth-century church of San Gennaro in Moenia, and hold early Christian frescoes and mosaics, newly restored and amazingly bright.

The Palazzo Reale di Capodimonte

At the top of the hill, accessible by bus #C40 from Piazza Garibaldi and Piazza Dante, the **Palazzo Reale di Capodimonte** – and its beautiful **park** (9am–1hr before dusk; free) – was the royal residence of the Bourbon King Charles III, built in 1738 and now housing the picture gallery of the Naples museum, the superb **Museo Nazionale di Capodimonte** (Tues–Sun 8.30am–7.30pm; €7.50). Probably the best collection of art in Italy after the Uffizi gallery in Florence, you could easily spend an entire day here. The vast holding contains many important works by Campanian and international artists, not least a grand collection of paintings by women, with works by Artemesia Gentileschi, Sofonisba Anguissola, Angelika Kauffmann and Elizabeth Vigee-Lebrun, as well as many curious *objets d'art* and some fine pieces of Capodimonte porcelain.

The three-storey museum is organized, not chronologically, but by collections: between them the Borgia, Farnese and Bourbon rulers amassed some superb **Renaissance and Flemish** works, including a couple of Brueghels – *The Misanthrope* and *The Parable of the Blind* – and two triptychs by Joos van Cleve. There are also canvases by Perugino and Pinturicchio, an elegant *Madonna and Child with Angels* by Botticelli and Lippi's soft, sensitive *Annunciation*. Later works include many Titians, with a number of paintings of the shrewd Farnese Pope Paul III in various states of ageing and the lascivious *Danae*; a Masaccio painting of the Crucifixion; a worldly *Clement VII* by Sebastiano del Piombo; Bellini's impressively coloured and composed *Transfiguration*; and one of Caravaggio's best known works, *The Flagellation*.

There is also an El Greco portrait of the Croatian-born illuminator Giulio Clovio, shown holding his masterpiece, *The Farnese Hours*, and a miniature by Clovio of one of the beauties of the Farnese court in the same gallery. The reputation of Clovio, in his time considered the equal of Michelangelo and Titian, has suffered from the fact that most of his works cannot be kept on permanent public view for conservation reasons.

On the top floor there are some outstanding Italian paintings from the fourteenth and fifteenth centuries, of which the most famous is the *St Louis of Anjou* by Simone Martini, a fascinating Gothic painting glowing with gold leaf. An overt work of propaganda, it depicts an enthroned Louis crowning Robert of Anjou and thereby legitimizing his rule. There is also a scattering of paintings and artworks from the **twentieth century**, of which the only famous work is a painting of Vesuvius in eruption by Andy Warhol; whatever you make of this spectacular daub, the rest of the works here are fairly forgettable.

If you have time to spare, take a walk around the **royal apartments** on the first floor, smaller and more downbeat than those at Caserta but in many ways more enjoyable, not least because you can actually walk through the rooms freely. High spots are the airy, mirrored ballroom, lined with portraits of various Bourbon monarchs and other European despots, an eccentric room entirely decorated with porcelain and sprouting Chinese scenes, monkeys and fruit and flowers in 3D, and a number of rooms of beautifully decorated plates, some painted with local scenes.

Chiaia, Villa Comunale, Mergellina and Posillipo

Via Chiaia leads west from Piazza Trieste e Trento into a quite different Naples from the congested *vicoli* of the *centro storico* or Quartieri Spagnoli, lined with the city's fanciest shops and bending down to the **Piazza dei Martiri** – named after the nineteenth-century revolutionary martyrs commemorated by the column in its centre. This part of town, the **Chiaia** neighbourhood, displays a sense of order and classical elegance that is quite absent from the rest of the city centre, its buildings well preserved, the people noticeably better heeled – although the upper part of the district, which spreads up the hill towards Vómero, is as maze-like and evocative as anywhere in the city.

From Piazza dei Martiri, you can stroll down to the waterfront and **Villa Comunale** (Mon–Sat 7am–10pm, Sun 7am–midnight; free), Naples' most central city park, richly adorned with Classical sculpture and the place from where it's possible to appreciate the city best as a port and seafront city, the views stretching right around the bay from the long lizard of its northern side to the distinctive silhouette of Vesuvius in the east, behind the cranes and far-off apartment blocks of the sprawling industrial suburbs. The park itself sometimes hosts a large antiques and bric-a-brac market on Sunday mornings, as well as contemporary art exhibitions in the Casina Pompeiana building, located in the middle of the park on the north side.

The road that skirts the park, **Via Caracciolo**, makes a nice way to walk around the bay to Mergellina, particularly in the early evening when the lights of the city enhance the views. On the way you might want to take in the Mediterranean marine life at the newly restored century-old **Aquarium** (La Stazione Zoologica; ☎081.583.3263; summer Tues–Sat 9am–6pm, Sun 9.30am–7pm; winter Tues–Sat 9am–5pm, Sun 9am–2pm; €1.50), which also features exhibits about endangered species such as coral and loggerhead sea turtles. Across from here, on the other side of Riviera di Chiaia, the gardens of the **Villa Pignatelli** (Wed–Mon 8.30am–1.30pm; €2, €5 including special exhibitions) are a peaceful alternative to the Villa Comunale, and the early nineteenth-century house itself, now a museum, is kept in much the same way as when it was the home of a prominent Naples family and a meeting place for the city's elite in the 1900s. It's tastefully furnished and by Naples standards low-key, its handful of rooms holding books, porcelain, the odd painting and a set of photos signed by various aristocrats and royal personages.

Villa Comunale stretches around the bay for a good mile, at the far end of which lie the harbour and main square – Piazza Sannazzaro – of the **Mergellina** district, a good place to come and eat at night and a terminus for hydrofoils to the bay's islands. There's not a lot else here, only the dense and lovely **Parco Virgiliano** (Tues–Sun 9am–1pm), north of Piazza Sannazzaro, where the supposed burial place of the Roman poet Virgil is marked by a Roman monument. Of the other neighbourhoods nearby, the **Fuorigrotta** district, the other side of the Mergellina hill, is not of interest unless you're going to a football match, since it's home to Napoli's **San Paolo** stadium (see p.906 for details). Ditto **Posillipo**, further along the shore, which is an upmarket suburb of the city stacked with fat villas and pockets – though, again, people do come out here to eat.

Vómero

Like Chiaia below and Mergellina to the west, **VÓMERO** – the district topping the hill immediately above the old city – is one of Naples' relatively modern additions, a light, airy and relatively peaceful quarter connected most directly with the teeming morass below by funicular railway. It's a large area but mostly residential, and you're unlikely to want to stray beyond the streets that fan out from each of the three funicular stations, centring on the grand symmetry of **Piazza Vanvitelli**.

Come up on the Montesanto funicular and you're well placed for a visit to two of the buildings that dominate Naples, way above the old city. Five minutes' walk away, the **Castel Sant'Elmo** (Tues–Sun 9am–7pm; €1) occupies Naples' highest point and is an impressive fortification, a fourteenth-century structure once used for incarcerating political prisoners and now lording it grandly over the streets below. Nowadays it houses libraries and archives and hosts exhibitions, concerts and antiques fairs, as well as boasting the very best views of Naples.

Beyond the castle, the fourteenth-century **Certosa San Martino** has the next-best views over the bay and is home to the **Museo Nazionale di San Martino** (daily except Wed 8.30am–7.30pm; €6). Much of the upstairs exhibitions are under restoration or closed simply for lack of personnel, but the monastery itself, thoroughly "Baroqued" in the seventeenth century, and the views from its cunningly constructed terraced gardens, are well worth the entrance fee – short of climbing Vesuvius as good a vista of the entire Bay of Naples as you'll get. The church, on the left of the entrance, is typically over-wrought Baroque, with a colourfully tortuous pavement and an *Adoration of the Shepherds* by Reni above the altar. In the museum proper, there are paintings by Neapolitan masters – Ribera, Stanzione, Vaccaro – and other rather dusty bits and pieces rescued from churches and the odd minor aristocrat, as well as historical and maritime sections displaying models of ships, and documents, coins and costumes recording the era of the Kingdom of Naples. The Baroque cloisters are lovely, though again rather gone to seed. The unparalleled collection of *presepi* or Christmas cribs (see box, p.895) is probably the most interesting aspect of the museum, though there is also a fine art gallery, with Ribera's *SS Sebastian* and *SS Girolamo* as its high points.

There's another museum up here, ten minutes' walk away in the Neoclassical **Villa Floridiana**, close to the Chiaia funicular, whose lush grounds (daily 9am–1hr before sunset) make a good place for a picnic. The **Museo Duca di Martina** (Wed–Mon 8.30am–2pm; €2.50) is, however, of fairly specialist interest, a porcelain collection varying from the beautifully simple to the outrageously kitsch – hideous teapots, ceramic asparagus sticks and the like. There are examples of Capodimonte and Meissen, and eighteenth-century English, French, German and Viennese work – as well as a handful of pieces of Qing-dynasty Chinese porcelain and Murano glass and exquisite non-ceramic items like inlaid ivory boxes and panels. On the whole, it's a small museum that's worth taking in before salivating over yet another view, this time from just below the villa.

Eating, drinking and nightlife

Neapolitan cuisine consists of simple dishes cooked with fresh, healthy ingredients (see box, p.882 for more on regional specialities). As Naples is not primarily a tourist-geared city, most restaurants are family-run places used by locals and as such generally serve good food at very reasonable prices. There's no better place in Italy to eat pizza, at a solid core of almost obsessively unchanging places that still serve only the (very few) traditional varieties. You're never far from a food stall for delectable snacks on the move, or you can always pick something up from the city's street markets in La Forcella or the fish market at Porta Nolana. For a quiet, though not necessarily cheap, evening meal, you could go to the Castel dell'Ovo on the seafront, lit up at night and clustered with bars and trattorias.

Restaurants and pizzerias

Al 53 Piazza Dante 53 ☏081.549.9372. A long-established restaurant with a superb selection of antipasti and mains from about €15. Try the *minestra maritata*. Daily.

Al Faretto Via Marechiaro 127, Posillipo ☏081.575.0407. Very atmospheric, romantic and smart, yet dinner averages only €30–40 each. Exceptionally fresh fish prepared and served with great style. Closed Mon.

Antonio & Antonio Via Francesco Crispi 89
T081.682.528. A cheery no-nonsense place which
dishes up enormous pizzas from €3.

Bellini Via Santa Maria di Constantinopoli 80
T081.459.774. One of the city's most famous
restaurants, with a great convivial outside terrace
screened by foliage. Delicious pizzas and seafood
dishes such as *linguine al cartoccio* for €13.50.
Closed Sun.

Bersagliera Borgo Marinaro 10–11
T081.764.6016. Fine food, especially seafood,
though inevitably you pay for the location, slap next
to the Castel dell'Ovo, and for the "O Sole Mio"
minstrels who wander between the tables outside.
The house special is *tagliatelle alla bersagliera*, at
about €11. Closed Sun.

Da Ciciotto Calata Ponticello a Marechiaro,
Posillipo T081.575.1165. Hole-in-the-wall place
where in fine weather you can sit outside and enjoy
the bay. Good seafood and fish. To get here, follow
Via Marechiaro to the end, where it opens out
onto a small piazza. Take the steps off the far end
that lead down to the sea. Turn sharp right at the
bottom of the first flight. Compulsory fixed-price
menus from €40. Daily.

Da Ettore Via Santa Lucia 56 T081.764.0498.
A popular neighbourhood restaurant, famous for
its *pagnotielli* – calzoni stuffed with mozzarella,
ham and mushrooms, for €6 (or €4 to take out).
Closed Sun.

Da Michele Via Cesare Sersale 1–3
T081.553.9204. Tucked away off Corso
Umberto I in the Forcella district, this is the most
determinedly traditional of all the Naples pizzerias,
offering just two varieties (allegedly the only two
worth eating) – *marinara* and *margherita* – for
about €3. Don't arrive late, as they sometimes run
out of dough. Closed Sun.

Da Pasqualino Piazza Sannazzaro 79
T081.681.524. Mergellina restaurant with outdoor
seating and great seafood; plate of mussels €5,
and pizzas from €3.50. Closed Tues.

Da Tonino Via Santa Teresa a Chiaia 47
T081.421.533. Friendly and frenetic restaurant
where you eat at large, communal tables. Try the
pasta e fagioli and *pasta e ceci* soups. Closed Sun.

Di Matteo Via dei Tribunali 94 T081.294.203. A
terrific and well-located pizzeria – one of the best
and most famous in the city. Photos advertise a
famous erstwhile customer – Bill Clinton. Pizzas
around €3. Closed Sun.

Gorizia Via Bernini 29 T081.578.2248. Unpretentious Vómero restaurant close to the Centrale and
Chiaia funicular stops that does good antipasti and
great mini-pizzas as well as a good selection of

main courses. Try the speciality of the house – veal
wrapped around prosciutto and mozzarella, at
about €12. Closed Mon.

Leon D'Oro Piazza Dante 48 T081.549.9404.
Great pizzas from €5 at a restaurant that's been
going strong since the 1950s. Closed Mon.

Lombardi a Santa Chiara Via B. Croce 59
T081.552.0780. Another well-known, well-
respected and moderately priced pizza
restaurant, and with a varied menu besides
pizza. Closed Mon.

Port'Alba Via Port'Alba 18 T081.459.713. Old-
established pizzeria (said to be the oldest in Italy)
just off Piazza Dante that has a wide-ranging menu
including very good fish dishes, besides its excellent pizza, Prices start at €3.10. Daily.

Sorbillo Via dei Tribunali 32 T081.446.643.
This freshly remodelled pizza joint is a favourite
with locals. Huge delicious pizzas average €4.
Closed Sun.

Umberto Via Alabardieri 30–31 T081.418.555. A
long-time popular choice among the professional
classes of the Chiaia district, serving marvellous
food in somewhat old-fashioned surroundings.
Pizza from €3.20, *spaghetti alle vongole* €9.50.
Closed Mon.

Zi' Carmela Via Tommaseo 11
T081.764.3581. On a quiet side street
between the Villa Comunale and the smart shoreline hotels, this family-run fish restaurant turns out
sumptuous seafood pastas and catch-of-the-day
dishes, from €12. Closed Mon.

Cakes, snacks, ice cream

Attanasio Vico Ferrovia, off Via Milano. Bakery that
specializes in delectable *sfogliatelle* (ricotta-stuffed
pastries).

Café Letterario Galleria Principe di Napoli 6–7.
An elegant café inside the *galleria*, within striking
distance of the Museo Nazionale. Also sells books
and posters, and has Internet access.

Gambrinus Via Chiaia 1–2. The oldest and
best-known of Neapolitan cafés, founded
in 1861. Not cheap, but its aura of chandeliered
gentility – and outside seating on Piazza Trieste e
Trento – makes it worth at least one visit.

Remy Gelo Via F. Galiani 29a. Off Via Caracciolo,
near the hydrofoil terminal, this place does superb
ice creams and *granite*.

Scaturchio Piazza San Domenico. Another
elegant old Naples standard, it's been
serving coffee and pastries in the heart of
Spaccanapoli for decades.

Bars, clubs and theatres

The old part of the city is crammed with **bars**; if you want to take pot luck try the sedate Chiaia district, where you'll find good wine bars like the *Enoteca Belledonne*, Vico Belledonne a Chiaia 18. For a more studenty crowd in the centre, check out the cheerful disco-pubs on Via Paladino. Most places close in July and August when discos move to the beach or out of town, and instead everyone congregates in the open air in Piazza del Gesù Nuovo and Piazza San Domenico Maggiore, or the gay-friendly cafés on Piazza Bellini, where tables spill out onto the square. Bear in mind though, that things don't really get going till at least 10pm.

For **nightclubs** you may – owing to the licensing laws – have to obtain a *tesserino* or membership card to gain entry, which can cost upwards of €10. For the best of the clubs head around the bay after 11pm, ideally with your own transport, to the places situated in the beach areas north or south of the city; *Zero*, a pamphlet available in bars, has listings, or for big events see Ⓦwww .angelsoflove.it, Italy's answer to the Ministry of Sound.

For more highbrow **culture** there's the Teatro San Carlo, whose opera season runs from October to May. You'll find tickets hard to come by, however, as they are mostly sold on subscription, but if you do manage to get hold of one, dress up. The rest of the year is given over to classical concerts and ballet (box office Sept–June Tues–Sun 10am–3pm; July Tues–Fri 10am–3pm & 1 hr before curtain; ℡081.797.2111 or 081.797.2412, Ⓦwww.teatrosancarlo.it). The Teatro Mercadante on Piazza Municipio (℡081.551.3396 or 081.551.3623, Ⓦwww .caspi.it/mercadante; tickets from €14) is a stunning little eighteenth-century building – although the facade was under restoration at the time of writing – featuring the best of touring Italian theatre.

Bars and clubs

Intra Moenia Piazza Bellini 70. A left-leaning "literary café" and one of several trendy haunts on Piazza Bellini, where tables spread across the square. A lovely place to sit and read under the wisteria on a sunny day. Substantial snacks and fancy ice creams are served, and there's Internet access. Daily 10am–2am.

Jail Via Sedile di Porto 65. One of the newer, larger clubs, popular with students. Usually a DJ holds forth, but there are also live shows, often featuring local death-metal bands, such as Burial in Sulphur and Black Death da Napoli.

Kinky Bar Via Cisterna dell'Olio 16. Popular reggae/African bar in the centre of Naples which doesn't offer what its name promises.

Madison Street Via Sgambati 30c. A huge upmarket disco with themed events and a gay night on Saturdays. Open till late.

My Way Via Cappella Vecchia 30c, off Piazza dei Martiri. A funky nightclub with a cave-like dance floor which plays a range of music, from salsa to house. Oct–April Thurs–Sat 10pm–4am.

New Dreamer Club Via Francesco de Sanctis 16. Currently the hottest new club in the historic centre, boasting all kinds of music and a youthful, international clientele.

Notting Hill Piazza Dante 88a. A non-mainstream club geared to Britpop plus garage and drum 'n' bass, with live music on Tues, Thurs and Sat. Oct–May Tues–Sun 10.30pm–5am.

Otto Jazz Club Piazzetta Cariati 23. A popular jazz club off Corso Vittorio Emanuele which also dips its toes into Neapolitan folk song. Has 200 cocktails on the menu. Daily 10pm–3am.

Rising South Via S Sebastiano 19 ℡0335.811.7107, Ⓦwww.risingsouth.com. The coolest club in Naples, with velveted baroque interior and fruit-based cocktails (try the refreshing Cucumber Slumber). You'll need to be on the list Thurs, Fri and Sat, so call in advance. Tues buffet and drink €5 from 9pm; Sun electrolounge and happy hour 10–11pm.

Virgilio Club Via Lucrezio Caro 6, just below the Parco della Rimembranza, Posillipo. A fun and leafy outdoor disco that gets jam-packed on summer nights. June–Sept Sat 11pm–4am.

Listings

Airlines Alitalia (☏848.865.643; Capodichino airport desk ☏081.751.1494); British Airways (☏848.812.266; Capodichino airport desk ☏081.712.266); Easyjet (☏848.887.766).

Car rental Avis, Via Piedigrotta 44 ☏081.761.1365; Europcar, Via Santa Lucia 54 ☏081.764.9838; Hertz, Via Ricciardi 5 ☏081.206.228; Maggiore, Via Cervantes 92 ☏081.552.1900. These agents also have desks at Stazione Centrale and at the airport.

Consulates Canada, Via Carducci 29 ☏081.401.338; UK, Via dei Mille 40 ☏081.423.8911; USA, Piazza della Repubblica ☏081.583.8111.

Exchange Outside normal banking hours you can change money and travellers' cheques at the booth inside Stazione Centrale (daily 8am–7.30pm).

Football The Stadio di San Paolo in Fuorigrotta is the home of the Napoli side. To get to the ground, take the Ferrovia Cumana from Montesanto to Mostra and the stadium is right in front of you. Tickets, available from the offices facing you as you approach, or from the club's outlets in town, cost from €12.

Hospital To call an ambulance, dial ☏118; hospital numbers include ☏081.747.1111 or 081.220.5797, or go to the Guardia Medica Permanente in the Palazzo Municipio, open 24hr.

Internet As well as the hotels, cafés and bars listed in this guide, try *Internet Café* in front of the station at Piazza Garibaldi 73 (Mon–Fri 9.30am–9pm, Sat 10am–5pm); and *Internet Napoli* near the Archeological Museum on Piazza Cavour 146 (daily 9am–11pm); both for around €2/hr.

Laundry Bolle Blu, Corso Novara 62–64, just up from the Stazione Centrale (Mon–Sat 8.30am–8pm).

Lottery Along with San Gennaro, the lottery is a fanatically observed institution in Naples. Winning the lottery is seen, in a way, as the ultimate triumph over the system, and superstitions around it are rife – to the extent that there's even a book, *La Smorfia*, which interprets the meaning behind each lottery number. There are also people, called *assisti* (literally "guided ones"), who claim to have supernatural access to knowledge of what the

winning numbers will be. The draw is made every Saturday noon at the Ufficio Lotto on Via San Biagio dei Librai, to the accompaniment of much hysteria.

Markets The Mercato dei Fiori (Flower Market) at Castel Nuovo kicks off every morning at sunrise, while Pignasecca on via Pignasecca is an atmospheric daily market, the stalls piled with fresh fruit, vegetables and seafood.

Pharmacies The pharmacy at Napoli Centrale is open 24 hr and there's a list of those open at night in the newspaper *Il Mattino*.

Police ☏112; you can speak to an operator in English. The main police station (*questura*) is at Via Medina 75 (☏081.794.1111); you can also report crimes at the small police station in Stazione Centrale. To report the theft of a car call ☏081.794.1435.

Post office The main post office is in the enormous building on Piazza Matteotti, just off Via Toledo (Mon–Sat 8.15am–7.20pm).

Taxis Radiotaxi ☏081.570.7070, ☏081.551.5151 or 081.556.4444.

Tours A "Neapolitan Legends" walk takes place every Sunday morning at 11am starting from Piazza San Domenico Maggiore (☏081.542.2088). You can also experience underground Naples on tours run by LAES (Sat & Sun 10am; ☏081.400.256, ⓦwww.lanapolisotterranea .it; €10.30), which leave from *Bar Gambrinus* on Piazza Trieste e Trento and take you through passageways and ancient streets 40 metres down that date back as far as 4000 years. In summer you can also cruise Naples harbour by boat, to the islands and back with LAES, and at night with Pelagus, Piazza Municipio 84 (☏081.552.0105; prices start at €135, including a meal on board); there are regular departures from Largo Nazario Sauro near Mergellina harbour between July and September.

Travel agents CTS, Via Mezzocannone 25 (☏081.552.7960), for discount tickets, budget flights and so on. You could also try Wasteels, Stazione Centrale (☏081.201.071; Mon–Sat 9am–7.30pm).

West from Naples: Pozzuoli and the Campi Flegrei

The area around Naples is one of the most geologically unstable in the world. Vesuvius is only the best known of the many and varied examples of volcanic activity in the province, the most concentrated instances – volcanic craters, hot springs, *fumaroles* – being west of the city in the region known as the **Campi Flegrei** (Fiery Fields). This is the Phlegrean Fields of classical times, a mysterious place in turn mythologized by Homer and Virgil as the entrance to Hades and eulogized as the Elysian Fields for its beauty. These days most of the mystery is gone – like most of the bay, the presence of Naples dominates in the form of new, mostly illegal, building – and much of the volcanic activity is extinct, or at least dormant. But parts of the area still retain some of the doomy associations that first drew the ancients here, and there are some substantial remains of their presence.

Pozzuoli and the Solfatara

The first town that can really be considered free of Naples' sprawl is **POZZUOLI**, which sits on a stout promontory jutting out from the slender crescent of volcanic hills behind. Despite achieving some glamour as the home town of Sophia Loren, it's an ordinary little place, nothing special but likeable enough, with ferry connections to the islands of Prócida and Ischia. And although you wouldn't want to stay here (unless you're a camper; see "Accommodation", p.890), it's a good first stop before travelling on to the rest of the Campi Flegrei. You can get here from Naples on the *metropolitana* from Piazza Garibaldi, or on the Ferrovia Cumana line from Montesanto station; both take about twenty minutes. Bus #152 also runs direct from Piazza Garibaldi.

Pozzuoli has suffered more than most of the towns around here from the area's volcanic activity and subsidence is still a major – and carefully monitored – problem. The best time to come is on Sunday, when the whole town turns out for the morning fish market, afterwards eating lunch in one of several waterfront **restaurants**: *Il Capitano* (℡081.526.2283; closed Tues), near the dock at Lungomare C. Colombo 10, is decent, and does a good *zuppa di pesce* for around €20; or there's *Don Antonio* (℡081.526.7941; closed Mon), up narrow Via Magazzini off the old port, at no. 20, which specializes in excellent fresh fish and seafood such as *spaghetti alle vongole* for €7. In town there are a number of relics of the Romans' liking for the place. The well-preserved **Anfiteatro Flavio** (daily 9am–1hr before sunset; €4 combined 2-day ticket with excavations at Baia and Cumae, closed Tues), on Via Domiziana just north of the centre, was at one time the third largest in Italy and is still reasonably intact. The subterranean chambers for gladiators and wild beasts are especially complete, and lying around everywhere is an abundance of beautifully carved architectural fragments. Not far from here, beyond the Cumana station between Via Roma and Via Sacchini, a **Temple of Serapide** sits enclosed within a small park, often flooded in winter, but, otherwise, accessible – and in fact since proved to be not a temple at all but a market hall from the first century AD. It's pretty ruined, but it is still possible to make out the shape of the building, its three freestanding marble columns eaten away halfway up by shellfish.

Just north of town, ten minutes' walk up the hill from the *metropolitana*/FS station (bus #152 from Piazza Garibaldi in Naples and the SEPSA M1 from the port stop outside), the **Solfatara** (daily 8.30am–1hr before sunset; €5.50) is further, and tangible, evidence of the volcanic nature of the area, the exposed crater of a semi-extinct volcano – into which you can walk – that hasn't erupted for a couple of thousand years; in fact, it was a major tourist attraction in Roman times too. Not surprisingly, it's a weird place: sulphur fumes rise from the rocks around and the grey-yellow ground is hot to the touch (and sounds hollow underfoot), emitting eerily silent jets or *fumaroles* that leave the air pungent with sulphurous fumes. In the 1800s some of the *fumaroles* were covered with brick, creating an almost unbearably warm, sauna-like environment into which you can bend if you can stand it, while others are just left open.

A short, three-minute walk further up the hill on the right, the sixteenth-century **Santuario di San Gennaro** (daily 9am–1pm & 4.30–7pm; free) was built on the supposed site of the martyrdom of Naples' patron saint and holds a stone stained with splashes of his blood (he was beheaded) that apparently glows when his blood liquefies in Naples, which it does three times a year – see "The Miracle of San Gennaro" box, p.893.

Baia and Cumae

The next town along from Pozzuoli, reached in fifteen minutes by train from the Cumana station, by the Temple of Serapide, is **Baia**, a small port with a tiny, rather unattractive bit of beach and a set of imperial-era Roman ruins piling up on the hill above. This was one of the bay's most favoured spots in Roman times, a trendy resort at which all the most fashionable of the city's patricians had villas: the Emperor Hadrian died here in 138 AD and Nero was rumoured to have murdered his mother in Baia. You can take a **tour** organized by the Associazione Aliseo (☎081.526.5780) in a glass-bottomed boat which explores the ruined substructures of submerged villas along the coastline at Baia. Trips run from March to November on Saturday at midday and 4pm, and on Sunday at 10.30am, midday and 4pm.

Immediately behind the station, remains of some enormous Roman baths leave you in no doubt of the town's function in ancient times. Steps lead up from the station square to the entrance to the **excavations** (Tues–Sun 9am–1hr before sunset; €4 combined ticket with Anfiteatro Flavio and Cumae) of a purported Roman palace of the first to the fourth century AD, structured across several levels and an evocative location. Follow the steps down from the entrance level to the first terrace of the palace: the rooms on the right contain patches of Roman stuccowork depicting birds and mythical creatures and a statue of Mercury, beheaded by vandals.. Below are the remains of a small theatre and an open space – a former *piscina* – bordered on one side by a pretty loggia.

There are more ruins inland from Baia at **Lago d'Averno**, where Agrippa constructed a military harbour in 37 BC. The lake itself is the Lake Avernus of antiquity, a volcanic crater that the Greeks believed – and Virgil later wrote – was the entrance to Hades: birds flying over were said to suffocate with the toxic fumes that rose from the lake's murky waters, and sacrifices were regularly made here to the dark deities that lurked beneath the gloomy surface. Today it's more cheerful, no longer surrounded by thick forest (this was cut down by Agrippa), although there's not really any other reason to come – the water of the nearby sea is much more enticing for a swim.

Further up the coast, the town of **Cumae** was the first Greek colony on the Italian mainland, a source of settlers for other colonies (Naples was originally settled by Greeks from Cumae) and a centre of Hellenistic civilization. Later it was home to the so-called Cumaean Sibyl, from whom Tarquinius purchased the Sibylline Books that laid down the laws for the Republic. The **site** (daily 9am–1hr before sunset; €4 combined ticket with Anfiteatro Flavio and Baia), a short walk from the bus stop, is spread over a large area and not at all comprehensively excavated. But the only part you're likely to want to see forms a tight nucleus close to the entrance. The best-known feature is the Cave of the Sibyl, a long, dark corridor that was home to the most famous of the ancient oracles. The cave is rectangular in shape, with light admitted from a series of openings in the western wall; the Sibyl used to dispense her wisdom from the three large chambers at the far end of the forty-foot passageway, the most famous occasion being when Aeneas came here to consult her – an event recorded by the lines of Virgil posted up either side of the entrance.

But the best of Cumae is still to come. Climb up the steps to the right of the cave entrance and follow the winding Via Sacra past a constructed belvedere on the left and the fairly scanty remains of a temple on the right to the Acropolis. Here you'll find the remains of a temple to Jupiter, but it's the **views** that you really come for: from the far side of the temple way south across the shellfish-filled **Lago Fusaro** and the bottom corner of the coast; and, if you clamber down from the other side of the temple, north up the curving coast to the Gulf of Gaeta.

East from Naples: Ercolano to Sorrento

The coast **east from Naples** is no better, perhaps even a little worse than the coast west of the city – the Circumvesuviana train edging out through derelict industrial buildings and dense housing that squeezes ever closer to the track. Most people come here for the ancient sights of **Herculaneum** and **Pompeii**, or to scale **Vesuvius** – or they skip the lot for the resort town of **Sorrento**. All are easy day-trips, and Sorrento, though overdeveloped, may be worth a little more time and makes a good springboard for seeing some of the Amalfi coast.

Ercolano: Vesuvius and the site of Herculaneum

East of Naples the first real point of any interest is the town of **ERCOLANO**, the modern offshoot of the ancient site of Herculaneum, which was destroyed by the eruption of Vesuvius on August 2, 79 AD. It's worth stopping here for two reasons: to see the excavations of the site and to climb to the summit of Vesuvius – to which buses run from outside the train station. A word of warning, though: if you're planning to both visit Herculaneum and scale Vesuvius in one day (and it is possible), be sure to see Vesuvius first, and set off reasonably early – buses stop running up the mountain at around lunchtime, leaving you the afternoon free to wander around the site.

Herculaneum
Situated at the seaward end of Ercolano's main street, the site of **Herculaneum** (daily: Apr–Oct 8.30am–7.30pm; Nov–Mar 8.30am–5pm; €11, or combined ticket with Pompeii and the Villa Oplontis, valid 3 days, €20; audio guide €7) was discovered in 1709, when a well-digger accidentally struck the stage of the buried theatre. Excavations were undertaken throughout the eighteenth and nineteenth centuries, during which period much of the marble and bronze from the site was carted off to Naples to decorate the city's palaces, and it wasn't until 1927 that digging and preservation began in earnest. Herculaneum was a residential town, much smaller than Pompeii, and as such it makes a more manageable site, less architecturally impressive and less outside the modern mainstream (Ercolano virtually abuts the site), but better preserved and more easily taken in on a single visit. Archeologists held for a long time that unlike in Pompeii, on the other side of the volcano, most of the inhabitants of Herculaneum managed to escape. However, recent discoveries of entangled skeletons found at what was the shoreline of the town suggest otherwise, and it's now believed that most of the population was buried by huge avalanches of volcanic

mud, which later hardened into the tufa-type rock that preserved much of the town so well. In early 2000 the remains of another 48 people were found; they were carrying coins, which suggests they were attempting to flee the disaster.

There are always plenty of **guides** hanging around, some English-speaking: it's a good way to get the most out of the site, but be sure to negotiate the fee before you start.

Because Herculaneum wasn't a commercial town, there was no central open space or forum, just streets of villas and shops, cut as usual by two very straight main thoroughfares that cross in the centre. Start your tour just inside the entrance at the bottom end of Cardo III, where you'll see the **House of the Argus** (Casa d'Argo) on the left, a very grand building judging by its once-impressive courtyard – although even this is upstaged by the size of the place across the street, the so-called **Hotel** (Casa del Albergo), which covers a huge area, though you can only really get a true impression of its size from the rectangle of stumpy columns that made up its atrium. Further up, Cardo III joins the Decumanus Inferiore, just beyond which it's the large **Thermae** or bath complex which dominates – the domed frigidarium of its men's section decorated with a floor mosaic of dolphins, its caldarium containing a plunge bath and a scallop-shell apse. Still intact are the benches where they sat and the wooden, partitioned shelves for clothing. The women's section has a well-preserved black and white mosaic of Triton and sea creatures, and original glass shards in its window. On the far side of the baths, across Cardo IV, the **Samnite House** (Casa Sannitica) has an attractive atrium, with a graceful loggia all the way round and a hole in the roof still decorated with animal spouts. Three doors down, the **House of Neptune and Amphitrite** (Casa di Nettuno ed Anfitrite) holds sparklingly preserved and richly ornamental wall mosaics featuring the gods themselves on one wall, hunting dogs and deer on a vibrant blue background on another. Adjacent is the **House of the Beautiful Courtyard** (Casa del Bel Cortile) where skeletons of bodies still lie in the positions they fell, and there's a **wine shop** (Casa con Botteghe), stocked with shelves of amphorae.

Turning right at the top of Cardo IV takes you around to Cardo V and most of the rest of the town's **shops** – a variety of places including a baker's, complete with ovens and grinding mills, a weaver's, with loom and bones, and a dyer's, with a huge pot for dyes. Behind the ones on the left you can see the **Palestra**, where public games were held, although it's not actually possible to reach this. Further down on the right, the shop on the corner of Cardo V and Decumanus Inferiore has a well-preserved counter and urns for cereals or some such merchandise; another, further down Cardo V on the right, has a Priapic painting behind its counter. Cutting through to Cardo IV from here takes you to the **House of the Wooden Partition** (Casa del Tramezzo di Legno) with its original partition doors (now under glass) – evidence that it was the home of a poorer class of person than many of the buildings here. The next-door **House of Opus Craticium** (Casa a Graticcio) is a plebeian artisans' residence, originally divided into separate apartments, and with an upper storey balcony overhanging the streetfront. The term *"opus craticium"* refers to the building method of using poor-quality material held together by wooden frames, of which this is a very well-preserved example. At the bottom end of Cardo IV, the **House of the Mosaic Atrium** (Casa del Atrio Mosaico) was a grand villa in its day and retains its mosaic-laid courtyard, corrugated by the force of the tufa. Behind here, the **House of the Deer** (Casa dei Cervi) on Cardo V was another luxury villa, its two storeys built around a central courtyard and containing corridors decorated with richly coloured still-lifes.

Close by, from the end of Cardo IV, a covered passageway leads down to another **baths** building on the left, which is in fact one of the most impressive – and intact – structures in Herculaneum, complete with extremely well-preserved stuccowork and a pretty much intact set of baths; it also has a complete original Roman door, the only one in Herculaneum that wasn't charred by fire. If you find it open, the damp mustiness makes it certainly the most evocative stop on a tour of the site.

Mount Vesuvius

Since its first eruption in 79 AD, when it buried the towns and inhabitants of Pompeii and Herculaneum, **Mount Vesuvius** has dominated the lives of those who live on the Bay of Naples, its brooding bulk forming a stately backdrop to the ever-growing settlements that group around its lower slopes. It's still an active volcano, the only one on mainland Europe. There have been more than a hundred eruptions over the years, but only two others of real significance – one in December 1631 that engulfed many nearby towns and killed 3000 people; and the last, in March 1944, which caused widespread devastation in the towns around, though no one was actually killed. The people who live here still fear the reawakening of the volcano, and with good cause – scientists calculate it should erupt every thirty years or so, and it hasn't since 1944. It's carefully monitored, of course, and there is apparently no reason to expect any movement for some time. But the subsidence in towns like Ercolano below is a continuing reminder of the instability of the area, one of southern Italy's most densely populated: around half a million people would be immediately threatened by another eruption.

There are several ways of making the **ascent**. Easiest is to buy a package ticket from the Circumvesuviana booth at Napoli Centrale. It runs €20 and includes the train ticket to Pompeii Scavi, the bus up the volcano and back, and admission to the crater. Alternatively, buses are run from Pompeii by Trasporti Vesuviani (℡081.559.2582; April–Oct at 9am, 10.10am, 11.30am, 1.30pm & 2.10pm, last bus back 5.50pm; Nov–March at 10.30am, 11.30am, 12.40pm, last bus back 3pm; €3.10 return); buses also go up and back twice daily from the bar by the Ercolano train station. All buses drop you at the car park and huddle of souvenir shops and cafés close to the crater. There is a **charge** of €6 to approach the crater, which includes a brief explanatory talk (in English). The bus is much the cheapest way of doing things, but you can look out for minibus taxis which charge around €6 per person and wait while you see the crater. Or you can take the infrequent local bus (#5) from the roundabout near the train station to the end of the line and walk from there – a good couple of hours to the crater. The walk is certainly a pleasant one, winding through the fertile lower slopes of the volcano, covered with vines and olives, past the main lava flows of the 1944 eruption as far as the car park, which sits just above the greenery among the bare cinders of Vesuvius's main summit.

Walking up to the crater from the car park takes about half an hour, a stony stroll across reddened, barren gravel and rock on marked-out paths, though with nothing on your right to prevent you falling down the smooth side of the mountain – take care. At the top is a deep, wide, jagged ashtray of red rock swirled over by midges and emitting the odd plume of smoke, though since the last eruption effectively sealed up the main crevice this is much less evident than it once was.

The bay to Sorrento

Beyond Ercolano the bay doesn't really pick up: it's still hard to distinguish much countryside between the towns – most of which sadly seem more in tune with their proximity to the city than to the sea. **TORRE DEL GRECO**, the first place you reach, is famous for its coral industry, and you can still buy coral jewellery here, though these days the coral is imported from Tunisia and Japan and then turned into jewellery in workshops here.

Further along, **TORRE ANNUNZIATA** is much less appealing at first sight, though about half a kilometre down from the train station is the **Villa Oplontis** (April–Oct 8.30am–7.30pm, last entry 6pm; Nov–March 8.30am–5pm, last entry 3.30pm; €5.50, or combined ticket with Pompeii and Herculaneum, valid 3 days, €20), one of the best preserved of all Roman villas. Also a victim of the 79 AD eruption, this sumptuous residence is now thought to have belonged to Poppaea, the second wife of Emperor Nero, and is remarkable for the scale and beauty of its architecture, wall paintings and gardens. From the vast atrium, adorned with intricate architectural paintings of columns and shields, the vista extends right through the house, to the colonnaded portico surrounding it and the restored, formal gardens bordered with box hedges. Like villas of today, this one also had its own sun terrace and swimming pool, and bones discovered under the lawn suggest that a goat kept the grass in check. Inside, most striking is the bright-red and tawny-yellow caldarium in the bath complex where a pastoral painting portrays Hercules, draped in lion skin, in the garden of the Hesperides, while above him, astride a seahorse, sits a sultry Nereid. Frescoed walls in other rooms yield peacocks galore, bowls of figs and pomegranates, theatrical masks and impressionistic scenes of daily life.

The only reason for stopping at **CASTELLAMMARE DI STABIA**, a few kilometres further round the bay, is to take the funicular from Circumvesuvi-ana station (daily every 30min: mid-June to Aug 7.25am–7.15pm; rest of year 9.35am–4.25pm; €7.23 return) up to the top of **Monte Faito** (1100m), a ten-minute journey that gives predictably dazzling views, although you need to walk for fifteen minutes or so at the top to get clear of the trees. Alternatively, hurry on south to Salerno or west to Sorrento – both feasible jumping-off points for the Amalfi coast.

Pompeii

The other Roman town to be destroyed by Vesuvius – **Pompeii** – was a much larger affair than Herculaneum and one of Campania's most important commercial centres in its day. After a spell as a Greek colony, Pompeii came under the sway of the Romans in 200 BC, later functioning as both a moneyed resort for wealthy patricians and a trading town that exported wine and fish products, notably its own brand of fish sauce. A severe earthquake destroyed much of the city in 63 AD, and the eruption of Vesuvius sixteen years later only served to exacerbate what was already a desperate situation.

Vesuvius had been spouting smoke and ash for several days before the eruption and in fact most of the town had already been evacuated when disaster struck: out of a total population of 20,000 it's thought that only 2000 actually perished, asphyxiated by the toxic fumes of the volcanic debris, their homes buried in several metres of volcanic ash and pumice. **Pliny**, the Roman naturalist, was one of the casualties – he died at nearby Stabiae (now Castellammare) of a heart attack. But his nephew, Pliny the Younger, described the full horror of the scene in two vivid letters to the historian Tacitus, who was compiling a history of the disaster, writing that the sky turned dark like "a room when it is shut up, and the lamp put out".

In effect the eruption froze the way of life in Pompeii as it stood at the time – a way of life that subsequent excavations have revealed in precise and remarkable detail; indeed Pompeii has probably yielded more information about the ordinary life of Roman citizens during the imperial era than any other site: its social conventions, class structure, domestic arrangements and its (very high) standard of living. Some of the buildings are even covered with ancient graffiti, either referring to contemporary political events or simply to the romantic entanglements of the inhabitants; and the full horror of their way of death is apparent in plaster casts made from the shapes their bodies left in the volcanic ash – with faces tortured with agony, or shielding themselves from the dust and ashes.

The first parts of the town were discovered in 1600, but it wasn't until 1748 that **excavations** began, continuing more or less without interruption – after 1860 under the auspices of the Italian government – until the present day. Indeed, exciting discoveries are still being made, and a flood of new funds is being used to excavate a further twenty hectares of the site; it is hoped to resolve whether or not the survivors attempted, vainly, to resettle Pompeii after the eruption. A privately funded excavation some years ago revealed a covered heated swimming pool, whose erotic wall paintings have been deemed by the Vatican to be unsuitable for children. And, in a further development, a luxury "hotel" complex was uncovered in 2000 during the widening of a motorway, slabs of stacked cut marble suggesting it was still under construction when Vesuvius erupted.

Bear in mind that most of the best mosaics and murals (from Herculaneum too) are in the archeological museum in Naples (see p.899), and that as you can only see a small proportion of those found *in situ*, visits to both sites really need to be supplemented by an additional one to the museum.

△ Human remains at Pompeii

The site

The **site** of Pompeii (daily: April–Oct 8.30am–7.30pm, last entry 6pm; Nov–March 8.30am–5pm, last entry 3.30pm; €11, or combined ticket with Herculaneum and Villa Oplontis, valid 3 days, €20; Ⓦ www.pompeiisites.org) covers a wide area, and seeing it properly takes half a day at the very least; really you should devote most of a day to it and take plenty of breaks – unlike Herculaneum there's little shade, and the distances involved are quite large: flat, comfortable shoes are a must.

All of this makes Pompeii sound a bit of a chore – which it certainly isn't. But there is a lot to see, and you should be reasonably selective: many of the streets aren't lined by much more than foundations, and after a while one ruin begins to look much like another. Again, many of the most interesting structures are kept locked and only opened when a large group forms or a tip is handed over to one of the many custodians. It's worth studying the **site map**, which you'll find at every entrance – pins on the map indicate which areas are currently closed, as the site is in continuous restoration. To be sure of seeing as much as possible you could take a tour, although one of the pleasures of Pompeii is to escape the hordes and absorb the strangely still quality of the town, which, despite the large number of visitors, it is quite possible to do.

Entering the site from the Pompeii-Villa dei Misteri side, through the Porta Marina, the **Forum** is the first real feature of significance, a long, slim open space surrounded by the ruins of what would have been some of the town's most important official buildings – a basilica, temples to Apollo and Jupiter, and a market hall. Walking north from here, up the so-called Via di Mercurio, takes you towards some of the town's more luxurious houses. On the left, the **House of the Tragic Poet** (Casa del Poetica Tragico) is named for its mosaics of a theatrical production and a poet inside, though the "Cave Canem" (Beware of the Dog) mosaic by the main entrance is more eye-catching. Close by, the residents of the **House of the Faun** (Casa del Fauno) must have been a friendlier lot, its "Ave" (Welcome) mosaic outside beckoning you in to view the atrium and the copy of a tiny, bronze, dancing faun (the original is in Naples) that gives the villa its name.

On the street behind, the **House of the Vettii** (Casa dei Vettii) is one of the most delightful houses in Pompeii and one of the best maintained, a merchant villa ranged around a lovely central peristyle that gives the best possible impression of the domestic environment of the city's upper middle classes. The first room on the right off the peristyle holds the best of Pompeii's murals actually viewable on site: the one on the left shows the young Hercules struggling with serpents; another, in the corner, depicts Ixion tied to a wheel after offending Zeus; while a third shows Dirce being dragged to her death by the bull set on her by the sons of Antiope. There are more paintings beyond here, through the villa's kitchen in a small room that's normally kept locked – erotic works showing various techniques of lovemaking (Greek-style, woman on top; Roman-style, man on top) together with an absurdly potent-looking statue of Priapus from which women were supposed to drink to be fertile; phallic symbols were also, it's reckoned, believed to ward off the evil eye.

Cross over to the other side of the site for the so-called **new excavations**, which began in 1911 and actually uncovered some of the town's most important quarters, stretching along the main Via dell'Abbondanza. The **Grand Theatre**, for one, is very well preserved and is still used for performances, overlooking the small, grassy, column-fringed square of the **Gladiators' Barracks** (Caserma dei Gladiatori) – not in fact a barracks at all but a refectory and meeting-place for spectators from the nearby amphitheatre. Walk around to the far left side of the Grand Theatre, down the steps and up again, and you're in front of the **Little Theatre** – a smaller, more intimate venue also still used for summer performances and with a better-kept corridor behind the stage space. As for the **Amphitheatre**, it's one of Italy's most intact and accessible, and also its oldest, dating from 80 BC; it once had room for a crowd of some 12,000 – well over half the town's population. Next door, the **Palestra** is a vast parade ground that was used by Pompeii's youth for sport and exercise – still with its square of swimming pool in the centre. It must have been in use when the eruption struck Pompeii, since its southeast corner was found littered with the skeletons of young men trying to flee the disaster. Just north of the Palestra, off Via Abbondanza, is the **House of Loreius Tiburtinus** (Casa di Loreio Tiburtino), a gracious villa fronted by great bronze doors. Paintings of Narcissus gazing rapt at his reflection and Pyramus and Thisbe frame a water cascade; the water flowed down a channel and into the villa's lovely garden, which has been replanted with vines and shrubs.

One last place you shouldn't miss at Pompeii is the **Villa dei Misteri**. This is probably the best preserved of all Pompeii's palatial houses, an originally third-century BC structure with a warren of rooms and courtyards that derives its name from a series of paintings in one of its larger chambers: depictions of the initiation rites of a young woman into the Dionysiac Mysteries, an outlawed cult of the early imperial era. Not much is known about the cult itself, but the paintings are marvellously clear, remarkable for the surety of their execution and the brightness of their tones and colours. They follow an obvious narrative, starting with the left-hand wall and continuing around the room with a series of freeze-frames showing sacrifice, flagellation, dancing and other rituals, all under the serene gaze of the mistress of the house.

Practicalities

To **reach Pompeii from Naples**, take the Circumvesuviana east from Torre Annuziata to Pompeii-Villa dei Misteri – about thirty minutes; this leaves you right outside the western entrance to the site. The Circumvesuviana also runs to Pompeii-Santuario, outside the site's eastern entrance, or you can take the roughly hourly mainline train (direction Salerno) to the main Pompeii FS station, on the south side of the fairly characterless modern town. From the main station ignore the taxi drivers offering to take you to the entrance for an extortionate fee – it only takes around ten minutes to walk. Head away from the station towards the tall belltower, turning left at the main square to follow the signs to "Pompeii Scavi". After around 200m you come to the eastern entrance, Porta di Nuceria, on the right-hand side, the site itself screened by an avenue of trees.

If you want to make Pompeii an overnight stop, there are plenty of **hotels** and an excellent **youth hostel**, *Casa del Pellegrino*, Via Duca d'Aosta 4 (℡081.850.8644, www.hihostels.com; dorms €14), with family rooms (❷) as well, situated 300m from the Pompei-Santuario station. There are also a couple of handy **camp-sites** including *Camping Pompei* (℡081.862.2882, ⓦwww.campingpompei.com; from €4 per person, ❶ for a bungalow) at Via Plinio 113, south of the main entrance. Modern Pompei's **tourist office** at Via Sacra 1 (Mon–Sat 9am–3pm; ℡081.850.7255), just off the main square, has plans of the site.

Sorrento

Topping the rocky cliffs close to the end of its peninsula, 25km south of Pompeii, the last town of significance on this side of the bay, **SORRENTO** is

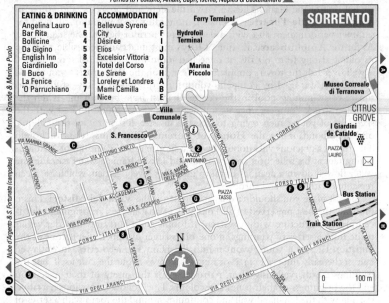

SORRENTO

EATING & DRINKING		ACCOMMODATION	
Angelina Lauro	1	Bellevue Syrene	C
Bar Rita	6	City	F
Bollicine	4	Désirée	I
Da Gigino	5	Elios	J
English Inn	8	Excelsior Vittoria	D
Giardiniello	3	Hotel del Corso	G
Il Buco	2	Le Sirene	H
La Fenice	9	Loreley et Londres	A
'O Parruchiano	7	Mami Camilla	B
		Nice	E

Ferry Terminal

Hydrofoil Terminal

Marina Piccolo

Museo Correale di Terranova

CITRUS GROVE

I Giardini de Cataldo

PIAZZA LAURO

Villa Comunale

S. Francesco

VIA LUIGI DE MAIO

VIA MARINA PICCOLA

VIA CORREALE

VIA VITTORIO VENETO

VIA S. PAOLO

VIA P.R. GIULIANI

PIAZZA S. ANTONINO

CORSO ITALIA

VIA S. MARIA DELLE GRAZIE

VIA ACCADEMIA

VIA S. MARIA DELLE GRAZIE

PIAZZA TASSO

Bus Station

VIA S. NICOLA

VIA S. CESAREO

VIA MARZIALE

VIA FUORO

VIA PIETÀ

Train Station

CORSO ITALIA

VIA SERSALE

VIA DEGLI ARANCI

VIA DEGLI ARANCI

VIA FUORIMURA

VIA MARZIALE

N

0   100 m

Marina Grande & Marina Puolo

Nube d'Argento & S. Fortunata (campsites)

13

CAMPANIA | East from Naples: Ercolano to Sorrento

solely and unashamedly a resort, its inspired location and mild climate draw-ing foreigners from all over Europe for close on 200 years. Ibsen wrote part of *Peer Gynt* in Sorrento, Wagner and Nietzsche had a well-publicized row here, and Maxim Gorky lived for over a decade in the town. Nowadays it's strictly package-tour territory, but not too much the worse for it, with little of the brashness of its Spanish and Greek equivalents but all of their vigour, a bright, lively place that retains its southern Italian roots. Cheap restaurants aren't too hard to find, nor – if you know where to look – is reasonably priced accom-modation; and it's a handy place outside Naples itself from which to explore the rugged peninsula (even parts of the Amalfi coast) and the islands of the bay. In fact, its main identity these days is as a transport hub for tourists going to more interesting places.

Sorrento's centre is **Piazza Tasso**, built astride the gorge that runs through the centre of town; it was named after the wayward sixteenth-century Italian poet to whom the town was home and has a statue of him in the far corner. There's nothing much to see in Sorrento itself, but it's nice to wander through the streets that feed into the square, some of which are pedestrianized for the lively evening *passeggiata*. The local **Museo Correale di Terranova**, housed in the airy former palace of a family of local counts at the far end of Via Correale (Mon & Wed–Sun 9am–2pm; €6), might kill an hour or so, with its exam-ples of the local inlaid wood *intarsio* work – most of it much nicer and more ingenious than the mass-produced stuff you see around town – along with various paintings of the Neapolitan school, the odd foreign canvas, includ-ing an obscure Rubens, lots of views of Sorrento and the Bay of Naples, and various locally unearthed archeological knick-knacks. Otherwise the town is entirely given over to pleasure and there's not much else to see, although it's nice to linger in the shady gardens of the **Villa Comunale**, whose terrace has lovely views out to sea, and peek into the small thirteenth-century cloister of the church of **San Francesco** just outside, planted with vines and bright bougainvillea – a peaceful escape from the bustle of the rest of Sorrento. The same applies to **I Giardini di Cataldo**, northern entrance at Via Correale 27 in the centre of Sorrento (daily 9am–7pm), an orange and lemon grove, across from which to the south, at Corso Italia 267, you can taste and buy delicious home-produced liqueurs.

Strange as it may seem, Sorrento isn't particularly well provided with **beaches**, and in the town itself you either have to make do with the small strips of sand of the **Marina Piccola** lido, right below the Villa Comunale gardens and accessible by a lift or steps, or the rocks and tiny, crowded strip of sand at **Marina Grande** – fifteen minutes' walk or a short bus ride (roughly every 30min) west of Piazza Tasso. Both places cost around €3 a head for the day, plus charges for parasol and chair rental, although there is a small patch of sand, immediately right of the lift exit at Marina Piccola, that is free. If you do come down to either of these spots, it's a good idea to rent a pedal-boat (from about €15 an hour) and get free of the shore, since both beaches can get busy.

If you don't fancy the crowds in Sorrento, you can try the beaches further west. Twenty minutes' walk from the centre of Sorrento along Via del Capo (which is the continuation of Corso Italia), or a short bus ride from Piazza Tasso, there are a couple of options. You can either walk ten minutes or so from the bus stop down the Ruderi Villa Romana Pollio to some nice rocks, swathed with walkways, around the ruins of a Roman villa; or you could stroll 100m further west and take a path off to the right past the *Hotel Dania*, which short-cuts in ten minutes or so to **Marina Puolo** – a short stretch of beach lined by fishing boats and a handful of trattorias.

Practicalities

Sorrento's **train station** is located in the centre of town, five minutes from the main Piazza Tasso along busy Corso Italia. There's a **tourist office** in the large yellow Circolo dei Forestieri building at Via Luigi de Maio 35, just off Piazza San Antonino (Mon–Sat 8.30am–6.30pm; ℡081.807.4033, Ⓦ www.sorrentotourism.com), which has maps, details on accommodation, transport and information about excursions. The travel offices on Piazza San Antonino can deal with bus and ferry enquiries and ticket reservations. If you don't want to rely on public transport, *Sorrento*, Corso Italia 210 (℡081.878.1386), close by the train station, rents out cars and scooters, and *Guarracino*, Via Sant'Antonino 19 (℡081.878.1728), just off the piazza of the same name, rents out bikes.

Accommodation

Accommodation isn't really a problem, although during peak season you should definitely book in advance. There's a private **youth hostel**, *Le Sirene*, Via degli Aranci 156 (℡081.807.2925, Ⓦ www.hostel.it; €20, including breakfast); it's fairly clean if a little cramped and noisy. To get there from the train station, turn left on the main road and Via degli Aranci is 200m down on the left. The closest of the **campsites** is the *Nube d'Argento* site, near the *Elios* hotel at Via del Capo 21 (℡081.878.1344, Ⓦ www.nubedargento.com; April–Dec; from €10 per person, ❸ for a bungalow for two); if that's full, try the cheaper *Santa Fortunata*, which comes with private beach, about 1.5km from the centre at Via del Capo 41 (℡081.807.3579, Ⓦ www.santafortunata .com; April–Oct; from €9 per person, ❷ for a two-person bungalow); both have superb sea views.

Bellevue Syrene Piazza della Vittoria 5 ℡081.878.1024, ℻081.878.3963, ⓦwww .bellevuesyrene.it. A lovely nineteenth-century hotel, built on the remains of a Roman villa. Boasts glorious views and a private beach. ❼

City Corso Italia 221 ℡ & ℻081.877.2210, ⓦwww.sorrentocity.com. Fairly basic, but recently remodelled and well placed for the action in town. ❹

Désirée Via Capo 31 ℡ & ℻081.878.1563, ⓦwww.desireehotelsorrento.com. Great option, beautifully situated on top of the cliff to the west of town, with stunning views and a private beach (accessible by lift). Rooms are stylish and the owners go out of their way to be helpful. Breakfast is included in the price. Closed mid-Nov to Feb. No credit cards. ❸

Elios Via del Capo 33 ℡081.878.1812. A good 15 minutes' walk from the centre to the west of town, the *Elios* has terrific sea views and private parking. Seaward rooms are quieter. Closed Dec–March. No credit cards. ❷

🏃 **Excelsior Vittoria** Piazza Tasso 34 ℡081.877.7111, ⓦwww.excelsiorvittoria .com. This fabulously grand hotel has been owned by the same family since 1834; it sits right in the centre of town in a formal garden with a lemon and orange grove and a large pool; the lift from the swish terrace bar plunges straight down to the seafront. Immaculate, friendly service. ❾

Hotel del Corso Corso Italia 134 ℡081.807.1016, ⓦwww.hoteldelcorso.com. Right by Piazza Tazzo, the *del Corso* is furnished in pleasant, modern style and has a breakfast terrace overlooking the street. ❺

Loreley et Londres Via Califano 2 ℡081.807.3187, ⓔinfo@sorrentohotelmigno.com. Situated in a beautiful ancient building high on the cliffs on the eastern edge of the town centre, this is wonderful value. Breakfast is included in the price. Closed mid-Nov to mid-March. ❸

Mami Camilla Via Cocomella 4 ℡081.878.2067, ⓦwww.mamicamilla.com. Hotel and cookery school rolled into one, with an exceptional family atmosphere and, as you'd expect, great food. B&B from €80 a night for two; book in advance to eat, from €15.

Nice Corso Italia 257 ℡081.878.1650, ⓦwww .hotelnice.it. A very convenient and centrally placed option; the attractive en-suite rooms are air condi-tioned, but a trifle noisy. Ask for one facing the citrus grove. ❸

Eating

Sorrento has no shortage of **restaurants**, but in the more touristy places service can be slow and the food not up to scratch. If you just want a snack, *Bar Rita*, Corso Italia 219, can't be bettered, with a wide array of sandwiches, cakes and other delicious lunch items.

Angelina Lauro Piazza Angelina Lauro 39 ℡081.807.4097. A self-service place with a *menù turistico* for €11. No credit cards. Closed Tues.

Da Gigino Via degli Archi 15 ℡081.878.1927. A great, no-nonsense choice, with excellent pizzas and good pasta and main courses; pizza from €7. Closed Tues except Aug.

Giardiniello Via Accademia 7 ℡081.878.4616. Just off Corso Italia, between Piazza Sant'Antonio and Via Tasso, this pizzeria-ristorante with a small garden specializes in fish, shellfish and barbecued meats; try the *gnocchi alla sorrentina*, in a spicy sauce of fresh tomato and basil leaves with chunks of *mozzarella di bufala* at €7. Closed Thurs.

Il Buco Rampa Marina Piccola 11, Piazza San Antonino ℡081.878.2354. This former monastic wine cellar does good fish; mains (€22) and *menù degustazione* (€75). Closed Wed.

La Fenice Via degli Aranci 11 ℡081.878.1652. A great place with a covered patio and lively atmos-phere, specializing in fish; mains around €20. Closed Mon.

'O Parruchiano Corso Italia 67 ℡081.878.13211. More of a conservatory than a restaurant, this vast place is very popular with locals and tour groups alike. The fine food is great value; try the *cannel-loni con la ricotta* at about €8.

Nightlife

For **drinking**, there's a glut of English-style pubs along Corso Italia, mainly frequented by Italians, such as the capacious *English Inn* at no. 55, with an outside dance floor, and *Chaplins*, almost opposite, at no. 18. Elsewhere, *Artis Domus*, Via S Nicola 56, is an elegant club with live music (open in summer only); *Bollicine*, Via Accademia 7, is a small, wood-panelled wine bar with a wide range of good Campanian wines; and *Matilda*, at Piazza

Tasso 1, is a huge, lively disco bar with nightly partying and Internet access (closed Tues).

The islands

Guarding each prong of the Bay of Naples, the islands of Cápri, Ischia and Prócida between them make up the best-known group of Italian islands. Each is a very different creature, though. **Cápri** is a place of legend, home to the mythical Sirens and a much-eulogized playground of the super-rich in the years since – though now settled down to a lucrative existence as a target for day-trippers from the mainland. Visit by all means, but bear in mind that you have to hunt hard these days to detect the origins of much of the purple prose. **Ischia** is a target for package tours (predominantly from Germany) and weekenders from Naples, but its size means that it doesn't feel as crowded as Cápri, and plentiful hot springs, sandy beaches and a green volcanic interior make the island well worth a few days' visit, especially as you can easily visit other sites in the bay (including Pompeii and Herculaneum, using the usual Circumvesuviana train connections from either Naples or Sorrento) by ferry from here. Pretty **Prócida**, the smallest of the islands and the least interesting – though the best venue for fairly peaceful lazing – remains reasonably untouched by the high season.

Cápri

Sheering out of the sea just off the far end of the Sorrentine peninsula, the island of **Cápri** has long been the most sought-after part of the Bay of Naples. During Roman times Augustus retreated to the island's gorgeous cliffbound scenery to escape the cares of office; later Tiberius moved the imperial capital here, indulging himself in legendarily debauched antics until his death in 37 AD. After the Romans left, Cápri was rather neglected until the early nineteenth century, when the discovery of the Blue Grotto and the island's remarkable natural landscape coincided nicely with the rise of tourism, and the island has never looked back, attracting a steady flow of artists, writers and, more recently, inquisitive tourists ever since. The English especially have always flocked here: D.H. Lawrence and George Bernard Shaw were among more illustrious visitors; Graham Greene and Gracie Fields had houses here; and even Lenin visited for a time after the failure of the 1905 uprising.

Cápri tends to get a mixed press these days, the consensus being that while it might have been an attractive place once, it's been pretty much ruined by the crowds and the prices. And Cápri *is* crowded, to the degree that in July and August, and on *all* summer weekends, it would be sensible to give it a miss. But reports that the island has been irreparably spoilt are overstated. Ischia is busy too, Prócida isn't nearly as interesting – or beautiful – and it would be hard to find a place with more inspiring views. It's expensive, though prices aren't really any higher than at other major Italian resorts, and you can find very reasonably priced and attractive accommodation in Anacápri or just visit on a day-trip, which should give you time enough to see the major sights of the island.

Marina Grande, Cápri town and around

Ferries and hydrofoils dock at **MARINA GRANDE**, the waterside extension of the island's main town, which perches on the hill above. You can take boats to the Blue Grotto (see p.922) from here, and there's a tourist office (see "Practicalities")

Ferries and hydrofoils to the islands operate from Naples, Pozzuoli and Sorrento, with some connections from Salerno, Amalfi and Positano. There are two departure points in Naples: the main harbour (the Molo Beverello) at the bottom of Piazza Municipio and the quayside at Mergellina. Whichever route you take, day-trips are quite feasible; usually the last connection delivers you back on the mainland in time for dinner. On foot, you can simply buy tickets when you turn up at the offices at the port; in general it's better to buy a single rather than a return ticket since it doesn't work out more expensive and you retain more flexibility on the time you come back. Having said that, on summer Sundays (especially on Cápri, and especially by hydrofoil), it's a good idea to buy your return ticket as soon as you arrive, to avoid the risk of finding the last boat or hydrofoil fully booked. If you're looking at price, the state-run ferry Caremar is usually the cheapest and slowest; tickets start at €5.60 compared with about €14 for the private hydrofoils.

The following gives a rough idea of frequencies during the summer (they're greatly reduced off-season). For specific timings you can look in *Il Mattino*, check with the local tourist office or look up the companies online: Caremar (℡081.551.3882, ⓦwww.caremar.it); Alilauro (℡081.761.1004, ⓦwww.alilauro.it); SNAV (℡081.428.5555, ⓦwww.snav.it); NLG (℡081.552.7209, ⓦwww.navlib.it); Prócida Lines (℡081.896.0328); and Traghetti Pozzuoli (℡081.526.7736).

Hydrofoils and fast ferries

Naples (Molo Beverello)–Cápri (25 daily; 40min).
Naples (Molo Beverello)–Casamicciola, Ischia (6 daily; 1hr).
Naples (Molo Beverello)–Forío, Ischia (9 daily; 50min).
Naples (Molo Beverello)–Ischia (22 daily; 40–60min).
Naples (Molo Beverello)–Prócida (6 daily; 35–40min).
Naples (Mergellina)–Cápri (6 daily; 35min).
Naples (Mergellina)–Casamicciola, Ischia (6 daily; 45min).
Naples (Mergellina)–Prócida (3 daily; 20min).
Casamicciola, Ischia–Prócida (10 daily; 20min).
Ischia–Prócida (4 daily; 15min).
Ischia–Cápri (1 daily; 50min).
Prócida–Ischia (4 daily; 15min).
Salerno–Cápri (2 daily; 2hr).
Sorrento–Ischia (via Naples: 4 daily; 1hr); also 1 daily direct, and 1 daily via Cápri.
Sorrento–Cápri (22 daily; 20–25min).

Ferries

Naples (Molo Beverello)–Cápri (3 daily; 1hr 20min).
Naples (Molo Beverello)–Ischia (7 daily; 1hr 30min).
Naples (Molo Beverello)–Prócida (6 daily; 1hr).
Pozzuoli–Ischia (3 daily; 1hr).
Pozzuoli–Casamicciola, Ischia (12 daily; 1hr 30min).
Pozzuoli–Prócida (13 daily; 35–50min).
Ischia–Prócida (6 daily; 25min).
Sorrento–Cápri (5 daily; 40min).
Salerno–Cápri (via Amalfi; 1 daily; 2hr).
Salerno–Ischia (via Amalfi and Positano: 1 daily; 2hr 30min).

that sells a map and hotel guide (€0.80), as well as any number of pricey waterside cafés and restaurants. It is, however, quickly exhausted, and you may as well take the **funicular** (daily 6.30am–9pm; till 12.30am June–Sept; €1.30

one-way) up the steep hill to Cápri town itself; if the funicular is too crowded (as it surely will be in high season) you can also walk, which takes about twenty minutes. Find the fountain in the middle of the harbour and from there steps, clearly marked, lead all the way up across the crisscrossing road.

CÁPRI is the main town of the island, nestled between its two mountains, its houses connected by winding, hilly alleyways that give onto the dinky main square of **Piazza Umberto**, crowded with café tables and lit by twinkling fairy lights in the evenings. On the far side of town is the **Certosa San Giacomo** (Tues–Sat 9am–2pm, Sun 9am–1pm; free; closed for restoration at the time of writing), a run-down old monastery with a multilingual lending library, a handful of German metaphysical paintings, a couple of shapeless Roman statues dredged up from the deep and an overgrown cloister. On past the monastery, at the other side of the island, the **Giardini di Augusto** give tremendous views of the coast below and the towering jagged cliffs above. The zigzag pathway down, Via Krupp, has been closed for restoration for years. However, if you find it reopened, you can wind down to either the beach (rocks really), or, beyond, to **MARINA PICCOLA** – a small huddle of houses and restaurants around patches of pebble beach: reasonably uncrowded out of season, though in July or August you might as well forget it. Marina Piccola is also accessible by bus from the Cápri town bus terminus.

Up above the Certosa, and a further pleasant walk fifteen minutes through Cápri town, the **Belvedere del Cannone** has marvellous views, especially over the **Faraglioni** rocks to the left and Marina Piccola to the right. Further out of Cápri town, there are two walks worth doing to the eastern edge of the island. One, up to the ruins of Tiberius's villa, the **Villa Jovis** (daily 9am–1hr before sunset; €2), is a steep thirty-minute hike from Piazza Umberto following Via Botteghe out of the square and Via Tiberio up the hill. It was here that Tiberius retired in 27 AD, reportedly to lead a life of vice and debauchery and to take revenge on his enemies, many of whom he apparently had thrown

△ Cápri

off the cliff face. You can see why he chose the site: it's among Cápri's most exhilarating, with incredible vistas of the Sorrentine Peninsula, including the Amalfi Coast, and the bay; on a clear day you can even see Salerno and beyond. There's not much left of the villa, but you can get a good sense of the shape and design of its various parts from the arched halls and narrow passageways that remain. Below, there's another villa, the more recent **Villa Fersen** of one Count Fersen-Adelsward, a gay Swedish millionaire writer who built the house in the early 1900s apparently to entertain his young Italian lovers, as well as his heroin and cocaine habits. The house is open to the public by guided morning tours in high season.

The other walk is to the **Arco Naturale**, an impressive natural rock formation at the end of a high, lush valley, a 25-minute walk from Cápri town, again following Via Botteghe out of the square but branching off up Via Matermania after ten minutes or so; just follow the signs. You can get quite close to the arch owing to the specially constructed viewing platforms. Just before the path descends towards the arch, steps lead down to the **Grotta di Matermania**, ten minutes away down quite a few steps – a dusty cutaway out of the rock that was converted to house a shrine to the goddess Cybele by the Romans. Steps lead on down from the cave, sheer through the trees, before flattening into a fine path that you can follow to the **Tragara Belvedere**, affording some of the island's best views along the way, and, eventually, back to Cápri town – reachable in about an hour.

Anacápri and around

The island's other main settlement, **ANACÁPRI**, is more sprawling than Cápri itself and less obviously picturesque, its main square, **Piazza Vittoria**, flanked by souvenir shops, bland fashion boutiques and restaurants decked with tourist menus – Cápri without the chic. A chair lift operates from Piazza Vittoria up to **Monte Solaro** (March–Oct daily 9.30am to sunset; Nov–Feb 10.30am–3pm; return €6, one-way €4.50), the island's highest point (596m). At the top there's only a ruined castle and a café, but the ride and the location are very tranquil and the 360-degree views are marvellous – the bay's very best.

A short walk away from Piazza Vittoria down Via G. Orlandi, the church of **San Michele** (April–June 9.30am–5pm; July–Oct 9.30am–7pm; Nov–March 10am–4.30pm; €1) is the village's principal sight, its tiled floor painted with an eighteenth-century depiction of the Fall that you view from an upstairs balcony – a lush work after a drawing by the Neapolitan painter **Solimena**, in rich blues and yellows, showing cats, unicorns and other creatures.

Continuing in the same direction, a good 45-minute hike away starting off down Via Lo Pozzo (or reachable by bus every twenty minutes from Piazza Vittoria), you come to the **Blue Grotto** or Grotta Azzurra, probably the island's best-known feature – though also its most exploitative, the boatmen here whisking visitors onto boats and in and out of the grotto in about five minutes flat (daily 9am–1hr before sunset, but not in case of adverse weather; €8.50 plus tip expected). The grotto is quietly impressive, the blue of its innards caused by sunlight entering the cave through the water, but it's rather overrated. Technically, you can swim into the cave – it's not the exclusive preserve of the boatmen, though they'll try to persuade you otherwise – but the route through is so busy that unless you're a strong swimmer it's only advisable to try at the end of the day after the tours have finished. You can also get here by boat direct from Marina Grande (€8–10 extra).

Time is much better spent walking in the opposite direction from Piazza Vittoria, past a long gauntlet of souvenir stalls to Axel Munthe's Villa **San Michele**

(May–Sept 9am–6pm; April & Oct 9am–5pm; March 9am–5.30pm; Nov–Feb 9am–3.30pm; €5; Ⓦwww.sanmichele.org), a light, airy house with lush and fragrant gardens that is one of the real highlights of the island. A nineteenth-century Swedish writer and physician to the elite, Munthe lived here for a number of years, and the place is filled with his furniture and knick-knacks, as well as Roman artefacts and columns plundered from a ruined villa on the site. Busts and bronzes abound: one statue of Hermes was given to Munthe by the city of Naples in thanks for his work in the city during the cholera epidemic of 1884; Corinthian capitals are converted to coffee tables, other surfaces topped with intricate Cosmati mosaic-work. His book *The Story of San Michele* – more the story of his life – is well worth reading. There's also an attractive, small natural history exhibition in the gardens, which fills you in on local flora and fauna, to the (recorded) accompaniment of the golden oriole and nightingale.

Island Practicalities

There are **tourist offices** in Marina Grande (May–Oct daily 8.30am–8.30pm; Nov–April Mon–Sat 9am–5pm; Ⓣ081.837.0634, Ⓦwww.capritourism.com), and on Piazza Umberto I in Cápri town (same hours; Ⓣ081.837.0686). In Anacápri the tourist office is at Via G. Orlandi 59 (May–Oct daily 8.30am–8.30pm; Nov–April Mon–Sat 9am–3pm; Ⓣ081.837.1524). You'll find an **Internet point** in Anacápri, the Cápri Internet Point at Piazza Vittoria 13 (Ⓣ081.837.3283; €2/hr). For **getting around** the island, there's a decent bus service connecting all the main centres – Marina Grande, Cápri, Marina Piccola, Anacápri – every fifteen minutes; buses also run regularly down to the Blue Grotto from Anacápri. Tickets cost €1.30 for a single trip, €2.10 for an hour and €6.70 for a day and are available from ticket booths and *tabacchi*. For travel in real style, however, go for one of the many (pricey) white, soft-top taxis that swish about the island (Ⓣ081.837.0543).

Accommodation

If you're contemplating **staying overnight** on Cápri in peak season – and the island is a lot quieter after the day-tripping crowds have gone home – book well ahead as space is extremely limited. Prices in Cápri itself can go through the roof, but there are a couple of very acceptable, cheaper alternatives in Anacápri.

In and around **Cápri town**, one of the easiest accommodation options to get to is the *Quattro Stagioni* at Via Marina Piccola 1 (Ⓣ & Ⓕ081.837.0041, Ⓦwww .hotel4stagionicapri.com; closed Nov–March; ❺) in a pretty location at the fork of the roads down to Marina Piccola and up to Anacápri. This place has friendly staff and offers a ten-percent discount to carriers of this book. Two other choices are found up the steps from the Piazzetta and through the arches along to Via Castello, where you'll find *La Prora*, at no. 6 (Ⓣ & Ⓕ081.837.0281, Ⓦwww .albergolaprora.it; closed Nov–March; ❻), an appealing, spic and span choice with great views from its balconies and a good breakfast. At Via Castello 13, there's the *Aranciera delle Teresiane* (Ⓣ081.838.2162; ❺), a tiny B&B in a historic building – very well decorated and located but with no views. One of the most economical choices is located directly across from the bus terminus, the *Stella Maris*, at Via Roma 27 (Ⓣ081.837.0452, F081.837.8682; ❹), unlovely but very convenient. Heading up to the left as you enter the Piazzetta is the *Villa Esperia*, at Via Sopramonte 41 (Ⓣ081.837.0262, Ⓕ081.837.0933; ❻), an intimate, family-run hotel, with lovely views from the rooms. Heading straight through the Piazzetta and past all the shops across to the other side of the island, you'll find two superior options, *Hotel Luna*, at Via Matteotti 3 (Ⓣ081.837.0433,

ⓦwww.lunahotel.com: ⓸), secluded and serene, near the gardens of Augustus, with a panoramic terrace and pool. Branching off to the other side of the Certosa, *La Scalinatella*, Casa Morgano Via Tragara 6/8 (ⓣ081.837.0633, ⓦwww.scalinatella.com; ⓸), is an airy, beautifully decorated five-star that locals say provides the best luxury stay on the island.

In **Anacápri**, two budget options stand out, both of them located down from the town towards the Blue Grotto. The *Bussola di Hermes*, Via Traversa La Vigna 14 (ⓣ & ⓕ081.838.2010, ⓦwww.bussolahermes.com; ⓹, no credit cards), is a very friendly hotel with an unofficial hostel (just a few dorm beds €30) as well as luxuriously appointed private rooms. ⚑ *Villa Eva*, Via La Fabbrica 8 (ⓣ081.837.1549, ⓦwww.villaeva.com; closed Nov–Feb; ⓸, no credit cards), is in a class by itself, a charming, eccentric house, with cottages and a large pool, all set in extensive gardens and designed and built by Eva's painter husband Vincenzo. It's a good twenty minutes on foot from Anacápri, but well worth it.

Eating

There are several good **places to eat** on the island, though you can always knock yourself up a **picnic** lunch if you prefer: in Cápri town there are a supermarket and bakery a little way down Via Botteghe, off Piazza Umberto, and a well-stocked *salumerie* at Via Roma 13 and 30. Dining in **Cápri town** can be a real gourmet experience and *Buca di Bacco "da Serafina"*, Via Longano 25 (ⓣ081.837.0723; closed Wed), is rated by locals as one of the best of the best; try the *spaghetti alla pescatora* for €16, or the fresh fish mains for around €22. Alternatively, on Via Roma, the main road coming into town, *Da Giorgio*, at no. 34 (ⓣ081.837.0898; closed Tues), is a surprisingly inexpensive (for Cápri) old favourite in a picturesque location; try the *linguine ai frutti di mare* at €12. Up to the left from the Piazzetta lie two additional finds. *La Capannina*, at Via Botteghe 12/14 (ⓣ081.837.0732; closed Wed & March–April & Oct), is considered by many as the island's top restaurant; fish main courses such as *pezzogna* (local red snapper) for around €28. Farther along, on the continuation of Via Botteghe, you'll find the humbler *Pizzeria Aurora* on Via Fuorlovado 18–22 (ⓣ081.837.0181; closed Tues), the longest-established place on the island, with tables outside and a crunchy speciality called *pizza all'acqua* (€6–8 depending on topping). A reliable choice in **Anacápri** is *Materita*, Via G. Orlandi 140, off Piazza Diaz (ⓣ081.837.3375), serving up Neapolitan-style wood-fired pizzas both lunch and dinner; €5 for a margherita.

Ischia

Largest of the islands in the Bay of Naples, **Ischia** rises out of the sea in a cone-shaped series of pointy green hummocks. German, Scandinavian and British tourists flocking in large numbers during peak season to its charming beach resorts, thermal springs and therapeutic sands. Its reputation has always been poorer than Cápri's: it is perhaps not so dramatically beautiful, but you can at least be sure of being alone in exploring parts of the mountainous interior, and **La Mortella**, the exotic garden cultivated by the British composer William Walton and his widow Susana, is an unmissable attraction. Indeed, if you're after some beach lounging, good walking and lively nightlife within striking distance of Naples and the rest of the bay, it might be just the place.

Public transport is regular and easy to negotiate: buses #CS (counter-clockwise) and #CD (clockwise) circle the island every thirty minutes, stopping just about everywhere. Tickets cost €1.20 and are valid for 90 minutes; day tickets are €4, two-day tickets €6.

Ischia Porto and Ischia Ponte

The main town of Ischia is **ISCHIA PORTO**, where the ferries dock, an appealing stretch of hotels, ritzy boutiques and beach shops planted with lemon trees and Indian figs fronted by golden sands: **Spiaggia San Pietro** is to the right of the port, accessible by following Via Buonocore off Via Roma. The inexplicably named **Spiaggia degli Inglesi**, on the other side of the port, is reachable by way of the narrow path that leads over the headland from the end of Via Jasolino.

Otherwise the main thing to do is to window-shop and stroll along the main Corso Vittoria Colonna, either branching off to a further beach, the Spiaggia **dei Pescatori**, or following it all the way down to the other part of Ischia's main town, **ISCHIA PONTE**, also reachable by bus #7, a quieter and less commercialized centre. Here the focus is the **Castello Aragonese** (March–Nov 9am to sunset; €8, includes the lift to the top), which crowns an offshore rock but is accessible from a short causeway; its stunningly distinctive pyramid was one of the backdrops in the film *The Talented Mr Ripley*. Vittoria Colonna, the Renaissance poet and close friend of Michelangelo, spent much of her life here, following the seizure of her family's land by Alexander VI. The citadel itself where she lived is rather tumbledown now and closed to the public, but below is a complex of buildings, almost a separate village really, around which you can stroll. There's the weird open shell of a cathedral destroyed by the British in 1806, a prison that once held political prisoners during the upheavals of the Unification, and the macabre remnants of a convent, in which a couple of dark rooms ringed with a set of commode-like seats served as a cemetery for the dead sisters – placed here to putrefy in front of the living members of the community.

Practicalities

Ischia Porto's helpful **tourist office** is right by the quayside ferry ticket offices (Mon–Sat 9am–2pm & 3–8pm; ℡081.507.4231, ⓦwww.ischia.it); the **bus terminus**, with buses going to all other parts of the island, is just behind here.

There is plenty of **accommodation**, though bear in mind that many places close in low season and those with their own spas are on the pricey side. Around the arrival docks of Ischia Porto, you'll find the prettily furnished *Antonio Macrì*, off the portside at Via Jasolino 96 (℡ & Ⓕ081.992.603; ❷), a good-value place handy for the lively nightlife. Close by, the very pleasant, idiosyncratically decorated *Locanda sul Mare*, Via Jasolino 68 (℡ & Ⓕ081.981.470, closed Dec–Feb; ❷), is a great bargain. Towards the pricier end of the scale is the *Hotel Continental Mare*, west of town at Via B. Cossa 25 (℡081.982.577, ⓦwww.continentalmare.it; ❺), which enjoys a splendid location above the sea and its own stretch of beach. Best of all, though, is luxurious *Il Moresco*, Via E. Gianturco 16 (℡081.981.355, ⓦwww.ilmoresco.it; ❾), housed in an elegant 1950s villa in the heart of Ischia Porto, although somehow it still manages to feel secluded. There are lovely swimming and thermal pools, and friendly, attentive service. For a **campsite**, *Eurocamping dei Pini*, Via delle Ginestre 28 (℡081.982.069), is not far from the port and also has bungalows from €45.

To the southeast of Ischia Porto 3km, at the farthest reach of Ischia Ponte, stands the island's landmark, Il Castello Aragonese, which includes the ♃ *Monastero*, high above the water on its own mini-island (℡081.992.435, ⓦwww.castelloaragonese.it; closed Nov–Feb; ❹), which is perfect if you fancy a bit of seclusion and tremendous views. The simple and elegantly furnished rooms were once the nuns' cells.

There's no shortage of eating options: *Mastu Peppe 'O Fraulese*, Via Jasolino 10 (℡081.981.912), is cheap and quite good, though the service can be slow; house speciality is *zuppa di pesce* for €20. Alternatively, try *Gennaro*, another seafood specialist across the harbour at Via Porto 59 (℡081.992.917), where a fish main course is €19. Better still is *Alberto*, right on the seafront on Viale C. Colombo (℡081.981.259) – the pretty restaurant, on stilts, over the sea, has immaculate service and beautifully presented seafood, main course around €20. In Ischia Ponte, *Cocò* (℡081.981.823), to the right of the causeway which leads to the *castello*, boasts lovely sea views and great seafood, such as *seppie in umido* for €10.

For nightlife, head for the lively run of late-night bars and cafés along Via Porto; best is the *Millennium Bar* at no. 86, which has a free dance floor as well as serving during the day as a café with Internet access (2pm till late). For clubs, in Forío the *Dolce Vita* and in Ischia the *Valentino* are worth a try.

Casamicciola Terme and Lacco Ameno

The island is at its most developed along its northern and western shores – heading west from Ischia Porto. The first village you reach, **CASAMICCI-OLA TERME**, is a spa centre with many hotels and a crowded central beach – though you can find a quieter one on the far side of the village. Ibsen spent a summer here, and the waters are said to be full of iodine (apparently beneficial for the skin and the nervous system), but otherwise you may as well push on to **LACCO AMENO**, a brighter little town, again with a beach and with spa waters that are said to be the most radioactive in Italy.

Above the main square away from the sea in Villa Arbusto is the **Museo Archeologico di Pithecusa** (Tues–Sun: April–Oct 9.30am–1pm & 3–7pm; €5; ⓦwww.pithecusae.it) with well-displayed finds from the acropolis of Monte di Vico, in continuous use from the eighth to the first centuries BC. Pithecusa (modern Ischia) was the first and northernmost Greek settlement in the West, a thriving and vital staging post at the western end of routes from the Aegean and the Levant – in addition to local artefacts, the museum displays grave goods imported from Syria, Egypt and Etruria. The epigram on the modest-looking Coppa di Nestore makes a light-hearted challenge to the cup mentioned in Homer's *Iliad*, while a shipwreck scene on a locally made bowl is thought to be the oldest example of figurative painting in Italy.

La Mortella

Between Lacco Ameno and Forío is one of Ischia's highlights: the stunning garden of **La Mortella** (April–Nov Tues, Thurs, Sat & Sun 9am–7pm; ⓦwww .ischia.it/mortella; €10, or €15 with concert; ask the bus driver to drop you off), created by the English composer William Walton and his Argentinian widow Susana, who still lives here. The Waltons moved to Ischia, then sparsely populated and little known to tourists, in 1949, forerunners of a coterie of writers and artists including Auden and Terence Rattigan. With the garden designer Russell Page they created La Mortella from an unpromising volcanic stone quarry, just the first phase of landscaping taking seven years to complete.

Paths wind up through the abundant site, which has some three hundred rare and exotic plants. Near the entrance is a glasshouse sheltering the world's largest water lily, **Victoria amazonica**, a gender-bending giant which flowers as a female with white petals, imprisons beetles for pollination purposes, and reopens later in the day with male organs developed and deep crimson petals. Above the glasshouse sits a charming terraced **tearoom/bar**, where the strains of Walton's music can be heard, and an enclosure with bright hummingbirds flitting about. Paths loop through luxuriant foliage to the pyramid-shaped rock that holds Walton's ashes, a cascade guarded by a sculpted crocodile and a pretty **Thai pavilion** surrounded by heavy-headed purple agapanthus. At the garden's summit, a belvedere provides superb views across the island.

Devotees of Walton's music shouldn't miss the prettily theatrical **museum** above the tearoom, which shows a video about the composer and features portraits by Cecil Beaton, a bust by Elizabeth Frink, and paintings and set-designs by John Piper. And it's well worth combining your visit to the garden with the **concerts** (April–July, Sept & Oct Sat & Sun 5pm), held in the adjoining recital hall, which provide a forum for students from Fiesole and Naples.

Forío

FORÍO sprawls around its bay, another growing resort that is quite pretty behind its seafront of bars and pizzerias, focusing around the busy main street of Corso Umberto. Out on the point on the far side of the old centre (turn right at the far end of Corso Umberto), the simple **Chiesa Soccorso** is a bold, whitewashed landmark from which to survey the town.

There are good **beaches** either side of Forío: the **Spiaggia di Chiaia**, a short walk to the north; to the south **Cava del Isola**, which is popular with a young crowd; and the **Spiaggia di Citara**, a somewhat longer walk to the south along Via G. Mazzella. Here you'll find the Giardini Poseidon (ⓣ081.908.7111, ⓦwww.giardiniposeidon.it; April–Oct daily 8.30am–7pm; €28 per day, €23 for a half-day, prices increase in August), an extensive complex of blissfully relaxing thermal baths on the seafront.

If you decide to stay, try the charming and central *Punta del Sole* on Piazza Maltese (ⓣ081.989.156, ⓦwww.casthotels.com; ❸), with balconied rooms set in a beautiful garden – or there's the more basic, but friendly, *Nettuno*, Via C. Piro 1 (ⓣ081.997.140, ⓕ081.507.1055; ❷). In the centre of Forío is the fun-loving ⚞ *Ring Hostel*, Via Gaetano Morgera 66 (ⓣ081.987.546, ⓦwww .ringhostel.com; from €18, private doubles from ❷), cheerfully run by three local brothers who all speak English and provide transport services.

There are some good eating options here too: head for the delightful *Umberto a Mare* (ⓣ081.997.171; closed Nov–April) tucked under the Chiesa Soccorso, whose pretty whitewashed interior looks out onto the sea; it's only open for dinner, except at weekends, and offers seasonal cuisine with lots of seafood, at around €25 for a main course. If you have a car, take the road to Monte Epomeo and head for *Peppina di Renato* (ⓣ081.998.312; closed Wed Nov–May) where you sit on barrel seats to consume great pizzas from €5 and *coniglio all'ischitana* for €26. Alternatively, just off the coast road heading south is *Il Melograno* (ⓣ081.998.450; closed Mon & Tues Nov–Dec), which does a modern take on traditional Ischia cuisine; specialities include a dish of raw fish and seafood for around €22.

Sant'Angelo and around

Ischia is most pleasant on its southern side, the landscape steeper and greener, with fewer people to enjoy it. **SANT'ANGELO** is probably its loveliest spot, a tiny fishing village crowded around a narrow isthmus linking with a humpy islet that's out of bounds to buses, which drop you right outside. It's inevitably quite developed, centring on a harbour and square crowded with café tables and surrounded by pricey boutiques, but if all you want to do is laze in the sun it's perhaps the island's most appealing spot to do so. There's a reasonable **beach** lining one side of the isthmus that connects Sant'Angelo to its islet, as well as the nearby stretch of the **Spiaggia dei Maronti**, 1km east, which is accessible by plentiful taxi boats from Sant'Angelo's harbour (around €5), or on foot in about 25 minutes – take the path from the top of the village.

Taxi boats will drop you at one of a number of specific features: one, the **Fumarole**, is where steam emerges from under the rocks in a kind of outdoor sauna, popular on moonlit nights; further along close by a couple of hotels is a path that cuts inland through a mini-gorge to the **Terme Cavascura**, the most historic hot springs on the island, used since Roman times (April–Oct, daily 8.30am–6pm; €10 for swim & sauna, €20 and upwards for mud treatments; ☎081.999.242, ⓦwww.cavascura.it).

Up above Sant'Angelo looms the craggy summit of Ischia's now dormant volcano, **Monte Epomeo**. Both CD and CS buses regularly stop at **FONTANA**, a superb ride up, with wonderful views back over the coast, from where you can climb up to the summit of the volcano. Follow the signposted road off to the left from the centre of Fontana: after about five minutes it joins a larger road; after another ten to fifteen minutes take the left fork, a stony track off the road, and follow this up to the summit – when in doubt, always fork left and you can't go wrong. It's a steep hour or so's climb, especially at the end when the path becomes no more than a channel cut out of the soft rock. However, there are a couple of scenically placed cafés in which to gather your energies at the top, where the views are stunning. Bear in mind, too, that you can drive to within about twenty minutes of the summit, leaving your vehicle by the signs for the military exclusion zone.

There are plenty of places to **stay** in and around Sant'Angelo; the cheaper places tend to be outside the village proper. Centrally situated, with balconies fronting the sea, *Casa Celestino* (☎081.999.213, ⓦwww.hotelcelestino.it; closed Oct–April; minimum stay 7 nights; ❻) is an attractive option. Up in Succhivo, ten minutes' walk back in the direction of Forío (the bus passes right by), *Casa Giuseppina*, on the main Via D'Iorio (☎ & ⓕ081.907.771, ⓦwww.casagiuseppina.it; minimum stay 3 nights; ❸), is excellent. On a rocky headland above Sant'Angelo itself, the ⚓ *San Michele* (☎081.999.276, ⓦwww.hoteltermesanmichele.it; closed Oct–April; ❼ with half board) is pricier but has a beautifully lush garden and terrace and a seawater pool.

When it comes to **eating**, you might be wise to walk up to the next village along from Succhivo, Panza, where the *Da Leopoldo* restaurant (☎081.907.086; closed Mon–Sat lunchtimes March–Oct, & Jan, Feb & Dec) is famous in these parts for its Ischian specialities (rabbit, great sausages and good antipasto table), cosy atmosphere and moderate prices. It is, however, a bit difficult to find: follow Via S. Gennaro from the main square of Panza for about ten minutes, and it's a little way past the *Hotel Al Bosco*. In Sant'Angelo itself you could do worse than stoke up on the fine pizzas (from €5) at the unpretentious *Da Pasquale*, Via Sant'Angelo 79 (☎081.904.208), up in the old centre of the village; everywhere else is much of a muchness.

Prócida

A serrated hunk of volcanic rock that's the smallest (population 10,000) and nearest island to Naples, **Prócida** has managed to fend off the kind of tourist numbers that have flooded into Cápri and Ischia. It lacks the spectacle, or variety, of both islands, though it compensates with extra room and extra peace. Its main town, **MARINA GRANDE**, where you arrive by ferry, is a slightly run-down but picturesque conglomeration of tall pastel-painted houses rising from the waterfront to a network of steep streets winding up to the fortified tip of the island – the so-called **Terra Murata**. Part of this was once given over to a rather forbidding prison, now abandoned, but it's worth walking up anyway to see the abbey church of **San Michele** (daily 9.45am–12.45pm & 3–5.30pm, closed Sun afternoon except when groups book; donation requested), whose domes are decorated with a stirring painting by Giordano of St Michael beating back the Turks from Prócida's shore. The views, too, from the nearby belvedere are among the region's best, taking in the whole of the Bay of Naples, from Capo Miseno bang in front of you right around to the end of the Sorrentine peninsula and Cápri on the far left. Look out for handwritten notes by the custodian lamenting thefts from the church.

For the rest, Prócida's appeal lies in its opportunities to swim and eat in relative peace. There are **beaches** in Marina Grande itself, on the far side of the jetty, and, in the opposite direction, beyond the fishing harbour, though both are fairly grubby. Similarly, **Spiaggia Chiaia**, just beyond the fishing harbour of nearby Coricella, is a reasonable bathing beach but isn't very large and can get crowded. You can walk there, or the Chiaiolella bus stops nearby.

On the whole if you want to swim you're better off making the fifteen-minute bus journey from Marina Grande to **CHIAIOLELLA**, where there's a handful of bars and **restaurants** around a pleasant, almost circular bay and a long stretch of sandy beach that is the island's best. By taking the road up from behind the beach you can cross the (officially closed) bridge onto the islet of **Vivara**, a nature reserve, very peaceful and overgrown. It's a refreshingly bucolic affair after the rest of the island, where the settlement is pretty much continuous, the narrow roads and constant traffic making walking uncomfortable.

Practicalities

The tourist office is on the port (☎081.810.1968, ⓦwww.isoladiprocida.it; daily 9.30am–1pm & 3–6pm,). For **getting around**, a bus service (€1.10 one-way, tickets sold on board) connects Marina Grande with Chiaiolella roughly every twenty minutes and coincides with all ferry and hydrofoil arrivals.

There's not much choice if you want to **stay** on the island: there are only a handful of hotels, together with a couple of *pensioni*. Note that at all of these places you *must* book in advance. Nicest, if your budget stretches to it, is *La Casa Sul Mare* (☎081.896.8799, ⓦwww.lacasasulmare.it; ❻), at Via Salita Castello 13, on the way to San Michele. Rooms are simple, fresh and elegant and all have a sea-view terrace. Alternatively, in Chiaiolella there is the *Riviera* hotel, ten minutes' walk from the beach at Via G. de Procida 36 (☎081.896.7197, ⓦwww .hotelrivieraprocida.it; closed Oct–March; ❷) – the bus goes right by. *Crescenzo*, at Via Marina Chiaiolella 33 (☎081.896.7255, ⓦwww.hotelcrescenzo.it; ❸), is a three-star with a fine *ristorante*-pizzeria whose speciality is spaghetti with crab meat and courgette. If these are full, there's the brand new ✠ *La Tonnara* round the marina, at no. 51/B (☎081.810.1052, ⓦwww.latonnarahotel.it; ❺), a pleasantly remodelled old tuna fishing factory, with spacious rooms and a good restaurant. For **camping**, there are six sites on the island, most within easy walking distance of the sea: best bet is *Vivara* on Via IV Novembre (☎081.896.9242; mid-June to mid-Sept) – 30m from the sea, with caravans for rent and a bar; to get there, take the Chiaiolella bus and get off at Piazza Olmo.

Eating is rather easier. In Marina Grande, restaurants line the waterfront Via Roma: *La Medusa*, opposite the ferry terminal at no. 112 (☎081.896.7481; closed Tues), is not cheap but is very good, with a house speciality of *spaghetti ai ricci di mare* at €10. Otherwise, there's the friendly *Il Cantinone*, Via Roma 53 (☎081.896.8811; closed Tues), a popular locals' joint where wood-panelled walls add to the marine flavour, the antipasto (€9) is unmissable and there's a great *linguine alla cantinone* for €12. In Chiaiolella, you could try *Il Galeone* (☎081.896.9622), right by the bus stop between the bay and the beach, with pizzas from €3. A number of **café–bars** in Marina Grande serve drinks and *gelati* – try *Capriccio* at Via Roma 99, which also acts as an **Internet** point – while the tiny *Number Two* on Via Libertà, which leads off Via Roma, is the main **nightclub**.

North of Naples: Caserta, Cápua and around

There's not much to draw you to the territory immediately north of Naples. The towns just outside the city – Casoria, Afragola, Acerra – are collectively known as the "**Triangle of Death**" for their Camorra connections and make up a bleak conurbation of poor housing and industrial messiness.

Caserta and the Palazzo Reale

Further inland, a short train or bus ride direct from Naples, **CASERTA**, incongruously surrounded by a sprawl of industrial complexes and warehouses that stretches all the way back to Naples, is known as the "Versailles of Naples" for its vast eighteenth-century **Palazzo Reale**, the only attraction in this otherwise completely nondescript modern town. Begun in 1752 for the Bourbon King Charles III to plans drawn up by Vanvitelli, and completed a little over twenty years later, it's an awesomely large complex, built around four courtyards, with a facade 245m long. However, it's a dull structure that generally substitutes size for inspiration. Only the majestic central staircases up to the **royal apartments** (Tues–Sun 8.30am–6.30pm; €4.20) hit exactly the right note. The apartments themselves are a grand parade of heavily painted and stuccoed rooms, sparsely furnished in French Empire style, some with great, overbearing classical statues and all, in their brazen, overstated display of wealth, pretty disgusting – not least in the smug portraits of the Bourbon dynasty, especially the one of the podgy Francis I with his brat-like children. There's little point in singling out anything of special significance: it's the feel of the building and its pitiless overstatement that are the real attractions.

Behind the palace, the **gardens** too (Tues–Sun 8.30am–5pm; €2) are classically ordered and on no less huge a scale, stretching out behind along one central three-kilometre-long axis and punctured by myth-inspired fountains. The main promenade is longer than it looks from the palace (it's a good half an hour's walk or a short bicycle ride), and regular buses make the round trip, dropping you off at selected intervals along the way and turning round by the main cascade at the top, completed in 1779, which depicts Diana turning Actaeon into a stag. Walk to the top, look back at the palace, hop on a bus . . . and depart.

Santa Maria Cápua Vetere and Cápua

Regular buses run from Caserta, either from the bus/train station or the stop just to the left as you exit the palace, for the 7km to **SANTA MARIA CÁPUA VETERE** – a not especially pleasant journey past signs, petrol stations and run-down housing, but worth the trip to see this historic town. In its day this originally Etruscan, later Samnite, city, then known as Cápua, was the second city of Italy, centre of the rich and important region of Campania and famous for its skill in working bronze. Its first-century AD **amphitheatre** was once the largest in Italy after the Colosseum, and a few very minimal parts of it remain on the far side of town, a right turn shortly after Piazza San Francesco d'Assisi. It held a reputed Roman gladiator school and barracks, and it was here that the gladiators' revolt, led by Spartacus, broke out in 73 BC – a revolt that was only put down after two years and four lost battles. The amphitheatre (Tues–Sun 9am–sunset; combined ticket with Mithraeum and Museo €2.50) now is much less well preserved than the one in Pozzuoli, having lost almost all of its marble and its surrounding tiers – with many of the remaining ones having been concreted over. But the network of tunnels underneath survives reasonably intact, and is partly accessible. The **Mithraeum** – about twenty minutes on foot, down Via Anfiteatro and then left hidden away down Via Morelli – is one of the best preserved in the country and redolent with the bizarre, bloodletting rites that accompanied the cult of Mithraism. It boasts a well-preserved fresco of Mithras himself in action. Ask for access at the **Museo Archeologico dell'Antica Cápua** on Via Roberto D'Angio 48 (Tues–Sun 9am–7pm; same ticket), most of whose rich collection of painted tombs survived bombing in the last war and are on display; to get here from the amphitheatre, cross the road, head left, then take the first right.

There are heaps of rubble and a handful of artefacts dotted around the amphitheatre, not least a large piece of mosaic, but most of the finds have made their way to the excellent **Museo Provinciale** in **CÁPUA**, 4km down the road at Via Roa 68 (Tues–Sat 9am–1.30pm, Sun 9am–1pm; €5), sited on the broad curve of the Volturno River and a more attractive place than Santa Maria. The museum holds a fascinating collection of **Madri Dei** or **Matres Matutae** – formidable votive figures of women holding children, statues found in a nearby shrine to the Mater Matuta, an ancient Italic divinity. Early effigies have two or three children in their arms, while later Roman-era statues have twelve, deemed by the Romans to be the ideal number. Opinion is divided about the purpose of the statues, whether to ask for children, give thanks for them, or to honour departed parents; in any case it seems likely the cult changed over time. The museum also contains remnants of statuary from the original Porta Federiciana, the "Gateway to the South" constructed in 1234 during the reign of Federico II, two towers of which can still be seen outside the town. The fragments include a bust of Federico's adviser, Pier della Vigna. Unfortunately, due to staff shortage, many of the forty rooms of exhibits are currently closed.

Benevento

Appealing **BENEVENTO**, further inland than Cápua or Caserta and reachable in about an hour and a half from Naples by bus or train (the private FBN line is quickest), was another important Roman settlement, a key point on the Via Appia between Rome and Bríndisi and as such a thriving trading town. Founded in 278 BC, it was at the time the farthest point from Rome to be colonized, and even now it has a remote air about it, circled by hills and with a centre that was (pointlessly) bombed to smithereens in the last war and even now seems only half rebuilt. Its climate also ranks among southern Italy's most extreme.

Buses from Naples drop you in a large parking lot, where you'll also find the **tourist office** on the corner of Via Sandro Bertini (daily 9am–1pm & 3.30–7.30pm; ☏0824.28.180 or toll-free 800.800.824), and from where Via

Rettori heads to the principle Piazza IV Novembre. From here, the main street, **Corso Garibaldi**, is pedestrian-only and leads off to the right. The first significant sight is the **Museo Sannio** (Tues–Sun 9am–1pm; €4), in the cloister behind the eighth-century church of Santa Sofia, which holds a good selection of Roman finds from the local area, including a number of artefacts from a temple of Isis – various sphinxes, bulls and a headless statue of Isis herself. There are also terracotta votive figurines from the fifth century BC, and the cloister itself has capitals carved with energetic scenes of animals, humans and strange beasts, hunting, riding and attacking. Further along Corso Garibaldi, off to the right, the **Arch of Trajan** is the major remnant of the Roman era, a marvellously preserved triumphal arch boasting much more distinct images than Rome's arches, and you can get close enough to study its friezes. Built to guard the entrance to Benevento from the Appian Way, it's actually as heavy-handed a piece of self-acclaim as there ever was, showing the Emperor Trajan in various scenes of triumph, power and generosity. Farther down, the city's **Duomo** is an almost total reconstruction of its thirteenth-century Romanesque original; what's left of its famous bronze doors, believed to be Byzantine, is now stashed inside.

There are more bits and pieces from Roman times scattered around the rather battered but picturesque old quarter of town, the **Triggio** – reached by following Via Carlo Torre off to the left of the main road beyond the cathedral. The **Bue Apis**, at the far end of Corso Dante, is another relic from the temple of Isis, a first-century BC sculpture of a bull. And in the heart of the old quarter there are the substantial remains of a **Teatro Romano** (daily 9am–sunset; €2; closed at the time of writing) built during the reign of Hadrian. In Hadrian's time it seated 20,000 people; it seats rather fewer today, rather less today but it's still an atmospheric sight – looking out over the green rolling countryside of the province beyond and, like most of Benevento, relatively unvisited by tourists.

The Amalfi coast

Occupying the southern side of Sorrento's peninsula, the **Costiera Amalfitana** lays claim to being Europe's most beautiful stretch of coast, its corniche road winding around the towering cliffs that slip almost sheer into the sea. By car or bus it's an incredible ride (though it can get mighty congested in summer), with some of the most spectacular stretches between Salerno and Amalfi. If you're staying in Sorrento especially it shouldn't be missed on any account; in any case the towns along here hold the beaches that Sorrento lacks. The coast as a whole has become rather developed, and these days it's in fact one of Italy's ritzier bits of shoreline, villas atop its precarious slopes fetching a bomb in both cash and kudos. While it's home to some of the most aesthetically lovely hotels in Italy, budget travellers should be aware that you certainly pay for what you get.

Coming **from Sorrento**, buses normally join the coast road a little way **west of Positano**. If the coast road is closed, however, which it is from time to time due to landslides and forest fires, the bus from Sorrento will take the alternative route, via Castellammare and Agerola, right over the backbone of the Sorrentine peninsula, which is itself a journey worth making – the bus zigzagging down the other side in a crazy helter-skelter of hairpin bends to join the road a few kilometres **west of Amalfi**.

Positano

There's not much to **POSITANO**, only a couple of decent beaches and a great many boutiques; the town has long specialized in clothes made from linen, georgette and cotton, as well as handmade shoes and sandals. But its location, heaped up in a pyramid high above the water, has inspired a thousand picture postcards and helped to make it a moneyed resort that runs a close second to Cápri in the celebrity stakes. Since John Steinbeck wrote up the place in glowing terms back in 1953, the village has enjoyed a fame quite out of proportion to its tiny size. Franco Zefferelli is just one of many famous names who have villas nearby, and the people who come here to lie on the beach consider themselves a cut above your average sun-worshipper.

Positano is, of course, expensive, although its beaches are nice enough and don't get too crowded – though do watch out for the jellyfish, abundant in these waters. The main beach, the Spiaggia Grande right in front of the village, is reasonable, although you'll be sunbathing among the fishing boats unless you want to pay over the odds for the pleasanter bit on the far left; there's also another, larger stretch of beach, Spiaggia del Fornillo, around the headland to the west, accessible in five minutes by a pretty path that winds around from above the hydrofoil jetty – although its central section is also a pay area. Nonetheless the bar-terrace of the *Puppetto* hotel (see p.934), which runs along much of its length, is a cheaper place to eat and drink than anywhere in Positano proper.

Positano practicalities

Buses to Positano drop off at the top of the village, from where it's a steep walk down or a short bus ride (every 30min) to the little square at the bottom end of Via Cristoforo Colombo, five minutes' walk from the seafront; **ferries** and **hydrofoils** from Cápri, Naples, Amalfi and Salerno pull in at the jetty just to the right of the main beach. Arriving by car you'll shell out a lot on garage space – up to €4 an hour – as parking is very limited. There's a busy **tourist office** just back from the beach by the church steps at Via del Saracino 2 (June–Oct Mon–Sat 8.30am–8pm; Nov–May Mon–Fri 8.30am–3pm; ☎089.875.067, ⓦwww.aziendaturismopositano.it).

Accommodation

Cheap **accommodation** does not come easily in chic Positano, but there is a **hostel**, the private *Ostello Brikette* at Via G. Marconi 358 (☎089.875.857, ⓦwww .brikette.com; €22, doubles ❷; midnight curfew, lockout 10am–4pm; closed Nov–March), a 200-metre walk uphill from the main bus stop at the Bar Internazionale on the coastal road. It's friendly and clean, with stunning Mediterranean views, bar and Internet access, but the dorms can be a bit airless. Other accommodation options can be pricey but there are a few mid-range possibilities.

Hotels

Casa Guadagno Via Fornillo 36 ☎089.875.042, ⓕ089.811.407. Delightfully fresh and colourful *pensione*, with a charming entrance hall, scenic terrace and some rooms with vistas of the sea and cliffs. Closed Nov–March. ❸

Il San Pietro di Positano Via Laurito 2 ☎089.875.455, ⓦwww.ilsanpietro.it. If money is truly no object, head a bit south of town on the corniche road. This is the area's most luxurious hotel, built down a rocky cliff face with plush, individually designed rooms and suites, fresh flowers, private beach and tennis court, and its own kitchen garden. Not to mention the breathtaking views. ❾

Maria Luisa Via Fornillo 42 ☎ & ⓕ089.875.023, ⓦwww.pensionemarialuisa.com. Lovely and old-fashioned, this homely *pensione* is pricey Positano's bargain, offering balconies, panoramic views and a plant-filled communal room with fridge. ❸

Palazzo Murat Via dei Mulini 23 ☎089.875.177, ⓦwww.palazzomurat.it. Housed in a beautiful,

shady eighteenth-century palace with a garden terrace, what's missing are full views of the sea, but the amenities, gorgeous rooms and superb restaurant make up for it. **⑧**
Pupetto Via Fornillo 37 ℡089.875.087, ⓦwww .hotelpupetto.it. Right on Fornillo beach and with access for guests, with full facilities, this bright spot offers a huge terrace and pastel rooms with sea views. Full-range restaurant, from wood-fired pizza to catch-of-the-day. Closed Jan–March. **⑥**
Vittoria Via Fornillo 35 ℡089.875.049, ⓦwww .hotelvitttoriapositano.com. Homelier sister hotel to the *Pupetto* (above) next door, this place offers sea views and beach access by elevator, along with a terrace restaurant and simple, airy rooms with balconies. **⑤**

Eating and drinking

For **food**, *Chez Black* on Positano's beach (℡089.875.036; closed Jan) is a long-established seafood restaurant, a bit over-branded these days, with pizzas for around €7. *Bar Bruno*, Via C. Colombo 157 (℡089.875.392), is a seafood restaurant with lovely views of the water at night, though you'll be sitting right on the road; main courses are around €16. *O' Capurale*, just around the corner (℡089.811.188; closed Nov–March), has a nicely painted fish-themed ceiling and does fish dishes for around €25. Fanciest of all is ⭐ *La Cambusa* (℡089.875.432), on the right as you approach the beach (closed Tues in winter), where a full fish blowout will set you back around €50–60 a head. By way of a bit of **nightlife**, *Zagara*, Via dei Mulini 8/10, is a late-night bar-cum-*pasticceria* with a leafy terrace and occasional live music, while *Music On The Rocks*, Via Grotte dell'Incanto 51, at the far end of the Spiaggia Grande (℡089.875.874), is the town's best club-restaurant with slick grotto-effect dance floor and sea views.

Praiano and the Grotta dello Smeraldo

PRAIANO is a little further along to the east, squeezed into a cleft in the rocks. Much smaller and very much quieter than Positano, it consists of two tiny centres – Véttica Maggiore on the Positano side and Marina di Praiano on the Amalfi side. There is a small patch of beach, together with a couple of sandy coves close by, but food and **rooms** are still fairly pricey. In Véttica Maggiore, the *Casa Colomba Pensione* (℡089.874.079, half board July & Aug; no credit cards; half board **③**), high above the main road just after the first tunnel, has great views from its location at the top of 180 steps. Conveniently sited by the bus stop, the *Continental* hotel (℡089.874.084, ⓦwww .continental.praiano.it; half board in Aug; closed mid-Nov to March; **③**) has a choice between frescoed rooms furnished with antiques in the main house or smart bungalows right on the cliff edge. It comes with a private beach, and on the terraces above it a **campsite**, *La Tranquillità* (℡089.874.084; closed Nov–April), which must be one of the best sited in the country. *Onda Verde* (℡089.874.143, ⓦwww.ondaverde.it; closed Nov–April; **④**) is similarly well placed, perched on the cliff edge at Marina di Praiano, or there are rooms to rent on the harbour front – ask at *La Conchiglia* restaurant in Marina di Praiano (℡089.874.313; **③**).

There's a concentration of **restaurants** in Véttica Maggiore; try the *Trattoria San Gennaro*, next to the church (℡089.874.293; closed Thurs), which serves huge portions of *antipasto di mare* and *primi* like *scialatilli con zucchine e gamberetti* (home-made pasta with courgettes and prawns) for €7; or *La Brace*, at Via Capriglione 146 (℡089.874.226; closed Tues Oct–March), with pizzas (from €2.60) straight from the wood-fired oven and fresh fish (around €10) which you can eat on the covered terrace.

Grotta dello Smeraldo

Shortly after Praiano you pass the **Furore** gorge, which gashes into the mountainside just above the coast road, and a little further along, about 4km out of Praiano (reachable direct by taxi boat from either Praiano or Amalfi), the **Grotta dello Smeraldo** (daily: March–Oct 9am–5pm; Nov–Feb 10am–4pm; €5), one of the most highly touted local natural features. A lift descends to the level of the grotto, where you can tour the interior by boat – a mildly impressive but certainly not unmissable sight that includes a rather startling sub-aquatic nativity scene.

Amalfi

Set in a wide cleft in the cliffs, **AMALFI**, a mere 4km or so further east, is the largest town and perhaps the highlight of the coast, and a good place to base yourself. It has been an established seaside resort since Edwardian times, when the British upper classes found the town a pleasant spot to spend their winters. Actually Amalfi's credentials go back much further: it was an independent republic during Byzantine times and one of the great naval powers, with a population of some 70,000; Webster's *Duchess of Malfi* was set here, and the city's traders established outposts all over the Mediterranean, setting up the Order of the Knights of St John of Jerusalem. Amalfi was finally vanquished by the Normans in 1131, and the town was devastated by an earthquake in 1343, but there is still the odd remnant of Amalfi's past glories around today, and the town has a crumbly attractiveness to its whitewashed courtyards and alleys that makes it fun to wander through.

The Town

The **Duomo** (daily: summer 9am–9pm; winter 10am–5pm; €5 for cloister & museum), at the top of a steep flight of steps, utterly dominates the town's main piazza, its tiered, almost gaudy facade topped by a glazed tiled cupola that's typical of the area. The bronze doors of the church came from Constantinople and date from 1066. Inside it's a mixture of Saracen and Romanesque styles, though now heavily restored, with a major relic in the body of St Andrew buried in its crypt. The cloister – the so-called **Chiostro del Paradiso** – is the most appealing part of the building, oddly Arabic in feel with its whitewashed arches and palms. There's an adjacent **museum** with various medieval and episcopal treasures, most intriguingly an eighteenth-century sedan chair from Macau, which was used by the bishop of Amalfi; a thirteenth-century mitre sewn with myriad seed pearls, gold panels and gems; and three silver reliquary heads – two gravely bearded and medieval, the third an altogether more relaxed and chubby Renaissance character, with elaborately braided hair.

Almost next door to the Duomo, in the small **museo civico** (Mon–Fri 8am–2pm; free), part of the Municipio, you can view the *Tavoliere Amalfitana*, the book of maritime laws that governed the republic, and the rest of the Mediterranean, until 1570. On the waterfront, the old **Arsenal** is a reminder of the military might of the Amalfi republic, and its ancient vaulted interior now hosts art exhibitions and suchlike. In the opposite direction you can follow the main street of **Via Genova** up through the heart of Amalfi and out the other side, to where the town peters out and the gorge narrows into the **Valle dei Mulini** (Valley of Mills), once the centre of Amalfi's high-quality paper industry. Apart from a rather over-hyped paper museum, there's not much to see here nowadays, despite the grandiose claims implied by the name, with only one mill that is still functioning.

Practicalities

Amalfi's most immediate focus is the seafront, a humming, cheerfully vigorous strand given over to street stalls, a car park for the town's considerable tourist traffic, and an acceptably crowded **beach**, although once again the best bits are pay areas only. The **tourist office**, at Corso Roma 19 (Mon–Fri 8am–1.30pm & 3–5pm, Sat 8am–1pm; ☎089.871.107, ⓦwww.amalfitouristoffice.it), is situated in the courtyard next to the **post office** in Corso Repubblica Marinara, the road that runs along the waterfront, and close to the *Bar Sirena* at no. 21, which provides **Internet** access. **Ferries** and **hydrofoils** to Salerno, Positano, Cápri and Ischia leave from the landing stage in the tiny harbour.

Amalfi is a fairly expensive place **to stay**, though there are a few reasonably priced options. Best bet is the *Lidomare*, tucked away to the left of the main square at Via Piccolomini 9 (☎089.871.332, ⓦwww.lidomare.it; ❹); a beautiful, family-run Ducal palace, it's nicely old-fashioned and full of antiques, though some bathrooms are equipped with modern hydromassage tubs. There's also the pretty *Sant'Andrea*, on the main square (☎089.871.145; closed Oct & Nov; ❸), stuffed full of pictures and ornaments and with some rooms boasting a view of the Duomo. Otherwise, you might consider staying in the adjacent village of Atrani (see below); if you're on a tight budget you could opt for the cosy **youth hostel** *Beata Solitudo*, located in Agerola, 16km north of Amalfi (☎081.802.5048, ⓦwww.beatasolitudo.it; €11, double bungalow ❷), which also has a small **campsite**; a regular bus connects with Amalfi. On the western edge of town is the swish *Hotel Santa Caterina* (☎089.871.012, ⓦwww .hotelsantacaterina.it; ❾), an elegant villa with period furnishings; it has a great lift that plummets down from the bougainvillea-wreathed terrace to an arc of rocky beach. Finally, the ⚔ *Hotel Luna Convento*, Via Pantaleone Comite 33, off the main road running out of Amalfi (☎089.871.002, ⓦwww.lunahotel.it; ❽), is a lovely five-star in a former convent dating from 1200, with a cloister and individual rooms fashioned from cells.

As for **eating**, *Trattoria da Gemma*, a short walk up Via Genova on the left (☎089.871.345; closed Wed), has a small, carefully considered menu, strong on fish and seafood with mains at around €25, and a lovely terrace overlooking the street. *Il Tari*, a little further up on the left after Via Genova has become Via P. Capuano (☎089.871.832; closed Tues), is cheap and not at all bad; a speciality is home-made *ravioli con atice e provola* at €13. Further up again, *Taverna Del Duca*, at Piazza Spirito Santo 26 (☎089.872.755; closed Thurs), has a cosy atmosphere, and its *felicelli allo scoglio con frutti di mare* (€14) is well worth a try; while *Il Mulino*, at the top of the main street ten minutes' walk from the Duomo (☎089.872.223; closed Mon), is a cheery family-run place that does good home-made pasta *alla pescatora* for around €10. If you fancy a bit of **nightlife**, carry on up the main street to *Il Roccoco Discopub* in the otherwise quiet Valle dei Mulini, one of the only places in town where you can get a dance.

Atrani

A short walk around the headland (take the path off to the right just before the tunnel through the *Zaccaria* restaurant), **ATRANI** is an extension of Amalfi really, and was indeed another part of the maritime republic, with a similarly styled church sporting another set of bronze doors from Constantinople, manufactured in 1086. It's a quiet place, which benefits from all the attention bestowed on its neighbour, with a pretty, almost entirely enclosed little square, Piazza Umberto, giving onto a usually gloriously peaceful (and free) patch of sandy **beach** – hard to believe the bustle of Amalfi is just around the corner. Another good reason for coming here is that it has a great **place to stay** in the *A'Scalinatella*, Piazza Umberto 1 (℡089.871.492, ⓦ www.hostelscalinatella .com), hostel and hotel – a friendly, family-run establishment that offers excellent-value hostel beds (Easter–Sept €21; Oct–Easter €10) and regular private rooms (❸) in various different buildings around town. For the reception, look for the telephone box and take the steps up to the right just beyond it. Otherwise, for **eating** try *A'Paranza*, Traversa Dragone 1/2 (℡089.871.840; closed Tues in low season), a friendly seafood trattoria with fabulous home-made pasta and a speciality of *zuppa di pesce*. You'll find the restaurant on the road that leads inland from the main square.

Ravello

The best views of the coast can be had inland, high above Amalfi in **RAVELLO**: another renowned spot "closer to the sky than the seashore", wrote André Gide – with some justification. Ravello was also an independent republic for a while, and for a time an outpost of the Amalfi city-state; now it's not much more than a large village, but its unrivalled location, spread across the top of one of the coast's mountains, 335m up, makes it more than worth the thirty-minute bus ride through the steeply cultivated terraces up from Amalfi – although, like most of this coast, the charms of Ravello haven't been recently discovered. Wagner set part of *Parsifal*, one of his last operas, in the place; D.H. Lawrence wrote some of *Lady Chatterley's Lover* here; John Huston filmed his languid movie *Beat the Devil* in town (a film in which the locations easily outshine the plot); and Gore Vidal is just one of the best known of many celebrities who used to spend at least part of the year here.

The Town

Buses drop off on the main **Piazza Vescovado**, outside the **Duomo**: a bright eleventh-century church, renovated in 1786, that's dedicated to St Pantaleone, a fourth-century saint whose blood – kept in a chapel on the left-hand side – is supposed to liquefy (like Naples' San Gennaro and others) once a year on July 27. It's a richly decorated church, with a pair of twelfth-century bronze doors, cast with 54 scenes of the Passion; inside, there are two monumental thirteenth-century ambones (pulpits), both wonderfully adorned with intricate and glittering mosaics. The more elaborate one to the right of the altar, the Gospel ambo, dated 1272, sports dragons and birds on spiral columns supported by six roaring lions, and with the coat of arms and the vivacious profiles of the Rufolo family, the donors, on each side. On the left, the Epistle ambo illustrates the story of Jonah and the whale. Downstairs in the crypt the **museo** (daily June–Sept 9am–7pm; Oct–May 9am–6pm; €2) holds the superb bust of Sigilgaita Rufolo and the silver reliquary of Saint Barbara, alongside a collection of highly decorative, fluid mosaic and marble reliefs from the same era.

The Rufolos figure again on the other side of the square, where various leftovers of their **Villa Rufolo** (daily: June–Sept 9am–8pm; Oct–May 9am–6pm; €5) lie scattered among rich gardens overlooking the precipitous coastline; this is the spectacular main venue for the prestigious open-air chamber concerts held from March to October. The programme is widely advertised and tickets cost €20 (details from the Ravello Concert Society ℡089.858.149, ⓦ www.ravelloarts.org); though there are plans to build a viewless modern auditorium for the festival on the same site, which critics fear could prove a triumph of acoustics over aesthetics.

If the crowds (best avoided by coming early in the morning) put you off, turn left by the entrance and walk up the steps over the tunnel for the best (free) view over the shore, from where it's a pleasant stroll through the back end of Ravello to the main square. Alternatively, walk in the opposite direction for ten minutes to the **Villa Cimbrone** (daily 9am–sunset; €5), whose formal gardens spread across the furthest tip of Ravello's ridge. Most of the villa itself, once frequented by the Bloomsbury Group as well as Greta Garbo, is now a freshly remodelled luxury hotel (℡089.857.459, Ⓦwww.villacimbrone.com; ❾), but you can peep into the flower-hung cloister as you go in. The gardens (open to the public daily 9am–sunset; €5) are on two levels, dotted with statues and little temples and leading down to what must be the most gorgeous spot in Ravello – a belvedere that looks down to Atrani below and the sea beyond.

Practicalities

Small orange SITA **buses** run up to Ravello from Amalfi roughly hourly from Piazza Flavio Gioià. If you can't tear yourself away, the **tourist office** in Piazza Duomo (Mon–Sat: May–Sept 8am–8pm; Oct–April 8am–7pm; ℡089.857.096, Ⓦwww.ravello.it/aziendaturismo) has information on **rooms**. If you have money to burn, the *Palumbo*, Via San Giovanni del Toro 16 (℡089.857.244, Ⓦwww.hotel-palumbo.it; ❾), is one of Italy's best opportunities to experience old-world luxury in a historic building incorporating columns from Paestum and handsomely decorated with antiques and works of art including a Guido Reni. More affordable, the *Parsifal*, back down the road (℡089.857.144, Ⓦwww.hotelparsifal.com; 5), is a former convent dating from 1288 with great views. The *Garden*, Via Boccaccio 4 (℡089.857.226, Ⓦwww.hotelgardenravello .it; 4), all of whose cool blue rooms have a terrace with a vista, is off the main piazza, and next to the cathedral, at Viale Wagner, the *Toro* (℡089.857.211,

△ Via dei Mercanti, Salerno

Ⓦ www.hoteltoro.it; 4) has cool rooms and makes up for lack of view with a lovely garden – highly recommended.

There are also some marvellous places to eat. The **restaurant** at the *Garden* hotel boasts a marvellous panoramic terrace and offers a seasonal menu with seafood around €12–20 for a main course, while *La Marra* at Via della Marra 7 (Ⓣ089.858.302; closed Tues Nov–March), full of abstract paintings and huge ceramic plates, has a tourist menu at €32. Finally, the *Cumpa Cosimo*, Via Roma 44 (Ⓣ089.857.156), has great local food, home-made pasta and wine at moderate prices, while fish mains are around €45.

Salerno

Capital of Campania's southernmost province, the lively port of **SALERNO** is much less pell-mell than Naples and, being well off most travellers' itineraries, has a good supply of cheap accommodation, making it an excellent base to hit both the Amalfi coast and the ancient site of Paestum further south. During medieval times the town's medical school was the most eminent in Europe. More recently, it was the site of the Allied landing of September 9, 1943 – a landing that reduced much of the centre to rubble. The subsequent rebuilding has restored neither charm nor efficiency to the town centre, which is an odd mixture of wide, rather characterless boulevards and a small medieval core full of intriguingly dark corners and alleys. It is, however, a lively, sociable place, with a busy seafront boulevard and plenty of nightlife and shops.

Arrival, information and accommodation

Salerno's **train station** lies at the southern end of the town centre on Piazza Vittorio Veneto. City and local **buses** pull up here; those from Paestum and further south arrive and leave from Piazza della Concordia, down by the waterside nearby; buses from Naples use the SITA bus station at Corso Garibaldi 119. **Ferries** and **hydrofoils** from Amalfi, Cápri and Positano arrive in the harbour.

For information, there's a **tourist office** at Via Roma 258 (Mon–Sat 9am–2pm & 3–8pm; Ⓣ089.224.744, Ⓦ www.salernocity.com, click on "Turismo" to find the English version); ask for a copy of the useful *Hello Salerno* booklet. The town's cheaper **hotels** are handily placed along (or just off) Corso V. Emanuele, which leads north into the town centre from the station: try the friendly, if ordinary, *Santa Rosa* at Corso V. Emanuele 16 (Ⓣ & Ⓕ089.225.346; ❷). Right by the station is the more upmarket Plaza, Piazza Vittorio Veneto 42 (Ⓣ089.224.477, Ⓦ www.plazasalerno.it; ❸), which has all mod cons. Alternatively, there's the Ave Gratia Plena, Via dei Canali (Ⓣ089.234.776, Ⓦ www.ostellodisalerno.it; €14–17.50; ❶), a clean, hotel-like HI **youth hostel**, with some doubles (❶), in an historic building a few minutes' walk west of the cathedral.

The Town

There isn't a great deal to see in Salerno, but it's pleasant to wander through the vibrant streets of the centre, especially the ramshackle old medieval quarter, which starts at the far end of **Corso V. Emanuele**, lined with designer shops and heaving with people (especially on Saturdays), and has **Via dei Mercanti** as its main axis. To the right of Via dei Mercanti, up Via Duomo, the **Duomo** (daily 7am–noon & 4–7.30pm; free) is Salerno's highlight, squeezed into the congested streets, an enormous church built in 1076 by Robert Guiscard and dedicated to St Matthew. The main features are yet another set of bronze doors from Constantinople and, in the heavily restored interior, two elegant mosaic pulpits dating from 1173, as well as the quietly expressive fifteenth-century tomb of Margaret of Anjou, wife of Charles III of Durazzo. The polychrome marble crypt holds the body of St Matthew himself, brought here in the tenth century. Outside, the courtyard is cool and shady, its columns plundered from Paestum, centring on a gently gurgling fountain.

From the cathedral, turn right at the bottom of the steps for the **Museo Diocesano** (daily 9am–6pm; free), which, although its opening times are erratic, is worth a hammer on the door to see its large altar-front, embellished with ivory panels in the late eleventh century and the largest work of its kind in the world. Failing that, turn left out of the church, left at the bottom of the steps, left again and then first right, and 100m or so further on is the **Museo Provinciale** (Mon–Sat 8am–1.15pm & 2–3pm, Sun 9am–1.30pm; ☎089.231.135; free) – a largely dull museum that occupies two floors of an over-restored Romanesque palace. It's worth heading upstairs though, past the deadening array of fossils and fragments of ancient sculpture, to see the sensual *Head of Apollo*, a Roman bronze fished from the Gulf of Salerno in the 1930s. Also worth visiting are the recently restored **Giardini della Minerva** on Via Ferrante Sanseverino (Tues–Sun 9am–3pm & 5–9pm; book on ☎089.222.237; free), dating from the twelfth century and thought to be the first botanic garden in Europe. It was reclaimed by the local council just a decade ago after several centuries in private hands.

Eating and drinking

Salerno is a sociable place, and while it's not a tourist town there are plenty of good places to **eat and drink**, especially along Via Roma, where you can pretty much take pot luck. Elsewhere, *Hostaria Il Brigante*, Via Fratelli Linguiti 4 (☎089.226.592), is a great, old-fashioned *osteria* near the Duomo with mains at around €10 – try its *zuppa dell'aglio* and *calamarata* pasta dishes. *Antica Pizzeria Vicolo delle Neve*, left off Via dei Mercanti about 50m past the Duomo (☎089.225.705; closed Wed & lunchtimes) – the oldest in the old city – is a deliciously downbeat place serving pizzas (from around €4) and local specialities, with a particularly good *calzone*. Just a block back from the *lungomare* promenade, the *Trattoria Peppe 'A Seccia*, Via Antica Corte 5, with tables outside in fine weather, offers pizzas starting at €3 (☎089.220.518; closed Mon). *Pasticceria Pantaleone*, Via dei Mercanti 73–75, housed in a deconsecrated chapel, does *scazzetta*, *millefoglie* and *pastiera* to die for. There are two good **bars** on Vicolo Giudaica: *Mennir*, at no. 50, is friendly, stylish and open for as long as its customers want to drink, while *La Cantinella*, at nos. 29–31, offers a more traditional Italian atmosphere and cheap drinks.

Salerno hosts what claims to be the oldest **fair** in Europe – the Fieravecchia – on the first weekend in May, when townsfolk parade in medieval gear, food stalls are set up along the waterfront and a 2000-egg omelette is cooked down at the beach on a giant metal contraption.

Paestum

About an hour's bus ride south of Salerno, the ancient site of **Paestum** (daily 9am–1hr before sunset; €4, €6.50 for site plus museum) spreads across a large area at the bottom end of the **Piana del Sele** – a wide, flat plain grazed by the buffalo that produce a good quantity of southern Italy's mozzarella cheese. Paestum, or Poseidonia as it was known, was founded by Greeks from Sybaris in the sixth century BC, and later, in 273 BC, colonized by the Romans, who Latinized the name. But by the ninth century a combination of malaria and Saracen raids had decimated the population and left the buildings deserted and gradually overtaken by thick forest, and the site wasn't rediscovered until the eighteenth century during the building of a road through here. It's a desolate, open place even now ("inexpressibly grand", Shelley called it), mostly unrecognizable ruin but with three golden-stoned **temples** that are among the best-preserved Doric temples in Europe. Of these, the Temple of Neptune, dating from about 450 BC, is the most complete, with only its roof and parts of the inner walls missing. The Basilica of Hera, built a century or so earlier, retains its double rows of columns, while the Temple of Ceres at the northern end of the site was used as a Christian church for a time. In between, the forum is little more than an open space, and the buildings around are mere foundations.

The splendid **museum** (daily 8.45am–7pm; closed first and third Mon every month; €4, €6.50 including site), across the road, holds Greek and Roman finds from the site and around. Straight ahead of you as you enter are some stunning sixth-century bronze vases (*hydriae*), decorated with rams, lions and sphinxes; behind them more bronze – gleaming helmets, breastplates and greaves. Make a point of seeing the rare Greek tomb paintings, the best of which are from the Tomb of the Diver, graceful and expressively naturalistic pieces of work, including a diver in mid-plunge, said to represent the passage from life to death, and male lovers banqueting. Attractive fourth-century terracotta plates depict all sorts of comestibles – fruit, sweets, fruit and cheese, and a set of weathered archaic period Greek metopes from another temple at the mouth of the Sele River, a few kilometres north, shows scenes of fighting and hunting. On the first floor, which is devoted to Roman finds, highlights are a statue of an abstracted-looking Pan with his pipes, a third-century relief showing a baby in pointed hat and amulets, and a sarcophagus cover of a tenderly embracing couple.

Practicalities

It's perfectly feasible to see Paestum on a day-trip from either Salerno or Agrópoli (see p.942) – it's much nearer to the latter. However, you can also stay in one of the many hotels or campsites that are strewn along the sandy shore beyond the site. The **tourist office** tucked away on a side street to the left of the museum at Via Magna Grecia 887 (Mon–Sat 9am–7pm, closes 5pm in winter, Sun 9am–1pm; ℡0828.811.016, @www.infopaestum.it) has details. For **hotels** just walk down to the beach (about 15min) and take your pick: close to the site to the left of where the main road hits the beach is *Calypso*, Via Mantegna 63 (℡0828.811.031, @www.calypsohotel.com; ❹), one of the few hotels around that can cope with vegan, macrobiotic and organic diets (with traditional food as well). The cheerful and very good value *Baia del Sole*, Via Torre 48 (℡ & ℻0828.811.119; @www.baiadelsolepaestum.it; ❷), is one of the few places that does not require half board in high season. If you prefer to be a little more secluded try *Villa Rita* (℡0828.811.081, @www.hotelvillarita.it; ❸), which is pleasantly situated in relaxing gardens with a pool just south of the archeological site. Or for a stopover in real style, head 4km northwards to the *Tenuta Seliano* (℡0828.724.544, @www.agriturismoseliano.it; ❹), a farm run by the Bellelli family, where the buffalo herd produces milk for mozzarella. You can either stay in the main house where the rooms are lined with antiques, or in more modern rooms near the rose garden and swimming pool; the food here is excellent and around €27 a head. Most of the **campsites** are much of a muchness: the *Intercamping Apollo* (☎0828.811.178; April–Sept) on Via Principe di Piemonte and the *Villaggio dei Pini* on Via Torre (☎0828.811.030; ⓦwww .campingvillaggiodeipini.com. open all year) are two of the most central and are well signposted.

There's some excellent **food** in the area, with the locally produced buffalo mozzarella featuring heavily on menus. You can get a list of manufacturers from the tourist office and at the weekend the roads are often jammed with people making a run down to buy the stuff fresh. One of the most popular producers is Vannulo, off the main superstrada SS18 towards Salerno (☎0828.724.765, ⓦwww.vannulo.it), which also has a buffalo yoghurt parlour on site. As for **restaurants**, try the excellent *Nettuno* on Via Principe di Piemonte; (☎0828.811.028) in an old building right by the temples, where the house speciality is crepes with buffalo mozzarella at €8; or the more intimate and upmarket *Ristorante Enoteca Tavernelle*, Via Tavernelle 14 (☎0828.722.440), about 1km out on the Salerno road, where main courses are around €15.

The Cilento coast

Immediately south of Paestum, the coastline bulges out into a broad mountainous hump of territory known as the **Cilento** – one of the remotest parts of Campania, thickly wooded with olives and chestnuts. **AGRÓPOLI**, the first town you reach, fifteen minutes out from Paestum and on the main Salerno–Reggio railway line, is a good base for the ruins (buses every hour), and its blend of the peaceful old quarter, heaped on a headland, and the new modern centre down below makes for a nice place to spend a few days, with a vivacious main-street *passeggiata*. The beaches aren't great, but you can swim from the flat rocks in the harbour and the water's perfectly clean. For accommodation, the *Hotel Carola* in the harbour (☎0974.826.422, ⓦwww.hotelcarola .it; ❸), on Via Carlo Pisacane, has attractive, freshly done-up double rooms with balconies, or there's the contemporary *Serenella*, Lungomare San Marco 150 (☎0974.823.333, ⓦwww.hotelserenella.it; usually full board in Aug, ❸), which has its own private beach. Agrópoli also has an HI **youth hostel**, *La Lanterna*, Via Lanterna 8 (☎0974.838.364, ⓦwww.hihostels.com; closed Nov–mid-March; €12), about 1km from the station and conveniently close to the bus stop for Paestum; as well as dorm beds it also offers family rooms (€11.50–16 per person) and does full dinners for €9.

Acciaroli, Marina d'Ascea and Velia
Buses run down to **ACCIAROLI**, about 25km south of Salerno – one of the Cilento's larger resorts and a port for the hydrofoils plying the coast during summer. The railway joins the shoreline again at **MARINA D'ASCEA**, a fairly indifferent resort but surrounded by hotels and campsites, especially along the lengthy sand beach that stretches north to Marina del Casalvelino.

Close by, **MARINA DI VELIA** gives access to the site of **Velia** (daily 9am–1hr before sunset; €2.50; tourist information ☎0974.972.230) – comprising the ruins of the Hellenistic town of Elea, founded around 540 BC and an important port and cultural centre, home to its own school of philosophy. Later it became a favourite holiday resort for wealthy Romans, Horace being just one of many who came here on the advice of his doctor. The decline of Velia parallels that of Paestum – malarial swamp rendering much of the area uninhabitable – though the upper reaches were lived in until the fifteenth century. There, however, the comparison ends: the remains of Velia are considerably more decimated than those of Paestum and the town was never as crucial a centre, with nothing like as many temples. At the centre of the ruins the "**Porta Rosa**", named after the wife of the archeologist who conducted the first investigations, is one of the earliest arches ever found – and the first indication to experts that the Greeks knew how to construct such things. Up from here, the **Acropolis** has relics of an amphitheatre and a temple, together with a massive Norman tower – visible for some distance around.

Palinuro

Cheerful **PALINURO**, too, further south, is worth a stop, named after the legendary pilot of the *Aeneid*, who is supposed to have drowned here. It's a much livelier place than anywhere else on the Cilento coast, and so can be packed out. But it's a good alternative to Agrópoli, both as a base for the site of Velia and a beach-bumming spot – the sea here is one of the cleanest spots on the coast – and the harbour area to the east of town retains a certain fishing port authenticity. From the harbour, you can explore the stunning craggy coast of the Capo Palinuro, studded with a series of caves, either by taking a guided **boat tour** (€8) or – more fun – by renting a **motorboat** (€25 for 2hr, plus around €10 for petrol).

The best **hotel** option is *Hotel Residence La Torre* (Via Porto 3, ☎0974.931.107, ☎0974.931.264; ❸), just 10m from the glorious sandy beach by the harbour, where you'll find a sociable bar – a great place for a sundowner. In town, the attractive central **campsite** provides shade and has a rudimentary restaurant, with access to a sandy beach where steps from a series of rock pools take you straight into the sea. A number of good unpretentious **eating** options line Via Indipendenza, the best of which is friendly *L'Ancora* at no. 115 (☎0974.931.373); its speciality is *zuppa di pesce* (around €30) and the wood-fired oven turns out large and delicious pizzas (from €3). Alternatively, blow your last few euros at the *Da Carmelo* restaurant (☎0974.931.138), 2km south of town at Località Isca, whose fish and seafood are said to be the best for miles around (main courses around €20).

Travel details

Metropolitana/FS Naples

Gianturco–Piazza Garibaldi–Piazza Cavour–Montesanto–Piazza Amedeo–Mergellina–Piazza Leopardi (Fuorigrotta)–Campi Flegrei–Cavalleggeri d'Aosta–Bagnoli–Pozzuoli. Trains every 8min. **Circumflegrea** (information ☎800.001.616). Connects Naples Montesanto to Cumae, Lido Fusaro and Torregaveta with 6 departures daily. Departures every 20min for all stations to Licola. **Circumvesuviana** (information ☎081.772.2444). This line runs between Naples and Sorrento, with many stops around the southern part of the bay, including Ercolano and Pompeii, every 30min, up to 40 daily from 5am to 11.30pm. **Ferrovia Cumana** (information ☎800.001.616). Connects Naples Montesanto with Fuorigrotta,

Agnano, Bagnoli, Pozzuoli, Baia, Fusaro and Torregaveta. Departures every 10min.

Trains

Benevento to: Fóggia (9 daily; 1hr 15min); Naples (18 daily; 1hr 5min–2hr 20min).
Naples to: Agrópoli (20 daily; 1hr 40min); Benevento (18 daily; 1hr 5min–2hr 20min); Caserta (every 30min; 35–45min); Fóggia (9 daily; via Caserta or Benevento 2hr 20min–5hr); Formia (every 30min; 1hr 20min); Paola (Calabria) (every 30min; 4hr); Rome (every 30min; 2hr); Salerno (every 30min; 50min); Santa Maria Cápua Vetere (every 30min; 50min); Sapri (hourly; 2hr 50min).
Salerno to: Paestum/Agrópoli (hourly; 35min); Sapri (every 30min; 2hr).

Buses

Agrópoli to: Acciaroli (6 daily; 1hr); Paestum (hourly; 10min); Salerno (hourly; 1hr 20min); Sapri (1 daily; 3hr 30min).

Naples to: Amalfi (5 daily; 1hr 55min); Benevento (6 daily; 1hr 30min); Cápua (hourly; 1hr 15min); Caserta (every 20min; 1hr); Salerno (every 15–30min; 1hr 5min); Sorrento (1 daily Mon–Sat at 8.45am; 1hr 20min); Pompeii Scavi (every 30min; 30min); Positano (1 daily Mon–Sat at 8.45am; 1hr 55min).

Naples Capodichino airport to: Sorrento (6 daily; 1hr).

Ravello to: Amalfi (15 daily; 30min).

Salerno to: Agrópoli (hourly; 1hr 20min); Amalfi (hourly; 1hr 10min); Naples (every 15–30min; 1hr 5min); Padula (2 daily; 1hr 50min–2hr); Paestum (hourly; 1hr); Positano (every 1–2hr; 2hr); Sorrento (every 1–2hr; 2hr 45min); Vietri (every 30min–1hr).

Sorrento to: Amalfi (18 daily; 1hr 30min); Naples (1 daily at 6.35pm; 1hr 20min); Naples Capodichino Airport (6 daily; 1hr); Positano (18 daily; 35min); Salerno (12 daily; 2hr 45min).

Ferries and hydrofoils

Naples to: Aeolian Islands/Milazzo (ferry: twice/thrice weekly in high season at 9pm; 9hr 30min/18hr 50min); Aeolian Islands (hydrofoil: June–Sept twice daily 4–6hr); Cágliari (ferry: weekly/twice weekly in high season at 7.15pm; 16hr 15min); Palermo (ferry: daily at 8.45pm; 9hr 45min and also twice weekly at 10am); Sorrento (7 daily hydrofoils; 35min).

Salerno to: Amalfi (April–Sept 6 daily hydrofoils; 35min); Positano (5 daily hydrofoils; 1hr 10min).

For details of ferry and hydrofoil connections between Naples, the Amalfi coast and Salerno and the islands, see box, p.920.

14

Puglia

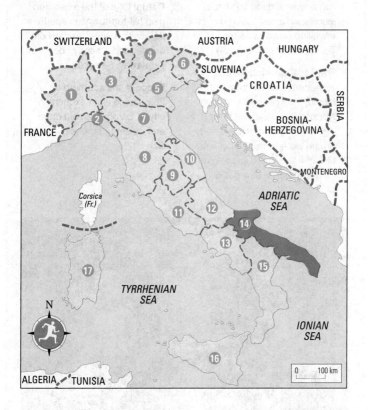

CHAPTER 14

Highlights

✳ **Castles** Puglia's Swabian castles are monuments to thirteenth-century engineering. See impressive examples at Lucera and Castel del Monte. **See p.952 & p.969**

✳ **Péschici and Vieste** For sun and sea, head for these resorts, with the option of travelling onwards to the Trémiti Islands. **See p.958**

✳ **Trani** The eleventh-century cathedral here is a gem, its interior restored to its original Norman state and the building itself impressively located on the waterfront of what was one of Italy's most important medieval ports. **See p.963**

✳ **Martina Franca** This lively town with its Moorish feel makes a good base for exploring the surrounding area's *trulli* – Puglia's traditional conical whitewashed buildings. **See box, p.974**

✳ **Ostuni** One of the most stunning hill-top towns in southern Italy, with a sun-bleached old quarter and a sandy coastline 7km away. **See p.983**

✳ **Lecce** In the southern tip of Italy, Lecce is an exuberant city of Baroque architecture and opulent churches. **See p.985**

△ Baroque detail in San Matteo church, Lecce

Puglia

Puglia is the long strip of land, 400km from north to south, that makes up the "heel" of Italy. For centuries it was a strategic province, colonized, invaded and conquered (like its neighbours, Calabria and Sicily) by just about every major power of the day – from the Greeks through to the Spanish. These days clean seas and reliable sunshine are the draw for holidaymakers both Italian and foreign, and acres of campsite-and-bungalow-type tourist villages stud the shoreline, though there are still quiet spots to be found. Low-cost flights to Bari and Bríndisi have opened up the area to English tourists, many of whom have been buying and doing up *trulli* (see p.973) as holiday accommodation. There's a brisk air of investment in many resorts, from the new top-of-the-range spa hotels in converted *masserias* (ancient, white farm estate houses) to agriturismo places, where you can holiday among olive groves and orchards and go horse riding or mountain biking. B&Bs have been springing up everywhere, often in the historic centres of towns, so a stay of a day or two is much more affordable than it used to be.

There's plenty of architectural interest throughout Puglia, as each ruling dynasty left its own distinctive mark on the landscape – the Romans their agricultural schemes and feudal lords their fortified medieval towns. Perhaps most distinctive are the Saracenic kasbah-like quarters of many towns and cities, the one at **Bari** being the biggest and most atmospheric. The Normans endowed Puglia with splendidly ornate cathedrals; there's one at **Trani** that skillfully blends the many strands of regional craft traditions from north and south. And the Baroque exuberance of towns like **Lecce** and **Martina Franca** are testament to the Spanish legacy. But if there's one symbol of Puglia that stands out, it's the imposing castles built by the Swabian Frederick II all over the province – foremost of which are the **Castel del Monte** and the remnants of the palace at **Lucera**.

Puglia's cities, generally visited only as transport hubs, merit some exploration nevertheless. **Táranto** and its surroundings have fought a losing battle with the local steel industry, but **Lecce** is worth a visit of a day or two for its crazed confection of Baroque churches and laid-back café life. Though **Bari** is not a traditional tourist destination, its maze-like old city makes for fascinating if slightly chancy wandering with excellent restaurants in all price brackets, while **Bríndisi**, best-known for its ferry connections with Greece, lies just 15km away from the beautiful **Torre Guaceto** nature reserve, a long stretch of uncontaminated sand dunes, *macchia* and clear water where you can cycle, walk or scuba dive.

The geographical diversity of Puglia is very attractive. The **Tavioliere** (table-land) of the north boasts mile after mile of wheatfields, while there's plenty of barren mountain scenery in the undulating plateau of **Le Murge**, in the centre

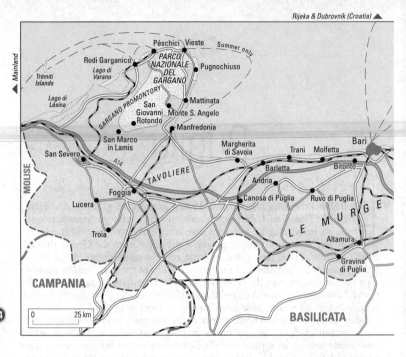

of the province. The hilly, forested **Gargano promontory** juts out to the east, and is fringed by gently shelving, sandy beaches, seaside hotels and campsite villages that make good places for a family holiday – though you'll need to catch a ferry to the **Trémiti islands** for the clearest sea. The best escape is to the southernmost tip, the **Salentine peninsula**, easier to visit now that a new bus service operates in summer. Here the terrain is rocky and dry, more Greek than Italian, and there are some beautiful coves and sea caves to swim in.

Getting around Puglia by public transport is fairly easy, at least as far as the main towns and cities go. FS **trains** connect nearly all the major places, while small, private lines head into previously remote areas – in the Gargano and on the edges of Le Murge. Most other places can be reached by **bus**, although isolated village services can be infrequent or inconveniently early – a problem that can only really be solved by taking, or renting, your own **car**. It's a thoroughly pleasant area to travel around: old-fashioned courtesy towards the traveller means that if you ask someone for information and they don't know the answer, they invariably make it their business to find out. It helps to speak a bit of Italian in these circumstances but you don't have to be fluent – people will respond if you make the effort.

Fóggia and the Tavoliere

The broad sweep of the **Tavoliere plain** stretches from the Basilicata border to the edge of the Gargano massif – flat, fertile lands that are southern Italy's wheat bowl, and the source of the country's best pasta. The Romans first attempted an

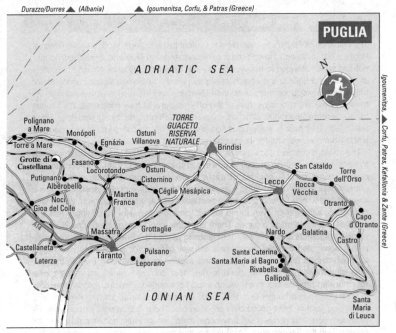

PUGLIA

ADRIATIC SEA

N

Polignano
a Mare   Monópoli   Ostuni   TORRE
                                            GUACETO
Torre a Mare   Egnázia   Villanova   RISERVA
                                            NATURALE   Brindisi
Grotte di   Fasano
Castellana
        Locorotondo   Ostuni   San Cataldo
Putignano   Cisternino   Torre
    Albèrobello   Lecce   dell'Orso
Noci   Martina   Céglie Mesápica   Rocca
Gioa del Colle   Franca   Vécchia
                                                                Otranto
                                                                    Capo
            Massafra   Grottaglie   d'Otranto
Castellàneta   Nardo   Galatina
                                                            Castro
    Laterza   Táranto   Pulsano
                        Leporano   Santa Caterina
                                    Santa Maria al Bagno
                                        Rivabella
                                        Gallipoli

IONIAN SEA

Santa
Maria
di Leuca

intense cultivation of the area, parcelling the land up into neat squares for distribution to its pensionable centurions. However, the gift was a mixed blessing: **Fóggia** province proved to be an unhealthy place, an earthquake-prone swampland rife with malarial mosquitoes, and settlements here suffered from disease and disaster in fairly equal proportions. It wasn't until the advent of irrigation schemes in the 1920s that the mosquitoes lost their malarial bite and the area began to take on its present rich appearance. As the transport hub of the province, Fóggia is somewhere you will probably pass through, though for more of an idea of what the Tavoliere is like, head for the walled town of **Lucera** or the little village of **Tróia**.

Fóggia

The Tavoliere's main town, **FÓGGIA**, looms out of the plain unexpectedly, a fine starting point for exploring northern Puglia and the Gargano promontory, though not an encouraging stop in itself. Although Fóggia flourished under Frederick II, who declared it an imperial residence and built a palace here, the town was devastated in turn by the French in 1528, an earthquake in 1731 and Allied bombs during World War II. Today the city's streets are all reassuringly earthquake-proof, wide and low-built, a modern layout that is handsome enough, but you're going to have to search hard in between the tree-lined boulevards for what is left of the old town.

Arrival and information

The **train station** is on Piazzale Vittorio Veneto, on the northern edge of town, a short walk from Piazza Cavour and the centre. FS services (☎0881.727.234) from here run to Manfredonia, while Ferrovie del Gargano (FG; ☎0881.587.211,

The influence of Puglia's former rulers is evident in the region's food. Like the **Greeks**, Pugliesi eat lamb and kid spit-roast over herb-scented fires and deep-fried dough-nut-like cakes steeped in honey; and like the **Spanish** they drink almond milk, *latte di mandorla*. Puglia is the source of eighty percent of Europe's pasta and most of Italy's fish; it produces more wine than Germany and more olive oil (even if it is not always of the finest quality) than all the other regions of Italy combined. It's famous for olives (from Cerignola), almonds (from Ruvo di Puglia), dark juicy tomatoes (often sun-dried), fava beans, voluptuous figs (fresh and dried), *cotognata* (a moulded jam made from quinces) and for its melons, grapes and green cauliflower.

The most distinctive local **pasta** is *orecchiette*, ear-shaped pasta that you will still see women making in their doorways in the old part of Bari. Look out too for *panzarotti alla barese*, pockets of pasta stuffed with *ragù* (meat sauce), egg and cheese or *ricotta* and *prosciutto* that are deep-fried in olive oil. Otherwise, there is a marked preference for short, stubby varieties of pasta, which you'll find served with peppers, cauliflower or even turnip leaves (*cime di rapa*). Not surprisingly, fish and shellfish dominate many a menu. There are some good fish soups (*zuppe di pesce*) whose ingredients and style vary from place to place – the Bríndisi version, for example, is dominated by eels. Vegetarians are well catered for with a variety of veggie antipasti dishes, and combining pasta and vegetables is a typically Puglian trait.

As elsewhere in the south, lamb is the most common **meat**, often roast over rosemary and thyme branches, which impart a wonderful flavour. A local speciality is *gnummerieddi*, a haggis-like dish, made by stuffing a lamb gut with minced offal, herbs and garlic – best grilled over an open fire. There is little beef or pork, poultry is uncommon, and game is virtually nonexistent; as a result, horsemeat is popular, especially in the Salento area. To confound your prejudices, go for *braciole di cavallo*, horsemeat steaks cooked in a good rich tomato sauce.

Cheeses are a strong point, including *ricotta*, *cacioricotta*, *mozzarella*, *burrata*, *caprini* (small fresh goat's cheeses preserved in olive oil) and *fagottini* (small smoked cheeses, a speciality of the Fóggia area). If you're in Andria, try *burrata*, a creamy soft cow's cheese.

Puglia is the land of the grape. In recent years the region has exploited its hot, fertile plain to become one of the wealthiest parts of the south, and while much of its **wine** is pretty basic (the vast majority is used in Torinese vermouths) there have recently been immense improvements. Yields have been severely reduced, grapes have been picked at precisely the right moment, and modern technology has been introduced to great advantage. Wine-maker Kym Milne, for example, has created an excellent Chardonnay del Salento and a huge red Salice Salentino. Other wines to look out for include Primitivo di Manduria (another important red) and Locorotondo, a straightforward, fresh white, as well as dessert wines.

ⓦ www.ferroviedelgargano.com; office to the left of the station entrance) trains go to Péschici Calanelle and their buses to Manfredonia and Vieste. SITA **buses**, which serve the whole region, arrive at and depart from just outside the train station; their ticket office (☎0881.773.117) is under the porticoes opposite the station; when this is closed, buy tickets at the *Kiwi Bar*, on the corner of Viale XXIV Maggio. The **tourist office** (Mon–Fri 8am–1pm, Tues & Thurs also 4–5.30pm; ☎0881.723.650, ⓦ www.pugliaturismo.com) is a twenty-minute walk into town, on the first floor at Via E. Perrone 17, off Piazzale Puglia and has a lot of good information on the whole province. If you are headed for the Gargano, it's worth picking up *Tutto Gargano* from a newsstand, a great resource for accommodation and information on festivals and events; check out its site at ⓦ www.tuttogargano.com, too.

Accommodation

Staying in Fóggia may be necessary if you arrive late or need to leave early: *Hotel Venezia*, Via Piave 40 (☎0881.770.903; ❷), is a good, three-star hotel that's been recently renovated; to get to it go down Viale XXIV Maggio from the station, then third right. *Hotel Europa*, Via Monfalcone 52 (☎0881.721.057, ⓦwww.hoteleuropefoggia.com; ❺), is more upmarket, with helpful staff – again it's down Viale XXIV Maggio from the station, then second right. The grandest place in town is *Cicolella*, at Viale XXIV Maggio 60 (☎0881.566.111, ⓦwww.hotelcicolella.it; ❼), a businesslike hotel with attentive service. Finally, *Cacciatore*, in the historic centre near the cathedral at Via Arrigotti 4 (☎0881.771.839; ❸), is a good, friendly, family-run *albergo* with restaurant. The only time that bed space will be short is at the beginning of May, during the **Fiera di Fóggia**, a huge international agricultural affair held on the outskirts of the town.

The Town

The old town lies scattered around the **Duomo**, which is to the left off Corso Vittorio Emanuele, the main drag that runs down from the central, fountained Piazza Cavour. The cathedral is an odd Romanesque–Baroque sandwich, the top part tacked on in the eighteenth century after the earthquake.

While you're here, take a look at the nearby **Museo Cívico** on Piazza Nigri (Sun–Fri 9am–1pm; €1.50), reached by walking down the Corso to Via Arpi. Incorporated into the side of the building are three portals, one of which – the Porta Grande, with the pensive-looking eagles – is all that remains of Frederick II's imperial palace. The museum underwent major renovations recently and with any luck will have reopened by the time you read this. Duck inside and there are the usual regional archeological finds and a more interesting section on local life and folklore. The modest **Museo di Storia Naturale** at Via Bellavia 1 (Tues–Sat 9am–1pm & 4–8pm; €2; take bus #12 from the train station) is dedicated to local flora and fauna, with a couple of dinosaur casts among the birds and insects on show.

That really is it as far as Fóggia's sights go, though there are enough green spaces and shopping streets in the new town to occupy any remaining time – something you might well have, as Fóggia is an important rail junction on the main Bologna–Lecce and Naples–Bari lines.

Eating and drinking

Good **food** options include *Osteria Chacaito*, near the Museo Civico at Via Arpi 62 (☎0881.708.104; closed Sun), a gourmet's delight offering seasonal dishes that might include *orecchie di ciuccio* ("donkey ear" pasta) with young courgette plants, salt-cod on a bed of bean puree flavoured with saffron, or milk-fed lamb, plus delicious desserts and an extensive wine list; expect to spend around €40 per head excluding wine. *Da Pompeo*, Vico al Piano 14 (☎0881.724.640; closed Sun & last 2 weeks of Aug), down Corso Vittorio Emanuele II and right at the Palazzo Vescovile, is another fine place to indulge in Pugliese specialities in a similar price bracket. For tasty dishes at lower prices (€20 for a four-course set menu), try *La Sciampagnotta*, Via San Domenico 1 (next to the Palazzo Vescovile), which serves up the likes of tagliatelle with asparagus, broad beans and ricotta, or *Il Rugantino*, Via Luigi Sturzo 23 (closed Mon) – head down Corso Roma and turn left at the sanatorium – which offers great pizzas and other dishes. For a **drink**, *Coniglio Mannaro* (closed Mon) is a pub-bar at Via Bruno 26 in the historic centre, with occasional live music and art exhibitions; the *Nessun Dorma* pub (closed Tues), Via Duomo 20, does snacks.

Lucera

Just 18km west, within easy reach of Fóggia (hourly buses), **LUCERA** (pronounced Loosh-airer) makes a wonderful and charming introduction to Puglia. A small town with a bright, bustling centre and a lively *passegiata* on summer evenings, it was once the capital of the Tavoliere – a thriving Saracen hub. Frederick II, having forced the Arabs out of Sicily, resettled 20,000 of them here, on the site of an abandoned Roman town, allowing them complete freedom in religious worship – an almost unheard act of liberalism for the early thirteenth century.

The **cathedral** was built in the early fourteenth century after Frederick II's death, when the Angevins arrived and a conflict with the Saracens began. The Angevins won and built the cathedral on the site of a mosque; by the end of their rule, few of the town's original Arab-influenced buildings were left. However, the Arabic layout of Lucera survived and there's a powerful atmosphere here – best appreciated by wandering the narrow streets of the old town, peering into the courtyards and alleyways.

The main sights are outside the old centre, most notably the vast **Castello** (Tues–Sun: summer 9am–2pm & 3–8pm; winter 9am–2pm; free), built by Frederick and designed to house a lavish court that included a collection of exotic wild beasts. To get there from Piazza Duomo follow Via Bovio and Via Federico II to Piazza Matteotti and look for the signs. The largest in southern Italy after Lagopésole in Basilicata, the castle commands spectacular views over the Tavoliere, stretching across to the foothills of the Apennines to the west and the mountains of Gargano to the east. Contained within the kilometre-long walls are the remains of Frederick's great palace, evocative fragments of mosaic work and fallen columns now surrounded by wild flowers. At the Roman **amphitheatre** (closed for restoration at time of writing) on the western edge of town, audiences of 18,000 once watched gladiatorial battles; today, smaller numbers gather for a series of classical music concerts in August.

Practicalities

Buses arrive at the train station (currently closed) and in Piazza del Popolo, from where it's only a short walk up Via Gramsci to the **Duomo**, which marks the centre of the medieval walled town.

Close to the cathedral is the **tourist office** on Via Luigi Zuppetta 5 (Tues–Sun 9am–2pm; March–Oct also Tues–Fri 3–8pm; ℡0881.522.762, ⓦwww .luceraweb.com).

You can **stay** in town at the businesslike *La Balconata 2* at Viale Ferrovia 15 (℡0881.520.998, ⓦwww.labalconata.it; ❸), just outside the gate into the old town. Or there's a B&B, *Masseria Mezzana Grande,* 5km outside Lucera, on the road to Bíccari (℡0881.529.915; ❼) A traditional farm house, it has large rooms filled with family antiques, modern bathrooms and a private kitchen and sitting room for guests. The B&B comes second to the farm's main business of growing grain, olives and almonds, so ring ahead. For **eating**, *La Tavernetta*, just behind the cathedral at Via Schiavone 7–9, is a good place for crispy pizzas cooked in a wood-fired oven, antipasti and local wine served at tables outside, while the pub-like *Lupus in Fabula*, Via Gramsci 10 (closed Tues in winter & July), also in the old town, offers a short menu of typically Luceran dishes and a good wine list at moderate prices.

Tróia

Frequent buses also make the short ride (from either Lucera or Fóggia) to **TRÓIA**, 18km due south of Lucera. The locals seem curiously blasé as to the origin of their village's name; it means "slut" in Italian, which probably has its origins in Helen of Troy, but no one is able to offer a logical connection with the village. Whatever the reason, the Tróiani atone for the name by having five patron saints, whose statues are paraded around town in a procession during the Gesta dei Santi Patroni every July 17.

At all other times of the year Tróia is a quiet, dusty village, its only sight the fine **Duomo**, an intriguing eleventh-century blend of Byzantine and Apulian–Romanesque styles, with a generous hint of Saracen influence. The great bronze doors are covered with reliefs of animals and biblical figures, while above, surrounded by a frenzy of carved lions frozen in stone, is an extraordinary rose window. Distinctly Saracen, the window resembles a finely worked piece of oriental ivory, being composed of eleven stone panels, each one delicately carved. There's more exact detail inside, too, including a curiously decorated pulpit and some ornate capitals.

Manfredonia

By Puglian standards, **MANFREDONIA** is a new town, a mere 600 years old, founded – as the name suggests – by Manfred, illegitimate son of Frederick II. The Austrians struck the first blow of World War I on Italian soil here by bombing the town's station in 1915, but this is really Manfredonia's only claim to fame. Heavy industry on the northern outskirts and the flat, featureless landscape ensure that for most visitors it's little more than a gateway to the Gargano promontory, and most people pass quickly through. Still, what the town lacks in ambience and historical sights is more than made up for by its sandy beaches, which stretch for miles down the coast.

The **Castello**, on Corso Manfredi, was begun by Manfred and later extended by the Angevins. The Spanish added huge bastions in 1607 to stave off a Turkish attack: they failed to do so, with the Turks landing in 1620, ravaging the hapless inhabitants and destroying much of the town – though most of the protective walls still survive. The castle now houses the **Museo Nazionale** (daily except first and last Mon of the month: 8.30am–1.30pm & 3.30–7.30pm; €4), largely devoted to Daunic finds from the seventh and sixth centuries BC. The prize exhibits are several stone stelae, thought to be tombstones, richly carved with images of armoured warriors, female figures and scenes from daily life. You can also see relics from a water-worshipping cult from the Grotta Scaloria – a reaction perhaps to the drought that struck the Tavoliere in Neolithic times.

Practicalities
The easiest way to reach Manfredonia is by train from Fóggia: from the **station** turn right and it's a short walk along Viale Aldo Moro to Piazza Marconi. Just across the square, Corso Manfredi leads up to the small **tourist office** in the *comune* building at Piazza del Popolo 10 (Mon–Fri 9am–1pm; ☎0884.519.319, ⓦwww.comune.manfredonia.fg.it), which has some information on the Gargano area. A **hydrofoil** service runs to the Trémiti Islands (see p.962) from the harbour in via Vieste; **tickets** can be bought from A Galli e Figlio, Corso Manfredi 4/6 (☎0884.582.520) in town or the harbourside Adriatica office (☎0892.123, ⓦwww.adriatica.it) at least thirty minutes before departure (June–Sept 1 daily; 2hr journey; €20.90 single). If you need to catch the hydrofoil, you will probably have to **stay** overnight; there are no central hotels – most places to stay are strung out along the gulf. *Panorama del Golfo*, Lungomare del

Sole (☎0884.542.944; ❸), on the seafront at the nearby resort of **Siponto** is a good option.

There are plenty of **restaurants** in Manfredonia, one of the best of which is *Coppola Rossa*, Via dei Celestini 13 (booking advisable ☎0884.582.522; closed all day Mon & Sun eve), where you can feast on grilled antipasti, *troccoli alla scoglio* (tiny pasta in a sauce of clams, eels, tomatoes and oil), *orecchiette* with scampi, or *ciambotta* (fish soup).

The Gargano promontory

Geographically and culturally different from the rest of Puglia, the **Gargano promontory** rises like an island from the flat plains of the Tavoliere. It has a remarkably diverse landscape: beaches and lagoons to the north, a rocky, indented eastern coast and a mountainous, green heartland of oaks and beech trees – reminiscent of a Germanic forest rather than a corner of southern Italy. For centuries the promontory was extremely isolated, visited only by pilgrims making their way along the valley to Monte Sant'Angelo and its shrine. Tourism has taken off in a big way, especially around the seaside resort of Vieste, but in 1991 the whole peninsula became a national park, helping to protect the Gargano from overbearing development and ensuring that much of the interior remains supremely unspoiled and quiet.

It may seem as though the promontory is one long strip of private beach, but bear in mind that by Italian law everyone has access to the actual seashore, as well as the 50m length between the reserved areas. Check with your hotel – often the price of a sunbed and umbrella at the nearest beach is included in the cost of an overnight stay.

Approaches to the promontory are pretty straightforward. **FS trains** run from Fóggia to Manfredonia on the southeast side of Gargano, from where it's only 16km by **bus** to Monte Sant'Angelo. Alternatively, in the north of the region, **Ferrovie del Gargano** (ⓦwww.ferroviedelgargano.com) operates trains between Fóggia and San Severo. You then change here for onward travel to Péschici-Calanelle, from where a bus connects with Péschici. Note that most FG stations are quite a distance from the towns and villages they serve, so always go for the connecting bus if there is one.

Getting around the interior can be a little more tortuous. **Buses** are run by two companies: SITA (☎0881.773.117, ⓦwww.sitabus.it) serves the inland towns and operates the inland route to Vieste; and FG (☎0881.725.188 or 0881.772.4918), which runs the trains and connecting buses in northern Gargano, including a coastal bus route to Vieste, via Manfredonia, Mattinata and Pugnochiuso. There is also a **ferry service** connecting Manfredonia, Vieste, Péschici, Rodi Garganico and most coastal towns, which continues the journey on to the Trémiti Islands (p.962).

Monte Sant'Angelo and the pilgrim route

Just north of Manfredonia, perched almost 800m up in the hills, **MONTE SANT'ANGELO** is the highest – and coldest – settlement in the Gargano. Pilgrims have trudged up the switchback paths and roads for centuries to visit the spot where the archangel Michael is said to have made four separate appearances, mostly at the end of the fifth century – making the sanctuary here one of the earliest Christian shrines in Europe and one of the most important in Italy. Today, the pilgrims come by bus, and the village is a bit

THE GARGANO PROMONTORY

Ferry
Hydrofoil

N

0   10 km

◄ *Trémiti Islands*

◄ *Trémiti Islands*

◄ *Termoli*

Vieste

Testa del Gargano

Pugnochiuso

Péschici

San Menaio

Vico del Gargano

Ischitella

Rodi Garganico

Summer only

Summer only

Summer only

Mattinata

FORESTA UMBRA

Park Visitor's Centre

Monte Sant'Angelo

Manfredonia

Siponto

Lago di Varano

Cagnano Varano

PARCO NAZIONALE DEL GARGANO

S. Maria di Pulsano

San Giovanni Rotondo

► *Bari*

Lago di Lesina

Sannicandro Garganico

San Marco in Lamis

► *Foggia*

► *Foggia*

Apricena

San Severo

► *Foggia*

Lucera

of a tourist trap. But the yearly major festivals on May 8 and September 28, 29 and 30 attract locals from miles around, some of whom turn up in traditional dress.

SITA **buses** (every two hours from Manfredonia) drop you in Piazza Duca d'Aosta, from where you should follow the road uphill to the edge of the old town and the Via Reale Basilica; here you'll find the famous **Santuario di San Michele Arcangelo** (July–Sept daily 7.30am–7.30pm; rest of year Sun & holidays only 7.30am–6pm). Apart from a lean, octagonal thirteenth-century campanile, the sanctuary is rather plain on the outside. From the small courtyard on the right a flight of stone steps leads down to the crypts – heralded by a magnificent pair of eleventh-century bronze doors, made in Constantinople – that form the entrance to the church built on the site of the cave in which the archangel first appeared (in 490). Opposite the campanile, another set of steps leads down to the nearby ruins of the **Chiesa di San Pietro**, behind which is the so-called **Tomba di Rotari** (March–Oct 9am–1pm; rest of year by appointment with the custodian in San Michele; €0.60) – an imposing domed tower once thought to be the tomb of Rothari, a seventh-century Lombard chieftain who was converted to Christianity. More prosaically, it's more likely to have been a twelfth-century baptistry; the large baptismal font is just on the right as you enter the tower. Little remains of the church itself, wrecked by an earthquake, but look out for the rose window – a Catherine wheel of entwined mermaids.

Back on Via Reale Basilica, it's an easy clamber up to the ruined Norman **Castello** (daily: July & Aug 8am–7pm; Sept–June 9am–1pm & 2.30–6pm; €1.70) for good views over the town and valley. From here, you can cut down through the narrow whitewashed streets of the old town to Piazza San Francesco d'Assisi and the **Museo Tancredi** (May–Sept Mon 8.30am–1pm, Tues–Fri 8.30am–1.30pm & 2.30–7.30pm, Sat & Sun 9am–1pm & 3.30–7pm; Oct–April Mon–Fri 8.30am–1.30pm, Tues & Thurs 4–7pm; €2), an arts and crafts museum with some sparse displays on the production of olive oil, wheat, wine and charcoal.

Practicalities

For overnight stays (though don't count on available beds at the main festival times) the only **hotels** are the peaceful *Rotary*, in a panoramic position 1km along the road to Pulsano (T0884.562.146, Wwww.hotelsantangelo.com; ❹); the *Sant'Angelo* nearby (T0884.565.536; ❺); and *Michael* (as in the Saint), Via R. Basilica 86 (T0884.565.519, Wwww.hotelmichael.com; ❹). There's a *foresteria* – accommodation run by a religious institution but open to everybody – on the hill into the old town: *Casa del Pellegrino*, Via Carlo d'Angio (T0884.562.396, Wwww.santuariosanmichele.it; ❶). The rooms are modern and well looked after, and there's a set lunch and dinner menu for €13, but you must be in by 11pm at the latest. For snacks, ignore the touristy places in the lower town and head instead for the bakery outside the castle, where they'll make you up a tasty sandwich and sell you a cold beer. One of the nicest **restaurants** in town is *Medio Evo*, Via Castelli 21 (T0884.565.356; closed Mon in winter), serving seasonal local dishes and home-made ice cream and liqueurs. Slightly more expensive is *Li Jalantuúmene* (T0884.565.484, Wwww .li-jalantuumene.it), on a tiny whitewashed piazza in the maze of streets opposite the Santuario, offering a menu based on local meat, cheeses and fruit – to get there, follow the brown signs for Itinerary no. 4, one of several local art history trails.

The pilgrim route: San Giovanni Rotondo

The ancient **pilgrim route** weaved its way along the Stignano Valley between San Severo in the west and Monte Sant'Angelo, and until comparatively recently was the only road that linked the villages of the Gargano interior. With your own transport, it's still a good route for exploring a couple of the region's most important religious centres. If you want to follow any part of the pilgrim route by bus, you'll have to plan your itinerary carefully and be prepared to travel in leisurely fashion.

Direct bus services between Monte Sant'Angelo and the first village on the route, **SAN GIOVANNI ROTONDO**, run every couple of hours, although the SITA bus from Manfredonia is much more frequent (around fourteen trips a day). Nestling under Monte Calvo, the highest peak hereabouts, San Giovanni Rotondo is a modern centre for pilgrimage on a massive scale: it's the burial place of Padre Pio, a local priest who died in 1968 and was canonized in 2002, and the location of his massive "Hospital for the Relief of Suffering". Pio received the stigmata and "appeared" before cardinals in Rome while asleep in San Giovanni Rotondo, and won an immense following – especially among Italian Catholics – for his model piety and legendary ability to heal the sick. There's no escaping his saintly portrait throughout the Gargano peninsula, but it's especially prominent in San Giovanni Rotondo. A whole industry has grown up here, fuelled by the seven million and more pilgrims who pass through every year, making it the most visited pilgrimage site in the world after Lourdes. It's steadily transforming the town: a striking, new, stadium-sized church by the renowned architect Renzo Piano dedicated to Padre Pio was inaugurated in July 2004. The town takes its name from the **Rotonda di San Giovanni**, a building of indeterminate origin on the edge of the old town – like the Tomba di Rotari (see opposite), it's thought to have been a baptistry, built on the site of an earlier pagan temple.

Nine kilometres further west, and looking splendidly out over the Tavoliere plain, **SAN MARCO IN LAMIS**, though considerably smaller than San Giovanni, is dominated by a huge sixteenth-century Convento di San Matteo, with a modern interior. Every Good Friday the town holds a noisy, lively – and originally pagan – affair called the **fracchie**, when huge bundles of burning wood are hauled through the streets to illuminate the town for the Madonna as she seeks Jesus.

Vieste and the Costa Garganica

About 15km north of Manfredonia, the road tunnels under a mountain to emerge in a softer, greener landscape. **MATTINATA**, a small resort with fine campsites, sits back from the coast, overlooking olive groves and pine trees that drop down gently to a long stretch of beach. You can **stay** at ✻ *Agriturismo Madonna Incoronata* (☏0884.582.317, ⓦwww.agriturismogargano.it; ⑥), 1.5km from the roundabout where the buses stop. It's a great base for exploring the Gargano offering well-furnished apartments with private terraces (minimum two-night stay) on an organic olive farm. Beyond Mattinata the road splits: one branch (which the SITA bus takes) winds its way through the eastern part of the Foresta Umbra (see p.962) to Vieste; the coastal route (and the FG bus) runs up to **PUGNOCHIUSO**, a panoramic bay dominated by a grim-looking holiday village surrounded by barbed-wire fences. One of the easiest of the local **hiking trails** starts close by. The path is clearly marked off the Mattinata–Pugnochiuso road, about 3km north of Baia di Zagare, and the trail (around 3km each way) runs sharply down to a beach, Spiaggia di Vignanótica. To reach the start of the trail, take the FG bus from Mattinata for Pugnochiuso/Vieste and ask to be let off at Località Mégoli.

Vieste

VIESTE juts out into the Adriatic on two promontories, the easternmost point of the Gargano peninsula. Fifty years ago there wasn't even a proper road here, but today Vieste, with its excellent beaches, is the holiday capital of Gargano, and the streets and sands are packed in August. Despite the crowds, it has managed to survive as a lively and inviting town, with an interesting historic core and active nightlife that warrant a stop of a day or two – particularly if you're planning to take the ferry from here to the Trémiti Islands.

Arrival, information and accommodation

You **arrive** by bus at Piazzale Manzoni, to the west of the town centre; bear right from here along Viale XXIV Maggio, which becomes Corso Lorenzo Fazzini – the main street. At no. 8 is the main **tourist office** (mid-June to mid-Sept Mon–Fri 8am–2pm & 3.30–9pm; rest of year Mon–Fri 8am–2pm, Tues & Thurs also 4–7pm; ℡0884.707.495, Ⓔvieste@pugliaturismo.com), and there's another at Piazza Kennedy, in the centre of the old town (June–Sept Mon–Sat 8am–1pm & 3.30–9pm; Oct–May Mon–Fri 8am–1pm, Tues & Thurs also 4–8pm; ℡0884.708.806). The website Ⓦwww.viesteonline.it is a good source of information.

There's no shortage of **accommodation** in Vieste but budget options in the old town are hard to come by if you want just one night's stay. First choice is the atmospheric *Pensione al Centro Storico*, Via Mafrolla 32 (℡0884.707.030, Ⓔcstorico@viesteonline.it; ❷), in the old town, with thirteen large, simple rooms, and a terrace overlooking the promontory where you can bring your own beer and take-out pizza and enjoy the sunset. People who come back year after year and those on a three-day to a weeks stay will be given prefer-ence, but if you call the day before, they will fit you in for one night if they

△ Vieste coastline

can. There's the same booking scenario with the more upmarket *Seggio* in the old town at Via Vesta 7 (℡0884.708.123, ⓦwww.hotelseggio.it; ➏; closed Nov–March), with vertiginous views down to its swimming pool, tiny private sandy beach and lagoon. The *Hotel Punta San Francesco* at Via D. Francesco 2 (℡0884.701.422, ⓦwww.hotelpuntasanfrancesco.it; ➍) enjoys a quiet position in the old town with lovely views over the promontory, though the decor is a little tired. Around 1.5km north of the castle along the shore, the good-value *Albergo Vela Velo*, Lungomare Europa 19 (℡0884.706.303; ➌), is perhaps a more standard choice. This small, friendly, modern two-star has private use of a section of San Lorenzo beach across the road (room rates include price of sunbed and umbrella included except in height of season) and it's an easy cycle into town on one of its mountain bikes (free to guests). For help finding **self-catering** accommodation (minimum stay of a week), ask at SOL (see p.960).

The Town

The **old town** sits on the easternmost of the two promontories, at the tip of which stands the **Chiesa di San Francesco**, once a thriving monastery, and a *trabucco* – used by fishermen to catch mullet. Probably Phoenician in origin, these cantilevered arrangements of wooden beams, winches and ropes are peculiar to the rocky Gargano coast. Exploiting the fact that mullet swim head to tail, a live mullet is attached to a line and used to entice others to swim over a net suspended below, which is then hoisted up to the platform.

From the church, climb up Via Mafrolla, walking through the old town to Piazza Seggio. Straight ahead, Via Duomo is the site of the so-called **Chianca Amara**, the "bitter stone", where as many as 5000 local people were beheaded when the Turks sacked the town in 1554. Further down, past the stone, the **Cattedrale**, eleventh century in origin but tampered with in the eighteenth century, provides a cool retreat from the fierce glare of the sun in the whitewashed streets.

Eating and drinking

Places to **eat** include cheap and cheerful pizzerias on the Piazza Vittorio Emanuele II, as well as the *Osteria degli Archi*, Via Ripe 2 (booking advisable; ℡0884.705.199; closed Mon in winter), at the Punta di San Francesco end of the old town. Occupying a restored stone building in the sea wall, it specializes in seafood and uses its own olive oil in its dishes. *Dragone*, via Duomo 8 (℡0884.701.212; closed Nov–March), located in a natural cave, is good for local fish dishes, such as smoked eel from nearby Lesina, and unusual desserts. It offers a four-course menu for €5, including drinks, or if you prefer something lighter, there are platters of Gargano cheeses and vegetables and regional wine by the glass. On the edge of the old town above the cathedral, *Piazzetta Petrone*, Via Mons. Palma 41 (℡0884.706.453; booking advisable in low season), has a lovely terrace, bakes its pizza in a wood-fired oven and uses the best of local

Getting to the Trémiti Islands

There are year-round catamaran and hydrofoil connections to the **Trémiti Islands** (Aug 3 daily, rest of year 1 daily; 1hr; €3.60 single from Vieste); tickets are available from a number of agencies around town, including Gargáno Viaggi at Piazza Roma 7 (daily: July & Aug 9am–12.30pm & 5–11pm; June & Sept until 9pm; rest of year until 8pm; ℡0884.708.501, ⓦwww.garganoviaggi.it), or from the Adriatica office (ⓦwww .tirrenia.it) in the harbour (look for the "Navegargano" or "Adriatica" signs).

ingredients such as *caciocavallo* (a local cheese) and sausage. If you fancy a **drink**, the terrace bar at *Seggio* (see p.959) is a perfect place to chill before dinner.

Around Vieste

There are a number of day-trips worth making **around Vieste**. The most obvious move is to the **beaches**: head for the small one between the promontories or to the north, San Lorenzo, with fine, soft, gently shelving sand, or finally, just south of town, Pizzomunno, which is also sandy. They all go in for the grill-pan variety of sunbathing with rows and rows of sunbeds. Slightly less crowded, if you're lucky, is the marvellous Scialmarino beach, 4.5km up the coast towards Péschici. Nicest of all is the small Baia di San Felice, squeezed between two headlands and backed by pine trees, just before you get to the Testa del Gargano, several kilometres south of town.

If you want to swim away from the crowds, consider an organized boat trip to the grotto-ridden **coastline** around the "head" or Testa del Gargano. Boats leave for the three-hour grotto excursion from next to San Francesco church at around 9am and 2.30pm; tickets cost €5 and are available from Gargáno Viaggi (see box, p.959) and SOL (daily March–Oct 9am–1pm & 4–9pm; July & Aug until midnight; ☎340.906.2046, ⑩www.solvieste.it) at Via Trepiccioni 5. If you really want to get away from it you could rent your own boat for the day, from SOL.

⑭ Péschici and northern Gargano

Atop its rocky vantage point overlooking a beautiful sandy bay, **PÉSCHICI** is a little smaller than Vieste and one of the most attractive village resorts in the Gargano. Though originally built in 970 AD as a buffer against Saracen incursions, its labyrinth of tiny streets and houses sporting domed roofs has a distinctly Arabic flavour. Beach-lazing is the focus, although the town also makes a good base for exploring some of the caves and defensive medieval towers of the nearby coastline. The easiest trips are to the grotto at **San Nicola**, 3km east of town (some buses), or 5km west to the **Torre di Monte Pucci** for fine coastal views (and where there's a *trabucco* restaurant for refreshments).

Practicalities

The FG **train** line ends at Calanelle, a few kilometres west of Péschici, but there's a connection to the town by a **bus**. This, and other buses, drops you in the newer, beach resort part of Péschici, from where it's a short walk down to the main street – Corso Garibaldi – and the sea.

Ferries to the Trémiti Islands from Péschici (calling at Rodi Garganico on the way) leave at around 9am from the port, take 1hr 15min and cost €5 for the return trip (the ferry brings everyone back at around 5pm). You can buy tickets onshore next to the boat right up until departure.

Accommodation

Places to stay include the *Locanda Al Castello*, Via Castello 29 (☎0884.964.038; ❸), a stiff walk away up in the old town, down a narrow lane of whitewashed houses; it has a restaurant offering five or six daily specials. There are plenty of hotels in the newer part of town: *Hotel d'Amato* off the SS89 next to the beach (☎0884.963.415, ⑩www.hoteldamato.it; ❻) offers modern rooms, a restaurant, a bar and two swimming pools The *Elisa*, right next to the beach at Via Marina 20 (☎0884.964.012, ⑩www.hotelelisa.it; ❹), is a simple place with a so-so restaurant below. Also next to the sea is the well-kept *Villa a Mare*, Via Marina

1 (☎0884.963.414, ⓦwww.villaamare.it; ⑥), with a shady patio garden next to the car park. You can get cheaper rooms if you are prepared to be set back from the sea: *Piccolo Paradiso*, a family-run hotel in Località Vignola, a five-minute walk from the beach (☎0884.963.466, ⓦwww.hotelpiccoloparadiso.it; ❸), has magnificent sea views and a deservedly popular terrace restaurant. *La Collinetta* (☎0884.964.151) on the coast road to Vieste (closed Nov to mid-March) has half-board deals worth considering: prices range from €48 per person in April–June and September to €71 per person in July and August. There's also a choice of **campsites** – the *Baia San Nicola* (☎0884.964.231), 2km east along the coast at Punta San Nicola, and *Baia Calenella* (☎0884.968.212, ⓦwww .baiacalenella.com, May–Sept), west along the SS89 coast road just past the train station at Péschici-Calenella, towards San Menaio.

Eating and drinking

There are scores of **restaurants**, pizzerias, *gelaterie* and **bars** in the old town, scene of a lively *passeggiata* that goes on all evening. In modest surroundings, the *Fra Stefano* at Via Forno 8 (☎0884.964.141; closed Nov–March) serves inexpensive delicious fish grilled over a wood fire, *ruoto* (kid with little onions and potatoes) and *capistrelli* (home-made pasta with seafood and white beans), all washed down with wine drawn from a barrel. For a more unusual setting, head for the *Grotta delle Rondini* (☎0884.964.007; closed Nov–March) situated in a natural cave near the port outside the old town: the antipasti is especially good. The hotel restaurant, *La Collinetta* (☎0884.964.151), serves reasonably priced fish dishes such as seafood gratin and red mullet baked in foil.

⑭

West along the coast and onwards

A string of white sandy beaches stretch from San Menaio to **RODI GARGAN- ICO** – originally a Greek settlement ("Rodi" is derived from Rhodes) and nowadays, with its beaches and fast hydrofoil links with the Trémiti Islands, a highly popular resort in summer. It's busy and expensive in August, but go a couple of months either side and it can be delightful. **SAN MENAIO** is much quieter than Rodi – more compact and with fewer villas – and even in high season it's easy to get away from it all by walking a few hundred metres south along the strand. *Sole,* Lungomare 2 (☎0884.963.415, ⓦwww.hoteldamato .it; ⑥), is an attractive 1920s resort **hotel** built right next to the sea, and room prices include a sunlounger and umbrella on the private sandy beach. There's also a pleasant, shady **campsite** called *Di Monte* (☎0884.968.528), just off the SS89, a few minutes' walk from the beach.

From Rodi Garganico, both road and rail skirt the large **Lago di Varano**, a once-malarial swamp that swallowed the ancient Athenian town of Uria in the fourth century BC. The preserve of eel fishermen, it's the least-visited region on the Gargano promontory, and consequently attracts a great variety of birdlife, particularly curlews and warblers. Further west, the thin **Lago di Lésina** is a highly saline shallow lagoon, cut off from the sea by a 27-kilometre stretch of sand dunes. It's still mercifully free from development – unlike the northern spit of Varano, which is slowly beginning to fill with campsites.

Inland Gargano: Vico del Gargano and the Foresta Umbra

The **interior** of the Gargano promontory can make a cool break from its busy coast, and though there's not much public transport, apart from the odd bus from Vieste, San Menaio and Rodi Garganico, you can rent mountain bikes or fix up jeep safaris or pony trekking (℡0884.568.911, ⓦwww.parcogargano.it). The SOL agency (see p.960) also arranges tours and hire out cars and mountain bikes. **DEL GARGANO** is the nicest of the villages and firmly off the beaten track, sited on a hill surrounded by citrus groves and with a creakingly ancient centre full of steep, tangled streets. It's on the edge of the **Foresta Umbra** (Forest of Shadows), which stretches right across the centre of the Gargano massif: 11,000 hectares of pines, oaks, beeches and yew, sheltering a rich variety of wildlife, especially roe deer, it is the last remnant of an ancient forest which once covered most of Puglia. Even if you're not a botanist or a birdwatcher you'll appreciate the amazing biodiversity of the forest, safeguarded by its designation as a national park in 1991. There are more than seventy species of orchid in the park and, if you're lucky, you may see wild-boar piglets rooting around by the side of the road. If you fancy following any of the marked woodland **walks**, head for the **Centro Visitatori** (April–Oct daily 9am–7pm; ℡0884.88.055, ⓦwww.mediterraneambiente.it) in the middle of the forest, where road 528 meets the road to Péschici and Vieste; the centre doles out maps and rents out mountain bikes.

The Trémiti Islands

A small group of Islands 40km off the Gargano coast, the **Trémiti Islands** – Isole Trémiti – are almost entirely given over to tourism in the summer, when the tiny population is swamped by visitors. Despite this, they remain relatively unspoilt and the sea crystal clear. The main Trémiti group consists of three Islands: **San Nicola**, **San Domino** – the biggest – and **Capraia**, of which only the first two are inhabited.

The Islands were traditionally a place of exile and punishment. Augustus banished his granddaughter Julia to the Islands, while Charlemagne packed his father-in-law off here (minus eyes and limbs) in the eighth century. Monks from Montecassino, on the mainland, first set about building a formidable fortress-abbey on one of the Islands in the eleventh century, which managed to withstand frequent assault by the Turks. Later, during the eighteenth century, the Islands returned to their old role as a place of confinement for political prisoners, though the Bourbons, concerned at the decline in the local population, shipped in two hundred women from the Neapolitan taverns to encourage a recovery.

Most **ferries** arrive at **SAN NICOLA**, where you can wander around the monastic fortress and the tiny church of **Santa Maria a Mare**, built by the monks in the eleventh century on the site of an earlier ninth-century hermitage. San Nicola is rugged and rocky with no beaches, although there is nude bathing on its east side and good swimming off the whole Island.

Ignore the offers of pricey boat trips to the other Islands and instead jump on the regular ferry that takes about a minute to cross to **SAN DOMINO**. It's a greener island than its neighbour, its pines offering welcome shade from

Getting to the Trémiti islands

Hydrofoils and catamarans run to San Nicola from Vieste (see p.959) all year round. There's also a summer service from Manfredonia (see p.953), Vasto (see p.870) and Ortona (see p.870). **Ferries** and **monostabs** (fast ferries) for foot passengers run throughout the year from Térmoli (see p.876). **Tourist motor cruisers** from Péschici and Rodi Gargánico also offer day trips to the Islands during the holiday season.

the heat. Although there's a sandy **beach** – Cala delle Arene – right where the ferry lands on the northeast side of the Island, it's packed in the summer. Your best bet is to follow the signs for the *Villaggio TCI* (see below) and make for the west of the Island and the quieter coves, such as Cala dello Spido. For **walking**, head for the Punta di Diamante; maps are pinned up in some of the bars or can be bought from souvenir shops.

Practicalities

Accommodation on the Islands is limited to San Domino and is largely full board in high season: count on paying €50–60 a night per person. The *municipio* on San Domino holds a list of private rooms, or you could try the most appealing of the small hotels, *Pensione Pineta* (☎0882.463.202; ❸), a whitewashed villa surrounded by pine trees, near some peaceful rocky coves just outside the tiny village centre. Alternatively, there are two places in the village: *Al Faro* at Via Cantina Sperimentale (☎0882.463.424; ❸), with purple bougainvillaea clambering over the outside and a brightly painted interior, and *Albergo Gabbiano* (☎0882.463.410; ❻) ensconced in greenery at Piazza Belvedere; it's essential to book ahead for all three. Camping is now forbidden on the Islands so the former *Villaggio TCI* (☎0882.463.402, ⓦwww.touringclub.it) campsite now rents out **cabins** by the week; for a stay of less than seven nights, call a couple of days beforehand to ask about vacancies. Bear in mind that mosquitoes tend to be a serious problem in the summer months and that, as provisions have to be ferried across from the mainland, eating out can be a costly exercise – buy some picnic food before you get on the boat.

Along the coast to Bari

The first part of the coastal route south from Manfredonia is unremarkable, with flat lands given up to saline extraction. You won't be able to come this way by train or bus anyway – though there is a direct coastal road. First stop, by rail at least, isn't until **MARGHERITA DI SAVOIA**, at the edge of Tavoliere, a small town that boasts the country's oldest working salt pans, dating to the third century BC. Pink flamingos, cranes and kingfishers are among 40,000 bird species that overwinter in the internationally recognised wetlands. Beyond here, the rest of the coastline is easily accessible by public transport; most places have stations on the main Bologna–Lecce rail line.

Among them is **TRANI**, a place with an usually cosmopolitan air. One of the most important medieval Italian ports, it was a prosperous trading centre with a large mercantile and Jewish community; during the Middle Ages it rivalled Bari as a commercial port, and in the fourteenth century was powerful enough to take on the domineering Venetians.

Modern-day Trani is still a prosperous place, its elegant buildings spruce and smart. Centrepiece of the town is the cream-coloured, eleventh-century **Duomo** (daily 8.30am–noon & 3–6pm), right on the sea at the edge of the old town. Dedicated to San Nicola Pellegrino, it consists of no fewer than three churches, stacked on top of each other like an inverted wedding cake – the facade austere but lightened by a pretty rose window. The interior has been restored to its original Norman state, the stark nave displaying a timbered ceiling, while fragments of a twelfth-century mosaic have been uncovered near the presbytery. Below the vaulted crypt, the marble Roman columns of the earlier Santa Maria della Scala church are visible, while still lower you can see a sixth-century, early Christian underground chamber.

A wander through the adjacent streets gives an impression of the medieval city, not least in the names that echo the town's mercantile and Jewish origins – Via Sinagoga, Via Doge Vecchia and Via Cambio (Street of the Moneychangers). The **Chiesa di Ognissanti**, close by, was a twelfth-century chapel of the Knights Templar, once part of a hospital for injured Crusaders. Sadly, it's unlikely to be open, but if you hang around, someone may appear with a key.

The rail line continues south to **MOLFETTA**, a working port, unashamedly non-touristy and all the better for it; the waterfront is active with visiting ships and thronged by an evening *passeggiata* that sweeps down to the docks to watch the sunset.

Bari

The commercial and administrative capital of Puglia, a university town and southern Italy's second city, **BARI** has its fair share of interest. But although it's an economically vibrant place, the town harbours no pretensions to being a major tourist attraction. People come here primarily for work or to leave for Greece on its many ferries.

Bari was already a thriving centre when the Romans arrived. Later, the city was the seat of the Byzantine governor of southern Italy, while, under the Normans, Bari rivalled Venice both as a maritime centre and, following the seizure of the remains of St Nicholas, as a place of pilgrimage. Since those heady days, Bari has declined considerably. Its fortunes revived briefly in 1813 when the king of Naples foisted a planned expansion on the city – giving the centre its contemporary gridded street pattern, wide avenues and piazzas. And Mussolini instituted a university and left a legacy of strident Fascist architecture. However, the city was heavily bombed during the last war, and today its compact and dynamic centre is a symbol of the south's zeal for commercial growth.

Arrival, information and accommodation

Bari's **airport** (℡080.5800.200, ⓦwww.seap-puglia.it) is 25km north-west from the city centre and is served by low-cost airlines from the UK; a shuttle bus connects it with the central train station roughly hourly between 5.10am and 11.20pm daily (30min; €4.15 one way; ℡080.521.9172, ⓦwww.autoservizitempesta.it).

There are three train stations. **Stazione Centrale** in Piazza Aldo Moro is on the southern edge of the modern centre and serves regular FS trains and those of the private Ferrovia del Sud-Est line (℡080.546.2111, ⓦwww.fseonline.it), which run down to Táranto via Alberobello, Locorotondo and Martina Franca (see p.972 for more on this route). Just to the west, also on Piazza Aldo Moro, the separate **Stazione Bari-Nord** is for trains run by the private FerroTramViaria company (℡080.523.2202, ⓦwww.ferrovienordbarese.it/), connecting Bari with Andria, Barletta, Bitonto and Ruvo di Puglia. Adjacent to this, on Corso Italia, is the **Stazione FAL Apulo-Lucane**; trains and buses from here are run by Ferrovia Appulo-Lucane (℡080.572.5229, ⓦwww.fal-srl.it/home.php) and go to Altamura, Gravina, and Matera and Potenza in Basilicata.

Buses complicate the issue even further: from the coastal towns north of Bari you'll arrive at Piazza Eroi del Mare; SITA buses from inland and southern towns pull up in Largo Sorrentino (behind the train station); Marozzi buses from Rome arrive either here or on Piazza Aldo Moro. Buses belonging to the

BARI

Porto Nuovo

PIAZZALE
C. COLOMBO

EATING & DRINKING
Ai 2 Ghiottoni	7
Al Pescatore	2
El Pedro	5
La Credenze	1
La Locanda di Federico	3
Le Travi	4
Terranima	6

ACCOMMODATION
Adria	B
Costa	A
Giulia	A

MOLO S. VITO

Stazione
Marrittima

Porto
Sen. Antonio
de Tullio

PIAZZA
S. PIETRO

Chiesa di
San Gregorio

PIAZZA
S. NICOLA

Basilica di
San Nicola

OLD CITY

N

CORSO SEN. ANTONIO DE TULLIO

Palese & Airport

Cattedrale
di San Sabino ❶

Castello
Normanno-
Svevo ❷

PIAZZA
ODEGITRIA

Colonna della
Giustizia ❸

PIAZZA
MERCANTILE

MOLO SANT' ANTONIO

PIAZZA ISABELLA
D'ARAGONA

PIAZZA FEDERICO II

PIAZZA MASSARI

Palazzo
Sedile

VIA G. MURAT

VIA S. FRANCESCO D'ASSISI

LARGO CHIURLIA

PIAZZA
FERRARESE

Porto Vecchio

❹

LUNGOMARE IMPERATORE AUGUSTO

MOLO S. NICOLA

CORSO VITTORIO EMANUELE II

VIA PICCINNI

LUNGOMARE DI CROLLALANZA

VIA MARCHESE DI MONTRONE

❺

VIA ABATE GIMMA

Bus
Station

VIA CALEFATI

VIA DE ROSSI

VIA CAIROLI

VIA PUTIGNANI

VIA ROBERTO DA BARI

VIA SPARANO

VIA AGIRO

VIA MELO

❼

CORSO CAVOUR

Teatro
Petruzzelli

VIA COGNETTI

Pinacoteca Provinciale (300m)

VIA QUINTINO SELLA

❻

VIA PRINCIPE AMEDEO

VIA DANTE ALIGHIERI

VIA IMBRIANI

VIA DE GIOSA

VIA CARDASSI

VIA NICOLAI

VIA BEATILLO

Università
& Museo
Archeologico

PIAZZA UMBERTO I

VIA CRISANZIO

Ⓐ

VIA SPARANO

VIA P. PETRONI

@

VIA CORNARI

VIA

Stazione FAL
Apulo-
Lucane

Stazione
Bari-Nord

PIAZZA ALDO MORO

ⓘ

Stazione FSR (Largo Ciaia)

CORSO ITALIA

0   100 m

VIA ZUPPETTA

Ⓑ

Stazione Centrale (FS)

⑭

PUGLIA | Bari

private rail line FAL, from Basilicata, arrive at the station on Corso Italia, while FSE buses from Bríndisi pull in at their station on Largo Ciaia.

Ferries from Albania, Croatia, Turkey, Israel, Montenegro and Greece (Igoumenitsa, Corfu and Patras) all use the Stazione Maríttima, next to the old city, which is connected with the main FS train station by bus #20.

Getting around, your best bet is to walk – not a bad option in such a small city. The **tourist office** is at Piazza Aldo Moro 33a, in a small cul-de-sac to the right as you come out of the main train station (Mon–Sat 8am–2pm, Tues & Thurs also 3–6pm; ℡080.524.2329, ⓦwww.pugliaturismo.com/aptbari).

Several handy and affordable **hotels** are found one block from the station in the apartment building at Via Crisanzio 12: *Costa* (℡080.521.9015; ❸) is the nicest, with simple but attractive rooms. Next door, *Giulia* (℡080.521.6630, ⓦwww.hotelpensionegiulia.it; ❷), run by a pleasant couple, has Internet access and some en-suite rooms. In the same area is the *Adria*, right out of the station on Via Zuppetta (℡080.524.6699, ⓦwww.adriahotelbari.com; ❹; some cheaper rooms are available).

The City

There's not a lot to the "**new town**" of Bari, bar a good museum or two. The straight streets are lined with shops and offices, relieved occasionally by the odd bit of greenery and piazza, best of which is the starting point of the evening *passeggiata*, **Piazza Umberto I**. Off the piazza, the university building houses an excellent **Museo Archeologico**, currently closed for restoration. If it's reopened by the time of your visit, it's well worth a look: it holds a good selection of Greek and Puglian ceramics and a solid collection of artefacts from the Daunic, Messapian and Peucetic peoples – Puglia's earliest inhabitants. Afterwards, cut east for **Corso Cavour**, Bari's main commercial street bordered with trees, which leads down to the waterfront. Right along Corso Cavour, in the Palazzo della Provincia, the **Pinacoteca Provinciale** (Tues–Sat 9.30am–1pm & 4–7pm, Sun 9am–1pm; €2.58) contains mostly southern Italian art ranging from the twelfth to nineteenth centuries, but there are also works by Tintoretto and Paolo Veronese that were moved from the cathedral, and a small collection of paintings by the twentieth-century Bolognese painter, Giorgio Morandi.

The old city

Even if you're only in Bari to catch a ferry, try to make time for a wander around the **old city**, an entrancing jumble of streets that's possibly the most perplexing place to walk around in southern Italy. Situated at the far end of Corso Cavour, its labyrinth of seemingly endless passages weaving through courtyards and under arches was originally designed to spare the inhabitants from the wind and throw invaders into a state of confusion. This it still does admirably, and even with the best of maps you're going to get lost. Life is lived very much outdoors, and on summer evenings it's full of people sitting outside their kitchen doors.

International ferry services run from Bari to Greece, Albania and Croatia; for information and timetables call ☎800.573.738 or visit ⓦ www.porto.bari.it. Travel agents often have special offers on **tickets**; as a general rule, you will save twenty percent if you buy a return ticket. Once you've got your ticket, you must report to the relevant desk at the Stazione Maríttima at least two hours before departure. Prices given below are for travel in high season.

Albania

Hydrofoil services to **Albania** operated by Quality Lines are bookable through P. Lorusso & Co, Via Piccinni 133 (☎080.521.7699, ⓦ www.agenzialorusso.it), and at the Stazione Maríttima (☎080.521.2840), departing Bari at least once daily in summer; the journey takes 3hr 30min and costs €80 one way.

Adriatica and Ventouris run car ferries to Durazzo/Durres in Albania daily all year round; the journey takes nine hours overnight (from €55 one way, €60 for a reclining seat). Adriatica has offices at Via Liside 4 (☎892.123 from Italy only, ⓦ www.tirrenia .it). Ventouris timetables and prices are listed at ⓦ www.ferries.gr. Embarkation tax of €0.75 per person, €4.80 for a car from Bari, is also payable; check whether it's included in your ticket price or not.

Croatia

Jadrolinija operates a service to Rijeka in **Croatia**, departing late evening for a night crossing of the Adriatic and stopping en route at the coastal towns of Dubrovnik, Korcula, Stari Grad and Split throughout the following day. The ship arrives at Rijeka early in the morning of the second day after departure. Ferries operate twice weekly in July and August. For the full timetable visit ⓦ www.jadrolinija.hr. Contact Jadrolinija and buy tickets (€50.50 for the full voyage one way) through P. Lorusso & Co (contact details as above) or at ⓔ jadrolinija@agenzialorusso.it.

Greece

Ferry services to **Greece** are operated by Ventouris, Agoudimos, Superfast and Superfast's sister company Blue Star. Ventouris and Agoudimos tickets are bookable at ⓦ www.ferries.gr or through P. Lorusso & Co (contact details as above). Superfast ferries can be booked on ⓦ www.superfast.com or through Portrans at Corso A. de Tullio 6 (☎080.521.1416) or at the Stazione Maríttima (☎080.528.2828). Ventouris runs two services daily to Corfu (end July to mid-Aug) and Igoumenitsa (mid-June to Dec), with three weekly sailings the rest of the year; one-way prices start at €58 per person, €69 extra for a car, plus port fees. The service to Igoumenitsa takes 11hr 30min and the service to Corfu takes 11hr. Superfast runs a daily overnight sailing to both Igoumenitsa (except Sun) and Patras (except Fri, Sat & Sun) year-round and the seats cost from €67 (cars €49); the journeys take 9hr 30min and 15hr 30min respectively.

Specific sights are few. The **Basilica di San Nicola** (daily 9am–1pm & 4–7pm; museum Tues–Fri 10am–noon; free), in the heart of the old city, was, as an inscription at the side of the main door testifies, consecrated in 1197 to house the relics of the saint plundered a century earlier from southern Turkey. From the outside it all looks thoroughly Norman, especially the twin fortress-like towers, but it's a misleading impression: the right-hand tower predates the church, the other was added later for balance, and even the simple nave is shattered by three great arches and an ornate seventeenth-century ceiling. The real beauty of the church lies in its stonework, with the twelfth-century altar canopy one of the finest in Italy. The motifs around the capitals are the work of stonemasons from Como, whilst the lovely twelfth-century carved doorway and simple, striking mosaic floor behind the altar are heavily influenced by the Saracens. Best of all is the twelfth-century episcopal throne behind the altar, a superb piece of work supported by small figures wheezing beneath its weight. Down in the crypt are the remains of the saint – patron of pawnbrokers – and sailors (and of Russians, who made the pilgrimage here until 1917). Behind the tomb-altar, the richly decorated fourteenth-century icon of the saint was a present from the King of Serbia.

It's not far from the basilica to Bari's other important church, the **Cattedrale di San Sabino** (daily 8.30am–7.30pm; free), off Piazza Odegitria, dedicated to the original patron saint of Bari, before he was usurped by Nicholas, and built at the end of the twelfth century. Come just for the contrast: uncluttered by arches, it retains its original medieval atmosphere and – unlike the basilica – a timbered roof. The cathedral houses an eighth-century icon known as the *Madonna Odegitria*, brought here for safety from Constantinople by Byzantine monks. It's said to be the most authentic likeness of the Madonna in existence, having been taken from an original sketch by Luke the Apostle, and it's paraded around the city at religious festivals.

Across the piazza Odegitria, the **Castello Normanno–Svevo** (Tues–Sat 9am–1pm & 3.30–7pm, Sun 9am–1pm; €2) sits on the site of an earlier Roman fort. Built by Frederick II, much of it is closed to the public, but it has a vaulted hall that provides a cool escape from the afternoon sun. You can also see a gathering of some of the best of past Puglian artistry in a display of plaster-cast reproductions from churches and buildings throughout the region – particularly from the Castel del Monte, the cathedral at Altamura, and an animated frieze of griffins devouring serpents, from the church of San Leonardo at Siponto.

Eating and drinking

There are lots of atmospheric choices of places to eat in and around the old town of Bari. Most offer traditional Pugliese dishes and seafood, along with the Bari speciality of little ear-shaped pasta, *orechiette*, which is a firm favourite.

Ai 2 Ghiottoni Via Putignani 11b ☎080.523.2240. One of the town's top restaurants serves good shellfish and a refined version of Pugliese cuisine in attractive surroundings just outside the old city. Closed Sun.

Al Pescatore Via Federico II di Svevia 8 ☎080.523.7039. A couple of blocks east of the castle (watch your bag in this area), this no-nonsense choice serves fine fish for around €25–30 a head.

El Pedro Via Piccinni 152 Closed Sun. Good self-service restaurant serving a variety of traditional Italian dishes. Closed Sun.

La Credenze Via Verrone 25/Arco Sant'Onofrio, This simple option in the old city offers typical Barese fare like *orecchiette* with cauliflower or broad beans with wild chicory. Closed Mon.

La Locanda di Federico Piazza Mercantile 63 ☎080.5227.705. There's a good wine list to accompany the home cooking at this relatively upmarket choice with outside tables on the traffic-free square. Closed Mon.

Le Travi Largo Chiurlia ☎530.840.438. Don't miss the excellent anitpasti buffet at this old-town trattoria serving authentic local food in pleasing surroundings. Closed Mon.

Terranima Via Putignani 213–215 ☎080.521.9725. Informal café/restaurant serving a daily changing menu of regional specialities for around €18, without drinks. There's often live music in the evenings. Closed Sun.

Listings

Airport information Bari Palese ☎080.583.5200, ⓦwww.seap-puglia.it.

Beach The nearest beach is north of the city; take bus #1 from Teatro Petruzzelli to Palese/Santo

Spirito. To the south, there are beaches at Torre a Mare and San Giorgio – both reached on bus #12 from Stazione Centrale or #12 from Teatro Petruzzelli. **Exchange** Outside banking hours in Piazza Aldo Moro, inside Stazione Centrale.

Police Via G. Murat ℡080.549.1331.
Post office The main office is behind the university in Piazza Battisti (Mon–Fri 8am–7.30pm, Sat 8.30am–noon).
Taxis Radio Taxi ℡080.554.3333 (24hr).

Le Murge

Rising gently from the Adriatic coast, **Le Murge** – a low limestone plateau – dominates the landscape to the south and west of Bari. The towns in the region are not natural holiday destinations: the area is sparsely populated and the small settlements that exist are rural backwaters with a slow pace of life. But they do make an interesting day out or a good stopover if you're heading for the region of Basilicata. There are some buses and trains from Bari, but, as always, in Puglia without your own car travelling very extensively can be difficult.

The Low Murge

Easily reached from Barletta or Bari, the main town of the Low Murge is **ANDRIA**, a large agricultural centre at its best during its Monday morning market – otherwise it has little to hold you. It was, though, a favourite haunt of Frederick II, who was responsible for the major local attraction these days, the **Castel del Monte**, 17km south – the most extraordinary of all Puglia's castles and one of the finest surviving examples of Swabian architecture (daily: March–Sept 10.15am–7.45pm; Oct–Feb 9am–6.30pm; ticket office closes 30min earlier; €3; ℡0883.569.997). There are free tours in English, although donations are appreciated; from April to September the official guides are based at the castle's Pro Loco cabin but from October to March contact the Pro Loco office at Via Vespucci 14 in Andria (℡0883.592.283, ⓦwww.proloco.andria.ba.it). Sadly, there is only an infrequent bus service from Andria – contact either Pro Loco office for timetables.

Begun by Frederick in the 1240s, the Castel is a high, isolated fortress built around an octagonal courtyard in two storeys of eight rooms. A mystery surrounds its intended purpose. Although there was once an iron gate that could be lowered over the main entrance, there are no other visible signs of fortification, and the castle may have served as merely a hunting lodge. Nonetheless, the mathematical precision involved in its construction, and the preoccupation with the number eight, have excited writers for centuries. It's argued the castle is in fact an enormous astrological calendar, or that Frederick may have had the octagonal Omar mosque in Jerusalem in mind when he designed it; yet, despite his recorded fascination with the sciences, no one really knows the truth. There is only one record of its use. The defeat of Manfred, Frederick's illegitimate son, at the battle of Benevento in 1266 signalled the end of Swabian power in Puglia; and Manfred's sons and heirs were imprisoned in the castle for over thirty years – a lonely place to be incarcerated.

East of Andria (but best reached by hourly bus from Molfetta), the old centre of **RUVO DI PUGLIA** is an attractive stop, with a quiet, timeless atmosphere. In the autumn, the pavements of the old town are traditionally strewn with almonds, spread out to dry in the sun. Just across from the **tourist office** on Via Vittorio Veneto 48 (Mon–Sat 9.30am–12.30pm & 4.30–7.30pm, Sun 9.30am–12.30pm; ℡080.361.5419), the **Museo Jatta** in Piazza Bovio (Mon–Thurs & Sun 8.30am–1.30pm, Fri–Sat 8.30am–7.30pm; ⓦwww.palazzojatta.org;

14

PUGLIA | Le Murge

△ Castel del Monte

free but small charge for tours in English) houses a dusty collection of local copies of ancient Greek pottery as well as some beautiful originals, including a fifth-century-BC crater depicting the death of Talos. Ruvo's thirteenth-century **Duomo**, tucked into the tightly packed streets of the town's old quarter, is also well worth a look. Its beautiful portal is guarded by animated griffins balancing on fragile columns, with a staggering amount of decoration on the outer walls, a fine rose window and arches that taper off into human and animal heads.

The High Murge

Around 45km south of Bari (and reachable by train), **ALTAMURA** is the largest town in the High Murge, originally a fifth-century-BC Peucetian settlement – you can still see some parts of the old town. Given its many historical layers, it's perhaps appropriate that Altamura is home to one of southern Italy's best **archeological museums** (Mon–Sat 8.30am–7.30pm, Sun 8.30am–1.30pm; €2; ℡080.314.6409) on Via Santeramo 88. The collection here traces the history of the people of the Murge from prehistory to late medieval times, with plenty of exciting finds from all over the peninsula.

Altamura's most striking feature is its **Duomo**, a mixture of styles varying from Apulian-Romanesque to Gothic and Baroque. Take a look, too, at the tiny church of **San Niccolò dei Greci** on Corso Federico di Svevia; built by the Greek colonists in the thirteenth century, it housed their Orthodox religious ceremonies for more than 400 years.

Some 12km west, not far from the border with Basilicata, lies **GRAVINA DI PUGLIA** – a fortified town clinging to the edge of a deep ravine. During the early Barbarian invasions the locals took refuge in the caves along the sides of the gully, a move that seems to have paid off until the arrival of the Saracens, who promptly massacred every cave-dwelling inhabitant. Under the Normans, the shattered town settled down to a quieter life as a fiefdom of the wealthy pope-producing Orsini family, whose emblem – an enormous spread eagle – is all over town. In the dilapidated old quarter, the cave-church of **San Michele delle Grotte**, a dark, dank affair hewn out of the rock, holds bones that are said to be the remains of victims of the last Saracen attack, almost a thousand years old. The **Santomasi museum** (Tues–Sat 9am–1pm & 4–6pm, Sun 9am–1pm; €5; ⓦwww.fondazionesantomasi.it) in Piazza Santomasi contains archeological finds including Roman coins, Bourbon arms and uniforms as well as sixteenth- and seventeenth-century paintings, but more engaging, certainly if you couldn't get into San Michele, is the reconstruction of San Vito Vecchio, another cave-church, set up on the ground floor with some remarkable thirteenth- to fourteenth-century frescoes.

Down the coast from Bari

The coast south of Bari is a craggy stretch, with rock-hewn villages towering above tiny sandy coves. Just ten minutes by FS train from Bari (or bus #12 from Piazza Aldo Moro), **TORRE A MARE** is one of the easiest escapes from the city, situated on a rocky ledge high above two large caves. Being so close to Bari, the village can become quite crowded, but there will be fewer people around another twenty minutes on, at **POLIGNANO A MARE**, which, despite a newfound popularity, remains fairly low-key. It's a small port with a whitewashed medieval centre sprinkled with bars, souvenir and *foccacciarie* shops, perched on the edge of the limestone cliffs, and where people head for on a Sunday to watch the waves crashing against the rocks or to sunbathe on the clifftops. If you don't have a car it is best reached by train, although there is a bus service, run by FSE, from Largo Ciaia in Bari. If you'd like to **stay**, head for the appealing *Covo dei Saraceni*, Via Conversano 1A (☎080.424.1177, ⓦwww .covodeisaraceni.com/; ❺), which sits right above the rocks and has comfort- able rooms – some with large balconies and private terraces – a restaurant with panoramic views, and a businesslike atmosphere. If you're feeling flush, don't miss a meal in the ⚑ **cave restaurant** (May–Oct; booking advisable on ☎080.424.0677), high above the crashing waves at the *Hotel Grotta Palazzese* in the old town. Carved out by a local lord to create a party venue in the 1700s, the restaurant serves extremely well on seafood, with a good choice of Pugliese fish dishes such as tagliolini with courgette flowers and eel. *Cala Porto* is a cheaper option, a self-styled American bar-bistro at the base of the bridge on the northern edge of the town centre (follow the flares down the cobble- stone path towards the sea). The menu includes pasta, salads, simple meat dishes and *piadine* (flat bread with a filling) – you can eat out on one of several, small candle-lit terraces or drink in the bar.

Egnázia and Fasano

Some 8km beyond Polignano a Mare lies the commercial port of **MONÓPOLI**, with a nice old town, but not much else to see. There's more interest south, at the site of the ancient city of **Egnázia** (March 27 to Sept 30 daily 8.30am– 7.30pm; last entry 7pm; €3 including museum; ⓦhttp://xoomer.alice.it /egnazia); if you don't have your own transport, it's best reached by bus from **Fasano** (call Fasano's tourist office for timetable; ☎080.441.3086). Right next to the seafront excavations, the water is tempting and clear, so bring swimming stuff and a picnic. Egnázia (also known as Gnathia) was an important Messapian centre during the fifth century BC, fortified with over 2km of walls, large parts of which still stand in the northern corner of the ruined town – up to 7m high. It was later colonized by the Greeks and then the Romans (in 244 BC), who built a forum, amphitheatre, a colonnaded public hall and temples: one was dedicated to Syria, a popular early Roman goddess, who, according to Lucian, was worshipped by men dressed as women. Horace is known to have dropped by here to see the city's famous altar, which ignited wood without a flame.

At the turn of the first century AD, the Emperor Trajan constructed the **Via Egnázia**, a road that ran down to Bríndisi and continued from what is now Durres in Albania, via Thessaloniki, all the way to Constantinople, marking Egnázia's importance as a military and commercial centre. Parts of the road survive (labelled as "Via Traiana" at the site), running alongside the Roman public buildings. With the collapse of the Roman Empire, the city fell to subsequent barbarian invasions, and was almost completely destroyed by the Gothic king Totila in 545 AD. A community struggled on here, seeking refuge in the Messapian tombs, until the tenth century when the settlement was finally abandoned. There's an on-site **museum** (same hours and ticket as above) housing an array of artefacts, including examples of the distinctive earthenware for which the ancient town was prized.

Places to stay in **Selva di Fasano** include a hill station of villas in lush gardens above the town of Fasano. Try *La Silvana*, Viale dei Pini 87 (℡080.433.1161, Ⓦ www.lasilvanahotel.it/; ❸), an unpretentious hotel with large, simply decorated rooms, balconies and plenty of terrace space. Alternatively, there's the modern, glitzy *Sierra Silvana*, Via Don Bartolo Boggia (℡080.433.1322, Ⓦ www.jpmoser.com/sierrasilvana.html; ❹), with both regular rooms and *trulli* in the grounds that you can stay in; it's the perfect place to lounge by the pool for the day or take the free shuttle bus to the beach 15km away.

The FSE line: Castellana Grotte to Martina Franca

Meandering lazily down towards the **Valle d'Itria**, the Ferrovia Sud-Est train passes through some of the prettiest of Puglia's landscapes. Olives gradually lose ground to vineyards and cherry and peach orchards, neatly partitioned by dry-stone walls. The barren limestone terrain of Le Murge swallows rivers whole (south of the Ofanto, near Barletta, few rivers make it to the sea), producing a landscape cut by deep ravines and pitted with caverns and grottoes. About 40km out of Bari are the **Grotte di Castellana**, a spectacular set of underground caves (mid-March to early Nov, Dec 26 to Jan 6 & Feb carnival time tours hourly 8.30am–1pm & 2.30–7pm; rest of year tours 9.30am–12.30pm; €13 for a full 3km/2hr tour, €8 for 1km/50min tour excluding Grotta Bianca; ℡080.499.8211). Check out the site Ⓦ www.grottedicastellana.it for full information on when tours depart; at the time of writing there were no tours in English. A lift takes you down to the largest of the caverns, La Grave, 60m below ground, which was used as the local rubbish dump until its accidental discovery in 1938. From here, there's over 1km of strangely formed caves to explore, ending in the most impressive of them all, the Grotta Bianca – a shimmering sea of white stalagmites and stalactites. To **get to the caves**, simply follow the signs from the Castellana-Grotte station, from where it's about 500m to the grotto.

Alberobello

Beyond **PUTIGNANO**, traditional *trulli* (see box opposite) buildings dominate the landscape. If you want to take a closer look, head for **ALBEROBELLO**. Around 1500 *trulli* pack the narrow streets; most are south of the town centre, on and around Largo Martellotta. You can pick up a town map from the **tourist**

Curious-looking **trulli** are dotted throughout the Murge area of Puglia. Cylindrical, whitewashed buildings with grey conical roofs tapering out to a point or sphere, they are often adorned with painted symbols. Unique to Puglia, their ancient origins are obscure, but are probably connected to feudal lords who made people working their land build their houses without mortar so they could easily be pulled down if tax inspectors came round. The thick walls insulate equally against the cold in winter and the summer heat, while local limestone is used to make the two-layered roofs water-tight. Most *trulli* have just one room but when more space was needed, a hole was simply knocked in the wall and an identical structure built next door. Although originally they were both dwellings and store houses, these days they're being snapped up by Italians and foreigners as holiday homes, and some are rented out as self-catering or B&B accommodation.

office in the central Piazza Ferdinando IV (Mon–Fri 8am–2pm, Tues & Thurs also 3–6.30pm; ℡080.432.5171, Ⓔalberobello.trulli@mbox.it.net), about a ten-minute walk from the station; for information Ⓦwww.tuttoalberobello.it is a useful site. Inevitably, a rampant tourist industry has grown up around the cute conical stone huts, and the proprietors of *trulli* given over to displays of woolly shawls, liqueurs and other souvenirs practically drag in passers-by and don't let them go until they've bought something.

If you want to complete the *trulli* experience by **staying** in one, look at Ⓦwww.trullinet.com/alberghi, which lists private *trulli* for rent; or check in at *Hotel Dei Trulli*, Via Cadore 31 (℡080.432.3555; ❻), which comprises a dozen or so of the conical cottages, shaded by pine trees. Otherwise, a five-minute stroll from the *trulli* area of town is *Casa Albergo S Antonio*, Via Isonzo 8a (℡080.432.2913; ❷), with bright, simply furnished rooms in a former seminary run by a religious institution – a good bet if budget is more important than ambience. A more central choice is the spick-and-span *Lanzillotta* at Piazza Ferdinando IV 31 (℡080.432.1511, Ⓦwww.hotellanzillotta.it; ❷), while if you have your own transport and would like to be in the countryside, consider *Fascino Antico* (℡080.432.5089, Ⓔinfo@fascinoantico.com; ❸), a nice B&B beside the SS172 between Alberobello and Locorotondo; it has air-conditioned rooms equipped with fridge and TV. Further afield, there's a really special place in the depths of the countryside south of **Noci**, about a twenty-minute drive from Alberobello. Attached to a dairy farm, ☘ *Masseria Murgia Albanese* (℡080.497.5676 or 347.229.8907, Ⓦwww.murgiaalbanese.it; ❷) is surrounded by arable fields crisscrossed by dry-stone walls. The guest accommodation in the eighteenth-century Neoclassical manor house (with its own separate chapel) is choc-full of family heirlooms. The owners are extremely hospitable and have a knack of producing an *aperitivo* on the weathered stone terrace at just the right moment. You can eat with the family, cook for yourself if you take the self-catering apartment, or visit one of the good restaurants in the area.

For **food** in Alberobello, *Il Poeta Contadino*, at Via Indipendenza 21 (Sept–June; closed Mon), has specialities including *purè di fave con cicoria* (broad beans with wild chicory) and *cavatelli con cime di rapa* (pasta with turnip tops). Wine buffs shouldn't pass up a browse around the *Enoteca Anima del Vino*, on Largo Martellota 93, with its assortment of local **wines** and excellent *cotognata* from Maglie. *Bar Ailanto* (across the way) serves a delicious **coffee** *granita*.

Just a few kilometres south, **LOCOROTONDO**, which owes its name to its circular layout, has good views over the whole area, speckled with red- and grey-roofed *trulli* in a sea of vines and olive and almond trees. It's a great place to wander for an hour or so, and to eat **local specialities**: check out 🎵 *Centro Storico* at Via Eroi di Dogali 6 (closed Wed in winter), an excellent trattoria where you can savour hearty *orecchiette* served with meat sauce and creamy white cheese (*ragù e caciotta*) washed down with the local DOC wine. There's a **B&B** at *Trullo Castaldo*, Contrada Pignataro 67 (☎347.630.3999, ⓦwww .mediasuditalia.com/trullo; ❸), a restored *trullo* 2km from Locorotondo. Between Locorotondo and Fasano, it's difficult to find, so call ahead and the owner, Paolo, will meet you.

Finally, on the road between Locorotondo and Ostuni, **CISTERNINO** rejoices in the nickname "La Vera" (the Real Thing) and is a marvellous antidote to touristy Alberobello: it's a pleasure to wander around the tiny, whitewashed alleyways of its old town. Two series of **open-air concerts** are held in the main square, Piazza Vittorio Emanuele, between late June and September: the *Pietre che Cantano* (The Stones that Sing) around 10.30pm at the weekend, the *Aperitivo Classico* on Sundays at midday.

Martina Franca

The *trulli* are still plentiful by the time you reach **MARTINA FRANCA**, a surprising town with a tangible Moorish flavour and a lively *passeggiata* at weekends. It is reputed to have been founded by Tarentine settlers fed up with constant Saracen attacks during the tenth century, but it was the Angevin prince of Táranto who bolstered the community in the early fourteenth century by granting it certain tax privileges. The town derives its name from this – *franca* meaning duty or stamp. Today its medieval core is adorned with some of the most subtle and least overbearing examples of architecture from the Baroque period you'll find.

Through the **Porta di Santo Stefano**, which marks the entrance to the old town, Piazza Roma is dominated by the vast **Palazzo Ducale**, which dates from 1688, and is now the town hall. A handful of rooms are open to the public most mornings – most of them smothered in classical eighteenth-century Arcadian murals. Just across the square, the narrow Via Vittorio Emanuele leads right into the old town and Piazza Plebiscito, fronted by the vast Baroque facade of the **Chiesa di San Martino**, an eighteenth-century church built on the site of an earlier Romanesque structure, of which only the campanile survives. From adjacent Piazza Immacolata you can either bear left down Via Cavour, with its Baroque *palazzi* and balconied streets, or wander further into the old town; the roads running around the edge of the surviving fourteenth-century town walls offer an excellent panorama of the Valle d'Itria, with its neatly ordered fields dotted with *trulli*.

Southern Italy's top performing arts festival, the **Festival della Valle d'Itria** (☎080.480.5100, ⓦwww.euro-festival.net), takes place in Martina Franca in late July/early August every year. On a par with the *Maggio Musicale* in Florence, the festival is mainly operatic, with performances in the appropriately grand Palazzo Ducale. It's a congenial and unpretentious event, though tickets aren't cheap, they're available from the festival office in the Palazzo Ducale.

Practicalities

There's a spasmodic bus service from the **FSE train station** up to the centre of town; otherwise you'll have to walk for fifteen minutes – go left out of the station and up Viale della Libertà to Corso Italia, which leads to the old town centre. The **tourist office** on Piazza Roma 35 (Mon–Fri 9am–1pm &

5–7.30pm, Sat 9am–12.30pm; ℡080.480.5702) has good maps of the town. The cheapest **hotel** is the *Hotel da Luigi* on Via Táranto, Zona G25 (℡080.485.60.66; ①), though this is 2km out of town and at festival time you won't get a room here. Pricier, but in town, is the comfortable *Dell'Erba*, Via dei Cedri 1 (℡080.430.1055, ✉hoteldellerba@italiainrete.net; ④), with a swimming pool, restaurant and plenty of sun terraces. For more atmospheric and cost-effective accommodation, consider renting a traditional apartment in the old town. Studio apartments work out at €37.50 per person per night for two sharing, plus linen charge (no minimum stay); contact *Villaggio In* at Via Arco Grassi 8 (℡080.480.5911, ⓦwww.villaggioin.it).

An excellent **restaurant** is *La Cantina*, Vico 1 Lanucara 12 (closed Mon), sign-posted off Piazza Settembre, the main gate to the old town – try the *bucatini con fagioli* (pasta with beans) or *agnello con fave e cicoria* (lamb and broad beans with wild chicory). Or head straight for the town's best pizzas at *La Panca* (closed Mon), Via Principe Umberto 51, which leads off the main square in the old town, Piazza M. Immacolata. For refined, upscale Pugliese cooking, don't miss *Ritrovo degli Amici* on Corso Messapia (closed Sun evening & Mon), just off Piazza XX Settembre on a little, flower-filled passageway – it's expensive but worth it. If you're after **snacks** or picnic food, try *Fratelli Ricci*, the butcher at Via Cavour 19 (closed Mon). They sell the wonderful *capocollo*, a local cured pork salami.

Táranto

There are numerous legends connected with the origins of **TÁRANTO**: it was variously founded by the Spartan deity Phalanthus, or by Taras, the son of Neptune, or – perhaps more likely – illegitimate Spartans born while their fathers were away fighting. Whatever the truth is, Taras, as it was known to the Greeks, was a well-chosen site and soon became the first city of Magna Graecia (the area of southern Italy colonized by the Greeks) renowned for its wool, oysters, mussels and dyes – the imperial purple was the product of decayed Tarentine molluscs. Resplendent with temples, its acropolis harboured a vast bronze of Poseidon that was one of the wonders of the ancient world. Sadly, little remains of ancient Taras or even of later Roman Tarentum, their monuments and relics confined to the great museum in the modern city. After being destroyed by the Romans, Táranto was for years little more than a small fishing port, its strategic position on the sea only being recognized in Napoleonic times. It was home to the Italian fleet after Unification, and consequently heavily bombed during World War II; attempts to rejuvenate the town have left its medieval heart girdled by heavy industry, including the vast Italsider steel plant that throws its flames and lights into the skies above.

Finding your way around is easy. The city divides neatly into three distinct parts: the northern spur is the industrial area, home of the steel works and train station. Cross the Ponte di Porta Napoli and you're on the central Island containing the old town. The southern spur holds the modern city centre (Borgo Nuovo), the administrative and commercial hub of Táranto, linked to the old town by a swing-bridge.

Arrival, information and accommodation

Buses generally arrive at and depart from Piazza Castello, except FS connections with Metaponto and Potenza, which arrive at Piazza Duca d'Aosta, just outside the **train station**. National bus services, run by Marozzi, stop at Porto

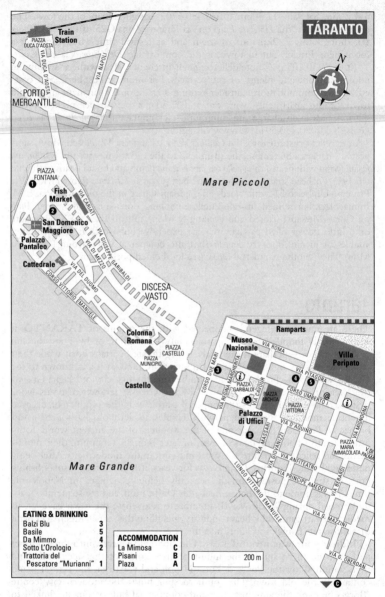

TÁRANTO

PIAZZA
DUCA D'AOSTA
Train
Station
VIA DUCA D'AOSTA
VIA NAPOLI
PORTO
MERCANTILE

Mare Piccolo

PIAZZA
FONTANA ❶
Fish
Market ❷
VIA CARIATI
San Domenico
Maggiore
VIA GIUSEPPE GARIBALDI
VIA D. MEZZO
Palazzo
Pantaleo
Cattedrale
VIA DEL DUOMO
CORSO VITTORIO EMANUELE

DISCESA
VASTO

Colonna
Romana
PIAZZA
CASTELLO
PIAZZA
MUNICIPIO
Castello

Ramparts
Museo
Nazionale
VIA ROMA
Villa
Peripato
CORSO DUE MARI
VIA REGINA MARGHERITA
❸ ⓘ
PIAZZA
GARIBALDI
VIA CAVOUR
Ⓐ
VIA PITAGORA
❹ ❺
CORSO UMBERTO I
PIAZZA
ARCHITA
@
ⓘ
VIA MIGNOGNA
PIAZZA
VITTORIA
Palazzo
di Uffici
Ⓑ
VIA D'AQUINO
PIAZZA
MARIA
IMMACOLATA
V. DI
PALMA
VIA MASSARI
VIA GIOVINAZZI
VIA ANFITEATRO
VIA BERARDI
LUNGO VITTORIO EMANUELE
VIA PRINCIPE AMEDEO
VIA G. MAZZINI
VIA G. OBERDAN

Mare Grande

EATING & DRINKING

Balzi Blu	3
Basile	5
Da Mimmo	4
Sotto L'Orologio	2
Trattoria del	
Pescatore "Murianni"	1

ACCOMMODATION

La Mimosa	C
Pisani	B
Plaza	A

0   200 m

▼ Ⓒ

Mercantile and the Discesa Vasto in the old town. For information about different departure points, call Consorzio Trasporto Pubblico on ☎099.730.5507. You can save yourself the half-hour walk in from the train station by hopping on bus #1, #3, #8 or #25 which run to Corso Umberto in the modern city. Get off just after Palazzo di Uffici and you're close to the **tourist office** on Corso Umberto I at no. 113 (Mon–Fri 9am–1pm & 4.30–6.30pm, Sat 9am–noon;

☎099.453.2392, ✉apttaranto@pugliaturismo.com). There's another mini tourist office at Piazza Garibaldi in a kiosk opposite the *Plaza* hotel (Mon–Fri 8.30am–1pm & 3–6.30pm, Sat 8.30am–1pm; ☎099.452.1359). Timetables for **city buses** are posted in the AMAT office just around the corner on Via Margherita 34. There's **Internet** access at *Chiocciolina.it*, Corso Umberto I 85 (Mon–Sat 10am–1pm & 4.30–9pm; winter closed Mon morning, summer closed Sat afternoon; ☎099.453.8051).

Finding **accommodation** can be a headache, as Táranto isn't really geared up for tourism: a central, inexpensive hotel is *Plaza*, Via d'Aquino 46 (☎099.459.0775, ⓦwww.hotelplazataranto.com; ❸), while just around the corner, at the end of an alleyway with potted plants, the basic *Pisani*, Via Cavour 43 (☎099.453.4087; ❶), has clean en-suite rooms. The simple B&B, *La Mimosa*, is a little way out of the centre at Via Istria 80 (☎099.335.549; ❶): take bus #3 or #28 from the train station or Piazza Vittoria, or call for a lift from the owners.

The City

In Greek times the island holding the **old town** wasn't an island at all but part of the southern peninsula, connected by an isthmus to the southern spur. The Greeks raised temples and the acropolis here, while further south lay the residential districts. There's one extant fragment of ancient Táranto – the Doric **columns**, re-erected in a corner of **Piazza Castello**, which once adorned a temple of Poseidon. The rest of the tiny island is a mass of poky streets and alleyways, buttressed by scaffolding seemingly to prevent the whole place from falling down. The Aragonese **Castello** (now owned by the navy) at the southern end surveys the comings and goings of warships and fishing boats. The narrow canal they slide through, between the city's two inland "seas", was built in the late nineteenth century, on the site of the castle's old moat. "Seas" is a bit of a misnomer: the Mare Piccolo is really a large lagoon, home to Táranto's famous oysters and the Italian navy; and the Mare Grande is actually a vast bay, protected by sea walls and the offshore fortified Island of San Pietro.

At the heart of the old town lies the eleventh-century **Cattedrale**, which once did duty as a mosque – dedicated to Táranto's patron saint, Cataldo (Cathal), a seventh-century Irish monk who on returning from a pilgrimage to the Holy Land was so shocked by the licentiousness of the town's inhabitants that he decided to stay and clean the place up. His remains lie under the altar of a small chapel – "a jovial nightmare in stone", Norman Douglas thought. As for the rest of the church, restoration has stripped away most of the Baroque alterations, and fragments of a Byzantine mosaic floor have been revealed. The columns of the nave, too, are ancient, pillaged from the temples that once stood on the island, their delicately carved capitals depicting tiny birds nestling among the stone foliage.

A few blocks away, check out the city's **fish market**, on Via Cariati, a lively affair where the best of the local catch is displayed at the crack of dawn: octopuses lie dazed, clams spit defiantly at you, while other less definable creatures seem preoccupied with making a last dash for freedom before the restaurateurs arrive – some of the city's finest restaurants are just across the road.

It's a short walk across the swing-bridge Táranto's **modern centre** – though this, like Bari's, has limited charms, its wide streets laid out on a grid pattern that forms the focus of the city's *passeggiata*, around piazzas Vittoria and Archita. Nearby, the **Villa Peripato** was *the* place for the Tarentini to take their early-evening stroll at the beginning of the last century, but today's gardeners seem to be fighting a losing battle with the ponds and undergrowth.

The only real attraction in this part of town – and it's a gem when it's fully functioning – is the **Museo Nazionale** on Corso Umberto I at no. 41 (Tues–Sun 9am–2pm; ⓦwww.museotaranto.it), which offers a fascinating insight into the splendour of ancient Taras. With something in excess of 50,000 pieces of Greek terracotta alone, it's one of the largest collections in the world. The museum has been undergoing restoration and expansion for several years so, at the time of writing, only temporary exhibitions and some of its collection is on view at **Palazzo Pantaleo**, near the church of San Domenico in the old town at Via Pantaleo and Corso Vittorio Emanuele II (daily 8.30am–7.30pm; €2). The work of the goldsmiths of Taras is a particular highlight, which give just a hint of Magna Graecia's wealth. They crafted earrings, necklaces, tiaras and bracelets with minute precision, all delicately patterned and finely worked in gold filigree. Several finds from Greek tombs are also worth a look, including a tiny terracotta model of Aphrodite emerging from the sea (dated end of fourth, early third century BC), and some fifth-century red-and-black Lekythos pots decorated with athletes. There's an informative commentary in English that gives some insight into Greek aristocratic culture, explaining that athleticism was considered a gift from the gods.

Eating and drinking

For **meals**, *Trattoria del Pescatore "Murianni"*, in the old city on Piazza Fontana, is a popular, convivial place for seafood at low to moderate prices – the fish comes fresh from the market just around the corner (booking advisable ☎099.470.7121; closed Sun). One of the city's oldest trattorias (passed down through two generations) is *Sotto L'Orologio*, Largo San Nicola 5, just by Piazza Fontana (closed Sat eve & Sun). The name comes from its position next to a tiny church with a clocktower, but the sign above the entrance simply says "Trattoria". A small place with no more than twelve tables, it serves interesting, fresh and good-value seafood. To sample from over 300 local and international wines, head for *Balzi Blu* on Corso Due Mari opposite the swing-bridge and castle in the new part of town; a very affordable *enoteca*, pizzeria and *pasticceria*, it has outdoor seating in summer for views onto the old city. You can also check out the €15 tourist menu at *Ristorante Basile*, Via Pitagora 76 (closed Sat), and the delicious – and very fairly priced – local specialities at *Da Mimmo*, one block up at Via Giovinazzi 18 (closed Wed).

Northwest of Táranto

Inland and **northwest** of Táranto, the scenery changes dramatically, with gorges and ravines marking a landscape that's closer to that of Basilicata than Puglia. **MASSAFRA**, about 15km from Táranto (regular trains and FSE buses from Piazza Castello), is split in two by a ravine, the Gravina di San Marco, lined with grottoes dating mainly from the ninth to the fourteenth centuries. Many contain cave-churches, hewn out of the rock by Greek monks and decorated with lavish frescoes. All such sites in Massafra are visitable only by guided tours arranged with the **tourist office** at Via Vittorio Veneto 15 (Mon–Fri 9.30am–noon & 4–7pm; ☎099.880.4695 or 338.565.9601). The **Santuario della Madonna della Scala** is built onto an earlier cave-church; a Baroque staircase runs down to the eighteenth-century church, which features a beautiful fresco of a Madonna and Child, dating from the twelfth to the thirteenth centuries; more steps lead down to an eighth-century crypt. The nearby **Cripta**

della Buona Nuova houses a thirteenth-century fresco of the Madonna and a striking painting of Christ Pantocrator. About 200m away, at the bottom of the ravine, is a mass of interconnected caves known as the **Farmacia del Mago Greguro**, now in a pretty pitiful state but once used by the medieval monks as a herbalist's workshop.

Easily the most spectacular of the ravine towns is **LATERZA**, close to the border of Basilicata, reachable by bus from Táranto's Piazza Castello and situated on the Puglian equivalent of the Grand Canyon, complete with buzzards and kites.

Bríndisi

Across the peninsula, 60km east of Táranto on the opposite coast, lies **BRÍNDISI**, once a bridging point for crusading knights and still a town that

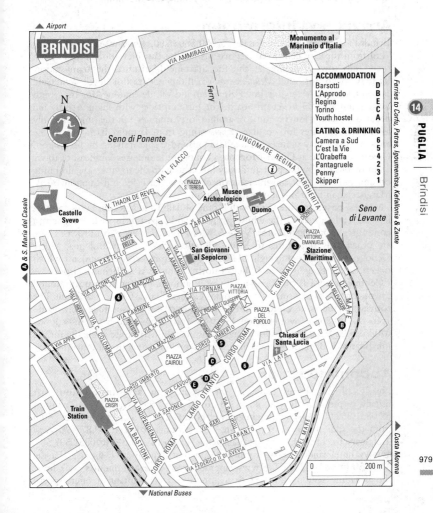

▲ Airport

BRÍNDISI

Monumento al Marinaio d'Italia

VIA AMMIRAGLIO

Ferry

N

Seno di Ponente

LUNGOMARE REGINA MARGHERITA

ACCOMMODATION

Barsotti	D
L'Approdo	B
Regina	E
Torino	C
Youth hostel	A

EATING & DRINKING

Camera a Sud	6
C'est la Vie	5
L'Orabeffa	4
Pantagruele	2
Penny	3
Skipper	1

VIA L. FLACCO

V. THAON DE REVEL

PIAZZA S. TERESA

Museo Archeologico

Duomo

Castello Svevo

VIA TARANTINI

VIA DUOMO

C. DONIS

PIAZZA VITTORIO EMANUELE

Seno di Levante

Stazione Marittima

CORTE DELLA

VIA CASTELLO

VIA SAN BENEDETTO

VIA ARENGULO

VIA LAURO

San Giovanni al Sepolcro

VIALE LIBERTÀ

VIA TAGGONE NICOLO

VIA MARCONI

VIA CARMINE

VIA PALMITI

VIA XX SETTEMBRE

VIA FORNARI

VIA OROATIA

PISANELLI GIUSEPPE

VIA BRINDISI SERGIO

VIA TRTSI DACRE

PIAZZA VITTORIA

C. GARIBALDI

VIA DEL MARE

PIAZZA DEL POPOLO

Chiesa di Santa Lucia

VIA APPIA

VIA C. COLOMBO

VIA MAZZINI

CORSO UMBERTO

CORSO ROMA

VIA LATA

PIAZZA CAIROLI

VIA CAVOUR

LARGO D'ORANTO

Train Station

PIAZZA CRISPI

VIA INDIPENDENZA

VIA SAPONEA

VIA BARI

VIA GALIPOLI

VIA DEL MARE

VIA BASTIONE

CORSO ROMA

VIA TARANTO

VIA FEDERICO II DI SVEVIA

0   200 m

▲ & S. Maria del Casale

▲ A & S. Maria del Casale

▼ National Buses

makes its living from people passing through. The natural harbour here, the safest on the Adriatic coast, made Bríndisi an ideal choice for early settlers. In Roman times, the port became the main crossing point between eastern and western empires, and later, under the Normans, there came a steady stream of pilgrims heading east towards the Holy Land. The route is still open, and now Bríndisi – primarily – is where you come if you're **heading for Greece** from Italy. On arrival, you may well think that the entire town is full of shipping agents: this, when all is said and done, is the town's main business. But even if you're leaving the same night you'll almost certainly end up with time on your hands. You could just while away time in a bar or restaurant in the old town – it is pretty compact and, although it isn't brimming with ancient monuments, has a pleasant, almost oriental flavour about it, and a few hidden gems tucked down its narrow streets. If you decide to stay, you will find that Bríndisi's youth hostel is a fun place to base yourself for day-trips to the beach, Ostuni or the Torre Guaceto, a lovely nature reserve for biking and swimming.

Arrival and information

Bríndisi's **airport**, Papola-Casale (☎080.580.0200, ⒲www.seap-puglia.it) is 7km from the city centre; an airport bus run by Bus Navetta STP goes from there into town, stopping at the the Stazione Maríttima, the train station, Viale A. Moro (for hotel *Mediterraneo*), Via Indipendenza (for hotels *Torino* and *Barsotti*), Via del Mare (for hotel *Approdo*) and Via de Simone (for the youth hostel); buy the €3 ticket on board. The bus coincides with flight arrivals and departures, with a journey time of around forty minutes, but the timetable only allows five minutes for possible delays going from Bríndisi back out to the airport so you may prefer to take a taxi (around €15). Arriving by **ferry** from Greece leaves you at **Costa Morena**, a couple of kilometres southeast of town; a shuttle bus run by the port authority links this with the town centre, dropping off and picking up at the intersection of Corso Garibaldi and Lungomare R. Margherita, in front of the maritime station.

Marozzi **buses** link the town with Rome (4 daily) and Miccolis buses connect it with Naples (3 daily); these buses arrive at, and depart from, Viale P. Togliatti, a continuation of Corso Roma/Viale A. Moro into the new part of town. There are other daily departures to Siena, Florence, Pisa, Rimini, Bologna, Milan, Genova and Palermo, and eight SITA bus to and from Lecce (45min), for which tickets can be bought at the Ufficio Informazioni SEAP at Bríndisi airport.

Central Bríndisi is small enough to walk around, but for **transport** around town, lots of buses run down Corso Umberto and Corso Garibaldi. The **tourist office** is at Lungomare R. Margherita 43/44 (summer daily 9am–1pm & 3–9.30pm; winter Mon–Fri 9am–1pm & 3–8pm, Sat 9am–1.30pm; ☎0831.523.072, ✉aptbrindisi@pugliaturismo.com). A website primarily for the inhabitants of Bríndisi, ⒲www.brindisiweb.com, has some useful tourism links.

Accommodation

Nearly all the ferries leave in the evening, so **accommodation** isn't usually a problem. If you do need to stay, try the *Regina*, Via Cavour 5 (☎0831.562.001, ⒲www.hotelreginaweb.com; ❸), down a quiet side street 150m from the station; the nearby *Barsotti*, Via Cavour 1 (☎0831.560.877, ⒲www.hotelbarsotti.com; ❸), or the smaller *Torino*, Largo Palumbo 6 (☎0831.597.587, ⒲www.hotelbrindisi.it:8080/torino/; ❷), a few steps away. *L'Approdo*, Via del Mare 50 (☎0831.529.667, ⒲www.lapprodo.it; ❸), is several minutes' walk from the maritime station and next to a popular pizza restaurant; it offers special deals on triple and quadruple rooms. All the hotels mentioned here have air conditioning. The best budget choice is the friendly 🛏 **youth hostel**, 2km out of town in Casale at Via Brandi 2 (☎0831.418.418, ⊛www.hostelcarpediem .it; €15), with no lock-out and a lively atmosphere. You can rent a bed for the day (€6) if you've got a night departure, with full use of the facilities, including hot power-showers, laundry, bike rental, book exchange, bar and pool table. If you email ahead to book and give your flight arrival time the hostel minibus will be at the airport to pick you up. Otherwise, take bus #3 or #4 from the train station, or walk for fifteen minutes, following the yellow signs through town. If you call in advance, the manager, Maurizio, might be able to pick you up from town.

The Town

The top of **Scalinata Virgiliana** (Virgil's Steps) marks the end of the ancient Via Appia, which ran all the way from the Porta Capena in Rome. Two columns stood here for years – useful navigation points for ships coming into harbour. The single column that remains has been restored, as has the area around it. A marble tablet in the corner of the piazza marks the supposed site of the house in which Virgil died, in 19 BC. Via Colonne, with its seventeenth- and eighteenth-century *palazzi*, runs up to the **Duomo** – a remarkable building, if only for the fact that it's survived seven earthquakes since its construction in the eleventh century. Just outside is the **Museo Archeologico Provinciale** (Mon–Sat 9am–1.30pm, Tues also 3.30–6.30pm; summer also sometimes Thurs evening & Sat; free). In addition to ornaments and statues from the necropolises that lined the Via Appia in Roman times, several rooms accommodate bronzes recovered in underwater exploration nearby, as well as finds from the excavations at Egnázia (see p.971). Follow Via Tarentini from here and bear left for the tiny round church of **San Giovanni al Sepolcro**, an eleventh-century baptistry. It's a little dark and decrepit inside, but you can just make out some of the original thirteenth-century frescoes. And there are more frescoes, this time a century older, in the **Chiesa di Santa Lucia**, just off Piazza del Popolo.

Bríndisi's most important medieval monument is further afield: the **Chiesa di Santa Maria del Casale** (check with the tourist office for hours and ring for entrance at the gate) – a three-kilometre bus ride towards the airport from town; take bus #4, from the train station, and ask the driver when to get off. Built by Philip of Anjou at the end of the thirteenth century, it's an odd mixture of styles: the facade is adorned with an Arabic mass of geometric patterns, worked in two shades of sandstone, and the portal has an almost Art Deco touch to it. The stark interior is rescued from gloom by some fourteenth-century frescoes depicting frightening allegorical scenes relating to the Day of Judgement, a vision of hell designed to scare the living daylights out of the less devout.

Eating and drinking

It's not difficult to **eat and drink** cheaply in Bríndisi: *C'est la Vie* on Via Conserva, a small, tree-lined street near Piazza del Popolo, serves decent food inside and out throughout the day. It's open until 2am and sometimes has a DJ on Friday and Saturday nights. *Camera a Sud*, at the junction of Largo Otanto and Corso Roma, is a chic little café-cum-wine bar, tea room and bookshop, open until at least midnight (closed Sun morning). *L'Orabeffa*, towards the castle at Via Marconi 33, is a pub with live music, open till 3am. For a pleasant sit-down meal in a **restaurant**, stroll around Piazza Dionisi and you will soon be accosted by waiters doing the hard sell. Highly recommended is *Skipper*

Onwards to Albania and Greece: routes, prices and some tips

Agents

A staggering array of **agents** sell ferry tickets to Albania and Greece, and you should take care to avoid getting ripped off. Ignore the touts clustered around the train station in high season, who specialize in selling imaginary places on non-existent boats, and *always* buy your ticket direct from the company's office or an approved agent. Among the **reliable general agencies** are Adriatic Mediterranean Lines, Via B. S. Giorgio 2 (℡0831.528.554, ⒲www.adriaticmedierraneanlines.com), opposite the station; Utac Viaggi, Bastione San Giacomo 70 (℡0831.524.921, ⒲www.utacviaggi .it), and Grecian Travel, near the harbour at Corso Garibaldi 79 (℡0831.568.333). Discovery, Corso Garibaldi 49 (℡0831.527.667, ⒠discovership@libero.it), also sells onward ferry tickets to the Cyclades and Crete, while Italian Ferries, Corso Garibaldi 96–98 (℡0831.590.840 or 0831.562.730), sells its own tickets and those of Adriatic Seaway. Appia Travel, Via Regina Margherita 8/9 (℡0831.521.684), offers rail and bus tickets to Rome and other destinations, as well as ferry tickets.

Routes

A variety of **routes** operate most of the year, although service is reduced outside the peak season – roughly defined as between mid-July and mid-August. **Services** – including some high-speed catamarans – sail to Vlore in Albania and Corfu, Igoumenitsa, Patras, Cephallonia and Zante in Greece. Visit ⒲www.ferries.gr or ⒲www.traghettiamo.it for **timetables** and **prices**. As a rule (though there are exceptions), nearly all the reliable companies sail in the evening.

Prices and boarding

Prices vary considerably according to season but there's not much difference between the companies: you'll be looking at a one-way, high-season fare to Corfu/Igoumenitsa for around €3 per person on deck or €63 for a reclining seat (cabins are available for a higher charge); from €60 extra for a car. High-speed links are more expensive. There are reductions of around 10–20 percent on the return fare if you book with the same company you travel out with. InterRail and Eurail **passes** are subject to high-season supplements and sometimes it is an uphill struggle to persuade ferry companies that your pass is valid – the tourist board is currently in negotiation with all ferry companies and agencies to make sure they accept passes in future. Likewise, holders of Italian rail passes get discounts on some services. Check on purchase whether your ticket includes **embarkation tax** – currently €10 per person or per car.

Leaving Italy, you must present your boarding card to the authorities at Costa Morena, the landing and embarkation stage for all sailings; you should arrive at least one hour – preferably two in high season – before your ship's departure. Allow enough time to get there by the free shuttle bus from Stazione Maríttima (the journey takes around 20min but find out beforehand when the shuttles depart) and make sure that any stopover you are making on the way to Patras is clearly marked on your ticket. It's advisable to **stock up on food and drink** in Bríndisi's supermarkets, as there are the inevitable mark-ups once on board.

---

pizzeria (closed Fri) at number 2, which has its own shady garden planted with large stands of bamboo. *Ristorante Penny* (closed Mon; ℡0831.563.013), in a thirteenth-century *palazzo* by the port at Via S. Francesco 1, is pricier but serves delicious *tagliolini* with crabmeat and calamari, and has a vast wine list. You can have an equally memorable meal at the acclaimed *Trattoria Pantagruele*, Via Salita di Ripalta 13 (℡0831.560.605; closed all day Mon & Sun evening, plus weekends in July & Aug), which serves excellent local dishes, especially seafood.

Listings

Airport information Papola Casale
☎080.580.0200, ⓦwww.seap-puglia.it.
Car rental at the airport: Avis ☎0831.418.826;
Europcar ☎0831.412.061; Maggiore
☎0831.418.155; Sixt ☎0831.411.253; Thrifty
☎0831.413.711.
Police station ☎0831.543.111.

Post office Main office on Piazza Vittoria (Mon–Fri
8.30am–6pm).
Train station ☎0831.521.975; train information
(number functions in Italy only) ☎848.88088;
timetables and prices on ⓦwww.fs-on-line.it.
Taxis ☎0831.597.901 & ☎0831.597.503.

Northwest of Bríndisi: Ostuni

Just 15km northwest of Bríndisi is a beautiful nature reserve and protected marine area known as **Torre Guaceto**. You'll need a car to get here, but it's a lovely spot for biking through maquis and olive groves, scuba diving over small reefs of coral and sea grass, or chilling out on the sandy beach; to visit, book at the Serranova visitor's centre (☎0831.989.885, ⓦwww.riservaditorreguaceto.it).

OSTUNI, 40km northwest of Bríndisi (35min by train), is known as "the white city" and is one of southern Italy's most stunning small towns. Situated on three hills at the southernmost edge of Le Murge, it was an important Greco-Roman city in the first century AD. The old centre spreads across the highest of the hills, a gleaming white splash of sun-bleached streets and cobbled alleyways, dominating the plains below. Seven kilometres away, the popular sandy coastline has Blue Flag beaches.

Arrival, information and accommodation

The maze of well-preserved winding streets provides a fascinating amble, and there are some exceptional views – particularly from Largo Castello over the woods to the north. Bits of cavorting Baroque twist out of unexpected places, including an ornamented eighteenth-century obelisk, 21m high, dedicated to Saint Oronzo, which stands in Piazza della Libertà (or Piazza Saint Oronzo) on the southern edge of the old town. This is the focal point on summer Saturday nights for hordes of people who drive in from the countryside, meet their friends and pack out the bars and cafés. The **Chiesa delle Monacelle**, on the main cobbled street leading off Piazza della Liberta up into the old town, has displays on prehistory (summer daily 9.30am–12.30pm & 4.30–7.30pm; July & Aug until 9pm; €2), the highlight of which is "Delia", the skeleton of a young pregnant woman found in a crouched position, her bones decorated before burial.

The Town

The **train station** is some way out of town, though there's a connecting bus service. Pullman **buses** to and from Bríndisi terminate outside the sports centre, from where there are buses into the town centre, or it's around a twenty-minute walk. You'll find the **tourist office** at Corso Mazzini 8 just off Piazza della Liberta (July & Aug daily 8am–2pm & 5.30–8.30pm; June & Sept Mon–Sat 8am–2pm & 4.30–7.30pm; Oct–May Mon–Fri 8am–2pm & 3.30–6.30pm; ☎0831.301.268).

Ostuni's proximity to the coast makes budget **accommodation** tricky to find, even if you go for a B&B. Central B&Bs include *Colucci Grazia* in the old town at Via Palmieri 16 (☎0831.302.997; ❸), *SoleBlu*, just off Piazza Liberta at Corso Emanuele II 16 (☎0831.303.856; ❸), *Morelli Luciana*, on Via Procida 16 (☎335.619.9734; ❸), just behind the post office and town hall off Corso

Mazzini, and *Pannofino Bagnardi Nonna Isa*, next to the public gardens at Via Alfieri 9 (℡0831.332.515; ❷).

Cheap, central **hotels** include the *Hotel Orchidea Nera* on Corso Mazzini 118 (℡0831.301.366; ❷) and the *Tre Torri*, at Via Vittorio Emanuele 298 (℡0831.331.114; ❷). Infinitely preferable, if your credit card can stand the shock, is the stunning, minimalist *La Sommita*, Via Scipione Petrarolo 7 (℡0831.305.925, ⓦwww.lasommita.relaisculti.com; ❾), in a sixteenth-century palace behind the cathedral. The rooms are elegant and luxurious, although five in particular have panoramic views over ancient olive groves to the sea. Spa treatments are available, and there's a small grove of orange and lemon trees where you can dine or just relax.

An alternative is to stay in one of the many excellent **agriturismo** places out of town: *Il Frantoio* (℡0831.330.276, ⓦwww.trecolline.it; ❼) on the SS16 towards Fasano at the km874 milestone is a traditional white farmhouse in 72 hectares of olive grove, with eight rooms furnished with family furniture and heirlooms. The estate produces organic olive oil, fruit and vegetables, and the owners, Armando and Rosalba Balestrazzi, are passionate advocates of ancient Puglian cuisine. Horse riding is available and rates include access to a private beach. *Masseria La Salinola* (℡0831.330.683, ⓦwww.agriturismo.com/Salinola; ❺) has doubles and small apartments on an estate surrounded by olive groves, with a swimming pool (in high season), bikes and a good restaurant serving Pugliese specialities; there's a one-week minimum stay.

Eating and drinking

Ostuni has some excellent **restaurants**, but they are comparatively expensive: try the wonderful local fare at the much-feted ⅋ *Osteria del Tempo Perso*, sign-posted up in the old town at Via Tanzarella 47 (closed all day Mon & lunchtimes except Sun; booking necessary ℡0831.303.320, ⓦwww.osteriadeltempoperso .com). *Vecchia Ostuni,* Largo Lanza 9, just off Piazza della Libertà (℡0831. 303.308), has a vast array of antipasti including deep-fried courgette flowers, snails in a piquant tomato sauce, twists of mozzarella, and pickled peppers. *Porto Nova,* Via Gaspare Petrarolo 38 (℡0831.338.983; closed Wed; signposted from near the cathedral), set in a fifteenth-century stone city gate overlooking olive groves and the sea, serves very good shellfish and some elaborate fish, pasta and vegetable combinations. In the old town, *La Locanda dei Sette Peccati*, at Via F. Campana 3, is cheaper, good fun and does sandwiches as well as large meals and pizzas. *L'Angolo Divino*, tucked into a corner of Piazza Liberta at no. 57 (closed Wed), serves simple, sound dishes at low prices, with a €15 set menu including drinks. The old town is full of **pubs and bars** and you can get pizza by the slice in Piazza Liberta; *Casbah*, off the same square, has a little balcony for people-watching – primarily a bar, it does snacks too.

Lecce and the Salentine peninsula

Some 40km south from Bríndisi, Baroque **Lecce** is a place to linger, with a few diverting Roman remains and a wealth of fine architecture scattered about an appealing old town. It's also a good starting point for excursions further into the **Salentine peninsula**, which begins south of the city. Here the landscape begins to take on a distinctive Greek flavour, a mildly undulating region planted with carob, prickly pear and tobacco. The Adriatic coast is pitted with cliffs topped with ruined watchtowers, and rugged coves and caves trail right the way down to the **southern cape**. The hinterland, by comparison, is more barren, although again there's a Greek feel to it, with tiny, sun-blasted villages growing out of the dry, stony, red earth and flat-roofed houses painted in bright pastel colours.

Lecce

Whether or not you're a fan of Baroque, you can't fail to be impressed by the exuberant building styles on display in **LECCE** – though the fact that they are firmly in the grip of a largely unremarkable modern city does detract from the enjoyment. The arrival of religious orders (Jesuits, the Teatini and Franciscans) at the end of the sixteenth century brought an influx of wealth which paid for the opulent churches and *palazzi* that still pervade today's city. The flowery style of "Leccese Baroque" owed as much to the materials to hand as to the skills of the architects: the soft local sandstone could be intricately carved and then became hard with age. Unfortunately, modern pollution is in danger of ruining many of the buildings, keeping the mass of Lecce's stonemasons and carpenters well occupied.

Arrival and information

Regional **buses** arrive at the Porta Napoli, the FSE bus station (ⓣ0832.347.634) on Viale Torre del Parco, or the STP bus station on Via Adua. FSE and FS **trains** (ⓣ0832.303.403) use the same station, 1km south of the centre at the end of Via Oronzo Quarta. Between late June and mid-September, **Salento-in-Bus** services depart from several places in town – including the City Terminal (near the *Tiziano* hotel), Viale Torre del Parco (near the train station) and the Museo Provinciale – and head to Otranto, Santa Maria di Leuca (via Gallipoli) and the seaside resort of Porto Cesareo, among other destinations. Ask for more information from the **tourist office** at Via Vittorio Emanuele II 24 (Mon–Fri 9am–1pm, Tues & Thurs also 4.30–6pm; ⓣ0832.248.092, Ⓦwww.turismo.provincia.le.it). There's another office at the Castello Carlo V, Via 25 Luglio 23 (daily 10am–1pm & 4–8pm; ⓣ0832.244.845, Ⓔinfo@abitalecce.it), and a third, CTC (Centro Turismo Culturale), in Palazzo dei Celestini, Via Principe Umberto I 13 (daily 9am–1pm & 4.30–7pm; ⓣ0832.683.417, Ⓔinfoturismo@provincia.le.it), right next to the church of Santa Croce.

Accommodation

The cheapest **place to stay** is *Cappello*, Via Montegrappa 4 (ⓣ0832.308.881, Ⓦwww.hotelcapello.it; ❶), a couple of minutes' walk from the station – for once, a fairly salubrious area. It's a large, friendly and efficiently run hotel with air conditioning and private bathrooms. At the other end of the scale, *Tiziano*, Viale Porta Europa (ⓣ0832.272.111, Ⓦwww.grandhoteltiziano.it; ❺), an impersonal conference hotel, has a nice swimming pool and is very handy for the airport bus from Bríndisi, which stops right outside, and the nearby City Terminal. Alternatively, there are many appealing **B&B** choices including *Centro Storico*, Via Vignes 2b (ⓣ0832.242.828, Ⓦwww.bedandbreakfast.lecce.it; ❷), a sixteenth-century building with vaulted ceilings, balconies, a reading room and a sun terrace looking out over the city's monuments; *Il Delfino*, Via del Delfino 20 (ⓣ338.394.0125, Ⓦwww.lecceholiday.com; ❹), also in the historic centre, or *Villa de Giorgi*, Via S. Fili 110, Monteroni di Lecce (ⓣ0832.327.065, Ⓦwww.villadegiorgi.it; ❸), in an old country house just over 7km southwest of the city. Otherwise, the tourist offices can help you find a reasonably priced private **room** in an historic building in the old town and on the outskirts (from around €60 per night); you could also search Ⓦwww.bedandbreakfast.lecce.it, Ⓦwww.abitalecce.it

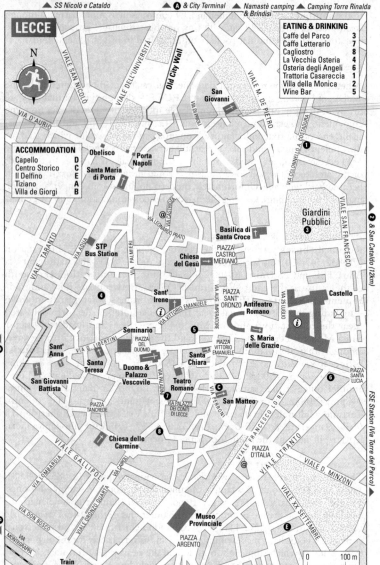

LECCE

N

EATING & DRINKING

Caffe del Parco	3
Caffe Letterario	7
Cagliostro	8
La Vecchia Osteria	4
Osteria degli Angeli	6
Trattoria Casareccia	1
Villa della Monica	2
Wine Bar	5

ACCOMMODATION

Capello	D
Centro Storico	C
Il Delfino	E
Tiziano	A
Villa de Giorgi	B

0   100 m

or Ⓦ www.caffelletto.it. The closest **campsites** are *Namastè* (☏ 0832.329.647,
Ⓦ www.camping-lecce.it) on the road to **NOVOLI** (at the 4.5km marker; take
bus #26 from Lecce train station) and *Camping Torre Rinalda* (☏ 0832.382.161,
Ⓦ www.torrerinalda.it) at **TORRE RINALDA** on the Salentine coast 10km
north of Lecce; hourly buses run from the Piazza Sant'Oronzo.

The City

Start in **Piazza Sant'Oronzo**, the hub of the old town, named after the first-century bishop of Lecce who went to the lions under Nero. His bronze statue lurches unsteadily from the top of the **Colonna di Sant'Oronzo** that once stood at the end of the Via Appia in Bríndisi (see p.981). It reappeared here in 1666 to honour Oronzo, who was credited with having spared the town from plague ten years earlier. The south side of the piazza is taken up by the **Anfiteatro Romano**, which probably dates from the time of Hadrian. In its heyday it seated 20,000 spectators, and it's still used for occasional summer concerts and the Christmas nativity scene. Sadly, most of its decorative bas-reliefs of fighting gladiators and wild beasts have been removed to the town's museum for safe-keeping, and nowadays it looks rather depleted.

The best of Lecce's Baroque churches are all a short distance from Piazza Sant'Oronzo. The finest – and certainly the most ornate – is the **Basilica di Santa Croce**, just to the north, whose florid facade was the work of the local architect Antonio Zimbalo and took around 150 years to complete; its upper half is a riot of decorative garlands and flowers around a central rose window. The **Church of Santa Chiara**, on Piazza Vittorio Emanuele, is an essential stop, loaded down with ornament and its interior full of little chapels groaning with garlands and gilt. There's more Baroque extravagance on Via Vittorio Emanuele, where the **Church of Sant'Irene** houses the most sumptuous of Lecce's altars – lavishly frosted and gilded, and smothered with decoration. Nearby, facing onto Piazza del Duomo, the **Seminario** holds an impressively ornate well, with carved stone masquerading as delicately wrought iron. Next door, the balconied **Palazzo Vescovile** adjoins the **Duomo** itself, twelfth-century in origin but rebuilt entirely in the mid-seventeenth century by Zimbalo. He tacked on two complex facades and an enormous five-storeyed campanile that towers 70m above the square. The plain **Castello di Carlo V** (closed for restoration at the time of writing) to the east of Piazza Sant'Oronzo, hosts temporary art exhibitions (contact the tourist office for details).

There's further work by Zimbalo in the **Church of San Giovanni Battista** (or del Rosario), by the Porta Rudiae in the southwest corner of town. The ornate facade and twisting columns front some extremely odd altars, while dumpy cherubim dive for cover amid scenes resembling an exploding fruit bowl. But if the Baroque trappings of the town are beginning to pall, you might want to check out the odd relic from other eras too, not least a well-preserved **Teatro Romano** near the church of Santa Chiara, the only one of its kind to be found in Puglia, with rows of seats and orchestra floor still remarkably intact. There's also the fine Romanesque church of **Santi Nicolò e Cataldo** (entrance through the cemetery gate; generally open mornings) built by the Normans in 1190. Its cool interior reveals a generous hint of Saracen in the arches and the octagonal rounded dome. Little remains of the frescoes that once covered its walls, though an image of St Nicolò can be found on the south side, together with a delicately carved portal. One more stop to make is the **Museo Provinciale Castromediano** (daily 9am–1.30pm, Mon & Sat also 2.30–7.30pm; free) near the train station on the other side of town, which has finds from the old Roman town, including decorative panels from the amphitheatre and some religious gold- and silverwork.

Eating and drinking

Lecce's **bar and café scene** is flourishing: an arty little book-café, *Caffè Letterario* (closed Aug), Via G. Paladini 46, serves tasty snacks from breakfast through to 2am, with a DJ or live music usually on Wednesday or Friday nights. *Cagliostro*, a few doors away at Via Cairoli 25, is a laid-back cocktail bar and eatery. A really nice place for a sit down, *Caffè del Parco* at Giardini Pubblici Lecce, offers the only patch of green in the city centre – though note that it sometimes shuts in the hottest hours of the day in mid-August. Tucked away in Antica Corte dei Pandolfi, a little courtyard near Santa Chiara, is the *Wine Bar* – a great place to try a large selection of wines. Check out *E-book Libreria Multimediale* (Mon–Sat 9am–1.30pm & 5–8.30pm), Piazza d'Italia 19, a very small, rather New Age **Internet** café and bookshop near Porta San Biagio, which offers *aperitivi astrologici* (prepared according to the customer's star sign).

For **meals**, it's worth tracking down *Villa della Monica*, Via SS. Giacomo e Filippo 40 (℡0832.548.432; closed Tues); in summer you can sit in the gleaming, fountain-studded marble courtyard for a full meal or a drink. Specialities include pasta with crayfish, beef with rocket and parmesan, Salentine chickpea soup, and grilled smoked *scamorza* cheese. For less expensive, more homely cuisine, head for *Trattoria Casareccia* on Via Colonnello A. Costadura 19 (℡0832.245.178; closed all day Mon & Sun evening); or *La Vecchia Osteria* on Via da Sumno (book at weekends ℡0832.308.057; closed Mon), which serves great antipasti and inexpensive simple dishes at low prices. *Osteria degli Angeli*, opposite the castle at Via Cavour 4 (℡0832. 244.250; closed Sun in summer and Tues in winter), is a good choice for antipasto and a pizza (around €15).

The eastern peninsula: Otranto and the southern cape

The quickest escape from Lecce to the coast is to **SAN CATALDO**, with sandy beaches popular with locals, and served by buses from Lecce's Villa Comunale. An inviting place, with an illuminated waterfront promenade studded with candlelit restaurants, it's an inexpensive base, boasting a council-run youth hostel in a great location across from the beach at Lungomare San Cataldo ℡0832.650.890 or 347.879.4378; ❶). Beds cost €15 per person per night in quads, or €20 in doubles and guests receive a discount at *Alex Bar*, Via A. Vespucci 41, a spacious pizzeria and restaurant at the hostel's entrance (daily; closed Nov & Jan), with outdoor tables looking onto the waterfront.

Even without a car, the summer Salento-in-Bus service (see p.985) means you can get to most of the coast south of San Cataldo, right down to Otranto and the tip of the southern cape. It's a pleasant route along a rocky shoreline littered with ruined towers, a legacy of the defences erected against Turkish incursions. An alternative road inland – for which you do need a car – takes you via **MARTANO**, a small town where you'll find the **Liquoreria Monastero SM della Consolazione** at Via Borgagne (daily 9am–noon & 3.30–6pm) the monastery's shop selling herbal teas and liqueurs made by the monks themselves. One of their prized products is *le gocce imperiali*, a kind of cure-all tonic with a high alcohol content. The original monastery dates from the sixteenth century although there are large post-World War II additions – there's also an interesting **herbal museum** (same hours as shop; free; advisable to call ahead on ℡0832.575.214).

Otranto

OTRANTO, a minuscule town nestling around a harbour, is only an hour by train from Lecce (change at Maglie), set in an arid, rocky and windblown landscape, with translucent seas to swim in. The port overflows with tourists in summer, when the population more or less triples, but the coastline around is still comparatively undeveloped. Otranto's history, however, is decidedly grim. One of the last Byzantine towns to fall to the Normans in 1070, it remained a thriving port for Crusaders, pilgrims and traders. But in 1480 a Turkish fleet laid siege to the town, which held out for fifteen days before capitulating. It's said that as a punishment the archbishop, on capture, suffered the indignity of being sawn in half, a popular Turkish spectacle at that time. Nearly 12,000 people lost their lives and the 800 survivors, refusing to convert, were taken up a nearby hill and beheaded. Otranto never really recovered, though the town does feature one glorious survivor of the Turkish attack inside its cathedral (down a small alleyway just to the left of the castle): an extraordinary **mosaic floor**.

Information and accommodation

The **tourist office** Piazza Castello (July & Aug daily 9am–1.30pm & 4–8.30pm; Sept–June Mon–Sat 9am–1.30pm, Tues & Thurs also 4–6pm; ℡0836.801.436, ⓦwww.comune.otranto.le.it) has all the usual information, including where to rent **bicycles** and scooters.

If **staying** in Otranto, your best bet is the light, modern *Bellavista*,Via Vittorio Emanuele 19 (℡0836.801.058; ❷), right in the centre of things near the beach just outside the old town. Alternatively, the **B&B** *Ad Est*, Via Riviera degli Heathey (℡338.461.5454; ❹; May–Sept & Easter on request), is another good choice: its large terrace gives 360-degree views over the city and the sea, and the owner speaks some English. The nearest **campsite**, *Camping Idrusa*, on Via del Porto (℡0836.801.255; May–Sept), is a little run-down but central – signposted from the port and cool among pine trees.

The Town

The marble-columned nave in the Romanesque **Cattedrale di Santa Maria Annunziata** (daily 8am–noon & 3–6pm; free) is adorned by an incredible multicoloured tapestry in stone. The central theme is the "Tree of Life". Historical and animal figures are shown as a mix of myth and reality – Alexander the Great, King Arthur, the Queen of Sheba, crabs, fish, serpents and mermaids. The work of a twelfth-century monk, its rough simplicity provides a captivating picture, empowered by a delightful child-like innocence. The rose window was added in the fifteenth century.

It's worthwhile getting hold of the key from the **Museo Diocesano**, Piazza Basilica 3 (Tues–Sun 10am–1pm & 4–8pm; €2.50) and heading up the stepped street to the **Basilica di San Pietro e Paolo**. One of the most important Byzantine monuments in the Salento, this tiny chapel has frescoes, some with Greek inscriptions dating from the tenth to the thirteenth centuries, including a Last Supper.

Not far from the cathedral, the town's Aragonese **Castello** (Sat & Sun 9.30am–12.30 & 3–5.30pm; €2) juts out into the bay, defending the harbour. Its walls incorporate fragments of Roman and medieval inscriptions, while Charles V's coat of arms looms from its portal. Out on the southern edge of town is the cypress-tree-covered hill, where the survivors of the Turkish siege were beheaded. At the top of the hill, the sixteenth-century **Chiesa di San Francesco di Paola** holds the names of the victims, together with a vivid description of the terrible events of July 1480.

A variety of musical and theatrical events are held in Otranto throughout the summer, usually centred around the castle, along with an annual **festival** commemorating the "800 Martyrs" on August 13–15.

Eating and drinking

There are some excellent **restaurants**: *Atlantis* (☎0836.804.401; closed winter), on the opposite side of the bay from the old town, complete with romantic Moroccan lamps and straw chairs, serves unusual antipasti and seafood at moderate to expensive prices. To get there, follow Via Riviera degli Heathey to the lighthouse and turn left onto the beach. *Ai Bastioni* on the harbourside below the old town (☎0836.801.557; closed Oct–March & Wed April–June), serves mainly fish – part of the dining room is on a pier above the water, with huge windows on three sides; a meal here will cost around €25. For local dishes try *Da Sergio* on Corso Garibaldi (☎0836.801.575; closed Wed in winter plus Nov & Feb), where an average meal costs €40, or the mid-range *La Duchesca* at Piazza Castello 17 (closed Mon in winter). The air-conditioned self-service restaurant *Boomerang*, at 13/14 Via Vittorio Emanuele II, by the park next to the beach, serves delicious, low-priced, simple meals, as well as fresh antipasti and pasta. Alternatively, in nearby Tenuta Frassanito, along the road to San Cataldo, *Da Umberto* (☎0836.803.072; closed Wed) does great fish dishes – its speciality is *tagliolini all'aragosta* (pasta with lobster) – a meal comes to around €35 per head.

To the southern cape

From Otranto, all the way down to the cape at Santa Maria di Leuca, the coastline is steep and rugged. The unmissable journey along the winding road takes you past one spectacular view of sheer cliffs and blue sea after another. **CAPO D'OTRANTO**, 5km south of Otranto, is the easternmost point on the Italian peninsula, topped by a lighthouse and the rather desolate ruins of a seventh-century abbey. This is the first place in Italy to see the sun rise, and is a popular place to welcome in the New Year. On clear mornings there's a commanding view across the straits – the mountains of Albania are visible about 80km away – and on seriously clear days they say you can even see Corfu, 100km away. The relative remoteness of the coast has allowed refugees from Albania, as well as Pakistanis, Kurds and North Africans who passed through Greece, to head for Otranto's coast regularly. Numbers have declined, but their beach landings in inflatable dinghies have been known to make a bizarre and poignant contrast to the happy crowds on Sunday outings.

Places to stay along this route have some stunning views: *Camping Porto Miggiano* (☎0836.944.303; June–Sept) 16km from Otranto, just south of **SANTA CESAREA TERME**, is a small, simple but beautiful campsite among olive trees, situated about 200m from the cliffs with 114 steps leading down to the beach. Small bungalows are also available, and there's a restaurant on site. Heading south a further 7km brings you to the marina at **CASTRO**, where *La Tartana*, Via IV Novembre 151 (☎0836.943.513; ❷), has nice, fresh rooms plus big balconies, and a restaurant with a view over the sea and the old town. If all this is giving you vertigo, head for Castro town itself and the B&B *La Ritunna*, Via Mons Capreoli (☎333.846.0828, ⓦwww.laritunna.com; ❷), which has large balconies for chilling out on.

There isn't really much to draw you down as far as **SANTA MARIA DI LEUCA**, a somewhat barren spot, with a scattering of Neolithic remains and an uninspiring marina. The once-supposed "end of the world" is marked by the tiny church of **Santa Maria Finibus Terrae**, built on the site of an ancient temple dedicated to Minerva, perched on the white limestone cliffs. In actual fact, the cape isn't really Italy's southernmost point: that distinction goes to the Punta Ristola, a little to the west. Nonetheless, this is a lovely place to rent a boat for the afternoon and swim in the seacaves along the coast: try Sailorman,

Via Doppia Croce (℡0833.758.813, Ⓦwww.sailorman.it), at the harbour. Prices start at €7 per person for a ninety-minute trip with a swimming stop, and there are longer trips including night dives. You can get down this far, or at least as far as **Gagliano del Capo**, by train: it's at the end of the FSE rail line, just 5km from the cape; the Salento-in-Bus service runs to the cape from Otranto (and from Lecce via Gallipoli or inland via Maglie).

The western peninsula: Galatina and Gallipoli

About half an hour down the rail line from Lecce, **GALATINA** is an intriguing Salentine town on the edge of an area known as Grecia Salentina, a key Greek colony in medieval times, and which has retained Greek customs and language up until the present. It's an important centre of the Italian tobacco industry today, with much of the weed grown in the fields around. It's also famed for its excellent local **wine**; stop by at *Bellone* on Via Soleto 2 (closed Thurs afternoon & all day Sun) for good pasta and wine, including hard-to-find local pasta shapes that are produced in-house. In the old part of town, the church of **Santa Caterina in Galatina** (daily 9am–noon & 4.30–7pm; free) is also well worth a look for the stunning fourteenth-century frescoes that cover its interior.

Most interestingly, Galatina is the prime place in the Salentine where the phenomenon of **tarantism** is still remembered. Once a year, on the feast day of Saints Peter and Paul (June 28–29), musicians, dancers, academics, photographers and curious bystanders gather at the chapel of St Paul near the cathedral for performances and polemic. Up until as recently as the 1950s, victims of an unexplained illness with various conflicting symptoms that could range from lassitude to paranoia and a compulsion to dance were brought to the chapel to be cured. The sickness was commonly attributed to the dreaded tarantula bite, and those who were cured by going into a sort of music-inspired trance-dance would then come here every year to give thanks to St Paul, who is seen as patron saint of the *tarantate* and protector against poisonous animals. Modern scholars say that the sufferers – mostly women – usually hadn't been bitten but that the ruse of the "spider bite" was a metaphor for poisoning and entrapment at an existential level. Various medical explanations have been put forward, with other theories linking it to

The pizzica revival

The beat of the tambourine is a vital feature of *pizzica* music, whether it is played at *festas* for couples or groups to dance to for fun, as accompaniment to a knife or sword dance traditionally used as a way of settling disputes, or in the trance-dance enacted by the sick to get over their illnesses. Resurging regional pride has given rise to a contemporary *pizzica* style played at such events as the all-night music festival "the night of the tarantula" (*la notte della taranta*) held in mid-August at Melpignano (between Galatina and Otranto), that apparently drew a 50,000-strong crowd in 2003. *Pizzica* has gained popularity not just throughout Italy, with efforts being made to create a niche for it in the world-music market: in summer 2004, Stewart Copeland (ex-percussionist of 1980s band The Police) toured various European cities with the line-up of the previous year's *notte della taranta*, of which he'd been musical director. Every August 15, another *festa*, this time in honour of St Rocco in the small village of Torrepaduli (25km southeast of Galatina, near Ruffano), is the scene for a mass *pizzica* dance, accompanied by musicians of all ages who beat their tambourines, it is said, until their fingers bleed.

exorcism and ecstatic religion. These days the *festa* is enjoying something of a revival, due in part to the resurgence of the Salentine *pizzica* music (see box, p.991). You should get to Galatina by 4.30am or 5am on June 29 for the most intriguing part of the action – this may range from music and dancing outside the doors of the candle-lit chapel (open only on the days of the *festa*) to some present-day *tarantati* shyly turning up to pay their respects to St Paul before the crowds arrive for the official early morning mass at the church next door at around 6am. A huge fair of rides and market stalls then takes over the town with the festivities going on until late.

The **tourist office** at Via V. Emanuele II (Mon–Fri 9am–8pm; ℡0836.569.984, ⓦwww.comune.galatina.le.it) will give the lowdown on events surrounding the *festa*, which is gaining a higher profile these days after years of "discouragement" by both the church and the municipality; it also offers free bike rental (you'll need to leave ID). The plush, elegant *Palazzo Baldi*, in a courtyard a few steps from the cathedral at Corte Baldi (℡0836.568.345, ⓦwww.hotelpalazzobaldi .com; ❹), is the only central **hotel**, but there are a couple of agreeable, central **B&Bs**: *Safi*, Via Ottavio Scalfo 70/74 (℡0836.569.401; ❸), a Baroque town house 200m from the tourist office; and *Grand*, up a slightly uninviting alleyway at Vico del Monte 21 (℡0836.563.950; ❷), round the corner from the tourist office. As for **eating and drinking**, *Il Covo della Taranta*, Corso Garibaldi 13, four doors down from the chapel of St Paul is a pub-trattoria that serves lunch and dinner accompanied by occasional world-music jam sessions (info on ℡0836.567.617). At *Il Borgo Antico*, Via Siciliani 80, you can eat a good home-cooked meal for under €15, excluding drinks (closed evenings Mon–Wed; booking advisable ℡0836.566.800).

First impressions of **GALLIPOLI** (not the World War I battlefield in Turkey) are fairly uninspiring. The new town sprouted on the mainland once the population outgrew its original island site in the eighteenth century, and all that remains of the once-beautiful Greek city (the Kalli-pollis) is a rather weather-beaten fountain, which sits in the new town near the bridge. Over the bridge, things are more interesting: the old town itself is a maze of meandering and twisting whitewashed streets, with tiny tomatoes hanging on the walls to dry, providing a sudden blaze of colour alongside the fishing nets. Only the Aragonese castle, which squats in one corner of the island, still retains an Italian air in the town.

For **accommodation**, try *Pescatore* on Riviera C. Colombo 39 (℡0833.263.656; ❸), an attractive hotel in the old quarter with some rooms overlooking the sea and a good restaurant (closed Mon in winter) serving home-cooked seafood at low-to-moderate prices. Alternatively, there's the simpler *Le Conchiglie*, Via delle Perle 12 (℡0833.209.039; ❷), outside the centre at Località Conchiglie. Decent B&Bs include *Palazzo de Tomasi*, in the historic centre at Riviera A. Diaz 99 (℡380.505.3335, ⓦwww.salanitro .it; ❺), and *Salanitro*, SV Patitari (℡347.600.8262, ⓦwww.salanitro.it; ❺), at the town entrance when coming by autostrada from Lecce, just 350m from the sea. There's a good **campsite** 5km to the north: *La Vecchia Torre* (℡0833.209.083, ⓦwww.lavecchiatorre.it; June–Sept) at Rivabella on the coast road to Santa Maria al Bagno. Other than *Pescatore*, a fine place to **eat** in Gallipoli's old quarter is *Il Bastione*, Riviera N. Sauro 28 (℡0833.263.836), where you can sample *tagliolini tricolore* (pasta coloured with squid ink and courgettes to make the colours of the Italian flag) served with a seafood sauce, on a seafront terrace.

Travel details

Trains

Altamura to: Gravina in Puglia (7 daily; 10min).
Bari to: Alberobello (FSE, 15 daily; 1hr 30min);
Altamura (13 daily; 1hr 10min); Andria (hourly; 1hr);
Barletta (hourly; 55min); Bitonto (hourly; 20min);
Bríndisi (hourly; 1hr–1hr 30min); Fasano (20 daily;
40min–1hr); Gravina in Puglia (3 daily; 1hr 15min);
Grotte di Castellana (FSE, hourly; 50min); Lecce
(hourly; 1hr 30min–2hr); Locorotondo (FSE, 15
daily; 1hr 40min); Martina Franca (FSE, 15 daily;
1hr 45min); Molfetta (hourly; 30min); Naples (2
daily; 3hr 45min); Ostuni (hourly; 1hr); Péschici
(1 daily, change at Rodi Gargánico; 5hr 20min);
Polignano a Mare (hourly; 45min); Putignano (FSE,
hourly; 1hr); Rome (9 daily; 4hr 30min–5hr 30min);
Ruvo di Puglia (hourly; 40min); Spinazzola (3 daily;
1hr 15min–1hr 45min); Táranto (11 fast trains
daily; 1hr 5min–1hr 26min); Torre a Mare (hourly;
10min); Trani (hourly; 40min).
Bríndisi to: Fasano (hourly; 37min); Lecce
(27 daily; 24–52min); Ostuni (22 daily; 20–28min).
Fóggia to: Bari (hourly; 1hr–1hr 30min); Barletta
(17 daily; 30min); Bríndisi (16 daily; 2hr 50min);
Fasano (17 daily; 2hr 15min); Manfredonia (9 daily;
30min); Molfetta (hourly; 1hr 5min); Ostuni
(17 daily; 2hr 30min); Péschici (4 daily; 2hr 8min);
San Severo (5 daily; 25min); Trani (hourly; 50min).
Lecce to: Bari (hourly; 1hr 30min–2hr); Gallipoli
(9 daily; 1hr); Gagliano del Capo (10 daily; 1hr
30min); Otranto (8 daily; 1hr); Rome (6 daily; 6hr
15min–7hr).
Martina Franca to: Táranto (9 daily; 40min).
San Severo to: Péschici (3 daily; 2hr 25min).
Táranto to: Bari (15 daily; 1hr 15min); Bríndisi
(12 daily; 1hr 7min–1hr 20min); Grottaglie
(12 daily; 14–25min); Martina Franca (9 daily;
40–55min); Massafra (13 daily; 12–55min);
Metaponto (21 daily; 30–55min); Naples (4 direct
trains daily; 4hr–4hr 35min); Reggio di Calabria
(4 direct trains daily; 5hr 12min–6hr 46min).

Buses

NB: Bus services on Sundays are drastically
reduced.
Bari to: Andria (6–7 daily; 1hr 30min); Barletta
(3–4 hourly; 1hr 25min); Canosa di Puglia
(10 daily; 2hr 10min); Margherita di Savoia (8 daily;
1hr 45min); Molfetta (3–4 hourly; 40min); Trani
(3–4 hourly; 1hr 5min).

Fasano to: Martina Franca (12 daily; 20min);
Savelletri and Egnázia (6 daily; 20 min); Selva
Fasano (4 daily; 10min).
Fóggia to: Lucera (at least hourly; 30min); Manfre-
donia (12 daily; 50min); Mattinata (10 daily; 1hr
15min); Monte S. Angelo (7 daily; 1hr 35min); San
Severo (6 daily; 45min); Troia (hourly; 40min);
Vieste (5 daily; 2hr 45min).
Lecce Salento-in-Bus (late June to mid-Sept only)
to: Gallipoli (6 daily 1hr & 8 daily 2hr); Otranto
(8 daily; 1hr); Porto Cesareo (8 daily; 50min); San
Cataldo (8 daily; 32min); Santa Maria di Leuca
(7 daily; 2hr 45min).
Manfredonia to: Bari (1 daily; 2hr 20min);
Mattinata (10 daily; 30min); Monte Sant'Angelo
(every 2hr; 55min); San Giovanni Rotondo (14 daily;
40min); San Marco in Lamis (10 daily; 1hr); Vico
del Gargano (2 daily; 2hr 15min); Vieste (2 daily;
1hr 55min).
Molfetta to: Ruvo di Puglia (hourly; 30min).
Péschici to: Rome (2 daily; 6hr 40min); Vico del
Gârgano (1 daily; 45min); Vieste (12 daily; 45min).
Rodi Gârgánico to: Foresta Umbra (2 daily; 1hr
5min); Vico del Gârgano (2 daily; 40min).
Vico del Gârgano to: Ischitella (9 daily; 15min).
Vieste to: Fóggia (1 daily; 2hr 40min); Manfredonia
(3 daily; 1hr 40min); Péschici (9 daily; 45min);
Rome (2 daily; 7hr 15min).

Ferries, hydrofoils and Monostabs (fast ferries)

Manfredonia to: Vieste (June–Sept 1 daily;
45min).
Péschici to: Trémiti via Rodi Gargánico (June–Sept
1 daily; 1hr 15min).
Trémiti Islands to: Manfredonia (June, July &
Sept 1 daily; 2hr); Ortona (end June to early Sept
1 daily; 2hr); Térmoli (June–Sept 2–3 daily; 50min;
ferries rest of year 2–3 weekly; 1hr 40min); Vasto
(end June to early Sept 1 daily; 1hr); Vieste (June,
July & Sept 1 daily; Aug 3 daily; 1hr; Monostabs
April & May 1 daily; 1hr 10min; and ferries rest
of year).
Vieste to: Trémiti (Jan–March & Oct–Dec 1 weekly;
2hr 15min).

International ferries

Bari to: Corfu (daily end July to mid Aug, rest of
year 3 weekly; 10hr); Durres/Durazzo, Albania (at
least daily; 3hr 30min–9hr); Igoumenitsa (daily;

from 9hr 30min); Patras (daily; from 15hr 30min); Rijeka via Dubrovnik, Korcula, Stari Grad and Split in Croatia (July & Aug 2 weekly; 32hr).

Brindisi to: Avlona (March–Dec 1 daily; 8hr 30min); Çesme (July & Aug 1 weekly; from 29hr 45min); Corfu (at least 1 daily in summer; from 8hr); Igoumenitsa (at least 1 daily in summer; 8hr); Kefallonia (13 sailings through July & Aug; 14hr); Patras (at least 1 daily in summer; 14hr); Zante (11 sailings through July & Aug; 21hr).

Calabria and Basilicata

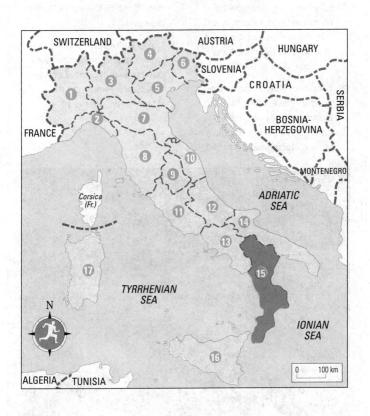

CHAPTER 15

Highlights

* **Giganti della Sila** Over 350 years old, and more than 40m high, these beautiful ancient pines are one of the many attractions in the Sila National Park. See p.1003

* **Tropea promontory** This region has it all – white sandy beaches, turquoise water, hills tumbling down to the coast and – in Tropea town and Pizzo – two of the most characterful old centres in Calabria. See p.1007

* **Bronzi di Riace** Two extra-ordinary seven-foot-high, bronze statues of Greek athletes housed in Reggio's Museo Nazionale. See p.1010

* **Matera** Sliced by a ravine containing thousands of *sassi* – cave dwellings gouged out of rock – Matera's unique landscape never ceases to astonish. See p.1015

* **Purple Codex, Rossano** An illustrated manuscript from the sixth century with early depictions of the life of Christ. See p.1021

* **Capo Colonna** A solitary Doric column marks the spot of what was the most impor-tant Greek temple on the Ionian coast. See p.1024

△ Matera

Calabria and Basilicata

ore than any other of the regions of the Italian South, **Calabria** and
Basilicata represent the quintessence of the *mezzogiorno*, the southern
regions of Italy that are traditionally poor. Underdeveloped and
– owing to emigration – sparsely populated, these rural regions were
long considered only good for taxation, and even then they were mismanaged.
Although agriculture was systematized to an extent when these lands formed a
part of Magna Graecia, by the time the Normans arrived in the eleventh century
there was little infrastructure or defence against the depredations of maritime
raiders. The feudal era didn't really die here until the Bourbons were ejected at
Unification, and remnants of the older society persist in the widespread system
of patronage and an exaggerated use of titles. Respect for authority coexists with
a deep scepticism and an apathy and inertia vividly described by Carlo Levi in
Christ Stopped at Eboli – a book that opened many Italians' eyes to the very deep
problems besetting the *mezzogiorno*. Levi describes a south where malaria is
endemic and the peasants' way of life seems to be basically pagan.

While malaria has now been eradicated, if anything this area is even more
marginalized than it was before Unification, when it was at least the geographical
centre of the Bourbon state. It's only in these southern regions that you really
appreciate talk of the Two Nations of Italy, seeing how different they are from
the emphatically European north. Since the war, a massive channelling of funds
to finance huge irrigation and land-reclamation schemes, industrial development
and a modern system of communications has brought built-up sprawl to previously isolated towns such as **Crotone** – often hand in hand with the forces of
organized crime and with frequently dire consequences for the environment.

In Calabria the **'ndrangheta** mafia maintains a stranglehold across much
of the region. Having moved on from kidnappings and localized extortion to
become an international network that deals in heroin and supposedly even
nuclear waste, these days it's thought to be far more powerful and dangerous
than the Sicilian Cosa Nostra.

The **landscape** and **seaside resorts** provide the main reasons to come to
Basilicata and Calabria. Although they're among the poorest and least fertile
regions in Italy, the combination of mountain grandeur, a relatively unspoilt
coastline and cheap but excellent food give them an appeal that is only beginning to be exploited by the tourist industry.

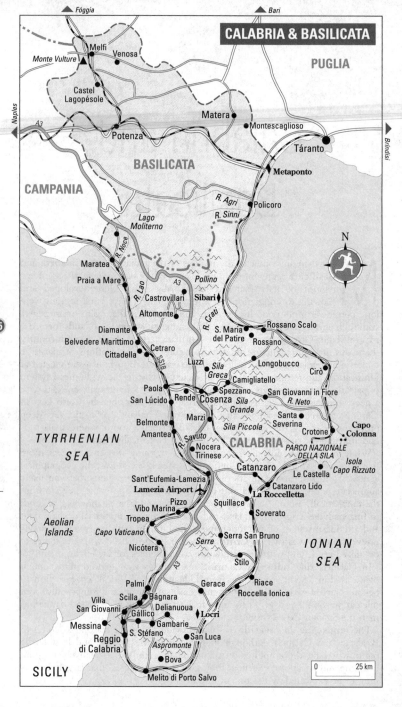

CALABRIA & BASILICATA

PUGLIA

Fóggia

Bari

Monte Vulture

Melfi

Venosa

Castel
Lagopésole

Matera

Montescaglioso

Naples

A3

Potenza

Táranto

BASILICATA

Metaponto

CAMPANIA

R. Agri

Policoro

R. Sinni

Lago
Moliterno

R. Noce

Maratea

Praia a Mare

R. Lao

A3

Pollino

Sibari

Castrovillari

Altomonte

R. Crati

Diamante

S. Maria
del Patire

Rossano Scalo

Belvedere Marittimo

Rossano

Cetraro

Cittadella

Luzzi

Sila
Greca

Longobucco

Ciró

Camigliatello

Paola

Spezzano

San Giovanni in Fiore

San Lúcido

Rende

Cosenza

Sila
Grande

R. Neto

Belmonte

Marzi

Santa
Severina

Amantea

Sila Piccola

Capo
Colonna

R. Savuto

Crotone

TYRRHENIAN
SEA

Nocera
Tirinese

CALABRIA

PARCO NAZIONALE
DELLA SILA

Catanzaro

Isola
Capo Rizzuto

Le Castella

Sant'Eufemia-Lamezia

Lamezia Airport

Catanzaro Lido
La Roccelletta

Pizzo

Squillace

Vibo Marina

Soverato

Tropea

Aeolian
Islands

Capo Vaticano

Serre

Serra San Bruno

Nicótera

IONIAN
SEA

Stilo

A3

Palmi

Gerace

Riace

Scilla

Bágnara

Roccella Ionica

Villa
San Giovanni

Delianuoua

Gállico

Locri

Messina

Gambarie

Reggio
di Calabria

S. Stéfano

San Luca

Aspromonte

Bova

N

998

SICILY

Melito di Porto Salvo

0   25 km

Brindisi

The food of **Calabria** is similar to that of Campania, but tends to have a rougher approach. **Greek influence** still pervades in the form of aubergines, swordfish and desserts incorporating figs, almonds and honey; otherwise it has the common trademarks of the south – plenty of pasta and pork (try the *sorpressata* salami, and cheeses such as *mozzarella*, *caciocavallo*, mature *provolone* and *pecorino*). Look out for spicy food with lots of chili, such as '**Nduia**, a spicy *peperoncino* and pork fat spread, and *rosmarina*, an equally spicy fish and chili paste. For sweets, try *mostacciolo*, a honeyed nut bread, or anything containing *bergamotto*, the fruit of a citrus tree similar to the orange that grows along the south coast. The *cedro* fruit grown in Calabria is used in liqueurs and candies, and draws Jewish rabbis in mid-September in search of the perfect fruit for use in the Feast of the Tabernacles.

Basilicata is another poor region, mountainous and sparsely populated, relying on pasta, tomatoes, bread, olives and pork. A fondness for **spicy food** shows in the popularity of all types of peppers and, unusually in Italy, ginger (*zenzero*), which is thrown into many dishes. **Strong cheeses**, like matured or smoked ricotta – to match the strength of other ingredients – are favoured.

Cirò is the success story of Calabrian wine making, an old **wine** that has been given some modern touches and now shifts bottles outside its home territory. Lento is also a good local *vino*. Not surprisingly, given its far-south position, Calabria also turns out sweet whites such as Greco di Bianco. The **aglianico** grape makes a star appearance in Basilicata: Aglianico del Vulture is the region's only DOC, but other wines worth trying are the sweet, sparkling Malvasia and Moscato.

In Basilicata, the greatest draw is **Matera**, whose distinctive *sassi* – cavelike dwellings in the heart of the town – give it a uniquely dramatic setting. Of the coasts, it's the **Tyrrhenian** that is most engaging, with spots like **Maratea**, **Tropea** and **Scilla** favourite hideaway resorts for discerning Italian and foreign visitors. The **Ionian** coast, on the other hand, can be bleak and is visited mainly for its **ancient sites** – relics of the once mighty states that comprised the Greek colonies known as Magna Graecia.

Good **transport** services exist, but in hilly and coastal areas a car is useful. Be warned that if you're planning on driving, the roads tend to be narrow and provincial and you should allow more time than you think you'll need. There's a mine of information on the regions at Ⓦ www.aptbasilicata.it.

The northern Tyrrhenian coast

The northern stretch of the Tyrrhenian coast takes in both Calabria and Basilicata, of which the latter – a brief mountainous slice – is the most inspiring stretch and probably the most visited part of the entire region, its sheer cliffs and rocky coves refreshingly unspoilt by the holiday industry.

The obvious stop here is **Maratea**, hemmed in by the mountains and offering some first-rate beaches that get overcrowded in summer. Once you're in Calabria, the holiday complexes intrude on the mainly mountainous littoral, though there are some absorbing places to break the journey, notably the towns of **Diamante**, **Belvedere** and, further south, **Paola**. Following the coast down, the main SS18 runs alongside the railway line, though the frequent trains don't always stop at smaller places.

Maratea

The only town on Basilicata's Tyrrhenian seaboard, **MARATEA** is a pictur-esque cluster of localities scattered along the cliffy coastline, mostly dedicated to the holiday industry during summer but perfectly peaceful outside the peak period. The old inland centre, known simply as **Maratea Paese**, is a knot of steep, narrow alleys and squares worth nosing around, though lacking any vital attractions. More compelling are the straggling, long-abandoned ruins of **Maratea Antica** behind and above town up the five-kilometre road to **Monte San Biagio** (624m), from which memorable views extend over the Golfo di Policastro. The peak is dominated by the **Redentore**, an enormous marble Christ, arms akimbo, symbolically positioned with its back to the sea, looking towards the mountains of the interior. Opposite the statue, and looking as if it were about to be crushed under the giant's feet, is an eighteenth-century church dedicated to the town's patron saint, the **Santuario di San Biagio**, built on the site of a pagan temple dedicated to Minerva and now the destina-tion of a procession during the town's main festivities on the second Sunday of May, when a statue of the patron saint is carried up the hill.

Maratea's chief allure, however, is the beautiful rocky **coastline** hereabouts and the string of coastal offshoots where the hotels and restaurants are located. Most of the action – and accommodation – is in or around the little seaside area of **Fiumicello**, 5km north of Maratea Paese, though the chic elite who have colonized much of the area prefer to be seen in the snazzier bars and restaurants of **Maratea Porto**, directly below Maratea Paese – if nothing else, a pleasant place to stroll around and gawp at the yachts. The whole area is well endowed with sandy **beaches**, including a good one below Fiumicello; most are well signposted, but don't hesitate to explore the less obvious ones.

Practicalities

Most **trains** stop at the main Maratea station, at the bottom of Maratea Paese, from where it's a five-minute minibus or taxi ride (or a fifteen-minute walk) to Fiumicello. There's a second, less-used station, Maratea Scalo (at Marina di Maratea), 5km south of the main station. For **getting around**, a July and August-only minibus service (up to four a day, tickets bought on board) connects Maratea Porto, Fiumicello and Maratea Paese in that order. The **tourist office** is on Fiumicello's main square (Mon–Sat: July & Aug 8.30am–2pm & 3.30–8pm; Sept–June 8.30am–2pm & 3–6pm; ☎0973.876.908, @www.costadimaratea.it).

Accommodation can be hard to come by at any time, and in high season is often expensive, with many hotels requiring half board during the peak period. To avoid this, you may do better to rent rooms – ask for a list from the tourist office. The most distinctive hotel in Maratea is the *Capo Casale*, Via Capo Casale 10, sited in a tastefully restored old house in the upper part of the *centro storico* (☎0973.871.308, @www.capocasale.it; ❹). More functional and cheaper is *Fiorella*, Via Santa Venere 21 (☎0973.876.921; ❶), a spacious and basic hotel, open all year round, just outside Fiumicello near the petrol station. *Settebello*, Via Fiumicello 52 (☎0973.876.277, @www.costadimaratea.com/settebello; ❸; late April to mid-Oct), overlooks the beach at Fiumicello. If you'd prefer to stay in a B&B, try the *Giovanni Talarico* on Via Santa Venere (☎0973.877.040; ❶; July & Aug) which has spotless accommodation with sparkling views across to the mountains. Even nicer, the B&B *Da Zio Pino* (☎0973.877.293 or 339.397.4700; ❷), also on Via Santa Venere, has six comfortable bedrooms, all with private bathrooms, and kind, welcoming owners. On the edge of Fiumicello, at Via Rasi 4c, *B&B Laino* (☎0973.876.506 or 329.240.4320; ❷) has six rooms, two apartments and a swimming pool.

There are dozens of **restaurants** in the area. Some of the best are in Fiumicello, where, on the main Via Santa Venere, *El Sol's* pizzas and seafood dishes such as mussels and swordfish, generally pull in a big local crowd (☎0973.876.928). Also on Via Santa Venere, opposite the Grand Hotel S. Venere, *Pub Listrico's* is a pub, restaurant and pizzeria with a terrace and a garden; it has a good-value fish menu for €20 (excluding drinks). Twenty metres along the road from *Da Zio Pino*, there's **Internet** access at InfoPoint, which also offers boat tours along the coast (☎0973.871.704 or 347.802.1537).

Into Calabria

South of Maratea the road drops to reveal the flat coast of Calabria on the other side of the River Noce, where, about 40km down the SS18, you arrive at the chic seaside town of **DIAMANTE**. Glistening on its small promontory, the town's narrow whitewashed lanes have been adorned with striking modern murals, making it a fascinating place for a wander, and there are a couple of good, moderately priced fish **restaurants** with outside seating down by the seafront at Spiaggia Piccola (beyond the jetty). Most relaxed is the *Taverna del Pescatore* (☎0985.81.482; closed Tues), with views over the small port – expect to pay around €40 for a full meal, excluding drinks. If you want **to stay**, try the ✴*Ferretti Hotel* on the seafront at Via Poseidone 1 (☎0985.81.428, ⓦwww .ferrettihotel.it; ❻), a luxurious modern place with its own swimming pool, restaurant, tennis court, private beach and excellent service (open May–Sept).

BELVEDERE MARITTIMO, some 10km further down the coast, overlooks its unexceptional marina from a spur a little way inland. It's an imposing and elegant town, full of greenery and having little of the air of neglect typical of Calabria's older centres. At the top, an impressive **castle** stands guard, originally a Norman construction but rebuilt under the Aragonese, whose coat of arms can be seen above the main gate. The inside has been gutted, however, and it's closed to the public. Down in **Belvedere Marina**, the best place to eat is the *Milleluci* on Via Grossi (☎0985.82.229; closed Tues), which serves pizzas baked in a wood-fired oven alongside such specialities as *gnocchi di patata alla pescatora* (potato gnocchi with seafood) for around €7.

Paola

About 40km further down the coast, the sizeable town of **PAOLA** is an important rail and road junction for Cosenza, and the site of the **Santuario di San Francesco di Paola**, in a ravine above the town. Not to be confused with Francis of Assisi, this St Francis spent most of his life here in Paola and, as Calabria's principal saint, is venerated throughout the south. People visit the shrine at all times of year, but particularly during the week leading up to the May 4 **festa** when a fair occupies the town, with daily festivities culminating in the carrying of his statue into the sea and a grand display of fireworks on the beach at midnight.

There are several reasonably priced **hotels** and **trattorias** around the station by the sea, but Paola's bargain is the hotel *Casa del Pellegrino Hotel San Francesco*, a neat two-star at Via Valle della Timpa aimed at pilgrims but open to all (☎0982.611.457, ⓦwww.hotelsanfrancescodipaola.it; ❶). There are also a couple of good **places to eat** near the central piazza above the *Casa del Pellegrino*: the *Eureka*, in Via del Cannone (☎0982.587.356; closed Tues), which does good fish from around €10 for a main course and has outdoor seating in summer, and pizzeria *Le Arcate* (☏0982.585.377), through the arch at Via Valitutti 5, where a Margherita costs €3.50.

Cosenza and around

COSENZA, a burgeoning city with a small and clean historic centre, is the region's capital. Largely ruined by rings of featureless modern construction, the result of a boom over the past twenty years, there are few attractions to draw you here, though you may need to pass through on your way to the Sila mountains. The one thing worth seeing is its stately **Duomo** in the historic town centre on the main street, Corso Telesio. Consecrated on the occasion of Frederick II's visit to the city in 1222, it contains the lovely tomb of Isabella of Aragon, who died in Cosenza in 1271 while returning with her husband Philip III – seen kneeling beside her – from an abortive Crusade in Tunisia, and a copy of a thirteenth-century Byzantine icon, the *Madonna del Pilerio*, which was once carried around the country during times of plague.

Tradition has it that under the Busento River in Cosenza is the burial place of **Alaric the Goth**, the barbarian who gave the western world a jolt when he prised open the gates of Rome in 410 AD. Struck down for his sins by malaria while journeying south, he was interred here along with his booty, and the course of the river deviated to cover the traces, lending Cosenza a place in history and giving rise to countless, fruitless projects to discover the tomb's whereabouts.

Practicalities

The **bus station** is below Piazza Fera, from where it's a twenty-minute walk down the length of Corso Mazzini to the hotels and the *centro storico*. Arriving by train, you have to take a bus (every 20min) from the **train station** a little way outside town – buy your ticket from the bar inside the station. The main **tourist office** is at Corso Mazzini 92 (Mon & Thurs 8am–1.30pm & 3–5pm, Tues, Wed & Fri 8am–1.30pm; ☏0984.27.271), and there's an office specifically for the *centro storico* behind the *duomo* in Via Toscano (Mon & Thurs 8.30am–1.30pm & 3.15–6pm, Tues, Wed & Fri 8.30am–1.30pm; ☏0984.813.336). The town's **Internet** point is at the *Casa della Cultura* on Corso Telesio in the historic centre.

Hotels are mostly expensive, business-traveller places, but there are one or two nicer alternatives. The *Excelsior* on Piazza Matteotti (☏0984.74.383, ⓦwww .italiaabc.it/a/excelsior; ❷) is a spacious, comfortable and well-furnished hotel, close to the historic centre and offering great value for money, or try the more business-like *Grisaro*, Viale Trieste (☏0984.27.838, ⓦwww.paginegialle.it /htlgrisaro; ❷). For **eating** try *Calabria Bella*, (☏0984.793531) in the old town on Piazza Duomo, which has outside seating in summer and serves traditional local dishes; a generous mixed plate of antipasti can be had for about €8. There are numerous cafés and pubs, but the best aperitif is to be had at the old-fashioned *Gran Caffè Renzelli*, up past the *duomo* on Corso Telesio.

Around Cosenza

People spending any time in Cosenza will be mostly interested in excursions into the **Sila** highlands (see opposite), but some of the villages dotted around the surrounding hills, where most of the Cosentine population have their roots and family homes, shouldn't be ignored. In summer, the streets are lively until late, and at night the views over the bowl of the valley are magnificent, with glittering threads and clusters of light. It's also in the summer that the village **festas** normally take place, with each *comune* vying to outdo the others in terms of spectacle and expense.

The hilltop village of **RENDE** holds the prize for the tidiest village in the region: it has good views and an absorbing little **museum** (Tues–Sun 9.30am–12.30pm & 5–8pm; free) in the Palazzo Zagarese, on Via de Bartolo, devoted to local folk art, costumes, cuisine, music, the Albanian community and emigration. Rende also boasts a decent choice of places to **eat** and drink, including the good-value pizzeria, *L'Arco*, at Via Costa 4 (☎0984.443.228; evenings only, closed Tues), with a panoramic terrace, where pizzas start at €4. Northeast of Cosenza, above the village of **LUZZI**, stands the **Abbazia di Sambucina**. A Cistercian abbey founded in the twelfth century and long the centre of this order of monks throughout the south, it has a beautiful, lightly pointed portal (rebuilt in the fifteenth century) and the original presbytery.

Buses for the villages depart from the **bus station** in Cosenza, below Piazza Fera, but to get the most out of these places you ideally need your own transport, as services normally stop at nightfall. An interesting (but slow) way to get to the villages in the Presila mountains during the day (and beyond, into the Sila) is by **train**, on the Calabro-Lucane (FCL) line: this leaves twice a day from the small train station east of Cosenza's Piazza Matteotti for Camigliatello, offering marvellous glimpses over the Cosenza valley as it twists and grinds up the mountain through woods and over rivers.

The Sila

Covering the widest part of the Calabrian peninsula, the **Sila** massif is more of an extensive plateau than a mountain range, though the peaks on its western flank reach heights of nearly 2000m. It's divided into three main groups, the Sila Greca, Sila Grande and Sila Piccola.

At one time the Sila was one huge forest and was exploited from earliest times to provide fuel and material for the construction of fleets, fortresses and even for church-building in Rome, resulting in a deforestation that helped bring about the malarial conditions that for centuries laid much of Calabria low. The cutting of trees is now strictly controlled, and **ancient pines** (the so-called **Giganti della Sila**), which can live for several hundred years, are among the region's chief attractions. There's plenty here too for the outdoors enthusiast: in summer the area provides relief from the heat of the towns; and in winter there's downhill and cross-country skiing.

The Sila Greca

Deforestation has had the most devastating effect on the **Sila Greca**, the northernmost part of the massif, leaving mainly cultivated rolling highlands in place of once dense woods. But the area is easily accessible from the Ionian coast or the main road inland, and if you have a car it's worth the detour to investigate some of the **Albanian villages** scattered around these hills, originally settled in the fifteenth century by colonies of Albanians in flight from Muslim invasions. **SAN DEMETRIO CORONE** is the most interesting, containing an Italo-Albanian *Collegio* charged with the task of guarding what remains of the Albanian heritage. Annexed to this is the church of **Sant'Adriano**, a structure that still shows elements of its Byzantine and Norman origins. Really, though, it's the annual festivals that show these villages at their best. Along with the opportunity to see their elaborate costumes and hear some gutsy singing, going to one may be the only chance of hearing the authentic language – a fifteenth-century version of modern Albanian – that has only recently been replaced by the *calabrese* dialect as the everyday language in these parts. Festivals take place in the villages of **Santa Sofia** (July 15 & 16), **San Cosmo** (Sept 26 & 27), **Vaccarizzo** (March 31 to April 2) and **San Giorgio** (April 2).

The Sila Grande

Densely forested, and the highest, most extensive part of the Sila range, the **Sila Grande** is home to Calabria's main **ski slopes** as well as the region's three principal **lakes** – all artificial (for hydroelectric purposes) and much loved by fishing enthusiasts, who come out in force at weekends. If you want to spend any time up here, the **campsites** enjoy good lakeside locations, while the hotels are mainly in the towns and villages, and many close out of season.

Camigliatello

The towns vary greatly. **SAN GIOVANNI IN FIORE**, in the heart of the Sila, is the area's biggest, but also the dreariest. For winter-sports enthusiasts and summer trekkers alike, **CAMIGLIATELLO** is the best known of the resorts, a functional place that's well connected by bus with Cosenza, though it lacks any intrinsic charm. Centred on Via Roma, the town has three ski slopes of its own and another at Moccone (3km west), plus a confusion of hotels, restaurants and souvenir shops. If you fancy **skiing**, you will find the slopes have facilities for renting equipment (from €15–20 per day) and offer tuition (group lessons from €15–25 per person per hour). For information call Sci La Baita (℡338.309.6063) or the inappropriately named *Summer Sila* (℡328.957.0993). The Sila terrain also makes ideal **riding** country, though most stables are open in summer only; try Maneggio il Viviere (℡0984.578.466), 3km from Camigiliatello at Moccone. If you want to **stay**, try the plain but inexpensive *Miramonti* on Via Forgitelle (℡0984.579.067, ⓦwww.miramontisila.it; ❶) or the comfortable and just slightly pricier *Meranda*, Via Roma, Camigliatello (℡0984.578.022, ⓦwww .consorziocamigliatello.it; ❶)

For a **snack** in Camigliatello, *Lo Spuntino* on Via Repaci, off the other side of Via Roma, has excellent panini and other fast food, while Moccone has a great-value **trattoria**, *Da Fulvio* (closed Mon), which has a well-deserved reputation for good-value, simple local cooking, using lots of wild mushrooms and wild boar (set menu €13). The Pro Loco **tourist office** at the top of Via Roma keeps slightly erratic opening hours (in theory daily 9am–1pm & 3–6pm; ℡0984.579.159), and has suggestions for **walking routes** in the area.

Aound Camigliatello

From Camigliatello, some of the oldest **pine forests** are to be found just a short distance away at **Croci di Megara**. Alternatively, you could hike for 15km – or take the bus – to **Lago Cecita**, the best starting-place for expeditions to **La Fossiata**, a conservation area that resembles a national park on the American model, with tidy wooden fences along the roads and numerous picnic spots. It's always possible to find your own space, but it's equally a good idea to follow the clearly defined routes set out by the *Corpo Forestale* to make sure you don't get lost (maps at the Camigliatello Pro Loco). One of the most interesting leads to an old brigand stronghold: descend the steep slope from La

Fossiata to the remote hamlet of **LONGOBUCCO**, atmospherically enclosed at the bottom of a narrow valley. If you want to stay, book in advance at the only local **hotel**, *Hotel Stella* (T 0983.72.082 or 338.415.6116; ●), a simple place with a restaurant.

Camigliatello is also a useful starting-point for a tough hike that takes in the area's highest peaks, following the *strada delle vette* ("road of the peaks") for 13km through pine and beech woods before forking off and up to the three **peaks** of Monte Scuro, Monte Curcio and, highest of all, Monte Botte Donato (1928m). The trail, which is often snowbound between December and May, continues on down to **Lago Arvo** and the resort of **LORICA**, from where it's a shorter distance than following the *strada delle vette* to reach Botte Donato. Or you can save the sweat and take the chair lift from the località Cavaliere, just outside town. Lorica, like Camigliatello, is dedicated to tourism in the height of the winter and summer seasons, but its lakeside location makes it a more relaxed spot, with lots of places for picnicking under the pines and observing the antics of the black squirrels that inhabit them. Lorica also boasts a comfortable four-star hotel, *Park 108* at Via Nazionale 86 (T 0984.537.077, W www.hotelpark108.it; ●), that doesn't ask for half board in high season and was revamped in 2004 with a sauna and fitness centre.

The town is connected with Cosenza by **bus**, arriving in the morning and returning in the afternoon,

The Sila Piccola

Bounded by Lago Ampollino in the north, Catanzaro and the Ionian coast in the south, the **Sila Piccola** is the region's most densely forested section, centred on the **Foresta di Gariglione**, thick with fir, beech and the gigantic turkey oak from which it derives its name. It's not so well adapted for walking as La Fossiata, though, and apart from the odd resort it's a thinly populated area, and most of its villages are in any case unattractive.

More interesting than most is **BELCASTRO**, on the southern fringes of the range. Watched over by a Norman castle, it's claimed to be the birthplace of St Thomas Aquinas, whose family once held the town in fief. Further west, on the SS109, the mountain village of **TAVERNA** has long historical associations but is best-known today as the home of Calabria's foremost seventeenth-century painter, **Mattia Preti**, whose Spanish-looking works can be seen in four of the local churches, notably **San Domenico**.

The southern Tyrrhenian coast

The province of Catanzaro begins at the Savuto River, and from here down to Reggio the SS18, autostrada and main rail line all run parallel along the coast, apart from the stretch of the Tropea promontory. Immediately south of the river, a few kilometres inland from the resort of Lido di Falerna, the hill-village of **NOCERA TIRINESE** (buses run from the Falerna train station on the coast) is famed for the flagellants who – literally – paint the streets red every Easter during a rather gruesome religious festival that grips the whole village with fervour. Wailing processions sway through the streets, and teams of two sprint between churches, one holding a cross, the other beating himself with a spiked brush; his freely flowing blood is then splashed over the doors of the houses to protect those within – not to be washed off until it happens naturally with the rain. One of the few examples of this kind of ritual bloodletting still to be found in the south, and not at all a mere tourist event, it's worth catching if you're around here at the right time.

Thirteen kilometres further down the coast, between Capo Suvero (marked by its lighthouse) and Lido di Gizzeria, is a fine **swimming spot**, a sandy spit with a freshwater lake close by, surrounded by palms and bamboo. The plain that stretches east from here, the **Piana di Sant'Eufemia**, is the narrowest part of the Calabrian peninsula, much of it reclaimed only in the last hundred years from malarial swamp: the mosquitoes remain but they no longer carry the disease. **LAMEZIA** has Calabria's main **airport** (ⓦwww.sacal.it), while **SANT'EUFEMIA-LAMEZIA** is the **rail and road junction** for Catanzaro and the Ionian coast. Heading south on the highway you begin a slow ascent on the long viaduct that is one of the engineering feats of the Autostrada del Sole, the views growing more inspiring as it rises above the coast to the high tableland of the Tropea promontory.

Pizzo

Following the railway or the SS18, you might want to spend some time in the picturesque little town of **PIZZO**, neatly placed for the **beaches** around Tropea and site of a small **castle** (daily 9am–12.30pm & 3–7.30pm; €2; ⓦwww .murat.it) overlooking the sea just off the main Piazza della Repubblica. Built in 1486 by Ferdinand I of Aragon, it holds the room in which the French general **Murat** was imprisoned, with some of his personal effects and copies of the last letters he wrote, and the terrace where he was shot in October 1815. Murat, Napoleon's brother-in-law and one of his ablest generals, met his ignominious end here after attempting to rouse the people against the Bourbons to reclaim the throne of Naples given to him by Napoleon; the people of Pizzo ignored his haughty entreaties, and he was arrested and court-martialled.

A couple of kilometres north of the centre, you might drop in on the **Chiesetta di Piedigrotta** (daily 9am–1pm & 3–7pm; tickets €2 from the bar or the tobacconist's opposite), a curious rock-hewn church next to a sandy beach, signposted off the coastal SS22. Created in the seventeenth century by Neapolitan sailors rescued from a shipwreck, the church was later enlarged and its interior festooned with eccentric statuary depicting episodes from the Bible. Most of this was the work of a local father-and-son team, and it was augmented by another scion of the family in 1969, who restored the works and contributed a scene of his own, a double portrait of Pope John XXIII and President Kennedy.

Pizzo has a Pro Loco **tourist information** office located over the arches at the bottom of Piazza della Repubblica (erratic opening hours, but officially Mon–Sat 10am–noon & 4.30–8pm; ☎0963.531.310).

There are good **places to stay** in Pizzo, though as it's a beach resort booking is essential in the summer. Close to the Chiesetta at Riviera Prangi 136 is the little B&B *Piedigrotta* (☎0963.531.760 or 347.616.5771; ❶). Another good option is *A Casa Janca* (☎0963.264.364 or 349.574.7135), a first-rate agriturismo on the main road out of town north towards Marinella (200m before the Agip station.) Furnished in traditional rustic style, the place is locally renowned for its **restaurant**, where non-guests can also dine for around €25–35 on Calabrian specialities such as *zuppa di cipolla* (onion soup); half board here costs €110 for two.

There's a good choice of **places to eat** in the centre of town including a trattoria under the arcade in Piazza della Repubblica, *Il Porticato* (closed Wed) where you can eat dishes such as *stranguggi* (fresh pasta) with beans and locally grown *peperoncino*. They have a tourist menu priced at €18. Also on the piazza is the *Pizzeria La Ruota* (☎0963.532.427, closed Wed) where pizzas cost between €3.50 and €7 – try the house speciality, La Ruota, with local tuna, olives and peppers. Alternatively, walk down to the port area for a range of seafood restaurants, one of them, *La Nave* (☎0963.532.211; closed Wed), in the form of a ship. Between April and July sample the **tuna** or **swordfish**, for which Pizzo is a fishing centre. Make sure you also try the famous local **ice cream**, *tartufo di Pizzo* – a portion is a bit like eating a whole box of chocolate truffles.

Tropea and around

Southwest of Pizzo, **TROPEA** can claim to be the prettiest town on the whole of the southern Tyrrhenian coast, built right on the edge of steep cliffs, towering high over its beach. It is also (after Maratea) the most fashionable, with a seaside charm missing from many of the other Calabrian resorts, and not yet entirely eroded by the annual influx of tourists. There are numerous beaches around the town, all within easy walking distance of the town centre, and the buildings have character without being twee – see particularly the lovely Norman **cathedral** at the bottom of Via Roma, whose interior harbours a couple of unexploded American bombs from the last war (one accompanied by a grateful prayer to the Madonna), a Renaissance ciborium and a statue of the Madonna and Child from the same period. The central apse also has a much-venerated fourteenth-century icon of the Virgin Maria of Romania. The views from the upper town over the sea and the church of **Santa Maria dell'Isola** on its rock (closed for restoration) are superb, and on a clear day you can see the cone of Strómboli and sometimes other Aeolian Islands looming on the horizon.

Practicalities

The Pro Loco **tourist office** is in Piazza Ercole (daily 9am–1pm & 4.30–7pm; ☎0963.61.475). Check out ⓦwww.tropea.biz for a full accommodation list

△ Tropea's coastline road

and lots of background information about the local area. For **Internet** access there's *Quellila della Bottega Artigiana*, in the historic centre on Largo Ruffa 5 (Mon–Sat 10am–1pm & 5–10pm, Sun 5–10pm).

Accommodation

In August it is vital to book **accommodation** ahead; Tropea is the best-known resort on the Calabrian coast and consequently expensive, too. *Virgilio*, on Viale Tondo (℡0963.61.978, Ⓦwww.hotel-virgilio.com; ❷), is a blandly furnished but welcoming family-run three-star that requires half or full board in high season. You may do better to rent an apartment – the *Gurnella* (℡0963.61.427, Ⓦwww.gurnella.it), just outside the centre, has several clean and modern apartments with lovely views over the town and out to sea. Prices start at €240 a week for a two-room apartment in mid-season; in high season expect to pay around €400. Otherwise, there are two **campsites** right on the beach in the centre of town: *Camping Marina dell'Isola* on Via Marina dell'Isola (℡0963.61.970, Ⓦwww.maregrande.it) and *Camping Marina del Convento* on Via Marina del Convento (℡0963.62.501, Ⓦwww.marinadelconvento.it).

Eating and nightlife

Tropea has more **trattorias** per square metre than any other town in Calabria, often with budget-priced tourist menus. **Nightlife**, meanwhile, is tranquil, with good wine bars and ice-cream parlours in which to while away the evening.

La Cantina del Principe Largo Galluppi 19 ℡0963.61.400. Typical, moderately priced Calabrese food in this beautifully converted cellar; mains from about €10, though prices rise for the month of August.
La Munizione Largo Duomo 12. *Enoteca* behind the cathedral, with a roof terrace boasting excellent views. It serves around 130 wines and cocktails from €5.
Le Volpi e L'Uva Via Pelliccia 2/4, signed off Corso Vittorio Emanuele. Around 300 wines and

good snacks, around the €5 mark, in an intimate *enoteca*.
Osteria del Pescatore Via del Monte. Excellent, good-value fish served up in a vaulted cellar around the corner from the cathedral; a big plate of *spaghetti alla tropeana* is around €4.50. Closed winter.
Vecchio Forno Via Caivano, off Corso Vittorio Emanuele III. The most historic place to eat in town, serving crisp, fresh pizza for around €4 – the smell of *peperoncino* is heavenly.

Capo Vaticano and Nicótera

Further around the promontory, **CAPO VATICANO** holds some of the area's most popular beaches, including **Grotticelle** and **Tonicello**, both spacious enough to allow you to get away from the bustle. Grotticelle has a **campsite** immediately above it, *Quattro Scoglie*, where you can rent self-contained **apartments** (℡0963.663.126; May–Oct). The nearest **hotel** to this beach, the *Grotticelle* (℡0963.663.157, Ⓦwww.grotticelle.it; half board obligatory in August; ❷), lies a few minutes' walk further up the road, but if you have transport it's worth phoning to see if the very special agriturismo *Donna Orsola* (℡0983.663.057; ❸) has reopened. If it has, you can expect a warm welcome, great food, and, for anyone interested, to be invited to share in the cooking. It's about 2km outside Tropea, on the edge of the hamlet of **Brivadi**, where there's a small Pro Loco tourist office on Via Vaisette (Mon–Fri 8.30am–12.30pm & 4–8pm, Sat & Sun 8.30am–12.30pm; ℡0983.663.119).

Beyond Capo Vaticano, the road teeters high above the sea before reaching **NICÓTERA**, 11km south, built in its present position by Robert Guiscard, "the Norman conqueror of southern Italy". The Castello Ruffo here contains a small **archeological museum** displaying finds from the area and a collection of folkloric items (both free), but keeps very irregular hours; you're most likely to find someone to let you in during the mornings. There's also a **cathedral**, with works by Antonello Gagini, and far-reaching views south over the **Piana**, Calabria's second plain of any size, mostly dedicated to olive cultivation. Directly below the town, Nicótera's marina has wide beaches with a couple of summer-only **campsites** at their southern end.

South to Reggio

The Mesima River marks the border of the province of Reggio di Calabria. The towns around here are mostly new and unattractive, partly owing to the fact that the area is one of the most seismically active in Italy – the epicentre of the notorious 1783 earthquake was at nearby Oppido. The small Tropea rail line connects with the main line at Rosarno, 18km beyond which is the bustling town of **Palmi**. Situated a little way above the town (take Via San Giorgio, close to the exit onto the SS18) is the excellent museum complex in **La Casa della Cultura Leonida Repaci** (Mon & Thurs 8am–1.45pm & 3–5.45pm, Tues, Wed & Fri 8am–1.45pm; €1.55; ☎0966.262.250), named after a local writer and artist. It incorporates an archeological section, holding pieces of pottery and various excavations from the sea bed; paintings including work by Tintoretto and Guercino; a gallery of modern art and sculpture; a section devoted to local composer Francesco Cilea; and Calabria's best collection of folklore items.

From Palmi the tall TV mast on Sicily's northern tip is already visible, but the best view of the Island and the Calabrian coast is some 5km down the road at **Monte Sant'Elia**, the first elevation of the Aspromonte massif. The spot is believed to have been named after St Elia Speleotes, who lived in these parts (in a cave, which can be visited on the road leading into Aspromonte from Melicucca) and whose body, when he died aged 94, proved unburnable by the Saracens. From this balcony, perched on cliffs that plunge vertically down to the sea, you can see the two volcanoes of Etna and Strómboli on a clear day; there's a **campsite** behind and a tourist village.

Heading south, looking out to sea, the proximity of Sicily becomes the dominant feature, and the stretch of the autostrada that dives down to the town of Villa San Giovanni can claim to be one of the most panoramic in Italy, burrowing high up through mountains with the Straits of Messina glittering below. Travelling by train or following the old coastal road, you skirt the so-called Costa Viola, passing through the small town of **Bagnara**, famous for its swordfish, and **SCILLA**, ancient Scylla, with a fine sandy **beach** and lots of action in the summer. This was the legendary location of a six-headed cave monster, one of two hazards to mariners mentioned in the **Odyssey**, the other being the whirlpool Charybdis, corresponding to the modern Cariddi located 6km away on the other side of the Strait. Crowning a hefty rock, a **castle** separates the main beach from the fishing village of Scilla to the north. The most popular **place to stay** in town is the *Pensione Le Sirene* (booking advisable in summer, ☎0965.754.121; ❶–❷): try to get one of the four front rooms facing the sea – the others are just mediocre. There are several good fish **restaurants** along the seafront, including *Il Pirata di U Bais* (☎0965.704.292; closed Wed), which does excellent *maccheroncini con pesce spada* (pasta with swordfish). There's also a fixed-price menu at €30.

From Scilla it's just 9km to **VILLA SAN GIOVANNI**, worth stopping at only as a point of embarkation for Sicily. The state-run FS **ferries** (☎892021, ⓦ www.trenitalia.it) leave from directly behind the train station about every thirty minutes and arrive at the train station in Messina in about forty minutes; if you're travelling by **car** it's more convenient to catch one of the private Caronte ferries, (☎800.627.414, ⓦwww.carontetourist.it), under the train tracks to the right of the station, which leave approximately every fifteen minutes and pull in closer to the entrance to the autostrada. Both companies charge around €1 for foot passengers and €21 for cars. If you're heading for Reggio, take a train or one of the hourly Salzone **buses** from outside the station.

Reggio di Calabria and around

As you approach **REGGIO DI CALABRIA**, the provincial capital, you travel through some of the most extreme landscapes in the South. Dilapidated villages lie stranded among mountains, which are themselves torn apart by wide *fiumare*, or riverbeds – empty or reduced to a trickle for most of the year, but swelling with the melting of the winter snows to destructive torrents. Reggio itself was one of the first ancient Greek settlements on the Italian mainland; today, it's Calabria's biggest town by some distance, with a population of over 180,000 – but also one that's been synonymous for years with urban decline and subject to violent earthquakes that have left little of historic value standing.

Reggio's grim suburbs, with their half-finished housing and potholed streets, are testament to its enduring and deep-seated social problems, specifically the stranglehold that the Calabrian Mafia, or **'ndrangheta**, continues to have on the town. Locally this phenomenon is referred to as the *piovra*, or octopus, whose tentacles penetrate all aspects of the city's life, although the bloody feuds between rival families over control of the drugs trade which have periodically convulsed the city seem to be on the decline. Although efforts to regenerate the city are evident wherever you look, there's little to detain you here.

The Town

The **Museo Nazionale** at the northern end of Corso Garibaldi (Tues–Sun 9am–7.30pm; €8) is Reggio's main draw. It holds the most important collection of archeological finds in Calabria, full of items dating from the Hellenic period, with examples from all the major Greek sites in Calabria, including the famous *pinakes* or carved tablets from the sanctuary of Persephone at Locri. The most renowned exhibits in the museum are the **Bronzi di Riace**: two bronze statues dragged out of the Ionian Sea in 1972 near the village of Riace. They are shapely examples of the highest period of Greek art (fifth century BC), attributed to Phidias or followers of his school, and especially prized because there are so few finds from this period in such a good state of repair. Around them are detailed explanations of the recovery and cleaning-up of the statues that preceded their tour around the country, when they caused a minor sensation. Now they seem almost forgotten in the well-lit basement they share with another prize exhibit – a philosopher's head from the fourth century BC. Upstairs, you can see examples of Byzantine and Renaissance art, including two works by Antonello da Messina.

The other must-see attraction in Reggio di Calabria is the **Piccolo Museo di San Paolo** at Via Reggio Campi 4 (Tues–Sat 9.30am–noon; free; ☎0965.892.426), an impressive private collection of religious art including some 160 Russian icons and a *St Michael* attributed to Antonello da Messina. A stroll along the **lungomare** seaside esplanade along the sandy beach rounds off a visit to Reggio, affording wonderful views of the Sicilian coastline and Mount Etna.

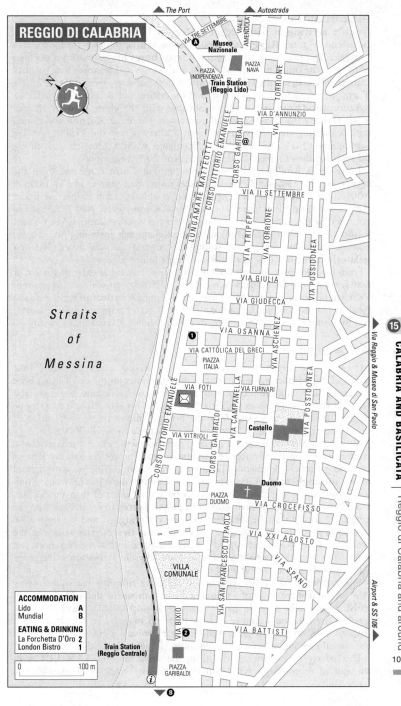

REGGIE DI CALABRIA

The Port ▲   ▲ Autostrada

VIA TRE SETTEMBRE
VIALE AMENDOLA
🅐 **Museo Nazionale**
PIAZZA NAVA
PIAZZA INDIPENDENZA
Train Station (Reggio Lido)
VIA D'ANNUNZIO

CORSO VITTORIO EMANUELE
CORSO GARIBALDI
VIA TORRIONE
@

VIA II SETTEMBRE

LUNGAMARE MATTEOTTI

VIA TRIPEPI
VIA TORRIONE
VIA POSSIDONEA

VIA GIULIA

VIA GIUDECCA

Straits

of

Messina

VIA OSANNA
VIA ASCHENEZ
❶
VIA CATTÓLICA DEL GRECI
PIAZZA ITALIA
VIA FOTI
VIA FURNARI
✉
VIA CAMPANELLA
CORSO VITTORIO EMANUELE
CORSO GARIBALDI
Castello
VIA POSSIDONEA
VIA VITRIOLI

Duomo ✝
PIAZZA DUOMO
VIA CROCEFISSO

VIA XXI AGOSTO

VIA SPANO

VILLA COMUNALE

VIA SAN FRANCESCO DI PAOLA
VIA BIXIO
❷
VIA BATTISTI

Train Station (Reggio Centrale)

PIAZZA GARIBALDI
ℹ
▼🅑

ACCOMMODATION
Lido **A**
Mundial **B**

EATING & DRINKING
La Forchetta D'Oro **2**
London Bistro **1**

0   100 m

Practicalities

If you're **arriving** by train, get off at **Reggio Lido** for the port or museum. Buses end up at the **Reggio Centrale** station, 1km or so down the long Corso Garibaldi. You may want to make use of **city buses** for getting from one end of town to the other; tickets cost €0.80 from kiosks and *tabacchi*. There's a small **tourist office** inside the Centrale station (Mon–Sat 8am–8pm; ℡0965.27.120). There are several Internet points around the station and along Via Garibaldi.

Accommodation options are reasonable with the clean, modern *Mundial* at Via Gaeta 9 (℡0965.332.255, ℮carmeloce@virgilio.it; ❷), near the central station, offering the best value in town. Otherwise try the *Lido* at Via Tre Settembre 6 (℡0965.25.001, ⓦwww.hotellidorc.it; ❸), a three-star with cheerful rooms at the other end of the Corso, near the Lido station.

There are a handful of **eating** places around Corso Garibaldi, from the very good *La Forchetta D'Oro* near the main train station at Via Bixio 5 (℡0965.896.048; closed Wed), where you could eat a fish dinner for under €25 a head, or meat dishes such as *maccheroncini* with spicy local *salsiccia* (sausage), to the *London Bistro* some way further up the Corso at Via Osanna 9 (℡0965.892.908; closed Mon) with its excellent fish, including *fiori di zucca e scampi* (courgette flowers and scampi) for around the same price. The best **gelateria** in town is *Cesare*, a kiosk on Piazza Indipendenza.

From Reggio's port you can reach Messina in fifteen minutes by *nave veloce*, or **fast ferry** (Mon–Sat 12 daily, Sun 6 daily; €1.50); by car you have to go from Villa San Giovanni (see p.1009). There are also regular **hydrofoil** services to the Aeolian Islands (summer up to 5 daily to each island; winter 1 daily; €17–31) run by Ústica Lines (℡0965.29568 or 346.011.6552, ⓦwww.usticalines.it).

Aspromonte

Most visitors to Reggio province leave without having ventured into the great massif of **Aspromonte**, the last spur of the Apennines on the tip of Italy's boot displaying an even more pronounced dialogue between mountain scenery and seascape than elsewhere in Calabria. You can be on a beach and a ski slope within the same hour, passing from the brilliant, almost tropical vegetation of the coast to dense forests of beech and pine that rise to nearly 2000m.

Although it recently became a national park (ⓦwww.parks.it/parco.nazionale .aspromonte), the thickly forested mountain has not yet shown any sign of becoming a tourist destination. There's a good reason for that: it's a stronghold of the '**ndrangheta**, the Calabrian mafia, and as such most Italians would think you insane for going there. Thought to be more powerful than the Sicilian Cosa Nostra, the *'ndrangheta* is known to produce drugs in enclaves around the range. On top of this, the area remains virtually unsigned, and the oppressive tree cover rarely breaks to provide views. If you're in a car take notice of the *Strada Interotta* ("Road interrupted") signs that you'll find at the entrances: you should not even think about attempting the rocky dirt tracks across the range unless you are driving an off-road vehicle.

Aspromonte's best-known attraction is the large **fair** that takes place every year on the first two days of September at the **Santuario della Madonna di Polsi**, a 10km hike from the park entrance – an unashamedly pagan event that involves the sale and slaughter of large numbers of goats. Its popularity has a darker side, however: the fair is well known to provide a convenient cover for the annual meeting of *'ndrangheta* cells from all over the world.

The *'ndrangheta* network is run from the small town of **SAN LUCA** to the east of Aspromonte, with iron bars over the windows of tumbledown cottages speaking volumes about the conditions of life in the area. Former *mafiosi* have revealed that houses in the town have a series of connecting doors and tunnels between them that allow people to move around without ever emerging into the open air. The triangle of land between the villages of San Luca, Plati and Cimina is a favourite area for holding kidnap victims, often for months at a time, and is periodically – usually following accusations of apathy on the part of the government – a target for army operations to root out the hiding places.

If the walking and hiking still draws you, will find access to the Aspromonte range is easiest from the Tyrrhenian side, with several buses a day leaving Reggio's Piazza Garibaldi for Gambarie and winding their way up the highly scenic SS184 from Gallico, through profusely terraced groves of vine and citrus to the village of **SANTO STEFANO**, famous as the birthplace and final resting place of the last of the great brigands who roamed these parts, **Giuseppe Musolino** (1875–1956). Occupying a sort of Robin Hood role in the popular imagination, Musolino was a legend in his own lifetime, the last thirty years of which he spent in jail and, finally, a lunatic asylum – the penalty for having led the *Carabinieri* on a long and humiliating dance up and down the slopes of Aspromonte during his profitable career. Just above the village, in the cemetery, you can see Musolino's grave, now renovated but until recently daubed with the signatures of people come to pay their respects.

The south coast

The **coastal route** along Italy's toe-tip also offers some interesting excursions into the mountainous area inland from Aspromonte. Road and rail lines running south out of Reggio pass through a series of small nondescript towns adorned by a profusion of cactus, agave, banana trees and date palms, and surrounded by the extensive plantations of citrus that are a feature of the Reggio area. Look out in particular for the **bergamot**, a fruit resembling a yellow orange, whose essence is used as a base for expensive perfumes and was one of the principal exports of this area until recently. Because of the precise conditions required for its cultivation, it's not found anywhere else in the world.

Campsites abound along this coast, attached to sandy beaches in varying states of cleanliness, and mostly open only in summer. Visible inland is the village of **PENTEDÁTTILO**, which owes its name to the Greek word for "five-fingered", on account of the curiously shaped rock on which it stands. Edward Lear, travelling through the area in 1848, thought it "perfectly magical", though its old Byzantine centre has largely been abandoned in favour of a new and ugly town just below.

You are now in the **Zona Grecanica**, named after the villages on these southern slopes of Aspromonte that were settled by Greeks more than two thousand years ago and still retain some traces of the Greek language in the local dialect. One such village is **BOVA**, perched on a crag 15km inland from its seaside satellite, Bova Marina. Bova is a remote place, with a view justifiably described by Lear as "truly magnificent", although the thick oak forests he saw then no longer exist. From the remains of the **castello** at the top, you can map out some alluring excursions into the wild country around: there are no hotels here but the countryside is one of the loveliest and most isolated parts of Aspromonte.

Potenza and around

Way up in the northwest of Basilicata, its regional capital, **POTENZA**, has suffered more than most southern towns from the effects of earthquake and war, which have robbed it of much of its historical heritage. However, there are three **train stations** and a bus terminal, and should you find yourself obliged to stop here for a connection, a trip to the town's only attraction, visiting the **Museo Archeologico Nazionale** (Mon 2–8pm, Tues–Sun 9am–8pm; €2.50), next to the cathedral, is a good enough way to pass the time; it is home to the region's most important collection of finds from the prehistory of Lucania (the Roman name for Basilicata), plus some well-preserved ceramics, terracottas and statuettes from Greek Metapontum.

North of Potenza lie several towns from the Norman era with some good examples of their brand of hybrid architecture. All are connected by bus with Potenza, and most are on the main Potenza–Fóggia rail line.

Melfi

North of Potenza on the SS93, on the far side of the imposing Monte Vulture (1326m), is the historic town of **MELFI**, long a centre of strategic importance, taken by the Normans in 1041 and their first capital in the south of Italy. It was in the formidable **castle** (Mon 2–8pm, Tues–Sun 9am–8pm; €2.50) at the top of the town that Pope Nicholas II formally recognized the conquests of Robert Guiscard over the Byzantines and Saracens, thereby legitimizing the piratical Normans and confirming their place in the embattled history of the south. It was here also that Guiscard imprisoned his first wife Aberada, and from where, in 1231, Frederick II issued his *Constitutiones Augustales*, reckoned to be the most comprehensive body of legislation promulgated since the time of Charlemagne. Repeatedly damaged by earthquakes, the castle now contains a **museum** (same hours as castle, entry included in castle ticket) housing prehistoric finds and objects from the Greek, Roman and Byzantine eras, including ceramics, jewellery and a candelabra carved with the goddess Ea abducting the manly looking infant Kephalos. A separate door from the courtyard gives access to the museum's most celebrated item, an exquisitely carved Roman sarcophagus from the second century, the so-called *sarcofago di Rapolla*, showing the image of the dead girl for whom it was made, reclining on cushions, with five statuettes of gods and heroes on the sides.

In the centre of town off Via Vittorio Emanuele is the **Duomo**, originally twelfth-century but rebuilt following earthquakes. After the 1930 quake, a Byzantine-style Madonna and Child fresco was brought to light, which you can see to the left of the altar; a chapel on the right also has a Madonna, in her role as protector of the city – a copy of the original statue stolen from here in 1982. The cathedral's campanile has miraculously survived the various cataclysms: the two black stone griffins symbolized the Norman hegemony in the region and are visible everywhere in Melfi, having been adopted as the town's emblem.

Melfi has a decent, very cheap **hotel**, the *Savoia* at Viale Savoia 21 (☎0972.23.710; ❶), though it's rather difficult to find: behind the cathedral turn right at Piazza IV Novembre, then left at Via Camassa, then left again onto Viale Savoia. You'll find a pleasant **restaurant-pizzeria** a little way down from the cathedral at Via Vittorio Emanuele 29, the ⚘ *Delle Rose* (☎0972.21.682; closed Thurs), with outdoor seating in summer. The *baccala alla trainera*, salt cod with sundried tomatoes, scorched garlic and fresh cherry tomatoes, is particularly delicious. This and other local specialities feature on a *degustazione* menu (€25), while for those on a tight budget there's a *menu turistica* (€13).

Venosa

If Melfi preserves the appearance of a dark medieval town, nearby **VENOSA** has an attractive airiness; a harmonious place, it is rich with historical associations. Known in antiquity as Venusia, it was in its time the largest colony in the Roman world, and much is made of the fact that it was the birthplace of Quintus Horatius Flaccus, known to Italians as Orazio and to English speakers as **Horace** (65–8 BC); his supposed house lies past the cathedral on the right. The town's chief attraction is the ruined **Abbazia della Trinità**, a complex of churches begun in the eleventh century that was the resting place of various Norman bigwigs including Robert Guiscard. Now in a state of partial ruin, part of it is accessible from the archeological park at the bottom of Corso Vittorio Emanuele (daily 9am till one hour before sunset; €2).

Matera and around

The interior of the **province of Matera** has a great deal in common with Potenza province – a wide, empty terrain that's run-down and depopulated. Its bare clay hills appear, in Carlo Levi's words, "a sea of white, monotonous and treeless", dotted with solitary villages that are cut off from each other and the rest of the world. Little to recommend for an action-packed tour, then, but plenty of the timeless atmosphere portrayed by film-makers like Rosi and Bertolucci.

Matera

The town of **MATERA** itself is unique, with a degree of culture and elegance unusual by southern standards and, in its **sassi** – dwellings dug out of the ravine in tiers – one of the country's oddest urban features.

During the 1950s and 1960s, fifteen thousand people were forcibly removed from the *sassi* and rehoused in modern districts on the outskirts of town. Since then the area has been officially cleaned up and is being gradually repopulated with homes, B&Bs and workshops, and in 1993 was made a World Heritage Site. Nowadays it's hard to picture the squalor that previously existed here: in Carlo Levi's 1945 memoir *Christ Stopped at Eboli*, the author's sister compared the *sassi* to Dante's *Inferno*, so horrified was she by their disease-ridden inhabitants. "Never before have I seen such a spectacle of misery," she said. The children had "the wrinkled faces of old men, emaciated by hunger, with hair crawling with lice and encrusted with scabs. Most of them had swollen bellies and faces yellowed and stricken with malaria." Pursuing her, they begged not for coins but for quinine.

Nonetheless, the *sassi* are still largely abandoned and form an eerie troglodyte enclave with little to show that the twenty-first century has arrived, a quality exploited by Mel Gibson when he used the area as a set for Jerusalem in *The Passion of Christ*. Recently, the *sassi* have begun to be restored, some of them as hotels and B&Bs, leaving Matera with the finest choice of accommodation in Basilicata.

Arrival and information

Matera's **train station** is on Piazza Matteotti and is served by the FAL line, linked to Altamura (in Puglia, for connections to Bari and Gravina) and to

Ferrandina (for connections to Metaponto or Potenza); **buses** also stop here. Trailing down from Piazza Matteotti, Via Roma has the town's **tourist office** – actually just off it at Via de Viti de Marco 9 (Mon & Thurs 9am–1pm & 4–6.30pm, Tues, Wed, Fri & Sat 9am–1pm; ⊤0835.331.983 and 335.254.658, ⓦwww.aptbasilicata.it). There is **Internet** access at PCInfoPoint on Via delle Beccherie, near the Banco di Napoli.

Accommodation

Apart from Maratea, Matera is the only place in Basilicata where you might have difficulty finding **a room** for the night – booking a week or so in advance is highly recommended. There are a lot of new B&Bs and some beautiful hotels recently opened in the *sassi* themselves, which are probably the most atmospheric places to stay – although of course the swish furniture, modern plumbing and decor would be unrecognizable to any former *sasso* dweller.

🏃 **Antica Locanda di San Martino** Via San Martino 22 ⊤0835.256.600, ⓦwww .locandadisanmartino.it. The loveliest hotel in town (since opening in 2004) is a conversion of *sassi* including a former carpenter's workshop and a deconsecrated chapel. The rooms are beautifully furnished, fragrant and cool. ❸

🏃 **Capriotti** Via Gradoni Due Uomo ⊤0835.333.997, ⓦwww.capriotti-bed -breakfast.it. Three tastefully decorated, light-flooded rooms, each with its private entrance and own outdoor space, in the vaulted rooms of a restored sixteenth-century *sasso* close to the duomo. ❷

🏃 **Casa d'Imperio** Via d'Addozio 39 ⊤0835.330.503, ⓦwww.casadimperio.it. This B&B is in a beautifully refurbished sixteenth-century house and a bargain at the price. ❷

🏃 **Casa di Lucio** Via S Pietro Caveoso 66 ⊤0835.312.798, ⓦwww.lacasadilucio.it. A picturesque residence and B&B in a sixteenth-century house in the *sassi*, near the Madonna de Idris. The owners also run a good restaurant (see p.1018). ❹

Italia Via Ridola ⊤0835.333.561, ⓦwww .albergoitalia,com. Matera's most expensive hotel, where Mel Gibson and his cast stayed, and the best option if you don't fancy sleeping in a cave. ❸

Sassi Via San Giovanni Vecchio 89 ⊤0835.331.009, ⓦwww.hotelsassi.it. The first hotel to open in the *sassi*, this place, in the heart of the Sasso Barisano district, has rooms gouged out of the tufa and affording marvellous views. It also has an unofficial hostel with beds at €16 a night or €20 with breakfast. ❸

The Town

Most visitors to Matera head straight for the atmospheric *sassi* area and understandably so, but the old town is worthy of exploration, too, with a host of churches and a livelier feel.

The sassi

Divided into two sections – the Sasso Caveoso and Sasso Barisano – the **sassi** district can be entered from a number of different points around the centre of town, some signposted, some not. A word of warning: while there's a main street that weaves through both zones and is a useful reference point, you will need to leave this to penetrate the warren and its *chiese rupestri* or **rock-hewn churches**; there's no sun cover, flights of steps are unavoidable, and you'd do well to take some water. To get the most out of the whole area equip yourself with an *itinerario turistico* and a map, both available from the tourist office. Better still, for a commentary and access to parts of the *sassi* you might otherwise miss on your own, you can join a guided **tour** – the 🏃 *Nuovi Amici dei Sassi*, at Piazza Sedile 20 (⊤0835.331.011), charges around €10 per person for groups of four or more in Italian, and around €15 per person in English; alternatively, negotiate with one of the guides direct through contacts on ⓦwww.aptbasilicata.it.

The most spectacular church, **Madonna de Idris** (all *chiese rupestri* open daily: April–Oct 9.30am–1.30pm & 3–7pm; Nov–March 9.30am–1.30pm & 2.30–4.30pm; €2.50 each or €6 for all), perched on the conical Monte Errone that rises in the midst of the *sassi*, has frescoes dating from the fourteenth century. Another, the tenth-century **Santa Lucia alle Malve** in the so-called Albanian quarter (settled by refugees in the fifteenth century), has Byzantine-style frescoes dating from 1250. But possibly the most interesting interior is the **Convincinio S. Antonio**, further up from Santa Lucia. This complex of four interlinking thirteenth-century churches was turned into wine cellars in 1700 – look for the spouts for red and white wine emerging from what appears to be an altar – and later into houses. Of particular interest are tombs in the floor converted into water tanks that demonstrate considerable ingenuity: the porous stone had to be waterproofed, and rainwater channelled into the tanks.

Other churches have a more orthodox appearance but are worth a visit; **San Pietro Caveoso**, for example, at the centre of the Caveoso district (Santa Lucia alle Malve lies behind it), is rather over-zealously restored but has a fine wooden ceiling and frescoes.

For a fascinating glimpse of what life was like for the *sassi*-dwellers, head for the **Casa Grotta**, just below Madonna de Idris (daily 9am–1pm & 3–7pm; €2). Reconstructed inside a *sasso* with the help of the family who lived here until the 1950s and using original furniture, utensils and clothes, it gives an insight into how families with several children and livestock managed to live together in one-room cave dwellings. If you want to explore the **caves** and more *chiese rupestri* on the far side of the ravine, you can cross the river further up towards the Sasso Barisano, an excursion that will take up to an hour if you don't stray off the track.

The old town

The centre of the old town of Matera is **Piazza Vittorio Veneto**, a large and stately square which in the evening is cleared of traffic and given over to a long procession of shuffling promenaders. The *materani* take their evening *passeggiata* seriously, and the din of the crowds rising up out of this square can be like the noise from a stadium. Matera's modern quarters stretch out to the north and west of here, but most of the things worth seeing are along the Via San Biagio and Via del Corso.

Winding off from the bottom end of the piazza, the narrow Via del Corso leads down to the seventeenth-century church of **San Francesco d'Assisi**, whose ornate Baroque style was superimposed on two older churches, traces of which, including some eleventh-century frescoes, can be visited through a passage in the third chapel on the left. In the main church are eight panels of a polyptych by Bartolomeo Vivarini, set above the altar. From San Francesco, you can cut across neighbouring Piazza Sedile onto Via Duomo – a good place to view the sprawling *sassi* below. Further on, the **Duomo**, which effectively divides this area into two, was built in the late thirteenth century and retains a strong Apulian-Romanesque flavour. Between the figures of Peter and Paul on the facade is a sculpture of the patron of Matera, Madonna della Bruna. Her feast day, the Sagra di Santa Bruna, is celebrated on July 2, when her statue is carried in procession three times round the piazza before being stormed by the onlookers, who are allowed to break up the papier-mâché float and carry off bits as mementos. At the back of the building you can see a recently recovered fresco from 1270 showing scenes from the Last Judgement.

From Piazza San Francesco, continue down into Via Ridola to admire the elliptical facade of the **Chiesa del Purgatorio**, gruesomely decorated with skulls.

Eating and drinking

Thanks to the surge in tourism, there's plenty of choice for **eating** in Matera. You'll find lots of cafés and bars around Piazzetta S Pietro Caveoso and in the streets of the *sassi*.

Casa di Lucio Via S Pietro Caveoso 66 ☎0835.312.The owners of this B&B also run a good restaurant, serving only local dishes. Try *cavatelli con pepperoni cruschi* (home-made pasta with sundried peppers) or *maltagliati con cicerchi* (home-made pasta with an ancient and rare variety of chickpea). Meals from around €35 a head.

Il Castell In the remains of an Angevin castle above Via Lucana ☎0835.33.375. Pizzeria with outside tables in summer. Closed Sat.

Il Terrazzino Vico San Giuseppe 7 ☎0835.333.752. Enjoy the view over the *sassi* at this atmospheric spot. Try the oven-baked

orecchiette with local sausage, tomatoes and mozzarella, or *pignata*, a dish of oven-roasted lamb with vegetables and cheese. There's a tourist menu priced at €14; eating à la carte should cost €20–25. Closed Tues.

Trattoria Lucana Via Lucana 48 ☎0835.336.117. A good family-run place with great vegetable antipasti and typical lucana dishes such as pasta with fresh tomatoes, mushrooms, sausage and rocket, lasagna with aubergine and grilled lamb. Expect to pay between €25 and €40 per head, depending on what you choose. Closed Sun in winter.

Around Matera

Twenty kilometres southeast of Matera and served by buses from the town, the hilltop village of **MONTESCAGLIOSO** was once a Greek settlement and is now the site of a magnificent ruined eleventh-century Benedictine abbey (closed for restoration, call Matera tourist office on ☎0835.331.983 or 335.254.658 for information on reopening). There are good views from here over the Bradano Valley. Also reached by a fifteen-minute bus journey from Matera is the lively medieval town of **MIGLIÓNICO**, with a finely preserved fifteenth-century bastion at one end, and views all around. It was here in 1481 that the *congiura dei baroni* was held, a meeting of rebellious barons who formed a league in opposition to Ferdinand II of Aragon, from which the castle assumed the name *Castello del Malconsiglio* ("bad counsel").

The northern Ionian coast

From Táranto to Reggio at Italy's toe-tip, the **Ionian coast** is a mainly flat sandy strip, sometimes monotonous but less developed than the Tyrrhenian side of the peninsula, and with cleaner water. The **northern** section, from **Metaponto** to **Capo Colonna**, consists of a mountainous interior backing onto an empty seaboard, punctuated only by holiday resorts, a plethora of campsites – overflowing in the summer months with legions of Italians – and some notable historical sites. Of these, the most significant are connected with the periods of Greek occupation, the most recent of which was that of the Byzantines, who administered the area on and off for five hundred years, leaving their traces most strikingly in the hilltop town of **Rossano**. A thousand years earlier, the clutch of Greek colonies collectively known as **Magna Graecia** rose and fell, of which Metapontum, Sybaris and Kroton, all on this stretch of the Ionian coast, were some of the greatest. Although only the first of these has been properly excavated, there are museums in all, describing an era that was – culturally and intellectually – the brightest moment in the history of Basilicata and Calabria. All the coastal towns are well connected by rail and bus, while places inland are linked by local buses from the coast. The SS106 road, which skirts this coastline, is mostly straight and fast.

The Basilicata coast

The most extensively excavated of the Greek sites, and the only place of any real significance on the Ionian coast of Basilicata, is at **METAPONTO**, an important road and rail junction connecting the coastal routes between Táranto and Reggio with the interior of Basilicata – to Potenza by train and Matera by bus. Metapontum was settled in the eighth century BC and owed its subsequent prosperity to the fertility of the surrounding land – perfect for cereal production (symbolized by the ear of corn stamped on its coinage) and its position as a commercial centre. Pythagoras, banished from Kroton, established a school here in about 510 BC that contributed to an enduring philosophical tradition. The city's downfall came as a result of a series of catastrophes: absorbed by Rome, embroiled in the Punic Wars, sacked by the slave-rebel Spartacus, and later desolated by a combination of malaria and Saracen raids.

Lido di Metaponto and the Zona Archeologica

Metaponto today is a straggling, amorphous place, comprising train station, museum and ruins. Arriving at the station, you're 3km from the **LIDO DI METAPONTO**, where there are sandy, well-equipped **beaches**, numerous **campsites** and a handful of hotels. Of the campsites, the *Camping Internazionale* on Viale Magna Grecia (℡0835.741.916, ⓦwww.villageinternazionale .com) is clean and well equipped, very near the beach, and has bungalows as well as places for tents and campers. The best-value **hotel** *Kennedy,* at Via Jonio 1, about 1km from the station, off the Lido road (℡0835.741.960, ⓦwww .hotelresidencekennedy.it; ❸). It has some apartments as well as rooms, and may be half-board-only in high season.

For the first batch of ruins, head towards the Lido from the train station, take the next turning on the right after the Lido junction and follow the narrow lane down to the site signposted **Zona Archeologica**, which has the remains of a theatre and a Temple of Apollo Licius. The latter is a sixth-century BC construction that once possessed 32 columns, but you need some imagination to picture its original appearance. In a better state of preservation is the **Temple of Hera**, or Tavole Palatine, 2–3km north, where the main SS106 crosses the River Bradano (take one of the buses to Táranto from Metaponto station and ask to be dropped off at the site). With fifteen of its columns remaining, it is the most suggestive remnant of this once mighty state. A selection of other exhibits can be seen at the **Museo Archeologico Nazionale** (Mon 2–8pm, Tues–Sun 9am–8pm; €2.50; ℡0835.745.327), 2km outside town, accessible by bus from the train station. The exhibits are mainly fifth- and fourth-century statuary, ceramics and jewellery, and there's a fascinating section on the new insights revealed by the study of fingerprints on shards found in the artisans' quarter.

Policoro

There's a similar collection of antiquities at the **Museo Nazionale della Siritide**, 25km down the coast, just behind the village of **POLICORO**. The museum (Wed–Mon 9am–8pm, Tues 2–8pm; €2.50; ℡0835.972.154) contains clay figurines and jewel-bedecked skeletons among other material taken from the zone between the Sinni and Agri rivers, in its time one of the richest areas on this coast and site of the two Greek colonies of **Siris** and **Heraclea**. The first of these, after which the museum is named, reached such a position of wealth and eminence that the other colonies were persuaded to gang together in the middle of the sixth century BC to put an end to Sirian ambitions. Heraclea was founded on the same spot by Tarentines in 432 BC with the aim of driving a wedge between the Achaean cities of Metapontum and Sybaris to the north and south. It was here that Pyrrhus, king of Epirus, first introduced elephants to the Romans, and, although winning the first of two battles in 280 BC, suffered such high losses that he declared another such victory would cost him the war – so bequeathing to posterity the term "Pyrrhic victory".

Into Calabria

Shortly after crossing the Sinni River you enter Calabria and the mountainous slopes soon give way to the wide **Piana di Sibari**, the most extensive of the Calabrian coastal plains, bounded by Pollino to the north, the Sila Greca to the west and the Sila Grande in the south. The rivers flowing off these mountains, which for centuries kept the land well watered and rich, also helped to transform it into a stagnant and malarial mire, and although land reclamation has restored the area's fertility, without visiting the museum and excavations at **Sibari** you could pass through the area with no inkling of the civilization that once flourished on these shores. Southeast of here, two monastery complexes and **Crotone**, another ancient Greek city, provide a trio of points of interest as you travel along the coastline.

Sybaris

Long one of the great archeological mysteries tantalizing generations of scholars, the site of ancient **SYBARIS** was only definitely identified in the late 1960s, when aerial and X-ray photography confirmed that the site previously known to be that of Roman Thurium was also that of Sybaris. There are in fact three separate levels of construction that have been unearthed here, one Greek and two Roman, one on top of the other. Together these make up one of the world's largest archeological sites, covering 1000 hectares (compared with Pompeii's 50), though only 10 hectares have so far been dug up, and the great riches that the excavations were expected to yield have not yet come to light; there have been too many other settlements on this same spot, not to mention the marauders who regularly passed through the area.

The wealth of the city – said to number 100,000 in population and have dominion over half a million – was only one factor in its fame, around which myth and documentary evidence have combined to produce a colourful muddle of anecdotes. The city's laws and institutions were apparently made to ensure the greatest comfort and well-being of its citizens, including the banning from the city of all noisy traders, such as metalworkers, and the planting of trees along every street for shade. Cooks were so highly prized that they were apparently bought and sold in the marketplace for great sums and were allowed to patent their recipes, while inventions ascribed to the Sybarites include pasta and the chamberpot. This was all too much for the Crotonians, who, under their general Milo (more famous as a much-garlanded Olympic athlete) destroyed the city in 510 BC, diverting the waters of the river over the site to complete the job.

The **excavations** lie across the rail lines, some 4km south down the SS106, on the right-hand side (daily 9am–6.30pm, closing earlier in winter; free; ⓣ0981.79.166). Most of them belong to the Roman period, but something of the earlier site might still be turned up – the silt and sand of the river bed have yet to be explored properly, work having been effectively halted for much of the last twenty years owing to shortage of funds. Of the Roman city, the remains are at least impressively displayed and maintained, including baths, a patrician's house with mosaics, and a *decumanus* – main street – claimed to be the widest in existence. Just off the site, a small room contains individual finds including some Greek exhibits, mainly ceramic shards, though nothing that would have raised much excitement in the numerous enthusiasts who long sought this spot. There's more to be seen, from here and other local sites, at the **Museo della Sibarite** (Tues–Sun 9am–7pm; €2; ☎0981.79.391), down a left-turn about 1km before the excavations, on the banks of the River Crati.

Monastery of Pathirion and Rossano

There are remnants from more recent times further south, near the village of **SANTA MARIA DEL PATIRE**, where the twelfth-century **Monastery of Pathirion** sits among groves of olive and holm oak at the end of a road built by Austrian prisoners during World War I. Its well-preserved church – a simple basilica – has sweeping views over the Sibari plain and the mountains around, but is the only intact relic of the monastery, which lies in ruins below – an extensive complex that had its centre at nearby Rossano and rivaled the holy mountain of Athos in Greece as a centre of monastic learning.

Twelve kilometres away, the resort of **ROSSANO SCALO** has far outstripped its parent-town of **ROSSANO** in terms of size and bustle, and most of the holiday-makers who frequent its beaches never even get round to visiting the hilltop town, 7km up an awkward winding road – something that has helped to preserve the old centre from excessive development. The foremost Byzantine centre in the south, Rossano was the focus of a veritable renaissance of literature, theology and art between the eighth and eleventh centuries, a period to which the town's greatest treasures belong. Its majolica-tiled **Cattedrale** is an Angevin construction largely rebuilt after an 1836 earthquake, but it does have a much-venerated ninth-century Byzantine fresco, *Madonna Achiropita*, whose Greek epithet, meaning "not painted by hand", refers to its divine authorship. The over-decorated interior boasts a wooden ceiling and a mosaic floor near the altar, though most of the artworks here suffer from neglect. Next to the cathedral, the **Museo Diocesano** (summer daily 9am–1pm and 4.30–8.30pm; winter Tues–Sun 9.30am–12.30pm & 4–7pm; €2.50) contains the famed **codex purpureus Rossanensis**, or Purple Codex, a unique sixth-century manuscript on reddish-purple parchment illustrating the life of Christ. The book, which was brought from Palestine by monks fleeing the Muslim invasions, is open at one page, but you can leaf through a good copy and see, among other things, how the Last Supper was originally depicted, with Christ and his disciples not seated but reclining on cushions round the table, and all eating from the same plate. Other items in this tiny museum include a fifteenth-century icon painted on both sides and formerly at Pathirion, and several pieces of silverware of superb artistry.

In contrast to the cathedral's grandiosity, the diminutive church of **San Marco**, at the end of Corso Garibaldi on the edge of town, retains a primitive spirituality. The five cupolas of the tenth- or eleventh-century construction, surrounded by palms on a terrace that looks out over the gorge below, impart an almost Middle Eastern flavour. The stark white interior is enlivened only by six frail columns and two Byzantine frescoes. To visit, ask at the Cooperativa Neilos at Piazza Duomo 25 (☎0983.525.263). They are also equipped to supply **information** on the area.

Practicalities

Hotels are all in the modern lower town and most are neither especially cheap nor lovely. *Murano* on Lido Sant'Angelo (☎0983.511.788, ⓦwww.hotelmurano .it; ❸) is an attractive modern exception, with great sea views and a maritime

CALABRIA AND BASILICATA | The northern Ionian coast

feel, while *Scigliano* (☎0983.511.846, ⊛www.hotelscigliano.it; ➌), 50m up from the level crossing from Lido Sant'Angelo, is a family-run place with an award-winning restaurant. For **camping**, *Campeggio Torino* (☎0983.565.684) is 1km north of Rossano Scalo and has chalets for rent (➊).

Up in the old town, just off Piazza Anargiri in Via San Bartolomeo, you'll find the best **trattoria**, 🍴 *La Villa*, with alfresco eating in summer (☎0983.522.214; evenings only, closed Tues). It serves typical calabrese food, with lots of local sausage and tomatoes; prices range from about €15 to €30 a head. There's another, slightly cheaper, more casual evenings-only place, *La Bizantina* (☎0983.525.340), right outside San Marco, which has great antipasti (try *peperoni e patate*, roast red peppers and potatoes); alternatively, go to *Le Arcate* near the cathedral (☎0983.520.321; closed Mon) which does typical and inexpensive local fare such as handmade *orecchiette* with *gamberetti e porcini* (prawns and ceps) as well as pizzas in the evening.

Crotone and around

South of Rossano lies an empty stretch of beaches, with, inland, the vineyards of Cirò, the source of Calabria's best-known **wine**. Crossing the River Neto into the fertile **Marchesato** region, you'll have your approach to **Crotone** (the ancient Greek city of Kroton) blighted by a smoky industrial zone – not the most alluring entry into a city, but a rare thing in Calabria, and a reminder of the false hopes once vested in the industrialization of the region.

Crotone

The site of ancient **Kroton** has been entirely lost, but in its day this was among the most important colonial settlements of Magna Graecia, overshadowed by its more powerful neighbour Sybaris, but with a school of medicine that was famous throughout the classical world and closely linked with the prowess of the city's athletes, who regularly scooped all the honours at the Olympic Games back in Greece. In 530 BC the mathematician and metaphysician Pythagoras took up residence in Kroton and established an aristocratic party based on his ideas which eventually gained control, though the political turmoil that resulted

△ Olive groves in Calabria

from the sack of Sybaris led to their banishment from the city. Kroton went on to be the first of the Greek cities in Calabria but was increasingly destabilized by internal conflicts and the external threat of the encroaching tribes, eventually being destroyed by the Romans. A resurgence of sorts occurred in the thirteenth century when it was made the main town of the Marchesato region, a vast feudal domain extending from the Neto to the Simeri rivers, held by the powerful Ruffo family of Catanzaro. But its prosperity was always hindered by the scourge of malaria, which poisoned every initiative and debilitated its people, provoking the author George Gissing – himself a victim of malaria during his visit in 1897 – to condemn Crotone as "a squalid little town".

In recent times Crotone has been mired in drugs and crime, though since its elevation to provincial capital in 1995, the city council has worked to revitalize the town, giving it a proud new face with a sparkling new seafront and archeological museum to attract the tourists. The old centre retains an agreeable, unspoiled character, and the town makes a good base for the **beaches** that spread to the south and for the Greek ruins at Capo Colonna. The town's new **Museo Archeologico Nazionale** (Tues–Sun 9am–7.30pm; €2; ☎0982.23.082) on Via Risorgimento in the historic centre holds the best collection of finds from Magna Graecia on the Ionian coast. Alongside fragments from the excavations at Crotone and its various colonies, lists of the Olympic winners who hailed from the city, and maps of the digs (the most important one is right next to the main industrial complex), the cool and airy rooms display an array of items from Capo Colonna. Most noteworthy of these is the so-called **Treasure of Hera**, a beautifully restored group of bronze statuettes – including a sphinx, a gorgon, a horse, a winged siren and a very rare nuraghic boat from Sardinia – found in a tomb at Capo Colonna in 1987, and dating from the seventh to the fifth centuries BC. The most dazzling item is a gold diadem, expertly worked with garlands of leaves and sprigs of myrtle.

Practicalities

Arriving by **train** you may want to take a taxi or bus to cover the 1.5km to the centre of town, Piazza Pitagora, and most of the hotels. There's a **tourist office** at Via Torino 148, obscurely sited halfway between the station and the old town (Mon & Wed 9am–1pm & 3–5pm, Tues, Thurs & Fri 7.30am–1pm; ☎0962.23.185). The **bus** station is on Via Ruffo, a couple of streets east of Piazza Pitagora, where most provincial and regional buses arrive.

Nearby, the rather cramped *Pace*, Via Cutro 56 (☎0962.22.584; ❶), is central Crotone's cheapest **accommodation** choice. Better are the *Concordia* on Piazza Vittoria, just off Corso Vittorio Emanuele (☎0962.23.910; ❸), whose dingy entrance hall belies this eighteenth-century building's attractive rooms, and – for a bit of luxury – *Residence Casarossa*, Via per Capocolonna (☎0962.934.201, ⓦwww.casarossa.it; ❸), which boasts a private beach and all mod cons.

As for **eating**, Crotone is one of the best places in the region to eat fish, being blessed with some of the least over-fished waters in the Mediterranean and a couple of talented chefs. Head for the excellent ⅍ *Da Ercole* (☎0962.901.425, closed Sun) along the seafront at Viale Gramsci 122, owned by chef Ercole Villirillo, who runs cookery classes all over the world. It's one of the few places anywhere that you can sample such dishes as *linguine a pitagora* (which feature *prine*, a kind of sea anemone) or *ricciola* with wild artichokes (*ricciola con carciofi selvatici*) – a meal here will probably weigh in at about €50. Also on the seafront on Via Corrado Alvaro Palazzo, highly rated ⅍ *Sosta da Marcello* (☎0962.902.243) is blessed with another chef who creates seasonal dishes depending on the ingredients of the day. Both places are closed on Sundays, but in winter *Sosta da Marcello* opens for Sunday lunch. In the centre, *Caffè Italia* on Piazza Vittoria is one of Crotone's most historic cafés, good for a refreshing *latte di mandorla* (almond milk) or the local speciality of rose-shaped pastries.

Inland to Santa Severina

From Crotone's bus office on Via Ruffo there are a couple of departures daily to **SANTA SEVERINA**, on the eastern fringes of the Sila Piccola. A Byzantine fortified town built on a hilltop, it's well worth a detour, principally for the Norman castle that dominates it. Rebuilt by Robert Guiscard on the ruins of a Byzantine stronghold and remodelled by the Swabians and Angevins, the renovated castle holds a first-rate **museum** (Tues–Sun 9am–1pm & 3–7pm; €5 including entrance to Museo Diocesano), taking in all parts of the construction from the foundations to the first-floor rooms. Exhibits include Byzantine artefacts, sundry arms and artillery, and a scale model of the castle, as well as an informative overview of military architecture in Calabria and temporary exhibitions upstairs. From the stout battlemented walls long views extend over the hilly surroundings towards the mountains of the Sila, and nearer at hand over the elongated square of the old town. On the other side of the piazza, whose flagstones are studded with symbols of the zodiac, the **Duomo** lies adjacent to an eighth-century Byzantine **baptistry** (ask the cathedral's nuns to open it for you) which preserves traces of frescoes of the saints, Greek inscriptions on the capitals and its original font. On the other side of the duomo, the **Museo Diocesano** also repays a visit (Tues–Sun 9am–1pm & 3–7pm; €5 including entrance to Castello), containing a painfully graphic fifteenth-century Christ on the cross, an early printed edition of the Bible, and – its greatest treasure – the *Spilla Angioina*, a brooch from about 1300, studded with gold, pearls and rubies. The bars in the square serve snacks, and if you're looking for a full **meal** in Santa Severina, try the *Locanda del Re* (☎0962.51.662) on the steps below the castle which, thanks to serving as the mensa for the town police, is open every day. Food is rooted in the medieval traditions of the area, so expect handmade pasta, lots of wild mushroom, wild pig, ricotta and pecorino. The owners also have little **apartments to rent** (①) in a pretty old house in the *centro storico*.

A nice alternative, 3km outside town at Cerzeto off the SS107, is the ⚜ *Agriturismo Il Querceto* (☎0962.51.467 or 335.829.9370, ⊛www.agriturismoilquerceto .kr.it), a fifty-hectare organic farm which raises beef and grows citrus fruit and olives. They have rooms and apartments to rent, a swimming pool, and mountain bikes to hire. You can stay on a B&B basis (①) or half board (€40 per person).

Capo Colonna to Le Castella

Another worthwhile excursion from Crotone is to the famed column at **Capo Colonna** on Calabria's extreme eastern point, for which you have to drive or walk 11km along the coast. The column is a solitary remnant of a vast structure that served as the temple for all the Greeks in Calabria. Dedicated to Hera Lacinia, the temple originally possessed 48 of these Doric columns and was the repository of immense wealth before being repeatedly sacked as Magna Graecia and Hellenism itself declined.

There are some excellent **bathing spots** not far south of here. The so-called **ISOLA CAPO RIZZUTO** is a spit of land, not an island, with a choice of sandy or rocky inlets to swim from. During the winter the resort is dead, but it can get quite congested in the height of summer and difficult to find a place to stay. Nearby **LE CASTELLA** is another busy holiday spot, but not yet strangled by tourism. It would be hard to spoil the beautifully sited Aragonese **fortress**

(Tues–Sun 9am–7pm; €3) on an islet just off the main town. As the Golfo di Squillace's only anchorage for large ships, the site was fortified from the fourth century BC and was later held by the Aragonese and Angevins, sold in perpetuum to the Duke of Carafa for 9000 ducats in 1496, and, the target of repeated Turkish raids, was finally abandoned at the end of the eighteenth century. You could wander round the outside of the castle and swim off the rocks, though you'll probably be more tempted by the arc of beach to the south. If you're seduced into staying, you can't do better than *L'Aragonese* (☎0962.795.013; full board only in Aug; ❶), right opposite the castle, and with a restaurant below – ask for a sea-facing room.

The southern Ionian coast

The southern part of Calabria's Ionian seaboard is less developed than the rest of the region, perhaps because it's less interesting scenically and most of the seaside towns and villages strung along it are unappealing. If you like sandy **beaches**, though, this is where to find them – either wild and unpopulated or, if you prefer, glitzy and brochure-style, as at **Soverato**. At **Locri** there's the region's best collection of Greek ruins and, overlooking the coast a short way inland, the craggy medieval strongholds of **Squillace** and **Gerace**, and **Stilo**, with its jewel of Byzantine church-building, the **Cattolica**.

Catanzaro, La Roccelletta and Squillace

Despite its fine position, set high up in the foothills of the Sila and with good views out to sea, Calabria's regional capital, **CATANZARO**, has little innate charm. It's a crowded, overdeveloped, traffic-ridden city, within a short ride of some five-star beaches, but otherwise best avoided. There's more interest further on down the coast at the ruined basilica of Santa Maria della Roccella, or **La Roccelletta**, 100m down the road that branches off the SS106, signposted towards San Floro and Borgia. Half-hidden in an olive grove, this partly restored redbrick shell is all that remains of what was once the second-largest church in Calabria (after Gerace). Of uncertain date, though probably Norman in origin and founded by Basilian monks, it still has a mighty impact on the unsuspecting viewer. Much of the building material used in its construction came from the remains of the Roman town of Scolacium, the excavations of which can be seen in the **zona archeologica** (daily 9am till an hour before sunset; free) nestled among the olives behind the church. The best-preserved item here is a **theatre**, once able to hold some 3500 spectators, and thought to have been abandoned following a fire some time after 350 AD. Elsewhere on the site are the scant remains of baths, and an **antiquarium** displaying finds from the site – mainly statuary, pottery and coins.

Five kilometres further south along the coast, at Lido di Squillace, is the turn-off for the old town of **SQUILLACE**, 8km up in the hills, once an important centre but now just a mountain village, isolated on its high crag. There are lofty views to be enjoyed over the Gulf and beyond Catanzaro as far as the Sila Piccola, and the **Castle** (usually someone there Mon–Sat 9am–1pm, but if closed apply to the Comune on Piazza Municipio and they will give you access; ☎0961.912.306 or 0961.912.542) is one of the most romantic collections of ruins in Calabria. The place is probably most renowned for its associations with **Cassiodorus**, whose monastery was located in the vicinity – though all trace of it has long since disappeared. Cassiodorus (480–570), scholar and secretary to the Ostrogoth, Theodoric, used his position to preserve much of Italy's classical heritage against the onset of the Dark Ages and the book-burning propensities of the Christians. Retiring to spend the last thirty years of his life in seclusion here, Cassiodorus composed histories and collections of documents – of invaluable use to historians.

The coast to Locri

South of Squillace, the golden sands of **COPANELLO** and **SOVERATO** beckon, two resorts that are increasingly attracting the international market. The private lidos hold sway here, charging up to €10 for a day under a parasol on a clean **beach** with access to a bar, but it's easy to find free beaches if you fancy more seclusion. **Accommodation** options in Soverato include a couple of two-stars: *San Vincenzo*, Corso Umberto 296 (☎0967.21.106; ❶), in the centre of town; and the *Riviera* on Via Regina Elena (☎0967.25.738; ❷), with sea views. Slightly more upmarket are the well-equipped *Gli Ulivi*, Via Moro 1 (☎0967.21.487, ⓦ www.gliulivi.net; ❷), which has its own strip of beach and requires half board in peak season, and *Del Golfo* on Via Marina (☎0967.21.307; ❸), nicely positioned by the sea with a decent restaurant and generous breakfasts featuring lots of fresh fruit. *Campeggio Glauco* **campsite** at località San Nicola (☎0967.25.533, ⓦ www.campeggioglauco.it; open June–Sept) is 1km north of Soverato and faces onto the beach.

The coast south assumes a bare, empty look that it keeps until the outskirts of Reggio, though with views of the distant mountains of the Serre and Aspromonte to stave off monotony. Regular **buses and trains** connect the towns along the coast, and buses link inland villages. On the far side of Monasterace, a turn-off where the bus stops leads to the village of **STILO**, 11km up the side of the rugged Monte Consolino. An influential centre at different periods, Stilo is best known for the tiny tenth-century Byzantine temple, the **Cattolica** (daily: summer 8am–8pm; winter 7am–7pm; free), which can be reached by car by taking the first hairpin on the right at the end of the village, or on foot by climbing a series of alleys from the village's main street, Via Tommaso Campanella. Once a base for hermits and Basilian monks in the south of Calabria, this perfectly proportioned temple is reckoned to be the best-preserved monument of its kind, though little of its former glory remains inside, apart from some damaged frescoes and four slim, upturned columns taken from an older temple.

The name of **Tommaso Campanella** occurs everywhere in Stilo, a reminder of the village's links with this Dominican friar and utopian philosopher (1568–1639). Campanella was hounded by the Inquisition principally for his support of the Copernican model of the solar system, and spent some thirty years in prison for the heretical theories expounded in his book, *City of the Sun*. Eventually fleeing to Paris, he became the protégé of Cardinal Richelieu. The shell of **San Domenico** church, part of the convent where he lived, can be seen by following Via Campanella to the Porta Stefanina at the end of the village. Halfway along the road, look into the thirteenth-century **Duomo**, its Gothic portal the only part remaining from the original construction. Note, too, along with other Byzantine and Norman reliefs, the surreal pair of feet stuck onto the wall on the left of the door, taken from a pagan temple and symbolizing the triumph of the Church.

If you want **accommodation**, there's a brilliant place to stay in Stilo, the *San Giorgio*, Via Citarelli 8 (☎0964.775.047, ⓦ www.hotelsangiorgiostilo.it; ❷; May–Sept only), just off the main Via Campanella. Housed in the seventeenth-century palace of the Lamberti counts, it's furnished in nineteenth-century style, and has a garden, pool and restaurant (open part of the year). A rather more corporate though very clean and neat choice is *Citta del Sole*, on Viale Roma heading towards the Cattolica (☎0964.775.588, ⓦwww.cittadelsolehotel.it; ❷), which has modern rooms and facilities. For simple, reasonably priced **food** head for *Punto Ristoro da Mario*, on the way out of town.

Locri and Gerace

Continuing south, you soon come to the most famous classical site on this coast, **Locri Epizefiri** (daily 9am until one hour before sunset; free), some 3km beyond the resort town of **LOCRI**. Founded sometime in the seventh century BC, the city of Locris was responsible for the first written code of law throughout the Hellenic world. Its moment of glory came in the second half of the sixth century when, supposedly assisted by Castor and Pollux, 10,000 Locrians defeated 130,000 Crotonians on the banks of the River Sagra, 25km north. Founding colonies and gathering fame in the spheres of horse rearing and music, the city was an ally of Syracuse but eventually declined during Roman times. The walls of the city, traces of which can still be seen, measured some 8km in circumference, and the excavations within are now interspersed over a wide area among farms and orchards. Your own transport would be useful to reach some of the more far-flung features, though the most interesting can be visited on foot without too much effort, including a fifth-century BC Ionic temple, a Roman necropolis and a well-preserved Graeco-Roman theatre. In any case make a stop at the **museum** (Tues–Sun 9am–7.30pm; €2.50) to consult the plan of the site, and examine the most recent finds, including a good collection of **pinakes**, or votive ceramics – though most of the best items have been appropriated by the Museo Nazionale in Reggio.

After the Saracens devastated Locris in the seventh century AD, the survivors fled inland to found **GERACE**, on an impregnable site that was later occupied and strengthened by the Normans. At the end of a steep and tortuous road 10km up from modern Locri, its ruined **castle** stands at one end of the town on a sheer cliff; it's usually accessible, though officially the site is out of bounds due to the very precarious state of the paths and walls. Easier to visit is the **Duomo** (daily 8am–12.15pm & 3–6pm; free), founded in 1045 by Robert Guiscard, enlarged by Frederick II in 1222 and today still the biggest church in Calabria. Its simple and well-preserved interior has twenty columns of granite and marble, each different and with various capitals; the one on the right nearest the altar in *verde antico* marble that changes tone according to the weather. Two other churches from the same period that are worth a look are **San Francesco** and **San Giovanello**, at the end of Via Caduti sul Lavoro (to the left of the duomo's main entrance), both showing a nice mix of Norman, Byzantine and Saracenic influences. They're usually closed but ask at the nearby *tabacchi* about access. There's an attractive **hotel-restaurant** in Gerace, the *Casa di Gianna* (☎0964.355.024, ⓦwww.lacasadigianna.it; ❸) on Via Paolo Frasca 8, a gem of a four-star with just ten rooms and a terrace restaurant.

Travel details

Trains	

Cosenza to: Camigliatello (Ferrovia Calabro–Lucane; 2 daily; 1hr 20min); Naples

(6 direct daily; 4hr–4hr 50min; 9 daily via Paola; 3–6hr); Paola (27 daily; 20–30min); Rome (1 direct daily; 6hr 25min; 12 daily via Paola or Naples; 5hr–7hr 45min).

Matera to: Bari (Ferrovia Appulo–Lucane; 10 daily; 1hr 10min–1hr 30min).

Metaponto to: Bari (6 direct daily; 2–3hr; 12 daily via Táranto; 2hr 20min–3hr 40min); Cosenza (1 direct daily; 2hr 30min; 7 daily via Sibari 2hr 30min–6hr); Ferrandina (for Matera) (10 daily; 30–40min); Reggio (1 daily; 5hr); Sibari (19 daily; 1hr–1hr 30min); Táranto (21 daily; 45min–1hr 10min).

Paola to: Naples (20 daily; 2hr 30min–4hr 15min); Reggio (22 daily; 2hr); Rome (every 1–2hr; 2–4hr).

Potenza (Inferiore) to: Fóggia (every 2hr; 2hr); Metaponto (10 daily; 1hr 20min–1hr 45min); Salerno (15 daily; 1hr 30min–2hr); Táranto (8 daily; 2hr 30min).

Reggio to: Catanzaro via Lamezia (20 daily; 2hr 45min); Naples (13 daily; 4hr 20min–9hr 20min); Rome (16 daily; 6hr 20min–8hr).

Buses

Cosenza to: Camigliatello (hourly; 1hr); Catanzaro (Mon–Sat 8 daily; 1hr 45min); Naples (1 daily; 5hr); Rome (3 daily; 6hr).

Matera to: Metaponto (Mon–Sat 4 daily; 50min); Potenza (Mon–Sat 2 daily; 1hr 30min).

Potenza to: Matera (Mon–Sat 4 daily, university term time only; 1hr 30min); Naples (4 daily; 2hr); Rome (2 daily; 4hr 30min).

Reggio to: Florence (2 daily, 12hr); Rome (3 daily; 8 hr).

Tropea to: Capo Vaticano (June–Sept 4 daily; 20min).

Ferries and hydrofoils

Reggio to: Aeolian Islands (summer up to 5 daily to each island; winter 1 daily, from 2hr to Lípari to 3hr 30min to Alicudi); Messina (12 daily; 20min);.

Villa San Giovanni to: Messina (every 15min; 45min).

16

Sicily

CHAPTER 16

Highlights

✳ **Monreale** One of the greatest architectural marvels of the Middle Ages, the cathedral at Monreale is a testament to Sicily's rich mixture of Arab, Norman and Byzantine history, containing exquisite examples of columns, portals and towering golden mosaics.
See p.1047

✳ **The ascent of Etna** It's an eerie climb up the blackened lunar landscape of this smoking volcano, which dominates the landscape of eastern Sicily.
See p.1065

✳ **Performance in Siracusa's Teatro Greco** Choose between classical dramas or more modern productions, staged every summer in the city's spectacular Greek theatre. See p.1077

✳ **Noto** The apotheosis of Baroque town planning, Noto offers glorious golden vistas, from extravagant balconied *palazzi* to soaring church facades. See p.1081

✳ **Agrigento** The Valley of the Temples at Agrigento is a spectacular sight, especially at night when the towering Doric columns are washed in gorgeous amber light.
See p.1082

✳ **Villa Romana del Casale, Piazza Armerina** The vitality, colour and diversity of the grand-scale mosaics at this Roman villa are not to be missed. See p.1086

△ Monreale Cathedral

16

Sicily

I like Sicily extremely – a good on-the-brink feeling – one hop and you're out of Europe . . .

D. H. Lawrence in a letter to Lady Cynthia Asquith, 1920

The Sicilians aren't the only people to consider themselves, and their island, a separate entity. Coming from the Italian mainland, it's very noticeable that **Sicily** (Sicilia) has a different feel, that socially and culturally you *are* all but out of Europe. The largest island in the Mediterranean, and with a strategically vital position, Sicily has a history and outlook derived not from its modern parent but from its erstwhile foreign rulers – from the Greeks who first settled the east coast in the eighth century BC, through a dazzling array of Romans, Arabs, Normans, French and Spanish, to the Bourbons seen off by Garibaldi in 1860. Substantial **relics** of these ages remain: temples, theatres and churches are scattered about the whole island. But there are other, more immediate hints of Sicily's unique past. A hybrid Sicilian language, for a start, is still widely spoken in the countryside; the food is noticeably different, spicier and with more emphasis on fish and vegetables; even the flora echoes the change of temperament – oranges, lemons, olives and palms are ubiquitous.

A visit here still induces a real sense of **arrival**. The standard approach for those heading south from the mainland is to cross the Straits of Messina, from Villa San Giovanni or Reggio di Calabria: this way, the train-ferry pilots a course between *Scylla* and *Charybdis*, the twin hazards of rock and whirlpool that were a legendary threat to sailors. Coming in by plane, too, there are spectacular approaches to both the coastal airports at Palermo and Catania.

Once you're on land, deciding **where to go** is largely a matter of time. Inevitably, most points of interest are on the coast: the interior of the island is often mountainous, sparsely populated and relatively inaccessible. The capital, **Palermo**, is a memorable first stop, a bustling, noisy city with an unrivalled display of Norman art and architecture and Baroque churches, combined with a warren of medieval streets and markets. From modern and earthquake-ravaged **Messina**, the most obvious trips are to the chic resort of **Taormina** and the lava-built second city of **Catania**. A skirt around the foothills, and even up to the craters of **Mount Etna**, shouldn't be missed, while to the south sit **Siracusa**, once the most important city of the Greek world, and a Baroque group of towns centring on **Ragusa**. The south coast's greatest draw are the Greek temples at **Agrigento**, while inland, **Enna** is typical of the mountain towns that provided defence for a succession of the island's rulers. Close by is **Piazza Armerina** and its Roman mosaics, while to the west, most of Sicily's fishing industry – and much of the continuing Mafia activity – focuses on the area around **Trápani**. To see all these places, you'll need at least a couple of

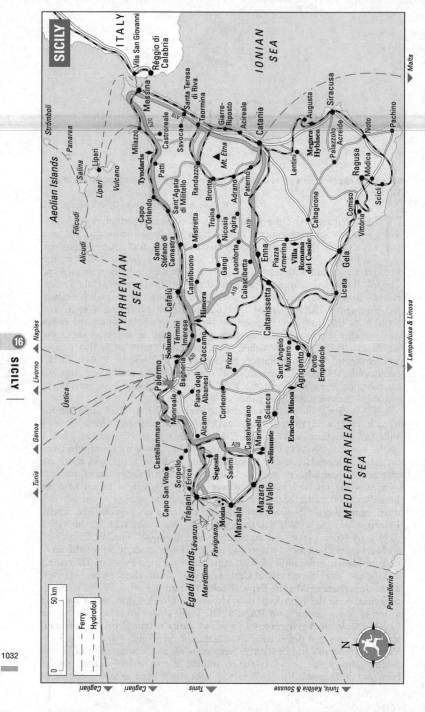

SICILY

ITALY

Villa San Giovanni

Réggio di Calabria

Messina

Santa Teresa di Riva

Taormina

Giarre-Riposto

Acireale

Catania

Augusta

Siracusa

Pachino

Noto

Palazzolo Acreide

Megara Hyblaea

Lentini

Ragusa

Módica

Scicli

Comiso

Vittória

Gela

Licata

IONIAN

SEA

Mt. Etna

Paternò

Adrano

Bronte

Randazzo

Sant'Agata di Militello

Savoca

Castroreale

Patti

Tyndaris

Milazzo

Capo d'Orlando

Santo Stéfano di Camastra

Mistretta

Troina

Nicosia

Agira

Leonforte

Gangi

Castelbuono

Cefalù

Himera

Términi Imerese

Solunto

Palermo

Bagheria

Monreale

Piana degli Albanesi

Caccamo

Prizzi

Corleone

Alcamo

Castelvetrano

Marinella

Selinunte

Sciacca

Eraclea Minoa

Santo Stéfano

Calascibetta

Enna

Piazza Armerina

Villa Romana del Casale

Caltanissetta

Sant'Angelo Muxaro

Agrigento

Porto Empédocle

Caltagirone

Strómboli

Panarea

Salina

Lipari

Lipari

Vulcano

Filicudi

Alicudi

Aeolian Islands

TYRRHENIAN

SEA

Ústica

Castellammare

Capo San Vito

Scopello

Érice

Trápani

Mózia

Marsala

Mazara del Vallo

Salemi

Segesta

Favignana

Lévanzo

Maréttimo

Égadi Islands

MEDITERRANEAN

SEA

Pantelleria

▲ Tunis   ▲ Genoa   ▲ Livorno   ▲ Naples

◀ Cagliari   ◀ Cagliari   ◀ Tunis   ◀ Tunis, Kélibia & Sousse

▶ Lampedusa & Linosa

▶ Malta

--- Ferry
--- Hydrofoil

0   50 km

N

weeks – more like a month if you want to travel extensively inland, a slower and more traditional experience altogether.

The Mafia

Whatever else the **Mafia** is, it isn't an organization that impinges upon the lives of tourists, and it's unlikely you'll come into contact with Mafia activity of any kind. That said, the Mafia does exist – and for very real historical and social reasons. But what began as an early medieval conspiracy, to protect the family from oppressive intrusions of the state, has developed along predictable lines. Alongside the endemic poverty, Sicily continues to endure a system of allegiance, preferment and patronage of massive self-perpetuating proportions, from which few local people profit. Most of the towns and villages of western Sicily are tainted, and Palermo and Trápani have been noted Mafia centres for decades. But travellers won't be much aware of the problem, due to the power of *omertà*, the law of silence. All this is not to say that **petty crime** won't make itself felt. Take all the usual precautions concerning your money and valuables, and be extra careful in the cities – Palermo and Catania in particular.

Getting around

Getting around Sicily can be a protracted business. **Trains** along the northern and eastern coasts (Messina–Palermo and Messina–Siracusa) are extensions of – or connected with – the "express" trains from Rome and Naples, which means that they are frequently late, with a delay of at least an hour considered normal. Also, Sicily's geography often conspires to place train stations miles away from the relevant town – check the text for details – and don't expect a rail pass to be as much use as on the mainland. **Buses** are generally quicker though more expensive. There's no single bus company – Interbus, SAIS and AST are the main three – but the local tourist office can point out where to catch what. Pick up timetables wherever you go and, despite the assertions to the contrary, expect there to be little (if any) service anywhere on a Sunday.

16

SICILY

Palermo and around

Unmistakably the capital of Sicily, **Palermo** is fast, brash, loud and exciting. Here the Sicilian fusion of all things foreign – art, architecture, culture and lifestyle – exists at its most extreme: elegant Baroque cheek by jowl with Arabic cupolas, high-fashion shops competing with Byzantine street markets, Vespas parked against Spanish *palazzi*. And all to a background of sputtering, swirling traffic.

You could easily spend two or three days in Palermo without ever leaving the city's limits. But make time for at least one day-trip: the capital has several traditional bolt holes if you want a break from the bustle, most obviously the heights of **Monte Pellegrino** and the fine beach at **Mondello**. If your interest has been fired by the city's great Norman heritage, you won't want to miss the famous medieval cathedral of **Monreale**, just a few kilometres west; or you might like to take one of the year-round ferries or hydrofoils to **Ústica**, 60km northwest of Palermo – a tiny volcanic island with enough impressive grottoes and coastal walks to occupy any remaining time.

Palermo

In its own wide bay underneath the limestone bulk of Monte Pellegrino, and fronting the broad, fertile Conca d'Oro (Golden Shell) Valley, **PALERMO** is stupendously sited. Originally a Phoenician, then a Carthaginian colony, this remarkable city was long considered a prize worth capturing. Named Panormus (All Harbour), its mercantile attractions were obvious, and under Saracen and Norman rule in the ninth to twelfth centuries Palermo became the greatest city in Europe – famed for the wealth of its court, and peerless as a centre of learning. There are plenty of relics from this era, but it's the rebuilding of the sixteenth and seventeenth centuries that shaped the city as you see it today.

Palermo has Sicily's greatest concentration of sights. Money from Rome and the EU has facilitated the regeneration of the historic centre – the signs are obvious – but the obstacles remain huge. This is partly owing to the age-old system of kickbacks for contracts and tenders to bent politicians and the Mafia, which have creamed off much of the money. One of the few to stand up against this state of affairs was **Leoluca Orlando**, who, following his deposition by his own Christian Democrat party in 1990, went on to found and lead the anti-Mafia and anti-Masonic party, **La Rete**. As Palermo's mayor (1993–2001), his prominence on the national stage forced attention on reform of the city's institutions and reversed the tendency of neglect and decay that had character-ized the city for centuries.

The essential sights are all pretty central and easy to cover on foot. Paramount are the hybrid **Cattedrale** and nearby **Palazzo dei Normanni** (Royal Palace), with its superb, mosaic-decorated chapel, the **Cappella Palatina**; the glorious Norman churches of **La Martorana** and **San Giovanni degli Eremiti**; the Baroque opulence of **San Giuseppe dei Teatini** and **Santa Caterina**; and first-class **museums** of art, archeology and ethnography.

This historical jumble of treasures has its downside. Many people have contin-ued to live in their medieval ghettos, unemployment is endemic, the old port largely idle and petty crime commonplace. Don't be paranoid, though: things are not significantly worse than in any other European city. By taking the usual precautions, not flashing bulging wallets or cameras around and avoiding any quiet neighbourhood, especially at night, you should feel perfectly safe.

Arrival, information and transport

Palermo's Falcone Borsellino **airport** (☎800.541.880, ⓦwww.gesap.it) is at Punta Raisi, 31km west of the city. Buses run every thirty minutes from the airport into the centre, stopping outside the Politeama Garibaldi theatre on Piazza Ruggero Settimo, then on to the Stazione Marittima, from which all ferries and hydrofoils depart, and finally outside the *Hotel Elena*, at the Stazione Centrale; buy your ticket on board. Buses run from 6.30am until the last incoming flight, and the journey time is 45 minutes (Prestia & Comandè buses; ☎091.580.457). For the return journey, departures are every thirty minutes from 5am to about 9.30pm from outside the *Hotel Elena*, and follow the same route. Trains run from the airport to Stazione Centrale every thirty minutes, between 6.30am and midnight from the airport (the last two trains wait for any delayed flights) and between 5am and 11pm from Stazione Centrale. The journey costs €5.

Trains all pull in at the Stazione Centrale (enquiries ☎091.603.3121), at the southern end of Via Roma, close to the city's cheaper accommodation; buses #101 and #102, and two circular minibus services – *linea gialla* and *linea rossa* – connect with the modern city from outside the station.

The majority of the country- and island-wide **buses** (including those in the following list) operate out of Via Paolo Balsamo beside the train station: AST (☎091.620.8111, ⓦwww.aziendasicilianatrasporti.it) serves Corleone, Modica and Ragusa; Cuffaro (☎091.616.1510, ⓦwww.cuffaro.info) serves Agrigento; Interbus (☎091.304.0900 or 091.616.7919, ⓦwww.interbus.it) serves Siracusa; SAIS (☎091.616.6028, ⓦwww.saisautolinee.it) serves Naples, Catania, Enna, Piazza Armerina and Messina; Salemi (☎091.617.5411 or 0923.981.120, ⓦwww.autoservizisalemi.it) serves Marsala and Mazara del Vallo; Segesta (☎091.616.9039, ⓦwww.segesta.it) serves Rome and Trápani.

All **ferry** and **hydrofoil** services dock at the Stazione Marittima, just off Via Francesco Crispi, from where it's a ten-minute walk up Via E. Amari to Piazza Castelnuovo; see p.1046 for details of ferry companies and destinations.

Driving in the city is best avoided if possible. Driving is anarchic, with over-taking on either side the norm, and indicating virtually unheard of. Parking attendants will guide you to a space and charge you a small amount per hour, and meters are installed over a large part of the centre. Renting a **bike** (see list-ings on p.1046) can be an exhilarating alternative for the steely nerved.

Information

Palermo's main **tourist office** is at Piazza Castelnuovo 34 (Mon–Fri 8.30am–2pm & 3–7pm, Sat 9am–1pm; ☎091 605.8531, ⓦwww.palermotourism.com); it has free maps of the city and province, the free booklets *Agenda* and *Guida all'Ospitalità* containing current events and transport information, and also provides a list of accommodation in and around the city. There are two smaller offices at the Stazione Centrale (same hours as above; ☎091.616.5914) and at the airport (daily 8.30am–midnight; ☎091.591.698). You'll also find numerous information kiosks dotted about the centre. For more complete **city listings** and a rundown of what's on, pick up a copy of the local paper, *Il Giornale di Sicilia*, or look out for the more youth-oriented *Lapis* (free), updated every few weeks.

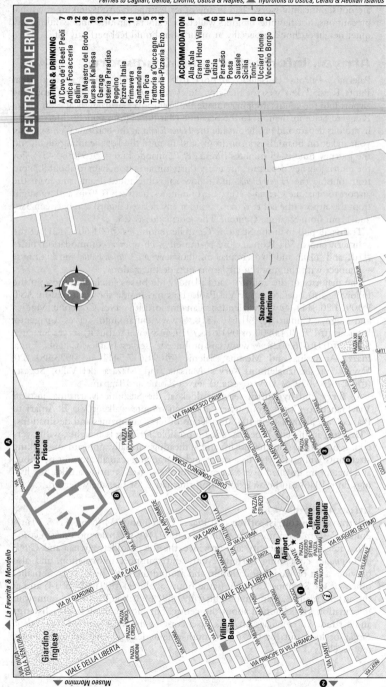

CENTRAL PALERMO

EATING & DRINKING

Al Covo de'i Beati Paoli	7
Antica Focacceria	9
Bellini	12
Dal Maestro del Brodo	8
Kursaal Kalhesa	10
Il Garage	13
Osteria Paradiso	2
Peppino	1
Pizzeria Italia	4
Primavera	11
Santandrea	6
Tina Pica	5
Trattoria a'Cuccagna	3
Trattoria-Pizzeria Enzo	14

ACCOMMODATION

Alla Kala	F
Grand Hotel Villa	A
Igiea	G
Letizia	H
Paradiso	E
Posta	J
Sausele	I
Sicilia	D
Tonic	B
Ucciard Home	C
Vecchio Borgo	

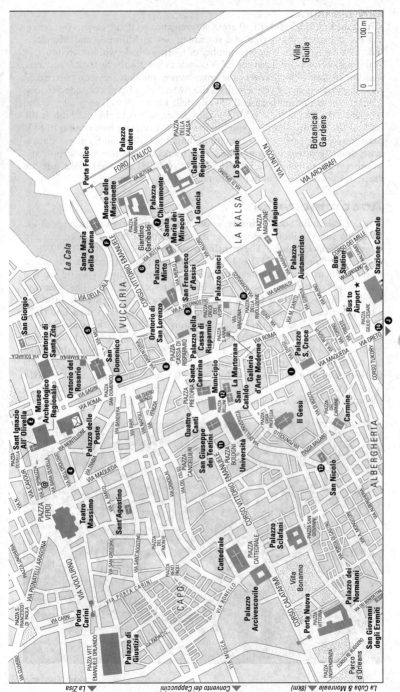

SICILY

1037

16

City transport

City buses (AMAT ☎091.690.2690, ⊛www.amat.pa.it) are easy to use, covering every corner of Palermo and stretching out to Monreale and Mondello. There's a flat fare of €1 for any number of journeys made within two hours, or you can buy an all-day ticket for €3.30, while tickets for the *linea gialla* and *rossa*, and the *circolare* (which covers the *centro storico*) minibus services, cost €0.52 for a day's use – all are available from the AMAT glass booths outside Stazione Centrale, or at the southern end of Viale della Libertà as well as in *tabacchi* and wherever else you see the AMAT sign; validate tickets in the machine at the back of the bus the first time you use them. The main city **bus rank** is outside Stazione Centrale and buses run until midnight (11.30pm on Sundays). Otherwise, don't be afraid to jump into a **taxi** (ranks outside the train station and in other main piazzas, or call ☎091.513.311 or ☎091.225.455); make sure the meter is switched on. The minimum fare is €4.50 per journey.

Accommodation

Most of Palermo's budget **hotels** lie on and around the southern ends of Via Maqueda and Via Roma, roughly in the area between Stazione Centrale and Corso Vittorio Emanuele. The **youth hostel** *Baia del Corallo* (☎091.679.7807, ⊛www.ostellionline.it; €17) is 12km northwest of the city, on Via Plauto out towards the airport; it's a fifteen-minute drive from the airport, so might be a feasible first or last night's stop, if you have a late or early flight. There are also family rooms (❶), access to the sea, and bikes for hire. To get there from the city centre take the metro to the Tommaso Natale stop and then bus #628 to the terminus. Alternatively, there's a university hostel, the *Casa Marconi*, much nearer the centre at Via Monfenera 140 (☎091.657.0611, ⊛www .casamarconi.it), which is cleaner and has private rooms (❷); to get there, take bus #246 from the station to the end of the line at the hospital, cross on to Via G. Basile and turn left into Via Monfenera. If you're **camping**, take bus #616 from Piazza Vittorio Veneto (itself reached by #101 or #106 along Viale della Libertà from Piazza Castelnuovo) out to Sferracavallo, 13km northwest, where

△ Palermo's mopeds out in force

there are two **year-round sites**: the *Trinacria* on the seafront on Via Barcarello (℡091.530.590, Ⓦwww.campingtrinacria.it) and the cheaper *Ulivi* on Via Pegaso (℡091.533.021, Ⓦwww.campingdegliulivi.com). For a wonderful range of distinctive **apartments** from €100 per night all over the *centro storico*, contact Orizzonte Rosso (℡333.663.8666, Ⓦwww.orizzonterosso.com) which also organizes upmarket boat trips and tailormade excursions all over Sicily.

Alla Kala Corso Vittorio Emanuele 71 ℡091.743.4763, Ⓦwww.allakala.it. Five stylish designer rooms with magnificent views of the sailing marina. ❹

Grand Hotel Villa Igiea Via Belmonte 43 ℡091.543.744, Ⓦwww.hilton.com. This classic Art Nouveau building, originally a villa of the Florio family (the people who pioneered tuna canning), was designed by Ernesto Basile in 1900. Sumptuous, and often full, so book ahead. ❼

Letizia Via dei Bottai 30 ℡091.589.110, Ⓦwww.hotelletizia.com. Each room in this charming hotel, just off Piazza Marina, has its own colour scheme and furnishings. There's an enclosed courtyard for breakfast, and free Internet for guests. ❸

Paradiso Via Schiavuzzo 65 ℡091.617.2825. The windows of this first-floor *pensione* overlook the Piazza della Rivoluzione. It's good and central, and its ten rooms without bath are among the cheapest in town. No credit cards. ❶

Posta Via Gagini 77 ℡091.587.338, Ⓦwww.hotelpostapalermo.it. On a street parallel to Via Roma, the hotel is central but quiet, with stylish modern rooms and polite service. It has traditionally been popular with theatre folk (most notably Dario Fo) and facilities include a reading room and library. Garage parking is available at €15 per day. ❹

Sausele Via V. Errante 12 ℡091.616.1308, Ⓦwww.hotelsausele.it. Well kept and secure, this Swiss-managed hotel is good value though can be noisy at night. Take the first right off Via Oreto, behind the station. Parking costs €10 a night. ❸

Sicilia Via Divisi 99 ℡091.616.8460, Ⓦwww.hotelsiciliapalermo.it. Pleasant management and good-value rooms with air conditioning; those around the small downstairs courtyard are quieter. There's parking nearby (€8). ❷

Tonic Via Mariano Stabile ℡091.581.754, Ⓦwww.hoteltonic.it. Smart, spacious hotel in the modern town. Caters mainly to the business fraternity (there's Internet connection in all rooms) ❸

Ucciard Home Via Enrico Albanese 34–36 ℡091.348.426, Ⓦwww.hotelucciardhome.com. Trendy new designer hotel opposite the prison. ❻

Vecchio Borgo Via Quintino Sella 1–7 ℡091.611.1446, Ⓦwww.classicahotels.com. A great find near the Piazza Politeama, this well-run four-star is on a quiet street at the entrance to one of Palermo's best weekend markets. The luxurious rooms here are plush, with all amenities (including Internet points in all rooms), and the breakfast buffet is excellent. Garage €15 a night, outdoor car park €7 a night. ❺

The City

Historical Palermo sits around a crossroads, the **Quattro Canti**, which is at the core of four distinct quarters. The **Albergheria** and the **Capo** quarter, the latter beyond the cathedral, lie roughly west of Via Maqueda; the **Vucciria** and old harbour of La Cala and the **La Kalsa** lie to the east, closest to the water. You'll find virtually all the surviving ancient monuments and buildings of the city in these areas.

Around the Quattro Canti

At the heart of the old city is the **Quattro Canti**, or "Four Corners", erected in 1611: a newly restored and gleaming Baroque crossroads that divides old Palermo into its quadrants. You'll pass this junction many times, and it's worth one turn around to check the tiered statues – respectively a season, a king of Sicily and a patron of the city – in each concave "corner".

On the southwest corner (entrance on Corso Vittorio Emanuele), **San Giuseppe dei Teatini** (Mon–Sat 7.30–11am & 6–8pm, Sun 8.30am–12.30pm & 6–8pm), begun in 1612, is the most harmonious of the city's Baroque churches. Inside there's a wealth of detail – especially in the lavish side chapels – given plenty of contrasting space by 22 enormous supporting columns in the nave and dome.

Outside, across Via Maqueda, is **Piazza Pretoria**, floodlit at night to highlight the nude figures of its great central fountain, a racy sixteenth-century Florentine design. The piazza also holds the restored **Municipio**, plaque-studded and pristine, while towering above both square and fountain is the massive flank of the recently restored **Santa Caterina** (open for services, or call ☎091.6162.488 for access), Sicilian Baroque at its most exuberant, every inch of the enormous interior covered in a wildly decorative, pustular relief-work, deep reds and yellows filling in between sculpted cherubs, Madonnas, lions and eagles.

Piazza Bellini, just around the corner, is the site of two more wildly contrasting churches. The little Saracenic red golfball domes belong to **San Cataldo**, a squat twelfth-century chapel on a palm-planted bank above the piazza (Mon–Fri 9.30am–1pm, 3.30–6pm, Sat & Sun 9.30am–1pm; €1). Never decorated, it retains a good mosaic floor in an otherwise bare and peaceful interior. The understatement of this little chapel is more than offset by the splendid intricacy of the adjacent **La Martorana** (Mon–Sat 8am–1pm & 3.30–7pm, Sun 8.30am–1pm; free) – one of the finest survivors of the medieval city. With a Norman foundation, the church received a Baroque going-over – and its curving northern facade – in 1588. Happily, the alterations don't detract from the power of the interior, entered through the slim twelfth-century campanile, which retains its ribbed arches and slender columns. A series of spectacular **mosaics**, animated twelfth-century Greek works, are laid on and around the columns supporting the main cupola. A gentle Christ dominates the dome, surrounded by angels, the Apostles and the Madonna to the sides. Two more original mosaic panels have been set in frames on the walls just inside the entrance to the church: a kneeling George of Antioch (the church's founder) dedicating La Martorana to the Virgin, and King Roger being crowned by Christ – the diamond-studded monarch contrasting with a larger, more dignified Christ. Tucked into the web of streets on the other side of Via Roma is Piazza S. Anna, where the former convent of Sant'Anna has been restored and is due to open shortly as an exhibition space as well as the home of the **Galleria d'Arte Moderne**, with a collection of twentieth-century Sicilian art and sculpture.

The Albergheria and the Palazzo dei Normanni

The district just to the northwest of the train station – the **Albergheria** – hasn't changed substantially for several hundred years. A maze of tiny streets and tall leaning buildings, it's an engaging place to wander, much of the central area taken up by a street market that all but conceals several fine churches. Via Ponticello leads down past the Baroque church of **Il Gesù**, or **Casa Professa** (Mon–Sat 7–11.30am & 5–6.30pm, Sun 7am–12.30pm & 5–6.30pm), the first Jesuit foundation in Sicily and gloriously decorated inside, to **Piazza Ballarò** – along with adjacent **Piazza del Carmine** the focus of a raucous daily **market**, with bulging vegetable stalls, unmarked drinking dens and some good snack stalls.

At the westernmost edge of the quarter, over Via Benedettini, is the Albergheria's quietest haven, the deconsecrated church of **San Giovanni degli Eremiti** (daily 9am–6.30pm; €4.50) – St John of the Hermits. Built in 1132, it's the most obviously Arabic of the city's Norman relics, with five ochre domes topping a small church that was built upon the remains of a mosque.

From San Giovanni it's a few paces to the main road, where, if you turn right and then veer left up the steps, you'll climb out of the fast traffic to gaze on the vast length of the **Palazzo dei Normanni**, or Palazzo Reale (entrance on Piazza Indipendenza). A royal palace has always occupied the high ground here, above medieval Palermo. Originally built by the Saracens, the palace was enlarged considerably by the Normans, under whom it housed the most magnificent of medieval European courts – a noted centre of poetic and artistic achievement. Sadly, there's little left from those times in the current structure. The long front was added by the Spanish in the seventeenth century and most of the interior is now taken up by the Sicilian regional Parliament (which explains the security guards and the limited opening hours). Be prepared to queue.

Of the **Royal Apartments**, the only part now open to the public is the sumptuous Sala di Ruggero (Mon, Fri & Sat 8.30am–12.30pm & 2–5pm, Tue, Wed, Thurs, Sun 8.30am–12.30pm; €6 includes entrance to Cappella Palatina), decorated with lively twelfth-century mosaics of hunting scenes. Descend a floor to the beautiful **Cappella Palatina** (Mon–Fri 9am–noon & 3–5pm, Sat & Sun 9–11.45am; €6 includes entrance to Royal Apartments), the private royal chapel of Roger II, and central Palermo's undisputed artistic gem. Built between 1132 and 1143, its interior is immediately overwhelming – cupola, three apses and nave entirely covered in twelfth-century **mosaics** of outstanding quality. As usual, it's the powerful representation of Christ as Pantocrator which dominates, bolstered here by other secondary images – Christ blessing, open book in hand, and Christ enthroned, between Peter (to whom the chapel is dedicated) and Paul. Unlike the bright pictures of La Martorana the mosaics here give a single, effective impression, fully expressing the faith that inspired their creation.

The Cattedrale, the Capo and the modern city

Spanning Corso Vittorio Emanuele, on the far side of the Palazzo dei Normanni, the early sixteenth-century **Porta Nuova** commemorates Charles V's Tunisian exploits, with suitably grim, turbaned figures adorning the western entrance. This gate marked the extent of the late medieval city, and the long road beyond heads to Monreale.

The Corso runs back towards the centre, past the huge bulk of the **Cattedrale** (daily 9.30am–5.30pm; free) – a more substantial Norman relic than the palace. It's an odd building, with the fine lines of the tawny stone spoilt by the late eighteenth-century addition of a completely out-of-character dome. Still, the triple-apsed eastern end and the lovely matching towers are all original, dating from 1185. And despite the Catalan-Gothic facade and arches, there's enough Norman carving and detail to rescue the exterior from mere curiosity value. The same is not true, however, of the inside: it is grand enough but cold and Neoclassical, and the only items of interest are the fine portal and wooden doors (both fifteenth-century) and the **royal tombs**, containing the mortal remains of some of Sicily's most famous monarchs – including Frederick II and his wife, Constance of Aragon. There's also a **treasury** (Mon–Sat 9.30am–5.30pm, Sun groups only; €2.50) to the right of the choir, the highlights of which are a jewel- and pearl-encrusted skull cap and three simple, precious rings, all enterprisingly removed from the tomb of Constance in the eighteenth century.

From the cathedral you can bear left, around the apses, and up into the **Capo** quarter, one of the oldest areas of Palermo and another tight web of impoverished streets, unrelieved by space or greenery. Just around the corner from Piazza del Monte is the fine church of **Sant'Agostino** (Mon–Sat 7am–noon & 4–6pm, Sun 7am–noon; free), built in the thirteenth century. Above its main door (on Via Raimondo) there's a gorgeous latticework rose window, and inside, some calm sixteenth-century cloisters. Further along Via Sant'Agostino, behind the market stalls, look out for a sculpted fifteenth-century doorway attributed to Domenico Gagini.

The stalls of the **clothes market** (daily 8am to around 8pm) along **Via Sant'Agostino** run all the way down to Via Maqueda and beyond, the streets off to the left gradually becoming wider and more nondescript as they broach the area around the late nineteenth-century **Teatro Massimo**. Strictly Neoclassical in style, this is a monumental structure, supposedly the largest theatre in Italy, and beautifully cleaned up after years of closure. To appreciate the interior fully take a **tour** (Tues–Sun every 30min 10.30am–3.30pm; €5), or attend one of the classical concerts or operas held here between October and June.

The theatre marks the dividing line between old and new Palermo and beyond here there's little that's vital, though plenty that is grand and modern. Via Maqueda becomes **Via Ruggero Settimo**, which cuts up through the gridded shopping streets to the huge double square made up of **Piazza Castelnuovo** and **Piazza Ruggero Settimo** (commonly referred to as Piazza Politeama). Dominating the whole lot is Palermo's other massive theatre, the **Politeama Garibaldi**, topped by a flambmoyant statue group of sword-brandishing figures on leaping horses.

The Vucciria, archeological museum and old harbour

Via Roma, running from Stazione Centrale, is a fairly modern addition to the city, all clothes and shoe shops. It's nothing like as interesting as the parallel **Via Maqueda**, consisting mostly of tall apartment blocks that conceal hotels, but stick with it as far as the church of Sant'Antonio. Behind here – down the steps – is the sprawling **Vucciria market** (daily 8am to around 8pm): winding streets radiating out from a small enclosed piazza, wet from the ice and waste of the fish stalls and where you'll find a couple of restaurants, some very basic bars and all manner of food and junk on sale.

The northern limit of the market is marked by the distinctive church of **San Domenico** (Tues–Sun 9am–11.30pm, Sat & Sun also 5–7pm; free), with a fine eighteenth-century facade and an interior of tombs containing a host of famous Sicilians. Parliamentarians, poets and painters, they're of little interest to foreigners except to explain the finer points behind Palermitan street naming. The **oratory** behind the church (Oratorio del Rosario; Mon–Fri 9am–1pm & 2–5.30pm, Sat 9am–1pm; free but tipping is usual) contains fine stuccowork by Serpotta and a masterful van Dyck altarpiece, painted in 1628 before the artist fled Palermo for Genoa to escape the plague.

From Piazza San Domenico, Via Roma continues north, passing (on the left) Palermo's main post office, the gargantuan **Palazzo delle Poste**. Built under Fascist rule in 1933, it's a severe concrete block, with a wide flight of steps running up to ten unfluted columns that run the length and height of the building itself.

The grandiosity of the post office is brought down to size by the sixteenth-century convent behind, which now houses the **Museo Archeologico Regionale** (Tues–Fri 8.30am–2pm & 2.30–6.45pm, Sat, Sun & Mon 8.30am–1.45pm; €6), a magnificent collection of artefacts, mainly from the western half of the island, displayed on three floors. Two cloisters hold anchors and other retrieved hardware from the sea off the Sicilian coast, Egyptian and Punic remains in rooms to either side, and Roman sculpture – notably a giant enthroned Zeus. In rooms at the far end of the cloisters are numerous stelae and other inscribed tablets, as well as reconstructions of the assembled stone **lion's head water spouts** from the so-called "Victory Temple" at Himera (fifth century BC), the fierce animal faces tempered by braided fur and a grooved tongue which channelled the water. There are also finds from the temple site of Selinunte, on the southwest coast of the island, highpoint of which – indeed of the museum – is the **Salone di Selinunte**, a room that gathers together the richly carved metopes from the various temples. Sculpted panels from the friezes which once adorned the temples, the metopes are appealing works of art depicting lively mythological scenes: the earliest, dating from the sixth century BC, are those representing the gods of Delphi, the Sphynx, the rape of Europa, and Hercules and the Bull. But it's the friezes from Temples C and F that really catch the eye, vivid fifth-century BC works – such as Perseus beheading the Medusa with a short sword. Upstairs has also plenty to reward a lengthy dawdle: some 12,000 votive terracotta figures, and two bronze sculptures – the life-like figure of an alert ram (third century BC), originally one of a pair, and the glistening, muscular study of Hercules subduing a stag, found at Pompeii. On the second floor, the beautifully preserved Roman mosaics from Piazza della Vittoria in Palermo are well worth seeing, too.

The juxtaposition of different styles begins again in earnest if you cross back over Via Roma and head towards the water. The church of **Santa Zita** (also known as Santa Cita or San Mamiliano), on quiet Via Squarcialupo, is justly known for its marvellous **oratory** (Mon–Fri 9am–1pm; ring the bell if closed, or ask in the church in front; €2): repository of one of Serpotta's finest works – the *Battle of Lepanto* – and some rich mother-of-pearl benches. From here streets spread back to the thumb-shaped inlet of **La Cala**, Palermo's **old harbour**. This was once the main port of Palermo, stretching as far inland as Via Roma, but during the sixteenth century silting caused the water to recede to its current position. All the heavy work eventually moved northwards to docks off the remodelled postwar streets, and La Cala now does duty as a yachting marina.

La Kalsa and the Galleria Regionale

This southeastern quarter of old Palermo was worst hit during the war, but, after years of decay, it's sloughing off its desolate image, as the numerous cranes and tiers of scaffolding testify. It's here that you'll find some of Palermo's most remarkable buildings and churches, as well as its only central park, **Villa Giulia**, just a few minutes' walk along Via Lincoln from the train station and home to an extensive botanical garden (Mon–Fri 9am–6pm, Sat & Sun 8.30am–1.30pm; €2).

Cutting back to Piazza Garibaldi and walking north, turn off down Via Magione for the church of **La Magione** (daily 9.30am–6.30pm; free), one of the city's more graceful spots, approached through a palm-lined drive. Built in 1151, the simple, sparse Norman church was subsequently given to the Teutonic knights as their headquarters by Henry VI. The beautiful cloisters are currently closed, but be sure to visit the adjacent chapel, where you'll find a rare plaster preparation of a crucifixion fresco and a lovely small Arab-Norman column carved with a Koranic inscription in Kufic Arabic. The church marks the edge of **La Kalsa** (its name is from the Arabic *khalisa*, meaning "pure"), an area subjected to saturation bombing during World War II, because of its proximity to the port. The worst of the bombsite is now greened over and a popular spot for football practice. Across the square, set back off Via Spasimo, is the complex of **Santa Maria dello Spasimo** (daily 8am–midnight; free), a former church, now roofless except for its Gothic apse, that holds atmospheric night-time jazz concerts. It is also one of the venues for the annual **KalsArt festival** (@www.kalsart.it; mid-June to mid-Sept), a huge cultural extravaganza of live music, theatre and cinema that takes place at a number of venues around this part of town.

Beyond Piazza della Kalsa is Via Alloro with, at its seaward end, the **Palazzo Abatellis**, a fifteenth-century palace that houses Sicily's **Galleria Regionale** (Tues–Fri 9am–1pm & 2.30–7pm, Sat–Mon 9am–1pm; €6), a stunning medieval art collection. Inside, there's a simple split: sculpture downstairs, and paintings upstairs, the one exception being a magnificent fifteenth-century fresco, the *Triumph of Death*, displayed in the former chapel, coating an entire wall. It's a chilling study by an unknown (possibly Flemish) painter in which Death is cast as a skeletal archer astride a galloping, spindly horse, trampling bodies planted by his arrows. The other masterpiece on the ground floor is among the works of fifteenth-century sculptor Francesco Laurana (room ❹), whose white marble bust of Eleonora of Aragon is a calm, perfectly studied portrait.

Upstairs there's no shortage of excellent Sicilian work, including a fourteenth-century Byzantine mosaic of the Madonna and Child, and paintings and frescoes from the fifteenth century vivid in their portrayal of the coronation of the Virgin, a favourite theme. This floor, too, contains a collection of works by Antonello da Messina (1430–79), including three small portraits of Saints Gregory, Jerome and Augustine and the celebrated *Annunciation*, a placid depiction of Mary, head and shoulders covered, right hand slightly raised.

Via Paternostro, which runs west off Via Alloro, curves north passing the striking thirteenth-century church of **San Francesco d'Assisi** (Mon–Fri 7am–noon & 4–6.30pm; free) whose portal, picked out with a zigzagged decoration, is topped by a wonderful rose window. To the side of the church, at Via Immacolatella 5, is the renowned **Oratorio di San Lorenzo** (Mon–Sat 9am–1pm; free), harbouring stucco scenes from the lives of St Lawrence and St Francis by Serpotta.

East of here on Via Merlo is the late eighteenth-century **Palazzo Mirto** (daily 9am–6.30pm; €3), one of the few *palazzi* in the city to have retained its imposing original fixtures and fittings. Passing through the Giardino Garibaldi and Piazza Marina brings you to Corso Vittorio Emanuele, which runs down to the water and ends in the Baroque gate, **Porta Felice**, begun in 1582 as a balance to the Porta Nuova to the west. The whole area beyond the gate was flattened in 1943, and has since been rebuilt as the ugly **Foro Italico** promenade, from where you can look back over the harbour to Monte Pellegrino. Back beyond the Porta Felice, around the corner from the **Palazzo Chiaramonte**, second-largest of Palermo's palaces and ex-headquarters of the Inquisition, is the engaging **Museo delle Marionette** off Via Butera at Novolo Niscemi 5 (Mon–Fri 9am–1pm & 3.30–6.30pm; ⓦ www.museomarionettepalermo .it; €5), the definitive collection of puppets, screens and painted scenery in Palermo. A traditional Sicilian entertainment, **puppet theatres** are now mainly staged for the benefit of tourists. The stories are usually based on the exploits of the hero Roland (Orlando), a dashing knight in combat against Saracen invaders, usually culminating in a great battle. It's all lots of fun, and in summer the museum puts on free shows (*Spettacolo dei pupi*); ring ⓣ 091.328.060, or ask the tourist office for the current schedule.

The outskirts

The **Museo Etnografico Pitrè** (Tues–Sat 9am–7.30pm, Sun 9am–12.30pm; €5) lies 3km north of Piazza Castelnuovo (bus #106 or #806 from Politeama or Viale della Libertà). Although its main attraction – the brightly painted Sicilian carts – are currently in the hands of the restorers, you'll still get a good insight into Sicilian folklore and culture. In addition to a reconstructed puppet theatre, expressive puppets and scenery backdrops, there's a whole series of intricately worked terracotta figures, dolls and games, bicycles, painted masks and even a great, flowery iron bedstead.

Tracking down the rest of Palermo's **Norman relics** entails a bit of a trek or using public transport. Bus #124 runs west from the Politeama to **La Zisa** (from the Arabic, *el aziz*, "magnificent"), a huge palace begun by William I in 1160, with a fine exterior and a rich, well-crafted Islamic interior (daily 9am–6.30pm; €2.50). Closer to the centre, about 1km beyond Porta Nuova at Corso Calatafimi 100, is **La Cuba**, the remains of a slightly later Norman pavilion that formed part of the same royal park as La Zisa, now tucked inside an army barracks, but well restored and open to the public (daily 9am–6.30pm; €2).

But for real attention-grabbing stuff, take bus #327 from Piazza Indipendenza southwest along Via dei Cappuccini as far as Via Pindemonte. Close by, in Piazza Cappuccini, the **Convento dei Cappuccini** (daily 9am–noon & 3–5.30pm; €1.50) retained its own burial ground for several hundred years, placing its dead in catacombs under the church. Later, right up until 1881, others were also interred here. The bodies (some eight thousand of them) were preserved by various chemical and drying processes – including the use of vinegar and arsenic baths – and then placed in niches along corridors, dressed in suits of clothes provided for the purpose. Descending into the catacombs is quite unnerving, especially if you arrive in a lull between coach parties. The rough-cut stone corridors are divided according to sex and status, different caverns reserved for men, women, the clergy, doctors, lawyers and surgeons. Suspended in individual niches, hand-written notes about their necks, the bodies have become vile, contorted, grinning figures – some decomposed beyond recognition, others complete with skin, hair and eyes fixing you with a steely stare; most harrowing are the tiny babies and children.

Eating

For **snacks**, the *Ferrara*, just to the left of the train station in Piazza Giulio Cesare, and the *Panineria*, Via Trabia 35, just across from the Teatro Massimo, are reliable options. You can eat good ice cream and snack lunches including *arancini* at *Mazzara*, a bar-*pasticceria* at Via Magliocco 15 (on the corner of Piazza Ungheria), while the *Antico Caffè*, Via Principe di Belmonte 111, is the perfect place for delicious cakes and ice cream with a piano accompaniment. You can also stock up from the **markets** of course; best are the Ballarò, in the Albergheria (see p.1040), and the Vucciria, off Via Roma (p.1042). There's also a GS **supermarket** on Piazza Marina (Mon–Sat 8.30am–8.30pm).

Al Covo de'i Beati Paoli Piazza Marina 50 ℡091.616.6634. Looking smack onto Piazza Garibaldi, this outdoor garden restaurant serves good-value pizzas and meat dishes: firsts cost about €7 and the scrumptious *stuzzicchini* (appetizers including olives and bruschetta) go for €4.50. It gets very crowded on weekend evenings.

Antica Focacceria San Francesco Via A. Paternostro 58 ℡091.320264. This old-fashioned place has been in the same family for five generations. Downstairs they serve traditional Palermitani street food, such as *focaccia schietta* (*focaccia* with offal and *caciocavallo*), *sfincione* (pizza with onion, tomato, *caciocavallo* and breadcrumbs), *cazzilli* (potato croquettes) and *panelle* (chick pea flour fritters). Upstairs you can eat full meals (try the *pasta con le sarde*, pasta with sardines). In summer you can eat outside. Closed Tues and Jan 7–21.

Bellini Piazza Bellini ℡091.615.5691. The best bet for alfresco pizzas (starting at €3); outdoor

tables are in the shadow of La Martorana church. Closed Mon and Dec.

Dal Maestro del Brodo Via Pannieri 7 ℡091.329.523. Great family-run place in the heart of the Vucciria market, named for its famously restorative broth, best tasted in their signature dish, *bollito di carne con patate e zaffarano*, meat broth with potatoes and saffron. No meat-eaters can be sure of spanking fresh fish. Closed Sun in summer, Mon in winter.

Il Garage Vicolo San Nicolo Albergheria 4 ℡333.490.6356. So called because the owner, Mario's, first restaurant in Palermo was in a converted garage, this small, eccentric Tunisian joint serves tasty, inexpensive fish, lamb and couscous dishes (never more than €7), and is also a nice place to sip a bottle of Peroni. Tough to find; ask around for Mario and most will know where it is. Closed Tues.

Osteria Paradiso Via Serradifalco 23. No phone. Typical family-run trattoria, to the north of La Zisa,

open only at lunchtime and specializing in fish. There is no written menu – the owner just tells you what's available that day. Specialities include fish cooked in seawater, raw prawns dressed with olive oil and lemon juice, and deep-fried *cicirello*, a long skinny silver fish. Arrive early to get a table. Closed Sun.
Peppino Piazza Castelnuovo 49 ☎091.324.195. There's a full restaurant menu as well as pizzas. It's touristy, but in a good location. Closed Wed & Aug.
Pizzeria Italia Via Orologio 54 (opposite Teatro Massimo) ☎091.589.885. Attracting large queues, this is the best place in town for light, oven-blistered pizzas (€3–10). Try the Palermitana with tomato, anchovies, onion, artichokes, *caciocavallo* cheese and breadcrumbs. Evenings only; closed Mon.
Primavera Piazza Bologni 4 ☎091.329.408. Not far from the cathedral, off Via Vittorio Emanuele, with outdoor seating in a lovely little piazza, this popular, reasonably priced trattoria serves home-style cooking such as *pasta con le sarde* and *bucatini con broccoli*. Bottles of good, inexpensive local wine as well. Closed Mon.

Santandrea Piazza Sant'Andrea ☎091.334.999. Chic, but not outrageously expensive restaurant a stone's throw from Piazza San Domenico and the Vucciria market. There are no menus, dishes are seasonal and generally delicious. Book early to eat alfresco. Closed Tues & Jan.
Trattoria a'Cuccagna Via Principe di Granatelli 21a, off Via Roma. This long-established, wood-panelled restaurant, whose walls are crammed with local memorabilia, serves authentic, if rather expensive, Sicilian food, along with innova-tions such as *linguine sabbiate* (literally "sandy linguini", with *cernia*, tomatoes, pine nuts, crunchy breadcrumbs and strands of fried chicory), a dish created for King Juan Carlos of Spain, and *pesce spada* (sword fish) grilled with citron, a sort of mild, very thick-skinned lemon (*cedro*).
Trattoria-Pizzeria Enzo Via Maurolico 17/19. The city's best bargain for three-course meals – hefty portions and daft prices: you can walk away very full and somewhat tipsy for under €10. Large range of salads. Closed Fri.

Bars and nightlife

The main focus of **nightlife** is currently the **Kalsa** area, in particular the streets between Piazza Garibaldi and Piazza Maggione, which are packed with styl-ish bars and pubs. Two places currently very "in" are ✴ *Kursaal Kalhesa*, Foro Umberto I 24 (closed Sun eve & Mon) a trendy wine-bar-cum-bookshop set within the ancient fortifications of Arabic Palermo, where they do a great Sunday brunch for €23; and the hip restaurant-club *Tina Pica*, Via Giovanni Meli 13 (closed Mon). In summer, most young people head for **Mondello** (see opposite), and buses run there and back till late.

Listings

American Express Via E. Amari 40 ☎091.587.144 (Mon–Fri 9am–1pm & 4–7pm, Sat 9am–1pm).
Bike rental Totò Cannatella, Via Papireto 14a ☎091.322.425, rents out regular bikes at €10 and mountain bikes at €13 a day.
Car rental Avis, Via Francesco Crispi 115 ☎091.586.940; Hertz, Via Messina 7c ☎091.323.439; Maggiore, Stazione Notarbartolo 79 ☎091.591.681; Sicily By Car, Via Mariano Stabile 6a ☎091.581.045. All of these also have desks at Punta Raisi airport.
Consulates Netherlands, Via Roma 489 ☎091.581.521; UK, Via Cavour 117 ☎091.326.412; USA, Via Vaccarini 1 ☎091.305.857. For nationals of most other coun-tries, the nearest consulates are in Naples or Rome.
Exchange There are exchange offices at Punta Raisi airport (Mon–Fri 9am–4pm) and the central

post office's BancoPosta at Via Roma 322 (bank hours).
Ferry and hydrofoil companies Grandi Navi Veloci (Grimaldi), services to Livorno, Rome and Tunis (at the port at Calata Marinai d'Italia ☎091.587.404, ⊚www.gnv.it); Siremar, to Ústica (Via F. Crispi 120; ☎091.749.3111, ⊚www .siremar.it) Ústica Lines, to the Aeolian Islands, Cefalù and Naples (Via Cap. di Bartolo 55 ☎091.844.9002 ⊚www.usticalines.it); Tirrenia, to Naples, Genoa and Cágliari (at the port on Via Molo ☎091.602.1111, ⊚www.tirrenia.it).
Gay and lesbian information ARCI Gay, Via Genova 7 ☎338.669.7407, ⊚www.arcigay.it. ARCI Donna ☎091.345.799, ⊚www.arcidonna.it.
Hospital Policlinica, Via Carmelo Lazzaro ☎091.655.1111. For an ambulance call ☎118.
Internet access Aboriginal Café, Via Spinuzza 51, opposite the Teatro Massimo ☎091.662.2229

or 328.933.0660, ⓦ www.aboriginalcafe.com (Mon–Sat 6pm–3am); International Point, Via Dante 5 ⓣ091.662.2085 (Mon–Sat 9am–1pm & 4–8pm). **Left luggage** Stazione Centrale by track 8 ⓣ091.603.3040 (daily 7am–11pm); Stazione Marittima ⓣ091.611.3257 (daily 7am–8pm). **Pharmacist** All-night service at Via Roma 1, Via Roma 207, and Via Mariano Stabile 177. There's also a list in Il Giornale di Sicilia. **Police** Central city station at Piazza Vittoria ⓣ112.

Post office Main post office is the Palazzo delle Poste on Via Roma (Mon–Sat 8am–6.30pm). Poste Restante closes at 1.30pm daily. **Travel agents** Compagnia Siciliana Turismo, Via E Amari 124 ⓣ091.743.9611 (for excursions in Sicily); CTS Viaggi Via Garzilli 28g ⓣ091.332.209 (Mon–Fri 9am–1pm & 3.30–7pm, Sat 9am–1pm); Pietro Barbaro, Via Principe di Belmonte 51/55 ⓣ091.333.333 (Mon–Fri 9am–1pm & 4–6pm, Sat 9am–1pm).

Monte Pellegrino and Mondello

Splitting the city from the bay at Mondello (see below) is **Monte Pellegrino**, a 609-metre-high mountain to which the ride itself is as good a reason as any to go (bus #812 from the Politeama theatre or Piazza Sturzo) – an impressive route through a green belt of trees, cacti and scrub, and with views over Palermo and its plain. The bus drops you at the **Santuario di Santa Rosalia** (daily 7am–8pm; ⓣ091.540.0326), a cave in the hillside where the bones of the city's patron were discovered. A chapel was promptly built over the entrance in 1625; supposedly miraculous water trickles down the walls, channelled and collected by steel plates, while fancy lighting illuminates a bier containing a statue of the saint, around which there's invariably a scrum. A small road to the right of the chapel leads to the summit, a half-hour's walk, affording more splendid views, while paths and trails cover the rest of the mountaintop.

If this isn't your bag, the other obvious trip from central Palermo is the short (11km) run to **MONDELLO**, a small seaside resort tucked under the northern bluff of Monte Pellegrino. It features one of Sicily's best stretches of sand (rather than the more usual stones), the two-kilometre **beach** curving round to a tiny working harbour and the remnants of a medieval tower. There's a line of **restaurants** overlooking the water that dish up temptingly fresh fish, while the posh and very expensive *Charleston*, at Viale Regina Elena ⓣ091.450.171, is Palermo's most celebrated restaurant serving exquisite Sicilian and continental cuisine such as home-made *gnocchetti* baked with tomato, basil, mozzarella and aubergine (closed Sun as well as all Jan & Feb). Alternatively, grab some of the excellent snack food from the waterfront stalls and hit the beach. Although often crowded, summer nights at Mondello are fun – the scene of Palermo's real *passeggiata*. In winter it's more laid-back, and rarely very busy, but the restaurants and snack stalls are still open. To get to Mondello, take bus #806, or #833 in summer, from the Politeama theatre or Viale della Libertà – a half-hour ride.

Monreale

The marvellous Monreale cloister…conjures up an impression of such grace as to make one want to stay there forever…

Guy de Maupassant

Even if you only have one spare day in your schedule, you shouldn't miss Sicily's most extraordinary medieval mosaics in the cathedral at **MONREALE** (Royal Mountain). This small hill-town, 8km southwest of Palermo, commands unsurpassed views down the Conca d'Oro Valley, with the capital shimmering in the distant bay. Buses #309 and #389 run frequently from Piazza dell'Indipendenza, and the journey up the valley takes twenty minutes. Monreale's Norman **Duomo** (daily: summer 8am–6pm, winter 8am–12.30pm & 3.30–6pm; free) flanks one side of Piazza Vittorio Emanuele. The rather severe, square-towered exterior – though handsome enough – is no preparation for what's inside: the most impressive and extensive area of Christian medieval mosaic work in the world, the apex of Sicilian-Norman art.

The cathedral, and the town that grew up around it in the twelfth century, both owe their existence to young King William II's rivalry with his powerful Palermitan archbishop, the Englishman Walter of the Mill. William endowed a new monastery in his royal grounds in 1174; the abbey church – this cathedral – was thrown up in a matter of years. This haste accounts for the splendid uniformity of the cathedral's galaxy of coloured mosaics, all bathed in a golden background.

The **mosaics** were almost certainly executed by Greek and Byzantine craftsmen, and they reveal a unitary plan and inspiration. What immediately draws your attention is the all-embracing half-figure of Christ in benediction in the central apse: an awesome and pivotal mosaic, the head and shoulders alone almost twenty metres high. Beneath sit an enthroned Madonna and Child, attendant angels and, below, ranks of saints, each individually and subtly coloured and identified by name. Worth singling out here is the figure of **Thomas à Becket** (marked *SCS Thomas Cantb*), canonized in 1173, just before the mosaics were begun, and presumably included as a show of support by William for the papacy. The nave mosaics are no less remarkable, an animated series that starts with the Creation (to the right of the altar) and runs around the whole church. Most scenes are instantly recognizable: Adam and Eve, Abraham on the point of sacrificing his son, a positively jaunty Noah's Ark; even the Creation, shown in a set of glorious, simplistic panels portraying God filling his world with animals, water, light . . . and people.

Ask at the desk by the entrance to climb the **tower** (daily 9.30am–6pm; €1.50) in the southwest corner of the cathedral. The steps give access to the roof and leave you standing right above the central apse – an unusual and precarious vantage point. It's also worth visiting the **cloisters** (same hours as duomo; €6), part of William's original Benedictine monastery. The formal garden is surrounded by an elegant arcaded quadrangle, 216 twin columns supporting slightly pointed arches – a legacy of the Arab influence. No two capitals are the same, each a riot of detail and imagination: armed hunters doing battle with winged beasts; flowers, birds, snakes and foliage. Entrance to the cloisters is from Piazza Guglielmo, in the corner by the right-hand tower of the cathedral.

If you want **to stay** over, try the *Carrubella Park Hotel*, Via Umberto I 233 (℡091.640.2187, ⓦwww.sicilyhotelsnet.it; ❹), a pleasant family-run place with great views over the valley of the Conca d'Oro, or the quaint B&B *La Ciambra*, Via Sanches 23 (℡091.640.9565, ⓦwww.laciambra.com; ❸), wedged into the web of streets behind the apse of the duomo.

A minute's walk from the duomo towards the belvedere, the **restaurant** *Dietro L'Angolo*, at Via Piave 5 (℡091.640.4067), also has spectacular views of the valley from its terrace, with spaghetti dishes at around €7.

Ústica

A volcanic, turtle-shaped island 60km northwest of Palermo, **ÚSTICA** is one of the more appealing destinations for a quick jaunt away from the city. Colonized originally by the Phoenicians, the island took its name from the Latin *ustum*, or "burnt", a reference to its blackened, lava-strewn appearance. Exposed and isolated, it had a rough time throughout the Middle Ages, its scant population repeatedly harried by pirates who used the island as a base. Even as late as the 1890s the few inhabitants were nearly all exiled prisoners. Today, Ústica's fertile uplands are just right for a day's ambling, while the rough coastline is touted as a skin-diver's paradise, the clear water bursting with fish, sponges, weed and coral. Less adventurous types can easily take a boat trip through Ústica's rugged grottoes and lava outcrops.

The small port of **Ústica town**, where the boats dock, features little more than a few bars, a bank, a dozen restaurants and a handful of places to stay. All these facilities sit around a sloping double piazza, just five minutes' walk uphill from the harbour. **Ferries** and **hydrofoils** operate roughly once or twice daily from the Stazione Marittima in Palermo. The cheapest summer crossing is €11.80 one-way by ferry, rising to €18.20 on the hydrofoils (tickets are from Siremar – see Palermo "Listings", p.1046). In summer Ústica Lines (see Palermo "Listings" p.1046) runs a service from Naples to Trápani via Ústica, Favignana and Levanzo (June and Sept Mon, Thurs & Sat; July & August Mon, Thurs, Fri & Sat). The fare between Naples and Ústica is €66, that between Ústica and Trápani €19.

Ústica town has a couple of good **hotel** choices: the attractive *Clelia*, at Via Magazzino 7 (☏091.844.9039, Ⓦwww.hotelclelia.it; ❸), with a roof terrace overlooking the sea, and the friendly but basic *Ariston*, Via della Vittoria 5 (☏091.844.9042, ❸), which offers rooms with views and can arrange diving and boat trips. Alternatively, look out for for signs advertising *camere* (rooms). For a **meal** with a view, dine at *La Luna sul Porto*, below the piazza and above the port, on Via Vittorio Emanuele (closed Sun in winter) or try local fare such as fish soup with tomatos, garlic and capers at the *Clelia's* restaurant.

The Tyrrhenian coast

From Palermo, the whole of the rugged **Tyrrhenian coast** is accessible by rail and road, offering at times a spectacular ride past deserted coves and rocky beaches. The first real attraction is **Cefalù**, a beach resort and cathedral town. There are few essential stops beyond, though the quiet seaside towns further east are all nice enough for a short break. Also, buses run inland from the larger resorts, providing access to the northern **mountain chains**, the **Madonie** and the **Nebrodi**, with their quiet hill-towns. Unfortunately, the easternmost part of the coast, around **Milazzo** – Sicily's second-largest port – is fairly grim and industrial. However, there's an easy escape route to the **Aeolian Islands**, visible from much of the Tyrrhenian coast and reached by ferries and hydrofoils from Milazzo, hydrofoils from Messina, and, during the summer, hydrofoils from Palermo and Cefalù.

Cefalù

Despite being one of Sicily's busiest international beach resorts, and a barrage of modern building outside town, **CEFALÙ** remains a fairly small-scale fishing port, partly by virtue of its geographical position – tucked onto every available inch of a shelf of land beneath a fearsome crag, **La Rocca**. Roger II founded a mighty cathedral here in 1131 and, as befitting one of the most influential early European rulers, his church dominates the skyline, the great twin towers of the facade rearing up above the flat roofs of the medieval quarter. Naturally, the fine curving sands are the major attraction in town – the main reason why the holiday companies have moved in in such great numbers in recent years – but still, it's a pleasant town, and nothing like as developed as Sicily's other package resort of Taormina.

Halfway along **Corso Ruggero**, the main pedestrianized road through the old town, stands the **duomo** (daily: summer 8am–7pm; winter 8am–5.30pm; free) built – partly at least – as Roger's thanks for fetching up at Cefalù's safe beach in a violent storm. Inside, covering the apse and presbytery, are the earliest and best preserved of the Sicilian church **mosaics**, dating from 1148. The mosaics follow a familiar pattern: Christ Pantocrator dominates the central apse, underneath is the Madonna flanked by archangels, and then the Apostles. Although minuscule in comparison with those at Monreale, these mosaics are just as appealing and, most interestingly, display a quite marked artistic tradition. Forty years earlier than those in William's cathedral, they are thoroughly Byzantine in concept: Christ's face is elongated, the powerful eyes set close together, the outstretched hand flexed and calming.

In high season, when Cefalù's tangibly Arabic central grid of streets is crowded with tourists, you'd do best to visit the cathedral early in the morning, before succumbing to the lure of the long sandy **beach** beyond the harbour. There are a couple of other places that are also worth venturing to: the **Museo Mandralisca** (daily 9am–7pm; €5), at Via Mandralisca 13 (across from Piazza Duomo), has a wry *Portrait of an Unknown Man* by the fifteenth-century Sicilian Master Antonello da Messina, and a huge shell collection; and **La Rocca**, the mountain above the town, holds the megalithic so-called Tempio di Diana, from where paths continue right around the crag, inside medieval walls, to the sketchy fortifications at the very top. If you want to stay over, try the best-priced **accommodation**, the clean, basic and small *Locanda Cangelosi*, centrally placed at Via Umberto I 26 (℡0921.421.591, ⓦwww.locandacangelosi.it; no credit cards; ❶);

Getting to the Aeolian Islands

Sailings **from Milazzo** operate daily and are frequent enough to make it unnecessary to book (unless you're taking a car), although bear in mind that there is a severely reduced service between October and May – and that even moderately rough weather can disrupt the schedules, except in the high season, when every effort is made to keep the hydrofoils running. The **shipping agencies** are down by the harbour and open usual working hours as well as just before all departures – Siremar (Via dei Mille 19; ℡090.928.3242, ⓦwww.siremar.it) for ferries and hydrofoils, Ústica Lines (Via dei Mille 32; ℡090.928.7821, ⓦwww.usticalines.it) for hydrofoils only, and NGI (Via dei Mille 26; ℡090.928.3415) for ferries only.

Hydrofoils are more frequent and twice as quick, but almost twice the price of the ferries: Milazzo to Lípari costs €7.60 one way on the ferry, €13.30 on the hydrofoil.

There are twice-weekly **ferries** throughout the year **from Naples**, and daily summer ferries and hydrofoils, too, from Naples and **Reggio di Calabria** on the Italian mainland; elsewhere in Sicily, services run once daily throughout the year **from Messina**, three weekly **from Palermo and Cefalù** (see "Travel details", p.1099, for an outline of schedules and crossing times).

it also has a handful of two-, three- and four-bed apartments with kitchens to rent. Alternatively, the very pleasant *B&B delle Rose* (T & F 0921.421.885; half board in July & Aug; ❷), at Via Gibilmanna, twenty minutes walk out of town along Umberto I, has rooms with private terraces, while *La Giara*, in the heart of the old town at Via Veterani 40 (T 0921.422.518, W www.hotel-lagiara.it; half board in Aug; ❷), is well equipped, with a big terrace and affable management. For **eating**, there's really nothing outstanding in town, though you'll eat adequately if you stick to *L'Antica Corte*, Corso Ruggero 193 (T 0921.423.228; closed Thurs & Nov), which serves pizza as well as full meals, or *Al Porticciolo*, Via Carlo Ortolani Bordonaro 66 & 92 (T 091. 921.981; closed Wed in winter), an atmospheric place for fish, with a terrace built right onto the rocky shore. The **tourist office** is at Corso Ruggero 77 (Mon–Sat 8am–7.30pm; summer also Sun 9am–1pm; T 0921.421.050, W www.cefalu-tour.pa.it), with free maps and accommodation lists. There are two **hydrofoils** daily to the Aeolian Islands from June to September.

The coast to Milazzo

East of Cefalù the train stops at several small seaside resorts, including **SANTA STEFANO DI CAMASTRA**, a ceramics town, and another 30km on, the fishing village of **SANT'AGATA DI MILITELLO**, popular with Italian holiday-makers. Further down the coast, rounding the cape, you'll find good beaches at **Capo d'Orlando** itself and also at **Oliveri**. From **Patti**'s main square you can catch a bus (3–5 daily) to **Tindari** and the best site along this stretch of coast, the ruins of ancient **Tyndaris** (daily 9am until 1hr before sunset; €2). Founded in 396 BC, it was one of the last Greek settlements in Sicily and retains its Greek walls. Most of the remains, though, are Roman, including some house ruins and a beautifully situated theatre. Visible on the hilltop as you approach the site is the **Santuario della Madonna Nera** (Mon–Sat 7am–noon & 3–6.30pm; free), a lavishly kitsch temple built in the 1960s, where pilgrims come for the Byzantine Black Madonna. From here there's a marvellous seaward view to the tongue of white sand and the Marinella lagoons.

Milazzo

At the base of a thin spit of land poking into the Tyrrhenian Sea, **MILAZZO** is not the sort of place you're likely to make a beeline for. Disfigured by a giant oil refinery, the coast around is noisy and smelly. However, it's the main port of departure for the **Aeolian Islands** (see box opposite for details of sailings), which means, at best, a couple of hours in town awaiting the ferry/hydrofoil – at worst a night in one of the hotels, which will at least give you time to wander the unexpectedly pleasant medieval **old town**, perched high on a hill above the new town, a ten- or fifteen-minute walk from the port.

The nicest place **to stay** is Italy's only eco-hotel, the friendly ✈ *Petit Hotel*, Via dei Mille 37 (T 090.9286.784, W www.petithotel.it; ❸), in a nineteenth-century building on the seafront overlooking the hydrofoil dock. The building was restored, and the hotel is run according to strong ecological principles, using sustainable woods, and tubes of cold water set into the walls as air conditioning in summer. Breakfasts include organic yogurt, eggs and jams.

Also near the dock, try the *California* at Via del Sole 9 (T 090.922.1389; no credit cards; ❶), which has basic rooms with private bathrooms, or *Jack's*, a couple of blocks back from the port at Via Colonnello Magistri 47

(T 090.928.3300, W www.jackshotel.it; ❷), offering clean functional rooms with bathrooms. A slightly more expensive option is *La Bussola*, Via XX Luglio 29 (T 090.928.2955, W www.hotellabussola.it; ❸), which is opposite the Mylarum 2 garage, a secure place to leave your car if you're heading for the islands (€10 per day). The local favourite for fish meals is *Il Covo del Pirata*, Lungomare Garibaldi 47–48 (closed Wed except Aug), while good for pizzas is *Da Tonino*, at Via Cavour 27 (closed Mon in winter), right in the centre. Another good option is *Al Bagatto*, Via M Regis 11 (T 090.922.4212; closed Wed) a wine bar where you can sample local salami and cheeses with a glass of wine, or eat a more substantial dish such as *tagliatelle ai funghi*, or rabbit baked with balsamic vinegar. **Buses** (including the Giuntabus service from Messina, whose timings are pretty much organized to tie in with hydrofoil arrivals and departures) stop on the port-side car park (turn right as you disembark from the hydrofoil). The **train station** is 3km south of the centre, but local buses run into town every thirty minutes during the day, dropping you on the quayside or further up in Piazza della Repubblica. Milazzo's helpful **tourist office** is at Piazza Duilio 20 (Mon–Sat 8am–2.30pm and possibly some afternoons; T 090.922.2865, W www.aastmilazzo.it), just back from the harbour.

If there's time to kill, you might like to poke around the streets of the **Borgo**, the old town on the top of the hill, where the restored **castle** (regular guided tours Tues–Sat: March–May & Sept 10am–5pm; June–Aug 10am–7pm; Oct–Feb 9.30am–3.30pm; €3.10) sits inside a much larger and older walled city, complete with its own cathedral. Dotted around the Borgo are plenty of pubs, open every evening in summer, but only from Wednesday to Sunday in winter. On a warm day, take the steps that run down the far side of the caste walls to the Spiaggia di Ponente, a long **beach** of grey gravel with crystal-clear waters.

The Aeolian Islands

Volcanic in origin, the **Aeolian Islands** lead a precarious existence in the buffeted waters off the northern Sicilian coast. They are named after Aeolus, the Greek god who kept the winds he controlled shut tight in one of the islands' many caves. According to Homer, Odysseus put into the Aeolians and was given a bag of wind to help him home, but his sailors opened it too soon and the ship was blown straight back to port. More verifiably, the islands were coveted for their mineral wealth, the mining of obsidian (hard, glass-like lava) providing the basis for early prosperity. Later their strategic importance attracted the Greeks, who settled on Lípari in 580 BC. The Greeks' powerful fleet kept rivals at bay until the islands fell to the Carthaginians, who in turn were pushed out by the Romans in 252 BC. Thereafter began a period of decline: the islands became a haven for pirates and a place of exile, a state of affairs that continued right into the twentieth century with the Fascists exiling their political opponents to Lípari.

It's only comparatively recently that the islanders stopped scratching a subsistence living and started welcoming tourists. Emigration had virtually depopulated some of the islands, and even now the more remote ones are sorely stretched to maintain a decent living. That said, you won't be alone if you come to the islands during the summer months: the central group of **Vulcano**, **Lípari**, **Panarea** and **Salina** are pretty well known to an increasing crowd of devotees, while the constant volcanic activity on **Strómboli** attracts tourists virtually year round. All the islands are **expensive** in high season, with prices in shops as well as restaurants reflecting the fact that just about all food is imported.

But get out to the minor isles or come in blustery winter for a taste of what life was like on the islands twenty – or a hundred – years ago: unsophisticated, rough and beautiful.

Getting here is easiest from Milazzo (see box, p.1050), with year-round ferries and hydrofoils connecting the port with all the islands. **Getting around** in summer is easy, as ferries (*traghetti*) and hydrofoils (*aliscafi*) link all the islands. In winter, services are reduced and in rough weather cancelled altogether, particularly on the routes out to Alicudi and Filicudi. A car might be worth taking to Lípari and Salina, but bikes are better and you can rent them on the spot.

In high season (Easter & July–Aug), **accommodation** is scarce and you'd be wise to phone in advance, especially if you want to visit Strómboli. You may also find that many places insist that you pay for half board. Most hotels and *pensioni* drop their prices by up to fifty percent from October to March, while renting **apartments** or **private rooms** is an economical option too. There are **campsites** on Vulcano, Salina and Lípari – but note that camping rough is illegal. In many places there's not always the option of a cheap pizzeria, so if money is tight, expect to do some self-catering.

There are **ATMs** on all the islands but Alicudi (though they frequently run out of cash), and you can change money in post offices, travel agencies and major hotels throughout the islands, though the rates aren't good. **Electricity** has only slowly come to some islands. Power cuts are still commonplace, usually caused by storms in winter, and in August simply by over-demand, and if you're spending any time on Alicudi, Filicudi or Strómboli, a torch is a good investment. Don't be surprised if hotels ask you to go sparingly with the **water** as it is imported by tanker.

Vulcano

Closest to the Sicilian mainland, **VULCANO** is the first port of call for ferries and hydrofoils – 45 minutes by hydrofoil, around an hour and a half on the slowest ferry crossing. From the harbour of **PORTO DI LEVANTE** you can walk up to the main crater of the volcano in around an hour; the last volcanic explosion here was in 1890. A second hike is to **Vulcanello**, the volcanic pimple just to the north of the port, spewed out of the sea in 183 BC, and there's good **walking** to be had around the rest of the island, too. Less energetically, just fifteen minutes' walk from Porto di Levante, across the neck of land separating it from Porto di Ponente, there's an excellent black-sand **beach**. On the way you'll pass Vulcano's sulphurous **mud baths** and **hot springs** bubbling into (and warming) the sea. If you opt for a wallow in the mud, be warned you'll reek of it for days afterwards, and don't wear any jewellery, because it will be stained and corroded.

A summer-only **tourist office** operates in the golfball-shaped building at Porto di Levante (June–Sept daily 8am–2pm; ☎090.985.2028) and provides information on rooms. There isn't a huge choice, but *La Giara* at Via Provinciale 18 is welcoming and quiet (☎090.985.2229 or ☎333.437.0802, ⓦwww .portaledelleeolie.it; ❸; closed Nov–March) and also has several apartments to rent, or there's the functional *Torre*, in the piazzetta near the mud baths (☎090.985.2342, ⓦwww.portaledelleeolie.it; no credit cards; ❶–❷). On the Porto Ponente side, *Residence Lanterna Bleu* (☎ & Ⓕ090.985.2178; ❶–❷; closed mid-Dec to mid-Jan) is a series of one- and two-bedroom apartments with kitchens and a small terrace. The cost of food on the island is exorbitant, and you have to choose carefully from the battery of **restaurants** (most of which close between November and Easter) along the road that bends around from the port. *Da Maurizio*, just beyond the Siremar agency, has a nice shady garden and a reasonable tourist menu, as does *Il Palmento*, just up from the mud baths. A more upmarket choice is the *Belvedere* (☎090.985.3047) in the Piano district between the port and Gelso.

Lípari

There are regular, daily hydrofoil services from Vulcano to **LÍPARI**, by far the most popular of the islands – and the most diverse. The group's main port and capital, **LÍPARI TOWN** is a thriving little place prettily bunched between two harbours: hydrofoils and ferries both dock at the **Marina Lunga**, a deep-water harbour curving around to the north as a long beach, while the smaller **Marina Corta**, a tiny harbour formed by a church-topped mole and dwarfed by the castle that crowns the hill above, is used for boats offering excursions to the surrounding islands.

The upper town within the fortress walls, the **Castello**, forms the main focus of interest. Finds from the site, which has been continuously occupied since Neolithic times, have enabled archeologists to date other Mediter-ranean cultures. Alongside the well-marked **excavations**, there's a tangle of dilapidated churches flanking the main cobbled street, and several buildings (including the seventeenth-century bishop's palace) that make up the separate arms of the **Museo Eoliano** (daily 9am–1.30pm & 3–7pm; €6) – a lavish collection of Neolithic pottery, late Bronze Age artefacts, and decorated Greek and Roman vases and statues, most of it dug up outside. Highlights are the towering banks of amphorae, a stunning array of Greek theatrical masks, and statuettes of dancers and actors – early Greek pin-ups. Down below, the streets wind around the base of the fortified hill and down to the harbours. The town relies on tourism these days – as the restaurants and craft shops testify – but it's all fairly small-scale.

The **tourist office** at Corso Vittorio Emanuele 202 (Mon–Fri 8.30am–1.30pm & 4.30–7.30pm; July & Aug also Sat 8.30am–1.30pm; ☎090.988.0095, ⓦwww.aasteolie.info) can provide the useful *Ospitalità in blu* booklet, which contains a list of hotels and information for all the Aeolian islands. In July and August it makes sense to listen to the offers of **rooms** as you step off the boat. Expect to pay around €25–40 per person in August, €20 at other times of the year, for something with a shower, kitchen and balcony or terrace. Otherwise, good places to try include *Enza Marturano*, Via Maurolico 35 (☎368.322.4997, ⓦwww.enzamarturano.it; no credit cards; ❷–❸), whose four bright rooms are ranged around a communal lounge/kitchen, and *Casa Vittorio*, Vico Sparviero (☎090.981.1523 or 338.392.3867, ⓦwww.casavittorio.it; ❷–❸), which rents out clean and plain rooms and apartments year round. Alternatively, ⚑ *Diana Brown*, at Vico Himera 3 (☎090.981.2584, ⓦwww.dianabrown.it; no credit cards; ❷–❸), is a spotlessly clean place with fridges, kettles, a book exchange and roof garden, run by a friendly South African expat, while the *Neri*, Via G. Marconi 43 (☎090.981.1413, ⓦwww.pensioneneri.it; open March–Sept; ❷), is a slightly dilapidated Liberty (Art Deco) mansion that serves breakfast on the terrace. There are also two nice rooms to rent from a lovely Frenchwoman, Christine Berart, the islands' vet, at Vico Montelbello 19 (☎090.9880.783 or 338.886.1297, ⓔchristine@eolnet.it; ❷). If you fancy staying in the lap of luxury, push the boat out at *Villa Meligunis*, Via Marte 7 (☎090.981.2426, ⓦwww.villameligunis.it; ❻–❽), a gorgeous converted *palazzo* with excellent views of the citadel and sea from its rooftop restaurant, and a pool along-side; it offers great discounts off-season. The nearest **campsite**, *Baia Unci*

(☎090.981.1909; mid-March to mid-Oct), is 3km away at the southern end of the fishing village of Canneto (see below); the bus from Lípari stops outside. There's a SISA **supermarket** and various *alimentari* and bakeries on the main Corso – if you're self-catering, head for the deli counter and fruit and veg section at the SISA, and buy your bread from the bakery opposite.

The town's numerous **restaurants and pizzerias** have (often poor, and inevitably over-priced) tourist menus at around €15–20, and even the cheaper places impose hefty fifteen or twenty percent service charges. *Bartolo*, Via Garibaldi 53 (closed Fri in winter, & Jan–March), makes great wood-fired pizzas, while *Trattoria d'Oro*, Via Umberto I 32 (closed Sun in winter), is a decent backstreet *trattoria* where you should be able to eat a full meal for around €20, including Sicilian dishes such as *pasta con muddiche* (pasta with anchoivies, garlic, cheese and breadcrumbs). For a gastronomic treat, the expensive *E'Pulera*, Via Diana (☎090.981.1158; closed Oct–April), specializes in traditional Aeolian food served in a romantic courtyard-garden. Try the fettucine with wild fennel and prawns.

The rest of the island is easy to reach on a network of regular **buses**, which leave from a stop by the Marina Lunga, opposite the service station. Around here too are a couple of **scooter and bike rental** outfits. Roberto (☎340.548.4396) rents out *motorinos* (€18 per day, rising to €25 in July and €35 in August) and also organizes **boat trips** on his little fishing boat, with or without delicious rough and ready food cooked from freshly caught fish and cooked on a single ring in the tiny galley. Typically, you'll pay around €35 for an all-day trip which lets you visit and swim off the island of Panarea and then see the evening explosions off Strómboli; day-trips to Panarea or Vulcano, allowing plenty of swimming, are around half that price.

CANNETO, a resort with a pebbled beach and a couple of hotels, also makes a pleasant excursion. From here the road climbs north, passing an excellent sandy beach (the Spiaggia Bianca) a couple of kilometres out of Canneto, before reaching the stony beach at Porticello. West of Lípari town, the road clambers up the hill to **Quattrocchi** ("Four Eyes"), a three-kilometre hike that ends in glorious and much-photographed views over Vulcano and the spiky faraglioni rocks that puncture the sea between the two islands. Keep on the road to **Pianoconte**, which has a couple of pizza restaurants that are popular in the evenings, and just after the village, a side road slinks off down to the old Roman thermal baths at **San Calogero**. This is a particularly fine walk, across a valley and skirting some impressive cliffs. It takes about half an hour from Pianoconte.

Salina

North of Lípari, **SALINA**'s two extinct volcanic cones rise out of a fertile land which produces capers and white malvasia wine by the bucketload. Again, it's excellent **walking** country (though there are bus services between the main villages) and you get some marvellous vantage points over the other islands.

The main island port is **SANTA MARINA DI SALINA** on the east coast – a relaxed enough spot ranged along a single, pedestrianized main street, with good swimming from a beach of large stones. You may be able to find private **rooms** here if you ask around, or try the *B&B Da Sabina*, at the far end of the village from the port at Via Risorgimento 5c (℡ 090.984.3134 or 333.272.6025, Ⓦ www.bbsalina.it; ❷–❸, rising to ❹–❺ in August), where there are three rooms with bath and a large terrace. The owner also offers cookery courses. The nicely furnished *Mamma Santina*, Via Sanità 40 (℡ 090.984.3054, Ⓦ www.mamma santina.it; ❺; open end March to Nov), signposted to the left off the main street of Via Risorgimento, has a great pool and one of the island's better restaurants. Down on the seafront is the new *Mercanti di Mare* (℡ 090.9843.536, Ⓦ www .hotelmercantidimare.it; ❹–❺), whose owner, Alberto, is author of a book of the same name, about the seafaring history of the islands (as well as running the local Siremar office). It has nine white, airy rooms and a terrace with views over the sea to Strómboli, Panarea and Lípari.

For **eating**, *Nni Lausto* (℡ 090.9843.486, open May–Oct), Via Risorgimento X, is a cool wine bar and restaurant whose New York-trained owner-chef brings an adventurous new twist to local dishes. Try the *tartare di tonno*, raw tuna dressed with wild fennel and capers, or spaghetti with raw sea urchin. The *Porto Bello* restaurant above the port (closed Wed in winter, & all Nov) serves excellent local antipasto, and beautifully prepared pasta and fish dishes.

LINGUA, sitting by a pretty lagoon 3km south, makes a pleasant alternative base, with a small ethnographic **museum** in front of the lagoon (July & Aug daily 9am–1pm & 5–8pm; Sept–June variable; free), displaying local prehistoric lavic rock utensils and the like, though the main draw is the tiny **bar** 🍴 *Da Alfredo*, on the seafront piazza, famous throughout Italy for its fresh fruit and nut granitas. They also do *pane cunzato*, a huge round of grilled bread piled with various combinations of home-cured tuna, capers, tomatos, baked ricotta and olives.

If you want to stay, try a new **hotel**, *La Salina*, with lovely rooms, many with private terraces, set in the buildings of the former salt works by the lagoon (℡ 090.9843.441, Ⓦ www.lasalinahotel.com; ❻). If you're on a tight budget, best value on the island is the assembly of half a dozen funky **apartments** known as the *Villagio* (℡ 335.666.0777 or 329.796.6120; ❶) on the main road through the village, overlooking the lagoon. You'll also find rooms at the restaurant '*A Cannata* (℡ 090.984.3161, Ⓦ www.acannata.it; ❷–❸), near the church, some of them with a terrace and wonderful views of Lípari. They also have **houses** to rent all over Lingua, the nicest right above the beach by the cemetery. There are nice rooms too at *Il Delfino*, right on the seafront at Via Garibaldi 19 (℡ 090.984.3024, Ⓦ www.ildelfinosalina.com; ❷–❸). Half board is compulsory at both '*A Cannata* and *Il Delfino* in August (a hefty €120 or so per person). Both have minibuses to ferry guests between the port and Lingua.

Walking trails cut right across Salina, in particular linking Santa Marina and Lingua with the peak of **Monte Fossa delle Felci** (962m), the sanctuary of **Madonna del Terzito** and the **south coast** at Rinella. There are trail heads signed from the road between Santa Marina and Lingua, and also from the Circonvalazione that cuts behind Santa Marina. If you want an easier time of it, all **buses** between Santa Marina/Malfa and Leni/Rinella pass right by the Madonna del Terzito – from where there's a broad easy-to-follow track. Don't go overloaded, wear strong shoes, and take plenty of water.

Most ferries and hydrofoils also call at the little port of **RINELLA**, on the island's south coast; if you want to move straight on, buses pretty much meet the boat arrivals on the quayside (and call here several times a day in addition). Notices at the port advertise **rooms** for rent and there's a very nice little **hotel**, too, *L'Ariana* (☎090.980.9075, ⊛www.hotelariana.it; half board in Aug; closed mid-Nov & Dec; ❷), occupying a turn-of-the-century villa with a frill of terracotta busts around its roof, just above the port to the left. You can eat well here, or try one of the two excellent **pizzerias**, *Da Marco*, just up the road from the Ariana, or *Le Tre Pietre*, on the main road out of the village. The village is also the site of the island's one **campsite**, *Tre Pini* (☎090.980.9155, ⊛www.trepini .com; April–Oct), right on the shore under pines.

Panarea

Only 3km by 1.5km, **PANAREA** is the smallest of the Aeolians but easily the most scenic. No cars can squeeze onto the island's narrow lanes to disturb the tranquillity, though heavily laden three-wheelers are common, and Panarea's cosy intimacy has made it into something of a ghetto for the idle rich. Nevertheless, either side of high season you can find reasonably priced accommodation if you persevere. Panarea's population divides itself among three hamlets on the eastern side of the island, Ditella, San Pietro and Drauto, with the boats docking at **SAN PIETRO**. It's always worth asking around for **rented rooms** – but bear in mind that the supply of accommodation on the island simply can't meet the demand in July and August. Possibilities include the *Trattoria da Francesco* (☎090.983.023; half board in Aug; closed Dec–Feb; ❸) on the harbourside, and several houses on Via San Pietro, up from the port; there are also five rooms with private bathroom at *Casa Nonna* (☎090.983.004, ⊛www .liscabianca.it; ❶) owned by the same people as the expensive *Lisca Bianca* hotel. Otherwise the two cheapest **hotels** are the *Casa Rodà* (☎090.983.006, ⓕ090.983.212; ❸), which also has some little apartments to rent, and the *Tesoriero* (☎090.983.098, ⊛www.hoteltesoriero.it; closed mid-Oct to mid-March; ❷), both on Via San Pietro, which has a minibus connecting it to the port. For a splurge, you could try one of the two more luxurious hotels at San Pietro, the *Raya* (☎090.983.013, ⊛www.hotelraya.it; ❾; closed Nov–March), on a hill to the left, or the nearby *Cincotta* (☎090.983.014, ⓕ090.983.211; ❻; closed mid-Oct to mid-April); both have wonderful terraces and facilities, and rates plummet outside high season. The hotels also house Panarea's best **restaurants**, though you can eat more modestly by the harbour at *Trattoria da Francesco*, while *Casa Rodà* has a garden-restaurant serving pizzas in the evenings (both closed in winter). The family-style *Da Paulino*, a ten-minute walk along Via San Pietro towards Ditella, also serves original, tasty meals.

Half an hour's walk south of San Pietro is the island's one sandy **beach** and, high above here on the other side, **Punta Milazzese**, where a Bronze Age village of 23 huts was discovered in 1948. The site is thought to have been inhabited since the fourteenth century BC, and pottery found here (displayed in Lípari's museum) shows a distinct Minoan influence. Elsewhere, there are **hot springs** at San Pietro and, at **Calcara** to the north, a beach and sea that sometimes steam – one effect of the island's fumaroles.

Strómboli

Despite the regularity of the volcanic explosions, people have always lived on **STRÓMBOLI**. Usually, little more than flashes and noise are thrown up, though sometimes the explosions are more serious, as in January 2003, when a burst of gas sent rocks into the sea and caused a tidal wave. A constant flow of lava is always to be seen, slowly sliding down the northwest side of the volcano into the sea. Most of the many hotels and rooms to let on the island are on the eastern side, in the adjacent parishes of San Vincenzo, San Bartolo and Piscità, often grouped together as **STRÓMBOLI TOWN** and something of a chic resort since Rossellini and Ingrid Bergman immortalized the place in the 1949 film *Strómboli*. From the quayside, the lower coastal road runs around to the main beaches of **FicograndE** and, further on, **Piscità**, the island's best ashy beach. It's around 25 minutes on foot from the port to here. The other road from the dock cuts up into the "village", where as Via Roma it runs to the church of **San Vincenzo**, whose square offers glorious views of the offshore islet of Strombolicchio. Beyond the square, along Via Vittorio Emanuele III, it's another fifteen minutes' walk to the second church of **San Bartolo**, above Piscità.

In summer, the quayside is thick with three-wheelers and touts offering **rooms**, waving their cards at you; prices start at around €25 per person. If you want to try and book a room in advance, the following places are all worth contacting: *Villa Petrusa*, Via Soldato Panettieri 4 (℡090.986.045, ℻090.986.126; closed Nov–March; ❸), with an attractive garden, or further out, and also with a garden, the friendly *Brasile*, Via Soldato Cincotta, in the Piscità district (℡090.986.008, ⓦwww.strombolialbergobrasile.it; closed Nov–March; ❷), where half board is required from mid-June to August, and the nearby *Casa del Sole*, at Via Soldato Cincotta (℡ & ℻090.986.017, ⓦwww.emmeti .it-casadelsole; closed Nov–Easter; no credit cards; ❷–❸), which has kitchen facilities and a sun terrace; off-season singles go for €22. The best **restaurant** in the village is *Il Canneto* (closed Oct–Easter), up from the port, though you'll find cheaper fare and good pizzas further up the road at *La Trottola*, a popular place where you can eat for well under €25 (closed Oct–Easter, though pizzas available in winter at weekends). At night, there's no better spot for lingering than *Bar Ingrid*, in the square by San Vincenzo church, open until 2am.

On the other side of the island, accessible by hydrofoil, the hamlet of **GINOSTRA** is a peaceful place of typical white Aeolian houses on terraces. There's excellent **accommodation** here, too, at the *Locanda Petrusa* (℡ & ℻090.981.2305; closed Oct–April; half board in July & Aug; no credit cards; ❸), which has three spacious rooms with terraces and a shared bathroom, and also serves meals. **Hydrofoils** run back to Strómboli town twice a day in summer (once daily in winter), but these are susceptible to cancellation because of rough waters.

Guides for the **ascent of the volcano** (depending on the level of activity) are readily available in Strómboli town and cost around €20 per person; try Magmatrek on Via Vittorio Emanuele (℡090.986.5768 or 333.906.6053; ⓦwww.magmatrek.it), where the guides are well informed and in constant radio contact with the volcanologists at the control centre. The climb up takes three hours; you get an hour or so at the top watching the pyrotechnics, and it then takes another two hours to descend. You should not attempt the climb alone, and do not consider spending the night on the volcano, as was popular some years ago. Not only is the volcano particularly volatile at present, but hoards of people sleeping rough did a lot of environmental damage. You need to be properly equipped: good shoes, a sunhat and plenty of water (a minimum of two litres per person) are essential, and for a night climb bring warm clothes and a torch.

The main **boat trips** offered are tours around the island, calling at Ginostra and Strombolicchio (3hr; €15), and trips out at night to see the Sciara del Fuoco (2hr 20min; €15). A friendly outfit is run by Pippo – of Società Navigazione Pippo (℡090.986.135 or 338.985.7883) – who has a stand in front of the *Beach Bar*. Alternatively, you can rent a boat from any of the outfits by the port.

The Ionian coast: Messina to Siracusa

It's Sicily's eastern **Ionian coast** which draws most visitors, attracted by some of the island's most exciting sights – natural and constructed. The most likely arrival point is **Messina**, which receives a constant stream of ferries bearing trains across the Straits from Calabria. **Taormina**, most chic of the island's resorts and famed for its remarkable Graeco-Roman theatre, is an hour's train ride south, and lava-built **Catania**, Sicily's second city, is another hour beyond: both places (indeed the whole of this part of the coast) are dominated by the massive presence of **Mount Etna**, Europe's highest volcano. A road and a narrow-gauge single-track railway circumnavigate the lower slopes of Etna, passing through a series of hardy towns surrounded by swirls of black rock spat from the volcano. Further south, out of the lee of Etna, lie traces of the **ancient Greek cities** that once lined the southeastern coast. **Megara Hyblaea** has the most extensive remains, and the route concludes in **Siracusa** – formerly the most important and beautiful city in the Hellenistic world.

Messina and south

MESSINA may well be your first sight of Sicily, and – from the ferry – it's a fine one, the glittering town spread up the hillside beyond the sickle-shaped harbour. Sadly, the image is shattered almost as soon as you step into the city, bombed and shaken to a shadow of its former self by a record number of disasters. Plague, cholera and earthquakes all struck throughout the eighteenth and nineteenth centuries, culminating in the great earthquake of 1908 that killed 84,000 people, levelled the city and made the shore sink by half a metre overnight. Allied bombing raids in 1943 didn't help, undoing much of the post-earthquake restoration.

Today, the remodelled city guards against future natural disasters, with wide streets and low, reinforced concrete buildings marching off in all directions. Not surprisingly, it's a pretty dull spectacle, and most of what interest there is resides in Messina's active **port area**. Take time at least to walk up Via I Settembre from the train station to **Piazza del Duomo**. The traffic-cluttered paved square was laid out in the eighteenth century, while the **duomo** itself (Mon–Sat 7am–7pm, Sun 7.30am–1pm, 4–7.30pm; free) is a faithful reconstruction of the medieval cathedral built by Roger II. The facade retains its grand doorways and some original sculpture: inside, most of what you see – from the marble floor to the painted wooden ceiling – has been retouched and rebuilt. The detached **campanile** reputedly contains the largest astronomical clock in the world. Be there at noon and you get the full show, a visually impressive panoply of moving gilt figures including a crowing cock, roaring lion and a succession of doves and angels accompanying the Madonna. You can climb the campanile if you want a closer look (mid-April to mid-Sept daily 9am–1pm & 4.30–6.30pm; mid-Sept to Oct daily 9am–1pm; Nov to mid-April open Mon–Sat for groups, by appointment only; ℡090.675.175).

Much of what was salvaged from the various disasters now resides in the **Museo Regionale** (Mon & Fri 9am–1.30pm, Tues, Thurs & Sat 9am–1.30pm & 3–5.30pm, Sun 9am–12.30pm, closed Wed; last entry 30min before closing; €4.50), 3km north of the centre – a 45-minute walk along Via della Libertà, or tram #28 to the terminus, Annunziata. A great deal has been painstakingly stuck and plastered back together in this beautifully laid-out museum, including a couple of **Caravaggio**s, commissioned by the city in 1604. There are also damaged works by Antonello da Messina, a few good Flemish pieces and the city's rescued archeological remains. Look out for the striking painting of St Peter by Girolamo Alibrandi and a writhing Scilla, adorned with lions' heads, a sixteenth-century sculpture by da Montorsoli.

If you're in Messina in mid-summer, you may coincide with the feast of the Assumption, or **ferragosto**, on August 15, when a towering carriage, the Vara – an elaborate column supporting dozens of papier-mâché putti and angels, topped by the figure of Christ stretching out his right arm to launch Mary heavenwards – is hauled through the city centre. Late at night, one of Sicily's best firework displays is held on the seafront near Via della Libertà.

Practicalities

Trains all use the Stazione Centrale by the harbour, adjacent to the **Stazione Marittima**, where the train-ferries from Calabria dock. Other **ferries** and **hydrofoils** (to and from Villa San Giovanni, Reggio di Calabria and the Aeolian Islands) dock at quays further to the north, on Via Vittorio Emanuele and Via della Libertà. Interbus and SAIS **buses** for Palermo, Rome and Catania leave from Piazza della Repubblica by the train station, while those for Milazzo (for onward connections to the Aeolian Islands) depart from the Giuntabus office at Via Terranova 8 (at the corner of Viale San Martino), a five-minute walk away. There are two **tourist offices** just outside the train station: one on Piazza della Repubblica (Mon–Thurs 9am–1.30pm & 3–5pm, Fri 9am–1.30pm; sometimes also opens Sat mornings; ℡090.672. 944), where good English is spoken, the other just beyond on Via Calabria (Mon–Sat 8am–6.30pm; ℡090.674.236, Ⓔaziendaturismo@aziendaturismomessina.it); both can supply you with free maps, Aeolian Islands ferry timetables and accommodation lists.

Unless you arrive late in the day, it's hardly necessary to stay over in Messina. Still, there are a couple of basic **accommodation** options on Via N. Scotto, an alley on the south side of Piazza della Repubblica, beyond the SAIS office: the *Mirage*, at no. 3 (℡090.293.8844; ❶–❷), which has fourteen rooms with and without bathrooms; and the sprucer *Touring*, at no. 17 (℡ & ℻090.293.8851;

●—❷), which also has rooms with or without bathroom. A slicker option is the modern *Excelsior* (℡090.293.1431, 🌐www.sicilyhotels.it; ❸), near Piazza Cairoli at Via Maddalena 32. There's a **campsite**, *Il Peloritano* (℡090.348.496), out beyond Punta del Faro on the northern coast; take bus #81 to Rodia from the train station.

Messina has a good choice of **restaurants**, many serving freshly caught swordfish from the straits; May and June are the height of the swordfish season. *Lungomare da Mario*, opposite the hydrofoil dock at Via Vittorio Emanuele 108 (℡090.42.477; closed Wed except Aug) has good fresh fish and an exceptional antipasto buffet, perfect for a quick lunch before catching the daily 1.50pm hydrofoil to the Aeolian islands; otherwise you can eat good pasta and not pay too much at the *Osteria del Campanile*, Via Loggia dei Mercanti 9 (℡090.711.418), off Piazza del Duomo (closed Sun except July & Aug) – try *spaghetti della stretta*, with swordfish, tomatos and olives. There's also the basic but good *Pizzeria del Capitano* at Via dei Mille 88 (℡090.661.748), close to Piazza Cairoli (closed Mon). Tasty panini and other cold **snacks** are on offer at *Salumeria Nucita*, an *alimentari* at Via Garibaldi 125 (closed Wed eve & Sun), while *Abbate*, Via Garibaldi 62 (℡090.774.064; closed Sun), serves fine wine, *crostini* and French cheese and a *tavola calda*. If it's breakfast you're after, head to Piazza Cairoli, where there are two good long-established café-*pasticcerias*: *Billé* at no. 7 (closed Tues) and *Irrera* at no. 12. For ice creams with a parrot and a view, head up to *Bar del Panorama*, next to the Santuario Cristo Re on Viale Principe Umberto. There's **Internet** access at Via dei Mille 200, off Piazza Cairoli (Mon–Sat 9am–1pm & 4–8pm), as well as the FastNet Café (which offers WiFi), Via Garibaldi 72 (same hours).

The coastal route south

Try to take the train, rather than the slower bus or road option, along the **coastal route south** from Messina, since the line follows the rough, stony shore pretty much all the way: on a clear day there are spanking views over to Calabria.

Santa Teresa Di Riva is the first recognizable resort, with an oversized beach, though it's nothing to shout about. The straggling village is more attractive as a jumping-off point for the foothills of the **Monti Peloritani**, the long mountain range that cuts south from Messina. Buses from Santa Teresa twist the 4km up to **SAVOCA**, a peaceful hill-village, evocatively situated up in the clouds. Houses and three churches perch precariously on the cliffsides in clumps, a tattered castle topping the pile. Signs in the village point you to the **Cappuccini monastery** whose catacombs (Tues–Sun: April–Sept 9am–1pm & 4–7pm; Oct–March 9am–noon & 3–7pm; donation requested) maintain a selection of mummified bodies, two to three hundred years old, in niches, dressed in their eighteenth-century finery, the skulls of less complete compatriots lining the walls above. More offbeat delight is at hand in the village's *Bar Vitelli*, used as the scene of Michael Corleone's betrothal in Coppola's film *The Godfather*.

Taormina

TAORMINA, high on Monte Tauro and dominating two grand sweeping bays below, is Sicily's best-known resort. The outstanding remains of its classical theatre, with Mount Etna as an unparalleled backdrop, arrested passing travellers when Taormina was no more than a medieval hill-village. Goethe and D.H.

Lawrence are the two big names touted by the tourist office; Lawrence was so enraptured that he lived here (1920–23) in a house at the top of the valley cleft behind the theatre. Although international tourism has taken its toll over recent years, Taormina still retains a lot of charm. The one main traffic-free street is an unbroken line of fifteenth- to nineteenth-century *palazzi* and small, intimate piazzas, and there is an agreeably crumbly castle and rows of flower-filled balconies. The downside is that between June and August it's virtually impossible to find anywhere to stay, and the narrow alleys are shoulder-to-shoulder with tourists. April, May or September are slightly better, but to avoid the crowds completely come between October and March, when it's often still warm enough to swim.

Arrival and information

Trains pull up at the handsome Taormina-Giardini station on the water's edge, way below town. It's a very steep thirty-minute walk up to Taormina (turn right out of the station and then, after 200m, left through a gap in the buildings, marked "Centro") and the road is extremely busy. Much better (certainly if you have luggage) is to take one of the fairly frequent local buses that pick up outside the train station, or else arrive by **bus** at the bus terminal, on Via Luigi Pirandello in Taormina itself: bear left up the road from the terminal, turn through the Porta Messina, and the main street, Corso Umberto I, lies before you. If you're arriving by **car** for the day, make for the Porta Catania multi-storey car park, situated below Piazza S. Antonio. The **tourist office** (Mon–Sat 8.30am–2pm & 4–7pm; ℡0942.23.243, ⓦwww.gat€2taormina.com) is in the fourteenth-century Palazzo Corvaja, off Piazza Vittorio Emanuele, the first square you come to. You'll find an **Internet** café at Corso Umberto 214, opposite the Municipio (daily 9am–9pm).

Accommodation

Finding **accommodation** in summer is a time-consuming business; only a handful of beds will be both available and affordable, so it's well worth booking ahead. The best prices are for **rented rooms**, though you'll find more comfort and great views at some of the town's **B&Bs** and **hotels** in choice locations. There's also a small **youth hostel**, *Taormona's Odyssey* (℡0942.24533; ⓦwww .taorminaodyssey.it; €16–18), just outside the centre at Traversa G. Martino 2 off Via Fontana Vecchia; book well ahead to secure a bed.

Diana Via di Giovanni 6 ℡0942.23.898. Tiny, centrally located *pensione* which has changed little since it was opened in 1960, and has a nice old-lady owner. No credit cards. ❶

Leone Via Bagnoli Croce 126 ℡ & ℻0942.23.878. Simple place close to the public gardens which also has one of the few no-frills bars in town (you can get a glass of wine for €1.30). No credit cards. ❶

Pensione Svizzera Via Pirandello 26 ℡0942.23.790, ⓦwww.pensionesvizzera.com. Just up from the bus terminal and cable car station this comfortable hotel has excellent views from its spacious rooms (with varying prices depending on size and view) and a shuttle service to a private beach. ❸–❺

🏃 **San Domenico Palace** Piazza San Domenico 5 ℡0942.613.111, ⓦwww.thi.it. The last word in luxury. One of the most celebrated hotels in Italy, housed in a fifteenth-century convent. ❾

Villa Belvedere Via Bagnoli Croce 79 ℡0942.23.791, ⓦwww.villabelvedere.it. Decent, if unexciting rooms, but a great pool in a lavish garden, and fantastic views. ❼

Villa Floresta Via Damiano Rosso 1 ℡0942.620.184, ⓦwww.villafloresta.it. Pleasant B&B in a nineteenth-century *palazzo* tucked into a courtyard with a crumbling fifteenth-century staircase behind Piazza del Duomo. ❷

Villa Greta Via Leonardo da Vinci 41 ℡0942.28.286, ⓦwww.villagreta.it. Family-run place fifteen minutes' walk out of town on the road up to Castelmola, with superb balcony views, as well as a dining room with good home cooking. In winter, tea with home-made cakes and biscuits is thrown in free. **3**

Villa Sara Via Leonardo da Vinci 55 ⊤0942.28.138, ⓦwww.villasara.net. Exceptional B&B a fifteen-minute walk (or a brief bus ride) up the road to Castelmola. It doesn't look much from the outside, but behind the bare walls is a gracious two-storey apartment where a friendly family rent out three spacious rooms, each with its own bathroom and its own large terrace commanding great views over Taormina, Etna and the sea. In the future there may also be a couple of self-catering apartments to rent. **2**

Villa Schuler Piazzetta Bastione ⊤0942.23.481, ⓦwww.villaschuler.com. This lovely old hotel has been in the same family of German émigrés for a century, and retains the feel of an elegant family-run *pensione* (they take no tour groups). There are great views from its rooms and terrace, and a beautiful garden behind. Worth checking the website for special offers. **5**

The Town

The **Teatro Greco** (daily 9am until 1hr before sunset; €6) – signposted from just about everywhere – is where you should make for first, not least for its panoramic views encompassing southern Calabria, the Sicilian coastline and snowcapped Etna. That it was founded by Greeks in the third century BC is the extent of the theatre's Hellenistic connections, as the visible remains are almost entirely Roman. It was rebuilt at the end of the first century AD, when Taormina thrived under imperial Roman rule, and the reconstruction changed the theatre's character entirely. The impressive Roman scene building, for example, is Sicily's only surviving example but can only have obscured the views of Etna – presumably a major reason for the theatre's original siting. Likewise, the stage and lower seats were cut back to provide more room and a deep trench dug in the orchestra to accommodate the animals and fighters used in Roman gladiatorial contests. Between July and August the theatre hosts an international **arts festival** including film, theatre and music (tickets and information from the tourist office).

There are a few other Roman vestiges around town, including a much smaller **Odeon** (originally used for musical recitations) next to the tourist office. Really, though, Taormina's attractions are all to do with strolling the flower-decked streets and alleys, and window-shopping in the converted ground floors of the mansions along the Corso. Centre of town is **Piazza IX Aprile**, with its restored twelfth-century **Torre dell'Orologio** and terrace overlooking Etna and the bay – though don't sit down at the inviting outdoor cafés unless you have a substantial bankroll. Give yourself time to hike up to the Castello by way of a stepped path leading up from the main road behind the tourist office, from where you can continue on to the little village of **Castelmola**, 5km above and seemingly growing out of its severe crag. It's about an hour's climb to get there (though there are buses), while another couple of hours beyond are the heights of **Monte Venere** (885m) – take the path behind Castelmola's cemetery – for the last word in local vistas.

Eating and drinking

Eating in Taormina can be an expensive business, though most places have tourist menus of varying standards and prices. Among the pizzerias, *Vecchia Taormina*, Vico Ebrei 3 (⊤0942.24.359), is the best, serving light, blistered pizzas from its wood-burning stove. The welcoming *Trattoria da Nino*, Via Luigi Pirandello 37 (⊤0942.21.265), is popular with locals for its good, fresh food: the mixed vegetable or mixed fish antipasto make a great lunch. *A' Zammara*, Via Fratelli Bandiera 15 (⊤0942.24.408), serves excellent local dishes including home-made tagliolini with prawns and pistacchios in a garden of orange trees. *A Duomo*, Vico Ebrei 11 (℡0942.625.656; closed Mon in winter), is an elegant place serving carefully researched traditional dishes such as pasta with sardines and wild fennel and *maccù*, a soup of broad beans. For snacks, head for the indoor **market** off Via Cappuccini (mornings only, Mon–Sat); alternatively, there's a good *rosticceria* just up from Porta Messina, on the corner of Via Timeo and Via Patricio, while *Mamma Mia*, a little *alimentari* at Via Bagnoli Croce 57, will make up sandwiches from its deli counter. Another option for a light lunch or snack is the wine bar *Al Grappola d'Uva*, Via Bagnoli Croce 6–8, a good place to sample Etna wines and local cheeses. They can also organize tours of Etna's vineyards.

For night-time **drinking**, head to the boho *Re di Bastoni* on Corso Umberto I (closed Mon in winter), the Irish pub *O'Seven*, Largo La Farina 6, or the *Wunderbar Café*, Piazza IX Aprile, once the haunt of Garbo and Fassbinder. The focus of Taormina's **gay scene** is the gorgeous Piazza Paladini, just off the Corso, where you'll find bars such as *Shatulle* and the super-cool minimalist *White Bar*, along with mixed bars *Casanova* and *Déja Vue*. In summertime, the most happening **club** is the *Panasia Beach* at Spisone, where you can dance the dawn in on the sand.

Taormina's beaches – and Naxos

The **coastline** below the town is unquestionably appealing – a mixture of grottoes and rocky coves – but too many of its **beaches** are either private lidos (paying) or simply too packed in summer to be much fun.

The closest beach to town is at **Mazzarò** with its much-photographed islet. There's a **cable car** service down to the beach (€1.80 single, €3 return) that runs every fifteen minutes from Via Pirandello (the road that encircles old Taormina) and a steep path that starts just below the cable car station. If you're still searching for a bed, you will find a dozen small **hotels** here, though get the tourist office to phone first. The beach-bars and restaurants at **Spisone**, north again, are also reachable by path from Taormina, this time from below the cemetery in town. From Spisone, the coast opens out and the beach gets wider. With more time you might explore **Letojanni**, a little resort in its own right with rather more ordinary bars and shops, a few fishing boats on a sand beach, and regular buses and trains back to Taormina. For **campers** there's a site called *Paradise International* (℡0942.36.306, ⓦwww.campingparadise.it; April–Sept), 1km north along the SS114 coast road (at km 41) near Letojanni.

Roomier and better for swimming are the sands south of Taormina at **GIARDINI-NAXOS**, and to a lesser extent at the holiday village of **Recanati**, beyond. Be prepared to pay to use the beach. The wide curving bay of Giardini – easily seen from Taormina's terraces – was the launching-point of Garibaldi's attack on the Bourbon troops in Calabria (1860) and, as significantly, the site of the first Greek colony in Sicily. An obvious stop for ships running between Greece and southern Italy, it was the site of a settlement in 734 BC, named Naxos after the Naxian colonists. It was never very important, and the extensive **excavations** (daily 9am to 1hr before sunset; €2) are very low-key – a long section of ancient, lava-built city wall, two covered kilns and a sketchy temple. But it's a pleasant walk there through the lemon groves (bus from Taormina to Naxos/Recanati and follow the "Scavi" signs), and you can see some of the finds in a **Museo Archeologico** by the entrance to the site (same ticket).

GIARDINI itself, the long town backing the good beach, is an excellent alternative source of accommodation and food. Prices tend to be a good bit cheaper than in Taormina, and in high season, if you arrive by train, it's probably worth trying here first. There's a good **tourist office** at Via Tysandros 54 (summer: Mon–Fri 8am–2pm & 4.40–7.30pm, Sat 8am–2pm; winter Mon–Fri 8am–2pm & 3.30–6.30pm, Sat 8am–2pm; ☎0942.51010, ⊛www .aasgtgiardininaxos.it). Recommended **places to stay** are *La Sirena*, Via Schisò 36 (☎0942.51.853; ❷), by the pier with views over the bay (open March–Oct), and *Villa Mora*, Via Naxos 47 (☎0942.51.839, ⊛www.hotelvillamare.com; ❸), near the tourist office (open March–Jan 6), both of which require half board in August. For **eating**, the best and the cheapest is the restaurant-pizzeria attached to the seafront *Lido d'Angelo* on Via Tysandros (☎0942.51902, closed Wed), while good pizzas and fresh pasta are also to be had at *Fratelli Marano*, Via Naxos 181. Buses run half-hourly to Giardini from Taormina, the last one returning from the station at 10.15pm.

Mount Etna

Mount Etna's massive bulk looms over much of the coastal route south from Taormina. One of the world's largest volcanoes, it really demands a separate visit, but if you're pushed for time you'll have to content yourself with the ever more imminent views of its eastern flank as you head along the coast to Catania. With time, you can make the circular route to Catania on the slow train around the volcano, the **Circumetnea** – one of Sicily's most interesting rides – and stop off on the volcano itself. Reaching the lower craters below the summit is eminently possible, on foot or by mountain-bus – either way a thrilling experience.

The Circumetnea railway: Giarre-Riposto to Catania

If you don't have the time to reach the summit of Etna, travel on the **Circumetnea railway**, which provides alternative volcanic thrills. A private line, 114km long, it runs around the base of the volcano through fertile vegetation and strewn lava – a marvellous ride. The line begins in the twin town of **Giarre-Riposto**, thirty minutes by train or bus from Taormina; mainline FS trains will drop you at Giarre, the second stop of the Circumetnea line. Rail passes are not valid on this route, and if you make the entire trip to Catania, allow five hours; tickets cost €5.65 one-way. There are frequent departures: nine daily in summer and sixteen daily in winter (more in winter because of the skiing).

The closest town to the summit is dark, medieval **RANDAZZO**, built entirely of lava. Although dangerously near Etna, Randazzo has never been engulfed; when the 1981 eruption took it to the point of evacuation, the lava-flow finally stopped just outside town. Poke around the gloomy streets – dingily authentic despite the fact that much of the town has been heavily restored after being bombed to bits in 1943, when it figured as the last Sicilian stronghold of the Axis forces. The **Museo Vagliasindi** in Via Castello (daily 9am–1pm & 3–7pm; €2), housed in the former castle, has good displays of small-scale objects mainly from nearby Greek metropolis, and ranks of dangling puppets.

If you want to break the journey around Etna, then Randazzo is probably the place to **stay**. Try the tidy *Scrivano* (☎095.921.126, ⓕ095.921.433; ❸), behind the Agip petrol station on Via Regina Margherita.

Mount Etna: the ascent

The bleak lava wilderness around the summit of **Etna** is one of the most memorable landscapes Italy has to offer. While circling its lower slopes by road or rail is fine for the views, it can only be second best to the spectacular ascent. At 3323m, Etna is a fairly substantial mountain, and one of the world's biggest active volcanoes. Some of its eruptions have been disastrous: in 1169, 1329 and 1381 the lava reached the sea and in 1669 Catania was wrecked and its castle surrounded by molten rock. The Circumetnea railway line has been repeatedly ruptured by lava flows: nine people were killed on the edge of the main crater in 1979 and in 2001 military helicopters were called in to water-bomb blazing fires.

This unpredictability means that it is no longer possible to get close to the main crater. An eruption in 1971 destroyed the observatory supposed to give warning of just such an event, and the volcano has been in an almost continual **state of eruption** since 1998, the most recent being in late 2002 when the resort of Piano Provenzana on the northern side was engulfed with lava. If you do attempt the summit, be sure to heed the warnings as you get closer to the top.

Nicolosi

There are several **approaches** to the volcano. If you have a car you can enjoy some of the best scenery, on the north side of the volcano, by taking the road that leads up from **Linguaglossa**. On public transport, though, you'll need to come via **NICOLOSI**, on the southern side of Etna and an hour from Catania by bus. A winter ski resort and last main stop before the steeper slopes begin, it's a good place to pick up information – from the small **tourist office** at Via Garibaldi 63 (Mon–Sat 9am–1pm & 3.30–8pm; ☎095.911.505, ⓦwww .aast-nicolosi.it), the main road that runs through Nicolosi. If you want to arrange to go on a **guided tour** up the mountain, go to Arcobaleno Vacanze, Via Garibaldi 5 (☎095.911.241 or ☎3430.001.7749).

There are several **hotels** too, a couple in town, the rest on the road out, as well as a **campsite** – all signposted and detailed on full lists available from the information office. There is also an outstanding (and hugely popular) **pizzeria**, ⚘*Antichi Proverbi*, Via M Rapisardi 2 (☎347.955.1683 or 329.615.5351, closed Mon), which serves light, oven-blistered pizzas in an atmospheric old house.

The refuge and beyond

Although there are frequent **buses** to Nicolosi from Catania, only one (around 8am from outside Catania train station) continues to the **Hotel/Rifugio Sapienza**, which marks the end of the negotiable road up the south side of Etna. In the summer of 2001 and winter of 2002 this was a scene of frenetic activity, when dams and channels were cut to contain the molten lava which threatened to engulf the whole area. However, the row of souvenir shops, the couple of restaurants, and the totally refurbished *Hotel/Rifugio Sapienza* (☎095.915.321; ❶) are still standing, but surrounded by rills of lava. Arriving on the early-morning bus, you should have enough time to make the top and get back for the return bus to Catania – it leaves around 4.30pm from the hotel.

There are two ways **up the volcano** from the refuge, by foot or cable car. Now open again after being destroyed in the last eruption, **cable cars** run between 9am and sunset, weather permitting (€45 return). The price includes a minibus from the top cable car station to just below the main crater, though many people prefer to walk from here. Really it all depends on finances and time: **walking up** all the way from *Rifugio Sapienza* will take around four hours, the return obviously a little less. However you go, at whatever time of year, take warm clothes, gloves, good shoes or boots and glasses to keep the flying grit out of your eyes (it's best not to wear contact lenses). You can rent boots and jackets (€1 each) from the cable-car station. Food up the mountain is poor and overpriced, so bring provisions.

The lower slopes have been newly planted with trees; higher up, the cindery texture of previous eruptions is in sharp contrast with the darker new crust of buckled folds and jagged piles. The highest you're allowed to get (on foot or in the bus) is currently 2760m, where signs forbid further access. To go further would be a foolish act – gaseous explosions and molten rock are common this far up. From here you can feel the heat through your feet and view the new **fumaroles** exuding smoke. Higher still is the main crater and, depending on weather conditions, you may see smoke from here too. Disappointingly, there's often haze or cloud which mars the unsurpassed panorama to the sea.

Catania

Bang in the middle of the Ionian coast, **CATANIA** is Sicily's second-largest city and despite the ever-looming presence of Etna – even the city's main street is named after the volcano – and the ubiquitous black-grey volcanic stone in pavements and buildings, there's more openness and space than in the island's capital. A major transport hub, Catania is not only a businesslike, commercial centre, but also the cultural capital of Sicily – a lively, open and energetic place with a more radical, international outlook than Palermo, and a dynamic night scene to boot. It's also, if you take time to explore, one of the island's most historic and intriguing cities.

Some of the island's first **Greek colonists** settled the site as early as 729 BC, becoming so influential that their laws were eventually adopted by all the Greek colonies on the Ionian coast (collectively known as Magna Graecia). Later, a series of natural disasters helped shape the city as it appears today: **Etna erupted** in 1669, engulfing the city, the lava swamping the harbour, which was then topped by an **earthquake** in 1693 that devastated the whole of southeastern Sicily. The swift **rebuilding** was on a grand scale, and making full use of the local building material, Giovanni Vaccarini, the eighteenth-century architect, gave the city a lofty, noble air. Despite the neglect of many of the churches and the disintegrating, grey mansions, there's still much of interest in what, at first, might seem a rather dour city. Delving about throws up lava-encrusted Roman relics, surviving alongside some of the finest Baroque work on the island.

Arrival and information

The **airport**, Fontanarossa (℡095.340.505, ⓦwww.aeroporto.catania.it), is 5km south of the centre. The Alibus (5am–midnight every 20min; €0.80) runs from right outside to the central Piazza Stesicoro (on Via Etnea) and to Stazione Centrale in around twenty minutes. A taxi from the rank outside the airport will cost around €18 for the same journey. If you're heading straight **to the Aeolian Islands**, catch the one direct bus that leaves daily from May to September from the airport to the port of Milazzo at around 4pm.

The **Stazione Centrale** (℡892.021), where all mainline trains arrive, is in Piazza Giovanni XXIII, northeast of the centre. To get into the centre, take one of the AMT city buses from the ranks outside the station: #1/4, #4/7, #432 and #448 run along Via VI Aprile and Via Vittorio Emanuele to Piazza del Duomo. Alternatively, if you're changing on to the round-Etna train, you'll need to head

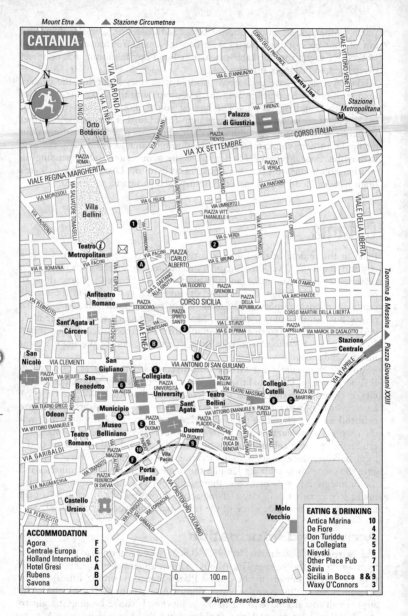

CATANIA

N

Taormina & Messina ▲ Piazza Giovanni XXIII

ACCOMMODATION

Agora	F
Centrale Europa	E
Holland International	C
Hotel Gresi	A
Rubens	B
Savona	D

EATING & DRINKING

Antica Marina	10
De Fiore	4
Don Turiddu	2
La Collegiata	5
Nievski	6
Other Place Pub	7
Savia	1
Sicilia in Bocca	8 & 9
Waxy O'Connors	3

0   100 m

▼ Airport, Beaches & Campsites

to the **Stazione Circumetnea** (☎095.541.250) at Via Caronda, at the northern end of Via Etnea, by the Borgo metro station.

All **buses**, both regional from Catania province and island-wide, stop at
various points in Piazza Giovanni XXIII, across from the train station. Of
the bus companies, AST (☎095.746.1096, ⊛www.aziendasicilianatrasporti
.it), whose timetables are pinned to posts and whose ticket office is at Via L.

Sturzo 230, on the east side of the square, stops opposite the station and serves Etna (*Hotel/Rifugio Sapienza*), Nicolosi and Siracusa; Interbus/Etna Trasporti (T 095.532.716, W www.interbus.it) leaves from Via d'Amico 185, at the back of the piazza, for Enna, Giardini-Naxos, Noto, Piazza Armerina, Ragusa, Rome, Siracusa and Taormina; SAIS (T 095.536.201, W www.saisautolinee.it) to Agrigento, Enna, Messina, Palermo and Rome also leaves from Via d'Amico.

There's a **tourist office** (Mon–Sat 8am–8pm, Sun 8am–2pm; T 095.730.6255) inside Stazione Centrale, but the main office (same times; T 095.730.6211 or 095.730.6233, W www.apt.catania.it) is signposted off Via Etnea, at Via Cimarosa 10. There's also a branch at the airport (same hours; T 095.730.6266). For **what's on** check out Catania's daily newspaper, *La Sicilia*, and the free fortnightly arts and entertainment guide, *Lapis*.

City transport

Catania is served by a network of AMT **city buses**, whose main ranks are outside the Stazione Centrale. Other central pick-up points are Piazza del Duomo, Piazza Stesicoro, and Piazza Borsellino (below Piazza del Duomo), where there's a stop for the airport Alibus and for buses #4/57 and #4/27L, which serve the campsites. Tickets (€0.80) are valid for any number of journeys within ninety minutes and are available from *tabacchi*, the newsagents inside Stazione Centrale or the booth outside the station. The same outlets also sell a *biglietto giornaliero* (€2), valid for one-day's unlimited travel on all local AMT bus routes.

The city has a **metro** system (T 095.534.323), which operates every fifteen minutes (7am–8.20pm) on a limited route running from the main Stazione Centrale (beyond Platform 11) south to Catania Porto and north and northwest to Catania Borgo, the terminal for the Stazione Circumetnea on Via Caronda. Tickets cost €0.80 for any number of journeys within ninety minutes, and are available from *tabacchi* at the train station. All tickets must be punched at machines before boarding the train. There are **taxi ranks** at Stazione Centrale, Piazza del Duomo and Via Etnea (Piazza Stesicoro); call T 095.330.966 or 095.338.282 for 24-hour service. **Driving** and parking in Catania is a stressful experience: ask your hotel where to park.

Accommodation

There's a fairly good choice of **places to stay** in Catania, though it's always wise to book ahead in summer. As well as the places listed below, there's a private **hostel**, the *Agora*, on Piazza Currò (T 095.723.3010, W www .agorahostel.com), offering dorm bunks (€18) and a couple of doubles (❶), with Internet access and laundry facilities. It also owns one of Catania's most popular and atmospheric pubs, the *Agora*, where you can eat and drink outside or in an underground grotto with a river running through it from morning till the early hours.

There are also three **campsites** (with lidos and cabins available) a short way south of the city on Lungomare Kennedy; take bus #4/57 and #4/27L (the latter service operates in summer only) from the train station or Via Etnea.

Centrale Europa Via Vittorio Emanuele 167 T 095.311.309, W www.hotelcentraleuropa.it. Spic-and-span rooms in a prime location right on Piazza del Duomo. Bit noisy at night. ❸

Holland International Via Vittorio Emanuele 8 T 095.533.605, W www.hollandintrooms.it.

Convenient for the station, and competitive prices for rooms on the first floor of an old *palazzo* with vaulted frescoed ceilings. There are rooms with and without bathroom (❶ for the latter). The Dutch owner speaks good English. ❷

The City

Catania's main square, **Piazza del Duomo**, is a handy orientation point
and a stop for most city buses: **Via Etnea** steams off north, lined with the
city's most fashionable shops and cafés; fish market and port lie behind to the
south; train station to the east; the best of the Baroque quarter to the west.
It's also one of Sicily's most attractive city squares, rebuilt completely in the
first half of the eighteenth century by Vaccarini and surrounded with fine
Baroque structures. Most striking of these is the **Municipio** on the northern
side of the piazza, finished in 1741, though to admire it properly you'll have
to gain the central reserve of the piazza. Here, the **elephant fountain** is the
city's symbol, the eighteenth-century lava elephant supporting an Egyptian
obelisk on its back.

Cross back for the **duomo** (daily 9.30am–12.30pm & 4–6.30pm; free) on
the piazza's eastern flank. Apart from the marvellous volcanic-rock medieval
apses (seen through the gate at Via Vittorio Emanuele 159), this was pretty
much entirely remodelled by Vaccarini, whose heavy Baroque touch is readily
apparent from the imposing facade on which he tagged granite columns from
Catania's Roman amphitheatre (see opposite). The interior is no less grand,
adorned by a rich series of chapels, notably the Cappella di Sant'Agata to the
right of the choir, which conceals the relics paraded through the city on the
saint's festival at the beginning of February.

Nearby is Catania's open-air **market**, with slabs and buckets full of twitch-
ing fish, eels and shellfish and endless lanes full of vegetable and fruit stalls, as
well as one or two excellent lunchtime trattorias. From here you can wind
through an atmospheric, if dilapidated, neighbourhood to an open space
punctured by the **Castello Ursino**, once the proud fortress of Frederick II.
Originally the castle stood on a rocky cliff, over the beach, but following the
1669 eruption, which reclaimed this entire area from the sea, all that remains
is the blackened keep. The **Museo Civico** inside is undergoing a lengthy
restoration – when it eventually reopens you'll find a delightful range of items
inside, including retrieved mosaic fragments, some tombstones, a lovely Greek
terracotta statuette of two goddesses being pulled in a sea carriage by mythical
beasts, and a seventeenth-century French pistol, inlaid in silver and depicting
rabbits, fish and cherubs.

Back towards the centre, dingy **Piazza Mazzini** heralds perhaps the most
interesting section of the city. Everything close by is big and Baroque, and
Via Crociferi – which strikes north from the main road, under an arch
– is lined with some of the most arresting religious and secular examples,
best seen on a slow amble, peering in the eighteenth-century courtyards
and churches. At the bottom of the narrow street, the house where the
composer Vincenzo Bellini was born in 1801 now houses the **Museo
Belliniano** (undergoing restoration, but due to reopen shortly;
☎095.715.0535), an agreeable collection of photographs, original scores, his
death mask and other memorabilia. A local boy, Bellini notches up several

tributes around the city, including a piazza, theatre and park named after him, a berth in the duomo and the ultimate accolade, *spaghetti alla Norma*. Cooked with tomato, ricotta and aubergine sauce, and named after one of Bellini's operas, it's a Catanian speciality.

West from here, the **Teatro Romano** (Mon–Sat 9am–1pm & 3–7pm, Sun 9am–1pm; free) was built of lava in the second century AD on the site of an earlier Greek theatre, and much of the seating and the underground passageways are preserved, though all the marble which originally covered it has disappeared. Further west, down Via Teatro Greco, the pretty crescent of Piazza Dante stares out over the unfinished facade of **San Nicolò** (daily 9am–1pm; free), the biggest church in Sicily, stark and empty of detail both outside and in – save for a meridian line drawn across the floor of the transept – following its partial eighteenth-century restoration.

Nearby, a few minutes' walk north, the little twelfth-century church of **Sant'Agata al Carcere** was built on the site of the prison where St Agatha was confined before her martyrdom. From here, you drop down into **Piazza Stesicoro**, the enormous square that marks the modern centre of Catania, one half of which is almost entirely occupied by the closed-off, sunken, black remains of Catania's **Anfiteatro Romano**, dating back to the second or third century AD. In its heyday, the amphitheatre could hold around sixteen thousand spectators, and from the church steps above you can see the seating quite clearly, supported by long vaults.

Eating and drinking

You'll rarely do better for **eating** than in Catania, where **fresh fish** is a speciality. The best place to sample it at lunchtime is around the markets, though **restaurants** here often close at night. One that is open for both lunch and dinner is the good-value *Antica Marina*, Via Pardo 29 (℡095.348.197; closed Wed), where you can eat excellent fish. A cosy family trattoria where you can eat good fresh fish is the moderately priced *De Fiore*, Via Coppola 24 (℡095.316.283; closed Mon). The more expensive *Sicilia in Bocca*, with branches at Piazza Pietro Lupo 16–18 (closed Wed) and in an old warehouse on Via Dusmet (closed Mon), is lively and popular and has fresh crustaceans in a tank. *At Don Turiddu*, Via Musumeci 50, there's no menu, just a splendid array of antipasti and fish for you to choose from (closed Sun & Aug).

For **snacks**, try the markets in Piazza Carlo Alberto and the streets through the Porta Uzeda, to the south of the duomo, which make great places to wander and munch from a variety of fresh-fruit stalls, stand-up cafés and snack bars. And don't miss *Savia*, Via Etnea 302 (closed Mon), opposite the main entrance to the Villa Bellini, one of the town's finest stand-up **café-bars**, which has been open since 1899.

Catania's student population ensures a fair choice of youthful **bars and pubs** – some with live music – which stay open late. *La Collegiata*, Via Collegiata 3, has a pleasant terrace for a night-time drink, and the *Nievski*, Via Alessi 15 (closed Sun lunch & Mon), offers organic food at lunchtime. The *Other Place Pub*, Via E Reina 18, is exactly like a pub, and always lively, as is *Waxy O'Connors* on Piazza Santo Spirito. *Tertulia*, Via Rapisardo 1, is a café-bar bookshop with a radical tradition; it stays open till the small hours. In addition, the *commune* operates **café-concerto** periods during the summer, when the streets and squares of the old town, between Piazza Università and Piazza Bellini, are closed to traffic between 9pm and 2am. The bars here all spill tables out onto the squares and alleys, and live bands keep things swinging until late.

Car rental Avis at the airport and Via V Cágliari 1, central booking line ☏ 0645.2108.391, ⊛ www .avis.co.uk or ⊛ www.avisautonoleggio.it; Sixt at airport ☏ 095.340.252 and Via Umberto 294B ☏ 095.538.831, ⊛ www.e-sixt.co.uk or ⊛ www .sixt.it; Hertz at airport ☏ 095.341.595 and Via Toselli ☏ 095.322.560, ⊛ www.hertz.co.uk or ⊛ www .hertz.it; Holiday Car Rental at airport ☏ 095.346.769, ⊛ www.holidaycarrental.it; Maggiore at airport ☏ 095.340.594 and Piazza G Verga ☏ 095.536.927, ⊛ www.maggiore.com or ⊛ www.maggiore.it.
Emergencies ☏ 113 for all emergency services.
Hospital Ospedale Garibaldi, Piazza Maria di Gesù 7, Pronto Soccorso ☏ 095.759.4368.
Internet access Internetteria, Via Penninello 44, just off Via Etnea ☏ 095.310.139. Open Mon–Sat 10am–10pm, Sun (winter only) 5–10pm.

Pharmacies Caltabiano, Piazza Stesicoro 36 ☏ 095.327.647; Croce Rossa, Via Etnea 274 ☏ 095.317.053; Cutelli, Via Vittorio Emanuele II 54 ☏ 095.531.400; Europa, Corso Italia 111 ☏ 095.383.536. The last three are open all night.
Police Emergencies ☏ 112; Carabinieri, Piazza Giovanni Verga 8, or Vigili Urbani, Via Veniero 7 ☏ 095.531.333. The Questura (police station) is in Piazza S. Nicolella 8 ☏ 095.736.7111.
Post office Main post office and poste restante at Via Etnea 215, close to the Villa Bellini (Mon–Sat 8.15am–6.30pm).
Travel agents La Duca Viaggi, Piazza Europa 2 ☏ 095.722.2295; G. W. Munzone, Corso Martiri della Libertà 186–88 ☏ 095.539.983.

Siracusa

It's hardly surprising that **SIRACUSA** (ancient Syracuse) – an easily defend-able offshore island with fertile plains across on the mainland and two natural harbours – should attract the early **Greek** colonists who settled the site in 733 BC. Within a hundred years, the city was so powerful that it was sending out its own colonists to the south and west, and soon became the power base of ancient Sicily's most famous and effective rulers.

Syracuse first assumed its almost mythic eminence under **Gelon**, the tyrant of Gela, who began work on the city's Temple of Athena, later to become the Christian cathedral of Syracuse. It was an unparalleled period of Greek prosper-ity and power in Sicily, though this growing influence troubled Athens, and in 415 BC a fleet of 134 triremes was dispatched to take Syracuse – only to be blockaded and the fleet destroyed. Those who weren't slaughtered as they ran were imprisoned in the city's stone quarries.

Under **Dionysius the Elder**, the city became a great military base, the tyrant building the first of the Euryalus forts and erecting strong city walls. As the leading European power, Syracuse more or less retained its prime position for two hundred years until it was attacked by the **Romans** in 215 BC. The subsequent **two-year siege** was made long and hazardous for the attackers by the mechanical devices contrived by Archimedes – who, as the Romans finally forced victory, was killed by a foot soldier.

From this time, Syracuse withered in importance. It became, briefly, a major religious centre in the early **Christian period**, but for the most part its days as a power were done: it was sacked by the Saracens and most of its later Norman buildings fell in the 1693 earthquake. Passed by until the twentieth century, the city suffered a double blow in World War II when it was **bombed** by the Allies and then, after its capture, by the Luftwaffe in 1943. Luckily, the extensive ancient remains were little damaged, and although decay and new development have reduced the attractions of the modern city, it's an essential stop on any tour of the island.

Some **orientation** pointers are useful. The original Greek settlement was on the fortified island of **Ortygia**, compact enough to see in a good half-day's stroll

It's worth buying a **combined ticket** (valid two days) if you're planning to see Siracusa's major sights: a ticket for the Parco Archeologico and the Museo Archeologico costs €10.

and almost completely late-medieval in character. The Greek city spread onto the mainland in four distinct areas: **Achradina**, over the water from Ortygia, was the city's commercial and administrative centre and today encompasses the new streets that radiate out from the train station; **Tyche**, to the northeast, was residential and now holds the archeological museum and the city's extensive catacombs; **Neapolis**, to the west, is the site of the fascinating archeological park based on ancient Syracuse's public and social amenities; while **Epipolae** stretches way to the northwest, to the city's outer defensive walls and the Euryalus fort.

Arrival and information

The **train station** is on the mainland, about a twenty-minute walk from either Ortygia or Neapolis. AST city and regional **buses** (☎0931.462.711) arrive in Piazza (or Riva) delle Poste, just over the bridge on Ortygia, or else in Piazzale Marconi, in the modern town; the Interbus office (☎0931.66.710) and their regional buses stop in Via Trieste, round the corner from Piazza delle Poste.

The main **city bus stops** are in Piazza Archimede and Largo XXV Luglio on Ortygia, and along Corso Umberto on the mainland; tickets cost €0.80, valid for ninety minutes. **Drivers** will find the city a breeze after Palermo and Catania, and parking places relatively easy to come by. For maps, accommodation listings, details of performances in the Greek theatre, and other information, visit the **tourist office** at Via Maestranza 33 in Ortygia (summer Mon–Sat 8.30am–1.45pm & 4.30–7pm; winter Mon–Fri 8.30am–1.45pm & 3–5.30pm, Sat 8.30am–1.45pm; ☎0931.464.255, ⓦwww.apt-siracusa) or at Via San Sebastiano 43, near the catacombs in Tyche (Mon–Fri 8.30am–1.30pm & 3–6pm, Sat 8.30am–1pm; ☎0931.67.710). The main **post office** is in Piazza delle Poste and there's an **Internet** point in the centre of Ortygia at the Libreria Gabo, Corso Matteotti 38 (Mon–Sat 9.15am–1pm & 4.30–8pm; ☎0931.66.255).

Accommodation

There's a fair spread of **accommodation** choices, but in high season it's wise to book in advance. The cheaper hotels are all on the mainland, while the nearest **campsite**, *Agriturist Rinaura* (☎0931.721.224), is 5km away – take bus #21, #22 or #23 from Corso Umberto or Piazza delle Poste. They also have cabins to rent (❷).

Casa Mia Corso Umberto 112 ☎0931.463.349, ⓦwww.bbcasamia.it. A decent B&B not far from Ortygia with antique beds, eleven rooms and an inner terrace for breakfast. ❷

Domus Mariae Via Vittorio Veneto 76 ☎0931.24.858, ⓦwww.sistemia.it/domusmariae. Elegant hotel on Ortygia, efficiently run by nuns and with views to the sea. The swish rooms have TVs, bathrooms and a/c. There's a solarium, a reading room and a chapel too. ❺–❻

Grand Hotel Viale Mazzini 12 ☎0931.464.600, ⓦwww.grandhotelsr.it. This veteran haunt of the rich and famous enjoys a prime position in Ortygia

overlooking the Porto Grande. Access to a private beach, lavish furnishings and all the refinements you'd expect at the price. ❼

Gutowski Lungomare Vittorini 26 ☎0931.465.861, ⓦwww.guthotel.it. Lovely hotel overlooking the sea on Ortygia's east side, with tastefully bare but comfortable rooms and good bathrooms. Great breakfasts, with freshly squeezed orange juice and, in summer, home-made almond granita. ❸

L'Approdo delle Sirene Riva Garibaldi 15 ☎0931.24.857, ⓦwww.apprododellesirene .com. A recently opened B&B in a tastefully renovated waterfront building in Ortygia, just across

▲ Catania

Latomia
dei Cappuccini

VIA POLITI LAUDIEN

PIAZZA
CAPPUCCINI

N

VIALE TERACATI

VIA SAN SEBASTIANO

Catacombs

VIA AUGUSTO VON PLATEN

Museo
Archeologico

TYCHE

❶

VIALE TEÓCRITO

VIALE TEÓCRITO

Stadio
Comunale

VIA TORINO

RIVIERA DIONISIO IL GRANDE

Hospital

VIA DEL SANTUARIO

✝ Madonna
delle Lacrime

PIAZZA
VITTORIA
(excavations)

VIA GORIZIA

VIA BIGNAMI

Santa
Lucia

VIA TESTAFERRATA

VIA DI NATALE

CORSO GELONE

VIA A. M. CARABELLI

VIALE LUIGI CADORNA

CORSO TIMOLEONE

VIA ENNA

VIA RAGUSA

VIA AGRIGENTO

VIA MONTE GRAPPA

PIAZZA
S. LUCIA

VIA ELISELETTO

VIA TRAPANI

VIA MOSCO

VIA STATELLO

ACHRADINA

VIA D'ARSENALE

Train
Station

V. EPICARMO

VIALE A. DIAZ

Arsenale

Porto Piccolo

CORSO UMBERTO I

CRISPI

PIAZZA
MARCONI

Ⓐ

VIA T

VIA R. MARGHERITA

VIA DANTE

Ginnasio
Romano

Foro
Siracusano

Ⓑ

VIA ELORINA

CORSO UMBERTO

VIA PALERMO

VIA ERITREA

PIAZZA
DELLA
POSTA

VIA TRIESTE

VIA TRENTO

❷

Ponte
Nuovo

VIA MALTA

VIA BENGASI

VIA RÓDI

PIAZZA
PANCALI

LARGO
XXV
LUGLIO

Tempio
di Apollo

VIA RESALIBERA

LUNGOMARE DI LEVANTE

VIA GABRIELE

VIA XX SETTEMBRE

VIA DEI MILLE

CORSO MATTEOTTI

VIA MIRABELLA

ORTYGIA

Ⓒ

VIA VITTORIO VENETO

Ⓕ

VIA G. PICALCO

Ⓔ Ⓓ ❸

VIA S. MAZZINI

Porta
Marina

❹

❺

VIA AMALFITANIA

Palazzo
Montalto

PIAZZA
ARCHIMEDE

ⓘ

VIA MAESTRANZA

Porto Grande

VIA
GEMMELLARO

❻

Municipio

❼

VIA GIUDECCA

Palazzo
Beneventano

PIAZZA
DEL
DUOMO

FORO ITALICO

Duomo

VIA LARGA

Santa Lucia
alla Badia

Fonte Aretusa ⵉ

VIA PICHERALE

VIA CAPODIECI

Museo Regionale
d'Arte Medioevale
e Moderna

San Martino

LUNGOMARE ORTIGIA

VIA CASTELLO MANIACE

Castello
Maniace

◄ Neapolis & Parco Archeologico

◄ Noto

1074

0   200 m

ACCOMMODATION	
Casa Mia	B
Domus Mariae	F
Grand Hotel	D
Gutowski	C
L'Approdo delle Sirene	E
Sorella Luna	A

EATING & DRINKING	
Gran Caffè del Duomo	7
L'Ancora	2
La Siciliana	3
Pescomare	6
Ristorante Jonico	1
Spaghetteria do Scogghiu	5
Trattoria Archimede	4

the bridge from the mainland. Great home-made breakfasts are served on a terrace overlooking the sea, and the hotel has a boat for excursions and canoes for hire. You can also borrow bikes, free of charge. ❸–❹

Sorella Luna Via F Crispi 23 ☎0931.21178, ⓦwww.sorellalunasrl.it. New B&B with nicely decorated and furnished rooms and a spacious roof terrace. ❸

Central Siracusa: Ortygia and Achradina

A fist of land with the thumb downturned, **ORTYGIA** stuffs more than 2700 years of history into a space barely 1km long and 0.5km across. The island was connected to the mainland at different times by causeway or by bridge: today you approach over the wide **Ponte Nuovo** to Piazza Pancali, where the sandstone remnants of the **Tempio di Apollo** sit in a little green park surrounded by railings. Erected around 570 BC in the colony's early years, it was the first grand Doric temple to be built in Sicily, though there's not much left: a few column stumps, part of the inner sanctuary wall and the stereobate can be made out.

Follow Via Savoia towards the water and you fetch up on the **harbourfront**, an active place overlooking the main harbour, the Porto Grande. Set back from the water, a curlicued fifteenth-century limestone gateway, the **Porta Marina**, provides one entrance into the webbed streets of the **old town**. The walk uphill ends on a terrace looking over the harbour, from where you slip down to a piazza encircling the **Fonte Aretusa**, probably the most enduring of Siracusa's romantic locations. The freshwater spring – now neither fresh nor a spring – fuelled an attractive Greek myth: the nymph Arethusa, chased by the river god Alpheus, was changed into a spring by the goddess Artemis and, jumping into the sea off the Peloponnese, reappeared as a fountain in Siracusa. Actually, there are natural freshwater springs all over Ortygia, but the landscaped, papyrus-covered fountain – complete with fish and ducks – is undeniably pretty. Admiral Nelson took on water supplies here before the Battle of the Nile, though you'd be advised to sip a coffee in one of the cafés nearby.

The old town's roads lead on, down the "thumb" of Ortygia, as far as the **Castello Maniace** on the island's southern tip. Thrown up by Frederick II in 1239, the solid square keep is now a barracks and is off-limits to visitors. Back on the main chunk of Ortygia, the severe thirteenth-century Palazzo Bellomo houses the **Museo Regionale d'Arte Medioevale e Moderna** (closed for restoration), an outstanding collection of medieval art. There are some wonderful pieces in here, including notable works by the omnipresent Gagini family and a damaged fifteenth-century *Annunciation* by Antonello da Messina, the museum's most famous exhibit.

Ortygia's most obvious attractions, though, surround the **Piazza del Duomo**, the island's most appealing spot. The piazza is an elongated space from which impressive buildings radiate out up either flank, including the seventeenth-century **Municipio** with the remains of an early Ionic temple in its basement. This was abandoned when work began on the most ambitious of all Siracusa's temples, the **Tempio di Atena**, which was raised in the fifth century BC and now forms the basis of the duomo. In the normal run of things it might be expected to have suffered the eventual ruination that befell most of the Greek temples in Sicily. Yet much of it survives, thanks to the foundation in the seventh century AD of a Christian church which incorporated the temple in its structure – thus keeping the masonry scavengers at bay. The **duomo** itself (daily 8am–noon & 4–8pm; free) makes the grandest statement about Ortygia's continuous settlement, with twelve of the temple's fluted columns, and their architrave, embedded in its battlemented Norman wall. Inside, the nave of the Christian church was formed by hacking eight arches in the cella walls.

Buses run from Largo XXV Luglio over Ponte Nuovo and into **ACHRADINA**, the important commercial centre of ancient Syracuse. Although nowadays there's little of interest here, you may find yourself staying in one of the hotels scattered around its modern streets. The **Foro Siracusano** was the site of the *agora*, the market place and public square, and there are a few remains still to be seen – though the dominant feature is the war memorial in its garden, a Fascist monument of 1936. The only other ancient attraction left in the area is the **Ginnasio Romano**, off Via Elorina behind the train station: not a gymnasium at all, but a small first-century AD Roman theatre – partly sunken under moss-covered water – and a few pieces of a temple and altar.

Tyche and Neapolis: the archeological museum and park

TYCHE, north of the train station, is mainly new and commercial, and if you want to see the best of Siracusa's archeological delights you might as well take the bus straight from Ortygia and save your legs. Buses #3, #5, #12 and #15 leave from Largo XXV Luglio – all running up Corso Gelone. Get off at Viale Teocrito and signposts point you east for the archeological museum and west for Neapolis. It's best to take the museum first: it's good for putting the site into perspective and is unlikely to be packed first thing in the morning.

The **Museo Archeologico** (Tues–Sat 9am–7pm; last entry 1hr before closing; €6 or combined ticket with Parco Archeologico €10) holds a wealth of material, starting with geological and prehistoric finds, moving through entire rooms devoted to the Chalcidesian colonies (Naxos, Lentini, Zancle) and to Megara Hyblaea, and finally to the main body of the collection: an immensely detailed catalogue of life in ancient Syracuse and its sub-colonies. The most famous exhibit is the **Venus**, at the entrance to the Syracuse section: a headless figure arising from the sea, the clear white marble almost palpably dripping. Look out, too, for the section dealing with the temples of Syracuse; fragments from each (like the seven lion-gargoyles from the Tempio di Atena) are displayed alongside model and video reconstructions. There's an explanatory diagram at the entrance to the circular building and everything is colour coded: pick the sector you're interested in and follow the arrows, prehistory starting just to the left of the entrance.

Tyche is riddled with **catacombs**, since the Romans forbade burial within the walls of a city. All are now inaccessible apart from those beneath the **Basilica di San Giovanni**, a stone's throw from the archeological museum off Viale Teocrito (Tues–Sun 9am–1pm & 2.30–6pm; tour of catacombs €3.50), built over the burial site of Roman martyr St Marcian. The presence of the saint made this a hugely popular burial place, and there are literally thousands of niches hollowed into the walls to contain the remains of Roman Siracusa's Christians.

Opposite the museum, across Viale Teocrito, the monolithic Santuario della Madonna delle Lacrime (daily 7am–12.30pm & 4–7pm; free) is the newest and most would say least harmonious addition to the city's skyline. Completed in 1994 to house a statue of the Madonna that allegedly wept for five days in 1953, it was designed to resemle a giant teardrop.

NEAPOLIS, to the west, is now contained within a large **Parco Archeologico** (daily 9am until 1hr before sunset). Although you don't pay to see the initial excavations, seeing the Greek theatre and quarries – easily the most interesting parts – costs €6, paid at a separate entrance (€10 with entrance to Museo Archeologico). The **Ara di Ierone II**, an enormous altar of the third century BC on a solid white plinth, is the first thing you see, across the way from which is the entrance to the theatre and quarries. The **Teatro Greco** is very prettily sited, cut out of the rock and looking down into trees below. It's much bigger than the one at Taormina, capable of holding around fifteen thousand people, though less impressive scenically. But the theatre's pedigree is impeccable: Aeschylus put on works here, and around the top of the middle gangway are a set of carved names which marked the various seat blocks occupied by the royal family. Greek dramas are still played here in May and June, as wooden planking over the surviving seats testifies.

Walk back through the theatre and another path leads down into a leafy quarry, the **Latomia del Paradiso**, best known for its unusually shaped cavern that Dionysius is supposed to have used as a prison. This, the **Orecchio di Dionigi** (or "Ear of Dionysius"), is a high, S-shaped cave 65m long: Caravaggio, a visitor in 1586, coined the name after the shape of the entrance, but the acoustic properties are such that it's not impossible to imagine Dionysius eavesdropping on his prisoners from a vantage point above. A second cave, the **Grotta dei Cordari**, used by the ancient city's ropemakers, is shored up at present.

Keep your ticket from the theatre and Latomia del Paradiso, as it will also get you into the elliptical **Anfiteatro Romano**, back up the main path past the altar and through a gate on your right; you have to see this last. A late building, dating from the third century AD, it's a substantial relic with the tunnels for animals and gladiators clearly visible. Again, some of the seats are inscribed with the owners' names.

Note that the site is pretty extensive, and worth at least half a day of your time. At the least, bring water, at best a picnic.

Castello Eurialo

For terrific views over the city and relief on hot and crowded days, it's worth the brief excursion a few kilometres west of Siracusa to the military and defensive works begun under Dionysius the Elder to defend the port from land attack. Added to and adapted over a couple of centuries, they basically consisted of a **great wall** which defended the ridge of Epipolae (the city's western limit), and the massive **Castello Euriale** (daily until 1hr before sunset; free) – the major extant Greek fortification in the Mediterranean. There are three defensive trenches, the innermost leading off into a system of tunnels and passages. Climb up to the castle proper and you'll be rewarded with hearty **views** from its long keep and lower walls and towers down to the oil refineries and tankers of the coast north of the city, and over Siracusa itself.

Bars and **pizzerias** share the view, and make this a viable place for an evening out. **Buses** #9, #11 and #25 run from the Corso Gelone, outside the archeological park, to the village of Belvedere; the site is just before the village, on the right, a fifteen-minute ride.

Eating, drinking and nightlife

Many of Siracusa's **restaurants** are overpriced, but there are some good-value places. *Spaghetteria do Scogghiu*, Via Scina 11 (no credit cards; closed Mon), has a huge pasta selection, while *La Siciliana*, Via Savoia 17 (no credit cards; closed Mon), is a no-frills pizzeria. For fish, the *Trattoria Archimede*, Via Gemmellaro 8 (closed Sun), is popular with locals, and does a great *cavatelli* (home-made pasta) with swordfish, sea urchins, tomatoes and zucchini. *Pescomare* (closed Mon), just off Piazza del Duomo at Via Landolina 6, serves pizza as well as fish, in an atmospheric, plant-filled old courtyard. The reasonably priced *L'Ancora di Giancarlo Russo*, Via Pemo 7, specializes in inventive dishes such as raw shrimp marinaded in orange juice, while for a real splash-out, take a taxi out to the rustic *Ristorante Jonico*, Riviera Dionisio il Grande 194 (℡ 0931.65.540; closed Tues), where a meal of superb antipasti and fresh fish will cost up to €40. Try the tiny potato gnocchi with swordfish, wild fennel, pink peppercorns and cherry tomatos.

Good **bars** and **cafés** are easy to find. In the daytime, the *Gran Caffè del Duomo*, right in front of the cathedral, is the place to sit and sup, while in the evening, Ortygia's tiny **Piazzetta San Rocco**, and the streets around it, are the focus of Siracusa's **night scene**.

The southern coast and the interior

It's tempting to give Sicily's long **southern coast** a miss, especially if you're short on time, as there are few major sites. But to do so would be to ignore some of the most appealing places on the island. The whole region, coast and hinterland, marks a welcome break from the volcanic fixation of the blacker lands to the north: here the towns are largely spacious and bright, strung across a gentler, unscarred landscape that rolls down to the sea.

Sicily's southeastern bulge was devastated by a calamitous seventeenth-century earthquake and the inland rebuilding, over the next century, was almost entirely Baroque in concept and execution. **Ragusa** dominates, a splendid town on two levels, the older town still with its share of grandiose buildings. Elsewhere, similar vigorous Baroque towns mushroomed, like little **Modica** to the south and – the undisputed gem – **Noto** to the east.

Down on the coast itself there's a line of small-town resorts which stretches from the southeastern cape, **Capo Passero**. There are decent beaches but often the coastline is marred by industrial development and pollution. More vital, further west, is **Agrigento**, sitting on a rise overlooking the sea above its famed series of Greek temples.

Slow cross-country trains and limited exit motorways do little to encourage stopping in the island's **interior**, but it's only here that you really begin to get off the tourist trail. Much of the land is burned dry during the long summer months, sometimes a dreary picture, but in compensation the region boasts some of Sicily's most curious towns. **Enna** is the obvious target, as central as you can get, the blustery mountain town a pace apart from the dry hills below. There are easy trips to be made from here, north into the hills and south to **Piazza Armerina** and the fabulous Roman mosaics.

Ragusa and the southeast

The **earthquake of 1693**, which destroyed utterly the towns and villages of southeastern Sicily, had one positive and lasting effect. Where there were ruins, a new generation of confident architects raised new planned towns in an opulent Baroque style. All were harmonious creations, Catania the grandest, **Noto** the most eagerly promoted by the tourist board. But there's a bagful of other towns too, like **Ragusa**, **Comiso** and **Modica** – less visited but all providing surprising pockets of grandeur amid the bare hills and deep valleys of the region.

Ragusa

RAGUSA is a busy and likeable provincial capital with an encouraging, friendly atmosphere. The earthquake split the city in two: the old town of **Ragusa Ibla**, on a jut of land above its valley, was flattened, and within a few years a **new town** emerged, on the higher ridge to the west. Ibla was stubbornly rebuilt around its medieval ruins, while its new rival developed along grander, planned lines. All the business and industry relocated to the prosperous upper town, where oil is the latest venture – derricks are scattered around modern Ragusa's higher reaches.

You'll arrive here, in the **upper town**: all buses stop outside the train station, and a left turn takes you along the main road and over the exposed **Ponte Nuovo**, spanning a huge cleft in the ridge. All the interest in "modern" Ragusa is on the other side, the gridded Baroque town slipping off to right and left on either side of the steeply sloping **Corso Italia**. To the right, down the Corso on a wide terrace above Piazza San Giovanni, stands the **Duomo**, conceived on a grand, symmetrical scale. Finished in 1774, its tapered columns and fine doorways are a fairly sombre background to the vigorous small-town atmosphere around. Back towards the train station, underneath the Ponte Nuovo, there's an important **Museo Archeologico** (daily 9am–1.30pm & 4–7.30pm; €2) dealing mainly with finds from the archeological site of Kamarina (sixth century BC) on the coast to the southwest.

But it's **RAGUSA IBLA**, the original **lower town**, where you'll probably while away much of the day, its weather-beaten roofs straddling the outcrop of rock about twenty minutes' walk away. The main attraction, situated in the newly restored and gleaming central core of the town, is the church of **San Giorgio** (undergoing restoration, but you can call Padre Floridia for details, ☎0932.210.085). Stridently placed at the top of Piazza Duomo, it's one of the masterpieces of Sicilian Baroque, built by Rosario Gagliardi and finished in 1784. The glorious three-tiered facade, sets of triple columns climbing up the wedding cake exterior to a balconied belfry, is an imaginative work, though typically not much enhanced by venturing inside. As with Gagliardi's other important church in Modica (see p.1080), all the beauty is in the immediacy of the powerful exterior.

The whole town – deathly quiet at lunchtime – is ripe for aimless wandering. Gagliardi gets another credit for the elegant rounded facade of the church of **San Giuseppe** in Piazza Pola, a few steps below the duomo, while Corso XXV Aprile continues down past abandoned *palazzi* to the **Giardino Ibleo** (daily 8am–8pm), gardens occupying the very edge of the spur on which the town is built. If you can't face the walk back to the upper town, the **bus navetta** from Largo Kamerina plies between the upper and lower towns every thirty minutes or so.

Ragusa's **train station**, which is also where **buses** arrive, is in the upper town, five minutes' walk from Ponte Nuovo. There are two **tourist offices**, both in Ragusa Ibla: one at Via Capitano Bocchieri 33 (daily 8.30am–2pm, Tues also 4–6pm; ☎0932.221.511), with information covering the whole province, and the more local Pro Loco on Largo Camerina (May–Sept Tues–Sun 9am–1pm & 4–8pm; Oct–April Sat & Sun 9am–1pm & 3–7pm; ☎0932.244.473).

The town offers a good choice of **accommodation**, including some nice B&Bs **in Ragusa Ibla**. One of them, *Ai Giardini Iblea*, Via Normanni 4 (☎338.640.1238 or 338.286.1058, Ⓦwww.aigiardini.it; ❷), has three rooms close to the Giardini and a kitchen for guests' use. Another, *Giardini di Pietra*, Vicolo Chiasso Guerra, off Via XI Febbraio (☎0932.621809, 333.708.5448, Ⓦwww.giardinodi pietra.com; ❷), offers panoramic views from its four rooms and terrace. ⚞ *Palazzo Castro al Duomo*, Piazza Duomo 2 ☎0932.621.887 or 349.266.0528, Ⓦwww.palazzocastro.it; ❷), features lovely rooms with frescoed ceilings next to the duomo, and a courtyard garden. *La Signoria*, Via Alloro 31 (☎0932.622.496, Ⓦwww.lasignoria.it; ❷), has cool airy and simply furnished rooms housed in a baroque warehouse. If you really want to splash out try ⚞ *Locanda Don Serafino*, Via XI Febbraio 15 (☎0932.222.0065, Ⓦwww.locanda donserafino.it; ❻), a small, excusive hotel beautifully set within the hefty stone walls of a nineteenth-century mansion, with an expensive and extremely refined restaurant. Another fine choice for those in search of style and comfort is the ⚞ *Eremo della Giubiliana* (☎0932.669.119, Ⓦwww.eremodellegiubiliane.it; ❼), an upmarket agriturismo (with its own 700m private airstrip no less) housed in the restored buildings of a feudal estate dating back to the twelfth century. The grounds are gorgeous, and you can dine on their own organically grown food. It's 7.5km out of Ragusa, along the road to Marina di Ragusa.

As for **eating**, the good, traditional *Ristorante Orfeo* in the upper town, at Via S. Anna 117 (☎0932. 621.035; closed Sun), serves dishes such as *maccù* (a soup made with broad beans) and pasta with sundried tomatos, while in Ibla, *U Saracinu* (☎0932.246.976; closed Sun), on Via del Convento, near the duomo, does decent Sicilian dishes with North African touches, such as couscous. Also in Ragusa Ibla, you can eat very well at *Cucina e Vino*, Via Orfanotrofio 91 (☎0932.686.447). Housed on the first floor of a nineteenth-century *palazzo*, dishes include lamb with artichokes, and delicious *nodini*, little balls of mozzarella stuffed with ricotta and served with an intense cherry tomato conserve. For breakfast, *Caffè Trieste*, Corso Italia 76–78, is a decent café-bar with an enticing savoury snack and pastry selection.

Comiso and Modica

The best of the rest of the Baroque southeast can be seen in easy trips from Ragusa. If you came from the west you might already have passed through **COMISO**, its green centre dominated by the twin domes of two impressive churches. If you didn't, the journey in itself is worth making, up over a barren 600-metre-high plateau looking away to the distant sea. The wild countryside hereabouts continues to impress as you head beyond Ragusa, the route to **MODICA**, half an hour to the south, a case in point. As the bus swirls down past Ragusa Ibla and climbs through some rugged hills, all the vegetation seems to have been pulled into the valleys below, the tiered slopes bare and rocky. Modica itself is an enjoyable place to spend half a day. A powerful medieval base of the Chiaramonte, the upper town is watched over by the magnificent eighteenth-century facade of **San Giorgio**, a worthy rival to the church of the same name in Ragusa Ibla. It's thought that Gagliardi was responsible for this too: the elliptical facade is topped by a belfry, the church approached by a symmetrical double staircase which switchbacks up across the upper roads of the town.

Noto

The real highlight of any tour of the Baroque southeast, despite the collapse of its duomo, is further afield at **NOTO**. It is easily the most harmonious town of those rebuilt after the earthquake, and for a time, in the mid-nineteenth century, it replaced Siracusa as provincial capital. Indeed, despite its architectural identification with the Baroque towns around Ragusa, Noto is best reached from Siracusa – around half an hour's journey by bus or train. Planned and laid out by Giovanni Battista Landolina and adorned by Gagliardi, there's not a town to touch Noto for uniform excellence in design and execution. Each year sees an increase in the number of monuments to have shaken off the grime of traffic pollution and regained their original honey-coloured facades.

The pedestrianized main Corso is lined with some of Sicily's most captivating buildings, from the flat-fronted church of **San Francesco**, on the right, along as far as Piazza XVI Maggio and the graceful, curving church of **San Domenico**. And **Piazza Municipio** is arguably Sicily's finest piazza with its perfectly proportioned, tree-planted expanses. The **duomo**, finished in 1770, has been closed since the collapse of the dome in 1996, but is due to reopen in 2007. Opposite, the **Municipio** (or Palazzo Ducezio) is flanked by its own green spaces, the arcaded building presenting a lovely, simple facade of columns and long stone balconies. Head up the steep Via Corrado Nicolaci, an eighteenth-century street that contains the extraordinary **Palazzo Villadorata** at no. 18 (closed for restoration until at least late 2007), its six balconies supported by a panoply of griffins, galloping horses and fat-cheeked cherubs.

Staying in Noto wouldn't be a bad alternative to Siracusa, though you'll need to book ahead in high season. The **tourist office** in Piazza XVI Maggio (Mon–Fri 8.30am–1.45pm, Sat 9am–1pm; ☎0931.836.744, ⓦwww.apt-siracusa.it) has details of numerous **rented rooms** and **B&B** places. Among them are *B&B Gulliver*, Via Tasca 2 (☎0931.894.119, ⓦwww.bbgulliver.it; ❶–❷), which has four comfortable rooms with bathrooms, fridge-bars and kitchens; otherwise there's the friendly *B&B Centro Storico*, Corso Vittorio Emanuele 54 (☎0931.573.967, ⓦwww.centro-storico.com; no credit cards; ❷), or the slightly more expensive *L'Arca*, Via Rococco Pirri 14 (☎0931.838.656, ⓦwww.notobarocca.com/arcarooms; no credit cards; ❷). There'a also an excellent **youth hostel**, *Il Castello*, housed in a converted *palazzo* on Via Fratelli Bandiera in the upper part of town (☎0931.571.534, 392.415.7899 or 335.523.5469, ⓦwww.notobarocca.com/ostello; €15). If you prefer a **hotel**, try the charming new *Albergo della Fontanella*, Via Pilo Rosolino 3 (☎0931.894.735, ⓦwww.albergolafontanella.it; ❷), in a restored nineteenth-century *palazzo* in the *centro storico*. A good alternative in summer is to stay on the coast at **Noto Marina**, 8km southeast, so you can spend days in the beach and evenings sightseeing. There's a cluster of holiday hotels here.

In Noto, you can **eat** at the bustling straightforward *Trattoria Giglio*, just to the side of the town hall at Piazza Municipio 8–10 (☎0931.838.640), where the cooking has a Spanish flavour, the small *Trattoria del Carmine*, Via Ducezio 9 (☎0931.838.705), for *cucina casalinga* at low prices, or more expensively at *Ristorante Neas*, Via Rocco Pirri 30 (☎0931.573.538; closed Tues in winter), a knock-out for fish dishes (try the *pesce spada*, swordfish, with herbs from Monte Iblei) and a good place to sample the local wine *moscato di Noto*.

Agrigento

Though handsome, well sited and awash with medieval atmosphere, **AGRI-GENTO** is rarely visited for the town itself. The interest instead focuses on the substantial **remains** of Pindar's "most beautiful city of mortals", a couple of kilometres below. Here, strung out along a ridge facing the sea, is a series of **Doric temples** – the most captivating of Sicilian Greek remains and a grouping unique outside Greece.

The site

In 581 BC colonists from nearby Gela and from Rhodes founded the city of **Akragas** between the rivers of Hypsas and Akragas. They surrounded it with a mighty wall, formed in part by a higher ridge on which stood the acropolis (and, today, the modern town). The southern limit of the ancient city was a second, lower ridge and it was here, in the so-called "**Valley of the Temples**", that the city architects erected their sacred buildings during the fifth century BC.

A road winds down from the modern city to the **VALLE DEI TEMPLI**, with buses stopping at a car park between the two separate sections of **archeological remains** (the eastern and western zones), and the museum (see below). Entrance to both the eastern and western temple sites costs €8, or €12 including the museum (daily 9am to 1hr before sunset). Guided tours are sometimes offered in English – ask at the information kiosk in the car park for details. The **eastern zone** is unenclosed and is at its crowd-free best in early morning or late evening. A path climbs up to the oldest of Akragas's temples, the **Tempio di Ercole** (Hercules). Probably begun in the last decades of the sixth century BC, nine of the original 38 columns have been re-erected, everything else scattered around like a waiting jigsaw puzzle. Retrace your steps back to the path which leads to the glorious **Tempio della Concordia**, dated to around 430 BC: perfectly preserved and beautifully sited, with fine views to the city and the sea, the tawny stone lending the structure warmth and strength. That it's still so complete is explained by its conversion (in the sixth century AD) to a Christian church. Restored to its (more or less) original layout in the eighteenth century, it's kept its lines and slightly tapering columns, although it's fenced off to keep the crowds at bay. The path continues, following the line of the ancient city walls, to the **Tempio di Giunone** (or Hera), an engaging half-ruin standing at the very edge of the ridge. The patches of red visible here and there on the masonry denote fire damage, probably from the sack of Akragas by the Carthaginians in 406 BC.

The **western zone**, back along the path and beyond the car park, is less impressive, a vast tangle of stone and fallen masonry from a variety of temples. Most notable is the mammoth construction that was the **Tempio di Giove**, or Temple of Olympian Zeus. The largest Doric temple ever known, it was never completed, left in ruins by the Carthaginians and further damaged by earthquakes. Still, the stereobate remains, while on the ground, face to the sky, lies an eight-metre-high *telamone*: a supporting column sculpted as a male figure, arms raised and bent to bear the temple's weight. Other scattered remains litter the area, including the so-called **Tempio dei Dioscuri** (Castor and Pollux), rebuilt in 1832 and actually made up of unrelated pieces from the confused rubble on the ground.

Via dei Templi leads back to the town from the car park via the excellent **Museo Nazionale Archeologico** (Tues–Sat 9am–7pm, Mon & Sun 9am–1pm; €6) – the bus passes by outside. The extraordinarily rich collection is devoted to finds from the city and the surrounding area; the best displays are the cases of vases (sixth to third century BC) and a reassembled *telamone* stacked against one wall. Nip over the road on the way out for the **Hellenistic-Roman quarter** (daily 9am until 1hr before sunset; free), which contains lines of houses, inhabited intermittently until the fifth century AD, many with mosaic designs still discernible.

The modern town

It would be a mistake not to scout round **the town** of Agrigento, modern only in comparison with the temples. Thoroughly medieval at its heart, its tiny stepped streets and fine churches look down over the Valle dei Templi (dramatically floodlit at night) and beyond to the sea. The main street, **Via Atenea**, starts at the eastern edge of the old town, above the train station, the streets off to the right harbouring ramshackle *palazzi* and the church of **Santa Maria dei Greci**. Built over a Greek temple of the fifth century BC, the flattened columns are visible in the nave, while an underground tunnel reveals the stylobate and column stumps, all part of the church's foundations.

When you're done with the ruins and the old town, you could always head out to the local beach resort of **SAN LEONE**, a pleasant, low-key place 6km away, served by half-hourly buses from outside the train station.

Practicalities

Trains arrive at Agrigento Centrale station at the edge of the old town; don't get out at Agrigento Bassa, as it's 3km north of town. **Regional** buses use the terminal in Piazza Roselli, near the post office, while **city buses** to the temples and the beach at San Leone leave from Piazza Marconi, outside the train station. Buy city bus tickets (€1) from kiosks or *tabacchi*. The old town stretches west of the three main interlocking squares, piazzas Marconi, Aldo Moro and Vittorio Emanuele. Via Atenea is Agrigento's principal artery, running west from Piazza Aldo Moro, off which runs Via Empedocle with the **tourist office** at no. 73 (Mon–Fri 8am–2pm plus Wed 3.30–6pm; ☎800.236.837).

Finding **accommodation** in Agrigento shouldn't be a problem, except perhaps in peak season. The best option is *Camere a Sud*, Via Ficani 6 (☎349.638.4424, ⓦwww.camereasud.it; ❷), a quiet, new B&B off Via Atenea with very comfortable rooms and a roof terrace. The *Bella Napoli*, Piazza Lena 6 (☎0922.20.435, ⓦwww.hotelbellanapoli.com; ❷), at the western end of the old town, is a reasonable budget choice, but can be a little noisy; otherwise try the unexciting but clean *Belvedere*, Via San Vito 20 (☎ & Ⓕ0922.20.051; ❶), or the obliging and smart *Amici* (☎0922.402.831, ⓦwww.hotelamici.com; ❷–❸) just by the train station, which also has rooms in a nearby B&B. For real luxury, stay at the *Villa Athena*, Via dei Templi (☎0922.596.288, ⓦwww.athenahotels.com; ❻–❼), right in the archeological zone, with a pool, garden, restaurant and big windows soaking up the views. You can **camp** 6km away at the coastal resort of San Leone, at Internazionale San Leone (☎0922.416.121); bus #2 from outside the train station (every 30min until 9pm).

As for **eating**, there's the budget *Atenea* (☎0922.20.247), a friendly family-run trattoria at Via Ficani 32, in a quiet courtyard just off the Via Atenea (no credit cards; closed Sun). In the same neighbourhood, at Via Giambertoni 2, the folksy *Ambasciata di Sicilia* (☎0922.20.526; closed Mon) is small but has a view-laden terrace and serves good *antipasto rustico* and fresh fish. For the best pizzas head for the basic *Chez Jean 2* in Via Cicerone (☎0922.29651, no credit cards), or *Trattoria Caico* (☎0922.412.788), on Via Nettuno in San Leone, near the temples, which is the locals' choice for pasta and pizza.

Eraclea Minoa

From Agrigento you're well positioned for moving on into western Sicily, and frequent buses get you to Sciacca in around two and a half hours. If you can, though, first drop in on the other important local Greek site, **ERACLEA MINOA** – originally named Minoa after the Cretan king Minos, who chased Daedalus from Crete to Sicily and founded a city where he landed. The Greeks settled here in the sixth century, later adding the tag Heraklea. A buffer between the two great cities at Akragas, 40km to the east, and Selinus, 60km west, Eraclea Minoa was dragged into endless border disputes, but in spite of this it flourished. Most of the remains date from the fourth century BC, Eraclea Minoa's most important period, three hundred years or so before the town declined.

The **site** (daily 9am until 1hr before sunset; €2) is finely situated right on the coast, at the mouth of the River Platani. Apart from the good **walls**, once 6km long, which survive in interrupted sections, the main attraction is the sandstone **theatre**; some of the finds are held in a small on-site **museum**. While you're here, you'll be hard put to resist a trip down to the **beach**, one of the best on Sicily's southern coast, backed by pine trees and chalky cliffs. At the foot of the road from the site, a couple of **bar-restaurants** sit right on the beach with **rooms** advertised – *Rido Gabbiano* is a good option here, with rooms and apartments (☎0922.846.061 or 339.813.7907; ❶) – and there's a **campsite** nearby, *Eraclea Minoa Village* (☎0922.847.310, ⓦ www.eracleaminoavillage.it; May–Sept), with cabins. Without your own transport, you can get here between June and September by **buses** from Cattolica Eraclea or from the SS115, both accessible from Agrigento, but outside the summer months you're going to have to do some tough walking: take any bus running between Agrigento and Sciacca and ask the driver to let you off at the turning; it's 5km west of Montallegro, on the SS115, and the site is another 3.5km from there. Heading on, walk west from the site turning and you should be able to flag down a bus going to Sciacca.

Inland to Enna

The most scenically rewarding parts of Sicily's **interior** are in the east, primarily the hill-towns and villages that lie in a wide half-circle to the north of Enna – which is where you should head if you want to see the region by public transport.

From Agrigento, however, there are several worthwhile routes – most only practicable for travellers with transport. One route goes by way of **Sant'Angelo Muxaro** (daily buses from Agrigento), beyond which begins the most convoluted approach to Palermo, the twisting road climbing up to 1000m at Prizzi, from where there are occasional bus services down to **Corleone**. A fairly large town for these parts, it lent Mario Puzo's fictional Godfather, Don Corleone, his adopted family name – and it's the name of one of Sicily's most notorious real-life Mafia clans. There's a bus from Corleone to Palermo, another 60km.

The other option from Agrigento, better if you want to head on to the most appealing parts of the interior, is the **route to Enna**. There's a local bus service that connects up the nearer places, while trains make the journey, too, up through gentle, tree-planted slopes and then across the hilltops. At Canicatti the line splits, trains running south to Licata, on the coast.

Enna

From a bulging V-shaped ridge almost 1000m up, **ENNA** lords it over the surrounding hills of central Sicily. The approach to this doughty mountain stronghold is still as formidable as ever, the bus climbing slowly out of the valley and looping across the solid crag to the summit and the town. For obvious strategic reasons, Enna was a magnet for successive hostile armies, who in turn besieged and fortified the town, each doing their damnedest to disprove Livy's description of Enna as *inexpugnabilis*.

Despite the destructive attention, most of Enna's remains are medieval and in good shape, with the prize exhibit the thirteenth-century **Castello di Lombardia** (Easter–Oct daily 8am–8pm; free), dominating the easternmost spur of town. A mighty construction with its strong walls complete, it guards the steep slopes on either side of Enna, its six surviving towers (out of an original twenty) providing lookouts. From the tallest, the **Torre Pisana**, the magnificent **views** take in Enna itself, some rugged countryside in all directions and, if you're lucky, Mount Etna.

In the centre of town virtually all the accredited sights lie stretched out along and around **Via Roma**, which descends from the castle. It's a narrow street, broken by small piazzas – one of which fronts the hemmed-in **duomo**, dating in part from 1307. The spacious sixteenth-century interior (9am–noon & 4–7pm; free) features huge supporting alabaster columns, the bases of which are covered with an amorphous writhing mass of carved figures. There's a museum worth seeing as well, the **Museo Varisano** (Tues–Fri 8am–7pm; €2), just over the way in Piazza Mazzini, covering Neolithic to Roman times and including a fine series of painted Greek vases.

Via Roma slopes down to the rectangular **Piazza Vittorio Emanuele**, focal point of the evening *passeggiata*. Off here, there's a long cliff-edge belvedere, while the bottom of the piazza is marked by the plain, high wall of the **Chiesa di San Francesco**, whose massive sixteenth-century tower previously formed part of the town's system of watchtowers. This linked the castle with the **Torre di Federico**, which stands in isolation in its little park in the largely modern south of the town. An octagonal tower, 24m high, it's a survivor of the alterations to the city made by Frederick of Aragon who added a (now hidden) underground passage linking it to the *castello*.

Practicalities

All long-distance and most local **buses** use the bus terminal on Viale Diaz in the new town – turn right out of the terminal, right again down Corso Sicilia and it's around a ten-minute walk to Piazza Vittorio Emanuele. Enna's **train station** is 5km below town – a local bus runs roughly hourly to the centre (less frequently on Sundays), while a taxi will cost €8. You can reach everywhere in Enna itself very easily on foot, though should you need to take a local bus (to nearby Pergusa, for example – see p.1086), tickets (€0.80) can be bought from *tabacchi* and are valid for one hour. Information, as well as a good, free map of Enna, is available from the **tourist office** at Via Roma 413 (Mon–Sat 9am–1pm & 3–7pm; closed Sat in winter; ☎0935.528.928, ⓦwww.vivienna.it).

There's only one **hotel** in Enna, the dead-central *Grande Albergo Sicilia* in Piazza Colaianni (☎0935.500.850, ⓦwww.hotelsiciliaenna.it; ❸), which has bright, well-furnished rooms, some with views. There's also a pleasant B&B place, *Da Pietro* (☎ & ⓕ0935.33.647; no credit cards; ❶), with a garden, 4km from Enna on Contrada Longobardi (1km before neighbouring Calascibetta, and accessible by frequent buses). Alternatively, you can head out to the nearby lake **PERGUSA**, supposedly the site of Hades' abduction of Persephone to the underworld; buses (#5; roughly hourly, Mon–Sat 6.55am–10pm, Sun 9am–10pm) leave from outside San Francesco church. These days the famed Lago di Pergusa is encircled by a motor-racing track, alongside which are several hotels, including the the *Riviera* (☎0935.541.267, ⓦwww.hotelrivieraenna.it; ❸), with its own swimming pool.

For **meals** in Enna, *Tiffany*, near the cathedral at Via Roma 487 (closed Thurs), has reasonably priced pizzas and pastas. *La Fontana*, Via Vulturo 6 (closed Fri in winter), is friendly and has good-value meals such as home-made pasta with tomato, basil, mushrooms and aubergines; or there's the pricier, more refined *Ristorante Ariston*, Via Roma 353 (closed Sun), which also does good home-made pasta. The **market** in Enna is held on Tuesdays (8am–2pm) in Piazza Europa, below the Torre di Federico II.

Piazza Armerina and around

To the south of Enna, less than an hour away by bus, **PIAZZA ARMERINA** lies amid thick tree-planted hills, a quiet, unassuming place mainly seventeenth and eighteenth century in appearance, its skyline pierced by towers, the houses huddled together under the joint protection of castle and cathedral. All in all, it's a thoroughly pleasant place to idle around, though the real local draw is an imperial **Roman villa** that stands in rugged countryside at Casale, 5km south-west of Piazza Armerina. Hidden under mud for seven hundred years, the excavated remains reveal a rich villa, probably a hunting lodge and summer home, decorated with polychromatic mosaic floors that are unique in the Roman world for their quality and extent.

Buses drop you in Piazza Sen. Marescalchi, in the lower town. The old town is up the hill, centred around Piazza Garibaldi, off which is the **tourist office**, at Via Cavour 15 (Mon–Fri 7.45am–2.15pm, plus Wed 3–6.30pm; ☎0935.680.201, ⓦwww.piazza-armerina.it). The only central **hotel** choices are the rather noisily sited *Villa Romana*, Via A. de Gasperi 18 (☎0935.682.911, ⓦwww.piazza-armerina.it/hotelvillaromana; ❸), or a refurbished fifteenth-century monastery, the *Ostello del Borgo*, Largo San Giovanni 6 (☎0935.687.019, ⓦwww.ostellodelborgo.it; ❷, €16.50 in dormitory with AIG card, available here for €3). There are several options out of town: signposted everywhere by a red fox is the *agriturismo Agricasale* (☎0935.686.034, ⓦwww.agricasale.it; half board only; ❸), a good spot with peaceful rooms, a large swimming pool, and great organic food; you can also camp here. The *Mosaici da Battiato*, in Contrada Paratore (☎0935.685.453, ⓦwww.paginegialle.it/hotelmosaici; closed late Nov to late Dec; ❶), is just at the turn-off to the villa, which is a further 1km from the hotel, and has a grill-restaurant popular with tour groups during the day. The bus to the villa passes right by. Immediately across from here, *La Ruota* (☎0935.680.542; March–Oct) has space for **camping**.

For **eating**, *La Tavernetta*, in town at Via Cavour 14 (☎0935.685.883; closed Sun), has fish dishes for €8–13, while *Da Pepito*, Via Roma 140 (☎0935.685.737; closed Tues in winter), opposite the park, serves tasty Sicilian dishes.

The Villa Romana del Casale

A regular **bus service** runs to the villa between May and September from Piazza Sen. Marescalchi in Piazza Armerina, leaving at 9am, 10am, 11am, noon, 3pm, 4pm, 5pm and 6pm, returning from the villa half an hour later.

Otherwise you'll have to take a **taxi** (around €25 there and back, including waiting time) or **walk** the 6km: head down Via Matteotti or Via Principato and follow the signs; it takes around an hour on foot and is an attractive walk. It's also feasible to visit on a day-trip **from Enna**, but check the bus schedules before setting out.

The **Villa Romana** (daily 8am until 1hr before sunset; July & Aug often open till midnight; €6) dates from the early fourth century BC and was used right up until the twelfth century when a mudslide left it largely covered until comprehensive excavations in the 1950s. It's been covered again since to protect the mosaics, with a hard plastic and metal roof and walls designed to indicate the original size and shape, while walkways lead visitors through the rooms in as logical an order as possible. The **mosaics** themselves are identifiable as fourth-century Roman-African school, which explains many of the more exotic scenes and animals portrayed; they also point to the villa having had an important owner, possibly Maximianus Herculeus, co-emperor with Diocletian.

The **main entrance** leads into a wide courtyard with fountains, where the **thermae** (baths) group around an octagonal *frigidarium* and a central mosaic showing a lively marine scene. A walkway leads out of the baths and into the villa proper, to the massive central court or **peristyle**, whose surrounding corridors are decorated with animal head mosaics. From here, a balcony looks down on one of the villa's most interesting pictures, a boisterous circus scene showing a chariot race. Small rooms beyond, on either side of the peristyle, reveal only fragmentary geometric patterns, although one contains probably the villa's most famous image, a two-tiered scene of ten realistically muscular **Roman girls in "bikinis"**, taking part in various gymnastic and athletic activities.

Beyond the peristyle, a long, covered corridor contains the most extraordinary of the mosaics: the **great hunting scene**, which sets armed and shield-bearing hunters against a panoply of wild animals. Along the entire sixty-metre length of the mosaic are tigers, ostriches, elephants, even a rhino, being trapped, bundled up and down gangplanks and into cages, destined for the Games back in Rome. The square-hatted figure overseeing the operation is probably Maximianus himself: his personal area of responsibility in the imperial Tetrarchy was North Africa, where much of the scene is set.

Other rooms beyond are nearly all on a grand scale. The **triclinium**, a dining room with three apses, features the labours of Hercules, and a path leads around the back to the **private apartments**, based around a large basilica. The best mosaics here are a children's circus, where tiny chariots are drawn by colourful birds, and a children's hunt, the kids chased and pecked by the hares and peacocks they're supposed to snare.

Trápani and the west

The **west** of Sicily is a land apart. Skirting around the coast from **Trápani** – easily the largest town in the region – it looks immediately different: the cubic whitewashed houses, palm trees, active fishing harbours and sunburned lowlands seem more akin to Africa than Europe; and historically, the west of the island has always looked south. The earliest of all Sicilian sites, the mountain haunt of **Érice**, was dominated by Punic influence, the Carthaginians themselves entrenched in **Marsala**, at Sicily's westernmost point, for several hundred years; while the Saracen invaders took their first steps on the island at **Mazara del Vallo**, a town still strongly Arabic at heart. The Greeks never secured the same foothold in Sicily's west as elsewhere, although the remains at **Segesta** and **Selinunte** count among the island's best. Also worth seeing are the three islands of the **Egadi** archipelago, and the stunning stretch of coastline protected by the **Riserva Naturale dello Zingaro**.

Trápani

Out on something of a limb, **TRÁPANI** is an attractive enough town, though with little to keep you long – more a stopover, perhaps, en route to the offshore Egadi Islands (see p.1092) or inland to Érice (see p.1090). A rich trading centre throughout the early Middle Ages, halfway point for Tunis and Africa, Trápani has suffered years of decline since then, and today suffers from its remote position on Sicily's western tip, despite the revitalization of the huge salt pans to the south of town.

The Town

Trápani's **old town**, broadly speaking the area west of the train station, sports a mix of often incongruous architectural styles, something that harks back to Trápani's past as a complex medieval Mediterranean trading centre. It's particularly true of the medieval **Jewish quarter**, a wedge of hairline streets and alleys that holds one of the city's most characteristic buildings, the **Palazzo della Giudecca** on Via Giudecca – sixteenth-century, with a stone-studded tower and finely wrought Spanish-style Plateresque windows. Just up from here, Trápani is at its most engaging, Corso Italia preceding a confused set of three piazzas, enlivened by their surrounding churches: one doorway of the sixteenth-century **Chiesa di Santa Maria di Gesù** (Via San Pietro) is defiantly Renaissance in execution, and further up, on Piazzetta Saturno, the church of **Sant'Agostino** is even earlier, fourteenth-century and retaining a Gothic portal and delicate rose window.

Off the Piazzetta, Via Torrearsa neatly splits the old town. West of here Trápani's layout becomes more regularly planned, while the main drag and shopping street, the elegant **Corso Vittorio Emanuele**, changes name to Via Carolina and then Via Torre di Ligny as it runs towards the **Torre di Ligny** – utmost point of the scimitar of land that holds the old town. Finish off your circuit at the daily **market**, at the northern end of Via Torrearsa – fish, fruit and veg sold from the arcaded Piazza Mercato di Pesce, and with several lively bars in the area.

Celebrations and processions at Easter in Trápani are given added piquancy by the carriage around town on Good Friday of the **Misteri**, a group of life-sized eighteenth-century wooden figures representing scenes from the Passion. At other times they are on display in the exuberantly sculpted **Chiesa del Purgatorio** (call ☏347.4063 for access; free), on Via Domenico Giglio, near the junction with Via Francesco d'Assisi.

Except on arrival, you hardly need to set foot in the newer parts of the city. The only incentive is the interesting **Museo Regionale Pepoli** (daily

9am–1.30pm; €4), a good three-kilometre bus ride away in the drab heart of modern Trápani: take bus #24, #25 or #30 from Corso Vittorio Emanuele, Via Libertà or Via Garibaldi, and get off at the park, Villa Pepoli, outside the Santuario dell'Annunziata, the fourteenth-century convent whose cloisters house the museum. The convent's Cappella della Madonna contains the city's sacred statue, the **Madonna di Trápani**, attributed to Nino Pisano, which stands under a grandiose marble canopy by Antonello Gagini. Approached through bird-filled cloisters, the museum includes a bit of everything, from local archeological finds to delicate seventeenth-century coral craftwork and a good medieval art section. Look out for the grim wooden guillotine of 1789 downstairs and the eighteenth-century majolica-tiled scene of *La Mattanza* (the annual tuna-fish kill).

Practicalities

Come to Trápani by land from the east of the island and you'll arrive in the modern part of town: most **buses** (including those to and from Érice) pull up at the terminal in Piazza Malta; **trains** stop just around the corner in Piazza Umberto I. If you're heading straight off to the Egadi islands, note that the fast buses from Palermo, Palermo Airport and Agrigento stop at the ferry and hydrofoil terminals as well as the bus station. **Ferries** for the Egadi Islands, Pantelleria, Cágliari and Tunis dock at the Molo di Sanità, while **hydrofoils** for the Egadi Islands, Ústica and Naples dock to the east of the Molo, on Via A. Stati. Trápani's **airport**, 15km south of the centre at Birgi, has flights from Italian cities and Pantelleria.

The grumpy **tourist office** in the Casina delle Palme behind the waterfront (July & Aug Mon–Sat 8am–8pm, Sun 9am–noon; ☎0923.29.000, ⊛www.apt .Trápani.it) can provide information leaflets in English, accommodation listings and free maps, and there's **Internet** access at Piazza Garibaldi 28 (on the sea front not far from the port), and at M Point, Corso Vittorio Emanuele II 17 in the old town.

Finding somewhere to stay at Easter will be tricky, unless you book well in advance, but at other times rooms are easy to come by. Cheapest of the **hotels** is the *Messina*, Corso Vittorio Emanuele 71 (☎0923.21.198; no credit cards; ❶); it's clean but a bit dingy and often booked up. Alternatively, try the bright *Nuovo Russo* at Via Tintori 4 (☎0923.22.166, ⊛www.nuovoalbergorusso.it; ❷). The **youth hostel** is currently closed, but worth calling as they're renting out little apartments in the *centro storico* (☎0923.522.964; ❶). The nearest **campsite**, *Lido Valderice*, is a twenty-minute bus ride away in Bonagia (summer ☎0923.573.477, winter ☎0923.573.086, ⊛www.campinglidovalderice.com; open all year) – there are around eight buses daily (except Sun in winter) to the turn-off, from where it's a fifteen-minute walk.

Eating is particularly enjoyable in Trápani. The *Trattoria Safina*, opposite the train station at Piazza Umberto I (closed Fri except July & Aug), is a real bargain; for fine pizzas seek out *Calvino*, Via N. Nasi 77 (no credit cards; closed Tues), parallel to the corso; try the speciality *rianata* (literally Sicilian for "oregano-ated"). For good, quite reasonably priced fish head to the *Trattoria del Porto*, Via A. Stati 45 (☎0923.547.842). Better-class meals are on offer at *P&G*, Via Spalti 1, near the station (☎0923.547.701; closed Sun & Aug), a semi-formal place with local *busiate* pasta. The best ice creams in town are at *Sebastiano*, Via Roma 15, and for a quiet **drink** outside, a rarity in Trápani, head to one of the little bars or cafés along the recently pedestrianized Via Garibaldi, which runs between the old town and the new.

Érice

The nearest and most exhilarating ride from Trápani is to **ÉRICE**, fifteen minutes away by a new **cable car** (*funivia*). It's a mountain town with creeping hillside alleys, stone buildings, silent charm and powerful associations. Founded by Elymnians, who claimed descent from the Trojans, the original city was known to the ancient world as Eryx, and a magnificent temple, dedicated to Venus Erycina, Mediterranean goddess of fertility, once topped the mountain. Though the city was considered impregnable, Carthaginian, Roman, Arab and Norman invaders all forced entry over the centuries. But all respected the sanctity of Érice: the Romans rebuilt the temple and set two hundred soldiers to serve as guardians of the shrine, while the Arabs renamed the town Gebel-Hamed, or Mohammed's mountain.

When it's fine, the **views** from the terraces of Érice are stupendous – over Trápani, the slumbering whales of the Egadi Islands and on very clear days as far as Cape Bon in Tunisia. Scout around the town at random: the most convoluted of routes is only going to take you a couple of hours and every street and piazza is a delight. You enter through the Norman **Porta Trápani**, just inside which the battlemented fourteenth-century campanile of the **duomo** did service as a lookout tower for Frederick III of Aragon. From here there's no set route, though passing through pretty **Piazza Umberto** with its couple of outdoor bars is a good idea; and a natural start or finish could be made at the ivy-clad **Norman Castello** at the far end of town. This was built on the site of the famed ancient temple, chunks of which are incorporated in the walls.

Practicalities

To **get to** Érice from Trápani, take bus #22 or #23 (direction Ospedale S. Antonio Abbate) and get off at the stop before the hospital, from where it's a short walk to the **funivia station** (if you're driving, there's a car park). The return trip costs €3.75 and you arrive at the Porta Trápani in Érice. The cable car operates Mon 2–8.30pm, Tues–Fri 7.30am–8.30pm, Sat & Sun 9.30am–midnight, longer hours in summer. Nearby on Viale Conte Pepoli, Érice's helpful **tourist office** (Mon–Fri 9am–2pm; ℡0923.869.388) dishes out maps, and can help with **accommodation**. The most reasonable choices are the smart *Edelweiss*, in Cortile Padre Vincenzo, a cobbled alley off Piazzetta San Domenico (℡0923.869.420, ℮edelweiss@libero.it; ❸), or the character-ful rooms in the beautifully restored *palazzo Elimo*, Corso Vittorio Emanuele 75 (℡0923.869.377, ⓦwww.charmerelax.it; ❺–❻). Alternatively, just outside town, there's the *Ermione*, Via Pineta Comunale 43 (℡0923.869.138, ⓦwww.ermionehotel.com; ❸), whose Soviet-looking exterior belies its cheerful interior, and has a pool.

If you're coming for the day you may want to bring a picnic since **restaurant** prices in Érice are vastly inflated – the gardens near the Torretta Pepoli make a lovely picnic spot, with great views of the Egadi Islands, especially at sunset. Otherwise, for evening pizzas and regular trattoria fare, *La Vetta*, Via G. Fontana (closed Thurs), has tables outside in summer, or there's higher-quality fare at the moderately priced *La Pentolaccia*, Via Guarnotti 17 (℡0923.869.099), housed in an old monastery (closed Tues) and offering great home-made pasta (try it *alla Pentolaccia*, with tomato, aubergine, almonds, pine nuts and ricotta salata). Alternatively, there's the more formal and pricier *Monte San Giuliano*, entered through a medieval gateway at Vicolo San Rocco 7 (℡0923.869.595; closed Mon & two weeks in Nov & Jan). Finally, don't leave town without a visit to the *Caffè Maria* at Corso Vittorio Emanuele 4 or its sister *pasticceria* a few doors down, for the marzipan goodies and exquisite *cannoli*. The café's founder, Maria Grammatico, learned her trade as a girl in a convent, and has co-written a recipe book with writer Mary Taylor Simeti.

The Temple of Segesta

If time is limited, it's hard to know which to recommend most: the heights of Érice or Trápani's other local attraction, the temple at **SEGESTA** (daily 9am until 1hr before sunset; €6), 35km southeast of Trápani. Although unfinished, this Greek construction of 424 BC is one of the most inspiring of Doric temples anywhere and, along with the theatre, virtually the only relic of an ancient city whose roots – like those of Érice – go back to the twelfth century BC. Unlike Érice, though, ancient Segesta was eventually Hellenized and spent most of the later period disputing its borders with Selinus to the south. The temple dates from a time of prosperous alliance with Athens, the building abandoned when a new dispute broke out with Selinus in 416 BC.

The **temple** itself crowns a low hill, beyond a café and car park. From a distance you could be forgiven for thinking that it's complete: the 36 regular white stone columns, entablature and pediment are all intact, and all it lacks is a roof. However, get closer and you see just how unfinished the building is: stone studs, always removed on completion, still line the stylobate, the tall columns are unfluted and the cella walls are missing. Below the car park, a road winds up through slopes of wild fennel to the small **theatre** on a higher hill beyond; there's a half-hourly **minibus** service if you don't fancy the twenty-minute climb. The view from the top is justly lauded, across green slopes and the plain to the sea, the deep blue of the bay a lovely contrast to the theatre's white stone – not much damaged by the stilted motorway snaking away below.

Without your own transport, **getting to Segesta** involves a twenty-minute uphill walk from Segesta-Tempio town, to which there are at least four **buses**

△ The Temple of Segesta

(Mon–Sat 8am, noon, 2pm, 5pm) from Piazza Malta in Trápani, the last one returning at around 6.30pm; there is no service on Sundays. **Trains** to Segesta-Tempio are infrequent, but there are more regular trains connecting Trápani and Palermo with the station of **CALATAFIMI**, about a two-kilometre walk from the temple. There's also a cheap and modern **hotel** in Calatafimi (though note that the town itself is 4km from the train station), the *Mille Pini*, Piazza F. Vivona 4 (℡0924.951.260, ⓦwww.hotelmillepini.com; ❷), if you want to stay the night in the quiet surroundings.

The Egadi Islands

Of the various islands, islets and rock stacks that fan out from the west coast of Sicily, the three **Egadi Islands** (Isole Egadi) are best for a quick jaunt – connected by ferry and hydrofoil with Trápani. Saved from depopulation by tourism, in season at least you're not going to be alone, certainly on the main island, **Favignana**, where in August every scrap of flat rock and sand is filled. But a tour of the islands is worthwhile, not least for the caves that perforate the splintered coastlines. Out of season things are noticeably quieter, and in May or June you may witness the bloody **Mattanza**, an age-old slaughter in this noted centre of tuna fishing: its future, however, is unsure, due to bureaucratic wrangling and in-fighting between two factions of *tonnaroti* (tuna fishermen).

   Ferries to the islands depart from Trápani's Molo di Sanità; **hydrofoils** from further east along Via Ammiraglio Staiti. Though less frequent, ferries are, as always, much cheaper.

Favignana

FAVIGNANA, island and port town, is first stop for the boats from Trápani, and makes a good base since it has virtually all the accommodation and the Egadi's only campsites. Only 25 minutes by hydrofoil from the mainland, the island attracts a lot of day-trippers, keen to get onto its few rocky beaches. But get out of the main port and, outside August, it's easy enough to escape the crowds, even easier with a bike (which can be rented for €6 a day from Isidoro, at Via Mazzini 40). **Caves** all over the island bear prehistoric traces and many are accessible if you're determined enough. Otherwise, the two wings of the island invite separate **walks**; best is the circuit around the eastern part, past the bizarre ancient quarries at Cala Rossa, over the cliffs to Cala Azzura and then following the coast past the ugly new tourist village at Punta Fanfalo to Lido Burrone, the island's best beach, only 1km from the port.

   The most unusual **accommodation** on the island is at the striking *Hotel delle Cave*, a designer hotel with just nine rooms built on the lip of an abandoned quarry out at Zona Cavallo (℡0923.925.423, ⓦwww.hoteldellecave.it; ❸), with its gardens and restaurant inside the quarry itself. Top choices in town include the very nice *Aegusa*, at Via Garibaldi 11 (℡0923.922.430, Ⓕ0923.922.440; ❸), and the new and very pleasant *Hotel Favignana*, Contrada Badia 8 (℡0923.925.449, ⓦwww.favignanahotel.com; ❸). There are two **campsites** outside town, both an easy walk and both well signposted.

Levanzo

LEVANZO, to the north, looks immediately inviting, its white houses against the turquoise sea reminiscent of the Greek islands. The steep coast is full of inlets and, again, is riddled with caves. One, the **Grotta del Genovese**, was discovered in 1949 and contains some remarkable Paleolithic incised drawings, six thousand years old, as well as later Neolithic pictures. To arrange to see the cave you'll have to contact the guardian, Natale Castiglione, who lives at Via Calvario 11 (☎0923.924.032, ⓦwww.grottadelgenovese.it; daily in summer; weekends only in winter, tours €15, by jeep in winter, by boat in summer), near the hydrofoil quay. The island's **interior** has some great **walks** along old cart tracks, and there's a paved (and virtually traffic-free) cornice road leading to a lovely white pebble **beach** by the jagged rocks of the Faraglioni.

There are two **hotels** on Levanzo, both just above the only road and with good views over the sea, and both requiring half or full board in summer – the *Paradiso* (☎0923.924.080, ⓦwww.isoladilevanzo.it; ❶), and a little further up the side road, the fancier *Pensione Dei Fenici* (☎0923.924.083, ⓦwww.emmeti .it; no credit cards; ❷). You should also be able to get **rooms** in private houses if you ask around the port. Both hotels have restaurants.

Maréttimo

MARÉTTIMO, furthest out of the Egadi Islands, is the place to come for solitude. Very much off the beaten track, it's reached by only a few tourists. More white houses are scattered across the rocky island, while there's a bar in the main piazza and two restaurants. The spectacular fragmented coastline is pitted with rocky coves sheltering hideaway **beaches**, and there are numerous gentle **walks** which will take you all over the island.

To organize **rooms** before you come, call *Rosa dei Venti* (☎0923.923.249, 368.768.1571 or 333.675.8893; 1) which has half a dozen with bathrooms, as well as apartments with cooking facilities, and can also arrange **boat trips**. Alternatively, try the *Maréttimo Residence* (☎0923.923.202, ⓦwww.marettimo residence.it; ❷), a little cluster of resort cottages, usually rented weekly, above a stony beach south of the main port, or ask at the café in the main square.

San Vito Lo Capo, Scopello and the Riserva Nazionale dello Zingaro

Frequent buses run north from Trápani, cutting away from the coast until reaching the popular seaside resort of **SAN VITO LO CAPO** at the very nib of the northwestern headland. There are some good sands nearby, while the cape itself is only a stride away. There are several **campsites** too; good options include the central *La Fata* (☎348.000.0303, ⓦwww.trapaniweb.it/lafata; open all year) and *La Pineta* (☎0923.972.818, 0923.974.074 or 347.786.6827, ⓦwww .campinglapineta.it; open all year except Nov), a twenty-minute walk towards Scopello. San Vito is a popular local holiday spot and has several fairly good *pensioni* in the village, as well as trattorias and bars catering to the summer crowds. The best-value **accommodation** choice is the nicely furnished *Eden*, Via Mulino 62, a ten-minute walk from the beach (☎0923.972.460; closed Nov–Feb; no credit cards; ❶), while the *Sabbia* d'Oro, Via Cavour 90 (☎0923.972.508, ⓦwww.hotelsabbiadoro.com; ❸), has pleasant rooms. The main Via Savoia has at least three places offering rooms, with the cheapest being the *Costa Gaia* (☎0923.972.268, ⓦwww.albergocostagaia.com; no credit cards; ❸). *Hotel Capo San Vito*, right on the beach at Via San Vito 3 (☎0923.972.1220, ⓦwww.hotelcaposanvito.it; ❻; closed Dec–March), is unprepossessing from the outside, but pukka within, and has a Moorish-style terrace restaurant. Most of the hotels require at least half board in July and August. There's no shortage of good **restaurants**; couscous is the thing to try here. Head for *Santareddu*, Piazza Marinella 3 (℡0923.974.350), which serves spanking fresh fish, and prepares its couscous in the traditional Arab way, lacing it with almonds and cinnamon.

From San Vito, you have to return to Trápani for onward transport. **Buses** or, more frequently, trains cut across the headland to **CASTELLAMMARE DEL GOLFO**, another popular resort built on and around a hefty rocky promontory which is guarded by the squat remains of an Aragonese **castle**. The local **train station** is 4km east of town; a bus meets arrivals and shuttles you into Castellammare.

However, if you're looking for an atmospheric place to stay you could do much better by moving the 10km west up the coast to hamlet of **SCOPELLO**; there are four buses a day (Mon–Sat) from Castellammare's bus station on Via della Repubblica off the main Via Segesta.

The road to Scopello from Castellammare forks just before the village, with one strand running the few hundred metres down to the **Tonnara do Scopello**, set in its own tiny cove. This old tuna fishery is where the writer Gavin Maxwell lived and worked in the 1950s, basing his *Ten Pains of Death* on his experiences here. It's almost too picturesque to be true – not least the row of abandoned buildings on the quayside and the ruined old watchtowers tottering on jagged pinnacles of rock above the sea. The actual village of Scopello perches on a ridge a couple of hundred metres above the coastline, comprising little more than a paved square and a fountain, off which run a couple of alleys. In summer, particularly, you'd do well to book in advance if you want **to stay** here. ⚘ *La Tranchina*, at Via A. Diaz 7 (℡ & 🖷0924.541.099; ❸), has comfortable rooms with a friendly English-speaking owner. You eat well here too – fresh fish, and interesting pasta dishes such as pasta with peppers and home-cured *bottarga* (tuna fish egg roe). *La Tavernetta*, next door at no. 3 (℡ & 🖷0924.541.129; ❸), has similarly pleasant rooms, some with distant sea views, and also has a restaurant. The nearest **campsite** is *Baia di Guidaloca* (℡0924.541.262; April–Sept), 3km south of Scopello and a stone's throw from the lovely bay of **Cala Bianca**, where there's good swimming; the bus from Castellammare passes right by.

Just 2km from Scopello (no buses but it's a nice, easy walk) is the southern entrance to the **Riserva Naturale dello Zingaro**, Sicily's first nature reserve, comprising a completely unspoiled seven-kilometre stretch of **coastline** backed by steep mountains. At the entrance, there's an **information hut**, where you can pick up a plan showing the **trails** through the reserve. It's less than twenty minutes to the first beach, Punta della Capreria, and 3km to the successive coves of Disa, Berretta and Marinella, which should be a little more secluded.

Mozia, Marsala and Mazara del Vallo

Around 15km south of Trápani, the unique Phoenician settlement of **MOZIA** (also known as Mothia or Motya) lies just offshore from the crystalline patchwork of saltpans which line this part of the coast. Situated on one of the islands in the shallow **Stagnone lagoon**, it was excavated in the late nineteenth century by an Englishman, Joseph Whitaker. You can explore the **ruins** (summer daily 9am until 1hr before sunset; €6) and visit the **museum** he established, which is worth a visit for its magnificent and sensual sculpture alone, *Il Giovannetto di Mozia*. If you're reliant on public transport, the island is more easily reached from Marsala: regular **buses** run from Piazza del Popolo to the ferry landing. And should you want **to stay** in the area, the peaceful agriturismo *Baglio Vajarassa* (℡0923.968.628, ⓦwww.bagliovajarassa.com; no credit cards; ❸, half board €60 per person) on Contrada Spagnola 176, a couple of kilometres south of the ferry landing, offers rooms furnished with antiques, and typical local dishes for dinner around a communal table.

Bypassing Mozia, and pretty much keeping within sight of the sea all the way, the western rail loop runs down the coast from Trápani to **MARSALA**, a distance of around 25km. The city, which takes its name from the Arabic Marsah-el-Allah, the port of Allah, was once the main Saracenic base in Sicily, but since the late eighteenth century it has been better known for the dessert wine that carries its name, something every bar and restaurant will sell you.

The centre of Marsala is extremely attractive, a clean sixteenth-century layout that's free of traffic and littered with high, ageing buildings and arcaded courtyards. But, pleasant as the town is, save your energy for two excellent museums. The most central, behind the cathedral at Via Garraffa 57, is the **Museo degli Arazzi** (Tues–Sat 9.30am–1pm & 4.30–6pm, Sun 9.30am–1pm; €2.50), whose sole display is a series of eight enormous hand-stitched wool and silk **tapestries** depicting the capture of Jerusalem – sixteenth-century and beautifully rich, in burnished red, gold and green. Afterwards, walk out to the cape (follow the main Via XI Maggio to Piazza della Vittoria and bear left towards the water); one of the stone-vaulted warehouses that line the promenade holds the equally impressive **Museo Archeologico e della Nave Punica** (daily 9am–6pm; €3). An archeological museum of quality, its major exhibit is a reconstructed Punic war ship once rowed by 68 oarsmen, probably sunk during the First Punic War, and rediscovered in 1971. Other bits and pieces on display are from the excavated site (mostly Roman) of Lilybaeum. If you want a **meal** in Marsala, head for the wood-panelled *Trattoria Garibaldi* at Piazza Addolorata 5 (closed Mon) for good local dishes, or to *Eubes* (℡0923.99.62.31), in front of the *imbarcadero*, where you can eat good fish.

Half an hour's driving further on, **MAZARA DEL VALLO** is Sicily's most important fishing port and a place of equal distinction for the Arabs and Normans who dominated the island a thousand years ago. The first Saracen gain in Sicily, Mazara was Arabic for 250 years until captured by Count Roger in 1075: the island's first Norman parliament met in the town 22 years later, and a relic of that period is the tiny pink-domed Norman chapel of **San Nicolò**, on the edge of the harbour. North Africans crew the colourful fishing boats that block the harbour and river, the old city kasbah once more houses a Tunisian community. Wandering around the **harbour** area is the most rewarding thing to do in Mazara, although you can also spend an enjoyable hour or so pottering around the town. There's a remodelled Norman **duomo**, which shelters some Roman and Byzantine remains, and in nearby Piazza del Plebiscito, the fifteenth-century church of Sant'Egido has recently been transformed into the **Museo del Satiro** (daily 9am–6.30pm; €6.50), home of a somewhat risqué fourth-century BC bronze satyr captured in the ecstatic throes of an orgiastic Dionysian dance. It was hauled up by a Mazara fishing boat, the *Captain Ciccio*, in the waters between Pantelleria and Cape Bon, Tunisia, in 1998. Sadly, as the fishermen brought the catch aboard, one of the arms broke off and has so far not been recovered. Across the square is the **Museo Civico**, which has been closed for restoration for several years (call the *Comune* for information; ℡0923.671.111).

The town's most central **hotel** is the dauntingly large but very comfortable *Hopps Hotel*, at Via G. Hopps 29 (℡0923.946.133; ⓦwww.elorogroup.com; ❸), at the eastern end of the Lungomare Mazzini, and there's a line of **restaurants** near the public gardens, each offering varieties of fish couscous and all with tables outside. Of these, *Lo Scoiattolo* ("The Squirrel"), at Via N Tortorici 9, has a fine antipasto buffet and daily fish specials, while *La Bettola*, Via Maccagnone 32 (closed Wed), is a small, intimate place with a great local wine list.

Marinella, Selinunte and Sciacca

There's little else to stop for around the western coast; even less inland, which is crossed by one major road, the SS188, running from Marsala to **Salemi**, centre of a prosperous wine-making region. But the southernmost chunk of Sicily's western bulge is easily reached by train and has several places worth more than a cursory glance if you have the time.

Seaside **MARINELLA**, together with the nearby Greek **ruins of Selinunte**, is one of them. To get there you'll need to take a **bus** from Piazza Reina Margherita (5 daily; 25min) in **Castelvetrano**, itself thirty minutes by bus from Mazara del Vallo. Marinella, right next to the Greek ruins of Selinunte, is no longer the isolated place it once was, with new buildings in the centre and the seafront slightly top-heavy with trattorias and *pensioni* these days. But it remains an attractive place, certainly if you're planning to make use of the fine sand **beach** that stretches west from the village to the ruins. **Buses** pull up on the road that leads down to the seafront, where the main **hotels** and restaurants are situated. First choice here is the *Lido Azzurro*, Via Marco Polo 98 (℡ & ℻0924.46.256; half board in July & Aug; ❷), a charming villa with sea-facing balconies and an owner who speaks good English. Opposite the temple car park, the sign pointing to "Chiesa" leads to the old abandoned train station, just before which you'll find *Il Pescatore*, at Via Castore e Polluce 31 (℡0924.46.303; no credit cards; ❶), with a very genial host, fruit breakfasts (€3) on the terrace and rooftop camping. There are also two **campsites** virtually next to each other on the main road, 1500m north of the village: the *Athena* (℡0924.46.132) and *Il Maggiolino* (℡0924.46.044, ⓦwww.campingmaggiolino.it); the bus from Castelvetrano passes right by them. Via Marco Polo, the road above the west beach, is where all the best **eating and drinking** places are, starting down at the little harbour where a couple of bars put out tables from where you can watch the sun set – *Cala Nnino*, here, is worth a visit for its sea urchin (*ricci*). Alternatively, if you're feeling energetic, walk the 3km head to the restaurant *La Pineta* on the east beach, **Mare Pineta**, for its great location, fish dishes and speciality bread.

Selinunte: the site

The westernmost of the Hellenic colonies, the Greek city of Selinus – **Selinunte** in modern Italian – reached its peak in the fifth century BC when a series of mighty temples was erected. A bitter rival of Segesta, whose lands lay adjacent to the north, the powerful city and its fertile plain attracted enemies hand over fist, and it was only a matter of time before Selinus caught the eye of Segesta's ally, Carthage. Geographically vulnerable, the city was sacked by Carthaginians, any recovery forestalled by earthquakes that later razed the city. Despite the destruction, which left the site completely abandoned until it was rediscovered in the sixteenth century, the ruins of Selinus have exerted a romantic hold ever since.

The **site of Selinus** is set back behind the main part of Marinella village, split into two parts with **temples** in each, known only as Temples A–G. The two parts are enclosed within the same site, with the car park and entrance (summer daily 9am until 1hr before sunset; €6) lying through the landscaped earthbanks that preclude views of the east group of temples from the road. The first stop is at the **East Group**. Shrouded in the wild celery which gave the ancient city its name, the temples are in various stages of ruin: the most complete is the one nearest the sea (Temple E), while the northernmost (Temple G) is a tangle of columned wreckage six metres high in places. The road leads down from here, across the (now buried) site of the old harbour to the second part of excavated Selinus, the **acropolis** (where there is another car park), a site containing what remains of the other temples (five in all), as well as the well-preserved city streets and massive, stepped walls which rise above the duned beach below. Temple C stands on the highest point of the acropolis, and there are glorious views from its stones out over the sparkling sea: from this temple were removed some of the best metopes, now on show in Palermo's archeological museum.

Sciacca

FS buses leave from outside Castelvetrano train station three times daily (1 on Sun) for the atmospheric port of **SCIACCA**, picking up at the abandoned Selinunte station in Marinella village. Sciacca's **upper town** is skirted by medieval walls which form high sides to the steep streets, rising to a ruined Spanish **castle**. Below, the **lower town** sits on a clifftop terrace overlooking the harbour, where it's easy to while away time drinking in the coastal views. There are also some wonderful **Roman hot springs**, still in operation next to the *Grand Hotel delle Terme* (Mon–Fri 8am–1pm as long as there are no patients), and a helpful **tourist office** at Corso Vittorio Emanuele 84 (Mon–Sat 9am–2pm; ℡0925.22.744).

With an active harbour and some good beaches close by, Sciacca makes a nice place to stay over, though there's precious little choice of **accommodation** – the only central budget option being the *Paloma Bianca* at Via Figuli 5 (℡0925.25.130; ❸), a rather uninspiring business-travellers' hotel, but comfortable enough. Alternatively, you could splash out on the plusher *Grand Hotel delle Terme*, Viale Nuove Terme 1 (℡0925.23.133, ⓦwww.grandhoteldelleterme .com; ❹), on the cliffs to the east of town, set in its own park with outstanding views out to sea. The nearest **campsite**, *Baia Makauda* (℡0925.997.001, ⓦwww .makaudabeach.com), 9km east of town at località San Giorgio Tranchina, also has bungalows and is best reached by taxi if you don't have your own transport.

Pantelleria

Forty kilometres nearer to Tunisia than to Sicily, **PANTELLERIA** is the most singular of Sicily's outlying volcanic islands. Settled since Neolithic times and later supporting a Phoenician colony in the seventh century BC, the island's strategic position kept it in the mainstream of Sicilian history for years. Nowadays the most visible sign of its past is the gloomy black **Castello Barabacane**, whose origins are Roman, but whose present appearance owes most to the Spanish. The island was used as one of the main Mediterranean bases by the Fascists during World War II, and was bombed without mercy by the Allies in May 1943 as they advanced from North Africa. In part, this explains the morose appearance of the island's main town (also called Pantelleria) – thrown up in unedifying concrete.

There are no beaches of any kind in Pantelleria, its rough **black coastline** mainly jagged rocks, but the **swimming** is still pretty good in some exceptionally scenic spots. Inland, the largely mountainous country offers plenty of rambling opportunities, all an easy moped- or bus-ride from the port. If you're spending any length of time on Pantelleria, you may want to stay in one of the local **dammuso** houses: a throwback to the buildings of Neolithic times, their strong walls and domed roofs keep the temperature down indoors. Many are available for rent through Call Tour, Via Cágliari 52 (☎0923.911.065, ⓦwww .calltour.net), or look at ⓦwww.pantelleriatravel.com.

The island's main drawback is the cost of living: there are only a few hotels, where there may be a minimum three-day stay in July and August, while food (and water) is mostly imported and therefore relatively expensive. The best times to visit are May/June or September/October, to avoid the summer's ferocious heat.

Getting to Pantelleria

Siremar (☎0923.545.455, ⓦwww.siremar.it) runs **ferries** to Pantelleria from Trápani (June–Sept 1 daily; Oct–May Sun–Fri 1 daily, returning Mon–Sat 1 daily; 5hr 45min; high season €22.60, low season €18.70 each way). Ústica Lines (☎0923.22.000, ⓦwww.usticalines.it) also operates a daily **hydrofoil** service from Trápani, which takes 2hr 30min (daily mid-June to mid-Sept; €34 each way) and a fast ferry from Mazara del Vallo (late June to Sept daily except Wed; 90min; €32.40 each way).

Pantelleria is a thirty-minute **flight** from Trápani (1–3 daily), and a fifty-minute flight from Palermo (1–2 daily); the normal one-way fare from either is around €80, but with special offers on the web, you can end up paying less than half that (ⓦwww.expedia.it is a good starting point).

Pantelleria Town

PANTELLERIA TOWN is the site of most of the island's accommodation and facilities. For online information, consult ⓦwww.pantelleria.it. The **airport** is 5km southeast of town; a bus connects with flight arrivals and drops you in the central Piazza Cavour. **Arriving by sea**, you'll disembark right in the centre of town, unless bad weather forces a landing at Scauri, a smaller port on the island's southwestern side, from where a bus takes foot passengers into town.

The few **hotels** in town include the *Miryam*, Corso Umberto I, at the far end of the port, near the castle (☎0923.911.374, ☎0932.911.777; ❸), which is bright and pleasant inside despite rather glum external appearances; the *Port Hotel* (☎0923.911.299, ⓦwww.pantelleriahotel.it; ❸), nearer the dock at Via Borgo Italia 6, with harbour-facing rooms; and the nearby *Khamma*, at Via Borgo Italia 24 (☎0923.912.680, ☎0923.912.570; ❸). Prices soar, however, in high season. There's no campsite on the island.

The best places **to eat** in town are *La Pergola*, Via Contrada Suvaki (☎0923.918.420; closed Tues), which has good, fresh local food, and is open all year, and *Il Cappero*, Via Roma 31 (☎0923.912.601), just off the main piazza (no credit cards; closed Mon in winter), which serves local ravioli stuffed with *tumma* (a light cheese), fresh fish (including large tuna steaks) and popular pizzas. There's a good antipasto table too. The best-placed trattoria in town is *Il Dammuso*, Via Borgo Italia (near the Miryam), a trendy spot with large windows opening right onto the harbour; its long menu includes great fish and pizzas.

Around the island

Local buses leave from Piazza Cavour, with regular departures to all the main villages on the island – but note that there are no services on Sundays. There are seven daily buses along the **southwest coast** to the village of **Scauri**, passing on the way the first of the island's strange **sesi**, massive black Neolithic funeral mounds of piled rock, with low passages leading inside. On foot, it's just over an hour from the sesi to **Sataria**, where concrete steps lead down to a tiny square-cut **sea pool**. In the cave behind are more pools where warm water bubbles through, reputed to be good for curing rheumatism and skin diseases.

Along the **northeast coast** to the villages of Kamma and Tracino (4 daily buses), get the bus to drop you at the top of the route down into **Gadir**, a small anchorage with just a few houses hemmed in by volcanic pricks of rock. From here it's an easy, fairly flat hour's stroll to the charming **Cala Levante**, a huddle of houses around another tiny fishing harbour. Where the road peters out, bear right along the path at the second anchorage and keep along the coast for another five minutes until the **Arco dell'Elefante**, or "Elephant Arch", hoves into view, named after the hooped formation of rock that resembles an elephant stooping to drink.

The principal inland destination is Pantelleria's main volcano, the **Montagna Grande**, whose summit is the island's most distinctive feature seen from out at sea. Buses (3 daily) run from the port for the crumbly old village of **Siba**, perched on a ridge below the volcano. To climb the peak of Montagna Grande (836m), keep left at the telephone sign by the *tabacchi* here, and strike off the main road. From Siba, another (signposted) path – on the left as you follow the road through the village – brings you in around twenty minutes to the **Sauna Naturale** (or Bagno Asciutto). It's little more than a slit in the rock-face, where you can crouch in absolute darkness, breaking out into a heavy sweat as soon as you enter.

Travel details

Trains

Services are drastically reduced on Sundays and holidays.

Agrigento to: Palermo (12 daily; 2hr).

Catania to: Enna (Mon–Sat 7 daily; 1hr 20min); Messina (20 daily; 1hr 30min); Palermo (3 daily; 3hr 45min); Siracusa (12 daily; 1hr 30min); Taormina (at least 1 hourly; 40min).

Enna to: Catania (7 daily; 1hr 20min); Palermo (5 daily; 2hr 10min–2hr 50min).

Messina to: Catania (20 daily; 1hr 30min); Cefalù (13 daily; 2–3hr); Milan (12 daily; 13–18hr); Milazzo (21 daily; 25min–1hr); Naples (11 daily; 5hr 50–6hr 30min); Palermo (up to 14 daily; 2hr 30min–4hr 30min); Rome (18 daily; 7–9hr); Taormina (at least 1 hourly; 40min–1hr).

Palermo to: Agrigento (12 daily; 2hr); Catania (3 daily; 3hr 45min); Cefalù (20 daily; 40min–1hr); Enna (5 daily; 2hr 10min–2hr 50min); Marsala (7 daily; 2hr 30min–3hr 30min); Mazara del Vallo (8 daily; 2hr 30min–4hr); Messina (hourly; 3hr–4hr 25min); Milazzo (13 daily; 2hr 30min–3hr); Trápani (9 daily; 1hr 45min–3hr 40min).

Ragusa to: Modica (8 daily; 20min); Noto (5 daily; 1hr 30min–1hr 45min).

Segesta Tempio to: Trápani (4 daily; 20min).

Siracusa to: Catania (12 daily; 1hr 30min); Messina (9 daily; 2hr 40min–3hr 50min); Noto (12 daily; 30min); Ragusa (4 daily; 2hr 5min–2hr 40min); Taormina (9 daily; 1hr 50min–2hr 20min).

Trápani to: Marsala (14 daily; 30min); Mazara del Vallo (13 daily; 45min–1hr); Palermo (9 daily; 2hr 45min–3hr 40min); Segesta–Tempio (3 daily; 20min).

Circumetnea trains

Catania to: Paternò/Adrano/Bronte/Maletto/Randazzo (9 daily in summer, 16 daily in winter; 35min/1hr/1hr 35min/1hr 50min/2hr).

Randazzo to: Linguaglossa/Giarre–Riposto (7 daily in summer, 10 daily in winter; 30min/1hr).

Buses

Schedules below are for Monday–Saturday services; on Sundays, services are either drastically reduced or non-existent.

Agrigento to: Catania (14 daily; 3hr); Palermo (10 daily; 2hr); Trápani (4 daily; 3hr 30min–4hr).

Catania to: Agrigento (14 daily; 3hr); Enna (8 daily; 1hr 20min); Messina (1–2 hourly; 1hr 35min);

Nicolosi (hourly; 40min); Noto (8 daily; 2hr 25min–2hr 15min); Palermo (hourly; 2hr 40min); Piazza Armerina (6 daily; 1hr 45min); Ragusa (10 daily; 2hr); Rifugio Sapienza (1 daily; 2hr); Rome (2–3 daily; 11hr); Siracusa (approx hourly; 1hr 20min); Taormina (15 daily; 1hr 10min).

Enna to: Catania (8–11 daily Mon–Sat, 3 daily Sun; 1hr 20min); Piazza Armerina (9 daily; 40min).

Messina to: Catania (1–2 hourly Mon–Sat; 1hr 35min); Catania airport (16 daily; 1hr 50min); Giardini-Naxos (7 daily Mon–Sat; 55min); Milazzo (approx hourly Mon–Sat; 50min); Palermo (6 daily Mon–Sat; 2hr 40min); Randazzo (2 daily; 1hr 50min); Taormina (11 daily; 1hr–1hr 40min).

Milazzo to: Messina (approx hourly; 50min).

Palermo to: Agrigento (10 daily; 2hr); Catania (hourly; 2hr 40min); Cefalù (3 daily; 1hr); Marsala (hourly; 2hr 30min); Messina (6 daily Mon–Sat; 2hr 40min); Siracusa (3 daily; 3hr 15min); Trápani (15 daily; 2hr).

Piazza Armerina to: Enna (9 daily; 40min); Palermo (5 daily Mon–Sat; 2hr 15min).

Siracusa to: Catania (approx hourly; 1hr 20min); Catania airport (9 daily; 1hr 10min); Noto (7 daily; 55min); Piazza Armerina (1 daily; 2hr 30min); Ragusa (5 daily Mon–Sat; 2hr 15min); Rome (1 daily and 3 weekly; 13hr).

Taormina to: Catania (15 daily; 1hr 10min); Catania airport (6 daily Mon–Sat; 1hr 25min).

Trápani to: Agrigento (4 daily Mon–Sat; 3hr 30min–4hr); Érice (10 daily; 40min); San Vito Lo Capo (8 daily Mon–Sat, 4 daily Sun; 1hr 20min).

Ferries

The services detailed here refer to the period from June to September; you should expect frequencies to be greatly reduced or suspended outside these months, especially to the Aeolian Islands.

Lípari to: Alicudi (5 weekly; 3hr 10min–3hr 50min); Filicudi (5 weekly; 2hr–2hr 45min); Milazzo (7 daily; 2hr); Naples (5 weekly; 14hr); Panarea (1–2 daily; 1hr 45min–2hr); Salina (2 daily; 50min); Strómboli (1–2 daily; 3hr–4hr 15min); Vulcano (3 daily; 25min).

Messina to: Lípari (4 daily; 1hr 40min–3hr); Villa San Giovanni (every 20min; 40min).

Milazzo to: Alicudi (2 daily; 6hr); Filicudi (2 daily; 4hr 55min); Ginostra (5–8 weekly; 6hr); Lípari (6–9 daily; 2hr); Naples (6 weekly; 16hr 30min); Panarea (6–10 weekly; 4–5hr); Rinella (6–8 weekly; 3hr 40min); Santa Marina (6 daily; 3hr–3hr 40min); Strómboli (6–10 weekly; 5hr 10min–7hr); Vulcano (3–6 daily; 1hr 30min).

Palermo to: Cágliari (1 weekly; 14hr 30min); Genoa (1 daily; 20hr); Livorno (3 weekly; 17hr);

Naples (2 daily; 11hr); Tunis (1 weekly; 9hr); Ústica (1 daily; 2hr 20min).

Trápani to: Cágliari (1 weekly; 11hr); Favignana (3 daily; 55min–1hr 25min); Levanzo (3 daily; 50min–1hr 30min); Maréttimo (1 daily; 2hr 35min); Pantelleria (1 daily; 5hr 45min).

Hydrofoils and fast ferries

Again, most of the services listed are greatly reduced or suspended outside the summer season.

Cefalù to: Lípari (3 weekly; 3hr 15min); Palermo (3 weekly; 1hr); Vulcano (3 weekly; 3hr).

Lípari to: Alicudi (6 daily; 1hr–2hr 45min); Cefalù (1 daily; 2hr 10min); Filicudi (6 daily; 1hr); Ginostra (3 daily; 1hr–1hr 25min); Messina (5 daily; 1hr 50min–2hr 10min); Milazzo (approx hourly; 45min–1hr); Naples (1 daily; 6hr); Palermo (2 daily; 3hr 30min); Panarea (4 daily; 1hr); Reggio di Calabria (2 daily; 1hr 55min); Salina (approx hourly; 20min); Strómboli (4 daily; 1hr 15min–1hr 45min); Vulcano (approx hourly; 10min).

Messina to: Lípari (2 daily June–Sept; 1 daily Oct–May 1hr 40min); Reggio di Calabria (2 daily June–Sept, 1 daily Oct–May; 15–25min); Vulcano (2 daily June–Sept; 1 daily Oct–May; 1hr 20min–3hr 10min).

Milazzo to: Alicudi (4 daily; 2hr 55min); Filicudi (4 daily; 2hr 20min); Ginostra (3 daily; 1hr 45min–2hr 30min); Lípari (approx hourly; 45min–1hr); Panarea (6 daily; 1hr 45min–2hr 10min); Rinella (7 daily; 1hr 40min); Santa Marina (approx hourly; 1hr 20min–3hr); Strómboli (6 daily; 1hr 25min–2hr 20min); Vulcano (approx hourly; 45min).

Palermo to: Aeolian Islands (2 daily, 3–8hr); Cefalù (3 weekly; 1hr); Naples (1 daily; 4hr); Ústica (3 daily; 1hr 15min).

Pantelleria to: Mazara del Vallo (6 weekly in summer; 90min); Trápani (1 daily in summer; 2hr 30min).

Trápani to: Favignana (14 daily; 25min); Levanzo (10 daily; 35min); Maréttimo (3 daily; 1hr); Naples (3 weekly; 6hr 45min); Pantelleria (1 daily in summer; 2hr 30min); Ústica (3 weekly; 2hr 30min).

Ústica to: Favignana (3 weekly; 2hr); Naples (3 weekly; 4hr); Trápani (3 weekly; 2hr 30min).

Flights

Palermo to: Pantelleria (1–2 daily; 50min).
Trápani to: Pantelleria (1–3 daily; 30min).

International ferries and catamarans

Catania to: Malta (3–6 weekly July & Aug, 1–2 weekly March–June & Sept to early Oct; 3hr).
Palermo to: Tunis (1 weekly; 9hr).
Trápani to: Tunis (1 weekly; 8hr 15min).

Sardinia

CHAPTER 17

Highlights

* **Cágliari's old town** Cágliari's Castello quarter is the most atmospheric part of town, a dense warren of alleys girded by thick walls. See p.1108

* **Nora** Although much of this Carthaginian and Roman archeological site is submerged under the sea, what remains – including mosaics, a theatre and baths – gives a good indication of the town's former importance. See p.1115

* **Chia** On the island's southern tip, the area around Chia combines idyllic beaches with Sardinia's classic rocky coastline. See p.1115

* **Nuraghe Su Nuraxi** Sardinia's mysterious prehistoric *nuraghi* are strewn throughout the island, and this is one of the most impressive. See p.1115

* **Sa Sartiglia, Oristano** One of the island's most spectacular festivals, involving brilliant feats of equestrian prowess, fabulous costumes and lashings of medieval pageantry. See p.1119

* **Tiscali** A vast mountain cave housing the remains of a prehistoric village. See p.1127

△ La Maddalena Island, Costa Smeralda

Sardinia

A little under 200km from the Italian mainland, slightly more than that from the North African coast at Tunisia, **Sardinia** is way off most tourist itineraries of Italy: D.H. Lawrence found it exotically different when he passed through here in 1921 – "lost", as he put it, "between Europe and Africa and belonging to nowhere." Your reasons for coming will probably be a combination of plain curiosity and a yearning for clean beaches. The island is relatively free of large cities or heavy industry, and its beaches are indeed some of the cleanest in Italy and on the whole uncrowded, except perhaps for peak season, when ferries bring in a steady stream of sun-worshippers from what the islanders call *il continente*, or mainland Italy. But Sardinia offers plenty besides sun and sea – the more so if you are prepared to venture into its lesser-known interior.

Although not famed for its cultural riches, the island does hold some surprises, not least the remains of the various civilizations that passed through here. Its central Mediterranean position ensured that it was never left alone for long, and from the Carthaginians onwards the island was ravaged by a succession of

Regional food and wine

Sardinian cooking revolves around scintillatingly fresh ingredients simply prepared: seafood – especially **lobster** – is grilled over open fires scented with myrtle and juniper, as is meltingly tender **suckling pig**. This means that there is little pork left to be made into salami and other cured meats, although a few wild boar escape the fire long enough to be made into *prosciutto di cinghiale*, a ham with a strong flavour of game. Being surrounded by sparkling seas, Sardinians also make rich, Spanish-inspired **fish stews** and produce **bottarga**, a version of caviar made with mullet eggs. **Pasta** is substantial here, taking the form of *culurgiones* (massive ravioli filled with cheese and egg) or *malloreddus* (saffron-flavoured, *gnocchi*-like shapes), while cheeses tend to be made from ewe's milk and are either fresh and herby or pungent and salty – like the famous **pecorino sardo**. The island is also famous for the quality and variety of its bread, ranging from parchment-like *carta da musica* wafers to chunky rustic loaves intended to sustain shepherds on the hills. As in Sicily, there is an abundance of light and airy **pastries**, frequently flavoured with lemon, almonds or orange flower water.

Vernaccia is the most famous Sardinian wine: a hefty drink reminiscent of sherry and treated in a similar way – the bone-dry version as an **aperitif** and the sweet variant as a **dessert wine**. Other wines worth seeking out are Mandrolasi, an easy-drinking **red**, and Cannonau di Sardegna, a heady number much favoured by locals. Among the **whites**, look out for dry Torbato or the full-flavoured Trebbiano Sardo, both perfect accompaniments to local fish and seafood.

Civitavecchia, Livorno ▶ & Fiumicino ▶ Genoa, Livorno, Piombino & Civitavecchia ▶ Genoa, Fiumicino & Civitavecchia

I. La Maddalena
Santa Teresa di Gallura
Porto Pollo
I. Caprera
Palau
Porto Cervo
Cannigione
Costa Smeralda
Arzachena
Golfo Aranci
Olbia

I. Asinara
Punta Falcone
La Pelosa
Stintino
Castelsardo
Tempio Pausania
GALLURA

Porto Torres
Sássari
Posada
Anghelu Ruju
Chilivani
Siniscola

Capo Caccia
Alghero
Torralba
Nuoro
Orosei

Bosa
Macomer
Oliena
Cala Gonone
Dorgali
Mamoiada
Tiscali
Abbasanta
Orgósolo

Fonni
BARBAGIA
Gola Su Gorroppu
Sinis
Sórgono
Désulo
Monte La Mármora
Baunei
Tonara
MONTI DEL GENNARGENTU
Tortolì
Arbatax
Oristano
Samugheo
Aritzo

Tharros

Laconi
Giara di Gesturi
Ísili
Su Nuraxi
Gesturi
Barúmini
Las Plassas
Mandas

Sanluri
SS131

Muravera

Iglésias
SS130

Portoscuso
I. di San Pietro
Carloforte
Carbonia
Cágliari
Villasimius
Calasetta
Sant' Antioco
Pula
Nora
I. di Sant'Antioco
Chia
Capo Spartivento

N

17
SARDINIA

invaders, each of them leaving some imprint behind: Roman and Carthagini-an ruins, Genoan fortresses, a string of elegant Pisan churches, not to mention some impressive Gothic and Spanish Baroque architecture. Perhaps most striking of all, however, are the remnants of Sardinia's only significant native culture, known as the **nuraghic** civilization after the 7000-odd *nuraghi* that litter the landscape. These mysterious, stone-built constructions, unique to Sardinia, are often in splendid isolation, which means they're fairly difficult to get to without your own transport, but make the effort to see at least one during your stay – or failing that, drop in on the museums of Cágliari or Sássari to view the lovely statuettes and domestic objects left by this culture.

On the whole, Sardinia's smaller centres are the most attractive, but the capital, **Cágliari** – for many the arrival point – shouldn't be written off. With good accommodation and restaurants, it makes a useful base for exploring the southern third of the island. The other main ferry port is **Olbia** in the north, little more than a transit town but conveniently close to pristine beaches of the jagged northern coast. The Costa Smeralda, a few kilometres distant, is Sardinia's best-known resort area and lives up to its reputation for glitzy opulence. The prices here may preclude anything more than a brief visit, although there are campsites for those outside the ranks of the super-rich.

Both Olbia and Cágliari have airports, as does the vibrant resort of **Alghero** – a fishing port in the northwest of the island that has been known to British holiday-makers for years, yet retains a friendly, unspoiled air. It has a different feel from the rest of the island, with its Spanish atmosphere being a legacy of the long years in which the town was a Catalan enclave. Sardinia's biggest interior town, **Nuoro** has an impressive ethnographical museum, and makes a useful stopover for visiting some of the remoter mountain areas. Of these, the **Gennargentu** range, covering the heart of the island, holds the highest peaks and provides rich evidence of the island's traditional culture, in particular the numerous village **festivals**.

Some history

Of all the phases in Sardinia's chequered history, the most intriguing is the prehistoric **Nuraghic era**, when the island's indigenous culture enjoyed relative prosperity and peace. Although little is known about the society, plenty of traces survive, most conspicuous of which are the rough constructions known as *nuraghi*, mainly built between 1500 and 500 BC both for defensive purposes and as dwellings. They can be seen everywhere in Sardinia, the biggest one in the heart of the island: at **Su Nuraxi**, between Cágliari and Oristano.

This nuraghic culture peaked between the tenth and eighth centuries BC, trading with the **Phoenicians**, among others, from the eastern Mediterranean. But from the sixth century BC, the more warlike **Carthaginians** settled on the island, with their capital less than 200km away near present-day Tunis, and their occupation continued gradually until it was challenged by the emergence of **Rome**. Caught in the middle, the Sards fought on both sides until their decisive defeat by the Romans in 177–6 BC, during which some 27,000 islanders were slaughtered. A core of survivors fled into the impenetrable central and eastern mountains, where they retained their independence in an area called Barbaria by the Romans, known today as the **Barbágia**.

The most impressive remains left by the Romans can be seen in **Cágliari**, on the coast south of the capital at **Nora**, and at **Tharros**, west of Oristano – all Carthaginian sites later enlarged by Roman settlers – and strong Latin traces still survive in the Sard dialect today. After the Roman withdrawal around the fifth century, the destructive effects of malaria and corsair raids from North Africa prompted the abandonment of the island's coasts in favour of more secure inland settlements. The numerous coastal watchtowers which can still be seen today testify to the constant threat of piracy and invasion.

In the eleventh century ecclesiastical rights over Sardinia were granted to the rising city-state of Pisa. **Pisan** influence was mainly concentrated in the south, based in **Cágliari**, where the defences they built still stand, and Pisan churches can be found throughout Sardinia, often marooned in the middle of the countryside. By the end of the thirteenth century, however, Pisa's rival **Genoa** had established itself in the north of the island, with power-bases in Sássari and on the coast, while the situation was further complicated in 1297, when Pope Boniface VIII gave James II of Aragon exclusive rights over both Sardinia and Corsica in exchange for surrendering his claims to Sicily. Local resistance to the Aragonese was led by **Arborea**, the area around present-day Oristano, and championed in particular by **Eleanor of Arborea**, a warrior whose forces succeeded in stemming the Spanish advance. Following her death in 1404, however, Sardinian opposition crumbled, beginning three centuries of **Spanish occupation** of the island. Traces of Spain's long dominion survive in Sardinia's dialects and in the sprinkling of Gothic and Baroque churches and palaces, with **Alghero**, in particular, still boasting a strong Catalan dialect and the air of a Spanish enclave. Nearby **Sássari** also shows strong Spanish influence.

In the wake of the War of the Spanish Succession (1701–20), the island was ceded first to Austria, then to Victor Amadeus, Duke of Savoy, whose united possessions became the new **Kingdom of Sardinia**. The years that followed saw a new emphasis on reconstruction, with the opening of schools, investment in industry and agriculture, and the building of roads, most famously the **Carlo Felice highway** which runs the length of the island – today the SS131. But Savoy's quarrels became Sardinia's, and the island found itself threatened by **Napoleon**, who led an unsuccessful attempt at invasion in 1793. Later, **Nelson** spent fifteen months hovering around the island's coasts in the hunt for the French fleet that led up to the rout at Trafalgar in 1805.

Garibaldi embarked on both his major expeditions from his farm on one of Sardinia's outlying islands, **Caprera**, and the Kingdom of Sardinia ended with the **Unification of Italy** in 1861. Since then, Sardinia's integration into the modern nation-state has not always been easy. Outbreaks of **banditry**, for example, associated with the hinterland and the Gennargentu mountains in particular, were ruthlessly suppressed, but there was little money available to address the root causes of the problem, nor much interest in doing so. The island benefited from the **land reforms** of Mussolini, however, which included the harnessing and damming of rivers, the draining of land, and the introduction of agricultural colonies from the mainland.

After World War II, Sardinia was granted semi-autonomous status, giving it control over such areas as transport, tourism, police, industry and agriculture. The *Cassa per il Mezzogiorno* fund was extended to Sardinia, and the island was saturated with enough DDT to rid it of malaria forever. Such improvements, together with the increasing revenues from tourism, have helped marginalize local opposition towards the central government, eroding the support of such separatist groups as the **Partito Sardo d'Azione** to the more remote inland mountain areas.

Getting to Sardinia

If you're coming direct from the UK, you'll find the regular **flights** operated by Ryanair to **Alghero** and by easyJet to **Olbia** and **Cágliari** hard to beat for price. From the Italian mainland there are frequent daily flights to all three of the island's airports from Rome, Milan and Bologna, with less frequent connections from smaller centres. Most routes are served by Alitalia, Air One and Meridiana; prices start at around €75 for a one-way Rome–Olbia ticket, and there are a myriad of special deals and weekend discounts available.

A cheaper option is the **ferries** from mainland Italy, as well as from Sicily, Corsica and France (see box below). You should make bookings several months in advance for summer crossings, even if you're on foot; August sailings can be fully booked up by May. Basic prices range from about €30 to €100 per person, depending on the season and the route taken: pricier tickets include use of a reclining armchair, while the cheapest tickets "*Ponte*" involve sleeping on deck. A **berth** provides a better night's sleep, but adds another €20 or so. The charge for a vehicle starts at around €70 for a small **car** in low season. Fares on

Ferries to Sardinia

From	To	Line	No. per week	Duration
Ajaccio	Porto Torres	SNCM/CMN	1–2	4–5hr
Bonifacio	S. Teresa di Gallura	Saremar & Moby Lines	3–49	1hr
Civitavécchia	Arbatax	Tirrenia	2	10hr 30min
Civitavécchia	Cágliari	Tirrenia	7	14hr 30min–17hr
Civitavécchia	Golfo Aranci	Sardinia	7–21	3hr 40min–7hr
Civitavécchia	Olbia	Tirrenia, Moby Lines & SNAV	12–56	5hr–8hr 30min
Fiumicino	Arbatax	Tirrenia	2 (late July to Aug only)	4hr
Fiumicino	Golfo Aranci	Tirrenia	7 (mid-June to mid-Sept only)	4hr 30min
Genoa	Arbatax	Tirrenia	2	16–19hr
Genoa	Olbia	Tirrenia, Grandi Navi Veloci & Moby Lines	3–22	9hr–13hr 15min
Genoa	Palau	Enermar	3–4 (June to late Sept only)	12–13hr
Genoa	Porto Torres	Tirrenia & Grandi Navi Veloci	7–21	8–11hr
Livorno	Cágliari	Linee dei Golfi	1	19hr
Livorno	Golfo Aranci	Sardinia	7–21	6–10hr
Livorno	Olbia	Linee dei Golfi & Moby Lines	12–27	6–11hr
Marseille	Porto Torres	SNCM/CMN	2–4	14–17hr
Naples	Cágliari	Tirrenia	1–2	16hr 15min
Naples	Palau	Linee Lauro	1 (mid-June to mid-Sept only)	13hr 30min
Palermo	Cágliari	Tirrenia	1	13hr 30min
Piombino	Olbia	Linee dei Golfi	10–14	7hr
Porto Vecchio	Palau	Linee Lauro	1 (mid-June to mid-Sept only)	2hr
Propriano	Porto Torres	SNCM/CMN	1–5	3–4hr
Trápani	Cágliari	Tirrenia	1	10hr–11hr 30min

the **high-speed ferries** (*mezzi veloci*) are €30–90 travelling second-class (up to 50 percent more in the peak season), plus €50–120 for a small car. Look out for discounts applying to return tickets bought in advance within certain periods, and for special deals for a car plus two or three passengers.

Getting around the island

Once on the island, a good network of public transport covers most localities. There is an island-wide **bus** service run by ARST, while FdS and FMS are concentrated in specific areas and FdS additionally covers the longer hauls between towns. **Trains** connect the major towns of Cágliari, Oristano, Sássari and Olbia, while smaller narrow-gauge lines link Nuoro and Alghero with the main network.

Cágliari and the south

Cágliari has been Sardinia's capital at least since Roman times and is still its biggest town, with the busiest port and the greatest concentration of industry. Despite this, the city is considerably less frenetic than any one of equivalent size on the Italian mainland, with most of its quarter-million population housed in mushrooming apartment blocks away from the centre. In any case, you won't want to stray far out of the old centre above the port, which is compact enough to negotiate on foot, and offers both sophistication and charm in the raggle-taggle of narrow lanes crammed into its high citadel.

Cágliari's main attractions are the **archeological museum** with its unique collection of nuraghic statuettes, the city walls with their two **Pisan towers** looking down over the port, and the **cathedral** – all within easy distance of each other. There is also a sprinkling of Roman remains, including an impressive **amphitheatre**. Forty kilometres down the coast, more ruins from this period can be seen at **Nora**, the most complete ancient site on the island. Other places worth visiting from Cágliari include the majestic nuraghic complex of **Su Nuraxi**, a compelling sight surrounded by the brown hills of the interior, and the islands of **Sant'Antíoco** and **San Pietro**, moored off the coast west of Cágliari.

Cágliari

Viewing **CÁGLIARI** from the sea at the start of his Sardinian sojourn in 1921, D.H. Lawrence compared it to Jerusalem: "strange and rather wonderful, not a bit like Italy", and the city still makes a striking impression today. Crowned by its historic nucleus squeezed within a protective ring of Pisan fortifica-tions, its setting is enhanced by the calm lagoons (*stagni*) west of the city and along the airport road, the habitat for cranes, cormorants and flamingos. In the centre, the evening promenades along Via Manno are the smartest you'll see in Sardinia, dropping down to the noisier Piazza Yenne and Largo Carlo Felice, around which most of the shops, restaurants, banks and hotels are located. At the bottom of the town, the arcades of Via Roma shelter more shops and bars, across from the port.

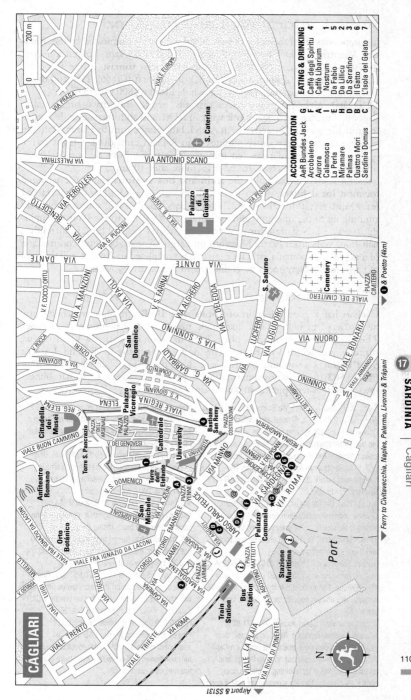

CÁGLIARI

ACCOMMODATION	
AeF Bundes Jack	G
Arcobaleno	F
Aurora	A
Calamosca	I
La Perla	E
Miramare	H
Palmas	D
Quattro Mori	B
Sardinia Domus	C

EATING & DRINKING	
Caffè degli Spiritu	4
Caffè Libarium	1
Nostrum	5
Da Fabio	2
Da Lillicu	3
Da Serafino	6
Il Gatto	7
L'Isola del Gelato	C

0   200 m

▼ Ferry to Civitavecchia, Naples, Palermo, Livorno & Trápani

▼ Airport & SS131

Arrival, information and transport

Just steps away from the heart of town, Cágliari's port is dominated by the **Stazione Maríttima**, which houses an information desk (daily 9am–1.30pm & 3–6pm; ☎070.668.352). Piazza Matteotti has the city's main **tourist office** (Mon–Fri 8.30am–1.30pm & 2–8pm, Sat & Sun 8.30am–8pm; ☎070.669.255), and there's also a toll-free information line for the whole island (☎800.013.153).

Cágliari's **airport** (ⓦ www.sogaer.it) sits beside the city's largest *stagno* (lagoon): facilities include a **bank** with an ATM, and an information desk open to coincide with flight arrivals. An ARST bus service runs to Piazza Matteotti in town at least every thirty minutes from 8.45am until the last flight arrival – about 11pm – and takes ten minutes (tickets €1 from the airport shop); otherwise a taxi ride costs around €15, more after 10pm.

Piazza Matteotti also holds the **train** and **bus stations** and is the terminus for most **local buses**, tickets for which are sold at a booth in the piazza (€1 for 90min, €1.50 for 2hr or €2.30 for a day's travel); useful routes include #7 running up to the museums and cathedral, and #8 going to the Roman amphitheatre. The FdS station, for slow trains to Arbatax (see p.1130), is currently a half-hour walk from Piazza Matteotti on Largo Gennari, but after construction of a new Metropolitana, or tram network, is completed in 2008, it will shift out of town to Monserrato, to be connected to the centre by Metro.

Accommodation

Cágliari has a good selection of **hotels and B&Bs**, though availability may be restricted in high season, and single rooms are at a premium at all times. The biggest concentration of places is on or around the narrow Via Sardegna, running parallel to Via Roma. The nearest **campsite** is beyond **Quartu Sant'Elena**, a 45-minute bus ride east along the coast, where the *Pini e Mare* (☎070.803.103, ⓦ www.web.tiscalinet.it/piniemare; Easter–Oct) has bungalows as well as tent pitches in woods close to the sea.

AeR Bundes Jack Via Roma 75 ☎070.657.970, ⓔ hotel.aerbundesjack @libero.it. Centrally located above the arcades on the third floor (there's a lift), this hotel has spotless, air-conditioned rooms, mostly en suite. Breakfast (€5) is available from May to September. The friendly host family also runs an adjacent B&B (❷). No credit cards. ❷

Arcobaleno Via Sardegna 38 ☎070.684.8325, ⓦ www.soggiornoarcobaleno.com. Clean and comfortable rooms, some with exposed brickwork, all with telephone, TV, a/c and en-suite bathrooms, and there's Internet access. ❸

Aurora Salita Santa Chiara 19 ☎070.658.625. A modest *pensione* in a dilapidated *palazzo* behind Piazza Yenne. The tastefully restored rooms, mostly en suite, are always popular so it's best to book ahead. ❶

Calamosca Viale Calamosca ☎070.371.628, ⓦ www.hotelcalamosca.it. Right on the sea, overlooking a secluded cove and small beach on Capo Sant'Elia, this is the nearest hotel to Poetto, and an excellent choice for avoiding Cágliari's noisy centre, 2km away. There's a restaurant, and a good

pizzeria next door. From the centre, take bus "PF" or "PQ", changing to the frequent #11 at Stadio Amsicora (on Sun take #5/11, running direct from Piazza Matteotti). ❸

La Perla Via Sardegna 18 ☎070.669.446. Very similar to its neighbour *Palmas*, though smaller and more old-fashioned. En-suite bathrooms are planned for 2007. No credit cards. ❶

Miramare Via Roma 59 ☎ & ⓕ070.664.021, ⓦ www.hotelmiramareCágliari.it. Located on the second floor of a block facing the port (but with no lift), this hotel has period trappings. Some rooms are small, but each has bathroom, air conditioning and TV. Rooms with views cost more. ❸

Palmas Via Sardegna 14 ☎070.651.679. Good value at this cheapie on the main tourist strip, with box showers in some rooms but no private WCs. ❶

Sardinia Domus Largo Carlo Felice 26 ☎070.659.783, ⓦ www.sardiniadomus.it. Pleasant, professionally run B&B in an old apartment given a modern makeover. Spacious, air-conditioned and en-suite rooms have TVs and Internet connections. ❷

The City

Almost all the sightseeing you will want to do in Cágliari is encompassed within the old Castello quarter, on the hill overlooking the port. The most evocative entry to this is from the monumental **Bastione San Remy** on Piazza Costituzione, whose nineteenth-century imperialist tone is tempered by the graffiti and weeds sprouting out of its walls. It's worth the haul up the grandiose flight of steps inside for Cágliari's best views over the port and the lagoons beyond. Sunset is a good time to be here, or whenever you feel like a rest, its shady benches conducive to a snatched siesta.

From the Bastione, you can wander off in any direction to explore the intricate maze of Cágliari's citadel, traditionally the seat of the administration, aristocracy and highest ecclesiastical offices. It has been little altered since the Middle Ages, though the tidy Romanesque facade on the **Cattedrale** (Mon–Sat 8am–12.30pm & 4–7pm, Sun 8am–1pm & 4–8pm) in Piazza Palazzo is in fact a fake, added in the twentieth century in the old Pisan style. The structure dates originally from the thirteenth century but has gone through what Lawrence called "the mincing machine of the ages, and oozed out Baroque and sausagey".

Inside, a pair of massive stone **pulpits** flank the main doors: they were crafted as a single piece in around 1160 to grace Pisa's cathedral, but were later presented to Cágliari along with the same sculptor's set of lions, which now adorn the outside of the building. Other features of the cathedral include the ornate seventeenth-century **tomb** of Martin II of Aragon (in the left transept), the **aula capitolare** (off the right transept), containing some good religious art, and, under the altar, a densely adorned **crypt**. Hewn out of the rock, little of this subterranean chamber has been left undecorated, and there are carvings by Sicilian artists of the Sardinian saints whose ashes were said to have been found under the church of San Saturno in 1617. Also here are the tombs of the wife of Louis XVIII of France, Marie-Josephine of Savoy, and the infant son of Vittorio Emanuele I of Savoy and Maria-Teresa of Austria, Carlo Emanuele, who died in 1799.

The cathedral stands in one corner of the square, to the left of which are the archbishop's palace and – also eighteenth-century – the **Palazzo Viceregio** or Governor's Palace (Tues–Fri 8.30am–2pm & 3–7pm, Sat 8.30am–2pm; free), used by the Piedmontese kings of Sardinia (though rarely inhabited by them), its stately rooms today holding meetings of the provincial assembly and occasional exhibitions. Behind the cathedral on Via Fossario, the **Museo del Duomo** (daily 10am–12.30pm & 4.30–7pm; €2) is primarily worth seeing for two items: the fifteenth-century *Tríttico di Clemente VII*, a painting of unknown authorship, but possibly a copy of a lost painting by Rogier van der Weyden, and the powerful *Retablo della Crocefissione*, a six-panelled polyptych attributed to Michele Cavaro (1517–84) or, more probably, to his workshop.

At the far end of Piazza Palazzo a road leads into the smaller Piazza Indipendenza, location of the **Torre San Pancrazio**, one of the main bulwarks of the city's defences erected by Pisa after it had wrested the city from the Genoans in 1305 (though these did not prevent the Aragonese from walking in just fifteen years later). It's worth ascending the tower (Tues–Sun: May–Oct 9am–1pm & 3.30–7.30pm; Nov–April 9am–4.30pm; €2) for the magnificent views seawards over the old town and port. From here it's only a short walk southwest to Via dell'Università and the city's second major bulwark, the **Torre dell'Elefante** (same hours as above; €2), named after a small carving of an elephant on one side. Like the other tower, it has a half-finished look, with the side facing the old town completely open.

Through the arch at the top of Piazza Indipendenza, Piazza dell'Arsenale holds a plaque recording the visit made by Cervantes to Cágliari in 1573, shortly before his capture and imprisonment by Moorish pirates. Across the square, the **Cittadella dei Musei** stands on the site of the former royal arsenal, housing the city's principal museums. The main attraction is the **Museo Archeologico** (Tues–Sun 9am–8pm; €4, or €5 with Pinacoteca), a must for anyone interested in Sardinia's past. The island's most important Phoenician, Carthaginian and Roman finds are gathered here, including busts and statues of muses and gods, jewellery and coins, and funerary items from the sites of Nora and Tharros. But everything pales beside the museum's greatest pieces, from Sardinia's **nuraghic** culture. Of these, the most eye-catching is a series of bronze statuettes, ranging from about thirty to ninety centimetres in height, spindly and highly stylized but packed with invention and quirky humour. The main source of information about this phase of the island's history, these figures represent warriors and hunters, athletes, shepherds, nursing mothers, bulls, horses and wild animals.

Most were votive offerings, made to decorate the inside of temples, later buried to protect them from the hands of foreign predators.

The Cittadella's other museums, all very different, are also worth exploring. The smallest and most surprising is the **Mostra di Cere Anatomiche** (Tues–Sat 9am–1pm & 4–7pm, Sun 9am–1pm; €1.55), which displays 23 wax models of anatomical sections, gruesome reproductions of works made by the Florentine Clemente Susini at the start of the nineteenth century. Further up, the **Museo d'Arte Siamese** (Tues–Sun 9am–1pm & 4–8pm, mid-Sept to mid-June 3.30–7.30pm; €3) holds a fascinating assemblage of items from Southeast Asia – the collection of a local engineer who spent twenty years in the region – including

△ A Cágliari street

Siamese paintings of Hindu and Buddhist legends, Chinese bowls and boxes, Japanese statuettes and a fearsome array of weaponry. Lastly, the excellent **Pinacoteca** (Tues–Sun 9am–8pm; €2, or €5 with Museo Archeologico) contains mostly Catalan and Italian religious art from the fifteenth and sixteenth centuries. Look out in particular for the trio of panel paintings next to each other on the top level: the *Retablo di San Bernardino* by Joan Figuera and Rafael Thomas, *Annunciation* by Joan Mates, and *Visitation* by Joan Barcelo.

From Piazza dell'Arsenale Viale Buon Cammino leads to Viale Fra Ignazio and the entrance to the **Anfiteatro Romano** (Tues–Sun: April–Oct 9.30am–1.30pm & 3.30–6.30pm; Nov–March 10am–4pm; €3.30). Cut out of solid rock in the second century AD, the amphitheatre could hold the entire city's population of about 20,000. Despite the decay, with much of the site cannibalized to build churches in the Middle Ages, you can still see the trenches for the animals, the underground passages and several rows of seats. Music, dance and theatre performances take place here in the summer months (tickets from the booth at the entrance). Turn left out of the amphitheatre and walk a few minutes down Viale Fra Ignazio da Laconi to the **Orto Botánico** (daily: April–Oct 8am–1.30pm & 3–7pm; Nov–March 8am–1.30pm; €2), one of Italy's most famous botanical gardens, with over five hundred species of Mediterranean and tropical plants – a shady spot on a sizzling afternoon.

East of the centre there's little to see in Cágliari's traffic-thronged modern quarters beyond the banks and businesses, the one exception being the fifth-century church of **San Saturno** (Mon–Sat 9am–1pm), Sardinia's oldest and one of the most important surviving examples of early Christian architecture in the Mediterranean. Set in its own piazza off the busy Via Dante, looking Middle Eastern with its palm trees and cupola, the basilica was erected on the spot where the Christian martyr Saturninus met his fate during the reign of Diocletian. Around the sturdy walls, which withstood severe bombardment during World War II, lie various pieces of flotsam from the past: four cannon-balls, fragments of Roman sarcophagi and slabs of stone carved with Latin inscriptions. The interior is bare of decoration, though it's impressive none-theless, with tall glass walls added to the sides, through which you can see an excavated necropolis.

Poetto

If you need a break and a bathe, head for the suburb of **Poetto**, a fifteen-minute bus ride from Piazza Matteotti past Cágliari's Sant'Elia football stadium. Poetto has 6km of fine sandy **beach**, with small bars and showers conveniently nearby; some stretches are lidos where you pay a standard daily rate for entry (about €5), and deckchairs and parasols are available for rent, along with pedalos and wind-surfing equipment.

Rearing above a small marina, the western end of the strip is dominated by the **Sella del Diávolo** ("Devil's Saddle"), a massive outcrop jutting into the sea; most of it is now a military zone and therefore off limits. The name is connected with a legend relating how the Archangel Gabriel won a battle here against the devil himself. The name of Cágliari's gulf, Golfo degli Angeli, is also a reference to this celestial tussle.

Eating, drinking and nightlife

Cágliari has a great range of **restaurants**, many clustered around Via Sardegna, and often with competitively priced tourist menus. For a morning **coffee** or afternoon tea, Piazza Yenne makes a pleasant, relatively traffic-free alternative to the bustling cafés on Via Roma, while, outside the centre, Poetto is a blitz of bars, fairgrounds and ice-cream kiosks – a good place for a summer evening outing. Cágliari also has a couple of lively places for **ice creams** and late-night **drinking**, listed below.

Caffè degli Spiritu Bastione San Remy. This is a fun place to be on a summer evening, and there are DJs and live music until late at weekends. It's mostly outside, and food includes pizzas and steaks.

Caffè Libarium Nostrum Via Santa Croce 33. With tables outside right on the old city walls, affording marvellous views, this is a great place for a snack and a drink from early morning to late at night. Closed Mon in winter.

Da Fabio Via Sardegna 90, on the corner with Via Concezione. Easy-going trattoria which offers tourist menus and pizzas and has an English-speaking boss. Mains €5–12. Closed Mon & two weeks in Nov.

Da Lillicu Via Sardegna 78 ☎070.652.970. Serves sensational antipasti followed by a small selection of authentic Sard specialities (€8–15) on plain marble tables. It's popular with locals, so you'll need to book ahead. Closed Sun lunch.

Da Serafino at Via Sardegna 109 and Via Lepanto 6. Honest, local dishes, informally served, are extremely good value with mains at €5–10. Closed Thurs.

Il Gatto Viale Trieste 15 ☎070.652.970. Away from the port, and with a smarter feel than the places there, this spacious, vaulted restaurant offers innovative seafood and meat dishes for €8–15, as well as pizzas and imported beers. Closed lunch Sat & Sun.

L'Isola del Gelato Piazza Yenne 35. Cágliari's top ice-cream parlour offers a range of scrumptious concoctions, as well as yoghurt with fresh fruit, making this a great breakfast stop too. Closed Mon Nov–Feb.

Quattro Mori Via Angioy 93 ☎070.650.269. One of Cágliari's best eateries, with a solid reputation for its endless courses of delectable Sard dishes, especially seafood. Despite relatively high prices, there's usually a full house and the atmosphere gets quite merry. Booking essential. Closed Sun eve & Mon.

Listings

Airlines Air One ☎199.207.080, ⓦwww.flyairone.it; Alitalia ☎06.2222, ⓦwww.alitalia.it; Alpi Eagles ☎899.500.058, ⓦwww.alpieagles.com; Easyjet ☎848.887.766, ⓦwww.easyjet.com; Meridiana ☎892.928, ⓦwww.meridiana.it; Ryanair ☎899.678.910, ⓦwww.ryanair.com.

Bus operators ARST, for places within the province excluding Sulcis (☎800.865.042, ⓦwww.arst.sardegna.it); FdS, for Oristano, Sássari and Nuoro (☎070.5793.0361, ⓦwww.ferrovie sardegna.it); FMS, for Sulcis (☎800.044.553, ⓦwww.ferroviemeridionalisarde.it); TURMO for Olbia and Santa Teresea di Gallura (☎0789.21.487, ⓦwww.turmotravel.it).

Car rental Hertz, Piazza Matteotti 8 ☎070.651.078 and airport ☎070.240.037, ⓦwww.hertz.it; Ruvioli, Via dei Mille 9 ☎070.658.955 & airport ☎070.240.323, ⓦwww.ruvioli.it; Sixt, Aeroporto di Elmas ☎070.212.045, ⓦwww.e-sixt.it. Scooters are also available from Ruvioli from about €50 a day.

Consulates Britain, Viale Colombia 160, Quartu Sant'Elena ☎070.828.628; Denmark, Via Roma 127 ☎070.668.208; Germany, Via R. Garzia 9 ☎070.307.229; Holland, Viale Armando Diaz ☎070.303.873.

Ferries Tirrenia, Stazione Maríttima ☎199.123.199, ⓦwww.tirrenia.it.

Festivals Sant'Efisio: May 1–4, including a procession to the saint's church at Nora.

Hospital Via Peretti 21 ☎070.543.266.

Internet access Bips, Via Sicilia 23 (daily 8.30am–10pm), also long-distance calls from here; Le Librerie della Costa, Via Roma 63–5 (Mon–Sat 9am–8.30pm, Sun 10am–1.30pm & 5.30–9pm).

Laundry Coin-operated *lavanderia* at Via Sicilia 23 (daily 8am–10pm, last wash at 9pm; €4/6kg). There are various service washes around town, charging around €3 each for trousers, shirts and skirts.

Left-luggage Ticket office at train station (daily 7am–7pm; €2.58 per bag for 12hr).

Post office Piazza del Cármine (Mon–Fri 8am–6.50pm, Sat 8am–1.15pm).

Taxis Rank at Piazza Matteotti; Coop Radio Taxi (☎070.400.101) operates 24hr.

Train information FS ☎892.021, ⓦwww.trenitalia.com; FdS ☎800.460.220, ⓦwww.ferroviesardegna.it.

Travel agents CTS, Via Balbo 12 ☎070.488.260; Sardamondial, Via Roma 9 ☎070.668.094; Viaggi Orrù, Via Roma 95 ☎070.659.858.

Nora

The easiest excursion you can make from Cágliari is to the waterside archeological site at **NORA**, 40km south of the city. In summer there's a bus service direct to the site; the rest of the year the nearest stop is the village of **PULA**, 3km away and served by hourly ARST buses (6 on Sun). It's worth going to Pula anyway, as the village **museum** (daily 9am–8pm; €5.50 including site at Nora) gives a good explanation of the Nora finds.

Founded by the Phoenicians and settled later by Carthaginians and Romans, **Nora** (daily 9am–dusk; €5.50 including museum) was abandoned around the third century AD, possibly as a result of a natural disaster. Now partly submerged under the sea, the remains on land include houses, Carthaginian warehouses, a temple, baths with some well-preserved mosaics, and a theatre in an equally good state of repair. The rest is rubble, though its position on the tip of a peninsula gives it plenty of atmosphere.

Outside the site stands the rather ordinary-looking eleventh-century church of Sant'Efisio, site of the saint's martyrdom and the ultimate destination of Cágliari's four-day May Day procession. Behind the church is an exquisite sandy bay, lapped by crystal-clear water, but packed with day-trippers in season. There's a fine **hotel** 1km away on the road back to Pula, *Su Gunventeddu* (☎070.920.9092, ⓦ www.sugunventeddu.com; ❸), just 100m from a good beach, with bright, quiet rooms and a recommended restaurant also open to non-residents. In Pula itself there's the good-value, flower-bedecked *Quattro Mori* at Via Cágliari 10 (☎070.920.9124; ❶; no credit cards), and, further along the same road at no. 30, the larger and better-equipped *Sandalyon* (☎070.920.9151; ❸), where most rooms have a balcony. Off the central Piazza del Pópolo, you can **eat** well at *Sa Macinera* (closed Mon in winter), a ristorante-pizzeria where you can also eat *alfresco* in summer.

The coast south holds some of Sardinia's most exclusive hotels, biggest and flashiest of which is the *Forte Village*, spread over a wide area, and catering largely to package groups (☎070.92.171, ⓦ www.fortevillageresort.com; late March to Oct; ❸), though you may be more enticed by the nearby **campsites**, sheltered by pinewoods and right by the sea: *Flumendosa* (☎070.920.8364, ⓦ www.campingflumendosa.it) and *Cala d'Ostia* (April–Sept; ☎070.921.470, ⓔ cop.tur@tin.it). There are fine beaches all down this coast, especially around **Chia**, while beyond **Capo Spartivento**, the coastal road offers terrific views over a deserted cliff-hung coastline, sheltering a few small sand beaches which are accessible on an infrequent bus service in summer.

Su Nuraxi and around

If you only have time to see one of Sardinia's *nuraghi*, you should make it **Su Nuraxi** (daily 9am–dusk; €5), the biggest and most famous of them, and a good taste of the primitive grandeur of the island's only indigenous civilization. The snag is access: the site lies 1km outside the village of **BARÚMINI**, 50km north of Cágliari, to which there are only two–three daily ARST buses, calling en route to Láconi, Désulo and Samugheo. The site lies fifteen minutes' walk west of the main crossroads at Barúmini's centre.

Su Nuraxi's dialect name means simply "the *nuragh*", and not only is it the largest nuraghic complex on the island, but it's also thought to be the oldest, dating probably from around 1500 BC. Comprising a bulky fortress surrounded by the remains of a village, Su Nuraxi was a palace complex at the very least – possibly even a capital city. The central tower once reached 21m (now shrunk to less than 15m), and its outer defences and inner chambers are connected by passageways and stairs. The whole complex is thought to have been covered with earth by Sards and Carthaginians at the time of the Roman conquest, which may account for its excellent state of preservation: if it weren't for a torrential rainstorm that washed away the slopes in 1949, the site may never have been revealed at all.

If you want to stay in the area, you will find several **accommodation** possibilities in the village. Of these, the swankiest is 𝔄 *Sa Lolla* (☎070.936.8419, ⓦwww .wels.it/salolla; ❷), a rustic-style hotel on Via Cavour with a fantastic **restaurant** attached: it's open to non-residents, and worth a journey in itself. Barúmini also offers a choice of B&Bs, with a cluster near the post office on Viale Umberto, all of a similar standard and similarly priced (❶): try *Casa Sanna* at Viale Umberto 61 (☎070.936.8157 or 348.058.2175), *Casa del Rio*, Via IV Novembre 24 (☎070.936.8141 or 328.675.6025) or *Casa dei Fiori*, Via Dante 2 (☎070.936.8028). They are not marked so you may have to ask around to find them.

The skyline south of Barúmini is punctuated by the extraordinary conical hill of **Las Plassas**, its round peak strewn with the fragments of a twelfth-century **castle** sticking up like broken teeth – a landmark for miles around. North and west of the town extends the high plain of **Giara di Gésturi**, the last refuge of Sardinia's wild ponies. You'll need a little luck and a lot of cunning to spot these small, shy creatures, but in any case it's excellent high ground for walking, at an altitude of around 600m. Spring is the best season to visit, when the area is a stopover for migrating birds. Again, though, the problem is access. Dedicated hikers can explore a good part of the plain on foot from the village of Gésturi, a stop on the bus routes from Cágliari to Láconi, Désulo and Samugheo.

West of Cágliari: Sant'Antíoco and San Pietro

West of Cágliari, the landscape is mountainous and empty, but cut through by the fast SS130 and the rail line as far as the mining towns of Iglesias and Carbonia. FMS buses also run this way, crossing a causeway south of Carbonia to reach the island of **Sant'Antíoco**. This and the neighbouring isle of **San Pietro** – reachable on ferries – can just about be visited from Cágliari on a day-trip, but you'd do better staying over and sampling the local beaches. Although well-frequented holiday destinations in summer, the islands have not yet become over-developed; in fact accommodation is on the scarce side, and if you're thinking of staying, be sure to book ahead.

Sant'Antíoco

Measuring about 15km in length by 10km at its widest, the wedge-shaped **SANT'ANTÍOCO** is the larger of the southwest islands, served by four daily FMS buses from Cágliari, about a two-hour ride. The port area of the island's main town (also called Sant'Antíoco) is just the other side of the causeway. The sheltered harbour made this an important base for the Carthaginians and the Romans, allowing them to command the whole of Sardinia's southwest coast. More recently, Nelson's storm-damaged flagship, the *Vanguard*, put in here shortly before the Battle of the Nile in 1798.

It is the upper part of the town which holds all the interest, however, having been continuously inhabited since Phoenician times. Here, on Piazza Parrochia, at the top of Via Regina Margherita, the twelfth-century church of **Sant'Antíoco** was built over Christian **catacombs**, which were in turn enlarged from an existing Carthaginian burial place; you can visit these dingy corridors, with authentic skeletons and reproductions of ceramic objects unearthed during excavation, on a guided tour (Mon–Sat 9am–noon & 3–6pm, also 7–9pm in summer, Sun 10–11am & 3–6pm; €2.50). Near the entrance to the catacombs, the musty, rather cavernous church holds a statue of St Antiochus, plainly showing his Mauretanian origins; his feast day, on the second Sunday after Easter, is a four-day affair with traditional songs, poetry recitations, dancing, fireworks and a procession to the sea.

Sant'Antíoco's archeological zone is signposted up a side road outside the church, less than a kilometre's walk from the sea. The most impressive site is that of an extensive **Punic tophet**, or burial site (daily 9am–1pm & 3.30–7pm; €3), dedicated to the Carthaginian goddess Tanit and once covering the entire hill where the old city now stands. The numerous urns scattered about here (mostly modern reproductions) were long believed to contain the ashes of sacrificed first-born children, but this is now thought to have been Roman propaganda: the urns, it seems, contained the cremated remains of children still-born or dead from natural causes. Finds from here and from the Phoenician, Carthaginian and Roman cities are collected in the **Museo Archeologico** (same times as tophet; €4), at the bottom of the hill, though these represent a tiny fraction of the second-largest collection of Carthaginian discoveries after Carthage itself, the bulk of which is presently stored away. It's an impressive display nonetheless, including inscribed stelae, a plethora of Punic amphoras, plates, ceramics, and jewellery, and material from the Roman necropolis, notably some impressive mosaics – one in a North African style showing panthers apparently drinking from a plant pot.

Returning into the town on Via Necrópoli, you can use your ticket for the museum and archeological zone for a small but engrossing **Museo Etnográfico** (daily: April–Sept 9am–8pm; Oct–March 9am–1pm & 3–6pm; €1.50): one capacious room crammed to the rafters with examples of rural culture – tools, agricultural implements, craftwork, bread- and pasta-making equipment, most of them only recently superseded by modern machinery – all enthusiastically explained (in Italian) by a guide. A little further down the same road, the **villaggio ipogeo** or Punic necropolis (same times as ethnographic museum; €1.50) is also worth a glance, consisting of restored hypogea, or underground chambers that once held Carthaginian tombs and were later converted into bare and plain dwellings by the local people. Finally, the **Forte Su Pisu** (same times as tophet; €1.50), signposted between Sant'Antíoco church and the archeological zone, is a small fortification dating from 1812 and stormed by corsairs three years later, resulting in the massacre of the entire garrison. Tidily restored, it's a panoramic spot, but there's nothing inside apart from a pair of old cannons and some costumed mannequins. **Tickets** for necropolis and fort are sold at the major attractions; you can buy various combinations of tickets, for example entry into the ethnographic and archeological museums, tophet, Forte Su Pisu and necropolis for €8.

Practicalities

The **tourist office** is in the lower part of town, on Piazza Repubblica (March–Oct Mon–Fri 10am–1pm & 4–6pm; Nov–Feb Mon–Fri 10am–1pm & 5–9pm, Sat 10am–noon; ☎0781.82.031, ⓦwww.santantioconline.com).

Bikes and scooters can be rented nearby at Euromoto, Via Nazionale 57 (℡0781.840.907 or 347.880.3875), and you can log on to the **Internet** at Semantica, Via Eleonora d'Arborea 38 (Mon–Sat 10am–1pm & 5–9pm). Of the **hotels** in town, the only one in the upper town is the somewhat dowdy *Eden* (℡0781.840.768, ⊛www.albergoleden.com; ❸), right next to the church of Sant'Antíoco, but you'll do much better at either of two places on the main road through town: the *Hotel del Corso*, at Corso Vittorio Emanuele 32 (℡0781.800.265, ⊛www.hoteldelcorso.it; ❸), with a panoramic roof-terrace, or the more modest *Moderno* at Via Nazionale 82 (℡0781.83.105, ⊛www.web .tiscali.it/albergomoderno; ❸). If you want to stay near a beach, try *Scala Longa* (℡0781.817.202; mid-April to mid-Sept; ❶), which overlooks the sandy bay of **Maladroxia**, 6km south of town; the small port and resort of **Calasetta**, 10km north of town and the terminus for the FMS bus from Cágliari, has *Cala di Seta*, Via Regina Margherita 61 (℡0781.88.304, ⊛www.hotelcaladiseta .it; ❹), and the *Bellavista*, standing above a lovely arc of beach a short walk north of town (℡0781.88.211, ⊛www.calasettabellavista.it; ❸). Sant'Antíoco's sole **campsite**, *Tonnara* (April–Sept; ℡0781.809.058, ⊛www.camping.it/italy /sardegna/tonnara), is on the western side of the island at the sheltered inlet of Cala Sapone, with caravans and chalets available to rent.

San Pietro

Ferries from Calasetta make the five-kilometre crossing to the approximately ten-by-seven-kilometre island of **SAN PIETRO** roughly every hour (40min; €1.10–2.20). In summer, drivers should join the queue in good time – and make sure they get a return ticket. San Pietro's dialect is pure Piedmontese, two and a half centuries after the Savoyan king Carlo Emanuele III invited a colony of Genoans to settle here after their eviction from the island of Tabarca, near Tunisia. The settlers were later abducted and taken back to Tunisia in one of the last great pirate raids, but were returned once the ransom demands had been met. The island's only town, attractive **CARLOFORTE** (named after the king), is lively in summer and close to panoramic beauty spots and mainly rocky beaches.

The few **hotels** are concentrated in Carloforte, where the family-run *California*, at Via Cavallera 15 (℡0781.854.470, ⊛www.hotelcaliforniacarloforte.it; ❸), offers clean and comfortable rooms, a ten-minute walk left along the port: alternatively, the *Hieracon* at Corso Cavour 62 (℡0781.854.028, ⊛www.hotelhieracon.com; ❸) – right from the port, as you leave the ferry – has a stylish, old-fashioned ambience and requires half or full board in summer. Availability is extremely limited in the holiday season, and it's worth asking about **rooms for rent** at the **tourist office**, opposite the port on Piazza Carlo Alberto III (May–Sept Mon–Sat 9am–1pm & 4–8.30pm; Oct–April Mon–Fri 9am–1pm, Mon & Wed also 3.30–6pm; ℡0781.854.009, ⊛www.prolococarloforte.it).

Oristano, Bosa and around

The province of Oristano roughly corresponds to the much older entity of Arborea, the medieval *giudicato* which championed the Sardinian cause in the struggle against the Spaniards. Then as now, **Oristano** was the region's main town, and today it retains more than a hint of medieval atmosphere.

A short distance west of the centre, the Punic-Roman settlement of **Tharros** resembles Nora in appearance and is well worth a visit if you gave Nora a miss. Further north up the coast, the picturesque riverside town of **Bosa** lies within striking distance of some great beaches amid a beautiful stretch of undeveloped rocky coastline.

Oristano

ORISTANO is a flat, unprepossessing place, whose old walls have been mostly replaced by busy boulevards. However, the centre has a relaxed and sophisticated ambience, and although it is 4km from the sea, the town is attractively surrounded by water, its lagoons and irrigation canals helping to make this a richly productive agricultural zone. The southern lagoon, the **Stagno di Santa Giusta**, is the place to see a local colony of Sardinia's flamingo population and the occasional example of the coracle-like flat-bottomed boats associated with the lagoon's fishermen. Many people, however, come to Oristano simply to visit the nearby Sinis peninsula, home to the impressive Punic and Roman ruins of **Tharros** and a string of wild beaches.

The Town

In the heart of the town is Oristano's central symbol, the marble statue of **Eleonora d'Arborea**, presiding over the piazza named after her. Eleanor was the *giudice* of the Arborea region from 1384 to 1404 and is the best known and best loved of Sardinia's medieval rulers, having been the only one who enjoyed any success against the island's aggressors. Ensconced in the last of Sardinia's *giudicati* to remain independent of the Aragonese, Eleanor united local resistance and succeeded in negotiating a treaty in 1388 that guaranteed her a measure of independence. She later backed this up by a tactical alliance with the Genoans, and it was with Genoan help that her forces managed to re-occupy Sássari in 1390.

Sa Sartiglia

The rituals of Oristano's flamboyant **Sa Sartiglia** festival perhaps originated with knights on the Second Crusade, who in the eleventh century may well have imported the trappings of Saracen tournaments to Sardinia. In the period of the Spanish domination, similarly lavish feasts were held for the ruling knights at regular intervals throughout the year. In time, these celebrations took on a more theatrical aspect and became merged with the annual Carnival – the Sa Sartiglia is now a three-day festival that closes the Carnival period, ending on **Shrove Tuesday**. Highlights of this costumed pageant include horseback parades and trials of equestrian prowess, all judged by a white-masked arbiter known as **Su Componidori**. Selected from among the "knight" contestants, the *Componidori* represents the continuation of the *giudice*'s role and is decked out in a bizarre pastiche of medieval garb – the process of dressing him is itself a highly formal ceremony, conducted in public at the beginning of each day.

In fact all the participants are masked and costumed, and the whole affair exudes a drama unrivalled by Sardinia's other festivals. The climax of the proceedings is the joust after which the festival is named, when the mounted contestants attempt to lance a ring, or *sartiglia*, suspended in the air, charging towards it at full gallop.

Eleanor's military achievements collapsed soon after her death from plague in 1404, though the most enduring benefit of her reign survived her by several centuries: the formulation of a **Code of Laws** (*Carta di Logu*), first mooted by her father Mariano IV but embodied by Eleanor in a legal document in 1395. Covering every aspect of civil legislation, this document was adopted in 1421 by the Aragonese and extended throughout the island. As the eighteenth-century English lawyer and traveller John Tyndale put it: "The framing of a body of laws so far in advance of those of other countries, where greater civilizations existed, must ever be the brightest ornament in the diadem of the Giudicessa." Eleanor's statue, carved in 1881, shows her bearing the scroll on which the laws were written, while inset panels depict her various victories.

Although it's called the **Casa di Eleonora**, the fine house – now semi-derelict – at Via Parpaglia 6–12 (off Piazza Roma) could not in fact have been her home, as it was built over a century after her death. She is, however, unequivocally buried in the fourteenth-century church of **Santa Chiara**, in the parallel Via Garibaldi.

Off Via Parpaglia, Piazzetta Corrias holds Oristano's **Antiquarium Arborense** (daily 9am–2pm & 3–8pm; €3), one of Sardinia's most absorbing museums, housed in a sixteenth-century merchant's house. As well as rotating exhibitions of its extensive collection of nuraghic, Phoenician, Roman and Greek artefacts, there's a gallery of medieval and Renaissance art and scaled-down reconstructions of Oristano c.1290 and Roman Tharros.

At one end of Via Parpaglia, linked to Piazza Eleonora by the narrow pedestrianized Corso Umberto, is Piazza Roma, where pavement bars are clustered around the base of the **San Cristóforo** bastion, erected by the *giudice* Mariano II in 1291. This was the fulcrum of Oristano's fortifications, the only other survivor of which is the smaller **Portixedda** ("little gate") tower, at the bottom of Via Mazzini (off Via Roma). Both are open for visits during the summer, each holding a small display of odds and ends relating to local history.

Oristano's **Duomo** stands in a spacious square up Via Duomo, which is behind Piazza Eleonora. Though started in the thirteenth century, most of the present duomo is a Baroque reworking, retaining only parts of the apses from its original construction. With the fourteenth-century onion-roofed belltower and the next-door seminary, it forms an atmospheric ensemble.

At the other end of Via Duomo stands the nineteenth-century church of **San Francesco**, incorporating the remains of a much older Gothic building. The space in front, merging with Piazza Eleonora, forms the main arena for Oristano's annual **Sa Sartiglia** (see box, p.1119).

Practicalities

Oristano's **train station** is at the eastern end of town, a twenty-minute walk from the centre, also linked by local buses running every 20–35 minutes – buy tickets from the bar outside the station. The ARST **bus station** is on Via Cágliari, while long-distance FdS buses pull in at Via Lombardia, ten minutes from Piazza Roma down Via Tirso (tickets from *Blu Bar*). The **Pro Loco** is between Piazza Eleonora and the duomo at Via Ciutadella di Menorca 14 (Mon–Fri 9am–1pm & 4–7.30pm, 4.30–8pm in summer, Sat 9am–noon; ℡0783.70.621, ⓦwww.comune.oristano.it), while information for the whole province is available from the **EPT** at Piazza Eleonora 19 (Mon–Fri 8am–2pm & 4–7pm; ℡0783.36.831).

Accommodation

You'll need to book way ahead if you want to stay in Oristano during the Sa Sartiglia festivities, and in fact accommodation can be hard to come by at any time, with most of the **hotels** geared towards business travellers. The most central of these are the *Isa* on Piazza Mariano (℡ & Ⓕ0783.360.101; ❸), rather bland but with spacious and comfortable rooms, and the fancier *Duomo*, Via Vittorio Emanuele 34 (℡0783.778.061, ⓦwww.hotelduomo.net; ❹), a modern refurbishment of a seventeenth-century building just across from the duomo. The cheapest hotel is the friendly *Píccolo*, Via Martignano 19 (℡0783.71.500; ❷; no credit cards), tucked away in an area of unmarked streets between Via Crispi and Via del Cármine, near the bus station. You'll get more personal attention, however, at one of Oristano's excellent **B&Bs**: both *Eleonora*, at Piazza Eleonora 12 (℡0783.704.35 or 347.481.7976, ⓦwww.eleonora-bed-and-breakfast.com; ❶), and nearby *L'Arco*, Vico Ammirato 12, off Piazza Martini (℡0783.72.849 or 335.690.4240, ⓦwww.arcobedandbreakfast.it; ❶), are in tastefully restored old buildings, while, further out, a five-minute walk from Piazza Mariano, *Antonella*, Via Sardegna 140 (℡0783.73.863, ⓦwww.lamiacasa.sardegna.it; ❶), is more modern. None of the B&Bs accepts credit cards.

The nearest **campsites** lie 6km away at Marina di Torre Grande, Oristano's lido, accessible on frequent buses from Oristano's bus and train stations. The *Torre Grande* (℡0783.22.228) is 150m from the sea, while the better-equipped but pricier *Spinnaker* (℡0783.22.074, ⓦwww.campingspinnaker.com) is nearer the beach; both are open from April/May to September/October.

Eating and drinking

Most of Oristano's **restaurants** are scattered on or around Piazza Roma, including the reliable *Trattoria Gino*, Via Tirso 13 (closed Sun), which features traditional Sardinian dishes such as *ravioli sardi* (made with butter and sage) and *sebadas* (warm, cheese-filled pastry-cases topped with honey). In contrast, a few doors further up the street, the stylish *Cocco & Dessi* has quality meat and seafood dishes with mains at €18–20 and good lunchtime deals (closed Tues). For a cheap and basic pizza or pasta, *La Torre* on Piazza Roma (closed Mon) serves a range of pizzas, including its speciality, *ai funghi porcini*. You might like to finish your meal with a glass of Oristano's celebrated Vernaccia dessert wine. For daytime snacks or late-night **drinking**, the hip *Lolamundo Café* has tables in the quiet Piazzetta Corrias (closed Sun), while the *Old Town Pub*, nearby on Vico Antonio Garau, is a lively Irish-style pub that also stays open late (closed Mon and lunchtime on Sat & Sun).

Tharros

About 20km west of Oristano, the Punic and Roman ruins at **Tharros** are served by five ARST buses daily (July and August only). Like Nora (see p.1115), Tharros is pitched on a limb of land surrounded by water, though in this case it's a clenched fist, dominated by a sturdy Spanish watchtower. The peninsula, which forms the northern tip of the mouth of the Golfo di Oristano, was settled by Phoenicians as early as 800 BC. Tharros grew under Carthaginian occupation and then, after 238 BC, was revitalized by the Romans, who furnished it with the baths and streets that you see today. The town was finally abandoned in 1070 in favour of the more secure Oristano, then a small village.

The **site** (daily 9am–1hr before sunset; €4, including museum at Cabras, see below) consists mostly of Punic and Roman houses arranged on a grid of streets, of which the broad-slabbed Decumanus Maximus is the most impressive. Another, the Cardo Maximus, has a deep open sewer visible alongside it. But the things you'll notice immediately on entering the site are the solitary remnants of a first-century BC Roman temple, with only two of its four Corinthian columns still upright. There are also baths and fragments of mosaics from the Roman city, and a wall and remains of a tophet from the earlier Punic settlement. Like Nora, there is much more submerged underwater, as a result of subsidence.

Near the site stands the fifth-century church of **San Giovanni di Sinis**, which vies with Cágliari's San Saturno for the title of oldest Christian church in Sardinia. Further back up the road towards Oristano (signposted off the Tharros road) is the sanctuary of **San Salvatore**, whose main interest is in a subterranean fourth-century chamber dedicated to Mars and Venus, complete with faded frescoes of Venus, Cupid and Hercules – ask the custodian to let you see it. The sanctuary forms the focus of a wild **festival** on the first weekend of September, the main feature of which is a race run at dawn to the village of **Cabras**, 8km away, by the town's boys. Barefoot and clad in white shirts and shorts, they bear aloft the statue of San Salvatore in a re-enactment of a frantic rescue mission undertaken four centuries ago to save the saint from Moorish attackers. If you're in Cabras, drop in to the **Museo Cívico** at Via Tharros 190 (daily 9am–1pm & 4–8pm, 3–7pm in winter; €2, or €4 including Tharros), on the banks of the lagoon near the southwest entrance to town, for its shelves full of finds from Tharros and its sections on *fassonis* – the traditional rush-constructed boats – and the culture and ecoculture of the lagoon.

Bosa

A two-hour bus ride takes you to **BOSA**, huddled around a hilltop castle on the banks of the Temo river, 62km north of Oristano. From the riverside, the corridor-like lanes of the medieval **Sa Costa** district ascend the hillside, and can be explored by taking any road leading up from the **Cathedral**, at the northern end of Bosa's old bridge. Keep climbing for about twenty minutes to reach the

Castello Malaspina (May, June, Sept & Oct daily 10am–1pm & 3.30–6pm; July daily 10am–1pm & 4–7.30pm; Aug daily 10am–7.30pm; Nov–April usually Sat 10am–1pm & 3.30–6pm, Sun 3.30–6pm, but check first at ☏333.544.5675; €2), erected by the Malaspina family in 1122 – there's also a road that skirts round the back of town, leading to the castle gate. Within the ramparts, take a look inside the church to see some rare Catalan frescoes dating from around 1300. From the ramparts themselves, the panoramic view takes in town, river and sea, and you can pick out Bosa's former cathedral of **San Pietro**, an eleventh-century construction with a Gothic facade added by Cistercian monks a couple of hundred years later. For a closer look, follow the country road running parallel to the south bank of the river from the old bridge eastwards for about 1.5km (same times as castle, but closed Mon in May, June, Sept & Oct, and open Nov–April by prearrangement, call ☏333.544.5675; €1).

In the opposite direction, **BOSA MARINA** lies 5km downstream of the old bridge, on what was the town's original site before its inhabitants shifted to a more defensible position. Today it is a conventional minor resort with a small choice of hotels and bars, a broad swathe of sandy beach and a tiny port on the islet of Isola Rossa, now linked to the mainland and guarded by an old Spanish watchtower. Across the river, you can also swim from the rocks at the mouth of the Temo, or further north off the beautiful rocky coast accessible from the Alghero road. This undeveloped, highly panoramic stretch of coast is one the last habitats in Sardinia of the griffon vulture.

Practicalities

Buses stop at Piazza Zanetti, a short walk from Bosa's **Pro Loco** tourist office at Via Azuni 5 (Mon–Sat 10am–1pm, extended hours in summer; ☏0785.376.107, ⓦwww.infobosa.it). There's another tourist office in Bosa Marina, on the main Via C. Colombo (mid-June to mid-Sept daily 8.30am–12.30pm & 3.30–11pm; mid-Sept to mid-June Mon–Fri 8.30am–12.30pm & 3.30–7.30pm; ☏0785.377.108); the office is also the agent for the Trenino Verde, a narrow-track tourist train to Macomer, 30km inland, which leaves from here on summer weekends. In Bosa, **bikes** are available for rent from Euro Service, Via Azuni 23, and there's an **Internet point** at Via Gioberti 12 (Mon–Sat 9am–1pm & 5–8.30pm, closes at 7.30pm in winter).

Of the **hotels** in Bosa, the best choice is *Sa Pischedda* (☏0785.373.065, ⓦwww.hotelsapischedda.it; ❸), a fine old *palazzo* at the southern end of the old bridge, though the pricier *Corte Fiorita*, on the north bank of the river at Via Lungo Temo De Gasperi 45 (☏0785.377.058, ⓦwww.albergo-diffuso.it; ❹), also has plenty of atmosphere, with more opulent trimmings and bedrooms with balconies and riverside views (for a supplement). Just outside Bosa, on the road to San Pietro, there's an attractive **agriturismo** ⚘ *Bainas* (☏339.209.0967 or 338.306.0004; ❷; no credit cards), a peaceful spot surrounded by fields and orchards, with an excellent restaurant (see p.1124). While convenient for the beach, Bosa Marina has a fairly uninspiring bunch of hotels, the best of which is the friendly *Costa Corallo* on Via C. Colombo (☏0784.375.162; ❸). Opposite here, on Via Sardegna, is one of Sardinia's rare **youth hostels** (☏0785.375.009, ⓔbosa@ostellionline.org; €10.50), a quiet, modern place with friendly management. The nearest **campsite**, *Turas* (☏0785.359.270; June–Sept), lies a couple of kilometres south down the coast from Bosa Marina, and is connected by a bus in summer.

In Bosa itself, the *Sa Pischedda* hotel has an excellent **restaurant** with outdoor seating in summer, and also runs the riverside *Ponte Vecchio* restaurant nearby (mid-June to mid-Sept), both reasonably priced. The *Bainas* agriturismo (see p.1123) serves wholesome organic and vegetarian dishes, using its own homegrown produce, but you'll need to call ahead. Alternatively, the rustic but elegant *Borgo Sant'Ignazio*, in an alley above the Corso, Via Sant'Ignazio 33 (☎0785.374.129; closed Mon), offers delicious local specialities of a meatier nature, with main courses at €10–15. For lunchtime **snacks** and refreshments, avoid the pricey bars on the main Corso in favour of the *Taverna*, on Piazza Cármine (closed Sun in winter).

Nuoro, the interior and the eastern coast

Though little travelled by tourists, Sardinia's **interior** is in many ways the most interesting part of the island, dominated by thick forests, rugged peaks and roaming flocks of sheep. The region is dotted with small and isolated villages for which **Nuoro**, the largest town, makes a useful transport junction and base for excursions. The local inhabitants have retained a fierce sense of independence and loyalty to their traditions, and this is especially true in the ring of the once almost impenetrable **Gennargentu mountains**, centred on the island's highest peak, La Mármora (1834m). The range forms the core of the **Barbágia** region, called Barbaria by the Romans who, like their successors, were never able to subdue it, foiled by the guerrilla warfare for which its hidden recesses proved ideal.

Sardinia's long **eastern seaboard** is highly developed around the resorts of Siniscola and Posada, but further south it preserves its desolate beauty, virtually untouched apart from a couple of isolated spots around **Cala Golone**, and, further down, **Tortolì** and the small port of **Arbatax**.

Nuoro and around

"There is nothing to see in Nuoro: which to tell the truth, is always a relief. Sights are an irritating bore," wrote D.H. Lawrence of the town he visited in 1921, though he was impressed by its appearance to him "as if at the end of the world, mountains rising sombre behind". Superbly positioned beneath the soaring peak of Monte Ortobene and opposite the sheer and stark heights of Monte Corrasi, **NUORO** is also marked out by its distinguished literary heritage. The best-known Sard poet, **Sebastiano Satta** (1867–1914), was Nuorese, as was the author **Grazia Deledda** (1871–1936), who won the Nobel Prize for Literature in 1926 in recognition of a writing career devoted to recounting the day-to-day trials and passions of local villagers. For **Salvatore Satta** (1902–75) – no relation to Sebastiano – "Nuoro was nothing but a perch for the crows", as he wrote in his semi-autobiographical masterpiece, *The Day of Judgment*; his only work, it was published posthumously to great acclaim. The last century has witnessed few changes in this insular town, though it has not escaped an unsightly accretion of apartment blocks, administrative buildings and banks.

Nuoro's **old quarter** is the most compelling part of town, spread around the pedestrianized axis of **Corso Garibaldi**, along which a buzzing *passeggiata* injects a bit of life into the place. Just off here, on Via Satta, drop into the **Museo d'Arte Nuoro** (Tues–Sun 10am–1pm & 4.30–8.30pm; €3), a superb collection of twentieth-century and contemporary art from the whole island, with a preponderance of local artists. Displayed on four floors, the works are refreshingly diverse, and there are also temporary exhibitions of modern Italian art. At the top of the Corso, turn right past the duomo and along Via Mereu to reach the town's impressive **Museo della Vita e delle Tradizioni Popolari Sarde** (daily: mid-June to Sept 9am–8pm; Oct to mid-June 9am–1pm & 3–7pm; €3), which holds Sardinia's most comprehensive range of local costumes, jewellery, masks, carpets and other handicrafts. Examples and explanations of traditional musical instruments from around the island are also displayed, together with a fascinating array of old photographs. Turn left at the eastern end of the Corso and up Via Deledda for the **Casa di Grazia Deledda** (same hours as ethnographic museum; €3.50), the well-to-do home of Nuoro's literary star, restored and furnished and displaying various photos and mementoes. Turn south down Via Deledda to find the **Museo Archeólogico** (Tues & Thurs 9am–1.30pm & 3–5.30pm, Wed, Fri & Sat 9am–1.30pm; free), accessed from Via Mannu or Via Asproni. The well-presented collection takes in everything from rocks and skulls to carved vases, neolithic jewelry and nuraghic art.

Nuoro's biggest annual **festival**, the **Festa del Redentore**, is one of the most vibrant events on the island's calendar, taking place over the last ten days of August, when enthusiastic dancing and dialect singing culminate with a long procession to Mount Ortobene (see p.1126). It's a grand spectacle, and a unique opportunity to see as many as 3000 of Sardinia's local costumes, worn by participants from all over the island, in particular the villages of Barbágia (see p.1126).

Practicalities

You can reach Nuoro in an hour and a quarter on the narrow-gauge FdS line from Macomer, a stop on the main train line from Cágliari, or on an FdS bus from Cágliari or Sássari. Nuoro's **train station** is a twenty-minute walk from the centre of town along Via La Mármora, where frequent **city buses** stop (tickets from the shop inside the station). ARST and FdS **buses** stop at Via Sardegna, ten minutes' walk south of the station. The main **tourist office** is on Piazza Italia, on the edge of the old quarter (June–Sept daily 9am–7pm; Oct–May Mon–Fri 8.30am–1.30pm & 2.30–5.30pm; ☎0784.30.083. There's another private information office at Corso Garibaldi 155 (Mon–Fri 9am–1pm & 3.30–7pm, Sat 9am–1pm; ☎0784.38.777, ⒲www.puntoinforma.it), which can arrange excursions around Nuoro.

Nuoro has few **accommodation** options, and your best bet is to stay outside town on Monte Ortobene or even further afield in Oliena (see p.1127 for both). In town, the best hotels are the *Grillo*, near the ethnographic museum at Via Monsignor Melas 14 (☎0784.38.678, ⒲www.grillohotel.it; ❸), and the *Euro*, near the train station on Via Trieste (☎0784.34.071, ⒲www.eurohotelnuoro .it; ❸), though both are rather charmless business-class places.

The town is better off for **restaurants**, many of which feature regional specialities: the best is *Il Rifugio* at Via Mereu 28 (☎0784.232.355; closed Wed), where main courses are €7–15 and pizzas are also available. Other places include the arty

Tascusi, Via Aspromonte 13 (closed Sun), and *Su Nugoresu*, Piazza San Giovanni 5, a pleasant trattoria in traditional surroundings with tables on the piazza in summer (closed Mon), both off the top end of the Corso. There's a slightly more formal atmosphere and imaginative dishes at *Ciusa*, Viale Ciusa 55 (☏0784.257.052; closed Sun), at the western end of town. For a more casual meal, try the *Pit Stop*, a pizzeria-restaurant at Via Brofferio 19, between Corso Garibaldi and Via Roma (closed Sun). The town also has some good **bars**. For breakfast or a lunchtime snack, *Bar Nuovo* at the top of Corso Garibaldi has outdoor tables (closed Wed in winter), while *Bar Cambosu*, round the corner on Piazza Vittorio Emanuele, is more old-fashioned but equally agreeable for a leisurely sit-down (closed Mon in winter, Sun eve in summer). For shaken ice or evening **drinks**, *Café San Juan* on Piazza San Giovanni has cosy nooks in various rooms.

Monte Ortobene

Between mid-June to mid-September bus #8 runs every twenty minutes or so (with a much reduced service in winter) from Nuoro's Piazza Vittorio Emanuele up to the summit of **Monte Ortobene**, 8km away, from where there are striking views over the gorge separating Nuoro from the Supramonte massif. This is the venue for Nuoro's **Festa del Redentore** at the end of August, when a procession from town weaves up the mountain to the bronze **statue** of the Redeemer at the top (955m). Poised in an attitude of swirling motion, the statue is probably the best vantage point, with dizzying views down to the valley floor. The woods round about are perfect for walks and picnics, and there are possibilities for horse riding at Farcana, signposted left near the top, where there's also a grand open-air public swimming pool open in summer. There's an excellent **B&B** on the mountain, the friendly ⚑ *Casa Solotti* (☏0784.33.954 or 328.602.8975, ⊛www.casasolotti.it; ◗; no credit cards), just after the Farcana turn-off, offering wonderful mountain views and great breakfasts; ring ahead for directions or a pick-up from Nuoro.

The Barbágia and the east coast

South of Nuoro extends the mountainous region known as the **Barbágia**, characterized by forested slopes, lush meadows and a scattering of villages still much as Salvatore Satta described them a century ago, "minuscule settlements as remote from one another as are the stars". The elderly folk in these tight communities are just about the only people on the island who still routinely wear the traditional local costumes, which otherwise are likely to be seen only during one of the numerous small festivals that punctuate the year. Each village has at least one, for which preparations are made months in advance.

Barbágia's villages evolved primarily as shepherds' settlements, whose isolated circumstances and economic difficulties in the postwar years led to widescale emigration and, among those who stayed behind, a crime wave. Sheep-rustling and internecine feuding came to be replaced by the infinitely more lucrative practice of the **kidnapping** and ransoming of wealthy industrialists or their families. This phenomenon reached epidemic proportions during 1966–68 when scores of Carabinieri were drafted into the area to comb the mountains for the hide-outs, rarely with any success. Recent years, however, have seen a lull in the kidnaps, since the high-profile case of Farouk Kassam, an 8-year-old who was abducted on the Costa Smeralda and held for seven months in 1992, having part of his ear cut off by his kidnappers to accelerate the ransom payment.

Nowadays, shepherds send their children to university, or they go to seek work in mainland Italy and don't come back. They leave behind slowly atrophying communities whose salvation is deemed to lie in a greater awareness of their tourism potential. Without the pulling power of the coastal regions, however, the area has to rely on its appeal to outdoors enthusiasts; mountain hiking in particular is increasingly popular – ask at Oliena's tourist office for routes and lists of guides (see below).

Sardinia's **east coast** is in some ways as inhospitable as the interior, sealed off from the rest of the island by a sheer wall of mountains with few points of access. One area has opened up, however: the resort of **Cala Gonone**, where a range of bars, restaurants and accommodation caters for seasonal crowds attracted by the exquisite patches of sand at the base of the cliffs. The beaches along this stretch can be reached on foot or by boat from Cala Gonone, or the small port of **Arbatax**, further south.

Oliena and Tiscali

Visible across the valley, the nearest village to Nuoro is **OLIENA** (hourly buses), 12km southeast, famed as the haunt of bandits until relatively recent times. However, the village prefers its reputation as the producer of one of the island's best wines, a dry, almost black concoction that turns lighter and stronger over time. Oliena lies on the slopes of **Monte Corrasi**, a dramatically rugged limestone elevation which forms part of the Supramonte massif and rises to 1363m. There are numerous organized **excursions** you can make around its various caves and crags, the most famous of which is to the remote Valle Lanaittu and the nuraghic village of **Tiscali** (daily: May–Sept 9am–7pm; Oct–April 9am–5pm; €5), spectacularly sited within a vast mountain-top cavern, a half-day jaunt from Oliena. All hikes should be accompanied by a guide, which can be arranged through Oliena's helpful **tourist office** on the main Via Deledda (Mon–Sat 9am–1pm & 4–7pm; June–Aug also Sun 9am–1pm; ☏0784.286.078). Bilingual staff here can also book **accommodation** in the area: the best options are *Ci Kappa*, Via M. Luther King (☏0784.288.721, ⓦwww.cikappa.it; ❷), a functional hotel in the centre of the village, with a lively pizzeria below; *Su Marimundu* (☏388.338.4892, Ⓔmarimundu@lycos.it; ❷), a well-equipped agriturismo about 1km north of the village (call to be met); and *Cooperativa Turística Enis*, up a steep hill 3km south in località Maccione (☏0784.288.363, ⓦwww.coopenis .it; ❸), where there are also pitches for **camping** and a superb **restaurant** (closed Nov–March) with lofty views over the valley.

Dorgali and Cala Gonone

Centre of the renowned **Cannonau** wine-growing region, **DORGALI** attracts a lot of tourists in summer, both for its craftwork and as a starting point for excursions into the mountains, to places such as Tiscali (see above). Local information is handled at the **Pro Loco** at Via La Mármora 108 (Mon–Fri 9am–1pm & 4–8pm, 3.30–7.30pm in winter; ☏0784.96.243, ⓦwww.dorgali .it), and there's a good **hotel** signposted off the SS125 a couple of kilometres south of town, the *Sant'Elene* (☏0784.94.572, ⓦwww.hotelsantelene.it; ❸).

Ten kilometres east, the small port of **CALA GONONE** is reached by heading south on the SS125 and turning left into the long tunnel through the rock wall, from which the road plunges down to the bay. Beautifully sited at the base of the 900-metre-high mountains, this once tiny settlement was until recently accessible only by boat. Now hotels and villas dominate the scene, though these have not entirely spoilt the sense of isolation, and it is worth a visit if only to take advantage of the numerous boat tours to the secluded beaches up and down the coast. Among the best are **Cala Luna** and **Cala Sisine**, though if you are here for a short time you would do well to choose a tour that combines pauses at these swimming stops with exploration of the deep grottoes that pit the shore.

Most famous of these is the **Grotta del Bue Marino**, formerly home to a colony of Mediterranean monk seals, or "sea ox". It's among Sardinia's most spectacular caves, a luminescent gallery filled with remarkable natural sculptures, resembling organ pipes, wedding cakes and even human heads – one of them is known as *Dante*, after a fondly imagined resemblance to the poet. Boat trips from Cala Gonone cost around €16.50 including entry to the grotto.

Ticket offices for the various excursions are sold in the port area, and there's a summer-only **tourist office** on Via Bue Marino (daily: March–May 9am–noon & 3–7pm; June 9am–1pm & 3–7.30pm; July–Sept 9am–11pm; Dec–Feb 9am–noon; ☎0784.93.696, ⓦwww.calagonone.com). There's no lack of **hotels** hereabouts, with the bougainvillea-covered *Cala Luna,* on Lungomare Palmasera (☎0784.93.133, ⓦwww.hotelcalaluna.com; Easter–Nov; ❺), having direct access to the beach. The lively *Pop* (☎0784.93.185; ❸), by the harbour, also has some seafront views, while the fairly plain *Píccolo*, just up the hill from the harbour (☎0784.93.232; ❷), is the cheapest place in town. There's also an excellent, well-equipped **campsite**, a brief walk up from the beach and near the tourist office (☎0784.93.165, ⓦwww.campingcalagonone.it; April–Oct).

There's a good range of **places to eat** in town, including a few pricey gourmet seafood parlours along the waterfront (most close in winter). The trattoria attached to the *San Francisco* hotel on Via Magellano cooks up wonderful *ravioli* and gnocchi as well as fish and pizzas (closed Tues in winter), while the *Roadhouse Blues* birreria on Lungomare Palmasera serves snacks and beers till late (closed Tues in winter & all Dec–Feb).

Hikes from Cala Gonone and Dorgali

South of Cala Gonone lies one of Sardinia's last truly untouched tracts, a majestic mountain landscape, largely devoid of human life, cut through by the Flumineddu valley and, high above it, the highly panoramic SS125. There are several half- or full-day hikes which can be made in these wild parts, for example following the coast south **from Cala Gonone** to the beaches at Cala Luna and Cala Sisine. From Cala Sisine, the route wanders inland up the Sisine canyon, as far as the solitary church of San Pietro, from where a track leads down to Baunei. *Dorgali*'s Pro Loco can supply a list of guides for the Sisine canyon, for Tiscali (see p.1127), and for the **Gorroppu gorge**, one of southern Europe's deepest canyons. Provided conditions are good, you can explore the latter independently, though you'll need transport to reach the starting point, a car park about 10km south of Dorgali, past the *Sant'Elene* hotel and the church of Buoncammino. From the car park, it takes around ninety minutes to descend to the Flumineddu River and enter the gorge, where you can continue for as long as you are not obstructed by rockfalls or floods, which would require climbing skills, ropes and even dinghies to negotiate. Even for shorter hikes, you'll need hardy footwear with a secure grip and ankle support, and preferably some protection for your head against bumps and falls: the boulders can be extremely slippery, especially when wet.

Orgósolo and around

Deeper into the mountains, at the end of a straggly eighteen-kilometre road running south from Oliena, **ORGÓSOLO** is stuck with its label of bandit capital of the island. The clans of Orgósolo, whose menfolk used to spend the greater part of the year away from home with their flocks, have always nursed an animosity towards the settled crop-farmers on Barbágia's fringes, a tension that occasionally broke out into open warfare. On top of this there was tension between rival clans, which found expression in large-scale sheep-rustling and bloody vendettas, such as the one that broke out at the beginning of the last century and lasted for fourteen years, virtually exterminating the two families involved. Between 1901 and 1954, Orgósolo – population 4000 – clocked up an average of one murder every two months.

Perhaps the village's most infamous son is **Graziano Mesina**, the so-called "Scarlet Rose", who won local hearts in the 1960s by robbing only from the rich to give to the poor and only killing for revenge against those who had betrayed him. Roaming at will through the mountains, even granting interviews to reporters and television journalists, he was eventually captured and incarcerated in Sássari prison. Escaping in 1968, he was recaptured near Nuoro and flown by helicopter the same day to appear on television in Cágliari. He was finally freed in 2004 after forty years behind bars, and returned to live with his sisters in Orgósolo.

Visitors to the village won't find much evidence of its violent past amid the shabby grey, breeze-blocked houses, but they will come across a vivid collection of **murals**, some of them covering whole houses and shops, portraying village culture, most illustrating the oppression of the landless by the landowners, or demanding Sardinian independence.

Orgósolo has two **hotels**: the basic *Petit* on Via Mannu (☎0784.401.070; ❶; no credit cards) and the panoramic and slightly smarter *Sa 'e Jana*, on Via Lussu, at the southern edge of the village (☎0784.402.437; ❷), with great views. The two hotel **restaurants** are about the only places to eat around here, both with low prices.

The Gennargentu massif

The central region of the Barbágia holds the **Gennargentu** chain of mountains – the name means "silver gate", referring to the snow that covers them every winter. Here, you'll find the island's only skiing facilities on **Monte Bruncu Spina**, Sardinia's second-highest peak (1829m). In spring and summer, you can explore this and other areas on **mountain treks**, best undertaken in the company of guides for which the tourist office at Nuoro can supply a list. Along the way you may see wild pigs, vultures and deer, though you would be lucky to spot one of the rare mouflon, an elegant wild goat with long curved horns – its numbers have been decimated by hunting.

The nearby settlements make useful bases for both skiers and trekkers, for example **FONNI**, 13km due south of Mamoiada and at 1000m the island's highest village. Try to coincide your visit with one of Fonni's costumed festivals, principally the Madonna dei Mártiri, on the Monday following the first Sunday in June, and on San Giovanni's day on June 24. Of the **hotels** here, try the modern and clean *Cualbu* on Viale del Lavoro (☎0784.57.054, ⓦwww.hotelcualbu.com; ❸), or *Sa Orte*, Via Roma 14 (☎0784.58.020, ⓦwww.hotelsaorte.it; ❹), an elegantly restored granite building with period trappings; both have their own restaurants.

From **DÉSULO**, a further 26km south, it is possible to reach the area's highest peak, La Mármora, by a twelve-kilometre path. Two of the local **hotels** are currently being rebuilt, though a cheaper option remains open: the basic *La Nuova* on Via Lamármora (☎0784.619.251; ❶; no credit cards), which has shared bathrooms.

Other feasible bases for the area include **TONARA**, 14km west of Désulo, where the modern and spacious *Belvedere* (☎0784.610.054; ❷) and the family-run *Locanda del Muggianeddu* (☎0784.63.885; ❶; no credit cards) make good **accommodation** options: both have restaurants. There's also an independent **hostel** (☎0784.610.005; Easter to mid-Nov; €13), signposted on the northern edge of the village, with ample dormitory space as well as en-suite doubles (❶). Hostellers and others can enjoy wonderful views over wooded slopes from the outdoor tables at the **pizzeria** here (closed Tues in winter). Finally, **ARITZO**, 15km south, has a choice of several **hotels**: try the old-fashioned but comfortable *Moderno*, at the top of the village on Via Kennedy (☎0784.629.229, ⓦ www .hotelmodernoaritzo.it; ❷), with a small garden and restaurant, or the modern and plain *Castello*, on the main Corso Umberto (☎0784.629.266; ❶). For **bus** services linking these villages see "Travel Details", p.1143.

Tortolì and Arbatax

South of Cala Gonone and the majestic Gorroppu gorge the SS125 descends steeply to **TORTOLÌ**, 5km inland from the port of **ARBATAX**, a fairly nondescript port from which ferries ply twice weekly to Genoa, Civitavecchia and (summer only) Fiumicino. The small beach here is famous for its red rocks, but there are better bathing spots outside town – north around **Santa Maria Navarrese** and south at **Lido Orrì**. There's a seasonal **tourist office** at Arbatax station (June to mid-Sept Mon 4–10pm, Tues–Sat 7.20am–1.20pm & 4–10pm, Sun 7.20am–1.20pm; ☎0782.667.690) that has information on sea **excursions**, including to the Grotta del Bue Marino for around €40 (see p.1128), while Tortolì's Pro Loco on Via Mazzini is open year-round (June to mid-Sept Mon–Sat 9am–12.30pm & 5.30–8pm; mid-Sept to May Mon–Fri 9am–12.30pm; ☎0782.622.824, ⓦ www.provincia.ogliastra.it). **Ferry tickets** are available from the Tirrenia office near the port, on your right as you walk towards the station (Mon–Fri 8.30am–1pm & 4–7.30pm, Sat 8.30am–1pm, plus Wed & Sun 10–11pm; ☎0782.667.067).

Frequent daily **buses** connect Cágliari and Nuoro with Tortolì, which, along with Arbatax, is also on the narrow-gauge FdS railway. The train follows an inland route to Cágliari, with a change at Mandas; the full journey from the coast to Cágliari takes around seven dawdling hours (mid-June to mid-Sept only). A frequent summer shuttle **bus** connects Tortolì, Arbatax, Lido Orrì and Porto Frailis.

There are several small **hotels** in the Arbatax area, most of them difficult to reach on foot. The only reasonably priced one lies a couple of kilometres south of the port in the Porto Frailis district, near a good beach, the small *Gabbiano* (Easter–Sept; ☎0782.667.622; ❷; no credit cards). Otherwise, head towards Tortolì, where there is a small selection, including the *Splendor* on Viale Arbatax (☎0782.623.037; ❸) – opposite the Esso station on the other side of the rail tracks. There are several **campsites** in the area, including *Telis* at Porto Frailis (☎0782.667.140, ⓦ www.campingtelis.com; April–Oct) and *Orrì* at Lido Orrì (☎0782.624.695, ⓦ www.campingorri.it; mid-May to late Sept); both have bungalows or caravans to rent. As for **restaurants**, there are few places in Arbatax itself; head, instead, for the Porto Frailis district, where *Il Faro*, overlooking the beach, has a good choice of fish (☎0782.667.499; closed Mon in winter).

Olbia, Gallura and the Costa Smeralda

The largest town in Sardinia's northeastern wedge, **Olbia** owes its recent phenomenal growth to the huge influx of tourists bound for one of the Mediterranean's loveliest stretches of coast, the **Costa Smeralda**, whose five-star development in the 1960s helped to transform the economy of the entire island. Elsewhere on the coast it's still possible to have fun without stacks of money: there are miles of shoreline still undeveloped and a profusion of minor islands, over sixty in all, which you can explore on various boat tours. A daily ferry service from **Palau** links the biggest islands of **Maddalena** and **Caprera**, while further west **Santa Teresa di Gallura** boasts some superb coves and beaches.

This indented northern shore fringes the region of **Gallura**, whose raw red and wind-sculpted granite mountains imbue the area with its unique edge-of-the-wilderness appeal. There is a hidden world within here that most tourists never discover, thickly forested with the cork-oaks which, after tourism, provide most of Gallura's revenue.

Olbia

Awash with traffic and ugly apartment blocks, **OLBIA** is the least Sardinian of all the island's towns. Its port and airport, however, make it an inevitable stop for some and its numerous bars and restaurants are usually a-buzz with tourists, sailors from the port and US service personnel from the nearby NATO base.

If you're stuck for an afternoon here, you might as well visit the town's only item of historical interest, the little basilica of **San Símplicio** (daily 6.30am–1pm & 3.30–8pm), on the street of the same name. The simple granite structure is set in a piazza apart from Olbia's bustle, making it a good spot for a sit down. Claimed to be the most important medieval monument in the whole of Gallura – a region hardly famed for its artistic heritage – the church formed part of the great Pisan reconstruction programme of the eleventh and twelfth centuries, though, it must be said, it is the least interesting example of it. Its murky interior has three aisles separated by pillars and columns recycled from Roman constructions, and even the stoup for the holy water was formerly an urn that held cremated ashes.

The church is the venue for Olbia's biggest **festa**, six days of processions, costumed dancing, poetry recitations, traditional games and fireworks around May 15, commemorating San Símplicio's martyrdom in the fourth century.

Practicalities

Ferries from Civitavecchia, Piombino, Genoa and Livorno (see box on p.1107) dock at the island of Isola Bianca, connected to the mainland by a two-kilometre causeway; twice-hourly buses (#9) run into town (€0.80 from the information office, or €1.30 on board), or you can take one of the infrequent trains to Olbia's main station. Tirrenia offices at the port (daily 8.30am–1pm

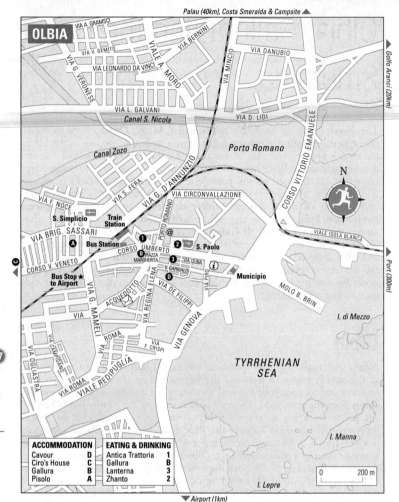

OLBIA

Palau (40km), Costa Smeralda & Campsite ▲

Golfo Aranci (20km) ▶

Port (300m) ▶

VIA A. GRAMSCI
VIA V. GEMITO
VIA G. VERONESE
VIA G. LEONARDO DA VINCI
VIALE A. MORO
VIA A. BERNINI
VIA DANUBIO
VIA MINCIO
VIA L. GALVANI
VIA D. LIDI
Canal S. Nicola
Porto Romano
CORSO VITTORIO EMANUELE
Canal Zozo
VIA S. FERA
VIA G. D'ANNUNZIO
VIA CIRCONVALLAZIONE
VIA F. NOCE
S. Simplicio
Train Station
VIA BRIG. SASSARI
Bus Station
CORSO V. VENETO
Bus Stop ★ to Airport
ACQUEDOTTO
PORTO ROMANO
CORSO UMBERTO
PIAZZA MARGHERITA
VIA OLBIA
VIA PIRO
S. Paolo
VIALE ISOLA BLANCA
V. GARIBALDI
Municipio
MOLO B. BRIN
I. di Mezzo
VIA G. MAMELI
VIA REGINA ELENA
VIA DE FILIPPI
VIA GENOVA
VIA
VIA CAMPIDANO
VIA OGLIASTRA
VIA ROMA
ROMA
VIALE REDIPUGLIA
VIA F. CRISPI
TYRRHENIAN SEA
I. Manna
I. Lepre
Airport (1km) ▼

N

ACCOMMODATION		EATING & DRINKING	
Cavour	D	Antica Trattoria	1
Ciro's House	C	Gallura	B
Gallura	B	Lanterna	3
Pisolo	A	Zhanto	2

0   200 m

& 4.45pm–12.15am; ☏199.123.199) and agencies at the bottom of Corso Umberto sell tickets for Tirrenia, Moby Lines and Sardinia Ferries services (all roughly Mon–Sat 8.30am–1pm & 4.30–7.30pm). Sardinia and some Tirrenia ferry services leave from Golfo Aranci, 15km up the coast (10 buses daily summer only, or regular trains). Book early for all departures.

Olbia's **airport** (Ⓦwww.olbiairport.it) is connected by buses #2 and #10 every twenty minutes (hourly on Sun) until 8pm, which take just ten minutes to reach the central Piazza Regina Margherita (tickets €0.80 from the bar or ticket machine in the terminal, or €1.30 on board). Taxis cost about €15. There is a summer-only bus service (6 daily) from the airport to the **resorts** of Arzachena, Palau and Santa Teresa di Gallura (see pp.1134–1136), so that you can avoid Olbia completely if you're bound for the beach-chequered coast or for Corsica.

⑰

SARDINIA | Olbia

Trains for Sássari and Cágliari run several times daily from the station just off Corso Umberto, while the ARST bus station is round the corner on the Corso (also reachable by walking along the train station platform).

The main tourist office is on Via Piro, a side street running off the main Corso (summer daily 8am–2pm & 3.30–6.30pm, winter Mon–Sat 8am–1pm; ☏0789.21.453, ⓦwww.olbia.it). There are also useful information desks at the airport (daily 8/8.30am until the last flight arrival; ☏0789.563.444), and the port (daily 6am–12.40pm & 2.30–10pm, reduced hours in winter; ☏0789.24.696), where there is also a left-luggage office. You can rent bikes and scooters from On the Road, Via Sássari 8 (☏0789.206.042), and there's Internet access at Intersmeraldo, Via Porto Romano 6b, both off the Corso.

Accommodation

Olbia has several good, central, though fairly pricey, hotels. The cheapest options include the *Hotel Cavour* on Via Cavour (☏0789.204.033, ⓦwww.cavourhotel .it; ❸) and the ⌇ *Gallura* at Corso Umberto 145 (☏0789.24.648; ❸), with great breakfasts included in the price and a first-class restaurant; both are comfortably equipped and have air conditioning. Alternatively, there are a couple of good B&Bs: the quiet, spacious *Ciro's House*, at Via Aspromonte 7 (☏0789.24.075 or 338.504.7598, ⓦwww.bbolbia.com; ❸), 2km west of the centre (buses #1 and #3 stop close by), and the more central *Pisolo*, Via Fiume d'Italia 6–8 (☏0789.209.115 or 340.243.0845, ⓔpisolo-olbia@libero.it; ❸), with two brightly coloured rooms and a shared bathroom; neither takes credit cards. The nearest campsite is at località Cugnana (☏0789.33.184, ⓦwww.campingcugnana.it; April–Sept), 10km north of town, with a pool and bungalows to rent (❺): it's also the closest campsite to the Costa Smeralda, and consequently can get crowded. Up to five buses daily (not Sun) from Olbia stop right outside.

Eating and drinking

As for eating, you'll find top-quality food, smart surroundings and plenty of locals at the *Gallura* (see above), though your final bill may be high. The nearby *Antica Trattoria*, Via Pala 6 (☏0789.25.725; closed Sun lunch & Mon in winter), is equally popular and has lower prices for its pastas, pizzas and seafood. *Zhanto*, just off the Corso on Via delle Terme (closed Sun), has an elegant atmosphere and a small garden, and serves pizzas as well as a regular restaurant menu (mains are €8–15), though if it's just a pizza you're after you may prefer the more casual tone of the subterranean *Lanterna*, Via Olbia 13 (closed Wed in winter), which also has several vegetarian options. The cafés on Piazza Margherita are good for coffees, fresh *cornetti* and drinks, with seating both inside and out.

The Costa Smeralda

The **Costa Smeralda** is a strictly defined ten-kilometre strip between the gulfs of Cugnana and Arzachena, beginning about 12km north of Olbia. Legend has it that the Aga Khan stumbled upon the charms of this jagged coast when his yacht took shelter from a storm in one of the narrow creeks here in 1958. Four years later the fabulously wealthy tycoon headed a consortium of businessmen with the aim of exploiting this wild coastal strip, and was easily able to persuade the local farmers to part with their largely uncultivable land – though stories have circulated ever since of the stratagems used to dupe the locals into selling their property for a fraction of its value.

The consortium's plans were on a massive scale, limited only by the conditions imposed by the regional government. These included proper sewage treatment and disposal, restrictions on building, and the insistence that the appearance of the landscape should not be unduly changed. On this last point the developers were only partly successful. Although you won't see any multistorey hotels, advertising hoardings, fast-food restaurants or garish filling stations, neither will you find a genuine fishing village surviving in these parts, nor anything like the kind of busy local markets you'll see in other parts of the island, and the luxurious holiday villages have a bland, almost suburban feel about them. This hasn't stopped the mega-rich from coming – Berlusconi owns six properties here, including Villa Certosa, where he entertains foreign dignitaries.

You can judge for yourself by taking a look at the "capital" of Costa Smeralda, **PORTO CERVO**, connected to Olbia by ARST buses (3–5 daily Mon–Sat). The "local"-style rustic-red architecture here embodies the dream of an idyllic Mediterranean village without any of the irritations of real life. Graffiti- and litter-free, Porto Cervo exults in its exclusivity, with a glittering yachting marina as its centrepiece. The ranks of sleek floating palaces here are overlooked by the **Stella Maris** church, a modern whitewashed design by the Roman architect Michel Busiri Vici, who was also responsible for the grotto-like shopping arcade in Porto Cervo's centre; inside there's a good *Mater Dolorosa* by El Greco.

Although the elite hotels are out of the range of most pockets, the sequestered sandy **beaches** are free to all, though you'll need your own transport to get to them. None is clearly marked; just follow any dirt track down to the sea – the rougher it is, the more promising. Try **Cappriccioli, Rena Bianca** and **Liscia Ruia**, dotted down the coast south of Porto Cervo.

The Golfo di Arzachena

At least five buses daily leave Olbia on the northward-bound SS125 that takes in Arzachena, Palau and Santa Teresa di Gallura. **ARZACHENA** is a not particularly inspiring inland town, though it has banks, stores, restaurants and a handful of pricey but characterless **hotels**. Most affordable of these, the *Citti*, lies on the edge of town on the main road to Palau at Viale Costa Smeralda 197 (☎0789.82.662, ⓦwww.hotelcitti.com; ④), with a small pool, while *Casa Mia*, on the other side of town off the Olbia road at Via Torricelli 3 (☎0789.82.790, ⓦwww.hotelcasamia.it; ⑤), has a garden and restaurant; both have significantly lower rates outside peak season.

Sharing many of the Costa Smeralda's natural features, the **Golfo di Arzachena** is a deep narrow bay with facilities concentrated in and around **CANNIGIONE**, a small fishing port and yachting resort linked to Arzachena by bus (Mon–Sat 5–8 daily). The region's main **tourist office** is here, at Lungomare Andrea Doria (Mon & Tues 8am–2pm & 3–6pm, Wed–Sat 8am–2pm; ☎0789.892.019), and there's also a private tourist office at Via Nazionale 47 (April–Oct Mon–Sat 9am–12.30pm & 6–8pm, Sun 9am–11.30pm; ☎0789.88.510). Virtually all Cannigione's hotels – including one owned by Peter Gabriel – are ⑥ and above; the cheapest one is *Hotel del Porto*, opposite the marina at Via Nazionale 94 (Jan–Oct; ☎0789.88.011, ⓦwww.hoteldelporto.com; ⑥), which has rooms with balconies and a good seafood restaurant. A cheaper option is to stay in one of the two local **campsites**: the inland *Golfo di Arzachena* (March–Oct; ☎0789.88.101, ⓦwww.campingarzachena.com), just south of the village, with a big pool and a free shuttle service to the beaches, and the preferable *Villaggio Isuledda* (mid-April to mid-Oct; ☎0789.86.003, ⓦwww.isuledda.it), a couple of kilometres north of Cannigione in **LACONIA**, right on the shore with excellent bathing spots. Both have a range of non-tent accommodation to rent (**②**–**④**).

The Maddalena Islands

From **PALAU**, 10km up the coast from Cannigione, ferries leave 2–4 times hourly (around €3.50 return per person, €22.50 return for two people in a medium-sized car) for the main island of the Maddalena archipelago, **La Maddalena**, from which you can reach **Caprera**, the island on which Garibaldi spent the last years of his life. In high season, drivers should book their crossings as early as possible.

La Maddalena

It takes twenty minutes to cross what Nelson called "Agincourt Sound" from Palau to the port and sole town on **LA MADDALENA**. The town, bearing the same name as the island, is a cheerful place with a population of about 15,000, swollen by a large number of Italian and US sailors. Their headquarters are on the eastern side of town, a drab area of barracks, though the main military installations and submarine base are situated on the neighbouring island of Santo Stéfano, briefly captured by Napoleon in 1793 in an abortive attempt to take Sardinia.

Most of the town's action takes place in the narrow lanes between Piazza Umberto I and Cala Gavetta (the marina for small boats), a five-minute walk from the ferry port (heading left) and site of the **tourist office** (Mon–Fri 8am–2pm, plus Mon & Wed 3.30–6.30pm, extended opening in summer; ☎0789.736.321). The town is not particularly well off for **hotels**. Cheapest are the *Arcipélago* at Via Indipendenza Traversa 2 (☎0789.727.328; **③**), a signposted fifteen-minute walk east from the ferry port, offering modern, quiet rooms, and, in the opposite direction, the *Gabbiano* at Via Giulio Césare 20 (☎0789.722.507, ⓦwww.hotel-ilgabbiano.it; **③**; closed Jan to mid-Feb), panoramically sited on the shore beyond Cala Gavetta; at least half board is required in August. There are also three **campsites**, all outside town and all closed outside the summer months: *Il Sole*, on Via Indipendenza (☎0789.727.727), *Maddalena*, in the Moneta district (☎0789.728.051, ⓦwww.campingmaddalena.it), and *Abbatoggia* (☎0789.739.173, ⓦwww.campingabbatoggia.it), close to some good beaches in the north of the island. The last two sites also have caravans and bungalows to rent (**④**–**⑤**), which need early booking.

Buses run to various parts of the island (and to Caprera) from the Colonna Garibaldi near Via Améndola and the port (every 30min–1hr in summer; every 1–2hr in winter). **Bikes** and **mopeds** can be rented from any of the outlets on the seafront towards Cala Gavetta for about €10 a day for a bike, or €50 for a scooter (prices drop outside peak season). The island invites aimless wandering and offers a variety of sandy and rocky beaches in mostly undeveloped coves. The **beaches** on the northern and western coasts are most attractive, particularly those around the tiny port of Madonetta, 5km west of La Maddalena, and at Cala Lunga, 5km north of town.

Caprera

Between October and May half of **CAPRERA** is closed off for military purposes, but there is always plenty of space left to roam this protected woody parkland, which is undeveloped apart from Garibaldi's house in the centre and a couple of secluded, self-contained tourist complexes.

Giuseppe Garibaldi (1807–82) came to live in Caprera in 1855, after a twenty-year exile from Italy. It was from here that he embarked on his spectacular conquest of Sicily and Naples in 1861, accompanied by his thousand Red-Shirts, and it was here that he returned after his campaigns to resume a simple farming life. Having bought the northern part of the island for £360, he spent much of his time writing his memoirs and some bad novels. His neighbour was an Englishman named Collins, with whom he had some celebrated disagreements concerning their wandering goat-herds, as a result of which Garibaldi built a wall dividing their properties, which can still be seen. After Collins's death in 1864 a group of English admirers provided the money for Garibaldi to buy the rest of Caprera from his ex-neighbour's family.

The **museum** (mid-June to mid-Sept Tues–Sat 9am–6.30pm, Sun 9am–1.30pm; mid-Sept to mid-June Tues–Sun 9am–1.30pm; €2) is in Garibaldi's old house, the elegant South American-style **Casa Bianca**, which has been preserved pretty much as he left it. Visitors are escorted past the bed where he slept, a smaller one where he died, various scrolls, manifestos and pronouncements, a pair of ivory-and-gold binoculars given to him by Edward VII and a letter from London, dated 1867, conferring on him honorary presidency of the National Reform League. A stopped clock and a wall-calendar indicate the precise time and date of his death.

The tour ends with Garibaldi's tomb in the garden, its rough granite contrasting with the more pompous tombs of his last wife and five of his children. Garibaldi had requested to be cremated, but following the wishes of his son Menotti his corpse was embalmed. In 1932, fifty years after his death, his tomb was opened to reveal the body perfectly intact.

Santa Teresa di Gallura and around

Heading northwest, the road from Olbia and Palau passes a succession of lovely bays, some dramatic rocky coastline, and a handful of campsites. Six kilometres west of Palau, **Porto Pollo** is Sardinia's busiest watersports centre, the slender isthmus ending in a thick knob of rock creating ideal conditions for **windsurfing** and **kitesurfing**. There are numerous surf schools and rental outfits, while the sheltered, dune-backed beaches will equally appeal to non-surfers. Fifteen kilometres further west, **SANTA TERESA DI GALLURA** is Sardinia's northernmost port. The town gets extremely animated in summer, with a buzzing nightlife, but the main draw is the **beaches**, many enjoying superb views over to Corsica, just 11km away. There's one stretch of sand right at the edge of town, but some of the finest bathing spots on the whole island are a short distance outside, with **Punta Falcone** and **La Marmorata** to the east, and the rocky promontory of **Capo Testa** 3km west of Santa Teresa.

Santa Teresa's **tourist office** is on the main Piazza Vittorio Emanuele (June–Sept daily 9am–1pm & 4.30–7.30pm; Oct–May Mon–Fri 9am–1pm & 3.30–6.30pm, Sat 9am–1pm; ☎0789.754.127, ⓦwww.comunesantateresagallura.it). From the port on the eastern side of town, Moby Lines and Saremar operate sailings to Bonifacio in Corsica (2–7 daily; 1hr; €14–16, vehicles extra). The town's plentiful **hotels** – most of which demand at least half board in July and August – include the central and elegant *Da Cecco*, at Via Po 3 (☎0789.754.220, ⓦwww .hoteldacecco.com; April–Oct; ❹), *Canne al Vento*, further out at Via Nazionale

23 (℡0789.754.219; April–Sept; ❷), with cool, tasteful rooms and a renowned restaurant, and the plainer, family-run *Scano* on Via Lázio (℡0789.754.447; ❸). Other hotels are situated outside town by the beaches, for example *Bocche di Bonifacio* (℡0789.754.202; April to mid-Oct; ❷) at Capo Testa, a relaxed place with a good restaurant; good-value **apartments** are also available here, though these are usually booked up in summer. The nearest **campsite** is *La Liccia* (mid-April to Sept; ℡0789.755.190, ⓦwww.campinglaliccia.com), 6km west, signposted off the Castelsardo road and near a beach. Santa Teresa has no shortage of bars and **restaurants**: for a good meal try *Canne al Vento* (see opposite) or, more centrally, *Papè Satan*, at Via Lamármora 20 (closed mid-Oct to mid-April), a backstreet pizzeria with a courtyard.

Sássari and Alghero

Sássari province is a green, fertile region, hilly but not so craggily scenic as Gallura. **Sássari** itself is for many the island's most interesting town, with its crowded medieval centre and secluded squares. As a holiday destination, however, this inland town has limited appeal, lacking enough entertainment to fill more than a couple of afternoons or evenings. More popular is **Alghero**, the island's oldest resort as well as its major fishing port.

Sássari

Sardinia's second city, **SÁSSARI**, combines an insular, traditional feel, as embodied in its well-preserved tangle of lanes in the old quarter, with a forward-looking, confident air that is most evident in its modern centre. Historically, while Cágliari was Pisa's base of operations during the Middle Ages, Sássari was the Genoan capital, ruled by the Doria family, whose power reached throughout the Mediterranean. Under the Aragonese it became an important centre of Spanish hegemony, and the Spanish stamp is still strong, not least in its churches. In the sixteenth century the Jesuits founded Sardinia's first **university** here, and the intellectual tradition has survived, particularly in the political sphere. In recent years, Sássari has produced two national presidents – Antonio Segni and Francesco Cossiga – as well as the Communist Party leader, Enrico Berlinguer (1922–84) – a cousin, incidentally, of the Christian Democrat Cossiga.

Arrival, information and accommodation

If you're coming to Sássari by **train**, you'll probably have to change at Ozieri-Chilivani station, outside the nondescript town of Chilivani, to arrive at Sássari **station**, at the bottom of the old town's Corso Vittorio Emanuele. There's a **left-luggage** office here (daily 8am–2.20pm), and also one at the **bus station** on Corso Vico, a right turn out of the train station, where all long-distance bus services arrive and depart, as well as the regular service linking the city

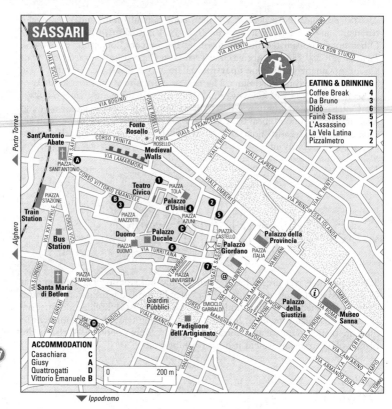

with **Fertilia airport** (ⓦwww.algheroairport.com). Sássari's **tourist office** is at Via Roma 62 (Mon–Thurs 9am–1.30pm & 4–6pm, Fri 9am–1.30pm; ⓣ079.231.777, ⓦwww.comune.sassari.it), and there's **Internet access** at the *Dream Bar*, Via Cavour 15.

Staying in Sássari can be a real problem, and you'd do well to phone ahead to ensure availability. The cheapest **hotel** is the lacklustre *Giusy* (ⓣ079.238.422; ❶; no credit cards), conveniently near the station on Piazza Sant'Antonio, though you'll have a more comfortable stay at the *Hotel Vittorio Emanuele*, Vittorio Emanuele 100 (ⓣ079.235.538, ⓦwww.hotelvittorioemanuele.ss.it; ❸), an old-town *palazzo* flashily renovated to appeal to business folk. On the whole you'd do better at one of Sássari's **B&Bs**, notably *Casachiara*, Vicolo Bertolinis 12 (ⓣ079.200.5052 or 333.695.7118, ⓦwww.casachiara.net; ❷), an apartment in the old quarter given a funky makeover, or *Quattrogatti*, Via Sant'Eligio 5 (ⓣ079.237.819 or 349.406.0481, ⓦwww.quattrogattibnb.it; ❸), where the three bright and spacious rooms come with DVD players and private bathrooms. Neither B&B accepts credit cards.

The City

Sássari's **old quarter**, a network of alleys and piazzas bisected by the main Corso Vittorio Emanuele, is a good area for strolling around. At the heart of it is the **duomo**, whose florid facade is Sardinia's most imposing example of Baroque architecture, added to a simpler Aragonese-Gothic base from the fifteenth and sixteenth centuries. Behind it, the eighteenth-century **Palazzo Ducale** now houses the town hall. On the other side of the Corso, **Piazza Tola** retains its medieval feel and is the venue of a daily market, overlooked by the Renaissance facade of the **Palazzo d'Usini**.

The only other item worth searching out in the old quarter is the late-Renaissance **Fonte Rosello** (Tues–Sat 9am–1pm & 5–8pm, Sun 9am–1pm; reduced hours in winter; free), at the bottom of a flight of grassy steps accessible from Corso Trinità, at the northern end of the old town. Fed by a spring in which the city's women once scrubbed their clothes, the fountain is elaborately carved with dolphins and four statues representing the seasons, the work of Genoese stonemasons. Next to it stands a reconstructed wash house.

Connected by a series of squares to the old quarter, the **newer town** is centred on the grandiose Piazza Italia. Leading off the piazza is Via Roma, location of the impressive **Museo Sanna** (Tues–Sun 9am–8pm; €2), Sardinia's second archeological museum; like the Cágliari museum (see p.1112), its most interesting exhibits are nuraghic sculptures.

Eating and drinking

Sássari has a good range of **restaurants**, including *La Vela Latina*, a smart, modern trattoria specializing in traditional Sard dishes, hidden away in the old town at Largo Sisini 3 (℡079.233.737; closed Sun). Nearby at Via Largo Pazzola 8, *Didò* (℡079.200.6089; closed Sun) has a range of pastas and good-value set menus at lunchtime, otherwise mains are €6–10. Among the old town's cheaper choices, try *L'Assassino*, a casual trattoria at Vicolo Ospizio Cappuccini 1, off Via Rosello (closed Sun), with, again, good fixed-price deals. For a snack, head for *Fainè Sassu*, off Piazza Castello at Via Usai 17 (closed Wed & June–Sept), where the menu is confined to a *sassarese* speciality, *fainè*, a sort of pancake made of chickpea flour, either plain or cooked with onions, sausage or anchovies. Alternatively, *Pizzalmetro*, across the street, serves **pizzas** by the metre to eat in or take away (closed Mon), while *Da Bruno*, a pizzeria on Piazza Matteotti, has inexpensive lunchtime menus and tables outside (no credit cards). For a breakfast, daytime snack or late drink, try *Coffee Break*, a cosy **bar** at Piazza Azuni 19 (closed Sun).

Sássari's festivals

One of Sardinia's showiest festivals – the **Cavalcata** – takes place in Sássari on the penultimate Sunday of May, the highlight of a month of cultural activities. Northern Sardinia's equivalent to Cágliari's Sant'Efisio festival, it attracts hundreds of richly costumed participants from villages throughout the province and beyond. Originally staged for the benefit of visiting Spanish kings or other dignitaries, it lapsed until its revival sixty years ago. The festival is divided into three stages, the morning featuring a horseback parade and a display of the embroidered and decorated costumes unique to each village, after which there is a show of stirring feats of horsemanship at the local race course, ending with traditional songs and dances back in Piazza Italia.

On the afternoon of **August 14** there is a much more local affair – **I Candelieri**, linked to the Pisan devotion to the Madonna of the Assumption. It became a regular event when an outbreak of plague in Sássari in 1652 mysteriously abated on the eve of the feast of the Assumption, since when the ritual has been repeated annually as a token of thanks. The rumbustious event involves bands of *gremi*, or medieval guilds of merchants, artisans and labourers, decked out in Spanish-style costumes and bearing gigantic wooden "candlesticks", 8m tall, through the old town.

Alghero

ALGHERO, 40km southwest of Sássari, is a very rare Italian phenomenon: a tourist town that is also a flourishing fishing port, giving it an economic base entirely independent of tourists. The predominant flavour here is Catalan, owing to a wholesale Hispanicization that followed the overthrow of the Doria family by Pedro IV of Aragon in 1354, a process so thorough that it became known as "Barcelonetta". The traces are still strong in the old town today, with its flamboyant churches and narrow cobbled streets named in both Italian and Catalan, all sheltered within a stout girdle of walls.

Arrival, information and accommodation

Visitors arriving at **Fertília airport** (@www.algheroairport.com) can catch local buses into the centre of town (tickets €0.70 from the shop at one end of the terminal), or direct services to Sássari, Nuoro and Cágliari. Taxis into Alghero cost around €20. Bus timetables and other information can be obtained from the airport's **tourist office** (daily 8.30am–1pm & 3.30–10pm; ☎079.935.124), or Alghero's main **tourist office** (Mon–Sat 8am–8pm, also Sun April–Sept 10am–1pm; ☎079.979.054, @www.comune.alghero.ss.it), at the top end of the Giardino Púbblico. **Trains** arrive some way out of the centre, but regular city buses (#AP and #AF) connect the station to the port. Out-of-town **buses** arrive on Via Catalogna, in the Giardino Púbblico. A good way to get around the town and its environs is by **bike**: Cicloexpress, off Via Garibaldi at the northern end of the port, charges €30–45 per day for a scooter, €8–15 for a bicycle.

Alghero's best-value **hotel**, and the only one located in the old town, is the 🏛 *San Francesco*, at Via Machin 2 (☎079.980.330, @www.sanfrancescohotel .com; ❸), just behind San Francesco church, with clean and quiet en-suite rooms grouped round a cloister. If it's full, try the basic but adequate *Normandie*, Via Enrico Mattei 6, south of the old town, between Via Kennedy and Via Giovanni XXIII (☎079.975.302, ✉nedved@hotmail.com; ❷; no credit cards). Alternatively, there's a small but very central **B&B** at Vicolo Adami 12, *Mamajuana* (☎079.973.5102 or 339.136.9791, @www.mamajuana.it; ❸), a smartly renovated traditional building in the heart of the old town, with all rooms en suite, or try *Catalan B&B*, Via Manzoni 41 (☎079.981.909 or 347.833.5230, @www.algherocasavacanze.it; ❷), an apartment in the modern town with shared bathrooms; neither B&B takes credit cards. There's a useful **hostel** 6km along the coast at Fertilia, reachable by local bus on Via Parenzo, off Via Zara (☎079.930.478, @www.ostellionline.org; €16). It's modern and clean with some family rooms; call first to check availability. There's a well-equipped **campsite** 2km north of Alghero, *La Mariposa* (☎079.950.360, @www .lamariposa.it; April–Oct), with direct access to the beach.

The Town

A walk around the old town should take in the circuit of seven defensive **towers** which dominate Alghero's centre and its surrounding walls. From the **Giardino Púbblico**, the **Porta Terra** is the first of these massive bulwarks – known as the Jewish Tower, it was erected at the expense of the prosperous Jewish community before their expulsion in 1492. Beyond is a puzzle of lanes, at the heart of which the pedestrianized Via Carlo Alberto, Via Principe Umberto and Via Roma have most of the town's bars and shops. At the bottom of Via Umberto stands Alghero's sixteenth-century **Cattedrale**, where Spanish viceroys stopped to

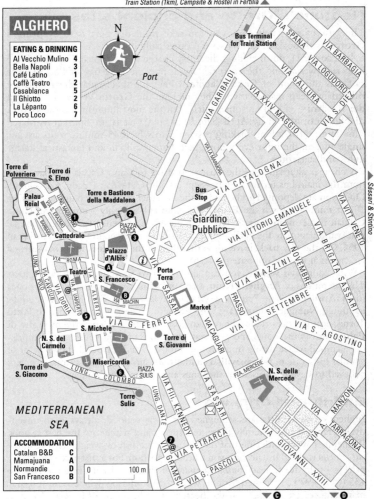

ALGHERO

EATING & DRINKING

Al Vecchio Mulino	4
Bella Napoli	3
Café Latino	1
Caffè Teatro	2
Casablanca	5
Il Ghiotto	2
La Lépanto	6
Poco Loco	7

ACCOMMODATION

Catalan B&B	C
Mamajuana	A
Normandie	D
San Francesco	B

swear a preliminary oath before taking office in Cágliari. Its incongruously Neoclassical entrance is round the other side on Via Manno; inside, the lofty nave's alternating pillars and columns rise to an impressive octagonal dome.

Most of Alghero's finest architecture dates from the same period and is built in a similar Catalan-Gothic style. Two of the best examples are a short walk away: the **Palazzo d'Albis** on Piazza Cívica and the elegantly austere Jewish palace **Palau Reial** in Via Sant'Erasmo (now a restaurant).

Outside the old quarter, most of the tourist activity revolves around the **port**, its wide quay nudged by rows of colourful fishing boats and bordered by bars. The town's beaches begin further north, backed by hotels, many of the older ones converted from villas formerly owned by the expatriate community of central Europeans who fled here after World War I.

17

SARDINIA | Alghero

Neptune's Grotto and ancient sites

The best of the excursions you can take from the port is to **Neptune's Grotto**, with boats departing several times daily between April and October: tickets cost €11, not including the entry charge to the grotto. The 45-minute boat ride west along the coast takes you past the long bay of Porto Conte as far as the point of **Capo Caccia**, where the spectacular sheer cliffs are riddled by deep marine caves. They include the **Grotta Verde** and **Grotta dei Ricami** – visited on some tours – but the most impressive is the **Grotta di Nettuno** itself (daily: April–Sept 9am–8pm; Oct 10am–6pm; Nov–March 9am–5pm; €10), a long snaking passage, into which 45-minute tours are led, single-file, on the hour every hour, past dramatically lit and fantastical stalagmites and stalactites.

A cheaper alternative to the boat is to drive to Capo Caccia or take a **bus** from the main bus terminal (June–Sept 3 daily; Oct–May 1 daily; €4; 50min). Once you are deposited at the end of the line, there's a 654-step descent (taking 10–15 minutes) down the **Escala del Cabirol**, a highly scenic route whose Catalan name means "goat's steps", presumably a reference to the only animal that could negotiate the perilous path before the construction of the stairway in 1954. On the way back, leave some time before the bus goes for a well-earned ice cream at the bar opposite the steps.

With your own vehicle, you can also visit two sites 10km outside Alghero. The necropolis of **Anghelu Ruju**, a pre-nuraghic cave complex of 36 hypogea (daily: April–Oct 9am–7pm; Nov–March 9.30am–4pm; €3, or €5 with guide; including Nuraghe Palmavera €5, or €8 with guides), is on the road to Porto Torres, near the airport. On the road to Porto Conte, you'll pass the **nuraghe di Palmavera** (same hours and prices as Anghelu Ruju) on your right, comprising a ruined palace dating from around 1100 BC and surrounded by fifty or so circular huts, one of which, with a central stool surrounded by a stone bench, is believed to have been used for meetings and religious gatherings.

Eating and drinking

Alghero's **restaurants** are renowned for their seafood, always fresh, inventively prepared and tastefully presented; spring and winter are the best seasons. Remember when ordering that most places price fish by weight: two-to-three *etti* (an *etto* is 100g) usually gets you a healthy portion. For a first-rate – and fairly pricey – fishy feast, head for *La Lépanto*, off Piazza Sulis at Via Carlo Alberto 135 (☏079.979.116; closed Mon in winter), also offering delicious meat dishes; main courses are €12–20. In the heart if the old town, *Al Vecchio Mulino*, at Via Don Deroma 3, deals out tasty sea- and land-based dishes in low-vaulted cellars (☏079.977.254; closed Nov & 2 weeks in Jan, also lunchtime & all day Tues in winter, open daily all day in July & Aug). For a straightforward pizza or pasta dish and a convivial atmosphere, head for *Casablanca*, with entrances on Via Principe Umberto 76 and Via Arduino 59, or *Bella Napoli*, Piazza Cívica 29, with traces of an ancient olive-mill inside; both have mains around €8–12 and are closed Wed in winter. Also on Piazza Cívica, *Il Ghiotto* offers a range of hot snacks, takeaway items and fine Sardinian wines (closed Nov).

There is an abundant supply of decent **bars**. The *Café Latino* (closed Tues Sept–June), with an entrance on Piazza Duomo, has parasols on the city wall overlooking the port, and serves ices and snacks as well as drinks, while *Poco Loco* on Via Gramsci has beers, pizzas, live music and **Internet** access (closed in day). You can also log on at the *Caffè Teatro*, Via Príncipe Umberto 23.

Stintino and around

The port and resort of **STINTINO**, on Sardinia's northwestern tip, was until recently nothing more than a remote jumble of fishermen's cottages jammed between two narrow harbours. Fortunately its discovery by the tourist industry has not resulted in any drastic alterations, and Stintino remains a small, laid-back village, the only one in the tongue of land forming the western arm of the **Golfo di Asinara**. Between two and six **buses** a day head here from Sássari, and there are organized bus trips from Alghero in the summer months.

Most of the peninsula's sunning and swimming takes place further up the coast at La Pelosa (see below), but the only reasonably priced **accommodation** in the area is in Stintino itself. The cheapest choices are the B&B *Il Porto Vecchio*, Via Tonnara 69 (℡079.523.212 or 339.435.3582, ⊛www.bbstintino .com; ❸; no credit cards), and the hotel *Lina*, overlooking the Porto Minori at Via Lepanto 38 (℡079.523.071, ⊛www.linahotel.it; ❸). If you want a touch more luxury, consider *Silvestrino* at Via Sássari 12 (April–Oct; ℡079.523.007, ⊛www.silvestrino.it; ❺), whose excellent restaurant specializes in lobster soup, or *Geranio Rosso*,Via XXI Aprile (℡079.523.292; ❸), which has a pizzeria on site: both require half or full board in high season. For stays of a week or more, you can rent an **apartment** in or around Stintino (up to €1200 per week for four), and you may be able to pick something up for just two or three days, especially outside peak season when prices are much lower: Stintours on Lungomare Colombo (℡079.523.160, ⊛www.stintours.com) can make bookings, and also rents out **cars** and **scooters**. The **Pro Loco** on Piazza dei Quarantacinque dispenses **tourist information** (April, May & late Sept Mon–Sat 9.30am–1pm; June to late Sept daily 9.30am–1pm & 5–8pm; Oct–March Mon, Wed. & Fri 9.30am–1pm; ℡079.520.081, ⊛www.infostintino.com), and there's **Internet** access at La Nassa,Via Tonnara 35.

Four kilometres up the road from Stintino a collection of tourist villages clutter up the otherwise idyllic promontory of **La Pelosa**, served by bus, otherwise taxi or rented transport from Stintino. Hotels and self-catering apartments back some of Sardinia's most deluxe **beaches**, with views out to the isles of Piana and the larger, elongated **Asinara**, the only known habitat of a miniature white ass from which the island takes its name, and previously a prison island. Between Easter and September, you can explore it on daily boat excursions from Stintino, leaving at 9.30am, returning at 4.30pm (or later in summer); the full visit including swimming-stops and guide costs around €30; bring your own lunch and water.You can book tickets on ℡800.561.166, at ⊛www.parcoasinara.it, or at Stintours (see above), and La Nassa,Via Tonnara 35 (℡079.520.060), in Stintino.

Travel details

Trains

Alghero to: Sássari (6–11 daily; 35min).
Arbatax to: Cágliari (mid-June to early Sept Tues–Sun 2 daily via Mandas; 6hr 45min).
Cágliari to: Arbatax (mid-June to early Sept Tues–Sun 2 daily via Mandas; 6hr 45min); Macomer** (8 daily; 1hr 40min–2hr 50min); Olbia** (5 daily; 3hr

40min–4hr 35min); Oristano (12 daily; 1hr 10min–1hr 35 min); Sássari** (4 daily; 3hr 20min–4hr).
Macomer to: Cágliari (9 daily; 1hr 40min–2hr 50min); Nuoro (Mon–Sat 6 daily; 1hr 15min).
Nuoro to: Macomer (Mon–Sat 7 daily; 1hr 15min).
Olbia to: Cágliari** (5 daily; 3hr 45min–4hr 30min); Golfo Aranci (4–6 daily; 25min); Oristano* (5 daily; 2hr 45min–3hr); Sássari** (4–5 daily; 2hr).

Oristano to: Cágliari (hourly; 1hr–1hr 40min); Macomer (8–9 daily; 45min–1hr 10min); Olbia* (5 daily; 2hr 40min–3hr); Sássari* (4 daily; 2hr 20min–2hr 45min).
Sássari to: Alghero (6–11 daily; 35min); Cágliari** (5 daily; 3hr 35min–4hr); Macomer (5 daily; 1hr 30min–1hr 50min); Olbia* (4–5 daily; 2hr); Oristano* (5 daily; 2hr 20min–2hr 40min).

*may involve changing trains at Ozieri-Chilivani
**may involve changing trains at Oristano and/or Ozieri-Chilivani

Buses

Alghero to: Bosa (2–4 daily; 1hr–1hr 40min); Nuoro (2 daily; 3hr 30min); Sássari (hourly; 1hr).
Cágliari to: Barúmini (2–3 daily; 1hr 30min); Nuoro (1 daily; 2hr 30min); Olbia (1–3 daily; 4hr 20min); Oristano (Mon–Sat 2 daily; 2hr); Sant'Antíoco (1–2 daily; 2hr–2hr 35min); Sássari (2–4 daily; 3hr 15min).
Nuoro to: Alghero (2 daily; 2hr); Aritzo (1 daily; 2hr); Cágliari (3 daily; 2hr 30min–4hr 50min); Désulo (Mon–Sat 1 daily; 1hr 20min); Fonni (5–11 daily; 30–40min); Olbia (4–8 daily; 2hr 30min–3hr 20min); Orgósolo (3–9 daily; 35min); Sássari (3–7 daily; 1hr 45min–2hr 45min); Tonara (1 daily; 1hr 30min).
Olbia to: Arzachena (8–14 daily; 40–50min); Nuoro (5–6 daily; 2hr 30min); Palau (8–12 daily; 1hr–1hr 10min); Porto Cervo (Mon–Sat 3–5 daily; 1hr 10min); Santa Teresa di Gallura (5–7 daily; 1hr 35min–2hr); Sássari (Mon–Sat 2 daily; 1hr 30min–2hr).
Oristano to: Bosa (Mon–Sat 4 daily; 2hr); Cágliari (Mon–Fri 2 daily; 2hr); Sássari (1 daily; 2hr).

Sássari to: Alghero (hourly; 50min); Bosa (3–7 daily; 1hr 50min–2hr 20min); Cágliari (4–5 daily; 2hr 30min–3hr 15min); Nuoro (3–5 daily; 1hr 45min–2hr 25min); Olbia (1 daily; 1hr 30min); Oristano (2–3 daily; 1hr 45min–2hr); Stintino (2–6 daily; 1hr 15min).

Ferries

Arbatax to: Civitavécchia (2 weekly; 10hr 30min); Fiumicino (late July to Aug 2 weekly; 5hr 30min); Genoa (2 weekly; 17hr 30min–20hr).
Cágliari to: Civitavécchia (1–2 daily; 14hr 30min–16hr 30min); Naples (1–2 weekly; 16hr); Palermo (1 weekly; 13hr 30min); Trápani (1 weekly; 11hr).
Calasetta to: San Pietro (7–13 daily; 40min).
Golfo Aranci to: Civitavécchia (early April to late Sept 1–3 daily; 3hr 45min–7hr); Fiumicino (mid-June to early Sept 1 daily; 4hr 30min); Livorno (2–5 daily; 5–10hr).
Olbia to: Civitavécchia (1–6 daily; 5–9hr); Genoa (3–21 weekly; 8hr–13hr 30min); Livorno (1–4 daily; 6–11hr); Piombino (1–2 daily; 7hr).
Palau to: Genoa (June–Sept 3–5 weekly; 12–13hr); La Maddalena (1–4 hourly; 20min); Naples (mid-June to mid-Sept 1 weekly; 13hr 30min).
Porto Torres to: Genoa (1–3 daily; 8–11hr).

International ferries

Palau to: Porto Vecchio, Corsica (mid-June to mid-Sept 1 weekly; 2hr).
Porto Torres to: Marseille, France (April–Oct 3–4 weekly; 10–17hr).
Santa Teresa di Gallura to: Bonifacio, Corsica (2–14 daily; 50min–1hr).

Contexts

Contexts

A history of Italy

A specific Italian history is hard to identify. Italy wasn't formally a united country until 1861, and the history of the peninsula after the Romans is more one of warring city states, colonization and annexation by foreign powers. It's almost inconceivable now that Italy should fragment once again, but the regional differences remain strong and have, in recent years, become a major factor in Italian politics.

Early times

A smattering of remains exist from the Neanderthals who occupied the Italian peninsula half a million years ago, but the main period of colonization began after the last Ice Age, with evidence of **Paleolithic** and **Neolithic** settlements dating from around 20,000 BC and 4000 BC respectively. More sophisticated tribes developed towards the end of the prehistoric period, between 2400 and 1800 BC; those who left the most visible traces were the **Ligurians** (who inhabited a much greater area than modern Liguria), the **Siculi** of southern Italy and Latium, and the **Sards**, who farmed and raised livestock on Sardinia. More advanced still were migrant groups from the eastern Mediterranean, who introduced the techniques of working copper. Later, various **Bronze Age** societies (1600–1000 BC) built a network of farms and villages in the Apennines, and on the Sicilian and southern coasts, the latter population trading with Mycenaeans in Greece.

Other tribes brought Indo-European languages into Italy. The Veneti, Latins and Umbrii moved down the peninsula from the north, while the Piceni and the Messapians in Puglia crossed the Adriatic from what is now Croatia. The artificial line between prehistory and history is drawn around the eighth century BC with the arrival of the **Phoenicians** and their trade links between Carthage and southern Italy. This soon encouraged the arrival of the **Carthaginians** in Sicily, Sardinia and the Latium coast – just when **Greeks** and **Etruscans** were gaining influence.

Etruscans and Greeks

Greek settlers colonized parts of the Tuscan coast and the Bay of Naples in the eighth century BC, moving on to **Naxos** on Sicily's Ionian coast, and founding the city of Syracuse in the year 736 BC. The colonies they established in Sicily and southern Italy came to be known as **Magna Graecia**. Along with Etruscan cities to the north they were the earliest Italian civilizations to leave substantial buildings and written records.

The Greek settlements were hugely successful, introducing the vine and the olive to Italy, and establishing a high-yielding agricultural system. Cities like **Syracuse** and **Tarentum** were wealthier and more sophisticated than those on mainland Greece, dominating trade in the central Mediterranean, despite competition from Carthage. Ruins such as the temples of **Agrigento** and **Selinunte**, the fortified walls around Gela, and the theatres at Syracuse and

Taormina on Sicily attest to a great prosperity, and Magna Graecia became an enriching influence on the culture of the Greek homeland – Archimedes, Aeschylus and Empedocles were all from Sicily. Yet these colonies suffered from the same factionalism as the Greek states, and the cities of Tarentum, Metapontum, Sybaris and Croton were united only when faced with the threat of outside invasion. From 400 BC, after Sybaris was razed to the ground, the other colonies went into irreversible economic decline, to become satellite states of Rome.

The **Etruscans** were the other major civilization of the period, mostly living in the area between the **Tiber** and **Arno** rivers. Their language, known mostly from funerary texts, is one of the last relics of an ancient language common to the Mediterranean. Some say they arrived in Italy around the ninth century BC from western Anatolia, others that they came from the north, and a third hypothesis places their origins in Etruria. Whatever the case, they set up a cluster of **twelve city states** in northern Italy, traded with Greek colonies to the south and were the most powerful people in northern Italy by the sixth century BC, edging out the indigenous population of Ligurians, Latins and Sabines. Tomb frescoes in Umbria and Lazio depict a refined and luxurious culture with highly developed systems of divination, based on the reading of animal entrails and the flight of birds. Herodotus wrote that the Etruscans recorded their ancestry along the female line, and tomb excavations in the nineteenth century revealed that women were buried in special sarcophagi carved with their names. Well-preserved chamber tombs with wall paintings exist at **Cerveteri** and **Tarquinia**, the two major sites in Italy. The Etruscans were technically advanced, creating new agricultural land through irrigation and building their cities on ramparted hilltops – a pattern of settlement that has left a permanent mark on central Italy. Their kingdom contracted, however, after invasions by the **Cumans**, **Syracusans** and **Gauls**, and was eventually forced into alliance with the embryonic Roman state. Almost none of their towns have survived the archeological record – the only exception being modern day Marzabotto or Misa, a fine example of Etruscan urban planning.

Roman Italy

The growth of **Rome**, a border town between the Etruscans and the Latins, gained impetus around 600 BC from a coalition of Latin and Sabine communities. The **Tarquins**, an Etruscan dynasty, oversaw the early expansion, but in 509 BC the Romans ejected the Etruscan royal family and became a **republic**, with power shared jointly between two consuls, both elected for one year. Further changes came half a century later, after a protracted class struggle that resulted in the **Law of the Twelve Tables**, which made patricians and plebeians equal. Thus stabilized, the Romans set out to systematically conquer the northern peninsula and, after the fall of Veii in 396 BC, succeeded in capturing **Sutri** and **Nepi**, towns which Livy considered the "barriers and gateways of Etruria". Various wars and truces with other cities brought about agreements to pay harsh tributes.

The **Gauls** captured Rome in 390, refusing to leave until they had received a vast payment, but this proved a temporary reversal. The Romans took **Campania** and the fertile land of Puglia after defeating the **Samnites** in battles over a period of 35 years. They then set their sights on the wealthy Greek colonies to the south, including Tarentum, whose inhabitants turned to the

Greek king, **Pyrrhus of Epirus**, for military support. He initially repelled the Roman invaders, but lost his advantage and was defeated at **Beneventum** in 275 BC. The Romans had by then established their rule in most of southern Italy, and now became a threat to Carthage. In 264 they had the chance of obtaining **Sicily**, when the Mamertines, a mercenary army in control of Messina, appealed to them for help against the Carthaginians. The Romans obliged – sparking off the **First Punic War** – and took most of the island, together with Sardinia and Corsica. With their victory in 222 BC over the Gauls in the Po Valley, all Italy was now under Roman control.

They also turned a subsequent military threat to their advantage, in what came to be known as the **Second Punic War**. The Carthaginians had watched the spread of Roman power across the Mediterranean with some alarm, and at the end of the third century BC they allowed **Hannibal** to make an Alpine crossing into Italy with his army of infantry, horsemen and elephants. Hannibal crushed the Roman legions at Lago Trasimeno and Cannae (216 BC), and then halted at Cápua. With remarkable cool, considering Hannibal's proximity, **Scipio** set sail on a retaliatory mission to the Carthaginian territory of **Spain**, taking Cartagena, and continuing his journey into **Africa**. It was another fifty years before Carthage was taken, closely followed by all of Spain, but the Romans were busy in the meantime adding **Macedonian Greece** to their territory.

These conquests gave Roman citizens a tax-free existence subsidized by captured treasure, but society was sharply divided into those enjoying the benefits, and those who were not. The former belonged mostly to the **senatorial party**, who ignored demands for reform by their opposition, the popular party. The radical reforms sponsored by the tribune **Gaius Gracchus** came too close to democracy for the senatorial party, whose declaration of martial law was followed by the assassination of Gracchus. The majority of people realized that the only hope of gaining influence was through the army, but **General Gaius Marius**, when put into power, was ineffective against the senatorial clique, who systematically picked off the new regime.

The first century BC saw civil strife on an unprecedented scale. Although Marius was still in power, another general, **Sulla**, was in the ascendancy, leading military campaigns against northern invaders and rebellious subjects in the south. Sulla subsequently took power and established his dictatorship in Rome, throwing out a populist government which had formed while he was away on a campaign in the east. Murder and exile were common, and cities which had sided with Marius during their struggle for power were punished with massacres and destruction. Thousands of Sulla's war veterans were given confiscated land, but much of it was laid to waste. In 73 BC a gladiator named **Spartacus** led 70,000 dispossessed farmers and escaped slaves in a revolt, which lasted for two years before they were defeated by the legions.

Julius Caesar and Augustus

Rome became calmer only after Sulla's death, when **Pompey**, another general, and **Licinus Crassus**, a rich builder, became masters of Rome. Pompey's interest lay in lucrative wars elsewhere, so his absence from the capital gave **Julius Caesar** the chance to make a name for himself as an orator and raiser of finance. When Pompey returned in 60 BC, he made himself, Crassus and Caesar rulers of the **first Triumvirate**.

Caesar bought himself the post of consul in 59 BC, then spent the next eight years on campaigns against the **Gauls**. His military success needled Pompey, and he eventually turned against his colleague, giving Caesar the chance to hit back. In 49 BC he crossed the river **Rubicon**, committing the offence of entering Roman territory with an army without first informing the Senate, but when he reached the city there was no resistance – everyone had fled, and Caesar became absolute ruler of Rome. He spent the next four years on civil reforms, writing his history of the Gallic wars, and chasing Pompey and his followers through Spain, Greece and Egypt. A group of enemies within the Senate, including his adopted son **Brutus**, conspired to murder him in 44 BC, a few months after he had been appointed ruler for life. **Octavian**, Caesar's nephew and heir, Lepidus and Marcus Antonius (**Mark Antony**) formed the **second Triumvirate** the following year. Again, the arrangement was fraught with tensions, the battle for power this time being between Antony and Octavian. While Antony was with **Cleopatra**, Octavian spent his time developing his military strength and the final, decisive battle took place at **Actium** in 31 BC, where Antony committed suicide.

As sole ruler of the new regime, Octavian, renaming himself **Augustus Caesar**, embarked on a series of reforms and public works, giving himself complete powers despite his unassuming official title of "First Citizen".

The emperors

Tiberius (AD 14–37), the successor to Augustus, ruled wisely, but thereafter began a period of decadence. During the psychopathic reign of **Caligula** (37–41) the civil service kept the empire running; **Claudius** (41–54) conquered southern Britain, and was succeeded by his stepson **Nero** (54–68), who violently persecuted the **Christians**. Nero committed suicide when threatened by a coup, leading to a rapid succession of four emperors in the year 68. The period of prosperity during the rule of the **Flavian** emperors (Vespasian and his sons Titus and Domitian) was a forerunner for the **Century of the Antonines**, a period named after the successful reigns of Nerva, Trajan, Hadrian, Antonius and **Marcus Aurelius**. These generals consolidated the empire's infrastructure, and created an encouraging environment for artistic achievement. A prime example is the formidable bronze equestrian statue of Marcus Aurelius in Rome – a work not equalled in sophistication until the Renaissance.

A troubled period followed under the rule of Marcus Aurelius' son **Commodus** (180–193) and his successors, none of whom were wholly in control of the legions. Artistic, intellectual and religious life stagnated, and the balance of economic development tilted in favour of the north, while the agricultural south grew ever more impoverished.

Barbarians and Byzantines

In the middle of the third century, incursions by **Goths** in Greece, the Balkans and Asia, and the **Franks** and **Alamanni** in Gaul foreshadowed the collapse of the empire. **Aurelian** (270–275) re-established some order after terrible civil wars, to be followed by **Diocletian** (284–305), whose persecution of Christians produced many of the Church's present-day saints. **Plagues** had decimated the population, but problems of a huge but static economy were compounded by the doubling in size of the army at this time to about half a million men. To ease administration, Diocletian **divided the empire** into two halves, east and west, basing himself as ruler of the western empire in Mediolanum (Milan). This measure brought about a relative recovery, coinciding with the rise of **Christianity**, which was declared the state religion during the reign of **Constantine** (306–337). **Constantinople**, capital of the eastern empire, became a thriving trading and manufacturing city, while Rome itself went into decline, as the enlargement of the senatorial estates and the impoverishment of the lower classes gave rise to something comparable to a primitive feudal system.

Barbarians (meaning outsiders, or foreigners) had been crossing the border into the empire since 376 AD, when the **Ostrogoths** were driven from their kingdom in southern Russia by the **Huns**, a tribe of ferocious horsemen. The Huns went on to attack the **Visigoths**, 70,000 of whom crossed the border and settled inside the empire. When the Roman aristocracy saw that the empire was no longer a shield against barbarian raids, they were less inclined to pay for its support, seeing that a more comfortable future lay in being on good terms with the barbarian successor states.

By the fifth century, many legions were made up of troops from conquered territories, and several posts of high command were held by outsiders. With little will or loyalty behind it, the **empire floundered**, and on New Year's Eve of 406, Vandals, Alans and Sueves crossed the frozen Rhine into Gaul, chased by the Huns from their kingdoms in what are now Hungary and Austria. By 408, the imperial government in Ravenna could no longer hold off **Alaric** (commander of Illyricum – now Croatia) who went on to **sack Rome** in 410, causing a crisis of morale in the west. "When the whole world perished in one city," wrote Saint Jerome, "then I was dumb with silence."

The bitter **end of the Roman Empire** in the west came after **Valentinian III**'s assassination in 455. His eight successors over the next twenty years were finally ignored by the Germanic troops in the army, who elected their general **Odoacer** as king. The remaining Roman aristocracy hated him, and the eastern emperor, **Zeno**, who in theory now ruled the whole empire, refused to recognize him. In 487, Zeno rid himself of the Ostrogoth leader **Theodoric** by persuading him to march on Odoacer in Italy. By 493, Theodoric succeeded, becoming ruler of the western territories.

A lull followed. The Senate in Rome and the civil service continued to function, and the remains of the empire were still administered under Roman law. Ostrogothic rule of the west continued after Theodoric's death, but in the 530s the eastern emperor, **Justinian**, began to plan the reunification of the Roman Empire "up to the two oceans". In 536 his general **Belisarius** landed in Sicily and moved north through Rome to Ravenna; complete reconquest of the Italian peninsula was achieved in 552, after which the Byzantines retained a presence in the south and in Sardinia for five hundred years.

During this time the **Christian Church** developed as a more or less independent authority, since the emperor was at a safe distance in Constantinople. Continual invasions had led to an uncertain political scene in which the **bishops of Rome** emerged with the strongest voice – justification of their primacy having already been given by Pope Leo I (440–461), who spoke of his right to "rule all who are ruled in the first instance by Christ". A confused period of rule followed, as armies from northern Europe tried to take more territory from the old empire.

Lombards and Franks

During the chaotic sixth century, the **Lombards**, a Germanic tribe, were driven southwest into Italy, and by the eighth century, when the **Franks** arrived from Gaul, they were extending their power throughout the peninsula. The Franks were orthodox Christians, and therefore acceptable to Gallo-Roman nobility, integrating quickly and taking over much of the provincial administration. They were ruled by the Merovingian royal family, but the mayors of the palace – the Carolingians – began to take power in real terms. Led by **Pepin the Short**, they saw an advantage in supporting the papacy, giving Rome large endowments and forcibly converting pagans in areas they conquered. When Pepin wanted to oust the Merovingians, and become King of the Franks, he appealed to the pope in Rome for his blessing, who was happy to agree, anointing the new Frankish king with holy oil.

This alliance was useful to both parties. In 755 the pope called on the Frankish army to confront the Lombards. The Franks forced them to hand over treasure and 22 cities and castles, which then became the northern part of the **Papal States**. Pepin died in 768, with the Church indebted to him. According to custom, he divided the kingdom between his two sons, one of whom died within three years. The other was Charles the Great, or **Charlemagne**.

An intelligent and innovative leader, Charlemagne was proclaimed King of the Franks and of the Lombards, and patrician of the Romans, after a decisive war against the Lombards in 774. On Christmas Day of the year 800, Pope Leo III expressed his gratitude for Charlemagne's political support by crowning him **Emperor of the Holy Roman Empire**, an investiture that forged an enduring link between the fortunes of Italy and those of northern Europe. By the time Charlemagne died, all of Italy from south of Rome to Lombardy, including Sardinia, was part of the huge **Carolingian Empire**. The parts that didn't come under his domain were Sicily and the southern coast, which were gradually being reconquered by Arabs from Tunisia; and Puglia and Calabria, colonized by Byzantines and Greeks.

The task of holding these gains was beyond Charlemagne's successors, and by the beginning of the tenth century the family was extinct and the rival Italian states had become prizes for which the western (French) and eastern (German) Frankish kingdoms competed. Power switched in 936 to **Otto**, king of the eastern Franks. Political disunity in Italy invited him to intervene, and in 962 he was crowned emperor; Otto's son and grandson (Ottos II and III) set the seal on the renewal of the Holy Roman Empire.

Popes and emperors

On the death of **Otto III** in 1002, Italy was again without a recognized ruler. In the north, noblemen jockeyed for power, and the papacy was manipulated by rival Roman families. The most decisive events were in the south, where Sicily, Calabria and Puglia were captured by the **Normans**, who proved effective administrators and synthesized their own culture with the existing half-Arabic, half-Italian south. In **Palermo** in the eleventh century they created the most dynamic culture of the Mediterranean world.

Meanwhile in Rome, a series of reforming popes began to strengthen the church. **Gregory VII**, elected in 1073, was the most radical, demanding the right to depose emperors if he so wished. **Emperor Henry IV** was equally determined for this not to happen. The inevitable quarrel broke out, over a key appointment to the archbishopric of Milan. Henry denounced Gregory as "now not pope, but false monk"; the pope responded by excommunicating him, thereby freeing his subjects from their allegiance. By 1077 Henry was aware of his tactical error and tried to make amends by visiting the pope at **Canossa**, where the emperor, barefoot and penitent, was kept waiting outside for three days. The formal reconciliation thus did nothing to heal the rift, and Henry's son, **Henry V**, continued the feud, eventually coming to a compromise in which the emperor kept control of bishops' land ownership, while giving up rights over their investiture.

After this symbolic victory, the papacy developed into the most comprehensive and advanced centralized government in Europe in the realms of law and finance, but it wasn't long before unity again came under attack. This time, the threat came from **Emperor Frederick I** (Barbarossa), who besieged many northern Italian cities from his base in Germany from 1154. **Pope Alexander III** responded with ambiguous pronouncements about the imperial crown being a "benefice" which the pope conferred, implying that the emperor was the pope's vassal. The issue of papal or imperial supremacy was to polarize the country for the next two hundred years, almost every part of Italy being torn by struggles between **Guelphs** (supporting the pope) and **Ghibellines** (supporting the emperor).

Henry VI's son, **Frederick II**, assumed the imperial throne at the age of three and a half, inheriting the Norman **Kingdom of Sicily**. Later linked by marriage to the great **Hohenstaufen** dynasty in Germany, he inevitably turned his attentions to northern Italy. However, his power base was small, and opposition from the Italian commune and the papacy snowballed into civil war. His sudden death in 1250 marked a major downturn in imperial fortunes.

The emergence of city states

Charles of Anjou, brother of King Louis IX of France, defeated Frederick II's heirs in southern Italy, and received **Naples** and **Sicily** as a reward from the pope. His oppressive government finally provoked an uprising on Easter Monday 1282, a revolt that came to be known as the **Sicilian Vespers**, as some two thousand occupying soldiers were murdered in Palermo at the sound of the bell for vespers. For the next twenty years the French were at war with **Peter of Aragon**, who took Sicily and then tried for the southern mainland.

If imperial power was on the defensive, the papacy was in even worse shape. Knowing that the pontiff had little military backing or financial strength left, **Philip of France** sent his men to the pope's summer residence in 1303, subjecting the old man to a degrading attack. Boniface died within a few weeks; his French successor, Clement V, promptly moved the papacy to **Avignon** in southern France.

The declining political power of the major rulers was countered by the growing autonomy of the cities. By 1300, a broad belt of some three hundred virtually **independent city states** stretched from central Italy to the northernmost edge of the peninsula. In the middle of the century the population of Europe was savagely depleted by the **Black Death** – brought into Europe by a Genoese ship returning from the Black Sea – but the city states survived, developing a concept of citizenship quite different from the feudal lord-and-vassal relationship. By the end of the fourteenth century the richer and more influential states had swallowed up the smaller **comune**, leaving four as clear political front runners. These were **Genoa** (controlling the Ligurian coast), **Florence** (ruling Tuscany), **Milan**, whose sphere of influence included Lombardy and much of central Italy, and **Venice**. Smaller principalities, such as Mantua and Ferrara, supported armies of mercenaries, ensuring their security by building impregnable fortress-palaces.

Perpetual vendettas between the propertied classes often induced the citizens to accept the overall rule of one **signore** in preference to the bloodshed of warring clans. A despotic form of government evolved, sanctioned by official titles from the emperor or pope, and by the fifteenth century most city states were under princely rather than republican rule. In the south of the fragmented peninsula was the **Kingdom of Naples**; the **States of the Church** stretched up from Rome through modern-day Marche, Umbria and the Romagna; **Siena**, **Florence**, **Modena**, **Mantua** and **Ferrara** were independent states, as were the **Duchy of Milan**, and the maritime republics of **Venice** and **Genoa**, with a few odd pockets of independence like Lucca, for example, and Rimini.

The commercial and secular city states of late medieval times were the seedbed for the **Renaissance**, when urban entrepreneurs (such as the Medici) and autocratic rulers (such as Federico da Montefeltro) enhanced their status through the financing of architectural projects, paintings and sculpture. It was also at this time that the Tuscan dialect – the language of Dante, Petrarch and Boccaccio – became established as Italy's literary language; it later became the nation's official spoken language.

By the mid-fifteenth century the five most powerful states – Naples, the papacy, Milan, and the republics of Venice and Florence – reached a tacit agreement to maintain the new balance of power. Yet though there was a balance of power at home, the history of each of the independent Italian states became inextricably bound up with the power politics of other European countries.

French and Spanish intervention

The inevitable finally happened when an Italian state invited a larger power in to defeat one of its rivals. In 1494, at the request of the Duke of Milan, **Charles VIII of France** marched south to renew the Angevin claim to the Kingdom of Naples. After the accomplishment of his mission, Charles stayed for three months in Naples, before heading back to France; the kingdom was then acquired by **Ferdinand II of Aragon**, subsequently ruler of all Spain.

The person who really established the Spanish in Italy was the Habsburg Charles V (1500–58), who within three years of inheriting both the Austrian and Spanish thrones bribed his way to being elected Holy Roman Emperor. In 1527 the imperial troops sacked **Rome**, a calamity widely interpreted at the time as God's punishment of the disorganized and dissolute Italians. The French remained troublesome opposition, but they were defeated at Pavia in 1526 and Naples in 1529. With the treaty of Cateau-Cambrésis in 1559, Spain held Sicily, Naples, Sardinia, the Duchy of Milan and some Tuscan fortresses, and they were to exert a stranglehold on Italian political life for the next 150 years. The remaining smaller states became satellites of either Spanish or French rule; only the papacy and Venice remained independent.

Social and economic troubles were as severe as the political upheavals. While the papacy combated the spread of the **Reformation** in northern Europe, the major manufacturing and trading centres were coming to terms with the opening up of the Atlantic and Indian Ocean trade routes – discoveries which meant that northern Italy would increasingly be bypassed. Mid-sixteenth-century **economic recession** prompted wealthy Venetian and Florentine merchants to invest in land rather than business, while in the south high taxes and repressive feudal regimes produced an upsurge of banditry and even the raising of peasant militias – resistance that was ultimately suppressed brutally by the Spanish.

The seventeenth century was a low point in Italian political life, with little room for manoeuvre between the papacy and colonial powers. The Spanish eventually lost control of Italy at the start of the eighteenth century when, as a result of the War of the Spanish Succession, Lombardy, Mantua, Naples and Sardinia all came under Austrian control. The machinations of the major powers led to **frequent realignments** in the first half of the century. Piemonte, ruled by the Duke of Savoy, Victor Amadeus II, was forced in 1720 to surrender Sicily to the Austrians in return for Sardinia. In 1734 Naples and Sicily passed to the Spanish Bourbons, and three years later the House of Lorraine acquired Tuscany on the extinction of the Medici.

Relatively enlightened Bourbon rule in the south did little to arrest the economic polarization of society, but the northern states advanced under the intelligent if autocratic rule of Austria's **Maria Theresa** (1740–80) and her son **Joseph II** (1780–90), who prepared the way for early industrialization. Lightning changes came in April 1796, when the French armies of Napoleon invaded northern Italy. Within a few years the French had been driven out again, but by 1810 Napoleon was in command of the whole peninsula, and his puppet regimes remained in charge until Waterloo. Napoleonic rule had profound effects, reducing the power of the papacy, reforming feudal land rights and introducing representative government to Italy. Elected assemblies were provided on the French model, giving the emerging middle class a chance for political discussion and action.

Unification

The fall of Napoleon led to the Vienna Settlement of 1815, by which the Austrians effectively restored the old ruling class. **Metternich**, the Austrian Chancellor, did all he could to foster any local loyalties that might weaken the appeal of unity, yet the years between 1820 and 1849 became years of revolution. Uprisings began in Sicily, Naples and Piemonte, when **King Ferdinand** introduced measures that restricted personal freedom and destroyed many farmers' livelihoods. A makeshift army quickly gained popular support in Sicily, and forced some concessions, before Ferdinand invited the Austrians in to help him crush the revolution. In the north, the oppressive laws enacted by **Vittorio Emanuele I** in the Kingdom of Piemonte sparked off student protests and army mutinies in Turin. Vittorio Emanuele abdicated in favour of his brother, Carlo Felice, and his son, **Carlo Alberto**; the latter initially gave some support to the radicals, but Carlo Felice then called in the Austrians, and thousands of revolutionaries were forced into exile. Carlo Alberto became King of Sardinia in 1831. A secretive, excessively devout and devious character, he did a major volte-face when he assumed the throne by forming an alliance with the Austrians.

In 1831 further uprisings occurred in Parma, Modena, the Papal States, Sicily and Naples. Their lack of coordination, and the readiness with which Austrian and papal troops intervened, ensured that revolution was short-lived. But even if these actions were unsustained, their influence grew.

One person profoundly influenced by these insurgencies was **Giuseppe Mazzini**. Arrested as Secretary of the Genoese branch of the Carbonari (a secret radical society) in 1827 and jailed for three months in 1830, he formulated his political ideology and set up "**Young Italy**" on his release. Among the many to whom the ideals of "Young Italy" appealed was **Giuseppe Garibaldi**, soon to play a central role in the **Risorgimento**, as the movement to reform and unite the country was known.

Crop failures in 1846 and 1847 produced widespread **famine** and **cholera outbreaks**. In Sicily an army of peasants marched on the capital, burning debt collection records, destroying property and freeing prisoners. Middle- and upper-class moderates were worried, and formed a government to control the uprising, but Sicilian **separatist** aims were realized in 1848. Fighting spread to Naples, where **Ferdinand II** made some temporary concessions, but nonetheless he retook Sicily the following year. At the same time as the southern revolution, serious disturbances took place in Tuscany, Piemonte and the Papal States. Rulers fled their duchies, and Carlo Alberto altered course again, prompted by Metternich's fall from power in Vienna: he granted his subjects a constitution and declared war on Austria. In Rome, the pope fled from rioting and Mazzini became a member of the city's republican triumvirate in 1849, with Garibaldi organizing the defences.

None of the uprisings lasted long. Twenty thousand revolutionaries were expelled from Rome, Carlo Alberto abdicated in favour of his son Vittorio Emanuele II after military defeats at the hands of the Austrians, and the dukes returned to Tuscany, Modena and Parma. One thing that survived was Piemonte's constitution, which throughout the 1850s attracted political refugees to the cosmopolitan state.

Cavour and Garibaldi

Nine years of radical change began when **Count Camillo Cavour** became Prime Minister of Piemonte in 1852. The involvement of Piemontese troops in the Crimean War brought Cavour into contact with Napoleon III at the Congress of Paris, at which the hostilities were ended, and in July 1858 the two men had secret talks on the "Italian question". Napoleon III had decided to support Italy in its fight against the Austrians – the only realistic way of achieving unification – as long as resistance was non-revolutionary. Having bargained over the division of territory, they waited for a chance to provoke Austria into war. This came in 1859, when Cavour wrote an emotive anti-Austrian speech for Vittorio Emanuele at the opening of parliament. His battle cry for an end to the **grido di dolore** (cry of pain) was taken up over Italy. The Austrians ordered demobilization by the Piemontese, who did the reverse.

The war was disastrous from the start, and thousands died at Magenta and Solferino. In July 1859, Napoleon III made a truce with the Austrians without consulting Cavour, who resigned in fury. Provisional governments remained in power in Tuscany, Modena and the Romagna. Cavour returned to government in 1860, and soon France, Piemonte and the papacy agreed to a series of plebiscites, a move that ensured that by mid-March of 1860, **Tuscany** and the new state of **Emilia** (duchies of Modena and Parma plus the Romagna) had voted for **union with Piemonte**. A secret treaty between Vittorio Emanuele and

Napoleon III ceded Savoy and Nice to France, subject to plebiscites. The result was as planned, no doubt due in part to the presence of the French Army during voting.

Garibaldi promptly set off for Nice with the aim of blowing up the ballot boxes, only to be diverted when he reached Genoa, where he heard of an **uprising in Sicily**. Commandeering two old paddle steamers and obtaining just enough rifles for his thousand Red Shirts, he headed south. More support came when they landed in Sicily, and Garibaldi's army outflanked the 12,000 Neapolitan troops to take the island. After that, they crossed to the mainland, easily occupied Naples, then struck out for Rome. Cavour, anxious that he might lose the initiative, hastily dispatched a Piemontese army to **annexe the Papal States**, except for the Patrimony around Rome. Worried by the possibility that the anti-Church revolutionaries who made up the Red Shirt army might stir up trouble, Cavour and Vittorio Emanuele travelled south to Rome, accompanied by their army, and arranged plebiscites in Sicily, Naples, Umbria and the Papal Marches that offered little alternative but to vote for annexation by Piemonte. After their triumphal parade through Naples, they thanked Garibaldi for his trouble, took command of all territories and held elections to a new parliament. In February 1861, the members formally announced the **Kingdom of Italy**.

Cavour died the same year, before the country was completely unified, since Rome and Venice were still outside the kingdom. Garibaldi marched unsuccessfully on Rome in 1862, and again five years later, by which time Venice had been subsumed. It wasn't until Napoleon III was defeated by Prussia in 1870 that the French troops were ousted from Rome. Thus by 1871 **Unification** was complete.

The world wars

After the Risorgimento, some things still hadn't changed. The ruling class were slow to move towards a broader based political system, while living standards actually worsened in some areas, particularly in Sicily. When Sicilian peasant farmers organized into **fasci** – forerunners of trade unions – the prime minister sent in 30,000 soldiers, closed down newspapers and interned suspected troublemakers without trial. In the 1890s capitalist methods and modern machinery in the Po Valley created a new social structure, with rich **agrari** at the top of the pile, a mass of farm labourers at the bottom, and an intervening layer of estate managers.

In the 1880s Italy's **colonial expansion** began, initially concentrated in bloody – and ultimately disastrous – campaigns in Abyssinia and Eritrea in 1886. In 1912 Italy wrested the Dodecanese islands and Libya from Turkey, a development deplored by many, including **Benito Mussolini**, who during this war was the radical secretary of the PSI (Partito Socialista Italiano) in Forlì.

World War I and the rise of Mussolini

Italy entered **World War I** in 1915 with the chief aims of settling old scores with Austria and furthering its colonial ambitions through French and British support. A badly equipped, poorly commanded army took three years to force Austria into defeat, finally achieved in the last month of the war at Vittorio Veneto. Some territory was gained – Trieste, Gorizia, and what became

Trentino-Alto Adige – but at the cost of over half a million dead, many more wounded, and a mountainous war debt.

The middle classes, disillusioned with the war's outcome and alarmed by inflation and social unrest, turned to Mussolini, now a figurehead of the Right. In 1921, recently elected to parliament, Mussolini formed the Partito Nazionale Fascista, whose **squadre** terrorized their opponents by direct personal attacks and the destruction of newspaper offices, printing shops, and socialist and trade union premises. By 1922 the party was in a position to carry out an insurrectionary "**March on Rome**". Plans for the march were leaked to Prime Minister Facta, who needed the king's signature on a martial law decree if the army were to meet the march. Fears of civil war led to the king's refusal. Facta resigned, Mussolini made it clear that he would not join any government he did not lead, and on October 29 **was awarded the premiership**. Only then did the march take place.

Zealous **squadristi** now urged Mussolini towards **dictatorship**, which he announced early in 1925. Political opposition and trade unions were outlawed, the free press disintegrated under censorship and Fascist takeovers, elected local governments were replaced by appointed officials, powers of arrest and detention were increased, and special courts were established for political crimes. In 1929, Mussolini ended a sixty-year feud between Church and State by reorganizing the **Vatican** as an autonomous Church state within the Kingdom of Italy. (As late as 1904, anyone involved in the new regime, even as a voter, had been automatically excommunicated.) By 1939, the motto "Everything within the State; nothing outside the State; nothing against the State" had become fact, with the government controlling the larger part of Italy's steel, iron and ship-building industries, as well as every aspect of political life.

World War II

Mussolini's involvement in the **Spanish Civil War** in 1936 brought about the formation of the "**Axis**" with Nazi Germany. Italy entered **World War II** totally unprepared and with outdated equipment, but in 1941 invaded Yugoslavia to gain control of the Adriatic coast. Before long, though, Mussolini was on the defensive. Tens of thousands of Italian troops were killed on the Russian front in the winter of 1942, and in July 1943 the Allied forces gained a first foothold in Europe, when Patton's American Seventh Army and the British Eighth Army under Montgomery landed in Sicily. A month later they controlled the island.

In the face of these and other reversals Mussolini was overthrown by his own Grand Council, who bundled him away to the isolated mountain resort of Gran Sasso, and replaced him with the perplexed **Marshal Badoglio**. The Allies wanted Italy's surrender, for which they secretly offered amnesty to the king, Vittorio Emanuele III, who had coexisted with the Fascist regime for 21 years. On September 8 a radio broadcast announced that an **armistice** had been signed, and on the following day the Allies crossed onto the mainland. As the Anglo-American army moved up through the peninsula, German divisions moved south to meet them, springing Mussolini from jail to set up the **republic of Salò** on Lago di Garda. It was a total failure, and increasing numbers of men and women from Communist, Socialist or Catholic parties swelled the opposing partisan forces to 450,000. In April 1945 Mussolini fled for his life, but was caught by partisans before reaching Switzerland. He and his lover, Claretta Petacci, were shot and strung upside down from a filling station roof in Milan's Piazzale Loreto.

The postwar years

A popular mandate declared Italy a republic in 1946, and Alcide de Gasperi's **Democrazia Cristiana** (DC) party formed a government. During the 1950s Italy became a front-rank industrial nation, massive firms such as Fiat and Olivetti helping to double the GDP and triple industrial production. American financial aid – the Marshall Plan – was an important factor in this expansion, as was the availability of a large and compliant workforce, a substantial proportion of which was drawn from the villages of the south.

The DC at first operated in alliance with other right-wing parties, but in 1963, in a move precipitated by the increased politicization of the blue-collar workers, they were obliged to share power for the first time with the **Partito Socialista Italiano** (PSI). The DC politician who was largely responsible for sounding out the socialists was **Aldo Moro**, the dominant figure of Italian politics in the 1960s. Moro was prime minister from 1963 to 1968, a period in which the economy was disturbed by inflation and the removal of vast sums of money by wealthy citizens alarmed by the arrival in power of the PSI. The decade ended with the "**autunno caldo**" ("hot autumn") of 1969, when strikes, occupations and demonstrations paralysed the country.

The 1970s and 1980s

In the 1970s the situation continued to worsen. More extreme forms of unrest broke out, instigated in the first instance by the far right, who were almost certainly behind a bomb which killed sixteen people in Piazza Fontana, Milan, in 1969, and the Piazza della Loggia bombing in Brescia five years later. **Neofascist terrorism** continued throughout the next decade, reaching its hideous climax in 1980, when 84 people were killed and 200 wounded in a bomb blast at Bologna train station. At the same time, a plethora of left-wing terrorist groups sprang up, many of them led by disaffected intellectuals at the northern universities. The most active of these were the **Brigate Rosse** (Red Brigades). They reached the peak of their notoriety in 1978, when a Red Brigade group kidnapped and killed Aldo Moro himself. A major police offensive in the early 1980s nullified most of the Brigate Rosse, but a number of hardline splinter groups from the various terrorist organizations are still in existence.

Inconsistencies and secrecy beset those trying to discover who was really responsible for the terrorist activity of the 1970s. One Red Brigade member who served eighteen years in jail for his part in the assassination of Aldo Moro recently asserted that it was spies working for the **Italian secret services** who masterminded the operation. A report prepared by the PDS (Italy's party of the democratic left) in 2000 stirred up further controversy: it alleged that in the 1970s and 1980s the Establishment pursued a "**strategy of tension**" and that indiscriminate bombing of the public and the threat of a right-wing coup were devices to stabilize centre-right political control of the country. The perpetrators of bombing campaigns were rarely caught, said the report, because "those massacres, those bombs, those military actions had been organized or promoted or supported by men inside Italian state institutions and, as has been discovered more recently, by men linked to the structures of United States intelligence". "Other bombing campaigns were attributed to the left to prevent the

Communist Party from achieving power by democratic means," said Valter Bielli, PDS MP, and one of the report's authors. The report drew furious rebuttals from centre-right groups and the US embassy in Rome.

By whatever means, the DC government certainly clung to power. It was partly sustained by the so-called "historic compromise" negotiated in 1976 with **Enrico Berlinguer**, leader of the **Partito Comunista Italiano** (PCI). By this arrangement the PCI – polling 34 percent of the national vote, just three points less than the DC – agreed to abstain from voting in parliament in order to maintain a government of national unity. The pact was rescinded in 1979, and after Berlinguer's death in 1984 the PCI's share of the vote dropped to around 27 percent. The combination of this withdrawal of popular support and the collapse of the Communist bloc led to a realignment of the PCI under the leadership of **Achille Occhetto**, who turned the party into a democratic socialist grouping along the lines of left-leaning parties in Germany or Sweden – a transformation encapsulated by the party's new name – the **Partito Democratico della Sinistra** ("Democratic Party of the Left").

In its efforts to exclude the left wing from power, the DC had been obliged to accede to demands from minor parties such as the **Radical Party**, which gained eighteen seats in the 1987 election, one of them going to the porn star Ilona Staller, better known as **La Cicciolina**. Furthermore, the DC's reputation was severely damaged in the early 1980s by a series of scandals, notably the furore surrounding the activities of the P2 Masonic lodge, when links were discovered between corrupt bankers, senior DC members, and fanatical right-wing groups. As its popularity fell, the DC was forced to offer the premiership to politicians from other parties. In 1981 Giovanni Spadolini of the Republicans became the first non-DC prime minister since the war, and in 1983 **Bettino Craxi** was installed as the first premier from the PSI, a position he held for four years.

Even through the upheavals of the 1970s the national income of Italy continued to grow, and there developed a national obsession with **Il Sorpasso**, a term signifying the country's overtaking of France and Britain in the economic league table. Experts disagreed as to whether *Il Sorpasso* actually happened (most thought it hadn't), and calculations were complicated by the huge scale of tax evasion and other illicit financial dealings in Italy. All strata of society were involved in the withholding of money from central government, but the ruling power in this **economia sommersa** (submerged economy) was, and to a certain extent still is, the **Mafia**, whose contacts penetrate to the highest levels in Rome. The most traumatic proof of the Mafia's infiltration of the political hierarchy came in May 1992, with the murders of anti-Mafia judges **Giovanni Falcone** and **Paolo Borsellino**, whose killers could only have penetrated the judges' security with the help of inside information.

To the present day

The murders of the immensely respected Falcone and Borsellino might well come to be seen as marking a fault line in the political history of modern Italy, and the late 1980s and early 1990s saw the rise of a number of new political parties, as people became disillusioned with the old DC-led consensus. One was the right-wing **Lega Nord** (Northern League), whose autocratic leader, **Umberto Bossi**, capitalized on northern frustration with the state, which they saw as supporting a corrupt south on the back of the hard-working, law-abiding north. The **Alleanza Democratica**, or Democratic Alliance, led by the more circumspect **Mario Segni**, offered a less divisive alternative to middle-of-the road voters, while the fascist MSI, renamed the **Alleanza Nazionale** (AN), or National Alliance, and now a wide coalition of right-wingers led by the persuasive Gianfranco Fini, has gained ground in recent years.

In 1992 the new government of **Giuliano Amato** – a politician untainted by any hint of corruption – instigated the biggest round-up of Mafia members in nearly a decade, leading to the arrest, at the beginning of 1993, of Salvatore "Toto" Riina, the Mafia **capo di tutti capi** (boss of bosses) and the man widely believed to have been behind the Falcone and Borsellino killings. The arrest of Riina followed the testimony of numerous supergrasses, who also implicated key members of the establishment in Mafia activities. For example, it was exposed that a murdered associate of the former prime minister **Giulio Andreotti** was the Mafia's man in Rome, a top-level fixer who would arrange acquittals from the Supreme Court in exchange for support. (Bettino Craxi once called Andreotti a fox, adding "sooner or later all foxes end up as fur coats".)

However, it was **Craxi** himself who was one of the first to fall from grace. Craxi was at the centre of the powerful Socialist establishment that ran the key city of Milan, when in February 1992 a minor party official was arrested on corruption charges. This represented just the tip of a long-established culture of kickbacks and bribes that went right to the top of the Italian political establishment, not just in Milan but across the entire country, and was nicknamed **tangentopoli** ("bribesville"). By the end of that year thousands were under arrest and the net was spreading. What came to be known as the **Mani Pulite** or "Clean Hands" investigation, led by the crusading Milan judge, Antonio di Pietro, was under way.

The established Italian parties, most notably the Christian Democrats and the Socialists, were almost entirely wiped out in the municipal elections of 1993. The establishment wasn't finished yet, however, and the national **elections of 1994** saw yet another political force emerge to fill the power vacuum: the centre-right **Forza Italia** or "Come On Italy", led by the media mogul **Silvio Berlusconi**, who used the power of his TV stations to build support, and swept to power as prime minister in a populist alliance – his "Freedom Pole" coalition – with Bossi's Lega Nord and the fascist National Alliance. The fact that Berlusconi was not a politician was perhaps his greatest asset, and most Italians, albeit briefly, saw this as a new beginning – the end of the old, corrupt regime, and the birth of a truly modern Italian state. However, as one of the country's top northern industrialists, and a former crony of Craxi, Berlusconi was as bound up with the old ways as anyone. Not only did he resist all attempts to reduce the scope of his media business, with which, as prime minister, there was a clear conflict of interest, but in time he himself came under investigation concerning the tax dealings of his Fininvest group. At the end of 1994 Berlusconi was himself forced to resign after the withdrawal of Bossi's Lega Nord from the coalition, and the government collapsed. The next administration, led by the relatively colourless finance man **Lamberto Dini**, managed to stagger on into 1995, but a year later things had once again descended into chaos, with none of a number of compromise candidates able to put together a government. In an attempt to break the deadlock, Scalfaro called elections for April 1996. For the first time in Italy's history a broad centre-left alliance was formed, known as the **ulivo** ("olive tree"), led by **Romano Prodi**, head of the small **Partito Popolare Italiano** (the PPI, or Italian People's Party). In terms of numbers, *l'ulivo* was made up mostly of the PDS, though in order to gain a majority in the Chamber of Deputies the government formed alliances with most of the other parties, including the Lega Nord and the newly created Italian Communist Party, the Rifondazione Comunista.

CONTEXTS | A history of Italy

Meanwhile, the trial of **Giulio Andreotti**, perhaps the most potent symbol of the sleazy postwar years, at last went ahead in Palermo and he had to answer charges of a long-term conspiracy with the Mafia. Andreotti, seven times prime minister of Italy and a senator for life, denied any association, and was acquitted in October 1999 aged 80. In 2002, however, he was back in court, this time charged with complicity in the murder of a journalist. Andreotti denied the charge, but was found guilty and sentenced to 24 years in prison. He is currently appealing, but even if he loses, the worst he can expect is house arrest – Italian law does not allow the jailing of anyone over 75 years old.

In January 1999, Craxi was convicted with twenty others of corruption in connection with kickbacks involving ENEL, the state electrical company. He was sentenced to five years in prison, but died a year later in exile in Tunisia. The most influential public figure to be tried in the late 1990s, however, was **Berlusconi**, who was **convicted** and sentenced in August 1998 to two years and nine months in jail. Perhaps not surprisingly, Berlusconi has since been acquitted of a number of the charges against him, and, although further offences have come to light (bribing the judiciary among them), the ongoing proceedings have served more as a background to his resurgent political career than anything else.

Compared with the turmoil of the early 1990s, the political situation had reached a fairly even plateau. The Christian Democratic party had dissolved; the shift from proportional representation to a first-past-the-post system had begun; and a trend towards two large coalitions – one on the centre-left and the other on the centre-right – indicated a major break from the fragmented, multiparty political landscape of the postwar era. In the mid- to late-1990s attention shifted to the economy and a series of austere measures to bring down inflation and reduce public spending began as a prelude to the entry of the lira into the **ERM**. In October 1998, the relatively prolonged period of stability ended when the Prodi government was defeated in a parliamentary vote of no confidence. President Scalfaro quickly appointed the former leader of the PDS, **Massimo D'Alema**, as prime minister designate. The government lasted for eighteen months before he quit after overwhelming defeat in regional elections in April 2000 and Giuliano Amato was re-appointed as Italy's 58th prime minister since World War II. The left coalition replaced him with **Francesco Rutelli**, the slick and successful ex-mayor of Rome, in the lead-up to the April 2001 elections, only to be crushingly defeated by Berlusconi's Forza Italia. In a televised interview Berlusconi made an unofficial agreement with the Italian people ("*contratto con gli italiani*") whereby he promised to accomplish various economic reforms including lowering taxes and increasing employment. However, with the Italian economy at zero growth, high inflation and the highest debts in the EU, he failed to fulfil any of his electoral promises – though a number of bills were passed that conveniently protected his own business interests and thwarted any attempts by the judiciary to pursue charges of corruption. In 2004 his economic minister, Guilio Tremonti, was forced to resign because of the incompetence of the government's economic policies. Berlusconi was also condemned by many Italians for his mismanagement of events at the G8 Summit in Genoa in 2001, during which demonstrator Carlo Giuliani was shot dead by a *carabiniere*. His support for the 2003 invasion of Iraq and his participation in the so-called "Coalition of the Willing", along with the deployment of Italian troops in Iraq, fuelled further disquiet, as did the machinations of his media division of Fininvest. Forza Italia's support was much reduced after the 2003 elections for the European Parliament, and, in 2005, Prodi's Union Party was successful in the local elections.

In 2006 Berlusconi was forced to call early elections and on April 9 he was narrowly defeated by Romano Prodi, who immediately pledged to withdraw troops from Iraq, to further links with Europe and to boost the economy by cutting both labour costs and the budget deficit. However, at the time of writing his progress had been slow and his approach timid.

The year 2006 also saw the death of Pope John Paul II and the accession of **cardinal Ratzinger**, who took the name of Benedict XVI on April 19. Known as a defender of traditional Catholic doctrine and values, he alienated many following a speech in which he made disparaging and controversial remarks about Islam – although his overall approach seems to be one of conciliation. The other great event of the year was the football **World Cup**, which Italy won for the fourth time, beating France on penalties in a contentious final that saw the French player Zinedine Zidane sent off for headbutting the Italian journeyman Marco Materazzi. It was an ironic but welcome relief from the **match-fixing scandal** that had transfixed the nation only a few months before. Whether the country follows the euphoric road of the World Cup over the next few years, or the dark path exemplified by the people who run football, remains to be seen.

Vernacular architecture

I talian **architecture** isn't just about palaces and churches: domestic architecture is also a source of interest, especially when taking into consideration the siting and layout of small towns and farming settlements, both of which have had as much impact on Italy's landscape as the country's better-known monuments and buildings.

The hill-towns

Throughout the Middle Ages, the countryside was unsafe, unhealthy and, in many places, uncultivated – either swamp or barren: as late as the fifteenth century, wolves still prowled within a few miles of Florence, in a landscape populated largely by brigands and deer. The topography of the countryside, with its abundance of hills and mountains rising steeply from fertile plains, provided natural sites for **fortified settlements** which could both remove the population from the malarial swamps and bandits and preserve the limited fertile land for cultivation.

In the period of their greatest expansion – between the twelfth and fourteenth centuries – **hill-towns** sprang up all over. Many were superimposed on early Etruscan cities – **Chiusi** and **Cortona** – or were cave dwellings, such as **Sorano**. **Matera**, in Basilicata, that grew from a very early settlement of grottoes formed by the natural erosion of volcanic rock (*tufa*) along the side of a high ravine. The houses that evolved from these caves (called *sassi* – literally "rocks") remained in use until 1952, when they were condemned. Though most hill-towns were built within high and sometimes battlemented perimeter walls, the fortress aspects of many sites obviated the need for additional protection. Houses in **Pitigliano** (in Tuscany), for example, rise like a natural extension of the rock outcropping on which they sit. The sheer drop afforded by these sites (often extended by the use of towers) enabled inhabitants to make good use of gravity by dropping a crushing blow onto the heads of enemies attempting to scale the walls. It was also a good way of dispatching the dead, as well as a simple form of rubbish disposal. After the revolution in fortifications between the thirteenth and fifteenth centuries, and the introduction of gunpowder and cannon reduced the need for enormous vertical drops, towers shrunk and were adapted to newer methods of warfare.

Although many hill-towns were genuinely self-contained communities, the countryside remained under the political and economic control of the cities and of the communes, and the Grand Dukes and Church officials who ran them, particularly in north and central Italy. Each city-state set up satellite towns of its own, to protect trade routes (whether at sea or on land), or to operate as garrisons for soldiers, weaponry and food in case of war (or civil insurrection). Siena established the fortified hill-town of **Monteriggioni** in the early thirteenth century along an important route from Rome into France, which also passed through **San Gimignano**. **San Miniato** was also set up as a fortified town by Emperor Frederick II (still quarrelling with the papacy) to take advantage of and protect this same route. At roughly the same time, Florence founded similar frontier outposts, setting up **San Giovanni Valdarno**, **Scarperia** and **Firenzuola**, all within ten years. Fewer towns emerged in the south during this period, partly because there were fewer cities: of the 26 Italian towns with populations of more than 20,000 in the thirteenth century, only three were in the south.

Hill-towns share many features, whatever the impetus for their original development. They are almost always densely built settlements, constructed with materials found on or near their site, which adds to the impression that they arise naturally from their geological foundations. They usually rely on just one or two simple dwelling types endlessly repeated. **Strómboli**, one of the Aeolian islands off the north coast of Sicily, is an example of the rich effects created by repetition of a single, very basic dwelling type, in this case a simple cube. In most hill-towns, houses are built right up to the edge of – and often open out directly onto – the narrow passageways and streets. This reflects the more integral links between the productive activities of the medieval household (carried out on the ground floor) and the street immediately outside which not only became an extension of the works inside but also served as a kind of shop, linked to a wider network of merchants, traders and exchange. Altogether, many more functions were carried out publicly in the streets, traces of which are still visible in the surviving evidence of public fountains and wash houses, wells and communal ovens. Streets in medieval hill-towns were even more crowded than they are today; houses had overhanging wooden balconies, used to dry and store a variety of foods. Supports for these balconies (or the holes which held them) can still be seen on the fronts of many houses.

Hill-towns still preserve a great deal of their medieval character today. Ironically, the very characteristics which made them useful for purposes of defence and isolation made them unsuitable for later growth and redevelopment in response to changing circumstances. There are exceptions though – in the late-fifteenth century the village of Corsignano near Montepulciano was transformed into the little Renaissance town of **Pienza** to commemorate the birthplace of Pope Pius II. But in general, there is little evidence of urban planning, or the country's more recent economic history, in hill-towns.

Settlements of the plain

Though variations abound, the basic types of **settlements** on the plains and in coastal areas reveal a great deal about the impact of urban political and economic activity. Distinct waves of development correspond to changes in the fortunes of city merchants and in the accumulation of capital required for agricultural investment. Accumulation, in turn, depended on economic prosperity and on relatively long and uninterrupted periods of peace.

The north

Just as the economic incentive for rural development derived from the towns, so did the building style. The **house-tower** (*la casa-torre*), which spread first through the Mugello, Chianti and Casentino districts between the thirteenth and fifteenth centuries, was really a transplanted version of the tall, square, fortified city house, and borrowed construction techniques from urban models, particularly from the fortified towns of Bologna, Perugia and Siena. The defensive nature of the house-tower is indicated by its tall, thick walls and the restricted openings high off the ground.

Over successive centuries, the house-tower gradually lost its defensive character, re-emerging as a **dove tower** (*la torre colombaia*), protruding from the centre of a new form of extended dwelling that had been wrapped around it. Doves and pigeons were not only adept at killing snakes and consuming weeds but also provided valuable meat for the table and manure for agricultural use. Though this functional role gradually fell away, the dove tower became a ubiquitous feature of domestic architecture across almost all of central and southern Italy, and still remains an important decorative element in contemporary villas.

The house to which the dove tower belongs is the **Casa della Mezzadria**, the classic Renaissance country villa, particularly widespread across Tuscany, Umbria and Marche. Usually square in plan, it was built using a combination of brick, stone and terracotta under a tent-like roof with the dove tower at its apex. Depending on its regional location, it might boast a portico at ground level (typically Florentine), and a loggia at first-floor level (typically Arentine), or neither a portico nor loggia but a flat wall on the front facade (more common in the area around Siena).

The house derives its name from the system of sharecropping by which most of the land was farmed. Under this system – *la mezzadria* (based on the word *mezza* – "half") – the peasant farmer yielded up half the annual produce to his landowner. This gave the landlord no incentive to invest in stock or to introduce new agricultural methods. At the same time, it impoverished the labour force, compelled by increasing debt to supply free labour – which was used, among other things, to build the main house. Used only occasionally by the landlord, the house was the primary residence of the estate manager (*il fattore*), who was the agent and overseer of urban capital invested in the countryside. Because this system paid workers in kind rather than in cash, it inevitably tied agriculture to the limited production of subsistence goods and so failed to encourage specialization (based on natural advantages) and the commercial innovations that modern agriculture required.

By contrast, the alluvial plain across north and central Italy encouraged specialization very early on. Large-scale investment in reclamation and irrigation was first undertaken by the Benedictines and Cistercians in the eleventh to thirteenth centuries and the consequential enterprises catered for commercial markets in rice, silk and dairy products. Square in plan and built around a massive enclosed courtyard which could extend for 150 metres or more, the architecture of the **farming complex** (*la cascina*) was stark, with high rectangular porticoes supported by square columns.

The estate accommodated four architecturally distinct elements: the owner-manager's house, which was more elaborate in design and often taller than the other buildings; housing for workers, tenement-like in character, with external balconies running along the upper floors used to dry and store crops like rice; cow barns; and stables for horses with hay lofts above, easily recognizable from a distance by the striking patterns of brickwork used to create large grates for the ventilation of hay. Today many of these courtyards are inhabited by independent small farmers, each cultivating their own smallholding. On the eastern side of the plain, around the Ferrara district, where agriculture has become most mechanized, the stables and storage areas of enclosed-court complexes have become truly vast.

At the more modest end of the spectrum, the house of the **independent farmer** (*la casa colonica*) is to be found all over Italy, adapted to local materials and customs. Of simpler construction, it often consists of a kitchen and bedrooms sitting on top of animal sheds and agricultural stores, but equally the barn and house might form separate wings or entirely separate buildings, as is typically found along the slopes of the Apennines running the entire length of the country.

The south

In southern Italy (particularly Campania and Puglia), the **masseria** is a more common type of farming settlement. These massive, complex structures dominate vast tracts of isolated countryside, entirely closed to the outside world. Consisting of a dense cluster of separate buildings, *masserie* were sometimes enclosed by a high-perimeter stone wall with defence towers built into it. They could, however, also consist of a lower grouping of buildings more loosely bound within a larger area. At its largest a *masseria* virtually operated as a self-contained village incorporating church, school, medical clinic and shop, in addition to accommodating the full range of agricultural requirements for stabling, housing (of day labourers called *braccianti*) and storage. In their purest, least-altered form, village *masserie* are still visible in parts of Sicily.

Trulli, found along the coast of Puglia and inland, form one of the most remote, curious and ancient types of farm settlement in Italy. Of uncertain origin (possibly Cretan or North African), and appearing in Italy some time between 2000 and 1000 BC, *trulli* consist of clusters of single circular rooms, each covered by a conical roof made of overlapping rough stone tiles and topped by decorative symbolic pinnacles. Built as primitive agricultural communities, the profusion of conical roofs (each dwelling contributing two or three) produces a startling effect on the landscape.

Cinema

From the earliest days of **cinema**, the Italians have always been passionate movie-lovers and movie-makers. But Italy's films really came to the forefront of world cinema in the postwar period; this was partly due to the location shift from studio-based films to the country's towns and landscape. Their style and technique were ground-breaking, and the use of real sites added a dimension, a mood, which made Italian cinema linger in the memory. The endless expanse of the Po Valley plain in *Obsession*, the steaming sulphur springs outside Naples in *Voyage to Italy*, the deserted, off-season seaside resort of Rimini in *I Vitelloni*, created an atmosphere that could never have been achieved in a studio.

The background

The Italians were once famous for their silent costume epics, pre-World War I dramas that had monumental backdrops and crowd scenes – a leftover from the Italian grand opera tradition. They were often set in the period of the Roman Empire, anticipating the Fascist nostalgia for ancient Rome by at least a decade. **Giovanni Pastrone**'s **Cabiria** (1914), set in ancient Carthage, was the most sophisticated and innovative of these, with spectacular sets and lighting effects that the American director D.W. Griffiths imitated in his masterpiece **Intolerance** (1916). This borrowing of Italian expertise by Hollywood gave the Taviani brothers the story for their **Good Morning Babylon** (1987).

Even in its early stages Italian cinema was handicapped by the economic problems that were destined to keep it lagging behind the American industry. The reason for this was not simply lack of funds, but also an inability on the part of the government to realize what a moneyspinner the indigenous film-making talent could be, and what the unregulated influx of foreign films into Italy would mean for the home market. In addition to this, the Americans themselves began making films in Italy, attracted by the cheap labour, the locations, and the quality of the light, thereby devastating the already fragile home-grown industry. An American film crew arrived in 1923 to make an epic version of **Ben Hur**. Three years prior to this, 220 films were made in Italy; by 1927 the number had dropped to around a dozen a year.

The **Fascist regime** (1922–43) was surprisingly slow to recognize the potential, in both economic and propaganda terms, of the cinema. But in 1934 Mussolini did begin to mete out financial support. He also limited the number of foreign imports, had film added to the arts festival in Venice, and in 1937 inaugurated "Cinecittà", the film studio complex just outside Rome. From 1938 to 1944 the proportion of Italian productions to imports rose rapidly, though home-produced films would never account for more than a third of the total number of films distributed in the country.

Films made during the Fascist period featured glorious victories from the past (the Romans again), and from the present – the war in Ethiopia, for example. During this time, although not all movies were vehicles for propaganda, no films could be made that were overtly critical of the regime. Most popular at the time were the escapist, sentimental, "white telephone" films, so-called because the heroine would have a gleaming white telephone in her boudoir, Hollywood-style – a touch of the exotic for the average Italian at the time, who rarely even saw such a thing, let alone owned one.

Italians were not, however, cut off from what was going on in world cinema between the wars, and the ideas and techniques of Eisenstein and, even more so, of **French directors**, particularly Renoir, Pagnol and Carné, began to filter through. As with literature, probably the biggest single influence on the emerging generation of Italian film-makers was the American novel. Hemingway, Faulkner and Steinbeck spoke directly to the young generation: their subjects were realistic, their stylistic approach was fresh, even raw, and the emotion seemed genuine.

It was not surprising, then, that the late 1930s and early 1940s saw an element of **documentary-style realism** creep into film-making. Contemporary social themes were addressed; non-professional actors were sometimes used. Directors – even those with the official stamp of approval – made the occasional realistic documentary, with none of the bombast or gloss of the typical Fascist film. It was on films such as these that future neo-realist directors such as Visconti, Rossellini and De Sica, and the writer Zavattini, worked their apprenticeships, learning techniques that they would draw on a few years later when they were allowed to unleash their creative imaginations.

A film made in 1943 caused a considerable stir. When it was first shown, Mussolini's son, Vittorio, walked out, exclaiming "This is not Italy!" But Mussolini allowed it to be distributed anyway, probably because there was nothing politically controversial in it. The film was **Luchino Visconti**'s **Obsession**, an unauthorized adaptation of the American novel **The Postman Always Rings Twice** by James M. Cain. Visconti transposed this low-life story of adultery and murder to northern Italy, the characters playing out their seedy tragedy in the relentlessly flat landscape of the Po Valley and among the surreal carnival floats in Ferrara. It showed two ordinary people in the grip of a violent passion, so obsessed with each other that they bring about their own destruction. The original negative was deliberately destroyed when the official film industry was moved north to Mussolini's Salò Republic on Lago di Garda. *Obsession* was something new in the Italian cinema: it had an honesty and intensity, a lack of glamour, that pointed the way to the "neo-realist" films of the immediate postwar period.

The neo-realists

The end of the war meant the end of Fascist domination of everything, including the film industry; but Italy was left emotionally as well as physically shattered. It now seemed important to film-makers to make sense of the intense experience the Italian people had undergone, to rebuild in some way what had been destroyed.

As the tanks were rolling out of Rome in 1945, **Roberto Rossellini** cobbled together the bare minimum of finances, crew and equipment and started shooting **Rome, Open City**. He used real locations, documentary footage, and low-grade film, and came up with a grainy, idiosyncratic style that influenced not only his Italian contemporaries, but also the American films noirs of the late 1940s, and the grittily realistic films of the early 1950s – as well as the French New Wave of the 1960s.

Neo-realism had no manifesto, but its main exponents – Rossellini, De Sica and Visconti – developed the following aims, even if they didn't always stick to them: to show real people rather than conventional heroes (using non-actors), real time, real light, real places (shooting on location, not in studios). Their intention was to present the everyday stuff of life and not romantic dreams.

Unusually for an "art" film, *Rome, Open City* was a box office hit. It had a good emotional, even melodramatic story, with touches of humour, and packed a terrific moral punch. Set in a downbeat quarter of occupied Rome, it is about a partisan priest and a communist who join forces to help the resistance. The Nazis are depicted as effeminate and depraved, while the partisans – including a band of children – are the true heroes, though Rossellini seems to pursue immediacy at the expense of making political statements.

This was the first in Rossellini's so-called "war trilogy". It was followed by **Paisà** (1946), which traced the Allied occupation north from Sicily to the Po Valley, in six self-contained episodes; and the desolate **Germany, Year Zero** (1947), set in the ruins of postwar Berlin, about a child whom circumstances push to suicide.

In these, as in other neo-realist films, children are seen as the innocent victims of adult corruption. **Vittorio De Sica**'s *Shoeshine* (1946) is an anatomy of a friendship between two Roman boys, destroyed first by black-marketeers, then by the police. A young boy is the witness to his father's humiliation in De Sica's **Bicycle Thieves** (1948) – also set in the poorer quarters of Rome – when he sees him steal a bicycle out of desperation (a bicycle will enable him to get his job back) and immediately get caught. The child's illusions are dashed, and the blame is laid on society for not providing the basic human requirements. At the time *Bicycle Thieves* was called the only truly communist film of the postwar decade, but in retrospect the message, as in *Rome, Open City*, seems politically ambiguous. Crowds are seen as hostile and claustrophobic, and the only hope seems to lie in the family unit, which the hero falls thankfully back on at the end.

The conflict between Catholic and Marxist ideology is a recurrent theme in Italian cinema, from Rossellini through to Pasolini, and the Taviani brothers in the 1980s, and it's often this that gives their films the necessary tension. More than anyone, Visconti exemplifies this dichotomy. Born an aristocrat in the famous Milanese family, and sentenced to death (though not executed) for being anti-Fascist in 1944, he was influenced by the writings of Antonio Gramsci, and right up until his death in 1976 veered between two milieux for his films – the honest, suffering sub-proletariat, and the decadent, suffering upper classes.

In 1948 Visconti made a version of the nineteenth-century Sicilian author Giovanni Verga's novel **The House by the Medlar Tree**, about a family of fishermen destroyed by circumstance, which he filmed as **The Earth Trembles**. It was shot on location on the stark Sicilian coast, using an entire village as cast, speaking in their native Sicilian (with an Italian voice-over and subtitles). He adapted the story to incorporate a Marxist perspective, but this fades from view in the pervading atmosphere of stoic fatalism, closer to Greek tragedy than to the party line. Something else that detracted from the intended message was the sophisticated visual style: stunning tableaux such as the one where the wives, dressed in black, stand waiting for their husbands on the skyline, looking out to sea, prompted Orson Welles to remark that Visconti shot fishermen as if they were Vogue models. Indeed, style constantly threatened to overtake content in Visconti's work, culminating in the emotionally slick **Death In Venice** (1971).

The end of neo-realism

By the **early 1950s**, neo-realism was on the way out. Social problems no longer occupied centre stage, and film-makers now concentrated on the psychological, the historical, even the magical side of life. There were several reasons for this, not least that the trauma of World War II had receded, and cities (and lives) were being rebuilt. As Rossellini said in 1954, "you can't go on making films about heroism among the rubble for ever". Directors wanted to move on to new themes. Another reason for the break was government intervention. The cinema industry was in the doldrums, and the Christian Democrat minister Giulio Andreotti had banned any more neo-realist films from being made on the grounds that social criticism equalled communism. The Cold War was just beginning.

Neo-realist films had in any case, with one or two exceptions, rarely been good box office. Of the Italian-made films, the general public tended to prefer farces, historical dramas or comedies. The Neapolitan comic actor Totò – who had a colossal career spanning scores of films and several decades – was a particular favourite. In **Totò looks for a Home** (1949), he and his family search for somewhere to live in the postwar ruins of Rome, in a comic variation on a neo-realist theme. It was a sign of the times that people preferred to laugh at their problems rather than confront them.

De Sica meanwhile had moved on from the unremitting pessimism of *Bicycle Thieves* to a fantastic fable set in Milan, **Miracle in Milan** (1951), about a young man who is given a white dove which possesses the power to grant the wishes of everyone living in his slummy suburb. Surreal special effects are used to create a startling impact, for example in a shot of the hero and heroine flying high above the pinnacles of Milan cathedral on a broomstick. The moral is still a neo-realist one, but with a change of emphasis: art and imagination can help your problems disappear for a while, but won't solve them.

In 1954 **Visconti** made **Senso**, another adaptation of a nineteenth-century novel but worlds away from **The Earth Trembles**. It opens to the strains of Verdi in the Venice opera house, La Fenice, one night in 1866, and is Visconti's view of the politically controversial Unification, portrayed through the lives of a few aristocratic individuals. It was a theme he would return to in **The Leopard** (1963). **Senso** was the first of Visconti's historical spectaculars, and the first major Italian film to be made in colour.

The Fifties and the next generation of directors

Neo-realism was dead, but the next generation of film-makers – Fellini, Pasolini, Bertolucci, Antonioni, Rosi – could not help but be influenced at first by its ideals and techniques, though the style each of them went on to evolve was highly personal.

Federico Fellini, for one, saw neo-realism as more a world-view than a "school". His early films, such as **La Strada** (1954), follow a recognizably realistic storyline (unlike his later movies), but the whole feeling is different from the films of the 1940s. His characters are motivated by human values rather than social ones – searching for love rather than solidarity. All through his long career Fellini used films as a kind of personal notebook in which to hark back to his youth. **I Vitelloni** (1953) is set in an unrecognizable Rimini, his birthplace, before the days of mass tourism; **Amarcord** (1973) is again set in Rimini, this time under Fascism. He also explores his own personal sexual fantasies and insecurities, as in **Casanova** (1976) and **The City of Women** (1980).

But Fellini isn't all nostalgia and sex. There are philosophical themes that run through his work, not least the gap between reality and illusion. The heroine of **The White Sheikh** (1952) falls in love with the Valentino-type actor playing the romantic lead for "photo romance" comics (being shot on the coast outside Rome), and has her illusions dashed when reality intervenes and he makes a bungling attempt to seduce her. *Casanova* too is an oddly (and deliberately) artificial-looking film. It wasn't actually shot in Venice, and the water in the lagoon is in fact a shaken plastic sheet – an odd backlash against the real landscapes of the neo-realists.

Religion is also a theme in Fellini's work, and he's at his best when satirizing the Roman Catholic Church, as in the grotesque clerical fashion parade in **Roma** (1972), or the malicious episode in **La Dolce Vita** (1960) where a couple of children claim to have had a vision of the Virgin Mary, and create the press event of the month.

Pier Paolo Pasolini, murdered in mysterious circumstances in 1975, was a practising Catholic, a homosexual and a Marxist, as well as a poet and novelist. His films reflected this cocktail of ideological and sexual tendencies, though in a less autobiographical way than Fellini's. They're also far more disturbing and challenging: **Theorem** (1968) intercuts shots of a spiritually empty middle-class Milanese family, into which a mysterious young stranger insinuates himself, with desolate scenes of a volcanic wasteland. **The Gospel According to Matthew** (1964) is a radical interpretation of a familiar story (and an excellent antidote to Zeffirelli's syrupy late-1970s **Jesus of Nazareth**) in which Jesus is not a man of peace but the champion of the sub-proletariat and the enemy of hypocrisy. It was filmed in the surprisingly biblical-looking landscape of the poorer regions of southern Italy – Puglia and Calabria – and used the peasants of the area in the cast. Pasolini's **Decameron** (1971) was a record hit at the box office because of its explicit sex scenes, though the director's intention had been political rather than salacious, with Boccaccio's fourteenth-century tales transposed from their original middle-class Florentine setting to the dispossessed of Naples.

Otherwise, the real box-office earners in the 1960s and 1970s were the so-called "spaghetti westerns", shot in the Arizona-look-alike interior of Sardinia, the best of which were directed by **Sergio Leone**.

Bernardo Bertolucci started out as Pasolini's assistant, and shared his politics, though his own films are more straightforward and accessible. **The Spider's Strategem** (1970), filmed in the strange, star-shaped Renaissance town of Sabbioneta near Mantua, was the first of many feature films sponsored by RAI, the Italian state TV network, and is about the anatomy of a destructive father-son relationship with constant flashbacks to the Fascist era. Another early film, **The Conformist** (1970), adapted from the novel by Alberto Moravia, had the spiritually empty hero (or rather, anti-hero) search for father-substitutes in Fascist Rome – again a dream-like jumble of flashbacks. **The Conformist** was Bertolucci's first step on the path to world recognition; subsequent projects, from **Last Tango in Paris** (1972), through **1900** (1976), **La Luna** (1979), the Oscar-winning **The Last Emperor** (1987) and the ill-judged **The Sheltering Sky** (1990), have made him one of the country's most commercially successful directors.

Michelangelo Antonioni again had a neo-realist background, but in the films he made in the 1960s and 1970s he shifted the emphasis from outward action and social realism to internal and psychological anguish. The locations he chose – the volcanic landscape of Sicily for **L'Avventura** (1960), the bleak townscape of industrial Milan in **La Notta** (1961), the impersonal Stock Exchange building in Rome for **The Eclipse** (1962), the alienating oil refineries and power plants at Ravenna for **The Red Desert** (1964) – made perfect settings for what were almost cinematic equivalents of existential novels.

The Neapolitan director **Francesco Rosi** made a series of semi-documentary "inquiry" films attacking various aspects of the Italian establishment: the Sicilian mafia in **Salvatore Giuliano** (1962), the construction industry mafia in Naples in **Hands Over the City** (1963), the army in **Many Wars Ago** (1970), and vested interests of all kinds in **The Mattei Affair** (1972). Not that these are dry analyses of Italian society: the viewer has to sort through the pieces of evidence – the newsreel footage, the half-heard comments, the absence of comment – to come to his or her own conclusions about the truth, in kind of do-it-yourself mystery stories.

Later on, in the late 1970s and 1980s, Rosi went in a more personal direction. **Christ Stopped at Eboli** (1979) is a surprisingly unincisive critique of "the problem of the south", set in a poverty-stricken mountain village in Basilicata. **Three Brothers** (1981) looks at three different political attitudes, as the brothers of the title, reunited for their mother's funeral back home in Puglia, argue, reminisce and dream. Oddly enough, in 1984 Rosi made a completely apolitical film of the opera **Carmen**.

Nostalgia... to the present

Italian cinema of the Seventies and Eighties was dominated by foreign co-productions and TV-sponsored films, which, like elsewhere, led to a loss of national identity. Audiences were steadily eroded by the successive onslaughts of television, video and TV deregulation. Some directors tried to address this problem by focusing on purely Italian themes, others by looking to the past.

Ermanno Olmi's **The Tree of Wooden Clogs** (1978) has a cast from Bergamo speaking dialect with Italian subtitles, and did well at the box office worldwide. Also prominent among Italian directors of the time were the **Taviani brothers**, whose **Padre Padrone** (1977), a mini-epic set in Sardinia that details the showdown between an overbearing father and his rebellious son, and **Kaos** (1984), an adaptation of Pirandello stories shot in scenic Sicily, are both loving of the Italian landscape and redolent of a time past. Together with **Good Morning Babylon** (1987), these films put the brothers' work centre-stage internationally.

Nostalgia was a keynote of the time. **Giuseppe Tornatore**'s Oscar-winning **Cinema Paradiso** (1988) was shot in the director's native village near Palermo, and tells its story through a series of flashbacks. The central figure, a successful film director named Salvatore, returns to the village for a funeral, only to find that the magical Cinema Paradiso of his childhood is about to be razed to make way for a car park. Similarly, in **Ettore Scola**'s **Splendor** (1989), the owner of the cinema in a small provincial town is forced to sell up to a property developer because of declining audiences and debt. In equally poignant vein, **Michael Radford**'s **Il Postino** (1994) is a humorous tale set in 1930s Italy, which follows the artistic and political awakening of the central character, played by Italian comic Massimo Troisi (who sadly died soon after the film's completion).

In this rather soul-searching period of Italian film-making, the films of **Gabriele Salvatores** dealt with groups of Italians abroad, often cut adrift, or seeking escape. His **Mediterraneo** (1991) shows eight reluctant Italian sailors stranded on a Greek island in 1941, and recounts their gradual integration into local life, while **Marrakech Express** (1989) has a group of seven setting off for Morocco in search of their friend, and **Puerto Escondido** (1992) explores life for an Italian in a commune in Mexico.

If the films best known outside Italy were rather escapist in their subject matter, it was a different story at home. During the late 1980s and early 1990s, film-makers began to address the major preoccupation of the time, namely the corruption at the heart of Italian society. The nicely titled **The Brownnose** (**Il Portaborse**; 1991) by **Daniele Luchetti** satirizes the favoured Italian way of outwitting the system and getting things done – the oiling of the wheels of bureaucracy by means of gifts and bribery involves the anti-hero in all manner of scrapes.

Gianni Amelio's political drama **Open Doors** (**Porte Aperte**; 1990), from Leonardo Sciascia's novel of the same name, is set in Fascist Palermo just before World War II, but its subject matter – a liberal judge being obstructed in his investigations of all-pervasive corruption – was particularly apposite at the time. The same director's **Stolen Children** (**Il Ladro di Bambini**; 1992) is a better-known film outside Italy, and deals with corrupt society as seen through the eyes of a child. Amelio made no new work for five years until **The Way We Laughed** (**Così Ridevamo**; 1998), the story of two brothers leaving rural Sicily for Turin in the late 1950s, a film which suggests that the present-day malaises that Italy is experiencing have their roots in the betrayals and violence in the late 1950s and early 1960s.

Films with a much more hard-hitting, realistic edge also began to emerge, among them **Mario Martone**'s **Rehearsal for War** (**Teatro di Guerra**; 1998), which examines the Yugoslav conflict and the power of the imagination in our perception of evil. Meanwhile, such directors as **Marco Risi** dealt with specific social problems – his **Mery per Sempre** (1989) follows the lives of half a dozen youngsters in prison, and its sequel, **Ragazzi Fuori** (1990), shows them fresh out of the clink.

More provocative still, **Daniele Cipri** and **Franco Maresco**'s **Toto Che Visse Due Volte** (**Totò And His Two Lives**; 1998), set in Sicily, ruffled a few feathers with its violation of religious and sexual taboos (including a depiction of a statue of the Virgin Mary being assaulted). Critics disliked the film's clumsiness, but this iconoclastic work didn't trouble the establishment. When the film censors banned its release, the deputy prime minister – a film buff – stepped in and disbanded their board.

A sea change

In the 1990s a sea change took place in Italian film as screenplay writers, cinematographers and directors began to shake free of nostalgia and corruption themes and explore contemporary life in an idiosyncratic, amusing and penetrating way. Director, actor and screenwriter **Nanni Moretti** achieved great acclaim with his **Dear Diary** (**Caro Diario**; 1993). In three parts, the film covers such diverse subjects as twentieth-century architecture, children and telephones, Pasolini's unsolved murder, the myth of rural idyll, as well as Moretti's own fight against cancer. Much of the film is spent following Moretti on his scooter through Rome, or travelling by ferry from one island to another. His latest film **The Son's Room** (**La Stanza del Figlio**; 2001), however, is a much darker work exploring a family's grief; the film won a Palme d'Or at Cannes and much critical attention.

In his films, Moretti appears to be continually questioning the worth of everything, including his own work; indeed, he went too far for some critics in **Aprile** (1998), which focuses on his inability to decide how to finish his films – or even whether to finish them. Although it wasn't as well received as his other works, it's still a very funny film; in it, Moretti feels obliged to make a film about Italian politics, but is continually sidetracked by his real passions, including the birth of his first child.

An Oscar-winning work by **Roberto Benigni**, known for such slapstick-style movies as **Johnny Stecchino** (1991) and **The Monster** (1994), marks another brave foray into new territory. Benigni's **Life is Beautiful** (**La Vita è Bella**; 1997) addresses the Holocaust and dares to combine comedy with genocide. A parent's desire to protect the innocence of their child, rather than the Holocaust itself, is the theme of the film, and Benigni (who also plays the lead role with his wife, Nicoletta Braschi, as his co-star) distinguishes between laughing *at* the Holocaust and laughing *in* the Holocaust; visual gags, dramatic tension and a poignancy that's almost unbearable at times permeate the film. In answer to critics who accuse him of treating a painful subject with too much levity, Benigni claims that Italian Holocaust survivors are only just beginning to talk about the events of more than fifty years ago and that a film like *La Vita è Bella* is justified if it opens up debate.

Film-makers have found a new assurance, and cinema audiences are flocking to the box office, not least because of the mediocrity (at best) of what's on TV. Benigni's **Pinocchio** (2002) grossed US$7m in its first weekend, a new record at the Italian box office. The story is adapted from the Italian writer Carlo Collodi's 1880 fable and, as he did in **Life is Beautiful**, Benigni doubles as star and director, playing opposite his wife, Braschi, who is the blue-haired fairy. True to the original story, the film is a moral tale in which the puppet who dreams of becoming a real boy has to learn honesty first through a series of adventures. Benigni's film represents a reclaiming of cultural property: Disney reportedly tried to trademark the character Pinocchio, claiming that it was their animation that everyone thought of first when they heard the name, but they lost their claim.

Other directors to have enjoyed success both at home and abroad include **Gabriele Muccino**, whose coming-of-age story **Come te nessuno mai** (**But Forever in My Mind**; 1999) is an interesting take on the US high-school comedy genre; his very Italian students are highly politicized youngsters, planning strikes and taking part in a 24-hour sit-in, both of which provide a backdrop for the inevitable angsting and first love. Muccino's romantic comedy **The Last Kiss** (**L'Ultimo Baccio**; 2001), a film dealing with panic at parenthood and the chasing of vanishing youth, won a flurry of awards and universal approval. He has recently directed a Hollywood movie, **The Pursuit of Happyness** (2006) starring Will Smith. **Ferzan Ozpetek**, a Turk who has lived in Rome for more than twenty years, made a name for himself with **Turkish Bath** (1997) and **Harem Sauré** (1999). His more mainstream film, **Ignorant Fairies** (**Le fate Ignoranti**; 2001), deals with the themes of love, loss and deception wrapped up in a soundtrack of Middle Eastern and Latin music. Commenting on the current changes in Italian film, Ozpetek says, "The public is more demanding now. At the same time, people have become more willing to experiment, to go to see quality Italian films with fully developed stories and interesting characters. Before they would have looked to foreign films for that type of cinema."

An example of one such quality film is **Giuseppe Piccioni**'s **Light of My Eyes** (**Luce Dei Miei Occhi**; 2001). Set in Rome, it's a haunting exploration of the alienation that many feel in their lives and their romantic relationships. The story is particularly strong thanks to the character of Maria, the female lead, free of the usual stereotypes and beautifully acted. **La Sconosciuta** (2006) by Tornature has an equally strong female lead; the story involves an East European prostitute forced to abandon her children as she tries to earn a living in an Italian town.

Many have been looking to Naples and Sicily as the most vibrant sector of the film industry, part of a general resurgence in artistic activity in southern Italy that's connected with a new pride in regional identity. **Vincenzo Marra**'s **Sailing Home** (**Tornando a Casa**; 2001) was made on a shoestring budget: it uses fishermen rather than professional actors, is spoken in Neapolitan dialect (at home it was released with Italian subtitles) and was shot in semi-documentary style. His follow up, **Vento to Terra** (2004), was also shot in Naples, as was **The Session Is Open**, a startling documentary about the trial of a notorious member of the Camorra.

More accessible to an international audience perhaps is Neapolitan director **Antonio Capuano**'s **Luna Rossa** (2001), a mesmerizing portrayal of a Camorra family from the inside, borrowing from Greek tragedy for its structure and with a soundtrack by indie-rockers Almamegretta. Visually rich, brooding, confusing and violent, the film is artistically assured in a way that few others have been in recent years. Another gritty film directed by Capuano's is **Mario's War** (2005), which looks at a well-to-do Neapolitan family who foster a disturbed boy.

Front of house

Film director **Martin Scorsese** has been active in restoring copies of the classic Italian movies and trying to work out a systematic distribution in the US and other English-speaking countries. His aim is to bring a whole new audience to Italian cinema, an aim that his epic documentary **My Voyage in Italy** (**Il Mio Viaggio in Italia**; 2001) supports. Growing up in New York's Little Italy in the 1940s, Scorsese remembers watching the Italian movies of the time with his extended family and neighbours who dropped by. "Italy had just come out of the devastation of World War II," he says "and these films were showing the war's harsh reality with images so intensely moving that my older relatives cried and we kids were overwhelmed." In his "voyage" he takes us through some of these films and in the process the viewer sees three stories unfolding: Scorsese's discovery of his family and his Italian roots, the shaping of his artistic vision, and an overview of some of the classic greats of Italian cinema – a four-hour marathon, and unmissable.

Revitalization has been taking place not just behind the camera, but also in front of the screen, with Rome foremost among Italian cities in wooing the public away from its TV and back into the cinemas. The city's old **cinema halls** of the 1930s, so deeply mourned in films like *Cinema Paradiso* and *Splendor*, are being brought back to life (if they haven't already been pulled down), financed by the film industry itself at the "encouragement" of the city council. New multiscreen complexes have supplemented the historic Pasquino and Nanni Moretti's Nuovo Sacher, and the redtape restricting filming on location in the city has been much reduced. By all accounts this has been a success: in the *Dolce Vita*-era there were three hundred cinema halls in the city – in 2000, this figure was exceeded and other Italian cities are reported to be set to follow the Roman example.

Books

A comprehensive background reading list for Italy would run on for dozens of pages, and would include a vast number of out-of-print (OP) titles. Most of our recommendations are in print, but those that aren't shouldn't be too difficult to track down. The book symbol (⚞) marks titles that are particularly recommended.

Travel and general

Anne Calcagno (ed) *Travelers' Tales: Italy*. Crammed with evocative period detail by the likes of H.V. Morton as well as contemporary writing specifically commissioned for this volume by Tim Parks, Lisa St Aubin de Terán and others, this makes a perfect introduction to the richness and variety of the country. See also *Tuscany: True Stories*, edited by Calcagno and Tara Austen Weaver, with a similar collection.

⚞ **Vincent Cronin** *The Golden Honeycomb*. Disguised as a quest for the mythical golden honeycomb of Daedalus, this is a searching account of a sojourn in Sicily in the 1950s. Although overwritten in parts, it has colourful descriptions of Sicily's art, architecture and folklore.

Charles Dickens *Pictures from Italy*. The classic mid-nineteenth-century Grand Tour, taking in the sights of Emilia, Tuscany, Rome and Naples, in elegant, measured and incisive prose.

⚞ **Norman Douglas** *Old Calabria*. A brilliant travel chronicle based on the author's wanderings around Calabria in the early twentieth century. Wide-ranging and digressive, it's a classic of the genre. See also *Siren Land* (OP) and the novel, *South Wind*, which focus on Cápri and the Bay of Naples.

Johann Wolfgang Von Goethe *Italian Journey*. Surprisingly readable account of a journey all through the peninsula at the end of the eighteenth century, a classic of travel writing and a decisive point in Goethe's own transition from Sturm und Drang to classicism.

Henry James *Italian Hours*. Urbane travel pieces from the young James; perceptive about particular monuments and works of art, superb on the different atmospheres of Italy.

Jonathan Keates *Italian Journeys*. Frank yet affectionate journey through the Italian social, cultural and historical landscape. Full of engaging anecdotes, its witty portraits get under the surface of Italy and its people.

⚞ **D.H. Lawrence** *D.H. Lawrence and Italy*. Lawrence's three Italian travelogues collected into one volume. *Sea and Sardinia* and *Twilight in Italy* combine the author's seemingly natural ill-temper when travelling with a genuine sense of regret for a way of life almost visibly passing away. *Etruscan Places*, published posthumously, consists of his more philosophical musings on Etruscan art and civilization, and remains one of the most illuminating books written on the period.

David Leavitt *Florence, A Delicate Case*. Though a book largely about Florence's expat community over the last 150 years may sound insular and antique, Leavitt injects a good deal of wit and sensitivity into this quirky portrait of Florence. Refreshingly free of cultural overload, the account focuses on the city's more shadowy side – its role as a destination for suicides and taboo-breakers – and there's a flamboyant cast of characters.

Norman Lewis *Naples '44.* Lewis was among the first Allied troops to move into Naples following the Italian surrender in World War II, and this is his diary of his experiences there. Part travelogue, part journalism, this is without question the finest thing you can read on World War II in Italy – and, despite its rather bleak subject matter, among the most entertaining. Lewis's more recent *In Sicily* is a broad contemporary portrait of the island he has married into and returns to frequently. Subjects range from reflections on Palermo's ruined *palazzi* to the impact of immigration, and there's plenty on the Mafia.

Charles Lister *Heel to Toe.* Firmly in the tradition of such English travelwriters as Douglas and Gissing, the author sets off on a bicycle, soon transferring to a moped, for a journey along the Ionian coast from Brindisi to Reggio. Mixing history and culture with strong opinions and copious digression, it's chatty and accessible, if somewhat over-written. In a similar style, Lister's *Between Two Seas* (OP) charts his walk along the Appian Way.

Mary McCarthy *The Stones of Florence/Venice Observed.* A mixture of high-class reporting on the contemporary cities and anecdotal detail on their histories; one of the few accounts of these two cities that doesn't read as if it's been written in a library.

Jan Morris *Venice* (titled *The World of Venice* in US). Some

people think this is the most acute modern book written about any Italian city, while others find it unbearably fey. At least give it a look. The author has more recently published what she claims is her final book, *Trieste and the Meaning of Nowhere*, an aptly elegiac salute to this curious frontier city.

H.V. Morton *A Traveller in Italy; A Traveller in Rome* and *A Traveller in Southern Italy.* Morton's leisurely and amiable books were written in the 1930s, long before modern tourism got into its stride, and their nostalgic charm has a lot to do with their enduring popularity. But they are also packed with learned details and vivid descriptions.

William Murray *Italy: the Fatal Gift* (OP). Murray spent several years in Italy shortly after the last war, and this is a collection of essays inspired by his time there, and many return visits since. Skilfully combining personal anecdote and contemporary Italian history and politics, it's one of the most insightful introductions to the country and its people you can buy.

Eric Newby *Love and War in the Apennines.* An anecdotal, oddly nostalgic account of the sheltering of the author by local people in the mountains of Emilia-Romagna in the closing months of World War II. Newby's *A Small Place in Italy*, recounting his life in a small farmhouse at the foot of the Alps, is equally evocative, and reads much more "authentically" than other expatriates-in-Italy tales.

History, politics and society

The Longman History of Italy This eight-volume series covers the history of Italy from the end of the Roman Empire to the present, each instalment comprising a range of essays on all aspects of political, social, economic and cultural history.

Invaluable if you've developed a special interest in a particular period.

Luigi Barzini *The Italians.* Long the most respected work on the Italian nation, and rightly so.

Barzini leaves no stone unturned in his quest to pinpoint the real Italy.

R.J.B. Bosworth *Mussolini*. This gripping account of modern Italy's most traumatic period paints a vivid picture of *Il Duce*. Achieving great understanding without succumbing to sympathy for the man, Bosworth explains the context of Fascism and examines Mussolini's legacy, warning of the strong fascination for him that still exists in Italy today. The same author's more recent *Mussolini's Italy* brings to life the realities for the Italian people during the same brutal period.

Jerome Carcopino *Daily Life in Ancient Rome*. Detailed but never dull, this is a seminal work of Roman social history, with background on everything from education and religion to domestic daily rituals.

John Cornwell *A Thief in the Night*. An investigation into the death of the "three-day pope", John Paul I, told as a fast-paced detective story. A good read for devotees of conspiracy theory, although more cynical types will probably wonder whether it isn't all a lot of fuss about nothing.

Giovanni Falcone *Men of Honour: The Truth about the Mafia* (OP). The most incisive analysis of the *mafioso* mentality by the investigating magistrate assassinated by the mob in May 1992.

Alan Friedman *Agnelli and the Network of Italian Power* (OP). Agnelli didn't like this book when it came out, and no wonder. Friedman's work was among the first pieces of journalism to pull no punches on the dynastic and anti-democratic power network that is at the heart of Italian society. If you're intrigued by the inertia of Italian postwar politics, it's a must.

Edward Gibbon *The Decline and Fall of the Roman Empire*. Awe-inspiring in its erudition, Gibbon's masterpiece is one of the greatest histories ever written, and one of the finest compositions of English prose. Penguin also publish an abridged version for those without the time to tackle the entire work.

Paul Ginsborg *A History of Contemporary Italy*. A very scholarly but readable account of postwar Italian history, illustrating the complexity of contending economic, social and political currents. Bringing the story up to date, Ginsborg's *Italy and its Discontents* unravels the knotty background to Berlusconi's rise to power and his tussles with the judiciary. It's essential reading for anyone intrigued by the present contradictions of Italian society.

Michael Grant *A History of Rome*. A straightforward and reliable summary of an impossibly complicated story.

Christopher Hibbert *Rome: The Biography of a City*. The history of Italy's capital made easy. As ever, Hibbert is readable and entertaining, but never superficial, providing by far the most comprehensive, yet concise, account of the city through the ages. The companion volumes, *Venice: The Biography of a City* (OP) and *Florence: The Biography of a City*, are particularly good on the changing social fabric in those cities, and have more coverage of the twentieth-century than most; excellent illustrations too. Another foray into an episode of Italian history, Hibbert's *Garibaldi and his Enemies* (OP) is a popular treatment of the life and revolutionary works of Giuseppe Garibaldi, thrillingly detailing the exploits of "The Thousand" in their lightning campaign from Marsala to Milazzo.

Tobias Jones *The Dark Heart of Italy*. Written during a three-year period in Parma, *The Dark Heart of Italy* consists of an interconnected sequence of essays dealing with various aspects of modern Italian society, from the legal and political systems to the media and football. Bewildered and fascinated at every turn, Jones reveals a culture in which evasiveness and ethical malleability are as significant as the much-celebrated virtues of vivacity, charm and sophistication – a culture exemplified above all by the character of Silvio Berlusconi, in effect the owner of the Italian state. An affectionate but clear-eyed corrective to the sentimentalizing claptrap perpetrated by so many English and American expats.

Norman Lewis *The Honoured Society*. Famous account of the Mafia, its origins, personalities and customs. Certainly the most enjoyable intro-duction to the subject available, though much of it is taken up with the story of banditry – really a separate issue – and his lack of accredited sources leaves you wondering how much is conjecture.

Valerio Lintner *A Traveller's History of Italy*. A brief history of the country, from the Etruscans right up to the present day. Well written and sensibly concise, it could be just the thing for the dilettante historian of the country. Lots of tables and chronolo-gies for easy reference.

Patrick McCarthy *The Crisis of the Italian State* (OP). Subtitled *From the Origins of the Cold War to the Fall of Berlusconi and Beyond*, this is a detailed but quite readable analysis of the root causes and major events of the "Clean Hands" political crisis of the Nineties.

John Julius Norwich *The Normans in Sicily*. Accessible, well-researched story of the Normans' explosive entry into the south of Italy and their creation in Sicily of one of the most brilliant medieval European civilizations. Just as stimulating is his *A History of Venice*, the most engrossing treatment of the subject available.

Giuliano Procacci *History of the Italian People*. A comprehensive history of the peninsula, charting the development of Italy as a nation-state.

Uta Ranke-Heinemann *Eunuchs for the Kingdom of Heaven* (OP). Entertaining, erudite and witty critique of the Catholic Church's attitude to sex.

Donald Sassoon *Contemporary Italy*. Slightly academic background on the country and its institutions.

Renate Siebert *Secrets of Life and Death: Women and the Mafia*, translated by Liz Heron. History and analysis of the patriarchal nature of Mafia organizations, which are held to be the apotheosis of the masculine society of Italy's south. Poignant first-person narratives give background to the account, exploding the myth of the Mafia as protecting the weak and defending women, who continue to be used as drug mules and decoys. The author is a German-born professor of sociology at the University of Calabria.

Denis Mack Smith *The Making of Italy 1796–1866*; *Italy and its Monarchy*. The former is an admirably lucid explanation of the various forces at work in the Unification of Italy, while the latter deals with Italy's short-lived monarchy, whose kings ruled the country for less than a century – it reveals Vittorio Emanuele II and co. as a bunch of irresponsible and rather dim buffoons that the country was glad to be rid of. The same author has also written a couple of excellent biographies, *Mazzini* and *Mussolini*.

Claire Sterling *The Mafia*. Thorough piece of Mafia scholarship, showing to a disturbing degree just how little Mafia power has been eroded by the state's onslaught of recent years.

Alexander Stille *Excellent Cadavers*. Stille traces the rise, successes, failures and eventual assassinations of anti-Mafia magistrates Giovanni Falcone and Paolo Borsellino, as well as dishing the dirt on Andreotti and Craxi.

Art, architecture and archeology

Michael Baxandall *Painting and Experience in Fifteenth-Century Italy*. An invaluable analysis, concentrating on the way in which the art of the period would have been perceived at the time.

Anthony Blunt *Artistic Theory in Italy 1450–1600*. A cogent summary of the aesthetic ground rules of Renaissance art, but – contrary to the impression given by the writer's patrician tone – far from the last word. The author's *Roman Baroque* is a broad examination of Rome's Baroque architecture in two volumes.

Jacob Burckhardt *The Civilization of the Renaissance in Italy*. A nineteenth-century classic of Renaissance scholarship.

Robert Etienne *Pompeii, The Day a City Died*. Archeologically and historically rigorous, yet highly accessible, account of the life and death of Pompeii.

J.R. Hale (ed) *Encyclopaedia of the Italian Renaissance*. Exemplary reference book, many of whose summaries are as informative as essays twice their length; covers individual artists, movements, cities, philosophical concepts, the lot.

Frederick Hartt *History of Italian Renaissance Art*. If one book on this vast subject can be said to be indispensable, this is it. In view of its comprehensiveness and acuity, and the range of its illustrations, it's something of a bargain.

Howard Hibbard *Bernini*. A standard overview of the life and work of the central figure of Roman Baroque.

Anthony Hughes *Michelangelo*. Part of the acclaimed Phaidon Art and Ideas series, this is an ideal single-volume introduction to arguably the greatest artist of the Renaissance.

Setting Michelangelo within his historical and political context, Hughes examines his work not only as the expression of an individual sensibility but also in the light of the often fraught relations between artist and patron. An accessible and stimulating read.

Peter Humfrey *Lorenzo Lotto*. A lavishly illustrated, scholarly reappraisal of the Renaissance painter who was a contemporary of Titian and Giorgione.

Ross King *Brunelleschi's Dome*. An intriguing account of the architectural innovations and intense rivalries behind the construction of Florence's duomo. It also paints an engaging picture of life in the medieval city.

Michael Levey *Early Renaissance*. (OP). Precise and fluently written, and well illustrated; probably the best introduction to the subject. Levey's *High Renaissance* (OP) continues the story in the same style.

Peter Murray *The Architecture of the Italian Renaissance*. Begins with Romanesque buildings and finishes with Palladio – valuable both as a gazetteer of the main monuments and as a synopsis of the underlying concepts.

Peter and Linda Murray *Art of the Renaissance*. Serviceable thumbnail sketch, useful for preparing the ground before a trip to Italy.

T.W. Potter *Roman Italy* (OP). A learned illustrated survey of Roman society based on archeological sources. Essential reading if you're interested in the period.

Catherine Puglisi *Caravaggio*. An intelligent and engaging study of one of the most innovative artists of the Renaissance, enhanced with sumptuous colour plates throughout.

Peter Robb *M.* This highly individual biography of Caravaggio – referred to as "M" throughout – tackles one of the most colourful figures of the late Renaissance. It's a passionately partisan and controversial study, with disconcerting inconsistencies of style, but ultimately hugely enjoyable, presenting an engrossing evocation of the period, rent boys and all.

John Shearman *Mannerism* (OP). The self-conscious art of sixteenth-century Mannerism is one of the most complex topics of Renaissance studies; Shearman's brief discussion analyses the main currents, yet never oversimplifies nor becomes pedantic.

Nigel Spivey *Etruscan Art.* An in-depth look at the art of the elusive Etruscans, whose history and lives are told through their tomb art. Sumptuously illustrated throughout, this is an intriguing story of a long lost race.

Giorgio Vasari *Lives of the Artists.* A new abridgement brought out by OUP of the sixteenth-century artist's classic work on his predecessors and contemporaries. Includes essays on Giotto, Brunelleschi, Mantegna, Leonardo, Michelangelo, Raphael and more. The first real work of art history and still among the most penetrating books you can read on Italian Renaissance art. The unabridged version was published in 1996 by Everyman's Library.

Specific guides

Helena Attlee and Alex Ramsay *Italian Gardens.* Evocatively photographed (by Alex Ramsay), this is a guide to more than sixty of the peninsula's most beautiful gardens. Both practical and up to date, the guide provides histories and descriptions, as well as detailed information on locations, facilities, opening times and accessibility.

Amanda Claridge *Oxford Archeological Guides: Rome.* A well-written and excellently conceived concise guide to the ancient city, a good investment if that is your particular area of interest.

Tim Jepson *Wild Italy.* Guide to the flora and fauna of the Italian peninsula by a *Rough Guide* contributor.

Gillian Price *Walking in the Dolomites.* A lively and informative specialized guide to the best walks in the Dolomites. Cicerone also publishes guides to Alta Via 1 & 2 and to various *Vie Ferrate* for more on these peculiarly Italian phenomena).

Victoria Pybus *Live and Work in Italy.* Accessible and informative handbook on all aspects of living and working in Italy, including regional differences.

Ancient literature

Catullus *The Poems of Catullus.* Although his name is associated primarily with the tortured love poems addressed to Lesbia, Catullus also produced some acerbic satirical verse; this collection does full justice to his range.

Cicero *Selected Works.* The rhetorical prose of Cicero was for many Renaissance scholars the paragon of

literary style, and his political ideas provided similarly fertile material for discussion.

Juvenal *The Sixteen Satires.* Savage attacks on the follies and excesses of Rome at the end of the first century and start of the second.

Livy *The Early History of Rome.* Lively chronicle of the city's evolution from the days of Romulus and Remus; Penguin also publishes later installments of those parts of Livy's history that have survived, including the gripping *War with Hannibal*.

Marcus Aurelius *Meditations*. The classic text of Stoic thought, written by one of the few Roman emperors it's easy to admire.

Ovid *Metamorphoses* and *Erotic Poems*. The mythical tales of the Metamorphoses have been so frequently quarried by artists that they can be enjoyed both as literature and as a key to some of the masterworks of Renaissance and later art. His elegiac love poems have a sexual candour that makes them seem almost modern.

Petronius *Satyricon*. Fragmentary, spicy narrative written by one of Nero's inner circle; Fellini's film of the same name gives a pretty accurate idea of the tone.

Plautus *Pot of Gold, and other plays*. The most popular playwright of his time, whose complicated plots provided a model for Renaissance comedies such as *The Comedy of Errors*.

Seneca *Four Tragedies and Octavia*. Violent, fast-paced drama from Nero's one-time tutor; the only plays to have survived from the Roman Empire.

Suetonius *The Twelve Caesars*. The inside story on such vile specimens as Caligula, Nero and Domitian; elegantly written and appalling.

Tacitus *Annals of Imperial Rome*. Covers much of the terrain dealt with by Suetonius, but from the stance of the diligent historian and serious moralist.

Virgil *The Aeneid*. The central work of Latin literature, depicting the adventures of Aeneas after the fall of Troy, and thus celebrating Rome's heroic lineage.

Italian classics

Dante Alighieri *The Divine Comedy*. No work in any other language bears comparison with Dante's poetic exegesis of the moral scheme of God's creation; in late medieval Italy it was venerated both as a book of almost scriptural authority and as the ultimate refinement of the vernacular Tuscan language. A new translation, by Mark Musa, is printed in full in *The Portable Dante*.

Ludovico Ariosto *Orlando Furioso*. Italy's chivalrous epic, set in Charlemagne's Europe; has its exciting moments, but most readers would be grateful for an abridged version. Penguin's verse translation is pacier and more accessible than Oxford's prose version.

Giovanni Boccaccio *The Decameron*. Set in the plague-racked Florence of 1348, this assembly of one hundred short stories is a fascinating social record as well as a constantly diverting comic sequence.

Baldassare Castiglione *The Book of the Courtier*. Written in the form of a series of dialogues held in the court of Urbino, this subtle, entertaining book defines all the qualities essential in the perfect gentleman; the idealistic converse of Machiavelli.

Benvenuto Cellini *Autobiography*. Shamelessly egocentric record of the travails and triumphs of the sculptor and goldsmith's career; one of the freshest literary productions of its time.

Giacomo Leopardi *Leopardi*, tr. Eamon Grennan. Generally considered the greatest Italian poet since Dante, and a formative influence on the poets who followed, Leopardi has never had a big following in the English-speaking world, a situation that may change with this new, gutsy translation by Grennan, an Irish poet, published by Dedalus Press.

Niccolò Machiavelli *The Prince*. A treatise on statecraft which actually did less to form the political thought of Italy than it did to form foreigners' perceptions of the country; there was far more to Machiavelli than the realpolitik of *The Prince*, as is shown by the selection of writings included in the anthology *The Portable Machiavelli*.

Alessandro Manzoni *The Betrothed*. No pool-side thriller, but a skilful melding of the romance of two young lovers and a sweeping historical drama, all suffused with an almost religious sense of human destiny. First published in 1823, but reissued in 1840 after Manzoni had improved the novel's diction through

study of the Tuscan dialect – a landmark in the transition towards linguistic nationalism.

Petrarch (Francesco Petrarca) *Selections from the Canzoniere*. Often described as the first modern poet, by virtue of his preoccupation with worldly fame and secular love, Petrarch wrote some of the Italian language's greatest lyrics. This slim selection at least hints at what is lost in translation.

Marco Polo *Travels*. Buttonholing account of Polo's journey to the court of Kublai Khan, and his seventeen-year stay there; engaging even when the stories are clearly fanciful.

Leonardo da Vinci *Notebooks*. Miscellany of speculation and observation from the universal genius of Renaissance Italy; essential to any understanding of the man.

Modern Italian literature

Giorgio Bassani *The Garden of the Finzi-Continis*. Gentle, elegiac novel, set in the Jewish community of Ferrara during the Fascist period, on the eve of the mass deportations to Germany. Infused with a sense of regret for a Europe that died with the war.

Cinzia Sartini Blum and Lara Trubowitz (eds). *Contemporary Italian Women Poets*. A bilingual selection of 25 very diverse poets working in the last half-century. Among the selections is verse by Dacia Maraini and Mariella Bettarini.

Enrico Brizzi *Jack Frusciante has Left the Band*. Pacy, unrequited-love story set in Bologna. Rebellious Alex D endures life with his parents (whom he calls Matron and The Chancellor) while not getting anywhere with his girlfriend, the enigmatic but totally insecure Aidi. Some great descriptions of the overpowering pressure to conform in an Italian provincial

town, the book is also memorably poignant at times.

Gesualdo Bufalino *The Keeper of Ruins* (OP); *The Plague Sower; Blind Argus* (OP) and *Night's Lies*. One of Sicily's most esteemed twentieth-century writers, Bufalino arrived late on the literary scene, publishing his first novel, *The Plague Sower*, when he was into his 60s. Most of his output has now been translated.

Aldo Busi *Seminar on Youth* (OP); *Standard Life of a Temporary Panty-Hose Salesman* and *Sodomies in Eleven Point*. Busi is something of an *enfant terrible* in the Italian literary world, but his tales of gay escapades around northern Italy go beyond the mere showy; indeed his somewhat impenetrable style masks a humanity and wit that is rare in much recent Italian fiction.

Ann and Michael Caesars (eds) *The Quality of Light*. Anthology of contemporary Italian writers, including work by Primo Levi and Gianni Celati, as well as many other less well-known writers like the starkly realistic Pier Vittorio Tondelli.

Italo Calvino *If on a Winter's Night a Traveller*. Calvino's fiction became increasingly concerned with the nature of fiction itself, and this involuted, witty novel marks the culmination of the process. Other titles include *The Castle of Crossed Destinies, Invisible Cities, Difficult Loves* and *Mr Palomar*.

Gianni Celati *Voices from the Plains*. Chance encounters on a walk down the Po provide the focus for these atmospheric tales. The four under-stated novellas in *Appearances* pay similarly close attention to the specific locales of Emilia-Romagna.

Gabriele D'Annunzio *Halcyon*. Self-regarding dandy, war hero and worshipper of Mussolini, D'Annunzio was perhaps the most complex figure of twentieth-century Italian literature; this extended lyric sequence – a troubled idyll set on the Tuscan coast – contains much of his finest poetry.

Umberto Eco *The Name of the Rose*. An allusive, tightly plotted monastic detective story. Check out also his equally hyped, though rather more impenetrable, *Foucault's Pendulum* and the allegorical *Island of the Day Before*. His most recent work, *Baudolino*, is another medieval fable, this time interspersed with reflections on the postmodern age.

Dario Fo *Plays I*. This collection includes a trio of Fo's most famous plays – *Mistero Buffo, Accidental Death of an Anarchist* and *Trumpets and Raspberries* – along with two previously unpublished short works. The Nobel Prize winner fabulously weaves together contemporary politics, surreal farce and the traditions of *commedia dell'arte*.

Carlo Emilio Gadda *That Awful Mess on Via Merulana* (OP). Superficially a detective story, this celebrated modernist novel is so dense a weave of physical reality and literary diversions that the reader is led away from a solution rather than towards it; it enjoys the sort of status in Italian fiction that *Ulysses* has in English.

Natalia Ginzburg *The Things We Used to Say*. The constraints of family life are a dominant theme in Ginzburg's writing, and her own upbringing is the source material for this characteristically rigorous yet lyrical work.

Giuseppe di Lampedusa *The Leopard*. The most famous Sicilian novel, written after the war but recounting the dramatic nineteenth-century transition from Bourbon to Piemontese rule from an aristocrat's point of view. A good character-study and rich with incidental detail, including some nice description of the Sicilian landscape.

Carlo Levi *Christ Stopped at Eboli*. First published in 1945, this memoir, describing Levi's exile to a remote region of Basilicata by the Fascists, was the first to awaken modern Italy to the plight of its southern regions.

Primo Levi *If This is a Man/ The Truce; The Periodic Table*. Levi's experiences in Auschwitz are the main subject of *If This is a Man*, while *The Truce* records his eight-month journey back to Turin after his liberation. Levi's training as a chemist forms the background of *Periodic Table*, a mixture of autobiographical reflections and practical observations. The amorality of the Third Reich and its repercussions are the recurrent subjects of Levi's later works, all of which show an unwavering exactitude of recollection and judgement.

Elsa Morante *History*. Capturing daily Roman life during the last war, this is probably the most vivid fictional picture of the conflict as seen from the city.

Alberto Moravia *Roman Tales* (OP). A collection of stories, first published in the Fifties, which show the underbelly of a rapidly changing city; it is evocative of both the city and its people. *The Conformist* is a psychological novel about a man sucked into the abyss of Fascism by his desperation to conform; *The Woman of Rome* is an earlier work, a teeming and sensual novel, centred on the activities of a Roman prostitute.

Pier Paolo Pasolini *A Violent Life*. Pasolini's writing is preoccupied with the demise of local, dialect-based cultures of agrarian Italy in the face of modernization. His supernaturalistic evocation of life in the slum areas of Rome caused a scandal when it was published in 1959, but is now considered one of the classics of Italian postwar fiction. See also the collection of short stories, *Roman Nights and Other Stories*, (OP) and *A Dream of Something* (OP) – Pasolini's pastoral tale of growing up in Friuli in the late Forties.

Cesare Pavese *Moon and the Bonfire*; *Devil in the Hills*. Exploring the difficulties of achieving an acceptance of one's past, *Moon and the Bonfire* was written shortly before Pavese's suicide at the age of 42; *Devil in the Hills* is an early collection of tales of adolescence in and around Turin.

Luigi Pirandello *Six Characters in Search of an Author*; *The Late Mattia Pascal* and *Eleven Short Stories*. His most famous and accomplished work, *Six Characters…*, written in 1921, contains many of the themes that dogged Pirandello throughout his writing career – the idea of a multiple personality and the quality of reality. *The Late Mattia Pascal* is an early novel (1904), entertainingly written despite its stylistic shortcomings; while the collection of short

stories is perhaps the best introduction to Pirandello's work.

Umberto Saba *Ernesto* (OP). A lyrical autobiographical novel by the Triestine poet, recollecting youth and homosexuality. Marvellous translation.

Leonardo Sciascia *Sicilian Uncles*; *The Wine Dark Sea*; *Candido* (OP) and *The Day of the Owl*. Writing again and again about his native Sicily, Sciascia has made of that island "a metaphor of the modern world". Economically written, Sciascia's short stories are packed with incisive insights, and infused with the author's humane and sympathetic views of its people. *The Moro Affair* is an illuminating account of the kidnapping of the ex-prime minister Aldo Moro by the Brigate Rosse in 1978.

Ignazio Silone *Fontamara*; *Bread and Wine*. From his exile in Switzerland, Silone wrote about his native Abruzzo, and about the struggle for social justice. *Fontamara* tells the tale of a small village driven to revolt against its landlords and the Fascist thugs sent to enforce their rule; *Bread and Wine*, a more introspective work, examines the parallels between Silone's political commitment and religious belief. The two works, together with *The Seed Beneath the Snow*, are published in one volume by Steerforth Press, titled *The Abruzzo Trilogy*.

Italo Svevo *Confessions of Zeno*. Complete critical indifference to his early efforts so discouraged Svevo that he gave up writing altogether, until encouraged by James Joyce, who taught him English in Trieste. The resultant novel is a unique creation, a comic portrait of a character at once wistful, helpless and irrepressible.

Giovanni Verga *Little Novels of Sicily* (*Sicilian Stories* in US); *Cavalleria*

Rusticana and *I Malavoglia, or The House by the Medlar Tree*. Verga, born in the nineteenth century in Catania, spent several years in various European salons before coming home to write his best work. Much of it is a reaction against the pseudo-sophistication of society circles, stressing the simple lives of ordinary people, though sometimes accompanied by a heavy smattering of "peasant passion", with much emotion, wounded honour and feuds to the death.

Elio Vittorini *Conversations in Sicily*. A Sicilian emigrant returns from the north of Italy after fifteen years to see his mother on her birthday. The conversations of the title are with the people he meets on the way, local villagers and his mother, and reveal a poverty- and disease-ridden Sicily, though the scenes are affectionately drawn. In the US, New Directions publishes an excellent anthology of his writings, *A Vittorini Omnibus*.

William Weaver (ed) *Open City: Seven Writers in Postwar Rome*. A nicely produced anthology of pieces by the cream of Italy's twentieth-century novelists – Bassani, Silone, Ginzburg, Moravia, among others – selected and with an introduction by one of the most eminent Italian translators of recent years.

An Italian miscellany

Lindsey Davis *Venus in Copper, The Jupiter Myth* and others. These crime novels set in the age of the Emperor Vespasian are shot through with sparkling comedy, and follow super-sleuth Marcus Didius Falco as he unpicks mysteries and dastardly doings. An omnibus containing three tales is also available: *Falco on his Metal*.

Michael Dibdin *Ratking, Vendetta, Cabal, Dead Lagoon*. Dibdin's Aurelio Zen is a classically eccentric loner detective, and this is a classic series of well-plotted detective yarns. However, Dibdin is as interested in the country as he is in his characters, and these novels tell us plenty about the way Italian society operates. Among the most recent in the series are *Cosi Fan Tutti*, set in Naples; *A Long Finish*, in which Zen is sent to Piemonte on the trail of the murderer of a noted wine-maker; and *Blood Rain*, set in Catania, with more of his own personal life revealed along the way. A supremely palatable way to read about Italy and Italians.

E.M. Forster *A Room with a View*. Set in and around Florence, this is the ultimate novel about how the nature of the Italian light, temperament and soul can make the English upper classes lose their heads.

Marius Gabriel *House of Many Rooms*. Psychological thriller and study of human relationships set in San Francisco and Italy.

Robert Graves *I Claudius* and *Claudius the God*. The classic book (and television serial) on the Imperial Caesars, from Augustus to Claudius. Having translated Suetonius' *Twelve Caesars*, Graves used the madness and corruption of the Imperial Age to create a gripping, if not necessarily historically accurate, tale. His *Count Belsarius* does the same for Roman Empire of the sixth century.

Annie Hawes *Extra Virgin*. Belonging to the Mayes/Mayle school of expats setting up in sunny rural climes, but superior to most of the genre in every way, this relates how two sisters overcome various adversities and much local incomprehension to find their idyll on a Ligurian mountain. It's funny and smart, interspersed with plenty of culinary culture and peasant lore.

Nathaniel Hawthorne *The Marble Faun.* A nineteenth-century take on the lives of Anglo-American expats in the Eternal City – sculptors, passionate lovers, devotees of Classical Purity – the usual mad mix and excessive goings-on that you'll still find today.

Ernest Hemingway *A Farewell To Arms.* Hemingway's first novel is partly based on his experiences as a teenage ambulance driver on Italy's northeast front during World War I – a terse account of the futility of this particular corner of the conflict.

Patricia Highsmith *The Talented Mr Ripley.* The novel follows the fortunes of the eponymous hero through Italy as he exchanges his own identity for that of the man he has murdered. Recently released as a movie, starring Gwyneth Paltrow and directed by Anthony Minghella.

Tom Holland *Rubicon.* An introduction to the Roman Republic from its founding to its demise (and that of Augustus). Its vivid descriptions put the flesh on the bones of this period of history.

Donna Leon *Death at La Fenice, A Venetian Reckoning, Fatal Remedies* and others. Venice-based crime thrillers featuring Guido Brunetti, the honest police commissario in a world of high-level intrigue and corruption. Public scandals and Brunetti's private life are absorbingly interwoven, and these atmospheric tales usually work on several different levels.

Thomas Mann *Death in Venice.* Irascible and ultra-traditional old novelist visits Venice to recover after a breakdown and becomes obsessed with a beautiful young boy, awakening an internal debate about the nature of beauty and art to which the city is a fitting and resonant backdrop.

Allan Massie *Augustus, Tiberius, Caesar.* A trilogy of novels that tells the stories of the three emperors as if they were recently discovered autobiographies. Massie's historical precision and careful dramatization hold up well.

Frances Mayes *Under the Tuscan Sun, Bella Tuscany.* Follow the trials and triumphs of American author and boyfriend as they renovate a farmhouse near Cortona, interspersed with recipes. The echoes of Peter Mayle in Provence will put many off.

Ian McEwan *The Comfort of Strangers.* An ordinary young English couple fall foul of a sexually ambiguous predator in a Venice which is never named, but evoked by means of arch little devices such as quotes from Ruskin.

John Mortimer *Summer's Lease.* The chattering classes revel in Chianti-shire. Not exactly profound, but hugely entertaining.

Magdalen Nabb *Death in Springtime* (OP), *Death in Autumn* and many other titles. Thrillers that make the most of their settings in low-life Florence and the wild Sardinian hills where shepherds dabble in a spot of kidnapping.

Michael Ondaatje *The English Patient.* The novel that inspired the Anthony Minghella film starring Juliette Binoche and Ralph Fiennes. A nurse cares for her patient, burnt beyond recognition, in an abandoned Italian monastery during World War II as his true identity, and the story of the passionate but doomed affair he has survived, are uncovered.

Tim Parks *Italian Neighbours, An Italian Education, Europa* and *A Season with Verona.* Novelist Tim Parks has lived in Italy since 1981. Through deftly told tales of family life, his books examine what it means to be Italian, and how national identity is absorbed. *Europa* is a bawdy, savage tale of love gone wrong, set among a group of academics travelling to lobby the European Parliament in Strasbourg, while *A Season with Verona* relates his passion for his local football team, but drawing in much more besides.

Daphne Phelps *A House in Sicily*. An Englishwoman inherits a villa in Taormina and turns it into a guesthouse to make ends meet. This allows vignettes of eminent guests – Bertrand Russell, Tennessee Williams, Roald Dahl – as well as of the locals, though her anglocentric and patronizing take on some of these, including the local Mafia don, grate.

Peter Robb *Midnight in Sicily*. The Australian Robb spent fifteen years in the Italian south tracing the contorted relations between organized crime and politics. Here, he focuses on the structure of the Mafia, the trials of the bosses in the 1980s, the high-profile assassinations that ensued, and the trial of Andreotti. It's a thorough, fast-paced study, providing deep insights into the dynamics of Sicilian society and an authentic portrait of Palermo.

Susan Sontag *The Volcano Lover*. A profound and surprising novel, based on the notorious affair between Nelson and Lady Hamilton, wife of the volcano-fixated English ambassador to Naples. The self-absorbed protagonists indulge their various obsessions – romantic and geological – as Vesuvius smoulders in the background and the Bourbon court wallows in dissolution and incompetence. An absolute must-read for visitors to Naples.

Stendhal *The Charterhouse of Parma*. Panoramic nineteenth-century French novel that dramatizes the struggles and intrigues of the Italian papal states before Unification. A wonderful read, and a good insight into the era to boot.

Irving Stone *The Agony and the Ecstasy*. Stone's dramatized life of Van Gogh is well known, filmed with a memorably angst-ridden Kirk Douglas in the title role. Here Stone gives the same treatment to Michelangelo, popular "faction" that is entertaining even if it doesn't exactly get to the root of the artist's work and times.

Lowri Turner *Gianni Versace: Fashion's Last Emperor*. Fashion editor Turner's "photo-biography" of the late designer suggests that Versace and the man who allegedly gunned him down were murdered by the Mafia. A strange mix of reportage, interspersed with ninety colour photographs of supermodels and Versace's own glamorous homes.

Barry Unsworth *After Hannibal* and *Stone Virgin*. The author lives in Umbria, where the former novel is set. *After Hannibal* is a black comedy of expat life, where a diverse cast of characters in the process of being betrayed each confide in the same local lawyer. The earlier *Stone Virgin*, set in Venice, is about a conservation expert who falls under the spell of a statue of the Madonna he is working on – and of a member of the family who owns it.

Roger Vailland *The Law*. This evocation of life in a small Pugliese town, of its people, etiquette and harsh tradition, is tight, considered and utterly convincing.

Salley Vickers *Miss Garnet's Angel*. The unique atmosphere of Venice is captured in this tale of a desiccated spinster awakened by the city to the finer things in life. The author's sound knowledge of the place and its art triumphs over a potentially hackneyed tale.

Edith Wharton *Roman Fever and Other Stories*. The title story of this collection recounts two old women's stingingly bitchy reminiscences about their adolescence in Rome.

Thornton Wilder *The Ides of March*
(OP). A suppositional reconstruction
of the last year of the life of Julius
Caesar through his letters, writings
and reports. A brilliant portrayal of the
burdens and isolation of leadership.

Jeanette Winterson *The Passion*.
Whimsical tale of the intertwined
lives of a member of Napoleon's
catering corps and a female
gondolier.

Food and drink

Burton Anderson *Wines of Italy*
and *Best Italian Wines*. The first is an
excellent pocket guide to the
regional wines and winemaking
techniques of Italy, the second an in-
depth look at the top two hundred
wines.

Antonio Carluccio *Carluccio's
Complete Italian Food*. Based on the
BBC TV series. Carluccio's passion
for food goes right back to basics; his
message is that a meal – however
humble or grand – is only as good as
the land or sea from which its ingredients come.

Elizabeth David *Italian Food*. The
writer who introduced Italian cuisine
– and ingredients – to Britain. Ahead
of its time when it was published in
the Fifties, and imbued with all the
enthusiasm and diversity of Italian
cookery. An inspirational book.

Patience Gray *Honey from a Weed*.
The author lived and worked in basic
conditions in various Mediterranean
countries, and in this intriguing
blend of cookbook and autobiography she describes roughing it and
cooking it.

Valentina Harris *Italia! Italia!*; *A
Passion for the Real Food of Italy*. All
the classics, pizzas and pastas, with
regional recipes and anecdotes from
local and regional tradiitions.

Marcella Hazan *The Classic
Italian Cookbook* (OP) and
Marcella Cucina. The best Italian
cookbook for the novice in the

kitchen, *The Classic Italian Cookbook*
is a step-by-step guide that never
compromises the spirit or authenticity of Hazan's subject. She draws
her recipes from all over the
peninsula, emphasizing the intrinsically regional nature of Italian food.
Her latest, the fully illustrated
Marcella Cucina, combines regional
dishes and anecdotes.

Fred Plotkin *Italy for the Gourmet
Traveller*. Comprehensive, region-by-
region guide to the best of Italian
cuisine, with a foodie's guide to
major towns and cities, a gazetteer of
restaurants and specialist food and
wine shops, and descriptions of local
dishes, with recipes.

Claudia Roden *The Food of
Italy*. A culinary classic, this
regional guide takes in local recipes
from the people for whom they are
second nature. Authentic and
accessible.

Arthur Schwartz *Naples at Table*.
Simple, authentic recipes from
Campania, all lavishly photographed.
There's impressive attention to detail
and care for local traditions, accom-
panied by entertaining commentary.

Mary Taylor Simeti *Sicilian Food*.
Starting with the oldest and most
elemental components of the Sicilian
diet, this book offers a collection of
recipes and evocations of the dishes'
origins: from the culinary innova-
tions of Arab and Norman invaders
to the ritual luxuries of Sicily's
aristocracy.

Language

Language

Italian

T he ability to speak English confers prestige in Italy, and there's often no shortage of people willing to show off their knowledge, especially in Rome. But using at least some Italian, however tentatively, can mark you out from the masses in a country used to hordes of tourists. The words and phrases below should help you master the basics. If you want a decent phrasebook, look no further than the *Rough Guide Italian Phrasebook*, which packs a huge amount of phrases and vocabulary into a handy dictionary format. There are lots of good pocket dictionaries – the Collins range represents probably the best all-round choice, with their Gem or Pocket formats perfect for travelling purposes.

Pronunciation

Italian is one of the easiest European languages to learn, especially if you already have a smattering of French or Spanish. Easiest of all is the **pronunciation**, since every word is spoken exactly as it's written, and is usually enunciated with exaggerated, open-mouthed clarity. All Italian words are stressed on the penultimate syllable unless an accent (´ or `) denotes otherwise.

The only difficulties you're likely to encounter are the few consonants that are different from English:

c before e or i is pronounced as in church, while **ch** before the same vowels is hard, as in cat.

sci or **sce** are pronounced as in sheet and shelter respectively.

The same goes with **g** – soft before e or i, as in geranium; hard before h, as in garlic.

gn has the ni sound of onion.

gl in Italian is softened to something like li in English, as in stallion.

h is not aspirated, as in honour.

When **speaking** to strangers, the third person is the polite form (ie lei instead of tu for "you"); using the second person is a mark of disrespect or stupidity. It's also worth remembering that Italians don't use "please" and "thank you" half as much as we do: it's all implied in the tone, though, if in doubt, err on the polite side.

Words and phrases

Basics

Buon giorno	Good morning	**Arrivederci**	Goodbye
Buona sera	Good afternoon/ evening	**Si**	Yes
		No	No
Buona notte	Good night	**Per favore**	Please
Ciao (informal; to strangers use phrases above)	Hello/goodbye	**Grázie (molte/mille grazie)**	Thank you (very much)

Prego	You're welcome
Va bene	All right/that's OK
Come stai/sta? (informal/formal)	How are you?
Bene	I'm fine
Parla inglese?	Do you speak English?
Non ho capito	I don't understand
Non lo so	I don't know
Mi scusi	Excuse me
Permesso (in a crowd)	Excuse me
Mi dispiace	I'm sorry
Sono qui in vacanza	I'm here on holiday
Sono inglese/ irlandese/scozzese	I'm English/Irish/ Scottish
americano/a	American
australiano/a	Australian
neozelandese/a	a New Zealander
Oggi	Today
Domani	Tomorrow
Dopodomani	Day after tomorrow
Ieri	Yesterday
Adesso	Now
Più tardi	Later
Aspetta!	Wait a minute!
Andiamo!	Let's go!
Di mattina	In the morning
Nel pomeriggio	In the afternoon
Di sera	In the evening
Qui/Là	Here/There
Buono/Cattivo	Good/Bad
Grande/Píccolo	Big/Small
Economico/Caro	Cheap/Expensive
Presto/Tardi	Early/Late
Caldo/Freddo	Hot/Cold
Vicino/Lontano	Near/Far
Velocemente/ Lentamente	Quickly/Slowly
Con/Senza	With/Without
Più/Meno	More/Less
Basta	Enough, no more
Signor/Signora/ Signorina	Mr/Mrs/Miss
Entrata/Uscita	Entrance/Exit
Ingresso líbero	Free entrance
Signori/Signore	Gentlemen/Ladies
Vietato fumare	No smoking
Gabinetto/Bagno	WC/Bathroom
Aperto/Chiuso	Open/Closed
Chiuso per restauro	Closed for restoration
Chiuso per ferie	Closed for holidays
Tirare/Spingere	Pull/Push
Cassa	Cash desk
Avanti	Go, walk
Alt	Stop, halt

Accommodation

Albergo	Hotel
C'è un albergo qui vicino?	Is there a hotel nearby?
Ha una cámera ...	Do you have a room ...
per una/due/tre persona/e	for one/two/three person/people
per una/due/ tre notteli	for one/two/three night/s
per una/due settimana/e	for one/two week/s
con un letto matrimoniale	with a double bed
con una doccia/ un bagno	with a shower/bath
con balcone	with a balcony
acqua calda/fredda	hot/cold water
Quanto costa?	How much is it?
È caro	It's expensive
È compresa la prima colazione?	Is breakfast included?
Ha qualcosa che costa di meno?	Do you have anything cheaper?
Pensione completa/ mezza pensione	Full/half board
Posso vedere la camera?	Can I see the room?
La prendo	I'll take it
Vorrei prenotare una camera	I'd like to book a room
Ho una prenotazione	I have a booking

Questions and directions

Dove?	Where?	Quant'è lontano a ...?	How far is it to ...?
(Dov'è/Dove sono ...?)	(Where is/Where are ...?)	Mi può dire dove scendere?	Can you tell me when to get off?
Quando?	When?	A che ora apre?	What time does it open?
Cosa? (Cos'è?)	What? (What is it?)		
Quanto/Quanti?	How much/many?	A che ora chiude?	What time does it close?
Perché?	Why?		
C'e ...?	It is/There is (Is it/Is there ...?)	Quanto costa? (Quanto cóstano?)	How much does it cost (do they cost?)
Che ore sono?	What time is it?	Come si chiama in italiano?	What's it called in Italian?
Per arrivare a ...?	How do I get to ...?		

Numbers

uno	1	venti	20
due	2	ventuno	21
tre	3	ventidue	22
quattro	4	trenta	30
cinque	5	quaranta	40
sei	6	cinquanta	50
sette	7	sessanta	60
otto	8	settanta	70
nove	9	ottanta	80
dieci	10	novanta	90
undici	11	cento	100
dodici	12	centuno	101
tredici	13	centodieci	110
quattordici	14	duecento	200
quindici	15	cinquecento	500
sedici	16	mille	1000
diciassette	17	cinquemila	5000
diciotto	18	diecimila	10000
diciannove	19	cinquantamila	50000

Food and drink

Il conto per favore?	The bill please?

Basics and snacks

Aceto	Vinegar	Burro	Butter
Aglio	Garlic	Caramelle	Sweets
Biscotti	Biscuits	Cioccolato	Chocolate

Formaggio	Cheese		Riso	Rice
Frittata	Omelette		Sale	Salt
Marmellata	Jam		Uova	Eggs
Olio	Oil		Yogurt	Yoghurt
Olive	Olives		Zucchero	Sugar
Pane	Bread		Zuppa	Soup
Pepe	Pepper			

The first course (il primo)

Brodo	Clear broth
Minestrina	Clear broth with small pasta shapes
Minestrone	Thick vegetable soup
Pasta al forno	Pasta baked with minced meat, eggs, tomato and cheese
Pasta e fagioli	Pasta with beans
Pastina in brodo	Pasta pieces in clear broth
Risotto	Cooked rice dish, with sauce
Stracciatella	Broth with egg

Pasta...

Bucatini Thick, hollow spaghetti-type pasta common in Rome and Lazio.

Cannelloni Thick pasta tubes usually filled with veal.

Capellini Thin noodles of pasta, thicker than *capelli d'angeli*.

Conchigliette Small shell-like shapes often used in soup.

Conchiglie Seashell-shaped pasta shapes, good for capturing thick sauces.

Farfalle Literally "butterflies", or bow ties.

Fettucini Flat ribbon egg noodles.

Fusilli Tight spirals of pasta.

Gnocchi Potato and pasta dumplings, often served "*alla Sorrentina*" or with tomato and basil sauce.

Lasagne Big squares of egg noodles, most commonly baked in the oven with white sauce and beef *ragú*.

Linguini Thin flat noodles, often served with seafood.

Macaroni Small tubes of pasta.

Maltagliati Flat triangles of pasta, often used in soup.

Orecchiette Small ear-shaped pieces of pasta.

Paccheri Large tubes of pasta.

Panzarotti Filled pasta shapes from Puglia.

Pappardelle Thick flat egg noodles.

Penne The most common tubes of pasta.

Penne rigate Ridged tubes of pasta – less common than regular *penne*.

Pennette Small *penne*.

Pici Thick Tuscan spaghetti.

Ravioli Literally "little turnips" – flat, square parcels of filled pasta.

Rigatoni Large, curved and ridged tubes of pasta – larger than *penne* but smaller than *paccheri*.

Spaghetti The most common pasta shape of all – long, thin, non-egg noodles.

Spaghettini Thin spaghetti.

Tagliatelle Flat ribbon egg noodles, slightly thinner than *fettucini*.

Tonnarelli Another name for bucatini.

Tortellini/Tortolloni Big and small rectanglar parcels of filled pasta.

Tortiglioni Narrow *rigatoni*.

Trenne Triangle-shaped *penne*.

Trennette Smaller *trenne*.

For more pasta types, see the Italian food colour section.

... and pasta sauce (salsa)

Amatriciana Cubed bacon and tomato sauce

Arrabbiata Spicy tomato sauce, with chillies ("Angry")

Bolognese Meat sauce

Burro Butter

Carbonara Cream, ham and beaten egg

Funghi Mushroom

Panna Cream

L

LANGUAGE | Food and drink

Parmigiano Parmesan cheese
Peperoncino Olive oil, garlic and fresh chillies
Pesto Sauce with ground basil, garlic and
  pine nuts
Pomodoro Tomato sauce

Puttanesca Tomato, anchovy, olive oil and
  oregano ("Whorish")
Ragù Meat sauce
Vongole Sauce with clams

The second course (il secondo)

meat (carne) ...

Agnello	Lamb
Bistecca	Steak
Carpaccio	Slices of raw beef
Cervello	Brain, usually calves'
Cinghiale	Wild boar
Coniglio	Rabbit
Costolette	Cutlet, chop
Fegato	Liver
Maiale	Pork
Manzo	Beef
Ossobuco	Shin of veal
Pancetta	Bacon
Pollo	Chicken
Polpette	Meatballs
Rognoni	Kidneys
Salsiccia	Sausage
Saltimbocca	Veal with ham
Spezzatino	Stew
Trippa	Tripe
Vitello	Veal

... fish (pesce) and shellfish (crostacei)

Acciughe	Anchovies
Anguilla	Eel
Aragosta	Lobster
Baccalà	Dried salted cod
Calamari	Squid
Cefalo	Grey mullet
Cozze	Mussels
Dentice	Sea bream
Gamberetti	Shrimps
Gamberi	Prawns
Granchio	Crab
Merluzzo	Cod
Ostriche	Oysters
Pesce spada	Swordfish
Polpo	Octopus
Rospo	Monkfish
Sampiero	John Dory
Sarde	Sardines
Sogliola	Sole
Tonno	Tuna
Trota	Trout
Vongole	Clams

Vegetables (contorni) and salad (insalata)

Asparagi	Asparagus	Funghi	Mushrooms
Carciofi	Artichokes	Insalata verde/mista	Green salad/mixed salad
Carciofini	Artichoke hearts		
Cavolfiori	Cauliflower	Lenticchie	Lentils
Cavolo	Cabbage	Melanzane	Aubergine
Cipolla	Onion	Patate	Potatoes
Erbe aromatiche	Herbs	Peperoni	Peppers
Fagioli	Beans	Piselli	Peas
Fagiolini	Green beans	Pomodori	Tomatoes
Finocchio	Fennel	Radicchio	Red salad leaves
		Spinaci	Spinach

Some terms and useful words

Al dente	Firm, not overcooked	Ben cotto	Well done
Al ferri	Grilled without oil	Bollito/lesso	Boiled
Al forno	Baked	Cotto	Cooked (not raw)
Al sangue	Rare	Crudo	Raw
Alla brace	Barbecued	Fritto	Fried
Alla griglia	Grilled	In umido	Stewed
Alla milanese	Fried in egg and breadcrumbs	Pizzaiola	Cooked with tomato sauce
Allo spiedo	On the spit	Ripieno	Stuffed
Arrosto	Roast	Stracotto	Braised, stewed

Cheese (formaggi)

Dolcelatte	Creamy blue cheese	Pecorino	Strong, hard sheep's cheese
Fontina	Northern Italian cheese, often used in cooking	Provola/Provolone	Smooth, round mild cheese, made from buffalo or sheep's milk; sometimes smoked
Gorgonzola	Soft, strong, blue-veined cheese		
Mozzarella	Soft white cheese, traditionally made from buffalo's milk	Ricotta	Soft, white sheep's cheese

Sweets (dolci), fruit (frutta) and nuts (noci)

Amaretti	Macaroons	Mandorle	Almonds
Ananas	Pineapple	Mele	Apples
Anguria/Coccomero	Watermelon	Melone	Melon
Arance	Oranges	Pere	Pears
Banane	Bananas	Pesche	Peaches
Cacchi	Persimmons	Pinoli	Pine nuts
Ciliegie	Cherries	Pistacchio	Pistachio nut
Fichi	Figs	Torta	Cake, tart
Fichi d'India	Prickly pears	Uva	Grapes
Fragole	Strawberries	Zabaglione	Dessert made with eggs, sugar and marsala wine
Gelato	Ice cream		
Limone	Lemon		
Macedonia	Fruit salad	Zuppa Inglese	Trifle

Drinks

Acqua minerale	Mineral water	Caffè	Coffee
Aranciata	Orangeade	Cioccolata calda	Hot chocolate
Bicchiere	Glass	Ghiaccio	Ice
Birra	Beer	Granita	Iced drink, with coffee or fruit
Bottiglia	Bottle		

Latte	Milk	Rosso	Red
Limonata	Lemonade	Bianco	White
Selz	Soda water	Rosato	Rosé
Spremuta	Fresh fruit juice	Secco	Dry
Spumante	Sparkling wine	Dolce	Sweet
Succo	Concentrated fruit juice with sugar	Litro	Litre
		Mezzo	Half
Tè	Tea	Quarto	Quarter
Tonica	Tonic water	Caraffa	Carafe
Vino	Wine	Salute!	Cheers!

Glossary of artistic and architectural terms

agora Square or marketplace in an ancient Greek city.

ambo A kind of simple pulpit, popular in Italian medieval churches.

apse Semicircular recess at the altar (usually eastern) end of a church.

architrave The lowest part of the entablature.

atrium Inner courtyard.

baldachino A canopy on columns, usually placed over the altar in a church.

basilica Originally a Roman administrative building, adapted for early churches; distinguished by lack of transepts.

belvedere A terrace or lookout point.

caldarium The steam room of a Roman bath.

campanile Belltower, sometimes detached, usually of a church.

capital Top of a column.

catalan-gothic Hybrid form of architecture, mixing elements of fifteenth-century Spanish and northern European styles.

cella Sanctuary of a temple.

chancel Part of a church containing the altar.

chiaroscuro The balance of light and shade in a painting, and the skill of the artist in depicting the contrast between the two.

ciborium Another word for baldachino, see above.

cornice The top section of a classical facade.

cortile Galleried courtyard or cloisters.

cosmati work Decorative mosaic work on marble, usually highly coloured, found in early Christian Italian churches, especially in Rome. Derives from the name Cosma, a common name among families of marble workers at the time.

crypt Burial place in a church, usually under the choir.

cryptoporticus Underground passageway.

cyclopean walls Fortifications built of huge, rough stone blocks, common in the pre-Roman settlements of Lazio.

decumanus maximus The main street of a Roman town. The second cross-street was known as the Decumanus Inferiore.

entablature The section above the capital on a classical building, below the cornice.

ex voto Artefact designed in thanksgiving to a saint. The adjective is ex votive.

fresco Wall-painting technique in which the artist applies paint to wet plaster for a more permanent finish.

loggia Roofed gallery or balcony.

metope A panel on the frieze of a Greek temple.

mithraism Pre-Christian cult associated with the Persian god of Light, who slew a bull and fertilized the world with its blood.

nave Central space in a church, usually flanked by aisles.

pantocrator Usually refers to an image of Christ, portrayed with outstretched arms.

piano nobile Main floor of a palace, usually the first.

polyptych Painting on several joined wooden panels.

portico Covered entrance to a building, or porch.

presepio A Christmas crib.

putti Cherubs.

reliquary Receptacle for a saint's relics, usually bones. Often highly decorated.

sgraffito Decorative technique whereby one layer of plaster is scratched to form a pattern. Popular in sixteenth-century Italy.

stereobate Visible base of any building, usually a Greek temple.

stucco Plaster made from water, lime, sand and powdered marble, used for decorative work.

thermae Baths, usually elaborate buildings in Roman villas.

triptych Painting on three joined wooden panels.

trompe l'oeil Work of art that deceives the viewer by means of tricks with perspective.

Glossary of words and acronyms

alimentari grocery shops

aliscafo hydrofoil

anfiteatro amphitheatre

autostazione bus station

autostrada motorway

biblioteca library

cappella chapel

castello castle

centro centre

chiesa church

comune an administrative area; also the local council or town hall

corso avenue or boulevard

duomo/cattedrale cathedral

entrata entrance

festa festival, holiday

fiume river

fumarola volcanic vapour emission from the ground

golfo gulf

lago lake

largo square

località neighbourhood or district

lungolago lakeside promenade

lungomare seafront road or promenade

mare sea

mercato market

municipio town hall

paese place, area, country village

palazzo palace, mansion, or block of flats

parco park

passeggiata the customary early evening walk

piano plain

piazza square

pinacoteca picture gallery

ponte bridge

santuario sanctuary

senso unico one-way street

sottopassaggio subway

spiaggia beach

stazione station

strada road

teatro theatre

tempio temple

torre tower

traghetto ferry

uscita exit

via road (always used with name, eg Via Roma)

Acronyms

AAST Azienda Autonoma di Soggiorno e Turismo

ACI Automobile Club d'Italia

APT Azienda Promozione Turistica

CAI Club Alpino Italiano

DC Democrazia Cristiana (the Christian Democrat party)

EPT Ente Provinciale per il Turismo (provincial tourist office); see also APT

FS Ferrovie dello Stato (Italian State Railways)

IVA Imposta Valore Aggiunto (VAT)

MSI Movimento Sociale Italiano (the Italian Fascist party)

PCI Partito Comunista Italiano; old name for the Italian Communist party

PDS Partito Democratico della Sinistra (new name for the Italian Communist party)

PSI Partito Socialista Italiano (the Italian Socialist party)

RAI The Italian state TV and radio network

SIP Italian state telephone company

SS Strada Statale; a major road, eg SS18

Glossary of street names

Italian streets form a kind of outdoor pantheon of historical figures. A jumble of artists, thinkers, politicians, generals and saints, in roughly equal proportions, intersect with each other in blind disregard for sense or chronology. The mad mix of heroes (and a very few heroines) constantly reminds the visitor of just how much Italians relish their past. Almost all of the following appear in every major Italian city.

Bassi, Ugo (1801–49). A priest from Bologna who, as a fervent and eloquent supporter of Garibaldi and his cause, became one of its most important martyrs when he was condemned to death and shot by the Austrians.

Bellini The name of both a Venetian family of fifteenth-century painters (Jacopo and sons Gentile and Giovanni) and a nineteenth-century Sicilian composer of operas (Vicenzo), best known for *Norma* and *La Sonnambula.*

Bertani, Agostino (1812–86). A Milanese doctor, who organized the medical and ambulance services for Garibaldi's campaigns and became one of his closest associates and shrewdest strategists.

Bixio, Nino (1821–73). Loyal companion-at-arms to Garibaldi, who enlisted and disciplined civilian volunteers to fight some of the critical battles of the Unification era.

Buonarroti, Filippo (1761–1837). Tuscan revolutionary and friend of Robespierre, who was involved with Gracchus Babeuf in the short-lived Conspiracy of Equals in Paris, May 1796.

Calatafimi First decisive battle in Garibaldi's Sicilian campaign, May 1860.

Cappuccini Monks whose characteristic brown robes and peaked white hoods have lent their names to the Italian coffee drink with hot milk.

Carducci, Giosue (1835–1907). Patriotic poet of the Risorgimento who won the Nobel Prize for literature in 1907.

Cavour, Camillo di (1810–61). Prime Minister of Piemonte who relied on diplomatic cunning to promote the interests of his northern kingdom in the Unification of Italy.

Crispi, Francesco (1819–1901). Reforming prime minister of the late nineteenth century.

D'Annunzio, Gabriele (1863–1938). Nationalist writer who refurbished Italy's past with sex and violence and who lived out some of his fantasies as a Fascist military adventurer.

Dante Alighieri (1265–1321). Medieval Italian poet known for his three-part poem, *The Divine Comedy.*

De Gasperi, Alcide (1881–1954). A prominent anti-Fascist imprisoned by Mussolini, and the first Catholic prime minister of modern Italy in 1945, aligning his country with the West by joining NATO.

Depretis, Agostino (1813–87). Italian prime minister on three occasions during the late nineteenth century. His administrations are remembered for the stagnation and corruption they engendered.

Foscolo, Ugo (1778–1827). Nineteenth-century poet, dramatist and critic who left Venice under Austrian rule to settle in England where he became a commentator on Petrarch, Dante and Boccaccio.

Garibaldi, Giuseppe (1807–82). Italy's unquestioned nationalist hero, and the tag on most Italian towns' most prominent boulevards or squares. Streets are full of his exploits and the supporting cast of comrades (see Bassi, Bertani, Bixio, Calatafimi, I Mille, Turr).

Giolitti, Giovanni (1842–1928). Prime minister five times between 1892 and 1921. He sponsored an electoral reform bill which extended male suffrage and won workers the right to organize and strike.

Goldoni, Carlo (1707–93). Venetian dramatist much influenced by Moliere, who wrote more than 250 comedies.

Gramsci, Antonio (1881–1937). One of the founders of the Italian Communist Party. Arrested by Mussolini in 1928 and held until just before his death, his influential writings from prison on the political role of culture and intellectuals remain controversial fifty years on.

I Mille (The Thousand). The name given to the largely untrained band of civilian volunteers (made up of students, workers, artists, journalists and every kind of adventurer) who were mobilized in 1860 for Garibaldi's successful Sicilian campaign.

Leopardi, Giacomo (1798–1837). A lyric poet plagued by ill-health and melancholy whose patriotic verses were taken up by the Unification.

Machiavelli, Niccolò (1469–1527). Political scientist and author of *The Prince* whose name outside Italy has become synonymous with unprincipled political opportunism.

Manin, Daniele (1804–57). Leader of a revolution in Venice which proclaimed a republic in March 1848 and was overrun by the Austrians shortly thereafter.

Manzoni, Alessandro (1785–1873). Liberal Catholic writer and playwright whose historical novel *I promesi sposi* (*The Betrothed*), set in seventeenth-century Milan, is still required reading in Italian schools.

Marconi, Guglielmo (1874–1937). Developer of the wireless system, sending messages across the Straits of Dover in 1899 and across the Atlantic in 1901.

Matteotti, Giacomo A Socialist in the Italian Parliament who was murdered by Fascist thugs for his public denunciation of the 1924 elections which gave Mussolini majority control. In what has become known as Mussolini's Watergate, the incident had a brief chance of stopping Il Duce in his tracks – but didn't.

Mazzini, Giuseppe (1805–72). Propagandist of Italian Unification whose influence was spread through the organization (Giovine Italia) Young Italy which he founded to promote the national cause.

Moro, Aldo Postwar prime minister who was kidnapped and murdered by the Brigate Rosse in May 1978.

Puccini, Giacomo (1858–1924). A member of the fifth generation of a family of professional musicians, and composer of many popular operas, including *Madame Butterfly*, *La Bohème* and *Tosca*.

Quattro Novembre (November 4). Anniversary of the 1918 victory in the war.

Ricasoli An ancient and distinguished Tuscan family name. The nineteenth-century Baron Ricasoli (an ally of Cavour and very briefly prime minister) has been eclipsed by the relatively greater prominence of his family's vineyards, known particularly for their Chianti.

Ricci, Matteo (1552–1610). Early Italian missionary to China.

Risorgimento The nineteenth-century movement to unify Italy and liberate the country from foreign domination.

Savonarola A fifteenth-century Dominican friar and prophet of doom, who inspired a famous book-burning (which included Boccaccio's *Decameron* among the forbidden texts), and was himself burned in 1498.

Togliatti (1893–1964). Cofounder (with Gramsci and others) of the Italian Communist Party, which, in 1956, adopted his programme for an "Italian Road to Socialism".

Turr, Stefan A Hungarian colonel in Garibaldi's army and close associate who helped acquire arms for the volunteer army (The Thousand) to mount the campaign in Sicily.

Umberto I and II Kings of Italy, respectively, between 1878 and 1900 and for a brief period in 1946.

Vasari, Giorgio (1511–74). The father of modern art history, whose *Lives of the Artists* traced the story of art from ancient Rome through to his own contemporary – and fellow Tuscan – Michelangelo.

Venti Settembre (September 20). The day Italian troops stormed into Rome in 1870, marking the final stage of Unification.

Venticinque Aprile (April 25). Anniversary of the 1945 liberation.

Ventiquattro Maggio (May 24). Date in 1915 when Italy declared war on Austria-Hungary.

Verdi, Giuseppe (1813–1901). Hugely popular and prolific composer of operas who became a national hero.

Vespri Siciliani Massacre of the Angevin French in Sicily in 1282, carried out (according to legend) while vesper bells were ringing, in retaliation for the savage colonization of the island by the Angevin. Verdi used the story for an opera in 1855.

Vittorio Emanuele II and III Respectively, the first king of unified Italy, from 1861 to 1878, and from 1900 until 1946. Very often the main street of towns are named after Vittorio Emanuele II – an overly grand accolade for a dull and unenlightened ruler.

Volturno A river near Cápua, and the name given to an important battle led by Garibaldi against the Bourbons in October 1860.

Small print and
Index

A Rough Guide to Rough Guides

Published in 1982, the first Rough Guide – to Greece – was a student scheme that became a publishing phenomenon. Mark Ellingham, a recent graduate in English from Bristol University, had been travelling in Greece the previous summer and couldn't find the right guidebook. With a small group of friends he wrote his own guide, combining a highly contemporary, journalistic style with a thoroughly practical approach to travellers' needs.

The immediate success of the book spawned a series that rapidly covered dozens of destinations. And, in addition to impecunious backpackers, Rough Guides soon acquired a much broader and older readership that relished the guides' wit and inquisitiveness as much as their enthusiastic, critical approach and value-for-money ethos.

These days, Rough Guides include recommendations from shoestring to luxury and cover more than 200 destinations around the globe, including almost every country in the Americas and Europe, more than half of Africa and most of Asia and Australasia. Our ever-growing team of authors and photographers is spread all over the world, particularly in Europe, the USA and Australia.

In the early 1990s, Rough Guides branched out of travel, with the publication of Rough Guides to World Music, Classical Music and the Internet. All three have become benchmark titles in their fields, spearheading the publication of a wide range of books under the Rough Guide name.

Including the travel series, Rough Guides now number more than 350 titles, covering: phrasebooks, waterproof maps, music guides from Opera to Heavy Metal, reference works as diverse as Conspiracy Theories and Shakespeare, and popular culture books from iPods to Poker. Rough Guides also produce a series of more than 120 World Music CDs in partnership with World Music Network.

Visit www.roughguides.com to see our latest publications.

Rough Guide travel images are available for commercial licensing at www.roughguidespictures.com

Rough Guide credits

Text editors: Lucy White, Lucy Ratcliffe and Melissa Graham
Layout: Jessica Subramanian
Cartography: Animesh Pathak, Katie Lloyd-Jones
Picture editor: Nicole Newman
Production: Katherine Owers
Proofreader: Susannah Wight, Megan McIntyre
Cover design: Chloë Roberts
Photographers: Helena Smith, Martin Richardson, Dylan Reisenberger, James McConnachie and Karen Trist
Editorial: **London** Kate Berens, Claire Saunders, Ruth Blackmore, Polly Thomas, Richard Lim, Alison Murchie, Karoline Densley, Andy Turner, Keith Drew, Edward Aves, Nikki Birrell, Alice Park, Sarah Eno, Jo Kirby, Samantha Cook, James Smart, Natasha Foges, Roisin Cameron, Joe Staines, Duncan Clark, Peter Buckley, Matthew Milton, Tracy Hopkins, Ruth Tidball; **New York** Andrew Rosenberg, Steven Horak, AnneLise Sorensen, Amy Hegarty, April Isaacs, Ella Steim, Anna Owens, Joseph Petta, Sean Mahoney
Design & Pictures: **London** Scott Stickland, Dan May, Diana Jarvis, Mark Thomas, Jj Luck, Harriet Mills; **Delhi** Umesh Aggarwal, Ajay Verma, Ankur Guha, Pradeep Thapliyal, Sachin Tanwar, Anita Singh, Madhavi Singh, Karen D'Souza
Production: Aimee Hampson
Cartography: **London** Maxine Repath, Ed Wright; **Delhi** Jai Prakash Mishra, Rajesh Chhibber, Ashutosh Bharti, Rajesh Mishra, Jasbir Sandhu, Karobi Gogoi, Amod Singh, Alakananda Bhattacharya, Athokpam Jotinkumar
Online: **New York** Jennifer Gold, Kristin Mingrone; **Delhi** Manik Chauhan, Narender Kumar, Rakesh Kumar, Amit Kumar, Amit Verma, Rahul Kumar, Ganesh Sharma, Debojit Borah
Marketing & Publicity: **London** Liz Statham, Niki Hanmer, Louise Maher, Jess Carter, Vanessa Godden, Anna Paynton, Vivienne Watton, Rachel Sprackett; **New York** Geoff Colquitt, Megan Kennedy, Katy Ball; **Delhi** Reem Khokhar
Special Projects Editor: Philippa Hopkins
Manager India: Punita Singh
Series Editor: Mark Ellingham
Reference Director: Andrew Lockett
Publishing Coordinator: Megan McIntyre
Publishing Director: Martin Dunford
Commercial Manager: Gino Magnotta
Managing Director: John Duhigg

Publishing information

This eighth edition published May 2007 by
Rough Guides Ltd,
80 Strand, London WC2R 0RL
345 Hudson St, 4th Floor,
New York, NY 10014, USA
14 Local Shopping Centre, Panchsheel Park,
New Delhi 110017, India
Distributed by the Penguin Group
Penguin Books Ltd,
80 Strand, London WC2R 0RL
Penguin Group (USA)
375 Hudson Street, NY 10014, USA
Penguin Group (Australia)
250 Camberwell Road, Camberwell,
Victoria 3124, Australia
Penguin Books Canada Ltd,
10 Alcorn Avenue, Toronto, Ontario,
Canada M4V 1E4
Penguin Group (NZ)
67 Apollo Drive, Mairangi Bay, Auckland 1310,
New Zealand
Cover concept by Peter Dyer.

Typeset in Bembo and Helvetica to an original design by Henry Iles.

Printed in Italy by Legoprint S.p.A.

© Ros Belford, Martin Dunford, Celia Woolfrey, Rob Andrews, Jules Brown, Jonathan Buckley and Tim Jepson 2007

No part of this book may be reproduced in any form without permission from the publisher except for the quotation of brief passages in reviews.

1224pp includes index

A catalogue record for this book is available from the British Library

ISBN: 9-78184-353-855-4

Help us update

We've gone to a lot of effort to ensure that the eighth edition of **The Rough Guide to Italy** is accurate and up to date. However, things change – places get "discovered", opening hours are notoriously fickle, restaurants and rooms raise prices or lower standards. If you feel we've got it wrong or left something out, we'd like to know, and if you can remember the address, the price, the time, the phone number, so much the better. We'll credit all contributions, and send a copy of the next edition (or any other Rough Guide if you prefer) for the best letters. Everyone who writes to us and isn't already a subscriber will receive a copy of our full-colour thrice-yearly newsletter. Please mark letters: "**Rough Guide Italy Update**" and send to: Rough Guides, 80 Strand, London WC2R 0RL, or Rough Guides, 345 Hudson St, 4th Floor, New York, NY 10014. Or send an email to mail@roughguides.com
Have your questions answered and tell others about your trip at
www.roughguides.atinfopop.com

Acknowledgements

Charles would like to thank Maria Teresa and Leonardo in Venice and Francesca and Bruna in Bassano for their assistance, the Veneto tourist offices for their patience, and Caroline and Molly for their help and vigilance.

Jeffrey would like to thank Paola Baratella, Giovanna Belluomini, Gianluca Borghese, Erika Carpaneto, Susanna Carpenter, Cefalo Family, Jolie Chain, Colella Family, Diletta Donati, Andrew Gallagher, Suzanne Hartley, Hanja Kochansky, Jean-François Martin, Adrian McCourt, Roberta Mencucci, Clare Merlo, Laura Mori, Frances Nacman, Elaine O'Reilly, Hanna & Aldo Parodi, Bruno Rota, Christine Salerno, Ev Small, Maria Rosa Subirana, Roseanne Ullman, Aloma Valentini, Andrea Veneziani, Robert Vente, Lila Yawn.

Lucy would like to thank Luca and Carlotta for all their help.

Martin would like to thank Lucy White for her skilful and above all patient editing; Victor Townley for help with Lazio; Flo Austin for her work on Italian Contexts; Katia and Sabrina and everyone at At Home; Kate and Jeremy and all the Austin-Tarrys for lovely days in Bracciano; Daisy and Caroline for heavenly days in Rome; Germana Colomba in Milan and the staff at the Distretto dei Laghi.

Nick wishes to thank Loredana Barindelli of Momentum Travel for sharing her local knowledge of Northern Italy.

Readers' letters

Thanks to all the readers who took the time to write in with comments and suggestions (and apologies if we've inadvertently omitted or misspelt anyone's name):

Philip Ainsworth, Edward Bacon, Carey Baff, Iain Baker, Kay and Enda Bannon, Ana Belén Martin, James Bigus, Alan Blandamer, Robert Bottomley, Roger Bowder, Mandi Brooker, John Brooks, René Brouwer, Diana Brown, Hans von Bülow, Adriana Buongiovanni, Mike Braide, Chris Burin, Stephen Buttimer, Pam Cantle, David Carr, Roger Carruthers, Joanne Carter, Lesley Chamberlain, John Close, Anna Comolli, Denise Cookson, Brian Cooney, Charles Daly, Rosena Davison, Gary Elflett, Ann Feltham, Bruno & Jelbrich Forment, M. Francis, Miranda Gardner, Dave Gilmour, Bill and Margaret Gray, Marla Gulley, Rich Hall, Alison Harris, Sue & Dave Hardwick, Bettina Hartas, Jeremy Hoult, Ken Howard, Roger Hunter, Emma Jones, Colm Kenneally, Michael & Marie-Madeleine Kenning, Martin Kenzie, Alex Klassmann, Hans Kleinen Hammans, Kurt & Catherine Kullmann, Sophia Lambert, Sarah Lane, Peter Lawton, Mark Lloyd, Kimberley Lomax, Jonas Ludvigsson, Bo Lundin, Ray Massey, Philip Melville, Anita Mokarram, Rachel Monk, Chris Moore, Lee Moore, Duncan Naughten, Danielle Neville, Norma Negrete, John Newton, Rosemary O'Connor, Geoff & Ann Obee, Martin Oldsberg, James Owen, J. Plumtree, Martin Price, Maarten Pullen, Mike Quirke, Mary-Elizabeth Raw, Jeffrey Robson, Enrico Russo, Helen Ryan, Loring Schwarz, Jonathan Sidaway Andrew Sides, Douglas Smith, Steve Soper, Simon & Bev Spears, Andreas Stegman, Antoinette Sutto, Sarah Sylbing, Geoff Taylor, Alastair Telford, David Thomas, Graham Thomas, Bill and Carolyn Thomas, Christen K. Thomsen, Jeanne Tift, G. Tillson, Michael Upshall, Michelle Villeneau, Monica de Vold, Karen Walker, Chris Wilkinson, Michael Williams, Judy Wood, Craig Wright, Michael Wyatt and Andrew Young.

SMALL PRINT

Photo credits

All photos © Rough Guides except the following:

Introduction
Twilight views of St. Peter's Church in Rome © Bob Krist/Corbis
Boats in harbor, Vernazza, Cinque Terre © Owen Franken/Corbis
Taking a break, Courmayeur © Sasha Gusov/Axiom
Cala Gonone, Sardinia © CuboImages/Robert Harding
The Colosseum at night © Doug McKinlay/Axiom

Things not to miss
01 Main Staircase, Musei Vaticani, Vatican City © Peter Adams/JAI/Corbis
02 Duomo, Piazza Sordello, Mantua © CuboImages/Robert Harding
03 Cathedral, Urbino © CuboImages/Robert Harding
04 Riomaggiore and Cinque Terre Coast © Blaine Harrington III/Corbis
05 Black truffles, Maratea, Basilicata © CuboImages/Robert Harding
06 Palazzo Dei Consoli, Gubbio © Travel Library/Robert Harding
07 Acquaviva coast, Portoferraio, Isle of Elba, Tuscany © CuboImages/Robert Harding
08 The Marriage of Mary and Joseph, Giotto di Bondone © Alinari Archives/Corbis
09 skiing, Veneto © CuboImages/Robert Harding
10 Matera, Basilicata © CuboImages/Robert Harding
11 Wild Grey wolf {Canis lupus} Abruzzo National Park © Angelo Gandolfi /naturepl.com
12 Statue on facade of Santa Croce, Lecce © John Heseltine/Corbis
13 Cala Mariolu, Sardinia © Robert Harding World Imagery/Corbis
14 Citta Alta, Bergamo © Tibor Bognar/Alamy
15 Greek theatre, Syracuse, Sicily © Michael Jenner/Robert Harding
16 The Last Supper © Getty Images/The Bridgeman Art Library
17 Palio Horse Race, Siena © Stefano Rellandini/Reuters/Corbis
18 25 Jul 2001, Mount Etna © Alfio Scigliano/Sygma/Corbis
19 Nettuno temple, Paestum archeological area, Campania © CuboImages/Robert Harding
20 Missoni at Milan Fashion Week 2007©Karlrouse/Catwalking/Getty Images
21 Duomo, Milan © Guenter Rossenbach/zefa/Corbis
23 Mosaic in Church of Sant' Apollinare Nuovo © Sandro Vannini/Corbis
24 Piazza San Lorenzo, Genoa © CuboImages/Robert Harding
25 Market selling peppers and mushrooms, Emilia-Romagna © Ellen Rooney/Axiom

26 Basilica of San Francesco © Elio Ciol/Corbis
28 Gran Paradiso National Park © Jason Friend/Alamy
30 Facade of Duomo, Orvieto, Umbria © Travel Library/Robert Harding
31 Amalfi Coast © AM Corporation/Alamy
33 Carnival, Venice © Guenter Rossenbach/zefa/Corbis
34 Courtyard at Certosa di Pavia Monastery © Francesco Venturi/Corbis
37 Basilica de San Marco © Mark Thomas
38 Fragment of staute of Constantine, Capitoline Museum © Martyn Vickery/Alamy

Black and whites
p.70 Gran Paradiso National Park, Valnontey Valley © Duncan Maxwell/Robert Harding
p.87 Aperitivo Snacks in Wine Bar © Bob Sacha/Corbis
p.92 Saluzzo, Piedmont © John Ferro Sims/Alamy
p.116 Casino Municipale © Bo Zaunders/Corbis
p.121 Via Garibaldi, Genoa © CuboImages/Robert Harding
p.145 Alassio © Gaetano Barone/zefa/Corbis
p.162 Riomaggiore, Cinque Terre © Grant Faint/Getty
p.170 Cycling, Lombardy © CuboImages/Alamy
p.261 Ice Man, Archeological Museum © Museo Archeologico Alto Adige/epa/Corbis
p.270 Piazza Duomo, Trento © CuboImages/Alamy
p.284 Gruppo del Sella © Les Gibbon/Alamy
p.308 Gondola under the Rialto Bridge © Roy Rainford/Robert Harding
p.348 Market in front of Santa Maria dei Miracoli © Cris Haigh/Alamy
p.408 Fusine upper lake in Tarvisio © PhotoDreams/Alamy
p.420 Grotta Gigante © CuboImages/Alamy
p.429 Cavour street, Udine © CuboImages/Robert Harding
p.440 Bologna © bobo/Alamy
p.475 Castello Estense in Ferrara © Paul Almasy/Corbis
p.492 Lucca © Michael Freeman/Corbis
p.527 Boboli Gardens © Mark Bolton/Corbis
p.582 The Palio horse race © Stefano Rellandini/Reuters/Corbis
p.594 Pitigliano defence walls © Andrzej Gorzkowski/Alamy
p.626 Gubbio, Umbria © Tony Gervis/Robert Harding
p.634 Piazza IV Novembre, Perugia © Tom Bean/Corbis
p.681 Duomo, Orvieto © Vince Streano/Corbis
p.690 Madonna and Child by Lorenzo Lotto © Alinari Archives/Corbis

p.697 Palazzo Ducale, Urbino © Angelo Hornak/ Corbis

p.713 Monte Conero © CuboImages/Robert Harding

p.778 Roman Forum viewed from the Capitoline Hill © Glyn Thomas/Alamy

p.794 Inside St. Peter's Basilica © Kazuyoshi Nomachi/Corbis

p.835 Abbey of Montecassino © Fulvio Roiter/ Corbis

p.946 Rocca di Calascio and views to Maiella mountains © Gillian Price/Alamy

p.954 Parco Nationale del Gran Sasso © Abruzzolan Cumming/Axiom

p.859 Woman Wearing Traditional Mourning Dress © Bob Krist/Corbis

p.880 Tomba del Tuffatore, Paestum archeological park © CuboImages/Robert Harding

p.938 Via dei Mercanti © CuboImages/Alamy

p.946 San Matteo church © CuboImages/Alamy

p.958 Coastline towards Vieste © Tony Gervis/ Robert Harding

p.970 Castel del Monte © CuboImages/Robert Harding

p.996 Matera © CuboImages/Robert Harding

p.1007 Tropea © Walter Bibikow/JAI/Corbis

p.1022 Olive grove, Calabria © imagebroker / Alamy

p.1030 Facade of Monreale Cathedral © Adam Woolfitt/Corbis

p.1038 Palermo © Frank Chmura/Alamy

p.1055 Lípari Town harbour © Ellen Rooney/ Robert Harding

p.1091 Temple, Segesta © CuboImages/Robert Harding

p.1102 La Maddalena Island, Costa Smeralda © Travel Library/Robert Harding

p.1112 Alleyway in Cágliari © Giraud Philippe/ Corbis Sygma

p.1120 Oristano, musicians in Sartiglia Carnival processio © Bruno Morandi/Getty

Italian football colour section

UEFA Champions League: Juventus v ArsenalLaurence © Griffiths/Getty Images

FIFA World Cup 2006 fans celebrating © Franco Origlia/Getty Images

Newspaper at kiosk © mediacolor's/Alamy

Italians Celebrate World Cup Win In Naples © Salvatore Laporta/Getty Images

AC Milan's striker Filippo Inzaghi waves a AC Milan flag © Reuters/Corbis

Luciano MoggiAP © Photo/Luca Bruno

Index

Map entries are in colour.

INDEX